Competitive Edge

A Guide to Graduate Business Programs

PETERSON'S

Publishing

Sustainability—Its Importance to Peterson's, a Nelnet company

What does sustainability mean to Peterson's? As a leading publisher, we are aware that our business has a direct impact on vital resources—most especially the trees that are used to make our books. Peterson's is proud that its products are made with fiber certified under the Sustainable Forestry Initiative® (SFI®) Standard and that this book is printed on paper that is 10 percent post-consumer waste.

Being a part of the Sustainable Forestry Initiative® (SFI®) means that all of our vendors—from paper suppliers to printers—have undergone rigorous audits to demonstrate that they are maintaining a sustainable environment.

Peterson's continually strives to find new ways to incorporate sustainability throughout all aspects of its business.

About Peterson's Publishing

To succeed on your lifelong educational journey, you will need accurate, dependable, and practical tools and resources. That is why Peterson's is everywhere education happens. Because whenever and however you need education content delivered, you can rely on Peterson's to provide the information, know-how, and guidance to help you reach your goals. Tools to match the right students with the right school. It's here. Personalized resources and expert guidance. It's here. Comprehensive and dependable education content—delivered whenever and however you need it. It's all here.

For more information, contact Peterson's Publishing, 2000 Lenox Drive, Lawrenceville, NJ 08648; 800-338-3282 Ext. 54229; or find us online at www.petersonspublishing.com.

Bernadette Webster, Director of Publishing; Jill C. Schwartz, Editor; Mark D. Snider, Editor; Ken Britschge, Research Project Manager; Nicole Gallo, Amy L. Weber, Research Associates; Phyllis Johnson, Software Engineer; Ray Golaszewski, Publishing Operations Manager; Linda M. Williams, Composition Manager; Karen Mount, Fulfillment Coordinator

ISBN-13: 978-0-7689-3438-0
ISBN-10: 0-7689-3438-9

Printed in the United States of America

10 9 8 7 6 5 4 3 2 1   13 12 11

First Edition

Contents

Contents

APPENDIX

SPECIAL ADVERTISING SECTION

A Note from the Editors at Peterson's Publishing

Looking for that *competitive edge* to get into a graduate business program? You've found the perfect guide! This brand new book offers you just what you need—application insight from admissions officials, tips from those in the know to help you determine the right business school, vital data on thousands of business programs in the United States and abroad, and a sample GMAT® practice exam to help boost your test-prep efforts.

Because advanced study in business is so popular, the types of schools offering these courses of study run the gamut from small private colleges with business schools enrolling only a few hundred students to large state schools whose student bodies can number in the tens of thousands. These days, you can also join the increasing number of students who take distance learning courses from their own home or attend a "virtual university," where opportunities for learning are shared online. If you're already employed, perhaps your company is one of the growing numbers of firms that offer on-site business courses in cooperation with local colleges. The possibilities are limitless. *Peterson's CompetitiveEdge: A Guide to Graduate Business Programs* is the perfect tool to help you narrow your choices and select the right program for you.

In the first part of the book, you'll find valuable articles to help you gain that *competitive edge*. In "Advice from Admissions Directors," you'll find extraordinarily helpful tips from the admissions directors at Penn's Wharton School, Penn State's Smeal College of Business, GWU's School of Business, Ohio State's Fisher College of Business, and Cornell's Samuel Curtis Johnson Graduate School of Management. Other articles include "Surviving the Application Process," "The Importance of Resumes" (includes a sample resume), "The Vital Role of Application Essays" (includes a sample MBA application essay), "Financial Support," "Returning to School," "Finding the Right MBA Program," "The MBA in Healthcare Management," and "Exciting Times in the Accounting Profession."

Whether or not you know precisely what field of business you want to study, you'll find a wealth of information in the second part of *CompetitiveEdge*. Each of the twenty-one sections of graduate business programs here begins with an overview—details on what the particular field entails, what courses may be required or available as electives, what the job outlook appears to be, a potential position in that field, and a list of some helpful organizations, publications, or blogs. Many of the sections also feature career insight from individuals whose graduate business degree led them to their current job. Each of the section profiles of graduate schools and programs are ideal for a quick reference of facts and figures.

The profiles provide essential information, including data on institution names, administrative units, degrees and fields of study, accreditation, jointly offered degrees, part-time and evening/weekend programs, postbaccalaureate distance learning degrees, faculty, students enrolled, degrees awarded, degree and entrance requirements, application deadlines, expenses and financial support, faculty research, and unit head and application contact info. Some schools even feature a display ad near the profile listing that highlights interesting aspects of their program.

The profile information published in this guide is collected through Peterson's Annual Survey of Graduate and Professional Institutions. While every effort has been made to ensure the accuracy and completeness of the data, information is sometimes unavailable or changes occur after publication deadlines. All usable information received in time has been included. Institutions that did not complete and submit the 2011 survey were not included in this guide. The omission of any particular item from a profile signifies either that the item is not applicable to the institution or program or that information was not available.

To be included in this guide, an institution must have full accreditation or be a candidate for accreditation (preaccreditation) status by an institutional or specialized accrediting body recognized by the U.S. Department of Education or the Council for Higher Education Accreditation (CHEA). Program registration by the New York State Board of Regents is considered to be the equivalent of institutional accreditation, since the board requires that all programs offered by an institution meet its standards before recognition is granted. A Canadian institution must be chartered and authorized to grant degrees by the provincial government, affiliated with a chartered institution, or accredited by a recognized U.S. accrediting body. This guide also includes institutions outside the United States that are accredited by these U.S. accrediting bodies. A full explanation of the accrediting process and complete information on recognized institutional (regional and national) and specialized accrediting bodies can be found online at www.chea.org or at www.ed.gov/admins/finaid/accred/index.html.

Following the profiles, certain sections contain in-depth write-ups (Close-ups) about certain graduate business schools or programs that chose to provide this additional information to help *you* gain a *competitive edge*. These Close-ups are more expansive and flexible than the profiles, and the administrators who have written them emphasize different aspects of their programs. In each Close-up, you will find information on programs of study, research facilities, faculty information, tuition and fees, financial aid, and application procedures. If an institution or program has submitted an in-depth article, a boldface cross-reference appears below its profile.

Toward the back of *CompetitiveEdge* in the Appendix, you'll find a sample GMAT test, with an answer key and explanations, from *Peterson's Master the GMAT 2012*. There are dozens of review questions for the quantitative and verbal sections as well as two analytical writing assessments. Please note that the practice test reflects the content of the GMAT exam at the time of this book's publication and does not include any practice questions that will appear on the new Integrated Reasoning section scheduled to be a part of the GMAT in June 2012. We hope the sample GMAT test will give you the additional practice you need to help you score high on the actual exam—an extra *competitive edge!*

At the end of the book, you'll find a special advertising section. The ads placed by these schools help make it possible for Peterson's Publishing to continue to provide you with the highest quality educational exploration, test-prep, financial aid, and career-preparation resources you need to succeed on your educational journey.

Peterson's publishes a full line of resources with information you need to guide you through the graduate admissions process. Peterson's publications can be found at college libraries and career centers and at your local bookstore or libraries. Peterson's books are now also available as eBooks. For more information, visit us online at www.petersonspublishing.com or find us on Facebook® at www.facebook.com/petersonspublishing.

We welcome any comments or suggestions you may have about this publication. Your feedback will help us to make education dreams possible for you—and others like you. The editors at Peterson's Publishing wish you the best of luck in your search for the right graduate business program for you!

In this article, admissions directors from The Wharton School at the University of Pennsylvania, the Smeal College of Business at Penn State University, The George Washington University School of Business, Fisher College of Business at The Ohio State University, and Samuel Curtis Johnson Graduate School of Management at Cornell University give you their perspectives on the value of an advanced degree in business. Their insight on what you should look for when choosing a business program and what admissions directors look for when reviewing business school applications will give you a *competitive edge.*

Ankur Kumar, Director
MBA Admissions & Financial Aid
The Wharton School
University of Pennsylvania
http://www.wharton.upenn.edu/

When is the right time for prospective students to start thinking about business school? Upon graduating from college? After a few years in the job market? Why?

There is no "right time" to start thinking about business school. Rather, the decision to go to business school is a personal one and will be different for everyone. Some candidates, while they are still in their undergrad studies, already know that they may plan to attend an MBA program. Others spend a few, or even more, years in a career first, gaining a better understanding of themselves and what they can gain out of business school. Business schools are aware of this, and, as such, tailor their recruiting programs to accommodate the varied timelines of *all* applicants. At whatever point they are at in their lives, once individuals have made that decision, our admissions officers are more than happy to help them with the next steps in the process.

What is the value of an advanced degree in business—in today's society and in the future?

The most fundamental thing about an MBA is that it is a degree for the long term. Many MBAs find themselves using different skills from their MBA at different points in their career. In other words, you may use your MBA to gain the basic skill set and network to make a career switch immediately upon graduation but then later use different skills when you are managing more people or making strategic decisions.

What makes an MBA so valuable is that it is so multi-purpose; it is a degree designed to help people lead people and organizations in a variety of industries and functions. In many ways, it is a form of insurance—it equips you with a skill set and network that can be used in many industries.

Certainly, though, we are at a unique time in business, in which we are experiencing much change, innovation, *and* instability. Given the

events of the recent years in the business world, there is much to learn from professors and other students (many of whom have first-hand experience with the financial crises, the downturn in the real estate market, and other events that have shaped today's economy) to better understand what will be required of successful and ethical business leaders in the future. Armed with this knowledge, students emerge from business school with a degree that will continue to benefit them for years to come.

What are the most important factors that a prospective student should consider when researching business programs?

There are many factors that prospective students must take into consideration before selecting a business program. First, it's important to take stock of your motivations for attending business school: Is it the desire to build a foundation of business knowledge? Is it to grow a professional network? Or is the degree simply essential for the next step in your career path?

As an applicant, you should also have an understanding of what your professional goals are, and you should, of course, seek programs that best support those goals. But you should also consider programs that offer opportunities and resources to explore other options—many, many MBA students end up changing their career focus upon arriving at business school and realizing the wealth of opportunities available to them. Other factors including structure of the program, location and cost are essential as well, and you should carefully consider these aspects when choosing a school. If possible, visit campuses and talk to current students, administrators, and faculty members to get a sense of a program's culture before making a decision on whether it would be a good fit for you.

How heavily does your program weigh the following five admissions criteria: undergraduate grades, GMAT scores, work experience, letters of recommendation, and essays? Why do you place the emphasis where you do?

Wharton's admissions evaluation process is a holistic one. There is no 'weight' given to any one piece of the application; rather, it is important that all the sections balance each other out and portray your strengths to the best of your abilities. Needless to say, Wharton cares about each piece of the application it requests from you, so be sure to deliver the best you can. Each of the elements of the application is taken into serious consideration and each plays an important role in portraying a well-rounded candidate.

How many essays does your program require the student to write? What kinds of questions do you ask? In your opinion, what is the difference between a good essay and a bad one? What do you look for when you read admissions essays?

Wharton requires candidates to write three essays, with an optional section to explain extenuating circumstances (only if necessary—most candidates are admitted without providing an optional fourth essay). The Admissions Committee is interested in getting to know candidates on both a professional *and* personal level. We encourage applicants to be introspective, candid, succinct, and most importantly, honest. Essays should be used to elaborate your candidacy, while answering the specific questions at hand.

What kind of work experience do you look for? Does it necessarily have to be in a business field?

One of the most rewarding aspects of business school is that students meet other students from myriad different professional backgrounds. As a result, Wharton seeks diversity in the professional backgrounds of its admitted students just as it does in all other parts of our applicants' profiles. No one industry is preferred more than another, and experience in a Fortune 500 company does not have higher value than experience in a start-up or in a public institution. While the median number of years of experience prior to enrollment is four years, there is certainly a range around that number. Wharton is more concerned with the depth and breadth of an individual's position, his or her contributions to the work environment, and the level of responsibility and progression rather than simply the number of years worked. To that end, Wharton is also interested in early career candidates, those with 3 or fewer years of full-time professional experience who exhibit strong managerial and professional potential.

What advice would you give students about whom to ask to write letters of recommendation?

Letters of recommendation are an effective way for applicants to give Wharton further insight into their professional accomplishment and leadership. You should choose people who can speak directly about your aptitude for, or accomplishments in, leadership and management. Thus, work-related recommendations are more valuable than academic ones. You should select two people who really know you and your work, who you believe can best address the questions asked.

An effective recommender will do more than check the right boxes and write a couple of sentences; he or she will include an example or two that illustrates his or her points. For many candidates, briefing your recommenders beforehand ensures their memory is refreshed as to your accomplishments, and that they are fully aware of your motivations for applying to business school. Applicants working in family businesses, entrepreneurial environments, or other non-traditional environments will need to be more creative in terms of choosing recommenders (and perhaps use the optional essay to allow us to understand how they made their choices). These applicants may wish to consider clients, mentors, or others they have worked with in the community.

Many applicants wonder if they should seek out Wharton alumni to write recommendations. Our strong recommendation is to seek the two people who are best-suited to give a thorough, thoughtful recommendation. Of course, if a Wharton graduate happens to be one of those two people, he or she may be able to use his or her understanding of Wharton to describe how you will fit into the Wharton culture. However, you should avoid seeking alumni who aren't truly qualified to write about you.

When you look at transcripts, do undergraduate business majors have an advantage over those with majors in other fields? If someone's major wasn't in a business or related field (economics, for example), what would your advice be?

Over two thirds of Wharton students did *not* major in business in undergrad. There are, in fact, many students who majored in the humanities and social sciences. Much like Wharton seeks diversity in the professional backgrounds of its students, so the same can be said of their academic backgrounds.

That being said, Wharton wants to make sure its students are academically prepared for the rigors of its business curriculum. When evaluating your transcripts of undergraduate work, Wharton is not simply considering the GPA; rather we are trying to put together a story of what you were like as a student and how you may fare in, and contribute to, our program.

If you have no business classes or quantitative classes in your undergraduate background, it may be advisable to pursue some basic business classes through continuing education. Classes such as calculus and/or statistics can provide an excellent grounding in business education and can help you understand the sort of curriculum you will be experiencing in business school, as well as show the Admissions Committee your aptitude for such study.

How important is timing in the admissions process? In other words, do students who apply early have an advantage over those who just meet the deadlines?

As applicants come from all walks of life, and hence decide to apply to business school at different times, Wharton offers three rounds of admission each year. However, we strongly encourage applicants serious about coming to business school in a given year to apply in one of the first two rounds of the application cycle. Applying earlier can have an added benefit for you, as receiving an earlier decision from Wharton may give you more clarity on the business school application process. In addition, if you are placed on the waitlist in an earlier round, you will have the opportunity to be considered for admission, again, in a subsequent round.

That said, a student should apply when he/she feels most confident and ready. Wharton is interested in the best applicants, not the earliest ones, and you are best served by taking the time to present the strongest application possible.

What words of wisdom do you have for students who are considering applying to business school?

Applying to business school is an introspective process, and it should not be rushed. You should carefully choose the schools that best fit you, and you should take the time to carefully put together an application that best represents your strengths as a potential student. It's also important to stay focused on *your* application; don't spend your energy worrying about other candidates' applications. Spend your time and energy putting together the application that best reflects the real you.

Stacey Dorang Peeler
MBA Admissions Director
**Smeal College of Business
Penn State University Park**
http://www.smeal.psu.edu/

When is the right time for prospective students to start thinking about business school? Upon graduating from college? After a few years in the job market? Why?

Most business schools prefer, if not require, applicants who have work experience. While it is never too early to start considering a career path and exploring advanced degree options, most people begin an in-depth search about eighteen months before they want to matriculate. However, timelines for pursuing business school certainly vary by individual situation. Looking ahead about a year and a half gives applicants time to visit programs in person, connect with faculty members, current students, and alumni as well as time to give the application the attention it warrants to be competitive in the MBA applicant pool. Planning a year or more ahead gives flexibility if the applicant intends to apply in the first round and wants to be considered for a full spectrum of financial aid opportunities, and it leaves room for error if he or she needs to take the GMAT more than once. It's important that applicants know all of the deadlines and requirements for each program they are applying to as programs will vary.

What is the value of an advanced degree in business—in today's society and in the future?

For many MBA students, an advanced degree is linked to opportunity and earning power. Many higher level and C-level positions will require an advanced degree. An MBA can be a bargaining chip in employment negotiations and will help an applicant differentiate him or herself from an often crowded and competitive pool of job seekers. While an advanced degree certainly won't guarantee anyone a job in any field, it will often give them a leg up and open up the most doors.

What are the most important factors that a prospective student should consider when researching business programs?

The single most important factor boils down to what we call "fit." In essence, is the program right for you? Candidates must ask themselves a series of questions including: What is my end career goal? Does the curriculum of the program match my academic needs? Does the program attract recruiters and place people in the field I want to pursue? Can I afford this school, and is aid available? What is the community like, and do I share the same values? What is daily life like, and will I like spending the next two years in this program? What is the best option for my spouse/partner/family? An MBA is a huge investment of resources. It's key that an applicant knows what he or she wants and the kind of environment in which he or she will be most successful.

How heavily does your program weigh the following five admissions criteria?

1. Undergraduate grades—*Very important*
2. GMAT scores—*Very important*
3. Work experience—*Very important*
4. Letters of recommendation—*Very important*
5. Essays—*Very important*

Why do you place the emphasis where you do?

At Smeal we have no "formula" or weighting system for application criteria. First, however, we need to ensure the candidate is academically prepared to succeed in a quantitatively rigorous program. While the GPA and GMAT scores are not the only factors used to make a decision, we need to see evidence that a candidate can handle the course work and ultimately graduate from the program. Work experience is also a significant factor. What can an applicant bring to the classroom, his/her team, and his/her own MBA experience? We look for applicants who have a strong sense of where they have been and where they are going. Not only is this reflected in the resume/work experience, but applicants are also given a chance to go into detail about their personal career path and goals in their essays. It's essential that the applicant's "story" ties together and makes sense. In addition, essays give important insight into an applicant's written communication skills and professionalism. They can also give us a look at things we might not see in other parts of the application (volunteer work, cultural background, unique experiences, and so on). Ultimately, we factor all of the application parts together to determine if the student will be a good fit for our program and if our program will be a good fit for the student.

How many essays does your program require the student to write? What kinds of questions do you ask? In your opinion, what is the difference between a good essay and a bad one? What do you look for when you read admissions essays?

Currently for the 2012 admissions cycle, we will require two essays. Our essays focus on career path and future goals as well as community fit and personal values. Good essays answer the question, follow the directions, are clear and concisely written, and give us insight into who the candidate is and why he or she should be admitted. Bad essays often are not proofread, lack direction and clarity, are off topic, and can sometimes cover inappropriate topics or demonstrate lack of professionalism. We look for candidates who have a strong sense of what they want to do and how Smeal can help them achieve their career goals. Again, this goes back to "fit". Do they share our program's values and will they be successful here? The essays are also used to assess written communication ability and, in the case of international students, to evaluate command of the English language.

What kind of work experience do you look for? Does it necessarily have to be in a business field?

The field of work experience isn't necessarily a factor. In many cases, MBA seekers are also career changers, so work experience to date might not be a good reflection of future goals. We do want to ensure a candidate has a career path that makes sense, promotions and/or a progressive addition of responsibilities, evidence of leadership roles, positions that have required teamwork and critical thinking, and an overall career story that fits together with the resume. Flags can be raised because of things like job jumping, backwards career moves (demotions or excessive lateral position changes), and lack of any career progression over a long period of time.

What advice would you give students about whom to ask to write letters of recommendation?

As we can already see academic records (GPA and transcripts), it is highly preferred if at least one, in most cases, BOTH letters of recommendation are acquired from professional sources, including a current supervisor. If there is no letter from a current supervisor, it should be noted why that is the case in the additional information section. In the case of applicants who do not have a supervisor, such as those working as independent contractors or those who are business owners, a client or coworker recommendation may be acceptable. In general, the admissions committee wants to know what it is like to work with the applicant. If in doubt, you can always ask the program what is preferred.

When you look at transcripts, do undergraduate business majors have an advantage over those with majors in other fields? If someone's major wasn't in a business or related field, what would your advice be?

At Smeal, we are more concerned about how the applicants performed during their undergraduate career and if they are academically capable of the rigors of an MBA program. Only about one third of our incoming class has an undergraduate degree in business. We are looking for people who have work experience in different functions, industries, and positions, and we want to ensure a class that is diverse in multiple ways. For those who do not have a strong quantitative background, we recommend taking a refresher math course, like MBA Math, during the summer prior to starting classes. Our orientation at Smeal also includes a mandatory pre-term accounting course, so all incoming students are up to speed on what will be expected in the classroom whether they've had business classes during their undergraduate study or not.

How important is timing in the admissions process? In other words, do students who apply early have an advantage over those who just meet the deadlines?

Many MBA programs, including Smeal's, have rolling admissions. This means we evaluate applications and make admissions decisions as we receive materials (versus waiting until a specific date to start). While still competitive, applicants may find they gain a bit of an edge by applying early in the cycle while there are still many seats in the class available. Applying early, while important, should NOT be done at the expense of submitting a subpar application. If your application is ready for the first round and you feel it is your best effort, apply. If not, it might be in the best interest of the candidate to wait until deadline two if he or she can significantly improve the quality of their application during the time between deadlines.

What words of wisdom do you have for students who are considering applying to business school?

Visit. While we realize this is often costly and time consuming, nothing can replace seeing a business school and meeting the students who attend the program in person. The Internet has allowed us the means to connect with people around the globe, but there is no substitute for physically setting foot on campus and seeing firsthand a school at which you will invest the next two years of your life. The MBA degree is a substantial investment in an applicant's future, so spending the extra time and money to make sure you are getting exactly what you need and want will be worth it in the long run.

Jason Garner, Assistant Director
MBA Admissions
**The George Washington University
School of Business**
http://business.gwu.edu/

When is the right time for prospective students to start thinking about business school? Upon graduating from college? After a few years in the job market? Why?

It is never too early for students to begin thinking about attending business school, but competitive applicants tend to have a few years in the job market. This is because many business schools are looking for students who can participate in the classroom and bring their first-person experience to the table.

What is the value of an advanced degree in business—in today's society and in the future?

An advanced degree in business holds so many possibilities in today's society and beyond. The basic skills of leadership and the management of both financial and human resources are more relevant today across industries and sectors than ever before.

What are the most important factors that a prospective student should consider when researching business programs?

The most important factor to consider is the "fit" for a program. Can you see yourself in this program and will it help you to achieve your personal, academic, and professional goals? This could encompass a variety of factors from student experience, location, cost, full-time vs. part-time, academic focus of the school, and many more.

How heavily does your program weigh the following five admissions criteria: undergraduate grades, GMAT scores, work experience, letters of recommendation, and essays? Why do you place the emphasis where you do?

Our application process is holistic as we search for candidates who will be happy and successful in our programs. Each piece of the application tells us something about the applicant. The GMAT score and the undergraduate grades can serve as indicators of how a student will perform academically. The work experience of an applicant can provide insight into future classroom participation and student leadership, as well as the employability of an applicant after graduation. The essays and letters of recommendation allow for a qualitative view of an applicant.

How many essays does your program require the student to write? What kinds of questions do you ask? In your opinion, what is the difference between a good essay and a bad one? What do you look for when you read admissions essays?

We ask for two essays about the student's professional goals and a personal life experience. In these essays we are looking for someone with clear and well-thought-out goals who can articulate why an MBA from our university will help him or her succeed in these goals. A good essay will be clear and concise, whereas a bad essay will lack focus. Proofread your essays, and ask someone else to read them for you. They should be able to tell you what the essay prompt was just by reading your essay.

What kind of work experience do you look for? Does it necessarily have to be in a business field?

We are looking for professional experience where the applicant has taken some sort of leadership role and has experienced working in teams. This experience is not necessarily always in a "traditional business field."

What advice would you give students about whom to ask to write letters of recommendation?

We recommend that students ask their current supervisor for a letter of recommendation. For the second letter, we encourage students to be willing to think outside the box and consider letters of recommendation from places they are involved in their communities.

When you look at transcripts, do undergraduate business majors have an advantage over those with majors in other fields? If someone's major wasn't in a business or related field, what would your advice be?

No, business majors do not have a distinct advantage over other majors. We believe that a variety of undergraduate education backgrounds bring different perspectives and viewpoints that we value in our classrooms.

How important is timing in the admissions process? In other words, do students who apply early have an advantage over those who just meet the deadlines?

It never hurts to apply early for a program, provided that your application is as strong as it can be at that time.

What words of wisdom do you have for students who are considering applying to business school?

Be honest with yourself about what you are looking for and why you are seeing it. Visit schools and interact with the faculty, students, and staff to determine if the school is the right fit for you personally and professionally.

Alison Merzel, Director of
MBA Admissions
**Fisher College of Business
The Ohio State University**
http://www.cob.ohio-state.edu/

When is the right time for prospective students to start thinking about business school? Why?

Ideally, prospective students should consider going to business school once they have decided how it will help them achieve their personal and professional goals. Generally, this happens once they have had a few years of postbaccalaureate work experience. Students who have had the chance to work on teams, manage people or projects, and develop some technical expertise or proficiency in a particular area find that they are more prepared to benefit from the business school education. These students can more clearly articulate their goals, identify their strengths and weaknesses, and focus on the potential career paths they would like to follow upon graduation.

What is the value of an advanced degree in business—in today's society and in the future?

If you aspire to attain a leadership role in an organization, an advanced degree in business is going to help you get there. It will help you maintain a competitive edge against other candidates, and it will demonstrate to potential employers that you have the skill set and knowledge that is required to do the job. The MBA will provide you with the solid foundation that you need in each of the core business functions so that you can add value to your organization and be an active contributor in conversations with individuals at all levels about any aspect of the business. It will give you credibility and empower you to make strategic decisions that can move an organization forward. These are valuable skills in today's struggling economy and will continue to be important in the future.

What are the most important factors that a prospective student should consider when researching business programs?

The factors that you should consider when researching programs are really personal. Consider your priorities and evaluate how closely the programs you are choosing meet those priorities. Are you willing to relocate for two years to do a full-time program, or do you want to look locally? Is financial aid important to you? Are you interested in studying with students who come from all over the world, or do you prefer to be among those who are primarily regional to the school? If you are looking to change careers, you are going to be much more interested in a program's career management resources, networking opportunities, and access to employers. If you are a working parent, you are likely going to be more concerned about geographic location, time management, part-time options, and so on. Decide what you want the degree to do for you, and look for programs that can deliver on those goals.

How heavily does your program weigh the admissions criteria of undergraduate grades, GMAT scores, work experience, letters of recommendation, and essays? Why do you place the emphasis where you do?

The goal of the admissions process is to identify candidates who are going to be academically successful in our program and who are going to thrive in our program's culture. We carefully evaluate all of the components of the application process to make this decision. We use undergraduate grades and the GMAT score to determine whether we think a candidate will be able to handle the academic rigor of the MBA program, particularly from a quantitative and analytical standpoint. The essay responses and letters of recommendation help us understand the motivation for pursuing the advanced degree and the "fit" of the candidate's personality and interests with our school and its offerings. The work experience enables us to evaluate the candidate's readiness for the program and whether he or she will be able to contribute to classroom discussions and team projects. We really do take a holistic approach to evaluate someone's potential. We are trying to create a class of diverse students who are interested in becoming active participants in the Fisher and Ohio State community.

How many essays does your program require the student to write? What kinds of questions do you ask? In your opinion, what is the difference between a good essay and a bad one? What do you look for when you read admissions essays?

We require three essays, although one of them offers a fair degree of latitude and enables the candidates to be rather creative with the response. The essays are the part of the application that brings the candidate to life, so to speak. We prefer that the applicants stays true to themselves and answer the questions being asked as *they* would answer rather than how they think we would want it to be answered. We really want to get to know the candidate through the essay responses. Good essays provide a window into the candidate's personality, previous experiences, interests, hobbies, goals, strengths, weaknesses, etc. They provide this information without always blatantly spelling it out, too. Through the telling of the applicant's story, we should learn these things. We shouldn't read an essay that could easily be written for another person. The essays should be unique to the candidate and should show that the person has seriously researched the program and has thoroughly evaluated why this particular program is a good match for his or her goals.

What kind of work experience do you look for? Does it necessarily have to be in a business field?

Any experience that has enabled a candidate to learn and grow is good experience. We see candidates coming from every imaginable background and industry. Many of our students do not have experience in business prior to entering the program. The diversity of undergraduate majors and jobs of the incoming students adds to the overall quality of the learning experience. Think about how boring it would be for every MBA student in the class to have come from the same major and job. So much of the learning in the MBA classroom comes from your peers, so having diverse perspectives and ideas completely enriches the experience for everyone involved.

Ideally MBA candidates have worked in a job that has provided them with the opportunity to manage projects or supervise other people,

but that isn't always the case. Many prospective MBA candidates are looking for those managerial level positions, and that is why they are pursuing the MBA program—we understand that. Experience working in teams is certainly valuable, but it's also something that is a large focus of the MBA program. Regardless of what kind of work experience someone has, we are looking for evidence that the candidate has been successful in his or her previous employment, that he or she has developed strong communication and interpersonal skills, and that he or she is a high-potential leader.

What advice would you give students about whom to ask to write letters of recommendation?

We prefer professional recommendations over academic recommendations unless you are a recent graduate or have maintained a strong relationship with a professor or faculty member that could really speak to your potential for success in business school. Our first choice is to receive letters of recommendation from current supervisors, but we understand that sometimes the student does not want to inform their current supervisor that they are applying to business school. In this case, a previous supervisor or current colleague could be other viable options. We also would be happy to receive letters from clients or from individuals with whom you work in a nonprofit or community organization or extracurricular activity, if there is one that would be appropriate.

When you look at transcripts, do undergraduate business majors have an advantage over those with majors in other fields? If someone's major wasn't in a business or related field, what would your advice be?

When we look at transcripts, we assess the courses you took while in college to determine whether we think you will be able to handle the quantitative rigor of the course work in the MBA program. Certainly undergraduate business majors may have an easier time demonstrating their academic aptitude in business courses than non-business students. If you did not take very many quantitative courses in college, we will look to your GMAT score and your current job duties to evaluate your readiness for the program from an academic standpoint. Some applicants choose to enroll in undergraduate continuing education courses in accounting, finance, or statistics to demonstrate to the admissions committee that they have the quantitative aptitude that is required of the MBA program. On your resume, you can certainly highlight the job functions you perform that utilize the knowledge and skills that we would be looking for in an MBA candidate.

How important is timing in the admissions process? In other words, do students who apply early have an advantage over those who just meet the deadlines?

This is specific to each school you are considering. At Fisher, we have a rolling admissions process, so we make admissions decisions throughout the application cycle. It would definitely be to your benefit to apply early, as we have all of the seats available at the beginning, but certainly not towards the end. Furthermore, applicants who apply at the beginning receive priority consideration for merit-based financial aid opportunities.

What words of wisdom do you have for students who are considering applying to business school?

Talk to as many people as you can who are affiliated with the school (current students, alumni, and faculty and staff members). Visit the school. Consult with your loved ones. Trust your instincts.

Christine E. Sneva, Director
Admissions and Financial Aid
**Samuel Curtis Johnson Graduate
    School of Management
Cornell University**
www.johnson.cornell.edu/

When is the right time for prospective students to start thinking about business school? Upon graduating from college? After a few years in the job market? Why?

The time to consider business school is a personal decision. It can start as early as high school, while in college, or after a few years of work experience. It's more important to consider *why* you want to go to business school. That motivation will drive the right set of decision making for a candidate.

What is the value of an advanced degree in business—in today's society and in the future?

This is an important question today. There are many advanced degree programs in higher education that are saturated with a utilitarian approach to decisions around academic major and careers. This will have two affects:

1. It will influence fewer people to pursue a liberal arts education that can showcase broader skill sets such as communication and writing.
2. It will cause more graduate-level students to question their career decision making at the wrong time or late in their studies.

The advanced degree in business is the true generalist degree to pursue. You do not need to have earned a specific major to qualify or have a particular amount of work experience for most programs. Advanced business education is for the visionaries, artists, and idealists as much as it is for consultants, bankers, and entrepreneurs. Business education will continue to be dynamic within the walls of the institution.

What are the most important factors that a prospective student should consider when researching business programs?

Again I think this is a personal decision because all of these factors coincide with fit. If someone wants to continue working and not leave his or her location, these will be different considerations in their particular order of importance. Each candidate should be honest about what will help them thrive and grow personally and professionally. Most of the time it surprises people where they end up and why, but if someone is open and flexible, the possibilities are endless in terms of which program may be right for you.

How heavily does your program weigh the admissions criteria of undergraduate grades, GMAT scores, work experience, letters of recommendation, and essays? Why do you place the emphasis where you do?

Each of these areas is very important because they are all telling us something different about someone. As gatekeepers, we are tasked with the difficult decision of deciding who will be successful academically and professionally—which isn't always an obvious answer. It is critical for applicants to acknowledge and self-assess their weaknesses carefully so admissions committees will see the potential.

When I look at this list of criteria, I group them in two categories—what a candidate can control and can't control. Undergraduate GPA and work experience is difficult to control, but the other criteria allow individuals to really take control of how they present themselves. I think that is uplifting and very positive for candidates who are considering business school later in their career.

How many essays does your program require the student to write? What kinds of questions do you ask? In your opinion, what is the difference between a good essay and a bad one? What do you look for when you read admissions essays?

Essays are an exciting piece to the application. We have to ask about your goals and where you see the resources of Johnson fitting into these. You have to make that connection, and it's the only place in the application to show this. Our favorite essay is where we ask applicants to write the chapter headings to their life story. This is where applicants can be creative and personal. Many have said they were challenged about what to write while at the same time it was the essay they looked forward to writing the most. We love that! Lastly, we ask about the legacy you want to leave at Johnson and our community. This question is really looking for how you see yourself linking to our community inside and outside the business school. At Johnson, the culture is inclusive of Cornell and the surrounding community of Ithaca.

What kind of work experience do you look for? Does it necessarily have to be in a business field?

Increasingly, we are seeing more unconventional candidates who don't fit that business school applicant model. It is important to show evidence of success from your previous role and how this translates into what you want to do. You will need to do this in front of employers, so it's important to perfect this pitch.

What advice would you give students about whom to ask to write letters of recommendation?

The request for letters of recommendation is the only time where we ask for an outside opinion. If someone only focuses on a person's title, then the quality of the letter will not resonate with the reader. Therefore, we encourage applicants to choose those who can speak to their experience, provide specific examples, and be supportive of their decision to pursue business school.

When you look at transcripts, do undergraduate business majors have an advantage over those with majors in other fields? If someone's major wasn't in a business or related field, what would your advice be?

An undergraduate business major doesn't translate into a successful business school student. In fact, there is little evidence that shows that the undergraduate major is a predictor of success. GPA is a more accurate measure, but non-business majors shouldn't discount that they chose that path for a reason, and what you have accomplished after college is just as relevant.

How important is timing in the admissions process? In other words, do students who apply early have an advantage over those who just meet the deadlines?

For Johnson, students who apply early will be reviewed earlier. We do our best to get through our applications as soon as possible and many times before the published notification date.

What words of wisdom do you have for students who are considering applying to business school?

Be yourself. Be introspective and reflective. Be certain about what you want and expect from a program. Be open and flexible about changing your mind. Your peers, professors, and new colleagues will teach you more than what you expected to get out of business school.

Finding the Right MBA Program

Dr. William L. Rhey, Dean
Barney Barnett School of Business and Economics
Florida Southern College

Guidebook rankings. Student-to-faculty ratios. Internships. How will you decide which MBA program is best for you?

If you are reading this essay then you have already begun to research the perfect program. But have you clearly defined your future career goals yet?

If you have not, try to do it before you choose an MBA program since each program is unique in how it will prepare you for success. Students seeking a job as an investment banker on Wall Street with JP Morgan Chase may be a perfect match for a Wharton MBA, while students seeking the skills needed to manage large projects for a national retailer or lead an entrepreneurial family business or run a nonprofit organization will likely be better off pursuing a program that focuses on developing leadership and communication skills as opposed to econometrics and financial modeling.

MBA programs are not "cookie-cutter" offerings, and sometimes, even the subject matter can vary among courses listed under the same name at different institutions.

Choose carefully. Each MBA program offers a wide variety of academic courses, real-world business connections, and styles of teaching and mentoring. Different schools offer different levels of degree prestige. How well you benefit from the program you choose will depend greatly on the career path you follow.

In fact, you may be considering an MBA even though you don't have an undergraduate degree in business. Some MBA programs, including the one that we offer at Florida Southern College, are very appealing to this type of student, and here's why.

At Florida Southern (FSC), we focus on developing the softer skills needed for success in organizational leadership, whether that's a "for profit" business or a nonprofit business, and regardless of the size and scope of that organization. Our courses and expert faculty provide students with a global perspective every step of the way. Developing exceptional communication skills—whether written, verbal, or non-verbal—is paramount in FSC'S business program. We have experts who teach courses in emotional intelligence, management, project management, and diplomacy.

Our graduates leave FSC with the ability to see the "big picture". They understand how to develop solid team-building skills whether they are leading the team or joining that team as a member for the first time. Our students know how to take a project from A to Z, assess the results, apply their knowledge, persuade others with respect to the meaning of the outcomes, and improve future performance.

How do we do it? Our students learn by "doing". Top-notch internship opportunities are the hallmark of a Florida Southern MBA and should be for any institution that you are considering for your education.

Why? Classroom learning is made even more powerful when combined with experience in the real world. If you really want to be prepared for today's competitive marketplace when you graduate with your MBA degree, this real-world experience is critical and will set you apart from other job applicants.

Last year, Florida Southern MBA students partnered with a large and well-regarded local nonprofit organization to provide an in-depth consultation service; they created and published a detailed analytic report outlining strategies and tactics that are the foundation for the future of the organization. Another class planned, organized, and hosted fundraisers for United Way and the SPCA, raising $22,500 for the organizations while gaining invaluable experience and community contacts. Right now, FSC students are interning with such world-renowned corporations as Goldman Sachs, GEICO, PricewaterhouseCoopers, The Walt Disney Company, Publix Super Markets, and OPEC.

That leads me to my next point—networking. Much of your success in the business world will be reliant upon building relationships, making connections, and knowing who to turn to for assistance. Developing a broad network takes time, talent, and commitment. Your MBA program should offer you solid networking opportunities before graduation. Look for programs like FSC's CEO Leadership series, where current industry leaders come to campus to inspire our students; the Executive Mentor program, which provides students with a professional guide through the graduate school process; and an "active classroom" approach, which allows students to constantly interact with peers and professors as they perfect their interpersonal communication skills.

Finally, there is something in a name. This year, Florida Southern College was very proud to name its business school for an exceptional businessman, Barney Barnett, Vice Chairman of Publix Super Markets. Schools that have earned the support of highly accomplished, internationally recognized business leaders like Mr. Barnett are definitely worth taking a good, long look at as you narrow down your search. A well-named business school is often the first and best indicator of the quality of education you will receive should you decide to enroll.

Most importantly, as I mentioned at the start, be realistic about your career goals and define them to the best of your ability. Once you have done that, you can choose the type of MBA program that will best prepare you for your desired career path and provide you with a solid foundation of academics, real-world experience, and networking connections on which you can stand throughout your life.

Dr. William L. Rhey became Dean of the Barney Barnett School of Business and Economics in June 2010. Previously, he was Director of Business Graduate Programs and Professor of Marketing at the Sykes College of Business at the University of Tampa. He earned his M.B.A. at Baylor University and his Ph.D. at the University of Mississippi at Oxford.

Exciting Times in the Accounting Profession

Donald E. Wygal, Ph.D.
Department of Accounting
Rider University

These are exciting times to be an accountant. In fact, students who want to pursue a career in accounting will find even more interesting and diverse opportunities as they enter the profession. This makes the selection of a graduate program (and the contents of this guide) all the more relevant and important.

For over a century, accounting has played an important role in our economy. Because the internal record-keeping system maintains and reports information on transactions of the company, accounting is often referred to as "the language of business." In addition, because businesses and other entities (for example, not-for-profit and governmental agencies) all need to monitor and report their activities, the demand for accounting professionals extends to every sector of the economy. In more recent years, the influence of accounting has expanded even more as companies do business on a "global" basis.

In addition, accounting information has become increasingly important to investors, creditors, and regulators (to name only several groups who value the services of accountants). As a result, there is a growing list of specialty areas that may be pursued in accounting, including taxation, information systems, auditing, and management accounting to name only a few. Another emerging area is in fraud and forensic applications that can link perspectives from accounting, finance, and law. There are many possible certifications in the accounting profession as well. These include CPA (sponsored by the American Institute of Certified Public Accountants), CMA (Certified Management Accountant, sponsored by the Institute of Management Accountants), and Certified Internal Auditor (sponsored by the Institute of Internal Auditors). These are three of the most prominent certifications, but there are many others that can meet your needs, too. Certain types of certification require an educational foundation (more credit hours of study) beyond the undergraduate level. You will find it to be helpful to consider these requirements as you are searching for the "right" graduate program—if certification is part of your career plans.

Another reason for excitement about entering the profession is that "accountants" can now play a more active role in company decision making. Businesses have always valued the ability of accounting professionals to "speak the language of business." In recent decades, accounting graduates have been called upon also to apply their abilities in many decision-making areas.

I have personally observed this expanding role for accountants during the fifteen-year period I served as chair of the Department of Accounting at Rider University. I learned that many of our graduates had achieved career success in accounting by becoming partners in local, regional, and national public accounting firms. Others have gained prominence in additional settings, including corporations, financial institutions, and governmental agencies.

In all of these examples, our graduates have noted the expanding opportunities to extend the benefits of their technical accounting knowledge by leveraging additional skills they had developed. These include written and oral communications, interpersonal abilities, and (more recently) proficiencies with information technology applications. In addition, many graduates have noted that they started their career as an "accountant" and then went on to perform in a decision-making role as an executive. It may surprise you to learn that many of these graduates have become the "chief executive officer" of a business.

This underscores the importance of your selection of a graduate program that is most appropriate for you. Regardless of any specialty area you may wish to pursue, I encourage you to pay attention to how programs identify the way they will address your skill-building needs in the courses they offer. Then, if you are sure now of your desire to specialize in a field of accounting (such as auditing or taxation), there are likely to be programs that will emphasize these areas and may be just right for you. However, do not be surprised if your career interests and opportunities change in the foreseeable future.

For that reason, I encourage you also to consider programs that may prepare you more generally for a variety of future career paths in accounting while enhancing your skills development in the process. For example, the Master of Accountancy (M.Acc.) program at Rider University enables students to take accounting course work that allows them to prepare for many certifications. In addition, course selection choices include many possible business electives that enable each student to pursue his or her own more specialized interests. This type of established focus plus flexible options could be just what you are looking for in a program. This type of program could enable you to build upon the knowledge and skills you have developed as an undergraduate student to seize upon new opportunities in the world of business that are only now being identified.

Your selection of a graduate program in accounting is an important next step in the exciting journey you are about to begin.

Donald E. Wygal, Ph.D., is Chair of the Department of Accounting in the College of Business Administration at Rider University. He received his M.B.A. and Ph.D. from the University of Pittsburgh.

The MBA in Healthcare Management

Peter Hilsenrath, Ph.D.
Eberhardt School of Business
University of the Pacific

There were an estimated 615,000 management positions in American healthcare in 2008. A master's degree is a credential recommended for many of the more senior and challenging positions in this field. The MBA with a focus in healthcare is one of the most accepted of these qualifications. The University of the Pacific's Eberhardt School of Business in Stockton, California, offers an MBA with a specialized track in healthcare management.

The University of the Pacific MBA offers core training in management, information systems, marketing, accounting, finance, human resource management, and management science. Students can then concentrate on taking courses with particular applicability to the health sector. These include health insurance, international healthcare systems, health economics, and health law. The University of the Pacific also offers a PharmD/MBA program. This is a dual degree providing a fast track to both qualifications. It is well suited for the changing world of pharmacy practice.

Managerial employment in the healthcare sector is expected to grow faster than average over the next ten years. Some of this job growth will be in hospitals, but faster growth is anticipated for outpatient care including group practices and home healthcare. Job opportunities also exist for the MBA in healthcare management in sectors related to health care. Government agencies and pharmaceutical firms are sources of growth. New and challenging positions will become available in managed care support and insurance services as well as health information systems.

Healthcare managers work in a dynamic and rapidly changing environment. New technologies, financial pressure, regulation, and a complex institutional environment create a remarkable dynamic with much opportunity for those looking into these positions. A wide range of skills and competencies is desirable. Business schools can provide a comparative advantage in core management competencies and arguably better prepare graduates for careers in healthcare finance, marketing, and management information systems. The primary alternative to the MBA is the Master in Health Administration (MHA), which is commonly offered by schools of public health or health professions. These programs have some advantages and offer a greater familiarity with the culture and operations of health services. They also commonly provide a population-based perspective, with courses in epidemiology and public health, which is important for HMOs and other organizations that manage care.

Figure 1 shows the changing mix of new members joining the American College of Healthcare Executives from 1970 to 2010. The relative share held by those trained in business, health science, and other settings has been shifting. Graduates of business programs gained "market share" among new members of the American College of Healthcare Executives (ACHE) until the early 1990s. This share has been relatively steady since. Graduate business degrees accounted for about 24 percent of new members in 2010, whereas those with graduate degrees in health or hospital administration accounted for about 47 percent. The share held by graduates of health and hospital administration programs has been in decline since 1970 when it accounted for 89 percent of new members. Those with clinical training have been gaining market share in recent years. This group includes graduates of nursing, medicine, and allied health programs. They accounted for 18 percent of new members in 2010. The ACHE is reasonably representative of healthcare management but is somewhat weighted toward hospital employees where the master's in hospital or health administration (MHA) has stronger roots. There is another reason Figure 1 understates market penetration of MBAs. Those with an MBA who also hold an MHA, M.D., or other advanced clinical degree are classified into the MHA or clinical degree categories.

Graduate health management education has been a natural experiment. Business and health science settings have been competing and evolving since the mid-20th century. The MHA has yielded as the dominant qualification for higher-level healthcare management positions. However, this evolution has not resulted in a clear verdict about which academic setting is preferable, at least not yet. There are advantages to both business and health science models of healthcare management education. Business schools are tuition dependent and have been more oriented toward enrollment. Health science centers rely largely on patient revenue and external grant funding and are less sensitive to student demand. Business schools can more easily assure a sound management curriculum, but public health and other academic health settings better promote research, at least for topics found suitable by government agencies and private foundations.

Derived demand from employers will determine long run market outcomes for graduate health management education. Employers are subject to environmental influence and will tend to conform to industry standards. They are likely to adhere to standards they know and what others in their respective professional communities do. The competition between business schools and health science centers to

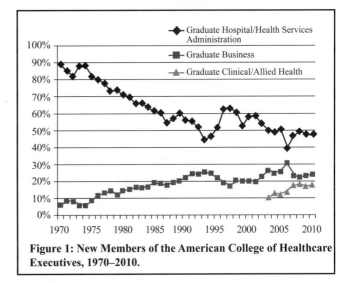

Figure 1: New Members of the American College of Healthcare Executives, 1970–2010.

produce managers will turn on how these standards and institutions evolve. The shape of the U.S. healthcare system remains unclear, in spite of recent landmark legislation. It is important to draw on what works best from each academic setting. Business schools should be more receptive to courses with substantial public health content, such as managerial epidemiology, behavioral health, and international health systems. In addition, there should be a more concerted effort to familiarize students with the culture and operations of health services. This may be problematic for business schools and may require collaboration with health service organizations. Business faculty accustomed to standardized MBA curriculum may not always readily accept sector specific offerings. However, such differentiation helps to meet the needs of students, society, and arguably the business schools themselves.

We welcome your interest in the University of the Pacific's Eberhardt MBA with a track in healthcare management. It helps provide the background necessary for management and leadership throughout the health and related sectors. The program, which integrates theory and practice, is accelerated and facilitates quicker and less costly completion of both degrees. New courses and opportunities are continually being developed. Contact us for additional information or questions.

––––––––––––––

Dr. Peter Hilsenrath is the Joseph M. Long Chair of Healthcare Management and Professor of Economics. He received his Ph.D. from the University of Texas at Austin. Prior to joining University of the Pacific in 2009, Dr. Hilsenrath was Professor and Department Chair of Health Management and Policy at the University of North Texas Health Science Center in Fort Worth. In addition, Dr. Hilsenrath served as Chief Economist for Syfrets Managed Assets in Cape Town in the mid-1990's and was on the research staff at the Center for Naval Analyses in Alexandria, Virginia, during the mid- to late-1980's. Dr. Hilsenrath teaches courses on finance, management, and economics in the health sector in the Eberhardt School of Business and the Thomas J. Long School of Pharmacy and Health Sciences.

Surviving the Application Process

Michele F. Kornegay

Different programs have different deadlines, so you'll need to stay organized throughout the application process. As you receive applications, you may want to file them in separate folders and note the program name and the deadline in a place where you can easily see them. Be sure to note whether the program has a rolling deadline, in which applications are reviewed as they are received and spots are filled until the program is full—or a firm deadline, for which your application must be submitted by a certain date.

Most schools and most business programs have a filing period for applications of about six to eight months. During this time, the department accepts applications, reviews them, and offers attractive candidates a spot in their program. With such a large window, are you better off applying earlier or later in the cycle?

Most admissions counselors advise that, when it comes to filing your application, earlier is better. In their opinion, an early application has a better chance for admission for several reasons. Most importantly, submitting your application early shows that you are really interested in the program—a surefire way to impress admissions committees.

Although it may not necessarily be the case, if you wait until the last minute to send in your application, it may leave the impression that you see the program as a last resort. If you take it down to the wire, there's also a greater chance that you may have to prepare your application hastily, something any admissions committee worth its salt is sure to notice, and view negatively. Remember, these people are professionals; they've reviewed thousands of applications over the years, so they'll recognize if you've rushed your application. This will not reflect well on your candidacy. The best applications are those that show readers that you have a well-thought-out plan for your future. A rushed application will make you look scattered and not very serious about the program.

Other good reasons for applying early: At the beginning of the process, there are more spots available. Inevitably, the majority of candidates wait until later on in the admissions window to apply, so as the deadline nears, you'll be competing for the (fewer) remaining spots with a greater number of applicants. Also, at the beginning of the application process, admissions directors have no idea about who will be applying to the program. This could work in your favor, since early on, your application will be judged more on its own merit than on how it compares with others.

TO HOW MANY SCHOOLS SHOULD YOU APPLY?

The business school application process can be fairly arduous, so you want to be sure that you apply to just the right number of schools. Too few and you may not be accepted to any; too many and you may go crazy filling out all those forms and writing all those essays! Make realistic choices. Look at the criteria of the schools in which you're interested and at your qualifications, and be honest with yourself. By all means, don't rule out your dream program if your GMAT is 10 points below their stated cutoff; however, if your GMAT is 50 points below the cutoff, your GPA is a point below their cutoff, and you don't have any real work experience, you might want to save yourself the effort.

Apply to a few reach schools (those that are long shots based on your academic record and other application materials), send more applications to probable schools (those to which you have a reasonable, realistic, and better-than-average chance of getting admitted), and send a few applications to your safety schools (those where you're sure you'll be accepted). Generally, safety schools won't be your first choices, but you may need to rely on them if you don't get accepted at your reach and probable schools. Don't, however, apply to any school that you wouldn't attend happily.

HOW DO BUSINESS SCHOOLS PICK STUDENTS?

When business schools review applications, they do not follow a magical formula, where GMAT + GPA + Work Experience + Personal Statement = Admissions. Schools are not just interested in the straight-A students with high GMAT scores. Most schools are looking to enroll an ideal community of students who will work well together in the program and benefit from the program's goals. Globalization in the field of business itself means that programs are looking for a more diverse student body that includes older students, women, minorities, international students, and students from small schools, big schools, Ivy League schools, and so on. This might all sound a little nebulous, but admissions directors want to enroll students that will be a good fit with their program. Every program has a different definition of what that good fit will be, based on a mix of professional, academic, and personal interests. If you've done your homework and are applying to those programs that you've determined will fulfill your career and personal goals, you're off to the right start. In other words, don't be discouraged from applying to a program just because your GMAT score falls slightly below the program's stated requirement. If all the other elements of your application show that you will be a valuable member of their team, your chances for admission will be favorable. By the same token, if you're an older applicant (more than 32 years old), you may feel that your chances for admission are lower because you do not represent the "typical" graduate student. On the contrary, in business school, older students are seen as offering professional experience, maturity, and real-world perspective—all highly valued in the business world.

So remember this when you're applying: At most schools, no single factor will count more than any other. As the old saying goes, "The whole is greater than the sum of its parts," and that's especially true in business school applications. Your tests scores, GPA, work experience, essays, and recommendations create a complete picture of your interests, strengths, and accolades. Weaknesses are over-shadowed easily by strengths in other areas, so be sure to show off those strengths.

THE ELEMENTS OF AN APPLICATION

Form and Fee

Application forms can be downloaded from a school's Web site, obtained through the mail, or submitted online. When filling out your application, whatever form it takes, remember that accuracy and neatness count. If you must handwrite it (and you should try at all costs to avoid this), make sure that your handwriting is legible. Check and double-check for typos, errors of punctuation, and other potentially embarrassing gaffs. You don't want to start off on the wrong foot with the admissions committee. You may want to photocopy the blank form several times and fill out a few drafts before you complete the copy that you'll submit.

Before you send the application, make a copy for your own records. Remember the fee. Ridiculous as it seems, admissions committees regularly receive lovingly prepared applications from well-meaning applicants who've forgotten to include the fee. No matter how well the rest of the application is prepared, this oversight simply doesn't look good.

Test Scores

Most business schools (but not all) require that prospective applicants submit scores from standardized tests, most often the GMAT, and the TOEFL, if you're an international student. The GRE is another admissions test that can help you get into grad business programs, including more and more MBA programs, throughout the world. When you take these tests, you'll be able to pick which schools you'd like your scores to be sent to; if you decide later on that you'd like your scores submitted to other schools, you'll need to make the proper arrangements to get them there.

Transcripts and Resume

You'll need to provide each program with a copy of your academic transcript from every school that you've attended. Don't forget to include transcripts from summer school programs, graduate work, or any classes you have taken since graduation. Allow at least a month to receive your transcript, and be ready to pay for each copy. Review your transcripts carefully to make sure that there are no mistakes, and remember to keep a copy for yourself.

Some programs will also ask you to include your resume or curriculum vitae (CV) as a summary of your work history. If you haven't updated your resume or CV lately, take the time to do so now. Include information about articles you have published or papers you have presented, volunteer work, and memberships and positions in professional societies. Have someone else review it for accuracy and spelling. Your resume or CV should highlight your accomplishments,

responsibilities, and career progression, if applicable. If possible, show evidence of managerial and leadership skills while portraying yourself as a team player.

For more information on resumes, along with a sample of a well organized MBA resume, check out **"The Importance of Resumes"** on page 17.

Letters of Recommendation

Most business programs will require you to submit two or three letters of recommendation from your present employer or professors. If you're not comfortable asking these people, you can submit recommendations from a coworker, a former boss, or someone else who can vouch for the quality of your work. When requesting recommendations, be sure to provide the recommendation writers with a summary of your accomplishments—perhaps your resume or academic transcripts—as well as some details about which programs you're applying to and the criteria by which you'll be judged. Supply them with labeled envelopes so they can seal the recommendations upon completing them. Give your recommendation writers plenty of time to write recommendations, as much as two or three months. Check in with them a month before the recommendations are due, and collect the recommendations from them yourselves; don't make them go to the trouble of mailing them for you.

Essays

By and large, all business programs ask candidates to respond to essay questions. The number varies from program to program; some ask candidates to provide just one personal statement that discusses their past and their goals, while others require candidates to respond to as many as five or more essay questions on separate topics. In general, admissions committees are looking for you to show them why you want to be admitted to their particular program, review your personal background and goals for the future, describe your accomplishments (and failures) and how they shaped you, and discuss activities that you enjoy outside of work and school.

Obviously, with some of these elements, you won't be able to exercise much control. The information you include on the form is basic information about you—your stats, so to speak, including your transcripts and test scores. You can't go back and change the grades you got in college (wouldn't it be great if we could do that?) or the scores you got on the GMAT. (Although you can take the test a few times, chances are that you won't improve your score that significantly with each try.) How, then, can you show the admissions committees who you really are—the brilliant person behind the so-so GPA from that little-known college in rural Any Town, USA? With your recommendations and your essays, that's how. You have total control over these elements. By choosing the perfect people to toot your horn and by doing some tooting of your own, you can turn an average application into an outstanding one and swing those admissions committees in your favor.

For more information on essays, along with a sample well-written essay, check out **"The Vital Role of Application Essays"** on page 20.

WHAT YOUR APPLICATIONS SHOULD SHOW ABOUT YOU

Academic Profile

Business programs want to admit those who can survive the rigors of their program. For this reason, they look at your undergraduate GPA, which reflects classroom achievement, and your GMAT score, which is an indicator of your aptitude. However, having a high GPA and GMAT score doesn't necessarily guarantee admission, nor does a lower GPA or GMAT score take you out of the picture. When reviewing your transcript, admissions committees will look not only at your overall GPA but also at the progression of your grades and the kinds of courses you took as an undergraduate. Did you work hard to improve your grades after a slow start—or did you lose steam in your final years? Did you take advanced courses as electives—or did you take easy introductory courses to beef up your GPA? Admissions committees will take note of this. They will also look to see if you've had any notable academic achievements or won any awards as an undergraduate or in the workplace. If this is the case, be sure that it's reflected on your application—if not in your transcripts, then in your essay, letters of recommendation, or resume.

Your undergraduate degree will have little effect on your chances for admission to most business schools, so don't think that your BA in English literature will be a hindrance. Remember that most advanced business degree programs offer, or even require, a core curriculum of basic business courses as part of the degree. However, you should be able to show that you have general skills in economics, calculus, and statistics. If you didn't take these courses as an undergraduate, show on your application that you are planning to do so before being admitted to the program.

Personal Qualities

Admissions committees want to see that you are a clear-headed individual who has taken the time to think about your future and your goals. For that reason, make sure that your application is consistent throughout—in what you're trying to say about yourself and your plans for the future. You'll be judged less favorably if you don't show a clear purpose or if you jump from idea to idea.

Along those lines, your application is a direct reflection of your ability to communicate with others—think of it as a high-level sales pitch. Communication skills are essential for business leaders. Your application is your only chance to show admissions committees how well you can communicate; this makes the essays especially important.

Your application should show that you have the motivation and commitment to complete graduate work in business.

Business programs are also looking for leaders who are capable of working as part of a team, so you'll need to show on your application that you have the right combination of initiative, ability to follow instructions, and capacity to work well with others.

Work Experience

The large majority of business programs want to see that you have a few years of solid work experience. In business school, you'll be called upon to contribute to class discussions and projects in meaningful ways, and work experience will provide a context for your interpretation of what you'll learn in the classroom. When reviewing your application, business schools will want to see not only where you worked, but what you did while you were there. Did you move up? Did you take initiative? How did your contributions to the companies you worked for make you invaluable to them? Obviously, if you rose up over the years from the mail room to the board room, this will show admissions committees that you've got what it takes to succeed not only in business but also in their program—initiative, drive, energy, and dedication. Committees also want to know about your membership in professional organizations, your positions within these organizations, and about research you've done in the field. All of this will paint a clear picture of you as a worker and, by extension, as a student.

Organization/Presentation

When you enter the world of business, you'll be called upon to present your ideas and the ideas of your company. How well you present yourself in your application will be an indication of how well you'll do at this task. Are you thorough? Did you supply the requested materials and the proper fee? Is everything spelled correctly? Check and double-check all the materials to make sure you haven't inadvertently sent the materials for another school. This is a huge mistake that will put a giant black mark on your application. Thoroughness and accuracy are key.

INTERVIEWS

Many schools require that you interview with admissions committees and faculty members before you are admitted to the program. If you're asked for an interview, you should be glad, since chances are that you've made it to the program's short list of candidates. Even if the program doesn't require it, going on an interview is another great way to take some initiative and swing the vote in your favor.

While interviewing, don't simply rehash your resume and transcripts. This is the perfect chance to tell the admissions committee something they *don't* know about you from your application. Before you go on the interview, think about the questions that you might be asked and how you'll answer them, especially the biggie: "Why do you want to go to school *here*?" Think about those things that you want the interviewer to remember about you. However, try not to prepare speeches, as this won't sound natural when you're sitting face-to-face with the interviewer. The interviewer wants to see that you'll fit into the program, so be yourself. You'll be more natural and appealing if you don't try to put on an act. However, even in a casual interview, certain things are *always* off limits: profanity, tasteless jokes, and discussions of sex or your love life.

Show the interviewer that you're well-versed about the program, and describe what you plan to contribute to it. Bring a copy of your resume or CV, your application (especially your essays), and any examples of your work that you feel are important. Don't ask about financial aid; the interview is not the time to discuss these details. Be proactive—before the interview, think of some questions that you'd like the interviewer to answer. Finally, dress professionally and be on time. The simplest rules are usually the most important. After you leave, be sure to write a thank-you note to the interviewer.

FIFTEEN TOUGH INTERVIEW QUESTIONS

1. Why an advanced business degree now?
2. Tell me why you think our program is the one that's right for you.
3. Describe some examples of how you've demonstrated leadership.
4. What are your career aspirations?
5. What do you do to relax?
6. Give three words that best describe you.
7. Why did you choose your undergraduate major? Do you regret it?
8. Describe instances where you've worked as a member of a team to get a job done.
9. What is your definition of success?
10. Describe someone who's been an inspiration to you.
11. Where do you see yourself five years from now? Ten years from now?
12. What do you find most frustrating about your present job?
13. Tell me about your biggest failure and how you rebounded from it.
14. What will you do if you're not accepted to this program?
15. So, tell me a little more about yourself....

DECIDING WHICH SCHOOL IS RIGHT FOR YOU

You've waged the battle, and the offers for admission are pouring in. Now it's time for you to decide which program you'll attend. With any number of attractive choices, you will face a daunting task. First, try to separate the hype from the reality. The programs that accept you will likely barrage you with phone calls, letters, and e-mails from admissions counselors, students, and faculty members. When they call, ask the questions that you've been dying to ask but could not in your interview. Now that they want you, the ball is in your court. Review the strategies that helped you pick schools. Of the schools that have accepted you, which meet the criteria you originally found most important? Have your criteria changed at all through the admissions process? Revisit each campus where you've been accepted, and really take a good look around. Attend special on-campus events that you've been invited to, and pick the brains of those in attendance. What do they like about the school? Do they think you'd be a good match there? Be sure to find out *all* the details about the costs of the program—and about any available sources of aid to help you pay for it—before you sign on the dotted line. Resist making a hasty decision; be sure that you've weighed all the facts before you make your final choice.

The Importance of Resumes

Darlene Zambruski, Managing Editor
ResumeEdge and JobInterviewEdge

With a wealth of candidates to consider and a limited number of slots available, admissions directors rely on more than test scores and essays to determine who will be the best fit for their school. Resumes play an important role in helping admissions directors arrive at their decision. A well-organized, professionally written resume that focuses on achievement rather than tasks can often mean the difference between acceptance and rejection.

Admissions directors, like hiring managers, know that past behavior is predictive of future behavior. Therefore, if you excelled in a school program, were selected for an internship, or held a leadership position in college, make sure you include that information on your resume. It proves to the admissions committee that you made good use of your time in school and added to the institution's prestige, which is certainly what they want for their programs.

Is a graduate school resume different from one you'd send to a hiring manager or a recruiter?

The answer is yes—in some cases. A notable exception is the MBA resume, which you can find a sample of on the following pages. Let's take a look at this kind of resume first.

A resume for an MBA program should be organized in much the same manner as one used to find a job. That is, you'd begin with an opening summary proving you're the ideal candidate for the position. Your proof should be demonstrated by including one, preferably two, recent, relevant, quantified accomplishments. It's not enough to say you're an expert in accounting. Perhaps you are. However, that statement is self-serving without proof to back it up. Therefore, you'd have to write something like this: Skilled accountant with expertise in IRS tax cases as demonstrated by saving XYZ company $200,000 in penalties during the 2010 tax season. With that one sentence, you've offered concrete evidence of your qualifications.

The next section of your MBA resume should include a special section with additional quantified accomplishments. If you've saved your company money or made it money, you need to showcase what you did and how you achieved it.

Following the accomplishments should be a Professional Experience section in reverse chronological order. That is, your most recent position listed first, followed by your next most recent and so on. Dates of employment, your job title, and your tasks should be included. In a resume for a hiring manager, you should include only 15 years of experience (10 if you're in IT). However, in an MBA resume, you can go back as far as you want provided the school doesn't have a page restriction for the resume. It's best to check each school to see what their guidelines are.

Lastly, on an MBA resume you'd list your educational experiences with your dates of graduation. High school information isn't necessary unless the school requires this information.

To see an example of an MBA resume, check out the sample on the following pages.

Graduate school resumes for other disciplines should be organized a bit differently. Although you'd begin with an opening summary proving that you would be an asset to the program, you should follow that section with information about your education, including GPA scores, internships, scholarships, etc. It's important to showcase how well you did in other school programs to prove that you will do well in a future class setting. As with the MBA resume, you can include an accomplishments section, but it's likely the achievements listed would focus on your academic success, rather than what you did professionally. Again, it's always wise to check with the schools' Web sites to determine what they most want to see in a resume.

Another detail to remember: There is no longer a one-size-fits-all-scenarios resume. This holds true for school admissions as much as it does for applying to jobs in the private or federal sectors.

Many individuals make the mistake of crafting one resume and using it to apply to any number of schools. Again, these institutions most likely have their own preference for resume length, what data is included or excluded, showcased, etc. It's unwise to ignore such directives. Your competition will surely not. Those candidates who will most likely enhance the school's reputation and programs will be selected. It certainly takes more time to tailor every resume to a particular school's preferences, but that kind of attention to detail will pay off in the long run.

Appearance is also important. Your resume should be formatted to align perfectly with your stated goal. If you're a creative person seeking to enter a graduate program in art or the performing arts, then your resume can be more visually stunning in appearance. If you're seeking an MBA or a graduate program in social work, psychiatry, mathematics, banking or the like, you'd be better served by a more conservative approach. First impressions are the most lasting; therefore, you want your resume to speak to your goal while at the targeted school. Even the choice of paper to print your resume on is important. Use a quality 20 lb stock with a watermark. Make certain that when you hold your resume up to a light source, the watermark is right-side up—that is, you can read it. Although it's a small detail, it does show professionalism.

Whatever graduate school program you're targeting, it's important to remember that a resume is a snapshot of you as the perfect candidate. If it's superbly organized, well written, error free and aesthetically pleasing, it can make an admissions director take notice of your application in what might be a sea of other equally qualified candidates.

Darlene Zambruski has been the managing editor of ResumeEdge since its inception in 2004, and the managing editor of JobInterviewEdge since it was launched in March 2010. She has authored more than 10,000 resumes/cover letters/CVs for clients at every career stage, from entry-level to corporate, and in every industry. She is also a featured expert on CareerSlingshot.com.

ZARA KAMAROV

774 First Street, #28 ~ Cambridge, Massachusetts 02138

617-555-1212   zkam@post.harvard.edu

HARVARD BUSINESS SCHOOL APPLICATION

Venture Capitalist ~ New Business Start-up ~ Executive Management

Dedicated, decisive, and unique Entrepreneur that started a company at 21 years old in 2001, and sold it for $3.5 Million to Timberline Venture Partners (NW Affiliates of Draper Fisher Jurvetson) in 2003, remaining on as CEO for two more years. As a holder of many patents and contributor to entrepreneurs, I have developed into a recognized consultant with early stage companies to help them obtain venture capital and develop strategies, business, operations, and lead them towards successful exit paths. Motivational leader and "hands-on" team contributor that develops trusting relationships through integrity, professional character, and industry expertise. Effective communicator and presenter that works with diverse individuals at every level.

Recognized for contributing in the following areas:

- ✓ Subject of case study for business students at Harvard, MIT, Babson, and Northeastern.
- ✓ Mentor for many entrepreneurs, including women in business, in the New England area.
- ✓ Contribute as a pre-business tutor at Harvard University and sat on career panels for undergraduate and graduate students.
- ✓ Member of The Indus Entrepreneurs (TiE) Network; invited to speak on venture creation; and contributed on an Expert Panel that evaluates business plans of other TiE members.
- ✓ Lecturer at the "Start-ups at MIT" class for undergraduates and business students at MIT.
- ✓ Active member of MIT's Entrepreneur's Club.
- ✓ Advisor to start-ups founded by Harvard Business School students and MIT Sloan students.
- ✓ Conduct networking sessions for Harvard undergraduates who have an interest in entrepreneurship.
- ✓ Review student business plans for Harvard and MIT's Entrepreneurship Contests.

PROFESSIONAL EXPERIENCE

VENTURE EXPERIENCE

SKYRIS NETWORKS, Cambridge, Massachusetts / Los Angeles, California   2001 - 2005
CEO and Member, Board of Directors, 2004-2005 (2-year contract post-acquisition)
Founder and CEO, Skyris Networks, 2001-2003 (sold company in 2003)

Operations and Entrepreneurial Management
- Raised funding and managed finances, legal, and corporate operations for this start-up company that developed distributed networking technology for digital media content distribution.
  - Recruited board of advisors, directors, engineers, sales, marketing and management team.
  - Grew this start-up and in two years sold to Timberline Venture Partners for $3.5 Million.
  - Stayed on as CEO for two years and grew venture capital backed company's products to generate business and revenues between $10-15 Million
  - Contributed as an Executive Team Member on Timberline Venture Partner's Stirling Bridge Holding Company and developed and wrote their Strategy and Operations Plan for 2004 and 2005.

Product Development and Management
- Executed business plan for a cost efficient content delivery solution for media distribution.
- Developed business relationships and tested products with Sony, IBM, Yahoo!, Don King Productions, MusicNet, Movielink, IFILM, Streamcast Networks, and Savantech.
- Created patent portfolio on distributed networking technologies and business models.
- Repositioned a free file sharing client as the cheapest and scalable channel for media and entertainment content distributors to connect directly online with a global consumer base.

HUB ANGELS INVESTMENT GROUP, Cambridge, Massachusetts   2004 - Present
Due Diligence / Investment Team Member
- Formulated recommendations and valuations for investments in early stage companies.
- Researched competitive landscapes and technologies in emerging markets.

PROFESSIONAL EXPERIENCE

VENTURE EXPERIENCE, (Continued)

HUB ANGELS INVESTMENT GROUP, continued
- Interviewed references to assess management teams and customer opportunities.
- Analyzed and reviewed business models, patents, contracts, and financials.
- Contributing as a personal investor in the Hub Angels Investment Fund in 2006.

STRATEGY AND BUSINESS DEVELOPMENT FOR START-UPS AND COMPANIES

SCAYLE, Seattle, Washington/San Francisco, California   2006 - Present
Founder and Consultant for Strategic Planning and Licensing
- Brought on to start this email infrastructure venture, co-founded by former investors and team members from Timberline Venture Partners, and credited by these investors as a Founder.

RELONA SEARCH TECHNOLOGIES, Boston, Massachusetts   2005 - Present
Strategy and Business Development Consultant
- Customized search technology with interactive web-browsing to capture and monetize interests and intents of web users and disrupt the web search market.
- Identified target buyers and led presentation and subsequent discussions regarding due diligence and terms for an acquisition.

VILLAGE SOFTWARE, Boston, Massachusetts   2005 - 2006
Sales Consultant
- Initiated and managed customer relationships with leading entertainment kiosk owners, suppliers, and manufacturers, which included $406 Million Photo-Me.
- Directed product design for wireless technology to remotely monitor, control, and service kiosks.
- Conducted demonstrations for digital imaging, games, and music downloads.

ENESUN INC., Needham, Massachusetts   2005 - Present
Director of Operations
- Oversee deployment of Content Distribution and Communications Network to save costs at the company.
- Work with CEO on unique and specific business development initiatives to increase revenues.

Advisor
- inoof (Online Web Services)
- Fundpeek (Financial portfolio management software)
- Pinya and Singlesnet (Online Social Networking Services)

EDUCATION

HARVARD UNIVERSITY, CAMBRIDGE, Massachusetts
A.B. Computer Science, June, 2001.
- Internships: IBM, India (1998); and Cisco Systems, San Jose, CA (2000)
- Co-invented, patented, distributed search and networking technology.
- Researched business models at HBS for distribution of media and entertainment content.
- Earned the distinction as Harvard Entrepreneurial Contest Runner Up.
- Wrote Business Plan for Skyris Networks.

COMMUNITY ACHIEVEMENTS

- *Nominated Finalist* for India New England Woman of the Year, 2005
- *Captained* India's State Basketball Team, 1989-1997
- *Participant,* Indian National Basketball Team, 1996

The Vital Role of Application Essays

Ryan Hickey, Managing Editor, EssayEdge.com

Applying to a graduate business program is no easy task. From recommendations and a resume to standardized test scores and transcripts, applicants must pull together a broad variety of information in support of their candidacy. Of all these distinct application components, nothing can benefit—or hurt—your chance of admission more than admissions essays.

While some may scoff at this notion, the application process today has evolved to place more and more emphasis on essays. With the number of highly qualified applicants to graduate business programs steadily increasing, admissions committees have had to adjust their methods of evaluating candidates and determining who to accept. Combined with a decrease in the weighting of standardized test scores, this means that your essays have never been more important. When an admissions committee is comparing two candidates with similar grades, scores, and work/education experience, essays are often the deciding factor in determining who receives a letter of acceptance and who is rejected or waitlisted.

Put yourself in the shoes of an admissions officer. Every year, you are faced with the daunting task of selecting an incoming class from thousands—more likely tens of thousands—of applications. If it were as easy as simply selecting the applicants with the best grades and scores, the job would be a breeze. In reality, however, graduate business programs receive applications from many more quantitatively qualified applicants than they have room for. That means they need other ways to separate applicants from one another and determine which ones will be the best additions to their programs. Essays are one of the application components they focus on most to make those difficult decisions.

Why are essays so vital? Simply put, they provide information that no other component of your application can. In addition, they provide that information in a distinctive form that tells the reader even more about you than general content alone. Everything from the stories you choose to share to the style and tone you write with gives the reader unique insights into your candidacy. While a resume can provide a great overview of your work and education history, along with a rundown of relevant skills, it does not provide intimate details about any of those elements. In an essay, on the other hand, you can share personal specifics about experiences that have shaped your life to this point. That is why so many essay prompts, particularly for business programs, ask you to talk about specific things that have happened to you in the past. From leadership positions and demonstrated teamwork to overcoming obstacles and mistakes, an essay should tell a unique story about something that has happened to you and how that event shaped your path toward a graduate business program. Information like that helps admissions officers who are reviewing your application get to know you beyond impersonal things like grades and test scores. They thus put substantial weight on the essays as they decide who is in and who is not.

For those reasons, it is imperative that you give your essays the time and attention they deserve. Submitting essays that are poorly written, contain dull stories, or include writing errors can have a substantial negative impact on your overall chance of admission. Because essays do not have to be scheduled in advance like a standardized test and because many applicants find it difficult to decide where to even begin writing, essays are all-too-often left until the last minute. Instead of making this mistake, recognize the importance of your essays and make them a priority as you complete your applications. By the time you apply to a graduate business program, it is too late to go back and increase your grades or test scores; instead, focus on writing outstanding essays that will capture a reader's attention and help your application stand out from the crowd.

If you are writing essays for a graduate business school application, there are three simple tips that can help you ensure that your finished work is as strong as it can be. These are relevant no matter where you are applying and no matter what you are writing about; every applicant should follow them in order to make the most of this vital part of the admissions packet.

1. **Give yourself time to write.** The earlier you start, the better your essays will be. Having more time means that you can try several different options before settling on a direction. Then, you can progress through multiple drafts of your essay to get everything just right for submission. Most importantly, writers who are not rushed find that ideas come more easily; removing the stress of working under an impending deadline will make the writing process more effective and enjoyable.

2. **Be personal.** Admissions officers do not want to read an essay that is simply your resume in essay form. Go beyond general listings of things you have done to share more detailed elements of those events. Focus on things like learning experiences, overcoming challenges, discovering or better understanding a passion (or even weakness), or establishing career goals to really capture the reader's attention.

3. **Proofread, proofread, proofread.** Too many applicants neglect this simple but vital advice and submit essays that include glaring, easy-to-catch errors with their applications. When you think your essay is perfect, proofread it one more time. Then, find a friend, colleague, or anyone else who is a good writer and have them proofread it. Finally, check it over once more yourself before you submit it. The small amount of extra time it takes will be completely worth it.

The following is an example of a very strong business school admissions essay. Like most essay prompts on business school applications, this one is very specific. It asks about a time in the candidate's life when he or she faced an ethical dilemma. As a result, writing a successful essay on a topic like this requires the applicant to be extremely detailed in describing a first-hand experience. Admissions committees want to be confident that applicants have faced the broad variety of situations one can expect to encounter in both business school and business careers; this means that the key to crafting a successful essay is showcasing your experience. Whether you are discussing an ethical dilemma, leadership position, team-based initiative, professional failure, or something totally different, be sure to focus on painting a vivid picture of what happened and how you handled it.

This author worked with an EssayEdge MBA specialist to revise the essay before submitting it. You can receive your own personalized guidance by visiting the EssayEdge Web site.

Because business school essays like this usually include a word limit—this one is a maximum of 400 words—applicants must also be economical in their writing. When this author started, his first draft was almost 700 words long. Through consultation with his EssayEdge editor, however, he was able to reduce it to roughly 380 words. Even though the finished essay was 300 words shorter, it was even more effective than the original because it did not include any unnecessary content. Submitting essays that exceed set word, character, or other length limits will negatively impact your application.

Business school essays need to sound professional, present clear evidence of your accomplishments and abilities, and not waste words. This one does all of those things and is a great example of a strong essay in this market.

———————————————

Ryan Hickey is the managing editor of EssayEdge.com, which has been the premier provider of admissions essay editing services on the Internet since 1997. EssayEdge has experienced, professional editors ready to help individuals make the most of their admissions essays—from a single proofread to multiple weeks of one-on-one writing consultation. Visit EssayEdge at http://www.essayedge.com.

Describe an ethical dilemma you have experienced firsthand. Discuss how you thought about and managed the situation. (400 words maximum)

While working at Kagan Networks, I experienced an extremely challenging ethical situation. The Kagan internship program entailed a rigorous selection process; those selected were then assigned to different teams within the company. The process was extremely competitive because outstanding interns had an excellent chance of being hired at the internship's conclusion. Team managers based hiring decisions on firsthand observations and feedback from the intern supervisor.

That year, I was asked to supervise the two interns assigned to my team, Avi and Kyle. I interacted with them daily, thus becoming friendly with both and keenly aware of their capabilities.

As the internship neared its end, our HR manager called me to his office. Assuming he simply wanted my input regarding the interns, I was surprised when the manger told me that he knew Kyle's family and had helped Kyle secure the internship due to his family's recent financial struggles. He then asked that I recommend Kyle over Avi since the firm only needed one of the two.

That meeting left me pondering a challenging ethical dilemma. On the one hand, I considered Avi the more deserving candidate and knew it was in the best interest of the company that I recommend him. On the other, I sincerely sympathized with Kyle. He was a solid candidate despite being less impressive than Avi, and I was confident he would do well over time. After carefully considering the matter, I ultimately decided to recommend Avi; regardless of how I felt about Kyle's family situation, it was my duty to provide an unbiased assessment of intern performance, act in the company's best interests, and reward Avi's excellence. Even after making this difficult decision, however, I also strived to help Kyle.

At that time, our firm had long planned to automate some test cases, which would require a specialized employee who would then be responsible for subsequently adding test cases to the test framework when new features were added. Because of a resource crunch, though, those plans had never come to fruition. Recognizing this as an opportunity, I discussed the issue with my manager and the engineering director, suggesting that since Kyle had worked on the test framework as part of his internship, he would be an ideal candidate to carry out the test automation. Thanks to my efforts, the director ultimately approved hiring both of my interns.

The range of financial support at the graduate level is very broad. The following descriptions will give you a general idea of what you might expect and what will be expected of you as a financial support recipient.

FELLOWSHIPS, SCHOLARSHIPS, AND GRANTS

These are usually outright awards of a few hundred to many thousands of dollars with no service to the institution required in return. Fellowships and scholarships are usually awarded on the basis of merit and are highly competitive. Grants are made on the basis of financial need or special talent in a field of study. Many fellowships, scholarships, and grants not only cover tuition, fees, and supplies but also include stipends for living expenses with allowances for dependents. However, the terms of each should be examined because some do not permit recipients to supplement their income with outside work. Fellowships, scholarships, and grants may vary in the number of years for which they are awarded.

In addition to the availability of these funds at the university or program level, many excellent fellowship programs are available at the national level and may be applied for before and during enrollment in a graduate program. A listing of many of these programs can be found at the Council of Graduate Schools' Web site: http://www.cgsnet.org. There is a wealth of information in the "Programs" and "Awards" sections.

ASSISTANTSHIPS AND INTERNSHIPS

Many graduate students receive financial support through assistantships, particularly involving teaching or research duties. It is important to recognize that such appointments should not be viewed simply as employment relationships but rather should constitute an integral and important part of a student's graduate education. As such, the appointments should be accompanied by strong faculty mentoring and increasingly responsible apprenticeship experiences. The specific nature of these appointments in a given program should be considered in selecting that graduate program.

Teaching Assistantships

These usually provide a salary and full or partial tuition remission and may also provide health benefits. Unlike fellowships, scholarships, and grants, which require no service to the institution, teaching assistantships require recipients to provide the institution with a specific amount of undergraduate teaching, ideally related to the student's field of study. Some teaching assistants are limited to grading papers, compiling bibliographies, taking notes, or monitoring laboratories. At some graduate schools, teaching assistants must carry lighter course loads than regular full-time students.

Research Assistantships

These are very similar to teaching assistantships in the manner in which financial assistance is provided. The difference is that recipients are given basic research assignments in their disciplines rather than teaching responsibilities. The work required is normally related to the student's field of study; in most instances, the assistantship supports the student's thesis or dissertation research.

Administrative Internships

These are similar to assistantships in application of financial assistance funds, but the student is given an assignment on a part-time basis, usually as a special assistant with one of the university's administrative offices. The assignment may not necessarily be directly related to the recipient's discipline.

Residence Hall and Counseling Assistantships

These assistantships are frequently assigned to graduate students in psychology, counseling, and social work, but they may be offered to students in other disciplines, especially if the student has worked in this capacity during his or her undergraduate years. Duties can vary from being available in a dean's office for a specific number of hours for consultation with undergraduates to living in campus residences and being responsible for both counseling and administrative tasks or advising student activity groups. Residence hall assistantships often include a room and board allowance and, in some cases, tuition assistance and stipends. Contact the Housing and Student Life Office for more information.

HEALTH INSURANCE

The availability and affordability of health insurance is an important issue and one that should be considered in an applicant's choice of institution and program. While often included with assistantships and fellowships, this is not always the case and, even if provided, the benefits may be limited. It is important to note that the U.S. government requires international students to have health insurance.

THE GI BILL

This provides financial assistance for students who are veterans of the United States armed forces. If you are a veteran, contact your local Veterans Administration (VA) office to determine your eligibility and to get full details about benefits. There are a number of programs that offer educational benefits to current military enlistees. Some states have tuition assistance programs for members of the National Guard. Contact the VA office at the college for more information.

FEDERAL WORK-STUDY PROGRAM (FWS)

Employment is another way some students finance their graduate studies. The federally funded Federal Work-Study Program provides eligible students with employment opportunities, usually in public and private nonprofit organizations. Federal funds pay up to 75 percent of the wages, with the remainder paid by the employing agency. FWS is available to graduate students who demonstrate financial need. Not all schools have these funds, and some only award them to undergraduates. Each school sets its application deadline and work-study earnings limits. Wages vary and are related to the type of work done. You must file the Free Application for Federal Student Aid (FAFSA) to be eligible for this program.

LOANS

Federal Direct Loans

Federal Direct Stafford Loans

The Federal Direct Stafford Loan Program offers low-interest loans to students with the Department of Education acting as the lender.

There are two components of the Federal Stafford Loan program. Under the *subsidized* component of the program, the federal government pays the interest on the loan while you are enrolled in graduate school on at least a half-time basis, during the six-month grace period after you drop below half-time enrollment, as well as during any period of deferment. Under the *unsubsidized* component of the program, you pay the interest on the loan from the day proceeds are issued. Eligibility for the federal subsidy is based on demonstrated financial need as determined by the financial aid office from the information you provide on the FAFSA. A cosigner is not required, since the loan is not based on creditworthiness.

Although *unsubsidized* Federal Direct Stafford Loans may not be as desirable as *subsidized* Federal Direct Stafford Loans from the student's perspective, they are a useful source of support for those who may not qualify for the subsidized loans or who need additional financial assistance.

Graduate students may borrow up to $20,500 per year through the Direct Stafford Loan Program, up to a cumulative maximum of $138,500, including undergraduate borrowing. This may include up to $8,500 in *subsidized* Direct Stafford Loans annually, depending on eligibility, up to a cumulative maximum of $65,500, including undergraduate borrowing. The amount of the loan borrowed through the *unsubsidized* Direct Stafford Loan Program equals the total amount of the loan (as much as $20,500) minus your eligibility for a *subsidized* Direct Loan (as much as $8,500). You may borrow up to the cost of attendance at the school in which you are enrolled or will attend, minus estimated financial assistance from other federal, state, and private sources, up to a maximum of $20,500.

Direct Stafford Loans made on or after July 1, 2006, carry a fixed interest rate of 6.8% both for in-school and in-repayment borrowers.

A fee is deducted from the loan proceeds upon disbursement. Loans with a first disbursement on or after July 1, 2010, have a borrower origination fee of 1 percent. The Department of Education offers a 0.5

percent origination fee rebate incentive. Borrowers must make their first twelve payments on time in order to retain the rebate.

Under the *subsidized* Federal Direct Stafford Loan Program, repayment begins six months after your last date of enrollment on at least a half-time basis. Under the *unsubsidized* program, repayment of interest begins within thirty days from disbursement of the loan proceeds, and repayment of the principal begins six months after your last enrollment on at least a half-time basis. Some borrowers may choose to defer interest payments while they are in school. The accrued interest is added to the loan balance when the borrower begins repayment. There are several repayment options.

Federal Perkins Loans

The Federal Perkins Loan is available to students demonstrating financial need and is administered directly by the school. Not all schools have these funds, and some may award them to undergraduates only. Eligibility is determined from the information you provide on the FAFSA. The school will notify you of your eligibility.

Eligible graduate students may borrow up to $6,000 per year, up to a maximum of $40,000, including undergraduate borrowing (even if your previous Perkins Loans have been repaid). The interest rate for Federal Perkins Loans is 5 percent, and no interest accrues while you remain in school at least half-time. There are no guarantee, loan, or disbursement fees. Repayment begins nine months after your last date of enrollment on at least a half-time basis and may extend over a maximum of ten years with no prepayment penalty.

Federal Direct Graduate PLUS Loans

Effective July 1, 2006, graduate and professional students are eligible for Graduate PLUS loans. This program allows students to borrow up to the cost of attendance, less any other aid received. These loans have a fixed interest rate of 7.9 percent, and interest begins to accrue at the time of disbursement. The PLUS loans do involve a credit check; a PLUS borrower may obtain a loan with a cosigner if his or her credit is not good enough. Grad PLUS loans may be deferred while a student in school and for the six months following a drop below half-time enrollment. For more information, contact your college financial aid office.

Deferring Your Federal Loan Repayments

If you borrowed under the Federal Direct Stafford Loan Program, Federal Direct PLUS Loan Program, or the Federal Perkins Loan Program for previous undergraduate or graduate study, your payments may be deferred when you return to graduate school, depending on when you borrowed and under which program.

There are other deferment options available if you are temporarily unable to repay your loan. Information about these deferments is provided at your entrance and exit interviews. If you believe you are eligible for a deferment of your loan payments, you must contact your lender or loan servicer to request a deferment. The deferment must be filed prior to the time your payment is due, and it must be refiled when it expires if you remain eligible for deferment at that time.

Supplemental (Private) Loans

Many lending institutions offer supplemental loan programs and other financing plans, such as the ones described here, to students seeking additional assistance in meeting their education expenses. Some loan programs target all types of graduate students; others are designed specifically for business, law, or medical students. In addition, you can use private loans not specifically designed for education to help finance your graduate degree.

If you are considering borrowing through a supplemental or private loan program, you should carefully consider the terms and be sure to "read the fine print." Check with the program sponsor for the most current terms that will be applicable to the amounts you intend to borrow for graduate study. Most supplemental loan programs for graduate study offer unsubsidized, credit-based loans. In general, a credit-ready borrower is one who has a satisfactory credit history or no credit history at all. A creditworthy borrower generally must pass a credit test to be eligible to borrow or act as a cosigner for the loan funds.

Many supplemental loan programs have minimum and maximum annual loan limits. Some offer amounts equal to the cost of attendance minus any other aid you will receive for graduate study. If you are planning to borrow for several years of graduate study, consider whether there is a cumulative or aggregate limit on the amount you may borrow. Often this cumulative or aggregate limit will include any amounts you borrowed and have not repaid for undergraduate or previous graduate study.

The combination of the annual interest rate, loan fees, and the repayment terms you choose will determine how much you will repay over time. Compare these features in combination before you decide which loan program to use. Some loans offer interest rates that are adjusted monthly, some quarterly and some annually. Some offer interest rates that are lower during the in-school, grace, and deferment periods and then increase when you begin repayment. Some programs include a loan "origination" fee, which is usually deducted from the principal amount you receive when the loan is disbursed and must be repaid along with the interest and other principal when you graduate, withdraw from school, or drop below half-time study. Sometimes the loan fees are reduced if you borrow with a qualified cosigner. Some programs allow you to defer interest and/or principal payments while you are enrolled in graduate school. Many programs allow you to capitalize your interest payments; the interest due on your loan is added to the outstanding balance of your loan, so you don't have to repay immediately, but this increases the amount you owe. Other programs allow you to pay the interest as you go, which reduces the amount you later have to repay. The private loan market is very competitive, and your financial aid office can help you evaluate these programs.

APPLYING FOR NEED-BASED FINANCIAL AID

Schools that award federal and institutional financial assistance based on need will require you to complete the FAFSA and, in some cases, an institutional financial aid application.

If you are applying for federal student assistance, you *must* complete the FAFSA. A service of the U.S. Department of Education, the FAFSA is free to all applicants. Most applicants apply online at www.fafsa.ed.gov. Paper applications are available at the financial aid office of your local college.

After your FAFSA information has been processed, you will receive a Student Aid Report (SAR). If you provided an e-mail address on the FAFSA, this will be sent to you electronically; otherwise, it will be mailed to your home address.

Follow the instructions on the SAR if you need to correct information reported on your original application. If your situation changes after you file your FAFSA, contact your financial aid officer to discuss amending your information. You can also appeal your financial aid award if you have extenuating circumstances.

If you would like more information on federal student financial aid, visit the FAFSA Web site or download the most recent version of *Funding Education Beyond High School: The Guide to Federal Student Aid* at http://studentaid.ed.gov/students/publications/student_guide/index.html. This guide is also available in Spanish.

The U.S. Department of Education also has a toll-free number for questions concerning federal student aid programs. The toll-free number is 800-4-FED AID (800-433-3243). If you are hearing impaired, you may call 800-730-8913 (toll-free).

SUMMARY

Remember that these are generalized statements about financial assistance at the graduate level. Because each institution allots its aid differently, you should communicate directly with the school and the specific department of interest to you. It is not unusual, for example, to find that an endowment vested within a specific department supports one or more fellowships. You may fit its requirements and specifications precisely.

Returning to School

Barbara B. Reinhold, Ed.D.
Former Director of Career Development
and Executive Education for Women
Smith College

Some decisions can be made and implemented quickly—you can often choose a new car, a new place to live, or even a new relationship rather impetuously and have it work out just fine. For the returning student, however, the process of deciding on and applying to school, and then earning an advanced business degree is seldom simple. It has to be done with a great deal of forethought.

The good news about being a mature student is that you'll probably get much more out of it, because there is more of you to take to the classroom—more experience, better judgment, clearer goals, and a greater appreciation for learning. The bad news is that your life will be more "squeezed" than it would have been before you took on all of life's responsibilities, particularly balancing work and family. In general, however, later is often better than sooner when it comes to getting a graduate-level business degree.

For mature women and men alike, there are many things to consider before upending your life to pursue an advanced business degree. First, be sure you really need one. It is silly to waste your time and resources being "retooled" in a graduate-level business program if your career goals could be accomplished just as easily by taking targeted courses, getting more training and supervision through your employer, or using your connections to enter a different field or organization and move up. If you are trying to determine whether an advanced business degree is really the key to where you want to go, find ways to network with people whose lives and career goals are similar to yours. You might discover that a variety of routes could lead you to your desired goal.

It's essential that you make your own decision about whether and where to apply, using a blend of logic and intuition. Though an advanced business degree requires strong quantitative skills, you'll also need good organizational, decision-making, and communication skills. For returning students, success in an advanced business degree program is often due more to life and work experience than technical knowledge alone. You have more information, more common sense, and more self-awareness at your disposal than you did as an undergraduate student. Use these assets along with your intuition in deciding whether this is really the right step for you.

It's also important to be an informed and demanding customer at the front end of the process. Be sure to ask hard questions about how well a school is prepared to respond to the particular concerns you might have, such as cultural openness, support for students who are also parents, and flexibility and accommodations of various types. The ball will be in their court later; in the first half of the game, however, be aggressive about getting the information you need. For more mature students, the philosophy, resources, and services of the school can be much more important than ranking or reputation.

The application stage is also a great time to practice your marketing skills. This may be the first of many times when you'll have to convince someone of your worth. For returning students this is often frightening. Some have been out of the job market for awhile, while others either want to change careers or are feeling stuck at a career plateau. Any of these situations is likely to leave you feeling less than competitive. This is a good time to figure out what you really have to offer to a particular school and to adjust to the notion of lifelong self-advocacy.

As you begin the difficult task of self-assessment, be honest about your strengths and weaknesses. If your technical, quantitative, or communication competencies are not what they should be in order for you to begin course work in a confident frame of mind, spend a year or so getting up to speed in these areas. You'll be expected to be familiar with the basics of accounting. Much of your work may be online and you'll be required to use programs such as Excel, Access, and PowerPoint. So use the time after you have completed your applications to do some studying on your own and become comfortable with these disciplines before you even enroll!

Once enrolled, you can do two things to make your life easier. First, take an honest look at your own learning style. Try to determine which methods work best for you; use methods that fit your personality—outlines, memorizing, listening to tapes, discussing concepts with other people, etc. Be proactive and establish a routine. As a returning student with many other responsibilities, you'll need to take a different approach to studying than you did in undergraduate school.

You'll also find that connecting with classmates is a critical part of doing well. You may be assigned to project teams, but it's a good idea to seek out your own support group as well. Join study groups and relevant student organizations, even though it may seem you can't spare the time. In business school, as in business itself, collaboration and networking are everything!

Becoming a student again is a great adventure—earning an advanced business degree will tax you, test you, stretch you, and reward you. But only you can know if it's right for you. When you applied to college as a high school student, you thought you had all the answers. What's different now is that, although you still don't have all the answers, you probably know much more than you think.

TEN TIPS FOR RETURNING STUDENTS

Deciding

1. Be sure an advanced business degree is the best route to where you're going—don't embark on a trip until your destination is clear.
2. Make your own decision, using a blend of logic and intuition.
3. Be a discerning customer; ask hard questions about which programs best meet your specific needs.

Arriving

4. Learn to market yourself; don't launch the campaign until you're ready.
5. Be sure your support system is in order—at home and at work.
6. Review your skills—technical, quantitative, written, and oral. If you're not really ready, take an extra year to polish those skills.
7. Measure your confidence level—if it's low, consider counseling to learn how to manage your anxieties and self-doubts.
8. Get your life in shape before you begin—paying attention to nutrition, exercise, relationships, and all the other things you'll need to sustain you.

Thriving

9. Ascertain your most effective learning style and design routines and study regimens that best fit that style.
10. Find a group of friends/colleagues right away; collaboration is the key to success and good health through one of the most demanding experiences you'll ever have.

Graduate Business Programs

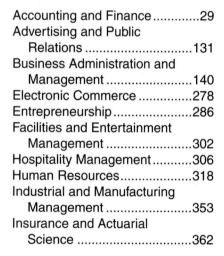

Accounting and Finance

OVERVIEW

The study of finance involves determining what to invest in, how much to invest, where to obtain funds, and how capital markets work. Accounting MBA programs concentrate on skills in the management of both fiscal and human resources within companies, making graduates an invaluable resource for not only private businesses, but also within public organizations and nonprofit groups. Students in an accounting MBA program gain in-depth knowledge in a variety of subjects including financial assessment and reporting, taxation, risk management, planning, and implementation. Most programs also offer courses focused on building and refining management and leadership skills. Graduates of accounting MBA programs are prepared to work in fast-paced and demanding positions in the accounting world, either within an existing company or through their own businesses. While an accounting MBA does not equate with being a professional auditor, it does prepare graduates to make decisions related to budgeting and accounting for planning purposes in myriad organizations.

Required courses may include study in:

- Business Law and Taxation for Accountants
- Corporate Finance
- Leadership and Teamwork
- Marketing Management
- Operations Management

Elective courses may include study in:

- Business Practicum
- Business Process Modeling
- Computer Concepts and Applications
- Enterprise Resource Planning
- Industry Analysis for Strategic Planning
- Lean Accounting Transformation for Accountants
- U.S. and International Accounting Practices

Accounting is an in-demand field, with businesses from large financial firms to small corporations needing accounting services to keep books, taxes, and other financial issues in order. Whether working with numbers or managing other accountants within a business, an accounting MBA prepares graduates for career opportunities managing the finances of industrial, commercial, and marketing enterprises; insurance companies; and government, hospitals, and other not-for-profit service institutions in roles such as public accountant, industrial accountant, and health-care auditor. For students with interests in the area of investment, career opportunities with investment banks, security dealers, brokerage firms, pension funds, insurance companies, and investment funds are all viable options. Specialized finance careers are also available with financial intermediaries such as commercial banks, savings and loans, and investment banks.

With an MBA in accounting, the career options are almost limitless. Any company that is looking to make a profit will benefit from an employee with a thorough understanding of accounting procedures, practices, and laws.

HELPFUL ORGANIZATIONS/ PUBLICATIONS/BLOGS

Financial Management Association International (FMA)

http://www.fma.org/

The Financial Management Association International (FMA) is the global leader in developing and disseminating knowledge about financial decision-making. FMA's members include academicians and practitioners worldwide. FMA serves the global finance community by:

- Promoting the development and understanding of high-quality basic and applied research and sound financial practices.
- Facilitating interaction and relationships among those who share a common interest in finance.
- Encouraging and supporting quality financial education.
- Sponsoring annual finance conferences that provide a chance to get together with colleagues, present current research and receive feedback, observe the presentations of others, and visit interesting places.

Financial Executives International (FEI)

http://www.financialexecutives.org/

Financial Executives International's (FEI) mission is to advance the success of senior-level financial executives, their organizations, and the profession. FEI strives to be recognized globally as the leading organization for senior-level financial executives. Since 1931, FEI has been connecting members through:

- Interaction by providing local and international forums for connecting with peers.
- Information by providing insight to assist with informed business decisions.
- Influence by providing authoritative representation for members' interests.
- Integrity by providing the tools to advance the profession through ethical leadership.

American Accounting Association

http://aaahq.org/index.cfm

The American Accounting Association promotes worldwide excellence in accounting education, research, and practice. Founded in 1916 as the American Association of University Instructors in Accounting, its present name was adopted in 1936. The Association is a voluntary organization of persons interested in accounting education and research.

American Institute of Certified Public Accountants (AICPA)

http://www.aicpa.org/

The American Institute of Certified Public Accountants (AICPA) is the world's largest association representing the accounting profession, with nearly 370,000 members in 128 countries. AICPA members represent many areas of practice, including business and industry, public practice, government, education and consulting; membership is also available to accounting students and CPA candidates. The AICPA sets ethical standards for the profession and U.S. auditing standards for audits of private companies, nonprofit organizations, and federal, state, and local governments. It develops and grades the Uniform CPA Examination.

CAREER ASPIRATIONS: A PROSPECTIVE POSITION

Regional CFO

Job Description

The Regional CFO will oversee several functions, including payroll, AP, and the client accounting team. The Regional CFO will manage the preparation of internal and external financial reporting for the U.S. operations and analyze and report variances. The Regional CFO must have experience in client compensation reconciliation.

Responsibilities

- Partner with global offices.
- Supervise tax reporting.
- Manage financial audits and credit analysis.
- Oversee monthly and quarterly SOX reporting.
- Play a significant role in developing business plans.
- Partner with senior leadership in the management of operating policies and procedures.
- Create cost-effective recommendations to strengthen operations and improve financial performance.
- Develop and implement new processes.
- Report directly to the CFO.
- Able to mobilize, elevate issues when needed, and interact effectively with all employees, vendors, corporate and clients.

Qualifications

- Bachelor's degree in accounting needed. CPA/MBA a plus.
- 10+ years of progressive finance experience.
- Excellent communication skills, both oral and written.
- Experience working in the advertising industry required.
- A minimum of 7 years managing a team.

Career Advice from Business Professionals

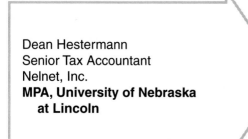

Dean Hestermann
Senior Tax Accountant
Nelnet, Inc.
**MPA, University of Nebraska
at Lincoln**

What drew you to this field?
I have an aptitude with numbers and enjoy problem solving and research.

What makes a day at your job interesting?
I enjoy interacting with people, problem solving, and research. The world of taxation, with all its rules and regulations, is still in many instances not black and white. From both a compliance and consulting aspect, the ability to communicate with associates and external individuals is a critical component. Effective communication and research is a baseline for successful problem solving.

How has your graduate education been important to your successes/accomplishments along your career path?
It has been very important. My graduate education has provided a baseline of knowledge and structure I can draw upon. An education does not prepare you for all obstacles in your future career, but it does create a foundation from both a knowledge and relationship perspective.

In your opinion, what does the future of your field hold for someone newly entering it?
There will always be opportunities to excel within the tax/accounting field, and the skill sets will provide leverage should you decide to become more active in company management. In addition, over the past generation, accounting has taken several strides forward from an efficiency standpoint via the utilization of technology. This will continue as new products/technologies enter the market place.

What are the exciting developments coming in the next five years?
As the business and financial worlds continue to become more complex, there continues to be a demand for more openness and a fallback to "ethics." In addition, from a tax perspective, as the various governmental entities need more revenues to balance budgets, there will be a continued focused on tax guidance and additional audit activity. Consequently, the field will continue to encounter more oversight from regulatory authorities.

Chad Stutzman
Tax Manager
Nelnet, Inc.
**MPA, University of Nebraska
at Lincoln**

What drew you to this field?
Initially, I enjoyed my accounting courses at the University. I had friends and family who were accountants, and they seemed to enjoy the field. CPA firms generally have a clear, defined career path, similar to engineers. I entered the Public Accounting field to receive my CPA license. Public accounting is a great place to learn about accounting and finance in a very efficient and real-world way. You're exposed to a variety of clients and transactions from which you learn.

What makes a day at your job interesting?
The work we do in the tax department actually saves Nelnet tax dollars, which is highly valued. Whether working at a corporation or a CPA firm, tax accountants look for ways to save businesses tax dollars. Tax accountants utilize both federal and state tax regulations to make the appropriate tax filings. In addition, various business decisions that need to be made may have a tax variable, and the data that tax accountants can provide may help to make those decisions easier (there may be an unforeseen tax consequence).

How has your graduate education been important to your successes/accomplishments along your career path?
It provided the foundation and terminology that served as a spring board once I entered the workforce. Ten years later, I still refer to books and notes from my graduate courses.

In your opinion, what does the future of your field hold for someone newly entering it?
Accounting will continue to provide stable, well paid careers. Change is constant.

What advice would you share with new graduates entering your field?
Do an internship with a CPA firm. It provides you with a "real-world" experience and gives you a good idea whether the field/career is for you. If it isn't, you'll know two to three years earlier than you would have.

ACCOUNTING

Abilene Christian University, Graduate School, College of Business Administration, Abilene, TX 79699-9100. Offers M Acc. *Accreditation:* AACSB. Part-time programs available. *Faculty:* 7 part-time/adjunct (0 women). *Students:* 32 full-time (14 women), 5 part-time (3 women); includes 2 Two or more races, non-Hispanic/Latino, 12 international. 23 applicants, 65% accepted, 14 enrolled. In 2010, 41 master's awarded. *Entrance requirements:* For master's, GMAT. Additional exam requirements/recommendations for international students: Required—TOEFL (minimum score 550 paper-based; 213 computer-based). *Application deadline:* For fall admission, 4/1 priority date for domestic students; for spring admission, 11/1 for domestic students. Applications are processed on a rolling basis. Application fee: $40. Electronic applications accepted. *Expenses:* Tuition: Full-time $12,906; part-time $717 per hour. Required fees: $1250; $61.50 per unit. *Financial support:* In 2010–11, 24 students received support; teaching assistantships, Federal Work-Study available. Support available to part-time students. Financial award application deadline: 4/1; financial award applicants required to submit FAFSA. *Faculty research:* Organizational structure, financial management, cost accounting, unit analysis management. *Unit head:* Bill Fowler, Department Chair, 325-674-2080, Fax: 325-674-2564, E-mail: bill.fowler@coba.acu.edu. *Application contact:* David Pittman, Graduate Admissions Counselor, 325-674-2656, Fax: 325-674-6717, E-mail: gradinfo@acu.edu.

Adelphi University, School of Business, Graduate Opportunity for Accelerated Learning MBA Program, Garden City, NY 11530-0701. Offers accounting (MBA); finance (MBA). *Accreditation:* AACSB. Part-time and evening/weekend programs available. *Students:* 14 full-time (8 women), 25 part-time (17 women); includes 7 Black or African American, non-Hispanic/Latino; 8 Asian, non-Hispanic/Latino; 3 Hispanic/Latino; 1 Two or more races, non-Hispanic/Latino, 1 international. Average age 40. In 2010, 14 master's awarded. *Entrance requirements:* For master's, GMAT, 2 letters of recommendation. Additional exam requirements/recommendations for international students: Required—TOEFL (minimum score 550 paper-based; 213 computer-based; 80 iBT). *Application deadline:* For fall admission, 4/1 for international students; for spring admission, 11/1 for international students. Applications are processed on a rolling basis. Application fee: $50. Electronic applications accepted. *Financial support:* Research assistantships with full and partial tuition reimbursements, career-related internships or fieldwork, Federal Work-Study, institutionally sponsored loans, scholarships/grants, and unspecified assistantships available. Financial award application deadline: 3/1; financial award applicants required to submit FAFSA. *Faculty research:* Capital market, executive compensation, business ethics, classical value theory, labor economics. *Unit head:* Rakesh Gupta, Chairperson, 516-877-4670, Fax: 516-877-4607, E-mail: gradbusinquiries@adelphi.edu. *Application contact:* Christine Murphy, Director of Admissions, 516-877-3050, Fax: 516-877-3039, E-mail: graduateadmissions@adelphi.edu.

Albany State University, College of Business, Albany, GA 31705-2717. Offers accounting (MBA); business administration (MBA). *Accreditation:* ACBSP. Part-time and evening/weekend programs available. *Faculty:* 5 full-time (1 woman), 1 part-time/adjunct (0 women). *Students:* 8 full-time (6 women), 25 part-time (17 women); includes 27 minority (all Black or African American, non-Hispanic/Latino), 2 international. Average age 31. 12 applicants, 92% accepted, 11 enrolled. In 2010, 8 master's awarded. *Degree requirements:* For master's, comprehensive exam. *Entrance requirements:* For master's, GMAT, minimum GPA of 2.5, 2 letters of reference. *Application deadline:* For fall admission, 7/15 for domestic students, 5/15 for international students; for spring admission, 11/15 for domestic students, 9/15 for international students. Applications are processed on a rolling basis. Application fee: $20. Electronic applications accepted. *Expenses:* Tuition, state resident: full-time $3060; part-time $170 per credit hour. Tuition, nonresident: full-time $12,204; part-time $678 per credit hour. Required fees: $1160. Part-time tuition and fees vary according to course load. *Financial support:* Application deadline: 4/15. *Faculty research:* Conceptual research, case study. *Unit head:* Dr. Kathaleena Monds, Interim Dean, 229-430-2749, Fax: 229-430-5119, E-mail: kathaleena.monds@asurams.edu. *Application contact:* Dr. Rani George, Dean, Graduate School, 229-430-5118, Fax: 229-430-6398, E-mail: rani.george@asurams.edu.

American Public University System, AMU/APU Graduate Programs, Charles Town, WV 25414. Offers accounting (MBA); administration and supervision (M Ed); air warfare (MA Military Studies); asymmetrical warfare (MA Military Studies); criminal justice (MA); emergency and disaster management (MA); entrepreneurship (MBA); environmental policy and management (MS); finance (MBA); general (MBA); global business management (MBA); guidance and counseling (M Ed); history (MA); homeland security (MA); homeland security resource allocation (MBA); humanities (MA); information technology (MS); information technology management (MBA); intelligence studies (MA); international relations and conflict resolution (MA); joint warfare (MA Military Studies); land warfare (MA Military Studies); legal studies (MA); management (MA), including defense mangement, general, human resource management, organizational leadership, public administration; marketing (MBA); military history (MA); national security studies (MA); naval warfare (MA Military Studies); nonprofit management (MBA);

political science (MA); psychology (MA); public administration (MA); public health (MA); security management (MA); space studies (MS); sports management (MS); strategic leadership (MA Military Studies); teaching (M Ed), including elementary, secondary social sciences; transportation and logistics management (MA). Programs offered via distance learning only. Part-time and evening/weekend programs available. Postbaccalaureate distance learning degree programs offered (no on-campus study). *Faculty:* 253 full-time (134 women), 1,208 part-time/adjunct (570 women). *Students:* 956 full-time (422 women), 8,476 part-time (2,821 women); includes 2,511 minority (1,218 Black or African American, non-Hispanic/Latino; 68 American Indian or Alaska Native, non-Hispanic/Latino; 219 Asian, non-Hispanic/Latino; 705 Hispanic/Latino; 46 Native Hawaiian or other Pacific Islander, non-Hispanic/Latino; 255 Two or more races, non-Hispanic/Latino), 107 international. Average age 35. 9,550 applicants, 100% accepted. In 2010, 1,688 master's awarded. *Degree requirements:* For master's, comprehensive exam or practicum. *Entrance requirements:* For master's, official transcript showing earned bachelor's degree from institution accredited by recognized accrediting body. Additional exam requirements/recommendations for international students: Required—TOEFL (minimum score 550 paper-based; 213 computer-based), IELTS (minimum score 6.5). *Application deadline:* Applications are processed on a rolling basis. Application fee: $0. Electronic applications accepted. *Financial support:* Applicants required to submit FAFSA. *Faculty research:* Military history, criminal justice, management performance, national security. *Unit head:* Dr. Frank McCluskey, Provost, 877-468-6268, Fax: 304-724-3780. *Application contact:* Terry Grant, Director of Enrollment Management, 877-468-6268, Fax: 304-724-3780, E-mail: info@apus.edu.

American University, Kogod School of Business, Master of Business Administration Program, Washington, DC 20016-8044. Offers accounting (MBA); consulting (MBA), including information technology, international business, management; corporate finance: commercial banking (MBA); corporate finance: corporate financial management (MBA); corporate finance: investment banking (MBA), including corporate finance and private equity, trading and selling; entrepreneurship (MBA); global emerging markets (MBA), including business, finance, information technology; international trade and global supply chain management (MBA); leadership (MBA); marketing management (MBA); marketing research (MBA); real estate (MBA); MBA/JD; MBA/LL M. Part-time and evening/weekend programs available. *Faculty:* 12 full-time (5 women). *Students:* 135 full-time (62 women), 104 part-time (38 women); includes 46 minority (18 Black or African American, non-Hispanic/Latino; 1 American Indian or Alaska Native, non-Hispanic/Latino; 12 Asian, non-Hispanic/Latino; 14 Hispanic/Latino; 1 Two or more races, non-Hispanic/Latino), 34 international. Average age 27. 467 applicants, 51% accepted, 70 enrolled. In 2010, 101 master's awarded. *Entrance requirements:* For master's, GMAT. Additional exam requirements/recommendations for international students: Required—TOEFL. *Application deadline:* For fall admission, 2/1 priority date for domestic students; for spring admission, 10/1 priority date for domestic students. Applications are processed on a rolling basis. Application fee: $100. *Expenses:* Contact institution. *Financial support:* In 2010–11, 19 students received support; fellowships, research assistantships with partial tuition reimbursements available, career-related internships or fieldwork, Federal Work-Study, and institutionally sponsored loans available. Support available to part-time students. Financial award application deadline: 2/1. *Faculty research:* Information technology, decision-aiding methodology, negotiation. *Unit head:* Dr. Stevan Holmberg, Chair, 202-885-6193, E-mail: sholmbe@american.edu. *Application contact:* Shannon Demko, Associate Director Graduate Admissions, 202-885-1994, Fax: 202-885-1108, E-mail: demko@american.edu.

Angelo State University, College of Graduate Studies, College of Business, Department of Accounting, Economics, and Finance, San Angelo, TX 76909. Offers accounting (MBA); professional accountancy (MPAC). Part-time and evening/weekend programs available. *Faculty:* 4 full-time (0 women), 1 part-time/adjunct (0 women). *Students:* 19 full-time (11 women), 4 part-time (all women); includes 4 Hispanic/Latino. Average age 24. 14 applicants, 29% accepted, 4 enrolled. In 2010, 11 master's awarded. *Entrance requirements:* For master's, GMAT or GRE. Additional exam requirements/recommendations for international students: Required—TOEFL or IELTS. *Application deadline:* For fall admission, 7/15 priority date for domestic students, 6/10 for international students; for spring admission, 12/1 priority date for domestic students, 11/1 for international students. Applications are processed on a rolling basis. Application fee: $40 ($50 for international students). Electronic applications accepted. *Expenses:* Tuition, state resident: full-time $4560; part-time $152 per credit hour. Tuition, nonresident: full-time $13,860; part-time $462 per credit hour. Required fees: $2132. Tuition and fees vary according to course load. *Financial support:* In 2010–11, 15 students received support. Career-related internships or fieldwork, Federal Work-Study, and scholarships/grants available. Support available to part-time students. Financial award application deadline: 3/1; financial award applicants required to submit FAFSA. *Unit head:* Dr. Thomas A. Bankston, Department Head, 325-942-2046 Ext. 248, Fax: 325-942-2285, E-mail: thomas.bankston@angelo.edu. *Application contact:* Dr. Norman A. Sunderman, Graduate Advisor, 325-942-2046 Ext. 245, E-mail: norman.sunderman@angelo.edu.

Appalachian State University, Cratis D. Williams Graduate School, Department of Accounting, Boone, NC 28608. Offers MS. Part-time programs available. *Faculty:* 12 full-time (5 women). *Students:* 44 full-time (16 women), 3 part-time (2 women); includes 1 Hispanic/Latino, 1 international. 78 applicants, 81% accepted, 30 enrolled. In 2010, 54 master's awarded. *Degree requirements:* For master's, comprehensive exam, thesis optional. *Entrance requirements:* For master's, GMAT, 3 letters of recommendation. Additional exam requirements/recommendations for international students: Required—TOEFL (minimum score 550 paper-based; 230 computer-based; 79 iBT), IELTS (minimum score 6.5). *Application deadline:* For fall admission, 7/1 for domestic students, 2/1 for international students; for spring admission, 11/1 for domestic students, 7/1 for international students. Applications are processed on a rolling basis. Application fee: $55. Electronic applications accepted. *Expenses:* Tuition, state resident: full-time $3428; part-time $428 per unit. Tuition, nonresident: full-time $14,518; part-time $1814 per unit. Required fees: $2320; $344 per unit. Tuition and fees vary according to campus/location. *Financial support:* In 2010–11, 17 research assistantships (averaging $4,000 per year) were awarded; fellowships, teaching assistantships, Federal Work-Study, scholarships/grants, and unspecified assistantships also available. Financial award application deadline: 4/1; financial award applicants required to submit FAFSA. *Faculty research:* Audit assurance risk, state taxation, financial accounting inconsistencies, management information systems, charitable contribution taxation. *Unit head:* Dr. Timothy Forsyth, Chairman, 828-262-2036, Fax: 828-262-6640. *Application contact:* Dr. William Pollard, Director, 828-262-6232, Fax: 828-262-6640, E-mail: pollardwb@appstate.edu.

Arizona State University, W. P. Carey School of Business, Program in Business Administration, Tempe, AZ 85287-4906. Offers accountancy (PhD); agribusiness (PhD); business administration (MBA); finance (PhD); financial management and markets (MBA); information management (MBA); information systems (PhD); management (PhD); marketing (PhD); strategic marketing and services leadership (MBA); supply chain financial management (MBA); supply chain management (MBA, PhD); JD/MBA; MBA/M Acc; MBA/M Arch. *Accreditation:* AACSB. Part-time and evening/weekend programs available. Postbaccalaureate distance learning degree programs offered (minimal on-campus study). *Faculty:* 84 full-time (22 women), 7 part-time/adjunct (2 women). *Students:* 1,302 full-time (379 women), 86 part-time (26 women); includes 241 minority (37 Black or African American, non-Hispanic/Latino; 11 American Indian or Alaska Native, non-Hispanic/Latino; 103 Asian, non-Hispanic/Latino; 76 Hispanic/Latino; 4 Native Hawaiian or other Pacific Islander, non-Hispanic/Latino; 10 Two or more races, non-Hispanic/Latino), 171 international. Average age 31. 1,795 applicants, 44% accepted, 525 enrolled. In 2010, 734 master's, 9 doctorates awarded. Terminal master's awarded for partial completion of doctoral program. *Degree requirements:* For master's, thesis or alternative, internship, interactive Program of Study (iPOS) submitted before completing 50 percent of required credit hours; for doctorate, comprehensive exam, thesis/dissertation, interactive Program of Study (iPOS) submitted before completing 50 percent of required credit hours. *Entrance requirements:* For master's, GMAT, minimum GPA of 3.0 in last 2 years of work leading to bachelor's degree, 2 letters of recommendation, professional resume, official transcripts, 3 essays; for doctorate, GMAT or GRE, minimum GPA of 3.0 in last 2 years of work leading to bachelor's degree, 3 letters of recommendation, resume, personal statement/essay. Additional exam requirements/recommendations for international students: Required—TOEFL (minimum score 550 paper-based; 213 computer-based; 80 iBT), IELTS (minimum score 6.5). Application fee: $70 ($90 for international students). Electronic applications accepted. *Expenses:* Contact institution. *Financial support:* In 2010–11, 17 research assistantships with full and partial tuition reimbursements (averaging $18,121 per year), 153 teaching assistantships with full and partial tuition reimbursements (averaging $9,176 per year) were awarded; fellowships with full and partial tuition reimbursements, career-related internships or fieldwork, institutionally sponsored loans, scholarships/grants, and tuition waivers (full and partial) also available. Support available to part-time students. Financial award application deadline: 3/1; financial award applicants required to submit FAFSA. Total annual research expenditures: $540,779. *Unit head:* Dr. Robert E. Mittelstaedt, Dean, 480-965-2468, Fax: 480-965-5539, E-mail: mittelsr@asu.edu. *Application contact:* Graduate Admissions, 480-965-6113.

Arizona State University, W. P. Carey School of Business, School of Accountancy, Tempe, AZ 85287-3606. Offers accountancy (M Acc, M Tax); business administration (accountancy) (PhD). *Accreditation:* AACSB. Part-time and evening/weekend programs available. *Faculty:* 28 full-time (11 women), 3 part-time/adjunct (0 women). *Students:* 145 full-time (68 women), 15 part-time (9 women); includes 32 minority (17 Asian, non-Hispanic/Latino; 15 Hispanic/Latino), 28 international. Average age 25. 431 applicants, 55% accepted, 145 enrolled. In 2010, 109 master's awarded. *Degree requirements:* For master's, thesis optional, interactive Program of Study (iPOS) submitted before completing 50 percent of required credit hours. *Entrance requirements:* For master's, GMAT (waivers may apply for ASU accountancy undergraduates), minimum GPA of 3.0 in last 2 years of work leading to bachelor's degree, 2 letters of recommendation, professional resume, official transcripts, responses to 3 essay questions. Additional exam requirements/recommendations for international students: Required—TOEFL (minimum score 550 paper-based; 213 computer-based; 80 iBT), IELTS (minimum score 6.5). *Application deadline:* For fall admission, 3/1 for domestic and international students. Application fee: $70 ($90 for international students). Electronic applications accepted. *Expenses:* Contact institution. *Financial support:* In 2010–11, 16 teaching assistantships with partial tuition reimbursements (averaging $6,491 per year) were awarded; fellowships with full and partial tuition reimbursements, research assistantships with partial tuition reimbursements, career-related internships or fieldwork, institutionally sponsored loans, scholarships/grants, and tuition waivers (full and partial) also available. Financial award application deadline: 3/1; financial award applicants required to submit FAFSA. Total annual research expenditures: $86,910. *Unit head:* Dr. Mike Mikhail, Director, 480-727-7198, Fax: 480-965-8392, E-mail: michael.mikhail@asu.edu. *Application contact:* Graduate Admissions, 480-965-6113.

Arkansas State University, Graduate School, College of Business, Department of Accounting, Jonesboro, State University, AR 72467. Offers accountancy (M Acc). Part-time programs available. *Faculty:* 5 full-time (2 women), 2 part-time/adjunct (1 woman). *Students:* 23 full-time (13 women), 17 part-time (12 women); includes 4 minority (2 Black or African American, non-Hispanic/Latino; 1 Asian, non-Hispanic/Latino; 1 Native Hawaiian or other Pacific Islander, non-Hispanic/Latino), 13 international. Average age 27. 29 applicants, 79% accepted, 17 enrolled. In 2010, 8 master's awarded. *Degree requirements:* For master's, comprehensive exam, thesis or alternative. *Entrance requirements:* For master's, GMAT, appropriate bachelor's degree, letters of reference, official transcript, immunization records. Additional exam requirements/recommendations for international students: Required—TOEFL (minimum score 550 paper-based; 253 computer-based; 79 iBT), IELTS (minimum score 6), PTE: Pearson Test of English Academic (56). *Application deadline:* For fall admission, 7/1 for domestic and international students; for spring admission, 11/15 for domestic students, 11/14 for international students. Applications are processed on a rolling basis. Application fee: $30 ($40 for international students). Electronic applications accepted. *Expenses:* Contact institution. *Financial support:* In 2010–11, 4 students received support. Career-related internships or fieldwork, scholarships/grants, and unspecified assistantships available. Financial award application deadline: 7/1; financial award applicants required to submit FAFSA. *Unit head:* Dr. John Robertson, Chair, 870-972-3038, Fax: 870-972-3868, E-mail: jfrobert@astate.edu. *Application contact:* Dr. Andrew Sustich, Dean of the Graduate School, 870-972-3029, Fax: 870-972-3857, E-mail: sustich@astate.edu.

Assumption College, Graduate School, Department of Business Studies, Worcester, MA 01609-1296. Offers accounting (MBA); business administration (CAGS); finance/economics (MBA); general business (MBA); human resources (MBA); international business (MBA); management (MBA); marketing (MBA); nonprofit leadership (MBA). Part-time and evening/weekend programs available. *Faculty:* 3 full-time (0 women), 13 part-time/adjunct (3 women). *Students:* 20 full-time (9 women), 135 part-time (70 women); includes 24 minority (19 Black or African American, non-Hispanic/Latino; 2 Asian, non-Hispanic/Latino; 3 Hispanic/Latino), 4 international. Average age 26. 85 applicants, 95% accepted. In 2010, 40 master's, 2 other advanced degrees awarded. *Entrance requirements:* For master's and CAGS, 3 letters of recommendation, resume, essay. Additional exam requirements/recommendations for international students: Required—TOEFL (minimum score 540 paper-based; 200 computer-based; 76 iBT), IELTS (minimum score 6). *Application deadline:* For fall admission, 6/1 priority date for domestic students, 5/1 priority date for international students; for spring admission, 11/1 priority date for domestic students, 9/1 priority date for international students. Applications are processed on a rolling basis. Application fee: $30. Electronic applications accepted. *Expenses:* Tuition: Part-time $503 per credit. Required fees: $20 per semester. One-time fee: $100. Part-time tuition and fees vary according to campus/location. *Financial support:* Application deadline: 6/1. *Faculty research:* Workplace diversity, dynamics of team interaction, utilization of leased employees. *Unit head:* Michael Lewis, Director, 508-767-7372, Fax: 508-767-7252, E-mail: milewis@assumption.edu. *Application contact:* Daniel Provost, Assistant Director of Graduate Student Services, 508-767-7426, Fax: 508-767-7030, E-mail: dprovost@assumption.edu.

Auburn University, Graduate School, College of Business, School of Accountancy, Auburn University, AL 36849. Offers M Acc. *Accreditation:* AACSB. Part-time programs available. *Faculty:* 15 full-time (5 women), 3 part-time/adjunct (2 women). *Students:* 51 full-time (36 women), 44 part-time (25 women); includes 2 Black or African American, non-Hispanic/Latino; 3 Asian, non-Hispanic/Latino; 1 Hispanic/Latino. Average age 28. 170 applicants, 47% accepted, 62 enrolled. In 2010, 48 master's awarded. *Entrance requirements:* For master's, GMAT, GRE General Test. Additional exam requirements/recommendations for international students: Required—TOEFL. *Application deadline:* For fall admission, 7/7 for domestic students; for spring admission, 11/24 for domestic students. Applications are processed on a rolling basis. Application fee: $50 ($60 for international students). Electronic applications accepted. *Expenses:* Tuition, state resident: full-time $7002. Tuition, nonresident: full-time $21,898. International tuition: $22,116 full-time. Required fees: $892. Tuition and fees vary according to course load and program. *Financial support:* Teaching assistantships, Federal Work-Study available. Support available to part-time students. Financial award application deadline: 3/15; financial award applicants required to submit FAFSA. *Unit* *head:* Norman H. Godwin, Director, 334-844-5340. *Application contact:* Dr. George Flowers, Dean of the Graduate School, 334-844-2125.

Avila University, School of Business, Kansas City, MO 64145-1698. Offers accounting (MBA); finance (MBA); general management (MBA); health care administration (MBA); international business (MBA); management information systems (MBA); marketing (MBA). Part-time and evening/weekend programs available. *Faculty:* 9 full-time (3 women), 24 part-time/adjunct (6 women). *Students:* 123 full-time (68 women), 87 part-time (52 women); includes 44 minority (30 Black or African American, non-Hispanic/Latino; 1 American Indian or Alaska Native, non-Hispanic/Latino; 6 Asian, non-Hispanic/Latino; 6 Hispanic/Latino; 1 Native Hawaiian or other Pacific Islander, non-Hispanic/Latino), 46 international. Average age 33. 62 applicants, 79% accepted, 49 enrolled. In 2010, 80 master's awarded. *Degree requirements:* For master's, comprehensive exam, capstone course. *Entrance requirements:* For master's, GMAT (minimum score 420), minimum GPA of 3.0, interview. Additional exam requirements/recommendations for international students: Required—TOEFL (minimum score 550 paper-based). *Application deadline:* For fall admission, 7/30 priority date for domestic students, 7/30 for international students; for winter admission, 11/30 priority date for domestic students, 11/30 for international students; for spring admission, 2/28 priority date for domestic students, 2/28 for international students. Applications are processed on a rolling basis. Application fee: $0. Electronic applications accepted. *Expenses:* Contact institution. *Financial support:* In 2010–11, 102 students received support. Career-related internships or fieldwork and Competitive Merit Scholarship available. Support available to part-time students. Financial award applicants required to submit FAFSA. *Faculty research:* Leadership characteristics, financial hedging, group dynamics. *Unit head:* Dr. Richard Woodall, Dean, 816-501-3720, Fax: 816-501-2463, E-mail: richard.woodall@avila.edu. *Application contact:* JoAnna Giffin, MBA Admissions Director, 816-501-3601, Fax: 816-501-2463, E-mail: joanna.giffin@avila.edu.

Babson College, F. W. Olin Graduate School of Business, Wellesley, Babson Park, MA 02457-0310. Offers accounting (MSA); advanced management (Certificate); business administration (MBA); global entrepreneurship (MS); technological entrepreneurship (MS). *Accreditation:* AACSB. Part-time and evening/weekend programs available. Postbaccalaureate distance learning degree programs offered (minimal on-campus study). *Faculty:* 142 full-time (39 women), 41 part-time/adjunct (9 women). *Students:* 486 full-time (145 women), 838 part-time (236 women); includes 199 minority (22 Black or African American, non-Hispanic/Latino; 1 American Indian or Alaska Native, non-Hispanic/Latino; 127 Asian, non-Hispanic/Latino; 29 Hispanic/Latino; 1 Native Hawaiian or other Pacific Islander, non-Hispanic/Latino; 19 Two or more races, non-Hispanic/Latino), 263 international. Average age 33. 877 applicants, 56% accepted, 283 enrolled. In 2010, 723 master's, 2 other advanced degrees awarded. *Entrance requirements:* For master's, GMAT, 2 years of work experience, resume, letters of recommendation. Additional exam requirements/recommendations for international students: Required—TOEFL (minimum score 100 iBT), IELTS (minimum score 6.5). *Application deadline:* For fall admission, 11/1 priority date for domestic and international students; for winter admission, 1/15 priority date for domestic and international students; for spring admission, 4/15 priority date for domestic students. Applications are processed on a rolling basis. Application fee: $100. Electronic applications accepted. *Expenses:* Tuition: Full-time $46,000; part-time $1220 per credit. Required fees: $1946. Full-time tuition and fees vary according to course load, program and student level. *Financial support:* In 2010–11, 286 students received support, including 48 fellowships (averaging $28,489 per year); career-related internships or fieldwork, Federal Work-Study, institutionally sponsored loans, scholarships/grants, health care benefits, and unspecified assistantships also available. Financial award application deadline: 4/15. *Faculty research:* Entrepreneurship, sustainability, global markets, process of innovation, social media and advertising. *Unit head:* Dr. Raghu Tadepalli, Dean, 781-239-5237, E-mail: rtadepalli@babson.edu. *Application contact:* Kathy Longee, Admission Services Team, 781-239-4317, Fax: 781-239-4194, E-mail: mbaadmission@babson.edu.

Baldwin-Wallace College, Graduate Programs, Division of Business, Program in Accounting, Berea, OH 44017-2088. Offers MBA. Part-time and evening/weekend programs available. *Students:* 24 full-time (16 women), 20 part-time (13 women); includes 8 minority (all Black or African American, non-Hispanic/Latino), 1 international. Average age 34. 15 applicants, 87% accepted, 7 enrolled. In 2010, 31 master's awarded. *Degree requirements:* For master's, minimum overall GPA of 3.0, completion of all required courses. *Entrance requirements:* For master's, GMAT, minimum GPA of 3.0, work experience, bachelor's degree in field, undergraduate accounting coursework. Additional exam requirements/recommendations for international students: Required—TOEFL (minimum score 523 paper-based; 193 computer-based; 70 iBT). *Application deadline:* For fall admission, 7/25 priority date for domestic students, 4/30 priority date for international students; for spring admission, 12/15 priority date for domestic students, 9/30 priority date for international students. Applications are processed on a rolling basis. Application fee: $25. Electronic applications accepted. *Expenses:* Contact institution. *Financial support:* Career-related internships or fieldwork available. Support available to part-time students. Financial award application deadline: 5/1. *Unit head:* Thomas Garvey, Director, 440-826-2438, Fax: 440-826-3868, E-mail:

tgarvey@bw.edu. *Application contact:* Laura Spencer, Graduate Application Specialist, 440-826-2191, Fax: 440-826-3868, E-mail: lspencer@bw.edu.

Ball State University, Graduate School, Miller College of Business, Department of Accounting, Muncie, IN 47306-1099. Offers MS. *Accreditation:* AACSB. *Faculty:* 11. *Students:* 28 full-time (8 women), 5 part-time (3 women), 11 international. Average age 25. 46 applicants, 72% accepted, 19 enrolled. In 2010, 11 master's awarded. Application fee: $50. *Expenses:* Tuition, state resident: full-time $6160; part-time $299 per credit hour. Tuition, nonresident: full-time $16,020; part-time $783 per credit hour. Required fees: $2278; $95 per credit hour. *Financial support:* In 2010–11, 5 teaching assistantships with full tuition reimbursements (averaging $9,085 per year) were awarded. Financial award application deadline: 3/1. *Unit head:* Dr. Lucinda Van Alst, Head, 765-285-5100, E-mail: lvanalst@bsu.edu. *Application contact:* Dr. Mark Myring, Information Contact, 765-285-5100, Fax: 765-285-8024.

Baylor University, Graduate School, Hankamer School of Business, Department of Accounting and Business Law, Waco, TX 76798. Offers M Acc, MT, JD/M Acc, JD/MT. *Accreditation:* AACSB. Part-time programs available. *Faculty:* 11 full-time (2 women). *Students:* 55 full-time (24 women), 7 part-time (5 women); includes 4 minority (1 Asian, non-Hispanic/Latino; 1 Hispanic/Latino; 2 Two or more races, non-Hispanic/Latino), 2 international. In 2010, 50 master's awarded. *Entrance requirements:* For master's, GMAT. *Application deadline:* For fall admission, 8/1 for domestic students; for spring admission, 12/1 for domestic students. Applications are processed on a rolling basis. Application fee: $25. *Financial support:* Research assistantships, career-related internships or fieldwork, Federal Work-Study, and institutionally sponsored loans available. *Faculty research:* Continuing professional education (CPE), accounting education, retirement plans. *Unit head:* Dr. Jane Baldwin, Adviser, 254-710-3536, Fax: 254-710-2421, E-mail: jane_baldwin@baylor.edu. Application contact: Vicky Todd, Administrative Assistant, 254-710-3718, Fax: 254-710-1066, E-mail: mba@hsb.baylor.edu.

Benedictine University, Graduate Programs, Program in Accountancy, Lisle, IL 60532-0900. Offers MS. Evening/weekend programs available. *Students:* 5 full-time (4 women), 32 part-time (21 women); includes 7 minority (2 Black or African American, non-Hispanic/Latino; 4 Asian, non-Hispanic/Latino; 1 Hispanic/Latino), 9 international. 29 applicants, 83% accepted, 16 enrolled. In 2010, 17 master's awarded. *Entrance requirements:* For master's, official transcripts, 2 letters of reference, resume. Additional exam requirements/recommendations for international students: Required—TOEFL. *Application deadline:* Applications are processed on a rolling basis. Electronic applications accepted. *Unit head:* Dr. Sharon Borowicz, Director, 630-829-6219, E-mail: sborowicz@ben.edu. *Application contact:* Kari Gibbons, Director, Admissions, 630-829-6200, Fax: 630-829-6584, E-mail: kgibbons@ben.edu.

Benedictine University, Graduate Programs, Program in Business Administration, Lisle, IL 60532-0900. Offers accounting (MBA); entrepreneurship and managing innovation (MBA); financial management (MBA); health administration (MBA); human resource management (MBA); information systems security (MBA); international business (MBA); management consulting (MBA); management information systems (MBA); marketing management (MBA); operations management and logistics (MBA); organizational leadership (MBA); MBA/MPH; MBA/MS. Part-time and evening/weekend programs available. Postbaccalaureate distance learning degree programs offered (minimal on-campus study). *Faculty:* 4 full-time (2 women), 24 part-time/adjunct (3 women). *Students:* 347 full-time (140 women), 672 part-time (360 women); includes 237 minority (155 Black or African American, non-Hispanic/Latino; 4 American Indian or Alaska Native, non-Hispanic/Latino; 43 Asian, non-Hispanic/Latino; 35 Hispanic/Latino), 21 international. Average age 34. 416 applicants, 88% accepted, 217 enrolled. In 2010, 355 master's awarded. *Entrance requirements:* For master's, GMAT. Additional exam requirements/recommendations for international students: Required—TOEFL (minimum score 550 paper-based; 213 computer-based). *Application deadline:* For fall admission, 9/1 for domestic students; for winter admission, 12/1 for domestic students; for spring admission, 2/15 for domestic students. Applications are processed on a rolling basis. Application fee: $40. Electronic applications accepted. *Financial support:* Career-related internships or fieldwork and health care benefits available. Support available to part-time students. *Faculty research:* Strategic leadership in professional organizations, sociology of professions, organizational change, social identity theory, applications to change management. *Unit head:* Dr. Sharon Borowicz, Director, 630-829-6219, E-mail: sborowicz@ben.edu. *Application contact:* Kari Gibbons, Director, Admissions, 630-829-6200, Fax: 630-829-6584, E-mail: kgibbons@ben.edu.

Bentley University, McCallum Graduate School of Business, Accountancy PhD Program, Waltham, MA 02452-4705. Offers PhD. Part-time programs available. *Faculty:* 74 full-time (22 women), 21 part-time/adjunct (5 women). *Students:* 10 full-time (5 women), 2 international. Average age 37. *Degree requirements:* For doctorate, comprehensive exam, thesis/dissertation. *Entrance requirements:* For doctorate, GMAT or GRE General Test. Additional exam requirements/recommendations for international students: Required—TOEFL (minimum score 650 paper-based; 250 computer-based; 100 iBT) or IELTS (minimum score 7). Application fee: $0. Electronic applications accepted. *Expenses:* Tuition: Full-time $28,224; part-time $1176 per credit. Required fees: $404. Part-time tuition and fees vary according to course load. *Financial support:* Scholarships/grants available. *Faculty research:* Accounting information systems, financial fraud, forensic accounting, enterprise risks and controls, managerial incentive systems, earnings management, auditor ethos and independence, audit team brainstorming, auditor-client negotiations, information technology auditing, corporate ethics and internal controls, corporate governance. *Unit head:* Dr. Sue Newell, Director, 781-891-2399, Fax: 781-891-3121, E-mail: snewell@bentley.edu. *Application contact:* Dr. Sue Newell, Director, 781-891-2399, Fax: 781-891-3121, E-mail: snewell@bentley.edu.

Bentley University, McCallum Graduate School of Business, Master's Program in Accounting, Waltham, MA 02452-4705. Offers MSA. *Accreditation:* AACSB. Part-time and evening/weekend programs available. *Faculty:* 74 full-time (22 women), 21 part-time/adjunct (5 women). *Students:* 170 full-time (117 women), 100 part-time (52 women); includes 37 minority (2 Black or African American, non-Hispanic/Latino; 2 American Indian or Alaska Native, non-Hispanic/Latino; 28 Asian, non-Hispanic/Latino; 5 Hispanic/Latino), 102 international. Average age 26. 557 applicants, 61% accepted, 160 enrolled. *Entrance requirements:* For master's, GMAT or GRE General Test. Additional exam requirements/recommendations for international students: Required—TOEFL (minimum score 600 paper-based; 250 computer-based; 100 iBT) or IELTS (minimum score 7). *Application deadline:* For fall admission, 12/1 priority date for domestic and international students. Application fee: $50. Electronic applications accepted. *Expenses:* Tuition: Full-time $28,224; part-time $1176 per credit. Required fees: $404. Part-time tuition and fees vary according to course load. *Financial support:* In 2010–11, 46 students received support. Scholarships/grants and unspecified assistantships available. Financial award application deadline: 6/1; financial award applicants required to submit CSS PROFILE or FAFSA. *Faculty research:* Audit risk assessment, ethics in accounting, corporate governance, accounting information systems and management control, tax policy, forensic accounting. *Unit head:* Dr. Martha Howe, Director, 781-891-2573, E-mail: mhowe@bentley.edu. *Application contact:* Sharon Hill, Director of Graduate Admissions, 781-891-2108, Fax: 781-891-2464, E-mail: bentleygraduate admissions@bentley.edu.

Boston College, Carroll School of Management, Programs in Accounting, Chestnut Hill, MA 02467-3800. Offers MSA. *Faculty:* 17 full-time (7 women), 17 part-time/adjunct (6 women). *Students:* 78 full-time (45 women); includes 7 Asian, non-Hispanic/Latino; 4 Hispanic/Latino, 22 international. Average age 26. 377 applicants, 36% accepted, 76 enrolled. In 2010, 76 master's awarded. *Entrance requirements:* For master's, GMAT, recommendations, resume. Additional exam requirements/recommendations for international students: Required—TOEFL (minimum score 600 paper-based; 250 computer-based; 100 iBT). *Application deadline:* For fall admission, 3/15 for domestic and international students; for spring admission, 2/15 for domestic and international students. Application fee: $100. Electronic applications accepted. *Financial support:* In 2010–11, 50 fellowships, 50 research assistantships were awarded; tuition waivers (partial) also available. *Faculty research:* Financial reporting, auditing, tax planning, financial statement analysis. *Unit head:* Dr. Jeffrey L. Ringuest, Associate Dean, Graduate Programs, 617-552-9100, Fax: 617-552-0514, E-mail: gsomdean@bc.edu. *Application contact:* Shelley A. Burt, Director of Graduate Enrollment, 617-552-3920, Fax: 617-552-8078, E-mail: bcmba@bc.edu.

Brenau University, Sydney O. Smith Graduate School, School of Business and Mass Communication, Gainesville, GA 30501. Offers accounting (MBA); business administration (MBA); healthcare management (MBA); organizational leadership (MS); project management (MBA). Part-time and evening/weekend programs available. Postbaccalaureate distance learning degree programs offered (no on-campus study). *Faculty:* 12 full-time (7 women), 24 part-time/adjunct (10 women). *Students:* 124 full-time (89 women), 348 part-time (250 women); includes 130 Black or African American, non-Hispanic/Latino; 2 American Indian or Alaska Native, non-Hispanic/Latino; 7 Asian, non-Hispanic/Latino; 13 Hispanic/Latino; 9 Two or more races, non-Hispanic/Latino, 42 international. Average age 35. In 2010, 125 master's awarded. *Degree requirements:* For master's, comprehensive exam (for some programs). *Entrance requirements:* For master's, resume, minimum undergraduate GPA of 2.5. Additional exam requirements/recommendations for international students: Required—TOEFL (minimum score 500 paper-based; 173 computer-based; 61 iBT); Recommended—IELTS (minimum score 5). *Application deadline:* Applications are processed on a rolling basis. Electronic applications accepted. *Expenses:* Contact institution. *Financial support:* In 2010–11, 1 student received support. Application deadline: 7/15. *Unit head:* Dr. William S. Lightfoot, Dean, 770-538-5330, Fax: 770-537-4701, E-mail: wlightfoot@ brenau.edu. *Application contact:* Christina White, Graduate Admissions Specialist, 770-718-5320, Fax: 770-718-5338, E-mail: cwhite@brenau.edu.

Brigham Young University, Graduate Studies, Marriott School of Management, Master of Accountancy Program, Provo, UT 84602. Offers M Acc, JD/M Acc. *Accreditation:* AACSB. *Faculty:* 26 full-time (2 women), 4 part-time/adjunct (2 women). *Students:* 178 full-time (36 women); includes 1 Black or African American, non-Hispanic/Latino; 2 Asian, non-Hispanic/Latino; 2 Hispanic/Latino, 14 international. Average age 24. 321 applicants,

56% accepted, 159 enrolled. In 2010, 164 master's awarded. *Entrance requirements:* For master's, GMAT, minimum GPA of 3.0 in last 60 hours. Additional exam requirements/recommendations for international students: Required—TOEFL (minimum score 580 paper-based; 230 computer-based). *Application deadline:* For fall admission, 3/1 for domestic and international students. Application fee: $50. Electronic applications accepted. *Expenses:* Contact institution. *Financial support:* In 2010–11, 97 students received support. Application deadline: 4/15. *Unit head:* Dr. Kevin D. Stocks, Director, 801-422-4613, Fax: 801-422-0621, E-mail: kevin stocks@byu.edu. Application contact: Julie Averett, Academic Advisor, 801-422-3951, Fax: 801-422-0621, E-mail: soa@byu.edu.

Brooklyn College of the City University of New York, Division of Graduate Studies, Department of Economics, Brooklyn, NY 11210-2889. Offers accounting (MS); business economics (MS), including economic analysis, global business and finance; economics (MA). Part-time and evening/weekend programs available. *Students:* 27 full-time (16 women), 163 part-time (76 women); includes 84 minority (60 Black or African American, non-Hispanic/Latino; 18 Asian, non-Hispanic/Latino; 6 Hispanic/Latino), 42 international. Average age 32. 184 applicants, 76% accepted, 68 enrolled. In 2010, 44 master's awarded. *Degree requirements:* For master's, comprehensive exam, thesis or alternative. *Entrance requirements:* For master's, GMAT (for MS), 2 letters of recommendation. Additional exam requirements/recommendations for international students: Required—TOEFL (minimum score 550 paper-based; 213 computer-based; 79 iBT). *Application deadline:* For fall admission, 3/1 priority date for domestic students, 2/1 priority date for international students; for spring admission, 11/1 priority date for domestic students, 10/1 priority date for international students. Applications are processed on a rolling basis. Application fee: $125. Electronic applications accepted. *Expenses:* Tuition, state resident: full-time $7360; part-time $310 per credit hour. Tuition, nonresident: full-time $13,800; part-time $575 per credit hour. Required fees: $190 per semester. *Financial support:* Career-related internships or fieldwork, Federal Work-Study, institutionally sponsored loans, and scholarships/grants available. Support available to part-time students. Financial award application deadline: 5/1; financial award applicants required to submit FAFSA. *Faculty research:* Econometrics, environmental economics, microeconomics, macroeconomics, taxation. *Unit head:* Dr. Emmanuel Thorne, Chairperson, 718-951-5317, E-mail: ethorne@brooklyn.cuny.edu. *Application contact:* Hernan Sierra, Graduate Admissions Coordinator, 718-951-4536, Fax: 718-951-4506, E-mail: grads@brooklyn.cuny.edu.

Bryant University, Graduate School of Business, Master of Professional Accountancy Program, Smithfield, RI 02917. Offers MPAC. Part-time programs available. *Faculty:* 12 full-time (2 women). *Students:* 68 full-time (35 women); includes 3 Black or African American, non-Hispanic/Latino; 4 Asian, non-Hispanic/Latino; 4 Hispanic/Latino, 2 international. Average age 24. 32 applicants, 75% accepted, 14 enrolled. In 2010, 74 master's awarded. *Entrance requirements:* For master's, GMAT, transcripts, resume, recommendation, personal statement. Additional exam requirements/recommendations for international students: Required—TOEFL (minimum score 580 paper-based; 237 computer-based; 95 iBT). *Application deadline:* For fall admission, 7/15 for domestic and international students; for spring admission, 11/15 for domestic students, 7/15 for international students. Applications are processed on a rolling basis. Application fee: $80. Electronic applications accepted. *Expenses:* Tuition: Full-time $32,580; part-time $2580 per course. One-time fee: $800. Tuition and fees vary according to program. *Financial support:* In 2010–11, 22 students received support, including 4 research assistantships (averaging $12,084 per year); scholarships/grants also available. Financial award application deadline: 2/15; financial award applicants required to submit FAFSA. *Faculty research:* Director compensation, public sector auditing, employee stock options, financial disclosure, XBRL. *Unit head:* Kristopher T. Sullivan, Assistant Dean of the Graduate School, 401-232-6320, Fax: 401-232-6494, E-mail: sullivan@bryant.edu. *Application contact:* Ellen Hudon, Assistant Director of Graduate Admission, 401-232-6529, Fax: 401-232-6494, E-mail: ehudon@bryant.edu.

California Baptist University, Program in Business Administration, Riverside, CA 92504-3206. Offers accounting (PhD); management (MBA). *Accreditation:* ACBSP. Part-time and evening/weekend programs available. *Faculty:* 8 full-time (2 women), 1 (woman) part-time/adjunct. *Students:* 37 full-time (19 women), 17 part-time (9 women); includes 7 Black or African American, non-Hispanic/Latino; 3 Asian, non-Hispanic/Latino; 10 Hispanic/Latino, 7 international. 24 applicants, 92% accepted, 16 enrolled. In 2010, 43 master's awarded. *Degree requirements:* For master's, thesis or alternative, capstone project. *Entrance requirements:* Additional exam requirements/recommendations for international students: Required—TOEFL (minimum score 575 paper-based; 230 computer-based; 89 iBT). *Application deadline:* For fall admission, 8/1 priority date for domestic students, 7/1 for international students; for spring admission, 12/1 priority date for domestic students, 10/15 for international students. Applications are processed on a rolling basis. Application fee: $45. Electronic applications accepted. *Expenses:* Contact institution. *Financial support:* Federal Work-Study and scholarships/grants available. Support available to part-time students. Financial award applicants required to submit FAFSA. *Unit head:* Dr. Andrew Herrity, Dean, School of Business, 951-343-4427, Fax: 951-343-4361, E-mail: aherrity@calbaptist.

edu. *Application contact:* Gail Ronveaux, Dean of Graduate Enrollment, 951-343-5045, Fax: 951-343-5095, E-mail: graduateadmissions@calbaptist.edu.

California State Polytechnic University, Pomona, Academic Affairs, College of Business Administration, Master of Science in Business Administration Program, Pomona, CA 91768-2557. Offers information systems auditing (MS). *Students:* 2 full-time (1 woman), 12 part-time (3 women); includes 10 minority (7 Asian, non-Hispanic/Latino; 3 Hispanic/Latino), 1 international. Average age 32. 20 applicants, 35% accepted, 5 enrolled. In 2010, 5 master's awarded. *Application deadline:* Applications are processed on a rolling basis. Application fee: $55. Electronic applications accepted. *Expenses:* Tuition, state resident: full-time $5386; part-time $2850 per year. Tuition, nonresident: full-time $12,082; part-time $248 per credit. Required fees: $577; $248 per credit. $577 per year. Tuition and fees vary according to course load and program. *Unit head:* Dr. Richard S. Lapidus, Dean, 909-869-2400, E-mail: rslapidus@csupomona.edu. *Application contact:* Dr. Steven Curl, Associate Dean, 909-869-4244, E-mail: scurl@csupomona.edu.

California State Polytechnic University, Pomona, Academic Affairs, College of Business Administration, Program in Accountancy, Pomona, CA 91768-2557. Offers MS. *Students:* 2 full-time (1 woman), 4 part-time (2 women); includes 2 minority (1 Asian, non-Hispanic/Latino; 1 Two or more races, non-Hispanic/Latino), 4 international. Average age 32. 41 applicants, 20% accepted, 2 enrolled. *Application deadline:* Applications are processed on a rolling basis. Application fee: $55. Electronic applications accepted. *Expenses:* Tuition, state resident: full-time $5386; part-time $2850 per year. Tuition, nonresident: full-time $12,082; part-time $248 per credit. Required fees: $577; $248 per credit. $577 per year. Tuition and fees vary according to course load and program. *Unit head:* Dr. Richard S. Lapidus, Dean, 909-869-2363, E-mail: rslapidus@csupomona.edu. *Application contact:* Dr. Steven Curl, Associate Dean, 909-869-4244, E-mail: scurl@csupomona.edu.

California State University, East Bay, Office of Academic Programs and Graduate Studies, College of Business and Economics, Department of Accounting and Finance, Option in Accounting/Finance, Hayward, CA 94542-3000. Offers MBA. *Degree requirements:* For master's, comprehensive exam or thesis. *Entrance requirements:* For master's, GMAT, minimum GPA of 2.75. Additional exam requirements/recommendations for international students: Required—TOEFL (minimum score 550 paper-based; 213 computer-based). *Application deadline:* For fall admission, 6/30 for domestic and international students. Applications are processed on a rolling basis. Application fee: $55. Electronic applications accepted. *Financial support:* Career-related internships or fieldwork, Federal Work-Study, and institutionally sponsored loans available. Support available to part-time students. Financial award application deadline: 3/1; financial award applicants required to submit FAFSA. *Unit head:* Prof. Micah Frankel, Graduate Adviser, 510-885-3397, Fax: 510-885-4796, E-mail: micah.frankel@csueastbay.edu. *Application contact:* Donna Wiley, Interim Associate Director, 510-885-2928, Fax: 510-885-4777, E-mail: donna.wiley@csueastbay.edu.

California State University, Fullerton, Graduate Studies, College of Business and Economics, Department of Accounting, Fullerton, CA 92834-9480. Offers accounting (MBA, MS); taxation (MS). *Accreditation:* AACSB. Part-time programs available. *Students:* 115 full-time (64 women), 97 part-time (59 women); includes 78 Asian, non-Hispanic/Latino; 14 Hispanic/Latino; 2 Two or more races, non-Hispanic/Latino, 58 international. Average age 29. 300 applicants, 49% accepted, 66 enrolled. In 2010, 57 master's awarded. *Degree requirements:* For master's, thesis or alternative, project. *Entrance requirements:* For master's, GMAT, minimum AACSB index of 950. *Application deadline:* Applications are processed on a rolling basis. Application fee: $55. Electronic applications accepted. *Financial support:* Career-related internships or fieldwork, Federal Work-Study, institutionally sponsored loans, and scholarships/grants available. Support available to part-time students. Financial award application deadline: 3/1; financial award applicants required to submit FAFSA. *Unit head:* Dr. Betty Chavis, Chair, 657-278-2225. *Application contact:* Admissions/Applications, 657-278-2371.

California State University, Los Angeles, Graduate Studies, College of Business and Economics, Department of Accounting, Los Angeles, CA 90032-8530. Offers accountancy (MS), including business taxation, financial accounting, information systems, management accounting; accounting (MBA). Part-time and evening/weekend programs available. *Faculty:* 5 full-time (1 woman), 2 part-time/adjunct (0 women). *Students:* 37 full-time (19 women), 72 part-time (49 women); includes 42 minority (35 Asian, non-Hispanic/Latino; 6 Hispanic/Latino; 1 Two or more races, non-Hispanic/Latino), 49 international. Average age 31. 76 applicants, 100% accepted, 48 enrolled. In 2010, 33 master's awarded. *Degree requirements:* For master's, comprehensive exam (MBA), thesis (MS). *Entrance requirements:* For master's, GMAT, minimum GPA of 2.5 during previous 2 years of course work. Additional exam requirements/recommendations for international students: Required—TOEFL (minimum score 550 paper-based; 213 computer-based). *Application deadline:* For fall admission, 5/1 for domestic and international students. Applications are processed on a rolling basis. Application fee: $55. Electronic applications accepted. *Financial support:* Career-related internships or fieldwork and Federal Work-Study available. Support available to part-time students. Financial award application deadline: 3/1. *Unit head:* Dr.

Greg Kunkel, Chair, 323-343-2830, Fax: 323-343-6439, E-mail: gkunkel@calstatela.edu. *Application contact:* Dr. Alan Muchlinski, Dean of Graduate Studies, 323-343-3820, Fax: 323-343-5653, E-mail: amuchli@exchange.calstatela.edu.

Canisius College, Graduate Division, Richard J. Wehle School of Business, Department of Accounting, Buffalo, NY 14208-1098. Offers accounting (MBA); forensic accounting (MS); professional accounting (MBA). Part-time and evening/weekend programs available. *Faculty:* 8 full-time (1 woman), 2 part-time/adjunct (0 women). *Students:* 48 full-time (15 women), 20 part-time (9 women); includes 7 minority (2 Black or African American, non-Hispanic/Latino; 3 Asian, non-Hispanic/Latino; 2 Hispanic/Latino), 6 international. Average age 27. 58 applicants, 69% accepted, 35 enrolled. In 2010, 4 master's awarded. *Entrance requirements:* For master's, GMAT, transcripts. Additional exam requirements/recommendations for international students: Required—TOEFL. *Application deadline:* For fall admission, 7/1 priority date for domestic students; for spring admission, 11/1 priority date for domestic students. Applications are processed on a rolling basis. Application fee: $25. Electronic applications accepted. *Expenses:* Tuition: Part-time $694 per credit hour. Required fees: $11 per credit hour. $90 per semester. *Financial support:* Career-related internships or fieldwork, Federal Work-Study, scholarships/grants, tuition waivers (partial), and unspecified assistantships available. Support available to part-time students. Financial award application deadline: 7/1; financial award applicants required to submit FAFSA. *Faculty research:* Auditing (process and operational factors), fraud from a global perspective, managing risk in software development, valuation of intellectual property. *Unit head:* Dr. Joseph B. O'Donnell, Chair/Professor, 716-888-2868, E-mail: odonnelj@canisius.edu. *Application contact:* Jim Bagwell, Director, Graduate Admissions, 716-888-2545, Fax: 716-888-3290, E-mail: bagwellj@canisius.edu.

Central Michigan University, College of Graduate Studies, College of Business Administration, School of Accounting, Mount Pleasant, MI 48859. Offers MBA. *Accreditation:* AACSB. Part-time and evening/weekend programs available. *Faculty:* 7 full-time (1 woman), 1 part-time/adjunct (0 women). *Degree requirements:* For master's, comprehensive exam (for some programs), thesis (for some programs). *Entrance requirements:* For master's, GMAT. *Application deadline:* For fall admission, 6/1 for international students; for spring admission, 10/1 for international students. Applications are processed on a rolling basis. Application fee: $35 ($45 for international students). Electronic applications accepted. *Expenses:* Tuition, state resident: full-time $8208; part-time $456 per credit hour. Tuition, nonresident: full-time $13,788; part-time $766 per credit hour. One-time fee: $25. *Financial support:* Fellowships with full tuition reimbursements, research assistantships with full and partial tuition reimbursements, teaching assistantships with full and partial tuition reimbursements, career-related internships or fieldwork, Federal Work-Study, unspecified assistantships, and out-of-state merit awards, non-resident graduate awards available. Financial award application deadline: 3/1. *Faculty research:* Accounting and financial reporting for local government, tax accounting for partnerships and small corporations, accounting for employee stock ownership plans. *Unit head:* Dr. Philip Kintzele, Chairperson, 989-774-3796, Fax: 989-774-3999, E-mail: philip.l.kintzele@cmich.edu. *Application contact:* Dr. Debasish Chakraborty, Director, MBA Program, 989-774-3337, Fax: 989-774-1320, E-mail: chakr1d@cmich.edu.

Clark Atlanta University, School of Business Administration, Department of Accounting, Atlanta, GA 30314. Offers MA. Part-time programs available. *Faculty:* 2 full-time (both women). *Students:* 20 full-time (15 women); includes 15 Black or African American, non-Hispanic/Latino; 1 Hispanic/Latino, 2 international. Average age 23. 16 applicants, 94% accepted, 9 enrolled. In 2010, 13 master's awarded. *Entrance requirements:* For master's, GMAT, minimum undergraduate GPA of 2.5. Additional exam requirements/recommendations for international students: Required—TOEFL (minimum score 500 paper-based; 173 computer-based; 61 iBT). *Application deadline:* For fall admission, 4/1 for domestic and international students; for spring admission, 11/1 for domestic and international students. Applications are processed on a rolling basis. Application fee: $40 ($55 for international students). Electronic applications accepted. *Expenses:* Tuition: Full-time $12,942; part-time $719 per credit hour. Required fees: $710; $355 per semester. *Financial support:* Career-related internships or fieldwork, Federal Work-Study, scholarships/grants, and unspecified assistantships available. Support available to part-time students. Financial award application deadline: 4/30; financial award applicants required to submit FAFSA. *Unit head:* Dr. Kasim Alli, Chairperson, 404-880-8740, E-mail: kalli@cau.edu. *Application contact:* Michelle Clark-Davis, Graduate Program Admissions, 404-880-6605, E-mail: cauadmissions@cau.edu.

Clark University, Graduate School, Graduate School of Management, Business Administration Program, Worcester, MA 01610-1477. Offers accounting (MBA); finance (MBA); global business (MBA); health care management (MBA); management (MBA); management of information technology (MBA); marketing (MBA). *Accreditation:* AACSB. Part-time and evening/weekend programs available. *Students:* 147 full-time (75 women), 126 part-time (54 women); includes 24 minority (10 Black or African American, non-Hispanic/Latino; 1 American Indian or Alaska Native, non-Hispanic/Latino; 6 Asian, non-Hispanic/Latino; 5 Hispanic/Latino; 2 Two or more races, non-Hispanic/Latino), 99 international. Average age 30. 382 applicants, 57% accepted, 89 enrolled. In 2010, 101 master's awarded. *Degree requirements:* For master's, thesis optional. *Application deadline:* For fall admission, 6/1 priority date for domestic students; for spring admission, 12/1 priority date for domestic students. Applications are processed on a rolling basis. Application fee: $50. Electronic applications accepted. *Expenses:* Tuition: Full-time $37,000; part-time $1156 per credit hour. Required fees: $30; $1156 per credit hour. *Financial support:* In 2010–11, research assistantships with partial tuition reimbursements (averaging $4,800 per year), teaching assistantships with partial tuition reimbursements (averaging $4,800 per year) were awarded; fellowships, career-related internships or fieldwork, Federal Work-Study, institutionally sponsored loans, and tuition waivers (partial) also available. Support available to part-time students. Financial award application deadline: 5/31. *Faculty research:* Organizational development, accounting, marketing, finance, human resource management. *Unit head:* Dr. Joseph Sarkis, Dean, 508-793-7406, Fax: 508-793-8822, E-mail: clarkmba@clarku.edu. *Application contact:* Lynn Davis, Enrollment and Marketing Director, 508-793-7406, Fax: 508-793-8822, E-mail: clarkmba@clarku.edu.

Cleary University, Online Program in Business Administration, Ann Arbor, MI 48105-2659. Offers financial planning (MBA); financial planning (Graduate Certificate); green business strategy (MBA, Graduate Certificate); management (MBA); nonprofit management (MBA, Graduate Certificate); organizational leadership (MBA); public accounting (MBA). Part-time and evening/weekend programs available. Postbaccalaureate distance learning degree programs offered (no on-campus study). *Faculty:* 1 (woman) full-time, 20 part-time/adjunct (8 women). *Students:* 1 (woman) full-time, 115 part-time (67 women); includes 30 minority (21 Black or African American, non-Hispanic/Latino; 1 American Indian or Alaska Native, non-Hispanic/Latino; 6 Asian, non-Hispanic/Latino; 2 Hispanic/Latino), 7 international. Average age 34. 62 applicants, 77% accepted, 36 enrolled. In 2010, 22 master's awarded. *Degree requirements:* For master's, thesis. *Entrance requirements:* For master's, bachelor's degree; minimum GPA of 2.5; professional resume indicating minimum 2 years management or related experience; undergraduate degree from an accredited college or university with at least 18 quarter hours (or 12 semester hours) of accounting study (for MBA in accounting). Additional exam requirements/recommendations for international students: Required—TOEFL (minimum score 550 paper-based; 213 computer-based; 79 iBT), Michigan English Language Assessment Battery (minimum score: 75). *Application deadline:* For fall admission, 8/15 for domestic students, 7/15 for international students; for spring admission, 4/2 for domestic students, 1/2 for international students. Applications are processed on a rolling basis. Application fee: $50. Electronic applications accepted. *Financial support:* In 2010–11, 80 students received support, including 80 fellowships (averaging $12,501 per year); Federal Work-Study and scholarships/grants also available. Support available to part-time students. Financial award application deadline: 8/15; financial award applicants required to submit FAFSA. *Unit head:* Dr. Vincent Linder, Provost and Vice President for Academic Affairs, 800-686-1883, Fax: 734-332-4646, E-mail: vlinder@cleary.edu. *Application contact:* Carrie Bonofiglio, Director of Student Recruiting, 800-686-1883, Fax: 517-552-7805, E-mail: cbono@cleary.edu.

Clemson University, Graduate School, College of Business and Behavioral Science, School of Accountancy and Finance, Clemson, SC 29634. Offers MP Acc. *Accreditation:* AACSB. Part-time programs available. *Faculty:* 17 full-time (6 women), 2 part-time/adjunct (1 woman). *Students:* 37 full-time (22 women), 3 part-time (all women); includes 1 Asian, non-Hispanic/Latino; 2 Hispanic/Latino; 1 Two or more races, non-Hispanic/Latino, 8 international. Average age 24. 132 applicants, 41% accepted, 30 enrolled. In 2010, 40 master's awarded. *Degree requirements:* For master's, oral final exam. *Entrance requirements:* For master's, GMAT, BS in accounting or equivalent, minimum GPA of 3.0. Additional exam requirements/recommendations for international students: Required—TOEFL. *Application deadline:* For fall admission, 5/1 priority date for domestic students, 4/15 for international students; for spring admission, 10/1 for domestic students, 9/15 for international students. Applications are processed on a rolling basis. Application fee: $70 ($80 for international students). Electronic applications accepted. *Expenses:* Tuition, state resident: full-time $6492; part-time $400 per credit hour. Tuition, non-resident: full-time $13,634; part-time $800 per credit hour. Required fees: $262 per semester. Part-time tuition and fees vary according to course load and program. *Financial support:* In 2010–11, 17 students received support, including 14 teaching assistantships with partial tuition reimbursements available (averaging $5,220 per year); fellowships with full and partial tuition reimbursements available, research assistantships with partial tuition reimbursements available, career-related internships or fieldwork, institutionally sponsored loans, scholarships/grants, health care benefits, and unspecified assistantships also available. Support available to part-time students. Financial award applicants required to submit FAFSA. *Unit head:* Dr. Ralph E. Welton, Director, 864-656-4881, Fax: 864-656-4892, E-mail: edwlsur@clemson.edu. *Application contact:* Dr. Thomas L. Dickens, Program Coordinator, 864-656-4890, Fax: 864-656-4892, E-mail: dickent@clemson.edu.

Cleveland State University, College of Graduate Studies, Nance College of Business Administration, Department of Accounting, Cleveland, OH 44115. Offers financial accounting/audit (M Acc); taxation (M Acc). *Accreditation:*

AACSB. Part-time and evening/weekend programs available. *Faculty:* 13 full-time (4 women), 11 part-time/adjunct (3 women). *Students:* 110 full-time (60 women), 130 part-time (76 women); includes 22 Black or African American, non-Hispanic/Latino; 12 Asian, non-Hispanic/Latino; 6 Hispanic/Latino; 1 Two or more races, non-Hispanic/Latino, 60 international. Average age 30. 87 applicants, 64% accepted, 19 enrolled. In 2010, 30 master's awarded. *Entrance requirements:* For master's, GMAT, minimum GPA of 2.75. Additional exam requirements/recommendations for international students: Required—TOEFL (minimum score 525 paper-based; 197 computer-based). *Application deadline:* For fall admission, 7/15 priority date for domestic students; for spring admission, 12/15 priority date for domestic students. Applications are processed on a rolling basis. Application fee: $30. *Expenses:* Tuition, state resident: full-time $8447; part-time $469 per credit hour. Tuition, nonresident: full-time $16,020; part-time $890 per credit hour. Required fees: $50. *Financial support:* In 2010–11, 3 research assistantships with full and partial tuition reimbursements (averaging $6,960 per year) were awarded; career-related internships or fieldwork, Federal Work-Study, scholarships/grants, and unspecified assistantships also available. Financial award applicants required to submit FAFSA. *Faculty research:* Internal auditing, computer auditing, accounting education, managerial accounting. *Unit head:* Bruce W. McClain, Chair, 216-687-3652, Fax: 216-687-9212, E-mail: b.mcclain@csuohio.edu. *Application contact:* Bruce Gottschalk, MBA Programs Administrator, 216-687-3730, Fax: 216-687-5311, E-mail: cbacsu@csuohio.edu.

Coastal Carolina University, Wall College of Business Administration, Conway, SC 29528-6054. Offers accounting (MBA); business (MBA). *Accreditation:* AACSB. Part-time and evening/weekend programs available. *Faculty:* 9 full-time (4 women). *Students:* 43 full-time (18 women), 13 part-time (5 women); includes 2 minority (both Black or African American, non-Hispanic/Latino), 6 international. Average age 27. 37 applicants, 68% accepted, 21 enrolled. In 2010, 25 master's awarded. *Entrance requirements:* For master's, GMAT, 2 letters of recommendation, resume, completion of prerequisites with minimum B average grade. Additional exam requirements/recommendations for international students: Required—TOEFL (minimum score 575 paper-based). *Application deadline:* For fall admission, 3/15 priority date for domestic and international students; for spring admission, 10/15 priority date for domestic and international students. Applications are processed on a rolling basis. Application fee: $45. Electronic applications accepted. *Expenses:* Contact institution. *Financial support:* Application deadline: 3/1. *Unit head:* John O. Lox, MBA Director, 843-349-2469, Fax: 843-349-2455, E-mail: jlox@coastal.edu. *Application contact:* Dr. Deborah A. Vrooman, Interim Director of Graduate Studies, 843-349-2783, Fax: 843-349-6444, E-mail: vroomand@coastal.edu.

The College at Brockport, State University of New York, Office of the Vice Provost, Department of Business Administration and Economics, Brockport, NY 14420-2997. Offers accounting (MS); forensic accounting (MS). Part-time programs available. *Students:* 15 full-time (9 women), 11 part-time (9 women); includes 1 Black or African American, non-Hispanic/Latino; 1 Asian, non-Hispanic/Latino. 28 applicants, 64% accepted, 16 enrolled. In 2010, 6 master's awarded. *Entrance requirements:* For master's, GMAT or GRE General Test, minimum GPA of 3.0, letters of recommendation, statement of objectives. Additional exam requirements/recommendations for international students: Required—TOEFL (minimum score 550 paper-based; 213 computer-based; 79 iBT). *Application deadline:* For fall admission, 7/15 priority date for domestic and international students; for spring admission, 11/1 priority date for domestic and international students. Application fee: $50. Electronic applications accepted. *Financial support:* Federal Work-Study, scholarships/grants, and unspecified assistantships available. Support available to part-time students. Financial award application deadline: 3/15; financial award applicants required to submit FAFSA. *Unit head:* Dr. John Keiser, Chairperson and Associate Professor, 585-395-2623, Fax: 585-395-2542, E-mail: jkeiser@brockport.edu. *Application contact:* Dr. D. Donald Kent, Graduate Director, 585-395-5521, Fax: 585-395-2542, E-mail: dkent@brockport.edu.

College of Charleston, Graduate School, School of Business, Program in Accountancy, Charleston, SC 29424-0001. Offers MS. *Accreditation:* AACSB. Part-time and evening/weekend programs available. *Faculty:* 12 full-time (5 women). *Students:* 24 full-time (15 women), 5 part-time (all women); includes 2 minority (1 Black or African American, non-Hispanic/Latino; 1 Hispanic/Latino), 1 international. Average age 24. 56 applicants, 55% accepted, 24 enrolled. In 2010, 46 master's awarded. *Entrance requirements:* For master's, GMAT, minimum GPA of 3.0 in last 60 hours of undergraduate course work, 24 hours of course work in accounting, 2 letters of reference. Additional exam requirements/recommendations for international students: Required—TOEFL (minimum score 81 iBT). *Application deadline:* For fall admission, 7/1 for domestic students. Applications are processed on a rolling basis. Application fee: $45. Electronic applications accepted. *Financial support:* In 2010–11, research assistantships (averaging $6,200 per year); Federal Work-Study, institutionally sponsored loans, scholarships/grants, and unspecified assistantships also available. Support available to part-time students. Financial award application deadline: 3/1; financial award applicants required to submit FAFSA. *Unit head:* Dr. Michael C. Cipriano, Director, 843-953-7166, Fax: 843-953-5697, E-mail: ciprianom@cofc.edu. *Application contact:* Susan

Hallatt, Director of Admissions, 843-953-5614, Fax: 843-953-1434, E-mail: hallatts@cofc.edu.

The College of William and Mary, Mason School of Business, Master of Accounting Program, Williamsburg, VA 23185. Offers M Acc. *Accreditation:* AACSB. *Faculty:* 13 full-time (4 women), 4 part-time/adjunct (1 woman). *Students:* 91 full-time (45 women); includes 12 minority (2 Black or African American, non-Hispanic/Latino; 7 Asian, non-Hispanic/Latino; 3 Hispanic/Latino), 17 international. Average age 23. 310 applicants, 44% accepted, 90 enrolled. In 2010, 68 master's awarded. *Entrance requirements:* For master's, GMAT, 2 written recommendations, interview. Additional exam requirements/recommendations for international students: Required—TOEFL (minimum score 620 paper-based; 260 computer-based; 102 iBT), IELTS (minimum score 7), TOEFL (minimum score 620 paper-based; 260 computer-based; 102 IBT) or IELTS (minimum score 7). *Application deadline:* Applications are processed on a rolling basis. Application fee: $80. Electronic applications accepted. *Expenses:* Contact institution. *Financial support:* In·2010–11, 12 research assistantships (averaging $4,000 per year) were awarded; fellowships, scholarships/grants and unspecified assistantships also available. Financial award application deadline: 3/15; financial award applicants required to submit FAFSA. *Faculty research:* Valuation, voluntary disclosure, auditing, taxation, executive compensation. *Unit head:* Linda Espahbodi, Director, 757-221-2953, Fax: 757-221-7862, E-mail: linda.espahbodi@mason.wm.edu. *Application contact:* Martha Howard, Associate Director, 757-221-2875, Fax: 757-221-7862, E-mail: martha.howard@mason.wm.edu.

Colorado State University, Graduate School, College of Business, Department of Accounting, Fort Collins, CO 80523-1271. Offers M Acc. Part-time programs available. *Faculty:* 10 full-time (3 women). *Students:* 46 full-time (27 women), 34 part-time (17 women); includes 5 minority (1 American Indian or Alaska Native, non-Hispanic/Latino; 3 Asian, non-Hispanic/Latino; 1 Hispanic/Latino), 10 international. Average age 36. 85 applicants, 74% accepted, 44 enrolled. In 2010, 26 master's awarded. *Degree requirements:* For master's, thesis or alternative. *Entrance requirements:* For master's, GMAT, minimum GPA of 3.0; BA/BS. Additional exam requirements/recommendations for international students: Required—TOEFL (minimum score 565 paper-based; 227 computer-based; 86 iBT). *Application deadline:* For fall admission, 7/15 for domestic students, 6/1 for international students; for spring admission, 11/15 for domestic students, 11/1 for international students. Applications are processed on a rolling basis. Application fee: $50. Electronic applications accepted. *Expenses:* Tuition, state resident: full-time $7434; part-time $413 per credit. Tuition, nonresident: full-time $19,022; part-time $1057 per credit. Required fees: $1729; $88 per credit. *Financial support:* Fellowships with partial tuition reimbursements, research assistantships with partial tuition reimbursements, unspecified assistantships available. Financial award application deadline: 3/1; financial award applicants required to submit FAFSA. *Faculty research:* Financial accounting and reporting, managerial accounting, earnings management, stock options, corporate social responsibility. *Unit head:* Dr. Bill Rankin, Department Head, 970-491-4244, Fax: 970-491-2676, E-mail: bill.rankin@business.colostate.edu. *Application contact:* Claire Pettner, Graduate Contact, 970-491-4612, Fax: 970-491-2676, E-mail: claire.pettner@colostate.edu.

Cornell University, Graduate School, Graduate Field of Management, Ithaca, NY 14853. Offers accounting (PhD); behavioral decision theory (PhD); finance (PhD); marketing (PhD); organizational behavior (PhD); production and operations management (PhD). *Accreditation:* AACSB. *Faculty:* 55 full-time (9 women). *Students:* 41 full-time (12 women); includes 5 Asian, non-Hispanic/Latino, 23 international. Average age 29. 436 applicants, 4% accepted, 12 enrolled. In 2010, 5 doctorates awarded. *Degree requirements:* For doctorate, comprehensive exam, thesis/dissertation. *Entrance requirements:* For doctorate, GMAT or GRE General Test. Additional exam requirements/recommendations for international students: Required—TOEFL (minimum score 600 paper-based; 250 computer-based; 77 iBT). *Application deadline:* For fall admission, 1/3 for domestic students. Application fee: $70. Electronic applications accepted. *Expenses:* Contact institution. *Financial support:* In 2010–11, 38 students received support, including 4 fellowships with full tuition reimbursements available, 34 research assistantships with full tuition reimbursements available, 1 teaching assistantship with full tuition reimbursement available; institutionally sponsored loans, scholarships/grants, health care benefits, tuition waivers (full and partial), and unspecified assistantships also available. Financial award applicants required to submit FAFSA. *Faculty research:* Operations and manufacturing. *Unit head:* Director of Graduate Studies, 607-255-3669. *Application contact:* Graduate Field Assistant, 607-255-9431, E-mail: js_phd@cornell.edu.

Daemen College, Department of Accounting/Information Systems, Amherst, NY 14226-3592. Offers global business (MS), including accounting, global business, management information systems, marketing. Part-time and evening/weekend programs available. *Faculty:* 1 full-time (0 women), 1 part-time/adjunct (0 women). *Students:* 19 full-time (16 women), 5 part-time (1 woman); includes 1 minority (Black or African American, non-Hispanic/Latino), 18 international. Average age 28. In 2010, 12 master's awarded. *Degree requirements:* For master's, minimum GPA of 3.0. *Entrance requirements:* For master's, GMAT if undergraduate GPA is less than 3.0, 2 letters of recommendation; goal statement; transcripts; demonstration of satisfactory oral and written English. Additional exam requirements/recommendations for international students: Required—TOEFL (minimum score 500 paper-based; 173 computer-based; 63 iBT), IELTS (minimum score 5.5). *Application deadline:* For fall admission, 3/1 priority date for domestic and international students; for spring admission, 10/1 priority date for domestic and international students. Applications are processed on a rolling basis. Application fee: $25. Electronic applications accepted. *Expenses:* Tuition: Part-time $830 per credit hour. Tuition and fees vary according to course load and reciprocity agreements. *Financial support:* Institutionally sponsored loans, scholarships/grants, and scholarships available. Financial award application deadline: 2/15; financial award applicants required to submit FAFSA. *Faculty research:* Internationalization of small business, cultural influences on business practices, international human resource practices. *Unit head:* S. Sgt. Sharlene S. Buszka, Chair, 716-839-8428, Fax: 716-839-8261, E-mail: sbuszka@daemen.edu. *Application contact:* Scott Rowe, Associate Director of Graduate Admissions, 716-839-8225, Fax: 716-839-8229, E-mail: srowe@daemen.edu.

DePaul University, Charles H. Kellstadt Graduate School of Business, School of Accountancy and Management Information Systems, Chicago, IL 60604-2287. Offers accountancy (M Acc, MSA); business information technology (MS); e-business (MBA, MS); financial management and control (MBA); management accounting (MBA); management information systems (MBA); taxation (MST). Part-time and evening/weekend programs available. *Faculty:* 30 full-time (9 women), 54 part-time/adjunct (7 women). *Students:* 207 full-time (112 women), 208 part-time (92 women); includes 7 Black or African American, non-Hispanic/Latino; 34 Asian, non-Hispanic/Latino; 19 Hispanic/Latino; 2 Two or more races, non-Hispanic/Latino, 76 international. In 2010, 141 master's awarded. *Entrance requirements:* For master's, GMAT, 2 letters of recommendation, resume. Additional exam requirements/recommendations for international students: Required—TOEFL (minimum score 550 paper-based; 213 computer-based). *Application deadline:* For fall admission, 7/1 for domestic students; for winter admission, 10/1 for domestic students; for spring admission, 2/1 for domestic students. Applications are processed on a rolling basis. Application fee: $60. *Financial support:* In 2010–11, 7 research assistantships with full tuition reimbursements (averaging $4,100 per year) were awarded; institutionally sponsored loans also available. Financial award application deadline: 4/2. *Faculty research:* Tax policy, property transactions, stock options as compensation, standards setting, activity-based costing in health care. *Unit head:* Kevin Stevens, Director, 312-362-6989, E-mail: kstevens@depaul.edu. *Application contact:* Christopher E. Kinsella, Director of Cohort MBA Programs, 312-362-8810, Fax: 312-362-6677, E-mail: kgsb@depaul.edu.

DeSales University, Graduate Division, Program in Business Administration, Center Valley, PA 18034-9568. Offers accounting (MBA); computer information systems (MBA); finance (MBA); health care systems management (MBA); health care systems management (online) (MBA); human resource management (MBA); management (MBA); management (online) (MBA); marketing (MBA); marketing (online) (MBA); physician's track (MBA); project management (MBA); project management (online) (MBA); self-design (MBA); self-design (online) (MBA); MSN/MBA. *Accreditation:* ACBSP. Part-time programs available. Postbaccalaureate distance learning degree programs offered (no on-campus study). *Entrance requirements:* For master's, GMAT, minimum GPA of 3.0, 2 years of work experience. Additional exam requirements/recommendations for international students: Required—TOEFL. *Application deadline:* Applications are processed on a rolling basis. Application fee: $35. Electronic applications accepted. *Expenses:* Tuition: Full-time $18,200; part-time $690 per credit. Required fees: $1200. *Faculty research:* Quality improvement, executive development, productivity, cross-cultural managerial differences, leadership. *Unit head:* Dr. David Gilfoil, Director, 610-282-1100 Ext. 1828, Fax: 610-282-2869, E-mail: david.gilfoil@desales.edu. *Application contact:* Caryn Stopper, Director of Graduate Admissions, 610-282-1100 Ext. 1768, Fax: 610-282-0525, E-mail: caryn.stopper@desales.edu.

Duquesne University, John F. Donahue Graduate School of Business, Pittsburgh, PA 15282-0001. Offers accountancy (MS); business administration (MBA); information systems management (MSISM); sustainability (MBA); JD/MBA; MBA/MA; MBA/MES; MBA/MHMS; MBA/MLLS; MBA/MS; MBA/MSN. *Accreditation:* AACSB. Part-time and evening/weekend programs available. *Faculty:* 24 full-time (5 women), 14 part-time/adjunct (0 women). *Students:* 97 full-time (45 women), 234 part-time (91 women); includes 5 Black or African American, non-Hispanic/Latino; 1 Asian, non-Hispanic/Latino; 2 Hispanic/Latino; 4 Native Hawaiian or other Pacific Islander, non-Hispanic/Latino, 29 international. Average age 31. 289 applicants, 43% accepted, 82 enrolled. In 2010, 120 master's awarded. *Entrance requirements:* For master's, GMAT, 2 letters of recommendation, current resume. Additional exam requirements/recommendations for international students: Required—TOEFL (minimum score 577 paper-based; 233 computer-based; 90 iBT); Recommended—TWE. *Application deadline:* For fall admission, 5/1 priority date for domestic students, 5/1 for international students; for spring admission, 10/1 for domestic and international students. Applications are processed on a rolling basis. Application fee: $0. Electronic applications accepted. *Expenses:* Tuition: Part-time $884 per credit. Required fees: $84 per credit. Tuition and fees vary according to course load. *Financial support:* In 2010–11,

40 students received support, including 12 fellowships with partial tuition reimbursements available, 28 research assistantships with partial tuition reimbursements available; career-related internships or fieldwork, scholarships/grants, and unspecified assistantships also available. Financial award application deadline: 7/1; financial award applicants required to submit FAFSA. *Faculty research:* International business, investment management, business ethics, technology management, supply chain management, business strategy, finance. *Unit head:* Alan R. Miciak, Dean, 412-396-5848, Fax: 412-396-5304, E-mail: miciaka@duq.edu. *Application contact:* Patricia Moore, Assistant Director, 412-396-6276, Fax: 412-396-1726, E-mail: moorep@duq.edu.

Eastern Michigan University, Graduate School, College of Business, Department of Accounting and Finance, Ypsilanti, MI 48197. Offers accounting (MS); accounting information systems (MS). Part-time and evening/weekend programs available. Postbaccalaureate distance learning degree programs offered (minimal on-campus study). *Faculty:* 23 full-time (7 women). *Students:* 44 full-time (24 women), 53 part-time (29 women); includes 11 minority (3 Black or African American, non-Hispanic/Latino; 7 Asian, non-Hispanic/Latino; 1 Hispanic/Latino), 11 international. Average age 30. 56 applicants, 54% accepted, 25 enrolled. In 2010, 55 master's awarded. *Entrance requirements:* For master's, GMAT. Additional exam requirements/recommendations for international students: Required—TOEFL. *Application deadline:* Applications are processed on a rolling basis. Application fee: $35. *Financial support:* Fellowships, research assistantships with full tuition reimbursements, teaching assistantships with full tuition reimbursements, career-related internships or fieldwork, Federal Work-Study, institutionally sponsored loans, scholarships/grants, tuition waivers (partial), and unspecified assistantships available. Support available to part-time students. Financial award applicants required to submit FAFSA. *Unit head:* Dr. Jens Stephan, Department Head, 734-487-3320, Fax: 734-482-0806, E-mail: jens.stephan@emich.edu. *Application contact:* Dr. Phil Lewis, Advisor, 734-487-6817, Fax: 734-482-0806, E-mail: plewis4@emich.edu.

East Tennessee State University, School of Graduate Studies, College of Business and Technology, Department of Accountancy, Johnson City, TN 37614. Offers M Acc. *Accreditation:* AACSB. Part-time and evening/weekend programs available. *Faculty:* 8 full-time (1 woman). *Students:* 44 full-time (25 women), 8 part-time (5 women); includes 4 minority (1 American Indian or Alaska Native, non-Hispanic/Latino; 2 Hispanic/Latino; 1 Two or more races, non-Hispanic/Latino), 10 international. Average age 25. 56 applicants, 64% accepted, 24 enrolled. In 2010, 21 master's awarded. *Degree requirements:* For master's, comprehensive exam, capstone and professional accounting experience. *Entrance requirements:* For master's, GMAT, minimum GPA of 2.5. Additional exam requirements/recommendations for international students: Required—TOEFL (minimum score 550 paper-based; 213 computer-based; 79 iBT). *Application deadline:* For fall admission, 6/1 priority date for domestic students, 4/30 for international students; for spring admission, 11/1 for domestic students, 9/30 for international students. Application fee: $25 ($35 for international students). Electronic applications accepted. *Financial support:* In 2010–11, 10 research assistantships with full tuition reimbursements (averaging $5,500 per year) were awarded; career-related internships or fieldwork, institutionally sponsored loans, scholarships/grants, and unspecified assistantships also available. Financial award application deadline: 7/1; financial award applicants required to submit FAFSA. *Faculty research:* Financial accounting, taxation, auditing, management accounting. *Unit head:* Dr. Paul E. Bayes, Chair, 423-439-8656, Fax: 423-439-5274, E-mail: bayes@etsu.edu. *Application contact:* Dr. Paul E. Bayes, Chair, 423-439-8656, Fax: 423-439-5274, E-mail: bayes@etsu.edu.

Edgewood College, Program in Business, Madison, WI 53711-1997. Offers accountancy (MS); business (MBA). *Accreditation:* ACBSP. Part-time and evening/weekend programs available. *Students:* 38 full-time (20 women), 98 part-time (42 women); includes 9 minority (1 Black or African American, non-Hispanic/Latino; 5 Asian, non-Hispanic/Latino; 1 Hispanic/Latino; 2 Two or more races, non-Hispanic/Latino), 6 international. Average age 33. In 2010, 45 master's awarded. *Entrance requirements:* For master's, GMAT (minimum score 425), minimum GPA of 2.75, 2 letters of recommendation. Additional exam requirements/recommendations for international students: Required—TOEFL (minimum score 213 computer-based). *Application deadline:* For fall admission, 8/26 for domestic students, 8/1 for international students; for spring admission, 1/10 for domestic students, 10/1 for international students. Applications are processed on a rolling basis. Application fee: $25. Electronic applications accepted. *Expenses:* Tuition: Part-time $719 per credit hour. *Financial support:* Career-related internships or fieldwork available. *Unit head:* Martin Preizler, Dean, 608-663-2898, Fax: 608-663-3291, E-mail: martinpreizler@edgewood.edu. *Application contact:* Joann Eastman, Admissions Counselor, 608-663-3250, Fax: 608-663-2214, E-mail: gps@edgewood.edu.

Elmhurst College, Graduate Programs, Program in Professional Accountancy, Elmhurst, IL 60126-3296. Offers MPA. Part-time and evening/weekend programs available. *Faculty:* 2 full-time (1 woman), 1 part-time/adjunct (0 women). *Students:* 4 full-time (1 woman), 17 part-time (7 women); includes 5 minority (1 Black or African American, non-Hispanic/Latino; 2 Asian, non-Hispanic/Latino; 1 Hispanic/Latino; 1 Two or more races, non-Hispanic/Latino). Average age 28. 15 applicants, 53% accepted, 7 enrolled. In 2010, 11 master's awarded. *Entrance requirements:* For master's, 3 recommendations, resume, statement of purpose. Additional exam requirements/recommendations for international students: Required—TOEFL (minimum score 550 paper-based; 213 computer-based). *Application deadline:* Applications are processed on a rolling basis. Application fee: $0. Electronic applications accepted. *Expenses:* Tuition: Part-time $785 per credit hour. Required fees: $60 per year. Tuition and fees vary according to program. *Financial support:* In 2010–11, 3 students received support. Federal Work-Study and scholarships/grants available. Support available to part-time students. Financial award application deadline: 6/1; financial award applicants required to submit FAFSA. *Unit head:* Elizabeth D. Kuebler, Director of Adult and Graduate Admission, 630-617-3300, Fax: 630-617-5501, E-mail: sal@elmhurst.edu. *Application contact:* Elizabeth D. Kuebler, Director of Adult and Graduate Admission, 630-617-3300, Fax: 630-617-5501, E-mail: sal@elmhurst.edu.

Emory University, Goizueta Business School, Doctoral Program in Business, Atlanta, GA 30322-1100. Offers accounting (PhD); finance (PhD); information systems (PhD); marketing (PhD); organization and management (PhD). *Faculty:* 55 full-time (11 women). *Students:* 32 full-time (17 women); includes 1 Black or African American, non-Hispanic/Latino; 17 Asian, non-Hispanic/Latino; 1 Hispanic/Latino. Average age 29. 218 applicants, 9% accepted, 9 enrolled. In 2010, 8 doctorates awarded. *Degree requirements:* For doctorate, comprehensive exam, thesis/dissertation. *Entrance requirements:* For doctorate, GMAT (strongly preferred) or GRE. Additional exam requirements/recommendations for international students: Required—TOEFL (minimum score 250 computer-based). *Application deadline:* For fall admission, 1/3 priority date for domestic students, 1/1 priority date for international students. Application fee: $50. Electronic applications accepted. *Expenses:* Tuition: Full-time $33,800. Required fees: $1300. *Financial support:* In 2010–11, 32 students received support. *Unit head:* Dr. Lawrence Benveniste, Dean, 404-727-6377, Fax: 404-727-0868, E-mail: larry benveniste@bus.emory.edu. Application contact: Allison Gilmore, Director of Admissions & Student Services, 404-727-6353, Fax: 404-727-5337, E-mail: phd@bus.emory.edu.

Fairfield University, Charles F. Dolan School of Business, Fairfield, CT 06824-5195. Offers accounting (MBA, MS, CAS); accounting information systems (MBA); entrepreneurship (MBA); finance (MBA, MS, CAS); general management (MBA, CAS); human resource management (MBA, CAS); information systems and operations (MBA); information systems and operations management (CAS); international business (MBA, CAS); marketing (MBA, CAS); taxation (MBA, CAS). *Accreditation:* AACSB. Part-time and evening/weekend programs available. *Faculty:* 42 full-time (15 women), 8 part-time/adjunct (1 woman). *Students:* 89 full-time (32 women), 127 part-time (54 women); includes 4 Black or African American, non-Hispanic/Latino; 2 Asian, non-Hispanic/Latino; 4 Hispanic/Latino; 1 Two or more races, non-Hispanic/Latino, 17 international. Average age 29. 108 applicants, 62% accepted, 46 enrolled. In 2010, 79 master's awarded. *Degree requirements:* For master's, capstone course. *Entrance requirements:* For master's, GMAT (minimum score 500), 2 letters of reference, resume, minimum GPA of 3.0. Additional exam requirements/recommendations for international students: Required—TOEFL (minimum score 550 paper-based; 213 computer-based; 80 iBT). *Application deadline:* For fall admission, 5/15 for international students; for spring admission, 10/15 for international students. Applications are processed on a rolling basis. Application fee: $60. Electronic applications accepted. *Expenses:* Contact institution. *Financial support:* In 2010–11, 48 students received support. Scholarships/grants, unspecified assistantships, and merit based one-time entrance scholarship available. Financial award applicants required to submit FAFSA. *Faculty research:* Optimization strategies, international finance, consumer behavior, financial market volatility, Internet marketing, supply chain analysis, tax issues. Total annual research expenditures: $50,000. *Unit head:* Dr. Norman A. Solomon, Dean, 203-254-4000 Ext. 4070, Fax: 203-254-4105, E-mail: nsolomon@fairfield.edu. *Application contact:* Marianne Gumpper, Director of Graduate and Continuing Studies Admissions, 203-254-4184, Fax: 203-254-4073, E-mail: gradadmis@fairfield.edu.

Fairleigh Dickinson University, College at Florham, Silberman College of Business, Department of Accounting, Law, and Tax, Program in Accounting, Madison, NJ 07940-1099. Offers MS. *Students:* 23 full-time (17 women), 28 part-time (8 women), 6 international. Average age 28. 27 applicants, 78% accepted, 16 enrolled. In 2010, 27 master's awarded. *Entrance requirements:* For master's, GMAT. *Application deadline:* Applications are processed on a rolling basis. Application fee: $40.

Fairleigh Dickinson University, Metropolitan Campus, Silberman College of Business, Department of Accounting, Law, and Tax, Program in Accounting, Teaneck, NJ 07666-1914. Offers MBA, MS, Certificate. *Students:* 96 full-time (31 women), 31 part-time (16 women), 35 international. Average age 28. 80 applicants, 76% accepted, 34 enrolled. In 2010, 74 master's awarded. *Application deadline:* Applications are processed on a rolling basis. Application fee: $40. *Faculty research:* Corporate accounting, legal issues. *Application contact:* Susan Brooman, University Director of Graduate Admissions, 201-692-2554, Fax: 201-692-2560, E-mail: globaleducation@fdu.edu.

Fitchburg State University, Division of Graduate and Continuing Education, Program in Business Administration, Fitchburg, MA 01420-2697. Offers accounting (MBA); human resource management (MBA);

management (MBA). Part-time and evening/weekend programs available. Postbaccalaureate distance learning degree programs offered (no on-campus study). *Students:* 24 full-time (11 women), 74 part-time (46 women); includes 6 Black or African American, non-Hispanic/Latino; 1 American Indian or Alaska Native, non-Hispanic/Latino; 5 Hispanic/Latino, 13 international. Average age 33. 42 applicants, 98% accepted, 33 enrolled. In 2010, 59 master's awarded. *Entrance requirements:* For master's, GMAT, minimum GPA of 2.8, letters of recommendation, resume. Additional exam requirements/recommendations for international students: Required—TOEFL (minimum score 550 paper-based; 213 computer-based; 79 iBT). *Application deadline:* Applications are processed on a rolling basis. Application fee: $25 ($50 for international students). *Expenses:* Tuition, area resident: Part-time $150 per credit. Tuition, state resident: part-time $150 per credit. Tuition, nonresident: part-time $150 per credit. Required fees: $127 per credit. *Financial support:* In 2010–11, research assistantships with partial tuition reimbursements (averaging $5,500 per year); Federal Work-Study, scholarships/grants, and unspecified assistantships also available. Support available to part-time students. Financial award application deadline: 3/1; financial award applicants required to submit FAFSA. *Unit head:* Joseph McAloon, Chair, 978-665-3745, Fax: 978-665-3658, E-mail: gce@fitchburgstate.edu. *Application contact:* Director of Admissions, 978-665-3144, Fax: 978-665-4540, E-mail: admissions@fitchburgstate.edu.

Florida Atlantic University, College of Business, School of Accounting, Boca Raton, FL 33431-0991. Offers M Ac, M Tax, PhD. *Accreditation:* AACSB. Part-time and evening/weekend programs available. Postbaccalaureate distance learning degree programs offered (minimal on-campus study). *Faculty:* 27 full-time (13 women), 21 part-time/adjunct (6 women). *Students:* 81 full-time (43 women), 320 part-time (195 women); includes 112 minority (42 Black or African American, non-Hispanic/Latino; 26 Asian, non-Hispanic/Latino; 41 Hispanic/Latino; 3 Two or more races, non-Hispanic/Latino), 6 international. Average age 31. 347 applicants, 46% accepted, 134 enrolled. In 2010, 153 master's awarded. *Degree requirements:* For master's, comprehensive exam, thesis optional. *Entrance requirements:* For master's, GMAT, BS in accounting or equivalent, minimum GPA of 3.0 in accounting. Additional exam requirements/recommendations for international students: Required—TOEFL (minimum score 600 paper-based; 250 computer-based). *Application deadline:* For fall admission, 7/1 priority date for domestic students, 2/15 priority date for international students; for spring admission, 11/1 priority date for domestic students, 7/15 priority date for international students. Applications are processed on a rolling basis. Application fee: $30. *Expenses:* Tuition, area resident: Part-time $319.96 per credit. Tuition, state resident: part-time $319.96 per credit. Tuition, nonresident: part-time $926.42 per credit. *Financial support:* Fellowships, research assistantships with partial tuition reimbursements, teaching assistantships, career-related internships or fieldwork, Federal Work-Study, institutionally sponsored loans, scholarships/grants, and tuition waivers (partial) available. Support available to part-time students. Financial award application deadline: 3/1. *Faculty research:* Systems and computer applications, accounting theory, information systems. *Unit head:* Dr. Somnath Bhattacharya, Director, 561-297-3638, Fax: 561-297-7023, E-mail: sbhatt@fau.edu. *Application contact:* Dr. Kim Dunn, Graduate Adviser, 561-297-3643, Fax: 561-297-1315, E-mail: kdunn@fau.edu.

Florida Gulf Coast University, Lutgert College of Business, Program in Accounting and Taxation, Fort Myers, FL 33965-6565. Offers MS. Part-time and evening/weekend programs available. *Faculty:* 64 full-time (21 women), 5 part-time/adjunct (1 woman). *Students:* 37 full-time (23 women), 27 part-time (14 women); includes 1 Black or African American, non-Hispanic/Latino; 1 American Indian or Alaska Native, non-Hispanic/Latino; 5 Asian, non-Hispanic/Latino; 10 Hispanic/Latino, 2 international. Average age 29. 47 applicants, 77% accepted, 26 enrolled. In 2010, 36 master's awarded. *Degree requirements:* For master's, thesis or alternative. *Entrance requirements:* For master's, GMAT, minimum GPA of 3.0. Additional exam requirements/recommendations for international students: Required—TOEFL (minimum score 550 paper-based; 213 computer-based). *Application deadline:* For fall admission, 6/1 priority date for domestic students; for spring admission, 11/1 for domestic students. Applications are processed on a rolling basis. Application fee: $30. Electronic applications accepted. *Expenses:* Tuition, state resident: part-time $322.08 per credit hour. Tuition, nonresident: part-time $1117.08 per credit hour. *Faculty research:* Stock petitions, mergers and acquisitions, deferred taxes, fraud and accounting regulations, graphical reporting practices. *Unit head:* Dr. Ara Volkan, Chair, 239-590-7380, Fax: 239-590-7330, E-mail: avolkan@fgcu.edu. *Application contact:* Marisa Ouverson, Director of Enrollment Management, 239-590-7403, Fax: 239-590-7330, E-mail: mouverso@fgcu.edu.

Florida Institute of Technology, Graduate Programs, Nathan M. Bisk College of Business, Online Programs, Melbourne, FL 32901-6975. Offers accounting (MBA); accounting and finance (MBA); finance (MBA); healthcare management (MBA); information technology (MS); information technology management (MBA); Internet marketing (MBA); management (MBA); marketing (MBA); project management (MBA). Part-time and evening/weekend programs available. Postbaccalaureate distance learning degree programs offered (no on-campus study). *Faculty:* 32 part-time/adjunct (8 women). *Students:* 4 full-time (1 woman), 1,062 part-time (499 women);

includes 373 minority (244 Black or African American, non-Hispanic/Latino; 8 American Indian or Alaska Native, non-Hispanic/Latino; 37 Asian, non-Hispanic/Latino; 76 Hispanic/Latino; 8 Native Hawaiian or other Pacific Islander, non-Hispanic/Latino), 39 international. Average age 37. 299 applicants, 167 enrolled. In 2010, 134 master's awarded. *Entrance requirements:* For master's, GMAT or resume showing 8 years of supervised experience, 2 letters of recommendation, resume, competency in math past college algebra. Additional exam requirements/recommendations for international students: Required—TOEFL (minimum score 550 paper-based; 213 computer-based; 79 iBT). *Application deadline:* For fall admission, 4/1 for international students; for spring admission, 9/30 for international students. Applications are processed on a rolling basis. Application fee: $50. Electronic applications accepted. *Expenses:* Contact institution. *Financial support:* Available to part-time students. Application deadline: 3/1. *Unit head:* Dr. Mary S. Bonhomme, Dean, Florida Tech Online Associate Provost for Online Learning, 321-674-8202, Fax: 321-674-8216, E-mail: bonhomme@fit.edu. *Application contact:* Carolyn Farrior, Director of Graduate Admissions Online Learning and Off Campus Programs, 321-674-7118, Fax: 321-674-8216, E-mail: cfarrior@fit.edu.

Florida International University, Alvah H. Chapman, Jr. Graduate School of Business, School of Accounting, Program in Accounting, Miami, FL 33199. Offers M Acc. *Accreditation:* AACSB. Part-time and evening/weekend programs available. *Students:* 69 full-time (41 women), 34 part-time (24 women); includes 10 Black or African American, non-Hispanic/Latino; 6 Asian, non-Hispanic/Latino; 70 Hispanic/Latino, 4 international. Average age 30. 277 applicants, 43% accepted. In 2010, 119 master's awarded. *Entrance requirements:* For master's, GMAT or GRE, minimum GPA of 3.0 (upper-level coursework); resume. Additional exam requirements/recommendations for international students: Required—TOEFL (minimum score 550 paper-based; 213 computer-based; 80 iBT) or IELTS (minimum score 6.5). *Application deadline:* For fall admission, 6/1 for domestic and international students; for spring admission, 10/1 for domestic students, 9/1 for international students. Applications are processed on a rolling basis. Application fee: $30. Electronic applications accepted. *Expenses:* Contact institution. *Financial support:* Institutionally sponsored loans and scholarships/grants available. Financial award application deadline: 3/1; financial award applicants required to submit FAFSA. *Faculty research:* Financial and managerial accounting. *Unit head:* Dr. Sharon Lassar, Director, School of Accounting, 305-348-3501, Fax: 305-348-2914, E-mail: sharon.lassar@fiu.edu. *Application contact:* Teresita Brunken, 305-348-4224, Fax: 305-348-2914, E-mail: brunkent@fiu.edu.

Florida State University, The Graduate School, College of Business, Tallahassee, FL 32306-1110. Offers accounting (M Acc), including accounting information services, assurance services, corporate accounting, taxation; business administration (MBA, PhD), including accounting (PhD), finance (PhD), management information systems (PhD), marketing (PhD), organizational behavior (PhD), risk management and insurance (PhD), strategic management (PhD); finance (MS); insurance (MSM); management information systems (MS); JD/MBA; MSW/MBA. *Accreditation:* AACSB. Part-time programs available. Postbaccalaureate distance learning degree programs offered (no on-campus study). *Faculty:* 107 full-time (31 women). *Students:* 196 full-time (76 women), 310 part-time (109 women); includes 27 Black or African American, non-Hispanic/Latino; 1 American Indian or Alaska Native, non-Hispanic/Latino; 31 Asian, non-Hispanic/Latino; 30 Hispanic/Latino. Average age 30. 702 applicants, 33% accepted, 205 enrolled. In 2010, 268 master's, 17 doctorates awarded. Terminal master's awarded for partial completion of doctoral program. *Degree requirements:* For doctorate, comprehensive exam, thesis/dissertation. *Entrance requirements:* For master's, GMAT, work experience (MBA, MS), minimum GPA of 3.0, letters of recommendation; for doctorate, GMAT, minimum graduate GPA of 3.5, letters of recommendation. Additional exam requirements/recommendations for international students: Required—TOEFL (minimum score 600 paper-based; 80 computer-based); Recommended—IELTS (minimum score 6.5). *Application deadline:* For fall admission, 6/1 for domestic students, 5/1 for international students; for spring admission, 10/1 for domestic students, 9/1 for international students. Applications are processed on a rolling basis. Application fee: $30. Electronic applications accepted. *Expenses:* Tuition, state resident: full-time $8238.24. *Financial support:* In 2010–11, 86 students received support, including 12 fellowships with full tuition reimbursements available (averaging $7,161 per year), 30 research assistantships with full tuition reimbursements available (averaging $6,000 per year), 43 teaching assistantships with full tuition reimbursements available (averaging $15,000 per year); career-related internships or fieldwork, scholarships/grants, health care benefits, tuition waivers (full and partial), and unspecified assistantships also available. Support available to part-time students. Financial award application deadline: 1/1. *Unit head:* Dr. Caryn Beck-Dudley, Dean, 850-644-3090, Fax: 850-644-0915. *Application contact:* Lisa Beverly, Director, Graduate Programs Admissions, 850-644-6458, Fax: 850-644-0588, E-mail: lbeverly@cob.fsu.edu.

Fontbonne University, Graduate Programs, College of Global Business and Professional Studies, Program in Accounting, St. Louis, MO 63105-3098. Offers MS. Part-time programs available. *Faculty:* 4 part-time/adjunct (3 women). *Students:* 9 full-time (5 women), 22 part-time (13 women); includes 5 Black or African American, non-Hispanic/Latino, 2 international. Average

age 34. In 2010, 14 master's awarded. *Entrance requirements:* For master's, GMAT. Additional exam requirements/recommendations for international students: Required—TOEFL (minimum score 197 computer-based; 71 iBT). *Expenses:* Tuition: Full-time $11,328. Full-time tuition and fees vary according to program. *Financial support:* Federal Work-Study and scholarships/grants available. Financial award application deadline: 4/1; financial award applicants required to submit FAFSA. *Unit head:* Dr. Linda Maurer, Dean of the College of Business and Professional Studies, 314-889-1423, E-mail: lmaurer@fontbonne.edu. *Application contact:* Fontbonne University OPTIONS, 314-863-2220, E-mail: options@fontbonne.edu.

Friends University, Graduate School, Wichita, KS 67213. Offers accounting (MBA); business administration (MBA); business law (MBL); Christian ministry (MACM); family therapy (MSFT); global leadership and management (MA); health care leadership (MHCL); management information systems (MMIS); operations management (MSOM); organization development (MSOD); teaching (MAT). Part-time and evening/weekend programs available. Postbaccalaureate distance learning degree programs offered (minimal on-campus study). *Faculty:* 14 full-time (5 women), 2 part-time/adjunct (1 woman). *Students:* 166 full-time (122 women), 507 part-time (290 women); includes 134 minority (64 Black or African American, non-Hispanic/Latino; 6 American Indian or Alaska Native, non-Hispanic/Latino; 24 Asian, non-Hispanic/Latino; 30 Hispanic/Latino; 1 Native Hawaiian or other Pacific Islander, non-Hispanic/Latino; 9 Two or more races, non-Hispanic/Latino). Average age 38. 445 applicants, 69% accepted, 236 enrolled. In 2010, 345 master's awarded. *Degree requirements:* For master's, research project. *Entrance requirements:* Additional exam requirements/recommendations for international students: Required—TOEFL (minimum score 560 paper-based; 220 computer-based). *Application deadline:* Applications are processed on a rolling basis. Application fee: $45 ($65 for international students). Electronic applications accepted. Tuition and fees vary according to course load, campus/location and program. *Financial support:* Applicants required to submit FAFSA. *Unit head:* Dr. Evelyn Hume, Dean, 800-794-6945 Ext. 5859, Fax: 316-295-5040, E-mail: evelyn hume@friends.edu. Application contact: Jeanette Hanson, Executive Director of Adult Recruitment, 800-794-6945, Fax: 316-295-5050, E-mail: jeanette@friends.edu.

Gannon University, School of Graduate Studies, College of Engineering and Business, School of Business, Program in Accounting, Erie, PA 16541-0001. Offers Certificate. Part-time and evening/weekend programs available. *Students:* 1 part-time (0 women). *Entrance requirements:* For degree, GMAT. Additional exam requirements/recommendations for international students: Required—TOEFL (minimum score 79 iBT). *Application deadline:* Applications are processed on a rolling basis. Application fee: $25. Electronic applications accepted. *Expenses:* Tuition: Full-time $14,670; part-time $815 per credit. Required fees: $430; $18 per credit. Tuition and fees vary according to class time, course load, degree level, campus/location and program. *Financial support:* Application deadline: 7/1. *Unit head:* Dr. Duane Prokop, Director, 814-871-7576, E-mail: prokop001@gannon.edu. *Application contact:* Kara Morgan, Assistant Director of Graduate Admissions, 814-871-5831, Fax: 814-871-5827, E-mail: graduate@gannon.edu.

George Mason University, School of Management, Program in Accounting, Fairfax, VA 22030. Offers MS. *Accreditation:* AACSB. *Faculty:* 80 full-time (26 women), 51 part-time/adjunct (15 women). *Students:* 8 full-time (6 women), 24 part-time (9 women); includes 12 Asian, non-Hispanic/Latino; 2 Hispanic/Latino, 3 international. Average age 26. 87 applicants, 31% accepted, 9 enrolled. In 2010, 13 master's awarded. *Entrance requirements:* For master's, GMAT, 2 letters of recommendation, resume. Additional exam requirements/recommendations for international students: Required—TOEFL (minimum score 570 paper-based; 230 computer-based; 88 iBT), IELTS. *Application deadline:* For fall admission, 3/15 priority date for domestic students; for spring admission, 10/15 for domestic students. Applications are processed on a rolling basis. Application fee: $100. Electronic applications accepted. *Expenses:* Tuition, state resident: full-time $8192; part-time $440 per credit hour. Tuition, nonresident: full-time $22,952; part-time $1055 per credit hour. Required fees: $2364; $99 per credit hour. *Financial support:* In 2010–11, 3 students received support, including 3 research assistantships with full and partial tuition reimbursements available (averaging $9,088 per year); career-related internships or fieldwork, Federal Work-Study, scholarships/grants, unspecified assistantships, and health care benefits (full-time research or teaching assistantship recipients) also available. Financial award application deadline: 3/1; financial award applicants required to submit FAFSA. *Faculty research:* Current leading global business issues, including offshore outsourcing, international financial risk, and comparative systems of innovation; business management/practices; emerging technology and generating new business. *Unit head:* Sarah Nutter, Accounting Chair, 703-993-1860, E-mail: snutter@gmu.edu. *Application contact:* Michelle Hanson, Program Coordinator, 703-993-1974, E-mail: mhanson1@gmu.edu.

The George Washington University, School of Business, Department of Accountancy, Washington, DC 20052. Offers M Accy, MBA, PhD. *Accreditation:* AACSB. Part-time and evening/weekend programs available. *Faculty:* 17 full-time (9 women), 7 part-time/adjunct (1 woman). *Students:* 128 full-time (77 women), 41 part-time (23 women); includes 2 Black or African American, non-Hispanic/Latino; 1 American Indian or Alaska Native, non-Hispanic/Latino; 11 Asian, non-Hispanic/Latino; 4 Hispanic/Latino; 1 Two or more races, non-Hispanic/Latino, 89 international. Average age 27. 238 applicants, 72% accepted, 72 enrolled. In 2010, 90 master's, 2 doctorates awarded. *Degree requirements:* For doctorate, thesis/dissertation. *Entrance requirements:* For master's, GMAT; for doctorate, GMAT or GRE. Additional exam requirements/recommendations for international students: Required—TOEFL. *Application deadline:* For fall admission, 4/1 priority date for domestic students; for spring admission, 10/1 for domestic students. Applications are processed on a rolling basis. Application fee: $75. *Financial support:* In 2010–11, 50 students received support; fellowships, teaching assistantships, career-related internships or fieldwork, Federal Work-Study, and institutionally sponsored loans available. Financial award application deadline: 4/1. *Faculty research:* Management accounting and capital markets, financial accounting and the analytic hierarchy process, ethics and accounting, accounting information systems. *Unit head:* Dr. Keith Smith, Chair, 202-994-7461, E-mail: kes@gwu.edu. *Application contact:* Louba Hatoum, Program Director, 202-994-4450, E-mail: lhatoum@gwu.edu.

Georgia College & State University, Graduate School, The J. Whitney Bunting School of Business, Milledgeville, GA 31061. Offers accountancy (MACCT); accounting (MBA); business (MBA); health services administration (MBA); information systems (MIS); management information services (MBA). *Accreditation:* AACSB. Part-time and evening/weekend programs available. Postbaccalaureate distance learning degree programs offered (no on-campus study). *Faculty:* 46 full-time (20 women). *Students:* 53 full-time (22 women), 157 part-time (53 women); includes 35 minority (18 Black or African American, non-Hispanic/Latino; 9 Asian, non-Hispanic/Latino; 5 Hispanic/Latino; 3 Two or more races, non-Hispanic/Latino), 11 international. Average age 30. 111 applicants, 83% accepted, 61 enrolled. In 2010, 121 master's awarded. *Entrance requirements:* For master's, GMAT or GRE. Additional exam requirements/recommendations for international students: Recommended—TOEFL (minimum score 550 paper-based; 213 computer-based; 79 iBT). *Application deadline:* For fall admission, 7/1 priority date for domestic students, 4/1 priority date for international students; for spring admission, 11/15 priority date for domestic students, 8/1 priority date for international students. Applications are processed on a rolling basis. Application fee: $40. Electronic applications accepted. *Expenses:* Tuition, state resident: full-time $4806; part-time $267 per hour. Tuition, nonresident: full-time $17,802; part-time $989 per hour. Tuition and fees vary according to course load. *Financial support:* In 2010–11, 33 research assistantships with full tuition reimbursements were awarded; career-related internships or fieldwork and unspecified assistantships also available. Support available to part-time students. Financial award application deadline: 3/1; financial award applicants required to submit FAFSA. *Unit head:* Dr. Matthew Liao-Troth, Dean, 478-445-5497, E-mail: matthew.liao-troth@gcsu.edu. *Application contact:* Lynn Hanson, Director of Graduate Programs, 478-445-5115, E-mail: lynn. hanson@gcsu.edu.

Georgian Court University, School of Business, Lakewood, NJ 08701-2697. Offers accounting (Certificate); business administration (MBA). *Accreditation:* ACBSP. Part-time and evening/weekend programs available. *Faculty:* 8 full-time (4 women), 7 part-time/adjunct (4 women). *Students:* 63 full-time (47 women), 65 part-time (42 women); includes 29 minority (14 Black or African American, non-Hispanic/Latino; 1 American Indian or Alaska Native, non-Hispanic/Latino; 2 Asian, non-Hispanic/Latino; 11 Hispanic/Latino; 1 Native Hawaiian or other Pacific Islander, non-Hispanic/Latino), 1 international. Average age 32. 85 applicants, 67% accepted, 41 enrolled. In 2010, 62 master's, 7 other advanced degrees awarded. *Entrance requirements:* For master's, GMAT or CPA exam, 3 letters of recommendation. Additional exam requirements/recommendations for international students: Required—TOEFL (minimum score 550 paper-based; 213 computer-based). *Application deadline:* For fall admission, 8/1 priority date for domestic students, 4/1 for international students; for spring admission, 1/1 priority date for domestic students, 7/1 for international students. Applications are processed on a rolling basis. Application fee: $40. Electronic applications accepted. *Expenses:* Tuition: Full-time $12,510; part-time $695 per credit. Required fees: $416 per year. Tuition and fees vary according to campus/location and program. *Financial support:* Scholarships/grants, health care benefits, and unspecified assistantships available. Financial award application deadline: 4/15; financial award applicants required to submit FAFSA. *Unit head:* Dr. Joseph Monahan, Dean, 732-987-2724, Fax: 732-987-2024, E-mail: monahanj@georgian.edu. *Application contact:* Patrick Givens, Assistant Director of Admissions, 732-987-2736, Fax: 732-987-2084, E-mail: graduateadmissions@georgian.edu.

Georgia Southern University, Jack N. Averitt College of Graduate Studies, College of Business Administration, School of Accountancy, Statesboro, GA 30460. Offers accounting (M Acc). *Accreditation:* AACSB. Part-time and evening/weekend programs available. *Students:* 90 full-time (35 women), 20 part-time (10 women); includes 16 Black or African American, non-Hispanic/Latino; 3 Asian, non-Hispanic/Latino; 1 Hispanic/Latino; 1 Two or more races, non-Hispanic/Latino, 16 international. Average age 25. 60 applicants, 83% accepted, 42 enrolled. In 2010, 43 master's awarded. *Entrance requirements:* For master's, GMAT. Additional exam requirements/recommendations for international students: Required—TOEFL (minimum score 550 paper-based; 213 computer-based; 80 iBT). *Application deadline:* For fall admission,

3/1 priority date for domestic and international students; for spring admission, 10/1 priority date for domestic students, 10/1 for international students. Applications are processed on a rolling basis. Application fee: $50. Electronic applications accepted. *Expenses:* Contact institution. *Financial support:* In 2010–11, 84 students received support, including research assistantships with partial tuition reimbursements available (averaging $7,200 per year), teaching assistantships with partial tuition reimbursements available (averaging $7,200 per year); career-related internships or fieldwork, Federal Work-Study, scholarships/grants, tuition waivers (partial), and unspecified assistantships also available. Support available to part-time students. Financial award application deadline: 4/15; financial award applicants required to submit FAFSA. *Faculty research:* Consolidation of fraud in the financial statement, reasons why firms switch auditions for the financial audit, internalization of accounting standards, pedagogy issues in accounting and law courses. *Unit head:* Dr. Mary Jill Lockwood, Director, 912-478-2228, Fax: 912-478-0105, E-mail: mjl@georgiasouthern.edu. *Application contact:* Dr. Charles Ziglar, Coordinator for Graduate Student Recruitment, 912-478-5365, Fax: 912-478-0740, E-mail: gradadmissions@georgiasouthern.edu.

Golden Gate University, Ageno School of Business, San Francisco, CA 94105-2968. Offers accounting (MBA); business administration (EMBA, MBA, PMBA, DBA); finance (MBA, MS, Certificate); financial planning (MS, Certificate); healthcare information systems (Certificate); human resource management (MBA, MS); human resources management (Certificate); information systems (MS); information technology (MBA); information technology management (Certificate); integrated marketing and communications (MS, Certificate); international business (MBA); management (MBA); marketing (MBA, MS, Certificate); operations supply chain management (Certificate); psychology (MA, Certificate); public administration (EMPA); public relations (MS, Certificate); technical market analysis (Certificate); JD/MBA. Part-time and evening/weekend programs available. *Faculty:* 16 full-time (4 women), 241 part-time/adjunct (72 women). *Students:* 421 full-time (235 women), 744 part-time (425 women); includes 526 minority (114 Black or African American, non-Hispanic/Latino; 2 American Indian or Alaska Native, non-Hispanic/Latino; 296 Asian, non-Hispanic/Latino; 73 Hispanic/Latino; 29 Native Hawaiian or other Pacific Islander, non-Hispanic/Latino; 12 Two or more races, non-Hispanic/Latino), 100 international. Average age 32. 681 applicants, 78% accepted, 270 enrolled. In 2010, 550 master's, 13 doctorates awarded. *Degree requirements:* For doctorate, thesis/dissertation. *Entrance requirements:* For master's, GMAT (MBA), minimum GPA of 2.5 (MS). Additional exam requirements/recommendations for international students: Required—TOEFL. *Application deadline:* For fall admission, 5/15 for domestic and international students; for winter admission, 1/15 for domestic and international students; for spring admission, 9/15 for domestic and international students. Applications are processed on a rolling basis. Application fee: $70 ($110 for international students). Electronic applications accepted. *Expenses:* Contact institution. *Financial support:* Career-related internships or fieldwork, Federal Work-Study, institutionally sponsored loans, and scholarships/grants available. Support available to part-time students. Financial award applicants required to submit FAFSA. *Unit head:* Dr. Paul Fouts, Dean, 415-442-7026, Fax: 415-442-6579. *Application contact:* Angela Melero, Enrollment Services, 415-442-7800, Fax: 415-442-7807, E-mail: info@ggu.edu.

Golden Gate University, School of Accounting, San Francisco, CA 94105-2968. Offers accounting (M Ac, Graduate Certificate); forensic (M Ac); forensic accounting (Graduate Certificate); taxation (M Ac). Part-time and evening/weekend programs available. *Faculty:* 5 full-time (2 women), 35 part-time/adjunct (12 women). *Students:* 129 full-time (84 women), 168 part-time (98 women); includes 127 minority (6 Black or African American, non-Hispanic/Latino; 1 American Indian or Alaska Native, non-Hispanic/Latino; 100 Asian, non-Hispanic/Latino; 15 Hispanic/Latino; 3 Native Hawaiian or other Pacific Islander, non-Hispanic/Latino; 2 Two or more races, non-Hispanic/Latino), 40 international. Average age 31. 132 applicants, 80% accepted, 52 enrolled. In 2010, 61 master's awarded. *Entrance requirements:* For master's, minimum GPA of 3.0. Additional exam requirements/recommendations for international students: Required—TOEFL. *Application deadline:* For fall admission, 5/15 for international students; for winter admission, 1/15 for international students; for spring admission, 9/15 for international students. Applications are processed on a rolling basis. Application fee: $70 ($110 for international students). Electronic applications accepted. *Financial support:* Career-related internships or fieldwork, Federal Work-Study, institutionally sponsored loans, and scholarships/grants available. Support available to part-time students. Financial award applicants required to submit FAFSA. *Faculty research:* Forensic accounting, audit, tax, CPA exam. *Unit head:* Mary Canning, 415-442-6559, Fax: 415-543-2607. *Application contact:* Angela Melero, Enrollment Services, 415-442-7800, Fax: 415-442-7807, E-mail: info@ggu.edu.

Grand Canyon University, College of Business, Phoenix, AZ 85017-1097. Offers accounting (MBA); corporate business administration (MBA); disaster preparedness and crisis management (MBA); executive fire service leadership (MS); finance (MBA); general management (MBA); government and policy (MPA); health care management (MPA); health systems management (MBA); human resource management (MBA); innovation (MBA); leadership (MBA,

MS); management of information system (MBA); marketing (MBA); project-based (MBA); six sigma (MBA); strategic human resource management (MBA). *Accreditation:* ACBSP. Part-time and evening/weekend programs available. Postbaccalaureate distance learning degree programs offered (no on-campus study). *Faculty:* 8 full-time (3 women), 147 part-time/adjunct (49 women). *Students:* 1 full-time (0 women), 2,121 part-time (1,165 women); includes 341 minority (249 Black or African American, non-Hispanic/Latino; 17 American Indian or Alaska Native, non-Hispanic/Latino; 15 Asian, non-Hispanic/Latino; 29 Hispanic/Latino; 4 Native Hawaiian or other Pacific Islander, non-Hispanic/Latino; 27 Two or more races, non-Hispanic/Latino), 20 international. Average age 38. In 2010, 569 master's awarded. *Entrance requirements:* For master's, equivalent of two years full-time professional work experience. Additional exam requirements/recommendations for international students: Required—TOEFL (minimum score 575 paper-based; 233 computer-based; 90 iBT), IELTS (minimum score 7). *Application deadline:* For fall admission, 8/21 for domestic students, 7/2 for international students; for spring admission, 12/24 for domestic students, 11/1 for international students. Applications are processed on a rolling basis. Application fee: $0. Electronic applications accepted. *Financial support:* Federal Work-Study available. Support available to part-time students. Financial award applicants required to submit FAFSA. *Unit head:* Kim Donaldson, Dean, 602-639-6597, E-mail: kdonaldson@gcu.edu. *Application contact:* Matt Tidwell, Enrollment Manager, 602-639-6020, E-mail: mtidwell@gcu.edu.

HEC Montreal, School of Business Administration, Diploma Programs in Administration, Program in Public Accountancy, Montréal, QC H3T 2A7, Canada. Offers Diploma. All courses are given in French. Part-time programs available. *Students:* 174 full-time (97 women), 42 part-time (26 women). 247 applicants, 76% accepted, 179 enrolled. In 2010, 173 Diplomas awarded. *Degree requirements:* For Diploma, one foreign language. *Entrance requirements:* For degree, bachelor's degree in accounting. *Application deadline:* For spring admission, 2/15 for domestic and international students. Application fee: $78 Canadian dollars. Electronic applications accepted. *Expenses:* Tuition, area resident: Part-time $68.93 per credit. Tuition, state resident: full-time $2481.48; part-time $188.92 per credit. Tuition, nonresident: full-time $6801; part-time $482.06 per course. International tuition: $17,354.16 full-time. Required fees: $1309.50; $30.28 per credit. $93.45 per term. Tuition and fees vary according to degree level and program. *Financial support:* Research assistantships, teaching assistantships, scholarships/grants available. Financial award application deadline: 9/2. *Unit head:* Silvia Ponce, Director, 514-340-6393, Fax: 514-340-6915, E-mail: silvia.ponce@hec.ca. *Application contact:* Marie Deshaies, Senior Student Advisor, 514-340-6135, Fax: 514-340-6411, E-mail: marie.deshaies@hec.ca.

HEC Montreal, School of Business Administration, Master of Science Programs in Administration, Program in Financial and Strategic Accounting, Montréal, QC H3T 2A7, Canada. Offers M Sc. Part-time programs available. *Students:* 2 full-time (1 woman), 1 part-time (0 women). 3 applicants, 67% accepted, 2 enrolled. *Degree requirements:* For master's, one foreign language, thesis. *Application deadline:* For fall admission, 3/15 for domestic and international students; for winter admission, 10/1 for domestic and international students. Application fee: $78. Electronic applications accepted. *Expenses:* Tuition, area resident: Part-time $68.93 per credit. Tuition, state resident: full-time $2481.48; part-time $188.92 per credit. Tuition, nonresident: full-time $6801; part-time $482.06 per course. International tuition: $17,354.16 full-time. Required fees: $1309.50; $30.28 per credit. $93.45 per term. Tuition and fees vary according to degree level and program. *Financial support:* Research assistantships, teaching assistantships, scholarships/grants available. Financial award application deadline: 9/2. *Unit head:* Claude Laurin, Director, 514-340-6847, Fax: 514-340-6880, E-mail: claude.laurin@hec.ca. *Application contact:* Francine Blais, Administrative Director, 514-340-6112, Fax: 514-340-6411, E-mail: francine.blais@hec.ca.

HEC Montreal, School of Business Administration, Master of Science Programs in Administration, Program in Management Control, Montréal, QC H3T 2A7, Canada. Offers M Sc. All courses are given in French. Part-time programs available. *Students:* 23 full-time (13 women), 9 part-time (6 women). 28 applicants, 50% accepted, 10 enrolled. In 2010, 5 master's awarded. *Degree requirements:* For master's, one foreign language, thesis. *Application deadline:* For fall admission, 3/15 for domestic and international students; for winter admission, 10/1 for domestic and international students. Application fee: $78 Canadian dollars. Electronic applications accepted. *Expenses:* Tuition, area resident: Part-time $68.93 per credit. Tuition, state resident: full-time $2481.48; part-time $188.92 per credit. Tuition, nonresident: full-time $6801; part-time $482.06 per course. International tuition: $17,354.16 full-time. Required fees: $1309.50; $30.28 per credit. $93.45 per term. Tuition and fees vary according to degree level and program. *Financial support:* Fellowships, research assistantships, teaching assistantships, scholarships/grants available. Financial award application deadline: 9/2. *Unit head:* Dr. Claude Laurin, Director, 514-340-6485, Fax: 514-340-6880, E-mail: claude.laurin@hec.ca. *Application contact:* Francine Blais, Administrative Director, 514-340-6112, Fax: 514-340-6411, E-mail: francine.blais@hec.ca.

HEC Montreal, School of Business Administration, Master of Science Programs in Administration, Program in Public Accounting, Montréal, QC H3T 2A7, Canada. Offers M Sc. Part-time programs available. *Students:* 6

full-time (3 women), 12 part-time (7 women). 1 applicant, 100% accepted, 0 enrolled. In 2010, 3 master's awarded. *Degree requirements:* For master's, one foreign language, thesis. *Application deadline:* For fall admission, 3/15 for domestic and international students; for winter admission, 10/1 for domestic and international students. Application fee: $78. Electronic applications accepted. *Expenses:* Tuition, area resident: Part-time $68.93 per credit. Tuition, state resident: full-time $2481.48; part-time $188.92 per credit. Tuition, nonresident: full-time $6801; part-time $482.06 per course. International tuition: $17,354.16 full-time. Required fees: $1309.50; $30.28 per credit. $93.45 per term. Tuition and fees vary according to degree level and program. *Financial support:* Research assistantships, teaching assistantships, scholarships/grants available. Financial award application deadline: 9/2. *Unit head:* Claude Laurin, Director, 514-340-6485, Fax: 514-340-6880, E-mail: claude.laurin@hec.ca. *Application contact:* Francine Blais, Administrative Director, 514-340-6112, Fax: 514-340-6411, E-mail: francine.blais@hec.ca.

Hofstra University, Frank G. Zarb School of Business, Programs in Accounting and Taxation, Hempstead, NY 11549. Offers accounting (MS, Advanced Certificate); business administration (MBA), including accounting, taxation; taxation (MS, Advanced Certificate). Part-time and evening/weekend programs available. Postbaccalaureate distance learning degree programs offered (minimal on-campus study). *Faculty:* 12 full-time (4 women), 3 part-time/adjunct (1 woman). *Students:* 107 full-time (52 women), 49 part-time (22 women); includes 19 minority (5 Black or African American, non-Hispanic/Latino; 9 Asian, non-Hispanic/Latino; 5 Hispanic/Latino), 45 international. Average age 26. 247 applicants, 73% accepted, 79 enrolled. In 2010, 37 master's awarded. *Degree requirements:* For master's, capstone course (for MBA); thesis (for MS). *Entrance requirements:* For master's, GMAT/GRE, 2 letters of recommendation; resume; essay. Additional exam requirements/recommendations for international students: Required—TOEFL (minimum score 550 paper-based; 213 computer-based; 80 iBT); Recommended—IELTS (minimum score 6). *Application deadline:* Applications are processed on a rolling basis. Application fee: $70 ($75 for international students). Electronic applications accepted. *Expenses:* Contact institution. *Financial support:* In 2010–11, 25 students received support, including 21 fellowships with full and partial tuition reimbursements available (averaging $10,613 per year), 1 research assistantship with full and partial tuition reimbursement available (averaging $9,594 per year); career-related internships or fieldwork, Federal Work-Study, institutionally sponsored loans, scholarships/grants, tuition waivers (full and partial), and unspecified assistantships also available. Support available to part-time students. Financial award applicants required to submit FAFSA. *Faculty research:* Corporate governance and executive compensation, Sarbanes-Oxley and certification compliance for financial statement, student performance and evaluation models, decomposing the elements of nonprofit organizational performance, accounting for international financial reporting standards. *Unit head:* Dr. Nathan S. Slavin, Chairperson, 516-463-5690, Fax: 516-463-4834, E-mail: actnzs@hofstra.edu. *Application contact:* Carol Drummer, Dean of Graduate Admissions, 516-463-4876, Fax: 516-463-4664, E-mail: gradstudent@hofstra.edu.

Hood College, Graduate School, Department of Economics and Management, Frederick, MD 21701-8575. Offers accounting (MBA); administration and management (MBA); finance (MBA); human resource management (MBA); information systems (MBA); marketing (MBA); public management (MBA). *Accreditation:* ACBSP. Part-time and evening/weekend programs available. *Faculty:* 4 full-time (1 woman), 9 part-time/adjunct (1 woman). *Students:* 16 full-time (9 women), 127 part-time (65 women); includes 17 Black or African American, non-Hispanic/Latino; 9 Asian, non-Hispanic/Latino; 5 Hispanic/Latino; 1 Two or more races, non-Hispanic/Latino, 10 international. Average age 32. 60 applicants, 62% accepted, 25 enrolled. In 2010, 56 master's awarded. *Degree requirements:* For master's, capstone/final research project. *Entrance requirements:* For master's, minimum GPA of 2.75, resume, letters of recommendation. Additional exam requirements/recommendations for international students: Required—TOEFL (minimum score 575 paper-based; 231 computer-based; 89 iBT). *Application deadline:* For fall admission, 7/15 for domestic and international students; for spring admission, 12/15 for domestic and international students. Applications are processed on a rolling basis. Application fee: $35. Electronic applications accepted. *Expenses:* Tuition: Full-time $6480; part-time $360 per credit. Required fees: $100; $50 per term. *Financial support:* Applicants required to submit FAFSA. *Faculty research:* Corporate strategy and sustainable competitive advantages, business ethics, entrepreneurship, investments management, economic development. *Unit head:* Dr. Anita Jose, Program Director, 301-696-3691, Fax: 301-696-3597, E-mail: jose@hood.edu. *Application contact:* Dr. Allen P. Flora, Dean of Graduate School, 301-696-3811, Fax: 301-696-3597, E-mail: gofurther@hood.edu.

Hunter College of the City University of New York, Graduate School, School of Arts and Sciences, Department of Economics, Program in Accounting, New York, NY 10021-5085. Offers MS. *Faculty:* 5 full-time (1 woman), 4 part-time/adjunct (0 women). *Students:* 16 full-time (8 women), 31 part-time (20 women); includes 5 Black or African American, non-Hispanic/Latino; 11 Asian, non-Hispanic/Latino; 2 Hispanic/Latino, 15 international. Average age 29. 66 applicants, 56% accepted, 22 enrolled. In 2010, 10 master's awarded. *Application deadline:* For fall admission, 4/1 for domestic students, 2/1 for international students; for spring admission, 11/1 for domestic students, 9/1 for international students. Application fee: $125. *Unit head:* Dr. Marjorie P. Honig, Chairperson, 212-772-5400, Fax: 212-772-5398, E-mail: mhonig@hunter.cuny.edu. *Application contact:* Dr. Tashiaki Mitsudome, Graduate Advisor, 212-772-5430, E-mail: tashiaki.mitsudome@hunter.cuny.edu.

Indiana University Northwest, School of Business and Economics, Gary, IN 46408-1197. Offers accountancy (M Acc); accounting (Certificate); business administration (MBA). *Accreditation:* AACSB. Part-time and evening/weekend programs available. *Faculty:* 5 full-time (0 women). *Students:* 54 full-time (15 women), 65 part-time (28 women); includes 43 minority (27 Black or African American, non-Hispanic/Latino; 7 Asian, non-Hispanic/Latino; 9 Hispanic/Latino). Average age 34. 64 applicants, 94% accepted, 55 enrolled. In 2010, 46 master's, 4 other advanced degrees awarded. *Entrance requirements:* For master's, GMAT, letter of recommendation. *Application deadline:* For fall admission, 7/15 priority date for domestic students; for spring admission, 11/15 for domestic students. Applications are processed on a rolling basis. Application fee: $25. *Expenses:* Contact institution. *Financial support:* In 2010–11, 9 students received support. Federal Work-Study, institutionally sponsored loans, and unspecified assistantships available. Support available to part-time students. Financial award application deadline: 7/15. *Faculty research:* International finance, wellness in the workplace, handicapped employment, MIS, regional economic forecasting. *Unit head:* Anna Rominger, Dean, 219-980-6636, Fax: 219-980-6916, E-mail: iunbiz@iun.edu. *Application contact:* John Gibson, Director of Graduate Program, 219-980-6635, Fax: 219-980-6916, E-mail: jagibson@iun.edu.

Indiana University–Purdue University Indianapolis, Kelley School of Business, Indianapolis, IN 46202-2896. Offers accounting (MSA); business (MBA). *Accreditation:* AACSB. Part-time and evening/weekend programs available. Postbaccalaureate distance learning degree programs offered (minimal on-campus study). *Faculty:* 20 full-time (4 women), 1 part-time/adjunct (0 women). *Students:* 128 full-time (57 women), 409 part-time (148 women); includes 85 minority (29 Black or African American, non-Hispanic/Latino; 40 Asian, non-Hispanic/Latino; 13 Hispanic/Latino; 3 Two or more races, non-Hispanic/Latino), 83 international. Average age 30. 221 applicants, 76% accepted, 113 enrolled. In 2010, 246 master's awarded. *Entrance requirements:* For master's, GMAT, previous course work in accounting, statistics. *Application deadline:* For fall admission, 4/15 priority date for domestic and international students; for spring admission, 11/1 priority date for domestic and international students. Application fee: $55 ($65 for international students). Electronic applications accepted. *Expenses:* Contact institution. *Financial support:* In 2010–11, 3 fellowships (averaging $16,193 per year), 1 teaching assistantship (averaging $9,000 per year) were awarded; Federal Work-Study, institutionally sponsored loans, and scholarships/grants also available. Support available to part-time students. Financial award application deadline: 3/1; financial award applicants required to submit FAFSA. *Unit head:* Phil Cochran, Associate Dean, Indianapolis Programs, 317-274-2481, Fax: 317-274-2483, E-mail: busugrad@iupui.edu. *Application contact:* Julie L. Moore, Recorder/Admission Coordinator, 317-274-4895, Fax: 317-274-2483, E-mail: mbaindy@iupui.edu.

Indiana University South Bend, School of Business and Economics, South Bend, IN 46634-7111. Offers accounting (MSA); business administration (MBA); management of information technologies (MS). Part-time and evening/weekend programs available. *Faculty:* 17 full-time (2 women), 3 part-time/adjunct (1 woman). *Students:* 61 full-time (26 women), 100 part-time (32 women); includes 16 minority (6 Black or African American, non-Hispanic/Latino; 1 American Indian or Alaska Native, non-Hispanic/Latino; 4 Asian, non-Hispanic/Latino; 4 Hispanic/Latino; 1 Two or more races, non-Hispanic/Latino), 51 international. Average age 32. 76 applicants, 58% accepted, 28 enrolled. In 2010, 67 master's awarded. *Entrance requirements:* For master's, GMAT. Additional exam requirements/recommendations for international students: Required—TOEFL (minimum score 550 paper-based; 213 computer-based). *Application deadline:* For fall admission, 7/1 priority date for domestic and international students; for spring admission, 11/1 priority date for domestic and international students. Applications are processed on a rolling basis. Application fee: $50 ($60 for international students). *Expenses:* Contact institution. *Financial support:* In 2010–11, 1 fellowship (averaging $3,846 per year) was awarded; Federal Work-Study and institutionally sponsored loans also available. Support available to part-time students. Financial award applicants required to submit FAFSA. *Faculty research:* Financial accounting, consumer research, capital budgeting research, business strategy research. *Unit head:* Robert H. Ducoffe, Dean, 574-520-4228, Fax: 574-520-4866. *Application contact:* Sharon Peterson, Secretary, 574-520-4138, Fax: 574-520-4866, E-mail: speterso@iusb.edu.

Iona College, Hagan School of Business, Department of Accounting, New Rochelle, NY 10801-1890. Offers MBA, PMC. Part-time and evening/weekend programs available. *Faculty:* 5 full-time (1 woman), 1 part-time/adjunct (0 women). *Students:* 28 full-time (16 women), 32 part-time (12 women); includes 15 minority (7 Black or African American, non-Hispanic/Latino; 1 Asian, non-Hispanic/Latino; 7 Hispanic/Latino). Average age 27. 32 applicants, 78% accepted, 21 enrolled. In 2010, 3 master's, 1 other advanced degree awarded. *Entrance requirements:* For master's, GMAT, two letters of recommendation; for PMC, GMAT. Additional exam requirements/

recommendations for international students: Required—TOEFL (minimum score 550 paper-based; 213 computer-based). *Application deadline:* Applications are processed on a rolling basis. Application fee: $50. Electronic applications accepted. *Expenses:* Tuition: Part-time $830 per credit. Required fees: $225 per credit. *Financial support:* Scholarships/grants, tuition waivers (partial), and unspecified assistantships available. Support available to part-time students. Financial award application deadline: 4/15; financial award applicants required to submit FAFSA. *Unit head:* Dr. Jeffry Haber, Chair, 914-633-2244, E-mail: jhaber@iona.edu. *Application contact:* Ben Fan, Director of MBA Admissions, 914-633-2289, Fax: 914-637-2708, E-mail: sfan@iona.edu.

Iowa State University of Science and Technology, Graduate College, College of Business, Department of Accounting, Ames, IA 50011. Offers M Acc. *Accreditation:* AACSB. *Faculty:* 13 full-time (5 women), 1 (woman) part-time/adjunct. *Students:* 43 full-time (24 women), 13 part-time (8 women); includes 1 Black or African American, non-Hispanic/Latino; 1 Asian, non-Hispanic/Latino, 19 international. 65 applicants, 45% accepted, 21 enrolled. In 2010, 42 master's awarded. *Degree requirements:* For master's, thesis or alternative. *Entrance requirements:* For master's, GMAT, resume. Additional exam requirements/recommendations for international students: Recommended—TOEFL (minimum score 600 paper-based; 100 iBT), IELTS (minimum score 7). *Application deadline:* For fall admission, 4/1 priority date for domestic and international students; for spring admission, 11/1 priority date for domestic and international students. Application fee: $40 ($90 for international students). Electronic applications accepted. *Financial support:* In 2010–11, 3 research assistantships with full and partial tuition reimbursements (averaging $4,056 per year) were awarded; teaching assistantships, career-related internships or fieldwork, scholarships/grants, health care benefits, and unspecified assistantships also available. *Unit head:* Dr. Frederick H. Dark, Interim Chair, 515-294-8118, E-mail: busgrad@iastate.edu. *Application contact:* Dr. Frederick H. Dark, Interim Chair, 515-294-8118, E-mail: busgrad@iastate.edu.

Ithaca College, Division of Graduate and Professional Studies, School of Business, Program in Professional Accountancy, Ithaca, NY 14850. Offers MBA. Part-time programs available. *Faculty:* 4 full-time (2 women). *Students:* 24 full-time (8 women), 1 (woman) part-time; includes 1 minority (Asian, non-Hispanic/Latino), 2 international. Average age 23. 33 applicants, 94% accepted, 23 enrolled. In 2010, 2 master's awarded. *Degree requirements:* For master's, thesis optional. *Entrance requirements:* For master's, GMAT, minimum GPA of 3.0. Additional exam requirements/recommendations for international students: Required—TOEFL (minimum score 550 paper-based; 213 computer-based; 80 iBT). *Application deadline:* For fall admission, 6/1 for domestic and international students; for spring admission, 12/1 for domestic and international students. Applications are processed on a rolling basis. Application fee: $40. Electronic applications accepted. *Expenses:* Contact institution. *Financial support:* In 2010–11, 12 students received support, including 9 fellowships (averaging $8,143 per year); career-related internships or fieldwork, Federal Work-Study, and scholarships/grants also available. Support available to part-time students. Financial award application deadline: 3/1; financial award applicants required to submit CSS PROFILE or FAFSA. *Unit head:* Dr. Joanne Burress, Chairperson, 607-274-3527, Fax: 607-274-1263, E-mail: gps@ithaca.edu. *Application contact:* Rob Gearhart, Dean, Graduate and Professional Studies, 607-274-3527, Fax: 607-274-1263, E-mail: gps@ithaca.edu.

Jackson State University, Graduate School, College of Business, Department of Accounting, Jackson, MS 39217. Offers MPA. *Accreditation:* AACSB. Part-time and evening/weekend programs available. *Faculty:* 4 full-time (0 women), 1 part-time/adjunct (0 women). *Students:* 13 full-time (9 women), 10 part-time (8 women); includes 21 Black or African American, non-Hispanic/Latino, 1 international. Average age 29. In 2010, 19 master's awarded. *Degree requirements:* For master's, comprehensive exam. *Entrance requirements:* For master's, GRE General Test, GMAT. Additional exam requirements/recommendations for international students: Required—TOEFL (minimum score 520 paper-based; 195 computer-based; 67 iBT). *Application deadline:* For fall admission, 3/1 priority date for domestic students, 3/1 for international students; for spring admission, 10/1 for domestic and international students. Applications are processed on a rolling basis. Application fee: $25. *Expenses:* Tuition, state resident: full-time $5050; part-time $281 per credit hour. Tuition, nonresident: full-time $12,380; part-time $689 per credit hour. *Financial support:* Career-related internships or fieldwork, Federal Work-Study, and tuition waivers (full and partial) available. Support available to part-time students. Financial award application deadline: 3/1. *Unit head:* Dr. Quinton Booker, Chair, 601-979-2414. *Application contact:* Sharlene Wilson, Director of Graduate Admissions, 601-979-2455, Fax: 601-979-4325, E-mail: sharlene.f.wilson@jsums.edu.

James Madison University, The Graduate School, College of Business, Program in Accounting, Harrisonburg, VA 22807. Offers MS. *Accreditation:* AACSB. Part-time and evening/weekend programs available. *Students:* 61 full-time (34 women), 4 part-time (1 woman); includes 14 minority (5 Black or African American, non-Hispanic/Latino; 4 Asian, non-Hispanic/Latino; 2 Hispanic/Latino; 3 Two or more races, non-Hispanic/Latino). Average age 27. In 2010, 70 master's awarded. *Entrance requirements:* For master's, GMAT or CPA exam. Additional exam requirements/recommendations for international

students: Required—TOEFL. *Application deadline:* For fall admission, 5/1 priority date for domestic students, 5/1 for international students; for spring admission, 9/1 priority date for domestic students, 9/1 for international students. Applications are processed on a rolling basis. Application fee: $55. Electronic applications accepted. *Financial support:* In 2010–11, 19 students received support. Federal Work-Study and 19 graduate assistantships ($7382) available. Financial award application deadline: 3/1; financial award applicants required to submit FAFSA. *Faculty research:* Controllership, government accounting. *Unit head:* Dr. Paul A. Copley, Academic Unit Head, 540-568-3081. *Application contact:* Dr. Nancy Nichols, Program Director, 540-568-3081.

Johnson & Wales University, The Alan Shawn Feinstein Graduate School, MBA Program in Global Business Leadership, Providence, RI 02903-3703. Offers accounting (MBA); enhanced accounting (MBA); hospitality (MBA). Part-time programs available. *Faculty:* 14 full-time (3 women), 18 part-time/adjunct (4 women). *Students:* 736 full-time (433 women), 359 part-time (237 women); includes 46 minority (18 Black or African American, non-Hispanic/Latino; 5 Asian, non-Hispanic/Latino; 22 Hispanic/Latino; 1 Native Hawaiian or other Pacific Islander, non-Hispanic/Latino), 640 international. Average age 29. 397 applicants, 76% accepted, 219 enrolled. In 2010, 329 master's awarded. *Entrance requirements:* For master's, minimum GPA of 2.75. Additional exam requirements/recommendations for international students: Required—TOEFL (minimum score 550 paper-based; 210 computer-based) or IELTS (recommended); Recommended—TWE. *Application deadline:* For fall admission, 8/15 priority date for domestic students, 6/28 priority date for international students; for winter admission, 11/10 priority date for domestic students, 9/20 priority date for international students; for spring admission, 2/5 priority date for domestic students, 12/20 priority date for international students. Applications are processed on a rolling basis. *Expenses:* Tuition: Part-time $1535 per course. Part-time tuition and fees vary according to degree level and program. *Financial support:* Tuition waivers (partial) and unspecified assistantships available. Support available to part-time students. Financial award application deadline: 5/1. *Faculty research:* International banking, global economy, international trade, cultural differences. *Unit head:* Dr. Frank Sargent, Director, 401-598-1033, Fax: 401-598-1125. *Application contact:* Graduate School Admissions, 401-598-1015, Fax: 401-598-1286, E-mail: gradadm@jwu.edu.

Kean University, College of Business and Public Management, Program in Accounting, Union, NJ 07083. Offers MS. Part-time and evening/weekend programs available. *Faculty:* 10 full-time (2 women). *Students:* 31 full-time (19 women), 38 part-time (23 women); includes 6 Black or African American, non-Hispanic/Latino; 5 Asian, non-Hispanic/Latino; 8 Hispanic/Latino, 17 international. Average age 30. 30 applicants, 93% accepted, 18 enrolled. In 2010, 45 master's awarded. *Entrance requirements:* For master's, GMAT, 2 letters of recommendation, interview, minimum GPA of 3.0, transcripts. *Application deadline:* For fall admission, 6/1 for domestic students; for spring admission, 11/1 for domestic students. Application fee: $75 ($150 for international students). Electronic applications accepted. *Expenses:* Tuition, state resident: full-time $10,872; part-time $500 per credit. Tuition, nonresident: full-time $14,736; part-time $614 per credit. Required fees: $2740.80; $125 per credit. Part-time tuition and fees vary according to course load and degree level. *Financial support:* In 2010–11, research assistantships with full tuition reimbursements (averaging $3,263 per year); unspecified assistantships also available. Financial award applicants required to submit FAFSA. *Unit head:* Dr. James Capone, Program Coordinator, 908-737-4110, E-mail: jcapone@kean.edu. *Application contact:* Reenat Hasan, Pre-Admissions Coordinator, 908-737-5923, Fax: 908-737-5925, E-mail: rhasan@exchange.kean.edu.

Keiser University, Master of Business Administration Program, Fort Lauderdale, FL 33309. Offers accounting (MBA); health services management (MBA); international business (MBA); leadership for managers (MBA); marketing (MBA). Leadership for Managers and International Business concentrations also offered in Spanish. Part-time programs available. Postbaccalaureate distance learning degree programs offered (minimal on-campus study). *Faculty:* 8 full-time (3 women), 7 part-time/adjunct (2 women). *Students:* 18 full-time (14 women), 83 part-time (51 women); includes 30 Black or African American, non-Hispanic/Latino; 2 American Indian or Alaska Native, non-Hispanic/Latino; 2 Asian, non-Hispanic/Latino; 17 Hispanic/Latino, 1 international. Average age 42. 30 applicants, 77% accepted, 18 enrolled. In 2010, 21 degrees awarded. *Entrance requirements:* For master's, minimum GPA of 2.7 from an accredited institution. Additional exam requirements/recommendations for international students: Required—TOEFL. *Application deadline:* Applications are processed on a rolling basis. Application fee: $50. Electronic applications accepted. *Financial support:* In 2010–11, 95 students received support. Federal Work-Study available. Financial award applicants required to submit FAFSA.

Kennesaw State University, Michael J. Coles College of Business, Program in Accounting, Kennesaw, GA 30144-5591. Offers M Acc. *Accreditation:* AACSB. Part-time and evening/weekend programs available. *Students:* 65 full-time (30 women), 55 part-time (25 women); includes 35 minority (18 Black or African American, non-Hispanic/Latino; 12 Asian, non-Hispanic/Latino; 2 Hispanic/Latino; 1 Native Hawaiian or other Pacific Islander, non-Hispanic/Latino; 2 Two or more races, non-Hispanic/Latino), 11 international.

Average age 32. 80 applicants, 33% accepted, 10 enrolled. In 2010, 57 master's awarded. *Entrance requirements:* For master's, GMAT, minimum GPA of 2.8. Additional exam requirements/recommendations for international students: Required—TOEFL (minimum score 550 paper-based; 213 computer-based; 80 iBT), IELTS (minimum score 6). *Application deadline:* For fall admission, 4/1 for domestic and international students. Applications are processed on a rolling basis. Application fee: $60. Electronic applications accepted. *Expenses:* Tuition, state resident: full-time $5500; part-time $225 per credit hour. Tuition, nonresident: full-time $16,100; part-time $813 per credit hour. Required fees: $673 per semester. *Financial support:* In 2010–11, 4 research assistantships with tuition reimbursements (averaging $4,000 per year) were awarded; unspecified assistantships also available. Financial award application deadline: 4/1. *Unit head:* Dr. Kathyrn Epps, Director, 770-423-6085, E-mail: kepps@kennesaw.edu. *Application contact:* Tamara Hutto, Admissions Counselor, 770-420-4377, Fax: 770-423-6885.

Kent State University, Graduate School of Management, Doctoral Program in Accounting, Kent, OH 44242. Offers PhD. *Faculty:* 10 full-time (4 women). *Students:* 5 full-time (0 women), 1 international. Average age 30. In 2010, 1 doctorate awarded. *Degree requirements:* For doctorate, comprehensive exam, thesis/dissertation, oral defense. *Entrance requirements:* For doctorate, GMAT. Additional exam requirements/recommendations for international students: Required—TOEFL (minimum score 600 paper-based; 250 computer-based; 100 iBT). *Application deadline:* For fall admission, 2/1 for domestic students, 1/1 for international students. Application fee: $30 ($60 for international students). Electronic applications accepted. *Expenses:* Tuition, state resident: full-time $7866; part-time $437 per credit hour. Tuition, nonresident: full-time $14,022; part-time $779 per credit hour. *Financial support:* In 2010–11, 3 students received support, including fellowships with full tuition reimbursements available (averaging $15,000 per year), 3 teaching assistantships with full tuition reimbursements available (averaging $15,000 per year); Federal Work-Study also available. Financial award application deadline: 2/1; financial award applicants required to submit FAFSA. *Faculty research:* Information economics, capital management, use of accounting information, curriculum design. *Unit head:* Dr. Linda Zucca, Chair and Associate Professor, 330-672-2545, Fax: 330-672-2548, E-mail: lzucca@kent.edu. *Application contact:* Felecia A. Urbanek, Coordinator, Graduate Programs, 330-672-2282, Fax: 330-672-7303, E-mail: gradbus@kent.edu.

Kent State University, Graduate School of Management, Master's Program in Accounting, Kent, OH 44242. Offers MS. Part-time programs available. *Faculty:* 10 full-time (4 women), 1 part-time/adjunct (0 women). *Students:* 42 full-time (22 women), 18 part-time (13 women); includes 1 Black or African American, non-Hispanic/Latino; 1 Asian, non-Hispanic/Latino, 20 international. Average age 23. 51 applicants, 86% accepted, 23 enrolled. In 2010, 25 master's awarded. *Degree requirements:* For master's, internship. *Entrance requirements:* For master's, GMAT, minimum GPA of 2.75. Additional exam requirements/recommendations for international students: Required—TOEFL (minimum score 550 paper-based; 213 computer-based; 79 iBT). *Application deadline:* For fall admission, 4/1 priority date for domestic students, 4/1 for international students; for spring admission, 12/1 for domestic students. Applications are processed on a rolling basis. Application fee: $30 ($60 for international students). Electronic applications accepted. *Expenses:* Tuition, state resident: full-time $7866; part-time $437 per credit hour. Tuition, nonresident: full-time $14,022; part-time $779 per credit hour. *Financial support:* In 2010–11, 8 students received support, including 8 research assistantships with full tuition reimbursements available (averaging $3,350 per year); Federal Work-Study also available. Financial award application deadline: 4/1; financial award applicants required to submit FAFSA. *Faculty research:* Financial accounting, managerial accounting, auditing, systems, nonprofit. *Unit head:* Dr. Linda Zucca, Chair and Associate Professor, 330-672-2545, Fax: 330-672-2548, E-mail: lzucca@kent.edu. *Application contact:* Louise M. Ditchey, Administrative Director, 330-672-2282, Fax: 330-672-7303, E-mail: gradbus@kent.edu.

Kentucky State University, College of Professional Studies, Frankfort, KY 40601. Offers business administration (MBA), including accounting, finance, management, marketing; public administration (MPA), including human resource management, international administration and development, management information systems, nonprofit management; special education (MA). Part-time and evening/weekend programs available. Postbaccalaureate distance learning degree programs offered (minimal on-campus study). *Faculty:* 12 full-time (4 women), 2 part-time/adjunct (both women). *Students:* 88 full-time (57 women), 79 part-time (42 women); includes 104 minority (101 Black or African American, non-Hispanic/Latino; 1 Asian, non-Hispanic/Latino; 2 Hispanic/Latino), 2 international. Average age 34. 124 applicants, 62% accepted, 45 enrolled. In 2010, 38 master's awarded. *Degree requirements:* For master's, comprehensive exam, thesis optional. *Entrance requirements:* For master's, GMAT, GRE. Additional exam requirements/recommendations for international students: Required—TOEFL (minimum score 525 paper-based; 173 computer-based). *Application deadline:* Applications are processed on a rolling basis. Application fee: $30 ($100 for international students). Electronic applications accepted. *Expenses:* Tuition, state resident: full-time $5886; part-time $352 per credit hour. Tuition, nonresident: full-time $9054; part-time $528 per credit hour. Required fees: $450; $26 per credit

hour. *Financial support:* In 2010–11, 46 students received support, including 4 research assistantships (averaging $10,975 per year); career-related internships or fieldwork, scholarships/grants, tuition waivers (partial), and unspecified assistantships also available. Financial award application deadline: 4/15; financial award applicants required to submit FAFSA. *Unit head:* Dr. Gashaw Lake, Dean, 502-597-6105, Fax: 502-597-6715, E-mail: gashaw.lake@kysu.edu. *Application contact:* Dr. Titilayo Ufomata, Acting Director of Graduate Studies, 502-597-6443, E-mail: titilayo.ufomata@kysu.edu.

Lamar University, College of Graduate Studies, College of Business, Beaumont, TX 77710. Offers accounting (MBA); experiential business and entrepreneurship (MBA); financial management (MBA); healthcare administration (MBA); information systems (MBA); management (MBA). *Accreditation:* AACSB. Part-time and evening/weekend programs available. *Faculty:* 17 full-time (4 women), 4 part-time/adjunct (0 women). *Students:* 79 full-time (37 women), 56 part-time (22 women); includes 14 Black or African American, non-Hispanic/Latino; 8 Asian, non-Hispanic/Latino; 12 Hispanic/Latino, 18 international. Average age 28. 103 applicants, 70% accepted, 40 enrolled. In 2010, 49 master's awarded. *Degree requirements:* For master's, comprehensive exam (for some programs), thesis optional. *Entrance requirements:* For master's, GMAT. Additional exam requirements/recommendations for international students: Required—TOEFL (minimum score 525 paper-based; 197 computer-based). *Application deadline:* For fall admission, 3/15 priority date for domestic students; for spring admission, 10/1 priority date for domestic students. Applications are processed on a rolling basis. Application fee: $25 ($50 for international students). *Expenses:* Tuition, state resident: full-time $4160; part-time $208 per credit hour. Tuition, nonresident: full-time $10,360; part-time $518 per credit hour. *Financial support:* In 2010–11, 12 students received support, including 4 research assistantships with partial tuition reimbursements available; fellowships with tuition reimbursements available, career-related internships or fieldwork, Federal Work-Study, institutionally sponsored loans, scholarships/grants, and tuition waivers (partial) also available. Support available to part-time students. Financial award application deadline: 4/1; financial award applicants required to submit FAFSA. *Faculty research:* Marketing, finance, quantitative methods, management information systems, legal, environmental. *Unit head:* Dr. Enrique R. Venta, Dean, 409-880-8604, Fax: 409-880-8088, E-mail: henry.venta@lamar.edu. *Application contact:* Dr. Brad Mayer, Professor and Associate Dean, 409-880-2383, Fax: 409-880-8605, E-mail: bradley.mayer@lamar.edu.

Lehigh University, College of Business and Economics, Department of Accounting, Bethlehem, PA 18015. Offers accounting and information analysis (MS). *Accreditation:* AACSB. *Faculty:* 8 full-time (0 women), 3 part-time/adjunct (1 woman). *Students:* 29 full-time (16 women), 6 part-time (4 women); includes 1 minority (Asian, non-Hispanic/Latino), 14 international. Average age 23. 162 applicants, 28% accepted, 31 enrolled. In 2010, 29 master's awarded. *Entrance requirements:* For master's, GMAT. Additional exam requirements/recommendations for international students: Required—TOEFL (minimum score 105 iBT). *Application deadline:* For fall admission, 5/1 for domestic and international students. Applications are processed on a rolling basis. Application fee: $100. Electronic applications accepted. *Expenses:* Contact institution. *Financial support:* In 2010–11, 6 research assistantships with partial tuition reimbursements (averaging $1,000 per year) were awarded; scholarships/grants and tuition waivers (partial) also available. Financial award application deadline: 1/15. *Faculty research:* Behavioral accounting, internal control, information systems, supply chain management, financial accounting. *Unit head:* Dr. Heibatollah Sami, Director, 610-758-3407, Fax: 610-758-6429, E-mail: hes205@lehigh.edu. *Application contact:* Corinn McBride, Director of Recruitment and Admissions, 610-758-3418, Fax: 610-758-5283, E-mail: com207@lehigh.edu.

Lewis University, College of Business, Graduate School of Management, Program in Business Administration, Romeoville, IL 60446. Offers accounting (MBA); custom elective option (MBA); e-business (MBA); finance (MBA); healthcare management (MBA); human resources management (MBA); information security (MBA); international business (MBA); management information systems (MBA); marketing (MBA); project management (MBA); technology and operations management (MBA). Part-time and evening/weekend programs available. *Students:* 119 full-time (66 women), 204 part-time (104 women); includes 55 Black or African American, non-Hispanic/Latino; 9 Asian, non-Hispanic/Latino; 30 Hispanic/Latino; 1 Native Hawaiian or other Pacific Islander, non-Hispanic/Latino, 9 international. Average age 28. In 2010, 111 master's awarded. *Entrance requirements:* For master's, interview, bachelor's degree, resume, 2 recommendations. Additional exam requirements/recommendations for international students: Required—TOEFL (minimum score 550 paper-based; 213 computer-based). *Application deadline:* For fall admission, 8/15 priority date for domestic students, 5/1 priority date for international students; for spring admission, 11/15 priority date for international students. Applications are processed on a rolling basis. Application fee: $40. Electronic applications accepted. *Expenses:* Tuition: Full-time $13,320; part-time $740 per credit hour. Tuition and fees vary according to program. *Financial support:* Career-related internships or fieldwork, Federal Work-Study, scholarships/grants, and unspecified assistantships available. Financial award application deadline: 5/1; financial award applicants required to submit FAFSA. *Unit head:* Dr. Maureen Culleeney, Academic Program Director,

815-838-0500 Ext. 5631, E-mail: culleema@lewisu.edu. *Application contact:* Michele Ryan, Director of Admission, 815-838-0500 Ext. 5384, E-mail: gsm@lewisu.edu.

Lindenwood University, Graduate Programs, School of Business and Entrepreneurship, St. Charles, MO 63301-1695. Offers accounting (MBA, MS); business administration (MBA); entrepreneurial studies (MBA, MS); finance (MBA, MS); human resource management (MBA); human resources (MS); international business (MBA, MS); management (MBA, MS); management information systems (MBA, MS); marketing (MBA, MS); public management (MBA, MS); sport management (MA). *Accreditation:* ACBSP. Part-time and evening/weekend programs available. *Faculty:* 20 full-time (8 women), 17 part-time/adjunct (5 women). *Students:* 179 full-time (73 women), 184 part-time (87 women); includes 27 minority (20 Black or African American, non-Hispanic/Latino; 3 Asian, non-Hispanic/Latino; 4 Hispanic/Latino), 146 international. Average age 28. 149 applicants, 73 enrolled. In 2010, 142 master's awarded. *Degree requirements:* For master's, comprehensive exam (for some programs), thesis (for some programs). *Entrance requirements:* For master's, interview, minimum GPA of 3.0, letter of recommendation. Additional exam requirements/recommendations for international students: Required—TOEFL (minimum score 550 paper-based; 213 computer-based; 80 iBT). *Application deadline:* For fall admission, 7/30 priority date for domestic students, 9/16 priority date for international students; for winter admission, 12/15 priority date for domestic and international students; for spring admission, 2/25 priority date for domestic students, 2/11 priority date for international students. Applications are processed on a rolling basis. Application fee: $30 ($100 for international students). Electronic applications accepted. *Expenses:* Tuition: Full-time $13,260; part-time $380 per credit hour. Required fees: $340. One-time fee: $30. Tuition and fees vary according to course level and course load. *Financial support:* In 2010–11, 209 students received support. Career-related internships or fieldwork, Federal Work-Study, institutionally sponsored loans, and tuition waivers (partial) available. Financial award application deadline: 6/30; financial award applicants required to submit FAFSA. *Unit head:* Roger Ellis, Dean, 636-949-4839, E-mail: rellis@lindenwood.edu. *Application contact:* Brett Barger, Dean of Evening Admissions and Extension Campuses, 636-949-4934, Fax: 636-949-4109, E-mail: adultadmissions@lindenwood.edu.

Lipscomb University, MBA Program, Nashville, TN 37204-3951. Offers accounting (MBA); business administration (general) (MBA); conflict management (MBA); financial services (MBA); healthcare management (MBA); leadership (MBA); nonprofit management (MBA); sports administration (MBA); sustainable practice (MBA). *Accreditation:* ACBSP. Part-time and evening/weekend programs available. *Faculty:* 17 full-time (5 women), 3 part-time/adjunct (0 women). *Students:* 52 full-time (30 women), 79 part-time (36 women); includes 20 Black or African American, non-Hispanic/Latino; 1 American Indian or Alaska Native, non-Hispanic/Latino; 1 Asian, non-Hispanic/Latino; 7 Hispanic/Latino. Average age 32. 151 applicants, 47% accepted, 45 enrolled. In 2010, 70 master's awarded. *Entrance requirements:* For master's, GMAT, interview, 2 references, resume. Additional exam requirements/recommendations for international students: Required—TOEFL (minimum score 570 paper-based; 230 computer-based). *Application deadline:* For fall admission, 2/1 for international students; for winter admission, 6/1 for international students. Applications are processed on a rolling basis. Application fee: $50 ($75 for international students). Electronic applications accepted. *Expenses:* Contact institution. *Financial support:* Career-related internships or fieldwork, Federal Work-Study, scholarships/grants, tuition waivers (partial), and unspecified assistantships available. Support available to part-time students. Financial award application deadline: 7/1; financial award applicants required to submit FAFSA. *Faculty research:* Impact of spirituality on organization commitment, leadership, psychological empowerment, training. *Unit head:* Dr. Mike Kendrick, Interim Chair of Graduate Business Studies, 615-966-1833, Fax: 615-966-1818, E-mail: mikekendrick@lipscomb.edu. *Application contact:* Emily Landsdell, 615-966-5284, E-mail: emily.lansdell@lipscomb.edu.

Lipscomb University, Program in Accountancy, Nashville, TN 37204-3951. Offers M Acc. Part-time and evening/weekend programs available. *Faculty:* 2 full-time (0 women), 1 part-time/adjunct (0 women). *Students:* 7 full-time (2 women), 13 part-time (7 women); includes 2 Black or African American, non-Hispanic/Latino. Average age 32. 34 applicants, 59% accepted, 5 enrolled. In 2010, 21 master's awarded. *Degree requirements:* For master's, internship. *Entrance requirements:* For master's, GMAT, 2 references, interview. Application fee: $50 ($75 for international students). *Expenses:* Contact institution. *Financial support:* Career-related internships or fieldwork, Federal Work-Study, scholarships/grants, and tuition waivers available. Support available to part-time students. Financial award application deadline: 7/1. *Faculty research:* Internal auditing, ethics and fraud. *Unit head:* Dr. Perry Moore, Director, 615-966-5795, Fax: 615-966-1818, E-mail: perry.moore@lipscomb.edu. *Application contact:* Emily B. Lansdell, Graduate Business Program Assistant, 615-966-5284, Fax: 615-966-1818, E-mail: emily.lansdell@lipscomb.edu.

Louisiana State University and Agricultural and Mechanical College, Graduate School, E. J. Ourso College of Business, Department of Accounting, Baton Rouge, LA 70803. Offers MS, PhD. *Faculty:* 10 full-time (4 women). *Students:* 87 full-time (47 women), 11 part-time (5 women); includes 3 Black or African American, non-Hispanic/Latino; 2 Asian, non-Hispanic/Latino; 1 Hispanic/Latino, 15 international. Average age 25. 119 applicants, 50% accepted, 14 enrolled. In 2010, 49 master's awarded. *Degree requirements:* For doctorate, thesis/dissertation. *Entrance requirements:* For master's, GMAT, minimum GPA of 3.2; for doctorate, GMAT, minimum GPA of 3.4. Additional exam requirements/recommendations for international students: Required—TOEFL (minimum score 550 paper-based; 213 computer-based; 79 iBT) or IELTS (minimum score 6.5). *Application deadline:* For fall admission, 1/25 priority date for domestic students, 5/15 for international students; for spring admission, 10/15 for international students. Applications are processed on a rolling basis. Application fee: $50 ($70 for international students). Electronic applications accepted. *Financial support:* In 2010–11, 53 students received support, including 3 research assistantships with full and partial tuition reimbursements available (averaging $15,333 per year), 18 teaching assistantships with full and partial tuition reimbursements available (averaging $13,205 per year); fellowships, Federal Work-Study, scholarships/grants, health care benefits, tuition waivers (full and partial), and unspecified assistantships also available. Support available to part-time students. Financial award application deadline: 4/15; financial award applicants required to submit FAFSA. *Faculty research:* Financial accounting, auditing fraud. Total annual research expenditures: $18,408. *Unit head:* Dr. Sam Tiras, Chair, 225-578-6202, Fax: 225-578-6201, E-mail: tiras@lsu.edu. *Application contact:* Dr. Jacquelyn Moffit, MS Program Advisor, 225-578-6211, Fax: 225-578-6201, E-mail: jsmoff22@lsu.edu.

Marquette University, Graduate School of Management, Program in Accounting, Milwaukee, WI 53201-1881. Offers MSA. *Accreditation:* AACSB. *Faculty:* 10 full-time (3 women), 5 part-time/adjunct (0 women). *Students:* 40 full-time (26 women), 9 part-time (5 women); includes 1 Asian, non-Hispanic/Latino, 30 international. Average age 24. 192 applicants, 41% accepted, 28 enrolled. In 2010, 7 master's awarded. *Entrance requirements:* For master's, GMAT, letters of recommendation (if applying for financial aid). Additional exam requirements/recommendations for international students: Required—TOEFL (minimum score 88 iBT). *Application deadline:* Applications are processed on a rolling basis. Application fee: $50. Electronic applications accepted. *Expenses:* Tuition: Full-time $16,290; part-time $905 per credit hour. Tuition and fees vary according to program. *Financial support:* In 2010–11, 2 teaching assistantships were awarded; fellowships, research assistantships also available. Financial award application deadline: 2/15. *Faculty research:* Financial (accounting) literacy, international perception of corruption, effect of carbon credits on accounting and tax transactions, targeted tax breaks. *Unit head:* Dr. Michael Akers, Chair, 414-288-1453. *Application contact:* Debra Leutermann, Admissions Coordinator, 414-288-8064, E-mail: debra.leutermann@marquette.edu.

Maryville University of Saint Louis, The John E. Simon School of Business, St. Louis, MO 63141-7299. Offers accounting (MBA, PGC); business studies (PGC); management (MBA, PGC); marketing (MBA, PGC); process and project management (MBA, PGC); sport and entertainment management (MBA, PGC). *Accreditation:* ACBSP. Part-time and evening/weekend programs available. *Faculty:* 7 full-time (4 women), 13 part-time/adjunct (5 women). *Students:* 16 full-time (8 women), 119 part-time (57 women); includes 15 minority (9 Black or African American, non-Hispanic/Latino; 3 Asian, non-Hispanic/Latino; 3 Hispanic/Latino), 5 international. Average age 31. In 2010, 60 master's awarded. *Entrance requirements:* For master's, GMAT (unless applicant possesses undergraduate business degree with minimum cumulative GPA of 3.0, or has completed master's degree from accredited university or one early access course prior to undergraduate degree). Additional exam requirements/recommendations for international students: Required—TOEFL (minimum score 563 paper-based; 85 iBT), If you took the revised TOEFL (after Sept. 24, 2005), you will be admitted into our MBA program with a speaking sub-score of 23, a writing sub-score of 20, reading and listening scores of 21 or higher and a combined score of 79 or higher. *Application deadline:* Applications are processed on a rolling basis. Application fee: $40 ($60 for international students). Electronic applications accepted. *Expenses:* Tuition: Full-time $21,100; part-time $633.50 per credit hour. Required fees: $150 per semester. *Financial support:* Career-related internships or fieldwork, Federal Work-Study, tuition waivers (partial), and campus employment available. Financial award application deadline: 3/1; financial award applicants required to submit FAFSA. *Faculty research:* International business, e-marketing, strategic planning, interpersonal management skills, financial analysis. *Unit head:* Dr. Pamela Horwitz, Dean, 314-529-9418, Fax: 314-529-9975, E-mail: horwitz@maryville.edu. *Application contact:* Kathy Dougherty, Director of MBA Programs, 314-529-9382, Fax: 314-529-9975, E-mail: business@maryville.edu.

McNeese State University, Doré School of Graduate Studies, College of Business, Master of Business Administration Program, Lake Charles, LA 70609. Offers accounting (MBA); business administration (MBA). *Accreditation:* AACSB. Evening/weekend programs available. *Faculty:* 17 full-time (1 woman). *Students:* 54 full-time (28 women), 33 part-time (17 women); includes 5 minority (3 Black or African American, non-Hispanic/Latino; 1 Asian, non-Hispanic/Latino; 1 Hispanic/Latino), 33 international. In 2010, 38 master's awarded. *Degree requirements:* For master's, written exam. *Entrance requirements:* For master's, GMAT. *Application deadline:* For fall admission, 5/15 priority date for domestic and international students; for spring admission, 10/15 priority date for domestic and international students. Applications are processed on a rolling basis. Application fee: $20 ($30 for international students). Tuition and fees vary according to course load. *Financial support:* Research assistantships, teaching assistantships, Federal Work-Study available. Support available to part-time students. Financial award application deadline: 5/1. *Faculty research:* Management development, integrating technology into the work force, union/management relations, economic development. *Unit head:* Dr. Akm Rahman, MBA Director, 337-475-5576, Fax: 337-475-5986, E-mail: mrahman@mcneese.edu. *Application contact:* Dr. Akm Rahman, MBA Director, 337-475-5576, Fax: 337-475-5986, E-mail: mrahman@mcneese.edu.

Mercy College, School of Business, Program in Public Accounting, Dobbs Ferry, NY 10522-1189. Offers MS. Part-time and evening/weekend programs available. *Students:* 23 full-time (13 women), 3 part-time (1 woman); includes 4 Black or African American, non-Hispanic/Latino; 3 Asian, non-Hispanic/Latino; 7 Hispanic/Latino. Average age 31. 8 applicants, 0% accepted, 0 enrolled. In 2010, 14 master's awarded. *Entrance requirements:* For master's, GMAT, two page written professional goals statement, resume, two letters of reference, interview, undergraduate transcripts. Additional exam requirements/recommendations for international students: Required—TOEFL (minimum score 600 paper-based; 250 computer-based; 100 iBT), IELTS (minimum score 8). *Application deadline:* For fall admission, 8/1 for international students. Applications are processed on a rolling basis. Application fee: $40. Electronic applications accepted. *Expenses:* Contact institution. *Financial support:* Career-related internships or fieldwork, Federal Work-Study, scholarships/grants, and unspecified assistantships available. Support available to part-time students. Financial award applicants required to submit FAFSA. *Faculty research:* Auditing, taxation, financial statements. *Unit head:* Lucretia Mann, Director, 914-674-7492, E-mail: accountinginfo@mercy.edu. *Application contact:* Valerie Peattie, Administrative Assistant, 914-674-7492, E-mail: vpeattie@mercy.edu.

Miami University, Graduate School, Farmer School of Business, Department of Accountancy, Oxford, OH 45056. Offers M Acc. *Accreditation:* AACSB. *Students:* 24 full-time (10 women); includes 2 minority (1 Hispanic/Latino; 1 Two or more races, non-Hispanic/Latino), 2 international. Average age 22. In 2010, 33 master's awarded. *Entrance requirements:* For master's, GMAT, minimum cumulative undergraduate GPA of 3.0. Additional exam requirements/recommendations for international students: Required—TOEFL. *Application deadline:* For fall admission, 1/1 for domestic students, 11/1 for international students. Application fee: $50. *Expenses:* Tuition, state resident: full-time $11,616; part-time $484 per credit hour. Tuition, nonresident: full-time $25,656; part-time $1069 per credit hour. Required fees: $528. *Financial support:* Fellowships with full tuition reimbursements, research assistantships, Federal Work-Study, health care benefits, tuition waivers (full), and unspecified assistantships available. Financial award application deadline: 3/1; financial award applicants required to submit FAFSA. *Unit head:* Marc Rubin, Chair, 513-529-6200, Fax: 513-529-4740, E-mail: rubinma@muohio.edu. *Application contact:* Gretchen Radler, Academic Program Director, 513-529-3372, E-mail: miamiacc@muohio.edu.

Middle Tennessee State University, College of Graduate Studies, Jennings A. Jones College of Business, Department of Accounting, Murfreesboro, TN 37132. Offers MS. *Accreditation:* AACSB. Part-time and evening/weekend programs available. Postbaccalaureate distance learning degree programs offered. *Faculty:* 11 full-time (4 women). *Students:* 11 full-time (3 women), 99 part-time (48 women); includes 13 Black or African American, non-Hispanic/Latino; 1 American Indian or Alaska Native, non-Hispanic/Latino; 16 Asian, non-Hispanic/Latino; 2 Hispanic/Latino; 1 Two or more races, non-Hispanic/Latino. Average age 29. 41 applicants, 78% accepted, 32 enrolled. In 2010, 45 master's awarded. *Entrance requirements:* Additional exam requirements/recommendations for international students: Required—TOEFL (minimum score 525 paper-based; 195 computer-based; 71 iBT) or IELTS (minimum score 6). *Application deadline:* For fall admission, 6/1 for domestic and international students. Applications are processed on a rolling basis. Application fee: $25 ($30 for international students). Electronic applications accepted. *Expenses:* Tuition, state resident: full-time $4632. Tuition, nonresident: full-time $11,520. *Financial support:* In 2010–11, 10 students received support. Institutionally sponsored loans available. Support available to part-time students. Financial award application deadline: 5/1; financial award applicants required to submit FAFSA. *Unit head:* Dr. G. Robert Smith, Chair, 615-898-2558, Fax: 615-898-5839, E-mail: smitty@mtsu.edu. *Application contact:* Dr. Michael Allen, Dean and Vice Provost for Research, 615-898-2840, Fax: 615-904-8020, E-mail: mallen@mtsu.edu.

Mississippi State University, College of Business, School of Accountancy, Mississippi State, MS 39762. Offers accounting (MBA); business administration (PhD); systems (MPA); taxation (MTX). MBA (accounting) only offered at the Meridian campus. *Accreditation:* AACSB. *Faculty:* 6 full-time (2 women), 2 part-time/adjunct (0 women). *Students:* 53 full-time (27 women), 13 part-time (10 women); includes 8 minority (3 Black or African American, non-Hispanic/Latino; 3 Asian, non-Hispanic/Latino; 2 Two or more races, non-Hispanic/Latino), 2 international. Average age 26. 59 applicants, 47% accepted, 21 enrolled. In 2010, 33 master's awarded. *Degree requirements:* For master's, comprehensive exam. *Entrance requirements:* For master's, GMAT (minimum score of 510), minimum GPA of 2.75 overall and in upper-level accounting, 3.0 in last 60 hours of course work; for doctorate, GMAT, minimum undergraduate GPA of 3.0, both cumulative and over the last 60 hours of undergraduate work; 3.25 on all prior graduate work. Additional exam requirements/recommendations for international students: Required—TOEFL (minimum score 575 paper-based; 233 computer-based; 84 iBT); Recommended—IELTS (minimum score 7). *Application deadline:* For fall admission, 7/1 for domestic students, 5/1 for international students; for spring admission, 11/1 for domestic students, 9/1 for international students. Applications are processed on a rolling basis. Application fee: $40. Electronic applications accepted. *Expenses:* Tuition, state resident: full-time $2730.50; part-time $304 per credit hour. Tuition, nonresident: full-time $6901; part-time $767 per credit hour. *Financial support:* Career-related internships or fieldwork, Federal Work-Study, institutionally sponsored loans, scholarships/grants, and unspecified assistantships available. Support available to part-time students. Financial award application deadline: 4/1; financial award applicants required to submit FAFSA. *Faculty research:* Income tax, financial accounting system, managerial accounting, auditing. *Unit head:* Dr. Jim Scheiner, Director, 662-325-1633, Fax: 662-325-1646, E-mail: jscheiner@cobilan.msstate.edu. *Application contact:* Dr. Barbara Spencer, Graduate Coordinator, 662-325-3710, Fax: 662-325-1646, E-mail: sac@cobilan.msstate.edu.

Molloy College, Graduate Business Program, Rockville Centre, NY 11571-5002. Offers accounting (MBA); accounting and management (MBA); management (MBA); personal financial planning and accounting (MBA); personal financial planning and management (MBA). Part-time programs available. *Faculty:* 5 full-time (0 women), 8 part-time/adjunct (2 women). *Students:* 26 full-time (15 women), 69 part-time (35 women); includes 19 Black or African American, non-Hispanic/Latino; 1 American Indian or Alaska Native, non-Hispanic/Latino; 7 Asian, non-Hispanic/Latino; 9 Hispanic/Latino. Average age 33. In 2010, 28 master's awarded. *Application deadline:* Applications are processed on a rolling basis. *Application contact:* Alina Haitz, Assistant Director of Graduate Admissions, 516-678-5000 Ext. 6399, Fax: 516-256-2247, E-mail: ahaitz@molloy.edu.

Monmouth University, The Graduate School, Leon Hess Business School, West Long Branch, NJ 07764-1898. Offers accounting (MBA, Post-Master's Certificate); business (MBA); finance (MBA); healthcare management (MBA, Post-Master's Certificate); real estate (MBA). *Accreditation:* AACSB. Part-time and evening/weekend programs available. *Faculty:* 27 full-time (9 women), 7 part-time/adjunct (1 woman). *Students:* 87 full-time (31 women), 144 part-time (69 women); includes 6 Black or African American, non-Hispanic/Latino; 14 Asian, non-Hispanic/Latino; 8 Hispanic/Latino; 2 Two or more races, non-Hispanic/Latino, 17 international. Average age 29. 181 applicants, 78% accepted, 81 enrolled. In 2010, 88 master's awarded. *Degree requirements:* For master's, capstone course. *Entrance requirements:* For master's, GMAT, minimum GPA of 3.0 in major, 2.75 overall. Additional exam requirements/recommendations for international students: Required—TOEFL (minimum score 550 paper-based; 213 computer-based; 79 iBT), IELTS (minimum score 5), Michigan English Language Assessment Battery (minimum score 77), Cambridge A, B, C. *Application deadline:* For fall admission, 7/15 priority date for domestic students, 6/1 for international students; for spring admission, 11/15 priority date for domestic students, 11/1 for international students. Applications are processed on a rolling basis. Application fee: $50. Electronic applications accepted. *Expenses:* Tuition: Full-time $19,572; part-time $816 per credit. Required fees: $628; $157 per semester. *Financial support:* In 2010–11, 166 students received support, including 161 fellowships (averaging $1,741 per year), 17 research assistantships (averaging $10,505 per year); career-related internships or fieldwork, scholarships/grants, and unspecified assistantships also available. Support available to part-time students. Financial award applicants required to submit FAFSA. *Faculty research:* Information technology and marketing, behavioral research in accounting, human resources, management of technology. *Unit head:* Douglas Stives, MBA Program Director, 732-263-5894, Fax: 732-263-5517, E-mail: dstives@monmouth.edu. *Application contact:* Kevin Roane, Director, Office of Graduate Admission, 732-571-3452, Fax: 732-263-5123, E-mail: gradadm@monmouth.edu.

Montana State University, College of Graduate Studies, College of Business, Bozeman, MT 59717. Offers professional accountancy (MP Ac). *Accreditation:* AACSB. Part-time programs available. *Faculty:* 25 full-time (8 women), 28 part-time/adjunct (12 women). *Students:* 41 full-time (25 women), 7 part-time (all women); includes 3 minority (1 Asian, non-Hispanic/Latino; 2 Hispanic/Latino). Average age 25. 27 applicants, 78% accepted, 18 enrolled. In 2010, 43 master's awarded. *Degree requirements:* For master's, comprehensive exam. *Entrance requirements:* For master's, GRE General Test, GMAT, minimum undergraduate GPA of 3.1 (preferred). Additional exam requirements/recommendations for international students: Required—TOEFL (minimum score 550 paper-based; 213 computer-based). *Application deadline:* For fall admission, 7/15 priority date for domestic students, 5/15 priority date for international students; for spring admission, 12/1 priority date for domestic students, 10/1 priority date for international students. Applications are processed on a rolling basis. Application fee: $30. Electronic applications accepted. *Expenses:* Tuition, state resident: full-time $5553.90. Tuition, nonresident: full-time $14,646. Required fees: $1233. *Financial support:* In 2010–11, 6 students received support, including 6 teaching assistantships with partial tuition reimbursements available (averaging $3,800 per year); career-related internships or fieldwork and tuition waivers (partial) also available. Financial award application deadline: 3/1; financial award applicants required to submit FAFSA. *Faculty research:* Tax research, accounting education, fraud issues, CPA exams. Total annual research expenditures: $37,898. *Unit head:* Dr. Dan Moshavi, Dean, 406-994-4423, Fax: 406-994-6206, E-mail: dmoshavi@montana.edu. *Application contact:* Dr. Carl A. Fox, Vice Provost for Graduate Education, 406-994-4145, Fax: 406-994-7433, E-mail: gradstudy@montana.edu.

Montclair State University, The Graduate School, School of Business, Department of Accounting, Law and Taxation, Montclair, NJ 07043-1624. Offers accounting (MBA, MS, Certificate). Part-time and evening/weekend programs available. *Faculty:* 16 full-time (5 women), 9 part-time/adjunct (2 women). *Students:* 43 full-time (22 women), 106 part-time (42 women); includes 11 Black or African American, non-Hispanic/Latino; 16 Asian, non-Hispanic/Latino; 11 Hispanic/Latino, 9 international. Average age 30. 75 applicants, 56% accepted, 21 enrolled. In 2010, 31 master's, 1 other advanced degree awarded. *Entrance requirements:* For master's, GMAT, 2 letters of recommendation, resume. Additional exam requirements/recommendations for international students: Required—TOEFL (minimum iBT score of 83) or IELTS. *Application deadline:* For fall admission, 6/1 for international students; for spring admission, 10/1 for international students. Applications are processed on a rolling basis. Application fee: $60. Electronic applications accepted. *Expenses:* Tuition, state resident: part-time $501.34 per credit. Tuition, nonresident: part-time $773.88 per credit. Required fees: $71.15 per credit. *Financial support:* In 2010–11, 2 research assistantships with full tuition reimbursements (averaging $7,000 per year) were awarded; Federal Work-Study and scholarships/grants also available. Support available to part-time students. Financial award application deadline: 3/1; financial award applicants required to submit FAFSA. *Faculty research:* International financial reporting, international transfer pricing issues, the popular ecology paradigm, tax fraud, measurement and reporting environmental accounting. *Unit head:* Prof. Frank Aquilino, Head, 973-655-4174. *Application contact:* Amy Aiello, Director of Graduate Admissions and Operations, 973-655-5147, Fax: 973-655-7869, E-mail: graduate.school@montclair.edu.

Moravian College, Moravian College Comenius Center, Business and Management Programs, Bethlehem, PA 18018-6650. Offers accounting (MBA); general management (MBA); health care management (MBA); human resource management (MBA); leadership (MSHRM); learning and performance management (MSHRM); supply chain management (MBA). Part-time and evening/weekend programs available. *Faculty:* 6 full-time (2 women), 10 part-time/adjunct (3 women). *Students:* 67 part-time (35 women). 24 applicants, 50% accepted, 12 enrolled. In 2010, 8 master's awarded. *Entrance requirements:* For master's, GMAT. Additional exam requirements/recommendations for international students: Required—TOEFL (minimum score 550 paper-based; 260 computer-based; 90 iBT). *Application deadline:* Applications are processed on a rolling basis. Application fee: $40. *Expenses:* Contact institution. *Financial support:* In 2010–11, 1 fellowship with full tuition reimbursement was awarded. *Faculty research:* Leadership, change management, human resources. *Unit head:* Dr. William A. Kleintop, Associate Dean for Business and Management Programs, 610-507-1400, Fax: 610-861-1400, E-mail: comenius@moravian.edu. *Application contact:* Linda J. Doyle, Information Contact, 610-861-1400, Fax: 610-861-1466, E-mail: mba@moravian.edu.

National University, Academic Affairs, School of Business and Management, Department of Accounting and Finance, La Jolla, CA 92037-1011. Offers accountancy (MS); corporate and international finance (MS). Part-time and evening/weekend programs available. Postbaccalaureate distance learning degree programs offered (no on-campus study). *Faculty:* 15 full-time (2 women), 149 part-time/adjunct (39 women). *Students:* 171 full-time (76 women), 410 part-time (202 women); includes 201 minority (40 Black or African American, non-Hispanic/Latino; 1 American Indian or Alaska Native, non-Hispanic/Latino; 67 Asian, non-Hispanic/Latino; 86 Hispanic/Latino; 1 Native Hawaiian or other Pacific Islander, non-Hispanic/Latino; 6 Two or more races, non-Hispanic/Latino), 147 international. Average age 33. 727 applicants, 100% accepted, 466 enrolled. In 2010, 58 master's awarded. *Degree requirements:* For master's, thesis. *Entrance requirements:* For master's, interview, minimum GPA of 2.5. Additional exam requirements/recommendations for international students: Required—TOEFL (minimum score 550 paper-based; 213 computer-based; 79 iBT), IELTS (minimum score 6). *Application deadline:* Applications are processed on a rolling basis. Application fee: $60 ($65 for international students). Electronic applications accepted. *Expenses:* Tuition: Full-time $9450; part-time $350 per unit. Required fees: $350 per unit. One-time fee: $60. *Financial support:* Career-related internships or fieldwork, institutionally sponsored loans, scholarships/grants, and tuition waivers (partial) available. Support available to part-time students. Financial award application deadline: 6/30; financial award applicants required to submit FAFSA. *Unit head:* Prof. Donald A. Schwartz, Chair and Associate Professor, 858-642-8420, Fax: 858-642-8740, E-mail: dschwartz@nu.edu.

Application contact: Dominick Giovanniello, Associate Regional Dean—San Diego, 800-NAT-UNIV, Fax: 858-541-7792, E-mail: dgiovann@nu.edu.

New Mexico State University, Graduate School, College of Business, Department of Accounting and Information Systems, Las Cruces, NM 88003-8001. Offers M Acct. *Accreditation:* AACSB. Part-time programs available. *Faculty:* 7 full-time (2 women). *Students:* 39 full-time (24 women), 15 part-time (13 women); includes 17 minority (2 Asian, non-Hispanic/Latino; 15 Hispanic/Latino), 10 international. Average age 29. 47 applicants, 87% accepted, 26 enrolled. In 2010, 21 master's awarded. *Degree requirements:* For master's, comprehensive exam, thesis optional. *Entrance requirements:* For master's, GMAT, minimum undergraduate accounting GPA of 3.0 (upper division). Additional exam requirements/recommendations for international students: Required—TOEFL (minimum score 530 paper-based; 197 computer-based). *Application deadline:* For fall admission, 7/1 priority date for domestic students, 3/1 priority date for international students; for spring admission, 11/1 priority date for domestic students. Applications are processed on a rolling basis. Application fee: $30 ($50 for international students). Electronic applications accepted. *Expenses:* Tuition, state resident: full-time $4536; part-time $242 per credit. Tuition, nonresident: full-time $15,816; part-time $712 per credit. Required fees: $636 per term. *Financial support:* In 2010–11, 6 students received support, including 2 research assistantships (averaging $6,925 per year), 14 teaching assistantships (averaging $5,361 per year); career-related internships or fieldwork, Federal Work-Study, and health care benefits also available. Support available to part-time students. Financial award application deadline: 3/1. *Faculty research:* Taxation, financial accounting, managerial accounting, accounting systems, accounting education. *Unit head:* Dr. Ed Scribner, Department Head, 575-646-4901, Fax: 575-646-1552, E-mail: escribne@nmsu.edu. *Application contact:* Dr. Cindy L. Seipel, Master of Accountancy Director, 575-646-5206, Fax: 575-646-1552, E-mail: cseipel@nmsu.edu.

New York Institute of Technology, Graduate Division, School of Management, Program in Business Administration, Old Westbury, NY 11568-8000. Offers accounting (Advanced Certificate); business administration (MBA); finance (Advanced Certificate); international business (Advanced Certificate); management of information systems (Advanced Certificate); marketing (Advanced Certificate). Part-time and evening/weekend programs available. *Students:* 454 full-time (188 women), 513 part-time (204 women); includes 49 minority (15 Black or African American, non-Hispanic/Latino; 23 Asian, non-Hispanic/Latino; 11 Hispanic/Latino), 268 international. Average age 29. In 2010, 435 master's, 1 other advanced degree awarded. *Degree requirements:* For master's, thesis (for some programs). *Entrance requirements:* For master's, minimum QPA of 2.85. Additional exam requirements/recommendations for international students: Required—TOEFL (minimum score 550 paper-based; 213 computer-based). *Application deadline:* For fall admission, 7/1 priority date for domestic students; for spring admission, 12/1 priority date for domestic students. Applications are processed on a rolling basis. Application fee: $50. Electronic applications accepted. *Expenses:* Tuition: Part-time $835 per credit. *Financial support:* Fellowships, research assistantships with partial tuition reimbursements, institutionally sponsored loans, tuition waivers (full and partial), and unspecified assistantships available. Support available to part-time students. Financial award applicants required to submit FAFSA. *Faculty research:* Instructor performance appraisal; relationship between TOEFL, GMAT, GRE, and performance in foreign students. *Unit head:* Dr. Stephen Hartman, Director, 516-686-7691, E-mail: shartman@nyit.edu. *Application contact:* Dr. Jacquelyn Nealon, Vice President for Enrollment Services, 516-686-7925, Fax: 516-686-7597, E-mail: jnealon@nyit.edu.

Northeastern Illinois University, Graduate College, College of Business and Management, Chicago, IL 60625-4699. Offers accounting (MSA); finance (MBA); management (MBA); marketing (MBA). Part-time and evening/weekend programs available. *Faculty:* 24 full-time (3 women), 13 part-time/adjunct (4 women). *Students:* 41 full-time (19 women), 69 part-time (32 women); includes 23 minority (4 Black or African American, non-Hispanic/Latino; 1 American Indian or Alaska Native, non-Hispanic/Latino; 11 Asian, non-Hispanic/Latino; 6 Hispanic/Latino; 1 Two or more races, non-Hispanic/Latino), 21 international. Average age 31. 112 applicants, 75% accepted, 80 enrolled. In 2010, 34 master's awarded. *Degree requirements:* For master's, thesis optional. *Entrance requirements:* For master's, GMAT, minimum GPA of 2.75. Additional exam requirements/recommendations for international students: Required—TOEFL (minimum score 550 paper-based; 213 computer-based; 79 iBT). *Application deadline:* For fall admission, 4/1 priority date for domestic students; for spring admission, 8/15 for domestic students. Applications are processed on a rolling basis. Application fee: $30. Electronic applications accepted. *Financial support:* In 2010–11, 20 students received support, including 6 research assistantships with full and partial tuition reimbursements available (averaging $6,600 per year); career-related internships or fieldwork, Federal Work-Study, institutionally sponsored loans, scholarships/grants, tuition waivers (full and partial), and unspecified assistantships also available. Support available to part-time students. *Faculty research:* Perception of accountants and non-accountants toward future of the accounting industry, asynchronous learning outcomes, cost and efficiency of financial markets, impact of deregulation on airline industry, analysis of derivational instruments.

Unit head: Dr. Amy B. Hietapelto, Dean, 773-442-6105. *Application contact:* Dr. Amy B. Hietapelto, Dean, 773-442-6105.

Northeastern State University, Graduate College, College of Business and Technology, Program in Accounting and Financial Analysis, Tahlequah, OK 74464-2399. Offers MS. Part-time and evening/weekend programs available. *Students:* 13 full-time (4 women), 56 part-time (36 women); includes 14 American Indian or Alaska Native, non-Hispanic/Latino; 3 Hispanic/Latino, 3 international. In 2010, 7 master's awarded. *Entrance requirements:* For master's, GMAT. Additional exam requirements/recommendations for international students: Required—TOEFL (minimum score 213 computer-based). *Application deadline:* For fall admission, 6/1 priority date for domestic students. Applications are processed on a rolling basis. Application fee: $0 ($25 for international students). Electronic applications accepted. *Expenses:* Tuition, state resident: part-time $144 per credit hour. Tuition, nonresident: part-time $384.05 per credit hour. Required fees: $34.90 per credit hour. Tuition and fees vary according to program. *Unit head:* Dr. Freeman Gary, Coordinator, 918-449-6524 Ext. 0000, E-mail: freemandg@nsuok.edu. *Application contact:* Dr. Freeman Gary, Coordinator, 918-449-6524 Ext. 0000, E-mail: freemandg@nsuok.edu.

Northeastern University, Graduate School of Professional Accounting, Boston, MA 02115-5096. Offers MS, MST, MS/MBA. Postbaccalaureate distance learning degree programs offered (no on-campus study). *Faculty:* 8 full-time (2 women), 6 part-time/adjunct (0 women). *Students:* 100 full-time (47 women), 77 part-time (31 women). Average age 26. 284 applicants, 58% accepted, 116 enrolled. In 2010, 127 master's awarded. *Entrance requirements:* For master's, GMAT, interview. Additional exam requirements/recommendations for international students: Required—TOEFL (minimum score 600 paper-based; 250 computer-based; 100 iBT). *Application deadline:* For fall admission, 8/1 for domestic students, 2/1 for international students; for winter admission, 11/15 for domestic and international students; for spring admission, 3/15 for domestic students. Application fee: $100. Electronic applications accepted. *Expenses:* Contact institution. *Financial support:* In 2010–11, 58 fellowships (averaging $8,295 per year) were awarded; career-related internships or fieldwork, Federal Work-Study, institutionally sponsored loans, and scholarships/grants also available. Support available to part-time students. Financial award application deadline: 3/1; financial award applicants required to submit FAFSA. *Unit head:* Kate Klepper, Associate Dean, Graduate Business Programs, 617-373-5417, Fax: 617-373-8564, E-mail: k.klepper@neu.edu. *Application contact:* Annarita Meeker, Director, Graduate Accounting and Tax Programs, 617-373-4621, Fax: 617-373-8564, E-mail: a.meeker@neu.edu.

Northern Illinois University, Graduate School, College of Business, Department of Accountancy, De Kalb, IL 60115-2854. Offers MAS, MST. *Accreditation:* AACSB. Part-time and evening/weekend programs available. *Faculty:* 14 full-time (4 women). *Students:* 165 full-time (49 women), 71 part-time (37 women); includes 29 minority (3 Black or African American, non-Hispanic/Latino; 17 Asian, non-Hispanic/Latino; 4 Hispanic/Latino; 1 Native Hawaiian or other Pacific Islander, non-Hispanic/Latino; 4 Two or more races, non-Hispanic/Latino), 45 international. Average age 27. 161 applicants, 58% accepted, 48 enrolled. In 2010, 171 master's awarded. *Degree requirements:* For master's, thesis optional. *Entrance requirements:* For master's, GMAT, minimum GPA of 2.75. Additional exam requirements/recommendations for international students: Required—TOEFL (minimum score 550 paper-based; 213 computer-based). *Application deadline:* For fall admission, 4/1 priority date for domestic students, 5/1 for international students; for spring admission, 9/15 priority date for domestic students, 10/1 for international students. Applications are processed on a rolling basis. Application fee: $30. Electronic applications accepted. *Expenses:* Tuition, state resident: full-time $7200; part-time $300 per credit hour. Tuition, nonresident: full-time $14,400; part-time $600 per credit hour. Required fees: $79 per credit hour. *Financial support:* In 2010–11, 28 research assistantships with full tuition reimbursements, 11 teaching assistantships with full tuition reimbursements were awarded; fellowships with full tuition reimbursements, career-related internships or fieldwork, Federal Work-Study, scholarships/grants, tuition waivers (full), and unspecified assistantships also available. Support available to part-time students. Financial award applicants required to submit FAFSA. *Faculty research:* Accounting fraud, governmental accounting, corporate income tax planning, auditing, ethics. *Unit head:* Dr. James C. Young, Chair, 815-753-1250, Fax: 815-753-8515. *Application contact:* Dr. Rowene Linden, Graduate Adviser, 815-753-6200.

Northern Kentucky University, Office of Graduate Programs, College of Business, Program in Accountancy, Highland Heights, KY 41099. Offers accountancy (M Acc); advanced taxation (Certificate). Part-time and evening/weekend programs available. *Faculty:* 5 full-time (1 woman), 2 part-time/adjunct (0 women). *Students:* 11 full-time (4 women), 49 part-time (27 women); includes 4 minority (1 American Indian or Alaska Native, non-Hispanic/Latino; 1 Asian, non-Hispanic/Latino; 2 Hispanic/Latino), 2 international. Average age 31. 51 applicants, 67% accepted, 22 enrolled. In 2010, 12 master's, 3 other advanced degrees awarded. *Degree requirements:* For master's, capstone course. *Entrance requirements:* For master's, GMAT (minimum score 450), minimum GPA of 2.5. Additional exam requirements/recommendations for international students: Required—TOEFL (minimum

score 550 paper-based; 213 computer-based; 79 iBT); Recommended—IELTS (minimum score 6.5). *Application deadline:* For fall admission, 8/1 for domestic students, 6/1 for international students; for spring admission, 12/1 for domestic students, 10/1 for international students. Applications are processed on a rolling basis. Application fee: $40. Electronic applications accepted. *Expenses:* Tuition, state resident: full-time $7254; part-time $403 per credit hour. Tuition, nonresident: full-time $12,492; part-time $694 per credit hour. Tuition and fees vary according to degree level and program. *Financial support:* Unspecified assistantships available. Financial award applicants required to submit FAFSA. *Faculty research:* Behavioral influences on accounting decisions, historical development of accounting, auditing and accounting failures. *Unit head:* Robert Salyer, Director, 859-572-7595, Fax: 859-572-7694, E-mail: salyerb@nku.edu. *Application contact:* Dr. Peg Griffin, Director of Graduate Programs, 859-572-6934, Fax: 859-572-6670, E-mail: griffinp@nku.edu.

Northwest Missouri State University, Graduate School, Melvin and Valorie Booth College of Business and Professional Studies, Program in Accounting, Maryville, MO 64468-6001. Offers MBA. *Faculty:* 3 full-time (0 women). In 2010, 3 master's awarded. *Degree requirements:* For master's, comprehensive exam. *Entrance requirements:* For master's, GMAT, minimum GPA of 2.5. Additional exam requirements/recommendations for international students: Required—TOEFL (minimum score 550 paper-based; 213 computer-based). *Application deadline:* For fall admission, 7/1 for domestic and international students; for spring admission, 12/1 for domestic students, 11/15 for international students. Applications are processed on a rolling basis. Application fee: $0 ($50 for international students). Electronic applications accepted. *Financial support:* In 2010–11, 3 research assistantships with full tuition reimbursements (averaging $6,000 per year) were awarded. Financial award application deadline: 4/1; financial award applicants required to submit FAFSA. *Unit head:* Dr. Rahnl Wood, Advisor, 660-562-1759. *Application contact:* Dr. Gregory Haddock, Dean of Graduate School, 660-562-1145, Fax: 660-562-1096, E-mail: gradsch@nwmissouri.edu.

Nova Southeastern University, H. Wayne Huizenga School of Business and Entrepreneurship, Doctoral Program in Business Administration, Fort Lauderdale, FL 33314-7796. Offers accounting (DBA); decision sciences (DBA); finance (DBA); human resource management (DBA); international business (DBA); management (DBA); marketing (DBA). Part-time and evening/weekend programs available. *Faculty:* 34 full-time (11 women), 2 part-time/adjunct (1 woman). *Students:* 2 full-time (1 woman), 93 part-time (32 women); includes 9 Black or African American, non-Hispanic/Latino; 4 Asian, non-Hispanic/Latino; 11 Hispanic/Latino, 8 international. Average age 47. 66 applicants, 14% accepted, 6 enrolled. In 2010, 29 doctorates awarded. *Degree requirements:* For doctorate, comprehensive exam, thesis/dissertation. *Entrance requirements:* For doctorate, GMAT. Additional exam requirements/recommendations for international students: Required—TOEFL (minimum score 600 paper-based; 250 computer-based; 100 iBT), IELTS (minimum score 7). *Application deadline:* Applications are processed on a rolling basis. Application fee: $50. Electronic applications accepted. *Financial support:* Available to part-time students. Applicants required to submit FAFSA. *Faculty research:* Reputation management, call centers, international social capital, corporate earnings guidance, corporate governance. *Unit head:* Kristie Tetrault, Director of Program Administration, 954-262-5120, Fax: 954-262-3849, E-mail: kristie@huizenga.nova.edu. *Application contact:* Karen Goldberg, Associate Director of Recruitment and Special Events, 954-262-5039, Fax: 954-262-3822, E-mail: karen@huizenga.nova.edu.

Nova Southeastern University, H. Wayne Huizenga School of Business and Entrepreneurship, Master's Program in Accounting, Fort Lauderdale, FL 33314-7796. Offers M Acc. Part-time and evening/weekend programs available. Postbaccalaureate distance learning degree programs offered (no on-campus study). *Faculty:* 4 full-time (0 women), 8 part-time/adjunct (4 women). *Students:* 30 full-time (21 women), 467 part-time (267 women); includes 330 minority (130 Black or African American, non-Hispanic/Latino; 1 American Indian or Alaska Native, non-Hispanic/Latino; 27 Asian, non-Hispanic/Latino; 168 Hispanic/Latino; 1 Native Hawaiian or other Pacific Islander, non-Hispanic/Latino; 3 Two or more races, non-Hispanic/Latino), 18 international. Average age 33. 188 applicants, 68% accepted, 98 enrolled. In 2010, 104 master's awarded. *Entrance requirements:* For master's, undergraduate degree in accounting, work experience. Additional exam requirements/recommendations for international students: Required—TOEFL (minimum score 550 paper-based; 213 computer-based; 79 iBT), IELTS (minimum score 6). *Application deadline:* For fall admission, 8/15 for domestic and international students; for winter admission, 12/10 for domestic and international students; for spring admission, 2/10 for domestic and international students. Applications are processed on a rolling basis. Application fee: $50. Electronic applications accepted. *Financial support:* Federal Work-Study and scholarships/grants available. Support available to part-time students. Financial award applicants required to submit FAFSA. *Unit head:* Dr. Preston Jones, Executive Associate Dean, 954-262-5127, Fax: 954-262-3960, E-mail: prestonj@huizenga.nova.edu. *Application contact:* Aimee Fernandez, Assistant Director, 954-262-5091, Fax: 954-262-3822, E-mail: aimee fernandez@huizenga.nova.edu.

The Ohio State University, Graduate School, Max M. Fisher College of Business, Department of Accounting and Management Information Systems, Columbus, OH 43210. Offers M Acc, MA, MS, PhD. *Accreditation:* AACSB. *Faculty:* 25. *Students:* 6 full-time (0 women), 5 part-time (2 women), 5 international. Average age 32. In 2010, 1 master's, 1 doctorate awarded. Terminal master's awarded for partial completion of doctoral program. *Degree requirements:* For doctorate, thesis/dissertation. *Entrance requirements:* For master's, GMAT (preferred) or GRE General Test; for doctorate, GMAT (preferred) or GRE. Additional exam requirements/recommendations for international students: Required—TOEFL (minimum score 600 paper-based; 250 computer-based). *Application deadline:* For fall admission, 8/15 priority date for domestic students, 7/1 priority date for international students; for winter admission, 12/1 priority date for domestic students, 11/1 priority date for international students; for spring admission, 3/1 priority date for domestic students, 2/1 priority date for international students. Applications are processed on a rolling basis. Application fee: $40 ($50 for international students). Electronic applications accepted. *Expenses:* Tuition, state resident: full-time $10,605. Tuition, nonresident: full-time $26,535. Tuition and fees vary according to course load and program. *Financial support:* Fellowships, research assistantships, teaching assistantships, career-related internships or fieldwork, Federal Work-Study, and institutionally sponsored loans available. Support available to part-time students. *Faculty research:* Artificial intelligence, protocol analysis, database design in decision-supporting systems. *Unit head:* Annette Beatty, Graduate Studies Committee Chair, 614-292-2081, Fax: 614-292-2118, E-mail: beatty.86@osu.edu. *Application contact:* 614-292-9444, Fax: 614-292-3895, E-mail: domestic.grad@osu.edu.

The Ohio State University, Graduate School, Max M. Fisher College of Business, Program in Accounting, Columbus, OH 43210. Offers M Acc, MA, MS. *Students:* 89 full-time (39 women), 8 part-time (all women); includes 3 Black or African American, non-Hispanic/Latino; 7 Asian, non-Hispanic/Latino; 2 Hispanic/Latino, 33 international. Average age 24. In 2010, 90 master's awarded. *Entrance requirements:* Additional exam requirements/recommendations for international students: Required—TOEFL. *Application deadline:* Applications are processed on a rolling basis. Application fee: $40 ($50 for international students). Electronic applications accepted. *Expenses:* Tuition, state resident: full-time $10,605. Tuition, nonresident: full-time $26,535. Tuition and fees vary according to course load and program. *Unit head:* Annette Beatty, Graduate Studies Committee Chair, 614-292-2081, Fax: 614-292-2118, E-mail: beatty.86@osu.edu. *Application contact:* Graduate Admissions, 614-292-9444, Fax: 614-292-3895, E-mail: domestic.grad@osu.edu.

Oklahoma State University, Spears School of Business, School of Accounting, Stillwater, OK 74078. Offers MS, PhD. *Accreditation:* AACSB. Part-time programs available. *Faculty:* 17 full-time (6 women), 2 part-time/adjunct (0 women). *Students:* 81 full-time (35 women), 33 part-time (17 women); includes 5 American Indian or Alaska Native, non-Hispanic/Latino, 14 international. Average age 26. 75 applicants, 44% accepted, 24 enrolled. In 2010, 44 master's, 1 doctorate awarded. *Degree requirements:* For master's, thesis or alternative; for doctorate, comprehensive exam, thesis/dissertation. *Entrance requirements:* For master's and doctorate, GRE or GMAT. Additional exam requirements/recommendations for international students: Required—TOEFL (minimum score 550 paper-based; 79 iBT). *Application deadline:* For fall admission, 3/1 priority date for international students; for spring admission, 8/1 priority date for international students. Applications are processed on a rolling basis. Application fee: $40 ($75 for international students). Electronic applications accepted. *Expenses:* Tuition, state resident: full-time $3716; part-time $154.85 per credit hour. Tuition, nonresident: full-time $14,892; part-time $621 per credit hour. Required fees: $2044; $85.20 per credit hour. One-time fee: $50. Tuition and fees vary according to course load and campus/location. *Financial support:* In 2010–11, 5 research assistantships (averaging $18,984 per year), 28 teaching assistantships (averaging $9,314 per year) were awarded; career-related internships or fieldwork, Federal Work-Study, scholarships/grants, health care benefits, tuition waivers (partial), and unspecified assistantships also available. Support available to part-time students. Financial award application deadline: 3/1; financial award applicants required to submit FAFSA. *Faculty research:* International accounting, accounting education, cost-management, taxation, oil and gas. *Unit head:* Dr. Don Hansen, Head, 405-744-5123, Fax: 405-744-1680. *Application contact:* Dr. Gordon Emslie, Dean, 405-744-6368, Fax: 405-744-0355, E-mail: grad-i@okstate.edu.

Old Dominion University, College of Business and Public Administration, Program in Accounting, Norfolk, VA 23529. Offers MS. *Accreditation:* AACSB. Part-time and evening/weekend programs available. *Faculty:* 12 full-time (4 women), 4 part-time/adjunct (2 women). *Students:* 24 full-time (14 women), 26 part-time (12 women); includes 9 minority (3 Black or African American, non-Hispanic/Latino; 4 Asian, non-Hispanic/Latino; 2 Hispanic/Latino), 11 international. Average age 29. 37 applicants, 68% accepted, 22 enrolled. In 2010, 24 master's awarded. *Degree requirements:* For master's, comprehensive exam. *Entrance requirements:* For master's, GMAT, minimum GPA of 3.0. Additional exam requirements/recommendations for international students: Required—TOEFL (minimum score 550 paper-based). *Application deadline:* For fall admission, 7/1 priority date for domestic students, 4/15 priority date for international students; for spring admission, 11/1 priority date for domestic students, 10/1 priority date for international students. Applications are processed on a rolling basis. Application fee: $50. *Expenses:* Tuition, state resident: full-time $8592; part-time $358 per credit. Tuition, nonresident: full-time $21,672; part-time $903 per credit. Required fees: $119 per semester. One-time fee: $50. *Financial support:* In 2010–11, 4 students received support, including 8 research assistantships with partial tuition reimbursements available (averaging $3,200 per year); career-related internships or fieldwork and unspecified assistantships also available. Financial award application deadline: 2/15; financial award applicants required to submit FAFSA. *Faculty research:* Assurance services, international accounting, strategic costing, business valuation. *Unit head:* Dr. Yin Xu, Graduate Program Director, 757-683-3554, Fax: 757-683-5639, E-mail: yxu@odu.edu. *Application contact:* Dr. Yin Xu, Graduate Program Director, 757-683-3554, Fax: 757-683-5639, E-mail: yxu@odu.edu.

Our Lady of the Lake University of San Antonio, School of Business and Leadership, Program in Accounting/Finance, San Antonio, TX 78207-4689. Offers MBA. Part-time and evening/weekend programs available. *Students:* 3 full-time (2 women), 55 part-time (35 women); includes 35 minority (8 Black or African American, non-Hispanic/Latino; 27 Hispanic/Latino), 2 international. Average age 32. In 2010, 33 master's awarded. *Expenses:* Tuition: Full-time $13,500; part-time $750 per contact hour. Required fees: $330. Tuition and fees vary according to course level, degree level and campus/location. *Unit head:* Dr. Robert Bisking, Dean, 210-434-6711, Fax: 210-434-0821. *Application contact:* Dr. Robert Bisking, Dean, 210-434-6711, Fax: 210-434-0821.

Pacific States University, College of Business, Los Angeles, CA 90006. Offers accounting (MBA); business administration (DBA); finance (MBA); international business (MBA); management of information technology (MBA); real estate management (MBA). Part-time and evening/weekend programs available. Postbaccalaureate distance learning degree programs offered (no on-campus study). *Faculty:* 4 full-time (1 woman), 13 part-time/adjunct (0 women). *Students:* 130 full-time (55 women); includes 1 Black or African American, non-Hispanic/Latino; 7 Asian, non-Hispanic/Latino; 3 Native Hawaiian or other Pacific Islander, non-Hispanic/Latino, 115 international. Average age 31. 42 applicants, 83% accepted, 33 enrolled. In 2010, 67 master's awarded. *Degree requirements:* For doctorate, comprehensive exam, thesis/dissertation. *Entrance requirements:* For master's, minimum undergraduate GPA of 2.5 during last 90 hours of course work. Additional exam requirements/recommendations for international students: Required—TOEFL (minimum score 133 computer-based; 45 iBT), IELTS (minimum score 4.5). *Application deadline:* For fall admission, 8/15 priority date for domestic students; for winter admission, 10/15 priority date for domestic students; for spring admission, 1/15 priority date for domestic students. Applications are processed on a rolling basis. Application fee: $100. *Expenses:* Tuition: Full-time $8280; part-time $345 per credit hour. Required fees: $150 per quarter. *Financial support:* Scholarships/grants available. Financial award applicants required to submit FAFSA. *Unit head:* Dr. Chase C. Lee, Director, 888-200-0383, Fax: 323-731-2383, E-mail: admission@psuca.edu. *Application contact:* Zolzaya Enkhbayar, Assistant Director of Admissions, 323-731-2383, Fax: 323-731-7276, E-mail: admissions@psuca.edu.

Prairie View A&M University, College of Business, Prairie View, TX 77446-0519. Offers accounting (MS); general business administration (MBA). *Accreditation:* AACSB. Part-time and evening/weekend programs available. *Faculty:* 14 full-time (5 women). *Students:* 55 full-time (33 women), 158 part-time (99 women); includes 166 Black or African American, non-Hispanic/Latino; 6 Asian, non-Hispanic/Latino; 8 Hispanic/Latino, 20 international. Average age 31. In 2010, 48 master's awarded. *Entrance requirements:* For master's, GMAT, minimum GPA of 2.45. Additional exam requirements/recommendations for international students: Required—TOEFL. *Application deadline:* For fall admission, 7/1 for domestic students, 6/1 priority date for international students; for spring admission, 11/1 for domestic students, 10/1 priority date for international students. Applications are processed on a rolling basis. Application fee: $50. Electronic applications accepted. *Expenses:* Tuition, state resident: full-time $3586.14; part-time $119.06 per credit hour. Tuition, nonresident: part-time $511.23 per credit hour. *Financial support:* In 2010–11, 9 research assistantships (averaging $6,240 per year), 7 teaching assistantships (averaging $6,240 per year) were awarded; career-related internships or fieldwork, Federal Work-Study, institutionally sponsored loans, and tuition waivers (partial) also available. Support available to part-time students. Financial award application deadline: 4/1; financial award applicants required to submit FAFSA. *Faculty research:* Operations, finance, marketing. Total annual research expenditures: $30,000. *Unit head:* Dr. Munir Quddus, Dean, 936-261-9217, Fax: 936-261-9241, E-mail: muquddus@pvamu.edu. *Application contact:* Dr. John Dyck, Director, Graduate Programs in Business, 936-261-9217, Fax: 936-261-9232, E-mail: jwdyck@pvamu.edu.

Providence College, Graduate Studies, School of Business, Providence, RI 02918. Offers accounting (MBA); entrepreneurship (MBA); finance (MBA); international business (MBA); management (MBA); marketing (MBA); not-for-profit organizations (MBA). Part-time and evening/weekend programs available. *Faculty:* 17 full-time (9 women), 10 part-time/adjunct (2 women). *Students:* 53 full-time (20 women), 57 part-time (22 women); includes 4 minority (1 Black or African American, non-Hispanic/Latino;

1 Asian, non-Hispanic/Latino; 2 Two or more races, non-Hispanic/Latino), 6 international. Average age 26. 72 applicants, 81% accepted. In 2010, 56 master's awarded. *Degree requirements:* For master's, thesis optional. *Entrance requirements:* For master's, GMAT. Additional exam requirements/recommendations for international students: Required—TOEFL (minimum score 550 paper-based; 213 computer-based; 80 iBT). *Application deadline:* For fall admission, 8/1 priority date for domestic and international students; for spring admission, 12/1 priority date for domestic and international students. Applications are processed on a rolling basis. Application fee: $55. *Expenses:* Contact institution. *Financial support:* In 2010–11, 34 research assistantships with full tuition reimbursements (averaging $8,400 per year) were awarded; Federal Work-Study, institutionally sponsored loans, and unspecified assistantships also available. Support available to part-time students. Financial award application deadline: 8/1; financial award applicants required to submit FAFSA. *Unit head:* Dr. MaryJane Lenon, Director, MBA Program, 401-865-2566, Fax: 401-865-2978, E-mail: mjlenon@providence.edu. *Application contact:* Katherine A. Follett, Administrative Coordinator, 401-865-2333, Fax: 401-865-2978, E-mail: kfollett@providence.edu.

Purdue University Calumet, Graduate Studies Office, School of Management, Hammond, IN 46323-2094. Offers accountancy (M Acc); business administration (MBA); business administration for executives (EMBA). Part-time and evening/weekend programs available. *Faculty:* 25 full-time (7 women). *Students:* 180 full-time, 15 part-time. In 2010, 80 master's awarded. *Entrance requirements:* For master's, GMAT. Additional exam requirements/recommendations for international students: Required—TOEFL. *Application deadline:* For fall admission, 8/20 priority date for domestic students; for spring admission, 1/15 priority date for domestic students. Applications are processed on a rolling basis. Application fee: $55. Electronic applications accepted. *Expenses:* Tuition, state resident: full-time $6867. Tuition, nonresident: full-time $14,157. *Financial support:* In 2010–11, 2 research assistantships with full tuition reimbursements (averaging $8,000 per year) were awarded. Financial award application deadline: 3/1. *Unit head:* Dr. Martine SuChatelet, Dean, 219-989-2606, E-mail: duchatel@purduecal.edu. *Application contact:* Kimberly Uhll, Graduate Adviser, 219-989-3150, E-mail: kuhll@purduecal.edu.

Queens College of the City University of New York, Division of Graduate Studies, Social Science Division, Department of Accounting, Flushing, NY 11367-1597. Offers MS. *Faculty:* 19 full-time (1 woman). *Students:* 31 full-time (16 women), 243 part-time (131 women); includes 18 Black or African American, non-Hispanic/Latino; 107 Asian, non-Hispanic/Latino; 20 Hispanic/Latino, 36 international. 215 applicants, 57% accepted, 80 enrolled. In 2010, 30 master's awarded. Application fee: $125. *Unit head:* Dr. Israel Blumenfrucht, Chairperson, 718-997-5070, E-mail: israel_blumenfrucht@qc.edu. Application contact: Mario Caruso, Director of Graduate Admissions, 718-997-5200, Fax: 718-997-5193, E-mail: graduate_admissions@qc.edu.

Rhode Island College, School of Graduate Studies, School of Management, Department of Accounting and Computer Information Systems, Providence, RI 02908-1991. Offers accounting (MP Ac); financial planning (CGS). Part-time and evening/weekend programs available. *Faculty:* 1 (woman) full-time. *Students:* 2 full-time (1 woman), 10 part-time (8 women); includes 1 minority (Asian, non-Hispanic/Latino), 1 international. Average age 29. In 2010, 5 master's awarded. *Entrance requirements:* For master's, GMAT (unless applicant is a CPA or has passed a state bar exam); for CGS, GMAT, bachelor's degree from an accredited college or university, official transcripts of all undergraduate and graduate records. Additional exam requirements/recommendations for international students: Recommended—TOEFL (minimum score 550 paper-based; 213 computer-based; 79 iBT). *Application deadline:* For fall admission, 3/1 for domestic students. Applications are processed on a rolling basis. Application fee: $50. *Expenses:* Tuition, state resident: full-time $8208; part-time $342 per credit hour. Tuition, nonresident: full-time $16,080; part-time $670 per credit hour. Required fees: $554; $20 per credit. $72 per term. *Financial support:* Federal Work-Study, scholarships/grants, and health care benefits available. Support available to part-time students. Financial award application deadline: 5/15; financial award applicants required to submit FAFSA. *Unit head:* Prof. David Filipek, Chair, 401-456-8009. *Application contact:* Graduate Studies, 401-456-8700.

Rhodes College, Department of Economics and Business Administration, Memphis, TN 38112-1690. Offers accounting (MS). Part-time programs available. *Faculty:* 5 full-time (3 women), 2 part-time/adjunct (0 women). *Students:* 18 full-time (5 women). Average age 22. In 2010, 10 master's awarded. *Entrance requirements:* For master's, GMAT. Additional exam requirements/recommendations for international students: Required—TOEFL (minimum score 550 paper-based). *Application deadline:* For fall admission, 3/1 for domestic students. Application fee: $25. *Expenses:* Tuition: Full-time $34,270; part-time $1440 per credit. Required fees: $310. *Financial support:* Career-related internships or fieldwork and scholarships/grants available. Financial award application deadline: 3/1; financial award applicants required to submit FAFSA. *Unit head:* Dr. Pamela H. Church, Program Director, 901-843-3863, Fax: 901-843-3798, E-mail: church@rhodes.edu. *Application contact:* Dr. Pamela H. Church, Program Director, 901-843-3863, Fax: 901-843-3798, E-mail: church@rhodes.edu.

Rider University, College of Business Administration, Program in Accountancy, Lawrenceville, NJ 08648-3001. Offers M Acc. *Accreditation:* AACSB. *Faculty:* 5 full-time (4 women), 2 part-time/adjunct (0 women). *Students:* 46 full-time (29 women), 50 part-time (28 women); includes 1 Black or African American, non-Hispanic/Latino; 6 Asian, non-Hispanic/Latino; 2 Hispanic/Latino, 38 international. Average age 28. In 2010, 35 master's awarded. *Entrance requirements:* For master's, GMAT, resume. Additional exam requirements/recommendations for international students: Required—TOEFL (minimum score 550 paper-based; 213 computer-based). *Application deadline:* For fall admission, 8/1 priority date for domestic students, 3/15 priority date for international students; for spring admission, 12/1 priority date for domestic students, 11/1 priority date for international students. Applications are processed on a rolling basis. Application fee: $50. Electronic applications accepted. *Expenses:* Tuition: Full-time $29,870; part-time $667.34 per credit. Required fees: $350; $11.60 per credit. Part-time tuition and fees vary according to program. *Financial support:* In 2010–11, 36 students received support. Career-related internships or fieldwork, Federal Work-Study, institutionally sponsored loans, and unspecified assistantships available. Support available to part-time students. Financial award applicants required to submit FAFSA. *Faculty research:* Financial reporting, corporate governance, information technology, ethics, pedagogy. *Unit head:* Dr. Marge O'Reilly-Allen, Chairperson, 609-895-3505, Fax: 609-896-5304. *Application contact:* Jamie L. Mitchell, Director of Graduate Admissions, 609-896-5036, Fax: 609-895-5680, E-mail: jmitchell@rider.edu.

Robert Morris University Illinois, Morris Graduate School of Management, Chicago, IL 60605. Offers accounting (MBA); accounting/finance (MBA); health care administration (MM); higher education administration (MM); human resource management (MBA); information systems (MIS); leadership (MBA); management/finance (MIS); management/human resource management (MBA). Part-time and evening/weekend programs available. *Faculty:* 9 full-time (2 women), 21 part-time/adjunct (6 women). *Students:* 275 full-time (151 women), 212 part-time (138 women); includes 170 Black or African American, non-Hispanic/Latino; 1 American Indian or Alaska Native, non-Hispanic/Latino; 21 Asian, non-Hispanic/Latino; 73 Hispanic/Latino; 2 Native Hawaiian or other Pacific Islander, non-Hispanic/Latino, 23 international. Average age 32. 172 applicants, 87% accepted, 105 enrolled. In 2010, 174 master's awarded. *Degree requirements:* For master's, 48 residency hours. *Entrance requirements:* Additional exam requirements/recommendations for international students: Required—TOEFL (minimum score 500 paper-based; 173 computer-based). *Application deadline:* Applications are processed on a rolling basis. Application fee: $50 ($100 for international students). Electronic applications accepted. *Expenses:* Tuition: Full-time $13,200; part-time $2200 per course. *Financial support:* Federal Work-Study, scholarships/grants, and tuition waivers available. Support available to part-time students. *Unit head:* Kayed Akkawi, Dean, 312-935-6025, Fax: 312-935-6020, E-mail: kakkawi@robertmorris.edu. *Application contact:* Courtney A. Kohn Sanders, Dean of Graduate Admissions, 312-935-4810, Fax: 312-935-6020, E-mail: ckohn@robertmorris.edu.

Rochester Institute of Technology, Graduate Enrollment Services, E. Philip Saunders College of Business, Graduate Business Programs, Program in Accounting, Rochester, NY 14623-5603. Offers MBA. Part-time and evening/weekend programs available. *Students:* 17 full-time (9 women), 7 part-time (2 women); includes 3 minority (1 Black or African American, non-Hispanic/Latino; 1 Asian, non-Hispanic/Latino; 1 Hispanic/Latino), 4 international. Average age 28. 52 applicants, 52% accepted, 15 enrolled. In 2010, 9 master's awarded. *Entrance requirements:* For master's, GMAT, minimum GPA of 2.5. Additional exam requirements/recommendations for international students: Required—TOEFL (minimum score 580 paper-based; 237 computer-based; 92 iBT) or IELTS (minimum score 7). *Application deadline:* For fall admission, 2/15 priority date for domestic and international students; for winter admission, 11/1 priority date for domestic students; for spring admission, 2/1 priority date for domestic students. Applications are processed on a rolling basis. Application fee: $50. *Expenses:* Tuition: Full-time $33,234; part-time $924 per credit hour. Required fees: $219. *Financial support:* In 2010–11, 21 students received support; research assistantships with partial tuition reimbursements available, teaching assistantships with partial tuition reimbursements available, career-related internships or fieldwork, scholarships/grants, and unspecified assistantships available. Support available to part-time students. Financial award applicants required to submit FAFSA. *Faculty research:* Formation and taxation of business entities, auditor independence: the conundrum of tax services, ethics in accounting and business or the lack thereof, accounting crisis: a curricular response. *Unit head:* Heather Krakehl, Graduate Program Director, 585-475-6916, Fax: 585-475-7450, E-mail: hmascb@rit.edu. *Application contact:* Diane Ellison, Assistant Vice President, Graduate Enrollment Services, 585-475-2229, Fax: 585-475-7164, E-mail: gradinfo@rit.edu.

Rocky Mountain College, Program in Accountancy, Billings, MT 59102-1796. Offers M Acc. Part-time programs available. *Faculty:* 2 full-time (1 woman), 1 part-time/adjunct (0 women). *Students:* 8 full-time (6 women), 1 international. In 2010, 6 master's awarded. *Entrance requirements:* Additional exam requirements/recommendations for international students: Required—TOEFL (minimum score 570 paper-based; 230 computer-based; 88 iBT),

IELTS (minimum score 6.5). *Application deadline:* Applications are processed on a rolling basis. Application fee: $35 ($40 for international students). Electronic applications accepted. *Expenses:* Tuition: Part-time $860 per credit. Required fees: $94 per semester. Part-time tuition and fees vary according to course load and program. *Financial support:* Federal Work-Study and scholarships/grants available. Financial award applicants required to submit FAFSA. *Unit head:* Anthony Piltz, Academic Vice President, 406-657-1020, Fax: 406-259-9751, E-mail: piltza@rocky.edu. *Application contact:* Kelly Edwards, Director of Admissions, 406-657-1026, Fax: 406-657-1189, E-mail: admissions@rocky.edu.

Rowan University, Graduate School, William G. Rohrer College of Business, Department of Accounting and Finance, Program in Accounting, Glassboro, NJ 08028-1701. Offers MBA. Part-time and evening/weekend programs available. *Students:* 5 full-time (1 woman), 12 part-time (6 women); includes 1 Black or African American, non-Hispanic/Latino; 1 Hispanic/Latino. Average age 30. 9 applicants, 78% accepted, 6 enrolled. In 2010, 4 master's awarded. *Degree requirements:* For master's, comprehensive exam, thesis. *Entrance requirements:* For master's, GRE General Test. Additional exam requirements/recommendations for international students: Required—TOEFL. *Application deadline:* Applications are processed on a rolling basis. Application fee: $65 ($200 for international students). Electronic applications accepted. *Expenses:* Tuition, area resident: Part-time $602 per semester hour. Tuition, nonresident: part-time $602 per semester hour. Required fees: $100 per semester hour. One-time fee: $10 part-time. *Financial support:* Career-related internships or fieldwork, Federal Work-Study, and unspecified assistantships available. Support available to part-time students. *Unit head:* Dr. Horacio Sosa, Dean, College of Graduate and Continuing Education, 856-256-4747, Fax: 856-256-5638, E-mail: sosa@rowan.edu. *Application contact:* Karen Haynes, Graduate Coordinator, 856-256-4052, E-mail: haynes@rowan.edu.

Rutgers, The State University of New Jersey, Newark, Graduate School, Program in Management, Newark, NJ 07102. Offers accounting (PhD); accounting information systems (PhD); computer information systems (PhD); finance (PhD); information technology (PhD); international business (PhD); management science (PhD); marketing (PhD); organization management (PhD). Program offered jointly with New Jersey Institute of Technology. *Accreditation:* AACSB. *Faculty:* 128 full-time (24 women), 4 part-time/adjunct (1 woman). *Students:* 95 full-time (34 women), 17 part-time (6 women); includes 9 Black or African American, non-Hispanic/Latino; 54 Asian, non-Hispanic/Latino; 3 Hispanic/Latino. 438 applicants, 14% accepted, 34 enrolled. In 2010, 10 doctorates awarded. *Degree requirements:* For doctorate, thesis/dissertation, cumulative exams. *Entrance requirements:* For doctorate, GMAT or GRE General Test, minimum undergraduate B average. Additional exam requirements/recommendations for international students: Required—TOEFL. *Application deadline:* For fall admission, 4/1 for domestic students; for spring admission, 11/1 for domestic students. Applications are processed on a rolling basis. Application fee: $60. Electronic applications accepted. *Expenses:* Tuition, state resident: part-time $600 per credit. Tuition, nonresident: full-time $10,694. *Financial support:* In 2010–11, 6 fellowships (averaging $18,000 per year), 4 research assistantships with full and partial tuition reimbursements (averaging $23,112 per year), 38 teaching assistantships with full and partial tuition reimbursements (averaging $23,112 per year) were awarded; institutionally sponsored loans and tuition waivers (full and partial) also available. Support available to part-time students. Financial award application deadline: 2/15. *Faculty research:* Technology management, leadership and teams, consumer behavior, financial and markets, logistics. *Unit head:* Dr. Glenn Shafer, Director, 973-353-1604, Fax: 973-353-5691, E-mail: gshafer@rbs.rutgers.edu. *Application contact:* Goncalo Filipe, Senior Academic Coordinator, 973-353-1002, Fax: 973-353-5691, E-mail: gfilipe@rbsmail.rutgers.edu.

Rutgers, The State University of New Jersey, Newark, Rutgers Business School–Newark and New Brunswick, Doctoral Programs in Management, Newark, NJ 07102. Offers accounting (PhD); accounting information systems (PhD); economics (PhD); finance (PhD); individualized study (PhD); information technology (PhD); international business (PhD); management science (PhD); marketing science (PhD); organizational management (PhD); science, technology and management (PhD); supply chain management (PhD). *Faculty:* 143 full-time (36 women), 2 part-time/adjunct (0 women). *Students:* 117 full-time (42 women), 1 (woman) part-time; includes 8 Black or African American, non-Hispanic/Latino; 14 Asian, non-Hispanic/Latino; 3 Hispanic/Latino, 68 international. Average age 33. 355 applicants, 14% accepted, 35 enrolled. In 2010, 8 doctorates awarded. *Degree requirements:* For doctorate, comprehensive exam, thesis/dissertation. *Entrance requirements:* For doctorate, GRE or GMAT. Additional exam requirements/recommendations for international students: Required—TOEFL (minimum score 550 paper-based; 213 computer-based; 79 iBT). *Application deadline:* For fall admission, 3/1 for domestic and international students; for spring admission, 10/15 for domestic and international students. Application fee: $65. Electronic applications accepted. *Expenses:* Tuition, state resident: part-time $600 per credit. Tuition, nonresident: full-time $10,694. *Financial support:* In 2010–11, 52 students received support, including 7 fellowships (averaging $18,000 per year), 4 research assistantships with tuition reimbursements available (averaging $23,112 per year), 41 teaching assistantships with tuition reimbursements

available (averaging $23,112 per year); health care benefits also available. Financial award application deadline: 3/1. *Unit head:* Dr. Glenn Shafer, Director, 973-353-1604, Fax: 973-353-5691, E-mail: gshafer@rbs.rutgers.edu. *Application contact:* Information Contact, 973-353-5371, Fax: 973-353-5691, E-mail: phdinfo@andromeda.rutgers.edu.

St. Ambrose University, College of Business, Program in Accounting, Davenport, IA 52803-2898. Offers MAC. Part-time and evening/weekend programs available. *Faculty:* 3 full-time (2 women), 1 part-time/adjunct (0 women). *Students:* 20 full-time (10 women), 17 part-time (7 women); includes 3 minority (1 Black or African American, non-Hispanic/Latino; 1 Asian, non-Hispanic/Latino; 1 Two or more races, non-Hispanic/Latino), 3 international. Average age 26. 21 applicants, 90% accepted, 15 enrolled. In 2010, 16 master's awarded. *Degree requirements:* For master's, comprehensive exam (for some programs), thesis or alternative, capstone seminar. *Entrance requirements:* For master's, GMAT. *Application deadline:* For fall admission, 8/15 priority date for domestic students; for winter admission, 12/15 priority date for domestic students; for spring admission, 1/1 priority date for domestic students. Applications are processed on a rolling basis. Application fee: $25. Electronic applications accepted. *Expenses:* Tuition: Full-time $13,230; part-time $735 per credit hour. Required fees: $60 per semester. Tuition and fees vary according to degree level, program and reciprocity agreements. *Financial support:* In 2010–11, 23 students received support, including 1 research assistantship with partial tuition reimbursement available (averaging $3,600 per year); career-related internships or fieldwork, scholarships/grants, tuition waivers (partial), and unspecified assistantships also available. Financial award application deadline: 3/15; financial award applicants required to submit FAFSA. *Unit head:* Lewis Marx, Director, 563-333-6186, Fax: 563-333-6243, E-mail: marxlewisd@sau.edu. *Application contact:* Deborah K. Bennett, Administrative Assistant, 563-333-6266, Fax: 563-333-6268, E-mail: bennettdeborahk@sau.edu.

St. Edward's University, School of Management and Business, Area of Business Administration, Austin, TX 78704. Offers accounting (MBA); business management (MBA); corporate finance (MBA, Certificate); global entrepreneurship (MBA); human resource management (Certificate); management information systems (MBA, Certificate); marketing (MBA, Certificate); operations management (MBA, Certificate). Part-time and evening/weekend programs available. *Faculty:* 17 full-time (7 women), 19 part-time/adjunct (4 women). *Students:* 41 full-time (21 women), 273 part-time (135 women); includes 111 minority (19 Black or African American, non-Hispanic/Latino; 1 American Indian or Alaska Native, non-Hispanic/Latino; 8 Asian, non-Hispanic/Latino; 78 Hispanic/Latino; 1 Native Hawaiian or other Pacific Islander, non-Hispanic/Latino; 4 Two or more races, non-Hispanic/Latino), 11 international. Average age 33. 101 applicants, 77% accepted, 50 enrolled. In 2010, 115 master's awarded. *Degree requirements:* For master's, minimum of 24 resident hours. *Entrance requirements:* For master's, GMAT or GRE General Test, minimum GPA of 2.75 in last 60 hours of course work. Additional exam requirements/recommendations for international students: Required—TOEFL (minimum score 550 paper-based; 213 computer-based; 79 iBT) or IELTS (minimum score 6). *Application deadline:* For fall admission, 7/1 for domestic and international students; for spring admission, 11/1 for domestic and international students. Applications are processed on a rolling basis. Application fee: $45 ($50 for international students). Electronic applications accepted. *Expenses:* Tuition: Full-time $16,200; part-time $900 per credit hour. Required fees: $50 per trimester. Full-time tuition and fees vary according to course load and program. *Financial support:* In 2010–11, 19 students received support. Scholarships/grants available. *Faculty research:* Ethics and corporate responsibility, new hire socialization, team performance, business strategy, non-traditional marketing, social media. *Unit head:* Dr. Stan Horner, Director, 512-428-1279, Fax: 512-448-8492, E-mail: stanleyh@stedwards.edu. *Application contact:* Kelly Luna, Graduate Admissions Coordinator, 512-233-1697, Fax: 512-428-1032, E-mail: kellyl@stedwards.edu.

St. Edward's University, School of Management and Business, Program in Accounting, Austin, TX 78704. Offers M Ac. Part-time and evening/weekend programs available. *Students:* 2 full-time (0 women), 28 part-time (16 women); includes 8 minority (2 Black or African American, non-Hispanic/Latino; 5 Hispanic/Latino; 1 Two or more races, non-Hispanic/Latino), 1 international. Average age 30. 34 applicants, 74% accepted, 12 enrolled. In 2010, 6 master's awarded. *Degree requirements:* For master's, minimum of 24 resident hours. *Entrance requirements:* For master's, GMAT or GRE General Test, minimum GPA of 2.75 in last 60 hours of course work and in accounting. Additional exam requirements/recommendations for international students: Required—TOEFL (minimum score 550 paper-based; 213 computer-based; 79 iBT) or IELTS (minimum score 6). *Application deadline:* For fall admission, 7/1 for domestic and international students; for spring admission, 11/1 for domestic and international students. Applications are processed on a rolling basis. Application fee: $45 ($50 for international students). Electronic applications accepted. *Expenses:* Tuition: Full-time $16,200; part-time $900 per credit hour. Required fees: $50 per trimester. Full-time tuition and fees vary according to course load and program. *Financial support:* Scholarships/grants available. *Unit head:* Dr. Louise E. Single, Director, 512-492-3114, Fax: 512-448-8492, E-mail: louises@stedwards.edu. *Application contact:* Kelly Luna, Graduate

Admissions Coordinator, 512-233-1697, Fax: 512-428-1032, E-mail: kellyl@stedwards.edu.

St. John's University, The Peter J. Tobin College of Business, Department of Accounting and Taxation, Program in Accounting, Queens, NY 11439. Offers MBA, MS, Adv C. *Accreditation:* AACSB. Part-time and evening/weekend programs available. *Students:* 260 full-time (165 women), 73 part-time (41 women); includes 54 minority (9 Black or African American, non-Hispanic/Latino; 31 Asian, non-Hispanic/Latino; 13 Hispanic/Latino; 1 Two or more races, non-Hispanic/Latino), 189 international. Average age 25. 459 applicants, 68% accepted, 160 enrolled. In 2010, 136 master's awarded. *Degree requirements:* For master's, comprehensive exam (for some programs), thesis optional. *Entrance requirements:* For master's, GMAT, 2 letters of recommendation, resume, transcripts, statement of goals; for Adv C, GMAT, 2 letters of recommendation, resume, undergraduate transcripts, essay. Additional exam requirements/recommendations for international students: Required—TOEFL (minimum score 600 paper-based; 250 computer-based; 100 iBT), IELTS (minimum score 5.5). *Application deadline:* For fall admission, 5/1 priority date for domestic and international students; for spring admission, 11/1 priority date for domestic and international students. Applications are processed on a rolling basis. Application fee: $70. Electronic applications accepted. *Expenses:* Contact institution. *Financial support:* Research assistantships available. Support available to part-time students. Financial award application deadline: 3/1; financial award applicants required to submit FAFSA. *Unit head:* Dr. Ardian Fitzsimons, Chair, 718-990-7306, Fax: 718-380-3803, E-mail: fitzsims@stjohns.edu. *Application contact:* Carol Swanberg, Assistant Dean, Director of Graduate Admissions, 718-990-1345, Fax: 718-990-5242, E-mail: tobingradnyc@stjohns.edu.

Saint Joseph's University, Erivan K. Haub School of Business, Professional MBA Program, Philadelphia, PA 19131-1395. Offers accounting (MBA); finance (MBA), including finance; general business (MBA); health and medical services administration (MBA); human resource management (MBA); international business (MBA); international marketing (MBA); management (MBA); marketing (MBA); DO/MBA. Do/MBA offered jointly with Philadelphia College of Osteopathic Medicine. Part-time and evening/weekend programs available. Postbaccalaureate distance learning degree programs offered (no on-campus study). *Students:* 47 full-time (35 women), 585 part-time (221 women); includes 92 minority (42 Black or African American, non-Hispanic/Latino; 1 American Indian or Alaska Native, non-Hispanic/Latino; 34 Asian, non-Hispanic/Latino; 12 Hispanic/Latino; 1 Native Hawaiian or other Pacific Islander, non-Hispanic/Latino; 2 Two or more races, non-Hispanic/Latino), 41 international. Average age 30. In 2010, 135 master's awarded. *Entrance requirements:* For master's, GMAT or GRE, 2 letters of recommendation, resume. Additional exam requirements/recommendations for international students: Required—TOEFL (minimum score: paper 550, computer 213, iBT 79) or IELTS (6.5), Pearson Test of English (minimum 60). *Application deadline:* For fall admission, 7/15 priority date for domestic students, 4/15 priority date for international students; for spring admission, 11/15 priority date for domestic students, 10/15 priority date for international students. Applications are processed on a rolling basis. Application fee: $35. Electronic applications accepted. *Expenses:* Tuition: Part-time $729 per credit. Tuition and fees vary according to course load, degree level and program. *Financial support:* Scholarships/grants and unspecified assistantships available. Financial award application deadline: 5/1; financial award applicants required to submit FAFSA. *Unit head:* Adele C. Foley, Associate Dean/Director, Graduate Business Programs, 610-660-1691, Fax: 610-660-1599, E-mail: afoley@sju.edu. *Application contact:* Janine N. Guerra, Assistant Director, MBA Program, 610-660-1695, Fax: 610-660-1599, E-mail: jguerra@sju.edu.

Saint Leo University, Graduate Business Studies, Saint Leo, FL 33574-6665. Offers accounting (MBA); business (MBA); health services management (MBA); human resource management (MBA); information security management (MBA); marketing (MBA); sport business (MBA). Part-time and evening/weekend programs available. Postbaccalaureate distance learning degree programs offered (no on-campus study). *Faculty:* 32 full-time (4 women), 53 part-time/adjunct (21 women). *Students:* 1,498 full-time (890 women), 10 part-time (6 women); includes 593 minority (465 Black or African American, non-Hispanic/Latino; 5 American Indian or Alaska Native, non-Hispanic/Latino; 23 Asian, non-Hispanic/Latino; 84 Hispanic/Latino; 2 Native Hawaiian or other Pacific Islander, non-Hispanic/Latino; 14 Two or more races, non-Hispanic/Latino), 14 international. Average age 38. In 2010, 557 master's awarded. *Entrance requirements:* For master's, GMAT (minimum score 500 if applicant does not have 5 years of professional work experience), bachelor's degree from regionally-accredited college or university with minimum GPA of 3.0 in the last 60 hours of coursework; 5 years of professional work experience; resume; 2 letters of recommendation. Additional exam requirements/recommendations for international students: Required—TOEFL (minimum score 550 paper-based; 213 computer-based; 80 iBT). *Application deadline:* For fall admission, 7/1 priority date for domestic and international students; for spring admission, 11/12 priority date for domestic students, 11/1 for international students. Applications are processed on a rolling basis. Application fee: $75. Electronic applications accepted. *Expenses:* Contact institution. *Financial support:* In 2010–11, 51 students received support. Career-related internships or fieldwork, Federal Work-Study, scholarships/grants, and health care benefits available. Financial award application deadline: 3/1; financial award applicants required to submit FAFSA. *Unit head:* Dr. Lorrie McGovern, Director, 352-588-7390, Fax: 352-588-8585, E-mail: mbaslu@saintleo.edu. *Application contact:* Jared Welling, Director, Graduate/Weekend and Evening Admission, 800-707-8846, Fax: 352-588-7873, E-mail: grad.admissions@saintleo.edu.

Saint Peter's College, Graduate Business Programs, Program in Accountancy, Jersey City, NJ 07306-5997. Offers MS, MBA/MS. Part-time and evening/weekend programs available. *Students:* 25 applicants, 72% accepted, 10 enrolled. *Entrance requirements:* Additional exam requirements/recommendations for international students: Required—TOEFL (minimum score 79 computer-based). *Application deadline:* Applications are processed on a rolling basis. Electronic applications accepted. *Financial support:* Applicants required to submit FAFSA. *Application contact:* Stephanie Autenrieth, Director, Graduate and Professional Studies Admission, 201-761-6474, Fax: 201-435-5270, E-mail: sautenrieth@spc.edu.

Salisbury University, Graduate Division, Department of Business Administration, Salisbury, MD 21801. Offers accounting track (MBA); general track (MBA). *Accreditation:* AACSB. Part-time and evening/weekend programs available. *Faculty:* 13 full-time (3 women), 1 part-time/adjunct (0 women). *Students:* 22 full-time (8 women), 42 part-time (16 women); includes 4 minority (1 Black or African American, non-Hispanic/Latino; 1 Asian, non-Hispanic/Latino; 2 Two or more races, non-Hispanic/Latino), 7 international. Average age 29. 59 applicants, 46% accepted, 26 enrolled. In 2010, 32 master's awarded. *Entrance requirements:* For master's, GMAT, resume; 2 recommendations. Additional exam requirements/recommendations for international students: Required—TOEFL (minimum score 550 paper-based; 213 computer-based; 79 iBT). *Application deadline:* For fall admission, 3/1 priority date for domestic students; for spring admission, 10/15 priority date for domestic students. Applications are processed on a rolling basis. Application fee: $45. Electronic applications accepted. *Financial support:* In 2010–11, 13 students received support. Institutionally sponsored loans, scholarships/grants, and unspecified assistantships available. Support available to part-time students. Financial award applicants required to submit FAFSA. *Unit head:* Yvonne Downie, MBA Director, 410-548-3983, Fax: 410-546-6208, E-mail: yxdownie@salisbury.edu. *Application contact:* Yvonne Downie, MBA Director, 410-548-3983, Fax: 410-546-6208, E-mail: yxdownie@salisbury.edu.

Sam Houston State University, College of Business Administration, Huntsville, TX 77341. Offers accounting (MS); business administration (MBA); general business and finance (MS), including finance. *Accreditation:* AACSB. Part-time and evening/weekend programs available. *Faculty:* 31 full-time (8 women). *Students:* 146 full-time (63 women), 150 part-time (71 women); includes 20 Black or African American, non-Hispanic/Latino; 2 American Indian or Alaska Native, non-Hispanic/Latino; 8 Asian, non-Hispanic/Latino; 24 Hispanic/Latino, 29 international. Average age 29. 141 applicants, 83% accepted, 78 enrolled. In 2010, 97 master's awarded. *Entrance requirements:* For master's, GMAT. Additional exam requirements/recommendations for international students: Required—TOEFL (minimum score 550 paper-based; 213 computer-based; 79 iBT). *Application deadline:* For fall admission, 8/1 for domestic students; for spring admission, 12/1 for domestic students. Applications are processed on a rolling basis. Application fee: $20. *Expenses:* Tuition, state resident: full-time $1363; part-time $163 per credit hour. Tuition, nonresident: full-time $3856; part-time $473 per credit hour. *Financial support:* Research assistantships, Federal Work-Study, institutionally sponsored loans, and unspecified assistantships available. Financial award application deadline: 5/31; financial award applicants required to submit FAFSA. *Unit head:* Dr. Mitchell J. Muehsam, Dean, 936-294-1254, Fax: 936-294-3612, E-mail: mmuehsam@shsu.edu. *Application contact:* Dr. Leroy Ashorn, Advisor, 936-294-1246, Fax: 936-294-3612, E-mail: busgrad@shsu.edu.

San Francisco State University, Division of Graduate Studies, College of Business, San Francisco, CA 94132-1722. Offers accountancy (MSA); business administration (MBA). *Unit head:* Dr. Caran Colvin, Dean, 415-405-3752. *Application contact:* Armaan Moattari, Assistant Director, Graduate Programs, 415-817-4314, E-mail: amoatt@sfsu.edu.

Santa Clara University, Leavey School of Business, Program in Business Administration, Santa Clara, CA 95053. Offers accounting (MBA); entrepreneurship (MBA); executive business administration (EMBA); finance (MBA); food and agribusiness (MBA); international business (MBA); leading people and organizations (MBA); managing technology and innovation (MBA); marketing management (MBA); supply chain management (MBA). *Accreditation:* AACSB. Part-time and evening/weekend programs available. *Students:* 229 full-time (80 women), 748 part-time (244 women); includes 354 minority (14 Black or African American, non-Hispanic/Latino; 1 American Indian or Alaska Native, non-Hispanic/Latino; 287 Asian, non-Hispanic/Latino; 42 Hispanic/Latino; 5 Native Hawaiian or other Pacific Islander, non-Hispanic/Latino; 5 Two or more races, non-Hispanic/Latino), 209 international. Average age 32. 334 applicants, 76% accepted, 191 enrolled. In 2010, 307 master's awarded. *Degree requirements:* For master's, thesis or alternative. *Entrance requirements:* For master's, GMAT, GRE. Additional exam requirements/

recommendations for international students: Required—TOEFL (minimum score 600 paper-based; 250 computer-based; 100 iBT). *Application deadline:* For fall admission, 6/1 for domestic and international students; for spring admission, 1/19 for domestic students, 1/17 for international students. Applications are processed on a rolling basis. Application fee: $75 ($100 for international students). Electronic applications accepted. *Expenses:* Contact institution. *Financial support:* In 2010–11, 350 students received support; fellowships with partial tuition reimbursements available, research assistantships with partial tuition reimbursements available, career-related internships or fieldwork, Federal Work-Study, institutionally sponsored loans, scholarships/grants, health care benefits, and unspecified assistantships available. Support available to part-time students. Financial award application deadline: 6/1; financial award applicants required to submit FAFSA. *Unit head:* Elizabeth B. Ford, Senior Assistant Dean, 408-554-2752, Fax: 408-554-4571, E-mail: eford@scu.edu. *Application contact:* Molly Mulally, Assistant Director, Graduate Business Admissions, 408-554-4539, Fax: 408-554-4571, E-mail: mbaadmissions@scu.edu.

Seton Hall University, Stillman School of Business, Department of Accounting, South Orange, NJ 07079-2697. Offers accounting (MS); professional accounting (MS); taxation (Certificate). Part-time and evening/weekend programs available. *Faculty:* 7 full-time (1 woman), 3 part-time/adjunct (1 woman). *Students:* 8 full-time (6 women), 36 part-time (7 women); includes 4 Black or African American, non-Hispanic/Latino; 10 Asian, non-Hispanic/Latino; 1 Hispanic/Latino. Average age 25. 105 applicants, 86% accepted, 44 enrolled. In 2010, 23 master's awarded. *Entrance requirements:* For master's, GMAT or CPA, Advanced degrees such as Ph.D., MD, JD, PharmD, DDS, DVM, MBA fro an AACSB institution, MS in a business discipline, and aminimum GPA of 3.0. Additional exam requirements/recommendations for international students: Required—TOEFL (minimum: 254 computer, 102 iBT), IELTS, or Pearson Test of English (PTE). *Application deadline:* For fall admission, 5/31 priority date for domestic students, 3/31 for international students; for spring admission, 10/31 for domestic students, 9/30 for international students. Applications are processed on a rolling basis. Application fee: $75. Electronic applications accepted. *Financial support:* In 2010–11, 2 students received support, including research assistantships with full tuition reimbursements available (averaging $35,610 per year); career-related internships or fieldwork, scholarships/grants, and unspecified assistantships also available. Support available to part-time students. Financial award application deadline: 6/30; financial award applicants required to submit FAFSA. *Faculty research:* Voluntary disclosure, international accounting, pension and retirement accounting, ethics in financial reporting. *Unit head:* Dr. Mark Holtzman, Chair, 973-761-9133, Fax: 973-761-9217, E-mail: mark.holtzman@shu.edu. *Application contact:* Catherine Bianchi, Director of Graduate Admissions, 973-761-9262, Fax: 973-761-9208, E-mail: catherine.bianchi@shu.edu.

Seton Hall University, Stillman School of Business, Programs in Business Administration, South Orange, NJ 07079-2697. Offers accounting (MBA); finance (MBA); information technology management (MBA); international business (MBA); management (MBA); marketing (MBA); sport management (MBA); supply chain management (MBA). Part-time and evening/weekend programs available. *Faculty:* 35 full-time (8 women), 11 part-time/adjunct (1 woman). *Students:* 93 full-time (33 women), 165 part-time (76 women); includes 26 Black or African American, non-Hispanic/Latino; 39 Asian, non-Hispanic/Latino; 8 Hispanic/Latino. Average age 29. 404 applicants, 74% accepted, 258 enrolled. In 2010, 203 master's awarded. *Degree requirements:* For master's, 20 hours of community service (Social Responsibility Project). *Entrance requirements:* For master's, GMAT or CPA, Advanced degree such as PhD, MD, JD, DVM, DDS, PharmD, MBA from an AACSB institution, MS in a business discipline and a minimum GPA of 3.0. Additional exam requirements/recommendations for international students: Required—TOEFL (minimum: 254 computer, 102 iBT), IELTS or Pearson Test of English (PTE). *Application deadline:* For fall admission, 5/31 priority date for domestic students, 3/31 priority date for international students; for spring admission, 10/31 priority date for domestic students, 9/30 priority date for international students. Applications are processed on a rolling basis. Application fee: $75. Electronic applications accepted. *Financial support:* In 2010–11, research assistantships with full tuition reimbursements (averaging $35,610 per year); career-related internships or fieldwork, Federal Work-Study, scholarships/grants, and unspecified assistantships also available. Support available to part-time students. Financial award application deadline: 6/30; financial award applicants required to submit FAFSA. *Faculty research:* Financial, hedge funds, international business, legal issues, disclosure and branding. *Unit head:* Dr. Joyce A. Strawser, Associate Dean for Undergraduate and MBA Curricula, 973-761-9225, Fax: 973-761-9217, E-mail: strawsjo@shu.edu. *Application contact:* Catherine Bianchi, Director of Graduate Admissions, 973-761-9262, Fax: 973-761-9208, E-mail: catherine.bianchi@shu.edu.

Shorter University, Professional Studies, Rome, GA 30165. Offers accountancy (MAC); business administration (MBA); curriculum and instruction (M Ed); leadership (MA). Evening/weekend programs available. *Faculty:* 9 full-time (3 women), 25 part-time/adjunct (9 women). *Students:* 330 full-time (212 women); includes 168 Black or African American, non-Hispanic/Latino; 5 American Indian or Alaska Native, non-Hispanic/Latino; 4 Asian, non-Hispanic/Latino; 5 Hispanic/Latino, 3 international. Average age 39. In

2010, 177 master's awarded. *Degree requirements:* For master's, project. *Entrance requirements:* For master's, minimum undergraduate GPA of 2.75 in last 60 hours, 3 years of work experience. Additional exam requirements/ recommendations for international students: Required—TOEFL (minimum score 550 paper-based; 213 computer-based; 79 iBT). *Application deadline:* Applications are processed on a rolling basis. Application fee: $50. *Expenses:* Tuition: Full-time $9840. Required fees: $360. One-time fee: $225 full-time. Tuition and fees vary according to course load and program. *Financial support:* Institutionally sponsored loans and scholarships/grants available. Financial award applicants required to submit FAFSA. *Faculty research:* Systems design, leadership, pedagogy using technology. *Unit head:* Jacqueline Avant, Dean of Students, 678-260-3538, E-mail: javant@shorter.edu. *Application contact:* Irene Barassa, Admissions Specialist, 678-260-3531, E-mail: ibarassa@shorter.edu.

Southeastern Louisiana University, College of Business, Hammond, LA 70402. Offers accounting (MBA); general (MBA); information systems for supply chain management (MBA). *Accreditation:* AACSB. Part-time and evening/weekend programs available. *Faculty:* 15 full-time (1 woman), 1 part-time/adjunct (0 women). *Students:* 52 full-time (29 women), 56 part-time (21 women); includes 12 minority (8 Black or African American, non-Hispanic/ Latino; 1 Asian, non-Hispanic/Latino; 2 Hispanic/Latino; 1 Two or more races, non-Hispanic/Latino), 8 international. Average age 28. 109 applicants, 40% accepted, 25 enrolled. In 2010, 62 master's awarded. *Entrance requirements:* For master's, GMAT (minimum score 450), minimum cumulative GPA of 2.75 for all undergraduate work attempted or 3.0 on all upper-division undergraduate coursework attempted. Additional exam requirements/recommendations for international students: Required—TOEFL (minimum score 525 paper-based; 195 computer-based; 61 iBT). *Application deadline:* For fall admission, 7/15 priority date for domestic students, 6/1 priority date for international students; for spring admission, 12/1 priority date for domestic students, 10/1 priority date for international students. Applications are processed on a rolling basis. Application fee: $20 ($30 for international students). Electronic applications accepted. *Expenses:* Tuition, state resident: full-time $3533. Tuition, nonresident: full-time $12,002. Required fees: $907. Tuition and fees vary according to degree level. *Financial support:* In 2010–11, 21 students received support, including 1 research assistantship (averaging $9,000 per year); career-related internships or fieldwork, Federal Work-Study, institutionally sponsored loans, scholarships/grants, and administrative assistantships, graduate professional services assistants also available. Support available to part-time students. Financial award application deadline: 5/1; financial award applicants required to submit FAFSA. *Faculty research:* Ethical decision-making in accounting, entrepreneurship and emerging information, leadership and organizational performance. *Unit head:* Dr. Randy Settoon, Dean, 985-549-2258, Fax: 985-549-5038, E-mail: rsettoon@selu.edu. *Application contact:* Sandra Meyers, Graduate Admissions Analyst, 985-549-5620, Fax: 985-549-5882, E-mail: admissions@selu.edu.

Southeast Missouri State University, School of Graduate Studies, Harrison College of Business, Cape Girardeau, MO 63701-4799. Offers accounting (MBA); entrepreneurship (MBA); environmental management (MBA); financial management (MBA); general management (MBA); health administration (MBA); industrial management (MBA); international business (MBA); sport management (MBA). *Accreditation:* AACSB. Part-time and evening/ weekend programs available. Postbaccalaureate distance learning degree programs offered (no on-campus study). *Faculty:* 31 full-time (10 women). *Students:* 51 full-time (24 women), 72 part-time (34 women); includes 4 minority (1 American Indian or Alaska Native, non-Hispanic/Latino; 3 Asian, non-Hispanic/Latino), 32 international. Average age 28. 71 applicants, 83% accepted, 33 enrolled. In 2010, 46 master's awarded. *Degree requirements:* For master's, variable foreign language requirement, applied research project; foreign language or 9 credit hours (for international business). *Entrance requirements:* For master's, GMAT (minimum score 400), minimum undergraduate GPA of 2.5, prerequisite courses for non-business undergraduate majors. Additional exam requirements/recommendations for international students: Required—TOEFL (minimum score 550 paper-based; 213 computer-based; 79 iBT); Recommended—IELTS (minimum score 6). *Application deadline:* For fall admission, 8/1 for domestic students, 6/1 for international students; for spring admission, 11/21 for domestic students, 10/1 for international students. Applications are processed on a rolling basis. Application fee: $25 ($35 for international students). Electronic applications accepted. *Expenses:* Tuition, state resident: full-time $4698; part-time $261 per credit hour. Tuition, nonresident: full-time $8379; part-time $465.50 per credit hour. *Financial support:* In 2010–11, 52 students received support, including 10 teaching assistantships with full tuition reimbursements available (averaging $7,600 per year); career-related internships or fieldwork, Federal Work-Study, institutionally sponsored loans, scholarships/grants, tuition waivers (full), and unspecified assistantships also available. Financial award application deadline: 6/30; financial award applicants required to submit FAFSA. *Faculty research:* Human resources, laws impacting accounting, advertising. *Unit head:* Dr. Kenneth A. Heischmidt, Director, Graduate Programs, 573-651-5116, Fax: 573-651-5032, E-mail: kheischmidt@semo.edu. *Application contact:* Gail Amick, Administrative Secretary, 573-651-2049, Fax: 573-651-2001, E-mail: gamick@semo.edu.

Southern Illinois University Edwardsville, Graduate School, School of Business, Department of Accounting, Edwardsville, IL 62026-0001. Offers accountancy (MSA); taxation (MSA). *Accreditation:* AACSB. Part-time and evening/weekend programs available. *Faculty:* 4 full-time (1 woman). *Students:* 15 full-time (7 women), 22 part-time (12 women); includes 3 minority (1 Asian, non-Hispanic/Latino; 1 Hispanic/Latino; 1 Two or more races, non-Hispanic/Latino), 2 international. Average age 26. 47 applicants, 47% accepted. In 2010, 22 master's awarded. *Degree requirements:* For master's, thesis or alternative, final exam. *Entrance requirements:* For master's, GMAT. Additional exam requirements/recommendations for international students: Required—TOEFL (minimum score 550 paper-based; 213 computer-based; 79 iBT), IELTS (minimum score 6.5). *Application deadline:* For fall admission, 7/22 for domestic students, 6/1 for international students; for spring admission, 12/10 for domestic students, 10/1 for international students. Applications are processed on a rolling basis. Application fee: $30. Electronic applications accepted. *Expenses:* Tuition, state resident: full-time $6012; part-time $1503 per semester. Tuition, nonresident: full-time $15,030; part-time $3758 per semester. Required fees: $1711; $675 per semester. *Financial support:* In 2010–11, 1 fellowship with full tuition reimbursement (averaging $8,370 per year), 8 teaching assistantships with full tuition reimbursements (averaging $8,064 per year) were awarded; research assistantships with full tuition reimbursements, career-related internships or fieldwork, Federal Work-Study, institutionally sponsored loans, scholarships/grants, traineeships, and unspecified assistantships also available. Support available to part-time students. Financial award application deadline: 3/1; financial award applicants required to submit FAFSA. *Unit head:* Dr. Michael Costigan, Chair, 618-650-2633, E-mail: mcostig@siue.edu. *Application contact:* Dr. Michael Costigan, Chair, 618-650-2633, E-mail: mcostig@siue.edu.

Southern Methodist University, Cox School of Business, MBA Program, Dallas, TX 75275. Offers accounting (MBA); finance (MBA); financial consulting (MBA); general business (MBA); information technology and operations management (MBA); management (MBA); marketing (MBA); real estate (MBA); strategy and entrepreneurship (MBA). Part-time and evening/weekend programs available. *Faculty:* 59 full-time (13 women), 30 part-time/adjunct (7 women). *Students:* 359 full-time (116 women), 592 part-time (154 women); includes 215 minority (44 Black or African American, non-Hispanic/Latino; 10 American Indian or Alaska Native, non-Hispanic/Latino; 118 Asian, non-Hispanic/Latino; 39 Hispanic/Latino; 2 Native Hawaiian or other Pacific Islander, non-Hispanic/Latino; 2 Two or more races, non-Hispanic/Latino), 92 international. Average age 30. In 2010, 486 master's awarded. *Entrance requirements:* For master's, GMAT. Additional exam requirements/recommendations for international students: Required—TOEFL. *Application deadline:* Applications are processed on a rolling basis. Application fee: $0. Electronic applications accepted. *Expenses:* Contact institution. *Financial support:* Applicants required to submit FAFSA. *Faculty research:* Corporate finance, financial reporting, modeling consumer decision-making, competition between national brands and store brands, institutional determinants of firms' strategy. *Unit head:* Dr. Marci Armstrong, Associate Dean for Master's Programs, 214-768-4486, Fax: 214-768-3956, E-mail: marci@cox.smu.edu. *Application contact:* Patti Cudney, Director of MBA Admissions, 214-768-3001, Fax: 214-768-3956, E-mail: pcudney@cox.smu.edu.

Southern Methodist University, Cox School of Business, Program in Accounting, Dallas, TX 75275. Offers MSA. Part-time programs available. *Faculty:* 14 full-time (4 women), 10 part-time/adjunct (4 women). *Students:* 65 applicants, 57% accepted. In 2010, 58 master's awarded. *Entrance requirements:* For master's, GMAT. Additional exam requirements/recommendations for international students: Required—TOEFL. *Application deadline:* For fall admission, 5/15 priority date for domestic students; for winter admission, 11/30 for domestic students. Application fee: $75. *Expenses:* Contact institution. *Financial support:* In 2010–11, 17 students received support, including 17 fellowships (averaging $3,800 per year); scholarships/grants and tuition waivers (partial) also available. Financial award application deadline: 5/15. *Faculty research:* Capital markets, taxation, business combinations, intangibles accounting, accounting history. *Unit head:* Joseph Magliolo, Head, 214-768-1678, Fax: 214-768-4099, E-mail: jmagliol@mail.cox.smu.edu. *Application contact:* Jeffrey R. Austin, Coordinator, 214-768-3630, Fax: 214-768-4099, E-mail: jraustin@mail.cox.smu.edu.

Southern Polytechnic State University, School of Engineering Technology and Management, Department of Business Administration, Marietta, GA 30060-2896. Offers accounting (MSA); business administration (MBA, Graduate Transition Certificate). *Accreditation:* ACBSP. Part-time and evening/weekend programs available. Postbaccalaureate distance learning degree programs offered (no on-campus study). *Faculty:* 9 full-time (2 women), 4 part-time/adjunct (2 women). *Students:* 87 full-time (51 women), 116 part-time (60 women); includes 66 Black or African American, non-Hispanic/Latino; 18 Asian, non-Hispanic/Latino; 5 Hispanic/Latino; 1 Two or more races, non-Hispanic/Latino, 46 international. Average age 32. 125 applicants, 95% accepted, 89 enrolled. In 2010, 64 master's awarded. *Degree requirements:* For master's, comprehensive exam, thesis or alternative. *Entrance requirements:* For master's, GMAT, letters of recommendation, statement of purpose, resume. Additional exam requirements/recommendations for international students: Required—TOEFL (minimum score 550

paper-based; 213 computer-based; 79 iBT), IELTS (minimum score 6.5). *Application deadline:* For fall admission, 7/1 priority date for domestic students, 5/1 priority date for international students; for spring admission, 11/1 priority date for domestic students, 9/1 priority date for international students. Applications are processed on a rolling basis. Application fee: $20. Electronic applications accepted. *Expenses:* Tuition, state resident: full-time $3690; part-time $205 per semester hour. Tuition, nonresident: full-time $13,428; part-time $746 per semester hour. Required fees: $598 per semester. *Financial support:* In 2010–11, 37 students received support, including 4 research assistantships with tuition reimbursements available (averaging $4,500 per year); career-related internships or fieldwork, scholarships/grants, and unspecified assistantships also available. Support available to part-time students. Financial award application deadline: 5/1; financial award applicants required to submit FAFSA. *Faculty research:* Ethics, virtual reality, sustainability, management of technology, quality management, capacity planning, human-computer interaction/interface, enterprise integration planning, economic impact of educational institutions, behavioral accounting, accounting ethics, taxation, information security, visualizational simulation, human-computer interaction. *Unit head:* Dr. Ronny Richardson, Chair, 678-915-7440, Fax: 678-915-4967, E-mail: rrichard@spsu.edu. *Application contact:* Nikki Palamiotis, Director of Graduate Studies, 678-915-4276, Fax: 678-915-7292, E-mail: npalamio@spsu.edu.

Southern Utah University, School of Business, Program in Accounting, Cedar City, UT 84720-2498. Offers M Acc. Part-time programs available. *Faculty:* 6 full-time (1 woman). *Students:* 39 full-time (7 women), 26 part-time (12 women); includes 2 Black or African American, non-Hispanic/Latino; 1 American Indian or Alaska Native, non-Hispanic/Latino; 1 Hispanic/Latino; 1 Native Hawaiian or other Pacific Islander, non-Hispanic/Latino. 50 applicants, 10% accepted, 5 enrolled. In 2010, 33 master's awarded. *Application deadline:* For fall admission, 8/1 priority date for domestic students. Applications are processed on a rolling basis. Application fee: $50 ($65 for international students). Electronic applications accepted. *Expenses:* Contact institution. *Financial support:* In 2010–11, 7 research assistantships with partial tuition reimbursements (averaging $1,300 per year) were awarded; career-related internships or fieldwork, institutionally sponsored loans, tuition waivers (full and partial), and unspecified assistantships also available. *Faculty research:* Cost accounting, intermediate accounting text, GAAP policy, statements on Standards for Accounting and Review Services (SSARS). *Unit head:* Dr. David Christensen, Chair, Accounting Department, 435-865-8058, Fax: 435-586-5493, E-mail: christensen@suu.edu. *Application contact:* Chris Proctor, Associate Director of Admissions, 435-586-7742, Fax: 435-865-8223, E-mail: alger@suu.edu.

State University of New York at Binghamton, Graduate School, School of Management, Program in Accounting, Binghamton, NY 13902-6000. Offers MS, PhD. Evening/weekend programs available. *Students:* 171 full-time (84 women), 19 part-time (15 women); includes 3 Black or African American, non-Hispanic/Latino; 39 Asian, non-Hispanic/Latino; 11 Hispanic/Latino, 72 international. Average age 24. 547 applicants, 29% accepted, 137 enrolled. In 2010, 80 master's awarded. *Degree requirements:* For doctorate, thesis/dissertation. *Entrance requirements:* For master's and doctorate, GMAT. Additional exam requirements/recommendations for international students: Required—TOEFL (minimum score 550 paper-based; 213 computer-based; 80 iBT). *Application deadline:* For fall admission, 3/1 priority date for domestic and international students; for spring admission, 10/15 priority date for domestic and international students. Applications are processed on a rolling basis. Application fee: $60. Electronic applications accepted. *Financial support:* In 2010–11, 10 students received support, including 3 teaching assistantships with full tuition reimbursements available (averaging $17,000 per year); career-related internships or fieldwork, Federal Work-Study, institutionally sponsored loans, scholarships/grants, health care benefits, and unspecified assistantships also available. Financial award application deadline: 2/15; financial award applicants required to submit FAFSA. *Unit head:* Dr. Upinder Dhillon, Dean of School of Management, 607-777-2314, E-mail: dhillon@binghamton.edu. *Application contact:* Catherine Smith, Recruiting and Admissions Coordinator, 607-777-2151, Fax: 607-777-2501, E-mail: cmsmith@binghamton.edu.

State University of New York at New Paltz, Graduate School, School of Business, New Paltz, NY 12561. Offers business administration (MBA); public accountancy (MBA). Part-time and evening/weekend programs available. *Faculty:* 11 full-time (4 women), 3 part-time/adjunct (2 women). *Students:* 45 full-time (19 women), 41 part-time (25 women); includes 2 Black or African American, non-Hispanic/Latino; 6 Asian, non-Hispanic/Latino; 6 Hispanic/Latino, 20 international. Average age 28. 64 applicants, 58% accepted, 31 enrolled. In 2010, 41 master's awarded. *Degree requirements:* For master's, internship. *Entrance requirements:* For master's, GMAT or GRE, minimum GPA of 3.0. Additional exam requirements/recommendations for international students: Required—TOEFL (minimum score 550 paper-based; 213 computer-based; 80 iBT), IELTS (minimum score 6.5). *Application deadline:* For fall admission, 5/15 priority date for domestic students, 5/15 for international students; for spring admission, 11/15 for domestic and international students. Applications are processed on a rolling basis. Application fee: $50. Electronic applications accepted. *Expenses:* Contact institution. *Financial support:* In 2010–11, 8 students received support, including 1 fellowship (averaging $2,500 per year), 6 research assistantships with partial tuition reimbursements available (averaging $5,000 per year), 1 teaching assistantship with partial tuition reimbursement available (averaging $5,000 per year); career-related internships or fieldwork, scholarships/grants, traineeships, and unspecified assistantships also available. Financial award application deadline: 8/1; financial award applicants required to submit FAFSA. *Faculty research:* Cognitive styles in management education, supporting SME e-commerce migration through e-learning, earnings management and board activity, trading future spread portfolio, global equity market correlation and volatility. *Unit head:* Dr. Hadi Salavitabar, Dean, 845-257-2930, E-mail: mba@newpaltz.edu. *Application contact:* Aaron Hines, Coordinator, 845-257-2968, E-mail: mba@newpaltz.edu.

State University of New York College at Geneseo, Graduate Studies, School of Business, Geneseo, NY 14454-1401. Offers accounting (MS). *Accreditation:* AACSB. *Faculty:* 3 full-time (1 woman), 1 part-time/adjunct (0 women). *Students:* 16 full-time (3 women). Average age 23. 33 applicants, 88% accepted, 16 enrolled. In 2010, 9 master's awarded. *Entrance requirements:* For master's, GMAT, bachelor's degree in accounting. *Application deadline:* For fall admission, 2/1 priority date for domestic students; for spring admission, 9/1 for domestic students. Application fee: $50. *Expenses:* Tuition, state resident: full-time $8370; part-time $349 per credit hour. Tuition, nonresident: full-time $13,780; part-time $574 per credit hour. Required fees: $725.52; $60.08 per credit hour. Tuition and fees vary according to program. *Financial support:* Application deadline: 4/1. *Unit head:* Dr. Michael Schinski, Interim Dean, 585-245-5367, Fax: 585-245-5467, E-mail: schinski@geneseo.edu. *Application contact:* Dr. Harry Howe, Director, Graduate Program, 585-245-5465, Fax: 585-245-5467, E-mail: howeh@geneseo.edu.

Stetson University, School of Business Administration, Program in Accounting, DeLand, FL 32723. Offers M Acc. *Accreditation:* AACSB. Part-time programs available. *Students:* 44 full-time (23 women), 22 part-time (17 women); includes 2 Black or African American, non-Hispanic/Latino; 1 Asian, non-Hispanic/Latino; 3 Hispanic/Latino, 1 international. Average age 36. In 2010, 32 master's awarded. *Entrance requirements:* For master's, GMAT. *Application deadline:* For fall admission, 7/1 for domestic students. Application fee: $25. *Financial support:* In 2010–11, 3 research assistantships were awarded; Federal Work-Study and institutionally sponsored loans also available. Support available to part-time students. Financial award application deadline: 3/15. *Unit head:* Dr. Judson P. Stryker, Director, 386-822-7410. *Application contact:* Kathryn Hannon, Assistant Director of Graduate Business Programs, 386-822-7410, Fax: 386-822-7413, E-mail: khannon@stetson.edu.

Suffolk University, Sawyer Business School, Department of Accounting, Boston, MA 02108-2770. Offers accounting (MSA, GDPA); taxation (MST); GDPA/MST; MBA/GDPA; MBA/MSA; MBA/MST. *Accreditation:* AACSB. Part-time and evening/weekend programs available. *Faculty:* 19 full-time (6 women), 3 part-time/adjunct (2 women). *Students:* 80 full-time (53 women), 150 part-time (77 women); includes 10 Black or African American, non-Hispanic/Latino; 1 American Indian or Alaska Native, non-Hispanic/Latino; 18 Asian, non-Hispanic/Latino; 2 Hispanic/Latino; 1 Two or more races, non-Hispanic/Latino, 74 international. Average age 29. 453 applicants, 71% accepted, 95 enrolled. In 2010, 86 master's, 5 GDPAs awarded. *Entrance requirements:* For master's, GMAT. Additional exam requirements/recommendations for international students: Required—TOEFL (minimum score 550 paper-based; 213 computer-based; 80 iBT). *Application deadline:* For fall admission, 6/15 priority date for domestic students, 6/15 for international students; for spring admission, 11/1 priority date for domestic students, 11/1 for international students. Applications are processed on a rolling basis. Application fee: $50. Electronic applications accepted. *Financial support:* In 2010–11, 91 students received support, including 45 fellowships with full and partial tuition reimbursements available (averaging $16,430 per year); career-related internships or fieldwork, Federal Work-Study, and institutionally sponsored loans also available. Support available to part-time students. Financial award application deadline: 4/1; financial award applicants required to submit CSS PROFILE. *Faculty research:* Tax policy, tax research, decision-making in accounting, accounting information systems, capital markets and strategic planning. *Unit head:* Lewis Shaw, Chair, 617-573-8615, Fax: 617-994-4260, E-mail: lshaw@suffolk.edu. *Application contact:* Judith Reynolds, Director of Graduate Admissions, 617-573-8302, Fax: 617-305-1733, E-mail: grad.admission@suffolk.edu.

Suffolk University, Sawyer Business School, Master of Business Administration Program, Boston, MA 02108-2770. Offers accounting (MBA); business administration (APC); corporate financial executive track (MBA); entrepreneurship (MBA); executive business administration (EMBA); finance (MBA); global business administration (GMBA); health administration (MBA); international business (MBA); marketing (MBA); organizational behavior (MBA); strategic management (MBA); taxation (MBA); JD/MBA; MBA/GDPA; MBA/MHA; MBA/MSA; MBA/MSF; MBA/MST. *Accreditation:* AACSB. Part-time and evening/weekend programs available. Postbaccalaureate distance learning degree programs offered (no on-campus study). *Faculty:* 97 full-time (30 women), 14 part-time/adjunct (3 women). *Students:* 179 full-time (65 women), 337 part-time (143 women); includes 16 Black or African American, non-Hispanic/Latino; 2 American Indian or Alaska Native, non-Hispanic/Latino; 22 Asian, non-Hispanic/Latino; 9 Hispanic/Latino; 1 Native Hawaiian or other Pacific Islander, non-Hispanic/Latino, 80 international. Average age 30. 431 applicants, 68% accepted, 128 enrolled. In 2010, 283 master's awarded. *Entrance requirements:* For master's, GMAT, minimum undergraduate GPA of 2.75 (MBA), 5 years of managerial experience (EMBA). Additional exam requirements/recommendations for international students: Required—TOEFL (minimum score 550 paper-based; 213 computer-based). *Application deadline:* For fall admission, 6/15 priority date for domestic students, 6/15 for international students; for spring admission, 11/1 priority date for domestic students, 11/1 for international students. Applications are processed on a rolling basis. Application fee: $50. Electronic applications accepted. *Financial support:* In 2010–11, 266 students received support, including 94 fellowships with full and partial tuition reimbursements available (averaging $12,635 per year); career-related internships or fieldwork, Federal Work-Study, and institutionally sponsored loans also available. Support available to part-time students. Financial award application deadline: 4/1; financial award applicants required to submit FAFSA. *Faculty research:* Foreign investments; career strategies and boundaryless careers; corporate ethics codes; interest rates, inflation, and growth options; innovation and product development performance. *Unit head:* Lillian Hallberg, Assistant Dean of Graduate Programs/Director of MBA Programs, 617-573-8306, E-mail: lhallber@suffolk.edu. *Application contact:* Judith Reynolds, Director of Graduate Admissions, 617-573-8302, Fax: 617-305-1733, E-mail: grad.admission@suffolk.edu.

Tennessee Technological University, Graduate School, College of Business, Cookeville, TN 38505. Offers accounting (MBA); finance (MBA); human resource management (MBA); international business (MBA); management information systems (MBA); risk management & insurance (MBA). *Accreditation:* AACSB. Part-time and evening/weekend programs available. *Faculty:* 28 full-time (5 women). *Students:* 58 full-time (18 women), 139 part-time (49 women); includes 10 Black or African American, non-Hispanic/Latino; 7 Asian, non-Hispanic/Latino; 7 Hispanic/Latino; 1 Native Hawaiian or other Pacific Islander, non-Hispanic/Latino. Average age 25. 211 applicants, 51% accepted, 59 enrolled. In 2010, 116 master's awarded. *Entrance requirements:* For master's, GMAT. Additional exam requirements/recommendations for international students: Required—TOEFL (minimum score 550 paper-based; 79 iBT), IELTS (minimum score 5.5). *Application deadline:* For fall admission, 8/1 for domestic and international students; for spring admission, 12/1 for domestic students, 10/1 for international students. Application fee: $25 ($30 for international students). Electronic applications accepted. *Expenses:* Tuition, state resident: full-time $7934; part-time $388 per credit hour. Tuition, nonresident: full-time $19,758; part-time $962 per credit hour. *Financial support:* In 2010–11, 5 fellowships (averaging $10,000 per year), 18 research assistantships (averaging $4,000 per year), teaching assistantships (averaging $4,000 per year) were awarded. Support available to part-time students. Financial award application deadline: 4/1. *Unit head:* Dr. Tom Timmerman, Director, 931-372-3600, Fax: 931-372-6249. *Application contact:* Shelia K. Kendrick, Coordinator of Graduate Admissions, 931-372-3808, Fax: 931-372-3497, E-mail: skendrick@tntech.edu.

Texas A&M International University, Office of Graduate Studies and Research, College of Business Administration, Division of International Banking and Finance Studies, Laredo, TX 78041-1900. Offers accounting (MP Acc); international banking (MBA). *Faculty:* 16 full-time (1 woman). *Students:* 53 full-time (29 women), 206 part-time (95 women); includes 2 Black or African American, non-Hispanic/Latino; 1 Asian, non-Hispanic/Latino; 178 Hispanic/Latino, 69 international. Average age 30. 137 applicants, 68% accepted, 71 enrolled. In 2010, 107 master's awarded. *Entrance requirements:* For master's, GMAT or GRE General Test. Additional exam requirements/recommendations for international students: Required—TOEFL (minimum score 550 paper-based; 213 computer-based; 79 iBT). *Application deadline:* For fall admission, 4/30 priority date for domestic students; for spring admission, 11/30 for domestic students, 10/1 for international students. Applications are processed on a rolling basis. Application fee: $25. *Financial support:* In 2010–11, 21 students received support, including 8 research assistantships. *Unit head:* Dr. Ken Hung, Chair, 956-326-2541, Fax: 956-326-2481, E-mail: ken.hung@tamiu.edu. *Application contact:* Imelda Lopez, Graduate Admissions Counselor, 956-326-2485, Fax: 956-326-2459, E-mail: lopez@tamiu.edu.

Texas A&M University, Mays Business School, Department of Accounting, College Station, TX 77843. Offers MS, PhD. *Accreditation:* AACSB. *Faculty:* 18. *Students:* 138 full-time (78 women), 4 part-time (2 women); includes 25 minority (5 Black or African American, non-Hispanic/Latino; 3 American Indian or Alaska Native, non-Hispanic/Latino; 8 Asian, non-Hispanic/Latino; 9 Hispanic/Latino), 8 international. Average age 27. In 2010, 106 master's, 1 doctorate awarded. Terminal master's awarded for partial completion of doctoral program. *Degree requirements:* For master's, comprehensive exam; for doctorate, thesis/dissertation. *Entrance requirements:* For master's, GMAT; for doctorate, GMAT or GRE General Test. Additional exam requirements/recommendations for international students: Required—TOEFL. *Application deadline:* For fall admission, 3/1 priority date for domestic students; for spring admission, 8/1 for domestic students. Applications are processed on a rolling basis. Application fee: $50 ($75 for international students). *Financial* *support:* In 2010–11, 100 students received support; fellowships, research assistantships, teaching assistantships, career-related internships or fieldwork and institutionally sponsored loans available. Financial award application deadline: 2/1. *Faculty research:* Financial reporting, taxation management, decision-making, accounting information systems, government accounting. *Unit head:* Dr. James J. Benjamin, Head, 979-845-0356, E-mail: jbenjamin@mays.tamu.edu. *Application contact:* Dr. James J. Benjamin, Head, 979-845-0356, E-mail: jbenjamin@mays.tamu.edu.

Texas Christian University, The Neeley School of Business at TCU, Program in Accounting, Fort Worth, TX 76129-0002. Offers M Ac. *Accreditation:* AACSB. *Entrance requirements:* For master's, GMAT, undergraduate degree in accounting from U.S.-accredited university. Additional exam requirements/recommendations for international students: Required—TOEFL (minimum score 600 paper-based; 250 computer-based; 100 iBT). *Application deadline:* For fall admission, 3/15 priority date for domestic students, 3/15 for international students; for spring admission, 9/15 priority date for domestic students, 9/15 for international students. Applications are processed on a rolling basis. Electronic applications accepted. *Expenses:* Tuition: Full-time $18,720; part-time $1040 per credit hour. Tuition and fees vary according to course load and program. *Financial support:* Tuition waivers (partial) and unspecified assistantships available. Financial award application deadline: 3/15; financial award applicants required to submit FAFSA. *Unit head:* Dr. Jerry L. Turner, Director, 817-257-7223, E-mail: jerry.turner@tcu.edu.

Texas State University–San Marcos, Graduate School, Emmett and Miriam McCoy College of Business Administration, Program in Accounting, San Marcos, TX 78666. Offers M Acy. Part-time programs available. *Faculty:* 9 full-time (6 women), 1 part-time/adjunct (0 women). *Students:* 70 full-time (42 women), 50 part-time (28 women); includes 26 minority (3 Black or African American, non-Hispanic/Latino; 10 Asian, non-Hispanic/Latino; 11 Hispanic/Latino; 1 Native Hawaiian or other Pacific Islander, non-Hispanic/Latino; 1 Two or more races, non-Hispanic/Latino), 9 international. Average age 28. 49 applicants, 88% accepted, 34 enrolled. In 2010, 65 master's awarded. *Degree requirements:* For master's, comprehensive exam. *Entrance requirements:* For master's, GMAT (minimum preferred score of 450 prior to admission decision), minimum GPA of 2.0 in last 60 hours of undergraduate work. Additional exam requirements/recommendations for international students: Required—TOEFL (minimum score 550 paper-based; 213 computer-based; 78 iBT). *Application deadline:* For fall admission, 6/1 for domestic and international students; for spring admission, 10/1 for domestic and international students. Applications are processed on a rolling basis. Application fee: $40 ($90 for international students). Electronic applications accepted. *Expenses:* Tuition, state resident: full-time $6024; part-time $251 per credit hour. Tuition, nonresident: full-time $13,536; part-time $564 per credit hour. Required fees: $1776; $50 per credit hour. $306 per semester. *Financial support:* In 2010–11, 39 students received support, including 2 research assistantships (averaging $5,076 per year), 8 teaching assistantships (averaging $5,092 per year); Federal Work-Study, institutionally sponsored loans, scholarships/grants, health care benefits, and unspecified assistantships also available. Support available to part-time students. Financial award application deadline: 4/1; financial award applicants required to submit FAFSA. *Unit head:* Dr. Robert Davis, Associate Dean, 512-245-3591, Fax: 512-245-7973, E-mail: rd23@txstate.edu. *Application contact:* Dr. Robert Davis, Associate Dean, 512-245-3591, Fax: 512-245-7973, E-mail: rd23@txstate.edu.

Texas State University–San Marcos, Graduate School, Emmett and Miriam McCoy College of Business Administration, Program in Accounting and Information Technology, San Marcos, TX 78666. Offers MS. *Faculty:* 7 full-time (2 women). *Students:* 11 full-time (3 women), 8 part-time (3 women); includes 6 minority (2 Black or African American, non-Hispanic/Latino; 2 Asian, non-Hispanic/Latino; 2 Hispanic/Latino), 3 international. Average age 32. 4 applicants, 100% accepted, 3 enrolled. In 2010, 7 master's awarded. *Degree requirements:* For master's, comprehensive exam. *Entrance requirements:* For master's, GMAT, official transcript from each college or university attended, 2 letters of recommendation, resume. Additional exam requirements/recommendations for international students: Required—TOEFL (minimum score 550 paper-based; 213 computer-based; 78 iBT). *Application deadline:* For fall admission, 6/1 for domestic and international students; for spring admission, 10/1 for domestic and international students. Application fee: $40 ($90 for international students). *Expenses:* Tuition, state resident: full-time $6024; part-time $251 per credit hour. Tuition, nonresident: full-time $13,536; part-time $564 per credit hour. Required fees: $1776; $50 per credit hour. $306 per semester. *Financial support:* In 2010–11, 5 students received support, including 6 teaching assistantships (averaging $5,098 per year); research assistantships, Federal Work-Study, institutionally sponsored loans, scholarships/grants, health care benefits, and unspecified assistantships also available. Support available to part-time students. *Unit head:* Dr. Robert Davis, Associate Dean, 512-245-3591, Fax: 512-245-7973, E-mail: rd23@txstate.edu. *Application contact:* Dr. J. Michael Willoughby, Dean of Graduate School, 512-245-2581, Fax: 512-245-8365, E-mail: gradcollege@txstate.edu.

Texas Tech University, Graduate School, Jerry S. Rawls College of Business Administration, Area of Accounting, Lubbock, TX 79409. Offers accounting (PhD); audit/financial reporting (MSA); taxation (MSA); JD/MSA. *Accreditation:* AACSB. Part-time programs available. *Faculty:* 15 full-time (3 women). *Students:* 134 full-time (72 women), 12 part-time (5 women); includes 17 minority (1 Black or African American, non-Hispanic/Latino; 3 American Indian or Alaska Native, non-Hispanic/Latino; 4 Asian, non-Hispanic/Latino; 8 Hispanic/Latino; 1 Two or more races, non-Hispanic/Latino), 1 international. Average age 23. 151 applicants, 72% accepted, 97 enrolled. In 2010, 37 master's, 3 doctorates awarded. Terminal master's awarded for partial completion of doctoral program. *Degree requirements:* For master's, capstone course; for doctorate, comprehensive exam, thesis/dissertation, qualifying exams. *Entrance requirements:* For master's and doctorate, GMAT, holistic profile of academic credentials. Additional exam requirements/recommendations for international students: Required—TOEFL (minimum score 550 paper-based; 213 computer-based; 79 iBT). *Application deadline:* For fall admission, 2/1 for domestic students, 1/15 for international students. Applications are processed on a rolling basis. Application fee: $50 ($75 for international students). Electronic applications accepted. *Expenses:* Tuition, state resident: full-time $5495.76; part-time $228.99 per credit hour. Tuition, nonresident: full-time $12,936; part-time $538.99 per credit hour. Required fees: $2674; $36 per credit hour. $905 per semester. *Financial support:* In 2010–11, 7 research assistantships (averaging $8,800 per year), 2 teaching assistantships (averaging $18,000 per year) were awarded; fellowships, career-related internships or fieldwork, Federal Work-Study, scholarships/grants, health care benefits, and unspecified assistantships also available. Financial award applicants required to submit FAFSA. *Faculty research:* Governmental and nonprofit accounting, managerial and financial accounting. *Unit head:* Dr. Robert Ricketts, Area Coordinator, 806-742-3180, Fax: 806-742-3182, E-mail: robert.ricketts@ttu.edu. *Application contact:* Cynthia D. Barnes, 806-742-3184, Fax: 806-742-3958, E-mail: ba_grad@ttu.edu.

Towson University, Joint Program in Accounting and Business Advisory Services, Towson, MD 21252-0001. Offers MS. Program offered jointly with University of Baltimore. *Accreditation:* AACSB. Part-time and evening/weekend programs available. *Students:* 31 full-time (21 women), 33 part-time (26 women); includes 9 minority (7 Black or African American, non-Hispanic/Latino; 1 American Indian or Alaska Native, non-Hispanic/Latino; 1 Asian, non-Hispanic/Latino), 19 international. Average age 29. In 2010, 16 master's awarded. *Entrance requirements:* For master's, GMAT, GRE General Test, minimum GPA of 3.0. *Application deadline:* Applications are processed on a rolling basis. Application fee: $50. Electronic applications accepted. *Expenses:* Tuition, state resident: part-time $324 per credit. Tuition, nonresident: part-time $681 per credit. Required fees: $95 per term. *Unit head:* Martin Freedman, Graduate Program Director, 410-704-4143, E-mail: mfreedman@towson.edu. *Application contact:* Carol Abraham, The Graduate School, 410-704-6163, Fax: 401-704-4675, E-mail: grads@towson.edu.

Troy University, Graduate School, College of Business, Program in Business Administration, Troy, AL 36082. Offers accounting (EMBA, MBA); criminal justice (EMBA); finance (MBA); general management (EMBA, MBA); healthcare management (EMBA); information systems (EMBA, MBA); international economic development (MBA). *Accreditation:* ACBSP. Part-time and evening/weekend programs available. *Students:* 351 full-time (198 women), 745 part-time (452 women); includes 589 minority (425 Black or African American, non-Hispanic/Latino; 13 American Indian or Alaska Native, non-Hispanic/Latino; 129 Asian, non-Hispanic/Latino; 21 Hispanic/Latino; 1 Two or more races, non-Hispanic/Latino). Average age 29. 748 applicants, 71% accepted. In 2010, 322 master's awarded. *Degree requirements:* For master's, minimum GPA 3.0, capstone course, research course. *Entrance requirements:* For master's, GMAT (minimum score 500) or GRE General Test (minimum score 900), minimum GPA of 2.5; letter of recommendation, bachelor's degree. Additional exam requirements/recommendations for international students: Required—TOEFL (minimum score 523 paper-based; 193 computer-based; 70 iBT), IELTS (minimum score 6), or ACT compass ESL (minimum Listening, Reading, and Grammar score: 270). *Application deadline:* Applications are processed on a rolling basis. Application fee: $50. *Expenses:* Tuition, state resident: full-time $4428; part-time $246 per credit hour. Tuition, nonresident: full-time $8856; part-time $492 per credit hour. Required fees: $432; $24 per credit hour. $50 per term. Tuition and fees vary according to program. *Unit head:* Dr. Henry M. Findley, Interim Chair/Professor, 334-670-3271, Fax: 334-670-3599, E-mail: hfindley@troy.edu. *Application contact:* Brenda K. Campbell, Director of Graduate Admissions, 334-670-3178, Fax: 334-670-3733, E-mail: bcamp@troy.edu.

Université de Sherbrooke, Faculty of Administration, Program in Accounting, Sherbrooke, QC J1K 2R1, Canada. Offers M Sc. *Faculty:* 11 full-time (9 women), 9 part-time/adjunct (7 women). *Students:* 120 applicants, 75% accepted, 71 enrolled. In 2010, 84 master's awarded. *Degree requirements:* For master's, one foreign language, thesis. *Entrance requirements:* For master's, No, Bachelor degree in related field Minimum GPA 3.0/4.3. *Application deadline:* For fall admission, 4/30 for domestic students, 1/15 for international students. Applications are processed on a rolling basis. Application fee: $70. Electronic applications accepted. *Faculty research:* Financial analysis, management accounting, certification, system and control. *Unit head:* Prof. Julien Bilodeau, Director, Graduate programs in business, 819-821-8000 Ext. 62355, E-mail: julien.bilodeau@usherbrooke.ca. *Application contact:* Marie-Claude Drouin, Programs Assistant Director, 819-821-8000 Ext. 63301.

Université du Québec en Outaouais, Graduate Programs, Program in Accounting, Gatineau, QC J8X 3X7, Canada. Offers MA, DESS, Diploma. Part-time and evening/weekend programs available. *Students:* 17 full-time, 44 part-time, 8 international. *Application deadline:* For fall admission, 6/1 for domestic students, 3/1 for international students; for winter admission, 11/1 for domestic students, 10/1 for international students. Application fee: $30 Canadian dollars. *Unit head:* Gilles Poirier, Director, 819-595-3900 Ext. 1755, Fax: 818-773-1760, E-mail: gilles.poirier@uqo.ca. *Application contact:* Registrar's Office, 819-773-1850, Fax: 819-773-1835, E-mail: registraire@uqo.ca.

Université du Québec en Outaouais, Graduate Programs, Program in Executive Certified Management Accounting, Gatineau, QC J8X 3X7, Canada. Offers MBA, DESS. Part-time and evening/weekend programs available. *Students:* 23 full-time, 45 part-time. *Degree requirements:* For master's, thesis (for some programs). *Application deadline:* For fall admission, 6/1 priority date for domestic students, 3/1 for international students; for winter admission, 11/1 priority date for domestic students, 10/1 for international students. Application fee: $30. *Unit head:* Gilles Poirier, Director, 819-595-3900 Ext. 1755, Fax: 819-773-1760, E-mail: gilles.poirier@uqo.ca. *Application contact:* Registrar's Office, 819-773-1850, Fax: 819-773-1835, E-mail: registraire@ugo.ca.

University at Buffalo, the State University of New York, Graduate School, School of Management, Buffalo, NY 14260. Offers accounting (MS); business administration (EMBA, MBA, PMBA); finance (MS), including financial engineering, financial management; information assurance (Certificate); management (PhD); management information systems (MS); supply chains and operations management (MS); Au D/MBA; JD/MBA; M Arch/MBA; MA/MBA; MD/MBA; MPH/MBA; MSW/MBA; Pharm D/MBA. *Accreditation:* AACSB. Part-time and evening/weekend programs available. *Faculty:* 65 full-time (18 women), 32 part-time/adjunct (8 women). *Students:* 626 full-time (229 women), 202 part-time (69 women); includes 43 minority (18 Black or African American, non-Hispanic/Latino; 2 American Indian or Alaska Native, non-Hispanic/Latino; 18 Asian, non-Hispanic/Latino; 5 Hispanic/Latino), 351 international. Average age 27. 1,553 applicants, 46% accepted, 400 enrolled. In 2010, 287 master's, 4 doctorates, 3 other advanced degrees awarded. *Degree requirements:* For master's, thesis (for some programs); for doctorate, comprehensive exam, thesis/dissertation. *Entrance requirements:* For master's, GMAT (MBA, MS in accounting), GRE or GMAT (for all other MS concentrations); for doctorate, GMAT or GRE. Additional exam requirements/recommendations for international students: Required—TOEFL (minimum score 230 computer-based; 95 iBT). *Application deadline:* For fall admission, 5/2 priority date for domestic students, 3/1 priority date for international students. Applications are processed on a rolling basis. Application fee: $100. Electronic applications accepted. *Expenses:* Contact institution. *Financial support:* In 2010–11, 91 students received support, including 5 fellowships with full and partial tuition reimbursements available (averaging $4,000 per year), 41 research assistantships with full and partial tuition reimbursements available (averaging $16,000 per year), 28 teaching assistantships with full and partial tuition reimbursements available (averaging $15,000 per year); career-related internships or fieldwork, Federal Work-Study, institutionally sponsored loans, scholarships/grants, health care benefits, and unspecified assistantships also available. Financial award application deadline: 2/15; financial award applicants required to submit FAFSA. *Faculty research:* Earnings management and electronic information assurance, supply chains and operations management, corporate financing and asset pricing, consumer behavior and quantitative modeling of marketing behavior, leadership and politics in organizations. Total annual research expenditures: $215,000. *Unit head:* David W. Frasier, Assistant Dean, 716-645-3204, Fax: 716-645-2341, E-mail: davidf@buffalo.edu. *Application contact:* David W. Frasier, Assistant Dean, 716-645-3204, Fax: 716-645-2341, E-mail: davidf@buffalo.edu.

The University of Akron, Graduate School, College of Business Administration, School of Accountancy, Akron, OH 44325. Offers accountancy (MS); accounting-information systems (MS); taxation (MT); JD/MT. *Accreditation:* AACSB. Part-time and evening/weekend programs available. *Faculty:* 15 full-time (4 women), 8 part-time/adjunct (0 women). *Students:* 71 full-time (37 women), 28 part-time (13 women); includes 4 Black or African American, non-Hispanic/Latino; 1 Asian, non-Hispanic/Latino; 1 Hispanic/Latino, 29 international. Average age 25. 76 applicants, 66% accepted, 31 enrolled. In 2010, 34 master's awarded. *Entrance requirements:* For master's, GMAT, minimum GPA of 2.75, two letters of recommendation, resume, statement of purpose. Additional exam requirements/recommendations for international students: Required—TOEFL (minimum score 550 paper-based; 213 computer-based; 79 iBT). *Application deadline:* For fall admission, 7/15 for domestic and international students; for spring admission, 11/15 for domestic and international students. Applications are processed on a rolling basis. Application fee: $30 ($40 for international students). Electronic applications accepted. *Expenses:* Tuition, state resident: full-time $6800; part-time $378 per credit hour. Tuition, nonresident: full-time $11,644; part-time $647 per credit hour. Required fees: $1265. One-time fee: $30 full-time. *Financial support:* In 2010–11, 5 research assistantships with full tuition reimbursements, 22 teaching assistantships with full tuition reimbursements were awarded. *Faculty research:* Financial reporting and management accounting auditing and assurance of financial information, business and information systems risk and security management, corporate governance and ethics, accounting education. Total annual research expenditures: $121,911. *Unit head:* Dr. Thomas Calderon, Chair, 330-972-6099, E-mail: tcalderon@uakron.edu. *Application contact:* Dr. Susan Hanlon, Director of Graduate Business Programs, 330-972-7043, Fax: 330-972-6588, E-mail: shanlon@uakron.edu.

The University of Alabama, Graduate School, Manderson Graduate School of Business, Culverhouse School of Accountancy, Tuscaloosa, AL 35487. Offers accounting (M Acc, PhD); tax accounting (MTA). *Accreditation:* AACSB. *Faculty:* 16 full-time (4 women). *Students:* 108 full-time (51 women), 3 part-time (2 women); includes 8 minority (5 Black or African American, non-Hispanic/Latino; 1 Asian, non-Hispanic/Latino; 1 Hispanic/Latino; 1 Two or more races, non-Hispanic/Latino), 1 international. Average age 24. 248 applicants, 49% accepted, 85 enrolled. In 2010, 99 master's, 1 doctorate awarded. *Degree requirements:* For doctorate, thesis/dissertation. *Entrance requirements:* For master's and doctorate, GMAT, minimum GPA of 3.0. Additional exam requirements/recommendations for international students: Required—TOEFL. *Application deadline:* For fall admission, 7/1 priority date for domestic students, 6/1 priority date for international students; for spring admission, 11/1 priority date for domestic students, 10/1 priority date for international students. Applications are processed on a rolling basis. Application fee: $50 ($60 for international students). Electronic applications accepted. *Expenses:* Tuition, state resident: full-time $7900. Tuition, nonresident: full-time $20,500. *Financial support:* In 2010–11, 99 students received support, including 6 fellowships with full tuition reimbursements available (averaging $15,000 per year), 21 research assistantships with full and partial tuition reimbursements available (averaging $6,065 per year), 18 teaching assistantships with full and partial tuition reimbursements available (averaging $6,065 per year); career-related internships or fieldwork, Federal Work-Study, institutionally sponsored loans, scholarships/grants, health care benefits, and unspecified assistantships also available. Financial award application deadline: 3/31. *Faculty research:* Corporate governance, audit decision making, earning management, valuation, executive compensation, not-for-profit. *Unit head:* Dr. Mary S. Stone, Director, 205-348-2915, Fax: 205-348-8453, E-mail: mstone@cba.ua.edu. *Application contact:* Sandy D. Davidson, Advisor, 205-348-8997, Fax: 205-348-8453, E-mail: sdavidso@cba.ua.edu.

The University of Alabama at Birmingham, School of Business, Program in Accounting, Birmingham, AL 35294. Offers M Acct. *Accreditation:* AACSB. *Students:* 17 full-time (6 women), 13 part-time (6 women); includes 5 minority (1 Black or African American, non-Hispanic/Latino; 4 Asian, non-Hispanic/Latino). Average age 27. 38 applicants, 58% accepted, 15 enrolled. In 2010, 7 master's awarded. *Expenses:* Tuition, state resident: full-time $5482. Tuition, nonresident: full-time $12,430. Tuition and fees vary according to program. *Unit head:* Dr. Jenice Prather-Kinsey, Director, 205-934-8880. *Application contact:* Dr. Jenice Prather-Kinsey, Director, 205-934-8880.

The University of Alabama in Huntsville, School of Graduate Studies, College of Business Administration, Department of Accounting and Finance, Huntsville, AL 35899. Offers accounting (M Acc), including CPA preparatory with an emphasis in taxation, CPA preparatory with emphasis in assurance and financial reporting, general accounting, information systems audit and control (ISAC). *Accreditation:* AACSB. Part-time and evening/weekend programs available. *Faculty:* 7 full-time (4 women), 2 part-time/adjunct (0 women). *Students:* 14 full-time (8 women), 27 part-time (14 women); includes 6 minority (all Black or African American, non-Hispanic/Latino), 3 international. Average age 33. 27 applicants, 56% accepted, 13 enrolled. In 2010, 8 master's awarded. *Degree requirements:* For master's, comprehensive exam, thesis or alternative. *Entrance requirements:* For master's, GMAT (minimum score 500), minimum AACSB index of 1080. Additional exam requirements/recommendations for international students: Required—TOEFL (minimum score 550 paper-based; 213 computer-based; 62 iBT). *Application deadline:* For fall admission, 8/1 for domestic students, 4/1 for international students; for spring admission, 12/1 for domestic students, 9/1 for international students. Applications are processed on a rolling basis. Application fee: $40 ($50 for international students). Electronic applications accepted. *Expenses:* Tuition, state resident: full-time $7250; part-time $407.75 per credit hour. Tuition, nonresident: full-time $17,358; part-time $970.05 per credit hour. Required fees: $246.80 per semester. Tuition and fees vary according to course load and program. *Financial support:* In 2010–11, 1 student received support, including 1 research assistantship with full tuition reimbursement available (averaging $14,400 per year), 1 teaching assistantship with full tuition reimbursement available (averaging $11,470 per year); career-related internships or fieldwork, Federal Work-Study, institutionally sponsored loans, scholarships/grants, health care benefits, and unspecified assistantships also available. Support available to part-time students. Financial award application deadline: 4/1; financial award applicants required to submit FAFSA. *Faculty research:* Accounting information systems, emerging technologies in accounting, behavioral accounting, state and local taxation, financial accounting. Total annual research expenditures: $17,511. *Unit head:* Dr. John Burnett, Interim Chair, 256-824-2923, Fax: 256-824-2929, E-mail: burnettj@uah.edu. *Application contact:* Jennifer Pettitt, Director of Graduate Programs, 256-824-6681, Fax: 256-824-7571, E-mail: jennifer.pettitt@uah.edu.

The University of Arizona, Eller College of Management, Department of Accounting, Tucson, AZ 85721. Offers M Ac. *Accreditation:* AACSB. Part-time programs available. *Faculty:* 10 full-time (3 women), 1 part-time/adjunct (0 women). *Students:* 57 full-time (36 women), 7 part-time (3 women); includes 1 American Indian or Alaska Native, non-Hispanic/Latino; 1 Asian, non-Hispanic/Latino; 9 Hispanic/Latino; 4 Two or more races, non-Hispanic/Latino, 5 international. Average age 26. 168 applicants, 39% accepted, 36 enrolled. In 2010, 41 master's awarded. *Degree requirements:* For master's, comprehensive exam, 1-year residency. *Entrance requirements:* For master's, GMAT (minimum score 550), 2 letters of recommendation, 3 writing samples, resume. Additional exam requirements/recommendations for international students: Required—TOEFL (minimum score 600 paper-based; 250 computer-based; 100 iBT). *Application deadline:* For fall admission, 3/1 priority date for domestic and international students; for spring admission, 10/1 priority date for domestic and international students. Applications are processed on a rolling basis. Application fee: $75. Electronic applications accepted. *Expenses:* Contact institution. *Financial support:* In 2010–11, 29 teaching assistantships with full tuition reimbursements (averaging $26,048 per year) were awarded; career-related internships or fieldwork, Federal Work-Study, scholarships/grants, health care benefits, tuition waivers (partial), and unspecified assistantships also available. Financial award application deadline: 3/15. *Faculty research:* Auditing, financial reporting and financial markets, taxation policy and markets, behavioral research in accounting. Total annual research expenditures: $35,764. *Unit head:* Dr. Dan S. Dhaliwal, Head, 520-621-2146, Fax: 520-621-3742, E-mail: dhaliwal@eller.arizona.edu. *Application contact:* Carol Plagman, Programs Coordinator, 520-621-3712, Fax: 520-621-3742, E-mail: accounting@eller.arizona.edu.

University of Arkansas, Graduate School, Sam M. Walton College of Business Administration, Department of Accounting, Fayetteville, AR 72701-1201. Offers M Acc. *Accreditation:* AACSB. *Students:* 56 full-time (26 women), 6 part-time (4 women); includes 8 minority (4 Black or African American, non-Hispanic/Latino; 1 American Indian or Alaska Native, non-Hispanic/Latino; 3 Asian, non-Hispanic/Latino), 5 international. 72 applicants, 65% accepted. In 2010, 37 master's awarded. *Entrance requirements:* For master's, GMAT. Application fee: $40 ($50 for international students). *Financial support:* In 2010–11, 10 fellowships with tuition reimbursements, 18 research assistantships, 3 teaching assistantships were awarded; career-related internships or fieldwork and Federal Work-Study also available. Support available to part-time students. Financial award application deadline: 4/1; financial award applicants required to submit FAFSA. *Unit head:* Dr. Vernon Richardson, Chair, 479-575-4051, Fax: 479-575-2863, E-mail: vrichardson@walton.uark.edu. *Application contact:* Dr. Gary Peters, Graduate Coordinator, 479-575-4117, Fax: 479-575-2863, E-mail: peters@uark.edu.

University of California, Berkeley, Graduate Division, Haas School of Business, PhD in Business Administration Program, Berkeley, CA 94720-1500. Offers accounting (PhD); business and public policy (PhD); finance (PhD); management of organizations (PhD); marketing (PhD); operations management (PhD); real estate (PhD). *Accreditation:* AACSB. *Students:* 78 full-time (25 women); includes 12 Asian, non-Hispanic/Latino; 2 Hispanic/Latino, 32 international. Average age 30. 526 applicants, 7% accepted, 17 enrolled. In 2010, 17 doctorates awarded. *Degree requirements:* For doctorate, comprehensive exam, thesis/dissertation, written preliminary exams, oral qualifying exam. *Entrance requirements:* For doctorate, GMAT or GRE, minimum GPA of 3.0 in undergraduate and graduate coursework. Additional exam requirements/recommendations for international students: Required—TOEFL (minimum score 570 paper-based; 230 computer-based; 70 iBT), IELTS (minimum score 7). *Application deadline:* For fall admission, 12/10 for domestic and international students. Application fee: $70 ($90 for international students). Electronic applications accepted. *Financial support:* In 2010–11, 63 students received support, including 58 fellowships with full and partial tuition reimbursements available (averaging $26,000 per year); research assistantships with full and partial tuition reimbursements available, teaching assistantships with full and partial tuition reimbursements available, scholarships/grants, health care benefits, tuition waivers (full), unspecified assistantships, and transit pass, travel grants also available. Financial award application deadline: 12/10; financial award applicants required to submit FAFSA. *Faculty research:* Accounting, business and public policy, finance, management of organizations, marketing, operations and information technology management, real estate526. *Unit head:* Dr. Sunil Dutta, Director, 510-642-1229, Fax: 510-643-4255, E-mail: kimg@haas.berkeley.edu. *Application contact:* Kim Guilfoyle, Director, Student Affairs, 510-642-3944, Fax: 510-643-4255, E-mail: kimg@haas.berkeley.edu.

University of California, Los Angeles, Graduate Division, UCLA Anderson School of Management, Los Angeles, CA 90095-1481. Offers accounting (PhD); business administration (MBA); decisions, operations and technology management (PhD); finance (PhD); financial engineering (MFE); global economics and management (PhD); human resources and organizational behavior (PhD); marketing (PhD); strategy and policy (PhD); DDS/MBA; MBA/JD; MBA/MD; MBA/MLAS; MBA/MLIS; MBA/MPH; MBA/MPP; MBA/MSCS; MBA/MSN; MBA/MUP. *Accreditation:* AACSB. Part-time programs available. *Faculty:* 102 full-time (17 women), 43 part-time/adjunct (6 women). *Students:* 833 full-time (270 women), 1,052 part-time (271 women);

includes 592 minority (25 Black or African American, non-Hispanic/Latino; 3 American Indian or Alaska Native, non-Hispanic/Latino; 482 Asian, non-Hispanic/Latino; 60 Hispanic/Latino; 6 Native Hawaiian or other Pacific Islander, non-Hispanic/Latino; 16 Two or more races, non-Hispanic/Latino), 445 international. In 2010, 735 master's, 10 doctorates awarded. *Degree requirements:* For master's, comprehensive exam, field study consulting project (for MBA); thesis/dissertation (for MFE); for doctorate, comprehensive exam, thesis/dissertation, oral and written qualifying exams. *Entrance requirements:* For master's, GMAT (MBA); GMAT or GRE General Test (MFE), minimum undergraduate GPA of 3.0; for doctorate, GMAT or GRE General Test, minimum undergraduate GPA of 3.0. Additional exam requirements/recommendations for international students: Required—TOEFL (minimum score 560 paper-based; 220 computer-based; 87 iBT), IELTS (minimum score 7). *Application deadline:* For fall admission, 10/20 for domestic and international students; for winter admission, 1/5 for domestic and international students; for spring admission, 4/13 for domestic and international students. Application fee: $200. Electronic applications accepted. *Expenses:* Contact institution. *Financial support:* Fellowships, research assistantships, teaching assistantships, career-related internships or fieldwork, institutionally sponsored loans, scholarships/grants, health care benefits, and tuition waivers (partial) available. Financial award application deadline: 3/2; financial award applicants required to submit FAFSA. *Unit head:* Judy D. Olian, Dean, UCLA Anderson School of Management, 310-825-7982, Fax: 310-206-2073. *Application contact:* Mae Jennifer Shores, Assistant Dean and Director of Full-time MBA Admissions and Financial Aid, 310-825-6944, Fax: 310-825-8582, E-mail: mba.admissions@anderson.ucla.edu.

University of Central Arkansas, Graduate School, College of Business Administration, Program in Accounting, Conway, AR 72035-0001. Offers M Acc. Part-time programs available. *Students:* 17 full-time (9 women), 5 part-time (4 women). Average age 25. In 2010, 15 master's awarded. *Degree requirements:* For master's, capstone course. *Entrance requirements:* For master's, GMAT, minimum GPA of 2.7. Additional exam requirements/recommendations for international students: Required—TOEFL (minimum score 550 paper-based; 213 computer-based). *Application deadline:* For fall admission, 3/1 for domestic and international students; for spring admission, 10/1 for domestic and international students. Applications are processed on a rolling basis. Application fee: $25 ($50 for international students). *Financial support:* In 2010–11, 4 research assistantships with partial tuition reimbursements (averaging $5,000 per year) were awarded; career-related internships or fieldwork, Federal Work-Study, scholarships/grants, tuition waivers (partial), and unspecified assistantships also available. Support available to part-time students. Financial award application deadline: 2/15. *Unit head:* Dr. Tom Oxner, Interim Chair, 501-450-5333, Fax: 501-450-5302. *Application contact:* Brenda Herring, Admissions Assistant, 501-450-3124, Fax: 501-450-5678, E-mail: bherring@uca.edu.

University of Central Florida, College of Business Administration, Kenneth G. Dixon School of Accounting, Orlando, FL 32816. Offers MSA, MST. *Accreditation:* AACSB. Part-time and evening/weekend programs available. *Faculty:* 21 full-time (9 women), 2 part-time/adjunct (1 woman). *Students:* 108 full-time (47 women), 114 part-time (56 women); includes 10 Black or African American, non-Hispanic/Latino; 22 Asian, non-Hispanic/Latino; 16 Hispanic/Latino; 2 Native Hawaiian or other Pacific Islander, non-Hispanic/Latino, 10 international. Average age 28. 166 applicants, 58% accepted, 69 enrolled. In 2010, 89 master's awarded. *Degree requirements:* For master's, comprehensive exam. *Entrance requirements:* For master's, GMAT, minimum GPA of 3.0 in last 60 hours. Additional exam requirements/recommendations for international students: Required—TOEFL. *Application deadline:* For fall admission, 6/15 priority date for domestic students; for spring admission, 11/1 priority date for domestic students. Electronic applications accepted. *Expenses:* Tuition, state resident: part-time $256.56 per credit hour. Tuition, nonresident: part-time $1011.52 per credit hour. Part-time tuition and fees vary according to program. *Financial support:* In 2010–11, 7 students received support, including 1 research assistantship (averaging $7,100 per year), 6 teaching assistantships with partial tuition reimbursements available (averaging $6,400 per year); career-related internships or fieldwork, Federal Work-Study, institutionally sponsored loans, tuition waivers (partial), and unspecified assistantships also available. Financial award application deadline: 3/1; financial award applicants required to submit FAFSA. *Unit head:* Dr. Sean Robb, Director, 407-823-2871, Fax: 407-823-3881, E-mail: srobb@bus.ucf.edu. *Application contact:* Dr. Sean Robb, Director, 407-823-2871, Fax: 407-823-3881, E-mail: srobb@bus.ucf.edu.

University of Charleston, Executive Master of Forensic Accounting Program, Charleston, WV 25304-1099. Offers EMFA. Part-time and evening/weekend programs available. *Faculty:* 6 part-time/adjunct (1 woman). *Students:* 7 full-time (4 women). Average age 35. 12 applicants, 83% accepted. In 2010, 9 master's awarded. *Entrance requirements:* For master's, undergraduate degree from regionally-accredited institution; minimum GPA of 3.0 in undergraduate work (recommended); three years of work experience since receiving undergraduate degree (recommended); minimum of two professional recommendations, one from current employer, addressing career potential and ability to do graduate work. Additional exam requirements/recommendations for international students: Required—TOEFL. *Application deadline:* Applications are processed on a rolling basis. Application fee: $50. Electronic applications accepted. Part-time tuition and fees vary according to course load and program. *Financial support:* In 2010–11, 1 student received support. Applicants required to submit FAFSA. *Unit head:* Dr. Robert B. Bliss, Associate Dean, 304-357-4865, Fax: 304-357-4872, E-mail: robertbliss@ucwv.edu. *Application contact:* Dr. Robert B. Bliss, Associate Dean, 304-357-4865, Fax: 304-357-4872, E-mail: robertbliss@ucwv.edu.

University of Chicago, Booth School of Business, Full-Time MBA Program, Chicago, IL 60637. Offers accounting (MBA); analytic finance (MBA); analytic management (MBA); econometrics and statistics (MBA); economics (MBA); entrepreneurship (MBA); finance (MBA); general management (MBA); human resource management (MBA); international business (MBA); managerial and organizational behavior (MBA); marketing management (MBA); operations management (MBA); strategic management (MBA); MBA/AM; MBA/JD; MBA/MA; MBA/MD; MBA/MPP. *Accreditation:* AACSB. Part-time and evening/weekend programs available. *Faculty:* 157 full-time, 35 part-time/adjunct. *Students:* 1,177 full-time (417 women); includes 301 minority (62 Black or African American, non-Hispanic/Latino; 1 American Indian or Alaska Native, non-Hispanic/Latino; 164 Asian, non-Hispanic/Latino; 55 Hispanic/Latino; 19 Two or more races, non-Hispanic/Latino), 403 international. Average age 28. 4,299 applicants, 22% accepted, 579 enrolled. In 2010, 1,374 master's awarded. *Entrance requirements:* For master's, GMAT, 2 letters of recommendation, 3 essays, resume, interview, transcripts. Additional exam requirements/recommendations for international students: Required—TOEFL (minimum score 600 paper-based; 250 computer-based), IELTS. *Application deadline:* For fall admission, 10/10 priority date for domestic students, 10/13 priority date for international students; for winter admission, 1/5 for domestic and international students; for spring admission, 4/13 for domestic and international students. Application fee: $200. Electronic applications accepted. *Expenses:* Contact institution. *Financial support:* Fellowships available. Financial award applicants required to submit FAFSA. *Faculty research:* Finance, economics, entrepreneurship, strategy, management. *Unit head:* Stacey Kole, Deputy Dean, 773-702-7121. *Application contact:* Kurt Ahlm, Associate Dean of Admissions and Financial Aid, 773-702-7369, Fax: 773-702-9085, E-mail: admissions@chicagobooth.edu.

University of Cincinnati, Graduate School, College of Business, MS Program, Cincinnati, OH 45221. Offers accounting (MS); information systems (MS); marketing (MS); quantitative analysis (MS). Part-time and evening/weekend programs available. *Faculty:* 79 full-time (22 women), 71 part-time/adjunct (24 women). *Students:* 130 full-time (46 women), 87 part-time (38 women); includes 12 minority (2 Black or African American, non-Hispanic/Latino; 3 Asian, non-Hispanic/Latino; 4 Hispanic/Latino; 3 Two or more races, non-Hispanic/Latino), 89 international. 407 applicants, 53% accepted, 110 enrolled. *Degree requirements:* For master's, thesis (for some programs). *Entrance requirements:* For master's, GMAT, GRE, resume, transcripts, essays, letters of recommendation. Additional exam requirements/recommendations for international students: Required—TOEFL (minimum score 600 paper-based; 250 computer-based; 100 iBT). *Application deadline:* For fall admission, 1/15 priority date for domestic students, 4/1 for international students. Applications are processed on a rolling basis. Application fee: $45. Electronic applications accepted. *Expenses:* Contact institution. *Financial support:* In 2010–11, 10 teaching assistantships with full and partial tuition reimbursements (averaging $5,400 per year) were awarded; scholarships/grants, tuition waivers (full and partial), and unspecified assistantships also available. Financial award application deadline: 2/1; financial award applicants required to submit FAFSA. *Unit head:* Dr. David Szymanski, Dean, 513-556-7001, Fax: 513-556-4891, E-mail: will.mcintosh@uc.edu. *Application contact:* Dona Clary, Director, Graduate Programs Office, 513-556-3546, Fax: 513-558-7006, E-mail: dona.clary@uc.edu.

University of Cincinnati, Graduate School, College of Business, PhD Program, Cincinnati, OH 45221. Offers accounting (PhD); finance (PhD); information systems (PhD); management (PhD); marketing (PhD); quantitative analysis and operations management (PhD). *Faculty:* 56 full-time (13 women). *Students:* 32 full-time (12 women), 9 part-time (3 women); includes 2 minority (both Hispanic/Latino), 23 international. 119 applicants, 12% accepted, 9 enrolled. In 2010, 8 doctorates awarded. *Degree requirements:* For doctorate, comprehensive exam, thesis/dissertation. *Entrance requirements:* For doctorate, GMAT, GRE, transcripts, essays, resume, letters of recommendation. Additional exam requirements/recommendations for international students: Required—TOEFL (minimum score 600 paper-based; 250 computer-based; 100 iBT). *Application deadline:* For fall admission, 2/1 for domestic and international students. Application fee: $45. Electronic applications accepted. *Expenses:* Contact institution. *Financial support:* In 2010–11, 38 students received support, including 29 research assistantships with full and partial tuition reimbursements available (averaging $14,640 per year); scholarships/grants, tuition waivers (full and partial), and unspecified assistantships also available. Financial award application deadline: 2/15; financial award applicants required to submit FAFSA. *Unit head:* Dr. Suzanne Masterson, Director, PhD Programs, 513-556-7125, Fax: 513-556-5499, E-mail: suzanne.masterson@uc.edu. *Application contact:* Deborah Schildknecht, Assistant Director, PhD Programs, 513-556-7190, Fax: 513-558-7006, E-mail: deborah.schildknecht@uc.edu.

University of Colorado Boulder, Leeds School of Business, Division of Business Administration, Boulder, CO 80309. Offers accounting (PhD); finance (PhD); information systems (PhD); marketing (PhD); operations (PhD); strategic, organizational, and entrepreneurial studies (PhD). Part-time and evening/weekend programs available. *Students:* 110 full-time (42 women), 2 part-time (1 woman); includes 6 minority (5 Asian, non-Hispanic/Latino; 1 Hispanic/Latino), 24 international. Average age 28. 342 applicants, 24 enrolled. In 2010, 48 master's, 12 doctorates awarded. *Entrance requirements:* For master's, GMAT, minimum undergraduate GPA of 3.0. *Application deadline:* For fall admission, 3/31 for domestic and international students; for spring admission, 10/31 for domestic and international students. Application fee: $50 ($60 for international students). Electronic applications accepted. *Financial support:* In 2010–11, 16 fellowships (averaging $1,038 per year), 26 research assistantships (averaging $17,558 per year), 11 teaching assistantships (averaging $12,576 per year) were awarded; career-related internships or fieldwork, Federal Work-Study, scholarships/grants, and unspecified assistantships also available. Financial award applicants required to submit FAFSA.

University of Colorado Denver, Business School, Program in Accounting, Denver, CO 80217. Offers auditing and forensic accounting (MS); financial accounting (MS); information systems audit control (MS); taxation (MS). *Accreditation:* AACSB. Part-time and evening/weekend programs available. *Students:* 120 full-time (68 women), 33 part-time (21 women); includes 6 Black or African American, non-Hispanic/Latino; 13 Asian, non-Hispanic/Latino; 6 Hispanic/Latino, 18 international. Average age 30. 71 applicants, 66% accepted, 30 enrolled. In 2010, 46 master's awarded. *Degree requirements:* For master's, 30 semester hours. *Entrance requirements:* For master's, GMAT. Additional exam requirements/recommendations for international students: Required—TOEFL (minimum score 525 paper-based; 197 computer-based; 71 iBT). *Application deadline:* For fall admission, 4/1 for domestic students, 3/15 for international students; for spring admission, 10/1 for domestic and international students. Application fee: $50 ($75 for international students). Electronic applications accepted. *Expenses:* Contact institution. *Financial support:* Federal Work-Study and scholarships/grants available. Support available to part-time students. Financial award application deadline: 4/1; financial award applicants required to submit FAFSA. *Faculty research:* Transfer pricing, behavioral accounting, environmental accounting, health services, international auditing. *Unit head:* Bruce Neumann, Professor, 303-315-8473, E-mail: bruce.neumann@ucdenver.edu. *Application contact:* Shelly Townley, Admissions Coordinator, 303-315-8202, E-mail: shelly.townley@ucdenver.edu.

University of Dayton, Graduate School, School of Business Administration, Dayton, OH 45469-1300. Offers accounting (MBA); business intelligence (MBA); cyber security (MBA); entrepreneurship (MBA); finance (MBA); international business (MBA); marketing (MBA); MIS (MBA); operations management (MBA); technology-enhanced business/e-commerce (MBA); JD/MBA. *Accreditation:* AACSB. Part-time and evening/weekend programs available. *Faculty:* 25 full-time (7 women), 14 part-time/adjunct (2 women). *Students:* 184 full-time (72 women), 110 part-time (34 women); includes 23 minority (7 Black or African American, non-Hispanic/Latino; 7 Asian, non-Hispanic/Latino; 8 Hispanic/Latino; 1 Two or more races, non-Hispanic/Latino), 31 international. Average age 28. 220 applicants, 85% accepted, 103 enrolled. In 2010, 113 master's awarded. *Entrance requirements:* For master's, GMAT or GRE. Additional exam requirements/recommendations for international students: Required—TOEFL (minimum score 550 paper-based; 213 computer-based; 79 iBT); Recommended—IELTS (minimum score 6.5). *Application deadline:* For fall admission, 3/1 priority date for international students; for winter admission, 7/1 priority date for international students; for spring admission, 1/1 priority date for international students. Applications are processed on a rolling basis. Application fee: $0 ($50 for international students). Electronic applications accepted. *Expenses:* Contact institution. *Financial support:* In 2010–11, 15 research assistantships with full and partial tuition reimbursements (averaging $7,020 per year) were awarded; career-related internships or fieldwork, institutionally sponsored loans, scholarships/grants, health care benefits, and unspecified assistantships also available. Support available to part-time students. Financial award application deadline: 3/15; financial award applicants required to submit FAFSA. *Faculty research:* Management information systems, economics, finance, entrepreneurship, marketing. *Unit head:* Janice M. Glynn, Director, MBA Program, 937-229-3733, Fax: 937-229-3882, E-mail: glynn@udayton.edu. *Application contact:* Jeffrey Carter, Assistant Director, MBA Program, 937-229-3733, Fax: 937-229-3882, E-mail: jeff.carter@notes.udayton.edu.

University of Denver, Daniels College of Business, School of Accountancy, Denver, CO 80208. Offers accountancy (M Acc); accounting (MBA). *Accreditation:* AACSB. Part-time and evening/weekend programs available. *Faculty:* 15 full-time (5 women), 5 part-time/adjunct (1 woman). *Students:* 26 full-time (17 women), 73 part-time (54 women); includes 9 minority (3 Asian, non-Hispanic/Latino; 6 Hispanic/Latino), 58 international. Average age 26. 291 applicants, 53% accepted, 57 enrolled. In 2010, 51 master's awarded. *Entrance requirements:* For master's, GRE General Test or GMAT. Additional exam requirements/recommendations for international students:

Required—TOEFL (minimum score 570 paper-based; 88 iBT). *Application deadline:* For fall admission, 11/15 priority date for domestic students; for spring admission, 10/15 priority date for domestic students. Applications are processed on a rolling basis. Application fee: $100. Electronic applications accepted. *Expenses:* Tuition: Full-time $35,604; part-time $29,670 per year. Required fees: $687 per year. Tuition and fees vary according to program. *Financial support:* In 2010–11, 11 teaching assistantships with full and partial tuition reimbursements (averaging $1,493 per year) were awarded; career-related internships or fieldwork, Federal Work-Study, institutionally sponsored loans, scholarships/grants, and unspecified assistantships also available. Support available to part-time students. Financial award application deadline: 3/15; financial award applicants required to submit FAFSA. *Faculty research:* Management accounting, activity-based management, benchmarking, financial management and human services, derivatives. *Unit head:* Dr. Sharon Lassar, Director, 303-871-2032, E-mail: slassar@du.edu. *Application contact:* Victoria Chen, Graduate Admissions Manager, 303-871-3826, E-mail: victoria.chen@du.edu.

University of Florida, Graduate School, Warrington College of Business Administration, Fisher School of Accounting, Gainesville, FL 32611. Offers M Acc, PhD, JD/M Acc. *Accreditation:* AACSB. Part-time programs available. *Faculty:* 9 full-time (2 women). *Students:* 223 full-time (94 women), 12 part-time (6 women); includes 5 Black or African American, non-Hispanic/Latino; 22 Asian, non-Hispanic/Latino; 31 Hispanic/Latino, 7 international. Average age 29. 314 applicants, 43% accepted, 101 enrolled. In 2010, 119 master's awarded. *Degree requirements:* For master's, comprehensive exam, thesis optional; for doctorate, comprehensive exam, thesis/dissertation. *Entrance requirements:* For master's, GRE General Test (minimum combined 1100, 550 verbal, 550 quantitative), GMAT, minimum GPA of 3.0; for doctorate, GRE (minimum scores: verbal 550, quantitative 550), GMAT (taken within last 3 years), minimum GPA of 3.0, BS. Additional exam requirements/recommendations for international students: Required—TOEFL (minimum score 80 iBT), IELTS (minimum score 6). *Application deadline:* Applications are processed on a rolling basis. Application fee: $30. Electronic applications accepted. *Expenses:* Tuition, state resident: full-time $10,915.92. Tuition, nonresident: full-time $28,309. *Financial support:* In 2010–11, 4 students received support, including 4 research assistantships (averaging $23,782 per year); Federal Work-Study and unspecified assistantships also available. Support available to part-time students. Financial award application deadline: 1/15; financial award applicants required to submit FAFSA. *Faculty research:* Financial reporting, managerial accounting, auditing, taxation. *Unit head:* Dr. Gary McGill, Associate Dean, 352-273-0219, Fax: 352-392-7962, E-mail: mcgill@ufl.edu. *Application contact:* Dominique A. DeSantiago, Associate Director, 352-273-0200, Fax: 352-392-7962, E-mail: dom.desantiago@cba.ufl.edu.

University of Florida, Graduate School, Warrington College of Business Administration, Hough Graduate School of Business, Programs in Business Administration, Gainesville, FL 32611. Offers accounting (MBA); arts administration (MBA); business strategy and public policy (MBA); competitive strategy (MBA); decision and information sciences (MBA); electronic commerce (MBA); finance (MBA); general business (MBA); global management (MBA); Graham-Buffett security analysis (MBA); health administration (MBA); human resources management (MBA); international studies (MBA); Latin American business (MBA); management (MBA); marketing (MBA); sports administration (MBA); JD/MBA; MBA/MS; MBA/PhD; MBA/Pharm D; MD/MBA. *Accreditation:* AACSB. Part-time and evening/weekend programs available. *Faculty:* 71 full-time (10 women). *Students:* 187 full-time (44 women), 305 part-time (83 women); includes 25 Black or African American, non-Hispanic/Latino; 2 American Indian or Alaska Native, non-Hispanic/Latino; 52 Asian, non-Hispanic/Latino; 54 Hispanic/Latino, 11 international. Average age 31. 919 applicants, 33% accepted, 225 enrolled. In 2010, 492 master's awarded. *Degree requirements:* For master's, capstone course. *Entrance requirements:* For master's, GMAT, minimum GPA of 3.0, interview. Additional exam requirements/recommendations for international students: Required—TOEFL (minimum score 550 paper-based; 213 computer-based; 80 iBT), IELTS (minimum score 6). *Application deadline:* For fall admission, 7/1 for domestic students, 1/1 for international students; for spring admission, 12/1 for domestic and international students. Applications are processed on a rolling basis. Application fee: $30. Electronic applications accepted. *Expenses:* Tuition, state resident: full-time $10,915.92. Tuition, nonresident: full-time $28,309. *Financial support:* In 2010–11, 1 student received support, including 1 teaching assistantship (averaging $20,600 per year); career-related internships or fieldwork, scholarships/grants, and unspecified assistantships also available. Support available to part-time students. Financial award applicants required to submit FAFSA. *Faculty research:* Accounting, finance, insurance, management, real estate, urban analysis marketing. *Unit head:* Prof. Alexander D. Sevilla, Assistant Dean and Director MBA Programs, 352-273-3252 Ext. 1206, E-mail: alex.sevilla@warrington.ufl.edu. *Application contact:* Prof. Kelli Gust, Associate Director of MBA Programs, 352-273-3255, Fax: 352-392-8791, E-mail: kelly.gust@ warrington.ufl.edu.

University of Georgia, Terry College of Business, J. M. Tull School of Accounting, Athens, GA 30602. Offers M Acc, JD/M Acc. *Accreditation:* AACSB. *Faculty:* 17 full-time (7 women). *Students:* 138 full-time (80 women),

8 part-time (5 women); includes 6 Black or African American, non-Hispanic/Latino; 11 Asian, non-Hispanic/Latino; 2 Hispanic/Latino; 2 Two or more races, non-Hispanic/Latino, 7 international. 199 applicants, 32% accepted, 45 enrolled. In 2010, 104 master's awarded. *Entrance requirements:* For master's, GMAT. *Application deadline:* For fall admission, 7/1 priority date for domestic students; for spring admission, 11/15 for domestic students. Application fee: $50. Electronic applications accepted. *Expenses:* Tuition, state resident: full-time $7200; part-time $344 per credit hour. Tuition, nonresident: full-time $21,900; part-time $944 per credit hour. Tuition and fees vary according to course load and program. *Financial support:* Fellowships, research assistantships, teaching assistantships, unspecified assistantships available. *Unit head:* Dr. Benjamin C. Ayers, Director, 706-542-1616, Fax: 706-542-3630, E-mail: bayers@terry.uga.edu. *Application contact:* Dr. E. Michael Bamber, Graduate Coordinator, 706-542-3601, E-mail: mbamber@terry.uga.edu.

University of Hawaii at Manoa, Graduate Division, Shidler College of Business, Program in Accounting, Honolulu, HI 96822. Offers accounting (M Acc); accounting law (M Acc); information systems (M Acc); taxation (M Acc). Part-time programs available. *Faculty:* 9 full-time (2 women). *Students:* 45 full-time (22 women), 33 part-time (22 women); includes 41 minority (28 Asian, non-Hispanic/Latino; 5 Native Hawaiian or other Pacific Islander, non-Hispanic/Latino; 8 Two or more races, non-Hispanic/Latino), 21 international. Average age 32. 144 applicants, 78% accepted, 72 enrolled. In 2010, 38 master's awarded. *Entrance requirements:* For master's, GMAT, bachelor's degree in accounting, minimum GPA of 3.0. Additional exam requirements/recommendations for international students: Required—TOEFL (minimum score 550 paper-based; 213 computer-based; 79 iBT), IELTS (minimum score 5). *Application deadline:* For fall admission, 5/1 for domestic students, 3/1 for international students; for spring admission, 11/1 for domestic students, 10/1 for international students. Application fee: $60. *Financial support:* In 2010–11, 24 fellowships (averaging $4,662 per year), 7 research assistantships (averaging $16,478 per year) were awarded; career-related internships or fieldwork, Federal Work-Study, and tuition waivers (full) also available. *Faculty research:* International accounting, current tax topics, insurance industry financial reporting, behavioral accounting, auditing. *Application contact:* Liming Guan, Graduate Chair, 808-956-7332, Fax: 808-956-9888, E-mail: lguan@hawaii.edu.

University of Hawaii at Manoa, Graduate Division, Shidler College of Business, Program in International Management, Honolulu, HI 96822. Offers Asian finance (PhD); global information technology management (PhD); international accounting (PhD); international marketing (PhD); international organization and strategy (PhD). Part-time programs available. *Students:* 30 full-time (11 women), 3 part-time (0 women); includes 7 minority (5 Asian, non-Hispanic/Latino; 2 Two or more races, non-Hispanic/Latino), 18 international. Average age 36. 65 applicants, 18% accepted, 5 enrolled. In 2010, 4 doctorates awarded. *Degree requirements:* For doctorate, comprehensive exam, thesis/dissertation. *Entrance requirements:* For doctorate, GMAT or GRE General Test, minimum GPA of 3.0. Additional exam requirements/recommendations for international students: Required—TOEFL (minimum score 600 paper-based; 250 computer-based; 100 iBT), IELTS (minimum score 7). *Application deadline:* For fall admission, 3/1 for domestic and international students. Application fee: $60. *Expenses:* Contact institution. *Financial support:* In 2010–11, 29 students received support, including 3 fellowships (averaging $5,491 per year), 25 research assistantships (averaging $17,750 per year), 1 teaching assistantship (averaging $15,558 per year). *Application contact:* Erica Okada, Graduate Chair, 808-956-6723, Fax: 808-956-6889, E-mail: imphd@hawaii.edu.

University of Houston, Bauer College of Business, Accountancy and Taxation Program, Houston, TX 77204. Offers accountancy (MS Accy); accountancy and taxation (PhD). *Accreditation:* AACSB. Part-time and evening/weekend programs available. *Faculty:* 11 full-time (4 women), 17 part-time/adjunct (3 women). *Students:* 216 full-time (116 women), 91 part-time (43 women); includes 134 minority (15 Black or African American, non-Hispanic/Latino; 1 American Indian or Alaska Native, non-Hispanic/Latino; 78 Asian, non-Hispanic/Latino; 35 Hispanic/Latino; 1 Native Hawaiian or other Pacific Islander, non-Hispanic/Latino; 4 Two or more races, non-Hispanic/Latino), 56 international. Average age 26. 237 applicants, 55% accepted, 107 enrolled. In 2010, 155 degrees awarded. *Degree requirements:* For master's, 30 hours completed in residence, minimum cumulative GPA of 3.0 at UH, no more than 11 semester hours of 'C' grades or below in graduate courses taken at UH; for doctorate, continuous full time enrollment, dissertation defense within 6 years of entering the program. *Entrance requirements:* For master's, GMAT, official transcripts from all higher education institutions attended, letters of recommendation, resume, goals statement; for doctorate, GMAT or GRE, letter of financial backing, statement of understanding, reference letters, statement of academic and research interests. Additional exam requirements/recommendations for international students: Required—TOEFL (minimum score 550 paper-based; 213 computer-based; 79 iBT), IELTS (minimum score 6.5), Pearson Test of English (minimum score: 70). *Application deadline:* For fall admission, 6/1 for domestic students, 5/1 for international students; for spring admission, 11/15 for domestic students, 10/1 for international students. Applications are processed on a rolling basis. Application fee: $75 ($150 for international students). Electronic applications accepted. *Expenses:* Tuition, state resident:

full-time $8592; part-time $358 per credit hour. Tuition, nonresident: full-time $16,032; part-time $668 per credit hour. Required fees: $2889. Tuition and fees vary according to course load and program. *Financial support:* In 2010–11, 1 teaching assistantship with partial tuition reimbursement (averaging $667 per year) was awarded; career-related internships or fieldwork, Federal Work-Study, institutionally sponsored loans, scholarships/grants, and unspecified assistantships also available. Support available to part-time students. Financial award application deadline: 2/1; financial award applicants required to submit FAFSA. *Faculty research:* Accountancy and taxation, finance, international business, management. *Unit head:* Dr. Kaye Newberry, Chairperson, 713-743-0849, Fax: 713-743-4828, E-mail: kjnewberry@uh.edu.

University of Houston–Victoria, School of Business Administration, Victoria, TX 77901-4450. Offers accounting (MBA); economic development and entrepreneurship (MS); finance (GMBA, MBA); general business (MBA); international business (MBA); management (GMBA, MBA); marketing (MBA). *Accreditation:* AACSB. Part-time and evening/weekend programs available. Postbaccalaureate distance learning degree programs offered (minimal on-campus study). *Faculty:* 37 full-time (11 women). *Students:* 234 full-time (108 women), 714 part-time (303 women); includes 542 minority (215 Black or African American, non-Hispanic/Latino; 1 American Indian or Alaska Native, non-Hispanic/Latino; 197 Asian, non-Hispanic/Latino; 124 Hispanic/Latino; 1 Native Hawaiian or other Pacific Islander, non-Hispanic/Latino; 4 Two or more races, non-Hispanic/Latino), 115 international. Average age 34. 362 applicants, 65% accepted, 147 enrolled. In 2010, 181 master's awarded. *Entrance requirements:* For master's, GMAT. Additional exam requirements/recommendations for international students: Required—TOEFL (minimum score 550 paper-based; 213 computer-based). *Application deadline:* For fall admission, 6/1 for international students; for spring admission, 10/1 for international students. Applications are processed on a rolling basis. Application fee: $0. Electronic applications accepted. *Expenses:* Tuition, state resident: full-time $4050; part-time $225 per credit hour. Tuition, nonresident: full-time $8730; part-time $485 per credit hour. Required fees: $810; $54 per credit hour. Tuition and fees vary according to course load. *Financial support:* In 2010–11, research assistantships with partial tuition reimbursements (averaging $2,000 per year), teaching assistantships with partial tuition reimbursements (averaging $2,000 per year) were awarded; Federal Work-Study, scholarships/grants, and unspecified assistantships also available. Support available to part-time students. Financial award application deadline: 4/15; financial award applicants required to submit FAFSA. *Faculty research:* Economic development, marketing, finance. *Unit head:* Dr. Farhang Niroomand, Dean, 361-570-4230, Fax: 361-580-5599, E-mail: niroomandf@uhv.edu. *Application contact:* Jane Mims, Assistant Dean, 361-570-4639, Fax: 361-580-5529, E-mail: mims@uhv.edu.

University of Idaho, College of Graduate Studies, College of Business and Economics, Department of Accounting, Moscow, ID 83844-2282. Offers accountancy (M Acct). *Accreditation:* AACSB. *Faculty:* 5 full-time. *Students:* 13 full-time, 4 part-time. Average age 29. In 2010, 22 master's awarded. *Degree requirements:* For master's, comprehensive exam. *Entrance requirements:* For master's, minimum GPA of 3.0. *Application deadline:* For fall admission, 8/1 for domestic students; for spring admission, 12/15 for domestic students. Applications are processed on a rolling basis. Application fee: $60. Electronic applications accepted. *Expenses:* Tuition, nonresident: part-time $580 per credit. Required fees: $306 per credit. *Financial support:* Research assistantships, teaching assistantships available. Financial award applicants required to submit FAFSA. *Unit head:* Dr. Marla Kraut, Head, 208-885-6453, Fax: 208-885-6296, E-mail: amberg@uidaho.edu. *Application contact:* Dr. Marla Kraut, Head, 208-885-6453, Fax: 208-885-6296, E-mail: amberg@uidaho.edu.

University of Illinois at Urbana–Champaign, Graduate College, College of Business, Department of Accountancy, Champaign, IL 61820. Offers accountancy (MAS, MS, PhD); taxation (MS); MAS/JD. *Accreditation:* AACSB. *Faculty:* 28 full-time (8 women), 4 part-time/adjunct (1 woman). *Students:* 406 full-time (229 women), 11 part-time (5 women); includes 6 Black or African American, non-Hispanic/Latino; 47 Asian, non-Hispanic/Latino; 2 Hispanic/Latino; 3 Two or more races, non-Hispanic/Latino, 167 international. 1,022 applicants, 46% accepted, 365 enrolled. In 2010, 398 master's, 1 doctorate awarded. *Entrance requirements:* For master's, GMAT (for MAS program), minimum GPA of 3.0; for doctorate, GMAT, minimum GPA of 3.0. Additional exam requirements/recommendations for international students: Required—TOEFL. *Application deadline:* Applications are processed on a rolling basis. Application fee: $75 ($90 for international students). Electronic applications accepted. *Financial support:* In 2010–11, 16 fellowships, 17 research assistantships, 85 teaching assistantships were awarded; tuition waivers (full and partial) also available. *Unit head:* Ira Solomon, Head, 217-333-3808, Fax: 217-244-0902, E-mail: isolomon@illinois.edu. *Application contact:* Yvonne Harden, Assistant Director, 217-333-4572, Fax: 217-244-0902, E-mail: yaharden@illinois.edu.

The University of Iowa, Henry B. Tippie College of Business, Department of Accounting, Iowa City, IA 52242-1316. Offers accounting (M Ac, PhD), including accountancy (M Ac), business administration (PhD); JD/M Ac. *Accreditation:* AACSB. Part-time programs available. *Faculty:* 16 full-time (4 women), 2 part-time/adjunct (0 women). *Students:* 43 full-time (22 women), 7 part-time (5 women); includes 3 Asian, non-Hispanic/Latino; 1 Hispanic/Latino, 15 international. Average age 25. 261 applicants, 16% accepted, 26 enrolled. In 2010, 45 master's awarded. *Entrance requirements:* For master's, GMAT. Additional exam requirements/recommendations for international students: Required—TOEFL (minimum score 600 paper-based; 250 computer-based; 100 iBT) or IELTS (minimum score 7). *Application deadline:* For fall admission, 7/15 for domestic students, 4/15 for international students; for spring admission, 12/1 for domestic students, 10/1 for international students. Application fee: $60 ($100 for international students). Electronic applications accepted. *Financial support:* In 2010–11, fellowships with full tuition reimbursements (averaging $20,000 per year), research assistantships with partial tuition reimbursements (averaging $16,277 per year), teaching assistantships with partial tuition reimbursements (averaging $16,277 per year) were awarded; career-related internships or fieldwork, Federal Work-Study, institutionally sponsored loans, scholarships/grants, and unspecified assistantships also available. Financial award applicants required to submit FAFSA. *Faculty research:* Corporate financial reporting issues; financial statement information and capital markets; cost structure: analysis, estimation, and management; experimental and prediction economics; income taxes and interaction of financial and tax reporting systems. *Unit head:* Prof. Douglas V. DeJong, Department Executive Officer, 319-335-0910, Fax: 319-335-1956, E-mail: douglas-dejong@uiowa.edu. *Application contact:* Prof. Thomas J. Carroll, Director, Master of Accountancy Program, 319-335-2727, Fax: 319-335-1956, E-mail: thomas-carroll@uiowa.edu.

The University of Kansas, Graduate Studies, School of Business, Program in Accounting, Lawrence, KS 66045. Offers M Acc. *Accreditation:* AACSB. *Faculty:* 20. *Students:* 127 full-time (59 women), 18 part-time (9 women); includes 17 minority (9 Asian, non-Hispanic/Latino; 4 Hispanic/Latino; 4 Two or more races, non-Hispanic/Latino), 9 international. Average age 24. 141 applicants, 72% accepted, 83 enrolled. In 2010, 121 master's awarded. *Degree requirements:* For master's, 30 credits. *Entrance requirements:* For master's, GMAT. Additional exam requirements/recommendations for international students: Required—TOEFL (minimum score 53 paper-based; 20 computer-based); Recommended—IELTS (minimum score 6). *Application deadline:* For fall admission, 3/1 priority date for domestic students, 2/27 priority date for international students; for spring admission, 11/1 for domestic students, 10/1 for international students. Applications are processed on a rolling basis. Application fee: $65. Electronic applications accepted. *Expenses:* Tuition, state resident: full-time $7092; part-time $295.50 per credit hour. Tuition, nonresident: full-time $16,590; part-time $691.25 per credit hour. Required fees: $858; $71.49 per credit hour. Tuition and fees vary according to course load, campus/location and program. *Financial support:* Fellowships, research assistantships with partial tuition reimbursements, teaching assistantships with full and partial tuition reimbursements, career-related internships or fieldwork, Federal Work-Study, institutionally sponsored loans, scholarships/grants, and unspecified assistantships available. Financial award application deadline: 6/1; financial award applicants required to submit FAFSA. *Faculty research:* Audit; artificial intelligence; agency theory; compensation; production, regulation, and use of accounting information. *Unit head:* Dr. James A. Heintz, Director, Accounting and Information Systems, 785-864-4500, Fax: 785-864-5328, E-mail: jheintz@ku.edu. *Application contact:* Dee Steinle, Administrative Director of Master's Programs, 785-864-7596, Fax: 785-864-5376, E-mail: dsteinle@ku.edu.

University of La Verne, College of Business and Public Management, Graduate Programs in Business Administration, La Verne, CA 91750-4443. Offers accounting (MBA); executive management (MBA-EP); finance (MBA, MBA-EP); health services management (MBA); information technology (MBA, MBA-EP); international business (MBA, MBA-EP); leadership (MBA-EP); managed care (MBA); management (MBA, MBA-EP); marketing (MBA, MBA-EP). Part-time and evening/weekend programs available. *Faculty:* 34 full-time (12 women), 36 part-time/adjunct (9 women). *Students:* 412 full-time (207 women), 200 part-time (96 women); includes 423 minority (32 Black or African American, non-Hispanic/Latino; 5 American Indian or Alaska Native, non-Hispanic/Latino; 294 Asian, non-Hispanic/Latino; 92 Hispanic/Latino), 6 international. Average age 29. In 2010, 229 master's awarded. *Entrance requirements:* For master's, minimum undergraduate GPA of 3.0, 2 letters of recommendation, resume. Additional exam requirements/recommendations for international students: Required—TOEFL (minimum score 550 paper-based; 213 computer-based). *Application deadline:* Applications are processed on a rolling basis. Application fee: $50. *Expenses:* Contact institution. *Financial support:* Career-related internships or fieldwork, institutionally sponsored loans, and scholarships/grants available. Financial award application deadline: 3/2; financial award applicants required to submit FAFSA. *Unit head:* Dr. Abe Helou, Chairperson, 909-593-3511 Ext. 4211, Fax: 909-392-2704, E-mail: ihelou@laverne.edu. *Application contact:* Rina Lazarian, Program and Admission Specialist, 909-593-3511 Ext. 4819, Fax: 909-392-2704, E-mail: cbpm@ulv.edu.

University of Louisville, Graduate School, College of Business, School of Accountancy, Louisville, KY 40292-0001. Offers MAC. *Accreditation:* AACSB. Part-time and evening/weekend programs available. *Faculty:* 7 full-time (1 woman). *Students:* 33 part-time (17 women); includes 2 Black or African American, non-Hispanic/Latino, 6 international. Average age 29.

28 applicants, 50% accepted, 12 enrolled. In 2010, 10 master's awarded. *Entrance requirements:* For master's, GMAT, 2 letters of reference, resume, personal statement, transcript. Additional exam requirements/recommendations for international students: Required—TOEFL (minimum score 550 paper-based; 213 computer-based; 83 iBT). *Application deadline:* For fall admission, 7/15 priority date for domestic students; for winter admission, 11/15 priority date for domestic students; for spring admission, 4/15 priority date for domestic students. Applications are processed on a rolling basis. Application fee: $50. *Expenses:* Tuition, state resident: full-time $9144; part-time $508 per credit hour. Tuition, nonresident: full-time $19,026; part-time $1057 per credit hour. Tuition and fees vary according to program and reciprocity agreements. *Financial support:* In 2010–11, 3 students received support, including 1 fellowship (averaging $3,000 per year), 2 research assistantships with full tuition reimbursements available (averaging $11,000 per year); health care benefits and unspecified assistantships also available. Financial award application deadline: 3/15; financial award applicants required to submit FAFSA. *Faculty research:* Audit judgment and decision-making, information systems, taxation, cost and managerial accounting. Total annual research expenditures: $221,322. *Unit head:* Dr. Charles Moyer, Dean, 502-852-6443, Fax: 502-852-7557, E-mail: charlie.moyer@louisville.edu. *Application contact:* Joshua M. Philpot, Graduate Programs Manager, 502-852-7257, Fax: 502-852-4901, E-mail: josh.philpot@louisville.edu.

University of Maine, Graduate School, College of Business, Public Policy and Health, The Maine Business School, Orono, ME 04469. Offers accounting (MBA); business and sustainability (MBA); finance (MBA); management (MBA). *Accreditation:* AACSB. Part-time and evening/weekend programs available. *Faculty:* 23 full-time (8 women), 2 part-time/adjunct (both women). *Students:* 53 full-time (24 women), 15 part-time (5 women); includes 4 minority (1 American Indian or Alaska Native, non-Hispanic/Latino; 2 Asian, non-Hispanic/Latino; 1 Hispanic/Latino), 3 international. Average age 29. 42 applicants, 69% accepted, 25 enrolled. In 2010, 25 degrees awarded. *Entrance requirements:* For master's, GMAT. Additional exam requirements/recommendations for international students: Required—TOEFL (minimum score 550 paper-based; 213 computer-based). *Application deadline:* For fall admission, 6/1 priority date for domestic and international students; for spring admission, 11/1 priority date for domestic and international students. Applications are processed on a rolling basis. Application fee: $65. Electronic applications accepted. *Expenses:* Contact institution. *Financial support:* In 2010–11, 16 students received support, including 4 teaching assistantships with tuition reimbursements available (averaging $12,790 per year); career-related internships or fieldwork, Federal Work-Study, institutionally sponsored loans, scholarships/grants, tuition waivers (full and partial), and unspecified assistantships also available. Financial award application deadline: 3/1. *Faculty research:* Entrepreneurship, investment management, international markets, decision support systems, strategic planning. *Unit head:* Dr. Nory Jones, Director of Graduate Programs, 207-581-1971, Fax: 207-581-1930, E-mail: mba@maine.edu. *Application contact:* Scott G. Delcourt, Associate Dean of the Graduate School, 207-581-3291, Fax: 207-581-3232, E-mail: graduate@maine.edu.

University of Mary, Gary Tharaldson School of Business, Bismarck, ND 58504-9652. Offers accountancy (MBA); business administration (MBA); health care (MBA); human resource management (MBA); management (MBA); project management (MPM); strategic leadership (MSSL). Part-time and evening/weekend programs available. *Faculty:* 2 full-time (0 women), 73 part-time/adjunct (27 women). *Students:* 232 full-time (123 women), 226 part-time (115 women); includes 63 minority (30 Black or African American, non-Hispanic/Latino; 23 American Indian or Alaska Native, non-Hispanic/Latino; 5 Asian, non-Hispanic/Latino; 3 Hispanic/Latino; 1 Native Hawaiian or other Pacific Islander, non-Hispanic/Latino; 1 Two or more races, non-Hispanic/Latino), 20 international. Average age 36. 209 applicants, 98% accepted, 189 enrolled. In 2010, 265 master's awarded. *Degree requirements:* For master's, strategic planning seminar. *Entrance requirements:* For master's, minimum GPA of 2.5. Additional exam requirements/recommendations for international students: Required—TOEFL (minimum score 500 paper-based; 197 computer-based; 71 iBT). *Application deadline:* Applications are processed on a rolling basis. Application fee: $40. *Expenses:* Tuition: Full-time $10,800; part-time $450 per credit. Tuition and fees vary according to course load, degree level, program and student level. *Financial support:* Application deadline: 8/1. *Unit head:* Dr. Shanda Traiser, Director of the School of Accelerated and Distance Education, 701-355-8160, Fax: 701-255-7687, E-mail: straiser@umary.edu. *Application contact:* Wayne G. Maruska, Graduate Program Advisor, 701-355-8134, Fax: 701-255-7687, E-mail: wmaruska@umary.edu.

University of Mary Hardin-Baylor, Graduate Studies in Business Administration, Belton, TX 76513. Offers accounting (MBA); information systems management (MBA); management (MBA). Part-time and evening/weekend programs available. *Faculty:* 6 full-time (3 women), 2 part-time/adjunct (0 women). *Students:* 29 full-time (10 women), 26 part-time (13 women); includes 12 minority (3 Black or African American, non-Hispanic/Latino; 9 Hispanic/Latino), 23 international. Average age 29. 71 applicants, 72% accepted, 27 enrolled. In 2010, 7 master's awarded. *Degree requirements:* For master's, comprehensive exam. *Entrance requirements:* For master's, GMAT, minimum GPA of 3.0, work experience, interview. *Application deadline:* For fall admission, 6/1 priority date for domestic students; for spring

admission, 11/1 for domestic students. Applications are processed on a rolling basis. Application fee: $35 ($135 for international students). Electronic applications accepted. *Financial support:* Federal Work-Study and scholarships (for some active duty military personnel only) available. Financial award applicants required to submit FAFSA. *Unit head:* Dr. Terry Fox, Program Director, 254-295-5406, E-mail: terry.fox@umhb.edu. *Application contact:* Dr. Terry Fox, Program Director, 254-295-5406, E-mail: terry.fox@umhb.edu.

University of Maryland University College, Graduate School of Management and Technology, Program in Accounting and Financial Management, Adelphi, MD 20783. Offers MS, Certificate. *Accreditation:* AACSB. Part-time and evening/weekend programs available. Postbaccalaureate distance learning degree programs offered (no on-campus study). *Students:* 13 full-time (7 women), 557 part-time (363 women); includes 283 minority (197 Black or African American, non-Hispanic/Latino; 47 Asian, non-Hispanic/Latino; 33 Hispanic/Latino; 1 Native Hawaiian or other Pacific Islander, non-Hispanic/Latino; 5 Two or more races, non-Hispanic/Latino), 25 international. Average age 35. 139 applicants, 100% accepted, 80 enrolled. In 2010, 103 master's awarded. *Degree requirements:* For master's, thesis or alternative, capstone course. *Application deadline:* Applications are processed on a rolling basis. Application fee: $50. Electronic applications accepted. *Financial support:* Federal Work-Study and scholarships/grants available. Support available to part-time students. Financial award application deadline: 6/1; financial award applicants required to submit FAFSA. *Unit head:* Dr. James Howard, Director, 240-684-2400, Fax: 240-684-2401, E-mail: jhoward@umuc.edu. *Application contact:* Coordinator, Graduate Admissions, 800-888-8682, Fax: 240-684-2151, E-mail: newgrad@umuc.edu.

University of Maryland University College, Graduate School of Management and Technology, Program in Accounting and Information Technology, Adelphi, MD 20783. Offers MS, Certificate. *Accreditation:* AACSB. Part-time and evening/weekend programs available. Postbaccalaureate distance learning degree programs offered (no on-campus study). *Students:* 7 full-time (4 women), 211 part-time (125 women); includes 125 minority (101 Black or African American, non-Hispanic/Latino; 15 Asian, non-Hispanic/Latino; 9 Hispanic/Latino), 3 international. Average age 35. 109 applicants, 100% accepted, 49 enrolled. In 2010, 36 master's, 6 other advanced degrees awarded. *Degree requirements:* For master's, thesis or alternative, capstone course. *Application deadline:* Applications are processed on a rolling basis. Application fee: $50. Electronic applications accepted. *Financial support:* Federal Work-Study and scholarships/grants available. Support available to part-time students. Financial award application deadline: 6/1; financial award applicants required to submit FAFSA. *Unit head:* Dr. Kathryn Klose, Director, 240-684-2400, Fax: 240-684-2401, E-mail: kklose@umuc.edu. *Application contact:* Coordinator, Graduate Admissions, 800-888-8682, Fax: 240-684-2151, E-mail: newgrad@umuc.edu.

University of Massachusetts Amherst, Graduate School, Isenberg School of Management, Program in Accounting, Amherst, MA 01003. Offers MSA. *Accreditation:* AACSB. Part-time programs available. *Students:* 20 full-time (9 women), 23 part-time (16 women); includes 7 minority (1 Black or African American, non-Hispanic/Latino; 3 Asian, non-Hispanic/Latino; 3 Hispanic/Latino), 1 international. Average age 23. 65 applicants, 82% accepted, 43 enrolled. In 2010, 61 master's awarded. *Entrance requirements:* For master's, GMAT. Additional exam requirements/recommendations for international students: Required—TOEFL (minimum score 550 paper-based; 213 computer-based; 80 iBT), IELTS (minimum score 6.5). *Application deadline:* For fall admission, 2/1 for domestic and international students. Applications are processed on a rolling basis. Application fee: $50 ($65 for international students). Electronic applications accepted. *Expenses:* Tuition, state resident: full-time $2640. Required fees: $8282. One-time fee: $357 full-time. *Unit head:* Dr. James F. Smith, Graduate Program Director, 413-545-5645, Fax: 413-545-3858. *Application contact:* Jean M. Ames, Supervisor of Admissions, 413-545-0722, Fax: 413-577-0010, E-mail: gradadm@grad.umass.edu.

University of Massachusetts Dartmouth, Graduate School, Charlton College of Business, Program in Business Administration, North Dartmouth, MA 02747-2300. Offers accounting (Postbaccalaureate Certificate); business administration (MBA); e-commerce (PMC); finance (PMC); general management (PMC); leadership (PMC); management (Postbaccalaureate Certificate); marketing (PMC); supply chain management (PMC). *Accreditation:* AACSB. Part-time programs available. *Faculty:* 40 full-time (13 women), 28 part-time/adjunct (8 women). *Students:* 99 full-time (38 women), 123 part-time (62 women); includes 4 Black or African American, non-Hispanic/Latino; 2 American Indian or Alaska Native, non-Hispanic/Latino; 3 Asian, non-Hispanic/Latino; 8 Hispanic/Latino; 1 Two or more races, non-Hispanic/Latino, 45 international. Average age 30. 185 applicants, 76% accepted, 79 enrolled. In 2010, 79 master's, 12 other advanced degrees awarded. *Entrance requirements:* For master's, GMAT, resume, letters of recommendation. Additional exam requirements/recommendations for international students: Required—TOEFL (minimum score 500 paper-based; 200 computer-based; 72 iBT). *Application deadline:* For fall admission, 6/1 for domestic students, 5/1 for international students; for spring admission, 10/1 for domestic students, 8/1 for international students. Application fee: $40 ($60 for international students). Electronic applications accepted. *Expenses:* Tuition, state resident: full-time $2071; part-time $86 per credit. Tuition, nonresident:

full-time $8099; part-time $337 per credit. Required fees: $9446; $394 per credit. One-time fee: $75. Part-time tuition and fees vary according to class time, course load, degree level and reciprocity agreements. *Financial support:* In 2010–11, 1 research assistantship with full tuition reimbursement (averaging $6,000 per year) was awarded; teaching assistantships, Federal Work-Study and unspecified assistantships also available. Support available to part-time students. Financial award application deadline: 3/1; financial award applicants required to submit FAFSA. *Faculty research:* Global business environment, e-commerce, managing diversity, agile manufacturing, green business. Total annual research expenditures: $29,538. *Unit head:* Dr. Norm Barber, Assistant Dean, 508-999-8543, E-mail: nbarber@umassd.edu. *Application contact:* Elan Turcotte-Shamski, Graduate Admissions Officer, 508-999-8604, Fax: 508-999-8183, E-mail: graduate@umassd.edu.

University of Memphis, Graduate School, Fogelman College of Business and Economics, Program in Business Administration, Memphis, TN 38152. Offers accounting (MBA, PhD); economics (MBA, PhD); executive business administration (MBA); finance (PhD); finance, insurance, and real estate (MBA, MS); international business administration (IMBA); management (MBA, MS, PhD); management information systems (MBA, MS, PhD); management science (MBA); marketing (MBA, MS); marketing and supply chain management (PhD); real estate development (MS); JD/MBA. *Accreditation:* AACSB. *Faculty:* 44 full-time (9 women), 5 part-time/adjunct (0 women). *Students:* 263 full-time (106 women), 181 part-time (66 women); includes 46 Black or African American, non-Hispanic/Latino; 3 American Indian or Alaska Native, non-Hispanic/Latino; 16 Asian, non-Hispanic/Latino; 5 Hispanic/Latino, 109 international. Average age 31. 374 applicants, 73% accepted, 119 enrolled. In 2010, 140 master's, 17 doctorates awarded. *Degree requirements:* For master's, comprehensive exam; for doctorate, comprehensive exam, thesis/dissertation. *Entrance requirements:* For master's, GMAT, resume; for doctorate, GMAT, interview, minimum GPA of 3.4, resume, letter of recommendation. Additional exam requirements/recommendations for international students: Required—TOEFL (minimum score 550 paper-based; 220 computer-based). *Application deadline:* For fall admission, 8/1 for domestic students; for spring admission, 12/1 for domestic students. Application fee: $35 ($60 for international students). *Financial support:* In 2010–11, 164 students received support; research assistantships with full tuition reimbursements available, teaching assistantships with full tuition reimbursements available, career-related internships or fieldwork, Federal Work-Study, scholarships/grants, and unspecified assistantships available. Financial award application deadline: 2/15; financial award applicants required to submit FAFSA. *Faculty research:* Competitive business strategy, finance microstructures, supply chain management innovations, health care economics, litigation risks and corporate audits. *Unit head:* Rajiv Grover, Dean, 901-678-3759, E-mail: rgrover@memphis.edu. *Application contact:* Dr. Carol V. Danehower, Associate Dean, 901-678-5402, Fax: 901-678-3579, E-mail: fcbegp@memphis.edu.

University of Memphis, Graduate School, Fogelman College of Business and Economics, School of Accountancy, Memphis, TN 38152. Offers accounting (MS); accounting systems (MS); taxation (MS). *Accreditation:* AACSB. *Faculty:* 10 full-time (2 women), 1 part-time/adjunct (0 women). *Students:* 25 full-time (10 women), 21 part-time (14 women); includes 7 Black or African American, non-Hispanic/Latino; 2 Asian, non-Hispanic/Latino; 1 Hispanic/Latino, 10 international. Average age 29. 33 applicants, 76% accepted, 9 enrolled. In 2010, 27 master's awarded. *Degree requirements:* For master's, comprehensive exam. *Entrance requirements:* For master's, GMAT. *Application deadline:* For fall admission, 8/1 for domestic students; for spring admission, 12/1 for domestic students. Application fee: $35 ($60 for international students). *Financial support:* In 2010–11, 32 students received support; research assistantships with full tuition reimbursements available, teaching assistantships with full tuition reimbursements available, Federal Work-Study, scholarships/grants, and unspecified assistantships available. Financial award application deadline: 2/15; financial award applicants required to submit FAFSA. *Faculty research:* Financial accounting, corporate governance, EDP auditing, evolution of system analysis, investor behavior and investment decisions. *Unit head:* Dr. Carolyn Callahan, Director, 901-678-4022, E-mail: cmcllhan@memphis.edu. *Application contact:* Dr. Craig Langstraat, Program Coordinator, 901-678-4577, E-mail: cjlngstr@memphis.edu.

University of Michigan–Dearborn, School of Management, Dearborn, MI 48128-1491. Offers accounting (MBA, MS); finance (MBA, MS); information systems (MS); international business (MBA); management (MBA); management information systems (MBA); marketing (MBA); supply chain management (MBA); MBA/MHSA; MBA/MSE; MBA/MSF. *Accreditation:* AACSB. Part-time and evening/weekend programs available. Postbaccalaureate distance learning degree programs offered (no on-campus study). *Faculty:* 40 full-time (17 women), 2 part-time/adjunct (1 woman). *Students:* 71 full-time (26 women), 403 part-time (134 women); includes 68 minority (19 Black or African American, non-Hispanic/Latino; 1 American Indian or Alaska Native, non-Hispanic/Latino; 39 Asian, non-Hispanic/Latino; 6 Hispanic/Latino; 1 Native Hawaiian or other Pacific Islander, non-Hispanic/Latino; 2 Two or more races, non-Hispanic/Latino), 89 international. Average age 30. 185 applicants, 51% accepted, 67 enrolled. In 2010, 150 master's awarded. *Entrance requirements:* For master's, GMAT, 2 years of work experience (MBA); course work in computer applications, statistics,

and pre-calculus or finite mathematics; 18 credits of accounting course work beyond introductory courses (MS in accounting). Additional exam requirements/recommendations for international students: Required—TOEFL (minimum score 560 paper-based; 220 computer-based; 84 iBT). *Application deadline:* For fall admission, 8/1 priority date for domestic students, 6/1 for international students; for winter admission, 12/1 priority date for domestic students, 10/1 for international students; for spring admission, 4/1 priority date for domestic students, 2/1 for international students. Applications are processed on a rolling basis. Application fee: $60. Electronic applications accepted. *Expenses:* Contact institution. *Financial support:* Career-related internships or fieldwork, Federal Work-Study, and scholarships/grants available. Support available to part-time students. Financial award application deadline: 9/1; financial award applicants required to submit FAFSA. *Faculty research:* Cultural diversity, buyer-supplier relations, error detection in data, economic evolution. *Unit head:* Dr. Kim Schatzel, Dean, 313-593-5248, Fax: 313-271-9835, E-mail: schatzel@umd.umich.edu. *Application contact:* Joan Doherty, Academic Advisor/Counselor, 313-593-5460, Fax: 313-271-9838, E-mail: gradbusiness@umd.umich.edu.

University of Minnesota, Twin Cities Campus, Carlson School of Management, Doctoral Program in Business Administration, Minneapolis, MN 55455-0213. Offers accounting (PhD); finance (PhD); information and decision sciences (PhD); marketing and logistics management (PhD); operations and management science (PhD); strategic management and organization (PhD). *Faculty:* 100 full-time (27 women). *Students:* 73 full-time (28 women); includes 3 Asian, non-Hispanic/Latino; 3 Hispanic/Latino, 53 international. Average age 30. 319 applicants, 6% accepted, 16 enrolled. In 2010, 8 doctorates awarded. *Degree requirements:* For doctorate, comprehensive exam, thesis/dissertation, written and oral preliminary exams, proposal defense, final defense. *Entrance requirements:* For doctorate, GMAT, GRE General Test. Additional exam requirements/recommendations for international students: Required—TOEFL (minimum score 600 paper-based; 250 computer-based; 100 iBT), IELTS (minimum score 7.5). *Application deadline:* For fall admission, 12/31 for domestic students, 12/31 priority date for international students. Applications are processed on a rolling basis. Application fee: $75 ($95 for international students). Electronic applications accepted. *Financial support:* In 2010–11, 68 students received support, including 134 fellowships with full tuition reimbursements available (averaging $6,622 per year), 63 research assistantships with full tuition reimbursements available (averaging $6,750 per year), 57 teaching assistantships with full tuition reimbursements available (averaging $6,750 per year); institutionally sponsored loans, scholarships/grants, health care benefits, and unspecified assistantships also available. Financial award application deadline: 12/31. *Faculty research:* Corporate strategy, finance, entrepreneurship, marketing, information and decision science, operations, accounting, quality management. *Unit head:* Dr. Shawn P. Curley, Director of Graduate Studies and PhD Program Director, 612-624-6546, Fax: 612-624-8221, E-mail: curley@umn.edu. *Application contact:* Earlene K. Bronson, Assistant Director, PhD Program, 612-624-0875, Fax: 612-624-8221, E-mail: brons003@umn.edu.

University of Minnesota, Twin Cities Campus, Carlson School of Management, Master's Program in Accountancy, Minneapolis, MN 55455-0213. Offers M Acc. *Accreditation:* AACSB. Part-time and evening/weekend programs available. *Faculty:* 15 full-time (3 women), 5 part-time/adjunct (1 woman). *Students:* 55 full-time (33 women), 3 part-time (2 women); includes 4 Asian, non-Hispanic/Latino, 31 international. Average age 23. 244 applicants, 22% accepted, 41 enrolled. In 2010, 31 master's awarded. *Entrance requirements:* For master's, GMAT, letters of recommendation. Additional exam requirements/recommendations for international students: Required—TOEFL (minimum score 550 paper-based; 213 computer-based; 79 iBT), IELTS (minimum score 6.5). *Application deadline:* For fall admission, 4/30 priority date for domestic students, 2/28 priority date for international students; for spring admission, 10/15 priority date for domestic and international students. Applications are processed on a rolling basis. Application fee: $75 ($95 for international students). Electronic applications accepted. *Expenses:* Contact institution. *Financial support:* In 2010–11, 13 students received support, including 13 fellowships (averaging $1,500 per year), 6 teaching assistantships with partial tuition reimbursements available (averaging $6,600 per year); institutionally sponsored loans also available. Financial award applicants required to submit FAFSA. *Faculty research:* Capitol market-based accounting, cognitive skill acquisition in auditing, incentives and control in organizations, economic consequences of securities regulation, earnings management. *Unit head:* Larry Kallio, Director of Graduate Studies, 612-624-9818, Fax: 612-626-7795, E-mail: kalli008@umn.edu. *Application contact:* Larry Kallio, Director of Graduate Studies, 612-624-9818, Fax: 612-626-7795, E-mail: kalli008@umn.edu.

University of Mississippi, Graduate School, School of Accountancy, Oxford, University, MS 38677. Offers accountancy (M Acc, PhD); taxation accounting (M Tax). *Accreditation:* AACSB. *Faculty:* 14 full-time (5 women), 3 part-time/adjunct (1 woman). *Students:* 112 full-time (43 women), 16 part-time (12 women); includes 12 minority (7 Black or African American, non-Hispanic/Latino; 1 American Indian or Alaska Native, non-Hispanic/Latino; 2 Asian, non-Hispanic/Latino; 2 Two or more races, non-Hispanic/Latino), 5 international. In 2010, 70 master's awarded. *Degree requirements:* For doctorate, thesis/dissertation. *Entrance requirements:* For master's, GMAT, minimum GPA of 3.0; for doctorate, GMAT. Additional exam requirements/recommendations for international students: Required—TOEFL. *Application deadline:* For fall admission, 4/1 for domestic students; for spring admission, 10/1 for domestic students. Applications are processed on a rolling basis. Application fee: $25. *Financial support:* Scholarships/grants available. Financial award application deadline: 3/1; financial award applicants required to submit FAFSA. *Unit head:* Dr. Mark Wilder, Interim Dean, 662-915-7468, Fax: 662-915-7483, E-mail: umaccy@olemiss.edu. *Application contact:* Dr. Christy M. Wyandt, Associate Dean, 662-915-7474, Fax: 662-915-7577, E-mail: cwyandt@olemiss.edu.

University of Missouri–Kansas City, Henry W. Bloch School of Management, Kansas City, MO 64110-2499. Offers accounting (MS); business administration (MBA); entrepreneurship and innovation (PhD); public affairs (MPA, PhD); JD/MBA; LL M/MPA. PhD (interdisciplinary) offered through the School of Graduate Studies. *Accreditation:* AACSB; NASPAA. Part-time and evening/weekend programs available. *Faculty:* 49 full-time (16 women), 21 part-time/adjunct (5 women). *Students:* 280 full-time (134 women), 435 part-time (193 women); includes 91 minority (44 Black or African American, non-Hispanic/Latino; 19 Asian, non-Hispanic/Latino; 23 Hispanic/Latino; 5 Two or more races, non-Hispanic/Latino), 50 international. Average age 30. 426 applicants, 255 enrolled. In 2010, 254 master's awarded. Terminal master's awarded for partial completion of doctoral program. *Entrance requirements:* For master's, GMAT, GRE, 2 writing essays, 2 references and support of employer; for doctorate, GRE, minimum GPA of 3.0. Additional exam requirements/recommendations for international students: Required—TOEFL (minimum score 550 paper-based; 213 computer-based; 80 iBT). *Application deadline:* For fall admission, 5/1 priority date for domestic and international students; for spring admission, 10/1 priority date for domestic and international students. Applications are processed on a rolling basis. Application fee: $45 ($50 for international students). Electronic applications accepted. *Expenses:* Tuition, state resident: full-time $5522.40; part-time $306.80 per credit hour. Tuition, nonresident: full-time $7128; part-time $792 per credit hour. Required fees: $261.15 per term. *Financial support:* In 2010–11, 26 research assistantships with partial tuition reimbursements (averaging $7,767 per year), 5 teaching assistantships with partial tuition reimbursements (averaging $8,430 per year) were awarded; career-related internships or fieldwork, Federal Work-Study, institutionally sponsored loans, scholarships/grants, tuition waivers (full and partial), and unspecified assistantships also available. Support available to part-time students. Financial award application deadline: 3/1; financial award applicants required to submit FAFSA. *Faculty research:* Entrepreneurship, finance, non-profit, risk management. *Unit head:* Dr. Teng-Kee Tan, Dean, 816-235-2215, Fax: 816-235-2206. *Application contact:* 816-235-1111, E-mail: admit@umkc.edu.

University of Missouri–St. Louis, College of Business Administration, Program in Accounting, St. Louis, MO 63121. Offers M Acc. *Accreditation:* AACSB. Part-time and evening/weekend programs available. *Faculty:* 9 full-time (4 women). *Students:* 56 full-time (31 women), 53 part-time (34 women); includes 13 minority (4 Black or African American, non-Hispanic/Latino; 1 American Indian or Alaska Native, non-Hispanic/Latino; 7 Asian, non-Hispanic/Latino; 1 Hispanic/Latino), 10 international. Average age 27. 85 applicants, 65% accepted, 32 enrolled. In 2010, 38 master's awarded. *Entrance requirements:* For master's, GMAT, 2 letters of recommendation. Additional exam requirements/recommendations for international students: Required—TOEFL (minimum score 550 paper-based; 213 computer-based). *Application deadline:* For fall admission, 3/15 for domestic and international students; for spring admission, 10/15 for domestic and international students. Application fee: $35 ($40 for international students). Electronic applications accepted. *Expenses:* Tuition, state resident: full-time $5522; part-time $306.80 per credit hour. Tuition, nonresident: full-time $14,253; part-time $792.10 per credit hour. Required fees: $658; $49 per credit hour. One-time fee: $12. Tuition and fees vary according to program. *Financial support:* Career-related internships or fieldwork, Federal Work-Study, and institutionally sponsored loans available. Support available to part-time students. Financial award application deadline: 4/1; financial award applicants required to submit FAFSA. *Faculty research:* Accounting information in contracts, financial reporting issues, empirical valuation issues. *Unit head:* Karl Kottemann, Assistant Director, 314-516-5885, Fax: 314-516-6420, E-mail: mba@umsl.edu. *Application contact:* 314-516-5458, Fax: 314-516-6996, E-mail: gradadm@umsl.edu.

University of Missouri–St. Louis, College of Business Administration, Program in Business Administration, St. Louis, MO 63121. Offers accounting (MBA); business administration (Certificate); finance (MBA); human resource management (Certificate); information systems (MBA); local government (Certificate); logistics and supply chain management (MBA, Certificate); marketing (MBA); marketing management (Certificate); operations management (MBA). *Accreditation:* AACSB. Part-time and evening/weekend programs available. *Faculty:* 30 full-time (5 women), 11 part-time/adjunct (2 women). *Students:* 132 full-time (57 women), 306 part-time (122 women); includes 55 minority (21 Black or African American, non-Hispanic/Latino; 20 Asian, non-Hispanic/Latino; 11 Hispanic/Latino; 1 Native Hawaiian or other Pacific Islander, non-Hispanic/Latino; 2 Two or more races, non-Hispanic/Latino), 6 international. Average age 30. 219 applicants, 60% accepted, 88 enrolled.

In 2010, 114 master's, 9 other advanced degrees awarded. *Entrance requirements:* For master's, GMAT, 2 letters of recommendation. Additional exam requirements/recommendations for international students: Required—TOEFL (minimum score 550 paper-based; 213 computer-based). *Application deadline:* For fall admission, 7/1 for domestic students; for spring admission, 11/1 for domestic students. Applications are processed on a rolling basis. Application fee: $35 ($40 for international students). Electronic applications accepted. *Expenses:* Tuition, state resident: full-time $5522; part-time $306.80 per credit hour. Tuition, nonresident: full-time $14,253; part-time $792.10 per credit hour. Required fees: $658; $49 per credit hour. One-time fee: $12. Tuition and fees vary according to program. *Financial support:* In 2010–11, 22 research assistantships with full and partial tuition reimbursements (averaging $7,414 per year), 4 teaching assistantships with full and partial tuition reimbursements (averaging $13,950 per year) were awarded; career-related internships or fieldwork, Federal Work-Study, and institutionally sponsored loans also available. Support available to part-time students. Financial award application deadline: 4/1; financial award applicants required to submit FAFSA. *Faculty research:* Human resources, strategic management, marketing strategy, consumer behavior product development, advertising. *Unit head:* Karl Kottemann, Assistant Director, 314-516-5885, Fax: 314-516-6420, E-mail: mba@umsl.edu. *Application contact:* 314-516-5458, Fax: 314-516-6996, E-mail: gradadm@umsl.edu.

University of Nebraska at Omaha, Graduate Studies, College of Business Administration, Department of Accounting, Omaha, NE 68182. Offers M Acc. Part-time and evening/weekend programs available. *Faculty:* 9 full-time (4 women). *Students:* 13 full-time (3 women), 20 part-time (14 women); includes 3 minority (1 Black or African American, non-Hispanic/Latino; 1 Asian, non-Hispanic/Latino; 1 Hispanic/Latino), 6 international. Average age 28. 34 applicants, 47% accepted, 15 enrolled. In 2010, 5 master's awarded. *Entrance requirements:* For master's, GMAT, minimum GPA of 3.0, resume. Additional exam requirements/recommendations for international students: Required—TOEFL (minimum score 600 paper-based; 213 computer-based; 100 iBT). *Application deadline:* For fall admission, 5/1 priority date for domestic students; for spring admission, 12/1 priority date for domestic students. Applications are processed on a rolling basis. Application fee: $45. Electronic applications accepted. *Financial support:* In 2010–11, 17 students received support; research assistantships with tuition reimbursements available, Federal Work-Study, institutionally sponsored loans, scholarships/grants, tuition waivers (partial), and unspecified assistantships available. Support available to part-time students. Financial award application deadline: 3/1; financial award applicants required to submit FAFSA. *Unit head:* Dr. Susan Eldridge, Chairperson, 402-554-3650. *Application contact:* Burch Kealey.

University of Nevada, Las Vegas, Graduate College, College of Business, Department of Accounting, Las Vegas, NV 89154-6003. Offers MS, Advanced Certificate, Certificate. *Accreditation:* AACSB. Part-time and evening/weekend programs available. *Faculty:* 11 full-time (3 women), 4 part-time/adjunct (1 woman). *Students:* 59 full-time (31 women), 46 part-time (29 women); includes 39 minority (3 Black or African American, non-Hispanic/Latino; 1 American Indian or Alaska Native, non-Hispanic/Latino; 14 Asian, non-Hispanic/Latino; 6 Hispanic/Latino; 15 Two or more races, non-Hispanic/Latino), 18 international. Average age 29. 54 applicants, 80% accepted, 30 enrolled. In 2010, 67 master's awarded. *Entrance requirements:* For master's, GMAT. Additional exam requirements/recommendations for international students: Required—TOEFL (minimum score 550 paper-based; 213 computer-based; 80 iBT), IELTS (minimum score 7). *Application deadline:* For fall admission, 8/1 priority date for domestic students, 6/1 for international students; for spring admission, 12/1 priority date for domestic students, 10/1 for international students. Applications are processed on a rolling basis. Application fee: $60 ($95 for international students). Electronic applications accepted. *Expenses:* Tuition, area resident: Part-time $239.50 per credit. Tuition, state resident: part-time $239.50 per credit. Tuition, nonresident: part-time $503 per credit. Required fees: $108 per semester. Tuition and fees vary according to course load, program and reciprocity agreements. *Financial support:* In 2010–11, 6 students received support, including 6 research assistantships with partial tuition reimbursements available (averaging $10,000 per year); institutionally sponsored loans, scholarships/grants, health care benefits, and unspecified assistantships also available. Financial award application deadline: 3/1. *Faculty research:* The study of auditor's judgments (psychology- and sociology-based), judgment biases, business processes, risk-based auditing. *Unit head:* Dr. Paulette Tandy, Chair/Associate Professor, 702-895-1559, Fax: 702-895-4306, E-mail: paulette.tandy@unlv.edu. *Application contact:* Graduate College Admissions Evaluator, 702-895-3320, Fax: 702-895-4180, E-mail: gradcollege@unlv.edu.

University of New Hampshire, Graduate School, Whittemore School of Business and Economics, Department of Accounting and Finance, Durham, NH 03824. Offers accounting (MS). Part-time programs available. *Faculty:* 8 full-time (2 women). *Students:* 29 full-time (16 women), 3 part-time (1 woman); includes 1 American Indian or Alaska Native, non-Hispanic/Latino, 2 international. Average age 30. 63 applicants, 44% accepted, 28 enrolled. In 2010, 24 master's awarded. *Entrance requirements:* For master's, GMAT. Additional exam requirements/recommendations for international students: Required—TOEFL (minimum score 550 paper-based; 213 computer-based;

80 iBT). *Application deadline:* For fall admission, 5/1 priority date for domestic students, 4/1 for international students; for spring admission, 12/1 for domestic students. Applications are processed on a rolling basis. Application fee: $65. *Financial support:* In 2010–11, 7 students received support; fellowships, research assistantships, teaching assistantships available. Financial award application deadline: 2/15. *Unit head:* Dr. Ahmad Etebari, Chairperson, 603-862-3359, E-mail: ahmad.etebari@unh.edu. *Application contact:* Lindsey Terestre, Administrative Assistant, 603-862-3326, E-mail: wsbe.grad@unh.edu.

University of New Haven, Graduate School, School of Business, Program in Accounting, West Haven, CT 06516-1916. Offers financial accounting (MS); managerial accounting (MS). *Students:* 18 full-time (10 women), 28 part-time (16 women); includes 11 Black or African American, non-Hispanic/Latino; 3 Asian, non-Hispanic/Latino; 4 Hispanic/Latino, 1 international. Average age 31. 36 applicants, 100% accepted, 17 enrolled. In 2010, 18 master's awarded. *Degree requirements:* For master's, thesis. *Application deadline:* Applications are processed on a rolling basis. Application fee: $50. *Financial support:* Research assistantships with partial tuition reimbursements, teaching assistantships with partial tuition reimbursements, Federal Work-Study available. Support available to part-time students. Financial award application deadline: 5/1; financial award applicants required to submit FAFSA. *Unit head:* Robert Wnek, Coordinator, 203-932-7111. *Application contact:* Eloise Gormley, Director of Graduate Admissions, 203-932-7449, Fax: 203-932-7137, E-mail: gradinfo@newhaven.edu.

University of New Haven, Graduate School, School of Business, Program in Business Administration, West Haven, CT 06516-1916. Offers accounting (MBA, Certificate), including CPA (MBA); business management (Certificate); business policy and strategy (MBA); finance (MBA), including CFA; global marketing (MBA); human resource management (Certificate); human resources management (MBA); international business (Certificate); marketing (Certificate); sports management (MBA); telecommunications management (Certificate); MBA/MPA. Part-time and evening/weekend programs available. *Students:* 158 full-time (80 women), 150 part-time (70 women); includes 36 Black or African American, non-Hispanic/Latino; 2 American Indian or Alaska Native, non-Hispanic/Latino; 19 Asian, non-Hispanic/Latino; 16 Hispanic/Latino, 82 international. Average age 32. 162 applicants, 99% accepted, 85 enrolled. In 2010, 141 master's, 16 other advanced degrees awarded. *Degree requirements:* For master's, thesis or alternative. *Entrance requirements:* For master's, GMAT. Additional exam requirements/recommendations for international students: Required—TOEFL (minimum score 520 paper-based; 190 computer-based; 70 iBT), IELTS (minimum score 5.5). *Application deadline:* For fall admission, 5/31 for international students; for winter admission, 10/15 for international students; for spring admission, 1/15 for international students. Applications are processed on a rolling basis. Application fee: $50. Electronic applications accepted. *Expenses:* Contact institution. *Financial support:* Research assistantships with partial tuition reimbursements, teaching assistantships with partial tuition reimbursements, Federal Work-Study, scholarships/grants, health care benefits, tuition waivers, and unspecified assistantships available. Support available to part-time students. Financial award applicants required to submit FAFSA. *Unit head:* Charles Coleman, Chairman, 203-932-7375. *Application contact:* Eloise Gormley, Director of Graduate Admissions, 203-932-7449, Fax: 203-932-7137, E-mail: gradinfo@newhaven.edu.

The University of North Carolina at Charlotte, Graduate School, Belk College of Business, Department of Accounting, Charlotte, NC 28223-0001. Offers M Acc. *Accreditation:* AACSB. Part-time and evening/weekend programs available. *Faculty:* 10 full-time (2 women), 2 part-time/adjunct (1 woman). *Students:* 67 full-time (35 women), 66 part-time (27 women); includes 22 minority (9 Black or African American, non-Hispanic/Latino; 8 Asian, non-Hispanic/Latino; 4 Hispanic/Latino; 1 Two or more races, non-Hispanic/Latino), 12 international. Average age 29. 153 applicants, 75% accepted, 67 enrolled. In 2010, 72 master's awarded. *Degree requirements:* For master's, thesis or alternative. *Entrance requirements:* For master's, GMAT, minimum GPA of 3.0 in undergraduate major, 2.8 overall. Additional exam requirements/recommendations for international students: Required—TOEFL (minimum score 557 paper-based; 220 computer-based; 83 iBT). *Application deadline:* For fall admission, 7/15 for domestic students, 5/1 for international students; for spring admission, 11/15 for domestic students, 10/1 for international students. Applications are processed on a rolling basis. Electronic applications accepted. *Expenses:* Tuition, state resident: full-time $3464. Tuition, nonresident: full-time $14,297. Required fees: $2094. Tuition and fees vary according to course load. *Financial support:* Research assistantships, career-related internships or fieldwork, institutionally sponsored loans, scholarships/grants, and unspecified assistantships available. Support available to part-time students. Financial award application deadline: 4/1; financial award applicants required to submit FAFSA. *Faculty research:* Corporate financial reporting trends, use of latest software for accounting and business applications, latest developments in federal and international taxation. *Unit head:* Dr. Jack Cathey, Interim Department Chair, 704-687-7690, Fax: 704-687-6938, E-mail: jmcathey@uncc.edu. *Application contact:* Kathy B. Giddings, Director of Graduate Admissions, 704-687-5503, Fax: 704-687-3279, E-mail: gradadm@uncc.edu.

The University of North Carolina Wilmington, School of Business, Program in Accountancy, Wilmington, NC 28403-3297. Offers MSA. *Students:* 65 full-time (37 women); includes 1 Black or African American, non-Hispanic/Latino; 1 American Indian or Alaska Native, non-Hispanic/Latino; 1 Asian, non-Hispanic/Latino; 1 Hispanic/Latino; 1 Native Hawaiian or other Pacific Islander, non-Hispanic/Latino, 1 international. Average age 25. 110 applicants, 51% accepted, 48 enrolled. In 2010, 60 master's awarded. *Degree requirements:* For master's, thesis or alternative, portfolio project. *Entrance requirements:* For master's, GMAT. Additional exam requirements/recommendations for international students: Required—TOEFL (minimum score 550 paper-based; 217 computer-based; 79 iBT), IELTS (minimum score 6.5). *Application deadline:* For fall admission, 5/1 for domestic students. Applications are processed on a rolling basis. Application fee: $60. *Financial support:* In 2010–11, 12 teaching assistantships with full and partial tuition reimbursements (averaging $9,000 per year) were awarded; career-related internships or fieldwork and Federal Work-Study also available. Support available to part-time students. Financial award application deadline: 3/15. *Unit head:* Dr. Randall Hanson, Department Chair, 910-962-3801, Fax: 910-962-3663, E-mail: hansonr@uncw.edu. *Application contact:* Dr. Karen Barnhill, Graduate Program Coordinator, 910-962-3903, E-mail: barnhillk@uncw.edu.

University of North Dakota, Graduate School, College of Business and Public Administration, Department of Accountancy, Grand Forks, ND 58202. Offers M Acc. Part-time programs available. *Faculty:* 10 full-time (4 women). *Students:* 4 full-time (1 woman), 2 part-time (1 woman), 3 international. Average age 28. 5 applicants, 0% accepted, 0 enrolled. *Degree requirements:* For master's, comprehensive exam, thesis or alternative, final exam. *Entrance requirements:* For master's, GMAT, minimum GPA of 3.0. Additional exam requirements/recommendations for international students: Required—TOEFL (minimum score 550 paper-based; 213 computer-based; 79 iBT), IELTS (minimum score 6.5). *Application deadline:* For fall admission, 8/1 priority date for domestic students, 8/1 for international students; for spring admission, 12/1 for domestic and international students. Applications are processed on a rolling basis. Application fee: $35. Electronic applications accepted. *Expenses:* Tuition, state resident: full-time $5857; part-time $306.74 per credit. Tuition, nonresident: full-time $15,666; part-time $729.77 per credit. Required fees: $53.42 per credit. Tuition and fees vary according to course load, program and reciprocity agreements. *Financial support:* In 2010–11, 4 students received support; fellowships with full and partial tuition reimbursements available, research assistantships with full and partial tuition reimbursements available, teaching assistantships with full and partial tuition reimbursements available, Federal Work-Study, institutionally sponsored loans, scholarships/grants, health care benefits, tuition waivers (full and partial), and unspecified assistantships available. Support available to part-time students. Financial award application deadline: 3/15; financial award applicants required to submit FAFSA. *Unit head:* Dr. Robert Dosch, Graduate Director, 701-777-4686, Fax: 701-777-5099, E-mail: robert.dosch@mail.business.und.edu. *Application contact:* Matt Anderson, Admissions Specialist, 701-777-2947, Fax: 701-777-3619, E-mail: matthew.anderson@gradschool.und.edu.

University of Northern Colorado, Graduate School, Monfort College of Business, Greeley, CO 80639. Offers accounting (MA). *Faculty:* 9 full-time (3 women). *Students:* 8 full-time (4 women). Average age 27. 10 applicants, 80% accepted, 6 enrolled. *Expenses:* Tuition, state resident: full-time $6199; part-time $344 per credit hour. Tuition, nonresident: full-time $14,834; part-time $824 per credit hour. Required fees: $1091; $60.60 per credit hour. Tuition and fees vary according to course load, degree level and program. *Unit head:* Donald Gudmundson, Dean, 970-351-1217, E-mail: don.gudmundson@unco.edu. *Application contact:* Linda Sisson, Graduate Student Admission Coordinator, 970-351-1807, Fax: 970-351-2371, E-mail: linda.sisson@unco.edu.

University of Northern Iowa, Graduate College, College of Business Administration, Program in Accounting, Cedar Falls, IA 50614. Offers M Acc. *Students:* 20 full-time (10 women), 2 part-time (0 women), 1 international. 33 applicants, 48% accepted, 16 enrolled. In 2010, 29 master's awarded. *Degree requirements:* For master's, thesis or alternative. *Entrance requirements:* For master's, GMAT. Additional exam requirements/recommendations for international students: Required—TOEFL (minimum score 575 paper-based; 230 computer-based; 89 iBT). *Application deadline:* For fall admission, 8/1 priority date for domestic students. Applications are processed on a rolling basis. Application fee: $50 ($70 for international students). *Financial support:* Application deadline: 2/1. *Unit head:* Dr. Martha Wartick, Head, 319-273-7754, Fax: 319-273-2922, E-mail: marty.wartick@uni.edu. *Application contact:* Laurie S. Russell, Record Analyst, 319-273-2623, Fax: 319-273-2885, E-mail: laurie.russell@uni.edu.

University of North Florida, Coggin College of Business, Master of Accountancy Program, Jacksonville, FL 32224. Offers M Acc. *Accreditation:* AACSB. Part-time and evening/weekend programs available. *Faculty:* 17 full-time (2 women), 1 part-time/adjunct (0 women). *Students:* 20 full-time (7 women), 38 part-time (20 women); includes 1 Black or African American, non-Hispanic/Latino; 3 Asian, non-Hispanic/Latino; 1 Hispanic/Latino; 1 Two or more races, non-Hispanic/Latino. Average age 29. 32 applicants, 56% accepted, 12 enrolled. In 2010, 37 master's awarded. *Entrance* *requirements:* For master's, GMAT or GRE, U.S. bachelor's degree from regionally-accredited university or equivalent foreign degree. Additional exam requirements/recommendations for international students: Required—TOEFL (minimum score 550 paper-based; 213 computer-based; 79 iBT). *Application deadline:* For fall admission, 7/1 priority date for domestic students, 5/1 for international students; for spring admission, 11/1 priority date for domestic students, 10/1 for international students. Applications are processed on a rolling basis. Application fee: $30. Electronic applications accepted. *Expenses:* Tuition, state resident: full-time $7646.40; part-time $318.60 per credit hour. Tuition, nonresident: full-time $23,502; part-time $979.24 per credit hour. Required fees: $1208.88; $50.37 per credit hour. Tuition and fees vary according to course load and program. *Financial support:* In 2010–11, 8 students received support; teaching assistantships, career-related internships or fieldwork, Federal Work-Study, and tuition waivers (partial) available. Financial award application deadline: 4/1; financial award applicants required to submit FAFSA. *Faculty research:* Enterprise-wide risk management, accounting input in the strategic planning process, accounting information systems, taxation issues in lawsuits and damage awards, database design. Total annual research expenditures: $20,469. *Unit head:* Dr. Charles Calhoun, Chair, 904-620-2630, Fax: 904-620-3861, E-mail: ccalhoun@unf.edu. *Application contact:* Lillith Richardson, Assistant Director, The Graduate School, 904-620-1360, Fax: 904-620-1362, E-mail: graduateschool@unf.edu.

University of North Florida, Coggin College of Business, MBA Program, Jacksonville, FL 32224. Offers accounting (MBA); construction management (MBA); e-commerce (MBA); economics (MBA); finance (MBA); human resource management (MBA); international business (MBA); logistics (MBA); management applications (MBA). *Accreditation:* AACSB. Part-time and evening/weekend programs available. *Faculty:* 17 full-time (5 women), 1 part-time/adjunct (0 women). *Students:* 137 full-time (56 women), 268 part-time (112 women); includes 17 Black or African American, non-Hispanic/Latino; 21 Asian, non-Hispanic/Latino; 12 Hispanic/Latino; 3 Two or more races, non-Hispanic/Latino, 29 international. Average age 30. 250 applicants, 57% accepted, 94 enrolled. In 2010, 173 master's awarded. *Entrance requirements:* For master's, GMAT or GRE, U.S. bachelor's degree from regionally-accredited university or equivalent foreign degree. Additional exam requirements/recommendations for international students: Required—TOEFL (minimum score 550 paper-based; 213 computer-based; 79 iBT). *Application deadline:* For fall admission, 7/1 priority date for domestic students, 5/1 for international students; for spring admission, 11/1 priority date for domestic students, 10/1 for international students. Applications are processed on a rolling basis. Application fee: $30. *Expenses:* Tuition, state resident: full-time $7646.40; part-time $318.60 per credit hour. Tuition, nonresident: full-time $23,502; part-time $979.24 per credit hour. Required fees: $1208.88; $50.37 per credit hour. Tuition and fees vary according to course load and program. *Financial support:* In 2010–11, 40 students received support; research assistantships, teaching assistantships, Federal Work-Study and tuition waivers (partial) available. Support available to part-time students. Financial award application deadline: 4/1; financial award applicants required to submit FAFSA. *Faculty research:* Performance measures, costing, and inventory issues in logistics and supply chain management; inter-organizational systems; international management and marketing practices; e-commerce; organizational learning and socialization processes. Total annual research expenditures: $9,024. *Unit head:* Dr. C. Bruce Kavan, Chair, 904-620-2780, Fax: 904-620-2832. *Application contact:* Cheryl Campbell, Graduate Advisor, 904-620-2575, Fax: 904-620-2832, E-mail: ccampbell@unf.edu.

University of North Texas, Toulouse Graduate School, College of Business Administration, Department of Accounting, Denton, TX 76203. Offers accounting (MS, PhD); taxation (MS). *Accreditation:* AACSB. Part-time programs available. *Degree requirements:* For master's, comprehensive exam; for doctorate, thesis/dissertation. *Entrance requirements:* For master's, GMAT or GRE General Test, essay, 3 letters of recommendation, resume; for doctorate, GMAT or GRE General Test, statement of purpose, resume, 3 letters of recommendation. Additional exam requirements/recommendations for international students: Recommended—TOEFL (minimum score 550 paper-based; 213 computer-based). *Application deadline:* Applications are processed on a rolling basis. Electronic applications accepted. *Expenses:* Tuition, state resident: full-time $4298; part-time $239 per credit hour. Tuition, nonresident: full-time $10,782; part-time $549 per credit hour. Required fees: $1292; $270 per credit hour. *Financial support:* Fellowships, career-related internships or fieldwork, Federal Work-Study, and institutionally sponsored loans available. Financial award applicants required to submit FAFSA. *Faculty research:* Empirical tax research issues, empirical financial accounting issues, problems and issues in public interest areas, historical perspective for accounting issues, behavioral issues in auditing and accounting systems. *Application contact:* Graduate Programs Office, 940-369-8977, Fax: 940-369-8978, E-mail: mbacob@unt.edu.

University of Notre Dame, Mendoza College of Business, Program in Accountancy, Notre Dame, IN 46556. Offers financial reporting and assurance services (MS); tax services (MS). *Accreditation:* AACSB. *Faculty:* 37 full-time (4 women), 14 part-time/adjunct (0 women). *Students:* 102 full-time (43 women); includes 7 minority (3 Asian, non-Hispanic/Latino; 4 Hispanic/Latino), 18 international. Average age 22. 353 applicants, 39% accepted, 102 enrolled. In 2010, 83 master's awarded. *Entrance requirements:* For master's, GMAT. Additional exam requirements/recommendations for international students: Required—TOEFL (minimum score 630 paper-based; 267 computer-based; 109 iBT). *Application deadline:* For fall admission, 11/1 for domestic and international students; for spring admission, 4/1 for domestic and international students. Applications are processed on a rolling basis. Application fee: $50 ($100 for international students). Electronic applications accepted. *Financial support:* In 2010–11, 97 students received support, including 97 fellowships (averaging $14,898 per year); scholarships/grants and unspecified assistantships also available. Financial award application deadline: 2/28; financial award applicants required to submit FAFSA. *Faculty research:* Stock valuation, accounting information in decision-making, choice of accounting method, taxes cost on capital. *Unit head:* Dr. Michael H. Morris, Director, 574-631-9732, Fax: 574-631-5300, E-mail: msacct.1@nd.edu. *Application contact:* Helen High, Assistant Director of Admissions and Student Services, 574-631-6499, Fax: 574-631-5300, E-mail: msacct.1@nd.edu.

University of Oklahoma, Michael F. Price College of Business, School of Accounting, Norman, OK 73019. Offers M Acc. *Accreditation:* AACSB. Part-time programs available. *Faculty:* 12 full-time (4 women), 1 part-time/adjunct (0 women). *Students:* 38 full-time (21 women), 11 part-time (5 women); includes 9 minority (1 Black or African American, non-Hispanic/Latino; 2 American Indian or Alaska Native, non-Hispanic/Latino; 5 Asian, non-Hispanic/Latino; 1 Two or more races, non-Hispanic/Latino), 5 international. Average age 26. 38 applicants, 39% accepted, 9 enrolled. In 2010, 16 master's awarded. *Degree requirements:* For master's, comprehensive exam. *Entrance requirements:* For master's, GMAT, minimum GPA of 3.0 in last 60 hours. Additional exam requirements/recommendations for international students: Required—TOEFL (minimum score 550 paper-based; 213 computer-based; 79 iBT). *Application deadline:* For fall admission, 6/15 for domestic students, 4/1 for international students; for spring admission, 11/15 for domestic students, 9/1 for international students. Applications are processed on a rolling basis. Application fee: $40 ($90 for international students). Electronic applications accepted. *Expenses:* Tuition, state resident: full-time $3893; part-time $162.20 per credit hour. Tuition, nonresident: full-time $14,167; part-time $590.30 per credit hour. Required fees: $2523; $94.60 per credit hour. Tuition and fees vary according to course load and degree level. *Financial support:* In 2010–11, 44 students received support, including 7 research assistantships with partial tuition reimbursements available (averaging $14,887 per year), 5 teaching assistantships with partial tuition reimbursements available (averaging $14,683 per year); career-related internships or fieldwork, scholarships/grants, and unspecified assistantships also available. Financial award application deadline: 4/1; financial award applicants required to submit FAFSA. *Faculty research:* Auditing, capital markets, corporate valuation, ethics, financial accounting. *Unit head:* Dr. Frances L. Ayres, Director, 405-325-4221, Fax: 405-325-2096, E-mail: fayres@ou.edu. *Application contact:* Amber Hasbrook, Academic Counselor, 405-325-4107, Fax: 405-325-7753, E-mail: amber.hasbrook@ou.edu.

University of Phoenix, School of Business, Phoenix, AZ 85034-7209. Offers accounting (MBA, MSA); business administration (MBA); energy management (MBA); global management (MBA); health care management (MBA); human resources management (MM); international management (MM); management (MM); marketing (MBA); project management (MBA); public administration (MPA); technology management (MBA). Programs are offered at the online campus. Evening/weekend programs available. Postbaccalaureate distance learning degree programs offered. *Students:* 20,237 full-time (12,641 women); includes 6,424 minority (4,376 Black or African American, non-Hispanic/Latino; 150 American Indian or Alaska Native, non-Hispanic/Latino; 546 Asian, non-Hispanic/Latino; 1,137 Hispanic/Latino; 155 Native Hawaiian or other Pacific Islander, non-Hispanic/Latino; 60 Two or more races, non-Hispanic/Latino), 1,149 international. Average age 39. *Entrance requirements:* For master's, minimum undergraduate GPA of 2.5 from accredited university, 3 years of work experience, citizen of the United States or have valid visa. Additional exam requirements/recommendations for international students: Required—TOEFL (minimum paper score 550, computer score 213, iBT 79), Test of English for International Communication, or IELTS. *Application deadline:* Applications are processed on a rolling basis. Application fee: $45. Electronic applications accepted. *Expenses:* Tuition: Full-time $16,440. One-time fee: $45 full-time. Full-time tuition and fees vary according to course load, degree level, campus/location and program. *Financial support:* Scholarships/grants available. Financial award applicants required to submit FAFSA. *Unit head:* Dr. Bill Berry, Director, 480-557-1824, E-mail: bill.berry@phoenix.edu. *Application contact:* Dr. Bill Berry, Director, 480-557-1824, E-mail: bill.berry@phoenix.edu.

University of Phoenix–Northern Virginia Campus, School of Business, Reston, VA 20190. Offers business administration (MBA); public accounting (MPA). Evening/weekend programs available. Postbaccalaureate distance learning degree programs offered. *Students:* 135 full-time (50 women); includes 43 Black or African American, non-Hispanic/Latino; 3 Asian, non-Hispanic/Latino; 3 Hispanic/Latino, 6 international. Average age 40. *Entrance requirements:* For master's, minimum undergraduate GPA of 2.5 from an accredited university, 3 years of work experience, must be a citizen of the United States or have a valid visa. Specific requirements may vary by program.

Additional exam requirements/recommendations for international students: Required—TOEFL (minimum score 213 paper, 79 iBT), TOEIC, IELTS or Berlitz. *Application deadline:* Applications are processed on a rolling basis. Application fee: $45. Electronic applications accepted. *Expenses:* Tuition: Full-time $16,440. One-time fee: $45 full-time. Full-time tuition and fees vary according to course load, degree level, campus/location and program. *Financial support:* Scholarships/grants available. Financial award applicants required to submit FAFSA. *Unit head:* Erik Greenberg, Campus Director, 703-376-6150, E-mail: erik.greenberg@phoenix.edu. *Application contact:* Erik Greenberg, Campus Director, 703-376-6150, E-mail: erik.greenberg@phoenix.edu.

University of Phoenix–Phoenix Campus, School of Business, Phoenix, AZ 85040-1958. Offers accounting (MSA); business administration (MBA); management (MM). Evening/weekend programs available. Postbaccalaureate distance learning degree programs offered. *Students:* 950 full-time (468 women); includes 194 minority (59 Black or African American, non-Hispanic/Latino; 11 American Indian or Alaska Native, non-Hispanic/Latino; 27 Asian, non-Hispanic/Latino; 84 Hispanic/Latino; 10 Native Hawaiian or other Pacific Islander, non-Hispanic/Latino; 3 Two or more races, non-Hispanic/Latino), 47 international. Average age 34. *Entrance requirements:* For master's, minimum undergraduate GPA of 2.5 from accredited university, 3 years of work experience, citizen of the United States or have valid visa. Additional exam requirements/recommendations for international students: Required—TOEFL (minimum paper score 500, computer score 213, iBT 79), Test of English for International Communication, or IELTS. *Application deadline:* Applications are processed on a rolling basis. Application fee: $45. Electronic applications accepted. *Expenses:* Tuition: Full-time $13,560. One-time fee: $45 full-time. Full-time tuition and fees vary according to course load, degree level, campus/location and program. *Financial support:* Scholarships/grants available. Financial award applicants required to submit FAFSA. *Unit head:* Bill Berry, Director, 480-557-1824, Fax: 480-557-1854, E-mail: bill.berry@phoenix.edu. *Application contact:* Campus Information Center, 800-766-0766.

University of Pittsburgh, Katz Graduate School of Business, Doctoral Program in Business Administration, Pittsburgh, PA 15260. Offers accounting (PhD); finance (PhD); information systems (PhD); marketing (PhD); operations/decision sciences/artificial intelligence (PhD); organizational behavior and human resource management (PhD); strategic planning (PhD). *Accreditation:* AACSB. *Faculty:* 50 full-time (15 women). *Students:* 51 full-time (22 women); includes 3 Black or African American, non-Hispanic/Latino; 4 Asian, non-Hispanic/Latino; 2 Hispanic/Latino, 18 international. 448 applicants, 5% accepted, 13 enrolled. In 2010, 4 doctorates awarded. *Degree requirements:* For doctorate, comprehensive exam, thesis/dissertation. *Entrance requirements:* For doctorate, GMAT or GRE, bachelor's degree, references, minimum GPA of 3.0. Additional exam requirements/recommendations for international students: Required—TOEFL, IELTS. *Application deadline:* For fall admission, 2/1 priority date for domestic and international students. Applications are processed on a rolling basis. Application fee: $50. Electronic applications accepted. *Expenses:* Tuition, state resident: full-time $17,304; part-time $701 per credit. Tuition, nonresident: full-time $29,554; part-time $1210 per credit. Required fees: $740; $214 per term. Tuition and fees vary according to program. *Financial support:* In 2010–11, 39 students received support, including 29 research assistantships with full tuition reimbursements available (averaging $1,900 per year), 10 teaching assistantships with full tuition reimbursements available (averaging $23,745 per year); fellowships, Federal Work-Study, scholarships/grants, health care benefits, and unspecified assistantships also available. Financial award application deadline: 2/1. *Faculty research:* Accounting statements and reporting, incentives and governance, corporate finance, mergers and acquisitions, information systems processes, structures and decision-making, organizational structure, knowledge management and corporate strategy, consumer behavior and marketing models. Total annual research expenditures: $362,777. *Unit head:* Dr. John E. Hulland, Director of Doctoral Program, 412-648-1534, Fax: 412-624-3633, E-mail: jhulland@katz.pitt.edu. *Application contact:* Carrie Woods, Assistant Director, Doctoral Office, 412-648-1525, Fax: 412-624-3633, E-mail: cawoods@katz.pitt.edu.

University of Pittsburgh, Katz Graduate School of Business, Master of Science in Accounting Program, Pittsburgh, PA 15260. Offers MS. Part-time programs available. *Faculty:* 15 full-time (8 women), 4 part-time/adjunct (2 women). *Students:* 41 full-time (23 women); includes 1 Black or African American, non-Hispanic/Latino; 2 Asian, non-Hispanic/Latino, 17 international. Average age 26. 282 applicants, 23% accepted, 27 enrolled. In 2010, 13 master's awarded. *Degree requirements:* For master's, minimum GPA of 3.0. *Entrance requirements:* For master's, GMAT, references, work experience relevant for program, interview, recommendations, essays, resume, transcripts. Additional exam requirements/recommendations for international students: Required—TOEFL or IELTS. *Application deadline:* For fall admission, 4/1 priority date for domestic students, 2/1 priority date for international students. Applications are processed on a rolling basis. Application fee: $50. Electronic applications accepted. *Expenses:* Contact institution. *Financial support:* In 2010–11, 30 students received support. Scholarships/grants available. *Faculty research:* Auditing and fraudulent reporting, management reporting, financial analysts' forecasts and investors' reactions, labor markets and employment

contracts, agency, performance measurement and incentive compensation, corporate governance, restructuring and organizational design. Total annual research expenditures: $11,721. *Unit head:* Dr. Karen Shastri, 412-648-1533, Fax: 412-624-5198, E-mail: kshastri@katz.pitt.edu. *Application contact:* Jessica Fick, Administrative Assistant, 412-624-0147, Fax: 412-624-5198, E-mail: macc@katz.pitt.edu.

University of Rhode Island, Graduate School, College of Business Administration, Kingston, RI 02881. Offers accounting (MS); business administration (MBA, PhD), including finance and insurance (PhD), management (PhD), marketing (PhD), operations and supply chain management (MBA); finance (MBA); general business (MBA); management (MBA); marketing (MBA); supply chain management (MBA). *Accreditation:* AACSB. Part-time and evening/weekend programs available. *Faculty:* 54 full-time (15 women), 3 part-time/adjunct (2 women). *Students:* 82 full-time (31 women), 218 part-time (77 women); includes 31 minority (6 Black or African American, non-Hispanic/Latino; 1 American Indian or Alaska Native, non-Hispanic/Latino; 13 Asian, non-Hispanic/Latino; 11 Hispanic/Latino), 29 international. In 2010, 78 master's, 3 doctorates awarded. *Degree requirements:* For master's, comprehensive exam (for some programs), thesis optional; for doctorate, comprehensive exam, thesis/dissertation. *Entrance requirements:* For master's, GMAT or GRE, 2 letters of recommendation, resume; for doctorate, GMAT or GRE, 3 letters of recommendation, resume. Additional exam requirements/recommendations for international students: Required—TOEFL (minimum score 575 paper-based; 233 computer-based; 91 iBT). Application fee: $65. Electronic applications accepted. *Expenses:* Tuition, state resident: full-time $9588; part-time $533 per credit hour. Tuition, nonresident: full-time $22,968; part-time $1276 per credit hour. Required fees: $1282; $68 per semester. Tuition and fees vary according to program. *Financial support:* In 2010–11, 13 teaching assistantships with full and partial tuition reimbursements (averaging $12,432 per year) were awarded. Financial award applicants required to submit FAFSA. Total annual research expenditures: $9,928. *Unit head:* Dr. Mark Higgins, Dean, 401-874-4244, Fax: 401-874-4312, E-mail: markhiggins@uri.edu. *Application contact:* Lisa Lancellotta, Coordinator, MBA Programs, 401-874-4241, Fax: 401-874-4312, E-mail: mba@uri.edu.

University of St. Thomas, Graduate Studies, Opus College of Business, Master of Science in Accountancy Program, Minneapolis, MN 55403. Offers MS. *Students:* 25 full-time (15 women); includes 1 minority (Asian, non-Hispanic/Latino), 1 international. Average age 23. 44 applicants, 61% accepted, 25 enrolled. In 2010, 21 master's awarded. *Entrance requirements:* For master's, GMAT. Additional exam requirements/recommendations for international students: Required—TOEFL (minimum 94 iBT), IELTS (minimum 7). *Application deadline:* For fall admission, 8/2 priority date for domestic students; for spring admission, 6/1 for domestic students, 4/1 for international students. Applications are processed on a rolling basis. Application fee: $30 ($90 for international students). Electronic applications accepted. *Financial support:* In 2010–11, 25 students received support. Career-related internships or fieldwork and scholarships/grants available. *Unit head:* Kristine Sharockman, Director, 651-962-4110, Fax: 651-962-4141, E-mail: msacct@stthomas.edu. *Application contact:* Cathy Davis, Program Manager, 651-962-4110, Fax: 651-962-4141, E-mail: msacct@stthomas.edu.

University of San Diego, School of Business Administration, Programs in Accountancy and Taxation, San Diego, CA 92110-2492. Offers accountancy (MS); taxation (MS). Part-time and evening/weekend programs available. *Students:* 15 full-time (10 women), 6 part-time (5 women); includes 4 Asian, non-Hispanic/Latino; 3 Hispanic/Latino, 5 international. Average age 26. In 2010, 23 master's awarded. *Entrance requirements:* For master's, GMAT (minimum score 550), minimum GPA of 3.0. Additional exam requirements/recommendations for international students: Required—TOEFL (minimum score 580 paper-based; 237 computer-based; 92 iBT), TWE. *Expenses:* Tuition: Full-time $21,744; part-time $1208 per unit. Required fees: $224. Full-time tuition and fees vary according to course load and degree level. *Financial support:* In 2010–11, 6 students received support. Career-related internships or fieldwork, Federal Work-Study, institutionally sponsored loans, scholarships/grants, and unspecified assistantships available. Support available to part-time students. Financial award application deadline: 4/1; financial award applicants required to submit FAFSA. *Faculty research:* Leadership and ethics. *Unit head:* Dr. Diane Pattison, Academic Director, Accountancy Programs, 619-260-4850, E-mail: pattison@sandiego.edu. *Application contact:* Stephen Pultz, Director of Admissions and Enrollment, 619-260-4506, Fax: 619-260-6836, E-mail: admissions@sandiego.edu.

The University of Scranton, College of Graduate and Continuing Education, Program in Business Administration, Scranton, PA 18510. Offers accounting (MBA); finance (MBA); general business administration (MBA); health care management (MBA); international business (MBA); management information systems (MBA); marketing (MBA); operations management (MBA). *Accreditation:* AACSB. Part-time and evening/weekend programs available. Postbaccalaureate distance learning degree programs offered (no on-campus study). *Faculty:* 34 full-time (8 women). *Students:* 251 full-time (91 women), 180 part-time (72 women); includes 41 Black or African American, non-Hispanic/Latino; 11 Asian, non-Hispanic/Latino; 7 Hispanic/Latino, 40 international. Average age 32. 386 applicants, 84% accepted. In 2010, 38 master's awarded. *Degree requirements:* For master's, capstone experience. *Entrance* *requirements:* For master's, GMAT, minimum GPA of 2.75. Additional exam requirements/recommendations for international students: Required—TOEFL (minimum score 500 paper-based; 173 computer-based), IELTS (minimum score 5.5). *Application deadline:* Applications are processed on a rolling basis. Application fee: $0. *Financial support:* In 2010–11, 13 students received support, including 13 teaching assistantships with full and partial tuition reimbursements available (averaging $6,430 per year); fellowships, career-related internships or fieldwork, Federal Work-Study, and unspecified assistantships also available. Support available to part-time students. Financial award application deadline: 3/1. *Faculty research:* Financial markets, strategic impact of total quality management, internal accounting controls, consumer preference, information systems and the Internet. *Unit head:* Dr. Murli Rajan, Director, 570-941-4043, Fax: 570-941-4342. *Application contact:* Joseph M. Roback, Director of Admissions, 570-941-4385, Fax: 570-941-5928, E-mail: robackj2@scranton.edu.

University of South Alabama, Graduate School, Mitchell College of Business, Program in Accounting, Mobile, AL 36688-0002. Offers M Acc. Part-time and evening/weekend programs available. *Faculty:* 4 full-time (1 woman). *Students:* 22 full-time (12 women), 4 part-time (3 women); includes 4 minority (3 Black or African American, non-Hispanic/Latino; 1 Hispanic/Latino), 2 international. 45 applicants, 53% accepted, 17 enrolled. In 2010, 9 master's awarded. *Degree requirements:* For master's, comprehensive exam. *Entrance requirements:* For master's, GMAT, minimum undergraduate GPA of 3.0. *Application deadline:* For fall admission, 7/15 priority date for domestic students, 6/15 priority date for international students; for spring admission, 12/1 priority date for domestic students, 11/1 priority date for international students. Applications are processed on a rolling basis. Application fee: $35. *Expenses:* Tuition, state resident: part-time $300 per credit hour. Tuition, non-resident: part-time $600 per credit hour. Required fees: $150 per semester. *Financial support:* Available to part-time students. Application deadline: 4/1. *Unit head:* Dr. John Gamble, Dean, Mitchell College of Business, 251-460-6180, Fax: 251-460-6529. *Application contact:* Dr. B. Keith Harrison, Dean of the Graduate School, 251-460-6310, Fax: 251-461-1513, E-mail: kharriso@usouthal.edu.

University of South Carolina, The Graduate School, Darla Moore School of Business, Master of Accountancy Program, Columbia, SC 29208. Offers business measurement and assurance (M Acc); JD/M Acc. *Accreditation:* AACSB. Part-time programs available. *Faculty:* 99 full-time (23 women), 10 part-time/adjunct (2 women). *Students:* 103 full-time (54 women); includes 2 Black or African American, non-Hispanic/Latino; 5 Asian, non-Hispanic/Latino, 12 international. Average age 25. 188 applicants, 76% accepted, 90 enrolled. In 2010, 39 master's awarded. *Degree requirements:* For master's, comprehensive exam. *Entrance requirements:* For master's, GMAT. Additional exam requirements/recommendations for international students: Required—TOEFL (minimum score 250 computer-based; 100 iBT); Recommended—IELTS. *Application deadline:* Applications are processed on a rolling basis. Application fee: $100. Electronic applications accepted. *Financial support:* Fellowships, career-related internships or fieldwork, Federal Work-Study, scholarships/grants, and unspecified assistantships available. *Faculty research:* Judgment modeling, international accounting, accounting information systems, behavioral accounting, cost/management accounting. *Unit head:* Christine LaCola, Managing Director, 803-777-2730, Fax: 803-777-0414, E-mail: christine.lacola@moore.sc.edu. *Application contact:* Scott King, Director, Graduate Admissions, 803-777-6749, Fax: 803-777-0414, E-mail: scott.king@moore.sc.edu.

University of Southern California, Graduate School, Marshall School of Business, Leventhal School of Accounting, Los Angeles, CA 90089. Offers accounting (M Acc); business taxation (MBT); JD/MBT. Part-time programs available. *Students:* 102 full-time (50 women), 2 part-time (both women); includes 32 minority (4 Black or African American, non-Hispanic/Latino; 20 Asian, non-Hispanic/Latino; 5 Hispanic/Latino; 3 Two or more races, non-Hispanic/Latino), 30 international. 971 applicants, 28% accepted. In 2010, 152 master's awarded. *Degree requirements:* For master's, 30-48 units of study. *Entrance requirements:* For master's, GMAT, undergraduate degree, communication skills. Additional exam requirements/recommendations for international students: Required—TOEFL (minimum score 100 computer-based). *Application deadline:* For fall admission, 3/31 for domestic students, 1/10 for international students; for spring admission, 11/1 for domestic students. Applications are processed on a rolling basis. Application fee: $85. Electronic applications accepted. *Expenses:* Tuition: Full-time $31,240; part-time $1420 per unit. Required fees: $600. One-time fee: $35 full-time. Full-time tuition and fees vary according to degree level and program. *Financial support:* In 2010–11, 92 students received support. Application deadline: 1/10. *Faculty research:* State and local taxation, Securities and Exchange Commission, governance, auditing fees, financial accounting, enterprise zones, women in business. *Unit head:* Shirley Maxey, Associate Dean, Accounting Masters Programs, 213-740-4838, E-mail: smaxey@marshall.usc.edu. *Application contact:* Jenna Buonanno, Associate Program Director, 213-740-4838, E-mail: buonanno@marshall.usc.edu.

University of Southern Mississippi, Graduate School, College of Business, School of Accountancy and Information Systems, Hattiesburg, MS 39406-0001. Offers accountancy (MPA). *Accreditation:* AACSB. Part-time and evening/weekend programs available. *Faculty:* 7 full-time (4 women), 2 part-time/adjunct (both women). *Students:* 21 full-time (13 women), 2 part-time (1 woman); includes 1 Black or African American, non-Hispanic/Latino, 1 international. Average age 26. 29 applicants, 79% accepted, 19 enrolled. In 2010, 14 master's awarded. *Degree requirements:* For master's, comprehensive exam. *Entrance requirements:* For master's, GMAT, minimum GPA of 2.75 on last 60 hours. Additional exam requirements/recommendations for international students: Required—TOEFL, IELTS. *Application deadline:* For fall admission, 7/15 priority date for domestic students, 7/15 for international students; for spring admission, 11/15 priority date for domestic students, 11/15 for international students. Applications are processed on a rolling basis. Application fee: $50. Electronic applications accepted. *Financial support:* In 2010–11, 7 research assistantships with full tuition reimbursements (averaging $7,200 per year) were awarded; Federal Work-Study, institutionally sponsored loans, scholarships/grants, health care benefits, and unspecified assistantships also available. Support available to part-time students. Financial award application deadline: 3/15; financial award applicants required to submit FAFSA. *Faculty research:* Bank liquidity, subchapter S corporations, internal auditing, governmental accounting, inflation accounting. *Unit head:* Dr. Skip Hughes, Director, 601-266-4322, Fax: 601-266-4639. *Application contact:* Dr. Michael Dugan, Director of Graduate Studies, 601-266-4641, Fax: 601-266-5814.

University of South Florida, Graduate School, College of Business, Department of Business Administration, Tampa, FL 33620-9951. Offers accounting (PhD); entrepreneurship (MBA); finance (PhD); information systems (PhD); leadership and organizational effectiveness (MSM); management and organization (MBA); marketing (PhD). *Accreditation:* AACSB. Part-time and evening/weekend programs available. *Faculty:* 1 (woman) full-time. *Students:* 148 full-time (48 women), 190 part-time (61 women); includes 70 minority (7 Black or African American, non-Hispanic/Latino; 1 American Indian or Alaska Native, non-Hispanic/Latino; 26 Asian, non-Hispanic/Latino; 36 Hispanic/Latino), 62 international. Average age 30. 452 applicants, 29% accepted, 80 enrolled. In 2010, 146 master's, 5 doctorates awarded. *Degree requirements:* For master's, comprehensive exam, thesis (for some programs); for doctorate, comprehensive exam, thesis/dissertation, 90 credit hours, minimum GPA of 3.0. *Entrance requirements:* For master's, GMAT, minimum GPA of 3.0 in last 60 hours of course work, 2 years of work experience, resume; for doctorate, GMAT, letters of recommendation, personal statement. Additional exam requirements/recommendations for international students: Required—TOEFL (minimum score 550 paper-based; 213 computer-based; 79 iBT). *Application deadline:* For fall admission, 6/1 for domestic students, 1/2 for international students; for spring admission, 10/15 for domestic students, 6/1 for international students. Application fee: $30. *Financial support:* Scholarships/grants, health care benefits, and unspecified assistantships available. Financial award applicants required to submit FAFSA. *Unit head:* Irene Hurst, Program Director, 813-974-3335, Fax: 813-974-4518, E-mail: hurst@coba.usf.edu. *Application contact:* Wendy Baker, Assistant Director, Graduate Studies, 813-974-3335, Fax: 813-974-4518, E-mail: wbaker@usf.edu.

University of South Florida, Graduate School, College of Business, School of Accounting, Tampa, FL 33620-9951. Offers accounting (M Acc); business administration (PhD), including accounting. *Accreditation:* AACSB. Part-time and evening/weekend programs available. *Faculty:* 3 full-time (all women). *Students:* 51 full-time (34 women), 31 part-time (20 women); includes 1 American Indian or Alaska Native, non-Hispanic/Latino; 7 Asian, non-Hispanic/Latino; 10 Hispanic/Latino; 1 Two or more races, non-Hispanic/Latino, 1 international. Average age 28. 122 applicants, 38% accepted, 28 enrolled. In 2010, 58 master's awarded. Terminal master's awarded for partial completion of doctoral program. *Degree requirements:* For master's, thesis or alternative, 30 credits, minimum GPA of 3.0; for doctorate, comprehensive exam, thesis/dissertation. *Entrance requirements:* For master's, GMAT, minimum GPA of 3.0 in upper-level accounting course work in last 5 years; for doctorate, GMAT, letters of recommendation, personal statement. Additional exam requirements/recommendations for international students: Required—TOEFL (minimum score 550 paper-based; 213 computer-based; 79 iBT). *Application deadline:* For fall admission, 6/1 for domestic students, 1/2 for international students; for spring admission, 10/15 for domestic students, 6/1 for international students. Application fee: $30. Electronic applications accepted. *Financial support:* In 2010–11, 17 teaching assistantships with tuition reimbursements (averaging $14,667 per year) were awarded; scholarships/grants, health care benefits, and unspecified assistantships also available. Financial award applicants required to submit FAFSA. *Faculty research:* Auditor independence, audit committee decisions, fraud detection and reporting, disclosure effects, effects of information technology on accounting, governmental accounting/auditing, accounting information systems, the reporting and use of financial information, fair value accounting issues, corporate governance and financial reporting quality. Total annual research expenditures: $279,601. *Unit head:* Dr. Stephanie Bryant, Chairperson, 813-974-4186, Fax: 813-974-6528, E-mail: sbryant2@usf.edu. *Application contact:* Christy Ward, Advisor, 813-974-4290, Fax: 813-974-2797, E-mail: cward@coba.usf.edu.

The University of Tampa, John H. Sykes College of Business, Tampa, FL 33606-1490. Offers accounting (MS); entrepreneurship (MBA); finance (MBA, MS); information systems management (MBA); innovation management (MBA); international business (MBA); marketing (MBA, MS); nonprofit management (MBA). *Accreditation:* AACSB. Part-time and evening/weekend programs available. *Faculty:* 67 full-time (24 women), 11 part-time/adjunct (4 women). *Students:* 235 full-time (89 women), 288 part-time (122 women); includes 74 minority (16 Black or African American, non-Hispanic/Latino; 2 American Indian or Alaska Native, non-Hispanic/Latino; 14 Asian, non-Hispanic/Latino; 34 Hispanic/Latino; 2 Native Hawaiian or other Pacific Islander, non-Hispanic/Latino; 6 Two or more races, non-Hispanic/Latino), 95 international. Average age 29. 457 applicants, 45% accepted, 175 enrolled. In 2010, 230 master's awarded. *Degree requirements:* For master's, capstone. *Entrance requirements:* For master's, GMAT or GRE, 4-year undergraduate degree, minimum GPA of 3.0, professional experience (for Executive MBA). Additional exam requirements/recommendations for international students: Required—TOEFL (minimum score 577 paper-based; 230 computer-based; 90 iBT); Recommended—IELTS (minimum score 7.5). *Application deadline:* Applications are processed on a rolling basis. Application fee: $40. Electronic applications accepted. *Expenses:* Tuition: Part-time $504 per credit hour. Required fees: $40 per term. *Financial support:* In 2010–11, 74 students received support. Career-related internships or fieldwork, scholarships/grants, unspecified assistantships, and grants available. Financial award applicants required to submit FAFSA. *Faculty research:* Management innovation, social marketing, value relevance of earnings and book value across industries, managerial finance, entrepreneurship. *Unit head:* Dennis Nostrand, Vice President, Enrollment/Admissions, 813-257-1808, E-mail: dnostrand@ut.edu. *Application contact:* Charlene Tobie, Associate Director of Admissions, 813-257-3566, E-mail: ctobie@ut.edu.

The University of Tennessee at Chattanooga, Graduate School, College of Business, Program in Accountancy, Chattanooga, TN 37403. Offers M Acc. *Accreditation:* AACSB. Part-time and evening/weekend programs available. *Faculty:* 5 full-time (1 woman), 2 part-time/adjunct (1 woman). *Students:* 18 full-time (8 women), 26 part-time (16 women); includes 7 minority (2 Black or African American, non-Hispanic/Latino; 3 Asian, non-Hispanic/Latino; 1 Hispanic/Latino; 1 Two or more races, non-Hispanic/Latino), 3 international. Average age 28. 32 applicants, 69% accepted, 18 enrolled. In 2010, 11 master's awarded. *Entrance requirements:* For master's, GMAT (minimum score 450). Additional exam requirements/recommendations for international students: Required—TOEFL (minimum score 550 paper-based; 213 computer-based; 79 iBT), IELTS (minimum score 6). *Application deadline:* For fall admission, 8/1 priority date for domestic students, 6/1 for international students; for spring admission, 12/1 priority date for domestic students, 10/1 for international students. Applications are processed on a rolling basis. Application fee: $35. Electronic applications accepted. *Financial support:* In 2010–11, 1 research assistantship with full and partial tuition reimbursement (averaging $5,500 per year) was awarded; career-related internships or fieldwork, scholarships/grants, and unspecified assistantships also available. Support available to part-time students. *Faculty research:* Performance measurement, auditing, income taxation, corporate efficiency, portfolio management and performance. *Unit head:* Dr. Stan Davis, Head, 423-425-4152, Fax: 423-425-5255, E-mail: stan-davis@utc.edu. *Application contact:* Dr. Jerald Ainsworth, Dean of Graduate Studies, 423-425-4478, Fax: 423-425-5223, E-mail: jerald-ainsworth@utc.edu.

The University of Texas at Arlington, Graduate School, College of Business, Accounting Department, Arlington, TX 76019. Offers accounting (MP Acc, MS, PhD); taxation (MS). *Accreditation:* AACSB. Part-time and evening/weekend programs available. *Faculty:* 12 full-time (3 women). *Students:* 98 full-time (54 women), 134 part-time (70 women); includes 53 minority (13 Black or African American, non-Hispanic/Latino; 1 American Indian or Alaska Native, non-Hispanic/Latino; 22 Asian, non-Hispanic/Latino; 14 Hispanic/Latino; 1 Native Hawaiian or other Pacific Islander, non-Hispanic/Latino; 2 Two or more races, non-Hispanic/Latino), 35 international. 154 applicants, 58% accepted, 56 enrolled. In 2010, 94 master's, 4 doctorates awarded. *Degree requirements:* For master's, thesis optional; for doctorate, comprehensive exam, thesis/dissertation. *Entrance requirements:* For master's, GMAT. Additional exam requirements/recommendations for international students: Required—TOEFL (minimum score 550 paper-based; 213 computer-based; 79 iBT). *Application deadline:* For fall admission, 6/1 for domestic students, 4/1 for international students; for spring admission, 10/15 for domestic students, 9/15 for international students. Applications are processed on a rolling basis. Application fee: $35 ($50 for international students). *Expenses:* Tuition, state resident: full-time $7500. Tuition, nonresident: full-time $13,080. International tuition: $13,250 full-time. *Financial support:* In 2010–11, 100 students received support, including 11 teaching assistantships (averaging $14,000 per year); fellowships, research assistantships, career-related internships or fieldwork, scholarships/grants, and unspecified assistantships also available. Financial award application deadline: 6/1; financial award applicants required to submit FAFSA. *Unit head:* Dr. LarrChandra Subramaniam, Chair, 817-272-7029, Fax: 817-282-5793, E-mail: subramaniam@uta.edu. *Application contact:* Carly S. Andrews, Graduate Advisor, 817-272-3047, Fax: 817-272-5793, E-mail: graduate.accounting.advisor@uta.edu.

The University of Texas at Arlington, Graduate School, College of Business, Program in Business Administration, Arlington, TX 76019. Offers accounting

(PhD); business statistics (PhD); finance (MBA, PhD); information systems (MBA, PhD); management (MBA, PhD); marketing (MBA, PhD); operations management (MBA, PhD); real estate (MBA). *Accreditation:* AACSB. Part-time and evening/weekend programs available. Postbaccalaureate distance learning degree programs offered (no on-campus study). *Students:* 555 full-time (197 women), 378 part-time (144 women); includes 179 minority (55 Black or African American, non-Hispanic/Latino; 1 American Indian or Alaska Native, non-Hispanic/Latino; 58 Asian, non-Hispanic/Latino; 55 Hispanic/Latino; 10 Two or more races, non-Hispanic/Latino), 410 international. 317 applicants, 93% accepted, 196 enrolled. In 2010, 468 master's, 1 doctorate awarded. Terminal master's awarded for partial completion of doctoral program. *Degree requirements:* For master's, thesis optional; for doctorate, comprehensive exam, thesis/dissertation. *Entrance requirements:* For master's, GMAT or GRE; for doctorate, GMAT, minimum GPA of 3.0 (undergraduate), 3.4 (graduate); 30 hours of graduate course work. Additional exam requirements/recommendations for international students: Required—TOEFL (minimum score 550 paper-based; 213 computer-based; 79 iBT). *Application deadline:* For fall admission, 6/1 for domestic students, 4/1 for international students; for spring admission, 10/15 for domestic students, 9/15 for international students. Applications are processed on a rolling basis. Application fee: $35 ($50 for international students). Electronic applications accepted. *Expenses:* Tuition, state resident: full-time $7500. Tuition, nonresident: full-time $13,080. International tuition: $13,250 full-time. *Financial support:* Career-related internships or fieldwork, scholarships/grants, and unspecified assistantships available. Financial award application deadline: 6/1; financial award applicants required to submit FAFSA. *Unit head:* Dr. Edmund Prater, Director of PhD Programs, 817-272-2131, Fax: 817-272-5799. *Application contact:* Melanie McGee, Director of MBA Program, 817-272-3005, Fax: 817-272-5799, E-mail: mwmcgee@uta.edu.

The University of Texas at Dallas, School of Management, Program in Accounting, Richardson, TX 75080. Offers audit and professional (MS); financial analysis (MS); information management (MS); international audit (MS); international services (MS); managerial (MS); taxation (MS). *Accreditation:* AACSB. *Faculty:* 17 full-time (4 women), 7 part-time/adjunct (2 women). *Students:* 412 full-time (270 women), 293 part-time (149 women); includes 164 minority (22 Black or African American, non-Hispanic/Latino; 1 American Indian or Alaska Native, non-Hispanic/Latino; 102 Asian, non-Hispanic/Latino; 37 Hispanic/Latino; 2 Two or more races, non-Hispanic/Latino), 283 international. Average age 28. 570 applicants, 68% accepted, 259 enrolled. In 2010, 273 master's awarded. *Entrance requirements:* For master's, GMAT, minimum GPA of 3.0 in upper-level course work in field. Additional exam requirements/recommendations for international students: Required—TOEFL (minimum score 550 paper-based; 215 computer-based). *Application deadline:* For fall admission, 7/15 for domestic students, 5/1 priority date for international students; for spring admission, 11/15 for domestic students, 9/1 priority date for international students. Applications are processed on a rolling basis. Application fee: $50 ($100 for international students). Electronic applications accepted. *Expenses:* Tuition, state resident: full-time $10,248; part-time $569 per credit hour. Tuition, nonresident: full-time $18,544; part-time $1030 per credit hour. Tuition and fees vary according to course load. *Financial support:* In 2010–11, 260 students received support, including 1 research assistantship with partial tuition reimbursement available (averaging $10,050 per year), 10 teaching assistantships with partial tuition reimbursements available (averaging $10,050 per year); career-related internships or fieldwork, Federal Work-Study, institutionally sponsored loans, scholarships/grants, and unspecified assistantships also available. Support available to part-time students. Financial award application deadline: 4/30; financial award applicants required to submit FAFSA. *Faculty research:* Privatization and accounting/auditing, corporate performance and executive compensation, risk management, information technology in accounting. *Unit head:* Amy Troutman, Assistant Director, 972-883-6719, Fax: 972-883-6823, E-mail: amybass@utdallas.edu. *Application contact:* James Parker, Assistant Director of Graduate Recruitment, 972-883-5842, E-mail: jparker@utdallas.edu.

The University of Texas at Dallas, School of Management, Programs in Management Science, Richardson, TX 75080. Offers accounting (PhD); finance (PhD); information systems (PhD); marketing (PhD); operations management (PhD). *Accreditation:* AACSB. Part-time and evening/weekend programs available. *Faculty:* 12 full-time (3 women), 3 part-time/adjunct (0 women). *Students:* 77 full-time (27 women), 11 part-time (4 women); includes 5 minority (all Asian, non-Hispanic/Latino), 72 international. Average age 32. 223 applicants, 9% accepted. In 2010, 16 doctorates awarded. *Degree requirements:* For doctorate, thesis/dissertation. *Entrance requirements:* For doctorate, GMAT, minimum GPA of 3.0. Additional exam requirements/recommendations for international students: Required—TOEFL (minimum score 550 paper-based; 215 computer-based). *Application deadline:* For fall admission, 7/15 for domestic students, 5/1 priority date for international students; for spring admission, 11/15 for domestic students, 9/1 priority date for international students. Applications are processed on a rolling basis. Application fee: $50 ($100 for international students). Electronic applications accepted. *Expenses:* Tuition, state resident: full-time $10,248; part-time $569 per credit hour. Tuition, nonresident: full-time $18,544; part-time $1030 per credit hour. Tuition and fees vary according to course load. *Financial support:* In 2010–11, 56 students received support, including 1 research assistantship with partial tuition reimbursement available (averaging $13,050 per year), 58 teaching assistantships with partial tuition reimbursements available (averaging $14,772 per year); career-related internships or fieldwork, Federal Work-Study, institutionally sponsored loans, scholarships/grants, and unspecified assistantships also available. Support available to part-time students. Financial award application deadline: 4/30; financial award applicants required to submit FAFSA. *Faculty research:* Empirical generalizations in marketing, diffusion of generations of technology, stochastic brand-choice theory, acceptance of trade deals by supermarkets, nonparametric estimations of market share response. *Unit head:* Dr. Sumit Sarkar, Program Director, 972-883-2745, Fax: 972-883-5977, E-mail: som phd.@utdallas.edu. Application contact: Dr. LeeAnne Sloane, Program Coordinator, 972-883-2745, Fax: 972-883-5977, E-mail: som_phd@utdallas.edu.

The University of Texas at El Paso, Graduate School, College of Business Administration, Department of Accounting, El Paso, TX 79968-0001. Offers M Acc. *Accreditation:* AACSB. Part-time and evening/weekend programs available. *Students:* 39 (20 women); includes 1 Black or African American, non-Hispanic/Latino; 1 Asian, non-Hispanic/Latino; 20 Hispanic/Latino, 6 international. Average age 34. In 2010, 18 master's awarded. *Entrance requirements:* For master's, GMAT, minimum GPA of 3.0. Additional exam requirements/recommendations for international students: Required—TOEFL; Recommended—IELTS. *Application deadline:* For fall admission, 8/1 priority date for domestic students, 3/1 for international students; for spring admission, 11/1 priority date for domestic students, 9/1 for international students. Applications are processed on a rolling basis. Application fee: $45 ($80 for international students). Electronic applications accepted. *Financial support:* In 2010–11, research assistantships with partial tuition reimbursements (averaging $18,750 per year), teaching assistantships with partial tuition reimbursements (averaging $15,000 per year) were awarded; fellowships with partial tuition reimbursements, institutionally sponsored loans, scholarships/grants, health care benefits, tuition waivers (partial), and unspecified assistantships also available. Support available to part-time students. Financial award application deadline: 3/15; financial award applicants required to submit FAFSA. *Faculty research:* International accounting, tax, not-for-profit accounting. *Unit head:* Dr. Ray Zimmerman, Chair, 915-747-5192, Fax: 915-747-8618, E-mail: rzimmer@utep.edu. *Application contact:* Dr. Patricia D. Witherspoon, Dean of the Graduate School, 915-747-5491, Fax: 915-747-5788, E-mail: withersp@utep.edu.

The University of Texas at San Antonio, College of Business, Department of Accounting, San Antonio, TX 78249-0617. Offers M Accy, PhD. *Accreditation:* AACSB. Part-time and evening/weekend programs available. *Faculty:* 11 full-time (4 women), 3 part-time/adjunct (0 women). *Students:* 57 full-time (23 women), 33 part-time (15 women); includes 40 minority (2 Black or African American, non-Hispanic/Latino; 2 Asian, non-Hispanic/Latino; 35 Hispanic/Latino; 1 Two or more races, non-Hispanic/Latino), 11 international. Average age 29. 65 applicants, 57% accepted, 31 enrolled. In 2010, 32 master's awarded. *Degree requirements:* For master's, comprehensive exam (for some programs), thesis (for some programs). *Entrance requirements:* For master's, GMAT. Additional exam requirements/recommendations for international students: Required—TOEFL (minimum score 500 paper-based; 173 computer-based; 61 iBT), IELTS (minimum score 5). *Application deadline:* For fall admission, 7/1 for domestic students, 4/1 for international students; for spring admission, 11/1 for domestic students, 9/1 for international students. Application fee: $45 ($80 for international students). *Expenses:* Tuition, state resident: full-time $4172; part-time $231.75 per credit hour. Tuition, nonresident: full-time $15,332; part-time $851.75 per credit hour. *Financial support:* In 2010–11, 17 students received support, including 9 research assistantships (averaging $11,332 per year), 15 teaching assistantships (averaging $8,107 per year); scholarships/grants, tuition waivers, and unspecified assistantships also available. Support available to part-time students. *Faculty research:* Financial reporting, auditing, tax, health care accounting. *Unit head:* Dr. James E. Groff, Chair, 210-458-5239, Fax: 210-458-4322, E-mail: james.groff@utsa.edu. *Application contact:* Dr. Jeff Boone, Advisor of Record Accounting Doctoral Programs, 210-458-7091, E-mail: jeff.boone@utsa.edu.

The University of Texas at San Antonio, College of Business, General Business Program, San Antonio, TX 78249-0617. Offers accounting (PhD); business (MBA); finance (PhD); information systems (MBA); information technology (PhD); international business (MBA); management accounting (MBA); management and organization studies (PhD); management of technology (MBA); marketing (PhD); marketing management (MBA); taxation (MBA). Part-time and evening/weekend programs available. *Students:* 159 full-time (59 women), 124 part-time (43 women); includes 82 minority (9 Black or African American, non-Hispanic/Latino; 2 American Indian or Alaska Native, non-Hispanic/Latino; 17 Asian, non-Hispanic/Latino; 50 Hispanic/Latino; 1 Native Hawaiian or other Pacific Islander, non-Hispanic/Latino; 3 Two or more races, non-Hispanic/Latino), 39 international. Average age 32. 330 applicants, 46% accepted, 105 enrolled. In 2010, 85 master's, 9 doctorates awarded. *Degree requirements:* For master's, comprehensive exam (for some programs), thesis (for some programs). *Entrance requirements:* For master's, GMAT. Additional exam requirements/recommendations for international students: Required—TOEFL (minimum score 500 paper-based; 173 computer-based; 61 iBT), IELTS (minimum score 5). *Application deadline:*

For fall admission, 7/1 for domestic students, 4/1 for international students; for spring admission, 11/1 for domestic students, 9/1 for international students. Application fee: $45 ($80 for international students). *Expenses:* Tuition, state resident: full-time $4172; part-time $231.75 per credit hour. Tuition, nonresident: full-time $15,332; part-time $851.75 per credit hour. *Financial support:* In 2010–11, 282 research assistantships (averaging $13,930 per year), 74 teaching assistantships (averaging $9,284 per year) were awarded; scholarships/grants, tuition waivers, and unspecified assistantships also available. Support available to part-time students. *Unit head:* Dr. Lynda Y. de la Vinna, Dean, 210-458-4317, Fax: 210-458-4308, E-mail: lynda.delavina@utsa.edu. *Application contact:* Veronica Ramirez, Assistant Dean of the Graduate School, 210-458-4330, Fax: 210-458-4332, E-mail: graduatestudies@utsa.edu.

University of the Incarnate Word, School of Graduate Studies and Research, H-E-B School of Business and Administration, Programs in Accounting, San Antonio, TX 78209-6397. Offers MS. Part-time and evening/weekend programs available. *Students:* 42 full-time (26 women), 32 part-time (20 women); includes 4 Black or African American, non-Hispanic/Latino; 2 Asian, non-Hispanic/Latino; 29 Hispanic/Latino, 5 international. Average age 30. In 2010, 25 master's awarded. *Entrance requirements:* For master's, GMAT. Additional exam requirements/recommendations for international students: Required—TOEFL (minimum score 560 paper-based; 220 computer-based; 83 iBT). *Application deadline:* Applications are processed on a rolling basis. Application fee: $20. Electronic applications accepted. *Expenses:* Tuition: Part-time $725 per contact hour. Required fees: $890 per semester. *Financial support:* Federal Work-Study and scholarships/grants available. Financial award applicants required to submit FAFSA. *Unit head:* Dr. Henry Elrod, 210-829-3184, Fax: 210-805-3564, E-mail: elrod@uiwtx.edu. *Application contact:* Andrea Cyterski-Acosta, Dean of Enrollment, 210-829-6005, Fax: 210-829-3921, E-mail: admis@uiwtx.edu.

The University of Toledo, College of Graduate Studies, College of Business and Innovation, Department of Accounting, Toledo, OH 43606-3390. Offers MSA. Part-time and evening/weekend programs available. *Faculty:* 5. *Students:* 33 full-time (18 women), 21 part-time (15 women); includes 2 Black or African American, non-Hispanic/Latino; 2 Hispanic/Latino, 16 international. Average age 27. 49 applicants, 71% accepted, 21 enrolled. In 2010, 20 master's awarded. *Entrance requirements:* For master's, GMAT, 2.7 GPA for all prior academic work. Three letters of recommendation, a statement of purpose, and transcripts from all prior institutions attended. Additional exam requirements/recommendations for international students: Required—TOEFL (minimum score 550 paper-based; 213 computer-based; 80 iBT), IELTS (minimum score 6.5). *Application deadline:* For fall admission, 1/15 priority date for domestic and international students. Applications are processed on a rolling basis. Application fee: $45 ($75 for international students). Electronic applications accepted. *Expenses:* Tuition, state resident: full-time $11,426; part-time $476 per credit hour. Tuition, nonresident: full-time $21,660; part-time $903 per credit hour. One-time fee: $62. *Financial support:* Research assistantships with tuition reimbursements, career-related internships or fieldwork, Federal Work-Study, institutionally sponsored loans, scholarships/grants, tuition waivers (full and partial), and unspecified assistantships available. Support available to part-time students. *Faculty research:* Estate gift tax, audit and legal liability, corporate tax, accounting information systems. *Unit head:* Dr. Donald Saftner, Chair. *Application contact:* Graduate School Office, 419-530-4723, Fax: 419-530-4724, E-mail: grdsch@utnet.utoledo.edu.

University of Tulsa, Graduate School, Collins College of Business, Master of Business Administration Program, Tulsa, OK 74104-3189. Offers accounting (MBA); business administration (MBA); energy management (MBA); finance (MBA); international business (MBA); management information systems (MBA); taxation (MBA); JD/MBA; MBA/MSCS; MBA/MSF. *Accreditation:* AACSB. Part-time and evening/weekend programs available. *Faculty:* 32 full-time (6 women). *Students:* 39 full-time (14 women), 40 part-time (16 women); includes 7 minority (1 Black or African American, non-Hispanic/Latino; 2 Asian, non-Hispanic/Latino; 4 Hispanic/Latino), 9 international. Average age 26. 73 applicants, 55% accepted, 18 enrolled. In 2010, 55 master's awarded. *Entrance requirements:* For master's, GMAT. Additional exam requirements/recommendations for international students: Required—TOEFL (minimum score 575 paper-based; 232 computer-based; 90 iBT), IELTS (minimum score 6.5). *Application deadline:* Applications are processed on a rolling basis. Application fee: $40. Electronic applications accepted. *Expenses:* Tuition: Full-time $16,902; part-time $939 per credit hour. Required fees: $1020; $4 per credit hour. Tuition and fees vary according to course load. *Financial support:* In 2010–11, 56 students received support, including 23 fellowships (averaging $4,872 per year), 4 research assistantships (averaging $9,323 per year), 29 teaching assistantships (averaging $10,642 per year); career-related internships or fieldwork, institutionally sponsored loans, scholarships/grants, health care benefits, tuition waivers (full and partial), and unspecified assistantships also available. Support available to part-time students. Financial award application deadline: 2/1; financial award applicants required to submit FAFSA. *Faculty research:* Accounting, energy management, finance, international business, management information systems, taxation. *Unit head:* Dr. Linda Nichols, Associate Dean of the Collins College of Business, 918-631-2242,

Fax: 918-631-2142, E-mail: linda-nichols@utulsa.edu. *Application contact:* Dr. Linda Nichols, Associate Dean of the Collins College of Business, 918-631-2242, Fax: 918-631-2142, E-mail: linda-nichols@utulsa.edu.

University of Utah, Graduate School, David Eccles School of Business, Business Administration Program, Salt Lake City, UT 84112. Offers accounting (PhD); business administration (EMBA, MBA, PMBA); statistics (M Stat). Part-time and evening/weekend programs available. *Faculty:* 18 full-time (8 women). *Students:* 608 full-time (118 women), 31 part-time (9 women); includes 53 minority (4 Black or African American, non-Hispanic/Latino; 2 American Indian or Alaska Native, non-Hispanic/Latino; 27 Asian, non-Hispanic/Latino; 15 Hispanic/Latino; 5 Two or more races, non-Hispanic/Latino), 47 international. Average age 32. 930 applicants, 45% accepted, 311 enrolled. In 2010, 256 master's, 8 doctorates awarded. Terminal master's awarded for partial completion of doctoral program. *Degree requirements:* For doctorate, thesis/dissertation, oral qualifying exams, written qualifying exams. *Entrance requirements:* For master's, GMAT, statistics course with minimum B grade, minimum undergraduate GPA of 3.0; for doctorate, GMAT or GRE General Test. Additional exam requirements/recommendations for international students: Required—TOEFL (minimum score 600 paper-based; 250 computer-based; 100 iBT), IELTS (minimum score 7). *Application deadline:* For fall admission, 2/15 priority date for domestic and international students. Applications are processed on a rolling basis. Application fee: $55 ($65 for international students). Electronic applications accepted. *Expenses:* Contact institution. *Financial support:* In 2010–11, 20 students received support, including 1 fellowship with partial tuition reimbursement available (averaging $9,000 per year), 58 teaching assistantships with partial tuition reimbursements available (averaging $6,350 per year); scholarships/grants and unspecified assistantships also available. Financial award application deadline: 2/15; financial award applicants required to submit FAFSA. *Faculty research:* Corporate finance, strategy services, consumer behavior, financial disclosures, operations. Total annual research expenditures: $60,805. *Unit head:* Linda Wells, Program Director of MBA Program, Fax: 801-581-3666. *Application contact:* Andrea Chmelik, Coordinator, 801-581-1719, Fax: 801-581-3666, E-mail: andrea.chmelik@business.utah.edu.

University of Utah, Graduate School, David Eccles School of Business, School of Accounting, Salt Lake City, UT 84112. Offers M Acc, PhD. *Accreditation:* AACSB. Part-time and evening/weekend programs available. *Faculty:* 16 full-time (7 women). *Students:* 95 full-time (33 women), 34 part-time (17 women); includes 7 minority (3 Asian, non-Hispanic/Latino; 3 Hispanic/Latino; 1 Two or more races, non-Hispanic/Latino), 4 international. Average age 28. 182 applicants, 64% accepted, 85 enrolled. In 2010, 83 master's awarded. *Degree requirements:* For doctorate, thesis/dissertation, oral qualifying exams, written qualifying exams. *Entrance requirements:* For master's, GMAT, minimum undergraduate GPA of 3.0; for doctorate, GMAT. Additional exam requirements/recommendations for international students: Required—TOEFL (minimum score 600 paper-based; 250 computer-based; 100 iBT), IELTS (minimum score 7). *Application deadline:* For fall admission, 3/1 priority date for domestic and international students; for spring admission, 11/1 for domestic and international students. Applications are processed on a rolling basis. Application fee: $55 ($65 for international students). Electronic applications accepted. *Expenses:* Contact institution. *Financial support:* In 2010–11, 15 students received support, including 8 fellowships with partial tuition reimbursements available (averaging $5,500 per year), 6 teaching assistantships with partial tuition reimbursements available (averaging $1,100 per year); research assistantships, Federal Work-Study, tuition waivers (full), and unspecified assistantships also available. Financial award application deadline: 4/1; financial award applicants required to submit FAFSA. *Faculty research:* Auditing, taxation, information systems, financial accounting, accounting theory, international accounting. Total annual research expenditures: $107,924. *Unit head:* Dr. Martha Eining, Chair, 801-581-7673, Fax: 801-581-3581, E-mail: martha.eining@utah.edu. *Application contact:* Andrea Chmelik, Admissions Coordinator, 801-585-1719, Fax: 801-581-3666, E-mail: andrea.chmelik@business.utah.edu.

University of Vermont, Graduate College, School of Business Administration, Program in Accounting, Burlington, VT 05405. Offers M Acc. *Students:* 12 (10 women); includes 1 Asian, non-Hispanic/Latino, 1 international. 45 applicants, 42% accepted, 7 enrolled. In 2010, 4 master's awarded. *Entrance requirements:* For master's, GMAT, GRE. Additional exam requirements/recommendations for international students: Required—TOEFL (minimum score 550 paper-based; 213 computer-based; 80 iBT). *Application deadline:* For fall admission, 4/1 for domestic and international students; for spring admission, 12/1 for domestic and international students. Applications are processed on a rolling basis. Application fee: $40. Electronic applications accepted. *Expenses:* Tuition, state resident: part-time $537 per credit hour. Tuition, nonresident: part-time $1355 per credit hour. *Unit head:* Dr. Michael Gurdon, Coordinator, 802-656-3177. *Application contact:* Dr. M. Gurdon, Coordinator, 802-656-0513.

University of Virginia, McIntire School of Commerce, Program in Accounting, Charlottesville, VA 22903. Offers MS. *Accreditation:* AACSB. *Students:* 106 full-time (48 women); includes 7 Black or African American, non-Hispanic/Latino; 11 Asian, non-Hispanic/Latino; 9 Hispanic/Latino; 3 Two or more races, non-Hispanic/Latino, 11 international. Average age 23.

183 applicants, 58% accepted, 68 enrolled. In 2010, 107 master's awarded. *Entrance requirements:* For master's, GMAT, 2 letters of recommendation, 12 hours of accounting courses. Additional exam requirements/recommendations for international students: Required—TOEFL (minimum score 600 paper-based; 250 computer-based; 100 iBT), IELTS (minimum score 7). *Application deadline:* For fall admission, 9/1 priority date for domestic students, 12/1 for international students. Applications are processed on a rolling basis. Application fee: $75. Electronic applications accepted. *Expenses:* Contact institution. *Financial support:* Fellowships, Federal Work-Study available. Financial award applicants required to submit FAFSA. *Unit head:* Carl P. Zeithaml, Dean, 434-924-3110. *Application contact:* Cathy Fox, Senior Associate Director for Graduate Admissions, 434-924-3571, E-mail: msaccounting@virginia.edu.

University of Washington, Tacoma, Graduate Programs, MBA Programs, Tacoma, WA 98402-3100. Offers accounting (MBA); business administration (MBA); certified financial analyst (MBA). Part-time and evening/weekend programs available. *Faculty:* 24 full-time (8 women), 3 part-time/adjunct (0 women). *Students:* 42 full-time (13 women), 14 part-time (4 women); includes 1 Black or African American, non-Hispanic/Latino; 8 Asian, non-Hispanic/Latino; 2 Hispanic/Latino, 1 international. Average age 32. 42 applicants, 76% accepted, 29 enrolled. In 2010, 18 master's awarded. *Entrance requirements:* For master's, GMAT, minimum GPA of 3.0 in final graded 90 quarter credits or 60 graded semester credits; at least 2 years of professional/management work experience. Additional exam requirements/recommendations for international students: Required—TOEFL (minimum score 580 paper-based; 237 computer-based; 92 iBT). *Application deadline:* For fall admission, 4/15 priority date for domestic students. Applications are processed on a rolling basis. Application fee: $65. Electronic applications accepted. *Expenses:* Contact institution. *Financial support:* Scholarships/grants available. *Faculty research:* International accounting, marketing, change management, investments, corporate social responsibility. *Unit head:* Dr. Shahrokh Saudagaran, Dean, 253-692-5630, Fax: 253-692-4523, E-mail: uwtmba@u.washington.edu. *Application contact:* Aubree Robinson, Academic Adviser, MBA and Undergraduate Programs, 253-692-5630, Fax: 253-692-4523, E-mail: uwtmba@u.washington.edu.

University of West Florida, College of Business, Department of Accounting, Pensacola, FL 32514-5750. Offers M Acc, MA. Part-time and evening/weekend programs available. *Faculty:* 10 full-time (0 women), 1 part-time/adjunct (0 women). *Students:* 13 full-time (6 women), 33 part-time (24 women); includes 2 Black or African American, non-Hispanic/Latino; 3 Asian, non-Hispanic/Latino; 2 Hispanic/Latino, 1 international. Average age 31. 37 applicants, 73% accepted, 17 enrolled. In 2010, 17 master's awarded. *Entrance requirements:* For master's, GMAT (minimum score 450) or equivalent GRE score, bachelor's degree, two letters of recommendation, resume. Additional exam requirements/recommendations for international students: Required—TOEFL (minimum score 550 paper-based; 213 computer-based). *Application deadline:* For fall admission, 6/30 priority date for domestic students, 5/15 for international students; for spring admission, 10/1 for domestic and international students. Application fee: $30. *Expenses:* Tuition, state resident: full-time $4982; part-time $208 per credit hour. Tuition, nonresident: full-time $20,059; part-time $836 per credit hour. Required fees: $1365; $57 per credit hour. *Financial support:* In 2010–11, 15 fellowships (averaging $520 per year), 3 research assistantships with partial tuition reimbursements (averaging $2,068 per year) were awarded; unspecified assistantships also available. Financial award application deadline: 4/15; financial award applicants required to submit FAFSA. *Faculty research:* Audit risk, tax legislation, product costing, bank core deposit intangibles, financial reporting. *Unit head:* Dr. Robert Fahnestock, Chairperson, 850-474-2738. *Application contact:* Terry McCray, Assistant Director of Graduate Admissions, 850-473-7718, Fax: 850-473-7714, E-mail: gradadmissions@uwf.edu.

University of West Georgia, Richards College of Business, Department of Accounting and Finance, Carrollton, GA 30118. Offers MP Acc. *Accreditation:* AACSB. Part-time and evening/weekend programs available. *Faculty:* 8 full-time (2 women). *Students:* 21 full-time (9 women), 9 part-time (6 women); includes 5 Black or African American, non-Hispanic/Latino; 2 Hispanic/Latino, 4 international. Average age 30. 26 applicants, 54% accepted, 3 enrolled. In 2010, 18 master's awarded. *Degree requirements:* For master's, comprehensive exam. *Entrance requirements:* For master's, GMAT, minimum GPA of 2.5. Additional exam requirements/recommendations for international students: Required—TOEFL (minimum score 550 paper-based; 213 computer-based). *Application deadline:* For fall admission, 7/17 for domestic students; for spring admission, 11/20 for domestic students. Applications are processed on a rolling basis. Application fee: $30. Electronic applications accepted. *Expenses:* Tuition, state resident: full-time $4130; part-time $173 per semester hour. Tuition, nonresident: full-time $16,524; part-time $689 per semester hour. Required fees: $1586; $44.01 per semester hour. $397 per semester. Tuition and fees vary according to program. *Financial support:* In 2010–11, 1 student received support, including 1 research assistantship with full tuition reimbursement available (averaging $4,500 per year); tuition waivers (partial) also available. Financial award application deadline: 7/1; financial award applicants required to submit FAFSA. *Faculty research:* Taxpayer insolvency, non-gap financial measures, deferred taxes, financial accounting issues. Total annual research expenditures: $40,000. *Unit head:* Dr. James R. Colley, Chair, 678-839-6469, Fax: 678-839-5041, E-mail: jcolley@westga.edu. *Application contact:* Dr. Charles W. Clark, Dean, 678-839-6508, E-mail: cclark@westga.edu.

University of Wisconsin–Madison, Graduate School, Wisconsin School of Business, Doctoral Program in Accounting and Information Systems, Madison, WI 53706-1380. Offers PhD. *Accreditation:* AACSB. *Faculty:* 12 full-time (4 women), 5 part-time/adjunct (2 women). *Students:* 11 full-time (6 women), 1 international. Average age 30. 82 applicants, 11% accepted, 5 enrolled. In 2010, 4 doctorates awarded. *Degree requirements:* For doctorate, comprehensive exam, thesis/dissertation. *Entrance requirements:* For doctorate, GMAT or GRE. Additional exam requirements/recommendations for international students: Required—Pearson Test of English (minimum score 73, written 80); Recommended—TOEFL (minimum score 623 paper-based; 263 computer-based; 106 iBT), IELTS (minimum score 7.5). *Application deadline:* For fall admission, 12/15 priority date for domestic and international students. Application fee: $56. Electronic applications accepted. *Expenses:* Tuition, state resident: full-time $9887; part-time $617.96 per credit. Tuition, nonresident: full-time $24,054; part-time $1503.40 per credit. Required fees: $67.63 per credit. Tuition and fees vary according to reciprocity agreements. *Financial support:* In 2010–11, 11 students received support, including 1 fellowship with full tuition reimbursement available (averaging $18,756 per year), research assistantships with full tuition reimbursements available (averaging $16,506 per year), 9 teaching assistantships with full tuition reimbursements available (averaging $14,088 per year); Federal Work-Study, institutionally sponsored loans, scholarships/grants, health care benefits, and unspecified assistantships also available. Financial award application deadline: 2/1. *Faculty research:* Auditing, financial reporting, economic theory, strategy, computer models. *Unit head:* Prof. Jon Davis, Chair, 608-263-4264. *Application contact:* Belle Heberling, Assistant Director for Research Programs, 608-262-3749, Fax: 608-890-0180, E-mail: phd@bus.wisc.edu.

Utica College, Program in Accountancy, Utica, NY 13502-4892. Offers MBA. Part-time and evening/weekend programs available. Postbaccalaureate distance learning degree programs offered. *Faculty:* 7 full-time (0 women). *Students:* 18 part-time (15 women); includes 1 Black or African American, non-Hispanic/Latino; 2 Hispanic/Latino. Average age 31. In 2010, 10 master's awarded. *Entrance requirements:* For master's, BS, minimum GPA of 3.0. Additional exam requirements/recommendations for international students: Required—TOEFL (minimum score 525 paper-based; 195 computer-based). *Application deadline:* Applications are processed on a rolling basis. Application fee: $50. Electronic applications accepted. *Expenses:* Contact institution. *Financial support:* Career-related internships or fieldwork, scholarships/grants, tuition waivers (partial), and unspecified assistantships available. Support available to part-time students. Financial award application deadline: 3/15; financial award applicants required to submit FAFSA. *Unit head:* Dr. Hartwell Herring, MBA Director, 315-792-3335, E-mail: hherring@utica.edu. *Application contact:* John D. Rowe, Director of Graduate Admissions, 315-792-3824, Fax: 315-792-3003, E-mail: jrowe@utica.edu.

Vanderbilt University, Owen Graduate School of Management and Graduate School, Master of Accountancy Program, Nashville, TN 37240-1001. Offers M Acc. *Accreditation:* AACSB. *Faculty:* 37 full-time (5 women), 25 part-time/adjunct (0 women). *Students:* 28 full-time (15 women); includes 1 Black or African American, non-Hispanic/Latino; 3 Asian, non-Hispanic/Latino. Average age 23. 159 applicants, 24% accepted, 28 enrolled. In 2010, 28 master's awarded. *Entrance requirements:* For master's, GMAT or GRE. Additional exam requirements/recommendations for international students: Required—TOEFL, IELTS. *Application deadline:* For fall admission, 10/11 priority date for domestic students, 10/11 for international students; for winter admission, 1/10 for domestic and international students; for spring admission, 3/1 for domestic students. Application fee: $50. Electronic applications accepted. *Expenses:* Contact institution. *Financial support:* Scholarships/grants and tuition waivers available. Financial award application deadline: 5/1; financial award applicants required to submit FAFSA. *Faculty research:* Financial marketing, operations, human resources. *Unit head:* Dr. Karl Hackbrack, Faculty, 615-322-3641, E-mail: karl.hackenbrack@owen.vanderbilt.edu. *Application contact:* Amy Johnson, Program Director, 615-322-6509, Fax: 615-343-1175, E-mail: ajohnson@owen.vanderbilt.edu.

Villanova University, Villanova School of Business, Master of Accountancy Program, Villanova, PA 19085. Offers MAC. *Accreditation:* AACSB. *Faculty:* 5 full-time (1 woman), 3 part-time/adjunct (2 women). *Students:* 41 part-time (17 women); includes 10 minority (5 Black or African American, non-Hispanic/Latino; 4 Asian, non-Hispanic/Latino; 1 Hispanic/Latino). Average age 25. In 2010, 44 master's awarded. *Degree requirements:* For master's, minimum cumulative GPA of 3.0. *Entrance requirements:* For master's, accounting major or the following pre-requisite courses: intermediate accounting I and II, federal income tax and auditing. Additional exam requirements/recommendations for international students: Required—TOEFL (minimum score 550 paper-based; 213 computer-based; 80 iBT). *Application deadline:* For spring admission, 3/31 for domestic and international students. Applications are processed on a rolling basis. Application fee: $50. Electronic applications accepted. *Expenses:* Tuition: Part-time $700 per credit. Part-time tuition and fees vary according to degree level and program. *Financial support:* Career-related internships or fieldwork and scholarships/grants available. Support available to part-time students. Financial award application deadline: 6/30; financial award applicants required to submit FAFSA. *Faculty research:* Global accounting standards, strategic planning and cost measurement, performance evaluation, the impact of e-business on the business value chain. *Unit head:* Meredith L. Kwiatek, Assistant Director, 610-519-7016, Fax: 610-519-6273, E-mail: meredith.kwiatek@villanova.edu. *Application contact:* Meredith L. Kwiatek, Assistant Director, 610-519-7016, Fax: 610-519-6273, E-mail: meredith.kwiatek@villanova.edu.

Virginia Commonwealth University, Graduate School, School of Business, Program in Accounting, Richmond, VA 23284-9005. Offers M Acc, MBA, PhD. *Accreditation:* AACSB. *Faculty:* 12 full-time (3 women). *Students:* 39 full-time (26 women), 17 part-time (9 women); includes 20 minority (13 Black or African American, non-Hispanic/Latino; 4 Asian, non-Hispanic/Latino; 1 Hispanic/Latino; 2 Two or more races, non-Hispanic/Latino), 11 international. 56 applicants, 64% accepted, 20 enrolled. In 2010, 27 master's awarded. *Degree requirements:* For doctorate, thesis/dissertation. *Entrance requirements:* For master's, GMAT; for doctorate, GMAT, relevant work experience. Additional exam requirements/recommendations for international students: Required—TOEFL (minimum score 600 paper-based; 250 computer-based; 100 iBT). *Application deadline:* For fall admission, 7/15 for domestic students; for spring admission, 11/15 for domestic students. Applications are processed on a rolling basis. Application fee: $50. Electronic applications accepted. *Expenses:* Tuition, state resident: full-time $4308; part-time $479 per credit hour. Tuition, nonresident: full-time $8942; part-time $994 per credit hour. Required fees: $2000; $85 per credit hour. Tuition and fees vary according to course level, course load, degree level, campus/location and program. *Financial support:* Fellowships, research assistantships, teaching assistantships, Federal Work-Study, institutionally sponsored loans, and tuition waivers (full and partial) available. Financial award application deadline: 3/15; financial award applicants required to submit FAFSA. *Unit head:* Dr. Carolyn S. Norman, Professor and Interim Chair of the Department of Accounting, 804-828-3160, E-mail: castrand@vcu.edu. *Application contact:* Jana P. McQuaid, Assistant Dean, Masters Programs, 804-828-4622, Fax: 804-828-7174, E-mail: jpmcquaid@vcu.edu.

Virginia Polytechnic Institute and State University, Graduate School, Pamplin College of Business, Department of Accounting and Information Systems, Blacksburg, VA 24061. Offers MACIS, PhD. *Accreditation:* AACSB. *Faculty:* 24 full-time (8 women). *Students:* 122 full-time (66 women), 7 part-time (4 women); includes 2 Black or African American, non-Hispanic/Latino; 8 Asian, non-Hispanic/Latino; 4 Hispanic/Latino, 39 international. Average age 26. 191 applicants, 55% accepted, 70 enrolled. In 2010, 75 master's, 5 doctorates awarded. *Degree requirements:* For master's, comprehensive exam (for some programs), thesis (for some programs); for doctorate, comprehensive exam (for some programs), thesis/dissertation (for some programs). *Entrance requirements:* For master's and doctorate, GRE. Additional exam requirements/recommendations for international students: Required—TOEFL (minimum score 550 paper-based; 213 computer-based). *Application deadline:* For fall admission, 7/1 for domestic and international students; for spring admission, 12/1 for domestic and international students. Applications are processed on a rolling basis. Application fee: $65. Electronic applications accepted. *Expenses:* Tuition, state resident: full-time $9399; part-time $488 per credit hour. Tuition, nonresident: full-time $17,854; part-time $957.75 per credit hour. Required fees: $1534. Full-time tuition and fees vary according to program. *Financial support:* In 2010–11, 3 fellowships with full tuition reimbursements (averaging $22,103 per year), 13 teaching assistantships with full tuition reimbursements (averaging $14,160 per year) were awarded; career-related internships or fieldwork, Federal Work-Study, scholarships/grants, health care benefits, and unspecified assistantships also available. Financial award application deadline: 1/15. *Faculty research:* Financial accounting, international accounting, management accounting. Total annual research expenditures: $225,770. *Unit head:* Dr. Robert M. Brown, UNIT HEAD, 540-231-6591, Fax: 540-231-2511, E-mail: acis@vt.edu. *Application contact:* Linda Wallace, Contact, 540-231-6328, Fax: 540-231-2511, E-mail: wallacel@vt.edu.

Wagner College, Division of Graduate Studies, Department of Business Administration, Program in Accounting, Staten Island, NY 10301-4495. Offers MS. Part-time programs available. *Faculty:* 3 full-time (all women), 1 part-time/adjunct (0 women). *Students:* 24 full-time (9 women), 9 part-time (4 women); includes 5 minority (1 Black or African American, non-Hispanic/Latino; 1 Asian, non-Hispanic/Latino; 2 Hispanic/Latino; 1 Two or more races, non-Hispanic/Latino). Average age 23. 29 applicants, 100% accepted, 24 enrolled. In 2010, 20 master's awarded. *Degree requirements:* For master's, thesis. *Entrance requirements:* For master's, bachelor's degree in accounting or business with a concentration in accounting. Additional exam requirements/recommendations for international students: Required—TOEFL (minimum score 550 paper-based; 217 computer-based; 79 iBT). *Application deadline:* For fall admission, 5/1 priority date for domestic students, 3/1 priority date for international students; for spring admission, 12/1 priority date for domestic students, 10/1 for international students. Applications are processed on a rolling basis. Application fee: $50 ($85 for international students). *Expenses:* Tuition: Full-time $15,570; part-time $865 per credit. *Financial* *support:* Career-related internships or fieldwork, unspecified assistantships, and alumni fellowship grant available. Financial award applicants required to submit FAFSA. *Unit head:* Prof. Margaret Horan, Director, 718-390-3437. *Application contact:* Patricia Clancy, Administrative Assistant, Admissions, 718-420-4464, Fax: 718-390-3105, E-mail: patricia.clancy@wagner.edu.

Wake Forest University, Schools of Business, MSA Program in Accountancy, Winston-Salem, NC 27106. Offers assurance services (MSA); tax consulting (MSA); transaction services (MSA). *Faculty:* 63 full-time (17 women), 30 part-time/adjunct (9 women). *Students:* 126 full-time (62 women); includes 22 minority (14 Black or African American, non-Hispanic/Latino; 1 American Indian or Alaska Native, non-Hispanic/Latino; 5 Asian, non-Hispanic/Latino; 2 Hispanic/Latino), 14 international. Average age 23. In 2010, 74 master's awarded. *Degree requirements:* For master's, 30 total credit hours. *Entrance requirements:* For master's, GMAT, letters of recommendation, official transcripts, current resume or curriculum vitae. Additional exam requirements/recommendations for international students: Required—TOEFL (minimum score 600 paper-based; 250 computer-based; 100 iBT), Pearson Test of English (PTE). *Application deadline:* For fall admission, 6/1 for domestic and international students. Applications are processed on a rolling basis. Application fee: $100. Electronic applications accepted. *Financial support:* In 2010–11, 103 students received support. Career-related internships or fieldwork and scholarships/grants available. Financial award application deadline: 2/15; financial award applicants required to submit FAFSA. *Faculty research:* The influence of personal relationships on business decision making and management of change; drivers of perceived value and consumer behavior; impact of accounting on auditing, financial, managerial, systems and taxation stakeholders; corporate governance and executive compensation; impact of operations strategies on competitiveness. *Unit head:* Yvonne Hinson, Director of Accountancy, 336-758-5305, Fax: 336-758-6133, E-mail: knappmm@wfu.edu. *Application contact:* Mary Knapp, Administrative Assistant, 336-758-5305, Fax: 336-758-6133, E-mail: knappmm@wfu.edu.

Walden University, Graduate Programs, School of Management, Minneapolis, MN 55401. Offers accounting (MS), including cpa emphasis, professional track, self-designed; accounting and management (MS), including self-designed, strategic management; applied management and decision sciences (PhD), including accounting, engineering management, finance, general applied management and decision sciences, information systems management, knowledge management, leadership and organizational change, learning management, operations research, self-designed program in applied management and design sciences; business information management (MISM); enterprise information security (MISM); entrepreneurship (MBA, DBA); finance (MBA, DBA); global management (MS); global supply chain management (DBA); health informatics (MISM); healthcare management (MBA, MS); healthcare system improvement (MBA); human resource management (MBA, MS), including functional human resource management (MS), human resource management (MS), integrating functional and strategic human resource management (MS), organizational strategy (MS); information systems (MS); information systems management (DBA); information technology (MS), including information security, software engineering; international business (MBA, DBA); IT strategy and governance (MISM); leadership (MBA, MS, DBA), including entrepreneurship (MS), general management (MS), human resources leadership (MS), innovation and technology (MS), leader development (MS), leading sustainability (MS), project management (MS), self-designed (MS); managers as leaders (MS); managing global software and service supply chains (MISM); marketing (MBA, DBA); project management (MBA, MS); research strategies (MS); risk management (MBA); self-designed (MBA, DBA); social impact management (DBA); strategy and operations (MS); sustainable futures (MBA); sustainable management (MS); technology (MBA); technology entrepreneurship (DBA); technology management (MS). Part-time and evening/weekend programs available. Postbaccalaureate distance learning degree programs offered (minimal on-campus study). *Faculty:* 22 full-time (8 women), 291 part-time/adjunct (100 women). *Students:* 3,705 full-time (1,956 women), 976 part-time (549 women); includes 2,432 minority (2,021 Black or African American, non-Hispanic/Latino; 32 American Indian or Alaska Native, non-Hispanic/Latino; 137 Asian, non-Hispanic/Latino; 193 Hispanic/Latino; 5 Native Hawaiian or other Pacific Islander, non-Hispanic/Latino; 44 Two or more races, non-Hispanic/Latino), 302 international. Average age 40. In 2010, 658 master's, 86 doctorates awarded. *Degree requirements:* For doctorate, thesis/dissertation (for some programs), residency. *Entrance requirements:* For master's, bachelor's degree or equivalent in related field; minimum GPA of 2.5; official transcripts; goal statement; access to computer and Internet; for doctorate, master's degree or equivalent in related field; minimum GPA of 3.0; 3 years of related professional/academic experience (preferred). Additional exam requirements/recommendations for international students: Required—TOEFL (minimum score 550 paper-based; 213 computer-based), IELTS (minimum score 6.5), Michigan English Language Assessment Battery (minimum score 82). *Application deadline:* Applications are processed on a rolling basis. Application fee: $50. Electronic applications accepted. *Expenses:* Tuition: Full-time $10,274; part-time $445 per credit. Tuition and fees vary according to course load, degree level and program. *Financial support:* Fellowships, Federal Work-Study, scholarships/grants, unspecified assistantships, and family tuition reduction, active duty/veteran tuition reduction, group tuition reduction, interest-free payment plans

available. Support available to part-time students. Financial award applicants required to submit FAFSA. *Unit head:* Dr. William Schulz, Associate Dean, 800-925-3368. *Application contact:* Jennifer Hall, Vice President of Enrollment Management, 866-4-WALDEN, E-mail: info@waldenu.edu.

Washington State University, Graduate School, College of Business, Business Administration Programs, Pullman, WA 99164. Offers business administration (MBA, PhD), including accounting (PhD), finance (PhD), management and operations (PhD), management information systems (PhD), marketing (PhD). *Accreditation:* AACSB. *Faculty:* 47. *Students:* 117 full-time (42 women), 117 part-time (30 women); includes 24 minority (1 Black or African American, non-Hispanic/Latino; 17 Asian, non-Hispanic/Latino; 5 Hispanic/Latino; 1 Two or more races, non-Hispanic/Latino), 48 international. Average age 32. 347 applicants, 19% accepted, 43 enrolled. In 2010, 58 master's, 5 doctorates awarded. *Degree requirements:* For master's, comprehensive exam (for some programs), thesis (for some programs), final presentation; for doctorate, comprehensive exam, thesis/dissertation, oral and written exams. *Entrance requirements:* For master's and doctorate, GMAT, minimum GPA of 3.0, 3 letters of recommendation. Additional exam requirements/recommendations for international students: Required—TOEFL. *Application deadline:* For fall admission, 3/1 priority date for domestic students, 3/1 for international students; for spring admission, 6/1 priority date for domestic students, 6/1 for international students. Applications are processed on a rolling basis. Application fee: $50. Electronic applications accepted. *Expenses:* Tuition, state resident: full-time $8552; part-time $443 per credit. Tuition, nonresident: full-time $21,650; part-time $1083 per credit. Required fees: $846. *Financial support:* In 2010–11, 102 students received support, including 36 teaching assistantships with full and partial tuition reimbursements available (averaging $18,204 per year); career-related internships or fieldwork, Federal Work-Study, institutionally sponsored loans, health care benefits, tuition waivers (partial), unspecified assistantships, and teaching associateships also available. Financial award application deadline: 4/1. Total annual research expenditures: $344,000. *Unit head:* Dr. Eric Spangenberg, Dean, 509-335-8150, E-mail: ers@wsu.edu. *Application contact:* Graduate School Admissions, 800-GRADWSU, Fax: 509-335-1949, E-mail: gradsch@wsu.edu.

Washington State University, Graduate School, College of Business, Department of Accounting, Pullman, WA 99164. Offers accounting and information systems (M Acc); accounting and taxation (M Acc). *Accreditation:* AACSB. *Faculty:* 9. *Students:* 47 full-time (25 women), 13 part-time (5 women); includes 7 minority (2 American Indian or Alaska Native, non-Hispanic/Latino; 4 Asian, non-Hispanic/Latino; 1 Hispanic/Latino), 19 international. Average age 27. 123 applicants, 37% accepted, 45 enrolled. In 2010, 28 master's awarded. *Degree requirements:* For master's, comprehensive exam (for some programs), thesis (for some programs), oral exam, research paper. *Entrance requirements:* For master's, GMAT (minimum score of 600), resume; statement of purpose identifying area of interest, experiences, and intended research focus; minimum GPA of 3.25. Additional exam requirements/recommendations for international students: Required—TOEFL (minimum score 580 paper-based; 237 computer-based), IELTS. *Application deadline:* For fall admission, 1/10 priority date for domestic students, 1/10 for international students. Applications are processed on a rolling basis. Application fee: $50. Electronic applications accepted. *Expenses:* Tuition, state resident: full-time $8552; part-time $443 per credit. Tuition, nonresident: full-time $21,650; part-time $1083 per credit. Required fees: $846. *Financial support:* In 2010–11, research assistantships (averaging $13,917 per year), 7 teaching assistantships with tuition reimbursements (averaging $18,204 per year) were awarded; Federal Work-Study, institutionally sponsored loans, tuition waivers (partial), and teaching associateships also available. Financial award application deadline: 3/1. *Faculty research:* Ethics, taxation, auditing. *Unit head:* Dr. John Sweeney, Chair, 509-335-8541, Fax: 509-335-4275, E-mail: jtsweeney@wsu.edu. *Application contact:* Graduate School Admissions, 800-GRADWSU, Fax: 509-335-1949, E-mail: gradsch@wsu.edu.

Washington University in St. Louis, Olin Business School, Program in Accounting, St. Louis, MO 63130-4899. Offers MS. Part-time programs available. *Faculty:* 79 full-time (17 women), 42 part-time/adjunct (7 women). *Students:* 45 full-time (29 women); includes 3 minority (2 Asian, non-Hispanic/Latino; 1 Two or more races, non-Hispanic/Latino), 35 international. Average age 24. 358 applicants, 21% accepted, 44 enrolled. In 2010, 36 master's awarded. *Entrance requirements:* For master's, GMAT or GRE. Additional exam requirements/recommendations for international students: Required—TOEFL. *Application deadline:* For fall admission, 11/8 for domestic and international students; for winter admission, 2/7 for domestic and international students; for spring admission, 3/7 for domestic students. Application fee: $100. Electronic applications accepted. *Financial support:* Applicants required to submit FAFSA. *Unit head:* Joseph Peter Fox, Associate Dean and Director of MBA Programs, 314-935-6322, Fax: 314-935-4464, E-mail: fox@wustl.edu. *Application contact:* Dr. Gary Hochberg, Director, Specialized Master's Programs, 314-935-6380, Fax: 314-935-4464, E-mail: hochberg@wustl.edu.

Wayne State University, School of Business Administration, Detroit, MI 48202. Offers accounting (MSA); business administration (MBA, PhD); taxation (MST); JD/MBA. *Accreditation:* AACSB. Part-time and evening/

weekend programs available. Postbaccalaureate distance learning degree programs offered. *Faculty:* 40 full-time (10 women), 8 part-time/adjunct (0 women). *Students:* 240 full-time (99 women), 800 part-time (419 women); includes 325 minority (180 Black or African American, non-Hispanic/Latino; 1 American Indian or Alaska Native, non-Hispanic/Latino; 118 Asian, non-Hispanic/Latino; 22 Hispanic/Latino; 4 Two or more races, non-Hispanic/Latino), 152 international. Average age 28. 529 applicants, 71% accepted, 287 enrolled. In 2010, 345 degrees awarded. *Entrance requirements:* For master's, GMAT, minimum undergraduate GPA of 2.5. Additional exam requirements/recommendations for international students: Required—TOEFL (minimum score 550 paper-based; 213 computer-based); Recommended—TWE (minimum score 6). *Application deadline:* For fall admission, 6/1 for domestic students, 3/1 for international students; for winter admission, 10/1 for domestic students, 6/1 for international students; for spring admission, 2/1 for domestic students, 10/1 for international students. Applications are processed on a rolling basis. Application fee: $50. Electronic applications accepted. *Expenses:* Tuition, state resident: full-time $7662; part-time $478.85 per credit hour. Tuition, nonresident: full-time $16,920; part-time $1057.55 per credit hour. Required fees: $571.20; $35.70 per credit hour. $188.05 per semester. Tuition and fees vary according to course load and program. *Financial support:* In 2010–11, 17 research assistantships (averaging $15,000 per year) were awarded; career-related internships or fieldwork, Federal Work-Study, and scholarships/grants also available. Support available to part-time students. Financial award applicants required to submit FAFSA. *Faculty research:* Corporate financial valuation, strategic advertising, information technology effectiveness, financial accounting and taxation, organizational performance and effectiveness. *Unit head:* Dr. Margaret Williams, Interim Dean, 313-577-4501, Fax: 313-577-4557. *Application contact:* Linda Zaddach, Assistant Dean, 313-577-4510, E-mail: l.s.zaddach@wayne.edu.

Western Connecticut State University, Division of Graduate Studies and External Programs, Ancell School of Business, Program in Business Administration, Danbury, CT 06810-6885. Offers accounting (MBA); business administration (MBA). Part-time programs available. *Students:* 5 full-time (1 woman), 45 part-time (22 women); includes 2 Asian, non-Hispanic/Latino; 3 Hispanic/Latino. Average age 34. In 2010, 13 master's awarded. *Degree requirements:* For master's, comprehensive exam, completion of program within 8 years. *Entrance requirements:* For master's, GMAT. Additional exam requirements/recommendations for international students: Recommended—TOEFL (minimum score 550 paper-based; 213 computer-based; 79 iBT), IELTS (minimum score 6). *Application deadline:* For fall admission, 8/5 priority date for domestic students; for spring admission, 1/5 priority date for domestic students. Applications are processed on a rolling basis. Application fee: $50. *Expenses:* Tuition, state resident: full-time $5012; part-time $417 per credit hour. Tuition, nonresident: full-time $13,962; part-time $423 per credit hour. Required fees: $3886. Full-time tuition and fees vary according to course load, degree level and program. *Financial support:* In 2010–11, 1 student received support. Application deadline: 5/1. *Unit head:* Dr. Fred Tesch, MBA Coordinator, 203-837-8654, Fax: 203-837-8527. *Application contact:* Chris Shankle, Associate Director of Graduate Studies, 203-837-9005, Fax: 203-837-8326, E-mail: shanklec@wcsu.edu.

Western Illinois University, School of Graduate Studies, College of Business and Technology, Department of Accountancy, Macomb, IL 61455-1390. Offers M Acct. *Accreditation:* AACSB. Part-time programs available. *Students:* 16 full-time (6 women), 5 part-time (2 women), 3 international. Average age 24. 16 applicants, 50% accepted. In 2010, 13 master's awarded. *Degree requirements:* For master's, thesis or alternative. *Entrance requirements:* For master's, GMAT. Additional exam requirements/recommendations for international students: Required—TOEFL (minimum score 550 paper-based; 213 computer-based; 80 iBT). *Application deadline:* Applications are processed on a rolling basis. Application fee: $30. Electronic applications accepted. *Expenses:* Tuition, state resident: full-time $6370; part-time $265.40 per credit hour. Tuition, nonresident: full-time $12,740; part-time $530.80 per credit hour. Required fees: $75.67 per credit hour. *Financial support:* In 2010–11, 8 students received support, including 8 research assistantships with full tuition reimbursements available (averaging $7,280 per year). Financial award applicants required to submit FAFSA. *Unit head:* Dr. John Elfrink, Chairperson, 309-298-1152. *Application contact:* Evelyn Hoing, Assistant Director of Graduate Studies, 309-298-1806, Fax: 309-298-2345, E-mail: grad-office@wiu.edu.

Western New England University, School of Business, Program in Accounting, Springfield, MA 01119. Offers MSA. Part-time and evening/weekend programs available. *Students:* 51 part-time (31 women); includes 5 Black or African American, non-Hispanic/Latino; 1 Asian, non-Hispanic/Latino; 1 Hispanic/Latino. In 2010, 21 master's awarded. *Entrance requirements:* For master's, GMAT, 2 letters of reference, resume. *Application deadline:* Applications are processed on a rolling basis. Application fee: $30. *Expenses:* Tuition: Full-time $35,582. *Financial support:* Available to part-time students. Application deadline: 4/1. *Unit head:* Dr. William Bosworth, Chair, Accounting and Finance, 413-782-1231, E-mail: wboswort@wnec.edu. *Application contact:* Matt Fox, Director of Recruiting and Marketing for Adult Learners, 413-782-1249, Fax: 413-782-1779, E-mail: ce@wnec.edu.

Westminster College, The Bill and Vieve Gore School of Business, Salt Lake City, UT 84105-3697. Offers accountancy (M Acc); business administration (MBA, Certificate); technology management (MBATM). *Accreditation:* ACBSP. Part-time and evening/weekend programs available. Postbaccalaureate distance learning degree programs offered (minimal on-campus study). *Faculty:* 35 full-time (9 women), 22 part-time/adjunct (4 women). *Students:* 175 full-time (44 women), 242 part-time (61 women); includes 2 Black or African American, non-Hispanic/Latino; 2 American Indian or Alaska Native, non-Hispanic/Latino; 8 Asian, non-Hispanic/Latino; 6 Hispanic/Latino; 2 Two or more races, non-Hispanic/Latino, 6 international. Average age 32. 342 applicants, 46% accepted, 113 enrolled. In 2010, 196 master's, 75 other advanced degrees awarded. *Degree requirements:* For master's, international trip, minimum grade of C in all classes. *Entrance requirements:* For master's, GMAT, 2 professional recommendations, employer letter of support, personal resume, essay questions, official transcripts. Additional exam requirements/recommendations for international students: Required—TOEFL (minimum score 600 paper-based; 250 computer-based; 100 iBT), IELTS (minimum score 7). *Application deadline:* Applications are processed on a rolling basis. Application fee: $50. Electronic applications accepted. *Expenses:* Contact institution. *Financial support:* In 2010–11, 222 students received support. Career-related internships or fieldwork and tuition reimbursement, tuition remission available. Support available to part-time students. Financial award applicants required to submit FAFSA. *Faculty research:* Innovation and entrepreneurship, business strategy and change, financial analysis and capital budgeting, leadership development. Total annual research expenditures: $100,000. *Unit head:* Gary Daynes, Dean, 801-832-2600, Fax: 801-832-3106, E-mail: gdaynes@westminstercollege.edu. *Application contact:* Joel Bauman, Vice President of Enrollment Services, 801-832-2200, Fax: 801-832-3101, E-mail: admission@westminstercollege.edu.

Wichita State University, Graduate School, W. Frank Barton School of Business, School of Accountancy, Wichita, KS 67260. Offers M Acc. *Accreditation:* AACSB. Part-time and evening/weekend programs available. *Unit head:* Dr. Paul D. Harrison, Director, 316-978-3215, Fax: 316-978-3660, E-mail: paul.harrison@wichita.edu. *Application contact:* Michael B. Flores, Assistant Director and Graduate Advisor, 316-978-3724, E-mail: michael.flores@wichita.edu.

Widener University, School of Business Administration, Program in Accounting Information Systems, Chester, PA 19013-5792. Offers MS. Part-time and evening/weekend programs available. *Faculty:* 6 full-time (2 women), 3 part-time/adjunct (0 women). *Students:* 4 part-time (2 women). Average age 36. 9 applicants, 100% accepted. In 2010, 5 master's awarded. *Entrance requirements:* For master's, Certified Management Accountant Exam, Certified Public Accountant Exam, or GMAT, minimum GPA of 2.5. *Application deadline:* For fall admission, 8/1 priority date for domestic students; for spring admission, 12/1 for domestic students. Applications are processed on a rolling basis. Application fee: $25 ($300 for international students). Electronic applications accepted. *Financial support:* Application deadline: 5/1. *Unit head:* Frank C. Lordi, Head, 610-499-4308, E-mail: frank.c.lordi@widener.edu. *Application contact:* Ann Seltzer, Graduate Enrollment Administrator, 610-499-4305, E-mail: apseltzer@widener.edu.

Wilfrid Laurier University, Faculty of Graduate and Postdoctoral Studies, School of Business and Economics, Department of Business, Waterloo, ON N2L 3C5, Canada. Offers accounting (PhD); finance (M Fin); financial economics (PhD); marketing (PhD); operations and supply chain management (PhD); organizational behavior and human resource management (M Sc); organizational behaviour and human resource management (PhD); supply chain management (M Sc); technology management (EMTM). Part-time and evening/weekend programs available. *Faculty:* 67 full-time (20 women), 12 part-time/adjunct (4 women). *Students:* 20 full-time (11 women), 1 part-time (0 women), 5 international. 80 applicants, 28% accepted, 3 enrolled. In 2010, 6 master's, 1 doctorate awarded. *Degree requirements:* For master's, thesis optional; for doctorate, comprehensive exam, thesis/dissertation. *Entrance requirements:* For master's, GMAT, 4-year honors degree with minimum B+ average; for doctorate, GMAT, master's degree, minimum B+ average. Additional exam requirements/recommendations for international students: Required—TOEFL (minimum score 89 iBT). *Application deadline:* For fall admission, 1/15 priority date for domestic and international students. Application fee: $125. Electronic applications accepted. Tuition and fees charges are reported in Canadian dollars. *Expenses:* Tuition, area resident: Full-time $15,300 Canadian dollars; part-time $1200 Canadian dollars per credit. International tuition: $21,300 Canadian dollars full-time. Required fees: $650 Canadian dollars; $100 Canadian dollars per credit. Tuition and fees vary according to course load, degree level, campus/location and program. *Financial support:* In 2010–11, 27 fellowships, 1 research assistantship, 27 teaching assistantships were awarded; career-related internships or fieldwork, scholarships/grants, health care benefits, and unspecified assistantships also available. *Faculty research:* Financial economics, management and organizational behavior, operations and supply chain management. *Unit head:* Dr. Hamid Noori, Director, 519-884-0710 Ext. 2571, Fax: 519-884-2357, E-mail: sbephdmasters@wlu.ca. *Application contact:* Jennifer Williams, Graduate Admission and Records Officer, 519-884-0710 Ext. 3536, Fax: 519-884-1020, E-mail: gradstudies@wlu.ca.

Wilkes University, College of Graduate and Professional Studies, Jay S. Sidhu School of Business and Leadership, Wilkes-Barre, PA 18766-0002. Offers accounting (MBA); entrepreneurship (MBA); finance (MBA); health care administration (MBA); human resource management (MBA); international business (MBA); marketing (MBA); operations management (MBA); organizational leadership and development (MBA). *Accreditation:* ACBSP. Part-time and evening/weekend programs available. *Students:* 39 full-time (16 women), 146 part-time (71 women); includes 5 Black or African American, non-Hispanic/Latino; 2 Asian, non-Hispanic/Latino; 1 Hispanic/Latino; 1 Two or more races, non-Hispanic/Latino, 16 international. Average age 30. In 2010, 85 master's awarded. *Entrance requirements:* For master's, GMAT. Additional exam requirements/recommendations for international students: Required—TOEFL (minimum score 550 paper-based; 213 computer-based; 79 iBT). *Application deadline:* Applications are processed on a rolling basis. Application fee: $45 ($65 for international students). Electronic applications accepted. *Expenses:* Contact institution. *Financial support:* Federal Work-Study and unspecified assistantships available. Financial award application deadline: 3/1; financial award applicants required to submit FAFSA. *Unit head:* Dr. Paul Browne, Dean, 570-408-4701, Fax: 570-408-7846, E-mail: paul.browne@wilkes.edu. *Application contact:* Kathleen Houlihan, Director of Graduate Studies, 570-408-3235, Fax: 570-408-7846, E-mail: kathleen.houlihan@wilkes.edu.

Worcester State University, Graduate Studies, Program in Management, Worcester, MA 01602-2597. Offers accounting (MS); managerial leadership (MS). Part-time and evening/weekend programs available. *Faculty:* 1 (woman) full-time, 1 part-time/adjunct (0 women). *Students:* 7 full-time (2 women), 12 part-time (5 women); includes 1 Black or African American, non-Hispanic/Latino; 1 Two or more races, non-Hispanic/Latino, 4 international. Average age 28. 21 applicants, 76% accepted, 11 enrolled. In 2010, 4 master's awarded. *Degree requirements:* For master's, comprehensive exam (for some programs), thesis optional. *Entrance requirements:* Additional exam requirements/recommendations for international students: Required—TOEFL (minimum score 500 paper-based; 61 iBT). *Application deadline:* Applications are processed on a rolling basis. Application fee: $40. Electronic applications accepted. *Expenses:* Tuition, state resident: full-time $2700; part-time $150 per credit. Tuition, nonresident: full-time $2700; part-time $150 per credit. Required fees: $2016; $112 per credit. *Financial support:* In 2010–11, 2 students received support, including 2 research assistantships with full tuition reimbursements available (averaging $4,800 per year); career-related internships or fieldwork, scholarships/grants, and unspecified assistantships also available. Financial award application deadline: 3/1; financial award applicants required to submit FAFSA. *Unit head:* Dr. Laurie Dahlin, Coordinator, 508-929-8084, Fax: 508-929-8048, E-mail: ldahlin@worcester.edu. *Application contact:* Sara Grady, Assistant Dean of Continuing Education, 508-929-8787, Fax: 508-929-8100, E-mail: sara.grady@worcester.edu.

Yale University, Yale School of Management and Graduate School of Arts and Sciences, Doctoral Program in Management, New Haven, CT 06520. Offers accounting (PhD); financial economics (PhD); marketing (PhD); organizations and management (PhD). *Accreditation:* AACSB. *Faculty:* 68 full-time (12 women), 1 (woman) part-time/adjunct. *Students:* 32 full-time (9 women); includes 3 Asian, non-Hispanic/Latino, 16 international. Average age 28. 441 applicants, 4% accepted, 6 enrolled. In 2010, 9 doctorates awarded. *Degree requirements:* For doctorate, comprehensive exam, thesis/dissertation. *Entrance requirements:* For doctorate, GMAT or GRE General Test. Additional exam requirements/recommendations for international students: Required—TOEFL, IELTS. *Application deadline:* For fall admission, 1/2 for domestic and international students. Application fee: $100. Electronic applications accepted. *Expenses:* Contact institution. *Financial support:* In 2010–11, 30 students received support, including 30 fellowships with full tuition reimbursements available, 30 research assistantships with full tuition reimbursements available, 30 teaching assistantships with full tuition reimbursements available; institutionally sponsored loans, scholarships/grants, and health care benefits also available. Financial award application deadline: 1/2. *Faculty research:* Pricing of options and futures, term structure of interest rates, use of accounting numbers in debt contracts, product differentiation, e-commerce and marketing, behavioral finance. *Unit head:* Carla Mills, Registrar, 203-432-3955, Fax: 203-432-0342, E-mail: carla.mills@yale.edu. *Application contact:* Carla Mills, Registrar, 203-432-3955, Fax: 203-432-0342, E-mail: carla.mills@yale.edu.

York College of Pennsylvania, Department of Business Administration, York, PA 17405-7199. Offers accounting (MBA); continuous improvement (MBA); finance (MBA); management (MBA); marketing (MBA). *Accreditation:* ACBSP. Part-time and evening/weekend programs available. *Faculty:* 11 full-time (2 women), 5 part-time/adjunct (1 woman). *Students:* 20 full-time (6 women), 111 part-time (44 women); includes 4 Black or African American, non-Hispanic/Latino; 1 Asian, non-Hispanic/Latino; 4 Hispanic/Latino, 2 international. Average age 30. 53 applicants, 91% accepted, 40 enrolled. In 2010, 45 master's awarded. *Entrance requirements:* For master's, GMAT. Additional exam requirements/recommendations for international students: Required—TOEFL (minimum score 530 paper-based; 200 computer-based; 72 iBT). *Application deadline:* For fall admission, 7/15 priority date for domestic students; for spring admission, 12/15 priority date for domestic

students. Applications are processed on a rolling basis. Application fee: $60. Electronic applications accepted. *Expenses:* Tuition: Full-time $11,520; part-time $640 per credit hour. Required fees: $1500; $660 per year. *Financial support:* Scholarships/grants available. Financial award application deadline: 4/15; financial award applicants required to submit FAFSA. *Unit head:* Dr. David Greisler, MBA Director, 717-815-6410, Fax: 717-600-3999, E-mail: dgreisle@ycp.edu. *Application contact:* Brenda Adams, Assistant Director, MBA Program, 717-815-1749, Fax: 717-600-3999, E-mail: badams@ycp.edu.

FINANCE AND BANKING

Adelphi University, School of Business, Graduate Opportunity for Accelerated Learning MBA Program, Garden City, NY 11530-0701. Offers accounting (MBA); finance (MBA). *Accreditation:* AACSB. Part-time and evening/weekend programs available. *Students:* 14 full-time (8 women), 25 part-time (17 women); includes 7 Black or African American, non-Hispanic/Latino; 8 Asian, non-Hispanic/Latino; 3 Hispanic/Latino; 1 Two or more races, non-Hispanic/Latino, 1 international. Average age 40. In 2010, 14 master's awarded. *Entrance requirements:* For master's, GMAT, 2 letters of recommendation. Additional exam requirements/recommendations for international students: Required—TOEFL (minimum score 550 paper-based; 213 computer-based; 80 iBT). *Application deadline:* For fall admission, 4/1 for international students; for spring admission, 11/1 for international students. Applications are processed on a rolling basis. Application fee: $50. Electronic applications accepted. *Financial support:* Research assistantships with full and partial tuition reimbursements, career-related internships or fieldwork, Federal Work-Study, institutionally sponsored loans, scholarships/grants, and unspecified assistantships available. Financial award application deadline: 3/1; financial award applicants required to submit FAFSA. *Faculty research:* Capital market, executive compensation, business ethics, classical value theory, labor economics. *Unit head:* Rakesh Gupta, Chairperson, 516-877-4670, Fax: 516-877-4607, E-mail: gradbusinquiries@adelphi.edu. *Application contact:* Christine Murphy, Director of Admissions, 516-877-3050, Fax: 516-877-3039, E-mail: graduateadmissions@adelphi.edu.

Adelphi University, School of Business, MBA Program, Garden City, NY 11530-0701. Offers finance (MBA); management information systems (MBA); management/human resource management (MBA); marketing/e-commerce (MBA). *Accreditation:* AACSB. Part-time and evening/weekend programs available. *Students:* 131 full-time (59 women), 173 part-time (73 women); includes 25 Black or African American, non-Hispanic/Latino; 20 Asian, non-Hispanic/Latino; 17 Hispanic/Latino; 3 Two or more races, non-Hispanic/Latino, 10 international. Average age 29. In 2010, 86 master's awarded. *Degree requirements:* For master's, capstone course. *Entrance requirements:* For master's, GMAT, 2 letters of recommendation. Additional exam requirements/recommendations for international students: Required—TOEFL (minimum score 550 paper-based; 213 computer-based; 80 iBT). *Application deadline:* For fall admission, 4/1 for international students; for spring admission, 11/1 for international students. Applications are processed on a rolling basis. Application fee: $50. Electronic applications accepted. *Financial support:* Research assistantships with full and partial tuition reimbursements, career-related internships or fieldwork, Federal Work-Study, institutionally sponsored loans, scholarships/grants, and unspecified assistantships available. Financial award application deadline: 3/1; financial award applicants required to submit FAFSA. *Faculty research:* Supply chain management, distribution channels, productivity benchmark analysis, data envelopment analysis, financial portfolio analysis. *Unit head:* Rakesh Gupta, 516-877-4670, Fax: 516-877-4607, E-mail: gradbusinquiries@adelphi.edu. *Application contact:* Christine Murphy, Director of Admissions, 516-877-3050, Fax: 516-877-3039, E-mail: graduateadmissions@adelphi.edu.

The American College, Graduate Programs, Bryn Mawr, PA 19010-2105. Offers financial services (MSFS); leadership (MSM). Part-time and evening/weekend programs available. Postbaccalaureate distance learning degree programs offered (minimal on-campus study). *Faculty:* 20 full-time, 7 part-time/adjunct. *Students:* 629 part-time (141 women). *Application deadline:* Applications are processed on a rolling basis. Application fee: $335. Electronic applications accepted. *Financial support:* Scholarships/grants available. Support available to part-time students. *Faculty research:* Retirement counseling, social security, aging, family composition, inflation. *Unit head:* Dr. Walter J. Woerheide, Vice President for Academics and Dean, 610-526-1398, Fax: 610-526-1359, E-mail: walt.woerheide@theamericancollege.edu. *Application contact:* Joanne F. Patterson, Associate Director of Graduate School Administration, 610-526-1366, Fax: 610-526-1359, E-mail: joanne.patterson@theamericancollege.edu.

American Public University System, AMU/APU Graduate Programs, Charles Town, WV 25414. Offers accounting (MBA); administration and supervision (M Ed); air warfare (MA Military Studies); asymmetrical warfare (MA Military Studies); criminal justice (MA); emergency and disaster management (MA); entrepreneurship (MBA); environmental policy and management (MS); finance (MBA); general (MBA); global business management (MBA); guidance and counseling (M Ed); history (MA); homeland security

(MA); homeland security resource allocation (MBA); humanities (MA); information technology (MS); information technology management (MBA); intelligence studies (MA); international relations and conflict resolution (MA); joint warfare (MA Military Studies); land warfare (MA Military Studies); legal studies (MA); management (MA), including defense mangement, general, human resource management, organizational leadership, public administration; marketing (MBA); military history (MA); national security studies (MA); naval warfare (MA Military Studies); nonprofit management (MBA); political science (MA); psychology (MA); public administration (MA); public health (MA); security management (MA); space studies (MS); sports management (MS); strategic leadership (MA Military Studies); teaching (M Ed), including elementary, secondary social sciences; transportation and logistics management (MA). Programs offered via distance learning only. Part-time and evening/weekend programs available. Postbaccalaureate distance learning degree programs offered (no on-campus study). *Faculty:* 253 full-time (134 women), 1,208 part-time/adjunct (570 women). *Students:* 956 full-time (422 women), 8,476 part-time (2,821 women); includes 2,511 minority (1,218 Black or African American, non-Hispanic/Latino; 68 American Indian or Alaska Native, non-Hispanic/Latino; 219 Asian, non-Hispanic/Latino; 705 Hispanic/Latino; 46 Native Hawaiian or other Pacific Islander, non-Hispanic/Latino; 255 Two or more races, non-Hispanic/Latino), 107 international. Average age 35. 9,550 applicants, 100% accepted. In 2010, 1,688 master's awarded. *Degree requirements:* For master's, comprehensive exam or practicum. *Entrance requirements:* For master's, official transcript showing earned bachelor's degree from institution accredited by recognized accrediting body. Additional exam requirements/recommendations for international students: Required—TOEFL (minimum score 550 paper-based; 213 computer-based), IELTS (minimum score 6.5). *Application deadline:* Applications are processed on a rolling basis. Application fee: $0. Electronic applications accepted. *Financial support:* Applicants required to submit FAFSA. *Faculty research:* Military history, criminal justice, management performance, national security. *Unit head:* Dr. Frank McCluskey, Provost, 877-468-6268, Fax: 304-724-3780. *Application contact:* Terry Grant, Director of Enrollment Management, 877-468-6268, Fax: 304-724-3780, E-mail: info@apus.edu.

American University, Kogod School of Business, Master of Business Administration Program, Washington, DC 20016-8044. Offers accounting (MBA); consulting (MBA), including information technology, international business, management; corporate finance: commercial banking (MBA); corporate finance: corporate financial management (MBA); corporate finance: investment banking (MBA), including corporate finance and private equity, trading and selling; entrepreneurship (MBA); global emerging markets (MBA), including business, finance, information technology; international trade and global supply chain management (MBA); leadership (MBA); marketing management (MBA); marketing research (MBA); real estate (MBA); MBA/JD; MBA/LL M. Part-time and evening/weekend programs available. *Faculty:* 12 full-time (5 women). *Students:* 135 full-time (62 women), 104 part-time (38 women); includes 46 minority (18 Black or African American, non-Hispanic/Latino; 1 American Indian or Alaska Native, non-Hispanic/Latino; 12 Asian, non-Hispanic/Latino; 14 Hispanic/Latino; 1 Two or more races, non-Hispanic/Latino), 34 international. Average age 27. 467 applicants, 51% accepted, 70 enrolled. In 2010, 101 master's awarded. *Entrance requirements:* For master's, GMAT. Additional exam requirements/recommendations for international students: Required—TOEFL. *Application deadline:* For fall admission, 2/1 priority date for domestic students; for spring admission, 10/1 priority date for domestic students. Applications are processed on a rolling basis. Application fee: $100. *Expenses:* Contact institution. *Financial support:* In 2010–11, 19 students received support; fellowships, research assistantships with partial tuition reimbursements available, career-related internships or fieldwork, Federal Work-Study, and institutionally sponsored loans available. Support available to part-time students. Financial award application deadline: 2/1. *Faculty research:* Information technology, decision-aiding methodology, negotiation. *Unit head:* Dr. Stevan Holmberg, Chair, 202-885-6193, E-mail: sholmbe@american.edu. *Application contact:* Shannon Demko, Associate Director Graduate Admissions, 202-885-1994, Fax: 202-885-1108, E-mail: demko@american.edu.

American University, School of Public Affairs, Department of Public Administration, Washington, DC 20016-8070. Offers advanced organization development (Certificate); fundamentals of organization development (Certificate); key executive leadership (MPA); leadership for organizational change (Certificate); non-profit management (Certificate); organization development (MSOD); organizational change (Certificate); public administration (MPA, PhD); public financial management (Certificate); public management (Certificate); public policy (MPP); public policy analysis (Certificate); LL M/MPA; MPA/JD; MPP/JD; MPP/LL M. Part-time and evening/weekend programs available. *Faculty:* 22 full-time (12 women), 12 part-time/adjunct (5 women). *Students:* 220 full-time (135 women), 248 part-time (159 women); includes 107 minority (71 Black or African American, non-Hispanic/Latino; 4 American Indian or Alaska Native, non-Hispanic/Latino; 18 Asian, non-Hispanic/Latino; 14 Hispanic/Latino), 19 international. Average age 30. 858 applicants, 73% accepted, 175 enrolled. In 2010, 205 master's, 8 doctorates awarded. *Degree requirements:* For master's, comprehensive exam; for doctorate, comprehensive exam, thesis/dissertation. *Entrance requirements:* For master's, GRE, statement of purpose; 2 recommendations; for doctorate, GRE, 3 recommendations; for Certificate, bachelor's degree. Additional exam requirements/recommendations for international students: Required—TOEFL. *Application deadline:* For fall admission, 2/1 for domestic students; for spring admission, 11/1 for domestic students. Application fee: $55. *Financial support:* Fellowships, research assistantships, teaching assistantships, career-related internships or fieldwork, Federal Work-Study, and institutionally sponsored loans available. Financial award application deadline: 2/1. *Faculty research:* Urban management, conservation politics, state and local budgeting, tax policy. *Unit head:* Dr. Robert Durant, Chair, 202-885-2509, E-mail: durant@american.edu. *Application contact:* Dr. Robert Durant, Chair, 202-885-2509, E-mail: durant@american.edu.

Arizona State University, W. P. Carey School of Business, Program in Business Administration, Tempe, AZ 85287-4906. Offers accountancy (PhD); agribusiness (PhD); business administration (MBA); finance (PhD); financial management and markets (MBA); information management (MBA); information systems (PhD); management (PhD); marketing (PhD); strategic marketing and services leadership (MBA); supply chain financial management (MBA); supply chain management (MBA, PhD); JD/MBA; MBA/M Acc; MBA/M Arch. *Accreditation:* AACSB. Part-time and evening/weekend programs available. Postbaccalaureate distance learning degree programs offered (minimal on-campus study). *Faculty:* 84 full-time (22 women), 7 part-time/adjunct (2 women). *Students:* 1,302 full-time (379 women), 86 part-time (26 women); includes 241 minority (37 Black or African American, non-Hispanic/Latino; 11 American Indian or Alaska Native, non-Hispanic/Latino; 103 Asian, non-Hispanic/Latino; 76 Hispanic/Latino; 4 Native Hawaiian or other Pacific Islander, non-Hispanic/Latino; 10 Two or more races, non-Hispanic/Latino), 171 international. Average age 31. 1,795 applicants, 44% accepted, 525 enrolled. In 2010, 734 master's, 9 doctorates awarded. Terminal master's awarded for partial completion of doctoral program. *Degree requirements:* For master's, thesis or alternative, internship, interactive Program of Study (iPOS) submitted before completing 50 percent of required credit hours; for doctorate, comprehensive exam, thesis/dissertation, interactive Program of Study (iPOS) submitted before completing 50 percent of required credit hours. *Entrance requirements:* For master's, GMAT, minimum GPA of 3.0 in last 2 years of work leading to bachelor's degree, 2 letters of recommendation, professional resume, official transcripts, 3 essays; for doctorate, GMAT or GRE, minimum GPA of 3.0 in last 2 years of work leading to bachelor's degree, 3 letters of recommendation, resume, personal statement/essay. Additional exam requirements/recommendations for international students: Required—TOEFL (minimum score 550 paper-based; 213 computer-based; 80 iBT), IELTS (minimum score 6.5). Application fee: $70 ($90 for international students). Electronic applications accepted. *Expenses:* Contact institution. *Financial support:* In 2010–11, 17 research assistantships with full and partial tuition reimbursements (averaging $18,121 per year), 153 teaching assistantships with full and partial tuition reimbursements (averaging $9,176 per year) were awarded; fellowships with full and partial tuition reimbursements, career-related internships or fieldwork, institutionally sponsored loans, scholarships/grants, and tuition waivers (full and partial) also available. Support available to part-time students. Financial award application deadline: 3/1; financial award applicants required to submit FAFSA. Total annual research expenditures: $540,779. *Unit head:* Dr. Robert E. Mittelstaedt, Dean, 480-965-2468, Fax: 480-965-5539, E-mail: mittelsr@asu.edu. *Application contact:* Graduate Admissions, 480-965-6113.

Assumption College, Graduate School, Department of Business Studies, Worcester, MA 01609-1296. Offers accounting (MBA); business administration (CAGS); finance/economics (MBA); general business (MBA); human resources (MBA); international business (MBA); management (MBA); marketing (MBA); nonprofit leadership (MBA). Part-time and evening/weekend programs available. *Faculty:* 3 full-time (0 women), 13 part-time/adjunct (3 women). *Students:* 20 full-time (9 women), 135 part-time (70 women); includes 24 minority (19 Black or African American, non-Hispanic/Latino; 2 Asian, non-Hispanic/Latino; 3 Hispanic/Latino), 4 international. Average age 26. 85 applicants, 95% accepted. In 2010, 40 master's, 2 other advanced degrees awarded. *Entrance requirements:* For master's and CAGS, 3 letters of recommendation, resume, essay. Additional exam requirements/recommendations for international students: Required—TOEFL (minimum score 540 paper-based; 200 computer-based; 76 iBT), IELTS (minimum score 6). *Application deadline:* For fall admission, 6/1 priority date for domestic students, 5/1 priority date for international students; for spring admission, 11/1 priority date for domestic students, 9/1 priority date for international students. Applications are processed on a rolling basis. Application fee: $30. Electronic applications accepted. *Expenses:* Tuition: Part-time $503 per credit. Required fees: $20 per semester. One-time fee: $100. Part-time tuition and fees vary according to campus/location. *Financial support:* Application deadline: 6/1. *Faculty research:* Workplace diversity, dynamics of team interaction, utilization of leased employees. *Unit head:* Michael Lewis, Director, 508-767-7372, Fax: 508-767-7252, E-mail: milewis@assumption.edu. *Application contact:* Daniel Provost, Assistant Director of Graduate Student Services, 508-767-7426, Fax: 508-767-7030, E-mail: dprovost@assumption.edu.

Auburn University, Graduate School, College of Business, Department of Finance, Auburn University, AL 36849. Offers MS. *Faculty:* 15 full-time (2 women), 4 part-time/adjunct (3 women). *Students:* 23 full-time (12 women),

5 part-time (3 women); includes 3 Black or African American, non-Hispanic/Latino, 10 international. Average age 25. 72 applicants, 71% accepted, 19 enrolled. In 2010, 9 master's awarded. Application fee: $50 ($60 for international students). *Expenses:* Tuition, state resident: full-time $7002. Tuition, nonresident: full-time $21,898. International tuition: $22,116 full-time. Required fees: $892. Tuition and fees vary according to course load and program. *Financial support:* Applicants required to submit FAFSA. *Unit head:* Dr. John S. Jahera, Head, 334-844-5344. *Application contact:* Dr. George Flowers, Dean of the Graduate School, 334-844-2125.

Avila University, School of Business, Kansas City, MO 64145-1698. Offers accounting (MBA); finance (MBA); general management (MBA); health care administration (MBA); international business (MBA); management information systems (MBA); marketing (MBA). Part-time and evening/weekend programs available. *Faculty:* 9 full-time (3 women), 24 part-time/adjunct (6 women). *Students:* 123 full-time (68 women), 87 part-time (52 women); includes 44 minority (30 Black or African American, non-Hispanic/Latino; 1 American Indian or Alaska Native, non-Hispanic/Latino; 6 Asian, non-Hispanic/Latino; 6 Hispanic/Latino; 1 Native Hawaiian or other Pacific Islander, non-Hispanic/Latino), 46 international. Average age 33. 62 applicants, 79% accepted, 49 enrolled. In 2010, 80 master's awarded. *Degree requirements:* For master's, comprehensive exam, capstone course. *Entrance requirements:* For master's, GMAT (minimum score 420), minimum GPA of 3.0, interview. Additional exam requirements/recommendations for international students: Required—TOEFL (minimum score 550 paper-based). *Application deadline:* For fall admission, 7/30 priority date for domestic students, 7/30 for international students; for winter admission, 11/30 priority date for domestic students, 11/30 for international students; for spring admission, 2/28 priority date for domestic students, 2/28 for international students. Applications are processed on a rolling basis. Application fee: $0. Electronic applications accepted. *Expenses:* Contact institution. *Financial support:* In 2010–11, 102 students received support. Career-related internships or fieldwork and Competitive Merit Scholarship available. Support available to part-time students. Financial award applicants required to submit FAFSA. *Faculty research:* Leadership characteristics, financial hedging, group dynamics. *Unit head:* Dr. Richard Woodall, Dean, 816-501-3720, Fax: 816-501-2463, E-mail: richard.woodall@avila.edu. *Application contact:* JoAnna Giffin, MBA Admissions Director, 816-501-3601, Fax: 816-501-2463, E-mail: joanna.giffin@avila.edu.

Azusa Pacific University, School of Business and Management, Azusa, CA 91702-7000. Offers business administration (MBA); diversity for strategic advantage (MA); entrepreneurship (MBA); finance (MBA); human and organizational development (MA); human resources and organizational development (MBA); human resources management (MA); international business (MBA); marketing (MBA); non-profit management (MA); organizational development and change (MA); performance improvement (MA); public administration (MA); strategic management (MBA). Part-time and evening/weekend programs available. *Faculty:* 19 full-time (5 women), 2 part-time/adjunct (1 woman). *Students:* 75 full-time (41 women), 96 part-time (46 women); includes 65 minority (15 Black or African American, non-Hispanic/Latino; 15 Asian, non-Hispanic/Latino; 34 Hispanic/Latino; 1 Native Hawaiian or other Pacific Islander, non-Hispanic/Latino), 17 international. Average age 30. In 2010, 82 master's awarded. *Degree requirements:* For master's, thesis (for some programs), final project. *Entrance requirements:* For master's, GMAT, minimum GPA of 3.0. Additional exam requirements/recommendations for international students: Required—TOEFL (minimum score 600 paper-based). *Application deadline:* For fall admission, 8/15 priority date for domestic students. Applications are processed on a rolling basis. Application fee: $45 ($65 for international students). *Expenses:* Contact institution. *Financial support:* Scholarships/grants available. *Faculty research:* Gender issues, financial risk, leadership and ethics, marketing strategy. *Unit head:* Dr. Ilene Bezjian, Dean, 626-815-3090, Fax: 626-815-3802, E-mail: ibezjian@apu.edu. *Application contact:* Dr. Ilene Bezjian, Dean, 626-815-3090, Fax: 626-815-3802, E-mail: ibezjian@apu.edu.

Benedictine University, Graduate Programs, Program in Business Administration, Lisle, IL 60532-0900. Offers accounting (MBA); entrepreneurship and managing innovation (MBA); financial management (MBA); health administration (MBA); human resource management (MBA); information systems security (MBA); international business (MBA); management consulting (MBA); management information systems (MBA); marketing management (MBA); operations management and logistics (MBA); organizational leadership (MBA); MBA/MPH; MBA/MS. Part-time and evening/weekend programs available. Postbaccalaureate distance learning degree programs offered (minimal on-campus study). *Faculty:* 4 full-time (2 women), 24 part-time/adjunct (3 women). *Students:* 347 full-time (140 women), 672 part-time (360 women); includes 237 minority (155 Black or African American, non-Hispanic/Latino; 4 American Indian or Alaska Native, non-Hispanic/Latino; 43 Asian, non-Hispanic/Latino; 35 Hispanic/Latino), 21 international. Average age 34. 416 applicants, 88% accepted, 217 enrolled. In 2010, 355 master's awarded. *Entrance requirements:* For master's, GMAT. Additional exam requirements/recommendations for international students: Required—TOEFL (minimum score 550 paper-based; 213 computer-based). *Application deadline:* For fall admission, 9/1 for domestic students; for winter admission, 12/1 for domestic students; for spring admission, 2/15 for domestic students. Applications are processed on a rolling basis. Application fee: $40. Electronic applications accepted. *Financial support:* Career-related internships or fieldwork and health care benefits available. Support available to part-time students. *Faculty research:* Strategic leadership in professional organizations, sociology of professions, organizational change, social identity theory, applications to change management. *Unit head:* Dr. Sharon Borowicz, Director, 630-829-6219, E-mail: sborowicz@ben.edu. *Application contact:* Kari Gibbons, Director, Admissions, 630-829-6200, Fax: 630-829-6584, E-mail: kgibbons@ben.edu.

Bentley University, McCallum Graduate School of Business, Master's Program in Financial Planning, Waltham, MA 02452-4705. Offers MSFP. Part-time and evening/weekend programs available. Postbaccalaureate distance learning degree programs offered (no on-campus study). *Faculty:* 74 full-time (22 women), 21 part-time/adjunct (5 women). *Students:* 8 full-time (1 woman), 29 part-time (8 women); includes 4 minority (1 Black or African American, non-Hispanic/Latino; 3 American Indian or Alaska Native, non-Hispanic/Latino), 1 international. Average age 37. 25 applicants, 72% accepted, 12 enrolled. *Entrance requirements:* For master's, GMAT or GRE General Test. Additional exam requirements/recommendations for international students: Required—TOEFL (minimum score 600 paper-based; 250 computer-based; 100 iBT) or IELTS (minimum score 7). *Application deadline:* For fall admission, 12/1 priority date for domestic and international students; for spring admission, 10/1 priority date for domestic and international students. Application fee: $50. Electronic applications accepted. *Expenses:* Tuition: Full-time $28,224; part-time $1176 per credit. Required fees: $404. Part-time tuition and fees vary according to course load. *Financial support:* In 2010–11, 4 students received support. Scholarships/grants and tuition waivers available. Financial award application deadline: 6/1; financial award applicants required to submit CSS PROFILE or FAFSA. *Faculty research:* International financial planning, compensation and benefits, retirement planning. *Unit head:* John E. Lynch, Director, 781-891-2624, E-mail: jlynch@bentley.edu. *Application contact:* Sharon Hill, Director of Graduate Admissions, 781-891-2108, Fax: 781-891-2464, E-mail: bentleygraduateadmissions@bentley.edu.

Bentley University, McCallum Graduate School of Business, Program in Finance, Waltham, MA 02452-4705. Offers MSF. Part-time and evening/weekend programs available. *Faculty:* 74 full-time (22 women), 21 part-time/adjunct (5 women). *Students:* 85 full-time (47 women), 46 part-time (21 women); includes 11 minority (2 Black or African American, non-Hispanic/Latino; 1 American Indian or Alaska Native, non-Hispanic/Latino; 6 Asian, non-Hispanic/Latino; 2 Hispanic/Latino), 82 international. Average age 25. 389 applicants, 45% accepted, 75 enrolled. *Entrance requirements:* For master's, GMAT or GRE General Test. Additional exam requirements/recommendations for international students: Required—TOEFL (minimum score 600 paper-based; 250 computer-based; 100 iBT) or IELTS (minimum score 7). *Application deadline:* For fall admission, 12/1 priority date for domestic and international students; for spring admission, 10/1 priority date for domestic students, 10/1 for international students. Application fee: $50. Electronic applications accepted. *Expenses:* Tuition: Full-time $28,224; part-time $1176 per credit. Required fees: $404. Part-time tuition and fees vary according to course load. *Financial support:* In 2010–11, 21 students received support. Scholarships/grants and unspecified assistantships available. Financial award application deadline: 6/1; financial award applicants required to submit CSS PROFILE or FAFSA. *Faculty research:* Management of financial institutions; corporate governance and executive compensation; asset valuation; international mergers and acquisitions; hedging, risk management and derivatives. *Unit head:* Brandon J. Bonghi, Director, 781-891-2384, E-mail: bbonghi@bentley.edu. *Application contact:* Sharon Hill, Director of Graduate Admissions, 781-891-2108, Fax: 781-891-2464, E-mail: bentleygraduateadmissions@bentley.edu.

Boston College, Carroll School of Management, Graduate Finance Programs, Chestnut Hill, MA 02467-3800. Offers MSF, PhD, MBA/MSF. Part-time programs available. *Faculty:* 23 full-time (4 women), 15 part-time/adjunct (3 women). *Students:* 68 full-time (25 women), 43 part-time (13 women); includes 2 Black or African American, non-Hispanic/Latino; 9 Asian, non-Hispanic/Latino, 45 international. Average age 26. 689 applicants, 17% accepted, 55 enrolled. In 2010, 84 master's, 13 doctorates awarded. *Degree requirements:* For doctorate, thesis/dissertation. *Entrance requirements:* For master's, GMAT, resume, recommendations; for doctorate, GMAT or GRE, curriculum vitae, recommendations. Additional exam requirements/recommendations for international students: Required—TOEFL (minimum score 600 paper-based; 250 computer-based; 100 iBT). *Application deadline:* For fall admission, 3/15 for domestic and international students; for spring admission, 10/15 for domestic and international students. Application fee: $100. Electronic applications accepted. *Financial support:* In 2010–11, 42 fellowships with partial tuition reimbursements, 36 research assistantships with tuition reimbursements were awarded; teaching assistantships with tuition reimbursements, Federal Work-Study, scholarships/grants, and unspecified assistantships also available. Financial award application deadline: 3/1; financial award applicants required to submit FAFSA. *Faculty research:* Security and derivative markets, financial institutions, corporate finance and capital markets, market macrostructure, investments, portfolio analysis. *Unit head:* Dr. Jeffrey L. Ringuest, Associate Dean for Graduate Programs, 617-552-9100, Fax:

617-552-0541, E-mail: gsomdean@bc.edu. *Application contact:* Shelley A. Burt, Director of Graduate Enrollment, 617-552-3920, Fax: 617-552-8078, E-mail: bcmba@bc.edu.

Boston University, Metropolitan College, Department of Administrative Sciences, Boston, MA 02215. Offers banking and financial management (MSM); business continuity in emergency management (MSM); economics development and tourism management (MSAS); electronic commerce, systems, and technology (MSAS); financial economics (MSAS); innovation and technology (MSAS); insurance management (MSM); international market management (MSM); multinational commerce (MSAS); project management (MSM). *Accreditation:* AACSB. Part-time and evening/weekend programs available. Postbaccalaureate distance learning degree programs offered (no on-campus study). *Faculty:* 14 full-time (2 women), 22 part-time/adjunct (2 women). *Students:* 107 full-time (51 women), 786 part-time (356 women); includes 130 minority (55 Black or African American, non-Hispanic/Latino; 1 American Indian or Alaska Native, non-Hispanic/Latino; 30 Asian, non-Hispanic/Latino; 36 Hispanic/Latino; 1 Native Hawaiian or other Pacific Islander, non-Hispanic/Latino; 7 Two or more races, non-Hispanic/Latino), 175 international. Average age 33. 398 applicants, 87% accepted, 180 enrolled. In 2010, 154 master's awarded. *Degree requirements:* For master's, thesis optional. *Entrance requirements:* For master's, 1 year of work experience, minimum GPA of 3.0. Additional exam requirements/recommendations for international students: Required—TOEFL (minimum score 560 paper-based; 220 computer-based; 84 iBT). *Application deadline:* Applications are processed on a rolling basis. Application fee: $70. Electronic applications accepted. *Expenses:* Tuition: Full-time $39,314; part-time $1228 per credit. Required fees: $40 per semester. *Financial support:* In 2010–11, 15 students received support, including 7 research assistantships with partial tuition reimbursements available (averaging $10,000 per year); career-related internships or fieldwork, Federal Work-Study, and unspecified assistantships also available. *Faculty research:* International business, innovative process. *Unit head:* Dr. Kip Becker, Chairman, 617-353-3016, E-mail: adminsc@bu.edu. *Application contact:* Lucille Dicker, Administrative Sciences Department, 617-353-3016, E-mail: adminsc@bu.edu.

Boston University, School of Law, Boston, MA 02215. Offers American law (LL M); banking (LL M); intellectual property law (LL M); law (JD); taxation (LL M); JD/LL M; JD/MA; JD/MBA; JD/MPH; JD/MS. *Accreditation:* ABA. *Faculty:* 65 full-time (26 women), 88 part-time/adjunct (32 women). *Students:* 973 full-time (490 women), 66 part-time (32 women); includes 235 minority (44 Black or African American, non-Hispanic/Latino; 5 American Indian or Alaska Native, non-Hispanic/Latino; 84 Asian, non-Hispanic/Latino; 79 Hispanic/Latino; 2 Native Hawaiian or other Pacific Islander, non-Hispanic/Latino; 21 Two or more races, non-Hispanic/Latino), 131 international. Average age 26. 7,660 applicants, 23% accepted, 271 enrolled. In 2010, 206 first professional degrees, 207 master's awarded. *Degree requirements:* For master's, thesis (for some programs); for JD, thesis/dissertation, research project resulting in a paper. *Entrance requirements:* For JD, LSAT; for master's, JD. Additional exam requirements/recommendations for international students: Required—TOEFL (minimum score 600 paper-based; 250 computer-based; 100 iBT). *Application deadline:* For fall admission, 3/1 for domestic and international students. Applications are processed on a rolling basis. Application fee: $75. Electronic applications accepted. *Expenses:* Tuition: Full-time $39,314; part-time $1228 per credit. Required fees: $40 per semester. *Financial support:* In 2010–11, 533 students received support. Career-related internships or fieldwork, Federal Work-Study, institutionally sponsored loans, and scholarships/grants available. Financial award application deadline: 3/1; financial award applicants required to submit FAFSA. *Faculty research:* Litigation and dispute resolution, intellectual property law, business organizations and finance law, international law, health law. *Unit head:* Maureen A. O'Rourke, Dean, 617-353-3112, Fax: 617-353-7400, E-mail: lawdean@bu.edu. *Application contact:* Alissa Leonard, Director of Admissions and Financial Aid, 617-353-3100, Fax: 617-353-0578, E-mail: bulawadm@bu.edu.

Brigham Young University, Graduate Studies, Marriott School of Management, Master of Public Administration Program, Provo, UT 84602. Offers finance (MPA); human resources (MPA); local government (MPA); nonprofit management (MPA); JD/MPA. *Faculty:* 12 full-time (1 woman), 5 part-time/adjunct (0 women). *Students:* 121 full-time (58 women); includes 3 Black or African American, non-Hispanic/Latino; 1 American Indian or Alaska Native, non-Hispanic/Latino; 11 Asian, non-Hispanic/Latino; 8 Hispanic/Latino. Average age 27. 137 applicants, 64% accepted, 61 enrolled. In 2010, 47 master's awarded. *Entrance requirements:* For master's, GRE, GMAT, minimum GPA of 3.0. Additional exam requirements/recommendations for international students: Required—TOEFL (minimum score 580 paper-based; 85 iBT), IELTS (minimum score 7). *Application deadline:* For fall admission, 2/1 for domestic and international students. Application fee: $50. Electronic applications accepted. *Expenses:* Tuition: Full-time $5580; part-time $310 per credit hour. Tuition and fees vary according to program and student's religious affiliation. *Financial support:* In 2010–11, 73 students received support. Career-related internships or fieldwork and scholarships/grants available. Financial award application deadline: 4/15; financial award applicants required to submit FAFSA. *Faculty research:* Taxes, budgeting,

nonprofit, ethics, decision modeling, work balance, organizational behavior. *Unit head:* Dr. David W. Hart, Director, 801-422-4221, Fax: 801-422-0311, E-mail: mpa@byu.edu. *Application contact:* Catherine Cooper, Director of Student Services, 801-422-4221, E-mail: mpa@byu.edu.

Brooklyn College of the City University of New York, Division of Graduate Studies, Department of Economics, Brooklyn, NY 11210-2889. Offers accounting (MS); business economics (MS), including economic analysis, global business and finance; economics (MA). Part-time and evening/weekend programs available. *Students:* 27 full-time (16 women), 163 part-time (76 women); includes 84 minority (60 Black or African American, non-Hispanic/Latino; 18 Asian, non-Hispanic/Latino; 6 Hispanic/Latino), 42 international. Average age 32. 184 applicants, 76% accepted, 68 enrolled. In 2010, 44 master's awarded. *Degree requirements:* For master's, comprehensive exam, thesis or alternative. *Entrance requirements:* For master's, GMAT (for MS), 2 letters of recommendation. Additional exam requirements/recommendations for international students: Required—TOEFL (minimum score 550 paper-based; 213 computer-based; 79 iBT). *Application deadline:* For fall admission, 3/1 priority date for domestic students, 2/1 priority date for international students; for spring admission, 11/1 priority date for domestic students, 10/1 priority date for international students. Applications are processed on a rolling basis. Application fee: $125. Electronic applications accepted. *Expenses:* Tuition, state resident: full-time $7360; part-time $310 per credit hour. Tuition, nonresident: full-time $13,800; part-time $575 per credit hour. Required fees: $190 per semester. *Financial support:* Career-related internships or fieldwork, Federal Work-Study, institutionally sponsored loans, and scholarships/grants available. Support available to part-time students. Financial award application deadline: 5/1; financial award applicants required to submit FAFSA. *Faculty research:* Econometrics, environmental economics, microeconomics, macroeconomics, taxation. *Unit head:* Dr. Emmanuel Thorne, Chairperson, 718-951-5317, E-mail: ethorne@brooklyn.cuny.edu. *Application contact:* Hernan Sierra, Graduate Admissions Coordinator, 718-951-4536, Fax: 718-951-4506, E-mail: grads@brooklyn.cuny.edu.

California College of the Arts, Graduate Programs, Program in Design Strategy, San Francisco, CA 94107. Offers MBA. *Accreditation:* NASAD. *Faculty:* 4 full-time (1 woman), 17 part-time/adjunct (6 women). *Students:* 72 full-time (39 women), 2 part-time (both women); includes 26 minority (5 Black or African American, non-Hispanic/Latino; 15 Asian, non-Hispanic/Latino; 6 Hispanic/Latino), 8 international. Average age 32. 151 applicants, 58% accepted, 51 enrolled. In 2010, 23 master's awarded. *Degree requirements:* For master's, thesis. *Entrance requirements:* Additional exam requirements/recommendations for international students: Required—TOEFL (minimum score 600 paper-based; 250 computer-based; 100 iBT). *Application deadline:* For fall admission, 1/5 for domestic and international students. Application fee: $70. *Expenses:* Tuition: Full-time $38,550; part-time $1285 per unit. One-time fee: $185 full-time. *Financial support:* In 2010–11, 3 fellowships (averaging $18,000 per year) were awarded. *Unit head:* Nathan Shedroff, Program Chair, 800-447-1ART, E-mail: nshedroff@cca.edu. *Application contact:* Heidi Geis, Assistant Director of Graduate Admissions, 415-703-9523 Ext. 9533, Fax: 415-703-9539, E-mail: hgeis@cca.edu.

California Lutheran University, Graduate Studies, School of Management, Thousand Oaks, CA 91360-2787. Offers business (IMBA); computer science (MS); econometrics (MBA); economics (MS); entrepreneurship (MBA, Certificate); finance (MBA, Certificate); financial planning (MBA, Certificate); information systems and technology (MS); information technology management (MBA, Certificate); international business (MBA, Certificate); management and organization behavior (MBA); management and organizational behavior (Certificate); marketing (MBA, Certificate); microeconomics (MBA); nonprofit and social enterprise (MBA). Part-time and evening/weekend programs available. Postbaccalaureate distance learning degree programs offered (no on-campus study). *Faculty:* 12 full-time (3 women), 27 part-time/adjunct (6 women). *Students:* 350 full-time (162 women), 262 part-time (99 women); includes 21 Black or African American, non-Hispanic/Latino; 44 Asian, non-Hispanic/Latino; 56 Hispanic/Latino; 4 Native Hawaiian or other Pacific Islander, non-Hispanic/Latino; 12 Two or more races, non-Hispanic/Latino, 185 international. Average age 32. 379 applicants, 74% accepted, 138 enrolled. In 2010, 231 master's awarded. *Entrance requirements:* For master's, GMAT, interview, minimum GPA of 3.0. *Application deadline:* Applications are processed on a rolling basis. Application fee: $50. *Expenses:* Contact institution. *Unit head:* Dr. Charles Maxey, Dean, 805-493-3360. *Application contact:* 805-493-3127, Fax: 805-493-3542, E-mail: clugrad@clunet.edu.

California State University, East Bay, Office of Academic Programs and Graduate Studies, College of Business and Economics, Department of Accounting and Finance, Option in Accounting/Finance, Hayward, CA 94542-3000. Offers MBA. *Degree requirements:* For master's, comprehensive exam or thesis. *Entrance requirements:* For master's, GMAT, minimum GPA of 2.75. Additional exam requirements/recommendations for international students: Required—TOEFL (minimum score 550 paper-based; 213 computer-based). *Application deadline:* For fall admission, 6/30 for domestic and international students. Applications are processed on a rolling basis. Application fee: $55. Electronic applications accepted. *Financial support:* Career-related internships or fieldwork, Federal Work-Study, and institutionally sponsored loans available. Support available to part-time students. Financial award application deadline: 3/1; financial award applicants required to submit FAFSA. *Unit head:* Prof. Micah Frankel, Graduate Adviser, 510-885-3397, Fax: 510-885-4796, E-mail: micah.frankel@csueastbay.edu. *Application contact:* Donna Wiley, Interim Associate Director, 510-885-2928, Fax: 510-885-4777, E-mail: donna.wiley@csueastbay.edu.

California State University, East Bay, Office of Academic Programs and Graduate Studies, College of Business and Economics, MBA Program, Hayward, CA 94542-3000. Offers entrepreneurship (MBA); finance (MBA); human resources and organizational behavior (MBA); information technology management (MBA); marketing management (MBA); operations and supply chain management (MBA); strategy and international business (MBA). Part-time and evening/weekend programs available. Postbaccalaureate distance learning degree programs offered (no on-campus study). *Faculty:* 33 full-time (9 women). *Students:* 121 full-time (58 women), 133 part-time (67 women); includes 7 Black or African American, non-Hispanic/Latino; 63 Asian, non-Hispanic/Latino; 11 Hispanic/Latino; 3 Native Hawaiian or other Pacific Islander, non-Hispanic/Latino; 5 Two or more races, non-Hispanic/Latino, 87 international. Average age 30. 284 applicants, 47% accepted, 55 enrolled. In 2010, 241 master's awarded. *Degree requirements:* For master's, comprehensive exam or thesis. *Entrance requirements:* For master's, GMAT (minimum 20th percentile verbal and quantitative section), bachelor's degree, minimum GPA of 2.75. Additional exam requirements/recommendations for international students: Required—TOEFL (minimum score 550 paper-based; 213 computer-based; 79 iBT). *Application deadline:* For fall admission, 6/30 for domestic and international students. Applications are processed on a rolling basis. Application fee: $55. Electronic applications accepted. *Financial support:* Career-related internships or fieldwork, Federal Work-Study, institutionally sponsored loans, and scholarships/grants available. Support available to part-time students. Financial award application deadline: 3/2; financial award applicants required to submit FAFSA. *Unit head:* Dr. Terri Swartz, Dean, 510-885-3291, Fax: 510-885-4884, E-mail: terri.swartz@csueastbay.edu. *Application contact:* Dr. Donna Wiley, Interim Associate Director, 510-885-2928, Fax: 510-885-4777, E-mail: donna.wiley@csueastbay.edu.

California State University, Fullerton, Graduate Studies, College of Business and Economics, Department of Finance, Fullerton, CA 92834-9480. Offers MBA. Part-time programs available. *Students:* 65 full-time (30 women), 62 part-time (18 women); includes 2 Black or African American, non-Hispanic/Latino; 36 Asian, non-Hispanic/Latino; 12 Hispanic/Latino, 42 international. Average age 29. 82 applicants, 39% accepted, 19 enrolled. In 2010, 57 master's awarded. *Degree requirements:* For master's, project or thesis. *Entrance requirements:* For master's, GMAT, minimum AACSB index of 950. Application fee: $55. *Financial support:* Career-related internships or fieldwork, Federal Work-Study, institutionally sponsored loans, and scholarships/grants available. Support available to part-time students. Financial award application deadline: 3/1; financial award applicants required to submit FAFSA. *Unit head:* Dr. John Erickson, Chair, 657-278-2217. *Application contact:* Admissions/Applications, 657-278-2371.

California State University, Los Angeles, Graduate Studies, College of Business and Economics, Department of Finance and Law, Los Angeles, CA 90032-8530. Offers finance and banking (MBA, MS). Part-time and evening/weekend programs available. *Faculty:* 2 full-time (0 women). *Students:* 3 full-time (1 woman), 14 part-time (4 women); includes 5 minority (1 Black or African American, non-Hispanic/Latino; 3 Asian, non-Hispanic/Latino; 1 Hispanic/Latino), 9 international. Average age 31. 13 applicants, 100% accepted, 6 enrolled. In 2010, 24 master's awarded. *Degree requirements:* For master's, comprehensive exam (MBA), thesis (MS). *Entrance requirements:* For master's, GMAT, minimum GPA of 2.5 during previous 2 years of course work. Additional exam requirements/recommendations for international students: Required—TOEFL (minimum score 550 paper-based; 213 computer-based). *Application deadline:* For fall admission, 5/1 for domestic and international students. Applications are processed on a rolling basis. Application fee: $55. Electronic applications accepted. *Financial support:* Career-related internships or fieldwork and Federal Work-Study available. Support available to part-time students. Financial award application deadline: 3/1. *Unit head:* Dr. Hsing Fang, Chair, 323-343-2870, Fax: 323-343-2885, E-mail: hfang@calstatela.edu. *Application contact:* Dr. Alan Muchlinski, Dean of Graduate Studies, 323-343-3820, Fax: 323-343-5653, E-mail: amuchli@exchange.calstatela.edu.

California State University, Stanislaus, College of Business Administration, Department of Accounting and Finance, Turlock, CA 95382. Offers MS. Part-time and evening/weekend programs available. *Students:* 4 full-time (1 woman); includes 1 minority (Asian, non-Hispanic/Latino), 1 international. Average age 29. 8 applicants, 100% accepted, 4 enrolled. In 2010, 4 master's awarded. *Degree requirements:* For master's, comprehensive exam, thesis or alternative. *Entrance requirements:* For master's, GMAT or GRE, minimum GPA 2.50, 3 letters of reference, personal statement. Additional exam requirements/recommendations for international students: Required—TOEFL (minimum score 550 paper-based; 213 computer-based). *Application deadline:* For fall admission, 5/1 for domestic students; for spring admission, 1/7 for domestic students. Application fee: $55. Electronic applications accepted. Tuition and fees vary according to program. *Financial support:* Career-related internships or fieldwork available. Financial award application

deadline: 3/1; financial award applicants required to submit FAFSA. *Unit head:* Dr. Andrew Wagner, MSBA Director, 209-667-3118, Fax: 209-667-3080, E-mail: awagner@csustan.edu. *Application contact:* Graduate School, 209-667-3129, Fax: 209-664-7025, E-mail: graduate_school@csustan.edu.

Central European University, CEU Business School, Budapest, Hungary. Offers executive business administration (EMBA); finance (MBA); general management (MBA); information technology management (MBA); marketing (MBA); real estate management (MBA). Part-time and evening/weekend programs available. *Faculty:* 16 full-time (4 women), 2 part-time/adjunct (1 woman). *Students:* 71 full-time (30 women), 142 part-time (47 women). Average age 34. 144 applicants, 36% accepted, 32 enrolled. In 2010, 64 master's awarded. *Degree requirements:* For master's, one foreign language. *Entrance requirements:* For master's, GMAT. Additional exam requirements/recommendations for international students: Required—TOEFL (minimum score 570 paper-based; 230 computer-based); Recommended—IELTS (minimum score 6.5). *Application deadline:* For fall admission, 5/15 priority date for domestic students, 5/22 for international students; for winter admission, 11/15 priority date for domestic students, 11/10 for international students. Applications are processed on a rolling basis. Application fee: $0. Electronic applications accepted. Tuition and fees charges are reported in euros. *Expenses:* Tuition: Full-time 11,000 euros. Required fees: 250 euros. One-time fee: 200 euros full-time. Tuition and fees vary according to degree level, program, reciprocity agreements and student level. *Financial support:* In 2010–11, 4 students received support. Tuition waivers (partial) available. *Faculty research:* Social and ethical business, marketing. *Unit head:* Dr. Mel Horwitch, Dean and Managing Director, 361-887-5050, E-mail: mhorwitch@ceubusiness.com. *Application contact:* Agnes Schram, MBA Program Manager, 361-887-5511, Fax: 361-887-5133, E-mail: mba@ceubusiness.com.

Central Michigan University, College of Graduate Studies, College of Business Administration, Department of Finance and Law, Mount Pleasant, MI 48859. Offers finance (MBA). Part-time and evening/weekend programs available. *Faculty:* 4 full-time (1 woman), 1 part-time/adjunct (0 women). *Degree requirements:* For master's, thesis or alternative. *Entrance requirements:* For master's, GMAT. *Application deadline:* Applications are processed on a rolling basis. Application fee: $35 ($45 for international students). Electronic applications accepted. *Expenses:* Tuition, state resident: full-time $8208; part-time $456 per credit hour. Tuition, nonresident: full-time $13,788; part-time $766 per credit hour. One-time fee: $25. *Financial support:* Fellowships with tuition reimbursements, research assistantships with tuition reimbursements, unspecified assistantships and out-of-state merit awards available. *Faculty research:* Investments, commercial banking, financial management. *Unit head:* Dr. James Felton, Chairperson, 989-774-3362, Fax: 989-774-6456, E-mail: felto1jm@cmich.edu. *Application contact:* Dr. Debasish Chakraborty, Director, MBA Program, 989-774-3678, Fax: 989-774-1320, E-mail: chakr1d@cmich.edu.

Christian Brothers University, School of Business, Memphis, TN 38104-5581. Offers business (MBA); financial planning (Certificate); project management (Certificate). Part-time and evening/weekend programs available. *Faculty:* 1 full-time (0 women), 5 part-time/adjunct (1 woman). *Students:* 11 full-time (4 women), 180 part-time (67 women); includes 57 minority (40 Black or African American, non-Hispanic/Latino; 8 Asian, non-Hispanic/Latino; 7 Hispanic/Latino; 2 Two or more races, non-Hispanic/Latino), 9 international. Average age 35. In 2010, 46 master's awarded. *Entrance requirements:* For master's, GMAT, GRE. Additional exam requirements/recommendations for international students: Required—TOEFL. *Application deadline:* Applications are processed on a rolling basis. Application fee: $50. *Expenses:* Tuition: Full-time $11,520; part-time $640 per credit hour. Required fees: $140; $140 per course. $70 per semester. Tuition and fees vary according to program. *Financial support:* Institutionally sponsored loans available. Support available to part-time students. *Unit head:* Dr. Scott Lawyer, Director, 901-321-3104, Fax: 901-321-3566, E-mail: mlawyer@cbu.edu. *Application contact:* Dr. Scott Lawyer, Director, Graduate Business Programs, 901-321-3104, Fax: 901-321-3566, E-mail: mlawyer@cbu.edu.

Claremont McKenna College, Robert Day School of Economics and Finance, Claremont, CA 91711. Offers finance (MAF). *Faculty:* 9 full-time (2 women), 1 part-time/adjunct (0 women). *Students:* 17 (3 women); includes 2 Asian, non-Hispanic/Latino, 5 international. Average age 23. 125 applicants, 16% accepted, 17 enrolled. In 2010, 20 master's awarded. *Entrance requirements:* For master's, GMAT or GRE, 2 letters of recommendation, resume, interview. Additional exam requirements/recommendations for international students: Required—TOEFL. *Application deadline:* For fall admission, 11/2 for domestic and international students; for winter admission, 1/15 for domestic students; for spring admission, 3/9 for domestic students, 2/10 for international students. Application fee: $70. Electronic applications accepted. *Expenses:* Tuition: Full-time $46,725. *Financial support:* In 2010–11, 17 students received support, including 17 fellowships with full and partial tuition reimbursements available. Financial award applicants required to submit FAFSA. *Faculty research:* Investments, corporate finance, financial reporting, entrepreneurship, decision-making metrics. *Unit head:* Brock Blomberg, Dean, 909-607-9597, E-mail: bblomberg@cmc.edu. *Application contact:* Kevin Arnold, Director of Graduate Programs, 909-607-3347, E-mail: karnold@cmc.edu.

Clark University, Graduate School, Graduate School of Management, Business Administration Program, Worcester, MA 01610-1477. Offers accounting (MBA); finance (MBA); global business (MBA); health care management (MBA); management (MBA); management of information technology (MBA); marketing (MBA). *Accreditation:* AACSB. Part-time and evening/weekend programs available. *Students:* 147 full-time (75 women), 126 part-time (54 women); includes 24 minority (10 Black or African American, non-Hispanic/Latino; 1 American Indian or Alaska Native, non-Hispanic/Latino; 6 Asian, non-Hispanic/Latino; 5 Hispanic/Latino; 2 Two or more races, non-Hispanic/Latino), 99 international. Average age 30. 382 applicants, 57% accepted, 89 enrolled. In 2010, 101 master's awarded. *Degree requirements:* For master's, thesis optional. *Application deadline:* For fall admission, 6/1 priority date for domestic students; for spring admission, 12/1 priority date for domestic students. Applications are processed on a rolling basis. Application fee: $50. Electronic applications accepted. *Expenses:* Tuition: Full-time $37,000; part-time $1156 per credit hour. Required fees: $30; $1156 per credit hour. *Financial support:* In 2010–11, research assistantships with partial tuition reimbursements (averaging $4,800 per year), teaching assistantships with partial tuition reimbursements (averaging $4,800 per year) were awarded; fellowships, career-related internships or fieldwork, Federal Work-Study, institutionally sponsored loans, and tuition waivers (partial) also available. Support available to part-time students. Financial award application deadline: 5/31. *Faculty research:* Organizational development, accounting, marketing, finance, human resource management. *Unit head:* Dr. Joseph Sarkis, Dean, 508-793-7406, Fax: 508-793-8822, E-mail: clarkmba@clarku.edu. *Application contact:* Lynn Davis, Enrollment and Marketing Director, 508-793-7406, Fax: 508-793-8822, E-mail: clarkmba@clarku.edu.

Clark University, Graduate School, Graduate School of Management, Program in Finance, Worcester, MA 01610-1477. Offers MSF. *Students:* 215 full-time (120 women), 7 part-time (3 women), 218 international. Average age 24. 911 applicants, 63% accepted, 126 enrolled. In 2010, 82 master's awarded. *Degree requirements:* For master's, thesis optional. *Application deadline:* For fall admission, 6/1 priority date for domestic students; for spring admission, 12/1 priority date for domestic students. Applications are processed on a rolling basis. Application fee: $50. Electronic applications accepted. *Expenses:* Tuition: Full-time $37,000; part-time $1156 per credit hour. Required fees: $30; $1156 per credit hour. *Financial support:* In 2010–11, research assistantships with partial tuition reimbursements (averaging $4,800 per year), teaching assistantships with partial tuition reimbursements (averaging $4,800 per year) were awarded; fellowships, tuition waivers (partial) also available. Financial award application deadline: 5/31. *Unit head:* Dr. Joseph Sarkis, Dean, 508-793-7406, Fax: 508-793-8822, E-mail: clarkmba@clarku.edu. *Application contact:* Lynn Davis, Enrollment and Marketing Director, 508-793-7406, Fax: 508-793-8822, E-mail: clarkmba@clarku.edu.

Cleary University, Online Program in Business Administration, Ann Arbor, MI 48105-2659. Offers financial planning (MBA); financial planning (Graduate Certificate); green business strategy (MBA, Graduate Certificate); management (MBA); nonprofit management (MBA, Graduate Certificate); organizational leadership (MBA); public accounting (MBA). Part-time and evening/weekend programs available. Postbaccalaureate distance learning degree programs offered (no on-campus study). *Faculty:* 1 (woman) full-time, 20 part-time/adjunct (8 women). *Students:* 1 (woman) full-time, 115 part-time (67 women); includes 30 minority (21 Black or African American, non-Hispanic/Latino; 1 American Indian or Alaska Native, non-Hispanic/Latino; 6 Asian, non-Hispanic/Latino; 2 Hispanic/Latino), 7 international. Average age 34. 62 applicants, 77% accepted, 36 enrolled. In 2010, 22 master's awarded. *Degree requirements:* For master's, thesis. *Entrance requirements:* For master's, bachelor's degree; minimum GPA of 2.5; professional resume indicating minimum 2 years management or related experience; undergraduate degree from an accredited college or university with at least 18 quarter hours (or 12 semester hours) of accounting study (for MBA in accounting). Additional exam requirements/recommendations for international students: Required—TOEFL (minimum score 550 paper-based; 213 computer-based; 79 iBT), Michigan English Language Assessment Battery (minimum score: 75). *Application deadline:* For fall admission, 8/15 for domestic students, 7/15 for international students; for spring admission, 4/2 for domestic students, 1/2 for international students. Applications are processed on a rolling basis. Application fee: $50. Electronic applications accepted. *Financial support:* In 2010–11, 80 students received support, including 80 fellowships (averaging $12,501 per year); Federal Work-Study and scholarships/grants also available. Support available to part-time students. Financial award application deadline: 8/15; financial award applicants required to submit FAFSA. *Unit head:* Dr. Vincent Linder, Provost and Vice President for Academic Affairs, 800-686-1883, Fax: 734-332-4646, E-mail: vlinder@cleary.edu. *Application contact:* Carrie Bonofiglio, Director of Student Recruiting, 800-686-1883, Fax: 517-552-7805, E-mail: cbono@cleary.edu.

Cleveland State University, College of Graduate Studies, Maxine Goodman Levin College of Urban Affairs, Program in Environmental Studies, Cleveland, OH 44115. Offers environmental studies (MAES); geographic information systems (Certificate); urban real estate development and finance (Certificate); JD/MAES. Part-time and evening/weekend programs available. *Faculty:* 26 full-time (10 women), 3 part-time/adjunct (0 women). *Students:* 12 full-time (5 women), 23 part-time (12 women); includes 1 Asian, non-Hispanic/Latino, 4 international. 16 applicants, 50% accepted, 6 enrolled. In 2010, 7 master's awarded. *Degree requirements:* For master's, thesis or alternative, exit project. *Entrance requirements:* For master's, GRE General Test (minimum score: verbal and quantitative 40th percentile, analytical writing 4.0), minimum GPA of 3.0. Additional exam requirements/recommendations for international students: Required—TOEFL (minimum score 525 paper-based; 197 computer-based; 65 iBT). *Application deadline:* For fall admission, 7/15 priority date for domestic students, 5/15 for international students; for spring admission, 11/1 for international students. Applications are processed on a rolling basis. Application fee: $30. Electronic applications accepted. *Expenses:* Tuition, state resident: full-time $8447; part-time $469 per credit hour. Tuition, nonresident: full-time $16,020; part-time $890 per credit hour. Required fees: $50. *Financial support:* In 2010–11, 1 student received support, including 1 research assistantship with full and partial tuition reimbursement available (averaging $6,960 per year); career-related internships or fieldwork, Federal Work-Study, scholarships/grants, tuition waivers (full and partial), and unspecified assistantships also available. Support available to part-time students. Financial award application deadline: 3/1; financial award applicants required to submit FAFSA. *Faculty research:* Environmental policy and administration, environmental planning, geographic information systems (GIS), urban sustainability planning and management, energy policy, land re-use. *Unit head:* Dr. Sanda Kaufman, Director, 216-687-2367, Fax: 216-687-9342, E-mail: s.kaufman@csuohio.edu. *Application contact:* Joan Demko, Graduate Academic Support Specialist, 216-523-7522, Fax: 216-687-5398, E-mail: urbanprograms@csuohio.edu.

Cleveland State University, College of Graduate Studies, Maxine Goodman Levin College of Urban Affairs, Program in Urban Planning, Design, and Development, Cleveland, OH 44115. Offers geographic information systems (Certificate); local and urban management (Certificate); urban economic development (Certificate); urban planning, design, and development (MUPDD); urban real estate development and finance (Certificate); JD/MUPDD. *Accreditation:* ACSP. Part-time and evening/weekend programs available. *Faculty:* 32 full-time (19 women), 8 part-time/adjunct (4 women). *Students:* 30 full-time (10 women), 28 part-time (17 women); includes 6 Black or African American, non-Hispanic/Latino; 3 Hispanic/Latino, 5 international. Average age 38. 72 applicants, 56% accepted, 21 enrolled. In 2010, 24 master's, 9 Certificates awarded. *Degree requirements:* For master's, thesis or alternative, project or thesis. *Entrance requirements:* For master's, GRE General Test (minimum 50th percentile verbal and quantitative, 4.0 analytical writing), minimum GPA of 3.0. Additional exam requirements/recommendations for international students: Required—TOEFL (minimum score 525 paper-based; 197 computer-based; 65 iBT). *Application deadline:* For fall admission, 7/15 priority date for domestic students, 5/15 for international students; for spring admission, 11/1 for international students. Applications are processed on a rolling basis. Application fee: $30. Electronic applications accepted. *Expenses:* Tuition, state resident: full-time $8447; part-time $469 per credit hour. Tuition, nonresident: full-time $16,020; part-time $890 per credit hour. Required fees: $50. *Financial support:* In 2010–11, 15 students received support, including 10 research assistantships with full and partial tuition reimbursements available (averaging $6,960 per year), 5 teaching assistantships with full and partial tuition reimbursements available (averaging $6,960 per year); career-related internships or fieldwork, Federal Work-Study, tuition waivers (full and partial), and unspecified assistantships also available. Support available to part-time students. Financial award application deadline: 3/1. *Faculty research:* Housing and neighborhood development, urban housing policy, environmental sustainability, economic development, metropolitan change, GIS and planning decision support, PPGIS. *Unit head:* Dr. Dennis Keating, Director, 216-687-2298, Fax: 216-687-2013, E-mail: w.keating@csuohio.edu. *Application contact:* Joan Demkow, Graduate Program Coordinator, 216-523-7522, Fax: 216-687-5398, E-mail: urban programs@csuohio.edu.

Cleveland State University, College of Graduate Studies, Maxine Goodman Levin College of Urban Affairs, Program in Urban Studies, Cleveland, OH 44115. Offers geographic information systems (Certificate); local and urban management (Certificate); nonprofit management (Certificate); urban economic development (Certificate); urban real estate development and finance (Certificate); urban studies (MS); urban studies and public affairs (PhD). PhD program offered jointly with The University of Akron. Part-time and evening/weekend programs available. *Faculty:* 26 full-time (10 women), 20 part-time/adjunct (11 women). *Students:* 16 full-time (10 women), 35 part-time (18 women); includes 7 Black or African American, non-Hispanic/Latino, 17 international. Average age 37. 90 applicants, 38% accepted, 18 enrolled. In 2010, 6 master's, 7 doctorates, 6 other advanced degrees awarded. *Degree requirements:* For master's, thesis or alternative, exit project, capstone course; for doctorate, comprehensive exam, thesis/dissertation. *Entrance requirements:* For master's, GRE General Test, minimum GPA of 3.0; for doctorate, GRE General Test, minimum GPA of 3.5. Additional exam requirements/recommendations for international students: Required—TOEFL (minimum score 525 paper-based; 197 computer-based; 65 iBT). *Application deadline:* For fall admission, 7/15 priority date for domestic students, 5/15 for international students; for spring admission, 11/1 for international students. Applications are processed on a rolling basis. Application fee: $30. Electronic applications accepted. *Expenses:* Tuition, state resident: full-time $8447; part-time $469 per credit hour. Tuition, nonresident: full-time $16,020; part-time $890 per credit hour. Required fees: $50. *Financial support:* In 2010–11, 15 students received support, including 11 research assistantships with full tuition reimbursements available (averaging $7,000 per year), 4 teaching assistantships with full and partial tuition reimbursements available (averaging $7,000 per year); career-related internships or fieldwork, Federal Work-Study, institutionally sponsored loans, scholarships/grants, tuition waivers (full and partial), and unspecified assistantships also available. Support available to part-time students. Financial award application deadline: 3/1; financial award applicants required to submit FAFSA. *Faculty research:* Environmental issues, economic development, urban and public policy, public management. *Unit head:* Dr. Sugie Lee, Director, 216-687-2381, Fax: 216-687-9342, E-mail: s.lee56@csuohio.edu. *Application contact:* Joan Demko, Graduate Academic Support Specialist, 216-523-7522, Fax: 216-687-5398, E-mail: urbanprograms@csuohio.edu.

Cleveland State University, College of Graduate Studies, Nance College of Business Administration, Doctor of Business Administration (DBA) Program, Cleveland, OH 44115. Offers business administration (DBA); finance (DBA); information systems (DBA); marketing (DBA); operations management (DBA). *Accreditation:* AACSB. Part-time and evening/weekend programs available. *Faculty:* 50 full-time (11 women). *Students:* 6 full-time (2 women), 31 part-time (6 women); includes 3 Black or African American, non-Hispanic/Latino; 2 Asian, non-Hispanic/Latino, 7 international. Average age 44. 7 applicants. *Degree requirements:* For doctorate, comprehensive exam, thesis/dissertation, oral dissertation defense. *Entrance requirements:* For doctorate, GMAT, MBA or equivalent. Additional exam requirements/recommendations for international students: Required—TOEFL (minimum score 550 paper-based; 213 computer-based; 79 iBT). *Application deadline:* For spring admission, 2/28 priority date for domestic and international students. Application fee: $30. Electronic applications accepted. *Expenses:* Tuition, state resident: full-time $8447; part-time $469 per credit hour. Tuition, nonresident: full-time $16,020; part-time $890 per credit hour. Required fees: $50. *Financial support:* In 2010–11, 5 research assistantships with full tuition reimbursements (averaging $11,700 per year), 1 teaching assistantship with full tuition reimbursement (averaging $11,700 per year) were awarded; tuition waivers (full) and unspecified assistantships also available. *Faculty research:* Supply chain management, international business, strategic management, risk analysis. *Unit head:* Dr. Raj Shekhar G. Javalgi, Director, 216-687-3786, Fax: 216-687-9354, E-mail: r.javalgi@csuohio.edu. *Application contact:* Brenda Wade, Administrative Secretary, 216-687-6952, Fax: 216-687-9257, E-mail: b.wade@csuohio.edu.

College for Financial Planning, Graduate Programs, Greenwood Village, CO 80111. Offers finance (MSF); financial analysis (MSF); personal financial planning (MS). Part-time and evening/weekend programs available. Postbaccalaureate distance learning programs offered (no on-campus study). *Degree requirements:* For master's, capstone course or thesis. *Entrance requirements:* Additional exam requirements/recommendations for international students: Required—TOEFL (minimum score 550 paper-based; 213 computer-based). *Application deadline:* Applications are processed on a rolling basis. Electronic applications accepted. *Expenses:* Tuition: Full-time $4875. *Financial support:* In 2010–11, 5 students received support. *Application contact:* Brett Sanborn, Director of Enrollment, 303-220-4951, Fax: 303-220-1810, E-mail: brett.sanborn@cffp.edu.

Colorado State University, Graduate School, College of Business, Program in Financial Risk Management, Fort Collins, CO 80523-0015. Offers MSBA. *Entrance requirements:* For master's, GMAT or GRE, undergraduate degree with minimum GPA of 3.0; coursework in business finance, probability and statistics, and differential equations; academic experience with computer programming; current resume; 3 letters of recommendation. Additional exam requirements/recommendations for international students: Required—TOEFL (minimum score 565 paper-based; 227 computer-based; 86 iBT) or IELTS (minimum score 6.5). *Application deadline:* For fall admission, 7/1 for domestic students, 6/1 for international students. Application fee: $50. Electronic applications accepted. *Expenses:* Tuition, state resident: full-time $7434; part-time $413 per credit. Tuition, nonresident: full-time $19,022; part-time $1057 per credit. Required fees: $1729; $88 per credit. *Unit head:* Dr. John Hoxmeier, Associate Dean, 970-491-2142, Fax: 970-491-0596, E-mail: john.hoxmeier@colostate.edu. *Application contact:* Rachel Stoll, Admissions Coordinator, 970-491-3704, Fax: 970-491-3481, E-mail: rachel.stoll@colostate.edu.

Cornell University, Graduate School, Graduate Field of Management, Ithaca, NY 14853. Offers accounting (PhD); behavioral decision theory (PhD); finance (PhD); marketing (PhD); organizational behavior (PhD); production and operations management (PhD). *Accreditation:* AACSB. *Faculty:* 55 full-time (9 women). *Students:* 41 full-time (12 women); includes 5 Asian, non-Hispanic/Latino, 23 international. Average age 29. 436 applicants, 4% accepted, 12 enrolled. In 2010, 5 doctorates awarded. *Degree requirements:* For doctorate, comprehensive exam, thesis/dissertation. *Entrance requirements:* For doctorate, GMAT or GRE General Test. Additional exam requirements/recommendations for international students: Required—TOEFL (minimum score 600 paper-based; 250 computer-based; 77 iBT). *Application*

deadline: For fall admission, 1/3 for domestic students. Application fee: $70. Electronic applications accepted. *Expenses:* Contact institution. *Financial support:* In 2010–11, 38 students received support, including 4 fellowships with full tuition reimbursements available, 34 research assistantships with full tuition reimbursements available, 1 teaching assistantship with full tuition reimbursement available; institutionally sponsored loans, scholarships/grants, health care benefits, tuition waivers (full and partial), and unspecified assistantships also available. Financial award applicants required to submit FAFSA. *Faculty research:* Operations and manufacturing. *Unit head:* Director of Graduate Studies, 607-255-3669. *Application contact:* Graduate Field Assistant, 607-255-9431, E-mail: js_phd@cornell.edu.

Cornell University, Graduate School, Graduate Fields of Arts and Sciences, Field of Economics, Ithaca, NY 14853-0001. Offers applied economics (PhD); basic analytical economics (PhD); econometrics and economic statistics (PhD); economic development and planning (PhD); economic theory (PhD); industrial organization and control (PhD); international economics (PhD); labor economics (PhD); monetary and macroeconomics (PhD); public finance (PhD). *Faculty:* 78 full-time (10 women). *Students:* 100 full-time (40 women); includes 1 Black or African American, non-Hispanic/Latino; 4 Asian, non-Hispanic/Latino; 1 Hispanic/Latino, 61 international. Average age 27. 742 applicants, 10% accepted, 20 enrolled. In 2010, 21 doctorates awarded. *Degree requirements:* For doctorate, comprehensive exam, thesis/dissertation. *Entrance requirements:* For doctorate, GRE General Test, 3 letters of recommendation. Additional exam requirements/recommendations for international students: Required—TOEFL (minimum score 550 paper-based; 213 computer-based; 77 iBT). *Application deadline:* For fall admission, 1/15 priority date for domestic students. Application fee: $80. Electronic applications accepted. *Expenses:* Tuition: Full-time $29,500. Required fees: $76. Tuition and fees vary according to degree level and program. *Financial support:* In 2010–11, 20 fellowships with full tuition reimbursements, 16 research assistantships with full tuition reimbursements, 50 teaching assistantships with full tuition reimbursements were awarded; institutionally sponsored loans, scholarships/grants, health care benefits, tuition waivers (full and partial), and unspecified assistantships also available. Financial award applicants required to submit FAFSA. *Faculty research:* Learning and games, economics of education, political economy, transfer payments, time series and nonparametrics. *Unit head:* Director of Graduate Studies, 607-255-4893, Fax: 607-255-2818. *Application contact:* Graduate Field Assistant, 607-255-4893, Fax: 607-255-2818, E-mail: econ_phd@cornell.edu.

Curry College, Graduate Studies, Program in Business Administration, Milton, MA 02186-9984. Offers business administration (MBA); finance (Certificate). Part-time and evening/weekend programs available. *Faculty:* 5 full-time (1 woman), 2 part-time/adjunct (0 women). *Students:* 111 part-time (68 women). Average age 36. 44 applicants, 89% accepted, 39 enrolled. In 2010, 49 master's awarded. *Degree requirements:* For master's, capstone applied project. *Entrance requirements:* For master's, resume, recommendations, interview, written statement. Additional exam requirements/recommendations for international students: Required—TOEFL (minimum score 550 paper-based; 213 computer-based; 80 iBT). *Application deadline:* For fall admission, 8/1 priority date for domestic students, 6/1 for international students; for winter admission, 10/1 for international students; for spring admission, 12/15 priority date for domestic students, 1/28 for international students. Applications are processed on a rolling basis. Application fee: $50. *Expenses:* Contact institution. *Unit head:* Dr. Gail Arch, Director and Professor, 617-333-2197. *Application contact:* John Bresnahan, Director of Graduate Enrollment and Student Services, 617-333-2243, Fax: 617-979-3535, E-mail: jbresnah0104@curry.edu.

DePaul University, Charles H. Kellstadt Graduate School of Business, Department of Finance, Chicago, IL 60604-2287. Offers behavioral finance (MBA); computational finance (MS); finance (MBA, MSF); financial analysis (MBA); financial management and control (MBA); international marketing and finance (MBA); managerial finance (MBA); real estate (MS); real estate finance and investment (MBA); strategy, execution and valuation (MBA). Part-time and evening/weekend programs available. *Faculty:* 26 full-time (5 women), 23 part-time/adjunct (2 women). *Students:* 454 full-time (138 women), 190 part-time (41 women); includes 85 minority (13 Black or African American, non-Hispanic/Latino; 53 Asian, non-Hispanic/Latino; 17 Hispanic/Latino; 2 Two or more races, non-Hispanic/Latino), 129 international. In 2010, 239 master's awarded. *Entrance requirements:* For master's, GMAT, 2 letters of recommendation, resume. Additional exam requirements/recommendations for international students: Required—TOEFL (minimum score 550 paper-based; 213 computer-based; 80 iBT). *Application deadline:* For fall admission, 7/1 for domestic students, 6/1 for international students; for winter admission, 10/1 for domestic students, 9/1 for international students; for spring admission, 2/1 for domestic students, 1/1 for international students. Applications are processed on a rolling basis. Application fee: $60. Electronic applications accepted. *Financial support:* In 2010–11, 8 students received support, including 6 research assistantships with partial tuition reimbursements available (averaging $4,340 per year); scholarships/grants and unspecified assistantships also available. Financial award application deadline: 4/1; financial award applicants required to submit FAFSA. *Faculty research:* Derivatives, valuation, international finance, real estate, corporate finance. *Unit head:* Ali M. Fatemi, Professor and Chair, 312-362-8826, Fax: 312-362-6566, E-mail: afatemi@depaul.edu. *Application contact:* Christopher E. Kinsella, Director of Cohort MBA Programs, 312-362-8810, Fax: 312-362-6677, E-mail: kgsb@depaul.edu.

DePaul University, Charles H. Kellstadt Graduate School of Business, School of Accountancy and Management Information Systems, Chicago, IL 60604-2287. Offers accountancy (M Acc, MSA); business information technology (MS); e-business (MBA, MS); financial management and control (MBA); management accounting (MBA); management information systems (MBA); taxation (MST). Part-time and evening/weekend programs available. *Faculty:* 30 full-time (9 women), 54 part-time/adjunct (7 women). *Students:* 207 full-time (112 women), 208 part-time (92 women); includes 7 Black or African American, non-Hispanic/Latino; 34 Asian, non-Hispanic/Latino; 19 Hispanic/Latino; 2 Two or more races, non-Hispanic/Latino, 76 international. In 2010, 141 master's awarded. *Entrance requirements:* For master's, GMAT, 2 letters of recommendation, resume. Additional exam requirements/recommendations for international students: Required—TOEFL (minimum score 550 paper-based; 213 computer-based). *Application deadline:* For fall admission, 7/1 for domestic students; for winter admission, 10/1 for domestic students; for spring admission, 2/1 for domestic students. Applications are processed on a rolling basis. Application fee: $60. *Financial support:* In 2010–11, 7 research assistantships with full tuition reimbursements (averaging $4,100 per year) were awarded; institutionally sponsored loans also available. Financial award application deadline: 4/2. *Faculty research:* Tax policy, property transactions, stock options as compensation, standards setting, activity-based costing in health care. *Unit head:* Kevin Stevens, Director, 312-362-6989, E-mail: kstevens@depaul.edu. *Application contact:* Christopher E. Kinsella, Director of Cohort MBA Programs, 312-362-8810, Fax: 312-362-6677, E-mail: kgsb@depaul.edu.

DePaul University, School of Public Service, Chicago, IL 60604. Offers financial administration management (Certificate); health administration (Certificate); health law and policy (MS); international public services (MS); leadership and policy studies (MS); metropolitan planning (Certificate); public administration (MPA); public service management (MS), including association management, fundraising and philanthropy, healthcare administration, higher education administration, metropolitan planning; public services (Certificate); JD/MS. Part-time and evening/weekend programs available. Postbaccalaureate distance learning degree programs offered (minimal on-campus study). *Faculty:* 14 full-time (3 women), 43 part-time/adjunct (24 women). *Students:* 372 full-time (256 women), 324 part-time (237 women); includes 156 Black or African American, non-Hispanic/Latino; 33 Asian, non-Hispanic/Latino; 65 Hispanic/Latino; 18 Two or more races, non-Hispanic/Latino, 18 international. Average age 26. 162 applicants, 100% accepted, 94 enrolled. In 2010, 108 master's awarded. *Degree requirements:* For master's, thesis or integrative seminar. *Entrance requirements:* For master's, minimum GPA of 2.7. Additional exam requirements/recommendations for international students: Required—TOEFL (minimum score 550 paper-based; 213 computer-based; 80 iBT), IELTS (minimum score 6.5). *Application deadline:* Applications are processed on a rolling basis. Application fee: $40. Electronic applications accepted. *Financial support:* In 2010–11, 60 students received support, including 3 research assistantships with full tuition reimbursements available (averaging $7,000 per year); career-related internships or fieldwork, Federal Work-Study, institutionally sponsored loans, scholarships/grants, tuition waivers (partial), and unspecified assistantships also available. Support available to part-time students. Financial award application deadline: 7/1; financial award applicants required to submit FAFSA. *Faculty research:* Government financing, transportation, leadership, health care, volunteerism and organizational behavior, non-profit organizations. Total annual research expenditures: $20,000. *Unit head:* Dr. J. Patrick Murphy, Director, 312-362-5608, Fax: 312-362-5506, E-mail: jpmurphy@depaul.edu. *Application contact:* Megan B. Balderston, Director of Admissions and Marketing, 312-362-5565, Fax: 312-362-5506, E-mail: pubserv@depaul.edu.

DeSales University, Graduate Division, Program in Business Administration, Center Valley, PA 18034-9568. Offers accounting (MBA); computer information systems (MBA); finance (MBA); health care systems management (MBA); health care systems management (online) (MBA); human resource management (MBA); management (MBA); management (online) (MBA); marketing (MBA); marketing (online) (MBA); physician's track (MBA); project management (MBA); project management (online) (MBA); self-design (MBA); self-design (online) (MBA); MSN/MBA. *Accreditation:* ACBSP. Part-time programs available. Postbaccalaureate distance learning degree programs offered (no on-campus study). *Entrance requirements:* For master's, GMAT, minimum GPA of 3.0, 2 years of work experience. Additional exam requirements/recommendations for international students: Required—TOEFL. *Application deadline:* Applications are processed on a rolling basis. Application fee: $35. Electronic applications accepted. *Expenses:* Tuition: Full-time $18,200; part-time $690 per credit. Required fees: $1200. *Faculty research:* Quality improvement, executive development, productivity, cross-cultural managerial differences, leadership. *Unit head:* Dr. David Gilfoil, Director, 610-282-1100 Ext. 1828, Fax: 610-282-2869, E-mail: david.gilfoil@desales.edu. *Application contact:* Caryn Stopper, Director of Graduate Admissions, 610-282-1100 Ext. 1768, Fax: 610-282-0525, E-mail: caryn.stopper@desales.edu.

Dowling College, School of Business, Oakdale, NY 11769-1999. Offers aviation management (MBA, Certificate); banking and finance (MBA, Certificate); corporate finance (MBA); financial planning (Certificate); health care management (MBA, Certificate); human resource management (Certificate); information systems management (MBA); management and leadership (MBA); marketing (Certificate); project management (Certificate); public management (MBA, Certificate); sport, event and entertainment management (Certificate); JD/MBA. Part-time and evening/weekend programs available. *Faculty:* 10 full-time (4 women), 56 part-time/adjunct (7 women). *Students:* 295 full-time (131 women), 460 part-time (206 women); includes 219 minority (97 Black or African American, non-Hispanic/Latino; 14 Asian, non-Hispanic/Latino; 35 Hispanic/Latino; 73 Native Hawaiian or other Pacific Islander, non-Hispanic/Latino), 3 international. Average age 33. 327 applicants, 85% accepted, 160 enrolled. In 2010, 33 master's, 1 other advanced degree awarded. *Degree requirements:* For master's, comprehensive exam, thesis optional. *Entrance requirements:* For master's, minimum GPA of 2.8, 2 letters of recommendation, courses in accounting and finance or seminar in accounting/finance, resume. Additional exam requirements/recommendations for international students: Required—TOEFL (minimum score 550 paper-based). *Application deadline:* For fall admission, 9/1 priority date for domestic students; for winter admission, 1/1 priority date for domestic students; for spring admission, 2/1 priority date for domestic students. Applications are processed on a rolling basis. Application fee: $50. Electronic applications accepted. *Expenses:* Tuition: Part-time $884 per credit hour. Part-time tuition and fees vary according to degree level and campus/location. *Financial support:* Career-related internships or fieldwork and Federal Work-Study available. Support available to part-time students. Financial award application deadline: 6/30; financial award applicants required to submit FAFSA. *Faculty research:* International finance, computer applications, labor relations, executive development. *Unit head:* Antonia Loschiavo, Assistant Dean, 631-244-3266, Fax: 631-244-1018, E-mail: loschiat@dowling.edu. *Application contact:* Ronnie S. Macdonald, Assistant Vice President for Enrollment Services/Dean of Admissions, 631-244-3357, Fax: 631-244-1059, E-mail: macdonar@dowling.edu.

Eastern Michigan University, Graduate School, College of Business, Programs in Business Administration, Ypsilanti, MI 48197. Offers business administration (MBA, Graduate Certificate); computer information systems (Graduate Certificate); e-business (MBA, Graduate Certificate); enterprise business intelligence (MBA); entrepreneurship (MBA, Graduate Certificate); finance (MBA, Graduate Certificate); human resources (MBA); human resources management (Graduate Certificate); information systems (MBA); internal auditing (MBA); international business (MBA, Graduate Certificate); marketing management (Graduate Certificate); nonprofit management (MBA); organizational development (Graduate Certificate); supply chain management (MBA, Graduate Certificate). *Accreditation:* AACSB. Part-time programs available. Postbaccalaureate distance learning degree programs offered (no on-campus study). *Students:* 149 full-time (66 women), 456 part-time (232 women); includes 146 minority (109 Black or African American, non-Hispanic/Latino; 4 American Indian or Alaska Native, non-Hispanic/Latino; 27 Asian, non-Hispanic/Latino; 6 Hispanic/Latino), 105 international. Average age 32. 330 applicants, 64% accepted, 150 enrolled. In 2010, 128 master's, 53 other advanced degree awarded. *Entrance requirements:* For master's, GMAT (minimum score 450), minimum cumulative undergraduate GPA of 2.75. Additional exam requirements/recommendations for international students: Required—TOEFL. *Application deadline:* For fall admission, 5/15 for domestic students, 5/1 for international students; for winter admission, 10/15 for domestic students, 10/1 for international students; for spring admission, 3/15 for domestic students, 3/1 for international students. Applications are processed on a rolling basis. Application fee: $35. *Financial support:* Fellowships, research assistantships with full tuition reimbursements, teaching assistantships with full tuition reimbursements, career-related internships or fieldwork, Federal Work-Study, institutionally sponsored loans, scholarships/grants, tuition waivers (partial), and unspecified assistantships available. Support available to part-time students. Financial award applicants required to submit FAFSA. *Unit head:* K. Michelle Henry, Interim Director, Graduate Programs, 734-487-4444, Fax: 734-483-1316, E-mail: mhenry1@emich.edu. *Application contact:* Beste Windes, Advisor, 734-487-4444, Fax: 734-483-1316, E-mail: bwindes@emich.edu.

East Tennessee State University, School of Graduate Studies, College of Arts and Sciences, Department of Economics, Finance, and Urban Studies, Johnson City, TN 37614. Offers city management (MCM); not-for-profit (MPA); planning and development (MPA); public financial management (MPA). Part-time programs available. *Faculty:* 1 full-time (0 women). *Students:* 15 full-time (5 women), 8 part-time (4 women); includes 1 Black or African American, non-Hispanic/Latino, 2 international. Average age 30. 19 applicants, 42% accepted, 7 enrolled. In 2010, 14 master's awarded. *Degree requirements:* For master's, comprehensive exam, internship, capstone, research report. *Entrance requirements:* For master's, GRE General Test, minimum GPA of 2.5. Additional exam requirements/recommendations for international students: Required—TOEFL (minimum score 550 paper-based;

213 computer-based; 79 iBT). *Application deadline:* For fall admission, 6/1 priority date for domestic students, 4/30 for international students; for spring admission, 11/1 for domestic students, 9/30 for international students. Application fee: $25 ($35 for international students). Electronic applications accepted. *Financial support:* In 2010–11, 9 research assistantships with full tuition reimbursements (averaging $5,500 per year) were awarded; career-related internships or fieldwork, institutionally sponsored loans, scholarships/grants, and unspecified assistantships also available. Financial award application deadline: 7/1; financial award applicants required to submit FAFSA. Total annual research expenditures: $6,519. *Unit head:* Dr. Weixing Chen, Chair, 423-439-6632, Fax: 423-439-4348, E-mail: chen@etsu.edu. *Application contact:* Dr. Weixing Chen, Chair, 423-439-6632, Fax: 423-439-4348, E-mail: chen@etsu.edu.

Emory University, Goizueta Business School, Doctoral Program in Business, Atlanta, GA 30322-1100. Offers accounting (PhD); finance (PhD); information systems (PhD); marketing (PhD); organization and management (PhD). *Faculty:* 55 full-time (11 women). *Students:* 32 full-time (17 women); includes 1 Black or African American, non-Hispanic/Latino; 17 Asian, non-Hispanic/Latino; 1 Hispanic/Latino. Average age 29. 218 applicants, 9% accepted, 9 enrolled. In 2010, 8 doctorates awarded. *Degree requirements:* For doctorate, comprehensive exam, thesis/dissertation. *Entrance requirements:* For doctorate, GMAT (strongly preferred) or GRE. Additional exam requirements/recommendations for international students: Required—TOEFL (minimum score 250 computer-based). *Application deadline:* For fall admission, 1/3 priority date for domestic students, 1/1 priority date for international students. Application fee: $50. Electronic applications accepted. *Expenses:* Tuition: Full-time $33,800. Required fees: $1300. *Financial support:* In 2010–11, 32 students received support. *Unit head:* Dr. Lawrence Benveniste, Dean, 404-727-6377, Fax: 404-727-0868, E-mail: larry benveniste@bus.emory.edu. Application contact: Allison Gilmore, Director of Admissions & Student Services, 404-727-6353, Fax: 404-727-5337, E-mail: phd@bus.emory.edu.

Fairfield University, Charles F. Dolan School of Business, Fairfield, CT 06824-5195. Offers accounting (MBA, MS, CAS); accounting information systems (MBA); entrepreneurship (MBA); finance (MBA, MS, CAS); general management (MBA, CAS); human resource management (MBA, CAS); information systems and operations (MBA); information systems and operations management (CAS); international business (MBA, CAS); marketing (MBA, CAS); taxation (MBA, CAS). *Accreditation:* AACSB. Part-time and evening/weekend programs available. *Faculty:* 42 full-time (15 women), 8 part-time/adjunct (1 woman). *Students:* 89 full-time (32 women), 127 part-time (54 women); includes 4 Black or African American, non-Hispanic/Latino; 2 Asian, non-Hispanic/Latino; 4 Hispanic/Latino; 1 Two or more races, non-Hispanic/Latino, 17 international. Average age 29. 108 applicants, 62% accepted, 46 enrolled. In 2010, 79 master's awarded. *Degree requirements:* For master's, capstone course. *Entrance requirements:* For master's, GMAT (minimum score 500), 2 letters of reference, resume, minimum GPA of 3.0. Additional exam requirements/recommendations for international students: Required—TOEFL (minimum score 550 paper-based; 213 computer-based; 80 iBT). *Application deadline:* For fall admission, 5/15 for international students; for spring admission, 10/15 for international students. Applications are processed on a rolling basis. Application fee: $60. Electronic applications accepted. *Expenses:* Contact institution. *Financial support:* In 2010–11, 48 students received support. Scholarships/grants, unspecified assistantships, and merit based one-time entrance scholarship available. Financial award applicants required to submit FAFSA. *Faculty research:* Optimization strategies, international finance, consumer behavior, financial market volatility, Internet marketing, supply chain analysis, tax issues. Total annual research expenditures: $50,000. *Unit head:* Dr. Norman A. Solomon, Dean, 203-254-4000 Ext. 4070, Fax: 203-254-4105, E-mail: nsolomon@fairfield.edu. *Application contact:* Marianne Gumpper, Director of Graduate and Continuing Studies Admissions, 203-254-4184, Fax: 203-254-4073, E-mail: gradadmis@fairfield.edu.

Fairleigh Dickinson University, College at Florham, Silberman College of Business, Department of Economics, Finance, and International Business, Program in Finance, Madison, NJ 07940-1099. Offers MBA, Certificate. *Students:* 16 full-time (5 women), 54 part-time (19 women), 4 international. Average age 30. 39 applicants, 67% accepted, 13 enrolled. In 2010, 48 master's awarded. *Application deadline:* Applications are processed on a rolling basis. Application fee: $40.

Fairleigh Dickinson University, Metropolitan Campus, Silberman College of Business, Department of Economics, Finance and International Business, Program in Finance, Teaneck, NJ 07666-1914. Offers MBA, Certificate. *Students:* 47 full-time (21 women), 15 part-time (6 women), 50 international. Average age 26. 78 applicants, 49% accepted, 12 enrolled. In 2010, 51 master's awarded. *Application deadline:* Applications are processed on a rolling basis. Application fee: $40. *Application contact:* Susan Brooman, University Director of Graduate Admissions, 201-692-2554, Fax: 201-692-2560, E-mail: globaleducation@fdu.edu.

Florida Atlantic University, College of Business, Department of Finance, Boca Raton, FL 33431-0991. Offers MS, PhD. *Faculty:* 15 full-time (2 women), 1 part-time/adjunct (0 women). In 2010, 1 master's awarded. *Degree requirements:* For master's, comprehensive exam, thesis optional. *Entrance*

requirements: For master's, GMAT or GRE General Test, minimum GPA of 3.0. Additional exam requirements/recommendations for international students: Required—TOEFL (minimum score 600 paper-based; 250 computer-based). *Application deadline:* For fall admission, 7/1 priority date for domestic students, 2/15 priority date for international students; for winter admission, 11/1 priority date for domestic students, 8/15 priority date for international students; for spring admission, 4/1 priority date for domestic students, 1/15 priority date for international students. Applications are processed on a rolling basis. Application fee: $30. *Expenses:* Tuition, area resident: Part-time $319.96 per credit. Tuition, state resident: part-time $319.96 per credit. Tuition, non-resident: part-time $926.42 per credit. *Unit head:* Dr. Emilio R. Zarruk, Chair, 561-297-3995. *Application contact:* Fredrick G. Taylor, Graduate Adviser, 561-297-3196, Fax: 561-297-1315, E-mail: ftaylor@fau.edu.

Florida Institute of Technology, Graduate Programs, Nathan M. Bisk College of Business, Online Programs, Melbourne, FL 32901-6975. Offers accounting (MBA); accounting and finance (MBA); finance (MBA); healthcare management (MBA); information technology (MS); information technology management (MBA); Internet marketing (MBA); management (MBA); marketing (MBA); project management (MBA). Part-time and evening/weekend programs available. Postbaccalaureate distance learning degree programs offered (no on-campus study). *Faculty:* 32 part-time/adjunct (8 women). *Students:* 4 full-time (1 woman), 1,062 part-time (499 women); includes 373 minority (244 Black or African American, non-Hispanic/Latino; 8 American Indian or Alaska Native, non-Hispanic/Latino; 37 Asian, non-Hispanic/Latino; 76 Hispanic/Latino; 8 Native Hawaiian or other Pacific Islander, non-Hispanic/Latino; 39 international. Average age 37. 299 applicants, 167 enrolled. In 2010, 134 master's awarded. *Entrance requirements:* For master's, GMAT or resume showing 8 years of supervised experience, 2 letters of recommendation, resume, competency in math past college algebra. Additional exam requirements/recommendations for international students: Required—TOEFL (minimum score 550 paper-based; 213 computer-based; 79 iBT). *Application deadline:* For fall admission, 4/1 for international students; for spring admission, 9/30 for international students. Applications are processed on a rolling basis. Application fee: $50. Electronic applications accepted. *Expenses:* Contact institution. *Financial support:* Available to part-time students. Application deadline: 3/1. *Unit head:* Dr. Mary S. Bonhomme, Dean, Florida Tech Online Associate Provost for Online Learning, 321-674-8202, Fax: 321-674-8216, E-mail: bonhomme@fit.edu. *Application contact:* Carolyn Farrior, Director of Graduate Admissions Online Learning and Off Campus Programs, 321-674-7118, Fax: 321-674-8216, E-mail: cfarrior@fit.edu.

Florida International University, Alvah H. Chapman, Jr. Graduate School of Business, Department of Finance and Real Estate, Miami, FL 33199. Offers finance (MSF); international real estate (MS); real estate (MS). Part-time and evening/weekend programs available. *Faculty:* 19 full-time (3 women), 10 part-time/adjunct (2 women). *Students:* 74 full-time (22 women), 3 part-time (2 women); includes 6 Black or African American, non-Hispanic/Latino; 1 Asian, non-Hispanic/Latino; 31 Hispanic/Latino, 18 international. Average age 29. 317 applicants, 30% accepted. In 2010, 121 master's awarded. *Entrance requirements:* For master's, GMAT or GRE, minimum GPA of 3.0 (upper-level coursework); letter of intent; resume. Additional exam requirements/recommendations for international students: Required—TOEFL (minimum score 550 paper-based; 213 computer-based; 80 iBT) or IELTS (minimum score 6.5). *Application deadline:* For fall admission, 6/1 for domestic students, 4/1 for international students; for spring admission, 10/1 for domestic students, 9/1 for international students. Applications are processed on a rolling basis. Application fee: $30. Electronic applications accepted. *Expenses:* Contact institution. *Financial support:* Institutionally sponsored loans and scholarships/grants available. Financial award application deadline: 3/1; financial award applicants required to submit FAFSA. *Faculty research:* Investment, corporate and international finance, commercial real estate. *Unit head:* Dr. Chun-Hao Chang, Chair, Finance and Real Estate Department, 305-348-2680, Fax: 305-348-4245, E-mail: chun-hao.chang@fiu.edu. *Application contact:* Isabel Lopez, Assistant Director, Finance and Real Estate Graduate Programs, 305-348-4198, E-mail: lopezi@fiu.edu.

Florida State University, The Graduate School, College of Business, Tallahassee, FL 32306-1110. Offers accounting (M Acc), including accounting information services, assurance services, corporate accounting, taxation; business administration (MBA, PhD), including accounting (PhD), finance (PhD), management information systems (PhD), marketing (PhD), organizational behavior (PhD), risk management and insurance (PhD), strategic management (PhD); finance (MS); insurance (MSM); management information systems (MS); JD/MBA; MSW/MBA. *Accreditation:* AACSB. Part-time programs available. Postbaccalaureate distance learning degree programs offered (no on-campus study). *Faculty:* 107 full-time (31 women). *Students:* 196 full-time (76 women), 310 part-time (109 women); includes 27 Black or African American, non-Hispanic/Latino; 1 American Indian or Alaska Native, non-Hispanic/Latino; 31 Asian, non-Hispanic/Latino; 30 Hispanic/Latino. Average age 30. 702 applicants, 33% accepted, 205 enrolled. In 2010, 268 master's, 17 doctorates awarded. Terminal master's awarded for partial completion of doctoral program. *Degree requirements:* For doctorate, comprehensive exam, thesis/dissertation. *Entrance requirements:* For master's, GMAT, work experience (MBA, MS), minimum GPA of 3.0, letters of recommendation; for doctorate, GMAT, minimum graduate GPA of 3.5, letters of recommendation. Additional exam requirements/recommendations for international students: Required—TOEFL (minimum score 600 paper-based; 80 computer-based); Recommended—IELTS (minimum score 6.5). *Application deadline:* For fall admission, 6/1 for domestic students, 5/1 for international students; for spring admission, 10/1 for domestic students, 9/1 for international students. Applications are processed on a rolling basis. Application fee: $30. Electronic applications accepted. *Expenses:* Tuition, state resident: full-time $8238.24. *Financial support:* In 2010–11, 86 students received support, including 12 fellowships with full tuition reimbursements available (averaging $7,161 per year), 30 research assistantships with full tuition reimbursements available (averaging $6,000 per year), 43 teaching assistantships with full tuition reimbursements available (averaging $15,000 per year); career-related internships or fieldwork, scholarships/grants, health care benefits, tuition waivers (full and partial), and unspecified assistantships also available. Support available to part-time students. Financial award application deadline: 1/1. *Unit head:* Dr. Caryn Beck-Dudley, Dean, 850-644-3090, Fax: 850-644-0915. *Application contact:* Lisa Beverly, Director, Graduate Programs Admissions, 850-644-6458, Fax: 850-644-0588, E-mail: lbeverly@cob.fsu.edu.

Gannon University, School of Graduate Studies, College of Engineering and Business, School of Business, Program in Finance, Erie, PA 16541-0001. Offers Certificate. Part-time and evening/weekend programs available. *Entrance requirements:* For degree, GMAT. Additional exam requirements/recommendations for international students: Required—TOEFL (minimum score 79 iBT). *Application deadline:* Applications are processed on a rolling basis. Application fee: $25. Electronic applications accepted. *Expenses:* Tuition: Full-time $14,670; part-time $815 per credit. Required fees: $430; $18 per credit. Tuition and fees vary according to class time, course load, degree level, campus/location and program. *Financial support:* Application deadline: 7/1. *Unit head:* Dr. Duane Prokop, Director, 814-871-7576, E-mail: prokop001@gannon.edu. *Application contact:* Kara Morgan, Assistant Director of Graduate Admissions, 814-871-5831, Fax: 814-871-5827, E-mail: graduate@gannon.edu.

George Fox University, School of Business, Newberg, OR 97132-2697. Offers finance (MBA); management (DBA); management/general (MBA); marketing (DBA); organizational strategy (MBA); strategic human resource management (MBA). MBA offered part-time and full-time, also offered in Portland, OR, and Boise, ID. Part-time and evening/weekend programs available. Postbaccalaureate distance learning degree programs offered (minimal on-campus study). *Faculty:* 9 full-time (2 women), 8 part-time/adjunct (3 women). *Students:* 21 full-time (7 women), 247 part-time (87 women); includes 4 Black or African American, non-Hispanic/Latino; 2 American Indian or Alaska Native, non-Hispanic/Latino; 13 Asian, non-Hispanic/Latino; 13 Hispanic/Latino; 2 Two or more races, non-Hispanic/Latino, 12 international. Average age 37. 101 applicants, 93% accepted, 72 enrolled. In 2010, 82 master's awarded. *Degree requirements:* For master's, capstone project; for doctorate, credit-applied research project. *Entrance requirements:* For master's, resume (5 years professional experience required); 3 professional references; interview; financial e-learning course; for doctorate, GRE or GMAT, resume; personal mission statement; academic research writing sample; official transcript from each college/university attended; three professional references. Additional exam requirements/recommendations for international students: Required—TOEFL (minimum score 577 paper-based; 233 computer-based; 90 iBT) or IELTS (minimum score 7). *Application deadline:* For fall admission, 8/1 for domestic and international students; for spring admission, 12/1 for domestic and international students. Applications are processed on a rolling basis. Application fee: $40. Electronic applications accepted. *Expenses:* Contact institution. *Financial support:* In 2010–11, 2 students received support. Applicants required to submit FAFSA. *Unit head:* Dr. Dirk Barram, Professor/Dean, 800-631-0921. *Application contact:* Robin Halverson, Admissions Counselor, 800-493-4937, Fax: 503-554-6111, E-mail: mba@georgefox.edu.

The George Washington University, Columbian College of Arts and Sciences, Trachtenberg School of Public Policy and Public Administration, Washington, DC 20052. Offers public administration (MPA), including budget and public finance, managing state and local governments; JD/MPP; MPA/JD; PhD/MPP. Part-time and evening/weekend programs available. *Faculty:* 37 full-time (13 women), 19 part-time/adjunct (10 women). *Students:* 286 full-time (182 women), 163 part-time (123 women); includes 18 Black or African American, non-Hispanic/Latino; 1 American Indian or Alaska Native, non-Hispanic/Latino; 30 Asian, non-Hispanic/Latino; 12 Hispanic/Latino; 1 Native Hawaiian or other Pacific Islander, non-Hispanic/Latino. Average age 26. 1,102 applicants, 49% accepted, 146 enrolled. In 2010, 113 master's awarded. *Entrance requirements:* For master's, GRE General Test, minimum GPA of 3.0. Additional exam requirements/recommendations for international students: Required—TOEFL (minimum score 600 paper-based; 250 computer-based; 100 iBT). *Application deadline:* For fall admission, 1/15 priority date for domestic and international students; for spring admission, 10/1 priority date for domestic students, 9/1 priority date for international students. Application fee: $60. Electronic applications accepted. *Financial support:* In 2010–11, 65 students received support; fellowships, research assistantships,

teaching assistantships available. Financial award application deadline: 1/15. *Faculty research:* Education policy, budget and finance, health policy, regulatory policy. *Unit head:* Dr. Kathyrn E. Newcomer, Director, 202-994-3959, Fax: 202-994-3959, E-mail: newcomer@gwu.edu. *Application contact:* Bethany Pope, Program Coordinator, 202-994-6295, Fax: 202-994-6295, E-mail: tspppa@gwu.edu.

The George Washington University, School of Business, Department of Finance, Washington, DC 20052. Offers finance (MSF, PhD); finance and investments (MBA); real estate and urban development (MBA). Part-time and evening/weekend programs available. *Faculty:* 17 full-time (4 women), 9 part-time/adjunct (2 women). *Students:* 71 full-time (27 women), 42 part-time (15 women); includes 7 Black or African American, non-Hispanic/Latino; 8 Asian, non-Hispanic/Latino; 5 Hispanic/Latino; 1 Two or more races, non-Hispanic/Latino, 64 international. Average age 30. 602 applicants, 23% accepted, 65 enrolled. In 2010, 52 master's awarded. *Degree requirements:* For doctorate, thesis/dissertation. *Entrance requirements:* For master's, GMAT; for doctorate, GMAT or GRE. Additional exam requirements/recommendations for international students: Required—TOEFL. *Application deadline:* For fall admission, 4/1 priority date for domestic students; for spring admission, 10/1 for domestic students. Applications are processed on a rolling basis. Application fee: $75. *Financial support:* In 2010–11, 38 students received support; fellowships, teaching assistantships, career-related internships or fieldwork, Federal Work-Study, and institutionally sponsored loans available. Financial award application deadline: 4/1. *Unit head:* Mark S. Klock, Chair, 202-994-5996, E-mail: klock@gwu.edu. *Application contact:* Kristin Williams, Asst VP Gradpec Enrlmnt Mgmt, 202-994-0467, Fax: 202-994-0371, E-mail: ksw@gwu.edu.

Golden Gate University, Ageno School of Business, San Francisco, CA 94105-2968. Offers accounting (MBA); business administration (EMBA, MBA, PMBA, DBA); finance (MBA, MS, Certificate); financial planning (MS, Certificate); healthcare information systems (Certificate); human resource management (MBA, MS); human resources management (Certificate); information systems (MS); information technology (MBA); information technology management (Certificate); integrated marketing and communications (MS, Certificate); international business (MBA); management (MBA); marketing (MBA, MS, Certificate); operations supply chain management (Certificate); psychology (MA, Certificate); public administration (EMPA); public relations (MS, Certificate); technical market analysis (Certificate); JD/MBA. Part-time and evening/weekend programs available. *Faculty:* 16 full-time (4 women), 241 part-time/adjunct (72 women). *Students:* 421 full-time (235 women), 744 part-time (425 women); includes 526 minority (114 Black or African American, non-Hispanic/Latino; 2 American Indian or Alaska Native, non-Hispanic/Latino; 296 Asian, non-Hispanic/Latino; 73 Hispanic/Latino; 29 Native Hawaiian or other Pacific Islander, non-Hispanic/Latino; 12 Two or more races, non-Hispanic/Latino), 100 international. Average age 32. 681 applicants, 78% accepted, 270 enrolled. In 2010, 550 master's, 13 doctorates awarded. *Degree requirements:* For doctorate, thesis/dissertation. *Entrance requirements:* For master's, GMAT (MBA), minimum GPA of 2.5 (MS). Additional exam requirements/recommendations for international students: Required—TOEFL. *Application deadline:* For fall admission, 5/15 for domestic and international students; for winter admission, 1/15 for domestic and international students; for spring admission, 9/15 for domestic and international students. Applications are processed on a rolling basis. Application fee: $70 ($110 for international students). Electronic applications accepted. *Expenses:* Contact institution. *Financial support:* Career-related internships or fieldwork, Federal Work-Study, institutionally sponsored loans, and scholarships/grants available. Support available to part-time students. Financial award applicants required to submit FAFSA. *Unit head:* Dr. Paul Fouts, Dean, 415-442-7026, Fax: 415-442-6579. *Application contact:* Angela Melero, Enrollment Services, 415-442-7800, Fax: 415-442-7807, E-mail: info@ggu.edu.

Goldey-Beacom College, Graduate Program, Wilmington, DE 19808-1999. Offers business administration (MBA); finance (MS); financial management (MBA); human resource management (MBA); information technology (MBA); international business management (MBA); major finance (MBA); major taxation (MBA); management (MM); marketing management (MBA); taxation (MBA, MS). *Accreditation:* ACBSP. Part-time and evening/weekend programs available. *Faculty:* 20 full-time (8 women), 28 part-time/adjunct (10 women). *Students:* 55 full-time (28 women), 393 part-time (164 women); includes 252 minority (51 Black or African American, non-Hispanic/Latino; 2 American Indian or Alaska Native, non-Hispanic/Latino; 183 Asian, non-Hispanic/Latino; 13 Hispanic/Latino; 1 Native Hawaiian or other Pacific Islander, non-Hispanic/Latino; 2 Two or more races, non-Hispanic/Latino). Average age 27. In 2010, 231 master's awarded. *Entrance requirements:* For master's, GMAT, MAT, GRE, minimum GPA of 3.0. Additional exam requirements/recommendations for international students: Required—TOEFL (minimum score 65 computer-based); Recommended—IELTS (minimum score 5). *Application deadline:* Applications are processed on a rolling basis. Electronic applications accepted. *Expenses:* Tuition: Full-time $14,796; part-time $822 per credit. Required fees: $180; $10 per credit. *Financial support:* Scholarships/grants available. Support available to part-time students. Financial award application deadline: 4/1; financial award applicants required to submit FAFSA. *Unit head:* Larry W. Eby, Director of Admissions, 302-225-6289,

Fax: 302-996-5408, E-mail: ebylw@gbc.edu. *Application contact:* Ashley E. Mashington, Graduate Admissions Representative, 302-225-6259, Fax: 302-996-5408, E-mail: mashina@gbc.edu.

Grand Canyon University, College of Business, Phoenix, AZ 85017-1097. Offers accounting (MBA); corporate business administration (MBA); disaster preparedness and crisis management (MBA); executive fire service leadership (MS); finance (MBA); general management (MBA); government and policy (MPA); health care management (MPA); health systems management (MBA); human resource management (MBA); innovation (MBA); leadership (MBA, MS); management of information system (MBA); marketing (MBA); project-based (MBA); six sigma (MBA); strategic human resource management (MBA). *Accreditation:* ACBSP. Part-time and evening/weekend programs available. Postbaccalaureate distance learning degree programs offered (no on-campus study). *Faculty:* 8 full-time (3 women), 147 part-time/adjunct (49 women). *Students:* 1 full-time (0 women), 2,121 part-time (1,165 women); includes 341 minority (249 Black or African American, non-Hispanic/Latino; 17 American Indian or Alaska Native, non-Hispanic/Latino; 15 Asian, non-Hispanic/Latino; 29 Hispanic/Latino; 4 Native Hawaiian or other Pacific Islander, non-Hispanic/Latino; 27 Two or more races, non-Hispanic/Latino), 20 international. Average age 38. In 2010, 569 master's awarded. *Entrance requirements:* For master's, equivalent of two years full-time professional work experience. Additional exam requirements/recommendations for international students: Required—TOEFL (minimum score 575 paper-based; 233 computer-based; 90 iBT), IELTS (minimum score 7). *Application deadline:* For fall admission, 8/21 for domestic students, 7/2 for international students; for spring admission, 12/24 for domestic students, 11/1 for international students. Applications are processed on a rolling basis. Application fee: $0. Electronic applications accepted. *Financial support:* Federal Work-Study available. Support available to part-time students. Financial award applicants required to submit FAFSA. *Unit head:* Kim Donaldson, Dean, 602-639-6597, E-mail: kdonaldson@gcu.edu. *Application contact:* Matt Tidwell, Enrollment Manager, 602-639-6020, E-mail: mtidwell@gcu.edu.

HEC Montreal, School of Business Administration, Diploma Programs in Administration, Program in Professional Finance, Montréal, QC H3T 2A7, Canada. Offers Diploma. Part-time programs available. *Students:* 29 full-time (8 women), 1 part-time (0 women). 111 applicants, 40% accepted, 26 enrolled. In 2010, 14 Diplomas awarded. *Application deadline:* For fall admission, 4/15 for domestic and international students. Application fee: $78. Electronic applications accepted. *Expenses:* Tuition, area resident: Part-time $68.93 per credit. Tuition, state resident: full-time $2481.48; part-time $188.92 per credit. Tuition, nonresident: full-time $6801; part-time $482.06 per course. International tuition: $17,354.16 full-time. Required fees: $1309.50; $30.28 per credit. $93.45 per term. Tuition and fees vary according to degree level and program. *Financial support:* Research assistantships, teaching assistantships, scholarships/grants available. Financial award application deadline: 9/2. *Unit head:* Silvia Ponce, Academic Supervisor, 514-340-6393, Fax: 514-340-6915, E-mail: silvia.ponce@hec.ca. *Application contact:* Marie Deshaies, Senior Student Advisor, 514-340-6135, Fax: 514-340-6411, E-mail: marie.deshaies@hec.ca.

HEC Montreal, School of Business Administration, Master of Science Programs in Administration, Program in Applied Financial Economics, Montréal, QC H3T 2A7, Canada. Offers M Sc. Part-time programs available. *Students:* 20 full-time (8 women), 2 part-time (1 woman). 19 applicants, 63% accepted, 8 enrolled. In 2010, 8 master's awarded. *Degree requirements:* For master's, one foreign language, thesis. *Application deadline:* For fall admission, 3/15 for domestic and international students; for winter admission, 9/15 for domestic and international students. Application fee: $78 Canadian dollars. Electronic applications accepted. *Expenses:* Tuition, area resident: Part-time $68.93 per credit. Tuition, state resident: full-time $2481.48; part-time $188.92 per credit. Tuition, nonresident: full-time $6801; part-time $482.06 per course. International tuition: $17,354.16 full-time. Required fees: $1309.50; $30.28 per credit. $93.45 per term. Tuition and fees vary according to degree level and program. *Financial support:* Fellowships, research assistantships, teaching assistantships, scholarships/grants available. Financial award application deadline: 9/2. *Unit head:* Dr. Claude Laurin, Director, 514-340-6485, Fax: 514-340-6880, E-mail: claude.laurin@hec.ca. *Application contact:* Francine Blais, Administrative Director, 514-340-6112, Fax: 514-340-6411, E-mail: francine.blais@hec.ca.

HEC Montreal, School of Business Administration, Master of Science Programs in Administration, Program in Finance, Montréal, QC H3T 2A7, Canada. Offers M Sc. All courses are given in French. Part-time programs available. *Students:* 78 full-time (14 women), 16 part-time (2 women). 146 applicants, 49% accepted, 37 enrolled. In 2010, 21 master's awarded. *Degree requirements:* For master's, one foreign language. *Application deadline:* For fall admission, 3/15 for domestic and international students; for winter admission, 10/1 for domestic and international students. Application fee: $78 Canadian dollars. Electronic applications accepted. *Expenses:* Tuition, area resident: Part-time $68.93 per credit. Tuition, state resident: full-time $2481.48; part-time $188.92 per credit. Tuition, nonresident: full-time $6801; part-time $482.06 per course. International tuition: $17,354.16 full-time. Required fees: $1309.50; $30.28 per credit. $93.45 per term. Tuition and fees vary according to degree level and program. *Financial support:* Fellowships,

research assistantships, teaching assistantships, scholarships/grants available. Financial award application deadline: 9/2. *Unit head:* Dr. Claude Laurin, Director, 514-340-6485, Fax: 514-340-6880, E-mail: claude.laurin@hec.ca. *Application contact:* Francine Blais, Administrative Director, 514-340-6112, Fax: 514-340-6411, E-mail: francine.blais@hec.ca.

Hofstra University, Frank G. Zarb School of Business, Department of Finance, Hempstead, NY 11549. Offers banking (Advanced Certificate); business administration (MBA), including finance, real estate management; corporate finance (Advanced Certificate); finance (MS); investment management (Advanced Certificate); quantitative finance (MS). Part-time and evening/weekend programs available. Postbaccalaureate distance learning degree programs offered (minimal on-campus study). *Faculty:* 12 full-time (2 women), 2 part-time/adjunct (1 woman). *Students:* 180 full-time (68 women), 99 part-time (26 women); includes 24 minority (6 Black or African American, non-Hispanic/Latino; 10 Asian, non-Hispanic/Latino; 8 Hispanic/Latino), 13 international. Average age 27. 329 applicants, 73% accepted, 102 enrolled. In 2010, 76 master's awarded. *Degree requirements:* For master's, capstone course (for MBA); thesis (for MS). *Entrance requirements:* For master's, GMAT/GRE, 2 letters of recommendation; resume; essay. Additional exam requirements/recommendations for international students: Required—TOEFL (minimum score 550 paper-based; 213 computer-based; 80 iBT); Recommended—IELTS (minimum score 6). *Application deadline:* Applications are processed on a rolling basis. Application fee: $70 ($75 for international students). Electronic applications accepted. *Expenses:* Contact institution. *Financial support:* In 2010–11, 41 students received support, including 38 fellowships with full and partial tuition reimbursements available (averaging $10,353 per year), 1 research assistantship with full and partial tuition reimbursement available (averaging $9,375 per year); Federal Work-Study, institutionally sponsored loans, scholarships/grants, and tuition waivers (full and partial) also available. Support available to part-time students. Financial award applicants required to submit FAFSA. *Faculty research:* International finance, investments, banking, real estate, derivatives. *Unit head:* Dr. Nancy W. White, Chairperson, 516-463-5699, Fax: 516-463-4834, E-mail: finnwh@hofstra.edu. *Application contact:* Carol Drummer, Dean of Graduate Admissions, 516-463-4876, Fax: 516-463-4664, E-mail: gradstudent@hofstra.edu.

Holy Family University, Division of Extended Learning, Philadelphia, PA 19114. Offers business administration (MBA); finance (MBA); health care administration (MBA). *Accreditation:* ACBSP. Part-time and evening/weekend programs available. *Faculty:* 78 part-time/adjunct (32 women). *Students:* 116 part-time (71 women); includes 10 Black or African American, non-Hispanic/Latino; 6 Asian, non-Hispanic/Latino; 2 Hispanic/Latino. Average age 35. 46 applicants, 93% accepted, 41 enrolled. In 2010, 47 master's awarded. *Entrance requirements:* For master's, interview, essay. Additional exam requirements/recommendations for international students: Required—TOEFL. *Application deadline:* Applications are processed on a rolling basis. Application fee: $50. Electronic applications accepted. *Expenses:* Tuition: Full-time $14,400; part-time $600 per credit hour. Required fees: $85 per term. *Financial support:* Applicants required to submit FAFSA. *Unit head:* Honour Moore, Associate Vice President, 267-341-5008, Fax: 215-633-0558, E-mail: hmoore@holyfamily.edu. *Application contact:* Don Reinmold, Director of Admissions for Division of Extended Learning, 267-341-5001 Ext. 3230, Fax: 215-633-0558, E-mail: dreinmold@holyfamily.edu.

Holy Names University, Graduate Division, Department of Business, Oakland, CA 94619-1699. Offers energy and environment management (MBA); finance (MBA); management and leadership (MBA); marketing (MBA); sports management (MBA). Part-time and evening/weekend programs available. *Faculty:* 3 full-time (2 women), 4 part-time/adjunct (1 woman). *Students:* 67 full-time (40 women); includes 28 Black or African American, non-Hispanic/Latino; 7 Asian, non-Hispanic/Latino; 5 Hispanic/Latino, 2 international. Average age 33. 24 applicants, 75% accepted, 7 enrolled. In 2010, 29 master's awarded. *Entrance requirements:* For master's, minimum undergraduate GPA of 2.6 overall, 3.0 in major. Additional exam requirements/recommendations for international students: Required—TOEFL (minimum score 550 paper-based; 213 computer-based; 80 iBT). *Application deadline:* For fall admission, 8/1 priority date for domestic students, 8/1 for international students; for spring admission, 12/1 priority date for domestic students, 12/1 for international students. Applications are processed on a rolling basis. Application fee: $0. *Expenses:* Tuition: Full-time $13,788; part-time $766 per credit. Required fees: $340; $170 per semester. *Financial support:* In 2010–11, 19 students received support. Available to part-time students. Application deadline: 3/2. *Faculty research:* Business ethics, sustainable economics, accounting models, cross-cultural management, diversity in organizations. *Unit head:* Dr. Marcia Frideger, Program Director, 510-436-1205, E-mail: frideger@hnu.edu. *Application contact:* 800-430-1351, Fax: 510-436-1325, E-mail: admissions@hnu.edu.

Hood College, Graduate School, Department of Economics and Management, Frederick, MD 21701-8575. Offers accounting (MBA); administration and management (MBA); finance (MBA); human resource management (MBA); information systems (MBA); marketing (MBA); public management (MBA). *Accreditation:* ACBSP. Part-time and evening/weekend programs available. *Faculty:* 4 full-time (1 woman), 9 part-time/adjunct (1 woman). *Students:* 16 full-time (9 women), 127 part-time (65 women); includes 17 Black or

African American, non-Hispanic/Latino; 9 Asian, non-Hispanic/Latino; 5 Hispanic/Latino; 1 Two or more races, non-Hispanic/Latino, 10 international. Average age 32. 60 applicants, 62% accepted, 25 enrolled. In 2010, 56 master's awarded. *Degree requirements:* For master's, capstone/final research project. *Entrance requirements:* For master's, minimum GPA of 2.75, resume, letters of recommendation. Additional exam requirements/recommendations for international students: Required—TOEFL (minimum score 575 paper-based; 231 computer-based; 89 iBT). *Application deadline:* For fall admission, 7/15 for domestic and international students; for spring admission, 12/15 for domestic and international students. Applications are processed on a rolling basis. Application fee: $35. Electronic applications accepted. *Expenses:* Tuition: Full-time $6480; part-time $360 per credit. Required fees: $100; $50 per term. *Financial support:* Applicants required to submit FAFSA. *Faculty research:* Corporate strategy and sustainable competitive advantages, business ethics, entrepreneurship, investments management, economic development. *Unit head:* Dr. Anita Jose, Program Director, 301-696-3691, Fax: 301-696-3597, E-mail: jose@hood.edu. *Application contact:* Dr. Allen P. Flora, Dean of Graduate School, 301-696-3811, Fax: 301-696-3597, E-mail: gofurther@hood.edu.

Illinois Institute of Technology, Chicago-Kent College of Law, Chicago, IL 60661-3691. Offers family law (LL M); financial services (LL M); international intellectual property (LL M); international law (LL M); law (JD); taxation (LL M); JD/LL M; JD/MBA; JD/MPA; JD/MPH; JD/MS. *Accreditation:* ABA. Part-time and evening/weekend programs available. *Faculty:* 70 full-time (24 women), 146 part-time/adjunct (35 women). *Students:* 889 full-time (417 women), 206 part-time (88 women); includes 214 minority (41 Black or African American, non-Hispanic/Latino; 64 Asian, non-Hispanic/Latino; 67 Hispanic/Latino; 26 Native Hawaiian or other Pacific Islander, non-Hispanic/Latino; 16 Two or more races, non-Hispanic/Latino), 112 international. Average age 27. 3,923 applicants, 47% accepted, 374 enrolled. In 2010, 297 first professional degrees, 128 master's awarded. *Entrance requirements:* LSAT, LSDAS. Additional exam requirements/recommendations for international students: Required—TOEFL (minimum score 600 paper-based; 250 computer-based; 100 iBT); Recommended—IELTS (minimum score 7). *Application deadline:* For fall admission, 3/1 priority date for domestic students, 2/1 priority date for international students. Applications are processed on a rolling basis. Application fee: $60 ($75 for international students). Electronic applications accepted. *Expenses:* Contact institution. *Financial support:* In 2010–11, 607 students received support. Career-related internships or fieldwork, Federal Work-Study, institutionally sponsored loans, scholarships/grants, and tuition waivers (full) available. Support available to part-time students. Financial award application deadline: 3/15; financial award applicants required to submit FAFSA. *Faculty research:* Constitutional law, bioethics, environmental law. Total annual research expenditures: $663,877. *Unit head:* Harold J. Krent, Dean, 312-906-5010, Fax: 312-906-5335, E-mail: hkrent@kentlaw.edu. *Application contact:* Nicole Vilches, Assistant Dean, 312-906-5020, Fax: 312-906-5274, E-mail: admissions@kentlaw.edu.

Illinois Institute of Technology, Stuart School of Business, Program in Business Administration, Chicago, IL 60616-3793. Offers financial management (MBA); innovation and emerging enterprises (MBA); management science (MBA); marketing (MBA); sustainability (MBA); JD/MBA; M Des/MBA; MBA/MS. *Accreditation:* AACSB. Part-time and evening/weekend programs available. *Faculty:* 37 full-time (4 women), 21 part-time/adjunct (5 women). *Students:* 153 full-time (66 women), 30 part-time (12 women); includes 17 minority (3 Black or African American, non-Hispanic/Latino; 9 Asian, non-Hispanic/Latino; 3 Hispanic/Latino; 2 Two or more races, non-Hispanic/Latino), 119 international. Average age 27. 334 applicants, 77% accepted, 63 enrolled. In 2010, 40 master's awarded. *Entrance requirements:* For master's, GRE (minimum score 1000) or GMAT (500). Additional exam requirements/recommendations for international students: Required—TOEFL (minimum score 600 paper-based; 85 iBT); Recommended—IELTS (minimum score 7). *Application deadline:* For fall admission, 8/1 for domestic students, 5/1 for international students; for spring admission, 12/15 for domestic students, 10/15 for international students. Applications are processed on a rolling basis. Application fee: $75. Electronic applications accepted. *Expenses:* Contact institution. *Financial support:* Career-related internships or fieldwork, Federal Work-Study, institutionally sponsored loans, scholarships/grants, traineeships, health care benefits, and tuition waivers (partial) available. Support available to part-time students. Financial award applicants required to submit FAFSA. *Faculty research:* Global management and marketing strategy, technological innovation, management science, financial management, knowledge management. *Unit head:* M. Krishna Erramilli, Interim Director, 312-906-6573, Fax: 312-906-6549. *Application contact:* Deborah Gibson, Director, Graduate Admission, 866-472-3448, Fax: 312-472-3448, E-mail: inquiry.grad@iit.edu.

Illinois Institute of Technology, Stuart School of Business, Program in Finance, Chicago, IL 60616-3793. Offers MS, JD/MS, MBA/MS. Part-time and evening/weekend programs available. *Faculty:* 37 full-time (4 women), 21 part-time/adjunct (5 women). *Students:* 352 full-time (158 women), 51 part-time (20 women); includes 6 minority (4 Asian, non-Hispanic/Latino; 2 Native Hawaiian or other Pacific Islander, non-Hispanic/Latino), 360 international. Average age 24. 825 applicants, 80% accepted, 200 enrolled. In 2010, 184

master's awarded. *Entrance requirements:* For master's, GRE (minimum score 1200) or GMAT (600). Additional exam requirements/recommendations for international students: Required—TOEFL (minimum score 600 paper-based; 85 iBT); Recommended—IELTS (minimum score 7). *Application deadline:* For fall admission, 8/1 for domestic students, 5/1 for international students; for spring admission, 12/15 for domestic students, 10/15 for international students. Applications are processed on a rolling basis. Application fee: $75. Electronic applications accepted. *Expenses:* Contact institution. *Financial support:* In 2010–11, 1 fellowship with full tuition reimbursement (averaging $4,800 per year) was awarded; career-related internships or fieldwork, Federal Work-Study, institutionally sponsored loans, scholarships/grants, traineeships, health care benefits, and tuition waivers (partial) also available. Support available to part-time students. Financial award applicants required to submit FAFSA. *Faculty research:* Factor models for investment management, credit rating and credit risk management, hedge fund performance analysis, option trading and risk management, global asset allocation strategies. *Unit head:* John Bilson, Director, 312-906-6538, Fax: 312-906-6549, E-mail: bilson@stuart.iit.edu. *Application contact:* Deborah Gibson, Director, Graduate Admission, 866-472-3448, Fax: 312-567-3138, E-mail: inquiry.grad@iit.edu.

Indiana University Bloomington, School of Public and Environmental Affairs, Public Affairs Programs, Bloomington, IN 47405-7000. Offers comparative and international affairs (MPA); economic development (MPA); energy (MPA); environmental policy (PhD); environmental policy and natural resource management (MPA); information systems (MPA); local government management (MPA); nonprofit management (MPA, Certificate); policy analysis (MPA); public finance (PhD); public financial administration (MPA); public management (MPA, PhD); public policy analysis (PhD); specialized public affairs (MPA); sustainability and sustainable development (MPA); JD/MPA; MPA/MIS; MPA/MLS; MSES/MPA. *Accreditation:* NASPAA (one or more programs are accredited). Part-time programs available. *Faculty:* 31 full-time, 15 part-time/adjunct. *Students:* 466 full-time (261 women); includes 11 Black or African American, non-Hispanic/Latino; 2 American Indian or Alaska Native, non-Hispanic/Latino; 42 Asian, non-Hispanic/Latino; 1 Hispanic/Latino, 65 international. Average age 26. 650 applicants, 218 enrolled. In 2010, 166 master's, 10 doctorates awarded. *Degree requirements:* For master's, core classes, capstone; for doctorate, comprehensive exam, thesis/dissertation. *Entrance requirements:* For master's, GRE General Test or GMAT, official transcripts, 3 letters of recommendation, resume, personal statement, departmental questions; for doctorate, GRE General Test or LSAT, official transcripts, 3 letters of recommendation, resume or curriculum vitae, statement of purpose. Additional exam requirements/recommendations for international students: Required—TOEFL (minimum score 600 paper-based; 96 iBT); Recommended—IELTS (minimum score 7). *Application deadline:* For fall admission, 5/1 priority date for domestic students, 12/1 priority date for international students. Applications are processed on a rolling basis. Application fee: $55 ($65 for international students). Electronic applications accepted. *Financial support:* Fellowships with partial tuition reimbursements, research assistantships with partial tuition reimbursements, teaching assistantships with partial tuition reimbursements, career-related internships or fieldwork, Federal Work-Study, scholarships/grants, health care benefits, unspecified assistantships, and Service Corps programs available. Financial award application deadline: 2/1; financial award applicants required to submit FAFSA. *Faculty research:* Comparative and international affairs, environmental policy and resource management, policy analysis, public finance, public management, urban management, nonprofit management, energy policy, social policy, public finance. *Unit head:* Jennifer Forney, Director of Graduate Student Services, 812-855-9485, Fax: 812-856-3665, E-mail: speampo@indiana.edu. *Application contact:* Audrey Whitaker, Admissions Assistant, 812-855-2840, E-mail: speaapps@indiana.edu.

Indiana University Southeast, School of Business, New Albany, IN 47150-6405. Offers business administration (MBA); strategic finance (MS). *Accreditation:* AACSB. *Faculty:* 11 full-time (2 women). *Students:* 11 full-time (4 women), 222 part-time (88 women); includes 19 minority (4 Black or African American, non-Hispanic/Latino; 8 Asian, non-Hispanic/Latino; 2 Hispanic/Latino; 3 Native Hawaiian or other Pacific Islander, non-Hispanic/Latino; 2 Two or more races, non-Hispanic/Latino), 4 international. Average age 31. 41 applicants, 100% accepted, 37 enrolled. In 2010, 74 master's awarded. *Degree requirements:* For master's, community service. *Entrance requirements:* For master's, GMAT, work experience. Additional exam requirements/recommendations for international students: Required—TOEFL. Application fee: $35. *Expenses:* Contact institution. *Financial support:* In 2010–11, 2 teaching assistantships (averaging $4,500 per year) were awarded. *Unit head:* Dr. Jay White, Dean, 812-941-2362, Fax: 812-941-2672. *Application contact:* Dr. Jay White, Dean, 812-941-2362, Fax: 812-941-2672.

Iona College, Hagan School of Business, Department of Finance, Business Economics and Legal Studies, New Rochelle, NY 10801-1890. Offers financial management (MBA, PMC). Part-time and evening/weekend programs available. *Faculty:* 12 full-time (4 women), 2 part-time/adjunct (0 women). *Students:* 30 full-time (14 women), 82 part-time (27 women); includes 21 minority (6 Black or African American, non-Hispanic/Latino; 5 Asian, non-Hispanic/Latino; 10 Hispanic/Latino), 4 international. Average age 29. 31 applicants, 68% accepted, 21 enrolled. In 2010, 71 master's awarded.

Entrance requirements: For master's, GMAT, 2 letters of recommendation. Additional exam requirements/recommendations for international students: Required—TOEFL (minimum score 550 paper-based; 213 computer-based). *Application deadline:* Applications are processed on a rolling basis. Application fee: $50. Electronic applications accepted. *Expenses:* Contact institution. *Financial support:* Scholarships/grants, tuition waivers (partial), and unspecified assistantships available. Support available to part-time students. Financial award application deadline: 4/15; financial award applicants required to submit FAFSA. *Faculty research:* Options, insurance financing, asset depreciation ranges, international finance, emerging markets. *Unit head:* Dr. Anand Shetty, Chairman, 914-633-2284, E-mail: ashetty@iona.edu. *Application contact:* Ben Fan, Director of MBA Admissions, 914-633-2289, Fax: 914-637-2708, E-mail: sfan@iona.edu.

The Johns Hopkins University, Carey Business School, Finance Programs, Baltimore, MD 21218-2699. Offers finance (MS); financial management (Certificate); investments (Certificate). Part-time and evening/weekend programs available. *Faculty:* 29 full-time (6 women), 135 part-time/adjunct (29 women). *Students:* 73 full-time (25 women), 112 part-time (32 women); includes 56 minority (15 Black or African American, non-Hispanic/Latino; 1 American Indian or Alaska Native, non-Hispanic/Latino; 31 Asian, non-Hispanic/Latino; 7 Hispanic/Latino; 1 Native Hawaiian or other Pacific Islander, non-Hispanic/Latino; 1 Two or more races, non-Hispanic/Latino), 65 international. Average age 30. 148 applicants, 72% accepted, 57 enrolled. In 2010, 65 master's, 19 other advanced degrees awarded. *Degree requirements:* For master's, 36 credits including final project. *Entrance requirements:* For master's, GMAT or GRE (recommended), minimum GPA of 3.0, resume, work experience, two letters of recommendation; for Certificate, minimum GPA of 3.0, resume, work experience, two letters of recommendation. Additional exam requirements/recommendations for international students: Required—TOEFL (minimum score 600 paper-based; 250 computer-based; 100 iBT). *Application deadline:* For fall admission, 4/1 for international students; for spring admission, 9/15 for international students. Applications are processed on a rolling basis. Application fee: $100. Electronic applications accepted. *Financial support:* In 2010–11, 9 students received support. Scholarships/grants available. Support available to part-time students. Financial award application deadline: 4/15; financial award applicants required to submit FAFSA. *Faculty research:* Financial econometrics, high frequency data modeling, corporate finance. *Unit head:* Dr. Dipankar Chakravarti, Vice Dean of Programs, 410-234-9311, E-mail: dipankar.chakravarti@jhu.edu. *Application contact:* Robin Greenberg, Admissions Coordinator, 410-234-9227, Fax: 443-529-1554, E-mail: carey.admissions@jhu.edu.

Kent State University, Graduate School of Management, Doctoral Program in Finance, Kent, OH 44242-0001. Offers PhD. *Faculty:* 8 full-time (2 women). *Students:* 16 full-time (9 women); includes 1 Black or African American, non-Hispanic/Latino, 3 international. Average age 34. 40 applicants, 25% accepted, 3 enrolled. In 2010, 2 doctorates awarded. *Degree requirements:* For doctorate, comprehensive exam, thesis/dissertation, oral defense. *Entrance requirements:* For doctorate, GMAT. Additional exam requirements/recommendations for international students: Required—TOEFL (minimum score 600 paper-based; 250 computer-based; 100 iBT). *Application deadline:* For fall admission, 2/1 for domestic students, 1/1 for international students. Application fee: $30 ($60 for international students). Electronic applications accepted. *Expenses:* Tuition, state resident: full-time $7866; part-time $437 per credit hour. Tuition, nonresident: full-time $14,022; part-time $779 per credit hour. *Financial support:* In 2010–11, 12 students received support, including fellowships with full tuition reimbursements available (averaging $15,000 per year), 12 teaching assistantships with full tuition reimbursements available (averaging $15,000 per year); Federal Work-Study also available. Financial award application deadline: 2/1; financial award applicants required to submit FAFSA. *Faculty research:* Corporate finance, investments, international finance, futures and options, risk and insurance. *Unit head:* Dr. John Thornton, Chair and Associate Professor, 330-672-2426, Fax: 330-672-9806, E-mail: jthornt5@kent.edu. *Application contact:* Felecia A. Urbanek, Coordinator, Graduate Programs, 330-672-2282, Fax: 330-672-7303, E-mail: gradbus@kent.edu.

Kentucky State University, College of Professional Studies, Frankfort, KY 40601. Offers business administration (MBA), including accounting, finance, management, marketing; public administration (MPA), including human resource management, international administration and development, management information systems, nonprofit management; special education (MA). Part-time and evening/weekend programs available. Postbaccalaureate distance learning degree programs offered (minimal on-campus study). *Faculty:* 12 full-time (4 women), 2 part-time/adjunct (both women). *Students:* 88 full-time (57 women), 79 part-time (42 women); includes 104 minority (101 Black or African American, non-Hispanic/Latino; 1 Asian, non-Hispanic/Latino; 2 Hispanic/Latino), 2 international. Average age 34. 124 applicants, 62% accepted, 45 enrolled. In 2010, 38 master's awarded. *Degree requirements:* For master's, comprehensive exam, thesis optional. *Entrance requirements:* For master's, GMAT, GRE. Additional exam requirements/recommendations for international students: Required—TOEFL (minimum score 525 paper-based; 173 computer-based). *Application deadline:* Applications are processed on a rolling basis. Application fee: $30 ($100 for international

students). Electronic applications accepted. *Expenses:* Tuition, state resident: full-time $5886; part-time $352 per credit hour. Tuition, nonresident: full-time $9054; part-time $528 per credit hour. Required fees: $450; $26 per credit hour. *Financial support:* In 2010–11, 46 students received support, including 4 research assistantships (averaging $10,975 per year); career-related internships or fieldwork, scholarships/grants, tuition waivers (partial), and unspecified assistantships also available. Financial award application deadline: 4/15; financial award applicants required to submit FAFSA. *Unit head:* Dr. Gashaw Lake, Dean, 502-597-6105, Fax: 502-597-6715, E-mail: gashaw.lake@kysu.edu. *Application contact:* Dr. Titilayo Ufomata, Acting Director of Graduate Studies, 502-597-6443, E-mail: titilayo.ufomata@kysu.edu.

Lamar University, College of Graduate Studies, College of Business, Beaumont, TX 77710. Offers accounting (MBA); experiential business and entrepreneurship (MBA); financial management (MBA); healthcare administration (MBA); information systems (MBA); management (MBA). *Accreditation:* AACSB. Part-time and evening/weekend programs available. *Faculty:* 17 full-time (4 women), 4 part-time/adjunct (0 women). *Students:* 79 full-time (37 women), 56 part-time (22 women); includes 14 Black or African American, non-Hispanic/Latino; 8 Asian, non-Hispanic/Latino; 12 Hispanic/Latino, 18 international. Average age 28. 103 applicants, 70% accepted, 40 enrolled. In 2010, 49 master's awarded. *Degree requirements:* For master's, comprehensive exam (for some programs), thesis optional. *Entrance requirements:* For master's, GMAT. Additional exam requirements/recommendations for international students: Required—TOEFL (minimum score 525 paper-based; 197 computer-based). *Application deadline:* For fall admission, 3/15 priority date for domestic students; for spring admission, 10/1 priority date for domestic students. Applications are processed on a rolling basis. Application fee: $25 ($50 for international students). *Expenses:* Tuition, state resident: full-time $4160; part-time $208 per credit hour. Tuition, nonresident: full-time $10,360; part-time $518 per credit hour. *Financial support:* In 2010–11, 12 students received support, including 4 research assistantships with partial tuition reimbursements available; fellowships with tuition reimbursements available, career-related internships or fieldwork, Federal Work-Study, institutionally sponsored loans, scholarships/grants, and tuition waivers (partial) also available. Support available to part-time students. Financial award application deadline: 4/1; financial award applicants required to submit FAFSA. *Faculty research:* Marketing, finance, quantitative methods, management information systems, legal, environmental. *Unit head:* Dr. Enrique R. Venta, Dean, 409-880-8604, Fax: 409-880-8088, E-mail: henry.venta@lamar.edu. *Application contact:* Dr. Brad Mayer, Professor and Associate Dean, 409-880-2383, Fax: 409-880-8605, E-mail: bradley.mayer@lamar.edu.

Lehigh University, College of Business and Economics, Department of Finance, Bethlehem, PA 18015. Offers analytical finance (MS). *Faculty:* 8 full-time (2 women). *Students:* 55 full-time (31 women), 26 part-time (8 women); includes 7 minority (6 Asian, non-Hispanic/Latino; 1 Native Hawaiian or other Pacific Islander, non-Hispanic/Latino), 46 international. Average age 26. 367 applicants, 18% accepted, 40 enrolled. In 2010, 36 master's awarded. *Degree requirements:* For master's, capstone project. *Entrance requirements:* For master's, GMAT or GRE, bachelor's degree from a mathematically rigorous program, minimum GPA of 3.0. Additional exam requirements/recommendations for international students: Required—TOEFL (minimum score 600 paper-based; 250 computer-based; 94 iBT). *Application deadline:* For fall admission, 7/15 for domestic students, 2/15 for international students. Applications are processed on a rolling basis. Application fee: $100. Electronic applications accepted. *Expenses:* Contact institution. Total annual research expenditures: $67,063. *Unit head:* Richard Kish, Department Chair, 610-758-4205, E-mail: rjk7@lehigh.edu. *Application contact:* Corinn McBride, Director of Recruitment and Admissions, 610-758-3418, Fax: 610-758-5283, E-mail: com207@lehigh.edu.

Lewis University, College of Business, Graduate School of Management, Program in Business Administration, Romeoville, IL 60446. Offers accounting (MBA); custom elective option (MBA); e-business (MBA); finance (MBA); healthcare management (MBA); human resources management (MBA); information security (MBA); international business (MBA); management information systems (MBA); marketing (MBA); project management (MBA); technology and operations management (MBA). Part-time and evening/weekend programs available. *Students:* 119 full-time (66 women), 204 part-time (104 women); includes 55 Black or African American, non-Hispanic/Latino; 9 Asian, non-Hispanic/Latino; 30 Hispanic/Latino; 1 Native Hawaiian or other Pacific Islander, non-Hispanic/Latino, 9 international. Average age 28. In 2010, 111 master's awarded. *Entrance requirements:* For master's, interview, bachelor's degree, resume, 2 recommendations. Additional exam requirements/recommendations for international students: Required—TOEFL (minimum score 550 paper-based; 213 computer-based). *Application deadline:* For fall admission, 8/15 priority date for domestic students, 5/1 priority date for international students; for spring admission, 11/15 priority date for international students. Applications are processed on a rolling basis. Application fee: $40. Electronic applications accepted. *Expenses:* Tuition: Full-time $13,320; part-time $740 per credit hour. Tuition and fees vary according to program. *Financial support:* Career-related internships or fieldwork, Federal Work-Study, scholarships/grants, and unspecified assistantships available. Financial award application deadline: 5/1; financial award applicants required to submit

FAFSA. *Unit head:* Dr. Maureen Culleeney, Academic Program Director, 815-838-0500 Ext. 5631, E-mail: culleema@lewisu.edu. *Application contact:* Michele Ryan, Director of Admission, 815-838-0500 Ext. 5384, E-mail: gsm@lewisu.edu.

Lewis University, College of Business, Graduate School of Management, Program in Finance, Romeoville, IL 60446. Offers MS. Part-time and evening/weekend programs available. *Students:* 14 full-time (3 women), 14 part-time (6 women); includes 4 Black or African American, non-Hispanic/Latino; 1 Hispanic/Latino, 3 international. Average age 29. In 2010, 8 master's awarded. *Entrance requirements:* For master's, bachelor's degree, interview, resume, 2 recommendations, minimum GPA of 2.75. Additional exam requirements/recommendations for international students: Required—TOEFL (minimum score 550 paper-based; 213 computer-based). *Application deadline:* For fall admission, 5/1 priority date for international students; for spring admission, 11/15 priority date for international students. Applications are processed on a rolling basis. Application fee: $40. Electronic applications accepted. *Expenses:* Tuition: Full-time $13,320; part-time $740 per credit hour. Tuition and fees vary according to program. *Financial support:* Career-related internships or fieldwork, Federal Work-Study, scholarships/grants, and unspecified assistantships available. Support available to part-time students. Financial award application deadline: 5/1; financial award applicants required to submit FAFSA. *Unit head:* Dr. Robert Atra, Academic Program Director, 815-838-0500 Ext. 5804, E-mail: atraro@lewisu.edu. *Application contact:* Michele Ryan, Director of Admission, 815-838-0500 Ext. 5384, E-mail: gsm@lewisu.edu.

Lincoln University, Graduate Studies, Oakland, CA 94612. Offers finance and investments (DBA); finance management and investment banking (MBA); general business (MBA); human resource management (MBA, DBA); international business (MBA); management information systems (MBA). Part-time and evening/weekend programs available. *Faculty:* 9 full-time (2 women), 11 part-time/adjunct (1 woman). *Students:* 297 full-time (134 women), 2 part-time (0 women). In 2010, 124 master's awarded. *Degree requirements:* For master's, research project (thesis), internship report, or comprehensive exam; for doctorate, comprehensive exam, thesis/dissertation. *Entrance requirements:* For master's, minimum GPA of 2.7; for doctorate, GMAT (minimum score: 550), GRE (minimum score: 1000), or equivalent test results (waived for master's degree with minimum cumulative GPA of 3.3). Additional exam requirements/recommendations for international students: Required—TOEFL (525 paper, 195 computer, 71 iBT) or IELTS (5.5) for MBA; TOEFL (550 paper, 213 computer, 79 iBT) or IELTS (6.0) for DBA; Recommended—IELTS. *Application deadline:* For fall admission, 7/2 priority date for domestic and international students; for spring admission, 11/25 priority date for domestic students, 11/26 priority date for international students. Applications are processed on a rolling basis. Application fee: $75. Electronic applications accepted. *Expenses:* Tuition: Full-time $6930. Required fees: $195 per semester. *Financial support:* In 2010–11, 1 teaching assistantship was awarded; career-related internships or fieldwork and scholarships/grants also available. *Unit head:* Dr. Marshall Burak, Director of Graduate Programs, 510-628-8016, Fax: 510-628-8012, E-mail: mburak@lincolnuca.edu. *Application contact:* Peggy Au, Director of Admissions and Records, 510-628-8010, Fax: 510-628-8012, E-mail: admissions@lincolnuca.edu.

Lindenwood University, Graduate Programs, School of Business and Entrepreneurship, St. Charles, MO 63301-1695. Offers accounting (MBA, MS); business administration (MBA); entrepreneurial studies (MBA, MS); finance (MBA, MS); human resource management (MBA); human resources (MS); international business (MBA, MS); management (MBA, MS); management information systems (MBA, MS); marketing (MBA, MS); public management (MBA, MS); sport management (MA). *Accreditation:* ACBSP. Part-time and evening/weekend programs available. *Faculty:* 20 full-time (8 women), 17 part-time/adjunct (5 women). *Students:* 179 full-time (73 women), 184 part-time (87 women); includes 27 minority (20 Black or African American, non-Hispanic/Latino; 3 Asian, non-Hispanic/Latino; 4 Hispanic/Latino), 146 international. Average age 28. 149 applicants, 73 enrolled. In 2010, 142 master's awarded. *Degree requirements:* For master's, comprehensive exam (for some programs), thesis (for some programs). *Entrance requirements:* For master's, interview, minimum GPA of 3.0, letter of recommendation. Additional exam requirements/recommendations for international students: Required—TOEFL (minimum score 550 paper-based; 213 computer-based; 80 iBT). *Application deadline:* For fall admission, 7/30 priority date for domestic students, 9/16 priority date for international students; for winter admission, 12/15 priority date for domestic and international students; for spring admission, 2/25 priority date for domestic students, 2/11 priority date for international students. Applications are processed on a rolling basis. Application fee: $30 ($100 for international students). Electronic applications accepted. *Expenses:* Tuition: Full-time $13,260; part-time $380 per credit hour. Required fees: $340. One-time fee: $30. Tuition and fees vary according to course level and course load. *Financial support:* In 2010–11, 209 students received support. Career-related internships or fieldwork, Federal Work-Study, institutionally sponsored loans, and tuition waivers (partial) available. Financial award application deadline: 6/30; financial award applicants required to submit FAFSA. *Unit head:* Roger Ellis, Dean, 636-949-4839, E-mail: rellis@lindenwood.edu. *Application contact:* Brett Barger, Dean of Evening Admissions and Extension Campuses, 636-949-4934, Fax: 636-949-4109, E-mail: adultadmissions@lindenwood.edu.

Lipscomb University, MBA Program, Nashville, TN 37204-3951. Offers accounting (MBA); business administration (general) (MBA); conflict management (MBA); financial services (MBA); healthcare management (MBA); leadership (MBA); nonprofit management (MBA); sports administration (MBA); sustainable practice (MBA). *Accreditation:* ACBSP. Part-time and evening/weekend programs available. *Faculty:* 17 full-time (5 women), 3 part-time/adjunct (0 women). *Students:* 52 full-time (30 women), 79 part-time (36 women); includes 20 Black or African American, non-Hispanic/Latino; 1 American Indian or Alaska Native, non-Hispanic/Latino; 1 Asian, non-Hispanic/Latino; 7 Hispanic/Latino. Average age 32. 151 applicants, 47% accepted, 45 enrolled. In 2010, 70 master's awarded. *Entrance requirements:* For master's, GMAT, interview, 2 references, resume. Additional exam requirements/recommendations for international students: Required—TOEFL (minimum score 570 paper-based; 230 computer-based). *Application deadline:* For fall admission, 2/1 for international students; for winter admission, 6/1 for international students. Applications are processed on a rolling basis. Application fee: $50 ($75 for international students). Electronic applications accepted. *Expenses:* Contact institution. *Financial support:* Career-related internships or fieldwork, Federal Work-Study, scholarships/grants, tuition waivers (partial), and unspecified assistantships available. Support available to part-time students. Financial award application deadline: 7/1; financial award applicants required to submit FAFSA. *Faculty research:* Impact of spirituality on organization commitment, leadership, psychological empowerment, training. *Unit head:* Dr. Mike Kendrick, Interim Chair of Graduate Business Studies, 615-966-1833, Fax: 615-966-1818, E-mail: mikekendrick@lipscomb.edu. *Application contact:* Emily Landsdell, 615-966-5284, E-mail: emily.lansdell@lipscomb.edu.

Long Island University, Rockland Graduate Campus, Graduate School, Masters of Business Administration Program, Orangeburg, NY 10962. Offers business administration (Post Master's Certificate); entrepreneurship (MBA); finance (MBA); healthcare sector management (MBA); management (MBA). Part-time and evening/weekend programs available. *Faculty:* 12 part-time/adjunct (2 women). *Students:* 42 part-time (26 women). In 2010, 12 master's awarded. *Entrance requirements:* For master's, GMAT, college transcripts, two letters of recommendation, personal statement, resume. *Application deadline:* Applications are processed on a rolling basis. Application fee: $30. *Expenses:* Tuition: Part-time $1028 per credit. Required fees: $340 per semester. *Financial support:* In 2010–11, 34 students received support. Scholarships/grants available. Support available to part-time students. Financial award applicants required to submit FAFSA. *Unit head:* Dr. Lynn Johnson, Program Director, 845-359-7200 Ext. 5436, Fax: 845-359-7248, E-mail: lynn.johnson@liu.edu. *Application contact:* Peter S. Reiner, Director of Admissions and Marketing, 845-359-7200, Fax: 845-359-7248, E-mail: peter.reiner@liu.edu.

Louisiana State University and Agricultural and Mechanical College, Graduate School, E. J. Ourso College of Business, Department of Finance, Baton Rouge, LA 70803. Offers business administration (PhD), including finance (MS). *Faculty:* 11 full-time (3 women), 1 part-time/adjunct (0 women). *Students:* 35 full-time (10 women), 5 part-time (0 women); includes 1 Asian, non-Hispanic/Latino, 15 international. Average age 27. 106 applicants, 25% accepted, 1 enrolled. In 2010, 20 master's, 2 doctorates awarded. *Degree requirements:* For master's, thesis or alternative; for doctorate, thesis/dissertation. *Entrance requirements:* For master's and doctorate, GMAT. Additional exam requirements/recommendations for international students: Required—TOEFL (minimum score 550 paper-based; 213 computer-based; 79 iBT) or IELTS (minimum score 6.5). *Application deadline:* For fall admission, 1/25 priority date for domestic students, 5/15 for international students; for spring admission, 10/15 for international students. Applications are processed on a rolling basis. Application fee: $50 ($70 for international students). *Financial support:* In 2010–11, 25 students received support, including 12 research assistantships with full and partial tuition reimbursements (averaging $17,033 per year), 3 teaching assistantships with full and partial tuition reimbursements available (averaging $12,267 per year); fellowships, career-related internships or fieldwork, Federal Work-Study, scholarships/grants, health care benefits, and unspecified assistantships also available. Support available to part-time students. Financial award application deadline: 4/1; financial award applicants required to submit FAFSA. *Faculty research:* Derivatives and risk management, capital structure, asset pricing, spatial statistics, financial institutions and underwriting. Total annual research expenditures: $16,334. *Unit head:* Dr. Vestor Carlos Slawson, Interim Chair, 225-578-6367, Fax: 225-578-6366, E-mail: cslawson@lsu.edu. *Application contact:* Dr. Vestor Carlos Slawson, Interim Chair, 225-578-6367, Fax: 225-578-6366, E-mail: cslawson@lsu.edu.

Manhattanville College, Graduate Programs, Humanities and Social Sciences Programs, Program in Finance, Purchase, NY 10577-2132. Offers MS. Part-time and evening/weekend programs available. *Students:* 8 part-time (4 women); includes 1 Black or African American, non-Hispanic/Latino. *Entrance requirements:* Additional exam requirements/recommendations for international students: Required—TOEFL. *Application deadline:* Applications are processed on a rolling basis. Application fee: $75. Electronic applications accepted. *Expenses:* Tuition: Full-time $16,110; part-time $895 per credit. Required fees: $50 per semester. *Financial support:* Career-related internships or fieldwork, Federal Work-Study, scholarships/grants, and unspecified assistantships available. Financial award application deadline: 3/1; financial award applicants required to submit FAFSA. *Unit head:* Donald Richards, Interim Dean, School of Graduate and Professional Studies, 914-323-5469, Fax: 914-694-3488, E-mail: gps@mville.edu. *Application contact:* Office of Admissions for Graduate and Professional Studies, 914-323-5418, E-mail: gps@mville.edu.

Marquette University, Graduate School of Management, Executive MBA Program, Milwaukee, WI 53201-1881. Offers economics (MBA); finance (MBA); human resources (MBA); international business (MBA); management information systems (MBA); marketing (MBA); operations and supply chain management (MBA); sports business (MBA). *Accreditation:* AACSB. *Faculty:* 3 full-time (1 woman), 2 part-time/adjunct (0 women). *Students:* 43 full-time (11 women); includes 6 minority (1 Black or African American, non-Hispanic/Latino; 4 Asian, non-Hispanic/Latino; 1 Hispanic/Latino), 3 international. Average age 37. 47 applicants, 74% accepted, 29 enrolled. In 2010, 13 master's awarded. *Degree requirements:* For master's, international trip. *Entrance requirements:* For master's, GMAT, two letters of recommendation, official transcripts from current and previous colleges/universities. Additional exam requirements/recommendations for international students: Required—TOEFL (minimum score 530 paper-based; 78 computer-based). *Application deadline:* Applications are processed on a rolling basis. Application fee: $50. Electronic applications accepted. *Expenses:* Contact institution. *Financial support:* Application deadline: 2/15. *Faculty research:* International trade and finance, customer relationship management, consumer satisfaction, customer service. *Unit head:* Dr. Jeanne Simmons, Graduate Director, 414-288-7145, Fax: 414-288-1660, E-mail: jeanne.simmons@marquette.edu. *Application contact:* Erin Fox, Assistant Director for Recruitment, 414-288-5319, Fax: 414-288-1902, E-mail: erin.fox@marquette.edu.

Marquette University, Graduate School of Management, Program in Business Administration, Milwaukee, WI 53201-1881. Offers business administration (MBA); economics (MBA); finance (MBA); human resources (MBA); international business (MBA); management information systems (MBA); marketing (MBA); operations and supply chain management (MBA); sports business (MBA); JD/MBA; MBA/MA; MBA/MSN. *Accreditation:* AACSB. Part-time and evening/weekend programs available. *Faculty:* 38 full-time (9 women), 24 part-time/adjunct (8 women). *Students:* 44 full-time (17 women), 368 part-time (105 women); includes 36 minority (4 Black or African American, non-Hispanic/Latino; 2 American Indian or Alaska Native, non-Hispanic/Latino; 20 Asian, non-Hispanic/Latino; 10 Hispanic/Latino), 30 international. Average age 31. 256 applicants, 60% accepted, 98 enrolled. In 2010, 117 master's awarded. *Entrance requirements:* For master's, GMAT, letters of recommendation. Additional exam requirements/recommendations for international students: Required—TOEFL (minimum score 530 paper-based; 78 computer-based). *Application deadline:* Applications are processed on a rolling basis. Application fee: $50. Electronic applications accepted. *Expenses:* Tuition: Full-time $16,290; part-time $905 per credit hour. Tuition and fees vary according to program. *Financial support:* In 2010–11, 4 fellowships, 11 teaching assistantships were awarded; research assistantships, Federal Work-Study, institutionally sponsored loans, scholarships/grants, and tuition waivers (full and partial) also available. Support available to part-time students. Financial award application deadline: 2/15. *Faculty research:* Ethics in the professions, services marketing, technology impact on decision-making, mentoring. *Unit head:* Dr. Jeanne Simmons, Graduate Director, 414-288-7145, Fax: 414-288-1660, E-mail: jeanne.simmons@marquette.edu. *Application contact:* Debra Leutermann, Admissions Coordinator, 414-288-8064, Fax: 414-288-1902, E-mail: debra.leutermann@marquette.edu.

Marylhurst University, Department of Business Administration, Marylhurst, OR 97036-0261. Offers finance (MBA); general management (MBA); government policy and administration (MBA); green development (MBA); health care management (MBA); marketing (MBA); natural and organic resources (MBA); nonprofit management (MBA); organizational behavior (MBA); real estate (MBA); renewable energy (MBA); sustainable business (MBA). Part-time and evening/weekend programs available. Postbaccalaureate distance learning degree programs offered (no on-campus study). *Faculty:* 3 full-time (0 women), 36 part-time/adjunct (6 women). *Students:* 27 full-time (13 women), 727 part-time (373 women); includes 167 minority (47 Black or African American, non-Hispanic/Latino; 6 American Indian or Alaska Native, non-Hispanic/Latino; 36 Asian, non-Hispanic/Latino; 51 Hispanic/Latino; 6 Native Hawaiian or other Pacific Islander, non-Hispanic/Latino; 21 Two or more races, non-Hispanic/Latino), 7 international. Average age 38. 262 applicants, 91% accepted, 194 enrolled. In 2010, 289 master's awarded. *Degree requirements:* For master's, comprehensive exam, capstone course. *Entrance requirements:* For master's, GMAT (if GPA less than 3.0 and fewer than 5 years of work experience), interview, resume, 2 letters of recommendation. Additional exam requirements/recommendations for international students: Recommended—TOEFL (minimum score 550 paper-based; 213 computer-based; 80 iBT). *Application deadline:* For fall admission, 9/11 priority date for domestic and international students; for winter admission, 12/15 priority date for domestic and international students; for spring admission, 3/15 priority date for domestic students, 3/17 priority date for international students. Applications are processed on a rolling basis. Application fee: $50. Electronic applications accepted. *Expenses:* Tuition: Full-time $13,932; part-time $516 per credit. Tuition and fees vary according to course load and program. *Financial support:* Scholarships/grants available. Support available to part-time students. Financial award applicants required to submit FAFSA. *Unit head:* Bob Hanks, Director of Business and Real Estate Programs, 503-636-8141, Fax: 503-697-5597, E-mail: mba@marylhurst.edu. *Application contact:* Maruska Lynch, Graduate Admissions Specialist, 800-634-9982 Ext. 6322, Fax: 503-699-6320, E-mail: admissions@marylhurst.edu.

Mississippi State University, College of Business, Department of Finance and Economics, Mississippi State, MS 39762. Offers applied economics (PhD); business administration (PhD), including finance; economics (MA); finance (MSBA). Part-time programs available. *Faculty:* 10 full-time (2 women). *Students:* 14 full-time (3 women), 3 part-time (1 woman); includes 1 minority (Black or African American, non-Hispanic/Latino), 10 international. Average age 31. 63 applicants, 11% accepted, 6 enrolled. In 2010, 1 master's, 2 doctorates awarded. Terminal master's awarded for partial completion of doctoral program. *Degree requirements:* For master's, comprehensive exam, thesis optional; for doctorate, comprehensive exam, thesis/dissertation. *Entrance requirements:* For master's and doctorate, GMAT, GRE General Test. Additional exam requirements/recommendations for international students: Required—TOEFL (minimum score 575 paper-based; 233 computer-based; 90 iBT); Recommended—IELTS (minimum score 6.5). *Application deadline:* For fall admission, 7/1 for domestic students, 5/1 for international students; for spring admission, 11/1 for domestic students, 10/1 for international students. Applications are processed on a rolling basis. Application fee: $40. Electronic applications accepted. *Expenses:* Tuition, state resident: full-time $2730.50; part-time $304 per credit hour. Tuition, nonresident: full-time $6901; part-time $767 per credit hour. *Financial support:* In 2010–11, 3 teaching assistantships with tuition reimbursements (averaging $14,677 per year) were awarded; Federal Work-Study, scholarships/grants, health care benefits, and unspecified assistantships also available. Financial award application deadline: 4/1; financial award applicants required to submit FAFSA. *Faculty research:* Economics development, mergers, event studies, economic education, bank performance. Total annual research expenditures: $961,000. *Unit head:* Dr. Mike Highfield, Department Head, 662-325-1984, Fax: 662-325-1977, E-mail: m.highfield@msstate.edu. *Application contact:* Dr. Benjamin F. Blair, Associate Professor/Graduate Coordinator, 662-325-1980, Fax: 662-325-1977, E-mail: bblair@cobilan.msstate.edu.

Molloy College, Graduate Business Program, Rockville Centre, NY 11571-5002. Offers accounting (MBA); accounting and management (MBA); management (MBA); personal financial planning and accounting (MBA); personal financial planning and management (MBA). Part-time programs available. *Faculty:* 5 full-time (0 women), 8 part-time/adjunct (2 women). *Students:* 26 full-time (15 women), 69 part-time (35 women); includes 19 Black or African American, non-Hispanic/Latino; 1 American Indian or Alaska Native, non-Hispanic/Latino; 7 Asian, non-Hispanic/Latino; 9 Hispanic/Latino. Average age 33. In 2010, 28 master's awarded. *Application deadline:* Applications are processed on a rolling basis. *Application contact:* Alina Haitz, Assistant Director of Graduate Admissions, 516-678-5000 Ext. 6399, Fax: 516-256-2247, E-mail: ahaitz@molloy.edu.

Monmouth University, The Graduate School, Leon Hess Business School, West Long Branch, NJ 07764-1898. Offers accounting (MBA, Post-Master's Certificate); business (MBA); finance (MBA); healthcare management (MBA, Post-Master's Certificate); real estate (MBA). *Accreditation:* AACSB. Part-time and evening/weekend programs available. *Faculty:* 27 full-time (9 women), 7 part-time/adjunct (1 woman). *Students:* 87 full-time (31 women), 144 part-time (69 women); includes 6 Black or African American, non-Hispanic/Latino; 14 Asian, non-Hispanic/Latino; 8 Hispanic/Latino; 2 Two or more races, non-Hispanic/Latino, 17 international. Average age 29. 181 applicants, 78% accepted, 81 enrolled. In 2010, 88 master's awarded. *Degree requirements:* For master's, capstone course. *Entrance requirements:* For master's, GMAT, minimum GPA of 3.0 in major, 2.75 overall. Additional exam requirements/recommendations for international students: Required—TOEFL (minimum score 550 paper-based; 213 computer-based; 79 iBT), IELTS (minimum score 5), Michigan English Language Assessment Battery (minimum score 77), Cambridge A, B, C. *Application deadline:* For fall admission, 7/15 priority date for domestic students, 6/1 for international students; for spring admission, 11/15 priority date for domestic students, 11/1 for international students. Applications are processed on a rolling basis. Application fee: $50. Electronic applications accepted. *Expenses:* Tuition: Full-time $19,572; part-time $816 per credit. Required fees: $628; $157 per semester. *Financial support:* In 2010–11, 166 students received support, including 161 fellowships (averaging $1,741 per year), 17 research assistantships (averaging $10,505 per year); career-related internships or fieldwork, scholarships/grants, and unspecified assistantships also available. Support available to part-time students. Financial award applicants required to submit FAFSA. *Faculty research:* Information technology and marketing, behavioral research in accounting, human resources, management of technology. *Unit head:* Douglas Stives, MBA Program Director, 732-263-5894, Fax: 732-263-5517, E-mail: dstives@monmouth.edu. *Application contact:* Kevin Roane,

Director, Office of Graduate Admission, 732-571-3452, Fax: 732-263-5123, E-mail: gradadm@monmouth.edu.

Montclair State University, The Graduate School, School of Business, Department of Economics and Finance, Montclair, NJ 07043-1624. Offers finance (MBA, Certificate). Part-time and evening/weekend programs available. *Faculty:* 16 full-time (5 women), 9 part-time/adjunct (3 women). *Students:* 18 full-time (9 women), 74 part-time (31 women); includes 9 Black or African American, non-Hispanic/Latino; 9 Asian, non-Hispanic/Latino; 6 Hispanic/Latino; 1 Two or more races, non-Hispanic/Latino, 5 international. Average age 30. 49 applicants, 61% accepted, 20 enrolled. In 2010, 33 master's awarded. *Entrance requirements:* For master's, GRE General Test, 2 letters of recommendation, resume. Additional exam requirements/recommendations for international students: Required—TOEFL (minimum iBT score of 83) or IELTS. *Application deadline:* For fall admission, 6/1 for international students; for spring admission, 10/1 for international students. Applications are processed on a rolling basis. Application fee: $60. Electronic applications accepted. *Expenses:* Tuition, state resident: part-time $501.34 per credit. Tuition, nonresident: part-time $773.88 per credit. Required fees: $71.15 per credit. *Financial support:* In 2010–11, 4 research assistantships with full tuition reimbursements (averaging $7,000 per year) were awarded; Federal Work-Study, scholarships/grants, and unspecified assistantships also available. Support available to part-time students. Financial award application deadline: 3/1; financial award applicants required to submit FAFSA. *Faculty research:* Foreign direct investment, central banking and inflation, African economic development, intraday trade, working capital management. *Unit head:* Dr. Richard Lord, Chair, 973-655-5255. *Application contact:* Amy Aiello, Director of Graduate Admissions and Operations, 973-655-5147, Fax: 973-655-7869, E-mail: graduate.school@montclair.edu.

Mount Saint Mary College, Division of Business, Newburgh, NY 12550-3494. Offers business (MBA); financial planning (MBA). Part-time and evening/weekend programs available. *Faculty:* 5 full-time (1 woman), 6 part-time/adjunct (2 women). *Students:* 35 full-time (21 women), 52 part-time (31 women); includes 20 minority (4 Black or African American, non-Hispanic/Latino; 4 Asian, non-Hispanic/Latino; 10 Hispanic/Latino; 2 Two or more races, non-Hispanic/Latino), 20 international. Average age 30. 22 applicants, 95% accepted, 10 enrolled. In 2010, 45 master's awarded. *Degree requirements:* For master's, thesis or alternative. *Entrance requirements:* For master's, GMAT or minimum undergraduate GPA of 2.7. *Application deadline:* Applications are processed on a rolling basis. Application fee: $45. *Expenses:* Tuition: Full-time $13,356; part-time $742 per credit. Required fees: $70 per semester. *Financial support:* In 2010–11, 25 students received support. Unspecified assistantships available. Financial award application deadline: 4/15; financial award applicants required to submit FAFSA. *Faculty research:* Financial reform, entrepreneurship and small business development, global business relations, technology's impact on business decision-making, college-assisted business education. *Unit head:* Dr. James Gearity, Graduate Coordinator, 845-569-3121, Fax: 845-562-6762, E-mail: james.gearity@msmc.edu. *Application contact:* Kathryn Sharp, Secretary, 845-569-3582, Fax: 845-569-3885, E-mail: ksharp@msmc.edu.

National University, Academic Affairs, College of Letters and Sciences, Department of Professional Studies, La Jolla, CA 92037-1011. Offers forensic science (MFS), including criminalistics and investigation; public administration (MPA), including alternative dispute resolution, human resource management, organizational leadership, public finance. Part-time and evening/weekend programs available. Postbaccalaureate distance learning degree programs offered (no on-campus study). *Faculty:* 10 full-time (3 women), 110 part-time/adjunct (22 women). *Students:* 189 full-time (117 women), 284 part-time (167 women); includes 259 minority (101 Black or African American, non-Hispanic/Latino; 2 American Indian or Alaska Native, non-Hispanic/Latino; 33 Asian, non-Hispanic/Latino; 104 Hispanic/Latino; 7 Native Hawaiian or other Pacific Islander, non-Hispanic/Latino; 12 Two or more races, non-Hispanic/Latino). Average age 38. 305 applicants, 100% accepted, 192 enrolled. In 2010, 160 master's awarded. *Degree requirements:* For master's, thesis. *Entrance requirements:* For master's, interview, minimum GPA of 2.5. Additional exam requirements/recommendations for international students: Required—TOEFL (minimum score 550 paper-based; 213 computer-based; 79 iBT), IELTS (minimum score 6). *Application deadline:* Applications are processed on a rolling basis. Application fee: $60 ($65 for international students). Electronic applications accepted. *Expenses:* Tuition: Full-time $9450; part-time $350 per unit. Required fees: $350 per unit. One-time fee: $60. *Financial support:* Career-related internships or fieldwork, institutionally sponsored loans, scholarships/grants, and tuition waivers (partial) available. Support available to part-time students. Financial award application deadline: 6/30; financial award applicants required to submit FAFSA. *Unit head:* James G. Larsen, Associate Professor and Chair, 858-642-8418, Fax: 858-642-8715, E-mail: jlarson@nu.edu. *Application contact:* Dominick Giovanniello, Associate Regional Dean—San Diego, 800-NAT-UNIV, Fax: 858-541-7792, E-mail: dgiovann@nu.edu.

National University, Academic Affairs, School of Business and Management, Department of Accounting and Finance, La Jolla, CA 92037-1011. Offers accountancy (MS); corporate and international finance (MS). Part-time and evening/weekend programs available. Postbaccalaureate distance learning degree programs offered (no on-campus study). *Faculty:* 15 full-time (2 women), 149 part-time/adjunct (39 women). *Students:* 171 full-time (76 women), 410 part-time (202 women); includes 201 minority (40 Black or African American, non-Hispanic/Latino; 1 American Indian or Alaska Native, non-Hispanic/Latino; 67 Asian, non-Hispanic/Latino; 86 Hispanic/Latino; 1 Native Hawaiian or other Pacific Islander, non-Hispanic/Latino; 6 Two or more races, non-Hispanic/Latino), 147 international. Average age 33. 727 applicants, 100% accepted, 466 enrolled. In 2010, 58 master's awarded. *Degree requirements:* For master's, thesis. *Entrance requirements:* For master's, interview, minimum GPA of 2.5. Additional exam requirements/recommendations for international students: Required—TOEFL (minimum score 550 paper-based; 213 computer-based; 79 iBT), IELTS (minimum score 6). *Application deadline:* Applications are processed on a rolling basis. Application fee: $60 ($65 for international students). Electronic applications accepted. *Expenses:* Tuition: Full-time $9450; part-time $350 per unit. Required fees: $350 per unit. One-time fee: $60. *Financial support:* Career-related internships or fieldwork, institutionally sponsored loans, scholarships/grants, and tuition waivers (partial) available. Support available to part-time students. Financial award application deadline: 6/30; financial award applicants required to submit FAFSA. *Unit head:* Prof. Donald A. Schwartz, Chair and Associate Professor, 858-642-8420, Fax: 858-642-8740, E-mail: dschwartz@nu.edu. *Application contact:* Dominick Giovanniello, Associate Regional Dean—San Diego, 800-NAT-UNIV, Fax: 858-541-7792, E-mail: dgiovann@nu.edu.

National University, Academic Affairs, School of Business and Management, Department of Leadership and Business Administration, La Jolla, CA 92037-1011. Offers alternative dispute resolution (MBA); e-business (MBA); financial management (MBA); human resource management (MBA); human resources management (MA); international business (MBA); knowledge management (MS); marketing (MBA); organizational leadership (MBA, MS); technology management (MBA). Part-time and evening/weekend programs available. Postbaccalaureate distance learning degree programs offered (no on-campus study). *Faculty:* 16 full-time (4 women), 126 part-time/adjunct (39 women). *Students:* 119 full-time (81 women), 410 part-time (202 women); includes 176 minority (81 Black or African American, non-Hispanic/Latino; 1 American Indian or Alaska Native, non-Hispanic/Latino; 31 Asian, non-Hispanic/Latino; 52 Hispanic/Latino; 4 Native Hawaiian or other Pacific Islander, non-Hispanic/Latino; 7 Two or more races, non-Hispanic/Latino), 183 international. Average age 38. 219 applicants, 100% accepted, 160 enrolled. In 2010, 95 master's awarded. *Degree requirements:* For master's, thesis. *Entrance requirements:* For master's, interview, minimum GPA of 2.5. Additional exam requirements/recommendations for international students: Required—TOEFL (minimum score 550 paper-based; 213 computer-based; 79 iBT), IELTS (minimum score 6). *Application deadline:* Applications are processed on a rolling basis. Application fee: $60 ($65 for international students). Electronic applications accepted. *Expenses:* Tuition: Full-time $9450; part-time $350 per unit. Required fees: $350 per unit. One-time fee: $60. *Financial support:* Career-related internships or fieldwork, institutionally sponsored loans, scholarships/grants, and tuition waivers (partial) available. Support available to part-time students. Financial award application deadline: 6/30; financial award applicants required to submit FAFSA. *Unit head:* Dr. Bruce Buchowicz, Chair, 858-642-8439, Fax: 858-642-8406, E-mail: bbuchowicz@nu.edu. *Application contact:* Dominick Giovanniello, Associate Regional Dean—San Diego, 800-NAT-UNIV, Fax: 858-541-7792, E-mail: dgiovann@nu.edu.

Newman University, MBA Program, Wichita, KS 67213-2097. Offers finance (MBA); international business (MBA); leadership (MBA); management (MBA); technology (MBA). Part-time programs available. *Faculty:* 4 full-time (2 women), 7 part-time/adjunct (2 women). *Students:* 33 full-time (14 women), 92 part-time (37 women); includes 28 minority (7 Black or African American, non-Hispanic/Latino; 6 Asian, non-Hispanic/Latino; 12 Hispanic/Latino; 1 Native Hawaiian or other Pacific Islander, non-Hispanic/Latino; 2 Two or more races, non-Hispanic/Latino), 24 international. Average age 32. 80 applicants, 83% accepted, 45 enrolled. In 2010, 72 master's awarded. *Degree requirements:* For master's, thesis optional. *Entrance requirements:* For master's, interview; minimum GPA of 3.0; 3 letters of recommendation; course work in algebra, statistics, macroeconomics, and financial accounting. Additional exam requirements/recommendations for international students: Required—TOEFL (minimum score 600 paper-based; 250 computer-based; 100 iBT). *Application deadline:* For fall admission, 8/1 priority date for domestic students, 7/15 priority date for international students; for winter admission, 1/1 priority date for domestic students; for spring admission, 1/1 priority date for domestic students, 11/15 priority date for international students. Applications are processed on a rolling basis. Application fee: $25 ($40 for international students). Electronic applications accepted. *Expenses:* Contact institution. *Financial support:* In 2010–11, 29 students received support. Federal Work-Study available. Financial award application deadline: 8/15; financial award applicants required to submit FAFSA. *Unit head:* Dr. George Goetz, Dean of the College of Professional Studies/Director, 316-942-4291 Ext. 2205, Fax: 316-942-4483, E-mail: smithge@newmanu.edu. *Application contact:* Linda Kay Sabala, Director of Graduate Admissions, 316-942-4291 Ext. 2230, Fax: 316-942-4483, E-mail: sabalal@newmanu.edu.

New York Institute of Technology, Graduate Division, School of Management, Program in Business Administration, Old Westbury, NY 11568-8000. Offers accounting (Advanced Certificate); business administration (MBA); finance (Advanced Certificate); international business (Advanced Certificate); management of information systems (Advanced Certificate); marketing (Advanced Certificate). Part-time and evening/weekend programs available. *Students:* 454 full-time (188 women), 513 part-time (204 women); includes 49 minority (15 Black or African American, non-Hispanic/Latino; 23 Asian, non-Hispanic/Latino; 11 Hispanic/Latino), 268 international. Average age 29. In 2010, 435 master's, 1 other advanced degree awarded. *Degree requirements:* For master's, thesis (for some programs). *Entrance requirements:* For master's, minimum QPA of 2.85. Additional exam requirements/recommendations for international students: Required—TOEFL (minimum score 550 paper-based; 213 computer-based). *Application deadline:* For fall admission, 7/1 priority date for domestic students; for spring admission, 12/1 priority date for domestic students. Applications are processed on a rolling basis. Application fee: $50. Electronic applications accepted. *Expenses:* Tuition: Part-time $835 per credit. *Financial support:* Fellowships, research assistantships with partial tuition reimbursements, institutionally sponsored loans, tuition waivers (full and partial), and unspecified assistantships available. Support available to part-time students. Financial award applicants required to submit FAFSA. *Faculty research:* Instructor performance appraisal; relationship between TOEFL, GMAT, GRE, and performance in foreign students. *Unit head:* Dr. Stephen Hartman, Director, 516-686-7691, E-mail: shartman@nyit.edu. *Application contact:* Dr. Jacquelyn Nealon, Vice President for Enrollment Services, 516-686-7925, Fax: 516-686-7597, E-mail: jnealon@nyit.edu.

New York Law School, Graduate Programs, New York, NY 10013. Offers financial services (LL M); law (JD); mental disability law (MA); real estate (LL M); taxation (LL M); JD/MBA. JD/MBA offered jointly with Bernard M. Baruch College of the City University of New York. *Accreditation:* ABA. Part-time and evening/weekend programs available. Postbaccalaureate distance learning degree programs offered. *Faculty:* 75 full-time (26 women), 100 part-time/adjunct (40 women). *Students:* 1,547 full-time (824 women), 491 part-time (214 women); includes 488 minority (145 Black or African American, non-Hispanic/Latino; 11 American Indian or Alaska Native, non-Hispanic/Latino; 67 Asian, non-Hispanic/Latino; 233 Hispanic/Latino; 1 Native Hawaiian or other Pacific Islander, non-Hispanic/Latino; 31 Two or more races, non-Hispanic/Latino). Average age 28. 5,405 applicants, 45% accepted, 550 enrolled. In 2010, 539 first professional degrees, 9 master's awarded. *Entrance requirements:* LSAT, letters of recommendation, resume. Additional exam requirements/recommendations for international students: Recommended—TOEFL (minimum score 600 paper-based; 250 computer-based; 100 iBT). *Application deadline:* For fall admission, 4/1 priority date for domestic and international students. Applications are processed on a rolling basis. Application fee: $65. Electronic applications accepted. *Expenses:* Tuition: Full-time $44,860; part-time $34,500 per year. Required fees: $1600. *Financial support:* In 2010–11, 682 students received support, including 202 research assistantships (averaging $3,920 per year), 5 teaching assistantships (averaging $1,000 per year); career-related internships or fieldwork, Federal Work-Study, institutionally sponsored loans, and scholarships/grants also available. Support available to part-time students. Financial award application deadline: 4/2; financial award applicants required to submit FAFSA. *Unit head:* Richard A. Matasar, President and Dean, 212-431-2840, Fax: 212-219-3752, E-mail: rmatasar@nyls.edu. *Application contact:* William D. Perez, Assistant Dean for Admissions and Financial Aid, 212-431-2888, Fax: 212-966-1522, E-mail: wperez@nyls.edu.

New York University, Robert F. Wagner Graduate School of Public Service, Program in Public Administration, New York, NY 10012-1019. Offers public administration (PhD); public and nonprofit management and policy (MPA, Advanced Certificate), including developmental administration (Advanced Certificate), financial management and public finance, human resources management (Advanced Certificate), international administration (Advanced Certificate), management (MPA), management for public and nonprofit organizations (Advanced Certificate), public policy analysis, quantitative analysis and computer applications (Advanced Certificate), urban public policy (Advanced Certificate); JD/MPA; MBA/MPA; MPA/MA. *Accreditation:* NASPAA (one or more programs are accredited). Part-time and evening/weekend programs available. *Faculty:* 32 full-time (13 women), 41 part-time/adjunct (22 women). *Students:* 400 full-time (301 women), 206 part-time (156 women); includes 43 Black or African American, non-Hispanic/Latino; 58 Asian, non-Hispanic/Latino; 36 Hispanic/Latino, 65 international. Average age 28. 1,230 applicants, 54% accepted, 219 enrolled. In 2010, 210 master's, 5 doctorates awarded. *Degree requirements:* For master's, thesis or alternative, capstone end event; for doctorate, one foreign language, thesis/dissertation. *Entrance requirements:* For master's, minimum undergraduate GPA of 3.0; for doctorate, GMAT or GRE General Test, minimum GPA of 3.5. Additional exam requirements/recommendations for international students: Required—TOEFL (minimum score 600 paper-based; 250 computer-based; 100 iBT), IELTS (minimum score 7.5), TWE (minimum score 4). *Application deadline:* For fall admission, 1/15 for domestic students, 1/4 for international students; for spring admission, 11/15 for domestic students, 10/1 for international students. Applications are processed on a rolling basis. Application fee: $80. Electronic applications accepted. *Expenses:* Contact institution. *Financial support:* In 2010–11, 176 students received support, including 171 fellowships (averaging $14,022 per year), 5 research assistantships with full

tuition reimbursements available (averaging $22,440 per year); career-related internships or fieldwork, Federal Work-Study, institutionally sponsored loans, scholarships/grants, health care benefits, and unspecified assistantships also available. Support available to part-time students. Financial award application deadline: 1/5; financial award applicants required to submit FAFSA. *Unit head:* Katty Jones, Director, Program Services, 212-998-7411, Fax: 212-995-4164, E-mail: katty.jones@nyu.edu. *Application contact:* Christopher Alexander, Administrative Aide, Enrollment, 212-998-7414, Fax: 212-995-4611, E-mail: wagner.admissions@nyu.edu.

New York University, School of Continuing and Professional Studies, The Preston Robert Tisch Center for Hospitality, Tourism, and Sports Management, Program in Hospitality Industry Studies, New York, NY 10012-1019. Offers brand strategy (MS); hospitality industry studies (Advanced Certificate); hotel finance (MS). Part-time and evening/weekend programs available. *Faculty:* 12 full-time (5 women), 17 part-time/adjunct (3 women). *Students:* 11 full-time (9 women), 25 part-time (16 women); includes 1 Black or African American, non-Hispanic/Latino; 1 American Indian or Alaska Native, non-Hispanic/Latino; 5 Asian, non-Hispanic/Latino; 4 Hispanic/Latino, 8 international. Average age 29. 104 applicants, 24% accepted, 8 enrolled. In 2010, 19 master's, 1 other advanced degree awarded. *Degree requirements:* For master's, thesis. *Entrance requirements:* For master's, GMAT or GRE General Test (for recent graduates), resume, 2 letters of recommendation, essay, professional experience. Additional exam requirements/recommendations for international students: Required—TOEFL (minimum score 600 paper-based; 250 computer-based; 100 iBT), TWE. *Application deadline:* For fall admission, 2/1 priority date for domestic and international students; for spring admission, 10/15 priority date for domestic students, 8/15 priority date for international students. Applications are processed on a rolling basis. Application fee: $75. Electronic applications accepted. *Financial support:* In 2010–11, 17 students received support, including 17 fellowships (averaging $3,186 per year); career-related internships or fieldwork, Federal Work-Study, institutionally sponsored loans, and scholarships/grants also available. Support available to part-time students. Financial award application deadline: 3/1; financial award applicants required to submit FAFSA. *Unit head:* Bjorn Hanson, Divisional Dean, Clinical Professor, HVS Chair, 212-998-9100, Fax: 212-995-4676, E-mail: lalia.rach@nyu.edu. *Application contact:* Sandra Dove-Lowther, Academic Services Director, 212-992-9087, Fax: 212-995-4676, E-mail: sd2@nyu.edu.

New York University, School of Continuing and Professional Studies, Schack Institute of Real Estate, Program in Real Estate, New York, NY 10012-1019. Offers business of development (MS); finance and investment (MS); global real estate (MS); real estate (Advanced Certificate); strategic real estate management (MS); sustainable development (MS). Part-time and evening/weekend programs available. *Faculty:* 11 full-time (3 women), 74 part-time/adjunct (8 women). *Students:* 94 full-time (17 women), 282 part-time (63 women); includes 16 Black or African American, non-Hispanic/Latino; 2 American Indian or Alaska Native, non-Hispanic/Latino; 30 Asian, non-Hispanic/Latino; 17 Hispanic/Latino, 62 international. Average age 30. 298 applicants, 68% accepted, 111 enrolled. In 2010, 184 master's, 48 other advanced degrees awarded. *Degree requirements:* For master's, thesis, capstone. *Entrance requirements:* For master's, GRE General Test or GMAT (for recent graduates), resume, 2 letters of recommendation, essay, professional experience. Additional exam requirements/recommendations for international students: Required—TOEFL (minimum score 600 paper-based; 250 computer-based; 100 iBT), TWE. *Application deadline:* For fall admission, 2/1 priority date for domestic and international students; for spring admission, 10/15 priority date for domestic students, 8/15 priority date for international students. Applications are processed on a rolling basis. Application fee: $75. Electronic applications accepted. *Financial support:* In 2010–11, 186 students received support, including 186 fellowships (averaging $2,423 per year); scholarships/grants also available. Support available to part-time students. Financial award application deadline: 3/1; financial award applicants required to submit FAFSA. *Faculty research:* Economics and market cycles, international property rights, comparative metropolitan economies, current market trends. *Unit head:* James Stuckey, Divisional Dean, 212-992-3335, Fax: 212-992-3686, E-mail: james.stuckey@nyu.edu. *Application contact:* Jennifer Monahan, Director of Administration and Student Services, 212-992-3335, Fax: 212-992-3686, E-mail: jm189@nyu.edu.

North Central College, Graduate and Continuing Education Programs, Department of Business, Program in Business Administration, Naperville, IL 60566-7063. Offers change management (MBA); finance (MBA); human resource management (MBA); management (MBA); marketing (MBA). Part-time and evening/weekend programs available. *Faculty:* 14 full-time (4 women), 5 part-time/adjunct (1 woman). *Students:* 46 full-time (17 women), 101 part-time (46 women); includes 6 Black or African American, non-Hispanic/Latino; 1 American Indian or Alaska Native, non-Hispanic/Latino; 4 Asian, non-Hispanic/Latino; 7 Hispanic/Latino, 3 international. Average age 31. In 2010, 46 master's awarded. *Degree requirements:* For master's, project. *Entrance requirements:* For master's, interview. Additional exam requirements/recommendations for international students: Required—TOEFL (minimum score 577 paper-based; 233 computer-based; 90 iBT). *Application deadline:* For fall admission, 8/15 for domestic students; for winter admission, 12/1 for domestic students; for spring admission, 2/1 for domestic students. Application fee: $25. *Financial support:* Scholarships/grants available. Support available to part-time students. *Unit head:* Dr. Jean Clifton, MBA Program Coordinator, 630-637-5244, E-mail: jmclifton@noctrl.edu. *Application contact:* Wendy Kulpinski, Director and Graduate and Continuing Education Admission, 630-637-5808, Fax: 630-637-5844, E-mail: wekulpinski@noctrl.edu.

Northeastern Illinois University, Graduate College, College of Business and Management, Chicago, IL 60625-4699. Offers accounting (MSA); finance (MBA); management (MBA); marketing (MBA). Part-time and evening/weekend programs available. *Faculty:* 24 full-time (3 women), 13 part-time/adjunct (4 women). *Students:* 41 full-time (19 women), 69 part-time (32 women); includes 23 minority (4 Black or African American, non-Hispanic/Latino; 1 American Indian or Alaska Native, non-Hispanic/Latino; 11 Asian, non-Hispanic/Latino; 6 Hispanic/Latino; 1 Two or more races, non-Hispanic/Latino), 21 international. Average age 31. 112 applicants, 75% accepted, 80 enrolled. In 2010, 34 master's awarded. *Degree requirements:* For master's, thesis optional. *Entrance requirements:* For master's, GMAT, minimum GPA of 2.75. Additional exam requirements/recommendations for international students: Required—TOEFL (minimum score 550 paper-based; 213 computer-based; 79 iBT). *Application deadline:* For fall admission, 4/1 priority date for domestic students; for spring admission, 8/15 for domestic students. Applications are processed on a rolling basis. Application fee: $30. Electronic applications accepted. *Financial support:* In 2010–11, 20 students received support, including 6 research assistantships with full and partial tuition reimbursements available (averaging $6,600 per year); career-related internships or fieldwork, Federal Work-Study, institutionally sponsored loans, scholarships/grants, tuition waivers (full and partial), and unspecified assistantships also available. Support available to part-time students. *Faculty research:* Perception of accountants and non-accountants toward future of the accounting industry, asynchronous learning outcomes, cost and efficiency of financial markets, impact of deregulation on airline industry, analysis of derivational instruments. *Unit head:* Dr. Amy B. Hietapelto, Dean, 773-442-6105. *Application contact:* Dr. Amy B. Hietapelto, Dean, 773-442-6105.

Northeastern State University, Graduate College, College of Business and Technology, Program in Accounting and Financial Analysis, Tahlequah, OK 74464-2399. Offers MS. Part-time and evening/weekend programs available. *Students:* 13 full-time (4 women), 56 part-time (36 women); includes 14 American Indian or Alaska Native, non-Hispanic/Latino; 3 Hispanic/Latino, 3 international. In 2010, 7 master's awarded. *Entrance requirements:* For master's, GMAT. Additional exam requirements/recommendations for international students: Required—TOEFL (minimum score 213 computer-based). *Application deadline:* For fall admission, 6/1 priority date for domestic students. Applications are processed on a rolling basis. Application fee: $0 ($25 for international students). Electronic applications accepted. *Expenses:* Tuition, state resident: part-time $144 per credit hour. Tuition, nonresident: part-time $384.05 per credit hour. Required fees: $34.90 per credit hour. Tuition and fees vary according to program. *Unit head:* Dr. Freeman Gary, Coordinator, 918-449-6524 Ext. 0000, E-mail: freemandg@nsuok.edu. *Application contact:* Dr. Freeman Gary, Coordinator, 918-449-6524 Ext. 0000, E-mail: freemandg@nsuok.edu.

Norwich University, School of Graduate and Continuing Studies, Program in Business Administration, Northfield, VT 05663. Offers finance (MBA); organizational leadership (MBA); project management (MBA). *Accreditation:* ACBSP. Evening/weekend programs available. *Faculty:* 26 part-time/adjunct (0 women). *Students:* 108 full-time (45 women); includes 17 minority (5 Black or African American, non-Hispanic/Latino; 3 American Indian or Alaska Native, non-Hispanic/Latino; 4 Asian, non-Hispanic/Latino; 5 Hispanic/Latino), 4 international. Average age 36. 187 applicants, 84% accepted, 95 enrolled. In 2010, 389 master's awarded. *Degree requirements:* For master's, comprehensive exam (for some programs), thesis optional. *Entrance requirements:* For master's, minimum undergraduate GPA of 2.75. Additional exam requirements/recommendations for international students: Required—TOEFL (minimum score 550 paper-based; 213 computer-based; 83 iBT). *Application deadline:* For fall admission, 8/10 for domestic and international students; for winter admission, 11/7 for domestic and international students; for spring admission, 2/6 for domestic and international students. Application fee: $50. *Expenses:* Tuition: Full-time $17,380; part-time $645 per credit. Tuition and fees vary according to program. *Financial support:* Scholarships/grants available. Financial award applicants required to submit FAFSA. *Unit head:* Dr. Jose Cordova, Faculty Director, 802-485-2567, Fax: 802-485-2533, E-mail: jcordova@norwich.edu. *Application contact:* Bernice Fousek, Student Services Coordinator, 802-485-2748, Fax: 802-485-2533, E-mail: bfousek@norwich.edu.

Notre Dame de Namur University, Division of Academic Affairs, School of Business and Management, Department of Business Administration, Belmont, CA 94002-1908. Offers business administration (MBA); finance (MBA); human resource management (MBA); marketing (MBA). Part-time and evening/weekend programs available. *Faculty:* 7 full-time (1 woman), 6 part-time/adjunct (0 women). *Students:* 46 full-time (24 women), 79 part-time (54 women); includes 54 minority (3 Black or African American, non-Hispanic/Latino; 28 Asian, non-Hispanic/Latino; 20 Hispanic/Latino; 2 Native Hawaiian or other Pacific Islander, non-Hispanic/Latino; 1 Two or more races, non-Hispanic/Latino), 22 international. Average age 34. 129 applicants, 53%

accepted, 37 enrolled. In 2010, 28 master's awarded. *Entrance requirements:* For master's, minimum GPA of 2.5. Additional exam requirements/recommendations for international students: Required—TOEFL (minimum score 550 paper-based; 213 computer-based; 79 iBT). *Application deadline:* For fall admission, 8/1 priority date for domestic students; for spring admission, 12/1 priority date for domestic students. Applications are processed on a rolling basis. Application fee: $60. Electronic applications accepted. *Expenses:* Tuition: Full-time $14,220; part-time $790 per credit. Required fees: $35 per semester. Tuition and fees vary according to program. *Financial support:* Available to part-time students. Applicants required to submit FAFSA. *Unit head:* Jordan Holtzman, Director, 650-508-3637, E-mail: jholtzman@ndnu.edu. *Application contact:* Candace Hallmark, Associate Director of Admissions, 650-508-3600, Fax: 650-508-3426, E-mail: grad.admit@ndnu.edu.

Nova Southeastern University, H. Wayne Huizenga School of Business and Entrepreneurship, Doctoral Program in Business Administration, Fort Lauderdale, FL 33314-7796. Offers accounting (DBA); decision sciences (DBA); finance (DBA); human resource management (DBA); international business (DBA); management (DBA); marketing (DBA). Part-time and evening/weekend programs available. *Faculty:* 34 full-time (11 women), 2 part-time/adjunct (1 woman). *Students:* 2 full-time (1 woman), 93 part-time (32 women); includes 9 Black or African American, non-Hispanic/Latino; 4 Asian, non-Hispanic/Latino; 11 Hispanic/Latino, 8 international. Average age 47. 66 applicants, 14% accepted, 6 enrolled. In 2010, 29 doctorates awarded. *Degree requirements:* For doctorate, comprehensive exam, thesis/dissertation. *Entrance requirements:* For doctorate, GMAT. Additional exam requirements/recommendations for international students: Required—TOEFL (minimum score 600 paper-based; 250 computer-based; 100 iBT), IELTS (minimum score 7). *Application deadline:* Applications are processed on a rolling basis. Application fee: $50. Electronic applications accepted. *Financial support:* Available to part-time students. Applicants required to submit FAFSA. *Faculty research:* Reputation management, call centers, international social capital, corporate earnings guidance, corporate governance. *Unit head:* Kristie Tetrault, Director of Program Administration, 954-262-5120, Fax: 954-262-3849, E-mail: kristie@huizenga.nova.edu. *Application contact:* Karen Goldberg, Associate Director of Recruitment and Special Events, 954-262-5039, Fax: 954-262-3822, E-mail: karen@huizenga.nova.edu.

Ohio University, Graduate College, College of Arts and Sciences, Department of Economics, Athens, OH 45701-2979. Offers applied economics (MA); financial economics (MFE). Part-time and evening/weekend programs available. *Students:* 65 full-time (16 women), 18 part-time (10 women); includes 10 minority (6 Black or African American, non-Hispanic/Latino; 3 Asian, non-Hispanic/Latino; 1 Two or more races, non-Hispanic/Latino), 46 international. 55 applicants, 42% accepted, 11 enrolled. In 2010, 42 master's awarded. *Degree requirements:* For master's, thesis or alternative. *Entrance requirements:* For master's, GRE or GMAT (recommended), minimum GPA of 3.0. Additional exam requirements/recommendations for international students: Required—TOEFL (minimum score 550 paper-based; 80 iBT) or IELTS (minimum score 6.5). *Application deadline:* For fall admission, 2/15 priority date for domestic and international students; for winter admission, 12/1 for domestic students, 10/1 priority date for international students. Application fee: $50 ($55 for international students). Electronic applications accepted. *Financial support:* Research assistantships with full and partial tuition reimbursements, Federal Work-Study, tuition waivers (partial), and unspecified assistantships available. Financial award application deadline: 2/15. *Faculty research:* Macroeconomics, public finance, international economics and finance, monetary theory, healthcare economics. *Unit head:* Dr. Rosmary Rossiter, Chair, 740-593-2040, E-mail: rossiter@ohio.edu. *Application contact:* Dr. K. Doroodian, Graduate Chair, 740-593-2046, E-mail: doroodia@ohio.edu.

Oklahoma State University, Spears School of Business, Department of Finance, Stillwater, OK 74078. Offers finance (PhD); quantitative financial economics (MS). Part-time programs available. *Faculty:* 13 full-time (1 woman), 5 part-time/adjunct (0 women). *Students:* 20 full-time (8 women), 9 part-time (2 women); includes 1 Black or African American, non-Hispanic/Latino; 1 Asian, non-Hispanic/Latino, 14 international. Average age 29. 59 applicants, 32% accepted, 8 enrolled. In 2010, 9 master's, 1 doctorate awarded. *Degree requirements:* For master's, thesis or alternative; for doctorate, comprehensive exam, thesis/dissertation. *Entrance requirements:* For master's and doctorate, GRE or GMAT. Additional exam requirements/recommendations for international students: Required—TOEFL (minimum score 550 paper-based; 79 iBT). *Application deadline:* For fall admission, 3/1 priority date for international students; for spring admission, 8/1 priority date for international students. Applications are processed on a rolling basis. Application fee: $40 ($75 for international students). Electronic applications accepted. *Expenses:* Tuition, state resident: full-time $3716; part-time $154.85 per credit hour. Tuition, nonresident: full-time $14,892; part-time $621 per credit hour. Required fees: $2044; $85.20 per credit hour. One-time fee: $50. Tuition and fees vary according to course load and campus/location. *Financial support:* In 2010–11, 13 research assistantships (averaging $8,749 per year), 5 teaching assistantships (averaging $21,587 per year) were awarded; career-related internships or fieldwork, Federal Work-Study, scholarships/grants, health care benefits, tuition waivers (partial), and unspecified assistantships also available. Support available to part-time students. Financial award application deadline: 3/1; financial award applicants required to submit FAFSA. *Faculty research:* Corporate risk management, derivatives banking, investments and securities issuance, corporate governance, banking. *Unit head:* Dr. John Polonchek, Head, 405-744-5199, Fax: 405-744-5180. *Application contact:* Dr. Gordon Emslie, Dean, 405-744-6368, Fax: 405-744-0355, E-mail: grad-i@okstate.edu.

Old Dominion University, College of Business and Public Administration, Doctoral Program in Business Administration, Norfolk, VA 23529. Offers finance (PhD); information technology (PhD); marketing (PhD); strategic management (PhD). *Accreditation:* AACSB. *Faculty:* 21 full-time (2 women). *Students:* 36 full-time (13 women), 1 part-time (0 women); includes 5 minority (2 Black or African American, non-Hispanic/Latino; 2 Asian, non-Hispanic/Latino; 1 Native Hawaiian or other Pacific Islander, non-Hispanic/Latino), 28 international. Average age 35. 42 applicants, 69% accepted, 10 enrolled. In 2010, 5 doctorates awarded. *Degree requirements:* For doctorate, comprehensive exam, thesis/dissertation. *Entrance requirements:* For doctorate, GMAT. Additional exam requirements/recommendations for international students: Required—TOEFL (minimum score 550 paper-based; 213 computer-based; 79 iBT). *Application deadline:* For fall admission, 4/1 priority date for domestic and international students. Application fee: $50. Electronic applications accepted. *Expenses:* Tuition, state resident: full-time $8592; part-time $358 per credit. Tuition, nonresident: full-time $21,672; part-time $903 per credit. Required fees: $119 per semester. One-time fee: $50. *Financial support:* In 2010–11, 27 students received support, including 2 fellowships with full tuition reimbursements available (averaging $7,500 per year), 32 research assistantships with full tuition reimbursements available (averaging $7,500 per year), 12 teaching assistantships with full tuition reimbursements available (averaging $7,500 per year); scholarships/grants and unspecified assistantships also available. Financial award application deadline: 4/1; financial award applicants required to submit FAFSA. *Faculty research:* International business, buyer behavior, financial markets, strategy, operations research. *Unit head:* Dr. John B. Ford, Graduate Program Director, 757-683-3587, Fax: 757-683-4076, E-mail: jford@odu.edu. *Application contact:* Katrina Davenport, Program Coordinator, 757-683-5138, Fax: 757-683-4076, E-mail: kdavenpo@odu.edu.

Old Dominion University, College of Business and Public Administration, MBA Program, Norfolk, VA 23529. Offers business and economic forecasting (MBA); financial analysis and valuation (MBA); information technology and enterprise integration (MBA); international business (MBA); maritime and port management (MBA); public administration (MBA). *Accreditation:* AACSB. Part-time and evening/weekend programs available. *Faculty:* 66 full-time (15 women), 6 part-time/adjunct (1 woman). *Students:* 74 full-time (32 women), 166 part-time (62 women); includes 45 minority (21 Black or African American, non-Hispanic/Latino; 1 American Indian or Alaska Native, non-Hispanic/Latino; 8 Asian, non-Hispanic/Latino; 10 Hispanic/Latino; 1 Native Hawaiian or other Pacific Islander, non-Hispanic/Latino; 4 Two or more races, non-Hispanic/Latino), 19 international. Average age 31. 169 applicants, 52% accepted, 61 enrolled. In 2010, 100 master's awarded. *Entrance requirements:* For master's, GMAT, letter of reference, resume, coursework in calculus, essay. Additional exam requirements/recommendations for international students: Required—TOEFL (minimum score 550 paper-based; 213 computer-based; 80 iBT). *Application deadline:* For fall admission, 6/1 priority date for domestic students, 4/15 priority date for international students; for spring admission, 11/1 priority date for domestic students, 10/1 priority date for international students. Applications are processed on a rolling basis. Application fee: $50. Electronic applications accepted. *Expenses:* Tuition, state resident: full-time $8592; part-time $358 per credit. Tuition, nonresident: full-time $21,672; part-time $903 per credit. Required fees: $119 per semester. One-time fee: $50. *Financial support:* In 2010–11, 44 students received support, including 90 research assistantships with partial tuition reimbursements available (averaging $3,200 per year); career-related internships or fieldwork, scholarships/grants, and unspecified assistantships also available. Support available to part-time students. Financial award application deadline: 2/15; financial award applicants required to submit FAFSA. *Faculty research:* International business, buyer behavior, financial markets, strategy, operations research. *Unit head:* Dr. Larry Filer, Graduate Program Director, 757-683-3585, Fax: 757-683-5750, E-mail: mbainfo@odu.edu. *Application contact:* Shanna Wood, MBA Program Manager, 757-683-3585, Fax: 757-683-5750, E-mail: mbainfo@odu.edu.

Our Lady of the Lake University of San Antonio, School of Business and Leadership, Program in Accounting/Finance, San Antonio, TX 78207-4689. Offers MBA. Part-time and evening/weekend programs available. *Students:* 3 full-time (2 women), 55 part-time (35 women); includes 35 minority (8 Black or African American, non-Hispanic/Latino; 27 Hispanic/Latino), 2 international. Average age 32. In 2010, 33 master's awarded. *Expenses:* Tuition: Full-time $13,500; part-time $750 per contact hour. Required fees: $330. Tuition and fees vary according to course level, degree level and campus/location. *Unit head:* Dr. Robert Bisking, Dean, 210-434-6711, Fax: 210-434-0821. *Application contact:* Dr. Robert Bisking, Dean, 210-434-6711, Fax: 210-434-0821.

Pacific States University, College of Business, Los Angeles, CA 90006. Offers accounting (MBA); business administration (DBA); finance (MBA); international business (MBA); management of information technology (MBA); real estate management (MBA). Part-time and evening/weekend programs available. Postbaccalaureate distance learning degree programs offered (no on-campus study). *Faculty:* 4 full-time (1 woman), 13 part-time/adjunct (0 women). *Students:* 130 full-time (55 women); includes 1 Black or African American, non-Hispanic/Latino; 7 Asian, non-Hispanic/Latino; 3 Native Hawaiian or other Pacific Islander, non-Hispanic/Latino, 115 international. Average age 31. 42 applicants, 83% accepted, 33 enrolled. In 2010, 67 master's awarded. *Degree requirements:* For doctorate, comprehensive exam, thesis/dissertation. *Entrance requirements:* For master's, minimum undergraduate GPA of 2.5 during last 90 hours of course work. Additional exam requirements/recommendations for international students: Required—TOEFL (minimum score 133 computer-based; 45 iBT), IELTS (minimum score 4.5). *Application deadline:* For fall admission, 8/15 priority date for domestic students; for winter admission, 10/15 priority date for domestic students; for spring admission, 1/15 priority date for domestic students. Applications are processed on a rolling basis. Application fee: $100. *Expenses:* Tuition: Full-time $8280; part-time $345 per credit hour. Required fees: $150 per quarter. *Financial support:* Scholarships/grants available. Financial award applicants required to submit FAFSA. *Unit head:* Dr. Chase C. Lee, Director, 888-200-0383, Fax: 323-731-2383, E-mail: admission@psuca.edu. *Application contact:* Zolzaya Enkhbayar, Assistant Director of Admissions, 323-731-2383, Fax: 323-731-7276, E-mail: admissions@psuca.edu.

Pepperdine University, Graziadio School of Business and Management, MS in Applied Finance Program, Malibu, CA 90263. Offers MS. *Students:* 48 full-time (32 women); includes 1 minority (Asian, non-Hispanic/Latino), 45 international. 376 applicants, 46% accepted, 47 enrolled. In 2010, 18 master's awarded. *Entrance requirements:* For master's, GMAT or GRE, two letters of recommendation. Additional exam requirements/recommendations for international students: Required—TOEFL. *Application deadline:* For fall admission, 1/10 for domestic students. Application fee: $100. *Unit head:* Dr. Linda A. Livingstone, Dean, Graziadio School of Business and Management, 310-568-5689, Fax: 310-568-5766, E-mail: linda.livingstone@pepperdine.edu. *Application contact:* Darrell Eriksen, Director of Admission and Student Accounts, Graziadio School of Business and Management, 310-568-5525, E-mail: darrell.eriksen@pepperdine.edu.

Polytechnic Institute of NYU, Department of Finance and Risk Engineering, Brooklyn, NY 11201-2990. Offers financial engineering (MS, Advanced Certificate), including capital markets (MS), computational finance (MS), financial technology (MS); financial technology management (Advanced Certificate); organizational behavior (Advanced Certificate); risk management (Advanced Certificate); technology management (Advanced Certificate). Part-time and evening/weekend programs available. *Faculty:* 6 full-time (1 woman), 24 part-time/adjunct (5 women). *Students:* 126 full-time (45 women), 61 part-time (15 women); includes 4 Black or African American, non-Hispanic/Latino; 17 Asian, non-Hispanic/Latino; 1 Hispanic/Latino, 130 international. Average age 27. 528 applicants, 44% accepted, 67 enrolled. In 2010, 154 master's awarded. *Degree requirements:* For master's, comprehensive exam (for some programs), thesis (for some programs). *Entrance requirements:* For master's, GMAT, minimum B average in undergraduate course work. Additional exam requirements/recommendations for international students: Required—TOEFL (minimum score 550 paper-based; 213 computer-based; 80 iBT); Recommended—IELTS (minimum score 6.5). *Application deadline:* For fall admission, 7/31 priority date for domestic students, 4/30 priority date for international students; for spring admission, 12/31 priority date for domestic students, 11/30 priority date for international students. Applications are processed on a rolling basis. Application fee: $75. Electronic applications accepted. *Expenses:* Tuition: Full-time $21,492; part-time $1194 per credit. Required fees: $385 per semester. Tuition and fees vary according to course load. *Financial support:* Institutionally sponsored loans, scholarships/grants, and unspecified assistantships available. Support available to part-time students. Financial award applicants required to submit FAFSA. *Unit head:* Prof. Charles S. Tapiero, Academic Director, 718-260-3653, Fax: 718-260-3874, E-mail: ctapiero@poly.edu. *Application contact:* JeanCarlo Bonilla, Director, Graduate Enrollment Management, 718-260-3182, Fax: 718-260-3624.

Polytechnic Institute of NYU, Westchester Graduate Center, Graduate Programs, Department of Finance and Risk Engineering, Major in Financial Engineering, Hawthorne, NY 10532-1507. Offers capital markets (MS); computational finance (MS); financial engineering (AC); financial technology (MS); financial technology management (AC); information management (AC). *Students:* 1 (woman) part-time, all international. Average age 25. In 2010, 8 master's awarded. *Degree requirements:* For master's, comprehensive exam (for some programs), thesis (for some programs). *Entrance requirements:* Additional exam requirements/recommendations for international students: Required—TOEFL (minimum score 550 paper-based; 213 computer-based; 80 iBT); Recommended—IELTS (minimum score 6.5). *Application deadline:* For fall admission, 7/31 priority date for domestic students, 4/30 priority date for international students; for spring admission, 12/31 priority date for domestic students, 11/30 priority date for international students. Applications are processed on a rolling basis. Application fee: $75. Electronic applications accepted. *Expenses:* Tuition: Full-time $21,492; part-time $1194 per credit. Required fees: $385 per semester. Tuition and fees vary according to course load. *Financial support:* Institutionally sponsored loans, scholarships/grants, and unspecified assistantships available. Support available to part-time students. *Unit head:* Dr. Charles S. Tapiero, Department Head, 718-260-3653, E-mail: ctapiero@poly.edu. *Application contact:* JeanCarlo Bonilla, Director of Graduate Enrollment Management, 718-260-3182, Fax: 718-260-3624, E-mail: gradinfo@poly.edu.

Portland State University, Graduate Studies, School of Business Administration, Master of Science in Financial Analysis Program, Portland, OR 97207-0751. Offers MSFA. Part-time and evening/weekend programs available. *Students:* 42 full-time (25 women), 37 part-time (17 women); includes 13 minority (3 Black or African American, non-Hispanic/Latino; 8 Asian, non-Hispanic/Latino; 2 Hispanic/Latino), 30 international. Average age 30. 46 applicants, 91% accepted, 40 enrolled. In 2010, 54 master's awarded. *Entrance requirements:* For master's, GMAT, minimum GPA of 2.75, 2 recommendations, resume, interview. Additional exam requirements/recommendations for international students: Required—TOEFL (minimum score 550 paper-based; 213 computer-based). *Application deadline:* For fall admission, 4/1 priority date for domestic students, 3/1 priority date for international students. Applications are processed on a rolling basis. Application fee: $50. *Expenses:* Tuition, state resident: full-time $8505; part-time $315 per credit. Tuition, nonresident: full-time $13,284; part-time $492 per credit. Required fees: $1482; $21 per credit. $99 per term. One-time fee: $120. Part-time tuition and fees vary according to course load and program. *Financial support:* Research assistantships with full tuition reimbursements, career-related internships or fieldwork, Federal Work-Study, and scholarships/grants available. Financial award application deadline: 3/1; financial award applicants required to submit FAFSA. *Unit head:* Dr. Berrin Erdogan, Coordinator, 503-725-3798, Fax: 503-725-5850, E-mail: berrine@sba.pdx.edu. *Application contact:* Pam Mitchell, Administrator, 503-725-3730, Fax: 503-725-5850, E-mail: pamm@sba.pdx.edu.

Providence College, Graduate Studies, School of Business, Providence, RI 02918. Offers accounting (MBA); entrepreneurship (MBA); finance (MBA); international business (MBA); management (MBA); marketing (MBA); not-for-profit organizations (MBA). Part-time and evening/weekend programs available. *Faculty:* 17 full-time (9 women), 10 part-time/adjunct (2 women). *Students:* 53 full-time (20 women), 57 part-time (22 women); includes 4 minority (1 Black or African American, non-Hispanic/Latino; 1 Asian, non-Hispanic/Latino; 2 Two or more races, non-Hispanic/Latino), 6 international. Average age 26. 72 applicants, 81% accepted. In 2010, 56 master's awarded. *Degree requirements:* For master's, thesis optional. *Entrance requirements:* For master's, GMAT. Additional exam requirements/recommendations for international students: Required—TOEFL (minimum score 550 paper-based; 213 computer-based; 80 iBT). *Application deadline:* For fall admission, 8/1 priority date for domestic and international students; for spring admission, 12/1 priority date for domestic and international students. Applications are processed on a rolling basis. Application fee: $55. *Expenses:* Contact institution. *Financial support:* In 2010–11, 34 research assistantships with full tuition reimbursements (averaging $8,400 per year) were awarded; Federal Work-Study, institutionally sponsored loans, and unspecified assistantships also available. Support available to part-time students. Financial award application deadline: 8/1; financial award applicants required to submit FAFSA. *Unit head:* Dr. MaryJane Lenon, Director, MBA Program, 401-865-2566, Fax: 401-865-2978, E-mail: mjlenon@providence.edu. *Application contact:* Katherine A. Follett, Administrative Coordinator, 401-865-2333, Fax: 401-865-2978, E-mail: kfollett@providence.edu.

Purdue University, Graduate School, Krannert School of Management, Master of Science in Finance Program, West Lafayette, IN 47907. Offers MSF. *Faculty:* 98 full-time (27 women), 22 part-time/adjunct (4 women). *Students:* 30 full-time (9 women), 24 international. Average age 26. 717 applicants, 8% accepted, 30 enrolled. In 2010, 22 master's awarded. *Entrance requirements:* For master's, GMAT or GRE, minimum GPA of 3.0, four-year baccalaureate degree, essays, letters of recommendation. Additional exam requirements/recommendations for international students: Required—TOEFL (minimum score 550 paper-based; 213 computer-based; 77 iBT). *Application deadline:* For fall admission, 1/10 priority date for domestic students, 2/1 for international students. Applications are processed on a rolling basis. Application fee: $55. Electronic applications accepted. *Expenses:* Contact institution. *Financial support:* Application deadline: 3/1. *Unit head:* Dr. Gerald J. Lynch, Interim Dean, 765-494-4366. *Application contact:* Charles R. Johnson, Executive Director, Krannert Executive Education Programs, 765-494-0773, Fax: 765-494-9841, E-mail: krannertmasters@purdue.edu.

Quinnipiac University, School of Business, MBA Program, Hamden, CT 06518-1940. Offers chartered financial analyst (MBA); finance (MBA); healthcare management (MBA); information systems management (MBA); marketing (MBA); supply chain management (MBA); JD/MBA. *Accreditation:* AACSB. Part-time and evening/weekend programs available. *Faculty:* 25 full-time (2 women), 3 part-time/adjunct (all women). *Students:* 87 full-time (24 women), 121 part-time (46 women); includes 12 minority (1 Black or African American, non-Hispanic/Latino; 7 Asian, non-Hispanic/Latino; 4 Hispanic/Latino), 14 international. Average age 29. 119 applicants,

81% accepted, 81 enrolled. In 2010, 70 master's awarded. *Entrance requirements:* For master's, GMAT or GRE, minimum GPA of 3.0. Additional exam requirements/recommendations for international students: Required—TOEFL (minimum score 575 paper-based; 233 computer-based; 90 iBT), IELTS (minimum score 6.5). *Application deadline:* For fall admission, 7/30 priority date for domestic students, 4/30 priority date for international students; for spring admission, 12/15 priority date for domestic students, 9/15 priority date for international students. Applications are processed on a rolling basis. Application fee: $45. Electronic applications accepted. *Expenses:* Tuition: Part-time $810 per credit. Required fees: $35 per credit. *Financial support:* In 2010–11, 110 students received support. Federal Work-Study, tuition waivers (partial), and unspecified assistantships available. Support available to part-time students. Financial award application deadline: 4/15; financial award applicants required to submit FAFSA. *Faculty research:* Equity compensation, marketing relationships and public policy, corporate governance, international business, supply chain management. *Unit head:* Lisa Braiewa, MBA Program Director, 203-582-3710, Fax: 203-582-8664, E-mail: lisa.braiewa@quinnipiac.edu. *Application contact:* Jennifer Boutin, 800-462-1944, Fax: 203-582-3443, E-mail: jennifer.boutin@quinnipiac.edu.

Rhode Island College, School of Graduate Studies, School of Management, Department of Accounting and Computer Information Systems, Providence, RI 02908-1991. Offers accounting (MP Ac); financial planning (CGS). Part-time and evening/weekend programs available. *Faculty:* 1 (woman) full-time. *Students:* 2 full-time (1 woman), 10 part-time (8 women); includes 1 minority (Asian, non-Hispanic/Latino), 1 international. Average age 29. In 2010, 5 master's awarded. *Entrance requirements:* For master's, GMAT (unless applicant is a CPA or has passed a state bar exam); for CGS, GMAT, bachelor's degree from an accredited college or university, official transcripts of all undergraduate and graduate records. Additional exam requirements/recommendations for international students: Recommended—TOEFL (minimum score 550 paper-based; 213 computer-based; 79 iBT). *Application deadline:* For fall admission, 3/1 for domestic students. Applications are processed on a rolling basis. Application fee: $50. *Expenses:* Tuition, state resident: full-time $8208; part-time $342 per credit hour. Tuition, nonresident: full-time $16,080; part-time $670 per credit hour. Required fees: $554; $20 per credit. $72 per term. *Financial support:* Federal Work-Study, scholarships/grants, and health care benefits available. Support available to part-time students. Financial award application deadline: 5/15; financial award applicants required to submit FAFSA. *Unit head:* Prof. David Filipek, Chair, 401-456-8009. *Application contact:* Graduate Studies, 401-456-8700.

Robert Morris University Illinois, Morris Graduate School of Management, Chicago, IL 60605. Offers accounting (MBA); accounting/finance (MBA); health care administration (MM); higher education administration (MM); human resource management (MBA); information systems (MIS); leadership (MBA); management/finance (MIS); management/human resource management (MBA). Part-time and evening/weekend programs available. *Faculty:* 9 full-time (2 women), 21 part-time/adjunct (6 women). *Students:* 275 full-time (151 women), 212 part-time (138 women); includes 170 Black or African American, non-Hispanic/Latino; 1 American Indian or Alaska Native, non-Hispanic/Latino; 21 Asian, non-Hispanic/Latino; 73 Hispanic/Latino; 2 Native Hawaiian or other Pacific Islander, non-Hispanic/Latino, 23 international. Average age 32. 172 applicants, 87% accepted, 105 enrolled. In 2010, 174 master's awarded. *Degree requirements:* For master's, 48 residency hours. *Entrance requirements:* Additional exam requirements/recommendations for international students: Required—TOEFL (minimum score 500 paper-based; 173 computer-based). *Application deadline:* Applications are processed on a rolling basis. Application fee: $50 ($100 for international students). Electronic applications accepted. *Expenses:* Tuition: Full-time $13,200; part-time $2200 per course. *Financial support:* Federal Work-Study, scholarships/grants, and tuition waivers available. Support available to part-time students. *Unit head:* Kayed Akkawi, Dean, 312-935-6025, Fax: 312-935-6020, E-mail: kakkawi@robertmorris.edu. *Application contact:* Courtney A. Kohn Sanders, Dean of Graduate Admissions, 312-935-4810, Fax: 312-935-6020, E-mail: ckohn@robertmorris.edu.

Rochester Institute of Technology, Graduate Enrollment Services, E. Philip Saunders College of Business, Graduate Business Programs, Program in Finance, Rochester, NY 14623-5603. Offers MS. Part-time and evening/weekend programs available. *Students:* 31 full-time (18 women), 12 part-time (3 women); includes 3 minority (1 Black or African American, non-Hispanic/Latino; 1 American Indian or Alaska Native, non-Hispanic/Latino; 1 Asian, non-Hispanic/Latino), 32 international. Average age 26. 182 applicants, 49% accepted, 28 enrolled. In 2010, 20 master's awarded. *Degree requirements:* For master's, comprehensive exam (for some programs), thesis (for some programs). *Entrance requirements:* For master's, GMAT, minimum GPA of 2.5. Additional exam requirements/recommendations for international students: Required—TOEFL (minimum score 580 paper-based; 237 computer-based; 92 iBT) or IELTS (minimum score 7). *Application deadline:* For fall admission, 2/15 priority date for domestic and international students; for winter admission, 11/1 priority date for domestic students; for spring admission, 2/1 priority date for domestic students. Applications are processed on a rolling basis. Application fee: $50. *Expenses:* Tuition: Full-time $33,234; part-time $924 per credit hour. Required fees: $219. *Financial support:* In 2010–11,

20 students received support; research assistantships with partial tuition reimbursements available, teaching assistantships with partial tuition reimbursements available, career-related internships or fieldwork, scholarships/grants, and unspecified assistantships available. Support available to part-time students. Financial award applicants required to submit FAFSA. *Faculty research:* Formation and taxation of business entities, modeling demand, production and cost functions in computerized business and economic simulations, economic games and educational software. *Unit head:* Heather Krakehl, Graduate Program Director, 585-475-6916, Fax: 585-475-7450, E-mail: hmascb@rit.edu. *Application contact:* Diane Ellison, Assistant Vice President, Graduate Enrollment Services, 585-475-2229, Fax: 585-475-7164, E-mail: gradinfo@rit.edu.

Rollins College, Crummer Graduate School of Business, Winter Park, FL 32789-4499. Offers entrepreneurship (MBA); finance (MBA); international business (MBA); management (MBA); marketing (MBA); operations and technology management (MBA). *Accreditation:* AACSB. Part-time and evening/weekend programs available. Postbaccalaureate distance learning degree programs offered (minimal on-campus study). *Faculty:* 22 full-time (3 women), 5 part-time/adjunct (3 women). *Students:* 303 full-time (117 women), 130 part-time (49 women); includes 111 minority (30 Black or African American, non-Hispanic/Latino; 1 American Indian or Alaska Native, non-Hispanic/Latino; 29 Asian, non-Hispanic/Latino; 50 Hispanic/Latino; 1 Two or more races, non-Hispanic/Latino; 29 international. Average age 32. 484 applicants, 42% accepted, 131 enrolled. In 2010, 223 master's awarded. *Entrance requirements:* For master's, GMAT, interview. Additional exam requirements/recommendations for international students: Required—TOEFL (minimum score 550 paper-based; 213 computer-based; 80 iBT). *Application deadline:* Applications are processed on a rolling basis. Application fee: $50. Electronic applications accepted. *Expenses:* Contact institution. *Financial support:* In 2010–11, 112 students received support, including 95 fellowships, 56 research assistantships (averaging $2,400 per year); career-related internships or fieldwork, scholarships/grants, and unspecified assistantships also available. Support available to part-time students. Financial award applicants required to submit FAFSA. *Faculty research:* Sustainability, world financial markets, international business, market research, strategic marketing. *Unit head:* Dr. Craig M. McAllaster, Dean, 407-646-2249, Fax: 407-646-1550, E-mail: cmcallaster@rollins.edu. *Application contact:* Linda Puritz, Student Admissions Office, 407-646-2405, Fax: 407-646-1550, E-mail: mba admissions@rollins.edu.

Rowan University, Graduate School, William G. Rohrer College of Business, Department of Accounting and Finance, Program in Finance, Glassboro, NJ 08028-1701. Offers MBA. Part-time and evening/weekend programs available. *Students:* 9 full-time (4 women), 7 part-time (2 women); includes 2 Black or African American, non-Hispanic/Latino. Average age 28. 4 applicants, 50% accepted, 1 enrolled. *Degree requirements:* For master's, comprehensive exam, thesis. *Entrance requirements:* For master's, GRE General Test. Additional exam requirements/recommendations for international students: Required—TOEFL. *Application deadline:* Applications are processed on a rolling basis. Application fee: $65 ($200 for international students). Electronic applications accepted. *Expenses:* Tuition, area resident: Part-time $602 per semester hour. Tuition, nonresident: part-time $602 per semester hour. Required fees: $100 per semester hour. One-time fee: $10 part-time. *Financial support:* Career-related internships or fieldwork, Federal Work-Study, and unspecified assistantships available. Support available to part-time students. *Unit head:* Dr. Horacio Sosa, Dean, College of Graduate and Continuing Education, 856-256-4747, Fax: 856-256-5638, E-mail: sosa@rowan.edu. *Application contact:* Karen Haynes, Graduate Coordinator, 856-256-4052, E-mail: haynes@rowan.edu.

Rutgers, The State University of New Jersey, Newark, Graduate School, Program in Management, Newark, NJ 07102. Offers accounting (PhD); accounting information systems (PhD); computer information systems (PhD); finance (PhD); information technology (PhD); international business (PhD); management science (PhD); marketing (PhD); organization management (PhD). Program offered jointly with New Jersey Institute of Technology. *Accreditation:* AACSB. *Faculty:* 128 full-time (24 women), 4 part-time/adjunct (1 woman). *Students:* 95 full-time (34 women), 17 part-time (6 women); includes 9 Black or African American, non-Hispanic/Latino; 54 Asian, non-Hispanic/Latino; 3 Hispanic/Latino. 438 applicants, 14% accepted, 34 enrolled. In 2010, 10 doctorates awarded. *Degree requirements:* For doctorate, thesis/dissertation, cumulative exams. *Entrance requirements:* For doctorate, GMAT or GRE General Test, minimum undergraduate B average. Additional exam requirements/recommendations for international students: Required—TOEFL. *Application deadline:* For fall admission, 4/1 for domestic students; for spring admission, 11/1 for domestic students. Applications are processed on a rolling basis. Application fee: $60. Electronic applications accepted. *Expenses:* Tuition, state resident: part-time $600 per credit. Tuition, nonresident: full-time $10,694. *Financial support:* In 2010–11, 6 fellowships (averaging $18,000 per year), 4 research assistantships with full and partial tuition reimbursements (averaging $23,112 per year), 38 teaching assistantships with full and partial tuition reimbursements (averaging $23,112 per year) were awarded; institutionally sponsored loans and tuition waivers (full and partial) also available. Support available to part-time students. Financial

award application deadline: 2/15. *Faculty research:* Technology management, leadership and teams, consumer behavior, financial and markets, logistics. *Unit head:* Dr. Glenn Shafer, Director, 973-353-1604, Fax: 973-353-5691, E-mail: gshafer@rbs.rutgers.edu. *Application contact:* Goncalo Filipe, Senior Academic Coordinator, 973-353-1002, Fax: 973-353-5691, E-mail: gfilipe@rbsmail.rutgers.edu.

Rutgers, The State University of New Jersey, Newark, Rutgers Business School–Newark and New Brunswick, Doctoral Programs in Management, Newark, NJ 07102. Offers accounting (PhD); accounting information systems (PhD); economics (PhD); finance (PhD); individualized study (PhD); information technology (PhD); international business (PhD); management science (PhD); marketing science (PhD); organizational management (PhD); science, technology and management (PhD); supply chain management (PhD). *Faculty:* 143 full-time (36 women), 2 part-time/adjunct (0 women). *Students:* 117 full-time (42 women), 1 (woman) part-time; includes 8 Black or African American, non-Hispanic/Latino; 14 Asian, non-Hispanic/Latino; 3 Hispanic/Latino, 68 international. Average age 33. 355 applicants, 14% accepted, 35 enrolled. In 2010, 8 doctorates awarded. *Degree requirements:* For doctorate, comprehensive exam, thesis/dissertation. *Entrance requirements:* For doctorate, GRE or GMAT. Additional exam requirements/recommendations for international students: Required—TOEFL (minimum score 550 paper-based; 213 computer-based; 79 iBT). *Application deadline:* For fall admission, 3/1 for domestic and international students; for spring admission, 10/15 for domestic and international students. Application fee: $65. Electronic applications accepted. *Expenses:* Tuition, state resident: part-time $600 per credit. Tuition, nonresident: full-time $10,694. *Financial support:* In 2010–11, 52 students received support, including 7 fellowships (averaging $18,000 per year), 4 research assistantships with tuition reimbursements available (averaging $23,112 per year), 41 teaching assistantships with tuition reimbursements available (averaging $23,112 per year); health care benefits also available. Financial award application deadline: 3/1. *Unit head:* Dr. Glenn Shafer, Director, 973-353-1604, Fax: 973-353-5691, E-mail: gshafer@rbs.rutgers.edu. *Application contact:* Information Contact, 973-353-5371, Fax: 973-353-5691, E-mail: phdinfo@andromeda.rutgers.edu.

Sage Graduate School, Graduate School, School of Management, Program in Business Administration, Troy, NY 12180-4115. Offers business strategy (MBA); finance (MBA); human resources (MBA); marketing (MBA); JD/MBA. Part-time and evening/weekend programs available. *Faculty:* 4 full-time (2 women), 8 part-time/adjunct (3 women). *Students:* 8 full-time (4 women), 67 part-time (45 women); includes 10 Black or African American, non-Hispanic/Latino; 2 Asian, non-Hispanic/Latino; 3 Hispanic/Latino, 1 international. Average age 31. 45 applicants, 64% accepted, 19 enrolled. In 2010, 24 master's awarded. *Entrance requirements:* For master's, minimum GPA of 2.75, resume, 2 letters of recommendation. Additional exam requirements/recommendations for international students: Required—TOEFL (minimum score 550 paper-based; 213 computer-based). *Application deadline:* Applications are processed on a rolling basis. Application fee: $40. *Expenses:* Tuition: Full-time $10,980; part-time $610 per credit hour. Tuition and fees vary according to course load, degree level and program. *Financial support:* Fellowships, research assistantships, Federal Work-Study, scholarships/grants, and unspecified assistantships available. Support available to part-time students. Financial award application deadline: 3/1; financial award applicants required to submit FAFSA. *Unit head:* Dr. Daniel Robeson, Dean, School of Management, 518-292-8637, Fax: 518-292-1964, E-mail: robesd@sage.edu. *Application contact:* Wendy D. Diefendorf, Director of Graduate and Adult Admission, 518-244-2443, Fax: 518-244-6880, E-mail: diefew@sage.edu.

St. Edward's University, School of Management and Business, Area of Business Administration, Austin, TX 78704. Offers accounting (MBA); business management (MBA); corporate finance (MBA, Certificate); global entrepreneurship (MBA); human resource management (Certificate); management information systems (MBA, Certificate); marketing (MBA, Certificate); operations management (MBA, Certificate). Part-time and evening/weekend programs available. *Faculty:* 17 full-time (7 women), 19 part-time/adjunct (4 women). *Students:* 41 full-time (21 women), 273 part-time (135 women); includes 111 minority (19 Black or African American, non-Hispanic/Latino; 1 American Indian or Alaska Native, non-Hispanic/Latino; 8 Asian, non-Hispanic/Latino; 78 Hispanic/Latino; 1 Native Hawaiian or other Pacific Islander, non-Hispanic/Latino; 4 Two or more races, non-Hispanic/Latino), 11 international. Average age 33. 101 applicants, 77% accepted, 50 enrolled. In 2010, 115 master's awarded. *Degree requirements:* For master's, minimum of 24 resident hours. *Entrance requirements:* For master's, GMAT or GRE General Test, minimum GPA of 2.75 in last 60 hours of course work. Additional exam requirements/recommendations for international students: Required—TOEFL (minimum score 550 paper-based; 213 computer-based; 79 iBT) or IELTS (minimum score 6). *Application deadline:* For fall admission, 7/1 for domestic and international students; for spring admission, 11/1 for domestic and international students. Applications are processed on a rolling basis. Application fee: $45 ($50 for international students). Electronic applications accepted. *Expenses:* Tuition: Full-time $16,200; part-time $900 per credit hour. Required fees: $50 per trimester. Full-time tuition and fees vary according to course load and program. *Financial support:* In 2010–11, 19 students received support. Scholarships/grants available. *Faculty research:*

Ethics and corporate responsibility, new hire socialization, team performance, business strategy, non-traditional marketing, social media. *Unit head:* Dr. Stan Horner, Director, 512-428-1279, Fax: 512-448-8492, E-mail: stanleyh@ stedwards.edu. *Application contact:* Kelly Luna, Graduate Admissions Coordinator, 512-233-1697, Fax: 512-428-1032, E-mail: kellyl@stedwards. edu.

St. John's University, The Peter J. Tobin College of Business, Department of Economics and Finance, Program in Finance, Queens, NY 11439. Offers MBA, Adv C. Part-time and evening/weekend programs available. *Students:* 113 full-time (41 women), 66 part-time (27 women); includes 34 minority (10 Black or African American, non-Hispanic/Latino; 13 Asian, non-Hispanic/ Latino; 9 Hispanic/Latino; 2 Two or more races, non-Hispanic/Latino), 68 international. Average age 27. 144 applicants, 67% accepted, 50 enrolled. In 2010, 81 master's awarded. *Degree requirements:* For master's, comprehensive exam (for some programs), thesis optional. *Entrance requirements:* For master's, GMAT, 2 letters of recommendation, resume, transcripts, essay; for Adv C, GMAT, 2 letters of recommendation, resume, undergraduate transcripts, essay. Additional exam requirements/recommendations for international students: Required—TOEFL (minimum score 600 paper-based; 250 computer-based; 100 iBT), IELTS (minimum score 5.5). *Application deadline:* For fall admission, 5/1 priority date for domestic and international students; for spring admission, 11/1 priority date for domestic and international students. Applications are processed on a rolling basis. Application fee: $70. Electronic applications accepted. *Expenses:* Contact institution. *Financial support:* Research assistantships, scholarships/grants available. Support available to part-time students. Financial award application deadline: 3/1; financial award applicants required to submit FAFSA. *Unit head:* Dr. Vipul K. Bansal, Chair, 718-990-2113, E-mail: bansalv@stjohns.edu. *Application contact:* Carol Swanberg, Assistant Dean, Director of Graduate Admissions, 718-990-1345, Fax: 718-990-5242, E-mail: tobingradnyc@stjohns.edu.

Saint Joseph's University, Erivan K. Haub School of Business, MS in Financial Services Program, Philadelphia, PA 19131-1395. Offers MS. Part-time and evening/weekend programs available. Postbaccalaureate distance learning degree programs offered (no on-campus study). *Students:* 28 full-time (20 women), 49 part-time (13 women); includes 4 minority (2 Black or African American, non-Hispanic/Latino; 1 Asian, non-Hispanic/Latino; 1 Hispanic/Latino), 31 international. Average age 28. In 2010, 27 master's awarded. *Entrance requirements:* For master's, GMAT or GRE, 2 letters of recommendation, resume, personal statement. Additional exam requirements/ recommendations for international students: Required—TOEFL (minimum score: paper 550, computer 213, iBT 79) or IELTS (6.5), Pearson Test of English (minimum 60). *Application deadline:* For fall admission, 7/15 priority date for domestic students, 5/15 priority date for international students; for spring admission, 11/15 priority date for domestic students, 10/15 priority date for international students. Applications are processed on a rolling basis. Application fee: $35. Electronic applications accepted. *Expenses:* Tuition: Part-time $729 per credit. Tuition and fees vary according to course load, degree level and program. *Financial support:* Research assistantships, scholarships/grants and unspecified assistantships available. Financial award applicants required to submit FAFSA. *Unit head:* David Benglian, Director, 610-660-1626, Fax: 610-660-1599, E-mail: david.benglian@sju.edu.

Saint Joseph's University, Erivan K. Haub School of Business, Professional MBA Program, Philadelphia, PA 19131-1395. Offers accounting (MBA); finance (MBA), including finance; general business (MBA); health and medical services administration (MBA); human resource management (MBA); international business (MBA); international marketing (MBA); management (MBA); marketing (MBA); DO/MBA. Do/MBA offered jointly with Philadelphia College of Osteopathic Medicine. Part-time and evening/weekend programs available. Postbaccalaureate distance learning degree programs offered (no on-campus study). *Students:* 47 full-time (35 women), 585 part-time (221 women); includes 92 minority (42 Black or African American, non-Hispanic/ Latino; 1 American Indian or Alaska Native, non-Hispanic/Latino; 34 Asian, non-Hispanic/Latino; 12 Hispanic/Latino; 1 Native Hawaiian or other Pacific Islander, non-Hispanic/Latino; 2 Two or more races, non-Hispanic/Latino), 41 international. Average age 30. In 2010, 135 master's awarded. *Entrance requirements:* For master's, GMAT or GRE, 2 letters of recommendation, resume. Additional exam requirements/recommendations for international students: Required—TOEFL (minimum score: paper 550, computer 213, iBT 79) or IELTS (6.5), Pearson Test of English (minimum 60). *Application deadline:* For fall admission, 7/15 priority date for domestic students, 4/15 priority date for international students; for spring admission, 11/15 priority date for domestic students, 10/15 priority date for international students. Applications are processed on a rolling basis. Application fee: $35. Electronic applications accepted. *Expenses:* Tuition: Part-time $729 per credit. Tuition and fees vary according to course load, degree level and program. *Financial support:* Scholarships/grants and unspecified assistantships available. Financial award application deadline: 5/1; financial award applicants required to submit FAFSA. *Unit head:* Adele C. Foley, Associate Dean/Director, Graduate Business Programs, 610-660-1691, Fax: 610-660-1599, E-mail: afoley@sju. edu. *Application contact:* Janine N. Guerra, Assistant Director, MBA Program, 610-660-1695, Fax: 610-660-1599, E-mail: jguerra@sju.edu.

Saint Peter's College, Graduate Business Programs, MBA Program, Jersey City, NJ 07306-5997. Offers finance (MBA); health care administration (MBA); human resource management (MBA); international business (MBA); management (MBA); management information systems (MBA); marketing (MBA); risk management (MBA); MBA/MS. Part-time and evening/weekend programs available. *Students:* 108 applicants, 81% accepted, 62 enrolled. *Entrance requirements:* Additional exam requirements/recommendations for international students: Required—TOEFL (minimum score 79 computer-based). *Application deadline:* Applications are processed on a rolling basis. Electronic applications accepted. *Financial support:* Career-related internships or fieldwork, Federal Work-Study, and institutionally sponsored loans available. Financial award applicants required to submit FAFSA. *Faculty research:* Finance, health care management, human resource management, international business, management, management information systems, marketing, risk management. *Application contact:* Stephanie Autenrieth, Director, Graduate and Professional Studies Admission, 201-761-6474, Fax: 201-435-5270, E-mail: sautenrieth@spc.edu.

Sam Houston State University, College of Business Administration, Department of General Business and Finance, Huntsville, TX 77341. Offers finance (MS). *Faculty:* 11 full-time (4 women). *Students:* 114 full-time (42 women), 144 part-time (66 women); includes 17 Black or African American, non-Hispanic/Latino; 2 American Indian or Alaska Native, non-Hispanic/ Latino; 7 Asian, non-Hispanic/Latino; 20 Hispanic/Latino, 25 international. Average age 29. 124 applicants, 81% accepted, 65 enrolled. In 2010, 73 master's awarded. *Entrance requirements:* For master's, GMAT. Additional exam requirements/recommendations for international students: Required—TOEFL (minimum score 550 paper-based; 213 computer-based; 79 iBT). *Application deadline:* For fall admission, 8/1 for domestic students; for spring admission, 12/1 for domestic students. Application fee: $20. *Expenses:* Tuition, state resident: full-time $1363; part-time $163 per credit hour. Tuition, nonresident: full-time $3856; part-time $473 per credit hour. *Financial support:* Application deadline: 5/31. *Unit head:* Dr. Bala Maniam, Chair, 936-294-1290, E-mail: maniam@shsu.edu. *Application contact:* Dr. Leroy Ashorn, Advisor, 936-294-4040, Fax: 936-294-3612, E-mail: busgrad@shsu.edu.

Santa Clara University, Leavey School of Business, Program in Business Administration, Santa Clara, CA 95053. Offers accounting (MBA); entrepreneurship (MBA); executive business administration (EMBA); finance (MBA); food and agribusiness (MBA); international business (MBA); leading people and organizations (MBA); managing technology and innovation (MBA); marketing management (MBA); supply chain management (MBA). *Accreditation:* AACSB. Part-time and evening/weekend programs available. *Students:* 229 full-time (80 women), 748 part-time (244 women); includes 354 minority (14 Black or African American, non-Hispanic/Latino; 1 American Indian or Alaska Native, non-Hispanic/Latino; 287 Asian, non-Hispanic/Latino; 42 Hispanic/Latino; 5 Native Hawaiian or other Pacific Islander, non-Hispanic/ Latino; 5 Two or more races, non-Hispanic/Latino), 209 international. Average age 32. 334 applicants, 76% accepted, 191 enrolled. In 2010, 307 master's awarded. *Degree requirements:* For master's, thesis or alternative. *Entrance requirements:* For master's, GMAT, GRE. Additional exam requirements/ recommendations for international students: Required—TOEFL (minimum score 600 paper-based; 250 computer-based; 100 iBT). *Application deadline:* For fall admission, 6/1 for domestic and international students; for spring admission, 1/19 for domestic students, 1/17 for international students. Applications are processed on a rolling basis. Application fee: $75 ($100 for international students). Electronic applications accepted. *Expenses:* Contact institution. *Financial support:* In 2010–11, 350 students received support; fellowships with partial tuition reimbursements available, research assistantships with partial tuition reimbursements available, career-related internships or fieldwork, Federal Work-Study, institutionally sponsored loans, scholarships/ grants, health care benefits, and unspecified assistantships available. Support available to part-time students. Financial award application deadline: 6/1; financial award applicants required to submit FAFSA. *Unit head:* Elizabeth B. Ford, Senior Assistant Dean, 408-554-2752, Fax: 408-554-4571, E-mail: eford@scu.edu. *Application contact:* Molly Mulally, Assistant Director, Graduate Business Admissions, 408-554-4539, Fax: 408-554-4571, E-mail: mbaadmissions@scu.edu.

Seton Hall University, Stillman School of Business, Programs in Business Administration, South Orange, NJ 07079-2697. Offers accounting (MBA); finance (MBA); information technology management (MBA); international business (MBA); management (MBA); marketing (MBA); sport management (MBA); supply chain management (MBA). Part-time and evening/weekend programs available. *Faculty:* 35 full-time (8 women), 11 part-time/adjunct (1 woman). *Students:* 93 full-time (33 women), 165 part-time (76 women); includes 26 Black or African American, non-Hispanic/Latino; 39 Asian, non-Hispanic/Latino; 8 Hispanic/Latino. Average age 29. 404 applicants, 74% accepted, 258 enrolled. In 2010, 203 master's awarded. *Degree requirements:* For master's, 20 hours of community service (Social Responsibility Project). *Entrance requirements:* For master's, GMAT or CPA, Advanced degree such as PhD, MD, JD, DVM, DDS, PharmD, MBA from an AACSB institution, MS in a business discipline and a minimum GPA of 3.0. Additional exam requirements/recommendations for international students: Required—TOEFL (minimum: 254 computer, 102 iBT), IELTS or Pearson Test of English (PTE).

Application deadline: For fall admission, 5/31 priority date for domestic students, 3/31 priority date for international students; for spring admission, 10/31 priority date for domestic students, 9/30 priority date for international students. Applications are processed on a rolling basis. Application fee: $75. Electronic applications accepted. *Financial support:* In 2010–11, research assistantships with full tuition reimbursements (averaging $35,610 per year); career-related internships or fieldwork, Federal Work-Study, scholarships/grants, and unspecified assistantships also available. Support available to part-time students. Financial award application deadline: 6/30; financial award applicants required to submit FAFSA. *Faculty research:* Financial, hedge funds, international business, legal issues, disclosure and branding. *Unit head:* Dr. Joyce A. Strawser, Associate Dean for Undergraduate and MBA Curricula, 973-761-9225, Fax: 973-761-9217, E-mail: strawsjo@shu.edu. *Application contact:* Catherine Bianchi, Director of Graduate Admissions, 973-761-9262, Fax: 973-761-9208, E-mail: catherine.bianchi@shu.edu.

Southeast Missouri State University, School of Graduate Studies, Harrison College of Business, Cape Girardeau, MO 63701-4799. Offers accounting (MBA); entrepreneurship (MBA); environmental management (MBA); financial management (MBA); general management (MBA); health administration (MBA); industrial management (MBA); international business (MBA); sport management (MBA). *Accreditation:* AACSB. Part-time and evening/weekend programs available. Postbaccalaureate distance learning degree programs offered (no on-campus study). *Faculty:* 31 full-time (10 women). *Students:* 51 full-time (24 women), 72 part-time (34 women); includes 4 minority (1 American Indian or Alaska Native, non-Hispanic/Latino; 3 Asian, non-Hispanic/Latino), 32 international. Average age 28. 71 applicants, 83% accepted, 33 enrolled. In 2010, 46 master's awarded. *Degree requirements:* For master's, variable foreign language requirement, applied research project; foreign language or 9 credit hours (for international business). *Entrance requirements:* For master's, GMAT (minimum score 400), minimum undergraduate GPA of 2.5, prerequisite courses for non-business undergraduate majors. Additional exam requirements/recommendations for international students: Required—TOEFL (minimum score 550 paper-based; 213 computer-based; 79 iBT); Recommended—IELTS (minimum score 6). *Application deadline:* For fall admission, 8/1 for domestic students, 6/1 for international students; for spring admission, 11/21 for domestic students, 10/1 for international students. Applications are processed on a rolling basis. Application fee: $25 ($35 for international students). Electronic applications accepted. *Expenses:* Tuition, state resident: full-time $4698; part-time $261 per credit hour. Tuition, nonresident: full-time $8379; part-time $465.50 per credit hour. *Financial support:* In 2010–11, 52 students received support, including 10 teaching assistantships with full tuition reimbursements available (averaging $7,600 per year); career-related internships or fieldwork, Federal Work-Study, institutionally sponsored loans, scholarships/grants, tuition waivers (full), and unspecified assistantships also available. Financial award application deadline: 6/30; financial award applicants required to submit FAFSA. *Faculty research:* Human resources, laws impacting accounting, advertising. *Unit head:* Dr. Kenneth A. Heischmidt, Director, Graduate Programs, 573-651-5116, Fax: 573-651-5032, E-mail: kheischmidt@semo.edu. *Application contact:* Gail Amick, Administrative Secretary, 573-651-2049, Fax: 573-651-2001, E-mail: gamick@semo.edu.

Southern Illinois University Edwardsville, Graduate School, School of Business, Department of Economics and Finance, Edwardsville, IL 62026. Offers MA, MS. Part-time and evening/weekend programs available. *Faculty:* 13 full-time (3 women). *Students:* 22 full-time (5 women), 12 part-time (3 women); includes 1 minority (Black or African American, non-Hispanic/Latino), 10 international. Average age 26. 36 applicants, 72% accepted. In 2010, 14 master's awarded. *Degree requirements:* For master's, thesis or alternative, final exam, portfolio. *Entrance requirements:* For master's, GMAT or GRE. Additional exam requirements/recommendations for international students: Required—TOEFL (minimum score 550 paper-based; 213 computer-based; 79 iBT), IELTS (minimum score 6.5). *Application deadline:* For fall admission, 7/22 for domestic students, 6/1 for international students; for spring admission, 12/10 for domestic students, 10/1 for international students. Applications are processed on a rolling basis. Application fee: $30. Electronic applications accepted. *Expenses:* Tuition, state resident: full-time $6012; part-time $1503 per semester. Tuition, nonresident: full-time $15,030; part-time $3758 per semester. Required fees: $1711; $675 per semester. *Financial support:* In 2010–11, 1 fellowship with full tuition reimbursement (averaging $8,370 per year), 16 teaching assistantships with full tuition reimbursements (averaging $8,064 per year) were awarded; research assistantships with full tuition reimbursements, career-related internships or fieldwork, Federal Work-Study, institutionally sponsored loans, scholarships/grants, traineeships, and unspecified assistantships also available. Support available to part-time students. Financial award application deadline: 3/1; financial award applicants required to submit FAFSA. *Unit head:* Dr. Rik Hafer, Chair, 618-650-2542, E-mail: rhafer@siue.edu. *Application contact:* Dr. Ali Kutan, Director, 618-650-3473, E-mail: akutan@siue.edu.

Southern Methodist University, Cox School of Business, MBA Program, Dallas, TX 75275. Offers accounting (MBA); finance (MBA); financial consulting (MBA); general business (MBA); information technology and operations management (MBA); management (MBA); marketing (MBA); real estate (MBA); strategy and entrepreneurship (MBA). Part-time and evening/weekend programs available. *Faculty:* 59 full-time (13 women), 30 part-time/adjunct (7 women). *Students:* 359 full-time (116 women), 592 part-time (154 women); includes 215 minority (44 Black or African American, non-Hispanic/Latino; 10 American Indian or Alaska Native, non-Hispanic/Latino; 118 Asian, non-Hispanic/Latino; 39 Hispanic/Latino; 2 Native Hawaiian or other Pacific Islander, non-Hispanic/Latino; 2 Two or more races, non-Hispanic/Latino), 92 international. Average age 30. In 2010, 486 master's awarded. *Entrance requirements:* For master's, GMAT. Additional exam requirements/recommendations for international students: Required—TOEFL. *Application deadline:* Applications are processed on a rolling basis. Application fee: $0. Electronic applications accepted. *Expenses:* Contact institution. *Financial support:* Applicants required to submit FAFSA. *Faculty research:* Corporate finance, financial reporting, modeling consumer decision-making, competition between national brands and store brands, institutional determinants of firms' strategy. *Unit head:* Dr. Marci Armstrong, Associate Dean for Master's Programs, 214-768-4486, Fax: 214-768-3956, E-mail: marci@cox.smu.edu. *Application contact:* Patti Cudney, Director of MBA Admissions, 214-768-3001, Fax: 214-768-3956, E-mail: pcudney@cox.smu.edu.

State University of New York at Binghamton, Graduate School, School of Arts and Sciences, Department of Economics, Binghamton, NY 13902-6000. Offers economics (MA, PhD); economics and finance (MA, PhD). *Faculty:* 20 full-time (5 women), 2 part-time/adjunct (0 women). *Students:* 45 full-time (20 women), 33 part-time (11 women); includes 1 Black or African American, non-Hispanic/Latino; 4 Asian, non-Hispanic/Latino; 1 Hispanic/Latino, 58 international. Average age 28. 152 applicants, 48% accepted, 29 enrolled. In 2010, 12 master's, 5 doctorates awarded. Terminal master's awarded for partial completion of doctoral program. *Degree requirements:* For doctorate, thesis/dissertation. *Entrance requirements:* For master's and doctorate, GRE General Test. Additional exam requirements/recommendations for international students: Required—TOEFL (minimum score 550 paper-based; 213 computer-based; 80 iBT). *Application deadline:* For fall admission, 8/1 priority date for domestic and international students. Applications are processed on a rolling basis. Application fee: $60. Electronic applications accepted. *Financial support:* In 2010–11, 29 students received support, including 8 fellowships with full tuition reimbursements available (averaging $14,500 per year), 27 teaching assistantships with full tuition reimbursements available (averaging $14,500 per year); career-related internships or fieldwork, Federal Work-Study, institutionally sponsored loans, scholarships/grants, health care benefits, tuition waivers (full and partial), and unspecified assistantships also available. Financial award application deadline: 2/15; financial award applicants required to submit FAFSA. *Unit head:* Dr. Susan Wolcott, Chairperson, 607-777-2339, E-mail: swolcott@binghamton.edu. *Application contact:* Catherine Smith, Recruiting and Admissions Coordinator, 607-777-2151, Fax: 607-777-2501, E-mail: cmsmith@binghamton.edu.

Stony Brook University, State University of New York, Graduate School, College of Business, Program in Business Administration, Stony Brook, NY 11794. Offers finance (MBA, Certificate); health care management (MBA, Certificate); human resource management (Certificate); human resources (MBA); information systems management (MBA, Certificate); management (MBA); marketing (MBA). *Faculty:* 14 full-time (2 women), 27 part-time/adjunct (6 women). *Students:* 182 full-time (103 women), 117 part-time (35 women); includes 11 Black or African American, non-Hispanic/Latino; 35 Asian, non-Hispanic/Latino; 10 Hispanic/Latino; 2 Two or more races, non-Hispanic/Latino, 88 international. 281 applicants, 60% accepted, 102 enrolled. In 2010, 95 master's, 1 other advanced degree awarded. Application fee: $100. *Expenses:* Tuition, state resident: full-time $8370; part-time $349 per credit. Tuition, nonresident: full-time $13,780; part-time $574 per credit. Required fees: $994. *Financial support:* In 2010–11, 2 teaching assistantships were awarded. *Unit head:* Dr. Manuel London, Interim Dean, 631-632-7180. *Application contact:* Dr. Aristotle Lekacos, Director, Graduate Program, 631-632-7171, E-mail: aristotle.lekacost@notes.cc.sunysb.edu.

Suffolk University, Sawyer Business School, Master of Business Administration Program, Boston, MA 02108-2770. Offers accounting (MBA); business administration (APC); corporate financial executive track (MBA); entrepreneurship (MBA); executive business administration (EMBA); finance (MBA); global business administration (GMBA); health administration (MBA); international business (MBA); marketing (MBA); organizational behavior (MBA); strategic management (MBA); taxation (MBA); JD/MBA; MBA/GDPA; MBA/MHA; MBA/MSA; MBA/MSF; MBA/MST. *Accreditation:* AACSB. Part-time and evening/weekend programs available. Postbaccalaureate distance learning degree programs offered (no on-campus study). *Faculty:* 97 full-time (30 women), 14 part-time/adjunct (3 women). *Students:* 179 full-time (65 women), 337 part-time (143 women); includes 16 Black or African American, non-Hispanic/Latino; 2 American Indian or Alaska Native, non-Hispanic/Latino; 22 Asian, non-Hispanic/Latino; 9 Hispanic/Latino; 1 Native Hawaiian or other Pacific Islander, non-Hispanic/Latino, 80 international. Average age 30. 431 applicants, 68% accepted, 128 enrolled. In 2010, 283 master's awarded. *Entrance requirements:* For master's, GMAT, minimum undergraduate GPA of 2.75 (MBA), 5 years of managerial experience (EMBA). Additional exam requirements/recommendations for international students: Required—TOEFL (minimum score 550 paper-based;

213 computer-based). *Application deadline:* For fall admission, 6/15 priority date for domestic students, 6/15 for international students; for spring admission, 11/1 priority date for domestic students, 11/1 for international students. Applications are processed on a rolling basis. Application fee: $50. Electronic applications accepted. *Financial support:* In 2010–11, 266 students received support, including 94 fellowships with full and partial tuition reimbursements available (averaging $12,635 per year); career-related internships or fieldwork, Federal Work-Study, and institutionally sponsored loans also available. Support available to part-time students. Financial award application deadline: 4/1; financial award applicants required to submit FAFSA. *Faculty research:* Foreign investments; career strategies and boundaryless careers; corporate ethics codes; interest rates, inflation, and growth options; innovation and product development performance. *Unit head:* Lillian Hallberg, Assistant Dean of Graduate Programs/Director of MBA Programs, 617-573-8306, E-mail: lhallber@suffolk.edu. *Application contact:* Judith Reynolds, Director of Graduate Admissions, 617-573-8302, Fax: 617-305-1733, E-mail: grad.admission@suffolk.edu.

Suffolk University, Sawyer Business School, Program in Finance, Boston, MA 02108-2770. Offers MSF, MSFSB, CPASF, JD/MSF. *Accreditation:* AACSB. Part-time and evening/weekend programs available. *Faculty:* 16 full-time (2 women). *Students:* 51 part-time (21 women); includes 1 Black or African American, non-Hispanic/Latino; 1 Asian, non-Hispanic/Latino, 17 international. Average age 28. 179 applicants, 24% accepted, 22 enrolled. In 2010, 35 master's awarded. *Entrance requirements:* For master's, GMAT, interview. Additional exam requirements/recommendations for international students: Required—TOEFL (minimum score 550 paper-based; 213 computer-based; 80 iBT). *Application deadline:* For fall admission, 6/15 priority date for domestic students, 6/15 for international students; for spring admission, 11/1 priority date for domestic students, 11/1 for international students. Applications are processed on a rolling basis. Application fee: $50. Electronic applications accepted. *Expenses:* Contact institution. *Financial support:* In 2010–11, 34 students received support, including 15 fellowships (averaging $20,077 per year); career-related internships or fieldwork, Federal Work-Study, and institutionally sponsored loans also available. Support available to part-time students. Financial award application deadline: 4/1; financial award applicants required to submit FAFSA. *Faculty research:* Financial institutions, corporate finance, ownership structure, dividend policy, corporate restructuring. *Unit head:* Dr. Ki Han, Director of Graduate Programs in Finance, 617-573-8641, E-mail: msf@suffolk.edu. *Application contact:* Judith Reynolds, Director of Graduate Admissions, 617-573-8302, Fax: 617-305-1733, E-mail: grad.admission@suffolk.edu.

Tennessee Technological University, Graduate School, College of Business, Cookeville, TN 38505. Offers accounting (MBA); finance (MBA); human resource management (MBA); international business (MBA); management information systems (MBA); risk management & insurance (MBA). *Accreditation:* AACSB. Part-time and evening/weekend programs available. *Faculty:* 28 full-time (5 women). *Students:* 58 full-time (18 women), 139 part-time (49 women); includes 10 Black or African American, non-Hispanic/Latino; 7 Asian, non-Hispanic/Latino; 7 Hispanic/Latino; 1 Native Hawaiian or other Pacific Islander, non-Hispanic/Latino. Average age 25. 211 applicants, 51% accepted, 59 enrolled. In 2010, 116 master's awarded. *Entrance requirements:* For master's, GMAT. Additional exam requirements/recommendations for international students: Required—TOEFL (minimum score 550 paper-based; 79 iBT), IELTS (minimum score 5.5). *Application deadline:* For fall admission, 8/1 for domestic and international students; for spring admission, 12/1 for domestic students, 10/1 for international students. Application fee: $25 ($30 for international students). Electronic applications accepted. *Expenses:* Tuition, state resident: full-time $7934; part-time $388 per credit hour. Tuition, nonresident: full-time $19,758; part-time $962 per credit hour. *Financial support:* In 2010–11, 5 fellowships (averaging $10,000 per year), 18 research assistantships (averaging $4,000 per year), teaching assistantships (averaging $4,000 per year) were awarded. Support available to part-time students. Financial award application deadline: 4/1. *Unit head:* Dr. Tom Timmerman, Director, 931-372-3600, Fax: 931-372-6249. *Application contact:* Shelia K. Kendrick, Coordinator of Graduate Admissions, 931-372-3808, Fax: 931-372-3497, E-mail: skendrick@tntech.edu.

Texas A&M International University, Office of Graduate Studies and Research, College of Business Administration, Division of International Banking and Finance Studies, Laredo, TX 78041-1900. Offers accounting (MP Acc); international banking (MBA). *Faculty:* 16 full-time (1 woman). *Students:* 53 full-time (29 women), 206 part-time (95 women); includes 2 Black or African American, non-Hispanic/Latino; 1 Asian, non-Hispanic/Latino; 178 Hispanic/Latino, 69 international. Average age 30. 137 applicants, 68% accepted, 71 enrolled. In 2010, 107 master's awarded. *Entrance requirements:* For master's, GMAT or GRE General Test. Additional exam requirements/recommendations for international students: Required—TOEFL (minimum score 550 paper-based; 213 computer-based; 79 iBT). *Application deadline:* For fall admission, 4/30 priority date for domestic students; for spring admission, 11/30 for domestic students, 10/1 for international students. Applications are processed on a rolling basis. Application fee: $25. *Financial support:* In 2010–11, 21 students received support, including 8 research assistantships. *Unit head:* Dr. Ken Hung, Chair, 956-326-2541, Fax: 956-326-2481,

E-mail: ken.hung@tamiu.edu. *Application contact:* Imelda Lopez, Graduate Admissions Counselor, 956-326-2485, Fax: 956-326-2459, E-mail: lopez@tamiu.edu.

Texas A&M University, Mays Business School, Department of Finance, College Station, TX 77843. Offers MS, PhD. *Faculty:* 17. *Students:* 158 full-time (45 women), 7 part-time (2 women); includes 22 minority (1 Black or African American, non-Hispanic/Latino; 15 Asian, non-Hispanic/Latino; 6 Hispanic/Latino), 12 international. Average age 27. 110 applicants, 33% accepted. In 2010, 150 master's, 1 doctorate awarded. Terminal master's awarded for partial completion of doctoral program. *Degree requirements:* For master's, comprehensive exam; for doctorate, thesis/dissertation. *Entrance requirements:* For master's, GMAT; for doctorate, GMAT or GRE General Test. Additional exam requirements/recommendations for international students: Required—TOEFL. *Application deadline:* For fall admission, 3/1 priority date for domestic students; for spring admission, 8/1 for domestic students. Applications are processed on a rolling basis. Application fee: $50 ($75 for international students). *Financial support:* In 2010–11, 30 students received support; fellowships, research assistantships, teaching assistantships, career-related internships or fieldwork and institutionally sponsored loans available. Financial award application deadline: 2/1. *Unit head:* Sorin Sorescu, Head, 979-458-0380, Fax: 979-845-3884, E-mail: smsorescu@mays.tamu.edu. *Application contact:* Timothy Dye, Assistant Head, 979-845-3446, E-mail: tdye@mays.tamu.edu.

Texas A&M University–San Antonio, School of Business, San Antonio, TX 78224. Offers business administration (MBA); enterprise resource planning systems (MBA); finance (MBA); healthcare management (MBA); human resources management (MBA); information assurance and security (MBA); international business (MBA); project management (MBA); supply chain management (MBA). Part-time and evening/weekend programs available. *Faculty:* 18 full-time (6 women), 1 part-time/adjunct (0 women). *Students:* 49 full-time (21 women), 195 part-time (107 women). In 2010, 20 master's awarded. *Entrance requirements:* For master's, GMAT. Additional exam requirements/recommendations for international students: Required—TOEFL (minimum score 550 paper-based; 213 computer-based; 80 iBT), IELTS (minimum score 6). *Application deadline:* For fall admission, 7/1 priority date for domestic students, 6/1 priority date for international students; for spring admission, 11/15 priority date for domestic students, 10/1 priority date for international students. Applications are processed on a rolling basis. Application fee: $35 ($50 for international students). Electronic applications accepted. *Expenses:* Tuition, state resident: full-time $2899; part-time $161 per credit hour. Tuition, nonresident: full-time $8479; part-time $471 per credit hour. Required fees: $1056; $61 per credit hour. $368 per semester. *Financial support:* Application deadline: 3/31. *Unit head:* Dr. Tracy Hurley, MBA Coordinator, 210-932-6200, E-mail: tracy.hurley@tamusa.tamus.edu. *Application contact:* Melissa A. Villanueva, Graduate Admissions Specialist, 210-932-6200, Fax: 210-932-6209, E-mail: melissa.villanueva@tamusa.tamus.edu.

Texas Tech University, Graduate School, Jerry S. Rawls College of Business Administration, Area of Finance, Lubbock, TX 79409. Offers MS, PhD. Part-time programs available. *Faculty:* 13 full-time (1 woman). *Students:* 37 full-time (6 women), 8 part-time (1 woman); includes 1 minority (Hispanic/Latino), 26 international. Average age 27. 51 applicants, 65% accepted, 26 enrolled. In 2010, 14 master's awarded. Terminal master's awarded for partial completion of doctoral program. *Degree requirements:* For master's, capstone course; for doctorate, comprehensive exam, thesis/dissertation, qualifying exams. *Entrance requirements:* For master's and doctorate, GMAT, holistic review of academic credentials. Additional exam requirements/recommendations for international students: Required—TOEFL (minimum score 550 paper-based; 213 computer-based; 79 iBT). *Application deadline:* For fall admission, 4/1 priority date for domestic students, 1/15 for international students; for spring admission, 9/1 priority date for domestic students, 6/15 for international students. Applications are processed on a rolling basis. Application fee: $50 ($75 for international students). Electronic applications accepted. *Expenses:* Tuition, state resident: full-time $5495.76; part-time $228.99 per credit hour. Tuition, nonresident: full-time $12,936; part-time $538.99 per credit hour. Required fees: $2674; $36 per credit hour. $905 per semester. *Financial support:* In 2010–11, 9 research assistantships (averaging $8,800 per year), 2 teaching assistantships (averaging $18,000 per year) were awarded; Federal Work-Study and scholarships/grants also available. Support available to part-time students. Financial award applicants required to submit FAFSA. *Faculty research:* Portfolio theory, banking and financial institutions, corporate finance, securities and options futures. *Unit head:* Dr. Drew Winters, Area Coordinator, 806-742-3350, Fax: 806-742-2099, E-mail: drew.winters@ttu.edu. *Application contact:* Cynthia D. Barnes, Director, Graduate Services Center, 806-742-3184, Fax: 806-742-3958, E-mail: ba_grad@ttu.edu.

Tiffin University, Program in Business Administration, Tiffin, OH 44883-2161. Offers finance (MBA); general management (MBA); healthcare administration (MBA); human resources (MBA); international business (MBA); leadership (MBA); marketing (MBA); sports management (MBA). *Accreditation:* ACBSP. Part-time and evening/weekend programs available. Postbaccalaureate distance learning degree programs offered (no on-campus study). *Faculty:* 18 full-time (9 women), 22 part-time/adjunct (6 women). *Students:* 186 full-time (93 women), 250 part-time (124 women). Average

age 31. 532 applicants, 86% accepted, 229 enrolled. In 2010, 340 master's awarded. *Entrance requirements:* For master's, minimum undergraduate GPA of 2.5, work experience. Additional exam requirements/recommendations for international students: Required—TOEFL (minimum score 550 paper-based; 213 computer-based). *Application deadline:* For fall admission, 8/15 for domestic students, 8/1 for international students; for spring admission, 1/9 for domestic students, 12/1 for international students. Applications are processed on a rolling basis. Application fee: $0. Electronic applications accepted. *Financial support:* In 2010–11, 94 students received support. Available to part-time students. Application deadline: 7/31. *Faculty research:* Small business, executive development operations, research and statistical analysis, market research, management information systems. *Unit head:* Dr. Lillian Schumacher, Dean of the School of Business, 419-448-3053, Fax: 419-443-5002, E-mail: schumacherlb@tiffin.edu. *Application contact:* Kristi Krintzline, Director of Graduate Admissions and Student Services, 800-968-6446 Ext. 3445, Fax: 419-443-5002, E-mail: krintzlineka@tiffin.edu.

Troy University, Graduate School, College of Business, Program in Business Administration, Troy, AL 36082. Offers accounting (EMBA, MBA); criminal justice (EMBA); finance (MBA); general management (EMBA, MBA); healthcare management (EMBA); information systems (EMBA, MBA); international economic development (MBA). *Accreditation:* ACBSP. Part-time and evening/weekend programs available. *Students:* 351 full-time (198 women), 745 part-time (452 women); includes 589 minority (425 Black or African American, non-Hispanic/Latino; 13 American Indian or Alaska Native, non-Hispanic/Latino; 129 Asian, non-Hispanic/Latino; 21 Hispanic/Latino; 1 Two or more races, non-Hispanic/Latino). Average age 29. 748 applicants, 71% accepted. In 2010, 322 master's awarded. *Degree requirements:* For master's, minimum GPA 3.0, capstone course, research course. *Entrance requirements:* For master's, GMAT (minimum score 500) or GRE General Test (minimum score 900), minimum GPA of 2.5; letter of recommendation, bachelor's degree. Additional exam requirements/recommendations for international students: Required—TOEFL (minimum score 523 paper-based; 193 computer-based; 70 iBT), IELTS (minimum score 6), or ACT compass ESL (minimum Listening, Reading, and Grammar score: 270). *Application deadline:* Applications are processed on a rolling basis. Application fee: $50. *Expenses:* Tuition: state resident: full-time $4428; part-time $246 per credit hour. Tuition, nonresident: full-time $8856; part-time $492 per credit hour. Required fees: $432; $24 per credit hour. $50 per term. Tuition and fees vary according to program. *Unit head:* Dr. Henry M. Findley, Interim Chair/Professor, 334-670-3271, Fax: 334-670-3599, E-mail: hfindley@troy.edu. *Application contact:* Brenda K. Campbell, Director of Graduate Admissions, 334-670-3178, Fax: 334-670-3733, E-mail: bcamp@troy.edu.

TUI University, College of Business Administration, Program in Business Administration, Cypress, CA 90630. Offers business administration (PhD); conflict and negotiation management (MBA); criminal justice administration (MBA); entrepreneurship (MBA); finance (MBA); general management (MBA); government accounting (MBA); human resource management (MBA); information security and digital assurance management (MBA); information technology management (MBA); international business (MBA); logistics management (MBA); marketing (MBA); project management (MBA); public management (MBA); quality management (MBA); strategic leadership (MBA). Part-time and evening/weekend programs available. Postbaccalaureate distance learning degree programs offered (no on-campus study). *Students:* 741 full-time (200 women), 1,585 part-time (410 women). 379 applicants, 81% accepted, 300 enrolled. In 2010, 752 master's, 28 doctorates awarded. *Degree requirements:* For doctorate, comprehensive exam, thesis/dissertation, defense of dissertation. *Entrance requirements:* For master's, minimum GPA of 2.5 (students with GPA 3.0 or greater may transfer up to 30% of graduate level credits); for doctorate, minimum GPA of 3.4, curriculum vitae, course work in research methods or statistics. Additional exam requirements/recommendations for international students: Required—TOEFL. *Application deadline:* For fall admission, 10/3 for domestic and international students; for winter admission, 12/22 for domestic and international students; for spring admission, 4/3 for domestic and international students. Applications are processed on a rolling basis. Application fee: $75. Electronic applications accepted. *Expenses:* Tuition: Full-time $11,040; part-time $345 per semester hour. *Unit head:* Paul Watkins, Dean, College of Business Administration, 800-375-9878, E-mail: pwatkins@tuiu.edu. *Application contact:* Wei Ren-Finaly, Registrar, 800-375-9878, Fax: 714-827-7407, E-mail: registration@tuiu.edu.

Union Graduate College, School of Management, Schenectady, NY 12308-3107. Offers business administration (MBA); financial management (Certificate); general management (Certificate); health systems administration (MBA, Certificate); human resources (Certificate). *Accreditation:* AACSB. Part-time and evening/weekend programs available. *Faculty:* 16 full-time (3 women), 7 part-time/adjunct (2 women). *Students:* 129 full-time (61 women), 86 part-time (42 women); includes 27 minority (4 Black or African American, non-Hispanic/Latino; 2 Asian, non-Hispanic/Latino; 4 Hispanic/Latino; 2 Two or more races, non-Hispanic/Latino), 17 international. Average age 27. 115 applicants, 77% accepted, 71 enrolled. In 2010, 78 master's, 17 other advanced degrees awarded. *Degree requirements:* For master's, internship, capstone course. *Entrance requirements:* For master's, GMAT, minimum GPA

of 3.0, 3 letters of recommendation. Additional exam requirements/recommendations for international students: Required—TOEFL (minimum score 550 paper-based; 213 computer-based). *Application deadline:* Applications are processed on a rolling basis. Application fee: $60. *Expenses:* Tuition: Part-time $750 per credit. One-time fee: $350 part-time. Tuition and fees vary according to course load and program. *Financial support:* Research assistantships, career-related internships or fieldwork, Federal Work-Study, scholarships/grants, health care benefits, and tuition waivers (partial) available. Support available to part-time students. Financial award applicants required to submit FAFSA. *Unit head:* Dr. Eric Lewis, Dean, 518-631-9890, Fax: 518-631-9902, E-mail: lewise@uniongraduatecollege.edu. *Application contact:* Diane Trzaskos, Admissions Coordinator, 518-631-9837, Fax: 518-631-9901, E-mail: trzaskod@uniongraduatecollege.edu.

United States International University, School of Business Administration, Nairobi, Kenya. Offers business administration (GEMBA); entrepreneurship (MBA); finance (MBA); human resource management (MBA); information technology management (MBA); integrated studies (MBA); international business administration (MBA); management and organizational development (MS); marketing (MBA); organizational development (EMS); strategic management (MBA). Part-time and evening/weekend programs available. *Faculty:* 42 full-time (8 women), 64 part-time/adjunct (14 women). *Students:* 423 full-time (227 women), 129 part-time (63 women). Average age 29. 110 applicants, 79% accepted, 78 enrolled. In 2010, 164 master's awarded. *Degree requirements:* For master's, thesis. *Entrance requirements:* For master's, GMAT, 2 letters of reference, resume. Additional exam requirements/recommendations for international students: Required—TOEFL (minimum score 550 paper-based; 213 computer-based). *Application deadline:* For fall admission, 6/30 priority date for domestic and international students; for spring admission, 9/30 for domestic and international students. Applications are processed on a rolling basis. Application fee: $50. *Financial support:* In 2010–11, 30 students received support, including 8 research assistantships (averaging $1,400 per year), 4 teaching assistantships (averaging $1,400 per year); career-related internships or fieldwork, scholarships/grants, and unspecified assistantships also available. Support available to part-time students. Financial award application deadline: 6/30; financial award applicants required to submit FAFSA. *Faculty research:* Marketing in small business enterprises, total quality management in Kenya. *Unit head:* Dr. Damary Sikalieh, Dean, 254-02-3606-415, E-mail: dsikalieh@usiu.ac.ke. *Application contact:* George Lumbasi, Director of Admissions, 254-02-3606563, Fax: 254-02-3606100, E-mail: glumbasi@usiu.ac.ke.

Université de Sherbrooke, Faculty of Administration, Program in Finance, Sherbrooke, QC J1K 2R1, Canada. Offers M Sc. *Faculty:* 6 full-time (1 woman), 9 part-time/adjunct (1 woman). *Students:* 58 full-time (8 women). Average age 23. 230 applicants, 49% accepted, 52 enrolled. In 2010, 32 master's awarded. *Degree requirements:* For master's, one foreign language, thesis. *Entrance requirements:* For master's, Bachelor degree in related field Minimum GPA 3.0/4.3. *Application deadline:* For fall admission, 4/30 for domestic students, 1/15 for international students. Applications are processed on a rolling basis. Application fee: $70. Electronic applications accepted. *Faculty research:* Public projects analysis, financial econometrics, risk management, portfolio management. *Unit head:* Prof. Julien Bilodeau, Director, Graduate programs in business, 819-821-8000 Ext. 62355. *Application contact:* Marie-Claude Drouin, Assistant Programs Director, 819-821-8000 Ext. 63301.

Université du Québec en Outaouais, Graduate Programs, Program in Financial Services, Gatineau, QC J8X 3X7, Canada. Offers MBA, DESS, Diploma. Part-time and evening/weekend programs available. *Students:* 46 full-time, 46 part-time, 8 international. *Degree requirements:* For master's, thesis (for some programs). *Application deadline:* For fall admission, 6/1 priority date for domestic students, 3/1 for international students; for winter admission, 11/1 priority date for domestic students, 10/1 for international students. Application fee: $30. *Unit head:* Francois-Eric Racicot, Director, 819-595-3900 Ext. 1727, Fax: 819-773-1747, E-mail: francois-eric.racicot@uqo.ca. *Application contact:* Registrar's Office, 819-773-1850, Fax: 819-773-1835, E-mail: registraire@ugo.ca.

University at Buffalo, the State University of New York, Graduate School, School of Management, Buffalo, NY 14260. Offers accounting (MS); business administration (EMBA, MBA, PMBA); finance (MS), including financial engineering, financial management; information assurance (Certificate); management (PhD); management information systems (MS); supply chains and operations management (MS); Au D/MBA; JD/MBA; M Arch/MBA; MA/MBA; MD/MBA; MPH/MBA; MSW/MBA; Pharm D/MBA. *Accreditation:* AACSB. Part-time and evening/weekend programs available. *Faculty:* 65 full-time (18 women), 32 part-time/adjunct (8 women). *Students:* 626 full-time (229 women), 202 part-time (69 women); includes 43 minority (18 Black or African American, non-Hispanic/Latino; 2 American Indian or Alaska Native, non-Hispanic/Latino; 18 Asian, non-Hispanic/Latino; 5 Hispanic/Latino), 351 international. Average age 27. 1,553 applicants, 46% accepted, 400 enrolled. In 2010, 287 master's, 4 doctorates, 3 other advanced degrees awarded. *Degree requirements:* For master's, thesis (for some programs); for doctorate, comprehensive exam, thesis/dissertation. *Entrance requirements:* For master's, GMAT (MBA, MS in accounting), GRE or GMAT (for all other MS concentrations); for doctorate, GMAT or GRE. Additional exam requirements/ recommendations for international students: Required—TOEFL (minimum score 230 computer-based; 95 iBT). *Application deadline:* For fall admission, 5/2 priority date for domestic students, 3/1 priority date for international students. Applications are processed on a rolling basis. Application fee: $100. Electronic applications accepted. *Expenses:* Contact institution. *Financial support:* In 2010–11, 91 students received support, including 5 fellowships with full and partial tuition reimbursements available (averaging $4,000 per year), 41 research assistantships with full and partial tuition reimbursements available (averaging $16,000 per year), 28 teaching assistantships with full and partial tuition reimbursements available (averaging $15,000 per year); career-related internships or fieldwork, Federal Work-Study, institutionally sponsored loans, scholarships/grants, health care benefits, and unspecified assistantships also available. Financial award application deadline: 2/15; financial award applicants required to submit FAFSA. *Faculty research:* Earnings management and electronic information assurance, supply chains and operations management, corporate financing and asset pricing, consumer behavior and quantitative modeling of marketing behavior, leadership and politics in organizations. Total annual research expenditures: $215,000. *Unit head:* David W. Frasier, Assistant Dean, 716-645-3204, Fax: 716-645-2341, E-mail: davidf@buffalo.edu. *Application contact:* David W. Frasier, Assistant Dean, 716-645-3204, Fax: 716-645-2341, E-mail: davidf@buffalo.edu.

The University of Akron, Graduate School, College of Business Administration, Department of Finance, Akron, OH 44325. Offers MBA, JD/MBA. Part-time and evening/weekend programs available. *Faculty:* 12 full-time (3 women), 10 part-time/adjunct (0 women). *Students:* 26 full-time (6 women), 37 part-time (8 women); includes 1 Asian, non-Hispanic/Latino; 1 Hispanic/Latino, 16 international. Average age 29. 58 applicants, 67% accepted, 16 enrolled. In 2010, 33 master's awarded. *Entrance requirements:* For master's, GMAT, minimum GPA of 2.75, two letters of recommendation, statement of purpose, resume. Additional exam requirements/ recommendations for international students: Required—TOEFL (minimum score 550 paper-based; 213 computer-based; 79 iBT). *Application deadline:* For fall admission, 7/15 for domestic and international students; for spring admission, 11/15 for domestic and international students. Application fee: $30 ($40 for international students). Electronic applications accepted. *Expenses:* Tuition, state resident: full-time $6800; part-time $378 per credit hour. Tuition, nonresident: full-time $11,644; part-time $647 per credit hour. Required fees: $1265. One-time fee: $30 full-time. *Financial support:* In 2010–11, 3 research assistantships with full tuition reimbursements, 10 teaching assistantships with full tuition reimbursements were awarded. *Faculty research:* Corporate finance, financial markets and institutions, investment and equity market analysis, personal financial planning, real estate. *Unit head:* David A. Redle, Chair, 330-972-6329, E-mail: dredle@uakron.edu. *Application contact:* Dr. Susan Hanlon, Director of Graduate Business Programs, 330-972-7043, Fax: 330-972-6588, E-mail: shanlon@uakron.edu.

The University of Alabama, Graduate School, College of Human Environmental Sciences, Program in Human Environmental Science, Tuscaloosa, AL 35487. Offers family financial planning and counseling (MS); interactive technology (MS); quality management (MS); restaurant and meeting management (MS); rural community health (MS); sport management (MS). *Faculty:* 1 full-time (0 women). *Students:* 67 full-time (39 women), 86 part-time (52 women); includes 47 minority (40 Black or African American, non-Hispanic/Latino; 3 Hispanic/Latino; 4 Two or more races, non-Hispanic/Latino), 1 international. Average age 34. 112 applicants, 78% accepted, 64 enrolled. In 2010, 64 master's awarded. *Degree requirements:* For master's, comprehensive exam. *Entrance requirements:* For master's, GRE (for some specializations), minimum GPA of 3.0. Additional exam requirements/recommendations for international students: Required—TOEFL. *Application deadline:* Applications are processed on a rolling basis. Application fee: $50 ($60 for international students). Electronic applications accepted. *Expenses:* Tuition, state resident: full-time $7900. Tuition, nonresident: full-time $20,500. *Faculty research:* Hospitality management, sports medicine education, technology and education. *Unit head:* Dr. Milla D. Boschung, Dean, 205-348-6250, Fax: 205-348-1786, E-mail: mboschun@ches.ua.edu. *Application contact:* Dr. Stuart Usdan, Associate Dean, 205-348-6150, Fax: 205-348-3789, E-mail: susdan@ches.ua.edu.

The University of Alabama, Graduate School, Manderson Graduate School of Business, Economics, Finance and Legal Studies Department, Tuscaloosa, AL 35487. Offers economics (MA, PhD); finance (MS, PhD). *Faculty:* 28 full-time (2 women). *Students:* 89 full-time (24 women), 7 part-time (3 women); includes 17 minority (9 Black or African American, non-Hispanic/Latino; 3 Asian, non-Hispanic/Latino; 3 Hispanic/Latino; 2 Two or more races, non-Hispanic/Latino), 19 international. Average age 27. 252 applicants, 34% accepted, 32 enrolled. In 2010, 46 master's, 7 doctorates awarded. Terminal master's awarded for partial completion of doctoral program. *Degree requirements:* For master's, comprehensive exam (MA), thesis (MS); for doctorate, comprehensive exam, thesis/dissertation. *Entrance requirements:* For master's, GMAT, GRE; for doctorate, GRE or GMAT. Additional exam requirements/recommendations for international students: Required—TOEFL (minimum score 550 paper-based; 213 computer-based). *Application deadline:* For fall admission, 7/1 priority date for domestic students, 1/15 for

international students; for spring admission, 11/1 priority date for domestic students, 6/1 for international students. Applications are processed on a rolling basis. Application fee: $50 ($60 for international students). Electronic applications accepted. *Expenses:* Tuition, state resident: full-time $7900. Tuition, nonresident: full-time $20,500. *Financial support:* In 2010–11, 10 fellowships (averaging $10,000 per year), 21 research assistantships with full and partial tuition reimbursements (averaging $12,000 per year), 15 teaching assistantships with full and partial tuition reimbursements (averaging $12,000 per year) were awarded; Federal Work-Study, institutionally sponsored loans, and unspecified assistantships also available. *Faculty research:* Taxation, futures market, monetary theory and policy, income distribution. *Unit head:* Prof. Billy P. Helms, Head, 205-348-8067, E-mail: bhelms@cba.ua.edu. *Application contact:* Debra F. Wheatley, 205-348-6683, Fax: 205-348-0590, E-mail: dwheatle@cba.ua.edu.

The University of Alabama in Huntsville, School of Graduate Studies, College of Business Administration, Department of Accounting and Finance, Huntsville, AL 35899. Offers accounting (M Acc), including CPA preparatory with an emphasis in taxation, CPA preparatory with emphasis in assurance and financial reporting, general accounting, information systems audit and control (ISAC). *Accreditation:* AACSB. Part-time and evening/weekend programs available. *Faculty:* 7 full-time (4 women), 2 part-time/adjunct (0 women). *Students:* 14 full-time (8 women), 27 part-time (14 women); includes 6 minority (all Black or African American, non-Hispanic/Latino), 3 international. Average age 33. 27 applicants, 56% accepted, 13 enrolled. In 2010, 8 master's awarded. *Degree requirements:* For master's, comprehensive exam, thesis or alternative. *Entrance requirements:* For master's, GMAT (minimum score 500), minimum AACSB index of 1080. Additional exam requirements/ recommendations for international students: Required—TOEFL (minimum score 550 paper-based; 213 computer-based; 62 iBT). *Application deadline:* For fall admission, 8/1 for domestic students, 4/1 for international students; for spring admission, 12/1 for domestic students, 9/1 for international students. Applications are processed on a rolling basis. Application fee: $40 ($50 for international students). Electronic applications accepted. *Expenses:* Tuition, state resident: full-time $7250; part-time $407.75 per credit hour. Tuition, nonresident: full-time $17,358; part-time $970.05 per credit hour. Required fees: $246.80 per semester. Tuition and fees vary according to course load and program. *Financial support:* In 2010–11, 1 student received support, including 1 research assistantship with full tuition reimbursement available (averaging $14,400 per year), 1 teaching assistantship with full tuition reimbursement available (averaging $11,470 per year); career-related internships or fieldwork, Federal Work-Study, institutionally sponsored loans, scholarships/grants, health care benefits, and unspecified assistantships also available. Support available to part-time students. Financial award application deadline: 4/1; financial award applicants required to submit FAFSA. *Faculty research:* Accounting information systems, emerging technologies in accounting, behavioral accounting, state and local taxation, financial accounting. Total annual research expenditures: $17,511. *Unit head:* Dr. John Burnett, Interim Chair, 256-824-2923, Fax: 256-824-2929, E-mail: burnettj@uah.edu. *Application contact:* Jennifer Pettitt, Director of Graduate Programs, 256-824-6681, Fax: 256-824-7571, E-mail: jennifer.pettitt@uah.edu.

The University of Alabama in Huntsville, School of Graduate Studies, College of Business Administration, Department of Management and Marketing, Huntsville, AL 35899. Offers management (MBA), including acquisition management, finance, human resource management, logistics and supply chain management, marketing, project management. *Accreditation:* AACSB. Part-time and evening/weekend programs available. *Faculty:* 11 full-time (2 women), 4 part-time/adjunct (1 woman). *Students:* 41 full-time (17 women), 159 part-time (69 women); includes 32 minority (15 Black or African American, non-Hispanic/Latino; 6 American Indian or Alaska Native, non-Hispanic/Latino; 7 Asian, non-Hispanic/Latino; 3 Hispanic/Latino; 1 Two or more races, non-Hispanic/Latino), 14 international. Average age 31. 141 applicants, 65% accepted, 79 enrolled. In 2010, 66 master's awarded. *Degree requirements:* For master's, comprehensive exam, thesis or alternative. *Entrance requirements:* For master's, GMAT (minimum score 500), minimum AACSB index of 1080. Additional exam requirements/recommendations for international students: Required—TOEFL (minimum score 550 paper-based; 213 computer-based; 62 iBT). *Application deadline:* For fall admission, 8/1 for domestic students, 4/1 for international students; for spring admission, 12/1 for domestic students, 9/1 for international students. Applications are processed on a rolling basis. Application fee: $40 ($50 for international students). Electronic applications accepted. *Expenses:* Tuition, state resident: full-time $7250; part-time $407.75 per credit hour. Tuition, nonresident: full-time $17,358; part-time $970.05 per credit hour. Required fees: $246.80 per semester. Tuition and fees vary according to course load and program. *Financial support:* In 2010–11, 3 students received support, including 1 research assistantship with full tuition reimbursement available (averaging $8,550 per year), 2 teaching assistantships with full tuition reimbursements available (averaging $8,000 per year); career-related internships or fieldwork, Federal Work-Study, institutionally sponsored loans, scholarships/grants, health care benefits, and unspecified assistantships also available. Support available to part-time students. Financial award application deadline: 4/1; financial award applicants required to submit FAFSA. *Faculty research:* Strategic human resources, corporate governance, cross-function integration and the management of research and development, determinants of team performance. Total annual research expenditures: $3 million. *Unit head:* Dr. Brent Wren, Chair, 256-824-6408, Fax: 256-824-6328, E-mail: wrenb@uah.edu. *Application contact:* Jennifer Pettitt, Director of Graduate Programs, 256-824-6681, Fax: 256-824-7571, E-mail: jennifer.pettitt@uah.edu.

University of Alaska Fairbanks, School of Management, Department of Business Administration, Fairbanks, AK 99775-6080. Offers capital markets (MBA); general management (MBA). *Accreditation:* AACSB. Part-time programs available. *Faculty:* 10 full-time (2 women), 1 part-time/adjunct (0 women). *Students:* 22 full-time (9 women), 33 part-time (23 women); includes 15 minority (5 Black or African American, non-Hispanic/Latino; 5 American Indian or Alaska Native, non-Hispanic/Latino; 3 Asian, non-Hispanic/Latino; 1 Hispanic/Latino; 1 Native Hawaiian or other Pacific Islander, non-Hispanic/Latino), 4 international. Average age 31. 32 applicants, 69% accepted, 18 enrolled. In 2010, 25 master's awarded. *Degree requirements:* For master's, comprehensive exam, thesis or alternative. *Entrance requirements:* For master's, GMAT. Additional exam requirements/recommendations for international students: Required—TOEFL (minimum score 550 paper-based; 213 computer-based; 80 iBT). *Application deadline:* For fall admission, 6/1 priority date for domestic students, 2/1 for international students; for spring admission, 10/15 priority date for domestic students, 9/1 for international students. Applications are processed on a rolling basis. Application fee: $60. Electronic applications accepted. *Expenses:* Tuition, state resident: full-time $5688; part-time $316 per credit. Tuition, nonresident: full-time $11,628; part-time $646 per credit. Required fees: $289 per semester. Tuition and fees vary according to course load and reciprocity agreements. *Financial support:* In 2010–11, 2 research assistantships with tuition reimbursements (averaging $11,939 per year), 5 teaching assistantships with tuition reimbursements (averaging $8,450 per year) were awarded; fellowships with tuition reimbursements, career-related internships or fieldwork, Federal Work-Study, scholarships/grants, health care benefits, and unspecified assistantships also available. Support available to part-time students. Financial award application deadline: 2/15; financial award applicants required to submit FAFSA. *Faculty research:* Consumer behavior, marketing, international finance and business, strategic risk, organization theory. Total annual research expenditures: $20,946. *Unit head:* Dr. Ping Lan, Director, MBA Program, 907-474-7688, Fax: 907-474-5219, E-mail: plan@alaska.edu. *Application contact:* Dr. Ping Lan, Director, MBA Program, 907-474-7688, Fax: 907-474-5219, E-mail: plan@alaska.edu.

The University of Arizona, Eller College of Management, Department of Finance, Tucson, AZ 85721. Offers MS, PhD. Part-time programs available. *Faculty:* 7 full-time (2 women). Terminal master's awarded for partial completion of doctoral program. *Degree requirements:* For master's, project; for doctorate, comprehensive exam, thesis/dissertation. *Entrance requirements:* Additional exam requirements/recommendations for international students: Required—TOEFL (minimum score 550 paper-based; 213 computer-based; 79 iBT). *Application deadline:* For fall admission, 2/15 for domestic and international students. Applications are processed on a rolling basis. Application fee: $75. Electronic applications accepted. *Expenses:* Contact institution. *Financial support:* In 2010–11, 5 research assistantships with full tuition reimbursements (averaging $24,795 per year), 6 teaching assistantships with full tuition reimbursements (averaging $22,952 per year) were awarded; health care benefits, tuition waivers (partial), and unspecified assistantships also available. Financial award application deadline: 3/15. *Faculty research:* Corporate finance, banking, investments, stock market. *Unit head:* Dr. Chris Lamoureux, Head, 520-621-7488, Fax: 520-621-1261, E-mail: lamoureu@lamfin.eller.arizona.edu. *Application contact:* Kay Ross, Program Coordinator, 520-621-1520, Fax: 520-621-1261, E-mail: kross@eller.arizona.edu.

University of California, Berkeley, Graduate Division, Haas School of Business, PhD in Business Administration Program, Berkeley, CA 94720-1500. Offers accounting (PhD); business and public policy (PhD); finance (PhD); management of organizations (PhD); marketing (PhD); operations management (PhD); real estate (PhD). *Accreditation:* AACSB. *Students:* 78 full-time (25 women); includes 12 Asian, non-Hispanic/Latino; 2 Hispanic/Latino, 32 international. Average age 30. 526 applicants, 7% accepted, 17 enrolled. In 2010, 17 doctorates awarded. *Degree requirements:* For doctorate, comprehensive exam, thesis/dissertation, written preliminary exams, oral qualifying exam. *Entrance requirements:* For doctorate, GMAT or GRE, minimum GPA of 3.0 in undergraduate and graduate coursework. Additional exam requirements/recommendations for international students: Required—TOEFL (minimum score 570 paper-based; 230 computer-based; 70 iBT), IELTS (minimum score 7). *Application deadline:* For fall admission, 12/10 for domestic and international students. Application fee: $70 ($90 for international students). Electronic applications accepted. *Financial support:* In 2010–11, 63 students received support, including 58 fellowships with full and partial tuition reimbursements available (averaging $26,000 per year); research assistantships with full and partial tuition reimbursements available, teaching assistantships with full and partial tuition reimbursements available, scholarships/grants, health care benefits, tuition waivers (full), unspecified assistantships, and transit pass, travel grants also available. Financial award application deadline: 12/10; financial award applicants required to submit FAFSA. *Faculty research:* Accounting, business and public policy, finance, management of organizations, marketing, operations and information

technology management, real estate526. *Unit head:* Dr. Sunil Dutta, Director, 510-642-1229, Fax: 510-643-4255, E-mail: kimg@haas.berkeley.edu. *Application contact:* Kim Guilfoyle, Director, Student Affairs, 510-642-3944, Fax: 510-643-4255, E-mail: kimg@haas.berkeley.edu.

University of California, Los Angeles, Graduate Division, UCLA Anderson School of Management, Los Angeles, CA 90095-1481. Offers accounting (PhD); business administration (MBA); decisions, operations and technology management (PhD); finance (PhD); financial engineering (MFE); global economics and management (PhD); human resources and organizational behavior (PhD); marketing (PhD); strategy and policy (PhD); DDS/MBA; MBA/JD; MBA/MD; MBA/MLAS; MBA/MLIS; MBA/MPH; MBA/MPP; MBA/MSCS; MBA/MSN; MBA/MUP. *Accreditation:* AACSB. Part-time programs available. *Faculty:* 102 full-time (17 women), 43 part-time/adjunct (6 women). *Students:* 833 full-time (270 women), 1,052 part-time (271 women); includes 592 minority (25 Black or African American, non-Hispanic/Latino; 3 American Indian or Alaska Native, non-Hispanic/Latino; 482 Asian, non-Hispanic/Latino; 60 Hispanic/Latino; 6 Native Hawaiian or other Pacific Islander, non-Hispanic/Latino; 16 Two or more races, non-Hispanic/Latino), 445 international. In 2010, 735 master's, 10 doctorates awarded. *Degree requirements:* For master's, comprehensive exam, field study consulting project (for MBA); thesis/dissertation (for MFE); for doctorate, comprehensive exam, thesis/dissertation, oral and written qualifying exams. *Entrance requirements:* For master's, GMAT (MBA); GMAT or GRE General Test (MFE), minimum undergraduate GPA of 3.0; for doctorate, GMAT or GRE General Test, minimum undergraduate GPA of 3.0. Additional exam requirements/recommendations for international students: Required—TOEFL (minimum score 560 paper-based; 220 computer-based; 87 iBT), IELTS (minimum score 7). *Application deadline:* For fall admission, 10/20 for domestic and international students; for winter admission, 1/5 for domestic and international students; for spring admission, 4/13 for domestic and international students. Application fee: $200. Electronic applications accepted. *Expenses:* Contact institution. *Financial support:* Fellowships, research assistantships, teaching assistantships, career-related internships or fieldwork, institutionally sponsored loans, scholarships/grants, health care benefits, and tuition waivers (partial) available. Financial award application deadline: 3/2; financial award applicants required to submit FAFSA. *Unit head:* Judy D. Olian, Dean, UCLA Anderson School of Management, 310-825-7982, Fax: 310-206-2073. *Application contact:* Mae Jennifer Shores, Assistant Dean and Director of Full-time MBA Admissions and Financial Aid, 310-825-6944, Fax: 310-825-8582, E-mail: mba.admissions@anderson.ucla.edu.

University of California, Santa Cruz, Division of Graduate Studies, Division of Social Sciences, Program in Applied Economics and Finance, Santa Cruz, CA 95064. Offers MS. *Students:* 32 full-time (11 women); includes 7 Asian, non-Hispanic/Latino; 4 Hispanic/Latino, 12 international. Average age 25. 112 applicants, 65% accepted, 24 enrolled. In 2010, 12 master's awarded. *Degree requirements:* For master's, thesis or alternative, project. *Entrance requirements:* For master's, GRE General Test, GRE Subject Test. Additional exam requirements/recommendations for international students: Required—TOEFL (minimum score 550 paper-based; 220 computer-based; 83 iBT); Recommended—IELTS (minimum score 8). *Application deadline:* For fall admission, 12/15 for domestic and international students. Application fee: $70 ($90 for international students). Electronic applications accepted. *Financial support:* Research assistantships, teaching assistantships, institutionally sponsored loans and tuition waivers available. Financial award applicants required to submit FAFSA. *Faculty research:* Economic decision-making skills for the design and operation of complex institutional systems. *Unit head:* Sandra Reebie, Graduate Program Coordinator, 831-459-2219, E-mail: screebie@ucsc.edu. *Application contact:* Sandra Reebie, Graduate Program Coordinator, 831-459-2219, E-mail: screebie@ucsc.edu.

University of Chicago, Booth School of Business, Full-Time MBA Program, Chicago, IL 60637. Offers accounting (MBA); analytic finance (MBA); analytic management (MBA); econometrics and statistics (MBA); economics (MBA); entrepreneurship (MBA); finance (MBA); general management (MBA); human resource management (MBA); international business (MBA); managerial and organizational behavior (MBA); marketing management (MBA); operations management (MBA); strategic management (MBA); MBA/AM; MBA/JD; MBA/MA; MBA/MD; MBA/MPP. *Accreditation:* AACSB. Part-time and evening/weekend programs available. *Faculty:* 157 full-time, 35 part-time/adjunct. *Students:* 1,177 full-time (417 women); includes 301 minority (62 Black or African American, non-Hispanic/Latino; 1 American Indian or Alaska Native, non-Hispanic/Latino; 164 Asian, non-Hispanic/Latino; 55 Hispanic/Latino; 19 Two or more races, non-Hispanic/Latino), 403 international. Average age 28. 4,299 applicants, 22% accepted, 579 enrolled. In 2010, 1,374 master's awarded. *Entrance requirements:* For master's, GMAT, 2 letters of recommendation, 3 essays, resume, interview, transcripts. Additional exam requirements/recommendations for international students: Required—TOEFL (minimum score 600 paper-based; 250 computer-based), IELTS. *Application deadline:* For fall admission, 10/10 priority date for domestic students, 10/13 priority date for international students; for winter admission, 1/5 for domestic and international students; for spring admission, 4/13 for domestic and international students. Application fee: $200. Electronic applications accepted. *Expenses:* Contact institution.

Financial support: Fellowships available. Financial award applicants required to submit FAFSA. *Faculty research:* Finance, economics, entrepreneurship, strategy, management. *Unit head:* Stacey Kole, Deputy Dean, 773-702-7121. *Application contact:* Kurt Ahlm, Associate Dean of Admissions and Financial Aid, 773-702-7369, Fax: 773-702-9085, E-mail: admissions@chicagobooth.edu.

University of Cincinnati, Graduate School, College of Business, PhD Program, Cincinnati, OH 45221. Offers accounting (PhD); finance (PhD); information systems (PhD); management (PhD); marketing (PhD); quantitative analysis and operations management (PhD). *Faculty:* 56 full-time (13 women). *Students:* 32 full-time (12 women), 9 part-time (3 women); includes 2 minority (both Hispanic/Latino), 23 international. 119 applicants, 12% accepted, 9 enrolled. In 2010, 8 doctorates awarded. *Degree requirements:* For doctorate, comprehensive exam, thesis/dissertation. *Entrance requirements:* For doctorate, GMAT, GRE, transcripts, essays, resume, letters of recommendation. Additional exam requirements/recommendations for international students: Required—TOEFL (minimum score 600 paper-based; 250 computer-based; 100 iBT). *Application deadline:* For fall admission, 2/1 for domestic and international students. Application fee: $45. Electronic applications accepted. *Expenses:* Contact institution. *Financial support:* In 2010–11, 38 students received support, including 29 research assistantships with full and partial tuition reimbursements available (averaging $14,640 per year); scholarships/grants, tuition waivers (full and partial), and unspecified assistantships also available. Financial award application deadline: 2/15; financial award applicants required to submit FAFSA. *Unit head:* Dr. Suzanne Masterson, Director, PhD Programs, 513-556-7125, Fax: 513-556-5499, E-mail: suzanne.masterson@uc.edu. *Application contact:* Deborah Schildknecht, Assistant Director, PhD Programs, 513-556-7190, Fax: 513-558-7006, E-mail: deborah.schildknecht@uc.edu.

University of Colorado Boulder, Leeds School of Business, Division of Business Administration, Boulder, CO 80309. Offers accounting (MS, PhD); finance (PhD); information systems (PhD); marketing (PhD); operations (PhD); strategic, organizational, and entrepreneurial studies (PhD). Part-time and evening/weekend programs available. *Students:* 110 full-time (42 women), 2 part-time (1 woman); includes 6 minority (5 Asian, non-Hispanic/Latino; 1 Hispanic/Latino), 24 international. Average age 28. 342 applicants, 24 enrolled. In 2010, 48 master's, 12 doctorates awarded. *Entrance requirements:* For master's, GMAT, minimum undergraduate GPA of 3.0. *Application deadline:* For fall admission, 3/31 for domestic and international students; for spring admission, 10/31 for domestic and international students. Application fee: $50 ($60 for international students). Electronic applications accepted. *Financial support:* In 2010–11, 16 fellowships (averaging $1,038 per year), 26 research assistantships (averaging $17,558 per year), 11 teaching assistantships (averaging $12,576 per year) were awarded; career-related internships or fieldwork, Federal Work-Study, scholarships/grants, and unspecified assistantships also available. Financial award applicants required to submit FAFSA.

University of Colorado Denver, Business School, Program in Finance, Denver, CO 80217. Offers MS, MS/MBA. Part-time and evening/weekend programs available. *Students:* 77 full-time (23 women), 24 part-time (4 women); includes 1 American Indian or Alaska Native, non-Hispanic/Latino; 4 Asian, non-Hispanic/Latino; 5 Hispanic/Latino, 20 international. Average age 30. 115 applicants, 39% accepted, 26 enrolled. In 2010, 55 master's awarded. *Degree requirements:* For master's, 30 semester hours (18 of required core courses, 9 of finance electives, and 3 of free elective). *Entrance requirements:* For master's, GMAT. Additional exam requirements/recommendations for international students: Required—TOEFL (minimum score 525 paper-based; 197 computer-based; 70 iBT). *Application deadline:* For fall admission, 4/1 priority date for domestic students, 3/15 priority date for international students; for spring admission, 10/1 priority date for domestic and international students. Application fee: $50 ($75 for international students). Electronic applications accepted. *Expenses:* Contact institution. *Financial support:* Federal Work-Study and scholarships/grants available. Support available to part-time students. Financial award application deadline: 4/1; financial award applicants required to submit FAFSA. *Faculty research:* Corporate governance, debt maturity policies, regulation and financial markets, option management strategies. *Unit head:* Dr. Ajeyo Banerjee, Associate Professor/Director, 303-315-8456, E-mail: ajeyo.banerjee@ucdenver.edu. *Application contact:* Shelly Townley, Admissions Director, Graduate Programs, 303-315-8202, E-mail: shelly.townley@ucdenver.edu.

University of Colorado Denver, Business School, Program in Health Administration, Denver, CO 80217. Offers financial management (MS); health information technology management (MS); international health management and policy (MS). *Accreditation:* CAHME. Part-time and evening/weekend programs available. *Students:* 11 full-time (5 women); includes 1 Asian, non-Hispanic/Latino. Average age 29. 16 applicants, 44% accepted, 4 enrolled. In 2010, 2 master's awarded. *Degree requirements:* For master's, 33 credit hours. *Entrance requirements:* For master's, GMAT. Additional exam requirements/recommendations for international students: Required—TOEFL (minimum score 525 paper-based; 197 computer-based; 71 iBT). *Application deadline:* For fall admission, 4/1 priority date for domestic students, 3/15 priority date for international students; for spring admission, 10/1 priority date for domestic and international students. Application fee: $50 ($75 for international students). Electronic applications accepted. *Expenses:* Contact institution. *Financial support:* Federal Work-Study and scholarships/grants available. Support available to part-time students. Financial award application deadline: 4/1; financial award applicants required to submit FAFSA. *Faculty research:* Cost containment, financial management, governance, rural health-care delivery systems. *Unit head:* Dr. Blair Gifford, Associate Professor/Director, 303-315-8400, E-mail: blair.gifford@ucdenver.edu. *Application contact:* Shelly Townley, Admissions Director, Graduate Programs, 303-315-8202, E-mail: shelly.townley@ucdenver.edu.

University of Dayton, Graduate School, School of Business Administration, Dayton, OH 45469-1300. Offers accounting (MBA); business intelligence (MBA); cyber security (MBA); entrepreneurship (MBA); finance (MBA); international business (MBA); marketing (MBA); MIS (MBA); operations management (MBA); technology-enhanced business/e-commerce (MBA); JD/MBA. *Accreditation:* AACSB. Part-time and evening/weekend programs available. *Faculty:* 25 full-time (7 women), 14 part-time/adjunct (2 women). *Students:* 184 full-time (72 women), 110 part-time (34 women); includes 23 minority (7 Black or African American, non-Hispanic/Latino; 7 Asian, non-Hispanic/Latino; 8 Hispanic/Latino; 1 Two or more races, non-Hispanic/Latino), 31 international. Average age 28. 220 applicants, 85% accepted, 103 enrolled. In 2010, 113 master's awarded. *Entrance requirements:* For master's, GMAT or GRE. Additional exam requirements/recommendations for international students: Required—TOEFL (minimum score 550 paper-based; 213 computer-based; 79 iBT); Recommended—IELTS (minimum score 6.5). *Application deadline:* For fall admission, 3/1 priority date for international students; for winter admission, 7/1 priority date for international students; for spring admission, 1/1 priority date for international students. Applications are processed on a rolling basis. Application fee: $0 ($50 for international students). Electronic applications accepted. *Expenses:* Contact institution. *Financial support:* In 2010–11, 15 research assistantships with full and partial tuition reimbursements (averaging $7,020 per year) were awarded; career-related internships or fieldwork, institutionally sponsored loans, scholarships/grants, health care benefits, and unspecified assistantships also available. Support available to part-time students. Financial award application deadline: 3/15; financial award applicants required to submit FAFSA. *Faculty research:* Management information systems, economics, finance, entrepreneurship, marketing. *Unit head:* Janice M. Glynn, Director, MBA Program, 937-229-3733, Fax: 937-229-3882, E-mail: glynn@udayton.edu. *Application contact:* Jeffrey Carter, Assistant Director, MBA Program, 937-229-3733, Fax: 937-229-3882, E-mail: jeff.carter@notes.udayton.edu.

University of Denver, Daniels College of Business, Reiman School of Finance, Denver, CO 80208. Offers IMBA, MBA, MS. Part-time and evening/weekend programs available. *Faculty:* 15 full-time (3 women), 4 part-time/adjunct (2 women). *Students:* 47 full-time (13 women), 80 part-time (32 women); includes 7 minority (1 Black or African American, non-Hispanic/Latino; 5 Asian, non-Hispanic/Latino; 1 Hispanic/Latino), 82 international. Average age 26. 518 applicants, 32% accepted, 41 enrolled. In 2010, 92 master's awarded. *Entrance requirements:* For master's, GRE General Test or GMAT. Additional exam requirements/recommendations for international students: Required—TOEFL (minimum score 570 paper-based; 88 iBT). *Application deadline:* For fall admission, 11/15 priority date for domestic students; for spring admission, 10/15 priority date for domestic students. Applications are processed on a rolling basis. Application fee: $100. Electronic applications accepted. *Expenses:* Tuition: Full-time $35,604; part-time $29,670 per year. Required fees: $687 per year. Tuition and fees vary according to program. *Financial support:* In 2010–11, 17 teaching assistantships with partial tuition reimbursements (averaging $1,425 per year) were awarded; career-related internships or fieldwork, Federal Work-Study, institutionally sponsored loans, scholarships/grants, and unspecified assistantships also available. Support available to part-time students. Financial award application deadline: 3/15; financial award applicants required to submit FAFSA. *Unit head:* Dr. Ron Rizzuto, Co-Director, 303-871-2010, E-mail: ronald.rizzuto@du.edu. *Application contact:* Tara Stenbakken, Graduate Admissions Manager, 303-871-4211, E-mail: tara.stenbakken@du.edu.

University of Florida, Graduate School, Warrington College of Business Administration, Hough Graduate School of Business, Department of Finance, Insurance and Real Estate, Gainesville, FL 32611. Offers business administration (MS), including entrepreneurship, real estate and urban analysis; finance (PhD); financial services (Certificate); real estate and urban analysis (PhD); JD/MBA. *Faculty:* 13 full-time (0 women). *Students:* 56 full-time (13 women), 2 part-time (0 women); includes 2 Black or African American, non-Hispanic/Latino; 2 Asian, non-Hispanic/Latino; 1 Hispanic/Latino, 16 international. Average age 27. 245 applicants, 34% accepted, 58 enrolled. In 2010, 105 master's awarded. Terminal master's awarded for partial completion of doctoral program. *Degree requirements:* For master's, comprehensive exam, thesis; for doctorate, comprehensive exam, thesis/dissertation. *Entrance requirements:* For master's, GMAT or GRE General Test, minimum GPA of 3.0 for last 60 hours of undergraduate degree, work experience (preferred); for doctorate, GMAT or GRE General Test, minimum GPA of 3.0. Additional exam requirements/recommendations for international students: Required—TOEFL (minimum score 550 paper-based; 213 computer-based; 80 iBT), IELTS (minimum score 6). *Application deadline:* For fall admission,

1/15 priority date for domestic students, 1/15 for international students. Applications are processed on a rolling basis. Application fee: $30. Electronic applications accepted. *Expenses:* Tuition, state resident: full-time $10,915.92. Tuition, nonresident: full-time $28,309. *Financial support:* In 2010–11, 18 students received support, including 6 fellowships, 12 research assistantships (averaging $20,699 per year), 2 teaching assistantships; career-related internships or fieldwork, scholarships/grants, and unspecified assistantships also available. Financial award application deadline: 1/15; financial award applicants required to submit FAFSA. *Faculty research:* Banking, empirical corporate finance, hedge funds. *Unit head:* Dr. Mahendrarajah Nimalendran, Chair, 352-392-9526, Fax: 352-392-0301, E-mail: nimal@ufl.edu. *Application contact:* Mark J. Flannery, Graduate Coordinator, 352-392-3184, Fax: 352-392-0301, E-mail: flannery@ufl.edu.

University of Florida, Graduate School, Warrington College of Business Administration, Hough Graduate School of Business, Programs in Business Administration, Gainesville, FL 32611. Offers accounting (MBA); arts administration (MBA); business strategy and public policy (MBA); competitive strategy (MBA); decision and information sciences (MBA); electronic commerce (MBA); finance (MBA); general business (MBA); global management (MBA); Graham-Buffett security analysis (MBA); health administration (MBA); human resources management (MBA); international studies (MBA); Latin American business (MBA); management (MBA); marketing (MBA); sports administration (MBA); JD/MBA; MBA/MS; MBA/PhD; MBA/Pharm D; MD/MBA. *Accreditation:* AACSB. Part-time and evening/weekend programs available. *Faculty:* 71 full-time (10 women). *Students:* 187 full-time (44 women), 305 part-time (83 women); includes 25 Black or African American, non-Hispanic/Latino; 2 American Indian or Alaska Native, non-Hispanic/Latino; 52 Asian, non-Hispanic/Latino; 54 Hispanic/Latino, 11 international. Average age 31. 919 applicants, 33% accepted, 225 enrolled. In 2010, 492 master's awarded. *Degree requirements:* For master's, capstone course. *Entrance requirements:* For master's, GMAT, minimum GPA of 3.0, interview. Additional exam requirements/recommendations for international students: Required—TOEFL (minimum score 550 paper-based; 213 computer-based; 80 iBT), IELTS (minimum score 6). *Application deadline:* For fall admission, 7/1 for domestic students, 1/1 for international students; for spring admission, 12/1 for domestic and international students. Applications are processed on a rolling basis. Application fee: $30. Electronic applications accepted. *Expenses:* Tuition, state resident: full-time $10,915.92. Tuition, nonresident: full-time $28,309. *Financial support:* In 2010–11, 1 student received support, including 1 teaching assistantship (averaging $20,600 per year); career-related internships or fieldwork, scholarships/grants, and unspecified assistantships also available. Support available to part-time students. Financial award applicants required to submit FAFSA. *Faculty research:* Accounting, finance, insurance, management, real estate, urban analysis marketing. *Unit head:* Prof. Alexander D. Sevilla, Assistant Dean and Director MBA Programs, 352-273-3252 Ext. 1206, E-mail: alex.sevilla@warrington.ufl.edu. *Application contact:* Prof. Kelli Gust, Associate Director of MBA Programs, 352-273-3255, Fax: 352-392-8791, E-mail: kelly.gust@ warrington.ufl.edu.

University of Hawaii at Manoa, Graduate Division, Shidler College of Business, Program in Business Administration, Honolulu, HI 96822. Offers Asian business studies (MBA); Chinese business studies (MBA); decision sciences (MBA); entrepreneurship (MBA); finance (MBA); finance and banking (MBA); human resources management (MBA); information management (MBA); information technology (MBA); international business (MBA); Japanese business studies (MBA); marketing (MBA); organizational behavior (MBA); organizational management (MBA); real estate (MBA); student-designed track (MBA). *Accreditation:* AACSB. Part-time and evening/weekend programs available. *Faculty:* 53 full-time (12 women). *Students:* 162 full-time (63 women), 102 part-time (43 women); includes 135 minority (1 Black or African American, non-Hispanic/Latino; 81 Asian, non-Hispanic/Latino; 5 Hispanic/Latino; 18 Native Hawaiian or other Pacific Islander, non-Hispanic/Latino; 30 Two or more races, non-Hispanic/Latino), 44 international. Average age 34. 361 applicants, 57% accepted, 172 enrolled. In 2010, 153 master's awarded. *Degree requirements:* For master's, thesis optional. *Entrance requirements:* For master's, GMAT, minimum GPA of 3.0. Additional exam requirements/recommendations for international students: Required—TOEFL (minimum score 600 paper-based; 250 computer-based; 100 iBT), IELTS (minimum score 7). *Application deadline:* For fall admission, 5/1 for domestic students, 3/1 for international students. Application fee: $60. *Expenses:* Contact institution. *Financial support:* In 2010–11, 83 fellowships (averaging $5,547 per year), 1 research assistantship (averaging $16,824 per year) were awarded. Total annual research expenditures: $427,000. *Application contact:* Daniel Port, Graduate Chair, 808-956-5565, Fax: 808-956-6889, E-mail: daniel.port@hawaii.edu.

University of Hawaii at Manoa, Graduate Division, Shidler College of Business, Program in International Management, Honolulu, HI 96822. Offers Asian finance (PhD); global information technology management (PhD); international accounting (PhD); international marketing (PhD); international organization and strategy (PhD). Part-time programs available. *Students:* 30 full-time (11 women), 3 part-time (0 women); includes 7 minority (5 Asian, non-Hispanic/Latino; 2 Two or more races, non-Hispanic/Latino), 18 international. Average age 36. 65 applicants, 18% accepted, 5 enrolled. In 2010,

4 doctorates awarded. *Degree requirements:* For doctorate, comprehensive exam, thesis/dissertation. *Entrance requirements:* For doctorate, GMAT or GRE General Test, minimum GPA of 3.0. Additional exam requirements/recommendations for international students: Required—TOEFL (minimum score 600 paper-based; 250 computer-based; 100 iBT), IELTS (minimum score 7). *Application deadline:* For fall admission, 3/1 for domestic and international students. Application fee: $60. *Expenses:* Contact institution. *Financial support:* In 2010–11, 29 students received support, including 3 fellowships (averaging $5,491 per year), 25 research assistantships (averaging $17,750 per year), 1 teaching assistantship (averaging $15,558 per year). *Application contact:* Erica Okada, Graduate Chair, 808-956-6723, Fax: 808-956-6889, E-mail: imphd@hawaii.edu.

University of Houston, Bauer College of Business, Finance Program, Houston, TX 77204. Offers MS. Part-time and evening/weekend programs available. *Faculty:* 12 full-time (1 woman), 8 part-time/adjunct (3 women). *Students:* 29 full-time (9 women), 33 part-time (1 woman); includes 1 Black or African American, non-Hispanic/Latino; 1 American Indian or Alaska Native, non-Hispanic/Latino; 8 Asian, non-Hispanic/Latino; 4 Hispanic/Latino, 23 international. Average age 28. 56 applicants, 70% accepted, 24 enrolled. In 2010, 24 master's awarded. *Degree requirements:* For master's, 30 hours completed in residence, minimum cumulative GPA of 3.0 at UH, no more than 11 semester hours of 'C' grades or below in graduate courses taken at UH. *Entrance requirements:* For master's, GMAT or GRE, official transcripts from all higher education institutions attended, resume, goal statement, letters of recommendation. Additional exam requirements/recommendations for international students: Required—TOEFL (minimum score 620 paper-based; 260 computer-based; 105 iBT), IELTS (minimum score 7.5). *Application deadline:* For fall admission, 6/1 for domestic students, 4/1 for international students; for spring admission, 11/1 for domestic students, 10/1 for international students. Applications are processed on a rolling basis. Application fee: $75 ($150 for international students). Electronic applications accepted. *Expenses:* Tuition, state resident: full-time $8592; part-time $358 per credit hour. Tuition, nonresident: full-time $16,032; part-time $668 per credit hour. Required fees: $2889. Tuition and fees vary according to course load and program. *Financial support:* In 2010–11, 5 fellowships with partial tuition reimbursements (averaging $2,400 per year), 2 research assistantships with partial tuition reimbursements (averaging $8,800 per year), 21 teaching assistantships with partial tuition reimbursements (averaging $13,832 per year) were awarded; career-related internships or fieldwork, Federal Work-Study, institutionally sponsored loans, scholarships/grants, health care benefits, and unspecified assistantships also available. Support available to part-time students. Financial award application deadline: 2/1; financial award applicants required to submit FAFSA. *Faculty research:* Accountancy and taxation, finance, international business, management. *Unit head:* Dr. Praveen Kumar, Chairperson, 713-743-4772, Fax: 713-743-4789, E-mail: pkumar@uh.edu.

University of Houston–Victoria, School of Business Administration, Victoria, TX 77901-4450. Offers accounting (MBA); economic development and entrepreneurship (MS); finance (GMBA, MBA); general business (MBA); international business (MBA); management (GMBA, MBA); marketing (MBA). *Accreditation:* AACSB. Part-time and evening/weekend programs available. Postbaccalaureate distance learning degree programs offered (minimal on-campus study). *Faculty:* 37 full-time (11 women). *Students:* 234 full-time (108 women), 714 part-time (303 women); includes 542 minority (215 Black or African American, non-Hispanic/Latino; 1 American Indian or Alaska Native, non-Hispanic/Latino; 197 Asian, non-Hispanic/Latino; 124 Hispanic/Latino; 1 Native Hawaiian or other Pacific Islander, non-Hispanic/Latino; 4 Two or more races, non-Hispanic/Latino), 115 international. Average age 34. 362 applicants, 65% accepted, 147 enrolled. In 2010, 181 master's awarded. *Entrance requirements:* For master's, GMAT. Additional exam requirements/recommendations for international students: Required—TOEFL (minimum score 550 paper-based; 213 computer-based). *Application deadline:* For fall admission, 6/1 for international students; for spring admission, 10/1 for international students. Applications are processed on a rolling basis. Application fee: $0. Electronic applications accepted. *Expenses:* Tuition, state resident: full-time $4050; part-time $225 per credit hour. Tuition, nonresident: full-time $8730; part-time $485 per credit hour. Required fees: $810; $54 per credit hour. Tuition and fees vary according to course load. *Financial support:* In 2010–11, research assistantships with partial tuition reimbursements (averaging $2,000 per year), teaching assistantships with partial tuition reimbursements (averaging $2,000 per year) were awarded; Federal Work-Study, scholarships/grants, and unspecified assistantships also available. Support available to part-time students. Financial award application deadline: 4/15; financial award applicants required to submit FAFSA. *Faculty research:* Economic development, marketing, finance. *Unit head:* Dr. Farhang Niroomand, Dean, 361-570-4230, Fax: 361-580-5599, E-mail: niroomandf@ uhv.edu. *Application contact:* Jane Mims, Assistant Dean, 361-570-4639, Fax: 361-580-5529, E-mail: mims@uhv.edu.

University of Illinois at Urbana–Champaign, Graduate College, College of Business, Department of Finance, Champaign, IL 61820. Offers MS, PhD. *Faculty:* 18 full-time (1 woman), 2 part-time/adjunct (0 women). *Students:* 148 full-time (64 women), 5 part-time (3 women); includes 3 Black or African American, non-Hispanic/Latino; 10 Asian, non-Hispanic/Latino, 120 international. 826 applicants, 24% accepted, 115 enrolled. In 2010, 111 master's awarded. *Entrance requirements:* For master's and doctorate, GMAT or GRE, minimum GPA of 3.0. Additional exam requirements/recommendations for international students: Required—TOEFL. *Application deadline:* Applications are processed on a rolling basis. Application fee: $75 ($90 for international students). Electronic applications accepted. *Financial support:* In 2010–11, 6 fellowships, 19 research assistantships, 4 teaching assistantships were awarded; tuition waivers (full and partial) also available. *Unit head:* Charles M. Kahn, Chair, 217-333-2813, Fax: 217-244-3102, E-mail: c-kahn@illinois.edu. *Application contact:* Karen Lynn Brunner, Office Manager, 217-244-0252, Fax: 217-244-9867, E-mail: kclark2@illinois.edu.

The University of Iowa, Henry B. Tippie College of Business, Department of Finance, Iowa City, IA 52242-1316. Offers business administration (PhD), including finance. *Faculty:* 22 full-time (2 women). *Students:* 14 full-time (8 women), 11 international. Average age 29. 96 applicants, 5% accepted, 2 enrolled. In 2010, 1 doctorate awarded. *Degree requirements:* For doctorate, comprehensive exam, thesis/dissertation, thesis defense. *Entrance requirements:* For doctorate, GMAT or GRE. Additional exam requirements/recommendations for international students: Required—TOEFL (minimum score 600 paper-based; 250 computer-based; 100 iBT). *Application deadline:* For fall admission, 1/15 for domestic and international students. Applications are processed on a rolling basis. Application fee: $60 ($100 for international students). Electronic applications accepted. *Financial support:* In 2010–11, 14 students received support, including 14 fellowships with full tuition reimbursements available (averaging $6,000 per year), 14 teaching assistantships with full tuition reimbursements available (averaging $16,575 per year); institutionally sponsored loans, scholarships/grants, health care benefits, and unspecified assistantships also available. Financial award application deadline: 1/15. *Faculty research:* International finance, real estate finance, theoretical and empirical corporate finance, theoretical and empirical asset pricing bond pricing and derivatives. *Unit head:* Prof. Paul Weller, Department Executive Officer, 319-335-0929, Fax: 319-335-3690, E-mail: paul-weller@uiowa.edu. *Application contact:* Renea L. Jay, PhD Program Coordinator, 319-335-0830, Fax: 319-335-1956, E-mail: renea-jay@uiowa.edu.

The University of Iowa, Henry B. Tippie College of Business, Henry B. Tippie School of Management, Iowa City, IA 52242-1316. Offers corporate finance (MBA); investment management (MBA); marketing (MBA); process and operations excellence (MBA); strategic management and innovation (MBA); JD/MBA; MBA/MA; MBA/MD; MBA/MHA; MBA/MSN. *Accreditation:* AACSB. Part-time and evening/weekend programs available. *Faculty:* 110 full-time (25 women), 19 part-time/adjunct (1 woman). *Students:* 242 full-time (46 women), 809 part-time (277 women); includes 95 minority (15 Black or African American, non-Hispanic/Latino; 3 American Indian or Alaska Native, non-Hispanic/Latino; 56 Asian, non-Hispanic/Latino; 21 Hispanic/Latino), 132 international. Average age 31. 652 applicants, 66% accepted, 380 enrolled. In 2010, 333 master's awarded. *Degree requirements:* For master's, minimum GPA of 2.75. *Entrance requirements:* For master's, GMAT, quality work experience and leadership as shown through resume, references, and essays. Additional exam requirements/recommendations for international students: Required—TOEFL (minimum score 600 paper-based; 250 computer-based; 100 iBT), IELTS (minimum score 7). *Application deadline:* For fall admission, 7/30 for domestic students, 4/15 for international students; for spring admission, 12/15 for domestic and international students. Applications are processed on a rolling basis. Application fee: $60 ($100 for international students). Electronic applications accepted. *Expenses:* Contact institution. *Financial support:* In 2010–11, 111 students received support, including 121 fellowships (averaging $8,285 per year), 87 research assistantships with partial tuition reimbursements available (averaging $8,288 per year), 25 teaching assistantships with partial tuition reimbursements available (averaging $11,326 per year); career-related internships or fieldwork, scholarships/grants, health care benefits, and unspecified assistantships also available. Financial award application deadline: 4/15; financial award applicants required to submit FAFSA. *Faculty research:* Capital markets, econometrics, optimization, investments and empirical corporate finance, Iowa electronic markets. *Unit head:* Prof. Jarjisu Sa-Aadu, Associate Dean, MBA Programs, 800-622-4692, Fax: 319-335-3604, E-mail: jsa-aadu@uiowa.edu. *Application contact:* Jodi Schafer, Director of Admissions and Financial Aid, 319-335-0864, Fax: 319-335-3604, E-mail: jodi-schafer@uiowa.edu.

University of La Verne, College of Business and Public Management, Graduate Programs in Business Administration, La Verne, CA 91750-4443. Offers accounting (MBA); executive management (MBA-EP); finance (MBA, MBA-EP); health services management (MBA); information technology (MBA, MBA-EP); international business (MBA, MBA-EP); leadership (MBA-EP); managed care (MBA); management (MBA, MBA-EP); marketing (MBA, MBA-EP). Part-time and evening/weekend programs available. *Faculty:* 34 full-time (12 women), 36 part-time/adjunct (9 women). *Students:* 412 full-time (207 women), 200 part-time (96 women); includes 423 minority (32 Black or African American, non-Hispanic/Latino; 5 American Indian or Alaska Native, non-Hispanic/Latino; 294 Asian, non-Hispanic/Latino; 92 Hispanic/Latino), 6 international. Average age 29. In 2010, 229 master's awarded. *Entrance requirements:* For master's, minimum undergraduate GPA of 3.0, 2 letters of recommendation, resume. Additional

exam requirements/recommendations for international students: Required—TOEFL (minimum score 550 paper-based; 213 computer-based). *Application deadline:* Applications are processed on a rolling basis. Application fee: $50. *Expenses:* Contact institution. *Financial support:* Career-related internships or fieldwork, institutionally sponsored loans, and scholarships/grants available. Financial award application deadline: 3/2; financial award applicants required to submit FAFSA. *Unit head:* Dr. Abe Helou, Chairperson, 909-593-3511 Ext. 4211, Fax: 909-392-2704, E-mail: ihelou@laverne.edu. *Application contact:* Rina Lazarian, Program and Admission Specialist, 909-593-3511 Ext. 4819, Fax: 909-392-2704, E-mail: cbpm@ulv.edu.

University of Maine, Graduate School, College of Business, Public Policy and Health, The Maine Business School, Orono, ME 04469. Offers accounting (MBA); business and sustainability (MBA); finance (MBA); management (MBA). *Accreditation:* AACSB. Part-time and evening/weekend programs available. *Faculty:* 23 full-time (8 women), 2 part-time/adjunct (both women). *Students:* 53 full-time (24 women), 15 part-time (5 women); includes 4 minority (1 American Indian or Alaska Native, non-Hispanic/Latino; 2 Asian, non-Hispanic/Latino; 1 Hispanic/Latino), 3 international. Average age 29. 42 applicants, 69% accepted, 25 enrolled. In 2010, 25 degrees awarded. *Entrance requirements:* For master's, GMAT. Additional exam requirements/recommendations for international students: Required—TOEFL (minimum score 550 paper-based; 213 computer-based). *Application deadline:* For fall admission, 6/1 priority date for domestic and international students; for spring admission, 11/1 priority date for domestic and international students. Applications are processed on a rolling basis. Application fee: $65. Electronic applications accepted. *Expenses:* Contact institution. *Financial support:* In 2010–11, 16 students received support, including 4 teaching assistantships with tuition reimbursements available (averaging $12,790 per year); career-related internships or fieldwork, Federal Work-Study, institutionally sponsored loans, scholarships/grants, tuition waivers (full and partial), and unspecified assistantships also available. Financial award application deadline: 3/1. *Faculty research:* Entrepreneurship, investment management, international markets, decision support systems, strategic planning. *Unit head:* Dr. Nory Jones, Director of Graduate Programs, 207-581-1971, Fax: 207-581-1930, E-mail: mba@maine.edu. *Application contact:* Scott G. Delcourt, Associate Dean of the Graduate School, 207-581-3291, Fax: 207-581-3232, E-mail: graduate@maine.edu.

University of Maryland University College, Graduate School of Management and Technology, Program in Accounting and Financial Management, Adelphi, MD 20783. Offers MS, Certificate. *Accreditation:* AACSB. Part-time and evening/weekend programs available. Postbaccalaureate distance learning degree programs offered (no on-campus study). *Students:* 13 full-time (7 women), 557 part-time (363 women); includes 283 minority (197 Black or African American, non-Hispanic/Latino; 47 Asian, non-Hispanic/Latino; 33 Hispanic/Latino; 1 Native Hawaiian or other Pacific Islander, non-Hispanic/Latino; 5 Two or more races, non-Hispanic/Latino), 25 international. Average age 35. 139 applicants, 100% accepted, 80 enrolled. In 2010, 103 master's awarded. *Degree requirements:* For master's, thesis or alternative, capstone course. *Application deadline:* Applications are processed on a rolling basis. Application fee: $50. Electronic applications accepted. *Financial support:* Federal Work-Study and scholarships/grants available. Support available to part-time students. Financial award application deadline: 6/1; financial award applicants required to submit FAFSA. *Unit head:* Dr. James Howard, Director, 240-684-2400, Fax: 240-684-2401, E-mail: jhoward@umuc.edu. *Application contact:* Coordinator, Graduate Admissions, 800-888-8682, Fax: 240-684-2151, E-mail: newgrad@umuc.edu.

University of Maryland University College, Graduate School of Management and Technology, Program in Financial Management and Information Systems, Adelphi, MD 20783. Offers MS, Certificate. Part-time and evening/weekend programs available. Postbaccalaureate distance learning degree programs offered (no on-campus study). *Students:* 7 full-time (2 women), 168 part-time (84 women); includes 112 minority (89 Black or African American, non-Hispanic/Latino; 17 Asian, non-Hispanic/Latino; 5 Hispanic/Latino; 1 Two or more races, non-Hispanic/Latino), 4 international. Average age 33. 39 applicants, 100% accepted, 28 enrolled. In 2010, 30 master's awarded. *Degree requirements:* For master's, thesis or alternative. *Application deadline:* Applications are processed on a rolling basis. Application fee: $50. Electronic applications accepted. *Financial support:* Federal Work-Study and scholarships/grants available. Support available to part-time students. Financial award application deadline: 6/1; financial award applicants required to submit FAFSA. *Unit head:* Dr. Jayanta Sen, Director, 240-684-2400, Fax: 240-684-2401, E-mail: jsen@umuc.edu. *Application contact:* Coordinator, Graduate Admissions, 800-888-8682, Fax: 240-684-2151, E-mail: newgrad@umuc.edu.

University of Massachusetts Dartmouth, Graduate School, Charlton College of Business, Program in Business Administration, North Dartmouth, MA 02747-2300. Offers accounting (Postbaccalaureate Certificate); business administration (MBA); e-commerce (PMC); finance (PMC); general management (PMC); leadership (PMC); management (Postbaccalaureate Certificate); marketing (PMC); supply chain management (PMC). *Accreditation:* AACSB. Part-time programs available. *Faculty:* 40 full-time (13 women), 28 part-time/adjunct (8 women). *Students:* 99 full-time (38 women), 123 part-time (62 women); includes 4 Black or African American, non-Hispanic/Latino; 2 American Indian or Alaska Native, non-Hispanic/

Latino; 3 Asian, non-Hispanic/Latino; 8 Hispanic/Latino; 1 Two or more races, non-Hispanic/Latino, 45 international. Average age 30. 185 applicants, 76% accepted, 79 enrolled. In 2010, 79 master's, 12 other advanced degrees awarded. *Entrance requirements:* For master's, GMAT, resume, letters of recommendation. Additional exam requirements/recommendations for international students: Required—TOEFL (minimum score 500 paper-based; 200 computer-based; 72 iBT). *Application deadline:* For fall admission, 6/1 for domestic students, 5/1 for international students; for spring admission, 10/1 for domestic students, 8/1 for international students. Application fee: $40 ($60 for international students). Electronic applications accepted. *Expenses:* Tuition, state resident: full-time $2071; part-time $86 per credit. Tuition, nonresident: full-time $8099; part-time $337 per credit. Required fees: $9446; $394 per credit. One-time fee: $75. Part-time tuition and fees vary according to class time, course load, degree level and reciprocity agreements. *Financial support:* In 2010–11, 1 research assistantship with full tuition reimbursement (averaging $6,000 per year) was awarded; teaching assistantships, Federal Work-Study and unspecified assistantships also available. Support available to part-time students. Financial award application deadline: 3/1; financial award applicants required to submit FAFSA. *Faculty research:* Global business environment, e-commerce, managing diversity, agile manufacturing, green business. Total annual research expenditures: $29,538. *Unit head:* Dr. Norm Barber, Assistant Dean, 508-999-8543, E-mail: nbarber@umassd.edu. *Application contact:* Elan Turcotte-Shamski, Graduate Admissions Officer, 508-999-8604, Fax: 508-999-8183, E-mail: graduate@umassd.edu.

University of Memphis, Graduate School, Fogelman College of Business and Economics, Program in Business Administration, Memphis, TN 38152. Offers accounting (MBA, PhD); economics (MBA, PhD); executive business administration (MBA); finance (PhD); finance, insurance, and real estate (MBA, MS); international business administration (IMBA); management (MBA, MS, PhD); management information systems (MBA, MS, PhD); management science (MBA); marketing (MBA, MS); marketing and supply chain management (PhD); real estate development (MS); JD/MBA. *Accreditation:* AACSB. *Faculty:* 44 full-time (9 women), 5 part-time/adjunct (0 women). *Students:* 263 full-time (106 women), 181 part-time (66 women); includes 46 Black or African American, non-Hispanic/Latino; 3 American Indian or Alaska Native, non-Hispanic/Latino; 16 Asian, non-Hispanic/Latino; 5 Hispanic/Latino, 109 international. Average age 31. 374 applicants, 73% accepted, 119 enrolled. In 2010, 140 master's, 17 doctorates awarded. *Degree requirements:* For master's, comprehensive exam; for doctorate, comprehensive exam, thesis/dissertation. *Entrance requirements:* For master's, GMAT, resume; for doctorate, GMAT, interview, minimum GPA of 3.4, resume, letter of recommendation. Additional exam requirements/recommendations for international students: Required—TOEFL (minimum score 550 paper-based; 220 computer-based). *Application deadline:* For fall admission, 8/1 for domestic students; for spring admission, 12/1 for domestic students. Application fee: $35 ($60 for international students). *Financial support:* In 2010–11, 164 students received support; research assistantships with full tuition reimbursements available, teaching assistantships with full tuition reimbursements available, career-related internships or fieldwork, Federal Work-Study, scholarships/grants, and unspecified assistantships available. Financial award application deadline: 2/15; financial award applicants required to submit FAFSA. *Faculty research:* Competitive business strategy, finance microstructures, supply chain management innovations, health care economics, litigation risks and corporate audits. *Unit head:* Rajiv Grover, Dean, 901-678-3759, E-mail: rgrover@memphis.edu. *Application contact:* Dr. Carol V. Danehower, Associate Dean, 901-678-5402, Fax: 901-678-3579, E-mail: fcbegp@memphis.edu.

University of Michigan–Dearborn, School of Management, Dearborn, MI 48128-1491. Offers accounting (MBA, MS); finance (MBA, MS); information systems (MS); international business (MBA); management (MBA); management information systems (MBA); marketing (MBA); supply chain management (MBA); MBA/MHSA; MBA/MSE; MBA/MSF. *Accreditation:* AACSB. Part-time and evening/weekend programs available. Postbaccalaureate distance learning degree programs offered (no on-campus study). *Faculty:* 40 full-time (17 women), 2 part-time/adjunct (1 woman). *Students:* 71 full-time (26 women), 403 part-time (134 women); includes 68 minority (19 Black or African American, non-Hispanic/Latino; 1 American Indian or Alaska Native, non-Hispanic/Latino; 39 Asian, non-Hispanic/Latino; 6 Hispanic/Latino; 1 Native Hawaiian or other Pacific Islander, non-Hispanic/Latino; 2 Two or more races, non-Hispanic/Latino), 89 international. Average age 30. 185 applicants, 51% accepted, 67 enrolled. In 2010, 150 master's awarded. *Entrance requirements:* For master's, GMAT, 2 years of work experience (MBA); course work in computer applications, statistics, and pre-calculus or finite mathematics; 18 credits of accounting course work beyond introductory courses (MS in accounting). Additional exam requirements/recommendations for international students: Required—TOEFL (minimum score 560 paper-based; 220 computer-based; 84 iBT). *Application deadline:* For fall admission, 8/1 priority date for domestic students, 6/1 for international students; for winter admission, 12/1 priority date for domestic students, 10/1 for international students; for spring admission, 4/1 priority date for domestic students, 2/1 for international students. Applications are processed on a rolling basis. Application fee: $60. Electronic applications accepted. *Expenses:* Contact institution. *Financial support:* Career-related internships or fieldwork, Federal Work-Study, and scholarships/grants available. Support

available to part-time students. Financial award application deadline: 9/1; financial award applicants required to submit FAFSA. *Faculty research:* Cultural diversity, buyer-supplier relations, error detection in data, economic evolution. *Unit head:* Dr. Kim Schatzel, Dean, 313-593-5248, Fax: 313-271-9835, E-mail: schatzel@umd.umich.edu. *Application contact:* Joan Doherty, Academic Advisor/Counselor, 313-593-5460, Fax: 313-271-9838, E-mail: gradbusiness@umd.umich.edu.

University of Minnesota, Twin Cities Campus, Carlson School of Management, Carlson Full-Time MBA Program, Minneapolis, MN 55455. Offers finance (MBA); information technology (MBA); management (MBA); marketing (MBA); medical industry orientation (MBA); supply chain and operations (MBA); JD/MBA; MBA/MPP; MD/MBA; MHA/MBA; Pharm D/MBA. *Accreditation:* AACSB. *Faculty:* 52 full-time (14 women), 20 part-time/adjunct (3 women). *Students:* 170 full-time (62 women); includes 1 Black or African American, non-Hispanic/Latino; 1 American Indian or Alaska Native, non-Hispanic/Latino; 9 Asian, non-Hispanic/Latino; 8 Hispanic/Latino, 36 international. Average age 28. 452 applicants, 30% accepted, 71 enrolled. In 2010, 105 master's awarded. *Entrance requirements:* For master's, GMAT. Additional exam requirements/recommendations for international students: Required—TOEFL (minimum score 580 paper-based; 240 computer-based; 84 iBT), IELTS (minimum score 7), or Pearson Test of English (PTE). *Application deadline:* For fall admission, 4/1 for domestic students, 2/1 for international students. Application fee: $60 ($90 for international students). Electronic applications accepted. *Expenses:* Contact institution. *Financial support:* In 2010–11, 95 students received support, including 95 fellowships with full and partial tuition reimbursements available (averaging $21,235 per year); research assistantships with partial tuition reimbursements available, teaching assistantships with partial tuition reimbursements available, career-related internships or fieldwork, Federal Work-Study, institutionally sponsored loans, scholarships/grants, health care benefits, and unspecified assistantships also available. Financial award application deadline: 4/1; financial award applicants required to submit FAFSA. *Faculty research:* Finance and accounting: financial reporting, asset pricing models and corporate finance; information and decision sciences: on-line auctions, information transparency and recommender systems; marketing: psychological influences on consumer behavior, brand equity, pricing and marketing channels; operations: lean manufacturing, quality management and global supply chains; strategic management and organization: global strategy, networks, entrepreneurship and innovation, sustainability. *Unit head:* Kathryn J. Carlson, Assistant Dean, MBA Programs and Graduate Business Career Center, 612-625-5555, Fax: 612-625-1012, E-mail: mba@umn.edu. *Application contact:* Daniel Bursch, Director of Admissions & Recruiting, 612-625-5555, Fax: 612-625-1012, E-mail: mba@umn.edu.

University of Minnesota, Twin Cities Campus, Carlson School of Management, Carlson Part-Time MBA Program, Minneapolis, MN 55455. Offers finance (MBA); information technology (MBA); management (MBA); marketing (MBA); supply chain and operations (MBA). Part-time and evening/weekend programs available. *Faculty:* 67 full-time (18 women), 23 part-time/adjunct (2 women). *Students:* 1,520 part-time (490 women); includes 16 Black or African American, non-Hispanic/Latino; 3 American Indian or Alaska Native, non-Hispanic/Latino; 87 Asian, non-Hispanic/Latino; 14 Hispanic/Latino, 94 international. Average age 29. 306 applicants, 70% accepted, 186 enrolled. In 2010, 401 master's awarded. *Entrance requirements:* For master's, GMAT. Additional exam requirements/recommendations for international students: Required—TOEFL (minimum score 580 paper-based; 240 computer-based; 84 iBT), IELTS (minimum score 7), or Pearson Test of English (PTE). *Application deadline:* For fall admission, 5/1 priority date for domestic and international students; for spring admission, 11/1 priority date for domestic and international students. Application fee: $60 ($90 for international students). Electronic applications accepted. *Expenses:* Contact institution. *Financial support:* Applicants required to submit FAFSA. *Faculty research:* Finance and accounting: financial reporting, asset pricing models and corporate finance; information and decision sciences: on-line auctions, information transparency and recommender systems; marketing: psychological influences on consumer behavior, brand equity, pricing and marketing channels; operations: lean manufacturing, quality management and global supply chains; strategic management and organization: global Strategy, networks, entrepreneurship and innovation, sustainability. *Unit head:* Kathryn J. Carlson, Assistant Dean, MBA Programs and Graduate Business Career Center, 612-624-2039, Fax: 612-625-1012, E-mail: mba@umn.edu. *Application contact:* Daniel Bursch, Director of Admissions & Recruiting, 612-625-5555, Fax: 612-625-1012, E-mail: mba@umn.edu.

University of Minnesota, Twin Cities Campus, Carlson School of Management, Doctoral Program in Business Administration, Minneapolis, MN 55455-0213. Offers accounting (PhD); finance (PhD); information and decision sciences (PhD); marketing and logistics management (PhD); operations and management science (PhD); strategic management and organization (PhD). *Faculty:* 100 full-time (27 women). *Students:* 73 full-time (28 women); includes 3 Asian, non-Hispanic/Latino; 3 Hispanic/Latino, 53 international. Average age 30. 319 applicants, 6% accepted, 16 enrolled. In 2010, 8 doctorates awarded. *Degree requirements:* For doctorate, comprehensive exam, thesis/dissertation, written and oral preliminary exams, proposal defense, final defense. *Entrance requirements:* For doctorate, GMAT, GRE General

Test. Additional exam requirements/recommendations for international students: Required—TOEFL (minimum score 600 paper-based; 250 computer-based; 100 iBT), IELTS (minimum score 7.5). *Application deadline:* For fall admission, 12/31 for domestic students, 12/31 priority date for international students. Applications are processed on a rolling basis. Application fee: $75 ($95 for international students). Electronic applications accepted. *Financial support:* In 2010–11, 68 students received support, including 134 fellowships with full tuition reimbursements available (averaging $6,622 per year), 63 research assistantships with full tuition reimbursements available (averaging $6,750 per year), 57 teaching assistantships with full tuition reimbursements available (averaging $6,750 per year); institutionally sponsored loans, scholarships/grants, health care benefits, and unspecified assistantships also available. Financial award application deadline: 12/31. *Faculty research:* Corporate strategy, finance, entrepreneurship, marketing, information and decision science, operations, accounting, quality management. *Unit head:* Dr. Shawn P. Curley, Director of Graduate Studies and PhD Program Director, 612-624-6546, Fax: 612-624-8221, E-mail: curley@umn.edu. *Application contact:* Earlene K. Bronson, Assistant Director, PhD Program, 612-624-0875, Fax: 612-624-8221, E-mail: brons003@umn.edu.

University of Missouri–St. Louis, College of Business Administration, Program in Business Administration, St. Louis, MO 63121. Offers accounting (MBA); business administration (Certificate); finance (MBA); human resource management (Certificate); information systems (MBA); local government (Certificate); logistics and supply chain management (MBA, Certificate); marketing (MBA); marketing management (Certificate); operations management (MBA). *Accreditation:* AACSB. Part-time and evening/weekend programs available. *Faculty:* 30 full-time (5 women), 11 part-time/adjunct (2 women). *Students:* 132 full-time (57 women), 306 part-time (122 women); includes 55 minority (21 Black or African American, non-Hispanic/Latino; 20 Asian, non-Hispanic/Latino; 11 Hispanic/Latino; 1 Native Hawaiian or other Pacific Islander, non-Hispanic/Latino; 2 Two or more races, non-Hispanic/Latino), 6 international. Average age 30. 219 applicants, 60% accepted, 88 enrolled. In 2010, 114 master's, 9 other advanced degrees awarded. *Entrance requirements:* For master's, GMAT, 2 letters of recommendation. Additional exam requirements/recommendations for international students: Required—TOEFL (minimum score 550 paper-based; 213 computer-based). *Application deadline:* For fall admission, 7/1 for domestic students; for spring admission, 11/1 for domestic students. Applications are processed on a rolling basis. Application fee: $35 ($40 for international students). Electronic applications accepted. *Expenses:* Tuition, state resident: full-time $5522; part-time $306.80 per credit hour. Tuition, nonresident: full-time $14,253; part-time $792.10 per credit hour. Required fees: $658; $49 per credit hour. One-time fee: $12. Tuition and fees vary according to program. *Financial support:* In 2010–11, 22 research assistantships with full and partial tuition reimbursements (averaging $7,414 per year), 4 teaching assistantships with full and partial tuition reimbursements (averaging $13,950 per year) were awarded; career-related internships or fieldwork, Federal Work-Study, and institutionally sponsored loans also available. Support available to part-time students. Financial award application deadline: 4/1; financial award applicants required to submit FAFSA. *Faculty research:* Human resources, strategic management, marketing strategy, consumer behavior product development, advertising. *Unit head:* Karl Kottemann, Assistant Director, 314-516-5885, Fax: 314-516-6420, E-mail: mba@umsl.edu. *Application contact:* 314-516-5458, Fax: 314-516-6996, E-mail: gradadm@umsl.edu.

University of Nevada, Las Vegas, Graduate College, College of Business, Department of Finance, Las Vegas, NV 89154. Offers Certificate. *Students:* 1 part-time (0 women); minority (Black or African American, non-Hispanic/Latino). Average age 33. 1 applicant, 100% accepted, 1 enrolled. *Expenses:* Tuition, area resident: Part-time $239.50 per credit. Tuition, state resident: part-time $239.50 per credit. Tuition, nonresident: part-time $503 per credit. Required fees: $108 per semester. Tuition and fees vary according to course load, program and reciprocity agreements. *Faculty research:* Financial markets, preferred stock, and stock re-purchases; hospitality industry finance and corporate finance; mergers and acquisitions; real estate; executive compensation. *Unit head:* Dr. Paul Thistle, Chair/Professor, 702-895-3856, E-mail: paul.thistle@unlv.edu. *Application contact:* Graduate College Admissions Evaluator, 702-895-3320, Fax: 702-895-4180, E-mail: gradcollege@unlv.edu.

University of New Haven, Graduate School, School of Business, Program in Business Administration, West Haven, CT 06516-1916. Offers accounting (MBA, Certificate), including CPA (MBA); business management (Certificate); business policy and strategy (MBA); finance (MBA), including CFA; global marketing (MBA); human resource management (Certificate); human resources management (MBA); international business (Certificate); marketing (Certificate); sports management (MBA); telecommunications management (Certificate); MBA/MPA. Part-time and evening/weekend programs available. *Students:* 158 full-time (80 women), 150 part-time (70 women); includes 36 Black or African American, non-Hispanic/Latino; 2 American Indian or Alaska Native, non-Hispanic/Latino; 19 Asian, non-Hispanic/Latino; 16 Hispanic/Latino; 82 international. Average age 32. 162 applicants, 99% accepted, 85 enrolled. In 2010, 141 master's, 16 other advanced degrees awarded. *Degree requirements:* For master's, thesis or alternative. *Entrance requirements:* For master's, GMAT. Additional exam requirements/

recommendations for international students: Required—TOEFL (minimum score 520 paper-based; 190 computer-based; 70 iBT), IELTS (minimum score 5.5). *Application deadline:* For fall admission, 5/31 for international students; for winter admission, 10/15 for international students; for spring admission, 1/15 for international students. Applications are processed on a rolling basis. Application fee: $50. Electronic applications accepted. *Expenses:* Contact institution. *Financial support:* Research assistantships with partial tuition reimbursements, teaching assistantships with partial tuition reimbursements, Federal Work-Study, scholarships/grants, health care benefits, tuition waivers, and unspecified assistantships available. Support available to part-time students. Financial award applicants required to submit FAFSA. *Unit head:* Charles Coleman, Chairman, 203-932-7375. *Application contact:* Eloise Gormley, Director of Graduate Admissions, 203-932-7449, Fax: 203-932-7137, E-mail: gradinfo@newhaven.edu.

University of New Haven, Graduate School, School of Business, Program in Finance and Financial Services, West Haven, CT 06516-1916. Offers finance (Certificate); finance and financial services (MS). *Students:* 27 full-time (12 women), 13 part-time (4 women); includes 3 Black or African American, non-Hispanic/Latino; 4 Asian, non-Hispanic/Latino; 1 Hispanic/Latino, 22 international. Average age 28. 40 applicants, 98% accepted, 13 enrolled. In 2010, 20 master's awarded. *Application deadline:* Applications are processed on a rolling basis. Application fee: $50. *Financial support:* Research assistantships with partial tuition reimbursements, teaching assistantships with partial tuition reimbursements, career-related internships or fieldwork and Federal Work-Study available. Financial award application deadline: 5/1; financial award applicants required to submit FAFSA. *Unit head:* Dr. S. Shapiro, Coordinator, 203-932-7496. *Application contact:* Eloise Gormley, Director of Graduate Admissions, 203-932-7449, Fax: 203-932-7137, E-mail: gradinfo@newhaven.edu.

University of New Mexico, Graduate School, College of Arts and Sciences, Department of Economics, Albuquerque, NM 87131-2039. Offers environmental/natural resources (MA, PhD); international/development (MA, PhD); labor/human resources (MA, PhD); public finance (MA, PhD). Part-time programs available. *Faculty:* 26 full-time (9 women), 7 part-time/adjunct (1 woman). *Students:* 47 full-time (14 women), 17 part-time (5 women); includes 2 American Indian or Alaska Native, non-Hispanic/Latino; 2 Asian, non-Hispanic/Latino; 8 Hispanic/Latino, 18 international. Average age 34. 75 applicants, 51% accepted, 15 enrolled. In 2010, 14 master's, 1 doctorate awarded. Terminal master's awarded for partial completion of doctoral program. *Degree requirements:* For master's, comprehensive exam, thesis (for some programs); for doctorate, comprehensive exam, thesis/dissertation. *Entrance requirements:* For master's and doctorate, GRE General Test, 3 letters of recommendation, letter of intent. Additional exam requirements/recommendations for international students: Required—TOEFL (minimum score 520 paper-based; 190 computer-based; 68 iBT). *Application deadline:* For fall admission, 3/1 priority date for domestic students, 3/1 for international students. Applications are processed on a rolling basis. Application fee: $50. Electronic applications accepted. *Expenses:* Tuition, state resident: full-time $5991; part-time $251 per credit hour. Tuition, nonresident: full-time $14,405; part-time $800.20 per credit hour. Tuition and fees vary according to course level, course load, program and reciprocity agreements. *Financial support:* In 2010–11, 47 students received support, including 3 fellowships with tuition reimbursements available (averaging $3,611 per year), 14 research assistantships with tuition reimbursements available (averaging $7,791 per year), 15 teaching assistantships (averaging $7,467 per year); career-related internships or fieldwork, Federal Work-Study, scholarships/grants, health care benefits, and unspecified assistantships also available. Support available to part-time students. Financial award application deadline: 3/1; financial award applicants required to submit FAFSA. *Faculty research:* Core theory, econometrics, public finance, international/development economics, labor/human resource economics, environmental/natural resource economics. Total annual research expenditures: $1.8 million. *Unit head:* Dr. Robert Berrens, Chair, 505-277-5304, Fax: 505-277-9445, E-mail: rberrens@unm.edu. *Application contact:* Shoshana Handel, Academic Advisor, 505-277-3056, Fax: 505-277-9445, E-mail: shandel@unm.edu.

The University of North Carolina at Charlotte, Graduate School, College of Arts and Sciences, Department of Political Science, Charlotte, NC 28223-0001. Offers emergency management (Certificate); non-profit management (Certificate); public administration (MPA, PhD), including arts administration (MPA), emergency management (MPA), non-profit management (MPA), public finance (MPA), urban management and policy (PhD); public finance (Certificate); public policy (PhD); urban management and policy (Certificate). *Accreditation:* NASPAA. Part-time and evening/weekend programs available. *Faculty:* 19 full-time (8 women), 3 part-time/adjunct (2 women). *Students:* 51 full-time (37 women), 75 part-time (49 women); includes 32 minority (26 Black or African American, non-Hispanic/Latino; 1 Asian, non-Hispanic/Latino; 2 Hispanic/Latino; 3 Two or more races, non-Hispanic/Latino), 11 international. Average age 29. 99 applicants, 72% accepted, 42 enrolled. In 2010, 15 master's, 5 doctorates awarded. *Degree requirements:* For master's, thesis or alternative; for doctorate, thesis/dissertation. *Entrance requirements:* For master's, GRE General Test or MAT, minimum GPA of 3.0 in undergraduate major, 2.75 overall. Additional exam requirements/recommendations for international students: Required—TOEFL (minimum score 557 paper-based; 220 computer-based; 83 iBT). *Application deadline:* For fall admission, 7/1 for domestic students, 5/1 for international students; for spring admission, 11/1 for domestic students, 10/1 for international students. Applications are processed on a rolling basis. Application fee: $55. Electronic applications accepted. *Expenses:* Tuition, state resident: full-time $3464. Tuition, nonresident: full-time $14,297. Required fees: $2094. Tuition and fees vary according to course load. *Financial support:* In 2010–11, 22 students received support, including 16 research assistantships (averaging $6,943 per year), 6 teaching assistantships (averaging $9,380 per year); career-related internships or fieldwork, Federal Work-Study, institutionally sponsored loans, scholarships/grants, unspecified assistantships, and administrative assistantship also available. Support available to part-time students. Financial award application deadline: 4/1; financial award applicants required to submit FAFSA. *Faculty research:* Terrorism, public administration, nonprofit and arts administration, educational policy, social policy. Total annual research expenditures: $242,404. *Unit head:* Dr. Theodore S. Arrington, Chair, 704-687-2571, Fax: 704-687-3497, E-mail: tarrngtn@uncc.edu. *Application contact:* Kathy B. Giddings, Director of Graduate Admissions, 704-687-5503, Fax: 704-687-3279, E-mail: gradadm@uncc.edu.

University of North Florida, Coggin College of Business, MBA Program, Jacksonville, FL 32224. Offers accounting (MBA); construction management (MBA); e-commerce (MBA); economics (MBA); finance (MBA); human resource management (MBA); international business (MBA); logistics (MBA); management applications (MBA). *Accreditation:* AACSB. Part-time and evening/weekend programs available. *Faculty:* 17 full-time (5 women), 1 part-time/adjunct (0 women). *Students:* 137 full-time (56 women), 268 part-time (112 women); includes 17 Black or African American, non-Hispanic/Latino; 21 Asian, non-Hispanic/Latino; 12 Hispanic/Latino; 3 Two or more races, non-Hispanic/Latino; 29 international. Average age 30. 250 applicants, 57% accepted, 94 enrolled. In 2010, 173 master's awarded. *Entrance requirements:* For master's, GMAT or GRE, U.S. bachelor's degree from regionally-accredited university or equivalent foreign degree. Additional exam requirements/recommendations for international students: Required—TOEFL (minimum score 550 paper-based; 213 computer-based; 79 iBT). *Application deadline:* For fall admission, 7/1 priority date for domestic students, 5/1 for international students; for spring admission, 11/1 priority date for domestic students, 10/1 for international students. Applications are processed on a rolling basis. Application fee: $30. *Expenses:* Tuition, state resident: full-time $7646.40; part-time $318.60 per credit hour. Tuition, nonresident: full-time $23,502; part-time $979.24 per credit hour. Required fees: $1208.88; $50.37 per credit hour. Tuition and fees vary according to course load and program. *Financial support:* In 2010–11, 40 students received support; research assistantships, teaching assistantships, Federal Work-Study and tuition waivers (partial) available. Support available to part-time students. Financial award application deadline: 4/1; financial award applicants required to submit FAFSA. *Faculty research:* Performance measures, costing, and inventory issues in logistics and supply chain management; inter-organizational systems; international management and marketing practices; e-commerce; organizational learning and socialization processes. Total annual research expenditures: $9,024. *Unit head:* Dr. C. Bruce Kavan, Chair, 904-620-2780, Fax: 904-620-2832. *Application contact:* Cheryl Campbell, Graduate Advisor, 904-620-2575, Fax: 904-620-2832, E-mail: ccampbell@unf.edu.

University of North Texas, Toulouse Graduate School, College of Business Administration, Department of Finance, Insurance, Real Estate, and Law, Denton, TX 76203. Offers finance (PhD); finance, insurance, real estate, and law (MS); real estate (MS). Part-time programs available. *Degree requirements:* For master's, thesis optional; for doctorate, comprehensive exam, thesis/dissertation. *Entrance requirements:* For master's, GMAT; for doctorate, GMAT or GRE General Test. Additional exam requirements/recommendations for international students: Recommended—TOEFL (minimum score 550 paper-based; 213 computer-based; 79 iBT). *Expenses:* Tuition, state resident: full-time $4298; part-time $239 per credit hour. Tuition, nonresident: full-time $10,782; part-time $549 per credit hour. Required fees: $1292; $270 per credit hour. *Financial support:* Fellowships, research assistantships, teaching assistantships, career-related internships or fieldwork and tuition waivers (partial) available. Financial award application deadline: 4/1; financial award applicants required to submit FAFSA. *Faculty research:* Financial impact of regulation, risk management, taxes and valuation, bankruptcy, real financial options. *Application contact:* PhD Advisor, 940-565-2511, Fax: 940-565-4234, E-mail: john.kensinger@unt.edu.

University of Pittsburgh, Katz Graduate School of Business, Doctoral Program in Business Administration, Pittsburgh, PA 15260. Offers accounting (PhD); finance (PhD); information systems (PhD); marketing (PhD); operations/decision sciences/artificial intelligence (PhD); organizational behavior and human resource management (PhD); strategic planning (PhD). *Accreditation:* AACSB. *Faculty:* 50 full-time (15 women). *Students:* 51 full-time (22 women); includes 3 Black or African American, non-Hispanic/Latino; 4 Asian, non-Hispanic/Latino; 2 Hispanic/Latino, 18 international. 448 applicants, 5% accepted, 13 enrolled. In 2010, 4 doctorates awarded. *Degree requirements:* For doctorate, comprehensive exam, thesis/dissertation. *Entrance requirements:* For doctorate, GMAT or GRE, bachelor's degree,

references, minimum GPA of 3.0. Additional exam requirements/recommendations for international students: Required—TOEFL, IELTS. *Application deadline:* For fall admission, 2/1 priority date for domestic and international students. Applications are processed on a rolling basis. Application fee: $50. Electronic applications accepted. *Expenses:* Tuition, state resident: full-time $17,304; part-time $701 per credit. Tuition, nonresident: full-time $29,554; part-time $1210 per credit. Required fees: $740; $214 per term. Tuition and fees vary according to program. *Financial support:* In 2010–11, 39 students received support, including 29 research assistantships with full tuition reimbursements available (averaging $1,900 per year), 10 teaching assistantships with full tuition reimbursements available (averaging $23,745 per year); fellowships, Federal Work-Study, scholarships/grants, health care benefits, and unspecified assistantships also available. Financial award application deadline: 2/1. *Faculty research:* Accounting statements and reporting, incentives and governance, corporate finance, mergers and acquisitions, information systems processes, structures and decision-making, organizational structure, knowledge management and corporate strategy, consumer behavior and marketing models. Total annual research expenditures: $362,777. *Unit head:* Dr. John E. Hulland, Director of Doctoral Program, 412-648-1534, Fax: 412-624-3633, E-mail: jhulland@katz.pitt.edu. *Application contact:* Carrie Woods, Assistant Director, Doctoral Office, 412-648-1525, Fax: 412-624-3633, E-mail: cawoods@katz.pitt.edu.

University of Pittsburgh, Katz Graduate School of Business, Master of Business Administration Programs, Pittsburgh, PA 15260. Offers finance (MBA); information systems (MBA); marketing (MBA); operations management (MBA); organizational behavior and human resource management (MBA); organizational leadership (Certificate); six sigma (Certificate); strategy, environment and organizations (MBA); technology, innovation and entrepreneurship (Certificate); MBA/JD; MBA/MIB; MBA/MPIA; MBA/MSE; MBA/MSIS; MID/MBA. *Accreditation:* AACSB. Part-time and evening/weekend programs available. *Faculty:* 60 full-time (18 women), 22 part-time/adjunct (5 women). *Students:* 232 full-time (75 women), 458 part-time (158 women); includes 34 Black or African American, non-Hispanic/Latino; 1 American Indian or Alaska Native, non-Hispanic/Latino; 20 Asian, non-Hispanic/Latino; 9 Hispanic/Latino, 105 international. Average age 29. 697 applicants, 50% accepted, 174 enrolled. In 2010, 263 master's awarded. *Degree requirements:* For master's, minimum GPA of 3.0. *Entrance requirements:* For master's, GMAT, recommendations, undergraduate transcripts, essay responses, resume, interview, bachelor's degree. Additional exam requirements/recommendations for international students: Required—TOEFL (minimum 600 paper, 250 computer, 100 iBT) or IELTS. *Application deadline:* For fall admission, 4/1 priority date for domestic students, 2/1 priority date for international students. Application fee: $50. Electronic applications accepted. *Expenses:* Tuition, state resident: full-time $17,304; part-time $701 per credit. Tuition, nonresident: full-time $29,554; part-time $1210 per credit. Required fees: $740; $214 per term. Tuition and fees vary according to program. *Financial support:* In 2010–11, 52 students received support. Career-related internships or fieldwork and scholarships/grants available. Financial award application deadline: 3/1; financial award applicants required to submit FAFSA. *Faculty research:* Accounting statements and reporting, incentives and governance, corporate finance, mergers and acquisitions, information systems processes, structures and decision-making, organizational structure, knowledge management and corporate strategy, consumer behavior and marketing models. *Unit head:* William T. Valenta, Assistant Dean, MBA Program Director, 412-648-1610, Fax: 412-648-1659, E-mail: wtvalenta@katz.pitt.edu. *Application contact:* Cliff McCormick, Director MBA Admissions, 412-648-1700, Fax: 412-648-1659, E-mail: mba@katz.pitt.edu.

University of Portland, Dr. Robert B. Pamplin, Jr. School of Business, Portland, OR 97203-5798. Offers business administration (MBA); entrepreneurship (MBA); finance (MBA, MS); health care management (MBA); marketing (MBA); nonprofit management (EMBA); operations and technology management (MBA); sustainability (MBA). *Accreditation:* AACSB. Part-time and evening/weekend programs available. *Faculty:* 12 full-time (2 women), 7 part-time/adjunct (2 women). *Students:* 55 full-time (24 women), 81 part-time (29 women); includes 18 minority (2 Black or African American, non-Hispanic/Latino; 8 Asian, non-Hispanic/Latino; 5 Hispanic/Latino; 3 Two or more races, non-Hispanic/Latino), 23 international. Average age 30. In 2010, 55 master's awarded. *Entrance requirements:* For master's, GMAT, minimum GPA of 3.0, resume, 2 letters of recommendation. Additional exam requirements/recommendations for international students: Required—TOEFL (minimum score 570 paper-based; 89 iBT), IELTS (minimum score 7). *Application deadline:* For fall admission, 7/15 priority date for domestic and international students; for spring admission, 12/15 priority date for domestic and international students. Applications are processed on a rolling basis. Application fee: $50. *Expenses:* Contact institution. *Financial support:* Federal Work-Study, scholarships/grants, and tuition waivers (partial) available. Support available to part-time students. Financial award application deadline: 3/1; financial award applicants required to submit FAFSA. *Unit head:* Dr. Howard Feldman, Associate Dean, 503-943-7224, E-mail: feldman@up.edu. *Application contact:* Melissa McCarthy, Academic Specialist, 503-943-7225, E-mail: mccarthy@up.edu.

University of Puerto Rico, Mayagüez Campus, Graduate Studies, College of Business Administration, Mayagüez, PR 00681-9000. Offers business administration (MBA); finance (MBA); human resources (MBA); industrial management (MBA). Part-time and evening/weekend programs available. *Students:* 47 full-time (28 women), 36 part-time (16 women); includes 79 Hispanic/Latino, 4 international. 19 applicants, 47% accepted, 4 enrolled. In 2010, 15 master's awarded. *Degree requirements:* For master's, comprehensive exam. *Entrance requirements:* For master's, GMAT or EXADEP, bachelor's degree with courses in calculus, microeconomics, accounting and statistics. Additional exam requirements/recommendations for international students: Required—TOEFL (minimum score 500 paper-based; 173 computer-based). *Application deadline:* For fall admission, 2/15 for domestic and international students; for spring admission, 9/15 for domestic and international students. Applications are processed on a rolling basis. Application fee: $25. *Expenses:* Tuition, state resident: full-time $1188. Tuition, non-resident: full-time $1188. International tuition: $6126 full-time. Tuition and fees vary according to course level and course load. *Financial support:* In 2010–11, fellowships (averaging $12,000 per year), 2 research assistantships (averaging $15,000 per year), teaching assistantships (averaging $8,500 per year) were awarded; Federal Work-Study and institutionally sponsored loans also available. *Faculty research:* Organizational studies, management, accounting. Total annual research expenditures: $20,000. *Unit head:* Dr. Rosario Ortiz, Graduate Student Coordinator, 787-265-3800, Fax: 787-832-5320, E-mail: rosario.ortiz@upr.edu. *Application contact:* Milagros Soto, Student Administrator, 787-265-3887, Fax: 787-832-5320, E-mail: milagros.soto1@upr.edu.

University of Rhode Island, Graduate School, College of Business Administration, Kingston, RI 02881. Offers accounting (MS); business administration (MBA, PhD), including finance and insurance (PhD), management (PhD), marketing (PhD), operations and supply chain management (MBA); finance (MBA); general business (MBA); management (MBA); marketing (MBA); supply chain management (MBA). *Accreditation:* AACSB. Part-time and evening/weekend programs available. *Faculty:* 54 full-time (15 women), 3 part-time/adjunct (2 women). *Students:* 82 full-time (31 women), 218 part-time (77 women); includes 31 minority (6 Black or African American, non-Hispanic/Latino; 1 American Indian or Alaska Native, non-Hispanic/Latino; 13 Asian, non-Hispanic/Latino; 11 Hispanic/Latino), 29 international. In 2010, 78 master's, 3 doctorates awarded. *Degree requirements:* For master's, comprehensive exam (for some programs), thesis optional; for doctorate, comprehensive exam, thesis/dissertation. *Entrance requirements:* For master's, GMAT or GRE, 2 letters of recommendation, resume; for doctorate, GMAT or GRE, 3 letters of recommendation, resume. Additional exam requirements/recommendations for international students: Required—TOEFL (minimum score 575 paper-based; 233 computer-based; 91 iBT). Application fee: $65. Electronic applications accepted. *Expenses:* Tuition, state resident: full-time $9588; part-time $533 per credit hour. Tuition, nonresident: full-time $22,968; part-time $1276 per credit hour. Required fees: $1282; $68 per semester. Tuition and fees vary according to program. *Financial support:* In 2010–11, 13 teaching assistantships with full and partial tuition reimbursements (averaging $12,432 per year) were awarded. Financial award applicants required to submit FAFSA. Total annual research expenditures: $9,928. *Unit head:* Dr. Mark Higgins, Dean, 401-874-4244, Fax: 401-874-4312, E-mail: markhiggins@uri.edu. *Application contact:* Lisa Lancellotta, Coordinator, MBA Programs, 401-874-4241, Fax: 401-874-4312, E-mail: mba@uri.edu.

University of San Francisco, College of Arts and Sciences, Department of Economics, Program in Financial Analysis, San Francisco, CA 94117-1080. Offers MS, MS/MBA. *Faculty:* 8 full-time (2 women), 9 part-time/adjunct (3 women). *Students:* 120 full-time (60 women), 4 part-time (1 woman); includes 26 minority (22 Asian, non-Hispanic/Latino; 2 Hispanic/Latino; 2 Two or more races, non-Hispanic/Latino), 71 international. Average age 27. 459 applicants, 39% accepted, 64 enrolled. In 2010, 86 master's awarded. *Expenses:* Tuition: Full-time $20,070; part-time $1115 per credit hour. Tuition and fees vary according to course load, degree level and program. *Financial support:* In 2010–11, 68 students received support. *Unit head:* Dr. John Veitch. *Application contact:* Information Contact, 415-422-5135, Fax: 415-422-6983, E-mail: asgraduate@usfca.edu.

University of San Francisco, College of Arts and Sciences, Investor Relations Program, San Francisco, CA 94117-1080. Offers MA. *Faculty:* 9 full-time (2 women), 11 part-time/adjunct (3 women). *Students:* 6 full-time (3 women); includes 1 minority (Asian, non-Hispanic/Latino), 4 international. Average age 28. 28 applicants, 32% accepted, 6 enrolled. In 2010, 6 master's awarded. *Expenses:* Tuition: Full-time $20,070; part-time $1115 per credit hour. Tuition and fees vary according to course load, degree level and program. *Financial support:* In 2010–11, 4 students received support. *Unit head:* John Veitch, Chair, 415-422-6784, Fax: 415-422-5784. *Application contact:* Information Contact, 415-422-5135, Fax: 415-422-2217, E-mail: asgraduate@usfca.edu.

University of San Francisco, School of Business and Professional Studies, Masagung Graduate School of Management, Program in Business Administration, San Francisco, CA 94117-1080. Offers business economics (MBA); e-business (MBA); entrepreneurship (MBA); finance (MBA); international business (MBA); management (MBA); marketing (MBA); telecommunications management and policy (MBA); JD/MBA; MSN/MBA.

Accreditation: AACSB. *Faculty:* 17 full-time (4 women), 16 part-time/adjunct (7 women). *Students:* 263 full-time (130 women), 11 part-time (6 women); includes 98 minority (3 Black or African American, non-Hispanic/Latino; 65 Asian, non-Hispanic/Latino; 18 Hispanic/Latino; 3 Native Hawaiian or other Pacific Islander, non-Hispanic/Latino; 9 Two or more races, non-Hispanic/Latino), 43 international. Average age 29. 503 applicants, 60% accepted, 80 enrolled. In 2010, 115 master's awarded. *Entrance requirements:* For master's, GMAT, minimum undergraduate GPA of 3.2. Additional exam requirements/recommendations for international students: Required—TOEFL. *Application deadline:* For fall admission, 7/1 priority date for domestic students; for spring admission, 11/30 for domestic students. Applications are processed on a rolling basis. Application fee: $55 ($65 for international students). *Expenses:* Tuition: Full-time $20,070; part-time $1115 per credit hour. Tuition and fees vary according to course load, degree level and program. *Financial support:* In 2010–11, 156 students received support; fellowships available. Financial award application deadline: 3/2; financial award applicants required to submit FAFSA. *Faculty research:* International financial markets, technology transfer licensing, international marketing, strategic planning. Total annual research expenditures: $50,000. *Unit head:* Kelly Brookes, Director, 415-422-2221, Fax: 415-422-6315. *Application contact:* Director, MBA Program, 415-422-2221, Fax: 415-422-6315, E-mail: mba@usfca.edu.

The University of Scranton, College of Graduate and Continuing Education, Program in Business Administration, Scranton, PA 18510. Offers accounting (MBA); finance (MBA); general business administration (MBA); health care management (MBA); international business (MBA); management information systems (MBA); marketing (MBA); operations management (MBA). *Accreditation:* AACSB. Part-time and evening/weekend programs available. Postbaccalaureate distance learning degree programs offered (no on-campus study). *Faculty:* 34 full-time (8 women). *Students:* 251 full-time (91 women), 180 part-time (72 women); includes 41 Black or African American, non-Hispanic/Latino; 11 Asian, non-Hispanic/Latino; 7 Hispanic/Latino, 40 international. Average age 32. 386 applicants, 84% accepted. In 2010, 38 master's awarded. *Degree requirements:* For master's, capstone experience. *Entrance requirements:* For master's, GMAT, minimum GPA of 2.75. Additional exam requirements/recommendations for international students: Required—TOEFL (minimum score 500 paper-based; 173 computer-based), IELTS (minimum score 5.5). *Application deadline:* Applications are processed on a rolling basis. Application fee: $0. *Financial support:* In 2010–11, 13 students received support, including 13 teaching assistantships with full and partial tuition reimbursements available (averaging $6,430 per year); fellowships, career-related internships or fieldwork, Federal Work-Study, and unspecified assistantships also available. Support available to part-time students. Financial award application deadline: 3/1. *Faculty research:* Financial markets, strategic impact of total quality management, internal accounting controls, consumer preference, information systems and the Internet. *Unit head:* Dr. Murli Rajan, Director, 570-941-4043, Fax: 570-941-4342. *Application contact:* Joseph M. Roback, Director of Admissions, 570-941-4385, Fax: 570-941-5928, E-mail: robackj2@scranton.edu.

University of South Florida, Graduate School, College of Business, Department of Business Administration, Tampa, FL 33620-9951. Offers accounting (PhD); entrepreneurship (MBA); finance (PhD); information systems (PhD); leadership and organizational effectiveness (MSM); management and organization (MBA); marketing (PhD). *Accreditation:* AACSB. Part-time and evening/weekend programs available. *Faculty:* 1 (woman) full-time. *Students:* 148 full-time (48 women), 190 part-time (61 women); includes 70 minority (7 Black or African American, non-Hispanic/Latino; 1 American Indian or Alaska Native, non-Hispanic/Latino; 26 Asian, non-Hispanic/Latino; 36 Hispanic/Latino), 62 international. Average age 30. 452 applicants, 29% accepted, 80 enrolled. In 2010, 146 master's, 5 doctorates awarded. *Degree requirements:* For master's, comprehensive exam, thesis (for some programs); for doctorate, comprehensive exam, thesis/dissertation, 90 credit hours, minimum GPA of 3.0. *Entrance requirements:* For master's, GMAT, minimum GPA of 3.0 in last 60 hours of course work, 2 years of work experience, resume; for doctorate, GMAT, letters of recommendation, personal statement. Additional exam requirements/recommendations for international students: Required—TOEFL (minimum score 550 paper-based; 213 computer-based; 79 iBT). *Application deadline:* For fall admission, 6/1 for domestic students, 1/2 for international students; for spring admission, 10/15 for domestic students, 6/1 for international students. Application fee: $30. *Financial support:* Scholarships/grants, health care benefits, and unspecified assistantships available. Financial award applicants required to submit FAFSA. *Unit head:* Irene Hurst, Program Director, 813-974-3335, Fax: 813-974-4518, E-mail: hurst@coba.usf.edu. *Application contact:* Wendy Baker, Assistant Director, Graduate Studies, 813-974-3335, Fax: 813-974-4518, E-mail: wbaker@usf.edu.

University of South Florida, Graduate School, College of Business, Department of Finance, Tampa, FL 33620-9951. Offers business (PhD), including finance; finance (MS); real estate (MS). Part-time and evening/weekend programs available. *Faculty:* 2 full-time (0 women). *Students:* 30 full-time (11 women), 10 part-time (4 women); includes 2 Black or African American, non-Hispanic/Latino; 5 Asian, non-Hispanic/Latino; 1 Hispanic/Latino, 9 international. Average age 27. 119 applicants, 40% accepted,

20 enrolled. In 2010, 4 master's, 1 doctorate awarded. Terminal master's awarded for partial completion of doctoral program. *Degree requirements:* For master's, thesis or alternative, 30 credits, minimum GPA of 3.0; for doctorate, comprehensive exam, thesis/dissertation. *Entrance requirements:* For master's, GMAT, minimum GPA of 3.0; for doctorate, GMAT, letters of recommendation, personal statement. Additional exam requirements/recommendations for international students: Required—TOEFL (minimum score 550 paper-based; 213 computer-based; 79 iBT). *Application deadline:* For fall admission, 6/1 for domestic students, 1/2 for international students; for spring admission, 10/15 for domestic students, 6/1 for international students. Application fee: $30. Electronic applications accepted. *Financial support:* In 2010–11, 10 research assistantships (averaging $14,943 per year), 6 teaching assistantships with tuition reimbursements (averaging $14,943 per year) were awarded; scholarships/grants, health care benefits, and unspecified assistantships also available. Financial award application deadline: 6/30. *Faculty research:* Corporate governance, international finance, asset pricing models, risk management, market efficiency. Total annual research expenditures: $110,581. *Unit head:* Dr. Scott Besley, Chairperson, 813-974-2081, Fax: 813-974-3084, E-mail: sbesley@coba.usf.edu. *Application contact:* Dr. Scott Besley, Chairperson, 813-974-2081, Fax: 813-974-3084, E-mail: sbesley@coba.usf.edu.

The University of Tampa, John H. Sykes College of Business, Tampa, FL 33606-1490. Offers accounting (MS); entrepreneurship (MBA); finance (MBA, MS); information systems management (MBA); innovation management (MBA); international business (MBA); marketing (MBA, MS); non-profit management (MBA). *Accreditation:* AACSB. Part-time and evening/weekend programs available. *Faculty:* 67 full-time (24 women), 11 part-time/adjunct (4 women). *Students:* 235 full-time (89 women), 288 part-time (122 women); includes 74 minority (16 Black or African American, non-Hispanic/Latino; 2 American Indian or Alaska Native, non-Hispanic/Latino; 14 Asian, non-Hispanic/Latino; 34 Hispanic/Latino; 2 Native Hawaiian or other Pacific Islander, non-Hispanic/Latino; 6 Two or more races, non-Hispanic/Latino), 95 international. Average age 29. 457 applicants, 45% accepted, 175 enrolled. In 2010, 230 master's awarded. *Degree requirements:* For master's, capstone. *Entrance requirements:* For master's, GMAT or GRE, 4-year undergraduate degree, minimum GPA of 3.0, professional experience (for Executive MBA). Additional exam requirements/recommendations for international students: Required—TOEFL (minimum score 577 paper-based; 230 computer-based; 90 iBT); Recommended—IELTS (minimum score 7.5). *Application deadline:* Applications are processed on a rolling basis. Application fee: $40. Electronic applications accepted. *Expenses:* Tuition: Part-time $504 per credit hour. Required fees: $40 per term. *Financial support:* In 2010–11, 74 students received support. Career-related internships or fieldwork, scholarships/grants, unspecified assistantships, and grants available. Financial award applicants required to submit FAFSA. *Faculty research:* Management innovation, social marketing, value relevance of earnings and book value across industries, managerial finance, entrepreneurship. *Unit head:* Dennis Nostrand, Vice President, Enrollment/Admissions, 813-257-1808, E-mail: dnostrand@ut.edu. *Application contact:* Charlene Tobie, Associate Director of Admissions, 813-257-3566, E-mail: ctobie@ut.edu.

The University of Texas at Arlington, Graduate School, College of Business, Department of Finance and Real Estate, Arlington, TX 76019. Offers finance (PhD); quantitative finance (MS); real estate (MS). Part-time and evening/weekend programs available. *Faculty:* 3 full-time (1 woman). *Students:* 48 full-time (10 women), 31 part-time (9 women); includes 18 minority (1 Black or African American, non-Hispanic/Latino; 1 American Indian or Alaska Native, non-Hispanic/Latino; 11 Asian, non-Hispanic/Latino; 4 Hispanic/Latino; 1 Two or more races, non-Hispanic/Latino), 28 international. 37 applicants, 70% accepted, 18 enrolled. In 2010, 24 master's, 1 doctorate awarded. *Degree requirements:* For master's, thesis optional; for doctorate, comprehensive exam, thesis/dissertation. *Entrance requirements:* For master's, GMAT, minimum GPA of 3.0. Additional exam requirements/recommendations for international students: Required—TOEFL (minimum score 550 paper-based; 213 computer-based; 79 iBT). *Application deadline:* For fall admission, 6/1 priority date for domestic students, 4/1 for international students; for spring admission, 10/15 for domestic students, 9/15 for international students. Applications are processed on a rolling basis. Application fee: $35 ($50 for international students). *Expenses:* Tuition, state resident: full-time $7500. Tuition, nonresident: full-time $13,080. International tuition: $13,250 full-time. *Financial support:* In 2010–11, 10 teaching assistantships (averaging $14,000 per year) were awarded; career-related internships or fieldwork, Federal Work-Study, institutionally sponsored loans, and unspecified assistantships also available. Financial award application deadline: 6/1; financial award applicants required to submit FAFSA. *Unit head:* Dr. David Diltz, Chair, 817-272-3705, Fax: 817-272-2252, E-mail: diltz@uta.edu. *Application contact:* Dr. Fred Forgey, Graduate Advisor, 817-272-0359, Fax: 817-272-2252, E-mail: realestate@uta.edu.

The University of Texas at Arlington, Graduate School, College of Business, Program in Business Administration, Arlington, TX 76019. Offers accounting (PhD); business statistics (PhD); finance (MBA, PhD); information systems (MBA, PhD); management (MBA, PhD); marketing (MBA, PhD); operations management (MBA, PhD); real estate (MBA). *Accreditation:* AACSB.

Part-time and evening/weekend programs available. Postbaccalaureate distance learning degree programs offered (no on-campus study). *Students:* 555 full-time (197 women), 378 part-time (144 women); includes 179 minority (55 Black or African American, non-Hispanic/Latino; 1 American Indian or Alaska Native, non-Hispanic/Latino; 58 Asian, non-Hispanic/Latino; 55 Hispanic/Latino; 10 Two or more races, non-Hispanic/Latino), 410 international. 317 applicants, 93% accepted, 196 enrolled. In 2010, 468 master's, 1 doctorate awarded. Terminal master's awarded for partial completion of doctoral program. *Degree requirements:* For master's, thesis optional; for doctorate, comprehensive exam, thesis/dissertation. *Entrance requirements:* For master's, GMAT or GRE; for doctorate, GMAT, minimum GPA of 3.0 (undergraduate), 3.4 (graduate); 30 hours of graduate course work. Additional exam requirements/recommendations for international students: Required—TOEFL (minimum score 550 paper-based; 213 computer-based; 79 iBT). *Application deadline:* For fall admission, 6/1 for domestic students, 4/1 for international students; for spring admission, 10/15 for domestic students, 9/15 for international students. Applications are processed on a rolling basis. Application fee: $35 ($50 for international students). Electronic applications accepted. *Expenses:* Tuition, state resident: full-time $7500. Tuition, nonresident: full-time $13,080. International tuition: $13,250 full-time. *Financial support:* Career-related internships or fieldwork, scholarships/grants, and unspecified assistantships available. Financial award application deadline: 6/1; financial award applicants required to submit FAFSA. *Unit head:* Dr. Edmund Prater, Director of PhD Programs, 817-272-2131, Fax: 817-272-5799. *Application contact:* Melanie McGee, Director of MBA Program, 817-272-3005, Fax: 817-272-5799, E-mail: mwmcgee@uta.edu.

The University of Texas at Dallas, School of Management, Program in Accounting, Richardson, TX 75080. Offers audit and professional (MS); financial analysis (MS); information management (MS); international audit (MS); international services (MS); managerial (MS); taxation (MS). *Accreditation:* AACSB. *Faculty:* 17 full-time (4 women), 7 part-time/adjunct (2 women). *Students:* 412 full-time (270 women), 293 part-time (149 women); includes 164 minority (22 Black or African American, non-Hispanic/Latino; 1 American Indian or Alaska Native, non-Hispanic/Latino; 102 Asian, non-Hispanic/Latino; 37 Hispanic/Latino; 2 Two or more races, non-Hispanic/Latino), 283 international. Average age 28. 570 applicants, 68% accepted, 259 enrolled. In 2010, 273 master's awarded. *Entrance requirements:* For master's, GMAT, minimum GPA of 3.0 in upper-level course work in field. Additional exam requirements/recommendations for international students: Required—TOEFL (minimum score 550 paper-based; 215 computer-based). *Application deadline:* For fall admission, 7/15 for domestic students, 5/1 priority date for international students; for spring admission, 11/15 for domestic students, 9/1 priority date for international students. Applications are processed on a rolling basis. Application fee: $50 ($100 for international students). Electronic applications accepted. *Expenses:* Tuition, state resident: full-time $10,248; part-time $569 per credit hour. Tuition, nonresident: full-time $18,544; part-time $1030 per credit hour. Tuition and fees vary according to course load. *Financial support:* In 2010–11, 260 students received support, including 1 research assistantship with partial tuition reimbursement available (averaging $10,050 per year), 10 teaching assistantships with partial tuition reimbursements available (averaging $10,050 per year); career-related internships or fieldwork, Federal Work-Study, institutionally sponsored loans, scholarships/grants, and unspecified assistantships also available. Support available to part-time students. Financial award application deadline: 4/30; financial award applicants required to submit FAFSA. *Faculty research:* Privatization and accounting/auditing, corporate performance and executive compensation, risk management, information technology in accounting. *Unit head:* Amy Troutman, Assistant Director, 972-883-6719, Fax: 972-883-6823, E-mail: amybass@utdallas.edu. *Application contact:* James Parker, Assistant Director of Graduate Recruitment, 972-883-5842, E-mail: jparker@utdallas.edu.

The University of Texas at Dallas, School of Management, Program in Finance, Richardson, TX 75080. Offers finance (MS); financial analysis (MS); financial engineering and risk management (MS); investment management (MS). Part-time and evening/weekend programs available. *Faculty:* 14 full-time (3 women), 3 part-time/adjunct (1 woman). *Students:* 229 full-time (105 women), 55 part-time (18 women); includes 36 minority (4 Black or African American, non-Hispanic/Latino; 25 Asian, non-Hispanic/Latino; 7 Hispanic/Latino), 190 international. Average age 26. 447 applicants, 67% accepted, 158 enrolled. In 2010, 39 master's awarded. *Entrance requirements:* For master's, GMAT. Additional exam requirements/recommendations for international students: Required—TOEFL (minimum score 550 paper-based; 215 computer-based). *Application deadline:* For fall admission, 7/15 for domestic students, 5/1 priority date for international students; for spring admission, 11/15 for domestic students, 9/1 priority date for international students. Applications are processed on a rolling basis. Application fee: $50 ($100 for international students). Electronic applications accepted. *Expenses:* Tuition, state resident: full-time $10,248; part-time $569 per credit hour. Tuition, nonresident: full-time $18,544; part-time $1030 per credit hour. Tuition and fees vary according to course load. *Financial support:* In 2010–11, 101 students received support, including 3 teaching assistantships with partial tuition reimbursements available (averaging $10,050 per year); research assistantships with partial tuition reimbursements available, career-related internships or fieldwork, Federal Work-Study, institutionally sponsored loans, scholarships/grants, and unspecified assistantships also available. Support available to part-time students. Financial award application deadline: 4/30; financial award applicants required to submit FAFSA. *Faculty research:* Econometrics, industrial organization, auction theory, file-sharing copyrights and bundling, international financial management, entrepreneurial finance. *Unit head:* Dr. H. Joe Wells, Director, 972-883-4897, E-mail: hjoewells@utdallas.edu. *Application contact:* James Parker, Assistant Director, 972-883-5842, E-mail: jparker@utdallas.edu.

The University of Texas at Dallas, School of Management, Program in Management and Administrative Sciences, Richardson, TX 75080. Offers electronic commerce (MS); finance (MS); healthcare administration (MS); information systems (MS); innovation and entrepreneurship (MS); international management (MS); leadership in organizations (MS); marketing (MS); operations (MS); organizations (MS); real estate (MS); strategy (MS). *Accreditation:* AACSB. Part-time and evening/weekend programs available. *Faculty:* 18 full-time (3 women), 8 part-time/adjunct (0 women). *Students:* 57 full-time (32 women), 107 part-time (49 women); includes 53 minority (14 Black or African American, non-Hispanic/Latino; 30 Asian, non-Hispanic/Latino; 8 Hispanic/Latino; 1 Two or more races, non-Hispanic/Latino), 25 international. Average age 32. 161 applicants, 67% accepted, 51 enrolled. In 2010, 27 master's awarded. *Degree requirements:* For master's, thesis optional. *Entrance requirements:* For master's, GMAT. Additional exam requirements/recommendations for international students: Required—TOEFL (minimum score 550 paper-based; 215 computer-based). *Application deadline:* For fall admission, 7/15 for domestic students, 5/1 priority date for international students; for spring admission, 11/15 for domestic students, 9/1 priority date for international students. Applications are processed on a rolling basis. Application fee: $50 ($100 for international students). Electronic applications accepted. *Expenses:* Tuition, state resident: full-time $10,248; part-time $569 per credit hour. Tuition, nonresident: full-time $18,544; part-time $1030 per credit hour. Tuition and fees vary according to course load. *Financial support:* In 2010–11, 26 students received support, including 38 teaching assistantships with partial tuition reimbursements available (averaging $11,528 per year); research assistantships with partial tuition reimbursements available, career-related internships or fieldwork, Federal Work-Study, institutionally sponsored loans, scholarships/grants, and unspecified assistantships also available. Support available to part-time students. Financial award application deadline: 4/30; financial award applicants required to submit FAFSA. *Faculty research:* Integrated and detailed knowledge of functional areas of management, analytical tools for effective appraisal and decision making. *Unit head:* Dr. Doug Eckel, Assistant Dean, 972-883-5923, E-mail: doug.eckel@utdallas.edu. *Application contact:* James Parker, Assistant Director, 972-883-5842, E-mail: jparker@utdallas.edu.

The University of Texas at Dallas, School of Management, Programs in Management Science, Richardson, TX 75080. Offers accounting (PhD); finance (PhD); information systems (PhD); marketing (PhD); operations management (PhD). *Accreditation:* AACSB. Part-time and evening/weekend programs available. *Faculty:* 12 full-time (3 women), 3 part-time/adjunct (0 women). *Students:* 77 full-time (27 women), 11 part-time (4 women); includes 5 minority (all Asian, non-Hispanic/Latino), 72 international. Average age 32. 223 applicants, 9% accepted. In 2010, 16 doctorates awarded. *Degree requirements:* For doctorate, thesis/dissertation. *Entrance requirements:* For doctorate, GMAT, minimum GPA of 3.0. Additional exam requirements/recommendations for international students: Required—TOEFL (minimum score 550 paper-based; 215 computer-based). *Application deadline:* For fall admission, 7/15 for domestic students, 5/1 priority date for international students; for spring admission, 11/15 for domestic students, 9/1 priority date for international students. Applications are processed on a rolling basis. Application fee: $50 ($100 for international students). Electronic applications accepted. *Expenses:* Tuition, state resident: full-time $10,248; part-time $569 per credit hour. Tuition, nonresident: full-time $18,544; part-time $1030 per credit hour. Tuition and fees vary according to course load. *Financial support:* In 2010–11, 56 students received support, including 1 research assistantship with partial tuition reimbursement available (averaging $13,050 per year), 58 teaching assistantships with partial tuition reimbursements available (averaging $14,772 per year); career-related internships or fieldwork, Federal Work-Study, institutionally sponsored loans, scholarships/grants, and unspecified assistantships also available. Support available to part-time students. Financial award application deadline: 4/30; financial award applicants required to submit FAFSA. *Faculty research:* Empirical generalizations in marketing, diffusion of generations of technology, stochastic brand-choice theory, acceptance of trade deals by supermarkets, nonparametric estimations of market share response. *Unit head:* Dr. Sumit Sarkar, Program Director, 972-883-2745, Fax: 972-883-5977, E-mail: som phd.@utdallas.edu. Application contact: Dr. LeeAnne Sloane, Program Coordinator, 972-883-2745, Fax: 972-883-5977, E-mail: som_phd@utdallas.edu.

The University of Texas at San Antonio, College of Business, Department of Finance, San Antonio, TX 78249-0617. Offers business finance (MBA); construction science and management (MS); finance (MS); real estate finance (MBA). Part-time and evening/weekend programs available. *Faculty:* 10 full-time (1 woman). *Students:* 24 full-time (6 women), 58 part-time (11 women); includes 21 minority (1 Black or African American, non-Hispanic/Latino;

4 Asian, non-Hispanic/Latino; 15 Hispanic/Latino; 1 Two or more races, non-Hispanic/Latino), 8 international. Average age 29. 56 applicants, 52% accepted, 17 enrolled. In 2010, 38 master's awarded. *Degree requirements:* For master's, comprehensive exam (for some programs), thesis (for some programs). *Entrance requirements:* For master's, GMAT, minimum GPA of 3.0. Additional exam requirements/recommendations for international students: Required—TOEFL (minimum score 500 paper-based; 173 computer-based; 61 iBT), IELTS (minimum score 5). *Application deadline:* For fall admission, 7/1 for domestic students, 4/1 for international students; for spring admission, 11/1 for domestic students, 9/1 for international students. Applications are processed on a rolling basis. Application fee: $45 ($85 for international students). Electronic applications accepted. *Expenses:* Tuition, state resident: full-time $4172; part-time $231.75 per credit hour. Tuition, nonresident: full-time $15,332; part-time $851.75 per credit hour. *Financial support:* In 2010–11, 6 students received support, including 7 research assistantships (averaging $16,052 per year), 38 teaching assistantships (averaging $9,767 per year); career-related internships or fieldwork, scholarships/grants, tuition waivers, and unspecified assistantships also available. Support available to part-time students. *Faculty research:* Capital markets, corporate finance, asset pricing and investments, international finance, real estate, finance. *Unit head:* Dr. Lalatendu Misra, Chair, 210-458-6315, Fax: 210-458-6320, E-mail: kfairchild@utsa.edu. *Application contact:* Veronica Ramirez, Assistant Dean of the Graduate School, 210-458-4330, Fax: 210-458-4332, E-mail: graduatestudies@utsa.edu.

The University of Texas at San Antonio, College of Business, General Business Program, San Antonio, TX 78249-0617. Offers accounting (PhD); business (MBA); finance (PhD); information systems (MBA); information technology (PhD); international business (MBA); management accounting (MBA); management and organization studies (PhD); management of technology (MBA); marketing (PhD); marketing management (MBA); taxation (MBA). Part-time and evening/weekend programs available. *Students:* 159 full-time (59 women), 124 part-time (43 women); includes 82 minority (9 Black or African American, non-Hispanic/Latino; 2 American Indian or Alaska Native, non-Hispanic/Latino; 17 Asian, non-Hispanic/Latino; 50 Hispanic/Latino; 1 Native Hawaiian or other Pacific Islander, non-Hispanic/Latino; 3 Two or more races, non-Hispanic/Latino), 39 international. Average age 32. 330 applicants, 46% accepted, 105 enrolled. In 2010, 85 master's, 9 doctorates awarded. *Degree requirements:* For master's, comprehensive exam (for some programs), thesis (for some programs). *Entrance requirements:* For master's, GMAT. Additional exam requirements/recommendations for international students: Required—TOEFL (minimum score 500 paper-based; 173 computer-based; 61 iBT), IELTS (minimum score 5). *Application deadline:* For fall admission, 7/1 for domestic students, 4/1 for international students; for spring admission, 11/1 for domestic students, 9/1 for international students. Application fee: $45 ($80 for international students). *Expenses:* Tuition, state resident: full-time $4172; part-time $231.75 per credit hour. Tuition, nonresident: full-time $15,332; part-time $851.75 per credit hour. *Financial support:* In 2010–11, 282 research assistantships (averaging $13,930 per year), 74 teaching assistantships (averaging $9,284 per year) were awarded; scholarships/grants, tuition waivers, and unspecified assistantships also available. Support available to part-time students. *Unit head:* Dr. Lynda Y. de la Vinna, Dean, 210-458-4317, Fax: 210-458-4308, E-mail: lynda.delavina@utsa.edu. *Application contact:* Veronica Ramirez, Assistant Dean of the Graduate School, 210-458-4330, Fax: 210-458-4332, E-mail: graduatestudies@utsa.edu.

The University of Toledo, College of Graduate Studies, College of Business and Innovation, Department of Finance, Toledo, OH 43606-3390. Offers MBA. Part-time and evening/weekend programs available. *Faculty:* 2. *Students:* 34 full-time (16 women), 28 part-time (5 women); includes 1 Black or African American, non-Hispanic/Latino; 2 Two or more races, non-Hispanic/Latino, 19 international. Average age 27. 47 applicants, 68% accepted, 21 enrolled. In 2010, 41 master's awarded. *Entrance requirements:* For master's, GMAT, 2.7 GPA on all prior academic work. Three letters of recommendation, a statement of purpose, and transcripts from all prior institutions attended. Additional exam requirements/recommendations for international students: Required—TOEFL (minimum score 550 paper-based; 213 computer-based; 80 iBT), IELTS (minimum score 6.5). *Application deadline:* For fall admission, 1/15 priority date for domestic and international students. Applications are processed on a rolling basis. Application fee: $45 ($75 for international students). Electronic applications accepted. *Expenses:* Tuition, state resident: full-time $11,426; part-time $476 per credit hour. Tuition, nonresident: full-time $21,660; part-time $903 per credit hour. One-time fee: $62. *Financial support:* Research assistantships with tuition reimbursements, career-related internships or fieldwork, Federal Work-Study, institutionally sponsored loans, scholarships/grants, tuition waivers (full and partial), unspecified assistantships, and administrative assistantships available. Support available to part-time students. *Faculty research:* Financial management, banking, international finance, investments. *Unit head:* Dr. Mark Vonderembse, Chair. *Application contact:* Graduate School Office, 419-530-4723, Fax: 419-530-4724, E-mail: grdsch@utnet.utoledo.edu.

University of Tulsa, Graduate School, Collins College of Business, Finance/Applied Mathematics Program, Tulsa, OK 74104-3189. Offers MS/MS.

Part-time and evening/weekend programs available. *Students:* 2 full-time (both women). Average age 24. 11 applicants, 73% accepted, 1 enrolled. *Entrance requirements:* Additional exam requirements/recommendations for international students: Required—TOEFL (minimum score 575 paper-based; 231 computer-based), IELTS (minimum score 6.5). *Application deadline:* Applications are processed on a rolling basis. Application fee: $40. Electronic applications accepted. *Expenses:* Tuition: Full-time $16,902; part-time $939 per credit hour. Required fees: $1020; $4 per credit hour. Tuition and fees vary according to course load. *Financial support:* In 2010–11, 2 students received support, including 2 teaching assistantships (averaging $7,961 per year); fellowships, career-related internships or fieldwork, Federal Work-Study, institutionally sponsored loans, scholarships/grants, health care benefits, tuition waivers (full and partial), and unspecified assistantships also available. Support available to part-time students. Financial award application deadline: 2/1; financial award applicants required to submit FAFSA. *Unit head:* Linda Nichols, Associate Dean, 918-631-2242, Fax: 918-631-2142, E-mail: linda-nichols@utulsa.edu. *Application contact:* Linda Nichols, Associate Dean, 918-631-2242, Fax: 918-631-2142, E-mail: linda-nichols@utulsa.edu.

University of Tulsa, Graduate School, Collins College of Business, Master of Business Administration Program, Tulsa, OK 74104-3189. Offers accounting (MBA); business administration (MBA); energy management (MBA); finance (MBA); international business (MBA); management information systems (MBA); taxation (MBA); JD/MBA; MBA/MSCS; MBA/MSF. *Accreditation:* AACSB. Part-time and evening/weekend programs available. *Faculty:* 32 full-time (6 women). *Students:* 39 full-time (14 women), 40 part-time (16 women); includes 7 minority (1 Black or African American, non-Hispanic/Latino; 2 Asian, non-Hispanic/Latino; 4 Hispanic/Latino), 9 international. Average age 26. 73 applicants, 55% accepted, 18 enrolled. In 2010, 55 master's awarded. *Entrance requirements:* For master's, GMAT. Additional exam requirements/recommendations for international students: Required—TOEFL (minimum score 575 paper-based; 232 computer-based; 90 iBT), IELTS (minimum score 6.5). *Application deadline:* Applications are processed on a rolling basis. Application fee: $40. Electronic applications accepted. *Expenses:* Tuition: Full-time $16,902; part-time $939 per credit hour. Required fees: $1020; $4 per credit hour. Tuition and fees vary according to course load. *Financial support:* In 2010–11, 56 students received support, including 23 fellowships (averaging $4,872 per year), 4 research assistantships (averaging $9,323 per year), 29 teaching assistantships (averaging $10,642 per year); career-related internships or fieldwork, institutionally sponsored loans, scholarships/grants, health care benefits, tuition waivers (full and partial), and unspecified assistantships also available. Support available to part-time students. Financial award application deadline: 2/1; financial award applicants required to submit FAFSA. *Faculty research:* Accounting, energy management, finance, international business, management information systems, taxation. *Unit head:* Dr. Linda Nichols, Associate Dean of the Collins College of Business, 918-631-2242, Fax: 918-631-2142, E-mail: linda-nichols@utulsa.edu. *Application contact:* Dr. Linda Nichols, Associate Dean of the Collins College of Business, 918-631-2242, Fax: 918-631-2142, E-mail: linda-nichols@utulsa.edu.

University of Tulsa, Graduate School, Collins College of Business, MBA/MS Program in Finance, Tulsa, OK 74104-3189. Offers MBA/MS. Part-time and evening/weekend programs available. *Students:* 2 full-time (1 woman), 1 international. Average age 28. 2 applicants, 50% accepted, 0 enrolled. *Entrance requirements:* Additional exam requirements/recommendations for international students: Required—TOEFL (minimum score 575 paper-based; 231 computer-based), IELTS (minimum score 6.5). *Application deadline:* Applications are processed on a rolling basis. Application fee: $40. Electronic applications accepted. *Expenses:* Tuition: Full-time $16,902; part-time $939 per credit hour. Required fees: $1020; $4 per credit hour. Tuition and fees vary according to course load. *Financial support:* In 2010–11, 2 fellowships (averaging $6,667 per year), 1 teaching assistantship (averaging $11,942 per year) were awarded; career-related internships or fieldwork, Federal Work-Study, institutionally sponsored loans, scholarships/grants, health care benefits, tuition waivers, and unspecified assistantships also available. Support available to part-time students. Financial award application deadline: 2/1. *Unit head:* Linda Nichols, Associate Dean, 918-631-2242, Fax: 918-631-2142, E-mail: linda-nichols@utulsa.edu. *Application contact:* Linda Nichols, Associate Dean, 918-631-2242, Fax: 918-631-2142, E-mail: linda-nichols@utulsa.edu.

University of Tulsa, Graduate School, Collins College of Business, Program in Finance, Tulsa, OK 74104-3189. Offers corporate finance (MS); investments and portfolio management (MS); risk management (MS); JD/MSF; MBA/MSF; MSF/MSAM. Part-time and evening/weekend programs available. *Faculty:* 10 full-time (1 woman). *Students:* 21 full-time (10 women), 4 part-time (2 women), 12 international. Average age 25. 87 applicants, 51% accepted, 11 enrolled. In 2010, 16 master's awarded. *Degree requirements:* For master's, thesis optional. *Entrance requirements:* For master's, GMAT. Additional exam requirements/recommendations for international students: Required—TOEFL (minimum score 575 paper-based; 231 computer-based), IELTS (minimum score 6.5). *Application deadline:* Applications are processed on a rolling basis. Application fee: $40. Electronic applications accepted. *Expenses:* Tuition: Full-time $16,902; part-time $939 per credit hour. Required fees: $1020; $4 per credit hour. Tuition and fees vary according to course load. *Financial support:* In 2010–11, 9 students received support, including 2 fellowships with full and partial tuition reimbursements available (averaging $8,750 per year), 2 research assistantships with full and partial tuition reimbursements available (averaging $9,286 per year), 5 teaching assistantships with full and partial tuition reimbursements available (averaging $8,815 per year); career-related internships or fieldwork, Federal Work-Study, institutionally sponsored loans, scholarships/grants, health care benefits, tuition waivers (full and partial), and unspecified assistantships also available. Support available to part-time students. Financial award application deadline: 2/1; financial award applicants required to submit FAFSA. *Unit head:* Dr. Linda Nichols, Associate Dean, 918-631-2242, Fax: 918-631-2142, E-mail: linda-nichols@utulsa.edu. *Application contact:* Dr. Linda Nichols, Associate Dean, 918-631-2242, Fax: 918-631-2142, E-mail: linda-nichols@utulsa.edu.

University of Utah, Graduate School, David Eccles School of Business, Department of Finance, Salt Lake City, UT 84112. Offers MS, PhD. *Faculty:* 14 full-time (2 women), 1 part-time/adjunct (0 women). *Students:* 51 full-time (17 women), 19 part-time (5 women); includes 9 minority (1 Black or African American, non-Hispanic/Latino; 1 American Indian or Alaska Native, non-Hispanic/Latino; 3 Asian, non-Hispanic/Latino; 3 Hispanic/Latino; 1 Two or more races, non-Hispanic/Latino), 31 international. Average age 27. 119 applicants, 51% accepted, 33 enrolled. In 2010, 38 master's awarded. Terminal master's awarded for partial completion of doctoral program. *Degree requirements:* For master's, comprehensive exam; for doctorate, thesis/dissertation, oral qualifying exams, written qualifying exams, research paper. *Entrance requirements:* For master's, GMAT, minimum undergraduate GPA of 3.0; for doctorate, GMAT/GRE. Additional exam requirements/recommendations for international students: Required—TOEFL (minimum score 600 paper-based; 250 computer-based; 100 iBT), IELTS (minimum score 7). *Application deadline:* For fall admission, 3/1 priority date for domestic and international students. Applications are processed on a rolling basis. Application fee: $55 ($65 for international students). Electronic applications accepted. *Expenses:* Tuition, area resident: Part-time $179.19 per credit hour. Tuition, state resident: full-time $4384. Tuition, nonresident: full-time $16,684; part-time $630.67 per credit hour. Required fees: $350 per semester. Tuition and fees vary according to course load, degree level and program. *Financial support:* In 2010–11, 11 students received support, including 7 teaching assistantships (averaging $7,950 per year); fellowships, research assistantships, tuition waivers (full and partial) and unspecified assistantships also available. Financial award application deadline: 4/1; financial award applicants required to submit FAFSA. *Faculty research:* Investment, managerial finance, corporate finance, capital budgeting, risk management. Total annual research expenditures: $113,812. *Unit head:* Dr. Uri Loewenstein, Chair, 801-581-4419, Fax: 801-581-3956, E-mail: uri.lowenstein@business.utah.edu. *Application contact:* Andrea Chmelik, Admissions and Program Coordinator, 801-585-1719, Fax: 801-581-3666, E-mail: andrea.chmelik@business.utah.edu.

University of Virginia, McIntire School of Commerce, Program in Commerce, Charlottesville, VA 22903. Offers financial services (MSC); marketing and management (MSC). *Students:* 85 full-time (36 women); includes 4 Asian, non-Hispanic/Latino; 3 Hispanic/Latino; 4 Two or more races, non-Hispanic/Latino, 11 international. Average age 22. 193 applicants, 68% accepted. In 2010, 42 master's awarded. *Entrance requirements:* For master's, GMAT, 2 letters of recommendation; prerequisite course work in financial accounting, microeconomics, and introduction to business. Additional exam requirements/recommendations for international students: Required—TOEFL (minimum score 600 paper-based; 250 computer-based; 100 iBT), IELTS (minimum score 7). *Application deadline:* For fall admission, 9/15 priority date for domestic students, 1/15 priority date for international students. Applications are processed on a rolling basis. Application fee: $75. Electronic applications accepted. *Expenses:* Contact institution. *Financial support:* Scholarships/grants available. Financial award application deadline: 3/1; financial award applicants required to submit CSS PROFILE or FAFSA. *Unit head:* Ira C. Harris, Head, 434-924-8816, Fax: 434-924-7074, E-mail: ich3x@comm.virginia.edu. *Application contact:* Emma Jean Candelier, Assistant Director, Commerce Graduate Marketing and Admissions, 434-243-4992, Fax: 434-924-7074, E-mail: mscommerce@virginia.edu.

University of Washington, Graduate School, School of Public Health, Department of Health Services, Seattle, WA 98195. Offers bioinformatics (PhD); cancer prevention and control (PhD); clinical research (MS); community oriented public health practice (MPH); economics or finance (PhD); evaluation sciences (PhD); executive program (MHA); health behavior and health promotion (PhD); health care and population health research (MPH); health policy analysis and process (PhD); health policy and analysis and process (MPH); health services (MS, PhD); health services administration (EMHA, MHA); in residence program (MHA); maternal and child health (MPH, PhD); occupational health (PhD); population health and social determinants (PhD); social and behavioral sciences (MPH); sociology and demography (PhD); JD/MHA; MHA/MBA; MHA/MD; MHA/MPA; MPH/JD; MPH/MD; MPH/MN; MPH/MPA; MPH/MS; MPH/MSD; MPH/MSW; MPH/PhD. Part-time and evening/weekend programs available. Postbaccalaureate distance learning degree programs offered (minimal on-campus study). *Faculty:* 36 full-time (18 women), 59 part-time/adjunct (26 women). *Students:* 107 full-time (82 women), 101 part-time (82 women); includes 1 Black or African

American, non-Hispanic/Latino; 1 American Indian or Alaska Native, non-Hispanic/Latino; 27 Asian, non-Hispanic/Latino; 10 Hispanic/Latino, 4 international. Average age 34. 426 applicants, 41% accepted, 106 enrolled. In 2010, 37 master's, 11 doctorates awarded. Terminal master's awarded for partial completion of doctoral program. *Degree requirements:* For master's, thesis (for some programs), practicum (MPH); for doctorate, comprehensive exam, thesis/dissertation. *Entrance requirements:* For master's and doctorate, GRE General Test, minimum GPA of 3.0. Additional exam requirements/recommendations for international students: Required—TOEFL (minimum score 580 paper-based; 237 computer-based; 92 iBT), IELTS (minimum score 7). *Application deadline:* For fall admission, 1/1 for domestic students, 11/1 for international students. Application fee: 75 Albanian leks. Electronic applications accepted. *Financial support:* In 2010–11, 47 students received support, including 10 fellowships with full and partial tuition reimbursements available (averaging $22,000 per year), 10 research assistantships with full and partial tuition reimbursements available (averaging $18,700 per year), 3 teaching assistantships with full and partial tuition reimbursements available (averaging $4,575 per year); institutionally sponsored loans, traineeships, and health care benefits also available. Financial award application deadline: 2/28; financial award applicants required to submit FAFSA. *Faculty research:* Public health practice, health promotion and disease prevention, maternal and child health, organizational behavior and culture, health policy. *Unit head:* Dr. Larry Kessler, Chair, 206-543-2930. *Application contact:* Kitty A. Andert, MPH/MS/PhD Program Manager, 206-616-2926, Fax: 206-543-3964, E-mail: kitander@u.washington.edu.

University of Washington, Tacoma, Graduate Programs, MBA Programs, Tacoma, WA 98402-3100. Offers accounting (MBA); business administration (MBA); certified financial analyst (MBA). Part-time and evening/weekend programs available. *Faculty:* 24 full-time (8 women), 3 part-time/adjunct (0 women). *Students:* 42 full-time (13 women), 14 part-time (4 women); includes 1 Black or African American, non-Hispanic/Latino; 8 Asian, non-Hispanic/Latino; 2 Hispanic/Latino, 1 international. Average age 32. 42 applicants, 76% accepted, 29 enrolled. In 2010, 18 master's awarded. *Entrance requirements:* For master's, GMAT, minimum GPA of 3.0 in final graded 90 quarter credits or 60 graded semester credits; at least 2 years of professional/management work experience. Additional exam requirements/recommendations for international students: Required—TOEFL (minimum score 580 paper-based; 237 computer-based; 92 iBT). *Application deadline:* For fall admission, 4/15 priority date for domestic students. Applications are processed on a rolling basis. Application fee: $65. Electronic applications accepted. *Expenses:* Contact institution. *Financial support:* Scholarships/grants available. *Faculty research:* International accounting, marketing, change management, investments, corporate social responsibility. *Unit head:* Dr. Shahrokh Saudagaran, Dean, 253-692-5630, Fax: 253-692-4523, E-mail: uwtmba@u.washington.edu. *Application contact:* Aubree Robinson, Academic Adviser, MBA and Undergraduate Programs, 253-692-5630, Fax: 253-692-4523, E-mail: uwtmba@u.washington.edu.

University of Wisconsin–Madison, Graduate School, Wisconsin School of Business, Doctoral Program in Finance, Investment and Banking, Madison, WI 53706-1380. Offers PhD. *Faculty:* 14 full-time (1 woman), 4 part-time/adjunct (1 woman). *Students:* 10 full-time (2 women), 9 international. Average age 30. 95 applicants, 3% accepted, 1 enrolled. In 2010, 1 doctorate awarded. *Degree requirements:* For doctorate, comprehensive exam, thesis/dissertation. *Entrance requirements:* For doctorate, GMAT or GRE. Additional exam requirements/recommendations for international students: Required—Pearson Test of English (minimum score 73, written 80); Recommended—TOEFL (minimum score 623 paper-based; 263 computer-based; 106 iBT), IELTS (minimum score 7.5). *Application deadline:* For fall admission, 12/15 priority date for domestic and international students. Application fee: $56. Electronic applications accepted. *Expenses:* Tuition, state resident: full-time $9887; part-time $617.96 per credit. Tuition, nonresident: full-time $24,054; part-time $1503.40 per credit. Required fees: $67.63 per credit. Tuition and fees vary according to reciprocity agreements. *Financial support:* In 2010–11, 10 students received support, including 1 fellowship with full tuition reimbursement available (averaging $18,756 per year), research assistantships with full tuition reimbursements available (averaging $16,506 per year), 9 teaching assistantships with full tuition reimbursements available (averaging $14,088 per year); Federal Work-Study, institutionally sponsored loans, scholarships/grants, health care benefits, and unspecified assistantships also available. Financial award application deadline: 2/1; financial award applicants required to submit FAFSA. *Faculty research:* Banking and financial institutions, business cycles, investments, derivatives, corporate finance. *Unit head:* Prof. Robert Krainer, Chair, 608-263-1253, Fax: 608-265-4195, E-mail: rkrainer@bus.wisc.edu. *Application contact:* Belle Heberling, Assistant Director for Research Programs, 608-262-3749, Fax: 608-890-0180, E-mail: phd@bus.wisc.edu.

University of Wisconsin–Madison, Graduate School, Wisconsin School of Business, Wisconsin Full-Time MBA Program, Madison, WI 53706-1380. Offers applied security analysis (MBA); arts administration (MBA); brand and product management (MBA); corporate finance and investment banking (MBA); entrepreneurial management (MBA); marketing research (MBA); operations and technology management (MBA); real estate (MBA); risk management and insurance (MBA); strategic human resource management (MBA);

strategic management in the life and engineering sciences (MBA); supply chain management (MBA). *Faculty:* 32 full-time (4 women), 17 part-time/adjunct (3 women). *Students:* 242 full-time (74 women); includes 16 Black or African American, non-Hispanic/Latino; 3 American Indian or Alaska Native, non-Hispanic/Latino; 16 Asian, non-Hispanic/Latino; 12 Hispanic/Latino, 29 international. Average age 28. 526 applicants, 32% accepted, 117 enrolled. In 2010, 106 master's awarded. *Entrance requirements:* For master's, GMAT, bachelor's or equivalent degree, 2 years of work experience, letters of recommendation. Additional exam requirements/recommendations for international students: Required—TOEFL (minimum score 600 paper-based; 250 computer-based; 100 iBT), IELTS. *Application deadline:* For fall admission, 11/4 for domestic students, 11/1 for international students; for winter admission, 2/5 for domestic and international students; for spring admission, 5/15 for domestic students, 4/5 for international students. Applications are processed on a rolling basis. Application fee: $56. Electronic applications accepted. *Expenses:* Tuition, state resident: full-time $9887; part-time $617.96 per credit. Tuition, nonresident: full-time $24,054; part-time $1503.40 per credit. Required fees: $67.63 per credit. Tuition and fees vary according to reciprocity agreements. *Financial support:* In 2010–11, 103 students received support, including 13 fellowships with full and partial tuition reimbursements available (averaging $15,000 per year), 53 research assistantships with full tuition reimbursements available (averaging $8,000 per year), 35 teaching assistantships with full tuition reimbursements available (averaging $11,000 per year); scholarships/grants, health care benefits, and unspecified assistantships also available. Financial award application deadline: 4/5; financial award applicants required to submit FAFSA. *Faculty research:* Market consequences of International Financial Reporting Standards (IFRS), inter-firm relationships and strategic partnerships, application of Bayesian statistical methods and applied probability models to understanding individuals' behaviors in the context of customer relationship management (CRM) applications, liquidity provision and the structure of financial markets, strategic management of global startups. *Unit head:* Dr. Kenneth A. Kavajecz, Associate Dean of Master's Programs, 608-265-3494, Fax: 608-265-4192, E-mail: kkavajecz@bus.wisc.edu. *Application contact:* Maria Reis, Assistant Director of MBA Marketing and Recruiting, 608-262-4000, Fax: 608-265-4192, E-mail: mreis@bus.wisc.edu.

Valparaiso University, Graduate School, Program in International Economics and Finance, Valparaiso, IN 46383. Offers MS. Part-time and evening/weekend programs available. *Students:* 31 full-time (15 women), 11 part-time (2 women); includes 2 minority (1 Asian, non-Hispanic/Latino; 1 Hispanic/Latino), 35 international. Average age 23. In 2010, 9 master's awarded. *Entrance requirements:* For master's, 1 semester of college level calculus; 1 statistics or quantitative methods class; 2 semesters of introductory economics; 1 introductory accounting course; minimum undergraduate GPA of 3.0; 2 letters of recommendation. Additional exam requirements/recommendations for international students: Required—TOEFL (minimum score 550 paper-based; 213 computer-based; 80 iBT). Application fee: $30 ($50 for international students). *Expenses:* Tuition: Full-time $9540; part-time $530 per credit hour. Required fees: $292; $95 per semester. Tuition and fees vary according to program. *Financial support:* Available to part-time students. Applicants required to submit FAFSA. *Unit head:* Dr. David L. Rowland, Dean, Graduate School and Continuing Education/Associate Provost, 219-464-5313, Fax: 219-464-5381, E-mail: david.rowland@valpo.edu. *Application contact:* Laura Groth, Coordinator of Student Services and Support, 219-464-5313, Fax: 219-464-5381, E-mail: laura.groth@valpo.edu.

Vanderbilt University, Owen Graduate School of Management, MS in Finance Program, Nashville, TN 37240-1001. Offers MSF. *Faculty:* 34 full-time (6 women). *Students:* 38 full-time (9 women); includes 2 Black or African American, non-Hispanic/Latino; 12 Asian, non-Hispanic/Latino, 12 international. Average age 26. 590 applicants, 14% accepted, 38 enrolled. In 2010, 38 master's awarded. *Entrance requirements:* For master's, GMAT and/or GRE. Additional exam requirements/recommendations for international students: Required—TOEFL (minimum score 640 paper-based; 105 computer-based). *Application deadline:* For fall admission, 11/15 priority date for domestic and international students; for winter admission, 1/15 priority date for domestic and international students; for spring admission, 3/1 priority date for domestic students, 3/1 for international students. Application fee: $55. Electronic applications accepted. *Financial support:* Scholarships/grants available. Financial award applicants required to submit FAFSA. *Unit head:* Dr. Kate Barraclough, Director, 615-343-8108, E-mail: kate.barraclough@owen.vanderbilt.edu. *Application contact:* John Roeder, Program Director, 615-343-6109, Fax: 615-343-1175, E-mail: john.roeder@owen.vanderbilt.edu.

Villanova University, Villanova School of Business, Master of Science in Finance Program, Villanova, PA 19085-1699. Offers MSF. *Faculty:* 6 full-time (1 woman), 1 part-time/adjunct (0 women). *Students:* 30 full-time (4 women); includes 4 minority (1 Black or African American, non-Hispanic/Latino; 2 Asian, non-Hispanic/Latino; 1 Two or more races, non-Hispanic/Latino). Average age 24. In 2010, 27 master's awarded. *Degree requirements:* For master's, minimum cumulative GPA of 3.0. *Entrance requirements:* For master's, GMAT, prerequisite course in principles of finance. Additional exam requirements/recommendations for international students: Required—TOEFL (minimum score 550 paper-based; 213 computer-based; 80 iBT). *Application deadline:* For spring admission, 3/31 for domestic and international students.

Applications are processed on a rolling basis. Application fee: $50. Electronic applications accepted. *Expenses:* Tuition: Part-time $700 per credit. Part-time tuition and fees vary according to degree level and program. *Financial support:* In 2010–11, 4 research assistantships (averaging $6,550 per year) were awarded; scholarships/grants and unspecified assistantships also available. Support available to part-time students. Financial award application deadline: 6/30; financial award applicants required to submit FAFSA. *Faculty research:* Derivatives, applied corporate finance, financial modeling, corporate risk management. *Unit head:* Meredith L. Kwiatek, Director of Graduate Recruitment & Marketing, 610-519-7016, Fax: 610-519-6273, E-mail: meredith.kwiatek@villanova.edu. *Application contact:* Meredith L. Kwiatek, Assistant Director, 610-519-7016, Fax: 610-519-6273, E-mail: meredith.kwiatek@villanova.edu.

Villanova University, Villanova School of Business, MBA—The Fast Track Program, Villanova, PA 19085. Offers finance (MBA); health care management (MBA); international business (MBA); management information systems (MBA); marketing (MBA); real estate (MBA); strategic management (MBA). *Accreditation:* AACSB. Part-time and evening/weekend programs available. *Faculty:* 15 full-time (2 women), 5 part-time/adjunct (0 women). *Students:* 118 part-time (34 women); includes 13 minority (2 Black or African American, non-Hispanic/Latino; 8 Asian, non-Hispanic/Latino; 3 Hispanic/Latino). Average age 30. In 2010, 35 master's awarded. *Degree requirements:* For master's, minimum GPA of 3.0. *Entrance requirements:* For master's, GMAT. Additional exam requirements/recommendations for international students: Required—TOEFL (minimum score 550 paper-based; 213 computer-based; 80 iBT). *Application deadline:* For fall admission, 6/30 for domestic and international students. Application fee: $50. Electronic applications accepted. *Expenses:* Tuition: Part-time $700 per credit. Part-time tuition and fees vary according to degree level and program. *Financial support:* Scholarships/grants available. Support available to part-time students. Financial award application deadline: 6/30; financial award applicants required to submit FAFSA. *Faculty research:* Developing and leveraging technology, ethical business practices, managing for innovation and creativity, the global political economy, strategic marketing management. *Unit head:* Meredith L. Kwiatek, Director of Graduate Recruitment & Marketing, 610-519-7016, Fax: 610-519-6273, E-mail: rachel.garonzik@villanova.edu. *Application contact:* Meredith L. Kwiatek, Assistant Director, 610-519-7016, Fax: 610-519-6273, E-mail: meredith.kwiatek@villanova.edu.

Villanova University, Villanova School of Business, MBA—The Flex Track Program, Villanova, PA 19085. Offers finance (MBA); health care management (MBA); international business (MBA); management information systems (MBA); marketing (MBA); real estate (MBA); strategic management (MBA); JD/MBA. *Accreditation:* AACSB. Part-time and evening/weekend programs available. Postbaccalaureate distance learning degree programs offered (minimal on-campus study). *Faculty:* 31 full-time (5 women), 22 part-time/adjunct (2 women). *Students:* 15 full-time (6 women), 443 part-time (150 women); includes 46 minority (5 Black or African American, non-Hispanic/Latino; 35 Asian, non-Hispanic/Latino; 6 Hispanic/Latino). Average age 30. In 2010, 133 master's awarded. *Degree requirements:* For master's, minimum GPA of 3.0. *Entrance requirements:* For master's, GMAT. Additional exam requirements/recommendations for international students: Required—TOEFL (minimum score 550 paper-based; 213 computer-based; 80 iBT). *Application deadline:* For fall admission, 6/30 for domestic and international students; for winter admission, 11/15 for domestic and international students; for spring admission, 3/30 for domestic students, 3/31 for international students. Applications are processed on a rolling basis. Application fee: $50. Electronic applications accepted. *Expenses:* Tuition: Part-time $700 per credit. Part-time tuition and fees vary according to degree level and program. *Financial support:* In 2010–11, 15 research assistantships with full tuition reimbursements (averaging $13,100 per year) were awarded; scholarships/grants and unspecified assistantships also available. Support available to part-time students. Financial award application deadline: 6/30; financial award applicants required to submit FAFSA. *Faculty research:* Developing and leveraging technology, ethical business practices, managing for innovation and creativity, the global political economy, strategic marketing management. *Unit head:* Meredith L. Kwiatek, Director of Graduate Recruitment and Marketing, 610-519-7016, Fax: 610-519-6273, E-mail: meredith.kwiatek@villanova.edu. *Application contact:* Meredith L. Kwiatek, Assistant Director, 610-519-7016, Fax: 610-519-6273, E-mail: meredith.kwiatek@villanova.edu.

Virginia Commonwealth University, Graduate School, School of Business, Program in Finance, Insurance, and Real Estate, Richmond, VA 23284-9005. Offers MS. *Faculty:* 11 full-time (0 women). *Entrance requirements:* For master's, GMAT (GRE for Finance). Additional exam requirements/recommendations for international students: Required—TOEFL (minimum score 600 paper-based; 250 computer-based; 100 iBT); Recommended—IELTS (minimum score 6.5). *Application deadline:* For fall admission, 6/1 for domestic students; for spring admission, 11/1 for domestic students. Applications are processed on a rolling basis. Application fee: $50. Electronic applications accepted. *Expenses:* Tuition, state resident: full-time $4308; part-time $479 per credit hour. Tuition, nonresident: full-time $8942; part-time $994 per credit hour. Required fees: $2000; $85 per credit hour. Tuition and fees vary according to course level, course load, degree level, campus/location and program. *Financial support:* Fellowships, research assistantships,

teaching assistantships, Federal Work-Study, institutionally sponsored loans, and tuition waivers (full and partial) available. Financial award application deadline: 3/15; financial award applicants required to submit FAFSA. *Unit head:* Ed Grier, Dean, 804-828-1595, Fax: 804-828-7174, E-mail: busdean@vcu.edu. *Application contact:* Jana P. McQuaid, Assistant Dean, Masters Programs, 804-828-4622, Fax: 804-828-7174, E-mail: jpmcquaid@vcu.edu.

Virginia Polytechnic Institute and State University, Graduate School, Pamplin College of Business, Department of Finance, Blacksburg, VA 24061. Offers MS, PhD. *Faculty:* 24 full-time (1 woman). *Students:* 9 full-time (3 women), 1 part-time (0 women), all international. Average age 31. 61 applicants, 3% accepted, 2 enrolled. *Degree requirements:* For master's, comprehensive exam (for some programs), thesis (for some programs); for doctorate, comprehensive exam (for some programs), thesis/dissertation (for some programs). *Entrance requirements:* For master's and doctorate, GRE. Additional exam requirements/recommendations for international students: Required—TOEFL (minimum score 550 paper-based; 213 computer-based). *Application deadline:* For fall admission, 7/1 for domestic and international students; for spring admission, 12/1 for domestic and international students. Applications are processed on a rolling basis. Application fee: $65. Electronic applications accepted. *Expenses:* Tuition, state resident: full-time $9399; part-time $488 per credit hour. Tuition, nonresident: full-time $17,854; part-time $957.75 per credit hour. Required fees: $1534. Full-time tuition and fees vary according to program. *Financial support:* In 2010–11, 7 teaching assistantships with full tuition reimbursements (averaging $14,068 per year) were awarded; career-related internships or fieldwork, Federal Work-Study, scholarships/grants, health care benefits, and unspecified assistantships also available. Financial award application deadline: 1/15. *Faculty research:* Capital markets, corporate finance, investment banking, derivatives, international finance. Total annual research expenditures: $45,571. *Unit head:* Dr. Raman Kumar, UNIT HEAD, 540-231-5700, Fax: 540-231-4487, E-mail: rkumar@vt.edu. *Application contact:* Dilip Shome, Contact, 540-231-3607, Fax: 540-231-4487, E-mail: dilip@vt.edu.

Wagner College, Division of Graduate Studies, Department of Business Administration, Program in Finance, Staten Island, NY 10301-4495. Offers MBA. Part-time and evening/weekend programs available. *Faculty:* 4 full-time (3 women), 2 part-time/adjunct (1 woman). *Students:* 21 full-time (3 women), 10 part-time (3 women); includes 3 minority (1 Hispanic/Latino; 2 Two or more races, non-Hispanic/Latino), 1 international. Average age 24. 18 applicants, 100% accepted, 17 enrolled. In 2010, 5 master's awarded. *Degree requirements:* For master's, thesis optional. *Entrance requirements:* For master's, GMAT, minimum GPA of 2.6, computer and math proficiency. Additional exam requirements/recommendations for international students: Required—TOEFL (minimum score 550 paper-based; 217 computer-based; 79 iBT). *Application deadline:* For fall admission, 4/1 priority date for domestic students, 3/1 priority date for international students; for spring admission, 12/1 priority date for domestic students, 10/1 priority date for international students. Applications are processed on a rolling basis. Application fee: $50 ($85 for international students). *Expenses:* Tuition: Full-time $15,570; part-time $865 per credit. *Financial support:* Career-related internships or fieldwork, unspecified assistantships, and alumni fellowship grant available. Financial award applicants required to submit FAFSA. *Unit head:* Dr. Donald Crooks, 718-390-3942, Fax: 718-420-4274. *Application contact:* Patricia Clancy, Administrative Assistant, Admissions, 718-420-4464, Fax: 718-390-3105, E-mail: patricia.clancy@wagner.edu.

Wake Forest University, Schools of Business, Full-time MBA Program, Winston-Salem, NC 27106. Offers consulting/general management (MBA); entrepreneurship (MBA); finance (MBA); health (MBA); marketing (MBA); operations management (MBA); JD/MBA; MD/MBA; MSA/MBA. *Accreditation:* AACSB. *Faculty:* 63 full-time (17 women), 30 part-time/adjunct (9 women). *Students:* 123 full-time (22 women); includes 9 Black or African American, non-Hispanic/Latino; 4 Asian, non-Hispanic/Latino; 2 Hispanic/Latino; 1 Two or more races, non-Hispanic/Latino, 25 international. Average age 28. In 2010, 83 master's awarded. *Degree requirements:* For master's, 65.5 total credit hours. *Entrance requirements:* For master's, GMAT or GRE, letters of recommendation, official transcripts, current resume or curriculum vitae, 2 years of work experience. Additional exam requirements/recommendations for international students: Required—TOEFL (minimum score 600 paper-based; 250 computer-based; 100 iBT), Pearson Test of English (PTE). *Application deadline:* For fall admission, 4/15 for domestic and international students. Applications are processed on a rolling basis. Application fee: $100. Electronic applications accepted. *Expenses:* Contact institution. *Financial support:* In 2010–11, 76 students received support. Career-related internships or fieldwork, scholarships/grants, and unspecified assistantships available. Financial award application deadline: 2/15; financial award applicants required to submit FAFSA. *Faculty research:* The influence of personal relationships on business decision making and management of change; drivers of perceived value and consumer behavior; impact of accounting on auditing, financial, managerial, systems and taxation stakeholders; corporate governance and executive compensation; impact of operations strategies on competitiveness. *Unit head:* Sherry Moss, Director, 336-758-5422, Fax: 336-758-5830, E-mail: admissions@mba.wfu.edu. *Application contact:* Tamara

Paquee, Administrative Assistant, 336-758-5422, Fax: 336-758-5830, E-mail: admissions@mba.wfu.edu.

Walden University, Graduate Programs, School of Management, Minneapolis, MN 55401. Offers accounting (MS), including cpa emphasis, professional track, self-designed; accounting and management (MS), including self-designed, strategic management; applied management and decision sciences (PhD), including accounting, engineering management, finance, general applied management and decision sciences, information systems management, knowledge management, leadership and organizational change, learning management, operations research, self-designed program in applied management and design sciences; business information management (MISM); enterprise information security (MISM); entrepreneurship (MBA, DBA); finance (MBA, DBA); global management (MS); global supply chain management (DBA); health informatics (MISM); healthcare management (MBA, MS); healthcare system improvement (MBA); human resource management (MBA, MS), including functional human resource management (MS), human resource management (MS), integrating functional and strategic human resource management (MS), organizational strategy (MS); information systems (MS); information systems management (DBA); information technology (MS), including information security, software engineering; international business (MBA, DBA); IT strategy and governance (MISM); leadership (MBA, MS, DBA), including entrepreneurship (MS), general management (MS), human resources leadership (MS), innovation and technology (MS), leader development (MS), leading sustainability (MS), project management (MS), self-designed (MS); managers as leaders (MS); managing global software and service supply chains (MISM); marketing (MBA, DBA); project management (MBA, MS); research strategies (MS); risk management (MBA); self-designed (MBA, DBA); social impact management (DBA); strategy and operations (MS); sustainable futures (MBA); sustainable management (MS); technology (MBA); technology entrepreneurship (DBA); technology management (MS). Part-time and evening/weekend programs available. Postbaccalaureate distance learning degree programs offered (minimal on-campus study). *Faculty:* 22 full-time (8 women), 291 part-time/adjunct (100 women). *Students:* 3,705 full-time (1,956 women), 976 part-time (549 women); includes 2,432 minority (2,021 Black or African American, non-Hispanic/Latino; 32 American Indian or Alaska Native, non-Hispanic/Latino; 137 Asian, non-Hispanic/Latino; 193 Hispanic/Latino; 5 Native Hawaiian or other Pacific Islander, non-Hispanic/Latino; 44 Two or more races, non-Hispanic/Latino), 302 international. Average age 40. In 2010, 658 master's, 86 doctorates awarded. *Degree requirements:* For doctorate, thesis/dissertation (for some programs), residency. *Entrance requirements:* For master's, bachelor's degree or equivalent in related field; minimum GPA of 2.5; official transcripts; goal statement; access to computer and Internet; for doctorate, master's degree or equivalent in related field; minimum GPA of 3.0; 3 years of related professional/academic experience (preferred). Additional exam requirements/recommendations for international students: Required—TOEFL (minimum score 550 paper-based; 213 computer-based), IELTS (minimum score 6.5), Michigan English Language Assessment Battery (minimum score 82). *Application deadline:* Applications are processed on a rolling basis. Application fee: $50. Electronic applications accepted. *Expenses:* Tuition: Full-time $10,274; part-time $445 per credit. Tuition and fees vary according to course load, degree level and program. *Financial support:* Fellowships, Federal Work-Study, scholarships/grants, unspecified assistantships, and family tuition reduction, active duty/veteran tuition reduction, group tuition reduction, interest-free payment plans available. Support available to part-time students. Financial award applicants required to submit FAFSA. *Unit head:* Dr. William Schulz, Associate Dean, 800-925-3368. *Application contact:* Jennifer Hall, Vice President of Enrollment Management, 866-4-WALDEN, E-mail: info@waldenu.edu.

Washington State University, Graduate School, College of Business, Business Administration Programs, Pullman, WA 99164. Offers business administration (MBA, PhD), including accounting (PhD), finance (PhD), management and operations (PhD), management information systems (PhD), marketing (PhD). *Accreditation:* AACSB. *Faculty:* 47. *Students:* 117 full-time (42 women), 117 part-time (30 women); includes 24 minority (1 Black or African American, non-Hispanic/Latino; 17 Asian, non-Hispanic/Latino; 5 Hispanic/Latino; 1 Two or more races, non-Hispanic/Latino), 48 international. Average age 32. 347 applicants, 19% accepted, 43 enrolled. In 2010, 58 master's, 5 doctorates awarded. *Degree requirements:* For master's, comprehensive exam (for some programs), thesis (for some programs), final presentation; for doctorate, comprehensive exam, thesis/dissertation, oral and written exams. *Entrance requirements:* For master's and doctorate, GMAT, minimum GPA of 3.0, 3 letters of recommendation. Additional exam requirements/recommendations for international students: Required—TOEFL. *Application deadline:* For fall admission, 3/1 priority date for domestic students, 3/1 for international students; for spring admission, 6/1 priority date for domestic students, 6/1 for international students. Applications are processed on a rolling basis. Application fee: $50. Electronic applications accepted. *Expenses:* Tuition, state resident: full-time $8552; part-time $443 per credit. Tuition, nonresident: full-time $21,650; part-time $1083 per credit. Required fees: $846. *Financial support:* In 2010–11, 102 students received support, including 36 teaching assistantships with full and partial tuition reimbursements available (averaging $18,204 per year); career-related internships or fieldwork, Federal Work-Study, institutionally sponsored loans, health care

benefits, tuition waivers (partial), unspecified assistantships, and teaching associateships also available. Financial award application deadline: 4/1. Total annual research expenditures: $344,000. *Unit head:* Dr. Eric Spangenberg, Dean, 509-335-8150, E-mail: ers@wsu.edu. *Application contact:* Graduate School Admissions, 800-GRADWSU, Fax: 509-335-1949, E-mail: gradsch@wsu.edu.

Washington University in St. Louis, Olin Business School, Program in Finance, St. Louis, MO 63130-4899. Offers MS. Part-time programs available. *Faculty:* 79 full-time (17 women), 42 part-time/adjunct (7 women). *Students:* 85 full-time (43 women), 4 part-time (1 woman); includes 12 minority (11 Asian, non-Hispanic/Latino; 1 Two or more races, non-Hispanic/Latino), 65 international. Average age 24. 937 applicants, 11% accepted, 62 enrolled. In 2010, 33 master's awarded. *Entrance requirements:* For master's, GMAT or GRE. Additional exam requirements/recommendations for international students: Required—TOEFL. *Application deadline:* For fall admission, 11/15 for domestic and international students; for winter admission, 2/15 for domestic students, 2/14 for international students; for spring admission, 3/21 for domestic students. Application fee: $100. Electronic applications accepted. *Expenses:* Contact institution. *Financial support:* Applicants required to submit FAFSA. *Unit head:* Joseph Peter Fox, Associate Dean and Director of MBA Programs, 314-935-6322, Fax: 314-935-4464, E-mail: fox@wustl.edu. *Application contact:* Dr. Gary Hochberg, Director, Specialized Master's Programs, 314-935-6380, Fax: 314-935-4464, E-mail: hochberg@wustl.edu.

Wilfrid Laurier University, Faculty of Graduate and Postdoctoral Studies, School of Business and Economics, Department of Business, Waterloo, ON N2L 3C5, Canada. Offers accounting (PhD); finance (M Fin); financial economics (PhD); marketing (PhD); operations and supply chain management (PhD); organizational behavior and human resource management (M Sc); organizational behaviour and human resource management (PhD); supply chain management (M Sc); technology management (EMTM). Part-time and evening/weekend programs available. *Faculty:* 67 full-time (20 women), 12 part-time/adjunct (4 women). *Students:* 20 full-time (11 women), 1 part-time (0 women), 5 international. 80 applicants, 28% accepted, 3 enrolled. In 2010, 6 master's, 1 doctorate awarded. *Degree requirements:* For master's, thesis optional; for doctorate, comprehensive exam, thesis/dissertation. *Entrance requirements:* For master's, GMAT, 4-year honors degree with minimum B+ average; for doctorate, GMAT, master's degree, minimum B+ average. Additional exam requirements/recommendations for international students: Required—TOEFL (minimum score 89 iBT). *Application deadline:* For fall admission, 1/15 priority date for domestic and international students. Application fee: $125. Electronic applications accepted. Tuition and fees charges are reported in Canadian dollars. *Expenses:* Tuition, area resident: Full-time $15,300 Canadian dollars; part-time $1200 Canadian dollars per credit. International tuition: $21,300 Canadian dollars full-time. Required fees: $650 Canadian dollars; $100 Canadian dollars per credit. Tuition and fees vary according to course load, degree level, campus/location and program. *Financial support:* In 2010–11, 27 fellowships, 1 research assistantship, 27 teaching assistantships were awarded; career-related internships or fieldwork, scholarships/grants, health care benefits, and unspecified assistantships also available. *Faculty research:* Financial economics, management and organizational behavior, operations and supply chain management. *Unit head:* Dr. Hamid Noori, Director, 519-884-0710 Ext. 2571, Fax: 519-884-2357, E-mail: sbephdmasters@wlu.ca. *Application contact:* Jennifer Williams, Graduate Admission and Records Officer, 519-884-0710 Ext. 3536, Fax: 519-884-1020, E-mail: gradstudies@wlu.ca.

Wilkes University, College of Graduate and Professional Studies, Jay S. Sidhu School of Business and Leadership, Wilkes-Barre, PA 18766-0002. Offers accounting (MBA); entrepreneurship (MBA); finance (MBA); health care administration (MBA); human resource management (MBA); international business (MBA); marketing (MBA); operations management (MBA); organizational leadership and development (MBA). *Accreditation:* ACBSP. Part-time and evening/weekend programs available. *Students:* 39 full-time (16 women), 146 part-time (71 women); includes 5 Black or African American, non-Hispanic/Latino; 2 Asian, non-Hispanic/Latino; 1 Hispanic/Latino; 1 Two or more races, non-Hispanic/Latino, 16 international. Average age 30. In 2010, 85 master's awarded. *Entrance requirements:* For master's, GMAT. Additional exam requirements/recommendations for international students: Required—TOEFL (minimum score 550 paper-based; 213 computer-based; 79 iBT). *Application deadline:* Applications are processed on a rolling basis. Application fee: $45 ($65 for international students). Electronic applications accepted. *Expenses:* Contact institution. *Financial support:* Federal Work-Study and unspecified assistantships available. Financial award application deadline: 3/1; financial award applicants required to submit FAFSA. *Unit head:* Dr. Paul Browne, Dean, 570-408-4701, Fax: 570-408-7846, E-mail: paul.browne@wilkes.edu. *Application contact:* Kathleen Houlihan, Director of Graduate Studies, 570-408-3235, Fax: 570-408-7846, E-mail: kathleen.houlihan@wilkes.edu.

Xavier University, Williams College of Business, Master of Business Administration Program, Cincinnati, OH 45207-3221. Offers business administration (Exec MBA, MBA); business intelligence (MBA); finance (MBA); international business (MBA); management information systems (MBA); marketing (MBA); MBA/MHSA; MSN/MBA. *Accreditation:* AACSB.

Part-time and evening/weekend programs available. *Faculty:* 37 full-time (13 women), 9 part-time/adjunct (2 women). *Students:* 200 full-time (60 women), 735 part-time (239 women); includes 128 minority (48 Black or African American, non-Hispanic/Latino; 3 American Indian or Alaska Native, non-Hispanic/Latino; 54 Asian, non-Hispanic/Latino; 22 Hispanic/Latino; 1 Native Hawaiian or other Pacific Islander, non-Hispanic/Latino; 32 international. Average age 30. 223 applicants, 85% accepted, 139 enrolled. In 2010, 323 master's awarded. *Degree requirements:* For master's, capstone course. *Entrance requirements:* For master's, GMAT. Additional exam requirements/recommendations for international students: Required—TOEFL (minimum score 550 paper-based; 213 computer-based; 80 iBT). *Application deadline:* For fall admission, 8/1 priority date for domestic students, 5/1 for international students; for spring admission, 12/1 priority date for domestic students, 9/1 for international students. Applications are processed on a rolling basis. Application fee: $35. Electronic applications accepted. *Expenses:* Contact institution. *Financial support:* In 2010–11, 176 students received support. Scholarships/grants, tuition waivers (partial), and unspecified assistantships available. Financial award application deadline: 3/1; financial award applicants required to submit FAFSA. *Unit head:* Dr. Hema Krishnan, Associate Dean, 513-745-3206, Fax: 513-745-3455, E-mail: krishnan@xavier.edu. *Application contact:* Anna Marie Whelan, Assistant Director, MBA Programs, 513-745-3525, Fax: 513-745-2929, E-mail: whelana@xavier.edu.

Yale University, Yale School of Management and Graduate School of Arts and Sciences, Doctoral Program in Management, New Haven, CT 06520. Offers accounting (PhD); financial economics (PhD); marketing (PhD); organizations and management (PhD). *Accreditation:* AACSB. *Faculty:* 68 full-time (12 women), 1 (woman) part-time/adjunct. *Students:* 32 full-time (9 women); includes 3 Asian, non-Hispanic/Latino, 16 international. Average age 28. 441 applicants, 4% accepted, 6 enrolled. In 2010, 9 doctorates awarded. *Degree requirements:* For doctorate, comprehensive exam, thesis/dissertation. *Entrance requirements:* For doctorate, GMAT or GRE General Test. Additional exam requirements/recommendations for international students: Required—TOEFL, IELTS. *Application deadline:* For fall admission, 1/2 for domestic and international students. Application fee: $100. Electronic applications accepted. *Expenses:* Contact institution. *Financial support:* In 2010–11, 30 students received support, including 30 fellowships with full tuition reimbursements available, 30 research assistantships with full tuition reimbursements available, 30 teaching assistantships with full tuition reimbursements available; institutionally sponsored loans, scholarships/grants, and health care benefits also available. Financial award application deadline: 1/2. *Faculty research:* Pricing of options and futures, term structure of interest rates, use of accounting numbers in debt contracts, product differentiation, e-commerce and marketing, behavioral finance. *Unit head:* Carla Mills, Registrar, 203-432-3955, Fax: 203-432-0342, E-mail: carla.mills@yale.edu. *Application contact:* Carla Mills, Registrar, 203-432-3955, Fax: 203-432-0342, E-mail: carla.mills@yale.edu.

York College of Pennsylvania, Department of Business Administration, York, PA 17405-7199. Offers accounting (MBA); continuous improvement (MBA); finance (MBA); management (MBA); marketing (MBA). *Accreditation:* ACBSP. Part-time and evening/weekend programs available. *Faculty:* 11 full-time (2 women), 5 part-time/adjunct (1 woman). *Students:* 20 full-time (6 women), 111 part-time (44 women); includes 4 Black or African American, non-Hispanic/Latino; 1 Asian, non-Hispanic/Latino; 4 Hispanic/Latino, 2 international. Average age 30. 53 applicants, 91% accepted, 40 enrolled. In 2010, 45 master's awarded. *Entrance requirements:* For master's, GMAT. Additional exam requirements/recommendations for international students: Required—TOEFL (minimum score 530 paper-based; 200 computer-based; 72 iBT). *Application deadline:* For fall admission, 7/15 priority date for domestic students; for spring admission, 12/15 priority date for domestic students. Applications are processed on a rolling basis. Application fee: $60. Electronic applications accepted. *Expenses:* Tuition: Full-time $11,520; part-time $640 per credit hour. Required fees: $1500; $660 per year. *Financial support:* Scholarships/grants available. Financial award application deadline: 4/15; financial award applicants required to submit FAFSA. *Unit head:* Dr. David Greisler, MBA Director, 717-815-6410, Fax: 717-600-3999, E-mail: dgreisle@ycp.edu. *Application contact:* Brenda Adams, Assistant Director, MBA Program, 717-815-1749, Fax: 717-600-3999, E-mail: badams@ycp.edu.

INVESTMENT MANAGEMENT

Boston University, School of Management, Boston, MA 02215. Offers business administration (MBA); executive business administration (EMBA); investment management (MS); management (PhD); mathematical finance (MS, PhD); JD/MBA; MBA/MA; MBA/MPH; MBA/MS; MBA/MSIS; MD/MBA; MS/MBA. *Accreditation:* AACSB. Part-time and evening/weekend programs available. *Faculty:* 185 full-time (49 women), 60 part-time/adjunct (15 women). *Students:* 525 full-time (206 women), 743 part-time (272 women); includes 14 Black or African American, non-Hispanic/Latino; 134 Asian, non-Hispanic/Latino; 19 Hispanic/Latino, 247 international. Average age 30. 1,387 applicants, 28% accepted, 160 enrolled. In 2010, 532 master's, 5 doctorates awarded. *Degree requirements:* For doctorate, comprehensive

exam, thesis/dissertation. *Entrance requirements:* For master's, GMAT (for MBA and MS in investment management); GMAT or GRE General Test (for MS in mathematical finance), resume, 2 letters of recommendation; for doctorate, GMAT or GRE General Test, resume, personal statement, 3 letters of recommendation, 3 essays, official transcripts. *Application deadline:* For fall admission, 1/5 for domestic and international students; for spring admission, 11/1 for domestic students. Application fee: $125. Electronic applications accepted. *Expenses:* Tuition: Full-time $39,314; part-time $1228 per credit. Required fees: $40 per semester. *Financial support:* Career-related internships or fieldwork, Federal Work-Study, institutionally sponsored loans, scholarships/grants, and tuition waivers (partial) available. Financial award applicants required to submit FAFSA. *Faculty research:* Innovation policy and productivity, corporate social responsibility, risk management, information systems, entrepreneurship, clean energy, sustainability. *Unit head:* Kenneth W. Freeman, Allen Questrom Professor and Dean, 617-353-9720, Fax: 617-353-5581, E-mail: kfreeman@bu.edu. *Application contact:* Patti Cudney, Assistant Dean, Graduate Admissions, 617-353-2670, Fax: 617-353-7368, E-mail: mba@bu.edu.

Gannon University, School of Graduate Studies, College of Engineering and Business, School of Business, Program in Investments, Erie, PA 16541-0001. Offers Certificate. Part-time and evening/weekend programs available. In 2010, 1 Certificate awarded. *Entrance requirements:* For degree, GMAT. Additional exam requirements/recommendations for international students: Required—TOEFL (minimum score 79 iBT). *Application deadline:* Applications are processed on a rolling basis. Application fee: $25. Electronic applications accepted. *Expenses:* Tuition: Full-time $14,670; part-time $815 per credit. Required fees: $430; $18 per credit. Tuition and fees vary according to class time, course load, degree level, campus/location and program. *Financial support:* Application deadline: 7/1. *Unit head:* Dr. Duane Prokop, Director, 814-871-7576, E-mail: prokop001@gannon.edu. *Application contact:* Kara Morgan, Assistant Director of Graduate Admissions, 814-871-5831, Fax: 814-871-5827, E-mail: graduate@gannon.edu.

The George Washington University, School of Business, Department of Finance, Washington, DC 20052. Offers finance (MSF, PhD); finance and investments (MBA); real estate and urban development (MBA). Part-time and evening/weekend programs available. *Faculty:* 17 full-time (4 women), 9 part-time/adjunct (2 women). *Students:* 71 full-time (27 women), 42 part-time (15 women); includes 7 Black or African American, non-Hispanic/Latino; 8 Asian, non-Hispanic/Latino; 5 Hispanic/Latino; 1 Two or more races, non-Hispanic/Latino, 64 international. Average age 30. 602 applicants, 23% accepted, 65 enrolled. In 2010, 52 master's awarded. *Degree requirements:* For doctorate, thesis/dissertation. *Entrance requirements:* For master's, GMAT; for doctorate, GMAT or GRE. Additional exam requirements/recommendations for international students: Required—TOEFL. *Application deadline:* For fall admission, 4/1 priority date for domestic students; for spring admission, 10/1 for domestic students. Applications are processed on a rolling basis. Application fee: $75. *Financial support:* In 2010–11, 38 students received support; fellowships, teaching assistantships, career-related internships or fieldwork, Federal Work-Study, and institutionally sponsored loans available. Financial award application deadline: 4/1. *Unit head:* Mark S. Klock, Chair, 202-994-5996, E-mail: klock@gwu.edu. *Application contact:* Kristin Williams, Asst VP Gradpec Enrlmnt Mgmt, 202-994-0467, Fax: 202-994-0371, E-mail: ksw@gwu.edu.

Hofstra University, Frank G. Zarb School of Business, Department of Finance, Hempstead, NY 11549. Offers banking (Advanced Certificate); business administration (MBA), including finance, real estate management; corporate finance (Advanced Certificate); finance (MS); investment management (Advanced Certificate); quantitative finance (MS). Part-time and evening/weekend programs available. Postbaccalaureate distance learning degree programs offered (minimal on-campus study). *Faculty:* 12 full-time (2 women), 2 part-time/adjunct (1 woman). *Students:* 180 full-time (68 women), 99 part-time (26 women); includes 24 minority (6 Black or African American, non-Hispanic/Latino; 10 Asian, non-Hispanic/Latino; 8 Hispanic/Latino), 13 international. Average age 27. 329 applicants, 73% accepted, 102 enrolled. In 2010, 76 master's awarded. *Degree requirements:* For master's, capstone course (for MBA); thesis (for MS). *Entrance requirements:* For master's, GMAT/GRE, 2 letters of recommendation; resume; essay. Additional exam requirements/recommendations for international students: Required—TOEFL (minimum score 550 paper-based; 213 computer-based; 80 iBT); Recommended—IELTS (minimum score 6). *Application deadline:* Applications are processed on a rolling basis. Application fee: $70 ($75 for international students). Electronic applications accepted. *Expenses:* Contact institution. *Financial support:* In 2010–11, 41 students received support, including 38 fellowships with full and partial tuition reimbursements available (averaging $10,353 per year), 1 research assistantship with full and partial tuition reimbursement available (averaging $9,375 per year); Federal Work-Study, institutionally sponsored loans, scholarships/grants, and tuition waivers (full and partial) also available. Support available to part-time students. Financial award applicants required to submit FAFSA. *Faculty research:* International finance, investments, banking, real estate, derivatives. *Unit head:* Dr. Nancy W. White, Chairperson, 516-463-5699, Fax: 516-463-4834, E-mail: finnwh@hofstra.edu. *Application contact:* Carol Drummer, Dean of Graduate Admissions, 516-463-4876, Fax: 516-463-4664, E-mail: gradstudent@hofstra.edu.

The Johns Hopkins University, Carey Business School, Finance Programs, Baltimore, MD 21218-2699. Offers finance (MS); financial management (Certificate); investments (Certificate). Part-time and evening/weekend programs available. *Faculty:* 29 full-time (6 women), 135 part-time/adjunct (29 women). *Students:* 73 full-time (25 women), 112 part-time (32 women); includes 56 minority (15 Black or African American, non-Hispanic/Latino; 1 American Indian or Alaska Native, non-Hispanic/Latino; 31 Asian, non-Hispanic/Latino; 7 Hispanic/Latino; 1 Native Hawaiian or other Pacific Islander, non-Hispanic/Latino; 1 Two or more races, non-Hispanic/Latino), 65 international. Average age 30. 148 applicants, 72% accepted, 57 enrolled. In 2010, 65 master's, 19 other advanced degrees awarded. *Degree requirements:* For master's, 36 credits including final project. *Entrance requirements:* For master's, GMAT or GRE (recommended), minimum GPA of 3.0, resume, work experience, two letters of recommendation; for Certificate, minimum GPA of 3.0, resume, work experience, two letters of recommendation. Additional exam requirements/recommendations for international students: Required—TOEFL (minimum score 600 paper-based; 250 computer-based; 100 iBT). *Application deadline:* For fall admission, 4/1 for international students; for spring admission, 9/15 for international students. Applications are processed on a rolling basis. Application fee: $100. Electronic applications accepted. *Financial support:* In 2010–11, 9 students received support. Scholarships/grants available. Support available to part-time students. Financial award application deadline: 4/15; financial award applicants required to submit FAFSA. *Faculty research:* Financial econometrics, high frequency data modeling, corporate finance. *Unit head:* Dr. Dipankar Chakravarti, Vice Dean of Programs, 410-234-9311, E-mail: dipankar.chakravarti@jhu.edu. *Application contact:* Robin Greenberg, Admissions Coordinator, 410-234-9227, Fax: 443-529-1554, E-mail: carey.admissions@jhu.edu.

Lincoln University, Graduate Studies, Oakland, CA 94612. Offers finance and investments (DBA); finance management and investment banking (MBA); general business (MBA); human resource management (MBA, DBA); international business (MBA); management information systems (MBA). Part-time and evening/weekend programs available. *Faculty:* 9 full-time (2 women), 11 part-time/adjunct (1 woman). *Students:* 297 full-time (134 women), 2 part-time (0 women). In 2010, 124 master's awarded. *Degree requirements:* For master's, research project (thesis), internship report, or comprehensive exam; for doctorate, comprehensive exam, thesis/dissertation. *Entrance requirements:* For master's, minimum GPA of 2.7; for doctorate, GMAT (minimum score: 550), GRE (minimum score: 1000), or equivalent test results (waived for master's degree with minimum cumulative GPA of 3.3). Additional exam requirements/recommendations for international students: Required—TOEFL (525 paper, 195 computer, 71 iBT) or IELTS (5.5) for MBA; TOEFL (550 paper, 213 computer, 79 iBT) or IELTS (6.0) for DBA; Recommended—IELTS. *Application deadline:* For fall admission, 7/2 priority date for domestic and international students; for spring admission, 11/25 priority date for domestic students, 11/26 priority date for international students. Applications are processed on a rolling basis. Application fee: $75. Electronic applications accepted. *Expenses:* Tuition: Full-time $6930. Required fees: $195 per semester. *Financial support:* In 2010–11, 1 teaching assistantship was awarded; career-related internships or fieldwork and scholarships/grants also available. *Unit head:* Dr. Marshall Burak, Director of Graduate Programs, 510-628-8016, Fax: 510-628-8012, E-mail: mburak@lincolnuca.edu. *Application contact:* Peggy Au, Director of Admissions and Records, 510-628-8010, Fax: 510-628-8012, E-mail: admissions@lincolnuca.edu.

Quinnipiac University, School of Business, MBA—Chartered Financial Analyst Track, Hamden, CT 06518-1940. Offers MBA. *Faculty:* 25 full-time (2 women), 3 part-time/adjunct (all women). *Entrance requirements:* For master's, GMAT or GRE, minimum GPA of 3.0. Additional exam requirements/recommendations for international students: Required—TOEFL (minimum score 575 paper-based; 233 computer-based; 90 iBT). *Application deadline:* For fall admission, 7/30 priority date for domestic students; for spring admission, 12/15 for domestic students. Applications are processed on a rolling basis. Application fee: $45. Electronic applications accepted. *Expenses:* Tuition: Part-time $810 per credit. Required fees: $35 per credit. *Unit head:* Lisa Braiewa, MBA Director, 203-582-3710, Fax: 203-582-8664, E-mail: lisa.braiewa@quinnipiac.edu. *Application contact:* Jennifer Boutin, 800-462-1944, Fax: 203-582-3443, E-mail: jennifer.boutin@quinnipiac.edu.

Quinnipiac University, School of Business, MBA Program, Hamden, CT 06518-1940. Offers chartered financial analyst (MBA); finance (MBA); healthcare management (MBA); information systems management (MBA); marketing (MBA); supply chain management (MBA); JD/MBA. *Accreditation:* AACSB. Part-time and evening/weekend programs available. *Faculty:* 25 full-time (2 women), 3 part-time/adjunct (all women). *Students:* 87 full-time (24 women), 121 part-time (46 women); includes 12 minority (1 Black or African American, non-Hispanic/Latino; 7 Asian, non-Hispanic/Latino; 4 Hispanic/Latino), 14 international. Average age 29. 119 applicants, 81% accepted, 81 enrolled. In 2010, 70 master's awarded. *Entrance requirements:* For master's, GMAT or GRE, minimum GPA of 3.0. Additional exam requirements/recommendations for international students: Required—TOEFL (minimum score 575 paper-based; 233 computer-based; 90 iBT), IELTS (minimum score 6.5). *Application deadline:* For fall admission, 7/30 priority

date for domestic students, 4/30 priority date for international students; for spring admission, 12/15 priority date for domestic students, 9/15 priority date for international students. Applications are processed on a rolling basis. Application fee: $45. Electronic applications accepted. *Expenses:* Tuition: Part-time $810 per credit. Required fees: $35 per credit. *Financial support:* In 2010–11, 110 students received support. Federal Work-Study, tuition waivers (partial), and unspecified assistantships available. Support available to part-time students. Financial award application deadline: 4/15; financial award applicants required to submit FAFSA. *Faculty research:* Equity compensation, marketing relationships and public policy, corporate governance, international business, supply chain management. *Unit head:* Lisa Braiewa, MBA Program Director, 203-582-3710, Fax: 203-582-8664, E-mail: lisa.braiewa@quinnipiac.edu. *Application contact:* Jennifer Boutin, 800-462-1944, Fax: 203-582-3443, E-mail: jennifer.boutin@quinnipiac.edu.

St. John's University, The Peter J. Tobin College of Business, Department of Economics and Finance, Queens, NY 11439. Offers finance (MBA, Adv C); investment management (MS). Part-time and evening/weekend programs available. *Students:* 113 full-time (41 women), 66 part-time (27 women); includes 34 minority (10 Black or African American, non-Hispanic/Latino; 13 Asian, non-Hispanic/Latino; 9 Hispanic/Latino; 2 Two or more races, non-Hispanic/Latino), 68 international. Average age 27. 144 applicants, 67% accepted, 50 enrolled. In 2010, 81 master's awarded. *Degree requirements:* For master's, comprehensive exam (for some programs), thesis optional. *Entrance requirements:* For master's, GMAT, 2 letters of recommendation, resume, transcripts, essay; for Adv C, GMAT, 2 letters of recommendation, resume, undergraduate transcripts, essay. Additional exam requirements/recommendations for international students: Required—TOEFL (minimum score 600 paper-based; 250 computer-based; 100 iBT), IELTS (minimum score 5.5). *Application deadline:* For fall admission, 5/1 priority date for domestic and international students; for spring admission, 11/1 priority date for domestic and international students. Applications are processed on a rolling basis. Application fee: $70. Electronic applications accepted. *Expenses:* Contact institution. *Financial support:* Research assistantships, scholarships/grants available. Support available to part-time students. Financial award application deadline: 3/1; financial award applicants required to submit FAFSA. *Faculty research:* Exchange rate exposure, corporate default likelihood, credit derivatives, information production, emerging markets. *Unit head:* Dr. Vipul K. Bansal, Chair, 718-990-2113, E-mail: bansalv@stjohns.edu. *Application contact:* Carol Swanberg, Assistant Dean, Director of Graduate Admissions, 718-990-1345, Fax: 718-990-5242, E-mail: tobingradnyc@stjohns.edu.

The University of Iowa, Henry B. Tippie College of Business, Henry B. Tippie School of Management, Iowa City, IA 52242-1316. Offers corporate finance (MBA); investment management (MBA); marketing (MBA); process and operations excellence (MBA); strategic management and innovation (MBA); JD/MBA; MBA/MA; MBA/MD; MBA/MHA; MBA/MSN. *Accreditation:* AACSB. Part-time and evening/weekend programs available. *Faculty:* 110 full-time (25 women), 19 part-time/adjunct (1 woman). *Students:* 242 full-time (46 women), 809 part-time (277 women); includes 95 minority (15 Black or African American, non-Hispanic/Latino; 3 American Indian or Alaska Native, non-Hispanic/Latino; 56 Asian, non-Hispanic/Latino; 21 Hispanic/Latino), 132 international. Average age 31. 652 applicants, 66% accepted, 380 enrolled. In 2010, 333 master's awarded. *Degree requirements:* For master's, minimum GPA of 2.75. *Entrance requirements:* For master's, GMAT, quality work experience and leadership as shown through resume, references, and essays. Additional exam requirements/recommendations for international students: Required—TOEFL (minimum score 600 paper-based; 250 computer-based; 100 iBT), IELTS (minimum score 7). *Application deadline:* For fall admission, 7/30 for domestic students, 4/15 for international students; for spring admission, 12/15 for domestic and international students. Applications are processed on a rolling basis. Application fee: $60 ($100 for international students). Electronic applications accepted. *Expenses:* Contact institution. *Financial support:* In 2010–11, 111 students received support, including 121 fellowships (averaging $8,285 per year), 87 research assistantships with partial tuition reimbursements available (averaging $8,288 per year), 25 teaching assistantships with partial tuition reimbursements available (averaging $11,326 per year); career-related internships or fieldwork, scholarships/grants, health care benefits, and unspecified assistantships also available. Financial award application deadline: 4/15; financial award applicants required to submit FAFSA. *Faculty research:* Capital markets, econometrics, optimization, investments and empirical corporate finance, Iowa electronic markets. *Unit head:* Prof. Jarjisu Sa-Aadu, Associate Dean, MBA Programs, 800-622-4692, Fax: 319-335-3604, E-mail: jsa-aadu@uiowa.edu. *Application contact:* Jodi Schafer, Director of Admissions and Financial Aid, 319-335-0864, Fax: 319-335-3604, E-mail: jodi-schafer@uiowa.edu.

University of San Francisco, College of Arts and Sciences, Risk Management Graduate Program, San Francisco, CA 94117-1080. Offers MS. *Expenses:* Tuition: Full-time $20,070; part-time $1115 per credit hour. Tuition and fees vary according to course load, degree level and program. *Unit head:* John Veitch, Director, 415-422-5555, Fax: 415-422-5784. *Application contact:* John Veitch, Director, 415-422-5555, Fax: 415-422-5784.

The University of Texas at Dallas, School of Management, Program in Finance, Richardson, TX 75080. Offers finance (MS); financial analysis (MS);

financial engineering and risk management (MS); investment management (MS). Part-time and evening/weekend programs available. *Faculty:* 14 full-time (3 women), 3 part-time/adjunct (1 woman). *Students:* 229 full-time (105 women), 55 part-time (18 women); includes 36 minority (4 Black or African American, non-Hispanic/Latino; 25 Asian, non-Hispanic/Latino; 7 Hispanic/Latino), 190 international. Average age 26. 447 applicants, 67% accepted, 158 enrolled. In 2010, 39 master's awarded. *Entrance requirements:* For master's, GMAT. Additional exam requirements/recommendations for international students: Required—TOEFL (minimum score 550 paper-based; 215 computer-based). *Application deadline:* For fall admission, 7/15 for domestic students, 5/1 priority date for international students; for spring admission, 11/15 for domestic students, 9/1 priority date for international students. Applications are processed on a rolling basis. Application fee: $50 ($100 for international students). Electronic applications accepted. *Expenses:* Tuition, state resident: full-time $10,248; part-time $569 per credit hour. Tuition, nonresident: full-time $18,544; part-time $1030 per credit hour. Tuition and fees vary according to course load. *Financial support:* In 2010–11, 101 students received support, including 3 teaching assistantships with partial tuition reimbursements available (averaging $10,050 per year); research assistantships with partial tuition reimbursements available, career-related internships or fieldwork, Federal Work-Study, institutionally sponsored loans, scholarships/grants, and unspecified assistantships also available. Support available to part-time students. Financial award application deadline: 4/30; financial award applicants required to submit FAFSA. *Faculty research:* Econometrics, industrial organization, auction theory, file-sharing copyrights and bundling, international financial management, entrepreneurial finance. *Unit head:* Dr. H. Joe Wells, Director, 972-883-4897, E-mail: hjoewells@utdallas.edu. *Application contact:* James Parker, Assistant Director, 972-883-5842, E-mail: jparker@utdallas.edu.

University of Tulsa, Graduate School, Collins College of Business, Program in Finance, Tulsa, OK 74104-3189. Offers corporate finance (MS); investments and portfolio management (MS); risk management (MS); JD/MSF; MBA/MSF; MSF/MSAM. Part-time and evening/weekend programs available. *Faculty:* 10 full-time (1 woman). *Students:* 21 full-time (10 women), 4 part-time (2 women), 12 international. Average age 25. 87 applicants, 51% accepted, 11 enrolled. In 2010, 16 master's awarded. *Degree requirements:* For master's, thesis optional. *Entrance requirements:* For master's, GMAT. Additional exam requirements/recommendations for international students: Required—TOEFL (minimum score 575 paper-based; 231 computer-based), IELTS (minimum score 6.5). *Application deadline:* Applications are processed on a rolling basis. Application fee: $40. Electronic applications accepted. *Expenses:* Tuition: Full-time $16,902; part-time $939 per credit hour. Required fees: $1020; $4 per credit hour. Tuition and fees vary according to course load. *Financial support:* In 2010–11, 9 students received support, including 2 fellowships with full and partial tuition reimbursements available (averaging $8,750 per year), 2 research assistantships with full and partial tuition reimbursements available (averaging $9,286 per year), 5 teaching assistantships with full and partial tuition reimbursements available (averaging $8,815 per year); career-related internships or fieldwork, Federal Work-Study, institutionally sponsored loans, scholarships/grants, health care benefits, tuition waivers (full and partial), and unspecified assistantships also available. Support available to part-time students. Financial award application deadline: 2/1; financial award applicants required to submit FAFSA. *Unit head:* Dr. Linda Nichols, Associate Dean, 918-631-2242, Fax: 918-631-2142, E-mail: linda-nichols@utulsa.edu. *Application contact:* Dr. Linda Nichols, Associate Dean, 918-631-2242, Fax: 918-631-2142, E-mail: linda-nichols@utulsa.edu.

University of Wisconsin–Madison, Graduate School, Wisconsin School of Business, Doctoral Program in Finance, Investment and Banking, Madison, WI 53706-1380. Offers PhD. *Faculty:* 14 full-time (1 woman), 4 part-time/adjunct (1 woman). *Students:* 10 full-time (2 women), 9 international. Average age 30. 95 applicants, 3% accepted, 1 enrolled. In 2010, 1 doctorate awarded. *Degree requirements:* For doctorate, comprehensive exam, thesis/dissertation. *Entrance requirements:* For doctorate, GMAT or GRE. Additional exam requirements/recommendations for international students: Required—Pearson Test of English (minimum score 73, written 80); Recommended—TOEFL (minimum score 623 paper-based; 263 computer-based; 106 iBT), IELTS (minimum score 7.5). *Application deadline:* For fall admission, 12/15 priority date for domestic and international students. Application fee: $56. Electronic applications accepted. *Expenses:* Tuition, state resident: full-time $9887; part-time $617.96 per credit. Tuition, nonresident: full-time $24,054; part-time $1503.40 per credit. Required fees: $67.63 per credit. Tuition and fees vary according to reciprocity agreements. *Financial support:* In 2010–11, 10 students received support, including 1 fellowship with full tuition reimbursement available (averaging $18,756 per year), research assistantships with full tuition reimbursements available (averaging $16,506 per year), 9 teaching assistantships with full tuition reimbursements available (averaging $14,088 per year); Federal Work-Study, institutionally sponsored loans, scholarships/grants, health care benefits, and unspecified assistantships also available. Financial award application deadline: 2/1; financial award applicants required to submit FAFSA. *Faculty research:* Banking and financial institutions, business cycles, investments, derivatives, corporate finance. *Unit head:* Prof. Robert Krainer, Chair, 608-263-1253, Fax: 608-265-4195, E-mail: rkrainer@bus.wisc.

edu. *Application contact:* Belle Heberling, Assistant Director for Research Programs, 608-262-3749, Fax: 608-890-0180, E-mail: phd@bus.wisc.edu.

University of Wisconsin–Milwaukee, Graduate School, Sheldon B. Lubar School of Business, Milwaukee, WI 53201. Offers business administration (MBA); enterprise resource planning (Certificate); investment management (Certificate); management science (MS, PhD); nonprofit management and leadership (MS, Certificate); state and local taxation (Certificate); MS/MBA. *Accreditation:* AACSB. Part-time and evening/weekend programs available. *Faculty:* 59 full-time (13 women). *Students:* 343 full-time (125 women), 345 part-time (146 women); includes 18 Black or African American, non-Hispanic/Latino; 2 American Indian or Alaska Native, non-Hispanic/Latino; 37 Asian, non-Hispanic/Latino; 4 Hispanic/Latino, 66 international. Average age 32. 560 applicants, 57% accepted, 155 enrolled. In 2010, 295 master's, 4 doctorates awarded. *Degree requirements:* For master's, comprehensive exam (for some programs); for doctorate, comprehensive exam, thesis/dissertation. *Entrance requirements:* For master's and doctorate, GMAT or GRE General Test. Additional exam requirements/recommendations for international students: Required—TOEFL (minimum score 550 paper-based; 79 iBT), IELTS (minimum score 6.5). *Application deadline:* For fall admission, 1/1 priority date for domestic students; for spring admission, 9/1 for domestic students. Applications are processed on a rolling basis. Application fee: $56 ($96 for international students). Electronic applications accepted. *Expenses:* Contact institution. *Financial support:* In 2010–11, 5 fellowships with full tuition reimbursements, 2 research assistantships with full tuition reimbursements, 41 teaching assistantships with full tuition reimbursements were awarded; career-related internships or fieldwork, Federal Work-Study, health care benefits, unspecified assistantships, and project assistantships also available. Support available to part-time students. Financial award application deadline: 4/15; financial award applicants required to submit FAFSA. *Faculty research:* Applied management research in finance, MIS, marketing, operations research, organizational sciences. Total annual research expenditures: $689,994. *Unit head:* Timothy L. Smunt, Dean, 414-229-6256, Fax: 414-229-2372, E-mail: tsmunt@uwm.edu. *Application contact:* Matthew Jensen, 414-229-5403, E-mail: mba-ms@uwm.edu.

TAXATION

Bentley University, McCallum Graduate School of Business, Master's Program in Taxation, Waltham, MA 02452-4705. Offers MST. Part-time and evening/weekend programs available. Postbaccalaureate distance learning degree programs offered (no on-campus study). *Faculty:* 74 full-time (22 women), 21 part-time/adjunct (5 women). *Students:* 45 full-time (22 women), 156 part-time (71 women); includes 34 minority (3 Black or African American, non-Hispanic/Latino; 5 American Indian or Alaska Native, non-Hispanic/Latino; 19 Asian, non-Hispanic/Latino; 7 Hispanic/Latino). Average age 31. 109 applicants, 90% accepted, 70 enrolled. *Entrance requirements:* For master's, GMAT or GRE General Test. Additional exam requirements/recommendations for international students: Required—TOEFL (minimum score 600 paper-based; 250 computer-based; 100 iBT) or IELTS (minimum score 7). *Application deadline:* For fall admission, 12/1 priority date for domestic and international students; for spring admission, 10/1 priority date for domestic and international students. Application fee: $50. Electronic applications accepted. *Expenses:* Tuition: Full-time $28,224; part-time $1176 per credit. Required fees: $404. Part-time tuition and fees vary according to course load. *Financial support:* In 2010–11, 29 students received support. Scholarships/grants and unspecified assistantships available. Financial award application deadline: 6/1; financial award applicants required to submit CSS PROFILE or FAFSA. *Faculty research:* Taxation of intellectual property, tax dispute resolution, corporate tax planning and advocacy, estate and financial planning. *Unit head:* John Lynch, Director, 781-891-2624, E-mail: jlynch@bentley.edu. *Application contact:* Sharon Hill, Director of Graduate Admissions, 781-891-2108, Fax: 781-891-2464, E-mail: bentleygraduateadmissions@bentley.edu.

Boston University, School of Law, Boston, MA 02215. Offers American law (LL M); banking (LL M); intellectual property law (LL M); law (JD); taxation (LL M); JD/LL M; JD/MA; JD/MBA; JD/MPH; JD/MS. *Accreditation:* ABA. *Faculty:* 65 full-time (26 women), 88 part-time/adjunct (32 women). *Students:* 973 full-time (490 women), 66 part-time (32 women); includes 235 minority (44 Black or African American, non-Hispanic/Latino; 5 American Indian or Alaska Native, non-Hispanic/Latino; 84 Asian, non-Hispanic/Latino; 79 Hispanic/Latino; 2 Native Hawaiian or other Pacific Islander, non-Hispanic/Latino; 21 Two or more races, non-Hispanic/Latino), 131 international. Average age 26. 7,660 applicants, 23% accepted, 271 enrolled. In 2010, 206 first professional degrees, 207 master's awarded. *Degree requirements:* For master's, thesis (for some programs); for JD, thesis/dissertation, research project resulting in a paper. *Entrance requirements:* For JD, LSAT; for master's, JD. Additional exam requirements/recommendations for international students: Required—TOEFL (minimum score 600 paper-based; 250 computer-based; 100 iBT). *Application deadline:* For fall admission, 3/1 for domestic and international students. Applications are processed on a rolling basis. Application fee: $75. Electronic applications accepted. *Expenses:* Tuition: Full-time $39,314; part-time $1228 per credit. Required fees: $40 per semester. *Financial support:* In 2010–11, 533 students received support. Career-related internships or fieldwork, Federal Work-Study, institutionally sponsored loans, and scholarships/grants available. Financial award application deadline: 3/1; financial award applicants required to submit FAFSA. *Faculty research:* Litigation and dispute resolution, intellectual property law, business organizations and finance law, international law, health law. *Unit head:* Maureen A. O'Rourke, Dean, 617-353-3112, Fax: 617-353-7400, E-mail: lawdean@bu.edu. *Application contact:* Alissa Leonard, Director of Admissions and Financial Aid, 617-353-3100, Fax: 617-353-0578, E-mail: bulawadm@bu.edu.

Bryant University, Graduate School of Business, Master of Science in Taxation Program, Smithfield, RI 02917. Offers MST. Part-time and evening/weekend programs available. *Faculty:* 3 full-time (0 women), 10 part-time/adjunct (0 women). *Students:* 75 part-time (30 women); includes 1 Black or African American, non-Hispanic/Latino; 1 Asian, non-Hispanic/Latino; 3 Hispanic/Latino, 2 international. Average age 33. 13 applicants, 92% accepted, 10 enrolled. In 2010, 10 master's awarded. *Entrance requirements:* For master's, GMAT, recommendation, resume. Additional exam requirements/recommendations for international students: Required—TOEFL (minimum score 580 paper-based; 237 computer-based; 95 iBT). *Application deadline:* For fall admission, 7/15 for domestic and international students; for spring admission, 11/15 for domestic and international students. Applications are processed on a rolling basis. Application fee: $80. Electronic applications accepted. *Expenses:* Contact institution. *Financial support:* In 2010–11, 1 student received support. Application deadline: 2/15. *Faculty research:* Tax efficiencies of mutual funds, cost segregation studies, taxation of partnerships, property transactions. *Unit head:* Kristopher T. Sullivan, Assistant Dean of the Graduate School, 401-232-6230, Fax: 401-232-6494, E-mail: sullivan@bryant.edu. *Application contact:* Ellen Hudon, Assistant Director of Graduate Admission, 401-232-6230, Fax: 401-232-6494, E-mail: ehudon@bryant.edu.

California Polytechnic State University, San Luis Obispo, Orfalea College of Business, Graduate Programs in Business, San Luis Obispo, CA 93407. Offers business (MBA); taxation (MSA). *Faculty:* 5 full-time (2 women). *Students:* 38 full-time (14 women), 13 part-time (6 women); includes 8 minority (4 Asian, non-Hispanic/Latino; 3 Hispanic/Latino; 1 Native Hawaiian or other Pacific Islander, non-Hispanic/Latino). Average age 26. 111 applicants, 46% accepted, 37 enrolled. In 2010, 68 master's awarded. *Degree requirements:* For master's, comprehensive exam (for some programs), thesis or alternative. *Entrance requirements:* For master's, GMAT. Additional exam requirements/recommendations for international students: Required—TOEFL (minimum score 550 paper-based; 213 computer-based) or IELTS (minimum score 6). *Application deadline:* For fall admission, 7/1 for domestic students, 11/30 for international students. Applications are processed on a rolling basis. Application fee: $55. Electronic applications accepted. *Expenses:* Tuition, state resident: full-time $5386; part-time $3124 per year. Tuition, nonresident: full-time $11,160; part-time $248 per unit. Required fees: $2250; $614 per term. One-time fee: $2250 full-time; $1842 part-time. *Financial support:* Career-related internships or fieldwork, Federal Work-Study, institutionally sponsored loans, scholarships/grants, and unspecified assistantships available. Support available to part-time students. Financial award application deadline: 3/2; financial award applicants required to submit FAFSA. *Faculty research:* International business, organizational behavior, graphic communication document systems management, commercial development of innovative technologies, effective communication skills for managers. *Unit head:* Dr. Bradford Anderson, Associate Dean/Graduate Coordinator, 805-756-5210, Fax: 805-756-0110, E-mail: bpanders@calpoly.edu. *Application contact:* Dr. Bradford Anderson, Associate Dean/Graduate Coordinator, 805-756-5210, Fax: 805-756-0110, E-mail: bpanders@calpoly.edu.

California State University, East Bay, Office of Academic Programs and Graduate Studies, College of Business and Economics, Department of Accounting and Finance, Program in Taxation, Hayward, CA 94542-3000. Offers MS. Part-time and evening/weekend programs available. Postbaccalaureate distance learning degree programs offered. *Faculty:* 2 full-time (0 women), 1 (woman) part-time/adjunct. *Students:* 14 full-time (8 women), 18 part-time (14 women); includes 3 Black or African American, non-Hispanic/Latino; 13 Asian, non-Hispanic/Latino; 1 Hispanic/Latino. Average age 37. 36 applicants, 92% accepted, 18 enrolled. In 2010, 7 master's awarded. *Degree requirements:* For master's, final project. *Entrance requirements:* For master's, GMAT, U.S. CPA exam or Enrolled Agents Exam, minimum GPA of 2.75. Additional exam requirements/recommendations for international students: Required—TOEFL (minimum score 550 paper-based; 213 computer-based). *Application deadline:* For fall admission, 6/30 for domestic and international students. Application fee: $55. Electronic applications accepted. *Financial support:* Career-related internships or fieldwork, Federal Work-Study, and institutionally sponsored loans available. Support available to part-time students. Financial award application deadline: 3/2; financial award applicants required to submit FAFSA. *Unit head:* Dr. Micah Frankel, Chair, Accounting and Finance, 510-885-3397, Fax: 510-885-4796, E-mail: gary.mcbride@csueastbay.edu. *Application contact:* Dr. Gary McBride, Graduate Advisor, 510-885-3307, Fax: 510-885-4796, E-mail: gary.mcbride@csueastbay.edu.

California State University, Fullerton, Graduate Studies, College of Business and Economics, Department of Accounting, Fullerton, CA 92834-9480. Offers accounting (MBA, MS); taxation (MS). *Accreditation:* AACSB. Part-time programs available. *Students:* 115 full-time (64 women), 97 part-time (59 women); includes 78 Asian, non-Hispanic/Latino; 14 Hispanic/Latino; 2 Two or more races, non-Hispanic/Latino, 58 international. Average age 29. 300 applicants, 49% accepted, 66 enrolled. In 2010, 57 master's awarded. *Degree requirements:* For master's, thesis or alternative, project. *Entrance requirements:* For master's, GMAT, minimum AACSB index of 950. *Application deadline:* Applications are processed on a rolling basis. Application fee: $55. Electronic applications accepted. *Financial support:* Career-related internships or fieldwork, Federal Work-Study, institutionally sponsored loans, and scholarships/grants available. Support available to part-time students. Financial award application deadline: 3/1; financial award applicants required to submit FAFSA. *Unit head:* Dr. Betty Chavis, Chair, 657-278-2225. *Application contact:* Admissions/Applications, 657-278-2371.

California State University, Los Angeles, Graduate Studies, College of Business and Economics, Department of Accounting, Los Angeles, CA 90032-8530. Offers accountancy (MS), including business taxation, financial accounting, information systems, management accounting; accounting (MBA). Part-time and evening/weekend programs available. *Faculty:* 5 full-time (1 woman), 2 part-time/adjunct (0 women). *Students:* 37 full-time (19 women), 72 part-time (49 women); includes 42 minority (35 Asian, non-Hispanic/Latino; 6 Hispanic/Latino; 1 Two or more races, non-Hispanic/Latino), 49 international. Average age 31. 76 applicants, 100% accepted, 48 enrolled. In 2010, 33 master's awarded. *Degree requirements:* For master's, comprehensive exam (MBA), thesis (MS). *Entrance requirements:* For master's, GMAT, minimum GPA of 2.5 during previous 2 years of course work. Additional exam requirements/recommendations for international students: Required—TOEFL (minimum score 550 paper-based; 213 computer-based). *Application deadline:* For fall admission, 5/1 for domestic and international students. Applications are processed on a rolling basis. Application fee: $55. Electronic applications accepted. *Financial support:* Career-related internships or fieldwork and Federal Work-Study available. Support available to part-time students. Financial award application deadline: 3/1. *Unit head:* Dr. Greg Kunkel, Chair, 323-343-2830, Fax: 323-343-6439, E-mail: gkunkel@calstatela.edu. *Application contact:* Dr. Alan Muchlinski, Dean of Graduate Studies, 323-343-3820, Fax: 323-343-5653, E-mail: amuchli@exchange.calstatela.edu.

Chapman University, Graduate Studies, School of Law, Orange, CA 92866. Offers advocacy and dispute resolution (JD); entertainment law (JD); environmental, land use, and real estate (JD); international law (JD); law (LL M), including business law and economics, entertainment and media law, international and comparative law; prosecutorial science (LL M); tax law (JD); taxation (LL M); JD/MBA; JD/MFA. *Accreditation:* ABA. Part-time and evening/weekend programs available. *Faculty:* 57 full-time (25 women), 26 part-time/adjunct (4 women). *Students:* 580 full-time (283 women), 64 part-time (22 women); includes 132 minority (5 Black or African American, non-Hispanic/Latino; 1 American Indian or Alaska Native, non-Hispanic/Latino; 77 Asian, non-Hispanic/Latino; 37 Hispanic/Latino; 1 Native Hawaiian or other Pacific Islander, non-Hispanic/Latino; 11 Two or more races, non-Hispanic/Latino), 8 international. Average age 27. 2,779 applicants, 28% accepted, 212 enrolled. In 2010, 173 first professional degrees, 19 master's awarded. *Entrance requirements:* LSAT, minimum undergraduate GPA of 2.75. Additional exam requirements/recommendations for international students: Required—TOEFL (minimum score 600 paper-based; 213 computer-based; 80 iBT). *Application deadline:* For fall admission, 4/15 priority date for domestic students. Applications are processed on a rolling basis. Application fee: $65. Electronic applications accepted. *Expenses:* Contact institution. *Financial support:* Fellowships, Federal Work-Study and scholarships/grants available. Financial award applicants required to submit FAFSA. *Unit head:* Dr. Tom Campbell, Dean, 714-628-2500. *Application contact:* Marissa Vargas, Assistant Director of Admission and Financial Aid, 877-CHAPLAW, E-mail: mvargas@chapman.edu.

Cleveland State University, College of Graduate Studies, Nance College of Business Administration, Department of Accounting, Cleveland, OH 44115. Offers financial accounting/audit (M Acc); taxation (M Acc). *Accreditation:* AACSB. Part-time and evening/weekend programs available. *Faculty:* 13 full-time (4 women), 11 part-time/adjunct (3 women). *Students:* 110 full-time (60 women), 130 part-time (76 women); includes 22 Black or African American, non-Hispanic/Latino; 12 Asian, non-Hispanic/Latino; 6 Hispanic/Latino; 1 Two or more races, non-Hispanic/Latino, 60 international. Average age 30. 87 applicants, 64% accepted, 19 enrolled. In 2010, 30 master's awarded. *Entrance requirements:* For master's, GMAT, minimum GPA of 2.75. Additional exam requirements/recommendations for international students: Required—TOEFL (minimum score 525 paper-based; 197 computer-based). *Application deadline:* For fall admission, 7/15 priority date for domestic students; for spring admission, 12/15 priority date for domestic students. Applications are processed on a rolling basis. Application fee: $30. *Expenses:* Tuition, state resident: full-time $8447; part-time $469 per credit hour. Tuition, nonresident: full-time $16,020; part-time $890 per credit hour. Required fees: $50. *Financial support:* In 2010–11, 3 research assistantships with full and partial tuition reimbursements (averaging $6,960 per year) were awarded; career-related internships or fieldwork, Federal Work-Study, scholarships/grants, and unspecified assistantships also available. Financial award applicants required to submit FAFSA. *Faculty research:* Internal auditing, computer auditing, accounting education, managerial accounting. *Unit head:* Bruce W. McClain, Chair, 216-687-3652, Fax: 216-687-9212, E-mail: b.mcclain@csuohio.edu. *Application contact:* Bruce Gottschalk, MBA Programs Administrator, 216-687-3730, Fax: 216-687-5311, E-mail: cbacsu@csuohio.edu.

DePaul University, Charles H. Kellstadt Graduate School of Business, School of Accountancy and Management Information Systems, Chicago, IL 60604-2287. Offers accountancy (M Acc, MSA); business information technology (MS); e-business (MBA, MS); financial management and control (MBA); management accounting (MBA); management information systems (MBA); taxation (MST). Part-time and evening/weekend programs available. *Faculty:* 30 full-time (9 women), 54 part-time/adjunct (7 women). *Students:* 207 full-time (112 women), 208 part-time (92 women); includes 7 Black or African American, non-Hispanic/Latino; 34 Asian, non-Hispanic/Latino; 19 Hispanic/Latino; 2 Two or more races, non-Hispanic/Latino, 76 international. In 2010, 141 master's awarded. *Entrance requirements:* For master's, GMAT, 2 letters of recommendation, resume. Additional exam requirements/recommendations for international students: Required—TOEFL (minimum score 550 paper-based; 213 computer-based). *Application deadline:* For fall admission, 7/1 for domestic students; for winter admission, 10/1 for domestic students; for spring admission, 2/1 for domestic students. Applications are processed on a rolling basis. Application fee: $60. *Financial support:* In 2010–11, 7 research assistantships with full tuition reimbursements (averaging $4,100 per year) were awarded; institutionally sponsored loans also available. Financial award application deadline: 4/2. *Faculty research:* Tax policy, property transactions, stock options as compensation, standards setting, activity-based costing in health care. *Unit head:* Kevin Stevens, Director, 312-362-6989, E-mail: kstevens@depaul.edu. *Application contact:* Christopher E. Kinsella, Director of Cohort MBA Programs, 312-362-8810, Fax: 312-362-6677, E-mail: kgsb@depaul.edu.

Fairfield University, Charles F. Dolan School of Business, Fairfield, CT 06824-5195. Offers accounting (MBA, MS, CAS); accounting information systems (MBA); entrepreneurship (MBA); finance (MBA, MS, CAS); general management (MBA, CAS); human resource management (MBA, CAS); information systems and operations (MBA); information systems and operations management (CAS); international business (MBA, CAS); marketing (MBA, CAS); taxation (MBA, CAS). *Accreditation:* AACSB. Part-time and evening/weekend programs available. *Faculty:* 42 full-time (15 women), 8 part-time/adjunct (1 woman). *Students:* 89 full-time (32 women), 127 part-time (54 women); includes 4 Black or African American, non-Hispanic/Latino; 2 Asian, non-Hispanic/Latino; 4 Hispanic/Latino; 1 Two or more races, non-Hispanic/Latino, 17 international. Average age 29. 108 applicants, 62% accepted, 46 enrolled. In 2010, 79 master's awarded. *Degree requirements:* For master's, capstone course. *Entrance requirements:* For master's, GMAT (minimum score 500), 2 letters of reference, resume, minimum GPA of 3.0. Additional exam requirements/recommendations for international students: Required—TOEFL (minimum score 550 paper-based; 213 computer-based; 80 iBT). *Application deadline:* For fall admission, 5/15 for international students; for spring admission, 10/15 for international students. Applications are processed on a rolling basis. Application fee: $60. Electronic applications accepted. *Expenses:* Contact institution. *Financial support:* In 2010–11, 48 students received support. Scholarships/grants, unspecified assistantships, and merit based one-time entrance scholarship available. Financial award applicants required to submit FAFSA. *Faculty research:* Optimization strategies, international finance, consumer behavior, financial market volatility, Internet marketing, supply chain analysis, tax issues. Total annual research expenditures: $50,000. *Unit head:* Dr. Norman A. Solomon, Dean, 203-254-4000 Ext. 4070, Fax: 203-254-4105, E-mail: nsolomon@fairfield.edu. *Application contact:* Marianne Gumpper, Director of Graduate and Continuing Studies Admissions, 203-254-4184, Fax: 203-254-4073, E-mail: gradadmis@fairfield.edu.

Fairleigh Dickinson University, College at Florham, Silberman College of Business, Department of Accounting, Law, and Tax, Program in Taxation, Madison, NJ 07940-1099. Offers MS, Certificate. *Students:* 2 full-time (1 woman), 79 part-time (36 women), 3 international. Average age 37. 31 applicants, 84% accepted, 15 enrolled. In 2010, 17 master's awarded. *Application deadline:* Applications are processed on a rolling basis. Application fee: $40.

Fairleigh Dickinson University, Metropolitan Campus, Silberman College of Business, Department of Accounting, Law, and Tax, Program in Taxation, Teaneck, NJ 07666-1914. Offers MS. *Application deadline:* Applications are processed on a rolling basis. Application fee: $40. *Application contact:* Susan Brooman, University Director of Graduate Admissions, 201-692-2554, Fax: 201-692-2560, E-mail: globaleducation@fdu.edu.

Florida Atlantic University, College of Business, School of Accounting, Program in Taxation, Boca Raton, FL 33431-0991. Offers M Tax. Part-time and evening/weekend programs available. Postbaccalaureate distance learning degree programs offered (minimal on-campus study). *Faculty:* 22 full-time (10 women), 12 part-time/adjunct (1 woman). *Students:* 7 full-time (1 woman), 15 part-time (8 women); includes 5 minority (3 Black or African

American, non-Hispanic/Latino; 1 Hispanic/Latino; 1 Two or more races, non-Hispanic/Latino). Average age 30. 73 applicants, 44% accepted. In 2010, 29 master's awarded. *Degree requirements:* For master's, comprehensive exam, thesis optional. *Entrance requirements:* For master's, GMAT, minimum GPA of 3.0. Additional exam requirements/recommendations for international students: Required—TOEFL (minimum score 600 paper-based; 250 computer-based). *Application deadline:* For fall admission, 7/1 priority date for domestic students, 2/15 priority date for international students; for spring admission, 11/1 priority date for domestic students, 7/15 priority date for international students. Applications are processed on a rolling basis. Application fee: $30. *Expenses:* Tuition, area resident: Part-time $319.96 per credit. Tuition, state resident: part-time $319.96 per credit. Tuition, nonresident: part-time $926.42 per credit. *Financial support:* Career-related internships or fieldwork, Federal Work-Study, institutionally sponsored loans, scholarships/grants, tuition waivers (full and partial), and unspecified assistantships available. Support available to part-time students. Financial award application deadline: 3/1. *Application contact:* Fredrick G. Taylor, Graduate Adviser, 561-297-3196, Fax: 561-297-1315, E-mail: ftaylor@fau.edu.

Florida Gulf Coast University, Lutgert College of Business, Program in Accounting and Taxation, Fort Myers, FL 33965-6565. Offers MS. Part-time and evening/weekend programs available. *Faculty:* 64 full-time (21 women), 5 part-time/adjunct (1 woman). *Students:* 37 full-time (23 women), 27 part-time (14 women); includes 1 Black or African American, non-Hispanic/Latino; 1 American Indian or Alaska Native, non-Hispanic/Latino; 5 Asian, non-Hispanic/Latino; 10 Hispanic/Latino, 2 international. Average age 29. 47 applicants, 77% accepted, 26 enrolled. In 2010, 36 master's awarded. *Degree requirements:* For master's, thesis or alternative. *Entrance requirements:* For master's, GMAT, minimum GPA of 3.0. Additional exam requirements/recommendations for international students: Required—TOEFL (minimum score 550 paper-based; 213 computer-based). *Application deadline:* For fall admission, 6/1 priority date for domestic students; for spring admission, 11/1 for domestic students. Applications are processed on a rolling basis. Application fee: $30. Electronic applications accepted. *Expenses:* Tuition, state resident: part-time $322.08 per credit hour. Tuition, nonresident: part-time $1117.08 per credit hour. *Faculty research:* Stock petitions, mergers and acquisitions, deferred taxes, fraud and accounting regulations, graphical reporting practices. *Unit head:* Dr. Ara Volkan, Chair, 239-590-7380, Fax: 239-590-7330, E-mail: avolkan@fgcu.edu. *Application contact:* Marisa Ouverson, Director of Enrollment Management, 239-590-7403, Fax: 239-590-7330, E-mail: mouverso@fgcu.edu.

Florida International University, Alvah H. Chapman, Jr. Graduate School of Business, School of Accounting, Program in Taxation, Miami, FL 33199. Offers MST. Part-time and evening/weekend programs available. *Students:* 60 full-time (37 women), 1 part-time (0 women); includes 5 Black or African American, non-Hispanic/Latino; 1 Asian, non-Hispanic/Latino; 49 Hispanic/Latino, 1 international. Average age 30. 116 applicants, 63% accepted. In 2010, 45 master's awarded. *Entrance requirements:* For master's, GMAT or GRE, minimum GPA of 3.0; resume. Additional exam requirements/recommendations for international students: Required—TOEFL (minimum score 550 paper-based; 213 computer-based; 80 iBT) or IELTS (minimum score 6.5). *Application deadline:* For fall admission, 4/1 for domestic and international students; for spring admission, 10/1 for domestic students, 9/1 for international students. Applications are processed on a rolling basis. Application fee: $30. Electronic applications accepted. *Expenses:* Contact institution. *Financial support:* Institutionally sponsored loans, scholarships/grants, and traineeships available. Financial award application deadline: 3/1; financial award applicants required to submit FAFSA. *Faculty research:* Corporate taxation, small business taxation. *Unit head:* Dr. Sharon Lassar, Director, School of Accounting, 305-348-3501, Fax: 305-348-2914, E-mail: sharon.lassar@fiu.edu. *Application contact:* Teresita Brunken, 305-348-4224, Fax: 305-348-2914, E-mail: brunken@fiu.edu.

Florida State University, The Graduate School, College of Business, Tallahassee, FL 32306-1110. Offers accounting (M Acc), including accounting information services, assurance services, corporate accounting, taxation; business administration (MBA, PhD), including accounting (PhD), finance (PhD), management information systems (PhD), marketing (PhD), organizational behavior (PhD), risk management and insurance (PhD), strategic management (PhD); finance (MS); insurance (MSM); management information systems (MS); JD/MBA; MSW/MBA. *Accreditation:* AACSB. Part-time programs available. Postbaccalaureate distance learning degree programs offered (no on-campus study). *Faculty:* 107 full-time (31 women). *Students:* 196 full-time (76 women), 310 part-time (109 women); includes 27 Black or African American, non-Hispanic/Latino; 1 American Indian or Alaska Native, non-Hispanic/Latino; 31 Asian, non-Hispanic/Latino; 30 Hispanic/Latino. Average age 30. 702 applicants, 33% accepted, 205 enrolled. In 2010, 268 master's, 17 doctorates awarded. Terminal master's awarded for partial completion of doctoral program. *Degree requirements:* For doctorate, comprehensive exam, thesis/dissertation. *Entrance requirements:* For master's, GMAT, work experience (MBA, MS), minimum GPA of 3.0, letters of recommendation; for doctorate, GMAT, minimum graduate GPA of 3.5, letters of recommendation. Additional exam requirements/recommendations for international students: Required—TOEFL (minimum score 600 paper-based; 80 computer-based);

Recommended—IELTS (minimum score 6.5). *Application deadline:* For fall admission, 6/1 for domestic students, 5/1 for international students; for spring admission, 10/1 for domestic students, 9/1 for international students. Applications are processed on a rolling basis. Application fee: $30. Electronic applications accepted. *Expenses:* Tuition, state resident: full-time $8238.24. *Financial support:* In 2010–11, 86 students received support, including 12 fellowships with full tuition reimbursements available (averaging $7,161 per year), 30 research assistantships with full tuition reimbursements available (averaging $6,000 per year), 43 teaching assistantships with full tuition reimbursements available (averaging $15,000 per year); career-related internships or fieldwork, scholarships/grants, health care benefits, tuition waivers (full and partial), and unspecified assistantships also available. Support available to part-time students. Financial award application deadline: 1/1. *Unit head:* Dr. Caryn Beck-Dudley, Dean, 850-644-3090, Fax: 850-644-0915. *Application contact:* Lisa Beverly, Director, Graduate Programs Admissions, 850-644-6458, Fax: 850-644-0588, E-mail: lbeverly@cob.fsu.edu.

Fontbonne University, Graduate Programs, College of Global Business and Professional Studies, Program in Taxation, St. Louis, MO 63105-3098. Offers MST. Part-time and evening/weekend programs available. *Faculty:* 4 part-time/adjunct (3 women). *Students:* 12 part-time (5 women); includes 2 Black or African American, non-Hispanic/Latino; 1 Asian, non-Hispanic/Latino. Average age 40. In 2010, 3 master's awarded. *Entrance requirements:* For master's, minimum GPA of 2.5. Additional exam requirements/recommendations for international students: Required—TOEFL (minimum score 197 computer-based; 71 iBT). *Application deadline:* For fall admission, 9/1 priority date for domestic students; for spring admission, 4/15 priority date for domestic students. Applications are processed on a rolling basis. Application fee: $25. *Expenses:* Tuition: Full-time $11,328. Full-time tuition and fees vary according to program. *Financial support:* Application deadline: 4/1. *Unit head:* Dr. Linda Maurer, Dean of College of Business and Professional Studies, 314-889-1423, E-mail: lmaurer@fontbonne.edu. *Application contact:* Fontbonne University OPTIONS, 314-863-2220, Fax: 314-963-0327, E-mail: options@fontbonne.edu.

George Mason University, School of Management, Fairfax, VA 22030. Offers accounting (MS); business administration (EMBA, MBA); real estate development (MS); taxation (MS); technology management (MS). Part-time and evening/weekend programs available. *Faculty:* 80 full-time (26 women), 51 part-time/adjunct (15 women). *Students:* 188 full-time (70 women), 353 part-time (111 women); includes 18 Black or African American, non-Hispanic/Latino; 1 American Indian or Alaska Native, non-Hispanic/Latino; 52 Asian, non-Hispanic/Latino; 17 Hispanic/Latino; 2 Two or more races, non-Hispanic/Latino, 40 international. Average age 31. 467 applicants, 58% accepted, 164 enrolled. In 2010, 203 master's awarded. *Entrance requirements:* For master's, GMAT. Additional exam requirements/recommendations for international students: Required—TOEFL (minimum score 570 paper-based; 230 computer-based; 88 iBT). *Application deadline:* Applications are processed on a rolling basis. Application fee: $100. Electronic applications accepted. *Expenses:* Tuition, state resident: full-time $8192; part-time $440 per credit hour. Tuition, nonresident: full-time $22,952; part-time $1055 per credit hour. Required fees: $2364; $99 per credit hour. *Financial support:* In 2010–11, 38 students received support, including 21 research assistantships with full and partial tuition reimbursements available (averaging $7,176 per year), 20 teaching assistantships with full and partial tuition reimbursements available (averaging $7,255 per year); career-related internships or fieldwork, Federal Work-Study, scholarships/grants, unspecified assistantships, and health care benefits (full-time research or teaching assistantship recipients) also available. Support available to part-time students. Financial award application deadline: 3/1; financial award applicants required to submit FAFSA. *Faculty research:* Current leading global issues: offshore outsourcing, international financial risk, comparative systems of innovation. Total annual research expenditures: $482,158. *Unit head:* Jorge Haddock, Dean, 703-993-1875, E-mail: jhaddock@gmu.edu. *Application contact:* Melanie Pflugshaupt, Administrative Coordinator to Dean's Office, 703-993-3638, E-mail: mpflugsh@gmu.edu.

Golden Gate University, School of Accounting, San Francisco, CA 94105-2968. Offers accounting (M Ac, Graduate Certificate); forensic (M Ac); forensic accounting (Graduate Certificate); taxation (M Ac). Part-time and evening/weekend programs available. *Faculty:* 5 full-time (2 women), 35 part-time/adjunct (12 women). *Students:* 129 full-time (84 women), 168 part-time (98 women); includes 127 minority (6 Black or African American, non-Hispanic/Latino; 1 American Indian or Alaska Native, non-Hispanic/Latino; 100 Asian, non-Hispanic/Latino; 15 Hispanic/Latino; 3 Native Hawaiian or other Pacific Islander, non-Hispanic/Latino; 2 Two or more races, non-Hispanic/Latino), 40 international. Average age 31. 132 applicants, 80% accepted, 52 enrolled. In 2010, 61 master's awarded. *Entrance requirements:* For master's, minimum GPA of 3.0. Additional exam requirements/recommendations for international students: Required—TOEFL. *Application deadline:* For fall admission, 5/15 for international students; for winter admission, 1/15 for international students; for spring admission, 9/15 for international students. Applications are processed on a rolling basis. Application fee: $70 ($110 for international students). Electronic applications accepted. *Financial support:* Career-related internships or fieldwork, Federal Work-Study, institutionally sponsored loans, and scholarships/grants available. Support available to part-time students. Financial award applicants required to submit FAFSA. *Faculty research:* Forensic accounting, audit, tax, CPA exam. *Unit head:* Mary Canning, 415-442-6559, Fax: 415-543-2607. *Application contact:* Angela Melero, Enrollment Services, 415-442-7800, Fax: 415-442-7807, E-mail: info@ggu.edu.

Golden Gate University, School of Law, San Francisco, CA 94105-2968. Offers environmental law (LL M); intellectual property law (LL M); international legal studies (LL M, SJD); law (JD); taxation (LL M); U. S. legal studies (LL M); JD/MBA; JD/PhD. *Accreditation:* ABA. Part-time and evening/weekend programs available. *Faculty:* 41 full-time (19 women), 67 part-time/adjunct (27 women). *Students:* 612 full-time (346 women), 253 part-time (127 women); includes 230 minority (30 Black or African American, non-Hispanic/Latino; 5 American Indian or Alaska Native, non-Hispanic/Latino; 147 Asian, non-Hispanic/Latino; 48 Hispanic/Latino), 83 international. In 2010, 249 first professional degrees, 60 master's, 9 doctorates awarded. *Degree requirements:* For doctorate, thesis/dissertation. *Entrance requirements:* LSAT, personal statement, letters of recommendation. Additional exam requirements/recommendations for international students: Required—TOEFL (minimum score 600 paper-based; 250 computer-based). *Application deadline:* For fall admission, 4/1 for domestic and international students. Applications are processed on a rolling basis. Application fee: $60. Electronic applications accepted. *Expenses:* Contact institution. *Financial support:* Fellowships, research assistantships, teaching assistantships, career-related internships or fieldwork, Federal Work-Study, institutionally sponsored loans, scholarships/grants, tuition waivers (full and partial), and unspecified assistantships available. Support available to part-time students. Financial award application deadline: 3/1; financial award applicants required to submit FAFSA. *Faculty research:* International law, intellectual property law, environmental law, real estate, civil rights. *Unit head:* Drucilla Ramey, Dean, 415-442-6600, Fax: 415-442-6609. *Application contact:* Greg Egertson, Associate Dean and Director of Admissions, 415-442-6636, Fax: 415-442-6609, E-mail: lawadmit@ggu.edu.

Golden Gate University, School of Taxation, San Francisco, CA 94105-2968. Offers advanced studies in taxation (Certificate); estate planning (Certificate); international tax (Certificate); tax (Certificate); taxation (MS). Part-time and evening/weekend programs available. *Faculty:* 6 full-time (1 woman), 65 part-time/adjunct (15 women). *Students:* 66 full-time (39 women), 641 part-time (359 women); includes 238 minority (20 Black or African American, non-Hispanic/Latino; 165 Asian, non-Hispanic/Latino; 35 Hispanic/Latino; 15 Native Hawaiian or other Pacific Islander, non-Hispanic/Latino; 3 Two or more races, non-Hispanic/Latino), 22 international. Average age 37. 337 applicants, 87% accepted, 148 enrolled. In 2010, 242 master's awarded. *Entrance requirements:* For master's, minimum GPA of 3.0. Additional exam requirements/recommendations for international students: Required—TOEFL. *Application deadline:* For fall admission, 5/15 for international students; for winter admission, 1/15 for international students; for spring admission, 9/15 for international students. Applications are processed on a rolling basis. Application fee: $70 ($110 for international students). Electronic applications accepted. *Expenses:* Contact institution. *Financial support:* Career-related internships or fieldwork, Federal Work-Study, institutionally sponsored loans, and scholarships/grants available. Support available to part-time students. Financial award applicants required to submit FAFSA. *Unit head:* Mary Canning, Dean, 415-442-7885, Fax: 415-442-7807. *Application contact:* Angela Melero, Enrollment Services, 415-442-7800, Fax: 415-442-7807, E-mail: info@ggu.edu.

Goldey-Beacom College, Graduate Program, Wilmington, DE 19808-1999. Offers business administration (MBA); finance (MS); financial management (MBA); human resource management (MBA); information technology (MBA); international business management (MBA); major finance (MBA); major taxation (MBA); management (MM); marketing management (MBA); taxation (MBA, MS). *Accreditation:* ACBSP. Part-time and evening/weekend programs available. *Faculty:* 20 full-time (8 women), 28 part-time/adjunct (10 women). *Students:* 55 full-time (28 women), 393 part-time (164 women); includes 252 minority (51 Black or African American, non-Hispanic/Latino; 2 American Indian or Alaska Native, non-Hispanic/Latino; 183 Asian, non-Hispanic/Latino; 13 Hispanic/Latino; 1 Native Hawaiian or other Pacific Islander, non-Hispanic/Latino; 2 Two or more races, non-Hispanic/Latino). Average age 27. In 2010, 231 master's awarded. *Entrance requirements:* For master's, GMAT, MAT, GRE, minimum GPA of 3.0. Additional exam requirements/recommendations for international students: Required—TOEFL (minimum score 65 computer-based); Recommended—IELTS (minimum score 5). *Application deadline:* Applications are processed on a rolling basis. Electronic applications accepted. *Expenses:* Tuition: Full-time $14,796; part-time $822 per credit. Required fees: $180; $10 per credit. *Financial support:* Scholarships/grants available. Support available to part-time students. Financial award application deadline: 4/1; financial award applicants required to submit FAFSA. *Unit head:* Larry W. Eby, Director of Admissions, 302-225-6289, Fax: 302-996-5408, E-mail: ebylw@gbc.edu. *Application contact:* Ashley E. Mashington, Graduate Admissions Representative, 302-225-6259, Fax: 302-996-5408, E-mail: mashina@gbc.edu.

HEC Montreal, School of Business Administration, Diploma Programs in Administration, Program in Taxation, Montréal, QC H3T 2A7, Canada. Offers

Diploma. All courses are given in French. Part-time programs available. *Students:* 40 full-time (20 women), 90 part-time (43 women). 98 applicants, 57% accepted, 39 enrolled. In 2010, 16 Diplomas awarded. *Degree requirements:* For Diploma, one foreign language. *Entrance requirements:* For degree, work experience in Canadian taxation system. *Application deadline:* For fall admission, 4/1 for domestic and international students; for winter admission, 9/15 for domestic and international students. Application fee: $78 Canadian dollars. Electronic applications accepted. *Expenses:* Tuition, area resident: Part-time $68.93 per credit. Tuition, state resident: full-time $2481.48; part-time $188.92 per credit. Tuition, nonresident: full-time $6801; part-time $482.06 per course. International tuition: $17,354.16 full-time. Required fees: $1309.50; $30.28 per credit. $93.45 per term. Tuition and fees vary according to degree level and program. *Financial support:* Research assistantships, teaching assistantships, scholarships/grants available. Financial award application deadline: 9/2. *Unit head:* Silvia Ponce, Director, 514-340-6393, Fax: 514-340-6915, E-mail: silvia.ponce@hec.ca. *Application contact:* Marie Deshaies, Senior Student Advisor, 514-340-6135, Fax: 514-340-6411, E-mail: marie.deshaies@hec.ca.

Hofstra University, Frank G. Zarb School of Business, Programs in Accounting and Taxation, Hempstead, NY 11549. Offers accounting (MS, Advanced Certificate); business administration (MBA), including accounting, taxation; taxation (MS, Advanced Certificate). Part-time and evening/weekend programs available. Postbaccalaureate distance learning degree programs offered (minimal on-campus study). *Faculty:* 12 full-time (4 women), 3 part-time/adjunct (1 woman). *Students:* 107 full-time (52 women), 49 part-time (22 women); includes 19 minority (5 Black or African American, non-Hispanic/Latino; 9 Asian, non-Hispanic/Latino; 5 Hispanic/Latino), 45 international. Average age 26. 247 applicants, 73% accepted, 79 enrolled. In 2010, 37 master's awarded. *Degree requirements:* For master's, capstone course (for MBA); thesis (for MS). *Entrance requirements:* For master's, GMAT/GRE, 2 letters of recommendation; resume; essay. Additional exam requirements/recommendations for international students: Required—TOEFL (minimum score 550 paper-based; 213 computer-based; 80 iBT); Recommended—IELTS (minimum score 6). *Application deadline:* Applications are processed on a rolling basis. Application fee: $70 ($75 for international students). Electronic applications accepted. *Expenses:* Contact institution. *Financial support:* In 2010–11, 25 students received support, including 21 fellowships with full and partial tuition reimbursements available (averaging $10,613 per year), 1 research assistantship with full and partial tuition reimbursement available (averaging $9,594 per year); career-related internships or fieldwork, Federal Work-Study, institutionally sponsored loans, scholarships/grants, tuition waivers (full and partial), and unspecified assistantships also available. Support available to part-time students. Financial award applicants required to submit FAFSA. *Faculty research:* Corporate governance and executive compensation, Sarbanes-Oxley and certification compliance for financial statement, student performance and evaluation models, decomposing the elements of nonprofit organizational performance, accounting for international financial reporting standards. *Unit head:* Dr. Nathan S. Slavin, Chairperson, 516-463-5690, Fax: 516-463-4834, E-mail: actnzs@hofstra.edu. *Application contact:* Carol Drummer, Dean of Graduate Admissions, 516-463-4876, Fax: 516-463-4664, E-mail: gradstudent@hofstra.edu.

Illinois Institute of Technology, Chicago-Kent College of Law, Chicago, IL 60661-3691. Offers family law (LL M); financial services (LL M); international intellectual property (LL M); international law (LL M); law (JD); taxation (LL M); JD/LL M; JD/MBA; JD/MPA; JD/MPH; JD/MS. *Accreditation:* ABA. Part-time and evening/weekend programs available. *Faculty:* 70 full-time (24 women), 146 part-time/adjunct (35 women). *Students:* 889 full-time (417 women), 206 part-time (88 women); includes 214 minority (41 Black or African American, non-Hispanic/Latino; 64 Asian, non-Hispanic/Latino; 67 Hispanic/Latino; 26 Native Hawaiian or other Pacific Islander, non-Hispanic/Latino; 16 Two or more races, non-Hispanic/Latino), 112 international. Average age 27. 3,923 applicants, 47% accepted, 374 enrolled. In 2010, 297 first professional degrees, 128 master's awarded. *Entrance requirements:* LSAT, LSDAS. Additional exam requirements/recommendations for international students: Required—TOEFL (minimum score 600 paper-based; 250 computer-based; 100 iBT); Recommended—IELTS (minimum score 7). *Application deadline:* For fall admission, 3/1 priority date for domestic students, 2/1 priority date for international students. Applications are processed on a rolling basis. Application fee: $60 ($75 for international students). Electronic applications accepted. *Expenses:* Contact institution. *Financial support:* In 2010–11, 607 students received support. Career-related internships or fieldwork, Federal Work-Study, institutionally sponsored loans, scholarships/grants, and tuition waivers (full) available. Support available to part-time students. Financial award application deadline: 3/15; financial award applicants required to submit FAFSA. *Faculty research:* Constitutional law, bioethics, environmental law. Total annual research expenditures: $663,877. *Unit head:* Harold J. Krent, Dean, 312-906-5010, Fax: 312-906-5335, E-mail: hkrent@kentlaw.edu. *Application contact:* Nicole Vilches, Assistant Dean, 312-906-5020, Fax: 312-906-5274, E-mail: admissions@kentlaw.edu.

John Marshall Law School, Graduate and Professional Programs, Chicago, IL 60604-3968. Offers comparative legal studies (LL M); employee benefits (LL M, MS); information technology (LL M, MS); intellectual property (LL M); international business and trade (LL M); law (JD); real estate (LL M, MS); taxation (LL M, MS); JD/LL M; JD/MA; JD/MBA; JD/MPA. JD/MBA offered jointly with Dominican University, JD/MA and JD/MPA with Roosevelt University. *Accreditation:* ABA. Part-time and evening/weekend programs available. *Faculty:* 65 full-time (21 women), 152 part-time/adjunct (48 women). *Students:* 1,237 full-time (567 women), 373 part-time (181 women); includes 464 minority (138 Black or African American, non-Hispanic/Latino; 12 American Indian or Alaska Native, non-Hispanic/Latino; 96 Asian, non-Hispanic/Latino; 125 Hispanic/Latino; 11 Native Hawaiian or other Pacific Islander, non-Hispanic/Latino; 82 Two or more races, non-Hispanic/Latino), 39 international. Average age 27. 3,523 applicants, 44% accepted, 351 enrolled. In 2010, 387 first professional degrees, 8 master's awarded. *Degree requirements:* For JD, 90 credits. *Entrance requirements:* For JD, LSAT; for master's, JD. Additional exam requirements/recommendations for international students: Required—TOEFL. *Application deadline:* For fall admission, 3/1 priority date for domestic and international students; for spring admission, 10/15 priority date for domestic and international students. Applications are processed on a rolling basis. Application fee: $60. Electronic applications accepted. *Expenses:* Contact institution. *Financial support:* In 2010–11, 1,350 students received support. Scholarships/grants and tuition waivers (full and partial) available. Support available to part-time students. Financial award application deadline: 6/1; financial award applicants required to submit FAFSA. *Unit head:* John Corkery, Dean, 312-427-2737. *Application contact:* William B. Powers, Associate Dean of Admission and Student Affairs, 800-537-4280, Fax: 312-427-5136, E-mail: admission@jmls.edu.

Loyola Marymount University, Loyola Law School Los Angeles, Los Angeles, CA 90015. Offers law (JD); taxation (LL M); JD/MBA. *Accreditation:* ABA. Part-time and evening/weekend programs available. *Faculty:* 74 full-time (35 women), 55 part-time/adjunct (13 women). *Students:* 1,034 full-time (541 women), 283 part-time (116 women); includes 515 minority (51 Black or African American, non-Hispanic/Latino; 4 American Indian or Alaska Native, non-Hispanic/Latino; 231 Asian, non-Hispanic/Latino; 159 Hispanic/Latino; 2 Native Hawaiian or other Pacific Islander, non-Hispanic/Latino; 68 Two or more races, non-Hispanic/Latino), 15 international. Average age 26. 7,869 applicants, 20% accepted, 403 enrolled. In 2010, 388 first professional degrees, 38 master's awarded. *Entrance requirements:* For JD, LSAT; for master's, JD. *Application deadline:* For fall admission, 2/1 priority date for domestic and international students. Applications are processed on a rolling basis. Application fee: $65. Electronic applications accepted. *Financial support:* In 2010–11, 322 students received support; research assistantships, Federal Work-Study and scholarships/grants available. Financial award application deadline: 3/12; financial award applicants required to submit FAFSA. *Unit head:* Victor Gold, Dean, 213-736-1062, Fax: 213-487-6736, E-mail: victor.gold@lls.edu. *Application contact:* Jannell Lundy Roberts, Assistant Dean, Admissions, 213-736-1074, Fax: 213-736-6523, E-mail: admissions@lls.edu.

Mississippi State University, College of Business, School of Accountancy, Mississippi State, MS 39762. Offers accounting (MBA); business administration (PhD); systems (MPA); taxation (MTX). MBA (accounting) only offered at the Meridian campus. *Accreditation:* AACSB. *Faculty:* 6 full-time (2 women), 2 part-time/adjunct (0 women). *Students:* 53 full-time (27 women), 13 part-time (10 women); includes 8 minority (3 Black or African American, non-Hispanic/Latino; 3 Asian, non-Hispanic/Latino; 2 Two or more races, non-Hispanic/Latino), 2 international. Average age 26. 59 applicants, 47% accepted, 21 enrolled. In 2010, 33 master's awarded. *Degree requirements:* For master's, comprehensive exam. *Entrance requirements:* For master's, GMAT (minimum score of 510), minimum GPA of 2.75 overall and in upper-level accounting, 3.0 in last 60 hours of course work; for doctorate, GMAT, minimum undergraduate GPA of 3.0, both cumulative and over the last 60 hours of undergraduate work; 3.25 on all prior graduate work. Additional exam requirements/recommendations for international students: Required—TOEFL (minimum score 575 paper-based; 233 computer-based; 84 iBT); Recommended—IELTS (minimum score 7). *Application deadline:* For fall admission, 7/1 for domestic students, 5/1 for international students; for spring admission, 11/1 for domestic students, 9/1 for international students. Applications are processed on a rolling basis. Application fee: $40. Electronic applications accepted. *Expenses:* Tuition, state resident: full-time $2730.50; part-time $304 per credit hour. Tuition, nonresident: full-time $6901; part-time $767 per credit hour. *Financial support:* Career-related internships or fieldwork, Federal Work-Study, institutionally sponsored loans, scholarships/grants, and unspecified assistantships available. Support available to part-time students. Financial award application deadline: 4/1; financial award applicants required to submit FAFSA. *Faculty research:* Income tax, financial accounting system, managerial accounting, auditing. *Unit head:* Dr. Jim Scheiner, Director, 662-325-1633, Fax: 662-325-1646, E-mail: jscheiner@cobilan.msstate.edu. *Application contact:* Dr. Barbara Spencer, Graduate Coordinator, 662-325-3710, Fax: 662-325-1646, E-mail: sac@cobilan.msstate.edu.

New York Law School, Graduate Programs, New York, NY 10013. Offers financial services (LL M); law (JD); mental disability law (MA); real estate (LL M); taxation (LL M); JD/MBA. JD/MBA offered jointly with Bernard M. Baruch College of the City University of New York. *Accreditation:* ABA. Part-time and evening/weekend programs available. Postbaccalaureate distance learning degree programs offered. *Faculty:* 75 full-time (26 women), 100 part-time/adjunct (40 women). *Students:* 1,547 full-time (824 women), 491 part-time (214 women); includes 488 minority (145 Black or African American, non-Hispanic/Latino; 11 American Indian or Alaska Native, non-Hispanic/Latino; 67 Asian, non-Hispanic/Latino; 233 Hispanic/Latino; 1 Native Hawaiian or other Pacific Islander, non-Hispanic/Latino; 31 Two or more races, non-Hispanic/Latino). Average age 28. 5,405 applicants, 45% accepted, 550 enrolled. In 2010, 539 first professional degrees, 9 master's awarded. *Entrance requirements:* LSAT, letters of recommendation, resume. Additional exam requirements/recommendations for international students: Recommended—TOEFL (minimum score 600 paper-based; 250 computer-based; 100 iBT). *Application deadline:* For fall admission, 4/1 priority date for domestic and international students. Applications are processed on a rolling basis. Application fee: $65. Electronic applications accepted. *Expenses:* Tuition: Full-time $44,860; part-time $34,500 per year. Required fees: $1600. *Financial support:* In 2010–11, 682 students received support, including 202 research assistantships (averaging $3,920 per year), 5 teaching assistantships (averaging $1,000 per year); career-related internships or fieldwork, Federal Work-Study, institutionally sponsored loans, and scholarships/grants also available. Support available to part-time students. Financial award application deadline: 4/2; financial award applicants required to submit FAFSA. *Unit head:* Richard A. Matasar, President and Dean, 212-431-2840, Fax: 212-219-3752, E-mail: rmatasar@nyls.edu. *Application contact:* William D. Perez, Assistant Dean for Admissions and Financial Aid, 212-431-2888, Fax: 212-966-1522, E-mail: wperez@nyls.edu.

New York University, School of Law, New York, NY 10012-1019. Offers law (JD, LL M, JSD); law and business (Advanced Certificate); taxation (Advanced Certificate); JD/LL B; JD/LL M; JD/MA; JD/MBA; JD/MPA; JD/MPP; JD/MSW; JD/MUP; JD/PhD. *Accreditation:* ABA. Part-time programs available. *Faculty:* 125 full-time (36 women), 70 part-time/adjunct (23 women). *Students:* 1,427 full-time (628 women); includes 88 Black or African American, non-Hispanic/Latino; 3 American Indian or Alaska Native, non-Hispanic/Latino; 150 Asian, non-Hispanic/Latino; 91 Hispanic/Latino, 44 international. 7,272 applicants, 450 enrolled. In 2010, 471 first professional degrees, 534 master's, 3 doctorates awarded. *Entrance requirements:* LSAT. *Application deadline:* For fall admission, 2/1 for domestic students. Application fee: $75. Electronic applications accepted. *Expenses:* Contact institution. *Financial support:* Fellowships, research assistantships, teaching assistantships, career-related internships or fieldwork, Federal Work-Study, institutionally sponsored loans, scholarships/grants, tuition waivers (partial), and loan repayment assistance available. Financial award application deadline: 4/15; financial award applicants required to submit FAFSA. *Faculty research:* International law, environmental law, corporate law, globalization of law, philosophy of law. *Unit head:* Richard L. Revesz, Dean, 212-998-6000, Fax: 212-995-3150. *Application contact:* Kenneth J. Kleinrock, Assistant Dean for Admissions, 212-998-6060, Fax: 212-995-4527.

Northern Illinois University, Graduate School, College of Business, Department of Accountancy, De Kalb, IL 60115-2854. Offers MAS, MST. *Accreditation:* AACSB. Part-time and evening/weekend programs available. *Faculty:* 14 full-time (4 women). *Students:* 165 full-time (49 women), 71 part-time (37 women); includes 29 minority (3 Black or African American, non-Hispanic/Latino; 17 Asian, non-Hispanic/Latino; 4 Hispanic/Latino; 1 Native Hawaiian or other Pacific Islander, non-Hispanic/Latino; 4 Two or more races, non-Hispanic/Latino), 45 international. Average age 27. 161 applicants, 58% accepted, 48 enrolled. In 2010, 171 master's awarded. *Degree requirements:* For master's, thesis optional. *Entrance requirements:* For master's, GMAT, minimum GPA of 2.75. Additional exam requirements/recommendations for international students: Required—TOEFL (minimum score 550 paper-based; 213 computer-based). *Application deadline:* For fall admission, 4/1 priority date for domestic students, 5/1 for international students; for spring admission, 9/15 priority date for domestic students, 10/1 for international students. Applications are processed on a rolling basis. Application fee: $30. Electronic applications accepted. *Expenses:* Tuition, state resident: full-time $7200; part-time $300 per credit hour. Tuition, nonresident: full-time $14,400; part-time $600 per credit hour. Required fees: $79 per credit hour. *Financial support:* In 2010–11, 28 research assistantships with full tuition reimbursements, 11 teaching assistantships with full tuition reimbursements were awarded; fellowships with full tuition reimbursements, career-related internships or fieldwork, Federal Work-Study, scholarships/grants, tuition waivers (full), and unspecified assistantships also available. Support available to part-time students. Financial award applicants required to submit FAFSA. *Faculty research:* Accounting fraud, governmental accounting, corporate income tax planning, auditing, ethics. *Unit head:* Dr. James C. Young, Chair, 815-753-1250, Fax: 815-753-8515. *Application contact:* Dr. Rowene Linden, Graduate Adviser, 815-753-6200.

Northern Kentucky University, Office of Graduate Programs, College of Business, Program in Accountancy, Highland Heights, KY 41099. Offers accountancy (M Acc); advanced taxation (Certificate). Part-time and evening/weekend programs available. *Faculty:* 5 full-time (1 woman), 2 part-time/adjunct (0 women). *Students:* 11 full-time (4 women), 49 part-time (27 women); includes 4 minority (1 American Indian or Alaska Native, non-Hispanic/Latino; 1 Asian, non-Hispanic/Latino; 2 Hispanic/Latino), 2

international. Average age 31. 51 applicants, 67% accepted, 22 enrolled. In 2010, 12 master's, 3 other advanced degrees awarded. *Degree requirements:* For master's, capstone course. *Entrance requirements:* For master's, GMAT (minimum score 450), minimum GPA of 2.5. Additional exam requirements/recommendations for international students: Required—TOEFL (minimum score 550 paper-based; 213 computer-based; 79 iBT); Recommended—IELTS (minimum score 6.5). *Application deadline:* For fall admission, 8/1 for domestic students, 6/1 for international students; for spring admission, 12/1 for domestic students, 10/1 for international students. Applications are processed on a rolling basis. Application fee: $40. Electronic applications accepted. *Expenses:* Tuition, state resident: full-time $7254; part-time $403 per credit hour. Tuition, nonresident: full-time $12,492; part-time $694 per credit hour. Tuition and fees vary according to degree level and program. *Financial support:* Unspecified assistantships available. Financial award applicants required to submit FAFSA. *Faculty research:* Behavioral influences on accounting decisions, historical development of accounting, auditing and accounting failures. *Unit head:* Robert Salyer, Director, 859-572-7695, Fax: 859-572-7694, E-mail: salyerb@nku.edu. *Application contact:* Dr. Peg Griffin, Director of Graduate Programs, 859-572-6934, Fax: 859-572-6670, E-mail: griffinp@nku.edu.

Nova Southeastern University, H. Wayne Huizenga School of Business and Entrepreneurship, Program in Taxation, Fort Lauderdale, FL 33314-7796. Offers M Tax. Part-time and evening/weekend programs available. Postbaccalaureate distance learning degree programs offered. *Faculty:* 2 full-time (1 woman), 5 part-time/adjunct (0 women). *Students:* 6 full-time (5 women), 158 part-time (85 women); includes 51 Black or African American, non-Hispanic/Latino; 4 Asian, non-Hispanic/Latino; 49 Hispanic/Latino; 2 Two or more races, non-Hispanic/Latino, 3 international. Average age 36. 69 applicants, 70% accepted, 34 enrolled. In 2010, 42 master's awarded. *Entrance requirements:* Additional exam requirements/recommendations for international students: Required—TOEFL (minimum score 550 paper-based; 213 computer-based; 79 iBT), IELTS (minimum score 6). *Application deadline:* For fall admission, 8/15 for domestic and international students; for winter admission, 12/10 for domestic and international students; for spring admission, 2/10 for domestic and international students. Applications are processed on a rolling basis. Application fee: $50. Electronic applications accepted. *Financial support:* Federal Work-Study and scholarships/grants available. Support available to part-time students. Financial award applicants required to submit FAFSA. *Unit head:* Dr. Preston Jones, Executive Associate Dean, 954-262-5127, Fax: 954-262-3960, E-mail: prestonj@huizenga.nova.edu. *Application contact:* Aimee Fernandez, Assistant Director, 954-262-5091, Fax: 954-262-3822, E-mail: aimeefernandez@huizenga.nova.edu.

St. John's University, The Peter J. Tobin College of Business, Department of Accounting and Taxation, Program in Taxation, Queens, NY 11439. Offers MBA, MS, Adv C. Part-time and evening/weekend programs available. *Students:* 49 full-time (24 women), 34 part-time (12 women); includes 40 minority (12 Black or African American, non-Hispanic/Latino; 19 Asian, non-Hispanic/Latino; 8 Hispanic/Latino; 1 Two or more races, non-Hispanic/Latino), 3 international. Average age 26. 153 applicants, 68% accepted, 53 enrolled. In 2010, 45 master's awarded. *Degree requirements:* For master's, comprehensive exam (for some programs), thesis optional. *Entrance requirements:* For master's, GMAT (waived for MS applicants who have successfully completed the CPA exam), 2 letters of recommendation, resume, transcripts, statement of goals; for Adv C, 2 letters of recommendation, resume, undergraduate transcripts, essay. Additional exam requirements/recommendations for international students: Required—TOEFL (minimum score 600 paper-based; 250 computer-based; 100 iBT), IELTS (minimum score 5.5). *Application deadline:* For fall admission, 5/1 priority date for domestic and international students; for spring admission, 11/1 priority date for domestic and international students. Applications are processed on a rolling basis. Application fee: $70. Electronic applications accepted. *Expenses:* Contact institution. *Financial support:* Research assistantships available. Support available to part-time students. Financial award application deadline: 3/1; financial award applicants required to submit FAFSA. *Unit head:* Dr. Adrian Fitzsimons, Chair, 718-990-7306, Fax: 718-380-3803, E-mail: fitzsims@stjohns.edu. *Application contact:* Carol Swanberg, Assistant Dean, Director of Graduate Admissions, 718-990-1345, Fax: 718-990-5242, E-mail: tobingradnyc@stjohns.edu.

Seton Hall University, Stillman School of Business, Department of Accounting, South Orange, NJ 07079-2697. Offers accounting (MS); professional accounting (MS); taxation (Certificate). Part-time and evening/weekend programs available. *Faculty:* 7 full-time (1 woman), 3 part-time/adjunct (1 woman). *Students:* 8 full-time (6 women), 36 part-time (7 women); includes 4 Black or African American, non-Hispanic/Latino; 10 Asian, non-Hispanic/Latino; 1 Hispanic/Latino. Average age 25. 105 applicants, 86% accepted, 44 enrolled. In 2010, 23 master's awarded. *Entrance requirements:* For master's, GMAT or CPA, Advanced degrees such as Ph.D., MD, JD, PharmD, DDS, DVM, MBA fro an AACSB institution, MS in a business discipline, and aminimum GPA of 3.0. Additional exam requirements/recommendations for international students: Required—TOEFL (minimum: 254 computer, 102 iBT), IELTS, or Pearson Test of English (PTE). *Application deadline:* For fall admission, 5/31 priority date for domestic students, 3/31 for international students; for spring admission, 10/31 for domestic students, 9/30 for international students. Applications are processed on a rolling basis. Application fee: $75. Electronic applications accepted. *Financial support:* In 2010–11, 2 students received support, including research assistantships with full tuition reimbursements available (averaging $35,610 per year); career-related internships or fieldwork, scholarships/grants, and unspecified assistantships also available. Support available to part-time students. Financial award application deadline: 6/30; financial award applicants required to submit FAFSA. *Faculty research:* Voluntary disclosure, international accounting, pension and retirement accounting, ethics in financial reporting. *Unit head:* Dr. Mark Holtzman, Chair, 973-761-9133, Fax: 973-761-9217, E-mail: mark.holtzman@shu.edu. *Application contact:* Catherine Bianchi, Director of Graduate Admissions, 973-761-9262, Fax: 973-761-9208, E-mail: catherine.bianchi@shu.edu.

Seton Hall University, Stillman School of Business, Department of Taxation, South Orange, NJ 07079-2697. Offers MS. Part-time and evening/weekend programs available. *Faculty:* 1 full-time (0 women), 2 part-time/adjunct (0 women). *Students:* 5 part-time (3 women). Average age 30. 8 applicants, 88% accepted, 5 enrolled. In 2010, 18 master's awarded. *Entrance requirements:* For master's, GMAT or CPA, Advanced degree such as JD, PhD, PharmD, MD, DDS, DVM, MBA from an AACSB institution, MS in a business discipline and a minimum GPA of 3.0. Additional exam requirements/recommendations for international students: Required—TOEFL (minimum: 550 paper, 254 computer, 102 iBT), IELTS or Pearson Test of English (PTE). *Application deadline:* For fall admission, 6/1 priority date for domestic students, 4/11 for international students; for spring admission, 11/1 priority date for domestic students, 10/1 for international students. Application fee: $75 ($100 for international students). Electronic applications accepted. *Expenses:* Contact institution. *Financial support:* In 2010–11, 3 students received support, including research assistantships with full tuition reimbursements available (averaging $35,610 per year); career-related internships or fieldwork, scholarships/grants, and unspecified assistantships also available. Support available to part-time students. Financial award application deadline: 6/1; financial award applicants required to submit FAFSA. *Faculty research:* Issues affecting cost capitalization, estate valuation discounts, qualified terminable interest property elections, eastern European tax initiatives, realigning the capital structure of closely-held business enterprises. *Unit head:* Dr. Mark Holtzman, Department Chair, 973-761-9133, Fax: 973-761-9217, E-mail: eastonre@shu.edu. *Application contact:* Catherine Bianchi, Director of Graduate Admissions, 973-761-9220, Fax: 973-761-9208, E-mail: catherine.bianchi@shu.edu.

Southern Illinois University Edwardsville, Graduate School, School of Business, Department of Accounting, Edwardsville, IL 62026-0001. Offers accountancy (MSA); taxation (MSA). *Accreditation:* AACSB. Part-time and evening/weekend programs available. *Faculty:* 4 full-time (1 woman). *Students:* 15 full-time (7 women), 22 part-time (12 women); includes 3 minority (1 Asian, non-Hispanic/Latino; 1 Hispanic/Latino; 1 Two or more races, non-Hispanic/Latino), 2 international. Average age 26. 47 applicants, 47% accepted. In 2010, 22 master's awarded. *Degree requirements:* For master's, thesis or alternative, final exam. *Entrance requirements:* For master's, GMAT. Additional exam requirements/recommendations for international students: Required—TOEFL (minimum score 550 paper-based; 213 computer-based; 79 iBT), IELTS (minimum score 6.5). *Application deadline:* For fall admission, 7/22 for domestic students, 6/1 for international students; for spring admission, 12/10 for domestic students, 10/1 for international students. Applications are processed on a rolling basis. Application fee: $30. Electronic applications accepted. *Expenses:* Tuition, state resident: full-time $6012; part-time $1503 per semester. Tuition, nonresident: full-time $15,030; part-time $3758 per semester. Required fees: $1711; $675 per semester. *Financial support:* In 2010–11, 1 fellowship with full tuition reimbursement (averaging $8,370 per year), 8 teaching assistantships with full tuition reimbursements (averaging $8,064 per year) were awarded; research assistantships with full tuition reimbursements, career-related internships or fieldwork, Federal Work-Study, institutionally sponsored loans, scholarships/grants, traineeships, and unspecified assistantships also available. Support available to part-time students. Financial award application deadline: 3/1; financial award applicants required to submit FAFSA. *Unit head:* Dr. Michael Costigan, Chair, 618-650-2633, E-mail: mcostig@siue.edu. *Application contact:* Dr. Michael Costigan, Chair, 618-650-2633, E-mail: mcostig@siue.edu.

Southern Methodist University, Dedman School of Law, Dallas, TX 75275-0110. Offers foreign law school graduates (LL M); law (JD, SJD); law-general (LL M); taxation (LL M); JD/MA; JD/MBA. *Accreditation:* ABA. Part-time and evening/weekend programs available. *Faculty:* 40 full-time (17 women), 50 part-time/adjunct (11 women). *Students:* 963 full-time (433 women), 58 part-time (26 women); includes 50 Black or African American, non-Hispanic/Latino; 12 American Indian or Alaska Native, non-Hispanic/Latino; 76 Asian, non-Hispanic/Latino; 80 Hispanic/Latino; 1 Two or more races, non-Hispanic/Latino, 79 international. Average age 27. 3,015 applicants, 26% accepted, 309 enrolled. In 2010, 270 first professional degrees, 58 master's awarded. *Degree requirements:* For master's, thesis optional; for doctorate, thesis/dissertation; for JD, 30 hours of public service. *Entrance requirements:* For JD, LSAT, 2 letters of recommendation, resume, personal statement; for master's, JD; for doctorate, LL M. Additional exam requirements/recommendations for international students: Required—TOEFL (minimum score 575 paper-based; 233

computer-based; 91 iBT). *Application deadline:* For fall admission, 2/15 priority date for domestic students. Applications are processed on a rolling basis. Application fee: $75. Electronic applications accepted. *Expenses:* Contact institution. *Financial support:* Career-related internships or fieldwork, Federal Work-Study, and scholarships/grants available. Financial award application deadline: 2/15; financial award applicants required to submit FAFSA. *Faculty research:* Corporate law, intellectual property, international law, commercial law, dispute resolution. *Unit head:* John B. Attanasio, Dean, 214-768-8999, Fax: 214-768-2182, E-mail: jba@mail.smu.edu. *Application contact:* Virginia Keehan, Assistant Dean for Admissions, 214-768-2550, Fax: 214-768-2549, E-mail: lawadmit@smu.edu.

Suffolk University, Sawyer Business School, Department of Accounting, Boston, MA 02108-2770. Offers accounting (MSA, GDPA); taxation (MST); GDPA/MST; MBA/GDPA; MBA/MSA; MBA/MST. *Accreditation:* AACSB. Part-time and evening/weekend programs available. *Faculty:* 19 full-time (6 women), 3 part-time/adjunct (2 women). *Students:* 80 full-time (53 women), 150 part-time (77 women); includes 10 Black or African American, non-Hispanic/Latino; 1 American Indian or Alaska Native, non-Hispanic/Latino; 18 Asian, non-Hispanic/Latino; 2 Hispanic/Latino; 1 Two or more races, non-Hispanic/Latino, 74 international. Average age 29. 453 applicants, 71% accepted, 95 enrolled. In 2010, 86 master's, 5 GDPAs awarded. *Entrance requirements:* For master's, GMAT. Additional exam requirements/recommendations for international students: Required—TOEFL (minimum score 550 paper-based; 213 computer-based; 80 iBT). *Application deadline:* For fall admission, 6/15 priority date for domestic students, 6/15 for international students; for spring admission, 11/1 priority date for domestic students, 11/1 for international students. Applications are processed on a rolling basis. Application fee: $50. Electronic applications accepted. *Financial support:* In 2010–11, 91 students received support, including 45 fellowships with full and partial tuition reimbursements available (averaging $16,430 per year); career-related internships or fieldwork, Federal Work-Study, and institutionally sponsored loans also available. Support available to part-time students. Financial award application deadline: 4/1; financial award applicants required to submit CSS PROFILE. *Faculty research:* Tax policy, tax research, decision-making in accounting, accounting information systems, capital markets and strategic planning. *Unit head:* Lewis Shaw, Chair, 617-573-8615, Fax: 617-994-4260, E-mail: lshaw@suffolk.edu. *Application contact:* Judith Reynolds, Director of Graduate Admissions, 617-573-8302, Fax: 617-305-1733, E-mail: grad.admission@suffolk.edu.

Suffolk University, Sawyer Business School, Master of Business Administration Program, Boston, MA 02108-2770. Offers accounting (MBA); business administration (APC); corporate financial executive track (MBA); entrepreneurship (MBA); executive business administration (EMBA); finance (MBA); global business administration (GMBA); health administration (MBA); international business (MBA); marketing (MBA); organizational behavior (MBA); strategic management (MBA); taxation (MBA); JD/MBA; MBA/GDPA; MBA/MHA; MBA/MSA; MBA/MSF; MBA/MST. *Accreditation:* AACSB. Part-time and evening/weekend programs available. Postbaccalaureate distance learning degree programs offered (no on-campus study). *Faculty:* 97 full-time (30 women), 14 part-time/adjunct (3 women). *Students:* 179 full-time (65 women), 337 part-time (143 women); includes 16 Black or African American, non-Hispanic/Latino; 2 American Indian or Alaska Native, non-Hispanic/Latino; 22 Asian, non-Hispanic/Latino; 9 Hispanic/Latino; 1 Native Hawaiian or other Pacific Islander, non-Hispanic/Latino, 80 international. Average age 30. 431 applicants, 68% accepted, 128 enrolled. In 2010, 283 master's awarded. *Entrance requirements:* For master's, GMAT, minimum undergraduate GPA of 2.75 (MBA), 5 years of managerial experience (EMBA). Additional exam requirements/recommendations for international students: Required—TOEFL (minimum score 550 paper-based; 213 computer-based). *Application deadline:* For fall admission, 6/15 priority date for domestic students, 6/15 for international students; for spring admission, 11/1 priority date for domestic students, 11/1 for international students. Applications are processed on a rolling basis. Application fee: $50. Electronic applications accepted. *Financial support:* In 2010–11, 266 students received support, including 94 fellowships with full and partial tuition reimbursements available (averaging $12,635 per year); career-related internships or fieldwork, Federal Work-Study, and institutionally sponsored loans also available. Support available to part-time students. Financial award application deadline: 4/1; financial award applicants required to submit FAFSA. *Faculty research:* Foreign investments; career strategies and boundaryless careers; corporate ethics codes; interest rates, inflation, and growth options; innovation and product development performance. *Unit head:* Lillian Hallberg, Assistant Dean of Graduate Programs/Director of MBA Programs, 617-573-8306, E-mail: lhallber@suffolk.edu. *Application contact:* Judith Reynolds, Director of Graduate Admissions, 617-573-8302, Fax: 617-305-1733, E-mail: grad.admission@suffolk.edu.

Temple University, James E. Beasley School of Law, Philadelphia, PA 19122. Offers law (JD); legal education (SJD); taxation (LL M); transnational law (LL M); trial advocacy (LL M); JD/LL M; JD/MBA. *Accreditation:* ABA. Part-time and evening/weekend programs available. *Faculty:* 61 full-time (25 women), 94 part-time/adjunct (35 women). *Students:* 798 full-time (351 women), 186 part-time (76 women); includes 246 minority (71 Black or

African American, non-Hispanic/Latino; 9 American Indian or Alaska Native, non-Hispanic/Latino; 85 Asian, non-Hispanic/Latino; 74 Hispanic/Latino; 7 Two or more races, non-Hispanic/Latino), 4 international. Average age 25. 4,682 applicants, 39% accepted, 326 enrolled. In 2010, 295 first professional degrees awarded. *Entrance requirements:* LSAT, Credential Assembly Service (CAS). *Application deadline:* For fall admission, 3/1 for domestic and international students. Applications are processed on a rolling basis. Application fee: $60. Electronic applications accepted. *Expenses:* Contact institution. *Financial support:* In 2010–11, 680 students received support, including research assistantships (averaging $5,500 per year), teaching assistantships (averaging $5,500 per year); Federal Work-Study, scholarships/grants, tuition waivers (full and partial), and unspecified assistantships also available. Support available to part-time students. Financial award application deadline: 3/1; financial award applicants required to submit FAFSA. *Faculty research:* Evidence, gender issues, health care law, immigration law, and intellectual property law. *Unit head:* JoAnne A. Epps, Dean, 215-204-7863, Fax: 215-204-1185, E-mail: law@temple.edu. *Application contact:* Johanne L. Johnston, Assistant Dean for Admissions & Financial Aid, 800-560-1428, Fax: 215-204-9319, E-mail: lawadmis@temple.edu.

Texas Tech University, Graduate School, Jerry S. Rawls College of Business Administration, Area of Accounting, Lubbock, TX 79409. Offers accounting (PhD); audit/financial reporting (MSA); taxation (MSA); JD/MSA. *Accreditation:* AACSB. Part-time programs available. *Faculty:* 15 full-time (3 women). *Students:* 134 full-time (72 women), 12 part-time (5 women); includes 17 minority (1 Black or African American, non-Hispanic/Latino; 3 American Indian or Alaska Native, non-Hispanic/Latino; 4 Asian, non-Hispanic/Latino; 8 Hispanic/Latino; 1 Two or more races, non-Hispanic/Latino), 1 international. Average age 23. 151 applicants, 72% accepted, 97 enrolled. In 2010, 37 master's, 3 doctorates awarded. Terminal master's awarded for partial completion of doctoral program. *Degree requirements:* For master's, capstone course; for doctorate, comprehensive exam, thesis/dissertation, qualifying exams. *Entrance requirements:* For master's and doctorate, GMAT, holistic profile of academic credentials. Additional exam requirements/recommendations for international students: Required—TOEFL (minimum score 550 paper-based; 213 computer-based; 79 iBT). *Application deadline:* For fall admission, 2/1 for domestic students, 1/15 for international students. Applications are processed on a rolling basis. Application fee: $50 ($75 for international students). Electronic applications accepted. *Expenses:* Tuition, state resident: full-time $5495.76; part-time $228.99 per credit hour. Tuition, nonresident: full-time $12,936; part-time $538.99 per credit hour. Required fees: $2674; $36 per credit hour. $905 per semester. *Financial support:* In 2010–11, 7 research assistantships (averaging $8,800 per year), 2 teaching assistantships (averaging $18,000 per year) were awarded; fellowships, career-related internships or fieldwork, Federal Work-Study, scholarships/grants, health care benefits, and unspecified assistantships also available. Financial award applicants required to submit FAFSA. *Faculty research:* Governmental and nonprofit accounting, managerial and financial accounting. *Unit head:* Dr. Robert Ricketts, Area Coordinator, 806-742-3180, Fax: 806-742-3182, E-mail: robert.ricketts@ttu.edu. *Application contact:* Cynthia D. Barnes, 806-742-3184, Fax: 806-742-3958, E-mail: ba_grad@ttu.edu.

Thomas M. Cooley Law School, Graduate Programs, Lansing, MI 48901-3038. Offers corporate law and finance (LL M); general, self-directed (LL M); insurance (LL M); intellectual property (LL M); law (JD); taxation (LL M); U. S. law for foreign attorneys (LL M). *Accreditation:* ABA. Part-time and evening/weekend programs available. Postbaccalaureate distance learning degree programs offered. *Faculty:* 127 full-time (53 women), 196 part-time/adjunct (78 women). *Students:* 718 full-time (342 women), 3,283 part-time (1,607 women); includes 1,071 minority (532 Black or African American, non-Hispanic/Latino; 19 American Indian or Alaska Native, non-Hispanic/Latino; 207 Asian, non-Hispanic/Latino; 219 Hispanic/Latino; 10 Native Hawaiian or other Pacific Islander, non-Hispanic/Latino; 84 Two or more races, non-Hispanic/Latino), 215 international. Average age 26. 4,922 applicants, 83% accepted, 1583 enrolled. In 2010, 918 first professional degrees awarded. *Degree requirements:* For master's, thesis optional; for JD, minimum of 3 credits of clinical experience. *Entrance requirements:* For JD, LSAT, CAS; for master's, JD or LL B. Additional exam requirements/recommendations for international students: Required—TOEFL. *Application deadline:* For fall admission, 9/1 for domestic and international students; for winter admission, 1/1 for domestic and international students; for spring admission, 5/1 for domestic and international students. Applications are processed on a rolling basis. Application fee: $0. Electronic applications accepted. *Expenses:* Tuition: Full-time $30,604; part-time $2186 per credit hour. Required fees: $40. *Financial support:* In 2010–11, 2,187 students received support. Federal Work-Study and scholarships/grants available. Support available to part-time students. Financial award applicants required to submit FAFSA. *Faculty research:* Wrongful convictions, civil rights, environmental law, litigation techniques, death penalty. *Unit head:* Don LeDuc, President and Dean, 517-371-5140. *Application contact:* Stephanie Gregg, Assistant Dean of Admissions, 517-371-5140, Fax: 517-334-5718, E-mail: greggs@cooley.edu.

Troy University, Graduate School, College of Business, Program in Taxation, Troy, AL 36082. Offers MTX, Certificate. Part-time and evening/weekend programs available. *Students:* 6 part-time (5 women); all minorities (4 Black or African American, non-Hispanic/Latino; 2 Hispanic/Latino). Average age 38. 7 applicants, 100% accepted. *Degree requirements:* For master's, minimum GPA of 3.0, research paper, capstone course. *Entrance requirements:* For master's, GMAT (minimum score of 500), minimum GPA of 2.5; letter of recommendation; bachelor's degree, CPA, or CFP. Additional exam requirements/recommendations for international students: Required—TOEFL (minimum score 523 paper-based; 193 computer-based; 70 iBT), IELTS (minimum score 6), or ACT compass ESL (minimum Listening, Reading, and Grammar score: 270). *Application deadline:* Applications are processed on a rolling basis. Application fee: $50. Electronic applications accepted. *Expenses:* Tuition, state resident: full-time $4428; part-time $246 per credit hour. Tuition, nonresident: full-time $8856; part-time $492 per credit hour. Required fees: $432; $24 per credit hour. $50 per term. Tuition and fees vary according to program. *Unit head:* Dr. Kay Sheridan, Interim Dean, 334-670-3143, Fax: 334-670-3708, E-mail: ksheridan@troy.edu. *Application contact:* Brenda K. Campbell, Director of Graduate Admissions, 334-670-3178, Fax: 334-670-3733, E-mail: bcamp@troy.edu.

Université de Sherbrooke, Faculty of Administration, Program in Taxation, Sherbrooke, QC J1K 2R1, Canada. Offers M Tax, Diploma. Part-time and evening/weekend programs available. *Faculty:* 12 full-time (2 women), 68 part-time/adjunct (26 women). *Students:* 57 full-time (26 women), 49 part-time (22 women). Average age 28. 226 applicants, 65% accepted, 106 enrolled. In 2010, 97 master's awarded. *Degree requirements:* For master's, one foreign language, thesis. *Entrance requirements:* For master's, No, Bachelor Degree in business, law or economics Basis knowledge in canadian taxation (2 courses). *Application deadline:* For fall admission, 4/30 priority date for domestic students, 4/5 priority date for international students; for winter admission, 10/15 priority date for domestic and international students. Applications are processed on a rolling basis. Application fee: $70. Electronic applications accepted. *Faculty research:* Taxation research, public finances. *Unit head:* Chantal Amiot, Director, 819-821-8000 Ext. 63731, Fax: 819-821-7364, E-mail: chantal.amiot@usherbrooke.ca. *Application contact:* Linda Papin, assistant to the director, 819-821-8000 Ext. 63427, Fax: 819-821-7364, E-mail: linda.pepin@usherbrooke.ca.

The University of Akron, Graduate School, College of Business Administration, School of Accountancy, Program in Taxation, Akron, OH 44325. Offers MT. *Students:* 17 full-time (10 women), 37 part-time (15 women); includes 1 Black or African American, non-Hispanic/Latino; 1 Asian, non-Hispanic/Latino, 1 international. Average age 37. 33 applicants, 91% accepted, 25 enrolled. In 2010, 36 master's awarded. *Entrance requirements:* For master's, GMAT, minimum GPA of 2.75, two letters of recommendation, resume, statement of purpose. Additional exam requirements/recommendations for international students: Required—TOEFL (minimum score 550 paper-based; 213 computer-based; 79 iBT). *Application deadline:* For fall admission, 7/15 for domestic and international students; for spring admission, 11/15 for domestic and international students. Application fee: $30 ($40 for international students). Electronic applications accepted. *Expenses:* Tuition, state resident: full-time $6800; part-time $378 per credit hour. Tuition, nonresident: full-time $11,644; part-time $647 per credit hour. Required fees: $1265. One-time fee: $30 full-time. *Unit head:* Coordinator. *Application contact:* Dr. Susan Hanlon, Director of Graduate Business Programs, 330-972-7043, Fax: 330-972-6588, E-mail: shanlon@uakron.edu.

The University of Alabama, Graduate School, Manderson Graduate School of Business, Culverhouse School of Accountancy, Tuscaloosa, AL 35487. Offers accounting (M Acc, PhD); tax accounting (MTA). *Accreditation:* AACSB. *Faculty:* 16 full-time (4 women). *Students:* 108 full-time (51 women), 3 part-time (2 women); includes 8 minority (5 Black or African American, non-Hispanic/Latino; 1 Asian, non-Hispanic/Latino; 1 Hispanic/Latino; 1 Two or more races, non-Hispanic/Latino), 1 international. Average age 24. 248 applicants, 49% accepted, 85 enrolled. In 2010, 99 master's, 1 doctorate awarded. *Degree requirements:* For doctorate, thesis/dissertation. *Entrance requirements:* For master's and doctorate, GMAT, minimum GPA of 3.0. Additional exam requirements/recommendations for international students: Required—TOEFL. *Application deadline:* For fall admission, 7/1 priority date for domestic students, 6/1 priority date for international students; for spring admission, 11/1 priority date for domestic students, 10/1 priority date for international students. Applications are processed on a rolling basis. Application fee: $50 ($60 for international students). Electronic applications accepted. *Expenses:* Tuition, state resident: full-time $7900. Tuition, nonresident: full-time $20,500. *Financial support:* In 2010–11, 99 students received support, including 6 fellowships with full tuition reimbursements available (averaging $15,000 per year), 21 research assistantships with full and partial tuition reimbursements available (averaging $6,065 per year), 18 teaching assistantships with full and partial tuition reimbursements available (averaging $6,065 per year); career-related internships or fieldwork, Federal Work-Study, institutionally sponsored loans, scholarships/grants, health care benefits, and unspecified assistantships also available. Financial award application deadline: 3/31. *Faculty research:* Corporate governance, audit decision making, earning management, valuation, executive compensation, not-for-profit. *Unit head:* Dr. Mary S. Stone, Director, 205-348-2915, Fax: 205-348-8453, E-mail: mstone@cba.ua.edu. *Application contact:* Sandy D. Davidson, Advisor, 205-348-8997, Fax: 205-348-8453, E-mail: sdavidso@cba.ua.edu.

The University of Alabama in Huntsville, School of Graduate Studies, College of Business Administration, Department of Accounting and Finance, Huntsville, AL 35899. Offers accounting (M Acc), including CPA preparatory with an emphasis in taxation, CPA preparatory with emphasis in assurance and financial reporting, general accounting, information systems audit and control (ISAC). *Accreditation:* AACSB. Part-time and evening/weekend programs available. *Faculty:* 7 full-time (4 women), 2 part-time/adjunct (0 women). *Students:* 14 full-time (8 women), 27 part-time (14 women); includes 6 minority (all Black or African American, non-Hispanic/Latino), 3 international. Average age 33. 27 applicants, 56% accepted, 13 enrolled. In 2010, 8 master's awarded. *Degree requirements:* For master's, comprehensive exam, thesis or alternative. *Entrance requirements:* For master's, GMAT (minimum score 500), minimum AACSB index of 1080. Additional exam requirements/recommendations for international students: Required—TOEFL (minimum score 550 paper-based; 213 computer-based; 62 iBT). *Application deadline:* For fall admission, 8/1 for domestic students, 4/1 for international students; for spring admission, 12/1 for domestic students, 9/1 for international students. Applications are processed on a rolling basis. Application fee: $40 ($50 for international students). Electronic applications accepted. *Expenses:* Tuition, state resident: full-time $7250; part-time $407.75 per credit hour. Tuition, nonresident: full-time $17,358; part-time $970.05 per credit hour. Required fees: $246.80 per semester. Tuition and fees vary according to course load and program. *Financial support:* In 2010–11, 1 student received support, including 1 research assistantship with full tuition reimbursement available (averaging $14,400 per year), 1 teaching assistantship with full tuition reimbursement available (averaging $11,470 per year); career-related internships or fieldwork, Federal Work-Study, institutionally sponsored loans, scholarships/grants, health care benefits, and unspecified assistantships also available. Support available to part-time students. Financial award application deadline: 4/1; financial award applicants required to submit FAFSA. *Faculty research:* Accounting information systems, emerging technologies in accounting, behavioral accounting, state and local taxation, financial accounting. Total annual research expenditures: $17,511. *Unit head:* Dr. John Burnett, Interim Chair, 256-824-2923, Fax: 256-824-2929, E-mail: burnettj@uah.edu. *Application contact:* Jennifer Pettitt, Director of Graduate Programs, 256-824-6681, Fax: 256-824-7571, E-mail: jennifer.pettitt@uah.edu.

University of Central Florida, College of Business Administration, Kenneth G. Dixon School of Accounting, Program in Taxation, Orlando, FL 32816. Offers MST. Part-time and evening/weekend programs available. *Students:* 28 full-time (12 women), 15 part-time (8 women); includes 3 Black or African American, non-Hispanic/Latino; 3 Asian, non-Hispanic/Latino; 2 Hispanic/Latino, 1 international. Average age 27. 30 applicants, 77% accepted, 16 enrolled. In 2010, 21 master's awarded. *Degree requirements:* For master's, comprehensive exam. *Entrance requirements:* For master's, GMAT, minimum GPA of 3.0 in last 60 hours of course work. Additional exam requirements/recommendations for international students: Required—TOEFL. *Application deadline:* For fall admission, 2/1 priority date for domestic students; for spring admission, 11/1 priority date for domestic students. Application fee: $30. Electronic applications accepted. *Expenses:* Tuition, state resident: part-time $256.56 per credit hour. Tuition, nonresident: part-time $1011.52 per credit hour. Part-time tuition and fees vary according to program. *Financial support:* In 2010–11, 7 students received support; research assistantships, teaching assistantships with partial tuition reimbursements available, career-related internships or fieldwork, Federal Work-Study, institutionally sponsored loans, tuition waivers (partial), and unspecified assistantships available. Financial award application deadline: 3/1; financial award applicants required to submit FAFSA. *Unit head:* Dr. Sean Robb, Director. *Application contact:* Dr. Sean Robb, Director.

University of Denver, Sturm College of Law, Taxation Program, Denver, CO 80208. Offers LL M, MT. Part-time and evening/weekend programs available. *Faculty:* 7 full-time (1 woman), 4 part-time/adjunct (1 woman). *Students:* 68 full-time (19 women), 88 part-time (26 women); includes 23 minority (7 Black or African American, non-Hispanic/Latino; 10 Asian, non-Hispanic/Latino; 4 Hispanic/Latino; 2 Two or more races, non-Hispanic/Latino), 7 international. Average age 32. 155 applicants, 100% accepted, 79 enrolled. In 2010, 105 master's awarded. *Entrance requirements:* For master's, LSAT (for LL M), JD from ABA-approved institution (for LL M). Additional exam requirements/recommendations for international students: Required—TOEFL (minimum score 550 paper-based; 80 iBT). *Application deadline:* Applications are processed on a rolling basis. Application fee: $30. *Expenses:* Contact institution. *Financial support:* Federal Work-Study, institutionally sponsored loans, scholarships/grants, and tuition waivers (full and partial) available. Support available to part-time students. Financial award application deadline: 6/30; financial award applicants required to submit FAFSA. *Unit head:* Dr. Mark A. Vogel, Director, 303-871-6239, Fax: 303-871-6358, E-mail: mvogel@du.edu. *Application contact:* Information Contact, 303-871-6239, Fax: 303-871-6358, E-mail: gtp@du.edu.

University of Florida, Levin College of Law, Gainesville, FL 32611. Offers comparative law (LL M); environmental law (LL M); international taxation (LL M); law (JD); taxation (LL M, SJD). *Accreditation:* ABA. *Faculty:* 77 full-time (37 women), 36 part-time/adjunct (10 women). *Students:* 1,175 full-time (518 women), 10 part-time (1 woman); includes 74 Black or African American, non-Hispanic/Latino; 16 American Indian or Alaska Native, non-Hispanic/Latino; 73 Asian, non-Hispanic/Latino; 112 Hispanic/Latino, 33 international. Average age 24. 3,357 applicants, 24% accepted, 310 enrolled. In 2010, 382 first professional degrees awarded. *Degree requirements:* For JD, thesis/dissertation or alternative. *Entrance requirements:* LSAT. *Application deadline:* For fall admission, 1/15 for domestic and international students. Applications are processed on a rolling basis. Application fee: $30. Electronic applications accepted. *Expenses:* Tuition, state resident: full-time $10,915.92. Tuition, nonresident: full-time $28,309. *Financial support:* In 2010–11, 261 students received support, including 30 research assistantships (averaging $8,580 per year); Federal Work-Study, institutionally sponsored loans, scholarships/grants, health care benefits, and unspecified assistantships also available. Financial award application deadline: 4/7; financial award applicants required to submit FAFSA. *Faculty research:* Environmental and land use law, taxation, family law, international law, Constitutional law. *Unit head:* Robert Jerry, Dean, 352-273-0600, Fax: 352-392-8727, E-mail: jerryr@law.ufl.edu. *Application contact:* Michelle Adorno, Assistant Dean for Admissions, 352-273-0890, Fax: 352-392-4087, E-mail: madorno@law.ufl.edu.

University of Hawaii at Manoa, Graduate Division, Shidler College of Business, Program in Accounting, Honolulu, HI 96822. Offers accounting (M Acc); accounting law (M Acc); information systems (M Acc); taxation (M Acc). Part-time programs available. *Faculty:* 9 full-time (2 women). *Students:* 45 full-time (22 women), 33 part-time (22 women); includes 41 minority (28 Asian, non-Hispanic/Latino; 5 Native Hawaiian or other Pacific Islander, non-Hispanic/Latino; 8 Two or more races, non-Hispanic/Latino), 21 international. Average age 32. 144 applicants, 78% accepted, 72 enrolled. In 2010, 38 master's awarded. *Entrance requirements:* For master's, GMAT, bachelor's degree in accounting, minimum GPA of 3.0. Additional exam requirements/recommendations for international students: Required—TOEFL (minimum score 550 paper-based; 213 computer-based; 79 iBT), IELTS (minimum score 5). *Application deadline:* For fall admission, 5/1 for domestic students, 3/1 for international students; for spring admission, 11/1 for domestic students, 10/1 for international students. Application fee: $60. *Financial support:* In 2010–11, 24 fellowships (averaging $4,662 per year), 7 research assistantships (averaging $16,478 per year) were awarded; career-related internships or fieldwork, Federal Work-Study, and tuition waivers (full) also available. *Faculty research:* International accounting, current tax topics, insurance industry financial reporting, behavioral accounting, auditing. *Application contact:* Liming Guan, Graduate Chair, 808-956-7332, Fax: 808-956-9888, E-mail: lguan@hawaii.edu.

University of Houston, Law Center, Houston, TX 77204-6060. Offers energy, environment, and natural resources (LL M); health law (LL M); intellectual property and information law (LL M); international law (LL M); law (JD, LL M); tax law (LL M). *Accreditation:* ABA. Part-time and evening/weekend programs available. *Faculty:* 40 full-time (9 women), 85 part-time/adjunct (32 women). *Students:* 734 full-time (319 women), 241 part-time (116 women); includes 285 minority (71 Black or African American, non-Hispanic/Latino; 5 American Indian or Alaska Native, non-Hispanic/Latino; 94 Asian, non-Hispanic/Latino; 100 Hispanic/Latino; 2 Native Hawaiian or other Pacific Islander, non-Hispanic/Latino; 13 Two or more races, non-Hispanic/Latino), 45 international. Average age 28. 1,059 applicants, 100% accepted, 361 enrolled. In 2010, 284 first professional degrees, 59 master's awarded. *Entrance requirements:* LSAT. Additional exam requirements/recommendations for international students: Required—TOEFL (minimum score 600 paper-based; 100 iBT). *Application deadline:* For fall admission, 11/15 priority date for domestic and international students. Applications are processed on a rolling basis. Application fee: $70. Electronic applications accepted. *Expenses:* Contact institution. *Financial support:* In 2010–11, 3 fellowships with partial tuition reimbursements (averaging $5,000 per year), 2 teaching assistantships with partial tuition reimbursements (averaging $7,720 per year) were awarded; career-related internships or fieldwork, Federal Work-Study, institutionally sponsored loans, scholarships/grants, health care benefits, and unspecified assistantships also available. Support available to part-time students. Financial award application deadline: 3/10; financial award applicants required to submit FAFSA. *Faculty research:* Health law, international, tax, environmental/energy, information law/intellectual property. *Unit head:* Raymond Nimmer, Dean, 713-743-2100, Fax: 713-743-2122, E-mail: rnimmer@uh.edu. *Application contact:* Jamie Dillon, Assistant Dean for Admissions, 713-743-2280, Fax: 713-743-2194, E-mail: jdillon@central.uh.edu.

University of Illinois at Urbana–Champaign, Graduate College, College of Business, Department of Accountancy, Champaign, IL 61820. Offers accountancy (MAS, MS, PhD); taxation (MS); MAS/JD. *Accreditation:* AACSB. *Faculty:* 28 full-time (8 women), 4 part-time/adjunct (1 woman). *Students:* 406 full-time (229 women), 11 part-time (5 women); includes 6 Black or African American, non-Hispanic/Latino; 47 Asian, non-Hispanic/Latino; 2 Hispanic/Latino; 3 Two or more races, non-Hispanic/Latino, 167 international. 1,022 applicants, 46% accepted, 365 enrolled. In 2010, 398 master's, 1 doctorate awarded. *Entrance requirements:* For master's, GMAT (for MAS program), minimum GPA of 3.0; for doctorate, GMAT, minimum GPA of 3.0. Additional exam requirements/recommendations for international students: Required—TOEFL. *Application deadline:* Applications are processed on a rolling basis.

Application fee: $75 ($90 for international students). Electronic applications accepted. *Financial support:* In 2010–11, 16 fellowships, 17 research assistantships, 85 teaching assistantships were awarded; tuition waivers (full and partial) also available. *Unit head:* Ira Soloman, Head, 217-333-3808, Fax: 217-244-0902, E-mail: isolomon@illinois.edu. *Application contact:* Yvonne Harden, Assistant Director, 217-333-4572, Fax: 217-244-0902, E-mail: yaharden@illinois.edu.

University of Memphis, Graduate School, Fogelman College of Business and Economics, School of Accountancy, Memphis, TN 38152. Offers accounting (MS); accounting systems (MS); taxation (MS). *Accreditation:* AACSB. *Faculty:* 10 full-time (2 women), 1 part-time/adjunct (0 women). *Students:* 25 full-time (10 women), 21 part-time (14 women); includes 7 Black or African American, non-Hispanic/Latino; 2 Asian, non-Hispanic/Latino; 1 Hispanic/Latino, 10 international. Average age 29. 33 applicants, 76% accepted, 9 enrolled. In 2010, 27 master's awarded. *Degree requirements:* For master's, comprehensive exam. *Entrance requirements:* For master's, GMAT. *Application deadline:* For fall admission, 8/1 for domestic students; for spring admission, 12/1 for domestic students. Application fee: $35 ($60 for international students). *Financial support:* In 2010–11, 32 students received support; research assistantships with full tuition reimbursements available, teaching assistantships with full tuition reimbursements available, Federal Work-Study, scholarships/grants, and unspecified assistantships available. Financial award application deadline: 2/15; financial award applicants required to submit FAFSA. *Faculty research:* Financial accounting, corporate governance, EDP auditing, evolution of system analysis, investor behavior and investment decisions. *Unit head:* Dr. Carolyn Callahan, Director, 901-678-4022, E-mail: cmcllhan@memphis.edu. *Application contact:* Dr. Craig Langstraat, Program Coordinator, 901-678-4577, E-mail: cjlngstr@memphis.edu.

University of Michigan, Law School, Ann Arbor, MI 48109-1215. Offers comparative law (MCL); international tax (LL M); law (JD, LL M, SJD); JD/MA; JD/MBA; JD/MHSA; JD/MPH; JD/MPP; JD/MS; JD/MSI; JD/MSW; JD/MUP; JD/PhD. *Accreditation:* ABA. *Faculty:* 87 full-time (26 women), 40 part-time/adjunct (14 women). *Students:* 1,134 full-time (506 women); includes 46 Black or African American, non-Hispanic/Latino; 22 American Indian or Alaska Native, non-Hispanic/Latino; 133 Asian, non-Hispanic/Latino; 42 Hispanic/Latino; 1 Native Hawaiian or other Pacific Islander, non-Hispanic/Latino, 24 international. 6,312 applicants, 19% accepted, 379 enrolled. In 2010, 358 first professional degrees, 43 master's, 2 doctorates awarded. *Entrance requirements:* For JD, master's, and doctorate, LSAT. Additional exam requirements/recommendations for international students: Required—TOEFL. *Application deadline:* For fall admission, 2/15 for domestic students. Applications are processed on a rolling basis. Application fee: $75. Electronic applications accepted. *Expenses:* Contact institution. *Financial support:* In 2010–11, 808 students received support. Career-related internships or fieldwork, Federal Work-Study, institutionally sponsored loans, and scholarships/grants available. Financial award applicants required to submit FAFSA. *Unit head:* Evan H. Caminker, Dean, 734-764-1358. *Application contact:* Sarah C. Zearfoss, Assistant Dean and Director of Admissions, 734-764-0537, Fax: 734-647-3218, E-mail: law.jd.admissions@umich.edu.

University of Minnesota, Twin Cities Campus, Carlson School of Management, Master's Program in Business Taxation, Minneapolis, MN 55455-0213. Offers MBT. Part-time and evening/weekend programs available. *Faculty:* 3 full-time (1 woman), 14 part-time/adjunct (4 women). *Students:* 37 full-time (21 women), 80 part-time (44 women); includes 2 Black or African American, non-Hispanic/Latino; 13 Asian, non-Hispanic/Latino; 3 Hispanic/Latino, 18 international. Average age 32. 59 applicants, 88% accepted, 45 enrolled. In 2010, 43 master's awarded. *Entrance requirements:* For master's, GMAT or LSAT. Additional exam requirements/recommendations for international students: Required—TOEFL (minimum score 550 paper-based; 213 computer-based; 79 iBT), IELTS (minimum score 6.5). *Application deadline:* For fall admission, 6/15 priority date for domestic and international students; for spring admission, 10/15 priority date for domestic and international students. Applications are processed on a rolling basis. Application fee: $75 ($95 for international students). Electronic applications accepted. *Expenses:* Contact institution. *Financial support:* In 2010–11, 8 students received support, including 8 fellowships (averaging $1,750 per year), 2 teaching assistantships with partial tuition reimbursements available (averaging $6,600 per year); career-related internships or fieldwork and institutionally sponsored loans also available. Financial award application deadline: 8/1; financial award applicants required to submit FAFSA. *Faculty research:* Partnership taxation, tax theory, corporate taxation. *Unit head:* Mark Sellner, Director of Graduate Studies, 612-624-1050, Fax: 612-626-7795, E-mail: selln001@umn.edu. *Application contact:* Mark Sellner, Director of Graduate Studies, 612-624-1050, Fax: 612-626-7795, E-mail: selln001@umn.edu.

University of Mississippi, Graduate School, School of Accountancy, Oxford, University, MS 38677. Offers accountancy (M Acc, PhD); taxation accounting (M Tax). *Accreditation:* AACSB. *Faculty:* 14 full-time (5 women), 3 part-time/adjunct (1 woman). *Students:* 112 full-time (43 women), 16 part-time (12 women); includes 12 minority (7 Black or African American, non-Hispanic/Latino; 1 American Indian or Alaska Native, non-Hispanic/Latino; 2 Asian, non-Hispanic/Latino; 2 Two or more races, non-Hispanic/Latino),

5 international. In 2010, 70 master's awarded. *Degree requirements:* For doctorate, thesis/dissertation. *Entrance requirements:* For master's, GMAT, minimum GPA of 3.0; for doctorate, GMAT. Additional exam requirements/recommendations for international students: Required—TOEFL. *Application deadline:* For fall admission, 4/1 for domestic students; for spring admission, 10/1 for domestic students. Applications are processed on a rolling basis. Application fee: $25. *Financial support:* Scholarships/grants available. Financial award application deadline: 3/1; financial award applicants required to submit FAFSA. *Unit head:* Dr. Mark Wilder, Interim Dean, 662-915-7468, Fax: 662-915-7483, E-mail: umaccy@olemiss.edu. *Application contact:* Dr. Christy M. Wyandt, Associate Dean, 662-915-7474, Fax: 662-915-7577, E-mail: cwyandt@olemiss.edu.

University of Missouri–Kansas City, School of Law, Kansas City, MO 64110-2499. Offers law (JD, LL M), including general (LL M), taxation (LL M); JD/LL M; JD/MBA; LL M/MPA. *Accreditation:* ABA. Part-time programs available. *Faculty:* 31 full-time (15 women), 5 part-time/adjunct (2 women). *Students:* 476 full-time (186 women), 51 part-time (21 women); includes 67 minority (29 Black or African American, non-Hispanic/Latino; 3 American Indian or Alaska Native, non-Hispanic/Latino; 15 Asian, non-Hispanic/Latino; 20 Hispanic/Latino), 23 international. Average age 27. 967 applicants, 22% accepted, 201 enrolled. In 2010, 156 first professional degrees, 32 master's awarded. *Degree requirements:* For master's, thesis (general). *Entrance requirements:* For JD, LSAT; for master's, LSAT, minimum GPA of 3.0 (general), 2.7 (taxation). Additional exam requirements/recommendations for international students: Required—TOEFL (minimum score 550 paper-based; 213 computer-based; 80 iBT). *Application deadline:* For fall admission, 3/1 priority date for domestic and international students. Applications are processed on a rolling basis. Application fee: $50. Electronic applications accepted. *Expenses:* Contact institution. *Financial support:* In 2010–11, 40 teaching assistantships with partial tuition reimbursements (averaging $2,133 per year) were awarded; career-related internships or fieldwork, Federal Work-Study, institutionally sponsored loans, scholarships/grants, and tuition waivers (full and partial) also available. Support available to part-time students. Financial award application deadline: 3/1; financial award applicants required to submit FAFSA. *Faculty research:* Family and children's issues, litigation, estate planning, urban law, business, tax entrepreneurial law. *Unit head:* Ellen Y. Suni, Dean, 816-235-1677, Fax: 816-235-5276, E-mail: sunie@umkc.edu. *Application contact:* Debbie Brooks, Director of Admissions, 816-235-1672, Fax: 816-235-5276, E-mail: brooksdv@umkc.edu.

University of New Haven, Graduate School, School of Business, Program in Taxation, West Haven, CT 06516-1916. Offers MS. Part-time and evening/weekend programs available. *Students:* 52 part-time (30 women); includes 11 Black or African American, non-Hispanic/Latino; 3 Asian, non-Hispanic/Latino; 4 Hispanic/Latino, 1 international. Average age 37. 17 applicants, 100% accepted, 13 enrolled. In 2010, 5 master's awarded. *Degree requirements:* For master's, thesis or alternative. *Entrance requirements:* For master's, GMAT. Additional exam requirements/recommendations for international students: Required—TOEFL (minimum score 520 paper-based; 190 computer-based; 70 iBT); Recommended—IELTS (minimum score 5.5). *Application deadline:* For fall admission, 5/31 for international students; for winter admission, 10/15 for international students; for spring admission, 1/15 for international students. Applications are processed on a rolling basis. Application fee: $50. Electronic applications accepted. *Expenses:* Contact institution. *Financial support:* Research assistantships with partial tuition reimbursements, teaching assistantships with partial tuition reimbursements, career-related internships or fieldwork, Federal Work-Study, scholarships/grants, tuition waivers, and unspecified assistantships available. Support available to part-time students. Financial award application deadline: 5/1; financial award applicants required to submit FAFSA. *Unit head:* Prof. Robert E. Wnek, Coordinator, 203-932-7111. *Application contact:* Eloise Gormley, Director of Graduate Admissions, 203-932-7449, Fax: 203-932-7137, E-mail: gradinfo@newhaven.edu.

University of North Texas, Toulouse Graduate School, College of Business Administration, Department of Accounting, Denton, TX 76203. Offers accounting (MS, PhD); taxation (MS). *Accreditation:* AACSB. Part-time programs available. *Degree requirements:* For master's, comprehensive exam; for doctorate, thesis/dissertation. *Entrance requirements:* For master's, GMAT or GRE General Test, essay, 3 letters of recommendation, resume; for doctorate, GMAT or GRE General Test, statement of purpose, resume, 3 letters of recommendation. Additional exam requirements/recommendations for international students: Recommended—TOEFL (minimum score 550 paper-based; 213 computer-based). *Application deadline:* Applications are processed on a rolling basis. Electronic applications accepted. *Expenses:* Tuition, state resident: full-time $4298; part-time $239 per credit hour. Tuition, nonresident: full-time $10,782; part-time $549 per credit hour. Required fees: $1292; $270 per credit hour. *Financial support:* Fellowships, career-related internships or fieldwork, Federal Work-Study, and institutionally sponsored loans available. Financial award applicants required to submit FAFSA. *Faculty research:* Empirical tax research issues, empirical financial accounting issues, problems and issues in public interest areas, historical perspective for accounting issues, behavioral issues in auditing and accounting systems. *Application contact:* Graduate Programs Office, 940-369-8977, Fax: 940-369-8978, E-mail: mbacob@unt.edu.

University of Notre Dame, Mendoza College of Business, Program in Accountancy, Notre Dame, IN 46556. Offers financial reporting and assurance services (MS); tax services (MS). *Accreditation:* AACSB. *Faculty:* 37 full-time (4 women), 14 part-time/adjunct (0 women). *Students:* 102 full-time (43 women); includes 7 minority (3 Asian, non-Hispanic/Latino; 4 Hispanic/Latino), 18 international. Average age 22. 353 applicants, 39% accepted, 102 enrolled. In 2010, 83 master's awarded. *Entrance requirements:* For master's, GMAT. Additional exam requirements/recommendations for international students: Required—TOEFL (minimum score 630 paper-based; 267 computer-based; 109 iBT). *Application deadline:* For fall admission, 11/1 for domestic and international students; for spring admission, 4/1 for domestic and international students. Applications are processed on a rolling basis. Application fee: $50 ($100 for international students). Electronic applications accepted. *Financial support:* In 2010–11, 97 students received support, including 97 fellowships (averaging $14,898 per year); scholarships/grants and unspecified assistantships also available. Financial award application deadline: 2/28; financial award applicants required to submit FAFSA. *Faculty research:* Stock valuation, accounting information in decision-making, choice of accounting method, taxes cost on capital. *Unit head:* Dr. Michael H. Morris, Director, 574-631-9732, Fax: 574-631-5300, E-mail: msacct.1@nd.edu. *Application contact:* Helen High, Assistant Director of Admissions and Student Services, 574-631-6499, Fax: 574-631-5300, E-mail: msacct.1@nd.edu.

University of San Diego, School of Business Administration, Program in Taxation, San Diego, CA 92110-2492. Offers MS. *Expenses:* Tuition: Full-time $21,744; part-time $1208 per unit. Required fees: $224. Full-time tuition and fees vary according to course load and degree level. *Unit head:* Dr. David Pyke, Interim Dean, 619-260-4886, E-mail: sbadean@sandiego.edu. *Application contact:* Stephen Pultz, Director of Admissions and Enrollment, 619-260-4506, Fax: 619-260-6836, E-mail: admissions@sandiego.edu.

University of San Diego, School of Business Administration, Programs in Accountancy and Taxation, San Diego, CA 92110-2492. Offers accountancy (MS); taxation (MS). Part-time and evening/weekend programs available. *Students:* 15 full-time (10 women), 6 part-time (5 women); includes 4 Asian, non-Hispanic/Latino; 3 Hispanic/Latino, 5 international. Average age 26. In 2010, 23 master's awarded. *Entrance requirements:* For master's, GMAT (minimum score 550), minimum GPA of 3.0. Additional exam requirements/recommendations for international students: Required—TOEFL (minimum score 580 paper-based; 237 computer-based; 92 iBT), TWE. *Expenses:* Tuition: Full-time $21,744; part-time $1208 per unit. Required fees: $224. Full-time tuition and fees vary according to course load and degree level. *Financial support:* In 2010–11, 6 students received support. Career-related internships or fieldwork, Federal Work-Study, institutionally sponsored loans, scholarships/grants, and unspecified assistantships available. Support available to part-time students. Financial award application deadline: 4/1; financial award applicants required to submit FAFSA. *Faculty research:* Leadership and ethics. *Unit head:* Dr. Diane Pattison, Academic Director, Accountancy Programs, 619-260-4850, E-mail: pattison@sandiego.edu. *Application contact:* Stephen Pultz, Director of Admissions and Enrollment, 619-260-4506, Fax: 619-260-6836, E-mail: admissions@sandiego.edu.

University of San Diego, School of Law, San Diego, CA 92110. Offers business and corporate law (LL M); comparative law (LL M); general studies (LL M); international law (LL M); law (JD); taxation (LL M, Diploma); JD/IMBA; JD/MA; JD/MBA. *Accreditation:* ABA. Part-time and evening/weekend programs available. *Faculty:* 50 full-time (21 women), 66 part-time/adjunct (18 women). *Students:* 881 full-time (435 women), 226 part-time (96 women); includes 336 minority (13 Black or African American, non-Hispanic/Latino; 3 American Indian or Alaska Native, non-Hispanic/Latino; 161 Asian, non-Hispanic/Latino; 113 Hispanic/Latino; 2 Native Hawaiian or other Pacific Islander, non-Hispanic/Latino; 44 Two or more races, non-Hispanic/Latino), 30 international. Average age 26. 4,808 applicants, 32% accepted, 295 enrolled. In 2010, 318 first professional degrees, 72 master's awarded. *Entrance requirements:* For JD, LSAT, bachelor's degree; for master's, JD, LLB or equivalent from an ABA-accredited law school. Additional exam requirements/recommendations for international students: Required—TOEFL (minimum score 600 paper-based; 250 computer-based; 98 iBT). *Application deadline:* For fall admission, 2/1 priority date for domestic students. Applications are processed on a rolling basis. Application fee: $50. Electronic applications accepted. *Expenses:* Contact institution. *Financial support:* In 2010–11, 973 students received support. Career-related internships or fieldwork, Federal Work-Study, institutionally sponsored loans, and scholarships/grants available. Support available to part-time students. Financial award application deadline: 3/1; financial award applicants required to submit FAFSA. *Unit head:* Kevin Cole, Dean, 619-260-2330, Fax: 619-260-2218. *Application contact:* Carl J. Eging, Director of Admissions and Financial Aid, 619-260-4528, Fax: 619-260-2218, E-mail: eging@sandiego.edu.

University of Southern California, Graduate School, Marshall School of Business, Leventhal School of Accounting, Los Angeles, CA 90089. Offers accounting (M Acc); business taxation (MBT); JD/MBT. Part-time programs available. *Students:* 102 full-time (50 women), 2 part-time (both women); includes 32 minority (4 Black or African American, non-Hispanic/Latino; 20 Asian, non-Hispanic/Latino; 5 Hispanic/Latino; 3 Two or more races, non-Hispanic/Latino), 30 international. 971 applicants, 28% accepted. In 2010, 152

master's awarded. *Degree requirements:* For master's, 30-48 units of study. *Entrance requirements:* For master's, GMAT, undergraduate degree, communication skills. Additional exam requirements/recommendations for international students: Required—TOEFL (minimum score 100 computer-based). *Application deadline:* For fall admission, 3/31 for domestic students, 1/10 for international students; for spring admission, 11/1 for domestic students. Applications are processed on a rolling basis. Application fee: $85. Electronic applications accepted. *Expenses:* Tuition: Full-time $31,240; part-time $1420 per unit. Required fees: $600. One-time fee: $35 full-time. Full-time tuition and fees vary according to degree level and program. *Financial support:* In 2010–11, 92 students received support. Application deadline: 1/10. *Faculty research:* State and local taxation, Securities and Exchange Commission, governance, auditing fees, financial accounting, enterprise zones, women in business. *Unit head:* Shirley Maxey, Associate Dean, Accounting Masters Programs, 213-740-4838, E-mail: smaxey@marshall.usc.edu. *Application contact:* Jenna Buonanno, Associate Program Director, 213-740-4838, E-mail: buonanno@marshall.usc.edu.

The University of Texas at Arlington, Graduate School, College of Business, Accounting Department, Arlington, TX 76019. Offers accounting (MP Acc, MS, PhD); taxation (MS). *Accreditation:* AACSB. Part-time and evening/weekend programs available. *Faculty:* 12 full-time (3 women). *Students:* 98 full-time (54 women), 134 part-time (70 women); includes 53 minority (13 Black or African American, non-Hispanic/Latino; 1 American Indian or Alaska Native, non-Hispanic/Latino; 22 Asian, non-Hispanic/Latino; 14 Hispanic/Latino; 1 Native Hawaiian or other Pacific Islander, non-Hispanic/Latino; 2 Two or more races, non-Hispanic/Latino), 35 international. 154 applicants, 58% accepted, 56 enrolled. In 2010, 94 master's, 4 doctorates awarded. *Degree requirements:* For master's, thesis optional; for doctorate, comprehensive exam, thesis/dissertation. *Entrance requirements:* For master's, GMAT. Additional exam requirements/recommendations for international students: Required—TOEFL (minimum score 550 paper-based; 213 computer-based; 79 iBT). *Application deadline:* For fall admission, 6/1 for domestic students, 4/1 for international students; for spring admission, 10/15 for domestic students, 9/15 for international students. Applications are processed on a rolling basis. Application fee: $35 ($50 for international students). *Expenses:* Tuition, state resident: full-time $7500. Tuition, nonresident: full-time $13,080. International tuition: $13,250 full-time. *Financial support:* In 2010–11, 100 students received support, including 11 teaching assistantships (averaging $14,000 per year); fellowships, research assistantships, career-related internships or fieldwork, scholarships/grants, and unspecified assistantships also available. Financial award application deadline: 6/1; financial award applicants required to submit FAFSA. *Unit head:* Dr. LarrChandra Subramaniam, Chair, 817-272-7029, Fax: 817-282-5793, E-mail: subramaniam@uta.edu. *Application contact:* Carly S. Andrews, Graduate Advisor, 817-272-3047, Fax: 817-272-5793, E-mail: graduate.accounting.advisor@uta.edu.

The University of Texas at Dallas, School of Management, Program in Accounting, Richardson, TX 75080. Offers audit and professional (MS); financial analysis (MS); information management (MS); international audit (MS); international services (MS); managerial (MS); taxation (MS). *Accreditation:* AACSB. *Faculty:* 17 full-time (4 women), 7 part-time/adjunct (2 women). *Students:* 412 full-time (270 women), 293 part-time (149 women); includes 164 minority (22 Black or African American, non-Hispanic/Latino; 1 American Indian or Alaska Native, non-Hispanic/Latino; 102 Asian, non-Hispanic/Latino; 37 Hispanic/Latino; 2 Two or more races, non-Hispanic/Latino), 283 international. Average age 28. 570 applicants, 68% accepted, 259 enrolled. In 2010, 273 master's awarded. *Entrance requirements:* For master's, GMAT, minimum GPA of 3.0 in upper-level course work in field. Additional exam requirements/recommendations for international students: Required—TOEFL (minimum score 550 paper-based; 215 computer-based). *Application deadline:* For fall admission, 7/15 for domestic students, 5/1 priority date for international students; for spring admission, 11/15 for domestic students, 9/1 priority date for international students. Applications are processed on a rolling basis. Application fee: $50 ($100 for international students). Electronic applications accepted. *Expenses:* Tuition, state resident: full-time $10,248; part-time $569 per credit hour. Tuition, nonresident: full-time $18,544; part-time $1030 per credit hour. Tuition and fees vary according to course load. *Financial support:* In 2010–11, 260 students received support, including 1 research assistantship with partial tuition reimbursement available (averaging $10,050 per year), 10 teaching assistantships with partial tuition reimbursements available (averaging $10,050 per year); career-related internships or fieldwork, Federal Work-Study, institutionally sponsored loans, scholarships/grants, and unspecified assistantships also available. Support available to part-time students. Financial award application deadline: 4/30; financial award applicants required to submit FAFSA. *Faculty research:* Privatization and accounting/auditing, corporate performance and executive compensation, risk management, information technology in accounting. *Unit head:* Amy Troutman, Assistant Director, 972-883-6719, Fax: 972-883-6823, E-mail: amybass@utdallas.edu. *Application contact:* James Parker, Assistant Director of Graduate Recruitment, 972-883-5842, E-mail: jparker@utdallas.edu.

The University of Texas at San Antonio, College of Business, General Business Program, San Antonio, TX 78249-0617. Offers accounting (PhD);

business (MBA); finance (PhD); information systems (MBA); information technology (PhD); international business (MBA); management accounting (MBA); management and organization studies (PhD); management of technology (MBA); marketing (PhD); marketing management (MBA); taxation (MBA). Part-time and evening/weekend programs available. *Students:* 159 full-time (59 women), 124 part-time (43 women); includes 82 minority (9 Black or African American, non-Hispanic/Latino; 2 American Indian or Alaska Native, non-Hispanic/Latino; 17 Asian, non-Hispanic/Latino; 50 Hispanic/Latino; 1 Native Hawaiian or other Pacific Islander, non-Hispanic/Latino; 3 Two or more races, non-Hispanic/Latino), 39 international. Average age 32. 330 applicants, 46% accepted, 105 enrolled. In 2010, 85 master's, 9 doctorates awarded. *Degree requirements:* For master's, comprehensive exam (for some programs), thesis (for some programs). *Entrance requirements:* For master's, GMAT. Additional exam requirements/recommendations for international students: Required—TOEFL (minimum score 500 paper-based; 173 computer-based; 61 iBT), IELTS (minimum score 5). *Application deadline:* For fall admission, 7/1 for domestic students, 4/1 for international students; for spring admission, 11/1 for domestic students, 9/1 for international students. Application fee: $45 ($80 for international students). *Expenses:* Tuition, state resident: full-time $4172; part-time $231.75 per credit hour. Tuition, nonresident: full-time $15,332; part-time $851.75 per credit hour. *Financial support:* In 2010–11, 282 research assistantships (averaging $13,930 per year), 74 teaching assistantships (averaging $9,284 per year) were awarded; scholarships/grants, tuition waivers, and unspecified assistantships also available. Support available to part-time students. *Unit head:* Dr. Lynda Y. de la Vinna, Dean, 210-458-4317, Fax: 210-458-4308, E-mail: lynda.delavina@utsa.edu. *Application contact:* Veronica Ramirez, Assistant Dean of the Graduate School, 210-458-4330, Fax: 210-458-4332, E-mail: graduatestudies@utsa.edu.

University of the Pacific, McGeorge School of Law, Sacramento, CA 95817. Offers advocacy (JD); criminal justice (JD); experiential law teaching (LL M); intellectual property (JD); international legal studies (JD); international water resources law (LL M, JSD); law (JD); public law and policy (JD); public policy and law (LL M); tax (JD); transnational business practice (LL M); JD/MBA; JD/MPPA. *Accreditation:* ABA. Part-time and evening/weekend programs available. *Faculty:* 49 full-time (22 women), 45 part-time/adjunct (15 women). *Students:* 756 full-time (362 women), 303 part-time (148 women); includes 27 Black or African American, non-Hispanic/Latino; 19 American Indian or Alaska Native, non-Hispanic/Latino; 150 Asian, non-Hispanic/Latino; 60 Hispanic/Latino, 27 international. Average age 27. 3,209 applicants, 42% accepted, 344 enrolled. In 2010, 307 first professional degrees, 36 master's awarded. *Degree requirements:* For master's, thesis (for some programs); for doctorate, thesis/dissertation. *Entrance requirements:* For JD, LSAT; for master's, JD; for doctorate, LL M. Additional exam requirements/recommendations for international students: Required—TOEFL (minimum score 600 paper-based; 250 computer-based; 100 iBT). *Application deadline:* For fall admission, 3/15 priority date for domestic students. Applications are processed on a rolling basis. Application fee: $50. Electronic applications accepted. *Expenses:* Contact institution. *Financial support:* Fellowships, research assistantships, teaching assistantships, career-related internships or fieldwork, Federal Work-Study, institutionally sponsored loans, and scholarships/grants available. Support available to part-time students. Financial award applicants required to submit FAFSA. *Faculty research:* International legal studies, public policy and law, advocacy, intellectual property law, taxation, criminal law. *Unit head:* Elizabeth Rindskopf Parker, Dean, 916-739-7151, E-mail: elizabeth@pacific.edu. *Application contact:* 916-739-7105, Fax: 916-739-7301, E-mail: mcgeorge@pacific.edu.

University of Tulsa, Graduate School, Collins College of Business, Master of Business Administration Program, Tulsa, OK 74104-3189. Offers accounting (MBA); business administration (MBA); energy management (MBA); finance (MBA); international business (MBA); management information systems (MBA); taxation (MBA); JD/MBA; MBA/MSCS; MBA/MSF. *Accreditation:* AACSB. Part-time and evening/weekend programs available. *Faculty:* 32 full-time (6 women). *Students:* 39 full-time (14 women), 40 part-time (16 women); includes 7 minority (1 Black or African American, non-Hispanic/Latino; 2 Asian, non-Hispanic/Latino; 4 Hispanic/Latino), 9 international. Average age 26. 73 applicants, 55% accepted, 18 enrolled. In 2010, 55 master's awarded. *Entrance requirements:* For master's, GMAT. Additional exam requirements/recommendations for international students: Required—TOEFL (minimum score 575 paper-based; 232 computer-based; 90 iBT), IELTS (minimum score 6.5). *Application deadline:* Applications are processed on a rolling basis. Application fee: $40. Electronic applications accepted. *Expenses:* Tuition: Full-time $16,902; part-time $939 per credit hour. Required fees: $1020; $4 per credit hour. Tuition and fees vary according to course load. *Financial support:* In 2010–11, 56 students received support, including 23 fellowships (averaging $4,872 per year), 4 research assistantships (averaging $9,323 per year), 29 teaching assistantships (averaging $10,642 per year); career-related internships or fieldwork, institutionally sponsored loans, scholarships/grants, health care benefits, tuition waivers (full and partial), and unspecified assistantships also available. Support available to part-time students. Financial award application deadline: 2/1; financial award applicants required to submit FAFSA. *Faculty research:* Accounting, energy management, finance, international business, management information systems, taxation. *Unit head:* Dr. Linda Nichols, Associate Dean of the Collins College of Business, 918-631-2242, Fax: 918-631-2142, E-mail: linda-nichols@utulsa.edu. *Application contact:* Dr. Linda Nichols, Associate Dean of the Collins College of Business, 918-631-2242, Fax: 918-631-2142, E-mail: linda-nichols@utulsa.edu.

University of Tulsa, Graduate School, Collins College of Business, Online Program in Taxation, Tulsa, OK 74104-3189. Offers M Tax, JD/M Tax. Part-time and evening/weekend programs available. Postbaccalaureate distance learning degree programs offered (no on-campus study). *Faculty:* 4 full-time (2 women), 1 part-time/adjunct (0 women). *Students:* 2 full-time (both women), 33 part-time (15 women), 1 international. Average age 38. 16 applicants, 50% accepted, 7 enrolled. In 2010, 12 master's awarded. *Entrance requirements:* For master's, GMAT or LSAT. Additional exam requirements/recommendations for international students: Required—TOEFL (minimum score 575 paper-based; 231 computer-based; 91 iBT), IELTS (minimum score 6.5). *Application deadline:* Applications are processed on a rolling basis. Application fee: $40. Electronic applications accepted. *Expenses:* Tuition: Full-time $16,902; part-time $939 per credit hour. Required fees: $1020; $4 per credit hour. Tuition and fees vary according to course load. *Financial support:* In 2010–11, 2 students received support, including 2 fellowships (averaging $780 per year); research assistantships, teaching assistantships with partial tuition reimbursements available, career-related internships or fieldwork, Federal Work-Study, institutionally sponsored loans, scholarships/grants, health care benefits, tuition waivers (full and partial), and unspecified assistantships also available. Support available to part-time students. Financial award application deadline: 2/1; financial award applicants required to submit FAFSA. *Unit head:* Dr. Linda Nichols, Associate Dean of the Collins College of Business, 918-631-2242, Fax: 918-631-2142, E-mail: linda-nichols@utulsa.edu. *Application contact:* Dr. Linda Nichols, Associate Dean of the Collins College of Business, 918-631-2242, Fax: 918-631-2142, E-mail: linda-nichols@utulsa.edu.

University of Wisconsin–Milwaukee, Graduate School, Sheldon B. Lubar School of Business, Milwaukee, WI 53201. Offers business administration (MBA); enterprise resource planning (Certificate); investment management (Certificate); management science (MS, PhD); nonprofit management and leadership (MS, Certificate); state and local taxation (Certificate); MS/MBA. *Accreditation:* AACSB. Part-time and evening/weekend programs available. *Faculty:* 59 full-time (13 women). *Students:* 343 full-time (125 women), 345 part-time (146 women); includes 18 Black or African American, non-Hispanic/Latino; 2 American Indian or Alaska Native, non-Hispanic/Latino; 37 Asian, non-Hispanic/Latino; 4 Hispanic/Latino, 66 international. Average age 32. 560 applicants, 57% accepted, 155 enrolled. In 2010, 295 master's, 4 doctorates awarded. *Degree requirements:* For master's, comprehensive exam (for some programs); for doctorate, comprehensive exam, thesis/dissertation. *Entrance requirements:* For master's and doctorate, GMAT or GRE General Test. Additional exam requirements/recommendations for international students: Required—TOEFL (minimum score 550 paper-based; 79 iBT), IELTS (minimum score 6.5). *Application deadline:* For fall admission, 1/1 priority date for domestic students; for spring admission, 9/1 for domestic students. Applications are processed on a rolling basis. Application fee: $56 ($96 for international students). Electronic applications accepted. *Expenses:* Contact institution. *Financial support:* In 2010–11, 5 fellowships with full tuition reimbursements, 2 research assistantships with full tuition reimbursements, 41 teaching assistantships with full tuition reimbursements were awarded; career-related internships or fieldwork, Federal Work-Study, health care benefits, unspecified assistantships, and project assistantships also available. Support available to part-time students. Financial award application deadline: 4/15; financial award applicants required to submit FAFSA. *Faculty research:* Applied management research in finance, MIS, marketing, operations research, organizational sciences. Total annual research expenditures: $689,994. *Unit head:* Timothy L. Smunt, Dean, 414-229-6256, Fax: 414-229-2372, E-mail: tsmunt@uwm.edu. *Application contact:* Matthew Jensen, 414-229-5403, E-mail: mba-ms@uwm.edu.

Virginia Commonwealth University, Graduate School, School of Business, Program in Taxation, Richmond, VA 23284-9005. Offers M Tax. *Students:* 2 full-time (1 woman), 19 part-time (8 women); includes 4 minority (2 Asian, non-Hispanic/Latino; 1 Hispanic/Latino; 1 Two or more races, non-Hispanic/Latino), 3 international. 11 applicants, 91% accepted, 6 enrolled. In 2010, 5 master's awarded. *Entrance requirements:* For master's, GMAT. Additional exam requirements/recommendations for international students: Required—TOEFL (minimum score 600 paper-based; 250 computer-based; 100 iBT); Recommended—IELTS (minimum score 6.5). *Application deadline:* For fall admission, 7/15 for domestic students; for spring admission, 11/15 for domestic students. Applications are processed on a rolling basis. Application fee: $50. Electronic applications accepted. *Expenses:* Tuition, state resident: full-time $4308; part-time $479 per credit hour. Tuition, nonresident: full-time $8942; part-time $994 per credit hour. Required fees: $2000; $85 per credit hour. Tuition and fees vary according to course level, course load, degree level, campus/location and program. *Financial support:* Fellowships, research assistantships, teaching assistantships, Federal Work-Study, institutionally sponsored loans, and tuition waivers (full and partial) available. Financial award application deadline: 3/15; financial award applicants required to submit FAFSA. *Unit head:* Dr. Carloyn Strand Norman, Interim Chair, 804-828-3160,

E-mail: castrand@vcu.edu. *Application contact:* Jana P. McQuaid, Assistant Dean, Masters Programs, 804-828-4622, Fax: 804-828-7174, E-mail: jpmcquaid@vcu.edu.

Wake Forest University, Schools of Business, MSA Program in Accountancy, Winston-Salem, NC 27106. Offers assurance services (MSA); tax consulting (MSA); transaction services (MSA). *Faculty:* 63 full-time (17 women), 30 part-time/adjunct (9 women). *Students:* 126 full-time (62 women); includes 22 minority (14 Black or African American, non-Hispanic/Latino; 1 American Indian or Alaska Native, non-Hispanic/Latino; 5 Asian, non-Hispanic/Latino; 2 Hispanic/Latino), 14 international. Average age 23. In 2010, 74 master's awarded. *Degree requirements:* For master's, 30 total credit hours. *Entrance requirements:* For master's, GMAT, letters of recommendation, official transcripts, current resume or curriculum vitae. Additional exam requirements/recommendations for international students: Required—TOEFL (minimum score 600 paper-based; 250 computer-based; 100 iBT), Pearson Test of English (PTE). *Application deadline:* For fall admission, 6/1 for domestic and international students. Applications are processed on a rolling basis. Application fee: $100. Electronic applications accepted. *Financial support:* In 2010–11, 103 students received support. Career-related internships or fieldwork and scholarships/grants available. Financial award application deadline: 2/15; financial award applicants required to submit FAFSA. *Faculty research:* The influence of personal relationships on business decision making and management of change; drivers of perceived value and consumer behavior; impact of accounting on auditing, financial, managerial, systems and taxation stakeholders; corporate governance and executive compensation; impact of operations strategies on competitiveness. *Unit head:* Yvonne Hinson, Director of Accountancy, 336-758-5305, Fax: 336-758-6133, E-mail: knappmm@wfu.edu. *Application contact:* Mary Knapp, Administrative Assistant, 336-758-5305, Fax: 336-758-6133, E-mail: knappmm@wfu.edu.

Washington State University, Graduate School, College of Business, Department of Accounting, Pullman, WA 99164. Offers accounting and information systems (M Acc); accounting and taxation (M Acc). *Accreditation:* AACSB. *Faculty:* 9. *Students:* 47 full-time (25 women), 13 part-time (5 women); includes 7 minority (2 American Indian or Alaska Native, non-Hispanic/Latino; 4 Asian, non-Hispanic/Latino; 1 Hispanic/Latino), 19 international. Average age 27. 123 applicants, 37% accepted, 45 enrolled. In 2010, 28 master's awarded. *Degree requirements:* For master's, comprehensive exam (for some programs), thesis (for some programs), oral exam, research paper. *Entrance requirements:* For master's, GMAT (minimum score of 600), resume; statement of purpose identifying area of interest, experiences, and intended research focus; minimum GPA of 3.25. Additional exam requirements/recommendations for international students: Required—TOEFL (minimum score 580 paper-based; 237 computer-based), IELTS. *Application deadline:* For fall admission, 1/10 priority date for domestic students, 1/10 for international students. Applications are processed on a rolling basis. Application fee: $50. Electronic applications accepted. *Expenses:* Tuition, state resident: full-time $8552; part-time $443 per credit. Tuition, nonresident: full-time $21,650; part-time $1083 per credit. Required fees: $846. *Financial support:* In 2010–11, research assistantships (averaging $13,917 per year), 7 teaching assistantships with tuition reimbursements (averaging $18,204 per year) were awarded; Federal Work-Study, institutionally sponsored loans, tuition waivers (partial), and teaching associateships also available. Financial award application deadline: 3/1. *Faculty research:* Ethics, taxation, auditing. *Unit head:* Dr. John

Sweeney, Chair, 509-335-8541, Fax: 509-335-4275, E-mail: jtsweeney@wsu.edu. *Application contact:* Graduate School Admissions, 800-GRADWSU, Fax: 509-335-1949, E-mail: gradsch@wsu.edu.

Wayne State University, School of Business Administration, Detroit, MI 48202. Offers accounting (MSA); business administration (MBA, PhD); taxation (MST); JD/MBA. *Accreditation:* AACSB. Part-time and evening/weekend programs available. Postbaccalaureate distance learning degree programs offered. *Faculty:* 40 full-time (10 women), 8 part-time/adjunct (0 women). *Students:* 240 full-time (99 women), 800 part-time (419 women); includes 325 minority (180 Black or African American, non-Hispanic/Latino; 1 American Indian or Alaska Native, non-Hispanic/Latino; 118 Asian, non-Hispanic/Latino; 22 Hispanic/Latino; 4 Two or more races, non-Hispanic/Latino), 152 international. Average age 28. 529 applicants, 71% accepted, 287 enrolled. In 2010, 345 degrees awarded. *Entrance requirements:* For master's, GMAT, minimum undergraduate GPA of 2.5. Additional exam requirements/recommendations for international students: Required—TOEFL (minimum score 550 paper-based; 213 computer-based); Recommended—TWE (minimum score 6). *Application deadline:* For fall admission, 6/1 for domestic students, 3/1 for international students; for winter admission, 10/1 for domestic students, 6/1 for international students; for spring admission, 2/1 for domestic students, 10/1 for international students. Applications are processed on a rolling basis. Application fee: $50. Electronic applications accepted. *Expenses:* Tuition, state resident: full-time $7662; part-time $478.85 per credit hour. Tuition, nonresident: full-time $16,920; part-time $1057.55 per credit hour. Required fees: $571.20; $35.70 per credit hour. $188.05 per semester. Tuition and fees vary according to course load and program. *Financial support:* In 2010–11, 17 research assistantships (averaging $15,000 per year) were awarded; career-related internships or fieldwork, Federal Work-Study, and scholarships/grants also available. Support available to part-time students. Financial award applicants required to submit FAFSA. *Faculty research:* Corporate financial valuation, strategic advertising, information technology effectiveness, financial accounting and taxation, organizational performance and effectiveness. *Unit head:* Dr. Margaret Williams, Interim Dean, 313-577-4501, Fax: 313-577-4557. *Application contact:* Linda Zaddach, Assistant Dean, 313-577-4510, E-mail: l.s.zaddach@wayne.edu.

Widener University, School of Business Administration, Program in Taxation, Chester, PA 19013-5792. Offers MS. Part-time and evening/weekend programs available. *Faculty:* 2 full-time (1 woman), 2 part-time/adjunct (1 woman). *Students:* 5 full-time (3 women), 46 part-time (25 women); includes 7 Black or African American, non-Hispanic/Latino; 1 American Indian or Alaska Native, non-Hispanic/Latino; 6 Asian, non-Hispanic/Latino; 1 Hispanic/Latino; 1 Two or more races, non-Hispanic/Latino, 4 international. Average age 35. 34 applicants, 94% accepted. In 2010, 11 master's awarded. *Entrance requirements:* For master's, Certified Public Accountant Exam or GMAT. *Application deadline:* For fall admission, 8/1 priority date for domestic students; for spring admission, 12/1 for domestic students. Applications are processed on a rolling basis. Application fee: $25 ($300 for international students). Electronic applications accepted. *Financial support:* Available to part-time students. Application deadline: 5/1. *Faculty research:* Financial planning, taxation fraud. *Unit head:* Frank C. Lordi, Head, 610-499-4308, E-mail: frank.c.lordi@widener.edu. *Application contact:* Ann Seltzer, Graduate Enrollment Administrator, 610-499-4305, E-mail: apseltzer@widener.edu.

Advertising and Public Relations

OVERVIEW

Advertising has become so omnipresent today that companies have to work harder than ever to capture the attention and loyalty of consumers. Advertising comes down to having a conversation with consumers. Effective advertising requires extensive planning, execution, and management of a group of programs designed to bring products and services to consumers, and also, to get those consumers to purchase those products. Because advertising is a part of every corporation's strategic plans, experienced professionals who specialize in advertising are in high demand. For those with an interest in advertising, seeing it as an important element of the product and service lifecycle, the MBA in advertising degree can be an opportunity to further advance your career. This MBA concentration is designed for students who plan to, or already work in, management and executive positions in the public relations, advertising, integrated marketing communications, or comprehensive marketing professions and industries.

Some of the areas students may cover as part of the advertising MBA include development of consumer audiences, consumer behavior, market research, the analysis of demand, strategic planning, marketing campaigns, consumer relations, advertising, studying the market, and cost volume and profits.

Required courses of study may include:

- Business Law
- Communication Skills
- Finance
- Global Economics
- Human Resources Management
- Management Information Systems
- Management Skills
- Managerial Accounting
- Mass Media Strategy, Planning, and Media Law
- Negotiation
- Organizational Behavior
- Organizational Communication
- Practical Applications in Public Relations
- Public Relations and Advertising
- Public Speaking and Public Communication
- Quantitative Business Methods
- Strategic Management

Elective courses of study may include:

- Advertising strategy
- Copywriting
- Crisis Communication
- Crisis Management Seminar
- Global Public Relations
- Legal and Ethical Issues in Global Communications
- Public Relations Campaigns
- Public Relations Techniques
- Public Relations Theory and Practice
- Relationship Marketing
- Special Events Promotion

Graduates with a specialized MBA in advertising often pursue careers as advertising purchasers, media analysts, project managers, media researchers, or account executives.

HELPFUL ORGANIZATIONS/ PUBLICATIONS/BLOGS

Inkblot

http://blog.aaaa.org/

Less of a blog and more of a journal of ideas and observations, this is a place where industry professionals can share their thoughts on the state of the industry; where consumers can learn more about the creators of the products, brands, and campaigns they interact with every day; where advertising executives can mete out their knowledge and expertise; and where clients can visit to gain perspective on the effectiveness of campaigns.

International Advertising Association (IAA)

http://www.iaaglobal.org/#home

The International Advertising Association (IAA) is a worldwide network of the most influential and inspirational marketing and advertising professionals who set and maintain the standards in the industry. Founded in the 1930s, the International Advertising Association has never been more relevant. With so many changes in the way people use advertising to communicate, it's important for everyone in the industry to have a trusted body they can turn to for advice and support. With members in 76 countries, the International Advertising Association works together to:

- Promote freedom of commercial speech.
- Fight unwarranted regulation.
- Champion advertising as a growth engine of free market societies.
- Encourage the exchange of knowledge and expertise amongst marketing peers around the world.
- Support self-regulation and provide an exchange of information and best practices.
- Provide professional development through education and training.
- Create industry forums that tackle issues with a single global voice.

Public Relations Society of America (PRSA)

http://www.prsa.org/

Chartered in 1947, the Public Relations Society of America (PRSA) is the world's largest and foremost organization of public relations professionals. PRSA provides professional development, sets standards of excellence, and upholds principles of ethics for its members and, more broadly, the multi-billion dollar global public relations profession. PRSA also advocates for greater understanding and adoption of public relations services and acts as one of the industry's leading voices on the important business and professional issues of our time.

PRSA is a community of more than 21,000 public relations and communications professionals across the United States, from recent college graduates to the leaders of the world's largest multinational firms. PRSA members represent nearly every practice area and professional and academic setting within the public relations field. In addition, there are more than 10,000 students who are members of the Public Relations Student Society of America (PRSSA) at colleges and universities in the United States and abroad.

CAREER ASPIRATIONS: A PROSPECTIVE POSITION

Consumer Relationship Marketing Director

Job Description

The Consumer Relationship Marketing Director has responsibility for growing sales of consumer products by planning and executing integrated CRM strategies and tactics across lines of business and in collaboration with key retailers and licensees. This entails:

- Turning key growth objectives into business-building CRM initiatives.
- Setting the marketing objectives and calendar of priorities for all CRM activities.
- Identifying customer data collection needs and driving initiatives to capture the data.
- Forging effective relationships with key business partners: LOBs, licensees, creative agencies to plan and execute CRM initiatives.
- Establishing business criteria and ROI parameters and measurements.
- Partnering with digital and social media departments to create full and robust communication integration.

Responsibilities

- Develop annual plan for loyalty programs and direct marketing campaigns that span all business categories inclusive of strategic input from corporate CRM, lines of business, sales, franchise marketing, and synergy.
- Outline programs/benefits/initiatives that resonate with customers.
- Ensure consumer engagement programs reflect the priorities of the company and third-party partners as applicable.
- Develop, execute, and manage annual plan.
- Create and implement CRM tools and toolkits.
- Define and develop lists for targeting, prospecting, and mining databases.
- Establish repeatable processes to execute CRM campaigns.
- Train others on these processes.
- Develop and manage budgets.
- Manage, engage, and measure performance of outside agencies to pre-set objectives and budgets.
- Lead and manage marketing projects requiring cross-functional involvement and coordination.

Qualifications

- MBA from top-tier business school preferred.
- 7+ years of work experience with at least 4+ years experience in digital marketing, including Web site development and online marketing; direct marketing, including targeted mail, e-mail, and mobile marketing; CRM, including management of ongoing loyalty marketing initiatives such as rewards or best customer programs; core consumer segmentation and insights, including consumer research and data analytics.
- Experience in effective consumer communication, including creative strategy and messaging.
- Proven success of strong leadership, creativity, innovation, and priority-setting.
- Negotiation and partner management skills.
- Experience interfacing effectively with multiple levels of management, ranging from senior executives to line managers.
- Strong, proven cross-functional leadership skills, including experience managing complex projects and integrating new initiatives across an organization.
- Excellent written and oral communication skills and negotiation skills, particularly within large organizations.
- Self-motivated, results-driven with excellent attention to detail.
- Leadership and team management experience.

ADVERTISING AND PUBLIC RELATIONS

Academy of Art University, Graduate Program, School of Advertising, San Francisco, CA 94105-3410. Offers MFA. Part-time programs available. Postbaccalaureate distance learning degree programs offered (no on-campus study). *Faculty:* 9 full-time (2 women), 51 part-time/adjunct (17 women). *Students:* 201 full-time (123 women), 95 part-time (64 women); includes 24 Black or African American, non-Hispanic/Latino; 20 Asian, non-Hispanic/Latino; 14 Hispanic/Latino, 115 international. Average age 28. 87 applicants. In 2010, 38 master's awarded. *Degree requirements:* For master's, thesis, final review. *Entrance requirements:* For master's, minimum GPA of 3.0, portfolio. *Application deadline:* For fall admission, 9/7 for domestic and international students; for spring admission, 2/2 for domestic and international students. Applications are processed on a rolling basis. Application fee: $100 ($500 for international students). Electronic applications accepted. *Expenses:* Tuition: Full-time $20,160; part-time $840 per semester hour. Required fees: $45 per semester. *Financial support:* Career-related internships or fieldwork and Federal Work-Study available. Support available to part-time students. Financial award application deadline: 8/10; financial award applicants required to submit FAFSA. *Application contact:* 800-544-ARTS, Fax: 415-263-4130, E-mail: info@academyart.edu.

Ball State University, Graduate School, College of Communication, Information, and Media, Department of Journalism, Muncie, IN 47306-1099. Offers journalism (MA); public relations (MA). *Faculty:* 14. *Students:* 31 full-time (18 women), 32 part-time (23 women); includes 1 Black or African American, non-Hispanic/Latino, 14 international. Average age 26. 83 applicants, 54% accepted, 22 enrolled. In 2010, 35 master's awarded. *Entrance requirements:* For master's, resume. Application fee: $50. *Expenses:* Tuition, state resident: full-time $6160; part-time $299 per credit hour. Tuition, nonresident: full-time $16,020; part-time $783 per credit hour. Required fees: $2278; $95 per credit hour. *Financial support:* In 2010–11, 10 teaching assistantships with full tuition reimbursements (averaging $8,381 per year) were awarded; career-related internships or fieldwork also available. Financial award application deadline: 3/1. *Faculty research:* Image studies, readership surveys, audience perception studies. *Unit head:* William J. Willis, Chairperson, 765-285-8200, Fax: 765-285-7997. *Application contact:* Dan Waechter, Information Contact, 765-285-8200, Fax: 765-285-7997, E-mail: dwaechter@bsu.edu.

Boston University, College of Communication, Department of Mass Communication, Advertising, and Public Relations, Boston, MA 02215. Offers advertising (MS); communication research (MS); communication studies (MS); public relations (MS); JD/MS. Part-time programs available. *Faculty:* 21 full-time, 28 part-time/adjunct. *Students:* 91 full-time (75 women), 44 part-time (29 women); includes 13 minority (3 Black or African American, non-Hispanic/Latino; 4 Asian, non-Hispanic/Latino; 6 Hispanic/Latino), 23 international. Average age 25. In 2010, 18 master's awarded. *Degree requirements:* For master's, comprehensive exam (for some programs), thesis (for some programs). *Entrance requirements:* For master's, GRE General Test, samples of written work. Additional exam requirements/recommendations for international students: Required—TOEFL (minimum score 600 paper-based; 250 computer-based; 100 iBT). *Application deadline:* For fall admission, 2/1 for domestic and international students. Application fee: $70. Electronic applications accepted. *Expenses:* Tuition: Full-time $39,314; part-time $1228 per credit. Required fees: $40 per semester. *Financial support:* Research assistantships, teaching assistantships with partial tuition reimbursements, career-related internships or fieldwork, Federal Work-Study, institutionally sponsored loans, scholarships/grants, and unspecified assistantships available. Support available to part-time students. Financial award application deadline: 2/1; financial award applicants required to submit FAFSA. *Unit head:* T. Barton Carter, Chairman, 617-353-3482, E-mail: comlaw@bu.edu. *Application contact:* Jennifer Healey, Administrator of Graduate Services, 617-353-3481, Fax: 617-358-0399, E-mail: comgrad@bu.edu.

Boston University, Metropolitan College, Program in Advertising, Boston, MA 02215. Offers MS. Part-time and evening/weekend programs available. *Faculty:* 8 part-time/adjunct (1 woman). *Students:* 32 part-time (21 women); includes 1 minority (Black or African American, non-Hispanic/Latino). Average age 28. In 2010, 39 master's awarded. *Entrance requirements:* For master's, undergraduate degree in appropriate field of study. *Application deadline:* Applications are processed on a rolling basis. Application fee: $70. Electronic applications accepted. *Expenses:* Tuition: Full-time $39,314; part-time $1228 per credit. Required fees: $40 per semester. *Financial support:* Unspecified assistantships available. Support available to part-time students. Financial award applicants required to submit FAFSA. *Faculty research:* Communication and advertising. *Unit head:* Dr. Christopher Cakebread, Associate Professor, 617-353-3476, E-mail: ccakebr@bu.edu. *Application contact:* Sonia M. Parker, Assistant Dean, 617-353-2975, Fax: 617-353-2686, E-mail: soparker@bu.edu.

California State University, Fullerton, Graduate Studies, College of Communications, Department of Communications, Fullerton, CA 92834-9480.

Offers advertising (MA); communications (MFA); entertainment and tourism (MA); journalism (MA); public relations (MA). Part-time programs available. *Students:* 24 full-time (15 women), 39 part-time (27 women); includes 2 Two or more races, non-Hispanic/Latino. Average age 29. 119 applicants, 40% accepted, 29 enrolled. In 2010, 30 master's awarded. *Degree requirements:* For master's, project or thesis. *Entrance requirements:* For master's, GRE General Test. Application fee: $55. *Financial support:* Teaching assistantships, career-related internships or fieldwork, Federal Work-Study, institutionally sponsored loans, and scholarships/grants available. Support available to part-time students. Financial award application deadline: 3/1; financial award applicants required to submit FAFSA. *Unit head:* Dr. Tony Fellow, Chair, 657-278-3517. *Application contact:* Coordinator, 657-278-3832.

Central Connecticut State University, School of Graduate Studies, School of Arts and Sciences, Department of Communication, New Britain, CT 06050-4010. Offers organizational communication (MS); public relations/promotions (Certificate). Part-time and evening/weekend programs available. *Faculty:* 12 full-time (4 women), 8 part-time/adjunct (2 women). *Students:* 12 full-time (6 women), 17 part-time (12 women); includes 5 minority (2 Black or African American, non-Hispanic/Latino; 1 Asian, non-Hispanic/Latino; 2 Hispanic/Latino). Average age 28. 19 applicants, 42% accepted, 5 enrolled. In 2010, 16 master's awarded. *Degree requirements:* For master's, comprehensive exam, thesis or alternative; for Certificate, qualifying exam. *Entrance requirements:* For master's, minimum undergraduate GPA of 3.0. Additional exam requirements/recommendations for international students: Required—TOEFL. *Application deadline:* For fall admission, 7/1 for domestic students; for spring admission, 12/1 for domestic students. Applications are processed on a rolling basis. Application fee: $50. Electronic applications accepted. *Expenses:* Tuition, area resident: Full-time $5012; part-time $470 per credit. Tuition, state resident: full-time $7518; part-time $482 per credit. Tuition, nonresident: full-time $13,962; part-time $482 per credit. Required fees: $3772. One-time fee: $62 part-time. *Financial support:* In 2010–11, 4 students received support, including 2 research assistantships; career-related internships or fieldwork, Federal Work-Study, scholarships/grants, and unspecified assistantships also available. Support available to part-time students. Financial award application deadline: 2/15; financial award applicants required to submit FAFSA. *Faculty research:* Organizational communication, mass communication, intercultural communication, political communication, information management. *Unit head:* Dr. Serafin Mendez-Mendez, Chair, 860-832-2690. *Application contact:* Dr. Serafin Mendez-Mendez, Chair, 860-832-2690.

Colorado State University, Graduate School, College of Liberal Arts, Department of Journalism and Technical Communication, Fort Collins, CO 80523-1785. Offers public communication and technology (MS, PhD); technical communication (MS). Part-time programs available. *Faculty:* 17 full-time (7 women), 1 (woman) part-time/adjunct. *Students:* 31 full-time (23 women), 34 part-time (23 women); includes 6 minority (4 Hispanic/Latino; 2 Two or more races, non-Hispanic/Latino), 2 international. Average age 33. 56 applicants, 50% accepted, 21 enrolled. In 2010, 14 master's awarded. *Degree requirements:* For master's, variable foreign language requirement, comprehensive exam (for some programs), thesis (for some programs); for doctorate, variable foreign language requirement, comprehensive exam (for some programs), thesis/dissertation (for some programs). *Entrance requirements:* For master's, GRE General Test, samples of written work, letters of recommendation, resume or curriculum vitae, 3 writing/communication projects; for doctorate, GRE General Test, master's degree, minimum GPA of 3.0, scholarly/professional work, letters of recommendation, statement of career plans, resume. Additional exam requirements/recommendations for international students: Required—TOEFL (minimum score 550 paper-based; 213 computer-based; 80 iBT). *Application deadline:* For fall admission, 2/15 priority date for domestic students, 12/15 priority date for international students; for spring admission, 6/15 priority date for domestic students. Applications are processed on a rolling basis. Application fee: $50. Electronic applications accepted. *Expenses:* Tuition, state resident: full-time $7434; part-time $413 per credit. Tuition, nonresident: full-time $19,022; part-time $1057 per credit. Required fees: $1729; $88 per credit. *Financial support:* In 2010–11, 35 students received support, including 2 research assistantships with full and partial tuition reimbursements available (averaging $9,269 per year), 33 teaching assistantships with partial tuition reimbursements available (averaging $10,636 per year); fellowships with partial tuition reimbursements available, career-related internships or fieldwork, Federal Work-Study, institutionally sponsored loans, scholarships/grants, traineeships, and unspecified assistantships also available. Support available to part-time students. Financial award application deadline: 3/1; financial award applicants required to submit FAFSA. *Faculty research:* Technical/science communication, public relations, health/risk communication, Web/new media technologies, environmental communication. Total annual research expenditures: $250,177. *Unit head:* Dr. Greg Luft, Chair, 970-491-1979, Fax: 970-491-2908, E-mail: greg.luft@colostate.edu. *Application contact:* Dr. Craig Trumbo, Graduate Program Coordinator, 970-491-2077, Fax: 970-491-2908, E-mail: craig.trumbo@colostate.edu.

DePaul University, College of Communication, Chicago, IL 60614. Offers journalism (MA); media, culture and society (MA); organizational and multicultural communication (MA); public relations and advertising (MA).

Part-time and evening/weekend programs available. *Faculty:* 31 full-time (17 women), 15 part-time/adjunct (7 women). *Students:* 170 full-time (129 women), 70 part-time (52 women); includes 29 Black or African American, non-Hispanic/Latino; 9 Asian, non-Hispanic/Latino; 20 Hispanic/Latino; 7 Two or more races, non-Hispanic/Latino, 17 international. Average age 29. 354 applicants, 44% accepted, 79 enrolled. In 2010, 64 master's awarded. *Degree requirements:* For master's, comprehensive exam (for some programs), final exam or thesis/project. *Entrance requirements:* For master's, GRE General Test (public relations and advertising), minimum GPA of 3.0, writing sample, letters of recommendation, resume. Additional exam requirements/recommendations for international students: Required—TOEFL (minimum score 590 paper-based; 243 computer-based; 96 iBT). Application fee: $40. Electronic applications accepted. *Financial support:* In 2010–11, 8 students received support, including 4 research assistantships with partial tuition reimbursements available, 2 teaching assistantships with full tuition reimbursements available (averaging $12,000 per year); fellowships with full tuition reimbursements available, career-related internships or fieldwork, scholarships/grants, and tuition waivers (partial) also available. Support available to part-time students. Financial award applicants required to submit FAFSA. *Faculty research:* Intercultural communication, corporate culture, diversity in the working place, organizational socialization, critical cultural studies. *Unit head:* Dr. Jacqueline Taylor, Dean, 773-325-7216, Fax: 773-325-7584, E-mail: jtaylor@depaul.edu. *Application contact:* Ann Spittle, Director of Graduate Admission, 773-325-7315, Fax: 773-325-2395, E-mail: gradcom@depaul.edu.

George Mason University, College of Visual and Performing Arts, Program in Arts Management, Fairfax, VA 22030. Offers arts entrepreneurship (Certificate); arts management (MA); fund raising and development in the arts (Certificate); public relations and marketing in the arts (Certificate); special events management in the arts (Certificate). *Accreditation:* NASAD. *Faculty:* 1 (woman) full-time, 9 part-time/adjunct (5 women). *Students:* 50 full-time (44 women), 41 part-time (36 women); includes 4 Black or African American, non-Hispanic/Latino; 2 Asian, non-Hispanic/Latino; 4 Hispanic/Latino; 1 Two or more races, non-Hispanic/Latino, 8 international. Average age 29. 90 applicants, 61% accepted, 29 enrolled. In 2010, 38 master's awarded. *Entrance requirements:* For master's, GRE (recommended), minimum GPA of 3.0, 2 letters of recommendation, personal interview, resume, work experience. Additional exam requirements/recommendations for international students: Required—TOEFL. *Application deadline:* For fall admission, 3/1 priority date for domestic students; for spring admission, 10/1 for domestic students. Applications are processed on a rolling basis. Application fee: $100. Electronic applications accepted. *Expenses:* Tuition, state resident: full-time $8192; part-time $440 per credit hour. Tuition, nonresident: full-time $22,952; part-time $1055 per credit hour. Required fees: $2364; $99 per credit hour. *Financial support:* Application deadline: 3/1. *Faculty research:* Information technology for arts managers, special topics in arts management, directions in gallery management, arts in society, public relations/marketing strategies for art organizations. *Unit head:* William Reeder, Dean, 703-993-8624, Fax: 703-993-8883. *Application contact:* Richard Kamenitzer, Director, 703-993-9194, E-mail: rkamenit@gmu.edu.

Golden Gate University, Ageno School of Business, San Francisco, CA 94105-2968. Offers accounting (MBA); business administration (EMBA, MBA, PMBA, DBA); finance (MBA, MS, Certificate); financial planning (MS, Certificate); healthcare information systems (Certificate); human resource management (MBA, MS); human resources management (Certificate); information systems (MS); information technology (MBA); information technology management (Certificate); integrated marketing and communications (MS, Certificate); international business (MBA); management (MBA); marketing (MBA, MS, Certificate); operations supply chain management (Certificate); psychology (MA, Certificate); public administration (EMPA); public relations (MS, Certificate); technical market analysis (Certificate); JD/MBA. Part-time and evening/weekend programs available. *Faculty:* 16 full-time (4 women), 241 part-time/adjunct (72 women). *Students:* 421 full-time (235 women), 744 part-time (425 women); includes 526 minority (114 Black or African American, non-Hispanic/Latino; 2 American Indian or Alaska Native, non-Hispanic/Latino; 296 Asian, non-Hispanic/Latino; 73 Hispanic/Latino; 29 Native Hawaiian or other Pacific Islander, non-Hispanic/Latino; 12 Two or more races, non-Hispanic/Latino, 100 international. Average age 32. 681 applicants, 78% accepted, 270 enrolled. In 2010, 550 master's, 13 doctorates awarded. *Degree requirements:* For doctorate, thesis/dissertation. *Entrance requirements:* For master's, GMAT (MBA), minimum GPA of 2.5 (MS). Additional exam requirements/recommendations for international students: Required—TOEFL. *Application deadline:* For fall admission, 5/15 for domestic and international students; for winter admission, 1/15 for domestic and international students; for spring admission, 9/15 for domestic and international students. Applications are processed on a rolling basis. Application fee: $70 ($110 for international students). Electronic applications accepted. *Expenses:* Contact institution. *Financial support:* Career-related internships or fieldwork, Federal Work-Study, institutionally sponsored loans, and scholarships/grants available. Support available to part-time students. Financial award applicants required to submit FAFSA. *Unit head:* Dr. Paul Fouts, Dean, 415-442-7026, Fax: 415-442-6579. *Application contact:* Angela Melero, Enrollment Services, 415-442-7800, Fax: 415-442-7807, E-mail: info@ggu.edu.

Immaculata University, College of Graduate Studies, Program in Applied Communication, Immaculata, PA 19345. Offers MA. Part-time and evening/weekend programs available. *Faculty:* 2 full-time (both women). *Students:* 1 (woman) full-time, 9 part-time (8 women). 17 applicants, 82% accepted, 8 enrolled. *Entrance requirements:* For master's, GRE, MAT. Additional exam requirements/recommendations for international students: Required—TOEFL, IELTS. *Application deadline:* Applications are processed on a rolling basis. Application fee: $50. Electronic applications accepted. *Financial support:* Applicants required to submit FAFSA. *Unit head:* Dr. Stacy Skirvin, Program Director, 610-647-4400 Ext. 3488. *Application contact:* Sandra A. Rollison, Director of Graduate Admission, 610-647-4400 Ext. 3215, Fax: 610-993-8550, E-mail: srollison@immaculata.edu.

Iona College, School of Arts and Science, Department of Mass Communication, New Rochelle, NY 10801-1890. Offers journalism (MS); public relations (MA). *Accreditation:* ACEJMC (one or more programs are accredited). Part-time and evening/weekend programs available. *Faculty:* 6 full-time (2 women), 3 part-time/adjunct (2 women). *Students:* 6 full-time (5 women), 44 part-time (38 women); includes 11 minority (6 Black or African American, non-Hispanic/Latino; 1 Asian, non-Hispanic/Latino; 4 Hispanic/Latino), 3 international. Average age 27. 34 applicants, 59% accepted, 11 enrolled. In 2010, 16 master's awarded. *Degree requirements:* For master's, comprehensive exam or thesis. *Entrance requirements:* For master's, GRE General Test, minimum GPA of 3.0. Additional exam requirements/recommendations for international students: Required—TOEFL (minimum score 550 paper-based; 213 computer-based). *Application deadline:* Applications are processed on a rolling basis. Application fee: $50. Electronic applications accepted. *Expenses:* Contact institution. *Financial support:* Career-related internships or fieldwork, tuition waivers (partial), and unspecified assistantships available. Support available to part-time students. Financial award application deadline: 4/15; financial award applicants required to submit FAFSA. *Faculty research:* Media ecology, new media, corporate communication, media images, organizational learning in public relations. *Unit head:* Br. Raymond Smith, Chair, 914-633-2354, E-mail: rrsmith@iona.edu. *Application contact:* Veronica Jarek-Prinz, Director of Graduate Admissions, 914-633-2420, Fax: 914-633-2277, E-mail: vjarekprinz@iona.edu.

Lasell College, Graduate and Professional Studies in Communication, Newton, MA 02466-2709. Offers integrated marketing communication (MSC, Graduate Certificate); public relations (MSC, Graduate Certificate). Part-time and evening/weekend programs available. Postbaccalaureate distance learning degree programs offered (minimal on-campus study). *Faculty:* 2 full-time (both women), 2 part-time/adjunct (both women). *Students:* 8 full-time (all women), 25 part-time (22 women); includes 3 minority (all Black or African American, non-Hispanic/Latino), 2 international. Average age 28. 24 applicants, 83% accepted, 13 enrolled. In 2010, 10 master's awarded. *Entrance requirements:* For master's and Graduate Certificate, bachelor's degree from an accredited institution. Additional exam requirements/recommendations for international students: Required—TOEFL (minimum score 550 paper-based; 213 computer-based; 75 iBT), IELTS. *Application deadline:* For fall admission, 8/31 priority date for domestic students, 6/30 priority date for international students; for spring admission, 12/31 priority date for domestic students, 10/31 priority date for international students. Applications are processed on a rolling basis. Application fee: $40. Electronic applications accepted. *Expenses:* Tuition: Part-time $550 per credit hour. Required fees: $55 per semester. *Financial support:* In 2010–11, 2 students received support. Available to part-time students. Application deadline: 8/31. *Unit head:* Dr. Joan Dolamore, Dean of Graduate and Professional Studies, 617-243-2485, Fax: 617-243-2450, E-mail: gradinfo@lasell.edu. *Application contact:* Adrienne Franciosi, Director of Graduate Admission, 617-243-2214, Fax: 617-243-2450, E-mail: gradinfo@lasell.edu.

Lasell College, Graduate and Professional Studies in Management, Newton, MA 02466-2709. Offers elder care administration (MSM, Graduate Certificate); elder care marketing (MSM, Graduate Certificate); fundraising management (MSM, Graduate Certificate); human resource management (Graduate Certificate); human resources management (MSM); management (MSM, Graduate Certificate); marketing (MSM, Graduate Certificate); non-profit management (MSM, Graduate Certificate); project management (MSM, Graduate Certificate); public relations (MSM). Part-time and evening/weekend programs available. Postbaccalaureate distance learning degree programs offered (no on-campus study). *Faculty:* 8 full-time (5 women), 7 part-time/adjunct (5 women). *Students:* 25 full-time (21 women), 97 part-time (67 women); includes 16 minority (6 Black or African American, non-Hispanic/Latino; 2 American Indian or Alaska Native, non-Hispanic/Latino; 4 Asian, non-Hispanic/Latino; 4 Hispanic/Latino), 17 international. Average age 33. 56 applicants, 52% accepted, 19 enrolled. In 2010, 65 master's, 7 other advanced degrees awarded. *Entrance requirements:* For master's and Graduate Certificate, bachelor's degree from an accredited institution. Additional exam requirements/recommendations for international students: Required—TOEFL (minimum score 550 paper-based; 213 computer-based; 75 iBT). *Application deadline:* For fall admission, 8/31 priority date for domestic students, 6/30 priority date for international students; for spring admission, 12/31 priority date for domestic students, 10/31 priority date for international students. Applications are processed on a rolling basis. Application fee: $40. Electronic applications accepted. *Expenses:* Tuition: Part-time $550 per credit hour. Required fees: $55 per semester. *Financial support:* In 2010–11, 40 students received support. Available to part-time students. Application deadline: 8/31. *Unit head:* Dr. Joan Dolamore, Dean of Graduate and Professional Studies, 617-243-2485, Fax: 617-243-2450, E-mail: gradinfo@lasell.edu. *Application contact:* Adrienne Franciosi, Director of Graduate Admission, 617-243-2214, Fax: 617-243-2450, E-mail: gradinfo@lasell.edu.

Marquette University, Graduate School, College of Communication, Milwaukee, WI 53201-1881. Offers advertising and public relations (MA); broadcasting and electronic communications (MA); communications studies (MA); digital storytelling (Certificate); health, environment, science and sustainability (MA); journalism (MA); mass communications (MA). *Accreditation:* ACEJMC (one or more programs are accredited). Part-time and evening/weekend programs available. *Faculty:* 33 full-time (18 women), 30 part-time/adjunct (16 women). *Students:* 35 full-time (20 women), 31 part-time (25 women); includes 5 minority (2 Black or African American, non-Hispanic/Latino; 1 Hispanic/Latino; 2 Two or more races, non-Hispanic/Latino), 4 international. Average age 28. 97 applicants, 52% accepted, 21 enrolled. In 2010, 16 master's, 5 other advanced degrees awarded. *Degree requirements:* For master's, comprehensive exam, thesis or alternative. *Entrance requirements:* For master's, GRE, official transcripts from all current and previous colleges/universities except Marquette, three letters of recommendation, statement of academic and professional goals. Additional exam requirements/recommendations for international students: Required—TOEFL (minimum score 530 paper-based; 78 computer-based). *Application deadline:* Applications are processed on a rolling basis. Application fee: $50. Electronic applications accepted. *Expenses:* Tuition: Full-time $16,290; part-time $905 per credit hour. Tuition and fees vary according to program. *Financial support:* In 2010–11, 2 fellowships, 7 research assistantships, 12 teaching assistantships were awarded; career-related internships or fieldwork, Federal Work-Study, institutionally sponsored loans, scholarships/grants, and tuition waivers (full and partial) also available. Support available to part-time students. Financial award application deadline: 2/15. *Faculty research:* Urban journalism, gender and communication, intercultural communication, religious communication. Total annual research expenditures: $3,088. *Unit head:* Dr. Lori Bergen, Dean, 414-288-7133, Fax: 414-288-1578. *Application contact:* Erin Fox, Assistant Director for Recruitment, 414-288-5319, Fax: 414-288-1902, E-mail: erin.fox@marquette.edu.

Monmouth University, The Graduate School, Department of Corporate and Public Communication, West Long Branch, NJ 07764-1898. Offers corporate and public communication (MA); human resources communication (Certificate); public relations (Certificate); public service communication specialist (Certificate). Part-time and evening/weekend programs available. *Faculty:* 8 full-time (5 women). *Students:* 11 full-time (9 women), 37 part-time (28 women); includes 2 Black or African American, non-Hispanic/Latino; 3 Hispanic/Latino; 1 Two or more races, non-Hispanic/Latino, 2 international. Average age 32. 28 applicants, 93% accepted, 15 enrolled. In 2010, 15 master's awarded. *Degree requirements:* For master's, comprehensive exam, project. *Entrance requirements:* For master's, GRE, minimum GPA of 3.0 in major, 2.75 overall. Additional exam requirements/recommendations for international students: Required—TOEFL (minimum score 550 paper-based; 213 computer-based; 79 iBT), IELTS (minimum score 5), Michigan English Language Assessment Battery (minimum score 77), Cambridge A, B, C. *Application deadline:* For fall admission, 7/15 priority date for domestic students, 6/1 for international students; for spring admission, 11/15 priority date for domestic students, 11/1 for international students. Applications are processed on a rolling basis. Application fee: $50. Electronic applications accepted. *Expenses:* Tuition: Full-time $19,572; part-time $816 per credit. Required fees: $628; $157 per semester. *Financial support:* In 2010–11, 24 students received support, including 23 fellowships (averaging $1,176 per year), 5 research assistantships (averaging $7,578 per year); scholarships/grants and unspecified assistantships also available. Support available to part-time students. Financial award applicants required to submit FAFSA. *Faculty research:* Service-learning, history of television, feminism and the media, executive communication, public relations pedagogy. *Unit head:* Dr. Shelia McAllister-Spooner, Program Director, 732-571-7553, Fax: 732-571-3609, E-mail: smcallis@monmouth.edu. *Application contact:* Kevin Roane, Director, Office of Graduate Admission, 732-571-3452, Fax: 732-263-5123, E-mail: gradadm@monmouth.edu.

Montclair State University, The Graduate School, School of the Arts, Department of Communication Studies, Montclair, NJ 07043-1624. Offers public and organizational relations (MA). Part-time and evening/weekend programs available. *Faculty:* 6 full-time (2 women), 41 part-time/adjunct (23 women). *Students:* 16 full-time (14 women), 19 part-time (16 women); includes 3 Black or African American, non-Hispanic/Latino; 1 Asian, non-Hispanic/Latino; 4 Hispanic/Latino, 3 international. Average age 30. 26 applicants, 54% accepted, 9 enrolled. In 2010, 14 master's awarded. *Degree requirements:* For master's, comprehensive exam. *Entrance requirements:* For master's, GRE General Test, 2 letters of recommendation. Additional exam requirements/recommendations for international students: Required—TOEFL (minimum iBT score of 83) or IELTS. *Application deadline:* For fall admission, 6/1 for international students; for spring admission, 10/1 for international students. Applications are processed on a rolling basis. Application fee: $60. Electronic applications accepted. *Expenses:* Tuition, state resident: part-time $501.34 per credit. Tuition, nonresident: part-time $773.88 per credit. Required fees: $71.15 per credit. *Financial support:* In 2010–11, 3 research assistantships with full tuition reimbursements (averaging $7,000 per year) were awarded; Federal Work-Study, scholarships/grants, and unspecified assistantships also available. Support available to part-time students. Financial award application deadline: 3/1; financial award applicants required to submit FAFSA. *Unit head:* Dr. Harry Haines, Chair, 973-655-4200. *Application contact:* Amy Aiello, Director of Graduate Admissions and Operations, 973-655-5147, Fax: 973-655-7869, E-mail: graduate.school@montclair.edu.

New York University, School of Continuing and Professional Studies, Division of Programs in Business, Program in Public Relations and Corporate Communication, New York, NY 10012-1019. Offers corporate and organizational communications (MS); public relations management (MS). Part-time and evening/weekend programs available. *Faculty:* 1 full-time (0 women), 44 part-time/adjunct (21 women). *Students:* 36 full-time (30 women), 74 part-time (60 women); includes 10 Black or African American, non-Hispanic/Latino; 8 Asian, non-Hispanic/Latino; 12 Hispanic/Latino. Average age 28. 199 applicants, 34% accepted, 35 enrolled. In 2010, 43 master's awarded. *Degree requirements:* For master's, thesis. *Entrance requirements:* For master's, GRE General Test or GMAT (for recent graduates), 2 letters of recommendation, resume, essay, professional experience. Additional exam requirements/recommendations for international students: Required—TOEFL (minimum score 600 paper-based; 250 computer-based; 100 iBT), TWE. *Application deadline:* For fall admission, 2/1 priority date for domestic and international students; for spring admission, 10/15 priority date for domestic students, 8/15 priority date for international students. Applications are processed on a rolling basis. Application fee: $75. Electronic applications accepted. *Financial support:* In 2010–11, 85 students received support, including 85 fellowships (averaging $2,490 per year); institutionally sponsored loans and scholarships/grants also available. Financial award application deadline: 3/1; financial award applicants required to submit FAFSA. *Unit head:* John Doorley, Director, 212-992-3221, Fax: 212-992-3676. *Application contact:* Angrand Fadia, Assistant Director, 212-992-3221, Fax: 212-992-3676, E-mail: fs20@nyu.edu.

Northern Kentucky University, Office of Graduate Programs, College of Informatics, Program in Communication, Highland Heights, KY 41099. Offers communication (MA); communication teaching (Certificate); documentary studies (Certificate); public relations (Certificate); relationships (Certificate). Part-time and evening/weekend programs available. *Faculty:* 7 full-time (3 women), 1 part-time/adjunct (0 women). *Students:* 10 full-time (4 women), 36 part-time (15 women); includes 7 minority (3 Black or African American, non-Hispanic/Latino; 2 Asian, non-Hispanic/Latino; 2 Hispanic/Latino). Average age 29. 29 applicants, 62% accepted, 14 enrolled. In 2010, 11 master's, 2 other advanced degrees awarded. *Degree requirements:* For master's, thesis (for some programs), capstone experience, internship. *Entrance requirements:* For master's, GRE, minimum GPA of 3.0, 3 letters of recommendation, letter of intent. Additional exam requirements/recommendations for international students: Required—TOEFL (minimum score 550 paper-based; 213 computer-based; 79 iBT); Recommended—IELTS (minimum score 6.5). *Application deadline:* For fall admission, 2/1 for domestic students, 6/1 for international students; for spring admission, 7/1 for domestic students, 10/1 for international students. Applications are processed on a rolling basis. Application fee: $40. Electronic applications accepted. *Expenses:* Tuition, state resident: full-time $7254; part-time $403 per credit hour. Tuition, nonresident: full-time $12,492; part-time $694 per credit hour. Tuition and fees vary according to degree level and program. *Financial support:* Unspecified assistantships available. Financial award applicants required to submit FAFSA. *Faculty research:* Business/organizational communication, interpersonal/relational communication, public relations, communication teaching/pedagogy, media (production, criticism, popular culture). Total annual research expenditures: $29,000. *Unit head:* Dr. Jimmy Manning, Director, 859-572-1329, E-mail: manningj1@nku.edu. *Application contact:* Dr. Peg Griffin, Director of Graduate Programs, 859-572-6934, Fax: 859-572-6670, E-mail: griffinp@nku.edu.

Quinnipiac University, School of Communications, Program in Public Relations, Hamden, CT 06518-1940. Offers MS. Part-time programs available. *Faculty:* 6 full-time (3 women), 6 part-time/adjunct (3 women). *Students:* 14 full-time (all women), 3 part-time (all women); includes 3 minority (2 Black or African American, non-Hispanic/Latino; 1 Two or more races, non-Hispanic/Latino). 25 applicants, 88% accepted, 15 enrolled. *Entrance requirements:* For master's, GRE. Additional exam requirements/recommendations for international students: Required—TOEFL (minimum score 575 paper-based; 233 computer-based; 90 iBT), IELTS (minimum score 6.5). *Application deadline:* For fall admission, 7/31 priority date for domestic students; for spring admission, 12/15 priority date for domestic students. Applications are processed on a rolling basis. Application fee: $45. Electronic applications accepted. *Expenses:* Tuition: Part-time $810 per credit. Required fees: $35 per credit. *Financial support:* Federal Work-Study and unspecified assistantships available. Financial award application deadline: 4/30; financial award applicants required to submit FAFSA. *Unit head:* Kathy Fitzpatrick, Professor, 203-582-3808, Fax: 203-582-3443, E-mail: graduate@quinnipiac.edu. *Application* *contact:* Scott Farber, Information Contact, 203-582-8672, E-mail: graduate@quinnipiac.edu.

Rowan University, Graduate School, College of Communication, Program in Public Relations, Glassboro, NJ 08028-1701. Offers MA. Part-time and evening/weekend programs available. *Faculty:* 1 full-time (0 women), 2 part-time/adjunct (1 woman). *Students:* 19 full-time (15 women), 8 part-time (7 women); includes 2 Black or African American, non-Hispanic/Latino; 1 Asian, non-Hispanic/Latino; 3 Hispanic/Latino. Average age 27. 23 applicants, 83% accepted, 13 enrolled. In 2010, 10 master's awarded. *Degree requirements:* For master's, thesis. *Entrance requirements:* For master's, GRE General Test. Additional exam requirements/recommendations for international students: Required—TOEFL. *Application deadline:* Applications are processed on a rolling basis. Application fee: $65 ($200 for international students). Electronic applications accepted. *Expenses:* Tuition, area resident: Part-time $602 per semester hour. Tuition, nonresident: part-time $602 per semester hour. Required fees: $100 per semester hour. One-time fee: $10 part-time. *Financial support:* Career-related internships or fieldwork available. Support available to part-time students. *Unit head:* Dr. Horacio Sosa, Dean, College of Graduate and Continuing Education, 856-256-4747, Fax: 856-256-5638, E-mail: sosa@rowan.edu. *Application contact:* Karen Haynes, Graduate Coordinator, 856-256-4052, E-mail: haynesk@rowan.edu.

Savannah College of Art and Design, Graduate School, Program in Advertising Design, Savannah, GA 31402-3146. Offers MA, MFA. Part-time programs available. *Faculty:* 12 full-time (4 women), 5 part-time/adjunct (2 women). *Students:* 37 full-time (22 women), 9 part-time (8 women); includes 2 Black or African American, non-Hispanic/Latino; 1 Hispanic/Latino, 12 international. Average age 26. In 2010, 30 master's awarded. *Degree requirements:* For master's, thesis, internships. *Entrance requirements:* For master's, interview, portfolio. Additional exam requirements/recommendations for international students: Required—TOEFL (minimum score 450 paper-based; 133 computer-based). *Application deadline:* For fall admission, 4/1 priority date for domestic and international students. Applications are processed on a rolling basis. Application fee: $35. Electronic applications accepted. *Expenses:* Tuition: Full-time $29,520; part-time $3280 per quarter. Tuition and fees vary according to campus/location. *Financial support:* Fellowships, career-related internships or fieldwork, Federal Work-Study, and scholarships/grants available. Financial award application deadline: 4/1; financial award applicants required to submit FAFSA. *Unit head:* Stephen Hall, Chair, 912-525-5974. *Application contact:* Elizabeth Mathis, Director of Graduate and International Enrollment, 912-525-5965, Fax: 912-525-5985, E-mail: emathis@scad.edu.

Southern Methodist University, Meadows School of the Arts, Temerlin Advertising Institute, Dallas, TX 75275. Offers MA. *Faculty:* 10 full-time (5 women), 4 part-time/adjunct (0 women). *Students:* 27 full-time (24 women); includes 5 Hispanic/Latino, 2 international. Average age 24. 33 applicants, 61% accepted. *Entrance requirements:* For master's, GRE, GMAT. Additional exam requirements/recommendations for international students: Required—TOEFL (minimum score 550 paper-based; 213 computer-based; 80 iBT). *Application deadline:* For fall admission, 3/15 for domestic students. Electronic applications accepted. *Financial support:* In 2010–11, 12 students received support, including 5 research assistantships (averaging $8,000 per year). Financial award application deadline: 4/1; financial award applicants required to submit FAFSA. *Unit head:* Dr. Patricia Alvey, Director, 214-768-3090, E-mail: palvey@mail.smu.edu. *Application contact:* Joe S. Hoselton, Graduate Admissions and Records Coordinator, 214-768-3765, Fax: 214-768-3272, E-mail: hoselton@smu.edu.

Suffolk University, College of Arts and Sciences, Department of Communication, Boston, MA 02108-2770. Offers communication studies (MAC); integrated marketing communication (MAC); organizational communication (MAC); public relations and advertising (MAC). Part-time and evening/weekend programs available. *Faculty:* 20 full-time (10 women), 1 part-time/adjunct (0 women). *Students:* 17 full-time (15 women), 18 part-time (13 women); includes 1 Asian, non-Hispanic/Latino, 3 international. Average age 26. 110 applicants, 54% accepted, 19 enrolled. In 2010, 23 master's awarded. *Degree requirements:* For master's, thesis optional. *Entrance requirements:* For master's, GRE General Test, MAT, or GMAT, 2 letters of recommendation, resume. Additional exam requirements/recommendations for international students: Required—TOEFL (minimum score 550 paper-based; 213 computer-based; 80 iBT). *Application deadline:* For fall admission, 6/15 priority date for domestic students, 6/15 for international students; for spring admission, 11/1 priority date for domestic students, 11/1 for international students. Applications are processed on a rolling basis. Application fee: $50. Electronic applications accepted. *Expenses:* Contact institution. *Financial support:* In 2010–11, 28 students received support, including 18 fellowships with partial tuition reimbursements available (averaging $5,403 per year); career-related internships or fieldwork, Federal Work-Study, and institutionally sponsored loans also available. Support available to part-time students. Financial award application deadline: 4/1; financial award applicants required to submit FAFSA. *Faculty research:* New media and new markets for advertising, First Amendment issues with the Internet, gender and intercultural communication, organizational development. *Unit head:* Dr. Robert Rosenthal, Chair, 617-573-8502, Fax: 617-742-6982, E-mail: rrosenth@suffolk.edu.

Application contact: Judith Reynolds, Director of Graduate Admissions, 617-573-8302, Fax: 617-305-1733, E-mail: grad.admission@suffolk.edu.

Syracuse University, S. I. Newhouse School of Public Communications, Program in Advertising, Syracuse, NY 13244. Offers MA. *Students:* 13 full-time (11 women), 1 (woman) part-time; includes 4 minority (3 Black or African American, non-Hispanic/Latino; 1 American Indian or Alaska Native, non-Hispanic/Latino), 7 international. Average age 23. 69 applicants, 51% accepted, 12 enrolled. In 2010, 1 master's awarded. *Degree requirements:* For master's, capstone course. *Entrance requirements:* For master's, GRE General Test. Additional exam requirements/recommendations for international students: Required—TOEFL (minimum score 600 paper-based; 250 computer-based; 100 iBT). *Application deadline:* For fall admission, 2/1 priority date for domestic and international students. Application fee: $45. Electronic applications accepted. *Expenses:* Tuition: Part-time $1162 per credit. *Financial support:* Fellowships with full tuition reimbursements, research assistantships with partial tuition reimbursements, teaching assistantships with full tuition reimbursements available. Financial award application deadline: 1/1. *Unit head:* James Tsao, Chair, 315-443-7401, Fax: 315-443-3946, E-mail: pcgrad@syr.edu. *Application contact:* Graduate Records Office, 315-443-5749, Fax: 315-443-1834, E-mail: pcgrad@syr.edu.

Syracuse University, S. I. Newhouse School of Public Communications, Program in Public Relations, Syracuse, NY 13244. Offers MS. *Students:* 49 full-time (41 women), 3 part-time (2 women); includes 17 minority (7 Black or African American, non-Hispanic/Latino; 5 Asian, non-Hispanic/Latino; 4 Hispanic/Latino; 1 Two or more races, non-Hispanic/Latino), 9 international. Average age 24. 210 applicants, 41% accepted, 38 enrolled. In 2010, 31 master's awarded. *Degree requirements:* For master's, thesis (for some programs). *Entrance requirements:* For master's, GRE General Test. Additional exam requirements/recommendations for international students: Required—TOEFL (minimum score 600 paper-based; 250 computer-based; 100 iBT). *Application deadline:* For fall admission, 2/1 priority date for domestic and international students. Application fee: $45. Electronic applications accepted. *Expenses:* Tuition: Part-time $1162 per credit. *Financial support:* Fellowships with full tuition reimbursements, research assistantships with partial tuition reimbursements, teaching assistantships with partial tuition reimbursements available. Financial award application deadline: 2/1. *Unit head:* Brenda M. Wrigley, Chair, 315-443-1911, E-mail: newhouse@syr.edu. *Application contact:* Martha Coria, Graduate Records Office, 315-443-5749, Fax: 315-443-1834, E-mail: pcgrad@syr.edu.

Texas Christian University, College of Communication, Schieffer School of Journalism, Fort Worth, TX 76129-0002. Offers advertising/public relations (MS); news-editorial (MS). Part-time and evening/weekend programs available. *Degree requirements:* For master's, thesis optional, written exam. *Entrance requirements:* For master's, GRE General Test. Additional exam requirements/recommendations for international students: Required—TOEFL. *Application deadline:* For fall admission, 3/1 for domestic and international students; for spring admission, 10/1 for domestic and international students. Applications are processed on a rolling basis. Application fee: $50. *Expenses:* Tuition: Full-time $18,720; part-time $1040 per credit hour. Tuition and fees vary according to course load and program. *Financial support:* Tuition waivers (full and partial) and unspecified assistantships available. Financial award application deadline: 3/1. *Unit head:* John Lumpkin, Director, 817-257-4908, E-mail: j.lumpkin@tcu.edu. *Application contact:* Dr. John Tisdale, Associate Director, 817-257-7425, E-mail: j.tisdale@tcu.edu.

Towson University, Program in Strategic Public Relations and Integrated Communications, Towson, MD 21252-0001. Offers Certificate. Evening/weekend programs available. Postbaccalaureate distance learning degree programs offered (no on-campus study). *Students:* 3 part-time (all women); includes 1 minority (Black or African American, non-Hispanic/Latino). In 2010, 6 Certificates awarded. *Entrance requirements:* For degree, 24 credits in related course work, minimum GPA of 3.0. *Application deadline:* For fall admission, 1/15 for domestic students. Application fee: $50. Electronic applications accepted. *Expenses:* Tuition, state resident: part-time $324 per credit. Tuition, nonresident: part-time $681 per credit. Required fees: $95 per term. *Financial support:* Fellowships, teaching assistantships, career-related internships or fieldwork, Federal Work-Study, and unspecified assistantships available. Support available to part-time students. Financial award application deadline: 4/1; financial award applicants required to submit FAFSA. *Unit head:* Theodora Carabas, Graduate Program Director, 410-704-4855, E-mail: tcarabas@towson.edu. *Application contact:* 410-704-2501, Fax: 410-704-4675, E-mail: grads@towson.edu.

The University of Alabama, Graduate School, College of Communication and Information Sciences, Department of Advertising and Public Relations, Tuscaloosa, AL 35487-0172. Offers MA. Part-time programs available. *Faculty:* 14 full-time (7 women). *Students:* 27 full-time (20 women), 9 part-time (5 women); includes 1 minority (Black or African American, non-Hispanic/Latino), 2 international. Average age 24. 111 applicants, 30% accepted, 18 enrolled. In 2010, 19 master's awarded. *Degree requirements:* For master's, comprehensive exam, thesis or alternative. *Entrance requirements:* For master's, GRE (minimum 1000 verbal plus quantitative, 400 in each; 4.0 in writing), minimum undergraduate GPA of 3.0 (for last 60 hours). Additional exam requirements/recommendations for international students: Required—TOEFL (minimum score 600 paper-based; 100 computer-based). *Application deadline:* For fall admission, 3/1 priority date for domestic and international students. Applications are processed on a rolling basis. Application fee: $50 ($60 for international students). Electronic applications accepted. *Expenses:* Tuition, state resident: full-time $7900. Tuition, nonresident: full-time $20,500. *Financial support:* In 2010–11, 7 students received support, including 4 research assistantships with partial tuition reimbursements available, 3 teaching assistantships with full tuition reimbursements available; career-related internships or fieldwork, scholarships/grants, health care benefits, and unspecified assistantships also available. Financial award application deadline: 3/1. *Faculty research:* Advertising and public relations management, public opinion, political communication, advertising media, international communication. Total annual research expenditures: $36,503. *Unit head:* Dr. Joseph Edward Phelps, Professor and Chairman, 205-348-8646, Fax: 205-348-2401, E-mail: phelps@apr.ua.edu. *Application contact:* Dr. Yorgo Pasadeos, Professor, 205-348-8641, Fax: 205-348-2401, E-mail: pasadeos@apr.ua.edu.

University of Denver, Division of Arts, Humanities and Social Sciences, Department of Media, Film and Journalism Studies, Denver, CO 80208. Offers advertising management (MS); digital media studies (MA); international and intercultural communication (MA); media, film, and journalism studies (MA); strategic communication (MS). Part-time programs available. *Faculty:* 14 full-time (7 women), 5 part-time/adjunct (3 women). *Students:* 28 full-time (24 women), 36 part-time (26 women); includes 12 minority (1 Black or African American, non-Hispanic/Latino; 3 Asian, non-Hispanic/Latino; 6 Hispanic/Latino; 2 Two or more races, non-Hispanic/Latino), 2 international. Average age 26. 155 applicants, 58% accepted, 32 enrolled. In 2010, 36 master's awarded. *Degree requirements:* For master's, thesis (for some programs). *Entrance requirements:* For master's, GRE General Test. Additional exam requirements/recommendations for international students: Required—TOEFL (minimum score 550 paper-based; 80 iBT). *Application deadline:* Applications are processed on a rolling basis. Application fee: $60. Electronic applications accepted. *Expenses:* Tuition: Full-time $35,604; part-time $29,670 per year. Required fees: $687 per year. Tuition and fees vary according to program. *Financial support:* In 2010–11, 4 teaching assistantships with full and partial tuition reimbursements (averaging $14,000 per year) were awarded; career-related internships or fieldwork, Federal Work-Study, institutionally sponsored loans, scholarships/grants, and unspecified assistantships also available. Support available to part-time students. Financial award application deadline: 3/1; financial award applicants required to submit FAFSA. *Faculty research:* Youth and civic engagement. *Unit head:* Dr. Renee Botta, Chair, 303-871-7918, Fax: 303-871-4949, E-mail: rbotta@du.edu. *Application contact:* Information Contact, 303-871-2166, E-mail: mfjs@du.edu.

University of Denver, University College, Denver, CO 80208. Offers arts and culture (MLS, Certificate), including art, literature, and culture, arts development and program management (Certificate), creative writing; environmental policy and management (MAS, Certificate), including energy and sustainability (Certificate), environmental assessment of nuclear power (Certificate), environmental health and safety (Certificate), environmental management, natural resource management (Certificate); geographic information systems (MAS, Certificate); global affairs (MLS, Certificate), including translation studies, world history and culture; healthcare leadership (MPH, Certificate), including healthcare policy, law, and ethics, medical and healthcare information technologies, strategic management of healthcare; information and communications technology (MCIS, Certificate), including database design and administration (Certificate), geographic information systems (MCIS), information security systems security (Certificate), information systems security (MCIS), project management (MCIS, MPS, Certificate), software design and administration (Certificate), software design and programming (MCIS), technology management, telecommunications technology (MCIS), Web design and development; leadership and organizations (MPS, Certificate), including human capital in organizations, philanthropic leadership, project management (MCIS, MPS, Certificate), strategic innovation and change; organizational and professional communication (MPS, Certificate), including alternative dispute resolution, organizational communication, organizational development and training, public relations and marketing; security management (MAS, Certificate), including emergency planning and response, information security (MAS), organizational security; strategic human resource management (MPS, Certificate), including global human resources (MPS), human resource management and development (MPS). Part-time and evening/weekend programs available. Postbaccalaureate distance learning degree programs offered (no on-campus study). *Faculty:* 7 full-time (2 women), 212 part-time/adjunct (83 women). *Students:* 52 full-time (19 women), 1,044 part-time (625 women); includes 196 minority (81 Black or African American, non-Hispanic/Latino; 7 American Indian or Alaska Native, non-Hispanic/Latino; 30 Asian, non-Hispanic/Latino; 66 Hispanic/Latino; 3 Native Hawaiian or other Pacific Islander, non-Hispanic/Latino; 9 Two or more races, non-Hispanic/Latino), 76 international. Average age 36. 488 applicants, 91% accepted, 339 enrolled. In 2010, 286 master's, 130 other advanced degrees awarded. *Entrance requirements:* Additional exam requirements/recommendations for international students: Required—TOEFL (minimum score 550 paper-based; 80 iBT). *Application deadline:* For fall admission, 6/22 priority date for domestic students, 6/10 priority date for international students; for winter admission, 9/15 priority date for domestic students, 9/6 priority date for international students; for spring admission, 2/3 priority date for domestic students, 12/15 priority date for international students. Applications are processed on a rolling basis. Application fee: $75. Electronic applications accepted. *Expenses:* Contact institution. *Financial support:* Applicants required to submit FAFSA. *Unit head:* Dr. James Davis, Dean, 303-871-2291, Fax: 303-871-4047, E-mail: jdavis@du.edu. *Application contact:* Information Contact, 303-871-3155, Fax: 303-871-4047, E-mail: ucolinfo@du.edu.

University of Florida, Graduate School, College of Journalism and Communications, Department of Advertising, Gainesville, FL 32611. Offers M Adv. *Faculty:* 3 full-time (0 women). *Students:* 13 full-time (12 women), 3 part-time (2 women); includes 4 Asian, non-Hispanic/Latino; 1 Hispanic/Latino, 8 international. Average age 24. 87 applicants, 26% accepted, 6 enrolled. In 2010, 12 master's awarded. *Degree requirements:* For master's, thesis or terminal project. *Entrance requirements:* For master's, GRE General Test, minimum GPA of 3.0. Additional exam requirements/recommendations for international students: Required—TOEFL (minimum score 550 paper-based; 213 computer-based; 80 iBT), IELTS (minimum score 6). *Application deadline:* For fall admission, 4/1 for domestic students, 1/30 for international students. Applications are processed on a rolling basis. Application fee: $30. Electronic applications accepted. *Expenses:* Tuition, state resident: full-time $10,915.92. Tuition, nonresident: full-time $28,309. *Financial support:* Applicants required to submit FAFSA. *Faculty research:* Branding, information flow between clients and suppliers, message and media strategies, emotional response. *Unit head:* Dr. John C. Sutherland, Chair, 352-392-4046, Fax: 352-846-3015, E-mail: jsutherland@jou.ufl.edu. *Application contact:* Robyn Goodman, Graduate Coordinator, 352-392-2704, Fax: 352-392-1794, E-mail: rgoodman@jou.ufl.edu.

University of Florida, Graduate School, College of Journalism and Communications, Department of Public Relations, Gainesville, FL 32611. Offers MAMC. *Faculty:* 7 full-time (4 women). *Entrance requirements:* For master's, GRE General Test, minimum GPA of 3.0. Additional exam requirements/recommendations for international students: Required—TOEFL (minimum score 550 paper-based; 213 computer-based; 80 iBT), IELTS (minimum score 6). *Application deadline:* For fall admission, 4/1 for domestic students, 1/30 for international students. Applications are processed on a rolling basis. Application fee: $30. *Expenses:* Tuition, state resident: full-time $10,915.92. Tuition, nonresident: full-time $28,309. *Financial support:* Applicants required to submit FAFSA. *Faculty research:* Social media/interactive media adoption and communication strategy; health and science communication, nonprofits, social marketing, public communications, and philanthropy; public relationships, partnerships and coalitions; strategic communication. Total annual research expenditures: $32,000. *Unit head:* Spiro K. Kiousis, Chair, 352-273-1222, E-mail: skiousis@jou.ufl.edu. *Application contact:* Juan C. Molleda, Graduate Coordinator, 352-273-1223, Fax: 352-392-3952, E-mail: jmolleda@jou.ufl.edu.

University of Houston, College of Liberal Arts and Social Sciences, School of Communication, Houston, TX 77204. Offers health communication (MA); mass communication studies (MA); public relations studies (MA); speech communication (MA). Part-time programs available. *Faculty:* 11 full-time (6 women), 2 part-time/adjunct (0 women). *Students:* 47 full-time (39 women), 46 part-time (36 women); includes 15 Black or African American, non-Hispanic/Latino; 2 American Indian or Alaska Native, non-Hispanic/Latino; 3 Asian, non-Hispanic/Latino; 16 Hispanic/Latino, 19 international. Average age 28. 54 applicants, 70% accepted, 24 enrolled. In 2010, 20 master's awarded. *Degree requirements:* For master's, comprehensive exam (for some programs), thesis (for some programs), 30-33 hours. *Entrance requirements:* For master's, GRE. Additional exam requirements/recommendations for international students: Required—TOEFL. *Application deadline:* For fall admission, 6/1 for domestic students, 4/1 for international students; for spring admission, 11/1 for domestic students, 10/1 for international students. Applications are processed on a rolling basis. Application fee: $50 ($100 for international students). Electronic applications accepted. *Expenses:* Tuition, state resident: full-time $8592; part-time $358 per credit hour. Tuition, nonresident: full-time $16,032; part-time $668 per credit hour. Required fees: $2889. Tuition and fees vary according to course load and program. *Financial support:* In 2010–11, 28 teaching assistantships with full tuition reimbursements (averaging $8,111 per year) were awarded; career-related internships or fieldwork, Federal Work-Study, institutionally sponsored loans, scholarships/grants, health care benefits, and unspecified assistantships also available. Support available to part-time students. Financial award application deadline: 2/1. *Unit head:* Dr. Beth Olson, Chairperson, 713-743-2873, Fax: 713-743-2876, E-mail: bolson@uh.edu. *Application contact:* Dr. Martha Haun, Director of Graduate Studies, 713-743-2886, E-mail: mhaun@uh.edu.

University of Illinois at Urbana–Champaign, Graduate College, College of Media, Department of Advertising, Champaign, IL 61820. Offers MS. *Faculty:* 6 full-time (3 women), 1 (woman) part-time/adjunct. *Students:* 14 full-time (all women), 1 (woman) part-time; includes 1 Two or more races, non-Hispanic/Latino, 6 international. 111 applicants, 13% accepted, 13 enrolled. In 2010, 14 master's awarded. *Entrance requirements:* For master's, GMAT or GRE General Test, minimum GPA of 3.0. Additional exam requirements/recommendations for international students: Required—TOEFL (minimum score 610 paper-based; 253 computer-based; 102 iBT) or IELTS (minimum score 6.5). *Application deadline:* Applications are processed on a rolling basis. Application fee: $75 ($90 for international students). Electronic applications accepted. *Financial support:* In 2010–11, 8 teaching assistantships were awarded; fellowships, research assistantships, tuition waivers (full and partial) also available. *Faculty research:* Consumer behavior, persuasive communication. *Unit head:* Janet S. Slater, Interim Head, 217-333-1602, Fax: 217-244-3348, E-mail: slaterj@illinois.edu. *Application contact:* Roberta Price, Office Administrator, 217-333-1602, Fax: 217-244-3348, E-mail: rlprice@illinois.edu.

University of Maryland, College Park, Academic Affairs, College of Arts and Humanities, Department of Communication, College Park, MD 20742. Offers MA, PhD. *Faculty:* 25 full-time (15 women), 7 part-time/adjunct (4 women). *Students:* 61 full-time (45 women), 2 part-time (both women); includes 1 Black or African American, non-Hispanic/Latino; 5 Asian, non-Hispanic/Latino, 13 international. 232 applicants, 3% accepted, 7 enrolled. In 2010, 7 master's, 8 doctorates awarded. *Degree requirements:* For master's, thesis optional; for doctorate, comprehensive exam, thesis/dissertation. *Entrance requirements:* For master's, GRE General Test, minimum GPA of 3.0, sample of scholarly writing, 3 letters of recommendation; for doctorate, GRE General Test. Additional exam requirements/recommendations for international students: Required—TOEFL. *Application deadline:* For fall admission, 2/1 for domestic and international students. Applications are processed on a rolling basis. Application fee: $75. Electronic applications accepted. *Expenses:* Tuition, state resident: part-time $471 per credit hour. Tuition, nonresident: part-time $1016 per credit hour. Required fees: $337 per term. *Financial support:* In 2010–11, 3 fellowships with partial tuition reimbursements (averaging $8,000 per year), 46 teaching assistantships with tuition reimbursements (averaging $16,047 per year) were awarded; Federal Work-Study, scholarships/grants, and unspecified assistantships also available. Support available to part-time students. Financial award applicants required to submit FAFSA. *Faculty research:* Health communication, interpersonal communication, persuasion, intercultural communication, contemporary rhetoric theory. Total annual research expenditures: $30,560. *Unit head:* Dr. Elizabeth L. Toth, Chair, 301-405-0870, Fax: 301-314-9471, E-mail: eltoth@umd.edu. *Application contact:* Dean of Graduate School, 301-405-0376, Fax: 301-314-9305.

The University of North Carolina at Charlotte, Graduate School, College of Arts and Sciences, Department of Communication Studies, Charlotte, NC 28223-0001. Offers health communication (MA); media/rhetorical critical studies (MA); organizational communication (MA); public relations (MA). Part-time and evening/weekend programs available. *Faculty:* 12 full-time (5 women), 1 (woman) part-time/adjunct. *Students:* 6 full-time (5 women), 19 part-time (17 women); includes 7 minority (6 Black or African American, non-Hispanic/Latino; 1 Asian, non-Hispanic/Latino). Average age 27. 554 applicants, 4% accepted, 12 enrolled. In 2010, 12 master's awarded. Terminal master's awarded for partial completion of doctoral program. *Degree requirements:* For master's, project, thesis, or comprehensive exam. *Entrance requirements:* For master's, GRE General Test, minimum GPA of 2.75 overall. Additional exam requirements/recommendations for international students: Required—TOEFL (minimum score 557 paper-based; 220 computer-based; 83 iBT). *Application deadline:* For fall admission, 3/15 for domestic students, 5/1 for international students; for spring admission, 11/15 for domestic students, 10/1 for international students. Applications are processed on a rolling basis. Application fee: $55. Electronic applications accepted. *Expenses:* Tuition, state resident: full-time $3464. Tuition, nonresident: full-time $14,297. Required fees: $2094. Tuition and fees vary according to course load. *Financial support:* In 2010–11, 9 students received support, including 1 research assistantship (averaging $18,000 per year), 8 teaching assistantships (averaging $15,529 per year); career-related internships or fieldwork, institutionally sponsored loans, scholarships/grants, and unspecified assistantships also available. Support available to part-time students. Financial award application deadline: 4/1; financial award applicants required to submit FAFSA. *Faculty research:* Health literacy, systems of care and mental illness, the communication of emotions in gendered workplaces, international constructs of public relations managerial responsibilities, sports culture and the construction of social contracts, African-American oratory. Total annual research expenditures: $25,636. *Unit head:* Dr. Richard W. Leeman, Chair, 704-687-2086, Fax: 704-687-6900, E-mail: rwleeman@uncc.edu. *Application contact:* Kathy B. Giddings, Director of Graduate Admissions, 704-687-5503, Fax: 704-687-3279, E-mail: gradadm@uncc.edu.

University of Oklahoma, Gaylord College of Journalism and Mass Communication, Program in Journalism and Mass Communication, Norman, OK 73019-0390. Offers advertising and public relations (MA); information gathering and distribution (MA); mass communication management and policy (MA); professional writing (MA); telecommunications and new technologies (MA). Part-time programs available. *Students:* 21 full-time (16 women), 26 part-time (13 women); includes 7 minority (4 Black or African American, non-Hispanic/Latino; 2 American Indian or Alaska Native, non-Hispanic/Latino; 1 Hispanic/Latino), 6 international. Average age 27. 29 applicants, 76% accepted, 10 enrolled. In 2010, 20 master's awarded. *Degree requirements:* For master's, thesis optional. *Entrance requirements:* For master's, GRE General Test, minimum GPA of 3.2, 9 hours of course work in journalism, course work in statistics. Additional exam requirements/recommendations for international students: Required—TOEFL (minimum score 600 paper-based; 250 computer-based; 100 iBT), TWE (minimum score 5). *Application deadline:* For fall admission, 2/1 for domestic students, 4/1 for international students; for spring admission, 11/1 for domestic students, 9/1 for international students. Application fee: $40 ($90 for international students). Electronic applications accepted. *Expenses:* Tuition, state resident: full-time $3893; part-time $162.20 per credit hour. Tuition, nonresident: full-time $14,167; part-time $590.30 per credit hour. Required fees: $2523; $94.60 per credit hour. Tuition and fees vary according to course load and degree level. *Financial support:* In 2010–11, 30 students received support. Career-related internships or fieldwork, scholarships/grants, health care benefits, and unspecified assistantships available. *Faculty research:* Organizational management, strategic communications, rhetorical theories and mass communication, interactive messaging and audience response; mass media history and law. *Unit head:* Dr. Joe Foote, Dean, 405-325-2721, Fax: 405-325-7565, E-mail: jfoote@ou.edu. *Application contact:* Kelly Storm, Graduate Advisor, 405-325-2722, Fax: 405-325-7565, E-mail: kstorm@ou.edu.

University of Southern California, Graduate School, Annenberg School for Communication and Journalism, School of Journalism, Program in Strategic Public Relations, Los Angeles, CA 90089. Offers MA. Part-time programs available. *Students:* 100 full-time, 3 part-time; includes 8 Black or African American, non-Hispanic/Latino; 12 Asian, non-Hispanic/Latino; 11 Hispanic/Latino; 1 Native Hawaiian or other Pacific Islander, non-Hispanic/Latino, 30 international. Average age 24. 142 applicants, 59% accepted, 55 enrolled. In 2010, 32 master's awarded. *Degree requirements:* For master's, comprehensive exam (for some programs), thesis optional. *Entrance requirements:* For master's, GRE General Test, resume, writing samples, letters of recommendation, statement of purpose. Additional exam requirements/recommendations for international students: Required—TOEFL (minimum score 280 computer-based; 114 iBT). *Application deadline:* For fall admission, 1/3 for domestic and international students. Application fee: $85. Electronic applications accepted. *Expenses:* Tuition: Full-time $31,240; part-time $1420 per unit. Required fees: $600. One-time fee: $35 full-time. Full-time tuition and fees vary according to degree level and program. *Financial support:* In 2010–11, 4 fellowships (averaging $27,200 per year) were awarded; career-related internships or fieldwork, Federal Work-Study, institutionally sponsored loans, scholarships/grants, health care benefits, and unspecified assistantships also available. Support available to part-time students. Financial award application deadline: 1/15; financial award applicants required to submit FAFSA. *Unit head:* Jerry Swerling, Director, 213-821-1275, E-mail: swerling@usc.edu. *Application contact:* Allyson Hill, Assistant Dean, Admissions, 213-821-0770, Fax: 213-740-1933, E-mail: ascadm@usc.edu.

University of Southern Mississippi, Graduate School, College of Arts and Letters, School of Mass Communication and Journalism, Hattiesburg, MS 39406-0001. Offers mass communication (MA, MS, PhD); public relations (MS). Part-time programs available. *Faculty:* 10 full-time (3 women), 1 part-time/adjunct (0 women). *Students:* 28 full-time (21 women), 40 part-time (29 women); includes 12 Black or African American, non-Hispanic/Latino; 3 Hispanic/Latino; 4 Two or more races, non-Hispanic/Latino, 6 international. Average age 34. 37 applicants, 62% accepted, 13 enrolled. In 2010, 26 master's, 4 doctorates awarded. *Degree requirements:* For master's, comprehensive exam, thesis optional; for doctorate, comprehensive exam, thesis/dissertation. *Entrance requirements:* For master's, GRE General Test, minimum GPA of 3.0 in field of study, 2.75 in last 2 years; for doctorate, GRE General Test, minimum GPA of 3.5. Additional exam requirements/recommendations for international students: Required—TOEFL, IELTS. *Application deadline:* For fall admission, 3/1 priority date for domestic students, 3/1 for international students; for spring admission, 1/10 priority date for domestic and international students. Applications are processed on a rolling basis. Application fee: $50. *Financial support:* In 2010–11, 18 students received support, including 12 teaching assistantships with full tuition reimbursements available (averaging $8,000 per year); fellowships with full tuition reimbursements available, research assistantships with full tuition reimbursements available, career-related internships or fieldwork, Federal Work-Study, institutionally sponsored loans, scholarships/grants, health care benefits, and unspecified assistantships also available. Financial award application deadline: 3/15; financial award applicants required to submit FAFSA. *Unit head:* Dr. Christopher Campbell, Director, 601-266-5650, Fax: 601-266-4263. *Application contact:* Dr. Fei Xue, Graduate Coordinator, 601-266-5652, Fax: 601-266-6473, E-mail: fei.xue@usm.edu.

Virginia Commonwealth University, Graduate School, College of Humanities and Sciences, School of Mass Communications, Brandcenter, Richmond, VA 23284-9005. Offers art direction (MS); communication strategy (MS); copywriting (MS); creative brand management (MS); creative media planning (MS). *Students:* 181 applicants, 50% accepted, 82 enrolled. *Degree requirements:* For master's, comprehensive exam, thesis optional. *Entrance requirements:* For master's, GRE or GMAT, interview, portfolio. Additional exam requirements/recommendations for international students: Required—TOEFL (minimum score 600 paper-based; 250 computer-based; 100 iBT); Recommended—IELTS (minimum score 6.5). *Application deadline:* For fall admission, 6/1 for domestic students, 4/15 for international students. Application fee: $50. Electronic applications accepted. *Expenses:* Tuition, state resident: full-time $4308; part-time $479 per credit hour. Tuition, nonresident: full-time $8942; part-time $994 per credit hour. Required fees: $2000; $85 per credit hour. Tuition and fees vary according to course level, course load, degree level, campus/location and program. *Financial support:* Career-related internships or fieldwork and Federal Work-Study available. Support available to part-time students. *Faculty research:* Art direction, copywriting, communications strategy, creative brand management, creative technology. *Unit head:* Rick Boyko, Director, VCU Brandcenter, 804-828-8384, E-mail: brandcenter@vcu.edu. *Application contact:* Karen Berndt, Admissions Coordinator, 804-828-8384, E-mail: berndtke@vcu.edu.

Virginia Commonwealth University, Graduate School, College of Humanities and Sciences, School of Mass Communications, Program in Mass Communications, Richmond, VA 23284-9005. Offers multimedia journalism (MS); strategic public relations (MS). *Students:* 62 applicants, 53% accepted, 26 enrolled. *Degree requirements:* For master's, comprehensive exam, thesis optional. *Entrance requirements:* For master's, GRE General Test. Additional exam requirements/recommendations for international students: Required—TOEFL (minimum score 600 paper-based; 250 computer-based; 100 iBT); Recommended—IELTS (minimum score 6.5). *Application deadline:* For fall admission, 3/15 for domestic students. Applications are processed on a rolling basis. Application fee: $50. Electronic applications accepted. *Expenses:* Tuition, state resident: full-time $4308; part-time $479 per credit hour. Tuition, nonresident: full-time $8942; part-time $994 per credit hour. Required fees: $2000; $85 per credit hour. Tuition and fees vary according to course level, course load, degree level, campus/location and program. *Financial support:* Teaching assistantships, career-related internships or fieldwork, Federal Work-Study, institutionally sponsored loans, and tuition waivers (full and partial) available. Support available to part-time students. Financial award applicants required to submit FAFSA. *Faculty research:* Multimedia journalism, strategic public relations. *Unit head:* Dr. Terry Oggel, Interim Director, School of Mass Communications, 804-828-2660, Fax: 804-828-9175, E-mail: masscomm@vcu.edu. *Application contact:* June O. Nicholson, Director of Graduate Studies, 804-827-0251, Fax: 804-828-9175, E-mail: jonichol@vcu.edu.

Wayne State University, College of Fine, Performing and Communication Arts, Department of Communication, Detroit, MI 48202. Offers communication studies (MA, PhD); public relations and organizational communication (MA); radio-TV-film (MA, PhD); speech communication (MA, PhD). *Faculty:* 25 full-time (11 women), 4 part-time/adjunct (1 woman). *Students:* 64 full-time (43 women), 107 part-time (73 women); includes 44 minority (36 Black or African American, non-Hispanic/Latino; 2 American Indian or Alaska Native, non-Hispanic/Latino; 1 Asian, non-Hispanic/Latino; 5 Hispanic/Latino), 7 international. Average age 32. 65 applicants, 66% accepted, 31 enrolled. In 2010, 37 master's, 7 doctorates awarded. *Degree requirements:* For master's, thesis, essay, or comprehensive exam; for doctorate, thesis/dissertation. *Entrance requirements:* For master's, minimum GPA of 3.0, sample of academic writing; for doctorate, GRE, minimum GPA of 3.3, MA; letters of recommendation; personal statement; sample of written scholarship. Additional exam requirements/recommendations for international students: Required—TOEFL (minimum score 550 paper-based; 213 computer-based); Recommended—TWE (minimum score 6). *Application deadline:* For fall admission, 4/1 for domestic students, 6/1 for international students; for winter admission, 10/1 for international students; for spring admission, 2/1 for international students. Applications are processed on a rolling basis. Application fee: $30 ($50 for international students). Electronic applications accepted. *Expenses:* Tuition, state resident: full-time $7662; part-time $478.85 per credit hour. Tuition, nonresident: full-time $16,920; part-time $1057.55 per credit hour. Required fees: $571.20; $35.70 per credit hour. $188.05 per semester. Tuition and fees vary according to course load and program. *Financial support:* In 2010–11, 22 students received support, including 8 fellowships with tuition reimbursements available (averaging $14,956 per year), 1 research assistantship with tuition reimbursement available (averaging $23,000 per year), 19 teaching assistantships with tuition reimbursements available (averaging $14,620 per year); career-related internships or fieldwork also available. Financial award application deadline: 2/1. *Faculty research:* Rhetorical theory and criticism; mass media theory and research; argumentation; organizational communication; risk and crisis communication; interpersonal, family, and health communication. *Unit head:* Dr. Matthew Seeger, Chair, 313-577-2959, Fax: 313-577-6300, E-mail: aa4331@wayne.edu. *Application contact:* Hayg Oshagan, Associate Professor, 313-577-0429, E-mail: ad4570@wayne.edu.

OVERVIEW

The Masters of Business Administration (MBA) is a postgraduate degree in business communication and thought to be one of the most prestigious and sought-after degrees in the world. An MBA degree benefits those in positions in business and management, especially those in executive and managerial positions.

At the core of MBA programs is the valuable knowledge about business—both strategies and concepts. Through the training and internship required in an MBA program, students learn how to use these skills in practical life and in day-to-day business operations. An MBA degree program entails rigorous training, assignments, reports, presentations, and group projects, all of which contribute to developing the leadership abilities students will need in real-life business situations. And notably, alliances formed with fellow classmates and MBA program instructors are deemed one of the most important and valuable takeaways of an MBA program. MBA graduates often remark that the associations and networks formed during the MBA program of study are invaluable resources to be drawn upon year after year after having received their MBA degrees.

Required courses may include study in:

- Accounting
- Financial Reporting
- Human Resources
- Leadership and Organizational Behavior
- Marketing
- Operations Management
- Technology and Operations Management

Elective courses may include study in:

- Advanced Corporate Finance
- Advanced Real Estate Investment and Analysis
- Competitive Strategy
- Consumer Behavior
- Entrepreneurship and Venture Initiation
- Fixed Income Securities
- Information: Industry Structure and Competitive Strategy
- Innovation, Change, and Entrepreneurship
- International Development Strategy
- Negotiation and Dispute Resolution
- The Political Economy of the Public Sector
- Political Environment of the Multinational Firm
- Private Equity in Emerging Markets
- Privatization: International Perspective
- Probability Modeling in Marketing
- Speculative Markets
- Urban Fiscal Policy
- Urban Real Estate Economics
- Venture Capital and Private Equity Finance

Students of MBA programs study the theory and application of business and management principles, which equip them with knowledge that can be applied to a variety of real-world business situations and career options. Typically, employers of MBA degree holders are companies, nonprofits, universities, government, and schools; however, graduates have also found success working in the health-care, entertainment, and sports industries. Other possible employment industries include media, insurance, and legal, as well as self-employment options. Some of the most prevalent career options for an MBA graduate are financial controller, project manager, and financial analyst, although potential careers include everything from a civil engineer to a marketing director to an accountant to a social worker. Career opportunities are also available in specific areas of management, such as business management, human resources management, operations management, and supply chain management.

IN THIS SECTION

You'll find profiles of institutions offering graduate programs in the following fields:

You'll also find Close-Ups—in-depth information—from the following institutions:

HELPFUL ORGANIZATIONS/ PUBLICATIONS/BLOGS

Chartered Association of Business Administrators (CABA)

http://www.charteredaba.org/

Chartered Association of Business Administrators (CABA) is a not-for-profit professional body chartered federally under Letters Patent granted by the Government of Canada. The vision of the Association is to become the leading global professional body in providing "The Global Business Credential," and the mission of the Association is to promote the development and best practice in international business management.

International Association of Business and Management Professionals (IABMP)

http://iabmp.org/

International Association of Business and Management Professionals (IABMP) is a professional association of business and management practitioners from around the world. The professional and corporate members of IABMP come from numerous countries, including the United States, the United Kingdom, China, Australia, Japan, the Philippines, and Saudi Arabia.

The idea of IABMP was first conceived in 1987 and is now focused on providing professional collaboration and credibility among and between its members. Today, IABMP continues to have strong professional and corporate members who are recognized as the leading authority in their fields. The International Association of Business and Management Professionals believes that continued professional and personal development will change the way people do business and manage resources. IABMP sets the stage for knowledge-sharing and the exchange of ideas and information—both valuable to the development of better business professionals and management professionals in the community and society.

Academy of Management (AOM)

http://www.aomonline.org/

The Academy of Management (AOM) is a leading professional association for scholars at colleges, universities, and research institutions, as well as practitioners with scholarly interests from business, government, and not-for-profit organizations—all dedicated to creating and disseminating knowledge about management and organizations. Founded in 1936 by two professors, the Academy of Management is the oldest and largest scholarly management association in the world. Today, the Academy is the professional home for 19,063 members from 105 nations. The Academy of Management is guided by the vision of inspiring and enabling a better world through scholarship and teaching about management and organizations. Their mission is to build a vibrant and supportive community of scholars by markedly expanding opportunities to connect and explore ideas.

CAREER ASPIRATIONS: A PROSPECTIVE POSITION
Senior Consultant, Business Strategy & Analysis

Job Description

We are looking for an experienced consultant who is deeply interested in business, organizational, and process transformation through the use of technology-based solutions that engage the user and facilitate good work practices, effective decision making, and efficient, successful process execution. The right candidate enjoys thinking rigorously and creatively about business models, business operations, online solutions, and associated work practices has the ability to deliver consulting products, and thinks comprehensively about the online solution—the overall on/off-line operating model, logical structures of the solution, technology enablers and constraints, the user experience, and visual elements. The candidate is proficient at creating diverse analytical and design work products (e.g., business strategy clarification, process analysis, and conceptual models) and gets things done through organization and doing the work. The candidate works effectively and independently with client executives and senior managers to understand and clarify business strategy, goals, and issues in order to define and develop online solutions. The candidate will:

- Lead strategy and early design projects that transform the business model for all or part of an enterprise.
- Develop and/or customize best practice methodologies and tools to meet specific project needs.
- Develop detailed analysis and create both business models and portal design requirements.
- Lead analytic teams and/or project tracks and serve as a project manager for smaller projects.
- Guide user experience, content, technology, and visual design professionals.

Requirements

- Converse broadly and insightfully about business operations and priorities and articulate them effectively through summary analysis and representative models.
- Conduct interviews with practitioners, subject matter experts, managers, and executives.
- Define and translate business needs into online solution requirements, initial design concepts, "rationalized" business and functional requirements, and specifications for online solutions (addressing user, business, and technology needs or constraints).
- Work closely with colleagues to ensure that their work products effectively address business needs and solution requirements.
- Facilitate teams and meetings at all levels of stakeholder/constituent seniority.
- Demonstrate a strong sense of ownership over individual and team's work products.
- Demonstrate a strong, practical understanding of how online solutions are effectively operationalized
- Demonstrate substantial knowledge of portal technology, including functional capabilities and structural nature.

Qualifications

- Minimum of 10 years consulting experience, preferably 7 in a consulting firm
- At least 10 to 15 years total experience in relevant business-oriented roles
- Experience in the implementation of online solution recommendations and change management
- Master's degree in the business and/or information technology fields, such as business administration (MBA), operations management, organizational development, or human resources

Career Advice from Business Professionals

Nicki DeFeo
Product Manager, Wellness
Boston Heart Diagnostics
MBA, Boston University

What drew you to pursue your MBA in this field?
I have always been interested in the sciences and health care, but I realized early in my career that being a lab scientist or a health-care provider did not fully capitalize on my strengths as a project manager and strategic planner. Instead, I found that an MBA would enable me to add more value to the life science and health-care industries by teaching me how to streamline the processes that transform ideas into products or services that benefit patients. There are tremendous opportunities right now in the health-care industry. Companies are looking for well-rounded students who not only understand business principles but also how they can be applied to drive innovation and deliver sustainable results.

If you are balancing a career and pursuing your MBA, what tips do you have for juggling both?
It is incredibly important to open the lines of communication with your manager from the start. Look at your syllabus and be honest, as early as possible, about the work sacrifices you may have to make because of school. At the same time, emphasize the benefits that your employer will get as you learn new frameworks and skills in an MBA program. Offer to take on reach projects that fit in with your coursework or share case studies and articles with your manager that could enhance the performance of your team.

What career opportunities opened up to you as a result of earning your MBA?
Pursuing my MBA has completely changed my career path. Before starting the program I had hit a ceiling at my previous company, not able to move up or to a different department. I was in human resources and operations and wanted to move into an area that gave me more access to the patient, but I didn't have the skills or experience that could facilitate that transition. After my first year in the MBA program, thanks to the connections I had made in the program and the strong health-sector foundation I had established, I was awarded an internship where I helped design a program that allows patients to monitor and improve their diagnostic test results, diets, and overall well-being. With this experience, I have successfully shifted the path of my career and will be able to continue on that path after graduation.

How has your graduate education been important to your successes/accomplishments along your career path?
The Boston University Health Sector MBA program has a strong reputation in Boston. Already, I have made lasting connections with classmates, professors, and alums at some of the premiere health-care, diagnostic, and pharmaceutical companies in Boston. I believe this network will help me become an informed and competitive member of the health-care industry.

What advice would you share with new graduates considering an MBA program in your field?
I recommend that students looking into a health-sector program look closely at the professors teaching in that program. The relationships students make with their professors and their professors' colleagues are influential in guiding the student's career.

Jim Kreutzmann
JBK Consulting
MBA in Marketing
University of Wisconsin

What drew you to this field?
I started my career as a sales engineer with The Trane Company, manufacturers of large central plant equipment. As the years went by and I began to move into sales/marketing management, I realized that an MBA would allow me greater job flexibility and would open new doors to advancement.

How has your graduate education been important to your successes/accomplishments along your career path?
Having the MBA has given me more opportunities for lateral and vertical job-related moves than I expected, and, in retrospect, investing the time and effort to obtain the degree was absolutely the right thing to do. In addition, having the MBA has allowed me to accept more varied and challenging assignments than would otherwise have been the case. My career has definitely been more interesting as a result.

In your opinion, what does the future of your field hold for someone newly entering it?
Given the rate of change of technical and communication advancements in recent years, and realizing that the rate will only increase in the future, I believe that for those who are interested in technical sales, marketing management, strategic planning, and financial analysis, an MBA is now a prerequisite.

What advice would you share with new graduates considering an MBA program in your field?
My advice to new undergraduates is to take a job in your field of interest for a few years and then embark on an MBA program. Work experience will enhance your MBA education. My advice to new MBA graduates is to subscribe to The Wall Street Journal or equivalent and read, read, read to stay current with business trends and issues.

Nancy Piatt, CEO
The Piatt Group LLC
MBA, Ellis College of New York Institute of Technology

What drew you to this field?
I had thought about getting a master's degree for many years but wasn't sure of the particular degree that would serve me best. When I decided to leave the corporate arena and become an entrepreneur, it became clear that the MBA would benefit me the most. Having a stronger background in marketing, finance, strategic decision-making, and leadership has helped me tremendously both when I started my business and now as I continue to position it for growth and success.

What makes a day at your job interesting?
Every day of my job is interesting because every day is different. Depending on the client, I could be facilitating a learning event at Ford, developing assessments for a financial services giant, or creating competency models for a health maintenance organization. Both the work and the people make my job, even on the not-so-great days, rewarding.

How has your graduate education been important to your successes/accomplishments along your career path?
I took a different path in that I went back to school in my 40s. The program's curriculum was largely case-based, so interpret that as light on theory, heavy on application. I appreciated that because that's really what matters in the end. Can you use what you've learned, or did you just memorize a bunch of formulae to pass a test? I continue to tap into several of my books and notes for my work with various clients.

What does the future of your field hold for someone newly entering it? What are the exciting developments coming in the next five years?
There will always be opportunities for entrepreneurs who have a vision and who are willing to work incredibly hard to make that vision a reality. You have to make a lot of personal sacrifices—like a regular paycheck!—and believe in yourself and your ability to outshine everyone. That takes a lot of blood, sweat, tears, and guts. Does having an MBA help? It will if it taught you how to think independently, look at problems from different vantage points, and collaborate when it makes good business sense.

What advice would you share with new graduates entering your field?
If you're entering the training and development/human resources field, where I began my career, concentrate on learning "the business of the business." Learning your job responsibilities is a given, so make it your mission to understand your business' core products and opportunities and how you can contribute. If you want to start your own business, believe in yourself, work harder than you've ever worked before, and make sure you're having fun because life's way too short to not be having fun at work.

Jennifer K. Rosado
Director of Strategic Initiatives
Matrix, a Division of L'Oreal
MBA, Harvard Business School

What drew you to this field?
I was drawn to this field by a passion for beauty products and an interest in empowering hairdressers to be better business people.

What makes a day at your job interesting?
Being told by a hairdresser, field sales person, or employee how I've inspired or helped them achieve something.

How has your graduate education been important to your successes/accomplishments along your career path?
It's helped me to refine my strategic and critical thinking to be a creative problem-solver, and then to have the confidence and people management ability to empower my team or colleagues to execute something with me. Prior to business school, I was able to see the bigger picture, but I didn't know how to take action and influence others to achieve bigger strategic initiatives.

In your opinion, what does the future of your field hold for someone newly entering it?
There's greater opportunity for newly graduating MBAs to participate in this part of the beauty industry than in earlier years when I transitioned into the professional salon hair care industry in 2006. Previously, the industry didn't know "what to do" with MBAs, and MBAs didn't really know that this aspect of the industry even existed. The right MBA graduate who is looking for a more nontraditional path within the beauty industry can apply his or her business skills towards helping the small business owner/hairdresser become more successful.

What are the exciting developments coming in the next five years?
One exciting development in my field is the thinning of the lines between distribution channels. Professional salon hair care is no longer "exclusively sold at salons" on purpose. The overlap of distribution channels like Sephora and Ulta with professional salons, and even with mass channels, is a young but growing area within the industry and offers a great opportunity for MBAs to help companies strategically navigate through these new waters.

What advice would you share with new graduates entering your field?
Be flexible, be open, and go against the tide of what other MBA graduates are doing. Find your passion and pursue it.

BUSINESS ADMINISTRATION AND MANAGEMENT

Adelphi University, School of Business, Graduate Opportunity for Accelerated Learning MBA Program, Garden City, NY 11530-0701. Offers accounting (MBA); finance (MBA). *Accreditation:* AACSB. Part-time and evening/weekend programs available. *Students:* 14 full-time (8 women), 25 part-time (17 women); includes 7 Black or African American, non-Hispanic/Latino; 8 Asian, non-Hispanic/Latino; 3 Hispanic/Latino; 1 Two or more races, non-Hispanic/Latino, 1 international. Average age 40. In 2010, 14 master's awarded. *Entrance requirements:* For master's, GMAT, 2 letters of recommendation. Additional exam requirements/recommendations for international students: Required—TOEFL (minimum score 550 paper-based; 213 computer-based; 80 iBT). *Application deadline:* For fall admission, 4/1 for international students; for spring admission, 11/1 for international students. Applications are processed on a rolling basis. Application fee: $50. Electronic applications accepted. *Financial support:* Research assistantships with full and partial tuition reimbursements, career-related internships or fieldwork, Federal Work-Study, institutionally sponsored loans, scholarships/grants, and unspecified assistantships available. Financial award application deadline: 3/1; financial award applicants required to submit FAFSA. *Faculty research:* Capital market, executive compensation, business ethics, classical value theory, labor economics. *Unit head:* Rakesh Gupta, Chairperson, 516-877-4670, Fax: 516-877-4607, E-mail: gradbusinquiries@adelphi.edu. *Application contact:* Christine Murphy, Director of Admissions, 516-877-3050, Fax: 516-877-3039, E-mail: graduateadmissions@adelphi.edu.

Adelphi University, School of Business, MBA Program, Garden City, NY 11530-0701. Offers finance (MBA); management information systems (MBA); management/human resource management (MBA); marketing/e-commerce (MBA). *Accreditation:* AACSB. Part-time and evening/weekend programs available. *Students:* 131 full-time (59 women), 173 part-time (73 women); includes 25 Black or African American, non-Hispanic/Latino; 20 Asian, non-Hispanic/Latino; 17 Hispanic/Latino; 3 Two or more races, non-Hispanic/Latino, 110 international. Average age 29. In 2010, 86 master's awarded. *Degree requirements:* For master's, capstone course. *Entrance requirements:* For master's, GMAT, 2 letters of recommendation. Additional exam requirements/recommendations for international students: Required—TOEFL (minimum score 550 paper-based; 213 computer-based; 80 iBT). *Application deadline:* For fall admission, 4/1 for international students; for spring admission, 11/1 for international students. Applications are processed on a rolling basis. Application fee: $50. Electronic applications accepted. *Financial support:* Research assistantships with full and partial tuition reimbursements, career-related internships or fieldwork, Federal Work-Study, institutionally sponsored loans, scholarships/grants, and unspecified assistantships available. Financial award application deadline: 3/1; financial award applicants required to submit FAFSA. *Faculty research:* Supply chain management, distribution channels, productivity benchmark analysis, data envelopment analysis, financial portfolio analysis. *Unit head:* Rakesh Gupta, 516-877-4670, Fax: 516-877-4607, E-mail: gradbusinquiries@adelphi.edu. *Application contact:* Christine Murphy, Director of Admissions, 516-877-3050, Fax: 516-877-3039, E-mail: graduateadmissions@adelphi.edu.

Albany State University, College of Business, Program in Business Administration, Albany, GA 31705-2717. Offers MBA. Part-time and evening/weekend programs available. *Faculty:* 5 full-time (1 woman), 1 part-time/adjunct (0 women). *Students:* 8 full-time (6 women), 25 part-time (17 women); includes 27 Black or African American, non-Hispanic/Latino, 2 international. Average age 31. 12 applicants, 92% accepted, 11 enrolled. In 2010, 8 master's awarded. *Degree requirements:* For master's, comprehensive exam. *Entrance requirements:* For master's, GMAT, minimum overall undergraduate GPA of 2.5, bachelor's degree in any field from accredited college or university, 2 letters of references that focus on candidate's potential success in graduate education, official copy of transcript, ASU medical and immunization forms. *Application deadline:* For fall admission, 7/15 for domestic students, 5/15 for international students; for spring admission, 11/15 for domestic students, 9/15 for international students. Applications are processed on a rolling basis. Application fee: $20. Electronic applications accepted. *Expenses:* Tuition, state resident: full-time $3060; part-time $170 per credit hour. Tuition, nonresident: full-time $12,204; part-time $678 per credit hour. Required fees: $1160. Part-time tuition and fees vary according to course load. *Financial support:* Application deadline: 4/15. *Faculty research:* Conceptual research, case study. *Unit head:* Dr. Jonathan Elimimian, Dean, 229-430-4772, Fax: 229-430-5119, E-mail: jonathan.elimimian@asurams.edu. *Application contact:* Dr. Rani George, Dean, Graduate School, 229-430-5118, Fax: 229-430-6398, E-mail: rani.george@asurams.edu.

Albertus Magnus College, Program in Leadership, New Haven, CT 06511-1189. Offers MA. *Faculty:* 4 full-time (2 women). *Students:* 16 full-time (11 women), 11 part-time (6 women); includes 6 Black or African American, non-Hispanic/Latino; 1 Asian, non-Hispanic/Latino; 4 Hispanic/Latino. 4 applicants, 75% accepted, 2 enrolled. *Degree requirements:* For master's, thesis optional. *Entrance requirements:* For master's, interview. Application

fee: $35. *Expenses:* Tuition: Full-time $12,582; part-time $2097 per course. Required fees: $90; $25 per course. *Unit head:* Dr. Howard Fero, Director, 203-977-7100, Fax: 203-777-2112, E-mail: hfero@albertus.edu. *Application contact:* Joseph Chadwick, Director of Program Development, 203-777-0800 Ext. 114, Fax: 203-777-2112.

Albertus Magnus College, Program in Management, New Haven, CT 06511-1189. Offers business administration (MBA); management (MSM). Program also offered in East Hartford, CT. Evening/weekend programs available. *Faculty:* 9 full-time (4 women), 37 part-time/adjunct (16 women). *Students:* 245 full-time (131 women), 22 part-time (14 women); includes 77 Black or African American, non-Hispanic/Latino; 2 American Indian or Alaska Native, non-Hispanic/Latino; 3 Asian, non-Hispanic/Latino; 20 Hispanic/Latino. Average age 35. 93 applicants, 83% accepted, 70 enrolled. In 2010, 233 master's awarded. *Degree requirements:* For master's, thesis. *Entrance requirements:* For master's, 3 years of management or related experience, minimum GPA of 2.5. Additional exam requirements/recommendations for international students: Required—TOEFL. *Application deadline:* Applications are processed on a rolling basis. Application fee: $75. *Expenses:* Tuition: Full-time $12,582; part-time $2097 per course. Required fees: $90; $25 per course. *Financial support:* Available to part-time students. *Unit head:* Dr. John Donohue, Provost and Vice President, Academic Affairs, 203-773-8068, Fax: 203-773-8525, E-mail: jdonohue@albertus.edu. *Application contact:* Dr. Irene Rios, Dean of New Dimensions, 203-777-7100 Ext. 108, Fax: 203-777-2112, E-mail: iriosi@albertus.edu.

Alverno College, School of Business, Milwaukee, WI 53234-3922. Offers MBA. Evening/weekend programs available. *Faculty:* 4 full-time (1 woman), 2 part-time/adjunct (both women). *Students:* 83 full-time (74 women), 5 part-time (all women); includes 24 minority (10 Black or African American, non-Hispanic/Latino; 2 American Indian or Alaska Native, non-Hispanic/Latino; 2 Asian, non-Hispanic/Latino; 8 Hispanic/Latino; 2 Two or more races, non-Hispanic/Latino), 1 international. Average age 36. 68 applicants, 43% accepted, 26 enrolled. In 2010, 39 master's awarded. *Entrance requirements:* For master's, 3 or more years relevant work experience. Additional exam requirements/recommendations for international students: Required—TOEFL. *Application deadline:* For fall admission, 7/15 priority date for domestic and international students; for spring admission, 12/15 priority date for domestic and international students. Applications are processed on a rolling basis. Application fee: $50. Electronic applications accepted. *Expenses:* Contact institution. *Financial support:* Federal Work-Study available. Support available to part-time students. Financial award application deadline: 4/15; financial award applicants required to submit FAFSA. *Unit head:* Patricia Jensen, MBA Program Director, 414-382-6321, E-mail: patricia.jensen@alverno.edu. *Application contact:* Carolyn Wise, Graduate Recruiter, 414-382-6045, Fax: 414-382-6354, E-mail: carolyn.wise@alverno.edu.

The American College, Graduate Programs, Bryn Mawr, PA 19010-2105. Offers financial services (MSFS); leadership (MSM). Part-time and evening/weekend programs available. Postbaccalaureate distance learning degree programs offered (minimal on-campus study). *Faculty:* 20 full-time, 7 part-time/adjunct. *Students:* 629 part-time (141 women). *Application deadline:* Applications are processed on a rolling basis. Application fee: $335. Electronic applications accepted. *Financial support:* Scholarships/grants available. Support available to part-time students. *Faculty research:* Retirement counseling, social security, aging, family composition, inflation. *Unit head:* Dr. Walter J. Woerheide, Vice President for Academics and Dean, 610-526-1398, Fax: 610-526-1359, E-mail: walt.woerheide@theamericancollege.edu. *Application contact:* Joanne F. Patterson, Associate Director of Graduate School Administration, 610-526-1366, Fax: 610-526-1359, E-mail: joanne.patterson@theamericancollege.edu.

American Graduate University, Program in Acquisition Management, Covina, CA 91724. Offers MAM, Certificate. Part-time programs available. Postbaccalaureate distance learning degree programs offered (no on-campus study). *Faculty:* 2 full-time (1 woman), 15 part-time/adjunct (2 women). *Students:* 366 part-time. In 2010, 49 master's, 10 Certificates awarded. *Entrance requirements:* Additional exam requirements/recommendations for international students: Required—TOEFL. *Application deadline:* Applications are processed on a rolling basis. Application fee: $50. Electronic applications accepted. *Expenses:* Tuition: Part-time $275 per credit. *Unit head:* Paul McDonald, President, 626-966-4576 Ext. 1006, E-mail: paulmcdonald@agu.edu. *Application contact:* Marie Sirney, Admissions Director, 626-966-4576 Ext. 1003, Fax: 626-915-1709, E-mail: mariesirney@agu.edu.

American Graduate University, Program in Business Administration, Covina, CA 91724. Offers MBA. Part-time programs available. Postbaccalaureate distance learning degree programs offered (no on-campus study). *Faculty:* 2 full-time (1 woman), 15 part-time/adjunct (2 women). *Students:* 235 part-time. In 2010, 27 master's awarded. *Entrance requirements:* Additional exam requirements/recommendations for international students: Required—TOEFL. *Application deadline:* Applications are processed on a rolling basis. Application fee: $50. Electronic applications accepted. *Expenses:* Tuition: Part-time $275 per credit. *Unit head:* Paul McDonald, President, 626-966-4576 Ext. 1006, E-mail: paulmcdonald@agu.edu. *Application contact:* Marie

J. Sirney, Executive Vice President, 626-966-4576, Fax: 626-915-1709, E-mail: mariesirney@agu.edu.

American Graduate University, Program in Contract Management, Covina, CA 91724. Offers MCM, Certificate. Part-time programs available. Postbaccalaureate distance learning degree programs offered (no on-campus study). *Faculty:* 2 full-time (1 woman), 15 part-time/adjunct (2 women). *Students:* 250 part-time. In 2010, 27 master's awarded. *Entrance requirements:* Additional exam requirements/recommendations for international students: Required—TOEFL. *Application deadline:* Applications are processed on a rolling basis. Application fee: $50. Electronic applications accepted. *Expenses:* Tuition: Part-time $275 per credit. *Unit head:* Paul McDonald, President, 626-966-4576 Ext. 1006, E-mail: paulmcdonald@agu.edu. *Application contact:* Marie Sirney, 626-966-4576 Ext. 1003, Fax: 626-915-1709, E-mail: mariesirney@agu.edu.

American Public University System, AMU/APU Graduate Programs, Charles Town, WV 25414. Offers accounting (MBA); administration and supervision (M Ed); air warfare (MA Military Studies); asymmetrical warfare (MA Military Studies); criminal justice (MA); emergency and disaster management (MA); entrepreneurship (MBA); environmental policy and management (MS); finance (MBA); general (MBA); global business management (MBA); guidance and counseling (M Ed); history (MA); homeland security (MA); homeland security resource allocation (MBA); humanities (MA); information technology (MS); information technology management (MBA); intelligence studies (MA); international relations and conflict resolution (MA); joint warfare (MA Military Studies); land warfare (MA Military Studies); legal studies (MA); management (MA), including defense mangement, general, human resource management, organizational leadership, public administration; marketing (MBA); military history (MA); national security studies (MA); naval warfare (MA Military Studies); nonprofit management (MBA); political science (MA); psychology (MA); public administration (MA); public health (MA); security management (MA); space studies (MS); sports management (MS); strategic leadership (MA Military Studies); teaching (M Ed), including elementary, secondary social sciences; transportation and logistics management (MA). Programs offered via distance learning only. Part-time and evening/weekend programs available. Postbaccalaureate distance learning degree programs offered (no on-campus study). *Faculty:* 253 full-time (134 women), 1,208 part-time/adjunct (570 women). *Students:* 956 full-time (422 women), 8,476 part-time (2,821 women); includes 2,511 minority (1,218 Black or African American, non-Hispanic/Latino; 68 American Indian or Alaska Native, non-Hispanic/Latino; 219 Asian, non-Hispanic/Latino; 705 Hispanic/Latino; 46 Native Hawaiian or other Pacific Islander, non-Hispanic/Latino; 255 Two or more races, non-Hispanic/Latino), 107 international. Average age 35. 9,550 applicants, 100% accepted. In 2010, 1,688 master's awarded. *Degree requirements:* For master's, comprehensive exam or practicum. *Entrance requirements:* For master's, official transcript showing earned bachelor's degree from institution accredited by recognized accrediting body. Additional exam requirements/recommendations for international students: Required—TOEFL (minimum score 550 paper-based; 213 computer-based), IELTS (minimum score 6.5). *Application deadline:* Applications are processed on a rolling basis. Application fee: $0. Electronic applications accepted. *Financial support:* Applicants required to submit FAFSA. *Faculty research:* Military history, criminal justice, management performance, national security. *Unit head:* Dr. Frank McCluskey, Provost, 877-468-6268, Fax: 304-724-3780. *Application contact:* Terry Grant, Director of Enrollment Management, 877-468-6268, Fax: 304-724-3780, E-mail: info@apus.edu.

American University, Kogod School of Business, Master of Business Administration Program, Washington, DC 20016-8044. Offers accounting (MBA); consulting (MBA), including information technology, international business, management; corporate finance: commercial banking (MBA); corporate finance: corporate financial management (MBA); corporate finance: investment banking (MBA), including corporate finance and private equity, trading and selling; entrepreneurship (MBA); global emerging markets (MBA), including business, finance, information technology; international trade and global supply chain management (MBA); leadership (MBA); marketing management (MBA); marketing research (MBA); real estate (MBA); MBA/JD; MBA/LL M. Part-time and evening/weekend programs available. *Faculty:* 12 full-time (5 women). *Students:* 135 full-time (62 women), 104 part-time (38 women); includes 46 minority (18 Black or African American, non-Hispanic/Latino; 1 American Indian or Alaska Native, non-Hispanic/Latino; 12 Asian, non-Hispanic/Latino; 14 Hispanic/Latino; 1 Two or more races, non-Hispanic/Latino), 34 international. Average age 27. 467 applicants, 51% accepted, 70 enrolled. In 2010, 101 master's awarded. *Entrance requirements:* For master's, GMAT. Additional exam requirements/recommendations for international students: Required—TOEFL. *Application deadline:* For fall admission, 2/1 priority date for domestic students; for spring admission, 10/1 priority date for domestic students. Applications are processed on a rolling basis. Application fee: $100. *Expenses:* Contact institution. *Financial support:* In 2010–11, 19 students received support; fellowships, research assistantships with partial tuition reimbursements available, career-related internships or fieldwork, Federal Work-Study, and institutionally sponsored loans available. Support available to part-time students. Financial award application deadline: 2/1. *Faculty research:* Information technology, decision-aiding methodology,

negotiation. *Unit head:* Dr. Stevan Holmberg, Chair, 202-885-6193, E-mail: sholmbe@american.edu. *Application contact:* Shannon Demko, Associate Director Graduate Admissions, 202-885-1994, Fax: 202-885-1108, E-mail: demko@american.edu.

American University, School of Public Affairs, Department of Public Administration, Washington, DC 20016-8070. Offers advanced organization development (Certificate); fundamentals of organization development (Certificate); key executive leadership (MPA); leadership for organizational change (Certificate); non-profit management (Certificate); organization development (MSOD); organizational change (Certificate); public administration (MPA, PhD); public financial management (Certificate); public management (Certificate); public policy (MPP); public policy analysis (Certificate); LL M/MPA; MPA/JD; MPP/JD; MPP/LL M. Part-time and evening/weekend programs available. *Faculty:* 22 full-time (12 women), 12 part-time/adjunct (5 women). *Students:* 220 full-time (135 women), 248 part-time (159 women); includes 107 minority (71 Black or African American, non-Hispanic/Latino; 4 American Indian or Alaska Native, non-Hispanic/Latino; 18 Asian, non-Hispanic/Latino; 14 Hispanic/Latino; 19 international. Average age 30. 858 applicants, 73% accepted, 175 enrolled. In 2010, 205 master's, 8 doctorates awarded. *Degree requirements:* For master's, comprehensive exam; for doctorate, comprehensive exam, thesis/dissertation. *Entrance requirements:* For master's, GRE, statement of purpose; 2 recommendations; for doctorate, GRE, 3 recommendations; for Certificate, bachelor's degree. Additional exam requirements/recommendations for international students: Required—TOEFL. *Application deadline:* For fall admission, 2/1 for domestic students; for spring admission, 11/1 for domestic students. Application fee: $55. *Financial support:* Fellowships, research assistantships, teaching assistantships, career-related internships or fieldwork, Federal Work-Study, and institutionally sponsored loans available. Financial award application deadline: 2/1. *Faculty research:* Urban management, conservation politics, state and local budgeting, tax policy. *Unit head:* Dr. Robert Durant, Chair, 202-885-2509, E-mail: durant@american.edu. *Application contact:* Dr. Robert Durant, Chair, 202-885-2509, E-mail: durant@american.edu.

American University of Beirut, Graduate Programs, Olayan School of Business, The Executive MBA Program, Beirut, Lebanon. Offers EMBA. *Faculty:* 15 full-time (3 women), 6 part-time/adjunct (2 women). *Students:* 49 full-time (11 women). Average age 40. 87 applicants, 72% accepted, 49 enrolled. In 2010, 17 master's awarded. *Degree requirements:* For master's, one foreign language. *Entrance requirements:* For master's, letters of recommendation, interview. Additional exam requirements/recommendations for international students: Required—TOEFL (minimum score 600 paper-based; 250 computer-based; 100 iBT), IELTS (minimum score 7.5). *Application deadline:* Applications are processed on a rolling basis. Application fee: $75. *Expenses:* Tuition: Full-time $12,294; part-time $683 per credit. Required fees: $499; $499 per credit. Tuition and fees vary according to course load and program. *Unit head:* Riad Dimeshkie, Director, 961-135-0000 Ext. 3724, Fax: 961-175-0214, E-mail: rd28@aub.edu.lb. *Application contact:* Rula Murtada-Karam, Executive MBA Officer, 961-135-0000 Ext. 3946, Fax: 961-175-0214, E-mail: rm04@aub.edu.lb.

American University of Beirut, Graduate Programs, Olayan School of Business, The MBA Program, Beirut, Lebanon. Offers MBA. Part-time and evening/weekend programs available. *Faculty:* 12 full-time (2 women), 2 part-time/adjunct (0 women). *Students:* 37 full-time (19 women), 40 part-time (22 women). Average age 27. 99 applicants, 35% accepted, 21 enrolled. In 2010, 9 master's awarded. *Degree requirements:* For master's, one foreign language, thesis, final project. *Entrance requirements:* For master's, GMAT, letters of recommendation. Additional exam requirements/recommendations for international students: Required—TOEFL (minimum score 600 paper-based; 250 computer-based; 100 iBT), IELTS (minimum score 7.5). *Application deadline:* For fall admission, 4/30 for domestic and international students; for spring admission, 11/1 for domestic and international students. Application fee: $50. *Expenses:* Tuition: Full-time $12,294; part-time $683 per credit. Required fees: $499; $499 per credit. Tuition and fees vary according to course load and program. *Financial support:* In 2010–11, 23 students received support. Unspecified assistantships available. Financial award application deadline: 2/2. *Faculty research:* Capital acquisition/mergers and acquisition, corporate governance and financial reporting, organizational behavior, entrepreneurship. *Unit head:* Dr. Salim Chahine, Director, 961-137-4374 Ext. 3722, Fax: 961-175-0214, E-mail: sc09@aub.edu.lb. *Application contact:* Dr. Salim Chahine, Director, 961-137-4374 Ext. 3722, Fax: 961-175-0214, E-mail: sc09@aub.edu.lb.

The American University of Paris, Graduate Programs, Paris, France. Offers cross-cultural and sustainable business management (MA); cultural translation (MA); global communications (MA); global communications and civil society (MA); international affairs, conflict resolution and civil society development (MA); Middle East and Islamic studies (MA); Middle East and Islamic studies and international affairs (MA); public policy and international affairs (MA); public policy and international law (MA). *Faculty:* 14 full-time (3 women). *Students:* 151 full-time (110 women), 56 part-time (43 women). 271 applicants, 83% accepted, 104 enrolled. In 2010, 67 master's awarded. *Degree requirements:* For master's, thesis. *Entrance requirements:* For master's, minimum undergraduate GPA of 3.0. Additional exam requirements/

recommendations for international students: Recommended—IELTS. *Application deadline:* For fall admission, 4/15 priority date for international students; for spring admission, 11/15 priority date for international students. Applications are processed on a rolling basis. Application fee: $75. Electronic applications accepted. *Financial support:* Scholarships/grants available. Financial award applicants required to submit FAFSA. *Unit head:* Dr. Celeste Schenck, President, 33-1 40 62 06 59, E-mail: president@aup.fr. *Application contact:* International Admissions Counselor, 33-1 40 62 07 20, Fax: 33-1 47 05 34 32, E-mail: admissions@aup.edu.

Anderson University, College of Business, Anderson, SC 29621-4035. Offers MBA. *Accreditation:* ACBSP. *Students:* 7 full-time (0 women), 1 part-time (0 women). *Expenses:* Tuition: Part-time $320 per semester hour. *Unit head:* Dr. Douglas Goodwin, MBA Director/Associate Dean, 864-MBA-6000. *Application contact:* Dr. Douglas Goodwin, MBA Director/Associate Dean, 864-MBA-6000.

Angelo State University, College of Graduate Studies, College of Business, Department of Management and Marketing, San Angelo, TX 76909. Offers business administration (MBA). *Accreditation:* ACBSP. Part-time and evening/weekend programs available. *Faculty:* 6 full-time (1 woman). *Students:* 9 full-time (1 woman), 28 part-time (11 women); includes 1 Black or African American, non-Hispanic/Latino; 2 Hispanic/Latino, 5 international. Average age 28. 29 applicants, 66% accepted, 18 enrolled. In 2010, 14 master's awarded. *Entrance requirements:* For master's, GMAT or GRE. Additional exam requirements/recommendations for international students: Required—TOEFL or IELTS. *Application deadline:* For fall admission, 7/15 priority date for domestic students, 6/10 for international students; for spring admission, 12/1 priority date for domestic students, 11/1 for international students. Applications are processed on a rolling basis. Application fee: $40 ($50 for international students). Electronic applications accepted. *Expenses:* Tuition, state resident: full-time $4560; part-time $152 per credit hour. Tuition, nonresident: full-time $13,860; part-time $462 per credit hour. Required fees: $2132. Tuition and fees vary according to course load. *Financial support:* In 2010–11, 21 students received support. Career-related internships or fieldwork, Federal Work-Study, and scholarships/grants available. Support available to part-time students. Financial award application deadline: 3/1; financial award applicants required to submit FAFSA. *Unit head:* Dr. Tom F. Badgett, Department Head, 325-942-2383 Ext. 225, Fax: 325-942-2384, E-mail: tom.badgett@angelo.edu. *Application contact:* Dr. Carol B. Diminnie, Graduate Advisor, 325-942-2383 Ext. 229, Fax: 325-942-2194, E-mail: carol.diminnie@angelo.edu.

Antioch University Midwest, Graduate Programs, Individualized Liberal and Professional Studies Program, Yellow Springs, OH 45387-1609. Offers liberal and professional studies (MA), including counseling, creative writing, education, film studies, liberal studies, management, modern literature, psychology, theatre, visual arts. Part-time and evening/weekend programs available. Postbaccalaureate distance learning degree programs offered (minimal on-campus study). *Faculty:* 2 full-time (1 woman), 2 part-time/adjunct (both women). *Students:* 15 full-time (11 women), 34 part-time (22 women); includes 11 minority (8 Black or African American, non-Hispanic/Latino; 3 Hispanic/Latino). Average age 40. 13 applicants, 69% accepted, 5 enrolled. In 2010, 18 master's awarded. *Degree requirements:* For master's, thesis or alternative. *Entrance requirements:* For master's, resume, goal statement, interview. *Application deadline:* For fall admission, 8/1 for domestic students; for winter admission, 12/1 for domestic students; for spring admission, 3/10 for domestic students. Applications are processed on a rolling basis. Application fee: $50. Electronic applications accepted. *Expenses:* Contact institution. *Financial support:* Federal Work-Study available. Financial award applicants required to submit FAFSA. *Unit head:* Dr. Joseph Cronin, Chair, 937-769-1894, Fax: 937-769-1807, E-mail: jcronin@antioch.edu. *Application contact:* Seth Gordon, Assistant Director of Admissions, 937-769-1800 Ext. 1825, Fax: 937-769-1804, E-mail: sgordon@antioch.edu.

Antioch University Midwest, Graduate Programs, Program in Management, Yellow Springs, OH 45387-1609. Offers MA. Part-time and evening/weekend programs available. Postbaccalaureate distance learning degree programs offered (minimal on-campus study). *Faculty:* 1 full-time (0 women), 4 part-time/adjunct (1 woman). *Students:* 33 full-time (16 women), 4 part-time (3 women); includes 2 Black or African American, non-Hispanic/Latino; 11 Hispanic/Latino. Average age 38. 18 applicants, 83% accepted, 14 enrolled. In 2010, 17 master's awarded. *Entrance requirements:* For master's, resume, goal statement, interview. *Application deadline:* For fall admission, 9/1 for domestic students; for winter admission, 12/1 for domestic students; for spring admission, 3/10 for domestic students. Applications are processed on a rolling basis. Application fee: $50. Electronic applications accepted. *Expenses:* Contact institution. *Financial support:* Federal Work-Study available. Financial award applicants required to submit FAFSA. *Unit head:* Dr. Stephen Brzezinski, Chair, 937-769-1860, Fax: 937-769-1807, E-mail: sbrzezinski@antioch.edu. *Application contact:* Rob McLaughlin, Enrollment Services Manager, 937-769-1816, Fax: 937-769-1804, E-mail: rmclaughlin@antioch.edu.

Appalachian State University, Cratis D. Williams Graduate School, Program in Business Administration, Boone, NC 28608. Offers MBA. *Accreditation:* AACSB. Part-time programs available. Postbaccalaureate distance learning degree programs offered (no on-campus study). *Faculty:* 34 full-time (8 women), 6 part-time/adjunct (0 women). *Students:* 52 full-time (19 women), 36 part-time (18 women); includes 9 minority (1 Black or African American, non-Hispanic/Latino; 1 American Indian or Alaska Native, non-Hispanic/Latino; 7 Asian, non-Hispanic/Latino), 3 international. 83 applicants, 87% accepted, 55 enrolled. In 2010, 40 master's awarded. *Degree requirements:* For master's, comprehensive exam. *Entrance requirements:* For master's, GMAT, 3 letters of recommendation. Additional exam requirements/recommendations for international students: Required—TOEFL (minimum score 550 paper-based; 230 computer-based; 79 iBT), IELTS (minimum score 6.5). *Application deadline:* For fall admission, 3/1 for domestic students, 2/1 for international students; for spring admission, 7/1 for international students. Applications are processed on a rolling basis. Application fee: $55. Electronic applications accepted. *Expenses:* Tuition, state resident: full-time $3428; part-time $428 per unit. Tuition, nonresident: full-time $14,518; part-time $1814 per unit. Required fees: $2320; $344 per unit. Tuition and fees vary according to campus/location. *Financial support:* In 2010–11, 10 research assistantships (averaging $8,000 per year) were awarded; fellowships, teaching assistantships, career-related internships or fieldwork, Federal Work-Study, scholarships/grants, and unspecified assistantships also available. Financial award application deadline: 4/1; financial award applicants required to submit FAFSA. Total annual research expenditures: $166,000. *Unit head:* Dr. Joseph Cazier, Director and Assistant Dean, College of Business, 828-262-2922, E-mail: cazierja@appstate.edu. *Application contact:* Sandy Krause, Director of Admissions, 828-262-2130, Fax: 828-262-2709, E-mail: krausesl@appstate.edu.

Aquinas College, School of Management, Grand Rapids, MI 49506-1799. Offers M Mgt. Part-time and evening/weekend programs available. *Faculty:* 11 full-time (3 women), 7 part-time/adjunct (0 women). *Students:* 11 full-time (6 women), 59 part-time (36 women); includes 7 minority (3 Black or African American, non-Hispanic/Latino; 1 Asian, non-Hispanic/Latino; 3 Hispanic/Latino). Average age 35. 79 applicants, 90% accepted, 37 enrolled. In 2010, 20 master's awarded. *Entrance requirements:* For master's, GMAT, minimum undergraduate GPA of 2.75, 2 years of work experience. Additional exam requirements/recommendations for international students: Required—TOEFL (minimum score 550 paper-based; 213 computer-based). *Application deadline:* Applications are processed on a rolling basis. *Expenses:* Contact institution. *Financial support:* In 2010–11, 26 students received support. Scholarships/grants available. Support available to part-time students. Financial award application deadline: 3/15; financial award applicants required to submit FAFSA. *Unit head:* Brian DiVita, Director, 616-632-2922, Fax: 616-732-4489, E-mail: vangecyn@aquinas.edu. *Application contact:* Lynn Atkins-Rykert, Executive Assistant, 616-632-2924, Fax: 616-732-4489, E-mail: atkinlyn@aquinas.edu.

Arcadia University, Graduate Studies, Program in Business Administration, Glenside, PA 19038-3295. Offers MBA. *Accreditation:* ACBSP. *Students:* 28 full-time (10 women), 107 part-time (61 women); includes 31 minority (25 Black or African American, non-Hispanic/Latino; 4 Asian, non-Hispanic/Latino; 1 Hispanic/Latino; 1 Two or more races, non-Hispanic/Latino), 32 international. Average age 33. In 2010, 46 master's awarded. Application fee: $50. *Expenses:* Contact institution. *Unit head:* Dr. Tony Muscia, Executive Director, 215-579-2789. *Application contact:* Office of Enrollment Management, 215-572-2910, Fax: 215-572-4049, E-mail: admiss@arcadia.edu.

Arizona State University, W. P. Carey School of Business, Program in Business Administration, Tempe, AZ 85287-4906. Offers accountancy (PhD); agribusiness (PhD); business administration (MBA); finance (PhD); financial management and markets (MBA); information management (MBA); information systems (PhD); management (PhD); marketing (PhD); strategic marketing and services leadership (MBA); supply chain financial management (MBA); supply chain management (MBA, PhD); JD/MBA; MBA/M Acc; MBA/M Arch. *Accreditation:* AACSB. Part-time and evening/weekend programs available. Postbaccalaureate distance learning degree programs offered (minimal on-campus study). *Faculty:* 84 full-time (22 women), 7 part-time/adjunct (2 women). *Students:* 1,302 full-time (379 women), 86 part-time (26 women); includes 241 minority (37 Black or African American, non-Hispanic/Latino; 11 American Indian or Alaska Native, non-Hispanic/Latino; 103 Asian, non-Hispanic/Latino; 76 Hispanic/Latino; 4 Native Hawaiian or other Pacific Islander, non-Hispanic/Latino; 2 Two or more races, non-Hispanic/Latino), 171 international. Average age 31. 1,795 applicants, 44% accepted, 525 enrolled. In 2010, 734 master's, 9 doctorates awarded. Terminal master's awarded for partial completion of doctoral program. *Degree requirements:* For master's, thesis or alternative, internship, interactive Program of Study (iPOS) submitted before completing 50 percent of required credit hours; for doctorate, comprehensive exam, thesis/dissertation, interactive Program of Study (iPOS) submitted before completing 50 percent of required credit hours. *Entrance requirements:* For master's, GMAT, minimum GPA of 3.0 in last 2 years of work leading to bachelor's degree, 2 letters of recommendation, professional resume, official transcripts, 3 essays; for doctorate, GMAT or GRE, minimum GPA of 3.0 in last 2 years of work leading to bachelor's degree, 3 letters of recommendation, resume, personal statement/essay. Additional exam requirements/recommendations for international students: Required—TOEFL (minimum score 550 paper-based; 213 computer-based; 80 iBT), IELTS (minimum score 6.5). Application fee: $70 ($90 for international students). Electronic applications accepted. *Expenses:* Contact institution. *Financial support:* In 2010–11, 17 research assistantships with full and partial tuition reimbursements (averaging $18,121 per year), 153 teaching assistantships with full and partial tuition reimbursements (averaging $9,176 per year) were awarded; fellowships with full and partial tuition reimbursements, career-related internships or fieldwork, institutionally sponsored loans, scholarships/grants, and tuition waivers (full and partial) also available. Support available to part-time students. Financial award application deadline: 3/1; financial award applicants required to submit FAFSA. Total annual research expenditures: $540,779. *Unit head:* Dr. Robert E. Mittelstaedt, Dean, 480-965-2468, Fax: 480-965-5539, E-mail: mittelsr@asu.edu. *Application contact:* Graduate Admissions, 480-965-6113.

Arkansas State University, Graduate School, College of Business, Department of Economics and Finance, Jonesboro, State University, AR 72467. Offers business administration (MBA). *Accreditation:* AACSB. Part-time programs available. *Faculty:* 12 full-time (2 women). *Students:* 58 full-time (29 women), 103 part-time (39 women); includes 13 minority (6 Black or African American, non-Hispanic/Latino; 4 Asian, non-Hispanic/Latino; 1 Hispanic/Latino; 2 Two or more races, non-Hispanic/Latino), 59 international. Average age 28. 169 applicants, 83% accepted, 75 enrolled. In 2010, 38 master's awarded. *Degree requirements:* For master's, comprehensive exam, thesis or alternative. *Entrance requirements:* For master's, GMAT, appropriate bachelor's degree, letters of reference, official transcripts, immunization records. Additional exam requirements/recommendations for international students: Required—TOEFL (minimum score 550 paper-based; 253 computer-based; 79 iBT), IELTS (minimum score 6), PTE: Pearson Test of English Academic (56). *Application deadline:* For fall admission, 7/1 for domestic and international students; for spring admission, 11/15 for domestic students, 11/14 for international students. Applications are processed on a rolling basis. Application fee: $30 ($40 for international students). Electronic applications accepted. *Expenses:* Contact institution. *Financial support:* In 2010–11, 22 students received support. Career-related internships or fieldwork, scholarships/grants, and unspecified assistantships available. Financial award application deadline: 7/1; financial award applicants required to submit FAFSA. *Unit head:* Dr. Jeffrey Pittman, Chair, 870-972-2280, Fax: 870-972-3863, E-mail: pittman@astate.edu. *Application contact:* Dr. Andrew Sustich, Dean of the Graduate School, 870-972-3029, Fax: 870-972-3857, E-mail: sustich@astate.edu.

Ashland University, Dauch College of Business and Economics, Ashland, OH 44805-3702. Offers MBA. *Accreditation:* ACBSP. Part-time and evening/weekend programs available. *Faculty:* 16 full-time (5 women), 21 part-time/adjunct (6 women). *Students:* 305 full-time (131 women), 290 part-time (125 women); includes 83 minority (59 Black or African American, non-Hispanic/Latino; 5 American Indian or Alaska Native, non-Hispanic/Latino; 6 Asian, non-Hispanic/Latino; 9 Hispanic/Latino; 3 Native Hawaiian or other Pacific Islander, non-Hispanic/Latino; 1 Two or more races, non-Hispanic/Latino), 80 international. Average age 33. 205 applicants, 98% accepted, 146 enrolled. In 2010, 191 master's awarded. *Degree requirements:* For master's, thesis optional. *Entrance requirements:* For master's, 2 years of full-time work experience. Additional exam requirements/recommendations for international students: Required—TOEFL. *Application deadline:* For fall admission, 8/1 priority date for domestic students; for spring admission, 12/1 priority date for domestic students. Applications are processed on a rolling basis. Application fee: $30. Electronic applications accepted. *Expenses:* Contact institution. *Financial support:* In 2010–11, 21 students received support. Tuition waivers (partial) and unspecified assistantships available. Financial award application deadline: 4/15; financial award applicants required to submit FAFSA. *Faculty research:* Human resource management, statistical analysis, global business issues, organizational development, government and business. Total annual research expenditures: $36,410. *Unit head:* Dr. Beverly Heimann, Chair, 419-289-5216, E-mail: bheimann@ashland.edu. *Application contact:* Stephen W. Krispinsky, Executive Director of MBA Program, 419-289-5236, Fax: 419-289-5910, E-mail: skrispin@ashland.edu.

Ashworth College, Graduate Programs, Norcross, GA 30092. Offers business administration (MBA); criminal justice (MS); health care administration (MBA, MS); human resource management (MBA, MS); international business (MBA); management (MS); marketing (MBA, MS). *Faculty:* 5 part-time/adjunct (1 woman). *Students:* 299. *Expenses:* Tuition: Full-time $9230; part-time $250 per credit hour. *Unit head:* Dr. Leslie A. Gargiulo, Vice President of Education, 770-729-8400, E-mail: lgargiulo@ashworthcollege.edu. *Application contact:* Dr. Leslie A. Gargiulo, Vice President of Education, 770-729-8400, E-mail: lgargiulo@ashworthcollege.edu.

Assumption College, Graduate School, Department of Business Studies, Worcester, MA 01609-1296. Offers accounting (MBA); business administration (CAGS); finance/economics (MBA); general business (MBA); human resources (MBA); international business (MBA); management (MBA); marketing (MBA); nonprofit leadership (MBA). Part-time and evening/weekend programs available. *Faculty:* 3 full-time (0 women), 13 part-time/adjunct (3 women). *Students:* 20 full-time (9 women), 135 part-time (70 women); includes 24 minority (19 Black or African American, non-Hispanic/Latino; 2 Asian, non-Hispanic/Latino; 3 Hispanic/Latino), 4 international. Average age 26. 85 applicants, 95% accepted. In 2010, 40 master's, 2 other advanced degrees awarded. *Entrance requirements:* For master's and CAGS, 3 letters of recommendation, resume, essay. Additional exam requirements/recommendations for international students: Required—TOEFL (minimum score 540 paper-based; 200 computer-based; 76 iBT), IELTS (minimum score 6). *Application deadline:* For fall admission, 6/1 priority date for domestic students, 5/1 priority date for international students; for spring admission, 11/1 priority date for domestic students, 9/1 priority date for international students. Applications are processed on a rolling basis. Application fee: $30. Electronic applications accepted. *Expenses:* Tuition: Part-time $503 per credit. Required fees: $20 per semester. One-time fee: $100. Part-time tuition and fees vary according to campus/location. *Financial support:* Application deadline: 6/1. *Faculty research:* Workplace diversity, dynamics of team interaction, utilization of leased employees. *Unit head:* Michael Lewis, Director, 508-767-7372, Fax: 508-767-7252, E-mail: milewis@assumption.edu. *Application contact:* Daniel Provost, Assistant Director of Graduate Student Services, 508-767-7426, Fax: 508-767-7030, E-mail: dprovost@assumption.edu.

Auburn University, Graduate School, College of Business, Department of Management, Auburn University, AL 36849. Offers human resource management (PhD); management (MS, PhD); management information systems (MS, PhD). *Accreditation:* AACSB. Part-time programs available. *Faculty:* 34 full-time (7 women), 5 part-time/adjunct (0 women). *Students:* 12 full-time (4 women), 12 part-time (2 women); includes 1 Black or African American, non-Hispanic/Latino; 2 Asian, non-Hispanic/Latino, 5 international. Average age 34. 137 applicants, 28% accepted, 20 enrolled. In 2010, 9 master's, 6 doctorates awarded. *Degree requirements:* For master's, thesis (for some programs); for doctorate, thesis/dissertation. *Entrance requirements:* For master's, GMAT, GRE General Test (MS); for doctorate, GMAT, GRE General Test. Additional exam requirements/recommendations for international students: Required—TOEFL. *Application deadline:* For fall admission, 7/7 for domestic students; for spring admission, 11/24 for domestic students. Applications are processed on a rolling basis. Application fee: $50 ($60 for international students). Electronic applications accepted. *Expenses:* Tuition, state resident: full-time $7002. Tuition, nonresident: full-time $21,898. International tuition: $22,116 full-time. Required fees: $892. Tuition and fees vary according to course load and program. *Financial support:* Teaching assistantships, Federal Work-Study available. Support available to part-time students. Financial award application deadline: 3/15; financial award applicants required to submit FAFSA. *Unit head:* Dr. Sharon Oswald, Head, 334-844-4071. *Application contact:* Dr. George Flowers, Dean of the Graduate School, 334-844-2125.

Auburn University, Graduate School, College of Business, Program in Business Administration, Auburn University, AL 36849. Offers MBA. *Accreditation:* AACSB. Part-time programs available. *Faculty:* 61 full-time (10 women), 11 part-time/adjunct (3 women). *Students:* 73 full-time (22 women), 340 part-time (89 women); includes 30 Black or African American, non-Hispanic/Latino; 3 American Indian or Alaska Native, non-Hispanic/Latino; 16 Asian, non-Hispanic/Latino; 17 Hispanic/Latino, 18 international. Average age 34. 363 applicants, 51% accepted, 124 enrolled. In 2010, 158 master's awarded. *Entrance requirements:* For master's, GMAT. *Application deadline:* For fall admission, 7/7 for domestic students; for spring admission, 11/24 for domestic students. Applications are processed on a rolling basis. Application fee: $50 ($60 for international students). Electronic applications accepted. *Expenses:* Tuition, state resident: full-time $7002. Tuition, nonresident: full-time $21,898. International tuition: $22,116 full-time. Required fees: $892. Tuition and fees vary according to course load and program. *Financial support:* Federal Work-Study available. Support available to part-time students. Financial award application deadline: 3/15; financial award applicants required to submit FAFSA. *Unit head:* Dr. Daniel M. Gropper, Director, 334-844-4060. *Application contact:* Dr. George Flowers, Dean of the Graduate School, 334-844-2125.

Aurora University, College of Professional Studies, Dunham School of Business, Aurora, IL 60506-4892. Offers MBA. Part-time and evening/weekend programs available. *Faculty:* 11 full-time (2 women), 15 part-time/adjunct (5 women). *Students:* 50 full-time (23 women), 109 part-time (52 women); includes 27 Black or African American, non-Hispanic/Latino; 2 Asian, non-Hispanic/Latino; 12 Hispanic/Latino. Average age 33. 59 applicants, 92% accepted, 37 enrolled. In 2010, 72 master's awarded. *Entrance requirements:* For master's, minimum GPA of 2.75, 2 years of work experience. Additional exam requirements/recommendations for international students: Required—TOEFL (minimum score 550 paper-based; 213 computer-based). *Application deadline:* For fall admission, 8/15 priority date for domestic students, 3/1 for international students; for spring admission, 12/15 for domestic students, 7/1 for international students. Applications are processed on a rolling basis. Application fee: $25. Electronic applications accepted. *Expenses:* Contact institution. *Financial support:* In 2010–11, 35 students received support. Federal Work-Study and scholarships/grants available. Support available to part-time students. Financial award application deadline: 4/15; financial award applicants required to submit FAFSA. *Unit head:* Charles Edwards, Director, 630-844-3847, Fax: 630-844-7830, E-mail: cedwards@aurora.edu. *Application contact:* Marcia Koenen, Director of Adult and Graduate Studies, 800-742-5281, Fax: 630-844-6854, E-mail: auadmission@aurora.edu.

Austin Peay State University, College of Graduate Studies, College of Business, Clarksville, TN 37044. Offers management (MS). Part-time and evening/weekend programs available. Postbaccalaureate distance learning degree programs offered (no on-campus study). *Faculty:* 5 full-time (0 women). *Students:* 7 full-time (4 women), 79 part-time (49 women); includes 30 minority (21 Black or African American, non-Hispanic/Latino; 1 American Indian or Alaska Native, non-Hispanic/Latino; 1 Asian, non-Hispanic/Latino; 5 Hispanic/Latino; 2 Two or more races, non-Hispanic/Latino). Average age 34. 37 applicants, 95% accepted, 23 enrolled. In 2010, 46 master's awarded. *Degree requirements:* For master's, comprehensive exam. *Entrance requirements:* For master's, GMAT, 3 letters of recommendation. Additional exam requirements/recommendations for international students: Required—TOEFL (minimum score 500 paper-based; 173 computer-based). *Application deadline:* For fall admission, 7/27 priority date for domestic students; for spring admission, 12/17 priority date for domestic students. Applications are processed on a rolling basis. Application fee: $25. Electronic applications accepted. *Expenses:* Tuition, state resident: full-time $6480; part-time $324 per credit hour. Tuition, nonresident: full-time $17,960; part-time $898 per credit hour. Required fees: $1244; $61.20 per credit hour. *Financial support:* In 2010–11, research assistantships with full tuition reimbursements (averaging $5,174 per year); career-related internships or fieldwork, Federal Work-Study, institutionally sponsored loans, scholarships/grants, and unspecified assistantships also available. Support available to part-time students. Financial award application deadline: 3/1; financial award applicants required to submit FAFSA. *Unit head:* Dr. William Rupp, Dean, 931-221-7674, Fax: 931-221-7355, E-mail: ruppw@apsu.edu. *Application contact:* Dr. Dixie Dennis, Dean, College of Graduate Studies, 931-221-7662, Fax: 931-221-7641, E-mail: dennisdi@apsu.edu.

Averett University, Program in Business Administration, Danville, VA 24541. Offers MBA. Part-time programs available. *Faculty:* 10 full-time (1 woman), 22 part-time/adjunct (3 women). *Students:* 125 full-time (79 women), 383 part-time (219 women); includes 209 Black or African American, non-Hispanic/Latino; 2 American Indian or Alaska Native, non-Hispanic/Latino; 8 Asian, non-Hispanic/Latino; 11 Hispanic/Latino. Average age 37. 164 applicants, 99% accepted, 135 enrolled. In 2010, 159 master's awarded. *Entrance requirements:* For master's, minimum cumulative GPA of 3.0 for last 60 undergraduate credit hours, 3 letters of recommendation, resume, 3 years of work experience. Additional exam requirements/recommendations for international students: Required—TOEFL (minimum score 600 paper-based; 250 computer-based). *Application deadline:* Applications are processed on a rolling basis. Application fee: $50. *Financial support:* Institutionally sponsored loans available. Support available to part-time students. *Unit head:* Dr. Eugene Steadman, 434-791-5600, E-mail: eugene.steadman@averett.edu. *Application contact:* Dr. Eugene Steadman, 434-791-5600, E-mail: eugene.steadman@averett.edu.

Avila University, School of Business, Kansas City, MO 64145-1698. Offers accounting (MBA); finance (MBA); general management (MBA); health care administration (MBA); international business (MBA); management information systems (MBA); marketing (MBA). Part-time and evening/weekend programs available. *Faculty:* 9 full-time (3 women), 24 part-time/adjunct (6 women). *Students:* 123 full-time (68 women), 87 part-time (52 women); includes 44 minority (30 Black or African American, non-Hispanic/Latino; 1 American Indian or Alaska Native, non-Hispanic/Latino; 6 Asian, non-Hispanic/Latino; 6 Hispanic/Latino; 1 Native Hawaiian or other Pacific Islander, non-Hispanic/Latino), 46 international. Average age 33. 62 applicants, 79% accepted, 49 enrolled. In 2010, 80 master's awarded. *Degree requirements:* For master's, comprehensive exam, capstone course. *Entrance requirements:* For master's, GMAT (minimum score 420), minimum GPA of 3.0, interview. Additional exam requirements/recommendations for international students: Required—TOEFL (minimum score 550 paper-based). *Application deadline:* For fall admission, 7/30 priority date for domestic students, 7/30 for international students; for winter admission, 11/30 priority date for domestic students, 11/30 for international students; for spring admission, 2/28 priority date for domestic students, 2/28 for international students. Applications are processed on a rolling basis. Application fee: $0. Electronic applications accepted. *Expenses:* Contact institution. *Financial support:* In 2010–11, 102 students received support. Career-related internships or fieldwork and Competitive Merit Scholarship available. Support available to part-time students. Financial award applicants required to submit FAFSA. *Faculty research:* Leadership characteristics, financial hedging, group dynamics. *Unit head:* Dr. Richard Woodall, Dean, 816-501-3720, Fax: 816-501-2463, E-mail: richard.woodall@avila.edu. *Application contact:* JoAnna Giffin, MBA Admissions Director, 816-501-3601, Fax: 816-501-2463, E-mail: joanna.giffin@avila.edu.

Azusa Pacific University, School of Business and Management, Program in Business Administration, Azusa, CA 91702-7000. Offers MBA. *Students:* 36 full-time (16 women), 57 part-time (24 women); includes 26 minority (4 Black or African American, non-Hispanic/Latino; 8 Asian, non-Hispanic/Latino; 14 Hispanic/Latino), 9 international. Average age 29. In 2010, 50 master's awarded. *Unit head:* Dr. Ilene Bezjian, Dean, 626-815-3090, Fax: 626-815-3802, E-mail: ibezjian@apu.edu. *Application contact:* Dr. Ilene Bezjian, Dean, 626-815-3090, Fax: 626-815-3802, E-mail: ibezjian@apu.edu.

Babson College, F. W. Olin Graduate School of Business, Wellesley, Babson Park, MA 02457-0310. Offers accounting (MSA); advanced management (Certificate); business administration (MBA); global entrepreneurship (MS); technological entrepreneurship (MS). *Accreditation:* AACSB. Part-time and evening/weekend programs available. Postbaccalaureate distance learning degree programs offered (minimal on-campus study). *Faculty:* 142 full-time (39 women), 41 part-time/adjunct (9 women). *Students:* 486 full-time (145 women), 838 part-time (236 women); includes 199 minority (22 Black or African American, non-Hispanic/Latino; 1 American Indian or Alaska Native, non-Hispanic/Latino; 127 Asian, non-Hispanic/Latino; 29 Hispanic/Latino; 1 Native Hawaiian or other Pacific Islander, non-Hispanic/Latino; 19 Two or more races, non-Hispanic/Latino), 263 international. Average age 33. 877 applicants, 56% accepted, 283 enrolled. In 2010, 723 master's, 2 other advanced degrees awarded. *Entrance requirements:* For master's, GMAT, 2 years of work experience, resume, letters of recommendation. Additional exam requirements/recommendations for international students: Required—TOEFL (minimum score 100 iBT), IELTS (minimum score 6.5). *Application deadline:* For fall admission, 11/1 priority date for domestic and international students; for winter admission, 1/15 priority date for domestic and international students; for spring admission, 4/15 priority date for domestic students. Applications are processed on a rolling basis. Application fee: $100. Electronic applications accepted. *Expenses:* Tuition: Full-time $46,000; part-time $1220 per credit. Required fees: $1946. Full-time tuition and fees vary according to course load, program and student level. *Financial support:* In 2010–11, 286 students received support, including 48 fellowships (averaging $28,489 per year); career-related internships or fieldwork, Federal Work-Study, institutionally sponsored loans, scholarships/grants, health care benefits, and unspecified assistantships also available. Financial award application deadline: 4/15. *Faculty research:* Entrepreneurship, sustainability, global markets, process of innovation, social media and advertising. *Unit head:* Dr. Raghu Tadepalli, Dean, 781-239-5237, E-mail: rtadepalli@babson.edu. *Application contact:* Kathy Longee, Admission Services Team, 781-239-4317, Fax: 781-239-4194, E-mail: mbaadmission@babson.edu.

Baker University, School of Professional and Graduate Studies, Programs in Business, Baldwin City, KS 66006-0065. Offers MBA, MSM. Programs also offered in Lee's Summit, MO; Overland Park, KS; Topeka, KS; and Wichita, KS. *Accreditation:* ACBSP. Evening/weekend programs available. Postbaccalaureate distance learning degree programs offered (minimal on-campus study). *Students:* 262 full-time (132 women), 404 part-time (207 women); includes 136 minority (69 Black or African American, non-Hispanic/Latino; 11 American Indian or Alaska Native, non-Hispanic/Latino; 18 Asian, non-Hispanic/Latino; 34 Hispanic/Latino; 1 Native Hawaiian or other Pacific Islander, non-Hispanic/Latino; 3 Two or more races, non-Hispanic/Latino). Average age 34. In 2010, 390 master's awarded. *Degree requirements:* For master's, comprehensive exam. *Entrance requirements:* For master's, 2 years of full-time work experience. Additional exam requirements/recommendations for international students: Required—TOEFL (minimum score 600 paper-based; 250 computer-based; 100 iBT). *Application deadline:* Applications are processed on a rolling basis. Application fee: $45. *Financial support:* Applicants required to submit FAFSA. *Unit head:* Dr. Peggy Harris, Vice President and Dean, 785-594-8492, Fax: 785-594-8363, E-mail: peggy.harris@bakeru.edu. *Application contact:* Kelly Belk, Director of Marketing, 913-491-4432, Fax: 913-491-0470, E-mail: kbelk@bakeru.edu.

Bakke Graduate University, Programs in Pastoral Ministry and Business, Seattle, WA 98104. Offers business (MBA); global urban leadership (MA); social and civic entrepreneurship (MA); transformational leadership for the global city (D Min). Part-time programs available. Postbaccalaureate distance learning degree programs offered (minimal on-campus study). *Faculty:* 7 full-time (2 women), 30 part-time/adjunct (4 women). *Students:* 78 full-time (15 women), 301 part-time (105 women); includes 199 minority (99 Black or African American, non-Hispanic/Latino; 1 American Indian or Alaska Native, non-Hispanic/Latino; 90 Asian, non-Hispanic/Latino; 9 Hispanic/Latino). Average age 38. 41 applicants, 98% accepted, 25 enrolled. In 2010, 11 master's, 37 doctorates awarded. *Degree requirements:* For master's, thesis; for doctorate, thesis/dissertation. *Entrance requirements:* For master's, 2 years of ministry experience, BA in Biblical studies or theology; for doctorate, 3 years of ministry experience, M Div. Additional exam requirements/recommendations for international students: Required—TOEFL (minimum score 60 computer-based). *Application deadline:* For fall admission, 7/1 priority date for domestic students; for winter admission, 12/1 for domestic students; for spring admission, 3/15 for domestic students. Applications are processed on a rolling basis. Application fee: $75. Electronic applications accepted. *Expenses:* Tuition: Full-time $5000; part-time $500 per credit. Required fees: $175; $50 per course. *Financial support:* In 2010–11, 140 students received support. Scholarships/grants and tuition waivers (partial) available. Financial award applicants required to submit FAFSA. *Faculty research:* Theological systems, church management, worship. *Unit head:* Dr. Gwen Dewey, Academic Dean, 206-264-9100 Ext. 119, Fax: 206-264-8828, E-mail: gwend@bgu.edu. *Application contact:* Addie Tolle, Registrar, 206-246-9100 Ext. 110, Fax: 206-264-8828.

Baldwin-Wallace College, Graduate Programs, Division of Business, Program in Business Administration-Systems Management, Berea, OH

44017-2088. Offers MBA. Part-time and evening/weekend programs available. Postbaccalaureate distance learning degree programs offered (minimal on-campus study). *Students:* 96 full-time (49 women), 110 part-time (52 women); includes 35 minority (22 Black or African American, non-Hispanic/Latino; 1 American Indian or Alaska Native, non-Hispanic/Latino; 4 Asian, non-Hispanic/Latino; 5 Hispanic/Latino; 3 Two or more races, non-Hispanic/Latino), 1 international. Average age 34. 65 applicants, 74% accepted, 32 enrolled. In 2010, 75 master's awarded. *Degree requirements:* For master's, minimum overall GPA of 3.0, completion of all required courses. *Entrance requirements:* For master's, GMAT, bachelor's degree in field, work experience, minimum GPA of 3.0. Additional exam requirements/recommendations for international students: Required—TOEFL (minimum score 523 paper-based; 193 computer-based; 70 iBT). *Application deadline:* For fall admission, 7/25 priority date for domestic students, 4/30 priority date for international students; for spring admission, 12/15 priority date for domestic students, 9/30 priority date for international students. Applications are processed on a rolling basis. Application fee: $25. Electronic applications accepted. *Expenses:* Contact institution. *Financial support:* Career-related internships or fieldwork available. Support available to part-time students. Financial award application deadline: 5/1. *Unit head:* Dale Kramer, Director of MBA/EMBA, 440-826-2392, Fax: 440-826-3868, E-mail: dkramer@bw.edu. *Application contact:* Laura Spencer, Graduate Application Specialist, 440-826-2191, Fax: 440-826-3868, E-mail: lspencer@bw.edu.

Baldwin-Wallace College, Graduate Programs, Division of Business, Program in Executive Management, Berea, OH 44017-2088. Offers MBA. Part-time and evening/weekend programs available. *Students:* 30 full-time (9 women), 1 part-time (0 women); includes 5 minority (2 Black or African American, non-Hispanic/Latino; 1 American Indian or Alaska Native, non-Hispanic/Latino; 2 Hispanic/Latino). Average age 41. 19 applicants, 84% accepted, 11 enrolled. In 2010, 15 master's awarded. *Degree requirements:* For master's, project, minimum overall GPA of 3.0, completion of all required courses. *Entrance requirements:* For master's, interview, 10 years of work experience, current professional or managerial position, bachelor's degree in any field. Additional exam requirements/recommendations for international students: Required—TOEFL (minimum score 523 paper-based; 193 computer-based; 70 iBT). *Application deadline:* For fall admission, 7/25 priority date for domestic students, 4/30 priority date for international students; for spring admission, 12/15 priority date for domestic students, 9/30 priority date for international students. Applications are processed on a rolling basis. Application fee: $25. Electronic applications accepted. *Expenses:* Contact institution. *Financial support:* Career-related internships or fieldwork available. Support available to part-time students. Financial award application deadline: 5/1; financial award applicants required to submit FAFSA. *Unit head:* Dale Kramer, Director of MBA/EMBA, 440-826-2392, Fax: 440-826-3868, E-mail: dkramer@bw.edu. *Application contact:* Laura Spencer, Graduate Application Specialist, 440-826-2191, Fax: 440-826-3868, E-mail: lspencer@bw.edu.

Ball State University, Graduate School, Miller College of Business, Interdepartmental Program in Business Administration, Muncie, IN 47306-1099. Offers MBA. *Accreditation:* AACSB. *Students:* 69 full-time (23 women), 169 part-time (66 women); includes 2 Black or African American, non-Hispanic/Latino; 1 Asian, non-Hispanic/Latino; 2 Two or more races, non-Hispanic/Latino, 13 international. Average age 27. 155 applicants, 61% accepted, 73 enrolled. In 2010, 78 master's awarded. *Entrance requirements:* For master's, GMAT, resume. Application fee: $50. *Expenses:* Tuition, state resident: full-time $6160; part-time $299 per credit hour. Tuition, nonresident: full-time $16,020; part-time $783 per credit hour. Required fees: $2278; $95 per credit hour. *Financial support:* In 2010–11, 22 teaching assistantships (averaging $9,085 per year) were awarded. Financial award application deadline: 3/1. *Unit head:* Jennifer Bott, Graduate Coordinator, 765-285-1931, Fax: 765-285-8818. *Application contact:* Tamara Estep, Graduate Coordinator, 765-285-1931, Fax: 765-285-8818, E-mail: testep@bsu.edu.

Baylor University, Graduate School, Hankamer School of Business, Program in Business Administration, Waco, TX 76798. Offers MBA, JD/MBA, MBA/MSIS. *Accreditation:* AACSB. Part-time programs available. *Students:* 193 full-time (44 women), 3 part-time (0 women); includes 44 minority (9 Black or African American, non-Hispanic/Latino; 1 American Indian or Alaska Native, non-Hispanic/Latino; 10 Asian, non-Hispanic/Latino; 20 Hispanic/Latino; 4 Two or more races, non-Hispanic/Latino), 17 international. In 2010, 136 master's awarded. *Entrance requirements:* For master's, GMAT, minimum AACSB index of 1050. *Application deadline:* For fall admission, 8/1 for domestic students; for spring admission, 12/1 for domestic students. Applications are processed on a rolling basis. Application fee: $25. *Expenses:* Contact institution. *Financial support:* Research assistantships, teaching assistantships, career-related internships or fieldwork, Federal Work-Study, and institutionally sponsored loans available. *Unit head:* Dr. Gary Carini, Associate Dean, 254-710-3718, Fax: 254-710-1092, E-mail: gary_carini@baylor.edu. Application contact: Laurie Wilson, Director, Graduate Business Programs, 254-710-4163, Fax: 254-710-1066, E-mail: laurie_wilson@baylor.edu.

Belhaven University, School of Business, Jackson, MS 39202-1789. Offers business administration (MBA); leadership (MSL); public administration (MPA). MBA program also offered in Houston, TX, Memphis, TN and Orlando, FL. Evening/weekend programs available. *Faculty:* 13 full-time (3 women), 24 part-time/adjunct (6 women). *Students:* 316 full-time (231 women), 39 part-time (25 women); includes 15 Black or African American, non-Hispanic/Latino; 1 Hispanic/Latino. Average age 36. 329 applicants, 54% accepted, 124 enrolled. In 2010, 103 master's awarded. *Degree requirements:* For master's, comprehensive exam (for some programs), thesis (for some programs). *Entrance requirements:* For master's, GMAT, GRE General Test or MAT, minimum GPA of 2.8. *Application deadline:* Applications are processed on a rolling basis. Application fee: $25. Electronic applications accepted. *Expenses:* Tuition: Full-time $6456; part-time $538 per credit hour. Tuition and fees vary according to campus/location. *Financial support:* Applicants required to submit FAFSA. *Unit head:* Dr. Ralph Mason, Dean, 601-968-8949, Fax: 601-968-8951, E-mail: cmason@belhaven.edu. *Application contact:* Dr. Audrey Kelleher, Vice President of Adult and Graduate Marketing and Development, 407-804-1424, Fax: 407-620-5210, E-mail: akelleher@belhaven.edu.

Bellarmine University, W. Fielding Rubel School of Business, Louisville, KY 40205-0671. Offers EMBA, MBA. *Accreditation:* AACSB. Part-time and evening/weekend programs available. *Faculty:* 10 full-time (2 women), 7 part-time/adjunct (0 women). *Students:* 81 full-time (31 women), 108 part-time (40 women); includes 11 Black or African American, non-Hispanic/Latino; 3 Asian, non-Hispanic/Latino; 1 Hispanic/Latino, 1 international. Average age 30. In 2010, 84 master's awarded. *Degree requirements:* For master's, comprehensive exam. *Entrance requirements:* For master's, GMAT, baccalaureate degree from accredited institution. Additional exam requirements/recommendations for international students: Required—TOEFL (minimum score 550 paper-based; 213 computer-based; 80 iBT). *Application deadline:* Applications are processed on a rolling basis. Application fee: $25. Electronic applications accepted. *Expenses:* Contact institution. *Financial support:* Career-related internships or fieldwork, scholarships/grants, and unspecified assistantships available. Support available to part-time students. Financial award application deadline: 7/1. *Faculty research:* Marketing, management, small business and entrepreneurship, finance, economics. *Unit head:* Dr. Daniel L. Bauer, Dean, 800-274-4723 Ext. 8026, Fax: 502-272-8013, E-mail: dbauer@bellarmine.edu. *Application contact:* Dr. Sara Pettingill, Dean of Graduate Admission, 800-274-4723 Ext. 8258, Fax: 502-272-8002, E-mail: spettingill@bellarmine.edu.

Belmont University, Jack C. Massey Graduate School of Business, Nashville, TN 37212-3757. Offers M Acc, MBA. *Accreditation:* AACSB. Part-time and evening/weekend programs available. *Faculty:* 34 full-time (11 women), 6 part-time/adjunct (2 women). *Students:* 45 full-time (23 women), 212 part-time (98 women); includes 43 minority (20 Black or African American, non-Hispanic/Latino; 1 American Indian or Alaska Native, non-Hispanic/Latino; 13 Asian, non-Hispanic/Latino; 9 Hispanic/Latino), 2 international. Average age 29. 181 applicants, 54% accepted, 72 enrolled. In 2010, 112 master's awarded. *Entrance requirements:* For master's, GMAT, 2 years of work experience (MBA). Additional exam requirements/recommendations for international students: Required—TOEFL (minimum score 550 paper-based; 213 computer-based). *Application deadline:* For fall admission, 7/1 for domestic and international students; for spring admission, 11/1 for domestic and international students. Applications are processed on a rolling basis. Application fee: $50. Electronic applications accepted. *Expenses:* Contact institution. *Financial support:* In 2010–11, 22 students received support. Scholarships/grants, tuition waivers (partial), and unspecified assistantships available. Financial award application deadline: 7/1; financial award applicants required to submit FAFSA. *Faculty research:* Music business, strategy, ethics, finance, accounting systems. *Unit head:* Dr. Patrick Raines, Dean, 615-460-6480, Fax: 615-460-6455, E-mail: patraines@belmont.edu. *Application contact:* Tonya Hollin, Admissions Assistant, 615-460-6480, Fax: 615-460-6353, E-mail: masseyadmissions@.belmont.edu.

Benedictine College, Executive Master of Business Administration Program, Atchison, KS 66002-1499. Offers EMBA. Evening/weekend programs available. *Faculty:* 5 full-time (0 women), 7 part-time/adjunct (2 women). *Students:* 20 full-time (6 women); includes 8 minority (all Black or African American, non-Hispanic/Latino). Average age 37. 22 applicants, 91% accepted, 20 enrolled. In 2010, 12 master's awarded. *Entrance requirements:* For master's, 5 years of management experience, interview. Additional exam requirements/recommendations for international students: Required—TOEFL (minimum score 533 paper-based). *Application deadline:* For fall admission, 7/15 priority date for domestic students, 7/1 for international students; for spring admission, 4/15 priority date for domestic students, 4/1 for international students. Applications are processed on a rolling basis. Application fee: $100. Electronic applications accepted. *Expenses:* Contact institution. *Financial support:* In 2010–11, 6 students received support. Scholarships/grants and tuition waivers (full and partial) available. Financial award application deadline: 4/15; financial award applicants required to submit FAFSA. *Faculty research:* Banking, strategic planning, ethics, leadership and entrepreneurship. *Unit head:* Dave Geenens, Executive Director, Graduate Business Programs, 913-367-5340 Ext. 7633, Fax: 913-360-7301, E-mail: emba@benedictine.edu. *Application contact:* Donna Bonnel, Administrator of Graduate Programs, 913-367-5340 Ext. 7589, Fax: 913-360-7301, E-mail: dbonnel@benedictine.edu.

Benedictine College, Traditional Business Administration Program, Atchison, KS 66002. Offers MBA. Part-time and evening/weekend programs available. *Faculty:* 2 full-time (1 woman), 4 part-time/adjunct (0 women). *Students:* 9 full-time (7 women), 16 part-time (5 women); includes 3 minority (2 Asian, non-Hispanic/Latino; 1 Hispanic/Latino). Average age 22. 28 applicants, 89% accepted, 25 enrolled. In 2010, 18 master's awarded. *Degree requirements:* For master's, comprehensive exam. *Entrance requirements:* For master's, GMAT. Additional exam requirements/recommendations for international students: Required—TOEFL (minimum score 533 paper-based; 200 computer-based; 72 iBT). *Application deadline:* For fall admission, 8/1 priority date for domestic students, 7/1 priority date for international students; for winter admission, 1/7 priority date for domestic students, 12/1 priority date for international students; for spring admission, 5/1 priority date for domestic students, 4/1 priority date for international students. Applications are processed on a rolling basis. Application fee: $50. Electronic applications accepted. *Expenses:* Contact institution. *Financial support:* In 2010–11, 7 students received support. Scholarships/grants and unspecified assistantships available. Support available to part-time students. Financial award application deadline: 3/15; financial award applicants required to submit FAFSA. *Unit head:* Dave Geenens, Executive Director, Graduate Business Programs, 913-367-5340 Ext. 7633, Fax: 913-360-7301, E-mail: emba@benedictine.edu. *Application contact:* Donna Bonnel, Administrative Specialist, 913-360-7589, Fax: 913-360-7301, E-mail: dbonnel@benedictine.edu.

Benedictine University, Graduate Programs, Program in Business Administration, Lisle, IL 60532-0900. Offers accounting (MBA); entrepreneurship and managing innovation (MBA); financial management (MBA); health administration (MBA); human resource management (MBA); information systems security (MBA); international business (MBA); management consulting (MBA); management information systems (MBA); marketing management (MBA); operations management and logistics (MBA); organizational leadership (MBA); MBA/MPH; MBA/MS. Part-time and evening/weekend programs available. Postbaccalaureate distance learning degree programs offered (minimal on-campus study). *Faculty:* 4 full-time (2 women), 24 part-time/adjunct (3 women). *Students:* 347 full-time (140 women), 672 part-time (360 women); includes 237 minority (155 Black or African American, non-Hispanic/Latino; 4 American Indian or Alaska Native, non-Hispanic/Latino; 43 Asian, non-Hispanic/Latino; 35 Hispanic/Latino), 21 international. Average age 34. 416 applicants, 88% accepted, 217 enrolled. In 2010, 355 master's awarded. *Entrance requirements:* For master's, GMAT. Additional exam requirements/recommendations for international students: Required—TOEFL (minimum score 550 paper-based; 213 computer-based). *Application deadline:* For fall admission, 9/1 for domestic students; for winter admission, 12/1 for domestic students; for spring admission, 2/15 for domestic students. Applications are processed on a rolling basis. Application fee: $40. Electronic applications accepted. *Financial support:* Career-related internships or fieldwork and health care benefits available. Support available to part-time students. *Faculty research:* Strategic leadership in professional organizations, sociology of professions, organizational change, social identity theory, applications to change management. *Unit head:* Dr. Sharon Borowicz, Director, 630-829-6219, E-mail: sborowicz@ben.edu. *Application contact:* Kari Gibbons, Director, Admissions, 630-829-6200, Fax: 630-829-6584, E-mail: kgibbons@ben.edu.

Benedictine University, Graduate Programs, Program in Management and Organizational Behavior, Lisle, IL 60532-0900. Offers MS, MBA/MS, MPH/MS. Part-time and evening/weekend programs available. *Faculty:* 1 full-time (0 women), 15 part-time/adjunct (7 women). *Students:* 42 full-time (27 women), 122 part-time (90 women); includes 40 minority (29 Black or African American, non-Hispanic/Latino; 1 American Indian or Alaska Native, non-Hispanic/Latino; 5 Asian, non-Hispanic/Latino; 5 Hispanic/Latino), 4 international. Average age 40. 75 applicants, 85% accepted, 31 enrolled. In 2010, 33 master's awarded. *Entrance requirements:* For master's, GMAT. Additional exam requirements/recommendations for international students: Required—TOEFL (minimum score 550 paper-based; 213 computer-based). *Application deadline:* For fall admission, 9/1 for domestic students; for winter admission, 12/1 for domestic students; for spring admission, 2/15 for domestic students. Applications are processed on a rolling basis. Application fee: $40. Electronic applications accepted. *Financial support:* Career-related internships or fieldwork and health care benefits available. Support available to part-time students. *Faculty research:* Organizational change, transformation, development, learning organizations, career transitions for academics. *Unit head:* Dr. Peter F. Sorensen, Director, 630-829-6220, Fax: 630-960-1126, E-mail: psorensen@ben.edu. *Application contact:* Kari Gibbons, Director, Admissions, 630-829-6200, Fax: 630-829-6584, E-mail: kgibbons@ben.edu.

Bentley University, McCallum Graduate School of Business, Business PhD Program, Waltham, MA 02452-4705. Offers PhD. Part-time programs available. *Faculty:* 74 full-time (22 women), 21 part-time/adjunct (5 women). *Students:* 23 full-time (11 women), 1 (woman) part-time; includes 3 minority (1 Black or African American, non-Hispanic/Latino; 2 Hispanic/Latino), 9 international. Average age 40. *Degree requirements:* For doctorate, comprehensive exam, thesis/dissertation. *Entrance requirements:* For doctorate, GMAT or GRE General Test. Additional exam requirements/recommendations for international students: Required—TOEFL (minimum score 600 paper-based;

250 computer-based; 100 iBT) or IELTS (minimum score 7). Application fee: $0. Electronic applications accepted. *Expenses:* Tuition: Full-time $28,224; part-time $1176 per credit. Required fees: $404. Part-time tuition and fees vary according to course load. *Financial support:* Scholarships/grants available. *Faculty research:* Information systems, management (including organization behavior, strategy, entrepreneurship, business ethics), marketing, business analytics. *Unit head:* Dr. Sue Newell, Director, 781-891-2399, Fax: 781-891-3121, E-mail: snewell@bentley.edu. *Application contact:* Dr. Sue Newell, Director, 781-891-2399, Fax: 781-891-3121, E-mail: snewell@bentley.edu.

Bentley University, McCallum Graduate School of Business, Evening MBA Program, Waltham, MA 02452-4705. Offers MBA. *Accreditation:* AACSB. Part-time and evening/weekend programs available. *Faculty:* 74 full-time (22 women), 21 part-time/adjunct (5 women). *Students:* 433 part-time (170 women); includes 43 minority (6 Black or African American, non-Hispanic/Latino; 4 American Indian or Alaska Native, non-Hispanic/Latino; 21 Asian, non-Hispanic/Latino; 11 Hispanic/Latino; 1 Two or more races, non-Hispanic/Latino), 29 international. Average age 28. 207 applicants, 84% accepted, 108 enrolled. *Entrance requirements:* For master's, GMAT or GRE General Test. Additional exam requirements/recommendations for international students: Required—TOEFL (minimum score 600 paper-based; 250 computer-based; 100 iBT) or IELTS (minimum score 7). *Application deadline:* For fall admission, 6/1 for domestic students, 6/1 priority date for international students; for spring admission, 11/1 for domestic students, 10/1 for international students. Application fee: $50. Electronic applications accepted. *Expenses:* Tuition: Full-time $28,224; part-time $1176 per credit. Required fees: $404. Part-time tuition and fees vary according to course load. *Financial support:* In 2010–11, 44 students received support. Scholarships/grants available. Financial award application deadline: 6/1; financial award applicants required to submit CSS PROFILE or FAFSA. *Faculty research:* Strategy and innovation; corporate social responsibility; IT strategy; business process management; organizational change and knowledge management; discipline-specific research in accountancy, finance, information design and communication, IT, marketing and taxation. *Unit head:* Dr. David Schwarzkopf, MBA Program Director, 781-891-2783, Fax: 781-891-2464, E-mail: dschwarzkopf@bentley.edu. *Application contact:* Sharon Hill, Director of Graduate Admissions, 781-891-2108, Fax: 781-891-2464, E-mail: bentleygraduateadmissions@bentley.edu.

Bentley University, McCallum Graduate School of Business, Graduate Business Certificate Program, Waltham, MA 02452-4705. Offers accounting (GBC); accounting information systems (GBC); business (GSS); business ethics (GBC); data analysis (GBC); financial planning (GBC); fraud and forensic accounting (GBC); marketing analytics (GBC); taxation (GBC). *Accreditation:* AACSB. Part-time and evening/weekend programs available. *Faculty:* 74 full-time (22 women), 21 part-time/adjunct (5 women). *Students:* 21 part-time (10 women); includes 1 minority (Asian, non-Hispanic/Latino). Average age 40. 15 applicants, 87% accepted, 7 enrolled. *Entrance requirements:* For degree, GMAT or GRE General Test. Additional exam requirements/recommendations for international students: Required—TOEFL (minimum score 600 paper-based; 250 computer-based; 100 iBT) or IELTS (minimum score 7). *Application deadline:* For fall admission, 6/1 priority date for domestic and international students; for spring admission, 10/1 priority date for domestic and international students. Applications are processed on a rolling basis. Application fee: $50. Electronic applications accepted. *Expenses:* Tuition: Full-time $28,224; part-time $1176 per credit. Required fees: $404. Part-time tuition and fees vary according to course load. *Financial support:* Application deadline: 6/1. *Unit head:* Dr. Roy A. Wiggins, Dean, 781-891-3166. *Application contact:* Sharon Hill, Director of Graduate Admissions, 781-891-2108, Fax: 781-891-2464, E-mail: bentleygraduateadmissions@bentley.edu.

Bentley University, McCallum Graduate School of Business, MBA Program, Waltham, MA 02452-4705. Offers MBA. *Accreditation:* AACSB. *Faculty:* 74 full-time (22 women), 21 part-time/adjunct (5 women). *Students:* 75 full-time (28 women); includes 6 minority (4 Asian, non-Hispanic/Latino; 2 Hispanic/Latino), 40 international. Average age 27. 211 applicants, 56% accepted, 33 enrolled. *Entrance requirements:* For master's, GMAT or GRE General Test. Additional exam requirements/recommendations for international students: Required—TOEFL (minimum score 600 paper-based; 250 computer-based; 100 iBT) or IELTS (minimum score 7). *Application deadline:* For fall admission, 12/1 priority date for domestic and international students. Application fee: $50. Electronic applications accepted. *Expenses:* Tuition: Full-time $28,224; part-time $1176 per credit. Required fees: $404. Part-time tuition and fees vary according to course load. *Financial support:* In 2010–11, 39 students received support, including 39 research assistantships (averaging $17,545 per year); scholarships/grants and unspecified assistantships also available. Financial award application deadline: 6/1; financial award applicants required to submit CSS PROFILE or FAFSA. *Faculty research:* Strategy and innovation, business process management, corporate social responsibility, IT strategy, organizational change and knowledge management. *Unit head:* Dr. David Schwarzkopf, MBA Program Director, 781-891-2783, Fax: 781-891-2464, E-mail: dschwarzkopf@bentley.edu. *Application contact:* Sharon Hill, Director of Graduate Admissions, 781-891-2108, Fax: 781-891-2464, E-mail: bentleygraduateadmissions@bentley.edu.

Bentley University, McCallum Graduate School of Business, MS and MBA Program, Waltham, MA 02452-4705. Offers MS/MBA. *Accreditation:* AACSB. *Faculty:* 74 full-time (22 women), 21 part-time/adjunct (5 women). *Students:* 13 full-time (6 women), 6 international. Average age 27. 20 applicants, 60% accepted, 5 enrolled. *Entrance requirements:* Additional exam requirements/recommendations for international students: Required—TOEFL (minimum score 600 paper-based; 250 computer-based; 100 iBT) or IELTS (minimum score 7). *Application deadline:* For fall admission, 12/1 priority date for domestic and international students; for spring admission, 10/1 priority date for domestic and international students. Application fee: $50. Electronic applications accepted. *Expenses:* Tuition: Full-time $28,224; part-time $1176 per credit. Required fees: $404. Part-time tuition and fees vary according to course load. *Financial support:* In 2010–11, 12 students received support. Scholarships/grants and unspecified assistantships available. Financial award application deadline: 6/1; financial award applicants required to submit CSS PROFILE or FAFSA. *Faculty research:* Strategy and innovation, business process management, corporate social responsibility, IT strategy, organizational change and knowledge management. *Unit head:* Dr. David Schwarzkopf, MBA Program Director, 781-891-2783, Fax: 781-891-2464, E-mail: dschwarzkopf@bentley.edu. *Application contact:* Sharon Hill, Director of Graduate Admissions, 781-891-2108, Fax: 781-891-2464, E-mail: bentleygraduateadmissions@bentley.edu.

Berry College, Graduate Programs, Campbell School of Business, Mount Berry, GA 30149-0159. Offers MBA. *Accreditation:* AACSB. Part-time and evening/weekend programs available. *Faculty:* 6 part-time/adjunct (2 women). *Students:* 4 full-time (2 women), 27 part-time (13 women); includes 3 minority (2 Black or African American, non-Hispanic/Latino; 1 American Indian or Alaska Native, non-Hispanic/Latino), 1 international. Average age 27. In 2010, 15 master's awarded. *Degree requirements:* For master's, thesis. *Entrance requirements:* For master's, GMAT, minimum GPA of 3.0, essay/goals statement. Additional exam requirements/recommendations for international students: Required—TOEFL (minimum score 550 paper-based; 213 computer-based). *Application deadline:* For fall admission, 7/22 for domestic students; for spring admission, 12/9 for domestic students. Applications are processed on a rolling basis. Application fee: $25 ($30 for international students). *Expenses:* Contact institution. *Financial support:* In 2010–11, 17 students received support, including 14 research assistantships with full tuition reimbursements available (averaging $4,376 per year); scholarships/grants, tuition waivers (partial), and unspecified assistantships also available. Support available to part-time students. Financial award application deadline: 4/1; financial award applicants required to submit FAFSA. *Faculty research:* Marketing, risk management, accounting strategies, business law, entrepreneurship. *Unit head:* Dr. John Grout, Dean, 706-236-2233, Fax: 706-802-6728, E-mail: jgrout@berry.edu. *Application contact:* Brett Kennedy, Director of Admissions, 706-236-2215, Fax: 706-290-2178, E-mail: admissions@berry.edu.

Bethel College, Division of Graduate Studies, Program in Business Administration, Mishawaka, IN 46545-5591. Offers MBA. Part-time and evening/weekend programs available. *Faculty:* 4 part-time/adjunct (1 woman). *Students:* 6 full-time (2 women), 37 part-time (17 women); includes 5 minority (3 Black or African American, non-Hispanic/Latino; 1 Hispanic/Latino; 1 Two or more races, non-Hispanic/Latino). 26 applicants, 88% accepted, 20 enrolled. In 2010, 21 master's awarded. *Entrance requirements:* For master's, GMAT. Additional exam requirements/recommendations for international students: Required—TOEFL (minimum score 540 paper-based; 207 computer-based). *Application deadline:* For fall admission, 5/1 for international students; for spring admission, 10/1 for international students. Applications are processed on a rolling basis. Application fee: $25. Electronic applications accepted. Tuition and fees vary according to program. *Financial support:* Career-related internships or fieldwork available. Financial award applicants required to submit FAFSA. *Faculty research:* Marketing. *Unit head:* Dawn Goellner, Director, 574-257-3485, E-mail: goellnd2@bethelcollege.edu. *Application contact:* Dawn Goellner, Director, 574-257-3485, E-mail: goellnd2@bethelcollege.edu.

Bethel University, Graduate Programs, McKenzie, TN 38201. Offers administration and supervision (MA Ed); business administration (MBA); conflict resolution (MA); physician assistant studies (MS). Part-time and evening/weekend programs available. *Faculty:* 7 full-time (4 women), 2 part-time/adjunct (both women). *Students:* 93 full-time (68 women), 27 part-time (18 women); includes 42 minority (27 Black or African American, non-Hispanic/Latino; 15 Asian, non-Hispanic/Latino). Average age 32. 120 applicants, 100% accepted, 120 enrolled. *Degree requirements:* For master's, thesis (for some programs). *Entrance requirements:* For master's, GRE General Test or MAT, minimum undergraduate GPA of 2.5. *Application deadline:* For fall admission, 8/23 priority date for domestic and international students; for spring admission, 1/11 priority date for domestic and international students. Applications are processed on a rolling basis. Application fee: $30. *Financial support:* In 2010–11, 61 students received support. Career-related internships or fieldwork available. Support available to part-time students. Financial award application deadline: 6/1; financial award applicants required to submit FAFSA. *Unit head:* J. Bentley Rawdon, Dean of Graduate Studies, 731-352-4028, Fax:

731-352-4097. *Application contact:* Dr. Ben G. McClure, Chair, Division of Education and Health Sciences, 731-352-4025, Fax: 731-352-4097.

Bethel University, Graduate School, The Bethel MBA, St. Paul, MN 55112-6999. Offers MBA. Part-time and evening/weekend programs available. Postbaccalaureate distance learning degree programs offered (minimal on-campus study). *Faculty:* 4 full-time (0 women), 33 part-time/adjunct (11 women). *Students:* 128 full-time (61 women), 111 part-time (52 women); includes 7 Black or African American, non-Hispanic/Latino; 1 American Indian or Alaska Native, non-Hispanic/Latino; 6 Asian, non-Hispanic/Latino; 4 Hispanic/Latino; 1 Two or more races, non-Hispanic/Latino, 5 international. Average age 36. 75 applicants, 99% accepted, 49 enrolled. In 2010, 110 master's awarded. *Degree requirements:* For master's, thesis or alternative, capstone. *Entrance requirements:* For master's, baccalaureate degree, letters of reference, accounting prerequisite, minimum GPA of 3.0, interview. Additional exam requirements/recommendations for international students: Required—TOEFL (minimum score 550 paper-based; 213 computer-based; 80 iBT). *Application deadline:* For fall admission, 5/1 priority date for domestic students; for winter admission, 11/1 priority date for domestic students. Applications are processed on a rolling basis. Electronic applications accepted. *Expenses:* Contact institution. *Financial support:* Applicants required to submit FAFSA. *Unit head:* Nikki Daniels, Assistant Dean, 651-635-8000, Fax: 651-635-8039, E-mail: n-daniels@bethel.edu. *Application contact:* Paul Ives, Director of Admissions, 651-635-8000, Fax: 651-635-8004, E-mail: gs@bethel.edu.

Biola University, Crowell School of Business, La Mirada, CA 90639-0001. Offers MBA. *Accreditation:* ACBSP. Part-time and evening/weekend programs available. *Faculty:* 7 full-time (1 woman), 5 part-time/adjunct (0 women). *Students:* 25 part-time (7 women); includes 2 Black or African American, non-Hispanic/Latino; 10 Asian, non-Hispanic/Latino. 22 applicants, 73% accepted, 13 enrolled. In 2010, 8 master's awarded. *Entrance requirements:* For master's, GMAT, minimum GPA of 3.0, 3 years of professional experience, relevant undergraduate degree from a regionally accredited institution. Additional exam requirements/recommendations for international students: Required—TOEFL (minimum score 550 paper-based; 213 computer-based). *Application deadline:* For fall admission, 4/30 priority date for domestic students. Application fee: $45. Electronic applications accepted. *Financial support:* Institutionally sponsored loans and scholarships/grants available. Support available to part-time students. *Faculty research:* Integration of theology with business principles. *Unit head:* Larry D. Strand, Dean, 562-777-4015, Fax: 562-906-4545, E-mail: mba@biola.edu. *Application contact:* Christina Bullock, Program Coordinator, 562-777-4015, E-mail: mba@biola.edu.

Boston College, Carroll School of Management, Business Administration Program, Chestnut Hill, MA 02467-3800. Offers MBA, JD/MBA, MBA/MA, MBA/MS, MBA/MSA, MBA/MSF, MBA/MSW, MBA/PhD. *Accreditation:* AACSB. Part-time and evening/weekend programs available. *Students:* 208 full-time (63 women), 460 part-time (150 women); includes 6 Black or African American, non-Hispanic/Latino; 1 American Indian or Alaska Native, non-Hispanic/Latino; 53 Asian, non-Hispanic/Latino; 16 Hispanic/Latino; 79 international. Average age 27. 879 applicants, 43% accepted, 196 enrolled. In 2010, 246 master's awarded. *Entrance requirements:* For master's, GMAT, 2 letters of recommendation, resume. Additional exam requirements/recommendations for international students: Required—TOEFL (minimum score 600 paper-based; 250 computer-based; 100 iBT). *Application deadline:* For fall admission, 4/15 for domestic and international students; for spring admission, 10/15 for domestic students. Application fee: $100. Electronic applications accepted. *Financial support:* In 2010–11, 150 fellowships, 115 research assistantships with full and partial tuition reimbursements were awarded; career-related internships or fieldwork, Federal Work-Study, scholarships/grants, tuition waivers (full and partial), and unspecified assistantships also available. Support available to part-time students. Financial award application deadline: 3/1; financial award applicants required to submit FAFSA. *Faculty research:* Investments, e-commerce, corporate finance, management of financial services, strategic management. *Unit head:* Dr. Jeffrey L. Ringuest, Associate Dean for Graduate Programs, 617-552-9100, Fax: 617-552-0514, E-mail: jeffrey.ringuest@bc.edu. *Application contact:* Shelley A. Burt, Director of Graduate Enrollment, 617-552-3920, Fax: 617-552-8078, E-mail: bcmba@bc.edu.

Boston University, Metropolitan College, Department of Administrative Sciences, Boston, MA 02215. Offers banking and financial management (MSM); business continuity in emergency management (MSM); economics development and tourism management (MSAS); electronic commerce, systems, and technology (MSAS); financial economics (MSAS); innovation and technology (MSAS); insurance management (MSM); international market management (MSM); multinational commerce (MSAS); project management (MSM). *Accreditation:* AACSB. Part-time and evening/weekend programs available. Postbaccalaureate distance learning degree programs offered (no on-campus study). *Faculty:* 14 full-time (2 women), 22 part-time/adjunct (2 women). *Students:* 107 full-time (51 women), 786 part-time (356 women); includes 130 minority (55 Black or African American, non-Hispanic/Latino; 1 American Indian or Alaska Native, non-Hispanic/Latino; 30 Asian, non-Hispanic/Latino; 36 Hispanic/Latino; 1 Native Hawaiian or other Pacific Islander, non-Hispanic/Latino; 7 Two or more races, non-Hispanic/Latino), 175 international. Average age 33. 398 applicants, 87% accepted, 180 enrolled. In 2010, 154 master's awarded. *Degree requirements:* For master's, thesis optional. *Entrance requirements:* For master's, 1 year of work experience, minimum GPA of 3.0. Additional exam requirements/recommendations for international students: Required—TOEFL (minimum score 560 paper-based; 220 computer-based; 84 iBT). *Application deadline:* Applications are processed on a rolling basis. Application fee: $70. Electronic applications accepted. *Expenses:* Tuition: Full-time $39,314; part-time $1228 per credit. Required fees: $40 per semester. *Financial support:* In 2010–11, 15 students received support, including 7 research assistantships with partial tuition reimbursements available (averaging $10,000 per year); career-related internships or fieldwork, Federal Work-Study, and unspecified assistantships also available. *Faculty research:* International business, innovative process. *Unit head:* Dr. Kip Becker, Chairman, 617-353-3016, E-mail: adminsc@bu.edu. *Application contact:* Lucille Dicker, Administrative Sciences Department, 617-353-3016, E-mail: adminsc@bu.edu.

Boston University, Metropolitan College, Program in Gastronomy, Boston, MA 02215. Offers business (MLA); communications (MLA); food policy (MLA); history and culture (MLA). Part-time and evening/weekend programs available. *Faculty:* 1 (woman) full-time, 11 part-time/adjunct (5 women). *Students:* 7 full-time (all women), 64 part-time (52 women); includes 13 minority (3 Black or African American, non-Hispanic/Latino; 1 American Indian or Alaska Native, non-Hispanic/Latino; 6 Asian, non-Hispanic/Latino; 1 Hispanic/Latino; 2 Two or more races, non-Hispanic/Latino), 2 international. Average age 29. 30 applicants, 93% accepted, 26 enrolled. In 2010, 9 master's awarded. *Degree requirements:* For master's, thesis optional. *Entrance requirements:* Additional exam requirements/recommendations for international students: Required—TOEFL. *Application deadline:* Applications are processed on a rolling basis. Application fee: $70. Electronic applications accepted. *Expenses:* Tuition: Full-time $39,314; part-time $1228 per credit. Required fees: $40 per semester. *Financial support:* In 2010–11, 4 research assistantships with partial tuition reimbursements (averaging $2,500 per year), 1 teaching assistantship (averaging $2,500 per year) were awarded; career-related internships or fieldwork, scholarships/grants, and unspecified assistantships also available. Support available to part-time students. Financial award applicants required to submit FAFSA. *Faculty research:* Food studies. *Unit head:* Dr. Rachel Black, Assistant Professor, 617-353-6291, Fax: 617-353-4130, E-mail: rblack@bu.edu. *Application contact:* Dr. Rachel Black, Assistant Professor, 617-353-6291, Fax: 617-353-4130, E-mail: rblack@bu.edu.

Boston University, School of Management, Boston, MA 02215. Offers business administration (MBA); executive business administration (EMBA); investment management (MS); management (PhD); mathematical finance (MS, PhD); JD/MBA; MBA/MA; MBA/MPH; MBA/MS; MBA/MSIS; MD/MBA; MS/MBA. *Accreditation:* AACSB. Part-time and evening/weekend programs available. *Faculty:* 185 full-time (49 women), 60 part-time/adjunct (15 women). *Students:* 525 full-time (206 women), 743 part-time (272 women); includes 14 Black or African American, non-Hispanic/Latino; 134 Asian, non-Hispanic/Latino; 19 Hispanic/Latino, 247 international. Average age 30. 1,387 applicants, 28% accepted, 160 enrolled. In 2010, 532 master's, 5 doctorates awarded. *Degree requirements:* For doctorate, comprehensive exam, thesis/dissertation. *Entrance requirements:* For master's, GMAT (for MBA and MS in investment management); GMAT or GRE General Test (for MS in mathematical finance), resume, 2 letters of recommendation; for doctorate, GMAT or GRE General Test, resume, personal statement, 3 letters of recommendation, 3 essays, official transcripts. *Application deadline:* For fall admission, 1/5 for domestic and international students; for spring admission, 11/1 for domestic students. Application fee: $125. Electronic applications accepted. *Expenses:* Tuition: Full-time $39,314; part-time $1228 per credit. Required fees: $40 per semester. *Financial support:* Career-related internships or fieldwork, Federal Work-Study, institutionally sponsored loans, scholarships/grants, and tuition waivers (partial) available. Financial award applicants required to submit FAFSA. *Faculty research:* Innovation policy and productivity, corporate social responsibility, risk management, information systems, entrepreneurship, clean energy, sustainability. *Unit head:* Kenneth W. Freeman, Allen Questrom Professor and Dean, 617-353-9720, Fax: 617-353-5581, E-mail: kfreeman@bu.edu. *Application contact:* Patti Cudney, Assistant Dean, Graduate Admissions, 617-353-2670, Fax: 617-353-7368, E-mail: mba@bu.edu.

Brandeis University, The Heller School for Social Policy and Management, Program in Nonprofit Management, Waltham, MA 02454-9110. Offers child, youth, and family management (MBA); health care management (MBA); social impact management (MBA); social policy and management (MBA); sustainable development (MBA); MBA/MA; MBA/MD. MBA/MD program offered in conjunction with Tufts University School of Medicine. *Accreditation:* AACSB. Part-time programs available. *Faculty:* 36 full-time, 107 part-time/adjunct. *Students:* 58 full-time (39 women), 5 part-time (3 women); includes 2 Black or African American, non-Hispanic/Latino; 11 Asian, non-Hispanic/Latino; 2 Hispanic/Latino, 4 international. Average age 27. 116 applicants, 57% accepted, 34 enrolled. In 2010, 21 master's awarded. *Degree requirements:* For master's, team consulting project. *Entrance requirements:* For

master's, GMAT (preferred) or GRE, 2 letters of recommendation, problem statement analysis, 3-5 years of professional experience. Additional exam requirements/recommendations for international students: Required—TOEFL (minimum score 600 paper-based; 250 computer-based; 100 iBT). *Application deadline:* For fall admission, 3/15 for domestic and international students. Applications are processed on a rolling basis. Application fee: $55. Electronic applications accepted. *Expenses:* Contact institution. *Financial support:* Scholarships/grants and tuition waivers (partial) available. Financial award application deadline: 3/15; financial award applicants required to submit FAFSA. *Faculty research:* Health care; children and families; elder and disabled services; social impact management; organizations in the non-profit, for-profit, or public sector. *Unit head:* Dr. Brenda Anderson, Program Director, 781-736-8423, E-mail: banderson@brandeis.edu. *Application contact:* Shana Mongan, Assistant Director for Admissions and Financial Aid, 781-736-4229, E-mail: mongan@brandeis.edu.

Brenau University, Sydney O. Smith Graduate School, School of Business and Mass Communication, Gainesville, GA 30501. Offers accounting (MBA); business administration (MBA); healthcare management (MBA); organizational leadership (MS); project management (MBA). Part-time and evening/weekend programs available. Postbaccalaureate distance learning degree programs offered (no on-campus study). *Faculty:* 12 full-time (7 women), 24 part-time/adjunct (10 women). *Students:* 124 full-time (89 women), 348 part-time (250 women); includes 130 Black or African American, non-Hispanic/Latino; 2 American Indian or Alaska Native, non-Hispanic/Latino; 7 Asian, non-Hispanic/Latino; 13 Hispanic/Latino; 9 Two or more races, non-Hispanic/Latino, 42 international. Average age 35. In 2010, 125 master's awarded. *Degree requirements:* For master's, comprehensive exam (for some programs). *Entrance requirements:* For master's, resume, minimum undergraduate GPA of 2.5. Additional exam requirements/recommendations for international students: Required—TOEFL (minimum score 500 paper-based; 173 computer-based; 61 iBT); Recommended—IELTS (minimum score 5). *Application deadline:* Applications are processed on a rolling basis. Electronic applications accepted. *Expenses:* Contact institution. *Financial support:* In 2010–11, 1 student received support. Application deadline: 7/15. *Unit head:* Dr. William S. Lightfoot, Dean, 770-538-5330, Fax: 770-537-4701, E-mail: wlightfoot@brenau.edu. *Application contact:* Christina White, Graduate Admissions Specialist, 770-718-5320, Fax: 770-718-5338, E-mail: cwhite@brenau.edu.

Brigham Young University, Graduate Studies, Marriott School of Management, Executive Master of Business Administration Program, Provo, UT 84602. Offers MBA. *Accreditation:* AACSB. Part-time and evening/weekend programs available. *Faculty:* 17 full-time (0 women). *Students:* 131 part-time (9 women); includes 1 American Indian or Alaska Native, non-Hispanic/Latino; 9 Asian, non-Hispanic/Latino; 3 Hispanic/Latino, 2 international. Average age 36. 126 applicants, 62% accepted, 63 enrolled. In 2010, 68 master's awarded. *Entrance requirements:* For master's, GMAT, 5 years of management experience, minimum GPA of 3.0 in last 60 undergraduate hours. Additional exam requirements/recommendations for international students: Required—TOEFL (minimum score 590 paper-based; 240 computer-based; 94 iBT). *Application deadline:* For fall admission, 5/1 for domestic and international students. Applications are processed on a rolling basis. Application fee: $50. Electronic applications accepted. *Expenses:* Contact institution. *Financial support:* Applicants required to submit FAFSA. *Unit head:* Monte Swain, Director, 801-422-3500, Fax: 801-422-0513, E-mail: emba@byu.edu. *Application contact:* Yvette Anderson, MBA Program Admissions Director, 801-422-3500, Fax: 801-422-0513, E-mail: mba@byu.edu.

Brigham Young University, Graduate Studies, Marriott School of Management, Master of Business Administration Program, Provo, UT 84602. Offers MBA, JD/MBA, MBA/MS. *Accreditation:* AACSB. *Students:* 339 full-time (51 women); includes 2 Black or African American, non-Hispanic/Latino; 11 Asian, non-Hispanic/Latino; 10 Hispanic/Latino, 47 international. Average age 29. 482 applicants, 44% accepted, 160 enrolled. In 2010, 159 master's awarded. *Entrance requirements:* For master's, GMAT, minimum GPA of 3.0 in last 60 hours. Additional exam requirements/recommendations for international students: Required—TOEFL (minimum score 590 paper-based; 240 computer-based). *Application deadline:* For fall admission, 3/1 for domestic students, 1/15 for international students. Applications are processed on a rolling basis. Application fee: $50. Electronic applications accepted. *Expenses:* Contact institution. *Financial support:* In 2010–11, 229 students received support; teaching assistantships, career-related internships or fieldwork, institutionally sponsored loans, scholarships/grants, and unspecified assistantships available. Financial award application deadline: 4/15; financial award applicants required to submit FAFSA. *Faculty research:* Finance, organizational behavior/human relations, marketing, supply chain management, strategy. *Unit head:* Craig B. Merrill, Director, 801-422-3500, Fax: 801-422-0513, E-mail: mba@byu.edu. *Application contact:* Yvette Anderson, MBA Program Admissions Director, 801-422-3500, Fax: 801-422-0513, E-mail: mba@byu.edu.

Bryant University, Graduate School of Business, Master of Business Administration Program, Smithfield, RI 02917. Offers general business (MBA). *Accreditation:* AACSB. Part-time and evening/weekend programs available. *Faculty:* 28 full-time (9 women), 1 part-time/adjunct (0 women). *Students:* 35 full-time (9 women), 102 part-time (39 women); includes 3 Black or African American, non-Hispanic/Latino; 1 American Indian or Alaska Native, non-Hispanic/Latino; 1 Hispanic/Latino, 3 international. Average age 28. 161 applicants, 71% accepted, 65 enrolled. In 2010, 113 master's awarded. *Entrance requirements:* For master's, GMAT, transcripts, recommendation, resume, statement of objectives. Additional exam requirements/recommendations for international students: Required—TOEFL (minimum score 580 paper-based; 237 computer-based; 95 iBT). *Application deadline:* For fall admission, 7/15 for domestic and international students; for spring admission, 11/15 for domestic and international students. Applications are processed on a rolling basis. Application fee: $80. Electronic applications accepted. *Expenses:* Tuition: Full-time $32,580; part-time $2580 per course. One-time fee: $800. Tuition and fees vary according to program. *Financial support:* In 2010–11, 25 students received support, including 16 research assistantships (averaging $15,242 per year); unspecified assistantships also available. Financial award application deadline: 2/15; financial award applicants required to submit FAFSA. *Faculty research:* International business, information systems security, leadership, financial markets microstructure, commercial lending practice. *Unit head:* Kristopher T. Sullivan, Assistant Dean of the Graduate School, 401-232-6230, Fax: 401-232-6494, E-mail: gradprog@bryant.edu. *Application contact:* Ellen Hudon, Assistant Director of Graduate Admission, 401-232-6230, Fax: 401-232-6494, E-mail: ehudon@bryant.edu.

Butler University, College of Business Administration, Indianapolis, IN 46208-3485. Offers MBA, MP Acc. *Accreditation:* AACSB. Part-time and evening/weekend programs available. *Faculty:* 17 full-time (4 women), 4 part-time/adjunct (0 women). *Students:* 37 full-time (11 women), 163 part-time (53 women); includes 11 minority (7 Black or African American, non-Hispanic/Latino; 4 Asian, non-Hispanic/Latino), 13 international. Average age 32. 195 applicants, 53% accepted, 45 enrolled. In 2010, 94 master's awarded. *Entrance requirements:* For master's, GMAT, minimum AACSB index of 950. *Application deadline:* For fall admission, 8/15 priority date for domestic students. Applications are processed on a rolling basis. Application fee: $35. Electronic applications accepted. *Expenses:* Tuition: Full-time $29,740; part-time $1250 per credit. Required fees: $818; $430 per credit. Tuition and fees vary according to program. *Financial support:* Career-related internships or fieldwork and institutionally sponsored loans available. Support available to part-time students. Financial award application deadline: 7/15; financial award applicants required to submit FAFSA. *Faculty research:* Real estate law, international finance, total quality management, Web-based commerce, pricing policies. *Unit head:* Dr. Chuck Williams, Dean, 317-940-8491, Fax: 317-940-9455, E-mail: crwillia@butler.edu. *Application contact:* Stephanie Judge, Director of Marketing, 317-940-9886, Fax: 317-940-9455, E-mail: sjudge@butler.edu.

California Baptist University, Program in Business Administration, Riverside, CA 92504-3206. Offers accounting (PhD); management (MBA). *Accreditation:* ACBSP. Part-time and evening/weekend programs available. *Faculty:* 8 full-time (2 women), 1 (woman) part-time/adjunct. *Students:* 37 full-time (19 women), 17 part-time (9 women); includes 7 Black or African American, non-Hispanic/Latino; 3 Asian, non-Hispanic/Latino; 10 Hispanic/Latino, 7 international. 24 applicants, 92% accepted, 16 enrolled. In 2010, 43 master's awarded. *Degree requirements:* For master's, thesis or alternative, capstone project. *Entrance requirements:* Additional exam requirements/recommendations for international students: Required—TOEFL (minimum score 575 paper-based; 230 computer-based; 89 iBT). *Application deadline:* For fall admission, 8/1 priority date for domestic students, 7/1 for international students; for spring admission, 12/1 priority date for domestic students, 10/15 for international students. Applications are processed on a rolling basis. Application fee: $45. Electronic applications accepted. *Expenses:* Contact institution. *Financial support:* Federal Work-Study and scholarships/grants available. Support available to part-time students. Financial award applicants required to submit FAFSA. *Unit head:* Dr. Andrew Herrity, Dean, School of Business, 951-343-4427, Fax: 951-343-4361, E-mail: aherrity@calbaptist.edu. *Application contact:* Gail Ronveaux, Dean of Graduate Enrollment, 951-343-5045, Fax: 951-343-5095, E-mail: graduateadmissions@calbaptist.edu.

California Lutheran University, Graduate Studies, School of Management, Thousand Oaks, CA 91360-2787. Offers business (IMBA); computer science (MS); econometrics (MBA); economics (MS); entrepreneurship (MBA, Certificate); finance (MBA, Certificate); financial planning (MBA, Certificate); information systems and technology (MS); information technology management (MBA, Certificate); international business (MBA, Certificate); management and organization behavior (MBA); management and organizational behavior (Certificate); marketing (MBA, Certificate); microeconomics (MBA); nonprofit and social enterprise (MBA). Part-time and evening/weekend programs available. Postbaccalaureate distance learning degree programs offered (no on-campus study). *Faculty:* 12 full-time (3 women), 27 part-time/adjunct (6 women). *Students:* 350 full-time (162 women), 262 part-time (99 women); includes 21 Black or African American, non-Hispanic/Latino; 44 Asian, non-Hispanic/Latino; 56 Hispanic/Latino; 4 Native Hawaiian or other Pacific Islander, non-Hispanic/Latino; 12 Two or more races, non-Hispanic/Latino, 185 international. Average age 32. 379 applicants, 74% accepted, 138 enrolled. In 2010, 231 master's awarded. *Entrance requirements:* For master's, GMAT, interview, minimum GPA of 3.0. *Application deadline:* Applications are processed on a rolling basis. Application fee: $50. *Expenses:* Contact

institution. *Unit head:* Dr. Charles Maxey, Dean, 805-493-3360. *Application contact:* 805-493-3127, Fax: 805-493-3542, E-mail: clugrad@clunet.edu.

California Polytechnic State University, San Luis Obispo, Orfalea College of Business, Graduate Programs in Business, San Luis Obispo, CA 93407. Offers business (MBA); taxation (MSA). *Faculty:* 5 full-time (2 women). *Students:* 38 full-time (14 women), 13 part-time (6 women); includes 8 minority (4 Asian, non-Hispanic/Latino; 3 Hispanic/Latino; 1 Native Hawaiian or other Pacific Islander, non-Hispanic/Latino). Average age 26. 111 applicants, 46% accepted, 37 enrolled. In 2010, 68 master's awarded. *Degree requirements:* For master's, comprehensive exam (for some programs), thesis or alternative. *Entrance requirements:* For master's, GMAT. Additional exam requirements/recommendations for international students: Required—TOEFL (minimum score 550 paper-based; 213 computer-based) or IELTS (minimum score 6). *Application deadline:* For fall admission, 7/1 for domestic students, 11/30 for international students. Applications are processed on a rolling basis. Application fee: $55. Electronic applications accepted. *Expenses:* Tuition, state resident: full-time $5386; part-time $3124 per year. Tuition, nonresident: full-time $11,160; part-time $248 per unit. Required fees: $2250; $614 per term. One-time fee: $2250 full-time; $1842 part-time. *Financial support:* Career-related internships or fieldwork, Federal Work-Study, institutionally sponsored loans, scholarships/grants, and unspecified assistantships available. Support available to part-time students. Financial award application deadline: 3/2; financial award applicants required to submit FAFSA. *Faculty research:* International business, organizational behavior, graphic communication document systems management, commercial development of innovative technologies, effective communication skills for managers. *Unit head:* Dr. Bradford Anderson, Associate Dean/Graduate Coordinator, 805-756-5210, Fax: 805-756-0110, E-mail: bpanders@calpoly.edu. *Application contact:* Dr. Bradford Anderson, Associate Dean/Graduate Coordinator, 805-756-5210, Fax: 805-756-0110, E-mail: bpanders@calpoly.edu.

California State Polytechnic University, Pomona, Academic Affairs, College of Business Administration, Master of Science in Business Administration Program, Pomona, CA 91768-2557. Offers information systems auditing (MS). *Students:* 2 full-time (1 woman), 12 part-time (3 women); includes 10 minority (7 Asian, non-Hispanic/Latino; 3 Hispanic/Latino), 1 international. Average age 32. 20 applicants, 35% accepted, 5 enrolled. In 2010, 5 master's awarded. *Application deadline:* Applications are processed on a rolling basis. Application fee: $55. Electronic applications accepted. *Expenses:* Tuition, state resident: full-time $5386; part-time $2850 per year. Tuition, nonresident: full-time $12,082; part-time $248 per credit. Required fees: $577; $248 per credit. $577 per year. Tuition and fees vary according to course load and program. *Unit head:* Dr. Richard S. Lapidus, Dean, 909-869-2400, E-mail: rslapidus@csupomona.edu. *Application contact:* Dr. Steven Curl, Associate Dean, 909-869-4244, E-mail: scurl@csupomona.edu.

California State Polytechnic University, Pomona, Academic Affairs, College of Business Administration, MBA Program, Pomona, CA 91768-2557. Offers MBA. *Students:* 27 full-time (15 women), 129 part-time (54 women); includes 59 minority (2 Black or African American, non-Hispanic/Latino; 37 Asian, non-Hispanic/Latino; 19 Hispanic/Latino; 1 Two or more races, non-Hispanic/Latino), 43 international. Average age 32. 189 applicants, 39% accepted, 41 enrolled. In 2010, 40 master's awarded. *Application deadline:* Applications are processed on a rolling basis. Application fee: $55. *Expenses:* Tuition, state resident: full-time $5386; part-time $2850 per year. Tuition, nonresident: full-time $12,082; part-time $248 per credit. Required fees: $577; $248 per credit. $577 per year. Tuition and fees vary according to course load and program. *Unit head:* Dr. Richard S. Lapidus, Dean, 909-869-2400, E-mail: rslapidus@csupomona.edu. *Application contact:* Dr. Steven Curl, Associate Dean, 909-869-4244, E-mail: scurl@csupomona.edu.

California State University, Chico, Graduate School, College of Behavioral and Social Sciences, Department of Political Science, Program in Public Administration, Chico, CA 95929-0722. Offers health administration (MPA); local government management (MPA); public administration (MPA). *Accreditation:* NASPAA. Part-time programs available. *Students:* 28 full-time (13 women), 23 part-time (12 women); includes 4 Black or African American, non-Hispanic/Latino; 1 American Indian or Alaska Native, non-Hispanic/Latino; 5 Asian, non-Hispanic/Latino; 10 Hispanic/Latino, 4 international. Average age 31. 45 applicants, 71% accepted, 18 enrolled. In 2010, 9 master's awarded. *Entrance requirements:* For master's, 2 letters of recommendation. Additional exam requirements/recommendations for international students: Required—TOEFL (minimum score 550 paper-based; 213 computer-based; 80 iBT), IELTS (minimum score 6.5). *Application deadline:* For fall admission, 3/1 priority date for domestic students, 3/1 for international students; for spring admission, 9/15 priority date for domestic students, 9/15 for international students. Applications are processed on a rolling basis. Application fee: $55. Electronic applications accepted. *Financial support:* Fellowships, career-related internships or fieldwork available. *Unit head:* Dr. Donna Kemp, Graduate Coordinator, 530-898-5734. *Application contact:* Dr. Donna Kemp, Graduate Coordinator, 530-898-5734.

California State University, Chico, Graduate School, College of Business, Program in Business Administration, Chico, CA 95929-0722. Offers MBA. *Accreditation:* AACSB. Part-time programs available. *Students:* 53 full-time

(28 women), 33 part-time (15 women); includes 7 Asian, non-Hispanic/Latino; 2 Hispanic/Latino, 38 international. Average age 26. 97 applicants, 73% accepted, 44 enrolled. In 2010, 33 master's awarded. *Degree requirements:* For master's, thesis or alternative. *Entrance requirements:* For master's, GMAT, 3 letters of recommendation, resume. Additional exam requirements/ recommendations for international students: Required—TOEFL (minimum score 550 paper-based; 213 computer-based; 80 iBT), IELTS (minimum score 6.5). *Application deadline:* For fall admission, 3/1 for domestic and international students; for spring admission, 9/15 for domestic and international students. Applications are processed on a rolling basis. Application fee: $55. Electronic applications accepted. *Unit head:* Graduate Coordinator, 530-898-5895. *Application contact:* Dr. Ray Boykin, Head, 530-898-5895.

California State University, Dominguez Hills, College of Business Administration and Public Policy, Program in Business Administration, Carson, CA 90747-0001. Offers MBA. *Accreditation:* ACBSP. Part-time and evening/ weekend programs available. Postbaccalaureate distance learning degree programs offered (no on-campus study). *Faculty:* 71 full-time (4 women), 8 part-time/adjunct (3 women). *Students:* 48 full-time (16 women), 82 part-time (25 women); includes 9 Black or African American, non-Hispanic/Latino; 20 Asian, non-Hispanic/Latino; 18 Hispanic/Latino; 1 Native Hawaiian or other Pacific Islander, non-Hispanic/Latino, 8 international. Average age 34. 278 applicants, 50% accepted, 38 enrolled. In 2010, 58 master's awarded. *Entrance requirements:* For master's, GMAT, minimum GPA of 2.75. Additional exam requirements/recommendations for international students: Required—TOEFL (minimum score 570 paper-based; 230 computer-based; 88 iBT). *Application deadline:* For fall admission, 4/1 for domestic and international students; for spring admission, 11/1 for domestic students, 10/1 for international students. Application fee: $55. *Faculty research:* Management. *Unit head:* Kenneth Poertner, Program Director, 310-243-2714, Fax: 310-516-4178, E-mail: kpoertner@csudh.edu. *Application contact:* Eileen Hall, Graduate Advisor, 310-243-3465, E-mail: ehall@csudh.edu.

California State University, East Bay, Office of Academic Programs and Graduate Studies, College of Business and Economics, MBA Program, Hayward, CA 94542-3000. Offers entrepreneurship (MBA); finance (MBA); human resources and organizational behavior (MBA); information technology management (MBA); marketing management (MBA); operations and supply chain management (MBA); strategy and international business (MBA). Part-time and evening/weekend programs available. Postbaccalaureate distance learning degree programs offered (no on-campus study). *Faculty:* 33 full-time (9 women). *Students:* 121 full-time (58 women), 133 part-time (67 women); includes 7 Black or African American, non-Hispanic/Latino; 63 Asian, non-Hispanic/Latino; 11 Hispanic/Latino; 3 Native Hawaiian or other Pacific Islander, non-Hispanic/Latino; 5 Two or more races, non-Hispanic/ Latino, 87 international. Average age 30. 284 applicants, 47% accepted, 55 enrolled. In 2010, 241 master's awarded. *Degree requirements:* For master's, comprehensive exam or thesis. *Entrance requirements:* For master's, GMAT (minimum 20th percentile verbal and quantitative section), bachelor's degree, minimum GPA of 2.75. Additional exam requirements/recommendations for international students: Required—TOEFL (minimum score 550 paper-based; 213 computer-based; 79 iBT). *Application deadline:* For fall admission, 6/30 for domestic and international students. Applications are processed on a rolling basis. Application fee: $55. Electronic applications accepted. *Financial support:* Career-related internships or fieldwork, Federal Work-Study, institutionally sponsored loans, and scholarships/grants available. Support available to part-time students. Financial award application deadline: 3/2; financial award applicants required to submit FAFSA. *Unit head:* Dr. Terri Swartz, Dean, 510-885-3291, Fax: 510-885-4884, E-mail: terri.swartz@csueastbay. edu. *Application contact:* Dr. Donna Wiley, Interim Associate Director, 510-885-2928, Fax: 510-885-4777, E-mail: donna.wiley@csueastbay.edu.

California State University, Fullerton, Graduate Studies, College of Business and Economics, Department of Information Systems and Decision Sciences, Fullerton, CA 92834-9480. Offers information systems (MS); information systems (decision sciences) (MS); information systems (e-commerce) (MS); information technology (MS); management science (MBA). Part-time programs available. *Students:* 13 full-time (2 women), 72 part-time (16 women); includes 2 Black or African American, non-Hispanic/Latino; 24 Asian, non-Hispanic/Latino; 6 Hispanic/Latino; 3 Two or more races, non-Hispanic/ Latino, 10 international. Average age 35. 120 applicants, 34% accepted, 34 enrolled. In 2010, 23 master's awarded. *Degree requirements:* For master's, project or thesis. *Entrance requirements:* For master's, GMAT, minimum AACSB index of 950. Application fee: $55. *Financial support:* Career-related internships or fieldwork, Federal Work-Study, institutionally sponsored loans, and scholarships/grants available. Support available to part-time students. Financial award application deadline: 3/1; financial award applicants required to submit FAFSA. *Unit head:* Dr. Bhushan Kapoor, Chair, 657-278-2221. *Application contact:* Admissions/Applications, 657-278-2371.

California State University, Fullerton, Graduate Studies, College of Business and Economics, Department of Management, Fullerton, CA 92834-9480. Offers entrepreneurship (MBA); management (MBA). *Accreditation:* AACSB. Part-time programs available. *Students:* 39 full-time (23 women), 51 part-time (16 women); includes 2 Black or African American, non-Hispanic/ Latino; 1 American Indian or Alaska Native, non-Hispanic/Latino; 30 Asian,

non-Hispanic/Latino; 11 Hispanic/Latino, 18 international. Average age 28. 116 applicants, 42% accepted, 23 enrolled. In 2010, 23 master's awarded. *Degree requirements:* For master's, project or thesis. *Entrance requirements:* For master's, GMAT, minimum AACSB index of 950. Application fee: $55. *Financial support:* Career-related internships or fieldwork, Federal Work-Study, institutionally sponsored loans, and scholarships/grants available. Support available to part-time students. Financial award application deadline: 3/1; financial award applicants required to submit FAFSA. *Unit head:* Dr. Ellen Dumond, Chair, 657-278-2251. *Application contact:* Admissions/Applications, 657-278-2371.

California State University, Fullerton, Graduate Studies, College of Business and Economics, Program in Business Administration, Fullerton, CA 92834-9480. Offers e-commerce (MBA); international business (MBA). *Accreditation:* AACSB. Part-time programs available. *Students:* 70 full-time (34 women), 88 part-time (30 women); includes 2 Black or African American, non-Hispanic/Latino; 46 Asian, non-Hispanic/Latino; 8 Hispanic/Latino; 8 Two or more races, non-Hispanic/Latino, 40 international. Average age 28. 322 applicants, 43% accepted, 50 enrolled. In 2010, 29 master's awarded. *Degree requirements:* For master's, project or thesis. *Entrance requirements:* For master's, GMAT. *Financial support:* Career-related internships or fieldwork, Federal Work-Study, institutionally sponsored loans, and scholarships/grants available. Support available to part-time students. Financial award application deadline: 3/1; financial award applicants required to submit FAFSA. *Unit head:* Dr. Anil Puri, Dean, 657-773-2592. *Application contact:* Admissions/Applications, 657-278-2371.

California State University, Long Beach, Graduate Studies, College of Business Administration, Long Beach, CA 90840. Offers MBA. *Accreditation:* AACSB. Part-time and evening/weekend programs available. *Faculty:* 20 full-time (5 women), 6 part-time/adjunct (1 woman). *Students:* 69 full-time (28 women), 175 part-time (79 women); includes 6 Black or African American, non-Hispanic/Latino; 51 Asian, non-Hispanic/Latino; 27 Hispanic/ Latino, 33 international. Average age 30. 557 applicants, 36% accepted, 65 enrolled. In 2010, 147 master's awarded. *Entrance requirements:* For master's, GMAT. *Application deadline:* For fall admission, 3/30 for domestic students. Applications are processed on a rolling basis. Application fee: $55. Electronic applications accepted. *Financial support:* Career-related internships or fieldwork and scholarships/grants available. Financial award application deadline: 3/2; financial award applicants required to submit FAFSA. *Faculty research:* Attitude formation theory, consumer motivation, gift giving, derivative and synthetic securities, financial applications of artificial intelligence. *Unit head:* Dr. Michael E. Solt, Dean, 562-985-5306, Fax: 562-985-5742, E-mail: msolt@csulb.edu. *Application contact:* Dr. H. Michael Chung, Director, Graduate Programs and Executive Education, 562-985-5565, Fax: 562-985-5742, E-mail: hmchung@csulb.edu.

California State University, Los Angeles, Graduate Studies, College of Business and Economics, Department of Information Systems, Los Angeles, CA 90032-8530. Offers business information systems (MBA); management (MS); management information systems (MS); office management (MBA). Part-time and evening/weekend programs available. *Faculty:* 5 full-time (0 women), 1 part-time/adjunct (0 women). *Students:* 7 full-time (3 women), 14 part-time (3 women); includes 2 minority (1 Asian, non-Hispanic/Latino; 1 Hispanic/Latino), 12 international. Average age 30. 7 applicants, 100% accepted, 4 enrolled. In 2010, 10 master's awarded. *Degree requirements:* For master's, comprehensive exam (MBA), thesis (MS). *Entrance requirements:* For master's, GMAT, minimum GPA of 2.5 during previous 2 years of course work. Additional exam requirements/recommendations for international students: Required—TOEFL (minimum score 550 paper-based; 213 computer-based). *Application deadline:* For fall admission, 5/1 for domestic and international students. Applications are processed on a rolling basis. Application fee: $55. Electronic applications accepted. *Financial support:* Career-related internships or fieldwork and Federal Work-Study available. Support available to part-time students. Financial award application deadline: 3/1. *Unit head:* Dr. Adam Huarng, Chair, 323-343-2983, E-mail: ahuarng@ calstatela.edu. *Application contact:* Dr. Alan Muchlinski, Dean of Graduate Studies, 323-343-3820, Fax: 323-343-5653, E-mail: amuchli@exchange.cal-statela.edu.

California State University, Los Angeles, Graduate Studies, College of Business and Economics, Department of Management, Los Angeles, CA 90032-8530. Offers health care management (MS); management (MBA, MS). *Accreditation:* AACSB. Part-time and evening/weekend programs available. *Faculty:* 4 full-time (3 women), 2 part-time/adjunct (0 women). *Students:* 7 full-time (2 women), 39 part-time (24 women); includes 23 minority (1 Black or African American, non-Hispanic/Latino; 12 Asian, non-Hispanic/Latino; 9 Hispanic/Latino; 1 Two or more races, non-Hispanic/Latino), 11 international. Average age 32. 28 applicants, 100% accepted, 19 enrolled. In 2010, 36 master's awarded. *Entrance requirements:* For master's, GMAT, minimum GPA of 2.5 during previous 2 years of course work. Additional exam requirements/ recommendations for international students: Required—TOEFL (minimum score 550 paper-based; 213 computer-based). *Application deadline:* For fall admission, 5/1 for domestic and international students. Applications are processed on a rolling basis. Application fee: $55. Electronic applications accepted. *Financial support:* Application deadline: 3/1. *Unit head:* Dr. Paul

Washburn, Chair, 323-343-2890, Fax: 323-343-6461, E-mail: pwashbu@calstatela.edu. *Application contact:* Dr. Alan Muchlinski, Dean of Graduate Studies, 323-343-3820 Ext. 3827, Fax: 323-343-5653, E-mail: amuchli@exchange.calstatela.edu.

California State University, Stanislaus, College of Business Administration, Program in Business Administration (Executive MBA), Turlock, CA 95382. Offers EMBA. *Accreditation:* AACSB. Part-time and evening/weekend programs available. *Faculty:* 8. *Students:* 41 full-time (13 women); includes 9 minority (2 Black or African American, non-Hispanic/Latino; 4 Asian, non-Hispanic/Latino; 3 Hispanic/Latino), 2 international. Average age 34. 2 applicants, 100% accepted, 2 enrolled. In 2010, 36 master's awarded. *Degree requirements:* For master's, comprehensive exam, thesis or alternative. *Entrance requirements:* For master's, GMAT or GRE, minimum GPA of 2.50, 2 letters of reference, personal statement, interview. Additional exam requirements/recommendations for international students: Required—TOEFL (minimum score 550 paper-based; 213 computer-based). *Application deadline:* For fall admission, 7/31 for domestic students. Applications are processed on a rolling basis. Application fee: $55. Electronic applications accepted. *Expenses:* Contact institution. *Unit head:* Dr. Ashour Badal, EMBA Director, 209-664-6747, Fax: 209-667-3080, E-mail: abadal@csustan.edu. *Application contact:* Extended Education, 209-667-3111, E-mail: uee@csustan.edu.

California State University, Stanislaus, College of Business Administration, Program in Business Administration (MBA), Turlock, CA 95382. Offers MBA. *Accreditation:* AACSB. Part-time and evening/weekend programs available. *Faculty:* 14. *Students:* 44 full-time (20 women), 66 part-time (35 women); includes 47 minority (5 Black or African American, non-Hispanic/Latino; 1 American Indian or Alaska Native, non-Hispanic/Latino; 17 Asian, non-Hispanic/Latino; 18 Hispanic/Latino; 3 Native Hawaiian or other Pacific Islander, non-Hispanic/Latino; 3 Two or more races, non-Hispanic/Latino), 13 international. Average age 30. 120 applicants, 78% accepted, 46 enrolled. In 2010, 44 master's awarded. *Degree requirements:* For master's, comprehensive exam, thesis or alternative. *Entrance requirements:* For master's, GMAT or GRE, minimum GPA of 2.50, 3 letters of reference, personal statement. Additional exam requirements/recommendations for international students: Required—TOEFL (minimum score 550 paper-based; 213 computer-based). *Application deadline:* For fall admission, 4/30 for domestic students; for spring admission, 10/31 for domestic students. Application fee: $55. Electronic applications accepted. *Expenses:* Contact institution. *Financial support:* Fellowships, career-related internships or fieldwork and Federal Work-Study available. Financial award application deadline: 3/1; financial award applicants required to submit FAFSA. *Faculty research:* Teaching creativity, graduate operations management, curricula data mining, foreign direct investment. *Unit head:* Dr. Randall Brown, MBA Director, 209-667-3280, Fax: 209-667-3080, E-mail: mbaprogram@csustan.edu. *Application contact:* Graduate School, 209-667-3129, Fax: 209-664-7025, E-mail: graduate_school@csustan.edu.

Cambridge College, School of Management, Cambridge, MA 02138-5304. Offers business negotiation and conflict resolution (M Mgt); general business (M Mgt); health care informatics (M Mgt); health care management (M Mgt); leadership in human and organizational dynamics (M Mgt); non-profit and public organization management (M Mgt); small business development (M Mgt); technology management (M Mgt). Part-time and evening/weekend programs available. *Faculty:* 6 full-time (3 women), 54 part-time/adjunct (26 women). *Students:* 222 full-time (121 women), 175 part-time (110 women); includes 127 minority (89 Black or African American, non-Hispanic/Latino; 2 American Indian or Alaska Native, non-Hispanic/Latino; 9 Asian, non-Hispanic/Latino; 25 Hispanic/Latino; 2 Two or more races, non-Hispanic/Latino), 125 international. Average age 37. In 2010, 221 master's awarded. *Degree requirements:* For master's, thesis, seminars. *Entrance requirements:* For master's, resume, 2 professional references. Additional exam requirements/recommendations for international students: Required—TOEFL (minimum score 550 paper-based; 213 computer-based; 79 iBT); Recommended—IELTS (minimum score 6). *Application deadline:* Applications are processed on a rolling basis. Application fee: $30. Electronic applications accepted. *Expenses:* Contact institution. *Financial support:* Career-related internships or fieldwork, Federal Work-Study, and scholarships/grants available. Financial award applicants required to submit FAFSA. *Faculty research:* Negotiation, mediation and conflict resolution; leadership; management of diverse organizations; case studies and simulation methodologies for management education, digital as a second language: social networking for digital immigrants, non-profit and public management. *Unit head:* Dr. Mary Ann Joseph, Acting Dean, 617-873-0227, E-mail: maryann.joseph@cambridgecollege.edu. *Application contact:* Elaine M. Lapomardo, Dean of Enrollment Management, 617-873-0274, Fax: 617-349-3561, E-mail: elaine.lapomardo@cambridgecollege.edu.

Canisius College, Graduate Division, Richard J. Wehle School of Business, Department of Management and Marketing, Buffalo, NY 14208-1098. Offers accelerated business administration (1 year) (MBA); business administration (MBA); international business (MS). *Accreditation:* AACSB. Part-time and evening/weekend programs available. *Faculty:* 35 full-time (7 women), 5 part-time/adjunct (3 women). *Students:* 95 full-time (36 women), 171 part-time (70 women); includes 26 minority (15 Black or African American, non-Hispanic/Latino; 1 American Indian or Alaska Native, non-Hispanic/Latino; 8 Asian, non-Hispanic/Latino; 2 Hispanic/Latino), 9 international.

Average age 29. 149 applicants, 71% accepted, 82 enrolled. In 2010, 111 master's awarded. *Entrance requirements:* For master's, GMAT, transcripts. Additional exam requirements/recommendations for international students: Required—TOEFL. *Application deadline:* For fall admission, 7/1 priority date for domestic students; for spring admission, 11/1 priority date for domestic students. Applications are processed on a rolling basis. Application fee: $25. Electronic applications accepted. *Expenses:* Tuition: Part-time $694 per credit hour. Required fees: $11 per credit hour. $90 per semester. *Financial support:* Research assistantships, career-related internships or fieldwork, Federal Work-Study, scholarships/grants, and unspecified assistantships available. Support available to part-time students. Financial award application deadline: 7/1; financial award applicants required to submit FAFSA. *Faculty research:* Global leadership effectiveness, global supply chain management, quality management. *Unit head:* Dr. George Palumbo, Director, MBA Program, 716-888-2667, Fax: 716-888-3132, E-mail: palumbo@canisius.edu. *Application contact:* Jim Bagwell, Director, Graduate Programs, 716-888-2545, Fax: 716-888-3290, E-mail: bagwellj@canisius.edu.

Cape Breton University, Shannon School of Business, Sydney, NS B1P 6L2, Canada. Offers MBA. Part-time programs available. *Faculty:* 6 full-time (3 women). *Students:* 211 full-time (119 women). 251 applicants, 92% accepted. In 2010, 1 master's awarded. *Entrance requirements:* For master's, GMAT. Additional exam requirements/recommendations for international students: Required—TOEFL (minimum score 550 paper-based; 213 computer-based; 80 iBT), IELTS (minimum score 6.5). *Application deadline:* For fall admission, 5/31 for domestic and international students; for spring admission, 3/31 for domestic and international students. Applications are processed on a rolling basis. Application fee: $80. Electronic applications accepted. Tuition and fees charges are reported in Canadian dollars. *Expenses:* Tuition, area resident: Full-time $19,520 Canadian dollars; part-time $1220 Canadian dollars per course. International tuition: $28,848 Canadian dollars full-time. One-time fee: $480 Canadian dollars full-time. *Unit head:* Anne Michele Chiasson, MBA Program Coordinator, 902-563-1664, E-mail: anne_chiasson@cbu.ca. Application contact: Anne Michele Chiasson, MBA Program Coordinator, 902-563-1664, E-mail: anne_chiasson@cbu.ca.

Carlos Albizu University, Miami Campus, Graduate Programs, Miami, FL 33172-2209. Offers clinical psychology (Psy D); entrepreneurship (MBA); exceptional student education (MS); industrial/organizational psychology (MS); marriage and family therapy (MS); mental health counseling (MS); nonprofit management (MBA); organizational management (MBA); psychology (MS); school counseling (MS); teaching English as a second language (MS). *Accreditation:* APA. Part-time and evening/weekend programs available. *Faculty:* 21 full-time (12 women), 37 part-time/adjunct (18 women). *Students:* 496 full-time (400 women), 242 part-time (192 women); includes 590 minority (58 Black or African American, non-Hispanic/Latino; 2 American Indian or Alaska Native, non-Hispanic/Latino; 5 Asian, non-Hispanic/Latino; 523 Hispanic/Latino; 2 Two or more races, non-Hispanic/Latino), 15 international. Average age 36. 141 applicants, 84% accepted, 118 enrolled. In 2010, 159 master's, 20 doctorates awarded. Terminal master's awarded for partial completion of doctoral program. *Degree requirements:* For master's, one foreign language, comprehensive exam, integrative project (MBA), research project (exceptional student education, teaching English as a second language); for doctorate, one foreign language, comprehensive exam, internship, project. *Entrance requirements:* For master's, 3 letters of recommendation, interview, minimum GPA of 3.0, resume, statement of purpose, official transcripts; for doctorate, 3 letters of recommendation, minimum GPA of 3.0, resume, interview. *Application deadline:* For fall admission, 8/1 priority date for domestic students; for spring admission, 11/30 priority date for domestic students. Applications are processed on a rolling basis. Application fee: $50. Electronic applications accepted. *Expenses:* Tuition: Full-time $9360; part-time $520 per credit. Required fees: $298 per term. Tuition and fees vary according to course load, degree level and program. *Financial support:* In 2010–11, 106 students received support. Federal Work-Study, scholarships/grants, and tuition discounts available. Financial award application deadline: 6/1; financial award applicants required to submit FAFSA. *Faculty research:* Psychotherapy, forensic psychology, neuropsychology, marketing strategy, entrepreneurship, special education. *Unit head:* Dr. Carmen S. Roca, Chancellor, 305-593-1223 Ext. 120, Fax: 305-629-8052, E-mail: croca@albizu.edu. *Application contact:* Vanessa Almendarez, Secretary, 305-593-1223 Ext. 137, Fax: 305-593-1854, E-mail: valmendarez@albizu.edu.

Carlow University, School of Management, Pittsburgh, PA 15213-3165. Offers business administration (MBA). Part-time and evening/weekend programs available. Postbaccalaureate distance learning degree programs offered (no on-campus study). *Students:* 83 full-time (71 women), 18 part-time (14 women); includes 18 Black or African American, non-Hispanic/Latino; 1 American Indian or Alaska Native, non-Hispanic/Latino; 1 Asian, non-Hispanic/Latino; 1 Hispanic/Latino, 2 international. Average age 37. 91 applicants, 48% accepted, 38 enrolled. In 2010, 33 master's awarded. *Degree requirements:* For master's, strategic planning, capstone experience. *Entrance requirements:* For master's, interview, minimum GPA of 3.0, resume, 2 letters of recommendation. Additional exam requirements/recommendations for international students: Required—TOEFL (minimum score 550 paper-based; 213 computer-based). *Application deadline:* For fall admission, 6/15 priority date for domestic and international students; for spring admission, 11/15 priority date for domestic and international students. Applications are processed on a rolling basis. Application fee: $20. Electronic applications accepted. *Expenses:* Tuition: Full-time $9900; part-time $660 per credit. Tuition and fees vary according to course load, degree level and program. *Financial support:* Federal Work-Study and scholarships/grants available. Support available to part-time students. Financial award application deadline: 4/1; financial award applicants required to submit FAFSA. *Faculty research:* Learning styles and distance learning, women and distance learning, women and organizational behavior. *Unit head:* Dr. Enrique Mu, Director, MBA Program, 412-578-8729, Fax: 412-587-6367, E-mail: muex@carlow.edu. *Application contact:* Jo Danhires, Administrative Assistant, Admissions, 412-578-6088, Fax: 412-578-6321, E-mail: gradstudies@carlow.edu.

Carroll University, Program in Business Administration, Waukesha, WI 53186-5593. Offers MBA. Part-time programs available. *Faculty:* 2 full-time (both women). *Students:* 15 part-time (6 women). Average age 28. 54 applicants, 43% accepted. *Entrance requirements:* For master's, GRE, resume, transcripts. Additional exam requirements/recommendations for international students: Required—TOEFL. *Application deadline:* Applications are processed on a rolling basis. Electronic applications accepted. *Expenses:* Tuition: Full-time $24,749; part-time $440 per credit hour. Required fees: $550. *Unit head:* Dr. Richard J. Penlesky, Professor, 262-951-3023, E-mail: rpenlesk@carrollu.edu. *Application contact:* Tami Bartunek, Graduate Admission Counselor, 262-524-7643, E-mail: tbartune@carrollu.edu.

Carson-Newman College, Program in Business Administration, Jefferson City, TN 37760. Offers MBA. *Faculty:* 6 full-time (3 women). *Students:* 7 full-time (3 women), 22 part-time (11 women); includes 1 Black or African American, non-Hispanic/Latino; 1 Hispanic/Latino, 2 international. *Application deadline:* For fall admission, 7/15 priority date for domestic students. Application fee: $50. *Expenses:* Tuition: Full-time $6750; part-time $375 per credit hour. Required fees: $200. *Unit head:* Dr. Clyde Herring. *Application contact:* Graduate Admissions and Services Adviser, 865-473-3468, Fax: 865-472-3475.

The Catholic University of America, Metropolitan School of Professional Studies, Washington, DC 20064. Offers human resource management (MA); management (MSM). Part-time and evening/weekend programs available. *Faculty:* 44 part-time/adjunct (20 women). *Students:* 21 full-time (15 women), 153 part-time (88 women); includes 51 Black or African American, non-Hispanic/Latino; 1 American Indian or Alaska Native, non-Hispanic/Latino; 4 Asian, non-Hispanic/Latino; 16 Hispanic/Latino, 15 international. Average age 36. 176 applicants, 47% accepted, 65 enrolled. In 2010, 34 master's awarded. *Degree requirements:* For master's, minimum GPA of 3.0, capstone course. *Entrance requirements:* For master's, statement of purpose, official copies of academic transcripts, three letters of recommendation, resume. Additional exam requirements/recommendations for international students: Required—TOEFL (minimum score 237 computer-based; 93 iBT). *Application deadline:* For fall admission, 8/1 priority date for domestic students, 7/15 for international students; for spring admission, 12/1 priority date for domestic students, 10/15 for international students. Application fee: $55. *Expenses:* Tuition: Full-time $33,580; part-time $1315 per credit hour. Required fees: $80; $40 per semester hour. One-time fee: $425. *Unit head:* Dr. Sara Thompson, Dean, 202-319-5256, Fax: 202-319-6032, E-mail: thompsons@cua.edu. *Application contact:* Andrew Woodall, Director of Graduate Admissions, 202-319-5057, Fax: 202-319-6533, E-mail: cua-admissions@cua.edu.

The Catholic University of America, School of Arts and Sciences, Department of Business and Economics, Washington, DC 20064. Offers international political economics (MA). Part-time programs available. *Faculty:* 10 full-time (4 women), 15 part-time/adjunct (4 women). *Students:* 16 full-time (12 women); includes 1 Black or African American, non-Hispanic/Latino; 1 Asian, non-Hispanic/Latino; 1 Hispanic/Latino, 1 international. Average age 23. 19 applicants, 84% accepted, 16 enrolled. *Degree requirements:* For master's, comprehensive exam. *Entrance requirements:* For master's, GRE General Test, statement of purpose, official copies of academic transcripts, three letters of recommendation. Additional exam requirements/recommendations for international students: Required—TOEFL (minimum score 580 paper-based; 237 computer-based). *Application deadline:* For fall admission, 8/1 priority date for domestic students, 7/15 for international students; for spring admission, 12/1 priority date for domestic students, 10/15 for international students. Applications are processed on a rolling basis. Application fee: $55. Electronic applications accepted. *Expenses:* Tuition: Full-time $33,580; part-time $1315 per credit hour. Required fees: $80; $40 per semester hour. One-time fee: $425. *Financial support:* Fellowships, research assistantships, teaching assistantships, Federal Work-Study, scholarships/grants, tuition waivers (full and partial), and unspecified assistantships available. Financial award application deadline: 2/1; financial award applicants required to submit FAFSA. *Faculty research:* Integrity of the marketing process, economics of energy and the environment, emerging markets, social change, international finance and economic development. Total annual research expenditures: $6,459. *Unit head:* Dr. Andrew V. Abela, Chair, 202-319-5235, Fax: 202-319-4426, E-mail: abela@cua.edu. *Application contact:* Andrew Woodall, Director of Graduate Admissions, 202-319-5057, Fax: 202-319-6533, E-mail: cua-admissions@cua.edu.

Central European University, CEU Business School, Budapest, Hungary. Offers executive business administration (EMBA); finance (MBA); general management (MBA); information technology management (MBA); marketing (MBA); real estate management (MBA). Part-time and evening/weekend programs available. *Faculty:* 16 full-time (4 women), 2 part-time/adjunct (1 woman). *Students:* 71 full-time (30 women), 142 part-time (47 women). Average age 34. 144 applicants, 36% accepted, 32 enrolled. In 2010, 64 master's awarded. *Degree requirements:* For master's, one foreign language. *Entrance requirements:* For master's, GMAT. Additional exam requirements/recommendations for international students: Required—TOEFL (minimum score 570 paper-based; 230 computer-based); Recommended—IELTS (minimum score 6.5). *Application deadline:* For fall admission, 5/15 priority date for domestic students, 5/22 for international students; for winter admission, 11/15 priority date for domestic students, 11/10 for international students. Applications are processed on a rolling basis. Application fee: $0. Electronic applications accepted. Tuition and fees charges are reported in euros. *Expenses:* Tuition: Full-time 11,000 euros. Required fees: 250 euros. One-time fee: 200 euros full-time. Tuition and fees vary according to degree level, program, reciprocity agreements and student level. *Financial support:* In 2010–11, 4 students received support. Tuition waivers (partial) available. *Faculty research:* Social and ethical business, marketing. *Unit head:* Dr. Mel Horwitch, Dean and Managing Director, 361-887-5050, E-mail: mhorwitch@ceubusiness.com. *Application contact:* Agnes Schram, MBA Program Manager, 361-887-5511, Fax: 361-887-5133, E-mail: mba@ceubusiness.com.

Central Michigan University, Central Michigan University Off-Campus Programs, Program in Business Administration, Mount Pleasant, MI 48859. Offers logistics management (MBA, Certificate); SAP (MBA, Certificate); value-driven organization (MBA). Part-time and evening/weekend programs available. *Entrance requirements:* For master's, GMAT. *Expenses:* Tuition, state resident: full-time $8208; part-time $456 per credit hour. Tuition, nonresident: full-time $13,788; part-time $766 per credit hour. One-time fee: $25. *Financial support:* Scholarships/grants available. Support available to part-time students. *Unit head:* Dr. Debasish Chakraborty, 989-774-3678, E-mail: chakt1d@cmich.edu. *Application contact:* Off-Campus Programs Call Center, 877-268-4636.

Central Michigan University, College of Graduate Studies, College of Business Administration, Mount Pleasant, MI 48859. Offers accounting (MBA); business economics (MBA); business information systems (MS, Graduate Certificate), including business computing (Graduate Certificate), information systems (MS); economics (MA); finance and law (MBA), including finance; management (MBA), including consulting, general business, human resources management, international business; management information systems (MBA); management information systems/SAP (MBA); marketing and hospitality services administration (MBA), including marketing. *Accreditation:* AACSB. Part-time and evening/weekend programs available. *Faculty:* 43 full-time (9 women), 4 part-time/adjunct (0 women). *Students:* 144 full-time (56 women), 99 part-time (40 women); includes 3 Black or African American, non-Hispanic/Latino; 4 American Indian or Alaska Native, non-Hispanic/Latino; 6 Asian, non-Hispanic/Latino, 102 international. Average age 27. *Degree requirements:* For master's, thesis or alternative. *Entrance requirements:* For master's, GMAT (MBA). *Application deadline:* For fall admission, 6/1 for international students; for spring admission, 10/1 for international students. Applications are processed on a rolling basis. Application fee: $35 ($45 for international students). Electronic applications accepted. *Expenses:* Tuition, state resident: full-time $8208; part-time $456 per credit hour. Tuition, nonresident: full-time $13,788; part-time $766 per credit hour. One-time fee: $25. *Financial support:* Fellowships with tuition reimbursements, research assistantships with tuition reimbursements, teaching assistantships with tuition reimbursements, career-related internships or fieldwork, Federal Work-Study, unspecified assistantships, and out-of-state merit awards, non-resident graduate awards available. *Faculty research:* Economics, enterprise software, business information systems, management, marketing. *Unit head:* Dr. Charles T. Crespy, Dean, 989-774-3337, Fax: 989-774-1320, E-mail: cresp1ct@cmich.edu. *Application contact:* Dr. Daniel Vetter, Senior Associate Dean, 989-774-7966, Fax: 989-774-1329, E-mail: vette1de@cmich.edu.

Central Michigan University, College of Graduate Studies, Interdisciplinary Administration Programs, Mount Pleasant, MI 48859. Offers acquisitions administration (MSA, Graduate Certificate); general administration (MSA, Graduate Certificate); health services administration (MSA, Graduate Certificate); human resource administration (Graduate Certificate); human resources administration (MSA); information resource management (MSA, Graduate Certificate); international administration (MSA, Graduate Certificate); leadership (MSA, Graduate Certificate); organizational communication (MSA, Graduate Certificate); public administration (MSA, Graduate Certificate); recreation and park administration (MSA); sport administration (MSA). *Accreditation:* AACSB. Part-time and evening/weekend programs available. Postbaccalaureate distance learning degree programs offered (no on-campus study). *Students:* 102 full-time (50 women), 77 part-time (51 women); includes 10 Black or African American, non-Hispanic/Latino; 3 American Indian or Alaska Native, non-Hispanic/Latino; 5 Asian, non-Hispanic/Latino,

65 international. Average age 29. *Degree requirements:* For master's, thesis or alternative. *Entrance requirements:* For master's, bachelor's degree with minimum GPA of 2.7. *Application deadline:* For fall admission, 6/1 for international students; for spring admission, 10/1 for international students. Applications are processed on a rolling basis. Application fee: $35 ($45 for international students). Electronic applications accepted. *Expenses:* Tuition, state resident: full-time $8208; part-time $456 per credit hour. Tuition, non-resident: full-time $13,788; part-time $766 per credit hour. One-time fee: $25. *Financial support:* Fellowships with tuition reimbursements, research assistantships with tuition reimbursements, career-related internships or fieldwork, Federal Work-Study, unspecified assistantships, and out-of-state merit awards, non-resident graduate awards available. *Faculty research:* Interdisciplinary studies in acquisitions administration, health services administration, sport administration, recreation and park administration, and international administration. *Unit head:* Dr. Nana Korash, Director, 989-774-6525, Fax: 989-774-2575, E-mail: msa@cmich.edu. *Application contact:* Denise Schafer, Coordinator, 989-774-4373, Fax: 989-774-2575, E-mail: schaf1dr@cmich.edu.

Champlain College, Graduate Studies, Burlington, VT 05402-0670. Offers business (MBA); digital forensic management (MS); education (M Ed); emergent media (MFA); health care management (MS); law (MS); managing innovation and information technology (MS); mediation and applied conflict studies (MS). Part-time programs available. Postbaccalaureate distance learning degree programs offered (no on-campus study). *Faculty:* 14 full-time (0 women), 24 part-time/adjunct (9 women). *Students:* 304 full-time (144 women), 2 part-time (both women). Average age 30. 271 applicants, 90% accepted, 216 enrolled. In 2010, 8 master's awarded. *Degree requirements:* For master's, capstone project. *Entrance requirements:* Additional exam requirements/recommendations for international students: Required—TOEFL. *Application deadline:* For fall admission, 8/1 priority date for domestic and international students; for spring admission, 1/1 priority date for domestic and international students. Applications are processed on a rolling basis. Application fee: $50. Electronic applications accepted. *Expenses:* Tuition: Part-time $740 per credit hour. Part-time tuition and fees vary according to program. *Financial support:* Applicants required to submit FAFSA. *Unit head:* Dr. Donald Haggerty, Associate Provost, Graduate Studies, 802-865-6403, Fax: 802-865-6447. *Application contact:* Jon Walsh, Assistant Vice President, Graduate Admission, 800-570-5858, E-mail: walsh@champlain.edu.

Chapman University, Graduate Studies, The George L. Argyros School of Business and Economics, Orange, CA 92866. Offers business administration (Exec MBA, MBA); JD/MBA. *Accreditation:* AACSB. Part-time and evening/weekend programs available. *Faculty:* 52 full-time (11 women), 25 part-time/adjunct (4 women). *Students:* 153 full-time (53 women), 111 part-time (33 women); includes 63 minority (4 Black or African American, non-Hispanic/Latino; 26 Asian, non-Hispanic/Latino; 30 Hispanic/Latino; 1 Native Hawaiian or other Pacific Islander, non-Hispanic/Latino; 2 Two or more races, non-Hispanic/Latino), 23 international. Average age 29. 252 applicants, 62% accepted, 90 enrolled. In 2010, 125 master's awarded. *Entrance requirements:* For master's, GMAT, minimum undergraduate GPA of 2.5. Additional exam requirements/recommendations for international students: Required—TOEFL (minimum score 550 paper-based; 213 computer-based; 80 iBT). Application fee: $60. Electronic applications accepted. *Expenses:* Contact institution. *Financial support:* Fellowships, Federal Work-Study and scholarships/grants available. Financial award applicants required to submit FAFSA. *Unit head:* Dr. Arthur Kraft, Dean, 714-997-6684. *Application contact:* Debra Gonda, Associate Dean, 714-997-6894, E-mail: gonda@chapman.edu.

Christian Brothers University, School of Business, Memphis, TN 38104-5581. Offers business (MBA); financial planning (Certificate); project management (Certificate). Part-time and evening/weekend programs available. *Faculty:* 1 full-time (0 women), 5 part-time/adjunct (1 woman). *Students:* 11 full-time (4 women), 180 part-time (67 women); includes 57 minority (40 Black or African American, non-Hispanic/Latino; 8 Asian, non-Hispanic/Latino; 7 Hispanic/Latino; 2 Two or more races, non-Hispanic/Latino), 9 international. Average age 35. In 2010, 46 master's awarded. *Entrance requirements:* For master's, GMAT, GRE. Additional exam requirements/recommendations for international students: Required—TOEFL. *Application deadline:* Applications are processed on a rolling basis. Application fee: $50. *Expenses:* Tuition: Full-time $11,520; part-time $640 per credit hour. Required fees: $140; $140 per course. $70 per semester. Tuition and fees vary according to program. *Financial support:* Institutionally sponsored loans available. Support available to part-time students. *Unit head:* Dr. Scott Lawyer, Director, 901-321-3104, Fax: 901-321-3566, E-mail: mlawyer@cbu.edu. *Application contact:* Dr. Scott Lawyer, Director, Graduate Business Programs, 901-321-3104, Fax: 901-321-3566, E-mail: mlawyer@cbu.edu.

The Citadel, The Military College of South Carolina, Citadel Graduate College, School of Business Administration, Charleston, SC 29409. Offers MBA. *Accreditation:* AACSB. Part-time and evening/weekend programs available. *Faculty:* 16 full-time (3 women), 6 part-time/adjunct (1 woman). *Students:* 62 full-time (23 women), 204 part-time (77 women); includes 15 Black or African American, non-Hispanic/Latino; 1 American Indian or Alaska Native, non-Hispanic/Latino; 2 Asian, non-Hispanic/Latino; 2 Hispanic/Latino, 4 international. Average age 28. In 2010, 92 master's

awarded. *Entrance requirements:* For master's, GMAT (minimum score 410), minimum undergraduate GPA of 3.0, 2 letters of reference, resume detailing previous work experience. Additional exam requirements/recommendations for international students: Required—TOEFL (minimum score 550 paper-based; 213 computer-based; 79 iBT). *Application deadline:* For fall admission, 7/20 for domestic students; for spring admission, 12/1 for domestic students. Application fee: $30. Electronic applications accepted. *Expenses:* Tuition, state resident: part-time $460 per credit hour. Tuition, nonresident: part-time $756 per credit hour. Required fees: $40 per term. *Financial support:* Fellowships, career-related internships or fieldwork, health care benefits, and unspecified assistantships available. Support available to part-time students. Financial award application deadline: 7/1; financial award applicants required to submit FAFSA. *Faculty research:* Business statistics and regression analysis, mentoring university students, tax reform proposals, risk management data, teaching leadership, inventory costing methods, capitalism, ethics in behavioral accounting, ethics of neuro-marketing, European and Japanese business ethics, profit motives, team building, process costing, FIFO vs. weight average. *Unit head:* Dr. Ronald F. Green, Dean, 843-953-5056, Fax: 843-953-6764, E-mail: ron.green@citadel.edu. *Application contact:* Lt. Col. Kathy Jones, Director, MBA Program, 843-953-5257, Fax: 843-953-6764, E-mail: kathy.jones@citadel.edu.

Claflin University, Graduate Programs, Orangeburg, SC 29115. Offers biotechnology (MS); business administration (MBA). Part-time programs available. *Students:* 71 full-time (48 women), 18 part-time (11 women); includes 72 minority (all Black or African American, non-Hispanic/Latino), 15 international. *Entrance requirements:* For master's, GRE, GMAT, baccalaureate degree, 3 letters of recommendation. Additional exam requirements/recommendations for international students: Recommended—TOEFL (minimum score 550 paper-based; 213 computer-based). *Application deadline:* For fall admission, 8/1 for domestic students; for spring admission, 12/1 for domestic students. Application fee: $40 ($55 for international students). *Expenses:* Tuition: Full-time $8532; part-time $474 per credit hour. Required fees: $312. *Financial support:* Research assistantships, teaching assistantships available. Financial award application deadline: 4/15; financial award applicants required to submit FAFSA. *Unit head:* Dr. Gloria Seabrook, Interim Executive Director of Professional and Continuing Studies, 803-535-5574, Fax: 803-535-5576, E-mail: gseabrook@claflin.edu. *Application contact:* Dr. Gloria Seabrook, Interim Executive Director of Professional and Continuing Studies, 803-535-5574, Fax: 803-535-5576, E-mail: gseabrook@claflin.edu.

Claremont Graduate University, Graduate Programs, Peter F. Drucker and Masatoshi Ito Graduate School of Management, Claremont, CA 91711-6160. Offers EMBA, MA, MBA, MS, PhD, Certificate, MBA/MA, MBA/PhD. Part-time programs available. *Faculty:* 11 full-time (3 women), 3 part-time/adjunct (0 women). *Students:* 165 full-time (77 women), 90 part-time (34 women); includes 102 minority (10 Black or African American, non-Hispanic/Latino; 1 American Indian or Alaska Native, non-Hispanic/Latino; 46 Asian, non-Hispanic/Latino; 38 Hispanic/Latino; 1 Native Hawaiian or other Pacific Islander, non-Hispanic/Latino; 6 Two or more races, non-Hispanic/Latino), 45 international. Average age 35. In 2010, 99 master's, 1 doctorate, 71 other advanced degrees awarded. *Entrance requirements:* For doctorate, GMAT or GRE General Test. Additional exam requirements/recommendations for international students: Required—TOEFL (minimum score 550 paper-based; 213 computer-based; 80 iBT). *Application deadline:* For fall admission, 2/15 priority date for domestic students. Applications are processed on a rolling basis. Application fee: $60. Electronic applications accepted. *Expenses:* Contact institution. *Financial support:* Fellowships, research assistantships, teaching assistantships, Federal Work-Study, institutionally sponsored loans, and scholarships/grants available. Support available to part-time students. Financial award application deadline: 2/15; financial award applicants required to submit FAFSA. *Faculty research:* Strategy and leadership, brand management, cost management and control, organizational transformation, general management. *Unit head:* Ira A. Jackson, Dean/Professor, 909-607-9209, Fax: 909-621-8543, E-mail: ira.jackson@cgu.edu. *Application contact:* Albert Ramos, Program Coordinator, 909-621-8067, Fax: 909-621-8551, E-mail: albert.ramos@cgu.edu.

Clark Atlanta University, School of Business Administration, Department of Business Administration, Atlanta, GA 30314. Offers MBA. *Accreditation:* AACSB. Part-time programs available. *Faculty:* 15 full-time (4 women). *Students:* 53 full-time (23 women), 14 part-time (8 women); includes 55 Black or African American, non-Hispanic/Latino; 1 Asian, non-Hispanic/Latino, 8 international. Average age 27. 65 applicants, 88% accepted, 34 enrolled. In 2010, 41 master's awarded. *Degree requirements:* For master's, thesis (for some programs). *Entrance requirements:* For master's, GMAT. Additional exam requirements/recommendations for international students: Required—TOEFL (minimum score 500 paper-based; 173 computer-based; 61 iBT). *Application deadline:* For fall admission, 4/1 for domestic and international students; for spring admission, 11/1 for domestic and international students. Applications are processed on a rolling basis. Application fee: $40 ($55 for international students). Electronic applications accepted. *Expenses:* Tuition: Full-time $12,942; part-time $719 per credit hour. Required fees: $710; $355 per semester. *Financial support:* Career-related internships or fieldwork, Federal Work-Study, scholarships/grants, and unspecified assistantships available. Support available to part-time students. Financial award application deadline: 4/30; financial award applicants required to submit FAFSA. *Unit head:* Dr. Kasim Alli, Chairperson, 404-880-8740, E-mail: kalli@cau.edu. *Application contact:* Michelle Clark-Davis, Graduate Program Admissions, 404-880-6605, E-mail: cauadmissions@cau.edu.

Clarkson University, Graduate School, School of Business, One-Year MBA Program, Potsdam, NY 13699. Offers MBA. *Accreditation:* AACSB. *Faculty:* 38 full-time (10 women), 1 part-time/adjunct (0 women). *Students:* 62 full-time (18 women), 22 part-time (9 women); includes 3 minority (1 American Indian or Alaska Native, non-Hispanic/Latino; 1 Asian, non-Hispanic/Latino; 1 Two or more races, non-Hispanic/Latino), 16 international. Average age 25. 165 applicants, 67% accepted, 62 enrolled. In 2010, 35 master's awarded. *Entrance requirements:* For master's, GMAT or GRE, transcripts of all college coursework, resume, personal statement, three letters of recommendation. Additional exam requirements/recommendations for international students: Required—TOEFL (minimum score 550 paper-based; 213 computer-based; 80 iBT), IELTS (minimum score 6.5), TSE required for some. *Application deadline:* For fall admission, 1/30 priority date for domestic and international students; for spring admission, 9/1 priority date for domestic and international students. Applications are processed on a rolling basis. Application fee: $25 ($35 for international students). Electronic applications accepted. *Expenses:* Tuition: Part-time $1136 per credit hour. *Financial support:* In 2010–11, 63 students received support. Scholarships/grants available. *Faculty research:* Industrial organization and regulated industries, end-user computing, systems analysis and design, technological marketing, leadership development. *Unit head:* Dr. Boris Jukic, Director, 315-268-6613, Fax: 315-268-3810, E-mail: bjukic@clarkson.edu. *Application contact:* Karen Fuhr, Assistant to the Graduate Director, 315-268-6613, Fax: 315-268-3810, E-mail: fuhrk@clarkson.edu.

Clark University, Graduate School, Graduate School of Management, Business Administration Program, Worcester, MA 01610-1477. Offers accounting (MBA); finance (MBA); global business (MBA); health care management (MBA); management (MBA); management of information technology (MBA); marketing (MBA). *Accreditation:* AACSB. Part-time and evening/weekend programs available. *Students:* 147 full-time (75 women), 126 part-time (54 women); includes 24 minority (10 Black or African American, non-Hispanic/Latino; 1 American Indian or Alaska Native, non-Hispanic/Latino; 6 Asian, non-Hispanic/Latino; 5 Hispanic/Latino; 2 Two or more races, non-Hispanic/Latino), 99 international. Average age 30. 382 applicants, 57% accepted, 89 enrolled. In 2010, 101 master's awarded. *Degree requirements:* For master's, thesis optional. *Application deadline:* For fall admission, 6/1 priority date for domestic students; for spring admission, 12/1 priority date for domestic students. Applications are processed on a rolling basis. Application fee: $50. Electronic applications accepted. *Expenses:* Tuition: Full-time $37,000; part-time $1156 per credit hour. Required fees: $30; $1156 per credit hour. *Financial support:* In 2010–11, research assistantships with partial tuition reimbursements (averaging $4,800 per year), teaching assistantships with partial tuition reimbursements (averaging $4,800 per year) were awarded; fellowships, career-related internships or fieldwork, Federal Work-Study, institutionally sponsored loans, and tuition waivers (partial) also available. Support available to part-time students. Financial award application deadline: 5/31. *Faculty research:* Organizational development, accounting, marketing, finance, human resource management. *Unit head:* Dr. Joseph Sarkis, Dean, 508-793-7406, Fax: 508-793-8822, E-mail: clarkmba@clarku.edu. *Application contact:* Lynn Davis, Enrollment and Marketing Director, 508-793-7406, Fax: 508-793-8822, E-mail: clarkmba@clarku.edu.

Cleary University, Online Program in Business Administration, Ann Arbor, MI 48105-2659. Offers financial planning (MBA); financial planning (Graduate Certificate); green business strategy (MBA, Graduate Certificate); management (MBA); nonprofit management (MBA, Graduate Certificate); organizational leadership (MBA); public accounting (MBA). Part-time and evening/weekend programs available. Postbaccalaureate distance learning degree programs offered (no on-campus study). *Faculty:* 1 (woman) full-time, 20 part-time/adjunct (8 women). *Students:* 1 (woman) full-time, 115 part-time (67 women); includes 30 minority (21 Black or African American, non-Hispanic/Latino; 1 American Indian or Alaska Native, non-Hispanic/Latino; 6 Asian, non-Hispanic/Latino; 2 Hispanic/Latino), 7 international. Average age 34. 62 applicants, 77% accepted, 36 enrolled. In 2010, 22 master's awarded. *Degree requirements:* For master's, thesis. *Entrance requirements:* For master's, bachelor's degree; minimum GPA of 2.5; professional resume indicating minimum 2 years management or related experience; undergraduate degree from an accredited college or university with at least 18 quarter hours (or 12 semester hours) of accounting study (for MBA in accounting). Additional exam requirements/recommendations for international students: Required—TOEFL (minimum score 550 paper-based; 213 computer-based; 79 iBT), Michigan English Language Assessment Battery (minimum score: 75). *Application deadline:* For fall admission, 8/15 for domestic students, 7/15 for international students; for spring admission, 4/2 for domestic students, 1/2 for international students. Applications are processed on a rolling basis. Application fee: $50. Electronic applications accepted. *Financial support:* In 2010–11, 80 students received support, including 80 fellowships (averaging $12,501 per year); Federal Work-Study and scholarships/grants also available.

Support available to part-time students. Financial award application deadline: 8/15; financial award applicants required to submit FAFSA. *Unit head:* Dr. Vincent Linder, Provost and Vice President for Academic Affairs, 800-686-1883, Fax: 734-332-4646, E-mail: vlinder@cleary.edu. *Application contact:* Carrie Bonofiglio, Director of Student Recruiting, 800-686-1883, Fax: 517-552-7805, E-mail: cbono@cleary.edu.

Clemson University, Graduate School, College of Architecture, Arts, and Humanities, Department of Planning and Landscape Architecture and College of Business and Behavioral Science, Program in Real Estate Development, Clemson, SC 29634. Offers MRED. *Students:* 39 full-time (6 women), 1 part-time (0 women); includes 1 Hispanic/Latino. Average age 27. 54 applicants, 54% accepted, 20 enrolled. In 2010, 20 master's awarded. *Entrance requirements:* For master's, GRE or GMAT, 3 letters of recommendation, resume, personal statement. Additional exam requirements/recommendations for international students: Required—TOEFL (minimum score 600 paper-based). *Application deadline:* For fall admission, 2/15 priority date for domestic and international students. Applications are processed on a rolling basis. Application fee: $70 ($80 for international students). Electronic applications accepted. *Expenses:* Tuition, state resident: full-time $6492; part-time $400 per credit hour. Tuition, nonresident: full-time $13,634; part-time $800 per credit hour. Required fees: $262 per semester. Part-time tuition and fees vary according to course load and program. *Financial support:* In 2010–11, 1 student received support, including 1 fellowship with partial tuition reimbursement available (averaging $200 per year); research assistantships with partial tuition reimbursements available, teaching assistantships with partial tuition reimbursements available, career-related internships or fieldwork, scholarships/grants, health care benefits, and unspecified assistantships also available. *Faculty research:* Real estate education, real estate investment/finance, sustainability, public private partnership, historic preservation. *Unit head:* Dr. Elaine M. Worzala, Interim Director, 864-656-4258, Fax: 864-656-7519, E-mail: eworzal@clemson.edu. *Application contact:* Amy Matthews, Program Coordinator, 864-656-4257, Fax: 864-656-7519, E-mail: matthe3@clemson.edu.

Clemson University, Graduate School, College of Business and Behavioral Science, Program in Business Administration, Clemson, SC 29634. Offers MBA. *Accreditation:* AACSB. Part-time programs available. *Faculty:* 30 full-time (6 women). *Students:* 95 full-time (27 women), 147 part-time (44 women); includes 8 Black or African American, non-Hispanic/Latino; 3 Asian, non-Hispanic/Latino; 2 Hispanic/Latino; 2 Two or more races, non-Hispanic/Latino, 33 international. Average age 31. 217 applicants, 57% accepted, 88 enrolled. In 2010, 87 master's awarded. *Entrance requirements:* For master's, GMAT. Additional exam requirements/recommendations for international students: Required—TOEFL. *Application deadline:* For fall admission, 5/1 priority date for domestic students, 4/15 for international students; for spring admission, 9/15 for international students. Applications are processed on a rolling basis. Application fee: $70 ($80 for international students). Electronic applications accepted. *Expenses:* Tuition, state resident: full-time $6492; part-time $400 per credit hour. Tuition, nonresident: full-time $13,634; part-time $800 per credit hour. Required fees: $262 per semester. Part-time tuition and fees vary according to course load and program. *Financial support:* In 2010–11, 34 students received support, including 1 fellowship with full and partial tuition reimbursement available (averaging $8,000 per year), 24 research assistantships with partial tuition reimbursements available (averaging $6,969 per year), 2 teaching assistantships with partial tuition reimbursements available (averaging $11,000 per year); institutionally sponsored loans and scholarships/grants also available. Financial award application deadline: 5/1; financial award applicants required to submit FAFSA. *Unit head:* Dr. Gregory Pickett, Director, 864-656-3975, Fax: 864-656-0947. *Application contact:* Dr. Gregory Pickett, Director, 864-656-3975, Fax: 864-656-0947.

Cleveland State University, College of Graduate Studies, Nance College of Business Administration, Doctor of Business Administration (DBA) Program, Cleveland, OH 44115. Offers business administration (DBA); finance (DBA); information systems (DBA); marketing (DBA); operations management (DBA). *Accreditation:* AACSB. Part-time and evening/weekend programs available. *Faculty:* 50 full-time (11 women). *Students:* 6 full-time (2 women), 31 part-time (6 women); includes 3 Black or African American, non-Hispanic/Latino; 2 Asian, non-Hispanic/Latino, 7 international. Average age 44. 7 applicants. *Degree requirements:* For doctorate, comprehensive exam, thesis/dissertation, oral dissertation defense. *Entrance requirements:* For doctorate, GMAT, MBA or equivalent. Additional exam requirements/recommendations for international students: Required—TOEFL (minimum score 550 paper-based; 213 computer-based; 79 iBT). *Application deadline:* For spring admission, 2/28 priority date for domestic and international students. Application fee: $30. Electronic applications accepted. *Expenses:* Tuition, state resident: full-time $8447; part-time $469 per credit hour. Tuition, nonresident: full-time $16,020; part-time $890 per credit hour. Required fees: $50. *Financial support:* In 2010–11, 5 research assistantships with full tuition reimbursements (averaging $11,700 per year), 1 teaching assistantship with full tuition reimbursement (averaging $11,700 per year) were awarded; tuition waivers (full) and unspecified assistantships also available. *Faculty research:* Supply chain management, international business, strategic management, risk analysis. *Unit head:* Dr. Raj Shekhar G. Javalgi, Director, 216-687-3786, Fax:

216-687-9354, E-mail: r.javalgi@csuohio.edu. *Application contact:* Brenda Wade, Administrative Secretary, 216-687-6952, Fax: 216-687-9257, E-mail: b.wade@csuohio.edu.

Cleveland State University, College of Graduate Studies, Nance College of Business Administration, MBA Programs, Cleveland, OH 44115. Offers business administration (AMBA, MBA); executive business administration (EMBA); health care administration (MBA); off-campus programs (MBA); JD/MBA; MSN/MBA. *Accreditation:* AACSB. Part-time and evening/weekend programs available. *Faculty:* 33 full-time (9 women), 16 part-time/adjunct (2 women). *Students:* 263 full-time (106 women), 433 part-time (186 women); includes 49 Black or African American, non-Hispanic/Latino; 1 American Indian or Alaska Native, non-Hispanic/Latino; 23 Asian, non-Hispanic/Latino; 10 Hispanic/Latino; 87 international. Average age 38. 544 applicants, 65% accepted, 208 enrolled. In 2010, 263 master's awarded. *Entrance requirements:* For master's, GMAT or GRE. Additional exam requirements/recommendations for international students: Required—TOEFL (minimum score 550 paper-based; 213 computer-based; 79 iBT). *Application deadline:* For fall admission, 7/15 priority date for domestic students, 5/15 for international students; for spring admission, 12/15 priority date for domestic students, 11/1 for international students. Applications are processed on a rolling basis. Application fee: $30. *Expenses:* Tuition, state resident: full-time $8447; part-time $469 per credit hour. Tuition, nonresident: full-time $16,020; part-time $890 per credit hour. Required fees: $50. *Financial support:* In 2010–11, 45 research assistantships with full and partial tuition reimbursements (averaging $6,960 per year), 1 teaching assistantship with full and partial tuition reimbursement (averaging $7,800 per year) were awarded; tuition waivers (full) and unspecified assistantships also available. Financial award application deadline: 5/15; financial award applicants required to submit FAFSA. Total annual research expenditures: $70,000. *Unit head:* Bruce Gottschalk, MBA Programs Administrator, 216-687-3730, Fax: 216-687-5311, E-mail: cbacsu@csuohio.edu. *Application contact:* Patricia Hite, Director, Academic Program Support, 216-687-6925, Fax: 216-687-6888, E-mail: p.hite@csuohio.edu.

Coastal Carolina University, Wall College of Business Administration, Conway, SC 29528-6054. Offers accounting (MBA); business (MBA). *Accreditation:* AACSB. Part-time and evening/weekend programs available. *Faculty:* 9 full-time (4 women). *Students:* 43 full-time (18 women), 13 part-time (5 women); includes 2 minority (both Black or African American, non-Hispanic/Latino), 6 international. Average age 27. 37 applicants, 68% accepted, 21 enrolled. In 2010, 25 master's awarded. *Entrance requirements:* For master's, GMAT, 2 letters of recommendation, resume, completion of prerequisites with minimum B average grade. Additional exam requirements/recommendations for international students: Required—TOEFL (minimum score 575 paper-based). *Application deadline:* For fall admission, 3/15 priority date for domestic and international students; for spring admission, 10/15 priority date for domestic and international students. Applications are processed on a rolling basis. Application fee: $45. Electronic applications accepted. *Expenses:* Contact institution. *Financial support:* Application deadline: 3/1. *Unit head:* John O. Lox, MBA Director, 843-349-2469, Fax: 843-349-2455, E-mail: jlox@coastal.edu. *Application contact:* Dr. Deborah A. Vrooman, Interim Director of Graduate Studies, 843-349-2783, Fax: 843-349-6444, E-mail: vroomand@coastal.edu.

College of Charleston, Graduate School, School of Business, Program in Business Administration, Charleston, SC 29424-0001. Offers MBA. *Faculty:* 7 full-time (2 women). *Students:* 25 full-time (8 women); includes 1 Black or African American, non-Hispanic/Latino. Average age 24. 49 applicants, 53% accepted, 25 enrolled. *Entrance requirements:* For master's, GMAT. Additional exam requirements/recommendations for international students: Required—TOEFL (minimum score 81 iBT). *Application deadline:* For fall admission, 6/1 for domestic students. Application fee: $45. Electronic applications accepted. *Financial support:* Federal Work-Study, scholarships/grants, and unspecified assistantships available. Financial award application deadline: 4/1; financial award applicants required to submit FAFSA. *Unit head:* Dr. Alan Shao, Dean, 843-953-6651, Fax: 843-953-5697, E-mail: shaoa@cofc.edu. *Application contact:* Penny McKeever, Associate Director of Graduate Programs, School of Business, 843-953-8112, E-mail: mckeeverp@cofc.edu.

College of Saint Elizabeth, Department of Business Administration and Economics, Morristown, NJ 07960-6989. Offers management (MS). Part-time and evening/weekend programs available. *Students:* 10 full-time (all women), 62 part-time (51 women); includes 11 Black or African American, non-Hispanic/Latino; 5 Asian, non-Hispanic/Latino; 6 Hispanic/Latino; 1 Two or more races, non-Hispanic/Latino, 5 international. Average age 34. 38 applicants, 87% accepted, 21 enrolled. In 2010, 39 master's awarded. *Degree requirements:* For master's, capstone seminar. *Entrance requirements:* For master's, minimum GPA of 3.0, course work in principles of management. Additional exam requirements/recommendations for international students: Required—TOEFL (minimum score 550 paper-based). *Application deadline:* Applications are processed on a rolling basis. Application fee: $35. Electronic applications accepted. *Expenses:* Tuition: Part-time $857 per credit. Required fees: $70 per credit. *Financial support:* Career-related internships or fieldwork, tuition waivers (partial), and unspecified assistantships available. Support available to part-time students. Financial award application deadline: 3/15; financial

award applicants required to submit FAFSA. *Faculty research:* American business history, business developments in Eastern Europe, MIS/programming languages, marketing strategy, strategic planning. *Unit head:* Dr. Kathleen Reddick, Director of the Graduate Program in Management, 973-290-4041, Fax: 973-290-4177, E-mail: kreddick@cse.edu. *Application contact:* Dean Donna Tatarka, Dean of Admission, 973-290-4705, Fax: 973-290-4710, E-mail: dtatarka@cse.edu.

College of St. Joseph, Graduate Programs, Division of Business, Program in Business Administration, Rutland, VT 05701-3899. Offers MBA. Part-time and evening/weekend programs available. *Faculty:* 1 full-time (0 women), 3 part-time/adjunct (0 women). *Students:* 3 full-time (1 woman), 22 part-time (11 women); includes 1 Asian, non-Hispanic/Latino; 1 Hispanic/Latino. Average age 35. 12 applicants, 92% accepted, 10 enrolled. In 2010, 10 master's awarded. *Entrance requirements:* For master's, 2 letters of reference, interview. *Application deadline:* Applications are processed on a rolling basis. Application fee: $35. Electronic applications accepted. *Expenses:* Contact institution. *Financial support:* In 2010–11, 1 student received support, including teaching assistantships (averaging $3,000 per year). Financial award application deadline: 3/1. *Unit head:* Robert Foley, Chair, 802-773-5900 Ext. 3248, Fax: 802-776-5258, E-mail: rfoley@csj.edu. *Application contact:* Alan Young, Dean of Admissions, 802-773-5900 Ext. 3227, Fax: 802-776-5310, E-mail: alanyoung@csj.edu.

The College of St. Scholastica, Graduate Studies, Department of Management, Duluth, MN 55811-4199. Offers MA, Certificate. Part-time and evening/weekend programs available. Postbaccalaureate distance learning degree programs offered (minimal on-campus study). *Faculty:* 6 full-time (0 women), 2 part-time/adjunct (1 woman). *Students:* 159 full-time (99 women), 55 part-time (35 women); includes 14 minority (4 Black or African American, non-Hispanic/Latino; 7 American Indian or Alaska Native, non-Hispanic/Latino; 1 Asian, non-Hispanic/Latino; 2 Two or more races, non-Hispanic/Latino), 2 international. Average age 35. 125 applicants, 79% accepted, 65 enrolled. In 2010, 62 master's, 1 other advanced degree awarded. *Degree requirements:* For master's, thesis. *Entrance requirements:* For master's, minimum GPA of 2.8. Additional exam requirements/recommendations for international students: Required—TOEFL (minimum score 550 paper-based; 213 computer-based; 79 iBT). *Application deadline:* For fall admission, 8/1 priority date for domestic students, 8/1 for international students; for spring admission, 11/15 priority date for domestic students, 11/15 for international students. Applications are processed on a rolling basis. Application fee: $50. Electronic applications accepted. *Expenses:* Contact institution. *Financial support:* In 2010–11, 53 students received support. Scholarships/grants available. Support available to part-time students. Financial award applicants required to submit FAFSA. *Faculty research:* Violence in higher education and workplace, screening and selection procedures in law enforcement, Internet use in criminal justice, stress management in law enforcement. *Unit head:* Randal Zimmermann, Chair, 218-625-4929, Fax: 218-723-6290, E-mail: rzimmerm@css.edu. *Application contact:* Lindsay Lahti, Director of Graduate and Extended Studies Recruitment, 218-733-2240, Fax: 218-733-2275, E-mail: gradstudies@css.edu.

College of Staten Island of the City University of New York, Graduate Programs, Program in Business Management, Staten Island, NY 10314-6600. Offers MS. Evening/weekend programs available. *Faculty:* 4 full-time (1 woman), 3 part-time/adjunct (1 woman). *Students:* 2 full-time (0 women), 28 part-time (14 women); includes 3 minority (1 Black or African American, non-Hispanic/Latino; 1 Asian, non-Hispanic/Latino; 1 Hispanic/Latino), 6 international. Average age 29. 41 applicants, 32% accepted, 8 enrolled. In 2010, 10 master's awarded. *Entrance requirements:* For master's, GMAT, minimum undergraduate GPA of 3.0. Additional exam requirements/recommendations for international students: Required—TOEFL (minimum score 600 paper-based; 250 computer-based; 100 iBT), IELTS (minimum score 7). *Application deadline:* For fall admission, 8/1 for domestic students. Applications are processed on a rolling basis. Application fee: $125. Electronic applications accepted. *Expenses:* Tuition, state resident: full-time $7730; part-time $325 per credit. Tuition, nonresident: full-time $14,520; part-time $605 per credit. Required fees: $378. *Financial support:* In 2010–11, 1 student received support. Career-related internships or fieldwork, Federal Work-Study, and scholarships/grants available. Support available to part-time students. Financial award applicants required to submit FAFSA. Total annual research expenditures: $2,000. *Unit head:* Dr. Gene Garaventa, Coordinator, 718-982-2963, E-mail: eugene.garaventa@csi.cuny.edu. *Application contact:* Sasha Spence, Assistant Director of Graduate Recruitment and Admissions, 718-982-2699, Fax: 718-982-2500, E-mail: sasha.spence@csi.cuny.edu.

The College of William and Mary, Mason School of Business, Williamsburg, VA 23185. Offers accounting (M Acc); business administration (EMBA, MBA); JD/MBA; MBA/MPP. *Accreditation:* AACSB. Part-time and evening/weekend programs available. *Faculty:* 52 full-time (13 women), 11 part-time/adjunct (1 woman). *Students:* 324 full-time (124 women), 185 part-time (44 women); includes 52 minority (15 Black or African American, non-Hispanic/Latino; 19 Asian, non-Hispanic/Latino; 14 Hispanic/Latino; 2 Native Hawaiian or other Pacific Islander, non-Hispanic/Latino; 2 Two or more races, non-Hispanic/Latino), 91 international. Average age 29. 761 applicants, 51% accepted, 224 enrolled. In 2010, 255 master's awarded. *Degree* *requirements:* For master's, three domestic residencies and international trip (EMBA). *Entrance requirements:* For master's, GMAT or GRE. Additional exam requirements/recommendations for international students: Required—TOEFL (minimum score 600 paper-based; 250 computer-based; 100 iBT), IELTS (minimum score 6.5). *Application deadline:* For fall admission, 11/1 for domestic students, 11/6 for international students; for winter admission, 1/10 for domestic and international students; for spring admission, 3/5 for domestic students, 3/7 for international students. Application fee: $100. Electronic applications accepted. *Expenses:* Contact institution. *Financial support:* In 2010–11, 10 fellowships, 62 research assistantships with partial tuition reimbursements were awarded; career-related internships or fieldwork, scholarships/grants, and unspecified assistantships also available. Financial award application deadline: 3/7; financial award applicants required to submit FAFSA. *Faculty research:* Saving and asset allocation decisions in retirement accounts, supply chain management, virtual and networked organizations, healthcare informatics, sustainable business operations. Total annual research expenditures: $351,800. *Unit head:* Dr. Lawrence Pulley, Dean, 757-221-2891, Fax: 757-221-2937, E-mail: larry.pulley@mason.wm.edu. *Application contact:* Amanda K. Barth, Director, Full-time MBA Admissions, 757-221-2944, Fax: 757-221-2958, E-mail: amanda.barth@mason.wm.edu.

Colorado Christian University, Program in Business Administration, Lakewood, CO 80226. Offers corporate training (MBA); information security (MA); leadership (MBA); project management (MBA). Part-time and evening/weekend programs available. Postbaccalaureate distance learning degree programs offered (minimal on-campus study). *Faculty:* 10 full-time (7 women), 35 part-time/adjunct (17 women). *Students:* 65 full-time (33 women), 35 part-time (19 women); includes 6 Black or African American, non-Hispanic/Latino; 2 Asian, non-Hispanic/Latino; 9 Hispanic/Latino. Average age 37. 25 applicants, 20% accepted. *Degree requirements:* For master's, thesis optional. *Entrance requirements:* For master's, GMAT, 2 letters of recommendation, resume. Additional exam requirements/recommendations for international students: Required—TOEFL. *Application deadline:* For fall admission, 8/25 priority date for domestic and international students; for spring admission, 1/12 priority date for domestic and international students. Applications are processed on a rolling basis. Application fee: $40. Electronic applications accepted. *Expenses:* Contact institution. *Financial support:* In 2010–11, 27 students received support. Scholarships/grants and tuition waivers (full and partial) available. Support available to part-time students. Financial award application deadline: 3/1; financial award applicants required to submit FAFSA. *Unit head:* Dr. Mellani Day, Dean of Business and Technology, 303-963-3300, Fax: 303-963-3301, E-mail: agsadmission@ccu.edu. *Application contact:* Dr. Mellani Day, Dean of Business and Technology, 303-963-3300, Fax: 303-963-3301, E-mail: agsadmission@ccu.edu.

Colorado State University, Graduate School, College of Business, MBA Program, Fort Collins, CO 80523-1201. Offers MBA, MBA/DVM. *Accreditation:* AACSB. Part-time and evening/weekend programs available. *Faculty:* 15 full-time (4 women). *Students:* 330 full-time (110 women), 834 part-time (213 women); includes 220 minority (34 Black or African American, non-Hispanic/Latino; 5 American Indian or Alaska Native, non-Hispanic/Latino; 92 Asian, non-Hispanic/Latino; 67 Hispanic/Latino; 3 Native Hawaiian or other Pacific Islander, non-Hispanic/Latino; 19 Two or more races, non-Hispanic/Latino), 87 international. Average age 36. 514 applicants, 95% accepted, 405 enrolled. In 2010, 374 master's awarded. *Entrance requirements:* For master's, GMAT, minimum undergraduate GPA of 3.0, 4 years post-undergraduate professional work experience. Additional exam requirements/recommendations for international students: Required—TOEFL (minimum score 565 paper-based; 227 computer-based; 86 iBT); Recommended—IELTS (minimum score 6.5). *Application deadline:* For fall admission, 5/1 for domestic and international students. Application fee: $50. Electronic applications accepted. *Expenses:* Contact institution. *Financial support:* Fellowships, teaching assistantships with partial tuition reimbursements, career-related internships or fieldwork and unspecified assistantships available. Support available to part-time students. Financial award application deadline: 6/1; financial award applicants required to submit FAFSA. *Faculty research:* E-commerce, entrepreneurship, global leadership, corporate citizenship, marketing management. Total annual research expenditures: $10,208. *Application contact:* Matt Leland, Admissions Coordinator, 970-491-1917, Fax: 970-491-3481, E-mail: matt.leland@colostate.edu.

Columbia College, Master of Business Administration Program, Columbia, MO 65216-0002. Offers MBA. Evening/weekend programs available. Postbaccalaureate distance learning degree programs offered (no on-campus study). *Faculty:* 7 full-time (2 women), 48 part-time/adjunct (18 women). *Students:* 87 full-time (52 women), 480 part-time (278 women); includes 117 minority (75 Black or African American, non-Hispanic/Latino; 10 American Indian or Alaska Native, non-Hispanic/Latino; 7 Asian, non-Hispanic/Latino; 21 Hispanic/Latino; 4 Two or more races, non-Hispanic/Latino), 12 international. Average age 36. 157 applicants, 65% accepted, 55 enrolled. In 2010, 219 master's awarded. *Entrance requirements:* For master's, 3 letters of recommendation, minimum cumulative undergraduate GPA of 3.0, resume, goal statement. Additional exam requirements/recommendations for international students: Required—TOEFL (minimum score 550 paper-based; 213 computer-based; 79 iBT). *Application deadline:* For fall admission, 8/9 priority

date for domestic and international students; for spring admission, 12/27 priority date for domestic and international students. Applications are processed on a rolling basis. Application fee: $55. Electronic applications accepted. *Expenses:* Tuition: Part-time $299 per credit hour. Tuition and fees vary according to course load. *Financial support:* In 2010–11, 25 students received support. Federal Work-Study and scholarships/grants available. Financial award applicants required to submit FAFSA. *Unit head:* Dr. Diane Suhler, Coordinator, 573-875-7640, Fax: 573-876-4493, E-mail: drsuhler@ccis.edu. *Application contact:* Samantha White, Director of Admissions, 573-875-7352, Fax: 573-875-7506, E-mail: sjwhite@ccis.edu.

Columbus State University, Graduate Studies, D. Abbott Turner College of Business and Computer Science, Columbus, GA 31907-5645. Offers applied computer science (MS); business administration (MBA); modeling and simulation (Certificate); organizational leadership (MS). *Accreditation:* AACSB. *Faculty:* 15 full-time (2 women). *Students:* 36 full-time (9 women), 145 part-time (54 women); includes 43 minority (19 Black or African American, non-Hispanic/Latino; 3 American Indian or Alaska Native, non-Hispanic/Latino; 12 Asian, non-Hispanic/Latino; 3 Hispanic/Latino; 6 Two or more races, non-Hispanic/Latino), 11 international. Average age 33. 133 applicants, 61% accepted, 58 enrolled. In 2010, 59 master's awarded. *Entrance requirements:* For master's, GMAT, GRE. Additional exam requirements/recommendations for international students: Required—TOEFL (minimum score 550 paper-based; 213 computer-based; 79 iBT). *Application deadline:* For fall admission, 6/30 for domestic students, 5/1 for international students; for spring admission, 11/1 for domestic and international students. Applications are processed on a rolling basis. Application fee: $30. Electronic applications accepted. *Expenses:* Tuition, state resident: full-time $5573; part-time $232 per semester hour. Tuition, nonresident: full-time $13,968; part-time $582 per semester hour. Required fees: $1300; $650 per semester. Tuition and fees vary according to degree level and program. *Financial support:* In 2010–11, 62 students received support, including 11 research assistantships (averaging $3,000 per year). Financial award application deadline: 5/1. *Unit head:* Dr. Linda U. Hadley, Dean, 706-568-2044, Fax: 706-568-2184, E-mail: hadley_linda@colstate.edu. *Application contact:* Katie Thornton, Graduate Admissions Specialist, 706-568-2035, Fax: 706-568-2462, E-mail: thornton_katie@colstate.edu.

Concordia University, School of Business and Professional Studies, Irvine, CA 92612-3299. Offers business administration: business practice (MBA); international studies (MA). Part-time and evening/weekend programs available. *Faculty:* 3 full-time (0 women), 19 part-time/adjunct (3 women). *Students:* 80 full-time (37 women), 48 part-time (22 women); includes 28 minority (6 Black or African American, non-Hispanic/Latino; 12 Asian, non-Hispanic/Latino; 10 Hispanic/Latino), 8 international. Average age 30. 52 applicants, 44% accepted, 15 enrolled. In 2010, 66 master's awarded. *Degree requirements:* For master's, capstone project or thesis. *Entrance requirements:* For master's, official college transcript(s), signed statement of intent, resume, two references, interview (MBA); passport photo, photocopies of valid U.S. passport, and college diploma (MAIS). Additional exam requirements/recommendations for international students: Required—TOEFL. *Application deadline:* For fall admission, 8/1 for domestic students, 6/1 for international students; for spring admission, 1/1 for domestic students, 11/1 for international students. Application fee: $50 ($125 for international students). Electronic applications accepted. *Expenses:* Contact institution. *Financial support:* In 2010–11, 107 students received support. Tuition waivers (full and partial) and unspecified assistantships available. Financial award applicants required to submit FAFSA. *Unit head:* Dr. Timothy Peters, Dean, 949-214-3363, E-mail: tim.peters@cui.edu. *Application contact:* Sherry Powers, MBA Admissions Coordinator, 949-214-3032, Fax: 949-854-6894, E-mail: sherry.powers@cui.edu.

Concordia University, St. Paul, College of Business and Organizational Leadership, St. Paul, MN 55104-5494. Offers business and organizational leadership (MBA); criminal justice leadership (MA); health care management (MBA); human resources management (MA); leadership and management (MA). *Accreditation:* ACBSP. Evening/weekend programs available. Postbaccalaureate distance learning degree programs offered (minimal on-campus study). *Faculty:* 14 full-time (6 women), 30 part-time/adjunct (8 women). *Students:* 338 full-time (203 women), 2 part-time (1 woman); includes 24 Black or African American, non-Hispanic/Latino; 3 American Indian or Alaska Native, non-Hispanic/Latino; 11 Asian, non-Hispanic/Latino; 3 Hispanic/Latino; 3 Two or more races, non-Hispanic/Latino. Average age 34. 191 applicants, 65% accepted, 117 enrolled. In 2010, 125 master's awarded. *Application deadline:* Applications are processed on a rolling basis. Application fee: $50. Electronic applications accepted. *Expenses:* Tuition: Full-time $7500; part-time $460 per credit. Required fees: $460 per credit. Tuition and fees vary according to program. *Financial support:* Applicants required to submit FAFSA. *Unit head:* Dr. Bruce Corrie, Dean, 651-641-8226, Fax: 651-641-8807, E-mail: corrie@csp.edu. *Application contact:* Kimberly Craig, Director of Graduate and Cohort Admission, 651-603-6223, Fax: 651-603-6320, E-mail: craig@csp.edu.

Cornell University, Graduate School, Graduate Field of Management, Ithaca, NY 14853. Offers accounting (PhD); behavioral decision theory (PhD); finance (PhD); marketing (PhD); organizational behavior (PhD); production and operations management (PhD). *Accreditation:* AACSB. *Faculty:* 55 full-time (9 women). *Students:* 41 full-time (12 women); includes 5 Asian, non-Hispanic/Latino, 23 international. Average age 29. 436 applicants, 4% accepted, 12 enrolled. In 2010, 5 doctorates awarded. *Degree requirements:* For doctorate, comprehensive exam, thesis/dissertation. *Entrance requirements:* For doctorate, GMAT or GRE General Test. Additional exam requirements/recommendations for international students: Required—TOEFL (minimum score 600 paper-based; 250 computer-based; 77 iBT). *Application deadline:* For fall admission, 1/3 for domestic students. Application fee: $70. Electronic applications accepted. *Expenses:* Contact institution. *Financial support:* In 2010–11, 38 students received support, including 4 fellowships with full tuition reimbursements available, 34 research assistantships with full tuition reimbursements available, 1 teaching assistantship with full tuition reimbursement available; institutionally sponsored loans, scholarships/grants, health care benefits, tuition waivers (full and partial), and unspecified assistantships also available. Financial award applicants required to submit FAFSA. *Faculty research:* Operations and manufacturing. *Unit head:* Director of Graduate Studies, 607-255-3669. *Application contact:* Graduate Field Assistant, 607-255-9431, E-mail: js_phd@cornell.edu.

Cornell University, Johnson Graduate School of Management, Ithaca, NY 14853. Offers MBA, JD/MBA, M Eng/MBA, MBA/MILR. *Accreditation:* AACSB. *Faculty:* 47 full-time (9 women), 4 part-time/adjunct (0 women). *Students:* 989 full-time (264 women); includes 163 minority (29 Black or African American, non-Hispanic/Latino; 104 Asian, non-Hispanic/Latino; 25 Hispanic/Latino; 5 Two or more races, non-Hispanic/Latino), 330 international. Average age 32. 2,283 applicants, 501 enrolled. In 2010, 468 master's awarded. *Entrance requirements:* For master's, GMAT. Additional exam requirements/recommendations for international students: Required—TOEFL (minimum score 250 computer-based; 100 iBT); Recommended—IELTS (minimum score 7), TWE. *Application deadline:* For fall admission, 3/15 for domestic students, 1/1 for international students. Application fee: $200. Electronic applications accepted. *Expenses:* Contact institution. *Financial support:* Fellowships, research assistantships, career-related internships or fieldwork, Federal Work-Study, institutionally sponsored loans, and tuition waivers (full and partial) available. Financial award application deadline: 2/15; financial award applicants required to submit FAFSA. *Unit head:* Dr. L. Joseph Thomas, Dean, 607-255-4854, E-mail: ljt3@cornell.edu. *Application contact:* 800-847-2082, Fax: 607-255-0065, E-mail: mba@johnson.cornell.edu.

Creighton University, Graduate School, Eugene C. Eppley College of Business Administration, Omaha, NE 68178-0001. Offers business administration (MBA); information technology management (MS); securities and portfolio management (MSAPM); JD/MBA; MBA/INR; MBA/MS-ITM; MBA/MSAPM; MD/MBA; MS ITM/JD; Pharm D/MBA. *Accreditation:* AACSB. Part-time and evening/weekend programs available. Postbaccalaureate distance learning degree programs offered (minimal on-campus study). *Faculty:* 37 full-time (7 women). *Students:* 42 full-time (13 women), 268 part-time (51 women); includes 32 minority (17 Black or African American, non-Hispanic/Latino; 12 Asian, non-Hispanic/Latino; 3 Hispanic/Latino), 20 international. Average age 30. 133 applicants, 80% accepted, 100 enrolled. In 2010, 77 master's awarded. *Degree requirements:* For master's, thesis optional. *Entrance requirements:* For master's, GMAT, resume, 2 letters of recommendation. Additional exam requirements/recommendations for international students: Required—TOEFL (minimum score 550 paper-based; 213 computer-based; 80 iBT). *Application deadline:* For fall admission, 7/1 priority date for domestic students, 3/1 for international students; for winter admission, 10/1 priority date for domestic students, 7/1 for international students; for spring admission, 4/1 priority date for domestic students, 10/1 for international students. Applications are processed on a rolling basis. Application fee: $50. Electronic applications accepted. *Expenses:* Tuition: Full-time $12,168; part-time $676 per credit hour. Required fees: $131 per semester. Tuition and fees vary according to program. *Financial support:* In 2010–11, 10 fellowships with partial tuition reimbursements (averaging $8,112 per year) were awarded; career-related internships or fieldwork, tuition waivers (partial), and unspecified assistantships also available. Financial award application deadline: 3/1. *Faculty research:* Small business issues, economics. *Unit head:* Dr. Deborah Wells, Associate Dean for Graduate Programs, 402-280-2841, E-mail: deborahwells@creighton.edu. *Application contact:* Gail Hafer, Assistant Dean, 402-280-2829, Fax: 402-280-2172, E-mail: ghafer@creighton.edu.

Curry College, Graduate Studies, Program in Business Administration, Milton, MA 02186-9984. Offers business administration (MBA); finance (Certificate). Part-time and evening/weekend programs available. *Faculty:* 5 full-time (1 woman), 2 part-time/adjunct (0 women). *Students:* 111 part-time (68 women). Average age 36. 44 applicants, 89% accepted, 39 enrolled. In 2010, 49 master's awarded. *Degree requirements:* For master's, capstone applied project. *Entrance requirements:* For master's, resume, recommendations, interview, written statement. Additional exam requirements/recommendations for international students: Required—TOEFL (minimum score 550 paper-based; 213 computer-based; 80 iBT). *Application deadline:* For fall admission, 8/1 priority date for domestic students, 6/1 for international students; for winter admission, 10/1 for international students; for spring admission, 12/15 priority date for domestic students, 1/28 for international

students. Applications are processed on a rolling basis. Application fee: $50. *Expenses:* Contact institution. *Unit head:* Dr. Gail Arch, Director and Professor, 617-333-2197. *Application contact:* John Bresnahan, Director of Graduate Enrollment and Student Services, 617-333-2243, Fax: 617-979-3535, E-mail: jbresnah0104@curry.edu.

Daemen College, Program in Executive Leadership and Change, Amherst, NY 14226-3592. Offers business (MS); health professions (MS); not-for-profit organizations (MS). Part-time and evening/weekend programs available. *Faculty:* 1 full-time (0 women), 4 part-time/adjunct (1 woman). *Students:* 8 full-time (5 women), 12 part-time (9 women); includes 3 minority (all Black or African American, non-Hispanic/Latino). Average age 38. In 2010, 5 master's awarded. *Degree requirements:* For master's, thesis, cohort learning sequence (2 years for weekend cohort; 3 years for weeknight cohort). *Entrance requirements:* For master's, 2 letters of recommendation, interview, goal statement, official transcripts, resume. Additional exam requirements/recommendations for international students: Required—TOEFL (minimum score 500 paper-based; 173 computer-based; 63 iBT), IELTS (minimum score 5.5). *Application deadline:* For fall admission, 3/1 priority date for domestic and international students; for spring admission, 10/1 priority date for domestic and international students. Applications are processed on a rolling basis. Application fee: $25. Electronic applications accepted. *Expenses:* Tuition: Part-time $830 per credit hour. Tuition and fees vary according to course load and reciprocity agreements. *Financial support:* In 2010–11, 1 student received support. Institutionally sponsored loans available. Financial award application deadline: 2/15; financial award applicants required to submit FAFSA. *Unit head:* Dr. John S. Frederick, Executive Director, 716-839-8342, Fax: 716-839-8261, E-mail: jfrederi@daemen.edu. *Application contact:* Scott Rowe, Associate Director of Graduate Admissions, 716-839-8225, Fax: 716-839-8229, E-mail: srowe@daemen.edu.

Dartmouth College, Tuck School of Business at Dartmouth, Hanover, NH 03755. Offers MBA, MBA/MPH, MD/MBA, PhD/MBA. *Accreditation:* AACSB. *Faculty:* 46 full-time (11 women). *Students:* 537 full-time (181 women); includes 29 Black or African American, non-Hispanic/Latino; 50 Asian, non-Hispanic/Latino; 20 Hispanic/Latino, 170 international. Average age 28. 2,528 applicants, 20% accepted, 280 enrolled. In 2010, 253 master's awarded. *Entrance requirements:* For master's, GMAT or GRE, 2 letters of recommendation, resume/curriculum vitae. Additional exam requirements/recommendations for international students: Required—TOEFL. *Application deadline:* For fall admission, 10/15 for domestic and international students; for winter admission, 1/31 for domestic and international students; for spring admission, 4/1 for domestic and international students. Application fee: $225. Electronic applications accepted. *Expenses:* Contact institution. *Financial support:* In 2010–11, 387 students received support. Institutionally sponsored loans and scholarships/grants available. Financial award application deadline: 4/15; financial award applicants required to submit FAFSA. *Faculty research:* Database marketing, mutual fund investment performance, dynamic capabilities of firms, return on marketing investment, tradeoff between risk and return in international financial markets, strategic innovation in established firms. *Unit head:* Paul Danos, Dean, 603-646-2460, Fax: 603-646-1308, E-mail: tuck.public.relations@dartmouth.edu. *Application contact:* Dawna Clarke, Director of Admissions, 603-646-3162, Fax: 603-646-1441, E-mail: tuck.admissions@dartmouth.edu.

DeSales University, Graduate Division, Program in Business Administration, Center Valley, PA 18034-9568. Offers accounting (MBA); computer information systems (MBA); finance (MBA); health care systems management (MBA); health care systems management (online) (MBA); human resource management (MBA); management (MBA); management (online) (MBA); marketing (MBA); marketing (online) (MBA); physician's track (MBA); project management (MBA); project management (online) (MBA); self-design (MBA); self-design (online) (MBA); MSN/MBA. *Accreditation:* ACBSP. Part-time programs available. Postbaccalaureate distance learning degree programs offered (no on-campus study). *Entrance requirements:* For master's, GMAT, minimum GPA of 3.0, 2 years of work experience. Additional exam requirements/recommendations for international students: Required—TOEFL. *Application deadline:* Applications are processed on a rolling basis. Application fee: $35. Electronic applications accepted. *Expenses:* Tuition: Full-time $18,200; part-time $690 per credit. Required fees: $1200. *Faculty research:* Quality improvement, executive development, productivity, cross-cultural managerial differences, leadership. *Unit head:* Dr. David Gilfoil, Director, 610-282-1100 Ext. 1828, Fax: 610-282-2869, E-mail: david.gilfoil@desales.edu. *Application contact:* Caryn Stopper, Director of Graduate Admissions, 610-282-1100 Ext. 1768, Fax: 610-282-0525, E-mail: caryn.stopper@desales.edu.

DeVry University, Keller Graduate School of Management, Arlington, VA 22202. Offers MAFM, MBA, MHRM, MISM, MNCM, MPA, MPM. *Students:* 61 full-time (30 women), 216 part-time (89 women). In 2010, 36 master's awarded. *Application contact:* Student Application Contact, 703-414-4000.

DeVry University, Keller Graduate School of Management, Columbus, OH 43209-2705. Offers MAFM, MBA, MHRM, MISM, MNCM, MPA, MPM. *Students:* 55 full-time (29 women), 341 part-time (199 women). In 2010,

90 master's awarded. *Application contact:* Student Application Contact, 614-253-7291.

DeVry University, Keller Graduate School of Management, Decatur, GA 30030-2556. Offers MAFM, MBA, MHRM, MISM, MNCM, MPA, MPM. *Students:* 82 full-time (47 women), 369 part-time (241 women). In 2010, 132 master's awarded. *Application contact:* Student Application Contact, 404-270-2700.

DeVry University, Keller Graduate School of Management, Federal Way, WA 98001. Offers MAFM, MBA, MHRM, MISM, MNCM, MPA, MPM. *Students:* 24 full-time (13 women), 148 part-time (55 women). In 2010, 44 master's awarded. *Application contact:* Student Application Contact, 253-943-2800.

DeVry University, Keller Graduate School of Management, Fort Washington, PA 19034. Offers MAFM, MBA, MHRM, MISM, MNCM, MPA, MPM. *Students:* 32 full-time (18 women), 191 part-time (99 women). In 2010, 40 master's awarded. *Application contact:* Student Application Contact, 215-591-5700.

DeVry University, Keller Graduate School of Management, Houston, TX 77041. Offers MAFM, MBA, MHRM, MISM, MNCM, MPA, MPM. *Students:* 91 full-time (47 women), 295 part-time (165 women). In 2010, 74 master's awarded. *Application contact:* Student Application Contact, 713-973-3100.

DeVry University, Keller Graduate School of Management, Irving, TX 75063-2439. Offers MAFM, MBA, MHRM, MISM, MPM. *Students:* 87 full-time (35 women), 306 part-time (137 women). In 2010, 60 master's awarded. *Application contact:* Student Application Contact, 972-929-6777.

DeVry College of New York, Keller Graduate School of Management, Long Island City, NY 11101. Offers MAFM, MBA, MISM. *Students:* 68 full-time (33 women), 229 part-time (111 women). In 2010, 19 master's awarded.

DeVry University, Keller Graduate School of Management, Miramar, FL 33027-4150. Offers MAFM, MBA, MHRM, MISM, MNCM, MPA, MPM. *Students:* 57 full-time (33 women), 200 part-time (117 women). In 2010, 64 master's awarded. *Application contact:* Student Application Contact, 954-499-9700.

DeVry University, Keller Graduate School of Management, North Brunswick, NJ 08902-3362. Offers MBA. *Students:* 40 full-time (21 women), 92 part-time (46 women).

DeVry University, Keller Graduate School of Management, Orlando, FL 32839. Offers MAFM, MBA, MHRM, MISM, MNCM, MPA, MPM. *Students:* 56 full-time (24 women), 235 part-time (130 women). In 2010, 66 master's awarded. *Application contact:* Student Application Contact, 407-345-2800.

DeVry University, Keller Graduate School of Management, Phoenix, AZ 85021-2995. Offers MAFM, MBA, MHRM, MISM, MNCM, MPA, MPM. *Students:* 41 full-time (15 women), 237 part-time (120 women). In 2010, 83 master's awarded. *Application contact:* Student Application Contact, 602-870-9222.

DeVry University, Keller Graduate School of Management, Pomona, CA 91768-2642. Offers MAFM, MBA, MHRM, MISM, MNCM, MPA, MPM. *Students:* 73 full-time (31 women), 322 part-time (148 women). In 2010, 92 master's awarded. *Application contact:* Student Application Contact, 909-622-8866.

DeVry University Online, Keller Graduate School of Management, Addison, IL 60101-6106. Offers MAFM, MBA, MEE, MET, MHRM, MISM, MNCM, MPA, MPM. *Students:* 903 full-time (522 women), 5,326 part-time (3,245 women). In 2010, 1,422 master's awarded.

Doane College, Program in Management, Crete, NE 68333-2430. Offers MA. Part-time and evening/weekend programs available. *Faculty:* 2 full-time (1 woman), 21 part-time/adjunct (9 women). *Students:* 109 full-time (63 women), 11 part-time (6 women); includes 12 minority (5 Black or African American, non-Hispanic/Latino; 1 Asian, non-Hispanic/Latino; 5 Hispanic/Latino; 1 Two or more races, non-Hispanic/Latino). Average age 36. In 2010, 20 master's awarded. *Degree requirements:* For master's, thesis. *Entrance requirements:* For master's, minimum GPA of 3.0. *Application deadline:* Applications are processed on a rolling basis. Application fee: $25. *Expenses:* Contact institution. *Financial support:* Application deadline: 6/1. *Unit head:* Janice Hedfield, Dean, 880-333-6263, E-mail: janice.hedfield@doane.edu. *Application contact:* Janice Hedfield, Dean, 880-333-6263, E-mail: janice. hedfield@doane.edu.

Dominican College, MBA Program, Orangeburg, NY 10962-1210. Offers MBA. Evening/weekend programs available. *Students:* 2 full-time (both women), 19 part-time (9 women); includes 3 Asian, non-Hispanic/Latino; 3 Hispanic/Latino. In 2010, 5 master's awarded. *Entrance requirements:* For master's, GMAT, 2 letters of recommendation. Additional exam requirements/ recommendations for international students: Required—TOEFL. Electronic applications accepted. *Expenses:* Contact institution. *Unit head:* Ken Mias, MBA Director, 845-848-4102, E-mail: ken.mias@dc.edu. *Application contact:* Joyce Elbe, Director of Admissions, 845-848-7896 Ext. 15, Fax: 845-365-3150, E-mail: admissions@dc.edu.

Dominican University of California, Graduate Programs, School of Business and Leadership, Green Business Administration Program, San Rafael, CA 94901-2298. Offers sustainable enterprise (MBA). Part-time and evening/ weekend programs available. *Faculty:* 4 full-time (3 women), 12 part-time/ adjunct (7 women). *Students:* 56 full-time (30 women), 58 part-time (34 women); includes 28 minority (3 Black or African American, non-Hispanic/ Latino; 7 Asian, non-Hispanic/Latino; 11 Hispanic/Latino; 7 Two or more races, non-Hispanic/Latino). Average age 35. 46 applicants, 70% accepted, 21 enrolled. In 2010, 36 master's awarded. *Entrance requirements:* Additional exam requirements/recommendations for international students: Required— TOEFL (minimum score 550 paper-based; 213 computer-based; 80 iBT), IELTS (minimum score 7). *Application deadline:* For fall admission, 6/15 priority date for domestic and international students; for spring admission, 11/15 priority date for domestic and international students. Applications are processed on a rolling basis. Application fee: $40. Electronic applications accepted. *Financial support:* In 2010–11, 43 students received support; fellowships, scholarships/grants available. Financial award application deadline: 3/2; financial award applicants required to submit FAFSA. *Unit head:* Joey Shepp, Director, 415-482-1822, Fax: 415-459-3206, E-mail: joey.shepp@ dominican.edu. *Application contact:* Robbie Hayes, Assistant Director, 415-458-3771, Fax: 415-485-3214, E-mail: robbie.hayes@dominican.edu.

Dominican University of California, Graduate Programs, School of Business and Leadership, Program in Management, San Rafael, CA 94901-2298. Offers MAM. Program offered through strategic alliance with the California Management Institute (CMI). *Students:* 7 full-time (3 women), 3 part-time (1 woman), all international. Average age 28. In 2010, 14 master's awarded. *Unit head:* Dr. Francoise LePage, Program Director, 415-485-3284, E-mail: flepage@dominican.edu. *Application contact:* Larry Schwaltz, Director, 415-458-3748, Fax: 415-485-3214, E-mail: larry.schwaltz@dominican.edu.

Dowling College, School of Business, Oakdale, NY 11769-1999. Offers aviation management (MBA, Certificate); banking and finance (MBA, Certificate); corporate finance (MBA); financial planning (Certificate); health care management (MBA, Certificate); human resource management (Certificate); information systems management (MBA); management and leadership (MBA); marketing (Certificate); project management (Certificate); public management (MBA, Certificate); sport, event and entertainment management (Certificate); JD/MBA. Part-time and evening/weekend programs available. *Faculty:* 10 full-time (4 women), 56 part-time/adjunct (7 women). *Students:* 295 full-time (131 women), 460 part-time (206 women); includes 219 minority (97 Black or African American, non-Hispanic/Latino; 14 Asian, non-Hispanic/Latino; 35 Hispanic/Latino; 73 Native Hawaiian or other Pacific Islander, non-Hispanic/Latino), 3 international. Average age 33. 327 applicants, 85% accepted, 160 enrolled. In 2010, 33 master's, 1 other advanced degree awarded. *Degree requirements:* For master's, comprehensive exam, thesis optional. *Entrance requirements:* For master's, minimum GPA of 2.8, 2 letters of recommendation, courses in accounting and finance or seminar in accounting/finance, resume. Additional exam requirements/recommendations for international students: Required—TOEFL (minimum score 550 paper-based). *Application deadline:* For fall admission, 9/1 priority date for domestic students; for winter admission, 1/1 priority date for domestic students; for spring admission, 2/1 priority date for domestic students. Applications are processed on a rolling basis. Application fee: $50. Electronic applications accepted. *Expenses:* Tuition: Part-time $884 per credit hour. Part-time tuition and fees vary according to degree level and campus/location. *Financial support:* Career-related internships or fieldwork and Federal Work-Study available. Support available to part-time students. Financial award application deadline: 6/30; financial award applicants required to submit FAFSA. *Faculty research:* International finance, computer applications, labor relations, executive development. *Unit head:* Antonia Loschiavo, Assistant Dean, 631-244-3266, Fax: 631-244-1018, E-mail: loschiat@dowling.edu. *Application contact:* Ronnie S. Macdonald, Assistant Vice President for Enrollment Services/Dean of Admissions, 631-244-3357, Fax: 631-244-1059, E-mail: macdonar@dowling.edu.

Duke University, Graduate School, Department of Business Administration, Durham, NC 27708. Offers PhD. *Faculty:* 90 full-time. *Students:* 77 full-time (22 women); includes 2 Black or African American, non-Hispanic/Latino; 3 Asian, non-Hispanic/Latino; 1 Hispanic/Latino, 44 international. 627 applicants, 4% accepted, 15 enrolled. In 2010, 7 doctorates awarded. *Degree requirements:* For doctorate, thesis/dissertation. *Entrance requirements:* For doctorate, GMAT or GRE General Test. Additional exam requirements/recommendations for international students: Required—TOEFL (minimum score 550 paper-based; 213 computer-based; 83 iBT), IELTS (minimum score 7). *Application deadline:* For fall admission, 12/8 for domestic and international students. Application fee: $75. Electronic applications accepted. *Financial support:* Fellowships with full tuition reimbursements, research assistantships, career-related internships or fieldwork, Federal Work-Study, and institutionally sponsored loans available. Financial award application deadline: 12/8; financial award applicants required to submit FAFSA. *Unit head:* James Bettman, Director of Graduate Studies, 919-660-7862, Fax: 919-681-6245, E-mail: bobbiec@mail.duke.edu. *Application contact:* Elizabeth Hutton, Director, Graduate Admissions, 919-684-3913, Fax: 919-684-2277, E-mail: grad-admissions@duke.edu.

Duquesne University, John F. Donahue Graduate School of Business, Pittsburgh, PA 15282-0001. Offers accountancy (MS); business administration (MBA); information systems management (MSISM); sustainability (MBA); JD/MBA; MBA/MA; MBA/MES; MBA/MHMS; MBA/MLLS; MBA/MS; MBA/MSN. *Accreditation:* AACSB. Part-time and evening/weekend programs available. *Faculty:* 24 full-time (5 women), 14 part-time/adjunct (0 women). *Students:* 97 full-time (45 women), 234 part-time (91 women); includes 5 Black or African American, non-Hispanic/Latino; 1 Asian, non-Hispanic/Latino; 2 Hispanic/Latino; 4 Native Hawaiian or other Pacific Islander, non-Hispanic/Latino, 29 international. Average age 31. 289 applicants, 43% accepted, 82 enrolled. In 2010, 120 master's awarded. *Entrance requirements:* For master's, GMAT, 2 letters of recommendation, current resume. Additional exam requirements/recommendations for international students: Required—TOEFL (minimum score 577 paper-based; 233 computer-based; 90 iBT); Recommended—TWE. *Application deadline:* For fall admission, 5/1 priority date for domestic students, 5/1 for international students; for spring admission, 10/1 for domestic and international students. Applications are processed on a rolling basis. Application fee: $0. Electronic applications accepted. *Expenses:* Tuition: Part-time $884 per credit. Required fees: $84 per credit. Tuition and fees vary according to course load. *Financial support:* In 2010–11, 40 students received support, including 12 fellowships with partial tuition reimbursements available, 28 research assistantships with partial tuition reimbursements available; career-related internships or fieldwork, scholarships/grants, and unspecified assistantships also available. Financial award application deadline: 7/1; financial award applicants required to submit FAFSA. *Faculty research:* International business, investment management, business ethics, technology management, supply chain management, business strategy, finance. *Unit head:* Alan R. Miciak, Dean, 412-396-5848, Fax: 412-396-5304, E-mail: miciaka@duq.edu. *Application contact:* Patricia Moore, Assistant Director, 412-396-6276, Fax: 412-396-1726, E-mail: moorep@duq.edu.

See Display below and Close-Up on page 164.

Duquesne University, School of Leadership and Professional Advancement, Pittsburgh, PA 15282-0001. Offers leadership (MS), including business ethics, community leadership, global leadership, information technology, leadership, liberal studies, professional administration, sports leadership. Part-time and evening/weekend programs available. Postbaccalaureate distance learning degree programs offered (no on-campus study). *Faculty:* 1 full-time (0 women), 70 part-time/adjunct (35 women). *Students:* 275 full-time, 171 part-time; includes 20 Black or African American, non-Hispanic/

Latino; 1 American Indian or Alaska Native, non-Hispanic/Latino; 6 Asian, non-Hispanic/Latino; 3 Hispanic/Latino. Average age 31. 161 applicants, 73% accepted, 103 enrolled. In 2010, 108 master's awarded. *Degree requirements:* For master's, capstone course. *Entrance requirements:* For master's, professional work experience, 500-word essay. Additional exam requirements/recommendations for international students: Required—TOEFL. *Application deadline:* Applications are processed on a rolling basis. Application fee: $0. Electronic applications accepted. *Expenses:* Tuition: Part-time $884 per credit. Required fees: $84 per credit. Tuition and fees vary according to course load. *Financial support:* Applicants required to submit FAFSA. *Unit head:* Dr. Dorothy Bassett, Dean, 412-396-2141, Fax: 412-396-4711, E-mail: bassettd@duq.edu. *Application contact:* Marianne Leister, Director of Student Services, 412-396-4933, Fax: 412-396-5072, E-mail: leister@duq.edu.

D'Youville College, Department of Business, Buffalo, NY 14201-1084. Offers business administration (MBA); international business (MS). Part-time and evening/weekend programs available. *Faculty:* 4 full-time (1 woman), 7 part-time/adjunct (2 women). *Students:* 63 full-time (46 women), 31 part-time (15 women); includes 24 minority (14 Black or African American, non-Hispanic/Latino; 2 American Indian or Alaska Native, non-Hispanic/Latino; 1 Asian, non-Hispanic/Latino; 6 Hispanic/Latino; 1 Two or more races, non-Hispanic/Latino), 19 international. Average age 30. 86 applicants, 62% accepted, 22 enrolled. In 2010, 19 master's awarded. *Degree requirements:* For master's, one foreign language, project or thesis. *Entrance requirements:* For master's, minimum GPA of 3.0. Additional exam requirements/recommendations for international students: Required—TOEFL (minimum score 500 paper-based; 173 computer-based). *Application deadline:* For fall admission, 5/1 priority date for international students; for spring admission, 9/1 priority date for international students. Applications are processed on a rolling basis. Application fee: $25. Electronic applications accepted. *Expenses:* Tuition: Part-time $790 per credit hour. Part-time tuition and fees vary according to degree level. *Financial support:* In 2010–11, 1 research assistantship with partial tuition reimbursement (averaging $3,000 per year) was awarded; career-related internships or fieldwork, Federal Work-Study, and scholarships/grants also available. Support available to part-time students. Financial award application deadline: 3/1; financial award applicants required to submit FAFSA. *Faculty research:* Assessment, accreditation, supply chain, online learning, adult learning. *Unit head:* Dr. Susan Kowalewski, Chair, 716-829-7839, Fax: 716-829-7760. *Application contact:* Linda Fisher, Graduate Admissions Director, 716-829-8400, Fax: 716-829-7900, E-mail: graduateadmissions@dyc.edu.

Eastern Michigan University, Graduate School, College of Business, Department of Management, Ypsilanti, MI 48197. Offers human resources management and organizational development (MSHROD). Part-time and evening/weekend programs available. Postbaccalaureate distance learning degree programs offered (minimal on-campus study). *Faculty:* 20 full-time (9 women). *Students:* 25 full-time (13 women), 69 part-time (50 women); includes 29 minority (18 Black or African American, non-Hispanic/Latino; 1 American Indian or Alaska Native, non-Hispanic/Latino; 6 Asian, non-Hispanic/Latino; 4 Hispanic/Latino), 22 international. Average age 31. 47 applicants, 64% accepted, 12 enrolled. In 2010, 37 master's awarded. *Degree requirements:* For master's, thesis optional. *Entrance requirements:* For master's, GMAT. Additional exam requirements/recommendations for international students: Required—TOEFL. *Application deadline:* For fall admission, 5/15 priority date for domestic and international students; for winter admission, 10/15 priority date for domestic and international students; for spring admission, 3/15 priority date for domestic and international students. Applications are processed on a rolling basis. Application fee: $35. *Financial support:* Fellowships, research assistantships with full tuition reimbursements, teaching assistantships with full tuition reimbursements, career-related internships or fieldwork, Federal Work-Study, institutionally sponsored loans, scholarships/grants, tuition waivers (partial), and unspecified assistantships available. Support available to part-time students. Financial award applicants required to submit FAFSA. *Unit head:* Dr. Fraya Wagner-Marsh, Department Head, 734-487-3240, Fax: 734-487-4100, E-mail: fraya.wagner@emich.edu. *Application contact:* Dr. Fraya Wagner-Marsh, Department Head, 734-487-3240, Fax: 734-487-4100, E-mail: fraya.wagner@emich.edu.

Eastern Michigan University, Graduate School, College of Business, Programs in Business Administration, Ypsilanti, MI 48197. Offers business administration (MBA, Graduate Certificate); computer information systems (Graduate Certificate); e-business (MBA, Graduate Certificate); enterprise business intelligence (MBA); entrepreneurship (MBA, Graduate Certificate); finance (MBA, Graduate Certificate); human resources (MBA); human resources management (Graduate Certificate); information systems (MBA); internal auditing (MBA); international business (MBA, Graduate Certificate); marketing management (Graduate Certificate); nonprofit management (MBA); organizational development (Graduate Certificate); supply chain management (MBA, Graduate Certificate). *Accreditation:* AACSB. Part-time programs available. Postbaccalaureate distance learning degree programs offered (no on-campus study). *Students:* 149 full-time (66 women), 456 part-time (232 women); includes 146 minority (109 Black or African American, non-Hispanic/Latino; 4 American Indian or Alaska Native, non-Hispanic/Latino; 27 Asian, non-Hispanic/Latino; 6 Hispanic/Latino), 105 international. Average age 32. 330 applicants, 64% accepted, 150 enrolled. In 2010, 128 master's, 53 other advanced degrees awarded. *Entrance requirements:* For master's, GMAT (minimum score 450), minimum cumulative undergraduate GPA of 2.75. Additional exam requirements/recommendations for international students: Required—TOEFL. *Application deadline:* For fall admission, 5/15 for domestic students, 5/1 for international students; for winter admission, 10/15 for domestic students, 10/1 for international students; for spring admission, 3/15 for domestic students, 3/1 for international students. Applications are processed on a rolling basis. Application fee: $35. *Financial support:* Fellowships, research assistantships with full tuition reimbursements, teaching assistantships with full tuition reimbursements, career-related internships or fieldwork, Federal Work-Study, institutionally sponsored loans, scholarships/grants, tuition waivers (partial), and unspecified assistantships available. Support available to part-time students. Financial award applicants required to submit FAFSA. *Unit head:* K. Michelle Henry, Interim Director, Graduate Programs, 734-487-4444, Fax: 734-483-1316, E-mail: mhenry1@emich.edu. *Application contact:* Beste Windes, Advisor, 734-487-4444, Fax: 734-483-1316, E-mail: bwindes@emich.edu.

Eastern New Mexico University, Graduate School, College of Business, Portales, NM 88130. Offers MBA. *Accreditation:* ACBSP. Part-time and evening/weekend programs available. Postbaccalaureate distance learning degree programs offered (no on-campus study). *Faculty:* 12 full-time (2 women). *Students:* 25 full-time (12 women), 78 part-time (49 women); includes 31 minority (5 Black or African American, non-Hispanic/Latino; 1 American Indian or Alaska Native, non-Hispanic/Latino; 1 Asian, non-Hispanic/Latino; 20 Hispanic/Latino; 1 Native Hawaiian or other Pacific Islander, non-Hispanic/Latino; 3 Two or more races, non-Hispanic/Latino), 10 international. Average age 35. 49 applicants, 96% accepted, 34 enrolled. In 2010, 14 master's awarded. *Degree requirements:* For master's, comprehensive exam, comprehensive integrative project and presentation. *Entrance requirements:* For master's, GMAT (minimum score 450), minimum undergraduate GPA of 3.0. Additional exam requirements/recommendations for international students: Required—TOEFL (minimum score 550 paper-based; 213 computer-based; 79 iBT), IELTS (minimum score 6). *Application deadline:* For fall admission, 7/20 priority date for domestic students, 6/20 priority date for international students; for spring admission, 12/15 priority date for domestic students, 11/15 priority date for international students. Applications are processed on a rolling basis. Application fee: $10. Electronic applications accepted. *Expenses:* Tuition, state resident: full-time $3210; part-time $130 per credit hour. Tuition, nonresident: full-time $8652; part-time $360.50 per credit hour. Required fees: $1212; $50.50 per credit hour. Tuition and fees vary according to course load.

Financial support: In 2010–11, 10 research assistantships with partial tuition reimbursements (averaging $4,250 per year) were awarded; tuition waivers (partial) and unspecified assistantships also available. Support available to part-time students. Financial award applicants required to submit FAFSA. *Unit head:* Dr. Veena Parboteeah, MBA Graduate Coordinator, 575-562-2442, Fax: 575-562-4331, E-mail: veena.parboteeah@enmu.edu. *Application contact:* Dr. Veena Parboteeah, MBA Graduate Coordinator, 575-562-2442, Fax: 575-562-4331, E-mail: veena.parboteeah@enmu.edu.

East Tennessee State University, School of Graduate Studies, College of Business and Technology, Johnson City, TN 37614. Offers M Acc, MBA, MS, Certificate. *Accreditation:* AACSB. *Faculty:* 68 full-time (16 women). *Students:* 187 full-time (67 women), 91 part-time (32 women); includes 30 minority (9 Black or African American, non-Hispanic/Latino; 1 American Indian or Alaska Native, non-Hispanic/Latino; 5 Asian, non-Hispanic/Latino; 10 Hispanic/Latino; 5 Two or more races, non-Hispanic/Latino), 31 international. Average age 30. 280 applicants, 57% accepted, 103 enrolled. In 2010, 121 master's, 8 other advanced degrees awarded. *Entrance requirements:* Additional exam requirements/recommendations for international students: Required—TOEFL (minimum score 550 paper-based; 213 computer-based; 79 iBT). Application fee: $25 ($35 for international students). Electronic applications accepted. *Financial support:* In 2010–11, 27 research assistantships with full tuition reimbursements (averaging $6,000 per year) were awarded. Financial award application deadline: 7/1; financial award applicants required to submit FAFSA. *Faculty research:* Artificial intelligence and accounting, profit vs. non-profit hospital comparisons, environmental compliance issues in manufacturing, international finance, case law on Americans with disabilities. Total annual research expenditures: $225,815. *Unit head:* Dr. Linda Garceau, Dean, 423-439-5276, Fax: 423-439-5274, E-mail: garceaul@etsu.edu. *Application contact:* Dr. Linda Garceau, Dean, 423-439-5276, Fax: 423-439-5274, E-mail: garceaul@etsu.edu.

Edgewood College, Program in Business, Madison, WI 53711-1997. Offers accountancy (MS); business (MBA). *Accreditation:* ACBSP. Part-time and evening/weekend programs available. *Students:* 38 full-time (20 women), 98 part-time (42 women); includes 9 minority (1 Black or African American, non-Hispanic/Latino; 5 Asian, non-Hispanic/Latino; 1 Hispanic/Latino; 2 Two or more races, non-Hispanic/Latino), 6 international. Average age 33. In 2010, 45 master's awarded. *Entrance requirements:* For master's, GMAT (minimum score 425), minimum GPA of 2.75, 2 letters of recommendation. Additional exam requirements/recommendations for international students: Required—TOEFL (minimum score 213 computer-based). *Application deadline:* For fall admission, 8/26 for domestic students, 8/1 for international students; for spring admission, 1/10 for domestic students, 10/1 for international students. Applications are processed on a rolling basis. Application fee: $25. Electronic applications accepted. *Expenses:* Tuition: Part-time $719 per credit hour. *Financial support:* Career-related internships or fieldwork available. *Unit head:* Martin Preizler, Dean, 608-663-2898, Fax: 608-663-3291, E-mail: martinpreizler@edgewood.edu. *Application contact:* Joann Eastman, Admissions Counselor, 608-663-3250, Fax: 608-663-2214, E-mail: gps@edgewood.edu.

Elmhurst College, Graduate Programs, Program in Business Administration, Elmhurst, IL 60126-3296. Offers MBA. Part-time and evening/weekend programs available. *Faculty:* 1 full-time (0 women), 6 part-time/adjunct (0 women). *Students:* 67 part-time (26 women); includes 7 minority (3 Black or African American, non-Hispanic/Latino; 3 Asian, non-Hispanic/Latino; 1 Hispanic/Latino). Average age 31. 67 applicants, 63% accepted, 35 enrolled. In 2010, 35 master's awarded. *Entrance requirements:* For master's, 3 recommendations, resume, statement of purpose. Additional exam requirements/recommendations for international students: Required—TOEFL (minimum score 550 paper-based; 213 computer-based). *Application deadline:* Applications are processed on a rolling basis. Application fee: $0. Electronic applications accepted. *Expenses:* Contact institution. *Financial support:* In 2010–11, 9 students received support. Federal Work-Study and scholarships/grants available. Support available to part-time students. Financial award application deadline: 6/1; financial award applicants required to submit FAFSA. *Unit head:* Elizabeth D. Kuebler, Director of Adult and Graduate Admission, 630-617-3300, Fax: 630-617-5501, E-mail: sal@elmhurst.edu. *Application contact:* Director of Adult and Graduate Admission.

Elon University, Program in Business Administration, Elon, NC 27244-2010. Offers MBA. *Accreditation:* AACSB. Part-time and evening/weekend programs available. *Faculty:* 20 full-time (7 women), 1 (woman) part-time/adjunct. *Students:* 137 part-time (52 women); includes 11 Black or African American, non-Hispanic/Latino; 1 American Indian or Alaska Native, non-Hispanic/Latino; 7 Asian, non-Hispanic/Latino; 2 Hispanic/Latino, 10 international. Average age 31. 107 applicants, 63% accepted, 52 enrolled. In 2010, 53 master's awarded. *Entrance requirements:* For master's, GMAT. Additional exam requirements/recommendations for international students: Required—TOEFL (minimum score 550 paper-based; 213 computer-based; 79 iBT). *Application deadline:* For fall admission, 8/1 priority date for domestic students; for spring admission, 2/1 priority date for domestic students. Applications are processed on a rolling basis. Application fee: $50. Electronic applications accepted. *Financial support:* In 2010–11, 1 student received support. Federal Work-Study and scholarships/grants available. Support available to part-time students. Financial award application deadline: 3/15; financial award applicants required to submit FAFSA. *Faculty research:* Business ethics, international business and global economics, sales force management, sustainable business practices, consumer behavior. *Unit head:* Dr. William Burpitt, Director, 336-278-5949, Fax: 336-278-5952, E-mail: wburpitt@elon.edu. *Application contact:* Art Fadde, Director of Graduate Admissions, 800-334-8448 Ext. 3, Fax: 336-278-7699, E-mail: afadde@elon.edu.

Embry-Riddle Aeronautical University–Daytona, Daytona Beach Campus Graduate Program, Department of Business Administration, Daytona Beach, FL 32114-3900. Offers business administration (MBA); business administration aviation management (MBA-AM). *Accreditation:* ACBSP. Part-time programs available. Postbaccalaureate distance learning degree programs offered (minimal on-campus study). *Faculty:* 12 full-time (3 women), 3 part-time/adjunct (1 woman). *Students:* 102 full-time (29 women), 59 part-time (16 women); includes 19 minority (9 Black or African American, non-Hispanic/Latino; 4 Asian, non-Hispanic/Latino; 6 Hispanic/Latino), 56 international. Average age 29. 96 applicants, 50% accepted, 32 enrolled. In 2010, 39 master's awarded. *Degree requirements:* For master's, thesis or alternative. *Entrance requirements:* For master's, minimum GPA of 2.5. Additional exam requirements/recommendations for international students: Required—TOEFL (minimum score 550 paper-based; 213 computer-based; 79 iBT). *Application deadline:* For fall admission, 8/1 priority date for domestic students; for spring admission, 12/1 priority date for domestic students. Applications are processed on a rolling basis. Application fee: $50. *Expenses:* Tuition: Full-time $14,040; part-time $1170 per credit hour. *Financial support:* In 2010–11, 35 students received support, including 20 research assistantships with partial tuition reimbursements available (averaging $2,882 per year), 3 teaching assistantships (averaging $2,452 per year); career-related internships or fieldwork, Federal Work-Study, and unspecified assistantships also available. Support available to part-time students. Financial award application deadline: 4/15; financial award applicants required to submit FAFSA. *Faculty research:* Aircraft safety operations analysis, energy consumption analysis, statistical analysis of general aviation accidents, airport funding strategies, industry assessment and marketing analysis for ENAER aerospace. *Unit head:* Dr. Dawna Rhoades, MBA Program Coordinator, 386-226-7756, E-mail: dawna.rhoades@erau.edu. *Application contact:* Keith Deaton, Director, International and Graduate Admissions, 800-388-3728, Fax: 386-226-7070, E-mail: graduate.admissions@erau.edu.

Embry-Riddle Aeronautical University–Worldwide, Worldwide Headquarters, Program in Business Administration for Aviation, Daytona Beach, FL 32114-3900. Offers MBAA. *Faculty:* 4 full-time (1 woman), 50 part-time/adjunct (15 women). *Students:* 190 full-time (40 women), 198 part-time (26 women); includes 95 minority (34 Black or African American, non-Hispanic/Latino; 1 American Indian or Alaska Native, non-Hispanic/Latino; 12 Asian, non-Hispanic/Latino; 39 Hispanic/Latino; 1 Native Hawaiian or other Pacific Islander, non-Hispanic/Latino; 8 Two or more races, non-Hispanic/Latino), 5 international. Average age 33. 226 applicants, 65% accepted, 104 enrolled. In 2010, 28 master's awarded. *Degree requirements:* For master's, thesis (for some programs). Application fee: $50. *Financial support:* In 2010–11, 81 students received support. *Unit head:* Dr. Kees Rietsema, Department Chair, 602-904-1295, E-mail: kees.rietsema@erau.edu. *Application contact:* Linda Dammer, Director of Admissions, 386-226-6396 Ext. 1, Fax: 386-226-6984, E-mail: worldwide@erau.edu.

Emory University, Goizueta Business School, Doctoral Program in Business, Atlanta, GA 30322-1100. Offers accounting (PhD); finance (PhD); information systems (PhD); marketing (PhD); organization and management (PhD). *Faculty:* 55 full-time (11 women). *Students:* 32 full-time (17 women); includes 1 Black or African American, non-Hispanic/Latino; 17 Asian, non-Hispanic/Latino; 1 Hispanic/Latino. Average age 29. 218 applicants, 9% accepted, 9 enrolled. In 2010, 8 doctorates awarded. *Degree requirements:* For doctorate, comprehensive exam, thesis/dissertation. *Entrance requirements:* For doctorate, GMAT (strongly preferred) or GRE. Additional exam requirements/recommendations for international students: Required—TOEFL (minimum score 250 computer-based). *Application deadline:* For fall admission, 1/3 priority date for domestic students, 1/1 priority date for international students. Application fee: $50. Electronic applications accepted. *Expenses:* Tuition: Full-time $33,800. Required fees: $1300. *Financial support:* In 2010–11, 32 students received support. *Unit head:* Dr. Lawrence Benveniste, Dean, 404-727-6377, Fax: 404-727-0868, E-mail: larry benveniste@bus.emory.edu. Application contact: Allison Gilmore, Director of Admissions & Student Services, 404-727-6353, Fax: 404-727-5337, E-mail: phd@bus.emory.edu.

Emory University, Goizueta Business School, Evening MBA Program, Atlanta, GA 30322-1100. Offers MBA. Part-time and evening/weekend programs available. *Faculty:* 78 full-time (18 women), 16 part-time/adjunct (2 women). *Students:* 308 part-time (78 women); includes 79 minority (19 Black or African American, non-Hispanic/Latino; 48 Asian, non-Hispanic/Latino; 11 Hispanic/Latino; 1 Two or more races, non-Hispanic/Latino), 51 international. Average age 30. 180 applicants, 66% accepted, 84 enrolled. In 2010, 95 master's awarded. *Entrance requirements:* For master's, GMAT. Additional exam requirements/recommendations for international students: Required—TOEFL; Recommended—IELTS, TWE. *Application deadline:* For fall admission, 6/1 for domestic students. Applications are processed on a rolling basis. Application fee: $150. Electronic applications accepted. *Expenses:* Tuition:

Full-time $33,800. Required fees: $1300. *Financial support:* In 2010–11, 207 students received support. Application deadline: 4/1. *Unit head:* Dr. Lawrence Benveniste, Dean, 404-727-6377, Fax: 404-727-0868, E-mail: larry benveniste@bus.emory.edu. Application contact: Julie Barefoot, Associate Dean, 404-727-6311, Fax: 404-727-4612, E-mail: admissions@bus.emory.edu.

Emory University, Goizueta Business School, Executive MBA Program, Atlanta, GA 30322-1100. Offers MBA. Concentrations are not built into the Executive MBA Program, however, students may elect to take additional classes and complete a concentration; concentrations available are marketing, information systems, operations management, finance, organization and management, and entrepreneurship. Part-time and evening/weekend programs available. *Faculty:* 78 full-time (18 women), 16 part-time/adjunct (2 women). *Students:* 83 full-time (17 women); includes 10 Black or African American, non-Hispanic/Latino; 8 Asian, non-Hispanic/Latino; 1 Hispanic/Latino, 11 international. 85 applicants, 80% accepted, 40 enrolled. In 2010, 118 master's awarded. *Degree requirements:* For master's, completion of lock-step program with minimum of 54 credit hours, one elective course, global business practices with 10-day international travel component. *Entrance requirements:* For master's, GMAT. Additional exam requirements/recommendations for international students: Required—TOEFL (minimum score 600 paper-based; 250 computer-based; 100 iBT), IELTS (minimum score 7). *Application deadline:* For fall admission, 6/1 for domestic students; for winter admission, 10/1 for domestic students. Applications are processed on a rolling basis. Application fee: $150. Electronic applications accepted. *Expenses:* Tuition: Full-time $33,800. Required fees: $1300. *Financial support:* Applicants required to submit FAFSA. *Unit head:* Dr. Steve Walton, Associate Dean, Executive MBA Program, 404-727-3526, Fax: 404-727-4936, E-mail: steve walton@bus.emory.edu. Application contact: Joan Coonrod, Assistant Dean, Executive MBA, 404-727-6311, Fax: 404-727-4612, E-mail: joan_coonrod@bus.emory.edu.

Emory University, Goizueta Business School, Full Time MBA Program, Atlanta, GA 30322-1100. Offers MBA. *Faculty:* 74 full-time (10 women), 23 part-time/adjunct (12 women). *Students:* 366 full-time (115 women); includes 33 Black or African American, non-Hispanic/Latino; 1 American Indian or Alaska Native, non-Hispanic/Latino; 29 Asian, non-Hispanic/Latino; 18 Hispanic/Latino, 118 international. Average age 29. 1,094 applicants, 32% accepted, 134 enrolled. In 2010, 206 master's awarded. *Entrance requirements:* For master's, GMAT. Additional exam requirements/recommendations for international students: Required—TOEFL (minimum score 600 paper-based; 100 iBT), IELTS, Pearson Test of English (PTE). *Application deadline:* For fall admission, 12/1 for domestic and international students; for winter admission, 2/1 priority date for domestic and international students; for spring admission, 3/1 priority date for domestic students. Applications are processed on a rolling basis. Application fee: $150. Electronic applications accepted. *Expenses:* Tuition: Full-time $33,800. Required fees: $1300. *Financial support:* In 2010–11, 230 students received support; fellowships, research assistantships, teaching assistantships, career-related internships or fieldwork, Federal Work-Study, institutionally sponsored loans, scholarships/grants, and unspecified assistantships available. Financial award application deadline: 2/1; financial award applicants required to submit FAFSA. *Unit head:* Brian Mitchell, Associate Dean, 404-727-4824, Fax: 404-727-0868, E-mail: brian mitchell@bus.emory.edu. Application contact: Julie Barefoot, Associate Dean, 404-727-6311, Fax: 404-727-4612, E-mail: admissions@bus.emory.edu.

Emporia State University, Graduate School, School of Business, Department of Business Administration and Education, Emporia, KS 66801-5087. Offers business administration (MBA); business education (MS). *Accreditation:* NCATE (one or more programs are accredited). Part-time programs available. Postbaccalaureate distance learning degree programs offered (minimal on-campus study). *Faculty:* 18 full-time (6 women). *Students:* 95 full-time (55 women), 45 part-time (26 women); includes 8 minority (3 Black or African American, non-Hispanic/Latino; 3 Asian, non-Hispanic/Latino; 2 Hispanic/Latino), 80 international. 56 applicants, 66% accepted, 29 enrolled. In 2010, 32 master's awarded. *Entrance requirements:* For master's, GMAT (MBA), appropriate bachelor's degree. Additional exam requirements/recommendations for international students: Required—TOEFL (minimum score 520 paper-based; 133 computer-based; 68 iBT). *Application deadline:* For fall admission, 8/15 priority date for domestic students. Applications are processed on a rolling basis. Application fee: $30 ($75 for international students). Electronic applications accepted. *Expenses:* Tuition, state resident: full-time $4382; part-time $183 per credit hour. Tuition, nonresident: full-time $13,572; part-time $566 per credit hour. Required fees: $1022; $62 per credit hour. Tuition and fees vary according to course level, course load and campus/location. *Financial support:* In 2010–11, 5 research assistantships with full tuition reimbursements (averaging $6,353 per year) were awarded; career-related internships or fieldwork, Federal Work-Study, institutionally sponsored loans, health care benefits, and unspecified assistantships also available. Financial award application deadline: 3/15; financial award applicants required to submit FAFSA. *Unit head:* Dr. Jack Sterett, Chair, 620-341-5345, Fax: 620-341-6345, E-mail: jsteret@emporia.edu. *Application contact:* Dr. Donald Miller, Director, MBA Program, 620-341-5456, Fax: 620-341-6523, E-mail: dmiller1@emporia.edu.

Endicott College, Van Loan School of Graduate and Professional Studies, Program in Business Administration, Beverly, MA 01915-2096. Offers MBA. Part-time and evening/weekend programs available. *Faculty:* 3 full-time (1 woman), 22 part-time/adjunct (6 women). *Students:* 100 full-time (51 women), 65 part-time (32 women); includes 10 Black or African American, non-Hispanic/Latino; 2 Asian, non-Hispanic/Latino; 5 Hispanic/Latino, 13 international. Average age 33. 72 applicants, 74% accepted, 49 enrolled. In 2010, 82 master's awarded. *Degree requirements:* For master's, thesis, project. *Entrance requirements:* For master's, letters of recommendation, resume. Additional exam requirements/recommendations for international students: Required—TOEFL. *Application deadline:* Applications are processed on a rolling basis. Application fee: $50. *Expenses:* Contact institution. *Financial support:* Tuition waivers (full) available. Financial award applicants required to submit FAFSA. *Faculty research:* Adult learning and development, supply chain management, marketing, ethics. *Unit head:* Richard Benedetto, Associate Dean of Graduate School, 978-232-2744, Fax: 978-232-3000, E-mail: rbenedet@endicott.edu. *Application contact:* Richard Benedetto, Associate Dean of Graduate School, 978-232-2744, Fax: 978-232-3000, E-mail: rbenedet@endicott.edu.

Everest University, Program in Business Administration, Tampa, FL 33619. Offers MBA. Part-time and evening/weekend programs available. Postbaccalaureate distance learning degree programs offered (minimal on-campus study). *Faculty:* 1 (woman) part-time/adjunct. *Students:* 2 full-time (both women), 17 part-time (12 women); includes 12 minority (8 Black or African American, non-Hispanic/Latino; 3 Hispanic/Latino; 1 Two or more races, non-Hispanic/Latino). Average age 38. In 2010, 10 master's awarded. *Entrance requirements:* Additional exam requirements/recommendations for international students: Required—TOEFL (minimum score 550 paper-based; 213 computer-based). *Application deadline:* Applications are processed on a rolling basis. Application fee: $25. *Expenses:* Tuition: Full-time $12,120; part-time $55 per credit hour. Required fees: $60 per quarter. *Financial support:* Institutionally sponsored loans and scholarships/grants available. *Unit head:* James Jehs, Chair, 813-621-0041 Ext. 140, Fax: 813-623-5769, E-mail: jjehs@cci.edu. *Application contact:* Shandretta Pointer, Admissions Office, 813-621-0041 Ext. 106, Fax: 813-628-0919, E-mail: spointer@cci.edu.

Fairfield University, Charles F. Dolan School of Business, Fairfield, CT 06824-5195. Offers accounting (MBA, MS, CAS); accounting information systems (MBA); entrepreneurship (MBA); finance (MBA, MS, CAS); general management (MBA, CAS); human resource management (MBA, CAS); information systems and operations (MBA); information systems and operations management (CAS); international business (MBA, CAS); marketing (MBA, CAS); taxation (MBA, CAS). *Accreditation:* AACSB. Part-time and evening/weekend programs available. *Faculty:* 42 full-time (15 women), 8 part-time/adjunct (1 woman). *Students:* 89 full-time (32 women), 127 part-time (54 women); includes 4 Black or African American, non-Hispanic/Latino; 2 Asian, non-Hispanic/Latino; 4 Hispanic/Latino; 1 Two or more races, non-Hispanic/Latino, 17 international. Average age 29. 108 applicants, 62% accepted, 46 enrolled. In 2010, 79 master's awarded. *Degree requirements:* For master's, capstone course. *Entrance requirements:* For master's, GMAT (minimum score 500), 2 letters of reference, resume, minimum GPA of 3.0. Additional exam requirements/recommendations for international students: Required—TOEFL (minimum score 550 paper-based; 213 computer-based; 80 iBT). *Application deadline:* For fall admission, 5/15 for international students; for spring admission, 10/15 for international students. Applications are processed on a rolling basis. Application fee: $60. Electronic applications accepted. *Expenses:* Contact institution. *Financial support:* In 2010–11, 48 students received support. Scholarships/grants, unspecified assistantships, and merit based one-time entrance scholarship available. Financial award applicants required to submit FAFSA. *Faculty research:* Optimization strategies, international finance, consumer behavior, financial market volatility, Internet marketing, supply chain analysis, tax issues. Total annual research expenditures: $50,000. *Unit head:* Dr. Norman A. Solomon, Dean, 203-254-4000 Ext. 4070, Fax: 203-254-4105, E-mail: nsolomon@fairfield.edu. *Application contact:* Marianne Gumpper, Director of Graduate and Continuing Studies Admissions, 203-254-4184, Fax: 203-254-4073, E-mail: gradadmis@fairfield.edu.

Fairleigh Dickinson University, College at Florham, Anthony J. Petrocelli College of Continuing Studies, School of Administrative Science, Program in Administrative Science, Madison, NJ 07940-1099. Offers MAS. *Students:* 1 part-time (0 women). Average age 33.Application fee: $40. *Application contact:* Susan Brooman, University Director, Graduate Admissions, 973-443-8905, Fax: 973-443-8088, E-mail: grad@fdu.edu.

Fairleigh Dickinson University, College at Florham, Silberman College of Business, Madison, NJ 07940-1099. Offers EMBA, MBA, MS, Certificate, MA/MBA, MBA/MA. *Accreditation:* AACSB. Part-time and evening/weekend programs available. *Students:* 81 full-time (49 women), 305 part-time (112 women), 34 international. Average age 32. 163 applicants, 72% accepted, 62 enrolled. In 2010, 157 master's awarded. *Application deadline:* Applications are processed on a rolling basis. Application fee: $40. *Unit head:* Dr. William Moore, Dean, 973-443-8500. *Application contact:* Susan Brooman, University Director of Graduate Admissions.

Fairleigh Dickinson University, College at Florham, Silberman College of Business, Departments of Management, Marketing, and Entrepreneurial Studies, Program in Management, Madison, NJ 07940-1099. Offers evolving technology (Certificate); management (MBA); MBA/MA. *Students:* 7 full-time (5 women), 33 part-time (20 women), 4 international. Average age 30. 32 applicants, 72% accepted, 9 enrolled. In 2010, 14 master's awarded. *Application deadline:* Applications are processed on a rolling basis. Application fee: $40.

Fairleigh Dickinson University, College at Florham, Silberman College of Business, Executive MBA Programs, Executive MBA Program in Management, Madison, NJ 07940-1099. Offers EMBA. *Students:* 53 part-time (4 women), 3 international. Average age 39. 1 applicant, 100% accepted, 0 enrolled. *Application deadline:* Applications are processed on a rolling basis. Application fee: $40.

Fairleigh Dickinson University, Metropolitan Campus, Anthony J. Petrocelli College of Continuing Studies, School of Administrative Science, Program in Administrative Science, Teaneck, NJ 07666-1914. Offers MAS, Certificate. *Students:* 78 full-time (43 women), 422 part-time (197 women), 24 international. Average age 39. 191 applicants, 98% accepted, 127 enrolled. In 2010, 288 master's awarded. *Application deadline:* Applications are processed on a rolling basis. *Application contact:* Susan Brooman, University Director of Graduate Admissions, 201-692-2554, Fax: 201-692-2560, E-mail: globaleducation@fdu.edu.

Fairleigh Dickinson University, Metropolitan Campus, Silberman College of Business, Teaneck, NJ 07666-1914. Offers EMBA, MBA, MS, Certificate, MBA/MA. *Accreditation:* AACSB. *Students:* 338 full-time (136 women), 112 part-time (53 women), 221 international. Average age 28. 451 applicants, 60% accepted, 106 enrolled. In 2010, 199 master's awarded. *Entrance requirements:* For master's, GMAT. *Application deadline:* Applications are processed on a rolling basis. Application fee: $40. *Unit head:* Dr. William Moore, Dean, 201-692-2000. *Application contact:* Susan Brooman, University Director of Graduate Admissions, 201-692-2554, Fax: 201-692-2560, E-mail: global education@fdu.edu.

Fairleigh Dickinson University, Metropolitan Campus, Silberman College of Business, Departments of Management, Marketing, and Entrepreneurial Studies, Program in Management, Teaneck, NJ 07666-1914. Offers management (MBA); management information systems (Certificate). *Accreditation:* AACSB. *Students:* 28 full-time (11 women), 9 part-time (3 women), 22 international. Average age 28. 100 applicants, 52% accepted, 14 enrolled. In 2010, 18 master's awarded. *Application deadline:* Applications are processed on a rolling basis. Application fee: $40. *Application contact:* Susan Brooman, University Director of Graduate Admissions, 201-692-2554, Fax: 201-692-2560, E-mail: globaleducation@fdu.edu.

Fayetteville State University, Graduate School, Program in Business Administration, Fayetteville, NC 28301-4298. Offers MBA. *Accreditation:* AACSB. *Faculty:* 15 full-time (4 women). *Students:* 10 full-time (5 women), 36 part-time (18 women); includes 17 Black or African American, non-Hispanic/Latino; 3 Asian, non-Hispanic/Latino; 4 Hispanic/Latino; 1 Native Hawaiian or other Pacific Islander, non-Hispanic/Latino, 2 international. Average age 33. 13 applicants, 100% accepted, 11 enrolled. In 2010, 21 master's awarded. *Entrance requirements:* For master's, GMAT. *Application deadline:* For fall admission, 4/15 for domestic students; for spring admission, 10/15 for domestic students. *Faculty research:* Business ethics, optimization and business simulation, consumer behavior, e-commerce and supply chain management, financial institutions. Total annual research expenditures: $15,000. *Unit head:* Dr. Assad Tavakoli, MBA Director/Assistant Dean, 910-672-1527, Fax: 910-672-1849, E-mail: atavakoli@uncfsu.edu. *Application contact:* Katrina Hoffman, Graduate Admissions Officer, 910-672-1374, Fax: 910-672-1470, E-mail: khoffma1@uncfsu.edu.

Ferris State University, College of Business, Big Rapids, MI 49307. Offers application development (MSISM); business intelligence and informatics (MBA); database administration (MSISM); design and innovation management process (MBA); e-business (MSISM); networking (MSISM); quality management (MBA); security (MSISM). *Accreditation:* ACBSP. Part-time and evening/weekend programs available. *Faculty:* 10 full-time (3 women), 2 part-time/adjunct (both women). *Students:* 34 full-time (9 women), 112 part-time (55 women); includes 3 Black or African American, non-Hispanic/Latino; 4 American Indian or Alaska Native, non-Hispanic/Latino; 3 Asian, non-Hispanic/Latino; 3 Hispanic/Latino; 4 Two or more races, non-Hispanic/Latino, 16 international. Average age 32. 68 applicants, 35% accepted, 15 enrolled. In 2010, 62 master's awarded. *Degree requirements:* For master's, comprehensive exam, thesis (for MSISM). *Entrance requirements:* For master's, GRE or GMAT (waived if GPA is 3.5 or better), minimum GPA of 3.0 in junior/senior level classes, 2.75 overall; writing sample; 3 letters of reference; resume. Additional exam requirements/recommendations for international students: Required—TOEFL (minimum score 500 paper-based; 173 computer-based; 67 iBT). *Application deadline:* For fall admission, 7/1 priority date for domestic students, 6/15 for international students; for winter admission, 11/1 priority date for domestic students, 10/15 for international students; for spring admission, 3/1 priority date for domestic students, 2/15 for international students. Applications are processed on a rolling basis. Application fee: $30. Electronic applications accepted. *Financial support:*

Career-related internships or fieldwork, Federal Work-Study, scholarships/grants, and unspecified assistantships available. Support available to part-time students. Financial award application deadline: 3/15; financial award applicants required to submit FAFSA. *Faculty research:* Quality improvement, client/server end-user computing, information management and policy, security, digital forensics. *Unit head:* Dr. David Steenstra, Department Chair, 231-591-2168, Fax: 231-591-3548, E-mail: yosts@ferris.edu. *Application contact:* Shannon Yost, Department Secretary, 231-591-2168, Fax: 231-591-3548, E-mail: yosts@ferris.edu.

Fitchburg State University, Division of Graduate and Continuing Education, Program in Business Administration, Fitchburg, MA 01420-2697. Offers accounting (MBA); human resource management (MBA); management (MBA). Part-time and evening/weekend programs available. Postbaccalaureate distance learning degree programs offered (no on-campus study). *Students:* 24 full-time (11 women), 74 part-time (46 women); includes 6 Black or African American, non-Hispanic/Latino; 1 American Indian or Alaska Native, non-Hispanic/Latino; 5 Hispanic/Latino, 13 international. Average age 33. 42 applicants, 98% accepted, 33 enrolled. In 2010, 59 master's awarded. *Entrance requirements:* For master's, GMAT, minimum GPA of 2.8, letters of recommendation, resume. Additional exam requirements/recommendations for international students: Required—TOEFL (minimum score 550 paper-based; 213 computer-based; 79 iBT). *Application deadline:* Applications are processed on a rolling basis. Application fee: $25 ($50 for international students). *Expenses:* Tuition, area resident: Part-time $150 per credit. Tuition, state resident: part-time $150 per credit. Tuition, nonresident: part-time $150 per credit. Required fees: $127 per credit. *Financial support:* In 2010–11, research assistantships with partial tuition reimbursements (averaging $5,500 per year); Federal Work-Study, scholarships/grants, and unspecified assistantships also available. Support available to part-time students. Financial award application deadline: 3/1; financial award applicants required to submit FAFSA. *Unit head:* Joseph McAloon, Chair, 978-665-3745, Fax: 978-665-3658, E-mail: gce@fitchburgstate.edu. *Application contact:* Director of Admissions, 978-665-3144, Fax: 978-665-4540, E-mail: admissions@fitchburgstate.edu.

Florida Atlantic University, College of Business, Boca Raton, FL 33431-0991. Offers Exec MBA, M Ac, M Tax, MBA, MHA, MS, PhD, Certificate. *Accreditation:* AACSB. Part-time and evening/weekend programs available. Postbaccalaureate distance learning degree programs offered (minimal on-campus study). *Faculty:* 134 full-time (45 women), 87 part-time/adjunct (23 women). *Students:* 440 full-time (216 women), 825 part-time (414 women); includes 420 minority (138 Black or African American, non-Hispanic/Latino; 79 Asian, non-Hispanic/Latino; 182 Hispanic/Latino; 1 Native Hawaiian or other Pacific Islander, non-Hispanic/Latino; 20 Two or more races, non-Hispanic/Latino), 59 international. Average age 31. 860 applicants, 43% accepted, 289 enrolled. In 2010, 369 master's, 6 doctorates awarded. *Degree requirements:* For master's, thesis optional; for doctorate, comprehensive exam, thesis/dissertation. *Entrance requirements:* For master's, GMAT, minimum GPA of 3.0; for doctorate, GMAT, minimum graduate GPA of 3.5. Additional exam requirements/recommendations for international students: Required—TOEFL (minimum score 600 paper-based; 250 computer-based). *Application deadline:* For fall admission, 7/15 priority date for domestic students, 2/15 priority date for international students; for winter admission, 11/1 priority date for domestic students, 8/15 priority date for international students; for spring admission, 4/1 priority date for domestic students, 1/15 priority date for international students. Applications are processed on a rolling basis. Application fee: $30. *Expenses:* Tuition, area resident: Part-time $319.96 per credit. Tuition, state resident: part-time $319.96 per credit. Tuition, nonresident: part-time $926.42 per credit. *Financial support:* Fellowships with partial tuition reimbursements, research assistantships with partial tuition reimbursements, teaching assistantships with full tuition reimbursements, career-related internships or fieldwork, Federal Work-Study, institutionally sponsored loans, tuition waivers (full and partial), and unspecified assistantships available. Support available to part-time students. Financial award application deadline: 3/1. *Faculty research:* International business, MIS, financial decision-making, marketing policy, strategy. *Unit head:* Dr. Dennis Coates, Dean, 561-297-3635, Fax: 561-297-3686, E-mail: coates@fau.edu. *Application contact:* Fredrick G. Taylor, Graduate Adviser, 561-297-3196, Fax: 561-297-1315, E-mail: ftaylor@fau.edu.

Florida Gulf Coast University, Lutgert College of Business, Master of Business Administration Program, Fort Myers, FL 33965-6565. Offers MBA. *Accreditation:* AACSB. Part-time and evening/weekend programs available. *Faculty:* 64 full-time (21 women), 5 part-time/adjunct (1 woman). *Students:* 142 full-time (63 women), 48 part-time (23 women); includes 5 Black or African American, non-Hispanic/Latino; 1 American Indian or Alaska Native, non-Hispanic/Latino; 6 Asian, non-Hispanic/Latino; 16 Hispanic/Latino, 6 international. Average age 29. 112 applicants, 59% accepted, 43 enrolled. In 2010, 57 master's awarded. *Entrance requirements:* For master's, GMAT, minimum GPA of 3.0. Additional exam requirements/recommendations for international students: Required—TOEFL (minimum score 550 paper-based; 213 computer-based). *Application deadline:* For fall admission, 6/1 priority date for domestic students; for spring admission, 11/1 for domestic students. Applications are processed on a rolling basis. Application fee: $30. Electronic

applications accepted. *Expenses:* Tuition, state resident: part-time $322.08 per credit hour. Tuition, nonresident: part-time $1117.08 per credit hour. *Faculty research:* Fraud in audits, production planning in cell manufacturing systems, collaborative learning in distance courses, characteristics of minority and women-owned businesses. *Unit head:* Dr. Gerald Schoenfeld, Chair, 239-590-7300, Fax: 239-590-7330. *Application contact:* Marissa Ouverson, Director of Enrollment Management, 239-590-7403, Fax: 239-590-7330, E-mail: mouverso@fgcu.edu.

Florida Institute of Technology, Graduate Programs, Extended Studies Division, Melbourne, FL 32901-6975. Offers acquisition and contract management (MS); aerospace engineering (MS); business administration (MBA); computer information systems (MS); computer science (MS); electrical engineering (MS); engineering management (MS); human resources management (MS); logistics management (MS), including humanitarian and disaster relief logistics; management (MS), including acquisition and contract management, e-business, human resources management, information systems, logistics management, management, transportation management; material acquisition management (MS); mechanical engineering (MS); operations research (MS); project management (MS), including information systems, operations research; public administration (MPA); quality management (MS); software engineering (MS); space systems (MS); space systems management (MS); systems management (MS), including information systems, operations research. Part-time and evening/weekend programs available. Postbaccalaureate distance learning degree programs offered (no on-campus study). *Faculty:* 11 full-time (3 women), 118 part-time/adjunct (24 women). *Students:* 69 full-time (23 women), 907 part-time (369 women); includes 385 minority (242 Black or African American, non-Hispanic/Latino; 15 American Indian or Alaska Native, non-Hispanic/Latino; 44 Asian, non-Hispanic/Latino; 52 Hispanic/Latino; 3 Native Hawaiian or other Pacific Islander, non-Hispanic/Latino; 29 Two or more races, non-Hispanic/Latino), 17 international. 517 applicants, 49% accepted, 245 enrolled. In 2010, 430 degrees awarded. *Degree requirements:* For master's, comprehensive exam (for some programs), capstone course. *Entrance requirements:* For master's, GMAT or resume showing 8 years of supervised experience, minimum GPA of 3.0, 2 letters of recommendation, resume. Additional exam requirements/recommendations for international students: Required—TOEFL (minimum score 550 paper-based; 213 computer-based; 79 iBT). *Application deadline:* For fall admission, 4/1 for international students; for spring admission, 9/30 for international students. Applications are processed on a rolling basis. Application fee: $50. Electronic applications accepted. *Financial support:* Application deadline: 3/1. *Unit head:* Dr. Theodore Richardson, Senior Associate Dean, 321-674-8123, Fax: 321-674-7597, E-mail: trichardson@fit.edu. *Application contact:* Carolyn Farrior, Director of Graduate Admissions, Online Learning and Off-Campus Programs, 321-674-7118, Fax: 321-674-8216, E-mail: cfarrior@fit.edu.

Florida International University, Alvah H. Chapman, Jr. Graduate School of Business, Program in Business Administration, Miami, FL 33199. Offers EMBA, IMBA, MBA, PMBA, PhD. *Accreditation:* AACSB. Part-time and evening/weekend programs available. *Faculty:* 6 part-time/adjunct (5 women). *Students:* 703 full-time (347 women), 500 part-time (258 women); includes 140 Black or African American, non-Hispanic/Latino; 3 American Indian or Alaska Native, non-Hispanic/Latino; 42 Asian, non-Hispanic/Latino; 530 Hispanic/Latino; 1 Native Hawaiian or other Pacific Islander, non-Hispanic/Latino, 238 international. Average age 33. 2,101 applicants, 47% accepted, 830 enrolled. In 2010, 391 master's, 8 doctorates awarded. *Degree requirements:* For doctorate, comprehensive exam, thesis/dissertation. *Entrance requirements:* For master's, GMAT or GRE (depending on program), minimum GPA of 3.0 (upper-level coursework); for doctorate, GMAT or GRE, minimum GPA of 3.0 in post-secondary education; letter of intent; 3 letters of recommendation; resume. Additional exam requirements/recommendations for international students: Required—TOEFL (minimum score 550 paper-based; 213 computer-based; 80 iBT) or IELTS (minimum score 6.5). *Application deadline:* For fall admission, 6/1 for domestic students, 4/1 for international students; for spring admission, 10/1 for domestic students, 9/1 for international students. Applications are processed on a rolling basis. Application fee: $30. Electronic applications accepted. *Expenses:* Contact institution. *Financial support:* Institutionally sponsored loans, scholarships/grants, and unspecified assistantships available. Financial award application deadline: 3/1; financial award applicants required to submit FAFSA. *Faculty research:* Taxation, financial and managerial accounting, human resource management, multinational corporations, strategy, international business, auditing, artificial intelligence, international banking, investments, entrepreneurship. *Unit head:* Dr. Christos Koulamas, Senior Associate Dean, 305-348-2830, Fax: 305-348-4126, E-mail: koulamas@fiu.edu. *Application contact:* Anna Pietraszek, Director of Admissions and Recruiting, Chapman Graduate School of Business, 305-348-7299, Fax: 305-348-2368, E-mail: pietrasa@fiu.edu.

Florida Southern College, Program in Business Administration, Lakeland, FL 33801-5698. Offers MBA. Part-time and evening/weekend programs available. *Faculty:* 14 full-time (2 women), 1 part-time/adjunct (0 women). *Students:* 27 full-time (8 women), 16 part-time (8 women); includes 2 Black or African American, non-Hispanic/Latino; 1 Hispanic/Latino, 4 international.

Average age 26. 41 applicants, 51% accepted, 19 enrolled. In 2010, 9 master's awarded. *Entrance requirements:* For master's, GMAT or GRE General Test, 3 letters of reference, resume, personal statement. Additional exam requirements/recommendations for international students: Required—TOEFL (minimum score 550 paper-based). *Application deadline:* For fall admission, 6/1 for domestic and international students. Applications are processed on a rolling basis. Application fee: $30. *Expenses:* Contact institution. *Financial support:* In 2010–11, 6 students received support. Scholarships/grants available. Support available to part-time students. Financial award applicants required to submit FAFSA. *Unit head:* Dr. Larry Ross, Program Coordinator, 863-680-4285, Fax: 863-680-4355, E-mail: lross@flsouthern.edu. *Application contact:* Kathy Connelly, Evening Program Assistant Director, 863-680-4205, Fax: 863-680-3872, E-mail: cconnelly@flsouthern.edu.

See Display on this page and Close-Up on page 255.

Florida State University, The Graduate School, College of Business, Tallahassee, FL 32306-1110. Offers accounting (M Acc), including accounting information services, assurance services, corporate accounting, taxation; business administration (MBA, PhD), including accounting (PhD), finance (PhD), management information systems (PhD), marketing (PhD), organizational behavior (PhD), risk management and insurance (PhD), strategic management (PhD); finance (MS); insurance (MSM); management information systems (MS); JD/MBA; MSW/MBA. *Accreditation:* AACSB. Part-time programs available. Postbaccalaureate distance learning degree programs offered (no on-campus study). *Faculty:* 107 full-time (31 women). *Students:* 196 full-time (76 women), 310 part-time (109 women); includes 27 Black or African American, non-Hispanic/Latino; 1 American Indian or Alaska Native, non-Hispanic/Latino; 31 Asian, non-Hispanic/Latino; 30 Hispanic/Latino. Average age 30. 702 applicants, 33% accepted, 205 enrolled. In 2010, 268 master's, 17 doctorates awarded. Terminal master's awarded for partial completion of doctoral program. *Degree requirements:* For doctorate, comprehensive exam, thesis/dissertation. *Entrance requirements:* For master's, GMAT, work experience (MBA, MS), minimum GPA of 3.0, letters of recommendation; for doctorate, GMAT, minimum graduate GPA of 3.5, letters of recommendation. Additional exam requirements/recommendations for international students: Required—TOEFL (minimum score 600 paper-based; 80 computer-based); Recommended—IELTS (minimum score 6.5). *Application deadline:* For fall admission, 6/1 for domestic students, 5/1 for international students; for spring admission, 10/1 for domestic students, 9/1 for international students. Applications are processed on a rolling basis. Application fee: $30. Electronic applications accepted. *Expenses:* Tuition, state resident: full-time $8238.24. *Financial support:* In 2010–11, 86 students received support, including 12 fellowships with full tuition reimbursements available (averaging $7,161 per year), 30 research assistantships with full tuition reimbursements available (averaging $6,000 per year), 43 teaching assistantships with full tuition reimbursements available (averaging $15,000 per year); career-related internships or fieldwork, scholarships/grants, health care benefits, tuition waivers (full and partial), and unspecified assistantships also available. Support available to part-time students. Financial award application deadline: 1/1. *Unit head:* Dr. Caryn Beck-Dudley, Dean, 850-644-3090, Fax: 850-644-0915. *Application contact:* Lisa Beverly, Director, Graduate Programs Admissions, 850-644-6458, Fax: 850-644-0588, E-mail: lbeverly@cob.fsu.edu.

Fontbonne University, Graduate Programs, College of Global Business and Professional Studies, Options Program in Business Administration, St. Louis, MO 63105-3098. Offers MBA. *Accreditation:* ACBSP. Evening/weekend programs available. *Faculty:* 1 full-time (0 women), 11 part-time/adjunct (4 women). *Students:* 81 full-time (54 women), 118 part-time (77 women); includes 87 Black or African American, non-Hispanic/Latino; 1 American Indian or Alaska Native, non-Hispanic/Latino; 3 Asian, non-Hispanic/Latino; 1 Hispanic/Latino, 32 international. Average age 34. In 2010, 148 master's awarded. *Degree requirements:* For master's, applied management project. *Entrance requirements:* For master's, minimum GPA of 2.5. *Application deadline:* For fall admission, 8/1 priority date for domestic students. Applications are processed on a rolling basis. Application fee: $25. *Expenses:* Contact institution. *Financial support:* Application deadline: 4/1. *Unit head:* Dean Linda Maurer, Executive Director, 314-889-1423, E-mail: lmaurer@fontbonne.edu. *Application contact:* OPTIONS, 314-863-2220, E-mail: options@fontbonne.edu.

Fontbonne University, Graduate Programs, College of Global Business and Professional Studies, Options Program in Management, St. Louis, MO 63105-3098. Offers MM. *Accreditation:* ACBSP. Part-time and evening/weekend programs available. Postbaccalaureate distance learning degree programs offered. *Faculty:* 16 part-time/adjunct (4 women). *Students:* 36 full-time (31 women), 86 part-time (63 women); includes 67 Black or African American, non-Hispanic/Latino, 1 international. Average age 39. In 2010, 64 master's awarded. *Application deadline:* For fall admission, 8/1 priority date for domestic students. Applications are processed on a rolling basis. Application fee: $25. *Expenses:* Contact institution. *Financial support:* Application deadline: 4/1. *Unit head:* Dean Linda Maurer, Dean of the College of Global Business and Professional Studies, 314-889-1423, Fax: 314-963-0327, E-mail: lmaurer@fontbonne.edu. *Application contact:* Fontbonne University OPTIONS, 314-863-2220, E-mail: options@fontbonne.edu.

Fontbonne University, Graduate Programs, College of Global Business and Professional Studies, Program in Business Administration, St. Louis, MO 63105-3098. Offers MBA. *Accreditation:* ACBSP. Part-time and evening/weekend programs available. *Faculty:* 1 (woman) full-time, 18 part-time/adjunct (6 women). *Students:* 39 full-time (19 women), 21 part-time (10 women); includes 11 Black or African American, non-Hispanic/Latino; 1 Asian, non-Hispanic/Latino, 29 international. Average age 31. In 2010, 25 master's awarded. *Entrance requirements:* For master's, minimum GPA of 2.5. Additional exam requirements/recommendations for international students: Required—TOEFL (minimum score 450 paper-based; 133 computer-based; 45 iBT). *Application deadline:* For fall admission, 8/1 priority date for domestic and international students. Applications are processed on a rolling basis. Application fee: $25. *Expenses:* Tuition: Full-time $11,328. Full-time tuition and fees vary according to program. *Financial support:* Application deadline: 4/1. *Unit head:* Dr. Linda Maurer, Dean of College of Global Business and Professional Studies, 314-889-1423, E-mail: lmaurer@fontbonne.edu. *Application contact:* Fontbonne University OPTIONS, 314-863-2220, Fax: 314-963-0327, E-mail: options@fontbonne.edu.

Francis Marion University, Graduate Programs, School of Business, Florence, SC 29502-0547. Offers business (MBA); health management (MBA). *Accreditation:* AACSB. Part-time and evening/weekend programs available. *Faculty:* 17 full-time (4 women). *Students:* 9 full-time (6 women), 40 part-time (14 women); includes 11 Black or African American, non-Hispanic/Latino; 1 Hispanic/Latino, 3 international. Average age 30. 18 applicants, 100% accepted, 12 enrolled. In 2010, 15 master's awarded. *Degree requirements:* For master's, comprehensive exam. *Entrance requirements:* For master's, GMAT. *Application deadline:* For fall admission, 3/15 priority date for domestic students; for spring admission, 10/15 priority date for domestic students. Applications are processed on a rolling basis. Application fee: $30. *Expenses:* Tuition, state resident: full-time $8667; part-time $433.35 per credit hour. Tuition, nonresident: full-time $17,334; part-time $866.70 per credit hour. Required fees: $335; $12.25 per credit hour. $30 per semester. *Financial support:* Research assistantships, unspecified assistantships available. Support available to part-time students. Financial award application deadline: 3/1; financial award applicants required to submit FAFSA. *Faculty research:* Ethics, directions of MBA, international business, regional economics, environmental issues. *Unit head:* Dr. M. Barry O'Brien, Dean, 843-661-1419, Fax: 843-661-1432, E-mail: mbobrien@fmarion.edu. *Application contact:* Dr. M. Barry O'Brien, Dean, 843-661-1419, Fax: 843-661-1432, E-mail: mbobrien@fmarion.edu.

Franklin Pierce University, Graduate Studies, Rindge, NH 03461-0060. Offers curriculum and instruction (M Ed); emerging network technology (Graduate Certificate); health administration (MBA, Graduate Certificate); human resource management (MBA, Graduate Certificate); information technology management (MS); leadership (MBA, DA); nursing (MS); physical therapy (DPT); physician assistant studies (MPAS); special education (M Ed); sports management (MS). *Accreditation:* APTA. Part-time programs available. Postbaccalaureate distance learning degree programs offered (no on-campus study). *Faculty:* 28 full-time (18 women), 72 part-time/adjunct (44 women). *Students:* 100 full-time (63 women), 487 part-time (306 women); includes 42 minority (25 Black or African American, non-Hispanic/Latino; 10 Asian, non-Hispanic/Latino; 6 Hispanic/Latino; 1 Two or more races, non-Hispanic/Latino), 67 international. Average age 38. 227 applicants, 97% accepted, 185 enrolled. In 2010, 76 master's, 46 doctorates awarded. *Degree requirements:* For master's, concentrated original research projects; student teaching; fieldwork and/or internship; leadership project; PRAXIS I and II (for M Ed); for doctorate, concentrated original research projects, clinical fieldwork and/or internship, leadership project. *Entrance requirements:* For master's, minimum GPA of 2.5, 3 letters of recommendation; competencies in accounting, economics, statistics, and computer skills through life experience or undergraduate coursework (for MBA); certification/e-portfolio, minimum C grade in all education courses (for M Ed); license to practice as RN (for MS in nursing); for doctorate, GRE, BA/BS, 3 letters of recommendation, personal mission statement, interview; writing sample (for DA program)For DPT: 80 hours of observation/work in PT settings, completion of anatomy, chemistry, physics, an statistics, all > 3.0 GPAFor DA: 2.8 cum. GPA, Master's degree completion. Additional exam requirements/recommendations for international students: Required—TOEFL (minimum score 550 paper-based; 195 computer-based; 61 iBT). *Application deadline:* Applications are processed on a rolling basis. Application fee: $0. Electronic applications accepted. *Expenses:* Tuition: Part-time $573 per credit hour. Part-time tuition and fees vary according to degree level and program. *Financial support:* In 2010–11, 121 students received support, including 32 teaching assistantships with full and partial tuition reimbursements available (averaging $8,000 per year); career-related internships or fieldwork and unspecified assistantships also available. Support available to part-time students. Financial award applicants required to submit FAFSA. *Faculty research:* Evidence-based practice in sports physical therapy, human resource management in economic crisis, leadership in nursing, innovation in sports facility management, differentiated learning and understanding by design. *Unit head:* Dr. Patricia Brown, Interim Dean of Graduate and Professional Studies, 603-899-4316, Fax: 603-229-4580, E-mail: brownp@franklinpierce.edu.

Franklin University, Graduate School of Business, Columbus, OH 43215-5399. Offers MBA. Part-time and evening/weekend programs available. Postbaccalaureate distance learning degree programs offered (no on-campus study). *Students:* 585 full-time (316 women), 158 part-time (95 women); includes 132 minority (106 Black or African American, non-Hispanic/Latino; 18 Asian, non-Hispanic/Latino; 8 Hispanic/Latino), 65 international. Average age 33. In 2010, 368 master's awarded. *Entrance requirements:* For master's, minimum undergraduate GPA of 2.75. Additional exam requirements/recommendations for international students: Required—TOEFL (minimum score 550 paper-based; 213 computer-based). *Application deadline:* For fall admission, 9/1 priority date for domestic students, 6/1 for international students; for winter admission, 1/15 priority date for domestic students, 10/1 for international students; for spring admission, 4/15 priority date for domestic students, 2/1 for international students. Applications are processed on a rolling basis. Application fee: $30. Electronic applications accepted. *Expenses:* Tuition: Full-time $9720; part-time $540 per credit hour. One-time fee: $30. Tuition and fees vary according to program. *Financial support:* Application deadline: 6/15. *Unit head:* Dr. Doug Ross, Program Chair, 614-947-6149, Fax: 614-224-4025. *Application contact:* Graduate Services Office, 614-797-4700, Fax: 614-221-7723, E-mail: gradschl@franklin.edu.

Friends University, Graduate School, Wichita, KS 67213. Offers accounting (MBA); business administration (MBA); business law (MBL); Christian ministry (MACM); family therapy (MSFT); global leadership and management (MA); health care leadership (MHCL); management information systems (MMIS); operations management (MSOM); organization development (MSOD); teaching (MAT). Part-time and evening/weekend programs available. Postbaccalaureate distance learning degree programs offered (minimal on-campus study). *Faculty:* 14 full-time (5 women), 2 part-time/adjunct (1 woman). *Students:* 166 full-time (122 women), 507 part-time (290 women); includes 134 minority (64 Black or African American, non-Hispanic/Latino; 6 American Indian or Alaska Native, non-Hispanic/Latino; 24 Asian, non-Hispanic/Latino; 30 Hispanic/Latino; 1 Native Hawaiian or other Pacific Islander, non-Hispanic/Latino; 9 Two or more races, non-Hispanic/Latino). Average age 38. 445 applicants, 69% accepted, 236 enrolled. In 2010, 345 master's awarded. *Degree requirements:* For master's, research project. *Entrance requirements:* Additional exam requirements/recommendations for international students: Required—TOEFL (minimum score 560 paper-based; 220 computer-based). *Application deadline:* Applications are processed on a rolling basis. Application fee: $45 ($65 for international students). Electronic applications accepted. Tuition and fees vary according to course load, campus/location and program. *Financial support:* Applicants required to submit FAFSA. *Unit head:* Dr. Evelyn Hume, Dean, 800-794-6945 Ext. 5859, Fax: 316-295-5040, E-mail: evelyn hume@friends.edu. Application contact: Jeanette Hanson, Executive Director of Adult Recruitment, 800-794-6945, Fax: 316-295-5050, E-mail: jeanette@friends.edu.

Gannon University, School of Graduate Studies, College of Engineering and Business, School of Business, Program in Business Administration, Erie, PA 16541-0001. Offers MBA. *Accreditation:* ACBSP. Part-time and evening/weekend programs available. Postbaccalaureate distance learning degree programs offered (no on-campus study). *Students:* 49 full-time (25 women), 59 part-time (31 women); includes 5 minority (4 Black or African American, non-Hispanic/Latino; 1 Asian, non-Hispanic/Latino), 11 international. Average age 32. 143 applicants, 71% accepted, 23 enrolled. In 2010, 27 master's awarded. *Degree requirements:* For master's, comprehensive exam, thesis. *Entrance requirements:* For master's, GMAT or GRE. Additional exam requirements/recommendations for international students: Required—TOEFL (minimum score 79 iBT). *Application deadline:* Applications are processed on a rolling basis. Application fee: $25. Electronic applications accepted. *Expenses:* Tuition: Full-time $14,670; part-time $815 per credit. Required fees: $430; $18 per credit. Tuition and fees vary according to class time, course load, degree level, campus/location and program. *Financial support:* Career-related internships or fieldwork, scholarships/grants, and administrative assistantships available. Financial award application deadline: 7/1; financial award applicants required to submit FAFSA. *Unit head:* Dr. Duane Prokop, Director, 814-871-7576, E-mail: prokop001@gannon.edu. *Application contact:* Kara Morgan, Assistant Director of Graduate Admissions, 814-871-5831, Fax: 814-871-5827, E-mail: graduate@gannon.edu.

Gannon University, School of Graduate Studies, College of Engineering and Business, School of Business, Program in Risk Management, Erie, PA 16541-0001. Offers Certificate. Part-time and evening/weekend programs available. *Entrance requirements:* For degree, GMAT. Additional exam requirements/recommendations for international students: Required—TOEFL (minimum score 79 iBT). *Application deadline:* Applications are processed on a rolling basis. Application fee: $25. Electronic applications accepted. *Expenses:* Tuition: Full-time $14,670; part-time $815 per credit. Required fees: $430; $18 per credit. Tuition and fees vary according to class time, course load, degree level, campus/location and program. *Financial support:* Application deadline: 7/1. *Unit head:* Dr. Duane Prokop, Director, 814-871-7567, E-mail: prokop001@gannon.edu. *Application contact:* Kara Morgan, Assistant Director of Graduate Admissions, 814-871-5831, Fax: 814-871-5827, E-mail: graduate@gannon.edu.

Gardner-Webb University, Graduate School of Business, Boiling Springs, NC 28017. Offers IMBA, M Acc, MBA. *Accreditation:* ACBSP. Part-time and evening/weekend programs available. Postbaccalaureate distance learning degree programs offered (no on-campus study). *Faculty:* 14 full-time (3 women), 3 part-time/adjunct (0 women). *Students:* 38 full-time (16 women), 370 part-time (205 women); includes 87 Black or African American, non-Hispanic/Latino; 1 American Indian or Alaska Native, non-Hispanic/Latino; 9 Asian, non-Hispanic/Latino; 5 Hispanic/Latino, 3 international. Average age 35. 147 applicants, 80% accepted, 116 enrolled. In 2010, 145 master's awarded. *Entrance requirements:* For master's, GMAT, 2 semesters of course work each in economics, statistics, and accounting. *Application deadline:* For fall admission, 8/25 for domestic students; for spring admission, 1/15 for domestic students. Applications are processed on a rolling basis. Application fee: $40. Electronic applications accepted. *Expenses:* Contact institution. *Financial support:* In 2010–11, 23 students received support. Unspecified assistantships available. Support available to part-time students. Financial award applicants required to submit FAFSA. *Unit head:* Dr. Anthony Negbenebor, Director, 704-406-4622, Fax: 704-406-3895, E-mail: anegbenebor@gardner-webb.edu. *Application contact:* Jeremy J. Fern, Director of Admissions, 800-457-4622, Fax: 704-434-3895, E-mail: jfern@gardner-webb.edu.

George Fox University, School of Business, Newberg, OR 97132-2697. Offers finance (MBA); management (DBA); management/general (MBA); marketing (DBA); organizational strategy (MBA); strategic human resource management (MBA). MBA offered part-time and full-time, also offered in Portland, OR, and Boise, ID. Part-time and evening/weekend programs available. Postbaccalaureate distance learning degree programs offered (minimal on-campus study). *Faculty:* 9 full-time (2 women), 8 part-time/adjunct (3 women). *Students:* 21 full-time (7 women), 247 part-time (87 women); includes 4 Black or African American, non-Hispanic/Latino; 2 American Indian or Alaska Native, non-Hispanic/Latino; 13 Asian, non-Hispanic/Latino; 13 Hispanic/Latino; 2 Two or more races, non-Hispanic/Latino, 12 international. Average age 37. 101 applicants, 93% accepted, 72 enrolled. In 2010, 82 master's awarded. *Degree requirements:* For master's, capstone project; for doctorate, credit-applied research project. *Entrance requirements:* For master's, resume (5 years professional experience required); 3 professional references; interview; financial e-learning course; for doctorate, GRE or GMAT, resume; personal mission statement; academic research writing sample; official transcript from each college/university attended; three professional references. Additional exam requirements/recommendations for international students: Required—TOEFL (minimum score 577 paper-based; 233 computer-based; 90 iBT) or IELTS (minimum score 7). *Application deadline:* For fall admission, 8/1 for domestic and international students; for spring admission, 12/1 for domestic and international students. Applications are processed on a rolling basis. Application fee: $40. Electronic applications accepted. *Expenses:* Contact institution. *Financial support:* In 2010–11, 2 students received support. Applicants required to submit FAFSA. *Unit head:* Dr. Dirk Barram, Professor/Dean, 800-631-0921. *Application contact:* Robin Halverson, Admissions Counselor, 800-493-4937, Fax: 503-554-6111, E-mail: mba@georgefox.edu.

George Mason University, School of Management, Program in Business Administration, Fairfax, VA 22030. Offers MBA. *Accreditation:* AACSB. Part-time and evening/weekend programs available. *Faculty:* 80 full-time (26 women), 51 part-time/adjunct (15 women). *Students:* 86 full-time (41 women), 301 part-time (91 women); includes 9 Black or African American, non-Hispanic/Latino; 1 American Indian or Alaska Native, non-Hispanic/Latino; 30 Asian, non-Hispanic/Latino; 9 Hispanic/Latino; 2 Two or more races, non-Hispanic/Latino, 33 international. Average age 30. 328 applicants, 59% accepted, 112 enrolled. In 2010, 119 master's awarded. *Entrance requirements:* For master's, GMAT, college-level calculus course, 2 years of work experience, letters of recommendation, interview with director. Additional exam requirements/recommendations for international students: Required—TOEFL (minimum score 570 paper-based; 230 computer-based; 88 iBT). *Application deadline:* For fall admission, 3/15 priority date for domestic students. Applications are processed on a rolling basis. Application fee: $100. Electronic applications accepted. *Expenses:* Tuition, state resident: full-time $8192; part-time $440 per credit hour. Tuition, nonresident: full-time $22,952; part-time $1055 per credit hour. Required fees: $2364; $99 per credit hour. *Financial support:* In 2010–11, 34 students received support, including 17 research assistantships with full and partial tuition reimbursements available (averaging $7,088 per year), 19 teaching assistantships with full and partial tuition reimbursements available (averaging $7,226 per year); career-related internships or fieldwork, Federal Work-Study, scholarships/grants, unspecified assistantships, and health care benefits (full-time research or teaching assistantship recipients) also available. Support available to part-time students. Financial award application deadline: 3/1; financial award applicants required to submit FAFSA. *Faculty research:* Electronic commerce, marketing information systems, group decision making, corporate governance, risk management. *Unit head:* Angel Burgos, Director, 703-993-8949, Fax: 703-993-1778, E-mail: aburgos2@gmu.edu. *Application contact:* Lynda Carmichael, Program Manager, 703-993-4457, E-mail: lcarmic1@gmu.edu.

The George Washington University, School of Business, Washington, DC 20052. Offers M Accy, MBA, MS, MSF, MSIST, MTA, PMBA, PhD, Professional Certificate, JD/MBA, JD/MPA, MBA/MA. PMBA program also offered in Alexandria and Ashburn, VA. Part-time and evening/weekend programs available. *Faculty:* 126 full-time (40 women), 57 part-time/adjunct (15 women). *Students:* 961 full-time (448 women), 961 part-time (433 women); includes 458 minority (173 Black or African American, non-Hispanic/Latino; 11 American Indian or Alaska Native, non-Hispanic/Latino; 178 Asian, non-Hispanic/Latino; 87 Hispanic/Latino; 3 Native Hawaiian or other Pacific Islander, non-Hispanic/Latino; 6 Two or more races, non-Hispanic/Latino), 390 international. Average age 32. 2,544 applicants, 52% accepted, 662 enrolled. In 2010, 756 master's, 11 doctorates awarded. *Degree requirements:* For doctorate, thesis/dissertation. *Entrance requirements:* For doctorate, GMAT or GRE. Additional exam requirements/recommendations for international students: Required—TOEFL. *Application deadline:* For fall admission, 4/1 priority date for domestic students; for spring admission, 10/1 for domestic students. Applications are processed on a rolling basis. Application fee: $75. Electronic applications accepted. *Financial support:* In 2010–11, 194 students received support; fellowships with tuition reimbursements available, teaching assistantships with tuition reimbursements available, career-related internships or fieldwork, Federal Work-Study, institutionally sponsored loans, and tuition waivers (partial) available. Financial award application deadline: 4/1. *Unit head:* Dr. Susan M. Phillips, Dean, 202-994-6380, Fax: 202-994-6382. *Application contact:* Kristin Williams, Assistant Vice President for Graduate and Special Enrollment Management, 202-994-0467, Fax: 202-994-0371, E-mail: ksw@gwu.edu.

Georgia College & State University, Graduate School, The J. Whitney Bunting School of Business, Milledgeville, GA 31061. Offers accountancy (MACCT); accounting (MBA); business (MBA); health services administration (MBA); information systems (MIS); management information services (MBA). *Accreditation:* AACSB. Part-time and evening/weekend programs available. Postbaccalaureate distance learning degree programs offered (no on-campus study). *Faculty:* 46 full-time (20 women). *Students:* 53 full-time (22 women), 157 part-time (53 women); includes 35 minority (18 Black or African American, non-Hispanic/Latino; 9 Asian, non-Hispanic/Latino; 5 Hispanic/Latino; 3 Two or more races, non-Hispanic/Latino), 11 international. Average age 30. 111 applicants, 83% accepted, 61 enrolled. In 2010, 121 master's awarded. *Entrance requirements:* For master's, GMAT or GRE. Additional exam requirements/recommendations for international students: Recommended—TOEFL (minimum score 550 paper-based; 213 computer-based; 79 iBT). *Application deadline:* For fall admission, 7/1 priority date for domestic students, 4/1 priority date for international students; for spring admission, 11/15 priority date for domestic students, 8/1 priority date for international students. Applications are processed on a rolling basis. Application fee: $40. Electronic applications accepted. *Expenses:* Tuition, state resident: full-time $4806; part-time $267 per hour. Tuition, nonresident: full-time $17,802; part-time $989 per hour. Tuition and fees vary according to course load. *Financial support:* In 2010–11, 33 research assistantships with full tuition reimbursements were awarded; career-related internships or fieldwork and unspecified assistantships also available. Support available to part-time students. Financial award application deadline: 3/1; financial award applicants required to submit FAFSA. *Unit head:* Dr. Matthew Liao-Troth, Dean, 478-445-5497, E-mail: matthew.liao-troth@gcsu.edu. *Application contact:* Lynn Hanson, Director of Graduate Programs, 478-445-5115, E-mail: lynn.hanson@gcsu.edu.

Georgian Court University, School of Business, Lakewood, NJ 08701-2697. Offers accounting (Certificate); business administration (MBA). *Accreditation:* ACBSP. Part-time and evening/weekend programs available. *Faculty:* 8 full-time (4 women), 7 part-time/adjunct (4 women). *Students:* 63 full-time (47 women), 65 part-time (42 women); includes 29 minority (14 Black or African American, non-Hispanic/Latino; 1 American Indian or Alaska Native, non-Hispanic/Latino; 2 Asian, non-Hispanic/Latino; 11 Hispanic/Latino; 1 Native Hawaiian or other Pacific Islander, non-Hispanic/Latino), 1 international. Average age 32. 85 applicants, 67% accepted, 41 enrolled. In 2010, 62 master's, 7 other advanced degrees awarded. *Entrance requirements:* For master's, GMAT or CPA exam, 3 letters of recommendation. Additional exam requirements/recommendations for international students: Required—TOEFL (minimum score 550 paper-based; 213 computer-based). *Application deadline:* For fall admission, 8/1 priority date for domestic students, 4/1 for international students; for spring admission, 1/1 priority date for domestic students, 7/1 for international students. Applications are processed on a rolling basis. Application fee: $40. Electronic applications accepted. *Expenses:* Tuition: Full-time $12,510; part-time $695 per credit. Required fees: $416 per year. Tuition and fees vary according to campus/location and program. *Financial support:* Scholarships/grants, health care benefits, and unspecified assistantships available. Financial award application deadline: 4/15; financial award applicants required to submit FAFSA. *Unit head:* Dr. Joseph Monahan, Dean, 732-987-2724, Fax: 732-987-2024, E-mail: monahanj@georgian.edu. *Application contact:* Patrick Givens, Assistant Director of Admissions, 732-987-2736, Fax: 732-987-2084, E-mail: graduateadmissions@georgian.edu.

Georgia Southern University, Jack N. Averitt College of Graduate Studies, College of Business Administration, The Georgia WebMBA, Statesboro, GA 30460. Offers MBA. Part-time and evening/weekend programs available. Postbaccalaureate distance learning degree programs offered. *Students:* 88

part-time (37 women); includes 14 Black or African American, non-Hispanic/Latino; 4 Asian, non-Hispanic/Latino; 2 Hispanic/Latino; 1 Native Hawaiian or other Pacific Islander, non-Hispanic/Latino, 3 international. Average age 32. 71 applicants, 75% accepted, 37 enrolled. In 2010, 40 master's awarded. *Entrance requirements:* For master's, GMAT. Additional exam requirements/recommendations for international students: Required—TOEFL (minimum score 550 paper-based; 213 computer-based; 80 iBT). *Application deadline:* For fall admission, 3/1 priority date for domestic and international students. Applications are processed on a rolling basis. Application fee: $50. Electronic applications accepted. *Expenses:* Tuition, state resident: full-time $6000; part-time $250 per semester hour. Tuition, nonresident: full-time $23,976; part-time $999 per semester hour. Required fees: $1644. *Financial support:* In 2010–11, 50 students received support. Application deadline: 4/15. *Unit head:* Melissa Holland, Graduate Program Director, 912-478-2357, Fax: 912-478-0292, E-mail: mholland@georgiasouthern.edu. *Application contact:* Dr. Charles Ziglar, Coordinator for Graduate Student Recruitment, 912-478-5635, Fax: 912-478-0740, E-mail: gradadmissions@georgiasouthern.edu.

Georgia Southern University, Jack N. Averitt College of Graduate Studies, College of Business Administration, Program in Business Administration, Statesboro, GA 30460. Offers MBA. *Accreditation:* AACSB. Part-time and evening/weekend programs available. Postbaccalaureate distance learning degree programs offered. *Students:* 84 full-time (23 women), 89 part-time (46 women); includes 20 Black or African American, non-Hispanic/Latino; 2 Asian, non-Hispanic/Latino; 1 Hispanic/Latino; 1 Two or more races, non-Hispanic/Latino, 11 international. Average age 28. 84 applicants, 81% accepted, 40 enrolled. In 2010, 67 master's awarded. *Entrance requirements:* For master's, GMAT. Additional exam requirements/recommendations for international students: Required—TOEFL (minimum score 550 paper-based; 213 computer-based; 80 iBT). *Application deadline:* For fall admission, 3/1 priority date for domestic students, 6/1 priority date for international students; for spring admission, 10/1 priority date for domestic students, 10/1 for international students. Applications are processed on a rolling basis. Application fee: $50. Electronic applications accepted. *Expenses:* Tuition, state resident: full-time $6000; part-time $250 per semester hour. Tuition, nonresident: full-time $23,976; part-time $999 per semester hour. Required fees: $1644. *Financial support:* In 2010–11, 105 students received support, including research assistantships with partial tuition reimbursements available (averaging $7,200 per year), teaching assistantships with partial tuition reimbursements available (averaging $7,200 per year); career-related internships or fieldwork, Federal Work-Study, scholarships/grants, tuition waivers (partial), and unspecified assistantships also available. Support available to part-time students. Financial award application deadline: 4/15; financial award applicants required to submit FAFSA. *Faculty research:* Applied, discipline, pedagogical theory-based, empirical-based. *Unit head:* Melissa Holland, Director, 912-478-2357, Fax: 912-478-7480, E-mail: mholland@georgiasouthern.edu. *Application contact:* Dr. Charles Ziglar, Coordinator for Graduate Student Recruitment, 912-478-5365, Fax: 912-478-0740, E-mail: gradadmissions@georgiasouthern.edu.

Golden Gate University, Ageno School of Business, San Francisco, CA 94105-2968. Offers accounting (MBA); business administration (EMBA, MBA, PMBA, DBA); finance (MBA, MS, Certificate); financial planning (MS, Certificate); healthcare information systems (Certificate); human resource management (MBA, MS); human resources management (Certificate); information systems (MS); information technology (MBA); information technology management (Certificate); integrated marketing and communications (MS, Certificate); international business (MBA); management (MBA); marketing (MBA, MS, Certificate); operations supply chain management (Certificate); psychology (MA, Certificate); public administration (EMPA); public relations (MS, Certificate); technical market analysis (Certificate); JD/MBA. Part-time and evening/weekend programs available. *Faculty:* 16 full-time (4 women), 241 part-time/adjunct (72 women). *Students:* 421 full-time (235 women), 744 part-time (425 women); includes 526 minority (114 Black or African American, non-Hispanic/Latino; 2 American Indian or Alaska Native, non-Hispanic/Latino; 296 Asian, non-Hispanic/Latino; 73 Hispanic/Latino; 29 Native Hawaiian or other Pacific Islander, non-Hispanic/Latino; 12 Two or more races, non-Hispanic/Latino), 100 international. Average age 32. 681 applicants, 78% accepted, 270 enrolled. In 2010, 550 master's, 13 doctorates awarded. *Degree requirements:* For doctorate, thesis/dissertation. *Entrance requirements:* For master's, GMAT (MBA), minimum GPA of 2.5 (MS). Additional exam requirements/recommendations for international students: Required—TOEFL. *Application deadline:* For fall admission, 5/15 for domestic and international students; for winter admission, 1/15 for domestic and international students; for spring admission, 9/15 for domestic and international students. Applications are processed on a rolling basis. Application fee: $70 ($110 for international students). Electronic applications accepted. *Expenses:* Contact institution. *Financial support:* Career-related internships or fieldwork, Federal Work-Study, institutionally sponsored loans, and scholarships/grants available. Support available to part-time students. Financial award applicants required to submit FAFSA. *Unit head:* Dr. Paul Fouts, Dean, 415-442-7026, Fax: 415-442-6579. *Application contact:* Angela Melero, Enrollment Services, 415-442-7800, Fax: 415-442-7807, E-mail: info@ggu.edu.

Goldey-Beacom College, Graduate Program, Wilmington, DE 19808-1999. Offers business administration (MBA); finance (MS); financial management (MBA); human resource management (MBA); information technology (MBA); international business management (MBA); major finance (MBA); major taxation (MBA); management (MM); marketing management (MBA); taxation (MBA, MS). *Accreditation:* ACBSP. Part-time and evening/weekend programs available. *Faculty:* 20 full-time (8 women), 28 part-time/adjunct (10 women). *Students:* 55 full-time (28 women), 393 part-time (164 women); includes 252 minority (51 Black or African American, non-Hispanic/Latino; 2 American Indian or Alaska Native, non-Hispanic/Latino; 183 Asian, non-Hispanic/Latino; 13 Hispanic/Latino; 1 Native Hawaiian or other Pacific Islander, non-Hispanic/Latino; 2 Two or more races, non-Hispanic/Latino). Average age 27. In 2010, 231 master's awarded. *Entrance requirements:* For master's, GMAT, MAT, GRE, minimum GPA of 3.0. Additional exam requirements/recommendations for international students: Required—TOEFL (minimum score 65 computer-based); Recommended—IELTS (minimum score 5). *Application deadline:* Applications are processed on a rolling basis. Electronic applications accepted. *Expenses:* Tuition: Full-time $14,796; part-time $822 per credit. Required fees: $180; $10 per credit. *Financial support:* Scholarships/grants available. Support available to part-time students. Financial award application deadline: 4/1; financial award applicants required to submit FAFSA. *Unit head:* Larry W. Eby, Director of Admissions, 302-225-6289, Fax: 302-996-5408, E-mail: ebylw@gbc.edu. *Application contact:* Ashley E. Mashington, Graduate Admissions Representative, 302-225-6259, Fax: 302-996-5408, E-mail: mashina@gbc.edu.

Grand Canyon University, College of Business, Phoenix, AZ 85017-1097. Offers accounting (MBA); corporate business administration (MBA); disaster preparedness and crisis management (MBA); executive fire service leadership (MS); finance (MBA); general management (MBA); government and policy (MPA); health care management (MPA); health systems management (MBA); human resource management (MBA); innovation (MBA); leadership (MBA, MS); management of information system (MBA); marketing (MBA); project-based (MBA); six sigma (MBA); strategic human resource management (MBA). *Accreditation:* ACBSP. Part-time and evening/weekend programs available. Postbaccalaureate distance learning degree programs offered (no on-campus study). *Faculty:* 8 full-time (3 women), 147 part-time/adjunct (49 women). *Students:* 1 full-time (0 women), 2,121 part-time (1,165 women); includes 341 minority (249 Black or African American, non-Hispanic/Latino; 17 American Indian or Alaska Native, non-Hispanic/Latino; 15 Asian, non-Hispanic/Latino; 29 Hispanic/Latino; 4 Native Hawaiian or other Pacific Islander, non-Hispanic/Latino; 27 Two or more races, non-Hispanic/Latino), 20 international. Average age 38. In 2010, 569 master's awarded. *Entrance requirements:* For master's, equivalent of two years full-time professional work experience. Additional exam requirements/recommendations for international students: Required—TOEFL (minimum score 575 paper-based; 233 computer-based; 90 iBT), IELTS (minimum score 7). *Application deadline:* For fall admission, 8/21 for domestic students, 7/2 for international students; for spring admission, 12/24 for domestic students, 11/1 for international students. Applications are processed on a rolling basis. Application fee: $0. Electronic applications accepted. *Financial support:* Federal Work-Study available. Support available to part-time students. Financial award applicants required to submit FAFSA. *Unit head:* Kim Donaldson, Dean, 602-639-6597, E-mail: kdonaldson@gcu.edu. *Application contact:* Matt Tidwell, Enrollment Manager, 602-639-6020, E-mail: mtidwell@gcu.edu.

Grand Canyon University, College of Doctoral Studies, Phoenix, AZ 85017-1097. Offers business administration (DBA); general psychology (PhD), including cognition and instruction, industrial and organizational psychology; organizational leadership (Ed D, PhD), including behavioral health (PhD), education and effective schools (PhD), higher education (PhD), instructional leadership (PhD), organizational development (Ed D). *Faculty:* 2 full-time (1 woman), 12 part-time/adjunct (5 women). *Students:* 968 part-time (711 women); includes 316 minority (283 Black or African American, non-Hispanic/Latino; 12 American Indian or Alaska Native, non-Hispanic/Latino; 3 Asian, non-Hispanic/Latino; 11 Hispanic/Latino; 1 Native Hawaiian or other Pacific Islander, non-Hispanic/Latino; 6 Two or more races, non-Hispanic/Latino). *Degree requirements:* For doctorate, comprehensive exam, thesis/dissertation. *Entrance requirements:* For doctorate, minimum GPA of 3.4 on earned advanced degree from regionally-accredited institution; transcripts; goals statement. Application fee: $0. *Unit head:* Dr. Hank Radda, Dean, 602-639-7255, E-mail: hank.radda@gcu.edu. *Application contact:* Hector Leal, Associate Vice President of Internet Enrollment, 800-639-7144, E-mail: hector.leal@.gcu.edu.

Grantham University, Mark Skousen School of Business, Kansas City, MO 64153. Offers business administration (MBA); business intelligence (MS); information management (MBA); information management technology (MS); information technology (MS); performance improvement (MS); project management (MBA, MSIM). Part-time and evening/weekend programs available. Postbaccalaureate distance learning degree programs offered (no on-campus study). *Students:* 74 full-time (32 women), 565 part-time (177 women); includes 218 minority (142 Black or African American, non-Hispanic/Latino; 6 American Indian or Alaska Native, non-Hispanic/Latino; 31 Asian, non-Hispanic/Latino; 37 Hispanic/Latino; 1 Native Hawaiian or other Pacific Islander, non-Hispanic/Latino; 1 Two or more races, non-Hispanic/Latino). In 2010, 126 master's awarded. *Degree requirements:* For master's, capstone project. *Entrance requirements:* For master's, bachelor's degree from accredited degree-granting institution. Additional exam requirements/recommendations for international students: Required—TOEFL (minimum score 500 paper-based; 213 computer-based; 61 iBT). *Application deadline:* Applications are processed on a rolling basis. Application fee: $0. Electronic applications accepted. *Expenses:* Tuition: Full-time $7950; part-time $265 per credit hour. One-time fee: $30. *Financial support:* Institutionally sponsored loans and scholarships/grants available. *Unit head:* Niccole Buckley, Dean, 800-955-2527, Fax: 816-595-5757, E-mail: admissions@grantham.edu. *Application contact:* Dan King, Vice President of Admissions, 800-955-2527, Fax: 816-595-5757, E-mail: admissions@grantham.edu.

Hamline University, School of Business, St. Paul, MN 55104-1284. Offers business (MBA); nonprofit management (MA); public administration (MA, DPA); JD/MA; JD/MBA; LL M/MA; LL M/MBA; MA/MA; MBA/MA. Part-time and evening/weekend programs available. *Faculty:* 20 full-time (8 women), 42 part-time/adjunct (12 women). *Students:* 509 full-time (234 women), 130 part-time (74 women); includes 102 minority (55 Black or African American, non-Hispanic/Latino; 6 American Indian or Alaska Native, non-Hispanic/Latino; 29 Asian, non-Hispanic/Latino; 10 Hispanic/Latino; 2 Two or more races, non-Hispanic/Latino), 66 international. Average age 32. 244 applicants, 73% accepted, 139 enrolled. In 2010, 293 master's, 3 doctorates awarded. *Degree requirements:* For master's, thesis (for some programs); for doctorate, comprehensive exam, thesis/dissertation. *Entrance requirements:* For master's, personal statement, official transcripts, curriculum vitae, letters of recommendation, writing sample; for doctorate, personal statement, curriculum vitae, official transcripts, letters of recommendation, writing sample. Additional exam requirements/recommendations for international students: Required—TOEFL (minimum score 80 iBT). *Application deadline:* For fall admission, 6/1 for international students; for spring admission, 10/1 for international students. Applications are processed on a rolling basis. Application fee: $0. Electronic applications accepted. *Expenses:* Tuition: Full-time $7248; part-time $453 per credit hour. Required fees: $7 per credit hour. One-time fee: $210. Tuition and fees vary according to degree level, campus/location and program. *Financial support:* Federal Work-Study and scholarships/grants available. Support available to part-time students. Financial award applicants required to submit FAFSA. *Faculty research:* Liberal arts-based business programs, experiential learning, organizational process/politics, gender differences, social equity. *Unit head:* Nancy Hellerud, Interim Dean, 651-523-2284, Fax: 651-523-3098, E-mail: nhellerud@gw.hamline.edu. *Application contact:* Rae A. Lenway, Director, Graduate Recruitment and Admission, 651-523-2900, Fax: 651-523-3058, E-mail: rlenway@gw.hamline.edu.

Harding University, College of Business Administration, Searcy, AR 72149-0001. Offers health care management (MBA); information technology management (MBA); international business (MBA); leadership and organizational management (MBA). *Accreditation:* ACBSP. Part-time and evening/weekend programs available. Postbaccalaureate distance learning degree programs offered (no on-campus study). *Faculty:* 30 part-time/adjunct (6 women). *Students:* 85 full-time (49 women), 133 part-time (52 women); includes 35 minority (27 Black or African American, non-Hispanic/Latino; 1 American Indian or Alaska Native, non-Hispanic/Latino; 4 Asian, non-Hispanic/Latino; 1 Hispanic/Latino; 1 Native Hawaiian or other Pacific Islander, non-Hispanic/Latino; 1 Two or more races, non-Hispanic/Latino), 29 international. Average age 30. 52 applicants, 94% accepted, 44 enrolled. In 2010, 100 master's awarded. *Degree requirements:* For master's, portfolio. *Entrance requirements:* For master's, minimum GPA of 3.0, 2 letters of recommendation, resume. Additional exam requirements/recommendations for international students: Required—TOEFL (minimum score 550 paper-based; 213 computer-based; 80 iBT). *Application deadline:* For fall admission, 8/1 priority date for domestic and international students; for spring admission, 12/1 priority date for domestic and international students. Applications are processed on a rolling basis. Application fee: $35. *Expenses:* Tuition: Full-time $10,098; part-time $561 per credit hour. Required fees: $22.50 per credit hour. *Financial support:* In 2010–11, 19 students received support. Unspecified assistantships available. Financial award application deadline: 7/30; financial award applicants required to submit FAFSA. *Unit head:* Glen Metheny, Director of Graduate Studies, 501-279-5851, Fax: 501-279-4805, E-mail: gmetheny@harding.edu. *Application contact:* Melanie Kiihnl, Recruiting Manager/Director of Marketing, 501-279-4523, Fax: 501-279-4805, E-mail: mba@harding.edu.

Hardin-Simmons University, The Acton MBA in Entrepreneurship, Austin, TX 78701. Offers MBA. *Entrance requirements:* For master's, GMAT, letters of recommendation. Additional exam requirements/recommendations for international students: Required—TOEFL. *Application deadline:* For fall admission, 5/1 for domestic students, 2/25 for international students. Application fee: $150. *Expenses:* Tuition: Full-time $12,150; part-time $675 per credit hour. Required fees: $650; $110 per semester. Tuition and fees vary according to degree level. *Application contact:* Jessica Blanchard, Director of Recruiting, 512-703-1231, E-mail: jblanchard@actonmba.org.

Hardin-Simmons University, Graduate School, Kelley College of Business, Abilene, TX 79698-0001. Offers MBA. *Accreditation:* ACBSP. Part-time

and evening/weekend programs available. *Faculty:* 7 full-time (3 women), 2 part-time/adjunct (0 women). *Students:* 11 full-time (6 women), 13 part-time (6 women); includes 2 Black or African American, non-Hispanic/Latino; 1 Hispanic/Latino, 2 international. Average age 25. 20 applicants, 70% accepted, 12 enrolled. In 2010, 17 master's awarded. *Degree requirements:* For master's, thesis or alternative. *Entrance requirements:* For master's, GMAT, minimum GPA of 3.0 in upper level course work, resume, interview. Additional exam requirements/recommendations for international students: Required—TOEFL (minimum score 600 paper-based; 232 computer-based; 75 iBT). *Application deadline:* For fall admission, 8/15 priority date for domestic students, 4/1 for international students; for spring admission, 1/5 priority date for domestic students, 9/1 for international students. Applications are processed on a rolling basis. Application fee: $50. *Expenses:* Tuition: Full-time $12,150; part-time $675 per credit hour. Required fees: $650; $110 per semester. Tuition and fees vary according to degree level. *Financial support:* In 2010–11, 23 students received support; fellowships, scholarships/grants available. Support available to part-time students. Financial award application deadline: 6/30; financial award applicants required to submit FAFSA. *Unit head:* Dr. Nancy Kucinski, Director, 325-670-1503, Fax: 325-670-1523, E-mail: kucinski@hsutx.edu. *Application contact:* Dr. Nancy Kucinski, Dean of Graduate Studies, 325-670-1298, Fax: 325-670-1564, E-mail: gradoff@hsutx.edu.

HEC Montreal, School of Business Administration, Diploma Programs in Administration, Program in Management, Montréal, QC H3T 2A7, Canada. Offers Diploma. All courses are given in French. *Accreditation:* AACSB. Part-time programs available. *Students:* 63 full-time (34 women), 365 part-time (210 women). 245 applicants, 67% accepted, 123 enrolled. In 2010, 150 Diplomas awarded. *Degree requirements:* For Diploma, one foreign language. *Application deadline:* For fall admission, 4/1 for domestic and international students; for winter admission, 9/15 for domestic and international students; for spring admission, 2/15 for domestic and international students. Application fee: $78 Canadian dollars. Electronic applications accepted. *Expenses:* Tuition, area resident: Part-time $68.93 per credit. Tuition, state resident: full-time $2481.48; part-time $188.92 per credit. Tuition, nonresident: full-time $6801; part-time $482.06 per course. International tuition: $17,354.16 full-time. Required fees: $1309.50; $30.28 per credit. $93.45 per term. Tuition and fees vary according to degree level and program. *Financial support:* Scholarships/grants available. *Unit head:* Silvia Ponce, Director, 514-340-6393, Fax: 514-340-6915, E-mail: silvia.ponce@hec.ca. *Application contact:* Marie Deshaies, Senior Student Advisor, 514-340-6135, Fax: 514-340-6411, E-mail: marie.deshaies@hec.ca.

HEC Montreal, School of Business Administration, Diploma Programs in Administration, Program in Management and Sustainable Development, Montréal, QC H3T 2A7, Canada. Offers Diploma. Part-time programs available. *Students:* 16 full-time (8 women), 59 part-time (31 women). 80 applicants, 70% accepted, 36 enrolled. In 2010, 30 Diplomas awarded. *Degree requirements:* For Diploma, one foreign language. *Application deadline:* For fall admission, 4/15 for domestic students. Application fee: $78. Electronic applications accepted. *Expenses:* Tuition, area resident: Part-time $68.93 per credit. Tuition, state resident: full-time $2481.48; part-time $188.92 per credit. Tuition, nonresident: full-time $6801; part-time $482.06 per course. International tuition: $17,354.16 full-time. Required fees: $1309.50; $30.28 per credit. $93.45 per term. Tuition and fees vary according to degree level and program. *Financial support:* Research assistantships, teaching assistantships available. Financial award application deadline: 9/2. *Unit head:* Silvia Ponce, Director, 514-340-6393, Fax: 514-340-6915, E-mail: silvia.ponce@hec.ca. *Application contact:* Marie Deshaies, Senior Student Advisor, 514-340-6135, Fax: 514-340-6411, E-mail: marie.deshaies@hec.ca.

HEC Montreal, School of Business Administration, Doctoral Program in Administration, Montréal, QC H3T 2A7, Canada. Offers PhD. Program offered jointly with Concordia University, McGill University, and Université du Québec à Montréal. *Accreditation:* AACSB. *Students:* 150 full-time (67 women). 76 applicants, 36% accepted, 16 enrolled. In 2010, 23 doctorates awarded. *Degree requirements:* For doctorate, one foreign language, thesis/dissertation. *Entrance requirements:* For doctorate, GMAT, GRE, master's degree in administration or related field. *Application deadline:* For fall admission, 2/1 for domestic and international students; for winter admission, 9/1 for domestic and international students. Application fee: $78. Electronic applications accepted. *Expenses:* Tuition, area resident: Part-time $68.93 per credit. Tuition, state resident: full-time $2481.48; part-time $188.92 per credit. Tuition, nonresident: full-time $6801; part-time $482.06 per course. International tuition: $17,354.16 full-time. Required fees: $1309.50; $30.28 per credit. $93.45 per term. Tuition and fees vary according to degree level and program. *Financial support:* Research assistantships, teaching assistantships available. Financial award application deadline: 9/2. *Unit head:* Alain d'Astous, Director, 514-340-6416, Fax: 514-340-5690, E-mail: alain.dastous@hec.ca. *Application contact:* Francine Blais, Administrative Director, 514-340-6112, Fax: 514-340-6411, E-mail: francine.blais@hec.ca.

HEC Montreal, School of Business Administration, Master of Science Programs in Administration, Montréal, QC H3T 2A7, Canada. Offers applied economics (M Sc); applied financial economics (M Sc); business analytics (M Sc); business intelligence (M Sc); electronic commerce (M Sc); finance (M Sc); financial and strategic accounting (M Sc); financial engineering

(M Sc); human resources management (M Sc); information technologies (M Sc); international business (M Sc); logistics (M Sc); management (M Sc); management control (M Sc); marketing (M Sc); organizational development (M Sc); organizational studies (M Sc); production and operations management (M Sc); public accounting (M Sc); strategy (M Sc). *Accreditation:* AACSB. Part-time programs available. *Students:* 670 full-time (305 women), 163 part-time (81 women). 829 applicants, 56% accepted, 270 enrolled. In 2010, 209 master's awarded. *Degree requirements:* For master's, one foreign language, thesis. *Entrance requirements:* For master's, bachelor's degree in business administration or equivalent. Additional exam requirements/recommendations for international students: Required—GMAT or TAGE-MAGE and TFI. *Application deadline:* For fall admission, 3/15 for domestic and international students; for winter admission, 10/1 for domestic and international students. Application fee: $78 Canadian dollars. Electronic applications accepted. *Expenses:* Tuition, area resident: Part-time $68.93 per credit. Tuition, state resident: full-time $2481.48; part-time $188.92 per credit. Tuition, nonresident: full-time $6801; part-time $482.06 per course. International tuition: $17,354.16 full-time. Required fees: $1309.50; $30.28 per credit. $93.45 per term. Tuition and fees vary according to degree level and program. *Financial support:* Research assistantships, teaching assistantships, scholarships/grants available. Financial award application deadline: 9/2. *Unit head:* Dr. Claude Laurin, Director, 514-340-6536, Fax: 514-340-6880, E-mail: claude.laurin@hec.ca. *Application contact:* Francine Blais, Administrative Director, 514-340-6112, Fax: 514-340-6411, E-mail: francine.blais@hec.ca.

HEC Montreal, School of Business Administration, Master's Program in Business Administration and Management, Montréal, QC H3T 2A7, Canada. Offers MBA. Courses are given in French or English. *Accreditation:* AACSB. Part-time programs available. *Students:* 227 full-time (75 women), 318 part-time (96 women). 602 applicants, 52% accepted, 223 enrolled. In 2010, 259 master's awarded. *Degree requirements:* For master's, one foreign language. *Entrance requirements:* For master's, GMAT, 3 years of related work experience. Additional exam requirements/recommendations for international students: Required—TOEFL (minimum score 550 paper-based; 213 computer-based). *Application deadline:* For fall admission, 3/15 for domestic students, 2/1 for international students; for winter admission, 10/1 for domestic students. Application fee: $78 Canadian dollars. Electronic applications accepted. *Expenses:* Tuition, area resident: Part-time $68.93 per credit. Tuition, state resident: full-time $2481.48; part-time $188.92 per credit. Tuition, nonresident: full-time $6801; part-time $482.06 per course. International tuition: $17,354.16 full-time. Required fees: $1309.50; $30.28 per credit. $93.45 per term. Tuition and fees vary according to degree level and program. *Financial support:* Scholarships/grants available. *Unit head:* Michael Wybo, Director, 514-340-6830, Fax: 514-340-6132, E-mail: michael.wybo@hec.ca. *Application contact:* Julie Benoit, Administrative Director, 514-340-6137, Fax: 514-340-5640, E-mail: julie.benoit@hec.ca.

High Point University, Norcross Graduate School, High Point, NC 27262-3598. Offers business administration (MBA); educational leadership (M Ed); elementary education (M Ed); history (MA); nonprofit management (MA); secondary math (M Ed); special education (M Ed); strategic communication (MA); teaching elementary education k-6 (MAT); teaching secondary mathematics 9-12 (MAT). *Accreditation:* ACBSP; NCATE. Part-time and evening/weekend programs available. *Faculty:* 30 full-time (11 women), 5 part-time/adjunct (1 woman). *Students:* 17 full-time (10 women), 292 part-time (198 women); includes 107 minority (100 Black or African American, non-Hispanic/Latino; 1 Asian, non-Hispanic/Latino; 6 Hispanic/Latino), 19 international. 249 applicants, 69% accepted, 141 enrolled. *Degree requirements:* For master's, comprehensive exam (for some programs), thesis (for some programs). *Entrance requirements:* For master's, GMAT (MBA), GRE, MAT, minimum GPA of 3.0. Additional exam requirements/recommendations for international students: Required—TOEFL (minimum score 550 paper-based). *Application deadline:* For fall admission, 4/15 priority date for domestic and international students; for spring admission, 10/15 priority date for domestic and international students. Applications are processed on a rolling basis. Application fee: $50. Electronic applications accepted. *Expenses:* Tuition: Full-time $11,520; part-time $640 per hour. Required fees: $90; $150 per semester. Part-time tuition and fees vary according to program. *Financial support:* Federal Work-Study available. Support available to part-time students. Financial award application deadline: 3/1; financial award applicants required to submit FAFSA. *Unit head:* Tracy Collum, Associate Dean, 336-767-4840, Fax: 336-841-9024, E-mail: tcollum@highpoint.edu. *Application contact:* Tracy Collum, Associate Dean, 336-767-4840, Fax: 336-841-9024, E-mail: tcollum@highpoint.edu.

Hodges University, Graduate Programs, Naples, FL 34119. Offers business administration (MBA); computer information technology (MS); criminal justice (MCJ); education (MPS); information systems management (MIS); interdisciplinary (MPS); legal studies (MS); management (MSM); mental health counseling (MS); psychology (MPS); public administration (MPA). Part-time and evening/weekend programs available. Postbaccalaureate distance learning degree programs offered (no on-campus study). *Faculty:* 25 full-time (9 women), 5 part-time/adjunct (4 women). *Students:* 27 full-time (15 women), 228 part-time (146 women); includes 76 minority (35 Black or African American, non-Hispanic/Latino; 5 Asian, non-Hispanic/Latino; 36

Hispanic/Latino). Average age 36. 92 applicants, 91% accepted, 81 enrolled. In 2010, 92 master's awarded. *Degree requirements:* For master's, comprehensive exam (for some programs), thesis (for some programs). *Entrance requirements:* For master's, in-house entrance exam. *Application deadline:* Applications are processed on a rolling basis. Application fee: $50. Electronic applications accepted. *Expenses:* Tuition: Full-time $16,605; part-time $615 per credit hour. Required fees: $190 per trimester. *Financial support:* In 2010–11, 200 students received support. Federal Work-Study and scholarships/grants available. Financial award application deadline: 7/9; financial award applicants required to submit FAFSA. *Unit head:* Terry McMahan, President, 239-513-1122, Fax: 239-598-6253, E-mail: tmcmahan@hodges.edu. *Application contact:* Rita Lampus, Vice President of Student Enrollment Management, 239-513-1122, Fax: 239-598-6253, E-mail: rlampus@hodges.edu.

Hofstra University, Frank G. Zarb School of Business, Department of Finance, Hempstead, NY 11549. Offers banking (Advanced Certificate); business administration (MBA), including finance, real estate management; corporate finance (Advanced Certificate); finance (MS); investment management (Advanced Certificate); quantitative finance (MS). Part-time and evening/weekend programs available. Postbaccalaureate distance learning degree programs offered (minimal on-campus study). *Faculty:* 12 full-time (2 women), 2 part-time/adjunct (1 woman). *Students:* 180 full-time (68 women), 99 part-time (26 women); includes 24 minority (6 Black or African American, non-Hispanic/Latino; 10 Asian, non-Hispanic/Latino; 8 Hispanic/Latino), 13 international. Average age 27. 329 applicants, 73% accepted, 102 enrolled. In 2010, 76 master's awarded. *Degree requirements:* For master's, capstone course (for MBA); thesis (for MS). *Entrance requirements:* For master's, GMAT/GRE, 2 letters of recommendation; resume; essay. Additional exam requirements/recommendations for international students: Required—TOEFL (minimum score 550 paper-based; 213 computer-based; 80 iBT); Recommended—IELTS (minimum score 6). *Application deadline:* Applications are processed on a rolling basis. Application fee: $70 ($75 for international students). Electronic applications accepted. *Expenses:* Contact institution. *Financial support:* In 2010–11, 41 students received support, including 38 fellowships with full and partial tuition reimbursements available (averaging $10,353 per year), 1 research assistantship with full and partial tuition reimbursement available (averaging $9,375 per year); Federal Work-Study, institutionally sponsored loans, scholarships/grants, and tuition waivers (full and partial) also available. Support available to part-time students. Financial award applicants required to submit FAFSA. *Faculty research:* International finance, investments, banking, real estate, derivatives. *Unit head:* Dr. Nancy W. White, Chairperson, 516-463-5699, Fax: 516-463-4834, E-mail: finnwh@hofstra.edu. *Application contact:* Carol Drummer, Dean of Graduate Admissions, 516-463-4876, Fax: 516-463-4664, E-mail: gradstudent@hofstra.edu.

Hofstra University, Frank G. Zarb School of Business, Department of Information Technology and Quantitative Methods, Hempstead, NY 11549. Offers business administration (MBA), including information technology, quality management; information technology (MS, Advanced Certificate). Part-time and evening/weekend programs available. Postbaccalaureate distance learning degree programs offered (minimal on-campus study). *Faculty:* 10 full-time (1 woman), 2 part-time/adjunct (0 women). *Students:* 11 full-time (1 woman), 12 part-time (4 women); includes 6 minority (1 Black or African American, non-Hispanic/Latino; 5 Asian, non-Hispanic/Latino), 4 international. Average age 29. 28 applicants, 57% accepted, 8 enrolled. In 2010, 8 master's awarded. *Degree requirements:* For master's, capstone course (for MBA); thesis (for MS). *Entrance requirements:* For master's, GMAT/GRE, 2 letters of recommendation; resume; essay; for Advanced Certificate, GMAT/GRE, 2 letters of recommendation; resume. Additional exam requirements/recommendations for international students: Required—TOEFL (minimum score 550 paper-based; 213 computer-based; 80 iBT); Recommended—IELTS (minimum score 6). *Application deadline:* Applications are processed on a rolling basis. Application fee: $70 ($75 for international students). Electronic applications accepted. *Expenses:* Contact institution. *Financial support:* In 2010–11, 4 students received support, including 4 fellowships with full and partial tuition reimbursements available (averaging $11,496 per year); research assistantships with full and partial tuition reimbursements available, career-related internships or fieldwork, Federal Work-Study, institutionally sponsored loans, scholarships/grants, tuition waivers (full and partial), and unspecified assistantships also available. Support available to part-time students. Financial award applicants required to submit FAFSA. *Faculty research:* IT outsourcing, IT strategy, SAP and enterprise systems, data mining/electronic medical records, IT and crisis management, inventory theory and modeling, forecasting. *Unit head:* Dr. Mohammed H. Tafti, Chairperson, 516-463-5720, E-mail: acsmht@hofstra.edu. *Application contact:* Carol Drummer, Dean of Graduate Admissions, 516-463-4876, Fax: 516-463-4664, E-mail: gradstudent@hofstra.edu.

Hofstra University, Frank G. Zarb School of Business, Department of Management, Entrepreneurship and General Business, Hempstead, NY 11549. Offers business administration (MBA), including health services management, management, sports and entertainment management; general management (Advanced Certificate); human resource management (MS). Part-time and evening/weekend programs available. Postbaccalaureate distance learning degree programs offered (minimal on-campus study). *Faculty:* 7 full-time (1 woman), 6 part-time/adjunct (0 women). *Students:* 73 full-time (34 women), 169 part-time (79 women); includes 60 minority (23 Black or African American, non-Hispanic/Latino; 30 Asian, non-Hispanic/Latino; 7 Hispanic/Latino), 28 international. Average age 33. 176 applicants, 62% accepted, 62 enrolled. In 2010, 51 master's awarded. *Degree requirements:* For master's, thesis optional, capstone course (for MBA); thesis (for MS). *Entrance requirements:* For master's, GMAT/GRE, 2 letters of recommendation; resume; essay. Additional exam requirements/recommendations for international students: Required—TOEFL (minimum score 550 paper-based; 213 computer-based; 80 iBT); Recommended—IELTS (minimum score 6). *Application deadline:* Applications are processed on a rolling basis. Application fee: $70 ($75 for international students). Electronic applications accepted. *Expenses:* Contact institution. *Financial support:* In 2010–11, 12 students received support, including 11 fellowships with full and partial tuition reimbursements available (averaging $10,256 per year), 1 research assistantship with full and partial tuition reimbursement available (averaging $18,925 per year); career-related internships or fieldwork, Federal Work-Study, institutionally sponsored loans, scholarships/grants, tuition waivers (full and partial), and unspecified assistantships also available. Support available to part-time students. Financial award applicants required to submit FAFSA. *Faculty research:* Business/personal ethics, sustainability, innovation, decision-making, supply chains analysis, learning and pedagogical issues, family business, small business, entrepreneurship. *Unit head:* Dr. Mamdouh I. Farid, Chairperson, 516-463-5735, Fax: 516-463-4834, E-mail: mgbmif@hofstra.edu. *Application contact:* Carol Drummer, Dean of Graduate Admissions, 516-463-4876, Fax: 516-463-4664, E-mail: gradstudent@hofstra.edu.

Hofstra University, Frank G. Zarb School of Business, Department of Marketing and International Business, Hempstead, NY 11549. Offers business administration (MBA), including international business, marketing; marketing (MS); marketing research (MS). Part-time and evening/weekend programs available. Postbaccalaureate distance learning degree programs offered (minimal on-campus study). *Faculty:* 7 full-time (0 women), 2 part-time/adjunct (0 women). *Students:* 63 full-time (34 women), 47 part-time (24 women); includes 9 minority (1 Black or African American, non-Hispanic/Latino; 2 Asian, non-Hispanic/Latino; 6 Hispanic/Latino), 52 international. Average age 27. 150 applicants, 66% accepted, 36 enrolled. In 2010, 35 master's awarded. *Degree requirements:* For master's, capstone course (MBA), thesis (MS). *Entrance requirements:* For master's, GMAT or GRE, 2 letters of recommendation, resume, essay. Additional exam requirements/recommendations for international students: Required—TOEFL (minimum score 550 paper-based; 213 computer-based; 80 iBT); Recommended—IELTS (minimum score 6). *Application deadline:* Applications are processed on a rolling basis. Application fee: $70 ($75 for international students). Electronic applications accepted. *Expenses:* Contact institution. *Financial support:* In 2010–11, 22 students received support, including 21 fellowships with full and partial tuition reimbursements available (averaging $8,965 per year); research assistantships with full and partial tuition reimbursements available, career-related internships or fieldwork, Federal Work-Study, institutionally sponsored loans, scholarships/grants, tuition waivers (full and partial), and unspecified assistantships also available. Support available to part-time students. Financial award applicants required to submit FAFSA. *Faculty research:* Outsourcing, global alliances, retailing, Web marketing, cross-cultural age research. *Unit head:* Dr. Benny Barak, Chairperson, 516-463-5707, Fax: 516-463-4834, E-mail: mktbzb@hofstra.edu. *Application contact:* Carol Drummer, Dean of Graduate Admissions, 516-463-4876, Fax: 516-463-4664, E-mail: gradstudent@hofstra.edu.

Hofstra University, Frank G. Zarb School of Business, Executive Master's Program in Business Administration, Hempstead, NY 11549. Offers management (EMBA). Evening/weekend programs available. *Students:* 15 full-time (5 women), 10 part-time (5 women); includes 9 minority (2 Black or African American, non-Hispanic/Latino; 4 Asian, non-Hispanic/Latino; 3 Hispanic/Latino). Average age 34. 29 applicants, 76% accepted, 15 enrolled. In 2010, 11 master's awarded. *Entrance requirements:* For master's, 2 letters of recommendation; Minimum 7 years of management experience; Resume; Interview; Essay. Additional exam requirements/recommendations for international students: Required—TOEFL (minimum score 550 paper-based; 213 computer-based; 80 iBT); Recommended—IELTS (minimum score 6). *Application deadline:* Applications are processed on a rolling basis. Application fee: $70 ($75 for international students). Electronic applications accepted. *Expenses:* Contact institution. *Financial support:* In 2010–11, 8 students received support, including 6 fellowships with full and partial tuition reimbursements available (averaging $3,833 per year); research assistantships with full and partial tuition reimbursements available, Federal Work-Study, institutionally sponsored loans, scholarships/grants, and tuition waivers (full and partial) also available. Support available to part-time students. Financial award applicants required to submit FAFSA. *Faculty research:* Business strategy, international business, financial management, marketing management. *Unit head:* Dr. Barry Berman, Director, 516-463-5711, E-mail: mktbxb@hofstra.edu. *Application contact:* Carol Drummer, Dean of Graduate Admissions, 516-463-4876, Fax: 516-463-4664, E-mail: gradstudent@hofstra.edu.

Hofstra University, Frank G. Zarb School of Business, Programs in Accounting and Taxation, Hempstead, NY 11549. Offers accounting (MS, Advanced Certificate); business administration (MBA), including accounting, taxation; taxation (MS, Advanced Certificate). Part-time and evening/weekend programs available. Postbaccalaureate distance learning degree programs offered (minimal on-campus study). *Faculty:* 12 full-time (4 women), 3 part-time/adjunct (1 woman). *Students:* 107 full-time (52 women), 49 part-time (22 women); includes 19 minority (5 Black or African American, non-Hispanic/Latino; 9 Asian, non-Hispanic/Latino; 5 Hispanic/Latino), 45 international. Average age 26. 247 applicants, 73% accepted, 79 enrolled. In 2010, 37 master's awarded. *Degree requirements:* For master's, capstone course (for MBA); thesis (for MS). *Entrance requirements:* For master's, GMAT/GRE, 2 letters of recommendation; resume; essay. Additional exam requirements/recommendations for international students: Required—TOEFL (minimum score 550 paper-based; 213 computer-based; 80 iBT); Recommended—IELTS (minimum score 6). *Application deadline:* Applications are processed on a rolling basis. Application fee: $70 ($75 for international students). Electronic applications accepted. *Expenses:* Contact institution. *Financial support:* In 2010–11, 25 students received support, including 21 fellowships with full and partial tuition reimbursements available (averaging $10,613 per year), 1 research assistantship with full and partial tuition reimbursement available (averaging $9,594 per year); career-related internships or fieldwork, Federal Work-Study, institutionally sponsored loans, scholarships/grants, tuition waivers (full and partial), and unspecified assistantships also available. Support available to part-time students. Financial award applicants required to submit FAFSA. *Faculty research:* Corporate governance and executive compensation, Sarbanes-Oxley and certification compliance for financial statement, student performance and evaluation models, decomposing the elements of nonprofit organizational performance, accounting for international financial reporting standards. *Unit head:* Dr. Nathan S. Slavin, Chairperson, 516-463-5690, Fax: 516-463-4834, E-mail: actnzs@hofstra.edu. *Application contact:* Carol Drummer, Dean of Graduate Admissions, 516-463-4876, Fax: 516-463-4664, E-mail: gradstudent@hofstra.edu.

Holy Family University, Division of Extended Learning, Philadelphia, PA 19114. Offers business administration (MBA); finance (MBA); health care administration (MBA). *Accreditation:* ACBSP. Part-time and evening/weekend programs available. *Faculty:* 78 part-time/adjunct (32 women). *Students:* 116 part-time (71 women); includes 10 Black or African American, non-Hispanic/Latino; 6 Asian, non-Hispanic/Latino; 2 Hispanic/Latino. Average age 35. 46 applicants, 93% accepted, 41 enrolled. In 2010, 47 master's awarded. *Entrance requirements:* For master's, interview, essay. Additional exam requirements/recommendations for international students: Required—TOEFL. *Application deadline:* Applications are processed on a rolling basis. Application fee: $50. Electronic applications accepted. *Expenses:* Tuition: Full-time $14,400; part-time $600 per credit hour. Required fees: $85 per term. *Financial support:* Applicants required to submit FAFSA. *Unit head:* Honour Moore, Associate Vice President, 267-341-5008, Fax: 215-633-0558, E-mail: hmoore@holyfamily.edu. *Application contact:* Don Reinmold, Director of Admissions for Division of Extended Learning, 267-341-5001 Ext. 3230, Fax: 215-633-0558, E-mail: dreinmold@holyfamily.edu.

Holy Family University, Graduate School, School of Business Administration, Philadelphia, PA 19114. Offers human resources management (MS); information systems management (MS). *Accreditation:* ACBSP. Part-time and evening/weekend programs available. *Faculty:* 2 full-time (0 women), 10 part-time/adjunct (3 women). *Students:* 62 part-time (36 women); includes 3 Black or African American, non-Hispanic/Latino; 1 Asian, non-Hispanic/Latino; 1 Hispanic/Latino. Average age 34. 32 applicants, 75% accepted, 17 enrolled. In 2010, 24 master's awarded. *Degree requirements:* For master's, comprehensive exam, thesis optional. *Entrance requirements:* For master's, GMAT, GRE, or MAT, minimum GPA of 3.0. *Application deadline:* For fall admission, 8/1 priority date for domestic students; for winter admission, 1/1 priority date for domestic students. Applications are processed on a rolling basis. Application fee: $25. Electronic applications accepted. *Expenses:* Tuition: Full-time $14,400; part-time $600 per credit hour. Required fees: $85 per term. *Financial support:* Federal Work-Study available. Support available to part-time students. Financial award application deadline: 5/1; financial award applicants required to submit FAFSA. *Unit head:* Dr. Jan Duggar, Dean of the School of Business, 267-341-3373, Fax: 215-637-5937, E-mail: jduggar@holyfamily.edu. *Application contact:* Gidget Marie Montelibano, Graduate Admissions Counselor, 267-341-3558, Fax: 215-637-1478, E-mail: gmontelibano@holyfamily.edu.

Holy Names University, Graduate Division, Department of Business, Oakland, CA 94619-1699. Offers energy and environment management (MBA); finance (MBA); management and leadership (MBA); marketing (MBA); sports management (MBA). Part-time and evening/weekend programs available. *Faculty:* 3 full-time (2 women), 4 part-time/adjunct (1 woman). *Students:* 67 full-time (40 women); includes 28 Black or African American, non-Hispanic/Latino; 7 Asian, non-Hispanic/Latino; 5 Hispanic/Latino, 2 international. Average age 33. 24 applicants, 75% accepted, 7 enrolled. In 2010, 29 master's awarded. *Entrance requirements:* For master's, minimum undergraduate GPA of 2.6 overall, 3.0 in major. Additional exam requirements/recommendations for international students: Required—TOEFL (minimum score 550 paper-based;

213 computer-based; 80 iBT). *Application deadline:* For fall admission, 8/1 priority date for domestic students, 8/1 for international students; for spring admission, 12/1 priority date for domestic students, 12/1 for international students. Applications are processed on a rolling basis. Application fee: $0. *Expenses:* Tuition: Full-time $13,788; part-time $766 per credit. Required fees: $340; $170 per semester. *Financial support:* In 2010–11, 19 students received support. Available to part-time students. Application deadline: 3/2. *Faculty research:* Business ethics, sustainable economics, accounting models, cross-cultural management, diversity in organizations. *Unit head:* Dr. Marcia Frideger, Program Director, 510-436-1205, E-mail: frideger@hnu.edu. *Application contact:* 800-430-1351, Fax: 510-436-1325, E-mail: admissions@hnu.edu.

Hood College, Graduate School, Department of Economics and Management, Frederick, MD 21701-8575. Offers accounting (MBA); administration and management (MBA); finance (MBA); human resource management (MBA); information systems (MBA); marketing (MBA); public management (MBA). *Accreditation:* ACBSP. Part-time and evening/weekend programs available. *Faculty:* 4 full-time (1 woman), 9 part-time/adjunct (1 woman). *Students:* 16 full-time (9 women), 127 part-time (65 women); includes 17 Black or African American, non-Hispanic/Latino; 9 Asian, non-Hispanic/Latino; 5 Hispanic/Latino; 1 Two or more races, non-Hispanic/Latino, 10 international. Average age 32. 60 applicants, 62% accepted, 25 enrolled. In 2010, 56 master's awarded. *Degree requirements:* For master's, capstone/final research project. *Entrance requirements:* For master's, minimum GPA of 2.75, resume, letters of recommendation. Additional exam requirements/recommendations for international students: Required—TOEFL (minimum score 575 paper-based; 231 computer-based; 89 iBT). *Application deadline:* For fall admission, 7/15 for domestic and international students; for spring admission, 12/15 for domestic and international students. Applications are processed on a rolling basis. Application fee: $35. Electronic applications accepted. *Expenses:* Tuition: Full-time $6480; part-time $360 per credit. Required fees: $100; $50 per term. *Financial support:* Applicants required to submit FAFSA. *Faculty research:* Corporate strategy and sustainable competitive advantages, business ethics, entrepreneurship, investments management, economic development. *Unit head:* Dr. Anita Jose, Program Director, 301-696-3691, Fax: 301-696-3597, E-mail: jose@hood.edu. *Application contact:* Dr. Allen P. Flora, Dean of Graduate School, 301-696-3811, Fax: 301-696-3597, E-mail: gofurther@hood.edu.

Humboldt State University, Academic Programs, College of Professional Studies, School of Business, Arcata, CA 95521-8299. Offers MBA. Part-time and evening/weekend programs available. *Students:* 10 full-time (6 women), 3 part-time (0 women); includes 4 minority (1 Asian, non-Hispanic/Latino; 3 Hispanic/Latino), 3 international. Average age 32. 37 applicants, 95% accepted, 7 enrolled. In 2010, 20 master's awarded. *Degree requirements:* For master's, thesis or alternative. *Entrance requirements:* For master's, GMAT or GRE, minimum GPA of 2.5. Additional exam requirements/recommendations for international students: Required—TOEFL (minimum score 500 paper-based; 173 computer-based). *Application deadline:* For fall admission, 6/30 for domestic and international students; for spring admission, 12/15 for domestic and international students. Applications are processed on a rolling basis. Application fee: $55. *Expenses:* Contact institution. *Financial support:* Fellowships, Federal Work-Study available. Support available to part-time students. Financial award application deadline: 3/1; financial award applicants required to submit FAFSA. *Faculty research:* International business development, small town entrepreneurship, international trade: Pacific Rim. *Unit head:* Dr. Steven Hackett, Chair, 707-826-3846, Fax: 707-826-6666, E-mail: steve.hackett@humboldt.edu. *Application contact:* Dr. Kien-Quoc Van Pham, MBA Coordinator, 707-826-5665, Fax: 707-826-6666, E-mail: kv7@humboldt.edu.

Illinois Institute of Technology, Stuart School of Business, Program in Business Administration, Chicago, IL 60616-3793. Offers financial management (MBA); innovation and emerging enterprises (MBA); management science (MBA); marketing (MBA); sustainability (MBA); JD/MBA; M Des/MBA; MBA/MS. *Accreditation:* AACSB. Part-time and evening/weekend programs available. *Faculty:* 37 full-time (4 women), 21 part-time/adjunct (5 women). *Students:* 153 full-time (66 women), 30 part-time (12 women); includes 17 minority (3 Black or African American, non-Hispanic/Latino; 9 Asian, non-Hispanic/Latino; 3 Hispanic/Latino; 2 Two or more races, non-Hispanic/Latino), 119 international. Average age 27. 334 applicants, 77% accepted, 63 enrolled. In 2010, 40 master's awarded. *Entrance requirements:* For master's, GRE (minimum score 1000) or GMAT (500). Additional exam requirements/recommendations for international students: Required—TOEFL (minimum score 600 paper-based; 85 iBT); Recommended—IELTS (minimum score 7). *Application deadline:* For fall admission, 8/1 for domestic students, 5/1 for international students; for spring admission, 12/15 for domestic students, 10/15 for international students. Applications are processed on a rolling basis. Application fee: $75. Electronic applications accepted. *Expenses:* Contact institution. *Financial support:* Career-related internships or fieldwork, Federal Work-Study, institutionally sponsored loans, scholarships/grants, traineeships, health care benefits, and tuition waivers (partial) available. Support available to part-time students. Financial award applicants required to submit FAFSA. *Faculty research:* Global management and marketing strategy, technological

innovation, management science, financial management, knowledge management. *Unit head:* M. Krishna Erramilli, Interim Director, 312-906-6573, Fax: 312-906-6549. *Application contact:* Deborah Gibson, Director, Graduate Admission, 866-472-3448, Fax: 312-472-3448, E-mail: inquiry.grad@iit.edu.

Illinois Institute of Technology, Stuart School of Business, Program in Management Science, Chicago, IL 60616-3793. Offers PhD. *Accreditation:* AACSB. Part-time programs available. *Faculty:* 37 full-time (4 women), 21 part-time/adjunct (5 women). *Students:* 24 full-time (11 women), 16 part-time (3 women), 30 international. Average age 34. 49 applicants, 47% accepted, 11 enrolled. In 2010, 7 doctorates awarded. *Degree requirements:* For doctorate, comprehensive exam, thesis/dissertation. *Entrance requirements:* For doctorate, GRE (minimum score 1300) or GMAT (minimum score 650). Additional exam requirements/recommendations for international students: Required—TOEFL (minimum score 600 paper-based; 85 iBT). *Application deadline:* For fall admission, 5/1 for domestic and international students; for spring admission, 10/15 for domestic and international students. Applications are processed on a rolling basis. Application fee: $75. Electronic applications accepted. *Expenses:* Contact institution. *Financial support:* Career-related internships or fieldwork, Federal Work-Study, institutionally sponsored loans, scholarships/grants, traineeships, health care benefits, and tuition waivers (partial) available. Support available to part-time students. Financial award applicants required to submit FAFSA. *Faculty research:* Scheduling systems, queuing systems, optimization, quality systems, foreign exchange, enterprise risk management, credit risk modeling. *Unit head:* Dr. Zia Hassan, Professor and Dean, Emeritus, 312-906-6515, Fax: 312-906-6549, E-mail: hassan@stuart.iit.edu. *Application contact:* Deborah Gibson, Director, Graduate Admission, 866-472-3448, Fax: 312-567-3138, E-mail: inquiry.grad@iit.edu.

Indiana University Bloomington, Kelley School of Business, Bloomington, IN 47405-7000. Offers MBA, MPA, MS, DBA, PhD, DBA/MIS, JD/MBA, JD/MPA, MBA/MA, PhD/MIS. PhD offered through University Graduate School. *Accreditation:* AACSB. *Faculty:* 71 full-time (10 women). *Students:* 1,401 full-time (376 women), 452 part-time (101 women); includes 323 minority (61 Black or African American, non-Hispanic/Latino; 1 American Indian or Alaska Native, non-Hispanic/Latino; 200 Asian, non-Hispanic/Latino; 45 Hispanic/Latino; 1 Native Hawaiian or other Pacific Islander, non-Hispanic/Latino; 15 Two or more races, non-Hispanic/Latino), 358 international. Average age 31. 2,746 applicants, 43% accepted, 763 enrolled. In 2010, 960 master's, 6 doctorates awarded. *Degree requirements:* For doctorate, thesis/dissertation. *Entrance requirements:* For master's, GMAT; for doctorate, GMAT, GRE General Test. Additional exam requirements/recommendations for international students: Required—TOEFL. *Application deadline:* For fall admission, 1/15 priority date for domestic students, 12/1 priority date for international students; for winter admission, 3/1 priority date for domestic students; for spring admission, 4/15 for domestic students, 9/1 for international students. Application fee: $55 ($65 for international students). Electronic applications accepted. *Expenses:* Contact institution. *Financial support:* Fellowships with full and partial tuition reimbursements, research assistantships, teaching assistantships, career-related internships or fieldwork, Federal Work-Study, institutionally sponsored loans, tuition waivers (full and partial), and unspecified assistantships available. Support available to part-time students. Financial award application deadline: 3/1; financial award applicants required to submit FAFSA. Total annual research expenditures: $1.1 million. *Unit head:* Daniel Smith, Dean, 812-855-8100, Fax: 812-855-8679, E-mail: business@indiana.edu. *Application contact:* Director of Admissions and Financial Aid, 812-855-8006, Fax: 812-855-9039.

Indiana University Kokomo, School of Business, Kokomo, IN 46904-9003. Offers business administration (MBA). *Accreditation:* AACSB. Part-time and evening/weekend programs available. *Faculty:* 14 full-time (6 women). *Students:* 7 full-time (2 women), 19 part-time (6 women); includes 4 minority (2 Black or African American, non-Hispanic/Latino; 1 Asian, non-Hispanic/Latino; 1 Two or more races, non-Hispanic/Latino). Average age 35. 13 applicants, 92% accepted, 10 enrolled. In 2010, 24 master's awarded. *Degree requirements:* For master's, thesis optional, research project. *Entrance requirements:* For master's, GMAT. Additional exam requirements/recommendations for international students: Required—TOEFL (minimum score 550 paper-based; 213 computer-based). *Application deadline:* For fall admission, 8/1 priority date for domestic and international students; for spring admission, 12/15 priority date for domestic and international students. Applications are processed on a rolling basis. Application fee: $40 ($50 for international students). *Expenses:* Contact institution. *Financial support:* In 2010–11, 2 students received support, including 2 fellowships (averaging $500 per year); research assistantships, teaching assistantships, career-related internships or fieldwork and tuition waivers (partial) also available. *Faculty research:* Investments, outsourcing, technology, adoption. *Unit head:* Dr. Niranjan Pati, Dean, 756-455-9275, Fax: 756-455-9348, E-mail: npati@iuk.edu. *Application contact:* Dr. Linda Ficht, Director of MBA Program, 765-455-9275, Fax: 765-455-9348, E-mail: lficht@iuk.edu.

Indiana University Northwest, School of Business and Economics, Gary, IN 46408-1197. Offers accountancy (M Acc); accounting (Certificate); business administration (MBA). *Accreditation:* AACSB. Part-time and evening/weekend programs available. *Faculty:* 5 full-time (0 women). *Students:* 54 full-time (15 women), 65 part-time (28 women); includes 43 minority (27

Black or African American, non-Hispanic/Latino; 7 Asian, non-Hispanic/Latino; 9 Hispanic/Latino). Average age 34. 64 applicants, 94% accepted, 55 enrolled. In 2010, 46 master's, 4 other advanced degrees awarded. *Entrance requirements:* For master's, GMAT, letter of recommendation. *Application deadline:* For fall admission, 7/15 priority date for domestic students; for spring admission, 11/15 for domestic students. Applications are processed on a rolling basis. Application fee: $25. *Expenses:* Contact institution. *Financial support:* In 2010–11, 9 students received support. Federal Work-Study, institutionally sponsored loans, and unspecified assistantships available. Support available to part-time students. Financial award application deadline: 7/15. *Faculty research:* International finance, wellness in the workplace, handicapped employment, MIS, regional economic forecasting. *Unit head:* Anna Rominger, Dean, 219-980-6636, Fax: 219-980-6916, E-mail: iunbiz@iun.edu. *Application contact:* John Gibson, Director of Graduate Program, 219-980-6635, Fax: 219-980-6916, E-mail: jagibson@iun.edu.

Indiana University of Pennsylvania, School of Graduate Studies and Research, Eberly College of Business and Information Technology, Program in Business Administration, Indiana, PA 15705-1087. Offers business administration (MBA); executive business administration (MBA). *Accreditation:* AACSB. Part-time programs available. *Faculty:* 38 full-time (9 women). *Students:* 184 full-time (67 women), 74 part-time (27 women); includes 11 minority (3 Black or African American, non-Hispanic/Latino; 6 Asian, non-Hispanic/Latino; 1 Hispanic/Latino; 1 Two or more races, non-Hispanic/Latino), 172 international. Average age 26. 202 applicants, 65% accepted, 100 enrolled. In 2010, 192 master's awarded. *Degree requirements:* For master's, thesis optional. *Entrance requirements:* For master's, GMAT, 2 letters of recommendation. Additional exam requirements/recommendations for international students: Required—TOEFL. *Application deadline:* For fall admission, 7/1 priority date for domestic students; for spring admission, 11/1 for domestic students. Applications are processed on a rolling basis. Application fee: $40. *Financial support:* In 2010–11, 44 research assistantships with full and partial tuition reimbursements (averaging $1,991 per year) were awarded; fellowships, career-related internships or fieldwork and Federal Work-Study also available. Support available to part-time students. Financial award application deadline: 3/15; financial award applicants required to submit FAFSA. *Unit head:* Dr. Krish Krishnan, Graduate Coordinator, 724-357-2522, E-mail: krishnan@iup.edu. *Application contact:* Donna Griffith, Assistant Dean, 724-357-2222, Fax: 724-357-4862, E-mail: graduate-admissions@iup.edu.

Indiana University–Purdue University Fort Wayne, Doermer School of Business, Fort Wayne, IN 46805-1499. Offers business administration (MBA); business administration-accelerated (MBA). *Accreditation:* AACSB. Part-time programs available. *Faculty:* 32 full-time (13 women). *Students:* 43 full-time (12 women), 60 part-time (17 women); includes 12 minority (5 Black or African American, non-Hispanic/Latino; 4 Asian, non-Hispanic/Latino; 3 Hispanic/Latino), 6 international. Average age 32. 108 applicants, 66% accepted, 63 enrolled. In 2010, 66 master's awarded. *Entrance requirements:* For master's, GMAT, minimum GPA of 3.0, two letters of recommendation, essay, interview. Additional exam requirements/recommendations for international students: Required—TOEFL (minimum score 600 paper-based; 250 computer-based; 100 iBT). *Application deadline:* For fall admission, 7/15 for domestic students, 5/1 for international students; for spring admission, 11/15 for domestic students, 10/1 for international students. Applications are processed on a rolling basis. Application fee: $55. *Expenses:* Tuition, state resident: full-time $4824; part-time $268 per credit. Tuition, nonresident: full-time $11,625; part-time $646 per credit. Required fees: $555; $30.85 per credit. Tuition and fees vary according to course load. *Financial support:* In 2010–11, 9 teaching assistantships with partial tuition reimbursements (averaging $12,740 per year) were awarded; scholarships/grants and unspecified assistantships also available. Support available to part-time students. Financial award application deadline: 3/1; financial award applicants required to submit FAFSA. *Faculty research:* U. S. healthcare system, oil and pump prices, retirement savings, culture and communication. Total annual research expenditures: $17,641. *Unit head:* Dr. Otto Chang, Dean, 260-481-0219, Fax: 260-481-6879, E-mail: chango@ipfw.edu. *Application contact:* Dr. Lyman Lewis, MBA Program Administrator, 260-481-6474, Fax: 260-481-6879, E-mail: lewisl@ipfw.edu.

Indiana University–Purdue University Indianapolis, Kelley School of Business, Indianapolis, IN 46202-2896. Offers accounting (MSA); business (MBA). *Accreditation:* AACSB. Part-time and evening/weekend programs available. Postbaccalaureate distance learning degree programs offered (minimal on-campus study). *Faculty:* 20 full-time (4 women), 1 part-time/adjunct (0 women). *Students:* 128 full-time (57 women), 409 part-time (148 women); includes 85 minority (29 Black or African American, non-Hispanic/Latino; 40 Asian, non-Hispanic/Latino; 13 Hispanic/Latino; 3 Two or more races, non-Hispanic/Latino), 83 international. Average age 30. 221 applicants, 76% accepted, 113 enrolled. In 2010, 246 master's awarded. *Entrance requirements:* For master's, GMAT, previous course work in accounting, statistics. *Application deadline:* For fall admission, 4/15 priority date for domestic and international students; for spring admission, 11/1 priority date for domestic and international students. Application fee: $55 ($65 for international students). Electronic applications accepted. *Expenses:* Contact institution. *Financial support:* In 2010–11, 3 fellowships (averaging $16,193 per year), 1 teaching

assistantship (averaging $9,000 per year) were awarded; Federal Work-Study, institutionally sponsored loans, and scholarships/grants also available. Support available to part-time students. Financial award application deadline: 3/1; financial award applicants required to submit FAFSA. *Unit head:* Phil Cochran, Associate Dean, Indianapolis Programs, 317-274-2481, Fax: 317-274-2483, E-mail: busugrad@iupui.edu. *Application contact:* Julie L. Moore, Recorder/Admission Coordinator, 317-274-4895, Fax: 317-274-2483, E-mail: mbaindy@iupui.edu.

Indiana University South Bend, School of Business and Economics, South Bend, IN 46634-7111. Offers accounting (MSA); business administration (MBA); management of information technologies (MS). Part-time and evening/weekend programs available. *Faculty:* 17 full-time (2 women), 3 part-time/adjunct (1 woman). *Students:* 61 full-time (26 women), 100 part-time (32 women); includes 16 minority (6 Black or African American, non-Hispanic/Latino; 1 American Indian or Alaska Native, non-Hispanic/Latino; 4 Asian, non-Hispanic/Latino; 4 Hispanic/Latino; 1 Two or more races, non-Hispanic/Latino), 51 international. Average age 32. 76 applicants, 58% accepted, 28 enrolled. In 2010, 67 master's awarded. *Entrance requirements:* For master's, GMAT. Additional exam requirements/recommendations for international students: Required—TOEFL (minimum score 550 paper-based; 213 computer-based). *Application deadline:* For fall admission, 7/1 priority date for domestic and international students; for spring admission, 11/1 priority date for domestic and international students. Applications are processed on a rolling basis. Application fee: $50 ($60 for international students). *Expenses:* Contact institution. *Financial support:* In 2010–11, 1 fellowship (averaging $3,846 per year) was awarded; Federal Work-Study and institutionally sponsored loans also available. Support available to part-time students. Financial award applicants required to submit FAFSA. *Faculty research:* Financial accounting, consumer research, capital budgeting research, business strategy research. *Unit head:* Robert H. Ducoffe, Dean, 574-520-4228, Fax: 574-520-4866. *Application contact:* Sharon Peterson, Secretary, 574-520-4138, Fax: 574-520-4866, E-mail: speterso@iusb.edu.

Indiana University Southeast, School of Business, New Albany, IN 47150-6405. Offers business administration (MBA); strategic finance (MS). *Accreditation:* AACSB. *Faculty:* 11 full-time (2 women). *Students:* 11 full-time (4 women), 222 part-time (88 women); includes 19 minority (4 Black or African American, non-Hispanic/Latino; 8 Asian, non-Hispanic/Latino; 2 Hispanic/Latino; 3 Native Hawaiian or other Pacific Islander, non-Hispanic/Latino; 2 Two or more races, non-Hispanic/Latino), 4 international. Average age 31. 41 applicants, 100% accepted, 37 enrolled. In 2010, 74 master's awarded. *Degree requirements:* For master's, community service. *Entrance requirements:* For master's, GMAT, work experience. Additional exam requirements/recommendations for international students: Required—TOEFL. Application fee: $35. *Expenses:* Contact institution. *Financial support:* In 2010–11, 2 teaching assistantships (averaging $4,500 per year) were awarded. *Unit head:* Dr. Jay White, Dean, 812-941-2362, Fax: 812-941-2672. *Application contact:* Dr. Jay White, Dean, 812-941-2362, Fax: 812-941-2672.

Iona College, Hagan School of Business, New Rochelle, NY 10801-1890. Offers MBA, Certificate, PMC. *Accreditation:* AACSB. Part-time and evening/weekend programs available. *Faculty:* 33 full-time (7 women), 14 part-time/adjunct (3 women). *Students:* 115 full-time (58 women), 299 part-time (130 women); includes 71 minority (23 Black or African American, non-Hispanic/Latino; 14 Asian, non-Hispanic/Latino; 33 Hispanic/Latino; 1 Two or more races, non-Hispanic/Latino), 7 international. Average age 32. 152 applicants, 71% accepted, 99 enrolled. In 2010, 179 master's, 139 other advanced degrees awarded. *Entrance requirements:* For master's, GMAT, 2 letters of recommendation. Additional exam requirements/recommendations for international students: Required—TOEFL (minimum score 550 paper-based; 213 computer-based). *Application deadline:* For fall admission, 8/15 priority date for domestic students, 8/1 for international students; for winter admission, 11/15 priority date for domestic students, 11/1 for international students; for spring admission, 2/15 priority date for domestic students, 2/1 for international students. Applications are processed on a rolling basis. Application fee: $50. Electronic applications accepted. *Expenses:* Contact institution. *Financial support:* Fellowships with tuition reimbursements, Federal Work-Study, scholarships/grants, tuition waivers (partial), and unspecified assistantships available. Support available to part-time students. Financial award application deadline: 4/15; financial award applicants required to submit FAFSA. *Faculty research:* Artificial intelligence, financial services, value-based management, public policy, business ethics. *Unit head:* Dr. Vincent Calluzo, Dean, 914-633-2256, E-mail: vcalluzo@iona.edu. *Application contact:* Ben Fan, Director of MBA Admissions, 914-633-2289, Fax: 914-637-2708, E-mail: sfan@iona.edu.

See Display on the next page and Close-Up on page 258.

Iowa State University of Science and Technology, Graduate College, College of Business, Ames, IA 50011. Offers M Acc, MBA, MS, PhD, M Arch/MBA, MBA/MCRP, MBA/MS. *Accreditation:* AACSB. *Faculty:* 75 full-time (18 women), 1 (woman) part-time/adjunct. *Students:* 178 full-time (74 women), 130 part-time (41 women); includes 4 Black or African American, non-Hispanic/Latino; 8 Asian, non-Hispanic/Latino; 6 Hispanic/Latino, 85 international. 272 applicants, 44% accepted, 85 enrolled. In 2010, 129 master's, 1 doctorate awarded. *Entrance requirements:* For master's, GMAT, resume. Additional exam requirements/recommendations for international students: Required—TOEFL. Application fee: $40 ($90 for international students). Electronic applications accepted. *Expenses:* Contact institution. *Financial support:* In 2010–11, 49 research assistantships with full and partial tuition reimbursements (averaging $5,621 per year), 2 teaching assistantships with full and partial tuition reimbursements (averaging $4,440 per year) were awarded; scholarships/grants, health care benefits, and unspecified assistantships also available. *Unit head:* Dr. Labh S. Hira, Dean, 515-294-2422, E-mail: busgrad@iastate.edu. *Application contact:* Dr. Labh S. Hira, Dean, 515-294-2422, E-mail: busgrad@iastate.edu.

Ithaca College, Division of Graduate and Professional Studies, School of Business, Program in Business Administration, Ithaca, NY 14850. Offers MBA. *Accreditation:* AACSB. Part-time programs available. *Faculty:* 18 full-time (5 women). *Students:* 10 full-time (2 women), 7 part-time (2 women); includes 3 minority (1 Black or African American, non-Hispanic/Latino; 1 Asian, non-Hispanic/Latino; 1 Hispanic/Latino). Average age 28. 29 applicants, 72% accepted, 11 enrolled. In 2010, 2 master's awarded. *Degree requirements:* For master's, thesis optional. *Entrance requirements:* For master's, GMAT, minimum GPA of 3.0. Additional exam requirements/recommendations for international students: Required—TOEFL (minimum score 550 paper-based; 213 computer-based; 80 iBT). *Application deadline:* For fall admission, 6/1 for domestic and international students; for spring admission, 12/1 for domestic and international students. Applications are processed on a rolling basis. Application fee: $40. Electronic applications accepted. *Expenses:* Contact institution. *Financial support:* In 2010–11, 6 students received support, including 2 fellowships (averaging $3,064 per year), 4 teaching assistantships (averaging $5,516 per year); career-related internships or fieldwork, Federal Work-Study, and scholarships/grants also available. Support available to part-time students. Financial award application deadline: 3/1; financial award applicants required to submit CSS PROFILE or FAFSA. *Unit head:* Dr. Donald Eckrich, MBA Program Director, 607-274-3527, Fax: 607-274-1263, E-mail: gps@ithaca.edu. *Application contact:* Rob Gearhart, Dean, Graduate and Professional Studies, 607-274-3527, Fax: 607-274-1263, E-mail: gps@ithaca.edu.

Jackson State University, Graduate School, College of Business, Department of Economics, Finance and General Business, Jackson, MS 39217. Offers business administration (MBA, PhD). *Accreditation:* AACSB. Part-time and evening/weekend programs available. *Faculty:* 7 full-time (1 woman). *Students:* 23 full-time (11 women), 27 part-time (13 women); includes 35 Black or African American, non-Hispanic/Latino; 1 Asian, non-Hispanic/Latino, 4 international. Average age 35. In 2010, 21 master's, 6 doctorates awarded. *Degree requirements:* For master's, comprehensive exam, thesis. *Entrance requirements:* For master's, GRE General Test, GMAT; for doctorate, MAT, GMAT. Additional exam requirements/recommendations for international students: Required—TOEFL. *Application deadline:* For fall admission, 3/1 priority date for domestic students, 3/1 for international students; for spring admission, 10/1 for domestic and international students. Applications are processed on a rolling basis. *Expenses:* Tuition, state resident: full-time $5050; part-time $281 per credit hour. Tuition, nonresident: full-time $12,380; part-time $689 per credit hour. *Financial support:* Federal Work-Study, scholarships/grants, tuition waivers (full and partial), and unspecified assistantships available. Support available to part-time students. Financial award application deadline: 3/1. *Unit head:* Dr. Maury Granger, Chair, 601-979-2531, E-mail: maury.granger@jsums.edu. *Application contact:* Sharlene Wilson, Director of Graduate Admissions, 601-979-2455, Fax: 601-979-4325, E-mail: sharlene.f.wilson@jsums.edu.

James Madison University, The Graduate School, College of Business, Program in Business Administration, Harrisonburg, VA 22807. Offers MBA. *Accreditation:* AACSB. Part-time and evening/weekend programs available. Postbaccalaureate distance learning degree programs offered (no on-campus study). *Students:* 37 full-time (13 women), 39 part-time (11 women); includes 18 minority (4 Black or African American, non-Hispanic/Latino; 7 Asian, non-Hispanic/Latino; 1 Hispanic/Latino; 1 Native Hawaiian or other Pacific Islander, non-Hispanic/Latino; 5 Two or more races, non-Hispanic/Latino), 3 international. Average age 27. In 2010, 27 master's awarded. *Entrance requirements:* For master's, GMAT, resume, 2 letters of recommendation. Additional exam requirements/recommendations for international students: Required—TOEFL. *Application deadline:* For fall admission, 6/1 priority date for domestic students, 5/1 for international students; for spring admission, 6/1 for domestic students, 9/1 for international students. Applications are processed on a rolling basis. Application fee: $55. Electronic applications accepted. *Financial support:* In 2010–11, 1 student received support. Federal Work-Study and 1 athletic assistantships ($8664) available. Financial award application deadline: 3/1; financial award applicants required to submit FAFSA. *Unit head:* Dr. Paul E. Bierly, Director, 540-568-3009. *Application contact:* Lynette M. Bible, Director of Graduate Admissions, 540-568-6395, Fax: 540-568-7860, E-mail: biblelm@jmu.edu.

The Johns Hopkins University, Carey Business School, Management Programs, Baltimore, MD 21218-2699. Offers leadership development (Certificate); organization development and human resources (MS); skilled facilitator (Certificate). Evening/weekend programs available. *Faculty:* 29 full-time (6 women), 135 part-time/adjunct (29 women). *Students:* 1 (woman) full-time, 33 part-time (19 women); includes 25 minority (22 Black or African

American, non-Hispanic/Latino; 2 Asian, non-Hispanic/Latino; 1 Hispanic/Latino). Average age 35. 30 applicants, 100% accepted, 25 enrolled. In 2010, 18 master's, 26 other advanced degrees awarded. *Degree requirements:* For master's, 36 credits including final project. *Entrance requirements:* For master's and Certificate, minimum GPA of 3.0, resume, work experience, two letters of recommendation. Additional exam requirements/recommendations for international students: Required—TOEFL (minimum score 600 paper-based; 250 computer-based; 100 iBT). *Application deadline:* For fall admission, 4/1 for international students; for spring admission, 9/15 for international students. Applications are processed on a rolling basis. Application fee: $100. Electronic applications accepted. *Financial support:* In 2010–11, 9 students received support. Scholarships/grants available. Support available to part-time students. Financial award application deadline: 4/15; financial award applicants required to submit FAFSA. *Faculty research:* Agency theory and theory of the firm, technological entrepreneurship, technology policy and economic development, strategic human resources management, ethics and stakeholder theory. Total annual research expenditures: $57,832. *Unit head:* Dr. Dipankar Chakravarti, Vice Dean of Programs, 410-234-9311, E-mail: dipankar.chakravarti@jhu.edu. *Application contact:* Robin Greeberg, Admissions Coordinator, 410-234-9227, Fax: 443-529-1554, E-mail: carey.admissions@jhu.edu.

The Johns Hopkins University, Carey Business School, MBA Department, Baltimore, MD 21218-2699. Offers MBA, MBA/MA, MBA/MPH, MBA/MS, MBA/MSIS, MBA/MSN. Part-time and evening/weekend programs available. Postbaccalaureate distance learning degree programs offered (minimal on-campus study). *Faculty:* 29 full-time (6 women), 135 part-time/adjunct (29 women). *Students:* 221 full-time (94 women), 604 part-time (249 women); includes 296 minority (118 Black or African American, non-Hispanic/Latino; 1 American Indian or Alaska Native, non-Hispanic/Latino; 121 Asian, non-Hispanic/Latino; 43 Hispanic/Latino; 2 Native Hawaiian or other Pacific Islander, non-Hispanic/Latino; 11 Two or more races, non-Hispanic/Latino), 130 international. Average age 33. 512 applicants, 80% accepted, 268 enrolled. In 2010, 312 master's awarded. *Degree requirements:* For master's, capstone project (MBA). *Entrance requirements:* For master's, GMAT or GRE, minimum GPA of 3.0, resume, work experience, two letters of recommendation. Additional exam requirements/recommendations for international students: Required—TOEFL (minimum score 600 paper-based; 250 computer-based; 100 iBT). *Application deadline:* For fall admission, 4/1 for international students; for spring admission, 8/15 for international students. Applications are processed on a rolling basis. Application fee: $100. Electronic applications accepted. *Financial support:* In 2010–11, 92 students received support. Scholarships/grants available. Support available to part-time students. Financial award application deadline: 4/15; financial award applicants required to submit FAFSA. *Unit head:* Dr. Dipankar Chakravarti, Vice Dean of Programs, 410-234-9311, Fax: 410-516-2033, E-mail: dipankar.chakravarti@jhu.edu. *Application contact:* Robin Greenberg, Admissions Coordinator, 410-234-9227, Fax: 443-529-1554, E-mail: carey.admissions@jhu.edu.

The Johns Hopkins University, School of Education, Division of Public Safety Leadership, Baltimore, MD 21218. Offers intelligence analysis (MS); management (MS). Part-time and evening/weekend programs available. *Faculty:* 10 full-time (3 women), 23 part-time/adjunct (7 women). *Students:* 131 full-time (39 women), 12 part-time (1 woman); includes 52 minority (35 Black or African American, non-Hispanic/Latino; 4 Asian, non-Hispanic/Latino; 12 Hispanic/Latino; 1 Two or more races, non-Hispanic/Latino). Average age 40. 81 applicants, 75% accepted, 54 enrolled. In 2010, 95 master's awarded. *Entrance requirements:* For master's, minimum undergraduate GPA of 3.0, curriculum vitae/resume, interview, professional experience, endorsement letter (MS in management). Additional exam requirements/recommendations for international students: Required—TOEFL (minimum score 600 paper-based; 250 computer-based; 100 iBT). *Application deadline:* For fall admission, 5/1 for international students; for spring admission, 10/15 for international students. Applications are processed on a rolling basis. Application fee: $0. Electronic applications accepted. *Financial support:* Scholarships/grants available. Support available to part-time students. Financial award application deadline: 6/1; financial award applicants required to submit FAFSA. *Faculty research:* Campus and school safety, prevention and effective response to violence against women, counterterrorism training, leadership development for public safety and homeland security executives. *Unit head:* Dr. Sheldon Greenberg, Associate Dean, 410-516-9900, Fax: 410-290-1061, E-mail: psl@jhu.edu. *Application contact:* Jennifer Shaffer, Director of Admissions, 410-516-9797, Fax: 410-516-9799, E-mail: educationinfo@jhu.edu.

Kean University, Nathan Weiss Graduate College, Program in Educational Administration, Union, NJ 07083. Offers school business administration (MA); supervisors and principals (MA). *Accreditation:* NCATE. Part-time and evening/weekend programs available. *Faculty:* 5 full-time (2 women). *Students:* 10 full-time (3 women), 221 part-time (147 women); includes 75 minority (44 Black or African American, non-Hispanic/Latino; 1 American Indian or Alaska Native, non-Hispanic/Latino; 2 Asian, non-Hispanic/Latino; 26 Hispanic/Latino; 1 Native Hawaiian or other Pacific Islander, non-Hispanic/Latino; 1 Two or more races, non-Hispanic/Latino). Average age 37. 111 applicants, 99% accepted, 75 enrolled. In 2010, 95 master's awarded. *Degree requirements:* For master's, comprehensive exam, portfolio, field experience, research component, internship, teaching experience. *Entrance requirements:* For master's, GRE General Test or MAT, minimum GPA of 3.0, interview, 2 letters of recommendation, 1 year of teaching experience, teacher certification, transcripts. *Application deadline:* For fall admission, 6/1 for domestic students; for spring admission, 11/1 for domestic students. Application fee: $75 ($150 for international students). Electronic applications accepted. *Expenses:* Tuition, state resident: full-time $10,872; part-time $500 per credit. Tuition, nonresident: full-time $14,736; part-time $614 per credit. Required fees: $2740.80; $125 per credit. Part-time tuition and fees vary according to course load and degree level. *Financial support:* In 2010–11, 2 research assistantships with full tuition reimbursements (averaging $3,263 per year) were awarded; unspecified assistantships also available. Financial award applicants required to submit FAFSA. *Unit head:* Dr. Efthimia Christie, Program Coordinator, 908-737-5974, E-mail: echristie@kean.edu. *Application contact:* Ann-Marie Kay, Assistant Director of Graduate Admissions, 908-737-5922, Fax: 908-737-5925, E-mail: akay@kean.edu.

Keiser University, Master of Business Administration Program, Fort Lauderdale, FL 33309. Offers accounting (MBA); health services management (MBA); international business (MBA); leadership for managers (MBA); marketing (MBA). Leadership for Managers and International Business concentrations also offered in Spanish. Part-time programs available. Postbaccalaureate distance learning degree programs offered (minimal on-campus study). *Faculty:* 8 full-time (3 women), 7 part-time/adjunct (2 women). *Students:* 18 full-time (14 women), 83 part-time (51 women); includes 30 Black or African American, non-Hispanic/Latino; 2 American Indian or Alaska Native, non-Hispanic/Latino; 2 Asian, non-Hispanic/Latino; 17 Hispanic/Latino, 1 international. Average age 42. 30 applicants, 77% accepted, 18 enrolled. In 2010, 21 degrees awarded. *Entrance requirements:* For master's, minimum GPA of 2.7 from an accredited institution. Additional exam requirements/recommendations for international students: Required—TOEFL. *Application deadline:* Applications are processed on a rolling basis. Application fee: $50. Electronic applications accepted. *Financial support:* In 2010–11, 95 students received support. Federal Work-Study available. Financial award applicants required to submit FAFSA.

Kennesaw State University, Michael J. Coles College of Business, Doctor of Business Administration Program, Kennesaw, GA 30144-5591. Offers DBA. *Accreditation:* AACSB. Part-time programs available. *Students:* 17 full-time (6 women), 24 part-time (11 women); includes 6 minority (4 Black or African American, non-Hispanic/Latino; 2 Asian, non-Hispanic/Latino). Average age 48. *Degree requirements:* For doctorate, thesis/dissertation. *Entrance requirements:* Additional exam requirements/recommendations for international students: Required—TOEFL (minimum score 550 paper-based; 213 computer-based; 80 iBT), IELTS (minimum score 6). *Application deadline:* For spring admission, 10/1 for domestic and international students. Applications are processed on a rolling basis. Application fee: $100. Electronic applications accepted. *Expenses:* Tuition, state resident: full-time $5500; part-time $225 per credit hour. Tuition, nonresident: full-time $16,100; part-time $813 per credit hour. Required fees: $673 per semester. *Financial support:* Application deadline: 4/1. *Unit head:* Dr. Joe Hair, Director, 770-499-3280, E-mail: jhair3@kennesaw.edu. *Application contact:* Tamara Hutto, Admissions Counselor, 770-420-4377, Fax: 770-423-6885, E-mail: ksugrad@kennesaw.edu.

Kennesaw State University, Michael J. Coles College of Business, Program in Business Administration, Kennesaw, GA 30144-5591. Offers MBA. *Accreditation:* AACSB. Part-time and evening/weekend programs available. Postbaccalaureate distance learning degree programs offered (no on-campus study). *Students:* 224 full-time (88 women), 337 part-time (124 women); includes 148 minority (101 Black or African American, non-Hispanic/Latino; 1 American Indian or Alaska Native, non-Hispanic/Latino; 29 Asian, non-Hispanic/Latino; 15 Hispanic/Latino; 2 Two or more races, non-Hispanic/Latino), 38 international. Average age 34. 419 applicants, 53% accepted, 176 enrolled. In 2010, 318 master's awarded. *Entrance requirements:* For master's, GMAT (minimum score 500), minimum GPA of 2.8, 1 year of work experience. Additional exam requirements/recommendations for international students: Required—TOEFL (minimum score 550 paper-based; 213 computer-based; 80 iBT), IELTS (minimum score 6). *Application deadline:* For fall admission, 7/1 for domestic and international students; for spring admission, 12/1 for domestic and international students. Applications are processed on a rolling basis. Application fee: $60. Electronic applications accepted. *Expenses:* Tuition, state resident: full-time $5500; part-time $225 per credit hour. Tuition, nonresident: full-time $16,100; part-time $813 per credit hour. Required fees: $673 per semester. *Financial support:* In 2010–11, 4 research assistantships with tuition reimbursements (averaging $4,000 per year) were awarded; unspecified assistantships also available. Financial award application deadline: 4/1; financial award applicants required to submit FAFSA. *Unit head:* Dr. Sheb True, Director, 770-423-6087, E-mail: strue@kennesaw.edu. *Application contact:* Tamara Hutto, Admissions Counselor, 770-420-4377, Fax: 770-423-6885, E-mail: ksugrad@kennesaw.edu.

Kent State University, Graduate School of Management, Master's Program in Business Administration, Kent, OH 44242-0001. Offers MBA. *Accreditation:* AACSB. Part-time and evening/weekend programs available. *Faculty:* 57

full-time (15 women), 7 part-time/adjunct (4 women). *Students:* 102 full-time (52 women), 124 part-time (52 women); includes 6 Black or African American, non-Hispanic/Latino; 7 Asian, non-Hispanic/Latino; 1 Hispanic/Latino, 32 international. Average age 27. 146 applicants, 75% accepted, 61 enrolled. In 2010, 80 master's awarded. *Entrance requirements:* For master's, GMAT, minimum GPA of 2.75. Additional exam requirements/recommendations for international students: Required—TOEFL (minimum score 550 paper-based; 213 computer-based; 79 iBT). *Application deadline:* For fall admission, 6/1 for domestic students, 4/1 for international students; for spring admission, 12/1 for domestic students. Application fee: $30 ($60 for international students). Electronic applications accepted. *Expenses:* Tuition, state resident: full-time $7866; part-time $437 per credit hour. Tuition, nonresident: full-time $14,022; part-time $779 per credit hour. *Financial support:* In 2010–11, 22 students received support, including 22 research assistantships with full tuition reimbursements available (averaging $6,700 per year); fellowships, career-related internships or fieldwork, Federal Work-Study, and unspecified assistantships also available. Financial award application deadline: 4/1; financial award applicants required to submit FAFSA. *Unit head:* Louise M. Ditchey, Administrative Director, 330-672-2282, Fax: 330-672-7303, E-mail: gradbus@kent.edu. *Application contact:* Felecia A. Urbanek, Coordinator, Graduate Programs, 330-672-2282, Fax: 330-672-7303, E-mail: gradbus@kent.edu.

Kentucky State University, College of Professional Studies, Frankfort, KY 40601. Offers business administration (MBA), including accounting, finance, management, marketing; public administration (MPA), including human resource management, international administration and development, management information systems, nonprofit management; special education (MA). Part-time and evening/weekend programs available. Postbaccalaureate distance learning degree programs offered (minimal on-campus study). *Faculty:* 12 full-time (4 women), 2 part-time/adjunct (both women). *Students:* 88 full-time (57 women), 79 part-time (42 women); includes 104 minority (101 Black or African American, non-Hispanic/Latino; 1 Asian, non-Hispanic/Latino; 2 Hispanic/Latino), 2 international. Average age 34. 124 applicants, 62% accepted, 45 enrolled. In 2010, 38 master's awarded. *Degree requirements:* For master's, comprehensive exam, thesis optional. *Entrance requirements:* For master's, GMAT, GRE. Additional exam requirements/recommendations for international students: Required—TOEFL (minimum score 525 paper-based; 173 computer-based). *Application deadline:* Applications are processed on a rolling basis. Application fee: $30 ($100 for international students). Electronic applications accepted. *Expenses:* Tuition, state resident: full-time $5886; part-time $352 per credit hour. Tuition, nonresident: full-time $9054; part-time $528 per credit hour. Required fees: $450; $26 per credit hour. *Financial support:* In 2010–11, 46 students received support, including 4 research assistantships (averaging $10,975 per year); career-related internships or fieldwork, scholarships/grants, tuition waivers (partial), and unspecified assistantships also available. Financial award application deadline: 4/15; financial award applicants required to submit FAFSA. *Unit head:* Dr. Gashaw Lake, Dean, 502-597-6105, Fax: 502-597-6715, E-mail: gashaw.lake@kysu.edu. *Application contact:* Dr. Titilayo Ufomata, Acting Director of Graduate Studies, 502-597-6443, E-mail: titilayo.ufomata@kysu.edu.

Kettering University, Graduate School, Department of Business, Flint, MI 48504. Offers MBA, MS. *Accreditation:* ACBSP. Part-time and evening/weekend programs available. Postbaccalaureate distance learning degree programs offered (no on-campus study). *Faculty:* 8 full-time (3 women), 6 part-time/adjunct (0 women). *Students:* 8 full-time (2 women), 262 part-time (90 women); includes 52 minority (35 Black or African American, non-Hispanic/Latino; 1 American Indian or Alaska Native, non-Hispanic/Latino; 6 Asian, non-Hispanic/Latino; 10 Hispanic/Latino), 7 international. Average age 33. 80 applicants, 81% accepted, 31 enrolled. In 2010, 106 master's awarded. *Entrance requirements:* Additional exam requirements/recommendations for international students: Required—TOEFL (minimum score 550 paper-based; 213 computer-based; 79 iBT). *Application deadline:* For fall admission, 9/15 for domestic students, 6/15 for international students; for winter admission, 12/15 for domestic students, 9/15 for international students; for spring admission, 3/15 for domestic students, 12/15 for international students. Applications are processed on a rolling basis. Electronic applications accepted. *Expenses:* Tuition: Full-time $11,120; part-time $695 per credit hour. *Financial support:* In 2010–11, 108 students received support, including fellowships with full tuition reimbursements available (averaging $13,000 per year), research assistantships with full tuition reimbursements available (averaging $13,000 per year), teaching assistantships with full tuition reimbursements available (averaging $13,000 per year); Federal Work-Study, scholarships/grants, and tuition waivers (partial) also available. Support available to part-time students. Financial award application deadline: 7/15. *Faculty research:* Entrepreneurship. Total annual research expenditures: $19,876. *Unit head:* Dr. Tony Hain, Associate Provost, Graduate Studies, Continuing Education and Sponsored Research, 810-762-9616, Fax: 810-762-9935, E-mail: thain@kettering.edu. *Application contact:* Bonnie Switzer, Admissions Representative, 810-762-7953, Fax: 810-762-9935, E-mail: bswitzer@kettering.edu.

Keuka College, Program in Management, Keuka Park, NY 14478-0098. Offers MS. Evening/weekend programs available. *Faculty:* 3 full-time (1

woman), 15 part-time/adjunct (5 women). *Students:* 53 full-time (36 women), 64 part-time (46 women); includes 14 Black or African American, non-Hispanic/Latino; 1 American Indian or Alaska Native, non-Hispanic/Latino; 1 Asian, non-Hispanic/Latino; 4 Hispanic/Latino. 31 applicants, 100% accepted, 31 enrolled. In 2010, 54 master's awarded. *Degree requirements:* For master's, thesis. *Entrance requirements:* For master's, 2 letters of reference, minimum GPA of 3.0. Additional exam requirements/recommendations for international students: Required—TOEFL (minimum score 550 paper-based; 213 computer-based). *Application deadline:* For fall admission, 8/15 priority date for domestic students; for winter admission, 12/15 priority date for domestic students; for spring admission, 4/15 priority date for domestic students. Applications are processed on a rolling basis. Application fee: $30. *Expenses:* Contact institution. *Faculty research:* Leadership, adult education, decision making, strategic planning, business ethics. *Unit head:* Owen Borda, Chair, Division of Business and Management, 315-279-5352, E-mail: gsmith@mail.keuka.edu. *Application contact:* Jack Ferrel, Director of Admissions, 315-279-5413, Fax: 315-279-5386, E-mail: admissions@mail.keuka.edu.

Kutztown University of Pennsylvania, College of Business, Program in Business Administration, Kutztown, PA 19530-0730. Offers MBA. Part-time and evening/weekend programs available. *Faculty:* 10 full-time (2 women). *Students:* 38 full-time (15 women), 43 part-time (18 women); includes 13 minority (2 Black or African American, non-Hispanic/Latino; 2 Asian, non-Hispanic/Latino; 9 Hispanic/Latino), 13 international. Average age 31. 87 applicants, 46% accepted, 26 enrolled. In 2010, 24 master's awarded. *Degree requirements:* For master's, comprehensive exam, thesis (for some programs). *Entrance requirements:* For master's, GMAT. Additional exam requirements/recommendations for international students: Required—TOEFL (minimum score 550 paper-based; 79 iBT). *Application deadline:* For fall admission, 8/15 for domestic students, 8/15 priority date for international students; for spring admission, 12/15 for domestic students, 12/15 priority date for international students. Applications are processed on a rolling basis. Application fee: $35. Electronic applications accepted. *Expenses:* Tuition, state resident: full-time $6966; part-time $387 per credit. Tuition, nonresident: full-time $11,146; part-time $619 per credit hour. Required fees: $1499; $54 per credit. $68 per year. *Financial support:* Career-related internships or fieldwork, Federal Work-Study, scholarships/grants, tuition waivers (partial), and unspecified assistantships available. Financial award application deadline: 3/1; financial award applicants required to submit FAFSA. *Unit head:* Dr. William Dempsey, Interim Dean, 610-683-4575, Fax: 610-683-4573, E-mail: dempsey@kutztown.edu. *Application contact:* Kelly D. Burr, Associate Director, Graduate Admissions, 610-683-4200, Fax: 610-683-1393, E-mail: graduate@kutztown.edu.

Lake Erie College, Division of Management Studies, Painesville, OH 44077-3389. Offers general management (MBA); management healthcare administration (MBA). Part-time and evening/weekend programs available. *Faculty:* 7 full-time (3 women), 3 part-time/adjunct (0 women). *Students:* 23 full-time (8 women), 142 part-time (73 women); includes 17 minority (9 Black or African American, non-Hispanic/Latino; 4 Asian, non-Hispanic/Latino; 1 Hispanic/Latino; 3 Two or more races, non-Hispanic/Latino). Average age 36. 106 applicants, 71% accepted, 56 enrolled. In 2010, 79 master's awarded. *Entrance requirements:* For master's, GMAT or minimum GPA of 3.0, resume, references. Additional exam requirements/recommendations for international students: Required—TOEFL (minimum score 550 paper-based; 79 computer-based). *Application deadline:* For fall admission, 8/1 priority date for domestic students, 6/1 for international students; for spring admission, 12/15 for domestic students, 10/1 for international students. Applications are processed on a rolling basis. Application fee: $30. Electronic applications accepted. *Expenses:* Tuition: Full-time $9594; part-time $533 per credit hour. Required fees: $51 per credit hour. Tuition and fees vary according to program. *Financial support:* Career-related internships or fieldwork and unspecified assistantships available. Financial award applicants required to submit FAFSA. *Faculty research:* Organizational effectiveness. *Unit head:* Prof. Robert Trebar, Associate Dean, 440-375-7115, Fax: 440-375-7005, E-mail: rtrebar@lec.edu. *Application contact:* Christopher Harris, Dean of Admissions and Financial Aid, 800-533-4996, Fax: 440-375-7000, E-mail: admissions@lec.edu.

Lamar University, College of Graduate Studies, College of Business, Beaumont, TX 77710. Offers accounting (MBA); experiential business and entrepreneurship (MBA); financial management (MBA); healthcare administration (MBA); information systems (MBA); management (MBA). *Accreditation:* AACSB. Part-time and evening/weekend programs available. *Faculty:* 17 full-time (4 women), 4 part-time/adjunct (0 women). *Students:* 79 full-time (37 women), 56 part-time (22 women); includes 14 Black or African American, non-Hispanic/Latino; 8 Asian, non-Hispanic/Latino; 12 Hispanic/Latino, 18 international. Average age 28. 103 applicants, 70% accepted, 40 enrolled. In 2010, 49 master's awarded. *Degree requirements:* For master's, comprehensive exam (for some programs), thesis optional. *Entrance requirements:* For master's, GMAT. Additional exam requirements/recommendations for international students: Required—TOEFL (minimum score 525 paper-based; 197 computer-based). *Application deadline:* For fall admission, 3/15 priority date for domestic students; for spring admission, 10/1 priority date for domestic students. Applications are processed on a rolling basis. Application fee: $25 ($50 for international students). *Expenses:* Tuition, state resident:

full-time $4160; part-time $208 per credit hour. Tuition, nonresident: full-time $10,360; part-time $518 per credit hour. *Financial support:* In 2010–11, 12 students received support, including 4 research assistantships with partial tuition reimbursements available; fellowships with tuition reimbursements available, career-related internships or fieldwork, Federal Work-Study, institutionally sponsored loans, scholarships/grants, and tuition waivers (partial) also available. Support available to part-time students. Financial award application deadline: 4/1; financial award applicants required to submit FAFSA. *Faculty research:* Marketing, finance, quantitative methods, management information systems, legal, environmental. *Unit head:* Dr. Enrique R. Venta, Dean, 409-880-8604, Fax: 409-880-8088, E-mail: henry.venta@lamar.edu. *Application contact:* Dr. Brad Mayer, Professor and Associate Dean, 409-880-2383, Fax: 409-880-8605, E-mail: bradley.mayer@lamar.edu.

Lasell College, Graduate and Professional Studies in Management, Newton, MA 02466-2709. Offers elder care administration (MSM, Graduate Certificate); elder care marketing (MSM, Graduate Certificate); fundraising management (MSM, Graduate Certificate); human resource management (Graduate Certificate); human resources management (MSM); management (MSM, Graduate Certificate); marketing (MSM, Graduate Certificate); non-profit management (MSM, Graduate Certificate); project management (MSM, Graduate Certificate); public relations (MSM). Part-time and evening/weekend programs available. Postbaccalaureate distance learning degree programs offered (no on-campus study). *Faculty:* 8 full-time (5 women), 7 part-time/adjunct (5 women). *Students:* 25 full-time (21 women), 97 part-time (67 women); includes 16 minority (6 Black or African American, non-Hispanic/Latino; 2 American Indian or Alaska Native, non-Hispanic/Latino; 4 Asian, non-Hispanic/Latino; 4 Hispanic/Latino), 17 international. Average age 33. 56 applicants, 52% accepted, 19 enrolled. In 2010, 65 master's, 7 other advanced degrees awarded. *Entrance requirements:* For master's and Graduate Certificate, bachelor's degree from an accredited institution. Additional exam requirements/recommendations for international students: Required—TOEFL (minimum score 550 paper-based; 213 computer-based; 75 iBT). *Application deadline:* For fall admission, 8/31 priority date for domestic students, 6/30 priority date for international students; for spring admission, 12/31 priority date for domestic students, 10/31 priority date for international students. Applications are processed on a rolling basis. Application fee: $40. Electronic applications accepted. *Expenses:* Tuition: Part-time $550 per credit hour. Required fees: $55 per semester. *Financial support:* In 2010–11, 40 students received support. Available to part-time students. Application deadline: 8/31. *Unit head:* Dr. Joan Dolamore, Dean of Graduate and Professional Studies, 617-243-2485, Fax: 617-243-2450, E-mail: gradinfo@lasell.edu. *Application contact:* Adrienne Franciosi, Director of Graduate Admission, 617-243-2214, Fax: 617-243-2450, E-mail: gradinfo@lasell.edu.

Lawrence Technological University, College of Management, Southfield, MI 48075-1058. Offers business administration (MBA, DBA); business administration international (MBA); global leadership and management (MS); global operations and project management (MS); information systems (MS); information technology (DM); operations management (MS). *Accreditation:* ACBSP. Part-time and evening/weekend programs available. *Faculty:* 14 full-time (6 women), 53 part-time/adjunct (14 women). *Students:* 7 full-time (2 women), 584 part-time (258 women); includes 137 Black or African American, non-Hispanic/Latino; 2 American Indian or Alaska Native, non-Hispanic/Latino; 51 Asian, non-Hispanic/Latino; 10 Hispanic/Latino; 8 Two or more races, non-Hispanic/Latino, 48 international. Average age 35. 431 applicants, 54% accepted, 151 enrolled. In 2010, 216 master's, 12 doctorates awarded. *Degree requirements:* For master's, thesis (for some programs). *Entrance requirements:* For master's, GMAT. Additional exam requirements/recommendations for international students: Required—TOEFL (minimum score 550 paper-based; 213 computer-based; 79 iBT). *Application deadline:* For fall admission, 6/30 priority date for domestic students, 6/30 for international students; for spring admission, 11/15 priority date for domestic students, 11/15 for international students. Applications are processed on a rolling basis. Application fee: $50. Electronic applications accepted. *Financial support:* In 2010–11, 142 students received support. Federal Work-Study and institutionally sponsored loans available. Support available to part-time students. Financial award application deadline: 4/1; financial award applicants required to submit FAFSA. *Unit head:* Dr. Lou DeGennaro, Dean, 248-204-3050, E-mail: degennaro@ltu.edu. *Application contact:* Jane Rohrback, Director of Admissions, 248-204-3160, Fax: 248-204-2228, E-mail: admissions@ltu.edu.

Lebanon Valley College, Graduate Studies and Continuing Education, Program in Business Administration, Annville, PA 17003-1400. Offers MBA. Part-time and evening/weekend programs available. *Faculty:* 14 part-time/adjunct (7 women). *Students:* 149 part-time (62 women); includes 11 minority (4 Black or African American, non-Hispanic/Latino; 2 Asian, non-Hispanic/Latino; 5 Hispanic/Latino). Average age 35. In 2010, 37 master's awarded. *Entrance requirements:* For master's, 3 years of work experience. *Application deadline:* Applications are processed on a rolling basis. Application fee: $30. Electronic applications accepted. *Expenses:* Tuition: Part-time $420 per credit hour. Part-time tuition and fees vary according to degree level and program. *Financial support:* Application deadline: 5/1. *Unit head:* Jennifer Easter, Director of the MBA Program, 717-867-6335. *Application contact:* Hope

Witmer, Assistant Dean, Graduate Studies and Continuing Education, 717-867-6213, Fax: 717-867-6018, E-mail: witmer@lvc.edu.

Lehigh University, College of Business and Economics, Bethlehem, PA 18015. Offers accounting (MS), including accounting and information analysis; business administration (MBA); economics (MS, PhD), including economics, health and bio-pharmaceutical economics (MS); entrepreneurship (Certificate); finance (MS), including analytical finance; project management (Certificate); supply chain management (Certificate); MBA/E; MBA/M Ed. *Accreditation:* AACSB. Part-time and evening/weekend programs available. Postbaccalaureate distance learning degree programs offered (minimal on-campus study). *Faculty:* 43 full-time (10 women), 19 part-time/adjunct (4 women). *Students:* 164 full-time (82 women), 242 part-time (72 women); includes 37 minority (6 Black or African American, non-Hispanic/Latino; 25 Asian, non-Hispanic/Latino; 5 Hispanic/Latino; 1 Native Hawaiian or other Pacific Islander, non-Hispanic/Latino), 110 international. Average age 29. 790 applicants, 35% accepted, 158 enrolled. In 2010, 159 master's, 3 doctorates awarded. Terminal master's awarded for partial completion of doctoral program. *Degree requirements:* For master's, thesis optional; for doctorate, comprehensive exam, thesis/dissertation, proposal defense. *Entrance requirements:* For master's, GMAT, GRE General Test; MCAT, DAT (health and biopharmaceutical economics); for doctorate, GMAT or GRE General Test. Additional exam requirements/recommendations for international students: Required—TOEFL (minimum score 600 paper-based; 250 computer-based; 94 iBT). *Application deadline:* For fall admission, 7/15 for domestic students, 5/1 for international students; for spring admission, 12/1 for domestic and international students. Applications are processed on a rolling basis. Application fee: $100. Electronic applications accepted. *Expenses:* Contact institution. *Financial support:* In 2010–11, 93 students received support, including 2 fellowships with full tuition reimbursements available (averaging $16,000 per year), 39 research assistantships with full and partial tuition reimbursements available (averaging $2,269 per year), 17 teaching assistantships with full tuition reimbursements available (averaging $13,840 per year); career-related internships or fieldwork, scholarships/grants, health care benefits, tuition waivers (full and partial), and unspecified assistantships also available. Support available to part-time students. Financial award application deadline: 1/15. *Faculty research:* Public finance, energy, investments, activity-based costing, management information systems. *Unit head:* Paul R. Brown, Dean, 610-758-6725, Fax: 610-758-4499, E-mail: prb207@lehigh.edu. *Application contact:* Corinn McBride, Director of Recruitment and Admissions, 610-758-3418, Fax: 610-758-5283, E-mail: com207@lehigh.edu.

Le Moyne College, Division of Management, Syracuse, NY 13214. Offers MBA. *Accreditation:* AACSB. Part-time and evening/weekend programs available. *Faculty:* 14 full-time (3 women), 6 part-time/adjunct (1 woman). *Students:* 23 full-time (9 women), 76 part-time (34 women); includes 6 minority (2 Black or African American, non-Hispanic/Latino; 1 American Indian or Alaska Native, non-Hispanic/Latino; 3 Asian, non-Hispanic/Latino), 1 international. Average age 29. 81 applicants, 77% accepted, 62 enrolled. In 2010, 43 master's awarded. *Degree requirements:* For master's, capstone level course. *Entrance requirements:* For master's, GMAT, interview, bachelor's degree, minimum GPA of 3.0, resume, 2 letters of recommendation, personal statement, transcripts. Additional exam requirements/recommendations for international students: Required—TOEFL (minimum score 550 paper-based; 213 computer-based; 79 iBT). *Application deadline:* For fall admission, 7/1 priority date for domestic and international students; for spring admission, 11/1 priority date for domestic and international students. Applications are processed on a rolling basis. Application fee: $0. *Expenses:* Tuition: Full-time $11,790; part-time $655 per credit hour. Required fees: $25 per semester. *Financial support:* In 2010–11, 8 students received support. Career-related internships or fieldwork, scholarships/grants, health care benefits, and unspecified assistantships available. Support available to part-time students. Financial award applicants required to submit FAFSA. *Faculty research:* Performance evaluation outcomes assessment, technology outsourcing, international business, systems for Web-based information-seeking, non-profit business practices, business sustainability practices. *Unit head:* Dr. George Kulick, Associate Dean, 315-445-4786, Fax: 315-445-4787, E-mail: kulick@lemoyne.edu. *Application contact:* Kristen P. Trapasso, Director of Graduate Admission, 315-445-4265, Fax: 315-445-6027, E-mail: trapaskp@lemoyne.edu.

LeTourneau University, School of Graduate and Professional Studies, Longview, TX 75607-7001. Offers business administration (MBA); counseling (MA); curriculum and instruction (M Ed); educational administration (M Ed); engineering (M Sc); psychology (MA); strategic leadership (MSL); teaching and learning (M Ed). Part-time and evening/weekend programs available. Postbaccalaureate distance learning degree programs offered (no on-campus study). *Faculty:* 9 full-time (1 woman), 62 part-time/adjunct (26 women). *Students:* 329 full-time (233 women); includes 152 Black or African American, non-Hispanic/Latino; 1 American Indian or Alaska Native, non-Hispanic/Latino; 5 Asian, non-Hispanic/Latino; 23 Hispanic/Latino. Average age 36. 138 applicants, 90% accepted, 120 enrolled. In 2010, 129 master's awarded. *Entrance requirements:* For master's, GRE (for MA in counseling and M Sc in engineering), minimum GPA of 2.8. Additional exam requirements/recommendations for international students: Required—TOEFL. *Application* *deadline:* Applications are processed on a rolling basis. Application fee: $0. Electronic applications accepted. *Expenses:* Tuition: Full-time $13,020; part-time $620 per credit hour. *Financial support:* Applicants required to submit FAFSA. *Unit head:* Dr. Carol Green, Vice President, 903-233-4010, Fax: 903-233-3227, E-mail: carolgreen@letu.edu. *Application contact:* Chris Fontaine, Assistant Vice President for Enrollment Management and Marketing, 903-233-4071, Fax: 903-233-3227, E-mail: chrisfontaine@letu.edu.

Lewis University, College of Business, Graduate School of Management, Romeoville, IL 60446. Offers business administration (MBA), including accounting, custom elective option, e-business, finance, healthcare management, human resources management, information security, international business, management information systems, marketing, project management, technology and operations management; finance (MS); management (MS). *Accreditation:* ACBSP. Part-time and evening/weekend programs available. Postbaccalaureate distance learning degree programs offered (no on-campus study). In 2010, 132 master's awarded. Application fee: $40. *Expenses:* Tuition: Full-time $13,320; part-time $740 per credit hour. Tuition and fees vary according to program. *Financial support:* Applicants required to submit FAFSA. *Application contact:* Michele Ryan, Director of Admission, 815-836-5384, E-mail: gsm@lewisu.edu.

Lewis University, College of Nursing and Health Professions and College of Business, Program in Nursing/Business, Romeoville, IL 60446. Offers MSN/MBA. Part-time and evening/weekend programs available. *Students:* 9 full-time (7 women), 33 part-time (32 women); includes 13 Black or African American, non-Hispanic/Latino; 3 Asian, non-Hispanic/Latino; 7 Hispanic/Latino. Average age 38. *Entrance requirements:* Additional exam requirements/recommendations for international students: Required—TOEFL (minimum score 550 paper-based; 213 computer-based). *Application deadline:* For fall admission, 5/1 priority date for international students; for spring admission, 11/15 priority date for international students. Applications are processed on a rolling basis. Electronic applications accepted. *Expenses:* Tuition: Full-time $13,320; part-time $740 per credit hour. Tuition and fees vary according to program. *Financial support:* Scholarships/grants, tuition waivers (full and partial), and unspecified assistantships available. Financial award application deadline: 5/1; financial award applicants required to submit FAFSA. *Faculty research:* Cancer prevention, phenomenological methods, public policy analysis. Total annual research expenditures: $1,000. *Unit head:* Dr. Linda Niedringhaus, Interim Director, 815-838-0500 Ext. 5878, E-mail: niedrili@lewisu.edu. *Application contact:* Nancy Wiksten, Adult Admission Counselor, 815-838-0500 Ext. 5628, Fax: 815-836-5578, E-mail: wikstena@lewisu.edu.

Liberty University, School of Business, Lynchburg, VA 24502. Offers MBA, MS. Part-time programs available. Postbaccalaureate distance learning degree programs offered (minimal on-campus study). *Students:* 749 full-time (385 women), 2,142 part-time (1,019 women); includes 648 minority (490 Black or African American, non-Hispanic/Latino; 16 American Indian or Alaska Native, non-Hispanic/Latino; 37 Asian, non-Hispanic/Latino; 97 Hispanic/Latino; 7 Native Hawaiian or other Pacific Islander, non-Hispanic/Latino; 1 Two or more races, non-Hispanic/Latino), 60 international. Average age 34. In 2010, 559 master's awarded. *Entrance requirements:* For master's, minimum undergraduate GPA of 3.0. Additional exam requirements/recommendations for international students: Required—TOEFL (minimum score 600 paper-based; 250 computer-based; 100 iBT). *Application deadline:* For fall admission, 6/1 for domestic students; for spring admission, 11/1 for domestic students. Applications are processed on a rolling basis. Application fee: $50. Electronic applications accepted. *Expenses:* Contact institution. *Unit head:* Dr. Bruce K. Bell, Dean, 434-592-3863, Fax: 434-582-2366, E-mail: bkbell@liberty.edu. *Application contact:* Jay Bridge, Director of Graduate Admissions, 800-424-9595, Fax: 800-628-7977, E-mail: gradadmissions@liberty.edu.

Lincoln Memorial University, School of Business, Harrogate, TN 37752-1901. Offers MBA. Part-time and evening/weekend programs available. *Faculty:* 6 full-time (0 women), 1 part-time/adjunct (0 women). *Students:* 48 full-time (12 women), 148 part-time (69 women); includes 8 Black or African American, non-Hispanic/Latino; 2 Asian, non-Hispanic/Latino, 21 international. Average age 31. 48 applicants, 94% accepted, 38 enrolled. In 2010, 23 master's awarded. *Degree requirements:* For master's, comprehensive exam, thesis. *Entrance requirements:* For master's, GMAT, resume, letters of recommendation, interview. Additional exam requirements/recommendations for international students: Required—TOEFL (minimum score 500 paper-based). *Application deadline:* For fall admission, 7/15 for domestic and international students; for spring admission, 12/1 for domestic and international students. Applications are processed on a rolling basis. Application fee: $25. *Financial support:* Career-related internships or fieldwork, health care benefits, and unspecified assistantships available. Support available to part-time students. Financial award applicants required to submit FAFSA. *Unit head:* Dr. Jack McCann, Dean, 423-869-7085, Fax: 423-869-6298, E-mail: jack.mccann@lmunet.edu. *Application contact:* Dr. Michael E. Dillon, Director, MBA Program, 423-869-7141, E-mail: michael.dillon@lmunet.edu.

Lincoln University, Graduate Studies, Oakland, CA 94612. Offers finance and investments (DBA); finance management and investment banking (MBA); general business (MBA); human resource management (MBA,

DBA); international business (MBA); management information systems (MBA). Part-time and evening/weekend programs available. *Faculty:* 9 full-time (2 women), 11 part-time/adjunct (1 woman). *Students:* 297 full-time (134 women), 2 part-time (0 women). In 2010, 124 master's awarded. *Degree requirements:* For master's, research project (thesis), internship report, or comprehensive exam; for doctorate, comprehensive exam, thesis/dissertation. *Entrance requirements:* For master's, minimum GPA of 2.7; for doctorate, GMAT (minimum score: 550), GRE (minimum score: 1000), or equivalent test results (waived for master's degree with minimum cumulative GPA of 3.3). Additional exam requirements/recommendations for international students: Required—TOEFL (525 paper, 195 computer, 71 iBT) or IELTS (5.5) for MBA; TOEFL (550 paper, 213 computer, 79 iBT) or IELTS (6.0) for DBA; Recommended—IELTS. *Application deadline:* For fall admission, 7/2 priority date for domestic and international students; for spring admission, 11/25 priority date for domestic students, 11/26 priority date for international students. Applications are processed on a rolling basis. Application fee: $75. Electronic applications accepted. *Expenses:* Tuition: Full-time $6930. Required fees: $195 per semester. *Financial support:* In 2010–11, 1 teaching assistantship was awarded; career-related internships or fieldwork and scholarships/grants also available. *Unit head:* Dr. Marshall Burak, Director of Graduate Programs, 510-628-8016, Fax: 510-628-8012, E-mail: mburak@lincolnuca.edu. *Application contact:* Peggy Au, Director of Admissions and Records, 510-628-8010, Fax: 510-628-8012, E-mail: admissions@lincolnuca.edu.

Lindenwood University, Graduate Programs, College of Individualized Education, St. Charles, MO 63301-1695. Offers administration (MSA); business administration (MBA); communications (MA); criminal justice and administration (MS); gerontology (MA); health management (MS); human resource management (MS); information technology (MBA, Certificate); managing information technology (MS); writing (MFA). Part-time and evening/weekend programs available. *Faculty:* 15 full-time (8 women), 128 part-time/adjunct (53 women). *Students:* 828 full-time (527 women), 80 part-time (50 women); includes 284 minority (265 Black or African American, non-Hispanic/Latino; 3 American Indian or Alaska Native, non-Hispanic/Latino; 6 Asian, non-Hispanic/Latino; 10 Hispanic/Latino), 23 international. Average age 35. 223 applicants, 44% accepted, 87 enrolled. In 2010, 478 master's awarded. *Degree requirements:* For master's, thesis (for some programs), 1 colloquium per term. *Entrance requirements:* For master's, interview, minimum GPA of 3.0. Additional exam requirements/recommendations for international students: Required—TOEFL (minimum score 550 paper-based; 213 computer-based; 80 iBT). *Application deadline:* For fall admission, 10/2 priority date for domestic and international students; for winter admission, 1/8 priority date for domestic and international students; for spring admission, 4/8 priority date for domestic and international students. Applications are processed on a rolling basis. Application fee: $30 ($100 for international students). Electronic applications accepted. *Expenses:* Tuition: Full-time $13,260; part-time $380 per credit hour. Required fees: $340. One-time fee: $30. Tuition and fees vary according to course level and course load. *Financial support:* In 2010–11, 631 students received support. Career-related internships or fieldwork, institutionally sponsored loans, tuition waivers (partial), and unspecified assistantships available. Financial award application deadline: 6/30; financial award applicants required to submit FAFSA. *Unit head:* Dan Kemper, Dean, 636-949-4501, Fax: 636-949-4505, E-mail: dkemper@lindenwood.edu. *Application contact:* Brett Barger, Dean of Evening Admissions and Extension Campuses, 636-949-4934, Fax: 636-949-4109, E-mail: adultadmissions@lindenwood.edu.

Lindenwood University, Graduate Programs, School of Business and Entrepreneurship, St. Charles, MO 63301-1695. Offers accounting (MBA, MS); business administration (MBA); entrepreneurial studies (MBA, MS); finance (MBA, MS); human resource management (MBA); human resources (MS); international business (MBA, MS); management (MBA, MS); management information systems (MBA, MS); marketing (MBA, MS); public management (MBA, MS); sport management (MA). *Accreditation:* ACBSP. Part-time and evening/weekend programs available. *Faculty:* 20 full-time (8 women), 17 part-time/adjunct (5 women). *Students:* 179 full-time (73 women), 184 part-time (87 women); includes 27 minority (20 Black or African American, non-Hispanic/Latino; 3 Asian, non-Hispanic/Latino; 4 Hispanic/Latino), 146 international. Average age 28. 149 applicants, 73 enrolled. In 2010, 142 master's awarded. *Degree requirements:* For master's, comprehensive exam (for some programs), thesis (for some programs). *Entrance requirements:* For master's, interview, minimum GPA of 3.0, letter of recommendation. Additional exam requirements/recommendations for international students: Required—TOEFL (minimum score 550 paper-based; 213 computer-based; 80 iBT). *Application deadline:* For fall admission, 7/30 priority date for domestic students, 9/16 priority date for international students; for winter admission, 12/15 priority date for domestic and international students; for spring admission, 2/25 priority date for domestic students, 2/11 priority date for international students. Applications are processed on a rolling basis. Application fee: $30 ($100 for international students). Electronic applications accepted. *Expenses:* Tuition: Full-time $13,260; part-time $380 per credit hour. Required fees: $340. One-time fee: $30. Tuition and fees vary according to course level and course load. *Financial support:* In 2010–11, 209 students received support. Career-related internships or fieldwork, Federal Work-Study, institutionally sponsored loans, and tuition waivers (partial) available. Financial award application deadline: 6/30; financial award applicants required to submit FAFSA. *Unit head:* Roger Ellis, Dean, 636-949-4839, E-mail: rellis@lindenwood.edu. *Application contact:* Brett Barger, Dean of Evening Admissions and Extension Campuses, 636-949-4934, Fax: 636-949-4109, E-mail: adultadmissions@lindenwood.edu.

Lipscomb University, MBA Program, Nashville, TN 37204-3951. Offers accounting (MBA); business administration (general) (MBA); conflict management (MBA); financial services (MBA); healthcare management (MBA); leadership (MBA); nonprofit management (MBA); sports administration (MBA); sustainable practice (MBA). *Accreditation:* ACBSP. Part-time and evening/weekend programs available. *Faculty:* 17 full-time (5 women), 3 part-time/adjunct (0 women). *Students:* 52 full-time (30 women), 79 part-time (36 women); includes 20 Black or African American, non-Hispanic/Latino; 1 American Indian or Alaska Native, non-Hispanic/Latino; 1 Asian, non-Hispanic/Latino; 7 Hispanic/Latino. Average age 32. 151 applicants, 47% accepted, 45 enrolled. In 2010, 70 master's awarded. *Entrance requirements:* For master's, GMAT, interview, 2 references, resume. Additional exam requirements/recommendations for international students: Required—TOEFL (minimum score 570 paper-based; 230 computer-based). *Application deadline:* For fall admission, 2/1 for international students; for winter admission, 6/1 for international students. Applications are processed on a rolling basis. Application fee: $50 ($75 for international students). Electronic applications accepted. *Expenses:* Contact institution. *Financial support:* Career-related internships or fieldwork, Federal Work-Study, scholarships/grants, tuition waivers (partial), and unspecified assistantships available. Support available to part-time students. Financial award application deadline: 7/1; financial award applicants required to submit FAFSA. *Faculty research:* Impact of spirituality on organization commitment, leadership, psychological empowerment, training. *Unit head:* Dr. Mike Kendrick, Interim Chair of Graduate Business Studies, 615-966-1833, Fax: 615-966-1818, E-mail: mikekendrick@lipscomb.edu. *Application contact:* Emily Landsdell, 615-966-5284, E-mail: emily.lansdell@lipscomb.edu.

Long Island University, Rockland Graduate Campus, Graduate School, Masters of Business Administration Program, Orangeburg, NY 10962. Offers business administration (Post Master's Certificate); entrepreneurship (MBA); finance (MBA); healthcare sector management (MBA); management (MBA). Part-time and evening/weekend programs available. *Faculty:* 12 part-time/adjunct (2 women). *Students:* 42 part-time (26 women). In 2010, 12 master's awarded. *Entrance requirements:* For master's, GMAT, college transcripts, two letters of recommendation, personal statement, resume. *Application deadline:* Applications are processed on a rolling basis. Application fee: $30. *Expenses:* Tuition: Part-time $1028 per credit. Required fees: $340 per semester. *Financial support:* In 2010–11, 34 students received support. Scholarships/grants available. Support available to part-time students. Financial award applicants required to submit FAFSA. *Unit head:* Dr. Lynn Johnson, Program Director, 845-359-7200 Ext. 5436, Fax: 845-359-7248, E-mail: lynn.johnson@liu.edu. *Application contact:* Peter S. Reiner, Director of Admissions and Marketing, 845-359-7200, Fax: 845-359-7248, E-mail: peter.reiner@liu.edu.

Louisiana State University and Agricultural and Mechanical College, Graduate School, E. J. Ourso College of Business, Department of Finance, Baton Rouge, LA 70803. Offers business administration (PhD), including finance; finance (MS). *Faculty:* 11 full-time (3 women), 1 part-time/adjunct (0 women). *Students:* 35 full-time (10 women), 5 part-time (0 women); includes 1 Asian, non-Hispanic/Latino, 15 international. Average age 27. 106 applicants, 25% accepted, 1 enrolled. In 2010, 20 master's, 2 doctorates awarded. *Degree requirements:* For master's, thesis or alternative; for doctorate, thesis/dissertation. *Entrance requirements:* For master's and doctorate, GMAT. Additional exam requirements/recommendations for international students: Required—TOEFL (minimum score 550 paper-based; 213 computer-based; 79 iBT) or IELTS (minimum score 6.5). *Application deadline:* For fall admission, 1/25 priority date for domestic students, 5/15 for international students; for spring admission, 10/15 for international students. Applications are processed on a rolling basis. Application fee: $50 ($70 for international students). *Financial support:* In 2010–11, 25 students received support, including 12 research assistantships with full and partial tuition reimbursements available (averaging $17,033 per year), 3 teaching assistantships with full and partial tuition reimbursements available (averaging $12,267 per year); fellowships, career-related internships or fieldwork, Federal Work-Study, scholarships/grants, health care benefits, and unspecified assistantships also available. Support available to part-time students. Financial award application deadline: 4/1; financial award applicants required to submit FAFSA. *Faculty research:* Derivatives and risk management, capital structure, asset pricing, spatial statistics, financial institutions and underwriting. Total annual research expenditures: $16,334. *Unit head:* Dr. Vestor Carlos Slawson, Interim Chair, 225-578-6367, Fax: 225-578-6366, E-mail: cslawson@lsu.edu. *Application contact:* Dr. Vestor Carlos Slawson, Interim Chair, 225-578-6367, Fax: 225-578-6366, E-mail: cslawson@lsu.edu.

Louisiana State University and Agricultural and Mechanical College, Graduate School, E. J. Ourso College of Business, Department of Management, Baton Rouge, LA 70803. Offers business administration (PhD), including management. *Accreditation:* AACSB. *Faculty:* 10 full-time (2 women). *Students:* 6 full-time (3 women); includes 1 Asian, non-Hispanic/Latino, 2 international. Average age 32. 2 applicants, 100% accepted, 0 enrolled. In 2010, 4 doctorates awarded. *Degree requirements:* For doctorate, thesis/dissertation. *Entrance requirements:* For doctorate, GMAT. Additional exam requirements/recommendations for international students: Required—TOEFL (minimum score 550 paper-based; 213 computer-based; 79 iBT) or IELTS (minimum score 6.5). *Application deadline:* For fall admission, 1/25 priority date for domestic students, 5/15 for international students; for spring admission, 10/15 for international students. Applications are processed on a rolling basis. Application fee: $50 ($70 for international students). Electronic applications accepted. *Financial support:* In 2010–11, 6 students received support, including 3 research assistantships with full and partial tuition reimbursements available (averaging $22,167 per year), 3 teaching assistantships with full and partial tuition reimbursements available (averaging $16,500 per year); fellowships, Federal Work-Study, institutionally sponsored loans, scholarships/grants, health care benefits, and unspecified assistantships also available. Support available to part-time students. Financial award applicants required to submit FAFSA. *Faculty research:* Human resource management, organizational behavior, strategy. Total annual research expenditures: $22,303. *Unit head:* Dr. Timothy Chandler, Chair, 225-578-6101, Fax: 225-578-6983, E-mail: mgchan@lsu.edu. *Application contact:* Hettie Richardson, Graduate Adviser, 225-578-6146, Fax: 225-578-6140, E-mail: hricha4@lsu.edu.

Louisiana State University and Agricultural and Mechanical College, Graduate School, E. J. Ourso College of Business, Department of Marketing, Baton Rouge, LA 70803. Offers business administration (PhD), including marketing. Part-time programs available. *Faculty:* 10 full-time (2 women). *Students:* 6 full-time (5 women), 3 part-time (1 woman), 4 international. Average age 31. 1 applicant, 100% accepted, 1 enrolled. In 2010, 4 doctorates awarded. *Degree requirements:* For doctorate, thesis/dissertation. *Entrance requirements:* Additional exam requirements/recommendations for international students: Required—TOEFL (minimum score 550 paper-based; 213 computer-based; 79 iBT) or IELTS (minimum score 6.5). *Application deadline:* For fall admission, 1/25 priority date for domestic students, 5/15 for international students; for spring admission, 10/15 for international students. Applications are processed on a rolling basis. Application fee: $50 ($70 for international students). Electronic applications accepted. *Financial support:* In 2010–11, 8 students received support, including 6 teaching assistantships with full and partial tuition reimbursements available (averaging $16,800 per year); fellowships, research assistantships with partial tuition reimbursements available, career-related internships or fieldwork, Federal Work-Study, institutionally sponsored loans, scholarships/grants, health care benefits, and unspecified assistantships also available. Support available to part-time students. Financial award applicants required to submit FAFSA. *Faculty research:* Consumer behavior, marketing strategy, global marketing, e-commerce, branding/brand equity. Total annual research expenditures: $5,050. *Unit head:* Dr. Alvin C. Burns, Chair, 225-578-8786, Fax: 225-578-8616, E-mail: alburns@lsu.edu. *Application contact:* Dr. Ron Niedrich, Graduate Adviser, 225-578-9068, Fax: 225-578-8616, E-mail: niedrich@lsu.edu.

Louisiana State University and Agricultural and Mechanical College, Graduate School, E. J. Ourso College of Business, Flores MBA Program, Baton Rouge, LA 70803. Offers EMBA, MBA, PMBA. *Accreditation:* AACSB. *Students:* 213 full-time (69 women), 79 part-time (24 women); includes 16 Black or African American, non-Hispanic/Latino; 2 American Indian or Alaska Native, non-Hispanic/Latino; 5 Asian, non-Hispanic/Latino; 7 Hispanic/Latino; 9 Two or more races, non-Hispanic/Latino, 30 international. Average age 27. 349 applicants, 47% accepted, 55 enrolled. In 2010, 153 master's awarded. *Entrance requirements:* Additional exam requirements/recommendations for international students: Required—TOEFL (minimum score 550 paper-based; 213 computer-based; 79 iBT) or IELTS (minimum score 6.5). *Application deadline:* For fall admission, 1/25 priority date for domestic students, 5/15 for international students; for spring admission, 10/15 for international students. Application fee: $50 ($70 for international students). Electronic applications accepted. *Financial support:* In 2010–11, 193 students received support, including 3 fellowships (averaging $25,565 per year), 16 research assistantships with partial tuition reimbursements available (averaging $12,219 per year), 65 teaching assistantships with full and partial tuition reimbursements available (averaging $12,550 per year); Federal Work-Study, institutionally sponsored loans, scholarships/grants, health care benefits, and unspecified assistantships also available. Support available to part-time students. Financial award applicants required to submit FAFSA. Total annual research expenditures: $145,723. *Unit head:* Dr. Ed Watson, Director, 225-578-8867, Fax: 225-578-2421. *Application contact:* Dana Hart, 225-578-8867, Fax: 225-578-2421, E-mail: dhart@lsu.edu.

Louisiana State University in Shreveport, College of Business Administration, Program in Business Administration, Shreveport, LA 71115-2399. Offers MBA. *Accreditation:* ACBSP. Part-time and evening/weekend programs available. *Students:* 18 full-time (8 women), 88 part-time (37 women); includes 13 minority (11 Black or African American, non-Hispanic/Latino; 2 Hispanic/Latino), 6 international. Average age 32. 48 applicants, 100% accepted, 24 enrolled. In 2010, 19 master's awarded. *Degree requirements:* For master's, comprehensive exam. *Entrance requirements:* For master's, GMAT, minimum undergraduate GPA of 2.5, 2.75 for last 60 credits.

Additional exam requirements/recommendations for international students: Required—TOEFL (minimum score 500 paper-based; 173 computer-based; 61 iBT). *Application deadline:* For fall admission, 6/30 for domestic and international students; for spring admission, 11/30 for domestic and international students. Applications are processed on a rolling basis. Application fee: $10 ($20 for international students). *Expenses:* Tuition, state resident: full-time $3272; part-time $181.80 per credit hour. Tuition, nonresident: full-time $7902; part-time $471.19 per credit hour. Required fees: $850; $47 per credit hour. *Financial support:* In 2010–11, 1 fellowship, 4 research assistantships with full and partial tuition reimbursements (averaging $10,000 per year) were awarded; scholarships/grants also available. *Unit head:* Dr. Bill Bigler, Program Director, 318-797-5247, Fax: 318-797-5176, E-mail: bill.bigler@lsus.edu. *Application contact:* Yvonne Yarbrough, Secretary, Graduate Studies, 318-797-5247, Fax: 318-798-4120, E-mail: yyarbrou@lsus.edu.

Loyola Marymount University, College of Business Administration, Los Angeles, CA 90045-2659. Offers MBA, MBA/JD, MBA/MS. *Accreditation:* AACSB. *Expenses:* Contact institution. *Unit head:* Dr. Dennis Draper, Dean, 310-338-7504, E-mail: ddraper@lmu.edu. *Application contact:* Dr. Dennis Draper, Dean, 310-338-7504, E-mail: ddraper@lmu.edu.

Loyola University New Orleans, Joseph A. Butt, S. J., College of Business, Program in Business Administration, New Orleans, LA 70118-6195. Offers MBA, JD/MBA. *Accreditation:* AACSB. Part-time and evening/weekend programs available. Postbaccalaureate distance learning degree programs offered (minimal on-campus study). *Students:* 32 full-time (13 women), 41 part-time (21 women); includes 3 Black or African American, non-Hispanic/Latino; 2 American Indian or Alaska Native, non-Hispanic/Latino; 2 Asian, non-Hispanic/Latino; 1 Hispanic/Latino; 1 Two or more races, non-Hispanic/Latino. Average age 27. 63 applicants, 79% accepted, 31 enrolled. In 2010, 37 master's awarded. *Entrance requirements:* For master's, GMAT, minimum GPA of 3.0, resume, 2 letters of recommendation, work experience in field. Additional exam requirements/recommendations for international students: Required—TOEFL (minimum score 550 paper-based; 213 computer-based). *Application deadline:* For fall admission, 6/15 priority date for domestic and international students; for spring admission, 11/15 priority date for domestic and international students. Applications are processed on a rolling basis. Application fee: $50. Electronic applications accepted. *Financial support:* Research assistantships, scholarships/grants, tuition waivers (partial), and unspecified assistantships available. Financial award application deadline: 5/1; financial award applicants required to submit FAFSA. *Faculty research:* Ethics, international business, entrepreneurship, quality management, risk management. *Unit head:* William B. Locander, Dean, 504-864-7979, Fax: 504-864-7970, E-mail: locander@loyno.edu. *Application contact:* Stephanie L. Mansfield, Assistant Director, Graduate Programs, 504-864-7965, Fax: 504-864-7970, E-mail: smans@loyno.edu.

Lynchburg College, Graduate Studies, School of Business and Economics, Master of Business Administration Program, Lynchburg, VA 24501-3199. Offers MBA. Part-time and evening/weekend programs available. *Faculty:* 4 full-time (2 women), 1 part-time/adjunct (0 women). *Students:* 13 full-time (6 women), 45 part-time (11 women); includes 4 minority (3 Black or African American, non-Hispanic/Latino; 1 Hispanic/Latino), 1 international. Average age 32. 68 applicants, 60% accepted. In 2010, 32 master's awarded. *Degree requirements:* For master's, capstone course. *Entrance requirements:* For master's, GMAT (minimum score of 400) or GRE, official transcripts, personal essay, 3 letters of recommendation. Additional exam requirements/recommendations for international students: Required—TOEFL (minimum score 530 paper-based; 197 computer-based; 71 iBT), IELTS (minimum score 6.5). *Application deadline:* For fall admission, 7/31 for domestic students, 6/1 for international students; for spring admission, 11/30 for domestic students, 10/15 for international students. Applications are processed on a rolling basis. Application fee: $30. Electronic applications accepted. *Expenses:* Tuition: Full-time $7200; part-time $400 per credit hour. Required fees: $20; $5.10 per credit hour. $15 per term. Tuition and fees vary according to degree level and program. *Financial support:* Fellowships, Federal Work-Study, scholarships/grants, health care benefits, and unspecified assistantships available. Support available to part-time students. Financial award application deadline: 7/31; financial award applicants required to submit FAFSA. *Unit head:* Dr. Atul Gupta, Professor and Program Director, MBA, 434-522-8651, E-mail: gupta@lynchburg.edu. *Application contact:* Dr. Atul Gupta, Professor and Program Director, MBA, 434-522-8651, E-mail: gupta@lynchburg.edu.

Malone University, Graduate Program in Business, Canton, OH 44709. Offers MBA. *Accreditation:* ACBSP. Part-time and evening/weekend programs available. *Faculty:* 9 full-time (3 women), 7 part-time/adjunct (3 women). *Students:* 5 full-time (3 women), 93 part-time (36 women); includes 8 Black or African American, non-Hispanic/Latino; 1 Asian, non-Hispanic/Latino; 2 Hispanic/Latino, 1 international. Average age 34. 49 applicants, 61% accepted, 14 enrolled. In 2010, 61 master's awarded. *Entrance requirements:* For master's, institution's own math prerequisite diagnostic test, minimum GPA of 3.0. Additional exam requirements/recommendations for international students: Required—TOEFL (minimum score 550 paper-based; 213 computer-based; 79 iBT). *Application deadline:* Applications are processed on a rolling basis. Application fee: $25. *Expenses:* Contact institution. *Financial support:* Tuition waivers (partial) available. Support available to part-time students. Financial award application deadline: 6/30. *Faculty research:* Leadership, business ethics, sustainability, globalization, non-profit financial management. *Unit head:* Dr. Julia A. Frankland, Director, 330-471-8552, Fax: 330-471-8563, E-mail: jfrankland@malone.edu. *Application contact:* Mona J. McAuliffe, Corporate Recruiter for Graduate and Professional Studies, 330-471-8623, Fax: 330-471-8343, E-mail: mmcauliffe@malone.edu.

Marian University, Business Division, Fond du Lac, WI 54935-4699. Offers organizational leadership and quality (MS). Part-time and evening/weekend programs available. *Faculty:* 17 part-time/adjunct (1 woman). *Students:* 11 full-time (6 women), 111 part-time (79 women); includes 7 Black or African American, non-Hispanic/Latino; 3 Asian, non-Hispanic/Latino; 4 Hispanic/Latino. Average age 38. 36 applicants, 92% accepted, 33 enrolled. In 2010, 52 master's awarded. *Degree requirements:* For master's, comprehensive group project. *Entrance requirements:* For master's, 3 years of managerial experience, minimum GPA of 2.75, letters of professional reference. *Application deadline:* Applications are processed on a rolling basis. Application fee: $25. Electronic applications accepted. *Expenses:* Contact institution. *Financial support:* In 2010–11, 8 students received support. Institutionally sponsored loans available. Support available to part-time students. Financial award application deadline: 3/1; financial award applicants required to submit FAFSA. *Faculty research:* Organizational values, statistical decision making, learning organization, quality planning, customer research. *Unit head:* Donna Innes, Dean of PACE, 920-923-8760, Fax: 920-923-7167, E-mail: dinnes@marianuniversity.edu. *Application contact:* Tracy Qualman, Director of Marketing and Admission, 920-923-7159, Fax: 920-923-7167, E-mail: tqualmann@marianuniversity.edu.

Marlboro College, Graduate School, Program in Business Administration, Marlboro, VT 05344. Offers managing for sustainability (MBA). Part-time and evening/weekend programs available. Postbaccalaureate distance learning degree programs offered (minimal on-campus study). *Faculty:* 1 full-time (0 women), 9 part-time/adjunct (5 women). *Students:* 30 full-time (20 women), 7 part-time (2 women); includes 1 Black or African American, non-Hispanic/Latino. Average age 37. In 2010, 3 master's awarded. *Degree requirements:* For master's, 60 credits including capstone project. *Entrance requirements:* For master's, letter of intent, essay, transcripts, 2 letters of recommendation. *Application deadline:* For winter admission, 10/30 priority date for domestic students. Applications are processed on a rolling basis. Application fee: $0. Electronic applications accepted. *Expenses:* Tuition: Full-time $14,280; part-time $680 per credit. Tuition and fees vary according to course load and program. *Financial support:* In 2010–11, 1 student received support. Applicants required to submit FAFSA. *Unit head:* Ralph Meima, Program Director, 802-251-7690, Fax: 802-258-9201, E-mail: rmeima@gradschool.marlboro.edu. *Application contact:* Joe Heslin, Associate Director of Admissions, 802-258-9209, Fax: 802-258-9201, E-mail: jheslin@gradcenter.marlboro.edu.

Marquette University, Graduate School of Management, Executive MBA Program, Milwaukee, WI 53201-1881. Offers economics (MBA); finance (MBA); human resources (MBA); international business (MBA); management information systems (MBA); marketing (MBA); operations and supply chain management (MBA); sports business (MBA). *Accreditation:* AACSB. *Faculty:* 3 full-time (1 woman), 2 part-time/adjunct (0 women). *Students:* 43 full-time (11 women); includes 6 minority (1 Black or African American, non-Hispanic/Latino; 4 Asian, non-Hispanic/Latino; 1 Hispanic/Latino), 3 international. Average age 37. 47 applicants, 74% accepted, 29 enrolled. In 2010, 13 master's awarded. *Degree requirements:* For master's, international trip. *Entrance requirements:* For master's, GMAT, two letters of recommendation, official transcripts from current and previous colleges/universities. Additional exam requirements/recommendations for international students: Required—TOEFL (minimum score 530 paper-based; 78 computer-based). *Application deadline:* Applications are processed on a rolling basis. Application fee: $50. Electronic applications accepted. *Expenses:* Contact institution. *Financial support:* Application deadline: 2/15. *Faculty research:* International trade and finance, customer relationship management, consumer satisfaction, customer service. *Unit head:* Dr. Jeanne Simmons, Graduate Director, 414-288-7145, Fax: 414-288-1660, E-mail: jeanne.simmons@marquette.edu. *Application contact:* Erin Fox, Assistant Director for Recruitment, 414-288-5319, Fax: 414-288-1902, E-mail: erin.fox@marquette.edu.

Marquette University, Graduate School of Management, Program in Business Administration, Milwaukee, WI 53201-1881. Offers business administration (MBA); economics (MBA); finance (MBA); human resources (MBA); international business (MBA); management information systems (MBA); marketing (MBA); operations and supply chain management (MBA); sports business (MBA); JD/MBA; MBA/MA; MBA/MSN. *Accreditation:* AACSB. Part-time and evening/weekend programs available. *Faculty:* 38 full-time (9 women), 24 part-time/adjunct (8 women). *Students:* 44 full-time (17 women), 368 part-time (105 women); includes 36 minority (4 Black or African American, non-Hispanic/Latino; 2 American Indian or Alaska Native, non-Hispanic/Latino; 20 Asian, non-Hispanic/Latino; 10 Hispanic/Latino), 30 international. Average age 31. 256 applicants, 60% accepted, 98 enrolled. In 2010, 117 master's awarded. *Entrance requirements:* For master's, GMAT, letters of recommendation. Additional exam requirements/recommendations for international students: Required—TOEFL (minimum score 530 paper-based; 78 computer-based). *Application deadline:* Applications are processed on a rolling basis. Application fee: $50. Electronic applications accepted. *Expenses:* Tuition: Full-time $16,290; part-time $905 per credit hour. Tuition and fees vary according to program. *Financial support:* In 2010–11, 4 fellowships, 11 teaching assistantships were awarded; research assistantships, Federal Work-Study, institutionally sponsored loans, scholarships/grants, and tuition waivers (full and partial) also available. Support available to part-time students. Financial award application deadline: 2/15. *Faculty research:* Ethics in the professions, services marketing, technology impact on decision-making, mentoring. *Unit head:* Dr. Jeanne Simmons, Graduate Director, 414-288-7145, Fax: 414-288-1660, E-mail: jeanne.simmons@marquette.edu. *Application contact:* Debra Leutermann, Admissions Coordinator, 414-288-8064, Fax: 414-288-1902, E-mail: debra.leutermann@marquette.edu.

Marshall University, Academic Affairs Division, Lewis College of Business, Graduate School of Management, Program in Business Administration, Huntington, WV 25755. Offers IMBA, MBA. Part-time and evening/weekend programs available. *Students:* 139 full-time (43 women), 24 part-time (12 women); includes 4 Black or African American, non-Hispanic/Latino; 1 American Indian or Alaska Native, non-Hispanic/Latino; 2 Asian, non-Hispanic/Latino, 27 international. Average age 27. In 2010, 121 master's awarded. *Degree requirements:* For master's, comprehensive assessment. *Entrance requirements:* For master's, GMAT. *Application deadline:* Applications are processed on a rolling basis. Application fee: $40. *Financial support:* Tuition waivers (full) available. Support available to part-time students. Financial award applicants required to submit FAFSA. *Unit head:* Dr. Andrew Sikula, 304-746-1956, E-mail: sikula@marshall.edu. *Application contact:* Steven Shumlas, Information Contact, 304-746-8964, Fax: 304-746-1902, E-mail: shumlas@marshall.edu.

Marshall University, Academic Affairs Division, Lewis College of Business, Graduate School of Management, Program in Business Management Foundations, Huntington, WV 25755. Offers Graduate Certificate. *Students:* 19 full-time (8 women), 22 part-time (11 women); includes 5 Black or African American, non-Hispanic/Latino; 1 Asian, non-Hispanic/Latino; 1 Hispanic/Latino. Average age 29.*Unit head:* Dr. Andrew Sikula, Associate Dean, 304-746-1956, E-mail: sikula@marshall.edu. *Application contact:* Steven Shumlas, Academic Advisor, 304-746-8964, E-mail: shumlas@marshall.edu.

Maryland Institute College of Art, Graduate Studies, The Business of Art and Design Program, Baltimore, MD 21217. Offers MPS. Part-time programs available. Postbaccalaureate distance learning degree programs offered (minimal on-campus study). *Entrance requirements:* Additional exam requirements/recommendations for international students: Required—TOEFL (minimum score 550 paper-based; 213 computer-based; 80 iBT). *Application deadline:* For spring admission, 1/15 for domestic and international students. Application fee: $60. *Expenses:* Tuition: Full-time $34,550; part-time $1440 per credit hour. Required fees: $1140; $570 per term. *Financial support:* Applicants required to submit FAFSA. *Unit head:* Heather Bradbury, Manager, 410-225-2220, Fax: 410-225-2229, E-mail: hbradbury@mica.edu. *Application contact:* Scott G. Kelly, Associate Dean of Graduate Admission, 410-225-2256, Fax: 410-225-2408, E-mail: graduate@mica.edu.

Marylhurst University, Department of Business Administration, Marylhurst, OR 97036-0261. Offers finance (MBA); general management (MBA); government policy and administration (MBA); green development (MBA); health care management (MBA); marketing (MBA); natural and organic resources (MBA); nonprofit management (MBA); organizational behavior (MBA); real estate (MBA); renewable energy (MBA); sustainable business (MBA). Part-time and evening/weekend programs available. Postbaccalaureate distance learning degree programs offered (no on-campus study). *Faculty:* 3 full-time (0 women), 36 part-time/adjunct (6 women). *Students:* 27 full-time (13 women), 727 part-time (373 women); includes 167 minority (47 Black or African American, non-Hispanic/Latino; 6 American Indian or Alaska Native, non-Hispanic/Latino; 36 Asian, non-Hispanic/Latino; 51 Hispanic/Latino; 6 Native Hawaiian or other Pacific Islander, non-Hispanic/Latino; 21 Two or more races, non-Hispanic/Latino), 7 international. Average age 38. 262 applicants, 91% accepted. In 2010, 289 master's awarded. *Degree requirements:* For master's, comprehensive exam, capstone course. *Entrance requirements:* For master's, GMAT (if GPA less than 3.0 and fewer than 5 years of work experience), interview, resume, 2 letters of recommendation. Additional exam requirements/recommendations for international students: Recommended—TOEFL (minimum score 550 paper-based; 213 computer-based; 80 iBT). *Application deadline:* For fall admission, 9/11 priority date for domestic and international students; for winter admission, 12/15 priority date for domestic and international students; for spring admission, 3/15 priority date for domestic students, 3/17 priority date for international students. Applications are processed on a rolling basis. Application fee: $50. Electronic applications accepted. *Expenses:* Tuition: Full-time $13,932; part-time $516 per credit. Tuition and fees vary according to course load and program. *Financial support:* Scholarships/grants available. Support available to part-time students. Financial award applicants required to submit FAFSA. *Unit head:* Bob Hanks, Director of Business and Real Estate Programs, 503-636-8141, Fax: 503-697-5597, E-mail: mba@marylhurst.edu. *Application contact:* Maruska Lynch, Graduate Admissions Specialist, 800-634-9982 Ext. 6322, Fax: 503-699-6320, E-mail: admissions@marylhurst.edu.

Maryville University of Saint Louis, The John E. Simon School of Business, St. Louis, MO 63141-7299. Offers accounting (MBA, PGC); business studies (PGC); management (MBA, PGC); marketing (MBA, PGC); process and project management (MBA, PGC); sport and entertainment management (MBA, PGC). *Accreditation:* ACBSP. Part-time and evening/weekend programs available. *Faculty:* 7 full-time (4 women), 13 part-time/adjunct (5 women). *Students:* 16 full-time (8 women), 119 part-time (57 women); includes 15 minority (9 Black or African American, non-Hispanic/Latino; 3 Asian, non-Hispanic/Latino; 3 Hispanic/Latino), 5 international. Average age 31. In 2010, 60 master's awarded. *Entrance requirements:* For master's, GMAT (unless applicant possesses undergraduate business degree with minimum cumulative GPA of 3.0, or has completed master's degree from accredited university or one early access course prior to undergraduate degree). Additional exam requirements/recommendations for international students: Required—TOEFL (minimum score 563 paper-based; 85 iBT), If you took the revised TOEFL (after Sept. 24, 2005), you will be admitted into our MBA program with a speaking sub-score of 23, a writing sub-score of 20, reading and listening scores of 21 or higher and a combined score of 79 or higher. *Application deadline:* Applications are processed on a rolling basis. Application fee: $40 ($60 for international students). Electronic applications accepted. *Expenses:* Tuition: Full-time $21,100; part-time $633.50 per credit hour. Required fees: $150 per semester. *Financial support:* Career-related internships or fieldwork, Federal Work-Study, tuition waivers (partial), and campus employment available. Financial award application deadline: 3/1; financial award applicants required to submit FAFSA. *Faculty research:* International business, e-marketing, strategic planning, interpersonal management skills, financial analysis. *Unit head:* Dr. Pamela Horwitz, Dean, 314-529-9418, Fax: 314-529-9975, E-mail: horwitz@maryville.edu. *Application contact:* Kathy Dougherty, Director of MBA Programs, 314-529-9382, Fax: 314-529-9975, E-mail: business@maryville.edu.

McKendree University, Graduate Programs, Master of Business Administration Program, Lebanon, IL 62254-1299. Offers business administration (MBA); human resource management (MBA); international business (MBA). Part-time and evening/weekend programs available. Postbaccalaureate distance learning degree programs offered (no on-campus study). *Faculty:* 8 full-time (3 women), 19 part-time/adjunct (3 women). *Students:* 99 full-time (49 women), 155 part-time (63 women). Average age 36. In 2010, 37 master's awarded. *Entrance requirements:* For master's, official transcripts from all institutions attended, essay, minimum GPA of 3.0, three references, resume. Additional exam requirements/recommendations for international students: Required—TOEFL. *Application deadline:* Applications are processed on a rolling basis. Application fee: $0. Electronic applications accepted. *Expenses:* Tuition: Full-time $6750; part-time $375 per credit hour. One-time fee: $100. Tuition and fees vary according to program. *Financial support:* Application deadline: 6/30. *Unit head:* Dr. Frank Spreng, Director of MBA Program, 618-537-6902, E-mail: fspreng@mckendree.edu. *Application contact:* Patty L. Aubel, Graduate Admission Counselor, 618-537-6943, Fax: 618-537-6410, E-mail: plaubel@mckendree.edu.

McNeese State University, Doré School of Graduate Studies, College of Business, Master of Business Administration Program, Lake Charles, LA 70609. Offers accounting (MBA); business administration (MBA). *Accreditation:* AACSB. Evening/weekend programs available. *Faculty:* 17 full-time (1 woman). *Students:* 54 full-time (28 women), 33 part-time (17 women); includes 5 minority (3 Black or African American, non-Hispanic/Latino; 1 Asian, non-Hispanic/Latino; 1 Hispanic/Latino), 33 international. In 2010, 38 master's awarded. *Degree requirements:* For master's, written exam. *Entrance requirements:* For master's, GMAT. *Application deadline:* For fall admission, 5/15 priority date for domestic and international students; for spring admission, 10/15 priority date for domestic and international students. Applications are processed on a rolling basis. Application fee: $20 ($30 for international students). Tuition and fees vary according to course load. *Financial support:* Research assistantships, teaching assistantships, Federal Work-Study available. Support available to part-time students. Financial award application deadline: 5/1. *Faculty research:* Management development, integrating technology into the work force, union/management relations, economic development. *Unit head:* Dr. Akm Rahman, MBA Director, 337-475-5576, Fax: 337-475-5986, E-mail: mrahman@mcneese.edu. *Application contact:* Dr. Akm Rahman, MBA Director, 337-475-5576, Fax: 337-475-5986, E-mail: mrahman@mcneese.edu.

Medaille College, Program in Business Administration—Amherst, Amherst, NY 14221. Offers business administration (MBA); organizational leadership (MA). Evening/weekend programs available. *Faculty:* 8 full-time (3 women), 14 part-time/adjunct (4 women). *Students:* 222 full-time (126 women), 1 (woman) part-time; includes 24 Black or African American, non-Hispanic/Latino; 3 Asian, non-Hispanic/Latino; 6 Hispanic/Latino; 1 Two or more races, non-Hispanic/Latino. Average age 31. In 2010, 143 master's awarded. *Degree requirements:* For master's, thesis or alternative. *Entrance requirements:* For master's, GMAT, minimum undergraduate GPA of 2.7, 3 years of work experience. Additional exam requirements/recommendations for international students: Required—TOEFL (minimum score 550 paper-based; 213 computer-based). *Application deadline:* Applications are processed on a rolling basis. Application fee: $100. *Expenses:* Contact institution. *Financial* *support:* In 2010–11, 180 students received support. Federal Work-Study available. Financial award applicants required to submit FAFSA. *Unit head:* Jennifer Bavifard, Associate Dean for Special Programs, 716-631-1061 Ext. 150, Fax: 716-631-1380, E-mail: jbavifar@medaille.edu. *Application contact:* Jacqueline Matheny, Executive Director of Marketing and Enrollment, 716-932-2541, Fax: 716-632-1811, E-mail: jmatheny@medaille.edu.

Medaille College, Program in Business Administration—Rochester, Rochester, NY 14623. Offers business administration (MBA); organizational leadership (MA). Evening/weekend programs available. *Faculty:* 3 full-time (2 women), 40 part-time/adjunct (20 women). *Students:* 37 full-time (26 women); includes 9 Black or African American, non-Hispanic/Latino; 5 Hispanic/Latino. Average age 36. 31 applicants, 90% accepted, 25 enrolled. In 2010, 27 master's awarded. *Degree requirements:* For master's, thesis or alternative. *Entrance requirements:* For master's, GMAT, 3 years of work experience, minimum undergraduate GPA of 2.7. Additional exam requirements/recommendations for international students: Required—TOEFL (minimum score 550 paper-based; 213 computer-based). *Application deadline:* Applications are processed on a rolling basis. Application fee: $100. *Expenses:* Contact institution. *Financial support:* In 2010–11, 37 students received support. Federal Work-Study available. Financial award applicants required to submit FAFSA. *Unit head:* Jennifer Bavifard, Branch Campus Director, 716-932-2591, Fax: 716-631-1380, E-mail: jbavifard@medaille.edu. *Application contact:* Jane Rowlands, Marketing Support, 585-272-0030, Fax: 585-272-0057, E-mail: jrowlands@medaille.edu.

Mercer University, Graduate Studies, Cecil B. Day Campus, Eugene W. Stetson School of Business and Economics (Atlanta), Macon, GA 31207-0003. Offers business administration (MBA, XMBA); Pharm D/MBA. *Accreditation:* AACSB. Part-time and evening/weekend programs available. *Faculty:* 18 full-time (6 women), 4 part-time/adjunct (0 women). *Students:* 146 full-time (63 women), 91 part-time (43 women); includes 67 minority (44 Black or African American, non-Hispanic/Latino; 17 Asian, non-Hispanic/Latino; 6 Hispanic/Latino), 15 international. Average age 32. 169 applicants, 54% accepted, 64 enrolled. In 2010, 154 master's awarded. *Entrance requirements:* For master's, GMAT. Additional exam requirements/recommendations for international students: Required—TOEFL (minimum score 550 paper-based; 213 computer-based; 80 iBT). *Application deadline:* For fall admission, 7/1 priority date for domestic students, 7/1 for international students; for spring admission, 11/1 priority date for domestic students, 11/1 for international students. Applications are processed on a rolling basis. Application fee: $50 ($100 for international students). Electronic applications accepted. *Financial support:* Federal Work-Study available. Financial award application deadline: 5/1; financial award applicants required to submit FAFSA. *Faculty research:* Entrepreneurship, market studies, international business strategy, financial analysis. *Unit head:* Dr. Gina L. Miller, Associate Dean, 678-547-6177, Fax: 678-547-6337, E-mail: miller gl@mercer.edu. Application contact: Jamie Thomas, Graduate Enrollment Associate, 678-547-6177, Fax: 678-547-6337, E-mail: atlbusadm@mercer.edu.

Mercer University, Graduate Studies, Macon Campus, Eugene W. Stetson School of Business and Economics (Macon), Macon, GA 31207-0003. Offers MBA. *Accreditation:* AACSB. Part-time and evening/weekend programs available. *Faculty:* 10 full-time (5 women). *Students:* 8 full-time (1 woman), 29 part-time (12 women); includes 3 minority (all Black or African American, non-Hispanic/Latino). Average age 26. 15 applicants, 93% accepted, 14 enrolled. In 2010, 18 master's awarded. *Entrance requirements:* For master's, GMAT/GRE. Additional exam requirements/recommendations for international students: Required—TOEFL (minimum score 550 paper-based; 213 computer-based). *Application deadline:* For fall admission, 8/1 for domestic students; for spring admission, 12/1 for domestic students. Applications are processed on a rolling basis. Application fee: $50 ($100 for international students). *Faculty research:* Federal Reserve System, management of nurses, sales promotion, systems for common stock selection, interest rate premiums. *Unit head:* Dr. David Scott Davis, Dean, 478-301-2990, Fax: 478-301-2635, E-mail: davis ds@mercer.edu. Application contact: Robert Holland, Director/Academic Administrator, 478-301-2835, Fax: 478-301-2635, E-mail: holland_r@mercer.edu.

Mercy College, School of Business, Program in Business Administration, Dobbs Ferry, NY 10522-1189. Offers MBA. Part-time and evening/weekend programs available. Postbaccalaureate distance learning degree programs offered (no on-campus study). *Students:* 83 full-time (42 women), 25 part-time (18 women); includes 30 Black or African American, non-Hispanic/Latino; 5 Asian, non-Hispanic/Latino; 21 Hispanic/Latino; 2 Two or more races, non-Hispanic/Latino, 8 international. Average age 31. 155 applicants, 55% accepted, 59 enrolled. In 2010, 27 master's awarded. *Entrance requirements:* For master's, GMAT, interview, two letters of recommendation, undergraduate transcripts. Additional exam requirements/recommendations for international students: Required—TOEFL (minimum score 600 paper-based; 250 computer-based; 100 iBT), IELTS (minimum score 8). *Application deadline:* For fall admission, 8/1 for international students. Applications are processed on a rolling basis. Application fee: $40. Electronic applications accepted. *Expenses:* Tuition: Full-time $13,572; part-time $754 per credit hour. Required fees: $130 per term. *Financial support:* In 2010–11, 27 students received support. Career-related internships or fieldwork, Federal Work-Study, scholarships/

grants, and unspecified assistantships available. Support available to part-time students. Financial award applicants required to submit FAFSA. *Faculty research:* Marketing systems, international business, diverse management challenges, decision making. *Unit head:* Dr. Lucretia Mills, Dean for the School of Business, 914-674-7490, E-mail: lmann@mercy.edu. *Application contact:* Allison Gurdineer, Senior Associate Director of Recruitment, 914-674-7601, E-mail: agurdineer@mercy.edu.

Meredith College, John E. Weems Graduate School, School of Business, Raleigh, NC 27607-5298. Offers business administration (MBA). *Accreditation:* AACSB. Part-time and evening/weekend programs available. *Faculty:* 8 full-time (5 women), 1 part-time/adjunct (0 women). *Students:* 2 full-time (0 women), 90 part-time (64 women); includes 11 Black or African American, non-Hispanic/Latino; 6 Asian, non-Hispanic/Latino; 2 Hispanic/Latino. Average age 34. 48 applicants, 83% accepted, 34 enrolled. In 2010, 21 master's awarded. *Degree requirements:* For master's, thesis optional. *Entrance requirements:* For master's, GMAT, interview, minimum GPA of 2.5, letters of recommendation. Additional exam requirements/recommendations for international students: Required—TOEFL. *Application deadline:* For fall admission, 7/1 priority date for domestic and international students; for spring admission, 11/1 priority date for domestic and international students. Applications are processed on a rolling basis. Application fee: $50. Electronic applications accepted. *Financial support:* Career-related internships or fieldwork, institutionally sponsored loans, scholarships/grants, and tuition waivers (partial) available. Support available to part-time students. Financial award application deadline: 2/15; financial award applicants required to submit FAFSA. *Unit head:* Dr. Denise Rotundo, Dean, 919-760-8471, Fax: 919-760-8470. *Application contact:* Page Midyette, Coordinator, 919-760-2281, Fax: 919-760-2898, E-mail: midyette@meredith.edu.

Mesa State College, Department of Business, Grand Junction, CO 81501-3122. Offers MBA. Part-time and evening/weekend programs available. *Faculty:* 12 full-time (1 woman), 1 part-time/adjunct (0 women). *Students:* 17 full-time (10 women), 27 part-time (15 women); includes 3 Hispanic/Latino; 1 Native Hawaiian or other Pacific Islander, non-Hispanic/Latino. Average age 32. 32 applicants, 81% accepted, 19 enrolled. In 2010, 10 master's awarded. *Degree requirements:* For master's, thesis or research practicum, written comprehensive exams. *Entrance requirements:* For master's, GMAT, MAT, or GRE, minimum GPA of 3.0 for last 60 undergraduate hours, 2 letters of recommendation. Additional exam requirements/recommendations for international students: Required—TOEFL (minimum score 550 paper-based; 207 computer-based). *Application deadline:* For fall admission, 7/15 priority date for domestic students; for spring admission, 12/22 priority date for domestic students. Applications are processed on a rolling basis. Application fee: $50. Electronic applications accepted. *Expenses:* Tuition, state resident: full-time $5400; part-time $300 per credit hour. Tuition, nonresident: full-time $16,200; part-time $900 per credit hour. Required fees: $461; $25.61 per credit hour. Tuition and fees vary according to course load and program. *Financial support:* In 2010–11, 3 students received support. Scholarships/grants available. Financial award applicants required to submit FAFSA. *Unit head:* Dr. Morgan Bridge, Department Head, 970-248-1169, Fax: 970-248-1730, E-mail: mbridge@mesastate.edu. *Application contact:* Jane Sandoval, MBA Coordinator, 970-248-1778, Fax: 970-248-1730, E-mail: jsandova@mesastate.edu.

Metropolitan State University, College of Management, St. Paul, MN 55106-5000. Offers business administration (MBA, DBA); information assurance security (Graduate Certificate); management information systems (MMIS); MIS generalist (Graduate Certificate); MIS systems analysis and design (Graduate Certificate); nonprofit management (MPNA); project management (Graduate Certificate); public administration (MPNA). Part-time and evening/weekend programs available. *Students:* 158 full-time (74 women), 217 part-time (114 women); includes 31 Black or African American, non-Hispanic/Latino; 26 Asian, non-Hispanic/Latino; 10 Hispanic/Latino; 6 Two or more races, non-Hispanic/Latino, 47 international. Average age 35. In 2010, 100 master's, 7 other advanced degrees awarded. *Degree requirements:* For master's, thesis optional, computer language (MMIS). *Entrance requirements:* For master's, GMAT (MBA), resume. Additional exam requirements/recommendations for international students: Required—TOEFL (minimum score 550 paper-based; 213 computer-based). *Application deadline:* For fall admission, 7/15 for international students; for winter admission, 11/15 for international students; for spring admission, 3/15 for international students. Applications are processed on a rolling basis. Application fee: $20. Electronic applications accepted. *Expenses:* Tuition, state resident: full-time $5827; part-time $291 per credit hour. Tuition, nonresident: full-time $11,654; part-time $583 per credit hour. Required fees: $10 per credit hour. Tuition and fees vary according to degree level. *Financial support:* Research assistantships with partial tuition reimbursements, career-related internships or fieldwork and Federal Work-Study available. Support available to part-time students. Financial award applicants required to submit FAFSA. *Faculty research:* Yugoslav economic system, workers' cooperatives, participative management and job enrichment, global business systems. *Unit head:* Dr. Paul Huo, Graduate Director, 612-659-7271, Fax: 612-659-7268, E-mail: carol.bormann.young@metrostate.edu. *Application contact:* Gloria B. Marcus, Recruiter/Admissions Adviser, 612-659-7258, Fax: 612-659-7268, E-mail: gloria.marcus@metrostate.edu.

Miami University, Graduate School, Farmer School of Business, Oxford, OH 45056. Offers accountancy (M Acc); business administration (MBA); economics (MA). *Accreditation:* AACSB. Part-time and evening/weekend programs available. *Students:* 66 full-time (21 women), 1 part-time (0 women); includes 10 minority (2 Black or African American, non-Hispanic/Latino; 4 Asian, non-Hispanic/Latino; 2 Hispanic/Latino; 2 Two or more races, non-Hispanic/Latino), 16 international. Average age 26. In 2010, 69 master's awarded. *Entrance requirements:* For master's, GMAT, minimum undergraduate GPA of 3.0 during previous 2 years or 2.75 overall. Additional exam requirements/recommendations for international students: Required—TOEFL. *Application deadline:* For fall admission, 4/15 for domestic students, 2/15 for international students. Application fee: $50. *Expenses:* Tuition, state resident: full-time $11,616; part-time $484 per credit hour. Tuition, nonresident: full-time $25,656; part-time $1069 per credit hour. Required fees: $528. *Financial support:* Fellowships with tuition reimbursements, research assistantships, Federal Work-Study, tuition waivers (full), and unspecified assistantships available. Financial award application deadline: 3/1; financial award applicants required to submit FAFSA. *Unit head:* Dr. Roger Jenkins, Dean, 513-529-3631, Fax: 513-529-6992, E-mail: deanofbusiness@muohio.edu. *Application contact:* MBA Program Office, 513-529-6643, E-mail: miamimba@muohio.edu.

Middle Tennessee State University, College of Graduate Studies, Jennings A. Jones College of Business, Department of Management and Marketing, Murfreesboro, TN 37132. Offers MBA. *Accreditation:* AACSB. Part-time and evening/weekend programs available. Postbaccalaureate distance learning degree programs offered. *Faculty:* 18 full-time (4 women). *Students:* 33 full-time (6 women), 343 part-time (136 women); includes 53 Black or African American, non-Hispanic/Latino; 1 American Indian or Alaska Native, non-Hispanic/Latino; 38 Asian, non-Hispanic/Latino; 10 Hispanic/Latino; 3 Two or more races, non-Hispanic/Latino. Average age 29. 213 applicants, 66% accepted, 140 enrolled. In 2010, 109 master's awarded. *Degree requirements:* For master's, comprehensive exam. *Entrance requirements:* Additional exam requirements/recommendations for international students: Required—TOEFL (minimum score 525 paper-based; 195 computer-based; 71 iBT) or IELTS (minimum score 6). *Application deadline:* For fall admission, 6/1 for domestic and international students. Applications are processed on a rolling basis. Application fee: $25 ($30 for international students). Electronic applications accepted. *Expenses:* Tuition, state resident: full-time $4632. Tuition, nonresident: full-time $11,520. *Financial support:* In 2010–11, 8 students received support. Institutionally sponsored loans available. Support available to part-time students. Financial award application deadline: 5/1; financial award applicants required to submit FAFSA. *Faculty research:* International business, business strategy, organizational culture/leadership, consumer behavior, services marketing. *Unit head:* Dr. Jill M. Austin, Chair, 615-898-2736, Fax: 615-898-5308, E-mail: jaustin@mtsu.edu. *Application contact:* Dr. Michael Allen, Dean and Vice Provost for Research, 615-898-2840, Fax: 615-904-8020, E-mail: mallen@mtsu.edu.

Midwestern State University, Graduate Studies, College of Business Administration, Wichita Falls, TX 76308. Offers MBA. *Accreditation:* AACSB; ACBSP. Part-time and evening/weekend programs available. *Faculty:* 13 full-time (3 women). *Students:* 37 full-time (10 women), 44 part-time (20 women); includes 11 minority (2 Black or African American, non-Hispanic/Latino; 1 American Indian or Alaska Native, non-Hispanic/Latino; 1 Asian, non-Hispanic/Latino; 7 Hispanic/Latino), 27 international. Average age 29. 22 applicants, 77% accepted, 17 enrolled. In 2010, 27 master's awarded. *Degree requirements:* For master's, comprehensive exam, thesis optional. *Entrance requirements:* For master's, GMAT. Additional exam requirements/recommendations for international students: Required—TOEFL (minimum score 550 paper-based; 213 computer-based). *Application deadline:* For fall admission, 7/1 priority date for domestic students, 4/1 for international students; for spring admission, 11/1 priority date for domestic students, 8/1 for international students. Applications are processed on a rolling basis. Application fee: $35 ($50 for international students). Electronic applications accepted. *Expenses:* Tuition, state resident: full-time $1620; part-time $90 per credit hour. Tuition, nonresident: full-time $2160; part-time $120 per credit hour. International tuition: $7200 full-time. *Financial support:* In 2010–11, 32 students received support, including 1 teaching assistantship with partial tuition reimbursement available (averaging $2,667 per year); career-related internships or fieldwork, Federal Work-Study, institutionally sponsored loans, tuition waivers (partial), and unspecified assistantships also available. Support available to part-time students. Financial award application deadline: 3/1; financial award applicants required to submit FAFSA. *Faculty research:* Citizenship behavior, software solutions, mediations, sales force training, stock trading volume. *Unit head:* Dr. Barbara Nemecek, Dean, 940-397-4088, Fax: 940-397-4280, E-mail: barbar.nemecek@mwsu.edu. *Application contact:* Dr. Chris Shao, Director of Graduate Programs, 940-397-4366, Fax: 940-397-4280, E-mail: chris.shao@mwsu.edu.

Millikin University, Tabor School of Business, Decatur, IL 62522-2084. Offers MBA. *Accreditation:* ACBSP. Evening/weekend programs available. *Faculty:* 6 full-time (1 woman), 5 part-time/adjunct (0 women). *Students:* 13 full-time (6 women). Average age 36. 14 applicants, 100% accepted, 13 enrolled. In 2010, 20 master's awarded. *Entrance requirements:* For master's, GMAT, resume, 3 reference letters, interview. Additional exam requirements/recommendations for international students: Required—TOEFL (minimum score 550 paper-based; 79 iBT). *Application deadline:* For spring admission, 11/1 priority date for domestic students, 8/1 priority date for international students. Applications are processed on a rolling basis. Application fee: $0. Electronic applications accepted. *Expenses:* Tuition: Full-time $24,890; part-time $681 per credit hour. *Financial support:* Applicants required to submit FAFSA. *Faculty research:* E-commerce, international marketing, pedagogy, total quality management, auditing. *Unit head:* Dr. James G. Dahl, Dean, 217-420-6634, Fax: 217-424-6286, E-mail: jdahl@millikin.edu. *Application contact:* Dr. Anthony Liberatore, Director of MBA Program, 217-424-6338, E-mail: aliberatore@millikin.edu.

Mills College, Graduate Studies, Lori I. Lokey Graduate School of Business, Oakland, CA 94613-1000. Offers management (MBA). *Faculty:* 1 full-time (0 women), 9 part-time/adjunct (4 women). *Students:* 98 full-time (92 women), 11 part-time (10 women); includes 17 Black or African American, non-Hispanic/Latino; 2 American Indian or Alaska Native, non-Hispanic/Latino; 8 Asian, non-Hispanic/Latino; 17 Hispanic/Latino; 3 Two or more races, non-Hispanic/Latino. Average age 33. 62 applicants, 97% accepted, 39 enrolled. In 2010, 28 master's awarded. *Entrance requirements:* For master's, 3 letters of recommendation, 2 transcripts. Additional exam requirements/recommendations for international students: Required—TOEFL (minimum score 550 paper-based; 213 computer-based; 80 iBT), IELTS (minimum score 6). *Application deadline:* For fall admission, 2/1 priority date for domestic students, 12/15 for international students. Application fee: $50. *Expenses:* Tuition: Full-time $28,280; part-time $7070 per course. Required fees: $1058; $1058 per year. Tuition and fees vary according to program. *Financial support:* In 2010–11, 97 students received support, including 97 fellowships (averaging $7,106 per year); scholarships/grants also available. Support available to part-time students. Financial award applicants required to submit FAFSA. *Faculty research:* Information systems, corporate and financial planning, interest-based marketing, organizational behavior, international trade and finance. Total annual research expenditures: $223,771. *Unit head:* Nancy Thornborrow, Dean, 510-430-2344, Fax: 510-430-3314, E-mail: nancy@mills.edu. *Application contact:* Jessica King, Graduate Admission Specialist, 510-430-3305, Fax: 510-430-2159, E-mail: grad-studies@mills.edu.

Milwaukee School of Engineering, Rader School of Business, Milwaukee, WI 53202-3109. Offers engineering management (MS); marketing and export management (MS); medical informatics (MS); new product management (MS). Part-time and evening/weekend programs available. *Faculty:* 6 full-time (1 woman), 16 part-time/adjunct (3 women). *Students:* 8 full-time (1 woman), 106 part-time (32 women); includes 2 Black or African American, non-Hispanic/Latino; 1 American Indian or Alaska Native, non-Hispanic/Latino; 6 Asian, non-Hispanic/Latino; 4 Hispanic/Latino; 1 Two or more races, non-Hispanic/Latino, 10 international. Average age 25. 35 applicants, 69% accepted, 18 enrolled. In 2010, 32 master's awarded. *Degree requirements:* For master's, thesis (for some programs), thesis defense or capstone project. *Entrance requirements:* For master's, GMAT, GRE General Test, or MCAT, BS in engineering, science, business or related fields; 2 letters of recommendation. Additional exam requirements/recommendations for international students: Required—TOEFL (minimum score 79 iBT). *Application deadline:* Applications are processed on a rolling basis. Application fee: $30. Electronic applications accepted. *Expenses:* Tuition: Full-time $17,550; part-time $650 per credit. One-time fee: $75. *Financial support:* In 2010–11, 36 students received support, including 2 research assistantships (averaging $15,000 per year); career-related internships or fieldwork also available. Support available to part-time students. Financial award applicants required to submit FAFSA. *Faculty research:* Operations, project management, quality marketing, information technology, databases. *Unit head:* Dr. Steven Bialek, Chairman, 414-277-7364, Fax: 414-277-7479, E-mail: bialek@msoe.edu. *Application contact:* Sarah K. Winchowky, 800-321-6763, Fax: 414-277-7475, E-mail: wp@msoe.edu.

Minnesota State University Mankato, College of Graduate Studies, College of Business, Mankato, MN 56001. Offers MBA. *Accreditation:* AACSB. *Students:* 11 full-time (3 women), 71 part-time (21 women). *Entrance requirements:* For master's, GMAT, 2 letters of reference, resume. Additional exam requirements/recommendations for international students: Required—TOEFL. *Application deadline:* For fall admission, 7/1 for domestic students, 5/1 for international students; for spring admission, 11/1 for domestic students, 10/1 for international students. Electronic applications accepted. *Unit head:* Dr. Kevin Elliott, Graduate Coordinator, 507-389-5420. *Application contact:* Dr. Kevin Elliott, Graduate Coordinator, 507-389-5420.

Misericordia University, College of Professional Studies and Social Sciences, Master of Business Administration Program, Dallas, PA 18612-1098. Offers MBA. Part-time and evening/weekend programs available. Postbaccalaureate distance learning degree programs offered. *Faculty:* 5 full-time (2 women), 6 part-time/adjunct (0 women). *Students:* 77 part-time (43 women); includes 1 Black or African American, non-Hispanic/Latino, 1 international. Average age 32. 21 applicants, 76% accepted, 14 enrolled. In 2010, 21 master's awarded. *Entrance requirements:* For master's, GMAT, MAT, GRE (50th percentile or higher), or minimum undergraduate GPA of 2.79, interview. *Application deadline:* Applications are processed on a rolling basis. *Expenses:* Tuition:

Full-time $23,750; part-time $525 per credit. Required fees: $1240. *Financial support:* In 2010–11, 44 students received support. Scholarships/grants and tuition waivers available. Support available to part-time students. Financial award applicants required to submit FAFSA. *Unit head:* Dr. John Sumansky, Director of Graduate Business Programs, 570-674-6158, E-mail: jsumansk@misericordia.edu. *Application contact:* Larree Brown, Assistant Director of Admissions, Part-Time Undergraduate and Graduate Programs, 570-674-6451, Fax: 570-674-6232, E-mail: lbrown@misericordia.edu.

Mississippi State University, College of Business, Department of Management and Information Systems, Mississippi State, MS 39762. Offers business administration (PhD), including business information systems, management; information systems (MSIS). Part-time programs available. *Faculty:* 14 full-time (3 women). *Students:* 19 full-time (7 women), 7 part-time (2 women); includes 3 minority (1 Black or African American, non-Hispanic/Latino; 1 American Indian or Alaska Native, non-Hispanic/Latino; 1 Two or more races, non-Hispanic/Latino), 7 international. Average age 31. 55 applicants, 33% accepted, 11 enrolled. In 2010, 6 master's, 1 doctorate awarded. *Degree requirements:* For master's, comprehensive exam; for doctorate, comprehensive exam, thesis/dissertation. *Entrance requirements:* For master's, GMAT, minimum GPA of 3.0 in last 60 hours of course work; for doctorate, GMAT, minimum graduate GPA of 3.25 in last 60 hours. Additional exam requirements/recommendations for international students: Required—TOEFL (minimum score 575 paper-based; 233 computer-based; 90 iBT); Recommended—IELTS (minimum score 7). *Application deadline:* For fall admission, 7/1 for domestic students, 5/1 for international students; for spring admission, 11/1 for domestic students, 9/1 for international students. Applications are processed on a rolling basis. Application fee: $40. Electronic applications accepted. *Expenses:* Tuition, state resident: full-time $2730.50; part-time $304 per credit hour. Tuition, nonresident: full-time $6901; part-time $767 per credit hour. *Financial support:* In 2010–11, 5 teaching assistantships (averaging $13,088 per year) were awarded; Federal Work-Study and institutionally sponsored loans also available. Financial award applicants required to submit FAFSA. *Faculty research:* Electronic commerce, management of information technology. *Unit head:* Dr. Rodney Pearson, Department Head and Professor of Information Systems, 662-325-3928, Fax: 662-325-8651, E-mail: rodney.pearson@msstate.edu. *Application contact:* Dr. Barbara Spencer, Associate Dean for Research and Outreach, 662-325-1891, Fax: 662-325-8161, E-mail: bspencer@cobian.msstate.edu.

Mississippi State University, College of Business, Department of Marketing, Quantitative Analysis and Business Law, Mississippi State, MS 39762. Offers business administration (MBA, PhD), including marketing. Part-time and evening/weekend programs available. *Faculty:* 10 full-time (3 women). *Students:* 5 full-time (4 women); includes 1 minority (Black or African American, non-Hispanic/Latino), 1 international. Average age 28. 16 applicants, 6% accepted, 1 enrolled. *Degree requirements:* For doctorate, comprehensive exam, thesis/dissertation. *Entrance requirements:* For doctorate, GMAT, minimum GPA of 2.75 in last 60 undergraduate hours. Additional exam requirements/recommendations for international students: Required—TOEFL (minimum score 575 paper-based; 233 computer-based; 90 iBT); Recommended—IELTS (minimum score 6.5). *Application deadline:* For fall admission, 7/1 for domestic students, 5/1 for international students; for spring admission, 11/1 for domestic students, 9/1 for international students. Applications are processed on a rolling basis. Application fee: $40. Electronic applications accepted. *Expenses:* Tuition, state resident: full-time $2730.50; part-time $304 per credit hour. Tuition, nonresident: full-time $6901; part-time $767 per credit hour. *Financial support:* In 2010–11, 2 teaching assistantships (averaging $12,270 per year) were awarded; Federal Work-Study, institutionally sponsored loans, and scholarships/grants also available. Financial award application deadline: 4/1; financial award applicants required to submit FAFSA. *Unit head:* Dr. Jason Lueg, Associate Professor and Department Head, 662-325-3163, Fax: 662-325-7012, E-mail: jlueg@cobilan.msstate.edu. *Application contact:* Dr. Barbara Spencer, Associate Dean for Research and Outreach, 662-325-1891, Fax: 662-325-8161, E-mail: gsbi@cobilan.msstate.edu.

Mississippi State University, College of Business, Graduate Studies in Business, Mississippi State, MS 39762. Offers business administration (MBA); project management (MBA). *Accreditation:* AACSB. Part-time and evening/weekend programs available. Postbaccalaureate distance learning degree programs offered (no on-campus study). *Students:* 99 full-time (37 women), 245 part-time (79 women); includes 34 minority (17 Black or African American, non-Hispanic/Latino; 3 American Indian or Alaska Native, non-Hispanic/Latino; 1 Asian, non-Hispanic/Latino; 10 Hispanic/Latino; 1 Native Hawaiian or other Pacific Islander, non-Hispanic/Latino; 2 Two or more races, non-Hispanic/Latino), 20 international. Average age 29. 218 applicants, 64% accepted, 105 enrolled. In 2010, 154 master's awarded. Terminal master's awarded for partial completion of doctoral program. *Degree requirements:* For master's, comprehensive exam (for some programs), thesis optional. *Entrance requirements:* For master's, GMAT, minimum GPA of 3.0 in last 60 hours of course work. Additional exam requirements/recommendations for international students: Required—TOEFL (minimum score 575 paper-based; 233 computer-based; 90 iBT); Recommended—IELTS (minimum score 6.5). *Application deadline:* For fall admission, 7/1 for domestic students, 5/1 for international

students; for spring admission, 11/1 for domestic students, 9/1 for international students. Applications are processed on a rolling basis. Application fee: $40. Electronic applications accepted. *Expenses:* Tuition, state resident: full-time $2730.50; part-time $304 per credit hour. Tuition, nonresident: full-time $6901; part-time $767 per credit hour. *Financial support:* In 2010–11, 1 research assistantship with full tuition reimbursement (averaging $11,779 per year), 34 teaching assistantships with full tuition reimbursements (averaging $10,024 per year) were awarded; Federal Work-Study, institutionally sponsored loans, scholarships/grants, and unspecified assistantships also available. Financial award application deadline: 4/1; financial award applicants required to submit FAFSA. *Unit head:* Dr. Barbara Spencer, Director, 662-325-1891, Fax: 662-325-8161, E-mail: gsbi@cobilan.msstate.edu. *Application contact:* Dr. Barbara Spencer, Director, 662-325-1891, Fax: 662-325-8161, E-mail: gsbi@cobilan.msstate.edu.

Mississippi State University, College of Business, School of Accountancy, Mississippi State, MS 39762. Offers accounting (MBA); business administration (PhD); systems (MPA); taxation (MTX). MBA (accounting) only offered at the Meridian campus. *Accreditation:* AACSB. *Faculty:* 6 full-time (2 women), 2 part-time/adjunct (0 women). *Students:* 53 full-time (27 women), 13 part-time (10 women); includes 8 minority (3 Black or African American, non-Hispanic/Latino; 3 Asian, non-Hispanic/Latino; 2 Two or more races, non-Hispanic/Latino), 2 international. Average age 26. 59 applicants, 47% accepted, 21 enrolled. In 2010, 33 master's awarded. *Degree requirements:* For master's, comprehensive exam. *Entrance requirements:* For master's, GMAT (minimum score of 510), minimum GPA of 2.75 overall and in upper-level accounting, 3.0 in last 60 hours of course work; for doctorate, GMAT, minimum undergraduate GPA of 3.0, both cumulative and over the last 60 hours of undergraduate work; 3.25 on all prior graduate work. Additional exam requirements/recommendations for international students: Required—TOEFL (minimum score 575 paper-based; 233 computer-based; 84 iBT); Recommended—IELTS (minimum score 7). *Application deadline:* For fall admission, 7/1 for domestic students, 5/1 for international students; for spring admission, 11/1 for domestic students, 9/1 for international students. Applications are processed on a rolling basis. Application fee: $40. Electronic applications accepted. *Expenses:* Tuition, state resident: full-time $2730.50; part-time $304 per credit hour. Tuition, nonresident: full-time $6901; part-time $767 per credit hour. *Financial support:* Career-related internships or fieldwork, Federal Work-Study, institutionally sponsored loans, scholarships/grants, and unspecified assistantships available. Support available to part-time students. Financial award application deadline: 4/1; financial award applicants required to submit FAFSA. *Faculty research:* Income tax, financial accounting system, managerial accounting, auditing. *Unit head:* Dr. Jim Scheiner, Director, 662-325-1633, Fax: 662-325-1646, E-mail: jscheiner@cobilan.msstate.edu. *Application contact:* Dr. Barbara Spencer, Graduate Coordinator, 662-325-3710, Fax: 662-325-1646, E-mail: sac@cobilan.msstate.edu.

Molloy College, Graduate Business Program, Rockville Centre, NY 11571-5002. Offers accounting (MBA); accounting and management (MBA); management (MBA); personal financial planning and accounting (MBA); personal financial planning and management (MBA). Part-time programs available. *Faculty:* 5 full-time (0 women), 8 part-time/adjunct (2 women). *Students:* 26 full-time (15 women), 69 part-time (35 women); includes 19 Black or African American, non-Hispanic/Latino; 1 American Indian or Alaska Native, non-Hispanic/Latino; 7 Asian, non-Hispanic/Latino; 9 Hispanic/Latino. Average age 33. In 2010, 28 master's awarded. *Application deadline:* Applications are processed on a rolling basis. *Application contact:* Alina Haitz, Assistant Director of Graduate Admissions, 516-678-5000 Ext. 6399, Fax: 516-256-2247, E-mail: ahaitz@molloy.edu.

Monmouth University, The Graduate School, Leon Hess Business School, West Long Branch, NJ 07764-1898. Offers accounting (MBA, Post-Master's Certificate); business (MBA); finance (MBA); healthcare management (MBA, Post-Master's Certificate); real estate (MBA). *Accreditation:* AACSB. Part-time and evening/weekend programs available. *Faculty:* 27 full-time (9 women), 7 part-time/adjunct (1 woman). *Students:* 87 full-time (31 women), 144 part-time (69 women); includes 6 Black or African American, non-Hispanic/Latino; 14 Asian, non-Hispanic/Latino; 8 Hispanic/Latino; 2 Two or more races, non-Hispanic/Latino, 17 international. Average age 29. 181 applicants, 78% accepted, 81 enrolled. In 2010, 88 master's awarded. *Degree requirements:* For master's, capstone course. *Entrance requirements:* For master's, GMAT, minimum GPA of 3.0 in major, 2.75 overall. Additional exam requirements/recommendations for international students: Required—TOEFL (minimum score 550 paper-based; 213 computer-based; 79 iBT), IELTS (minimum score 5), Michigan English Language Assessment Battery (minimum score 77), Cambridge A, B, C. *Application deadline:* For fall admission, 7/15 priority date for domestic students, 6/1 for international students; for spring admission, 11/15 priority date for domestic students, 11/1 for international students. Applications are processed on a rolling basis. Application fee: $50. Electronic applications accepted. *Expenses:* Tuition: Full-time $19,572; part-time $816 per credit. Required fees: $628; $157 per semester. *Financial support:* In 2010–11, 166 students received support, including 161 fellowships (averaging $1,741 per year), 17 research assistantships (averaging $10,505 per year); career-related internships or fieldwork, scholarships/grants, and unspecified assistantships also available. Support available to part-time students. Financial award applicants required to submit FAFSA. *Faculty research:* Information technology and marketing, behavioral research in accounting, human resources, management of technology. *Unit head:* Douglas Stives, MBA Program Director, 732-263-5894, Fax: 732-263-5517, E-mail: dstives@monmouth.edu. *Application contact:* Kevin Roane, Director, Office of Graduate Admission, 732-571-3452, Fax: 732-263-5123, E-mail: gradadm@monmouth.edu.

Montclair State University, The Graduate School, College of Humanities and Social Sciences, Department of Political Science and Law, Montclair, NJ 07043-1624. Offers law and governance (MA), including conflict management and peace studies, governance, compliance and regulation, intellectual property, law and governance, legal management. Part-time and evening/weekend programs available. *Faculty:* 13 full-time (6 women), 25 part-time/adjunct (8 women). *Students:* 9 full-time (5 women), 26 part-time (15 women); includes 10 Black or African American, non-Hispanic/Latino; 4 Asian, non-Hispanic/Latino; 2 Hispanic/Latino. Average age 30. 19 applicants, 68% accepted, 10 enrolled. In 2010, 16 master's, 3 other advanced degrees awarded. *Degree requirements:* For master's, thesis or comprehensive exam. *Entrance requirements:* For master's, GRE, minimum cumulative GPA of 2.75 for undergraduate work. Additional exam requirements/recommendations for international students: Required—TOEFL (minimum iBT score of 83) or IELTS. *Expenses:* Tuition, state resident: part-time $501.34 per credit. Tuition, nonresident: part-time $773.88 per credit. Required fees: $71.15 per credit. *Financial support:* In 2010–11, 1 research assistantship with full tuition reimbursement (averaging $7,000 per year) was awarded; Federal Work-Study, scholarships/grants, and unspecified assistantships also available. Support available to part-time students. Financial award application deadline: 3/1. *Unit head:* Dr. William Berlin, Chair, 973-655-7576, E-mail: berlinw@mail.montclair.edu. *Application contact:* Amy Aiello, Director of Graduate Admissions and Operations, 973-655-5147, Fax: 973-655-7869, E-mail: graduate.school@montclair.edu.

Montclair State University, The Graduate School, School of Business, Montclair, NJ 07043-1624. Offers MBA, MS, Certificate. *Accreditation:* AACSB. Part-time and evening/weekend programs available. *Faculty:* 77 full-time (26 women), 39 part-time/adjunct (10 women). *Students:* 92 full-time (45 women), 296 part-time (124 women); includes 31 Black or African American, non-Hispanic/Latino; 35 Asian, non-Hispanic/Latino; 27 Hispanic/Latino; 1 Two or more races, non-Hispanic/Latino, 30 international. Average age 29. 209 applicants, 58% accepted, 65 enrolled. In 2010, 110 master's, 1 other advanced degree awarded. *Degree requirements:* For master's, comprehensive exam. *Entrance requirements:* For master's, GMAT, 2 letters of recommendation, resume. Additional exam requirements/recommendations for international students: Required—TOEFL (minimum iBT score of 83) or IELTS. *Application deadline:* For fall admission, 6/1 for international students; for spring admission, 10/1 for international students. Applications are processed on a rolling basis. Application fee: $60. Electronic applications accepted. *Expenses:* Tuition, state resident: part-time $501.34 per credit. Tuition, nonresident: part-time $773.88 per credit. Required fees: $71.15 per credit. *Financial support:* In 2010–11, 28 students received support, including 21 research assistantships with full tuition reimbursements available (averaging $7,000 per year); Federal Work-Study, scholarships/grants, and unspecified assistantships also available. Support available to part-time students. Financial award application deadline: 3/1; financial award applicants required to submit FAFSA. *Unit head:* Dr. E. LeBrent Chrite, Dean, 973-655-4304, E-mail: chritee@mail.montclair.edu. *Application contact:* Amy Aiello, Director of Graduate Admissions and Operations, 973-655-5147, Fax: 973-655-7869, E-mail: graduate.school@montclair.edu.

Montreat College, School of Professional and Adult Studies, Montreat, NC 28757-1267. Offers business administration (MBA); environmental education (MS); K-6 education (MA Ed); management and leadership (MS). Evening/weekend programs available. Postbaccalaureate distance learning degree programs offered. *Students:* 231 full-time (163 women), 1 part-time (0 women). Average age 34. In 2010, 117 degrees awarded. *Entrance requirements:* Additional exam requirements/recommendations for international students: Required—TOEFL (minimum score 500 paper-based; 190 computer-based). *Application deadline:* Applications are processed on a rolling basis. *Financial support:* Available to part-time students. Applicants required to submit FAFSA. *Application contact:* Joey Higgins, Director of Enrollment Marketing and Communication, 828-669-8012 Ext. 3782, Fax: 818-669-0120, E-mail: jhiggins@montreat.edu.

Moravian College, Moravian College Comenius Center, Business and Management Programs, Bethlehem, PA 18018-6650. Offers accounting (MBA); general management (MBA); health care management (MBA); human resource management (MBA); leadership (MSHRM); learning and performance management (MSHRM); supply chain management (MBA). Part-time and evening/weekend programs available. *Faculty:* 6 full-time (2 women), 10 part-time/adjunct (3 women). *Students:* 67 part-time (35 women). 24 applicants, 50% accepted, 12 enrolled. In 2010, 8 master's awarded. *Entrance requirements:* For master's, GMAT. Additional exam requirements/ recommendations for international students: Required—TOEFL (minimum score 550 paper-based; 260 computer-based; 90 iBT). *Application deadline:* Applications are processed on a rolling basis. Application fee: $40. *Expenses:*

Contact institution. *Financial support:* In 2010–11, 1 fellowship with full tuition reimbursement was awarded. *Faculty research:* Leadership, change management, human resources. *Unit head:* Dr. William A. Kleintop, Associate Dean for Business and Management Programs, 610-507-1400, Fax: 610-861-1400, E-mail: comenius@moravian.edu. *Application contact:* Linda J. Doyle, Information Contact, 610-861-1400, Fax: 610-861-1466, E-mail: mba@moravian.edu.

Mount Saint Mary College, Division of Business, Newburgh, NY 12550-3494. Offers business (MBA); financial planning (MBA). Part-time and evening/weekend programs available. *Faculty:* 5 full-time (1 woman), 6 part-time/adjunct (2 women). *Students:* 35 full-time (21 women), 52 part-time (31 women); includes 20 minority (4 Black or African American, non-Hispanic/Latino; 4 Asian, non-Hispanic/Latino; 10 Hispanic/Latino; 2 Two or more races, non-Hispanic/Latino), 20 international. Average age 30. 22 applicants, 95% accepted, 10 enrolled. In 2010, 45 master's awarded. *Degree requirements:* For master's, thesis or alternative. *Entrance requirements:* For master's, GMAT or minimum undergraduate GPA of 2.7. *Application deadline:* Applications are processed on a rolling basis. Application fee: $45. *Expenses:* Tuition: Full-time $13,356; part-time $742 per credit. Required fees: $70 per semester. *Financial support:* In 2010–11, 25 students received support. Unspecified assistantships available. Financial award application deadline: 4/15; financial award applicants required to submit FAFSA. *Faculty research:* Financial reform, entrepreneurship and small business development, global business relations, technology's impact on business decision-making, college-assisted business education. *Unit head:* Dr. James Gearity, Graduate Coordinator, 845-569-3121, Fax: 845-562-6762, E-mail: james.gearity@msmc.edu. *Application contact:* Kathryn Sharp, Secretary, 845-569-3582, Fax: 845-569-3885, E-mail: ksharp@msmc.edu.

Mount St. Mary's University, Program in Business Administration, Emmitsburg, MD 21727-7799. Offers MBA. Part-time and evening/weekend programs available. *Faculty:* 12 full-time (4 women), 7 part-time/adjunct (2 women). *Students:* 45 full-time (21 women), 182 part-time (76 women); includes 31 minority (15 Black or African American, non-Hispanic/Latino; 6 Asian, non-Hispanic/Latino; 8 Hispanic/Latino; 2 Two or more races, non-Hispanic/Latino), 9 international. Average age 31. 101 applicants, 78% accepted, 79 enrolled. In 2010, 107 master's awarded. *Degree requirements:* For master's, thesis. *Entrance requirements:* For master's, minimum undergraduate GPA of 2.75, 5 years' relevant professional business experience, or GMAT (minimum score of 500). Additional exam requirements/recommendations for international students: Required—TOEFL (minimum score 550 paper-based; 213 computer-based). *Application deadline:* Applications are processed on a rolling basis. Application fee: $35. *Expenses:* Tuition: Full-time $8640; part-time $480 per credit hour. Tuition and fees vary according to program. *Financial support:* Career-related internships or fieldwork and unspecified assistantships available. Financial award applicants required to submit FAFSA. *Faculty research:* Corporate social responsibility, socially responsible investing, leadership, Russian economics and law, knowledge management. *Unit head:* Dr. William Forgang, Dean, School of Business, 301-447-5326, Fax: 301-447-5335, E-mail: mbareq@msmary.edu. *Application contact:* Dr. William Forgang, Dean, School of Business, 301-447-5326, Fax: 301-447-5335, E-mail: mbareq@msmary.edu.

National-Louis University, College of Management and Business, Chicago, IL 60603. Offers business administration (MBA); human resource management and development (MS); management (MS). Part-time and evening/weekend programs available. *Students:* 125 full-time (80 women), 8 part-time (5 women); includes 59 minority (28 Black or African American, non-Hispanic/Latino; 1 American Indian or Alaska Native, non-Hispanic/Latino; 3 Asian, non-Hispanic/Latino; 26 Hispanic/Latino; 1 Two or more races, non-Hispanic/Latino). Average age 37. In 2010, 173 master's awarded. *Entrance requirements:* For master's, college-administered critical thinking and writing skills test, minimum GPA of 3.0, resume, 3 references. Additional exam requirements/recommendations for international students: Required—TOEFL (minimum score 550 paper-based; 213 computer-based; 79 iBT). *Application deadline:* Applications are processed on a rolling basis. Application fee: $40. *Financial support:* Federal Work-Study, institutionally sponsored loans, and scholarships/grants available. Support available to part-time students. Financial award applicants required to submit FAFSA. *Unit head:* Walter Roetlger, Executive Dean, 312-261-3073, Fax: 312-261-3073, E-mail: chris.multhauf@nl.edu. *Application contact:* Dr. Larry Poselli, Vice President of Enrollment and Student Services, 800-443-5522 Ext. 5718, Fax: 312-261-3550, E-mail: larry.polselli@nl.edu.

National University, Academic Affairs, School of Business and Management, La Jolla, CA 92037-1011. Offers MA, MBA, MS. Part-time and evening/weekend programs available. Postbaccalaureate distance learning degree programs offered (no on-campus study). *Faculty:* 31 full-time (6 women), 282 part-time/adjunct (82 women). *Students:* 654 full-time (322 women), 1,102 part-time (550 women); includes 658 minority (194 Black or African American, non-Hispanic/Latino; 6 American Indian or Alaska Native, non-Hispanic/Latino; 197 Asian, non-Hispanic/Latino; 230 Hispanic/Latino; 9 Native Hawaiian or other Pacific Islander, non-Hispanic/Latino; 22 Two or more races, non-Hispanic/Latino), 345 international. Average age 35. 1,108 applicants, 100% accepted, 764 enrolled. In 2010, 474 master's awarded.

Degree requirements: For master's, thesis. *Entrance requirements:* For master's, interview, minimum GPA of 2.5. Additional exam requirements/recommendations for international students: Required—TOEFL (minimum score 550 paper-based; 213 computer-based; 79 iBT), IELTS (minimum score 6). *Application deadline:* Applications are processed on a rolling basis. Application fee: $60 ($65 for international students). Electronic applications accepted. *Expenses:* Tuition: Full-time $9450; part-time $350 per unit. Required fees: $350 per unit. One-time fee: $60. *Financial support:* Career-related internships or fieldwork, scholarships/grants, and tuition waivers (partial) available. Support available to part-time students. Financial award application deadline: 6/30; financial award applicants required to submit FAFSA. *Unit head:* Dr. Ronald Uhlig, Interim Dean, 858-642-8400, Fax: 858-642-8740, E-mail: ruhlig@nu.edu. *Application contact:* Dominick Giovanniello, Associate Regional Dean—San Diego, 800-NAT-UNIV, Fax: 858-541-7792, E-mail: dgiovann@nu.edu.

New Jersey Institute of Technology, Office of Graduate Studies, School of Management, Program in Management of Business Administration, Newark, NJ 07102. Offers MBA. *Accreditation:* AACSB. Part-time and evening/weekend programs available. *Students:* 71 full-time (25 women), 18 part-time (11 women); includes 14 Black or African American, non-Hispanic/Latino; 18 Asian, non-Hispanic/Latino; 16 Hispanic/Latino, 15 international. Average age 32. 249 applicants, 51% accepted, 64 enrolled. In 2010, 80 master's awarded. *Entrance requirements:* For master's, GMAT. Additional exam requirements/recommendations for international students: Required—TOEFL (minimum score 550 paper-based; 213 computer-based; 79 iBT). *Application deadline:* For fall admission, 6/5 priority date for domestic students, 4/1 for international students; for spring admission, 11/15 for domestic and international students. Applications are processed on a rolling basis. Application fee: $65. Electronic applications accepted. *Expenses:* Tuition, state resident: full-time $14,724; part-time $818 per credit. Tuition, nonresident: full-time $20,304; part-time $1128 per credit. Required fees: $2272; $209 per credit. $103 per semester. One-time fee: $312 full-time; $212 part-time. *Financial support:* Fellowships with full and partial tuition reimbursements, research assistantships with full and partial tuition reimbursements, teaching assistantships with full and partial tuition reimbursements, career-related internships or fieldwork, Federal Work-Study, institutionally sponsored loans, and unspecified assistantships available. Financial award application deadline: 3/15. *Unit head:* Dr. Robert English, Chair, 973-596-3224, Fax: 973-596-3074, E-mail: robert.english@njit.edu. *Application contact:* Kathryn Kelly, Director of Admissions, 973-596-3300, Fax: 973-596-3461, E-mail: admissions@njit.edu.

Newman University, MBA Program, Wichita, KS 67213-2097. Offers finance (MBA); international business (MBA); leadership (MBA); management (MBA); technology (MBA). Part-time programs available. *Faculty:* 4 full-time (2 women), 7 part-time/adjunct (2 women). *Students:* 33 full-time (14 women), 92 part-time (37 women); includes 28 minority (7 Black or African American, non-Hispanic/Latino; 6 Asian, non-Hispanic/Latino; 12 Hispanic/Latino; 1 Native Hawaiian or other Pacific Islander, non-Hispanic/Latino; 2 Two or more races, non-Hispanic/Latino), 24 international. Average age 32. 80 applicants, 83% accepted, 45 enrolled. In 2010, 72 master's awarded. *Degree requirements:* For master's, thesis optional. *Entrance requirements:* For master's, interview; minimum GPA of 3.0; 3 letters of recommendation; course work in algebra, statistics, macroeconomics, and financial accounting. Additional exam requirements/recommendations for international students: Required—TOEFL (minimum score 600 paper-based; 250 computer-based; 100 iBT). *Application deadline:* For fall admission, 8/1 priority date for domestic students, 7/15 priority date for international students; for winter admission, 1/1 priority date for domestic students; for spring admission, 1/1 priority date for domestic students, 11/15 priority date for international students. Applications are processed on a rolling basis. Application fee: $25 ($40 for international students). Electronic applications accepted. *Expenses:* Contact institution. *Financial support:* In 2010–11, 29 students received support. Federal Work-Study available. Financial award application deadline: 8/15; financial award applicants required to submit FAFSA. *Unit head:* Dr. George Goetz, Dean of the College of Professional Studies/Director, 316-942-4291 Ext. 2205, Fax: 316-942-4483, E-mail: smithge@newmanu.edu. *Application contact:* Linda Kay Sabala, Director of Graduate Admissions, 316-942-4291 Ext. 2230, Fax: 316-942-4483, E-mail: sabalal@newmanu.edu.

New Mexico Highlands University, Graduate Studies, School of Business, Las Vegas, NM 87701. Offers business administration (MBA), including government nonprofit management, human resource management, international business, management, management information systems. *Accreditation:* ACBSP. *Faculty:* 14 full-time (3 women). *Students:* 71 full-time (44 women), 124 part-time (68 women); includes 119 minority (8 Black or African American, non-Hispanic/Latino; 18 American Indian or Alaska Native, non-Hispanic/Latino; 1 Asian, non-Hispanic/Latino; 89 Hispanic/Latino; 1 Native Hawaiian or other Pacific Islander, non-Hispanic/Latino; 2 Two or more races, non-Hispanic/Latino), 34 international. Average age 34. 128 applicants, 98% accepted, 34 enrolled. In 2010, 48 master's awarded. *Degree requirements:* For master's, comprehensive exam, thesis or alternative. *Entrance requirements:* For master's, minimum undergraduate GPA of 3.0. Additional exam requirements/recommendations for international students: Required—TOEFL (minimum score 540 paper-based; 207 computer-based). *Application deadline:*

For fall admission, 8/1 priority date for domestic students. Applications are processed on a rolling basis. Application fee: $15. *Expenses:* Tuition, state resident: full-time $2544. Required fees: $624; $132 per credit hour. *Financial support:* In 2010–11, 29 students received support. Career-related internships or fieldwork, Federal Work-Study, institutionally sponsored loans, scholarships/grants, tuition waivers (full and partial), and unspecified assistantships available. Support available to part-time students. Financial award application deadline: 3/1; financial award applicants required to submit FAFSA. *Faculty research:* Real estate valuation, studying expert judgments in complex accounting, decision environments, green marketing, environmentalism, marketing research methodology. *Unit head:* Dr. Margaret Young, Dean, 505-454-3522, Fax: 505-454-3354, E-mail: young_m@nmhu.edu. *Application contact:* Diane Trujillo, Administrative Assistant, Graduate Studies, 505-454-3266, Fax: 505-426-2117, E-mail: dtrujillo@nmhu.edu.

New Mexico State University, Graduate School, College of Arts and Sciences, Department of Biology, Las Cruces, NM 88003-8001. Offers biology (MS, PhD); biotechnology and business (MS). Part-time programs available. *Faculty:* 25 full-time (10 women). *Students:* 70 full-time (46 women), 12 part-time (8 women); includes 20 minority (3 Black or African American, non-Hispanic/Latino; 1 American Indian or Alaska Native, non-Hispanic/Latino; 16 Hispanic/Latino), 24 international. Average age 30. 71 applicants, 86% accepted, 25 enrolled. In 2010, 13 master's, 10 doctorates awarded. *Degree requirements:* For master's, thesis (for some programs), defense or oral exam; for doctorate, comprehensive exam, thesis/dissertation, qualifying exam, defense. *Entrance requirements:* Additional exam requirements/recommendations for international students: Required—TOEFL. *Application deadline:* For fall admission, 1/15 priority date for domestic students, 1/15 for international students; for spring admission, 10/4 priority date for domestic students, 10/4 for international students. Applications are processed on a rolling basis. Application fee: $30 ($50 for international students). Electronic applications accepted. *Expenses:* Tuition, state resident: full-time $4536; part-time $242 per credit. Tuition, nonresident: full-time $15,816; part-time $712 per credit. Required fees: $636 per term. *Financial support:* In 2010–11, 21 research assistantships (averaging $16,987 per year), 33 teaching assistantships (averaging $10,202 per year) were awarded; fellowships, Federal Work-Study and health care benefits also available. Support available to part-time students. Financial award application deadline: 1/15. *Faculty research:* Microbiology, cell and organismal physiology, ecology and ethology, evolution, genetics, developmental biology. *Unit head:* Dr. Michele Nishiguchi, Head, 575-646-3611, Fax: 575-646-5665, E-mail: nish@nmsu.edu. *Application contact:* Gloria Valencia, Administration Assistant, 575-646-3611, Fax: 575-646-5665, E-mail: gvalenci@nmsu.edu.

New Mexico State University, Graduate School, College of Business, Department of Management, Las Cruces, NM 88003-8001. Offers business administration (PhD), including management. *Faculty:* 13 full-time (2 women). *Students:* 15 full-time (5 women), 1 (woman) part-time; includes 2 minority (1 American Indian or Alaska Native, non-Hispanic/Latino; 1 Hispanic/Latino), 6 international. Average age 33. 39 applicants, 33% accepted, 3 enrolled. In 2010, 3 doctorates awarded. *Degree requirements:* For doctorate, comprehensive exam, thesis/dissertation. *Entrance requirements:* For doctorate, GMAT or GRE, references, writing sample. Additional exam requirements/recommendations for international students: Required—TOEFL (minimum score 530 paper-based; 197 computer-based). *Application deadline:* For fall admission, 2/15 priority date for domestic and international students. Application fee: $30 ($50 for international students). Electronic applications accepted. *Expenses:* Tuition, state resident: full-time $4536; part-time $242 per credit. Tuition, nonresident: full-time $15,816; part-time $712 per credit. Required fees: $636 per term. *Financial support:* In 2010–11, 10 students received support, including 1 research assistantship (averaging $4,000 per year), 12 teaching assistantships (averaging $17,567 per year); health care benefits and unspecified assistantships also available. *Faculty research:* Cross-cultured leadership, deviant behavior in the work place, quality management, transaction cost analysis, issues in post-modernism. *Unit head:* Dr. Bonnie F. Daily, Head, 575-646-1201, Fax: 575-646-1372, E-mail: bdaily@nmsu.edu. *Application contact:* Dr. Steven Elias, Associate Professor, 575-646-7642, Fax: 575-646-1372, E-mail: phddirector@business.nmsu.edu.

New Mexico State University, Graduate School, College of Business, Program in Business Administration, Las Cruces, NM 88003-8001. Offers MBA, PhD. *Accreditation:* AACSB. Part-time and evening/weekend programs available. *Students:* 84 full-time (37 women), 130 part-time (56 women); includes 92 minority (6 Black or African American, non-Hispanic/Latino; 2 American Indian or Alaska Native, non-Hispanic/Latino; 3 Asian, non-Hispanic/Latino; 78 Hispanic/Latino; 3 Two or more races, non-Hispanic/Latino), 28 international. Average age 31. 134 applicants, 95% accepted, 73 enrolled. In 2010, 125 master's awarded. *Degree requirements:* For master's, comprehensive exam, thesis optional. *Entrance requirements:* For master's, GMAT, graduate degree, work experience. Additional exam requirements/recommendations for international students: Required—TOEFL (minimum score 530 paper-based; 197 computer-based). *Application deadline:* For fall admission, 7/1 priority date for domestic students, 3/1 priority date for international students; for spring admission, 11/1 priority date for domestic students, 10/1 priority date for international students. Applications are processed on a rolling basis. Application fee: $30 ($50 for international students). Electronic applications accepted. *Expenses:* Tuition, state resident: full-time $4536; part-time $242 per credit. Tuition, nonresident: full-time $15,816; part-time $712 per credit. Required fees: $636 per term. *Financial support:* In 2010–11, 12 research assistantships with partial tuition reimbursements (averaging $12,181 per year), 23 teaching assistantships with partial tuition reimbursements (averaging $7,647 per year) were awarded; fellowships, Federal Work-Study, institutionally sponsored loans, scholarships/grants, health care benefits, and unspecified assistantships also available. Financial award application deadline: 3/1. *Faculty research:* Small business/entrepreneurship, human resources, global marketing and management, supply chain management. *Unit head:* John Shonk, MBA Advisor, 575-646-8003, Fax: 575-646-7977, E-mail: mba@nmsu.edu. *Application contact:* John Shonk, MBA Advisor, 575-646-8003, Fax: 575-646-7977, E-mail: mba@nmsu.edu.

New York Institute of Technology, Graduate Division, School of Management, Program in Business Administration, Old Westbury, NY 11568-8000. Offers accounting (Advanced Certificate); business administration (MBA); finance (Advanced Certificate); international business (Advanced Certificate); management of information systems (Advanced Certificate); marketing (Advanced Certificate). Part-time and evening/weekend programs available. *Students:* 454 full-time (188 women), 513 part-time (204 women); includes 49 minority (15 Black or African American, non-Hispanic/Latino; 23 Asian, non-Hispanic/Latino; 11 Hispanic/Latino, 268 international. Average age 29. In 2010, 435 master's, 1 other advanced degree awarded. *Degree requirements:* For master's, thesis (for some programs). *Entrance requirements:* For master's, minimum QPA of 2.85. Additional exam requirements/recommendations for international students: Required—TOEFL (minimum score 550 paper-based; 213 computer-based). *Application deadline:* For fall admission, 7/1 priority date for domestic students; for spring admission, 12/1 priority date for domestic students. Applications are processed on a rolling basis. Application fee: $50. Electronic applications accepted. *Expenses:* Tuition: Part-time $835 per credit. *Financial support:* Fellowships, research assistantships with partial tuition reimbursements, institutionally sponsored loans, tuition waivers (full and partial), and unspecified assistantships available. Support available to part-time students. Financial award applicants required to submit FAFSA. *Faculty research:* Instructor performance appraisal; relationship between TOEFL, GMAT, GRE, and performance in foreign students. *Unit head:* Dr. Stephen Hartman, Director, 516-686-7691, E-mail: shartman@nyit.edu. *Application contact:* Dr. Jacquelyn Nealon, Vice President for Enrollment Services, 516-686-7925, Fax: 516-686-7597, E-mail: jnealon@nyit.edu.

New York University, School of Law, New York, NY 10012-1019. Offers law (JD, LL M, JSD); law and business (Advanced Certificate); taxation (Advanced Certificate); JD/LL B; JD/LL M; JD/MA; JD/MBA; JD/MPA; JD/MPP; JD/MSW; JD/MUP; JD/PhD. *Accreditation:* ABA. Part-time programs available. *Faculty:* 125 full-time (36 women), 70 part-time/adjunct (23 women). *Students:* 1,427 full-time (628 women); includes 88 Black or African American, non-Hispanic/Latino; 3 American Indian or Alaska Native, non-Hispanic/Latino; 150 Asian, non-Hispanic/Latino; 91 Hispanic/Latino, 44 international. 7,272 applicants, 450 enrolled. In 2010, 471 first professional degrees, 534 master's, 3 doctorates awarded. *Entrance requirements:* LSAT. *Application deadline:* For fall admission, 2/1 for domestic students. Application fee: $75. Electronic applications accepted. *Expenses:* Contact institution. *Financial support:* Fellowships, research assistantships, teaching assistantships, career-related internships or fieldwork, Federal Work-Study, institutionally sponsored loans, scholarships/grants, tuition waivers (partial), and loan repayment assistance available. Financial award application deadline: 4/15; financial award applicants required to submit FAFSA. *Faculty research:* International law, environmental law, corporate law, globalization of law, philosophy of law. *Unit head:* Richard L. Revesz, Dean, 212-998-6000, Fax: 212-995-3150. *Application contact:* Kenneth J. Kleinrock, Assistant Dean for Admissions, 212-998-6060, Fax: 212-995-4527.

Niagara University, Graduate Division of Business Administration, Niagara Falls, Niagara University, NY 14109. Offers business (MBA); commerce (MBA). *Accreditation:* AACSB. Part-time and evening/weekend programs available. *Faculty:* 6 full-time (1 woman), 7 part-time/adjunct (1 woman). *Students:* 156 full-time (67 women), 64 part-time (25 women); includes 9 Black or African American, non-Hispanic/Latino; 7 Asian, non-Hispanic/Latino; 3 Hispanic/Latino, 22 international. Average age 33. 89 applicants, 73% accepted. In 2010, 74 master's awarded. *Entrance requirements:* For master's, GMAT. Additional exam requirements/recommendations for international students: Required—TOEFL. *Application deadline:* For fall admission, 8/1 for domestic students; for spring admission, 11/1 for domestic students. Applications are processed on a rolling basis. Application fee: $30. *Expenses:* Tuition: Full-time $13,230; part-time $735 per credit hour. Required fees: $50. One-time fee: $120 full-time. *Financial support:* In 2010–11, 3 fellowships, 2 research assistantships were awarded; career-related internships or fieldwork and Federal Work-Study also available. Support available to part-time students. Financial award application deadline: 8/1; financial award applicants required to submit FAFSA. *Faculty research:* Capital flows, Federal Reserve policy, human resource management, public policy, issues in marketing. *Unit head:* Dr. Peggy Choong, Director, 716-286-8178, Fax: 716-286-8206.

Application contact: Carlos Tejada, Associate Dean for Graduate Recruitment, 716-286-8769, Fax: 716-286-8170.

North Carolina State University, Graduate School, College of Management, Program in Business Administration, Raleigh, NC 27695. Offers biosciences management (MBA); entrepreneurship and technology commercialization (MBA); financial management (MBA); innovation management (MBA); marketing management (MBA); services management and consulting (MBA); supply chain management (MBA). *Accreditation:* AACSB. Part-time programs available. *Degree requirements:* For master's, thesis optional. *Entrance requirements:* For master's, GMAT, interview, 3 letters of recommendation. Additional exam requirements/recommendations for international students: Required—TOEFL (minimum score 600 paper-based; 250 computer-based; 100 iBT). Electronic applications accepted. *Faculty research:* Manufacturing strategy, information systems, technology commercialization, managing research and development, historical stock returns.

See Display on the next page and Close-Up on page 260.

North Central College, Graduate and Continuing Education Programs, Department of Business, Program in Business Administration, Naperville, IL 60566-7063. Offers change management (MBA); finance (MBA); human resource management (MBA); management (MBA); marketing (MBA). Part-time and evening/weekend programs available. *Faculty:* 14 full-time (4 women), 5 part-time/adjunct (1 woman). *Students:* 46 full-time (17 women), 101 part-time (46 women); includes 6 Black or African American, non-Hispanic/Latino; 1 American Indian or Alaska Native, non-Hispanic/Latino; 4 Asian, non-Hispanic/Latino; 7 Hispanic/Latino, 3 international. Average age 31. In 2010, 46 master's awarded. *Degree requirements:* For master's, project. *Entrance requirements:* For master's, interview. Additional exam requirements/recommendations for international students: Required—TOEFL (minimum score 577 paper-based; 233 computer-based; 90 iBT). *Application deadline:* For fall admission, 8/15 for domestic students; for winter admission, 12/1 for domestic students; for spring admission, 2/1 for domestic students. Application fee: $25. *Financial support:* Scholarships/grants available. Support available to part-time students. *Unit head:* Dr. Jean Clifton, MBA Program Coordinator, 630-637-5244, E-mail: jmclifton@noctrl.edu. *Application contact:* Wendy Kulpinski, Director and Graduate and Continuing Education Admission, 630-637-5808, Fax: 630-637-5844, E-mail: wekulpinski@noctrl.edu.

North Central College, Graduate and Continuing Education Programs, Department of Leadership Studies, Naperville, IL 60566-7063. Offers higher education leadership (MLS); professional leadership (MLS); social entrepreneurship (MLS); sports leadership (MLS). Part-time and evening/weekend programs available. *Faculty:* 7 full-time (1 woman), 7 part-time/adjunct (1 woman). *Students:* 28 full-time (15 women), 32 part-time (21 women); includes 5 Black or African American, non-Hispanic/Latino; 3 Hispanic/Latino; 1 Two or more races, non-Hispanic/Latino. Average age 28. In 2010, 2 master's awarded. *Degree requirements:* For master's, project. *Entrance requirements:* For master's, interview. Additional exam requirements/recommendations for international students: Required—TOEFL (minimum score 570 paper-based; 233 computer-based; 90 iBT). *Application deadline:* For fall admission, 8/15 for domestic students; for winter admission, 12/1 for domestic students; for spring admission, 2/1 for domestic students. Applications are processed on a rolling basis. Application fee: $25. *Expenses:* Contact institution. *Financial support:* Scholarships/grants available. Support available to part-time students. *Unit head:* Dr. Thomas Cavanagh, Head, 630-637-5285. *Application contact:* Wendy Kulpinski, Director and Graduate and Continuing Education Admissions, 630-637-5808, Fax: 630-637-5844, E-mail: wekulpinski@noctrl.edu.

Northcentral University, Graduate Studies, Prescott Valley, AZ 86314. Offers business (MBA, DBA, PhD, CAGS); education (M Ed, Ed D, PhD, CAGS); marriage and family therapy (MA, PhD); psychology (MA, PhD, CAGS). Evening/weekend programs available. Postbaccalaureate distance learning degree programs offered (no on-campus study). *Faculty:* 18 full-time (7 women), 449 part-time/adjunct (199 women). *Students:* 8,363 full-time (4,501 women); includes 896 minority (606 Black or African American, non-Hispanic/Latino; 35 American Indian or Alaska Native, non-Hispanic/Latino; 92 Asian, non-Hispanic/Latino; 142 Hispanic/Latino; 13 Native Hawaiian or other Pacific Islander, non-Hispanic/Latino; 8 Two or more races, non-Hispanic/Latino). Average age 43. In 2010, 367 master's, 150 doctorates, 33 other advanced degrees awarded. *Entrance requirements:* For master's, bachelor's degree from regionally-accredited institution, current resume; for doctorate and CAGS, master's degree from regionally-accredited university. Additional exam requirements/recommendations for international students: Required—TOEFL (minimum score 95 computer-based), IELTS (minimum score 7), Pearson Test of English (minimum score: 65). *Application deadline:* Applications are processed on a rolling basis. Application fee: $75. *Financial support:* Scholarships/grants available. *Unit head:* Dr. Clinton D. Gardner, President and Provost, 888-327-2877, Fax: 928-759-6381, E-mail: president@ncu.edu. *Application contact:* Kevin Lustig, Vice President, Enrollment Services, 480-478-7490, Fax: 928-759-6285, E-mail: klustig@ncu.edu.

North Dakota State University, College of Graduate and Interdisciplinary Studies, College of Business, Fargo, ND 58108. Offers MBA. *Accreditation:* AACSB. Part-time and evening/weekend programs available. *Faculty:* 25

full-time (5 women). *Students:* 64 full-time (22 women), 30 part-time (9 women); includes 1 Black or African American, non-Hispanic/Latino; 2 Asian, non-Hispanic/Latino; 1 Hispanic/Latino, 18 international. Average age 29. 55 applicants, 76% accepted, 38 enrolled. In 2010, 26 master's awarded. *Entrance requirements:* For master's, GMAT. Additional exam requirements/recommendations for international students: Required—TOEFL (minimum score 550 paper-based; 213 computer-based; 79 iBT). *Application deadline:* For fall admission, 7/15 priority date for domestic students; for spring admission, 11/15 for domestic students. Applications are processed on a rolling basis. Application fee: $45 ($60 for international students). *Financial support:* In 2010–11, 14 students received support, including 13 research assistantships, 1 teaching assistantship; institutionally sponsored loans and tuition waivers (partial) also available. Support available to part-time students. Financial award application deadline: 5/15; financial award applicants required to submit FAFSA. *Faculty research:* Labor management, operations, international finance, agency, Internet marketing. *Unit head:* Dr. Ron Johnson, Dean, 701-231-8805. *Application contact:* Paul R. Brown, Director, 701-231-7681, Fax: 701-231-7508, E-mail: paul.brown@ndsu.edu.

Northeastern Illinois University, Graduate College, College of Business and Management, Chicago, IL 60625-4699. Offers accounting (MSA); finance (MBA); management (MBA); marketing (MBA). Part-time and evening/weekend programs available. *Faculty:* 24 full-time (3 women), 13 part-time/adjunct (4 women). *Students:* 41 full-time (19 women), 69 part-time (32 women); includes 23 minority (4 Black or African American, non-Hispanic/Latino; 1 American Indian or Alaska Native, non-Hispanic/Latino; 11 Asian, non-Hispanic/Latino; 6 Hispanic/Latino; 1 Two or more races, non-Hispanic/Latino), 21 international. Average age 31. 112 applicants, 75% accepted, 80 enrolled. In 2010, 34 master's awarded. *Degree requirements:* For master's, thesis optional. *Entrance requirements:* For master's, GMAT, minimum GPA of 2.75. Additional exam requirements/recommendations for international students: Required—TOEFL (minimum score 550 paper-based; 213 computer-based; 79 iBT). *Application deadline:* For fall admission, 4/1 priority date for domestic students; for spring admission, 8/15 for domestic students. Applications are processed on a rolling basis. Application fee: $30. Electronic applications accepted. *Financial support:* In 2010–11, 20 students received support, including 6 research assistantships with full and partial tuition reimbursements available (averaging $6,600 per year); career-related internships or fieldwork, Federal Work-Study, institutionally sponsored loans, scholarships/grants, tuition waivers (full and partial), and unspecified assistantships also available. Support available to part-time students. *Faculty research:* Perception of accountants and non-accountants toward future of the accounting industry, asynchronous learning outcomes, cost and efficiency of financial markets, impact of deregulation on airline industry, analysis of derivational instruments. *Unit head:* Dr. Amy B. Hietapelto, Dean, 773-442-6105. *Application contact:* Dr. Amy B. Hietapelto, Dean, 773-442-6105.

Northeastern State University, Graduate College, College of Business and Technology, Program in Business Administration, Tahlequah, OK 74464-2399. Offers MBA. *Accreditation:* ACBSP. Part-time and evening/weekend programs available. *Faculty:* 9 full-time (2 women). *Students:* 14 full-time (7 women), 86 part-time (40 women); includes 7 Black or African American, non-Hispanic/Latino; 31 American Indian or Alaska Native, non-Hispanic/Latino; 2 Asian, non-Hispanic/Latino; 2 Hispanic/Latino, 6 international. In 2010, 18 master's awarded. *Degree requirements:* For master's, comprehensive exam, thesis, business plan, oral exam. *Entrance requirements:* For master's, GMAT, minimum GPA of 2.5. Additional exam requirements/recommendations for international students: Required—TOEFL (minimum score 213 computer-based). *Application deadline:* For fall admission, 6/1 priority date for domestic students. Applications are processed on a rolling basis. Application fee: $0 ($25 for international students). Electronic applications accepted. *Expenses:* Tuition, state resident: part-time $144 per credit hour. Tuition, nonresident: part-time $384.05 per credit hour. Required fees: $34.90 per credit hour. Tuition and fees vary according to program. *Financial support:* Teaching assistantships, Federal Work-Study available. Financial award application deadline: 3/1. *Unit head:* Dr. Sandra Edwards, Chair, 918-683-0400 Ext. 5219. *Application contact:* Dr. Sandra Edwards, Chair, 918-683-0400 Ext. 5219.

Northeastern University, Graduate School of Business Administration, Boston, MA 02115-5096. Offers EMBA, MBA, MS, CAGS, JD/MBA, MBA/MSN, MS/MBA. *Accreditation:* AACSB. Part-time and evening/weekend programs available. Postbaccalaureate distance learning degree programs offered (no on-campus study). *Faculty:* 46 full-time (7 women), 5 part-time/adjunct (0 women). *Students:* 200 full-time (80 women), 483 part-time (174 women). 955 applicants, 43% accepted, 259 enrolled. In 2010, 285 master's awarded. *Entrance requirements:* For master's, GMAT, interview. Additional exam requirements/recommendations for international students: Required—TOEFL (minimum score 600 paper-based; 250 computer-based; 100 iBT). *Application deadline:* For fall admission, 11/30 for domestic and international students; for winter admission, 2/1 for domestic and international students; for spring admission, 4/15 for domestic students. Application fee: $100. Electronic applications accepted. *Expenses:* Contact institution. *Financial support:* Federal Work-Study, institutionally sponsored loans, and scholarships/grants available. Support available to part-time students. Financial award application deadline: 3/1; financial award applicants required to submit FAFSA. *Unit head:* Kate

Klepper, Associate Dean, Graduate Business Programs, 617-373-5417, Fax: 617-373-8564, E-mail: k.klepper@neu.edu. *Application contact:* Evelyn Tate, Director, Graduate Admissions, 617-373-5992, Fax: 617-373-8564, E-mail: e.tate@neu.edu.

Northern Arizona University, Graduate College, NAU-Yuma, Master of Administration Program, Flagstaff, AZ 86011. Offers M Adm. Part-time programs available. Postbaccalaureate distance learning degree programs offered (no on-campus study). *Faculty:* 31 full-time (13 women). *Students:* 85 full-time (45 women), 357 part-time (194 women); includes 146 minority (26 Black or African American, non-Hispanic/Latino; 22 American Indian or Alaska Native, non-Hispanic/Latino; 8 Asian, non-Hispanic/Latino; 82 Hispanic/Latino; 2 Native Hawaiian or other Pacific Islander, non-Hispanic/Latino; 6 Two or more races, non-Hispanic/Latino), 1 international. Average age 25. 116 applicants, 94% accepted, 83 enrolled. In 2010, 131 master's awarded. *Degree requirements:* For master's, projects. *Entrance requirements:* For master's, five years' related work experience, minimum GPA of 3.0. Additional exam requirements/recommendations for international students: Required—TOEFL (minimum score 550 paper-based; 213 computer-based; 80 iBT), IELTS (minimum score 7). *Application deadline:* For fall admission, 3/1 priority date for international students; for spring admission, 9/15 priority date for international students. Applications are processed on a rolling basis. Application fee: $65. Electronic applications accepted. *Financial support:* Federal Work-Study and scholarships/grants available. Support available to part-time students. Financial award applicants required to submit FAFSA. *Unit head:* Dr. Alex Steenstra, Chair, 928-317-6083, E-mail: alex.steenstra@nau.edu. *Application contact:* Pam Torbico, Coordinator, 928-523-6694, E-mail: m.admin@nau.edu.

Northern Arizona University, Graduate College, The W. A. Franke College of Business, Flagstaff, AZ 86011. Offers MBA. *Accreditation:* AACSB. Part-time programs available. *Faculty:* 52 full-time (33 women). *Students:* 25 full-time (9 women), 3 part-time (1 woman); includes 5 minority (1 Black or African American, non-Hispanic/Latino; 2 Asian, non-Hispanic/Latino; 2 Two or more races, non-Hispanic/Latino), 2 international. Average age 32. 59 applicants, 27% accepted, 9 enrolled. In 2010, 31 master's awarded. *Entrance requirements:* For master's, GMAT. Additional exam requirements/recommendations for international students: Required—TOEFL (minimum score 550 paper-based; 213 computer-based; 80 iBT), IELTS (minimum score 7). *Application deadline:* For fall admission, 5/15 priority date for domestic students, 3/1 priority date for international students. Applications are processed on a rolling basis. Application fee: $65. Electronic applications accepted. *Expenses:* Contact institution. *Financial support:* In 2010–11, 6 research assistantships (averaging $9,479 per year) were awarded; Federal Work-Study, institutionally sponsored loans, scholarships/grants, health care benefits, tuition waivers (partial), and unspecified assistantships also available. Support available to part-time students. Financial award applicants required to submit FAFSA. *Faculty research:* Data processing applications for business situations and problems, accounting fraud, effects of sales tactics, self-efficacy and performance. *Unit head:* Dr. Marc Chopin, Dean, 928-523-3657, Fax: 928-523-7331, E-mail: marc.chopin@nau.edu. *Application contact:* Katie Poindexter, Coordinator, 928-523-7342, Fax: 928-523-6559, E-mail: mba@nau.edu.

Northern Illinois University, Graduate School, College of Business, MBA Program, De Kalb, IL 60115-2854. Offers MBA. *Accreditation:* AACSB. Part-time and evening/weekend programs available. *Faculty:* 53 full-time (17 women), 3 part-time/adjunct (0 women). *Students:* 93 full-time (30 women), 442 part-time (142 women); includes 28 Black or African American, non-Hispanic/Latino; 70 Asian, non-Hispanic/Latino; 23 Hispanic/Latino; 5 Two or more races, non-Hispanic/Latino, 21 international. Average age 32. 210 applicants, 65% accepted, 103 enrolled. In 2010, 195 master's awarded. *Degree requirements:* For master's, thesis optional, seminar. *Entrance requirements:* For master's, GMAT, minimum GPA of 2.75. Additional exam requirements/recommendations for international students: Required—TOEFL (minimum score 550 paper-based; 213 computer-based). *Application deadline:* For fall admission, 6/1 for domestic students, 5/1 for international students; for spring admission, 11/1 for domestic students, 10/1 for international students. Applications are processed on a rolling basis. Application fee: $30. Electronic applications accepted. *Expenses:* Tuition, state resident: full-time $7200; part-time $300 per credit hour. Tuition, nonresident: full-time $14,400; part-time $600 per credit hour. Required fees: $79 per credit hour. *Financial support:* In 2010–11, 13 research assistantships with full tuition reimbursements, 3 teaching assistantships with full tuition reimbursements were awarded; fellowships with full tuition reimbursements, career-related internships or fieldwork, Federal Work-Study, scholarships/grants, tuition waivers (full), and unspecified assistantships also available. Support available to part-time students. Financial award applicants required to submit FAFSA. *Unit head:* Jeff Probhaker, Associate Dean of Graduate Affairs, 815-753-6176, E-mail: hwright@niu.edu. *Application contact:* Office of Graduate Studies in Business, 815-753-6301.

Northern Kentucky University, Office of Graduate Programs, College of Business, Program in Business Administration, Highland Heights, KY 41099. Offers business administration (MBA, Certificate); JD/MBA. *Accreditation:* AACSB. Part-time and evening/weekend programs available. *Faculty:* 12 full-time (6 women), 3 part-time/adjunct (0 women). *Students:* 24 full-time (10 women), 107 part-time (38 women); includes 7 minority (1 Black or African American, non-Hispanic/Latino; 5 Asian, non-Hispanic/Latino; 1 Two or more races, non-Hispanic/Latino), 8 international. Average age 31. 125 applicants, 42% accepted, 29 enrolled. In 2010, 61 master's awarded. *Degree requirements:* For master's, thesis optional. *Entrance requirements:* For master's, GMAT, minimum GPA of 2.5, resume, statement of purpose. Additional exam requirements/recommendations for international students: Required—TOEFL (minimum score 550 paper-based; 213 computer-based; 79 iBT); Recommended—IELTS (minimum score 6.5). *Application deadline:* For fall admission, 7/1 for domestic students, 6/1 priority date for international students; for spring admission, 12/1 for domestic students, 10/1 priority date for international students. Applications are processed on a rolling basis. Application fee: $40. Electronic applications accepted. *Expenses:* Tuition, state resident: full-time $7254; part-time $403 per credit hour. Tuition, nonresident: full-time $12,492; part-time $694 per credit hour. Tuition and fees vary according to degree level and program. *Financial support:* Unspecified assistantships available. Financial award applicants required to submit FAFSA. *Unit head:* James Bast, Director of MBA Programs, 859-572-7695, Fax: 859-572-7694, E-mail: mbusiness@nku.edu. *Application contact:* Dr. Peg Griffin, Director of Graduate Programs, 859-572-6934, Fax: 859-572-6670, E-mail: griffinp@nku.edu.

Northern Kentucky University, Office of Graduate Programs, College of Business, Program in Executive Leadership and Organizational Change, Highland Heights, KY 41099. Offers MS. Part-time and evening/weekend programs available. *Students:* 47 part-time (26 women); includes 7 minority (5 Black or African American, non-Hispanic/Latino; 1 Asian, non-Hispanic/Latino; 1 Hispanic/Latino). Average age 40. 38 applicants, 66% accepted, 24 enrolled. In 2010, 20 master's awarded. *Degree requirements:* For master's, field research project. *Entrance requirements:* For master's, minimum GPA of 2.5; essay on professional career objective; 3 letters of recommendation, 1 from a current organization; 3 years of professional or managerial work experience. Additional exam requirements/recommendations for international students: Required—TOEFL (minimum score 600 paper-based; 213 computer-based; 79 iBT); Recommended—IELTS (minimum score 6.5). *Application deadline:* For fall admission, 6/15 for domestic students, 6/1 priority date for international students. Application fee: $40. Electronic applications accepted. *Expenses:* Tuition, state resident: full-time $7254; part-time $403 per credit hour. Tuition, nonresident: full-time $12,492; part-time $694 per credit hour. Tuition and fees vary according to degree level and program. *Financial support:* Unspecified assistantships available. Financial award applicants required to submit FAFSA. *Faculty research:* Leadership and development, organizational change, field research, team and conflict management, strategy development and systems thinking. *Unit head:* Dr. Kenneth Rhee, Program Director, 859-572-6310, Fax: 859-572-7694, E-mail: rhee@nku.edu. *Application contact:* Amberly Hurst-Nutini, Coordinator, 859-572-5947, Fax: 859-572-7694, E-mail: hurstam@nku.edu.

North Park University, School of Business and Nonprofit Management, Chicago, IL 60625-4895. Offers MBA, MHEA, MHRM, MM, MNA. Part-time and evening/weekend programs available. Postbaccalaureate distance learning degree programs offered (no on-campus study). *Faculty:* 12 full-time (5 women), 40 part-time/adjunct (22 women). *Students:* 12 full-time (5 women), 338 part-time (185 women). Average age 34. 130 applicants, 77% accepted, 87 enrolled. In 2010, 85 master's awarded. *Entrance requirements:* For master's, GMAT, GRE. Additional exam requirements/recommendations for international students: Required—TOEFL. *Application deadline:* For fall admission, 8/1 priority date for domestic students, 7/1 for international students; for spring admission, 12/15 for domestic students, 12/1 for international students. Applications are processed on a rolling basis. Application fee: $30. *Expenses:* Contact institution. *Financial support:* In 2010–11, 98 students received support. Scholarships/grants available. Support available to part-time students. Financial award application deadline: 8/15; financial award applicants required to submit FAFSA. *Unit head:* Dr. Wesley E. Lindahl, Dean, 773-784-3000. *Application contact:* Dr. Christopher Nicholson, Director of Admissions for Graduate and Continuing Education, 773-244-5518, Fax: 773-255-4953, E-mail: cnicholson@northpark.edu.

Northwest Christian University, School of Business and Management, Eugene, OR 97401-3745. Offers MBA. Part-time and evening/weekend programs available. *Faculty:* 1 full-time (0 women). *Students:* 39 full-time (23 women), 2 part-time (1 woman); includes 1 Black or African American, non-Hispanic/Latino; 2 Hispanic/Latino; 1 Native Hawaiian or other Pacific Islander, non-Hispanic/Latino, 1 international. 30 applicants, 73% accepted, 16 enrolled. In 2010, 10 master's awarded. *Degree requirements:* For master's, thesis. *Entrance requirements:* For master's, GMAT, GRE, MAT, interview, minimum undergraduate GPA of 3.0. *Application deadline:* For fall admission, 3/15 priority date for domestic students. Applications are processed on a rolling basis. Application fee: $50. Electronic applications accepted. *Unit head:* Dr. Michael Kennedy, Professor, 541-684-7243, Fax: 541-684-7333, E-mail: mkennedy@nwcu.edu.edu. *Application contact:* Kathy Wilson, Assistant Director of Admission, Graduate and Professional Studies, 541-684-7326, Fax: 541-684-7333, E-mail: kwilson@nwcu.edu.

Northwestern University, The Graduate School, Kellogg School of Management, MBA Programs, Evanston, IL 60208. Offers MBA, JD/MBA.

Accreditation: CAHME (one or more programs are accredited). Part-time and evening/weekend programs available. *Faculty:* 182 full-time, 112 part-time/adjunct. *Students:* 1,126 full-time, 1,020 part-time. Average age 28. 5,270 applicants, 19% accepted, 565 enrolled. In 2010, 532 master's awarded. *Entrance requirements:* For master's, GMAT, interview, 2 letters of recommendation, Kellogg Honor Code, college transcripts, resume, essays. Additional exam requirements/recommendations for international students: Required—TOEFL. Application fee: $250. Electronic applications accepted. *Expenses:* Contact institution. *Financial support:* Fellowships, career-related internships or fieldwork, institutionally sponsored loans, and scholarships/grants available. Support available to part-time students. Financial award applicants required to submit FAFSA. *Unit head:* Sally Blount, Dean. *Application contact:* Michele Rogers, Interim Director of Admissions and Financial Aid, 847-491-3308, Fax: 847-491-4960, E-mail: mbaadmissions@kellogg.northwestern.edu.

Northwest Missouri State University, Graduate School, Melvin and Valorie Booth College of Business and Professional Studies, Program in Business Administration, Maryville, MO 64468-6001. Offers MBA. *Accreditation:* ACBSP. *Faculty:* 22 full-time (5 women). *Students:* 43 full-time (22 women), 86 part-time (42 women); includes 14 minority (2 Black or African American, non-Hispanic/Latino; 2 American Indian or Alaska Native, non-Hispanic/Latino; 3 Asian, non-Hispanic/Latino; 2 Hispanic/Latino; 1 Native Hawaiian or other Pacific Islander, non-Hispanic/Latino; 4 Two or more races, non-Hispanic/Latino), 5 international. 72 applicants, 58% accepted, 28 enrolled. In 2010, 45 master's awarded. *Degree requirements:* For master's, comprehensive exam. *Entrance requirements:* For master's, GMAT, minimum GPA of 2.5. Additional exam requirements/recommendations for international students: Required—TOEFL (minimum score 550 paper-based; 213 computer-based). *Application deadline:* For fall admission, 7/1 for domestic and international students; for spring admission, 12/1 for domestic students, 11/15 for international students. Applications are processed on a rolling basis. Application fee: $0 ($50 for international students). Electronic applications accepted. *Financial support:* In 2010–11, 3 research assistantships with full tuition reimbursements (averaging $6,000 per year), 1 teaching assistantship with full tuition reimbursement (averaging $6,000 per year) were awarded; unspecified assistantships also available. Financial award application deadline: 4/1; financial award applicants required to submit FAFSA. *Unit head:* Dr. Mark Jelavich, Head, 660-562-1763. *Application contact:* Dr. Gregory Haddock, Dean of Graduate School, 660-562-1145, Fax: 660-562-1096, E-mail: gradsch@nwmissouri.edu.

Northwest Nazarene University, Graduate Studies, Program in Business Administration, Nampa, ID 83686-5897. Offers MBA. *Accreditation:* ACBSP. Part-time and evening/weekend programs available. *Faculty:* 11 full-time (3 women), 4 part-time/adjunct (2 women). *Students:* 97 full-time (40 women), 14 part-time (6 women); includes 8 minority (1 Black or African American, non-Hispanic/Latino; 2 Asian, non-Hispanic/Latino; 5 Hispanic/Latino), 3 international. Average age 35. In 2010, 50 master's awarded. *Entrance requirements:* For master's, GMAT, minimum GPA of 3.0. *Application deadline:* Applications are processed on a rolling basis. Application fee: $40. Electronic applications accepted. *Expenses:* Contact institution. *Unit head:* Dr. Ron Galloway, Director, 208-467-8415, Fax: 208-467-8440, E-mail: mba@nnu.edu. *Application contact:* MBA Program Administrator, 208-467-8123, Fax: 208-467-8440, E-mail: nnu-mba@nnu.edu.

Northwest University, School of Business and Management, Kirkland, WA 98033. Offers business administration (MBA); social entrepreneurship (MA). Evening/weekend programs available. *Faculty:* 6 full-time (1 woman), 7 part-time/adjunct (3 women). *Students:* 41 full-time (20 women), 3 part-time (1 woman); includes 10 minority (5 Black or African American, non-Hispanic/Latino; 3 Asian, non-Hispanic/Latino; 2 Hispanic/Latino), 9 international. Average age 34. 21 applicants, 86% accepted, 18 enrolled. In 2010, 11 master's awarded. *Degree requirements:* For master's, formalized research. *Entrance requirements:* For master's, GMAT, 4 foundation courses. Additional exam requirements/recommendations for international students: Required—TOEFL (minimum score 550 paper-based). *Application deadline:* For fall admission, 8/1 for domestic and international students; for spring admission, 12/1 for domestic and international students. Applications are processed on a rolling basis. Application fee: $75. Electronic applications accepted. Tuition and fees vary according to program. *Financial support:* Federal Work-Study, scholarships/grants, health care benefits, and tuition waivers (full) available. Financial award applicants required to submit FAFSA. *Unit head:* Dr. Teresa Gillespie, Dean, 425-889-5290, E-mail: teresa.gillespie@northwestu.edu. *Application contact:* Aaron Oosterwyk, Director of Graduate and Professional Studies Enrollment, 425-889-7799, Fax: 425-803-3059, E-mail: aaron.oosterwyk@northwestu.edu.

Norwich University, School of Graduate and Continuing Studies, Program in Business Administration, Northfield, VT 05663. Offers finance (MBA); organizational leadership (MBA); project management (MBA). *Accreditation:* ACBSP. Evening/weekend programs available. *Faculty:* 26 part-time/adjunct (0 women). *Students:* 108 full-time (45 women); includes 17 minority (5 Black or African American, non-Hispanic/Latino; 3 American Indian or Alaska Native, non-Hispanic/Latino; 4 Asian, non-Hispanic/Latino; 5 Hispanic/Latino), 4 international. Average age 36. 187 applicants, 84% accepted, 95

enrolled. In 2010, 389 master's awarded. *Degree requirements:* For master's, comprehensive exam (for some programs), thesis optional. *Entrance requirements:* For master's, minimum undergraduate GPA of 2.75. Additional exam requirements/recommendations for international students: Required—TOEFL (minimum score 550 paper-based; 213 computer-based; 83 iBT). *Application deadline:* For fall admission, 8/10 for domestic and international students; for winter admission, 11/7 for domestic and international students; for spring admission, 2/6 for domestic and international students. Application fee: $50. *Expenses:* Tuition: Full-time $17,380; part-time $645 per credit. Tuition and fees vary according to program. *Financial support:* Scholarships/grants available. Financial award applicants required to submit FAFSA. *Unit head:* Dr. Jose Cordova, Faculty Director, 802-485-2567, Fax: 802-485-2533, E-mail: jcordova@norwich.edu. *Application contact:* Bernice Fousek, Student Services Coordinator, 802-485-2748, Fax: 802-485-2533, E-mail: bfousek@norwich.edu.

Norwich University, School of Graduate and Continuing Studies, Program in Business Continuity, Northfield, VT 05663. Offers consultancy project (MS); continuity of government operations (MS); private sector continuity of operations (MS). *Expenses:* Tuition: Full-time $17,380; part-time $645 per credit. Tuition and fees vary according to program. *Unit head:* Dr. William Clements, Vice President of Academic Affairs and Dean of the School of Graduate and Continuing Studies, 802-485-2730. *Application contact:* Allison Crownson, Director of Admissions and Retention, 802-485-2720, Fax: 802-485-2533.

Notre Dame de Namur University, Division of Academic Affairs, School of Business and Management, Department of Business Administration, Belmont, CA 94002-1908. Offers business administration (MBA); finance (MBA); human resource management (MBA); marketing (MBA). Part-time and evening/weekend programs available. *Faculty:* 7 full-time (1 woman), 6 part-time/adjunct (0 women). *Students:* 46 full-time (24 women), 79 part-time (54 women); includes 54 minority (3 Black or African American, non-Hispanic/Latino; 28 Asian, non-Hispanic/Latino; 20 Hispanic/Latino; 2 Native Hawaiian or other Pacific Islander, non-Hispanic/Latino; 1 Two or more races, non-Hispanic/Latino), 22 international. Average age 34. 129 applicants, 53% accepted, 37 enrolled. In 2010, 28 master's awarded. *Entrance requirements:* For master's, minimum GPA of 2.5. Additional exam requirements/recommendations for international students: Required—TOEFL (minimum score 550 paper-based; 213 computer-based; 79 iBT). *Application deadline:* For fall admission, 8/1 priority date for domestic students; for spring admission, 12/1 priority date for domestic students. Applications are processed on a rolling basis. Application fee: $60. Electronic applications accepted. *Expenses:* Tuition: Full-time $14,220; part-time $790 per credit. Required fees: $35 per semester. Tuition and fees vary according to program. *Financial support:* Available to part-time students. Applicants required to submit FAFSA. *Unit head:* Jordan Holtzman, Director, 650-508-3637, E-mail: jholtzman@ndnu.edu. *Application contact:* Candace Hallmark, Associate Director of Admissions, 650-508-3600, Fax: 650-508-3426, E-mail: grad.admit@ndnu.edu.

Notre Dame de Namur University, Division of Academic Affairs, School of Business and Management, Department of Management, Belmont, CA 94002-1908. Offers MSM. Part-time and evening/weekend programs available. *Faculty:* 3 full-time (1 woman), 3 part-time/adjunct (1 woman). *Students:* 13 full-time (11 women), 41 part-time (34 women); includes 4 Black or African American, non-Hispanic/Latino; 4 Asian, non-Hispanic/Latino; 12 Hispanic/Latino; 1 Native Hawaiian or other Pacific Islander, non-Hispanic/Latino, 10 international. Average age 32. 35 applicants, 49% accepted, 14 enrolled. In 2010, 13 master's awarded. *Entrance requirements:* For master's, minimum GPA of 2.5. Additional exam requirements/recommendations for international students: Required—TOEFL (minimum score 550 paper-based; 213 computer-based). *Application deadline:* For fall admission, 8/1 priority date for domestic students; for spring admission, 12/1 priority date for domestic students. Applications are processed on a rolling basis. Application fee: $60. Electronic applications accepted. *Expenses:* Tuition: Full-time $14,220; part-time $790 per credit. Required fees: $35 per semester. Tuition and fees vary according to program. *Financial support:* Available to part-time students. Applicants required to submit FAFSA. *Unit head:* Jordan Holtzman, Director, 650-508-3637, E-mail: jholtzman@ndnu.edu. *Application contact:* Candace Hallmark, Associate Director of Admissions, 650-508-3600, Fax: 650-508-3426, E-mail: grad.admit@ndnu.edu.

Nova Southeastern University, H. Wayne Huizenga School of Business and Entrepreneurship, Doctoral Program in Business Administration, Fort Lauderdale, FL 33314-7796. Offers accounting (DBA); decision sciences (DBA); finance (DBA); human resource management (DBA); international business (DBA); management (DBA); marketing (DBA). Part-time and evening/weekend programs available. *Faculty:* 34 full-time (11 women), 2 part-time/adjunct (1 woman). *Students:* 2 full-time (1 woman), 93 part-time (32 women); includes 9 Black or African American, non-Hispanic/Latino; 4 Asian, non-Hispanic/Latino; 11 Hispanic/Latino, 8 international. Average age 47. 66 applicants, 14% accepted, 6 enrolled. In 2010, 29 doctorates awarded. *Degree requirements:* For doctorate, comprehensive exam, thesis/dissertation. *Entrance requirements:* For doctorate, GMAT. Additional exam requirements/recommendations for international students: Required—TOEFL (minimum score 600 paper-based; 250 computer-based; 100 iBT), IELTS (minimum score 7). *Application deadline:* Applications are processed on a rolling basis. Application fee: $50. Electronic applications accepted. *Financial support:* Available to part-time students. Applicants required to submit FAFSA. *Faculty research:* Reputation management, call centers, international social capital, corporate earnings guidance, corporate governance. *Unit head:* Kristie Tetrault, Director of Program Administration, 954-262-5120, Fax: 954-262-3849, E-mail: kristie@huizenga.nova.edu. *Application contact:* Karen Goldberg, Associate Director of Recruitment and Special Events, 954-262-5039, Fax: 954-262-3822, E-mail: karen@huizenga.nova.edu.

Nova Southeastern University, H. Wayne Huizenga School of Business and Entrepreneurship, Master's Program in Business Administration, Fort Lauderdale, FL 33314-7796. Offers business administration (MBA); JD/MBA; Pharm D/MBA. Part-time and evening/weekend programs available. Postbaccalaureate distance learning degree programs offered (minimal on-campus study). *Faculty:* 25 full-time (9 women), 78 part-time/adjunct (17 women). *Students:* 259 full-time (135 women), 1,777 part-time (998 women); includes 1,319 minority (634 Black or African American, non-Hispanic/Latino; 4 American Indian or Alaska Native, non-Hispanic/Latino; 84 Asian, non-Hispanic/Latino; 576 Hispanic/Latino; 1 Native Hawaiian or other Pacific Islander, non-Hispanic/Latino; 20 Two or more races, non-Hispanic/Latino), 119 international. Average age 31. 855 applicants, 71% accepted, 395 enrolled. In 2010, 758 master's awarded. *Degree requirements:* For master's, thesis optional. *Entrance requirements:* Additional exam requirements/recommendations for international students: Required—TOEFL (minimum score 550 paper-based; 213 computer-based; 79 iBT), IELTS (minimum score 6). *Application deadline:* For fall admission, 8/15 for domestic and international students; for winter admission, 12/10 for domestic and international students; for spring admission, 2/10 for domestic and international students. Applications are processed on a rolling basis. Application fee: $50. Electronic applications accepted. *Financial support:* Career-related internships or fieldwork, Federal Work-Study, and scholarships/grants available. Support available to part-time students. Financial award applicants required to submit FAFSA. *Unit head:* Dr. Preston Jones, Executive Associate Dean, 954-262-5127, Fax: 954-262-3960, E-mail: prestonj@huizenga.nova.edu. *Application contact:* Karen Goldberg, Associate Director of Recruitment and Special Events, 954-262-5039, Fax: 954-262-3822, E-mail: karen@nova.edu.

Nova Southeastern University, H. Wayne Huizenga School of Business and Entrepreneurship, Program in Leadership, Fort Lauderdale, FL 33314-7796. Offers MS. Part-time and evening/weekend programs available. Postbaccalaureate distance learning degree programs offered (minimal on-campus study). *Faculty:* 2 full-time (both women), 5 part-time/adjunct (3 women). *Students:* 1 full-time (0 women), 191 part-time (128 women); includes 124 minority (81 Black or African American, non-Hispanic/Latino; 2 Asian, non-Hispanic/Latino; 39 Hispanic/Latino; 2 Two or more races, non-Hispanic/Latino), 4 international. Average age 37. 81 applicants, 67% accepted, 41 enrolled. In 2010, 79 master's awarded. *Degree requirements:* For master's, situational leadership seminar. *Entrance requirements:* Additional exam requirements/recommendations for international students: Required—TOEFL (minimum score 550 paper-based; 213 computer-based; 79 iBT), IELTS (minimum score 6). *Application deadline:* For fall admission, 8/15 for domestic and international students; for winter admission, 12/10 for domestic and international students; for spring admission, 2/10 for domestic and international students. Applications are processed on a rolling basis. Application fee: $50. Electronic applications accepted. *Financial support:* Federal Work-Study and scholarships/grants available. Support available to part-time students. Financial award applicants required to submit FAFSA. *Unit head:* Dr. Preston Jones, Executive Associate Dean, 954-262-5127, Fax: 954-262-3960, E-mail: prestonj@huizenga.nova.edu. *Application contact:* Karen Goldberg, Associate Director of Recruitment and Special Events, 954-262-5039, Fax: 954-262-3822, E-mail: karen@nova.edu.

Nyack College, School of Business and Leadership, Nyack, NY 10960-3698. Offers business administration (MBA); organizational leadership (MS). Evening/weekend programs available. *Students:* 112 full-time (72 women), 7 part-time (5 women); includes 96 minority (83 Black or African American, non-Hispanic/Latino; 3 Asian, non-Hispanic/Latino; 7 Hispanic/Latino; 3 Two or more races, non-Hispanic/Latino), 6 international. Average age 40. In 2010, 53 master's awarded. *Degree requirements:* For master's, thesis (for some programs). *Entrance requirements:* For master's, GMAT (MBA only), resume. *Application deadline:* Applications are processed on a rolling basis. Application fee: $50. Electronic applications accepted. *Expenses:* Contact institution. *Unit head:* Dr. Anita Underwood, Dean, 845-675-4511, Fax: 845-353-5812. *Application contact:* Traci Piescki, Director of Admissions, 800-541-6891, Fax: 845-348-3912, E-mail: admissions.grad@nyack.edu.

Oakland City University, School of Adult and Extended Learning, Oakland City, IN 47660-1099. Offers MBA. Part-time and evening/weekend programs available. *Faculty:* 23 part-time/adjunct (2 women). *Students:* 40 part-time (14 women); includes 8 minority (7 Black or African American, non-Hispanic/Latino; 1 Two or more races, non-Hispanic/Latino). Average age 35. 23 applicants, 87% accepted, 18 enrolled. In 2010, 44 master's awarded. *Degree requirements:* For master's, thesis or alternative. *Entrance requirements:* For master's, GMAT, GRE, or MAT, appropriate bachelor's degree, computer literacy. Additional exam requirements/recommendations

for international students: Required—TOEFL. *Application deadline:* Applications are processed on a rolling basis. Application fee: $35. *Financial support:* Institutionally sponsored loans available. Financial award application deadline: 3/10; financial award applicants required to submit FAFSA. *Faculty research:* Leadership and management styles, international business, new technologies. *Unit head:* Dr. Michael Pelt, Dean, 812-749-1542, Fax: 812-749-1511, E-mail: mpelt@oak.edu.

Ohio Dominican University, Graduate Programs, Division of Business, Columbus, OH 43219-2099. Offers MBA, MS. Program also offered in Dayton, OH. *Accreditation:* ACBSP. Part-time and evening/weekend programs available. Postbaccalaureate distance learning degree programs offered (no on-campus study). *Students:* 354 full-time (185 women), 33 part-time (14 women); includes 128 minority (113 Black or African American, non-Hispanic/Latino; 1 American Indian or Alaska Native, non-Hispanic/Latino; 3 Asian, non-Hispanic/Latino; 7 Hispanic/Latino; 1 Native Hawaiian or other Pacific Islander, non-Hispanic/Latino; 3 Two or more races, non-Hispanic/Latino), 1 international. Average age 33. In 2010, 387 master's awarded. *Degree requirements:* For master's, thesis or alternative. *Entrance requirements:* For master's, minimum GPA of 3.0, 3 letters of recommendation. Additional exam requirements/recommendations for international students: Required—TOEFL (minimum score 550 paper-based; 213 computer-based), IELTS (minimum score 6.5). *Application deadline:* For fall admission, 7/15 priority date for domestic students, 7/18 priority date for international students; for spring admission, 12/18 priority date for domestic and international students. Applications are processed on a rolling basis. Application fee: $25. *Expenses:* Tuition: Part-time $485 per credit hour. *Financial support:* Applicants required to submit FAFSA. *Unit head:* Antonio R. Emanuel, Director of Graduate Business Programs, 614-251-4559, E-mail: emanu@ohiodominican.edu. *Application contact:* Jill M. Westerfeld, Assistant Director Graduate Admissions, 614-251-4725, Fax: 614-251-6654, E-mail: westerfj@ohiodominican.edu.

The Ohio State University, Graduate School, Max M. Fisher College of Business, Program in Business Administration, Columbus, OH 43210. Offers MA, MBA, PhD. *Accreditation:* AACSB. *Faculty:* 75. *Students:* 406 full-time (124 women), 262 part-time (69 women); includes 28 Black or African American, non-Hispanic/Latino; 3 American Indian or Alaska Native, non-Hispanic/Latino; 51 Asian, non-Hispanic/Latino; 13 Hispanic/Latino; 3 Two or more races, non-Hispanic/Latino, 137 international. Average age 31. In 2010, 321 master's, 12 doctorates awarded. *Degree requirements:* For doctorate, thesis/dissertation. *Entrance requirements:* For master's and doctorate, GMAT. Additional exam requirements/recommendations for international students: Required—TOEFL (minimum score 600 paper-based; 250 computer-based). *Application deadline:* For fall admission, 8/15 priority date for domestic students, 7/1 priority date for international students; for winter admission, 12/1 priority date for domestic students, 11/1 priority date for international students; for spring admission, 3/1 priority date for domestic students, 2/1 priority date for international students. Applications are processed on a rolling basis. Application fee: $40 ($50 for international students). Electronic applications accepted. *Expenses:* Tuition, state resident: full-time $10,605. Tuition, nonresident: full-time $26,535. Tuition and fees vary according to course load and program. *Financial support:* Fellowships, research assistantships, teaching assistantships, Federal Work-Study, institutionally sponsored loans, and unspecified assistantships available. Support available to part-time students. *Unit head:* Ingrid Werner, Head, 614-292-6040, Fax: 614-292-9006, E-mail: werner.47@osu.edu. *Application contact:* 614-292-9444, Fax: 614-292-3895, E-mail: domestic.grad@osu.edu.

The Ohio State University, Graduate School, Max M. Fisher College of Business, Program in Business Logistics Engineering, Columbus, OH 43210. Offers MBLE. *Students:* 32 full-time (19 women), 16 part-time (8 women), 46 international. Average age 24. In 2010, 26 master's awarded. *Entrance requirements:* For master's, GRE or GMAT. Additional exam requirements/recommendations for international students: Required—TOEFL. *Application deadline:* Applications are processed on a rolling basis. Application fee: $40 ($50 for international students). Electronic applications accepted. *Expenses:* Tuition, state resident: full-time $10,605. Tuition, nonresident: full-time $26,535. Tuition and fees vary according to course load and program. *Unit head:* Walter Zinn, Graduate Studies Committee Chair, 416-292-0797, Fax: 416-292-9006, E-mail: zinn.13@osu.edu. *Application contact:* Graduate Admissions, 614-292-9444, Fax: 614-292-3895, E-mail: domestic.grad@osu.edu.

Ohio University, Graduate College, College of Business, Executive Business Administration Program, Athens, OH 45701-2979. Offers EMBA. *Accreditation:* AACSB. Part-time and evening/weekend programs available. *Faculty:* 44 full-time (15 women), 16 part-time/adjunct (7 women). *Students:* 56 full-time (11 women); includes 4 Black or African American, non-Hispanic/Latino; 4 Asian, non-Hispanic/Latino. Average age 34. 48 applicants, 79% accepted. In 2010, 28 master's awarded. *Entrance requirements:* For master's, work experience in management (7-10 years). *Application deadline:* For fall admission, 6/1 priority date for domestic students. Applications are processed on a rolling basis. Application fee: $50 ($55 for international students). *Expenses:* Contact institution. *Faculty research:* Business, strategy, issues. *Application contact:* Virginia Finsterwald, Assistant Director, 740-593-2028, Fax: 740-593-0319, E-mail: finsterw@ohio.edu.

Ohio University, Graduate College, College of Business, Program in Business Administration, Athens, OH 45701-2979. Offers MBA. *Accreditation:* AACSB. Part-time and evening/weekend programs available. *Students:* 130 full-time (45 women), 1 part-time (0 women); includes 12 minority (5 Black or African American, non-Hispanic/Latino; 3 Asian, non-Hispanic/Latino; 2 Hispanic/Latino; 2 Two or more races, non-Hispanic/Latino), 4 international. 81 applicants, 53% accepted, 2 enrolled. In 2010, 233 master's awarded. *Entrance requirements:* For master's, GMAT (minimum score 500), minimum GPA of 3.0. Additional exam requirements/recommendations for international students: Required—TOEFL (minimum score 600 paper-based; 250 computer-based). *Application deadline:* For fall admission, 2/1 priority date for domestic students, 1/15 priority date for international students. Applications are processed on a rolling basis. Application fee: $50 ($55 for international students). Electronic applications accepted. *Expenses:* Contact institution. *Financial support:* In 2010–11, 20 research assistantships with full and partial tuition reimbursements (averaging $8,000 per year) were awarded; career-related internships or fieldwork and institutionally sponsored loans also available. Financial award application deadline: 2/1. *Application contact:* Jan Ross, Assistant Dean, 740-593-2007, Fax: 740-593-1388, E-mail: rossj@ohio.edu.

Oklahoma State University, Spears School of Business, Department of Management, Stillwater, OK 74078. Offers MBA, MS, PhD. Part-time programs available. *Faculty:* 24 full-time (9 women), 6 part-time/adjunct (3 women). *Students:* 5 full-time (0 women), 3 part-time (0 women), 2 international. Average age 33. In 2010, 3 doctorates awarded. *Degree requirements:* For master's, thesis or alternative; for doctorate, comprehensive exam, thesis/dissertation. *Entrance requirements:* For master's and doctorate, GRE or GMAT. Additional exam requirements/recommendations for international students: Required—TOEFL (minimum score 550 paper-based; 79 iBT). *Application deadline:* For fall admission, 3/1 priority date for international students; for spring admission, 8/1 priority date for international students. Applications are processed on a rolling basis. Application fee: $40 ($75 for international students). Electronic applications accepted. *Expenses:* Tuition, state resident: full-time $3716; part-time $154.85 per credit hour. Tuition, nonresident: full-time $14,892; part-time $621 per credit hour. Required fees: $2044; $85.20 per credit hour. One-time fee: $50. Tuition and fees vary according to course load and campus/location. *Financial support:* In 2010–11, 7 research assistantships (averaging $16,272 per year), 2 teaching assistantships (averaging $9,492 per year) were awarded; career-related internships or fieldwork, Federal Work-Study, scholarships/grants, health care benefits, tuition waivers (partial), and unspecified assistantships also available. Support available to part-time students. Financial award application deadline: 3/1; financial award applicants required to submit FAFSA. *Faculty research:* Telecommunications management, innovative decision support techniques, knowledge networking, organizational research methods, strategic planning. *Unit head:* Dr. Kenneth Eastman, Head, 405-744-5201, Fax: 405-744-5180. *Application contact:* Dr. Gordon Emslie, Dean, 405-744-6368, Fax: 405-744-0355, E-mail: grad-i@okstate.edu.

Oklahoma State University, Spears School of Business, Programs in Business Administration, Stillwater, OK 74078. Offers MBA, PhD. *Accreditation:* AACSB. Part-time programs available. Postbaccalaureate distance learning degree programs offered. *Faculty:* 2 full-time (0 women). *Students:* 167 full-time (54 women), 357 part-time (97 women); includes 13 Black or African American, non-Hispanic/Latino; 30 American Indian or Alaska Native, non-Hispanic/Latino; 10 Asian, non-Hispanic/Latino; 13 Hispanic/Latino, 27 international. Average age 30. 616 applicants, 35% accepted, 170 enrolled. In 2010, 158 master's awarded. *Degree requirements:* For master's, thesis or alternative; for doctorate, comprehensive exam, thesis/dissertation. *Entrance requirements:* For master's and doctorate, GMAT. Additional exam requirements/recommendations for international students: Required—TOEFL (minimum score 550 paper-based; 79 iBT). *Application deadline:* For fall admission, 3/1 priority date for international students; for spring admission, 8/1 priority date for international students. Applications are processed on a rolling basis. Application fee: $40 ($75 for international students). Electronic applications accepted. *Expenses:* Tuition, state resident: full-time $3716; part-time $154.85 per credit hour. Tuition, nonresident: full-time $14,892; part-time $621 per credit hour. Required fees: $2044; $85.20 per credit hour. One-time fee: $50. Tuition and fees vary according to course load and campus/location. *Financial support:* In 2010–11, 1 research assistantship (averaging $18,984 per year) was awarded; career-related internships or fieldwork, Federal Work-Study, scholarships/grants, health care benefits, tuition waivers, and unspecified assistantships also available. Support available to part-time students. Financial award application deadline: 3/1; financial award applicants required to submit FAFSA. *Unit head:* Dr. Sara Freedman, Dean, 405-744-5075. *Application contact:* Jan Analla, Assistant Director of Graduate Programs, 405-744-2951.

Old Dominion University, College of Business and Public Administration, Doctoral Program in Business Administration, Norfolk, VA 23529. Offers finance (PhD); information technology (PhD); marketing (PhD); strategic management (PhD). *Accreditation:* AACSB. *Faculty:* 21 full-time (2 women). *Students:* 36 full-time (13 women), 1 part-time (0 women); includes 5 minority (2 Black or African American, non-Hispanic/Latino; 2 Asian, non-Hispanic/

Latino; 1 Native Hawaiian or other Pacific Islander, non-Hispanic/Latino), 28 international. Average age 35. 42 applicants, 69% accepted, 10 enrolled. In 2010, 5 doctorates awarded. *Degree requirements:* For doctorate, comprehensive exam, thesis/dissertation. *Entrance requirements:* For doctorate, GMAT. Additional exam requirements/recommendations for international students: Required—TOEFL (minimum score 550 paper-based; 213 computer-based; 79 iBT). *Application deadline:* For fall admission, 4/1 priority date for domestic and international students. Application fee: $50. Electronic applications accepted. *Expenses:* Tuition, state resident: full-time $8592; part-time $358 per credit. Tuition, nonresident: full-time $21,672; part-time $903 per credit. Required fees: $119 per semester. One-time fee: $50. *Financial support:* In 2010–11, 27 students received support, including 2 fellowships with full tuition reimbursements available (averaging $7,500 per year), 32 research assistantships with full tuition reimbursements available (averaging $7,500 per year), 12 teaching assistantships with full tuition reimbursements available (averaging $7,500 per year); scholarships/grants and unspecified assistantships also available. Financial award application deadline: 4/1; financial award applicants required to submit FAFSA. *Faculty research:* International business, buyer behavior, financial markets, strategy, operations research. *Unit head:* Dr. John B. Ford, Graduate Program Director, 757-683-3587, Fax: 757-683-4076, E-mail: jford@odu.edu. *Application contact:* Katrina Davenport, Program Coordinator, 757-683-5138, Fax: 757-683-4076, E-mail: kdavenpo@odu.edu.

Old Dominion University, College of Business and Public Administration, MBA Program, Norfolk, VA 23529. Offers business and economic forecasting (MBA); financial analysis and valuation (MBA); information technology and enterprise integration (MBA); international business (MBA); maritime and port management (MBA); public administration (MBA). *Accreditation:* AACSB. Part-time and evening/weekend programs available. *Faculty:* 66 full-time (15 women), 6 part-time/adjunct (1 woman). *Students:* 74 full-time (32 women), 166 part-time (62 women); includes 45 minority (21 Black or African American, non-Hispanic/Latino; 1 American Indian or Alaska Native, non-Hispanic/Latino; 8 Asian, non-Hispanic/Latino; 10 Hispanic/Latino; 1 Native Hawaiian or other Pacific Islander, non-Hispanic/Latino; 4 Two or more races, non-Hispanic/Latino), 19 international. Average age 31. 169 applicants, 52% accepted, 61 enrolled. In 2010, 100 master's awarded. *Entrance requirements:* For master's, GMAT, letter of reference, resume, coursework in calculus, essay. Additional exam requirements/recommendations for international students: Required—TOEFL (minimum score 550 paper-based; 213 computer-based; 80 iBT). *Application deadline:* For fall admission, 6/1 priority date for domestic students, 4/15 priority date for international students; for spring admission, 11/1 priority date for domestic students, 10/1 priority date for international students. Applications are processed on a rolling basis. Application fee: $50. Electronic applications accepted. *Expenses:* Tuition, state resident: full-time $8592; part-time $358 per credit. Tuition, nonresident: full-time $21,672; part-time $903 per credit. Required fees: $119 per semester. One-time fee: $50. *Financial support:* In 2010–11, 44 students received support, including 90 research assistantships with partial tuition reimbursements available (averaging $3,200 per year); career-related internships or fieldwork, scholarships/grants, and unspecified assistantships also available. Support available to part-time students. Financial award application deadline: 2/15; financial award applicants required to submit FAFSA. *Faculty research:* International business, buyer behavior, financial markets, strategy, operations research. *Unit head:* Dr. Larry Filer, Graduate Program Director, 757-683-3585, Fax: 757-683-5750, E-mail: mbainfo@odu.edu. *Application contact:* Shanna Wood, MBA Program Manager, 757-683-3585, Fax: 757-683-5750, E-mail: mbainfo@odu.edu.

Our Lady of the Lake University of San Antonio, School of Business and Leadership, Program in Management, San Antonio, TX 78207-4689. Offers business administration (MBA); management (MBA). *Students:* 6 full-time (3 women), 141 part-time (77 women); includes 87 minority (12 Black or African American, non-Hispanic/Latino; 1 American Indian or Alaska Native, non-Hispanic/Latino; 3 Asian, non-Hispanic/Latino; 68 Hispanic/Latino; 1 Native Hawaiian or other Pacific Islander, non-Hispanic/Latino; 2 Two or more races, non-Hispanic/Latino), 1 international. Average age 34. In 2010, 48 master's awarded. *Expenses:* Tuition: Full-time $13,500; part-time $750 per contact hour. Required fees: $330. Tuition and fees vary according to course level, degree level and campus/location. *Unit head:* Dr. Robert Bisking, Dean, 210-434-6711, Fax: 210-434-0821, E-mail: rbisking@ollusa.edu. *Application contact:* Dr. Robert Bisking, Dean, 210-434-6711, Fax: 210-434-0821, E-mail: rbisking@ollusa.edu.

Pacific States University, College of Business, Los Angeles, CA 90006. Offers accounting (MBA); business administration (DBA); finance (MBA); international business (MBA); management of information technology (MBA); real estate management (MBA). Part-time and evening/weekend programs available. Postbaccalaureate distance learning degree programs offered (no on-campus study). *Faculty:* 4 full-time (1 woman), 13 part-time/adjunct (0 women). *Students:* 130 full-time (55 women); includes 1 Black or African American, non-Hispanic/Latino; 7 Asian, non-Hispanic/Latino; 3 Native Hawaiian or other Pacific Islander, non-Hispanic/Latino, 115 international. Average age 31. 42 applicants, 83% accepted, 33 enrolled. In 2010, 67 master's awarded. *Degree requirements:* For doctorate, comprehensive exam, thesis/dissertation. *Entrance requirements:* For master's, minimum undergraduate GPA of 2.5 during last 90 hours of course work. Additional exam requirements/recommendations for international students: Required—TOEFL (minimum score 133 computer-based; 45 iBT), IELTS (minimum score 4.5). *Application deadline:* For fall admission, 8/15 priority date for domestic students; for winter admission, 10/15 priority date for domestic students; for spring admission, 1/15 priority date for domestic students. Applications are processed on a rolling basis. Application fee: $100. *Expenses:* Tuition: Full-time $8280; part-time $345 per credit hour. Required fees: $150 per quarter. *Financial support:* Scholarships/grants available. Financial award applicants required to submit FAFSA. *Unit head:* Dr. Chase C. Lee, Director, 888-200-0383, Fax: 323-731-2383, E-mail: admission@psuca.edu. *Application contact:* Zolzaya Enkhbayar, Assistant Director of Admissions, 323-731-2383, Fax: 323-731-7276, E-mail: admissions@psuca.edu.

Palm Beach Atlantic University, Rinker School of Business, West Palm Beach, FL 33416-4708. Offers MBA. Part-time and evening/weekend programs available. *Faculty:* 10 full-time (3 women), 3 part-time/adjunct (1 woman). *Students:* 33 full-time (11 women), 80 part-time (43 women); includes 26 minority (15 Black or African American, non-Hispanic/Latino; 3 Asian, non-Hispanic/Latino; 8 Hispanic/Latino), 16 international. Average age 32. 48 applicants, 92% accepted, 40 enrolled. In 2010, 54 master's awarded. *Entrance requirements:* For master's, GMAT, minimum GPA of 3.0. Additional exam requirements/recommendations for international students: Required—TOEFL (minimum score 550 paper-based; 213 computer-based). *Application deadline:* For fall admission, 7/15 priority date for domestic students; for spring admission, 11/15 priority date for domestic students. Applications are processed on a rolling basis. Application fee: $45. Electronic applications accepted. *Expenses:* Tuition: Full-time $8280; part-time $460 per credit hour. Required fees: $99 per semester. Tuition and fees vary according to course load, degree level and campus/location. *Financial support:* Applicants required to submit FAFSA. *Unit head:* Dr. Edgar Langlois, MBA Program Director, 561-803-2456, E-mail: edgar langlois@pba.edu. Application contact: Graduate Admissions, 888-468-6722, Fax: 561-803-2115, E-mail: grad@pba.edu.

Penn State Erie, The Behrend College, Graduate School, Erie, PA 16563-0001. Offers business administration (MBA); engineering (M Eng). *Accreditation:* AACSB. Part-time programs available. *Students:* 48 full-time (9 women), 59 part-time (17 women). Average age 28. 70 applicants, 70% accepted, 35 enrolled. In 2010, 123 master's awarded. *Entrance requirements:* Additional exam requirements/recommendations for international students: Required—TOEFL (minimum score 550 paper-based; 213 computer-based; 80 iBT). *Application deadline:* Applications are processed on a rolling basis. Application fee: $65. Electronic applications accepted. *Financial support:* Federal Work-Study available. Financial award application deadline: 2/15; financial award applicants required to submit FAFSA. *Unit head:* Dr. John D. Burke, Chief Executive Officer/Dean, 814-898-6160, Fax: 814-898-6461, E-mail: jdb1@psu.edu. *Application contact:* Ann M. Burbules, Graduate Admissions Counselor, 814-898-7255, Fax: 814-898-6044, E-mail: amb29@psu.edu.

Penn State Great Valley, Graduate Studies, Management Division, Malvern, PA 19355-1488. Offers M Fin, MBA, MLD. *Accreditation:* AACSB. *Unit head:* Dr. Daniel Indro, Division Head, 610-725-5283, Fax: 610-725-5224, E-mail: dci1@psu.edu. *Application contact:* Dr. Daniel Indro, Division Head, 610-725-5283, Fax: 610-725-5224, E-mail: dci1@psu.edu.

Penn State Harrisburg, Graduate School, School of Business Administration, Program in Business Administration, Middletown, PA 17057-4898. Offers MBA, MBA/JD, MBA/PhD. *Accreditation:* AACSB. *Entrance requirements:* For master's, GMAT.

Penn State University Park, Graduate School, The Mary Jean and Frank P. Smeal College of Business Administration, State College, University Park, PA 16802-1503. Offers MBA, PhD. *Accreditation:* AACSB. *Students:* 256 full-time (91 women), 2 part-time (0 women). Average age 31. 1,130 applicants, 28% accepted, 160 enrolled. In 2010, 171 master's, 9 doctorates awarded. *Entrance requirements:* Additional exam requirements/recommendations for international students: Required—TOEFL (minimum score 550 paper-based; 213 computer-based; 80 iBT). *Application deadline:* Applications are processed on a rolling basis. Application fee: $65. Electronic applications accepted. *Financial support:* Fellowships, research assistantships, teaching assistantships available. Financial award applicants required to submit FAFSA. *Unit head:* Dr. James B. Thomas, Dean, 814-863-0448, Fax: 814-865-7064, E-mail: j2t@psu.edu. *Application contact:* Cynthia E. Nicosia, Director, Graduate Enrollment Services, 814-865-1795, Fax: 814-865-4627, E-mail: cey1@psu.edu.

Pepperdine University, Graziadio School of Business and Management, Executive MBA Program, Malibu, CA 90263. Offers Exec MBA. Part-time and evening/weekend programs available. *Students:* 111 full-time (40 women); includes 39 minority (11 Black or African American, non-Hispanic/Latino; 20 Asian, non-Hispanic/Latino; 8 Hispanic/Latino), 3 international. 74 applicants, 91% accepted, 46 enrolled. In 2010, 104 master's awarded. *Entrance requirements:* For master's, two personal interviews; two letters of nomination; minimum of seven years professional experience, including two years at a significant level of management. *Application deadline:* For fall

admission, 6/10 priority date for domestic students. Application fee: $100. *Unit head:* Dr. Linda A. Livingstone, Dean, Graziadio School of Business and Management, 310-568-5689, Fax: 310-568-5766, E-mail: linda.livingstone@pepperdine.edu. *Application contact:* Darrell Eriksen, Director of Admission and Student Accounts, Graziadio School of Business and Management, 310-568-5525, E-mail: darrell.eriksen@pepperdine.edu.

Pepperdine University, Graziadio School of Business and Management, Full-Time MBA Program, Malibu, CA 90263. Offers MBA. *Students:* 276 full-time (102 women), 2 part-time (0 women); includes 56 minority (8 Black or African American, non-Hispanic/Latino; 41 Asian, non-Hispanic/Latino; 6 Hispanic/Latino; 1 Two or more races, non-Hispanic/Latino), 77 international. 335 applicants, 49% accepted, 137 enrolled. In 2010, 156 master's awarded. *Entrance requirements:* For master's, GMAT or GRE, two letters of recommendation. Additional exam requirements/recommendations for international students: Required—TOEFL. *Application deadline:* For fall admission, 5/1 for domestic students, 4/1 for international students. Application fee: $75. Electronic applications accepted. *Unit head:* Dr. Linda A. Livingstone, Dean, Graziadio School of Business and Management, 310-568-5689, Fax: 310-568-5766, E-mail: linda.livingstone@pepperdine.edu. *Application contact:* Darrell Eriksen, Director of Admission and Student Accounts, Graziadio School of Business and Management, 310-568-5525, E-mail: darrell.eriksen@pepperdine.edu.

Pepperdine University, Graziadio School of Business and Management, Fully-Employed MBA Program, Malibu, CA 90263. Offers MBA. Part-time and evening/weekend programs available. *Students:* 250 full-time (111 women), 536 part-time (203 women); includes 274 minority (37 Black or African American, non-Hispanic/Latino; 6 American Indian or Alaska Native, non-Hispanic/Latino; 155 Asian, non-Hispanic/Latino; 71 Hispanic/Latino; 4 Native Hawaiian or other Pacific Islander, non-Hispanic/Latino; 1 Two or more races, non-Hispanic/Latino), 13 international. 227 applicants, 72% accepted, 130 enrolled. In 2010, 423 master's awarded. *Entrance requirements:* For master's, GMAT or GRE, professional recommendation. Additional exam requirements/recommendations for international students: Required—TOEFL. *Application deadline:* For fall admission, 6/25 for domestic students. Application fee: $75. Electronic applications accepted. *Unit head:* Dr. Linda A. Livingstone, Dean, Graziadio School of Business and Management, 310-568-5689, Fax: 310-568-5766, E-mail: linda.livingstone@pepperdine.edu. *Application contact:* Darrell Eriksen, Director of Admission and Student Accounts, Graziadio School of Business and Management, 310-568-5525, E-mail: darrell.eriksen@pepperdine.edu.

Pepperdine University, Graziadio School of Business and Management, MBA Program for Presidents and Key Executives, Malibu, CA 90263. Offers MBA. Part-time and evening/weekend programs available. *Students:* 45 full-time (9 women); includes 9 minority (2 Black or African American, non-Hispanic/Latino; 4 Asian, non-Hispanic/Latino; 3 Hispanic/Latino), 1 international. 12 applicants, 92% accepted, 8 enrolled. In 2010, 23 master's awarded. *Entrance requirements:* For master's, two letters of nomination; two personal interviews; minimum of 10 years of organizational or professional experience, including at least one year in a senior executive position. Additional exam requirements/recommendations for international students: Required—TOEFL. *Application deadline:* For fall admission, 6/15 priority date for domestic students. Application fee: $100. *Unit head:* Dr. Linda A. Livingstone, Dean, Graziadio School of Business and Management, 310-568-5689, Fax: 310-568-5766, E-mail: linda.livingstone@pepperdine.edu. *Application contact:* Darrell Eriksen, Director of Admission and Student Accounts, Graziadio School of Business and Management, 310-568-5525, E-mail: darrell.eriksen@pepperdine.edu.

Pepperdine University, Graziadio School of Business and Management, MS in Management and Leadership Program, Malibu, CA 90263. Offers MS. Part-time and evening/weekend programs available. *Students:* 48 full-time (33 women); includes 21 minority (9 Black or African American, non-Hispanic/Latino; 1 American Indian or Alaska Native, non-Hispanic/Latino; 10 Asian, non-Hispanic/Latino; 1 Hispanic/Latino), 1 international. 22 applicants, 86% accepted, 16 enrolled. In 2010, 18 master's awarded. *Entrance requirements:* For master's, GMAT or GRE, two letters of recommendation. *Application deadline:* For fall admission, 6/25 for domestic students. Application fee: $75. *Unit head:* Dr. Linda A. Livingstone, Dean, Graziadio School of Business and Management, 310-568-5689, Fax: 310-568-5766, E-mail: linda.livingstone@pepperdine.edu. *Application contact:* Darrell Eriksen, Director of Admission and Student Accounts, Graziadio School of Business and Management, 310-568-5525, E-mail: darrell.eriksen@pepperdine.edu.

Piedmont College, School of Business, Demorest, GA 30535-0010. Offers MBA. *Accreditation:* ACBSP. Part-time and evening/weekend programs available. *Faculty:* 9 full-time (1 woman). *Students:* 26 full-time (12 women), 76 part-time (42 women); includes 8 Black or African American, non-Hispanic/Latino; 1 American Indian or Alaska Native, non-Hispanic/Latino; 3 Hispanic/Latino, 2 international. 33 applicants, 79% accepted, 24 enrolled. In 2010, 50 master's awarded. *Degree requirements:* For master's, capstone. *Entrance requirements:* For master's, GMAT, GRE, minimum GPA of 2.75. Additional exam requirements/recommendations for international students: Required—TOEFL (minimum score 550 paper-based; 213 computer-based). *Application* *deadline:* For fall admission, 7/15 for domestic students; for spring admission, 12/1 for domestic students. Applications are processed on a rolling basis. Electronic applications accepted. *Financial support:* Federal Work-Study and unspecified assistantships available. Financial award applicants required to submit FAFSA. *Unit head:* Dr. John Misner, Dean, 706-778-3000 Ext. 1349, Fax: 706-778-0701, E-mail: jmisner@piedmont.edu. *Application contact:* Anthony J. Cox, Director of Graduate Admissions, 706-778-8500 Ext. 1118, Fax: 706-776-6635, E-mail: acox@piedmont.edu.

Point Park University, School of Business, Pittsburgh, PA 15222-1984. Offers business (MBA); organizational leadership (MA). Part-time and evening/weekend programs available. *Faculty:* 11 full-time, 14 part-time/adjunct. *Students:* 121 full-time (69 women), 272 part-time (137 women); includes 107 minority (86 Black or African American, non-Hispanic/Latino; 1 American Indian or Alaska Native, non-Hispanic/Latino; 9 Asian, non-Hispanic/Latino; 5 Hispanic/Latino; 6 Two or more races, non-Hispanic/Latino), 23 international. Average age 32. 356 applicants, 73% accepted, 166 enrolled. In 2010, 168 master's awarded. *Degree requirements:* For master's, comprehensive exam (for some programs), thesis or alternative. *Entrance requirements:* For master's, minimum QPA of 2.75; 2 letters of recommendation; resume (MA). Additional exam requirements/recommendations for international students: Required—TOEFL (minimum score 550 paper-based; 79 iBT). *Application deadline:* Applications are processed on a rolling basis. Application fee: $30. Electronic applications accepted. *Expenses:* Tuition: Full-time $12,456; part-time $692 per credit. Required fees: $630; $35 per credit. *Financial support:* In 2010–11, 48 students received support, including 5 teaching assistantships with full tuition reimbursements available (averaging $6,400 per year); scholarships/grants also available. Financial award application deadline: 4/15; financial award applicants required to submit FAFSA. *Faculty research:* Technology issues, foreign direct investment, multinational corporate issues, cross-cultural international organizations/administrations, regional integration issues. *Unit head:* Dr. Angela Isaac, Dean, 412-392-8011, Fax: 412-392-8048, E-mail: aisaac@pointpark.edu. *Application contact:* Marty M. Paonessa, Associate Director, Graduate and Adult Enrollment, 412-392-3915, Fax: 412-392-6164, E-mail: mpaonessa@pointpark.edu.

Polytechnic Institute of NYU, Department of Technology Management, Brooklyn, NY 11201-2990. Offers construction management (Advanced Certificate); electronic business management (Advanced Certificate); entrepreneurship (Advanced Certificate); human resources management (Advanced Certificate); information management (Advanced Certificate); management (MS); management of technology (MS); organizational behavior (MS, Advanced Certificate); project management (Advanced Certificate); technology management (MBA, PhD, Advanced Certificate); telecommunications and information management (MS); telecommunications management (Advanced Certificate). Part-time and evening/weekend programs available. *Faculty:* 7 full-time (2 women), 28 part-time/adjunct (4 women). *Students:* 224 full-time (93 women), 106 part-time (38 women); includes 15 Black or African American, non-Hispanic/Latino; 41 Asian, non-Hispanic/Latino; 10 Hispanic/Latino, 158 international. Average age 30. 370 applicants, 60% accepted, 120 enrolled. In 2010, 173 master's, 1 doctorate awarded. *Degree requirements:* For master's, comprehensive exam (for some programs), thesis (for some programs); for doctorate, comprehensive exam, thesis/dissertation. *Entrance requirements:* For master's, GMAT, minimum B average in undergraduate course work. Additional exam requirements/recommendations for international students: Required—TOEFL (minimum score 550 paper-based; 213 computer-based; 80 iBT); Recommended—IELTS (minimum score 6.5). *Application deadline:* For fall admission, 7/31 priority date for domestic students, 4/30 priority date for international students; for spring admission, 12/31 priority date for domestic students, 11/30 priority date for international students. Applications are processed on a rolling basis. Application fee: $75. Electronic applications accepted. *Expenses:* Tuition: Full-time $21,492; part-time $1194 per credit. Required fees: $385 per semester. Tuition and fees vary according to course load. *Financial support:* In 2010–11, 1 fellowship (averaging $26,400 per year) was awarded; research assistantships, teaching assistantships, institutionally sponsored loans, scholarships/grants, and unspecified assistantships also available. Support available to part-time students. *Unit head:* Prof. Bharadwaj Rao, Head, 718-260-3617, Fax: 718-260-3874, E-mail: brao@poly.edu. *Application contact:* JeanCarlo Bonilla, Director of Graduate Enrollment Management, 718-260-3182, Fax: 718-260-3624, E-mail: gradinfo@poly.edu.

Polytechnic Institute of NYU, Westchester Graduate Center, Graduate Programs, Department of Technology Management, Major in Management, Hawthorne, NY 10532-1507. Offers MS. Part-time and evening/weekend programs available. *Faculty:* 5 part-time/adjunct (1 woman). *Students:* 5 part-time (1 woman). Average age 35. 1 applicant, 100% accepted, 0 enrolled. In 2010, 13 master's awarded. *Degree requirements:* For master's, comprehensive exam (for some programs), thesis (for some programs). *Entrance requirements:* Additional exam requirements/recommendations for international students: Required—TOEFL (minimum score 550 paper-based; 213 computer-based; 80 iBT); Recommended—IELTS (minimum score 6.5). *Application deadline:* For fall admission, 7/31 priority date for domestic students, 4/30 priority date for international students; for spring admission, 12/31 priority date for domestic students, 11/30 priority date for international

students. Applications are processed on a rolling basis. Application fee: $75. Electronic applications accepted. *Expenses:* Tuition: Full-time $21,492; part-time $1194 per credit. Required fees: $385 per semester. Tuition and fees vary according to course load. *Financial support:* Institutionally sponsored loans, scholarships/grants, and unspecified assistantships available. Support available to part-time students. *Unit head:* Dr. Bharadwaj Rao, Department Head, 718-260-3617, E-mail: brao@poly.edu. *Application contact:* JeanCarlo Bonilla, Director of Graduate Enrollment Management, 718-260-3182, Fax: 718-260-3624, E-mail: gradinfo@poly.edu.

Portland State University, Graduate Studies, School of Business Administration, Program in Business Administration, Portland, OR 97207-0751. Offers MBA. Part-time and evening/weekend programs available. *Students:* 127 full-time (44 women), 190 part-time (66 women); includes 39 minority (1 Black or African American, non-Hispanic/Latino; 4 American Indian or Alaska Native, non-Hispanic/Latino; 26 Asian, non-Hispanic/Latino; 7 Hispanic/Latino; 1 Two or more races, non-Hispanic/Latino), 26 international. Average age 32. 149 applicants, 82% accepted, 116 enrolled. In 2010, 111 master's awarded. *Degree requirements:* For master's, one foreign language, project. *Entrance requirements:* For master's, GMAT, minimum GPA of 3.0 in upper-division course work, 2 recommendations, resume, interview. Additional exam requirements/recommendations for international students: Required—TOEFL (minimum score 550 paper-based; 213 computer-based). *Application deadline:* For fall admission, 4/1 priority date for domestic students, 3/1 priority date for international students. Applications are processed on a rolling basis. Application fee: $50. *Expenses:* Tuition, state resident: full-time $8505; part-time $315 per credit. Tuition, nonresident: full-time $13,284; part-time $492 per credit. Required fees: $1482; $21 per credit. $99 per term. One-time fee: $120. Part-time tuition and fees vary according to course load and program. *Financial support:* Research assistantships with full tuition reimbursements, teaching assistantships with full tuition reimbursements, career-related internships or fieldwork and Federal Work-Study available. Support available to part-time students. Financial award application deadline: 3/1; financial award applicants required to submit FAFSA. *Faculty research:* Quality management and organizational excellence, performance measurement, customer satisfaction, values, technology management and technology transfer. *Unit head:* Dr. Berrin Erdogan, Chair, 503-725-3798, Fax: 503-725-5850, E-mail: berrine@sba.pdx.edu. *Application contact:* Pam Mitchell, Administrator, 503-725-3730, Fax: 503-725-5850, E-mail: pamm@sba.pdx.edu.

Portland State University, Graduate Studies, Systems Science Program, Portland, OR 97207-0751. Offers computational intelligence (Certificate); computer modeling and simulation (Certificate); systems science (MS); systems science/anthropology (PhD); systems science/business administration (PhD); systems science/civil engineering (PhD); systems science/economics (PhD); systems science/engineering management (PhD); systems science/general (PhD); systems science/mathematical sciences (PhD); systems science/mechanical engineering (PhD); systems science/psychology (PhD); systems science/sociology (PhD). *Faculty:* 4 full-time (0 women), 1 part-time/adjunct (0 women). *Students:* 15 full-time (4 women), 35 part-time (11 women); includes 1 American Indian or Alaska Native, non-Hispanic/Latino; 1 Asian, non-Hispanic/Latino; 1 Two or more races, non-Hispanic/Latino, 4 international. Average age 39. 8 applicants, 88% accepted, 5 enrolled. In 2010, 2 master's, 4 doctorates awarded. *Degree requirements:* For doctorate, variable foreign language requirement, thesis/dissertation. *Entrance requirements:* For master's, 2 letters of recommendation; for doctorate, GMAT, GRE General Test, minimum undergraduate GPA of 3.0. Additional exam requirements/recommendations for international students: Required—TOEFL. *Application deadline:* For fall admission, 2/1 for domestic students; for spring admission, 11/1 for domestic students. Application fee: $50. *Expenses:* Tuition, state resident: full-time $8505; part-time $315 per credit. Tuition, nonresident: full-time $13,284; part-time $492 per credit. Required fees: $1482; $21 per credit. $99 per term. One-time fee: $120. Part-time tuition and fees vary according to course load and program. *Financial support:* In 2010–11, 1 research assistantship with full tuition reimbursement (averaging $7,704 per year) was awarded; teaching assistantships with full tuition reimbursements, career-related internships or fieldwork, Federal Work-Study, scholarships/grants, and unspecified assistantships also available. Support available to part-time students. Financial award application deadline: 3/1; financial award applicants required to submit FAFSA. *Faculty research:* Systems theory and methodology, artificial intelligence neural networks, information theory, nonlinear dynamics/chaos, modeling and simulation. *Unit head:* George Lendaris, Acting Director, 503-725-4960. *Application contact:* Dawn Sharafi, Administrative Assistant, 503-725-4960, E-mail: dawn@sysc.pdx.edu.

Prairie View A&M University, College of Business, Prairie View, TX 77446-0519. Offers accounting (MS); general business administration (MBA). *Accreditation:* AACSB. Part-time and evening/weekend programs available. *Faculty:* 14 full-time (5 women). *Students:* 55 full-time (33 women), 158 part-time (99 women); includes 166 Black or African American, non-Hispanic/Latino; 6 Asian, non-Hispanic/Latino; 8 Hispanic/Latino, 20 international. Average age 31. In 2010, 48 master's awarded. *Entrance requirements:* For master's, GMAT, minimum GPA of 2.45. Additional exam requirements/recommendations for international students: Required—TOEFL. *Application* *deadline:* For fall admission, 7/1 for domestic students, 6/1 priority date for international students; for spring admission, 11/1 for domestic students, 10/1 priority date for international students. Applications are processed on a rolling basis. Application fee: $50. Electronic applications accepted. *Expenses:* Tuition, state resident: full-time $3586.14; part-time $119.06 per credit hour. Tuition, nonresident: part-time $511.23 per credit hour. *Financial support:* In 2010–11, 9 research assistantships (averaging $6,240 per year), 7 teaching assistantships (averaging $6,240 per year) were awarded; career-related internships or fieldwork, Federal Work-Study, institutionally sponsored loans, and tuition waivers (partial) also available. Support available to part-time students. Financial award application deadline: 4/1; financial award applicants required to submit FAFSA. *Faculty research:* Operations, finance, marketing. Total annual research expenditures: $30,000. *Unit head:* Dr. Munir Quddus, Dean, 936-261-9217, Fax: 936-261-9241, E-mail: muquddus@pvamu.edu. *Application contact:* Dr. John Dyck, Director, Graduate Programs in Business, 936-261-9217, Fax: 936-261-9232, E-mail: jwdyck@pvamu.edu.

Providence College, Graduate Studies, School of Business, Providence, RI 02918. Offers accounting (MBA); entrepreneurship (MBA); finance (MBA); international business (MBA); management (MBA); marketing (MBA); not-for-profit organizations (MBA). Part-time and evening/weekend programs available. *Faculty:* 17 full-time (9 women), 10 part-time/adjunct (2 women). *Students:* 53 full-time (20 women), 57 part-time (22 women); includes 4 minority (1 Black or African American, non-Hispanic/Latino; 1 Asian, non-Hispanic/Latino; 2 Two or more races, non-Hispanic/Latino), 6 international. Average age 26. 72 applicants, 81% accepted. In 2010, 56 master's awarded. *Degree requirements:* For master's, thesis optional. *Entrance requirements:* For master's, GMAT. Additional exam requirements/recommendations for international students: Required—TOEFL (minimum score 550 paper-based; 213 computer-based; 80 iBT). *Application deadline:* For fall admission, 8/1 priority date for domestic and international students; for spring admission, 12/1 priority date for domestic and international students. Applications are processed on a rolling basis. Application fee: $55. *Expenses:* Contact institution. *Financial support:* In 2010–11, 34 research assistantships with full tuition reimbursements (averaging $8,400 per year) were awarded; Federal Work-Study, institutionally sponsored loans, and unspecified assistantships also available. Support available to part-time students. Financial award application deadline: 8/1; financial award applicants required to submit FAFSA. *Unit head:* Dr. MaryJane Lenon, Director, MBA Program, 401-865-2566, Fax: 401-865-2978, E-mail: mjlenon@providence.edu. *Application contact:* Katherine A. Follett, Administrative Coordinator, 401-865-2333, Fax: 401-865-2978, E-mail: kfollett@providence.edu.

Purdue University, Graduate School, Krannert School of Management, Doctoral Program in Management, West Lafayette, IN 47907-2056. Offers PhD. *Students:* 57 full-time (16 women); includes 2 Asian, non-Hispanic/Latino; 1 Hispanic/Latino, 41 international. Average age 34. 404 applicants, 4% accepted, 10 enrolled. In 2010, 9 doctorates awarded. *Degree requirements:* For doctorate, comprehensive exam, thesis/dissertation, first year summer paper, dissertation proposal, dissertation defense. *Entrance requirements:* For doctorate, GMAT or GRE. Additional exam requirements/recommendations for international students: Required—TOEFL (minimum score 575 paper-based; 233 computer-based); Recommended—TWE. *Application deadline:* For fall admission, 1/15 priority date for domestic and international students. Application fee: $55. Electronic applications accepted. *Financial support:* In 2010–11, fellowships with full tuition reimbursements (averaging $25,000 per year), research assistantships with partial tuition reimbursements (averaging $18,000 per year), teaching assistantships with full tuition reimbursements (averaging $10,000 per year) were awarded; institutionally sponsored loans, scholarships/grants, health care benefits, tuition waivers (full and partial), unspecified assistantships, and travel funds to present at a major conference also available. Financial award application deadline: 1/15. *Faculty research:* Accounting, finance, marketing, management information systems, operations management, organizational behavior and human resource management, quantitative methods/management science, strategic management. *Unit head:* Dr. Gerald J. Lynch, Dean, 765-494-4366. *Application contact:* Krannert Ph.D. Admissions, 765-494-4375, Fax: 765-494-0136, E-mail: krannertphd@purdue.edu.

Purdue University, Graduate School, Krannert School of Management, Executive MBA Program, West Lafayette, IN 47907. Offers MBA. *Faculty:* 12 full-time (0 women), 3 part-time/adjunct (0 women). *Students:* 21 full-time (4 women); includes 2 Black or African American, non-Hispanic/Latino; 1 Asian, non-Hispanic/Latino. Average age 39. 37 applicants, 68% accepted, 21 enrolled. In 2010, 17 master's awarded. *Entrance requirements:* For master's, GMAT. Additional exam requirements/recommendations for international students: Required—TOEFL (minimum score 77 computer-based). *Application deadline:* For fall admission, 6/1 for domestic and international students. Applications are processed on a rolling basis. Application fee: $55. Electronic applications accepted. *Financial support:* Application deadline: 6/1. *Unit head:* Dr. Gerald J. Lynch, Dean, 765-494-4366, E-mail: lynch@purdue.edu. *Application contact:* Lori Stout, Admissions Assistant, 765-494-2291, E-mail: krannertexec@purdue.edu.

Purdue University, Graduate School, Krannert School of Management, GISMA Program, Hannover, IN 30625, Germany. Offers general business

(MBA). *Faculty:* 25 full-time (3 women), 5 part-time/adjunct (0 women). *Students:* 53 full-time (22 women); includes 1 Black or African American, non-Hispanic/Latino; 2 Asian, non-Hispanic/Latino; 3 Hispanic/Latino, 35 international. Average age 26. 106 applicants, 66% accepted, 53 enrolled. In 2010, 53 master's awarded. *Entrance requirements:* For master's, GMAT, letters of recommendation. Additional exam requirements/recommendations for international students: Required—TOEFL (minimum score 550 paper-based; 213 computer-based; 77 iBT). *Application deadline:* For fall admission, 7/31 for domestic students, 8/1 for international students. Applications are processed on a rolling basis. Application fee: $55 ($60 for international students). *Expenses:* Contact institution. *Unit head:* Dr. David Schoorman, Dean/Professor of Organizational Behavior and Human Resource Management, 765-494-4391, E-mail: schoor@purdue.edu. *Application contact:* Monika Baer, Director of Admissions, 49-511 54609-36, E-mail: mbaer@gisma.com.

Purdue University, Graduate School, Krannert School of Management, Master of Business Administration Program, West Lafayette, IN 47907. Offers MBA. *Faculty:* 98 full-time (27 women), 22 part-time/adjunct (4 women). *Students:* 222 full-time (49 women); includes 10 Black or African American, non-Hispanic/Latino; 16 Asian, non-Hispanic/Latino; 5 Hispanic/Latino, 107 international. Average age 27. 771 applicants, 33% accepted, 108 enrolled. In 2010, 148 master's awarded. *Entrance requirements:* For master's, GMAT, four-year baccalaureate degree, minimum GPA of 3.0, essays, recommendation letters, work/internship experience. Additional exam requirements/recommendations for international students: Required—TOEFL (minimum 550 paper, 213 computer, 77 iBT), IELTS, or Pearson PTE. *Application deadline:* For fall admission, 1/10 priority date for domestic students, 2/1 for international students. Applications are processed on a rolling basis. Application fee: $55. Electronic applications accepted. *Financial support:* In 2010–11, 80 research assistantships, 20 teaching assistantships were awarded; scholarships/grants and unspecified assistantships also available. Financial award applicants required to submit FAFSA. *Faculty research:* Capital market imperfections and the sensitivity of investment to stock prices, identifying beneficial collaboration in decentralized logistics systems, performance periods and the dynamics of the performance-risk relationship, applications of global optimization to process and molecular design. *Unit head:* Dr. Gerald J. Lynch, Interim Dean, 765-494-4366. *Application contact:* Brenda Knebel, Director, Full-time Master's Admissions, 765-494-0773, Fax: 765-494-9841, E-mail: krannertmasters@purdue.edu.

Purdue University, Graduate School, Krannert School of Management, Weekend Master of Business Administration Program, West Lafayette, IN 47907. Offers MBA. Part-time and evening/weekend programs available. *Faculty:* 14 full-time (2 women), 3 part-time/adjunct (0 women). *Students:* 149 part-time (35 women); includes 12 Black or African American, non-Hispanic/Latino; 1 American Indian or Alaska Native, non-Hispanic/Latino; 21 Asian, non-Hispanic/Latino; 4 Hispanic/Latino, 27 international. 70 applicants, 91% accepted, 48 enrolled. In 2010, 52 master's awarded. *Entrance requirements:* For master's, GMAT. Additional exam requirements/recommendations for international students: Required—IELTS; Recommended—TOEFL (minimum score 77 iBT). *Application deadline:* For winter admission, 12/1 for domestic and international students. Applications are processed on a rolling basis. Electronic applications accepted. *Financial support:* Partial scholarships available. Financial award application deadline: 12/1; financial award applicants required to submit FAFSA. *Unit head:* Dr. Gerald J. Lynch, Interim Dean, 765-494-4366. *Application contact:* Erika L. Murphy, Associate Director, 765-494-1395, E-mail: murphy89@purdue.edu.

Purdue University Calumet, Graduate Studies Office, School of Management, Hammond, IN 46323-2094. Offers accountancy (M Acc); business administration (MBA); business administration for executives (EMBA). Part-time and evening/weekend programs available. *Faculty:* 25 full-time (7 women). *Students:* 180 full-time, 15 part-time. In 2010, 80 master's awarded. *Entrance requirements:* For master's, GMAT. Additional exam requirements/recommendations for international students: Required—TOEFL. *Application deadline:* For fall admission, 8/20 priority date for domestic students; for spring admission, 1/15 priority date for domestic students. Applications are processed on a rolling basis. Application fee: $55. Electronic applications accepted. *Expenses:* Tuition, state resident: full-time $6867. Tuition, nonresident: full-time $14,157. *Financial support:* In 2010–11, 2 research assistantships with full tuition reimbursements (averaging $8,000 per year) were awarded. Financial award application deadline: 3/1. *Unit head:* Dr. Martine SuChatelet, Dean, 219-989-2606, E-mail: duchatel@purduecal.edu. *Application contact:* Kimberly Uhll, Graduate Adviser, 219-989-3150, E-mail: kuhll@purduecal.edu.

Quincy University, Program in Business Administration, Quincy, IL 62301-2699. Offers business administration (MBA); human resource management (MBA). Part-time and evening/weekend programs available. *Faculty:* 5 full-time (3 women). *Students:* 8 full-time (6 women), 17 part-time (8 women); includes 1 Black or African American, non-Hispanic/Latino; 1 Hispanic/Latino. In 2010, 21 master's awarded. *Entrance requirements:* For master's, GMAT, previous course work in accounting, economics, finance, management or marketing, and statistics. Additional exam requirements/recommendations for international students: Required—TOEFL (minimum score 550 paper-based). *Application deadline:* Applications are processed on a rolling basis.

Application fee: $25. Electronic applications accepted. *Expenses:* Contact institution. *Financial support:* Available to part-time students. Applicants required to submit FAFSA. *Faculty research:* Macroeconomic forecasting, business ethics/social responsibility. *Unit head:* Dr. John Palmer, Director, 217-228-5432 Ext. 3070, E-mail: palmejo@quincy.edu. *Application contact:* Jennifer Bang, Coordinator of Adult Studies, 217-228-5404, Fax: 217-228-5479, E-mail: admissions@quincy.edu.

Quinnipiac University, School of Business, MBA Program, Hamden, CT 06518-1940. Offers chartered financial analyst (MBA); finance (MBA); healthcare management (MBA); information systems management (MBA); marketing (MBA); supply chain management (MBA); JD/MBA. *Accreditation:* AACSB. Part-time and evening/weekend programs available. *Faculty:* 25 full-time (2 women), 3 part-time/adjunct (all women). *Students:* 87 full-time (24 women), 121 part-time (46 women); includes 12 minority (1 Black or African American, non-Hispanic/Latino; 7 Asian, non-Hispanic/Latino; 4 Hispanic/Latino), 14 international. Average age 29. 119 applicants, 81% accepted, 81 enrolled. In 2010, 70 master's awarded. *Entrance requirements:* For master's, GMAT or GRE, minimum GPA of 3.0. Additional exam requirements/recommendations for international students: Required—TOEFL (minimum score 575 paper-based; 233 computer-based; 90 iBT), IELTS (minimum score 6.5). *Application deadline:* For fall admission, 7/30 priority date for domestic students, 4/30 priority date for international students; for spring admission, 12/15 priority date for domestic students, 9/15 priority date for international students. Applications are processed on a rolling basis. Application fee: $45. Electronic applications accepted. *Expenses:* Tuition: Part-time $810 per credit. Required fees: $35 per credit. *Financial support:* In 2010–11, 110 students received support. Federal Work-Study, tuition waivers (partial), and unspecified assistantships available. Support available to part-time students. Financial award application deadline: 4/15; financial award applicants required to submit FAFSA. *Faculty research:* Equity compensation, marketing relationships and public policy, corporate governance, international business, supply chain management. *Unit head:* Lisa Braiewa, MBA Program Director, 203-582-3710, Fax: 203-582-8664, E-mail: lisa.braiewa@quinnipiac.edu. *Application contact:* Jennifer Boutin, 800-462-1944, Fax: 203-582-3443, E-mail: jennifer.boutin@quinnipiac.edu.

Radford University, College of Graduate and Professional Studies, College of Business and Economics, Program in Business Administration, Radford, VA 24142. Offers MBA. *Accreditation:* AACSB. Part-time and evening/weekend programs available. *Faculty:* 38 full-time (6 women), 4 part-time/adjunct (1 woman). *Students:* 39 full-time (15 women), 44 part-time (15 women); includes 11 minority (6 Black or African American, non-Hispanic/Latino; 1 American Indian or Alaska Native, non-Hispanic/Latino; 1 Asian, non-Hispanic/Latino; 3 Hispanic/Latino), 9 international. Average age 30. 70 applicants, 67% accepted, 33 enrolled. In 2010, 50 master's awarded. *Degree requirements:* For master's, comprehensive exam. *Entrance requirements:* For master's, GMAT, minimum GPA of 2.75, 2 letters of reference. Additional exam requirements/recommendations for international students: Required—TOEFL (minimum score 550 paper-based; 213 computer-based; 79 iBT). *Application deadline:* For fall admission, 2/15 priority date for domestic students, 12/1 for international students; for spring admission, 7/1 for international students. Applications are processed on a rolling basis. Application fee: $50. Electronic applications accepted. *Expenses:* Tuition, state resident: full-time $5746; part-time $239 per credit hour. Tuition, nonresident: full-time $14,174; part-time $591 per credit hour. Required fees: $2634; $111 per credit hour. *Financial support:* In 2010–11, 21 students received support, including 14 research assistantships with partial tuition reimbursements available (averaging $8,000 per year), 4 teaching assistantships with partial tuition reimbursements available (averaging $8,700 per year); career-related internships or fieldwork, Federal Work-Study, institutionally sponsored loans, scholarships/grants, and unspecified assistantships also available. Financial award application deadline: 3/1; financial award applicants required to submit FAFSA. *Unit head:* Elizabeth C. Jamison, Director of MBA, 540-831-6712, Fax: 540-831-6655, E-mail: rumba@radford.edu. *Application contact:* Rebecca Conner, Graduate Admissions, 540-831-5431, Fax: 540-831-6061, E-mail: gradcollege@radford.edu.

Regent University, Graduate School, School of Global Leadership and Entrepreneurship, Virginia Beach, VA 23464-9800. Offers business administration (MBA); management (MA); organizational leadership (MA, PhD, Certificate); strategic foresight (MA); strategic leadership (DSL). Part-time and evening/weekend programs available. Postbaccalaureate distance learning degree programs offered (minimal on-campus study). *Faculty:* 13 full-time (3 women), 9 part-time/adjunct (3 women). *Students:* 30 full-time (11 women), 499 part-time (184 women); includes 125 Black or African American, non-Hispanic/Latino; 4 American Indian or Alaska Native, non-Hispanic/Latino; 10 Asian, non-Hispanic/Latino; 15 Hispanic/Latino, 93 international. Average age 41. 157 applicants, 66% accepted, 64 enrolled. In 2010, 86 master's, 30 doctorates awarded. *Degree requirements:* For master's, thesis or alternative, 3 credit hour culminating experience; for doctorate, thesis/dissertation. *Entrance requirements:* For master's, GRE, GMAT, minimum undergraduate GPA of 2.75, computer literacy survey, 2 recommendations, resume, transcripts, essay; for doctorate, GRE, GMAT, sample of writing, minimum 3 years of relevant experience, computer literacy survey, 2 recommendations, resume, essay,

transcripts; for Certificate, writing sample, resume, transcripts. Additional exam requirements/recommendations for international students: Required—TOEFL (minimum score 577 paper-based; 233 computer-based). *Application deadline:* For fall admission, 5/1 priority date for domestic students; for spring admission, 10/1 priority date for domestic students. Applications are processed on a rolling basis. Application fee: $50. Electronic applications accepted. *Expenses:* Contact institution. *Financial support:* Career-related internships or fieldwork, scholarships/grants, and tuition waivers (full and partial) available. Support available to part-time students. Financial award application deadline: 9/1. *Faculty research:* Servant leadership, ethics and values, telecommuting and family values, organizational communications, distance education. *Unit head:* Dr. Bruce Winston, Dean, 757-352-4306, Fax: 757-352-4634, E-mail: brucwin@regent.edu. *Application contact:* Matthew Chadwick, Director of Enrollment Support Services, 800-373-5504, Fax: 757-352-4381, E-mail: admissions@regent.edu.

Reinhardt University, Program in Business Administration, Alpharetta, GA 30005-4442. Offers MBA. Program offered on the Alpharetta Campus. Part-time and evening/weekend programs available. *Faculty:* 5 full-time (3 women). *Students:* 2 full-time (1 woman), 32 part-time (16 women); includes 4 Black or African American, non-Hispanic/Latino; 2 Asian, non-Hispanic/Latino. Average age 38. 57 applicants, 47% accepted, 23 enrolled. In 2010, 12 master's awarded. *Degree requirements:* For master's, comprehensive exam. *Entrance requirements:* For master's, GRE (upper 50th percentile) or GMAT (minimum score 500), bachelor's degree with minimum GPA of 2.75, current resume, interview, 3 professional references. Additional exam requirements/recommendations for international students: Required—TOEFL. *Application deadline:* For fall admission, 5/7 for domestic and international students; for spring admission, 8/9 for domestic and international students. Applications are processed on a rolling basis. Application fee: $25. Electronic applications accepted. *Expenses:* Tuition: Full-time $8400; part-time $350 per credit hour. Required fees: $125 per semester. *Financial support:* Application deadline: 5/1. *Unit head:* Ray Schumacher, Admissions Counselor, 770-993-6971, Fax: 770-475-0263, E-mail: res@reinhardt.edu. *Application contact:* Ray Schumacher, Admissions Counselor, 770-993-6971, Fax: 770-475-0263, E-mail: res@reinhardt.edu.

Rensselaer Polytechnic Institute, Graduate School, Lally School of Management and Technology, Troy, NY 12180-3590. Offers business (MBA); financial engineering and risk analysis (MS); management (MS, PhD); technology, commercialization, and entrepreneurship (MS). *Accreditation:* AACSB. Part-time and evening/weekend programs available. *Faculty:* 44 full-time (10 women), 19 part-time/adjunct (0 women). *Students:* 189 full-time (82 women), 162 part-time (40 women); includes 65 minority (22 Black or African American, non-Hispanic/Latino; 34 Asian, non-Hispanic/Latino; 9 Hispanic/Latino), 92 international. Average age 28. 507 applicants, 56% accepted, 150 enrolled. In 2010, 263 master's, 7 doctorates awarded. *Degree requirements:* For doctorate, thesis/dissertation. *Entrance requirements:* For master's, GMAT, 2 letters of recommendation, resume; for doctorate, GMAT or GRE General Test, 2 letters of recommendation. Additional exam requirements/recommendations for international students: Required—TOEFL (minimum score 600 paper-based; 250 computer-based; 100 iBT); Recommended—IELTS (minimum score 7). *Application deadline:* For fall admission, 3/15 priority date for domestic and international students. Applications are processed on a rolling basis. Application fee: $75. Electronic applications accepted. *Expenses:* Tuition: Full-time $39,600; part-time $1650 per credit. Required fees: $1896. *Financial support:* Fellowships with partial tuition reimbursements, career-related internships or fieldwork, institutionally sponsored loans, scholarships/grants, and assistantships are for Ph D students only available. Financial award application deadline: 3/15; financial award applicants required to submit FAFSA. *Faculty research:* Technological entrepreneurship, operations management, new product development and marketing, finance and financial engineering and risk analytics, information systems. *Unit head:* Dr. Iftekhar Hasan, Acting Dean/Professor, 518-276-6586, Fax: 518-276-2665, E-mail: lallymba@rpi.edu. *Application contact:* Michele M. Martens, Manager of Graduate Programs, 518-276-6586, Fax: 518-276-8190, E-mail: lallymba@rpi.edu.

The Richard Stockton College of New Jersey, School of Graduate and Continuing Studies, Program in Business Administration, Pomona, NJ 08240-0195. Offers MBA. Part-time and evening/weekend programs available. *Faculty:* 5 full-time (1 woman), 1 (woman) part-time/adjunct. *Students:* 15 full-time (8 women), 38 part-time (13 women); includes 7 minority (2 Black or African American, non-Hispanic/Latino; 3 Asian, non-Hispanic/Latino; 1 Hispanic/Latino; 1 Two or more races, non-Hispanic/Latino), 3 international. Average age 32. 26 applicants, 62% accepted, 13 enrolled. In 2010, 24 master's awarded. *Degree requirements:* For master's, project. *Entrance requirements:* For master's, GMAT. Additional exam requirements/recommendations for international students: Required—TOEFL. *Application deadline:* For fall admission, 7/1 for domestic and international students; for spring admission, 12/1 for domestic and international students. Applications are processed on a rolling basis. Application fee: $50. Electronic applications accepted. *Expenses:* Tuition, state resident: full-time $9310; part-time $517.25 per credit. Tuition, nonresident: full-time $14,332; part-time $796.23 per credit. Required fees: $2600; $144 per credit. $70 per semester. Tuition and fees vary according to degree level. *Financial support:* In 2010–11, 4 students received support, including 4 research assistantships with partial tuition reimbursements available; career-related internships or fieldwork, Federal Work-Study, scholarships/grants, and unspecified assistantships also available. Support available to part-time students. Financial award application deadline: 3/1; financial award applicants required to submit FAFSA. *Faculty research:* Business ethics, marketing channels development, event studies, total quality management. *Unit head:* Dr. Gurprit Chhatwal, Director, 609-652-4615, E-mail: mba@stockton.edu. *Application contact:* Tara Williams, Assistant Director of Graduate Enrollment Management, 609-626-3640, Fax: 609-626-6050, E-mail: gradschool@stockton.edu.

Rider University, College of Business Administration, Lawrenceville, NJ 08648-3001. Offers M Acc, MBA. *Accreditation:* AACSB. Part-time and evening/weekend programs available. *Faculty:* 18 full-time (5 women), 9 part-time/adjunct (3 women). *Students:* 123 full-time (61 women), 185 part-time (88 women); includes 12 Black or African American, non-Hispanic/Latino; 28 Asian, non-Hispanic/Latino; 8 Hispanic/Latino, 59 international. Average age 29. In 2010, 122 master's awarded. *Entrance requirements:* For master's, GMAT, minimum AACSB index of 1050, resume. Additional exam requirements/recommendations for international students: Required—TOEFL (minimum score 550 paper-based; 213 computer-based). *Application deadline:* For fall admission, 8/1 priority date for domestic students, 3/15 priority date for international students; for spring admission, 12/1 priority date for domestic students, 11/1 priority date for international students. Applications are processed on a rolling basis. Application fee: $50. Electronic applications accepted. *Expenses:* Contact institution. *Financial support:* Career-related internships or fieldwork, Federal Work-Study, institutionally sponsored loans, unspecified assistantships, and institutional work-study available. Support available to part-time students. Financial award applicants required to submit FAFSA. *Unit head:* Dr. John Farrell, MBA Program Director, 609-895-5776, Fax: 609-896-5304. *Application contact:* Jamie L. Mitchell, Director of Graduate Admissions, 609-896-5036, Fax: 609-895-5680, E-mail: jmitchell@rider.edu.

Rivier College, School of Graduate Studies, Department of Business Administration, Nashua, NH 03060. Offers MBA. Part-time and evening/weekend programs available. *Faculty:* 1 full-time (0 women), 8 part-time/adjunct (0 women). *Students:* 39 full-time (20 women), 72 part-time (41 women); includes 3 Black or African American, non-Hispanic/Latino; 10 Asian, non-Hispanic/Latino; 2 Hispanic/Latino. Average age 36. 49 applicants, 33% accepted, 9 enrolled. In 2010, 43 master's awarded. *Application deadline:* Applications are processed on a rolling basis. Application fee: $25. *Expenses:* Tuition: Part-time $456 per credit. *Financial support:* Available to part-time students. Application deadline: 2/1. *Unit head:* Maria Matarazzo, Division Chair, 603-897-8532, Fax: 603-897-8885, E-mail: mmatarazzo@rivier.edu. *Application contact:* Mathew Kittredge, Director of Graduate Admissions, 603-897-8229, Fax: 603-897-8810, E-mail: mkittredge@rivier.edu.

Robert Morris University Illinois, Morris Graduate School of Management, Chicago, IL 60605. Offers accounting (MBA); accounting/finance (MBA); health care administration (MM); higher education administration (MM); human resource management (MBA); information systems (MIS); leadership (MBA); management/finance (MIS); management/human resource management (MBA). Part-time and evening/weekend programs available. *Faculty:* 9 full-time (2 women), 21 part-time/adjunct (6 women). *Students:* 275 full-time (151 women), 212 part-time (138 women); includes 170 Black or African American, non-Hispanic/Latino; 1 American Indian or Alaska Native, non-Hispanic/Latino; 21 Asian, non-Hispanic/Latino; 73 Hispanic/Latino; 2 Native Hawaiian or other Pacific Islander, non-Hispanic/Latino, 23 international. Average age 32. 172 applicants, 87% accepted, 105 enrolled. In 2010, 174 master's awarded. *Degree requirements:* For master's, 48 residency hours. *Entrance requirements:* Additional exam requirements/recommendations for international students: Required—TOEFL (minimum score 500 paper-based; 173 computer-based). *Application deadline:* Applications are processed on a rolling basis. Application fee: $50 ($100 for international students). Electronic applications accepted. *Expenses:* Tuition: Full-time $13,200; part-time $2200 per course. *Financial support:* Federal Work-Study, scholarships/grants, and tuition waivers available. Support available to part-time students. *Unit head:* Kayed Akkawi, Dean, 312-935-6025, Fax: 312-935-6020, E-mail: kakkawi@robertmorris.edu. *Application contact:* Courtney A. Kohn Sanders, Dean of Graduate Admissions, 312-935-4810, Fax: 312-935-6020, E-mail: ckohn@robertmorris.edu.

Rochester Institute of Technology, Graduate Enrollment Services, E. Philip Saunders College of Business, Graduate Business Programs, Executive MBA Program, Rochester, NY 14623-5603. Offers Exec MBA. *Accreditation:* AACSB. Part-time and evening/weekend programs available. Postbaccalaureate distance learning degree programs offered (minimal on-campus study). *Students:* 92 full-time (20 women), 1 (woman) part-time; includes 10 minority (6 Black or African American, non-Hispanic/Latino; 3 Asian, non-Hispanic/Latino; 1 Hispanic/Latino), 4 international. Average age 39. 55 applicants, 96% accepted, 46 enrolled. In 2010, 24 master's awarded. *Degree requirements:* For master's, thesis. *Entrance requirements:* For master's, GMAT, minimum 6 years of work experience. Additional

exam requirements/recommendations for international students: Required—TOEFL (minimum score 580 paper-based; 237 computer-based; 92 iBT) or IELTS (minimum score 7). *Application deadline:* For fall admission, 6/30 priority date for domestic students, 2/15 priority date for international students. Applications are processed on a rolling basis. Application fee: $50. *Expenses:* Contact institution. *Financial support:* In 2010–11, 41 students received support. Scholarships/grants available. Support available to part-time students. Financial award applicants required to submit FAFSA. *Unit head:* Donna Scheid, Graduate Program Director, 585-475-7935, Fax: 585-475-7450, E-mail: djsbbu@rit.edu. *Application contact:* Diane Ellison, Assistant Vice President, Graduate Enrollment Services, 585-475-2229, Fax: 585-475-7164, E-mail: gradinfo@rit.edu.

Rochester Institute of Technology, Graduate Enrollment Services, E. Philip Saunders College of Business, Graduate Business Programs, Program in Business Administration, Rochester, NY 14623-5603. Offers MBA. *Accreditation:* AACSB. Part-time and evening/weekend programs available. *Students:* 95 full-time (31 women), 85 part-time (31 women); includes 15 minority (6 Black or African American, non-Hispanic/Latino; 6 Asian, non-Hispanic/Latino; 3 Hispanic/Latino), 60 international. Average age 30. 301 applicants, 37% accepted, 46 enrolled. In 2010, 108 master's awarded. *Degree requirements:* For master's, comprehensive exam (for some programs), thesis (for some programs). *Entrance requirements:* For master's, GMAT, minimum GPA of 2.5. Additional exam requirements/recommendations for international students: Required—TOEFL (minimum score 580 paper-based; 237 computer-based; 92 iBT) or IELTS (minimum score 7). *Application deadline:* For fall admission, 2/15 priority date for domestic and international students; for winter admission, 11/1 priority date for domestic students, 10/1 priority date for international students; for spring admission, 2/1 priority date for domestic students, 1/1 priority date for international students. Applications are processed on a rolling basis. *Expenses:* Tuition: Full-time $33,234; part-time $924 per credit hour. Required fees: $219. *Financial support:* In 2010–11, 111 students received support; research assistantships with partial tuition reimbursements available, teaching assistantships with partial tuition reimbursements available, career-related internships or fieldwork, scholarships/grants, and unspecified assistantships available. Support available to part-time students. Financial award applicants required to submit FAFSA. *Faculty research:* Strategic use of information technology to gain a competitive advantage, developing new statistical quality control techniques and revising the existing techniques to improve their performance, corporate governance. *Unit head:* Heather Krakehl, Graduate Program Director, 585-475-6916, E-mail: hmascb@rit.edu. *Application contact:* Diane Ellison, Assistant Vice President, Graduate Enrollment Services, 585-475-2229, Fax: 585-475-7164, E-mail: gradinfo@rit.edu.

Rockford College, Graduate Studies, Program in Business Administration, Rockford, IL 61108-2393. Offers MBA. Part-time and evening/weekend programs available. *Students:* 15 full-time (6 women), 46 part-time (21 women); includes 1 Black or African American, non-Hispanic/Latino; 3 Hispanic/Latino, 1 international. Average age 31. In 2010, 21 master's awarded. *Entrance requirements:* For master's, GMAT, 3 letters of recommendation. Additional exam requirements/recommendations for international students: Required—TOEFL (minimum score 550 paper-based; 213 computer-based; 79 iBT). *Application deadline:* Applications are processed on a rolling basis. Application fee: $50. Electronic applications accepted. *Expenses:* Tuition: Full-time $16,280; part-time $675 per hour. Required fees: $40 per semester. *Financial support:* Scholarships/grants and unspecified assistantships available. Support available to part-time students. Financial award application deadline: 3/1; financial award applicants required to submit FAFSA. *Faculty research:* Entrepreneurship, leadership, international business, services marketing, project management. *Unit head:* Prof. Jeff Fahrenwald, MBA Director, 815-226-4178, E-mail: jfahrenwald@rockford.edu. *Application contact:* Michele Mehren, Office Manager for Graduate Studies, 815-226-4041, E-mail: mmehren@rockford.edu.

Rockhurst University, Helzberg School of Management, Kansas City, MO 64110-2561. Offers MBA. *Accreditation:* AACSB. Part-time and evening/weekend programs available. *Faculty:* 24 full-time (5 women), 9 part-time/adjunct (4 women). *Students:* 116 full-time (35 women), 111 part-time (32 women); includes 25 minority (10 Black or African American, non-Hispanic/Latino; 10 Asian, non-Hispanic/Latino; 5 Hispanic/Latino), 3 international. Average age 30. 104 applicants, 51% accepted, 40 enrolled. In 2010, 197 master's awarded. *Entrance requirements:* For master's, GMAT. Additional exam requirements/recommendations for international students: Required—TOEFL (minimum score 550 paper-based; 213 computer-based; 79 iBT). *Application deadline:* For fall admission, 7/25 priority date for domestic students; for spring admission, 12/15 priority date for domestic students. Applications are processed on a rolling basis. Application fee: $0. Electronic applications accepted. Tuition and fees vary according to program. *Financial support:* Career-related internships or fieldwork available. Support available to part-time students. Financial award application deadline: 4/1; financial award applicants required to submit FAFSA. *Faculty research:* Offshoring/outsourcing, systems analysis/synthesis, work teams, multilateral trade, path dependencies/creation. *Unit head:* Dr. James Daley, Dean, 816-501-4201, Fax: 816-501-4650, E-mail:

james.daley@rockhurst.edu. *Application contact:* Michele Haggerty, Director of MBA Advising, 816-501-4823, E-mail: michele.haggerty@rockhurst.edu.

Rollins College, Crummer Graduate School of Business, Winter Park, FL 32789-4499. Offers entrepreneurship (MBA); finance (MBA); international business (MBA); management (MBA); marketing (MBA); operations and technology management (MBA). *Accreditation:* AACSB. Part-time and evening/weekend programs available. Postbaccalaureate distance learning degree programs offered (minimal on-campus study). *Faculty:* 22 full-time (3 women), 5 part-time/adjunct (3 women). *Students:* 303 full-time (117 women), 130 part-time (49 women); includes 111 minority (30 Black or African American, non-Hispanic/Latino; 1 American Indian or Alaska Native, non-Hispanic/Latino; 29 Asian, non-Hispanic/Latino; 50 Hispanic/Latino; 1 Two or more races, non-Hispanic/Latino), 29 international. Average age 32. 484 applicants, 42% accepted, 131 enrolled. In 2010, 223 master's awarded. *Entrance requirements:* For master's, GMAT, interview. Additional exam requirements/recommendations for international students: Required—TOEFL (minimum score 550 paper-based; 213 computer-based; 80 iBT). *Application deadline:* Applications are processed on a rolling basis. Application fee: $50. Electronic applications accepted. *Expenses:* Contact institution. *Financial support:* In 2010–11, 112 students received support, including 95 fellowships, 56 research assistantships (averaging $2,400 per year); career-related internships or fieldwork, scholarships/grants, and unspecified assistantships also available. Support available to part-time students. Financial award applicants required to submit FAFSA. *Faculty research:* Sustainability, world financial markets, international business, market research, strategic marketing. *Unit head:* Dr. Craig M. McAllaster, Dean, 407-646-2249, Fax: 407-646-1550, E-mail: cmcallaster@rollins.edu. *Application contact:* Linda Puritz, Student Admissions Office, 407-646-2405, Fax: 407-646-1550, E-mail: mbaadmissions@rollins.edu.

Roseman University of Health Sciences, MBA Program, Henderson, NV 89014. Offers MBA. Evening/weekend programs available. *Faculty:* 3 full-time (0 women), 19 part-time/adjunct (6 women). *Students:* 11 full-time (7 women); includes 1 American Indian or Alaska Native, non-Hispanic/Latino; 2 Asian, non-Hispanic/Latino; 1 Native Hawaiian or other Pacific Islander, non-Hispanic/Latino. Average age 38. 5 applicants, 0% accepted, 0 enrolled. In 2010, 5 master's awarded. *Degree requirements:* For master's, comprehensive exam, entrepreneurial project, summative assessment and capstone. *Entrance requirements:* For master's, GMAT or leveling course for applicants whose overall GPA is below 3.0, bachelor's degree. Additional exam requirements/recommendations for international students: Required—TOEFL (minimum score 550 paper-based; 213 computer-based; 79 iBT). *Application deadline:* Applications are processed on a rolling basis. Application fee: $100. *Expenses:* Contact institution. *Financial support:* Scholarships/grants available. Financial award application deadline: 3/1; financial award applicants required to submit FAFSA. *Faculty research:* Corporate leadership, economic development, dental practice management. *Unit head:* Dr. Okeleke Nzeogwu, Program Director, 702-968-1659, Fax: 702-968-1685, E-mail: onzeogwu@usn.edu. *Application contact:* Dr. Okeleke Nzeogwu, Program Director, 702-968-1659, Fax: 702-968-1685, E-mail: onzeogwu@usn.edu.

Rowan University, Graduate School, William G. Rohrer College of Business, Glassboro, NJ 08028-1701. Offers MBA. *Accreditation:* AACSB. Part-time and evening/weekend programs available. *Faculty:* 13 full-time (5 women), 4 part-time/adjunct (3 women). *Students:* 47 full-time (19 women), 114 part-time (69 women); includes 9 Black or African American, non-Hispanic/Latino; 10 Asian, non-Hispanic/Latino; 4 Hispanic/Latino. Average age 28. 63 applicants, 67% accepted, 33 enrolled. In 2010, 29 master's awarded. *Degree requirements:* For master's, thesis. *Entrance requirements:* For master's, GMAT, minimum GPA of 2.8. Additional exam requirements/recommendations for international students: Required—TOEFL. *Application deadline:* Applications are processed on a rolling basis. Application fee: $65 ($200 for international students). Electronic applications accepted. *Expenses:* Tuition, area resident: Part-time $602 per semester hour. Tuition, nonresident: part-time $602 per semester hour. Required fees: $100 per semester hour. One-time fee: $10 part-time. *Financial support:* Career-related internships or fieldwork, scholarships/grants, health care benefits, and unspecified assistantships available. *Unit head:* Dr. Horacio Sosa, Dean, College of Graduate and Continuing Education, 856-256-4747, E-mail: sosa@rowan.edu. *Application contact:* Karen Haynes, Graduate Coordinator, 856-256-4052, E-mail: haynes@rowan.edu.

Rutgers, The State University of New Jersey, Camden, School of Business, Camden, NJ 08102-1401. Offers MBA, JD/MBA. *Accreditation:* AACSB. Part-time and evening/weekend programs available. *Faculty:* 34 full-time, 5 part-time/adjunct. *Students:* 39 full-time (13 women), 212 part-time (70 women). Average age 28. 212 applicants, 61% accepted, 57 enrolled. *Entrance requirements:* For master's, GMAT, 2 letters of recommendation. Additional exam requirements/recommendations for international students: Required—TOEFL (minimum score 230 computer-based; 89 iBT). *Application deadline:* For fall admission, 7/1 priority date for domestic students, 2/1 for international students; for spring admission, 11/1 priority date for domestic students, 9/1 for international students. Applications are processed on a rolling basis. Application fee: $60. Electronic applications accepted. *Expenses:* Contact institution. *Financial support:* Research assistantships, career-related internships or fieldwork, Federal Work-Study, institutionally sponsored

loans, and scholarships/grants available. Support available to part-time students. Financial award application deadline: 8/1; financial award applicants required to submit FAFSA. *Faculty research:* Efficiency in utility industry, management information systems development, management/labor relations. *Unit head:* Dr. Jaishankar Ganesh, Dean, 856-225-6217, Fax: 856-225-6231, E-mail: jganesh@camden.rutgers.edu. *Application contact:* Dr. Rakesh B. Sambharya, Associate Dean, MBA Program, 856-225-6712, Fax: 856-225-6231, E-mail: sambhary@camden.rutgers.edu.

Rutgers, The State University of New Jersey, Newark, Graduate School, Program in Management, Newark, NJ 07102. Offers accounting (PhD); accounting information systems (PhD); computer information systems (PhD); finance (PhD); information technology (PhD); international business (PhD); management science (PhD); marketing (PhD); organization management (PhD). Program offered jointly with New Jersey Institute of Technology. *Accreditation:* AACSB. *Faculty:* 128 full-time (24 women), 4 part-time/adjunct (1 woman). *Students:* 95 full-time (34 women), 17 part-time (6 women); includes 9 Black or African American, non-Hispanic/Latino; 54 Asian, non-Hispanic/Latino; 3 Hispanic/Latino. 438 applicants, 14% accepted, 34 enrolled. In 2010, 10 doctorates awarded. *Degree requirements:* For doctorate, thesis/dissertation, cumulative exams. *Entrance requirements:* For doctorate, GMAT or GRE General Test, minimum undergraduate B average. Additional exam requirements/recommendations for international students: Required—TOEFL. *Application deadline:* For fall admission, 4/1 for domestic students; for spring admission, 11/1 for domestic students. Applications are processed on a rolling basis. Application fee: $60. Electronic applications accepted. *Expenses:* Tuition, state resident: part-time $600 per credit. Tuition, nonresident: full-time $10,694. *Financial support:* In 2010–11, 6 fellowships (averaging $18,000 per year), 4 research assistantships with full and partial tuition reimbursements (averaging $23,112 per year), 38 teaching assistantships with full and partial tuition reimbursements (averaging $23,112 per year) were awarded; institutionally sponsored loans and tuition waivers (full and partial) also available. Support available to part-time students. Financial award application deadline: 2/15. *Faculty research:* Technology management, leadership and teams, consumer behavior, financial and markets, logistics. *Unit head:* Dr. Glenn Shafer, Director, 973-353-1604, Fax: 973-353-5691, E-mail: gshafer@rbs.rutgers.edu. *Application contact:* Goncalo Filipe, Senior Academic Coordinator, 973-353-1002, Fax: 973-353-5691, E-mail: gfilipe@rbsmail.rutgers.edu.

Rutgers, The State University of New Jersey, Newark, Rutgers Business School–Newark and New Brunswick, Newark, NJ 07102. Offers MBA, MBA/MS, MD/MBA, MPH/MBA, MS/MBA. *Accreditation:* AACSB. Part-time and evening/weekend programs available. *Faculty:* 148 full-time (27 women), 124 part-time/adjunct (36 women). *Students:* 208 full-time (86 women), 1,004 part-time (343 women); includes 68 Black or African American, non-Hispanic/Latino; 2 American Indian or Alaska Native, non-Hispanic/Latino; 248 Asian, non-Hispanic/Latino; 64 Hispanic/Latino, 79 international. Average age 28. 635 applicants, 72% accepted, 313 enrolled. In 2010, 400 master's awarded. Terminal master's awarded for partial completion of doctoral program. *Degree requirements:* For master's, 60 total credits including capstone course. *Entrance requirements:* For master's, GMAT, GRE. Additional exam requirements/recommendations for international students: Required—TOEFL (minimum score 600 paper-based; 100 computer-based). *Application deadline:* For fall admission, 5/1 for domestic students, 3/15 for international students; for spring admission, 11/15 for domestic students. Applications are processed on a rolling basis. Application fee: $73. Electronic applications accepted. *Expenses:* Contact institution. *Financial support:* Fellowships with tuition reimbursements, teaching assistantships, career-related internships or fieldwork, Federal Work-Study, institutionally sponsored loans, and scholarships/grants available. Financial award application deadline: 3/15; financial award applicants required to submit FAFSA. *Faculty research:* Finance/economics, accounting, international business, operations research, marketing, organizational behavior, supply chain management, pharmaceutical management. *Unit head:* Dr. Michael Cooper, Dean, 973-353-5128, Fax: 973-353-1345. *Application contact:* Rita Galen, Assistant Dean of Admissions, 973-353-1234, Fax: 973-353-1592, E-mail: admit@business.rutgers.edu.

Sage Graduate School, Graduate School, School of Management, Program in Business Administration, Troy, NY 12180-4115. Offers business strategy (MBA); finance (MBA); human resources (MBA); marketing (MBA); JD/MBA. Part-time and evening/weekend programs available. *Faculty:* 4 full-time (2 women), 8 part-time/adjunct (3 women). *Students:* 8 full-time (4 women), 67 part-time (45 women); includes 10 Black or African American, non-Hispanic/Latino; 2 Asian, non-Hispanic/Latino; 3 Hispanic/Latino, 1 international. Average age 31. 45 applicants, 64% accepted, 19 enrolled. In 2010, 24 master's awarded. *Entrance requirements:* For master's, minimum GPA of 2.75, resume, 2 letters of recommendation. Additional exam requirements/recommendations for international students: Required—TOEFL (minimum score 550 paper-based; 213 computer-based). *Application deadline:* Applications are processed on a rolling basis. Application fee: $40. *Expenses:* Tuition: Full-time $10,980; part-time $610 per credit hour. Tuition and fees vary according to course load, degree level and program. *Financial support:* Fellowships, research assistantships, Federal Work-Study, scholarships/grants, and unspecified assistantships available. Support available to part-time students. Financial award application deadline: 3/1; financial award applicants required to submit FAFSA. *Unit head:* Dr. Daniel Robeson, Dean, School of Management, 518-292-8637, Fax: 518-292-1964, E-mail: robesd@sage.edu. *Application contact:* Wendy D. Diefendorf, Director of Graduate and Adult Admission, 518-244-2443, Fax: 518-244-6880, E-mail: diefew@sage.edu.

St. Ambrose University, College of Business, Program in Business Administration, Davenport, IA 52803-2898. Offers business administration (DBA); health care (MBA); human resources (MBA). *Accreditation:* ACBSP. Part-time and evening/weekend programs available. *Faculty:* 17 full-time (3 women), 9 part-time/adjunct (2 women). *Students:* 52 full-time (20 women), 221 part-time (110 women); includes 16 minority (5 Black or African American, non-Hispanic/Latino; 4 Asian, non-Hispanic/Latino; 7 Hispanic/Latino), 4 international. Average age 33. 79 applicants, 78% accepted, 51 enrolled. In 2010, 94 master's, 5 doctorates awarded. *Degree requirements:* For master's, comprehensive exam (for some programs), thesis or alternative, capstone seminar; for doctorate, comprehensive exam, thesis/dissertation, oral and written exams. *Entrance requirements:* For master's, GMAT; for doctorate, GMAT, master's degree. Additional exam requirements/recommendations for international students: Required—TOEFL. *Application deadline:* For fall admission, 8/15 priority date for domestic students; for winter admission, 12/15 for domestic students; for spring admission, 1/1 for domestic students. Applications are processed on a rolling basis. Application fee: $25. Electronic applications accepted. *Expenses:* Contact institution. *Financial support:* In 2010–11, 54 students received support, including 5 research assistantships with partial tuition reimbursements available (averaging $3,600 per year); career-related internships or fieldwork, scholarships/grants, tuition waivers (partial), and unspecified assistantships also available. Financial award application deadline: 3/15; financial award applicants required to submit FAFSA. *Unit head:* Dr. Linda K. Brown, MBA Director, 563-333-6343, Fax: 563-333-6243, E-mail: brownlindak@sau.edu. *Application contact:* Dr. Linda K. Brown, MBA Director, 563-333-6343, Fax: 563-333-6243, E-mail: brownlindak@sau.edu.

St. Bonaventure University, School of Graduate Studies, School of Business, St. Bonaventure, NY 14778-2284. Offers general business (MBA). *Accreditation:* AACSB. Part-time and evening/weekend programs available. *Faculty:* 22 full-time (5 women), 1 part-time/adjunct (0 women). *Students:* 76 full-time (30 women), 68 part-time (25 women); includes 8 minority (2 Black or African American, non-Hispanic/Latino; 2 American Indian or Alaska Native, non-Hispanic/Latino; 1 Asian, non-Hispanic/Latino; 2 Hispanic/Latino; 1 Native Hawaiian or other Pacific Islander, non-Hispanic/Latino), 7 international. Average age 31. 71 applicants, 96% accepted, 52 enrolled. In 2010, 102 master's awarded. *Entrance requirements:* For master's, GMAT, undergraduate degree, letters of recommendation. Additional exam requirements/recommendations for international students: Required—TOEFL (minimum score 550 paper-based; 213 computer-based). *Application deadline:* For fall admission, 3/15 priority date for domestic students, 2/1 priority date for international students; for spring admission, 10/1 priority date for domestic students, 7/1 priority date for international students. Applications are processed on a rolling basis. Application fee: $30. Electronic applications accepted. *Expenses:* Tuition: Part-time $670 per credit hour. *Financial support:* In 2010–11, 12 research assistantships with full and partial tuition reimbursements were awarded; career-related internships or fieldwork, Federal Work-Study, scholarships/grants, health care benefits, and unspecified assistantships also available. Support available to part-time students. Financial award application deadline: 4/15; financial award applicants required to submit FAFSA. *Unit head:* John B. Stevens, MBA Director, 716-375-7662, Fax: 716-375-2191, E-mail: jstevens@sbu.edu. *Application contact:* John B. Stevens, MBA Director, 716-375-7662, Fax: 716-375-2191, E-mail: jstevens@sbu.edu.

St. Edward's University, School of Management and Business, Austin, TX 78704. Offers M Ac, MA, MBA, MS, Certificate. Part-time and evening/weekend programs available. *Faculty:* 24 full-time (8 women), 30 part-time/adjunct (9 women). *Students:* 99 full-time (42 women), 396 part-time (198 women); includes 182 minority (33 Black or African American, non-Hispanic/Latino; 3 American Indian or Alaska Native, non-Hispanic/Latino; 14 Asian, non-Hispanic/Latino; 125 Hispanic/Latino; 1 Native Hawaiian or other Pacific Islander, non-Hispanic/Latino; 6 Two or more races, non-Hispanic/Latino), 15 international. Average age 33. 221 applicants, 78% accepted, 118 enrolled. In 2010, 183 master's awarded. *Degree requirements:* For master's, minimum of 24 hours in residence. *Entrance requirements:* For master's, GMAT or GRE General Test, minimum GPA of 2.75 in last 60 hours of course work. Additional exam requirements/recommendations for international students: Required—TOEFL (minimum score 550 paper-based; 213 computer-based; 79 iBT) or IELTS (minimum score 6). *Application deadline:* For fall admission, 7/1 for domestic and international students; for spring admission, 11/1 for domestic and international students. Applications are processed on a rolling basis. Application fee: $45 ($50 for international students). Electronic applications accepted. *Expenses:* Tuition: Full-time $16,200; part-time $900 per credit hour. Required fees: $50 per trimester. Full-time tuition and fees vary according to course load and program. *Financial support:* In 2010–11, 19 students received support. Scholarships/grants available. *Faculty research:* Ethics and corporate responsibility, spirituality and work, Asian (Eastern) ethics, new hire socialization, team performance, business

strategy, non-traditional marketing, social media, Birkman Method impact on college retention. *Unit head:* Marsha Kelliher, Dean, 512-448-8588, Fax: 512-448-8492, E-mail: marshak@stedwards.edu. *Application contact:* Kelly Luna, Graduate Admissions Coordinator, 512-233-1697, Fax: 512-428-1032, E-mail: kellyl@stedwards.edu.

Saint Francis University, Graduate School of Business and Human Resource Management, Loretto, PA 15940-0600. Offers business administration (MBA); human resource management (MHRM). Part-time and evening/weekend programs available. *Faculty:* 8 full-time (2 women), 25 part-time/adjunct (12 women). *Students:* 16 full-time (8 women), 141 part-time (66 women); includes 2 Black or African American, non-Hispanic/Latino. Average age 32. 40 applicants, 88% accepted, 25 enrolled. In 2010, 67 master's awarded. *Entrance requirements:* For master's, 2 letters of recommendation, minimum GPA of 2.75. Additional exam requirements/recommendations for international students: Required—TOEFL (minimum score 550 paper-based; 213 computer-based; 57 iBT). *Application deadline:* For fall admission, 8/1 priority date for domestic and international students; for spring admission, 12/1 priority date for domestic students, 12/1 for international students. Applications are processed on a rolling basis. Application fee: $30. *Expenses:* Contact institution. *Financial support:* Fellowships with partial tuition reimbursements, career-related internships or fieldwork and unspecified assistantships available. *Unit head:* Dr. Randy Frye, Director, 814-472-3041, Fax: 814-472-3174, E-mail: rfrye@francis.edu. *Application contact:* Dr. Peter Raymond Skoner, Associate Vice President for Academic Affairs, 814-472-3085, Fax: 814-472-3365, E-mail: pskoner@francis.edu.

St. John Fisher College, Ronald L. Bittner School of Business, MBA Program, Rochester, NY 14618-3597. Offers MBA. *Accreditation:* AACSB. Part-time and evening/weekend programs available. *Faculty:* 13 full-time (3 women), 5 part-time/adjunct (0 women). *Students:* 49 full-time (26 women), 90 part-time (49 women); includes 16 minority (4 Black or African American, non-Hispanic/Latino; 8 Asian, non-Hispanic/Latino; 2 Hispanic/Latino; 2 Two or more races, non-Hispanic/Latino). Average age 27. 105 applicants, 80% accepted, 59 enrolled. In 2010, 23 master's awarded. *Degree requirements:* For master's, capstone project. *Entrance requirements:* For master's, GMAT, 2 letters of recommendation, personal statement, current resume, interview. Additional exam requirements/recommendations for international students: Required—TOEFL (minimum score 575 paper-based; 233 computer-based; 80 iBT). *Application deadline:* Applications are processed on a rolling basis. Application fee: $30. Electronic applications accepted. *Expenses:* Tuition: Part-time $705 per credit hour. Required fees: $25 per semester. *Financial support:* In 2010–11, 77 students received support. Scholarships/grants available. Financial award applicants required to submit FAFSA. *Faculty research:* Business strategy, consumer behavior, cross-cultural management practices, international finance, organizational trust. *Unit head:* Lori Hollenbeck, Assistant Dean of the School of Business, 585-899-3707, Fax: 585-385-8094, E-mail: lhollenbeck@sjfc.edu. *Application contact:* Jose Perales, Director of Graduate Admissions, 585-385-8067, E-mail: jperales@sjfc.edu.

St. John's University, The Peter J. Tobin College of Business, Queens, NY 11439. Offers MBA, MS, Adv C, JD/MBA. *Accreditation:* AACSB. Part-time and evening/weekend programs available. *Faculty:* 94 full-time (22 women), 32 part-time/adjunct (5 women). *Students:* 629 full-time (337 women), 272 part-time (115 women); includes 202 minority (54 Black or African American, non-Hispanic/Latino; 1 American Indian or Alaska Native, non-Hispanic/Latino; 87 Asian, non-Hispanic/Latino; 49 Hispanic/Latino; 1 Native Hawaiian or other Pacific Islander, non-Hispanic/Latino; 10 Two or more races, non-Hispanic/Latino), 383 international. Average age 26. 1,105 applicants, 68% accepted, 384 enrolled. In 2010, 368 master's, 1 other advanced degree awarded. *Degree requirements:* For master's, comprehensive exam (for some programs), thesis optional. *Entrance requirements:* For master's, GMAT, 2 letters of recommendation, resume, statement of goals, minimum GPA of 3.0; for Adv C, GMAT, 2 letters of recommendation, resume, undergraduate transcripts, essay. Additional exam requirements/recommendations for international students: Required—TOEFL (minimum score 600 paper-based; 250 computer-based; 100 iBT), IELTS (minimum score 5.5). *Application deadline:* For fall admission, 5/1 priority date for domestic and international students; for spring admission, 11/1 priority date for domestic and international students. Applications are processed on a rolling basis. Application fee: $70. Electronic applications accepted. *Expenses:* Contact institution. *Financial support:* In 2010–11, 214 students received support, including 1 fellowship (averaging $23,115 per year), 55 research assistantships with full and partial tuition reimbursements available (averaging $16,637 per year), 2 teaching assistantships (averaging $11,870 per year); scholarships/grants also available. Support available to part-time students. Financial award application deadline: 3/1; financial award applicants required to submit FAFSA. *Unit head:* Dr. Victoria Shoaf, Dean, 718-990-6458, E-mail: shoafv@stjohns.edu. *Application contact:* Carol Swanberg, Assistant Dean, Director of grad Admissions, 718-990-1345, Fax: 718-990-5242, E-mail: tobingradnyc@stjohns.edu.

Saint Joseph College, Department of Business, West Hartford, CT 06117-2700. Offers management (MS). Part-time and evening/weekend programs available. *Students:* 28 full-time (25 women), 30 part-time (22 women); includes 9 Black or African American, non-Hispanic/Latino; 2 Asian, non-Hispanic/Latino; 4 Hispanic/Latino; 1 Two or more races, non-Hispanic/Latino,

1 international. *Entrance requirements:* For master's, 2 letters of recommendation. *Application deadline:* Applications are processed on a rolling basis. Application fee: $50. Electronic applications accepted. *Expenses:* Tuition: Full-time $11,340; part-time $630 per credit. Required fees: $540; $30 per credit. Tuition and fees vary according to course load, campus/location and program. *Financial support:* Career-related internships or fieldwork and unspecified assistantships available. Support available to part-time students. Financial award applicants required to submit FAFSA. *Application contact:* Graduate Admissions Assistant, 860-231-5261, E-mail: graduate@sjc.edu.

Saint Joseph's University, Erivan K. Haub School of Business, Philadelphia, PA 19131-1395. Offers MBA, MS, Post Master's Certificate, DO/MBA. *Accreditation:* AACSB. Part-time and evening/weekend programs available. Postbaccalaureate distance learning degree programs offered (no on-campus study). *Faculty:* 75 full-time (12 women), 41 part-time/adjunct (10 women). *Students:* 181 full-time (101 women), 932 part-time (374 women); includes 182 minority (90 Black or African American, non-Hispanic/Latino; 1 American Indian or Alaska Native, non-Hispanic/Latino; 59 Asian, non-Hispanic/Latino; 25 Hispanic/Latino; 1 Native Hawaiian or other Pacific Islander, non-Hispanic/Latino; 6 Two or more races, non-Hispanic/Latino), 111 international. Average age 32. In 2010, 307 master's awarded. *Entrance requirements:* For master's, GMAT, MAT, GRE, letters of recommendation, resume. Additional exam requirements/recommendations for international students: Required—TOEFL (minimum score: paper 550, computer 213, iBT 79) or IELTS (6.5), Pearson Test of English (minimum 60). *Application deadline:* For fall admission, 7/15 priority date for domestic students, 4/15 priority date for international students; for spring admission, 11/15 priority date for domestic students, 10/15 priority date for international students. Applications are processed on a rolling basis. Application fee: $35. Electronic applications accepted. *Expenses:* Tuition: Part-time $729 per credit. Tuition and fees vary according to course load, degree level and program. *Financial support:* In 2010–11, research assistantships with full and partial tuition reimbursements (averaging $4,000 per year), teaching assistantships with full and partial tuition reimbursements (averaging $4,000 per year) were awarded; fellowships, scholarships/grants and unspecified assistantships also available. Financial award application deadline: 5/1; financial award applicants required to submit FAFSA. *Faculty research:* Food marketing, agriculture, finance and accounting systems, advertising cues and effects. Total annual research expenditures: $598,365. *Unit head:* Dr. Joseph A. DiAngelo, Dean, 610-660-1645, Fax: 610-660-1649, E-mail: jodiange@sju.edu. *Application contact:* Janine N. Guerra, Assistant Director, MBA Program, 610-660-1695, Fax: 610-660-1599, E-mail: jguerra@sju.edu.

Saint Leo University, Graduate Business Studies, Saint Leo, FL 33574-6665. Offers accounting (MBA); business (MBA); health services management (MBA); human resource management (MBA); information security management (MBA); marketing (MBA); sport business (MBA). Part-time and evening/weekend programs available. Postbaccalaureate distance learning degree programs offered (no on-campus study). *Faculty:* 32 full-time (4 women), 53 part-time/adjunct (21 women). *Students:* 1,498 full-time (890 women), 10 part-time (6 women); includes 593 minority (465 Black or African American, non-Hispanic/Latino; 5 American Indian or Alaska Native, non-Hispanic/Latino; 23 Asian, non-Hispanic/Latino; 84 Hispanic/Latino; 2 Native Hawaiian or other Pacific Islander, non-Hispanic/Latino; 14 Two or more races, non-Hispanic/Latino), 14 international. Average age 38. In 2010, 557 master's awarded. *Entrance requirements:* For master's, GMAT (minimum score 500 if applicant does not have 5 years of professional work experience), bachelor's degree from regionally-accredited college or university with minimum GPA of 3.0 in the last 60 hours of coursework; 5 years of professional work experience; resume; 2 letters of recommendation. Additional exam requirements/recommendations for international students: Required—TOEFL (minimum score 550 paper-based; 213 computer-based; 80 iBT). *Application deadline:* For fall admission, 7/1 priority date for domestic and international students; for spring admission, 11/12 priority date for domestic students, 11/1 for international students. Applications are processed on a rolling basis. Application fee: $75. Electronic applications accepted. *Expenses:* Contact institution. *Financial support:* In 2010–11, 51 students received support. Career-related internships or fieldwork, Federal Work-Study, scholarships/grants, and health care benefits available. Financial award application deadline: 3/1; financial award applicants required to submit FAFSA. *Unit head:* Dr. Lorrie McGovern, Director, 352-588-7390, Fax: 352-588-8585, E-mail: mbaslu@saintleo.edu. *Application contact:* Jared Welling, Director, Graduate/Weekend and Evening Admission, 800-707-8846, Fax: 352-588-7873, E-mail: grad.admissions@saintleo.edu.

Saint Martin's University, Graduate Programs, School of Business, Lacey, WA 98503. Offers MBA. Part-time and evening/weekend programs available. *Faculty:* 5 full-time (0 women), 5 part-time/adjunct (0 women). *Students:* 45 full-time (29 women), 29 part-time (18 women); includes 8 Black or African American, non-Hispanic/Latino; 1 American Indian or Alaska Native, non-Hispanic/Latino; 6 Asian, non-Hispanic/Latino; 1 Hispanic/Latino; 2 Native Hawaiian or other Pacific Islander, non-Hispanic/Latino, 12 international. Average age 33. 34 applicants, 94% accepted, 28 enrolled. In 2010, 21 master's awarded. *Degree requirements:* For master's, thesis (for some programs). *Entrance requirements:* For master's, GMAT. Additional exam requirements/

recommendations for international students: Required—TOEFL (minimum score 525 paper-based; 197 computer-based; 71 iBT). *Application deadline:* Applications are processed on a rolling basis. Application fee: $35. *Financial support:* In 2010–11, 29 students received support. Career-related internships or fieldwork and scholarships/grants available. Support available to part-time students. Financial award application deadline: 3/1; financial award applicants required to submit FAFSA. *Unit head:* Dr. Heather Grob, Director, 360-438-4292, Fax: 360-438-4522, E-mail: hgrob@stmartin.edu. *Application contact:* Keri Olsen, Administrative Assistant, 360-438-4512, Fax: 360-438-4522, E-mail: kolsen@stmartin.edu.

Saint Mary's College of California, Graduate Business Programs, Evening MBA Program, Moraga, CA 94556. Offers MBA. Part-time and evening/weekend programs available. *Faculty:* 3 full-time (2 women), 6 part-time/adjunct (0 women). *Students:* 75 full-time (35 women), 36 part-time (13 women); includes 26 minority (4 Black or African American, non-Hispanic/Latino; 10 Asian, non-Hispanic/Latino; 12 Hispanic/Latino), 1 international. Average age 29. 32 applicants, 78% accepted, 21 enrolled. In 2010, 33 master's awarded. *Degree requirements:* For master's, 4 half-day management practica. *Entrance requirements:* For master's, GMAT. Additional exam requirements/recommendations for international students: Required—TOEFL. *Application deadline:* Applications are processed on a rolling basis. Application fee: $50. *Expenses:* Contact institution. *Financial support:* Available to part-time students. Application deadline: 3/2. *Application contact:* Bob Peterson, Director of Admissions, 925-631-4505, Fax: 925-376-6521, E-mail: smcmba@stmarys-ca.edu.

Saint Mary's College of California, Graduate Business Programs, Executive MBA Program, Moraga, CA 94556. Offers MBA. Part-time and evening/weekend programs available. Postbaccalaureate distance learning degree programs offered (minimal on-campus study). *Students:* 190 full-time (64 women), 1 part-time (0 women); includes 50 minority (9 Black or African American, non-Hispanic/Latino; 23 Asian, non-Hispanic/Latino; 18 Hispanic/Latino), 1 international. Average age 38. In 2010, 118 master's awarded. *Entrance requirements:* For master's, 5 years of management experience. Additional exam requirements/recommendations for international students: Required—TOEFL (minimum score 91 computer-based). *Application deadline:* Applications are processed on a rolling basis. Application fee: $50. *Expenses:* Contact institution. *Financial support:* Available to part-time students. Applicants required to submit FAFSA. *Unit head:* Dr. Guido Krickx, Program Director, 925-631-4514, Fax: 925-376-6521, E-mail: gak1@stmarys-ca.edu. *Application contact:* Bob Peterson, Director of Admissions, 925-631-4504, Fax: 925-376-6521, E-mail: bpeterso@stmarys-ca.edu.

Saint Mary's College of California, School of Liberal Arts, Leadership Studies Programs, Moraga, CA 94556. Offers MA. Part-time and evening/weekend programs available. Postbaccalaureate distance learning degree programs offered (minimal on-campus study). *Faculty:* 5 full-time (2 women), 12 part-time/adjunct (9 women). *Students:* 13 full-time (7 women), 43 part-time (25 women); includes 11 Black or African American, non-Hispanic/Latino; 8 Asian, non-Hispanic/Latino; 12 Hispanic/Latino. Average age 39. In 2010, 36 master's awarded. *Degree requirements:* For master's, research project. *Entrance requirements:* For master's, letters of recommendation, interview. *Application deadline:* For fall admission, 8/1 priority date for domestic students; for winter admission, 12/1 priority date for domestic students; for spring admission, 3/31 priority date for domestic students. Applications are processed on a rolling basis. Application fee: $50. Electronic applications accepted. *Expenses:* Contact institution. *Financial support:* Available to part-time students. Applicants required to submit FAFSA. *Faculty research:* Leadership, organizational change, values, adult learning, transformative learning. *Unit head:* Kenneth Otter, Program Director, 925-631-8692, Fax: 925-631-9214, E-mail: kotter@stmarys-ca.edu. *Application contact:* Tammy Cabading, Manager, Marketing and Admissions, 925-631-4541, Fax: 925-631-9214, E-mail: tappling@stmarys-ca.edu.

Saint Mary's University of Minnesota, Schools of Graduate and Professional Programs, Graduate School of Business and Technology, Business Administration Program, Winona, MN 55987-1399. Offers MBA. *Unit head:* Matthew Nowakowski, Director, 612-728-5142, Fax: 612-728-5121, E-mail: mjnowa05@smumn.edu. *Application contact:* Yasin Alsaidi, Director of Admissions for Graduate and Professional Programs, 612-728-5207, Fax: 612-728-5121, E-mail: yalsaidi@smumn.edu.

Saint Mary's University of Minnesota, Schools of Graduate and Professional Programs, Graduate School of Business and Technology, Management Program, Winona, MN 55987-1399. Offers MA. *Unit head:* Janet Dunn, Director, 612-238-4546, E-mail: jdunn@smumn.edu. *Application contact:* Yasin Alsaidi, Director of Admissions for Graduate and Professional Programs, 612-728-5207, Fax: 612-728-5121, E-mail: yalsaidi@smumn.edu.

Saint Peter's College, Graduate Business Programs, MBA Program, Jersey City, NJ 07306-5997. Offers finance (MBA); health care administration (MBA); human resource management (MBA); international business (MBA); management (MBA); management information systems (MBA); marketing (MBA); risk management (MBA); MBA/MS. Part-time and evening/weekend programs available. *Students:* 108 applicants, 81% accepted, 62 enrolled. *Entrance requirements:* Additional exam requirements/recommendations for international students: Required—TOEFL (minimum score 79 computer-based). *Application deadline:* Applications are processed on a rolling basis. Electronic applications accepted. *Financial support:* Career-related internships or fieldwork, Federal Work-Study, and institutionally sponsored loans available. Financial award applicants required to submit FAFSA. *Faculty research:* Finance, health care management, human resource management, international business, management, management information systems, marketing, risk management. *Application contact:* Stephanie Autenrieth, Director, Graduate and Professional Studies Admission, 201-761-6474, Fax: 201-435-5270, E-mail: sautenrieth@spc.edu.

Salem State University, School of Graduate Studies, Program in Business Administration, Salem, MA 01970-5353. Offers MBA. Part-time and evening/weekend programs available. *Students:* 16 full-time (9 women), 45 part-time (28 women); includes 3 Black or African American, non-Hispanic/Latino; 3 Asian, non-Hispanic/Latino; 1 Two or more races, non-Hispanic/Latino, 10 international. Average age 32. 20 applicants, 50% accepted, 10 enrolled. In 2010, 21 master's awarded. *Entrance requirements:* For master's, GMAT. Additional exam requirements/recommendations for international students: Required—TOEFL (minimum score 550 paper-based; 80 iBT) or IELTS (minimum score 5.5). *Application deadline:* For fall admission, 5/1 for domestic students; for spring admission, 11/1 for domestic students. Applications are processed on a rolling basis. Application fee: $50. *Expenses:* Tuition, state resident: full-time $2520; part-time $290 per credit hour. Tuition, nonresident: full-time $4140; part-time $380 per credit hour. Required fees: $2700. *Financial support:* Career-related internships or fieldwork, Federal Work-Study, scholarships/grants, and unspecified assistantships available. Support available to part-time students. Financial award application deadline: 5/1; financial award applicants required to submit FAFSA. *Unit head:* Raminder Luther, Coordinator, 978-542-2229, E-mail: rluther@salemstate.edu. *Application contact:* Dr. Lee A. Brossoit, Assistant Dean of Graduate Admissions, 978-542-6673, Fax: 978-542-7215, E-mail: lbrossoit@salemstate.edu.

Salisbury University, Graduate Division, Department of Business Administration, Salisbury, MD 21801. Offers accounting track (MBA); general track (MBA). *Accreditation:* AACSB. Part-time and evening/weekend programs available. *Faculty:* 13 full-time (3 women), 1 part-time/adjunct (0 women). *Students:* 22 full-time (8 women), 42 part-time (16 women); includes 4 minority (1 Black or African American, non-Hispanic/Latino; 1 Asian, non-Hispanic/Latino; 2 Two or more races, non-Hispanic/Latino), 7 international. Average age 29. 59 applicants, 46% accepted, 26 enrolled. In 2010, 32 master's awarded. *Entrance requirements:* For master's, GMAT, resume; 2 recommendations. Additional exam requirements/recommendations for international students: Required—TOEFL (minimum score 550 paper-based; 213 computer-based; 79 iBT). *Application deadline:* For fall admission, 3/1 priority date for domestic students; for spring admission, 10/15 priority date for domestic students. Applications are processed on a rolling basis. Application fee: $45. Electronic applications accepted. *Financial support:* In 2010–11, 13 students received support. Institutionally sponsored loans, scholarships/grants, and unspecified assistantships available. Support available to part-time students. Financial award applicants required to submit FAFSA. *Unit head:* Yvonne Downie, MBA Director, 410-548-3983, Fax: 410-546-6208, E-mail: yxdownie@salisbury.edu. *Application contact:* Yvonne Downie, MBA Director, 410-548-3983, Fax: 410-546-6208, E-mail: yxdownie@salisbury.edu.

Samford University, Brock School of Business, Birmingham, AL 35229. Offers M Acc, MBA, JD/M Acc, JD/MBA, M Div/MBA, MBA/M Acc, MBA/MSN. *Accreditation:* AACSB. Part-time and evening/weekend programs available. *Faculty:* 12 full-time (3 women). *Students:* 88 full-time (36 women), 21 part-time (7 women); includes 13 minority (9 Black or African American, non-Hispanic/Latino; 3 Asian, non-Hispanic/Latino; 1 Two or more races, non-Hispanic/Latino), 3 international. Average age 27. 109 applicants, 69% accepted, 66 enrolled. In 2010, 66 master's awarded. *Entrance requirements:* For master's, GMAT. Additional exam requirements/recommendations for international students: Recommended—TOEFL (minimum score 550 paper-based; 213 computer-based). *Application deadline:* For fall admission, 7/31 priority date for domestic students, 6/1 for international students; for spring admission, 12/1 priority date for domestic students, 10/1 for international students. Applications are processed on a rolling basis. Application fee: $25. *Expenses:* Tuition: Part-time $622 per credit. Required fees: $110 per semester. *Financial support:* In 2010–11, 32 students received support. Career-related internships or fieldwork, institutionally sponsored loans, scholarships/grants, and tuition waivers (partial) available. Support available to part-time students. Financial award applicants required to submit FAFSA. *Faculty research:* Entrepreneurship, accounting, finance, organizational behavior, leadership. *Unit head:* Dr. Jim Reburn, Acting Dean, 205-726-2364, Fax: 205-726-2464, E-mail: jpreburn@samford.edu. *Application contact:* Larron Harper, Director of Graduate Programs, 205-726-2931, Fax: 205-726-4555, E-mail: lcharper@samford.edu.

Sam Houston State University, College of Business Administration, Huntsville, TX 77341. Offers accounting (MS); business administration (MBA); general business and finance (MS), including finance. *Accreditation:* AACSB. Part-time and evening/weekend programs available. *Faculty:* 31 full-time (8 women). *Students:* 146 full-time (63 women), 150 part-time (71 women); includes 20 Black or African American, non-Hispanic/Latino; 2 American Indian or Alaska Native, non-Hispanic/Latino; 8 Asian, non-Hispanic/Latino; 24 Hispanic/Latino, 29 international. Average age 29. 141 applicants, 83% accepted, 78 enrolled. In 2010, 97 master's awarded. *Entrance requirements:* For master's, GMAT. Additional exam requirements/recommendations for international students: Required—TOEFL (minimum score 550 paper-based; 213 computer-based; 79 iBT). *Application deadline:* For fall admission, 8/1 for domestic students; for spring admission, 12/1 for domestic students. Applications are processed on a rolling basis. Application fee: $20. *Expenses:* Tuition, state resident: full-time $1363; part-time $163 per credit hour. Tuition, nonresident: full-time $3856; part-time $473 per credit hour. *Financial support:* Research assistantships, Federal Work-Study, institutionally sponsored loans, and unspecified assistantships available. Financial award application deadline: 5/31; financial award applicants required to submit FAFSA. *Unit head:* Dr. Mitchell J. Muehsam, Dean, 936-294-1254, Fax: 936-294-3612, E-mail: mmuehsam@shsu.edu. *Application contact:* Dr. Leroy Ashorn, Advisor, 936-294-1246, Fax: 936-294-3612, E-mail: busgrad@shsu.edu.

San Francisco State University, Division of Graduate Studies, College of Business, San Francisco, CA 94132-1722. Offers accountancy (MSA); business administration (MBA). *Unit head:* Dr. Caran Colvin, Dean, 415-405-3752. *Application contact:* Armaan Moattari, Assistant Director, Graduate Programs, 415-817-4314, E-mail: amoatt@sfsu.edu.

Santa Clara University, Leavey School of Business, Program in Business Administration, Santa Clara, CA 95053. Offers accounting (MBA); entrepreneurship (MBA); executive business administration (EMBA); finance (MBA); food and agribusiness (MBA); international business (MBA); leading people and organizations (MBA); managing technology and innovation (MBA); marketing management (MBA); supply chain management (MBA). *Accreditation:* AACSB. Part-time and evening/weekend programs available. *Students:* 229 full-time (80 women), 748 part-time (244 women); includes 354 minority (14 Black or African American, non-Hispanic/Latino; 1 American Indian or Alaska Native, non-Hispanic/Latino; 287 Asian, non-Hispanic/Latino; 42 Hispanic/Latino; 5 Native Hawaiian or other Pacific Islander, non-Hispanic/Latino; 5 Two or more races, non-Hispanic/Latino), 209 international. Average age 32. 334 applicants, 76% accepted, 191 enrolled. In 2010, 307 master's awarded. *Degree requirements:* For master's, thesis or alternative. *Entrance requirements:* For master's, GMAT, GRE. Additional exam requirements/recommendations for international students: Required—TOEFL (minimum score 600 paper-based; 250 computer-based; 100 iBT). *Application deadline:* For fall admission, 6/1 for domestic and international students; for spring admission, 1/19 for domestic students, 1/17 for international students. Applications are processed on a rolling basis. Application fee: $75 ($100 for international students). Electronic applications accepted. *Expenses:* Contact institution. *Financial support:* In 2010–11, 350 students received support; fellowships with partial tuition reimbursements available, research assistantships with partial tuition reimbursements available, career-related internships or fieldwork, Federal Work-Study, institutionally sponsored loans, scholarships/grants, health care benefits, and unspecified assistantships available. Support available to part-time students. Financial award application deadline: 6/1; financial award applicants required to submit FAFSA. *Unit head:* Elizabeth B. Ford, Senior Assistant Dean, 408-554-2752, Fax: 408-554-4571, E-mail: eford@scu.edu. *Application contact:* Molly Mulally, Assistant Director, Graduate Business Admissions, 408-554-4539, Fax: 408-554-4571, E-mail: mbaadmissions@scu.edu.

Savannah State University, Master of Business Administration Program, Savannah, GA 31404. Offers MBA. *Accreditation:* AACSB. Part-time programs available. *Students:* 11 full-time (6 women), 8 part-time (6 women); includes 16 Black or African American, non-Hispanic/Latino, 2 international. Average age 28. In 2010, 8 master's awarded. *Entrance requirements:* For master's, GMAT or GRE. Additional exam requirements/recommendations for international students: Required—TOEFL. *Application deadline:* For fall admission, 7/1 for domestic students, 5/15 for international students; for spring admission, 10/31 for domestic students, 10/1 for international students. Applications are processed on a rolling basis. Application fee: $25. Electronic applications accepted. *Expenses:* Tuition, state resident: full-time $4042. Tuition, nonresident: full-time $15,028. Required fees: $1350. *Financial support:* Career-related internships or fieldwork, Federal Work-Study, institutionally sponsored loans, scholarships/grants, and unspecified assistantships available. Financial award applicants required to submit FAFSA. *Unit head:* Dr. Mostafa Sarhan, Dean, 912-358-3388, E-mail: sarhanm@savannahstate.edu. *Application contact:* Emily Crawford, Interim Dean of Graduate Studies, 912-358-4183, E-mail: crawford@savannahstate.edu.

Seattle Pacific University, Master's Degree in Business Administration (MBA) Program, Seattle, WA 98119-1997. Offers MBA. *Accreditation:* AACSB. Part-time programs available. *Faculty:* 15 full-time (5 women), 1 part-time/adjunct (0 women). *Students:* 17 full-time (6 women), 80 part-time (31 women); includes 24 minority (3 Black or African American, non-Hispanic/Latino; 18 Asian, non-Hispanic/Latino; 2 Hispanic/Latino; 1 Two or more races, non-Hispanic/Latino), 15 international. Average age 31. 42 applicants, 26% accepted, 11 enrolled. In 2010, 38 master's awarded. *Entrance requirements:* For master's, GMAT, minimum GPA of 3.0. Additional exam requirements/recommendations for international students: Required—TOEFL (minimum score 225 computer-based). *Application deadline:* For fall admission, 8/1 for domestic and international students; for winter admission, 11/1 for domestic and international students; for spring admission, 2/1 for domestic and international students. Applications are processed on a rolling basis. Application fee: $50. Electronic applications accepted. *Financial support:* In 2010–11, 28 students received support. Scholarships/grants available. Financial award applicants required to submit FAFSA. *Unit head:* Gary Karns, Associate Dean for Graduate Studies, 206-281-2948, Fax: 206-281-2733. *Application contact:* Gary Karns, Associate Dean for Graduate Studies, 206-281-2948, Fax: 206-281-2733.

Seton Hall University, Stillman School of Business, South Orange, NJ 07079-2697. Offers MBA, MS, Certificate. *Accreditation:* AACSB. Part-time and evening/weekend programs available. *Faculty:* 35 full-time (8 women), 11 part-time/adjunct (1 woman). *Students:* 93 full-time (33 women), 165 part-time (76 women); includes 26 Black or African American, non-Hispanic/Latino; 39 Asian, non-Hispanic/Latino; 8 Hispanic/Latino. Average age 28. 404 applicants, 74% accepted, 258 enrolled. In 2010, 203 master's awarded. *Entrance requirements:* For master's, GMAT, Advanced degrees such as JD, MD, DVM, DDS, PharmD MBA from AACSB institution, MS in a business discipline, minimum GPA of 3.0. Additional exam requirements/recommendations for international students: Required—TOEFL (minimum: 607 paper, 254 computer, 102 iBT), IELTS or Pearson Test of English (PTE). *Application deadline:* For fall admission, 5/31 priority date for domestic students, 3/31 priority date for international students; for spring admission, 10/31 priority date for domestic students, 9/30 priority date for international students. Applications are processed on a rolling basis. Application fee: $75. Electronic applications accepted. *Expenses:* Contact institution. *Financial support:* In 2010–11, 16 students received support, including research assistantships with full tuition reimbursements available (averaging $34,404 per year); career-related internships or fieldwork, Federal Work-Study, scholarships/grants, and unspecified assistantships also available. Support available to part-time students. Financial award application deadline: 6/30; financial award applicants required to submit FAFSA. *Faculty research:* Financial, hedge funds, international business, legal issues, disclosure and branding. Total annual research expenditures: $500,000. *Unit head:* Dr. Joyce Strawser, Acting Dean, 973-761-9013, Fax: 973-275-2465, E-mail: joyce.strawser@shu.edu. *Application contact:* Catherine Bianchi, Director of Graduate Admissions, 973-761-9262, Fax: 973-761-9208, E-mail: catherine.bianchi@shu.edu.

Seton Hill University, Program in Business Administration, Greensburg, PA 15601. Offers entrepreneurship (MBA, Certificate); management (MBA). Part-time and evening/weekend programs available. *Faculty:* 5 full-time (3 women), 6 part-time/adjunct (0 women). *Students:* 25 full-time (14 women), 48 part-time (22 women); includes 6 minority (3 Black or African American, non-Hispanic/Latino; 1 American Indian or Alaska Native, non-Hispanic/Latino; 1 Asian, non-Hispanic/Latino; 1 Hispanic/Latino), 1 international. Average age 32. 107 applicants, 38% accepted, 31 enrolled. In 2010, 50 degrees awarded. *Entrance requirements:* For master's, resume, minimum GPA of 3.0, completion of prerequisite courses in statistics. Additional exam requirements/recommendations for international students: Required—TOEFL (minimum score 600 paper-based; 250 computer-based). *Application deadline:* For fall admission, 8/15 priority date for domestic students; for spring admission, 12/15 for domestic students. Applications are processed on a rolling basis. Application fee: $35. Electronic applications accepted. *Expenses:* Tuition: Full-time $13,050; part-time $725 per credit. Required fees: $700; $34 per credit. $50 per semester. Tuition and fees vary according to course load and program. *Financial support:* Federal Work-Study, scholarships/grants, tuition waivers (partial), and unspecified assistantships available. Support available to part-time students. Financial award application deadline: 8/15; financial award applicants required to submit FAFSA. *Faculty research:* Entrepreneurship, leadership and strategy, knowledge management. *Unit head:* Dr. Douglas Nelson, Director, 724-830-4738, E-mail: dnelson@setonhill.edu. *Application contact:* Laurel Komarny, Program Counselor, 724-838-4209, Fax: 724-830-1891, E-mail: lkomarny@setonhill.edu.

Shenandoah University, Byrd School of Business, Winchester, VA 22601-5195. Offers business administration (MBA); business administration essentials (Certificate). *Accreditation:* AACSB. Part-time and evening/weekend programs available. *Faculty:* 11 full-time (1 woman), 1 part-time/adjunct (0 women). *Students:* 47 full-time (26 women), 22 part-time (9 women); includes 7 minority (4 Black or African American, non-Hispanic/Latino; 2 American Indian or Alaska Native, non-Hispanic/Latino; 1 Asian, non-Hispanic/Latino), 29 international. Average age 30. 112 applicants, 43% accepted, 25 enrolled. In 2010, 35 master's, 7 other advanced degrees awarded. *Entrance requirements:* For master's and Certificate, 2 letters of recommendation, resume, interview, brief narrative. Additional exam requirements/recommendations for international students: Required—TOEFL (minimum score 550 paper-based; 213 computer-based; 79 iBT), IELTS (minimum score 6.5), Sakae Institute of Study Abroad (550). *Application deadline:* Applications are processed on a rolling basis. Application fee: $30. Electronic applications accepted. *Expenses:* Tuition: Full-time $17,352; part-time $723 per credit. Tuition and fees vary according to course load and program. *Financial support:* Career-related internships or fieldwork, institutionally sponsored loans, and unspecified

assistantships available. Support available to part-time students. Financial award application deadline: 3/15; financial award applicants required to submit FAFSA. *Unit head:* Dr. Randy Boxx, Dean, 540-665-4572, Fax: 540-665-5437, E-mail: rboxx@su.edu. *Application contact:* David Anthony, Dean of Admissions, 540-665-4581, Fax: 540-665-4627, E-mail: admit@su.edu.

Shippensburg University of Pennsylvania, School of Graduate Studies, College of Arts and Sciences, Department of Sociology and Anthropology, Shippensburg, PA 17257-2299. Offers organizational development and leadership (MS), including business, communications, education, environmental management, higher education, historical administration, individual and organizational development, public organizations, social structures and organizations. Part-time and evening/weekend programs available. *Faculty:* 3 full-time (all women). *Students:* 18 full-time (13 women), 46 part-time (33 women); includes 11 minority (6 Black or African American, non-Hispanic/Latino; 3 Asian, non-Hispanic/Latino; 2 Two or more races, non-Hispanic/Latino), 2 international. Average age 32. 56 applicants, 55% accepted, 20 enrolled. In 2010, 28 master's awarded. *Degree requirements:* For master's, capstone experience including internship. *Entrance requirements:* For master's, interview (if GPA less than 2.75), resume, personal goals statement. Additional exam requirements/recommendations for international students: Required—TOEFL (minimum score 580 paper-based; 237 computer-based); Recommended—IELTS (minimum score 6). *Application deadline:* For fall admission, 3/1 for international students; for spring admission, 7/1 for international students. Applications are processed on a rolling basis. Application fee: $30. Electronic applications accepted. *Expenses:* Tuition, state resident: full-time $6966. Tuition, nonresident: full-time $11,146. Required fees: $1802. *Financial support:* In 2010–11, 8 research assistantships with full tuition reimbursements (averaging $5,000 per year) were awarded; career-related internships or fieldwork, scholarships/grants, unspecified assistantships, and resident hall director and student payroll positions also available. Support available to part-time students. Financial award applicants required to submit FAFSA. *Unit head:* Dr. Barbara Denison, Chairperson, 717-477-1735, Fax: 717-477-4011, E-mail: bjdeni@ship.edu. *Application contact:* Jeremy R. Goshorn, Associate Dean of Graduate Admissions, 717-477-1231, Fax: 717-477-4016, E-mail: jrgoshorn@ship.edu.

Shippensburg University of Pennsylvania, School of Graduate Studies, John L. Grove College of Business, Shippensburg, PA 17257-2299. Offers advanced studies in business (Certificate); business administration (MBA). *Accreditation:* AACSB. Part-time and evening/weekend programs available. Postbaccalaureate distance learning degree programs offered (minimal on-campus study). *Faculty:* 20 full-time (11 women), 1 (woman) part-time/adjunct. *Students:* 11 full-time (5 women), 106 part-time (40 women); includes 10 minority (4 Black or African American, non-Hispanic/Latino; 1 American Indian or Alaska Native, non-Hispanic/Latino; 4 Asian, non-Hispanic/Latino; 1 Hispanic/Latino), 1 international. Average age 32. 132 applicants, 43% accepted, 36 enrolled. In 2010, 58 master's awarded. *Entrance requirements:* For master's, GMAT (minimum score 450 if less than 5 years post-graduate experience, including some mid-level management), resume; relevant work/classroom experience; personal goals statement; prerequisites of quantitative analysis, computer usage, oral and written communications; laptop. Additional exam requirements/recommendations for international students: Required—TOEFL (minimum score 580 paper-based; 237 computer-based); Recommended—IELTS (minimum score 6). *Application deadline:* For fall admission, 3/1 for international students; for spring admission, 7/1 for international students. Applications are processed on a rolling basis. Application fee: $30. Electronic applications accepted. *Expenses:* Tuition, state resident: full-time $6966. Tuition, nonresident: full-time $11,146. Required fees: $1802. *Financial support:* In 2010–11, 7 research assistantships with full tuition reimbursements (averaging $5,000 per year) were awarded; career-related internships or fieldwork, scholarships/grants, unspecified assistantships, and resident hall director and student payroll positions also available. Support available to part-time students. Financial award application deadline: 3/1; financial award applicants required to submit FAFSA. *Unit head:* Dr. Robert Stephens, Director of MBA Program, 717-477-1684, Fax: 717-477-4003, E-mail: rdstep@ship.edu. *Application contact:* Jeremy R. Goshorn, Associate Dean of Graduate Admissions, 717-477-1231, Fax: 717-477-4016, E-mail: jrgoshorn@ship.edu.

Shorter University, Professional Studies, Rome, GA 30165. Offers accountancy (MAC); business administration (MBA); curriculum and instruction (M Ed); leadership (MA). Evening/weekend programs available. *Faculty:* 9 full-time (3 women), 25 part-time/adjunct (9 women). *Students:* 330 full-time (212 women); includes 168 Black or African American, non-Hispanic/Latino; 5 American Indian or Alaska Native, non-Hispanic/Latino; 4 Asian, non-Hispanic/Latino; 5 Hispanic/Latino, 3 international. Average age 39. In 2010, 177 master's awarded. *Degree requirements:* For master's, project. *Entrance requirements:* For master's, minimum undergraduate GPA of 2.75 in last 60 hours, 3 years of work experience. Additional exam requirements/recommendations for international students: Required—TOEFL (minimum score 550 paper-based; 213 computer-based; 79 iBT). *Application deadline:* Applications are processed on a rolling basis. Application fee: $50. *Expenses:* Tuition: Full-time $9840. Required fees: $360. One-time fee: $225 full-time. Tuition and fees vary according to course load and program. *Financial *support:* Institutionally sponsored loans and scholarships/grants available. Financial award applicants required to submit FAFSA. *Faculty research:* Systems design, leadership, pedagogy using technology. *Unit head:* Jacqueline Avant, Dean of Students, 678-260-3538, E-mail: javant@shorter.edu. *Application contact:* Irene Barassa, Admissions Specialist, 678-260-3531, E-mail: ibarassa@shorter.edu.

Silver Lake College, Division of Graduate Studies, Program in Management and Organizational Behavior, Manitowoc, WI 54220-9319. Offers MS. Part-time and evening/weekend programs available. Postbaccalaureate distance learning degree programs offered (minimal on-campus study). *Faculty:* 27 part-time/adjunct (14 women). *Students:* 15 full-time (13 women), 52 part-time (31 women); includes 7 minority (6 American Indian or Alaska Native, non-Hispanic/Latino; 1 Asian, non-Hispanic/Latino). Average age 38. 33 applicants, 94% accepted, 18 enrolled. In 2010, 39 master's awarded. *Degree requirements:* For master's, thesis optional. *Entrance requirements:* For master's, minimum undergraduate GPA of 3.0, statement of purpose, three letters of recommendation, professional resume. Additional exam requirements/recommendations for international students: Required—TOEFL. *Application deadline:* For fall admission, 8/1 priority date for domestic students; for spring admission, 12/1 priority date for domestic students. Applications are processed on a rolling basis. Application fee: $0. Electronic applications accepted. *Expenses:* Tuition: Part-time $425 per credit. Required fees: $10 per semester. *Financial support:* Career-related internships or fieldwork, Federal Work-Study, and scholarships/grants available. Support available to part-time students. Financial award application deadline: 6/30; financial award applicants required to submit FAFSA. *Unit head:* Suzanne M. Lawrence, Director, 920-686-6198, Fax: 920-684-7082, E-mail: law@silver.sl.edu. *Application contact:* Cindy St. John, Interim Director of Admissions, 800-236-4752 Ext. 350, Fax: 920-686-6350, E-mail: cynthia.st.john@sl.edu.

Sonoma State University, School of Business and Economics, Rohnert Park, CA 94928. Offers MBA. *Accreditation:* AACSB. Part-time and evening/weekend programs available. *Faculty:* 6 full-time (2 women). *Students:* 7 full-time (6 women), 37 part-time (19 women); includes 1 American Indian or Alaska Native, non-Hispanic/Latino; 1 Asian, non-Hispanic/Latino; 8 Hispanic/Latino; 2 Two or more races, non-Hispanic/Latino. Average age 30. 38 applicants, 68% accepted, 12 enrolled. In 2010, 25 master's awarded. *Degree requirements:* For master's, thesis or alternative. *Entrance requirements:* For master's, GMAT. Additional exam requirements/recommendations for international students: Required—TOEFL (minimum score 500 paper-based; 173 computer-based). *Application deadline:* For fall admission, 1/31 priority date for domestic students; for spring admission, 8/31 for domestic students. Applications are processed on a rolling basis. Application fee: $55. *Financial support:* Career-related internships or fieldwork, Federal Work-Study, institutionally sponsored loans, and scholarships/grants available. Support available to part-time students. Financial award application deadline: 3/2; financial award applicants required to submit FAFSA. *Unit head:* Dr. William Silver, Coordinator, 707-664-2220, E-mail: silver@sonoma.edu. *Application contact:* Dr. Kris Wright, Associate Vice Provost, Academic Programs/Graduate Studies, 707-664-3954, E-mail: wright@sonoma.edu.

Southeastern Louisiana University, College of Business, Hammond, LA 70402. Offers accounting (MBA); general (MBA); information systems for supply chain management (MBA). *Accreditation:* AACSB. Part-time and evening/weekend programs available. *Faculty:* 15 full-time (1 woman), 1 part-time/adjunct (0 women). *Students:* 52 full-time (29 women), 56 part-time (21 women); includes 12 minority (8 Black or African American, non-Hispanic/Latino; 1 Asian, non-Hispanic/Latino; 2 Hispanic/Latino; 1 Two or more races, non-Hispanic/Latino), 8 international. Average age 28. 109 applicants, 40% accepted, 25 enrolled. In 2010, 62 master's awarded. *Entrance requirements:* For master's, GMAT (minimum score 450), minimum cumulative GPA of 2.75 for all undergraduate work attempted or 3.0 on all upper-division undergraduate coursework attempted. Additional exam requirements/recommendations for international students: Required—TOEFL (minimum score 525 paper-based; 195 computer-based; 61 iBT). *Application deadline:* For fall admission, 7/15 priority date for domestic students, 6/1 priority date for international students; for spring admission, 12/1 priority date for domestic students, 10/1 priority date for international students. Applications are processed on a rolling basis. Application fee: $20 ($30 for international students). Electronic applications accepted. *Expenses:* Tuition, state resident: full-time $3533. Tuition, nonresident: full-time $12,002. Required fees: $907. Tuition and fees vary according to degree level. *Financial support:* In 2010–11, 21 students received support, including 1 research assistantship (averaging $9,000 per year); career-related internships or fieldwork, Federal Work-Study, institutionally sponsored loans, scholarships/grants, and administrative assistantships, graduate professional services assistants also available. Support available to part-time students. Financial award application deadline: 5/1; financial award applicants required to submit FAFSA. *Faculty research:* Ethical decision-making in accounting, entrepreneurship and emerging information, leadership and organizational performance. *Unit head:* Dr. Randy Settoon, Dean, 985-549-2258, Fax: 985-549-5038, E-mail: rsettoon@selu.edu. *Application contact:* Sandra Meyers, Graduate Admissions Analyst, 985-549-5620, Fax: 985-549-5882, E-mail: admissions@selu.edu.

Southeastern Oklahoma State University, School of Business, Durant, OK 74701-0609. Offers MBA. *Accreditation:* AACSB; ACBSP. Part-time and evening/weekend programs available. *Faculty:* 13 full-time (6 women), 5 part-time/adjunct (0 women). *Students:* 11 full-time (5 women), 22 part-time (13 women); includes 9 American Indian or Alaska Native, non-Hispanic/Latino; 2 Asian, non-Hispanic/Latino, 4 international. Average age 32. 8 applicants, 100% accepted, 8 enrolled. *Degree requirements:* For master's, thesis optional. *Entrance requirements:* For master's, GMAT, minimum GPA of 3.0 in last 60 hours or 2.75 overall. Additional exam requirements/recommendations for international students: Required—TOEFL (minimum score 550 paper-based; 213 computer-based). *Application deadline:* For fall admission, 8/1 for domestic students, 6/1 for international students; for spring admission, 1/5 for domestic students, 11/1 for international students. Application fee: $20 ($55 for international students). Electronic applications accepted. *Financial support:* In 2010–11, 30 students received support, including 3 teaching assistantships with full tuition reimbursements available (averaging $5,000 per year); Federal Work-Study, institutionally sponsored loans, and tuition waivers (partial) also available. Support available to part-time students. Financial award application deadline: 6/15; financial award applicants required to submit FAFSA. *Unit head:* Dr. Buddy Gaster, Dean, 580-745-2030, Fax: 580-970-7479, E-mail: bgaster@se.edu. *Application contact:* Carrie Williamson, Graduate Secretary, 580-745-2200, Fax: 580-745-7474, E-mail: cwilliamson@se.edu.

Southeast Missouri State University, School of Graduate Studies, Harrison College of Business, Cape Girardeau, MO 63701-4799. Offers accounting (MBA); entrepreneurship (MBA); environmental management (MBA); financial management (MBA); general management (MBA); health administration (MBA); industrial management (MBA); international business (MBA); sport management (MBA). *Accreditation:* AACSB. Part-time and evening/weekend programs available. Postbaccalaureate distance learning degree programs offered (no on-campus study). *Faculty:* 31 full-time (10 women). *Students:* 51 full-time (24 women), 72 part-time (34 women); includes 4 minority (1 American Indian or Alaska Native, non-Hispanic/Latino; 3 Asian, non-Hispanic/Latino), 32 international. Average age 28. 71 applicants, 83% accepted, 33 enrolled. In 2010, 46 master's awarded. *Degree requirements:* For master's, variable foreign language requirement, applied research project; foreign language or 9 credit hours (for international business). *Entrance requirements:* For master's, GMAT (minimum score 400), minimum undergraduate GPA of 2.5, prerequisite courses for non-business undergraduate majors. Additional exam requirements/recommendations for international students: Required—TOEFL (minimum score 550 paper-based; 213 computer-based; 79 iBT); Recommended—IELTS (minimum score 6). *Application deadline:* For fall admission, 8/1 for domestic students, 6/1 for international students; for spring admission, 11/21 for domestic students, 10/1 for international students. Applications are processed on a rolling basis. Application fee: $25 ($35 for international students). Electronic applications accepted. *Expenses:* Tuition, state resident: full-time $4698; part-time $261 per credit hour. Tuition, nonresident: full-time $8379; part-time $465.50 per credit hour. *Financial support:* In 2010–11, 52 students received support, including 10 teaching assistantships with full tuition reimbursements available (averaging $7,600 per year); career-related internships or fieldwork, Federal Work-Study, institutionally sponsored loans, scholarships/grants, tuition waivers (full), and unspecified assistantships also available. Financial award application deadline: 6/30; financial award applicants required to submit FAFSA. *Faculty research:* Human resources, laws impacting accounting, advertising. *Unit head:* Dr. Kenneth A. Heischmidt, Director, Graduate Programs, 573-651-5116, Fax: 573-651-5032, E-mail: kheischmidt@semo.edu. *Application contact:* Gail Amick, Administrative Secretary, 573-651-2049, Fax: 573-651-2001, E-mail: gamick@semo.edu.

Southern Arkansas University–Magnolia, Graduate Programs, Magnolia, AR 71753. Offers agriculture (MS); business administration (MBA); computer and information sciences (MS); education (M Ed), including counseling and development, curriculum and instruction emphasis, educational administration and supervision, elementary education, middle level emphasis, reading emphasis, secondary education, TESOL emphasis; kinesiology (M Ed); library media and information specialist (M Ed); mental health and clinical counseling (MS); public administration (MPA); school counseling (M Ed); teaching (MAT). *Accreditation:* NCATE. Part-time and evening/weekend programs available. *Faculty:* 32 full-time (16 women), 6 part-time/adjunct (5 women). *Students:* 71 full-time (43 women), 364 part-time (275 women); includes 109 Black or African American, non-Hispanic/Latino; 1 American Indian or Alaska Native, non-Hispanic/Latino; 3 Asian, non-Hispanic/Latino, 19 international. Average age 33. 107 applicants, 71% accepted, 69 enrolled. In 2010, 157 master's awarded. *Degree requirements:* For master's, comprehensive exam, thesis optional. *Entrance requirements:* For master's, GRE, MAT or GMAT, minimum GPA of 2.75. *Application deadline:* For fall admission, 7/31 for domestic students; for winter admission, 12/1 for domestic students; for spring admission, 12/1 for domestic students. Applications are processed on a rolling basis. Application fee: $25. *Expenses:* Tuition, state resident: part-time $221 per hour. Tuition, nonresident: part-time $325 per hour. *Financial support:* Career-related internships or fieldwork, Federal Work-Study, scholarships/grants, tuition waivers (full), and unspecified assistantships available. Financial award applicants required to submit FAFSA. *Faculty research:* Alternative certification for teachers, supervision of instruction, instructional leadership, counseling. *Unit head:* Dr. Kim Bloss, Dean, Graduate Studies, 870-235-4150, Fax: 870-235-5227, E-mail: kkbloss@saumag.edu. *Application contact:* Dr. Kim Bloss, Dean, Graduate Studies, 870-235-4150, Fax: 870-235-5227, E-mail: kkbloss@saumag.edu.

Southern Connecticut State University, School of Graduate Studies, School of Business, Program in Business Administration, New Haven, CT 06515-1355. Offers MBA. Part-time and evening/weekend programs available. *Faculty:* 34 full-time (8 women). *Students:* 83 full-time (40 women), 109 part-time (54 women); includes 24 Black or African American, non-Hispanic/Latino; 2 American Indian or Alaska Native, non-Hispanic/Latino; 17 Asian, non-Hispanic/Latino; 11 Hispanic/Latino; 2 Two or more races, non-Hispanic/Latino, 8 international. 185 applicants, 30% accepted, 48 enrolled. In 2010, 57 master's awarded. *Entrance requirements:* For master's, GMAT, interview. *Application deadline:* For fall admission, 7/1 priority date for domestic students. Applications are processed on a rolling basis. Application fee: $50. Electronic applications accepted. *Expenses:* Tuition, state resident: full-time $5137; part-time $518 per credit. Tuition, nonresident: part-time $542 per credit. Required fees: $4008; $55 per semester. Tuition and fees vary according to program. *Financial support:* Application deadline: 4/15. *Unit head:* Dr. Wafeek Abdelsayed, Director, 203-392-5873, Fax: 203-392-5988, E-mail: abdelsayedw1@southernct.edu. *Application contact:* Dr. Wafeek Abdelsayed, Director, 203-392-5873, Fax: 203-392-5988, E-mail: abdelsayedw1@southernct.edu.

Southern Illinois University Edwardsville, Graduate School, School of Business, Program in Business Administration, Edwardsville, IL 62026. Offers management information systems (MBA); project management (MBA). *Accreditation:* AACSB. Part-time and evening/weekend programs available. *Students:* 25 full-time (12 women), 130 part-time (46 women); includes 14 minority (6 Black or African American, non-Hispanic/Latino; 1 Asian, non-Hispanic/Latino; 3 Hispanic/Latino; 1 Native Hawaiian or other Pacific Islander, non-Hispanic/Latino; 3 Two or more races, non-Hispanic/Latino), 9 international. Average age 26. 83 applicants, 63% accepted. In 2010, 59 master's awarded. *Degree requirements:* For master's, comprehensive exam. *Entrance requirements:* For master's, GMAT. Additional exam requirements/recommendations for international students: Required—TOEFL (minimum score 550 paper-based; 213 computer-based; 79 iBT), IELTS (minimum score 6.5). *Application deadline:* For fall admission, 7/22 for domestic students, 6/1 for international students; for spring admission, 12/10 for domestic students, 10/1 for international students. Applications are processed on a rolling basis. Application fee: $30. Electronic applications accepted. *Expenses:* Tuition, state resident: full-time $6012; part-time $1503 per semester. Tuition, nonresident: full-time $15,030; part-time $3758 per semester. Required fees: $1711; $675 per semester. *Financial support:* In 2010–11, 1 research assistantship with full tuition reimbursement (averaging $8,064 per year), 31 teaching assistantships with full tuition reimbursements (averaging $8,064 per year) were awarded; fellowships with full tuition reimbursements, career-related internships or fieldwork, Federal Work-Study, institutionally sponsored loans, scholarships/grants, traineeships, and unspecified assistantships also available. Support available to part-time students. Financial award application deadline: 3/1; financial award applicants required to submit FAFSA. *Unit head:* Dr. Janice Joplin, Director, 618-650-2485, E-mail: jjoplin@siue.edu. *Application contact:* Dr. Janice Joplin, Director, 618-650-2485, E-mail: jjoplin@siue.edu.

Southern Methodist University, Cox School of Business, Dallas, TX 75275. Offers accounting (MSA); business (Exec MBA); business administration (MBA), including accounting, finance, information technology and operations management, management, marketing, strategy and entrepreneurship; entrepreneurship (MS); management (MSM); JD/MBA. *Accreditation:* AACSB. Part-time and evening/weekend programs available. *Faculty:* 59 full-time (13 women), 30 part-time/adjunct (7 women). *Students:* 359 full-time (116 women), 592 part-time (154 women); includes 215 minority (44 Black or African American, non-Hispanic/Latino; 10 American Indian or Alaska Native, non-Hispanic/Latino; 118 Asian, non-Hispanic/Latino; 39 Hispanic/Latino; 2 Native Hawaiian or other Pacific Islander, non-Hispanic/Latino; 2 Two or more races, non-Hispanic/Latino), 92 international. Average age 30. In 2010, 486 master's awarded. *Entrance requirements:* For master's, GMAT. Additional exam requirements/recommendations for international students: Required—TOEFL, Pearson Test of English. *Application deadline:* Applications are processed on a rolling basis. Electronic applications accepted. *Expenses:* Contact institution. *Financial support:* Research assistantships available. Financial award application deadline: 3/1; financial award applicants required to submit FAFSA. *Faculty research:* Financial markets structure, international finance, accounting disclosure, corporate finance, leadership, change management, organizational behavior, entrepreneurship, strategic marketing, corporate strategy, product innovation, information systems, knowledge management, energy markets, customer relationship management. *Unit head:* Dr. Albert W. Niemi, Dean, 214-768-3012, Fax: 214-768-3713, E-mail: aniemi@mail.cox.smu.edu. *Application contact:* Patti Cudney, Director of MBA Admissions, 214-768-3001, Fax: 214-768-3956, E-mail: pcudney@cox.smu.edu.

Southern Oregon University, Graduate Studies, School of Business, Ashland, OR 97520. Offers MBA, MIM. Part-time and evening/weekend programs available. Postbaccalaureate distance learning degree programs offered (minimal on-campus study). *Faculty:* 15 full-time (4 women), 5 part-time/adjunct (1 woman). *Students:* 36 full-time (14 women), 99 part-time (41 women); includes 14 minority (2 Black or African American, non-Hispanic/Latino; 2 American Indian or Alaska Native, non-Hispanic/Latino; 3 Asian, non-Hispanic/Latino; 3 Hispanic/Latino; 2 Native Hawaiian or other Pacific Islander, non-Hispanic/Latino; 2 Two or more races, non-Hispanic/Latino), 20 international. Average age 36. 106 applicants, 82% accepted, 81 enrolled. In 2010, 43 master's awarded. *Degree requirements:* For master's, comprehensive exam. *Entrance requirements:* For master's, GMAT. *Application deadline:* Applications are processed on a rolling basis. Application fee: $50. Electronic applications accepted. *Expenses:* Tuition, state resident: full-time $9450; part-time $350 per credit. Tuition, nonresident: full-time $15,000; part-time $350 per credit. Required fees: $400 per quarter. *Financial support:* Career-related internships or fieldwork, Federal Work-Study, institutionally sponsored loans, scholarships/grants, and unspecified assistantships available. Support available to part-time students. *Unit head:* Rajeev Parikh, Dean, 541-552-6483, E-mail: parikhr@sou.edu. *Application contact:* Mark Bottorff, Director of Admissions, 541-552-6411, Fax: 541-552-8403, E-mail: admissions@sou.edu.

Southern Polytechnic State University, School of Engineering Technology and Management, Department of Business Administration, Marietta, GA 30060-2896. Offers accounting (MSA); business administration (MBA, Graduate Transition Certificate). *Accreditation:* ACBSP. Part-time and evening/weekend programs available. Postbaccalaureate distance learning degree programs offered (no on-campus study). *Faculty:* 9 full-time (2 women), 4 part-time/adjunct (2 women). *Students:* 87 full-time (51 women), 116 part-time (60 women); includes 66 Black or African American, non-Hispanic/Latino; 18 Asian, non-Hispanic/Latino; 5 Hispanic/Latino; 1 Two or more races, non-Hispanic/Latino, 46 international. Average age 32. 125 applicants, 95% accepted, 89 enrolled. In 2010, 64 master's awarded. *Degree requirements:* For master's, comprehensive exam, thesis or alternative. *Entrance requirements:* For master's, GMAT, letters of recommendation, statement of purpose, resume. Additional exam requirements/recommendations for international students: Required—TOEFL (minimum score 550 paper-based; 213 computer-based; 79 iBT), IELTS (minimum score 6.5). *Application deadline:* For fall admission, 7/1 priority date for domestic students, 5/1 priority date for international students; for spring admission, 11/1 priority date for domestic students, 9/1 priority date for international students. Applications are processed on a rolling basis. Application fee: $20. Electronic applications accepted. *Expenses:* Tuition, state resident: full-time $3690; part-time $205 per semester hour. Tuition, nonresident: full-time $13,428; part-time $746 per semester hour. Required fees: $598 per semester. *Financial support:* In 2010–11, 37 students received support, including 4 research assistantships with tuition reimbursements available (averaging $4,500 per year); career-related internships or fieldwork, scholarships/grants, and unspecified assistantships also available. Support available to part-time students. Financial award application deadline: 5/1; financial award applicants required to submit FAFSA. *Faculty research:* Ethics, virtual reality, sustainability, management of technology, quality management, capacity planning, human-computer interaction/interface, enterprise integration planning, economic impact of educational institutions, behavioral accounting, accounting ethics, taxation, information security, visualizational simulation, human-computer interaction. *Unit head:* Dr. Ronny Richardson, Chair, 678-915-7440, Fax: 678-915-4967, E-mail: rrichard@spsu.edu. *Application contact:* Nikki Palamiotis, Director of Graduate Studies, 678-915-4276, Fax: 678-915-7292, E-mail: npalamio@spsu.edu.

Southern Utah University, School of Business, Program in Business Administration, Cedar City, UT 84720-2498. Offers MBA. *Accreditation:* AACSB; ACBSP. Part-time programs available. *Faculty:* 8 full-time (1 woman), 2 part-time/adjunct (0 women). *Students:* 26 full-time (1 woman), 49 part-time (7 women); includes 5 minority (1 Black or African American, non-Hispanic/Latino; 1 Asian, non-Hispanic/Latino; 1 Hispanic/Latino; 2 Native Hawaiian or other Pacific Islander, non-Hispanic/Latino). 58 applicants, 93% accepted, 54 enrolled. In 2010, 55 master's awarded. *Degree requirements:* For master's, thesis or alternative. *Application deadline:* For fall admission, 8/1 priority date for domestic students. Applications are processed on a rolling basis. Application fee: $50 ($65 for international students). Electronic applications accepted. *Expenses:* Contact institution. *Financial support:* In 2010–11, 6 research assistantships with partial tuition reimbursements (averaging $1,375 per year) were awarded; career-related internships or fieldwork, institutionally sponsored loans, tuition waivers (full and partial), and unspecified assistantships also available. *Unit head:* Dr. Alan Hamlin, Chair, Management and Marketing Department, 435-586-5147, Fax: 435-586-5493, E-mail: hamlin@suu.edu. *Application contact:* Chris Proctor, Associate Director of Admissions, 435-586-7742, Fax: 435-865-8223, E-mail: alger@suu.edu.

Southern Wesleyan University, Program in Business Administration, Central, SC 29630-1020. Offers MBA. Evening/weekend programs available. *Faculty:* 6 full-time (1 woman), 13 part-time/adjunct (3 women). *Students:* 197 full-time (92 women); includes 78 minority (71 Black or African American, non-Hispanic/Latino; 1 American Indian or Alaska Native, non-Hispanic/Latino; 2 Asian, non-Hispanic/Latino; 4 Hispanic/Latino), 1 international. Average age 39. 37 applicants, 86% accepted, 16 enrolled. In 2010, 67 master's awarded. *Degree requirements:* For master's, comprehensive exam. *Entrance requirements:* For master's, GMAT, GRE, or MAT, minimum of 3 undergraduate semester credit hours each in accounting, economics, and statistics; minimum of 18 undergraduate semester credit hours in business administration; minimum of 2 years' significant work experience. Additional exam requirements/recommendations for international students: Required— TOEFL (minimum score 500 paper-based; 173 computer-based). *Application deadline:* Applications are processed on a rolling basis. Application fee: $50. *Expenses:* Tuition: Full-time $8925; part-time $425 per credit hour. Required fees: $1659; $230 per course. *Unit head:* Dr. Royce Caines, Dean, School of Business, 864-644-5349, Fax: 864-644-5958, E-mail: rcaines@swu.edu. *Application contact:* Corrie Creasman, Enrollment Services Coordinator, 877-644-5557, Fax: 864-644-5972, E-mail: ccreasman@swu.edu.

Southern Wesleyan University, Program in Management, Central, SC 29630-1020. Offers MSM. Evening/weekend programs available. *Faculty:* 5 full-time (1 woman), 7 part-time/adjunct (1 woman). *Students:* 43 full-time (30 women); includes 34 Black or African American, non-Hispanic/Latino. Average age 42. 22 applicants, 95% accepted, 21 enrolled. In 2010, 98 master's awarded. *Entrance requirements:* For master's, GMAT, GRE, or MAT, minimum of 18 undergraduate semester credit hours in business administration; minimum of 2 years significant work experience. Additional exam requirements/recommendations for international students: Required— TOEFL (minimum score 500 paper-based; 173 computer-based). *Application deadline:* Applications are processed on a rolling basis. Application fee: $50. *Expenses:* Contact institution. *Unit head:* Dr. Royce Caines, Dean, 864-644-5349, Fax: 864-644-5958, E-mail: rcaines@swu.edu. *Application contact:* Corrie Creasman, Enrollment Services Coordinator, 877-644-5557, Fax: 864-644-5972, E-mail: ccreasman@swu.edu.

Southwestern College, Fifth-Year Graduate Programs, Winfield, KS 67156-2499. Offers leadership (MS); management (MBA); music (MA), including education, performance. Part-time programs available. *Faculty:* 9 full-time (1 woman), 8 part-time/adjunct (2 women). *Students:* 9 full-time (3 women), 8 part-time (3 women), 6 international. Average age 25. 10 applicants, 90% accepted, 9 enrolled. In 2010, 26 master's awarded. *Entrance requirements:* For master's, baccalaureate degree, minimum GPA of 3.0. Additional exam requirements/recommendations for international students: Required— TOEFL (minimum score 550 paper-based; 213 computer-based). *Application deadline:* For fall admission, 4/1 priority date for domestic students; for spring admission, 12/1 priority date for domestic students. Applications are processed on a rolling basis. Electronic applications accepted. *Expenses:* Tuition: Full-time $7470; part-time $415 per credit hour. Tuition and fees vary according to program. *Financial support:* In 2010–11, 6 students received support. Federal Work-Study, tuition waivers (partial), and unspecified assistantships available. Financial award application deadline: 4/1; financial award applicants required to submit FAFSA. *Unit head:* Dr. James Sheppard, Vice President for Academic Affairs, 620-229-6227, Fax: 620-229-6224, E-mail: james.sheppard@sckans.edu. *Application contact:* Marla Sexson, Director of Admissions, 800-846-1543 Ext. 6364, Fax: 620-229-6344, E-mail: marla.sexson@sckans.edu.

Southwestern College, Professional Studies Programs, Wichita, KS 67207. Offers business administration (MBA); leadership (MS); management (MS); security administration (MS); specialized ministries (MA); theological studies (MA). Part-time and evening/weekend programs available. Postbaccalaureate distance learning degree programs offered (minimal on-campus study). *Faculty:* 12 part-time/adjunct (5 women). *Students:* 154 part-time (62 women); includes 29 minority (20 Black or African American, non-Hispanic/Latino; 1 American Indian or Alaska Native, non-Hispanic/Latino; 4 Hispanic/Latino; 4 Two or more races, non-Hispanic/Latino). Average age 35. 91 applicants, 66% accepted, 52 enrolled. In 2010, 112 master's awarded. *Degree requirements:* For master's, practicum/capstone project. *Entrance requirements:* For master's, baccalaureate degree; minimum GPA of 2.5, 3.0 for MBA. Additional exam requirements/recommendations for international students: Required—TOEFL (minimum score 550 paper-based; 213 computer-based). *Application deadline:* For fall admission, 8/1 for domestic students; for spring admission, 12/1 for domestic students. Applications are processed on a rolling basis. Application fee: $0. Electronic applications accepted. *Expenses:* Tuition: Full-time $7470; part-time $415 per credit hour. Tuition and fees vary according to program. *Financial support:* In 2010–11, 6 students received support. Federal Work-Study, tuition waivers (partial), and unspecified assistantships available. Financial award application deadline: 4/1; financial award applicants required to submit FAFSA. *Unit head:* Gail Cullen, Director of Academic Affairs, 888-684-5335 Ext. 203, Fax: 316-688-5218, E-mail: gail.cullen@sckans.edu. *Application contact:* Gail Cullen, Director of Academic Affairs, 888-684-5335 Ext. 203, Fax: 316-688-5218, E-mail: gail.cullen@sckans.edu.

Southwest Minnesota State University, Department of Business and Public Affairs, Marshall, MN 56258. Offers leadership (MBA); management (MBA); marketing (MBA). Part-time and evening/weekend programs available. Postbaccalaureate distance learning degree programs offered (no on-campus study). *Faculty:* 11 full-time (3 women), 1 (woman) part-time/adjunct. *Students:* 27 full-time (15 women), 82 part-time (38 women); includes 7 minority (3 Black or African American, non-Hispanic/Latino; 1 Asian, non-Hispanic/Latino; 2 Hispanic/Latino; 1 Two or more races, non-Hispanic/

Latino), 21 international. Average age 30. 49 applicants, 55% accepted, 18 enrolled. In 2010, 20 master's awarded. *Degree requirements:* For master's, thesis. *Entrance requirements:* For master's, GMAT (minimum score: 450). Additional exam requirements/recommendations for international students: Recommended—TOEFL (minimum score 550 paper-based; 213 computer-based; 79 iBT), IELTS. *Application deadline:* For fall admission, 8/28 for domestic students, 6/15 for international students; for spring admission, 1/15 for domestic students, 12/15 for international students. Applications are processed on a rolling basis. Application fee: $30. Electronic applications accepted. *Financial support:* Institutionally sponsored loans and unspecified assistantships available. Support available to part-time students. Financial award application deadline: 3/1; financial award applicants required to submit FAFSA. *Unit head:* Dr. Daniel Campagna, Dean of Professional Studies, 507-537-6251, E-mail: daniel.campagna@smsu.edu. *Application contact:* Cori Ann Dahlager, Graduate Office Coordinator, 507-537-6819, Fax: 507-537-6227, E-mail: coriann.dahlager@smsu.edu.

Spalding University, Graduate Studies, College of Business and Communication, Louisville, KY 40203-2188. Offers business communication (MS). Part-time and evening/weekend programs available. *Faculty:* 6 full-time (2 women), 7 part-time/adjunct (2 women). *Students:* 44 full-time (35 women), 41 part-time (32 women); includes 38 minority (27 Black or African American, non-Hispanic/Latino; 1 Asian, non-Hispanic/Latino; 1 Hispanic/Latino; 9 Two or more races, non-Hispanic/Latino). Average age 37. 41 applicants, 78% accepted, 31 enrolled. In 2010, 29 master's awarded. *Degree requirements:* For master's, project. *Entrance requirements:* For master's, GRE or GMAT, writing sample, interview, letters of recommendation, transcripts. Additional exam requirements/recommendations for international students: Required—TOEFL (minimum score 535 paper-based; 203 computer-based). *Application deadline:* Applications are processed on a rolling basis. Application fee: $30. *Financial support:* In 2010–11, 26 students received support. Application deadline: 3/15. *Faculty research:* Curriculum development, consumer behavior, interdisciplinary pedagogy. *Unit head:* Dr. Orville Blackman, Program Director, 502-585-9911 Ext. 2630, E-mail: cbc@spalding.edu. *Application contact:* Claire Rayburn, Administrative Assistant, 502-585-9911 Ext. 2120, E-mail: cbc@spalding.edu.

Spring Arbor University, Gainey School of Business, Spring Arbor, MI 49283-9799. Offers MBA. Part-time and evening/weekend programs available. Postbaccalaureate distance learning degree programs offered. *Faculty:* 7 full-time (2 women), 4 part-time/adjunct (1 woman). *Students:* 84 full-time (41 women), 5 part-time (3 women); includes 16 Black or African American, non-Hispanic/Latino; 1 American Indian or Alaska Native, non-Hispanic/Latino; 3 Asian, non-Hispanic/Latino. Average age 36. In 2010, 30 master's awarded. *Degree requirements:* For master's, thesis. *Entrance requirements:* For master's, minimum overall GPA of 3.0 for all undergraduate coursework, bachelor's degree from regionally-accredited college or university, two recommendation forms from professional/academic individuals. Additional exam requirements/recommendations for international students: Required—TOEFL (minimum score 600 paper-based; 220 computer-based). *Application deadline:* Applications are processed on a rolling basis. Application fee: $40. *Expenses:* Tuition: Full-time $6300; part-time $525 per credit hour. Required fees: $240; $120 per semester. Tuition and fees vary according to course load and program. *Financial support:* Career-related internships or fieldwork, scholarships/grants, and tuition waivers (partial) available. Support available to part-time students. Financial award application deadline: 8/25; financial award applicants required to submit FAFSA. *Unit head:* Dr. James Coe, Dean, 517-750-1200 Ext. 1569, Fax: 517-750-6624, E-mail: jcoe@arbor.edu. *Application contact:* Greg Bentle, Coordinator of Graduate Recruitment, 517-750-6763, Fax: 517-750-6624, E-mail: gbentle@arbor.edu.

Spring Hill College, Graduate Programs, Program in Business Administration, Mobile, AL 36608-1791. Offers MBA. *Accreditation:* ACBSP. Part-time and evening/weekend programs available. *Faculty:* 3 full-time (1 woman), 2 part-time/adjunct (1 woman). *Students:* 7 full-time (4 women), 16 part-time (6 women); includes 3 minority (all Black or African American, non-Hispanic/Latino), 2 international. Average age 29. In 2010, 8 master's awarded. *Degree requirements:* For master's, comprehensive exam, capstone course, completion of program within 6 calendar years. *Entrance requirements:* For master's, GMAT, bachelor's degree. Additional exam requirements/recommendations for international students: Required—TOEFL (minimum score 550 paper-based; 213 computer-based; 80 iBT), IELTS (minimum score 6.5), CPE or CAE (score: C), MELAB (score: 90). *Application deadline:* For fall admission, 8/1 priority date for domestic and international students; for spring admission, 12/1 priority date for domestic and international students. Applications are processed on a rolling basis. Application fee: $25 ($35 for international students). Electronic applications accepted. *Expenses:* Contact institution. *Financial support:* Applicants required to submit FAFSA. *Unit head:* Dr. Sergio Castello, Director, 251-380-4123, Fax: 251-460-2178, E-mail: scastello@shc.edu. *Application contact:* Donna B. Tarasavage, Director of Admissions, Graduate and Continuing Studies, 251-380-3067, Fax: 251-460-2190, E-mail: dtarasavage@shc.edu.

State University of New York at Binghamton, Graduate School, School of Management, Program in Business Administration, Binghamton, NY 13902-6000. Offers business administration (MBA, PhD); health care professional executive (MBA). *Accreditation:* AACSB. *Students:* 119 full-time (45 women), 21 part-time (3 women); includes 1 Black or African American, non-Hispanic/Latino; 13 Asian, non-Hispanic/Latino; 2 Hispanic/Latino, 46 international. Average age 27. 317 applicants, 33% accepted, 71 enrolled. In 2010, 116 master's, 2 doctorates awarded. *Degree requirements:* For doctorate, thesis/dissertation. *Entrance requirements:* For master's and doctorate, GMAT. Additional exam requirements/recommendations for international students: Required—TOEFL (minimum score 550 paper-based; 213 computer-based; 80 iBT). *Application deadline:* For fall admission, 3/1 priority date for domestic and international students; for spring admission, 10/15 priority date for domestic and international students. Applications are processed on a rolling basis. Application fee: $60. Electronic applications accepted. *Financial support:* In 2010–11, 20 students received support, including 3 fellowships with full tuition reimbursements available (averaging $17,000 per year), 2 research assistantships, 13 teaching assistantships with full tuition reimbursements available (averaging $17,000 per year); career-related internships or fieldwork, Federal Work-Study, institutionally sponsored loans, scholarships/grants, health care benefits, tuition waivers (full and partial), and unspecified assistantships also available. Financial award application deadline: 2/15; financial award applicants required to submit FAFSA. *Unit head:* Dr. George Bobinski, Associate Dean, 607-777-2315, E-mail: gbobins@binghamton.edu. *Application contact:* Catherine Smith, Recruiting and Admissions Coordinator, 607-777-2151, Fax: 607-777-2501, E-mail: cmsmith@binghamton.edu.

State University of New York at New Paltz, Graduate School, School of Business, New Paltz, NY 12561. Offers business administration (MBA); public accountancy (MBA). Part-time and evening/weekend programs available. *Faculty:* 11 full-time (4 women), 3 part-time/adjunct (2 women). *Students:* 45 full-time (19 women), 41 part-time (25 women); includes 2 Black or African American, non-Hispanic/Latino; 6 Asian, non-Hispanic/Latino; 6 Hispanic/Latino, 20 international. Average age 28. 64 applicants, 58% accepted, 31 enrolled. In 2010, 41 master's awarded. *Degree requirements:* For master's, internship. *Entrance requirements:* For master's, GMAT or GRE, minimum GPA of 3.0. Additional exam requirements/recommendations for international students: Required—TOEFL (minimum score 550 paper-based; 213 computer-based; 80 iBT), IELTS (minimum score 6.5). *Application deadline:* For fall admission, 5/15 priority date for domestic students, 5/15 for international students; for spring admission, 11/15 for domestic and international students. Applications are processed on a rolling basis. Application fee: $50. Electronic applications accepted. *Expenses:* Contact institution. *Financial support:* In 2010–11, 8 students received support, including 1 fellowship (averaging $2,500 per year), 6 research assistantships with partial tuition reimbursements available (averaging $5,000 per year), 1 teaching assistantship with partial tuition reimbursement available (averaging $5,000 per year); career-related internships or fieldwork, scholarships/grants, traineeships, and unspecified assistantships also available. Financial award application deadline: 8/1; financial award applicants required to submit FAFSA. *Faculty research:* Cognitive styles in management education, supporting SME e-commerce migration through e-learning, earnings management and board activity, trading future spread portfolio, global equity market correlation and volatility. *Unit head:* Dr. Hadi Salavitabar, Dean, 845-257-2930, E-mail: mba@newpaltz.edu. *Application contact:* Aaron Hines, Coordinator, 845-257-2968, E-mail: mba@newpaltz.edu.

State University of New York at Oswego, Graduate Studies, School of Business, Program in Business Administration, Oswego, NY 13126. Offers MBA. *Accreditation:* AACSB. Part-time and evening/weekend programs available. *Faculty:* 8 full-time (3 women), 7 part-time/adjunct (1 woman). *Students:* 72 full-time (32 women), 39 part-time (20 women); includes 2 Black or African American, non-Hispanic/Latino; 6 Asian, non-Hispanic/Latino; 2 Hispanic/Latino, 9 international. Average age 27. 101 applicants, 99% accepted. In 2010, 39 master's awarded. *Entrance requirements:* For master's, GMAT, minimum GPA of 2.6. Additional exam requirements/recommendations for international students: Required—TOEFL (minimum score 560 paper-based; 220 computer-based). *Application deadline:* For fall admission, 4/15 for domestic students; for spring admission, 10/1 for domestic students. Applications are processed on a rolling basis. Application fee: $50. *Expenses:* Tuition, state resident: full-time $8370; part-time $349 per credit hour. Tuition, nonresident: full-time $13,780; part-time $574 per credit hour. Required fees: $853; $22.59 per credit hour. *Financial support:* In 2010–11, 6 students received support, including 6 teaching assistantships with partial tuition reimbursements available (averaging $2,400 per year); career-related internships or fieldwork, Federal Work-Study, institutionally sponsored loans, scholarships/grants, health care benefits, tuition waivers (partial), and unspecified assistantships also available. Support available to part-time students. Financial award application deadline: 4/1; financial award applicants required to submit FAFSA. *Faculty research:* Marketing, industrial finance, technology. *Unit head:* Tammie Sullivan, Director, 315-312-2911, E-mail: tammie.sullivan@oswego.edu. *Application contact:* Dr. David W. King, Dean for Graduate Studies and Research, 315-312-3152, Fax: 315-312-3228, E-mail: tammie.sullivan@oswego.edu.

State University of New York College at Geneseo, Graduate Studies, School of Business, Geneseo, NY 14454-1401. Offers accounting (MS). *Accreditation:* AACSB. *Faculty:* 3 full-time (1 woman), 1 part-time/adjunct (0 women). *Students:* 16 full-time (3 women). Average age 23. 33 applicants, 88% accepted, 16 enrolled. In 2010, 9 master's awarded. *Entrance requirements:* For master's, GMAT, bachelor's degree in accounting. *Application deadline:* For fall admission, 2/1 priority date for domestic students; for spring admission, 9/1 for domestic students. Application fee: $50. *Expenses:* Tuition, state resident: full-time $8370; part-time $349 per credit hour. Tuition, nonresident: full-time $13,780; part-time $574 per credit hour. Required fees: $725.52; $60.08 per credit hour. Tuition and fees vary according to program. *Financial support:* Application deadline: 4/1. *Unit head:* Dr. Michael Schinski, Interim Dean, 585-245-5367, Fax: 585-245-5467, E-mail: schinski@geneseo.edu. *Application contact:* Dr. Harry Howe, Director, Graduate Program, 585-245-5465, Fax: 585-245-5467, E-mail: howeh@geneseo.edu.

Stephens College, Division of Graduate and Continuing Studies, Graduate Business Programs, Columbia, MO 65215-0002. Offers MBA, MSL. Part-time programs available. Postbaccalaureate distance learning degree programs offered (minimal on-campus study). *Faculty:* 1 (woman) full-time, 11 part-time/adjunct (5 women). *Students:* 65 full-time (55 women), 26 part-time (23 women); includes 9 Black or African American, non-Hispanic/Latino; 3 Asian, non-Hispanic/Latino; 4 Hispanic/Latino. Average age 37. 34 applicants, 53% accepted, 16 enrolled. In 2010, 28 master's awarded. *Entrance requirements:* For master's, minimum GPA of 3.0 in last 60 hours. Additional exam requirements/recommendations for international students: Required—TOEFL (minimum score 213 computer-based). *Application deadline:* For fall admission, 7/25 priority date for domestic and international students; for winter admission, 12/1 priority date for domestic and international students; for spring admission, 4/25 priority date for domestic and international students. Applications are processed on a rolling basis. Application fee: $40. Electronic applications accepted. *Financial support:* In 2010–11, 67 students received support, including 5 fellowships with full tuition reimbursements available (averaging $5,067 per year); scholarships/grants and unspecified assistantships also available. Financial award applicants required to submit FAFSA. *Unit head:* Susan Bartel, Department Chair, 800-388-7579. *Application contact:* Jennifer Deaver, Director of Recruitment, 800-388-7579, E-mail: online@stephens.edu.

Stetson University, School of Business Administration, Program in Business Administration, DeLand, FL 32723. Offers MBA, JD/MBA. *Accreditation:* AACSB. Part-time and evening/weekend programs available. *Students:* 66 full-time (24 women), 161 part-time (74 women); includes 12 Black or African American, non-Hispanic/Latino; 1 American Indian or Alaska Native, non-Hispanic/Latino; 5 Asian, non-Hispanic/Latino; 19 Hispanic/Latino; 4 Two or more races, non-Hispanic/Latino, 17 international. Average age 30. In 2010, 129 master's awarded. *Entrance requirements:* For master's, GMAT. *Application deadline:* For fall admission, 7/1 for domestic students. Application fee: $25. *Financial support:* Application deadline: 3/15. *Unit head:* Dr. Fred Augustine, Director, 386-822-7410. *Application contact:* Kathryn Hannon, Administrative Assistant, 386-822-7410, Fax: 386-822-7413, E-mail: khannon@stetson.edu.

Stevens Institute of Technology, Graduate School, Wesley J. Howe School of Technology Management, Program in Management, Hoboken, NJ 07030. Offers general management (MS); global innovation management (MS); human resource management (MS); information management (MS); project management (MS); technology commercialization (MS); technology management (MS). Part-time programs available. *Students:* 15 full-time (6 women), 35 part-time (15 women); includes 1 Black or African American, non-Hispanic/Latino; 5 Asian, non-Hispanic/Latino; 6 Hispanic/Latino, 12 international. Average age 31. *Degree requirements:* For master's, thesis optional. *Entrance requirements:* For master's, GMAT, GRE General Test. Additional exam requirements/recommendations for international students: Required—TOEFL. *Application deadline:* Applications are processed on a rolling basis. Application fee: $50. Electronic applications accepted. *Financial support:* Unspecified assistantships available. *Faculty research:* Industrial economics. *Unit head:* Elizabeth Watson, Director, 201-216-5081. *Application contact:* Graduate Admissions, 800-496-4935, Fax: 201-216-8044, E-mail: gradadmissions@stevens.edu.

Stony Brook University, State University of New York, Graduate School, College of Business, Program in Business Administration, Stony Brook, NY 11794. Offers finance (MBA, Certificate); health care management (MBA, Certificate); human resource management (Certificate); human resources (MBA); information systems management (MBA, Certificate); management (MBA); marketing (MBA). *Faculty:* 14 full-time (2 women), 27 part-time/adjunct (6 women). *Students:* 182 full-time (103 women), 117 part-time (35 women); includes 11 Black or African American, non-Hispanic/Latino; 35 Asian, non-Hispanic/Latino; 10 Hispanic/Latino; 2 Two or more races, non-Hispanic/Latino, 88 international. 281 applicants, 60% accepted, 102 enrolled. In 2010, 95 master's, 1 other advanced degree awarded. Application fee: $100. *Expenses:* Tuition, state resident: full-time $8370; part-time $349 per credit. Tuition, nonresident: full-time $13,780; part-time $574 per credit. Required fees: $994. *Financial support:* In 2010–11, 2 teaching assistantships were awarded. *Unit head:* Dr. Manuel London, Interim Dean, 631-632-7180. *Application contact:* Dr. Aristotle Lekacos, Director, Graduate Program, 631-632-7171, E-mail: aristotle.lekacost@notes.cc.sunysb.edu.

Suffolk University, Sawyer Business School, Master of Business Administration Program, Boston, MA 02108-2770. Offers accounting (MBA); business administration (APC); corporate financial executive track (MBA); entrepreneurship (MBA); executive business administration (EMBA); finance (MBA); global business administration (GMBA); health administration (MBA); international business (MBA); marketing (MBA); organizational behavior (MBA); strategic management (MBA); taxation (MBA); JD/MBA; MBA/GDPA; MBA/MHA; MBA/MSA; MBA/MSF; MBA/MST. *Accreditation:* AACSB. Part-time and evening/weekend programs available. Postbaccalaureate distance learning degree programs offered (no on-campus study). *Faculty:* 97 full-time (30 women), 14 part-time/adjunct (3 women). *Students:* 179 full-time (65 women), 337 part-time (143 women); includes 16 Black or African American, non-Hispanic/Latino; 2 American Indian or Alaska Native, non-Hispanic/Latino; 22 Asian, non-Hispanic/Latino; 9 Hispanic/Latino; 1 Native Hawaiian or other Pacific Islander, non-Hispanic/Latino, 80 international. Average age 30. 431 applicants, 68% accepted, 128 enrolled. In 2010, 283 master's awarded. *Entrance requirements:* For master's, GMAT, minimum undergraduate GPA of 2.75 (MBA), 5 years of managerial experience (EMBA). Additional exam requirements/recommendations for international students: Required—TOEFL (minimum score 550 paper-based; 213 computer-based). *Application deadline:* For fall admission, 6/15 priority date for domestic students, 6/15 for international students; for spring admission, 11/1 priority date for domestic students, 11/1 for international students. Applications are processed on a rolling basis. Application fee: $50. Electronic applications accepted. *Financial support:* In 2010–11, 266 students received support, including 94 fellowships with full and partial tuition reimbursements available (averaging $12,635 per year); career-related internships or fieldwork, Federal Work-Study, and institutionally sponsored loans also available. Support available to part-time students. Financial award application deadline: 4/1; financial award applicants required to submit FAFSA. *Faculty research:* Foreign investments; career strategies and boundaryless careers; corporate ethics codes; interest rates, inflation, and growth options; innovation and product development performance. *Unit head:* Lillian Hallberg, Assistant Dean of Graduate Programs/Director of MBA Programs, 617-573-8306, E-mail: lhallber@suffolk.edu. *Application contact:* Judith Reynolds, Director of Graduate Admissions, 617-573-8302, Fax: 617-305-1733, E-mail: grad.admission@suffolk.edu.

Sullivan University, School of Business, Louisville, KY 40205. Offers business administration (MBA); collaborative leadership (MSCL); conflict management (MSCM); dispute resolution (MSDR); executive business administration (EMBA); human resource leadership (MSHRL); information technology (MSMIT); management (PhD); management and information technology (MBIT); pharmacy (Pharm D). Part-time programs available. Postbaccalaureate distance learning degree programs offered (no on-campus study). *Faculty:* 13 full-time (7 women), 11 part-time/adjunct (4 women). *Students:* 429 full-time (239 women), 322 part-time (198 women); includes 244 minority (152 Black or African American, non-Hispanic/Latino; 5 American Indian or Alaska Native, non-Hispanic/Latino; 5 Hispanic/Latino; 56 Native Hawaiian or other Pacific Islander, non-Hispanic/Latino; 26 Two or more races, non-Hispanic/Latino), 15 international. In 2010, 133 master's awarded. *Entrance requirements:* Additional exam requirements/recommendations for international students: Required—TOEFL. *Application deadline:* Applications are processed on a rolling basis. Application fee: $100. *Unit head:* Dr. Eric S. Harter, Dean of Graduate School, 502-456-6504, Fax: 502-456-0040, E-mail: eharter@sullivan.edu. *Application contact:* Beverly Horsley, Admissions Officer, 502-456-6505, Fax: 502-456-0040, E-mail: bhorsley@sullivan.edu.

Taylor University, Master of Business Administration Program, Upland, IN 46989-1001. Offers emerging business strategies (MBA); global leadership (MBA). Part-time programs available. *Faculty:* 1 full-time (0 women), 8 part-time/adjunct (0 women). *Students:* 59 full-time (15 women), 4 part-time (1 woman); includes 2 Black or African American, non-Hispanic/Latino; 2 Hispanic/Latino; 1 Two or more races, non-Hispanic/Latino, 1 international. Average age 35. 28 applicants, 79% accepted, 17 enrolled. In 2010, 37 master's awarded. *Application deadline:* Applications are processed on a rolling basis. Application fee: $100. *Expenses:* Tuition: Full-time $10,260; part-time $570 per credit hour. Required fees: $72 per semester. One-time fee: $100. *Financial support:* Applicants required to submit FAFSA. *Unit head:* Dr. Evan Wood, Interim Chair, 260-627-9663, E-mail: evwood@taylor.edu. *Application contact:* Wendy Speakman, Program Director, 866-471-6062, Fax: 260-492-0452, E-mail: wnspeakman@taylor.edu.

Tennessee Technological University, Graduate School, College of Business, Cookeville, TN 38505. Offers accounting (MBA); finance (MBA); human resource management (MBA); international business (MBA); management information systems (MBA); risk management & insurance (MBA). *Accreditation:* AACSB. Part-time and evening/weekend programs available. *Faculty:* 28 full-time (5 women). *Students:* 58 full-time (18 women), 139 part-time (49 women); includes 10 Black or African American, non-Hispanic/Latino; 7 Asian, non-Hispanic/Latino; 7 Hispanic/Latino; 1 Native Hawaiian or other Pacific Islander, non-Hispanic/Latino. Average age 25. 211 applicants, 51% accepted, 59 enrolled. In 2010, 116 master's awarded. *Entrance requirements:* For master's, GMAT. Additional exam requirements/

recommendations for international students: Required—TOEFL (minimum score 550 paper-based; 79 iBT), IELTS (minimum score 5.5). *Application deadline:* For fall admission, 8/1 for domestic and international students; for spring admission, 12/1 for domestic students, 10/1 for international students. Application fee: $25 ($30 for international students). Electronic applications accepted. *Expenses:* Tuition, state resident: full-time $7934; part-time $388 per credit hour. Tuition, nonresident: full-time $19,758; part-time $962 per credit hour. *Financial support:* In 2010–11, 5 fellowships (averaging $10,000 per year), 18 research assistantships (averaging $4,000 per year), teaching assistantships (averaging $4,000 per year) were awarded. Support available to part-time students. Financial award application deadline: 4/1. *Unit head:* Dr. Tom Timmerman, Director, 931-372-3600, Fax: 931-372-6249. *Application contact:* Shelia K. Kendrick, Coordinator of Graduate Admissions, 931-372-3808, Fax: 931-372-3497, E-mail: skendrick@tntech.edu.

Texas A&M International University, Office of Graduate Studies and Research, College of Business Administration, Laredo, TX 78041-1900. Offers MBA, MP Acc, MSIS. *Accreditation:* AACSB. Part-time and evening/weekend programs available. *Faculty:* 29 full-time (2 women), 2 part-time/adjunct (0 women). *Students:* 91 full-time (35 women), 232 part-time (101 women); includes 5 Black or African American, non-Hispanic/Latino; 2 Asian, non-Hispanic/Latino; 190 Hispanic/Latino, 115 international. Average age 29. 236 applicants, 48% accepted, 84 enrolled. In 2010, 136 master's awarded. *Degree requirements:* For master's, thesis (for some programs). *Entrance requirements:* For master's, GMAT or GRE General Test. Additional exam requirements/recommendations for international students: Required—TOEFL (minimum score 550 paper-based; 213 computer-based). *Application deadline:* For fall admission, 4/30 priority date for domestic students; for spring admission, 11/30 for domestic students, 10/1 for international students. Applications are processed on a rolling basis. Application fee: $25. *Financial support:* In 2010–11, 27 students received support, including 8 research assistantships; Federal Work-Study, institutionally sponsored loans, and scholarships/grants also available. Support available to part-time students. Financial award application deadline: 11/1; financial award applicants required to submit FAFSA. *Unit head:* Dr. Stephen R. Sears, Dean, 956-326-2480, E-mail: steve.sears@tamiu.edu. *Application contact:* Imelda Lopez, Graduate Admissions Counselor, 956-326-2485, Fax: 956-326-2459, E-mail: lopez@tamiu.edu.

Texas A&M University, Mays Business School, Department of Management, College Station, TX 77843. Offers human resource management (MS); management (PhD). *Faculty:* 32. *Students:* 66 full-time (43 women), 2 part-time (1 woman); includes 14 minority (4 Black or African American, non-Hispanic/Latino; 1 American Indian or Alaska Native, non-Hispanic/Latino; 3 Asian, non-Hispanic/Latino; 6 Hispanic/Latino), 5 international. Average age 31. 76 applicants, 28% accepted. In 2010, 44 master's, 3 doctorates awarded. Terminal master's awarded for partial completion of doctoral program. *Degree requirements:* For master's, comprehensive exam; for doctorate, thesis/dissertation. *Entrance requirements:* For master's, GMAT or GRE; for doctorate, GMAT or GRE General Test. Additional exam requirements/recommendations for international students: Required—TOEFL. *Application deadline:* For fall admission, 3/1 priority date for domestic students; for spring admission, 8/1 for domestic students. Applications are processed on a rolling basis. Application fee: $50 ($75 for international students). *Financial support:* In 2010–11, 25 students received support; fellowships, research assistantships, teaching assistantships, career-related internships or fieldwork and institutionally sponsored loans available. Financial award application deadline: 2/1. *Faculty research:* Strategic and human resource management, business and public policy, organizational behavior, organizational theory. *Unit head:* Murray R. Barrick, Head, 979-845-0329, Fax: 979-845-9641, E-mail: mbarrick@mays.tamu.edu. *Application contact:* Kristi Mora, Senior Academic Advisor II, 979-845-6127, E-mail: kmora@mays.tamu.edu.

Texas A&M University, Mays Business School, Executive MBA Program, College Station, TX 77843. Offers EMBA. *Accreditation:* AACSB. *Application deadline:* Applications are processed on a rolling basis. Application fee: $50 ($75 for international students). Electronic applications accepted. *Expenses:* Contact institution. *Financial support:* Application deadline: 2/1. *Unit head:* Julie Orzabal, Director, 979-845-0361, Fax: 979-862-6296, E-mail: emba@tamu.edu. *Application contact:* Julie Orzabal, Director, 979-845-0361, Fax: 979-862-6296, E-mail: emba@tamu.edu.

Texas A&M University, Mays Business School, MBA Program, College Station, TX 77843. Offers MBA. *Accreditation:* AACSB. *Entrance requirements:* For master's, GMAT, minimum of two years of full-time work with management experience. Additional exam requirements/recommendations for international students: Required—TOEFL (minimum score 600 paper-based; 250 computer-based; 100 iBT), IELTS (minimum score 7). *Application deadline:* For fall admission, 11/1 for domestic and international students; for winter admission, 1/15 for domestic and international students; for spring admission, 3/15 for domestic and international students. Application fee: $50 ($75 for international students). Electronic applications accepted. *Expenses:* Contact institution. *Financial support:* Fellowships, research assistantships, career-related internships or fieldwork, Federal Work-Study, institutionally sponsored loans, scholarships/grants, health care benefits, and unspecified assistantships available. Financial award application deadline: 1/15. *Unit head:* Kelli Kilpatrick, Director, Full-Time MBA Program, 979-845-4714,

Fax: 979-862-2393, E-mail: kkilpatrick@mays.tamu.edu. *Application contact:* Wendy Flynn, Director of MBA and Executive MBA Admissions, 979-845-4714, Fax: 979-862-2393, E-mail: wflynn@mays.tamu.edu.

Texas A&M University–San Antonio, School of Business, San Antonio, TX 78224. Offers business administration (MBA); enterprise resource planning systems (MBA); finance (MBA); healthcare management (MBA); human resources management (MBA); information assurance and security (MBA); international business (MBA); project management (MBA); supply chain management (MBA). Part-time and evening/weekend programs available. *Faculty:* 18 full-time (6 women), 1 part-time/adjunct (0 women). *Students:* 49 full-time (21 women), 195 part-time (107 women). In 2010, 20 master's awarded. *Entrance requirements:* For master's, GMAT. Additional exam requirements/recommendations for international students: Required—TOEFL (minimum score 550 paper-based; 213 computer-based; 80 iBT), IELTS (minimum score 6). *Application deadline:* For fall admission, 7/1 priority date for domestic students, 6/1 priority date for international students; for spring admission, 11/15 priority date for domestic students, 10/1 priority date for international students. Applications are processed on a rolling basis. Application fee: $35 ($50 for international students). Electronic applications accepted. *Expenses:* Tuition, state resident: full-time $2899; part-time $161 per credit hour. Tuition, nonresident: full-time $8479; part-time $471 per credit hour. Required fees: $1056; $61 per credit hour. $368 per semester. *Financial support:* Application deadline: 3/31. *Unit head:* Dr. Tracy Hurley, MBA Coordinator, 210-932-6200, E-mail: tracy.hurley@tamusa.tamus.edu. *Application contact:* Melissa A. Villanueva, Graduate Admissions Specialist, 210-932-6200, Fax: 210-932-6209, E-mail: melissa.villanueva@tamusa.tamus.edu.

Texas Christian University, College of Science and Engineering, Department of Physics and Astronomy, Fort Worth, TX 76129-0002. Offers physics (MA, MS, PhD), including astrophysics (PhD), business (PhD), physics (PhD); PhD/MBA. Terminal master's awarded for partial completion of doctoral program. *Degree requirements:* For master's, comprehensive exam, thesis; for doctorate, comprehensive exam, thesis/dissertation, paper submitted to scientific journal. *Entrance requirements:* For master's and doctorate, GRE General Test, minimum GPA of 3.0. Additional exam requirements/recommendations for international students: Required—TOEFL (minimum score 600 paper-based). *Application deadline:* For fall admission, 2/1 for domestic and international students; for spring admission, 10/1 for domestic and international students. Applications are processed on a rolling basis. Application fee: $50. Electronic applications accepted. *Expenses:* Tuition: Full-time $18,720; part-time $1040 per credit hour. Tuition and fees vary according to course load and program. *Financial support:* In 2010–11, 11 teaching assistantships (averaging $18,000 per year) were awarded; tuition waivers also available. Financial award application deadline: 2/1. *Unit head:* Dr. T. W. Zerda, Chairperson, 817-257-7375 Ext. 7124, Fax: 817-257-7742, E-mail: t.zerda@tcu.edu. *Application contact:* Dr. Yuri Strzhemechny, Assistant Professor, 817-257-7375 Ext. 5793, Fax: 817-257-7742, E-mail: y.strzhemechny@tcu.edu.

Texas Christian University, The Neeley School of Business at TCU, Program in Business Administration, Fort Worth, TX 76129-0002. Offers MBA. *Accreditation:* AACSB. Part-time and evening/weekend programs available. *Entrance requirements:* For master's, GMAT, 3 hours of course work in college algebra. Additional exam requirements/recommendations for international students: Required—TOEFL (minimum score 600 paper-based; 250 computer-based; 100 iBT). *Application deadline:* For fall admission, 11/1 priority date for domestic and international students; for winter admission, 1/15 priority date for domestic and international students; for spring admission, 4/15 priority date for domestic and international students. Applications are processed on a rolling basis. Application fee: $100. Electronic applications accepted. *Expenses:* Tuition: Full-time $18,720; part-time $1040 per credit hour. Tuition and fees vary according to course load and program. *Financial support:* Career-related internships or fieldwork, Federal Work-Study, institutionally sponsored loans, scholarships/grants, and unspecified assistantships available. Support available to part-time students. Financial award application deadline: 5/1; financial award applicants required to submit FAFSA. *Faculty research:* Emerging financial markets, derivative trading activity, salesforce deployment, examining sales activity, litigation against tax practitioners. Total annual research expenditures: $2.5 million. *Unit head:* Dr. Bill Cron, Associate Dean, Graduate Programs, 817-257-7531, Fax: 817-257-6431. *Application contact:* Peggy Conway, Director, MBA Admissions, 817-257-7531, Fax: 817-257-6431, E-mail: mbainfo@tcu.edu.

Texas Southern University, Jesse H. Jones School of Business, Program in Business Administration, Houston, TX 77004-4584. Offers MBA. *Accreditation:* AACSB. Part-time and evening/weekend programs available. *Faculty:* 12 full-time (4 women), 2 part-time/adjunct (0 women). *Students:* 85 full-time (45 women), 140 part-time (68 women); includes 199 Black or African American, non-Hispanic/Latino; 8 Asian, non-Hispanic/Latino; 5 Hispanic/Latino, 7 international. Average age 32. 93 applicants, 99% accepted, 80 enrolled. In 2010, 112 master's awarded. *Degree requirements:* For master's, comprehensive exam. *Entrance requirements:* For master's, GMAT, minimum GPA of 2.5. *Application deadline:* For fall admission, 7/1 for domestic and international students; for spring admission, 11/1 for domestic and international students. Applications are processed on a rolling basis. Application fee: $50 ($75 for international students). Electronic applications accepted. *Expenses:* Tuition, state resident: full-time $1875; part-time $100 per credit hour. Tuition, nonresident: full-time $6641; part-time $343 per credit hour. Tuition and fees vary according to course level, course load and degree level. *Financial support:* In 2010–11, 1 research assistantship (averaging $2,500 per year), 8 teaching assistantships (averaging $2,505 per year) were awarded; fellowships, career-related internships or fieldwork, scholarships/grants, and unspecified assistantships also available. Financial award application deadline: 5/1. *Unit head:* Dr. Jeff Brice, Interim Chair, 713-313-7011 Ext. 1303, E-mail: bricejx@tsu.edu. *Application contact:* Bobbie J. Richardson, Executive Secretary, 713-313-7309, Fax: 713-313-7705, E-mail: richardson_bj@tsu.edu.

Texas State University–San Marcos, Graduate School, Emmett and Miriam McCoy College of Business Administration, Program in Business Administration, San Marcos, TX 78666. Offers MBA. *Accreditation:* AACSB. Part-time programs available. *Faculty:* 23 full-time (7 women), 2 part-time/adjunct (0 women). *Students:* 106 full-time (40 women), 225 part-time (82 women); includes 83 minority (17 Black or African American, non-Hispanic/Latino; 20 Asian, non-Hispanic/Latino; 42 Hispanic/Latino; 4 Two or more races, non-Hispanic/Latino), 15 international. Average age 30. 138 applicants, 84% accepted, 88 enrolled. In 2010, 96 master's awarded. *Degree requirements:* For master's, comprehensive exam, thesis optional. *Entrance requirements:* For master's, GMAT (minimum preferred score of 450 prior to admission decision), minimum GPA of 2.0 in last 60 hours of undergraduate work. Additional exam requirements/recommendations for international students: Required—TOEFL (minimum score 550 paper-based; 213 computer-based; 78 iBT). *Application deadline:* For fall admission, 6/1 for domestic and international students; for spring admission, 10/1 for domestic and international students. Applications are processed on a rolling basis. Application fee: $40 ($90 for international students). Electronic applications accepted. *Expenses:* Tuition, state resident: full-time $6024; part-time $251 per credit hour. Tuition, nonresident: full-time $13,536; part-time $564 per credit hour. Required fees: $1776; $50 per credit hour. $306 per semester. *Financial support:* In 2010–11, 69 students received support, including 7 research assistantships (averaging $5,081 per year), 13 teaching assistantships (averaging $5,122 per year); Federal Work-Study, institutionally sponsored loans, scholarships/grants, health care benefits, and unspecified assistantships also available. Support available to part-time students. Financial award application deadline: 4/1; financial award applicants required to submit FAFSA. *Unit head:* Dr. Robert Davis, Associate Dean, 512-245-3591, Fax: 512-245-7973, E-mail: rd23@txstate.edu. *Application contact:* Dr. J. Michael Willoughby, Dean of Graduate School, 512-245-2581, Fax: 512-245-8365, E-mail: gradcollege@txstate.edu.

Texas Tech University, Graduate School, Jerry S. Rawls College of Business Administration, Area of Management, Lubbock, TX 79409. Offers PhD. *Accreditation:* AACSB. Part-time programs available. *Faculty:* 12 full-time (2 women), 2 part-time/adjunct (0 women). *Students:* 14 full-time (7 women); includes 2 minority (both Black or African American, non-Hispanic/Latino), 5 international. Average age 30. 28 applicants, 18% accepted, 5 enrolled. In 2010, 2 doctorates awarded. *Degree requirements:* For doctorate, comprehensive exam, thesis/dissertation, qualifying exams. *Entrance requirements:* For doctorate, GMAT, holistic profile of academic credentials. Additional exam requirements/recommendations for international students: Required—TOEFL (minimum score 550 paper-based; 213 computer-based; 79 iBT). *Application deadline:* For fall admission, 2/1 priority date for domestic students, 1/15 for international students. Applications are processed on a rolling basis. Application fee: $50 ($75 for international students). Electronic applications accepted. *Expenses:* Tuition, state resident: full-time $5495.76; part-time $228.99 per credit hour. Tuition, nonresident: full-time $12,936; part-time $538.99 per credit hour. Required fees: $2674; $36 per credit hour. $905 per semester. *Financial support:* In 2010–11, 15 research assistantships (averaging $8,800 per year), 7 teaching assistantships (averaging $18,000 per year) were awarded; career-related internships or fieldwork, Federal Work-Study, and scholarships/grants also available. Financial award applicants required to submit FAFSA. *Faculty research:* Entrepreneurship, leadership, health care, organization theory. *Unit head:* Dr. William Gardner, Area Coordinator, 806-742-1055, Fax: 806-742-2308, E-mail: william.gardner@ttu.edu. *Application contact:* Cynthia D. Barnes, Director, Graduate Services Center, 806-742-3184, Fax: 806-742-3958, E-mail: ba_grad@ttu.edu.

Texas Tech University, Graduate School, Jerry S. Rawls College of Business Administration, Programs in Business Administration, Lubbock, TX 79409. Offers agricultural business (MBA); business administration (IMBA); business statistics (MBA); entrepreneurship and innovation (MBA); general business (MBA); health organization management (MBA); international business (MBA); management and leadership skills (MBA); management information systems (MBA); marketing (MBA); real estate (MBA); JD/MBA; MBA/M Arch; MBA/MA; MBA/MD; MBA/MS; MBA/Pharm D. Part-time and evening/weekend programs available. *Faculty:* 47 full-time (8 women), 5 part-time/adjunct (0 women). *Students:* 52 full-time (13 women), 531 part-time (152 women); includes 121 minority (28 Black or African American, non-Hispanic/Latino; 3 American Indian or Alaska Native, non-Hispanic/Latino; 31 Asian, non-Hispanic/Latino; 53 Hispanic/Latino; 6 Two or more races, non-Hispanic/Latino), 49 international. Average age 30. 437

applicants, 77% accepted, 258 enrolled. In 2010, 228 master's awarded. *Degree requirements:* For master's, capstone course. *Entrance requirements:* For master's, GMAT, holistic review of academic credentials. Additional exam requirements/recommendations for international students: Required—TOEFL (minimum score 550 paper-based; 213 computer-based; 79 iBT). *Application deadline:* For fall admission, 4/1 priority date for domestic students, 1/15 for international students; for spring admission, 9/1 priority date for domestic students, 6/15 for international students. Applications are processed on a rolling basis. Application fee: $50 ($75 for international students). Electronic applications accepted. *Expenses:* Tuition, state resident: full-time $5495.76; part-time $228.99 per credit hour. Tuition, nonresident: full-time $12,936; part-time $538.99 per credit hour. Required fees: $2674; $36 per credit hour. $905 per semester. *Financial support:* In 2010–11, 25 research assistantships (averaging $8,800 per year) were awarded; teaching assistantships, career-related internships or fieldwork, Federal Work-Study, scholarships/grants, health care benefits, and unspecified assistantships also available. Support available to part-time students. Financial award applicants required to submit FAFSA. *Unit head:* Dr. W. Jay Conover, Director, 806-742-1546, Fax: 806-742-3958, E-mail: jay.conover@ttu.edu. *Application contact:* Cynthia D. Barnes, Director, Graduate Services Center, 806-742-3184, Fax: 806-742-3958, E-mail: ba_grad@ttu.edu.

Texas Woman's University, Graduate School, College of Arts and Sciences, School of Management, Denton, TX 76201. Offers business administration (MBA); health systems management (MHSM). Part-time programs available. *Faculty:* 20 full-time (11 women). *Students:* 605 full-time (502 women), 457 part-time (367 women); includes 411 Black or African American, non-Hispanic/Latino; 9 American Indian or Alaska Native, non-Hispanic/Latino; 117 Asian, non-Hispanic/Latino; 107 Hispanic/Latino, 38 international. Average age 36. 365 applicants, 88% accepted, 83 enrolled. In 2010, 477 master's awarded. *Degree requirements:* For master's, thesis optional. *Entrance requirements:* For master's, 2 letters of reference, resume, minimum GPA of 3.0, 5 years relevant experience (EMBA only). Additional exam requirements/recommendations for international students: Required—TOEFL (minimum score 550 paper-based; 213 computer-based; 79 iBT). *Application deadline:* For fall admission, 8/1 priority date for domestic students, 3/1 for international students; for spring admission, 12/1 priority date for domestic students, 7/1 for international students. Applications are processed on a rolling basis. Application fee: $50 ($75 for international students). Electronic applications accepted. *Expenses:* Tuition, state resident: full-time $3834; part-time $213 per credit hour. Tuition, nonresident: full-time $9468; part-time $526 per credit hour. Required fees: $1247; $220 per credit hour. *Financial support:* In 2010–11, 116 students received support, including 16 research assistantships (averaging $11,520 per year); career-related internships or fieldwork, Federal Work-Study, institutionally sponsored loans, scholarships/grants, traineeships, health care benefits, and unspecified assistantships also available. Support available to part-time students. Financial award application deadline: 3/1; financial award applicants required to submit FAFSA. *Faculty research:* Tax research, privacy issues in Web-based marketing, multitasking, leadership, women in management, global comparative studies, corporate sustainability and responsibility. *Unit head:* Dr. P. Ann Hughes, Director, 940-898-2458, Fax: 940-898-2120, E-mail: som@twu.edu. *Application contact:* Dr. Samuel Wheeler, Assistant Director of Admissions, 940-898-3188, Fax: 940-898-3081, E-mail: wheelersr@twu.edu.

Thomas Edison State College, School of Business and Management, Program in Management, Trenton, NJ 08608-1176. Offers MSM. Part-time programs available. Postbaccalaureate distance learning degree programs offered (minimal on-campus study). *Students:* 300 part-time (114 women); includes 65 Black or African American, non-Hispanic/Latino; 2 American Indian or Alaska Native, non-Hispanic/Latino; 13 Asian, non-Hispanic/Latino; 18 Hispanic/Latino, 3 international. Average age 43. In 2010, 47 master's awarded. *Degree requirements:* For master's, final capstone project. *Entrance requirements:* For master's, bachelor's degree from a regionally-accredited college or university; minimum 2 letters of recommendation; 3-5 years of related working experience; current resume. Additional exam requirements/recommendations for international students: Required—TOEFL (minimum score 550 paper-based; 213 computer-based; 79 iBT). *Application deadline:* For fall admission, 8/15 priority date for domestic and international students; for winter admission, 11/15 priority date for domestic and international students; for spring admission, 2/15 priority date for domestic and international students. Applications are processed on a rolling basis. Application fee: $75. Electronic applications accepted. *Financial support:* Applicants required to submit FAFSA. *Unit head:* Dr. Susan Gilbert, Dean, School of Business and Management, 609-984-1130, Fax: 609-984-3898, E-mail: info@tesc.edu. *Application contact:* David Hoftiezer, Director of Admissions, 888-442-8372, Fax: 609-984-8447, E-mail: admissions@tesc.edu.

Thomas More College, Program in Business Administration, Crestview Hills, KY 41017-3495. Offers MBA. *Faculty:* 6 full-time (1 woman), 2 part-time/adjunct (0 women). *Students:* 117 full-time (53 women); includes 12 minority (5 Black or African American, non-Hispanic/Latino; 3 Asian, non-Hispanic/Latino; 3 Hispanic/Latino; 1 Native Hawaiian or other Pacific Islander, non-Hispanic/Latino). Average age 33. 47 applicants, 91% accepted, 41 enrolled. In 2010, 75 master's awarded. *Degree requirements:* For master's, comprehensive

exam, final project. *Entrance requirements:* For master's, GMAT, minimum GPA of 2.7. Additional exam requirements/recommendations for international students: Required—TOEFL (minimum score 600 paper-based; 250 computer-based; 100 iBT). *Application deadline:* Applications are processed on a rolling basis. Application fee: $25. Electronic applications accepted. *Expenses:* Tuition: Full-time $11,691; part-time $570 per credit hour. Tuition and fees vary according to program. *Financial support:* In 2010–11, 13 students received support. Federal Work-Study, institutionally sponsored loans, and scholarships/grants available. Financial award application deadline: 3/15; financial award applicants required to submit FAFSA. *Faculty research:* Comparison level and consumer satisfaction, history of U. S. business development, share price reaction, quality and competition, personnel development. *Unit head:* Nathan Hartman, Director of Lifelong Learning, 859-344-3333, Fax: 859-344-3686, E-mail: nathan.hartman@thomasmore.edu. *Application contact:* Judy Bautista, Enrollment Manager, 859-341-4554, Fax: 859-578-3589, E-mail: judy.bautista@apollogrp.edu.

Thunderbird School of Global Management, Master's Programs in Global Management, Glendale, AZ 85306-6000. Offers global affairs and management (MA); global management (MS). *Accreditation:* AACSB. *Faculty:* 48 full-time (13 women). *Students:* 139 full-time (74 women); includes 2 Black or African American, non-Hispanic/Latino; 1 American Indian or Alaska Native, non-Hispanic/Latino; 5 Asian, non-Hispanic/Latino; 2 Hispanic/Latino; 5 Two or more races, non-Hispanic/Latino, 68 international. 153 applicants, 45% accepted, 69 enrolled. In 2010, 55 master's awarded. *Degree requirements:* For master's, one foreign language. *Entrance requirements:* For master's, GMAT/GRE. Additional exam requirements/recommendations for international students: Required—TOEFL. *Application deadline:* For fall admission, 6/10 for domestic students, 4/30 for international students. Application fee: $125. *Expenses:* Tuition: Full-time $43,080; part-time $1436 per credit hour. Required fees: $300. Part-time tuition and fees vary according to program. *Financial support:* Career-related internships or fieldwork, Federal Work-Study, scholarships/grants, and unspecified assistantships available. *Unit head:* Dr. Glenn Fong, Unit Head, 602-978-7156. *Application contact:* Jay Bryant, Director of Admissions, 602-978-7294, Fax: 602-439-5432, E-mail: jay.bryant@thunderbird.edu.

Tiffin University, Program in Business Administration, Tiffin, OH 44883-2161. Offers finance (MBA); general management (MBA); healthcare administration (MBA); human resources (MBA); international business (MBA); leadership (MBA); marketing (MBA); sports management (MBA). *Accreditation:* ACBSP. Part-time and evening/weekend programs available. Postbaccalaureate distance learning degree programs offered (no on-campus study). *Faculty:* 18 full-time (9 women), 22 part-time/adjunct (6 women). *Students:* 186 full-time (93 women), 250 part-time (124 women). Average age 31. 532 applicants, 86% accepted, 229 enrolled. In 2010, 340 master's awarded. *Entrance requirements:* For master's, minimum undergraduate GPA of 2.5, work experience. Additional exam requirements/recommendations for international students: Required—TOEFL (minimum score 550 paper-based; 213 computer-based). *Application deadline:* For fall admission, 8/15 for domestic students, 8/1 for international students; for spring admission, 1/9 for domestic students, 12/1 for international students. Applications are processed on a rolling basis. Application fee: $0. Electronic applications accepted. *Financial support:* In 2010–11, 94 students received support. Available to part-time students. Application deadline: 7/31. *Faculty research:* Small business, executive development operations, research and statistical analysis, market research, management information systems. *Unit head:* Dr. Lillian Schumacher, Dean of the School of Business, 419-448-3053, Fax: 419-443-5002, E-mail: schumacherlb@tiffin.edu. *Application contact:* Kristi Krintzline, Director of Graduate Admissions and Student Services, 800-968-6446 Ext. 3445, Fax: 419-443-5002, E-mail: krintzlineka@tiffin.edu.

Trevecca Nazarene University, Graduate Division, Graduate Business Programs, Major in Business Administration, Nashville, TN 37210-2877. Offers MBA. Evening/weekend programs available. *Students:* 23 part-time (14 women); includes 7 minority (5 Black or African American, non-Hispanic/Latino; 1 American Indian or Alaska Native, non-Hispanic/Latino; 1 Two or more races, non-Hispanic/Latino). In 2010, 46 master's awarded. *Entrance requirements:* For master's, GMAT, proficiency exam (quantitative skills), minimum GPA of 2.5, resume, employer letter of recommendation, 2 letters of recommendation, written business analysis. Additional exam requirements/recommendations for international students: Required—TOEFL (minimum score 550 paper-based; 213 computer-based). *Application deadline:* Applications are processed on a rolling basis. Application fee: $25. *Expenses:* Contact institution. *Financial support:* Applicants required to submit FAFSA. *Unit head:* Dr. Jon Burch, Director of Graduate Management Program, 615-248-1529, E-mail: management@trevecca.edu. *Application contact:* College of Lifelong Learning, 615-248-1200, E-mail: cll@trevecca.edu.

Troy University, Graduate School, College of Business, Program in Business Administration, Troy, AL 36082. Offers accounting (EMBA, MBA); criminal justice (EMBA); finance (MBA); general management (EMBA, MBA); healthcare management (EMBA); information systems (EMBA, MBA); international economic development (MBA). *Accreditation:* ACBSP. Part-time and evening/weekend programs available. *Students:* 351 full-time (198 women), 745 part-time (452 women); includes 589 minority (425 Black or African

American, non-Hispanic/Latino; 13 American Indian or Alaska Native, non-Hispanic/Latino; 129 Asian, non-Hispanic/Latino; 21 Hispanic/Latino; 1 Two or more races, non-Hispanic/Latino). Average age 29. 748 applicants, 71% accepted. In 2010, 322 master's awarded. *Degree requirements:* For master's, minimum GPA 3.0, capstone course, research course. *Entrance requirements:* For master's, GMAT (minimum score 500) or GRE General Test (minimum score 900), minimum GPA of 2.5; letter of recommendation, bachelor's degree. Additional exam requirements/recommendations for international students: Required—TOEFL (minimum score 523 paper-based; 193 computer-based; 70 iBT), IELTS (minimum score 6), or ACT compass ESL (minimum Listening, Reading, and Grammar score: 270). *Application deadline:* Applications are processed on a rolling basis. Application fee: $50. *Expenses:* Tuition, state resident: full-time $4428; part-time $246 per credit hour. Tuition, nonresident: full-time $8856; part-time $492 per credit hour. Required fees: $432; $24 per credit hour. $50 per term. Tuition and fees vary according to program. *Unit head:* Dr. Henry M. Findley, Interim Chair/Professor, 334-670-3271, Fax: 334-670-3599, E-mail: hfindley@troy.edu. *Application contact:* Brenda K. Campbell, Director of Graduate Admissions, 334-670-3178, Fax: 334-670-3733, E-mail: bcamp@troy.edu.

Troy University, Graduate School, College of Business, Program in Management, Troy, AL 36082. Offers applied management (MSM); healthcare management (MSM); human resources management (MSM); information systems (MSM); international hospitality management (MSM); international management (MSM); leadership and organizational effectiveness (MSM); public management (MS, MSM). *Accreditation:* ACBSP. Evening/weekend programs available. *Students:* 101 full-time (62 women), 398 part-time (249 women); includes 308 minority (278 Black or African American, non-Hispanic/Latino; 8 American Indian or Alaska Native, non-Hispanic/Latino; 8 Asian, non-Hispanic/Latino; 13 Hispanic/Latino; 1 Two or more races, non-Hispanic/Latino). Average age 35. 218 applicants, 80% accepted. In 2010, 314 master's awarded. *Degree requirements:* For master's, Graduate Educational Testing Service Major Field Test, capstone exam, minimum GPA of 3.0. *Entrance requirements:* For master's, GMAT (minimum score 500) or GRE General Test (minimum score 900), minimum GPA of 2.5, bachelor's degree, letter of recommendation. Additional exam requirements/recommendations for international students: Required—TOEFL (minimum score 523 paper-based; 193 computer-based; 70 iBT), IELTS, or ACT compass ESL (minimum Listening, Reading, and Grammar score: 270). *Application deadline:* Applications are processed on a rolling basis. Application fee: $50. Electronic applications accepted. *Expenses:* Contact institution. *Unit head:* Dr. Henry M. Findley, Interim Chair/Professor, 334-670-3271, Fax: 334-670-3599, E-mail: hfindley@troy.edu. *Application contact:* Brenda K. Campbell, Director of Graduate Admissions, 334-670-3178, Fax: 334-670-3733, E-mail: bcamp@troy.edu.

TUI University, College of Business Administration, Program in Business Administration, Cypress, CA 90630. Offers business administration (PhD); conflict and negotiation management (MBA); criminal justice administration (MBA); entrepreneurship (MBA); finance (MBA); general management (MBA); government accounting (MBA); human resource management (MBA); information security and digital assurance management (MBA); information technology management (MBA); international business (MBA); logistics management (MBA); marketing (MBA); project management (MBA); public management (MBA); quality management (MBA); strategic leadership (MBA). Part-time and evening/weekend programs available. Postbaccalaureate distance learning degree programs offered (no on-campus study). *Students:* 741 full-time (200 women), 1,585 part-time (410 women). 379 applicants, 81% accepted, 300 enrolled. In 2010, 752 master's, 28 doctorates awarded. *Degree requirements:* For doctorate, comprehensive exam, thesis/dissertation, defense of dissertation. *Entrance requirements:* For master's, minimum GPA of 2.5 (students with GPA 3.0 or greater may transfer up to 30% of graduate level credits); for doctorate, minimum GPA of 3.4, curriculum vitae, course work in research methods or statistics. Additional exam requirements/recommendations for international students: Required—TOEFL. *Application deadline:* For fall admission, 10/3 for domestic and international students; for winter admission, 12/22 for domestic and international students; for spring admission, 4/3 for domestic and international students. Applications are processed on a rolling basis. Application fee: $75. Electronic applications accepted. *Expenses:* Tuition: Full-time $11,040; part-time $345 per semester hour. *Unit head:* Paul Watkins, Dean, College of Business Administration, 800-375-9878, E-mail: pwatkins@tuiu.edu. *Application contact:* Wei Ren-Finaly, Registrar, 800-375-9878, Fax: 714-827-7407, E-mail: registration@tuiu.edu.

Union Graduate College, School of Management, Schenectady, NY 12308-3107. Offers business administration (MBA); financial management (Certificate); general management (Certificate); health systems administration (MBA, Certificate); human resources (Certificate). *Accreditation:* AACSB. Part-time and evening/weekend programs available. *Faculty:* 16 full-time (3 women), 7 part-time/adjunct (2 women). *Students:* 129 full-time (61 women), 86 part-time (42 women); includes 27 minority (4 Black or African American, non-Hispanic/Latino; 16 Asian, non-Hispanic/Latino; 4 Hispanic/Latino; 3 Two or more races, non-Hispanic/Latino), 17 international. Average age 27. 115 applicants, 77% accepted, 71 enrolled. In 2010, 78 master's, 17 other

advanced degrees awarded. *Degree requirements:* For master's, internship, capstone course. *Entrance requirements:* For master's, GMAT, minimum GPA of 3.0, 3 letters of recommendation. Additional exam requirements/recommendations for international students: Required—TOEFL (minimum score 550 paper-based; 213 computer-based). *Application deadline:* Applications are processed on a rolling basis. Application fee: $60. *Expenses:* Tuition: Part-time $750 per credit. One-time fee: $350 part-time. Tuition and fees vary according to course load and program. *Financial support:* Research assistantships, career-related internships or fieldwork, Federal Work-Study, scholarships/grants, health care benefits, and tuition waivers (partial) available. Support available to part-time students. Financial award applicants required to submit FAFSA. *Unit head:* Dr. Eric Lewis, Dean, 518-631-9890, Fax: 518-631-9902, E-mail: lewise@uniongraduatecollege.edu. *Application contact:* Diane Trzaskos, Admissions Coordinator, 518-631-9837, Fax: 518-631-9901, E-mail: trzaskod@uniongraduatecollege.edu.

United States International University, School of Business Administration, Nairobi, Kenya. Offers business administration (GEMBA); entrepreneurship (MBA); finance (MBA); human resource management (MBA); information technology management (MBA); integrated studies (MBA); international business administration (MBA); management and organizational development (MS); marketing (MBA); organizational development (EMS); strategic management (MBA). Part-time and evening/weekend programs available. *Faculty:* 42 full-time (8 women), 64 part-time/adjunct (14 women). *Students:* 423 full-time (227 women), 129 part-time (63 women). Average age 29. 110 applicants, 79% accepted, 78 enrolled. In 2010, 164 master's awarded. *Degree requirements:* For master's, thesis. *Entrance requirements:* For master's, GMAT, 2 letters of reference, resume. Additional exam requirements/recommendations for international students: Required—TOEFL (minimum score 550 paper-based; 213 computer-based). *Application deadline:* For fall admission, 6/30 priority date for domestic and international students; for spring admission, 9/30 for domestic and international students. Applications are processed on a rolling basis. Application fee: $50. *Financial support:* In 2010–11, 30 students received support, including 8 research assistantships (averaging $1,400 per year), 4 teaching assistantships (averaging $1,400 per year); career-related internships or fieldwork, scholarships/grants, and unspecified assistantships also available. Support available to part-time students. Financial award application deadline: 6/30; financial award applicants required to submit FAFSA. *Faculty research:* Marketing in small business enterprises, total quality management in Kenya. *Unit head:* Dr. Damary Sikalieh, Dean, 254-02-3606-415, E-mail: dsikalieh@usiu.ac.ke. *Application contact:* George Lumbasi, Director of Admissions, 254-02-3606563, Fax: 254-02-3606100, E-mail: glumbasi@usiu.ac.ke.

Université de Moncton, Faculty of Administration, Moncton, NB E1A 3E9, Canada. Offers MBA, LL B/MBA. Part-time and evening/weekend programs available. Postbaccalaureate distance learning degree programs offered (no on-campus study). *Faculty:* 22 full-time (7 women), 20 part-time/adjunct (1 woman). *Students:* 32 full-time (5 women), 17 international. Average age 28. 142 applicants, 60% accepted, 20 enrolled. In 2010, 15 master's awarded. *Degree requirements:* For master's, one foreign language, thesis. *Entrance requirements:* For master's, minimum undergraduate GPA of 3.0. *Application deadline:* For fall admission, 6/1 for domestic students, 2/1 for international students; for winter admission, 11/15 for domestic students, 9/1 for international students; for spring admission, 3/31 for domestic students, 1/1 for international students. Applications are processed on a rolling basis. Application fee: $39. Electronic applications accepted. *Financial support:* In 2010–11, 7 fellowships (averaging $2,500 per year) were awarded; teaching assistantships, institutionally sponsored loans also available. Support available to part-time students. Financial award application deadline: 5/30. *Faculty research:* Service management, corporate reputation, financial management, accounting, supply chain. Total annual research expenditures: $150,000. *Unit head:* Dr. Nha Nguyen, Director, 506-858-4231, Fax: 506-858-4093, E-mail: nha.nguyen@umoncton.ca. *Application contact:* Natalie Allain, Admission Counselor, 506-858-4273, Fax: 506-858-4093, E-mail: natalie.allain@umoncton.ca.

Université de Sherbrooke, Faculty of Administration, Doctoral Program in Business Administration, Sherbrooke, QC J1K 2R1, Canada. Offers DBA. *Faculty:* 38 full-time (15 women). *Students:* 15 full-time (5 women). Average age 40. 51 applicants, 12% accepted, 14 enrolled. In 2010, 7 doctorates awarded. *Degree requirements:* For doctorate, one foreign language, comprehensive exam, thesis/dissertation. *Entrance requirements:* For doctorate, 3 years related work experience Interview Be fluent in french Advanced english english test good oral and written french comprehension (tested with an interview). *Application deadline:* For fall admission, 4/30 for domestic students, 1/15 for international students. Applications are processed on a rolling basis. Application fee: $70. Electronic applications accepted. *Financial support:* In 2010–11, 3 research assistantships (averaging $4,000 per year) were awarded; teaching assistantships. *Faculty research:* Change management, international business and finance, work organization, information technology implementation and impact on organizations, strategic management. *Unit head:* John Ingham, Program Director, 819-821-8000 Ext. 62330, Fax: 819-821-7364, E-mail: john.ingham@usherbrooke.ca. *Application contact:*

Marie-Claude Drouin, Assistant Programs Director, 819-821-8000 Ext. 63301, Fax: 819-821-7364, E-mail: marie-claude.drouin@usherbrooke.ca.

Université de Sherbrooke, Faculty of Administration, Master of Business Administration Program, Sherbrooke, QC J1K 2R1, Canada. Offers executive business administration (EMBA); general management (MBA). Part-time and evening/weekend programs available. *Faculty:* 16 full-time (2 women), 65 part-time/adjunct (21 women). *Students:* 66 full-time (30 women), 108 part-time (35 women). Average age 33. 354 applicants, 67% accepted, 169 enrolled. In 2010, 104 master's awarded. *Entrance requirements:* For master's, Bacc. degree with a minimum GPA of 2.7/4.3, minimum of two years of work experience, letter of motivation and recommendation letters. *Application deadline:* For fall admission, 4/30 priority date for domestic and international students. Application fee: $70. Electronic applications accepted. *Unit head:* Prof. Louis Cote, Director, 819-821-8000 Ext. 62836, Fax: 819-821-7364, E-mail: louis.cote2@usherbrooke.ca. *Application contact:* Lise Custeau, Assistant Director, 819-821-8000 Ext. 63834, Fax: 819-821-7364, E-mail: lise.custeau@usherbrooke.ca.

University at Buffalo, the State University of New York, Graduate School, School of Management, Buffalo, NY 14260. Offers accounting (MS); business administration (EMBA, MBA, PMBA); finance (MS), including financial engineering, financial management; information assurance (Certificate); management (PhD); management information systems (MS); supply chains and operations management (MS); Au D/MBA; JD/MBA; M Arch/MBA; MA/MBA; MD/MBA; MPH/MBA; MSW/MBA; Pharm D/MBA. *Accreditation:* AACSB. Part-time and evening/weekend programs available. *Faculty:* 65 full-time (18 women), 32 part-time/adjunct (8 women). *Students:* 626 full-time (229 women), 202 part-time (69 women); includes 43 minority (18 Black or African American, non-Hispanic/Latino; 2 American Indian or Alaska Native, non-Hispanic/Latino; 18 Asian, non-Hispanic/Latino; 5 Hispanic/Latino), 351 international. Average age 27. 1,553 applicants, 46% accepted, 400 enrolled. In 2010, 287 master's, 4 doctorates, 3 other advanced degrees awarded. *Degree requirements:* For master's, thesis (for some programs); for doctorate, comprehensive exam, thesis/dissertation. *Entrance requirements:* For master's, GMAT (MBA, MS in accounting), GRE or GMAT (for all other MS concentrations); for doctorate, GMAT or GRE. Additional exam requirements/recommendations for international students: Required—TOEFL (minimum score 230 computer-based; 95 iBT). *Application deadline:* For fall admission, 5/2 priority date for domestic students, 3/1 priority date for international students. Applications are processed on a rolling basis. Application fee: $100. Electronic applications accepted. *Expenses:* Contact institution. *Financial support:* In 2010–11, 91 students received support, including 5 fellowships with full and partial tuition reimbursements available (averaging $4,000 per year), 41 research assistantships with full and partial tuition reimbursements available (averaging $16,000 per year), 28 teaching assistantships with full and partial tuition reimbursements available (averaging $15,000 per year); career-related internships or fieldwork, Federal Work-Study, institutionally sponsored loans, scholarships/grants, health care benefits, and unspecified assistantships also available. Financial award application deadline: 2/15; financial award applicants required to submit FAFSA. *Faculty research:* Earnings management and electronic information assurance, supply chains and operations management, corporate financing and asset pricing, consumer behavior and quantitative modeling of marketing behavior, leadership and politics in organizations. Total annual research expenditures: $215,000. *Unit head:* David W. Frasier, Assistant Dean, 716-645-3204, Fax: 716-645-2341, E-mail: davidf@buffalo.edu. *Application contact:* David W. Frasier, Assistant Dean, 716-645-3204, Fax: 716-645-2341, E-mail: davidf@buffalo.edu.

The University of Akron, Graduate School, College of Business Administration, Department of Management, Akron, OH 44325. Offers electronic business (MBA); entrepreneurship (MBA); management (MBA); management of technology (MBA); management-health services administration (MSM); management-human resources (MSM); management-information systems (MSM); management-supply chain management (MSM); JD/MBA; JD/MSM. *Accreditation:* AACSB. Part-time and evening/weekend programs available. *Faculty:* 20 full-time (4 women), 11 part-time/adjunct (1 woman). *Students:* 67 full-time (25 women), 111 part-time (36 women); includes 6 Black or African American, non-Hispanic/Latino; 6 Asian, non-Hispanic/Latino; 2 Hispanic/Latino; 1 Two or more races, non-Hispanic/Latino, 36 international. Average age 30. 121 applicants, 57% accepted, 48 enrolled. In 2010, 56 master's awarded. *Entrance requirements:* For master's, GMAT, minimum GPA of 2.75, two letters of recommendation, statement of purpose, resume. Additional exam requirements/recommendations for international students: Required—TOEFL (minimum score 550 paper-based; 213 computer-based; 79 iBT). *Application deadline:* For fall admission, 7/15 for domestic and international students; for spring admission, 11/15 for domestic and international students. Application fee: $30 ($40 for international students). Electronic applications accepted. *Expenses:* Tuition, state resident: full-time $6800; part-time $378 per credit hour. Tuition, nonresident: full-time $11,644; part-time $647 per credit hour. Required fees: $1265. One-time fee: $30 full-time. *Financial support:* In 2010–11, 6 research assistantships with full tuition reimbursements, 25 teaching assistantships with full tuition reimbursements were awarded; career-related internships or fieldwork and Federal Work-Study also available. *Faculty research:* Human resource management, innovation,

entrepreneurship, technology management and technology transfer, artificial intelligence and belief functions. *Unit head:* Dr. Steve Ash, Interim Chair, 330-972-6086, Fax: 330-972-6588, E-mail: ash@uakron.edu. *Application contact:* Dr. Susan Hanlon, Director of Graduate Business Programs, 330-972-7043, Fax: 330-972-6588, E-mail: shanlon@uakron.edu.

The University of Alabama, Graduate School, Manderson Graduate School of Business, Department of Information Systems, Statistics, and Management Science, Program of Information Systems, Statistics, and Management Science—Operations Management, Tuscaloosa, AL 35487. Offers operations management (MS, PhD). *Accreditation:* AACSB. Part-time programs available. Postbaccalaureate distance learning degree programs offered (no on-campus study). *Faculty:* 22 full-time (4 women). *Students:* 33 full-time (7 women), 30 part-time (7 women); includes 7 minority (4 Black or African American, non-Hispanic/Latino; 2 Asian, non-Hispanic/Latino; 1 Hispanic/Latino), 12 international. Average age 32. 55 applicants, 62% accepted, 24 enrolled. In 2010, 30 master's, 2 doctorates awarded. Terminal master's awarded for partial completion of doctoral program. *Degree requirements:* For master's, comprehensive exam, business calculus; for doctorate, comprehensive exam, thesis/dissertation. *Entrance requirements:* For master's, GMAT or GRE; for doctorate, GRE or GMAT. Additional exam requirements/recommendations for international students: Required—TOEFL (minimum score 550 paper-based; 213 computer-based), IELTS (minimum score 6.5). *Application deadline:* For spring admission, 3/1 priority date for domestic and international students. Applications are processed on a rolling basis. Application fee: $50 ($60 for international students). Electronic applications accepted. *Expenses:* Tuition, state resident: full-time $7900. Tuition, nonresident: full-time $20,500. *Financial support:* In 2010–11, 11 students received support, including 7 teaching assistantships with full tuition reimbursements available (averaging $13,500 per year); scholarships/grants and health care benefits also available. Financial award application deadline: 3/1. *Faculty research:* Supply chain management, inventory, simulation, logistics. *Unit head:* Dr. Michael D. Conerly, Head, 205-348-8902, Fax: 205-348-0560, E-mail: mconerly@cba.ua.edu. *Application contact:* Dana Merchant, Administrative Secretary, 205-348-8904, E-mail: dmerchan@cba.ua.edu.

The University of Alabama, Graduate School, Manderson Graduate School of Business, Department of Management and Marketing, Program in Management, Tuscaloosa, AL 35487. Offers MA, MS, PhD. *Accreditation:* AACSB. Part-time and evening/weekend programs available. Postbaccalaureate distance learning degree programs offered (no on-campus study). *Faculty:* 25 full-time (7 women), 1 part-time/adjunct (0 women). *Students:* 36 full-time (13 women), 27 part-time (8 women); includes 8 minority (7 Black or African American, non-Hispanic/Latino; 1 Hispanic/Latino), 28 international. Average age 30. 57 applicants, 51% accepted, 19 enrolled. In 2010, 8 master's, 1 doctorate awarded. Terminal master's awarded for partial completion of doctoral program. *Degree requirements:* For master's, comprehensive exam (for some programs), thesis (for some programs), formal project paper; for doctorate, comprehensive exam, thesis/dissertation. *Entrance requirements:* For master's and doctorate, GMAT or GRE, minimum GPA of 3.0. Additional exam requirements/recommendations for international students: Required—TOEFL (minimum score 600 paper-based) or IELTS (minimum score 6.5). *Application deadline:* For fall admission, 6/30 priority date for domestic students, 1/31 for international students; for spring admission, 10/30 for domestic students. Applications are processed on a rolling basis. Application fee: $50 ($60 for international students). *Expenses:* Tuition, state resident: full-time $7900. Tuition, nonresident: full-time $20,500. *Financial support:* In 2010–11, 5 fellowships with full and partial tuition reimbursements (averaging $15,000 per year), 2 research assistantships (averaging $18,444 per year), 2 teaching assistantships (averaging $16,200 per year) were awarded; scholarships/grants, health care benefits, and unspecified assistantships also available. *Faculty research:* Leadership, entrepreneurship, health care management, organizational behavior, strategy. *Unit head:* Dr. Robert M. Morgan, Department Head, 205-348-6183, Fax: 205-348-6695, E-mail: rmorgan@cba.ua.edu. *Application contact:* Courtney Cox, Office Associate II, 205-348-6183, Fax: 205-348-6695, E-mail: crhodes@cba.ua.edu.

The University of Alabama, Graduate School, Manderson Graduate School of Business, Program in General Commerce and Business, Tuscaloosa, AL 35487. Offers EMBA, MBA. *Accreditation:* AACSB. Part-time programs available. *Students:* 231 full-time (60 women); includes 30 minority (12 Black or African American, non-Hispanic/Latino; 1 American Indian or Alaska Native, non-Hispanic/Latino; 8 Asian, non-Hispanic/Latino; 8 Hispanic/Latino; 1 Two or more races, non-Hispanic/Latino), 15 international. Average age 28. 227 applicants, 59% accepted, 96 enrolled. In 2010, 120 master's awarded. *Entrance requirements:* For master's, GMAT or GRE. Additional exam requirements/recommendations for international students: Required—TOEFL (minimum score 550 paper-based). *Application deadline:* For winter admission, 1/2 priority date for domestic students, 1/1 priority date for international students; for spring admission, 4/15 for domestic and international students. Applications are processed on a rolling basis. Application fee: $50 ($60 for international students). Electronic applications accepted. *Expenses:* Tuition, state resident: full-time $7900. Tuition, nonresident: full-time $20,500. *Financial support:* In 2010–11, 26 students received support, including 22 research assistantships (averaging $5,400 per year), 4 teaching assistantships; health care benefits also available. Financial award application deadline: 4/15. *Unit head:* Susan C. West, Assistant Dean and Director of MBA Programs, 205-348-0954, Fax: 205-348-0479, E-mail: swest@cba.ua.edu. *Application contact:* Blake Bedsole, Coordinator of Graduate Recruiting/Admissions, 205-348-9122, Fax: 205-348-4504, E-mail: bbedsole@cba.ua.edu.

The University of Alabama at Birmingham, School of Business, Birmingham, AL 35294. Offers M Acct, MBA. *Accreditation:* AACSB. *Students:* 123 full-time (38 women), 228 part-time (68 women); includes 56 minority (25 Black or African American, non-Hispanic/Latino; 23 Asian, non-Hispanic/Latino; 5 Hispanic/Latino; 3 Two or more races, non-Hispanic/Latino), 11 international. Average age 29. 143 applicants, 73% accepted, 68 enrolled. In 2010, 129 master's awarded. *Entrance requirements:* For master's, GMAT. *Application deadline:* Applications are processed on a rolling basis. Electronic applications accepted. *Expenses:* Tuition, state resident: full-time $5482. Tuition, nonresident: full-time $12,430. Tuition and fees vary according to program. *Financial support:* Fellowships, career-related internships or fieldwork available. *Unit head:* Dr. David R. Klock, Dean, 205-934-8800, Fax: 205-934-8886, E-mail: dklock@uab.edu. *Application contact:* Director, 205-934-8817.

The University of Alabama in Huntsville, School of Graduate Studies, College of Business Administration, Department of Management and Marketing, Huntsville, AL 35899. Offers management (MBA), including acquisition management, finance, human resource management, logistics and supply chain management, marketing, project management. *Accreditation:* AACSB. Part-time and evening/weekend programs available. *Faculty:* 11 full-time (2 women), 4 part-time/adjunct (1 woman). *Students:* 41 full-time (17 women), 159 part-time (69 women); includes 32 minority (15 Black or African American, non-Hispanic/Latino; 6 American Indian or Alaska Native, non-Hispanic/Latino; 7 Asian, non-Hispanic/Latino; 3 Hispanic/Latino; 1 Two or more races, non-Hispanic/Latino), 14 international. Average age 31. 141 applicants, 65% accepted, 79 enrolled. In 2010, 66 master's awarded. *Degree requirements:* For master's, comprehensive exam, thesis or alternative. *Entrance requirements:* For master's, GMAT (minimum score 500), minimum AACSB index of 1080. Additional exam requirements/recommendations for international students: Required—TOEFL (minimum score 550 paper-based; 213 computer-based; 62 iBT). *Application deadline:* For fall admission, 8/1 for domestic students, 4/1 for international students; for spring admission, 12/1 for domestic students, 9/1 for international students. Applications are processed on a rolling basis. Application fee: $40 ($50 for international students). Electronic applications accepted. *Expenses:* Tuition, state resident: full-time $7250; part-time $407.75 per credit hour. Tuition, nonresident: full-time $17,358; part-time $970.05 per credit hour. Required fees: $246.80 per semester. Tuition and fees vary according to course load and program. *Financial support:* In 2010–11, 3 students received support, including 1 research assistantship with full tuition reimbursement available (averaging $8,550 per year), 2 teaching assistantships with full tuition reimbursements available (averaging $8,000 per year); career-related internships or fieldwork, Federal Work-Study, institutionally sponsored loans, scholarships/grants, health care benefits, and unspecified assistantships also available. Support available to part-time students. Financial award application deadline: 4/1; financial award applicants required to submit FAFSA. *Faculty research:* Strategic human resources, corporate governance, cross-function integration and the management of research and development, determinants of team performance. Total annual research expenditures: $3 million. *Unit head:* Dr. Brent Wren, Chair, 256-824-6408, Fax: 256-824-6328, E-mail: wrenb@uah.edu. *Application contact:* Jennifer Pettitt, Director of Graduate Programs, 256-824-6681, Fax: 256-824-7571, E-mail: jennifer.pettitt@uah.edu.

University of Alaska Fairbanks, School of Management, Department of Business Administration, Fairbanks, AK 99775-6080. Offers capital markets (MBA); general management (MBA). *Accreditation:* AACSB. Part-time programs available. *Faculty:* 10 full-time (2 women), 1 part-time/adjunct (0 women). *Students:* 22 full-time (9 women), 33 part-time (23 women); includes 15 minority (5 Black or African American, non-Hispanic/Latino; 5 American Indian or Alaska Native, non-Hispanic/Latino; 3 Asian, non-Hispanic/Latino; 1 Hispanic/Latino; 1 Native Hawaiian or other Pacific Islander, non-Hispanic/Latino), 4 international. Average age 31. 32 applicants, 69% accepted, 18 enrolled. In 2010, 25 master's awarded. *Degree requirements:* For master's, comprehensive exam, thesis or alternative. *Entrance requirements:* For master's, GMAT. Additional exam requirements/recommendations for international students: Required—TOEFL (minimum score 550 paper-based; 213 computer-based; 80 iBT). *Application deadline:* For fall admission, 6/1 priority date for domestic students, 2/1 for international students; for spring admission, 10/15 priority date for domestic students, 9/1 for international students. Applications are processed on a rolling basis. Application fee: $60. Electronic applications accepted. *Expenses:* Tuition, state resident: full-time $5688; part-time $316 per credit. Tuition, nonresident: full-time $11,628; part-time $646 per credit. Required fees: $289 per semester. Tuition and fees vary according to course load and reciprocity agreements. *Financial support:* In 2010–11, 2 research assistantships with tuition reimbursements (averaging $11,939 per year), 5 teaching assistantships with tuition reimbursements (averaging $8,450 per year) were awarded; fellowships with tuition reimbursements, career-related internships or fieldwork, Federal Work-Study, scholarships/grants, health care benefits, and unspecified assistantships also available. Support available to part-time students. Financial award application deadline: 2/15; financial award applicants required to submit FAFSA. *Faculty research:* Consumer behavior, marketing, international finance and business, strategic risk, organization theory. Total annual research expenditures: $20,946. *Unit head:* Dr. Ping Lan, Director, MBA Program, 907-474-7688, Fax: 907-474-5219, E-mail: plan@alaska.edu. *Application contact:* Dr. Ping Lan, Director, MBA Program, 907-474-7688, Fax: 907-474-5219, E-mail: plan@alaska.edu.

The University of Arizona, Eller College of Management, Tucson, AZ 85721. Offers M Ac, MA, MBA, MPA, MS, PhD, JD/MA, JD/MBA, JD/PhD. *Accreditation:* AACSB. Evening/weekend programs available. *Faculty:* 67 full-time (18 women), 7 part-time/adjunct (1 woman). *Students:* 633 full-time (249 women), 67 part-time (22 women); includes 16 Black or African American, non-Hispanic/Latino; 4 American Indian or Alaska Native, non-Hispanic/Latino; 28 Asian, non-Hispanic/Latino; 70 Hispanic/Latino; 32 Two or more races, non-Hispanic/Latino, 177 international. Average age 31. 1,656 applicants, 46% accepted, 294 enrolled. In 2010, 407 master's, 23 doctorates awarded. *Degree requirements:* For doctorate, thesis/dissertation. *Entrance requirements:* Additional exam requirements/recommendations for international students: Required—TOEFL (minimum score 550 paper-based; 213 computer-based; 79 iBT). *Application deadline:* Applications are processed on a rolling basis. Application fee: $75. Electronic applications accepted. *Expenses:* Contact institution. *Financial support:* In 2010–11, 48 research assistantships with full tuition reimbursements (averaging $21,909 per year), 64 teaching assistantships with full tuition reimbursements (averaging $21,830 per year) were awarded; career-related internships or fieldwork, Federal Work-Study, scholarships/grants, health care benefits, tuition waivers (partial), and unspecified assistantships also available. Financial award application deadline: 3/15. Total annual research expenditures: $4.8 million. *Unit head:* Dr. Paul R. Portney, Dean, 520-621-2125, Fax: 520-621-8105, E-mail: pportney@email.arizona.edu. *Application contact:* Information Contact, 520-621-2165, Fax: 520-621-8105, E-mail: mbaadmissions@eller.arizona.edu.

University of Arkansas, Graduate School, Sam M. Walton College of Business Administration, Program in Business Administration, Fayetteville, AR 72701-1201. Offers MBA, PhD. *Accreditation:* AACSB. Part-time and evening/weekend programs available. Postbaccalaureate distance learning degree programs offered (minimal on-campus study). *Students:* 42 full-time (6 women), 98 part-time (24 women); includes 12 minority (2 Black or African American, non-Hispanic/Latino; 2 American Indian or Alaska Native, non-Hispanic/Latino; 5 Asian, non-Hispanic/Latino; 2 Hispanic/Latino; 1 Native Hawaiian or other Pacific Islander, non-Hispanic/Latino), 13 international. 67 applicants, 87% accepted. In 2010, 91 master's awarded. *Degree requirements:* For doctorate, thesis/dissertation. *Entrance requirements:* For master's and doctorate, GMAT. Application fee: $40 ($50 for international students). *Financial support:* In 2010–11, 25 research assistantships were awarded; fellowships with tuition reimbursements, teaching assistantships, career-related internships or fieldwork and Federal Work-Study also available. Support available to part-time students. Financial award application deadline: 4/1; financial award applicants required to submit FAFSA. *Unit head:* Dr. Alan Ellstrand, MBA Director, 479-575-2851, E-mail: aellstra@uark.edu. *Application contact:* Dr. Alan Ellstrand, MBA Director, 479-575-2851, E-mail: aellstra@uark.edu.

University of California, Berkeley, Graduate Division, Haas School of Business, Berkeley-Columbia Executive MBA Program, Berkeley, CA 94720-1500. Offers MBA. *Accreditation:* AACSB. Part-time programs available. *Faculty:* 237 full-time, 262 part-time/adjunct. *Students:* 146 part-time (35 women); includes 4 Black or African American, non-Hispanic/Latino; 1 American Indian or Alaska Native, non-Hispanic/Latino; 25 Asian, non-Hispanic/Latino; 5 Hispanic/Latino, 15 international. Average age 36. In 2010, 60 master's awarded. *Entrance requirements:* For master's, GMAT. Additional exam requirements/recommendations for international students: Required—TOEFL (minimum score 570 paper-based; 230 computer-based; 68 iBT). *Application deadline:* For winter admission, 1/5 priority date for domestic students, 1/6 priority date for international students; for spring admission, 2/1 priority date for domestic and international students. Application fee: $250. Electronic applications accepted. *Expenses:* Contact institution. *Financial support:* Available to part-time students. Applicants required to submit FAFSA. *Unit head:* Carol Lo, Executive Director, Berkeley-Columbia Executive MBA Program, Haas School of Business, 510-642-8705, Fax: 510-642-0631, E-mail: carol lo@haas.berkeley.edu. Application contact: Marjorie DeGraca, Berkeley-Columbia Executive MBA Admissions Office, 510-643-1046, Fax: 510-642-0631, E-mail: emba@haas.berkeley.edu.

University of California, Berkeley, Graduate Division, Haas School of Business and School of Law, Concurrent JD/MBA Program, Berkeley, CA 94720-1500. Offers JD/MBA. *Accreditation:* AACSB; ABA. *Students:* 1 full-time (0 women). *Entrance requirements:* Additional exam requirements/recommendations for international students: Required—TOEFL. Application fee: $200. Electronic applications accepted. *Financial support:* Application deadline: 3/1. *Unit head:* Julia Hwang, Director, MBA Program, 510-642-1405, Fax: 510-643-6659, E-mail: julia hwang@haas.berkeley.edu. Application contact: Office of Admissions, 510-642-1405, Fax: 510-643-6659, E-mail: admissions@boalt.berkeley.edu.

University of California, Berkeley, Graduate Division, Haas School of Business and School of Public Health, Concurrent MBA/MPH Program, Berkeley, CA 94720-1500. Offers MBA/MPH. *Accreditation:* AACSB; CEPH. *Students:* 43 full-time (26 women); includes 14 Asian, non-Hispanic/Latino, 7 international. Average age 28. *Entrance requirements:* Additional exam requirements/recommendations for international students: Required—TOEFL. Application fee: $200. Electronic applications accepted. *Financial support:* Fellowships with tuition reimbursements, teaching assistantships with tuition reimbursements, career-related internships or fieldwork, scholarships/grants, and unspecified assistantships available. Financial award applicants required to submit FAFSA. *Unit head:* Prof. Kristi Raube, Director, Health Services Management Program, 510-642-5023, Fax: 510-643-6659, E-mail: raube@haas.berkeley.edu. *Application contact:* Lee Forgue, Student Affairs Officer, 510-642-5023, Fax: 510-643-6659, E-mail: eilis@haas.berkeley.edu.

University of California, Berkeley, Graduate Division, Haas School of Business, Evening and Weekend MBA Program, Berkeley, CA 94720-1500. Offers MBA. *Accreditation:* AACSB. Part-time and evening/weekend programs available. *Faculty:* 90 full-time (21 women), 127 part-time/adjunct (20 women). *Students:* 783 part-time (207 women); includes 187 minority (5 Black or African American, non-Hispanic/Latino; 1 American Indian or Alaska Native, non-Hispanic/Latino; 155 Asian, non-Hispanic/Latino; 19 Hispanic/Latino; 7 Two or more races, non-Hispanic/Latino), 356 international. Average age 32. 678 applicants, 42% accepted, 240 enrolled. In 2010, 248 master's awarded. *Degree requirements:* For master's, academic retreat, experiential learning course. *Entrance requirements:* For master's, GMAT. Additional exam requirements/recommendations for international students: Required—TOEFL (minimum score 570 paper-based; 230 computer-based; 68 iBT). *Application deadline:* For fall admission, 11/3 for domestic students; for winter admission, 1/10 for domestic students; for spring admission, 3/15 for domestic students. Application fee: $200. Electronic applications accepted. *Expenses:* Contact institution. *Financial support:* Scholarships/grants and unspecified assistantships available. Support available to part-time students. Financial award application deadline: 3/1; financial award applicants required to submit FAFSA. *Faculty research:* Accounting, business and public policy, economic analysis and public policy, finance, management of organizations, marketing, operations and information technology management, real estate. *Unit head:* David Gent, Executive Director, Evening & Weekend MBA Program, 510-642-1406, Fax: 510-643-5902, E-mail: ewmbaadm@haas.berkeley.edu. *Application contact:* Evening & Weekend MBA Admissions Office, 510-643-5902, Fax: 510-643-5902, E-mail: ewmbaadm@haas.berkeley.edu.

University of California, Berkeley, Graduate Division, Haas School of Business, Full-Time MBA Program, Berkeley, CA 94720-1902. Offers MBA. *Accreditation:* AACSB. *Faculty:* 90 full-time (21 women), 127 part-time/adjunct (20 women). *Students:* 497 full-time (147 women); includes 107 minority (3 Black or African American, non-Hispanic/Latino; 80 Asian, non-Hispanic/Latino; 15 Hispanic/Latino; 1 Native Hawaiian or other Pacific Islander, non-Hispanic/Latino; 8 Two or more races, non-Hispanic/Latino), 167 international. Average age 29. 3,626 applicants, 12% accepted, 243 enrolled. In 2010, 243 master's awarded. *Degree requirements:* For master's, 51 units, one Innovative Leader Curriculum experiential learning course. *Entrance requirements:* For master's, GMAT, BA/BS. Additional exam requirements/recommendations for international students: Required—TOEFL (minimum score 570 paper-based; 230 computer-based; 68 iBT), IELTS. *Application deadline:* For fall admission, 10/12 for domestic and international students; for winter admission, 12/1 for domestic and international students; for spring admission, 3/7 for domestic and international students. Application fee: $200. Electronic applications accepted. *Expenses:* Contact institution. *Financial support:* In 2010–11, 215 students received support, including 215 fellowships with full tuition reimbursements available (averaging $24,238 per year), 16 research assistantships with partial tuition reimbursements available (averaging $6,111 per year), 199 teaching assistantships with partial tuition reimbursements available (averaging $6,111 per year); career-related internships or fieldwork, institutionally sponsored loans, and scholarships/grants also available. Financial award application deadline: 6/1; financial award applicants required to submit FAFSA. *Faculty research:* Accounting, business and public policy, finance, management of organizations, marketing, operations and information technology management, real estate. *Unit head:* Julia Hwang, Executive Director, 510-642-1407, Fax: 510-643-6659, E-mail: julia hwang@haas.berkeley.edu. Application contact: Stephanie Fujii, Executive Director, Full-Time MBA Admissions, 510-642-1405, Fax: 510-643-6659, E-mail: mbaadm@haas.berkeley.edu.

University of California, Berkeley, Graduate Division, Haas School of Business and Group in International and Area Studies, MBA/MA Program in International and Area Studies, Berkeley, CA 94720-1500. Offers MBA/MA. *Accreditation:* AACSB. *Entrance requirements:* Additional exam requirements/recommendations for international students: Required—TOEFL. Application fee: $200. *Financial support:* Fellowships with full tuition reimbursements, research assistantships, teaching assistantships with partial tuition reimbursements, career-related internships or fieldwork, scholarships/grants, and unspecified assistantships available. Financial award application deadline: 3/1; financial award applicants required to submit FAFSA. *Unit head:* Julia Hwang, Director, MBA Program, 510-642-1405, Fax: 510-643-6659, E-mail:

julia hwang@haas.berkeley.edu. Application contact: 510-642-1405, Fax: 510-643-6659.

University of California, Berkeley, Graduate Division, Haas School of Business, PhD in Business Administration Program, Berkeley, CA 94720-1500. Offers accounting (PhD); business and public policy (PhD); finance (PhD); management of organizations (PhD); marketing (PhD); operations management (PhD); real estate (PhD). *Accreditation:* AACSB. *Students:* 78 full-time (25 women); includes 12 Asian, non-Hispanic/Latino; 2 Hispanic/Latino, 32 international. Average age 30. 526 applicants, 7% accepted, 17 enrolled. In 2010, 17 doctorates awarded. *Degree requirements:* For doctorate, comprehensive exam, thesis/dissertation, written preliminary exams, oral qualifying exam. *Entrance requirements:* For doctorate, GMAT or GRE, minimum GPA of 3.0 in undergraduate and graduate coursework. Additional exam requirements/recommendations for international students: Required—TOEFL (minimum score 570 paper-based; 230 computer-based; 70 iBT), IELTS (minimum score 7). *Application deadline:* For fall admission, 12/10 for domestic and international students. Application fee: $70 ($90 for international students). Electronic applications accepted. *Financial support:* In 2010–11, 63 students received support, including 58 fellowships with full and partial tuition reimbursements available (averaging $26,000 per year); research assistantships with full and partial tuition reimbursements available, teaching assistantships with full and partial tuition reimbursements available, scholarships/grants, health care benefits, tuition waivers (full), unspecified assistantships, and transit pass, travel grants also available. Financial award application deadline: 12/10; financial award applicants required to submit FAFSA. *Faculty research:* Accounting, business and public policy, finance, management of organizations, marketing, operations and information technology management, real estate526. *Unit head:* Dr. Sunil Dutta, Director, 510-642-1229, Fax: 510-643-4255, E-mail: kimg@haas.berkeley.edu. *Application contact:* Kim Guilfoyle, Director, Student Affairs, 510-642-3944, Fax: 510-643-4255, E-mail: kimg@haas.berkeley.edu.

University of California, Davis, Graduate School of Management, Daytime MBA Program, Davis, CA 95616. Offers MBA, JD/MBA, M Engr/MBA, MBA/MPH, MBA/MS, MD/MBA. *Faculty:* 31 full-time (13 women), 29 part-time/adjunct (1 woman). *Students:* 117 full-time (41 women); includes 26 minority (1 Black or African American, non-Hispanic/Latino; 19 Asian, non-Hispanic/Latino; 3 Hispanic/Latino; 3 Two or more races, non-Hispanic/Latino), 21 international. Average age 29. 429 applicants, 25% accepted, 55 enrolled. *Entrance requirements:* For master's, GMAT, letters of recommendation, resume, essays, equivalent of a 4-year U.S. undergraduate degree. Additional exam requirements/recommendations for international students: Required—TOEFL (minimum score 600 paper-based; 250 computer-based; 100 iBT), IELTS (minimum score 7), Pearson Test of English (PTE) (minimum score 68). *Application deadline:* For fall admission, 3/1 priority date for domestic students, 3/6 priority date for international students. Applications are processed on a rolling basis. Application fee: $125. Electronic applications accepted. *Financial support:* In 2010–11, 101 students received support; research assistantships with partial tuition reimbursements available, teaching assistantships with partial tuition reimbursements available, career-related internships or fieldwork, Federal Work-Study, institutionally sponsored loans, scholarships/grants, tuition waivers (partial), and unspecified assistantships available. Financial award application deadline: 3/1; financial award applicants required to submit FAFSA. *Faculty research:* Technology management, finance, marketing, corporate governance and investor welfare, organizational behavior. *Unit head:* James Stevens, Assistant Dean of Student Affairs, 530-752-7658, Fax: 530-754-9355, E-mail: admissions@gsm.ucdavis.edu. *Application contact:* Heather O'Leary, Director, Admissions, 530-752-7658, Fax: 530-754-9355, E-mail: admissions@gsm.ucdavis.edu.

University of California, Davis, Graduate School of Management, Working Professional MBA Program, Davis, CA 95616. Offers MBA. Part-time and evening/weekend programs available. *Faculty:* 31 full-time (13 women), 29 part-time/adjunct (1 woman). *Students:* 432 part-time (124 women); includes 176 minority (8 Black or African American, non-Hispanic/Latino; 3 American Indian or Alaska Native, non-Hispanic/Latino; 128 Asian, non-Hispanic/Latino; 34 Hispanic/Latino; 2 Native Hawaiian or other Pacific Islander, non-Hispanic/Latino; 1 Two or more races, non-Hispanic/Latino), 42 international. Average age 32. 213 applicants, 74% accepted, 118 enrolled. *Entrance requirements:* For master's, GMAT, letters of recommendation, resume, equivalent of a 4 year undergraduate degree. Additional exam requirements/recommendations for international students: Required—TOEFL (minimum score 600 paper-based; 250 computer-based; 100 iBT), IELTS (minimum score 7), Pearson Test of English (PTE) (minimum score 68). *Application deadline:* For fall admission, 3/31 priority date for domestic and international students. Applications are processed on a rolling basis. Application fee: $125. Electronic applications accepted. *Expenses:* Contact institution. *Financial support:* In 2010–11, 24 students received support. Scholarships/grants available. Financial award application deadline: 3/31; financial award applicants required to submit FAFSA. *Faculty research:* Technology management, finance, marketing, corporate governance and investor welfare, organizational behavior. *Unit head:* James Stevens, Assistant Dean of Student Affairs, 530-752-7658, Fax: 530-754-9355, E-mail: admissions@gsm.ucdavis.edu.

Application contact: Heather O'Leary, Director, Admissions, 530-752-7658, Fax: 530-754-9355, E-mail: admissions@gsm.ucdavis.edu.

University of California, Irvine, The Paul Merage School of Business, Doctoral Program in Management, Irvine, CA 92697. Offers PhD. *Students:* 50 full-time (20 women); includes 8 minority (7 Asian, non-Hispanic/Latino; 1 Hispanic/Latino), 19 international. Average age 28. 273 applicants, 4% accepted, 8 enrolled. In 2010, 5 doctorates awarded. Application fee: $80 ($100 for international students). *Unit head:* Dr. Robin Keller, Director, 949-824-6348, Fax: 949-824-2835, E-mail: lrkeller@uci.edu. *Application contact:* Noelia Negrete, Assistant PhD Program Director, 949-824-8318, Fax: 949-824-1592, E-mail: nnegrete@uci.edu.

University of California, Irvine, The Paul Merage School of Business, Executive MBA Program, Irvine, CA 92697. Offers EMBA. *Students:* 38 full-time (9 women), 40 part-time (13 women); includes 28 minority (1 Black or African American, non-Hispanic/Latino; 22 Asian, non-Hispanic/Latino; 5 Hispanic/Latino), 5 international. Average age 28. 74 applicants, 77% accepted, 36 enrolled. In 2010, 28 master's awarded. Application fee: $80 ($100 for international students). *Unit head:* Anthony Hansford, Assistant Dean, 949-824-3801, E-mail: hansfora@uci.edu. *Application contact:* Sofia Trinidad Dang, Associate Director, Student Affairs, 949-824-5374, Fax: 949-824-0522, E-mail: sofia.dang@uci.edu.

University of California, Irvine, The Paul Merage School of Business, Full-Time MBA Program, Irvine, CA 92697. Offers MBA. *Students:* 156 full-time (49 women), 1 (woman) part-time; includes 35 minority (1 Black or African American, non-Hispanic/Latino; 2 American Indian or Alaska Native, non-Hispanic/Latino; 28 Asian, non-Hispanic/Latino; 4 Hispanic/Latino), 63 international. Average age 28. 842 applicants, 26% accepted, 86 enrolled. In 2010, 99 master's awarded. Application fee: $80 ($100 for international students). *Unit head:* Jaycee H. Chu, Associate Director, Full-Time MBA Program Services, 949-824-8809, Fax: 949-824-2235, E-mail: jhchu@uci.edu. *Application contact:* Bradley Derek Jong, Program Coordinator, Full-Time MBA Program, 949-824-4949, Fax: 949-824-2235, E-mail: bjong@merage.uci.edu.

University of California, Irvine, The Paul Merage School of Business, Fully Employed MBA Program, Irvine, CA 92697. Offers MBA. Part-time programs available. *Students:* 147 full-time (40 women), 294 part-time (95 women); includes 163 minority (4 Black or African American, non-Hispanic/Latino; 2 American Indian or Alaska Native, non-Hispanic/Latino; 140 Asian, non-Hispanic/Latino; 14 Hispanic/Latino; 3 Native Hawaiian or other Pacific Islander, non-Hispanic/Latino), 31 international. Average age 28. 224 applicants, 77% accepted, 104 enrolled. In 2010, 173 master's awarded. *Application deadline:* For fall admission, 7/11 for domestic students. Application fee: $80 ($100 for international students). *Unit head:* Mary Clark, Assistant Dean, 949-824-4207, Fax: 949-824-2235, E-mail: mary.clark@uci.edu. *Application contact:* Jon Masciana, Director, 949-824-0595, E-mail: jmascian@uci.edu.

University of California, Los Angeles, Graduate Division, UCLA Anderson School of Management, Los Angeles, CA 90095-1481. Offers accounting (PhD); business administration (MBA); decisions, operations and technology management (PhD); finance (PhD); financial engineering (MFE); global economics and management (PhD); human resources and organizational behavior (PhD); marketing (PhD); strategy and policy (PhD); DDS/MBA; MBA/JD; MBA/MD; MBA/MLAS; MBA/MLIS; MBA/MPH; MBA/MPP; MBA/MSCS; MBA/MSN; MBA/MUP. *Accreditation:* AACSB. Part-time programs available. *Faculty:* 102 full-time (17 women), 43 part-time/adjunct (6 women). *Students:* 833 full-time (270 women), 1,052 part-time (271 women); includes 592 minority (25 Black or African American, non-Hispanic/Latino; 3 American Indian or Alaska Native, non-Hispanic/Latino; 482 Asian, non-Hispanic/Latino; 60 Hispanic/Latino; 6 Native Hawaiian or other Pacific Islander, non-Hispanic/Latino; 16 Two or more races, non-Hispanic/Latino), 445 international. In 2010, 735 master's, 10 doctorates awarded. *Degree requirements:* For master's, comprehensive exam, field study consulting project (for MBA); thesis/dissertation (for MFE); for doctorate, comprehensive exam, thesis/dissertation, oral and written qualifying exams. *Entrance requirements:* For master's, GMAT (MBA); GMAT or GRE General Test (MFE), minimum undergraduate GPA of 3.0; for doctorate, GMAT or GRE General Test, minimum undergraduate GPA of 3.0. Additional exam requirements/recommendations for international students: Required—TOEFL (minimum score 560 paper-based; 220 computer-based; 87 iBT), IELTS (minimum score 7). *Application deadline:* For fall admission, 10/20 for domestic and international students; for winter admission, 1/5 for domestic and international students; for spring admission, 4/13 for domestic and international students. Application fee: $200. Electronic applications accepted. *Expenses:* Contact institution. *Financial support:* Fellowships, research assistantships, teaching assistantships, career-related internships or fieldwork, institutionally sponsored loans, scholarships/grants, health care benefits, and tuition waivers (partial) available. Financial award application deadline: 3/2; financial award applicants required to submit FAFSA. *Unit head:* Judy D. Olian, Dean, UCLA Anderson School of Management, 310-825-7982, Fax: 310-206-2073. *Application contact:* Mae Jennifer Shores, Assistant Dean and Director of Full-time MBA Admissions

and Financial Aid, 310-825-6944, Fax: 310-825-8582, E-mail: mba.admissions@anderson.ucla.edu.

See Display on next page and Close-Up on page 263.

University of California, Riverside, Graduate Division, A. Gary Anderson Graduate School of Management, Riverside, CA 92521-0102. Offers MBA. *Accreditation:* AACSB. Part-time and evening/weekend programs available. *Faculty:* 29 full-time (3 women), 14 part-time/adjunct (2 women). *Students:* 170 full-time (78 women), 5 part-time (3 women); includes 8 Black or African American, non-Hispanic/Latino; 34 Asian, non-Hispanic/Latino; 9 Hispanic/Latino; 1 Native Hawaiian or other Pacific Islander, non-Hispanic/Latino, 88 international. Average age 33. 311 applicants, 47% accepted, 64 enrolled. In 2010, 73 master's awarded. *Degree requirements:* For master's, thesis optional. *Entrance requirements:* For master's, GMAT, minimum GPA of 3.2. Additional exam requirements/recommendations for international students: Required—TOEFL (minimum score 550 paper-based; 213 computer-based; 80 iBT). *Application deadline:* For fall admission, 9/1 for domestic students, 5/1 for international students; for winter admission, 12/1 for domestic students, 9/1 for international students; for spring admission, 3/1 for domestic students, 10/1 for international students. Applications are processed on a rolling basis. Application fee: $100 ($125 for international students). *Expenses:* Contact institution. *Financial support:* In 2010–11, 44 students received support, including 44 fellowships with partial tuition reimbursements available (averaging $19,770 per year), 47 teaching assistantships with partial tuition reimbursements available (averaging $16,500 per year); research assistantships, career-related internships or fieldwork, institutionally sponsored loans, scholarships/grants, and tuition waivers (full) also available. Financial award application deadline: 5/1; financial award applicants required to submit FAFSA. *Faculty research:* Option pricing, marketing, decision modeling, new technologies in cost accounting, supply chain management, operations, production and inventory systems, entrepreneurial finance, e-commerce. *Unit head:* Dr. David W. Stewart, Dean, 951-827-6329, Fax: 951-827-3970, E-mail: mba@ucr.edu. *Application contact:* Dr. Yunzeng Wang, Associate Dean and Graduate Adviser, 951-827-2932, Fax: 951-827-3970, E-mail: mba@ucr.edu.

University of Central Arkansas, Graduate School, College of Business Administration, Program in Business Administration, Conway, AR 72035-0001. Offers MBA. *Accreditation:* AACSB. Part-time and evening/weekend programs available. *Students:* 28 full-time (8 women), 15 part-time (6 women); includes 7 minority (4 Black or African American, non-Hispanic/Latino; 1 American Indian or Alaska Native, non-Hispanic/Latino; 1 Asian, non-Hispanic/Latino; 1 Two or more races, non-Hispanic/Latino), 5 international. Average age 26. In 2010, 35 master's awarded. *Entrance requirements:* For master's, GMAT, minimum GPA of 2.7. Additional exam requirements/recommendations for international students: Required—TOEFL (minimum score 550 paper-based; 213 computer-based). *Application deadline:* For fall admission, 3/1 priority date for domestic and international students; for spring admission, 10/1 priority date for domestic and international students. Applications are processed on a rolling basis. Application fee: $25 ($50 for international students). *Financial support:* In 2010–11, 4 research assistantships with partial tuition reimbursements (averaging $5,000 per year) were awarded; career-related internships or fieldwork, Federal Work-Study, scholarships/grants, tuition waivers (partial), and unspecified assistantships also available. Support available to part-time students. Financial award application deadline: 2/15. *Unit head:* Dr. Michael Rubach, MBA Director, 501-450-5316, Fax: 501-450-5302, E-mail: mrubach@uca.edu. *Application contact:* Brenda Herring, Admissions Assistant, 501-450-3124, Fax: 501-450-5678, E-mail: bherring@uca.edu.

University of Central Florida, College of Business Administration, Department of Management, Orlando, FL 32816. Offers entrepreneurship (Graduate Certificate); management (MSM); technology ventures (Graduate Certificate). *Accreditation:* AACSB. *Faculty:* 25 full-time (9 women), 4 part-time/adjunct (1 woman). *Students:* 30 part-time (15 women); includes 4 Black or African American, non-Hispanic/Latino; 3 Asian, non-Hispanic/Latino; 3 Hispanic/Latino. Average age 31. 8 applicants, 88% accepted, 6 enrolled. In 2010, 23 master's, 9 other advanced degrees awarded. *Entrance requirements:* For master's, GMAT, minimum GPA of 3.0 in last 60 hours. *Application deadline:* For fall admission, 2/1 priority date for domestic students; for spring admission, 11/1 priority date for domestic students. Application fee: $30. Electronic applications accepted. *Expenses:* Tuition, state resident: part-time $256.56 per credit hour. Tuition, nonresident: part-time $1011.52 per credit hour. Part-time tuition and fees vary according to program. *Financial support:* Fellowships, research assistantships, teaching assistantships available. *Unit head:* Dr. Stephen Goodman, Chair, 407-823-5569, Fax: 407-823-3725, E-mail: sgoodman@bus.ucf.edu. *Application contact:* Dr. Stephen Goodman, Chair, 407-823-5569, Fax: 407-823-3725, E-mail: sgoodman@bus.ucf.edu.

University of Central Florida, College of Business Administration, Program in Business Administration, Orlando, FL 32816. Offers MBA, PhD. *Accreditation:* AACSB. Part-time and evening/weekend programs available. *Students:* 252 full-time (102 women), 301 part-time (110 women); includes 112 minority (28 Black or African American, non-Hispanic/Latino; 2 American Indian or Alaska Native, non-Hispanic/Latino; 33 Asian, non-Hispanic/Latino; 47 Hispanic/Latino; 1 Native Hawaiian or other Pacific Islander,

UCLA ANDERSON SCHOOL OF MANAGEMENT

Celebrating 75 Years of
Business Beyond Usual

anderson.ucla.edu

non-Hispanic/Latino; 1 Two or more races, non-Hispanic/Latino), 45 international. Average age 30. In 2010, 276 master's, 11 doctorates awarded. *Degree requirements:* For master's, exam; for doctorate, thesis/dissertation, departmental candidacy exam. *Entrance requirements:* For master's and doctorate, GMAT, minimum GPA of 3.0 in last 60 hours. Additional exam requirements/recommendations for international students: Required—TOEFL. *Application deadline:* For fall admission, 2/1 priority date for domestic students; for spring admission, 11/1 priority date for domestic students. Application fee: $30. Electronic applications accepted. *Expenses:* Tuition, state resident: part-time $256.56 per credit hour. Tuition, nonresident: part-time $1011.52 per credit hour. Part-time tuition and fees vary according to program. *Financial support:* In 2010–11, 68 students received support, including 13 fellowships with partial tuition reimbursements available (averaging $8,200 per year), 9 research assistantships with partial tuition reimbursements available (averaging $3,200 per year), 66 teaching assistantships with partial tuition reimbursements available (averaging $12,400 per year); career-related internships or fieldwork, Federal Work-Study, institutionally sponsored loans, tuition waivers (partial), and unspecified assistantships also available. Financial award application deadline: 3/1; financial award applicants required to submit FAFSA. *Unit head:* Dr. Foard L. Jones, Associate Dean, 407-823-2925, E-mail: foard.jones@bus.ucf.edu. *Application contact:* Judy Ryder, Director, Graduate Admissions, 407-823-2364, Fax: 407-823-0219, E-mail: judy.ryder@bus.ucf.edu.

University of Charleston, Executive Master of Business Administration Program, Charleston, WV 25304-1099. Offers EMBA. Part-time and evening/weekend programs available. *Faculty:* 4 full-time (0 women), 1 (woman) part-time/adjunct. *Students:* 57 full-time (22 women); includes 1 minority (Native Hawaiian or other Pacific Islander, non-Hispanic/Latino). Average age 34. 37 applicants, 89% accepted, 33 enrolled. In 2010, 38 master's awarded. *Degree requirements:* For master's, successful completion of practicum paper, minimum cumulative GPA of 3.0. *Entrance requirements:* For master's, GMAT, undergraduate degree from regionally-accredited institution; minimum GPA of 3.0 in undergraduate work (recommended); three years of work experience since receiving the undergraduate degree (recommended); minimum of two professional recommendations, one from current employer, addressing career potential and ability to do graduate work. Additional exam requirements/recommendations for international students: Required—TOEFL, IELTS. *Application deadline:* Applications are processed on a rolling basis. Application fee: $40. Electronic applications accepted. Part-time tuition and fees vary according to course load and program. *Financial support:* In 2010–11, 3 students received support. Scholarships/grants available. Support available to part-time students. Financial award application deadline: 3/1; financial award applicants required to submit FAFSA. *Unit head:* Dr. Robert B. Bliss, Associate Dean, 304-357-4865, Fax: 304-357-4872, E-mail: robertbliss@ucwv.edu. *Application contact:* Dr. Robert B. Bliss, Associate Dean, 304-357-4865, Fax: 304-357-4872, E-mail: robertbliss@ucwv.edu.

University of Charleston, Master of Business Administration and Leadership Program, Charleston, WV 25304-1099. Offers MBA. *Faculty:* 3 full-time (1 woman). *Students:* 24 full-time (12 women); includes 3 minority (all Black or African American, non-Hispanic/Latino), 7 international. Average age 23. 46 applicants, 57% accepted, 11 enrolled. In 2010, 10 master's awarded. *Degree requirements:* For master's, thesis, successful completion of professional portfolio, minimum cumulative GPA of 3.0. *Entrance requirements:* For master's, official transcripts for all undergraduate work; minimum GPA of 3.0; personal interview. Additional exam requirements/recommendations for international students: Required—TOEFL, IELTS. *Application deadline:* Applications are processed on a rolling basis. Application fee: $0. Electronic applications accepted. Part-time tuition and fees vary according to course load and program. *Financial support:* Career-related internships or fieldwork and scholarships/grants available. Financial award application deadline: 3/1; financial award applicants required to submit FAFSA. *Unit head:* Dr. J. Bart Morrison, Dean, 304-357-4373, E-mail: bartmorrison@ucwv.edu. *Application contact:* Cheryl Fout, Administrative Assistant to the Dean, 304-357-4373, E-mail: cherylfout@ucwv.edu.

University of Chicago, Booth School of Business, Full-Time MBA Program, Chicago, IL 60637. Offers accounting (MBA); analytic finance (MBA); analytic management (MBA); econometrics and statistics (MBA); economics (MBA); entrepreneurship (MBA); finance (MBA); general management (MBA); human resource management (MBA); international business (MBA); managerial and organizational behavior (MBA); marketing management (MBA); operations management (MBA); strategic management (MBA); MBA/AM; MBA/JD; MBA/MA; MBA/MD; MBA/MPP. *Accreditation:* AACSB. Part-time and evening/weekend programs available. *Faculty:* 157 full-time, 35 part-time/adjunct. *Students:* 1,177 full-time (417 women); includes 301 minority (62 Black or African American, non-Hispanic/Latino; 1 American Indian or Alaska Native, non-Hispanic/Latino; 164 Asian, non-Hispanic/Latino; 55 Hispanic/Latino; 19 Two or more races, non-Hispanic/Latino), 403 international. Average age 28. 4,299 applicants, 22% accepted, 579 enrolled. In 2010, 1,374 master's awarded. *Entrance requirements:* For master's, GMAT, 2 letters of recommendation, 3 essays, resume, interview, transcripts. Additional exam requirements/recommendations for international students: Required—TOEFL (minimum score 600 paper-based; 250 computer-based), IELTS. *Application deadline:* For fall admission, 10/10 priority date for domestic students, 10/13 priority date for international students; for winter admission, 1/5 for domestic and international students; for spring admission, 4/13 for domestic and international students. Application fee: $200. Electronic applications accepted. *Expenses:* Contact institution. *Financial support:* Fellowships available. Financial award applicants required to submit FAFSA. *Faculty research:* Finance, economics, entrepreneurship, strategy, management. *Unit head:* Stacey Kole, Deputy Dean, 773-702-7121. *Application contact:* Kurt Ahlm, Associate Dean of Admissions and Financial Aid, 773-702-7369, Fax: 773-702-9085, E-mail: admissions@chicagobooth.edu.

University of Cincinnati, Graduate School, College of Business, MBA Program, Cincinnati, OH 45221. Offers MBA. Part-time and evening/weekend programs available. *Faculty:* 79 full-time (22 women), 71 part-time/adjunct (24 women). *Students:* 93 full-time (33 women), 91 part-time (31 women); includes 19 minority (4 Black or African American, non-Hispanic/Latino; 11 Asian, non-Hispanic/Latino; 3 Hispanic/Latino; 1 Native Hawaiian or other Pacific Islander, non-Hispanic/Latino), 38 international. 231 applicants, 85% accepted, 112 enrolled. *Degree requirements:* For master's, capstone project. *Entrance requirements:* For master's, GMAT, resume, letters of recommendation, essays, official transcripts. Additional exam requirements/recommendations for international students: Required—TOEFL (minimum score 600 paper-based; 250 computer-based; 100 iBT). *Application deadline:* For fall admission, 1/15 priority date for domestic students, 4/1 for international students. Application fee: $45. Electronic applications accepted. *Expenses:* Contact institution. *Financial support:* Scholarships/grants, tuition waivers (full and partial), and unspecified assistantships available. Financial award application deadline: 2/1; financial award applicants required to submit FAFSA. *Unit head:* Dr. Robert Dwyer, Academic Program Director, 513-556-7103, E-mail: robert.dwyer@uc.edu. *Application contact:* Dona Clary, Director, Graduate Programs Office, 513-556-3546, Fax: 513-558-7006, E-mail: dona.clary@uc.edu.

University of Cincinnati, Graduate School, College of Business, PhD Program, Cincinnati, OH 45221. Offers accounting (PhD); finance (PhD); information systems (PhD); management (PhD); marketing (PhD); quantitative analysis and operations management (PhD). *Faculty:* 56 full-time (13 women). *Students:* 32 full-time (12 women), 9 part-time (3 women); includes 2 minority (both Hispanic/Latino), 23 international. 119 applicants, 12% accepted, 9 enrolled. In 2010, 8 doctorates awarded. *Degree requirements:* For doctorate, comprehensive exam, thesis/dissertation. *Entrance requirements:* For doctorate, GMAT, GRE, transcripts, essays, resume, letters of recommendation. Additional exam requirements/recommendations for international students: Required—TOEFL (minimum score 600 paper-based; 250 computer-based; 100 iBT). *Application deadline:* For fall admission, 2/1 for domestic and international students. Application fee: $45. Electronic applications accepted. *Expenses:* Contact institution. *Financial support:* In 2010–11, 38 students received support, including 29 research assistantships with full and partial tuition reimbursements available (averaging $14,640 per year); scholarships/grants, tuition waivers (full and partial), and unspecified assistantships also available. Financial award application deadline: 2/15; financial award applicants required to submit FAFSA. *Unit head:* Dr. Suzanne Masterson, Director, PhD Programs, 513-556-7125, Fax: 513-556-5499, E-mail: suzanne.masterson@uc.edu. *Application contact:* Deborah Schildknecht, Assistant Director, PhD Programs, 513-556-7190, Fax: 513-558-7006, E-mail: deborah.schildknecht@uc.edu.

University of Colorado at Colorado Springs, Graduate School of Business Administration, Colorado Springs, CO 80933-7150. Offers MBA. *Accreditation:* AACSB. Part-time and evening/weekend programs available. *Faculty:* 32 full-time (11 women), 8 part-time/adjunct (3 women). *Students:* 250 full-time (84 women), 94 part-time (39 women); includes 10 Black or African American, non-Hispanic/Latino; 1 American Indian or Alaska Native, non-Hispanic/Latino; 12 Asian, non-Hispanic/Latino; 16 Hispanic/Latino, 14 international. Average age 32. 169 applicants, 73% accepted, 68 enrolled. In 2010, 117 master's awarded. *Entrance requirements:* For master's, GMAT. *Application deadline:* For fall admission, 6/1 for domestic students; for spring admission, 11/1 for domestic students. Application fee: $60 ($75 for international students). *Expenses:* Contact institution. *Financial support:* Career-related internships or fieldwork, Federal Work-Study, and scholarships/grants available. Support available to part-time students. Financial award application deadline: 3/1; financial award applicants required to submit FAFSA. *Faculty research:* Quality financial reporting, investments and corporate governance, group support systems, environmental and project management, customer relationship management. *Unit head:* Dr. Venkateshwar Reddy, Dean, 719-255-3113, Fax: 719-255-3100, E-mail: vreddy@uccs.edu. *Application contact:* Windy Haddad, MBA Program Director, 719-255-3401, Fax: 719-255-3100, E-mail: whaddad@uccs.edu.

University of Colorado Boulder, Leeds School of Business, Master of Business Administration Program, Boulder, CO 80309. Offers MBA. *Accreditation:* AACSB. *Students:* 328 full-time (97 women), 4 part-time (3 women); includes 18 minority (1 Black or African American, non-Hispanic/Latino; 2 American Indian or Alaska Native, non-Hispanic/Latino; 12 Asian, non-Hispanic/Latino; 3 Hispanic/Latino), 22 international. Average age 30. In 2010, 151 master's awarded. *Entrance requirements:* For master's, GMAT,

minimum undergraduate GPA of 2.75. *Application deadline:* Applications are processed on a rolling basis. Application fee: $50 ($60 for international students). *Financial support:* In 2010–11, 79 fellowships (averaging $5,842 per year), 1 research assistantship (averaging $2,016 per year) were awarded. Financial award applicants required to submit FAFSA.

University of Colorado Denver, Business School, Master of Business Administration Program, Denver, CO 80217-3364. Offers business administration (MBA); health administration (MBA). *Accreditation:* AACSB. Part-time and evening/weekend programs available. Postbaccalaureate distance learning degree programs offered (no on-campus study). *Students:* 814 full-time (300 women), 182 part-time (73 women); includes 12 Black or African American, non-Hispanic/Latino; 6 American Indian or Alaska Native, non-Hispanic/Latino; 66 Asian, non-Hispanic/Latino; 48 Hispanic/Latino; 1 Two or more races, non-Hispanic/Latino, 44 international. Average age 31. 458 applicants, 72% accepted, 252 enrolled. In 2010, 340 master's awarded. *Degree requirements:* For master's, 48 semester hours, including 30 of core courses, 3 in international business, and 15 in electives from over 50 other graduate business courses. *Entrance requirements:* For master's, GMAT, resume, official transcripts. Additional exam requirements/recommendations for international students: Required—TOEFL (minimum score 525 paper-based; 197 computer-based; 71 iBT). *Application deadline:* For fall admission, 4/1 for domestic students, 3/15 for international students; for spring admission, 10/1 for domestic and international students. Applications are processed on a rolling basis. Application fee: $50 ($75 for international students). Electronic applications accepted. *Expenses:* Contact institution. *Financial support:* Scholarships/grants available. Support available to part-time students. Financial award application deadline: 4/1; financial award applicants required to submit FAFSA. *Faculty research:* Marketing, management, entrepreneurship, finance, health administration. *Unit head:* Elizabeth Cooperman, Professor of Finance and Managing for Sustainability/MBA Program Director, 303-315-8422, E-mail: elizabeth.cooperman@ucdenver.edu. *Application contact:* Shelly Townley, Admissions Director, Graduate Programs, 303-315-8202, E-mail: shelly.townley@ucdenver.edu.

University of Colorado Denver, Business School, Program in Management and Organization, Denver, CO 80217. Offers communications management (MS); enterprise technology management (MS); entrepreneurship and innovation (MS); global management (MS); human resources management (MS); leadership (MS); quantitative decision methods (MS); sports and entertainment management (MS); strategic management (MS); sustainability management (MS). *Accreditation:* AACSB. Part-time and evening/weekend programs available. Postbaccalaureate distance learning degree programs offered (no on-campus study). *Students:* 34 full-time (21 women), 9 part-time (2 women); includes 3 Asian, non-Hispanic/Latino; 5 Hispanic/Latino. Average age 33. 28 applicants, 61% accepted, 10 enrolled. In 2010, 20 master's awarded. *Degree requirements:* For master's, 30 semester hours (12 of required courses, 12 of management electives, and 6 of free electives). *Entrance requirements:* For master's, GMAT. Additional exam requirements/recommendations for international students: Required—TOEFL (minimum score 525 paper-based; 197 computer-based; 71 iBT). *Application deadline:* For fall admission, 4/1 priority date for domestic students, 3/15 priority date for international students; for spring admission, 10/1 priority date for domestic and international students. Application fee: $50 ($75 for international students). Electronic applications accepted. *Expenses:* Contact institution. *Financial support:* Federal Work-Study and scholarships/grants available. Support available to part-time students. Financial award application deadline: 4/1; financial award applicants required to submit FAFSA. *Faculty research:* Human resource management, management of catastrophe, turnaround strategies. *Unit head:* Dr. Kenneth Bettenhausen, Associate Professor/Director, 303-315-8425, E-mail: kenneth.bettehausen@ucdenver.edu. *Application contact:* Shelly Townley, Admissions Director, Graduate Programs, 303-315-8202, E-mail: shelly.townley@ucdenver.edu.

University of Connecticut, Graduate School, School of Business, Storrs, CT 06269. Offers accounting (MS, PhD); business administration (Exec MBA, MBA, PhD); finance (PhD); health care management and insurance studies (MBA); management (PhD); management consulting (MBA); marketing (PhD); marketing intelligence (MBA); MA/MBA; MBA/MSW. *Accreditation:* AACSB. *Degree requirements:* For master's, comprehensive exam; for doctorate, thesis/dissertation. *Entrance requirements:* For master's and doctorate, GMAT. Additional exam requirements/recommendations for international students: Required—TOEFL (minimum score 550 paper-based; 213 computer-based). Electronic applications accepted.

See Display on the next page and Close-Up on page 265.

University of Dayton, Graduate School, School of Business Administration, Dayton, OH 45469-1300. Offers accounting (MBA); business intelligence (MBA); cyber security (MBA); entrepreneurship (MBA); finance (MBA); international business (MBA); marketing (MBA); MIS (MBA); operations management (MBA); technology-enhanced business/e-commerce (MBA); JD/MBA. *Accreditation:* AACSB. Part-time and evening/weekend programs available. *Faculty:* 25 full-time (7 women), 14 part-time/adjunct (2 women). *Students:* 184 full-time (72 women), 110 part-time (34 women); includes 23 minority (7 Black or African American, non-Hispanic/Latino; 7 Asian, non-Hispanic/Latino; 8 Hispanic/Latino; 1 Two or more races, non-Hispanic/Latino), 31 international. Average age 28. 220 applicants, 85% accepted, 103 enrolled. In 2010, 113 master's awarded. *Entrance requirements:* For master's, GMAT or GRE. Additional exam requirements/recommendations for international students: Required—TOEFL (minimum score 550 paper-based; 213 computer-based; 79 iBT); Recommended—IELTS (minimum score 6.5). *Application deadline:* For fall admission, 3/1 priority date for international students; for winter admission, 7/1 priority date for international students; for spring admission, 1/1 priority date for international students. Applications are processed on a rolling basis. Application fee: $0 ($50 for international students). Electronic applications accepted. *Expenses:* Contact institution. *Financial support:* In 2010–11, 15 research assistantships with full and partial tuition reimbursements (averaging $7,020 per year) were awarded; career-related internships or fieldwork, institutionally sponsored loans, scholarships/grants, health care benefits, and unspecified assistantships also available. Support available to part-time students. Financial award application deadline: 3/15; financial award applicants required to submit FAFSA. *Faculty research:* Management information systems, economics, finance, entrepreneurship, marketing. *Unit head:* Janice M. Glynn, Director, MBA Program, 937-229-3733, Fax: 937-229-3882, E-mail: glynn@udayton.edu. *Application contact:* Jeffrey Carter, Assistant Director, MBA Program, 937-229-3733, Fax: 937-229-3882, E-mail: jeff.carter@notes.udayton.edu.

University of Denver, Daniels College of Business, Denver, CO 80208. Offers EMS, IMBA, M Acc, MBA, MS. *Accreditation:* AACSB. Part-time and evening/weekend programs available. *Faculty:* 117 full-time (27 women), 59 part-time/adjunct (19 women). *Students:* 540 full-time (193 women), 485 part-time (191 women); includes 103 minority (13 Black or African American, non-Hispanic/Latino; 4 American Indian or Alaska Native, non-Hispanic/Latino; 36 Asian, non-Hispanic/Latino; 44 Hispanic/Latino; 1 Native Hawaiian or other Pacific Islander, non-Hispanic/Latino; 5 Two or more races, non-Hispanic/Latino), 271 international. Average age 29. 1,870 applicants, 50% accepted, 381 enrolled. In 2010, 587 master's awarded. *Entrance requirements:* For master's, GMAT or GRE General Test. Additional exam requirements/recommendations for international students: Required—TOEFL (minimum score 570 paper-based; 88 iBT). *Application deadline:* For fall admission, 1/15 priority date for domestic students. Applications are processed on a rolling basis. Application fee: $60. Electronic applications accepted. *Expenses:* Tuition: Full-time $35,604; part-time $29,670 per year. Required fees: $687 per year. Tuition and fees vary according to program. *Financial support:* In 2010–11, 99 teaching assistantships with full and partial tuition reimbursements (averaging $1,669 per year) were awarded; career-related internships or fieldwork,

Federal Work-Study, institutionally sponsored loans, scholarships/grants, and unspecified assistantships also available. Support available to part-time students. Financial award application deadline: 2/15; financial award applicants required to submit FAFSA. *Unit head:* Dr. Chris Riordan, Dean, 303-871-4324, E-mail: christine.riordan@du.edu. *Application contact:* Admissions, 303-871-3416, Fax: 303-571-4466, E-mail: daniels@du.edu.

University of Evansville, Schroeder Family School of Business Administration, Evansville, IN 47722. Offers executive business administration (MBA). *Accreditation:* AACSB. Part-time and evening/weekend programs available. *Faculty:* 1 (woman) part-time/adjunct. *Students:* 9 full-time (2 women); includes 1 minority (Hispanic/Latino). Average age 41. 16 applicants, 81% accepted, 8 enrolled. In 2010, 6 master's awarded. *Entrance requirements:* For master's, GMAT or GRE (upon request), minimum 5 years professional experience, 2 letters of recommendation. Additional exam requirements/recommendations for international students: Required—TOEFL (minimum score 577 paper-based; 90 iBT). *Application deadline:* For fall admission, 6/1 for domestic students, 4/1 for international students. Applications are processed on a rolling basis. Application fee: $75. *Expenses:* Contact institution. *Financial support:* In 2010–11, 3 students received support. Application deadline: 6/1. *Unit head:* Dr. Peter Sherman, Interim Dean, 812-488-2851, Fax: 812-488-2872, E-mail: ps45@evansville.edu. *Application contact:* Dr. Peter Rosen, Chair, EMBA Admissions, 812-488-2851, Fax: 812-488-2872, E-mail: emba@evansville.edu.

The University of Findlay, Graduate and Professional Studies, College of Business, Findlay, OH 45840-3653. Offers health care management (MBA); hospitality management (MBA); organizational leadership (MBA); public management (MBA). Part-time and evening/weekend programs available. Postbaccalaureate distance learning degree programs offered (no on-campus study). *Faculty:* 20 full-time (5 women), 6 part-time/adjunct (0 women). *Students:* 25 full-time (11 women), 239 part-time (112 women); includes 15 minority (5 Black or African American, non-Hispanic/Latino; 9 Asian, non-Hispanic/Latino; 1 Hispanic/Latino), 98 international. Average age 25. 93 applicants, 86% accepted, 70 enrolled. In 2010, 283 master's awarded. *Degree requirements:* For master's, thesis, cumulative project. *Entrance requirements:* For master's, GMAT or GRE, minimum undergraduate GPA of 3.0. Additional exam requirements/recommendations for international students: Required—TOEFL (minimum score 550 paper-based; 213 computer-based; 80 iBT). *Application deadline:* Applications are processed on a rolling basis. Application fee: $25. Electronic applications accepted. *Expenses:* Contact institution. *Financial support:* In 2010–11, 8 research assistantships with full and partial tuition reimbursements (averaging $4,200 per year) were awarded;

career-related internships or fieldwork, Federal Work-Study, health care benefits, and unspecified assistantships also available. Financial award application deadline: 4/1; financial award applicants required to submit FAFSA. *Faculty research:* Health care management, operations and logistics management. *Unit head:* Dr. Paul Sears, Dean, College of Business, 419-434-4704, Fax: 419-434-4822. *Application contact:* Heather Riffle, Assistant Director, Graduate and Professional Studies, 419-434-4640, Fax: 419-434-5517, E-mail: riffle@findlay.edu.

University of Florida, Graduate School, Warrington College of Business Administration, Hough Graduate School of Business, Department of Finance, Insurance and Real Estate, Gainesville, FL 32611. Offers business administration (MS), including entrepreneurship, real estate and urban analysis; finance (PhD); financial services (Certificate); real estate and urban analysis (PhD); JD/MBA. *Faculty:* 13 full-time (0 women). *Students:* 56 full-time (13 women), 2 part-time (0 women); includes 2 Black or African American, non-Hispanic/Latino; 2 Asian, non-Hispanic/Latino; 1 Hispanic/Latino, 16 international. Average age 27. 245 applicants, 34% accepted, 58 enrolled. In 2010, 105 master's awarded. Terminal master's awarded for partial completion of doctoral program. *Degree requirements:* For master's, comprehensive exam, thesis; for doctorate, comprehensive exam, thesis/dissertation. *Entrance requirements:* For master's, GMAT or GRE General Test, minimum GPA of 3.0 for last 60 hours of undergraduate degree, work experience (preferred); for doctorate, GMAT or GRE General Test, minimum GPA of 3.0. Additional exam requirements/recommendations for international students: Required—TOEFL (minimum score 550 paper-based; 213 computer-based; 80 iBT), IELTS (minimum score 6). *Application deadline:* For fall admission, 1/15 priority date for domestic students, 1/15 for international students. Applications are processed on a rolling basis. Application fee: $30. Electronic applications accepted. *Expenses:* Tuition, state resident: full-time $10,915.92. Tuition, nonresident: full-time $28,309. *Financial support:* In 2010–11, 18 students received support, including 6 fellowships, 12 research assistantships (averaging $20,699 per year), 2 teaching assistantships; career-related internships or fieldwork, scholarships/grants, and unspecified assistantships also available. Financial award application deadline: 1/15; financial award applicants required to submit FAFSA. *Faculty research:* Banking, empirical corporate finance, hedge funds. *Unit head:* Dr. Mahendrarajah Nimalendran, Chair, 352-392-9526, Fax: 352-392-0301, E-mail: nimal@ufl.edu. *Application contact:* Mark J. Flannery, Graduate Coordinator, 352-392-3184, Fax: 352-392-0301, E-mail: flannery@ufl.edu.

University of Florida, Graduate School, Warrington College of Business Administration, Hough Graduate School of Business, Department of Management, Gainesville, FL 32611. Offers international business (MAIB); management (MSM, PhD). *Accreditation:* AACSB. Postbaccalaureate distance learning degree programs offered. *Faculty:* 11 full-time (2 women). *Students:* 223 full-time (103 women), 66 part-time (35 women); includes 12 Black or African American, non-Hispanic/Latino; 1 American Indian or Alaska Native, non-Hispanic/Latino; 16 Asian, non-Hispanic/Latino; 40 Hispanic/Latino, 42 international. Average age 28. 37 applicants, 59% accepted, 15 enrolled. In 2010, 234 master's, 3 doctorates awarded. *Degree requirements:* For master's, comprehensive exam, thesis; for doctorate, comprehensive exam, thesis/dissertation. *Entrance requirements:* For master's and doctorate, GMAT or GRE General Test, minimum GPA of 3.0. Additional exam requirements/recommendations for international students: Required—TOEFL (minimum score 550 paper-based; 213 computer-based; 80 iBT), IELTS (minimum score 6). *Application deadline:* For fall admission, 1/1 for domestic and international students. Applications are processed on a rolling basis. Application fee: $30. Electronic applications accepted. *Expenses:* Tuition, state resident: full-time $10,915.92. Tuition, nonresident: full-time $28,309. *Financial support:* In 2010–11, 18 students received support, including 10 fellowships, 4 research assistantships (averaging $21,839 per year), 4 teaching assistantships (averaging $15,288 per year); unspecified assistantships also available. Financial award applicants required to submit FAFSA. *Faculty research:* Job attitudes, personality and individual differences, organizational entry and exit, knowledge management, competitive dynamics. *Unit head:* Dr. Robert E. Thomas, Chair, 352-392-0136, Fax: 352-392-6020, E-mail: rethomas@ufl.edu. *Application contact:* Dr. Jason A. Colquitt, Graduate Coordinator, 352-846-0507, Fax: 352-392-6020, E-mail: colquitt@ufl.edu.

University of Florida, Graduate School, Warrington College of Business Administration, Hough Graduate School of Business, Programs in Business Administration, Gainesville, FL 32611. Offers accounting (MBA); arts administration (MBA); business strategy and public policy (MBA); competitive strategy (MBA); decision and information sciences (MBA); electronic commerce (MBA); finance (MBA); general business (MBA); global management (MBA); Graham-Buffett security analysis (MBA); health administration (MBA); human resources management (MBA); international studies (MBA); Latin American business (MBA); management (MBA); marketing (MBA); sports administration (MBA); JD/MBA; MBA/MS; MBA/PhD; MBA/Pharm D; MD/MBA. *Accreditation:* AACSB. Part-time and evening/weekend programs available. *Faculty:* 71 full-time (10 women). *Students:* 187 full-time (44 women), 305 part-time (83 women); includes 25 Black or African American, non-Hispanic/Latino; 2 American Indian or Alaska Native, non-Hispanic/Latino; 52 Asian, non-Hispanic/Latino; 54 Hispanic/Latino, 11

international. Average age 31. 919 applicants, 33% accepted, 225 enrolled. In 2010, 492 master's awarded. *Degree requirements:* For master's, capstone course. *Entrance requirements:* For master's, GMAT, minimum GPA of 3.0, interview. Additional exam requirements/recommendations for international students: Required—TOEFL (minimum score 550 paper-based; 213 computer-based; 80 iBT), IELTS (minimum score 6). *Application deadline:* For fall admission, 7/1 for domestic students, 1/1 for international students; for spring admission, 12/1 for domestic and international students. Applications are processed on a rolling basis. Application fee: $30. Electronic applications accepted. *Expenses:* Tuition, state resident: full-time $10,915.92. Tuition, non-resident: full-time $28,309. *Financial support:* In 2010–11, 1 student received support, including 1 teaching assistantship (averaging $20,600 per year); career-related internships or fieldwork, scholarships/grants, and unspecified assistantships also available. Support available to part-time students. Financial award applicants required to submit FAFSA. *Faculty research:* Accounting, finance, insurance, management, real estate, urban analysis marketing. *Unit head:* Prof. Alexander D. Sevilla, Assistant Dean and Director MBA Programs, 352-273-3252 Ext. 1206, E-mail: alex.sevilla@warrington.ufl.edu. *Application contact:* Prof. Kelli Gust, Associate Director of MBA Programs, 352-273-3255, Fax: 352-392-8791, E-mail: kelly.gust@warrington.ufl.edu.

University of Georgia, Terry College of Business, Program in Business Administration, Athens, GA 30602. Offers MA, MBA, PhD, JD/MBA. *Accreditation:* AACSB. *Students:* 171 full-time (46 women), 2 part-time (0 women); includes 9 Black or African American, non-Hispanic/Latino; 5 Asian, non-Hispanic/Latino; 3 Hispanic/Latino, 45 international. 632 applicants, 43% accepted. In 2010, 81 master's, 4 doctorates awarded. *Degree requirements:* For master's, thesis (MA); for doctorate, thesis/dissertation. *Entrance requirements:* For master's, GMAT (MBA), GRE General Test (MA); for doctorate, GMAT or GRE General Test. *Application deadline:* For fall admission, 7/1 priority date for domestic students; for spring admission, 11/15 for domestic students. Application fee: $50. Electronic applications accepted. *Expenses:* Tuition, state resident: full-time $7200; part-time $344 per credit hour. Tuition, nonresident: full-time $21,900; part-time $944 per credit hour. Tuition and fees vary according to course load and program. *Financial support:* Fellowships, research assistantships, teaching assistantships, unspecified assistantships available. *Unit head:* Dr. Richard L. Daniels, Director, 404-842-4862, Fax: 706-542-5351, E-mail: rdaniels@terry.uga.edu. *Application contact:* Interim Associate Dean.

University of Hawaii at Manoa, Graduate Division, Shidler College of Business, Executive MBA Programs, Honolulu, HI 96822. Offers executive business administration (EMBA); Vietnam focused business administration (EMBA). *Accreditation:* AACSB. Part-time programs available. *Entrance requirements:* For master's, GMAT, minimum GPA of 3.0. *Application deadline:* For fall admission, 5/1 for domestic and international students; for spring admission, 11/1 for domestic and international students. Application fee: $50. *Application contact:* Alice Li, Assistant Director, 808-956-8870, Fax: 808-956-3766, E-mail: emba@hawaii.edu.

University of Hawaii at Manoa, Graduate Division, Shidler College of Business, Program in Business Administration, Honolulu, HI 96822. Offers Asian business studies (MBA); Chinese business studies (MBA); decision sciences (MBA); entrepreneurship (MBA); finance (MBA); finance and banking (MBA); human resources management (MBA); information management (MBA); information technology (MBA); international business (MBA); Japanese business studies (MBA); marketing (MBA); organizational behavior (MBA); organizational management (MBA); real estate (MBA); student-designed track (MBA). *Accreditation:* AACSB. Part-time and evening/weekend programs available. *Faculty:* 53 full-time (12 women). *Students:* 162 full-time (63 women), 102 part-time (43 women); includes 135 minority (1 Black or African American, non-Hispanic/Latino; 81 Asian, non-Hispanic/Latino; 5 Hispanic/Latino; 18 Native Hawaiian or other Pacific Islander, non-Hispanic/Latino; 30 Two or more races, non-Hispanic/Latino), 44 international. Average age 34. 361 applicants, 57% accepted, 172 enrolled. In 2010, 153 master's awarded. *Degree requirements:* For master's, thesis optional. *Entrance requirements:* For master's, GMAT, minimum GPA of 3.0. Additional exam requirements/recommendations for international students: Required—TOEFL (minimum score 600 paper-based; 250 computer-based; 100 iBT), IELTS (minimum score 7). *Application deadline:* For fall admission, 5/1 for domestic students, 3/1 for international students. Application fee: $60. *Expenses:* Contact institution. *Financial support:* In 2010–11, 83 fellowships (averaging $5,547 per year), 1 research assistantship (averaging $16,824 per year) were awarded. Total annual research expenditures: $427,000. *Application contact:* Daniel Port, Graduate Chair, 808-956-5565, Fax: 808-956-6889, E-mail: daniel.port@hawaii.edu.

University of Houston, Bauer College of Business, Houston, TX 77204. Offers MBA, MS, MS Accy, PhD. *Accreditation:* AACSB. Part-time and evening/weekend programs available. *Faculty:* 52 full-time (10 women), 44 part-time/adjunct (9 women). *Students:* 774 full-time (311 women), 699 part-time (230 women); includes 533 minority (105 Black or African American, non-Hispanic/Latino; 4 American Indian or Alaska Native, non-Hispanic/Latino; 251 Asian, non-Hispanic/Latino; 159 Hispanic/Latino; 2 Native Hawaiian or other Pacific Islander, non-Hispanic/Latino; 12 Two or more races, non-Hispanic/Latino), 276 international. Average age 29. 1,173 applicants, 56% accepted,

481 enrolled. In 2010, 601 master's, 14 doctorates awarded. *Degree requirements:* For master's, 30 hours completed in residence, minimum cumulative GPA of 3.0 at UH, no more than 11 semester hours of 'C' grades or below in graduate courses taken at UH; for doctorate, comprehensive exam, thesis/dissertation, minimum GPA of 3.25, continuous full time enrollment, dissertation defense within 6 years of entering the program. *Entrance requirements:* For master's, GMAT or GRE (MBA), official transcripts from all higher education institutions attended, resume, letters of recommendation, self appraisal and goal statement (MBA); for doctorate, GMAT or GRE, letter of financial backing, statement of understanding, reference letters, statement of academic and research interests. Additional exam requirements/recommendations for international students: Required—TOEFL (minimum score 603 paper-based; 250 computer-based; 100 iBT), IELTS (minimum score 6.5), Pearson Test of English (minimum score: 70). *Application deadline:* For fall admission, 6/1 for domestic students, 4/1 for international students; for spring admission, 11/1 for domestic students, 10/1 for international students. Applications are processed on a rolling basis. Application fee: $75 ($150 for international students). Electronic applications accepted. *Expenses:* Tuition, state resident: full-time $8592; part-time $358 per credit hour. Tuition, nonresident: full-time $16,032; part-time $668 per credit hour. Required fees: $2889. Tuition and fees vary according to course load and program. *Financial support:* In 2010–11, 26 fellowships with partial tuition reimbursements (averaging $2,400 per year), 2 research assistantships with partial tuition reimbursements (averaging $8,800 per year), 54 teaching assistantships with partial tuition reimbursements (averaging $14,571 per year) were awarded; career-related internships or fieldwork, Federal Work-Study, institutionally sponsored loans, scholarships/grants, health care benefits, and unspecified assistantships also available. Support available to part-time students. Financial award application deadline: 2/1; financial award applicants required to submit FAFSA. *Faculty research:* Accountancy and taxation, finance, international business, management. *Unit head:* Dr. Latha Ramchand, Interim Dean, 713-743-4604, Fax: 713-743-4622, E-mail: ramchand@uh.edu. *Application contact:* Dr. Latha Ramchand, Interim Dean, 713-743-4604, Fax: 713-743-4622, E-mail: ramchand@uh.edu.

University of Houston–Victoria, School of Business Administration, Victoria, TX 77901-4450. Offers accounting (MBA); economic development and entrepreneurship (MS); finance (GMBA, MBA); general business (MBA); international business (MBA); management (GMBA, MBA); marketing (MBA). *Accreditation:* AACSB. Part-time and evening/weekend programs available. Postbaccalaureate distance learning degree programs offered (minimal on-campus study). *Faculty:* 37 full-time (11 women). *Students:* 234 full-time (108 women), 714 part-time (303 women); includes 542 minority (215 Black or African American, non-Hispanic/Latino; 1 American Indian or Alaska Native, non-Hispanic/Latino; 197 Asian, non-Hispanic/Latino; 124 Hispanic/Latino; 1 Native Hawaiian or other Pacific Islander, non-Hispanic/Latino; 4 Two or more races, non-Hispanic/Latino), 115 international. Average age 34. 362 applicants, 65% accepted, 147 enrolled. In 2010, 181 master's awarded. *Entrance requirements:* For master's, GMAT. Additional exam requirements/recommendations for international students: Required—TOEFL (minimum score 550 paper-based; 213 computer-based). *Application deadline:* For fall admission, 6/1 for international students; for spring admission, 10/1 for international students. Applications are processed on a rolling basis. Application fee: $0. Electronic applications accepted. *Expenses:* Tuition, state resident: full-time $4050; part-time $225 per credit hour. Tuition, nonresident: full-time $8730; part-time $485 per credit hour. Required fees: $810; $54 per credit hour. Tuition and fees vary according to course load. *Financial support:* In 2010–11, research assistantships with partial tuition reimbursements (averaging $2,000 per year), teaching assistantships with partial tuition reimbursements (averaging $2,000 per year) were awarded; Federal Work-Study, scholarships/grants, and unspecified assistantships also available. Support available to part-time students. Financial award application deadline: 4/15; financial award applicants required to submit FAFSA. *Faculty research:* Economic development, marketing, finance. *Unit head:* Dr. Farhang Niroomand, Dean, 361-570-4230, Fax: 361-580-5599, E-mail: niroomandf@uhv.edu. *Application contact:* Jane Mims, Assistant Dean, 361-570-4639, Fax: 361-580-5529, E-mail: mims@uhv.edu.

University of Idaho, College of Graduate Studies, College of Business and Economics, Department of Business and Economics, Moscow, ID 83844-2282. Offers economics (MS); general management (MBA). *Faculty:* 8 full-time, 1 part-time/adjunct. *Students:* 9 full-time, 7 part-time. Average age 41. In 2010, 9 master's awarded. *Application deadline:* For fall admission, 8/1 for domestic students; for spring admission, 12/15 for domestic students. Applications are processed on a rolling basis. Application fee: $60. Electronic applications accepted. *Expenses:* Tuition, nonresident: part-time $580 per credit. Required fees: $306 per credit. *Financial support:* Applicants required to submit FAFSA. *Unit head:* Dr. Mario Reyes, Associate Dean, 208-885-6478, E-mail: cbe@uidaho.edu. *Application contact:* Dr. Mario Reyes, Associate Dean, 208-885-6478, E-mail: cbe@uidaho.edu.

University of Illinois at Urbana–Champaign, Graduate College, College of Business, Department of Business Administration, Champaign, IL 61820. Offers business administration (MS, PhD); technology management (MS). *Accreditation:* AACSB. *Faculty:* 44 full-time (8 women), 5 part-time/adjunct (1 woman). *Students:* 98 full-time (36 women), 11 part-time (4 women); includes 6 Asian, non-Hispanic/Latino, 91 international. 344 applicants, 24% accepted, 58 enrolled. In 2010, 46 master's, 10 doctorates awarded. *Entrance requirements:* For master's, minimum GPA of 3.0; for doctorate, GMAT or GRE, minimum GPA of 3.0. Additional exam requirements/recommendations for international students: Required—TOEFL (minimum score 550 paper-based; 231 computer-based; 79 iBT) or IELTS (6.5). *Application deadline:* Applications are processed on a rolling basis. Application fee: $75 ($90 for international students). Electronic applications accepted. *Expenses:* Contact institution. *Financial support:* In 2010–11, 24 fellowships, 38 research assistantships, 16 teaching assistantships were awarded; tuition waivers (full and partial) also available. *Unit head:* William J. Qualls, Interim Head, 217-265-0794, Fax: 217-244-7969, E-mail: wqualls@illinois.edu. *Application contact:* J. E. Miller, Coordinator of Graduate Programs, 217-244-8002, Fax: 217-244-7969, E-mail: j-miller@illinois.edu.

University of Illinois at Urbana–Champaign, Graduate College, College of Business, Program in Business Administration, Champaign, IL 61820. Offers MBA, Ed M/MBA, JD/MBA, M Arch/MBA, MCS/MBA, MHRIR/MBA, MS/MBA, PhD/MBA. *Accreditation:* AACSB. Part-time programs available. *Students:* 628 full-time (192 women), 12 part-time (2 women); includes 48 Black or African American, non-Hispanic/Latino; 80 Asian, non-Hispanic/Latino; 10 Hispanic/Latino; 10 Two or more races, non-Hispanic/Latino, 176 international. 1,556 applicants, 24% accepted, 222 enrolled. *Entrance requirements:* For master's, GMAT. Additional exam requirements/recommendations for international students: Required—TOEFL. Application fee: $75 ($90 for international students). Electronic applications accepted. *Financial support:* In 2010–11, 3 fellowships, 1 research assistantship, 2 teaching assistantships were awarded. *Unit head:* Stig Lanneskog, Interim Associate Dean, 217-244-8019, Fax: 217-333-1156, E-mail: slanessk@illinois.edu. *Application contact:* Courtney Joan Hainline, Assistant Director, 217-265-7155, Fax: 217-333-1156, E-mail: hainline@illinois.edu.

University of Indianapolis, Graduate Programs, School of Business, Indianapolis, IN 46227-3697. Offers EMBA, MBA, Graduate Certificate. *Accreditation:* ACBSP. Part-time and evening/weekend programs available. *Faculty:* 4 full-time (2 women), 4 part-time/adjunct (1 woman). *Students:* 28 full-time (9 women), 185 part-time (62 women); includes 15 minority (8 Black or African American, non-Hispanic/Latino; 2 Asian, non-Hispanic/Latino; 5 Hispanic/Latino), 13 international. Average age 30. In 2010, 77 master's awarded. *Entrance requirements:* For master's, GMAT, interview, minimum GPA of 2.8, 2 letters of recommendation, resume. Additional exam requirements/recommendations for international students: Required—TOEFL (minimum score 550 paper-based; 213 computer-based). *Application deadline:* Applications are processed on a rolling basis. Application fee: $50. Tuition and fees vary according to course load, degree level and program. *Financial support:* Tuition waivers (full and partial) and unspecified assistantships available. Support available to part-time students. Financial award application deadline: 5/1; financial award applicants required to submit FAFSA. *Unit head:* Dr. Sheela Yadav, Dean, 317-788-3232, E-mail: syadav@uindy.edu. *Application contact:* Stephen A. Tokar, Director of Graduate Business Programs, 317-788-4905, E-mail: tokarsa@uindy.edu.

The University of Iowa, Henry B. Tippie College of Business, Department of Accounting, Iowa City, IA 52242-1316. Offers accounting (M Ac, PhD), including accountancy (M Ac), business administration (PhD); JD/M Ac. *Accreditation:* AACSB. Part-time programs available. *Faculty:* 16 full-time (4 women), 2 part-time/adjunct (0 women). *Students:* 43 full-time (22 women), 7 part-time (5 women); includes 3 Asian, non-Hispanic/Latino; 1 Hispanic/Latino, 15 international. Average age 25. 261 applicants, 16% accepted, 26 enrolled. In 2010, 45 master's awarded. *Entrance requirements:* For master's, GMAT. Additional exam requirements/recommendations for international students: Required—TOEFL (minimum score 600 paper-based; 250 computer-based; 100 iBT) or IELTS (minimum score 7). *Application deadline:* For fall admission, 7/15 for domestic students, 4/15 for international students; for spring admission, 12/1 for domestic students, 10/1 for international students. Application fee: $60 ($100 for international students). Electronic applications accepted. *Financial support:* In 2010–11, fellowships with full tuition reimbursements (averaging $20,000 per year), research assistantships with partial tuition reimbursements (averaging $16,277 per year), teaching assistantships with partial tuition reimbursements (averaging $16,277 per year) were awarded; career-related internships or fieldwork, Federal Work-Study, institutionally sponsored loans, scholarships/grants, and unspecified assistantships also available. Financial award applicants required to submit FAFSA. *Faculty research:* Corporate financial reporting issues; financial statement information and capital markets; cost structure: analysis, estimation, and management; experimental and prediction economics; income taxes and interaction of financial and tax reporting systems. *Unit head:* Prof. Douglas V. DeJong, Department Executive Officer, 319-335-0910, Fax: 319-335-1956, E-mail: douglas-dejong@uiowa.edu. *Application contact:* Prof. Thomas J. Carroll, Director, Master of Accountancy Program, 319-335-2727, Fax: 319-335-1956, E-mail: thomas-carroll@uiowa.edu.

The University of Iowa, Henry B. Tippie College of Business, Department of Finance, Iowa City, IA 52242-1316. Offers business administration (PhD), including finance. *Faculty:* 22 full-time (2 women). *Students:* 14 full-time

(8 women), 11 international. Average age 29. 96 applicants, 5% accepted, 2 enrolled. In 2010, 1 doctorate awarded. *Degree requirements:* For doctorate, comprehensive exam, thesis/dissertation, thesis defense. *Entrance requirements:* For doctorate, GMAT or GRE. Additional exam requirements/recommendations for international students: Required—TOEFL (minimum score 600 paper-based; 250 computer-based; 100 iBT). *Application deadline:* For fall admission, 1/15 for domestic and international students. Applications are processed on a rolling basis. Application fee: $60 ($100 for international students). Electronic applications accepted. *Financial support:* In 2010–11, 14 students received support, including 14 fellowships with full tuition reimbursements available (averaging $6,000 per year), 14 teaching assistantships with full tuition reimbursements available (averaging $16,575 per year); institutionally sponsored loans, scholarships/grants, health care benefits, and unspecified assistantships also available. Financial award application deadline: 1/15. *Faculty research:* International finance, real estate finance, theoretical and empirical corporate finance, theoretical and empirical asset pricing bond pricing and derivatives. *Unit head:* Prof. Paul Weller, Department Executive Officer, 319-335-0929, Fax: 319-335-3690, E-mail: paul-weller@uiowa.edu. *Application contact:* Renea L. Jay, PhD Program Coordinator, 319-335-0830, Fax: 319-335-1956, E-mail: renea-jay@uiowa.edu.

The University of Iowa, Henry B. Tippie College of Business, Department of Management and Organizations, Iowa City, IA 52242-1316. Offers business administration (PhD), including management and organizations. *Accreditation:* AACSB. *Faculty:* 21 full-time (8 women), 7 part-time/adjunct (1 woman). *Students:* 15 full-time (2 women); includes 3 minority (2 Asian, non-Hispanic/Latino; 1 Hispanic/Latino), 1 international. Average age 32. 60 applicants, 8% accepted, 5 enrolled. In 2010, 2 doctorates awarded. *Degree requirements:* For doctorate, comprehensive exam, thesis/dissertation, thesis defense. *Entrance requirements:* For doctorate, GMAT or GRE. Additional exam requirements/recommendations for international students: Required—TOEFL (minimum score 600 paper-based; 250 computer-based; 100 iBT). *Application deadline:* For fall admission, 1/15 for domestic and international students. Applications are processed on a rolling basis. Application fee: $60 ($100 for international students). Electronic applications accepted. *Financial support:* In 2010–11, 15 students received support, including 3 fellowships with full tuition reimbursements available (averaging $20,000 per year), 12 teaching assistantships with full tuition reimbursements available (averaging $16,575 per year); research assistantships, institutionally sponsored loans, scholarships/grants, health care benefits, unspecified assistantships, and 12 partial fellowships (averaging $6000 per year) also available. Financial award application deadline: 1/15; financial award applicants required to submit FAFSA. *Faculty research:* Decision making, human resources, personal selection, organizational behavior, training. *Unit head:* Prof. Jay Christensen-Szalanski, Department Executive Officer, 319-335-0927, Fax: 319-335-1956, E-mail: jay-christensen-szalanski@uiowa.edu. *Application contact:* Renea L. Jay, PhD Program Coordinator, 319-335-0830, Fax: 319-335-1956, E-mail: renea-jay@uiowa.edu.

The University of Iowa, Henry B. Tippie College of Business, Department of Management Sciences, Iowa City, IA 52242-1316. Offers business administration (PhD), including management sciences. *Accreditation:* AACSB. *Faculty:* 16 full-time (3 women), 3 part-time/adjunct (0 women). *Students:* 11 full-time (3 women), 2 part-time (1 woman), 10 international. Average age 28. 33 applicants, 21% accepted, 5 enrolled. In 2010, 3 doctorates awarded. *Degree requirements:* For doctorate, comprehensive exam, thesis/dissertation, thesis defense. *Entrance requirements:* For doctorate, GRE General Test or GMAT, minimum GPA of 3.0. Additional exam requirements/recommendations for international students: Required—TOEFL (minimum score 600 paper-based; 250 computer-based; 100 iBT). *Application deadline:* For fall admission, 2/1 for domestic and international students. Applications are processed on a rolling basis. Application fee: $60 ($100 for international students). Electronic applications accepted. *Financial support:* In 2010–11, 11 students received support, including 1 research assistantship with full tuition reimbursement available (averaging $16,575 per year), 8 teaching assistantships with full tuition reimbursements available (averaging $16,575 per year); institutionally sponsored loans, scholarships/grants, health care benefits, unspecified assistantships, and 11 partial fellowships (averaging $2750 per year) also available. Financial award application deadline: 2/1. *Faculty research:* Optimization, supply chain management, data mining, logistics, database management. *Unit head:* Prof. Kurt Anstreicher, Department Executive Officer, 319-335-0858, Fax: 319-335-1956, E-mail: kurt-anstreicher@uiowa.edu. *Application contact:* Renea L. Jay, PhD Program Coordinator, 319-335-0830, Fax: 319-335-1956, E-mail: renea-jay@uiowa.edu.

The University of Iowa, Henry B. Tippie College of Business, Henry B. Tippie School of Management, Iowa City, IA 52242-1316. Offers corporate finance (MBA); investment management (MBA); marketing (MBA); process and operations excellence (MBA); strategic management and innovation (MBA); JD/MBA; MBA/MA; MBA/MD; MBA/MHA; MBA/MSN. *Accreditation:* AACSB. Part-time and evening/weekend programs available. *Faculty:* 110 full-time (25 women), 19 part-time/adjunct (1 woman). *Students:* 242 full-time (46 women), 809 part-time (277 women); includes 95 minority (15 Black or African American, non-Hispanic/Latino; 3 American Indian or Alaska Native, non-Hispanic/Latino; 56 Asian, non-Hispanic/Latino; 21

Hispanic/Latino), 132 international. Average age 31. 652 applicants, 66% accepted, 380 enrolled. In 2010, 333 master's awarded. *Degree requirements:* For master's, minimum GPA of 2.75. *Entrance requirements:* For master's, GMAT, quality work experience and leadership as shown through resume, references, and essays. Additional exam requirements/recommendations for international students: Required—TOEFL (minimum score 600 paper-based; 250 computer-based; 100 iBT), IELTS (minimum score 7). *Application deadline:* For fall admission, 7/30 for domestic students, 4/15 for international students; for spring admission, 12/15 for domestic and international students. Applications are processed on a rolling basis. Application fee: $60 ($100 for international students). Electronic applications accepted. *Expenses:* Contact institution. *Financial support:* In 2010–11, 111 students received support, including 121 fellowships (averaging $8,285 per year), 87 research assistantships with partial tuition reimbursements available (averaging $8,288 per year), 25 teaching assistantships with partial tuition reimbursements available (averaging $11,326 per year); career-related internships or fieldwork, scholarships/grants, health care benefits, and unspecified assistantships also available. Financial award application deadline: 4/15; financial award applicants required to submit FAFSA. *Faculty research:* Capital markets, econometrics, optimization, investments and empirical corporate finance, Iowa electronic markets. *Unit head:* Prof. Jarjisu Sa-Aadu, Associate Dean, MBA Programs, 800-622-4692, Fax: 319-335-3604, E-mail: jsa-aadu@uiowa.edu. *Application contact:* Jodi Schafer, Director of Admissions and Financial Aid, 319-335-0864, Fax: 319-335-3604, E-mail: jodi-schafer@uiowa.edu.

The University of Kansas, Graduate Studies, School of Business, Program in Business, Lawrence, KS 66045. Offers PhD. *Accreditation:* AACSB. *Faculty:* 59 full-time (14 women), 49 part-time/adjunct (14 women). *Students:* 76 full-time (27 women); includes 16 minority (7 Black or African American, non-Hispanic/Latino; 1 American Indian or Alaska Native, non-Hispanic/Latino; 5 Asian, non-Hispanic/Latino; 3 Hispanic/Latino), 23 international. Average age 35. 248 applicants, 25% accepted, 44 enrolled. In 2010, 2 doctorates awarded. *Degree requirements:* For doctorate, comprehensive exam, thesis/dissertation, departmental qualifying exam. *Entrance requirements:* For doctorate, GMAT or GRE. Additional exam requirements/recommendations for international students: Required—TOEFL (minimum score 600 paper-based; 250 computer-based; 100 iBT). *Application deadline:* For fall admission, 1/10 for domestic and international students. Applications are processed on a rolling basis. Application fee: $65. Electronic applications accepted. *Expenses:* Tuition, state resident: full-time $7092; part-time $295.50 per credit hour. Tuition, nonresident: full-time $16,590; part-time $691.25 per credit hour. Required fees: $858; $71.49 per credit hour. Tuition and fees vary according to course load, campus/location and program. *Financial support:* Fellowships with full tuition reimbursements, research assistantships with full tuition reimbursements, teaching assistantships with full tuition reimbursements, scholarships/grants, health care benefits, tuition waivers (full), and unspecified assistantships available. *Faculty research:* Tax, mergers and acquisitions, risk analysis personality and work outcomes, services, marketing, business ethics, corporate turnarounds. *Unit head:* Charly Edmonds, Director, 785-864-3841, Fax: 785-864-5376, E-mail: bschoolphd@ku.edu. *Application contact:* Charly Edmonds, Director, 785-864-3841, E-mail: bschoolphd@ku.edu.

The University of Kansas, Graduate Studies, School of Business, Program in Business Administration and Management, Lawrence, KS 66045. Offers finance (MBA); human resources management (MBA); information systems (MBA); international business (MBA); management (MBA); marketing (MBA); strategic management (MBA); JD/MBA; MBA/MA; MBA/MM; MBA/MS; MBA/Pharm D. *Accreditation:* AACSB. Part-time programs available. *Faculty:* 57 full-time (12 women), 20 part-time/adjunct (13 women). *Students:* 204 full-time (51 women), 221 part-time (70 women); includes 56 minority (16 Black or African American, non-Hispanic/Latino; 2 American Indian or Alaska Native, non-Hispanic/Latino; 24 Asian, non-Hispanic/Latino; 13 Hispanic/Latino; 1 Two or more races, non-Hispanic/Latino), 48 international. Average age 29. 201 applicants, 76% accepted, 119 enrolled. In 2010, 108 master's awarded. *Degree requirements:* For master's, comprehensive exam (for some programs), thesis optional. *Entrance requirements:* For master's, GMAT, 2 years of professional work experience. Additional exam requirements/recommendations for international students: Required—TOEFL (minimum score 53 paper-based; 20 computer-based), TOEFL = part scores; Recommended—IELTS (minimum score 6). *Application deadline:* For fall admission, 6/1 priority date for domestic students, 5/1 priority date for international students; for spring admission, 11/1 priority date for domestic students, 10/1 for international students. Applications are processed on a rolling basis. Application fee: $65. Electronic applications accepted. *Expenses:* Tuition, state resident: full-time $7092; part-time $295.50 per credit hour. Tuition, nonresident: full-time $16,590; part-time $691.25 per credit hour. Required fees: $858; $71.49 per credit hour. Tuition and fees vary according to course load, campus/location and program. *Financial support:* Research assistantships, career-related internships or fieldwork, Federal Work-Study, institutionally sponsored loans, scholarships/grants, and unspecified assistantships available. Financial award application deadline: 6/1; financial award applicants required to submit FAFSA. *Faculty research:* Advanced audit technologies, real options and asset pricing, corporate governance, foreign direct investment, CEO characteristics and organizational innovation. *Unit head:* Dr. Charles Krider, Director of MBA Programs, 785-864-7543, E-mail: ckrider@

ku.edu. *Application contact:* Dee Steinle, Administrative Director of Master's Programs, 785-864-7596, Fax: 785-864-5376, E-mail: dsteinle@ku.edu.

University of La Verne, College of Business and Public Management, Graduate Programs in Business Administration, La Verne, CA 91750-4443. Offers accounting (MBA); executive management (MBA-EP); finance (MBA, MBA-EP); health services management (MBA); information technology (MBA, MBA-EP); international business (MBA, MBA-EP); leadership (MBA-EP); managed care (MBA); management (MBA, MBA-EP); marketing (MBA, MBA-EP). Part-time and evening/weekend programs available. *Faculty:* 34 full-time (12 women), 36 part-time/adjunct (9 women). *Students:* 412 full-time (207 women), 200 part-time (96 women); includes 423 minority (32 Black or African American, non-Hispanic/Latino; 5 American Indian or Alaska Native, non-Hispanic/Latino; 294 Asian, non-Hispanic/Latino; 92 Hispanic/Latino), 6 international. Average age 29. In 2010, 229 master's awarded. *Entrance requirements:* For master's, minimum undergraduate GPA of 3.0, 2 letters of recommendation, resume. Additional exam requirements/recommendations for international students: Required—TOEFL (minimum score 550 paper-based; 213 computer-based). *Application deadline:* Applications are processed on a rolling basis. Application fee: $50. *Expenses:* Contact institution. *Financial support:* Career-related internships or fieldwork, institutionally sponsored loans, and scholarships/grants available. Financial award application deadline: 3/2; financial award applicants required to submit FAFSA. *Unit head:* Dr. Abe Helou, Chairperson, 909-593-3511 Ext. 4211, Fax: 909-392-2704, E-mail: ihelou@laverne.edu. *Application contact:* Rina Lazarian, Program and Admission Specialist, 909-593-3511 Ext. 4819, Fax: 909-392-2704, E-mail: cbpm@ulv.edu.

University of La Verne, College of Business and Public Management, Program in Organizational Management and Leadership, La Verne, CA 91750-4443. Offers nonprofit management (Certificate); organizational leadership (Certificate); organizational management and leadership (MS). Part-time programs available. *Faculty:* 34 full-time (12 women), 36 part-time/adjunct (9 women). *Students:* 92 full-time (44 women), 70 part-time (46 women); includes 9 Black or African American, non-Hispanic/Latino; 31 Asian, non-Hispanic/Latino; 35 Hispanic/Latino. Average age 32. In 2010, 58 master's awarded. *Degree requirements:* For master's, thesis or research project. *Entrance requirements:* For master's, minimum undergraduate GPA of 2.75, 2 letters of recommendation, interview, resume. Additional exam requirements/recommendations for international students: Required—TOEFL (minimum score 550 paper-based; 213 computer-based). *Application deadline:* Applications are processed on a rolling basis. Application fee: $50. *Expenses:* Contact institution. *Financial support:* Institutionally sponsored loans available. Financial award application deadline: 3/2; financial award applicants required to submit FAFSA. *Unit head:* Dr. Kathy Duncan, Chairperson, 909-593-3511 Ext. 4415, E-mail: kduncan2@laverne.edu. *Application contact:* Program and Admissions Specialist, 909-593-3511 Ext. 4819, Fax: 909-392-2761, E-mail: cbpm@laverne.edu.

University of La Verne, Regional Campus Administration, Graduate Programs, Central Coast/Vandenberg Air Force Base Campuses, La Verne, CA 91750-4443. Offers business (MBA-EP), including health services management, information technology; health administration (MHA); leadership and management (MS). *Faculty:* 12 part-time/adjunct (7 women). *Students:* 26 full-time (13 women), 33 part-time (16 women); includes 18 minority (6 Black or African American, non-Hispanic/Latino; 2 American Indian or Alaska Native, non-Hispanic/Latino; 2 Asian, non-Hispanic/Latino; 8 Hispanic/Latino). Average age 36. In 2010, 4 master's awarded. *Entrance requirements:* For master's, 2 letters of recommendation, resume. *Application deadline:* Applications are processed on a rolling basis. Application fee: $50. *Expenses:* Contact institution. *Financial support:* Institutionally sponsored loans available. Financial award application deadline: 3/2; financial award applicants required to submit FAFSA. *Unit head:* Kitt Vincent, Director, Central Coast Campus, 805-542-9690 Ext. 6043, Fax: 805-542-9735, E-mail: kvincent@laverne.edu. *Application contact:* Kitt Vincent, Director, Central Coast Campus, 805-542-9690 Ext. 6043, Fax: 805-542-9735, E-mail: kvincent@laverne.edu.

University of La Verne, Regional Campus Administration, Graduate Programs, High Desert Campus, Victorville, CA 92392. Offers business (MBA). *Faculty:* 7 part-time/adjunct (3 women). *Students:* 12 full-time (7 women), 10 part-time (7 women); includes 10 minority (8 Black or African American, non-Hispanic/Latino; 2 Hispanic/Latino). Average age 39. In 2010, 6 master's awarded. *Entrance requirements:* For master's, 2 letters of recommendation, resume. *Application deadline:* Applications are processed on a rolling basis. Application fee: $50. *Expenses:* Contact institution. *Financial support:* Application deadline: 3/2. *Unit head:* Julie Roberts, Director, 760-843-0086 Ext. 222, Fax: 760-843-9505, E-mail: jroberts@laverne.edu. *Application contact:* Julie Roberts, Director, 760-843-0086 Ext. 222, Fax: 760-843-9505, E-mail: jroberts@laverne.edu.

University of La Verne, Regional Campus Administration, Graduate Programs, Inland Empire Campus, Rancho Cucamonga, CA 91730. Offers business (MBA-EP), including health services management, information technology, management, marketing; leadership and management (MS). *Faculty:* 3 full-time (2 women), 22 part-time/adjunct (9 women). *Students:* 27

full-time (17 women), 100 part-time (68 women); includes 14 Black or African American, non-Hispanic/Latino; 1 American Indian or Alaska Native, non-Hispanic/Latino; 22 Asian, non-Hispanic/Latino; 36 Hispanic/Latino. Average age 39. In 2010, 20 master's awarded. *Entrance requirements:* For master's, 2 letters of recommendation, resume. *Application deadline:* Applications are processed on a rolling basis. Application fee: $50. *Expenses:* Contact institution. *Financial support:* Institutionally sponsored loans available. Financial award application deadline: 3/2; financial award applicants required to submit FAFSA. *Unit head:* Allan Stout, Director, 909-484-3858 Ext. 6002, Fax: 909-484-9469, E-mail: astout@laverne.edu. *Application contact:* Allan Stout, Director, 909-484-3858 Ext. 6002, Fax: 909-484-9469, E-mail: astout@laverne.edu.

University of La Verne, Regional Campus Administration, Graduate Programs, Kern County Campus, Bakersfield, CA 93301. Offers business (MBA-EP); health administration (MHA); leadership and management (MS). *Faculty:* 16 part-time/adjunct (7 women). *Students:* 8 full-time (5 women), 7 part-time (2 women); includes 8 minority (1 Black or African American, non-Hispanic/Latino; 3 Asian, non-Hispanic/Latino; 4 Hispanic/Latino). Average age 35. In 2010, 2 master's awarded. *Entrance requirements:* For master's, 2 letters of recommendation, resume. *Application deadline:* Applications are processed on a rolling basis. Application fee: $50. *Expenses:* Contact institution. *Financial support:* Institutionally sponsored loans available. Financial award application deadline: 3/2; financial award applicants required to submit FAFSA. *Unit head:* Nora Dominguez, Interim Director, 661-328-1430 Ext. 6024, E-mail: ndominguez@laverne.edu. *Application contact:* Nora Dominguez, Interim Director, 661-328-1430 Ext. 6024, E-mail: ndominguez@laverne.edu.

University of La Verne, Regional Campus Administration, Graduate Programs, Orange County Campus, Garden Grove, CA 92840. Offers business (MBA); health administration (MHA); leadership and management (MS). *Faculty:* 1 (woman) full-time, 7 part-time/adjunct (4 women). *Students:* 24 full-time (13 women), 89 part-time (41 women); includes 65 minority (8 Black or African American, non-Hispanic/Latino; 5 American Indian or Alaska Native, non-Hispanic/Latino; 25 Asian, non-Hispanic/Latino; 27 Hispanic/Latino). Average age 38. In 2010, 22 master's awarded. *Entrance requirements:* For master's, 2 letters of recommendation, resume. *Application deadline:* Applications are processed on a rolling basis. Application fee: $50. *Expenses:* Contact institution. *Financial support:* Institutionally sponsored loans available. Financial award application deadline: 3/2; financial award applicants required to submit FAFSA. *Unit head:* Jane Courcy, Director, 714-505-1684 Ext. 6900, E-mail: jcourcy@laverne.edu. *Application contact:* Jane Courcy, Director, 714-505-1684 Ext. 6900, E-mail: jcourcy@laverne.edu.

University of La Verne, Regional Campus Administration, Graduate Programs, San Fernando Valley Campus, Burbank, CA 91505. Offers business (MBA-EP); leadership and management (MS). *Faculty:* 1 (woman) full-time, 14 part-time/adjunct (5 women). *Students:* 46 full-time (26 women), 124 part-time (78 women); includes 100 minority (36 Black or African American, non-Hispanic/Latino; 1 American Indian or Alaska Native, non-Hispanic/Latino; 14 Asian, non-Hispanic/Latino; 49 Hispanic/Latino). Average age 38. In 2010, 31 master's awarded. *Entrance requirements:* For master's, 2 letters of recommendation, resume. *Application deadline:* Applications are processed on a rolling basis. Application fee: $50. *Expenses:* Contact institution. *Financial support:* Institutionally sponsored loans available. Financial award application deadline: 3/2; financial award applicants required to submit FAFSA. *Unit head:* Nelly Kazman, Director, 818-846-4008 Ext. 6088, Fax: 818-566-1047, E-mail: nkazman@laverne.edu. *Application contact:* Nelly Kazman, Director, 818-846-4008 Ext. 6088, Fax: 818-566-1047, E-mail: nkazman@laverne.edu.

University of La Verne, Regional Campus Administration, Graduate Programs, Ventura County/Point Mugu Naval Air Station Campuses, La Verne, CA 91750-4443. Offers leadership and management (MS). *Faculty:* 3 full-time (1 woman), 26 part-time/adjunct (5 women). *Students:* 25 full-time (11 women), 28 part-time (10 women); includes 29 minority (4 Black or African American, non-Hispanic/Latino; 12 Asian, non-Hispanic/Latino; 13 Hispanic/Latino). Average age 38. In 2010, 10 master's awarded. *Entrance requirements:* For master's, 2 letters of recommendation, resume. Application fee: $50. *Expenses:* Contact institution. *Financial support:* Institutionally sponsored loans available. Financial award application deadline: 3/2; financial award applicants required to submit FAFSA. *Unit head:* Jamie Dempsey, Director, Point Mugu, 805-986-1783 Ext. 6955, Fax: 805-981-8033, E-mail: jdempsey@laverne.edu. *Application contact:* Jamie Dempsey, Director, Point Mugu, 805-986-1783 Ext. 6955, Fax: 805-981-8033, E-mail: jdempsey@laverne.edu.

University of La Verne, Regional Campus Administration, Graduate Program, ULV Online, La Verne, CA 91750-4443. Offers business administration (MBA). *Faculty:* 2 full-time (1 woman), 1 part-time/adjunct (0 women). *Students:* 37 full-time (24 women), 71 part-time (47 women); includes 51 minority (21 Black or African American, non-Hispanic/Latino; 7 Asian, non-Hispanic/Latino; 23 Hispanic/Latino). Average age 36. In 2010, 29 master's awarded. *Entrance requirements:* For master's, resume, 2 letters of recommendation. *Application deadline:* Applications are processed on a rolling basis. Application fee: $50. *Expenses:* Tuition: Part-time $620 per credit hour. Tuition and fees vary according to degree level and program. *Financial support:* Application deadline: 3/2. *Unit head:* Barbara Colley, Coordinator, 800-695-4858 Ext. 5322, E-mail: bcolley@ulv.edu. *Application contact:* Barbara Colley, Coordinator, 800-695-4858 Ext. 5322, E-mail: bcolley@ulv.edu.

University of Louisiana at Monroe, Graduate School, College of Business Administration, Monroe, LA 71209-0001. Offers MBA. *Accreditation:* AACSB. Part-time and evening/weekend programs available. *Faculty:* 18 full-time (6 women), 2 part-time/adjunct (both women). *Students:* 44 full-time (15 women), 36 part-time (17 women); includes 10 Black or African American, non-Hispanic/Latino; 5 Asian, non-Hispanic/Latino, 9 international. Average age 28. 90 applicants. In 2010, 30 master's awarded. *Degree requirements:* For master's, comprehensive exam. *Entrance requirements:* For master's, GMAT, minimum GPA of 2.5, minimum AACSB index of 950. Additional exam requirements/recommendations for international students: Required—TOEFL (minimum score 500 paper-based; 61 computer-based). *Application deadline:* For fall admission, 8/24 for domestic students, 7/1 for international students; for winter admission, 12/14 for domestic students; for spring admission, 1/19 for domestic students, 11/1 for international students. Applications are processed on a rolling basis. Application fee: $20 ($30 for international students). Electronic applications accepted. *Expenses:* Tuition, state resident: full-time $2991; part-time $197 per credit hour. Tuition, nonresident: full-time $2991; part-time $197 per credit hour. International tuition: $10,288 full-time. *Financial support:* In 2010–11, 12 research assistantships with full tuition reimbursements (averaging $2,500 per year), 1 teaching assistantship with full tuition reimbursement (averaging $2,500 per year) were awarded; career-related internships or fieldwork, Federal Work-Study, and unspecified assistantships also available. Financial award application deadline: 4/1; financial award applicants required to submit FAFSA. *Faculty research:* Information assurance framework, TPB in e-learning, bias in balanced scorecard. *Unit head:* Dr. Ronald Berry, Dean, 318-342-1100, Fax: 318-342-1101, E-mail: rberry@ulm.edu. *Application contact:* Dr. Donna Walton Luse, Program Chair, 318-342-1106, Fax: 318-342-1101, E-mail: luse@ulm.edu.

University of Louisville, Graduate School, College of Business, MBA Programs, Louisville, KY 40292-0001. Offers entrepreneurship (MBA); global business (PMBA); global business (full time) (MBA). The MBA degree is offered in both a full time and part time format. The full time program is a 13 month program paired with a paid internship. The part-time program is available in an evening as well as a Saturday format. All MBA programs are cohort-based and include an international learning experience. *Accreditation:* AACSB. Part-time and evening/weekend programs available. *Faculty:* 30 full-time (7 women), 2 part-time/adjunct (0 women). *Students:* 25 full-time (9 women), 185 part-time (54 women); includes 19 minority (6 Black or African American, non-Hispanic/Latino; 1 American Indian or Alaska Native, non-Hispanic/Latino; 8 Asian, non-Hispanic/Latino; 4 Hispanic/Latino), 8 international. Average age 29. 318 applicants, 42% accepted, 111 enrolled. In 2010, 104 master's awarded. *Entrance requirements:* For master's, GMAT, 2 letters of reference, personal interview, resume, personal statement, college transcript(s). Additional exam requirements/recommendations for international students: Required—TOEFL (minimum score 557 paper-based; 213 computer-based; 83 iBT). *Application deadline:* For fall admission, 7/31 for domestic students; for spring admission, 12/1 for domestic students. Applications are processed on a rolling basis. Application fee: $50. *Expenses:* Tuition, state resident: full-time $9144; part-time $508 per credit hour. Tuition, nonresident: full-time $19,026; part-time $1057 per credit hour. Tuition and fees vary according to program and reciprocity agreements. *Financial support:* In 2010–11, 16 students received support, including 6 fellowships (averaging $3,133 per year), 10 research assistantships with full tuition reimbursements available (averaging $12,000 per year); health care benefits and unspecified assistantships also available. Financial award application deadline: 3/31; financial award applicants required to submit FAFSA. *Faculty research:* Entrepreneurship, venture capital, retailing/franchising, corporate governance and leadership, supply chain management. Total annual research expenditures: $221,322. *Unit head:* Dr. R. Charles Moyer, Dean, 502-852-6443, Fax: 502-852-7557, E-mail: charlie.moyer@louisville.edu. *Application contact:* Joshua M. Philpot, Graduate Programs Manager, 502-852-7257, Fax: 502-852-4901, E-mail: josh.philpot@louisville.edu.

University of Maine, Graduate School, College of Business, Public Policy and Health, The Maine Business School, Orono, ME 04469. Offers accounting (MBA); business and sustainability (MBA); finance (MBA); management (MBA). *Accreditation:* AACSB. Part-time and evening/weekend programs available. *Faculty:* 23 full-time (8 women), 2 part-time/adjunct (both women). *Students:* 53 full-time (24 women), 15 part-time (5 women); includes 4 minority (1 American Indian or Alaska Native, non-Hispanic/Latino; 2 Asian, non-Hispanic/Latino; 1 Hispanic/Latino), 3 international. Average age 29. 42 applicants, 69% accepted, 25 enrolled. In 2010, 25 degrees awarded. *Entrance requirements:* For master's, GMAT. Additional exam requirements/recommendations for international students: Required—TOEFL (minimum score 550 paper-based; 213 computer-based). *Application deadline:* For fall admission, 6/1 priority date for domestic and international students; for spring admission, 11/1 priority date for domestic and international students. Applications are processed on a rolling basis. Application fee: $65. Electronic applications accepted. *Expenses:* Contact institution. *Financial support:* In 2010–11, 16 students received support, including 4 teaching assistantships with tuition reimbursements available (averaging $12,790 per year); career-related internships or fieldwork, Federal Work-Study, institutionally sponsored loans, scholarships/grants, tuition waivers (full and partial), and unspecified assistantships also available. Financial award application deadline: 3/1. *Faculty research:* Entrepreneurship, investment management, international markets, decision support systems, strategic planning. *Unit head:* Dr. Nory Jones, Director of Graduate Programs, 207-581-1971, Fax: 207-581-1930, E-mail: mba@maine.edu. *Application contact:* Scott G. Delcourt, Associate Dean of the Graduate School, 207-581-3291, Fax: 207-581-3232, E-mail: graduate@maine.edu.

University of Mary, Gary Tharaldson School of Business, Bismarck, ND 58504-9652. Offers accountancy (MBA); business administration (MBA); health care (MBA); human resource management (MBA); management (MBA); project management (MPM); strategic leadership (MSSL). Part-time and evening/weekend programs available. *Faculty:* 2 full-time (0 women), 73 part-time/adjunct (27 women). *Students:* 232 full-time (123 women), 226 part-time (115 women); includes 63 minority (30 Black or African American, non-Hispanic/Latino; 23 American Indian or Alaska Native, non-Hispanic/Latino; 5 Asian, non-Hispanic/Latino; 3 Hispanic/Latino; 1 Native Hawaiian or other Pacific Islander, non-Hispanic/Latino; 1 Two or more races, non-Hispanic/Latino), 20 international. Average age 36. 209 applicants, 98% accepted, 189 enrolled. In 2010, 265 master's awarded. *Degree requirements:* For master's, strategic planning seminar. *Entrance requirements:* For master's, minimum GPA of 2.5. Additional exam requirements/recommendations for international students: Required—TOEFL (minimum score 500 paper-based; 197 computer-based; 71 iBT). *Application deadline:* Applications are processed on a rolling basis. Application fee: $40. *Expenses:* Tuition: Full-time $10,800; part-time $450 per credit. Tuition and fees vary according to course load, degree level, program and student level. *Financial support:* Application deadline: 8/1. *Unit head:* Dr. Shanda Traiser, Director of the School of Accelerated and Distance Education, 701-355-8160, Fax: 701-255-7687, E-mail: straiser@umary.edu. *Application contact:* Wayne G. Maruska, Graduate Program Advisor, 701-355-8134, Fax: 701-255-7687, E-mail: wmaruska@umary.edu.

University of Mary Hardin-Baylor, Graduate Studies in Business Administration, Belton, TX 76513. Offers accounting (MBA); information systems management (MBA); management (MBA). Part-time and evening/weekend programs available. *Faculty:* 6 full-time (3 women), 2 part-time/adjunct (0 women). *Students:* 29 full-time (10 women), 26 part-time (13 women); includes 12 minority (3 Black or African American, non-Hispanic/Latino; 9 Hispanic/Latino), 23 international. Average age 29. 71 applicants, 72% accepted, 27 enrolled. In 2010, 7 master's awarded. *Degree requirements:* For master's, comprehensive exam. *Entrance requirements:* For master's, GMAT, minimum GPA of 3.0, work experience, interview. *Application deadline:* For fall admission, 6/1 priority date for domestic students; for spring admission, 11/1 for domestic students. Applications are processed on a rolling basis. Application fee: $35 ($135 for international students). Electronic applications accepted. *Financial support:* Federal Work-Study and scholarships (for some active duty military personnel only) available. Financial award applicants required to submit FAFSA. *Unit head:* Dr. Terry Fox, Program Director, 254-295-5406, E-mail: terry.fox@umhb.edu. *Application contact:* Dr. Terry Fox, Program Director, 254-295-5406, E-mail: terry.fox@umhb.edu.

University of Maryland, College Park, Academic Affairs, Joint Program in Business and Management/Public Policy, College Park, MD 20742. Offers MBA/MPM. *Accreditation:* AACSB. *Students:* 13 full-time (5 women), 2 part-time (0 women); includes 4 minority (1 Black or African American, non-Hispanic/Latino; 2 Asian, non-Hispanic/Latino; 1 Two or more races, non-Hispanic/Latino). 45 applicants, 20% accepted, 6 enrolled. *Application deadline:* For fall admission, 12/15 for domestic students, 2/1 for international students; for spring admission, 10/15 for domestic students, 6/1 for international students. Applications are processed on a rolling basis. Application fee: $75. Electronic applications accepted. *Expenses:* Tuition, state resident: part-time $471 per credit hour. Tuition, nonresident: part-time $1016 per credit hour. Required fees: $337 per term. *Financial support:* In 2010–11, 2 fellowships with full and partial tuition reimbursements (averaging $13,807 per year), 7 teaching assistantships (averaging $15,250 per year) were awarded; research assistantships. Financial award applicants required to submit FAFSA. *Unit head:* Dr. Charles Caramello, Dean of the Graduate School, 301-405-0358, Fax: 301-314-9305, E-mail: ccaramel@umd.edu. *Application contact:* Dean of Graduate School, 301-405-0358, Fax: 301-314-9305.

University of Maryland, College Park, Academic Affairs, Robert H. Smith School of Business, Combined MSW/MBA Program, College Park, MD 20742. Offers MSW/MBA. *Accreditation:* AACSB. *Students:* 1 (woman) full-time, all international. 7 applicants, 57% accepted, 1 enrolled. *Entrance requirements:* Additional exam requirements/recommendations for international students: Required—TOEFL. *Application deadline:* For fall admission, 5/1 priority date for domestic students, 2/1 for international students; for spring admission, 11/30 for domestic students, 6/1 for international students. Application fee: $75. *Expenses:* Tuition, state resident: part-time $471 per credit hour. Tuition, nonresident: part-time $1016 per credit hour. Required fees: $337 per term. *Financial support:* Fellowships available. *Application* *contact:* Dr. Charles A. Caramello, Dean of Graduate School, 301-405-0358, Fax: 301-314-9305, E-mail: ccaramel@umd.edu.

University of Maryland, College Park, Academic Affairs, Robert H. Smith School of Business, Executive MBA Program, College Park, MD 20742. Offers EMBA. *Accreditation:* AACSB. *Students:* 73 full-time (16 women), 3 part-time (1 woman); includes 20 minority (16 Black or African American, non-Hispanic/Latino; 2 Asian, non-Hispanic/Latino; 2 Hispanic/Latino), 4 international. 22 applicants, 86% accepted, 19 enrolled. In 2010, 97 master's awarded. *Entrance requirements:* For master's, minimum GPA of 3.0, 7-12 years professional experience. Additional exam requirements/recommendations for international students: Required—TOEFL. *Application deadline:* For fall admission, 5/1 priority date for domestic students, 2/1 for international students; for spring admission, 11/30 for domestic students, 6/1 for international students. Application fee: $75. *Expenses:* Tuition, state resident: part-time $471 per credit hour. Tuition, nonresident: part-time $1016 per credit hour. Required fees: $337 per term. *Financial support:* In 2010–11, 8 fellowships with full and partial tuition reimbursements (averaging $16,781 per year) were awarded. *Unit head:* Dr. Robert Krapfel, Associate Dean, 301-405-2198, E-mail: bkrapfel@umd.edu. *Application contact:* Dr. Charles A. Caramello, Dean of Graduate School, 301-405-0358, Fax: 301-314-9305, E-mail: ccaramel@umd.edu.

University of Maryland, College Park, Academic Affairs, Robert H. Smith School of Business, Joint Program in Business and Management, College Park, MD 20742. Offers MBA/MS. *Accreditation:* AACSB. *Students:* 24 full-time (8 women), 20 part-time (4 women); includes 15 minority (1 American Indian or Alaska Native, non-Hispanic/Latino; 10 Asian, non-Hispanic/Latino; 2 Hispanic/Latino; 2 Two or more races, non-Hispanic/Latino), 4 international. 14 applicants, 29% accepted, 2 enrolled. *Entrance requirements:* Additional exam requirements/recommendations for international students: Required— TOEFL. *Application deadline:* For fall admission, 5/1 for domestic students, 2/1 for international students; for spring admission, 11/30 for domestic students, 6/1 for international students. Applications are processed on a rolling basis. Application fee: $75. Electronic applications accepted. *Expenses:* Tuition, state resident: part-time $471 per credit hour. Tuition, nonresident: part-time $1016 per credit hour. Required fees: $337 per term. *Financial support:* In 2010–11, 2 teaching assistantships (averaging $14,772 per year) were awarded. *Unit head:* Dr. Anand Anandalingam, Dean, 301-405-0582, E-mail: ganand@umd.edu. *Application contact:* Dr. Charles A. Caramello, Dean of Graduate School, 301-405-0358, Fax: 301-314-9305, E-mail: ccaramel@umd.edu.

University of Maryland, College Park, Academic Affairs, Robert H. Smith School of Business, Program in Business Administration, College Park, MD 20742. Offers MBA. *Accreditation:* AACSB. Part-time and evening/weekend programs available. Postbaccalaureate distance learning degree programs offered. *Students:* 518 full-time (163 women), 700 part-time (235 women); includes 347 minority (106 Black or African American, non-Hispanic/Latino; 201 Asian, non-Hispanic/Latino; 30 Hispanic/Latino; 1 Native Hawaiian or other Pacific Islander, non-Hispanic/Latino; 9 Two or more races, non-Hispanic/Latino), 183 international. 1,490 applicants, 52% accepted, 473 enrolled. In 2010, 477 master's awarded. *Entrance requirements:* For master's, GMAT, minimum GPA of 3.0, resume, 3 letters of recommendation. Additional exam requirements/recommendations for international students: Required—TOEFL. *Application deadline:* For fall admission, 5/1 for domestic students, 2/1 for international students; for spring admission, 11/30 for domestic students, 6/1 for international students. Applications are processed on a rolling basis. Application fee: $75. Electronic applications accepted. *Expenses:* Tuition, state resident: part-time $471 per credit hour. Tuition, nonresident: part-time $1016 per credit hour. Required fees: $337 per term. *Financial support:* In 2010–11, 39 fellowships with full and partial tuition reimbursements (averaging $19,500 per year), 96 teaching assistantships (averaging $14,873 per year) were awarded. Financial award applicants required to submit FAFSA. *Faculty research:* Accounting, entrepreneurship, finance management and organization, management server and statistical information systems. *Unit head:* Robert Krapfel, Associate Dean, 301-405-2198, E-mail: bkrapfel@umd.edu. *Application contact:* Dr. Charles A. Caramello, Dean of Graduate School, 301-405-0358, Fax: 301-314-9305, E-mail: ccaramel@umd.edu.

University of Maryland, College Park, Academic Affairs, Robert H. Smith School of Business, Program in Business and Management, College Park, MD 20742. Offers MS, PhD. *Accreditation:* AACSB. Part-time programs available. *Students:* 252 full-time (117 women), 56 part-time (22 women); includes 62 minority (28 Black or African American, non-Hispanic/Latino; 29 Asian, non-Hispanic/Latino; 5 Hispanic/Latino), 176 international. 1,294 applicants, 18% accepted, 151 enrolled. In 2010, 68 master's, 13 doctorates awarded. *Degree requirements:* For master's, thesis optional; for doctorate, comprehensive exam, thesis/dissertation. *Entrance requirements:* For master's, GMAT, minimum GPA of 3.0, resume, 2 letters of recommendation; for doctorate, GMAT or GRE General Test, minimum GPA of 3.0, resume, 2 letters of recommendation. Additional exam requirements/recommendations for international students: Required—TOEFL. *Application deadline:* For fall admission, 12/15 for domestic and international students. Applications are processed on a rolling basis. Application fee: $75. Electronic applications accepted. *Expenses:* Tuition, state resident: part-time $471 per credit hour.

Tuition, nonresident: part-time $1016 per credit hour. Required fees: $337 per term. *Financial support:* In 2010–11, 2 fellowships with full and partial tuition reimbursements (averaging $12,900 per year), 1 research assistantship with tuition reimbursement (averaging $24,500 per year), 86 teaching assistantships with tuition reimbursements (averaging $20,674 per year) were awarded. Financial award applicants required to submit FAFSA. *Unit head:* Anand Anandallngam, Dean, 301-405-0582. *Application contact:* Dr. Charles A. Caramello, Dean of Graduate School, 301-405-0358, Fax: 301-314-9305, E-mail: ccaramel@umd.edu.

University of Maryland, College Park, Academic Affairs, Robert H. Smith School of Business, Program in Business Management/Law, College Park, MD 20742. Offers JD/MBA. *Accreditation:* AACSB. *Students:* 5 full-time (2 women), 1 part-time (0 women); includes 3 minority (1 Black or African American, non-Hispanic/Latino; 1 Asian, non-Hispanic/Latino; 1 Hispanic/Latino). 12 applicants, 67% accepted, 5 enrolled. *Entrance requirements:* Additional exam requirements/recommendations for international students: Required—TOEFL. *Application deadline:* For fall admission, 5/1 for domestic students, 2/1 for international students; for spring admission, 11/30 for domestic students, 6/1 for international students. Applications are processed on a rolling basis. Application fee: $75. *Expenses:* Tuition, state resident: part-time $471 per credit hour. Tuition, nonresident: part-time $1016 per credit hour. Required fees: $337 per term. *Financial support:* In 2010–11, 1 fellowship with full tuition reimbursement (averaging $19,845 per year) was awarded. Financial award applicants required to submit FAFSA. *Unit head:* Dr. Anand Anandalingam, Dean, 301-405-0582, E-mail: ganand@umd.edu. *Application contact:* Dr. Charles A. Caramello, Dean of Graduate School, 301-405-0358, Fax: 301-314-9305, E-mail: ccaramel@umd.edu.

University of Maryland University College, Graduate School of Management and Technology, Doctoral Program in Management, Adelphi, MD 20783. Offers DM. *Accreditation:* AACSB. Part-time programs available. *Students:* 322 part-time (146 women); includes 150 minority (118 Black or African American, non-Hispanic/Latino; 1 American Indian or Alaska Native, non-Hispanic/Latino; 15 Asian, non-Hispanic/Latino; 14 Hispanic/Latino; 2 Two or more races, non-Hispanic/Latino), 35 international. Average age 45. 141 applicants, 100% accepted, 19 enrolled. In 2010, 42 doctorates awarded. *Degree requirements:* For doctorate, comprehensive exam, thesis/dissertation. *Application deadline:* Applications are processed on a rolling basis. Application fee: $100. Electronic applications accepted. *Financial support:* Federal Work-Study and scholarships/grants available. Support available to part-time students. Financial award application deadline: 6/1; financial award applicants required to submit FAFSA. *Unit head:* Dr. Bryan Booth, Executive Director, 240-684-2400, Fax: 240-684-2401, E-mail: bbooth@umuc.edu. *Application contact:* Admissions Coordinator, 800-888-8682, Fax: 240-684-2151, E-mail: newgrad@umuc.edu.

University of Maryland University College, Graduate School of Management and Technology, Program in Business Administration, Adelphi, MD 20783. Offers MBA, Certificate. *Accreditation:* AACSB. Part-time and evening/weekend programs available. Postbaccalaureate distance learning degree programs offered (no on-campus study). *Students:* 5 full-time (2 women), 2,545 part-time (1,443 women); includes 1,413 minority (1,084 Black or African American, non-Hispanic/Latino; 7 American Indian or Alaska Native, non-Hispanic/Latino; 165 Asian, non-Hispanic/Latino; 122 Hispanic/Latino; 8 Native Hawaiian or other Pacific Islander, non-Hispanic/Latino; 27 Two or more races, non-Hispanic/Latino), 84 international. Average age 33. 1,296 applicants, 100% accepted, 493 enrolled. In 2010, 1,089 master's awarded. *Degree requirements:* For master's, thesis or alternative, capstone course. *Application deadline:* Applications are processed on a rolling basis. Application fee: $50. Electronic applications accepted. *Financial support:* Federal Work-Study and scholarships/grants available. Support available to part-time students. Financial award application deadline: 6/1; financial award applicants required to submit FAFSA. *Unit head:* Dr. Robert Goodwin, Chair, Business and Executive Programs, 240-684-2400, Fax: 240-684-2401, E-mail: rgoodwin@umuc.edu. *Application contact:* Coordinator, Graduate Admissions, 800-888-8682, Fax: 240-684-2151, E-mail: newgrad@umuc.edu.

University of Maryland University College, Graduate School of Management and Technology, Program in Management, Adelphi, MD 20783. Offers MS, Certificate. Offered evenings and weekends only. Part-time and evening/weekend programs available. Postbaccalaureate distance learning degree programs offered (no on-campus study). *Students:* 87 full-time (65 women), 3,395 part-time (2,306 women); includes 2,045 minority (1,665 Black or African American, non-Hispanic/Latino; 11 American Indian or Alaska Native, non-Hispanic/Latino; 173 Asian, non-Hispanic/Latino; 158 Hispanic/Latino; 6 Native Hawaiian or other Pacific Islander, non-Hispanic/Latino; 32 Two or more races, non-Hispanic/Latino), 75 international. Average age 34. 1,158 applicants, 100% accepted, 659 enrolled. In 2010, 563 master's, 130 other advanced degrees awarded. *Degree requirements:* For master's, thesis or alternative. *Application deadline:* Applications are processed on a rolling basis. Application fee: $50. Electronic applications accepted. *Financial support:* Federal Work-Study and scholarships/grants available. Support available to part-time students. Financial award application deadline: 6/1; financial award applicants required to submit FAFSA. *Unit head:* Dr. Alan Sutherland, Director, 240-684-2400, Fax: 240-684-2401, E-mail: asutherland@umuc.edu.

Application contact: Coordinator, Graduate Admissions, 888-888-8682, Fax: 240-684-2151, E-mail: newgrad@umuc.edu.

University of Mary Washington, College of Business, Fredericksburg, VA 22401-5300. Offers business administration (MBA); management information systems (MSMIS). Part-time and evening/weekend programs available. *Faculty:* 11 full-time (4 women), 9 part-time/adjunct (1 woman). *Students:* 107 full-time (57 women), 253 part-time (123 women); includes 78 Black or African American, non-Hispanic/Latino; 1 American Indian or Alaska Native, non-Hispanic/Latino; 8 Asian, non-Hispanic/Latino; 13 Hispanic/Latino, 5 international. Average age 36. 131 applicants, 56% accepted, 53 enrolled. In 2010, 85 master's awarded. *Entrance requirements:* For master's, GMAT or GRE, minimum GPA of 3.0. Additional exam requirements/recommendations for international students: Required—TOEFL (minimum score 570 paper-based; 230 computer-based; 88 iBT), IELTS (minimum score 6.5). *Application deadline:* For fall admission, 6/1 priority date for domestic students, 6/1 for international students; for spring admission, 10/1 for domestic and international students. Application fee: $50. Electronic applications accepted. *Financial support:* Available to part-time students. Application deadline: 3/15. *Faculty research:* Management of IT offshoring, boundary theory and co-creation matrix: hermeneutics perspectives, text and image mining, queuing theory and supply chain, organizational learning. *Unit head:* Dr. Larry W. Penwell, Acting Dean, 540-654-1561, E-mail: lpenwell@umw. edu. *Application contact:* Matthew E. Mejia, Associate Dean of Admissions, 540-286-8088, Fax: 540-286-8085, E-mail: mmejia@umw.edu.

University of Massachusetts Amherst, Graduate School, Interdisciplinary Programs, Program in Public Policy and Business Administration, Amherst, MA 01003. Offers MPPA/MBA. *Accreditation:* AACSB. Part-time programs available. *Students:* 7 full-time (6 women); includes 2 minority (1 Asian, non-Hispanic/Latino; 1 Two or more races, non-Hispanic/Latino). Average age 30. 12 applicants, 50% accepted, 3 enrolled. *Entrance requirements:* Additional exam requirements/recommendations for international students: Required—TOEFL (minimum score 600 paper-based; 250 computer-based; 100 iBT), IELTS (minimum score 7). *Application deadline:* For fall admission, 2/1 for domestic and international students. Applications are processed on a rolling basis. Application fee: $50 ($65 for international students). Electronic applications accepted. *Expenses:* Tuition, state resident: full-time $2640. Required fees: $8282. One-time fee: $357 full-time. *Financial support:* Career-related internships or fieldwork, Federal Work-Study, scholarships/grants, traineeships, health care benefits, tuition waivers (full), and unspecified assistantships available. Support available to part-time students. Financial award application deadline: 2/1; financial award applicants required to submit FAFSA. *Unit head:* Dr. M. V. Lee Badgett, Graduate Program Director, 413-545-3956, Fax: 413-545-1108. *Application contact:* Jean M. Ames, Supervisor of Admissions, 413-545-0722, Fax: 413-577-0010, E-mail: gradadm@grad.umass.edu.

University of Massachusetts Amherst, Graduate School, Isenberg School of Management, Part-time Master of Business Administration Program, Amherst, MA 01003. Offers MBA. *Accreditation:* AACSB. Part-time and evening/weekend programs available. Postbaccalaureate distance learning degree programs offered (no on-campus study). *Students:* 56 full-time (18 women), 1,034 part-time (284 women); includes 196 minority (31 Black or African American, non-Hispanic/Latino; 2 American Indian or Alaska Native, non-Hispanic/Latino; 116 Asian, non-Hispanic/Latino; 30 Hispanic/Latino; 3 Native Hawaiian or other Pacific Islander, non-Hispanic/Latino; 14 Two or more races, non-Hispanic/Latino), 63 international. Average age 36. 338 applicants, 87% accepted, 220 enrolled. In 2010, 286 master's awarded. *Entrance requirements:* For master's, GMAT. Additional exam requirements/recommendations for international students: Required—TOEFL (minimum score 600 paper-based; 250 computer-based; 100 iBT), IELTS (minimum score 7). *Application deadline:* For fall admission, 7/1 for domestic and international students; for spring admission, 12/1 for domestic and international students. Applications are processed on a rolling basis. Application fee: $50 ($65 for international students). Electronic applications accepted. *Expenses:* Tuition, state resident: full-time $2640. Required fees: $8282. One-time fee: $357 full-time. *Unit head:* Dr. Eric N. Berkowitz, Graduate Program Director, 413-545-5608, Fax: 413-577-2234, E-mail: gradprog@som.umass.edu. *Application contact:* Jean M. Ames, Supervisor of Admissions, 415-545-0722, Fax: 413-577-0010, E-mail: gradadm@grad.umass.edu.

University of Massachusetts Amherst, Graduate School, Isenberg School of Management, Program in Management, Amherst, MA 01003. Offers MBA, MS, PhD. *Accreditation:* AACSB. Part-time programs available. *Faculty:* 57 full-time (11 women). *Students:* 114 full-time (43 women), 4 part-time (2 women); includes 11 minority (2 Black or African American, non-Hispanic/ Latino; 6 Asian, non-Hispanic/Latino; 3 Hispanic/Latino), 48 international. Average age 32. 374 applicants, 21% accepted, 44 enrolled. In 2010, 32 master's, 9 doctorates awarded. Terminal master's awarded for partial completion of doctoral program. *Degree requirements:* For doctorate, comprehensive exam, thesis/dissertation. *Entrance requirements:* For master's and doctorate, GMAT. Additional exam requirements/recommendations for international students: Required—TOEFL (minimum score 550 paper-based; 213 computer-based; 80 iBT), IELTS (minimum score 6.5). *Application deadline:* For fall admission, 2/1 for domestic and international students. Applications are processed on a rolling basis. Application fee: $50 ($65 for international students).

Electronic applications accepted. *Expenses:* Tuition, state resident: full-time $2640. Required fees: $8282. One-time fee: $357 full-time. *Financial support:* In 2010–11, 15 fellowships with full tuition reimbursements (averaging $6,067 per year), 69 research assistantships with full tuition reimbursements (averaging $8,702 per year), 63 teaching assistantships with full tuition reimbursements (averaging $9,337 per year) were awarded; career-related internships or fieldwork, Federal Work-Study, scholarships/grants, traineeships, health care benefits, tuition waivers (full), and unspecified assistantships also available. Support available to part-time students. Financial award application deadline: 2/1; financial award applicants required to submit FAFSA. *Unit head:* Dr. William Wooldridge, Chair, 413-545-5675, Fax: 413-577-2234. *Application contact:* Jean M. Ames, Supervisor of Admissions, 413-545-0722, Fax: 413-577-0010, E-mail: gradadm@grad.umass.edu.

University of Massachusetts Dartmouth, Graduate School, Charlton College of Business, Program in Business Administration, North Dartmouth, MA 02747-2300. Offers accounting (Postbaccalaureate Certificate); business administration (MBA); e-commerce (PMC); finance (PMC); general management (PMC); leadership (PMC); management (Postbaccalaureate Certificate); marketing (PMC); supply chain management (PMC). *Accreditation:* AACSB. Part-time programs available. *Faculty:* 40 full-time (13 women), 28 part-time/adjunct (8 women). *Students:* 99 full-time (38 women), 123 part-time (62 women); includes 4 Black or African American, non-Hispanic/Latino; 2 American Indian or Alaska Native, non-Hispanic/Latino; 3 Asian, non-Hispanic/Latino; 8 Hispanic/Latino; 1 Two or more races, non-Hispanic/Latino, 45 international. Average age 30. 185 applicants, 76% accepted, 79 enrolled. In 2010, 79 master's, 12 other advanced degrees awarded. *Entrance requirements:* For master's, GMAT, resume, letters of recommendation. Additional exam requirements/recommendations for international students: Required—TOEFL (minimum score 500 paper-based; 200 computer-based; 72 iBT). *Application deadline:* For fall admission, 6/1 for domestic students, 5/1 for international students; for spring admission, 10/1 for domestic students, 8/1 for international students. Application fee: $40 ($60 for international students). Electronic applications accepted. *Expenses:* Tuition, state resident: full-time $2071; part-time $86 per credit. Tuition, nonresident: full-time $8099; part-time $337 per credit. Required fees: $9446; $394 per credit. One-time fee: $75. Part-time tuition and fees vary according to class time, course load, degree level and reciprocity agreements. *Financial support:* In 2010–11, 1 research assistantship with full tuition reimbursement (averaging $6,000 per year) was awarded; teaching assistantships, Federal Work-Study and unspecified assistantships also available. Support available to part-time students. Financial award application deadline: 3/1; financial award applicants required to submit FAFSA. *Faculty research:* Global business environment, e-commerce, managing diversity, agile manufacturing, green business. Total annual research expenditures: $29,538. *Unit head:* Dr. Norm Barber, Assistant Dean, 508-999-8543, E-mail: nbarber@umassd.edu. *Application contact:* Elan Turcotte-Shamski, Graduate Admissions Officer, 508-999-8604, Fax: 508-999-8183, E-mail: graduate@umassd.edu.

University of Memphis, Graduate School, Fogelman College of Business and Economics, Program in Business Administration, Memphis, TN 38152. Offers accounting (MBA, PhD); economics (MBA, PhD); executive business administration (MBA); finance (PhD); finance, insurance, and real estate (MBA, MS); international business administration (IMBA); management (MBA, MS, PhD); management information systems (MBA, MS, PhD); management science (MBA); marketing (MBA, MS); marketing and supply chain management (PhD); real estate development (MS); JD/MBA. *Accreditation:* AACSB. *Faculty:* 44 full-time (9 women), 5 part-time/adjunct (0 women). *Students:* 263 full-time (106 women), 181 part-time (66 women); includes 46 Black or African American, non-Hispanic/Latino; 3 American Indian or Alaska Native, non-Hispanic/Latino; 16 Asian, non-Hispanic/Latino; 5 Hispanic/Latino, 109 international. Average age 31. 374 applicants, 73% accepted, 119 enrolled. In 2010, 140 master's, 17 doctorates awarded. *Degree requirements:* For master's, comprehensive exam; for doctorate, comprehensive exam, thesis/dissertation. *Entrance requirements:* For master's, GMAT, resume; for doctorate, GMAT, interview, minimum GPA of 3.4, resume, letter of recommendation. Additional exam requirements/recommendations for international students: Required—TOEFL (minimum score 550 paper-based; 220 computer-based). *Application deadline:* For fall admission, 8/1 for domestic students; for spring admission, 12/1 for domestic students. Application fee: $35 ($60 for international students). *Financial support:* In 2010–11, 164 students received support; research assistantships with full tuition reimbursements available, teaching assistantships with full tuition reimbursements available, career-related internships or fieldwork, Federal Work-Study, scholarships/grants, and unspecified assistantships available. Financial award application deadline: 2/15; financial award applicants required to submit FAFSA. *Faculty research:* Competitive business strategy, finance microstructures, supply chain management innovations, health care economics, litigation risks and corporate audits. *Unit head:* Rajiv Grover, Dean, 901-678-3759, E-mail: rgrover@ memphis.edu. *Application contact:* Dr. Carol V. Danehower, Associate Dean, 901-678-5402, Fax: 901-678-3579, E-mail: fcbegp@memphis.edu.

University of Michigan–Dearborn, School of Management, Dearborn, MI 48128-1491. Offers accounting (MBA, MS); finance (MBA, MS); information systems (MS); international business (MBA); management

(MBA); management information systems (MBA); marketing (MBA); supply chain management (MBA); MBA/MHSA; MBA/MSE; MBA/MSF. *Accreditation:* AACSB. Part-time and evening/weekend programs available. Postbaccalaureate distance learning degree programs offered (no on-campus study). *Faculty:* 40 full-time (17 women), 2 part-time/adjunct (1 woman). *Students:* 71 full-time (26 women), 403 part-time (134 women); includes 68 minority (19 Black or African American, non-Hispanic/Latino; 1 American Indian or Alaska Native, non-Hispanic/Latino; 39 Asian, non-Hispanic/Latino; 6 Hispanic/Latino; 1 Native Hawaiian or other Pacific Islander, non-Hispanic/Latino; 2 Two or more races, non-Hispanic/Latino), 89 international. Average age 30. 185 applicants, 51% accepted, 67 enrolled. In 2010, 150 master's awarded. *Entrance requirements:* For master's, GMAT, 2 years of work experience (MBA); course work in computer applications, statistics, and pre-calculus or finite mathematics; 18 credits of accounting course work beyond introductory courses (MS in accounting). Additional exam requirements/recommendations for international students: Required—TOEFL (minimum score 560 paper-based; 220 computer-based; 84 iBT). *Application deadline:* For fall admission, 8/1 priority date for domestic students, 6/1 for international students; for winter admission, 12/1 priority date for domestic students, 10/1 for international students; for spring admission, 4/1 priority date for domestic students, 2/1 for international students. Applications are processed on a rolling basis. Application fee: $60. Electronic applications accepted. *Expenses:* Contact institution. *Financial support:* Career-related internships or fieldwork, Federal Work-Study, and scholarships/grants available. Support available to part-time students. Financial award application deadline: 9/1; financial award applicants required to submit FAFSA. *Faculty research:* Cultural diversity, buyer-supplier relations, error detection in data, economic evolution. *Unit head:* Dr. Kim Schatzel, Dean, 313-593-5248, Fax: 313-271-9835, E-mail: schatzel@umd.umich.edu. *Application contact:* Joan Doherty, Academic Advisor/Counselor, 313-593-5460, Fax: 313-271-9838, E-mail: gradbusiness@umd.umich.edu.

University of Minnesota, Twin Cities Campus, Carlson School of Management, Minneapolis, MN 55455. Offers EMBA, M Acc, MA, MBA, MBT, PhD, JD/MBA, MBA/MPP, MD/MBA, MHA/MBA, Pharm D/MBA. *Accreditation:* AACSB. Part-time and evening/weekend programs available. *Faculty:* 144 full-time (43 women), 83 part-time/adjunct (34 women). *Students:* 531 full-time (282 women), 1,695 part-time (604 women); includes 32 Black or African American, non-Hispanic/Latino; 4 American Indian or Alaska Native, non-Hispanic/Latino; 134 Asian, non-Hispanic/Latino; 33 Hispanic/Latino, 294 international. Average age 28. In 2010, 676 master's, 13 doctorates awarded. Terminal master's awarded for partial completion of doctoral program. *Degree requirements:* For doctorate, comprehensive exam, thesis/dissertation. Electronic applications accepted. *Expenses:* Contact institution. *Financial support:* Fellowships with full and partial tuition reimbursements, research assistantships with full tuition reimbursements, teaching assistantships with full and partial tuition reimbursements, career-related internships or fieldwork, Federal Work-Study, institutionally sponsored loans, scholarships/grants, health care benefits, tuition waivers (full and partial), and unspecified assistantships available. Support available to part-time students. Financial award application deadline: 4/1; financial award applicants required to submit FAFSA. *Faculty research:* Finance and accounting: financial reporting, asset pricing models and corporate finance; information and decision sciences: on-line auctions, information transparency and recommender systems; marketing: psychological influences on consumer behavior, brand equity, pricing and marketing channels; operations: lean manufacturing, quality management and global supply chains; strategic management and organization: global strategy, networks, entrepreneurship and innovation, sustainability. *Unit head:* Dr. Alison Davis-Blake, Dean, 612-626-9636, Fax: 612-624-6374, E-mail: csdean@umn.edu. *Application contact:* Dr. Alison Davis-Blake, Dean, 612-626-9636, Fax: 612-624-6374, E-mail: csdean@umn.edu.

University of Mississippi, Graduate School, School of Business Administration, Oxford, University, MS 38677. Offers business administration (MBA, PhD); systems management (MS); JD/MBA. *Accreditation:* AACSB. *Students:* 96 full-time (30 women), 49 part-time (8 women); includes 17 minority (8 Black or African American, non-Hispanic/Latino; 2 Asian, non-Hispanic/Latino; 2 Hispanic/Latino; 5 Two or more races, non-Hispanic/Latino), 16 international. In 2010, 46 master's, 9 doctorates awarded. *Degree requirements:* For doctorate, thesis/dissertation. *Entrance requirements:* For master's, GMAT, minimum GPA of 3.0; for doctorate, GMAT. Additional exam requirements/recommendations for international students: Required—TOEFL. *Application deadline:* For fall admission, 2/1 for domestic students; for spring admission, 10/1 for domestic students. Applications are processed on a rolling basis. Application fee: $25. Electronic applications accepted. *Financial support:* Fellowships, career-related internships or fieldwork, scholarships/grants, tuition waivers (full), and unspecified assistantships available. Financial award application deadline: 3/1; financial award applicants required to submit FAFSA. *Unit head:* Dr. Ken Cyree, Dean, 662-915-5820, Fax: 662-915-5821, E-mail: info@bus.olemiss.edu. *Application contact:* Dr. Christy M. Wyandt, Associate Dean, 662-915-7474, Fax: 662-915-7577, E-mail: cwyandt@olemiss.edu.

University of Missouri–Kansas City, Henry W. Bloch School of Management, Kansas City, MO 64110-2499. Offers accounting (MS); business administration

(MBA); entrepreneurship and innovation (PhD); public affairs (MPA, PhD); JD/MBA; LL M/MPA. PhD (interdisciplinary) offered through the School of Graduate Studies. *Accreditation:* AACSB; NASPAA. Part-time and evening/weekend programs available. *Faculty:* 49 full-time (16 women), 21 part-time/adjunct (5 women). *Students:* 280 full-time (134 women), 435 part-time (193 women); includes 91 minority (44 Black or African American, non-Hispanic/Latino; 19 Asian, non-Hispanic/Latino; 23 Hispanic/Latino; 5 Two or more races, non-Hispanic/Latino), 50 international. Average age 30. 426 applicants, 255 enrolled. In 2010, 254 master's awarded. Terminal master's awarded for partial completion of doctoral program. *Entrance requirements:* For master's, GMAT, GRE, 2 writing essays, 2 references and support of employer; for doctorate, GRE, minimum GPA of 3.0. Additional exam requirements/recommendations for international students: Required—TOEFL (minimum score 550 paper-based; 213 computer-based; 80 iBT). *Application deadline:* For fall admission, 5/1 priority date for domestic and international students; for spring admission, 10/1 priority date for domestic and international students. Applications are processed on a rolling basis. Application fee: $45 ($50 for international students). Electronic applications accepted. *Expenses:* Tuition, state resident: full-time $5522.40; part-time $306.80 per credit hour. Tuition, nonresident: full-time $7128; part-time $792 per credit hour. Required fees: $261.15 per term. *Financial support:* In 2010–11, 26 research assistantships with partial tuition reimbursements (averaging $7,767 per year), 5 teaching assistantships with partial tuition reimbursements (averaging $8,430 per year) were awarded; career-related internships or fieldwork, Federal Work-Study, institutionally sponsored loans, scholarships/grants, tuition waivers (full and partial), and unspecified assistantships also available. Support available to part-time students. Financial award application deadline: 3/1; financial award applicants required to submit FAFSA. *Faculty research:* Entrepreneurship, finance, non-profit, risk management. *Unit head:* Dr. Teng-Kee Tan, Dean, 816-235-2215, Fax: 816-235-2206. *Application contact:* 816-235-1111, E-mail: admit@umkc.edu.

University of Missouri–St. Louis, College of Business Administration, Program in Business Administration, St. Louis, MO 63121. Offers accounting (MBA); business administration (Certificate); finance (MBA); human resource management (Certificate); information systems (MBA); local government (Certificate); logistics and supply chain management (MBA, Certificate); marketing (MBA); marketing management (Certificate); operations management (MBA). *Accreditation:* AACSB. Part-time and evening/weekend programs available. *Faculty:* 30 full-time (5 women), 11 part-time/adjunct (2 women). *Students:* 132 full-time (57 women), 306 part-time (122 women); includes 55 minority (21 Black or African American, non-Hispanic/Latino; 20 Asian, non-Hispanic/Latino; 11 Hispanic/Latino; 1 Native Hawaiian or other Pacific Islander, non-Hispanic/Latino; 2 Two or more races, non-Hispanic/Latino), 6 international. Average age 30. 219 applicants, 60% accepted, 88 enrolled. In 2010, 114 master's, 9 other advanced degrees awarded. *Entrance requirements:* For master's, GMAT, 2 letters of recommendation. Additional exam requirements/recommendations for international students: Required—TOEFL (minimum score 550 paper-based; 213 computer-based). *Application deadline:* For fall admission, 7/1 for domestic students; for spring admission, 11/1 for domestic students. Applications are processed on a rolling basis. Application fee: $35 ($40 for international students). Electronic applications accepted. *Expenses:* Tuition, state resident: full-time $5522; part-time $306.80 per credit hour. Tuition, nonresident: full-time $14,253; part-time $792.10 per credit hour. Required fees: $658; $49 per credit hour. One-time fee: $12. Tuition and fees vary according to program. *Financial support:* In 2010–11, 22 research assistantships with full and partial tuition reimbursements (averaging $7,414 per year), 4 teaching assistantships with full and partial tuition reimbursements (averaging $13,950 per year) were awarded; career-related internships or fieldwork, Federal Work-Study, and institutionally sponsored loans also available. Support available to part-time students. Financial award application deadline: 4/1; financial award applicants required to submit FAFSA. *Faculty research:* Human resources, strategic management, marketing strategy, consumer behavior product development, advertising. *Unit head:* Karl Kottemann, Assistant Director, 314-516-5885, Fax: 314-516-6420, E-mail: mba@umsl.edu. *Application contact:* 314-516-5458, Fax: 314-516-6996, E-mail: gradadm@umsl.edu.

University of Missouri–St. Louis, Graduate School, Program in Public Policy Administration, St. Louis, MO 63121. Offers health policy (MPPA); local government management (MPPA); managing human resources and organization (MPPA); nonprofit organization management (MPPA); nonprofit organization management and leadership (Certificate); policy research and analysis (MPPA). *Accreditation:* NASPAA. Part-time and evening/weekend programs available. *Faculty:* 9 full-time (4 women), 8 part-time/adjunct (6 women). *Students:* 36 full-time (21 women), 59 part-time (33 women); includes 17 minority (13 Black or African American, non-Hispanic/Latino; 2 American Indian or Alaska Native, non-Hispanic/Latino; 1 Asian, non-Hispanic/Latino; 1 Hispanic/Latino), 11 international. Average age 31. 60 applicants, 68% accepted, 24 enrolled. In 2010, 23 master's, 17 Certificates awarded. *Entrance requirements:* For master's, 3 letters of recommendation. Additional exam requirements/recommendations for international students: Required—TOEFL (minimum score 550 paper-based; 213 computer-based). *Application deadline:* For fall admission, 7/1 priority date for domestic and international students; for spring admission, 12/1 priority date for domestic and international students. Applications are processed on a rolling basis. Application fee: $35 ($40 for international students). Electronic applications accepted. *Expenses:* Tuition, state resident: full-time $5522; part-time $306.80 per credit hour. Tuition, nonresident: full-time $14,253; part-time $792.10 per credit hour. Required fees: $658; $49 per credit hour. One-time fee: $12. Tuition and fees vary according to program. *Financial support:* In 2010–11, 3 research assistantships with full and partial tuition reimbursements (averaging $12,000 per year) were awarded; career-related internships or fieldwork also available. Financial award application deadline: 4/1; financial award applicants required to submit FAFSA. *Faculty research:* Urban policy, public finance, evaluation. *Unit head:* Dr. Brady Baybeck, Director, 314-516-5145, Fax: 314-516-5210, E-mail: baybeck@umsl.edu. *Application contact:* 314-516-5458, Fax: 314-516-6996, E-mail: gradadm@umsl.edu.

University of Mobile, Graduate Programs, Program in Business Administration, Mobile, AL 36613. Offers MBA. *Accreditation:* ACBSP. Part-time and evening/weekend programs available. *Faculty:* 3 full-time (all women), 2 part-time/adjunct (0 women). *Students:* 4 full-time (all women), 36 part-time (19 women); includes 16 Black or African American, non-Hispanic/Latino, 5 international. Average age 35. 21 applicants, 95% accepted, 20 enrolled. In 2010, 18 master's awarded. *Degree requirements:* For master's, comprehensive exam. *Entrance requirements:* For master's, GMAT. Additional exam requirements/recommendations for international students: Required—TOEFL (minimum score 550 paper-based; 213 computer-based; 80 iBT). *Application deadline:* For fall admission, 8/3 priority date for domestic students; for spring admission, 12/23 for domestic students. Applications are processed on a rolling basis. Application fee: $40 ($50 for international students). *Expenses:* Tuition: Full-time $3915; part-time $435 per credit hour. Required fees: $63 per semester. *Financial support:* Application deadline: 8/1. *Faculty research:* Management, personnel management, small business, diversity. *Unit head:* Dr. Jane Finley, Dean, School of Business, 251-442-2219, Fax: 251-442-2523, E-mail: jfinley@umobile.edu. *Application contact:* Tammy C. Eubanks, Administrative Assistant to Dean of Graduate Programs, 251-442-2270, Fax: 251-442-2523, E-mail: teubanks@umobile.edu.

University of Montevallo, Stephens College of Business, Montevallo, AL 35115. Offers MBA. *Accreditation:* AACSB. Part-time and evening/weekend programs available. *Students:* 6 full-time (3 women), 11 part-time (5 women); includes 4 minority (2 Black or African American, non-Hispanic/Latino; 1 Hispanic/Latino; 1 Two or more races, non-Hispanic/Latino). *Degree requirements:* For master's, comprehensive exam. *Entrance requirements:* Additional exam requirements/recommendations for international students: Required—TOEFL (minimum score 550 paper-based). *Application deadline:* For fall admission, 7/15 for domestic students; for spring admission, 11/15 for domestic students. Application fee: $25. *Expenses:* Tuition, state resident: full-time $6264; part-time $261 per credit hour. Tuition, nonresident: full-time $12,528; part-time $502 per credit hour. Required fees: $251 per semester. *Unit head:* Dr. Stephen H. Craft, Dean, 205-665-6540. *Application contact:* Rebecca Hartley, Coordinator for Graduate Studies, 205-665-6350, Fax: 205-665-6353, E-mail: hartleyrs@montevallo.edu.

University of Nebraska at Omaha, Graduate Studies, College of Business Administration, Program in Business Administration, Omaha, NE 68182. Offers EMBA, MBA. *Accreditation:* AACSB. Part-time and evening/weekend programs available. *Faculty:* 22 full-time (7 women). *Students:* 85 full-time (27 women), 243 part-time (76 women); includes 30 minority (9 Black or African American, non-Hispanic/Latino; 1 American Indian or Alaska Native, non-Hispanic/Latino; 12 Asian, non-Hispanic/Latino; 8 Hispanic/Latino), 18 international. Average age 33. 162 applicants, 48% accepted, 69 enrolled. In 2010, 121 master's awarded. *Degree requirements:* For master's, thesis (for some programs), capstone course. *Entrance requirements:* For master's, GMAT, minimum AACSB index of 1040, minimum GPA of 3.0, resume. Additional exam requirements/recommendations for international students: Required—TOEFL (minimum score 550 paper-based; 213 computer-based; 80 iBT). *Application deadline:* For fall admission, 7/1 for domestic students; for spring admission, 11/15 for domestic students. Applications are processed on a rolling basis. Application fee: $45. Electronic applications accepted. *Financial support:* In 2010–11, 106 students received support; research assistantships with tuition reimbursements available, Federal Work-Study, institutionally sponsored loans, scholarships/grants, tuition waivers (partial), and unspecified assistantships available. Support available to part-time students. Financial award application deadline: 3/1; financial award applicants required to submit FAFSA. *Unit head:* Dr. Lynn Harland, Associate Dean, 402-554-2303. *Application contact:* Lex Kaczmarek, Director, 402-554-2303.

University of Nevada, Las Vegas, Graduate College, College of Business, Program in Business Administration, Las Vegas, NV 89154-6031. Offers Exec MBA, MBA. *Accreditation:* AACSB. Part-time and evening/weekend programs available. *Faculty:* 21 full-time (1 woman), 1 (woman) part-time/adjunct. *Students:* 161 full-time (50 women), 77 part-time (30 women); includes 55 minority (19 Asian, non-Hispanic/Latino; 9 Hispanic/Latino; 27 Two or more races, non-Hispanic/Latino), 25 international. Average age 31. 129 applicants, 64% accepted, 55 enrolled. In 2010, 142 master's awarded. *Entrance requirements:* For master's, GMAT. Additional exam requirements/recommendations for international students: Required—TOEFL (minimum score 550 paper-based; 213 computer-based; 80 iBT), IELTS (minimum score 7). *Application deadline:* For fall admission, 6/1 priority date for domestic and international students; for spring admission, 11/15 priority date for domestic and international students. Applications are processed on a rolling basis. Application fee: $60 ($95 for international students). Electronic applications accepted. *Expenses:* Tuition, area resident: Part-time $239.50 per credit. Tuition, state resident: part-time $239.50 per credit. Tuition, nonresident: part-time $503 per credit. Required fees: $108 per semester. Tuition and fees vary according to course load, program and reciprocity agreements. *Financial support:* In 2010–11, 18 students received support, including 17 research assistantships with partial tuition reimbursements available (averaging $10,000 per year), 1 teaching assistantship with partial tuition reimbursement available (averaging $10,000 per year); institutionally sponsored loans, scholarships/grants, health care benefits, and unspecified assistantships also available. Financial award application deadline: 3/1. *Faculty research:* Economic effects on wages, benefits and economic effects of risk, uncertainty; asymmetric information: adverse selection, moral hazard; business processes. Total annual research expenditures: $10,671. *Unit head:* Dr. Reza Torkzadeh, Department Chair/ Professor/Associate Dean, 702-895-1832, Fax: 702-895-3655, E-mail: reza.torkzadeh@unlv.edu. *Application contact:* Graduate College Admissions Evaluator, 702-895-3320, Fax: 702-895-4180, E-mail: gradcollege@unlv.edu.

University of New Brunswick Fredericton, School of Graduate Studies, Faculty of Business Administration, Fredericton, NB E3B 5A3, Canada. Offers business administration (MBA); engineering management (MBA); entrepreneurship (MBA); sports and recreation management (MBA); MBA/LL B. Part-time programs available. *Faculty:* 23 full-time (3 women), 5 part-time/adjunct (2 women). *Students:* 43 full-time (18 women), 35 part-time (20 women). In 2010, 29 master's awarded. *Degree requirements:* For master's, thesis optional. *Entrance requirements:* For master's, GMAT (550 minimum score), minimum GPA of 3.0; 3-5 years work experience. Additional exam requirements/recommendations for international students: Required—TOEFL (minimum score 580 paper-based; 92 iBT), IELTS (minimum score 7), TOEFL or IELTS. *Application deadline:* For fall admission, 3/1 priority date for domestic students. Applications are processed on a rolling basis. Application fee: $50 Canadian dollars. *Expenses:* Tuition, area resident: Full-time $3708; part-time $927 per term. International tuition: $6300 full-time. Required fees: $50 per term. *Financial support:* In 2010–11, 4 research assistantships (averaging $4,500 per year), 13 teaching assistantships (averaging $2,250 per year) were awarded. *Faculty research:* Accounting and auditing practices, human resource management, the non-profit sector, marketing, strategic management, entrepreneurship, investment practices, supply chain management, and operations management. *Unit head:* Judy Roy, Director of Graduate Studies, 506-458-7307, Fax: 506-453-3561, E-mail: jroy@unb.ca. *Application contact:* Marilyn Davis, Acting Graduate Secretary, 506-453-4766, Fax: 506-453-3561, E-mail: mbacontact@unb.ca.

University of New Brunswick Saint John, Faculty of Business, Saint John, NB E2L 4L5, Canada. Offers administration (MBA); electronic commerce (MBA); international business (MBA); natural resource management (MBA). Part-time programs available. *Faculty:* 19 full-time (4 women), 14 part-time/adjunct (8 women). *Students:* 47 full-time (18 women), 55 part-time (21 women). 93 applicants, 78% accepted, 25 enrolled. In 2010, 36 master's awarded. *Entrance requirements:* For master's, GMAT, minimum GPA of 3.0. Additional exam requirements/recommendations for international students: Required—TOEFL (minimum score 580 paper-based; 237 computer-based), IELTS (minimum score 7), TWE (minimum score 4.5). *Application deadline:* For fall admission, 5/15 for domestic and international students. Applications are processed on a rolling basis. Application fee: $100. Electronic applications accepted. *Expenses:* Contact institution. *Financial support:* In 2010–11, 4 students received support. Career-related internships or fieldwork and scholarships/grants available. *Faculty research:* Business use of weblogs and podcasts to communicate, corporate governance, high-involvement work systems, international competitiveness, supply chain management and logistics. *Unit head:* Henryk Sterniczuk, Director of Graduate Studies, 506-648-5573, Fax: 506-648-5574, E-mail: sternicz@unbsj.ca. *Application contact:* Tammy Morin, Secretary, 506-648-5746, Fax: 506-648-5574, E-mail: tmorin@unbsj.ca.

University of New Hampshire, Center for Graduate and Professional Studies, Manchester, NH 03101. Offers business administration (MBA); counseling (M Ed); education (M Ed, MAT); educational administration and supervision (M Ed, Ed S); industrial statistics (Certificate); public administration (MPA); public health (MPH, Certificate); social work (MSW); software systems engineering (Certificate). Part-time and evening/weekend programs available. *Students:* 97 full-time (65 women), 159 part-time (85 women); includes 20 minority (11 Black or African American, non-Hispanic/Latino; 1 American Indian or Alaska Native, non-Hispanic/Latino; 6 Asian, non-Hispanic/Latino; 2 Hispanic/Latino), 2 international. 119 applicants, 71% accepted, 61 enrolled. In 2010, 79 master's, 1 other advanced degree awarded. *Degree requirements:* For master's, thesis or alternative. *Entrance requirements:* Additional exam requirements/recommendations for international students: Required—TOEFL (minimum score 550 paper-based; 213 computer-based; 80 iBT). *Application deadline:* For fall admission, 6/1 for domestic students, 4/1 for international students; for spring admission, 12/1 for domestic students. Applications are processed on a rolling basis. Application fee: $65. Electronic applications accepted. *Financial support:* In 2010–11, 21 students received support, including 1 fellowship, 1 teaching assistantship; research assistantships, Federal Work-Study, scholarships/grants, health care benefits, and unspecified assistantships also available. Support available to part-time students. Financial award application deadline: 3/1; financial award applicants required to submit FAFSA. *Unit head:* Kate Ferreira, Director, 603-641-4313, E-mail: unhm. gradcenter@unh.edu. *Application contact:* Graduate Admissions Office, 603-862-3000, Fax: 603-862-0275, E-mail: grad.school@unh.edu.

University of New Hampshire, Graduate School, Whittemore School of Business and Economics, Department of Business Administration, Durham, NH 03824. Offers business administration (MBA); executive business administration (MBA); health management (MBA); management of technology (MS, Postbaccalaureate Certificate). *Accreditation:* AACSB. Part-time and evening/weekend programs available. *Faculty:* 24 full-time (4 women). *Students:* 97 full-time (24 women), 84 part-time (21 women); includes 3 Black or African American, non-Hispanic/Latino; 1 American Indian or Alaska Native, non-Hispanic/Latino; 5 Asian, non-Hispanic/Latino; 1 Hispanic/Latino, 7 international. Average age 36. 142 applicants, 54% accepted, 65 enrolled. In 2010, 87 master's awarded. *Entrance requirements:* For master's, GMAT. Additional exam requirements/recommendations for international students: Required—TOEFL (minimum score 550 paper-based; 213 computer-based; 80 iBT). *Application deadline:* For fall admission, 7/1 priority date for domestic students, 4/1 for international students; for spring admission, 11/1 for domestic students. Applications are processed on a rolling basis. Application fee: $65. *Expenses:* Contact institution. *Financial support:* In 2010–11, 35 students received support; fellowships, research assistantships, teaching assistantships, career-related internships or fieldwork, Federal Work-Study, scholarships/grants, and tuition waivers (full and partial) available. Financial award application deadline: 2/15. *Unit head:* Christine Shea, Chairperson, 603-862-3316. *Application contact:* Rachel Hopkins, Administrative Assistant, 603-862-3316, E-mail: wsbe.grad@unh.edu.

University of New Haven, Graduate School, School of Business, Executive Program in Business Administration, West Haven, CT 06516-1916. Offers EMBA. Part-time and evening/weekend programs available. *Students:* 5 full-time (0 women), 2 part-time (both women); includes 1 Black or African American, non-Hispanic/Latino, 1 international. Average age 45. In 2010, 3 master's awarded. *Entrance requirements:* Additional exam requirements/recommendations for international students: Required—TOEFL (minimum score 520 paper-based; 190 computer-based; 70 iBT), IELTS (minimum score 5.5). *Application deadline:* For fall admission, 5/31 for international students; for winter admission, 10/15 for international students; for spring admission, 1/15 for international students. Applications are processed on a rolling basis. Application fee: $50. Electronic applications accepted. *Expenses:* Contact institution. *Financial support:* Research assistantships with partial tuition reimbursements, teaching assistantships with partial tuition reimbursements, career-related internships or fieldwork, Federal Work-Study, health care benefits, and unspecified assistantships available. Financial award application deadline: 5/1; financial award applicants required to submit FAFSA. *Unit head:* Linda Carlone, Coordinator, 203-932-7433. *Application contact:* Eloise Gormley, Director of Graduate Admissions, 203-932-7449, Fax: 203-932-7137, E-mail: gradinfo@newhaven.edu.

University of New Haven, Graduate School, School of Business, Program in Business Administration, West Haven, CT 06516-1916. Offers accounting (MBA, Certificate), including CPA (MBA); business management (Certificate); business policy and strategy (MBA); finance (MBA), including CFA; global marketing (MBA); human resource management (Certificate); human resources management (MBA); international business (Certificate); marketing (Certificate); sports management (MBA); telecommunications management (Certificate); MBA/MPA. Part-time and evening/weekend programs available. *Students:* 158 full-time (80 women), 150 part-time (70 women); includes 36 Black or African American, non-Hispanic/Latino; 2 American Indian or Alaska Native, non-Hispanic/Latino; 19 Asian, non-Hispanic/Latino; 16 Hispanic/Latino, 82 international. Average age 32. 162 applicants, 99% accepted, 85 enrolled. In 2010, 141 master's, 16 other advanced degrees awarded. *Degree requirements:* For master's, thesis or alternative. *Entrance requirements:* For master's, GMAT. Additional exam requirements/recommendations for international students: Required—TOEFL (minimum score 520 paper-based; 190 computer-based; 70 iBT), IELTS (minimum score 5.5). *Application deadline:* For fall admission, 5/31 for international students; for winter admission, 10/15 for international students; for spring admission, 1/15 for international students. Applications are processed on a rolling basis. Application fee: $50. Electronic applications accepted. *Expenses:* Contact institution. *Financial support:* Research assistantships with partial tuition reimbursements, teaching assistantships with partial tuition reimbursements, Federal Work-Study, scholarships/grants, health care benefits, tuition waivers, and unspecified assistantships available. Support available to part-time students. Financial award applicants required to submit FAFSA. *Unit head:* Charles Coleman, Chairman, 203-932-7375. *Application contact:* Eloise Gormley, Director of Graduate Admissions, 203-932-7449, Fax: 203-932-7137, E-mail: gradinfo@newhaven.edu.

University of North Alabama, College of Business, Florence, AL 35632-0001. Offers MBA. *Accreditation:* ACBSP. Part-time and evening/weekend programs available. *Faculty:* 3 full-time (0 women), 17 part-time/adjunct (4

women). *Students:* 248 full-time (113 women), 326 part-time (154 women); includes 288 minority (42 Black or African American, non-Hispanic/Latino; 5 American Indian or Alaska Native, non-Hispanic/Latino; 231 Asian, non-Hispanic/Latino; 3 Hispanic/Latino; 2 Native Hawaiian or other Pacific Islander, non-Hispanic/Latino; 5 Two or more races, non-Hispanic/Latino), 49 international. Average age 35. In 2010, 268 master's awarded. *Entrance requirements:* For master's, GMAT, minimum GPA of 2.75 in last 60 hours, 2.5 overall on a 3.0 scale; 27 hours of course work in business and economics. *Application deadline:* For fall admission, 7/1 priority date for domestic students; for spring admission, 12/1 for domestic students. Applications are processed on a rolling basis. Application fee: $25. Electronic applications accepted. *Expenses:* Tuition, state resident: full-time $5472; part-time $228 per credit hour. Tuition, nonresident: full-time $10,944; part-time $456 per credit hour. Required fees: $986. Tuition and fees vary according to course load. *Financial support:* Federal Work-Study available. Support available to part-time students. Financial award application deadline: 4/1. *Unit head:* Dr. Kerry Gatlin, Dean, 256-765-4261, Fax: 256-765-4170, E-mail: kpgatlin@una.edu. *Application contact:* Kim Mauldin, Director of Admissions, 256-765-4608, Fax: 256-765-4960, E-mail: komauldin@una.edu.

The University of North Carolina at Charlotte, Graduate School, Belk College of Business, Program in Business Administration, Charlotte, NC 28223-0001. Offers business administration (PhD); Hong Kong (MBA); MBA-plus (Post-Master's Certificate); Mexico (MBA); real estate finance and development (Certificate); sports marketing and management (MBA); Taiwan (MBA); U. S. (MBA). *Accreditation:* AACSB. Part-time and evening/weekend programs available. *Faculty:* 34 full-time (10 women). *Students:* 142 full-time (55 women), 307 part-time (96 women); includes 69 minority (33 Black or African American, non-Hispanic/Latino; 22 Asian, non-Hispanic/Latino; 12 Hispanic/Latino; 2 Two or more races, non-Hispanic/Latino), 145 international. Average age 30. 265 applicants, 82% accepted, 126 enrolled. In 2010, 227 master's, 1 doctorate awarded. *Degree requirements:* For master's, thesis or alternative; for doctorate, thesis/dissertation. *Entrance requirements:* For master's, GMAT, minimum GPA of 3.0 in undergraduate major, 2.8 overall. Additional exam requirements/recommendations for international students: Required—TOEFL (minimum score 557 paper-based; 220 computer-based; 83 iBT). *Application deadline:* For fall admission, 7/15 for domestic students, 5/1 for international students; for spring admission, 11/15 for domestic students, 10/1 for international students. Applications are processed on a rolling basis. Application fee: $55. Electronic applications accepted. *Expenses:* Tuition, state resident: full-time $3464. Tuition, nonresident: full-time $14,297. Required fees: $2094. Tuition and fees vary according to course load. *Financial support:* In 2010–11, 68 students received support, including 2 research assistantships (averaging $18,000 per year), 65 teaching assistantships (averaging $12,142 per year); career-related internships or fieldwork, Federal Work-Study, institutionally sponsored loans, scholarships/grants, and administrative assistantship also available. Support available to part-time students. Financial award application deadline: 4/1; financial award applicants required to submit FAFSA. Total annual research expenditures: $86,745. *Unit head:* Jeremiah Nelson, Interim Director, MBA Program, 704-687-6058, Fax: 704-687-4014, E-mail: jeremiah.nelson@uncc.edu. *Application contact:* Kathy B. Giddings, Director of Graduate Admissions, 704-687-5503, Fax: 704-687-3279, E-mail: gradadm@uncc.edu.

The University of North Carolina Wilmington, School of Business, Program in Business Administration, Wilmington, NC 28403-3297. Offers MBA. *Accreditation:* AACSB. Part-time and evening/weekend programs available. *Faculty:* 12 full-time (5 women). *Students:* 1 full-time (0 women), 78 part-time (22 women); includes 2 Black or African American, non-Hispanic/Latino; 4 Asian, non-Hispanic/Latino; 6 Hispanic/Latino; 2 Two or more races, non-Hispanic/Latino. Average age 32. 77 applicants, 70% accepted, 40 enrolled. In 2010, 57 master's awarded. *Degree requirements:* For master's, comprehensive exam, thesis (for some programs), final project. *Entrance requirements:* For master's, GMAT, 1 year of appropriate work experience. Additional exam requirements/recommendations for international students: Required—TOEFL (minimum score 550 paper-based; 217 computer-based; 79 iBT), IELTS (minimum score 6.5). *Application deadline:* For fall admission, 2/1 for domestic students. Applications are processed on a rolling basis. Application fee: $60. *Financial support:* In 2010–11, 1 teaching assistantship with full and partial tuition reimbursement (averaging $9,000 per year) was awarded; career-related internships or fieldwork and Federal Work-Study also available. Support available to part-time students. Financial award application deadline: 3/15. *Unit head:* Dr. Vince Howe, Coordinator, 910-962-3882, E-mail: howe@uncw.edu. *Application contact:* Dr. Karen Barnhill, Graduate Coordinator, 910-962-3903, E-mail: barnhillk@uncw.edu.

University of North Dakota, Graduate School, College of Business and Public Administration, Business Administration Program, Grand Forks, ND 58202. Offers MBA. *Accreditation:* AACSB. Part-time and evening/weekend programs available. Postbaccalaureate distance learning degree programs offered (minimal on-campus study). *Faculty:* 26 full-time (6 women). *Students:* 46 full-time (14 women), 49 part-time (22 women); includes 6 minority (3 Black or African American, non-Hispanic/Latino; 3 Asian, non-Hispanic/Latino), 12 international. Average age 29. 45 applicants, 62% accepted, 27 enrolled. In 2010, 45 master's awarded. *Degree requirements:* For master's, comprehensive exam, thesis or alternative, project. *Entrance requirements:* For master's, GMAT, minimum GPA of 3.25. Additional exam requirements/ recommendations for international students: Required—TOEFL (minimum score 550 paper-based; 213 computer-based; 79 iBT), IELTS (minimum score 6.5). *Application deadline:* For fall admission, 8/1 priority date for domestic students, 5/1 priority date for international students; for spring admission, 12/1 priority date for domestic students, 9/1 priority date for international students. Applications are processed on a rolling basis. Application fee: $35. Electronic applications accepted. *Expenses:* Tuition, state resident: full-time $5857; part-time $306.74 per credit. Tuition, nonresident: full-time $15,666; part-time $729.77 per credit. Required fees: $53.42 per credit. Tuition and fees vary according to course load, program and reciprocity agreements. *Financial support:* In 2010–11, 27 students received support; fellowships with full and partial tuition reimbursements available, research assistantships with full tuition reimbursements available, teaching assistantships with full and partial tuition reimbursements available, Federal Work-Study, institutionally sponsored loans, scholarships/grants, health care benefits, tuition waivers (full and partial), and unspecified assistantships available. Support available to part-time students. Financial award application deadline: 3/15; financial award applicants required to submit FAFSA. *Unit head:* Dr. Timothy P. O'Keefe, Graduate Director, 701-777-2135, Fax: 701-777-2019, E-mail: mba@mail.business.und.edu. *Application contact:* Matt Anderson, Admissions Specialist, 701-777-2947, Fax: 701-777-3619, E-mail: matthew.anderson@gradschool.und.edu.

University of Northern Iowa, Graduate College, College of Business Administration, Program in Business Administration, Cedar Falls, IA 50614. Offers MBA. *Accreditation:* AACSB. Part-time and evening/weekend programs available. *Students:* 17 full-time (6 women), 26 part-time (7 women); includes 3 minority (1 Black or African American, non-Hispanic/Latino; 2 Hispanic/Latino), 21 international. 74 applicants, 41% accepted, 17 enrolled. In 2010, 40 master's awarded. *Entrance requirements:* For master's, GMAT (minimum score 500), minimum GPA of 3.0. Additional exam requirements/ recommendations for international students: Required—TOEFL (minimum score 500 paper-based; 180 computer-based; 61 iBT). *Application deadline:* For fall admission, 8/1 priority date for domestic students. Applications are processed on a rolling basis. Application fee: $50 ($70 for international students). Electronic applications accepted. *Financial support:* Career-related internships or fieldwork, Federal Work-Study, scholarships/grants, and tuition waivers (full and partial) available. Support available to part-time students. Financial award application deadline: 2/1. *Unit head:* Dr. Leslie K. Wilson, Acting Associate Dean, 319-273-6240, Fax: 319-273-2922, E-mail: leslie.wilson@uni.edu. *Application contact:* Laurie S. Russell, Record Analyst, 319-273-2623, Fax: 319-273-2885, E-mail: laurie.russell@uni.edu.

University of North Florida, Coggin College of Business, MBA Program, Jacksonville, FL 32224. Offers accounting (MBA); construction management (MBA); e-commerce (MBA); economics (MBA); finance (MBA); human resource management (MBA); international business (MBA); logistics (MBA); management applications (MBA). *Accreditation:* AACSB. Part-time and evening/weekend programs available. *Faculty:* 17 full-time (5 women), 1 part-time/adjunct (0 women). *Students:* 137 full-time (56 women), 268 part-time (112 women); includes 17 Black or African American, non-Hispanic/Latino; 21 Asian, non-Hispanic/Latino; 12 Hispanic/Latino; 3 Two or more races, non-Hispanic/Latino, 29 international. Average age 30. 250 applicants, 57% accepted, 94 enrolled. In 2010, 173 master's awarded. *Entrance requirements:* For master's, GMAT or GRE, U.S. bachelor's degree from regionally-accredited university or equivalent foreign degree. Additional exam requirements/recommendations for international students: Required—TOEFL (minimum score 550 paper-based; 213 computer-based; 79 iBT). *Application deadline:* For fall admission, 7/1 priority date for domestic students, 5/1 for international students; for spring admission, 11/1 priority date for domestic students, 10/1 for international students. Applications are processed on a rolling basis. Application fee: $30. *Expenses:* Tuition, state resident: full-time $7646.40; part-time $318.60 per credit hour. Tuition, nonresident: full-time $23,502; part-time $979.24 per credit hour. Required fees: $1208.88; $50.37 per credit hour. Tuition and fees vary according to course load and program. *Financial support:* In 2010–11, 40 students received support; research assistantships, teaching assistantships, Federal Work-Study and tuition waivers (partial) available. Support available to part-time students. Financial award application deadline: 4/1; financial award applicants required to submit FAFSA. *Faculty research:* Performance measures, costing, and inventory issues in logistics and supply chain management; inter-organizational systems; international management and marketing practices; e-commerce; organizational learning and socialization processes. Total annual research expenditures: $9,024. *Unit head:* Dr. C. Bruce Kavan, Chair, 904-620-2780, Fax: 904-620-2832. *Application contact:* Cheryl Campbell, Graduate Advisor, 904-620-2575, Fax: 904-620-2832, E-mail: ccampbell@unf.edu.

University of North Texas, Toulouse Graduate School, College of Business Administration, Denton, TX 76203. Offers MBA, MS, PhD. *Accreditation:* AACSB. Part-time and evening/weekend programs available. *Degree requirements:* For master's, thesis or alternative; for doctorate, thesis/dissertation. *Entrance requirements:* For master's, GMAT or GRE General Test, resume, 3 letters of recommendation; for doctorate, GMAT or GRE General Test,

statement of purpose, resume, 3 letters of recommendation. Additional exam requirements/recommendations for international students: Required—proof of English language proficiency required for non-native English speakers; Recommended—TOEFL (minimum score 550 paper-based; 213 computer-based; 79 iBT). *Application deadline:* Applications are processed on a rolling basis. Electronic applications accepted. *Expenses:* Tuition, state resident: full-time $4298; part-time $239 per credit hour. Tuition, nonresident: full-time $10,782; part-time $549 per credit hour. Required fees: $1292; $270 per credit hour. *Financial support:* Fellowships, research assistantships, teaching assistantships, career-related internships or fieldwork, Federal Work-Study, and institutionally sponsored loans available. Financial award applicants required to submit FAFSA. *Faculty research:* Oil and gas accounting, expert systems, stock returns, occupational safety, service marketing. *Application contact:* Associate Dean for Graduate Programs, 940-565-8977, Fax: 940-369-8978, E-mail: mbacoba@unt.edu.

University of Notre Dame, Mendoza College of Business, Executive Master of Business Administration Program, Notre Dame, IN 46556. Offers MBA. *Accreditation:* AACSB. *Faculty:* 27 full-time (3 women), 7 part-time/ adjunct (0 women). *Students:* 252 full-time (58 women); includes 15 Black or African American, non-Hispanic/Latino; 2 American Indian or Alaska Native, non-Hispanic/Latino; 13 Asian, non-Hispanic/Latino; 10 Hispanic/ Latino; 3 Two or more races, non-Hispanic/Latino, 6 international. Average age 36. 2,267 applicants, 7% accepted, 128 enrolled. In 2010, 110 master's awarded. *Entrance requirements:* For master's, 5 years of work experience in management. *Application deadline:* For fall admission, 6/1 for domestic students; for winter admission, 11/1 for domestic students. Applications are processed on a rolling basis. Application fee: $100. Electronic applications accepted. *Expenses:* Contact institution. *Financial support:* In 2010–11, 12 students received support, including 9 fellowships (averaging $10,000 per year); institutionally sponsored loans also available. Financial award application deadline: 5/15; financial award applicants required to submit FAFSA. *Faculty research:* Exchange rates, compensation, market microstructure or volatility in foreign currency, ethical negotiation/decision making. *Unit head:* Paul C. Velasco, Director of Degree Programs, 574-631-8876, Fax: 574-631-6783, E-mail: pcvelasco@nd.edu. *Application contact:* Dr. Barry J. VanDyck, Director of Admissions and Recruiting, Executive MBA, 574-631-8351, Fax: 574-631-6783, E-mail: bvandyck@nd.edu.

University of Notre Dame, Mendoza College of Business, Master of Business Administration Program, Notre Dame, IN 46556. Offers MBA. *Accreditation:* AACSB. *Faculty:* 60 full-time (10 women), 18 part-time/adjunct (4 women). *Students:* 337 full-time (83 women); includes 59 minority (11 Black or African American, non-Hispanic/Latino; 8 American Indian or Alaska Native, non-Hispanic/Latino; 27 Asian, non-Hispanic/Latino; 13 Hispanic/Latino), 49 international. Average age 27. 888 applicants, 33% accepted, 133 enrolled. In 2010, 201 master's awarded. *Entrance requirements:* For master's, GMAT, GRE, work experience. Additional exam requirements/recommendations for international students: Required—TOEFL (minimum score 600 paper-based; 250 computer-based). *Application deadline:* For fall admission, 11/1 priority date for domestic and international students; for winter admission, 1/10 priority date for domestic and international students; for spring admission, 3/21 for domestic students, 5/21 for international students. Applications are processed on a rolling basis. Application fee: $100. Electronic applications accepted. *Financial support:* In 2010–11, 206 students received support, including fellowships with full and partial tuition reimbursements available (averaging $18,725 per year), research assistantships (averaging $3,000 per year), teaching assistantships (averaging $3,000 per year); career-related internships or fieldwork, Federal Work-Study, institutionally sponsored loans, scholarships/grants, and unspecified assistantships also available. Financial award application deadline: 2/15; financial award applicants required to submit FAFSA. *Faculty research:* Market micro-structure, marketing and public policy, corporate finance and accounting, corporate governance and ethical behavior, high performing organizations. *Unit head:* Dr. Edward J. Conlon, Associate Dean, Graduate Programs, 574-631-9295, Fax: 574-631-4825, E-mail: econlon@nd.edu. *Application contact:* Brian T. Lohr, Director of MBA Admissions, 574-631-8488, Fax: 574-631-8800, E-mail: blohr@nd.edu.

University of Oklahoma, Michael F. Price College of Business, Program in Business Administration, Norman, OK 73019. Offers MBA, PhD, JD/MBA, MBA/MS. *Accreditation:* AACSB. Part-time and evening/weekend programs available. *Students:* 142 full-time (38 women), 133 part-time (34 women); includes 30 minority (3 Black or African American, non-Hispanic/Latino; 9 American Indian or Alaska Native, non-Hispanic/Latino; 11 Asian, non-Hispanic/Latino; 4 Hispanic/Latino; 3 Two or more races, non-Hispanic/Latino), 47 international. Average age 28. 307 applicants, 45% accepted, 99 enrolled. In 2010, 72 master's, 6 doctorates awarded. Terminal master's awarded for partial completion of doctoral program. *Degree requirements:* For master's, comprehensive exam (for some programs); for doctorate, thesis/dissertation. *Entrance requirements:* For master's, minimum GPA of 3.2; for doctorate, GMAT. Additional exam requirements/recommendations for international students: Required—TOEFL (minimum score 550 paper-based; 213 computer-based; 79 iBT). *Application deadline:* For fall admission, 6/1 for domestic students, 4/1 for international students; for spring admission, 11/1 for domestic students, 9/1 for international students. Applications are processed on a rolling basis. Application fee: $40 ($90 for international students). Electronic applications accepted. *Expenses:* Tuition, state resident: full-time $3893; part-time $162.20 per credit hour. Tuition, nonresident: full-time $14,167; part-time $590.30 per credit hour. Required fees: $2523; $94.60 per credit hour. Tuition and fees vary according to course load and degree level. *Financial support:* In 2010–11, 170 students received support, including 13 fellowships (averaging $5,300 per year); career-related internships or fieldwork, scholarships/grants, health care benefits, unspecified assistantships, and support for special summer internships also available. Financial award applicants required to submit FAFSA. *Faculty research:* Corporate finance issues (capital structure, dividend policy and privatization); IT and organizational behavior; entrepreneurship and venture capital; corporate governance and risk management; earning management; behavior of intermediaries in real markets; strategy and firm performance; liquidity risk in financial markets; energy assets. *Unit head:* Dr. Kenneth Evans, Dean, 405-325-0100, Fax: 405-325-3421, E-mail: evansk@ou.edu. *Application contact:* Amber Hasbrook, Academic Counselor, 405-325-4107, Fax: 405-325-7753, E-mail: amber.hasbrook@ou.edu.

See Display on this page and Close-Up on page 268.

University of Phoenix, School of Advanced Studies, Phoenix, AZ 85034-7209. Offers business administration (DBA); education (Ed D); educational leadership (Ed D), including curriculum and instruction, educational technology; health administration (DHA); higher education administration (PhD); industrial organizational psychology (PhD); nursing (PhD); organizational leadership and technology (DM), including information systems and technology, organizational leadership. Evening/weekend programs available. Postbaccalaureate distance learning degree programs offered. *Students:* 6,882 full-time (4,598 women); includes 2,871 minority (2,251 Black or African American, non-Hispanic/Latino; 50 American Indian or Alaska Native, non-Hispanic/Latino; 133 Asian, non-Hispanic/Latino; 378 Hispanic/Latino; 46 Native Hawaiian or other Pacific Islander, non-Hispanic/Latino; 13 Two or more races, non-Hispanic/Latino), 375 international. Average age 46. *Degree requirements:* For doctorate, thesis/dissertation. *Entrance requirements:* For doctorate, master's degree from accredited university, minimum master's GPA of 3.0, 3 years' professional work experience, laptop computer, membership in research library. Additional exam requirements/recommendations for international students: Required—TOEFL (minimum paper score 550, computer score 213, iBT 79), Test of English for International Communication, or IELTS. *Application deadline:* Applications are processed on a rolling basis. Application fee: $45. Electronic applications accepted. *Expenses:* Contact institution. *Financial support:* Scholarships/grants available. Financial award applicants required to submit FAFSA. *Unit head:* Dr. Jeremy Moreland, Dean/Executive Director, 480-557-3231, E-mail: jeremy.moreland@phoenix.edu. *Application contact:* Dr. Jeremy Moreland, Dean/Executive Director, 480-557-3231, E-mail: jeremy.moreland@phoenix.edu.

University of Phoenix, School of Business, Phoenix, AZ 85034-7209. Offers accounting (MBA, MSA); business administration (MBA); energy management (MBA); global management (MBA); health care management (MBA); human resources management (MM); international management (MM); management (MM); marketing (MBA); project management (MBA); public administration (MPA); technology management (MBA). Programs are offered at the online campus. Evening/weekend programs available. Postbaccalaureate distance learning degree programs offered. *Students:* 20,237 full-time (12,641 women); includes 6,424 minority (4,376 Black or African American, non-Hispanic/Latino; 150 American Indian or Alaska Native, non-Hispanic/Latino; 546 Asian, non-Hispanic/Latino; 1,137 Hispanic/Latino; 155 Native Hawaiian or other Pacific Islander, non-Hispanic/Latino; 60 Two or more races, non-Hispanic/Latino), 1,149 international. Average age 39. *Entrance requirements:* For master's, minimum undergraduate GPA of 2.5 from accredited university, 3 years of work experience, citizen of the United States or have valid visa. Additional exam requirements/recommendations for international students: Required—TOEFL (minimum paper score 550, computer score 213, iBT 79), Test of English for International Communication, or IELTS. *Application deadline:* Applications are processed on a rolling basis. Application fee: $45. Electronic applications accepted. *Expenses:* Tuition: Full-time $16,440. One-time fee: $45 full-time. Full-time tuition and fees vary according to course load, degree level, campus/location and program. *Financial support:* Scholarships/grants available. Financial award applicants required to submit FAFSA. *Unit head:* Dr. Bill Berry, Director, 480-557-1824, E-mail: bill.berry@phoenix.edu. *Application contact:* Dr. Bill Berry, Director, 480-557-1824, E-mail: bill.berry@phoenix.edu.

University of Phoenix–Northern Virginia Campus, School of Business, Reston, VA 20190. Offers business administration (MBA); public accounting (MPA). Evening/weekend programs available. Postbaccalaureate distance learning degree programs offered. *Students:* 135 full-time (50 women); includes 43 Black or African American, non-Hispanic/Latino; 3 Asian, non-Hispanic/Latino; 3 Hispanic/Latino, 6 international. Average age 40. *Entrance requirements:* For master's, minimum undergraduate GPA of 2.5 from an accredited university, 3 years of work experience, must be a citizen of the United States or have a valid visa. Specific requirements may vary by program. Additional exam requirements/recommendations for international students: Required—TOEFL (minimum score 213 paper, 79 iBT), TOEIC, IELTS or

Berlitz. *Application deadline:* Applications are processed on a rolling basis. Application fee: $45. Electronic applications accepted. *Expenses:* Tuition: Full-time $16,440. One-time fee: $45 full-time. Full-time tuition and fees vary according to course load, degree level, campus/location and program. *Financial support:* Scholarships/grants available. Financial award applicants required to submit FAFSA. *Unit head:* Erik Greenberg, Campus Director, 703-376-6150, E-mail: erik.greenberg@phoenix.edu. *Application contact:* Erik Greenberg, Campus Director, 703-376-6150, E-mail: erik.greenberg@phoenix.edu.

University of Phoenix–Phoenix Campus, School of Business, Phoenix, AZ 85040-1958. Offers accounting (MSA); business administration (MBA); management (MM). Evening/weekend programs available. Postbaccalaureate distance learning degree programs offered. *Students:* 950 full-time (468 women); includes 194 minority (59 Black or African American, non-Hispanic/Latino; 11 American Indian or Alaska Native, non-Hispanic/Latino; 27 Asian, non-Hispanic/Latino; 84 Hispanic/Latino; 10 Native Hawaiian or other Pacific Islander, non-Hispanic/Latino; 3 Two or more races, non-Hispanic/Latino), 47 international. Average age 34. *Entrance requirements:* For master's, minimum undergraduate GPA of 2.5 from accredited university, 3 years of work experience, citizen of the United States or have valid visa. Additional exam requirements/recommendations for international students: Required—TOEFL (minimum paper score 500, computer score 213, iBT 79), Test of English for International Communication, or IELTS. *Application deadline:* Applications are processed on a rolling basis. Application fee: $45. Electronic applications accepted. *Expenses:* Tuition: Full-time $13,560. One-time fee: $45 full-time. Full-time tuition and fees vary according to course load, degree level, campus/location and program. *Financial support:* Scholarships/grants available. Financial award applicants required to submit FAFSA. *Unit head:* Bill Berry, Director, 480-557-1824, Fax: 480-557-1854, E-mail: bill.berry@phoenix.edu. *Application contact:* Campus Information Center, 800-766-0766.

University of Pittsburgh, Graduate School of Public and International Affairs, Public Policy and Management Program for Mid-Career Professionals, Pittsburgh, PA 15260. Offers development planning (MPPM); international development (MPPM); international political economy (MPPM); international security studies (MPPM); management of non profit organizations (MPPM); metropolitan management and regional development (MPPM); policy analysis and evaluation (MPPM). Part-time programs available. *Faculty:* 30 full-time (12 women), 67 part-time/adjunct (25 women). *Students:* 14 full-time (1 woman), 34 part-time (17 women), 8 international. Average age 38. 31 applicants, 74% accepted, 15 enrolled. In 2010, 14 master's awarded. *Degree requirements:* For master's, thesis optional, capstone seminar. *Entrance requirements:* For master's, 2 letters of recommendation, resume, 5 years of supervisory or budgetary experience. Additional exam requirements/recommendations for international students: Required—TOEFL (minimum score 600 paper-based; 250 computer-based; 100 iBT), TWE (minimum score 4); Recommended—IELTS (minimum score 7). *Application deadline:* For fall admission, 6/1 priority date for domestic students, 2/15 for international students; for spring admission, 1/1 priority date for domestic students, 8/1 for international students. Applications are processed on a rolling basis. Application fee: $50. Electronic applications accepted. *Expenses:* Tuition, state resident: full-time $17,304; part-time $701 per credit. Tuition, nonresident: full-time $29,554; part-time $1210 per credit. Required fees: $740; $214 per term. Tuition and fees vary according to program. *Financial support:* In 2010–11, 14 students received support. Scholarships/grants and tuition waivers (partial) available. Support available to part-time students. Financial award application deadline: 2/1. *Faculty research:* Nonprofit management, urban and regional affairs, policy analysis and evaluation, security and intelligence studies, global political economy, nongovernmental organizations, civil society, development planning and environmental sustainability, human security. Total annual research expenditures: $892,349. *Unit head:* Dr. George Dougherty, Director, Executive Education, 412-648-7603, Fax: 412-648-2605, E-mail: gwdjr@pitt.edu. *Application contact:* Michael T. Rizzi, Associate Director of Student Services, 412-648-7640, Fax: 412-648-7641, E-mail: rizzim@pitt.edu.

University of Pittsburgh, Katz Graduate School of Business, Doctoral Program in Business Administration, Pittsburgh, PA 15260. Offers accounting (PhD); finance (PhD); information systems (PhD); marketing (PhD); operations/decision sciences/artificial intelligence (PhD); organizational behavior and human resource management (PhD); strategic planning (PhD). *Accreditation:* AACSB. *Faculty:* 50 full-time (15 women). *Students:* 51 full-time (22 women); includes 3 Black or African American, non-Hispanic/Latino; 4 Asian, non-Hispanic/Latino; 2 Hispanic/Latino, 18 international. 448 applicants, 5% accepted, 13 enrolled. In 2010, 4 doctorates awarded. *Degree requirements:* For doctorate, comprehensive exam, thesis/dissertation. *Entrance requirements:* For doctorate, GMAT or GRE, bachelor's degree, references, minimum GPA of 3.0. Additional exam requirements/recommendations for international students: Required—TOEFL, IELTS. *Application deadline:* For fall admission, 2/1 priority date for domestic and international students. Applications are processed on a rolling basis. Application fee: $50. Electronic applications accepted. *Expenses:* Tuition, state resident: full-time $17,304; part-time $701 per credit. Tuition, nonresident: full-time $29,554; part-time $1210 per credit. Required fees: $740; $214 per term. Tuition and fees vary according to program. *Financial support:* In 2010–11, 39 students

received support, including 29 research assistantships with full tuition reimbursements available (averaging $1,900 per year), 10 teaching assistantships with full tuition reimbursements available (averaging $23,745 per year); fellowships, Federal Work-Study, scholarships/grants, health care benefits, and unspecified assistantships also available. Financial award application deadline: 2/1. *Faculty research:* Accounting statements and reporting, incentives and governance, corporate finance, mergers and acquisitions, information systems processes, structures and decision-making, organizational structure, knowledge management and corporate strategy, consumer behavior and marketing models. Total annual research expenditures: $362,777. *Unit head:* Dr. John E. Hulland, Director of Doctoral Program, 412-648-1534, Fax: 412-624-3633, E-mail: jhulland@katz.pitt.edu. *Application contact:* Carrie Woods, Assistant Director, Doctoral Office, 412-648-1525, Fax: 412-624-3633, E-mail: cawoods@katz.pitt.edu.

University of Pittsburgh, Katz Graduate School of Business, Executive MBA Program, Pittsburgh, PA 15260. Offers EMBA. *Accreditation:* AACSB. Evening/weekend programs available. *Faculty:* 36 full-time (5 women), 7 part-time/adjunct (2 women). *Students:* 64 full-time (14 women); includes 1 Black or African American, non-Hispanic/Latino; 4 Asian, non-Hispanic/Latino; 3 Hispanic/Latino, 37 international. Average age 37. 102 applicants, 68% accepted, 64 enrolled. In 2010, 62 master's awarded. *Entrance requirements:* For master's, GMAT (candidates with less than 10 years experience, GPA less than 3.0, or limited quantitative background), 3 credits of course work in college-level calculus, minimum 5 years management experience, references, interview, bachelor's degree. Additional exam requirements/recommendations for international students: Required—TOEFL, TOEFL or IELTS. *Application deadline:* For winter admission, 12/1 priority date for domestic students, 3/1 priority date for international students. Applications are processed on a rolling basis. Application fee: $0. Electronic applications accepted. *Expenses:* Contact institution. *Financial support:* In 2010–11, 17 students received support, including 2 fellowships (averaging $4,000 per year); scholarships/grants, tuition waivers (partial), and unspecified assistantships also available. Financial award application deadline: 12/1. *Faculty research:* Transitional economies, incentives and governance, corporate finance, mergers and acquisitions, global information systems and structures, consumer behavior and marketing models, entrepreneurship and globalization. *Unit head:* Anne M. Nemer, Executive Director for EMBA Worldwide, 412-648-1694, Fax: 412-648-1787, E-mail: annemer@katz.pitt.edu. *Application contact:* Kristen Carothers, Director, Executive MBA, 866-623-3622, Fax: 412-648-1787, E-mail: embaprogram@katz.pitt.edu.

University of Pittsburgh, Katz Graduate School of Business, Master of Business Administration Programs, Pittsburgh, PA 15260. Offers finance (MBA); information systems (MBA); marketing (MBA); operations management (MBA); organizational behavior and human resource management (MBA); organizational leadership (Certificate); six sigma (Certificate); strategy, environment and organizations (MBA); technology, innovation and entrepreneurship (Certificate); MBA/JD; MBA/MIB; MBA/MPIA; MBA/MSE; MBA/MSIS; MID/MBA. *Accreditation:* AACSB. Part-time and evening/weekend programs available. *Faculty:* 60 full-time (18 women), 22 part-time/adjunct (5 women). *Students:* 232 full-time (75 women), 458 part-time (158 women); includes 34 Black or African American, non-Hispanic/Latino; 1 American Indian or Alaska Native, non-Hispanic/Latino; 20 Asian, non-Hispanic/Latino; 9 Hispanic/Latino, 105 international. Average age 29. 697 applicants, 50% accepted, 174 enrolled. In 2010, 263 master's awarded. *Degree requirements:* For master's, minimum GPA of 3.0. *Entrance requirements:* For master's, GMAT, recommendations, undergraduate transcripts, essay responses, resume, interview, bachelor's degree. Additional exam requirements/recommendations for international students: Required—TOEFL (minimum 600 paper, 250 computer, 100 iBT) or IELTS. *Application deadline:* For fall admission, 4/1 priority date for domestic students, 2/1 priority date for international students. Application fee: $50. Electronic applications accepted. *Expenses:* Tuition, state resident: full-time $17,304; part-time $701 per credit. Tuition, nonresident: full-time $29,554; part-time $1210 per credit. Required fees: $740; $214 per term. Tuition and fees vary according to program. *Financial support:* In 2010–11, 52 students received support. Career-related internships or fieldwork and scholarships/grants available. Financial award application deadline: 3/1; financial award applicants required to submit FAFSA. *Faculty research:* Accounting statements and reporting, incentives and governance, corporate finance, mergers and acquisitions, information systems processes, structures and decision-making, organizational structure, knowledge management and corporate strategy, consumer behavior and marketing models. *Unit head:* William T. Valenta, Assistant Dean, MBA Program Director, 412-648-1610, Fax: 412-648-1659, E-mail: wtvalenta@katz.pitt.edu. *Application contact:* Cliff McCormick, Director MBA Admissions, 412-648-1700, Fax: 412-648-1659, E-mail: mba@katz.pitt.edu.

University of Pittsburgh, Katz Graduate School of Business, MBA/Juris Doctor Dual Degree Program, Pittsburgh, PA 15260. Offers MBA/JD. *Faculty:* 60 full-time (18 women), 22 part-time/adjunct (5 women). *Students:* 28 full-time (5 women); includes 1 Black or African American, non-Hispanic/Latino; 2 Asian, non-Hispanic/Latino. Average age 28. 15 applicants, 80% accepted, 7 enrolled. *Entrance requirements:* Additional exam requirements/recommendations for international students: Required—TOEFL (minimum 600 paper,

250 computer, 100 iBT) or IELTS. *Application deadline:* For fall admission, 4/1 priority date for domestic students, 2/1 priority date for international students. Application fee: $50. Electronic applications accepted. *Expenses:* Tuition, state resident: full-time $17,304; part-time $701 per credit. Tuition, nonresident: full-time $29,554; part-time $1210 per credit. Required fees: $740; $214 per term. Tuition and fees vary according to program. *Financial support:* In 2010–11, 2 students received support. Career-related internships or fieldwork and scholarships/grants available. Financial award application deadline: 3/1; financial award applicants required to submit FAFSA. *Faculty research:* Accounting statements and reporting; incentives and governance; corporate finance, mergers and acquisitions; information systems processes, structures, and decision-making; organizational structure, knowledge management, and corporate strategy; consumer behavior and marketing models. *Unit head:* William T. Valenta, Assistant Dean, Director of MBA Programs, 412-648-1610, Fax: 412-648-1659, E-mail: wtvalenta@katz.pitt.edu. *Application contact:* Cliff McCormick, Director MBA Admissions, 412-648-1700, Fax: 412-648-1659, E-mail: mba@katz.pitt.edu.

University of Pittsburgh, Katz Graduate School of Business, MBA/Master of International Development Joint Degree Program, Pittsburgh, PA 15260. Offers MID/MBA. *Accreditation:* AACSB. Part-time and evening/weekend programs available. *Faculty:* 60 full-time (18 women), 22 part-time/adjunct (5 women). *Students:* 2 full-time (both women). Average age 26. 2 applicants, 50% accepted, 0 enrolled. *Entrance requirements:* Additional exam requirements/recommendations for international students: Required—TOEFL (minimum 600 paper, 250 computer, 100 iBT) or IELTS. *Application deadline:* For fall admission, 4/1 priority date for domestic students, 2/1 priority date for international students. Application fee: $50. Electronic applications accepted. *Expenses:* Tuition, state resident: full-time $17,304; part-time $701 per credit. Tuition, nonresident: full-time $29,554; part-time $1210 per credit. Required fees: $740; $214 per term. Tuition and fees vary according to program. *Financial support:* Career-related internships or fieldwork and scholarships/grants available. Financial award application deadline: 3/1; financial award applicants required to submit FAFSA. *Faculty research:* Transitional economies, incentives and governance, corporate finance, mergers and acquisitions, global information systems and structures, consumer behavior and marketing models, entrepreneurship and globalization. *Unit head:* Wiliam T. Valenta, Assistant Dean, Director of MBA Program, 412-648-1610, Fax: 412-648-1659, E-mail: wtvalenta@katz.pitt.edu. *Application contact:* Cliff McCormick, Director of MBA Admissions, 412-648-1700, Fax: 412-648-1659, E-mail: mba@katz.pitt.edu.

University of Pittsburgh, Katz Graduate School of Business, MBA/Master of Public and International Affairs Dual-Degree Program, Pittsburgh, PA 15260. Offers MBA/MPIA. *Accreditation:* AACSB. Part-time and evening/weekend programs available. *Faculty:* 60 full-time (18 women), 22 part-time/adjunct (5 women). *Students:* 2 full-time (0 women), 1 (woman) part-time. Average age 27. 2 applicants, 0% accepted, 0 enrolled. *Entrance requirements:* Additional exam requirements/recommendations for international students: Required— TOEFL (minimum 600 paper, 250 computer, 100 iBT) or IELTS. *Application deadline:* For fall admission, 4/1 priority date for domestic students, 2/1 priority date for international students. Application fee: $50. Electronic applications accepted. *Expenses:* Tuition, state resident: full-time $17,304; part-time $701 per credit. Tuition, nonresident: full-time $29,554; part-time $1210 per credit. Required fees: $740; $214 per term. Tuition and fees vary according to program. *Financial support:* Career-related internships or fieldwork and scholarships/grants available. Financial award application deadline: 3/1; financial award applicants required to submit FAFSA. *Faculty research:* Transitional economies; incentives and governance; corporate finance, mergers and acquisitions; global information systems and structures, consumer behavior and marketing models; entrepreneurship and globalization. *Unit head:* William T. Valenta, Assistant Dean, Director of MBA Programs, 412-648-1610, Fax: 412-648-1659, E-mail: wtvalenta@katz.pitt.edu. *Application contact:* Cliff McCormick, Director MBA Admissions, 412-648-1700, Fax: 412-648-1659, E-mail: mba@katz.pitt.edu.

University of Pittsburgh, Katz Graduate School of Business, MBA/Master of Science in Engineering Dual-Degree Program, Pittsburgh, PA 15260. Offers MBA/MSE. *Accreditation:* AACSB. Part-time and evening/weekend programs available. *Faculty:* 60 full-time (18 women), 22 part-time/adjunct (5 women). *Students:* 12 full-time (2 women), 25 part-time (5 women); includes 1 Black or African American, non-Hispanic/Latino; 1 Hispanic/Latino. Average age 26. 33 applicants, 64% accepted, 11 enrolled. *Entrance requirements:* Additional exam requirements/recommendations for international students: Required—TOEFL (minimum 600 paper, 250 computer, 100 iBT) or IELTS. *Application deadline:* For fall admission, 4/1 for domestic students, 2/1 priority date for international students. Application fee: $50. Electronic applications accepted. *Expenses:* Tuition, state resident: full-time $17,304; part-time $701 per credit. Tuition, nonresident: full-time $29,554; part-time $1210 per credit. Required fees: $740; $214 per term. Tuition and fees vary according to program. *Financial support:* In 2010–11, 4 students received support. Career-related internships or fieldwork and scholarships/grants available. Financial award application deadline: 3/1; financial award applicants required to submit FAFSA. *Faculty research:* Diffusion of technology-driven innovation, customer-focused development of engineered and

high-tech products and services, logistics and operations research, global supply chains, value innovation and sustainable innovation—green products for the planet's population. *Unit head:* William T. Valenta, Assistant Dean, Director of MBA Programs, 412-648-1610, Fax: 412-648-1659, E-mail: wtvalenta@katz.pitt.edu. *Application contact:* Cliff McCormick, Director MBA Admissions, 412-648-1700, Fax: 412-648-1659, E-mail: mba@katz.pitt.edu.

University of Portland, Dr. Robert B. Pamplin, Jr. School of Business, Portland, OR 97203-5798. Offers business administration (MBA); entrepreneurship (MBA); finance (MBA, MS); health care management (MBA); marketing (MBA); nonprofit management (EMBA); operations and technology management (MBA); sustainability (MBA). *Accreditation:* AACSB. Part-time and evening/weekend programs available. *Faculty:* 12 full-time (2 women), 7 part-time/adjunct (2 women). *Students:* 55 full-time (24 women), 81 part-time (29 women); includes 18 minority (2 Black or African American, non-Hispanic/Latino; 8 Asian, non-Hispanic/Latino; 5 Hispanic/Latino; 3 Two or more races, non-Hispanic/Latino), 23 international. Average age 30. In 2010, 55 master's awarded. *Entrance requirements:* For master's, GMAT, minimum GPA of 3.0, resume, 2 letters of recommendation. Additional exam requirements/recommendations for international students: Required—TOEFL (minimum score 570 paper-based; 89 iBT), IELTS (minimum score 7). *Application deadline:* For fall admission, 7/15 priority date for domestic and international students; for spring admission, 12/15 priority date for domestic and international students. Applications are processed on a rolling basis. Application fee: $50. *Expenses:* Contact institution. *Financial support:* Federal Work-Study, scholarships/grants, and tuition waivers (partial) available. Support available to part-time students. Financial award application deadline: 3/1; financial award applicants required to submit FAFSA. *Unit head:* Dr. Howard Feldman, Associate Dean, 503-943-7224, E-mail: feldman@up.edu. *Application contact:* Melissa McCarthy, Academic Specialist, 503-943-7225, E-mail: mccarthy@up.edu.

University of Puerto Rico, Mayagüez Campus, Graduate Studies, College of Business Administration, Mayagüez, PR 00681-9000. Offers business administration (MBA); finance (MBA); human resources (MBA); industrial management (MBA). Part-time and evening/weekend programs available. *Students:* 47 full-time (28 women), 36 part-time (16 women); includes 79 Hispanic/Latino, 4 international. 19 applicants, 47% accepted, 4 enrolled. In 2010, 15 master's awarded. *Degree requirements:* For master's, comprehensive exam. *Entrance requirements:* For master's, GMAT or EXADEP, bachelor's degree with courses in calculus, microeconomics, accounting and statistics. Additional exam requirements/recommendations for international students: Required—TOEFL (minimum score 500 paper-based; 173 computer-based). *Application deadline:* For fall admission, 2/15 for domestic and international students; for spring admission, 9/15 for domestic and international students. Applications are processed on a rolling basis. Application fee: $25. *Expenses:* Tuition, state resident: full-time $1188. Tuition, nonresident: full-time $1188. International tuition: $6126 full-time. Tuition and fees vary according to course level and course load. *Financial support:* In 2010–11, fellowships (averaging $12,000 per year), 2 research assistantships (averaging $15,000 per year), teaching assistantships (averaging $8,500 per year) were awarded; Federal Work-Study and institutionally sponsored loans also available. *Faculty research:* Organizational studies, management, accounting. Total annual research expenditures: $20,000. *Unit head:* Dr. Rosario Ortiz, Graduate Student Coordinator, 787-265-3800, Fax: 787-832-5320, E-mail: rosario.ortiz@upr.edu. *Application contact:* Milagros Soto, Student Administrator, 787-265-3887, Fax: 787-832-5320, E-mail: milagros.soto1@upr.edu.

University of Regina, Faculty of Graduate Studies and Research, Kenneth Levene Graduate School of Business, Regina, SK S4S 0A2, Canada. Offers M Admin, MBA, MHRM, Master's Certificate. Part-time and evening/weekend programs available. *Faculty:* 51 full-time (14 women), 10 part-time/adjunct (0 women). *Students:* 85 full-time (28 women), 73 part-time (43 women). 191 applicants, 75% accepted. In 2010, 46 master's awarded. *Degree requirements:* For master's, project. *Entrance requirements:* For master's, GMAT, two years relevant work experience. Additional exam requirements/recommendations for international students: Required—TOEFL (minimum score 580 paper-based; 80 iBT). *Application deadline:* Applications are processed on a rolling basis. Application fee: $100. Electronic applications accepted. *Expenses:* Contact institution. *Financial support:* In 2010–11, 9 fellowships (averaging $18,000 per year), 2 research assistantships (averaging $16,500 per year), 8 teaching assistantships (averaging $6,759 per year) were awarded; scholarships/grants also available. Financial award application deadline: 6/15. *Faculty research:* Management of public and private sector organizations. *Unit head:* Dr. Anne Lavack, Dean, 306-585-4162, Fax: 306-585-4805, E-mail: anne.lavack@uregina.ca. *Application contact:* Steve Wield, Manager, 306-337-8463, Fax: 306-585-5361, E-mail: steve.wield@uregina.ca.

University of Rhode Island, Graduate School, College of Business Administration, Kingston, RI 02881. Offers accounting (MS); business administration (MBA, PhD), including finance and insurance (PhD), management (PhD), marketing (PhD), operations and supply chain management (MBA); finance (MBA); general business (MBA); management (MBA); marketing (MBA); supply chain management (MBA). *Accreditation:* AACSB. Part-time and evening/weekend programs available. *Faculty:* 54 full-time (15 women), 3 part-time/adjunct (2 women). *Students:* 82 full-time (31 women), 218 part-time (77 women); includes 31 minority (6 Black or African American, non-Hispanic/Latino; 1 American Indian or Alaska Native, non-Hispanic/Latino; 13 Asian, non-Hispanic/Latino; 11 Hispanic/Latino), 29 international. In 2010, 78 master's, 3 doctorates awarded. *Degree requirements:* For master's, comprehensive exam (for some programs), thesis optional; for doctorate, comprehensive exam, thesis/dissertation. *Entrance requirements:* For master's, GMAT or GRE, 2 letters of recommendation, resume; for doctorate, GMAT or GRE, 3 letters of recommendation, resume. Additional exam requirements/recommendations for international students: Required—TOEFL (minimum score 575 paper-based; 233 computer-based; 91 iBT). Application fee: $65. Electronic applications accepted. *Expenses:* Tuition, state resident: full-time $9588; part-time $533 per credit hour. Tuition, nonresident: full-time $22,968; part-time $1276 per credit hour. Required fees: $1282; $68 per semester. Tuition and fees vary according to program. *Financial support:* In 2010–11, 13 teaching assistantships with full and partial tuition reimbursements (averaging $12,432 per year) were awarded. Financial award applicants required to submit FAFSA. Total annual research expenditures: $9,928. *Unit head:* Dr. Mark Higgins, Dean, 401-874-4244, Fax: 401-874-4312, E-mail: markhiggins@uri.edu. *Application contact:* Lisa Lancellotta, Coordinator, MBA Programs, 401-874-4241, Fax: 401-874-4312, E-mail: mba@uri.edu.

University of St. Francis, College of Business and Health Administration, School of Business, Joliet, IL 60435-6169. Offers MBA, MSM. Part-time and evening/weekend programs available. Postbaccalaureate distance learning degree programs offered (no on-campus study). *Faculty:* 6 full-time (2 women), 7 part-time/adjunct (2 women). *Students:* 38 full-time (23 women), 115 part-time (64 women); includes 31 minority (22 Black or African American, non-Hispanic/Latino; 8 Hispanic/Latino; 1 Two or more races, non-Hispanic/Latino). Average age 37. 88 applicants, 59% accepted, 31 enrolled. In 2010, 58 master's awarded. *Entrance requirements:* Additional exam requirements/recommendations for international students: Required—TOEFL (minimum score 550 paper-based; 213 computer-based). *Application deadline:* Applications are processed on a rolling basis. Application fee: $30. Electronic applications accepted. *Expenses:* Tuition: Part-time $628 per credit. Part-time tuition and fees vary according to degree level, campus/location and program. *Financial support:* In 2010–11, 35 students received support. Federal Work-Study, scholarships/grants, and tuition waivers (partial) available. Support available to part-time students. Financial award applicants required to submit FAFSA. *Unit head:* Dr. Michael LaRocco, Dean, 815-740-5025, Fax: 815-774-2920, E-mail: mlarocco@stfrancis.edu. *Application contact:* Sandra Sloka, Director of Admissions for Graduate and Degree Completion Programs, 800-735-7500, Fax: 815-740-5032, E-mail: ssloka@stfrancis.edu.

University of St. Thomas, Cameron School of Business, Houston, TX 77006-4696. Offers MBA, MSA. *Accreditation:* ACBSP. Part-time and evening/weekend programs available. *Faculty:* 24 full-time (7 women), 3 part-time/adjunct (0 women). *Students:* 137 full-time (74 women), 235 part-time (123 women); includes 156 minority (44 Black or African American, non-Hispanic/Latino; 29 Asian, non-Hispanic/Latino; 81 Hispanic/Latino; 2 Two or more races, non-Hispanic/Latino), 80 international. Average age 30. 134 applicants, 95% accepted, 87 enrolled. In 2010, 179 master's awarded. *Degree requirements:* For master's, capstone (for some programs), additional course requirements for those sitting for state accountancy exam. *Entrance requirements:* For master's, GMAT or GRE, minimum GPA of 2.5, 3 letters of recommendation. Additional exam requirements/recommendations for international students: Required—TOEFL (minimum score 550 paper-based; 213 computer-based; 79 iBT), IELTS (minimum score 6.5). *Application deadline:* Applications are processed on a rolling basis. Application fee: $35. Electronic applications accepted. *Expenses:* Tuition: Full-time $15,696; part-time $872 per credit hour. Required fees: $236; $83 per term. One-time fee: $100. Tuition and fees vary according to course load, campus/location and program. *Financial support:* In 2010–11, 21 students received support. Federal Work-Study, scholarships/grants, unspecified assistantships, and state work-study, institutional employment available. Support available to part-time students. Financial award application deadline: 4/15; financial award applicants required to submit FAFSA. *Unit head:* Dr. Bahman Mirshab, Dean, 713-525-2100, Fax: 713-525-2110, E-mail: cameron@stthom.edu. *Application contact:* Sandra Flanagan, Assistant Director, 713-525-2100, Fax: 713-525-2110, E-mail: cameron@stthom.edu.

University of St. Thomas, Graduate Studies, Opus College of Business, Evening UST MBA Program, Minneapolis, MN 55403. Offers MBA. Part-time and evening/weekend programs available. *Students:* 1,053 part-time (421 women); includes 104 minority (23 Black or African American, non-Hispanic/Latino; 4 American Indian or Alaska Native, non-Hispanic/Latino; 53 Asian, non-Hispanic/Latino; 18 Hispanic/Latino; 1 Native Hawaiian or other Pacific Islander, non-Hispanic/Latino; 5 Two or more races, non-Hispanic/Latino), 27 international. Average age 31. 184 applicants, 98% accepted, 142 enrolled. In 2010, 340 master's awarded. *Entrance requirements:* For master's, GMAT. Additional exam requirements/recommendations for international students: Required—TOEFL (minimum 80 iBT), IELTS, or Michigan Language Assessment Battery. *Application deadline:* For fall admission, 6/1 priority date for domestic students; for spring admission, 11/1 priority date for domestic

students. Applications are processed on a rolling basis. Application fee: $60. Electronic applications accepted. *Financial support:* In 2010–11, 52 students received support. Scholarships/grants available. Financial award application deadline: 6/1. *Unit head:* Corey Eakins, Program Director, 651-962-4200, Fax: 651-962-4129, E-mail: eveningmba@stthomas.edu. *Application contact:* Corey Eakins, Program Director, 651-962-4200, Fax: 651-962-4129, E-mail: eveningmba@stthomas.edu.

University of St. Thomas, Graduate Studies, Opus College of Business, Executive UST MBA Program, Minneapolis, MN 55403. Offers MBA. Part-time and evening/weekend programs available. *Students:* 39 part-time (19 women); includes 5 minority (2 Black or African American, non-Hispanic/Latino; 1 American Indian or Alaska Native, non-Hispanic/Latino; 1 Asian, non-Hispanic/Latino; 1 Hispanic/Latino). Average age 42. 19 applicants, 100% accepted, 17 enrolled. In 2010, 32 master's awarded. *Entrance requirements:* For master's, five years of significant management or leadership experience. *Application deadline:* For fall admission, 10/7 for domestic and international students. Applications are processed on a rolling basis. Application fee: $100. Electronic applications accepted. *Expenses:* Contact institution. *Unit head:* Dr. John Militello, Director, 651-962-4230, Fax: 651-962-4235, E-mail: execmba@stthomas.edu. *Application contact:* Jean Trudeau, Manager, 651-962-4230, Fax: 651-962-4235, E-mail: execmba@stthomas.edu.

University of St. Thomas, Graduate Studies, Opus College of Business, Full-time UST MBA Program, Minneapolis, MN 55403. Offers MBA. *Students:* 119 full-time (42 women); includes 20 minority (5 Black or African American, non-Hispanic/Latino; 5 Asian, non-Hispanic/Latino; 8 Hispanic/Latino; 2 Two or more races, non-Hispanic/Latino), 21 international. Average age 27. 85 applicants, 85% accepted, 50 enrolled. In 2010, 67 master's awarded. *Entrance requirements:* For master's, GMAT. Additional exam requirements/recommendations for international students: Required—TOEFL (minimum 80 iBT), IELTS (minimum 7), or Michigan English Language Assessment Battery. *Application deadline:* For fall admission, 6/15 for domestic and international students. Applications are processed on a rolling basis. Application fee: $60. Electronic applications accepted. *Financial support:* In 2010–11, 84 students received support. Scholarships/grants, tuition waivers (full and partial), and unspecified assistantships available. Financial award application deadline: 4/15. *Unit head:* William Woodson, Assistant Dean, 651-962-8800, Fax: 651-962-4129, E-mail: ustmba@stthomas.edu. *Application contact:* Dustin Cornwell, Program Director, 651-962-8800, Fax: 651-962-4129, E-mail: dcornwell@stthomas.edu.

University of San Diego, School of Business Administration, San Diego, CA 92110-2492. Offers accountancy and taxation (MS), including accountancy, taxation; business administration (MBA); executive leadership (MS); global leadership (MS); international business administration (IMBA); real estate (MS); supply chain management (MS, Certificate); taxation (MS); JD/IMBA; JD/MBA; MBA/MSRE. *Accreditation:* AACSB. Part-time and evening/weekend programs available. *Faculty:* 33 full-time (7 women), 14 part-time/adjunct (6 women). *Students:* 207 full-time (85 women), 269 part-time (93 women); includes 98 minority (10 Black or African American, non-Hispanic/Latino; 2 American Indian or Alaska Native, non-Hispanic/Latino; 30 Asian, non-Hispanic/Latino; 46 Hispanic/Latino; 2 Native Hawaiian or other Pacific Islander, non-Hispanic/Latino; 8 Two or more races, non-Hispanic/Latino), 41 international. Average age 31. 591 applicants, 54% accepted, 216 enrolled. In 2010, 239 master's awarded. *Degree requirements:* For master's, variable foreign language requirement. *Entrance requirements:* For master's, GMAT, minimum GPA of 3.0. Additional exam requirements/recommendations for international students: Required—TOEFL (minimum score 580 paper-based; 237 computer-based; 92 iBT), TWE. Application fee: $80. Electronic applications accepted. *Expenses:* Tuition: Full-time $21,744; part-time $1208 per unit. Required fees: $224. Full-time tuition and fees vary according to course load and degree level. *Financial support:* In 2010–11, 247 students received support. Career-related internships or fieldwork, Federal Work-Study, institutionally sponsored loans, scholarships/grants, and unspecified assistantships available. Support available to part-time students. Financial award application deadline: 4/1; financial award applicants required to submit FAFSA. *Unit head:* Dr. David Pyke, Dean, 619-260-4886, E-mail: sbadean@sandiego.edu. *Application contact:* Stephen Pultz, Director of Admissions and Enrollment, 619-260-4506, Fax: 619-260-6836, E-mail: admissions@sandiego.edu.

University of San Francisco, School of Business and Professional Studies, Masagung Graduate School of Management, MBA for Executives Program, San Francisco, CA 94117-1080. Offers MBA. *Accreditation:* AACSB. *Faculty:* 10 full-time (3 women), 4 part-time/adjunct (2 women). *Students:* 58 full-time (23 women); includes 24 minority (4 Black or African American, non-Hispanic/Latino; 10 Asian, non-Hispanic/Latino; 7 Hispanic/Latino; 3 Two or more races, non-Hispanic/Latino), 2 international. Average age 37. 31 applicants, 71% accepted, 19 enrolled. In 2010, 40 master's awarded. Application fee: $50. *Expenses:* Contact institution. *Financial support:* In 2010–11, 44 students received support. Applicants required to submit FAFSA. *Unit head:* Dr. Karl Boedecker, Director, 415-422-2511, Fax: 415-422-6315. *Application contact:* Kelly Tarry, Secretary, 415-422-2525, E-mail: mbae@usfca.edu.

University of San Francisco, School of Business and Professional Studies, Masagung Graduate School of Management, Program in Business Administration, San Francisco, CA 94117-1080. Offers business economics (MBA); e-business (MBA); entrepreneurship (MBA); finance (MBA); international business (MBA); management (MBA); marketing (MBA); telecommunications management and policy (MBA); JD/MBA; MSN/MBA. *Accreditation:* AACSB. *Faculty:* 17 full-time (4 women), 16 part-time/adjunct (7 women). *Students:* 263 full-time (130 women), 11 part-time (6 women); includes 98 minority (3 Black or African American, non-Hispanic/Latino; 65 Asian, non-Hispanic/Latino; 18 Hispanic/Latino; 3 Native Hawaiian or other Pacific Islander, non-Hispanic/Latino; 9 Two or more races, non-Hispanic/Latino), 43 international. Average age 29. 503 applicants, 60% accepted, 80 enrolled. In 2010, 115 master's awarded. *Entrance requirements:* For master's, GMAT, minimum undergraduate GPA of 3.2. Additional exam requirements/recommendations for international students: Required—TOEFL. *Application deadline:* For fall admission, 7/1 priority date for domestic students; for spring admission, 11/30 for domestic students. Applications are processed on a rolling basis. Application fee: $55 ($65 for international students). *Expenses:* Tuition: Full-time $20,070; part-time $1115 per credit hour. Tuition and fees vary according to course load, degree level and program. *Financial support:* In 2010–11, 156 students received support; fellowships available. Financial award application deadline: 3/2; financial award applicants required to submit FAFSA. *Faculty research:* International financial markets, technology transfer licensing, international marketing, strategic planning. Total annual research expenditures: $50,000. *Unit head:* Kelly Brookes, Director, 415-422-2221, Fax: 415-422-6315. *Application contact:* Director, MBA Program, 415-422-2221, Fax: 415-422-6315, E-mail: mba@usfca.edu.

The University of Scranton, College of Graduate and Continuing Education, Program in Business Administration, Scranton, PA 18510. Offers accounting (MBA); finance (MBA); general business administration (MBA); health care management (MBA); international business (MBA); management information systems (MBA); marketing (MBA); operations management (MBA). *Accreditation:* AACSB. Part-time and evening/weekend programs available. Postbaccalaureate distance learning degree programs offered (no on-campus study). *Faculty:* 34 full-time (8 women). *Students:* 251 full-time (91 women), 180 part-time (72 women); includes 41 Black or African American, non-Hispanic/Latino; 11 Asian, non-Hispanic/Latino; 7 Hispanic/Latino, 40 international. Average age 32. 386 applicants, 84% accepted. In 2010, 38 master's awarded. *Degree requirements:* For master's, capstone experience. *Entrance requirements:* For master's, GMAT, minimum GPA of 2.75. Additional exam requirements/recommendations for international students: Required—TOEFL (minimum score 500 paper-based; 173 computer-based), IELTS (minimum score 5.5). *Application deadline:* Applications are processed on a rolling basis. Application fee: $0. *Financial support:* In 2010–11, 13 students received support, including 13 teaching assistantships with full and partial tuition reimbursements available (averaging $6,430 per year); fellowships, career-related internships or fieldwork, Federal Work-Study, and unspecified assistantships also available. Support available to part-time students. Financial award application deadline: 3/1. *Faculty research:* Financial markets, strategic impact of total quality management, internal accounting controls, consumer preference, information systems and the Internet. *Unit head:* Dr. Murli Rajan, Director, 570-941-4043, Fax: 570-941-4342. *Application contact:* Joseph M. Roback, Director of Admissions, 570-941-4385, Fax: 570-941-5928, E-mail: robackj2@scranton.edu.

University of South Alabama, Graduate School, Mitchell College of Business, Program in Business Management, Mobile, AL 36688-0002. Offers general management (MBA). *Accreditation:* AACSB. Part-time and evening/weekend programs available. *Faculty:* 9 full-time (5 women). *Students:* 69 full-time (24 women), 6 part-time (4 women); includes 9 minority (5 Black or African American, non-Hispanic/Latino; 1 American Indian or Alaska Native, non-Hispanic/Latino; 2 Asian, non-Hispanic/Latino; 1 Hispanic/Latino), 9 international. 130 applicants, 35% accepted, 30 enrolled. In 2010, 30 master's awarded. *Degree requirements:* For master's, comprehensive exam. *Entrance requirements:* For master's, GMAT, minimum undergraduate GPA of 3.0. *Application deadline:* For fall admission, 7/15 priority date for domestic students, 6/15 priority date for international students; for spring admission, 12/1 priority date for domestic students, 11/1 priority date for international students. Applications are processed on a rolling basis. Application fee: $35. *Expenses:* Tuition, state resident: part-time $300 per credit hour. Tuition, nonresident: part-time $600 per credit hour. Required fees: $150 per semester. *Financial support:* Research assistantships available. Support available to part-time students. Financial award application deadline: 4/1. *Unit head:* Dr. John Gamble, Director of Graduate Studies, 251-460-6418. *Application contact:* Dr. B. Keith Harrison, Dean of the Graduate School, 251-460-6310, Fax: 251-461-1513, E-mail: kharriso@usouthal.edu.

University of Southern California, Graduate School, Marshall School of Business, Los Angeles, CA 90089. Offers M Acc, MBA, MBT, MMM, MS, PhD, DDS/MBA, JD/MBT, MBA/Ed D, MBA/M Pl, MBA/MD, MBA/MRED, MBA/MS, MBA/MSW, MBA/Pharm D. *Accreditation:* AACSB. *Students:* 1,422 full-time (407 women), 586 part-time (173 women); includes 802 minority (45 Black or African American, non-Hispanic/Latino; 4 American Indian or Alaska Native, non-Hispanic/Latino; 623 Asian,

non-Hispanic/Latino; 100 Hispanic/Latino; 3 Native Hawaiian or other Pacific Islander, non-Hispanic/Latino; 27 Two or more races, non-Hispanic/Latino), 332 international. In 2010, 911 master's, 11 doctorates awarded. *Degree requirements:* For doctorate, thesis/dissertation. *Entrance requirements:* For master's, GMAT and/or CPA Exam; for doctorate, GMAT or GRE. Additional exam requirements/recommendations for international students: Required—TOEFL. Electronic applications accepted. *Expenses:* Tuition: Full-time $31,240; part-time $1420 per unit. Required fees: $600. One-time fee: $35 full-time. Full-time tuition and fees vary according to degree level and program. *Financial support:* Fellowships, research assistantships, teaching assistantships, institutionally sponsored loans and scholarships/grants available. *Unit head:* James Ellis, Dean, 213-740-6422, E-mail: dean@marshall.usc.edu. *Application contact:* James Ellis, Dean, 213-740-6422, E-mail: dean@marshall.usc.edu.

University of Southern Indiana, Graduate Studies, College of Business, Program in Business Administration, Evansville, IN 47712-3590. Offers MBA. *Accreditation:* AACSB. Part-time and evening/weekend programs available. *Faculty:* 11 full-time (2 women). *Students:* 14 full-time (2 women), 80 part-time (23 women), 10 international. Average age 30. 13 applicants, 92% accepted, 10 enrolled. In 2010, 28 master's awarded. *Entrance requirements:* For master's, GMAT, minimum GPA of 2.5, resume. Additional exam requirements/recommendations for international students: Required—TOEFL (minimum score 550 paper-based; 213 computer-based; 79 iBT), IELTS (minimum score 6). *Application deadline:* For fall admission, 8/15 for domestic students, 3/1 priority date for international students. Applications are processed on a rolling basis. Application fee: $25. Electronic applications accepted. *Expenses:* Tuition, state resident: full-time $4823; part-time $267.95 per credit hour. Tuition, nonresident: full-time $9515; part-time $528.62 per credit hour. Required fees: $220; $22.75 per term. Tuition and fees vary according to course load and reciprocity agreements. *Financial support:* In 2010–11, 4 students received support. Federal Work-Study, scholarships/grants, tuition waivers (full and partial), and unspecified assistantships available. Financial award application deadline: 3/1; financial award applicants required to submit FAFSA. *Unit head:* Dr. Brian L. McGuire, Program Director, 812-465-7031, E-mail: bmcguire@usi.edu. *Application contact:* Information Contact, 812-464-1803.

University of Southern Mississippi, Graduate School, College of Business, Department of Management and Marketing, Hattiesburg, MS 39406-0001. Offers business administration (MBA). *Accreditation:* AACSB. Part-time and evening/weekend programs available. *Faculty:* 61 full-time (27 women). *Students:* 24 full-time (11 women), 32 part-time (17 women); includes 4 Black or African American, non-Hispanic/Latino; 1 Asian, non-Hispanic/Latino; 2 Hispanic/Latino; 1 Two or more races, non-Hispanic/Latino, 4 international. Average age 29. 47 applicants, 53% accepted, 20 enrolled. In 2010, 60 master's awarded. *Degree requirements:* For master's, comprehensive exam. *Entrance requirements:* For master's, GMAT, minimum GPA of 2.75 on last 60 hours. Additional exam requirements/recommendations for international students: Required—TOEFL, IELTS. *Application deadline:* For fall admission, 7/15 priority date for domestic students, 7/15 for international students; for spring admission, 11/15 priority date for domestic students, 11/15 for international students. Application fee: $50. Electronic applications accepted. *Financial support:* In 2010–11, 14 research assistantships with full and partial tuition reimbursements (averaging $7,200 per year), 1 teaching assistantship with full tuition reimbursement (averaging $7,200 per year) were awarded; Federal Work-Study, institutionally sponsored loans, scholarships/grants, health care benefits, and unspecified assistantships also available. Support available to part-time students. Financial award application deadline: 3/15; financial award applicants required to submit FAFSA. *Faculty research:* Inflation accounting, self-esteem training, international trade policy, health care marketing, ethics in strategic planning. *Unit head:* Dr. Joseph Peyrefitte, Chair, 601-266-4659. *Application contact:* Dr. Joseph Peyrefitte, Associate Dean, 601-266-4659, Fax: 601-266-5814.

University of South Florida, Graduate School, College of Business, Department of Business Administration, Tampa, FL 33620-9951. Offers accounting (PhD); entrepreneurship (MBA); finance (PhD); information systems (PhD); leadership and organizational effectiveness (MSM); management and organization (MBA); marketing (PhD). *Accreditation:* AACSB. Part-time and evening/weekend programs available. *Faculty:* 1 (woman) full-time. *Students:* 148 full-time (48 women), 190 part-time (61 women); includes 70 minority (7 Black or African American, non-Hispanic/Latino; 1 American Indian or Alaska Native, non-Hispanic/Latino; 26 Asian, non-Hispanic/Latino; 36 Hispanic/Latino), 62 international. Average age 30. 452 applicants, 29% accepted, 80 enrolled. In 2010, 146 master's, 5 doctorates awarded. *Degree requirements:* For master's, comprehensive exam, thesis (for some programs); for doctorate, comprehensive exam, thesis/dissertation, 90 credit hours, minimum GPA of 3.0. *Entrance requirements:* For master's, GMAT, minimum GPA of 3.0 in last 60 hours of course work, 2 years of work experience, resume; for doctorate, GMAT, letters of recommendation, personal statement. Additional exam requirements/recommendations for international students: Required—TOEFL (minimum score 550 paper-based; 213 computer-based; 79 iBT). *Application deadline:* For fall admission, 6/1 for domestic students, 1/2 for international students; for spring admission,

10/15 for domestic students, 6/1 for international students. Application fee: $30. *Financial support:* Scholarships/grants, health care benefits, and unspecified assistantships available. Financial award applicants required to submit FAFSA. *Unit head:* Irene Hurst, Program Director, 813-974-3335, Fax: 813-974-4518, E-mail: hurst@coba.usf.edu. *Application contact:* Wendy Baker, Assistant Director, Graduate Studies, 813-974-3335, Fax: 813-974-4518, E-mail: wbaker@usf.edu.

University of South Florida, Graduate School, College of Business, Department of Management and Organization, Tampa, FL 33620-9951. Offers management (MS). *Accreditation:* AACSB. Part-time programs available. Postbaccalaureate distance learning degree programs offered (minimal on-campus study). *Faculty:* 3 full-time (0 women). *Students:* 4 full-time (3 women), 20 part-time (13 women); includes 1 Black or African American, non-Hispanic/Latino; 2 Hispanic/Latino; 1 Two or more races, non-Hispanic/Latino, 4 international. Average age 35. 25 applicants, 48% accepted, 7 enrolled. In 2010, 11 master's awarded. Terminal master's awarded for partial completion of doctoral program. *Degree requirements:* For master's, comprehensive exam. *Entrance requirements:* For master's, GRE General Test, minimum GPA of 3.0 in last 60 hours of coursework. Additional exam requirements/recommendations for international students: Required—TOEFL (minimum score 550 paper-based; 213 computer-based; 80 iBT). *Application deadline:* For fall admission, 6/1 for domestic students, 1/2 for international students. Application fee: $30. Electronic applications accepted. *Financial support:* Tuition waivers available. Financial award applicants required to submit FAFSA. Total annual research expenditures: $399,841. *Unit head:* Alan Balfour, Program Director, 813-974-1785, E-mail: abalfour@coba.usf.edu. *Application contact:* Alan Balfour, Program Director, 813-974-1785, E-mail: abalfour@coba.usf.edu.

University of South Florida, Graduate School, College of Business, Executive Program in Business Administration, Tampa, FL 33620-9951. Offers MBA. *Accreditation:* AACSB. Evening/weekend programs available. *Students:* 47 full-time (13 women); includes 4 Black or African American, non-Hispanic/Latino; 6 Asian, non-Hispanic/Latino; 5 Hispanic/Latino; 1 Two or more races, non-Hispanic/Latino, 3 international. Average age 30. 31 applicants, 87% accepted, 23 enrolled. In 2010, 31 master's awarded. *Degree requirements:* For master's, thesis or alternative. *Entrance requirements:* For master's, minimum 5 years of management/professional experience, minimum GPA of 3.0, interview, letters of recommendation. Additional exam requirements/recommendations for international students: Required—TOEFL (minimum score 550 paper-based; 213 computer-based). *Application deadline:* For fall admission, 5/31 for domestic students, 1/2 for international students. Applications are processed on a rolling basis. Application fee: $30. *Expenses:* Contact institution. *Financial support:* Applicants required to submit FAFSA. *Unit head:* Irene Hurst, Program Director, 813-974-3335, Fax: 813-974-4518, E-mail: ihurst@usf.edu. *Application contact:* Chris Williams, Program Administrator, 813-974-4876, Fax: 813-974-4518, E-mail: cmwilliams@usf.edu.

The University of Tampa, John H. Sykes College of Business, Tampa, FL 33606-1490. Offers accounting (MS); entrepreneurship (MBA); finance (MBA, MS); information systems management (MBA); innovation management (MBA); international business (MBA); marketing (MBA, MS); nonprofit management (MBA). *Accreditation:* AACSB. Part-time and evening/weekend programs available. *Faculty:* 67 full-time (24 women), 11 part-time/adjunct (4 women). *Students:* 235 full-time (89 women), 288 part-time (122 women); includes 74 minority (16 Black or African American, non-Hispanic/Latino; 2 American Indian or Alaska Native, non-Hispanic/Latino; 14 Asian, non-Hispanic/Latino; 34 Hispanic/Latino; 2 Native Hawaiian or other Pacific Islander, non-Hispanic/Latino; 6 Two or more races, non-Hispanic/Latino), 95 international. Average age 29. 457 applicants, 45% accepted, 175 enrolled. In 2010, 230 master's awarded. *Degree requirements:* For master's, capstone. *Entrance requirements:* For master's, GMAT or GRE, 4-year undergraduate degree, minimum GPA of 3.0, professional experience (for Executive MBA). Additional exam requirements/recommendations for international students: Required—TOEFL (minimum score 577 paper-based; 230 computer-based; 90 iBT); Recommended—IELTS (minimum score 7.5). *Application deadline:* Applications are processed on a rolling basis. Application fee: $40. Electronic applications accepted. *Expenses:* Tuition: Part-time $504 per credit hour. Required fees: $40 per term. *Financial support:* In 2010–11, 74 students received support. Career-related internships or fieldwork, scholarships/grants, unspecified assistantships, and grants available. Financial award applicants required to submit FAFSA. *Faculty research:* Management innovation, social marketing, value relevance of earnings and book value across industries, managerial finance, entrepreneurship. *Unit head:* Dennis Nostrand, Vice President, Enrollment/Admissions, 813-257-1808, E-mail: dnostrand@ut.edu. *Application contact:* Charlene Tobie, Associate Director of Admissions, 813-257-3566, E-mail: ctobie@ut.edu.

The University of Tennessee at Chattanooga, Graduate School, College of Business, Program in Business Administration, Chattanooga, TN 37403. Offers EMBA, MBA. *Accreditation:* AACSB. Part-time and evening/weekend programs available. *Faculty:* 9 full-time (3 women), 1 part-time/adjunct (0 women). *Students:* 112 full-time (40 women), 149 part-time (59 women); includes 14 Black or African American, non-Hispanic/Latino; 3 Asian,

non-Hispanic/Latino; 2 Hispanic/Latino; 3 Two or more races, non-Hispanic/Latino, 8 international. Average age 28. 147 applicants, 78% accepted, 96 enrolled. In 2010, 96 master's awarded. *Entrance requirements:* For master's, GMAT (minimum score 450) or GRE General Test (minimum score 1000). Additional exam requirements/recommendations for international students: Required—TOEFL (minimum score 550 paper-based; 213 computer-based; 79 iBT), IELTS (minimum score 6). *Application deadline:* For fall admission, 8/1 priority date for domestic students, 6/1 for international students; for spring admission, 12/1 priority date for domestic students, 10/1 for international students. Applications are processed on a rolling basis. Application fee: $35. Electronic applications accepted. *Financial support:* In 2010–11, 8 research assistantships with full and partial tuition reimbursements (averaging $5,500 per year) were awarded; career-related internships or fieldwork, scholarships/grants, tuition waivers (partial), and unspecified assistantships also available. Support available to part-time students. *Faculty research:* Diversity, operations/production management, entrepreneurial processes, customer satisfaction and retention, branding. *Unit head:* Lawrence Ettkin, Department Head, 423-425-4403, Fax: 423-425-5255, E-mail: lawrence-ettkin@utc.edu. *Application contact:* Dr. Jerald Ainsworth, Dean of Graduate Studies, 423-425-4478, Fax: 423-425-5223, E-mail: jerald-ainsworth@utc.edu.

The University of Tennessee at Martin, Graduate Programs, College of Business and Global Affairs, Program in Business, Martin, TN 38238-1000. Offers MBA. *Accreditation:* AACSB. Part-time programs available. Postbaccalaureate distance learning degree programs offered (no on-campus study). *Faculty:* 29. *Students:* 70 (22 women); includes 3 Black or African American, non-Hispanic/Latino; 1 Hispanic/Latino, 12 international. 48 applicants, 58% accepted, 21 enrolled. In 2010, 26 master's awarded. *Degree requirements:* For master's, comprehensive exam. *Entrance requirements:* For master's, GMAT, minimum GPA of 2.5, resume. Additional exam requirements/recommendations for international students: Required—TOEFL (minimum score 525 paper-based; 197 computer-based; 71 iBT). *Application deadline:* For fall admission, 8/1 priority date for domestic students, 8/1 for international students; for spring admission, 1/1 priority date for domestic students, 1/1 for international students. Applications are processed on a rolling basis. Application fee: $30 ($50 for international students). Electronic applications accepted. *Expenses:* Tuition, state resident: full-time $7164; part-time $400 per credit hour. Tuition, nonresident: full-time $19,574; part-time $1090 per credit hour. Required fees: $1044; $60 per credit hour. *Financial support:* In 2010–11, 13 students received support, including 12 research assistantships with full tuition reimbursements available (averaging $6,866 per year), 1 teaching assistantship (averaging $6,284 per year); career-related internships or fieldwork, scholarships/grants, and unspecified assistantships also available. Support available to part-time students. Financial award application deadline: 3/1. *Unit head:* Dr. Kevin Hammond, Coordinator, 731-881-7236, Fax: 731-881-7241, E-mail: bagrad@utm.edu. *Application contact:* Linda S. Arant, Student Services Specialist, 731-881-7012, Fax: 731-881-7499, E-mail: larant@utm.edu.

The University of Texas at Arlington, Graduate School, College of Business, Program in Business Administration, Arlington, TX 76019. Offers accounting (PhD); business statistics (PhD); finance (MBA, PhD); information systems (MBA, PhD); management (MBA, PhD); marketing (MBA, PhD); operations management (MBA, PhD); real estate (MBA). *Accreditation:* AACSB. Part-time and evening/weekend programs available. Postbaccalaureate distance learning degree programs offered (no on-campus study). *Students:* 555 full-time (197 women), 378 part-time (144 women); includes 179 minority (55 Black or African American, non-Hispanic/Latino; 1 American Indian or Alaska Native, non-Hispanic/Latino; 58 Asian, non-Hispanic/Latino; 55 Hispanic/Latino; 10 Two or more races, non-Hispanic/Latino), 410 international. 317 applicants, 93% accepted, 196 enrolled. In 2010, 468 master's, 1 doctorate awarded. Terminal master's awarded for partial completion of doctoral program. *Degree requirements:* For master's, thesis optional; for doctorate, comprehensive exam, thesis/dissertation. *Entrance requirements:* For master's, GMAT or GRE; for doctorate, GMAT, minimum GPA of 3.0 (undergraduate), 3.4 (graduate); 30 hours of graduate course work. Additional exam requirements/recommendations for international students: Required—TOEFL (minimum score 550 paper-based; 213 computer-based; 79 iBT). *Application deadline:* For fall admission, 6/1 for domestic students, 4/1 for international students; for spring admission, 10/15 for domestic students, 9/15 for international students. Applications are processed on a rolling basis. Application fee: $35 ($50 for international students). Electronic applications accepted. *Expenses:* Tuition, state resident: full-time $7500. Tuition, nonresident: full-time $13,080. International tuition: $13,250 full-time. *Financial support:* Career-related internships or fieldwork, scholarships/grants, and unspecified assistantships available. Financial award application deadline: 6/1; financial award applicants required to submit FAFSA. *Unit head:* Dr. Edmund Prater, Director of PhD Programs, 817-272-2131, Fax: 817-272-5799. *Application contact:* Melanie McGee, Director of MBA Program, 817-272-3005, Fax: 817-272-5799, E-mail: mwmcgee@uta.edu.

The University of Texas at Dallas, School of Management, Richardson, TX 75080. Offers EMBA, MBA, MS, PhD, MSEE/MBA. Part-time and evening/weekend programs available. Postbaccalaureate distance learning degree programs offered. *Faculty:* 78 full-time (14 women), 28 part-time/adjunct (6 women). *Students:* 1,471 full-time (676 women), 1,314 part-time (489 women); includes 643 minority (82 Black or African American, non-Hispanic/Latino; 6 American Indian or Alaska Native, non-Hispanic/Latino; 399 Asian, non-Hispanic/Latino; 147 Hispanic/Latino; 9 Two or more races, non-Hispanic/Latino), 1,065 international. Average age 30. 2,827 applicants, 57% accepted, 919 enrolled. In 2010, 964 master's, 17 doctorates awarded. *Degree requirements:* For doctorate, thesis/dissertation. *Entrance requirements:* For master's and doctorate, GMAT. Additional exam requirements/recommendations for international students: Required—TOEFL (minimum score 550 paper-based; 215 computer-based). *Application deadline:* For fall admission, 7/15 for domestic students, 5/1 priority date for international students; for spring admission, 11/15 for domestic students, 9/1 priority date for international students. Applications are processed on a rolling basis. Application fee: $50 ($100 for international students). Electronic applications accepted. *Expenses:* Tuition, state resident: full-time $10,248; part-time $569 per credit hour. Tuition, nonresident: full-time $18,544; part-time $1030 per credit hour. Tuition and fees vary according to course load. *Financial support:* In 2010–11, 837 students received support, including 6 research assistantships with partial tuition reimbursements available (averaging $11,239 per year), 170 teaching assistantships with partial tuition reimbursements available (averaging $12,706 per year); career-related internships or fieldwork, Federal Work-Study, institutionally sponsored loans, scholarships/grants, and unspecified assistantships also available. Support available to part-time students. Financial award application deadline: 4/30; financial award applicants required to submit FAFSA. *Faculty research:* Finance, marketing and organization, strategy, management education for physicians. Total annual research expenditures: $490,962. *Unit head:* Dr. Hasan Pirkul, Dean, 972-883-2705, Fax: 972-883-2799, E-mail: hpirkul@utdallas.edu. *Application contact:* David B. Ritchey, Director of Advising, 972-883-2750, Fax: 972-883-6425, E-mail: davidr@utdallas.edu.

See Display below and Close-Up on page 271.

The University of Texas at El Paso, Graduate School, College of Business Administration, Programs in Business Administration, El Paso, TX 79968-0001. Offers business administration (MBA, Certificate); international business (PhD). *Accreditation:* AACSB. Part-time and evening/weekend programs available. Postbaccalaureate distance learning degree programs offered (no on-campus study). *Students:* 277 (111 women); includes 8 Black or African American, non-Hispanic/Latino; 1 American Indian or Alaska Native, non-Hispanic/Latino; 4 Asian, non-Hispanic/Latino; 177 Hispanic/Latino, 23 international. Average age 34. In 2010, 126 master's awarded. *Entrance requirements:* For master's, GMAT, minimum GPA of 2.7. Additional exam requirements/recommendations for international students: Required—TOEFL. *Application deadline:* For fall admission, 7/1 priority date for domestic students, 3/1 for international students; for spring admission, 11/1 priority date for domestic students, 9/1 for international students. Applications are processed on a rolling basis. Application fee: $15 ($65 for international students). Electronic applications accepted. *Financial support:* In 2010–11, research assistantships with partial tuition reimbursements (averaging $18,750 per year), teaching assistantships with partial tuition reimbursements (averaging $15,000 per year) were awarded; Federal Work-Study, institutionally sponsored loans, and tuition waivers (partial) also available. Financial award application deadline: 3/15; financial award applicants required to submit FAFSA. *Unit head:* Laura M. Uribarri, Director, 915-747-5379, Fax: 915-747-5147, E-mail: mba@utep.edu. *Application contact:* Dr. Charles H. Ambler, Dean of the Graduate School, 915-747-5491 Ext. 7886, Fax: 915-747-5788, E-mail: cambler@utep.edu.

See Display on the next page and Close-Up on page 273.

The University of Texas at San Antonio, College of Business, Department of Management Science and Statistics, San Antonio, TX 78249-0617. Offers applied statistics (MS, PhD); management science (MBA). *Accreditation:* AACSB. Part-time and evening/weekend programs available. *Faculty:* 15 full-time (4 women), 1 part-time/adjunct (0 women). *Students:* 34 full-time (12 women), 23 part-time (6 women); includes 13 minority (2 Black or African American, non-Hispanic/Latino; 5 Asian, non-Hispanic/Latino; 5 Hispanic/Latino; 1 Native Hawaiian or other Pacific Islander, non-Hispanic/Latino), 16 international. Average age 31. 51 applicants, 67% accepted, 25 enrolled. In 2010, 15 master's, 1 doctorate awarded. *Degree requirements:* For master's, comprehensive exam (for some programs), thesis (for some programs). *Entrance requirements:* For master's, GMAT, minimum GPA of 3.0. Additional exam requirements/recommendations for international students: Required—TOEFL (minimum score 500 paper-based; 173 computer-based; 61 iBT). *Application deadline:* For fall admission, 7/1 for domestic students, 4/1 for international students; for spring admission, 11/1 for domestic students, 9/1 for international students. Applications are processed on a rolling basis. Application fee: $45 ($80 for international students). Electronic applications accepted. *Expenses:* Tuition, state resident: full-time $4172; part-time $231.75 per credit hour. Tuition, nonresident: full-time $15,332; part-time $851.75 per credit hour. *Financial support:* In 2010–11, 13 students received support, including 1 fellowship (averaging $45,000 per year), 79 research assistantships (averaging $13,264 per year), 8 teaching assistantships (averaging $8,000 per year). *Faculty research:* Applied statistics, biostatistics, supply chain management. Total annual research expenditures: $23,518. *Unit head:*

Dr. Raydel Tullous, Chair, 210-458-6345, Fax: 210-458-6350, E-mail: raydel.tullous@utsa.edu. *Application contact:* Veronica Ramirez, Assistant Dean of the Graduate School, 210-458-7841, Fax: 210-458-4332, E-mail: graduatestudies@utsa.edu.

The University of Texas at San Antonio, College of Business, General Business Program, San Antonio, TX 78249-0617. Offers accounting (PhD); business (MBA); finance (PhD); information systems (MBA); information technology (PhD); international business (MBA); management accounting (MBA); management and organization studies (PhD); management of technology (MBA); marketing (PhD); marketing management (MBA); taxation (MBA). Part-time and evening/weekend programs available. *Students:* 159 full-time (59 women), 124 part-time (43 women); includes 82 minority (9 Black or African American, non-Hispanic/Latino; 2 American Indian or Alaska Native, non-Hispanic/Latino; 17 Asian, non-Hispanic/Latino; 50 Hispanic/Latino; 1 Native Hawaiian or other Pacific Islander, non-Hispanic/Latino; 3 Two or more races, non-Hispanic/Latino), 39 international. Average age 32. 330 applicants, 46% accepted, 105 enrolled. In 2010, 85 master's, 9 doctorates awarded. *Degree requirements:* For master's, comprehensive exam (for some programs), thesis (for some programs). *Entrance requirements:* For master's, GMAT. Additional exam requirements/recommendations for international students: Required—TOEFL (minimum score 500 paper-based; 173 computer-based; 61 iBT), IELTS (minimum score 5). *Application deadline:* For fall admission, 7/1 for domestic students, 4/1 for international students; for spring admission, 11/1 for domestic students, 9/1 for international students. Application fee: $45 ($80 for international students). *Expenses:* Tuition, state resident: full-time $4172; part-time $231.75 per credit hour. Tuition, nonresident: full-time $15,332; part-time $851.75 per credit hour. *Financial support:* In 2010–11, 282 research assistantships (averaging $13,930 per year), 74 teaching assistantships (averaging $9,284 per year) were awarded; scholarships/grants, tuition waivers, and unspecified assistantships also available. Support available to part-time students. *Unit head:* Dr. Lynda Y. de la Vinna, Dean, 210-458-4317, Fax: 210-458-4308, E-mail: lynda.delavina@utsa.edu. *Application contact:* Veronica Ramirez, Assistant Dean of the Graduate School, 210-458-4330, Fax: 210-458-4332, E-mail: graduatestudies@utsa.edu.

University of the Cumberlands, Hutton School of Business, Williamsburg, KY 40769-1372. Offers MBA. Part-time programs available. Postbaccalaureate distance learning degree programs offered (no on-campus study). *Faculty:* 1 (woman) full-time, 9 part-time/adjunct (3 women). *Students:* 46 full-time (16 women), 12 part-time (5 women); includes 1 Asian, non-Hispanic/Latino; 1 Hispanic/Latino, 1 international. Average age 37. In 2010, 16 master's awarded. *Entrance requirements:* For master's, GMAT, GRE. Additional exam

requirements/recommendations for international students: Required—TOEFL. *Application deadline:* Applications are processed on a rolling basis. Application fee: $30. Electronic applications accepted. *Expenses:* Tuition: Full-time $6984; part-time $291 per credit hour. Required fees: $50 per term. Tuition and fees vary according to course level, course load and program. *Unit head:* Dr. Vonda Moore, Director, MBA and Business Online Programs, 606-539-4293, E-mail: vonda.moore@ucumberlands.edu. *Application contact:* Donna Stanfil, Director, Graduate Admissions, 606-549-2200 Ext. 4496, Fax: 606-539-4534, E-mail: donna.stanfill@cumberlandcollege.edu.

University of the Incarnate Word, Extended Academic Programs, Program in Administration, San Antonio, TX 78209-6397. Offers MAA. *Students:* 9 full-time (5 women), 149 part-time (91 women); includes 17 Black or African American, non-Hispanic/Latino; 2 Asian, non-Hispanic/Latino; 70 Hispanic/Latino. In 2010, 58 degrees awarded. *Degree requirements:* For master's, capstone experience. *Expenses:* Tuition: Part-time $725 per contact hour. Required fees: $890 per semester. *Unit head:* Dr. Cyndi Porter, Vice President, 877-603-1130, E-mail: porter@uiwtx.edu. *Application contact:* Julie Weber, Director of Marketing and Recruitment, 210-832-2100, Fax: 210-829-2756, E-mail: eapadmission@uiwtx.edu.

University of the Incarnate Word, Extended Academic Programs, Program in Business Administration, San Antonio, TX 78209-6397. Offers MBA. *Students:* 10 full-time (4 women), 169 part-time (85 women); includes 15 Black or African American, non-Hispanic/Latino; 1 American Indian or Alaska Native, non-Hispanic/Latino; 5 Asian, non-Hispanic/Latino; 89 Hispanic/Latino, 2 international. In 2010, 61 degrees awarded. *Expenses:* Tuition: Part-time $725 per contact hour. Required fees: $890 per semester. *Unit head:* Dr. Cyndi Porter, Vice President, 877-603-1130, E-mail: porter@uiwtx.edu. *Application contact:* Julie Weber, Director of Marketing and Recruitment, 210-832-2100, Fax: 210-829-2756, E-mail: eapadmission@uiwtx.edu.

University of the Incarnate Word, School of Graduate Studies and Research, H-E-B School of Business and Administration, Programs in Administration, San Antonio, TX 78209-6397. Offers adult education (MAA); applied administration (MAA); communication arts (MAA); healthcare administration (MAA); instructional technology (MAA); international business (Certificate); nutrition (MAA); organizational development (MAA, Certificate); project management (Certificate); sports management (MAA). Part-time and evening/weekend programs available. Postbaccalaureate distance learning degree programs offered (no on-campus study). *Students:* 30 full-time (20 women), 64 part-time (37 women); includes 10 Black or African American, non-Hispanic/Latino; 1 Asian, non-Hispanic/Latino; 48 Hispanic/Latino, 8 international. Average age 35. In 2010, 68 master's awarded. *Degree requirements:* For

master's, capstone. *Entrance requirements:* For master's, GRE, GMAT, undergraduate degree, minimum GPA of 2.5. Additional exam requirements/recommendations for international students: Required—TOEFL (minimum score 560 paper-based; 220 computer-based; 83 iBT). *Application deadline:* Applications are processed on a rolling basis. Application fee: $20. Electronic applications accepted. *Expenses:* Tuition: Part-time $725 per contact hour. Required fees: $890 per semester. *Financial support:* Federal Work-Study and scholarships/grants available. Financial award applicants required to submit FAFSA. *Unit head:* Dr. Daniel Dominguez, MAA Programs Director, 210-829-3180, Fax: 210-805-3564, E-mail: domingue@uiwtx.edu. *Application contact:* Andrea Cyterski-Acosta, Dean of Enrollment, 210-829-6005, Fax: 210-829-3921, E-mail: admis@uiwtx.edu.

University of the Incarnate Word, School of Graduate Studies and Research, H-E-B School of Business and Administration, Programs in Business Administration, San Antonio, TX 78209-6397. Offers general business (MBA); international business (MBA); international business strategy (MBA); sports management (MBA). *Accreditation:* ACBSP. Part-time and evening/weekend programs available. Postbaccalaureate distance learning degree programs offered. *Students:* 58 full-time (42 women), 32 part-time (20 women). Average age 32. In 2010, 111 master's awarded. *Degree requirements:* For master's, capstone. *Entrance requirements:* For master's, GMAT (minimum score 450), undergraduate degree with minimum overall GPA of 2.5. Additional exam requirements/recommendations for international students: Required—TOEFL (minimum score 560 paper-based; 220 computer-based; 83 iBT). *Application deadline:* Applications are processed on a rolling basis. Application fee: $20. Electronic applications accepted. *Expenses:* Tuition: Part-time $725 per contact hour. Required fees: $890 per semester. *Financial support:* Federal Work-Study and scholarships/grants available. Financial award applicants required to submit FAFSA. Total annual research expenditures: $177,763. *Unit head:* Dr. Jeannie Scott, MBA Director, 210-283-5002, Fax: 210-805-3564, E-mail: scott@uiwtx.edu. *Application contact:* Andrea Cyterski-Acosta, Dean of Enrollment, 210-829-6005, Fax: 210-829-3921, E-mail: admis@uiwtx.edu.

University of the Pacific, Eberhardt School of Business, Stockton, CA 95211-0197. Offers MBA, JD/MBA. *Accreditation:* AACSB. Part-time programs available. *Faculty:* 24 full-time (7 women), 1 (woman) part-time/adjunct. *Students:* 49 full-time (20 women), 1 (woman) part-time; includes 1 American Indian or Alaska Native, non-Hispanic/Latino; 19 Asian, non-Hispanic/Latino; 1 Hispanic/Latino, 14 international. Average age 25. 81 applicants, 60% accepted, 28 enrolled. In 2010, 28 master's awarded. *Entrance requirements:* For master's, GMAT. Additional exam requirements/recommendations for international students: Required—TOEFL (minimum score 475 paper-based; 150 computer-based). *Application deadline:* For fall admission, 7/31 priority date for domestic students; for spring admission, 11/30 for domestic students. Applications are processed on a rolling basis. Application fee: $75. *Financial support:* Fellowships, research assistantships, Federal Work-Study and institutionally sponsored loans available. Support available to part-time students. Financial award application deadline: 3/1; financial award applicants required to submit FAFSA. *Unit head:* Dr. Richard Flaherty, Dean, 209-946-2466, Fax: 209-946-2586. *Application contact:* Dr. Chris Lozano, MBA Recruiting Director, 209-946-2597, Fax: 209-946-2586, E-mail: clozano@pacific.edu.

See Display below and Close-Up on page 275.

University of the Southwest, Graduate Programs, Hobbs, NM 88240-9129. Offers business administration (MBA); curriculum and instruction (MSE); curriculum and instruction: reading (MSE); early childhood education (MSE); educational administration (MSE); educational diagnostician (MSE); mental health counseling (MSE); school counseling (MSE); special education (MSE); sports management (MBA). Part-time and evening/weekend programs available. Postbaccalaureate distance learning degree programs offered (no on-campus study). *Faculty:* 13 full-time (6 women), 28 part-time/adjunct (17 women). *Students:* 169 full-time (125 women), 59 part-time (42 women); includes 87 minority (16 Black or African American, non-Hispanic/Latino; 68 Hispanic/Latino; 3 Two or more races, non-Hispanic/Latino), 1 international. Average age 36. 94 applicants, 65% accepted, 36 enrolled. In 2010, 41 master's awarded. *Degree requirements:* For master's, comprehensive exam. *Application deadline:* For fall admission, 3/1 priority date for domestic students; for spring admission, 10/1 for domestic students. Applications are processed on a rolling basis. Application fee: $50. Electronic applications accepted. *Expenses:* Tuition: Part-time $512 per credit hour. *Financial support:* In 2010–11, 188 students received support; research assistantships with partial tuition reimbursements available, Federal Work-Study, scholarships/grants, and tuition waivers (partial) available. Support available to part-time students. Financial award application deadline: 4/1; financial award applicants required to submit FAFSA. *Unit head:* Dr. Mary Harris, Dean of Education, 575-492-2162 Ext. 2162, Fax: 575-392-6006, E-mail: mharris@usw.edu. *Application contact:* Melissa Mitchell, Graduate Program Advisor, 575-492-2142 Ext. 2142, Fax: 575-392-6006, E-mail: mmitchell@usw.edu.

The University of Toledo, College of Graduate Studies, College of Business and Innovation, Toledo, OH 43606-3390. Offers EMBA, MBA, MSA, DME, Certificate. *Accreditation:* AACSB. Part-time and evening/weekend programs available. *Faculty:* 37. *Students:* 248 full-time (99 women), 194 part-time (76 women); includes 19 Black or African American, non-Hispanic/Latino; 4

Asian, non-Hispanic/Latino; 8 Hispanic/Latino; 2 Two or more races, non-Hispanic/Latino, 169 international. Average age 27. 254 applicants, 67% accepted, 124 enrolled. In 2010, 238 master's, 4 doctorates, 1 other advanced degree awarded. *Degree requirements:* For doctorate, thesis/dissertation. *Entrance requirements:* For master's, doctorate, and Certificate, GMAT, 2.70 GPA for all prior academic work. Three letters of recommendation, a statement of purpose, and transcripts from all prior institutions attended. Additional exam requirements/recommendations for international students: Required—TOEFL (minimum score 550 paper-based; 213 computer-based; 80 iBT), IELTS (minimum score 6.5). *Application deadline:* For fall admission, 1/15 priority date for domestic and international students. Applications are processed on a rolling basis. Application fee: $45 ($75 for international students). Electronic applications accepted. *Expenses:* Tuition, state resident: full-time $11,426; part-time $476 per credit hour. Tuition, nonresident: full-time $21,660; part-time $903 per credit hour. One-time fee: $62. *Financial support:* In 2010–11, 47 research assistantships with full and partial tuition reimbursements (averaging $6,967 per year) were awarded; career-related internships or fieldwork, Federal Work-Study, institutionally sponsored loans, scholarships/grants, tuition waivers (full and partial), unspecified assistantships, and administrative assistantships also available. Support available to part-time students. *Unit head:* Dr. Thomas G. Gutteridge, Dean, 419-530-4060, Fax: 419-530-7260, E-mail: mba@uoft01.utoledo.edu. *Application contact:* Graduate School Office, 419-530-4723, Fax: 419-530-4724, E-mail: grdsch@utnet.utoledo.edu.

University of Tulsa, Graduate School, Collins College of Business, Business Administration/Computer Science Program, Tulsa, OK 74104-3189. Offers MBA/MS. Part-time programs available. *Students:* 1 full-time (0 women), 1 part-time (0 women). Average age 28. *Entrance requirements:* Additional exam requirements/recommendations for international students: Required—TOEFL (minimum score 575 paper-based; 231 computer-based; 79 iBT), IELTS (minimum score 6.5). *Application deadline:* Applications are processed on a rolling basis. Application fee: $40. Electronic applications accepted. *Expenses:* Tuition: Full-time $16,902; part-time $939 per credit hour. Required fees: $1020; $4 per credit hour. Tuition and fees vary according to course load. *Financial support:* In 2010–11, 1 student received support, including 1 teaching assistantship with full and partial tuition reimbursement available (averaging $11,594 per year); fellowships with full and partial tuition reimbursements available, research assistantships with full and partial tuition reimbursements available, career-related internships or fieldwork, Federal Work-Study, institutionally sponsored loans, scholarships/grants, health care benefits, tuition waivers, and unspecified assistantships also available. Support available to part-time students. Financial award application deadline: 2/1; financial award applicants required to submit FAFSA. *Unit head:* Dr. Linda Nichols, Associate Dean, 918-631-2242, Fax: 918-631-2142, E-mail: linda-nichols@utulsa.edu. *Application contact:* Information Contact, 918-631-2242, E-mail: graduate-business@utulsa.edu.

University of Tulsa, Graduate School, Collins College of Business, Master of Business Administration Program, Tulsa, OK 74104-3189. Offers accounting (MBA); business administration (MBA); energy management (MBA); finance (MBA); international business (MBA); management information systems (MBA); taxation (MBA); JD/MBA; MBA/MSCS; MBA/MSF. *Accreditation:* AACSB. Part-time and evening/weekend programs available. *Faculty:* 32 full-time (6 women). *Students:* 39 full-time (14 women), 40 part-time (16 women); includes 7 minority (1 Black or African American, non-Hispanic/Latino; 2 Asian, non-Hispanic/Latino; 4 Hispanic/Latino), 9 international. Average age 26. 73 applicants, 55% accepted, 18 enrolled. In 2010, 55 master's awarded. *Entrance requirements:* For master's, GMAT. Additional exam requirements/recommendations for international students: Required—TOEFL (minimum score 575 paper-based; 232 computer-based; 90 iBT), IELTS (minimum score 6.5). *Application deadline:* Applications are processed on a rolling basis. Application fee: $40. Electronic applications accepted. *Expenses:* Tuition: Full-time $16,902; part-time $939 per credit hour. Required fees: $1020; $4 per credit hour. Tuition and fees vary according to course load. *Financial support:* In 2010–11, 56 students received support, including 23 fellowships (averaging $4,872 per year), 4 research assistantships (averaging $9,323 per year), 29 teaching assistantships (averaging $10,642 per year); career-related internships or fieldwork, institutionally sponsored loans, scholarships/grants, health care benefits, tuition waivers (full and partial), and unspecified assistantships also available. Support available to part-time students. Financial award application deadline: 2/1; financial award applicants required to submit FAFSA. *Faculty research:* Accounting, energy management, finance, international business, management information systems, taxation. *Unit head:* Dr. Linda Nichols, Associate Dean of the Collins College of Business, 918-631-2242, Fax: 918-631-2142, E-mail: linda-nichols@utulsa.edu. *Application contact:* Dr. Linda Nichols, Associate Dean of the Collins College of Business, 918-631-2242, Fax: 918-631-2142, E-mail: linda-nichols@utulsa.edu.

University of Utah, Graduate School, David Eccles School of Business, Salt Lake City, UT 84112. Offers EMBA, M Acc, M Stat, MBA, MHA, MRED, MS, PMBA, PhD. *Accreditation:* AACSB. Part-time and evening/weekend programs available. *Faculty:* 69 full-time (21 women), 1 part-time/adjunct (0 women). *Students:* 796 full-time (174 women), 99 part-time (31 women); includes 75 minority (5 Black or African American, non-Hispanic/Latino;

3 American Indian or Alaska Native, non-Hispanic/Latino; 37 Asian, non-Hispanic/Latino; 23 Hispanic/Latino; 7 Two or more races, non-Hispanic/Latino), 90 international. Average age 31. 1,340 applicants, 49% accepted, 464 enrolled. In 2010, 383 master's, 8 doctorates awarded. *Degree requirements:* For doctorate, comprehensive exam, thesis/dissertation, oral and written qualifying exams. *Entrance requirements:* For master's, GMAT, GRE (for some programs), minimum undergraduate GPA of 3.0; for doctorate, GMAT, GRE. Additional exam requirements/recommendations for international students: Required—TOEFL (minimum score 600 paper-based; 250 computer-based; 100 iBT), IELTS (minimum score 7). Application fee: $55 ($65 for international students). Electronic applications accepted. *Expenses:* Contact institution. *Financial support:* In 2010–11, 50 students received support, including 8 fellowships with partial tuition reimbursements available, 13 teaching assistantships with partial tuition reimbursements available; career-related internships or fieldwork and health care benefits also available. Financial award applicants required to submit FAFSA. *Faculty research:* Information systems, investment, financial accounting, international strategy. Total annual research expenditures: $365,579. *Unit head:* Dr. Taylor Randall, Dean, 801-587-3860, Fax: 801-581-3074, E-mail: dean@business.utah.edu. *Application contact:* Andrea Chmelik, Program Coordinator, 801-581-7785, Fax: 801-581-3666, E-mail: andrea.chmelik@business.utah.edu.

University of Vermont, Graduate College, School of Business Administration, Burlington, VT 05405. Offers M Acc, MBA. *Accreditation:* AACSB. Part-time programs available. *Faculty:* 25. *Students:* 58 (21 women); includes 2 Black or African American, non-Hispanic/Latino; 2 Asian, non-Hispanic/Latino; 2 Hispanic/Latino, 4 international. 70 applicants, 66% accepted, 14 enrolled. In 2010, 16 master's awarded. *Entrance requirements:* For master's, GMAT. Additional exam requirements/recommendations for international students: Required—TOEFL (minimum score 550 paper-based; 213 computer-based; 80 iBT). *Application deadline:* For fall admission, 4/1 priority date for domestic students. Applications are processed on a rolling basis. Application fee: $40. Electronic applications accepted. *Expenses:* Tuition, state resident: part-time $537 per credit hour. Tuition, nonresident: part-time $1355 per credit hour. *Financial support:* Fellowships, teaching assistantships, Federal Work-Study available. Financial award application deadline: 3/1. *Unit head:* Dr. R. DeWitt, Dean, 802-656-0513. *Application contact:* Dr. Michael Gurdon, Coordinator, 802-656-4015.

University of Virginia, Darden Graduate School of Business Administration, Charlottesville, VA 22903. Offers MBA, PhD, MBA/JD, MBA/MA, MBA/MD, MBA/ME, MBA/MSN. *Accreditation:* AACSB. *Faculty:* 63 full-time (14 women), 5 part-time/adjunct (2 women). *Students:* 774 full-time (214 women), 2 part-time (0 women); includes 37 Black or African American, non-Hispanic/Latino; 2 American Indian or Alaska Native, non-Hispanic/Latino; 52 Asian, non-Hispanic/Latino; 33 Hispanic/Latino; 5 Two or more races, non-Hispanic/Latino, 174 international. Average age 29. 2,411 applicants, 27% accepted, 339 enrolled. In 2010, 387 master's, 3 doctorates awarded. *Degree requirements:* For doctorate, thesis/dissertation. *Entrance requirements:* For master's, GMAT, resume; 2 letters of recommendation; interview; for doctorate, GMAT, resume; essay; 2 letters of recommendation; interview. Additional exam requirements/recommendations for international students: Required—TOEFL. *Application deadline:* For fall admission, 3/1 for domestic students, 3/2 for international students. Applications are processed on a rolling basis. Application fee: $200. Electronic applications accepted. *Expenses:* Contact institution. *Financial support:* Career-related internships or fieldwork available. Financial award applicants required to submit FAFSA. *Unit head:* Robert F. Bruner, Dean, 434-924-3900, E-mail: darden@virginia.edu. *Application contact:* Sara Neher, Assistant Dean of MBA Admissions, 434-924-3900, E-mail: darden@virginia.edu.

University of Virginia, McIntire School of Commerce, Charlottesville, VA 22903. Offers accounting (MS); commerce (MSC), including financial services, marketing and management; management of information technology (MS). *Accreditation:* AACSB. *Faculty:* 61 full-time (19 women), 2 part-time/adjunct (1 woman). *Students:* 223 full-time (89 women), 35 part-time (9 women); includes 11 Black or African American, non-Hispanic/Latino; 26 Asian, non-Hispanic/Latino; 15 Hispanic/Latino; 8 Two or more races, non-Hispanic/Latino, 27 international. Average age 26. 376 applicants, 64% accepted, 154 enrolled. In 2010, 228 master's awarded. *Entrance requirements:* For master's, GMAT, 2 letters of recommendation. Additional exam requirements/recommendations for international students: Required—TOEFL (minimum score 600 paper-based; 250 computer-based; 100 iBT), IELTS (minimum score 7). *Application deadline:* Applications are processed on a rolling basis. Application fee: $75. Electronic applications accepted. *Expenses:* Contact institution. *Financial support:* Fellowships, research assistantships, teaching assistantships, career-related internships or fieldwork and Federal Work-Study available. Financial award applicants required to submit FAFSA. *Unit head:* Carl Zeithaml, Dean, 434-924-3110, Fax: 434-924-7074, E-mail: mcs@virginia.edu. *Application contact:* Carl Zeithaml, Dean, 434-924-3110, Fax: 434-924-7074, E-mail: mcs@virginia.edu.

University of Washington, Bothell, Business Program, Bothell, WA 98011-8246. Offers leadership (MBA); technology (MBA). Part-time and evening/weekend programs available. *Faculty:* 18 full-time (2 women), 4 part-time/adjunct (2 women). *Students:* 125 full-time (32 women), 1 part-time (0 women); includes 4 Black or African American, non-Hispanic/Latino; 20 Asian, non-Hispanic/Latino; 7 Hispanic/Latino, 3 international. Average age 33. 131 applicants, 53% accepted, 60 enrolled. In 2010, 36 master's awarded. *Degree requirements:* For master's, 74 total credits, minimum cumulative GPA of 3.0. *Entrance requirements:* For master's, GMAT or GRE General Test. Additional exam requirements/recommendations for international students: Required—TOEFL (minimum score 580 paper-based; 237 computer-based; 92 iBT), IELTS (minimum score 7). *Application deadline:* For fall admission, 4/16 priority date for domestic and international students. Application fee: $75. Electronic applications accepted. *Expenses:* Contact institution. *Financial support:* In 2010–11, 67 students received support. Federal Work-Study and scholarships/grants available. Financial award application deadline: 2/28; financial award applicants required to submit FAFSA. *Faculty research:* New product marketing, supply chain management, entrepreneurship, financial accounting, interactive marketing, corporate finance. *Unit head:* Prof. Sandeep Krishnamurthy, Director, 425-352-5229, Fax: 425-352-5277, E-mail: sandeep@uw.edu. *Application contact:* Kathryn Chester, MBA Admissions Coordinator, 425-352-3275, Fax: 425-352-5277, E-mail: kchester@uwb.edu.

University of Washington, Tacoma, Graduate Programs, MBA Programs, Tacoma, WA 98402-3100. Offers accounting (MBA); business administration (MBA); certified financial analyst (MBA). Part-time and evening/weekend programs available. *Faculty:* 24 full-time (8 women), 3 part-time/adjunct (0 women). *Students:* 42 full-time (13 women), 14 part-time (4 women); includes 1 Black or African American, non-Hispanic/Latino; 8 Asian, non-Hispanic/Latino; 2 Hispanic/Latino, 1 international. Average age 32. 42 applicants, 76% accepted, 29 enrolled. In 2010, 18 master's awarded. *Entrance requirements:* For master's, GMAT, minimum GPA of 3.0 in final graded 90 quarter credits or 60 graded semester credits; at least 2 years of professional/management work experience. Additional exam requirements/recommendations for international students: Required—TOEFL (minimum score 580 paper-based; 237 computer-based; 92 iBT). *Application deadline:* For fall admission, 4/15 priority date for domestic students. Applications are processed on a rolling basis. Application fee: $65. Electronic applications accepted. *Expenses:* Contact institution. *Financial support:* Scholarships/grants available. *Faculty research:* International accounting, marketing, change management, investments, corporate social responsibility. *Unit head:* Dr. Shahrokh Saudagaran, Dean, 253-692-5630, Fax: 253-692-4523, E-mail: uwtmba@u.washington.edu. *Application contact:* Aubree Robinson, Academic Adviser, MBA and Undergraduate Programs, 253-692-5630, Fax: 253-692-4523, E-mail: uwtmba@u.washington.edu.

University of West Florida, College of Business, Program in Business Administration, Pensacola, FL 32514-5750. Offers MBA. *Accreditation:* AACSB. Part-time and evening/weekend programs available. *Faculty:* 7 full-time (2 women), 4 part-time/adjunct (2 women). *Students:* 29 full-time (13 women), 89 part-time (36 women); includes 10 Black or African American, non-Hispanic/Latino; 2 American Indian or Alaska Native, non-Hispanic/Latino; 4 Asian, non-Hispanic/Latino; 5 Hispanic/Latino; 2 Two or more races, non-Hispanic/Latino, 18 international. Average age 29. 64 applicants, 72% accepted, 35 enrolled. In 2010, 62 master's awarded. *Degree requirements:* For master's, industry portfolio project based on information from five of the core MBA courses. *Entrance requirements:* For master's, GMAT (minimum score 450) or equivalent GRE score, bachelor's degree, two letters of recommendation, resume. Additional exam requirements/recommendations for international students: Required—TOEFL (minimum score 550 paper-based; 213 computer-based). *Application deadline:* For fall admission, 6/30 for domestic students, 5/15 for international students; for spring admission, 10/1 for domestic and international students. Applications are processed on a rolling basis. Application fee: $30. *Expenses:* Tuition, state resident: full-time $4982; part-time $208 per credit hour. Tuition, nonresident: full-time $20,059; part-time $836 per credit hour. Required fees: $1365; $57 per credit hour. *Financial support:* In 2010–11, 43 fellowships (averaging $500 per year), 46 research assistantships with partial tuition reimbursements (averaging $3,438 per year) were awarded; unspecified assistantships also available. Financial award application deadline: 4/15; financial award applicants required to submit FAFSA. *Faculty research:* Robotics, corporate behavior, international trade, franchising, counterfeiting. *Unit head:* Dr. W Timothy O'Keefe, Associate Dean and Director, 850-474-2348. *Application contact:* Cheryl Powell, Academic Advisor, 850-474-2348.

University of West Florida, College of Professional Studies, Department of Professional and Community Leadership, Program in Administration, Pensacola, FL 32514-5750. Offers acquisition and contract administration (MSA); biomedical/pharmaceutical (MSA); criminal justice administration (MSA); database administration (MSA); education leadership (MSA); healthcare administration (MSA); human performance technology (MSA); leadership (MSA); nursing administration (MSA); public administration (MSA); software engineering administration (MSA). Part-time and evening/weekend programs available. Postbaccalaureate distance learning degree programs offered (no on-campus study). *Students:* 26 full-time (24 women), 185 part-time (115 women); includes 30 Black or African American, non-Hispanic/Latino; 1 American Indian or Alaska Native, non-Hispanic/Latino; 5 Asian, non-Hispanic/Latino; 13 Hispanic/Latino; 1 Native Hawaiian or other Pacific Islander, non-Hispanic/Latino, 2 international. Average age 34. 139 applicants,

70% accepted, 80 enrolled. In 2010, 60 master's awarded. *Entrance requirements:* For master's, GRE General Test, letter of intent, names of references. Additional exam requirements/recommendations for international students: Required—TOEFL (minimum score 550 paper-based; 213 computer-based). *Application deadline:* For fall admission, 6/1 for domestic students, 5/15 for international students; for spring admission, 10/1 for domestic and international students. Applications are processed on a rolling basis. Application fee: $30. *Expenses:* Tuition, state resident: full-time $4982; part-time $208 per credit hour. Tuition, nonresident: full-time $20,059; part-time $836 per credit hour. Required fees: $1365; $57 per credit hour. *Financial support:* Unspecified assistantships available. Financial award application deadline: 4/15; financial award applicants required to submit FAFSA. *Unit head:* Dr. Karen Rasmussen, Chairperson, 850-474-2301, Fax: 850-474-2804, E-mail: krasmuss@uwf.edu. *Application contact:* Terry McCray, Assistant Director of Graduate Admissions, 850-473-7718, Fax: 850-473-7714, E-mail: gradadmissions@uwf.edu.

University of West Georgia, Richards College of Business, Program of Business Administration, Carrollton, GA 30118. Offers MBA. *Accreditation:* AACSB. Part-time and evening/weekend programs available. Postbaccalaureate distance learning degree programs offered (no on-campus study). *Faculty:* 10 full-time (3 women), 2 part-time/adjunct (0 women). *Students:* 31 full-time (17 women), 80 part-time (37 women); includes 16 Black or African American, non-Hispanic/Latino; 1 Asian, non-Hispanic/Latino; 2 Hispanic/Latino, 6 international. Average age 32. 67 applicants, 61% accepted, 12 enrolled. In 2010, 82 master's awarded. *Degree requirements:* For master's, comprehensive exam. *Entrance requirements:* For master's, GMAT, minimum GPA of 2.5. Additional exam requirements/recommendations for international students: Required—TOEFL. *Application deadline:* For fall admission, 7/17 for domestic students, 6/6 for international students; for spring admission, 11/20 for domestic students, 5/10 for international students. Applications are processed on a rolling basis. Application fee: $30. Electronic applications accepted. *Expenses:* Tuition, state resident: full-time $4130; part-time $173 per semester hour. Tuition, nonresident: full-time $16,524; part-time $689 per semester hour. Required fees: $1586; $44.01 per semester hour. $397 per semester. Tuition and fees vary according to program. *Financial support:* In 2010–11, 8 research assistantships with full tuition reimbursements (averaging $8,000 per year) were awarded; career-related internships or fieldwork, tuition waivers (partial), and unspecified assistantships also available. Support available to part-time students. Financial award application deadline: 7/1; financial award applicants required to submit FAFSA. *Faculty research:* Distance learning, small business development, e-commerce, computer self-efficacy. *Unit head:* Dr. Blaise J. Bergiel, Associate Dean/Interim MBA Director, 678-839-5252, E-mail: bbergiel@westga.edu. *Application contact:* Dr. Charles W. Clark, Dean, 678-839-6508, E-mail: cclark@westga.edu.

University of Wisconsin–Eau Claire, College of Business, Program in Business Administration, Eau Claire, WI 54702-4004. Offers MBA. *Accreditation:* AACSB. Part-time and evening/weekend programs available. Postbaccalaureate distance learning degree programs offered (no on-campus study). *Faculty:* 31 full-time (11 women). *Students:* 11 full-time (1 woman), 229 part-time (106 women); includes 30 minority (8 Black or African American, non-Hispanic/Latino; 2 American Indian or Alaska Native, non-Hispanic/Latino; 16 Asian, non-Hispanic/Latino; 3 Hispanic/Latino; 1 Two or more races, non-Hispanic/Latino). Average age 32. 135 applicants, 81% accepted, 51 enrolled. In 2010, 60 master's awarded. Terminal master's awarded for partial completion of doctoral program. *Degree requirements:* For master's, thesis optional, applied field project. *Entrance requirements:* For master's, GMAT or GRE, minimum GPA of 2.75 overall or 2.9 in final 10 credit hours. Additional exam requirements/recommendations for international students: Required—TOEFL (minimum score 550 paper-based; 213 computer-based; 79 iBT); Recommended—IELTS (minimum score 7). *Application deadline:* For fall admission, 7/1 priority date for domestic students, 6/1 priority date for international students; for spring admission, 12/1 priority date for domestic students, 11/1 priority date for international students. Applications are processed on a rolling basis. Application fee: $56. *Expenses:* Tuition, state resident: full-time $7001; part-time $389 per credit. Tuition, nonresident: full-time $16,771; part-time $932 per credit. Required fees: $1057; $58.49 per credit. *Financial support:* In 2010–11, 34 students received support, including 13 fellowships (averaging $2,340 per year); Federal Work-Study and unspecified assistantships also available. Financial award application deadline: 3/1; financial award applicants required to submit FAFSA. *Unit head:* Dr. Robert Erffmeyer, Director, 715-836-5509, Fax: 715-836-4014, E-mail: erffmerc@uwec.edu. *Application contact:* Dr. Robert Erffmeyer, Director, 715-836-5509, Fax: 715-836-4014, E-mail: erffmerc@uwec.edu.

University of Wisconsin–Green Bay, Graduate Studies, Program in Management, Green Bay, WI 54311-7001. Offers MS. Part-time programs available. *Faculty:* 4 full-time (1 woman), 1 part-time/adjunct (0 women). *Students:* 2 full-time (1 woman), 27 part-time (16 women); includes 4 minority (1 Black or African American, non-Hispanic/Latino; 1 American Indian or Alaska Native, non-Hispanic/Latino; 1 Asian, non-Hispanic/Latino; 1 Hispanic/Latino). Average age 30. 3 applicants, 67% accepted, 2 enrolled. In 2010, 9 master's awarded. *Degree requirements:* For master's, thesis or alternative. *Entrance requirements:* For master's, GMAT or GRE General Test, minimum GPA of 3.0. *Application deadline:* For fall admission, 8/1 for domestic students; for spring admission, 11/1 for domestic students. Applications are processed on a rolling basis. Application fee: $56. Electronic applications accepted. *Expenses:* Tuition, state resident: full-time $7001; part-time $389 per credit. Tuition, nonresident: full-time $16,771; part-time $932 per credit. Required fees: $1314; $110 per credit. Tuition and fees vary according to reciprocity agreements. *Financial support:* Career-related internships or fieldwork, Federal Work-Study, and institutionally sponsored loans available. Financial award application deadline: 7/15; financial award applicants required to submit FAFSA. *Faculty research:* Planning methods, budgeting, decision making, organizational behavior and theory, management. *Unit head:* Dr. Meir Russ, Chair, 920-465-2757, E-mail: russm@uwgb.edu. *Application contact:* Don McCartney, Adviser, 920-465-2520, E-mail: mccartnd@uwgb.edu.

University of Wisconsin–La Crosse, Office of University Graduate Studies, College of Business Administration, La Crosse, WI 54601-3742. Offers MBA. *Accreditation:* AACSB. Part-time and evening/weekend programs available. *Faculty:* 24 full-time (5 women). *Students:* 26 full-time (11 women), 34 part-time (12 women); includes 2 minority (1 Asian, non-Hispanic/Latino; 1 Hispanic/Latino), 25 international. Average age 29. 95 applicants, 38% accepted, 26 enrolled. In 2010, 32 master's awarded. *Degree requirements:* For master's, thesis optional. *Entrance requirements:* For master's, GMAT. Additional exam requirements/recommendations for international students: Required—TOEFL (minimum score 550 paper-based; 213 computer-based; 79 iBT). *Application deadline:* For fall admission, 6/15 priority date for domestic and international students; for spring admission, 11/15 priority date for domestic and international students. Applications are processed on a rolling basis. Application fee: $56. Electronic applications accepted. *Expenses:* Contact institution. *Financial support:* In 2010–11, 8 research assistantships with partial tuition reimbursements (averaging $5,011 per year) were awarded; Federal Work-Study, scholarships/grants, health care benefits, and tuition waivers (partial) also available. Support available to part-time students. Financial award application deadline: 3/15; financial award applicants required to submit FAFSA. *Faculty research:* Tax regulation, accounting standards, public sector information technology, corporate social responsibility, economics of sports. *Unit head:* Dr. Bruce May, Associate Dean, 608-785-8095, Fax: 608-785-6700, E-mail: may.bruce@uwlax.edu. *Application contact:* Amelia Dittman, Assistant to the Dean, 608-785-8092, Fax: 608-785-6700, E-mail: dittman.amel@uwlax.edu.

University of Wisconsin–Madison, Graduate School, Wisconsin School of Business, Wisconsin Evening MBA Program, Madison, WI 53706-1380. Offers MBA. Part-time and evening/weekend programs available. *Faculty:* 16 full-time (4 women), 1 part-time/adjunct (0 women). *Students:* 179 part-time (126 women); includes 4 Black or African American, non-Hispanic/Latino; 1 American Indian or Alaska Native, non-Hispanic/Latino; 14 Asian, non-Hispanic/Latino; 3 Hispanic/Latino, 8 international. Average age 31. 85 applicants, 81% accepted, 57 enrolled. In 2010, 57 master's awarded. *Entrance requirements:* For master's, GMAT, bachelor's degree, 2 years work experience. Additional exam requirements/recommendations for international students: Required—TOEFL (minimum score 600 paper-based; 250 computer-based; 100 iBT). *Application deadline:* For fall admission, 5/1 priority date for domestic and international students. Applications are processed on a rolling basis. Application fee: $56. Electronic applications accepted. *Expenses:* Contact institution. *Financial support:* Career-related internships or fieldwork and scholarships/grants available. Support available to part-time students. Financial award application deadline: 5/1; financial award applicants required to submit FAFSA. *Faculty research:* Regulation, housing economy, environmental issues on supply chain management, marketing strategy, cost management. *Unit head:* Jim Woodrum, Associate Dean for Wisconsin MBA Programs, 608-263-1169, E-mail: mbaenterprise@bus.wisc.edu. *Application contact:* Linda Uitvlugt, Executive Director, 608-263-1169, Fax: 608-262-3607, E-mail: mbaenterprise@bus.wisc.edu.

University of Wisconsin–Madison, Graduate School, Wisconsin School of Business, Wisconsin Executive MBA Program, Madison, WI 53706-1380. Offers MBA. Part-time and evening/weekend programs available. *Faculty:* 15 full-time (4 women), 3 part-time/adjunct (0 women). *Students:* 66 part-time (22 women); includes 3 Black or African American, non-Hispanic/Latino; 8 Asian, non-Hispanic/Latino; 1 Hispanic/Latino. Average age 38. 59 applicants, 73% accepted, 39 enrolled. In 2010, 33 master's awarded. *Entrance requirements:* For master's, 8 years professional work experience, 5 years leadership experience, minimum GPA of 3.0. *Application deadline:* For fall admission, 5/1 priority date for domestic and international students. Applications are processed on a rolling basis. Application fee: $56. Electronic applications accepted. *Expenses:* Tuition, state resident: full-time $9887; part-time $617.96 per credit. Tuition, nonresident: full-time $24,054; part-time $1503.40 per credit. Required fees: $67.63 per credit. Tuition and fees vary according to reciprocity agreements. *Financial support:* Scholarships/grants available. Support available to part-time students. Financial award application deadline: 5/1; financial award applicants required to submit FAFSA. *Faculty research:* Marketing strategy, housing markets, corporate governance, healthcare fiscal management, management in cross cultural boundaries. *Unit*

head: Jim Woodrum, Associate Dean for Enterprise MBA Programs, 608-263-1169, E-mail: mbaenterprise@bus.wisc.edu. *Application contact:* Linda Uitvlugt, Executive Director, 608-263-1169, Fax: 608-262-3607, E-mail: mabenterprise@bus.wisc.edu.

University of Wisconsin–Madison, Graduate School, Wisconsin School of Business, Wisconsin Full-Time MBA Program, Madison, WI 53706-1380. Offers applied security analysis (MBA); arts administration (MBA); brand and product management (MBA); corporate finance and investment banking (MBA); entrepreneurial management (MBA); marketing research (MBA); operations and technology management (MBA); real estate (MBA); risk management and insurance (MBA); strategic human resource management (MBA); strategic management in the life and engineering sciences (MBA); supply chain management (MBA). *Faculty:* 32 full-time (4 women), 17 part-time/adjunct (3 women). *Students:* 242 full-time (74 women); includes 16 Black or African American, non-Hispanic/Latino; 3 American Indian or Alaska Native, non-Hispanic/Latino; 16 Asian, non-Hispanic/Latino; 12 Hispanic/Latino, 29 international. Average age 28. 526 applicants, 32% accepted, 117 enrolled. In 2010, 106 master's awarded. *Entrance requirements:* For master's, GMAT, bachelor's or equivalent degree, 2 years of work experience, letters of recommendation. Additional exam requirements/recommendations for international students: Required—TOEFL (minimum score 600 paper-based; 250 computer-based; 100 iBT), IELTS. *Application deadline:* For fall admission, 11/4 for domestic students, 11/1 for international students; for winter admission, 2/5 for domestic and international students; for spring admission, 5/15 for domestic students, 4/5 for international students. Applications are processed on a rolling basis. Application fee: $56. Electronic applications accepted. *Expenses:* Tuition, state resident: full-time $9887; part-time $617.96 per credit. Tuition, nonresident: full-time $24,054; part-time $1503.40 per credit. Required fees: $67.63 per credit. Tuition and fees vary according to reciprocity agreements. *Financial support:* In 2010–11, 103 students received support, including 13 fellowships with full and partial tuition reimbursements available (averaging $15,000 per year), 53 research assistantships with full tuition reimbursements available (averaging $8,000 per year), 35 teaching assistantships with full tuition reimbursements available (averaging $11,000 per year); scholarships/grants, health care benefits, and unspecified assistantships also available. Financial award application deadline: 4/5; financial award applicants required to submit FAFSA. *Faculty research:* Market consequences of International Financial Reporting Standards (IFRS), inter-firm relationships and strategic partnerships, application of Bayesian statistical methods and applied probability models to understanding individuals' behaviors in the context of customer relationship management (CRM) applications, liquidity provision and the structure of financial markets, strategic management of global startups. *Unit head:* Dr. Kenneth A. Kavajecz, Associate Dean of Master's Programs, 608-265-3494, Fax: 608-265-4192, E-mail: kkavajecz@bus.wisc.edu. *Application contact:* Maria Reis, Assistant Director of MBA Marketing and Recruiting, 608-262-4000, Fax: 608-265-4192, E-mail: mreis@bus.wisc.edu.

University of Wisconsin–Milwaukee, Graduate School, Sheldon B. Lubar School of Business, Milwaukee, WI 53201. Offers business administration (MBA); enterprise resource planning (Certificate); investment management (Certificate); management science (MS, PhD); nonprofit management and leadership (MS, Certificate); state and local taxation (Certificate); MS/MBA. *Accreditation:* AACSB. Part-time and evening/weekend programs available. *Faculty:* 59 full-time (13 women). *Students:* 343 full-time (125 women), 345 part-time (146 women); includes 18 Black or African American, non-Hispanic/Latino; 2 American Indian or Alaska Native, non-Hispanic/Latino; 37 Asian, non-Hispanic/Latino; 4 Hispanic/Latino, 66 international. Average age 32. 560 applicants, 57% accepted, 155 enrolled. In 2010, 295 master's, 4 doctorates awarded. *Degree requirements:* For master's, comprehensive exam (for some programs); for doctorate, comprehensive exam, thesis/dissertation. *Entrance requirements:* For master's and doctorate, GMAT or GRE General Test. Additional exam requirements/recommendations for international students: Required—TOEFL (minimum score 550 paper-based; 79 iBT), IELTS (minimum score 6.5). *Application deadline:* For fall admission, 1/1 priority date for domestic students; for spring admission, 9/1 for domestic students. Applications are processed on a rolling basis. Application fee: $56 ($96 for international students). Electronic applications accepted. *Expenses:* Contact institution. *Financial support:* In 2010–11, 5 fellowships with full tuition reimbursements, 2 research assistantships with full tuition reimbursements, 41 teaching assistantships with full tuition reimbursements were awarded; career-related internships or fieldwork, Federal Work-Study, health care benefits, unspecified assistantships, and project assistantships also available. Support available to part-time students. Financial award application deadline: 4/15; financial award applicants required to submit FAFSA. *Faculty research:* Applied management research in finance, MIS, marketing, operations research, organizational sciences. Total annual research expenditures: $689,994. *Unit head:* Timothy L. Smunt, Dean, 414-229-6256, Fax: 414-229-2372, E-mail: tsmunt@uwm.edu. *Application contact:* Matthew Jensen, 414-229-5403, E-mail: mba-ms@uwm.edu.

Ursuline College, School of Graduate Studies, Program in Business Administration, Pepper Pike, OH 44124-4398. Offers MBA. *Faculty:* 1 part-time/adjunct (0 women). *Students:* 15 full-time (6 women), 14 part-time (12 women); includes 27 minority (22 Black or African American, non-Hispanic/

Latino; 1 American Indian or Alaska Native, non-Hispanic/Latino; 2 Asian, non-Hispanic/Latino; 1 Hispanic/Latino; 1 Native Hawaiian or other Pacific Islander, non-Hispanic/Latino). Average age 38. 40 applicants, 90% accepted. *Expenses:* Tuition: Full-time $15,138; part-time $841 per credit. Required fees: $240; $120 per semester. *Unit head:* Nancy Brown, Assistant Program Coordinator, 440-684-6038, Fax: 440-684-6088, E-mail: nbrown@ursuline.edu. *Application contact:* Melanie Steele, Graduate Admission Assistant, 440-646-8119, Fax: 440-684-6088, E-mail: graduateadmissions@ursuline.edu.

Ursuline College, School of Graduate Studies, Program in Management, Pepper Pike, OH 44124-4398. Offers MMT. Part-time programs available. *Students:* 2 full-time (1 woman); includes 1 minority (Black or African American, non-Hispanic/Latino). Average age 42. 2 applicants, 100% accepted, 1 enrolled. In 2010, 4 master's awarded. *Degree requirements:* For master's, project. *Entrance requirements:* For master's, minimum undergraduate GPA of 3.0. Additional exam requirements/recommendations for international students: Required—TOEFL (minimum score 500 paper-based; 173 computer-based). *Application deadline:* For fall admission, 8/1 priority date for domestic students. Applications are processed on a rolling basis. Application fee: $25. *Expenses:* Tuition: Full-time $15,138; part-time $841 per credit. Required fees: $240; $120 per semester. *Financial support:* Federal Work-Study available. Financial award application deadline: 3/1; financial award applicants required to submit FAFSA. *Unit head:* Nancy Brown, Assistant Program Coordinator, 440-684-6038, Fax: 440-684-6088, E-mail: nbrown@ursuline.edu. *Application contact:* Melanie Steele, Graduate Admission Assistant, 440-646-8199, Fax: 440-684-6138, E-mail: graduateadmissions@ursuline.edu.

Valdosta State University, Program in Business Administration, Valdosta, GA 31698. Offers MBA. *Accreditation:* AACSB. Part-time and evening/weekend programs available. Postbaccalaureate distance learning degree programs offered (no on-campus study). *Faculty:* 6 full-time (1 woman). *Students:* 4 full-time (0 women), 61 part-time (30 women); includes 6 Black or African American, non-Hispanic/Latino; 1 Asian, non-Hispanic/Latino; 2 Two or more races, non-Hispanic/Latino, 1 international. Average age 26. 52 applicants, 46% accepted, 21 enrolled. In 2010, 11 master's awarded. *Degree requirements:* For master's, comprehensive written and/or oral exams. *Entrance requirements:* For master's, GMAT, minimum GPA of 2.75. Additional exam requirements/recommendations for international students: Required—TOEFL (minimum score 523 paper-based; 193 computer-based). *Application deadline:* For fall admission, 7/1 for domestic and international students; for spring admission, 11/1 for domestic students. Applications are processed on a rolling basis. Application fee: $35. Electronic applications accepted. *Expenses:* Tuition, state resident: full-time $5256; part-time $197 per credit hour. Tuition, nonresident: full-time $14,490; part-time $710 per credit hour. Required fees: $855 per semester. Tuition and fees vary according to course load and campus/location. *Financial support:* In 2010–11, 5 students received support, including 5 research assistantships with full tuition reimbursements available (averaging $3,652 per year); institutionally sponsored loans and scholarships/grants also available. Support available to part-time students. Financial award application deadline: 7/1; financial award applicants required to submit FAFSA. *Unit head:* Dr. Mel Schnake, Director, 229-245-2233, Fax: 229-245-2795, E-mail: mschnake@valdosta.edu. *Application contact:* Jessica DeVane, Coordinator of Graduate Admissions, 229-333-5694, Fax: 229-245-3853, E-mail: rlwaters@valdosta.edu.

Valparaiso University, Graduate School, College of Business Administration, Valparaiso, IN 46383. Offers business administration (MBA); engineering management (MEM); management (Certificate); JD/MBA; MSN/MBA. *Accreditation:* AACSB. Part-time and evening/weekend programs available. Postbaccalaureate distance learning degree programs offered (minimal on-campus study). *Faculty:* 15 part-time/adjunct (4 women). *Students:* 25 full-time (11 women), 48 part-time (18 women); includes 10 minority (4 Black or African American, non-Hispanic/Latino; 1 Asian, non-Hispanic/Latino; 4 Hispanic/Latino; 1 Two or more races, non-Hispanic/Latino), 4 international. Average age 31. In 2010, 29 master's, 4 other advanced degrees awarded. *Entrance requirements:* For master's, GMAT, GRE, minimum GPA of 3.0. Additional exam requirements/recommendations for international students: Required—TOEFL (minimum score 550 paper-based; 213 computer-based; 80 iBT). *Application deadline:* Applications are processed on a rolling basis. Application fee: $30 ($50 for international students). Electronic applications accepted. *Expenses:* Contact institution. *Financial support:* Available to part-time students. Applicants required to submit FAFSA. *Unit head:* Bruce MacLean, Director of Graduate Programs in Management, 219-465-7952, Fax: 219-464-5789, E-mail: bruce.maclean@valpo.edu. *Application contact:* Cindy Scanlan, Assistant Director of Graduate Programs in Management, 219-465-7952, Fax: 219-464-5789, E-mail: cindy.scanlan@valpo.edu.

Vanderbilt University, Owen Graduate School of Management, Executive MBA Program, Nashville, TN 37240-1001. Offers EMBA. *Accreditation:* AACSB. Evening/weekend programs available. *Faculty:* 21 full-time (3 women), 7 part-time/adjunct (2 women). *Students:* 99 full-time (15 women); includes 9 minority (2 Black or African American, non-Hispanic/Latino; 6 Asian, non-Hispanic/Latino; 1 Two or more races, non-Hispanic/Latino), 5 international. Average age 36. 70 applicants, 87% accepted, 49 enrolled. In 2010, 46 master's awarded. *Entrance requirements:* For master's, GMAT, minimum of 5 years of professional work experience. *Application deadline:*

For fall admission, 6/1 for domestic and international students. Applications are processed on a rolling basis. Application fee: $150. Electronic applications accepted. *Expenses:* Contact institution. *Financial support:* In 2010–11, 1 student received support. Scholarships/grants available. Financial award application deadline: 3/31. *Unit head:* Tami Fassinger, Associate Dean of Executive Programs, 615-322-3120, Fax: 615-343-2293, E-mail: tami.fassinger@owen.vanderbilt.edu. *Application contact:* Juli Bennett, Director of Executive MBA and Americas MBA programs, 615-322-9865, Fax: 615-343-2293, E-mail: juli.bennett@owen.vanderbilt.edu.

Vanderbilt University, Owen Graduate School of Management, Full Time MBA Program, Nashville, TN 37203. Offers MBA, JD/MBA, MBA/M Div, MBA/MA, MBA/MD. Students in the 5-year MBA program enter as undergraduates. *Accreditation:* AACSB. *Faculty:* 42 full-time (5 women), 23 part-time/adjunct (0 women). *Students:* 366 full-time (95 women); includes 52 minority (14 Black or African American, non-Hispanic/Latino; 27 Asian, non-Hispanic/Latino; 9 Hispanic/Latino; 2 Native Hawaiian or other Pacific Islander, non-Hispanic/Latino), 83 international. Average age 28. 894 applicants, 36% accepted, 186 enrolled. In 2010, 249 master's awarded. *Entrance requirements:* For master's, GMAT, minimum 2 years of work experience (strongly recommended). Additional exam requirements/recommendations for international students: Required—TOEFL; Recommended—TWE. *Application deadline:* For fall admission, 11/15 priority date for domestic and international students; for winter admission, 1/15 priority date for domestic and international students; for spring admission, 3/1 priority date for domestic and international students. Applications are processed on a rolling basis. Application fee: $0. Electronic applications accepted. *Financial support:* In 2010–11, 200 students received support. Scholarships/grants and tuition waivers (full and partial) available. Financial award application deadline: 5/1; financial award applicants required to submit FAFSA. *Faculty research:* Financial markets, services marketing, operations, organization studies, health care. *Unit head:* John Roeder, Director of Admissions, 615-322-6469, Fax: 615-343-1175, E-mail: admissions@owen.vanderbilt.edu. *Application contact:* Cori Washington, Operations Manager, 615-322-6469, Fax: 615-343-1175, E-mail: admissions@owen.vanderbilt.edu.

Villanova University, Villanova School of Business, Executive MBA Program, Radnor, PA 19087. Offers EMBA. *Accreditation:* AACSB. Evening/weekend programs available. *Faculty:* 9 full-time (1 woman), 4 part-time/adjunct (1 woman). *Students:* 48 part-time (7 women); includes 3 Black or African American, non-Hispanic/Latino; 1 American Indian or Alaska Native, non-Hispanic/Latino; 1 Asian, non-Hispanic/Latino. Average age 37. In 2010, 38 master's awarded. *Degree requirements:* For master's, minimum cumulative GPA of 3.0, only two missed classes per module. *Entrance requirements:* For master's, significant managerial or executive work experience. Additional exam requirements/recommendations for international students: Required—TOEFL (minimum score 550 paper-based; 213 computer-based; 80 iBT). *Application deadline:* For fall admission, 6/30 for domestic and international students. Application fee: $50. Electronic applications accepted. *Expenses:* Contact institution. *Financial support:* Scholarships/grants available. Support available to part-time students. Financial award application deadline: 6/30; financial award applicants required to submit FAFSA. *Faculty research:* Leadership, management, corporate valuation, systems thinking, strategy. *Unit head:* Vincent DiFelice, Director, Executive Programs, 610-523-1737, Fax: 610-523-1737, E-mail: vincent.difeice@villanova.edu. *Application contact:* Vincent DiFelice, Director, Executive Programs, 610-523-1737, Fax: 610-523-1737, E-mail: vincent.difeice@villanova.edu.

Villanova University, Villanova School of Business, MBA—The Fast Track Program, Villanova, PA 19085. Offers finance (MBA); health care management (MBA); international business (MBA); management information systems (MBA); marketing (MBA); real estate (MBA); strategic management (MBA). *Accreditation:* AACSB. Part-time and evening/weekend programs available. *Faculty:* 15 full-time (2 women), 5 part-time/adjunct (0 women). *Students:* 118 part-time (34 women); includes 13 minority (2 Black or African American, non-Hispanic/Latino; 8 Asian, non-Hispanic/Latino; 3 Hispanic/Latino). Average age 30. In 2010, 35 master's awarded. *Degree requirements:* For master's, minimum GPA of 3.0. *Entrance requirements:* For master's, GMAT. Additional exam requirements/recommendations for international students: Required—TOEFL (minimum score 550 paper-based; 213 computer-based; 80 iBT). *Application deadline:* For fall admission, 6/30 for domestic and international students. Application fee: $50. Electronic applications accepted. *Expenses:* Tuition: Part-time $700 per credit. Part-time tuition and fees vary according to degree level and program. *Financial support:* Scholarships/grants available. Support available to part-time students. Financial award application deadline: 6/30; financial award applicants required to submit FAFSA. *Faculty research:* Developing and leveraging technology, ethical business practices, managing for innovation and creativity, the global political economy, strategic marketing management. *Unit head:* Meredith L. Kwiatek, Director of Graduate Recruitment & Marketing, 610-519-7016, Fax: 610-519-6273, E-mail: rachel.garonzik@villanova.edu. *Application contact:* Meredith L. Kwiatek, Assistant Director, 610-519-7016, Fax: 610-519-6273, E-mail: meredith.kwiatek@villanova.edu.

Villanova University, Villanova School of Business, MBA—The Flex Track Program, Villanova, PA 19085. Offers finance (MBA); health care management (MBA); international business (MBA); management information systems (MBA); marketing (MBA); real estate (MBA); strategic management (MBA); JD/MBA. *Accreditation:* AACSB. Part-time and evening/weekend programs available. Postbaccalaureate distance learning degree programs offered (minimal on-campus study). *Faculty:* 31 full-time (5 women), 22 part-time/adjunct (2 women). *Students:* 15 full-time (6 women), 443 part-time (150 women); includes 46 minority (5 Black or African American, non-Hispanic/Latino; 35 Asian, non-Hispanic/Latino; 6 Hispanic/Latino). Average age 30. In 2010, 133 master's awarded. *Degree requirements:* For master's, minimum GPA of 3.0. *Entrance requirements:* For master's, GMAT. Additional exam requirements/recommendations for international students: Required—TOEFL (minimum score 550 paper-based; 213 computer-based; 80 iBT). *Application deadline:* For fall admission, 6/30 for domestic and international students; for winter admission, 11/15 for domestic and international students; for spring admission, 3/30 for domestic students, 3/31 for international students. Applications are processed on a rolling basis. Application fee: $50. Electronic applications accepted. *Expenses:* Tuition: Part-time $700 per credit. Part-time tuition and fees vary according to degree level and program. *Financial support:* In 2010–11, 15 research assistantships with full tuition reimbursements (averaging $13,100 per year) were awarded; scholarships/grants and unspecified assistantships also available. Support available to part-time students. Financial award application deadline: 6/30; financial award applicants required to submit FAFSA. *Faculty research:* Developing and leveraging technology, ethical business practices, managing for innovation and creativity, the global political economy, strategic marketing management. *Unit head:* Meredith L. Kwiatek, Director of Graduate Recruitment and Marketing, 610-519-7016, Fax: 610-519-6273, E-mail: meredith.kwiatek@villanova.edu. *Application contact:* Meredith L. Kwiatek, Assistant Director, 610-519-7016, Fax: 610-519-6273, E-mail: meredith.kwiatek@villanova.edu.

Virginia Commonwealth University, Graduate School, School of Business, Program in Business Administration, Richmond, VA 23284-9005. Offers MBA, Postbaccalaureate Certificate. *Faculty:* 26 full-time (2 women). *Students:* 118 full-time (46 women), 220 part-time (71 women); includes 74 minority (35 Black or African American, non-Hispanic/Latino; 26 Asian, non-Hispanic/Latino; 9 Hispanic/Latino; 4 Two or more races, non-Hispanic/Latino), 24 international. 218 applicants, 60% accepted, 102 enrolled. In 2010, 143 master's, 5 other advanced degrees awarded. *Entrance requirements:* For master's, GMAT. Additional exam requirements/recommendations for international students: Required—TOEFL (minimum score 600 paper-based; 250 computer-based; 100 iBT). *Application deadline:* For fall admission, 7/1 for domestic students; for spring admission, 11/1 for domestic students. Applications are processed on a rolling basis. Application fee: $50. Electronic applications accepted. *Expenses:* Tuition, state resident: full-time $4308; part-time $479 per credit hour. Tuition, nonresident: full-time $8942; part-time $994 per credit hour. Required fees: $2000; $85 per credit hour. Tuition and fees vary according to course level, course load, degree level, campus/location and program. *Financial support:* Fellowships, research assistantships, teaching assistantships, Federal Work-Study, institutionally sponsored loans, and tuition waivers (full and partial) available. Financial award application deadline: 3/15; financial award applicants required to submit FAFSA. *Unit head:* Ed Grier, Dean, 804-828-1595, Fax: 804-828-8884. *Application contact:* Jana P. McQuaid, Assistant Dean, Masters Programs, 804-828-4622, Fax: 804-828-7174, E-mail: jpmcquaid@vcu.edu.

Virginia Commonwealth University, Graduate School, School of Business, Program in Management, Richmond, VA 23284-9005. Offers Certificate. *Application deadline:* Applications are processed on a rolling basis. Application fee: $50. *Expenses:* Tuition, state resident: full-time $4308; part-time $479 per credit hour. Tuition, nonresident: full-time $8942; part-time $994 per credit hour. Required fees: $2000; $85 per credit hour. Tuition and fees vary according to course level, course load, degree level, campus/location and program. *Financial support:* Fellowships, research assistantships, teaching assistantships, Federal Work-Study, institutionally sponsored loans, and tuition waivers (full and partial) available. Financial award application deadline: 3/15. *Unit head:* Dr. George R. Gray, Chair, 804-828-1732, Fax: 804-828-1600, E-mail: grgray@vcu.edu. *Application contact:* Jana P. McQuaid, Graduate Program Director, 804-828-4622, Fax: 804-828-7174, E-mail: jpmcquaid@vcu.edu.

Virginia Polytechnic Institute and State University, Graduate School, College of Science, Program in Biomedical Technology Development and Management, Blacksburg, VA 24061. Offers MS. *Students:* 5 part-time (4 women); includes 3 Asian, non-Hispanic/Latino. Average age 25. 2 applicants, 100% accepted, 2 enrolled. *Degree requirements:* For master's, comprehensive exam (for some programs), thesis (for some programs). *Entrance requirements:* For master's, GRE. Additional exam requirements/recommendations for international students: Required—TOEFL (minimum score 550 paper-based; 213 computer-based). *Application deadline:* For fall admission, 7/1 for domestic and international students; for spring admission, 12/1 for domestic and international students. Applications are processed on a rolling basis. Application fee: $65. Electronic applications accepted. *Expenses:* Tuition, state resident: full-time $9399; part-time $488 per credit hour. Tuition, nonresident: full-time $17,854; part-time $957.75 per credit hour. Required fees: $1534. Full-time tuition and fees vary according to program. *Financial*

support: Career-related internships or fieldwork, Federal Work-Study, scholarships/grants, health care benefits, and unspecified assistantships available. Total annual research expenditures: $289,400. *Unit head:* Dr. Kenneth H. Wong, UNIT HEAD, 703-518-2978, Fax: 540-231-7511, E-mail: khwong@vt.edu. *Application contact:* Jennifer LeFurgy, Contact, 703-518-2710, Fax: 540-231-7511, E-mail: jlefurgy@vt.edu.

Virginia Polytechnic Institute and State University, Graduate School, Pamplin College of Business, Department of Management, Blacksburg, VA 24061. Offers PhD. *Accreditation:* AACSB. *Faculty:* 19 full-time (7 women), 1 (woman) part-time/adjunct. *Students:* 10 full-time (2 women), 8 international. Average age 33. 21 applicants, 14% accepted, 2 enrolled. In 2010, 2 doctorates awarded. *Degree requirements:* For doctorate, comprehensive exam (for some programs), thesis/dissertation (for some programs). *Entrance requirements:* For doctorate, GRE. Additional exam requirements/recommendations for international students: Required—TOEFL (minimum score 550 paper-based; 213 computer-based). *Application deadline:* For fall admission, 7/1 for domestic and international students; for spring admission, 11/1 for domestic and international students. Applications are processed on a rolling basis. Application fee: $65. Electronic applications accepted. *Expenses:* Tuition, state resident: full-time $9399; part-time $488 per credit hour. Tuition, nonresident: full-time $17,854; part-time $957.75 per credit hour. Required fees: $1534. Full-time tuition and fees vary according to program. *Financial support:* In 2010–11, 7 teaching assistantships with full tuition reimbursements (averaging $14,758 per year) were awarded; career-related internships or fieldwork, Federal Work-Study, scholarships/grants, health care benefits, and unspecified assistantships also available. Financial award application deadline: 1/15. *Faculty research:* Compensation, organization effectiveness, selection, strategic planning, labor/management relations. Total annual research expenditures: $49,550. *Unit head:* Dr. Anju Seth, UNIT HEAD, 540-231-6353, Fax: 540-231-4487, E-mail: aseth@vt.edu. *Application contact:* Kevin Carlson, Contact, 540-231-4990, Fax: 540-231-4487, E-mail: kevinc@vt.edu.

Virginia Polytechnic Institute and State University, Graduate School, Pamplin College of Business, Program in Business Administration, Blacksburg, VA 24061. Offers MBA. *Accreditation:* AACSB. *Students:* 242 full-time (75 women), 96 part-time (32 women); includes 12 Black or African American, non-Hispanic/Latino; 25 Asian, non-Hispanic/Latino; 7 Hispanic/Latino, 57 international. Average age 31. 277 applicants, 51% accepted, 113 enrolled. In 2010, 187 master's awarded. *Degree requirements:* For master's, comprehensive exam (for some programs), thesis (for some programs). *Entrance requirements:* For master's, GRE. Additional exam requirements/recommendations for international students: Required—TOEFL (minimum score 550 paper-based; 213 computer-based). *Application deadline:* For fall admission, 7/1 for domestic and international students; for spring admission, 12/1 for domestic and international students. Applications are processed on a rolling basis. Application fee: $65. Electronic applications accepted. *Expenses:* Tuition, state resident: full-time $9399; part-time $488 per credit hour. Tuition, nonresident: full-time $17,854; part-time $957.75 per credit hour. Required fees: $1534. Full-time tuition and fees vary according to program. *Financial support:* In 2010–11, 5 teaching assistantships with full tuition reimbursements (averaging $9,210 per year) were awarded; career-related internships or fieldwork, Federal Work-Study, scholarships/grants, health care benefits, and unspecified assistantships also available. Financial award application deadline: 1/15. *Unit head:* Dr. Stephen J. Skripak, UNIT HEAD, 540-231-6152, Fax: 540-231-4487, E-mail: sskripak@vt.edu. *Application contact:* Melanie Johnston, Contact, 540-231-6904, Fax: 540-231-4487, E-mail: mjohnston@vt.edu.

Wagner College, Division of Graduate Studies, Department of Business Administration, Staten Island, NY 10301-4495. Offers accelerated business administration (MBA); accounting (MS); finance (MBA); health care administration (MBA); international business (MBA); management (Exec MBA, MBA); marketing (MBA). *Accreditation:* ACBSP. Part-time and evening/weekend programs available. *Faculty:* 8 full-time (3 women), 20 part-time/adjunct (2 women). *Students:* 112 full-time (42 women), 41 part-time (15 women); includes 44 minority (12 Black or African American, non-Hispanic/Latino; 1 American Indian or Alaska Native, non-Hispanic/Latino; 8 Asian, non-Hispanic/Latino; 20 Hispanic/Latino; 3 Two or more races, non-Hispanic/Latino), 2 international. Average age 30. 97 applicants, 99% accepted, 79 enrolled. In 2010, 69 master's awarded. *Degree requirements:* For master's, thesis optional. *Entrance requirements:* For master's, GMAT, minimum GPA of 2.75, proficiency in computers and math. Additional exam requirements/recommendations for international students: Required—TOEFL (minimum score 550 paper-based; 217 computer-based; 79 iBT). *Application deadline:* For fall admission, 5/1 priority date for domestic students, 3/1 priority date for international students; for spring admission, 12/1 for domestic students, 11/1 for international students. Applications are processed on a rolling basis. Application fee: $50 ($85 for international students). *Expenses:* Tuition: Full-time $15,570; part-time $865 per credit. *Financial support:* Career-related internships or fieldwork, unspecified assistantships, and alumni fellowship grant available. Financial award applicants required to submit FAFSA. *Unit head:* Prof. Donald Crooks, Director, 718-390-3429, Fax: 718-420-4274, E-mail: dcrooks@wagner.edu. *Application contact:* Patricia

Clancy, Administrative Assistant, 718-420-4464, Fax: 718-390-3105, E-mail: patricia.clancy@wagner.edu.

Wake Forest University, Schools of Business, Charlotte Evening MBA Program, Charlotte, NC 28211. Offers MBA. *Accreditation:* AACSB. Evening/weekend programs available. *Faculty:* 63 full-time (17 women), 30 part-time/adjunct (9 women). *Students:* 100 full-time (25 women); includes 16 minority (12 Black or African American, non-Hispanic/Latino; 2 Asian, non-Hispanic/Latino; 2 Hispanic/Latino), 4 international. Average age 31. In 2010, 47 master's awarded. *Degree requirements:* For master's, 54 total credit hours. *Entrance requirements:* For master's, GMAT or GRE, letters of recommendation, official transcripts, current resume or curriculum vitae, three years of work experience. Additional exam requirements/recommendations for international students: Required—TOEFL (minimum score 600 paper-based; 250 computer-based; 100 iBT), Pearson Test of English (PTE). *Application deadline:* For fall admission, 6/1 for domestic and international students. Applications are processed on a rolling basis. Application fee: $100. Electronic applications accepted. *Expenses:* Contact institution. *Financial support:* In 2010–11, 33 students received support. Scholarships/grants available. Financial award application deadline: 4/1; financial award applicants required to submit FAFSA. *Faculty research:* The influence of personal relationships on business decision making and management of change; drivers of perceived value and consumer behavior; impact of accounting on auditing, financial, managerial, systems and taxation stakeholders; corporate governance and executive compensation; impact of operations strategies on competitiveness. *Unit head:* Bill Davis, Associate Dean, Working Professional Programs, 704-365-1717, Fax: 704-365-3511, E-mail: clt.mba@mba.wfu.edu. *Application contact:* Judi Affeldt, Administrative Assistant, 704-365-1717, Fax: 704-365-3511, E-mail: clt.mba@mba.wfu.edu.

Wake Forest University, Schools of Business, Evening MBA Program–Winston-Salem, Winston-Salem, NC 27106. Offers MBA, PhD/MBA. *Accreditation:* AACSB. Evening/weekend programs available. *Faculty:* 63 full-time (17 women), 30 part-time/adjunct (9 women). *Students:* 67 full-time (23 women); includes 13 minority (7 Black or African American, non-Hispanic/Latino; 3 Asian, non-Hispanic/Latino; 2 Hispanic/Latino; 1 Two or more races, non-Hispanic/Latino), 2 international. Average age 33. In 2010, 39 master's awarded. *Degree requirements:* For master's, 54 total credit hours. *Entrance requirements:* For master's, GMAT or GRE, letters of recommendation, official transcripts, current resume or curriculum vitae, three years of work experience. Additional exam requirements/recommendations for international students: Required—TOEFL (minimum score 600 paper-based; 250 computer-based; 100 iBT), Pearson Test of English (PTE). *Application deadline:* For fall admission, 7/1 for domestic and international students. Applications are processed on a rolling basis. Application fee: $100. Electronic applications accepted. *Expenses:* Contact institution. *Financial support:* In 2010–11, 18 students received support. Scholarships/grants available. Financial award applicants required to submit FAFSA. *Faculty research:* The influence of personal relationships on business decision making and management of change; drivers of perceived value and consumer behavior; impact of accounting on auditing, financial, managerial, systems and taxation stakeholders; corporate governance and executive compensation; impact of operations strategies on competitiveness. *Unit head:* Bill Davis, Associate Dean, Working Professional Programs, 336-758-5422, Fax: 336-758-5830, E-mail: admissions@mba.wfu.edu. *Application contact:* Tamara Paquee, Administrative Assistant, 336-758-5422, Fax: 336-758-5830, E-mail: admissions@mba.wfu.edu.

Wake Forest University, Schools of Business, Full-time MBA Program, Winston-Salem, NC 27106. Offers consulting/general management (MBA); entrepreneurship (MBA); finance (MBA); health (MBA); marketing (MBA); operations management (MBA); JD/MBA; MD/MBA; MSA/MBA. *Accreditation:* AACSB. *Faculty:* 63 full-time (17 women), 30 part-time/adjunct (9 women). *Students:* 123 full-time (22 women); includes 9 Black or African American, non-Hispanic/Latino; 4 Asian, non-Hispanic/Latino; 2 Hispanic/Latino; 1 Two or more races, non-Hispanic/Latino, 25 international. Average age 28. In 2010, 83 master's awarded. *Degree requirements:* For master's, 65.5 total credit hours. *Entrance requirements:* For master's, GMAT or GRE, letters of recommendation, official transcripts, current resume or curriculum vitae, 2 years of work experience. Additional exam requirements/recommendations for international students: Required—TOEFL (minimum score 600 paper-based; 250 computer-based; 100 iBT), Pearson Test of English (PTE). *Application deadline:* For fall admission, 4/15 for domestic and international students. Applications are processed on a rolling basis. Application fee: $100. Electronic applications accepted. *Expenses:* Contact institution. *Financial support:* In 2010–11, 76 students received support. Career-related internships or fieldwork, scholarships/grants, and unspecified assistantships available. Financial award application deadline: 2/15; financial award applicants required to submit FAFSA. *Faculty research:* The influence of personal relationships on business decision making and management of change; drivers of perceived value and consumer behavior; impact of accounting on auditing, financial, managerial, systems and taxation stakeholders; corporate governance and executive compensation; impact of operations strategies on competitiveness. *Unit head:* Sherry Moss, Director, 336-758-5422, Fax: 336-758-5830, E-mail: admissions@mba.wfu.edu. *Application contact:* Tamara Paquee, Administrative Assistant, 336-758-5422, Fax: 336-758-5830, E-mail: admissions@mba.wfu.edu.

Wake Forest University, Schools of Business, MA in Management Program, Winston-Salem, NC 27106. Offers MA. *Faculty:* 63 full-time (17 women), 30 part-time/adjunct (9 women). *Students:* 93 full-time (41 women); includes 56 minority (44 Black or African American, non-Hispanic/Latino; 1 American Indian or Alaska Native, non-Hispanic/Latino; 2 Asian, non-Hispanic/Latino; 9 Hispanic/Latino), 6 international. Average age 22. In 2010, 91 master's awarded. *Degree requirements:* For master's, 43.5 total credit hours. *Entrance requirements:* For master's, GMAT or GRE, letters of recommendation, official transcripts, current resume or curriculum vitae. Additional exam requirements/recommendations for international students: Required—TOEFL (minimum score 600 paper-based; 250 computer-based; 100 iBT), Pearson Test of English (PTE). *Application deadline:* For fall admission, 6/15 for domestic and international students. Applications are processed on a rolling basis. Application fee: $100. Electronic applications accepted. *Financial support:* In 2010–11, 54 students received support. Scholarships/grants available. Financial award application deadline: 3/15; financial award applicants required to submit FAFSA. *Faculty research:* The influence of personal relationships on business decision making and management of change; drivers of perceived value and consumer behavior; impact of accounting on auditing, financial, managerial, systems and taxation stakeholders; corporate governance and executive compensation; impact of operations strategies on competitiveness. *Unit head:* Derrick Boone, Director, MA in Management, 336-758-5422, Fax: 336-758-5830, E-mail: admissions@mba.wfu.edu. *Application contact:* Tamara Paquee, Administrative Assistant, 336-758-5422, Fax: 336-758-5830, E-mail: admissions@mba.wfu.edu.

Wake Forest University, Schools of Business, Saturday MBA Program–Charlotte, Charlotte, NC 28211. Offers MBA. *Accreditation:* AACSB. Evening/weekend programs available. *Faculty:* 63 full-time (17 women), 30 part-time/adjunct (9 women). *Students:* 75 full-time (13 women); includes 22 minority (8 Black or African American, non-Hispanic/Latino; 7 Asian, non-Hispanic/Latino; 3 Hispanic/Latino; 4 Two or more races, non-Hispanic/Latino), 3 international. Average age 31. In 2010, 42 master's awarded. *Degree requirements:* For master's, 54 total credit hours. *Entrance requirements:* For master's, GMAT or GRE, letters of recommendation, official transcripts, current resume or curriculum vitae, three years of work experience. Additional exam requirements/recommendations for international students: Required—TOEFL (minimum score 600 paper-based; 250 computer-based; 100 iBT), Pearson Test of English (PTE). *Application deadline:* For spring admission, 11/1 for domestic and international students. Applications are processed on a rolling basis. Application fee: $100. Electronic applications accepted. *Expenses:* Contact institution. *Financial support:* In 2010–11, 8 students received support. Scholarships/grants available. Financial award application deadline: 9/1; financial award applicants required to submit FAFSA. *Faculty research:* The influence of personal relationships on business decision making and management of change; drivers of perceived value and consumer behavior; impact of accounting on auditing, financial, managerial, systems and taxation stakeholders; corporate governance and executive compensation; impact of operations strategies on competitiveness. *Unit head:* Bill Davis, Associate Dean, Working Professional Programs, 704-365-1717, Fax: 704-365-3511, E-mail: clt.mba@mba.wfu.edu. *Application contact:* Judi Affeldt, Administrative Assistant, 704-365-1717, Fax: 704-365-3511, E-mail: clt.mba@mba.wfu.edu.

Walden University, Graduate Programs, School of Management, Minneapolis, MN 55401. Offers accounting (MS), including cpa emphasis, professional track, self-designed; accounting and management (MS), including self-designed, strategic management; applied management and decision sciences (PhD), including accounting, engineering management, finance, general applied management and decision sciences, information systems management, knowledge management, leadership and organizational change, learning management, operations research, self-designed program in applied management and design sciences; business information management (MISM); enterprise information security (MISM); entrepreneurship (MBA, DBA); finance (MBA, DBA); global management (MS); global supply chain management (DBA); health informatics (MISM); healthcare management (MBA, MS); healthcare system improvement (MBA); human resource management (MBA, MS), including functional human resource management (MS), human resource management (MS), integrating functional and strategic human resource management (MS), organizational strategy (MS); information systems (MS); information systems management (DBA); information technology (MS), including information security, software engineering; international business (MBA, DBA); IT strategy and governance (MISM); leadership (MBA, MS, DBA), including entrepreneurship (MS), general management (MS), human resources leadership (MS), innovation and technology (MS), leader development (MS), leading sustainability (MS), project management (MS), self-designed (MS); managers as leaders (MS); managing global software and service supply chains (MISM); marketing (MBA, DBA); project management (MBA, MS); research strategies (MS); risk management (MBA); self-designed (MBA, DBA); social impact management (DBA); strategy and operations (MS); sustainable futures (MBA); sustainable management (MS); technology (MBA); technology entrepreneurship (DBA); technology management (MS).

Part-time and evening/weekend programs available. Postbaccalaureate distance learning degree programs offered (minimal on-campus study). *Faculty:* 22 full-time (8 women), 291 part-time/adjunct (100 women). *Students:* 3,705 full-time (1,956 women), 976 part-time (549 women); includes 2,432 minority (2,021 Black or African American, non-Hispanic/Latino; 32 American Indian or Alaska Native, non-Hispanic/Latino; 137 Asian, non-Hispanic/Latino; 193 Hispanic/Latino; 5 Native Hawaiian or other Pacific Islander, non-Hispanic/Latino; 44 Two or more races, non-Hispanic/Latino), 302 international. Average age 40. In 2010, 658 master's, 86 doctorates awarded. *Degree requirements:* For doctorate, thesis/dissertation (for some programs), residency. *Entrance requirements:* For master's, bachelor's degree or equivalent in related field; minimum GPA of 2.5; official transcripts; goal statement; access to computer and Internet; for doctorate, master's degree or equivalent in related field; minimum GPA of 3.0; 3 years of related professional/academic experience (preferred). Additional exam requirements/recommendations for international students: Required—TOEFL (minimum score 550 paper-based; 213 computer-based), IELTS (minimum score 6.5), Michigan English Language Assessment Battery (minimum score 82). *Application deadline:* Applications are processed on a rolling basis. Application fee: $50. Electronic applications accepted. *Expenses:* Tuition: Full-time $10,274; part-time $445 per credit. Tuition and fees vary according to course load, degree level and program. *Financial support:* Fellowships, Federal Work-Study, scholarships/grants, unspecified assistantships, and family tuition reduction, active duty/veteran tuition reduction, group tuition reduction, interest-free payment plans available. Support available to part-time students. Financial award applicants required to submit FAFSA. *Unit head:* Dr. William Schulz, Associate Dean, 800-925-3368. *Application contact:* Jennifer Hall, Vice President of Enrollment Management, 866-4-WALDEN, E-mail: info@waldenu.edu.

Walsh University, Graduate Studies, MBA Program, North Canton, OH 44720-3396. Offers health care management (MBA); integrated marketing communications (MBA); management (MBA). Part-time and evening/weekend programs available. *Faculty:* 8 full-time (3 women), 21 part-time/adjunct (4 women). *Students:* 22 full-time (8 women), 132 part-time (68 women); includes 13 minority (10 Black or African American, non-Hispanic/Latino; 3 Hispanic/Latino). Average age 34. 60 applicants, 98% accepted, 49 enrolled. In 2010, 57 master's awarded. *Entrance requirements:* For master's, GMAT, minimum GPA of 3.0. Additional exam requirements/recommendations for international students: Required—TOEFL (minimum score 500 paper-based; 173 computer-based; 61 iBT). *Application deadline:* For fall admission, 7/15 priority date for domestic students. Applications are processed on a rolling basis. Application fee: $25. Electronic applications accepted. *Expenses:* Tuition: Full-time $13,080; part-time $545 per credit hour. *Financial support:* In 2010–11, 98 students received support, including 9 research assistantships with partial tuition reimbursements available (averaging $5,518 per year); tuition waivers (partial), unspecified assistantships, and tuition discounts also available. Financial award application deadline: 12/31. *Faculty research:* Patient and physician satisfaction, advancing and improving learning with information technology, consumer-driven healthcare, branding and the service industry, service provider training and customer satisfaction. *Unit head:* Dr. Michael A. Petrochuk, Director of the MBA Program and Assistant Professor, 330-244-4764, Fax: 330-490-7359, E-mail: mpetrochuk@walsh.edu. *Application contact:* Christine Haver, Assistant Director for Graduate and Transfer Admissions, 330-490-7177, Fax: 330-244-4925, E-mail: chaver@walsh.edu.

Washington State University, Graduate School, College of Business, Business Administration Programs, Pullman, WA 99164. Offers business administration (MBA, PhD), including accounting (PhD), finance (PhD), management and operations (PhD), management information systems (PhD), marketing (PhD). *Accreditation:* AACSB. *Faculty:* 47. *Students:* 117 full-time (42 women), 117 part-time (30 women); includes 24 minority (1 Black or African American, non-Hispanic/Latino; 17 Asian, non-Hispanic/Latino; 5 Hispanic/Latino; 1 Two or more races, non-Hispanic/Latino), 48 international. Average age 32. 347 applicants, 19% accepted, 43 enrolled. In 2010, 58 master's, 5 doctorates awarded. *Degree requirements:* For master's, comprehensive exam (for some programs), thesis (for some programs), final presentation; for doctorate, comprehensive exam, thesis/dissertation, oral and written exams. *Entrance requirements:* For master's and doctorate, GMAT, minimum GPA of 3.0, 3 letters of recommendation. Additional exam requirements/recommendations for international students: Required—TOEFL. *Application deadline:* For fall admission, 3/1 priority date for domestic students, 3/1 for international students; for spring admission, 6/1 priority date for domestic students, 6/1 for international students. Applications are processed on a rolling basis. Application fee: $50. Electronic applications accepted. *Expenses:* Tuition, state resident: full-time $8552; part-time $443 per credit. Tuition, nonresident: full-time $21,650; part-time $1083 per credit. Required fees: $846. *Financial support:* In 2010–11, 102 students received support, including 36 teaching assistantships with full and partial tuition reimbursements available (averaging $18,204 per year); career-related internships or fieldwork, Federal Work-Study, institutionally sponsored loans, health care benefits, tuition waivers (partial), unspecified assistantships, and teaching associateships also available. Financial award application deadline: 4/1. Total annual research expenditures: $344,000. *Unit head:* Dr. Eric Spangenberg, Dean, 509-335-8150, E-mail: ers@wsu.edu. *Application contact:* Graduate

School Admissions, 800-GRADWSU, Fax: 509-335-1949, E-mail: gradsch@wsu.edu.

Washington State University Tri-Cities, Graduate Programs, College of Business, Richland, WA 99354. Offers business management (MBA). Part-time and evening/weekend programs available. *Faculty:* 56. *Students:* 11 full-time (5 women), 37 part-time (5 women); includes 1 American Indian or Alaska Native, non-Hispanic/Latino; 3 Asian, non-Hispanic/Latino; 2 Hispanic/Latino, 1 international. Average age 35. In 2010, 16 master's awarded. *Degree requirements:* For master's, thesis (for some programs), oral presentation exam. *Entrance requirements:* For master's, GMAT, minimum GPA of 3.0, 3 letters of recommendation. Additional exam requirements/recommendations for international students: Required—TOEFL (minimum score 550 paper-based; 213 computer-based). *Application deadline:* For fall admission, 1/10 priority date for domestic students, 1/10 for international students; for spring admission, 7/1 priority date for domestic students, 7/1 for international students. Application fee: $50. *Financial support:* In 2010–11, 17 students received support. *Faculty research:* Strategy, organizational transformation, technology and instructional effectiveness, market research effects of type (fonts), optimization of price structure, accounting ethic. *Unit head:* Dr. John Thornton, Director, 509-372-7246, Fax: 509-372-7354, E-mail: jthornt@tricity.wsu.edu. *Application contact:* Graduate School Admissions, 800-GRADWSU, Fax: 509-335-1949, E-mail: gradsch@wsu.edu.

Washington State University Vancouver, Graduate Programs, Program in Business Administration, Vancouver, WA 98686. Offers MBA. *Faculty:* 14. *Students:* 4 full-time (0 women), 46 part-time (14 women); includes 1 Black or African American, non-Hispanic/Latino; 5 Asian, non-Hispanic/Latino; 1 Hispanic/Latino. *Degree requirements:* For master's, comprehensive exam (for some programs), thesis (for some programs), final presentation, portfolio. *Entrance requirements:* For master's, GMAT, minimum GPA of 3.0, 3 letters of recommendation, resume. Additional exam requirements/recommendations for international students: Required—TOEFL. *Application deadline:* For fall admission, 1/10 priority date for domestic students; for spring admission, 7/1 priority date for domestic students, 7/1 for international students. Application fee: $50. *Financial support:* In 2010–11, research assistantships (averaging $14,634 per year), teaching assistantships with full tuition reimbursements (averaging $13,383 per year) were awarded. Financial award application deadline: 2/15. *Faculty research:* Liquidity, cost of capital and firm value, business ethics, corporate governance, finance and nonfinancial performance measurement, negotiations, project management. *Unit head:* Dr. Jane Cote, Academic Director, 360-546-9756, E-mail: cotej@vancouver.wsu.edu. *Application contact:* Graduate School Admissions, 800-GRADWSU, Fax: 509-335-1949, E-mail: gradsch@wsu.edu.

Washington University in St. Louis, Olin Business School, St. Louis, MO 63130-4899. Offers EMBA, M Acc, MBA, MS, PhD, JD/MBA, M Arch/MBA, M Eng/MBA, MBA/MA, MBA/MSW. *Accreditation:* AACSB. *Faculty:* 79 full-time (17 women), 42 part-time/adjunct (7 women). *Students:* 487 full-time (170 women), 503 part-time (127 women); includes 168 minority (34 Black or African American, non-Hispanic/Latino; 2 American Indian or Alaska Native, non-Hispanic/Latino; 93 Asian, non-Hispanic/Latino; 10 Hispanic/Latino; 29 Two or more races, non-Hispanic/Latino), 320 international. *Entrance requirements:* Additional exam requirements/recommendations for international students: Required—TOEFL. Electronic applications accepted. *Unit head:* Dr. Mahendra Gupta, Dean, 314-935-6344. *Application contact:* Dr. Mahendra Gupta, Dean, 314-935-6344.

Wayne State University, School of Business Administration, Detroit, MI 48202. Offers accounting (MSA); business administration (MBA, PhD); taxation (MST); JD/MBA. *Accreditation:* AACSB. Part-time and evening/weekend programs available. Postbaccalaureate distance learning degree programs offered. *Faculty:* 40 full-time (10 women), 8 part-time/adjunct (0 women). *Students:* 240 full-time (99 women), 800 part-time (419 women); includes 325 minority (180 Black or African American, non-Hispanic/Latino; 1 American Indian or Alaska Native, non-Hispanic/Latino; 118 Asian, non-Hispanic/Latino; 22 Hispanic/Latino; 4 Two or more races, non-Hispanic/Latino), 152 international. Average age 28. 529 applicants, 71% accepted, 287 enrolled. In 2010, 345 degrees awarded. *Entrance requirements:* For master's, GMAT, minimum undergraduate GPA of 2.5. Additional exam requirements/recommendations for international students: Required—TOEFL (minimum score 550 paper-based; 213 computer-based); Recommended—TWE (minimum score 6). *Application deadline:* For fall admission, 6/1 for domestic students, 3/1 for international students; for winter admission, 10/1 for domestic students, 6/1 for international students; for spring admission, 2/1 for domestic students, 10/1 for international students. Applications are processed on a rolling basis. Application fee: $50. Electronic applications accepted. *Expenses:* Tuition, state resident: full-time $7662; part-time $478.85 per credit hour. Tuition, nonresident: full-time $16,920; part-time $1057.55 per credit hour. Required fees: $571.20; $35.70 per credit hour. $188.05 per semester. Tuition and fees vary according to course load and program. *Financial support:* In 2010–11, 17 research assistantships (averaging $15,000 per year) were awarded; career-related internships or fieldwork, Federal Work-Study, and scholarships/grants also available. Support available to part-time students. Financial award applicants required to submit FAFSA. *Faculty research:* Corporate financial valuation, strategic advertising, information technology effectiveness, financial accounting and taxation, organizational performance and effectiveness. *Unit head:* Dr. Margaret Williams, Interim Dean, 313-577-4501, Fax: 313-577-4557. *Application contact:* Linda Zaddach, Assistant Dean, 313-577-4510, E-mail: l.s.zaddach@wayne.edu.

West Chester University of Pennsylvania, Office of Graduate Studies, College of Business and Public Affairs, Department of Management, West Chester, PA 19383. Offers business (Certificate); general business (MBA). *Accreditation:* AACSB. Part-time and evening/weekend programs available. *Students:* 69 part-time (23 women); includes 4 minority (1 Black or African American, non-Hispanic/Latino; 3 Asian, non-Hispanic/Latino), 2 international. Average age 31. 74 applicants, 39% accepted, 10 enrolled. In 2010, 29 master's, 13 other advanced degrees awarded. *Degree requirements:* For master's, minimum GPA of 3.0. *Entrance requirements:* For master's, GMAT, statement of professional goals, resume, two letters of recommendation, transcripts. Additional exam requirements/recommendations for international students: Required—TOEFL (minimum score 550 paper-based; 213 computer-based; 80 iBT). *Application deadline:* For fall admission, 4/15 priority date for domestic students, 3/15 for international students; for spring admission, 10/15 for domestic students, 9/1 for international students. Applications are processed on a rolling basis. Application fee: $35. Electronic applications accepted. *Expenses:* Tuition, state resident: full-time $6966; part-time $387 per credit. Tuition, nonresident: full-time $11,146; part-time $619 per credit. Required fees: $1614.40; $133.24 per credit. Part-time tuition and fees vary according to campus/location. *Financial support:* Unspecified assistantships available. Support available to part-time students. Financial award application deadline: 2/15; financial award applicants required to submit FAFSA. *Unit head:* Dr. Paul Christ, MBA Director and Graduate Coordinator, 610-425-5000 Ext. 3232, E-mail: mba@wcupa.edu. *Application contact:* Dr. Paul Christ, MBA Director and Graduate Coordinator, 610-425-5000 Ext. 3232, E-mail: mba@wcupa.edu.

Western Connecticut State University, Division of Graduate Studies and External Programs, Ancell School of Business, Program in Business Administration, Danbury, CT 06810-6885. Offers accounting (MBA); business administration (MBA). Part-time programs available. *Students:* 5 full-time (1 woman), 45 part-time (22 women); includes 2 Asian, non-Hispanic/Latino; 3 Hispanic/Latino. Average age 34. In 2010, 13 master's awarded. *Degree requirements:* For master's, comprehensive exam, completion of program within 8 years. *Entrance requirements:* For master's, GMAT. Additional exam requirements/recommendations for international students: Recommended—TOEFL (minimum score 550 paper-based; 213 computer-based; 79 iBT), IELTS (minimum score 6). *Application deadline:* For fall admission, 8/5 priority date for domestic students; for spring admission, 1/5 priority date for domestic students. Applications are processed on a rolling basis. Application fee: $50. *Expenses:* Tuition, state resident: full-time $5012; part-time $417 per credit hour. Tuition, nonresident: full-time $13,962; part-time $423 per credit hour. Required fees: $3886. Full-time tuition and fees vary according to course load, degree level and program. *Financial support:* In 2010–11, 1 student received support. Application deadline: 5/1. *Unit head:* Dr. Fred Tesch, MBA Coordinator, 203-837-8654, Fax: 203-837-8527. *Application contact:* Chris Shankle, Associate Director of Graduate Studies, 203-837-9005, Fax: 203-837-8326, E-mail: shanklec@wcsu.edu.

Western Illinois University, School of Graduate Studies, College of Business and Technology, Program in Business Administration, Macomb, IL 61455-1390. Offers MBA. *Accreditation:* AACSB. Part-time programs available. *Students:* 64 full-time (28 women), 54 part-time (19 women); includes 7 minority (4 Black or African American, non-Hispanic/Latino; 1 American Indian or Alaska Native, non-Hispanic/Latino; 1 Asian, non-Hispanic/Latino; 1 Hispanic/Latino), 7 international. Average age 30. 55 applicants, 55% accepted. In 2010, 39 master's awarded. *Degree requirements:* For master's, thesis or alternative. *Entrance requirements:* For master's, GMAT. Additional exam requirements/recommendations for international students: Required—TOEFL (minimum score 550 paper-based; 213 computer-based; 80 iBT). *Application deadline:* Applications are processed on a rolling basis. Application fee: $30. Electronic applications accepted. *Expenses:* Tuition, state resident: full-time $6370; part-time $265.40 per credit hour. Tuition, nonresident: full-time $12,740; part-time $530.80 per credit hour. Required fees: $75.67 per credit hour. *Financial support:* In 2010–11, 27 students received support, including 27 research assistantships with full tuition reimbursements available (averaging $7,280 per year). Financial award applicants required to submit FAFSA. *Unit head:* Dr. John Drea, Associate Dean, 309-298-2442. *Application contact:* Evelyn Hoing, Assistant Director of Graduate Studies, 309-298-1806, Fax: 309-298-2345, E-mail: grad-office@wiu.edu.

Western New England University, School of Business, Program in Business Administration (General), Springfield, MA 01119. Offers general business (MBA); sport management (MBA). *Accreditation:* AACSB. Part-time and evening/weekend programs available. *Students:* 107 part-time (44 women); includes 3 Black or African American, non-Hispanic/Latino; 1 Asian, non-Hispanic/Latino; 2 Hispanic/Latino; 1 Two or more races, non-Hispanic/Latino, 1 international. In 2010, 44 master's awarded. *Entrance requirements:* For master's, GMAT, 2 letters of reference, resume. *Application deadline:* Applications are processed on a rolling basis. Application fee: $30. *Expenses:* Tuition: Full-time $35,582. *Financial support:* Available to part-time students.

Applicants required to submit FAFSA. *Unit head:* Dr. Julie Siciliano, Dean, 413-782-1231. *Application contact:* Matt Fox, Director of Recruiting and Marketing for Adult Learners, 413-782-1249, Fax: 413-782-1779, E-mail: ce@wnec.edu.

Westminster College, The Bill and Vieve Gore School of Business, Salt Lake City, UT 84105-3697. Offers accountancy (M Acc); business administration (MBA, Certificate); technology management (MBATM). *Accreditation:* ACBSP. Part-time and evening/weekend programs available. Postbaccalaureate distance learning degree programs offered (minimal on-campus study). *Faculty:* 35 full-time (9 women), 22 part-time/adjunct (4 women). *Students:* 175 full-time (44 women), 242 part-time (61 women); includes 2 Black or African American, non-Hispanic/Latino; 2 American Indian or Alaska Native, non-Hispanic/Latino; 8 Asian, non-Hispanic/Latino; 6 Hispanic/Latino; 2 Two or more races, non-Hispanic/Latino, 6 international. Average age 32. 342 applicants, 46% accepted, 113 enrolled. In 2010, 196 master's, 75 other advanced degrees awarded. *Degree requirements:* For master's, international trip, minimum grade of C in all classes. *Entrance requirements:* For master's, GMAT, 2 professional recommendations, employer letter of support, personal resume, essay questions, official transcripts. Additional exam requirements/ recommendations for international students: Required—TOEFL (minimum score 600 paper-based; 250 computer-based; 100 iBT), IELTS (minimum score 7). *Application deadline:* Applications are processed on a rolling basis. Application fee: $50. Electronic applications accepted. *Expenses:* Contact institution. *Financial support:* In 2010–11, 222 students received support. Career-related internships or fieldwork and tuition reimbursement, tuition remission available. Support available to part-time students. Financial award applicants required to submit FAFSA. *Faculty research:* Innovation and entrepreneurship, business strategy and change, financial analysis and capital budgeting, leadership development. Total annual research expenditures: $100,000. *Unit head:* Gary Daynes, Dean, 801-832-2600, Fax: 801-832-3106, E-mail: gdaynes@westminstercollege.edu. *Application contact:* Joel Bauman, Vice President of Enrollment Services, 801-832-2200, Fax: 801-832-3101, E-mail: admission@westminstercollege.edu.

Wichita State University, Graduate School, W. Frank Barton School of Business, Department of Business, Wichita, KS 67260. Offers EMBA, MBA, MSN/MBA. *Accreditation:* AACSB. Part-time and evening/weekend programs available. *Unit head:* Angela Jones, Director, 316-978-3230, E-mail: angela.jones@wichita.edu. *Application contact:* Angela Jones, Director, 316-978-3230, E-mail: angela.jones@wichita.edu.

Widener University, School of Business Administration, Chester, PA 19013-5792. Offers MBA, MHA, MHR, MS, JD/MBA, MD/MBA, MD/MHA, ME/MBA, Psy D/MBA, Psy D/MHA, Psy D/MHR. *Accreditation:* AACSB. Part-time and evening/weekend programs available. *Faculty:* 14 full-time (6 women), 6 part-time/adjunct (2 women). *Students:* 25 full-time (12 women), 122 part-time (55 women); includes 34 minority (16 Black or African American, non-Hispanic/Latino; 2 American Indian or Alaska Native, non-Hispanic/Latino; 11 Asian, non-Hispanic/Latino; 3 Hispanic/Latino; 1 Native Hawaiian or other Pacific Islander, non-Hispanic/Latino; 1 Two or more races, non-Hispanic/Latino), 15 international. Average age 34. 254 applicants, 91% accepted. In 2010, 85 master's awarded. *Entrance requirements:* For master's, minimum GPA of 2.5. *Application deadline:* For fall admission, 8/1 priority date for domestic students; for spring admission, 12/1 for domestic students. Applications are processed on a rolling basis. Application fee: $25 ($300 for international students). Electronic applications accepted. *Expenses:* Contact institution. *Financial support:* In 2010–11, 11 research assistantships with full tuition reimbursements were awarded; career-related internships or fieldwork, Federal Work-Study, and traineeships also available. Support available to part-time students. Financial award application deadline: 5/1. *Faculty research:* Cost containment in health care, human resource management, productivity, globalization. *Unit head:* Dr. Savas Ozatalay, Dean, 610-499-4300, Fax: 610-499-4615. *Application contact:* Ann Seltzer, Graduate Enrollment Administrator, 610-499-4305, E-mail: apseltzer@widener.edu.

Wilfrid Laurier University, Faculty of Graduate and Postdoctoral Studies, School of Business and Economics, Business Administration Program, Waterloo, ON N2L 3C5, Canada. Offers co-op (MBA); full-time (MBA); part-time (MBA). *Accreditation:* AACSB. Part-time and evening/weekend programs available. *Faculty:* 67 full-time (20 women), 12 part-time/adjunct (4 women). *Students:* 156 full-time (62 women), 417 part-time (135 women), 14 international. 383 applicants, 61% accepted, 101 enrolled. In 2010, 247 master's awarded. *Degree requirements:* For master's, thesis. *Entrance requirements:* For master's, GMAT, minimum 2 years of business experience (for 12-month or part-time MBA formats), minimum B average in 4-year BA program. Additional exam requirements/recommendations for international students: Required—TOEFL (minimum score 89 iBT). *Application deadline:* For fall admission, 5/1 priority date for domestic students, 1/30 priority date for international students. Applications are processed on a rolling basis. Application fee: $125. Electronic applications accepted. Tuition and fees charges are reported in Canadian dollars. *Expenses:* Tuition, area resident: Full-time $15,300 Canadian dollars; part-time $1200 Canadian dollars per credit. International tuition: $21,300 Canadian dollars full-time. Required fees: $650 Canadian dollars; $100 Canadian dollars per credit. Tuition and fees vary according to course load, degree level, campus/location and program. *Financial support:* In

2010–11, 14 research assistantships were awarded; career-related internships or fieldwork, scholarships/grants, health care benefits, and unspecified assistantships also available. *Unit head:* Dr. Hugh Munroe, Director, 519-884-0710 Ext. 2556, Fax: 519-884-0210, E-mail: hmunro@wlu.ca. *Application contact:* Jennifer Williams, Graduate Admissions and Records Officer, 519-884-0710 Ext. 3536, Fax: 519-884-1020, E-mail: graduatestudies@wlu.ca.

Wilfrid Laurier University, Faculty of Graduate and Postdoctoral Studies, School of Business and Economics, Department of Business, Waterloo, ON N2L 3C5, Canada. Offers accounting (PhD); finance (M Fin); financial economics (PhD); marketing (PhD); operations and supply chain management (PhD); organizational behavior and human resource management (M Sc); organizational behaviour and human resource management (PhD); supply chain management (M Sc); technology management (EMTM). Part-time and evening/weekend programs available. *Faculty:* 67 full-time (20 women), 12 part-time/adjunct (4 women). *Students:* 20 full-time (11 women), 1 part-time (0 women), 5 international. 80 applicants, 28% accepted, 3 enrolled. In 2010, 6 master's, 1 doctorate awarded. *Degree requirements:* For master's, thesis optional; for doctorate, comprehensive exam, thesis/dissertation. *Entrance requirements:* For master's, GMAT, 4-year honors degree with minimum B+ average; for doctorate, GMAT, master's degree, minimum B+ average. Additional exam requirements/recommendations for international students: Required—TOEFL (minimum score 89 iBT). *Application deadline:* For fall admission, 1/15 priority date for domestic and international students. Application fee: $125. Electronic applications accepted. Tuition and fees charges are reported in Canadian dollars. *Expenses:* Tuition, area resident: Full-time $15,300 Canadian dollars; part-time $1200 Canadian dollars per credit. International tuition: $21,300 Canadian dollars full-time. Required fees: $650 Canadian dollars; $100 Canadian dollars per credit. Tuition and fees vary according to course load, degree level, campus/location and program. *Financial support:* In 2010–11, 27 fellowships, 1 research assistantship, 27 teaching assistantships were awarded; career-related internships or fieldwork, scholarships/grants, health care benefits, and unspecified assistantships also available. *Faculty research:* Financial economics, management and organizational behavior, operations and supply chain management. *Unit head:* Dr. Hamid Noori, Director, 519-884-0710 Ext. 2571, Fax: 519-884-2357, E-mail: sbephdmasters@wlu.ca. *Application contact:* Jennifer Williams, Graduate Admission and Records Officer, 519-884-0710 Ext. 3536, Fax: 519-884-1020, E-mail: gradstudies@wlu.ca.

Wilkes University, College of Graduate and Professional Studies, Jay S. Sidhu School of Business and Leadership, Wilkes-Barre, PA 18766-0002. Offers accounting (MBA); entrepreneurship (MBA); finance (MBA); health care administration (MBA); human resource management (MBA); international business (MBA); marketing (MBA); operations management (MBA); organizational leadership and development (MBA). *Accreditation:* ACBSP. Part-time and evening/weekend programs available. *Students:* 39 full-time (16 women), 146 part-time (71 women); includes 5 Black or African American, non-Hispanic/Latino; 2 Asian, non-Hispanic/Latino; 1 Hispanic/Latino; 1 Two or more races, non-Hispanic/Latino, 16 international. Average age 30. In 2010, 85 master's awarded. *Entrance requirements:* For master's, GMAT. Additional exam requirements/recommendations for international students: Required—TOEFL (minimum score 550 paper-based; 213 computer-based; 79 iBT). *Application deadline:* Applications are processed on a rolling basis. Application fee: $45 ($65 for international students). Electronic applications accepted. *Expenses:* Contact institution. *Financial support:* Federal Work-Study and unspecified assistantships available. Financial award application deadline: 3/1; financial award applicants required to submit FAFSA. *Unit head:* Dr. Paul Browne, Dean, 570-408-4701, Fax: 570-408-7846, E-mail: paul.browne@wilkes.edu. *Application contact:* Kathleen Houlihan, Director of Graduate Studies, 570-408-3235, Fax: 570-408-7846, E-mail: kathleen.houlihan@wilkes.edu.

Willamette University, George H. Atkinson Graduate School of Management, Salem, OR 97301-3931. Offers MBA, JD/MBA. *Accreditation:* AACSB; NASPAA. Part-time and evening/weekend programs available. *Faculty:* 17 full-time (4 women), 26 part-time/adjunct (8 women). *Students:* 203 full-time (85 women), 104 part-time (49 women); includes 43 minority (9 Black or African American, non-Hispanic/Latino; 1 American Indian or Alaska Native, non-Hispanic/Latino; 16 Asian, non-Hispanic/Latino; 13 Hispanic/Latino; 4 Two or more races, non-Hispanic/Latino), 73 international. Average age 28. 299 applicants, 86% accepted, 132 enrolled. In 2010, 100 master's awarded. *Degree requirements:* For master's, minimum cumulative GPA of 3.0. *Entrance requirements:* For master's, GMAT or GRE (for Early Career MBA and MBA for Career Change); GMAT (for MBA for Professionals only), essays, transcripts, references, resume, interview. Additional exam requirements/recommendations for international students: Required—TOEFL (minimum score 570 paper-based; 230 computer-based; 88 iBT), IELTS (minimum score 6.5). *Application deadline:* For fall admission, 1/10 priority date for domestic and international students; for winter admission, 3/1 priority date for domestic and international students; for spring admission, 5/1 priority date for domestic and international students. Applications are processed on a rolling basis. Application fee: $0. Electronic applications accepted. *Expenses:* Contact institution. *Financial support:* In 2010–11, 177 students received support, including 12 research assistantships with tuition reimbursements

available (averaging $1,500 per year); career-related internships or fieldwork, Federal Work-Study, scholarships/grants, unspecified assistantships, and scholarships are merit-based also available. Financial award application deadline: 5/1; financial award applicants required to submit FAFSA. *Faculty research:* Entrepreneurship, organizational behavior, social networks, general management, finance, marketing, public management, human resources, social networks, angel investing, public budgeting, operations. *Unit head:* Dr. Debra J. Ringold, Dean and JELD-WEN Professor of Free Enterprise, 503-370-6440, Fax: 503-370-3011, E-mail: dringold@willamette.edu. *Application contact:* Aimee Akimoff, Director of Recruitment, 503-370-6167, Fax: 503-370-3011, E-mail: aakimoff@willamette.edu.

Woodbury University, School of Business and Management, Burbank, CA 91504-1099. Offers business administration (MBA); organizational leadership (MA). *Accreditation:* ACBSP. Part-time and evening/weekend programs available. *Faculty:* 10 full-time (3 women), 8 part-time/adjunct (1 woman). *Students:* 178 full-time (109 women), 41 part-time (22 women); includes 66 minority (17 Black or African American, non-Hispanic/Latino; 12 Asian, non-Hispanic/Latino; 37 Hispanic/Latino), 45 international. Average age 30. 92 applicants, 54% accepted, 32 enrolled. In 2010, 84 master's awarded. *Entrance requirements:* For master's, GMAT, transcripts, resume. Additional exam requirements/recommendations for international students: Required—TOEFL (minimum score 550 paper-based; 220 computer-based; 83 iBT), IELTS (minimum score 6.5). *Application deadline:* For fall admission, 8/1 priority date for domestic students; for spring admission, 12/1 for domestic and international students. Applications are processed on a rolling basis. Application fee: $35 ($50 for international students). *Expenses:* Tuition: Full-time $10,548; part-time $879 per credit. Required fees: $8 per credit. $50 per semester. One-time fee: $110. *Financial support:* In 2010–11, 13 students received support. Scholarships/grants available. *Faculty research:* Total quality management, leadership. *Unit head:* Dr. Andre Van Niekerk, Dean, 818-767-0888 Ext. 264, Fax: 818-767-0032. *Application contact:* Ani Khukoyan, Assistant Director, Graduate Admissions, 818-767-0888 Ext. 224, Fax: 818-767-7520, E-mail: ani.khukoyan@woodbury.edu.

Worcester Polytechnic Institute, Graduate Studies, School of Business, Worcester, MA 01609-2280. Offers information technology (MS), including information security management; management (Graduate Certificate); marketing and technological innovation (MS); operations design and leadership (MS); technology (MBA). *Accreditation:* AACSB. Part-time and evening/weekend programs available. Postbaccalaureate distance learning degree programs offered (minimal on-campus study). *Faculty:* 13 full-time (7 women), 9 part-time/adjunct (2 women). *Students:* 112 full-time (53 women), 135 part-time (33 women); includes 5 Black or African American, non-Hispanic/Latino; 1 Hispanic/Latino; 15 Native Hawaiian or other Pacific Islander, non-Hispanic/Latino, 105 international. 396 applicants, 67% accepted, 79 enrolled. In 2010, 69 degrees awarded. *Degree requirements:* For master's, thesis optional. *Entrance requirements:* For master's, GMAT (MBA), GMAT or GRE General Test (MS), resume; for Graduate Certificate, GMAT or GRE General Test, statement of purpose, 3 letters of recommendation. Additional exam requirements/recommendations for international students: Required—TOEFL (minimum score 550 paper-based; 213 computer-based; 79 iBT), IELTS (minimum score 6.5). *Application deadline:* For fall admission, 6/1 priority date for domestic and international students; for spring admission, 11/1 priority date for domestic students, 10/1 priority date for international students. Applications are processed on a rolling basis. Application fee: $70. Electronic applications accepted. *Expenses:* Tuition: Full-time $20,862; part-time $1159 per term. One-time fee: $15. *Financial support:* Career-related internships or fieldwork, institutionally sponsored loans, scholarships/grants, and unspecified assistantships available. Financial award application deadline: 6/1; financial award applicants required to submit FAFSA. *Faculty research:* Organizational aesthetics, resistance in organizations, dynamics of product innovation, economic approaches to productivity, corporate earnings forecasts and value relevance, ERP implementation, improving Web accessibility, information quality assessment, measuring strategic and transactional IT, website quality, service operations modeling, healthcare operations and performance analysis, loan process design. *Unit head:* Dr. Mark Rice, Dean, 508-831-4665, Fax: 508-831-5218, E-mail: rice@wpi.edu. *Application contact:* Alyssa Bates, Director, Graduate Management Programs, 508-831-4665, Fax: 508-831-5720, E-mail: ajbates@wpi.edu.

Worcester State University, Graduate Studies, Program in Management, Worcester, MA 01602-2597. Offers accounting (MS); managerial leadership (MS). Part-time and evening/weekend programs available. *Faculty:* 1 (woman) full-time, 1 part-time/adjunct (0 women). *Students:* 7 full-time (2 women), 12 part-time (5 women); includes 1 Black or African American, non-Hispanic/Latino; 1 Two or more races, non-Hispanic/Latino, 4 international. Average age 28. 21 applicants, 76% accepted, 11 enrolled. In 2010, 4 master's awarded. *Degree requirements:* For master's, comprehensive exam (for some programs), thesis optional. *Entrance requirements:* Additional exam requirements/recommendations for international students: Required—TOEFL (minimum score 500 paper-based; 61 iBT). *Application deadline:* Applications are processed on a rolling basis. Application fee: $40. Electronic applications accepted. *Expenses:* Tuition, state resident: full-time $2700; part-time $150 per credit. Tuition, nonresident: full-time $2700; part-time $150 per credit. Required fees:

$2016; $112 per credit. *Financial support:* In 2010–11, 2 students received support, including 2 research assistantships with full tuition reimbursements available (averaging $4,800 per year); career-related internships or fieldwork, scholarships/grants, and unspecified assistantships also available. Financial award application deadline: 3/1; financial award applicants required to submit FAFSA. *Unit head:* Dr. Laurie Dahlin, Coordinator, 508-929-8084, Fax: 508-929-8048, E-mail: ldahlin@worcester.edu. *Application contact:* Sara Grady, Assistant Dean of Continuing Education, 508-929-8787, Fax: 508-929-8100, E-mail: sara.grady@worcester.edu.

Xavier University, Williams College of Business, Master of Business Administration Program, Cincinnati, OH 45207-3221. Offers business administration (Exec MBA, MBA); business intelligence (MBA); finance (MBA); international business (MBA); management information systems (MBA); marketing (MBA); MBA/MHSA; MSN/MBA. *Accreditation:* AACSB. Part-time and evening/weekend programs available. *Faculty:* 37 full-time (13 women), 9 part-time/adjunct (2 women). *Students:* 200 full-time (60 women), 735 part-time (239 women); includes 128 minority (48 Black or African American, non-Hispanic/Latino; 3 American Indian or Alaska Native, non-Hispanic/Latino; 54 Asian, non-Hispanic/Latino; 22 Hispanic/Latino; 1 Native Hawaiian or other Pacific Islander, non-Hispanic/Latino), 32 international. Average age 30. 223 applicants, 85% accepted, 139 enrolled. In 2010, 323 master's awarded. *Degree requirements:* For master's, capstone course. *Entrance requirements:* For master's, GMAT. Additional exam requirements/recommendations for international students: Required—TOEFL (minimum score 550 paper-based; 213 computer-based; 80 iBT). *Application deadline:* For fall admission, 8/1 priority date for domestic students, 5/1 for international students; for spring admission, 12/1 priority date for domestic students, 9/1 for international students. Applications are processed on a rolling basis. Application fee: $35. Electronic applications accepted. *Expenses:* Contact institution. *Financial support:* In 2010–11, 176 students received support. Scholarships/grants, tuition waivers (partial), and unspecified assistantships available. Financial award application deadline: 3/1; financial award applicants required to submit FAFSA. *Unit head:* Dr. Hema Krishnan, Associate Dean, 513-745-3206, Fax: 513-745-3455, E-mail: krishnan@xavier.edu. *Application contact:* Anna Marie Whelan, Assistant Director, MBA Programs, 513-745-3525, Fax: 513-745-2929, E-mail: whelana@xavier.edu.

Yale University, Yale School of Management and Graduate School of Arts and Sciences, Doctoral Program in Management, New Haven, CT 06520. Offers accounting (PhD); financial economics (PhD); marketing (PhD); organizations and management (PhD). *Accreditation:* AACSB. *Faculty:* 68 full-time (12 women), 1 (woman) part-time/adjunct. *Students:* 32 full-time (9 women); includes 3 Asian, non-Hispanic/Latino, 16 international. Average age 28. 441 applicants, 4% accepted, 6 enrolled. In 2010, 9 doctorates awarded. *Degree requirements:* For doctorate, comprehensive exam, thesis/dissertation. *Entrance requirements:* For doctorate, GMAT or GRE General Test. Additional exam requirements/recommendations for international students: Required—TOEFL, IELTS. *Application deadline:* For fall admission, 1/2 for domestic and international students. Application fee: $100. Electronic applications accepted. *Expenses:* Contact institution. *Financial support:* In 2010–11, 30 students received support, including 30 fellowships with full tuition reimbursements available, 30 research assistantships with full tuition reimbursements available, 30 teaching assistantships with full tuition reimbursements available; institutionally sponsored loans, scholarships/grants, and health care benefits also available. Financial award application deadline: 1/2. *Faculty research:* Pricing of options and futures, term structure of interest rates, use of accounting numbers in debt contracts, product differentiation, e-commerce and marketing, behavioral finance. *Unit head:* Carla Mills, Registrar, 203-432-3955, Fax: 203-432-0342, E-mail: carla.mills@yale.edu. *Application contact:* Carla Mills, Registrar, 203-432-3955, Fax: 203-432-0342, E-mail: carla.mills@yale.edu.

Yale University, Yale School of Management, Program in Business Administration, New Haven, CT 06520. Offers MBA, PhD, MBA/JD, MBA/M Arch, MBA/M Div, MBA/MA, MBA/MEM, MBA/MF, MBA/MFA, MBA/MPH, MBA/PhD, MD/MBA. *Accreditation:* AACSB. *Faculty:* 68 full-time (13 women), 27 part-time/adjunct (6 women). *Students:* 465 full-time (165 women). Average age 28. 2,963 applicants, 17% accepted, 231 enrolled. In 2010, 187 master's, 9 doctorates awarded. Terminal master's awarded for partial completion of doctoral program. *Degree requirements:* For master's, international experience; for doctorate, comprehensive exam, thesis/dissertation. *Entrance requirements:* For master's, GMAT or GRE; for doctorate, GMAT or GRE General Test (preferred). Additional exam requirements/recommendations for international students: Required—TOEFL, Pearson Test of English (PTE), or IELTS. *Application deadline:* For fall admission, 10/7 priority date for domestic and international students; for winter admission, 1/6 priority date for domestic and international students; for spring admission, 3/15 priority date for domestic students, 3/17 priority date for international students. Application fee: $220. Electronic applications accepted. *Expenses:* Contact institution. *Financial support:* Career-related internships or fieldwork, Federal Work-Study, institutionally sponsored loans, and scholarships/grants available. Financial award application deadline: 3/1; financial award applicants required to submit FAFSA. *Faculty research:* Finance, strategy, marketing, leadership, operations. *Application contact:* Bruce DelMonico, Director of Admissions, 203-432-5635, Fax: 203-432-7004, E-mail: mba.admissions@yale.edu.

York College of Pennsylvania, Department of Business Administration, York, PA 17405-7199. Offers accounting (MBA); continuous improvement (MBA); finance (MBA); management (MBA); marketing (MBA). *Accreditation:* ACBSP. Part-time and evening/weekend programs available. *Faculty:* 11 full-time (2 women), 5 part-time/adjunct (1 woman). *Students:* 20 full-time (6 women), 111 part-time (44 women); includes 4 Black or African American, non-Hispanic/Latino; 1 Asian, non-Hispanic/Latino; 4 Hispanic/Latino, 2 international. Average age 30. 53 applicants, 91% accepted, 40 enrolled. In 2010, 45 master's awarded. *Entrance requirements:* For master's, GMAT. Additional exam requirements/recommendations for international students: Required—TOEFL (minimum score 530 paper-based; 200 computer-based; 72 iBT). *Application deadline:* For fall admission, 7/15 priority date for domestic students; for spring admission, 12/15 priority date for domestic students. Applications are processed on a rolling basis. Application fee: $60. Electronic applications accepted. *Expenses:* Tuition: Full-time $11,520; part-time $640 per credit hour. Required fees: $1500; $660 per year. *Financial support:* Scholarships/grants available. Financial award application deadline: 4/15; financial award applicants required to submit FAFSA. *Unit head:* Dr. David Greisler, MBA Director, 717-815-6410, Fax: 717-600-3999, E-mail: dgreisle@ycp.edu. *Application contact:* Brenda Adams, Assistant Director, MBA Program, 717-815-1749, Fax: 717-600-3999, E-mail: badams@ycp.edu.

Master of Business Administration

Programs of Study

The Donahue Graduate School of Business at Duquesne University in Pittsburgh, Pennsylvania, prepares responsible leaders who are capable of transforming organizations, communities, and the world. The School challenges its students to reach their full potential, reflecting the University's century-long commitment to ethics and service, excellence, and innovation.

The Donahue School is among the elite 5 percent of graduate business schools accredited by AACSB International. It is ranked among the Global Top 20 by Beyond Grey Pinstripes for integrating social and environmental stewardship (Aspen Institute, 2009). The Princeton Review includes Duquesne among the most connected campuses in terms of its use of technology (2010), and in a recent survey by the Academy of Management Learning and Education, Duquesne was named one of the top three universities in the nation for infusing ethics content into the graduate business curriculum.

The Donahue School offers a portfolio of current and managerially relevant M.B.A. curricula for full-time students and working professionals.

The **Evening M.B.A.** program offers a traditional approach to M.B.A. course work and convenient evening and weekend classes for busy professionals. Duquesne's M.B.A. program has been providing professional business career preparation for over fifty years and enjoys a productive, ongoing relationship with high-profile employers in Western Pennsylvania.

Classes are offered at Duquesne's campus in the heart of Pittsburgh's downtown business district, as well as at the Regional Learning Alliance in Cranberry Township, a northern suburb and emergent office park community. Students may begin their studies in August or January, and classes are offered year-round. Students can complete the evening M.B.A. program in approximately two years if taking a full-time course load or three years if studying on a part-time basis. More details can be found at http://www.duq.edu/business/grad.

An accelerated, one-year daytime cohort program, the **M.B.A. Sustainability** explicitly focuses on managing social, environmental, and financial capital for prosperity today without compromising resources for tomorrow. This internationally recognized, 45-credit program integrates rigorous course work in all business disciplines with practical application of global best practices in sustainability through an innovative delivery model that features live consulting projects, team teaching, cross-functional integration, professional skill development, and international travel. Students begin their studies

in August and complete the program requirements at the end of the following July.

Two faculty-supervised consulting engagements anchor the M.B.A. Sustainability program and provide an unmatched proving ground for managing social, environmental, and financial resources. Through these contemporary problem-solving experiences, small teams of students make an immediate bottom line impact for multinational corporations, regional businesses, government, and not-for-profit organizations.

M.B.A. Sustainability students investigate international best practices firsthand, expand their perspectives by studying global economics at a partnering university abroad, and collaborate on field projects with students at a host university. They interface regularly with international thought leaders, corporate executives, and alumni advisers through their study trips, an annual sustainability symposium, ethics luncheons, Idea Cafes and Net Impact activities. Sustainability fellows, chosen on merit, support faculty research and coauthor papers for publication. Visit http://mba.sustainability.duq.edu for more inforrmation.

The newly launched, full-time **Master of Accountancy (M.Acc.)** is a unique program of study that responds to three emerging areas of critical importance to the accounting

profession: forensic accounting, ethics, and regulation and reporting. Students enrolled in the program will complete in-depth course work in these areas by taking classes such as Fraud Examination, SEC Reporting, Accounting Ethics, Advanced Forensic Techniques, and International Financial Reporting. Students will benefit significantly from face-to-face classroom interaction with award-winning, knowledgeable, and experienced accounting faculty members.

The **Master of Science in Information Systems Management (M.S.I.S.M.)** program prepares students for IS management and analytical positions involving the strategic role of information technology in modern business. Students graduating with an M.S.I.S.M. degree pursue careers as business/systems analysts, information systems managers, and IT auditors, among many others.

Research Facilities

The Gumberg Library's primary mission is to support the teaching, learning, and research of Duquesne students, faculty, and staff. The library's Web site (http://www.duq.edu/library) provides a convenient gateway to research databases, electronic journals and books, library services, and DuCat, the library's catalog. Reference librarians are available to provide assistance 24 hours a day, 365 days a year through Duquesne's online chat service, Ask A Librarian.

Duquesne's Investment Center offers students instant access to information and sophisticated analytical techniques in a classroom setting that mimics worldwide trading operations. The center provides data feeds that supply real-time news and market data on stocks, bonds, international markets, futures, and options and other securities. Also, a state-of-the-art technology center features three technology-rich classroom learning centers that provide access to enterprise resource planning (ERP) software applications, and a general computer laboratory available for use by students and faculty members in courses throughout the graduate curriculum.

Financial Aid

A limited number of graduate assistantships, which provide up to 9 credits of tuition remission each semester and a monthly cash stipend, are available to evening students who take a full-time course load.

The M.B.A. Sustainability program considers all applicants for merit scholarships, research fellowships, and graduate assistantships.

Cost of Study

Evening M.B.A. and M.Acc. programs are billed on a per-credit basis. Tuition for the 2011–12 academic year was $922 per credit. An $88 University fee was added per credit.

The M.B.A. Sustainability program is billed in three equal installments. For the 2011–12 academic year, tuition and fees were $14,947 per semester, totaling $44,841 for the three-semester program. Tuition and fees do not include airfare, incidentals, or some meals for the mandatory international study trip.

Living and Housing Costs

On-campus housing is available to graduate students. The cost of room and board varies depending on the student's living arrangements. Details are available at the Office of Residence Life Web site at http://www.duq.edu/residence-life.

Student Group

The student body of approximately 350 students is diverse. The typical evening student is a working professional with about five years of experience; however, a significant portion of evening M.B.A. students takes the equivalent of a full-time schedule in evening classes, in some cases while working at the University as graduate assistants. Part-time students bring a rich, real-world perspective to classroom discussion and activities.

The M.B.A. Sustainability program is small and selective, and students take their classes as a cohort. In a typical year, students hail from around the country and the world and bring a wide variety of educational backgrounds and work experience to the intensive, one-year program, which focuses on active learning.

Location

Long noted as one of the world's great business centers, Pittsburgh combines the features of big-city living with many of the charms and personal characteristics of a much smaller town. Pittsburgh has one of the largest concentrations of corporate headquarters in the United States and has developed a strong civic identity and sense of pride in its rebirth as a modern urban community. Students from Duquesne and other colleges and universities in the city can choose from a wide variety of cultural, social, and sporting events and programs.

The University

Nestled in a private 49-acre campus in the heart of Pittsburgh, Duquesne University provides a unique world-renowned education that continues to be grounded in the values of the Holy Spirit Fathers who founded it in 1878. Faculty members are recognized time and again both nationally and internationally for their instruction and research, and their support and encouragement provide an energetic and productive environment in which students thrive.

Applying

Required application materials for all programs include an online application form, official transcripts and GMAT scores, two professional references/ratings, personal essays (questions vary by program), and a resume or vitae. The Test of English as a Foreign Language (TOEFL) is required for international students. Additional information can be found at http://www.duq.edu/business/grad.

The Evening M.B.A. program accepts new students in fall and spring. Application deadlines are May 1 for fall enrollment and October 1 for spring admissions. A separate application is required for candidates interested in graduate assistantships.

The M.B.A. Sustainability program admits one cohort per academic year. Early decision applications are accepted from September through December, and the regular decision deadline is March 31 for enrollment in August. Scholarships, fellowships, and graduate assistantships are granted on a merit basis, and all applicants are considered based on the strength of application materials. Visit http://mba.sustainability.duq.edu for more details.

The M.Acc. program admits one cohort per academic year. The application deadline is May 1 for fall enrollment. Financial assistance may be available.

Correspondence and Information

John F. Donahue Graduate School of Business
704 Rockwell Hall
Duquesne University
600 Forbes Avenue
Pittsburgh, Pennsylvania 15282
United States
Phone: 412-396-6276
E-mail: grad-bus@duq.edu (Evening M.B.A. or joint degree programs)
         sustainablemba@duq.edu (M.B.A. Sustainability program)
         kollar@duq.edu (M.Acc.)
Web sites: http://www.duq.edu/business/grad
              http://mba.sustainability.duq.edu

The Faculty

The faculty members of the Donahue Graduate School of Business are committed to teaching excellence, scholarship that focuses on real business problems, and developing creative academic-business partnerships. The academic and professional experiences of the faculty members are complemented by the executive adjunct faculty members who teach classes in their areas of expertise, directly relating their daily experiences to the material covered in the courses. Graduate students benefit from exposure to a roster of executives who share their knowledge and experience.

Please refer to the Donahue Graduate School of Business Web site for additional information:
http://www.business.duq.edu/faculty/AllFaculty.asp.

Master of Business Administration

Programs of Study

In today's competitive and ever-changing global marketplace, not only are employers seeking individuals with a solid understanding of core business principles, they are demanding that their executive team possess the managerial and leadership skills needed to achieve organizational success. Students gain the expertise and experience needed to take their careers to the next level by earning their M.B.A. at Florida Southern College. Students choose from a full-time weekday option or a flexible and convenient Saturday option. The Florida Southern College M.B.A. program is transformational, open to graduates with a degree in any major, and obtainable in sixteen months.

Recognized as a national leader in engaged learning, Florida Southern provides students with hands-on experience through real-world business situations. Experiential learning is woven into all course work. Through collaborations with peers, faculty, and business leaders, students actively participate in large-scale projects—learning what it means to build a team, take risks, set goals, implement the plan, and assess the results.

Internships are an integral component of the weekday program. Through FSC's partnerships with premier national and international companies, students have plenty of opportunities to gain practical work experience. FSC students have interned with top-notch companies such as The Walt Disney Company, ESPN, GEICO, NASA, Merrill Lynch, Publix Super Markets, and MetLife. The M.B.A. placement director assists students directly with internship placements and job opportunities.

An intensive, yet integrated, core curriculum combined with an active classroom approach provides students with a solid foundation of universal business knowledge—accounting, finance, marketing, and statistics—while also developing the persuasion, communication, and managerial skills necessary for successful organizational leadership.

All students begin their journey with two 2-credit-hour foundations (Flying Start) courses, held prior to beginning the core course sequence. The program also includes six 4-credit-hour courses and 16 elective credits for a total of 44 credit hours.

Classes in the weekday option meet in late afternoon and early evening to allow for work experience and internships earlier in the day. The Saturday option allows even more flexibility.

The Mentor Program, part of the Florida Southern M.B.A., provides students with insight into the day-to-day challenges of specific fields. Students explore career paths, build relationships with nurturing professionals, and see firsthand what opportunities are available to them after graduation.

FSC's dynamic classroom approach helps M.B.A. students master the team-building and communication skills necessary to manage teams and lead organizations through in-depth group projects and case studies. Professional networking and peer experience sharing are also benefits of the program.

Global awareness is an integral aspect of the Florida Southern M.B.A. experience. Global issues are at the heart of many of the courses—allowing students to gain insights into the problems, opportunities, and challenges of business in an international context. Students are encouraged to take advantage of the College's many global opportunities.

For example, the M.B.A. program's optional international summer study experience—studying manufacturing in China, trade in Brazil, or marketing in Europe, among other options—is a great opportunity for students to gain a better sense of issues affecting the global business environment through hands-on experience.

Research Facilities

A computer lab in the Barney Barnett School of Business and Economics offers software tailored to the needs of graduate business students. In addition, M.B.A. students have access to the College's new state-of-the-art Rinker Technology Center, as well as the extensive resources of the Roux Library and McKay Archives Center.

Graduates of Florida Southern's M.B.A. program understand the challenges and complexities of today's global business environment and are well-prepared for a successful career.

Financial Aid

A limited number of graduate assistantships are offered. For more information, prospective students should contact Dr. Nick Nugent, M.B.A. director. In addition, students may apply for financial aid by completing the Free Application for Federal Student Aid (FAFSA). Students should contact the M.B.A. Admissions Office at 863-680-4205 or the Financial Aid Office at 800-205-1600 (toll-free) for more information.

Cost of Study

Earning an M.B.A. is an investment of both time and money, and Florida Southern's M.B.A. program is offered at an incredible value. The tuition cost for the entire sixteen-month program is $25,675. Additional costs include books and supplies, personal expenses, and travel for the optional international study program. M.B.A. students who wish to live on campus (depending on space availability) also should plan for room and board expenses.

Living and Housing Costs

Any student living in a College (double occupancy) residence hall room will pay $8808 in room and board for the academic year. All students, living on campus or off, have access to campus amenities such as the modern Hollis Wellness Center and competition pool, high-tech computer labs, libraries and archives, and free, on-campus entertainment programming.

Location

Florida Southern College is situated on a picturesque 100-acre campus in Lakeland, Florida, located 30 minutes from Tampa and 45 minutes from Orlando. The College is less than an hour away from many of Florida's world-class beaches. The campus is home to the world's largest single-site collection of Frank Lloyd Wright architecture. With beautiful Lake Hollingsworth just across the street, water-skiing, sailing, and kayaking are popular pastimes. A 3-mile walking and biking path around the lake stays busy day and night, year-round, as students and neighbors take advantage of the weather and spectacular scenery to make their workouts more enjoyable. Lakeland's vibrant downtown—brimming with museums, sidewalk cafés, and charming retail shops—is within walking or biking distance. The city also has an active arts community, with year-round live performances planned in local venues.

The College

Founded in 1885, Florida Southern is a private, comprehensive, Methodist-affiliated college that offers fifty undergraduate programs and distinctive graduate programs in business, nursing, and education. Florida Southern College is a rapidly rising star among the nation's best private colleges. The College enrolls 2,427 students from forty-four states and thirty-one countries. A national leader in engaged learning, FSC provides students with numerous opportunities for internships, study abroad, collaborative research, performance, and service learning. The College is committed to the development of the whole student through vibrant student life programs that prepare graduates to make a positive, consequential impact on society.

Applying

Compelling candidates for Florida Southern's M.B.A. program possess strong academic ability, excellent interpersonal skills, and a desire to succeed. Rather than applying traditional admission requirements, FSC uses a combination of a student's GPA, GRE or GMAT score, as well as previous work experience to determine acceptance to the program. The program is open to graduates with a degree in any major, and GRE/GMAT test scores may be waived for students who meet certain requirements.

International students are encouraged to apply. The M.B.A. program has a significant global component at its core, and FSC believes that the enrollment of international students provides for lively interaction, discussion, and peer learning.

The priority application date is April 15, and the application deadline is June 1 for the August program start date. Thereafter, applications will continue to be accepted, and prospective students will be considered for admission as space is available.

Correspondence and Information

M.B.A. Admissions Office
Florida Southern College
111 Lake Hollingsworth Drive
Lakeland, Florida 33801-5698
United States
Phone: 863-680-4205
E-mail: fscmba@flsouthern.edu
Web site: http://www.flsouthern.edu/mba

Full-time M.B.A. students at Florida Southern develop the skills necessary to lead an organization, a small business, or a large company through internships, FSC's CEO Lecture Series and Executive Mentor program, and an optional international field experience.

The Faculty

Bringing years of business and consulting experience to the classroom, Florida Southern's faculty members are people in the know. Through thought-provoking lectures and informal discussions, they emphasize the application of concepts and principles to the practical world of work. The College's faculty members keep pace with the latest trends in the world of business by serving on boards for corporations, nonprofits, and civic organizations; practicing as CPAs; operating their own businesses; and serving as consultants to both local and national companies. All business faculty members bring practical experience to the classroom. They include a former vice president of marketing for a furniture company, a former human resources manager, an attorney, a former chief financial officer for a health-care facility, an international business consultant, and the owner/operator of several Florida restaurants.

For additional information about Florida Southern's faculty members, visit:
http://www.flsouthern.edu/business/faculty2.htm

Hagan School of Business

Programs of Study

The Hagan School of Business at Iona College offers classes leading to the Master of Business Administration (M.B.A.) degree as well as advanced certificates and the Post-Master's Certificate (PMC) in business administration. The dean of the Hagan School of Business, Vincent J. Calluzzo, Ph.D., is accredited by AACSB International.

Programs are designed to meet the needs of both full-time and part-time students and are organized on a trimester basis during the academic year, September to May. Two summer sessions are also available in May and July.

The goal of the M.B.A. program is to prepare students for management careers in business and other organizations. Effective managers must know themselves, work in teams, lead organizational change, and understand the macro factors affecting the future. They must also appreciate the role of information technology, ethically and socially responsible decision making, and the globalization of business. The School's concentrations in accounting, financial management, health-care management, human resource management, information systems management, management, and marketing provide solid knowledge in a specific functional area of business. Required course work consists of 27 credits in the core curriculum and 30 credits in the major and related fields. Waivers are possible out of the core curriculum if certain criteria are met. Students must complete at least 33 credits of graduate work at Iona. The M.B.A. program is offered at the main campus at New Rochelle and the Rockland Graduate Center in Pearl River, New York.

The program also offers certificate options in business continuity and risk management, e-commerce, general accounting, health-care management, infrastructure management, international business, long-term care services management, public accounting, and sports and entertainment studies, which can be completed concurrently with the M.B.A. curriculum. A minimum of 15 credits is required to earn the New York State–approved certificate.

Research Facilities

The new Center for Financial Market Studies, with a state-of-the-art trading floor, housed on the main floor of the Hagan School of Business, is scheduled to open during the fall 2011 semester. The center will offer a fully equipped, simulated trading environment with twenty high-end networked trading desks, continuous live data feeds from Bloomberg, real-time market quotes, and computerized trading.

Financial Aid

Iona College serves graduate students through a variety of state, federal, and institutional programs that include loans, scholarships, and assistantships. Scholarships are available based on undergraduate GPA or GRE/GMAT scores. To be eligible for federal loans, students must complete the FAFSA and the Iona College loan application. Tuition scholarships based on exceptional GMAT scores are available.

Cost of Study

Tuition for 2011–12 was $872 per credit. The initial application fee is $50. A $225 registration fee is charged for each trimester; the fee is $80 for the summer sessions. Other charges depend on the course of study.

Living and Housing Costs

While Iona does not offer on-campus graduate housing, the Office of Off-Campus Housing provides information about living off campus, estimated apartment costs, and contact information for student-friendly real estate agents.

Iona College grad student studying in the newly renovated Ryan Library.

Student Group

There are approximately 350 students enrolled in the M.B.A. program; 85 percent are part-time students.

Location

Iona's main campus is located on 35 acres in New Rochelle, New York, 20 minutes north of Manhattan. New Rochelle is a beautiful suburb of 70,000 located on Long Island Sound and is well served by mass transportation and highways. Iona's Rockland Graduate Center is 3 miles from the Palisades Parkway in Pearl River. Both campuses offer plentiful parking for evening students. The location of both campuses in the NYC metropolitan area allows students to take advantage of the many cultural, internship, and employment opportunities available.

The College

Iona College is a comprehensive, coed, Catholic college, founded in 1940 by the Congregation of Christian Brothers. The overall enrollment is about 4,200 students, of whom 900 study at the graduate level.

Iona offers study in more than twenty graduate areas and is accredited by the Middle States Association of Colleges and Schools. The Hagan School is accredited by AACSB International–The Association to Advance Collegiate Schools of Business.

Applying

Applications are available by mail or can be completed online at http://www.iona.edu/admissions/applyTolona.cfm.

Candidates for the Hagan School of Business may enter the graduate program in the fall (September), winter (November), or spring (March) trimester or in the summer session. The completed application, with fee, must be accompanied by two letters of recommendation, official transcripts from all postsecondary schools, and GMAT scores. All documents must be received no later than two weeks prior to the start of the session for which the candidate is applying.

Correspondence and Information

Director of Admissions
Hagan School of Business
Iona College
New Rochelle, New York 10801
United States
Phone: 914-633-2288
Fax: 914-633-2012
Web site: http://www.iona.edu/hagan

The Faculty

The faculty members of the Hagan School continuously strive to be excellent teachers. Teaching excellence mandates that faculty have an active scholarly agenda. Faculty scholarship often focuses on student learning or on furthering knowledge in the faculty member's discipline.

The academic and intellectual development of the School's students is the focus of Hagan's 38 full-time faculty members who are organized into five departments: Accounting; Finance, Business Economics and Legal Studies; Information Systems; Management and Business Administration; and Marketing and International Business.

The School's commitment to Catholic Higher Education in the Christian Brothers' Tradition coupled with its AACSB International accreditation assures that the student is at the core of everything done. Iona's rich heritage affirms its commitment to academic excellence, intellectual inquiry, and the values of justice, peace, and service to others. The Hagan School of Business seeks to develop confident, competent, and complete professionals who will be involved in both local and global communities in service to others.

For more information, visit: http://www.iona.edu/academic/ hagan/contacts.cfm.

Ryan Library on the campus of Iona College.

North Carolina State University

JENKINS MBA

Programs of Study

The Master of Business Administration (M.B.A.) at North Carolina State University (NC State) emphasizes the management of innovation and technology. Students take an integrated core curriculum, with a focus on technology, business processes, and practical applications, in a collaborative learning environment. Through simulations, case studies, and projects, students learn from real-world examples and experiences. Full-time students take a course in managerial effectiveness, which emphasizes communication skills, networking, negotiations, team skills, ethics, and social responsibility.

Students begin the program by taking core courses. Students in the full- and part-time programs then choose a concentration from biosciences management, entrepreneurship, financial management, marketing management, product innovation management, services management, and supply chain management. Full-time students complete the program in twenty-one months; part-time students complete the program in thirty-three months, and online students complete the program in twenty-four months.

Biosciences management is an exciting area of specialization at NC State. Life sciences comprise one of today's fastest-growing business sectors, offering new opportunities for those who can provide managerial leadership in a technology-focused environment. This concentration was designed and is taught by faculty members with extensive experience in biotechnology and pharmaceuticals, working closely with industry leaders located right in the Research Triangle Park.

Services management is another area of concentration. Services are dominating the economy, providing about three-fourths of all jobs—a rising share of which are highly skilled and technology-intensive. This is fueling a growing need for managers skilled in outsourcing, consulting, and process re-engineering. NC State's management and engineering faculties are at the forefront of curriculum development and research in the evolving discipline of services science, management and engineering (SSME), working with IBM and a growing list of other company partners.

The entrepreneurship concentration within the M.B.A. teaches students how to turn technologies into business, using real technologies as live case studies. Supported by the National Science Foundation, the Kenan Institute, and several other organizations, graduate students and faculty members in the College of Management work closely in teams with their counterparts in the science and engineering disciplines to identify, evaluate, and commercialize promising technologies. The TEC curriculum follows the complete product-development cycle. Students gain evaluation skills for commercializing new technologies, along with an understanding of what it takes to start and run a high-technology business. Students also interact with business experts and entrepreneurs from outside the University.

Research Facilities

The Poole College of Management is headquartered in Nelson Hall, which houses classrooms, computer labs, and the offices of the faculty members and students. Classrooms feature tiered seating, laptop connections, a wireless network, and complete multimedia facilities. The Poole College of Management's computer lab houses 100 microcomputers connected to a campuswide network. Students have access to a wide range of spreadsheet, word processing, database, statistical, and econometric software, along with several large databases.

D. H. Hill Library, which is located near the center of the campus, offers access to millions of volumes of books and journals and an extensive and growing collection of CD-ROM and electronic databases. Graduate students also have borrowing privileges at Duke University, North Carolina Central University, and the University of North Carolina at Chapel Hill.

Financial Aid

Graduate assistantships and scholarships are available to full-time students through the M.B.A. program. Grants and loan programs are available through the Graduate School and the University's Financial Aid Office.

Group work is an important part of the M.B.A. experience.

Classes are offered on the main campus and in the Research Triangle Park (RTP).

Cost of Study

For full-time students who are North Carolina residents, tuition and fees in 2011–12 were $8379 per semester; the estimated total for living expenses, including tuition and fees, books, medical insurance, housing, food, clothing, transportation, and other miscellaneous items, was $15,000 per semester. Tuition and fees for full-time nonresidents were $14,646 per semester. Part-time students on the main campus who are North Carolina residents paid $6206 per semester for tuition and fees only; nonresidents paid $10,906. Part-time students on the RTP campus or in the online program who are North Carolina residents paid $4494; nonresidents paid $8168.

Living and Housing Costs

On-campus dormitory facilities are provided for unmarried graduate students. In 2011–12, the rent for double occupancy rooms started at $2420 per semester. Accommodations in the newest residence hall for graduate students cost $2755 per semester (Wolf Village). Apartments for married students in King Village rented for $560 per month for a studio, $620 for a one-bedroom apartment, and $715 for a two-bedroom apartment.

Student Group

Almost all M.B.A. students have professional work experience, many in high-technology industries, such as telecommunications or software, and others in industries such as health care or financial services, in which technology is the key to a competitive advantage. A technical background is not essential for the M.B.A., but all students must be willing to learn about technology and the management challenges it creates. More than 75 percent of M.B.A. students have undergraduate degrees in business, computer science, sciences, or engineering. The rest come from a variety of fields, including the social sciences and humanities.

The average full-time M.B.A. student has four years of work experience. The average part-time student has seven years of professional experience. Women comprise approximately 30 percent of each entering full-time class; members of minority groups account for approximately 15 percent; international students account for approximately 33 percent of the full-time class.

Student Outcomes

The placement and promotion of graduates is the strongest testament to the value of the NC State M.B.A. program. The program's alumni include managers, entrepreneurs, and innovators in all fields and in all sizes of companies. Recent employers include SAS Institute, IBM, Progress Energy, Red Hat, John Deere, GlaxoSmithKline, Cisco Systems, and several local start-up ventures.

Location

Raleigh, the state capital, has a population of 405,791. Nearby is the Research Triangle Park, one of the largest and fastest-growing research institutions of its type in the country. The Raleigh metro area population is 1,742,816. The University's concert series has more subscribers than any other in the United States. Excellent sports and recreational facilities are also available.

The University and The College

NC State was founded in 1889 as a land-grant institution. Within 100 years, it has become one of the nation's leading research universities. Located in the Research Triangle, a world-renowned center of research, industry, technology, and education, the College of Management is housed on the 623-acre main campus of NC State, which lies just west of downtown Raleigh, the state capital. NC State comprises eleven colleges and schools serving a total student population of more than 30,000. More than 5,000 of those students are in graduate programs.

Applying

M.B.A. students must have a baccalaureate degree from an accredited college or university and are strongly encouraged to have had courses in calculus, statistics, accounting, and economics. Calculus or statistics must be completed prior to enrollment, with a grade of C or better. Admissions decisions are based on previous academic performance, GMAT scores, essays, letters of reference, and previous work and volunteer experience. Applicants whose native language is not English, regardless of citizenship, must also submit TOEFL scores of at least 250 (computer-based) or an IELTS score of 7.5; applicants to the part-time programs may apply for a TOEFL waiver. Interviews are by invitation.

The NC State M.B.A. program accepts applications for the fall semester only for the full-time program, with application deadlines of October 4, January 15, and March 1. Part-time students may enter the program in either fall or spring, with application deadlines of October 3 for spring entry and February 13 and April 9 for fall entry. Online students may enter the program in the fall only, with application deadlines of February 13 and April 9. Once an application has been received and is complete, it is reviewed for admission.

This rolling admission process allows an applicant to receive an admission decision within six weeks of receipt of a completed application.

Correspondence and Information

Ms. Pam Bostic, Director
M.B.A. Program
North Carolina State University
Box 8114
Raleigh, North Carolina 27695
United States
Phone: 919-515-5584
Fax: 919-515-5073
E-mail: mba@ncsu.edu
Web site: http://www.mba.ncsu.edu

The Faculty

The graduate faculty members of the M.B.A. program are outstanding teachers and researchers. In recent years, faculty members have been selected for the University of North Carolina Board of Governors' Award, Alumni Distinguished Professorships, and the NC State Academy of Outstanding Teachers. They match their teaching methods to the subject material, using case discussions, group projects, lectures, class discussions, and guest speakers as appropriate. Several faculty members serve on the editorial boards of journals in accounting, finance, marketing, operations, project management, and strategy. They have been ranked in the top twenty nationally for publishing in the top economics and finance journals.

Many faculty members held positions in management before receiving their doctoral degrees and stay in touch with today's business world through consulting and executive education.

For more information, visit:
http://poole.ncsu.edu/mba/faculty-research

University of California, Los Angeles

UCLA Anderson School of Management M.B.A. Program

Programs of Study

Celebrating 75 years of Business Beyond Usual, UCLA Anderson School of Management is among the leading business schools in the world. UCLA Anderson faculty members are globally renowned for their teaching excellence and research in advancing management thinking. Each year, UCLA Anderson provides a distinctive approach to management education to more than 1,800 students enrolled in its MBA, Fully Employed MBA, Executive MBA, UCLA-NUS Global Executive MBA for Asia Pacific, UCLA–UAI Global Executive MBA for the Americas, Master of Financial Engineering, doctoral, and executive education programs. Combining selective admissions, varied and innovative learning programs, and a worldwide network of 37,000 alumni, UCLA Anderson develops and prepares global leaders. More information on the school, programs, alumni, and students can be found at www.anderson.ucla.edu.

Research Facilities

UCLA Anderson's Rosenfeld Library is ranked among the top U.S. business school libraries. Rosenfeld Library provides access to over 100 specialized databases, as well as to an expanding array of electronic journals and texts supporting all areas of business and management, such as accounting, business economics, strategy and policy, finance, human resources, marketing, and organizational behavior. It also delivers robust reference, consultation, course outreach, course reserves, facilities management, document delivery, and information fluency programs. The library's print collections support the UCLA Anderson curriculum in all areas of business and management and comprise 180,600 volumes, 2,900 currently received serial subscriptions, 633,000 microforms, and over 269,000 historical corporate reports. While the Rosenfeld Library's information sources are of particular value to the M.B.A. curriculum; Rosenfeld Library is one of twelve UCLA campus libraries whose vast resources are also available to the M.B.A. student. In addition, UCLA students, including Anderson M.B.A.'s, are part of the University of California Library system and have access to those information resources through a variety of programs ranging from licensed databases to interlibrary loan to borrowing print materials. The Rosenfeld Library also participates in an international interlibrary loan program that allows it to borrow materials M.B.A. students may need from libraries beyond the UC system.

Research programs and study centers associated with the School and its faculty include the Harold and Pauline Price Center for Entrepreneurial Studies, the Center for International Business Education and Research, the Richard S. Ziman Center for Real Estate, the UCLA Anderson Forecast, the Laurence D. and Lori W. Fink Center for Finance & Investments, and the Center for Management of Enterprise in Media, Entertainment, and Sports.

Financial Aid

Merit fellowships, donor fellowships, and need-based grants are available. Private education loans are available for international students who do not have a U.S. cosigner. A limited number of research and teaching assistantship positions are also available.

The UCLA Anderson School of Management Complex by Peden+Munk.

Cost of Study

For 2011–12, tuition and fees per academic year totaled $45,385 for California residents and $52,508 for nonresidents. These costs are subject to change.

Living and Housing Costs

Room and board for the 2011–12 academic year are estimated to be $14,040. Books and supplies are approximately $4900 (including a $2500 laptop computer allowance). These costs are for students living off campus in shared housing. Additional costs may include support of dependents and medical expenses. Married students should budget additional costs from personal resources as financial aid only covers the student's costs.

Student Group

UCLA Anderson has a vibrant student body whose extraordinary intellectual, cultural, social, and athletic energies spill out of the classroom into a plethora of nonacademic activities. The average age of the most recent entering class for the full-time M.B.A. program (class of 2012) is 28 and the average number of years postgraduate work experience is five years. Of this class, 31 percent are female and 33 percent are international.

Location

Los Angeles is among the world's most vibrant and exciting cities. In addition to being the entertainment capital of the world, businesses in Los Angeles create four times the gross domestic product and diversity of the Silicon Valley. The city is home to Fortune 500 companies and major industries ranging from financial services and health care to manufacturing and aerospace. The city hosts even more small businesses, which are a significant source of U.S. economic growth. Located in Southern California, Los Angeles serves as a gateway to both Asia and Latin America.

UCLA Anderson students enjoy access to extensive cultural and recreational opportunities with museums, sporting events, theaters, and countless other activities offered both on campus and throughout the city. Because the location is such a cultural crossroads, there are always opportunities to engage with people from various backgrounds and points of view. Students benefit from this interaction both professionally and personally, learning as they share cultural traditions with each other.

The School

UCLA Anderson's management education complex is a testament to the School's vision of the growing importance of superior management education. Continuing the School's reputation as a national leader in the use of computing in M.B.A. instruction, the eleven specially designed case study rooms have data ports at each seating station to integrate the instructional program of each faculty member with the School's central computing facility in the Rosenfeld Library.

UCLA Anderson's Rosenfeld Library houses three computer labs that are available to M.B.A. students, one of which includes twenty-three desktop computers and two networked printers. The other two collaborative labs are both wired and wireless and are capable of seating up to fifteen teams of 5 students. The Rosenfeld Library also provides M.B.A. students with access to a professional audio-visual presentation facility, known as the boardroom, as well as to twenty-four collaborative pods and rooms for team work.

Applying

Applicants may apply for fall 2012 admission through third rounds. The deadlines for these rounds are January 11, 2012 and April 18, 2012.

Correspondence and Information

Rob Weiler, Assistant Dean
Interim Director M.B.A. Admissions
Parker Career Management Center
UCLA Anderson School of Management
110 Westwood Plaza, Suite C201
Los Angeles, California 90095-1481
United States
Phone: 310-825-3325
E-mail: mba.admissions@anderson.ucla.edu
Web site: http://www.anderson.ucla.edu/programs/mba/

The Faculty

The mainstay of UCLA Anderson's high-quality management education programs is its esteemed, international faculty. Each year, UCLA Anderson faculty members publish papers in leading scholarly journals, receive recognition for research excellence, provide leadership in and beyond UCLA, and serve as inspirational teachers and mentors.

The UCLA Anderson faculty is organized into nine academic areas: Accounting; Decisions, Operations, & Technology Management; Finance; Global Economics and Management; HR and Organizational Behavior; Information Systems; Interdisciplinary Group in Behavioral Decision Making; Marketing; and Policy.

For an alphabetical list of faculty members (teaching and emeritus), visiting scholars, and program advisors, prospective student should visit: http://www.anderson.ucla.edu/x322.xml.

University of Connecticut

SCHOOL OF BUSINESS

M.B.A. Program

Program of Study

Educating leaders for over 130 years, the University of Connecticut (UConn) has been ranked among the top 5 percent of business schools worldwide by *Bloomberg Businessweek, Forbes,* and *U.S. News & World Report.*

UConn's flagship full-time M.B.A. program offers students a practical, comprehensive, and individualized business education that integrates basic business fundamentals, innovative experiential learning, and personal interests. This carefully blended curriculum differentiates UConn M.B.A. graduates and uniquely positions them for career success.

Essential to UConn's M.B.A. curriculum is the incorporation of innovative experiential learning accelerators, such as the SS&C Technologies Financial Accelerator, Innovation Accelerator, Student Managed Fund, Sustainable Community Outreach and Public Engagement (SCOPE) program, and the Stamford Learning Accelerator. These unique practice-based initiatives integrate traditional teaching and classroom experience with high-profile business partnering to close the gap between theory and practice.

The UConn M.B.A. program also offers a number of international learning opportunities that allow students to participate in a variety of international electives abroad. These one- to two-week courses are typically held in January, May, and during other break periods to minimize conflict with regular semester course work.

Year One of the program follows a lockstep format in which all students go through the core curriculum together—no exceptions. This ensures the same foundation of knowledge for every UConn M.B.A. student. The first-year core curriculum covers fundamentals across all business disciplines including preterm work on business law and ethics; a multisemester project, the Application of Core Teaching (ACT), the first formal exposure to experiential and integrated learning; and a non-credit seminar series focused on enhancing personal, team, and communication skills for the workplace.

In the spring of Year One, M.B.A. students develop an Individualized plan of study in consultation with an advisory committee comprised of business school faculty, career counselors, and alumni/experts in the field. A student's individualized plan of study consists of eight courses (24 credits) including a primary area of emphasis, one to two courses (3–6 credits) of experiential learning, and carefully selected electives. Ultimately, the approved plan is a strategic bundle of courses and experiences that best aligns with each student's personal career goals and objectives.

After fulfilling the summer Internship Milestone, M.B.A. students continue with Year Two, pursuing the customized plan of study developed and approved in Year One. Most, if not all, second-year course offerings will be delivered in Hartford, Stamford, and/or Waterbury to best coordinate with the experiential learning centers where students will be participating.

The integration of business fundamentals and experiential learning helps provide the real-world experience that today's global businesses demand.

UConn provides state-of-the-art experiential learning opportunities through such collaborative initiatives as the SS&C Technologies Financial Accelerator (above).

Research Facilities

UConn M.B.A. students study in state-of-the-art research and learning facilities. Classrooms and meeting spaces are outfitted with broad multimedia capability reflecting the School's commitment to meet the demands of the information era.

UConn's accelerator labs also serve as advanced business solution centers in which M.B.A. students, research faculty, and corporate managers jointly investigate and develop solutions to real-world, real-time, complex challenges facing business today.

The School's various centers—Connecticut Center for Entrepreneurship and Innovation, Center for Real Estate and Urban Economic Studies, Center for International Business Education and Research (CIBER), GE Global Learning Center, and the ING Center for Financial Services—provide specialized resources for students at the University of Connecticut.

The University of Connecticut libraries form the largest public research collection in the state. The collection contains some 3.6 million volumes; 51,000 currently received print and electronic periodicals; 4.3 million units of microform; 15,000 reference sources; 232,000 maps; sound and video recordings; musical scores; and a growing array of electronic resources, including e-books, e-sound recordings, and image databases.

Financial Aid

Although the cost of a UConn M.B.A. is among the most affordable, candidates often need financial assistance. Financial aid is available in the form of loans and scholarships. Most financial aid is awarded on the basis of established need, primarily determined through an analysis of an applicant's Free Application for Federal Student Aid (FAFSA). The School of Business also offers a limited number of merit-based graduate teaching assistantships. Out-of-state candidates who have demonstrated a high likelihood of success can also benefit from the Tuition Assistance Program. In this program, out-of-state students receive the benefit of paying in-state tuition fees. There are a limited number of these awards, so work experience and GMAT scores are important determinants. For more information, contact the University of Connecticut financial aid office at 860-486-2819 or visit the Web site at http://www.financialaid.uconn.edu.

Cost of Study

Tuition and fees for the 2011–12 academic year (two semesters) for the full-time M.B.A. program at UConn were $12,130 for Connecticut residents and $28,438 for nonresidents. Additional costs, including required health insurance, textbooks, mobile computer, laundry, and incidentals, can add up to an estimated $7500. Fees are subject to change without notice.

Living and Housing Costs

For a nine-month academic year, the approximate cost of living, in addition to tuition and fees, is estimated to be $12,104. Most M.B.A. students choose to live off campus, however some opt for graduate housing on campus. Specific information is available by contacting the Department of Residential Life at http://www.reslife.uconn.edu. A wide variety of off-campus housing is available to students. A visit to the area is recommended for all students interested in finding off-campus housing.

Student Group

UConn M.B.A. students come from a wide variety of undergraduate institutions, both domestic and international. Their undergraduate degrees represent majors in many diverse areas—from engineering and English, sciences and fine arts, to business to economics. In a typical class of students, 35 percent are women, the average age is 28, and approximately 30 percent are international students. Friendliness and familiarity characterize student life at the main campus. Social and professional organizations, including the Graduate Business Association (GBA), offer a variety of activities to satisfy the needs of students.

Student Outcomes

UConn's career-planning activities begin during orientation and continue throughout the M.B.A. Primary recruiters include General Electric, CIGNA, Aetna, IBM, United Technologies Corp., Wachovia, Hartford Financial Services, PricewaterhouseCoopers, Gerber Technologies, ESPN, and UBS. For the class of 2010, the mean base salary was $90,313.

Location

The University's span of more than 4,300 acres includes ten schools and colleges at its main campus in Storrs, separate schools of law and social work in Hartford, five regional campuses throughout the state, and schools of medicine and dental medicine at the UConn Health Center in Farmington. Right in the middle of Fortune 500 territory, the state capital and metropolitan area of Hartford is 30 minutes away, Boston is a 90-minute drive, and New York City is a 3-hour drive.

The University and The School

UConn has grown in recent years from a strong regional school to a prominent national academic institution with over 29,000 students and 190,000 alumni. The UConn School of Business is nationally accredited by AACSB International and is a member of the Graduate Management Admissions Council (GMAC) and the European Foundation for Management Development (EFMD). UConn is also accredited by the New England Association of Schools and Colleges (NEASC).

Applying

Admission to UConn's M.B.A. program is very competitive. The minimum requirements for admission include two years of postgraduate professional work experience; a minimum 3.0 GPA on a 4.0 scale, or the equivalent, from a four-year accredited institution; and a total GMAT score of at least 560. For international students whose native language is not English, a TOEFL score of at least 233 (computer-based) is required. The application deadline for international applicants is February 1. For domestic applicants the deadline is March 1.

Correspondence and Information

For the master's program:
Full-Time M.B.A. Director, Storrs
School of Business
University of Connecticut
2100 Hillside Road, Unit 1041
Storrs, Connecticut 06269-1041
United States
Phone: 860-486-2872
Fax: 860-486-5222
E-mail: UConnMBA@business.uconn.edu
Web site: http://mba.uconn.edu

For the Ph.D. program:
Ph.D. Director
School of Business
University of Connecticut
2100 Hillside Road, Unit 1041
Storrs, Connecticut 06269-1041
United States
Phone: 860-486-5822
Fax: 860-486-0270
E-mail: phdmail@business.uconn.edu
Web site: http://www.business.uconn.edu

The Faculty

As leaders in business education, UConn's world-class M.B.A. professors are critical to the learning process. In addition to teaching, many are actively involved in scholarly research activities or business consulting that enables them to stay current in, and contribute to, their fields of knowledge. When UConn faculty members introduce original research and practical experience into the classroom, students benefit from the intersection of cutting-edge knowledge and practice. This winning combination shortens the learning curve and equips students to immediately add value to hiring companies.

In addition to individual faculty research, the School's extensive network of centers and institutes assists in carrying out UConn's research and education mission, serving as a resource for businesses—both in the state of Connecticut and worldwide. As coalitions for innovation, UConn's centers bring together cross-disciplinary faculty perspectives and a strong interface between UConn and the business community. M.B.A. students not only benefit from the knowledge and research being developed by the centers and institutes, but also from the opportunities and relationships associated with them.

For more information about UConn's M.B.A. faculty, please visit http://www.business.uconn.edu/cms/p1065.

The University of Connecticut's $27-million School of Business facility opened its doors in 2001.

MBA

Programs of Study

The Price College of Business at the University of Oklahoma (OU) offers the following graduate programs: the Master of Business Administration (M.B.A.), the Master of Accountancy (M.Acc.), the Master of Science in Management Information Systems (M.S. in MIS), and the Doctor of Philosophy (Ph.D.). Dual-degree programs offered include the M.B.A./M.S. in MIS, M.B.A./J.D., M.B.A./M.Acc., M.Acc./M.S. in MIS, and generic dual degrees, which combine any other graduate program available at OU with the M.B.A. For the dual-degree programs, applicants must apply and be admitted to each program separately. Programs in the Price College of Business are fully accredited by AACSB International–The Association to Advance Collegiate Schools of Business.

The full-time M.B.A. is a 47-credit hour, sixteen-month program, with all courses taken at the graduate level. The full-time program facilitates the development of professional skills and broad business perspectives through opportunities such as unique summer internships in New York (Price Scholars), London (Dunham Scholars), Houston (Energy Scholars), and Dallas (Corporate Scholars) along with other domestic and international internships, case competitions, and working in teams on real-life cases. Interacting with excellent faculty members keeps OU M.B.A. students on the cutting edge of knowledge. A customized program in one of five specializations—finance, risk management, energy, entrepreneurship, or MIS—allows personal attention for each student. Students specializing in energy can spend a spring semester abroad, study at the Institute of French Petroleum, and receive an M.S. in energy economics, in addition to their OU M.B.A.Low tuition costs plus significant scholarship and assistantship opportunities make the OU M.B.A. an outstanding program for those looking to improve their professional opportunities and create a pathway to business leadership.

The professional part-time M.B.A. requires 47 credit hours, with all courses taken at the graduate level. Designed for the working professional, all courses are offered in the evening and are based in downtown Oklahoma City.

Both M.B.A. programs require that the student become familiar with the functional areas of business, the necessary tools for management decision making, and the environment in which business firms operate. Students from all undergraduate majors are encouraged to apply.

The M.Acc. is a 33-hour program for students with an undergraduate degree in accounting from a program accredited by AACSB International. Other students may enter this program,

but they must take a minimum of 24 hours of undergraduate accounting courses as well as other undergraduate business courses. The M.Acc. is a full-time program.

The M.S. in MIS is a 32-hour program designed for people with an undergraduate degree in a discipline other than MIS who wish to embark on a career as an information system analyst or designer. The program combines a solid base of business and organizational knowledge with in-depth exposure to information systems technologies. The curriculum contains 15 hours of graduate business courses and 17 hours of graduate MIS courses. In addition, candidates must demonstrate competency in two programming languages. The M.S. in MIS program admits a small number of highly qualified students.

The full-time Ph.D. program is small and research-oriented. The program requires a minimum of 90 graduate hours past a bachelor's degree. Eighteen hours of course work are stipulated; most degree requirements and major, in addition to supporting fields, are determined on an individual basis. Close association with faculty members, as well as early research involvement, is standard. Doctoral students normally receive financial aid. Doctoral majors are available in accounting, finance, management, and entrepreneurship, management information systems, and marketing/supply chain management. A master's degree is not required to enter the doctoral program.

The Oklahoma M.B.A. is a pathway to business leadership.

Princeton Review ranks OU among the best universities in the nation in terms of academic excellence and cost for students.

Research Facilities

Research facilities that are available to graduate students include an extensive university library, the Amoco Business Resource Information Center, a graduate computer lab, the Bass Business History Collection, the Oklahoma University Research Institute, the Center for Economic and Management Research, and extensive computer facilities including a new trading floor lab.

Financial Aid

Graduate assistantships of up to $18,700 a year, special instructorships, fellowships and scholarships, and tuition-waiver scholarships are available for qualified graduate students. Graduate assistantships may include a full waiver of resident and nonresident tuition.

Cost of Study

Tuition in 2011–12 for full-time state residents was $311 per credit hour; nonresident students paid $760 per credit hour. Books and supplies are estimated at $1250 per academic year; other fees vary by program.

Living and Housing Costs

Many graduate students live on campus in one of the university's three apartment complexes or in the residence halls. Prices for apartments vary from $475 to $1000 per month. Room and board rates for the residence halls are approximately $3662 for one semester. For more information, students should call 405-325-2511 or visit the Web site at http://www.housing.ou.edu.

Student Group

Typically, 45 percent of an M.B.A. class consists of business majors, 24 percent engineering majors, and the remainder science and humanities majors. More than 40 percent have two years or more of work experience. The average age is 27 and approximately 30 percent are women. There are generally 300 to 350 graduate students in the College.

Location

Although part of the Oklahoma City metropolitan area, Norman began and continues as an independent community with a permanent population of nearly 111,000. It has extensive parks and recreation programs, a 10,000-acre lake and park area, a community theater, an art center and art league, and other amenities of a university town. Norman is minutes from downtown Oklahoma City and 3 hours from Dallas. Summers are hot with high humidity, and winters are mild to cold.

The University

The University of Oklahoma, which was founded in 1890, is a doctoral degree-granting research university. The Norman campus serves as home to all of the university's academic programs, except health-related fields. Both the Norman and Health Sciences Center colleges offer programs at the Schusterman Center, the site of OU-Tulsa. OU enrolls more than 31,000 students, has more than 2,400 full-time faculty members, and has twenty colleges offering 163 majors at the baccalaureate level, 166 majors at the master's level, eighty-one majors at the doctoral level, twenty-seven majors at the first-professional level, and twenty-six graduate certificates.

Applying

There is a nonrefundable application processing fee of $40 for U.S. citizens and permanent residents and $90 for international applicants. Admission is open to qualified individuals holding a bachelor's degree from an accredited college or university who show high promise of success in graduate study. Applicants need not have undergraduate backgrounds in business. All applicants must submit satisfactory scores on the Graduate Management Admission Test (GMAT). International applicants must submit satisfactory scores on the Test of English as a Foreign Language (TOEFL) or the Cambridge IELTS. In addition, the Test of Spoken English (TSE) is required of international applicants to the Ph.D. program. Letters of recommendation are required for all applicants.

Students may enter the M.Acc. program in the fall semester beginning in late August, the spring semester beginning in early January, or the eight-week summer session beginning in early June. Students may enter the M.B.A. program, M.S. in MIS program, and doctoral program in the fall semester only.

Correspondence and Information

Graduate Programs Office
Price College of Business
1003 Asp Avenue, Suite 1040
University of Oklahoma
Norman, Oklahoma 73019-4302
United States
Phone: 405-325-4107
Fax: 405-325-7753
E-mail: oklahomamba@ou.edu
Web site: http://price.ou.edu/mba/

The Faculty

Faculty members in the Price College of Business are dedicated to students. As researchers in their respective fields, they bring real-world knowledge and experience to the classroom. Recognized nationally and internationally, Oklahoma MBA faculty members demonstrate extensive knowledge in their diverse teaching and research interests.

More information about the faculty of the Price College of Business can be found at http://www.ou.edu/content/price/left/faculty_research.htm.

Programs of Study

The School of Management's eleven dynamic master's programs answer the challenges facing today's business leaders. The curriculum for each of these degree programs is built around a strong core of classes with detailed study to address specific industry issues. These master's programs—accounting, finance, health-care management, information technology management, innovation and entrepreneurship, international management studies, management and administrative science, marketing, project management, supply chain management, and systems engineering and management—also prepare students to take national certification exams, including CPA, CFA, CFP, Certified Internal Auditor, and others.

Master's degree programs require 36 credit hours for completion. School of Management classes are offered year-round, with a full schedule of courses offered in the evening to accommodate working professionals.

The School of Management also offers eight different M.B.A. programs with concentrations in accounting, finance, healthcare administration, information systems, innovation and entrepreneurship, internal audit, international management, leadership in organizations, marketing, operations management, strategic management and supply chain management. Employers particularly like the strong analytical skills UT Dallas students develop during their M.B.A. studies, and students may focus their course work to match their individual career goals. These programs are nationally recognized and offer a terrific tuition value for in-state students. Several of these 53-hour programs include an international study trip, many offer opportunities to take classes online, and all develop cross-disciplinary skills sought by the most competitive employers in the nation and around the world. Representatives from many corporations—ranging from retail to transportation to banking, finance, health care and communications—partner with the School of Management. These industry executives sit on various advisory panels, provide financial and research support, and serve as mentors to undergraduate and graduate students. Faculty members seek these outside professionals as classroom speakers, adding real-life perspective to textbook learning.

Research Facilities

School of Management faculty has been recognized globally for its research productivity. The faculty ranks 15th in North America and 16th globally based on research contributions to major journals, according to *The UTD Top 100 Business School Research Rankings,* and ranks 22nd worldwide according to *Financial Times.* Research by the information systems faculty and operations management faculty ranks in the top 5 nationally in those respective fields. The School of Management also hosts twelve Centers of Excellence where faculty and students join to tackle real-world issues faced by local businesses. Students also have the opportunity to apply for internships with these centers and participate in the meetings and lectures they sponsor for industry professionals.

Financial Aid

The UT Dallas School of Management Scholarship Committee makes awards each fall based on merit, need, or a combination of the two. The annual Scholarship Breakfast most recently generated more than $100,000 in scholarships specifically for School of Management students at all levels. Students may also apply for the Dean's Excellence Scholarships, several of which are awarded each year. Full-time M.B.A. students with strong academic potential are eligible for significant scholarship and grant assistance. Last year, School of Management awarded more than $430,000 in scholarships to graduate students. Applications are available from the UT Dallas Office of Financial Aid. The University participates in most federal and state aid programs. Short-term loans are also available. Prospective students should visit the

The Atrium in the School of Management building provides a light-filled spot to study between classes.

School of Management's Web site at http://som.utdallas.edu for more information.

Cost of Study

Tuition for in-state full-time graduate students (9 hours) for fall 2011 was $5124. For graduate students attending school on a part-time basis, tuition was $2435 for 3 hours and $3888 for 6 hours. These prices excluded fees and other charges. The cost of obtaining a master's degree depends upon how many hours a student completes each semester. The Full-Time M.B.A. cost about $26,000 for students entering in fall 2011.

Living and Housing Costs

UT Dallas offers on-campus apartments, Waterview Park, which are operated by a private company. These apartments offer a variety of floorplans, are competitively priced, and fill quickly. Interested students should visit http://www.utdallas.edu for on-campus housing information. The surrounding metropolitan area offers many options for off-campus housing in a range of prices. An array of shopping and dining establishments, representing everything from large chains to small, single proprietor–run shops, are within bicycling distance of campus.

Student Group

About 60 percent of School of Management graduate students are working professionals seeking an advanced degree; they often take classes online, in the evening, and during the summer semester. The School's environment is both challenging and naturally diverse. About a third of the graduate students take 9 or more hours a semester. The School of Management, with almost 6,500 students, is the largest of the seven schools of UT Dallas. School of Management students are equally split between undergraduate and graduate studies.

Most graduate students have at least five years of work experience. Women make up about 40 percent of master's students, and minorities represent almost 30 percent of the student population. About 30 percent of the students are from another country. Students range in age from 20 to more than 70; the average age is 30.

Location

The University of Texas at Dallas campus, in Richardson, is convenient to the George Bush Turnpike, U.S. Highway 75 and the Dallas North Tollway. The Dallas-Fort Worth metro area features professional sports teams and venues, world-acclaimed museums and concert halls, a vibrant arts scene and special cultural events, and activities every week.

The University and The School

The University of Texas at Dallas was established in 1969 by the Texas Legislature. The School of Management is fully accredited by AACSB International–The Association to Advance Collegiate Schools of Business and occupies a 204,000-square-foot building that opened in 2003. Research centers at the School of Management seek graduate students to run studies and conduct research for corporate clients, offering students a high level of interaction with real-life business issues during their time in school.

Applying

Prerequisites for all graduate admissions include a bachelor's degree from an accredited institution, completion of an undergraduate calculus class, and spreadsheet proficiency. Undergraduate work in business courses is not required. Additional requirements include GMAT or GRE scores, a complete application, and three recent letters of reference. A TOEFL score is required from those for whom English is not the native language. Applicants are evaluated on personal qualities and academic backgrounds, following admission formula guidelines of the International Association for Management Education. Personal interviews are not required. Admission deadlines vary by program and according to the applicant's citizenship status. Application requirements and deadlines are available on the School's Web site at http://som.utdallas.edu. To receive an application, students should send an e-mail to grad-admission@utdallas.edu.

Most programs enroll students in the next semester after acceptance. Certain programs, including the Full-Time M.B.A. and Executive M.B.A., admit students only once each year.

Correspondence and Information

James Parker, Assistant Director of Graduate Recruiting
School of Management, SM40
The University of Texas at Dallas
Richardson, Texas 75080
United States
Phone: 972-883-5842
Fax: 972-883-4095
E-mail: jparker@utdallas.edu
Web site: http://som.utdallas.edu

The Faculty

Outstanding faculty members form the backbone of the School of Management and bring a wealth of intellectual capital. Recruited for their business, teaching, and research acumen, faculty members often come here because UT Dallas enthusiastically encourages and supports scholarly inquiry and innovative teaching that is at the cutting edge of the changing global economy. Faculty researchers' productivity is exceptional, both in quantity and in groundbreaking quality. This year, Financial Times ranked the UT Dallas School of Management faculty twenty-second in the world based on publications in the leading business journals. New discoveries, along with faculty members' long-held expertise, prompt and inform the School's academic programs at every level—undergraduate to MBA to post-doctorate.

For more information about the School of Management faculty members, visit http://som.utdallas.edu/facultyResearch/.

The University of Texas at El Paso

College of Business Administration
M.B.A. Program

Programs of Study

The Master of Business Administration (M.B.A.) program at the University of Texas at El Paso (UTEP) is designed for students from a wide range of backgrounds who are seeking a graduate business education with a dynamic international focus. By offering a menu of flexible schedules and class formats, the program meets the needs of both full-time students and working professionals. Students bring professional perspectives to the classroom from a range of industries: health care, engineering, education, cross-border business, and more.

The program awards the Master of Business Administration degree. The course of study offers concentrations in computer information systems, economics, finance, international business, management, supply chain management, and health systems. Students are enrolled in the program for 48 credit hours, which can be completed in the following three formats.

Full-Time M.B.A.: The 22-month full-time M.B.A. offers students courses in a traditional semester. Most students are engaged in corporate projects with multinational companies, nonprofits, and start-up businesses, which bring an experiential learning component to their classroom education. Language workshops in Spanish and Mandarin are features of this format.

Accelerated M.B.A.: The 24-month Accelerated M.B.A. is a cohort format that is designed for working professionals. The courses are taken in six-week modules during evenings and weekends, year-round.

Executive M.B.A.: The 18-month Executive M.B.A. is a cohort format for business leaders with at least eight years of management experience. The classes meet for two weekends (Friday and Saturday) a month. Courses are taken in topic-related modules with two courses completed every five sessions. Executive M.B.A. electives are specifically designed to augment and develop critical leadership skills.

Research Facilities

UTEP M.B.A. students enjoy exclusive access to a state-of-the-art downtown Graduate Business Center (GBC). In addition to the M.B.A. classrooms and student collaboration rooms, the GBC houses several of the College's applied research centers including the Center for Hispanic Entrepreneurship; the Centers for Entrepreneurial Development, Advancement, and Research and Support; and the M.B.A. Corporate Engagement Projects. The College of Business Administration is also home to the Center for Multicultural Management and Ethics and the Border Region Modeling Project.

Financial Aid

The M.B.A. program offers assistantship positions to more than half of the full-time M.B.A. students. Full-time M.B.A. applicants who meet certain qualifications are guaranteed an assistantship. In addition, domestic students have access to financial aid. Scholarship opportunities are available.

Cost of Study

In-state tuition and fees for the full-time and accelerated M.B.A. programs are approximately $1300 per course or $21,000 for the degree program. Tuition and fees for international students are $2100 per course and $32,500 for the degree program. International students who receive an assistantship are eligible for in-state tuition and fees.

Executive M.B.A. program costs, which include tuition, fees, books/course materials, and lodging and ground transportation for the international travel research course, are $35,000 for in-state and international students.

Living and Housing Costs

Although on-campus housing is available, most students commute from their established residences or find rental housing in the El Paso area.

Student Group

The UTEP M.B.A. program serves a diverse population of over 400 students from more than twenty countries. Many M.B.A. students are involved with the UTEP M.B.A. Student Association and the local chapter of the National Society of Hispanic MBAs. Through these organizations, students take part in networking events, community service projects, and other social activities.

Student Outcomes

UTEP M.B.A. graduates are employed by multinational corporations all over the world including JP Morgan Chase, Boeing, KPMG, Phillips, Lockheed Martin, Procter & Gamble, Amazon, ADP, Helen of Troy, and many others. Given the entrepreneurial spirit of the region, many UTEP M.B.A. graduates launch their own businesses as well.

M.B.A. students attend classes in the state-of-the-art UTEP Graduate Center located in downtown El Paso.

Location

El Paso is located in West Texas. It borders New Mexico and Mexico and has a population of more than 600,000. The University offers a picturesque campus within the shadows of the towering Franklin Mountains, from the top of which it is possible to see two countries and three states, all within a stone's throw of each other. This Paso del Norte region is one of the largest international communities in the world with a population of over 2 million. Along with its ruggedly beautiful environment, the city provides many creative international artists, hiking/biking trails, athletic events, great weather, and a host of entertainment opportunities.

The University and The College

The University of Texas at El Paso provides a living, breathing laboratory for research critical to the future, including border security, international business, and desalination projects. UTEP is the second-oldest academic component of the University of Texas system. It was founded by the Texas legislature in 1914 as the State School of Mines and Metallurgy, a name that reflected the scope of education offered at that time. UTEP's present 366-acre site features distinctive Bhutanese-style architecture. UTEP has become an internationally recognized research and doctoral university, with more than 21,000 students and 89,000 alumni. UTEP offers 181 bachelor's, master's, and doctoral degrees, all of which reflect a quality of education that has led major magazines to praise the University for the success of its business, engineering, and health sciences programs.

The College of Business Administration is accredited by the Association to Advance Collegiate Schools of Business International—the only school in the El Paso metropolitan area to be awarded this distinction. The UTEP M.B.A. program is ranked Number 1 by *Hispanic Business Magazine*.

Applying

Applicants should submit the following in order to be considered for admission to the M.B.A. program: online application for admission into a graduate degree program (accessible at mba.utep.edu), official transcript from an accredited institution demonstrating completion of a four-year bachelor's degree or equivalent and official transcripts from all colleges or universities attended, a one-page statement of purpose, resume, two letters of reference, GMAT score (for full-time and accelerated M.B.A. programs), and TOEFEL score of at least 250/600 (for international students). Applicants to the Accelerated M.B.A. program must have at least one year of professional work experience; Executive M.B.A. applicants must demonstrate at least eight years of managerial experience. Additional details are available online at http://mba.utep.edu.

All the materials listed above must be submitted before an admission decision can be made. Application deadlines vary by program; specific dates are available online at http://mba.utep.edu.

Correspondence and Information

Laura M. Uribarri, Assistant Dean for M.B.A. Programs
The University of Texas at El Paso
Graduate Business Center
El Paso, Texas 79968-0587
United States
Phone: 915-747-7727
Fax: 915-532-8213
E-mail: mba@utep.edu
Web site: http://www.business.utep.edu
 http://mba.utep.edu

The Faculty

Faculty members in the UTEP M.B.A. program hold doctoral degrees from top institutions worldwide. They bring to the classroom a global perspective and conduct research important to the global marketplace. Faculty members have recently been cited for high research productivity in the area of international business, leading their disciplines in creating relevant knowledge. Adjunct professors bring their vast industry experience to the M.B.A. learning experience as well.

For more information about the UTEP MBA faculty, visit: www.business.utep.edu/faculty.

University of the Pacific

Eberhardt School of Business

Program of Study

The University of the Pacific's AACSB-accredited Eberhardt School of Business offers a full-time 16-month M.B.A. program. The program is designed for early-career professionals who want to enhance their careers by adding advanced business knowledge and experience to their current skill sets, regardless of prior experience or educational field. Although short, the M.B.A. program is comprehensive and highly effective. The classes are small, interactive, and incorporate opportunities to gain hands-on experience. The dedicated faculty members pride themselves on working closely with students to enable them to reach their full potential.

The program begins in fall with an intensive business foundations semester. Students complete this semester equipped with the skills needed to succeed in advanced M.B.A. courses. The spring semester focuses on advanced business studies and is notable for its emphasis on real-world learning. Students may have the opportunity to write a business plan, conduct a feasibility study, write a market summary for a new product, or help manage the $2 million Eberhardt Student Investment Fund portfolio. Summer starts with a trip abroad to observe global business practices under the guidance of an Eberhardt School faculty member, and ends with a required summer internship. The focus of the final semester is on leadership and business strategy and includes many elective courses which are available in finance, marketing, health-care management, entrepreneurship, and sport management.

The Eberhardt School also offers a dual-degree J.D./M.B.A. with Pacific's McGeorge School of Law and a dual-degree Pharm.D./M.B.A. with Pacific's Thomas J. Long School of Pharmacy and Health Sciences. In addition, a Peace Corps/M.B.A. is offered in which students are given M.B.A. credit for service in the Peace Corps.

Research Facilities

The University Library subscribes to an extensive set of online business research resources including Business Source Complete (EBSCO), Factiva (Dow Jones), and LexisNexis. In addition, the University has substantial academic computing resources available to students, with multiple laboratories across the campus, including a dedicated lab and classroom in the Eberhardt School. Wireless access is available throughout the campus. Research expertise is available

through the Eberhardt School's Business Forecasting Center, a vibrant source of business and economic information for regional and state decision makers; the Westgate Center for Management Development, which provides management training for the regional business community; and through the Institute for Family Business, which assists family-owned businesses in finding and developing solutions to their unique business challenges.

Financial Aid

Financial assistance is available through several scholarships, graduate assistantships, and loans. Merit-based scholarships and graduate assistantships are available directly from the Eberhardt School. Typically 40 to 50 percent of M.B.A. students receive some form of merit-based financial assistance from the School. These awards are generally determined by May 1; upon acceptance to the M.B.A. program, all students will automatically be considered for possible assistance. Federal and private loans are also available and students are encouraged to complete the Free Application for Federal Student Aid (FAFSA).

The Eberhardt School of Business at the University of the Pacific is housed in Weber Hall (reminiscent of the red brick and ivy that can be found throughout the campus.

Cost of Study

The tuition and fees for the entire sixteen-month M.B.A. program are approximately $60,000 or $1118 per unit for the 53-unit full-time program. Fees include health center, university student association, and activity and recreation costs charged to all full-time students.

Living and Housing Costs

The cost of living in Stockton is relatively low for California, and students can find housing for about $800 to $1100 per month. Room and board expenses on the campus are approximately $12,000 per year, depending on the housing and meal plan options chosen. Additional student recreation and health center fees are required of all full-time students.

Student Group

The entering classes are organized around cohort groups of approximately 30 students. The Eberhardt M.B.A. provides a friendly, supportive environment that helps each individual adapt to the challenges of graduate management studies. A cohort approach also provides a format that fosters close student-faculty interaction. The average full-time student is 24 years of age, with less than two years of formal professional work experience. Women represent 45 percent of the student body, while 30 percent are international students.

The highest percentage of the students in the 16-month M.B.A. program have academic backgrounds in business, management, or economics, but the range of academic preparation typically encompasses engineering, pharmacy, natural sciences, social sciences, and the humanities. The blending of professional and liberal arts students provides a unique opportunity to develop teamwork and leadership skills in an academically diverse environment.

The M.B.A. Student Association (MBASA) is responsible for developing high-quality extracurricular activities for M.B.A. students. It provides formal and informal social events, professional programs, and student representation on governance committees within the business school and the University structure as a whole.

Student Outcomes

The Career Services Office is an integral part of each student's experience in the Eberhardt M.B.A. Students begin the process of launching their professional careers during orientation and continue year-round with workshops, mock interviews, on- and off-campus recruiting events, and internship placements. In addition to career development sessions, students have an online application and job-posting system available. Ninety-two percent of 2010 M.B.A. graduates accepted jobs within a few months of graduation, with medial total compensation of $55,000.

The Eberhardt MBA provides an intellectually challenging classroom experience that goes beyond traditional book- or case-based classes.

Location

The Eberhardt School of Business is on Pacific's main campus in Stockton, with its red-brick buildings and ivy-covered walls. The University is now in its 160th year. Strategically located in the heart of California near the San Francisco Bay area, Silicon Valley, and California's capital city of Sacramento, the University allows students direct access to companies and career opportunities. In addition, Yosemite National Park, Lake Tahoe, Napa Valley, and the California coastline are within a short drive, offering limitless activities, world-class cuisine, and unparalleled natural beauty.

The University

The University of the Pacific was established in 1851 as California's first chartered institution of higher education. The University's classic college environment combined with modern facilities provides students with the best of both worlds. The architecture and landscaping of the 175-acre main campus provide an Ivy League type of setting. The University also includes the Arthur A. Dugoni School of Dentistry in San Francisco and the McGeorge School of Law in Sacramento.

Applying

Admission to the Eberhardt M.B.A. program is competitive and based on criteria that indicate significant promise for a successful academic and professional career. Qualified candidates are admitted to the program on a rolling basis for the fall semester each year. The 16-month M.B.A. typically enrolls a cohort class of 25–30 students. A personalized review of each application is conducted, with each candidate's file evaluated on the basis of previous academic record and grade trends, standardized test scores (GMAT), professional and personal accomplishments, personal statements, letters of recommendation, and a required interview. The typical undergraduate upper-division GPA is 3.0 or higher, and GMAT scores are generally 540 and above. A score of 80 (Internet-based test) or better on the TOEFL is required for all international students for whom English is not their native language. In addition, international students must present proof of adequate funds to cover expenses for the first year of the M.B.A. program.

The application deadline is March 1 for the fall semester. Applicants seeking priority consideration for merit-based financial assistance are advised to submit their applications by January 15. M.B.A. admissions decisions are made on a rolling basis, and applicants are notified immediately when decisions have been made. To ensure a timely response, application packages should be submitted as a complete package.

Correspondence and Information

Christopher Lozano
Director of Student Recruitment and Admissions
Eberhardt School of Business
University of the Pacific
3601 Pacific Avenue
Stockton, California 95211
United States
Phone: 800-952-3179 (toll-free)
209-946-2629
Fax: 209-946-2586
Web site: http://www.pacific.edu/mba

The Faculty

The Eberhardt School of Business faculty is committed to teaching excellence. Faculty members pride themselves on their ability to establish long-lasting, close relationships with students and use this ability to help students reach the highest level of academic and professional achievement. Faculty research activities complement the teaching mission, and enable faculty members to offer instruction that is relevant and current. They integrate their real-world business experience that is relevant to current business practices. Through consulting activities, the Eberhardt School faculty continues to be engaged in the business community and, as a result, is able to provide students with exceptional real-world opportunities for experiential learning.

Electronic Commerce

OVERVIEW

The Internet and Web are transforming businesses around the world, facilitating new kinds of interactions between companies, suppliers, and customers, as well as within firms. The vast potential of this area has created a need for managers with a broad understanding of the key trends in technology-supported applications who can explore emerging new business models. The electronic commerce MBA specialization is designed for learners who want to become proficient in conducting business on the Web. Courses in e-commerce provide students with the basic knowledge of business practices, including management, finance, marketing, customer relations, and business strategies. They also help students translate all of those business skills into the online environment.

In addition to taking courses on Web design, database management, information security, IT, and even supply chain management, online marketing, and Web-based applications, courses on enabling methodologies and tools for online payment and transactions are often included in the curriculum. Drawing on real-world industry experience and the latest academic research exposes students to the tools necessary to analyze business functions and processes, formulate effective business strategies, and identify characteristics and implications of effective leadership and policy practices in a global and diverse business environment. The MBA e-commerce courses give graduates the fundamental skills needed to manage and lead enterprises that create value for stakeholders in a dynamic, global business environment.

Required courses may include study in:

- Accounting for E-Commerce
- E-Business Strategies
- E-Commerce for Entrepreneurs
- E-Commerce Law
- E-Commerce Systems Security and Firewall
- E-Marketing
- Information Technology Development and Innovation
- Internet-Based Systems Analysis and Development
- Internet Web Site Promotion
- Managerial Electronic Commerce
- Online Auctions
- Project Management

Elective courses may include study in:

- Data Mining
- E-Commerce: Business Models and Technology
- Managing the Real-Time Supply Chain
- Telecommunications and Technology Policy
- Web Commerce Security

Graduates of MBA programs in e-business land a variety of positions, including technology officer, information systems director, IT project manager, systems analyst, e-business consultant, and customer relationship manager.

HELPFUL ORGANIZATIONS/PUBLICATIONS/BLOGS

Women in e-Commerce™

http://www.wecai.org/

Women in e-Commerce™ is the original business and social networking community for social and professional networking and business development for successful women who want to take their businesses to a new level offline and online. This networking community offers tools, resources, and networking opportunities to build a strong foundation for future growth and expansion. As the voice of business, professional, and executive women, this community provides virtual and in-person opportunities for collaboration, networking, personal and professional development, leadership, and international recognition.

The goals of Women in e-Commerce are to empower women, promote business, create connections, network, and celebrate women's achievements around the globe through technology. With its vast internal and global network, they research tools and information and make recommendations that will help women do business on and off the Web. They are dedicated to providing women with the latest and best resources to build their online business, as well as give them a place where they can find other women entrepreneurs, professionals, and future business leaders with whom they can exchange ideas and create strategic alliances.

E-Commerce Times

http://www.ecommercetimes.com/?wlc=1313360689

Since its launch on the Internet in 1998, the *E-Commerce Times* has consistently ranked among the top technology news outlets in the world. It is a must-read for IT professionals and other key decision makers—from C-level executives at Fortune 1000 companies to owners of small and mid-size businesses—who need to keep up with the latest technology news and business trends in order to stay ahead of the competition.

Whether it's boardroom dramas, new enterprise IT applications, the latest security threats, developments in online entertainment, or the emergence of global trends, the *E-Commerce Times* offers fresh, original, and insightful coverage of breaking news, along with unique features and perspectives on business world affairs.

Electronic Commerce Branch of Industry Canada

http://www.ic.gc.ca/eic/site/ecic-ceac.nsf/eng/home

Canada recognizes the importance of the adoption, use, and development of e-business. The Electronic Commerce Branch of Industry Canada aims to build on its established foundation to support and facilitate continued growth of e-business in the Canadian economy by building trust in the digital economy; clarifying marketplace rules, both domestically and internationally; removing barriers for the use of e-commerce, in conjunction with the private sector; and benchmarking both firm-level and national performance in the digital economy.

The Electronic Commerce Branch is responsible for encouraging the development and adoption of e-business in Canada. This is accomplished through three main lines of business:

1. Policy Development and Harmonization: Helps to establish an orderly domestic and international marketplace and provides a favorable legal and regulatory environment for e-commerce.
2. Research and Analysis: Works in close collaboration with private-sector partners, academic researchers, Statistics Canada, and international organizations, among others, to better understand the economic, business, and social impact of the digital economy.
3. Broadband Canada: Connects rural Canadians and strives to make broadband service available to as many unserved and underserved households as possible.

CAREER ASPIRATIONS: A PROSPECTIVE POSITION

Manager of Operations & Customer Experience, E-commerce

Job Description

We are currently seeking a Manager of Operations & Customer Experience to actively participate in the e-commerce department's initiatives.

In this role, you will work with business leaders to ensure our customers are thoroughly satisfied with their e-commerce order experience by managing the relationships with our customer service, fulfillment, payment management, and fraud management partners, communicating issue resolution and new project requirements to the technical team and helping to oversee the timely execution of various enhancement projects.

Responsibilities

- Manage e-commerce call center and distribution center partner.
- Partner with e-commerce call center partner on customer experience initiatives, including call quality, product training, and enhancement projects to streamline processes, and improve customer experience and/or call center productivity.
- Responsible for e-commerce vendor relationships in areas such as payment and fraud management, package insert programs, store locator, and packaging supplies.
- Make recommendations and develops processes and tools to encourage continuous performance improvements.
- Research and make recommendations for user experience and back-end Web site enhancements.
- Take active role in user acceptance testing for new e-commerce site and process enhancements.
- Act as a team player sharing responsibility for achievement of goals and objectives.
- Accept accountability for individual and teams' performance and productivity.
- Develop and manage online customer experience improvement program for e-commerce.

Qualifications

- MBA preferred.
- 3+ years e-commerce experience with customer experience and/or operations required.
- Previous experience effectively managing outside resources and working with IT teams required.
- Must be self-sufficient and results-oriented, with strong hands-on project management background.
- Must have excellent facilitation skills and be an inherent team player.
- Must have a strong blend of process skills and business acumen.
- Attention to detail; ability to work independently in a fast-paced deadline-oriented environment necessary.

ELECTRONIC COMMERCE

Adelphi University, School of Business, MBA Program, Garden City, NY 11530-0701. Offers finance (MBA); management information systems (MBA); management/human resource management (MBA); marketing/e-commerce (MBA). *Accreditation:* AACSB. Part-time and evening/weekend programs available. *Students:* 131 full-time (59 women), 173 part-time (73 women); includes 25 Black or African American, non-Hispanic/Latino; 20 Asian, non-Hispanic/Latino; 17 Hispanic/Latino; 3 Two or more races, non-Hispanic/Latino, 110 international. Average age 29. In 2010, 86 master's awarded. *Degree requirements:* For master's, capstone course. *Entrance requirements:* For master's, GMAT, 2 letters of recommendation. Additional exam requirements/recommendations for international students: Required—TOEFL (minimum score 550 paper-based; 213 computer-based; 80 iBT). *Application deadline:* For fall admission, 4/1 for international students; for spring admission, 11/1 for international students. Applications are processed on a rolling basis. Application fee: $50. Electronic applications accepted. *Financial support:* Research assistantships with full and partial tuition reimbursements, career-related internships or fieldwork, Federal Work-Study, institutionally sponsored loans, scholarships/grants, and unspecified assistantships available. Financial award application deadline: 3/1; financial award applicants required to submit FAFSA. *Faculty research:* Supply chain management, distribution channels, productivity benchmark analysis, data envelopment analysis, financial portfolio analysis. *Unit head:* Rakesh Gupta, 516-877-4670, Fax: 516-877-4607, E-mail: gradbusinquiries@adelphi.edu. *Application contact:* Christine Murphy, Director of Admissions, 516-877-3050, Fax: 516-877-3039, E-mail: graduateadmissions@adelphi.edu.

Arkansas State University, Graduate School, College of Business, Department of Computer and Information Technology, Jonesboro, State University, AR 72467. Offers business education (SCCT); business technology education (MSE); information systems and e-commerce (MS). Part-time programs available. *Faculty:* 12 full-time (1 woman). *Students:* 11 full-time (6 women), 19 part-time (16 women). Average age 35. 15 applicants, 93% accepted, 13 enrolled. In 2010, 23 master's awarded. *Degree requirements:* For master's, comprehensive exam, thesis or alternative. *Entrance requirements:* For master's, GRE General Test or MAT, appropriate bachelor's degree, official transcript, immunization records. Additional exam requirements/recommendations for international students: Required—TOEFL (minimum score 550 paper-based; 253 computer-based; 79 iBT), IELTS (minimum score 6), PTE: Pearson Test of English Academic (56). *Application deadline:* For fall admission, 7/1 for domestic and international students; for spring admission, 11/15 for domestic students, 11/14 for international students. Applications are processed on a rolling basis. Application fee: $30 ($40 for international students). Electronic applications accepted. *Expenses:* Contact institution. *Financial support:* In 2010–11, 3 students received support. Career-related internships or fieldwork, scholarships/grants, and unspecified assistantships available. Financial award application deadline: 7/1; financial award applicants required to submit FAFSA. *Unit head:* Dr. John Robertson, Chair, 870-972-3416, Fax: 870-972-3868, E-mail: jfrobert@astate.edu. *Application contact:* Dr. Andrew Sustich, Dean of the Graduate School, 870-972-3029, Fax: 870-972-3857, E-mail: sustich@astate.edu.

Boston University, Metropolitan College, Department of Administrative Sciences, Boston, MA 02215. Offers banking and financial management (MSM); business continuity in emergency management (MSM); economics development and tourism management (MSAS); electronic commerce, systems, and technology (MSAS); financial economics (MSAS); innovation and technology (MSAS); insurance management (MSM); international market management (MSM); multinational commerce (MSAS); project management (MSM). *Accreditation:* AACSB. Part-time and evening/weekend programs available. Postbaccalaureate distance learning degree programs offered (no on-campus study). *Faculty:* 14 full-time (2 women), 22 part-time/adjunct (2 women). *Students:* 107 full-time (51 women), 786 part-time (356 women); includes 130 minority (55 Black or African American, non-Hispanic/Latino; 1 American Indian or Alaska Native, non-Hispanic/Latino; 30 Asian, non-Hispanic/Latino; 36 Hispanic/Latino; 1 Native Hawaiian or other Pacific Islander, non-Hispanic/Latino; 7 Two or more races, non-Hispanic/Latino), 175 international. Average age 33. 398 applicants, 87% accepted, 180 enrolled. In 2010, 154 master's awarded. *Degree requirements:* For master's, thesis optional. *Entrance requirements:* For master's, 1 year of work experience, minimum GPA of 3.0. Additional exam requirements/recommendations for international students: Required—TOEFL (minimum score 560 paper-based; 220 computer-based; 84 iBT). *Application deadline:* Applications are processed on a rolling basis. Application fee: $70. Electronic applications accepted. *Expenses:* Tuition: Full-time $39,314; part-time $1228 per credit. Required fees: $40 per semester. *Financial support:* In 2010–11, 15 students received support, including 7 research assistantships with partial tuition reimbursements available (averaging $10,000 per year); career-related internships or fieldwork, Federal Work-Study, and unspecified assistantships also available. *Faculty research:* International business, innovative process. *Unit head:* Dr. Kip Becker, Chairman, 617-353-3016, E-mail: adminsc@bu.edu. *Application contact:* Lucille Dicker, Administrative Sciences Department, 617-353-3016, E-mail: adminsc@bu.edu.

California State University, Fullerton, Graduate Studies, College of Business and Economics, Department of Information Systems and Decision Sciences, Fullerton, CA 92834-9480. Offers information systems (MS); information systems (decision sciences) (MS); information systems (e-commerce) (MS); information technology (MS); management science (MBA). Part-time programs available. *Students:* 13 full-time (2 women), 72 part-time (16 women); includes 2 Black or African American, non-Hispanic/Latino; 24 Asian, non-Hispanic/Latino; 6 Hispanic/Latino; 3 Two or more races, non-Hispanic/Latino, 10 international. Average age 35. 120 applicants, 34% accepted, 34 enrolled. In 2010, 23 master's awarded. *Degree requirements:* For master's, project or thesis. *Entrance requirements:* For master's, GMAT, minimum AACSB index of 950. Application fee: $55. *Financial support:* Career-related internships or fieldwork, Federal Work-Study, institutionally sponsored loans, and scholarships/grants available. Support available to part-time students. Financial award application deadline: 3/1; financial award applicants required to submit FAFSA. *Unit head:* Dr. Bhushan Kapoor, Chair, 657-278-2221. *Application contact:* Admissions/Applications, 657-278-2371.

California State University, Fullerton, Graduate Studies, College of Business and Economics, Program in Business Administration, Fullerton, CA 92834-9480. Offers e-commerce (MBA); international business (MBA). *Accreditation:* AACSB. Part-time programs available. *Students:* 70 full-time (34 women), 88 part-time (30 women); includes 2 Black or African American, non-Hispanic/Latino; 46 Asian, non-Hispanic/Latino; 8 Hispanic/Latino; 8 Two or more races, non-Hispanic/Latino, 40 international. Average age 28. 322 applicants, 43% accepted, 50 enrolled. In 2010, 29 master's awarded. *Degree requirements:* For master's, project or thesis. *Entrance requirements:* For master's, GMAT. *Financial support:* Career-related internships or fieldwork, Federal Work-Study, institutionally sponsored loans, and scholarships/grants available. Support available to part-time students. Financial award application deadline: 3/1; financial award applicants required to submit FAFSA. *Unit head:* Dr. Anil Puri, Dean, 657-773-2592. *Application contact:* Admissions/Applications, 657-278-2371.

Claremont Graduate University, Graduate Programs, School of Information Systems and Technology, Claremont, CA 91711-6160. Offers electronic commerce (MS, PhD); health information management (MS); information systems (Certificate); knowledge management (MS, PhD); systems development (MS, PhD); telecommunications and networking (MS, PhD); MBA/MS. Part-time programs available. *Faculty:* 6 full-time (1 woman), 1 part-time/adjunct (0 women). *Students:* 87 full-time (24 women), 22 part-time (8 women); includes 31 minority (6 Black or African American, non-Hispanic/Latino; 1 American Indian or Alaska Native, non-Hispanic/Latino; 18 Asian, non-Hispanic/Latino; 3 Hispanic/Latino; 1 Native Hawaiian or other Pacific Islander, non-Hispanic/Latino; 2 Two or more races, non-Hispanic/Latino), 37 international. Average age 37. In 2010, 30 master's, 6 doctorates awarded. *Degree requirements:* For doctorate, comprehensive exam, thesis/dissertation, portfolio. *Entrance requirements:* For master's and doctorate, GMAT, GRE General Test. Additional exam requirements/recommendations for international students: Required—TOEFL (minimum score 550 paper-based; 213 computer-based; 80 iBT). *Application deadline:* For fall admission, 2/1 priority date for domestic students. Applications are processed on a rolling basis. Application fee: $60. Electronic applications accepted. *Expenses:* Tuition: Full-time $35,748; part-time $1554 per unit. Required fees: $215 per semester. *Financial support:* Fellowships, research assistantships, teaching assistantships, Federal Work-Study, institutionally sponsored loans, and scholarships/grants available. Support available to part-time students. Financial award application deadline: 2/15; financial award applicants required to submit FAFSA. *Faculty research:* GPSS, man-machine interaction, organizational aspects of computing, implementation of information systems, information systems practice. *Unit head:* Terry Ryan, Dean, 909-607-9591, Fax: 909-621-8564, E-mail: terry.ryan@cgu.edu. *Application contact:* Matt Hutter, Director of External Affairs, 909-621-3180, Fax: 909-621-8564, E-mail: matt.hutter@cgu.edu.

DePaul University, Charles H. Kellstadt Graduate School of Business, School of Accountancy and Management Information Systems, Chicago, IL 60604-2287. Offers accountancy (M Acc, MSA); business information technology (MS); e-business (MBA, MS); financial management and control (MBA); management accounting (MBA); management information systems (MBA); taxation (MST). Part-time and evening/weekend programs available. *Faculty:* 30 full-time (9 women), 54 part-time/adjunct (7 women). *Students:* 207 full-time (112 women), 208 part-time (106 women); includes 7 Black or African American, non-Hispanic/Latino; 34 Asian, non-Hispanic/Latino; 19 Hispanic/Latino; 2 Two or more races, non-Hispanic/Latino, 76 international. In 2010, 141 master's awarded. *Entrance requirements:* For master's, GMAT, 2 letters of recommendation, resume. Additional exam requirements/recommendations for international students: Required—TOEFL (minimum score 550 paper-based; 213 computer-based). *Application deadline:* For fall admission, 7/1 for domestic students; for winter admission, 10/1 for domestic students; for spring admission, 2/1 for domestic students. Applications are processed on a rolling basis. Application fee: $60. *Financial support:* In 2010–11, 7 research assistantships with full tuition reimbursements (averaging $4,100 per year) were awarded; institutionally sponsored loans also available. Financial award application deadline: 4/2. *Faculty research:* Tax policy, property transactions, stock options as compensation, standards setting, activity-based costing in health care. *Unit head:* Kevin Stevens, Director, 312-362-6989, E-mail: kstevens@depaul.edu. *Application contact:* Christopher E. Kinsella, Director of Cohort MBA Programs, 312-362-8810, Fax: 312-362-6677, E-mail: kgsb@depaul.edu.

DePaul University, College of Computing and Digital Media, Chicago, IL 60604. Offers animation (MA, MFA); applied technology (MS); business information technology (MS); cinema (MFA); cinema production (MS); computational finance (MS); computer and information sciences (PhD); computer game development (MS); computer graphics and motion technology (MS); computer information and network security (MS); computer science (MS); e-commerce technology (MS); human-computer interaction (MS); information systems (MS); information technology (MA); information technology project management (MS); network engineering and management (MS); predictive analytics (MS); screenwriting (MFA); software engineering (MS); JD/MA; JD/MS. Part-time and evening/weekend programs available. Postbaccalaureate distance learning degree programs offered (no on-campus study). *Faculty:* 51 full-time (11 women), 50 part-time/adjunct (9 women). *Students:* 952 full-time (230 women), 927 part-time (226 women); includes 557 minority (205 Black or African American, non-Hispanic/Latino; 2 American Indian or Alaska Native, non-Hispanic/Latino; 167 Asian, non-Hispanic/Latino; 136 Hispanic/Latino; 7 Native Hawaiian or other Pacific Islander, non-Hispanic/Latino; 40 Two or more races, non-Hispanic/Latino), 292 international. Average age 31. 896 applicants, 70% accepted, 324 enrolled. In 2010, 417 master's, 6 doctorates awarded. *Degree requirements:* For master's, thesis (for some programs); for doctorate, comprehensive exam, thesis/dissertation. *Entrance requirements:* For master's, GRE or GMAT (MS in computational finance only), bachelor's degree, resume (MS in predictive analytics only), IT experience (MS in information technology project management only), portfolio review (MFA); for doctorate, GRE, master's degree in computer science. Additional exam requirements/recommendations for international students: Required—TOEFL (minimum score 550 paper-based; 213 computer-based; 80 iBT), IELTS (minimum score 6.5), Pearson Test of English (minimum score 53). *Application deadline:* For fall admission, 8/15 priority date for domestic students, 6/1 priority date for international students; for winter admission, 12/15 priority date for domestic students, 9/15 priority date for international students; for spring admission, 3/1 priority date for domestic students, 12/15 priority date for international students. Applications are processed on a rolling basis. Application fee: $25. Electronic applications accepted. *Expenses:* Contact institution. *Financial support:* In 2010–11, 102 students received support, including 4 fellowships with full tuition reimbursements available (averaging $24,435 per year), 6 research assistantships (averaging $21,100 per year), 92 teaching assistantships with full and partial tuition reimbursements available (averaging $6,904 per year); Federal Work-Study, scholarships/grants, tuition waivers (full and partial), and unspecified assistantships also available. Support available to part-time students. Financial award application deadline: 4/30; financial award applicants required to submit FAFSA. *Faculty research:* Bioinformatics, visual computing, graphics and animation, high performance and scientific computing, databases. Total annual research expenditures: $1.4 million. *Unit head:* Dr. David Miller, Dean, 312-362-8381, Fax: 312-362-5185. *Application contact:* Dr. Liz Friedman, Assistant Dean of Student Services, 312-362-8714, Fax: 312-362-5179, E-mail: efriedm2@cdm.depaul.edu.

Eastern Michigan University, Graduate School, College of Business, Programs in Business Administration, Ypsilanti, MI 48197. Offers business administration (MBA, Graduate Certificate); computer information systems (Graduate Certificate); e-business (MBA, Graduate Certificate); enterprise business intelligence (MBA); entrepreneurship (MBA, Graduate Certificate); finance (MBA, Graduate Certificate); human resources (MBA); human resources management (Graduate Certificate); information systems (MBA); internal auditing (MBA); international business (MBA, Graduate Certificate); marketing management (Graduate Certificate); nonprofit management (MBA); organizational development (Graduate Certificate); supply chain management (MBA, Graduate Certificate). *Accreditation:* AACSB. Part-time programs available. Postbaccalaureate distance learning degree programs offered (no on-campus study). *Students:* 149 full-time (66 women), 456 part-time (232 women); includes 146 minority (109 Black or African American, non-Hispanic/Latino; 4 American Indian or Alaska Native, non-Hispanic/Latino; 27 Asian, non-Hispanic/Latino; 6 Hispanic/Latino), 105 international. Average age 32. 330 applicants, 64% accepted, 150 enrolled. In 2010, 128 master's, 53 other advanced degrees awarded. *Entrance requirements:* For master's, GMAT (minimum score 450), minimum cumulative undergraduate GPA of 2.75. Additional exam requirements/recommendations for international students: Required—TOEFL. *Application deadline:* For fall admission, 5/15 for domestic students, 5/1 for international students; for winter admission, 10/15 for domestic students, 10/1 for international students; for spring admission, 3/15 for domestic students, 3/1 for international students. Applications are processed on a rolling basis. Application fee: $35. *Financial support:* Fellowships, research assistantships with full tuition reimbursements, teaching assistantships with full tuition reimbursements, career-related internships or fieldwork, Federal Work-Study, institutionally sponsored loans, scholarships/grants, tuition waivers (partial), and unspecified assistantships available. Support available to part-time students. Financial award applicants required to submit FAFSA. *Unit head:* K. Michelle Henry, Interim Director, Graduate

Programs, 734-487-4444, Fax: 734-483-1316, E-mail: mhenry1@emich.edu. *Application contact:* Beste Windes, Advisor, 734-487-4444, Fax: 734-483-1316, E-mail: bwindes@emich.edu.

Fairleigh Dickinson University, Metropolitan Campus, University College: Arts, Sciences, and Professional Studies, School of Computer Sciences and Engineering, Program in E-Commerce, Teaneck, NJ 07666-1914. Offers MS. *Students:* 7 full-time (3 women), 2 part-time (0 women), 6 international. Average age 29. 13 applicants, 69% accepted, 2 enrolled. In 2010, 1 master's awarded. *Application deadline:* Applications are processed on a rolling basis. Application fee: $40. *Application contact:* Susan Brooman, University Director of Graduate Admissions, 201-692-2554, Fax: 201-692-2560, E-mail: globaleducation@fdu.edu.

Ferris State University, College of Business, Big Rapids, MI 49307. Offers application development (MSISM); business intelligence and informatics (MBA); database administration (MSISM); design and innovation management process (MBA); e-business (MSISM); networking (MSISM); quality management (MBA); security (MSISM). *Accreditation:* ACBSP. Part-time and evening/weekend programs available. *Faculty:* 10 full-time (3 women), 2 part-time/adjunct (both women). *Students:* 34 full-time (9 women), 112 part-time (55 women); includes 3 Black or African American, non-Hispanic/Latino; 4 American Indian or Alaska Native, non-Hispanic/Latino; 3 Asian, non-Hispanic/Latino; 3 Hispanic/Latino; 4 Two or more races, non-Hispanic/Latino, 16 international. Average age 32. 68 applicants, 35% accepted, 15 enrolled. In 2010, 62 master's awarded. *Degree requirements:* For master's, comprehensive exam, thesis (for MSISM). *Entrance requirements:* For master's, GRE or GMAT (waived if GPA is 3.5 or better), minimum GPA of 3.0 in junior/senior level classes, 2.75 overall; writing sample; 3 letters of reference; resume. Additional exam requirements/recommendations for international students: Required—TOEFL (minimum score 500 paper-based; 173 computer-based; 67 iBT). *Application deadline:* For fall admission, 7/1 priority date for domestic students, 6/15 for international students; for winter admission, 11/1 priority date for domestic students, 10/15 for international students; for spring admission, 3/1 priority date for domestic students, 2/15 for international students. Applications are processed on a rolling basis. Application fee: $30. Electronic applications accepted. *Financial support:* Career-related internships or fieldwork, Federal Work-Study, scholarships/grants, and unspecified assistantships available. Support available to part-time students. Financial award application deadline: 3/15; financial award applicants required to submit FAFSA. *Faculty research:* Quality improvement, client/server end-user computing, information management and policy, security, digital forensics. *Unit head:* Dr. David Steenstra, Department Chair, 231-591-2168, Fax: 231-591-3548, E-mail: yosts@ferris.edu. *Application contact:* Shannon Yost, Department Secretary, 231-591-2168, Fax: 231-591-3548, E-mail: yosts@ferris.edu.

Florida Institute of Technology, Graduate Programs, Extended Studies Division, Melbourne, FL 32901-6975. Offers acquisition and contract management (MS); aerospace engineering (MS); business administration (MBA); computer information systems (MS); computer science (MS); electrical engineering (MS); engineering management (MS); human resources management (MS); logistics management (MS), including humanitarian and disaster relief logistics; management (MS), including acquisition and contract management, e-business, human resources management, information systems, logistics management, management, transportation management; material acquisition management (MS); mechanical engineering (MS); operations research (MS); project management (MS), including information systems, operations research; public administration (MPA); quality management (MS); software engineering (MS); space systems (MS); space systems management (MS); systems management (MS), including information systems, operations research. Part-time and evening/weekend programs available. Postbaccalaureate distance learning degree programs offered (no on-campus study). *Faculty:* 11 full-time (3 women), 118 part-time/adjunct (24 women). *Students:* 69 full-time (23 women), 907 part-time (369 women); includes 385 minority (242 Black or African American, non-Hispanic/Latino; 15 American Indian or Alaska Native, non-Hispanic/Latino; 44 Asian, non-Hispanic/Latino; 52 Hispanic/Latino; 3 Native Hawaiian or other Pacific Islander, non-Hispanic/Latino; 29 Two or more races, non-Hispanic/Latino), 17 international. 517 applicants, 49% accepted, 245 enrolled. In 2010, 430 degrees awarded. *Degree requirements:* For master's, comprehensive exam (for some programs), capstone course. *Entrance requirements:* For master's, GMAT or resume showing 8 years of supervised experience, minimum GPA of 3.0, 2 letters of recommendation, resume. Additional exam requirements/recommendations for international students: Required—TOEFL (minimum score 550 paper-based; 213 computer-based; 79 iBT). *Application deadline:* For fall admission, 4/1 for international students; for spring admission, 9/30 for international students. Applications are processed on a rolling basis. Application fee: $50. Electronic applications accepted. *Expenses:* Contact institution. *Financial support:* Application deadline: 3/1. *Unit head:* Dr. Theodore Richardson, Senior Associate Dean, 321-674-8123, Fax: 321-674-7597, E-mail: trichardson@fit.edu. *Application contact:* Carolyn Farrior, Director of Graduate Admissions, Online Learning and Off-Campus Programs, 321-674-7118, Fax: 321-674-8216, E-mail: cfarrior@fit.edu.

Florida Institute of Technology, Graduate Programs, Nathan M. Bisk College of Business, Online Programs, Melbourne, FL 32901-6975. Offers accounting (MBA); accounting and finance (MBA); finance (MBA); healthcare management (MBA); information technology (MS); information technology management (MBA); Internet marketing (MBA); management (MBA); marketing (MBA); project management (MBA). Part-time and evening/weekend programs available. Postbaccalaureate distance learning degree programs offered (no on-campus study). *Faculty:* 32 part-time/adjunct (8 women). *Students:* 4 full-time (1 woman), 1,062 part-time (499 women); includes 373 minority (244 Black or African American, non-Hispanic/Latino; 8 American Indian or Alaska Native, non-Hispanic/Latino; 37 Asian, non-Hispanic/Latino; 76 Hispanic/Latino; 8 Native Hawaiian or other Pacific Islander, non-Hispanic/Latino), 39 international. Average age 37. 299 applicants, 167 enrolled. In 2010, 134 master's awarded. *Entrance requirements:* For master's, GMAT or resume showing 8 years of supervised experience, 2 letters of recommendation, resume, competency in math past college algebra. Additional exam requirements/recommendations for international students: Required—TOEFL (minimum score 550 paper-based; 213 computer-based; 79 iBT). *Application deadline:* For fall admission, 4/1 for international students; for spring admission, 9/30 for international students. Applications are processed on a rolling basis. Application fee: $50. Electronic applications accepted. *Expenses:* Contact institution. *Financial support:* Available to part-time students. Application deadline: 3/1. *Unit head:* Dr. Mary S. Bonhomme, Dean, Florida Tech Online Associate Provost for Online Learning, 321-674-8202, Fax: 321-674-8216, E-mail: bonhomme@fit.edu. *Application contact:* Carolyn Farrior, Director of Graduate Admissions Online Learning and Off Campus Programs, 321-674-7118, Fax: 321-674-8216, E-mail: cfarrior@fit.edu.

George Mason University, Volgenau School of Engineering, Department of Computer Science, Fairfax, VA 22030. Offers biometrics (Certificate); computer games technology (Certificate); computer networking (Certificate); computer science (MS, PhD); data mining (Certificate); database management (Certificate); electronic commerce (Certificate); foundations of information systems (Certificate); information engineering (Certificate); information security and assurance (MS, Certificate); information systems (MS); intelligent agents (Certificate); software architecture (Certificate); software engineering (MS, Certificate); systems engineering (MS); Web-based software engineering (Certificate). MS program offered jointly with Old Dominion University, University of Virginia, Virginia Commonwealth University, and Virginia Polytechnic Institute and State University. Part-time and evening/weekend programs available. Postbaccalaureate distance learning degree programs offered. *Faculty:* 42 full-time (9 women), 20 part-time/adjunct (1 woman). *Students:* 124 full-time (37 women), 453 part-time (103 women); includes 14 Black or African American, non-Hispanic/Latino; 66 Asian, non-Hispanic/Latino; 13 Hispanic/Latino; 3 Two or more races, non-Hispanic/Latino, 206 international. Average age 30. 904 applicants, 53% accepted, 150 enrolled. In 2010, 203 master's, 4 doctorates, 20 other advanced degrees awarded. *Degree requirements:* For master's, thesis optional; for doctorate, comprehensive exam, thesis/dissertation. *Entrance requirements:* For master's, GRE General Test, minimum GPA of 3.0 in last 60 hours, 3 letters of recommendation; for doctorate, GRE, 4-year BA, academic work in computer science, 3 letters of recommendation, statement of career goals and aspirations. Additional exam requirements/recommendations for international students: Required—TOEFL (minimum score 570 paper-based; 230 computer-based; 88 iBT). *Application deadline:* For fall admission, 4/15 priority date for domestic students, 1/15 for international students; for spring admission, 11/15 for domestic students. Application fee: $100. Electronic applications accepted. *Expenses:* Tuition, state resident: full-time $8192; part-time $440 per credit hour. Tuition, nonresident: full-time $22,952; part-time $1055 per credit hour. Required fees: $2364; $99 per credit hour. *Financial support:* In 2010–11, 101 students received support, including 3 fellowships (averaging $18,000 per year), 52 research assistantships (averaging $15,078 per year), 47 teaching assistantships (averaging $10,983 per year); career-related internships or fieldwork, Federal Work-Study, scholarships/grants, unspecified assistantships, and health care benefits (full-time research or teaching assistantship recipients) also available. Financial award application deadline: 3/1; financial award applicants required to submit FAFSA. *Faculty research:* Artificial intelligence, image processing/graphics, parallel/distributed systems, software engineering systems. Total annual research expenditures: $1.3 million. *Unit head:* Dr. Arun Sood, Director, 703-993-1524, Fax: 703-993-1710, E-mail: asood@gmu.edu. *Application contact:* Jay Shapiro, Professor, 703-993-1485, E-mail: jshapiro@gmu.edu.

HEC Montreal, School of Business Administration, Diploma Programs in Administration, Program in E-Business, Montréal, QC H3T 2A7, Canada. Offers Diploma. All courses are given in French. Part-time programs available. *Students:* 16 full-time (3 women), 55 part-time (20 women). 56 applicants, 55% accepted, 26 enrolled. In 2010, 25 Diplomas awarded. *Degree requirements:* For Diploma, one foreign language. *Application deadline:* For fall admission, 4/15 for domestic and international students; for winter admission, 9/15 for domestic and international students. Application fee: $78 Canadian dollars. Electronic applications accepted. *Expenses:* Tuition, area resident: Part-time $68.93 per credit. Tuition, state resident: full-time $2481.48; part-time $188.92 per credit. Tuition, nonresident: full-time $6801; part-time

$482.06 per course. International tuition: $17,354.16 full-time. Required fees: $1309.50; $30.28 per credit. $93.45 per term. Tuition and fees vary according to degree level and program. *Financial support:* Scholarships/grants available. Financial award application deadline: 9/2. *Unit head:* Silvia Ponce, Director, 514-340-6393, E-mail: silvia.ponce@hec.ca. *Application contact:* Marie Deshaies, Senior Student Advisor, 514-340-6135, Fax: 514-340-6411, E-mail: marie.deshaies@hec.ca.

HEC Montreal, School of Business Administration, Master of Science Programs in Administration, Program in Electronic Commerce, Montréal, QC H3T 2A7, Canada. Offers M Sc. Program offered jointly with Université de Montréal. Part-time programs available. *Students:* 29 full-time (13 women), 19 part-time (7 women). 56 applicants, 50% accepted, 18 enrolled. In 2010, 15 master's awarded. *Degree requirements:* For master's, one foreign language. *Entrance requirements:* For master's, bachelor's degree in law, management, information systems or related field. *Application deadline:* For fall admission, 4/1 for domestic and international students. Application fee: $78 Canadian dollars. Electronic applications accepted. *Expenses:* Tuition, area resident: Part-time $68.93 per credit. Tuition, state resident: full-time $2481.48; part-time $188.92 per credit. Tuition, nonresident: full-time $6801; part-time $482.06 per course. International tuition: $17,354.16 full-time. Required fees: $1309.50; $30.28 per credit. $93.45 per term. Tuition and fees vary according to degree level and program. *Financial support:* Research assistantships, teaching assistantships available. Financial award application deadline: 9/2. *Unit head:* Olivier Gerbe, Co-Director, 514-340-6855, Fax: 514-340-6132, E-mail: olivier.gerbe@hec.ca. *Application contact:* Jo Anne Audet, Administrative Director, 514-340-1315, Fax: 514-340-6411, E-mail: joanne.audet@hec.ca.

Inter American University of Puerto Rico, Bayamón Campus, Graduate School, Bayamón, PR 00957. Offers biology (MS), including environmental sciences and ecology, molecular biotechnology; electronic commerce (MBA); human resources (MBA). Part-time and evening/weekend programs available. *Faculty:* 4 full-time (1 woman), 5 part-time/adjunct (4 women). *Students:* 115 part-time (84 women); includes 49 Hispanic/Latino. Average age 31. *Degree requirements:* For master's, comprehensive exam, research project. *Entrance requirements:* For master's, EXADEP, GRE General Test, letters of recommendation. *Application deadline:* For fall admission, 7/1 for domestic students, 5/1 priority date for international students; for winter admission, 11/15 priority date for domestic and international students; for spring admission, 2/15 priority date for domestic and international students. Application fee: $31. *Expenses:* Tuition: Full-time $4424; part-time $202 per credit. Required fees: $180 per trimester. *Unit head:* Prof. Juan F. Martinez, Chancellor, 787-279-1200 Ext. 2295, Fax: 787-279-2205, E-mail: jmartinez@bc.inter.edu. *Application contact:* Carlos Alicea, Director of Admission, 787-279-1200 Ext. 2017, Fax: 787-279-2205, E-mail: calicea@bc.inter.edu.

Lewis University, College of Business, Graduate School of Management, Program in Business Administration, Romeoville, IL 60446. Offers accounting (MBA); custom elective option (MBA); e-business (MBA); finance (MBA); healthcare management (MBA); human resources management (MBA); information security (MBA); international business (MBA); management information systems (MBA); marketing (MBA); project management (MBA); technology and operations management (MBA). Part-time and evening/weekend programs available. *Students:* 119 full-time (66 women), 204 part-time (104 women); includes 55 Black or African American, non-Hispanic/Latino; 9 Asian, non-Hispanic/Latino; 30 Hispanic/Latino; 1 Native Hawaiian or other Pacific Islander, non-Hispanic/Latino, 9 international. Average age 28. In 2010, 111 master's awarded. *Entrance requirements:* For master's, interview, bachelor's degree, resume, 2 recommendations. Additional exam requirements/recommendations for international students: Required—TOEFL (minimum score 550 paper-based; 213 computer-based). *Application deadline:* For fall admission, 8/15 priority date for domestic students, 5/1 priority date for international students; for spring admission, 11/15 priority date for international students. Applications are processed on a rolling basis. Application fee: $40. Electronic applications accepted. *Expenses:* Tuition: Full-time $13,320; part-time $740 per credit hour. Tuition and fees vary according to program. *Financial support:* Career-related internships or fieldwork, Federal Work-Study, scholarships/grants, and unspecified assistantships available. Financial award application deadline: 5/1; financial award applicants required to submit FAFSA. *Unit head:* Dr. Maureen Culleeney, Academic Program Director, 815-838-0500 Ext. 5631, E-mail: culleema@lewisu.edu. *Application contact:* Michele Ryan, Director of Admission, 815-838-0500 Ext. 5384, E-mail: gsm@lewisu.edu.

Mercy College, School of Liberal Arts, Program in Internet Business Systems, Dobbs Ferry, NY 10522-1189. Offers Web strategy and design (MS, Certificate). Part-time and evening/weekend programs available. Postbaccalaureate distance learning degree programs offered (no on-campus study). *Students:* 15 full-time (6 women), 3 part-time; includes 3 Black or African American, non-Hispanic/Latino; 1 Asian, non-Hispanic/Latino; 3 Hispanic/Latino, 3 international. Average age 35. 29 applicants, 52% accepted, 10 enrolled. In 2010, 7 master's awarded. *Entrance requirements:* For master's, interview, resume, 2 letters of recommendation, 2-page written personal statement. Additional exam requirements/recommendations for international students: Required—TOEFL (minimum score 600 paper-based; 250

computer-based; 100 iBT), IELTS (minimum score 8). *Application deadline:* For fall admission, 8/1 for international students. Applications are processed on a rolling basis. Application fee: $40. Electronic applications accepted. *Expenses:* Contact institution. *Financial support:* Career-related internships or fieldwork, Federal Work-Study, scholarships/grants, and unspecified assistantships available. Support available to part-time students. Financial award applicants required to submit FAFSA. *Faculty research:* Internet business systems, Internet marketing, Web design, Internet technologies. *Unit head:* John DiElsi, Program Director, 914-674-7306, E-mail: jdielsi@mercy.edu. *Application contact:* Allison Gurdineer, Senior Associate Director of Recruitment, 914-674-7601, E-mail: agurdineer@mercy.edu.

National University, Academic Affairs, School of Business and Management, Department of Leadership and Business Administration, La Jolla, CA 92037-1011. Offers alternative dispute resolution (MBA); e-business (MBA); financial management (MBA); human resource management (MBA); human resources management (MA); international business (MBA); knowledge management (MS); marketing (MBA); organizational leadership (MBA, MS); technology management (MBA). Part-time and evening/weekend programs available. Postbaccalaureate distance learning degree programs offered (no on-campus study). *Faculty:* 16 full-time (4 women), 126 part-time/adjunct (39 women). *Students:* 119 full-time (81 women), 410 part-time (202 women); includes 176 minority (81 Black or African American, non-Hispanic/Latino; 1 American Indian or Alaska Native, non-Hispanic/Latino; 31 Asian, non-Hispanic/Latino; 52 Hispanic/Latino; 4 Native Hawaiian or other Pacific Islander, non-Hispanic/Latino; 7 Two or more races, non-Hispanic/Latino), 183 international. Average age 38. 219 applicants, 100% accepted, 160 enrolled. In 2010, 95 master's awarded. *Degree requirements:* For master's, thesis. *Entrance requirements:* For master's, interview, minimum GPA of 2.5. Additional exam requirements/recommendations for international students: Required—TOEFL (minimum score 550 paper-based; 213 computer-based; 79 iBT), IELTS (minimum score 6). *Application deadline:* Applications are processed on a rolling basis. Application fee: $60 ($65 for international students). Electronic applications accepted. *Expenses:* Tuition: Full-time $9450; part-time $350 per unit. Required fees: $350 per unit. One-time fee: $60. *Financial support:* Career-related internships or fieldwork, institutionally sponsored loans, scholarships/grants, and tuition waivers (partial) available. Support available to part-time students. Financial award application deadline: 6/30; financial award applicants required to submit FAFSA. *Unit head:* Dr. Bruce Buchowicz, Chair, 858-642-8439, Fax: 858-642-8406, E-mail: bbuchowicz@nu.edu. *Application contact:* Dominick Giovanniello, Associate Regional Dean—San Diego, 800-NAT-UNIV, Fax: 858-541-7792, E-mail: dgiovann@nu.edu.

National University, Academic Affairs, School of Business and Management, Department of Management and Marketing, La Jolla, CA 92037-1011. Offers e-business (MS); knowledge management (MS); management (MA); organizational leadership (MS). Part-time and evening/weekend programs available. Postbaccalaureate distance learning degree programs offered (no on-campus study). *Faculty:* 16 full-time (4 women), 110 part-time/adjunct (34 women). *Students:* 364 full-time (165 women), 458 part-time (212 women); includes 278 minority (71 Black or African American, non-Hispanic/Latino; 4 American Indian or Alaska Native, non-Hispanic/Latino; 99 Asian, non-Hispanic/Latino; 91 Hispanic/Latino; 4 Native Hawaiian or other Pacific Islander, non-Hispanic/Latino; 9 Two or more races, non-Hispanic/Latino), 195 international. Average age 34. 157 applicants, 100% accepted, 134 enrolled. In 2010, 321 master's awarded. *Degree requirements:* For master's, thesis. *Entrance requirements:* For master's, interview, minimum GPA of 2.5. Additional exam requirements/recommendations for international students: Required—TOEFL (minimum score 550 paper-based; 213 computer-based; 79 iBT), IELTS (minimum score 6). *Application deadline:* Applications are processed on a rolling basis. Application fee: $60 ($65 for international students). Electronic applications accepted. *Expenses:* Tuition: Full-time $9450; part-time $350 per unit. Required fees: $350 per unit. One-time fee: $60. *Financial support:* Career-related internships or fieldwork, institutionally sponsored loans, scholarships/grants, and tuition waivers (partial) available. Support available to part-time students. Financial award application deadline: 6/30; financial award applicants required to submit FAFSA. *Unit head:* Dr. Ramon Corona, Chair and Professor, 858-642-8427, Fax: 858-642-8406, E-mail: rcorona@nu.edu. *Application contact:* Dominick Giovanniello, Associate Regional Dean—San Diego, 800-NAT-UNIV, Fax: 858-541-7792, E-mail: dgiovann@nu.edu.

Polytechnic Institute of NYU, Department of Technology Management, Brooklyn, NY 11201-2990. Offers construction management (Advanced Certificate); electronic business management (Advanced Certificate); entrepreneurship (Advanced Certificate); human resources management (Advanced Certificate); information management (Advanced Certificate); management (MS); management of technology (MS); organizational behavior (MS, Advanced Certificate); project management (Advanced Certificate); technology management (MBA, PhD, Advanced Certificate); telecommunications and information management (MS); telecommunications management (Advanced Certificate). Part-time and evening/weekend programs available. *Faculty:* 7 full-time (2 women), 28 part-time/adjunct (4 women). *Students:* 224 full-time (93 women), 106 part-time (38 women); includes 15 Black or African American, non-Hispanic/Latino; 41 Asian, non-Hispanic/Latino; 10 Hispanic/Latino, 158 international. Average age 30. 370 applicants, 60%

accepted, 120 enrolled. In 2010, 173 master's, 1 doctorate awarded. *Degree requirements:* For master's, comprehensive exam (for some programs), thesis (for some programs); for doctorate, comprehensive exam, thesis/dissertation. *Entrance requirements:* For master's, GMAT, minimum B average in undergraduate course work. Additional exam requirements/recommendations for international students: Required—TOEFL (minimum score 550 paper-based; 213 computer-based; 80 iBT); Recommended—IELTS (minimum score 6.5). *Application deadline:* For fall admission, 7/31 priority date for domestic students, 4/30 priority date for international students; for spring admission, 12/31 priority date for domestic students, 11/30 priority date for international students. Applications are processed on a rolling basis. Application fee: $75. Electronic applications accepted. *Expenses:* Tuition: Full-time $21,492; part-time $1194 per credit. Required fees: $385 per semester. Tuition and fees vary according to course load. *Financial support:* In 2010–11, 1 fellowship (averaging $26,400 per year) was awarded; research assistantships, teaching assistantships, institutionally sponsored loans, scholarships/grants, and unspecified assistantships also available. Support available to part-time students. *Unit head:* Prof. Bharadwaj Rao, Head, 718-260-3617, Fax: 718-260-3874, E-mail: brao@poly.edu. *Application contact:* JeanCarlo Bonilla, Director of Graduate Enrollment Management, 718-260-3182, Fax: 718-260-3624, E-mail: gradinfo@poly.edu.

Université de Sherbrooke, Faculty of Administration, Program in E-Commerce, Sherbrooke, QC J1K 2R1, Canada. Offers M Sc. *Faculty:* 4 full-time (0 women), 7 part-time/adjunct (1 woman). *Students:* 19 full-time (4 women). Average age 22. 55 applicants, 80% accepted, 19 enrolled. In 2010, 10 master's awarded. *Degree requirements:* For master's, one foreign language, thesis. *Entrance requirements:* For master's, No, Bachelor degree in related field Minimum GPA 3.0/4.3 Letters of references Fluent in french. *Application deadline:* For fall admission, 4/30 for domestic students, 1/15 for international students. Applications are processed on a rolling basis. Application fee: $70. Electronic applications accepted. *Faculty research:* RFID, B2B, Web social NW, Web value concept. *Unit head:* Prof. Julien Bilodeau, Director, Graduate programs in business, 819-821-8000 Ext. 62355, E-mail: julien.bilodeau@usherbrooke.ca. *Application contact:* Marie-Claude Drouin, Assistant to the director, 819-821-7685, Fax: 819-821-7966.

University at Buffalo, the State University of New York, Graduate School, College of Arts and Sciences, Department of Economics, Buffalo, NY 14260. Offers economics (MA, MS, PhD); financial economics (Certificate); health services (Certificate); information and Internet economics (Certificate); international economics (Certificate); law and regulation (Certificate); urban and regional economics (Certificate). Part-time programs available. *Faculty:* 19 full-time (3 women), 7 part-time/adjunct (2 women). *Students:* 264 full-time (124 women); includes 23 minority (3 Black or African American, non-Hispanic/Latino; 1 American Indian or Alaska Native, non-Hispanic/Latino; 16 Asian, non-Hispanic/Latino; 3 Hispanic/Latino), 177 international. Average age 24. 483 applicants, 48% accepted, 99 enrolled. In 2010, 82 master's, 7 doctorates, 3 other advanced degrees awarded. Terminal master's awarded for partial completion of doctoral program. *Degree requirements:* For master's, comprehensive exam; for doctorate, comprehensive exam, thesis/dissertation, field and theory exams. *Entrance requirements:* For master's, GRE or GMAT Test; for doctorate, GRE General Test. Additional exam requirements/recommendations for international students: Required—TOEFL (minimum score 550 paper-based; 213 computer-based; 79 iBT), TWE. *Application deadline:* For fall admission, 1/15 priority date for domestic and international students; for spring admission, 11/1 priority date for domestic and international students. Applications are processed on a rolling basis. Application fee: $75. Electronic applications accepted. *Financial support:* In 2010–11, 24 students received support, including 10 fellowships with full tuition reimbursements available (averaging $2,200 per year), 1 research assistantship with full tuition reimbursement available (averaging $13,500 per year), 12 teaching assistantships with full tuition reimbursements available (averaging $13,500 per year); Federal Work-Study, health care benefits, and unspecified assistantships also available. Financial award application deadline: 2/1; financial award applicants required to submit FAFSA. *Faculty research:* Human capital, international economics, econometrics, applied economics, urban economics, economic growth and development. *Unit head:* Dr. Isaac Ehrlich, Chair, 716-645-8670, Fax: 716-645-2127, E-mail: mgtehrl@buffalo.edu. *Application contact:* Dr. Nagesh Revankar, Director of Graduate Studies, 716-645-2121 Ext. 428, Fax: 716-645-2127, E-mail: ecorevan@buffalo.edu.

The University of Akron, Graduate School, College of Business Administration, Department of Management, Program in Electronic Business, Akron, OH 44325. Offers MBA. *Students:* 2 full-time (0 women), 1 part-time (0 women), all international. Average age 35. 2 applicants, 50% accepted. In 2010, 2 master's awarded. *Entrance requirements:* For master's, GMAT, minimum GPA of 2.75, two letters of recommendation, statement of purpose, resume. Additional exam requirements/recommendations for international students: Required—TOEFL (minimum score 550 paper-based; 213 computer-based; 79 iBT). *Application deadline:* For fall admission, 7/15 for domestic and international students; for spring admission, 11/15 for domestic and international students. Applications are processed on a rolling basis. Application fee: $30 ($40 for international students). Electronic applications accepted. *Expenses:* Tuition, state resident: full-time $6800; part-time $378 per credit hour. Tuition, nonresident: full-time $11,644; part-time $647 per credit hour. Required fees: $1265. One-time fee: $30 full-time. *Unit head:* Dr. B. S. Vijayaraman, Head, 330-972-5442, E-mail: bsv@uakron.edu. *Application contact:* Dr. Susan Hanlon, Director of Graduate Business Programs, 330-972-7043, Fax: 330-972-6588, E-mail: shanlon@uakron.edu.

University of Colorado Denver, Business School, Program in Marketing, Denver, CO 80217. Offers brand management and marketing communication (MS); global marketing (MS); high-tech/entrepreneurial marketing (MS); Internet marketing (MS); market research (MS); marketing and business intelligence (MS); marketing for sustainability (MS); marketing in nonprofit organizations (MS); sports and entertainment marketing (MS). Part-time and evening/weekend programs available. *Students:* 31 full-time (18 women), 8 part-time (4 women); includes 3 Hispanic/Latino, 5 international. Average age 29. 46 applicants, 63% accepted, 18 enrolled. In 2010, 11 master's awarded. *Degree requirements:* For master's, 30 semester hours (18 of marketing core courses, 12 of graduate marketing electives). *Entrance requirements:* For master's, GMAT. Additional exam requirements/recommendations for international students: Required—TOEFL (minimum score 525 paper-based; 197 computer-based; 71 iBT). *Application deadline:* For fall admission, 4/1 priority date for domestic students, 3/15 priority date for international students; for spring admission, 10/1 priority date for domestic and international students. Application fee: $50 ($75 for international students). Electronic applications accepted. *Expenses:* Contact institution. *Financial support:* Federal Work-Study and scholarships/grants available. Support available to part-time students. Financial award application deadline: 4/1; financial award applicants required to submit FAFSA. *Faculty research:* Marketing issues in the Chinese environment, impact of individual difference and contextual factors on the risk-taking behaviors of managers making new-business creation decisions, Attribution Theory perspective of conflict between marketers and engineers, organizational identity and identification, international market entry strategies. *Unit head:* Dr. David Forlani, Associate Professor/Director, 303-315-8420, E-mail: david.forlani@ucdenver.edu. *Application contact:* Shelly Townley, Admissions Director, Graduate Programs, 303-315-8202, E-mail: shelly.townley@ucdenver.edu.

University of Dayton, Graduate School, School of Business Administration, Dayton, OH 45469-1300. Offers accounting (MBA); business intelligence (MBA); cyber security (MBA); entrepreneurship (MBA); finance (MBA); international business (MBA); marketing (MBA); MIS (MBA); operations management (MBA); technology-enhanced business/e-commerce (MBA); JD/MBA. *Accreditation:* AACSB. Part-time and evening/weekend programs available. *Faculty:* 25 full-time (7 women), 14 part-time/adjunct (2 women). *Students:* 184 full-time (72 women), 110 part-time (34 women); includes 23 minority (7 Black or African American, non-Hispanic/Latino; 7 Asian, non-Hispanic/Latino; 8 Hispanic/Latino; 1 Two or more races, non-Hispanic/Latino), 31 international. Average age 28. 220 applicants, 85% accepted, 103 enrolled. In 2010, 113 master's awarded. *Entrance requirements:* For master's, GMAT or GRE. Additional exam requirements/recommendations for international students: Required—TOEFL (minimum score 550 paper-based; 213 computer-based; 79 iBT); Recommended—IELTS (minimum score 6.5). *Application deadline:* For fall admission, 3/1 priority date for international students; for winter admission, 7/1 priority date for international students; for spring admission, 1/1 priority date for international students. Applications are processed on a rolling basis. Application fee: $0 ($50 for international students). Electronic applications accepted. *Expenses:* Contact institution. *Financial support:* In 2010–11, 15 research assistantships with full and partial tuition reimbursements (averaging $7,020 per year) were awarded; career-related internships or fieldwork, institutionally sponsored loans, scholarships/grants, health care benefits, and unspecified assistantships also available. Support available to part-time students. Financial award application deadline: 3/15; financial award applicants required to submit FAFSA. *Faculty research:* Management information systems, economics, finance, entrepreneurship, marketing. *Unit head:* Janice M. Glynn, Director, MBA Program, 937-229-3733, Fax: 937-229-3882, E-mail: glynn@udayton.edu. *Application contact:* Jeffrey Carter, Assistant Director, MBA Program, 937-229-3733, Fax: 937-229-3882, E-mail: jeff.carter@notes.udayton.edu.

University of Denver, Daniels College of Business, Department of Information Technology and Electronic Commerce, Denver, CO 80208. Offers business intelligence (MS); information technology (IMBA, MBA). Part-time and evening/weekend programs available. *Faculty:* 6 full-time (1 woman). *Entrance requirements:* For master's, GRE General Test or GMAT. Additional exam requirements/recommendations for international students: Required—TOEFL (minimum score 570 paper-based; 88 iBT). *Application deadline:* For fall admission, 11/15 priority date for domestic students; for spring admission, 10/15 priority date for domestic students. Applications are processed on a rolling basis. Application fee: $100. Electronic applications accepted. *Expenses:* Tuition: Full-time $35,604; part-time $29,670 per year. Required fees: $687 per year. Tuition and fees vary according to program. *Financial support:* Career-related internships or fieldwork, Federal Work-Study, institutionally sponsored loans, and scholarships/grants available. Support available to part-time students. Financial award application deadline: 3/15. *Faculty research:* Cross-cultural research in information systems, electronic commerce, distributed project management, strategic information

systems, management of emerging technologies. *Unit head:* Dr. Paul Bauer, Chair, 303-871-3816, E-mail: paul.bauer@du.edu. *Application contact:* Allison Sharpe, Graduate Admissions Manager, 303-871-4212, E-mail: allison.sharpe@du.edu.

University of Florida, Graduate School, Warrington College of Business Administration, Hough Graduate School of Business, Programs in Business Administration, Gainesville, FL 32611. Offers accounting (MBA); arts administration (MBA); business strategy and public policy (MBA); competitive strategy (MBA); decision and information sciences (MBA); electronic commerce (MBA); finance (MBA); general business (MBA); global management (MBA); Graham-Buffett security analysis (MBA); health administration (MBA); human resources management (MBA); international studies (MBA); Latin American business (MBA); management (MBA); marketing (MBA); sports administration (MBA); JD/MBA; MBA/MS; MBA/PhD; MBA/Pharm D; MD/MBA. *Accreditation:* AACSB. Part-time and evening/weekend programs available. *Faculty:* 71 full-time (10 women). *Students:* 187 full-time (44 women), 305 part-time (83 women); includes 25 Black or African American, non-Hispanic/Latino; 2 American Indian or Alaska Native, non-Hispanic/Latino; 52 Asian, non-Hispanic/Latino; 54 Hispanic/Latino, 11 international. Average age 31. 919 applicants, 33% accepted, 225 enrolled. In 2010, 492 master's awarded. *Degree requirements:* For master's, capstone course. *Entrance requirements:* For master's, GMAT, minimum GPA of 3.0, interview. Additional exam requirements/recommendations for international students: Required—TOEFL (minimum score 550 paper-based; 213 computer-based; 80 iBT), IELTS (minimum score 6). *Application deadline:* For fall admission, 7/1 for domestic students, 1/1 for international students; for spring admission, 12/1 for domestic and international students. Applications are processed on a rolling basis. Application fee: $30. Electronic applications accepted. *Expenses:* Tuition, state resident: full-time $10,915.92. Tuition, nonresident: full-time $28,309. *Financial support:* In 2010–11, 1 student received support, including 1 teaching assistantship (averaging $20,600 per year); career-related internships or fieldwork, scholarships/grants, and unspecified assistantships also available. Support available to part-time students. Financial award applicants required to submit FAFSA. *Faculty research:* Accounting, finance, insurance, management, real estate, urban analysis marketing. *Unit head:* Prof. Alexander D. Sevilla, Assistant Dean and Director MBA Programs, 352-273-3252 Ext. 1206, E-mail: alex.sevilla@warrington.ufl.edu. *Application contact:* Prof. Kelli Gust, Associate Director of MBA Programs, 352-273-3255, Fax: 352-392-8791, E-mail: kelly.gust@warrington.ufl.edu.

University of Massachusetts Dartmouth, Graduate School, Charlton College of Business, Program in Business Administration, North Dartmouth, MA 02747-2300. Offers accounting (Postbaccalaureate Certificate); business administration (MBA); e-commerce (PMC); finance (PMC); general management (PMC); leadership (PMC); management (Postbaccalaureate Certificate); marketing (PMC); supply chain management (PMC). *Accreditation:* AACSB. Part-time programs available. *Faculty:* 40 full-time (13 women), 28 part-time/adjunct (8 women). *Students:* 99 full-time (38 women), 123 part-time (62 women); includes 4 Black or African American, non-Hispanic/Latino; 2 American Indian or Alaska Native, non-Hispanic/Latino; 3 Asian, non-Hispanic/Latino; 8 Hispanic/Latino; 1 Two or more races, non-Hispanic/Latino, 45 international. Average age 30. 185 applicants, 76% accepted, 79 enrolled. In 2010, 79 master's, 12 other advanced degrees awarded. *Entrance requirements:* For master's, GMAT, resume, letters of recommendation. Additional exam requirements/recommendations for international students: Required—TOEFL (minimum score 500 paper-based; 200 computer-based; 72 iBT). *Application deadline:* For fall admission, 6/1 for domestic students, 5/1 for international students; for spring admission, 10/1 for domestic students, 8/1 for international students. Application fee: $40 ($60 for international students). Electronic applications accepted. *Expenses:* Tuition, state resident: full-time $2071; part-time $86 per credit. Tuition, nonresident: full-time $8099; part-time $337 per credit. Required fees: $9446; $394 per credit. One-time fee: $75. Part-time tuition and fees vary according to class time, course load, degree level and reciprocity agreements. *Financial support:* In 2010–11, 1 research assistantship with full tuition reimbursement (averaging $6,000 per year) was awarded; teaching assistantships, Federal Work-Study and unspecified assistantships also available. Support available to part-time students. Financial award application deadline: 3/1; financial award applicants required to submit FAFSA. *Faculty research:* Global business environment, e-commerce, managing diversity, agile manufacturing, green business. Total annual research expenditures: $29,538. *Unit head:* Dr. Norm Barber, Assistant Dean, 508-999-8543, E-mail: nbarber@umassd.edu. *Application contact:* Elan Turcotte-Shamski, Graduate Admissions Officer, 508-999-8604, Fax: 508-999-8183, E-mail: graduate@umassd.edu.

University of New Brunswick Saint John, Faculty of Business, Saint John, NB E2L 4L5, Canada. Offers administration (MBA); electronic commerce (MBA); international business (MBA); natural resource management (MBA). Part-time programs available. *Faculty:* 19 full-time (4 women), 14 part-time/adjunct (8 women). *Students:* 47 full-time (18 women), 55 part-time (21 women). 93 applicants, 78% accepted, 25 enrolled. In 2010, 36 master's awarded. *Entrance requirements:* For master's, GMAT, minimum GPA of 3.0. Additional exam requirements/recommendations for international students: Required—TOEFL (minimum score 580 paper-based; 237 computer-based),

IELTS (minimum score 7), TWE (minimum score 4.5). *Application deadline:* For fall admission, 5/15 for domestic and international students. Applications are processed on a rolling basis. Application fee: $100. Electronic applications accepted. *Expenses:* Contact institution. *Financial support:* In 2010–11, 4 students received support. Career-related internships or fieldwork and scholarships/grants available. *Faculty research:* Business use of weblogs and podcasts to communicate, corporate governance, high-involvement work systems, international competitiveness, supply chain management and logistics. *Unit head:* Henryk Sterniczuk, Director of Graduate Studies, 506-648-5573, Fax: 506-648-5574, E-mail: sternicz@unbsj.ca. *Application contact:* Tammy Morin, Secretary, 506-648-5746, Fax: 506-648-5574, E-mail: tmorin@unbsj.ca.

University of North Florida, Coggin College of Business, MBA Program, Jacksonville, FL 32224. Offers accounting (MBA); construction management (MBA); e-commerce (MBA); economics (MBA); finance (MBA); human resource management (MBA); international business (MBA); logistics (MBA); management applications (MBA). *Accreditation:* AACSB. Part-time and evening/weekend programs available. *Faculty:* 17 full-time (5 women), 1 part-time/adjunct (0 women). *Students:* 137 full-time (56 women), 268 part-time (112 women); includes 17 Black or African American, non-Hispanic/Latino; 21 Asian, non-Hispanic/Latino; 12 Hispanic/Latino; 3 Two or more races, non-Hispanic/Latino, 29 international. Average age 30. 250 applicants, 57% accepted, 94 enrolled. In 2010, 173 master's awarded. *Entrance requirements:* For master's, GMAT or GRE, U.S. bachelor's degree from regionally-accredited university or equivalent foreign degree. Additional exam requirements/recommendations for international students: Required—TOEFL (minimum score 550 paper-based; 213 computer-based; 79 iBT). *Application deadline:* For fall admission, 7/1 priority date for domestic students, 5/1 for international students; for spring admission, 11/1 priority date for domestic students, 10/1 for international students. Applications are processed on a rolling basis. Application fee: $30. *Expenses:* Tuition, state resident: full-time $7646.40; part-time $318.60 per credit hour. Tuition, nonresident: full-time $23,502; part-time $979.24 per credit hour. Required fees: $1208.88; $50.37 per credit hour. Tuition and fees vary according to course load and program. *Financial support:* In 2010–11, 40 students received support; research assistantships, teaching assistantships, Federal Work-Study and tuition waivers (partial) available. Support available to part-time students. Financial award application deadline: 4/1; financial award applicants required to submit FAFSA. *Faculty research:* Performance measures, costing, and inventory issues in logistics and supply chain management; inter-organizational systems; international management and marketing practices; e-commerce; organizational learning and socialization processes. Total annual research expenditures: $9,024. *Unit head:* Dr. C. Bruce Kavan, Chair, 904-620-2780, Fax: 904-620-2832. *Application contact:* Cheryl Campbell, Graduate Advisor, 904-620-2575, Fax: 904-620-2832, E-mail: ccampbell@unf.edu.

University of San Francisco, School of Business and Professional Studies, Masagung Graduate School of Management, Program in Business Administration, San Francisco, CA 94117-1080. Offers business economics (MBA); e-business (MBA); entrepreneurship (MBA); finance (MBA); international business (MBA); management (MBA); marketing (MBA); telecommunications management and policy (MBA); JD/MBA; MSN/MBA. *Accreditation:* AACSB. *Faculty:* 17 full-time (4 women), 16 part-time/adjunct (7 women). *Students:* 263 full-time (130 women), 11 part-time (6 women); includes 98 minority (3 Black or African American, non-Hispanic/Latino; 65 Asian, non-Hispanic/Latino; 18 Hispanic/Latino; 3 Native Hawaiian or other Pacific Islander, non-Hispanic/Latino; 9 Two or more races, non-Hispanic/Latino), 43 international. Average age 29. 503 applicants, 60% accepted, 80 enrolled. In 2010, 115 master's awarded. *Entrance requirements:* For master's, GMAT, minimum undergraduate GPA of 3.2. Additional exam requirements/recommendations for international students: Required—TOEFL. *Application deadline:* For fall admission, 7/1 priority date for domestic students; for spring admission, 11/30 for domestic students. Applications are processed on a rolling basis. Application fee: $55 ($65 for international students). *Expenses:* Tuition: Full-time $20,070; part-time $1115 per credit hour. Tuition and fees vary according to course load, degree level and program. *Financial support:* In 2010–11, 156 students received support; fellowships available. Financial award application deadline: 3/2; financial award applicants required to submit FAFSA. *Faculty research:* International financial markets, technology transfer licensing, international marketing, strategic planning. Total annual research expenditures: $50,000. *Unit head:* Kelly Brookes, Director, 415-422-2221, Fax: 415-422-6315. *Application contact:* Director, MBA Program, 415-422-2221, Fax: 415-422-6315, E-mail: mba@usfca.edu.

The University of Texas at Dallas, School of Management, Program in Management and Administrative Sciences, Richardson, TX 75080. Offers electronic commerce (MS); finance (MS); healthcare administration (MS); information systems (MS); innovation and entrepreneurship (MS); international management (MS); leadership in organizations (MS); marketing (MS); operations (MS); organizations (MS); real estate (MS); strategy (MS). *Accreditation:* AACSB. Part-time and evening/weekend programs available. *Faculty:* 18 full-time (3 women), 8 part-time/adjunct (0 women). *Students:* 57 full-time (32 women), 107 part-time (49 women); includes 53 minority (14 Black or African American, non-Hispanic/Latino; 30 Asian, non-Hispanic/Latino; 8 Hispanic/Latino; 1 Two or more races, non-Hispanic/Latino), 25 international. Average age 32. 161 applicants, 67% accepted, 51 enrolled. In 2010, 27 master's awarded. *Degree requirements:* For master's, thesis optional. *Entrance requirements:* For master's, GMAT. Additional exam requirements/recommendations for international students: Required—TOEFL (minimum score 550 paper-based; 215 computer-based). *Application deadline:* For fall admission, 7/15 for domestic students, 5/1 priority date for international students; for spring admission, 11/15 for domestic students, 9/1 priority date for international students. Applications are processed on a rolling basis. Application fee: $50 ($100 for international students). Electronic applications accepted. *Expenses:* Tuition, state resident: full-time $10,248; part-time $569 per credit hour. Tuition, nonresident: full-time $18,544; part-time $1030 per credit hour. Tuition and fees vary according to course load. *Financial support:* In 2010–11, 26 students received support, including 38 teaching assistantships with partial tuition reimbursements available (averaging $11,528 per year); research assistantships with partial tuition reimbursements available, career-related internships or fieldwork, Federal Work-Study, institutionally sponsored loans, scholarships/grants, and unspecified assistantships also available. Support available to part-time students. Financial award application deadline: 4/30; financial award applicants required to submit FAFSA. *Faculty research:* Integrated and detailed knowledge of functional areas of management, analytical tools for effective appraisal and decision making. *Unit head:* Dr. Doug Eckel, Assistant Dean, 972-883-5923, E-mail: doug.eckel@utdallas.edu. *Application contact:* James Parker, Assistant Director, 972-883-5842, E-mail: jparker@utdallas.edu.

OVERVIEW

Entrepreneurship is an academic discipline and field of business concentrating on the development of new businesses and ideas. While degrees in entrepreneurship aren't usually available at the undergraduate level, ambitious students can earn an MBA or doctoral degree in this field. Graduate education in entrepreneurship covers a broad range of subjects in finance, economics, and marketing and introduces students to advanced concepts in the management and operation of new business ventures. Students pursuing an entrepreneurship MBA learn about financing new business ventures, developing burgeoning industries, and creating revenue streams from new ideas. Although programs may have similar core courses, some curricula allow students to focus on a specific area of entrepreneurship, such as high-tech enterprises or intrapreneurship (the development of new products or systems within established companies).

Required courses may include study in:

- Entrepreneurial Finance
- Forecasting Business Trends
- Managing Emerging Enterprises
- Organizational Behavior
- Strategic Management

Elective courses may include study in:

- Business Plan Review
- Corporate Venturing
- Creation of High Potential Ventures
- New Venture Creation
- New Venture Financing
- Strategic Growth of Emerging Companies
- Technology Entrepreneurship
- Technology Transfer and Commercialization
- Venture Capital for Investors and Entrepreneurs

Graduates with an MBA in entrepreneurship often find work in various segments of the business industry, whether to form their own start-up or to advance and improve the workings of a mature company. Some popular job titles include operations manager, financier, account executive, human resource manager, and business innovator.

HELPFUL ORGANIZATIONS/ PUBLICATIONS/BLOGS

National Association for the Self-Employed (NASE)

http://www.nase.org/Home.aspx

The National Association for the Self-Employed (NASE) was founded in 1981 to provide day-to-day support, including direct access to experts, benefits, and consolidated buying power that traditionally had been available only to large corporations. Today, the NASE represents hundreds of thousands of entrepreneurs and micro-businesses and is the largest nonprofit, nonpartisan association of its kind in the United States.

The NASE offers entrepreneurs a wide range of resources and tools to help run their businesses successfully. Members are automatically e-mailed every issue of the NASE's monthly e-newsletter, *SelfInformed*, and can access even more articles and resources online through the NASE's Learning Center. NASE members also have unlimited access to the NASE consultants to ask tax, finance, retirement, and/or operations questions.

NASE members can apply for an NASE Succeed Scholarship to help pay for university or college courses, business certification or training, and other courses and seminars to help improve their businesses. In addition, the NASE Scholarship Program provides annual financial scholarships to children and dependents of NASE members.

The NASE champions small businesses by providing a powerful voice backed by hundreds of thousands of members. Key federal legislative priorities include the economy and micro-business, fairness in tax compliance, access to affordable health coverage, self-employment tax on health insurance premiums, improving the health-care system, home office deduction simplification, tax cuts for small business, estate tax relief, retirement security, federal small-business programs, and tax-free Internet access.

The Entrepreneurs' Organization (EO)

http://www.eonetwork.org/Pages/welcome.aspx

The Entrepreneurs' Organization (EO) for entrepreneurs only is a dynamic, global network of more than 8,000 business owners in 40 countries. Founded in 1987 by a group of young entrepreneurs, EO is the catalyst that enables entrepreneurs to learn and grow from each other, leading to greater business success and an enriched personal life. Membership in one of EO's 120 chapters is by invitation only; the average member is 41 years old with annual revenues of $17.3 million (in U.S. dollars).

The EO's vision is to build the world's most influential community of entrepreneurs, and its mission is to engage leading entrepreneurs to learn and grow. The organization's core values encompass betting on each individual's own abilities, a thirst for learning, leaving a legacy, and building a safe haven for learning and growing, and creating.

TiE (The Indus Entrepreneurs)

http://www.tie.org/

TiE (The Indus Entrepreneurs) was founded in 1992 in Silicon Valley by a group of successful entrepreneurs, corporate executives, and senior professionals with roots in the Indus region of Pakistan. There are currently 13,000 members in 57 chapters across 14 countries. TiE's mission is to foster entrepreneurship globally through mentoring, networking, and education. Dedicated to the virtuous cycle of wealth creation and giving back to the community, TiE's focus is on generating and nurturing the next generation of entrepreneurs.

Besides its flagship event, TiECon—the largest professional conference for entrepreneurs—TIE now has a wide range of programs, including Special Interest Groups (SIGs), TiE Institute, Deal Flow Meetings, TiE Young Entrepreneurs (TYE), and, most recently, TiE Women's Forum and CEO Forum.

TiE counts among its achievements:

- Largest pool of intellectual capital anywhere.
- TiE brand is globally synonymous with entrepreneurship.
- TiE's annual professional conference, TiECon, is regarded as the largest entrepreneurial forum in the world.
- TiE has helped boost the economies of the communities in which it operates.
- Economic wealth creation estimated at $200 billion.
- Significant involvement in social entrepreneurship.
- Influenced liberalization of key economic sectors in India and Pakistan.

CAREER ASPIRATIONS: A PROSPECTIVE POSITION

Business Development Manager, Channel & Alliance

Job Description

The Business Development Manager will be responsible for identifying and developing new partners for the technology, consulting, and integration solutions (TCIS) channel organization.

Requirements

This person must be highly skilled and experienced with a wide range of professional attributes, including, but not limited to, the following:

Sales Skills

- The Channel & Alliance Manager must have a proven track record of selling in both a direct and indirect sales environment, including understanding value propositions, pipeline development, pipeline velocity, and the ability to manage the forecast process in an accurate and timely manner. These basic skills allow the Channel & Alliance Manager to empathize with the direct sales person, because some indirect selling models (and all alliance selling models) engage a direct sales person in the selling process.

Time Management

- The Channel & Alliance Manager must have a proven method for time management that allows for the highest levels of productivity. At any given moment, the Channel & Alliance Manager should be able to explain to management how time is managed and what tools and methodologies are utilized.

Creativity

- The Channel & Alliance Manager must constantly be thinking outside the box to generate programs to grow revenue. Related to this, and as important, is the ability to take these creative ideas and present them to management in an analytical manner that will enhance the chance of adoption and execution.

Marketing

- Proficiency and experience in marketing and the ability to create actionable, results-oriented go-to-marketing programs is critical to the success of both alliances and indirect sales channels. The Channel & Alliance Manager must have the skills and experience to create and execute a business plan based on solid market segmentation principles, understanding how to attract clients via a specific business need in the market.

(continued on next page)

Career Aspirations: A Prospective Position (continued)

Leadership

- This is an absolute necessity for the Channel & Alliance Manager. Success in this role is sometimes dependent on establishing a strong cooperative operating model with direct sales and services, which mandates leadership. Alliances and indirect sales channels can sometimes be viewed as secondary to sales and services, yet all three have dependencies necessary for the overall success of the company. Because of this, it takes an extremely strong individual to champion the alliance cause, deliver the expected results, and gain and maintain the respect of persons in other dependent organizations. The Channel & Alliance Manager must be mature enough to understand when to acquiesce to, and when to challenge, other organizations, yet do so in a style that fosters a strong teamwork environment.

Business Development

- This is the most essential skill required of the Channel & Alliance Manager. The skills required range from the basic (knowing how to contact and cold call a potential partner executive, presenting the value proposition in a concise manner, understanding the business goals of the potential partner) to the more sophisticated (developing a win/win proposition for both parties, creating the best terms and conditions for the company, defining specific targets based on a well-developed strategy).
- The best business development occurs when one embraces and acts in the role of entrepreneur and constantly takes initiative. The Channel & Alliance Manager must be able to look at the business as his/her own with an entrepreneurial passion that seeks opportunities for growth in diverse places. This passion is closely linked with creativity yet must be advanced with a keen analytical sense to efficiently understand the possibilities hidden within any potential partnering scenario.
- The Channel & Alliance Manager must also have the ability to maintain focus of mission and strategy and not be distracted by projects that are inconsistent with the defined strategy. Flexibility is required, but focus on the defined results must be of utmost importance and maintained at all times.

Qualifications

- 5–10 years direct and indirect sales environment.
- Minimum of 5 years selling new accounts; 10 years preferred.
- Ability to quickly understand company technology.
- Ability to grasp value propositions and be able to sell these to prospective new clients.
- Successful track record as being a self starter with the ability to take any and all initiatives required to maintain the sense of urgency to drive new business.
- BS degree (technical degree preferred), MBA preferred.

ENTREPRENEURSHIP

American Public University System, AMU/APU Graduate Programs, Charles Town, WV 25414. Offers accounting (MBA); administration and supervision (M Ed); air warfare (MA Military Studies); asymmetrical warfare (MA Military Studies); criminal justice (MA); emergency and disaster management (MA); entrepreneurship (MBA); environmental policy and management (MS); finance (MBA); general (MBA); global business management (MBA); guidance and counseling (M Ed); history (MA); homeland security (MA); homeland security resource allocation (MBA); humanities (MA); information technology (MS); information technology management (MBA); intelligence studies (MA); international relations and conflict resolution (MA); joint warfare (MA Military Studies); land warfare (MA Military Studies); legal studies (MA); management (MA), including defense mangement, general, human resource management, organizational leadership, public administration; marketing (MBA); military history (MA); national security studies (MA); naval warfare (MA Military Studies); nonprofit management (MBA); political science (MA); psychology (MA); public administration (MA); public health (MA); security management (MA); space studies (MS); sports management (MS); strategic leadership (MA Military Studies); teaching (M Ed), including elementary, secondary social sciences; transportation and logistics management (MA). Programs offered via distance learning only. Part-time and evening/weekend programs available. Postbaccalaureate distance learning degree programs offered (no on-campus study). *Faculty:* 253 full-time (134 women), 1,208 part-time/adjunct (570 women). *Students:* 956 full-time (422 women), 8,476 part-time (2,821 women); includes 2,511 minority (1,218 Black or African American, non-Hispanic/Latino; 68 American Indian or Alaska Native, non-Hispanic/Latino; 219 Asian, non-Hispanic/Latino; 705 Hispanic/Latino; 46 Native Hawaiian or other Pacific Islander, non-Hispanic/Latino; 255 Two or more races, non-Hispanic/Latino), 107 international. Average age 35. 9,550 applicants, 100% accepted. In 2010, 1,688 master's awarded. *Degree requirements:* For master's, comprehensive exam or practicum. *Entrance requirements:* For master's, official transcript showing earned bachelor's degree from institution accredited by recognized accrediting body. Additional exam requirements/recommendations for international students: Required—TOEFL (minimum score 550 paper-based; 213 computer-based), IELTS (minimum score 6.5). *Application deadline:* Applications are processed on a rolling basis. Application fee: $0. Electronic applications accepted. *Financial support:* Applicants required to submit FAFSA. *Faculty research:* Military history, criminal justice, management performance, national security. *Unit head:* Dr. Frank McCluskey, Provost, 877-468-6268, Fax: 304-724-3780. *Application contact:* Terry Grant, Director of Enrollment Management, 877-468-6268, Fax: 304-724-3780, E-mail: info@apus.edu.

American University, Kogod School of Business, Master of Business Administration Program, Washington, DC 20016-8044. Offers accounting (MBA); consulting (MBA), including information technology, international business, management; corporate finance: commercial banking (MBA); corporate finance: corporate financial management (MBA); corporate finance: investment banking (MBA), including corporate finance and private equity, trading and selling; entrepreneurship (MBA); global emerging markets (MBA), including business, finance, information technology; international trade and global supply chain management (MBA); leadership (MBA); marketing management (MBA); marketing research (MBA); real estate (MBA); MBA/JD; MBA/LL M. Part-time and evening/weekend programs available. *Faculty:* 12 full-time (5 women). *Students:* 135 full-time (62 women), 104 part-time (38 women); includes 46 minority (18 Black or African American, non-Hispanic/Latino; 1 American Indian or Alaska Native, non-Hispanic/Latino; 12 Asian, non-Hispanic/Latino; 14 Hispanic/Latino; 1 Two or more races, non-Hispanic/Latino), 34 international. Average age 27. 467 applicants, 51% accepted, 70 enrolled. In 2010, 101 master's awarded. *Entrance requirements:* For master's, GMAT. Additional exam requirements/recommendations for international students: Required—TOEFL. *Application deadline:* For fall admission, 2/1 priority date for domestic students; for spring admission, 10/1 priority date for domestic students. Applications are processed on a rolling basis. Application fee: $100. *Expenses:* Contact institution. *Financial support:* In 2010–11, 19 students received support; fellowships, research assistantships with partial tuition reimbursements available, career-related internships or fieldwork, Federal Work-Study, and institutionally sponsored loans available. Support available to part-time students. Financial award application deadline: 2/1. *Faculty research:* Information technology, decision-aiding methodology, negotiation. *Unit head:* Dr. Stevan Holmberg, Chair, 202-885-6193, E-mail: sholmbe@american.edu. *Application contact:* Shannon Demko, Associate Director Graduate Admissions, 202-885-1994, Fax: 202-885-1108, E-mail: demko@american.edu.

Arizona State University, College of Technology and Innovation, Department of Technology Management, Mesa, AZ 85212. Offers technology (aviation management and human factors) (MS); technology (environmental technology management) (MS); technology (global technology and development) (MS); technology (graphic information technology) (MS); technology (management of technology) (MS). Part-time and evening/weekend programs available. Postbaccalaureate distance learning degree programs

offered (minimal on-campus study). *Faculty:* 13 full-time (3 women), 6 part-time/adjunct (2 women). *Students:* 56 full-time (16 women), 212 part-time (95 women); includes 61 minority (14 Black or African American, non-Hispanic/Latino; 8 American Indian or Alaska Native, non-Hispanic/Latino; 14 Asian, non-Hispanic/Latino; 21 Hispanic/Latino; 4 Two or more races, non-Hispanic/Latino), 27 international. Average age 36. 124 applicants, 77% accepted, 58 enrolled. In 2010, 35 master's awarded. *Degree requirements:* For master's, thesis or applied project and oral defense; interactive Program of Study (iPOS) submitted before completing 50 percent of required credit hours. *Entrance requirements:* For master's, GRE, minimum GPA of 3.0 or equivalent in last 2 years of work leading to bachelor's degree. Additional exam requirements/recommendations for international students: Required—TOEFL, IELTS, or Pearson Test of English. *Application deadline:* For fall admission, 7/1 for domestic and international students; for spring admission, 12/1 for domestic and international students. Applications are processed on a rolling basis. Application fee: $70 ($90 for international students). Electronic applications accepted. *Expenses:* Tuition, state resident: full-time $8510; part-time $608 per credit. Tuition, nonresident: full-time $16,542; part-time $919 per credit. Required fees: $339; $110 per credit. Part-time tuition and fees vary according to course load. *Financial support:* In 2010–11, 3 research assistantships with full and partial tuition reimbursements (averaging $12,729 per year), 1 teaching assistantship with full and partial tuition reimbursement (averaging $14,125 per year) were awarded; career-related internships or fieldwork, Federal Work-Study, scholarships/grants, health care benefits, tuition waivers (full and partial), and unspecified assistantships also available. Support available to part-time students. Financial award application deadline: 3/1; financial award applicants required to submit FAFSA. *Faculty research:* Digital imaging, digital publishing, Internet development/e-commerce, information aviation human factors, pilot selection, databases, multimedia, commercial digital photography, digital workflow, computer graphics modeling and animation, information design, sociotechnology, visual and technical literacy, environmental management, quality management, project management, industrial ethics, hazardous materials, environmental chemistry. Total annual research expenditures: $755,686. *Unit head:* Dr. Mitzi Montoya, Vice Provost and Dean, 480-727-1955, Fax: 480-727-1538, E-mail: mitzi.montoya@asu.edu. *Application contact:* Graduate Admissions, 480-965-6113.

Azusa Pacific University, School of Business and Management, Azusa, CA 91702-7000. Offers business administration (MBA); diversity for strategic advantage (MA); entrepreneurship (MBA); finance (MBA); human and organizational development (MA); human resources and organizational development (MBA); human resources management (MA); international business (MBA); marketing (MBA); non-profit management (MA); organizational development and change (MA); performance improvement (MA); public administration (MA); strategic management (MBA). Part-time and evening/weekend programs available. *Faculty:* 19 full-time (5 women), 2 part-time/adjunct (1 woman). *Students:* 75 full-time (41 women), 96 part-time (46 women); includes 65 minority (15 Black or African American, non-Hispanic/Latino; 15 Asian, non-Hispanic/Latino; 34 Hispanic/Latino; 1 Native Hawaiian or other Pacific Islander, non-Hispanic/Latino), 17 international. Average age 30. In 2010, 82 master's awarded. *Degree requirements:* For master's, thesis (for some programs), final project. *Entrance requirements:* For master's, GMAT, minimum GPA of 3.0. Additional exam requirements/recommendations for international students: Required—TOEFL (minimum score 600 paper-based). *Application deadline:* For fall admission, 8/15 priority date for domestic students. Applications are processed on a rolling basis. Application fee: $45 ($65 for international students). *Expenses:* Contact institution. *Financial support:* Scholarships/grants available. *Faculty research:* Gender issues, financial risk, leadership and ethics, marketing strategy. *Unit head:* Dr. Ilene Bezjian, Dean, 626-815-3090, Fax: 626-815-3802, E-mail: ibezjian@apu.edu. *Application contact:* Dr. Ilene Bezjian, Dean, 626-815-3090, Fax: 626-815-3802, E-mail: ibezjian@apu.edu.

Babson College, F. W. Olin Graduate School of Business, Wellesley, Babson Park, MA 02457-0310. Offers accounting (MSA); advanced management (Certificate); business administration (MBA); global entrepreneurship (MS); technological entrepreneurship (MS). *Accreditation:* AACSB. Part-time and evening/weekend programs available. Postbaccalaureate distance learning degree programs offered (minimal on-campus study). *Faculty:* 142 full-time (39 women), 41 part-time/adjunct (9 women). *Students:* 486 full-time (145 women), 838 part-time (236 women); includes 199 minority (22 Black or African American, non-Hispanic/Latino; 1 American Indian or Alaska Native, non-Hispanic/Latino; 127 Asian, non-Hispanic/Latino; 29 Hispanic/Latino; 1 Native Hawaiian or other Pacific Islander, non-Hispanic/Latino; 19 Two or more races, non-Hispanic/Latino), 263 international. Average age 33. 877 applicants, 56% accepted, 283 enrolled. In 2010, 723 master's, 2 other advanced degrees awarded. *Entrance requirements:* For master's, GMAT, 2 years of work experience, resume, letters of recommendation. Additional exam requirements/recommendations for international students: Required—TOEFL (minimum score 100 iBT), IELTS (minimum score 6.5). *Application deadline:* For fall admission, 11/1 priority date for domestic and international students; for winter admission, 1/15 priority date for domestic and international students; for spring admission, 4/15 priority date for domestic students. Applications are processed on a rolling basis. Application fee: $100. Electronic applications accepted. *Expenses:* Tuition: Full-time $46,000; part-time $1220 per credit. Required fees: $1946. Full-time tuition and fees vary according to course load, program and student level. *Financial support:* In 2010–11, 286 students received support, including 48 fellowships (averaging $28,489 per year); career-related internships or fieldwork, Federal Work-Study, institutionally sponsored loans, scholarships/grants, health care benefits, and unspecified assistantships also available. Financial award application deadline: 4/15. *Faculty research:* Entrepreneurship, sustainability, global markets, process of innovation, social media and advertising. *Unit head:* Dr. Raghu Tadepalli, Dean, 781-239-5237, E-mail: rtadepalli@babson.edu. *Application contact:* Kathy Longee, Admission Services Team, 781-239-4317, Fax: 781-239-4194, E-mail: mbaadmission@babson.edu.

Bakke Graduate University, Programs in Pastoral Ministry and Business, Seattle, WA 98104. Offers business (MBA); global urban leadership (MA); social and civic entrepreneurship (MA); transformational leadership for the global city (D Min). Part-time programs available. Postbaccalaureate distance learning degree programs offered (minimal on-campus study). *Faculty:* 7 full-time (2 women), 30 part-time/adjunct (4 women). *Students:* 78 full-time (15 women), 301 part-time (105 women); includes 199 minority (99 Black or African American, non-Hispanic/Latino; 1 American Indian or Alaska Native, non-Hispanic/Latino; 90 Asian, non-Hispanic/Latino; 9 Hispanic/Latino). Average age 38. 41 applicants, 98% accepted, 25 enrolled. In 2010, 11 master's, 37 doctorates awarded. *Degree requirements:* For master's, thesis; for doctorate, thesis/dissertation. *Entrance requirements:* For master's, 2 years of ministry experience, BA in Biblical studies or theology; for doctorate, 3 years of ministry experience, M Div. Additional exam requirements/recommendations for international students: Required—TOEFL (minimum score 60 computer-based). *Application deadline:* For fall admission, 7/1 priority date for domestic students; for winter admission, 12/1 for domestic students; for spring admission, 3/15 for domestic students. Applications are processed on a rolling basis. Application fee: $75. Electronic applications accepted. *Expenses:* Tuition: Full-time $5000; part-time $500 per credit. Required fees: $175; $50 per course. *Financial support:* In 2010–11, 140 students received support. Scholarships/grants and tuition waivers (partial) available. Financial award applicants required to submit FAFSA. *Faculty research:* Theological systems, church management, worship. *Unit head:* Dr. Gwen Dewey, Academic Dean, 206-264-9100 Ext. 119, Fax: 206-264-8828, E-mail: gwend@bgu.edu. *Application contact:* Addie Tolle, Registrar, 206-246-9100 Ext. 110, Fax: 206-264-8828.

Baldwin-Wallace College, Graduate Programs, Division of Business, Program in Entrepreneurship, Berea, OH 44017-2088. Offers MBA. Part-time and evening/weekend programs available. *Students:* 19 full-time (6 women), 19 part-time (7 women); includes 8 minority (7 Black or African American, non-Hispanic/Latino; 1 Asian, non-Hispanic/Latino), 2 international. Average age 35. 14 applicants, 79% accepted, 9 enrolled. In 2010, 9 master's awarded. *Degree requirements:* For master's, minimum overall GPA of 3.0, completion of all required courses. *Entrance requirements:* For master's, GMAT, bachelor's degree in any field, work experience, minimum GPA of 3.0. Additional exam requirements/recommendations for international students: Required—TOEFL (minimum score 523 paper-based; 193 computer-based; 70 iBT). *Application deadline:* For fall admission, 7/25 priority date for domestic students, 4/30 priority date for international students; for spring admission, 12/15 priority date for domestic students, 9/30 priority date for international students. Applications are processed on a rolling basis. Application fee: $25. Electronic applications accepted. *Expenses:* Tuition: Full-time $16,750; part-time $712 per credit hour. Tuition and fees vary according to program. *Financial support:* Career-related internships or fieldwork available. Support available to part-time students. Financial award application deadline: 5/1. *Unit head:* Ven Ochaya, Director, 440-826-2391, Fax: 440-826-3868, E-mail: vochaya@bw.edu. *Application contact:* Laura Spencer, Graduate Application Specialist, 440-826-2191, Fax: 440-826-3868, E-mail: lspencer@bw.edu.

Benedictine University, Graduate Programs, Program in Business Administration, Lisle, IL 60532-0900. Offers accounting (MBA); entrepreneurship and managing innovation (MBA); financial management (MBA); health administration (MBA); human resource management (MBA); information systems security (MBA); international business (MBA); management consulting (MBA); management information systems (MBA); marketing management (MBA); operations management and logistics (MBA); organizational leadership (MBA); MBA/MPH; MBA/MS. Part-time and evening/weekend programs available. Postbaccalaureate distance learning degree programs offered (minimal on-campus study). *Faculty:* 4 full-time (2 women), 24 part-time/adjunct (3 women). *Students:* 347 full-time (140 women), 672 part-time (360 women); includes 237 minority (155 Black or African American, non-Hispanic/Latino; 4 American Indian or Alaska Native, non-Hispanic/Latino; 43 Asian, non-Hispanic/Latino; 35 Hispanic/Latino), 21 international. Average age 34. 416 applicants, 88% accepted, 217 enrolled. In 2010, 355 master's awarded. *Entrance requirements:* For master's, GMAT. Additional exam requirements/recommendations for international students: Required—TOEFL (minimum score 550 paper-based; 213 computer-based). *Application deadline:* For fall admission, 9/1 for domestic students; for winter admission, 12/1 for domestic students; for spring admission, 2/15 for domestic students.

Applications are processed on a rolling basis. Application fee: $40. Electronic applications accepted. *Financial support:* Career-related internships or fieldwork and health care benefits available. Support available to part-time students. *Faculty research:* Strategic leadership in professional organizations, sociology of professions, organizational change, social identity theory, applications to change management. *Unit head:* Dr. Sharon Borowicz, Director, 630-829-6219, E-mail: sborowicz@ben.edu. *Application contact:* Kari Gibbons, Director, Admissions, 630-829-6200, Fax: 630-829-6584, E-mail: kgibbons@ben.edu.

Brandeis University, Graduate School of Arts and Sciences, Program in Computer Science and IT Entrepreneurship, Waltham, MA 02454-9110. Offers MA. Part-time programs available. *Faculty:* 13 full-time (3 women), 4 part-time/adjunct (2 women). *Students:* 11 full-time (6 women), 1 (woman) part-time; includes 1 Asian, non-Hispanic/Latino, 9 international. 26 applicants, 81% accepted, 12 enrolled. *Degree requirements:* For master's, practicum. *Entrance requirements:* For master's, official transcript(s), 2 letters of recommendation, curriculum vitae or resume, statement of purpose. Additional exam requirements/recommendations for international students: Required—TOEFL (minimum score 600 paper-based; 250 computer-based; 100 iBT); Recommended—IELTS (minimum score 7). *Application deadline:* Applications are processed on a rolling basis. Application fee: $75. Electronic applications accepted. *Financial support:* In 2010–11, teaching assistantships with partial tuition reimbursements (averaging $3,200 per year); institutionally sponsored loans, scholarships/grants, and tuition waivers (partial) also available. Financial award application deadline: 4/15; financial award applicants required to submit FAFSA. *Faculty research:* Software development, IT entrepreneurship, business, computer science, innovation. *Unit head:* Prof. Fernando Colon Osorio, Director of Graduate Studies, 781-736-4586, E-mail: fcco@brandeis.edu. *Application contact:* David F. Cotter, Assistant Dean, Graduate School of Arts and Sciences, 781-736-3410, Fax: 781-736-3412, E-mail: gradschool@brandeis.edu.

California Lutheran University, Graduate Studies, School of Management, Thousand Oaks, CA 91360-2787. Offers business (IMBA); computer science (MS); econometrics (MBA); economics (MS); entrepreneurship (MBA, Certificate); finance (MBA, Certificate); financial planning (MBA, Certificate); information systems and technology (MS); information technology management (MBA, Certificate); international business (MBA, Certificate); management and organization behavior (MBA); management and organizational behavior (Certificate); marketing (MBA, Certificate); microeconomics (MBA); nonprofit and social enterprise (MBA). Part-time and evening/weekend programs available. Postbaccalaureate distance learning degree programs offered (no on-campus study). *Faculty:* 12 full-time (3 women), 27 part-time/adjunct (6 women). *Students:* 350 full-time (162 women), 262 part-time (99 women); includes 21 Black or African American, non-Hispanic/Latino; 44 Asian, non-Hispanic/Latino; 56 Hispanic/Latino; 4 Native Hawaiian or other Pacific Islander, non-Hispanic/Latino; 12 Two or more races, non-Hispanic/Latino, 185 international. Average age 32. 379 applicants, 74% accepted, 138 enrolled. In 2010, 231 master's awarded. *Entrance requirements:* For master's, GMAT, interview, minimum GPA of 3.0. *Application deadline:* Applications are processed on a rolling basis. Application fee: $50. *Expenses:* Contact institution. *Unit head:* Dr. Charles Maxey, Dean, 805-493-3360. *Application contact:* 805-493-3127, Fax: 805-493-3542, E-mail: clugrad@clunet.edu.

California State University, East Bay, Office of Academic Programs and Graduate Studies, College of Business and Economics, Department of Marketing, Option in Entrepreneurship, Hayward, CA 94542-3000. Offers MBA. *Entrance requirements:* Additional exam requirements/recommendations for international students: Required—TOEFL (minimum score 550 paper-based; 213 computer-based). *Application deadline:* For fall admission, 6/30 for domestic and international students. *Financial support:* Career-related internships or fieldwork, Federal Work-Study, institutionally sponsored loans, and scholarships/grants available. Support available to part-time students. Financial award applicants required to submit FAFSA. *Unit head:* Dr. Nan Maxwell, Chair, 510-885-4336, Fax: 510-885-4796, E-mail: nan.maxwell@csueastbay.edu. *Application contact:* Donna Wiley, Interim Associate Director, 510-885-2928, Fax: 510-885-4777, E-mail: donna.wiley@csueastbay.edu.

California State University, East Bay, Office of Academic Programs and Graduate Studies, College of Business and Economics, MBA Program, Hayward, CA 94542-3000. Offers entrepreneurship (MBA); finance (MBA); human resources and organizational behavior (MBA); information technology management (MBA); marketing management (MBA); operations and supply chain management (MBA); strategy and international business (MBA). Part-time and evening/weekend programs available. Postbaccalaureate distance learning degree programs offered (no on-campus study). *Faculty:* 33 full-time (9 women). *Students:* 121 full-time (58 women), 133 part-time (67 women); includes 7 Black or African American, non-Hispanic/Latino; 63 Asian, non-Hispanic/Latino; 11 Hispanic/Latino; 3 Native Hawaiian or other Pacific Islander, non-Hispanic/Latino; 5 Two or more races, non-Hispanic/Latino, 87 international. Average age 30. 284 applicants, 47% accepted, 55 enrolled. In 2010, 241 master's awarded. *Degree requirements:* For master's, comprehensive exam or thesis. *Entrance requirements:* For master's, GMAT (minimum 20th percentile verbal and quantitative section), bachelor's degree, minimum GPA of 2.75. Additional exam requirements/recommendations for international students: Required—TOEFL (minimum score 550 paper-based; 213 computer-based; 79 iBT). *Application deadline:* For fall admission, 6/30 for domestic and international students. Applications are processed on a rolling basis. Application fee: $55. Electronic applications accepted. *Financial support:* Career-related internships or fieldwork, Federal Work-Study, institutionally sponsored loans, and scholarships/grants available. Support available to part-time students. Financial award application deadline: 3/2; financial award applicants required to submit FAFSA. *Unit head:* Dr. Terri Swartz, Dean, 510-885-3291, Fax: 510-885-4884, E-mail: terri.swartz@csueastbay. edu. *Application contact:* Dr. Donna Wiley, Interim Associate Director, 510-885-2928, Fax: 510-885-4777, E-mail: donna.wiley@csueastbay.edu.

California State University, Fullerton, Graduate Studies, College of Business and Economics, Department of Management, Fullerton, CA 92834-9480. Offers entrepreneurship (MBA); management (MBA). *Accreditation:* AACSB. Part-time programs available. *Students:* 39 full-time (23 women), 51 part-time (16 women); includes 2 Black or African American, non-Hispanic/Latino; 1 American Indian or Alaska Native, non-Hispanic/Latino; 30 Asian, non-Hispanic/Latino; 11 Hispanic/Latino, 18 international. Average age 28. 116 applicants, 42% accepted, 23 enrolled. In 2010, 23 master's awarded. *Degree requirements:* For master's, project or thesis. *Entrance requirements:* For master's, GMAT, minimum AACSB index of 950. Application fee: $55. *Financial support:* Career-related internships or fieldwork, Federal Work-Study, institutionally sponsored loans, and scholarships/grants available. Support available to part-time students. Financial award application deadline: 3/1; financial award applicants required to submit FAFSA. *Unit head:* Dr. Ellen Dumond, Chair, 657-278-2251. *Application contact:* Admissions/Applications, 657-278-2371.

Cambridge College, School of Management, Cambridge, MA 02138-5304. Offers business negotiation and conflict resolution (M Mgt); general business (M Mgt); health care informatics (M Mgt); health care management (M Mgt); leadership in human and organizational dynamics (M Mgt); non-profit and public organization management (M Mgt); small business development (M Mgt); technology management (M Mgt). Part-time and evening/weekend programs available. *Faculty:* 6 full-time (3 women), 54 part-time/adjunct (26 women). *Students:* 222 full-time (121 women), 175 part-time (110 women); includes 127 minority (89 Black or African American, non-Hispanic/Latino; 2 American Indian or Alaska Native, non-Hispanic/Latino; 9 Asian, non-Hispanic/Latino; 25 Hispanic/Latino; 2 Two or more races, non-Hispanic/Latino), 125 international. Average age 37. In 2010, 221 master's awarded. *Degree requirements:* For master's, thesis, seminars. *Entrance requirements:* For master's, resume, 2 professional references. Additional exam requirements/recommendations for international students: Required—TOEFL (minimum score 550 paper-based; 213 computer-based; 79 iBT); Recommended—IELTS (minimum score 6). *Application deadline:* Applications are processed on a rolling basis. Application fee: $30. Electronic applications accepted. *Expenses:* Contact institution. *Financial support:* Career-related internships or fieldwork, Federal Work-Study, and scholarships/grants available. Financial award applicants required to submit FAFSA. *Faculty research:* Negotiation, mediation and conflict resolution; leadership; management of diverse organizations; case studies and simulation methodologies for management education, digital as a second language: social networking for digital immigrants, non-profit and public management. *Unit head:* Dr. Mary Ann Joseph, Acting Dean, 617-873-0227, E-mail: maryann.joseph@cambridgecollege.edu. *Application contact:* Elaine M. Lapomardo, Dean of Enrollment Management, 617-873-0274, Fax: 617-349-3561, E-mail: elaine.lapomardo@cambridgecollege.edu.

Carlos Albizu University, Miami Campus, Graduate Programs, Miami, FL 33172-2209. Offers clinical psychology (Psy D); entrepreneurship (MBA); exceptional student education (MS); industrial/organizational psychology (MS); marriage and family therapy (MS); mental health counseling (MS); nonprofit management (MBA); organizational management (MBA); psychology (MS); school counseling (MS); teaching English as a second language (MS). *Accreditation:* APA. Part-time and evening/weekend programs available. *Faculty:* 21 full-time (12 women), 37 part-time/adjunct (18 women). *Students:* 496 full-time (400 women), 242 part-time (192 women); includes 590 minority (58 Black or African American, non-Hispanic/Latino; 2 American Indian or Alaska Native, non-Hispanic/Latino; 5 Asian, non-Hispanic/Latino; 523 Hispanic/Latino; 2 Two or more races, non-Hispanic/Latino), 15 international. Average age 36. 141 applicants, 84% accepted, 118 enrolled. In 2010, 159 master's, 20 doctorates awarded. Terminal master's awarded for partial completion of doctoral program. *Degree requirements:* For master's, one foreign language, comprehensive exam, integrative project (MBA), research project (exceptional student education, teaching English as a second language); for doctorate, one foreign language, comprehensive exam, internship, project. *Entrance requirements:* For master's, 3 letters of recommendation, interview, minimum GPA of 3.0, resume, statement of purpose, official transcripts; for doctorate, 3 letters of recommendation, minimum GPA of 3.0, resume, interview. *Application deadline:* For fall admission, 8/1 priority date for domestic students; for spring admission, 11/30 priority date for domestic students. Applications are processed on a rolling basis. Application

fee: $50. Electronic applications accepted. *Expenses:* Tuition: Full-time $9360; part-time $520 per credit. Required fees: $298 per term. Tuition and fees vary according to course load, degree level and program. *Financial support:* In 2010–11, 106 students received support. Federal Work-Study, scholarships/grants, and tuition discounts available. Financial award application deadline: 6/1; financial award applicants required to submit FAFSA. *Faculty research:* Psychotherapy, forensic psychology, neuropsychology, marketing strategy, entrepreneurship, special education. *Unit head:* Dr. Carmen S. Roca, Chancellor, 305-593-1223 Ext. 120, Fax: 305-629-8052, E-mail: croca@albizu.edu. *Application contact:* Vanessa Almendarez, Secretary, 305-593-1223 Ext. 137, Fax: 305-593-1854, E-mail: valmendarez@albizu.edu.

DePaul University, Charles H. Kellstadt Graduate School of Business, Department of Management, Chicago, IL 60604-2287. Offers entrepreneurship (MBA); health sector management (MBA); human resource management (MBA, MSHR); leadership/change management (MBA); management planning and strategy (MBA); operations management (MBA). Part-time and evening/weekend programs available. *Faculty:* 36 full-time (7 women), 35 part-time/adjunct (16 women). *Students:* 267 full-time (116 women), 125 part-time (43 women); includes 76 minority (24 Black or African American, non-Hispanic/Latino; 1 American Indian or Alaska Native, non-Hispanic/Latino; 33 Asian, non-Hispanic/Latino; 13 Hispanic/Latino; 1 Native Hawaiian or other Pacific Islander, non-Hispanic/Latino; 4 Two or more races, non-Hispanic/Latino), 20 international. In 2010, 112 master's awarded. *Entrance requirements:* For master's, GMAT, GRE (MSHR), 2 letters of recommendation, resume. Additional exam requirements/recommendations for international students: Required—TOEFL (minimum score 550 paper-based; 213 computer-based). *Application deadline:* For fall admission, 7/1 for domestic students; for winter admission, 10/1 for domestic students; for spring admission, 2/1 for domestic students. Applications are processed on a rolling basis. Application fee: $60. Electronic applications accepted. *Financial support:* Research assistantships available. Financial award application deadline: 4/1. *Faculty research:* Growth management, creativity and innovation, quality management and business process design, entrepreneurship. *Application contact:* Christopher E. Kinsella, Director of Cohort MBA Programs, 312-362-8810, Fax: 312-362-6677, E-mail: kgsb@depaul.edu.

Eastern Michigan University, Graduate School, College of Business, Programs in Business Administration, Ypsilanti, MI 48197. Offers business administration (MBA, Graduate Certificate); computer information systems (Graduate Certificate); e-business (MBA, Graduate Certificate); enterprise business intelligence (MBA); entrepreneurship (MBA, Graduate Certificate); finance (MBA, Graduate Certificate); human resources (MBA); human resources management (Graduate Certificate); information systems (MBA); internal auditing (MBA); international business (MBA, Graduate Certificate); marketing management (Graduate Certificate); nonprofit management (MBA); organizational development (Graduate Certificate); supply chain management (MBA, Graduate Certificate). *Accreditation:* AACSB. Part-time programs available. Postbaccalaureate distance learning degree programs offered (no on-campus study). *Students:* 149 full-time (66 women), 456 part-time (232 women); includes 146 minority (109 Black or African American, non-Hispanic/Latino; 4 American Indian or Alaska Native, non-Hispanic/Latino; 27 Asian, non-Hispanic/Latino; 6 Hispanic/Latino), 105 international. Average age 32. 330 applicants, 64% accepted, 150 enrolled. In 2010, 128 master's, 53 other advanced degrees awarded. *Entrance requirements:* For master's, GMAT (minimum score 450), minimum cumulative undergraduate GPA of 2.75. Additional exam requirements/recommendations for international students: Required—TOEFL. *Application deadline:* For fall admission, 5/15 for domestic students, 5/1 for international students; for winter admission, 10/15 for domestic students, 10/1 for international students; for spring admission, 3/15 for domestic students, 3/1 for international students. Applications are processed on a rolling basis. Application fee: $35. *Financial support:* Fellowships, research assistantships with full tuition reimbursements, teaching assistantships with full tuition reimbursements, career-related internships or fieldwork, Federal Work-Study, institutionally sponsored loans, scholarships/grants, tuition waivers (partial), and unspecified assistantships available. Support available to part-time students. Financial award applicants required to submit FAFSA. *Unit head:* K. Michelle Henry, Interim Director, Graduate Programs, 734-487-4444, Fax: 734-483-1316, E-mail: mhenry1@emich.edu. *Application contact:* Beste Windes, Advisor, 734-487-4444, Fax: 734-483-1316, E-mail: bwindes@emich.edu.

East Tennessee State University, School of Graduate Studies, College of Business and Technology, Department of Technology and Geomatics, Johnson City, TN 37614. Offers digital media (MS); engineering technology (MS); entrepreneurial leadership (MS, Certificate). Part-time programs available. *Faculty:* 19 full-time (2 women). *Students:* 22 full-time (5 women), 27 part-time (8 women); includes 13 minority (8 Black or African American, non-Hispanic/Latino; 2 Asian, non-Hispanic/Latino; 2 Hispanic/Latino; 1 Two or more races, non-Hispanic/Latino), 3 international. Average age 35. 34 applicants, 71% accepted, 8 enrolled. In 2010, 21 master's, 2 other advanced degrees awarded. *Degree requirements:* For master's, comprehensive exam, thesis optional, strategic experience, capstone. *Entrance requirements:* For master's, bachelor's degree in technical or related area, minimum GPA of

3.0. Additional exam requirements/recommendations for international students: Required—TOEFL (minimum score 550 paper-based; 213 computer-based; 79 iBT). *Application deadline:* For fall admission, 6/1 priority date for domestic students, 4/30 for international students; for spring admission, 11/1 for domestic students, 9/30 for international students. Application fee: $25 ($35 for international students). Electronic applications accepted. *Financial support:* In 2010–11, 10 research assistantships with full tuition reimbursements (averaging $5,500 per year), 1 teaching assistantship with full tuition reimbursement (averaging $5,500 per year) were awarded; career-related internships or fieldwork, institutionally sponsored loans, scholarships/grants, and unspecified assistantships also available. Financial award application deadline: 7/1; financial award applicants required to submit FAFSA. *Faculty research:* Computer-integrated manufacturing, technology education, CAD/CAM, organizational change. Total annual research expenditures: $136,039. *Unit head:* Dr. Keith V. Johnson, Chair, 423-439-7813, Fax: 423-439-7750, E-mail: johnsonk@etsu.edu. *Application contact:* Dr. Keith V. Johnson, Chair, 423-439-7813, Fax: 423-439-7750, E-mail: johnsonk@etsu.edu.

Fairfield University, Charles F. Dolan School of Business, Fairfield, CT 06824-5195. Offers accounting (MBA, MS, CAS); accounting information systems (MBA); entrepreneurship (MBA); finance (MBA, MS, CAS); general management (MBA, CAS); human resource management (MBA, CAS); information systems and operations (MBA); information systems and operations management (CAS); international business (MBA, CAS); marketing (MBA, CAS); taxation (MBA, CAS). *Accreditation:* AACSB. Part-time and evening/weekend programs available. *Faculty:* 42 full-time (15 women), 8 part-time/adjunct (1 woman). *Students:* 89 full-time (32 women), 127 part-time (54 women); includes 4 Black or African American, non-Hispanic/Latino; 2 Asian, non-Hispanic/Latino; 4 Hispanic/Latino; 1 Two or more races, non-Hispanic/Latino, 17 international. Average age 29. 108 applicants, 62% accepted, 46 enrolled. In 2010, 79 master's awarded. *Degree requirements:* For master's, capstone course. *Entrance requirements:* For master's, GMAT (minimum score 500), 2 letters of reference, resume, minimum GPA of 3.0. Additional exam requirements/recommendations for international students: Required—TOEFL (minimum score 550 paper-based; 213 computer-based; 80 iBT). *Application deadline:* For fall admission, 5/15 for international students; for spring admission, 10/15 for international students. Applications are processed on a rolling basis. Application fee: $60. Electronic applications accepted. *Expenses:* Contact institution. *Financial support:* In 2010–11, 48 students received support. Scholarships/grants, unspecified assistantships, and merit based one-time entrance scholarship available. Financial award applicants required to submit FAFSA. *Faculty research:* Optimization strategies, international finance, consumer behavior, financial market volatility, Internet marketing, supply chain analysis, tax issues. Total annual research expenditures: $50,000. *Unit head:* Dr. Norman A. Solomon, Dean, 203-254-4000 Ext. 4070, Fax: 203-254-4105, E-mail: nsolomon@fairfield.edu. *Application contact:* Marianne Gumpper, Director of Graduate and Continuing Studies Admissions, 203-254-4184, Fax: 203-254-4073, E-mail: gradadmis@fairfield.edu.

Fairleigh Dickinson University, College at Florham, Silberman College of Business, Departments of Management, Marketing, and Entrepreneurial Studies, Program in Entrepreneurial Studies, Madison, NJ 07940-1099. Offers MBA, Certificate. *Students:* 7 full-time (5 women), 5 part-time (1 woman), 2 international. Average age 27. 7 applicants, 86% accepted, 2 enrolled. In 2010, 8 master's awarded. *Application deadline:* Applications are processed on a rolling basis. Application fee: $40.

Fairleigh Dickinson University, Metropolitan Campus, Silberman College of Business, Departments of Management, Marketing, and Entrepreneurial Studies, Program in Entrepreneurial Studies, Teaneck, NJ 07666-1914. Offers MBA, Certificate. *Students:* 7 full-time (3 women), 4 part-time (0 women), 5 international. Average age 26. 12 applicants, 50% accepted, 3 enrolled. In 2010, 1 master's awarded. *Application deadline:* Applications are processed on a rolling basis. Application fee: $40. *Application contact:* Susan Brooman, University Director of Graduate Admissions, 201-692-2554, Fax: 201-692-2560, E-mail: globaleducation@fdu.edu.

Florida Atlantic University, College of Business, Department of Management Programs, Boca Raton, FL 33431-0991. Offers global entrepreneurship (MBA); international business (MBA, MS); management (PhD). *Faculty:* 30 full-time (10 women), 23 part-time/adjunct (7 women). *Students:* 298 full-time (144 women), 447 part-time (192 women); includes 263 minority (81 Black or African American, non-Hispanic/Latino; 43 Asian, non-Hispanic/Latino; 124 Hispanic/Latino; 1 Native Hawaiian or other Pacific Islander, non-Hispanic/Latino; 14 Two or more races, non-Hispanic/Latino), 41 international. Average age 32. 455 applicants, 40% accepted, 138 enrolled. In 2010, 206 master's, 6 doctorates awarded. *Entrance requirements:* For master's, GMAT or GRE General Test, minimum GPA of 3.0 in last 60 hours of course work. Additional exam requirements/recommendations for international students: Required—TOEFL (minimum score 600 paper-based; 250 computer-based). *Application deadline:* For fall admission, 7/25 for domestic students, 2/15 for international students; for spring admission, 12/10 for domestic students, 7/15 for international students. Applications are processed on a rolling basis. Application fee: $30. Electronic applications accepted. *Expenses:* Tuition, area resident:

Part-time $319.96 per credit. Tuition, state resident: part-time $319.96 per credit. Tuition, nonresident: part-time $926.42 per credit. *Financial support:* Research assistantships with full tuition reimbursements, career-related internships or fieldwork, tuition waivers (partial), and unspecified assistantships available. *Faculty research:* Sports administration, healthcare, policy, finance, real estate, senior living. *Unit head:* Dr. Peggy Golden, Chair, 561-297-2675, E-mail: golden@fau.edu. *Application contact:* Dr. Peggy Golden, Chair, 561-297-2675, E-mail: golden@fau.edu.

George Mason University, College of Visual and Performing Arts, Program in Arts Management, Fairfax, VA 22030. Offers arts entrepreneurship (Certificate); arts management (MA); fund raising and development in the arts (Certificate); public relations and marketing in the arts (Certificate); special events management in the arts (Certificate). *Accreditation:* NASAD. *Faculty:* 1 (woman) full-time, 9 part-time/adjunct (5 women). *Students:* 50 full-time (44 women), 41 part-time (36 women); includes 4 Black or African American, non-Hispanic/Latino; 2 Asian, non-Hispanic/Latino; 4 Hispanic/Latino; 1 Two or more races, non-Hispanic/Latino, 8 international. Average age 29. 90 applicants, 61% accepted, 29 enrolled. In 2010, 38 master's awarded. *Entrance requirements:* For master's, GRE (recommended), minimum GPA of 3.0, 2 letters of recommendation, personal interview, resume, work experience. Additional exam requirements/recommendations for international students: Required—TOEFL. *Application deadline:* For fall admission, 3/1 priority date for domestic students; for spring admission, 10/1 for domestic students. Applications are processed on a rolling basis. Application fee: $100. Electronic applications accepted. *Expenses:* Tuition, state resident: full-time $8192; part-time $440 per credit hour. Tuition, nonresident: full-time $22,952; part-time $1055 per credit hour. Required fees: $2364; $99 per credit hour. *Financial support:* Application deadline: 3/1. *Faculty research:* Information technology for arts managers, special topics in arts management, directions in gallery management, arts in society, public relations/marketing strategies for art organizations. *Unit head:* William Reeder, Dean, 703-993-8624, Fax: 703-993-8883. *Application contact:* Richard Kamenitzer, Director, 703-993-9194, E-mail: rkamenit@gmu.edu.

Grand Canyon University, College of Business, Phoenix, AZ 85017-1097. Offers accounting (MBA); corporate business administration (MBA); disaster preparedness and crisis management (MBA); executive fire service leadership (MS); finance (MBA); general management (MBA); government and policy (MPA); health care management (MPA); health systems management (MBA); human resource management (MBA); innovation (MBA); leadership (MBA, MS); management of information system (MBA); marketing (MBA); project-based (MBA); six sigma (MBA); strategic human resource management (MBA). *Accreditation:* ACBSP. Part-time and evening/weekend programs available. Postbaccalaureate distance learning degree programs offered (no on-campus study). *Faculty:* 8 full-time (3 women), 147 part-time/adjunct (49 women). *Students:* 1 full-time (0 women), 2,121 part-time (1,165 women); includes 341 minority (249 Black or African American, non-Hispanic/Latino; 17 American Indian or Alaska Native, non-Hispanic/Latino; 15 Asian, non-Hispanic/Latino; 29 Hispanic/Latino; 4 Native Hawaiian or other Pacific Islander, non-Hispanic/Latino; 27 Two or more races, non-Hispanic/Latino), 20 international. Average age 38. In 2010, 569 master's awarded. *Entrance requirements:* For master's, equivalent of two years full-time professional work experience. Additional exam requirements/recommendations for international students: Required—TOEFL (minimum score 575 paper-based; 233 computer-based; 90 iBT), IELTS (minimum score 7). *Application deadline:* For fall admission, 8/21 for domestic students, 7/2 for international students; for spring admission, 12/24 for domestic students, 11/1 for international students. Applications are processed on a rolling basis. Application fee: $0. Electronic applications accepted. *Financial support:* Federal Work-Study available. Support available to part-time students. Financial award applicants required to submit FAFSA. *Unit head:* Kim Donaldson, Dean, 602-639-6597, E-mail: kdonaldson@gcu.edu. *Application contact:* Matt Tidwell, Enrollment Manager, 602-639-6020, E-mail: mtidwell@gcu.edu.

Harrisburg University of Science and Technology, Program in Information Systems Engineering and Management, Harrisburg, PA 17101. Offers digital government specialization (MS); digital health specialization (MS); entrepreneurship specialization (MS). Part-time programs available. *Faculty:* 1 full-time (0 women), 2 part-time/adjunct (0 women). *Students:* 4 full-time (2 women), 16 part-time (5 women); includes 5 Black or African American, non-Hispanic/Latino; 2 Hispanic/Latino. Average age 30. 18 applicants, 83% accepted, 11 enrolled. *Degree requirements:* For master's, comprehensive exam, thesis optional. *Entrance requirements:* For master's, baccalaureate degree. Additional exam requirements/recommendations for international students: Required—TOEFL (minimum score 520 paper-based; 200 computer-based; 80 iBT). *Application deadline:* For fall admission, 8/1 priority date for domestic students, 7/1 priority date for international students. Applications are processed on a rolling basis. Application fee: $0. Electronic applications accepted. *Expenses:* Tuition: Full-time $19,500; part-time $700 per credit hour. *Financial support:* In 2010–11, 2 students received support. Scholarships/grants available. Financial award applicants required to submit FAFSA. *Unit head:* Dr. Amjad Umar, Director and Professor, 717-901-5141, Fax: 717-901-3141, E-mail: aumar@harrisburgu.edu. *Application contact:*

Timothy Dawson, Information Contact, 717-901-5158, Fax: 717-901-3158, E-mail: admissions@harrisburgu.edu.

Lamar University, College of Graduate Studies, College of Business, Beaumont, TX 77710. Offers accounting (MBA); experiential business and entrepreneurship (MBA); financial management (MBA); healthcare administration (MBA); information systems (MBA); management (MBA). *Accreditation:* AACSB. Part-time and evening/weekend programs available. *Faculty:* 17 full-time (4 women), 4 part-time/adjunct (0 women). *Students:* 79 full-time (37 women), 56 part-time (22 women); includes 14 Black or African American, non-Hispanic/Latino; 8 Asian, non-Hispanic/Latino; 12 Hispanic/Latino, 18 international. Average age 28. 103 applicants, 70% accepted, 40 enrolled. In 2010, 49 master's awarded. *Degree requirements:* For master's, comprehensive exam (for some programs), thesis optional. *Entrance requirements:* For master's, GMAT. Additional exam requirements/recommendations for international students: Required—TOEFL (minimum score 525 paper-based; 197 computer-based). *Application deadline:* For fall admission, 3/15 priority date for domestic students; for spring admission, 10/1 priority date for domestic students. Applications are processed on a rolling basis. Application fee: $25 ($50 for international students). *Expenses:* Tuition, state resident: full-time $4160; part-time $208 per credit hour. Tuition, nonresident: full-time $10,360; part-time $518 per credit hour. *Financial support:* In 2010–11, 12 students received support, including 4 research assistantships with partial tuition reimbursements available; fellowships with tuition reimbursements available, career-related internships or fieldwork, Federal Work-Study, institutionally sponsored loans, scholarships/grants, and tuition waivers (partial) also available. Support available to part-time students. Financial award application deadline: 4/1; financial award applicants required to submit FAFSA. *Faculty research:* Marketing, finance, quantitative methods, management information systems, legal, environmental. *Unit head:* Dr. Enrique R. Venta, Dean, 409-880-8604, Fax: 409-880-8088, E-mail: henry.venta@lamar.edu. *Application contact:* Dr. Brad Mayer, Professor and Associate Dean, 409-880-2383, Fax: 409-880-8605, E-mail: bradley.mayer@lamar.edu.

Lindenwood University, Graduate Programs, School of Business and Entrepreneurship, St. Charles, MO 63301-1695. Offers accounting (MBA, MS); business administration (MBA); entrepreneurial studies (MBA, MS); finance (MBA, MS); human resource management (MBA); human resources (MS); international business (MBA, MS); management (MBA, MS); management information systems (MBA, MS); marketing (MBA, MS); public management (MBA, MS); sport management (MA). *Accreditation:* ACBSP. Part-time and evening/weekend programs available. *Faculty:* 20 full-time (8 women), 17 part-time/adjunct (5 women). *Students:* 179 full-time (73 women), 184 part-time (87 women); includes 27 minority (20 Black or African American, non-Hispanic/Latino; 3 Asian, non-Hispanic/Latino; 4 Hispanic/Latino), 146 international. Average age 28. 149 applicants, 73 enrolled. In 2010, 142 master's awarded. *Degree requirements:* For master's, comprehensive exam (for some programs), thesis (for some programs). *Entrance requirements:* For master's, interview, minimum GPA of 3.0, letter of recommendation. Additional exam requirements/recommendations for international students: Required—TOEFL (minimum score 550 paper-based; 213 computer-based; 80 iBT). *Application deadline:* For fall admission, 7/30 priority date for domestic students, 9/16 priority date for international students; for winter admission, 12/15 priority date for domestic and international students; for spring admission, 2/25 priority date for domestic students, 2/11 priority date for international students. Applications are processed on a rolling basis. Application fee: $30 ($100 for international students). Electronic applications accepted. *Expenses:* Tuition: Full-time $13,260; part-time $380 per credit hour. Required fees: $340. One-time fee: $30. Tuition and fees vary according to course level and course load. *Financial support:* In 2010–11, 209 students received support. Career-related internships or fieldwork, Federal Work-Study, institutionally sponsored loans, and tuition waivers (partial) available. Financial award application deadline: 6/30; financial award applicants required to submit FAFSA. *Unit head:* Roger Ellis, Dean, 636-949-4839, E-mail: rellis@lindenwood.edu. *Application contact:* Brett Barger, Dean of Evening Admissions and Extension Campuses, 636-949-4934, Fax: 636-949-4109, E-mail: adultadmissions@lindenwood.edu.

Long Island University, Rockland Graduate Campus, Graduate School, Masters of Business Administration Program, Orangeburg, NY 10962. Offers business administration (Post Master's Certificate); entrepreneurship (MBA); finance (MBA); healthcare sector management (MBA); management (MBA). Part-time and evening/weekend programs available. *Faculty:* 12 part-time/adjunct (2 women). *Students:* 42 part-time (26 women). In 2010, 12 master's awarded. *Entrance requirements:* For master's, GMAT, college transcripts, two letters of recommendation, personal statement, resume. *Application deadline:* Applications are processed on a rolling basis. Application fee: $30. *Expenses:* Tuition: Part-time $1028 per credit. Required fees: $340 per semester. *Financial support:* In 2010–11, 34 students received support. Scholarships/grants available. Support available to part-time students. Financial award applicants required to submit FAFSA. *Unit head:* Dr. Lynn Johnson, Program Director, 845-359-7200 Ext. 5436, Fax: 845-359-7248, E-mail: lynn.johnson@liu.edu. *Application contact:* Peter S. Reiner, Director

of Admissions and Marketing, 845-359-7200, Fax: 845-359-7248, E-mail: peter.reiner@liu.edu.

Marquette University, Graduate School of Management, Program in Entrepreneurship, Milwaukee, WI 53201-1881. Offers Graduate Certificate. *Students:* 5 part-time (3 women). Average age 26. 6 applicants, 83% accepted, 5 enrolled. *Entrance requirements:* Additional exam requirements/recommendations for international students: Required—TOEFL (minimum score 530 paper-based; 78 computer-based). *Application deadline:* Applications are processed on a rolling basis. Application fee: $50. Electronic applications accepted. *Expenses:* Tuition: Full-time $16,290; part-time $905 per credit hour. Tuition and fees vary according to program. *Financial support:* Application deadline: 2/15. *Unit head:* Dr. Jeanne Simmons, Associate Dean, 414-288-7145, Fax: 414-288-8078. *Application contact:* Debra Leutermann, Admissions Coordinator, 414-288-8064, Fax: 414-288-8078, E-mail: debra.leutermann@marquette.edu.

Northeastern University, School of Technological Entrepreneurship, Boston, MA 02115. Offers MS. Part-time programs available. *Faculty:* 7 full-time (2 women), 3 part-time/adjunct (0 women). *Students:* 22 full-time (10 women), 1 part-time (0 women). 38 applicants, 87% accepted, 22 enrolled. In 2010, 13 master's awarded. *Entrance requirements:* For master's, GRE or GMAT, BS, minimum GPA of 3.0. Additional exam requirements/recommendations for international students: Required—TOEFL. *Application deadline:* For fall admission, 7/1 for international students. Applications are processed on a rolling basis. Application fee: $50. Electronic applications accepted. *Unit head:* Dr. Paul M. Zavracky, Dean, 617-373-2788, Fax: 617-373-7490, E-mail: ste@neu.edu. *Application contact:* Information Contact, 617-373-2788, Fax: 617-373-7490, E-mail: ste@neu.edu.

Polytechnic Institute of NYU, Department of Chemical and Biological Sciences, Major in Biotechnology and Entrepreneurship, Brooklyn, NY 11201-2990. Offers MS. *Students:* 17 full-time (5 women), 5 part-time (0 women); includes 1 Asian, non-Hispanic/Latino, 18 international. Average age 24. 58 applicants, 43% accepted, 11 enrolled. In 2010, 17 master's awarded. *Entrance requirements:* Additional exam requirements/recommendations for international students: Required—TOEFL (minimum score 550 paper-based; 213 computer-based; 80 iBT); Recommended—IELTS (minimum score 6.5). *Application deadline:* For fall admission, 7/31 priority date for domestic students, 4/30 priority date for international students; for spring admission, 12/31 priority date for domestic students, 10/30 priority date for international students. Applications are processed on a rolling basis. Application fee: $75. Electronic applications accepted. *Expenses:* Tuition: Full-time $21,492; part-time $1194 per credit. Required fees: $385 per semester. Tuition and fees vary according to course load. *Financial support:* Institutionally sponsored loans, scholarships/grants, and unspecified assistantships available. Support available to part-time students. *Unit head:* Dr. Bruce Garetz, Department Head, 718-260-3287, E-mail: bgaretz@poly.edu. *Application contact:* JeanCarlo Bonilla, Director, Graduate Enrollment Management, 718-260-3182, Fax: 718-260-3624, E-mail: gradinfo@poly.edu.

Polytechnic Institute of NYU, Department of Technology Management, Brooklyn, NY 11201-2990. Offers construction management (Advanced Certificate); electronic business management (Advanced Certificate); entrepreneurship (Advanced Certificate); human resources management (Advanced Certificate); information management (Advanced Certificate); management (MS); management of technology (MS); organizational behavior (MS, Advanced Certificate); project management (Advanced Certificate); technology management (MBA, PhD, Advanced Certificate); telecommunications and information management (MS); telecommunications management (Advanced Certificate). Part-time and evening/weekend programs available. *Faculty:* 7 full-time (2 women), 28 part-time/adjunct (4 women). *Students:* 224 full-time (93 women), 106 part-time (38 women); includes 15 Black or African American, non-Hispanic/Latino; 41 Asian, non-Hispanic/Latino; 10 Hispanic/Latino, 158 international. Average age 30. 370 applicants, 60% accepted, 120 enrolled. In 2010, 173 master's, 1 doctorate awarded. *Degree requirements:* For master's, comprehensive exam (for some programs), thesis (for some programs); for doctorate, comprehensive exam, thesis/dissertation. *Entrance requirements:* For master's, GMAT, minimum B average in undergraduate course work. Additional exam requirements/recommendations for international students: Required—TOEFL (minimum score 550 paper-based; 213 computer-based; 80 iBT); Recommended—IELTS (minimum score 6.5). *Application deadline:* For fall admission, 7/31 priority date for domestic students, 4/30 priority date for international students; for spring admission, 12/31 priority date for domestic students, 11/30 priority date for international students. Applications are processed on a rolling basis. Application fee: $75. Electronic applications accepted. *Expenses:* Tuition: Full-time $21,492; part-time $1194 per credit. Required fees: $385 per semester. Tuition and fees vary according to course load. *Financial support:* In 2010–11, 1 fellowship (averaging $26,400 per year) was awarded; research assistantships, teaching assistantships, institutionally sponsored loans, scholarships/grants, and unspecified assistantships also available. Support available to part-time students. *Unit head:* Prof. Bharadwaj Rao, Head, 718-260-3617, Fax: 718-260-3874, E-mail: brao@poly.edu. *Application contact:* JeanCarlo Bonilla,

Director of Graduate Enrollment Management, 718-260-3182, Fax: 718-260-3624, E-mail: gradinfo@poly.edu.

Providence College, Graduate Studies, School of Business, Providence, RI 02918. Offers accounting (MBA); entrepreneurship (MBA); finance (MBA); international business (MBA); management (MBA); marketing (MBA); not-for-profit organizations (MBA). Part-time and evening/weekend programs available. *Faculty:* 17 full-time (9 women), 10 part-time/adjunct (2 women). *Students:* 53 full-time (20 women), 57 part-time (22 women); includes 4 minority (1 Black or African American, non-Hispanic/Latino; 1 Asian, non-Hispanic/Latino; 2 Two or more races, non-Hispanic/Latino), 6 international. Average age 26. 72 applicants, 81% accepted. In 2010, 56 master's awarded. *Degree requirements:* For master's, thesis optional. *Entrance requirements:* For master's, GMAT. Additional exam requirements/recommendations for international students: Required—TOEFL (minimum score 550 paper-based; 213 computer-based; 80 iBT). *Application deadline:* For fall admission, 8/1 priority date for domestic and international students; for spring admission, 12/1 priority date for domestic and international students. Applications are processed on a rolling basis. Application fee: $55. *Expenses:* Contact institution. *Financial support:* In 2010–11, 34 research assistantships with full tuition reimbursements (averaging $8,400 per year) were awarded; Federal Work-Study, institutionally sponsored loans, and unspecified assistantships also available. Support available to part-time students. Financial award application deadline: 8/1; financial award applicants required to submit FAFSA. *Unit head:* Dr. MaryJane Lenon, Director, MBA Program, 401-865-2566, Fax: 401-865-2978, E-mail: mjlenon@providence.edu. *Application contact:* Katherine A. Follett, Administrative Coordinator, 401-865-2333, Fax: 401-865-2978, E-mail: kfollett@providence.edu.

Regent University, Graduate School, School of Global Leadership and Entrepreneurship, Virginia Beach, VA 23464-9800. Offers business administration (MBA); management (MA); organizational leadership (MA, PhD, Certificate); strategic foresight (MA); strategic leadership (DSL). Part-time and evening/weekend programs available. Postbaccalaureate distance learning degree programs offered (minimal on-campus study). *Faculty:* 13 full-time (3 women), 9 part-time/adjunct (3 women). *Students:* 30 full-time (11 women), 499 part-time (184 women); includes 125 Black or African American, non-Hispanic/Latino; 4 American Indian or Alaska Native, non-Hispanic/Latino; 10 Asian, non-Hispanic/Latino; 15 Hispanic/Latino, 93 international. Average age 41. 157 applicants, 66% accepted, 64 enrolled. In 2010, 86 master's, 30 doctorates awarded. *Degree requirements:* For master's, thesis or alternative, 3 credit hour culminating experience; for doctorate, thesis/dissertation. *Entrance requirements:* For master's, GRE, GMAT, minimum undergraduate GPA of 2.75, computer literacy survey, 2 recommendations, resume, transcripts, essay; for doctorate, GRE, GMAT, sample of writing, minimum 3 years of relevant experience, computer literacy survey, 2 recommendations, resume, essay, transcripts; for Certificate, writing sample, resume, transcripts. Additional exam requirements/recommendations for international students: Required—TOEFL (minimum score 577 paper-based; 233 computer-based). *Application deadline:* For fall admission, 5/1 priority date for domestic students; for spring admission, 10/1 priority date for domestic students. Applications are processed on a rolling basis. Application fee: $50. Electronic applications accepted. *Expenses:* Contact institution. *Financial support:* Career-related internships or fieldwork, scholarships/grants, and tuition waivers (full and partial) available. Support available to part-time students. Financial award application deadline: 9/1. *Faculty research:* Servant leadership, ethics and values, telecommuting and family values, organizational communications, distance education. *Unit head:* Dr. Bruce Winston, Dean, 757-352-4306, Fax: 757-352-4634, E-mail: brucwin@regent.edu. *Application contact:* Matthew Chadwick, Director of Enrollment Support Services, 800-373-5504, Fax: 757-352-4381, E-mail: admissions@regent.edu.

Rensselaer Polytechnic Institute, Graduate School, Lally School of Management and Technology, Troy, NY 12180-3590. Offers business (MBA); financial engineering and risk analysis (MS); management (MS, PhD); technology, commercialization, and entrepreneurship (MS). *Accreditation:* AACSB. Part-time and evening/weekend programs available. *Faculty:* 44 full-time (10 women), 19 part-time/adjunct (0 women). *Students:* 189 full-time (82 women), 162 part-time (40 women); includes 65 minority (22 Black or African American, non-Hispanic/Latino; 34 Asian, non-Hispanic/Latino; 9 Hispanic/Latino), 92 international. Average age 28. 507 applicants, 56% accepted, 150 enrolled. In 2010, 263 master's, 7 doctorates awarded. *Degree requirements:* For doctorate, thesis/dissertation. *Entrance requirements:* For master's, GMAT, 2 letters of recommendation, resume; for doctorate, GMAT or GRE General Test, 2 letters of recommendation. Additional exam requirements/recommendations for international students: Required—TOEFL (minimum score 600 paper-based; 250 computer-based; 100 iBT); Recommended—IELTS (minimum score 7). *Application deadline:* For fall admission, 3/15 priority date for domestic and international students. Applications are processed on a rolling basis. Application fee: $75. Electronic applications accepted. *Expenses:* Tuition: Full-time $39,600; part-time $1650 per credit. Required fees: $1896. *Financial support:* Fellowships with partial tuition reimbursements, career-related internships or fieldwork, institutionally sponsored loans, scholarships/grants, and assistantships are for Ph D students only available. Financial

award application deadline: 3/15; financial award applicants required to submit FAFSA. *Faculty research:* Technological entrepreneurship, operations management, new product development and marketing, finance and financial engineering and risk analytics, information systems. *Unit head:* Dr. Iftekhar Hasan, Acting Dean/Professor, 518-276-6586, Fax: 518-276-2665, E-mail: lallymba@rpi.edu. *Application contact:* Michele M. Martens, Manager of Graduate Programs, 518-276-6586, Fax: 518-276-8190, E-mail: lallymba@rpi.edu.

Rollins College, Crummer Graduate School of Business, Winter Park, FL 32789-4499. Offers entrepreneurship (MBA); finance (MBA); international business (MBA); management (MBA); marketing (MBA); operations and technology management (MBA). *Accreditation:* AACSB. Part-time and evening/weekend programs available. Postbaccalaureate distance learning degree programs offered (minimal on-campus study). *Faculty:* 22 full-time (3 women), 5 part-time/adjunct (3 women). *Students:* 303 full-time (117 women), 130 part-time (49 women); includes 111 minority (30 Black or African American, non-Hispanic/Latino; 1 American Indian or Alaska Native, non-Hispanic/Latino; 29 Asian, non-Hispanic/Latino; 50 Hispanic/Latino; 1 Two or more races, non-Hispanic/Latino), 29 international. Average age 32. 484 applicants, 42% accepted, 131 enrolled. In 2010, 223 master's awarded. *Entrance requirements:* For master's, GMAT, interview. Additional exam requirements/recommendations for international students: Required—TOEFL (minimum score 550 paper-based; 213 computer-based; 80 iBT). *Application deadline:* Applications are processed on a rolling basis. Application fee: $50. Electronic applications accepted. *Expenses:* Contact institution. *Financial support:* In 2010–11, 112 students received support, including 95 fellowships, 56 research assistantships (averaging $2,400 per year); career-related internships or fieldwork, scholarships/grants, and unspecified assistantships also available. Support available to part-time students. Financial award applicants required to submit FAFSA. *Faculty research:* Sustainability, world financial markets, international business, market research, strategic marketing. *Unit head:* Dr. Craig M. McAllaster, Dean, 407-646-2249, Fax: 407-646-1550, E-mail: cmcallaster@rollins.edu. *Application contact:* Linda Puritz, Student Admissions Office, 407-646-2405, Fax: 407-646-1550, E-mail: mbaadmissions@rollins.edu.

Rowan University, Graduate School, William G. Rohrer College of Business, Department of Management, Program in Entrepreneurship, Glassboro, NJ 08028-1701. Offers MBA. Part-time and evening/weekend programs available. *Degree requirements:* For master's, comprehensive exam, thesis. *Entrance requirements:* For master's, GRE General Test. Additional exam requirements/recommendations for international students: Required—TOEFL. *Application deadline:* Applications are processed on a rolling basis. Application fee: $65 ($200 for international students). Electronic applications accepted. *Expenses:* Tuition, area resident: Part-time $602 per semester hour. Tuition, nonresident: part-time $602 per semester hour. Required fees: $100 per semester hour. One-time fee: $10 part-time. *Financial support:* Career-related internships or fieldwork, Federal Work-Study, and unspecified assistantships available. Support available to part-time students. *Unit head:* Dr. Horacio Sosa, Dean, College of Graduate and Continuing Education, 856-256-4747, Fax: 856-256-5638, E-mail: sosa@rowan.edu. *Application contact:* Karen Haynes, Graduate Coordinator, 856-256-4052, E-mail: haynes@rowan.edu.

Santa Clara University, Leavey School of Business, Program in Business Administration, Santa Clara, CA 95053. Offers accounting (MBA); entrepreneurship (MBA); executive business administration (EMBA); finance (MBA); food and agribusiness (MBA); international business (MBA); leading people and organizations (MBA); managing technology and innovation (MBA); marketing management (MBA); supply chain management (MBA). *Accreditation:* AACSB. Part-time and evening/weekend programs available. *Students:* 229 full-time (80 women), 748 part-time (244 women); includes 354 minority (14 Black or African American, non-Hispanic/Latino; 1 American Indian or Alaska Native, non-Hispanic/Latino; 287 Asian, non-Hispanic/Latino; 42 Hispanic/Latino; 5 Native Hawaiian or other Pacific Islander, non-Hispanic/Latino; 5 Two or more races, non-Hispanic/Latino), 209 international. Average age 32. 334 applicants, 76% accepted, 191 enrolled. In 2010, 307 master's awarded. *Degree requirements:* For master's, thesis or alternative. *Entrance requirements:* For master's, GMAT, GRE. Additional exam requirements/recommendations for international students: Required—TOEFL (minimum score 600 paper-based; 250 computer-based; 100 iBT). *Application deadline:* For fall admission, 6/1 for domestic and international students; for spring admission, 1/19 for domestic students, 1/17 for international students. Applications are processed on a rolling basis. Application fee: $75 ($100 for international students). Electronic applications accepted. *Expenses:* Contact institution. *Financial support:* In 2010–11, 350 students received support; fellowships with partial tuition reimbursements available, research assistantships with partial tuition reimbursements available, career-related internships or fieldwork, Federal Work-Study, institutionally sponsored loans, scholarships/grants, health care benefits, and unspecified assistantships available. Support available to part-time students. Financial award application deadline: 6/1; financial award applicants required to submit FAFSA. *Unit head:* Elizabeth B. Ford, Senior Assistant Dean, 408-554-2752, Fax: 408-554-4571, E-mail: eford@scu.edu. *Application contact:* Molly Mulally, Assistant Director,

Graduate Business Admissions, 408-554-4539, Fax: 408-554-4571, E-mail: mbaadmissions@scu.edu.

Seton Hill University, Program in Business Administration, Greensburg, PA 15601. Offers entrepreneurship (MBA, Certificate); management (MBA). Part-time and evening/weekend programs available. *Faculty:* 5 full-time (3 women), 6 part-time/adjunct (0 women). *Students:* 25 full-time (14 women), 48 part-time (22 women); includes 6 minority (3 Black or African American, non-Hispanic/Latino; 1 American Indian or Alaska Native, non-Hispanic/Latino; 1 Asian, non-Hispanic/Latino; 1 Hispanic/Latino), 1 international. Average age 32. 107 applicants, 38% accepted, 31 enrolled. In 2010, 50 degrees awarded. *Entrance requirements:* For master's, resume, minimum GPA of 3.0, completion of prerequisite courses in statistics. Additional exam requirements/recommendations for international students: Required—TOEFL (minimum score 600 paper-based; 250 computer-based). *Application deadline:* For fall admission, 8/15 priority date for domestic students; for spring admission, 12/15 for domestic students. Applications are processed on a rolling basis. Application fee: $35. Electronic applications accepted. *Expenses:* Tuition: Full-time $13,050; part-time $725 per credit. Required fees: $700; $34 per credit. $50 per semester. Tuition and fees vary according to course load and program. *Financial support:* Federal Work-Study, scholarships/grants, tuition waivers (partial), and unspecified assistantships available. Support available to part-time students. Financial award application deadline: 8/15; financial award applicants required to submit FAFSA. *Faculty research:* Entrepreneurship, leadership and strategy, knowledge management. *Unit head:* Dr. Douglas Nelson, Director, 724-830-4738, E-mail: dnelson@setonhill.edu. *Application contact:* Laurel Komarny, Program Counselor, 724-838-4209, Fax: 724-830-1891, E-mail: 1komarny@setonhill.edu.

Southeast Missouri State University, School of Graduate Studies, Harrison College of Business, Cape Girardeau, MO 63701-4799. Offers accounting (MBA); entrepreneurship (MBA); environmental management (MBA); financial management (MBA); general management (MBA); health administration (MBA); industrial management (MBA); international business (MBA); sport management (MBA). *Accreditation:* AACSB. Part-time and evening/weekend programs available. Postbaccalaureate distance learning degree programs offered (no on-campus study). *Faculty:* 31 full-time (10 women). *Students:* 51 full-time (24 women), 72 part-time (34 women); includes 4 minority (1 American Indian or Alaska Native, non-Hispanic/Latino; 3 Asian, non-Hispanic/Latino), 32 international. Average age 28. 71 applicants, 83% accepted, 33 enrolled. In 2010, 46 master's awarded. *Degree requirements:* For master's, variable foreign language requirement, applied research project; foreign language or 9 credit hours (for international business). *Entrance requirements:* For master's, GMAT (minimum score 400), minimum undergraduate GPA of 2.5, prerequisite courses for non-business undergraduate majors. Additional exam requirements/recommendations for international students: Required—TOEFL (minimum score 550 paper-based; 213 computer-based; 79 iBT); Recommended—IELTS (minimum score 6). *Application deadline:* For fall admission, 8/1 for domestic students, 6/1 for international students; for spring admission, 11/21 for domestic students, 10/1 for international students. Applications are processed on a rolling basis. Application fee: $25 ($35 for international students). Electronic applications accepted. *Expenses:* Tuition: Tuition, state resident: full-time $4698; part-time $261 per credit hour. Tuition, nonresident: full-time $8379; part-time $465.50 per credit hour. *Financial support:* In 2010–11, 52 students received support, including 10 teaching assistantships with full tuition reimbursements available (averaging $7,600 per year); career-related internships or fieldwork, Federal Work-Study, institutionally sponsored loans, scholarships/grants, tuition waivers (full), and unspecified assistantships also available. Financial award application deadline: 6/30; financial award applicants required to submit FAFSA. *Faculty research:* Human resources, laws impacting accounting, advertising. *Unit head:* Dr. Kenneth A. Heischmidt, Director, Graduate Programs, 573-651-5116, Fax: 573-651-5032, E-mail: kheischmidt@semo.edu. *Application contact:* Gail Amick, Administrative Secretary, 573-651-2049, Fax: 573-651-2001, E-mail: gamick@semo.edu.

Southern Methodist University, Cox School of Business, MBA Program, Dallas, TX 75275. Offers accounting (MBA); finance (MBA); financial consulting (MBA); general business (MBA); information technology and operations management (MBA); management (MBA); marketing (MBA); real estate (MBA); strategy and entrepreneurship (MBA). Part-time and evening/weekend programs available. *Faculty:* 59 full-time (13 women), 30 part-time/adjunct (7 women). *Students:* 359 full-time (116 women), 592 part-time (154 women); includes 215 minority (44 Black or African American, non-Hispanic/Latino; 10 American Indian or Alaska Native, non-Hispanic/Latino; 118 Asian, non-Hispanic/Latino; 39 Hispanic/Latino; 2 Native Hawaiian or other Pacific Islander, non-Hispanic/Latino; 2 Two or more races, non-Hispanic/Latino), 92 international. Average age 30. In 2010, 486 master's awarded. *Entrance requirements:* For master's, GMAT. Additional exam requirements/recommendations for international students: Required—TOEFL. *Application deadline:* Applications are processed on a rolling basis. Application fee: $0. Electronic applications accepted. *Expenses:* Contact institution. *Financial support:* Applicants required to submit FAFSA. *Faculty research:* Corporate finance, financial reporting, modeling consumer decision-making, competition between national brands and store brands, institutional determinants of firms' strategy. *Unit head:* Dr. Marci Armstrong, Associate Dean for Master's Programs, 214-768-4486, Fax: 214-768-3956, E-mail: marci@cox.smu.edu. *Application contact:* Patti Cudney, Director of MBA Admissions, 214-768-3001, Fax: 214-768-3956, E-mail: pcudney@cox.smu.edu.

Southern Methodist University, Cox School of Business, Program in Entrepreneurship, Dallas, TX 75275. Offers MS. *Faculty:* 7 full-time (3 women), 2 part-time/adjunct (0 women). In 2010, 11 master's awarded. *Unit head:* Dr. Albert W. Niemi, Dean, 214-768-3012, Fax: 214-768-3713, E-mail: aniemi@mail.cox.smu.edu. *Application contact:* Path Cudney, Director of MBA Admissions, 214-768-3001, Fax: 214-768-3956, E-mail: pcudney@mail.cox.smu.edu.

Suffolk University, Sawyer Business School, Master of Business Administration Program, Boston, MA 02108-2770. Offers accounting (MBA); business administration (APC); corporate financial executive track (MBA); entrepreneurship (MBA); executive business administration (EMBA); finance (MBA); global business administration (GMBA); health administration (MBA); international business (MBA); marketing (MBA); organizational behavior (MBA); strategic management (MBA); taxation (MBA); JD/MBA; MBA/GDPA; MBA/MHA; MBA/MSA; MBA/MSF; MBA/MST. *Accreditation:* AACSB. Part-time and evening/weekend programs available. Postbaccalaureate distance learning degree programs offered (no on-campus study). *Faculty:* 97 full-time (30 women), 14 part-time/adjunct (3 women). *Students:* 179 full-time (65 women), 337 part-time (143 women); includes 16 Black or African American, non-Hispanic/Latino; 2 American Indian or Alaska Native, non-Hispanic/Latino; 22 Asian, non-Hispanic/Latino; 9 Hispanic/Latino; 1 Native Hawaiian or other Pacific Islander, non-Hispanic/Latino, 80 international. Average age 30. 431 applicants, 68% accepted, 128 enrolled. In 2010, 283 master's awarded. *Entrance requirements:* For master's, GMAT, minimum undergraduate GPA of 2.75 (MBA), 5 years of managerial experience (EMBA). Additional exam requirements/recommendations for international students: Required—TOEFL (minimum score 550 paper-based; 213 computer-based). *Application deadline:* For fall admission, 6/15 priority date for domestic students, 6/15 for international students; for spring admission, 11/1 priority date for domestic students, 11/1 for international students. Applications are processed on a rolling basis. Application fee: $50. Electronic applications accepted. *Financial support:* In 2010–11, 266 students received support, including 94 fellowships with full and partial tuition reimbursements available (averaging $12,635 per year); career-related internships or fieldwork, Federal Work-Study, and institutionally sponsored loans also available. Support available to part-time students. Financial award application deadline: 4/1; financial award applicants required to submit FAFSA. *Faculty research:* Foreign investments; career strategies and boundaryless careers; corporate ethics codes; interest rates, inflation, and growth options; innovation and product development performance. *Unit head:* Lillian Hallberg, Assistant Dean of Graduate Programs/Director of MBA Programs, 617-573-8306, E-mail: lhallber@suffolk.edu. *Application contact:* Judith Reynolds, Director of Graduate Admissions, 617-573-8302, Fax: 617-305-1733, E-mail: grad.admission@suffolk.edu.

Syracuse University, School of Information Studies, Program in Information Innovation, Syracuse, NY 13244. Offers CAS. Part-time and evening/weekend programs available. Postbaccalaureate distance learning degree programs offered. *Entrance requirements:* Additional exam requirements/recommendations for international students: Required—TOEFL (minimum score 100 iBT). *Application deadline:* For fall admission, 2/1 priority date for domestic students, 1/1 priority date for international students. Applications are processed on a rolling basis. Application fee: $75. Electronic applications accepted. *Expenses:* Tuition: Part-time $1162 per credit. *Unit head:* Elizabeth Liddy, Dean, 315-443-2736. *Application contact:* Susan Corieri, Director of Enrollment Management, 315-443-2575, E-mail: ischool@syr.edu.

Texas Tech University, Graduate School, Jerry S. Rawls College of Business Administration, Programs in Business Administration, Lubbock, TX 79409. Offers agricultural business (MBA); business administration (IMBA); business statistics (MBA); entrepreneurship and innovation (MBA); general business (MBA); health organization management (MBA); international business (MBA); management and leadership skills (MBA); management information systems (MBA); marketing (MBA); real estate (MBA); JD/MBA; MBA/M Arch; MBA/MA; MBA/MD; MBA/MS; MBA/Pharm D. Part-time and evening/weekend programs available. *Faculty:* 47 full-time (8 women), 5 part-time/adjunct (0 women). *Students:* 52 full-time (13 women), 51 part-time (152 women); includes 121 minority (28 Black or African American, non-Hispanic/Latino; 3 American Indian or Alaska Native, non-Hispanic/Latino; 31 Asian, non-Hispanic/Latino; 53 Hispanic/Latino; 6 Two or more races, non-Hispanic/Latino), 49 international. Average age 30. 437 applicants, 77% accepted, 258 enrolled. In 2010, 228 master's awarded. *Degree requirements:* For master's, capstone course. *Entrance requirements:* For master's, GMAT, holistic review of academic credentials. Additional exam requirements/recommendations for international students: Required—TOEFL (minimum score 550 paper-based; 213 computer-based; 79 iBT). *Application deadline:* For fall admission, 4/1 priority date for domestic students, 1/15 for international students; for spring admission, 9/1 priority date for domestic students, 6/15 for international students. Applications are processed on a rolling basis. Application fee: $50 ($75 for international students). Electronic applications accepted. *Expenses:* Tuition, state resident: full-time $5495.76; part-time $228.99 per credit hour. Tuition, nonresident: full-time $12,936; part-time $538.99 per credit hour. Required fees: $2674; $36 per credit hour. $905 per semester. *Financial support:* In 2010–11, 25 research assistantships (averaging $8,800 per year) were awarded; teaching assistantships, career-related internships or fieldwork, Federal Work-Study, scholarships/grants, health care benefits, and unspecified assistantships also available. Support available to part-time students. Financial award applicants required to submit FAFSA. *Unit head:* Dr. W. Jay Conover, Director, 806-742-1546, Fax: 806-742-3958, E-mail: jay.conover@ttu.edu. *Application contact:* Cynthia D. Barnes, Director, Graduate Services Center, 806-742-3184, Fax: 806-742-3958, E-mail: ba_grad@ttu.edu.

United States International University, School of Business Administration, Nairobi, Kenya. Offers business administration (GEMBA); entrepreneurship (MBA); finance (MBA); human resource management (MBA); information technology management (MBA); integrated studies (MBA); international business administration (MBA); management and organizational development (MS); marketing (MBA); organizational development (EMS); strategic management (MBA). Part-time and evening/weekend programs available. *Faculty:* 42 full-time (8 women), 64 part-time/adjunct (14 women). *Students:* 423 full-time (227 women), 129 part-time (63 women). Average age 29. 110 applicants, 79% accepted, 78 enrolled. In 2010, 164 master's awarded. *Degree requirements:* For master's, thesis. *Entrance requirements:* For master's, GMAT, 2 letters of reference, resume. Additional exam requirements/recommendations for international students: Required—TOEFL (minimum score 550 paper-based; 213 computer-based). *Application deadline:* For fall admission, 6/30 priority date for domestic and international students; for spring admission, 9/30 for domestic and international students. Applications are processed on a rolling basis. Application fee: $50. *Financial support:* In 2010–11, 30 students received support, including 8 research assistantships (averaging $1,400 per year), 4 teaching assistantships (averaging $1,400 per year); career-related internships or fieldwork, scholarships/grants, and unspecified assistantships also available. Support available to part-time students. Financial award application deadline: 6/30; financial award applicants required to submit FAFSA. *Faculty research:* Marketing in small business enterprises, total quality management in Kenya. *Unit head:* Dr. Damary Sikalieh, Dean, 254-02-3606-415, E-mail: dsikalieh@usiu.ac.ke. *Application contact:* George Lumbasi, Director of Admissions, 254-02-3606563, Fax: 254-02-3606100, E-mail: glumbasi@usiu.ac.ke.

The University of Akron, Graduate School, College of Business Administration, Department of Management, Program in Entrepreneurship, Akron, OH 44325. Offers MBA. *Students:* 1 full-time, 1 part-time. Average age 27. 6 applicants, 33% accepted. In 2010, 2 master's awarded. *Entrance requirements:* For master's, GMAT, minimum GPA of 2.75, two letters of recommendation, statement of purpose, resume. Additional exam requirements/recommendations for international students: Required—TOEFL (minimum score 550 paper-based; 213 computer-based; 79 iBT). *Application deadline:* For fall admission, 7/15 for domestic and international students; for spring admission, 11/15 for domestic and international students. Application fee: $30 ($40 for international students). Electronic applications accepted. *Expenses:* Tuition, state resident: full-time $6800; part-time $378 per credit hour. Tuition, nonresident: full-time $11,644; part-time $647 per credit hour. Required fees: $1265. One-time fee: $30 full-time. *Unit head:* Dr. Steven Ash, Head, 330-972-6429, E-mail: ash@uakron.edu. *Application contact:* Dr. Susan Hanlon, Director of Graduate Business Programs, 330-972-7043, Fax: 330-972-6588, E-mail: shanlon@uakron.edu.

University of Central Florida, College of Business Administration, Department of Management, Orlando, FL 32816. Offers entrepreneurship (Graduate Certificate); management (MSM); technology ventures (Graduate Certificate). *Accreditation:* AACSB. *Faculty:* 25 full-time (9 women), 4 part-time/adjunct (1 woman). *Students:* 30 part-time (15 women); includes 4 Black or African American, non-Hispanic/Latino; 3 Asian, non-Hispanic/Latino; 3 Hispanic/Latino. Average age 31. 8 applicants, 88% accepted, 6 enrolled. In 2010, 23 master's, 9 other advanced degrees awarded. *Entrance requirements:* For master's, GMAT, minimum GPA of 3.0 in last 60 hours. *Application deadline:* For fall admission, 2/1 priority date for domestic students; for spring admission, 11/1 priority date for domestic students. Application fee: $30. Electronic applications accepted. *Expenses:* Tuition, state resident: part-time $256.56 per credit hour. Tuition, nonresident: part-time $1011.52 per credit hour. Part-time tuition and fees vary according to program. *Financial support:* Fellowships, research assistantships, teaching assistantships available. *Unit head:* Dr. Stephen Goodman, Chair, 407-823-5569, Fax: 407-823-3725, E-mail: sgoodman@bus.ucf.edu. *Application contact:* Dr. Stephen Goodman, Chair, 407-823-5569, Fax: 407-823-3725, E-mail: sgoodman@bus.ucf.edu.

University of Chicago, Booth School of Business, Full-Time MBA Program, Chicago, IL 60637. Offers accounting (MBA); analytic finance (MBA); analytic management (MBA); econometrics and statistics (MBA); economics

(MBA); entrepreneurship (MBA); finance (MBA); general management (MBA); human resource management (MBA); international business (MBA); managerial and organizational behavior (MBA); marketing management (MBA); operations management (MBA); strategic management (MBA); MBA/AM; MBA/JD; MBA/MA; MBA/MD; MBA/MPP. *Accreditation:* AACSB. Part-time and evening/weekend programs available. *Faculty:* 157 full-time, 35 part-time/adjunct. *Students:* 1,177 full-time (417 women); includes 301 minority (62 Black or African American, non-Hispanic/Latino; 1 American Indian or Alaska Native, non-Hispanic/Latino; 164 Asian, non-Hispanic/Latino; 55 Hispanic/Latino; 19 Two or more races, non-Hispanic/Latino), 403 international. Average age 28. 4,299 applicants, 22% accepted, 579 enrolled. In 2010, 1,374 master's awarded. *Entrance requirements:* For master's, GMAT, 2 letters of recommendation, 3 essays, resume, interview, transcripts. Additional exam requirements/recommendations for international students: Required—TOEFL (minimum score 600 paper-based; 250 computer-based), IELTS. *Application deadline:* For fall admission, 10/10 priority date for domestic students, 10/13 priority date for international students; for winter admission, 1/5 for domestic and international students; for spring admission, 4/13 for domestic and international students. Application fee: $200. Electronic applications accepted. *Expenses:* Contact institution. *Financial support:* Fellowships available. Financial award applicants required to submit FAFSA. *Faculty research:* Finance, economics, entrepreneurship, strategy, management. *Unit head:* Stacey Kole, Deputy Dean, 773-702-7121. *Application contact:* Kurt Ahlm, Associate Dean of Admissions and Financial Aid, 773-702-7369, Fax: 773-702-9085, E-mail: admissions@chicagobooth.edu.

University of Colorado Boulder, Leeds School of Business, Division of Business Administration, Boulder, CO 80309. Offers accounting (MS, PhD); finance (PhD); information systems (PhD); marketing (PhD); operations (PhD); strategic, organizational, and entrepreneurial studies (PhD). Part-time and evening/weekend programs available. *Students:* 110 full-time (42 women), 2 part-time (1 woman); includes 6 minority (5 Asian, non-Hispanic/Latino; 1 Hispanic/Latino), 24 international. Average age 28. 342 applicants, 24 enrolled. In 2010, 48 master's, 12 doctorates awarded. *Entrance requirements:* For master's, GMAT, minimum undergraduate GPA of 3.0. *Application deadline:* For fall admission, 3/31 for domestic and international students; for spring admission, 10/31 for domestic and international students. Application fee: $50 ($60 for international students). Electronic applications accepted. *Financial support:* In 2010–11, 16 fellowships (averaging $1,038 per year), 26 research assistantships (averaging $17,558 per year), 11 teaching assistantships (averaging $12,576 per year) were awarded; career-related internships or fieldwork, Federal Work-Study, scholarships/grants, and unspecified assistantships also available. Financial award applicants required to submit FAFSA.

University of Colorado Denver, Business School, Program in Management and Organization, Denver, CO 80217. Offers communications management (MS); enterprise technology management (MS); entrepreneurship and innovation (MS); global management (MS); human resources management (MS); leadership (MS); quantitative decision methods (MS); sports and entertainment management (MS); strategic management (MS); sustainability management (MS). *Accreditation:* AACSB. Part-time and evening/weekend programs available. Postbaccalaureate distance learning degree programs offered (no on-campus study). *Students:* 34 full-time (21 women), 9 part-time (2 women); includes 3 Asian, non-Hispanic/Latino; 5 Hispanic/Latino. Average age 33. 28 applicants, 61% accepted, 10 enrolled. In 2010, 20 master's awarded. *Degree requirements:* For master's, 30 semester hours (12 of required courses, 12 of management electives, and 6 of free electives). *Entrance requirements:* For master's, GMAT. Additional exam requirements/recommendations for international students: Required—TOEFL (minimum score 525 paper-based; 197 computer-based; 71 iBT). *Application deadline:* For fall admission, 4/1 priority date for domestic students, 3/15 priority date for international students; for spring admission, 10/1 priority date for domestic and international students. Application fee: $50 ($75 for international students). Electronic applications accepted. *Expenses:* Contact institution. *Financial support:* Federal Work-Study and scholarships/grants available. Support available to part-time students. Financial award application deadline: 4/1; financial award applicants required to submit FAFSA. *Faculty research:* Human resource management, management of catastrophe, turnaround strategies. *Unit head:* Dr. Kenneth Bettenhausen, Associate Professor/Director, 303-315-8425, E-mail: kenneth.bettehausen@ucdenver.edu. *Application contact:* Shelly Townley, Admissions Director, Graduate Programs, 303-315-8202, E-mail: shelly.townley@ucdenver.edu.

University of Colorado Denver, College of Engineering and Applied Science, Department of Bioengineering, Aurora, CO 80045-2560. Offers bioengineering (PhD); clinical imaging (MS); device design and entrepreneurship (MS); research (MS). Part-time programs available. *Faculty:* 3 full-time (1 woman). *Students:* 13 full-time (2 women), 1 part-time; includes 1 Black or African American, non-Hispanic/Latino; 1 Asian, non-Hispanic/Latino; 1 Hispanic/Latino. Average age 30. 15 applicants, 100% accepted, 12 enrolled. Terminal master's awarded for partial completion of doctoral program. *Degree requirements:* For master's, thesis or alternative, 30 credit hours; for doctorate, comprehensive exam, thesis/dissertation, 36 credit hours of classwork (18 core, 18 elective), additional 30 hours of thesis work, three formal examinations, approval of dissertations. *Entrance requirements:* For master's, GRE (recommended); for doctorate, GRE. Additional exam requirements/recommendations for international students: Required—TOEFL (minimum score 550 paper-based; 213 computer-based; 79 iBT), TOEFL (minimum 250 CBT/600 PBT/100IBT) for Ph D. *Application deadline:* For fall admission, 4/30 for domestic students. Application fee: $50. Electronic applications accepted. *Expenses:* Contact institution. *Financial support:* Fellowships, research assistantships, teaching assistantships, Federal Work-Study available. Financial award application deadline: 4/1; financial award applicants required to submit FAFSA. *Faculty research:* Imaging and biophotonics, cardiovascular biomechanics and hemodynamics, orthopedic biomechanics, ophthalmology, neuroscience engineering. *Unit head:* Dr. Robin Shandas, Chair, 303-724-4196, E-mail: robin.shandas@ucdenver.edu. *Application contact:* Dr. Robin Shandas, Chair, 303-724-4196, E-mail: robin.shandas@ucdenver.edu.

University of Dayton, Graduate School, School of Business Administration, Dayton, OH 45469-1300. Offers accounting (MBA); business intelligence (MBA); cyber security (MBA); entrepreneurship (MBA); finance (MBA); international business (MBA); marketing (MBA); MIS (MBA); operations management (MBA); technology-enhanced business/e-commerce (MBA); JD/MBA. *Accreditation:* AACSB. Part-time and evening/weekend programs available. *Faculty:* 25 full-time (7 women), 14 part-time/adjunct (2 women). *Students:* 184 full-time (72 women), 110 part-time (34 women); includes 23 minority (7 Black or African American, non-Hispanic/Latino; 7 Asian, non-Hispanic/Latino; 8 Hispanic/Latino; 1 Two or more races, non-Hispanic/Latino), 31 international. Average age 28. 220 applicants, 85% accepted, 103 enrolled. In 2010, 113 master's awarded. *Entrance requirements:* For master's, GMAT or GRE. Additional exam requirements/recommendations for international students: Required—TOEFL (minimum score 550 paper-based; 213 computer-based; 79 iBT); Recommended—IELTS (minimum score 6.5). *Application deadline:* For fall admission, 3/1 priority date for international students; for winter admission, 7/1 priority date for international students; for spring admission, 1/1 priority date for international students. Applications are processed on a rolling basis. Application fee: $0 ($50 for international students). Electronic applications accepted. *Expenses:* Contact institution. *Financial support:* In 2010–11, 15 research assistantships with full and partial tuition reimbursements (averaging $7,020 per year) were awarded; career-related internships or fieldwork, institutionally sponsored loans, scholarships/grants, health care benefits, and unspecified assistantships also available. Support available to part-time students. Financial award application deadline: 3/15; financial award applicants required to submit FAFSA. *Faculty research:* Management information systems, economics, finance, entrepreneurship, marketing. *Unit head:* Janice M. Glynn, Director, MBA Program, 937-229-3733, Fax: 937-229-3882, E-mail: glynn@udayton.edu. *Application contact:* Jeffrey Carter, Assistant Director, MBA Program, 937-229-3733, Fax: 937-229-3882, E-mail: jeff.carter@notes.udayton.edu.

University of Florida, Graduate School, Warrington College of Business Administration, Hough Graduate School of Business, Department of Finance, Insurance and Real Estate, Gainesville, FL 32611. Offers business administration (MS), including entrepreneurship, real estate and urban analysis; finance (PhD); financial services (Certificate); real estate and urban analysis (PhD); JD/MBA. *Faculty:* 13 full-time (0 women). *Students:* 56 full-time (13 women), 2 part-time (0 women); includes 2 Black or African American, non-Hispanic/Latino; 2 Asian, non-Hispanic/Latino; 1 Hispanic/Latino, 16 international. Average age 27. 245 applicants, 34% accepted, 58 enrolled. In 2010, 105 master's awarded. Terminal master's awarded for partial completion of doctoral program. *Degree requirements:* For master's, comprehensive exam, thesis; for doctorate, comprehensive exam, thesis/dissertation. *Entrance requirements:* For master's, GMAT or GRE General Test, minimum GPA of 3.0 for last 60 hours of undergraduate degree, work experience (preferred); for doctorate, GMAT or GRE General Test, minimum GPA of 3.0. Additional exam requirements/recommendations for international students: Required—TOEFL (minimum score 550 paper-based; 213 computer-based; 80 iBT), IELTS (minimum score 6). *Application deadline:* For fall admission, 1/15 priority date for domestic students, 1/15 for international students. Applications are processed on a rolling basis. Application fee: $30. Electronic applications accepted. *Expenses:* Tuition, state resident: full-time $10,915.92. Tuition, nonresident: full-time $28,309. *Financial support:* In 2010–11, 18 students received support, including 6 fellowships, 12 research assistantships (averaging $20,699 per year), 2 teaching assistantships; career-related internships or fieldwork, scholarships/grants, and unspecified assistantships also available. Financial award application deadline: 1/15; financial award applicants required to submit FAFSA. *Faculty research:* Banking, empirical corporate finance, hedge funds. *Unit head:* Dr. Mahendrarajah Nimalendran, Chair, 352-392-9526, Fax: 352-392-0301, E-mail: nimal@ufl.edu. *Application contact:* Mark J. Flannery, Graduate Coordinator, 352-392-3184, Fax: 352-392-0301, E-mail: flannery@ufl.edu.

University of Hawaii at Manoa, Graduate Division, Shidler College of Business, The Pacific Asian Center for Entrepreneurship and E-Business (PACE), Honolulu, HI 96822. Offers entrepreneurship (Graduate Certificate). Part-time programs available. *Entrance requirements:* Additional exam

requirements/recommendations for international students: Required—TOEFL (minimum score 500 paper-based; 61 iBT). *Application deadline:* For fall admission, 5/1 for domestic and international students. *Application contact:* John Butler, Dean, 808-956-8582, E-mail: jebutler@hawaii.edu.

University of Hawaii at Manoa, Graduate Division, Shidler College of Business, Program in Business Administration, Honolulu, HI 96822. Offers Asian business studies (MBA); Chinese business studies (MBA); decision sciences (MBA); entrepreneurship (MBA); finance (MBA); finance and banking (MBA); human resources management (MBA); information management (MBA); information technology (MBA); international business (MBA); Japanese business studies (MBA); marketing (MBA); organizational behavior (MBA); organizational management (MBA); real estate (MBA); student-designed track (MBA). *Accreditation:* AACSB. Part-time and evening/weekend programs available. *Faculty:* 53 full-time (12 women). *Students:* 162 full-time (63 women), 102 part-time (43 women); includes 135 minority (1 Black or African American, non-Hispanic/Latino; 81 Asian, non-Hispanic/Latino; 5 Hispanic/Latino; 18 Native Hawaiian or other Pacific Islander, non-Hispanic/Latino; 30 Two or more races, non-Hispanic/Latino), 44 international. Average age 34. 361 applicants, 57% accepted, 172 enrolled. In 2010, 153 master's awarded. *Degree requirements:* For master's, thesis optional. *Entrance requirements:* For master's, GMAT, minimum GPA of 3.0. Additional exam requirements/recommendations for international students: Required—TOEFL (minimum score 600 paper-based; 250 computer-based; 100 iBT), IELTS (minimum score 7). *Application deadline:* For fall admission, 5/1 for domestic students, 3/1 for international students. Application fee: $60. *Expenses:* Contact institution. *Financial support:* In 2010–11, 83 fellowships (averaging $5,547 per year), 1 research assistantship (averaging $16,824 per year) were awarded. Total annual research expenditures: $427,000. *Application contact:* Daniel Port, Graduate Chair, 808-956-5565, Fax: 808-956-6889, E-mail: daniel.port@hawaii.edu.

University of Houston–Victoria, School of Business Administration, Victoria, TX 77901-4450. Offers accounting (MBA); economic development and entrepreneurship (MS); finance (GMBA, MBA); general business (MBA); international business (MBA); management (GMBA, MBA); marketing (MBA). *Accreditation:* AACSB. Part-time and evening/weekend programs available. Postbaccalaureate distance learning degree programs offered (minimal on-campus study). *Faculty:* 37 full-time (11 women). *Students:* 234 full-time (108 women), 714 part-time (303 women); includes 542 minority (215 Black or African American, non-Hispanic/Latino; 1 American Indian or Alaska Native, non-Hispanic/Latino; 197 Asian, non-Hispanic/Latino; 124 Hispanic/Latino; 1 Native Hawaiian or other Pacific Islander, non-Hispanic/Latino; 4 Two or more races, non-Hispanic/Latino), 115 international. Average age 34. 362 applicants, 65% accepted, 147 enrolled. In 2010, 181 master's awarded. *Entrance requirements:* For master's, GMAT. Additional exam requirements/recommendations for international students: Required—TOEFL (minimum score 550 paper-based; 213 computer-based). *Application deadline:* For fall admission, 6/1 for international students; for spring admission, 10/1 for international students. Applications are processed on a rolling basis. Application fee: $0. Electronic applications accepted. *Expenses:* Tuition, state resident: full-time $4050; part-time $225 per credit hour. Tuition, nonresident: full-time $8730; part-time $485 per credit hour. Required fees: $810; $54 per credit hour. Tuition and fees vary according to course load. *Financial support:* In 2010–11, research assistantships with partial tuition reimbursements (averaging $2,000 per year), teaching assistantships with partial tuition reimbursements (averaging $2,000 per year) were awarded; Federal Work-Study, scholarships/grants, and unspecified assistantships also available. Support available to part-time students. Financial award application deadline: 4/15; financial award applicants required to submit FAFSA. *Faculty research:* Economic development, marketing, finance. *Unit head:* Dr. Farhang Niroomand, Dean, 361-570-4230, Fax: 361-580-5599, E-mail: niroomandf@uhv.edu. *Application contact:* Jane Mims, Assistant Dean, 361-570-4639, Fax: 361-580-5529, E-mail: mims@uhv.edu.

University of Louisville, Graduate School, College of Business, MBA Programs, Louisville, KY 40292-0001. Offers entrepreneurship (MBA); global business (PMBA); global business (full time) (MBA). The MBA degree is offered in both a full time and part time format. The full time program is a 13 month program paired with a paid internship. The part-time program is available in an evening as well as a Saturday format. All MBA programs are cohort-based and include an international learning experience. *Accreditation:* AACSB. Part-time and evening/weekend programs available. *Faculty:* 30 full-time (7 women), 2 part-time/adjunct (0 women). *Students:* 25 full-time (9 women), 185 part-time (54 women); includes 19 minority (6 Black or African American, non-Hispanic/Latino; 1 American Indian or Alaska Native, non-Hispanic/Latino; 8 Asian, non-Hispanic/Latino; 4 Hispanic/Latino), 8 international. Average age 29. 318 applicants, 42% accepted, 111 enrolled. In 2010, 104 master's awarded. *Entrance requirements:* For master's, GMAT, 2 letters of reference, personal interview, resume, personal statement, college transcript(s). Additional exam requirements/recommendations for international students: Required—TOEFL (minimum score 557 paper-based; 213 computer-based; 83 iBT). *Application deadline:* For fall admission, 7/31 for domestic students; for spring admission, 12/1 for domestic students.

Applications are processed on a rolling basis. Application fee: $50. *Expenses:* Tuition, state resident: full-time $9144; part-time $508 per credit hour. Tuition, nonresident: full-time $19,026; part-time $1057 per credit hour. Tuition and fees vary according to program and reciprocity agreements. *Financial support:* In 2010–11, 16 students received support, including 6 fellowships (averaging $3,133 per year), 10 research assistantships with full tuition reimbursements available (averaging $12,000 per year); health care benefits and unspecified assistantships also available. Financial award application deadline: 3/31; financial award applicants required to submit FAFSA. *Faculty research:* Entrepreneurship, venture capital, retailing/franchising, corporate governance and leadership, supply chain management. Total annual research expenditures: $221,322. *Unit head:* Dr. R. Charles Moyer, Dean, 502-852-6443, Fax: 502-852-7557, E-mail: charlie.moyer@louisville.edu. *Application contact:* Joshua M. Philpot, Graduate Programs Manager, 502-852-7257, Fax: 502-852-4901, E-mail: josh.philpot@louisville.edu.

University of Louisville, Graduate School, College of Business, PhD Program in Entrepreneurship, Louisville, KY 40292-0001. Offers PhD. *Faculty:* 12 full-time (4 women), 6 part-time/adjunct (0 women). *Students:* 12 full-time (2 women); includes 1 Asian, non-Hispanic/Latino, 6 international. Average age 34. 32 applicants, 34% accepted, 6 enrolled. In 2010, 2 doctorates awarded. *Degree requirements:* For doctorate, comprehensive exam, thesis/dissertation, paper of sufficient quality for journal publication. *Entrance requirements:* For doctorate, GMAT, 3 letters of recommendation, curriculum vitae, personal interview. Additional exam requirements/recommendations for international students: Required—TOEFL (minimum score 550 paper-based; 213 computer-based; 79 iBT). *Application deadline:* For fall admission, 3/31 for domestic and international students. Applications are processed on a rolling basis. Application fee: $50. Electronic applications accepted. *Expenses:* Tuition, state resident: full-time $9144; part-time $508 per credit hour. Tuition, nonresident: full-time $19,026; part-time $1057 per credit hour. Tuition and fees vary according to program and reciprocity agreements. *Financial support:* In 2010–11, 11 students received support, including 6 fellowships with full tuition reimbursements available (averaging $21,000 per year), 3 teaching assistantships with full tuition reimbursements available (averaging $21,000 per year); scholarships/grants, health care benefits, and unspecified assistantships also available. Financial award application deadline: 3/15; financial award applicants required to submit FAFSA. *Faculty research:* Entrepreneurship, supply chain management, venture capital, retailing/franchising, corporate governance. *Unit head:* Dr. Charles Moyer, Dean, 502-852-6443, Fax: 502-852-7557, E-mail: charlie.moyer@louisville.edu. *Application contact:* Dr. David Dubofsky, Director, 502-852-3016, Fax: 502-852-6072, E-mail: d.dubofsky@louisville.edu.

University of Missouri–Kansas City, Henry W. Bloch School of Management, Kansas City, MO 64110-2499. Offers accounting (MS); business administration (MBA); entrepreneurship and innovation (PhD); public affairs (MPA, PhD); JD/MBA; LL M/MPA. PhD (interdisciplinary) offered through the School of Graduate Studies. *Accreditation:* AACSB; NASPAA. Part-time and evening/weekend programs available. *Faculty:* 49 full-time (16 women), 21 part-time/adjunct (5 women). *Students:* 280 full-time (134 women), 435 part-time (193 women); includes 91 minority (44 Black or African American, non-Hispanic/Latino; 19 Asian, non-Hispanic/Latino; 23 Hispanic/Latino; 5 Two or more races, non-Hispanic/Latino), 50 international. Average age 30. 426 applicants, 255 enrolled. In 2010, 254 master's awarded. Terminal master's awarded for partial completion of doctoral program. *Entrance requirements:* For master's, GMAT, GRE, 2 writing essays, 2 references and support of employer; for doctorate, GRE, minimum GPA of 3.0. Additional exam requirements/recommendations for international students: Required—TOEFL (minimum score 550 paper-based; 213 computer-based; 80 iBT). *Application deadline:* For fall admission, 5/1 priority date for domestic and international students; for spring admission, 10/1 priority date for domestic and international students. Applications are processed on a rolling basis. Application fee: $45 ($50 for international students). Electronic applications accepted. *Expenses:* Tuition, state resident: full-time $5522.40; part-time $306.80 per credit hour. Tuition, nonresident: full-time $7128; part-time $792 per credit hour. Required fees: $261.15 per term. *Financial support:* In 2010–11, 26 research assistantships with partial tuition reimbursements (averaging $7,767 per year), 5 teaching assistantships with partial tuition reimbursements (averaging $8,430 per year) were awarded; career-related internships or fieldwork, Federal Work-Study, institutionally sponsored loans, scholarships/grants, tuition waivers (full and partial), and unspecified assistantships also available. Support available to part-time students. Financial award application deadline: 3/1; financial award applicants required to submit FAFSA. *Faculty research:* Entrepreneurship, finance, non-profit, risk management. *Unit head:* Dr. Teng-Kee Tan, Dean, 816-235-2215, Fax: 816-235-2206. *Application contact:* 816-235-1111, E-mail: admit@umkc.edu.

University of Nevada, Las Vegas, Graduate College, College of Business, Department of Management, Las Vegas, NV 89154. Offers management (Certificate); new venture management (Certificate). *Students:* 2 part-time (1 woman); includes 1 minority (Two or more races, non-Hispanic/Latino). Average age 28. 2 applicants, 50% accepted, 1 enrolled. *Expenses:* Tuition, area resident: Part-time $239.50 per credit. Tuition, state resident: part-time

$239.50 per credit. Tuition, nonresident: part-time $503 per credit. Required fees: $108 per semester. Tuition and fees vary according to course load, program and reciprocity agreements. *Faculty research:* Supply chain management, business strategy, human resource management, entrepreneurship, business ethics. *Unit head:* Dr. Keong Leong, Chair/Professor, 702-895-1762, E-mail: keong.leong@unlv.edu. *Application contact:* Graduate College Admissions Evaluator, 702-895-3320, Fax: 702-895-4180, E-mail: gradcollege@unlv.edu.

University of New Brunswick Fredericton, School of Graduate Studies, Faculty of Business Administration, Fredericton, NB E3B 5A3, Canada. Offers business administration (MBA); engineering management (MBA); entrepreneurship (MBA); sports and recreation management (MBA); MBA/LL B. Part-time programs available. *Faculty:* 23 full-time (3 women), 5 part-time/adjunct (2 women). *Students:* 43 full-time (18 women), 35 part-time (20 women). In 2010, 29 master's awarded. *Degree requirements:* For master's, thesis optional. *Entrance requirements:* For master's, GMAT (550 minimum score), minimum GPA of 3.0; 3-5 years work experience. Additional exam requirements/recommendations for international students: Required—TOEFL (minimum score 580 paper-based; 92 iBT), IELTS (minimum score 7), TOEFL or IELTS. *Application deadline:* For fall admission, 3/1 priority date for domestic students. Applications are processed on a rolling basis. Application fee: $50 Canadian dollars. *Expenses:* Tuition, area resident: Full-time $3708; part-time $927 per term. International tuition: $6300 full-time. Required fees: $50 per term. *Financial support:* In 2010–11, 4 research assistantships (averaging $4,500 per year), 13 teaching assistantships (averaging $2,250 per year) were awarded. *Faculty research:* Accounting and auditing practices, human resource management, the non-profit sector, marketing, strategic management, entrepreneurship, investment practices, supply chain management, and operations management. *Unit head:* Judy Roy, Director of Graduate Studies, 506-458-7307, Fax: 506-453-3561, E-mail: jroy@unb.ca. *Application contact:* Marilyn Davis, Acting Graduate Secretary, 506-453-4766, Fax: 506-453-3561, E-mail: mbacontact@unb.ca.

University of Portland, Dr. Robert B. Pamplin, Jr. School of Business, Portland, OR 97203-5798. Offers business administration (MBA); entrepreneurship (MBA); finance (MBA, MS); health care management (MBA); marketing (MBA); nonprofit management (EMBA); operations and technology management (MBA); sustainability (MBA). *Accreditation:* AACSB. Part-time and evening/weekend programs available. *Faculty:* 12 full-time (2 women), 7 part-time/adjunct (2 women). *Students:* 55 full-time (24 women), 81 part-time (29 women); includes 18 minority (2 Black or African American, non-Hispanic/Latino; 8 Asian, non-Hispanic/Latino; 5 Hispanic/Latino; 3 Two or more races, non-Hispanic/Latino), 23 international. Average age 30. In 2010, 55 master's awarded. *Entrance requirements:* For master's, GMAT, minimum GPA of 3.0, resume, 2 letters of recommendation. Additional exam requirements/recommendations for international students: Required—TOEFL (minimum score 570 paper-based; 89 iBT), IELTS (minimum score 7). *Application deadline:* For fall admission, 7/15 priority date for domestic and international students; for spring admission, 12/15 priority date for domestic and international students. Applications are processed on a rolling basis. Application fee: $50. *Expenses:* Contact institution. *Financial support:* Federal Work-Study, scholarships/grants, and tuition waivers (partial) available. Support available to part-time students. Financial award application deadline: 3/1; financial award applicants required to submit FAFSA. *Unit head:* Dr. Howard Feldman, Associate Dean, 503-943-7224, E-mail: feldman@up.edu. *Application contact:* Melissa McCarthy, Academic Specialist, 503-943-7225, E-mail: mccarthy@up.edu.

University of San Francisco, College of Arts and Sciences, Department of Computer Science, Program in Web Science, San Francisco, CA 94117-1080. Offers MS. *Faculty:* 5 full-time (1 woman). *Students:* 15 full-time (3 women), 2 part-time (0 women); includes 2 minority (both Black or African American, non-Hispanic/Latino), 11 international. Average age 30. 20 applicants, 75% accepted, 5 enrolled. In 2010, 4 master's awarded. *Expenses:* Tuition: Full-time $20,070; part-time $1115 per credit hour. Tuition and fees vary according to course load, degree level and program. *Financial support:* In 2010–11, 7 students received support. *Unit head:* Terence Parr, Graduate Director, 415-422-6530, Fax: 415-422-5800. *Application contact:* Mark Landerghini, Graduate Adviser, 415-422-5135, E-mail: asgraduate@usfca.edu.

University of San Francisco, School of Business and Professional Studies, Masagung Graduate School of Management, Joint Master of Global Entrepreneurship and Management Program, San Francisco, CA 94117-1080. Offers MGEM. Program offered jointly with IQS in Barcelona, Spain and Fu Jen Catholic University in Taipei, Taiwan. *Faculty:* 2 full-time (both women), 2 part-time/adjunct (0 women). *Students:* 29 full-time (17 women); includes 11 minority (1 Black or African American, non-Hispanic/Latino; 1 Asian, non-Hispanic/Latino; 6 Hispanic/Latino; 3 Two or more races, non-Hispanic/Latino), 12 international. Average age 23. 58 applicants, 71% accepted, 29 enrolled. In 2010, 29 master's awarded. *Expenses:* Tuition: Full-time $20,070; part-time $1115 per credit hour. Tuition and fees vary according to course load, degree level and program. *Financial support:* In 2010–11, 11 students received support. *Unit head:* Dr. Shenzhao Fu, 415-422-6771, Fax: 415-422-2502.

Application contact: Kelly Brookes, Director, MBA Program, 415-422-2221, Fax: 415-422-6315, E-mail: mba@usfca.edu.

University of San Francisco, School of Business and Professional Studies, Masagung Graduate School of Management, Program in Business Administration, San Francisco, CA 94117-1080. Offers business economics (MBA); e-business (MBA); entrepreneurship (MBA); finance (MBA); international business (MBA); management (MBA); marketing (MBA); telecommunications management and policy (MBA); JD/MBA; MSN/MBA. *Accreditation:* AACSB. *Faculty:* 17 full-time (4 women), 16 part-time/adjunct (7 women). *Students:* 263 full-time (130 women), 11 part-time (6 women); includes 98 minority (3 Black or African American, non-Hispanic/Latino; 65 Asian, non-Hispanic/Latino; 18 Hispanic/Latino; 3 Native Hawaiian or other Pacific Islander, non-Hispanic/Latino; 9 Two or more races, non-Hispanic/Latino), 43 international. Average age 29. 503 applicants, 60% accepted, 80 enrolled. In 2010, 115 master's awarded. *Entrance requirements:* For master's, GMAT, minimum undergraduate GPA of 3.2. Additional exam requirements/recommendations for international students: Required—TOEFL. *Application deadline:* For fall admission, 7/1 priority date for domestic students; for spring admission, 11/30 for domestic students. Applications are processed on a rolling basis. Application fee: $55 ($65 for international students). *Expenses:* Tuition: Full-time $20,070; part-time $1115 per credit hour. Tuition and fees vary according to course load, degree level and program. *Financial support:* In 2010–11, 156 students received support; fellowships available. Financial award application deadline: 3/2; financial award applicants required to submit FAFSA. *Faculty research:* International financial markets, technology transfer licensing, international marketing, strategic planning. Total annual research expenditures: $50,000. *Unit head:* Kelly Brookes, Director, 415-422-2221, Fax: 415-422-6315. *Application contact:* Director, MBA Program, 415-422-2221, Fax: 415-422-6315, E-mail: mba@usfca.edu.

University of South Florida, Graduate School, College of Business, Center for Entrepreneurship, Tampa, FL 33620-9951. Offers MS, Graduate Certificate. Part-time and evening/weekend programs available. *Faculty:* 1 full-time (0 women). *Students:* 46 full-time (19 women), 52 part-time (19 women); includes 12 Black or African American, non-Hispanic/Latino; 1 American Indian or Alaska Native, non-Hispanic/Latino; 3 Asian, non-Hispanic/Latino; 11 Hispanic/Latino; 1 Two or more races, non-Hispanic/Latino, 8 international. Average age 32. 75 applicants, 68% accepted, 37 enrolled. In 2010, 25 master's awarded. *Degree requirements:* For master's, thesis (for some programs). *Entrance requirements:* For master's, GMAT, minimum undergraduate GPA of 3.0 in last 2 years, recommendations, interview. Additional exam requirements/recommendations for international students: Required—TOEFL (minimum score 550 paper-based; 213 computer-based; 79 iBT). *Application deadline:* For fall admission, 2/15 for domestic students, 1/2 for international students; for spring admission, 10/15 for domestic students, 6/1 for international students. Applications are processed on a rolling basis. Application fee: $30. Electronic applications accepted. *Financial support:* Applicants required to submit FAFSA. *Unit head:* Dr. Michael W. Fountain, Director, 813-974-7900, Fax: 813-974-7663, E-mail: fountain@coba.usf.edu. *Application contact:* Dr. Michael W. Fountain, Director, 813-974-7900, Fax: 813-974-7663, E-mail: fountain@coba.usf.edu.

The University of Tampa, John H. Sykes College of Business, Tampa, FL 33606-1490. Offers accounting (MS); entrepreneurship (MBA); finance (MBA, MS); information systems management (MBA); innovation management (MBA); international business (MBA); marketing (MBA, MS); nonprofit management (MBA). *Accreditation:* AACSB. Part-time and evening/weekend programs available. *Faculty:* 67 full-time (24 women), 11 part-time/adjunct (4 women). *Students:* 235 full-time (89 women), 288 part-time (122 women); includes 74 minority (16 Black or African American, non-Hispanic/Latino; 2 American Indian or Alaska Native, non-Hispanic/Latino; 14 Asian, non-Hispanic/Latino; 34 Hispanic/Latino; 2 Native Hawaiian or other Pacific Islander, non-Hispanic/Latino; 6 Two or more races, non-Hispanic/Latino), 95 international. Average age 29. 457 applicants, 45% accepted, 175 enrolled. In 2010, 230 master's awarded. *Degree requirements:* For master's, capstone. *Entrance requirements:* For master's, GMAT or GRE, 4-year undergraduate degree, minimum GPA of 3.0, professional experience (for Executive MBA). Additional exam requirements/recommendations for international students: Required—TOEFL (minimum score 577 paper-based; 230 computer-based; 90 iBT); Recommended—IELTS (minimum score 7.5). *Application deadline:* Applications are processed on a rolling basis. Application fee: $40. Electronic applications accepted. *Expenses:* Tuition: Part-time $504 per credit hour. Required fees: $40 per term. *Financial support:* In 2010–11, 74 students received support. Career-related internships or fieldwork, scholarships/grants, unspecified assistantships, and grants available. Financial award applicants required to submit FAFSA. *Faculty research:* Management innovation, social marketing, value relevance of earnings and book value across industries, managerial finance, entrepreneurship. *Unit head:* Dennis Nostrand, Vice President, Enrollment/Admissions, 813-257-1808, E-mail: dnostrand@ut.edu. *Application contact:* Charlene Tobie, Associate Director of Admissions, 813-257-3566, E-mail: ctobie@ut.edu.

The University of Texas at Dallas, School of Management, Program in Innovation and Entrepreneurship, Richardson, TX 75080. Offers MS. Part-time and evening/weekend programs available. *Faculty:* 2 part-time/adjunct (0 women). *Students:* 2 full-time (0 women), 2 part-time (1 woman); includes 1 minority (Hispanic/Latino), 1 international. Average age 29. 19 applicants, 47% accepted, 4 enrolled. *Degree requirements:* For master's, thesis optional. *Entrance requirements:* For master's, GMAT, minimum GPA of 3.0 in upper-level course work in field. Additional exam requirements/recommendations for international students: Required—TOEFL (minimum score 550 paper-based; 215 computer-based). *Application deadline:* For fall admission, 7/15 for domestic students, 5/1 priority date for international students; for spring admission, 11/15 for domestic students, 9/1 priority date for international students. Applications are processed on a rolling basis. Application fee: $50 ($100 for international students). Electronic applications accepted. *Expenses:* Tuition, state resident: full-time $10,248; part-time $569 per credit hour. Tuition, nonresident: full-time $18,544; part-time $1030 per credit hour. Tuition and fees vary according to course load. *Financial support:* Research assistantships with partial tuition reimbursements, teaching assistantships with partial tuition reimbursements, career-related internships or fieldwork, Federal Work-Study, institutionally sponsored loans, scholarships/grants, and unspecified assistantships available. Support available to part-time students. Financial award application deadline: 4/30; financial award applicants required to submit FAFSA. *Unit head:* Dr. Joseph C. Picken, Program Director, 972-883-4986, E-mail: jpicken@utdallas.edu. *Application contact:* James Parker, Assistant Director, Graduate Recruitment, 972-883-5842, E-mail: jparker@utdallas.edu.

The University of Texas at Dallas, School of Management, Program in Management and Administrative Sciences, Richardson, TX 75080. Offers electronic commerce (MS); finance (MS); healthcare administration (MS); information systems (MS); innovation and entrepreneurship (MS); international management (MS); leadership in organizations (MS); marketing (MS); operations (MS); organizations (MS); real estate (MS); strategy (MS). *Accreditation:* AACSB. Part-time and evening/weekend programs available. *Faculty:* 18 full-time (3 women), 8 part-time/adjunct (0 women). *Students:* 57 full-time (32 women), 107 part-time (49 women); includes 53 minority (14 Black or African American, non-Hispanic/Latino; 30 Asian, non-Hispanic/Latino; 8 Hispanic/Latino; 1 Two or more races, non-Hispanic/Latino), 25 international. Average age 32. 161 applicants, 67% accepted, 51 enrolled. In 2010, 27 master's awarded. *Degree requirements:* For master's, thesis optional. *Entrance requirements:* For master's, GMAT. Additional exam requirements/recommendations for international students: Required—TOEFL (minimum score 550 paper-based; 215 computer-based). *Application deadline:* For fall admission, 7/15 for domestic students, 5/1 priority date for international students; for spring admission, 11/15 for domestic students, 9/1 priority date for international students. Applications are processed on a rolling basis. Application fee: $50 ($100 for international students). Electronic applications accepted. *Expenses:* Tuition, state resident: full-time $10,248; part-time $569 per credit hour. Tuition, nonresident: full-time $18,544; part-time $1030 per credit hour. Tuition and fees vary according to course load. *Financial support:* In 2010–11, 26 students received support, including 38 teaching assistantships with partial tuition reimbursements available (averaging $11,528 per year); research assistantships with partial tuition reimbursements available, career-related internships or fieldwork, Federal Work-Study, institutionally sponsored loans, scholarships/grants, and unspecified assistantships also available. Support available to part-time students. Financial award application deadline: 4/30; financial award applicants required to submit FAFSA. *Faculty research:* Integrated and detailed knowledge of functional areas of management, analytical tools for effective appraisal and decision making. *Unit head:* Dr. Doug Eckel, Assistant Dean, 972-883-5923, E-mail: doug.eckel@utdallas.edu. *Application contact:* James Parker, Assistant Director, 972-883-5842, E-mail: jparker@utdallas.edu.

University of the Incarnate Word, School of Graduate Studies and Research, Dreeben School of Education, Programs in Education, San Antonio, TX 78209-6397. Offers adult education (M Ed, MA); cross-cultural education (M Ed, MA); early childhood literacy (M Ed, MA); general education (M Ed, MA); higher education (PhD); instructional technology (M Ed, MA); international education and entrepreneurship (PhD); kinesiology (M Ed, MA); literacy (M Ed, MA); organizational leadership (PhD); organizational learning and learning (M Ed, MA); reading (M Ed, MA); special education (M Ed, MA); teacher leadership (M Ed, MA). Part-time and evening/weekend programs available. *Students:* 14 full-time (5 women), 230 part-time (151 women); includes 25 Black or African American, non-Hispanic/Latino; 2 American Indian or Alaska Native, non-Hispanic/Latino; 2 Asian, non-Hispanic/Latino; 98 Hispanic/Latino, 31 international. Average age 41. In 2010, 20 master's, 13 doctorates awarded. *Degree requirements:* For master's, capstone; for doctorate, thesis/dissertation, qualifying exam. *Entrance requirements:* For master's, baccalaureate degree; minimum foundation GPA of 2.5; interview; for doctorate, master's degree; interview; supervised writing sample. Additional exam requirements/recommendations for international students: Required—TOEFL (minimum score 560 paper-based; 220 computer-based; 83 iBT). *Application deadline:* Applications are processed on a rolling basis. Application fee: $20. Electronic applications accepted. *Expenses:*

Tuition: Part-time $725 per contact hour. Required fees: $890 per semester. *Financial support:* Federal Work-Study and scholarships/grants available. Financial award applicants required to submit FAFSA. *Unit head:* Dr. Denise Staudt, Dean, Dreeben School of Education, 210-829-2762, E-mail: staudt@uiwtx.edu. *Application contact:* Andrea Cyterski-Acosta, Dean of Enrollment, 210-829-6005, Fax: 210-829-3921, E-mail: admis@uiwtx.edu.

The University of Toledo, College of Graduate Studies, College of Business and Innovation, Department of Management, Toledo, OH 43606-3390. Offers administration (MBA); entrepreneurship (MBA); executive management (MBA); human resource management (MBA); leadership (MBA); management (MBA). Part-time and evening/weekend programs available. *Faculty:* 9. *Students:* 116 full-time (42 women), 100 part-time (36 women); includes 11 Black or African American, non-Hispanic/Latino; 1 Asian, non-Hispanic/Latino; 3 Hispanic/Latino; 99 international. Average age 27. 82 applicants, 72% accepted, 53 enrolled. In 2010, 133 master's awarded. *Entrance requirements:* For master's, GMAT, 2.7 GPA on all prior academic work. Three letters of recommendation, a statement of purpose, and transcripts from all prior institutions attended. Additional exam requirements/recommendations for international students: Required—TOEFL (minimum score 550 paper-based; 213 computer-based; 80 iBT), IELTS (minimum score 6.5). *Application deadline:* For fall admission, 1/15 priority date for domestic and international students. Applications are processed on a rolling basis. Application fee: $45 ($75 for international students). Electronic applications accepted. *Expenses:* Tuition, state resident: full-time $11,426; part-time $476 per credit hour. Tuition, nonresident: full-time $21,660; part-time $903 per credit hour. One-time fee: $62. *Financial support:* Research assistantships with tuition reimbursements, career-related internships or fieldwork, Federal Work-Study, institutionally sponsored loans, scholarships/grants, tuition waivers (full and partial), and unspecified assistantships available. Support available to part-time students. *Faculty research:* Stress, deviation, workplace, globalization, recruitment. *Unit head:* Dr. Sonny Ariss, Chair. *Application contact:* Graduate School Office, 419-530-4723, Fax: 419-530-4724, E-mail: grdsch@utnet.utoledo.edu.

University of Wisconsin–Madison, Graduate School, Wisconsin School of Business, Wisconsin Full-Time MBA Program, Madison, WI 53706-1380. Offers applied security analysis (MBA); arts administration (MBA); brand and product management (MBA); corporate finance and investment banking (MBA); entrepreneurial management (MBA); marketing research (MBA); operations and technology management (MBA); real estate (MBA); risk management and insurance (MBA); strategic human resource management (MBA); strategic management in the life and engineering sciences (MBA); supply chain management (MBA). *Faculty:* 32 full-time (4 women), 17 part-time/adjunct (3 women). *Students:* 242 full-time (74 women); includes 16 Black or African American, non-Hispanic/Latino; 3 American Indian or Alaska Native, non-Hispanic/Latino; 16 Asian, non-Hispanic/Latino; 12 Hispanic/Latino; 29 international. Average age 28. 526 applicants, 32% accepted, 117 enrolled. In 2010, 106 master's awarded. *Entrance requirements:* For master's, GMAT, bachelor's or equivalent degree, 2 years of work experience, letters of recommendation. Additional exam requirements/recommendations for international students: Required—TOEFL (minimum score 600 paper-based; 250 computer-based; 100 iBT), IELTS. *Application deadline:* For fall admission, 11/4 for domestic students, 11/1 for international students; for winter admission, 2/5 for domestic and international students; for spring admission, 5/15 for domestic students, 4/5 for international students. Applications are processed on a rolling basis. Application fee: $56. Electronic applications accepted. *Expenses:* Tuition, state resident: full-time $9887; part-time $617.96 per credit. Tuition, nonresident: full-time $24,054; part-time $1503.40 per credit. Required fees: $67.63 per credit. Tuition and fees vary according to reciprocity agreements. *Financial support:* In 2010–11, 103 students received support, including 13 fellowships with full and partial tuition reimbursements available (averaging $15,000 per year), 53 research assistantships with full tuition reimbursements available (averaging $8,000 per year), 35 teaching assistantships with full tuition reimbursements available (averaging $11,000 per year); scholarships/grants, health care benefits, and unspecified assistantships also available. Financial award application deadline: 4/5; financial award applicants required to submit FAFSA. *Faculty research:* Market consequences of International Financial Reporting Standards (IFRS), inter-firm relationships and strategic partnerships, application of Bayesian statistical methods and applied probability models to understanding individuals' behaviors in the context of customer relationship management (CRM) applications, liquidity provision and the structure of financial markets, strategic management of global startups. *Unit head:* Dr. Kenneth A. Kavajecz, Associate Dean of Master's Programs, 608-265-3494, Fax: 608-265-4192, E-mail: kkavajecz@bus.wisc.edu. *Application contact:* Maria Reis, Assistant Director of MBA Marketing and Recruiting, 608-262-4000, Fax: 608-265-4192, E-mail: mreis@bus.wisc.edu.

Wake Forest University, Schools of Business, Full-time MBA Program, Winston-Salem, NC 27106. Offers consulting/general management (MBA); entrepreneurship (MBA); finance (MBA); health (MBA); marketing (MBA); operations management (MBA); JD/MBA; MD/MBA; MSA/MBA. *Accreditation:* AACSB. *Faculty:* 63 full-time (17 women), 30 part-time/adjunct (9 women). *Students:* 123 full-time (22 women); includes 9 Black

or African American, non-Hispanic/Latino; 4 Asian, non-Hispanic/Latino; 2 Hispanic/Latino; 1 Two or more races, non-Hispanic/Latino, 25 international. Average age 28. In 2010, 83 master's awarded. *Degree requirements:* For master's, 65.5 total credit hours. *Entrance requirements:* For master's, GMAT or GRE, letters of recommendation, official transcripts, current resume or curriculum vitae, 2 years of work experience. Additional exam requirements/recommendations for international students: Required—TOEFL (minimum score 600 paper-based; 250 computer-based; 100 iBT), Pearson Test of English (PTE). *Application deadline:* For fall admission, 4/15 for domestic and international students. Applications are processed on a rolling basis. Application fee: $100. Electronic applications accepted. *Expenses:* Contact institution. *Financial support:* In 2010–11, 76 students received support. Career-related internships or fieldwork, scholarships/grants, and unspecified assistantships available. Financial award application deadline: 2/15; financial award applicants required to submit FAFSA. *Faculty research:* The influence of personal relationships on business decision making and management of change; drivers of perceived value and consumer behavior; impact of accounting on auditing, financial, managerial, systems and taxation stakeholders; corporate governance and executive compensation; impact of operations strategies on competitiveness. *Unit head:* Sherry Moss, Director, 336-758-5422, Fax: 336-758-5830, E-mail: admissions@mba.wfu.edu. *Application contact:* Tamara Paquee, Administrative Assistant, 336-758-5422, Fax: 336-758-5830, E-mail: admissions@mba.wfu.edu.

Walden University, Graduate Programs, School of Management, Minneapolis, MN 55401. Offers accounting (MS), including cpa emphasis, professional track, self-designed; accounting and management (MS), including self-designed, strategic management; applied management and decision sciences (PhD), including accounting, engineering management, finance, general applied management and decision sciences, information systems management, knowledge management, leadership and organizational change, learning management, operations research, self-designed program in applied management and design sciences; business information management (MISM); enterprise information security (MISM); entrepreneurship (MBA, DBA); finance (MBA, DBA); global management (MS); global supply chain management (DBA); health informatics (MISM); healthcare management (MBA, MS); healthcare system improvement (MBA); human resource management (MBA, MS), including functional human resource management (MS), human resource management (MS), integrating functional and strategic human resource management (MS), organizational strategy (MS); information systems (MS); information systems management (DBA); information technology (MS), including information security, software engineering; international business (MBA, DBA); IT strategy and governance (MISM); leadership (MBA, MS, DBA), including entrepreneurship (MS), general management (MS), human resources leadership (MS), innovation and technology (MS), leader development (MS), leading sustainability (MS), project management (MS), self-designed (MS); managers as leaders (MS); managing global software and service supply chains (MISM); marketing (MBA, DBA); project management (MBA, MS); research strategies (MS); risk management (MBA); self-designed (MBA, DBA); social impact management (DBA); strategy and operations (MS); sustainable futures (MBA); sustainable management (MS); technology (MBA); technology entrepreneurship (DBA); technology management (MS). Part-time and evening/weekend programs available. Postbaccalaureate distance learning degree programs offered (minimal on-campus study). *Faculty:* 22 full-time (8 women), 291 part-time/adjunct (100 women). *Students:* 3,705 full-time (1,956 women), 976 part-time (549 women); includes 2,432 minority (2,021 Black or African American, non-Hispanic/Latino; 32 American Indian or Alaska Native, non-Hispanic/Latino; 137 Asian, non-Hispanic/Latino; 193 Hispanic/Latino; 5 Native Hawaiian or other Pacific Islander, non-Hispanic/Latino; 44 Two or more races, non-Hispanic/Latino), 302 international. Average age 40. In 2010, 658 master's, 86 doctorates awarded. *Degree requirements:* For doctorate, thesis/dissertation (for some programs), residency. *Entrance requirements:* For master's, bachelor's degree or equivalent in related field; minimum GPA of 2.5; official transcripts; goal statement; access to computer and Internet; for doctorate, master's degree or equivalent in related field; minimum GPA of 3.0; 3 years of related professional/academic experience (preferred). Additional exam requirements/recommendations for international students: Required—TOEFL (minimum score 550 paper-based; 213 computer-based), IELTS (minimum score 6.5), Michigan English Language Assessment Battery (minimum score 82). *Application deadline:* Applications are processed on a rolling basis. Application fee: $50. Electronic applications accepted. *Expenses:* Tuition: Full-time $10,274; part-time $445 per credit. Tuition and fees vary according to course load, degree level and program. *Financial support:* Fellowships, Federal Work-Study, scholarships/grants, unspecified assistantships, and family tuition reduction, active duty/veteran tuition reduction, group tuition reduction, interest-free payment plans available. Support available to part-time students. Financial award applicants required to submit FAFSA. *Unit head:* Dr. William Schulz, Associate Dean, 800-925-3368. *Application contact:* Jennifer Hall, Vice President of Enrollment Management, 866-4-WALDEN, E-mail: info@waldenu.edu.

West Chester University of Pennsylvania, Office of Graduate Studies, College of Education, Department of Professional and Secondary Education, West Chester, PA 19383. Offers education for sustainability (Certificate);

entrepreneurial education (Certificate); secondary education (M Ed, Teaching Certificate); teaching and learning with technology (Certificate). Part-time and evening/weekend programs available. *Students:* 1 (woman) full-time, 32 part-time (17 women); includes 3 minority (2 Black or African American, non-Hispanic/Latino; 1 Asian, non-Hispanic/Latino). Average age 33. 26 applicants, 73% accepted, 2 enrolled. In 2010, 11 master's, 2 other advanced degrees awarded. *Degree requirements:* For master's, comprehensive exam, thesis (for some programs). *Entrance requirements:* For master's, GRE or MAT, teaching certificate. Additional exam requirements/recommendations for international students: Required—TOEFL (minimum score 550 paper-based; 213 computer-based; 80 iBT). *Application deadline:* For fall admission, 4/15 priority date for domestic students, 3/15 for international students; for spring admission, 10/15 priority date for domestic students, 9/1 for international students. Applications are processed on a rolling basis. Application fee: $35. Electronic applications accepted. *Expenses:* Tuition, state resident: full-time $6966; part-time $387 per credit. Tuition, nonresident: full-time $11,146; part-time $619 per credit. Required fees: $1614.40; $133.24 per credit. Part-time tuition and fees vary according to campus/location. *Financial support:* Unspecified assistantships available. Support available to part-time students. Financial award application deadline: 2/15; financial award applicants required to submit FAFSA. *Faculty research:* Technology integration: preparing our teachers for the twenty-first century. *Unit head:* Dr. John Elmore, Chair, 610-436-3057, E-mail: jelmore@wcupa.edu. *Application contact:* Dr. Cynthia Haggard, Graduate Coordinator, 610-436-6934, E-mail: chaggard@wcupa.edu.

Wilkes University, College of Graduate and Professional Studies, Jay S. Sidhu School of Business and Leadership, Wilkes-Barre, PA 18766-0002. Offers accounting (MBA); entrepreneurship (MBA); finance (MBA); health care administration (MBA); human resource management (MBA); international business (MBA); marketing (MBA); operations management (MBA); organizational leadership and development (MBA). *Accreditation:* ACBSP. Part-time and evening/weekend programs available. *Students:* 39 full-time (16 women), 146 part-time (71 women); includes 5 Black or African American, non-Hispanic/Latino; 2 Asian, non-Hispanic/Latino; 1 Hispanic/Latino; 1 Two or more races, non-Hispanic/Latino, 16 international. Average age 30. In 2010, 85 master's awarded. *Entrance requirements:* For master's, GMAT. Additional exam requirements/recommendations for international students: Required—TOEFL (minimum score 550 paper-based; 213 computer-based; 79 iBT). *Application deadline:* Applications are processed on a rolling basis. Application fee: $45 ($65 for international students). Electronic applications accepted. *Expenses:* Contact institution. *Financial support:* Federal Work-Study and unspecified assistantships available. Financial award application deadline: 3/1; financial award applicants required to submit FAFSA. *Unit head:* Dr. Paul Browne, Dean, 570-408-4701, Fax: 570-408-7846, E-mail: paul.browne@wilkes.edu. *Application contact:* Kathleen Houlihan, Director of Graduate Studies, 570-408-3235, Fax: 570-408-7846, E-mail: kathleen.houlihan@wilkes.edu.

OVERVIEW

Properties are an important cost factor for companies, and up-to-date integrated management of buildings and facilities is highly valued in any company's workforce. With an MBA in facilities management, graduates are poised to achieve the best possible results in the management of properties and facilities. The degree work features programs designed for individuals in control of budgets, those who are interested in comprehending the complexity of managing buildings and facilities, and professionals who manage in-sourced or out-sourced facilities for their own organization or provide facilities management services to other organizations. Core management topics cover technical subjects ranging from procuring technology for, and using technology within, buildings to setting up and managing facilities' projects and services.

An MBA program within the entertainment management field provides students with the capabilities to understand and manage the entire spectrum of the entertainment and media business—from its impact on the economy and the digital revolution to the global opportunities created by technology. Students in an entertainment management MBA program learn about the business of the entertainment industry, the ins and outs of media management, budgeting and financial management of special projects, and representation of, or managing, celebrities. With a focus on both the business and content aspects of the industry, these programs offer students a range of courses with practical and real-life application covering the marketing, finance, management, accounting, legal, and economic issues facing entertainment and media firms. Industries covered in the entertainment management MBA usually include film, home video, television, cable, music, sports, and publishing.

Courses for facilities management study may include:

- Aspects of Architecture and Construction Technology in Facility Management
- Data Structures and IT-Support in Facility Management
- Facility Management: Strategic, Tactical, and Operative
- Facility Services and Their Management
- Fundamentals of Facility Management
- Legal Compliance
- Management, Organization, and Organizational Development
- Project Management
- Tools of Business Administration

Courses for entertainment management study may include:

- The Art of Entertainment Industry Public Relations
- Economics for Decision-Making
- Entertainment Business Finance and Capitalization
- Entertainment Media Content Marketing and Distribution
- Financial Statement Analysis
- Marketing and Brand Management
- Project Production and Scheduling for Television and Film
- Problem Analysis and Research Methods
- Strategic Human Resource Management
- Strategic Management and Competitive Globalization
- Talent Representation and Artist Management

Graduates with an MBA in facilities management can look towards careers in senior levels of property and premises management, facilities management, and general management. Jobs in the industry include assistant facilities coordinator, facilities manager, support services manager (such as cleaning, catering, or security), and building maintenance personnel, as well as emerging jobs such as environmental management, sustainability in response to legislation and changes to building design, and risk management.

An MBA with an emphasis in entertainment management is designed to prepare graduates for careers in the business fields of entertainment, public relations, media promotion, marketing and distribution, talent search, management and organization, entertainment production, capitalization and financing, and artist management.

IN THIS SECTION

You'll find profiles of institutions offering graduate programs in the following fields:

HELPFUL ORGANIZATIONS/ PUBLICATIONS/BLOGS

International Facility Management Association (IFMA)
http://www.ifma.org/

International Facility Management Association (IFMA) is the world's largest and most widely recognized international association for professional facility managers, supporting more than 19,500 members in 78 countries. The association's members include 125 chapters and 16 industry councils worldwide, manage more than 37 billion square feet of property, and annually purchase more than $100 billion (U.S. dollars) in products and services.

Formed in 1980, IFMA certifies facility managers, conducts research, provides educational programs, recognizes facility management certificate programs, and produces World Workplace, the world's largest facility management conference and exposition.

Event & Entertainment Management Association (EEMA)
http://www.eemaindia.org/

The Event & Entertainment Management Association (EEMA) seeks to be the unified voice of the industry to government, statutory bodies, taxation authorities, and private licensing bodies and seeks to protect its members' interests in all these avenues. EEMA also seeks to lay down professional standards of management and interface between its members and clients, vendors, and artists across the country. EEMA is a repository of knowledge for its members in terms of providing a databank of venues, artists, and vendors and advising its members on safety standards, employee codes of conduct, and best practices of the industry. EEMA is committed to upgrading skills and knowledge levels of its members by organizing training programs and seminars and interfacing with international and local industry stalwarts.

APPA

http://www.appa.org/

APPA is the gathering place for those engaged in the field of educational facilities management and is dedicated to the ongoing evolution of its professionals into influential leaders in education. APPA has spent nearly 100 years applying experience, focus, and the power of member collaboration to their driving purpose: Elevating facilities professionals into influential leaders in education.

APPA promotes excellence in all phases of educational facilities management, including administration, planning, design, construction, energy/utilities, maintenance, and operations. Membership is open to all educational facilities professionals, including those from public and private, two-year and four-year colleges and universities; medical and law schools; seminaries; public and private K–12 schools and districts; museums and parks; military installations; federal, state, and city-county governments; and business partners who serve educational facilities.

APPA stands behind the values of:

- Vision in achieving continuous improvement and performance excellence.
- Transformation in providing ongoing leadership development and continuously setting the standard for credibility to transform the profession.
- Stewardship in sustaining and maintaining passionate commitment to the future of industry professionals and their facilities, wisely investing in intellectual capital, and producing results that enhance the credibility of the entire profession.
- Collaboration in networking, information sharing, celebrating achievements, and creating meaningful connections among all members.
- Leadership in implementing standards and processes and establishing the credentials that contribute to creating true leaders in educational facilities.

CAREER ASPIRATIONS: A PROSPECTIVE POSITION

Director, Business Planning and Facilities

Job Description

This position will support the head of business planning and facilities with analysis, communications, and project management specifically around operational improvements, short- and longer-term planning, executive communications, and facilities management.

Responsibilities

- Work with finance and the leadership team, assist development of annual operating budget and company's 5-year plan.
- Perform assessment of selected HR access functions, processes, and business operations capabilities.
- Perform regular external benchmarking, including participation in annual cost structure survey.
- Participate in the development of materials for management meetings, including the Board of Advisors' meeting, quarterly business reviews, and leadership team meetings and calls.
- Support the development of regular operating reports.
- Work with regions and countries to develop business plans, review the status of key actions, and create and review the status of annual leadership management business objectives.
- On a monthly basis, forecast the real estate requirements of current and future sites.
- Support the development and execution of the facilities plans in current and future sites.
- Forecast and manage seating capacity.
- Act as a primary point of facilities contact for the site.
- Work with the team to facilitate the relocation and building fit-out projects as required.

Qualifications

- 5 to 10 years of direct experience in or with a human resource outsourcing business in the United States or Western Europe required
- MBA preferred
- Detailed and current understanding of the HR product, service, and outsourcing markets and business practices in the United States and Western Europe
- Proficiency in space planning, project management, facility management, and finance/accounting
- Self-motivated, able to work with little or no supervision; demonstrate initiative, tenacity, adaptability, teamwork, and maturity under pressure; attention to detail; anticipate and resolve problems before they develop
- Ability to create and develop business planning and company presentations at the direction of the CEO and president
- Strong leadership skills in team management (including line management experience), project management, and interaction with all levels of the organization
- High integrity in dealing with sensitive information
- Excellent verbal and written presentation and communication skills; ability to synthesize complex information and present to audiences at all levels within organization
- Ability to manage conflict and crisis situations constructively and effectively

ENTERTAINMENT MANAGEMENT

Columbia College Chicago, Graduate School, Department of Arts, Entertainment and Media Management, Chicago, IL 60605-1996. Offers arts, entertainment and media management (MA), including media management, music business management, performing arts management, visual arts management. Evening/weekend programs available. *Students:* 68 full-time (53 women), 45 part-time (33 women); includes 44 minority (29 Black or African American, non-Hispanic/Latino; 1 American Indian or Alaska Native, non-Hispanic/Latino; 5 Asian, non-Hispanic/Latino; 9 Hispanic/Latino), 8 international. Average age 28. 252 applicants, 35% accepted, 31 enrolled. In 2010, 52 master's awarded. *Degree requirements:* For master's, thesis, internship. *Entrance requirements:* For master's, self-assessment essay. Additional exam requirements/recommendations for international students: Required—TOEFL (minimum score 550 paper-based; 213 computer-based). *Application deadline:* For fall admission, 1/15 for domestic and international students. Application fee: $55. Electronic applications accepted. *Expenses:* Tuition: Full-time $16,966; part-time $684 per credit. Required fees: $520; $113 per semester. One-time fee: $150 full-time. Tuition and fees vary according to course load and program. *Financial support:* Fellowships, career-related internships or fieldwork, Federal Work-Study, and scholarships/grants available. Support available to part-time students. Financial award application deadline: 8/13; financial award applicants required to submit FAFSA. *Unit head:* Prof. Dawn Larsen, Director of Graduate Studies, 312-369-7639, E-mail: dlarsen@colum.edu. *Application contact:* Cate Lagueux, Director of Graduate Admissions, 312-369-7260, Fax: 312-369-8047, E-mail: clagueux@colum.edu.

Dowling College, School of Business, Oakdale, NY 11769-1999. Offers aviation management (MBA, Certificate); banking and finance (MBA, Certificate); corporate finance (MBA); financial planning (Certificate); health care management (MBA, Certificate); human resource management (Certificate); information systems management (MBA); management and leadership (MBA); marketing (Certificate); project management (Certificate); public management (MBA, Certificate); sport, event and entertainment management (Certificate); JD/MBA. Part-time and evening/weekend programs available. *Faculty:* 10 full-time (4 women), 56 part-time/adjunct (7 women). *Students:* 295 full-time (131 women), 460 part-time (206 women); includes 219 minority (97 Black or African American, non-Hispanic/Latino; 14 Asian, non-Hispanic/Latino; 35 Hispanic/Latino; 73 Native Hawaiian or other Pacific Islander, non-Hispanic/Latino), 3 international. Average age 33. 327 applicants, 85% accepted, 160 enrolled. In 2010, 33 master's, 1 other advanced degree awarded. *Degree requirements:* For master's, comprehensive exam, thesis optional. *Entrance requirements:* For master's, minimum GPA of 2.8, 2 letters of recommendation, courses in accounting and finance or seminar in accounting/finance, resume. Additional exam requirements/recommendations for international students: Required—TOEFL (minimum score 550 paper-based). *Application deadline:* For fall admission, 9/1 priority date for domestic students; for winter admission, 1/1 priority date for domestic students; for spring admission, 2/1 priority date for domestic students. Applications are processed on a rolling basis. Application fee: $50. Electronic applications accepted. *Expenses:* Tuition: Part-time $884 per credit hour. Part-time tuition and fees vary according to degree level and campus/location. *Financial support:* Career-related internships or fieldwork and Federal Work-Study available. Support available to part-time students. Financial award application deadline: 6/30; financial award applicants required to submit FAFSA. *Faculty research:* International finance, computer applications, labor relations, executive development. *Unit head:* Antonia Loschiavo, Assistant Dean, 631-244-3266, Fax: 631-244-1018, E-mail: loschiat@dowling.edu. *Application contact:* Ronnie S. Macdonald, Assistant Vice President for Enrollment Services/Dean of Admissions, 631-244-3357, Fax: 631-244-1059, E-mail: macdonar@dowling.edu.

Hofstra University, Frank G. Zarb School of Business, Department of Management, Entrepreneurship and General Business, Hempstead, NY 11549. Offers business administration (MBA), including health services management, management, sports and entertainment management; general management (Advanced Certificate); human resource management (MS). Part-time and evening/weekend programs available. Postbaccalaureate distance learning degree programs offered (minimal on-campus study). *Faculty:* 7 full-time (1 woman), 6 part-time/adjunct (0 women). *Students:* 73 full-time (34 women), 169 part-time (79 women); includes 60 minority (23 Black or African American, non-Hispanic/Latino; 30 Asian, non-Hispanic/Latino; 7 Hispanic/Latino), 28 international. Average age 33. 176 applicants, 62% accepted, 62 enrolled. In 2010, 51 master's awarded. *Degree requirements:* For master's, thesis optional, capstone course (for MBA); thesis (for MS). *Entrance requirements:* For master's, GMAT/GRE, 2 letters of recommendation; resume; essay. Additional exam requirements/recommendations for international students: Required—TOEFL (minimum score 550 paper-based; 213 computer-based; 80 iBT); Recommended—IELTS (minimum score 6). *Application deadline:* Applications are processed on a rolling basis. Application fee: $70 ($75 for international students). Electronic applications accepted. *Expenses:* Contact institution. *Financial support:* In 2010–11, 12 students received support, including 11 fellowships with full and partial tuition reimbursements available (averaging $10,256 per year), 1 research assistantship with full and partial

tuition reimbursement available (averaging $18,925 per year); career-related internships or fieldwork, Federal Work-Study, institutionally sponsored loans, scholarships/grants, tuition waivers (full and partial), and unspecified assistantships also available. Support available to part-time students. Financial award applicants required to submit FAFSA. *Faculty research:* Business/personal ethics, sustainability, innovation, decision-making, supply chains analysis, learning and pedagogical issues, family business, small business, entrepreneurship. *Unit head:* Dr. Mamdouh I. Farid, Chairperson, 516-463-5735, Fax: 516-463-4834, E-mail: mgbmif@hofstra.edu. *Application contact:* Carol Drummer, Dean of Graduate Admissions, 516-463-4876, Fax: 516-463-4664, E-mail: gradstudent@hofstra.edu.

Maryville University of Saint Louis, The John E. Simon School of Business, St. Louis, MO 63141-7299. Offers accounting (MBA, PGC); business studies (PGC); management (MBA, PGC); marketing (MBA, PGC); process and project management (MBA, PGC); sport and entertainment management (MBA, PGC). *Accreditation:* ACBSP. Part-time and evening/weekend programs available. *Faculty:* 7 full-time (4 women), 13 part-time/adjunct (5 women). *Students:* 16 full-time (8 women), 119 part-time (57 women); includes 15 minority (9 Black or African American, non-Hispanic/Latino; 3 Asian, non-Hispanic/Latino; 3 Hispanic/Latino), 5 international. Average age 31. In 2010, 60 master's awarded. *Entrance requirements:* For master's, GMAT (unless applicant possesses undergraduate business degree with minimum cumulative GPA of 3.0, or has completed master's degree from accredited university or one early access course prior to undergraduate degree). Additional exam requirements/recommendations for international students: Required—TOEFL (minimum score 563 paper-based; 85 iBT), If you took the revised TOEFL (after Sept. 24, 2005), you will be admitted into our MBA program with a speaking sub-score of 23, a writing sub-score of 20, reading and listening scores of 21 or higher and a combined score of 79 or higher. *Application deadline:* Applications are processed on a rolling basis. Application fee: $40 ($60 for international students). Electronic applications accepted. *Expenses:* Tuition: Full-time $21,100; part-time $633.50 per credit hour. Required fees: $150 per semester. *Financial support:* Career-related internships or fieldwork, Federal Work-Study, tuition waivers (partial), and campus employment available. Financial award application deadline: 3/1; financial award applicants required to submit FAFSA. *Faculty research:* International business, e-marketing, strategic planning, interpersonal management skills, financial analysis. *Unit head:* Dr. Pamela Horwitz, Dean, 314-529-9418, Fax: 314-529-9975, E-mail: horwitz@maryville.edu. *Application contact:* Kathy Dougherty, Director of MBA Programs, 314-529-9382, Fax: 314-529-9975, E-mail: business@maryville.edu.

University of Massachusetts Amherst, Graduate School, Interdisciplinary Programs, Program in Civil Engineering and Business Administration, Amherst, MA 01003. Offers MSCE/MBA. Part-time programs available. *Students:* 1 applicant, 0% accepted, 0 enrolled. *Entrance requirements:* Additional exam requirements/recommendations for international students: Required—TOEFL (minimum score 600 paper-based; 250 computer-based; 100 iBT), IELTS (minimum score 7). *Application deadline:* For fall admission, 2/1 for domestic and international students. Applications are processed on a rolling basis. Application fee: $50 ($65 for international students). Electronic applications accepted. *Expenses:* Tuition, state resident: full-time $2640. Required fees: $8282. One-time fee: $357 full-time. *Financial support:* Career-related internships or fieldwork, Federal Work-Study, scholarships/grants, traineeships, health care benefits, tuition waivers (full), and unspecified assistantships available. Support available to part-time students. Financial award application deadline: 2/1; financial award applicants required to submit FAFSA. *Unit head:* Dr. David Ahlfeld, Graduate Program Director, 413-545-0686, Fax: 413-545-2840. *Application contact:* Jean M. Ames, Supervisor of Admissions, 413-545-0722, Fax: 413-577-0010, E-mail: gradadm@grad.umass.edu.

Valparaiso University, Graduate School, Program in Arts and Entertainment Administration, Valparaiso, IN 46383. Offers MA. Part-time and evening/weekend programs available. *Students:* 1 full-time (0 women), 1 (woman) part-time; both minorities (1 Hispanic/Latino; 1 Two or more races, non-Hispanic/Latino). Average age 37. *Degree requirements:* For master's, internship or research project. *Entrance requirements:* Additional exam requirements/recommendations for international students: Required—TOEFL (minimum score 550 paper-based; 213 computer-based; 80 iBT). *Application deadline:* Applications are processed on a rolling basis. Application fee: $30 ($50 for international students). Electronic applications accepted. *Expenses:* Tuition: Full-time $9540; part-time $530 per credit hour. Required fees: $292; $95 per semester. Tuition and fees vary according to program. *Financial support:* Available to part-time students. Applicants required to submit FAFSA. *Unit head:* Dr. David L. Rowland, Dean, Graduate School and Continuing Education/Associate Provost, 219-464-5313, Fax: 219-464-5381, E-mail: david.rowland@valpo.edu. *Application contact:* Laura Groth, Coordinator of Student Services and Support, 219-464-5313, Fax: 219-464-5381, E-mail: laura.groth@valpo.edu.

FACILITIES MANAGEMENT

Cornell University, Graduate School, Graduate Fields of Human Ecology, Field of Design and Environmental Analysis, Ithaca, NY 14853. Offers applied research in human-environment relations (MS); facilities planning and management (MS); housing and design (MS); human factors and ergonomics (MS); human-environment relations (MS); interior design (MA, MPS). *Faculty:* 15 full-time (6 women). *Students:* 27 full-time (22 women); includes 2 Black or African American, non-Hispanic/Latino; 6 Asian, non-Hispanic/Latino; 7 international. Average age 25. 83 applicants, 27% accepted, 21 enrolled. In 2010, 29 master's awarded. *Degree requirements:* For master's, thesis. *Entrance requirements:* For master's, GRE General Test, portfolio or slides of recent work; bachelor's degree in interior design, architecture or related design discipline; 2 letters of recommendation. Additional exam requirements/recommendations for international students: Required—TOEFL (minimum score 600 paper-based; 250 computer-based; 105 iBT). *Application deadline:* For fall admission, 2/1 priority date for domestic students. Application fee: $70. Electronic applications accepted. *Expenses:* Tuition: Full-time $29,500. Required fees: $76. Tuition and fees vary according to degree level and program. *Financial support:* In 2010–11, 13 students received support, including 3 fellowships with full tuition reimbursements available, 2 research assistantships with full tuition reimbursements available, 13 teaching assistantships with full tuition reimbursements available; institutionally sponsored loans, scholarships/grants, health care benefits, tuition waivers (full and partial), and unspecified assistantships also available. Financial award applicants required to submit FAFSA. *Faculty research:* Facility planning and management, environmental psychology, housing, interior design, ergonomics and human factors. *Unit head:* Director of Graduate Studies, 607-255-2168, Fax: 607-255-0305. *Application contact:* Graduate Field Assistant, 607-255-2168, Fax: 607-255-0305, E-mail: deagrad@cornell.edu.

Indiana University of Pennsylvania, School of Graduate Studies and Research, College of Health and Human Services, Department of Health and Physical Education, Indiana, PA 15705-1087. Offers aquatics administration and facilities management (MS); exercise science (MS); sport management (MS); sport science (MS). Part-time programs available. *Faculty:* 8 full-time (4 women), 1 (woman) part-time/adjunct. *Students:* 60 full-time (23 women), 22 part-time (11 women); includes 7 minority (6 Black or African American, non-Hispanic/Latino; 1 Two or more races, non-Hispanic/Latino), 5 international. Average age 25. 134 applicants, 45% accepted, 40 enrolled. In 2010, 65 master's awarded. *Degree requirements:* For master's, thesis optional. *Entrance requirements:* For master's, 2 letters of recommendation. Additional exam requirements/recommendations for international students: Required—TOEFL. *Application deadline:* For fall admission, 7/1 priority date for domestic students; for spring admission, 11/1 for domestic students. Applications are processed on a rolling basis. Application fee: $40. *Financial support:* In 2010–11, 11 research assistantships with full and partial tuition reimbursements (averaging $4,945 per year) were awarded; fellowships also available. Financial award application deadline: 3/15; financial award applicants required to submit FAFSA. *Unit head:* Dr. Elaine Blair, Chairperson, 724-357-2770, E-mail: eblair@iup.edu. *Application contact:* Dr. Elaine Blair, Chairperson, 724-357-2770, E-mail: eblair@iup.edu.

Indiana University–Purdue University Fort Wayne, College of Engineering, Technology, and Computer Science, Program in Technology, Fort Wayne, IN 46805-1499. Offers facilities and construction management (MS); industrial technology/manufacturing (MS); information technology/advanced computer applications (MS). Part-time programs available. *Faculty:* 12 full-time (6 women), 1 part-time/adjunct (0 women). *Students:* 4 full-time (2 women), 14 part-time (1 woman); includes 3 minority (2 Asian, non-Hispanic/Latino; 1 Hispanic/Latino), 2 international. Average age 32. 5 applicants, 100% accepted, 2 enrolled. In 2010, 4 master's awarded. *Entrance requirements:* For master's, minimum GPA of 3.0. Additional exam requirements/recommendations for international students: Required—TOEFL (minimum score 550 paper-based; 213 computer-based; 77 iBT), TWE. *Application deadline:* For fall admission, 7/15 for domestic students, 5/15 for international students; for spring admission, 12/1 for domestic students, 10/15 for international students. Applications are processed on a rolling basis. Application fee: $55 ($60 for international students). Electronic applications accepted. *Expenses:* Tuition, state resident: full-time $4824; part-time $268 per credit. Tuition, nonresident: full-time $11,625; part-time $646 per credit. Required fees: $555; $30.85 per credit. Tuition and fees vary according to course load. *Financial support:* Career-related internships or fieldwork, scholarships/grants, and unspecified assistantships available. Support available to part-time students. Financial award application deadline: 3/1; financial award applicants required to submit FAFSA. *Unit head:* Dr. Max Yen, Dean, 260-481-6839, Fax: 260-481-5734, E-mail: yens@ipfw.edu. *Application contact:* Dr. Gary Steffen, Chair, 260-481-6344, Fax: 260-481-5734, E-mail: steffen@ipfw.edu.

Pratt Institute, School of Architecture, Program in Facilities Management, New York, NY 10011. Offers MS. Part-time programs available. *Faculty:* 1 (woman) full-time, 5 part-time/adjunct (0 women). *Students:* 16 full-time (6 women), 2 part-time (0 women); includes 3 Black or African American, non-Hispanic/Latino; 1 Asian, non-Hispanic/Latino; 3 Hispanic/Latino, 5 international. Average age 32. 14 applicants, 86% accepted, 6 enrolled. In 2010,

3 master's awarded. *Degree requirements:* For master's, thesis. *Entrance requirements:* For master's, writing sample, bachelor's degree, transcripts, letters of recommendation, portfolio. Additional exam requirements/recommendations for international students: Required—TOEFL (minimum score 550 paper-based; 213 computer-based; 79 iBT). *Application deadline:* For fall admission, 1/5 for domestic and international students; for spring admission, 10/1 for domestic and international students. Applications are processed on a rolling basis. Application fee: $50 ($90 for international students). Electronic applications accepted. *Expenses:* Tuition: Full-time $22,734; part-time $1263 per credit. Required fees: $1280. *Financial support:* Career-related internships or fieldwork, Federal Work-Study, institutionally sponsored loans, scholarships/grants, health care benefits, and unspecified assistantships available. Support available to part-time students. Financial award application deadline: 2/1; financial award applicants required to submit FAFSA. *Faculty research:* Benchmarking, organizational studies, resource planning and management, computer-aided facilities management, value analysis. *Unit head:* Harriet Markis, Chairperson, 212-647-7524, Fax: 212-367-2497, E-mail: hmarkis@pratt.edu. *Application contact:* Young Hah, Director of Graduate Admissions, 718-636-3683, Fax: 718-399-4242, E-mail: yhah@pratt.edu.

The University of Kansas, Graduate Studies, School of Architecture, Design, and Planning, Program in Architecture, Lawrence, KS 66045. Offers academic track (MA); architecture (PhD); facility management (Certificate); management track (MA); professional track (M Arch); M Arch/MBA; M Arch/MUP. *Faculty:* 20 full-time (5 women). *Students:* 187 full-time (88 women), 24 part-time (10 women); includes 22 minority (4 Black or African American, non-Hispanic/Latino; 1 American Indian or Alaska Native, non-Hispanic/Latino; 3 Asian, non-Hispanic/Latino; 8 Hispanic/Latino; 6 Two or more races, non-Hispanic/Latino), 18 international. Average age 26. 137 applicants, 64% accepted, 47 enrolled. In 2010, 67 master's awarded. Terminal master's awarded for partial completion of doctoral program. *Degree requirements:* For master's, thesis or alternative, 1 summer abroad; for doctorate, comprehensive exam, thesis/dissertation. *Entrance requirements:* For master's, portfolio, minimum GPA of 3.0; for doctorate, GRE, portfolio. Additional exam requirements/recommendations for international students: Required—TOEFL. *Application deadline:* For fall admission, 3/1 priority date for domestic and international students; for spring admission, 11/1 priority date for domestic and international students. Applications are processed on a rolling basis. Application fee: $55 ($65 for international students). Electronic applications accepted. *Expenses:* Tuition, state resident: full-time $7092; part-time $295.50 per credit hour. Tuition, nonresident: full-time $16,590; part-time $691.25 per credit hour. Required fees: $858; $71.49 per credit hour. Tuition and fees vary according to course load, campus/location and program. *Financial support:* Fellowships, research assistantships with partial tuition reimbursements, teaching assistantships with full and partial tuition reimbursements, scholarships/grants, health care benefits, and unspecified assistantships available. Financial award application deadline: 2/1; financial award applicants required to submit FAFSA. *Faculty research:* Design build, sustainability, emergent technology, healthy places, urban design. *Unit head:* Prof. Nils Gore, Interim Chair, 785-864-2700, Fax: 785-864-5185, E-mail: archku@ku.edu. *Application contact:* Gera Elliott, Admissions Coordinator, 785-864-3167, Fax: 785-864-5185, E-mail: archku@ku.edu.

University of New Haven, Graduate School, School of Business, Program in Sports Management, West Haven, CT 06516-1916. Offers facility management (MS); management of sports industries (Certificate); sports management (MS). *Students:* 39 full-time (13 women), 9 part-time (5 women); includes 6 Black or African American, non-Hispanic/Latino; 1 Hispanic/Latino, 3 international. Average age 27. 31 applicants, 97% accepted, 17 enrolled. In 2010, 26 master's awarded. *Entrance requirements:* For master's, GMAT, minimum GPA of 2.7. Additional exam requirements/recommendations for international students: Required—TOEFL (minimum score 520 paper-based; 190 computer-based; 70 iBT); Recommended—IELTS (minimum score 5.5). *Application deadline:* For fall admission, 5/31 for international students; for winter admission, 10/15 for international students; for spring admission, 1/15 for international students. Applications are processed on a rolling basis. Application fee: $50. Electronic applications accepted. *Financial support:* Research assistantships with partial tuition reimbursements, teaching assistantships with partial tuition reimbursements, career-related internships or fieldwork, Federal Work-Study, scholarships/grants, tuition waivers, and unspecified assistantships available. Support available to part-time students. Financial award applicants required to submit FAFSA. *Unit head:* Dr. Gil B. Fried, Head, 203-932-7081. *Application contact:* Eloise Gormley, Director of Graduate Admissions, 203-932-7449, Fax: 203-932-7137, E-mail: gradinfo@newhaven.edu.

OVERVIEW

The hospitality and tourism industries are expected to grow at the rate of 8% through 2025. The diversity of experience in hotel management and tourism is greater than in any other profession.

Students in hospitality management MBA programs are prepared to better understand the needs of those who demand top quality services from industries such as restaurants, resorts, and hotels. An MBA hospitality management degree is generally aimed at giving students a solid background in customer service, employee development, and the business aspects of hospitality, such as accounting and human resources. Students in an MBA hospitality management program also focus on tourism, health care, international business, advertising, and marketing and learn about industry venues—cruise ships, amusement parks and centers, event facilities, and restaurants. Students hone their skills in how to recruit, hire, and train employees, how to manage money and funds associated with their venues, and how to identify and solve real-life problems and issues that often arise in the workplace.

Classes in an MBA program for hospitality management are designed to develop students' ability to apply business and leadership strategies to hospitality industry-specific situations. Likewise, an MBA in tourism provides a good understanding of the language and structure of tourism and hospitality management. Subjects in this program are designed to provide a sophisticated body of knowledge by integrating critical strategies and techniques with the principles of tourism and hospitality management, preparing graduates for tourism and hospitality management challenges in both the national and international arena.

Tourism MBA programs often explore the role of the tourism industry in society, including how tourism policy impacts governments and emerging technological and economic trends in international tourism. Subjects such as sustainable tourism, examining the part natural and cultural resources play in a country's ability to market itself as a tourist destination, financial strategies for tourism development, tourism product development, and cultural heritage tourism are also sometimes offered within the program.

Courses for hospitality management study may include:

- Business Communication
- Contemporary Tourism Management
- Economics
- Food and Beverage Cost Control
- Front Office Operations
- Hospitality Facilities Design
- Housekeeping Management
- Purchasing and Inventory Control
- Real Estate Finance and Investments
- Resort Development
- Retail and Consumer Behavior
- Revenue Management
- Sanitation and Safety
- Travel Agency and Tour Operations

Courses for travel and tourism study may include:

- Accounting and Finance
- Buffet-Organization Methods
- Entrepreneurship
- Event Management
- Finance
- Food Display and Presentation
- Front Desk/Office Skills
- Hotel and Resort Management Issues
- Human Resource Management
- Leadership
- Legal and Social Issues
- Sales and Marketing

Graduates of either of these programs will find themselves equipped with the skills to critically appraise a range of relevant practical tourism and hospitality management knowledge and business data and apply it to complex tourism and hospitality management issues.

The most popular career opportunities for graduates with an MBA in hospitality management include positions as hotel/resort managers, assistant managers, sales and marketing professionals, property managers, restaurant managers, convention services managers, general managers, food and beverage directors, front office managers, conference planners, human resource managers, convention planners, special event planners, travel agents, and group travel facilitators.

An MBA in tourism program prepares graduates to become managers of the day-to-day operations of large hotels, restaurants, and tourist attractions. Careers in such areas as tourism planning, tourism product development, and marketing are also options.

IN THIS SECTION

You'll find profiles of institutions offering graduate programs in the following fields:

HELPFUL ORGANIZATIONS/ PUBLICATIONS/BLOGS

British Hospitality Association (BHA)

http://www.bha.org.uk/

The British Hospitality Association (BHA) is the leading representative organization for the UK hospitality industry, representing hotels, restaurants, and food service providers. BHA promotes the interests of hotels, restaurants, and food service providers, delivering tangible results for their members by successfully championing the industry's priorities and partnering with the government to drive hospitality growth in the UK.

The British Hospitality Association has been representing the hotel, restaurant, and food service management industry for over 100 years.

With input from its members, BHA has identified the following five key areas in which to drive industry action and change:

1. Economy—to champion a supportive fiscal environment for the industry to prosper in the context of global competition
2. Employment—to bridge the gap between education and industry to build a skilled hospitality workforce
3. Intelligent Regulation—to advise the government to reduce the burden of costly regulation at national and local levels
4. Sustainability—to facilitate an industry-led effort to develop economic, social, and environmental success
5. Health—to proactively shape industry and public sector policy to enhance the wellness of consumers

World Travel & Tourism Council (WTTC)

http://www.wttc.org/

The World Travel & Tourism Council (WTTC) is the forum for business leaders in the travel and tourism industry. With chief executives of some 100 of the world's leading travel and tourism companies as its members, WTTC works to raise awareness of travel and tourism as one of the world's largest industries, supporting more than 258 million jobs and generating 9.1% of the world's GDP. WTTC undertakes extensive annual macro-economic research, assessing the current and projected impact of travel and tourism on a total of 181 national economies around the world.

WTTC addresses challenges and opportunities that affect all sectors of the global travel and tourism industry. It is empowered by its members to provide an effective voice for the industry and its dialogue with governments around the world. Global activities include Environment Initiative, the Global Travel & Tourism Summit, and the Tourism for Tomorrow Awards. WTTC regional activities are set up in the countries and regions with potential for travel and tourism development but lack the framework or resourcing to achieve growth. The objective of these initiatives is to translate WTTC's mission into action by working with governments, local leaders, and WTTC global members with a regional presence to identify and eliminate barriers to growth.

The International Society of Hospitality Consultants (ISHC)

http://www.ishc.com/

The International Society of Hospitality Consultants (ISHC) is the world's greatest source for hospitality expertise and counsel, represented by some 200 of the industry's most respected professionals from across six continents. As a whole, ISHC members have experience and expertise in over fifty different areas of specialty in the industry. Specialty areas include appraisals, arbitration, architectural and engineering services, asset management, construction and project management, executive search, feasibility, food service, franchise expertise, legal services, operational reviews, marketing and sales, organizational development, research, training, strategic planning, and technology. Members also have experience with various property types, including arenas and convention centers, boutique hotels, casino hotels, conference centers, extended-stay hotels, independent hotels, limited and full service hotels, marinas, mixed-use developments, resort hotels, theme parks and attractions, and time share and vacation clubs.

CAREER ASPIRATIONS: A PROSPECTIVE POSITION

Vice President, Fitness and Club Services

Job Description

The Vice President, Fitness and Club Services (VP, F&CS) will be responsible for the efficiency, effectiveness, and revenue growth of all of the company's ancillary fitness businesses. This position will report directly to the Senior Vice President (SVP) of Operations. The VP, F&CS will be responsible for reviewing and evaluating the overall experience of the fitness services businesses and club offerings and creating metrics to manage and monitor the success of these operations. The VP, F&CS will identify key performance metrics, build dashboards, perform competitive benchmarking, and present key insights and ensure that data drives action to improve the business. The VP, F&CS will partner with field leadership and industry associations closely to understand current offerings and trends, while aligning with current company brands, missions, and strategies.

Responsibilities

- Develop standard operation procedures.
- Develop dashboard metrics to measure results affecting revenues and pay-per-performance for field management and corporate reporting.
- Increase revenue and control expenses by optimizing current strategies and developing new ones according to business needs.
- Responsible for P & L and budget allocation.
- Strategic lead responsible for execution and delivery of fitness and club services.
- Set expectations and requirements to ensure company is offering the most efficient, state-of-the-art, and current trends.
- Work closely with corporate and field leadership to resolve issues for trainers, instructors, and club members.
- Partner with HR directors to ensure the attraction and retention of staff and establish guidelines for staffing and coaching of club training programs.
- Partner with field leadership to ensure fitness and club services are an integral part of club activity, member engagement, and operation.

Qualifications

- Bachelor's degree/MBA or MA preferred
- 10+ years managing P & L statements/revenue/EBITDA budget in the fitness, retail, and/or hospitality services
- 10+ years experience in sales, operations, budgeting and forecasting, and strategic development in a corporate-held position of a national and progressive service-oriented or retail business
- 10+ year's management experience in the fitness, retail, and/or hospitality services
- Multi-unit retail management experience with a proven track record for leading
- Excellent knowledge of current trends and practices relating to fitness services, as well as interaction with related networking associations
- Proven track record in leading successful lines of business with improved efficiencies, human capital, and revenue gains
- Ability to function within ambiguous guidelines
- Ability to define problems, collect and analyze data, establish facts, and recommend out-of-the-box solutions
- Ability to plan and manage annual budgets
- Experience presenting complex business information to senior leadership
- Ability to effectively function and lead with tight deadlines, independently and within a team environment, with little direction
- Knowledge of the health and fitness industry
- Strong relationship-building and leadership skills; works well with all levels of employees within all corporate and field departments
- Demonstrated strategic, management, analytical, organizational, and team development skills
- Highly developed interpersonal skills with the ability to communicate effectively at all levels of the organization
- Exceptional PC, Outlook, Excel, Word, and PowerPoint skills
- Ability to travel
- Exceptional written, oral, and presentation skills
- Proven leadership; visionary skills with innovative solutions
- Self-motivated, energetic, and forward thinking

HOSPITALITY MANAGEMENT

California State University, Long Beach, Graduate Studies, College of Health and Human Services, Department of Family and Consumer Sciences, Master of Science in Nutritional Science Program, Long Beach, CA 90840. Offers food science (MS); hospitality foodservice and hotel management (MS); nutritional science (MS). Part-time programs available. *Students:* 30 full-time (all women), 19 part-time (18 women); includes 1 Black or African American, non-Hispanic/Latino; 7 Asian, non-Hispanic/Latino; 4 Hispanic/Latino. Average age 26. 119 applicants, 39% accepted, 23 enrolled. In 2010, 11 master's awarded. *Degree requirements:* For master's, thesis, oral presentation of thesis or directed project. *Entrance requirements:* For master's, GRE, minimum GPA of 2.5 in last 60 units. *Application deadline:* For fall admission, 5/1 for domestic students. Applications are processed on a rolling basis. Application fee: $55. Electronic applications accepted. *Financial support:* Federal Work-Study, institutionally sponsored loans, and scholarships/grants available. Financial award application deadline: 3/2. *Faculty research:* Protein and water-soluble vitamins, sensory evaluation of foods, mineral deficiencies in humans, child nutrition, minerals and blood pressure. *Unit head:* Dr. M. Sue Stanley, Chair, 562-985-4484, Fax: 562-985-4414, E-mail: stanleym@csulb.edu. *Application contact:* Dr. Mary Jacob, Graduate Coordinator, 562-985-4484, Fax: 562-985-4414, E-mail: marjacob@csulb.edu.

Cornell University, Graduate School, Field of Hotel Administration, Ithaca, NY 14853. Offers hospitality management (MMH); hotel administration (MS, PhD). *Faculty:* 43 full-time (11 women). *Students:* 77 full-time (39 women); includes 1 Black or African American, non-Hispanic/Latino; 8 Asian, non-Hispanic/Latino; 5 Hispanic/Latino, 42 international. Average age 28. 236 applicants, 31% accepted, 73 enrolled. In 2010, 45 master's, 2 doctorates awarded. Terminal master's awarded for partial completion of doctoral program. *Degree requirements:* For master's, thesis (MS); for doctorate, comprehensive exam, thesis/dissertation. *Entrance requirements:* For master's and doctorate, GMAT, 1 academic and 1 employer letter of recommendation, 2 interviews. Additional exam requirements/recommendations for international students: Required—TOEFL (minimum score 600 paper-based; 250 computer-based). *Application deadline:* For fall admission, 2/1 for domestic students. Application fee: $70. Electronic applications accepted. *Expenses:* Tuition: Full-time $29,500. Required fees: $76. Tuition and fees vary according to degree level and program. *Financial support:* In 2010–11, 12 students received support, including 2 fellowships with full tuition reimbursements available, 6 teaching assistantships with full tuition reimbursements available; research assistantships with full tuition reimbursements available, institutionally sponsored loans, scholarships/grants, health care benefits, tuition waivers (full and partial), and unspecified assistantships also available. Financial award applicants required to submit FAFSA. *Faculty research:* Hospitality finance; property-asset management; real estate; management, strategy, and human resources; organizational communication. *Unit head:* Director of Graduate Studies, 607-255-7245. *Application contact:* Graduate Field Assistant, 607-255-6376, E-mail: mmh@cornell.edu.

Eastern Michigan University, Graduate School, College of Technology, School of Technology Studies, Program in Hotel and Restaurant Management, Ypsilanti, MI 48197. Offers MS, Graduate Certificate. Part-time and evening/weekend programs available. Postbaccalaureate distance learning degree programs offered (minimal on-campus study). *Students:* 3 full-time (all women), 9 part-time (8 women); includes 7 minority (4 Black or African American, non-Hispanic/Latino; 1 Asian, non-Hispanic/Latino; 2 Hispanic/Latino), 3 international. Average age 28. In 2010, 6 master's awarded. *Entrance requirements:* Additional exam requirements/recommendations for international students: Required—TOEFL. *Application deadline:* Applications are processed on a rolling basis. Application fee: $35. *Financial support:* Fellowships, research assistantships with full tuition reimbursements, teaching assistantships with full tuition reimbursements, career-related internships or fieldwork, Federal Work-Study, institutionally sponsored loans, scholarships/grants, tuition waivers (partial), and unspecified assistantships available. Support available to part-time students. Financial award applicants required to submit FAFSA. *Unit head:* Dr. Susan Gregory, Program Coordinator, 734-487-0845, Fax: 734-487-7690, E-mail: susan.gregory@emich.edu. *Application contact:* Dr. Susan Gregory, Program Coordinator, 734-487-0845, Fax: 734-487-7690, E-mail: susan.gregory@emich.edu.

Endicott College, Apicius International School of Hospitality, Florence, MA 50122, Italy. Offers organizational management (M Ed). Program held entirely in Florence, Italy. *Degree requirements:* For master's, thesis. *Entrance requirements:* For master's, MAT or GRE, 250-500 word essay explaining professional goals, official transcripts of all academic work, bachelor's degree, two letters of recommendation, personal interview. *Application deadline:* For fall admission, 6/30 for domestic and international students. Application fee: $50. *Financial support:* Applicants required to submit FAFSA. *Application contact:* Dr. Mary Huegel, Dean of Graduate and Professional Studies, 978-232-2084, Fax: 978-232-3000, E-mail: mhuegel@endicott.edu.

Fairleigh Dickinson University, College at Florham, Anthony J. Petrocelli College of Continuing Studies, International School of Hospitality and Tourism Management, Madison, NJ 07940-1099. Offers hospitality management (MS). *Students:* 4 full-time (all women), 33 part-time (16 women), 1 international. Average age 34. 13 applicants, 92% accepted, 10 enrolled. In 2010, 7 master's awarded. *Application deadline:* Applications are processed on a rolling basis. Application fee: $40. *Application contact:* Susan Brooman, University Director, Graduate Admissions, 973-443-8905, Fax: 973-443-8088, E-mail: grad@fdu.edu.

Fairleigh Dickinson University, Metropolitan Campus, Anthony J. Petrocelli College of Continuing Studies, International School of Hospitality and Tourism Management, Teaneck, NJ 07666-1914. Offers hospitality management (MS). *Students:* 11 full-time (10 women), 14 part-time (8 women), 14 international. Average age 32. 17 applicants, 71% accepted, 6 enrolled. In 2010, 8 master's awarded. *Application deadline:* Applications are processed on a rolling basis. Application fee: $40. *Unit head:* Dr. Richard Wisch, Director, 201-692-2000. *Application contact:* Susan Brooman, University Director of Graduate Admissions, 201-692-2554, Fax: 201-692-2560, E-mail: globaleducation@fdu.edu.

Florida International University, School of Hospitality and Tourism Management, Hospitality Management Program, Miami, FL 33199. Offers MS. Part-time and evening/weekend programs available. Postbaccalaureate distance learning degree programs offered. *Faculty:* 17 full-time (5 women), 23 part-time/adjunct (8 women). *Students:* 214 full-time (144 women), 86 part-time (56 women); includes 28 Black or African American, non-Hispanic/Latino; 1 American Indian or Alaska Native, non-Hispanic/Latino; 7 Asian, non-Hispanic/Latino; 47 Hispanic/Latino, 150 international. Average age 29. 528 applicants, 42% accepted, 197 enrolled. In 2010, 81 master's awarded. *Entrance requirements:* For master's, minimum GPA of 3.0, letters of recommendation, 5 years of management experience (for executive track). Additional exam requirements/recommendations for international students: Required—TOEFL (minimum score 550 paper-based; 213 computer-based). *Application deadline:* For fall admission, 6/1 for domestic students, 4/1 for international students; for spring admission, 10/1 for domestic students, 9/1 for international students. Applications are processed on a rolling basis. Electronic applications accepted. *Financial support:* Scholarships/grants available. *Unit head:* Dr. Mike Hampton, Dean, 305-919-4500, Fax: 305-919-4555, E-mail: mhampton@fiu.edu. *Application contact:* Nanett Rojas, Coordinator of Graduate Admissions, 305-348-7442, Fax: 305-348-7441, E-mail: gradadm@fiu.edu.

The George Washington University, School of Business, Department of Tourism and Hospitality Management, Washington, DC 20052. Offers event and meeting management (MTA); event management (Professional Certificate); hospitality management (MTA, Professional Certificate); sports business management (Professional Certificate); sports management (MTA); sustainable destination management (MTA); tourism administration (MTA); tourism and hospitality management (MBA); tourism destination management (Professional Certificate). Part-time programs available. Postbaccalaureate distance learning degree programs offered. *Faculty:* 9 full-time (5 women), 6 part-time/adjunct (4 women). *Students:* 84 full-time (62 women), 107 part-time (77 women); includes 27 Black or African American, non-Hispanic/Latino; 2 American Indian or Alaska Native, non-Hispanic/Latino; 5 Asian, non-Hispanic/Latino; 9 Hispanic/Latino, 38 international. Average age 30. 152 applicants, 74% accepted. In 2010, 69 master's awarded. *Degree requirements:* For master's, comprehensive exam, thesis. *Entrance requirements:* For master's, GRE General Test. Additional exam requirements/recommendations for international students: Required—TOEFL. *Application deadline:* For fall admission, 4/1 priority date for domestic students; for spring admission, 10/1 for domestic students. Applications are processed on a rolling basis. Application fee: $75. *Financial support:* In 2010–11, 32 students received support; fellowships, teaching assistantships, career-related internships or fieldwork, Federal Work-Study, institutionally sponsored loans, and tuition waivers (partial) available. Financial award application deadline: 4/1. *Faculty research:* Tourism policy, tourism impact forecasting, geotourism. *Unit head:* Susan M. Phillips, Dean, 202-994-6380, E-mail: gwsbdean@gwu.edu. *Application contact:* Kristin Williams, Assistant Vice President for Graduate and Special Enrollment Management, 202-994-0467, Fax: 202-994-0371, E-mail: ksw@gwu.edu.

Iowa State University of Science and Technology, Graduate College, College of Human Sciences, Department of Apparel, Education Studies, and Hospitality Management, Program in Foodservice and Lodging Management, Ames, IA 50011. Offers MFCS, MS, PhD. *Students:* 2 full-time (1 woman), 2 part-time (1 woman); includes 2 Black or African American, non-Hispanic/Latino; 1 Hispanic/Latino. In 2010, 3 master's, 1 doctorate awarded. *Degree requirements:* For master's, thesis or alternative; for doctorate, thesis/dissertation. *Application deadline:* For fall admission, 2/1 priority date for domestic and international students. Application fee: $40 ($90 for international students). Electronic applications accepted. *Financial support:* In 2010–11, 3 research assistantships with full and partial tuition reimbursements (averaging $12,304 per year), 5 teaching assistantships with full and partial tuition reimbursements (averaging $8,505 per year) were awarded; scholarships/grants also available. *Unit head:* Dr. Ann-Marie Fiore, Director of Graduate Education, 515-294-9303. *Application contact:* Dr. Ann-Marie Fiore, Director of Graduate Education, 515-294-9303.

Johnson & Wales University, The Alan Shawn Feinstein Graduate School, MAT Program in Teacher Education, Providence, RI 02903-3703. Offers business education and secondary special education (MAT); elementary education and elementary special education (MAT); elementary education and elementary/secondary special education (MAT); elementary education and secondary special education (MAT); food service education (MAT). Part-time and evening/weekend programs available. *Faculty:* 6 full-time (3 women), 3 part-time/adjunct (2 women). *Students:* 71 full-time (51 women), 1 part-time (0 women); includes 1 minority (Hispanic/Latino). Average age 31. 47 applicants, 72% accepted, 28 enrolled. In 2010, 38 master's awarded. *Entrance requirements:* For master's, MAT, minimum GPA of 2.75. Additional exam requirements/recommendations for international students: Required—TOEFL (minimum score 550 paper-based; 210 computer-based) or IELTS (recommended). *Application deadline:* For fall admission, 8/21 priority date for domestic students, 6/15 priority date for international students; for winter admission, 11/15 priority date for domestic students, 10/1 priority date for international students. Applications are processed on a rolling basis. Application fee: $0. *Expenses:* Tuition: Part-time $1535 per course. Part-time tuition and fees vary according to degree level and program. *Financial support:* Unspecified assistantships available. Financial award application deadline: 5/1. *Faculty research:* Secondary education, student teaching, educational reform, evaluation procedures. *Unit head:* Karen Swoboda, Director of Teacher Education, 401-598-1922, Fax: 401-598-1125. *Application contact:* Graduate School Admissions, 401-598-1015, Fax: 401-598-1286, E-mail: gradadm@jwu.edu.

Johnson & Wales University, The Alan Shawn Feinstein Graduate School, MBA Program in Global Business Leadership, Providence, RI 02903-3703. Offers accounting (MBA); enhanced accounting (MBA); hospitality (MBA). Part-time programs available. *Faculty:* 14 full-time (3 women), 18 part-time/adjunct (4 women). *Students:* 736 full-time (433 women), 359 part-time (237 women); includes 46 minority (18 Black or African American, non-Hispanic/Latino; 5 Asian, non-Hispanic/Latino; 22 Hispanic/Latino; 1 Native Hawaiian or other Pacific Islander, non-Hispanic/Latino), 640 international. Average age 29. 397 applicants, 76% accepted, 219 enrolled. In 2010, 329 master's awarded. *Entrance requirements:* For master's, minimum GPA of 2.75. Additional exam requirements/recommendations for international students: Required—TOEFL (minimum score 550 paper-based; 210 computer-based) or IELTS (recommended); Recommended—TWE. *Application deadline:* For fall admission, 8/15 priority date for domestic students, 6/28 priority date for international students; for winter admission, 11/10 priority date for domestic students, 9/20 priority date for international students; for spring admission, 2/5 priority date for domestic students, 12/20 priority date for international students. Applications are processed on a rolling basis. *Expenses:* Tuition: Part-time $1535 per course. Part-time tuition and fees vary according to degree level and program. *Financial support:* Tuition waivers (partial) and unspecified assistantships available. Support available to part-time students. Financial award application deadline: 5/1. *Faculty research:* International banking, global economy, international trade, cultural differences. *Unit head:* Dr. Frank Sargent, Director, 401-598-1033, Fax: 401-598-1125. *Application contact:* Graduate School Admissions, 401-598-1015, Fax: 401-598-1286, E-mail: gradadm@jwu.edu.

Kent State University, Graduate School of Education, Health, and Human Services, School of Foundations, Leadership and Administration, Program in Hospitality and Tourism Management, Kent, OH 44242-0001. Offers MS. Part-time programs available. *Faculty:* 6 full-time (4 women), 3 part-time/adjunct (1 woman). *Students:* 14 full-time (8 women), 2 part-time (1 woman). 23 applicants, 57% accepted. *Degree requirements:* For master's, thesis (for some programs). *Entrance requirements:* For master's, GRE, minimum GPA of 3.0, 3 letters of recommendation. Additional exam requirements/recommendations for international students: Required—TOEFL. *Application deadline:* Applications are processed on a rolling basis. Application fee: $30 ($60 for international students). Electronic applications accepted. *Expenses:* Tuition, state resident: full-time $7866; part-time $437 per credit hour. Tuition, nonresident: full-time $14,022; part-time $779 per credit hour. *Financial support:* In 2010–11, 4 students received support, including 1 fellowship (averaging $8,500 per year), research assistantships with full tuition reimbursements available (averaging $8,500 per year), Federal Work-Study, scholarships/grants, unspecified assistantships, and 3 administrative assistantships (averaging $8,500 per year) also available. Financial award application deadline: 2/1; financial award applicants required to submit FAFSA. *Faculty research:* Training human service workers, health care services for older adults, early adolescent development, care giving arrangements with aging families, peace and war23. *Unit head:* Barb Scheule, Coordinator, 330-672-3796, E-mail: bscheule@kent.edu. *Application contact:* Nancy Miller, Academic Program Coordinator, 330-672-2576, Fax: 330-672-9162, E-mail: ogs@kent.edu.

Lasell College, Graduate and Professional Studies in Sport Management, Newton, MA 02466-2709. Offers sport hospitality management (MS, Graduate Certificate); sport leadership (MS, Graduate Certificate); sport non-profit management (MS, Graduate Certificate). Part-time programs available. Postbaccalaureate distance learning degree programs offered (no on-campus study). *Faculty:* 1 full-time (0 women), 4 part-time/adjunct (3 women). *Students:* 3 full-time (2 women), 10 part-time (0 women); includes 1 minority (Black or African American, non-Hispanic/Latino). Average age 28. 12 applicants, 58% accepted, 4 enrolled. *Entrance requirements:* For master's and Graduate Certificate, bachelor's degree from an accredited institution. Additional exam requirements/recommendations for international students: Required—TOEFL (minimum score 550 paper-based; 213 computer-based; 75 iBT), IELTS. *Application deadline:* For fall admission, 8/31 priority date for domestic students, 6/30 priority date for international students; for spring admission, 12/31 priority date for domestic students, 10/31 priority date for international students. Applications are processed on a rolling basis. Application fee: $40. Electronic applications accepted. *Expenses:* Tuition: Part-time $550 per credit hour. Required fees: $55 per semester. *Financial support:* In 2010–11, 2 students received support. Available to part-time students. Application deadline: 8/31. *Unit head:* Dr. Joan Dolamore, Dean of Graduate and Professional Studies, 617-243-2485, Fax: 617-243-2450, E-mail: gradinfo@lasell.edu. *Application contact:* Adrienne Franciosi, Director of Graduate Admission, 617-243-2214, Fax: 617-243-2450, E-mail: gradinfo@lasell.edu.

New York University, School of Continuing and Professional Studies, The Preston Robert Tisch Center for Hospitality, Tourism, and Sports Management, Program in Hospitality Industry Studies, New York, NY 10012-1019. Offers brand strategy (MS); hospitality industry studies (Advanced Certificate); hotel finance (MS). Part-time and evening/weekend programs available. *Faculty:* 12 full-time (5 women), 17 part-time/adjunct (3 women). *Students:* 11 full-time (9 women), 25 part-time (16 women); includes 1 Black or African American, non-Hispanic/Latino; 1 American Indian or Alaska Native, non-Hispanic/Latino; 5 Asian, non-Hispanic/Latino; 4 Hispanic/Latino, 8 international. Average age 29. 104 applicants, 24% accepted, 8 enrolled. In 2010, 19 master's, 1 other advanced degree awarded. *Degree requirements:* For master's, thesis. *Entrance requirements:* For master's, GMAT or GRE General Test (for recent graduates), resume, 2 letters of recommendation, essay, professional experience. Additional exam requirements/recommendations for international students: Required—TOEFL (minimum score 600 paper-based; 250 computer-based; 100 iBT), TWE. *Application deadline:* For fall admission, 2/1 priority date for domestic and international students; for spring admission, 10/15 priority date for domestic students, 8/15 priority date for international students. Applications are processed on a rolling basis. Application fee: $75. Electronic applications accepted. *Financial support:* In 2010–11, 17 students received support, including 17 fellowships (averaging $3,186 per year); career-related internships or fieldwork, Federal Work-Study, institutionally sponsored loans, and scholarships/grants also available. Support available to part-time students. Financial award application deadline: 3/1; financial award applicants required to submit FAFSA. *Unit head:* Bjorn Hanson, Divisional Dean, Clinical Professor, HVS Chair, 212-998-9100, Fax: 212-995-4676, E-mail: lalia.rach@nyu.edu. *Application contact:* Sandra Dove-Lowther, Academic Services Director, 212-992-9087, Fax: 212-995-4676, E-mail: sd2@nyu.edu.

New York University, Steinhardt School of Culture, Education, and Human Development, Department of Nutrition, Food Studies, and Public Health, Program in Food Studies and Food Management, New York, NY 10012-1019. Offers food studies (MA), including food culture, food systems; food studies and food management (PhD). Part-time programs available. *Faculty:* 6 full-time (5 women). *Students:* 21 full-time (18 women), 138 part-time (117 women); includes 4 Black or African American, non-Hispanic/Latino; 15 Asian, non-Hispanic/Latino; 7 Hispanic/Latino, 13 international. Average age 31. 163 applicants, 45% accepted, 50 enrolled. In 2010, 26 master's awarded. *Degree requirements:* For master's, thesis (for some programs); for doctorate, thesis/dissertation. *Entrance requirements:* For doctorate, GRE General Test, interview. Additional exam requirements/recommendations for international students: Required—TOEFL. *Application deadline:* For fall admission, 12/1 priority date for domestic students, 12/1 for international students; for spring admission, 11/1 for domestic and international students. Applications are processed on a rolling basis. Application fee: $75. Electronic applications accepted. *Financial support:* Fellowships with full and partial tuition reimbursements, career-related internships or fieldwork, Federal Work-Study, institutionally sponsored loans, scholarships/grants, tuition waivers (partial), and unspecified assistantships available. Financial award application deadline: 2/1; financial award applicants required to submit FAFSA. *Faculty research:* Cultural and social history of food, food systems and agriculture, food and aesthetics, political economy of food. *Unit head:* Dr. Jennifer Berg, Director, 212-998-5580, Fax: 212-995-4194. *Application contact:* 212-998-5030, Fax: 212-995-4328, E-mail: steinhardt.gradadmissions@nyu.edu.

The Ohio State University, Graduate School, College of Education and Human Ecology, Department of Consumer Sciences, Columbus, OH 43210. Offers family resource management (MS, PhD); fashion and retail studies (MS, PhD); hospitality management (MS, PhD). *Students:* 22 full-time (17 women), 6 part-time (5 women); includes 2 Asian, non-Hispanic/Latino, 19 international. Average age 31. In 2010, 4 master's, 6 doctorates awarded. *Entrance requirements:* Additional exam requirements/recommendations for international students: Required—TOEFL. *Application deadline:* Applications are processed on a rolling basis. Application fee: $40 ($50 for international students). Electronic applications accepted. *Expenses:* Tuition, state resident: full-time $10,605. Tuition, nonresident: full-time $26,535. Tuition and fees vary according to course load and program. *Unit head:* Jonathan Fox,

Interim Chair, 614-292-4561, E-mail: jfox@ehe.osu.edu. *Application contact:* Jonathan Fox, Interim Chair, 614-292-4561, E-mail: jfox@ehe.osu.edu.

The Ohio State University, Graduate School, College of Education and Human Ecology, Department of Human Nutrition, Columbus, OH 43210. Offers food service management (MS, PhD); foods (MS, PhD); nutrition (MS, PhD). *Accreditation:* ADtA. *Faculty:* 18. *Students:* 25 full-time (19 women), 18 part-time (15 women); includes 2 Black or African American, non-Hispanic/Latino, 20 international. Average age 29. In 2010, 5 master's, 2 doctorates awarded. *Degree requirements:* For master's, thesis optional; for doctorate, thesis/dissertation. *Entrance requirements:* For master's and doctorate, GRE General Test. Additional exam requirements/recommendations for international students: Required—TOEFL (minimum score 577 paper-based; 233 computer-based). *Application deadline:* For fall admission, 8/15 priority date for domestic students, 7/1 priority date for international students; for winter admission, 12/1 priority date for domestic students, 11/1 priority date for international students; for spring admission, 3/1 priority date for domestic students, 2/1 priority date for international students. Applications are processed on a rolling basis. Application fee: $40 ($50 for international students). Electronic applications accepted. *Expenses:* Tuition, state resident: full-time $10,605. Tuition, nonresident: full-time $26,535. Tuition and fees vary according to course load and program. *Financial support:* Fellowships, research assistantships, teaching assistantships, Federal Work-Study and institutionally sponsored loans available. Support available to part-time students. *Unit head:* James E. Kinder, Chair, 614-292-4485, Fax: 614-292-8880, E-mail: kinder.15@osu.edu. *Application contact:* 614-292-9444, Fax: 614-292-3895, E-mail: domestic.grad@osu.edu.

Oklahoma State University, College of Human Sciences, School of Hotel and Restaurant Administration, Stillwater, OK 74078. Offers MS, PhD. *Faculty:* 10 full-time (3 women), 3 part-time/adjunct (0 women). *Students:* 21 full-time (15 women), 34 part-time (22 women); includes 3 Black or African American, non-Hispanic/Latino; 1 Asian, non-Hispanic/Latino; 3 Hispanic/Latino, 35 international. Average age 37. 30 applicants, 20% accepted, 3 enrolled. In 2010, 4 master's, 5 doctorates awarded. *Degree requirements:* For master's, thesis (for some programs); for doctorate, comprehensive exam, thesis/dissertation. *Entrance requirements:* For master's and doctorate, GRE or GMAT. Additional exam requirements/recommendations for international students: Required—TOEFL (minimum score 550 paper-based; 79 iBT). *Application deadline:* For fall admission, 3/1 priority date for international students; for spring admission, 8/1 priority date for international students. Applications are processed on a rolling basis. Application fee: $40 ($75 for international students). Electronic applications accepted. *Expenses:* Tuition, state resident: full-time $3716; part-time $154.85 per credit hour. Tuition, nonresident: full-time $14,892; part-time $621 per credit hour. Required fees: $2044; $85.20 per credit hour. One-time fee: $50. Tuition and fees vary according to course load and campus/location. *Financial support:* In 2010–11, 5 research assistantships (averaging $7,974 per year), 14 teaching assistantships (averaging $10,881 per year) were awarded; career-related internships or fieldwork, Federal Work-Study, scholarships/grants, health care benefits, tuition waivers (partial), and unspecified assistantships also available. Support available to part-time students. Financial award application deadline: 3/1; financial award applicants required to submit FAFSA. *Faculty research:* Hotel operations and management, restaurant/food service management, hospitality education, hospitality human resources management, tourism. *Unit head:* Dr. Bill Ryan, Director, 405-744-6713, Fax: 405-744-6299. *Application contact:* Dr. Gordon Emslie, Dean, 405-744-6368, Fax: 405-744-0355, E-mail: grad-i@okstate.edu.

Penn State University Park, Graduate School, College of Health and Human Development, School of Hospitality Management, State College, University Park, PA 16802-1503. Offers MS, PhD.

Rochester Institute of Technology, Graduate Enrollment Services, College of Applied Science and Technology, Department of Hospitality and Service Management, Program in Hospitality-Tourism Management, Rochester, NY 14623-5603. Offers MS. *Students:* 12 full-time (8 women), 5 part-time (3 women); includes 1 Asian, non-Hispanic/Latino, 13 international. Average age 27. 29 applicants, 86% accepted, 10 enrolled. In 2010, 6 master's awarded. *Degree requirements:* For master's, thesis or project. *Entrance requirements:* For master's, minimum GPA of 3.0. Additional exam requirements/recommendations for international students: Required—TOEFL (minimum score 550 paper-based; 213 computer-based; 79 iBT) or IELTS (minimum score 6.5). *Application deadline:* For fall admission, 2/15 priority date for domestic and international students; for winter admission, 11/1 priority date for domestic students, 10/1 priority date for international students; for spring admission, 2/1 priority date for domestic students, 1/1 priority date for international students. Applications are processed on a rolling basis. *Expenses:* Tuition: Full-time $33,234; part-time $924 per credit hour. Required fees: $219. *Financial support:* In 2010–11, 6 students received support; research assistantships with partial tuition reimbursements available, teaching assistantships with partial tuition reimbursements available, career-related internships or fieldwork, scholarships/grants, and unspecified assistantships available. Support available to part-time students. Financial award application deadline: 2/15; financial award applicants required to submit FAFSA. *Unit head:* Dr. Linda Underhill, Chair, 585-475-7359, Fax: 585-475-5099, E-mail: lmuism@rit.edu. *Application contact:* Diane Ellison, Assistant Vice President, Graduate Enrollment Services, 585-475-2229, Fax: 585-475-7164, E-mail: gradinfo@rit.edu.

Rochester Institute of Technology, Graduate Enrollment Services, College of Applied Science and Technology, Department of Hospitality and Service Management, Program in Service Leadership and Innovation, Rochester, NY 14623-5603. Offers MS. Part-time and evening/weekend programs available. *Students:* 15 full-time (10 women), 69 part-time (34 women); includes 1 Black or African American, non-Hispanic/Latino; 1 American Indian or Alaska Native, non-Hispanic/Latino, 10 international. Average age 29. 82 applicants, 54% accepted, 21 enrolled. In 2010, 31 master's awarded. *Degree requirements:* For master's, thesis or alternative. *Entrance requirements:* For master's, minimum GPA of 3.0. Additional exam requirements/recommendations for international students: Required—TOEFL (minimum score 550 paper-based; 213 computer-based; 79 iBT) or IELTS (minimum score 6.5). *Application deadline:* For fall admission, 2/15 priority date for domestic and international students; for winter admission, 11/1 for domestic and international students; for spring admission, 2/1 for domestic and international students. Applications are processed on a rolling basis. *Expenses:* Tuition: Full-time $33,234; part-time $924 per credit hour. Required fees: $219. *Financial support:* In 2010–11, 23 students received support; research assistantships with partial tuition reimbursements available, teaching assistantships with partial tuition reimbursements available, career-related internships or fieldwork, institutionally sponsored loans, scholarships/grants, and unspecified assistantships available. Support available to part-time students. Financial award application deadline: 2/15; financial award applicants required to submit FAFSA. *Faculty research:* Global resource development, service/product innovation and implementation. *Unit head:* Dr. James Jacobs, Graduate Program Director, 585-475-6017, E-mail: jwjism@rit.edu. *Application contact:* Diane Ellison, Assistant Vice President, Graduate Enrollment Services, 585-475-2229, Fax: 585-475-7164, E-mail: gradinfo@rit.edu.

Temple University, School of Tourism and Hospitality Management, Program in Tourism and Hospitality Management, Philadelphia, PA 19122-6096. Offers MTHM. Part-time and evening/weekend programs available. *Faculty:* 9 full-time (4 women). *Students:* 12 full-time (10 women), 7 part-time (all women); includes 1 Black or African American, non-Hispanic/Latino; 1 American Indian or Alaska Native, non-Hispanic/Latino; 3 Asian, non-Hispanic/Latino, 1 international. 62 applicants, 31% accepted, 7 enrolled. In 2010, 6 master's awarded. *Entrance requirements:* For master's, GRE General Test or MAT, minimum of 2 years professional experience, minimum undergraduate GPA of 3.0. Additional exam requirements/recommendations for international students: Required—TOEFL (minimum score 550 paper-based; 213 computer-based; 79 iBT). *Application deadline:* For fall admission, 4/1 priority date for domestic students, 12/15 for international students; for spring admission, 9/30 priority date for domestic students, 8/1 for international students. Application fee: $50. Electronic applications accepted. *Financial support:* Teaching assistantships available. Financial award application deadline: 1/15; financial award applicants required to submit FAFSA. *Unit head:* Dr. Wesley Roehl, Director, 215-204-5861, E-mail: wroehl@temple.edu. *Application contact:* Dr. Wesley Roehl, Director, 215-204-5861, E-mail: wroehl@temple.edu.

Texas Tech University, Graduate School, College of Human Sciences, Department of Nutrition, Hospitality, and Retailing, Program in Hospitality Administration, Lubbock, TX 79409. Offers PhD. *Students:* 32 full-time (13 women), 7 part-time (2 women); includes 1 Native Hawaiian or other Pacific Islander, non-Hispanic/Latino, 29 international. 17 applicants, 82% accepted, 8 enrolled. In 2010, 10 doctorates awarded. *Degree requirements:* For doctorate, thesis/dissertation. *Entrance requirements:* For doctorate, GRE General Test. Additional exam requirements/recommendations for international students: Required—TOEFL (minimum score 550 paper-based; 213 computer-based; 79 iBT). *Application deadline:* For fall admission, 6/1 priority date for domestic students, 1/15 priority date for international students; for spring admission, 9/1 priority date for domestic students, 6/15 priority date for international students. Applications are processed on a rolling basis. Application fee: $50 ($75 for international students). Electronic applications accepted. *Expenses:* Tuition, state resident: full-time $5495.76; part-time $228.99 per credit hour. Tuition, nonresident: full-time $12,936; part-time $538.99 per credit hour. Required fees: $2674; $36 per credit hour. $905 per semester. *Financial support:* Application deadline: 4/15. *Unit head:* Dr. Shane Blum, Chair, 806-742-3068 Ext. 253, Fax: 806-742-3042, E-mail: shane.blum@ttu.edu. *Application contact:* Dr. Debra Reed, Graduate Advisor, Nutritional Sciences, 806-742-3068 Ext. 251, Fax: 806-742-3042, E-mail: debra.reed@ttu.edu.

Texas Tech University, Graduate School, College of Human Sciences, Department of Nutrition, Hospitality, and Retailing, Program in Hospitality and Retail Management, Lubbock, TX 79409. Offers MS. Part-time programs available. Postbaccalaureate distance learning degree programs offered (minimal on-campus study). *Students:* 20 full-time (10 women), 3 part-time (2 women); includes 5 Hispanic/Latino, 3 international. Average age 27. 27 applicants, 74% accepted, 8 enrolled. In 2010, 15 master's awarded. *Degree requirements:* For master's, thesis or alternative. *Entrance requirements:* For master's, GRE General Test. Additional exam requirements/recommendations for international students: Required—TOEFL (minimum score 550 paper-based; 213 computer-based; 79 iBT). *Application deadline:* For fall admission, 6/1 priority date for domestic students, 1/15 priority date for international students; for spring admission, 9/1 priority date for domestic students, 6/15 priority date for international students. Applications are processed on a rolling basis. Application fee: $50 ($75 for international students). Electronic applications accepted. *Expenses:* Tuition, state resident: full-time $5495.76; part-time $228.99 per credit hour. Tuition, nonresident: full-time $12,936; part-time $538.99 per credit hour. Required fees: $2674; $36 per credit hour. $905 per semester. *Financial support:* Application deadline: 4/15. *Faculty research:* Community engagement and food supply development and security, tourism, lodging and human resource management, rural tourism. *Unit head:* Dr. Shane Blum, Chairperson, 806-742-3068 Ext. 253, Fax: 806-742-3042, E-mail: shane.blum@ttu.edu.

Troy University, Graduate School, College of Business, Program in Management, Troy, AL 36082. Offers applied management (MSM); healthcare management (MSM); human resources management (MSM); information systems (MSM); international hospitality management (MSM); international management (MSM); leadership and organizational effectiveness (MSM); public management (MS, MSM). *Accreditation:* ACBSP. Evening/weekend programs available. *Students:* 101 full-time (62 women), 398 part-time (249 women); includes 308 minority (278 Black or African American, non-Hispanic/Latino; 8 American Indian or Alaska Native, non-Hispanic/Latino; 8 Asian, non-Hispanic/Latino; 13 Hispanic/Latino; 1 Two or more races, non-Hispanic/Latino). Average age 35. 218 applicants, 80% accepted. In 2010, 314 master's awarded. *Degree requirements:* For master's, Graduate Educational Testing Service Major Field Test, capstone exam, minimum GPA of 3.0. *Entrance requirements:* For master's, GMAT (minimum score 500) or GRE General Test (minimum score 900), minimum GPA of 2.5, bachelor's degree, letter of recommendation. Additional exam requirements/recommendations for international students: Required—TOEFL (minimum score 523 paper-based; 193 computer-based; 70 iBT), IELTS, or ACT compass ESL (minimum Listening, Reading, and Grammar score: 270). *Application deadline:* Applications are processed on a rolling basis. Application fee: $50. Electronic applications accepted. *Expenses:* Contact institution. *Unit head:* Dr. Henry M. Findley, Interim Chair/Professor, 334-670-3271, Fax: 334-670-3599, E-mail: hfindley@troy.edu. *Application contact:* Brenda K. Campbell, Director of Graduate Admissions, 334-670-3178, Fax: 334-670-3733, E-mail: bcamp@troy.edu.

The University of Alabama, Graduate School, College of Human Environmental Sciences, Department of Human Nutrition and Hospitality Management, Tuscaloosa, AL 35487. Offers MSHES. Part-time programs available. Postbaccalaureate distance learning degree programs offered (no on-campus study). *Faculty:* 7 full-time (5 women). *Students:* 25 full-time (21 women), 64 part-time (63 women); includes 12 minority (9 Black or African American, non-Hispanic/Latino; 2 Asian, non-Hispanic/Latino; 1 Hispanic/Latino), 2 international. Average age 31. 53 applicants, 70% accepted, 29 enrolled. In 2010, 29 master's awarded. *Degree requirements:* For master's, comprehensive exam, thesis optional. *Entrance requirements:* For master's, minimum GPA of 3.0. Additional exam requirements/recommendations for international students: Required—TOEFL. *Application deadline:* For fall admission, 7/6 for domestic students. Applications are processed on a rolling basis. Application fee: $50 ($60 for international students). Electronic applications accepted. *Expenses:* Tuition, state resident: full-time $7900. Tuition, nonresident: full-time $20,500. *Financial support:* In 2010–11, 4 students received support, including 2 research assistantships (averaging $8,100 per year), 2 teaching assistantships (averaging $8,100 per year); career-related internships or fieldwork also available. Financial award application deadline: 3/15. *Faculty research:* Maternal and child nutrition, childhood obesity, community nutrition interventions, geriatric nutrition, family eating patterns. Total annual research expenditures: $12,180. *Unit head:* Dr. Olivia W. Kendrick, Chair and Associate Professor, 205-348-6150, Fax: 205-348-3789, E-mail: okendric@ches.ua.edu. *Application contact:* Dr. Olivia W. Kendrick, Chair and Associate Professor, 205-348-6150, Fax: 205-348-3789, E-mail: okendric@ches.ua.edu.

The University of Alabama, Graduate School, College of Human Environmental Sciences, Program in Human Environmental Science, Tuscaloosa, AL 35487. Offers family financial planning and counseling (MS); interactive technology (MS); quality management (MS); restaurant and meeting management (MS); rural community health (MS); sport management (MS). *Faculty:* 1 full-time (0 women). *Students:* 67 full-time (39 women), 86 part-time (52 women); includes 47 minority (40 Black or African American, non-Hispanic/Latino; 3 Hispanic/Latino; 4 Two or more races, non-Hispanic/Latino), 1 international. Average age 34. 112 applicants, 78% accepted, 64 enrolled. In 2010, 64 master's awarded. *Degree requirements:* For master's, comprehensive exam. *Entrance requirements:* For master's, GRE (for some specializations), minimum GPA of 3.0. Additional exam requirements/recommendations for international students: Required—TOEFL. *Application deadline:* Applications are processed on a rolling basis. Application fee: $50 ($60 for international students). Electronic applications accepted. *Expenses:* Tuition, state resident: full-time $7900. Tuition, nonresident: full-time $20,500. *Faculty research:* Hospitality management, sports medicine education, technology and education. *Unit head:* Dr. Milla D. Boschung,

Dean, 205-348-6250, Fax: 205-348-1786, E-mail: mboschun@ches.ua.edu. *Application contact:* Dr. Stuart Usdan, Associate Dean, 205-348-6150, Fax: 205-348-3789, E-mail: susdan@ches.ua.edu.

University of Central Florida, Rosen College of Hospitality Management, Orlando, FL 32816. Offers hospitality and tourism management (MS). *Faculty:* 35 full-time (12 women), 29 part-time/adjunct (12 women). *Students:* 45 full-time (30 women), 40 part-time (28 women); includes 3 Black or African American, non-Hispanic/Latino; 4 Asian, non-Hispanic/Latino; 3 Hispanic/Latino; 1 Two or more races, non-Hispanic/Latino, 13 international. Average age 28. 69 applicants, 58% accepted, 28 enrolled. In 2010, 25 master's awarded. *Degree requirements:* For master's, thesis or alternative. *Entrance requirements:* For master's, GMAT or GRE, minimum GPA of 3.0 in last 60 hours. Additional exam requirements/recommendations for international students: Required—TOEFL. *Application deadline:* For fall admission, 2/1 for domestic students. Application fee: $30. Electronic applications accepted. *Expenses:* Tuition, state resident: part-time $256.56 per credit hour. Tuition, nonresident: part-time $1011.52 per credit hour. Part-time tuition and fees vary according to program. *Financial support:* In 2010–11, 1 student received support, including 1 fellowship with partial tuition reimbursement available (averaging $10,000 per year). *Unit head:* Dr. Abraham C. Pizam, Dean, 407-903-8010, E-mail: apizam@mail.ucf.edu. *Application contact:* Dr. Abraham C. Pizam, Dean, 407-903-8010, E-mail: apizam@mail.ucf.edu.

The University of Findlay, Graduate and Professional Studies, College of Business, Findlay, OH 45840-3653. Offers health care management (MBA); hospitality management (MBA); organizational leadership (MBA); public management (MBA). Part-time and evening/weekend programs available. Postbaccalaureate distance learning degree programs offered (no on-campus study). *Faculty:* 20 full-time (5 women), 6 part-time/adjunct (0 women). *Students:* 25 full-time (11 women), 239 part-time (112 women); includes 15 minority (5 Black or African American, non-Hispanic/Latino; 9 Asian, non-Hispanic/Latino; 1 Hispanic/Latino), 98 international. Average age 25. 93 applicants, 86% accepted, 70 enrolled. In 2010, 283 master's awarded. *Degree requirements:* For master's, thesis, cumulative project. *Entrance requirements:* For master's, GMAT or GRE, minimum undergraduate GPA of 3.0. Additional exam requirements/recommendations for international students: Required—TOEFL (minimum score 550 paper-based; 213 computer-based; 80 iBT). *Application deadline:* Applications are processed on a rolling basis. Application fee: $25. Electronic applications accepted. *Expenses:* Contact institution. *Financial support:* In 2010–11, 8 research assistantships with full and partial tuition reimbursements (averaging $4,200 per year) were awarded; career-related internships or fieldwork, Federal Work-Study, health care benefits, and unspecified assistantships also available. Financial award application deadline: 4/1; financial award applicants required to submit FAFSA. *Faculty research:* Health care management, operations and logistics management. *Unit head:* Dr. Paul Sears, Dean, College of Business, 419-434-4704, Fax: 419-434-4822. *Application contact:* Heather Riffle, Assistant Director, Graduate and Professional Studies, 419-434-4640, Fax: 419-434-5517, E-mail: riffle@findlay.edu.

University of Houston, Conrad N. Hilton College of Hotel and Restaurant Management, Houston, TX 77204. Offers hospitality management (MS). Part-time programs available. *Faculty:* 11 full-time (3 women), 10 part-time/adjunct (3 women). *Students:* 76 full-time (55 women), 25 part-time (20 women); includes 6 Black or African American, non-Hispanic/Latino; 9 Asian, non-Hispanic/Latino; 7 Hispanic/Latino; 2 Two or more races, non-Hispanic/Latino, 44 international. Average age 26. 79 applicants, 80% accepted, 43 enrolled. In 2010, 21 master's awarded. *Degree requirements:* For master's, practicum or thesis. *Entrance requirements:* For master's, GMAT or GRE General Test. Additional exam requirements/recommendations for international students: Required—TOEFL (minimum score 100 iBT) or IELTS (minimum score 7). *Application deadline:* For fall admission, 5/1 for domestic students, 4/1 for international students; for spring admission, 11/1 for domestic students, 10/1 for international students. Applications are processed on a rolling basis. Application fee: $50 ($75 for international students). Electronic applications accepted. *Expenses:* Tuition, state resident: full-time $8592; part-time $358 per credit hour. Tuition, nonresident: full-time $16,032; part-time $668 per credit hour. Required fees: $2889. Tuition and fees vary according to course load and program. *Financial support:* In 2010–11, 4 research assistantships with partial tuition reimbursements (averaging $5,600 per year), 24 teaching assistantships with partial tuition reimbursements (averaging $6,224 per year) were awarded; career-related internships or fieldwork, Federal Work-Study, institutionally sponsored loans, scholarships/grants, health care benefits, and unspecified assistantships also available. Support available to part-time students. Financial award application deadline: 2/1. *Faculty research:* Catering, tourism, hospitality marketing, security and risk management, purchasing and financial information usage. *Unit head:* Dr. John Bowen, Dean, 713-743-2607, Fax: 713-743-2482, E-mail: jbowen@uh.edu. *Application contact:* Laura S. Gonzalez, Graduate Program Coordinator, 713-743-2457, Fax: 713-743-2218, E-mail: lgonzal3@central.uh.edu.

University of Massachusetts Amherst, Graduate School, Interdisciplinary Programs, Program in Hospitality and Tourism Management and Business Administration, Amherst, MA 01003. Offers MS/MBA. Part-time programs available. *Entrance requirements:* Additional exam requirements/

recommendations for international students: Required—TOEFL (minimum score 550 paper-based; 213 computer-based; 80 iBT), IELTS (minimum score 6.5). *Application deadline:* For fall admission, 2/1 for domestic and international students. Applications are processed on a rolling basis. Application fee: $50 ($65 for international students). Electronic applications accepted. *Expenses:* Tuition, state resident: full-time $2640. Required fees: $8282. One-time fee: $357 full-time. *Financial support:* Career-related internships or fieldwork, Federal Work-Study, scholarships/grants, traineeships, health care benefits, tuition waivers (full), and unspecified assistantships available. Support available to part-time students. *Unit head:* Dr. Atul Sheel, Graduate Program Director, 413-545-1389, Fax: 413-545-1235. *Application contact:* Jean M. Ames, Supervisor of Admissions, 413-545-0722, Fax: 413-577-0010, E-mail: gradadm@grad.umass.edu.

University of Massachusetts Amherst, Graduate School, Isenberg School of Management, Department of Hospitality and Tourism Management, Amherst, MA 01003. Offers MS, MS/MBA. Part-time programs available. *Faculty:* 12 full-time (3 women). *Students:* 9 full-time (8 women), 6 part-time (3 women), 11 international. Average age 26. 50 applicants, 74% accepted, 8 enrolled. In 2010, 7 master's awarded. *Degree requirements:* For master's, thesis or alternative. *Entrance requirements:* For master's, GMAT. Additional exam requirements/recommendations for international students: Required—TOEFL (minimum score 550 paper-based; 213 computer-based; 80 iBT), IELTS (minimum score 6.5). *Application deadline:* For fall admission, 2/1 for domestic and international students; for spring admission, 10/1 for domestic and international students. Applications are processed on a rolling basis. Application fee: $50 ($65 for international students). Electronic applications accepted. *Expenses:* Tuition, state resident: full-time $2640. Required fees: $8282. One-time fee: $357 full-time. *Financial support:* In 2010–11, 9 teaching assistantships with full tuition reimbursements (averaging $7,438 per year) were awarded; fellowships, research assistantships, career-related internships or fieldwork, Federal Work-Study, scholarships/grants, traineeships, health care benefits, tuition waivers (full), and unspecified assistantships also available. Support available to part-time students. Financial award application deadline: 2/1; financial award applicants required to submit FAFSA. *Unit head:* Dr. Atul Sheel, Graduate Program Director, 413-545-1389, Fax: 413-545-1235. *Application contact:* Jean M. Ames, Supervisor of Admissions, 413-545-0722, Fax: 413-577-0010, E-mail: gradadm@grad.umass.edu.

University of Missouri, Graduate School, College of Agriculture, Food and Natural Resources, Department of Food Science, Columbia, MO 65211. Offers food science (MS, PhD); foods and food systems management (MS); human nutrition (MS). *Faculty:* 17 full-time (4 women), 2 part-time/adjunct (0 women). *Students:* 28 full-time (12 women), 8 part-time (4 women); includes 1 minority (Hispanic/Latino), 19 international. Average age 27. 53 applicants, 40% accepted, 6 enrolled. In 2010, 9 master's, 2 doctorates awarded. Terminal master's awarded for partial completion of doctoral program. *Degree requirements:* For doctorate, comprehensive exam, thesis/dissertation. *Entrance requirements:* For master's, GRE General Test (minimum score: Verbal and Quantitative 1000 with neither section below 400, Analytical 3.5), minimum GPA of 3.0; BS in food science from accredited university; for doctorate, GRE General Test (minimum score: Verbal and Quantitative 1000 with neither section below 400, Analytical 3.5), minimum GPA of 3.0; BS and MS in food science from accredited university. Additional exam requirements/recommendations for international students: Required—TOEFL (minimum score 550 paper-based; 79 iBT). *Application deadline:* For fall admission, 4/1 priority date for domestic students; for winter admission, 10/1 priority date for domestic students. Applications are processed on a rolling basis. Application fee: $45 ($60 for international students). Electronic applications accepted. *Financial support:* Fellowships, research assistantships with tuition reimbursements, teaching assistantships with tuition reimbursements, institutionally sponsored loans, scholarships/grants, health care benefits, and unspecified assistantships available. Support available to part-time students. *Faculty research:* Food chemistry, food analysis, food microbiology, food engineering and process control, functional foods, meat science and processing technology. *Unit head:* Dr. Jinglu Tan, Department Chair, 573-882-2369, E-mail: tanj@missouri.edu. *Application contact:* JoAnn Lewis, 573-882-4113, E-mail: lewisj@missouri.edu.

University of Nevada, Las Vegas, Graduate College, William F. Harrah College of Hotel Administration, Program in Hotel Administration, Las Vegas, NV 89154-6013. Offers hospitality administration (MHA, PhD); hotel administration (MS). MHA program also offered in Singapore. Part-time programs available. Postbaccalaureate distance learning degree programs offered (no on-campus study). *Faculty:* 36 full-time (14 women), 7 part-time/adjunct (3 women). *Students:* 81 full-time (46 women), 85 part-time (43 women); includes 57 minority (1 Black or African American, non-Hispanic/Latino; 1 American Indian or Alaska Native, non-Hispanic/Latino; 2 Asian, non-Hispanic/Latino; 5 Hispanic/Latino; 2 Native Hawaiian or other Pacific Islander, non-Hispanic/Latino; 46 Two or more races, non-Hispanic/Latino), 60

international. Average age 33. 169 applicants, 54% accepted, 65 enrolled. In 2010, 39 master's, 5 doctorates awarded. *Degree requirements:* For master's, comprehensive exam, thesis (for some programs), professional paper; for doctorate, comprehensive exam, thesis/dissertation, dissertation defense, seminar. *Entrance requirements:* Additional exam requirements/recommendations for international students: Required—TOEFL (minimum score 550 paper-based; 213 computer-based; 80 iBT), IELTS (minimum score 7). *Application deadline:* For fall admission, 3/1 priority date for domestic and international students; for spring admission, 10/1 priority date for domestic and international students. Applications are processed on a rolling basis. Application fee: $60 ($95 for international students). Electronic applications accepted. *Expenses:* Tuition, area resident: Part-time $239.50 per credit. Tuition, state resident: part-time $239.50 per credit. Tuition, nonresident: part-time $503 per credit. Required fees: $108 per semester. Tuition and fees vary according to course load, program and reciprocity agreements. *Financial support:* In 2010–11, 27 students received support, including 26 research assistantships with partial tuition reimbursements available (averaging $11,961 per year), 1 teaching assistantship with partial tuition reimbursement available (averaging $12,000 per year); institutionally sponsored loans, scholarships/grants, health care benefits, and unspecified assistantships also available. Financial award application deadline: 3/1. *Faculty research:* Sustainable development and green strategies, self-service technology applications, branding and brand equity, employee engagement and leadership, pricing and loyalty in food-service operations. Total annual research expenditures: $257,351. *Unit head:* Dr. Pearl Brewer, Chair/Professor, 702-895-3643, Fax: 702-895-4872, E-mail: pearl.brewer@unlv.edu. *Application contact:* Graduate College Admissions Evaluator, 702-895-3320, Fax: 702-895-4180, E-mail: gradcollege@unlv.edu.

University of North Texas, Toulouse Graduate School, School of Merchandising and Hospitality Management, Denton, TX 76203. Offers hospitality management (MS); merchandising (MS). Part-time programs available. Postbaccalaureate distance learning degree programs offered (no on-campus study). *Degree requirements:* For master's, comprehensive exam, thesis or alternative. *Entrance requirements:* For master's, GRE General Test or GMAT, minimum GPA of 2.8, course work in major area, 3 references, resume. Additional exam requirements/recommendations for international students: Recommended—TOEFL (minimum score 550 paper-based; 213 computer-based; 79 iBT). *Application deadline:* Applications are processed on a rolling basis. Electronic applications accepted. *Expenses:* Tuition, state resident: full-time $4298; part-time $239 per credit hour. Tuition, nonresident: full-time $10,782; part-time $549 per credit hour. Required fees: $1292; $270 per credit hour. *Financial support:* Fellowships, research assistantships, teaching assistantships, career-related internships or fieldwork, Federal Work-Study, and institutionally sponsored loans available. Financial award application deadline: 4/1; financial award applicants required to submit FAFSA. *Faculty research:* Management, hospitality, merchandising, globalization, consumer behavior and experiences. *Application contact:* Coordinator, 940-565-4757, Fax: 940-565-4348, E-mail: kennon@smhm.unt.edu.

Virginia Polytechnic Institute and State University, Graduate School, Pamplin College of Business, Department of Hospitality and Tourism Management, Blacksburg, VA 24061. Offers MS, PhD. *Faculty:* 12 full-time (4 women), 1 part-time/adjunct (0 women). *Students:* 19 full-time (13 women), 5 part-time (3 women); includes 1 Black or African American, non-Hispanic/Latino; 3 Asian, non-Hispanic/Latino, 10 international. Average age 29. 25 applicants, 36% accepted, 8 enrolled. In 2010, 2 master's, 4 doctorates awarded. *Degree requirements:* For master's, comprehensive exam (for some programs), thesis (for some programs); for doctorate, comprehensive exam (for some programs), thesis/dissertation (for some programs). *Entrance requirements:* For master's and doctorate, GRE. Additional exam requirements/recommendations for international students: Required—TOEFL (minimum score 550 paper-based; 213 computer-based). *Application deadline:* For fall admission, 7/1 for domestic and international students; for spring admission, 12/1 for domestic and international students. Applications are processed on a rolling basis. Application fee: $65. Electronic applications accepted. *Expenses:* Tuition, state resident: full-time $9399; part-time $488 per credit hour. Tuition, nonresident: full-time $17,854; part-time $957.75 per credit hour. Required fees: $1534. Full-time tuition and fees vary according to program. *Financial support:* In 2010–11, 1 research assistantship with full tuition reimbursement (averaging $12,053 per year), 3 teaching assistantships with full tuition reimbursements (averaging $12,861 per year) were awarded; career-related internships or fieldwork, Federal Work-Study, scholarships/grants, health care benefits, and unspecified assistantships also available. Financial award application deadline: 1/15. *Faculty research:* Human resource management, service management, marketing, strategy and finance tourist behavior. Total annual research expenditures: $102,947. *Unit head:* Dr. Rick R. Perdue, UNIT HEAD, 540-231-3287, Fax: 540-231-8313, E-mail: perduerr@vt.edu. *Application contact:* Nancy McGehee, Contact, 540-231-1201, Fax: 540-231-8313, E-mail: nmcgehee@vt.edu.

TRAVEL AND TOURISM

Arizona State University, College of Public Programs, School of Community Resources and Development, Phoenix, AZ 85004-0685. Offers community resources and development (PhD); nonprofit leadership and management (Graduate Certificate); nonprofit studies (MNpS); recreation and tourism studies (MS). Part-time and evening/weekend programs available. *Faculty:* 19 full-time (8 women), 2 part-time/adjunct (both women). *Students:* 53 full-time (35 women), 72 part-time (55 women); includes 28 minority (6 Black or African American, non-Hispanic/Latino; 5 American Indian or Alaska Native, non-Hispanic/Latino; 1 Asian, non-Hispanic/Latino; 16 Hispanic/Latino), 12 international. Average age 33. 90 applicants, 73% accepted, 45 enrolled. In 2010, 37 master's, 3 other advanced degrees awarded. Terminal master's awarded for partial completion of doctoral program. *Degree requirements:* For master's, thesis or alternative, interactive Program of Study (iPOS) submitted before completing 50 percent of required credit hours; for doctorate, comprehensive exam, thesis/dissertation, interactive Program of Study (iPOS) submitted before completing 50 percent of required credit hours. *Entrance requirements:* For master's and doctorate, GRE, minimum GPA of 3.0 or equivalent in last 2 years of work leading to bachelor's degree. Additional exam requirements/recommendations for international students: Required—TOEFL, IELTS, or Pearson Test of English. *Application deadline:* For fall admission, 3/1 for domestic and international students; for spring admission, 10/1 for domestic and international students. Application fee: $70 ($90 for international students). Electronic applications accepted. *Expenses:* Contact institution. *Financial support:* In 2010–11, 6 research assistantships with full and partial tuition reimbursements (averaging $8,949 per year), 5 teaching assistantships with full and partial tuition reimbursements (averaging $9,774 per year) were awarded; fellowships with full tuition reimbursements, career-related internships or fieldwork, Federal Work-Study, institutionally sponsored loans, scholarships/grants, and tuition waivers (full and partial) also available. Financial award application deadline: 3/1; financial award applicants required to submit FAFSA. Total annual research expenditures: $2.5 million. *Unit head:* Dr. Kathleen Andereck, Director, 602-496-1056, E-mail: kandereck@asu.edu. *Application contact:* Graduate Admissions, 480-965-6113.

Boston University, Metropolitan College, Department of Administrative Sciences, Boston, MA 02215. Offers banking and financial management (MSM); business continuity in emergency management (MSM); economics development and tourism management (MSAS); electronic commerce, systems, and technology (MSAS); financial economics (MSAS); innovation and technology (MSAS); insurance management (MSM); international market management (MSM); multinational commerce (MSAS); project management (MSM). *Accreditation:* AACSB. Part-time and evening/weekend programs available. Postbaccalaureate distance learning degree programs offered (no on-campus study). *Faculty:* 14 full-time (2 women), 22 part-time/adjunct (2 women). *Students:* 107 full-time (51 women), 786 part-time (356 women); includes 130 minority (55 Black or African American, non-Hispanic/Latino; 1 American Indian or Alaska Native, non-Hispanic/Latino; 30 Asian, non-Hispanic/Latino; 36 Hispanic/Latino; 1 Native Hawaiian or other Pacific Islander, non-Hispanic/Latino; 7 Two or more races, non-Hispanic/Latino), 175 international. Average age 33. 398 applicants, 87% accepted, 180 enrolled. In 2010, 154 master's awarded. *Degree requirements:* For master's, thesis optional. *Entrance requirements:* For master's, 1 year of work experience, minimum GPA of 3.0. Additional exam requirements/recommendations for international students: Required—TOEFL (minimum score 560 paper-based; 220 computer-based; 84 iBT). *Application deadline:* Applications are processed on a rolling basis. Application fee: $70. Electronic applications accepted. *Expenses:* Tuition: Full-time $39,314; part-time $1228 per credit. Required fees: $40 per semester. *Financial support:* In 2010–11, 15 students received support, including 7 research assistantships with partial tuition reimbursements available (averaging $10,000 per year); career-related internships or fieldwork, Federal Work-Study, and unspecified assistantships also available. *Faculty research:* International business, innovative process. *Unit head:* Dr. Kip Becker, Chairman, 617-353-3016, E-mail: adminsc@bu.edu. *Application contact:* Lucille Dicker, Administrative Sciences Department, 617-353-3016, E-mail: adminsc@bu.edu.

California State University, East Bay, Office of Academic Programs and Graduate Studies, College of Education and Allied Studies, Department of Hospitality, Recreation and Tourism, Hayward, CA 94542-3000. Offers recreation and tourism (MS). Part-time and evening/weekend programs available. Postbaccalaureate distance learning degree programs offered (no on-campus study). *Faculty:* 7 full-time (4 women). *Students:* 29 full-time (20 women), 12 part-time (7 women); includes 6 Black or African American, non-Hispanic/Latino; 5 Asian, non-Hispanic/Latino; 5 Hispanic/Latino; 2 Two or more races, non-Hispanic/Latino, 1 international. Average age 33. 36 applicants, 69% accepted, 0 enrolled. In 2010, 5 master's awarded. *Degree requirements:* For master's, thesis optional. *Entrance requirements:* For master's, minimum GPA of 2.75; 2 years' related work experience. Additional exam requirements/recommendations for international students: Required—TOEFL (minimum score 550 paper-based; 237 computer-based). *Application deadline:* For fall admission, 6/30 for domestic and international students. Applications are processed on a rolling basis. Application fee: $55. Electronic applications

accepted. *Financial support:* Federal Work-Study, institutionally sponsored loans, and scholarships/grants available. Support available to part-time students. Financial award application deadline: 3/2; financial award applicants required to submit FAFSA. *Unit head:* Dr. Melany Spielman, Chair, 510-885-3043, E-mail: melany.spielman@csueastbay.edu. *Application contact:* Dr. Donna Wiley, Interim Associate Director, 510-885-2928, Fax: 510-885-4777, E-mail: donna.wiley@csueastbay.edu.

California State University, Fullerton, Graduate Studies, College of Communications, Department of Communications, Fullerton, CA 92834-9480. Offers advertising (MA); communications (MFA); entertainment and tourism (MA); journalism (MA); public relations (MA). Part-time programs available. *Students:* 24 full-time (15 women), 39 part-time (27 women); includes 2 Two or more races, non-Hispanic/Latino. Average age 29. 119 applicants, 40% accepted, 29 enrolled. In 2010, 30 master's awarded. *Degree requirements:* For master's, project or thesis. *Entrance requirements:* For master's, GRE General Test. Application fee: $55. *Financial support:* Teaching assistantships, career-related internships or fieldwork, Federal Work-Study, institutionally sponsored loans, and scholarships/grants available. Support available to part-time students. Financial award application deadline: 3/1; financial award applicants required to submit FAFSA. *Unit head:* Dr. Tony Fellow, Chair, 657-278-3517. *Application contact:* Coordinator, 657-278-3832.

Clemson University, Graduate School, College of Health, Education, and Human Development, Department of Parks, Recreation, and Tourism Management, Clemson, SC 29634. Offers MPRTM, MS, PhD. Part-time programs available. Postbaccalaureate distance learning degree programs offered (no on-campus study). *Faculty:* 16 full-time (6 women), 1 (woman) part-time/adjunct. *Students:* 51 full-time (29 women), 8 part-time (5 women); includes 1 Black or African American, non-Hispanic/Latino; 1 Hispanic/Latino, 17 international. Average age 32. 74 applicants, 49% accepted, 22 enrolled. In 2010, 11 master's, 11 doctorates awarded. *Degree requirements:* For master's, thesis (for some programs); for doctorate, thesis/dissertation. *Entrance requirements:* For master's, GRE General Test, minimum undergraduate GPA of 3.0; for doctorate, GRE General Test, minimum graduate GPA of 3.0. Additional exam requirements/recommendations for international students: Required—TOEFL. *Application deadline:* For fall admission, 5/1 priority date for domestic students; for spring admission, 10/1 for domestic students. Applications are processed on a rolling basis. Application fee: $70 ($80 for international students). Electronic applications accepted. *Expenses:* Tuition, state resident: full-time $6492; part-time $400 per credit hour. Tuition, non-resident: full-time $13,634; part-time $800 per credit hour. Required fees: $262 per semester. Part-time tuition and fees vary according to course load and program. *Financial support:* In 2010–11, 43 students received support, including 43 teaching assistantships with partial tuition reimbursements available (averaging $8,737 per year); fellowships with full and partial tuition reimbursements available, research assistantships with partial tuition reimbursements available, career-related internships or fieldwork, scholarships/grants, health care benefits, tuition waivers (partial), and unspecified assistantships also available. Support available to part-time students. Financial award application deadline: 1/15; financial award applicants required to submit FAFSA. *Faculty research:* Recreation resource management, leisure behavior, therapeutic recreation, community leisure services. Total annual research expenditures: $339,871. *Unit head:* Dr. Brett A. Wright, Chair, 864-656-3036, Fax: 864-656-2226, E-mail: wright@clemson.edu. *Application contact:* Dr. Denise M. Anderson, Graduate Coordinator, 864-656-5679, Fax: 864-656-2226, E-mail: dander2@clemson.edu.

Eastern Michigan University, Graduate School, College of Arts and Sciences, Department of Geography and Geology, Program in Historic Preservation, Ypsilanti, MI 48197. Offers heritage interpretation and tourism (MS); historic preservation (MS, Graduate Certificate). Part-time and evening/weekend programs available. Postbaccalaureate distance learning degree programs offered (minimal on-campus study). *Students:* 17 full-time (14 women), 59 part-time (44 women); includes 2 minority (both Black or African American, non-Hispanic/Latino), 1 international. Average age 35. In 2010, 14 master's, 4 other advanced degrees awarded. *Entrance requirements:* Additional exam requirements/recommendations for international students: Required—TOEFL. *Application deadline:* Applications are processed on a rolling basis. Application fee: $35. *Financial support:* Fellowships, research assistantships with full tuition reimbursements, teaching assistantships with full tuition reimbursements, career-related internships or fieldwork, Federal Work-Study, institutionally sponsored loans, scholarships/grants, tuition waivers (partial), and unspecified assistantships available. Support available to part-time students. Financial award applicants required to submit FAFSA. *Application contact:* Dr. Ted Ligibel, Program Advisor, 734-487-0232, Fax: 734-487-6979, E-mail: tligibel@emich.edu.

Florida Atlantic University, College of Design and Social Inquiry, School of Urban and Regional Planning, Boca Raton, FL 33431-0991. Offers economic development and tourism (Certificate); environmental planning (Certificate); sustainable community planning (Certificate); urban and regional planning (MURP); visual planning technology (Certificate). *Accreditation:* ACSP. Part-time and evening/weekend programs available. *Faculty:* 8 full-time (5 women), 2 part-time/adjunct (1 woman). *Students:* 24 full-time (18 women), 12 part-time (1 woman); includes 17 minority (4 Black or African American, non-Hispanic/Latino; 1 American Indian or Alaska Native, non-Hispanic/Latino; 12 Hispanic/Latino), 2 international. Average age 30. 55 applicants, 35% accepted, 12 enrolled. In 2010, 13 master's awarded. *Entrance requirements:* For master's, GRE General Test, minimum GPA of 3.0. Additional exam requirements/recommendations for international students: Required—TOEFL. *Application deadline:* For fall admission, 7/1 priority date for domestic students, 2/15 for international students; for spring admission, 11/1 priority date for domestic students, 7/15 for international students. Applications are processed on a rolling basis. Application fee: $30. *Expenses:* Tuition, area resident: Part-time $319.96 per credit. Tuition, state resident: part-time $319.96 per credit. Tuition, nonresident: part-time $926.42 per credit. *Financial support:* Fellowships with full tuition reimbursements, research assistantships, career-related internships or fieldwork, Federal Work-Study, institutionally sponsored loans, and tuition waivers (partial) available. Financial award application deadline: 4/1. *Faculty research:* Growth management, urban design, computer applications/geographical information systems, environmental planning. *Unit head:* Dr. Jaap Vos, Chair, 954-762-5653, Fax: 954-762-5673, E-mail: jvos@fau.edu. *Application contact:* Dr. Jaap Vos, Chair, 954-762-5653, Fax: 954-762-5673, E-mail: jvos@fau.edu.

The George Washington University, School of Business, Department of Tourism and Hospitality Management, Washington, DC 20052. Offers event and meeting management (MTA); event management (Professional Certificate); hospitality management (MTA, Professional Certificate); sports business management (Professional Certificate); sports management (MTA); sustainable destination management (MTA); tourism administration (MTA); tourism and hospitality management (MBA); tourism destination management (Professional Certificate). Part-time programs available. Postbaccalaureate distance learning degree programs offered. *Faculty:* 9 full-time (5 women), 6 part-time/adjunct (4 women). *Students:* 84 full-time (62 women), 107 part-time (77 women); includes 27 Black or African American, non-Hispanic/Latino; 2 American Indian or Alaska Native, non-Hispanic/Latino; 5 Asian, non-Hispanic/Latino; 9 Hispanic/Latino, 38 international. Average age 30. 152 applicants, 74% accepted. In 2010, 69 master's awarded. *Degree requirements:* For master's, comprehensive exam, thesis. *Entrance requirements:* For master's, GRE General Test. Additional exam requirements/recommendations for international students: Required—TOEFL. *Application deadline:* For fall admission, 4/1 priority date for domestic students; for spring admission, 10/1 for domestic students. Applications are processed on a rolling basis. Application fee: $75. *Financial support:* In 2010–11, 32 students received support; fellowships, teaching assistantships, career-related internships or fieldwork, Federal Work-Study, institutionally sponsored loans, and tuition waivers (partial) available. Financial award application deadline: 4/1. *Faculty research:* Tourism policy, tourism impact forecasting, geotourism. *Unit head:* Susan M. Phillips, Dean, 202-994-6380, E-mail: gwsbdean@gwu.edu. *Application contact:* Kristin Williams, Assistant Vice President for Graduate and Special Enrollment Management, 202-994-0467, Fax: 202-994-0371, E-mail: ksw@gwu.edu.

Indiana University Bloomington, School of Health, Physical Education and Recreation, Department of Recreation, Park, and Tourism Studies, Bloomington, IN 47405-7000. Offers leisure behavior (PhD); outdoor recreation (MS); recreation (Re Dir); recreation administration (MS); recreational sports administration (MS); therapeutic recreation (MS); tourism management (MS). *Faculty:* 16 full-time (6 women), 2 part-time/adjunct (both women). *Students:* 63 full-time (36 women), 23 part-time (18 women); includes 3 Black or African American, non-Hispanic/Latino; 1 Asian, non-Hispanic/Latino; 2 Hispanic/Latino; 3 Two or more races, non-Hispanic/Latino, 20 international. Average age 31. 62 applicants, 69% accepted, 24 enrolled. In 2010, 14 master's, 2 doctorates awarded. Terminal master's awarded for partial completion of doctoral program. *Degree requirements:* For master's and Re Dir, thesis optional; for doctorate, thesis/dissertation. *Entrance requirements:* For master's, GRE General Test, minimum GPA of 2.8; for doctorate, GRE General Test, minimum GPA of 3.0 (undergraduate), 3.5 (graduate). Additional exam requirements/recommendations for international students: Required—TOEFL. *Application deadline:* For fall admission, 1/1 for international students; for spring admission, 9/1 for international students. Applications are processed on a rolling basis. Application fee: $55 ($65 for international students). *Financial support:* Fellowships, research assistantships, teaching assistantships with partial tuition reimbursements, career-related internships or fieldwork, Federal Work-Study, institutionally sponsored loans, scholarships/grants, tuition waivers (partial), unspecified assistantships, and fee remissions available. Financial award application deadline: 3/1. *Faculty research:* Leisure counseling, gerontology, special populations, planning and development. *Unit head:* Bryce Smedley, Graduate Student Specialist, 812-855-4711, E-mail: bsmedley@indiana.edu. *Application contact:* Program Office, 812-855-1232, Fax: 812-855-3998.

Kent State University, Graduate School of Education, Health, and Human Services, School of Foundations, Leadership and Administration, Program in Hospitality and Tourism Management, Kent, OH 44242-0001. Offers MS. Part-time programs available. *Faculty:* 6 full-time (4 women), 3 part-time/adjunct (1 woman). *Students:* 14 full-time (8 women), 2 part-time (1 woman). 23 applicants, 57% accepted. *Degree requirements:* For master's, thesis (for some programs). *Entrance requirements:* For master's, GRE, minimum GPA

of 3.0, 3 letters of recommendation. Additional exam requirements/recommendations for international students: Required—TOEFL. *Application deadline:* Applications are processed on a rolling basis. Application fee: $30 ($60 for international students). Electronic applications accepted. *Expenses:* Tuition, state resident: full-time $7866; part-time $437 per credit hour. Tuition, nonresident: full-time $14,022; part-time $779 per credit hour. *Financial support:* In 2010–11, 4 students received support, including 1 fellowship (averaging $8,500 per year), research assistantships with full tuition reimbursements available (averaging $8,500 per year); Federal Work-Study, scholarships/grants, unspecified assistantships, and 3 administrative assistantships (averaging $8,500 per year) also available. Financial award application deadline: 2/1; financial award applicants required to submit FAFSA. *Faculty research:* Training human service workers, health care services for older adults, early adolescent development, care giving arrangements with aging families, peace and war23. *Unit head:* Barb Scheule, Coordinator, 330-672-3796, E-mail: bscheule@kent.edu. *Application contact:* Nancy Miller, Academic Program Coordinator, 330-672-2576, Fax: 330-672-9162, E-mail: ogs@kent.edu.

New York University, School of Continuing and Professional Studies, The Preston Robert Tisch Center for Hospitality, Tourism, and Sports Management, Program in Tourism Management, New York, NY 10012-1019. Offers MS, Advanced Certificate. Part-time and evening/weekend programs available. *Faculty:* 12 full-time (5 women), 12 part-time/adjunct (4 women). *Students:* 4 full-time (3 women), 6 part-time (2 women). Average age 32. 39 applicants, 41% accepted, 8 enrolled. In 2010, 5 master's, 1 other advanced degree awarded. *Degree requirements:* For master's, thesis. *Entrance requirements:* For master's, GMAT or GRE General Test (for recent graduates), resume, 2 letters of recommendation, essay, professional experience. Additional exam requirements/recommendations for international students: Required—TOEFL (minimum score 600 paper-based; 250 computer-based; 100 iBT), TWE. *Application deadline:* For fall admission, 2/1 priority date for domestic and international students; for spring admission, 10/15 priority date for domestic students, 8/15 priority date for international students. Applications are processed on a rolling basis. Application fee: $75. Electronic applications accepted. *Financial support:* In 2010–11, 6 students received support, including 6 fellowships (averaging $2,666 per year); research assistantships, career-related internships or fieldwork, Federal Work-Study, institutionally sponsored loans, and scholarships/grants also available. Support available to part-time students. Financial award application deadline: 3/1; financial award applicants required to submit FAFSA. *Faculty research:* Tourism planning for national parks and protected areas, leadership and organizational behavior issues. *Unit head:* Bjorn Hanson, Divisional Dean, Clinical Professor, HVS Chair, 212-998-9102, Fax: 212-995-4678, E-mail: lalia.rach@nyu.edu. *Application contact:* Sandra Dove-Lowther, Office of Admissions, 212-992-9087, Fax: 212-995-4676, E-mail: sd2@nyu.edu.

Old Dominion University, Darden College of Education, Program in Physical Education, Recreation and Tourism Studies Emphasis, Norfolk, VA 23529. Offers MS Ed. Part-time and evening/weekend programs available. Postbaccalaureate distance learning degree programs offered (minimal on-campus study). *Faculty:* 1 full-time (0 women). *Students:* 4 full-time (all women), 2 part-time (1 woman); includes 2 minority (1 Black or African American, non-Hispanic/Latino; 1 Asian, non-Hispanic/Latino). Average age 32. 10 applicants, 60% accepted, 5 enrolled. In 2010, 7 master's awarded. *Degree requirements:* For master's, comprehensive exam, thesis or alternative, internship, research project. *Entrance requirements:* For master's, GRE, minimum GPA of 2.8 overall, 3.0 in major. Additional exam requirements/recommendations for international students: Required—TOEFL (minimum score 500 paper-based; 200 computer-based). *Application deadline:* For fall admission, 6/1 for domestic students. Application fee: $40. Electronic applications accepted. *Expenses:* Tuition, state resident: full-time $8592; part-time $358 per credit. Tuition, nonresident: full-time $21,672; part-time $903 per credit. Required fees: $119 per semester. One-time fee: $50. *Financial support:* In 2010–11, 1 student received support, including 1 research assistantship with partial tuition reimbursement available (averaging $9,000 per year); career-related internships or fieldwork, scholarships/grants, and unspecified assistantships also available. Financial award application deadline: 3/1; financial award applicants required to submit FAFSA. *Faculty research:* Ethnicity and recreation, recreation programming, recreation and resiliency, tourism development, dog parks, sense of community and urban parks. Total annual research expenditures: $12,000. *Unit head:* Dr. Edwin Gomez, Graduate Program Director, 757-683-4995, Fax: 757-683-4270, E-mail: egomez@odu.edu. *Application contact:* Dr. Edwin Gomez, Graduate Program Director, 757-683-4995, Fax: 757-683-4270, E-mail: egomez@odu.edu.

Penn State University Park, Graduate School, College of Health and Human Development, Department of Recreation, Park and Tourism Management, State College, University Park, PA 16802-1503. Offers MS, PhD.

Rochester Institute of Technology, Graduate Enrollment Services, College of Applied Science and Technology, Department of Hospitality and Service Management, Program in Hospitality-Tourism Management, Rochester, NY 14623-5603. Offers MS. *Students:* 12 full-time (8 women), 5 part-time (3 women); includes 1 Asian, non-Hispanic/Latino, 13 international. Average age 27. 29 applicants, 86% accepted, 10 enrolled. In 2010, 6 master's awarded. *Degree requirements:* For master's, thesis or project. *Entrance requirements:*

For master's, minimum GPA of 3.0. Additional exam requirements/recommendations for international students: Required—TOEFL (minimum score 550 paper-based; 213 computer-based; 79 iBT) or IELTS (minimum score 6.5). *Application deadline:* For fall admission, 2/15 priority date for domestic and international students; for winter admission, 11/1 priority date for domestic students, 10/1 priority date for international students; for spring admission, 2/1 priority date for domestic students, 1/1 priority date for international students. Applications are processed on a rolling basis. *Expenses:* Tuition: Full-time $33,234; part-time $924 per credit hour. Required fees: $219. *Financial support:* In 2010–11, 6 students received support; research assistantships with partial tuition reimbursements available, teaching assistantships with partial tuition reimbursements available, career-related internships or fieldwork, scholarships/grants, and unspecified assistantships available. Support available to part-time students. Financial award application deadline: 2/15; financial award applicants required to submit FAFSA. *Unit head:* Dr. Linda Underhill, Chair, 585-475-7359, Fax: 585-475-5099, E-mail: lmuism@rit.edu. *Application contact:* Diane Ellison, Assistant Vice President, Graduate Enrollment Services, 585-475-2229, Fax: 585-475-7164, E-mail: gradinfo@rit.edu.

Rochester Institute of Technology, Graduate Enrollment Services, College of Applied Science and Technology, Department of Hospitality and Service Management, Program in Service Leadership and Innovation, Rochester, NY 14623-5603. Offers MS. Part-time and evening/weekend programs available. *Students:* 15 full-time (10 women), 69 part-time (34 women); includes 1 Black or African American, non-Hispanic/Latino; 1 American Indian or Alaska Native, non-Hispanic/Latino, 10 international. Average age 29. 82 applicants, 54% accepted, 21 enrolled. In 2010, 31 master's awarded. *Degree requirements:* For master's, thesis or alternative. *Entrance requirements:* For master's, minimum GPA of 3.0. Additional exam requirements/recommendations for international students: Required—TOEFL (minimum score 550 paper-based; 213 computer-based; 79 iBT) or IELTS (minimum score 6.5). *Application deadline:* For fall admission, 2/15 priority date for domestic and international students; for winter admission, 11/1 for domestic and international students; for spring admission, 2/1 for domestic and international students. Applications are processed on a rolling basis. *Expenses:* Tuition: Full-time $33,234; part-time $924 per credit hour. Required fees: $219. *Financial support:* In 2010–11, 23 students received support; research assistantships with partial tuition reimbursements available, teaching assistantships with partial tuition reimbursements available, career-related internships or fieldwork, institutionally sponsored loans, scholarships/grants, and unspecified assistantships available. Support available to part-time students. Financial award application deadline: 2/15; financial award applicants required to submit FAFSA. *Faculty research:* Global resource development, service/product innovation and implementation. *Unit head:* Dr. James Jacobs, Graduate Program Director, 585-475-6017, E-mail: jwjism@rit.edu. *Application contact:* Diane Ellison, Assistant Vice President, Graduate Enrollment Services, 585-475-2229, Fax: 585-475-7164, E-mail: gradinfo@rit.edu.

Temple University, School of Tourism and Hospitality Management, Program in Tourism and Hospitality Management, Philadelphia, PA 19122-6096. Offers MTHM. Part-time and evening/weekend programs available. *Faculty:* 9 full-time (4 women). *Students:* 12 full-time (10 women), 7 part-time (all women); includes 1 Black or African American, non-Hispanic/Latino; 1 American Indian or Alaska Native, non-Hispanic/Latino; 3 Asian, non-Hispanic/Latino, 1 international. 62 applicants, 31% accepted, 7 enrolled. In 2010, 6 master's awarded. *Entrance requirements:* For master's, GRE General Test or MAT, minimum of 2 years professional experience, minimum undergraduate GPA of 3.0. Additional exam requirements/recommendations for international students: Required—TOEFL (minimum score 550 paper-based; 213 computer-based; 79 iBT). *Application deadline:* For fall admission, 4/1 priority date for domestic students, 12/15 for international students; for spring admission, 9/30 priority date for domestic students, 8/1 for international students. Application fee: $50. Electronic applications accepted. *Financial support:* Teaching assistantships available. Financial award application deadline: 1/15; financial award applicants required to submit FAFSA. *Unit head:* Dr. Wesley Roehl, Director, 215-204-5861, E-mail: wroehl@temple.edu. *Application contact:* Dr. Wesley Roehl, Director, 215-204-5861, E-mail: wroehl@temple.edu.

University of Central Florida, Rosen College of Hospitality Management, Orlando, FL 32816. Offers hospitality and tourism management (MS). *Faculty:* 35 full-time (12 women), 29 part-time/adjunct (12 women). *Students:* 45 full-time (30 women), 40 part-time (28 women); includes 3 Black or African American, non-Hispanic/Latino; 4 Asian, non-Hispanic/Latino; 3 Hispanic/Latino; 1 Two or more races, non-Hispanic/Latino, 13 international. Average age 28. 69 applicants, 58% accepted, 28 enrolled. In 2010, 25 master's awarded. *Degree requirements:* For master's, thesis or alternative. *Entrance requirements:* For master's, GMAT or GRE, minimum GPA of 3.0 in last 60 hours. Additional exam requirements/recommendations for international students: Required—TOEFL. *Application deadline:* For fall admission, 2/1 for domestic students. Application fee: $30. Electronic applications accepted. *Expenses:* Tuition, state resident: part-time $256.56 per credit hour. Tuition, nonresident: part-time $1011.52 per credit hour. Part-time tuition and fees vary according to program. *Financial support:* In 2010–11, 1 student received support, including 1 fellowship with partial tuition reimbursement available

(averaging $10,000 per year). *Unit head:* Dr. Abraham C. Pizam, Dean, 407-903-8010, E-mail: apizam@mail.ucf.edu. *Application contact:* Dr. Abraham C. Pizam, Dean, 407-903-8010, E-mail: apizam@mail.ucf.edu.

University of Hawaii at Manoa, Graduate Division, School of Travel Industry Management, Honolulu, HI 96822. Offers MS. Part-time programs available. *Faculty:* 8 full-time (3 women). *Students:* 10 full-time (7 women), 2 part-time (1 woman); includes 4 minority (3 Asian, non-Hispanic/Latino; 1 Two or more races, non-Hispanic/Latino), 2 international. Average age 31. 56 applicants, 32% accepted, 8 enrolled. In 2010, 2 master's awarded. *Degree requirements:* For master's, thesis optional. *Entrance requirements:* For master's, GRE General Test, minimum GPA of 3.0. Additional exam requirements/recommendations for international students: Required—TOEFL (minimum score 560 paper-based; 220 computer-based; 83 iBT), IELTS (minimum score 5). *Application deadline:* For fall admission, 3/1 for domestic and international students. Applications are processed on a rolling basis. Application fee: $60. Electronic applications accepted. *Financial support:* In 2010–11, 1 fellowship with partial tuition reimbursement (averaging $6,000 per year) was awarded; career-related internships or fieldwork, scholarships/grants, tuition waivers (full and partial), and student assistantships also available. Financial award application deadline: 3/1. *Faculty research:* Travel information technology, tourism development and policy, transportation management and policy, hospitality management, sustainable tourism development. Total annual research expenditures: $85,000. *Application contact:* Dexter J. L. Choy, Graduate Chair, 808-956-9840, Fax: 808-956-5378, E-mail: djlchoy@hawaii.edu.

University of Massachusetts Amherst, Graduate School, Interdisciplinary Programs, Program in Hospitality and Tourism Management and Business Administration, Amherst, MA 01003. Offers MS/MBA. Part-time programs available. *Entrance requirements:* Additional exam requirements/recommendations for international students: Required—TOEFL (minimum score 550 paper-based; 213 computer-based; 80 iBT), IELTS (minimum score 6.5). *Application deadline:* For fall admission, 2/1 for domestic and international students. Applications are processed on a rolling basis. Application fee: $50 ($65 for international students). Electronic applications accepted. *Expenses:* Tuition, state resident: full-time $2640. Required fees: $8282. One-time fee: $357 full-time. *Financial support:* Career-related internships or fieldwork, Federal Work-Study, scholarships/grants, traineeships, health care benefits, tuition waivers (full), and unspecified assistantships available. Support available to part-time students. *Unit head:* Dr. Atul Sheel, Graduate Program Director, 413-545-1389, Fax: 413-545-1235. *Application contact:* Jean M. Ames, Supervisor of Admissions, 413-545-0722, Fax: 413-577-0010, E-mail: gradadm@grad.umass.edu.

University of Massachusetts Amherst, Graduate School, Isenberg School of Management, Department of Hospitality and Tourism Management, Amherst, MA 01003. Offers MS, MS/MBA. Part-time programs available. *Faculty:* 12 full-time (3 women). *Students:* 9 full-time (8 women), 6 part-time (3 women), 11 international. Average age 26. 50 applicants, 74% accepted, 8 enrolled. In 2010, 7 master's awarded. *Degree requirements:* For master's, thesis or alternative. *Entrance requirements:* For master's, GMAT. Additional exam requirements/recommendations for international students: Required—TOEFL (minimum score 550 paper-based; 213 computer-based; 80 iBT), IELTS (minimum score 6.5). *Application deadline:* For fall admission, 2/1 for domestic and international students; for spring admission, 10/1 for domestic and international students. Applications are processed on a rolling basis. Application fee: $50 ($65 for international students). Electronic applications accepted. *Expenses:* Tuition, state resident: full-time $2640. Required fees: $8282. One-time fee: $357 full-time. *Financial support:* In 2010–11, 9 teaching assistantships with full tuition reimbursements (averaging $7,438 per year) were awarded; fellowships, research assistantships, career-related internships or fieldwork, Federal Work-Study, scholarships/grants, traineeships, health care benefits, tuition waivers (full), and unspecified assistantships also available. Support available to part-time students. Financial award application deadline: 2/1; financial award applicants required to submit FAFSA. *Unit head:* Dr. Atul Sheel, Graduate Program Director, 413-545-1389, Fax: 413-545-1235. *Application contact:* Jean M. Ames, Supervisor of Admissions, 413-545-0722, Fax: 413-577-0010, E-mail: gradadm@grad.umass.edu.

Virginia Polytechnic Institute and State University, Graduate School, Pamplin College of Business, Department of Hospitality and Tourism Management, Blacksburg, VA 24061. Offers MS, PhD. *Faculty:* 12 full-time (4 women), 1 part-time/adjunct (0 women). *Students:* 19 full-time (13 women), 5 part-time (3 women); includes 1 Black or African American, non-Hispanic/Latino; 3 Asian, non-Hispanic/Latino, 10 international. Average age 29. 25 applicants, 36% accepted, 8 enrolled. In 2010, 2 master's, 4 doctorates awarded. *Degree requirements:* For master's, comprehensive exam (for some programs), thesis (for some programs); for doctorate, comprehensive exam (for some programs), thesis/dissertation (for some programs). *Entrance requirements:* For master's and doctorate, GRE. Additional exam requirements/recommendations for international students: Required—TOEFL (minimum score 550 paper-based; 213 computer-based). *Application deadline:* For fall admission, 7/1 for domestic and international students; for spring admission, 12/1 for domestic and international students. Applications are processed on a rolling basis. Application fee: $65. Electronic applications accepted. *Expenses:* Tuition, state resident: full-time $9399; part-time $488 per credit hour. Tuition, nonresident: full-time $17,854; part-time $957.75 per credit hour. Required fees: $1534. Full-time tuition and fees vary according to program. *Financial support:* In 2010–11, 1 research assistantship with full tuition reimbursement (averaging $12,053 per year), 3 teaching assistantships with full tuition reimbursements (averaging $12,861 per year) were awarded; career-related internships or fieldwork, Federal Work-Study, scholarships/grants, health care benefits, and unspecified assistantships also available. Financial award application deadline: 1/15. *Faculty research:* Human resource management, service management, marketing, strategy and finance tourist behavior. Total annual research expenditures: $102,947. *Unit head:* Dr. Rick R. Perdue, UNIT HEAD, 540-231-3287, Fax: 540-231-8313, E-mail: perduerr@vt.edu. *Application contact:* Nancy McGehee, Contact, 540-231-1201, Fax: 540-231-8313, E-mail: nmcgehee@vt.edu.

Western Illinois University, School of Graduate Studies, College of Education and Human Services, Department of Recreation, Park, and Tourism Administration, Macomb, IL 61455-1390. Offers MS. Part-time programs available. *Students:* 29 full-time (23 women), 10 part-time (6 women); includes 6 minority (4 Black or African American, non-Hispanic/Latino; 1 Hispanic/Latino; 1 Two or more races, non-Hispanic/Latino), 5 international. Average age 26. 19 applicants, 79% accepted. In 2010, 18 master's awarded. *Degree requirements:* For master's, thesis or alternative. *Entrance requirements:* Additional exam requirements/recommendations for international students: Required—TOEFL (minimum score 550 paper-based; 213 computer-based; 80 iBT). *Application deadline:* Applications are processed on a rolling basis. Application fee: $30. Electronic applications accepted. *Expenses:* Tuition, state resident: full-time $6370; part-time $265.40 per credit hour. Tuition, nonresident: full-time $12,740; part-time $530.80 per credit hour. Required fees: $75.67 per credit hour. *Financial support:* In 2010–11, 21 students received support, including 21 research assistantships with full tuition reimbursements available (averaging $7,280 per year). Financial award applicants required to submit FAFSA. *Unit head:* Dr. K. Dale Adkins, Chairperson, 309-298-1967. *Application contact:* Evelyn Hoing, Assistant Director of Graduate Studies, 309-298-1806, Fax: 309-298-2345, E-mail: grad-office@wiu.edu.

Human Resources

OVERVIEW

The human resources profession is no longer about hiring, policing, and pushing paper. In today's dynamic workplace, human resources professionals not only manage "traditional" human resource functions, they are expected to contribute to such key organizational challenges as facilitating mergers and acquisitions, improving productivity and quality, improving the ability of an organization to bring new products to market, and continuously improving the company's return on its greatest asset—its own workforce.

Human resources MBA degree programs prepare graduates with the skills they will need for working in leadership and management-level positions in human resources: recruiting and hiring employees, handling position alignment within the organization, handling compensation and budgeting, and creating practical and efficient strategic policies and plans for the organization. Throughout the program, students master the concepts around developing leadership skills, being able to manage a team, developing strong organizational skills, handling difficult personnel decisions, and being prepared for the real-life situations and issues that arise in any business environment. MBA human resources degree programs also teach students how important human resources are within a company or organization and how to work with other employees to boost employee productivity and morale. Graduates of MBA human resources degree programs have also most likely studied legal issues in the workplace, employee insurance and benefits, and ethical dimensions of business organizations.

Required courses of study may include:

- Accounting
- Business Strategy
- Corporate Management and Business Strategy
- Ethical Leadership
- Marketing
- Operations Management
- Organizational Behavior and Design
- Statistics

Elective courses of study may include:

- Current Perspectives in Training and Development
- Employee Relations
- Issues and Practices in Human Resources Management
- Job Analysis, Assessment, and Compensation
- Organizational Development and Change
- Recruitment and Selection

Graduates with a human resources MBA procure employment as human resources managers, training and development managers, executive recruiters, industrial relations analysts, union organizers, training specialists, and employee benefits administrators. Within HR circles, professionals can be employed in recruitment, training, and labor relations—with each area having its own specialties.

HELPFUL ORGANIZATIONS/ PUBLICATIONS/BLOGS

Society for Human Resource Management (SHRM)

http://www.shrm.org/Pages/default.aspx

The Society for Human Resource Management (SHRM) is the world's largest association devoted to human resource management. Representing more than 250,000 members in more than 140 countries, SHRM serves the needs of HR professionals and advances the interests of the HR profession. Founded in 1948, SHRM has more than 575 affiliated chapters within the United States and subsidiary offices in China and India. As part of SHRM's commitment to developing the HR profession globally, SHRM opened offices in Beijing, China, and Mumbai, India, to help establish important two-way relationships, provide education, and facilitate the advancement of HR. SHRM is running a pilot program to create Member Forums in selected countries to encourage local networking among SHRM members. SHRM is an active member of the North American Human Resource Management Association and the current secretariat for the World Federation of People Management Associations.

National Human Resources Association (NHRA)

http://www.humanresources.org/

Established in 1951, the National Human Resources Association (NHRA) is focused on advancing the development and leadership of human resource professionals. Through professional programs and services offered across the country, NHRA strives to support human resource professionals throughout their careers.

The mission of the NHRA Board of Directors is to serve and support the association members and affiliates by providing networking forums and professional development programs for the human resources community. NHRA provides professional development opportunities via live meetings in affiliate locations and via conferences and seminars delivered in conjunction with training partners. In addition, NHRA offers a wide range of on-demand, Webcast, and audiocast events.

International Public Management Association for Human Resources (IPMA-HR)

http://www.ipma-hr.org/

The International Public Management Association for Human Resources (IPMA-HR) is an organization that represents the interests of human resource professionals at the federal, state, and local levels of government and strives to promote excellence in HR management. Its goal is to provide information and assistance to help HR professionals increase their job performance and overall agency function by providing cost-effective products, services, and educational opportunities.

Serving HR professionals since 1906, IPMA-HR is the resource for comprehensive and timely HR industry news, jobs, policies, resources, education, and professional development opportunities. The organization is governed by an Executive Council and divided into more than 40 chapters, residing in four U.S. regions and abroad.

CAREER ASPIRATIONS: A PROSPECTIVE POSITION
Vice President Global Human Resources

Job Description

The VP Global Human Resources will have responsibility for leading global human resources for more than 1,700 associates located in 6 facilities. Through a team of direct reports, this role is responsible for providing strategic leadership in effectively developing and deploying human capital to achieve targeted business results while contributing to both departmental and company-wide HR strategies, policies, and procedures. Working as a critical member of the leadership team, he/she will define organizational needs, lead major change initiatives, identify training and development/management needs, determine hiring requirements, and track and exceed the appropriate HR metrics for strategic and operating plans. The successful candidate will identify business challenges/opportunities and develop effective people solutions in the form of processes, programs, and/or initiatives across the department.

This individual will be responsible for talent acquisition and retention, salary and benefit administration, performance management, succession planning, safety and worker's compensation, labor relations, and union avoidance. In addition, he/she will oversee the planning and initiation of all employee relations activities, including associate recognition and incentive plans for domestic and international associates, and will participate in all presentations to group and corporate executives (strategic planning and operations reviews).

Requirements

- Direct the development, implementation, and administration of policies and human resources programs.
- Manage employment procedures, wage and salary administration, benefits, safety, worker's compensation, employee development, training, and recruitment.
- Oversee the planning of associate relations activities and benefits plans, presentations, and programs such as associate recognition and incentive plans for domestic and international employees.
- Conduct group-level presentations and partnerships with the executive team on strategic planning and initiatives.
- Direct all labor relations situations and represents the company in unemployment hearings, worker's compensation hearings, and other legal forums.
- Ensure collaboration between multiple divisions, in terms of associate morale, general information, and any issues affecting morale and performance.

Qualifications

- Bachelor's degree in human resources or related field
- MBA or graduate degree in human resources or similar field
- 10+ years experience in human resources
- Experience in a global HR environment
- Strong business acumen, leadership, presentation skills
- Superior teamwork skills
- Superior communication skills
- Conflict management/composure
- Planning and organizing
- Initiative and follow-up

Career Advice from a Business Professional

Nicholas K. Iadevaio, Jr.
Vice President Human Resources
L'Oréal USA Professional
    Products Division
MBA in Human Resources
Adelphi University

What drew you to this field?

Early in my career, I was a general manager for a global supermarket company. I had a lot of exposure to human resources issues and challenges as a general manager (GM), and I realized what I was most passionate about was the people.

What makes a day at your job interesting?

The diversity of human resources issues, challenges, and opportunities that exist or could come up. As a true business partner to the business, I enjoy it most when I am close to the real business and working with the people to help them work in high-performing teams. I also enjoy coaching executives about their teams, their businesses, and themselves.

How has your graduate education been important to your successes/accomplishments along your career path?

It has provided me with an important framework to understand the many facets of human resources (HR) management. HR is not just about the people, but how the people make the business successful or not. To fully comprehend this, the well-rounded business background and education has helped me to this day to be able to speak to GMs about how strong HR strategies are the foundation of a successful business using their language—not HR-speak.

In your opinion, what does the future of your field hold for someone newly entering it?

With the advent of e-learning and new technologies everyday, the possibilities are endless in the field of HR management. Businesses are global, so HR issues have become more complex than ever in dealing with global employees.

What are the exciting developments coming in the next five years?

Digital media and the Internet continue to impact the way business is done, so consequently, it affects people's jobs, how they work, and how they interact. In addition, the global society that we live in makes it necessary for HR professionals to understand the complexity of the global issues. Legislation that is enacted will always impact how we service our business partners, as new laws impact what companies can and cannot do.

What advice would you share with new graduates entering your field?

I also teach HR at NYU in the Master's Program in Human Capital Management, and what I tell my students is simple… Make sure you understand your business completely:

- Read the *Wall Street Journal* or other business publications, so that you speak the "language of business."
- Get experience in managing or dealing with people, such as in retail, sales, or even restaurant service. Those types of experiences are extremely valuable as you look to move into HR, as they will have given you tough and real experiences in managing difficult and complex people issues.

Good luck!

HUMAN RESOURCES DEVELOPMENT

Abilene Christian University, Graduate School, College of Arts and Sciences, Department of Communication, Program in Organizational and Human Resource Development, Abilene, TX 79699-9100. Offers MS. Part-time and evening/weekend programs available. Postbaccalaureate distance learning degree programs offered (no on-campus study). *Students:* 10 full-time (6 women), 97 part-time (75 women); includes 21 Black or African American, non-Hispanic/Latino; 2 Asian, non-Hispanic/Latino; 8 Hispanic/Latino; 2 Two or more races, non-Hispanic/Latino, 3 international. 88 applicants, 44% accepted, 37 enrolled. In 2010, 14 master's awarded. *Degree requirements:* For master's, thesis. *Entrance requirements:* Additional exam requirements/recommendations for international students: Required—TOEFL (minimum score 550 paper-based; 213 computer-based). *Application deadline:* For fall admission, 4/1 priority date for domestic students; for spring admission, 11/1 for domestic students. Applications are processed on a rolling basis. Application fee: $100. Electronic applications accepted. *Expenses:* Tuition: Full-time $12,906; part-time $717 per hour. Required fees: $1250; $61.50 per unit. *Financial support:* Available to part-time students. Application deadline: 4/1. *Unit head:* Dr. Jonathan Camp, Graduate Advisor, 325-674-2136, E-mail: jwc03b@acu.edu. *Application contact:* David Pittman, Graduate Admissions Counselor, 325-674-2656, Fax: 325-674-6717, E-mail: gradinfo@acu.edu.

Azusa Pacific University, School of Business and Management, Program in Human and Organizational Development, Azusa, CA 91702-7000. Offers MA. Part-time and evening/weekend programs available. *Students:* 2 full-time (both women), 14 part-time (11 women); includes 2 Black or African American, non-Hispanic/Latino; 2 Asian, non-Hispanic/Latino; 3 Hispanic/Latino, 2 international. In 2010, 9 master's awarded. *Degree requirements:* For master's, comprehensive exam, final project. *Entrance requirements:* For master's, minimum GPA of 3.0. *Application deadline:* For fall admission, 8/15 priority date for domestic students. Applications are processed on a rolling basis. Application fee: $45 ($65 for international students). *Unit head:* Dr. Ilene Bezjian, Dean, 626-815-3090, Fax: 626-815-3802, E-mail: ibezjian@apu.edu. *Application contact:* Dr. Ilene Bezjian, Dean, 626-815-3090, Fax: 626-815-3802, E-mail: ibezjian@apu.edu.

Claremont Graduate University, Graduate Programs, School of Behavioral and Organizational Sciences, Department of Psychology, Claremont, CA 91711-6160. Offers advanced study in evaluation (Certificate); cognitive psychology (MA, PhD); developmental psychology (MA, PhD); evaluation and applied research methods (MA, PhD); health behavior research and evaluation (MA, PhD); human resource development and evaluation (MA); industrial/organizational psychology (MA, PhD); organizational behavior (MA, PhD); organizational psychology (MA, PhD); social psychology (MA, PhD); MBA/PhD. Part-time programs available. *Faculty:* 15 full-time (6 women), 5 part-time/adjunct (2 women). *Students:* 248 full-time (169 women), 15 part-time (9 women); includes 68 minority (14 Black or African American, non-Hispanic/Latino; 1 American Indian or Alaska Native, non-Hispanic/Latino; 27 Asian, non-Hispanic/Latino; 19 Hispanic/Latino; 2 Native Hawaiian or other Pacific Islander, non-Hispanic/Latino; 5 Two or more races, non-Hispanic/Latino), 29 international. Average age 30. In 2010, 45 master's, 21 doctorates, 4 other advanced degrees awarded. Terminal master's awarded for partial completion of doctoral program. *Entrance requirements:* For master's and doctorate, GRE General Test. Additional exam requirements/recommendations for international students: Required—TOEFL (minimum score 550 paper-based; 213 computer-based; 80 iBT). *Application deadline:* For fall admission, 1/15 priority date for domestic students. Applications are processed on a rolling basis. Application fee: $60. Electronic applications accepted. *Expenses:* Tuition: Full-time $35,748; part-time $1554 per unit. Required fees: $215 per semester. *Financial support:* Fellowships, research assistantships, teaching assistantships, Federal Work-Study, institutionally sponsored loans, scholarships/grants, and tuition waivers (full and partial) available. Support available to part-time students. Financial award application deadline: 2/15; financial award applicants required to submit FAFSA. *Faculty research:* Social intervention, diversity in organizations, eyewitness memory, aging and cognition, drug policy. *Unit head:* Stewart Donaldson, Dean, 909-607-9001, Fax: 909-621-8905, E-mail: stewart.donaldson@cgu.edu. *Application contact:* Paul Thomas, Director, External Affairs, 909-607-9016, Fax: 909-621-8905, E-mail: paul.thomas@cgu.edu.

Clemson University, Graduate School, College of Health, Education, and Human Development, Eugene T. Moore School of Education, Program in Human Resource Development, Clemson, SC 29634. Offers MHRD. Part-time and evening/weekend programs available. Postbaccalaureate distance learning degree programs offered (no on-campus study). *Students:* 2 full-time (1 woman), 70 part-time (49 women); includes 14 Black or African American, non-Hispanic/Latino; 1 American Indian or Alaska Native, non-Hispanic/Latino; 1 Hispanic/Latino. Average age 35. 51 applicants, 90% accepted, 41 enrolled. In 2010, 35 master's awarded. *Degree requirements:* For master's, comprehensive exam. *Entrance requirements:* For master's, GRE General Test, Keirsey Campbell. Additional exam requirements/recommendations

for international students: Required—TOEFL; Recommended—IELTS. *Application deadline:* For fall admission, 7/1 for domestic students. Application fee: $70 ($80 for international students). Electronic applications accepted. *Expenses:* Contact institution. *Financial support:* In 2010–11, 2 students received support. Application deadline: 6/1. *Faculty research:* Organizational development, human performance improvement, attachment theory, social constructivism, technology-mediated teaching and learning, corporate universities. *Unit head:* Dr. Michael J. Padilla, Director/Associate Dean, 864-656-4444, Fax: 864-656-0311, E-mail: pmcgee@clemson.edu. *Application contact:* Dr. David Fleming, Graduate Coordinator, 864-656-1881, Fax: 864-656-0311, E-mail: dflemin@clemson.edu.

Florida International University, College of Education, Department of Educational Leadership and Policy Studies, Miami, FL 33199. Offers adult education (MS); adult education in human resource development (Ed D); clinical mental health counseling (MS); conflict resolution and consensus building (Certificate); counselor education (MS); educational administration and supervision (Ed D); educational leadership (MS, Certificate, Ed S); higher education (Ed D); higher education administration (MS); human resource development (MS); instruction in urban settings (MS); international/intercultural education (MS); learning technologies (MS); multicultural-bilingual (MS); multicultural-TESOL (MS); recreation and sport management (MS); recreation therapy (MS); rehabilitation counseling (MS); school counseling (MS); school psychology (Ed S); urban education (MS). Part-time and evening/weekend programs available. *Students:* 164 full-time (124 women), 308 part-time (234 women); includes 107 Black or African American, non-Hispanic/Latino; 3 American Indian or Alaska Native, non-Hispanic/Latino; 8 Asian, non-Hispanic/Latino; 223 Hispanic/Latino, 12 international. Average age 31. 544 applicants, 41% accepted, 197 enrolled. In 2010, 123 master's, 5 doctorates, 16 other advanced degrees awarded. *Degree requirements:* For doctorate, thesis/dissertation. *Entrance requirements:* For master's, minimum GPA of 3.0; for doctorate and other advanced degree, GRE General Test. Additional exam requirements/recommendations for international students: Required—TOEFL (minimum score 550 paper-based; 213 computer-based; 80 iBT), IELTS (minimum score 6.3). *Application deadline:* For fall admission, 6/1 priority date for domestic students, 4/1 for international students; for winter admission, 10/1 priority date for domestic students, 9/1 for international students; for spring admission, 3/1 priority date for domestic students, 2/1 for international students. Applications are processed on a rolling basis. Application fee: $30. Electronic applications accepted. *Financial support:* Fellowships, research assistantships with full and partial tuition reimbursements, teaching assistantships with full and partial tuition reimbursements, Federal Work-Study and tuition waivers (full and partial) available. Support available to part-time students. Financial award applicants required to submit FAFSA. *Unit head:* Dr. Patricia Barbetta, Dean of Graduate Studies, 305-348-2835, Fax: 305-348-2081, E-mail: barbetta@fiu.edu. *Application contact:* Nanett Rojas, Graduate Admission, 305-348-7442, Fax: 305-348-7441, E-mail: nanett.rojas@fiu.edu.

Florida State University, The Graduate School, College of Education, Department of Educational Psychology and Learning Systems, Program in Instructional Systems, Tallahassee, FL 32306. Offers instructional systems (MS, PhD, Ed S); open and distance learning (MS); performance improvement and human resources (MS). *Faculty:* 8 full-time (5 women), 1 (woman) part-time/adjunct. *Students:* 62 full-time (43 women), 58 part-time (37 women); includes 14 minority (7 Black or African American, non-Hispanic/Latino; 6 Asian, non-Hispanic/Latino; 1 Hispanic/Latino), 35 international. Average age 37. 68 applicants, 71% accepted, 30 enrolled. In 2010, 33 master's, 3 doctorates, 2 other advanced degrees awarded. *Degree requirements:* For master's and Ed S, comprehensive exam, thesis optional; for doctorate, comprehensive exam, thesis/dissertation. *Entrance requirements:* For master's, doctorate, and Ed S, GRE General Test, minimum GPA of 3.0. Additional exam requirements/recommendations for international students: Required—TOEFL (minimum score 550 paper-based; 213 computer-based; 80 iBT). *Application deadline:* For fall admission, 7/1 for domestic and international students; for winter admission, 11/1 for domestic and international students; for spring admission, 3/1 for domestic and international students. Applications are processed on a rolling basis. Application fee: $30. Electronic applications accepted. *Expenses:* Tuition, state resident: full-time $8238.24. *Financial support:* Fellowships with full and partial tuition reimbursements, research assistantships with full and partial tuition reimbursements, teaching assistantships with full and partial tuition reimbursements, career-related internships or fieldwork available. Financial award applicants required to submit FAFSA. *Faculty research:* Human performance improvement, educational semiotics, development of software tools to measure online interaction among learners. *Unit head:* Dr. Vanessa Dennen, Program Coordinator, 850-644-8783, Fax: 850-644-8776, E-mail: vdennen@fsu.edu. *Application contact:* Mary Kate McKee, Program Coordinator, 850-644-8792, Fax: 850-644-8776, E-mail: mmckee@campus.fsu.edu.

Friends University, Graduate School, Wichita, KS 67213. Offers accounting (MBA); business administration (MBA); business law (MBL); Christian ministry (MACM); family therapy (MSFT); global leadership and management (MA); health care leadership (MHCL); management information systems (MMIS); operations management (MSOM); organization development

(MSOD); teaching (MAT). Part-time and evening/weekend programs available. Postbaccalaureate distance learning degree programs offered (minimal on-campus study). *Faculty:* 14 full-time (5 women), 2 part-time/adjunct (1 woman). *Students:* 166 full-time (122 women), 507 part-time (290 women); includes 134 minority (64 Black or African American, non-Hispanic/Latino; 6 American Indian or Alaska Native, non-Hispanic/Latino; 24 Asian, non-Hispanic/Latino; 30 Hispanic/Latino; 1 Native Hawaiian or other Pacific Islander, non-Hispanic/Latino; 9 Two or more races, non-Hispanic/Latino). Average age 38. 445 applicants, 69% accepted, 236 enrolled. In 2010, 345 master's awarded. *Degree requirements:* For master's, research project. *Entrance requirements:* Additional exam requirements/recommendations for international students: Required—TOEFL (minimum score 560 paper-based; 220 computer-based). *Application deadline:* Applications are processed on a rolling basis. Application fee: $45 ($65 for international students). Electronic applications accepted. Tuition and fees vary according to course load, campus/location and program. *Financial support:* Applicants required to submit FAFSA. *Unit head:* Dr. Evelyn Hume, Dean, 800-794-6945 Ext. 5859, Fax: 316-295-5040, E-mail: evelyn hume@friends.edu. Application contact: Jeanette Hanson, Executive Director of Adult Recruitment, 800-794-6945, Fax: 316-295-5050, E-mail: jeanette@friends.edu.

The George Washington University, Graduate School of Education and Human Development, Department of Counseling/Human and Organizational Studies, Programs in Human and Organizational Learning, Washington, DC 20052. Offers human and organizational learning (Ed D); human resource development (MA Ed); leadership development (Graduate Certificate). MA Ed program also offered in Alexandria and Newport News, VA, as well as in Singapore and Hong Kong. *Faculty:* 11 full-time (8 women). *Students:* 62 full-time (33 women), 72 part-time (49 women); includes 32 Black or African American, non-Hispanic/Latino; 1 American Indian or Alaska Native, non-Hispanic/Latino; 4 Asian, non-Hispanic/Latino; 4 Hispanic/Latino, 5 international. Average age 45. 54 applicants, 87% accepted, 33 enrolled. In 2010, 3 doctorates, 1 other advanced degree awarded. *Degree requirements:* For master's and Graduate Certificate, comprehensive exam; for doctorate, comprehensive exam, thesis/dissertation. *Entrance requirements:* For master's, GRE General Test or MAT, minimum GPA of 2.75; for doctorate, GRE General Test or MAT, interview, minimum GPA of 3.3; for Graduate Certificate, GRE General Test or MAT, minimum GPA of 3.3. *Application deadline:* For fall admission, 1/15 priority date for domestic students; for spring admission, 10/1 for domestic students. Applications are processed on a rolling basis. Application fee: $75. *Financial support:* Fellowships, research assistantships, teaching assistantships, career-related internships or fieldwork, Federal Work-Study, and tuition waivers (partial) available. Financial award application deadline: 1/15; financial award applicants required to submit FAFSA. *Faculty research:* Organizational learning, program evaluation. *Unit head:* David Schwandt, Program Manager, 703-726-8396, E-mail: chwandt@gwu.edu. *Application contact:* Sarah Lang, Director of Graduate Admissions, 202-994-1447, E-mail: slang@gwu.edu.

Grantham University, Mark Skousen School of Business, Kansas City, MO 64153. Offers business administration (MBA); business intelligence (MS); information management (MBA); information management technology (MS); information technology (MS); performance improvement (MS); project management (MBA, MSIM). Part-time and evening/weekend programs available. Postbaccalaureate distance learning degree programs offered (no on-campus study). *Students:* 74 full-time (32 women), 565 part-time (177 women); includes 218 minority (142 Black or African American, non-Hispanic/Latino; 6 American Indian or Alaska Native, non-Hispanic/Latino; 31 Asian, non-Hispanic/Latino; 37 Hispanic/Latino; 1 Native Hawaiian or other Pacific Islander, non-Hispanic/Latino; 1 Two or more races, non-Hispanic/Latino). In 2010, 126 master's awarded. *Degree requirements:* For master's, capstone project. *Entrance requirements:* For master's, bachelor's degree from accredited degree-granting institution. Additional exam requirements/recommendations for international students: Required—TOEFL (minimum score 500 paper-based; 213 computer-based; 61 iBT). *Application deadline:* Applications are processed on a rolling basis. Application fee: $0. Electronic applications accepted. *Expenses:* Tuition: Full-time $7950; part-time $265 per credit hour. One-time fee: $30. *Financial support:* Institutionally sponsored loans and scholarships/grants available. *Unit head:* Niccole Buckley, Dean, 800-955-2527, Fax: 816-595-5757, E-mail: admissions@grantham.edu. *Application contact:* Dan King, Vice President of Admissions, 800-955-2527, Fax: 816-595-5757, E-mail: admissions@grantham.edu.

Illinois Institute of Technology, Graduate College, College of Psychology, Chicago, IL 60616. Offers clinical psychology (PhD); industrial/organizational psychology (PhD); personnel/human resource development (MS); rehabilitation (PhD); rehabilitation counseling (MS). *Accreditation:* APA (one or more programs are accredited); CORE. Part-time and evening/weekend programs available. *Faculty:* 21 full-time (7 women), 6 part-time/adjunct (4 women). *Students:* 160 full-time (111 women), 39 part-time (33 women); includes 36 minority (8 Black or African American, non-Hispanic/Latino; 1 American Indian or Alaska Native, non-Hispanic/Latino; 15 Asian, non-Hispanic/Latino; 12 Hispanic/Latino), 16 international. Average age 29. 253 applicants, 40% accepted, 43 enrolled. In 2010, 31 master's, 14 doctorates awarded. Terminal master's awarded for partial completion of doctoral program. *Degree*

requirements: For master's, thesis (for some programs); for doctorate, comprehensive exam, thesis/dissertation, 96-108 credit hours, internship (for clinical and industrial/organizational specializations). *Entrance requirements:* For master's, GRE General Test (minimum score 900 Quantitative and Verbal, 2.5 Analytical Writing), minimum high school GPA of 3.0; at least 18 credit hours of undergraduate study in psychology with at least one course each in experimental psychology and statistics; official transcripts; 3 letters of recommendation; personal statement; for doctorate, GRE General Test (minimum score 1000 Quantitative and Verbal, 3.0 Analytical Writing), minimum high school GPA of 3.0; at least 18 credit hours of undergraduate study in psychology with at least one course each in experimental psychology and statistics; official transcripts; 3 letters of recommendation; personal statement. Additional exam requirements/recommendations for international students: Required—TOEFL (minimum score 550 paper-based; 213 computer-based; 80 iBT); Recommended—IELTS (minimum score 5.5). *Application deadline:* For fall admission, 1/15 for domestic and international students. Application fee: $50. Electronic applications accepted. *Expenses:* Tuition: Full-time $18,576; part-time $1032 per credit hour. Required fees: $583 per semester. One-time fee: $150. Tuition and fees vary according to program and student level. *Financial support:* In 2010–11, 23 research assistantships with full and partial tuition reimbursements (averaging $223 per year) were awarded; fellowships with full and partial tuition reimbursements, career-related internships or fieldwork, Federal Work-Study, institutionally sponsored loans, scholarships/grants, traineeships, health care benefits, tuition waivers (partial), and unspecified assistantships also available. Support available to part-time students. Financial award application deadline: 1/15; financial award applicants required to submit FAFSA. *Faculty research:* Health psychology, behavioral medicine, attachment, child social and emotional development, educational assessment. Total annual research expenditures: $1.6 million. *Unit head:* Dr. M. Ellen Mitchell, Dean, 312-567-3362, Fax: 312-567-3493, E-mail: mitchelle@iit.edu. *Application contact:* Institute of Psychology Graduate Admissions, 312-567-3500, Fax: 312-567-3493, E-mail: psychology@iit.edu.

Indiana University of Pennsylvania, School of Graduate Studies and Research, Eberly College of Business and Information Technology, Department of Technology Support and Training, Program in Business/Workforce Development, Indiana, PA 15705-1087. Offers M Ed. *Faculty:* 8 full-time (5 women). *Students:* 10 full-time (5 women), 18 part-time (12 women); includes 1 minority (Black or African American, non-Hispanic/Latino). Average age 37. 26 applicants, 31% accepted, 8 enrolled. In 2010, 13 master's awarded. *Degree requirements:* For master's, thesis optional. *Entrance requirements:* For master's, 2 letters of recommendation. Additional exam requirements/recommendations for international students: Required—TOEFL. *Application deadline:* For fall admission, 7/1 priority date for domestic students; for spring admission, 11/1 for domestic students. Applications are processed on a rolling basis. Application fee: $40. *Financial support:* In 2010–11, 7 research assistantships with full and partial tuition reimbursements (averaging $1,980 per year) were awarded; career-related internships or fieldwork and Federal Work-Study also available. Support available to part-time students. Financial award application deadline: 3/15; financial award applicants required to submit FAFSA. *Unit head:* Dr. Dawn Woodland, Graduate Coordinator, 724-357-5736, E-mail: woodland@iup.edu. *Application contact:* Dr. Dawn Woodland, Graduate Coordinator, 724-357-5736, E-mail: woodland@iup.edu.

Iowa State University of Science and Technology, Graduate College, College of Human Sciences, Department of Educational Leadership and Policy Studies, Ames, IA 50011. Offers counselor education (M Ed, MS); educational administration (M Ed, MS); educational leadership (PhD); higher education (M Ed, MS); organizational learning and human resource development (M Ed, MS); research and evaluation (MS). *Faculty:* 19 full-time (9 women), 16 part-time/adjunct (9 women). *Students:* 138 full-time (84 women), 278 part-time (158 women); includes 39 Black or African American, non-Hispanic/Latino; 3 American Indian or Alaska Native, non-Hispanic/Latino; 3 Asian, non-Hispanic/Latino; 22 Hispanic/Latino, 9 international. 182 applicants, 72% accepted, 69 enrolled. In 2010, 58 master's, 21 doctorates awarded. *Degree requirements:* For master's, thesis or alternative; for doctorate, thesis/dissertation. *Entrance requirements:* For master's and doctorate, GRE General Test. Additional exam requirements/recommendations for international students: Required—TOEFL (minimum score 560 paper-based; 83 iBT), IELTS (minimum score 6.5). *Application deadline:* For fall admission, 1/1 priority date for domestic and international students. Applications are processed on a rolling basis. Application fee: $40 ($90 for international students). Electronic applications accepted. *Financial support:* In 2010–11, 26 research assistantships with full and partial tuition reimbursements (averaging $13,109 per year), 2 teaching assistantships with full and partial tuition reimbursements (averaging $9,864 per year) were awarded; fellowships, scholarships/grants, health care benefits, and unspecified assistantships also available. *Unit head:* Dr. Laura Rendon, Chair, 515-294-7093, E-mail: lrendon@iastate.edu. *Application contact:* Dr. Daniel Robinson, Information Contact, 515-294-1241, E-mail: eldrshp@iastate.edu.

The Johns Hopkins University, Carey Business School, Management Programs, Baltimore, MD 21218-2699. Offers leadership development (Certificate); organization development and human resources (MS); skilled facilitator (Certificate). Evening/weekend programs available. *Faculty:* 29

full-time (6 women), 135 part-time/adjunct (29 women). *Students:* 1 (woman) full-time, 33 part-time (19 women); includes 25 minority (22 Black or African American, non-Hispanic/Latino; 2 Asian, non-Hispanic/Latino; 1 Hispanic/Latino). Average age 35. 30 applicants, 100% accepted, 25 enrolled. In 2010, 18 master's, 26 other advanced degrees awarded. *Degree requirements:* For master's, 36 credits including final project. *Entrance requirements:* For master's and Certificate, minimum GPA of 3.0, resume, work experience, two letters of recommendation. Additional exam requirements/recommendations for international students: Required—TOEFL (minimum score 600 paper-based; 250 computer-based; 100 iBT). *Application deadline:* For fall admission, 4/1 for international students; for spring admission, 9/15 for international students. Applications are processed on a rolling basis. Application fee: $100. Electronic applications accepted. *Financial support:* In 2010–11, 9 students received support. Scholarships/grants available. Support available to part-time students. Financial award application deadline: 4/15; financial award applicants required to submit FAFSA. *Faculty research:* Agency theory and theory of the firm, technological entrepreneurship, technology policy and economic development, strategic human resources management, ethics and stakeholder theory. Total annual research expenditures: $57,832. *Unit head:* Dr. Dipankar Chakravarti, Vice Dean of Programs, 410-234-9311, E-mail: dipankar.chakravarti@jhu.edu. *Application contact:* Robin Greeberg, Admissions Coordinator, 410-234-9227, Fax: 443-529-1554, E-mail: carey. admissions@jhu.edu.

Kentucky State University, College of Professional Studies, Frankfort, KY 40601. Offers business administration (MBA), including accounting, finance, management, marketing; public administration (MPA), including human resource management, international administration and development, management information systems, nonprofit management; special education (MA). Part-time and evening/weekend programs available. Postbaccalaureate distance learning degree programs offered (minimal on-campus study). *Faculty:* 12 full-time (4 women), 2 part-time/adjunct (both women). *Students:* 88 full-time (57 women), 79 part-time (42 women); includes 104 minority (101 Black or African American, non-Hispanic/Latino; 1 Asian, non-Hispanic/Latino; 2 Hispanic/Latino), 2 international. Average age 34. 124 applicants, 62% accepted, 45 enrolled. In 2010, 38 master's awarded. *Degree requirements:* For master's, comprehensive exam, thesis optional. *Entrance requirements:* For master's, GMAT, GRE. Additional exam requirements/recommendations for international students: Required—TOEFL (minimum score 525 paper-based; 173 computer-based). *Application deadline:* Applications are processed on a rolling basis. Application fee: $30 ($100 for international students). Electronic applications accepted. *Expenses:* Tuition, state resident: full-time $5886; part-time $352 per credit hour. Tuition, nonresident: full-time $9054; part-time $528 per credit hour. Required fees: $450; $26 per credit hour. *Financial support:* In 2010–11, 46 students received support, including 4 research assistantships (averaging $10,975 per year); career-related internships or fieldwork, scholarships/grants, tuition waivers (partial), and unspecified assistantships also available. Financial award application deadline: 4/15; financial award applicants required to submit FAFSA. *Unit head:* Dr. Gashaw Lake, Dean, 502-597-6105, Fax: 502-597-6715, E-mail: gashaw.lake@kysu.edu. *Application contact:* Dr. Titilayo Ufomata, Acting Director of Graduate Studies, 502-597-6443, E-mail: titilayo.ufomata@kysu.edu.

Lincoln Memorial University, Carter and Moyers School of Education, Harrogate, TN 37752-1901. Offers administration and supervision (M Ed, Ed S); counseling and guidance (M Ed); curriculum and instruction (M Ed, Ed D, Ed S); English (M Ed); executive leadership (Ed D); higher education administration (Ed D); human resource development (Ed D); leadership and administration (Ed D). Part-time and evening/weekend programs available. Postbaccalaureate distance learning degree programs offered. *Faculty:* 31 full-time (13 women), 22 part-time/adjunct (11 women). *Students:* 169 full-time (132 women), 1,288 part-time (1,004 women); includes 167 Black or African American, non-Hispanic/Latino; 2 American Indian or Alaska Native, non-Hispanic/Latino; 3 Asian, non-Hispanic/Latino; 6 Hispanic/Latino; 4 Two or more races, non-Hispanic/Latino, 2 international. Average age 37. 1,562 applicants, 96% accepted, 1457 enrolled. In 2010, 173 master's, 901 other advanced degrees awarded. *Degree requirements:* For master's, comprehensive exam, thesis optional; for Ed S, comprehensive exam. *Entrance requirements:* For master's, PRAXIS, NTE, GRE, MAT, letters of recommendation; for Ed S, graduate transcripts. *Application deadline:* For fall admission, 8/1 for domestic students, 8/10 for international students; for spring admission, 1/10 for domestic and international students. Application fee: $25. *Financial support:* In 2010–11, 973 students received support. Career-related internships or fieldwork, health care benefits, and unspecified assistantships available. Support available to part-time students. Financial award application deadline: 4/1; financial award applicants required to submit FAFSA. *Faculty research:* Brain compatible teaching and learning; poverty in Appalachia; leadership for change; ethics, moral responsibility and social justice; human and organizational learning. *Unit head:* Dr. Michael Clyburn, Dean, 423-869-6259, Fax: 423-869-6259, E-mail: michael.clyburn@lmunet.edu. *Application contact:* Terri Knuckles, Executive Assistant, Graduate Education, 423-869-6223, Fax: 423-869-6261, E-mail: terri.knuckles@lmunet.edu.

Louisiana State University and Agricultural and Mechanical College, Graduate School, College of Agriculture, School of Human Resource Education and Workforce Development, Baton Rouge, LA 70803. Offers agriculture and extension education and youth development (MS, PhD); career and technical education (MS, PhD); comprehensive vocational education (MS, PhD); extension and international education (MS, PhD); human resource and leadership development (MS, PhD); industrial education (MS); vocational agriculture education (MS, PhD); vocational business education (MS); vocational home economics education (MS). *Accreditation:* NCATE. Part-time programs available. *Faculty:* 11 full-time (6 women), 2 part-time/adjunct (0 women). *Students:* 43 full-time (30 women), 80 part-time (55 women); includes 15 Black or African American, non-Hispanic/Latino; 1 Asian, non-Hispanic/Latino; 4 Hispanic/Latino, 5 international. Average age 37. 42 applicants, 88% accepted, 13 enrolled. In 2010, 17 master's, 18 doctorates awarded. Terminal master's awarded for partial completion of doctoral program. *Degree requirements:* For master's, thesis (for some programs); for doctorate, thesis/dissertation. *Entrance requirements:* For master's and doctorate, GRE General Test, minimum GPA of 3.0. Additional exam requirements/recommendations for international students: Required—TOEFL (minimum score 550 paper-based; 213 computer-based; 79 iBT) or IELTS (minimum score 6.5). *Application deadline:* For fall admission, 1/25 priority date for domestic students, 5/15 for international students; for spring admission, 10/15 for international students. Applications are processed on a rolling basis. Application fee: $50 ($70 for international students). Electronic applications accepted. *Financial support:* In 2010–11, 73 students received support, including 3 fellowships with full and partial tuition reimbursements available (averaging $2,241 per year), 3 research assistantships with full and partial tuition reimbursements available (averaging $12,000 per year), 3 teaching assistantships with partial tuition reimbursements available (averaging $17,787 per year); career-related internships or fieldwork, Federal Work-Study, institutionally sponsored loans, health care benefits, tuition waivers (full and partial), and unspecified assistantships also available. Financial award application deadline: 3/1; financial award applicants required to submit FAFSA. *Faculty research:* Adult education, history and philosophy of vocational education, curriculum and instruction, career decision making. Total annual research expenditures: $53,300. *Unit head:* Dr. Michael F. Burnett, Director, 225-578-5748, Fax: 225-578-2526, E-mail: vocbur@lsu.edu. *Application contact:* Paula Beecher, Recruiting Coordinator, 225-578-2468, E-mail: pbeeche@lsu.edu.

Manhattanville College, Graduate Programs, Humanities and Social Sciences Programs, Program in Organizational Management and Human Resource Development, Purchase, NY 10577-2132. Offers MS. Part-time and evening/weekend programs available. In 2010, 25 master's awarded. *Degree requirements:* For master's, thesis. *Entrance requirements:* For master's, interview, 2 letters of recommendation. Additional exam requirements/recommendations for international students: Required—TOEFL. *Application deadline:* Applications are processed on a rolling basis. Application fee: $75. *Expenses:* Tuition: Full-time $16,110; part-time $895 per credit. Required fees: $50 per semester. *Financial support:* Career-related internships or fieldwork, Federal Work-Study, institutionally sponsored loans, and unspecified assistantships available. Financial award application deadline: 3/1; financial award applicants required to submit FAFSA. *Unit head:* Dr. Don Richards, Interim Dean, School of Graduate and Professional Studies, 914-323-5469, Fax: 914-694-3488, E-mail: gps@mivlle.edu. *Application contact:* Office of Admissions for Graduate and Professional Studies, 914-323-5418, E-mail: gps@mville.edu.

Marquette University, Graduate School of Management, Program in Human Resources, Milwaukee, WI 53201-1881. Offers MSHR. Part-time and evening/weekend programs available. *Faculty:* 4 full-time (3 women), 3 part-time/adjunct (2 women). *Students:* 18 full-time (11 women), 16 part-time (12 women); includes 3 minority (2 Black or African American, non-Hispanic/Latino; 1 Asian, non-Hispanic/Latino), 16 international. Average age 26. 68 applicants, 57% accepted, 15 enrolled. In 2010, 4 master's awarded. *Entrance requirements:* For master's, GMAT or GRE General Test, letters of recommendation. Additional exam requirements/recommendations for international students: Required—TOEFL (minimum score 530 paper-based; 78 computer-based). *Application deadline:* Applications are processed on a rolling basis. Application fee: $50. Electronic applications accepted. *Expenses:* Tuition: Full-time $16,290; part-time $905 per credit hour. Tuition and fees vary according to program. *Financial support:* In 2010–11, 3 teaching assistantships were awarded; fellowships, research assistantships, Federal Work-Study, institutionally sponsored loans, and tuition waivers (full and partial) also available. Support available to part-time students. Financial award application deadline: 2/15. *Faculty research:* Diversity, mentoring. *Unit head:* Dr. Timothy Keaveny, Management Chair, 414-288-3643. *Application contact:* Dr. Timothy Keaveny, Management Chair, 414-288-3643.

Midwestern State University, Graduate Studies, College of Education, Program in Counseling, Wichita Falls, TX 76308. Offers general counseling (MA); human resource development (MA); school counseling (M Ed); training and development (MA). Part-time and evening/weekend programs available. *Faculty:* 9 full-time (4 women), 1 (woman) part-time/adjunct. *Students:* 15 full-time (14 women), 59 part-time (49 women); includes 8 Black or African American, non-Hispanic/Latino; 1 American Indian or Alaska Native, non-Hispanic/Latino; 5 Hispanic/Latino; 1 Two or more races, non-Hispanic/Latino, 9 international. Average age 33. 17 applicants, 82% accepted, 13 enrolled. In 2010, 27 master's awarded. *Degree requirements:* For master's, comprehensive exam, thesis (for some programs). *Entrance requirements:* For master's, GRE General Test, MAT, or GMAT, valid teaching certificate (M Ed). Additional exam requirements/recommendations for international students: Required—TOEFL (minimum score 550 paper-based; 213 computer-based). *Application deadline:* For fall admission, 7/1 priority date for domestic students, 4/1 for international students; for spring admission, 11/1 priority date for domestic students, 8/1 for international students. Applications are processed on a rolling basis. Application fee: $35 ($50 for international students). Electronic applications accepted. *Expenses:* Tuition, state resident: full-time $1620; part-time $90 per credit hour. Tuition, nonresident: full-time $2160; part-time $120 per credit hour. International tuition: $7200 full-time. *Financial support:* In 2010–11, 23 students received support; teaching assistantships with partial tuition reimbursements available, career-related internships or fieldwork, Federal Work-Study, institutionally sponsored loans, scholarships/grants, tuition waivers (partial), and unspecified assistantships available. Support available to part-time students. Financial award application deadline: 3/1; financial award applicants required to submit FAFSA. *Faculty research:* Social development of students with disabilities, autism, criminal justice counseling, conflict resolution issues, leadership. *Unit head:* Dr. Michaelle Kitchen, Chair, 940-397-4141, Fax: 940-397-4694, E-mail: michaelle.kitchen@mwsu.edu. *Application contact:* 800-842-1922, Fax: 940-397-4672, E-mail: admissions@mwsu.edu.

Mississippi State University, College of Education, Department of Instructional Systems and Workforce Development, Mississippi State, MS 39762. Offers education (Ed D, Ed S), including technology; instructional systems and workforce development (PhD); instructional technology (MSIT); technology (MS). *Faculty:* 9 full-time (6 women), 1 part-time/adjunct (0 women). *Students:* 27 full-time (15 women), 83 part-time (62 women); includes 50 minority (48 Black or African American, non-Hispanic/Latino; 1 Asian, non-Hispanic/Latino; 1 Hispanic/Latino), 2 international. Average age 37. 34 applicants, 62% accepted, 15 enrolled. In 2010, 18 master's, 10 doctorates, 3 other advanced degrees awarded. *Degree requirements:* For master's, thesis optional, comprehensive oral or written exam; for doctorate, thesis/dissertation, comprehensive oral and written exam; for Ed S, thesis, comprehensive written exam. *Entrance requirements:* For master's, GRE, minimum GPA of 2.75 in junior and senior courses; for doctorate and Ed S, GRE. Additional exam requirements/recommendations for international students: Required—TOEFL (minimum score 550 paper-based; 213 computer-based; 79 iBT); Recommended—IELTS (minimum score 6.5). *Application deadline:* For fall admission, 7/1 for domestic students, 5/1 for international students; for spring admission, 11/1 for domestic students, 9/1 for international students. Applications are processed on a rolling basis. Application fee: $40. Electronic applications accepted. *Expenses:* Tuition, state resident: full-time $2730.50; part-time $304 per credit hour. Tuition, nonresident: full-time $6901; part-time $767 per credit hour. *Financial support:* In 2010–11, 2 teaching assistantships with full tuition reimbursements (averaging $10,800 per year) were awarded; Federal Work-Study, institutionally sponsored loans, and unspecified assistantships also available. Financial award application deadline: 4/1; financial award applicants required to submit FAFSA. *Faculty research:* Computer technology, nontraditional students, interactive video, instructional technology, educational leadership. *Unit head:* Dr. Linda Cornelius, Professor and Interim Head, 662-325-2281, Fax: 662-325-7599, E-mail: lcornelius@colled.msstate.edu. *Application contact:* Dr. Connie Forde, Professor and Graduate Coordinator, 662-325-2281, Fax: 662-325-7258, E-mail: cforde@colled.msstate.edu.

Moravian College, Moravian College Comenius Center, Business and Management Programs, Bethlehem, PA 18018-6650. Offers accounting (MBA); general management (MBA); health care management (MBA); human resource management (MBA); leadership (MSHRM); learning and performance management (MSHRM); supply chain management (MBA). Part-time and evening/weekend programs available. *Faculty:* 6 full-time (2 women), 10 part-time/adjunct (3 women). *Students:* 67 part-time (35 women). 24 applicants, 50% accepted, 12 enrolled. In 2010, 8 master's awarded. *Entrance requirements:* For master's, GMAT. Additional exam requirements/recommendations for international students: Required—TOEFL (minimum score 550 paper-based; 260 computer-based; 90 iBT). *Application deadline:* Applications are processed on a rolling basis. Application fee: $40. *Expenses:* Contact institution. *Financial support:* In 2010–11, 1 fellowship with full tuition reimbursement was awarded. *Faculty research:* Leadership, change management, human resources. *Unit head:* Dr. William A. Kleintop, Associate Dean for Business and Management Programs, 610-507-1400, Fax: 610-861-1400, E-mail: comenius@moravian.edu. *Application contact:* Linda J. Doyle, Information Contact, 610-861-1400, Fax: 610-861-1466, E-mail: mba@moravian.edu.

National-Louis University, College of Management and Business, Chicago, IL 60603. Offers business administration (MBA); human resource management and development (MS); management (MS). Part-time and evening/weekend programs available. *Students:* 125 full-time (80 women), 8 part-time (5 women); includes 59 minority (28 Black or African American, non-Hispanic/Latino; 1 American Indian or Alaska Native, non-Hispanic/Latino; 3 Asian, non-Hispanic/Latino; 26 Hispanic/Latino; 1 Two or more races, non-Hispanic/Latino). Average age 37. In 2010, 173 master's awarded. *Entrance*

requirements: For master's, college-administered critical thinking and writing skills test, minimum GPA of 3.0, resume, 3 references. Additional exam requirements/recommendations for international students: Required—TOEFL (minimum score 550 paper-based; 213 computer-based; 79 iBT). *Application deadline:* Applications are processed on a rolling basis. Application fee: $40. *Financial support:* Federal Work-Study, institutionally sponsored loans, and scholarships/grants available. Support available to part-time students. Financial award applicants required to submit FAFSA. *Unit head:* Walter Roetlger, Executive Dean, 312-261-3073, Fax: 312-261-3073, E-mail: chris.multhauf@nl.edu. *Application contact:* Dr. Larry Poselli, Vice President of Enrollment and Student Services, 800-443-5522 Ext. 5718, Fax: 312-261-3550, E-mail: larry.polselli@nl.edu.

New York University, School of Continuing and Professional Studies, Division of Programs in Business, Program in Leadership and Human Capital Management, New York, NY 10012-1019. Offers benefits and compensation (Advanced Certificate); human resource development (MS); human resource management (MS, Advanced Certificate); organizational and executive coaching (Advanced Certificate); organizational effectiveness (MS). Part-time and evening/weekend programs available. Postbaccalaureate distance learning degree programs offered (no on-campus study). *Faculty:* 52 part-time/adjunct (15 women). *Students:* 21 full-time (17 women), 123 part-time (107 women); includes 19 Black or African American, non-Hispanic/Latino; 2 American Indian or Alaska Native, non-Hispanic/Latino; 6 Asian, non-Hispanic/Latino; 15 Hispanic/Latino, 18 international. Average age 31. 119 applicants, 66% accepted, 42 enrolled. In 2010, 81 master's, 28 other advanced degrees awarded. Terminal master's awarded for partial completion of doctoral program. *Degree requirements:* For master's, thesis. *Entrance requirements:* For master's, GRE General Test or GMAT (for recent graduates), 2 letters of recommendation, resume, essay, professional experience. Additional exam requirements/recommendations for international students: Required—TOEFL (minimum score 600 paper-based; 250 computer-based; 100 iBT), TWE. *Application deadline:* For fall admission, 2/1 priority date for domestic and international students; for spring admission, 10/15 priority date for domestic students, 8/15 priority date for international students. Applications are processed on a rolling basis. Application fee: $75. Electronic applications accepted. *Financial support:* In 2010–11, 106 students received support, including 106 fellowships (averaging $2,430 per year); career-related internships or fieldwork, institutionally sponsored loans, and scholarships/grants also available. Support available to part-time students. Financial award application deadline: 3/1; financial award applicants required to submit FAFSA. *Unit head:* Stephanie Bonadio, Academic Director, 212-992-3633, Fax: 212-992-3650, E-mail: sgb259@nyu.edu. *Application contact:* Assistant Director, 212-992-3600, Fax: 212-992-3650, E-mail: scps.hrmdstudent@nyu.edu.

Northeastern Illinois University, Graduate College, College of Education, Department of Educational Leadership and Development, Program in Human Resource Development, Chicago, IL 60625-4699. Offers educational leadership (MA); human resource development (MA). Part-time and evening/weekend programs available. *Faculty:* 25 full-time (11 women), 22 part-time/adjunct (8 women). *Students:* 5 full-time (all women), 43 part-time (29 women); includes 25 minority (12 Black or African American, non-Hispanic/Latino; 1 American Indian or Alaska Native, non-Hispanic/Latino; 4 Asian, non-Hispanic/Latino; 8 Hispanic/Latino), 4 international. Average age 38. 30 applicants, 83% accepted, 15 enrolled. In 2010, 11 master's awarded. *Degree requirements:* For master's, comprehensive papers. *Entrance requirements:* For master's, minimum GPA of 2.75, BA in human resource development. Additional exam requirements/recommendations for international students: Required—TOEFL (minimum score 550 paper-based; 213 computer-based; 79 iBT). *Application deadline:* For fall admission, 4/1 priority date for domestic students; for spring admission, 8/15 for domestic students. Applications are processed on a rolling basis. Application fee: $30. Electronic applications accepted. *Financial support:* In 2010–11, 14 students received support, including 3 research assistantships with full and partial tuition reimbursements available (averaging $6,600 per year); career-related internships or fieldwork, Federal Work-Study, institutionally sponsored loans, scholarships/grants, tuition waivers (full and partial), and unspecified assistantships also available. Support available to part-time students. *Faculty research:* Analogics, development of expertise, case-based instruction, action science organizational development, theoretical model building. *Unit head:* Dr. Howard Bultinck, Department Chair. *Application contact:* Dr. Howard Bultinck, Department Chair.

Penn State University Park, Graduate School, College of the Liberal Arts, Department of Labor Studies and Employment Relations, State College, University Park, PA 16802-1503. Offers MPS, MS. Postbaccalaureate distance learning degree programs offered.

Rochester Institute of Technology, Graduate Enrollment Services, College of Applied Science and Technology, Department of Hospitality and Service Management, Program in Human Resources Development, Rochester, NY 14623-5603. Offers MS. Part-time and evening/weekend programs available. *Students:* 18 full-time (12 women), 26 part-time (17 women); includes 8 Black or African American, non-Hispanic/Latino; 2 Hispanic/Latino, 16 international. Average age 34. 62 applicants, 56% accepted, 19 enrolled. In 2010, 18 master's awarded. *Degree requirements:* For master's, thesis or alternative.

Entrance requirements: For master's, minimum GPA of 3.0. Additional exam requirements/recommendations for international students: Required—TOEFL (minimum score 550 paper-based; 213 computer-based; 79 iBT) or IELTS (minimum score 6.5). *Application deadline:* For fall admission, 2/15 priority date for domestic and international students; for winter admission, 11/1 for domestic and international students; for spring admission, 2/1 for domestic and international students. Applications are processed on a rolling basis. *Expenses:* Tuition: Full-time $33,234; part-time $924 per credit hour. Required fees: $219. *Financial support:* In 2010–11, 31 students received support; research assistantships with partial tuition reimbursements available, teaching assistantships with partial tuition reimbursements available, career-related internships or fieldwork, scholarships/grants, and unspecified assistantships available. Support available to part-time students. Financial award application deadline: 2/15; financial award applicants required to submit FAFSA. *Faculty research:* Global resource development, service/product innovation and implementation. *Unit head:* Dr. Linda Underhill, Chair, 585-475-7359, Fax: 585-475-5099, E-mail: lmuism@rit.edu. *Application contact:* Diane Ellison, Assistant Vice President, Graduate Enrollment Services, 585-475-2229, Fax: 585-475-7164, E-mail: gradinfo@rit.edu.

Rollins College, Hamilton Holt School, Program in Human Resources, Winter Park, FL 32789. Offers MA. Part-time and evening/weekend programs available. *Faculty:* 4 full-time (0 women), 2 part-time/adjunct (0 women). *Students:* 4 full-time (2 women), 52 part-time (46 women); includes 26 minority (13 Black or African American, non-Hispanic/Latino; 1 Asian, non-Hispanic/Latino; 12 Hispanic/Latino), 2 international. Average age 31. 42 applicants, 71% accepted, 26 enrolled. In 2010, 23 master's awarded. *Degree requirements:* For master's, thesis optional. *Entrance requirements:* For master's, GMAT or GRE, interview. Additional exam requirements/recommendations for international students: Required—TOEFL (minimum score 550 paper-based; 213 computer-based; 80 iBT). *Application deadline:* For fall admission, 4/1 for domestic students; for spring admission, 12/1 for domestic students. Application fee: $50. *Expenses:* Contact institution. *Financial support:* In 2010–11, 3 students received support. Career-related internships or fieldwork, scholarships/grants, and unspecified assistantships available. Support available to part-time students. Financial award applicants required to submit FAFSA. *Unit head:* Dr. Donald Rogers, Director, 407-646-2348, E-mail: drogers@rollins.edu. *Application contact:* Christian Ricaurte, Coordinator of Records and Registration, 407-646-2653, Fax: 407-646-1551, E-mail: cricaurte@rollins.edu.

St. John Fisher College, Ronald L. Bittner School of Business, Organizational Learning and Human Resource Development Program, Rochester, NY 14618-3597. Offers MS. Part-time and evening/weekend programs available. *Faculty:* 4 part-time/adjunct (2 women). *Students:* 1 (woman) full-time, 27 part-time (20 women); includes 6 minority (5 Black or African American, non-Hispanic/Latino; 1 American Indian or Alaska Native, non-Hispanic/Latino). Average age 31. 24 applicants, 75% accepted, 14 enrolled. In 2010, 21 master's awarded. *Degree requirements:* For master's, capstone project, professional portfolio. *Entrance requirements:* For master's, 2 letters of recommendation, personal statement, current resume. Additional exam requirements/recommendations for international students: Required—TOEFL (minimum score 575 paper-based; 233 computer-based; 80 iBT). *Application deadline:* Applications are processed on a rolling basis. Application fee: $30. Electronic applications accepted. *Expenses:* Tuition: Part-time $705 per credit hour. Required fees: $25 per semester. *Financial support:* In 2010–11, 22 students received support. Scholarships/grants available. Financial award applicants required to submit FAFSA. *Faculty research:* Empowerment, leadership, group dynamics, team learning, project management. *Unit head:* Edward Ciaschi, Program Director, 585-385-5266, E-mail: eciaschi@sjfc.edu. *Application contact:* Jose Perales, Director of Graduate Admissions, 585-385-8067, E-mail: jperales@sjfc.edu.

Suffolk University, College of Arts and Sciences, Department of Education and Human Services, Boston, MA 02108-2770. Offers administration of higher education (M Ed, CAGS), including administration of higher education (M Ed), leadership (CAGS); human resource, learning and performance (MS, CAGS, Graduate Certificate, including global human resources (Graduate Certificate), human resources (MS, Graduate Certificate), organizational development (CAGS, Graduate Certificate), organizational learning and development (MS, Graduate Certificate); mental health counseling (MS, CAGS); school counseling (M Ed, CAGS); school teaching (M Ed, CAGS), including foundations of education (M Ed), middle school teaching (M Ed), secondary school teaching (M Ed); MPA/MSMHC; MS/Certificate. Part-time and evening/weekend programs available. *Faculty:* 8 full-time (4 women), 9 part-time/adjunct (3 women). *Students:* 62 full-time (49 women), 126 part-time (94 women); includes 6 Black or African American, non-Hispanic/Latino; 1 American Indian or Alaska Native, non-Hispanic/Latino; 3 Asian, non-Hispanic/Latino; 5 Hispanic/Latino, 7 international. Average age 28. 170 applicants, 78% accepted, 61 enrolled. In 2010, 80 master's, 2 other advanced degrees awarded. *Entrance requirements:* For master's, GRE General Test or MAT, 2 letters of recommendation, resume. Additional exam requirements/recommendations for international students: Required—TOEFL (minimum score 550 paper-based; 213 computer-based; 80 iBT). *Application deadline:* For fall admission, 6/15 priority date for domestic students, 6/15 for international

students; for spring admission, 11/1 priority date for domestic students, 11/1 for international students. Applications are processed on a rolling basis. Application fee: $50. Electronic applications accepted. *Expenses:* Contact institution. *Financial support:* In 2010–11, 110 students received support, including 34 fellowships with full and partial tuition reimbursements available (averaging $10,596 per year); career-related internships or fieldwork, Federal Work-Study, and institutionally sponsored loans also available. Support available to part-time students. Financial award application deadline: 4/1; financial award applicants required to submit FAFSA. *Faculty research:* Predicting competent Head Start preschools, cultural differences. *Unit head:* Dr. Donna Qualters, Interim Chair & Director, 617-573-8264 Ext. 8261, Fax: 617-305-1743, E-mail: dqualters@suffolk.edu. *Application contact:* Judith Reynolds, Director of Graduate Admissions, 617-573-8302, Fax: 617-305-1733, E-mail: grad.admission@suffolk.edu.

Texas A&M University, College of Education and Human Development, Department of Educational Administration and Human Resource Development, College Station, TX 77843. Offers adult education (PhD); higher education administration (MS, PhD); human resource development (MS, PhD); public school administration (M Ed, Ed D, PhD). Part-time programs available. *Faculty:* 31. *Students:* 134 full-time (102 women), 281 part-time (159 women); includes 154 minority (69 Black or African American, non-Hispanic/Latino; 2 American Indian or Alaska Native, non-Hispanic/Latino; 12 Asian, non-Hispanic/Latino; 71 Hispanic/Latino), 25 international. Average age 37. In 2010, 58 master's, 34 doctorates awarded. *Degree requirements:* For master's, thesis optional; for doctorate, thesis/dissertation. *Entrance requirements:* For master's, GRE General Test, writing exam, interview, professional experience; for doctorate, GRE General Test, writing exam, interview/presentation, professional experience. Additional exam requirements/recommendations for international students: Required—TOEFL. *Application deadline:* For fall admission, 12/1 for domestic and international students; for spring admission, 8/15 for domestic and international students. Application fee: $50 ($75 for international students). Electronic applications accepted. *Financial support:* In 2010–11, fellowships (averaging $20,000 per year), research assistantships (averaging $12,000 per year) were awarded; career-related internships or fieldwork and institutionally sponsored loans also available. Support available to part-time students. Financial award application deadline: 3/1; financial award applicants required to submit FAFSA. *Faculty research:* Higher education administration, public school administration, student affairs. *Unit head:* Dr. Fred M. Nafukho, Head, 979-862-3395, Fax: 979-862-4347. *Application contact:* Joyce Nelson, Director of Academic Advising, 979-847-9098, Fax: 979-862-4347, E-mail: jnelson@tamu.edu.

Towson University, Program in Human Resource Development, Towson, MD 21252-0001. Offers MS. Part-time and evening/weekend programs available. *Students:* 64 full-time (48 women), 186 part-time (145 women); includes 65 minority (47 Black or African American, non-Hispanic/Latino; 2 American Indian or Alaska Native, non-Hispanic/Latino; 9 Asian, non-Hispanic/Latino; 6 Hispanic/Latino; 1 Two or more races, non-Hispanic/Latino), 8 international. Average age 30. In 2010, 99 master's awarded. *Degree requirements:* For master's, comprehensive exam, internship (educational leadership track). *Entrance requirements:* For master's, 2 letters of recommendation, minimum GPA of 3.0. Additional exam requirements/recommendations for international students: Required—TOEFL. *Application deadline:* Applications are processed on a rolling basis. Application fee: $50. Electronic applications accepted. *Expenses:* Tuition, state resident: part-time $324 per credit. Tuition, nonresident: part-time $681 per credit. Required fees: $95 per term. *Financial support:* In 2010–11, 1 research assistantship with full and partial tuition reimbursement was awarded; career-related internships or fieldwork, Federal Work-Study, and unspecified assistantships also available. Financial award application deadline: 4/1; financial award applicants required to submit FAFSA. *Faculty research:* Workforce training and development. *Unit head:* Alan Clardy, Graduate Program Director, 410-704-3069, E-mail: aclardy@towson.edu. *Application contact:* 410-704-2501, Fax: 410-704-4675, E-mail: grads@towson.edu.

University of California, Los Angeles, Graduate Division, UCLA Anderson School of Management, Los Angeles, CA 90095-1481. Offers accounting (PhD); business administration (MBA); decisions, operations and technology management (PhD); finance (PhD); financial engineering (MFE); global economics and management (PhD); human resources and organizational behavior (PhD); marketing (PhD); strategy and policy (PhD); DDS/MBA; MBA/JD; MBA/MD; MBA/MLAS; MBA/MLIS; MBA/MPH; MBA/MPP; MBA/MSCS; MBA/MSN; MBA/MUP. *Accreditation:* AACSB. Part-time programs available. *Faculty:* 102 full-time (17 women), 43 part-time/adjunct (6 women). *Students:* 833 full-time (270 women), 1,052 part-time (271 women); includes 592 minority (25 Black or African American, non-Hispanic/Latino; 3 American Indian or Alaska Native, non-Hispanic/Latino; 482 Asian, non-Hispanic/Latino; 60 Hispanic/Latino; 6 Native Hawaiian or other Pacific Islander, non-Hispanic/Latino; 16 Two or more races, non-Hispanic/Latino), 445 international. In 2010, 735 master's, 10 doctorates awarded. *Degree requirements:* For master's, comprehensive exam, field study consulting project (for MBA); thesis/dissertation (for MFE); for doctorate, comprehensive exam, thesis/dissertation, oral and written qualifying exams. *Entrance requirements:* For master's, GMAT (MBA); GMAT or GRE General Test (MFE), minimum undergraduate GPA of 3.0; for doctorate, GMAT or GRE General Test, minimum undergraduate GPA of 3.0. Additional exam requirements/recommendations for international students: Required—TOEFL (minimum score 560 paper-based; 220 computer-based; 87 iBT), IELTS (minimum score 7). *Application deadline:* For fall admission, 10/20 for domestic and international students; for winter admission, 1/5 for domestic and international students; for spring admission, 4/13 for domestic and international students. Application fee: $200. Electronic applications accepted. *Expenses:* Contact institution. *Financial support:* Fellowships, research assistantships, teaching assistantships, career-related internships or fieldwork, institutionally sponsored loans, scholarships/grants, health care benefits, and tuition waivers (partial) available. Financial award application deadline: 3/2; financial award applicants required to submit FAFSA. *Unit head:* Judy D. Olian, Dean, UCLA Anderson School of Management, 310-825-7982, Fax: 310-206-2073. *Application contact:* Mae Jennifer Shores, Assistant Dean and Director of Full-time MBA Admissions and Financial Aid, 310-825-6944, Fax: 310-825-8582, E-mail: mba.admissions@anderson.ucla.edu.

University of Denver, University College, Denver, CO 80208. Offers arts and culture (MLS, Certificate), including art, literature, and culture, arts development and program management (Certificate), creative writing; environmental policy and management (MAS, Certificate), including energy and sustainability (Certificate), environmental assessment of nuclear power (Certificate), environmental health and safety (Certificate), environmental management, natural resource management (Certificate); geographic information systems (MAS, Certificate); global affairs (MLS, Certificate), including translation studies, world history and culture; healthcare leadership (MPH, Certificate), including healthcare policy, law, and ethics, medical and healthcare information technologies, strategic management of healthcare; information and communications technology (MCIS, Certificate), including database design and administration (Certificate), geographic information systems (MCIS), information security systems security (Certificate), information systems security (MCIS), project management (MCIS, MPS, Certificate), software design and administration (Certificate), software design and programming (MCIS), technology management, telecommunications technology (MCIS), Web design and development; leadership and organizations (MPS, Certificate), including human capital in organizations, philanthropic leadership, project management (MCIS, MPS, Certificate), strategic innovation and change; organizational and professional communication (MPS, Certificate), including alternative dispute resolution, organizational communication, organizational development and training, public relations and marketing; security management (MAS, Certificate), including emergency planning and response, information security (MAS), organizational security; strategic human resource management (MPS, Certificate), including global human resources (MPS), human resource management and development (MPS). Part-time and evening/weekend programs available. Postbaccalaureate distance learning degree programs offered (no on-campus study). *Faculty:* 7 full-time (2 women), 212 part-time/adjunct (83 women). *Students:* 52 full-time (19 women), 1,044 part-time (625 women); includes 196 minority (81 Black or African American, non-Hispanic/Latino; 7 American Indian or Alaska Native, non-Hispanic/Latino; 30 Asian, non-Hispanic/Latino; 66 Hispanic/Latino; 3 Native Hawaiian or other Pacific Islander, non-Hispanic/Latino; 9 Two or more races, non-Hispanic/Latino), 76 international. Average age 36. 488 applicants, 91% accepted, 339 enrolled. In 2010, 286 master's, 130 other advanced degrees awarded. *Entrance requirements:* Additional exam requirements/recommendations for international students: Required—TOEFL (minimum score 550 paper-based; 80 iBT). *Application deadline:* For fall admission, 6/22 priority date for domestic students, 6/10 priority date for international students; for winter admission, 9/15 priority date for domestic students, 9/6 priority date for international students; for spring admission, 2/3 priority date for domestic students, 12/15 priority date for international students. Applications are processed on a rolling basis. Application fee: $75. Electronic applications accepted. *Expenses:* Contact institution. *Financial support:* Applicants required to submit FAFSA. *Unit head:* Dr. James Davis, Dean, 303-871-2291, Fax: 303-871-4047, E-mail: jdavis@du.edu. *Application contact:* Information Contact, 303-871-3155, Fax: 303-871-4047, E-mail: ucolinfo@du.edu.

University of Houston, College of Technology, Department of Human Development and Consumer Science, Houston, TX 77204. Offers future studies in commerce (MS); human resources development (MS). Part-time programs available. *Faculty:* 3 full-time (2 women), 6 part-time/adjunct (3 women). *Students:* 45 full-time (33 women), 54 part-time (36 women); includes 16 Black or African American, non-Hispanic/Latino; 1 American Indian or Alaska Native, non-Hispanic/Latino; 9 Asian, non-Hispanic/Latino; 11 Hispanic/Latino, 20 international. Average age 32. 47 applicants, 89% accepted, 30 enrolled. In 2010, 22 master's awarded. *Degree requirements:* For master's, project or thesis. *Entrance requirements:* For master's, GMAT, MAT. Additional exam requirements/recommendations for international students: Required—TOEFL (minimum score 550 paper-based; 79 iBT). *Application deadline:* For fall admission, 7/1 for domestic students, 4/1 for international students; for spring admission, 12/1 for domestic students, 10/1 for international students. Applications are processed on a rolling basis. Application fee: $75 ($150 for international students). Electronic applications accepted. *Expenses:* Tuition, state resident: full-time $8592; part-time $358 per credit hour. Tuition, nonresident: full-time $16,032; part-time $668 per credit hour. Required fees: $2889. Tuition and fees vary according to course load and program. *Financial support:* In 2010–11, 11 teaching assistantships with partial tuition reimbursements (averaging $8,400 per year) were awarded. *Unit head:* Carole Goodson, Chairperson, 713-743-4046, Fax: 713-743-4033, E-mail: cgoodson@uh.edu. *Application contact:* Tiffany Roosa, Academic Advisor, 713-743-4100, Fax: 713-743-4151, E-mail: troosa@uh.edu.

University of Illinois at Urbana–Champaign, Graduate College, College of Education, Department of Human Resource Education, Champaign, IL 61820. Offers Ed M, MS, Ed D, PhD, CAS, MBA/M Ed. Part-time and evening/weekend programs available. Postbaccalaureate distance learning degree programs offered (no on-campus study). *Faculty:* 6 full-time (1 woman). *Students:* 48 full-time (21 women), 118 part-time (81 women); includes 19 Black or African American, non-Hispanic/Latino; 6 Asian, non-Hispanic/Latino; 5 Hispanic/Latino, 38 international. 104 applicants, 63% accepted, 29 enrolled. In 2010, 87 master's, 9 doctorates, 3 other advanced degrees awarded. *Entrance requirements:* For master's, minimum GPA of 3.0; for doctorate, GRE, minimum GPA of 3.0. Additional exam requirements/recommendations for international students: Required—TOEFL (minimum score 96 iBT). *Application deadline:* Applications are processed on a rolling basis. Application fee: $75 ($90 for international students). Electronic applications accepted. *Financial support:* In 2010–11, 3 fellowships, 8 research assistantships, 11 teaching assistantships were awarded; tuition waivers (full and partial) also available. *Unit head:* Steven R. Aragon, Interim Head, 217-333-0807, Fax: 217-244-5632, E-mail: aragon@illinois.edu. *Application contact:* Laura Ketchum, Secretary, 217-333-0807, Fax: 217-244-5632, E-mail: lirle@illinois.edu.

University of Louisville, Graduate School, College of Education and Human Development, Department of Leadership, Foundations and Human Resource Education, Louisville, KY 40292-0001. Offers educational leadership and organizational development (Ed D, PhD); higher education (MA); human resource education (MS); P-12 educational administration (M Ed, Ed S). *Accreditation:* NCATE. Part-time and evening/weekend programs available. Postbaccalaureate distance learning degree programs offered. *Faculty:* 18 full-time (9 women), 9 part-time/adjunct (5 women). *Students:* 56 full-time (36 women), 200 part-time (140 women); includes 29 Black or African American, non-Hispanic/Latino; 2 Asian, non-Hispanic/Latino; 6 Hispanic/Latino; 1 Native Hawaiian or other Pacific Islander, non-Hispanic/Latino; 2 Two or more races, non-Hispanic/Latino, 7 international. Average age 38. 94 applicants, 78% accepted, 62 enrolled. In 2010, 23 master's, 29 doctorates, 11 other advanced degrees awarded. *Degree requirements:* For doctorate, comprehensive exam, thesis/dissertation. *Entrance requirements:* For master's, doctorate, and Ed S, GRE General Test. Additional exam requirements/recommendations for international students: Required—TOEFL (minimum score 560 paper-based; 210 computer-based; 83 iBT). *Application deadline:* Applications are processed on a rolling basis. Application fee: $50. Electronic applications accepted. *Expenses:* Tuition, state resident: full-time $9144; part-time $508 per credit hour. Tuition, nonresident: full-time $19,026; part-time $1057 per credit hour. Tuition and fees vary according to program and reciprocity agreements. *Financial support:* In 2010–11, 31 students received support; fellowships, research assistantships, teaching assistantships, career-related internships or fieldwork, Federal Work-Study, scholarships/grants, health care benefits, and unspecified assistantships available. Financial award application deadline: 6/1; financial award applicants required to submit FAFSA. *Faculty research:* Evaluation of methods and programs to improve elementary and secondary education; research on organizational and human resource development; student access, retention and success in post-secondary education; educational policy analysis; multivariate quantitative research methods. *Unit head:* Dr. Bridgette Pregliasco, Acting Chair, 502-852-6204, Fax: 502-852-4563, E-mail: bridgette.pregliasco@louisville.edu. *Application contact:* Libby Leggett, Director, Graduate Admissions, 502-852-3101, Fax: 502-852-6536, E-mail: gradadm@louisville.edu.

University of Minnesota, Twin Cities Campus, Graduate School, College of Education and Human Development, Department of Organizational Leadership, Policy and Development, Program in Human Resource Development, Minneapolis, MN 55455-0213. Offers M Ed, MA, Ed D, PhD, Certificate. *Students:* 32 full-time (24 women), 30 part-time (23 women); includes 9 Black or African American, non-Hispanic/Latino; 2 Asian, non-Hispanic/Latino; 1 Hispanic/Latino, 4 international. Average age 34. 65 applicants, 75% accepted, 44 enrolled. In 2010, 28 master's, 83 other advanced degrees awarded. *Unit head:* Dr. Rebecca Ropers-Huilman, Chair, 612-624-1006, Fax: 612-624-3377, E-mail: ropers@umn.edu. *Application contact:* Dr. Jennifer Engler, Assistant Dean, 612-626-2887, Fax: 612-626-7496, E-mail: engle009@umn.edu.

University of Missouri–St. Louis, Graduate School, Program in Public Policy Administration, St. Louis, MO 63121. Offers health policy (MPPA); local government management (MPPA); managing human resources and organization (MPPA); nonprofit organization management (MPPA); nonprofit organization management and leadership (Certificate); policy research and analysis (MPPA). *Accreditation:* NASPAA. Part-time and evening/weekend programs available. *Faculty:* 9 full-time (4 women), 8 part-time/adjunct (6 women). *Students:* 36 full-time (21 women), 59 part-time (33 women); includes 17 minority (13 Black or African American, non-Hispanic/Latino;

2 American Indian or Alaska Native, non-Hispanic/Latino; 1 Asian, non-Hispanic/Latino; 1 Hispanic/Latino), 11 international. Average age 31. 60 applicants, 68% accepted, 24 enrolled. In 2010, 23 master's, 17 Certificates awarded. *Entrance requirements:* For master's, 3 letters of recommendation. Additional exam requirements/recommendations for international students: Required—TOEFL (minimum score 550 paper-based; 213 computer-based). *Application deadline:* For fall admission, 7/1 priority date for domestic and international students; for spring admission, 12/1 priority date for domestic and international students. Applications are processed on a rolling basis. Application fee: $35 ($40 for international students). Electronic applications accepted. *Expenses:* Tuition, state resident: full-time $5522; part-time $306.80 per credit hour. Tuition, nonresident: full-time $14,253; part-time $792.10 per credit hour. Required fees: $658; $49 per credit hour. One-time fee: $12. Tuition and fees vary according to program. *Financial support:* In 2010–11, 3 research assistantships with full and partial tuition reimbursements (averaging $12,000 per year) were awarded; career-related internships or fieldwork also available. Financial award application deadline: 4/1; financial award applicants required to submit FAFSA. *Faculty research:* Urban policy, public finance, evaluation. *Unit head:* Dr. Brady Baybeck, Director, 314-516-5145, Fax: 314-516-5210, E-mail: baybeck@umsl.edu. *Application contact:* 314-516-5458, Fax: 314-516-6996, E-mail: gradadm@umsl.edu.

University of Oklahoma, College of Arts and Sciences, Department of Human Relations, Norman, OK 73019-0390. Offers human relations (MHR), including affirmative action, chemical addictions counseling, family relations, general, human resources, juvenile justice; human relations licensure (Graduate Certificate). Part-time and evening/weekend programs available. Postbaccalaureate distance learning degree programs offered (minimal on-campus study). *Faculty:* 25 full-time (16 women), 27 part-time/adjunct (13 women). *Students:* 315 full-time (216 women), 499 part-time (312 women); includes 258 minority (159 Black or African American, non-Hispanic/Latino; 39 American Indian or Alaska Native, non-Hispanic/Latino; 14 Asian, non-Hispanic/Latino; 24 Hispanic/Latino; 2 Native Hawaiian or other Pacific Islander, non-Hispanic/Latino; 20 Two or more races, non-Hispanic/Latino), 24 international. Average age 34. 262 applicants, 89% accepted, 151 enrolled. In 2010, 384 master's awarded. *Degree requirements:* For master's, thesis optional. *Entrance requirements:* For master's, minimum GPA of 3.0 in last 60 hours of undergraduate course work, resume, 3 letters of reference. Additional exam requirements/recommendations for international students: Required—TOEFL (minimum score 550 paper-based; 213 computer-based; 79 iBT). *Application deadline:* For fall admission, 4/1 priority date for domestic students, 4/1 for international students; for spring admission, 11/1 for domestic students, 9/1 for international students. Applications are processed on a rolling basis. Application fee: $40 ($90 for international students). Electronic applications accepted. *Expenses:* Tuition, state resident: full-time $3893; part-time $162.20 per credit hour. Tuition, nonresident: full-time $14,167; part-time $590.30 per credit hour. Required fees: $2523; $94.60 per credit hour. Tuition and fees vary according to course load and degree level. *Financial support:* In 2010–11, 201 students received support, including 12 research assistantships with partial tuition reimbursements available (averaging $10,699 per year), 1 teaching assistantship (averaging $10,800 per year); career-related internships or fieldwork, scholarships/grants, and unspecified assistantships also available. Financial award applicants required to submit FAFSA. *Faculty research:* Non-profit organizations, high risk youth, trauma, women's studies, impact of war on women and children. Total annual research expenditures: $30,549. *Unit head:* Dr. Susan Marcus-Mendoza, Dept Chair, 405-325-1756, Fax: 405-325-4402, E-mail: smmendoza@ou.edu. *Application contact:* Lawana Miller, Admissions Coordinator, 405-325-1756, Fax: 405-325-4402, E-mail: lmiller@ou.edu.

University of Regina, Faculty of Graduate Studies and Research, Faculty of Education, Department of Human Resources Development, Regina, SK S4S 0A2, Canada. Offers MHRD. Part-time programs available. *Faculty:* 3 full-time (2 women). *Students:* 6 full-time (all women), 15 part-time (12 women). 19 applicants, 74% accepted. In 2010, 5 master's awarded. *Degree requirements:* For master's, practicum, project, or thesis. *Entrance requirements:* For master's, 4-year B Ed, two years of teaching experience. Additional exam requirements/recommendations for international students: Required—TOEFL (minimum score 580 paper-based; 80 iBT). *Application deadline:* 2/15 for domestic and international students. Application fee: $100. Electronic applications accepted. Tuition and fees charges are reported in Canadian dollars. *Expenses:* Tuition, area resident: Full-time $3244.50 Canadian dollars; part-time $180.25 Canadian dollars per credit hour. International tuition: $4744.50 Canadian dollars full-time. Required fees: $494 Canadian dollars; $115.25 Canadian dollars per credit hour. $115.25 Canadian dollars per semester. Tuition and fees vary according to program. *Financial support:* In 2010–11, 2 fellowships (averaging $18,000 per year), 1 teaching assistantship (averaging $6,759 per year) were awarded; research assistantships, scholarships/grants also available. Financial award application deadline: 6/15. *Faculty research:* Foundations of adult development, theory and practice of adult education and human resource development; design and assessment of curriculum and instruction; planning and curriculum development; learning and the workplace. *Unit head:* Dr. Rod Dolmage, Associate Dean, Research and Graduate Programs, 306-585-4816, Fax: 306-585-5387, E-mail: rod.dolmage@uregina.

ca. *Application contact:* Tania Gates, Graduate Program Coordinator, 306-585-4506, Fax: 306-585-5387, E-mail: edgrad@uregina.ca.

University of St. Thomas, Graduate Studies, School of Education, Program in Organization Learning and Development, St. Paul, MN 55105-1096. Offers career development (Certificate); e-learning (Certificate); human resource development (Certificate); human resource management (Certificate); human resources and change leadership (MA); learning technology (Certificate); learning technology for learning development and change (MA); organization development (Ed D, Certificate). Part-time and evening/weekend programs available. Postbaccalaureate distance learning degree programs offered (minimal on-campus study). *Faculty:* 6 full-time (4 women), 15 part-time/adjunct (8 women). *Students:* 8 full-time (7 women), 156 part-time (118 women); includes 30 minority (12 Black or African American, non-Hispanic/Latino; 7 Asian, non-Hispanic/Latino; 7 Hispanic/Latino; 1 Native Hawaiian or other Pacific Islander, non-Hispanic/Latino; 3 Two or more races, non-Hispanic/Latino), 6 international. Average age 37. 165 applicants, 71% accepted, 102 enrolled. In 2010, 38 master's, 9 doctorates, 15 other advanced degrees awarded. *Degree requirements:* For doctorate, comprehensive exam, thesis/dissertation. *Entrance requirements:* For master's, minimum GPA of 3.0, 2 letters of reference, personal statement; for doctorate, minimum GPA of 3.5, interview; for Certificate, minimum graduate GPA of 3.25. Additional exam requirements/recommendations for international students: Required—TOEFL (minimum score 550 paper-based; 213 computer-based). *Application deadline:* For fall admission, 8/1 priority date for domestic and international students; for winter admission, 12/1 priority date for domestic students, 12/1 for international students; for spring admission, 12/1 priority date for domestic and international students. Applications are processed on a rolling basis. Application fee: $50. *Expenses:* Contact institution. *Financial support:* Fellowships, research assistantships, institutionally sponsored loans and scholarships/grants available. Support available to part-time students. Financial award applicants required to submit FAFSA. *Faculty research:* Workplace conflict, physician leaders, entrepreneurship education, mentoring. *Unit head:* Dr. David W. Jamieson, Department Chair, 651-962-4387, Fax: 651-962-4169, E-mail: jami9859@stthomas.edu. *Application contact:* Liz G. Knight, Department Coordinator, 651-962-4459, Fax: 651-962-4169, E-mail: egknight@stthomas.edu.

The University of Scranton, College of Graduate and Continuing Education, Department of Health Administration and Human Resources, Program in Human Resources, Scranton, PA 18510. Offers MS. Part-time and evening/weekend programs available. *Students:* 55 full-time (43 women), 17 part-time (9 women); includes 5 Black or African American, non-Hispanic/Latino; 3 Asian, non-Hispanic/Latino; 2 Hispanic/Latino. Average age 34. 46 applicants, 98% accepted. *Degree requirements:* For master's, capstone experience. *Entrance requirements:* Additional exam requirements/recommendations for international students: Required—TOEFL (minimum score 550 paper-based; 173 computer-based), IELTS (minimum score 5.5). Application fee: $0. *Financial support:* Fellowships, teaching assistantships, career-related internships or fieldwork available. Financial award application deadline: 3/1. *Unit head:* Dr. Daniel J. West, Chair, 570-941-4126, Fax: 570-941-4201, E-mail: westd1@scranton.edu. *Application contact:* Joseph M. Roback, Director of Admissions, 570-941-4385, Fax: 570-941-5928, E-mail: robackj2@scranton.edu.

The University of Scranton, College of Graduate and Continuing Education, Department of Health Administration and Human Resources, Program in Human Resources Administration, Scranton, PA 18510. Offers human resources (MS); human resources development (MS); organizational leadership (MS). Part-time and evening/weekend programs available. *Students:* 4 full-time (3 women), 6 part-time (5 women); includes 1 Hispanic/Latino. Average age 36. In 2010, 12 master's awarded. *Degree requirements:* For master's, capstone experience. *Entrance requirements:* For master's, minimum GPA of 2.75. Additional exam requirements/recommendations for international students: Required—TOEFL (minimum score 500 paper-based; 173 computer-based), IELTS (minimum score 5.5). *Application deadline:* Applications are processed on a rolling basis. Application fee: $0. *Financial support:* Fellowships, teaching assistantships, career-related internships or fieldwork, Federal Work-Study, and unspecified assistantships available. Support available to part-time students. Financial award application deadline: 3/1. *Unit head:* Dr. Daniel West, Director, 570-941-6218, E-mail: westd1@scranton.edu. *Application contact:* Joseph M. Roback, Director of Admissions, 570-941-4385, Fax: 570-941-5928, E-mail: robackj2@scranton.edu.

University of Wisconsin–Milwaukee, Graduate School, College of Letters and Sciences, Interdepartmental Program in Human Resources and Labor Relations, Milwaukee, WI 53201-0413. Offers human resources and labor relations (MHRLR); international human resources and labor relations (Certificate); mediation and negotiation (Certificate). Part-time programs available. *Students:* 17 full-time (13 women), 30 part-time (23 women); includes 5 Black or African American, non-Hispanic/Latino; 1 American Indian or Alaska Native, non-Hispanic/Latino, 5 international. Average age 30. 38 applicants, 58% accepted, 8 enrolled. In 2010, 20 master's awarded. *Entrance requirements:* For master's, GMAT or GRE General Test. Additional exam requirements/recommendations for international students: Required—TOEFL (minimum score 550 paper-based; 79 iBT), IELTS (minimum score

6.5). *Application deadline:* For fall admission, 1/1 priority date for domestic students; for spring admission, 9/1 for domestic students. Applications are processed on a rolling basis. Application fee: $56 ($96 for international students). Electronic applications accepted. *Financial support:* Career-related internships or fieldwork available. Support available to part-time students. Financial award application deadline: 4/15; financial award applicants required to submit FAFSA. *Unit head:* Susan M. Donohue-Davies, Representative, 414-299-4009, Fax: 414-229-5915, E-mail: suedono@uwm.edu. *Application contact:* General Information Contact, 414-229-4982, Fax: 414-229-6967, E-mail: gradschool@uwm.edu.

Villanova University, Graduate School of Liberal Arts and Sciences, Department of Human Resource Development, Villanova, PA 19085-1699. Offers MS. Part-time and evening/weekend programs available. *Faculty:* 21 part-time/adjunct (8 women). *Students:* 107 full-time (84 women), 189 part-time (135 women); includes 95 minority (49 Black or African American, non-Hispanic/Latino; 2 American Indian or Alaska Native, non-Hispanic/Latino; 13 Asian, non-Hispanic/Latino; 22 Hispanic/Latino; 9 Two or more races, non-Hispanic/Latino), 4 international. Average age 36. 199 applicants, 82% accepted, 141 enrolled. In 2010, 35 master's awarded. *Degree requirements:* For master's, comprehensive exam. *Entrance requirements:* For master's, GRE General Test, minimum GPA of 3.0. Additional exam requirements/recommendations for international students: Required—TOEFL. *Application deadline:* For fall admission, 2/1 priority date for domestic and international students; for spring admission, 11/15 priority date for domestic and international students. Applications are processed on a rolling basis. Application fee: $50. Electronic applications accepted. *Expenses:* Tuition: Part-time $700 per credit. Part-time tuition and fees vary according to degree level and program. *Financial support:* Research assistantships, career-related internships or fieldwork and Federal Work-Study available. Financial award applicants required to submit FAFSA. *Unit head:* Dr. David F. Bush, Director, 610-519-4746, E-mail: david.bush@villanova.edu. *Application contact:* Dr. Adele Lindenmeyr, Dean, Graduate School of Liberal Arts and Sciences, 610-519-7093, Fax: 610-519-7096.

Virginia Commonwealth University, Graduate School, School of Education, Program in Adult Learning, Richmond, VA 23284-9005. Offers adult literacy (M Ed); human resource development (M Ed); teaching and learning with technology (M Ed). *Accreditation:* NCATE. Part-time programs available. *Students:* 1 (woman) full-time, 22 part-time (16 women); includes 4 minority (all Black or African American, non-Hispanic/Latino), 1 international. 4 applicants, 75% accepted, 3 enrolled. In 2010, 6 master's awarded. *Entrance requirements:* For master's, GRE General Test or MAT. Additional exam requirements/recommendations for international students: Required—TOEFL (minimum score 600 paper-based; 250 computer-based; 100 iBT). *Application deadline:* For fall admission, 3/15 for domestic students; for spring admission, 11/1 for domestic students. Applications are processed on a rolling basis. Application fee: $50. Electronic applications accepted. *Expenses:* Tuition, state resident: full-time $4308; part-time $479 per credit hour. Tuition, nonresident: full-time $8942; part-time $994 per credit hour. Required fees: $2000; $85 per credit hour. Tuition and fees vary according to course level, course load, degree level, campus/location and program. *Financial support:* Career-related internships or fieldwork and Federal Work-Study available. Financial award application deadline: 3/1; financial award applicants required to submit FAFSA. *Faculty research:* Adult development and learning, program planning and evaluation. *Unit head:* Dr. Leila Christenbury, Interim Department Chair, 804-828-1306, Fax: 804-827-0676, E-mail: lchriste@vcu.edu. *Application contact:* Dr. Terry J. Carter, Adult Learning Program Coordinator, 804-827-2628, E-mail: tjcarter@vcu.edu.

Walden University, Graduate Programs, Richard W. Riley College of Education and Leadership, Minneapolis, MN 55401. Offers administrator leadership for teaching and learning (Ed D, Ed S); adult learning (MS), including developmental education, online teaching, teaching adults English as a second language, training and performance management; college teaching and learning (Postbaccalaureate Certificate); curriculum, instruction and assessment (Ed D, Postbaccalaureate Certificate); curriculum, instruction, and professional development (Ed S); early childhood education (birth-grade 3) (MAT); early childhood studies (MS), including administration, management and leadership, early childhood public policy and advocacy, teaching adults in the early childhood field, teaching and diversity; education (MS, PhD), including adolescent literacy and technology (grades 6-12) (MS), adult education leadership (PhD), community college leadership (PhD), curriculum, instruction, and assessment, early childhood education (PhD), educational leadership (MS), educational technology (PhD), elementary reading and literacy (MS), elementary reading and mathematics (MS), emotional/behavioral disorders (K-12) (MS), general program, higher education (PhD), integrating technology in the classroom (MS), K-12 educational leadership (PhD), leadership, policy and change (PhD), learning disabilities (K-12) (MS), learning, instruction and innovation (PhD), literacy and learning in the content areas (MS), mathematics (grades 6-8) (MS), mathematics (grades K-5) (MS), middle level education (grades 5-8) (MS), professional development (MS), science (grades K-8) (MS), self-designed (PhD), special education (PhD), special education (non-licensure) (MS), teacher leadership (grades K-12) (MS), teaching English language learners (grades K-12) (MS); educational leadership and administration (principal preparation) (Ed S); educational technology (Ed S); engaging culturally diverse learners (Postbaccalaureate Certificate); enrollment management and institutional marketing (Postbaccalaureate Certificate); higher education (MS), including college teaching and learning, enrollment management and institutional planning, global higher education, leadership for student success, online and distance learning; higher education and adult learning (Ed D); higher education leadership (Ed D); instructional design (Postbaccalaureate Certificate); instructional design and technology (MS), including general program (MS, PhD), online learning, training and performance improvement; integrating technology in the classroom (Postbaccalaureate Certificate); online learning (Postbaccalaureate Certificate); professional development (Postbaccalaureate Certificate); special education (Ed D, Ed S); special education: emotional/behavioral disorders (K-12) (MAT); special education: learning disabilities (K-12) (MAT); teacher leadership (Ed D, Ed S, Postbaccalaureate Certificate); training and performance management (Postbaccalaureate Certificate). Part-time and evening/weekend programs available. Postbaccalaureate distance learning degree programs offered (minimal on-campus study). *Faculty:* 61 full-time (44 women), 822 part-time/adjunct (539 women). *Students:* 13,130 full-time (10,679 women), 1,719 part-time (1,437 women); includes 5,153 minority (4,233 Black or African American, non-Hispanic/Latino; 89 American Indian or Alaska Native, non-Hispanic/Latino; 161 Asian, non-Hispanic/Latino; 542 Hispanic/Latino; 12 Native Hawaiian or other Pacific Islander, non-Hispanic/Latino; 116 Two or more races, non-Hispanic/Latino), 325 international. Average age 38. In 2010, 4,656 master's, 306 doctorates, 65 other advanced degrees awarded. *Degree requirements:* For doctorate, thesis/dissertation (for some programs), residency; for other advanced degree, residency (for some programs). *Entrance requirements:* For master's, bachelor's degree or equivalent in related field; minimum GPA of 2.5; official transcripts; goal statement; access to computer and Internet; for doctorate, master's degree or equivalent in related field; minimum GPA of 3.0; official transcripts; three years' related professional/academic experience (preferred); access to computer and Internet; for other advanced degree, master's degree or equivalent in related field; minimum GPA of 3.0; 3 years related professional/academic experience (preferred); access to computer and Internet (Ed S). Additional exam requirements/recommendations for international students: Required—TOEFL (minimum score 550 paper-based; 213 computer-based), IELTS (minimum score 6.5), TOEFL (minimum score 550 paper-based; 213 computer-based), IELTS (minimum score 6.5), or Michigan English Language Assessment Battery (minimum score 82). *Application deadline:* Applications are processed on a rolling basis. Application fee: $50. Electronic applications accepted. *Expenses:* Tuition: Full-time $10,274; part-time $445 per credit. Tuition and fees vary according to course load, degree level and program. *Financial support:* In 2010–11, 1 fellowship was awarded; Federal Work-Study, scholarships/grants, unspecified assistantships, and family tuition reduction, active duty/veteran tuition reduction, group tuition reduction, interest-free payment plans also available. Support available to part-time students. Financial award applicants required to submit FAFSA. *Unit head:* Dr. Kate Steffens, Dean, 800-925-3368. *Application contact:* Jennifer Hall, Vice President of Enrollment Management, 866-4-WALDEN, E-mail: info@waldenu.edu.

Western Seminary, Graduate Programs, Program in Ministry and Leadership, Portland, OR 97215-3367. Offers chaplaincy (MA); coaching (MA); Jewish ministry (MA); pastoral care to women (MA); youth ministry (MA). *Students:* 265 applicants, 77% accepted, 155 enrolled. In 2010, 93 master's awarded. *Degree requirements:* For master's, practicum. *Entrance requirements:* Additional exam requirements/recommendations for international students: Required—TOEFL. *Application deadline:* For fall admission, 7/18 priority date for domestic students; for winter admission, 11/7 priority date for domestic students; for spring admission, 3/13 priority date for domestic students. Applications are processed on a rolling basis. Application fee: $50. *Expenses:* Tuition: Part-time $425 per credit. *Financial support:* Applicants required to submit FAFSA. *Unit head:* Beverly Hislop, Director, 503-517-1881, E-mail: bhislop@westernseminary.edu. *Application contact:* Dr. Robert W. Wiggins, Registrar/Dean of Student Development, 503-517-1820, Fax: 503-517-1801, E-mail: rwiggins@westernseminary.edu.

Xavier University, College of Social Sciences, Health and Education, School of Education, Department of Educational Leadership and Human Resource Development, Program in Human Resource Development, Cincinnati, OH 45207. Offers MS. Evening/weekend programs available. *Faculty:* 2 full-time (both women), 3 part-time/adjunct (2 women). *Students:* 34 full-time (28 women), 28 part-time (20 women); includes 16 minority (13 Black or African American, non-Hispanic/Latino; 3 Asian, non-Hispanic/Latino). Average age 34. 38 applicants, 97% accepted, 33 enrolled. In 2010, 38 master's awarded. *Entrance requirements:* For master's, GRE or MAT, resume, goal statement, two references. Additional exam requirements/recommendations for international students: Required—TOEFL (minimum score 550 paper-based; 213 computer-based; 79 iBT). *Application deadline:* For fall admission, 8/1 priority date for domestic and international students. Application fee: $35. Electronic applications accepted. *Expenses:* Contact institution. *Financial support:* Teaching assistantships, unspecified assistantships available. Financial award applicants required to submit FAFSA. *Faculty research:* Graduate education, group dynamics, organizational behavior, reflection-in-action. *Unit head:* Dr.

Brenda Levya-Gardner, Associate Professor/Director, 513-745-4287, Fax: 513-745-1052, E-mail: gardner@xavier.edu. *Application contact:* Roger Bosse, Graduate Services Director, 513-745-3357, Fax: 513-745-1048, E-mail: bosse@xavier.edu.

HUMAN RESOURCES MANAGEMENT

Adelphi University, School of Business, Certificate Programs in Human Resources Management, Garden City, NY 11530-0701. Offers Certificate. Part-time and evening/weekend programs available. *Students:* 4 part-time (3 women); includes 2 Black or African American, non-Hispanic/Latino. Average age 37. *Entrance requirements:* For degree, GMAT or master's degree. Additional exam requirements/recommendations for international students: Required—TOEFL (minimum score 550 paper-based; 213 computer-based; 80 iBT). *Application deadline:* For fall admission, 4/1 for international students; for spring admission, 11/1 for international students. Applications are processed on a rolling basis. Application fee: $50. Electronic applications accepted. *Financial support:* Application deadline: 3/1. *Unit head:* Brian Rothschild, Assistant Dean, 516-877-4670, Fax: 516-877-4607, E-mail: gradbusinquiries@adelphi.edu. *Application contact:* Christine Murphy, Director of Admissions, 516-877-3050, Fax: 516-877-3039, E-mail: graduateadmissions@adelphi.edu.

Adelphi University, School of Business, MBA Program, Garden City, NY 11530-0701. Offers finance (MBA); management information systems (MBA); management/human resource management (MBA); marketing/e-commerce (MBA). *Accreditation:* AACSB. Part-time and evening/weekend programs available. *Students:* 131 full-time (59 women), 173 part-time (73 women); includes 25 Black or African American, non-Hispanic/Latino; 20 Asian, non-Hispanic/Latino; 17 Hispanic/Latino; 3 Two or more races, non-Hispanic/Latino, 110 international. Average age 29. In 2010, 86 master's awarded. *Degree requirements:* For master's, capstone course. *Entrance requirements:* For master's, GMAT, 2 letters of recommendation. Additional exam requirements/recommendations for international students: Required—TOEFL (minimum score 550 paper-based; 213 computer-based; 80 iBT). *Application deadline:* For fall admission, 4/1 for international students; for spring admission, 11/1 for international students. Applications are processed on a rolling basis. Application fee: $50. Electronic applications accepted. *Financial support:* Research assistantships with full and partial tuition reimbursements, career-related internships or fieldwork, Federal Work-Study, institutionally sponsored loans, scholarships/grants, and unspecified assistantships available. Financial award application deadline: 3/1; financial award applicants required to submit FAFSA. *Faculty research:* Supply chain management, distribution channels, productivity benchmark analysis, data envelopment analysis, financial portfolio analysis. *Unit head:* Rakesh Gupta, 516-877-4670, Fax: 516-877-4607, E-mail: gradbusinquiries@adelphi.edu. *Application contact:* Christine Murphy, Director of Admissions, 516-877-3050, Fax: 516-877-3039, E-mail: graduateadmissions@adelphi.edu.

Albany State University, College of Arts and Humanities, Program in Public Administration, Albany, GA 31705-2717. Offers community and economic development administration (MPA); criminal justice administration (MPA); fiscal management (MPA); general management (MPA); health administration and policy (MPA); human resources management (MPA); public policy (MPA); water resource management and policy (MPA). *Accreditation:* NASPAA. *Faculty:* 3 full-time (1 woman), 2 part-time/adjunct (0 women). *Students:* 13 full-time (7 women), 49 part-time (32 women); includes 58 Black or African American, non-Hispanic/Latino, 1 international. Average age 34. 18 applicants, 78% accepted, 12 enrolled. In 2010, 12 master's awarded. *Degree requirements:* For master's, professional public service internship, professional portfolio, capstone research project. *Entrance requirements:* For master's, GRE, MAT, or GMAT, baccalaureate degree from accredited college or university, two letters of recommendation, ASU medical and immunization form. *Application deadline:* For fall admission, 7/15 for domestic students, 5/15 for international students; for spring admission, 11/15 for domestic students, 9/15 for international students. Applications are processed on a rolling basis. Application fee: $20. Electronic applications accepted. *Expenses:* Tuition, state resident: full-time $3060; part-time $170 per credit hour. Tuition, nonresident: full-time $12,204; part-time $678 per credit hour. Required fees: $1160. Part-time tuition and fees vary according to course load. *Financial support:* Application deadline: 4/15. *Faculty research:* Public policy, strategic public human resources and human capital management, diversity management in the public sector and collective bargaining and labor relations in the public sector, e-government and public sector information systems, public administration pedagogy and business process modeling simulation, community development, nonprofit organizations, civic engagement and civic participation, healthcare disparities among minorities, poverty. Total annual research expenditures: $250. *Unit head:* Dr. Peter Ngwafu, Director, 229-430-4760, Fax: 229-430-7895, E-mail: peter.ngwafu@asurams.edu. *Application*

contact: Dr. Rani George, Dean, Graduate School, 229-430-5118, Fax: 229-430-6398, E-mail: rani.george@asurams.edu.

American Public University System, AMU/APU Graduate Programs, Charles Town, WV 25414. Offers accounting (MBA); administration and supervision (M Ed); air warfare (MA Military Studies); asymmetrical warfare (MA Military Studies); criminal justice (MA); emergency and disaster management (MA); entrepreneurship (MBA); environmental policy and management (MS); finance (MBA); general (MBA); global business management (MBA); guidance and counseling (M Ed); history (MA); homeland security (MA); homeland security resource allocation (MBA); humanities (MA); information technology (MS); information technology management (MBA); intelligence studies (MA); international relations and conflict resolution (MA); joint warfare (MA Military Studies); land warfare (MA Military Studies); legal studies (MA); management (MA), including defense mangement, general, human resource management, organizational leadership, public administration; marketing (MBA); military history (MA); national security studies (MA); naval warfare (MA Military Studies); nonprofit management (MBA); political science (MA); psychology (MA); public administration (MA); public health (MA); security management (MA); space studies (MS); sports management (MS); strategic leadership (MA Military Studies); teaching (M Ed), including elementary, secondary social sciences; transportation and logistics management (MA). Programs offered via distance learning only. Part-time and evening/weekend programs available. Postbaccalaureate distance learning degree programs offered (no on-campus study). *Faculty:* 253 full-time (134 women), 1,208 part-time/adjunct (570 women). *Students:* 956 full-time (422 women), 8,476 part-time (2,821 women); includes 2,511 minority (1,218 Black or African American, non-Hispanic/Latino; 68 American Indian or Alaska Native, non-Hispanic/Latino; 219 Asian, non-Hispanic/Latino; 705 Hispanic/Latino; 46 Native Hawaiian or other Pacific Islander, non-Hispanic/Latino; 255 Two or more races, non-Hispanic/Latino), 107 international. Average age 35. 9,550 applicants, 100% accepted. In 2010, 1,688 master's awarded. *Degree requirements:* For master's, comprehensive exam or practicum. *Entrance requirements:* For master's, official transcript showing earned bachelor's degree from institution accredited by recognized accrediting body. Additional exam requirements/recommendations for international students: Required—TOEFL (minimum score 550 paper-based; 213 computer-based), IELTS (minimum score 6.5). *Application deadline:* Applications are processed on a rolling basis. Application fee: $0. Electronic applications accepted. *Financial support:* Applicants required to submit FAFSA. *Faculty research:* Military history, criminal justice, management performance, national security. *Unit head:* Dr. Frank McCluskey, Provost, 877-468-6268, Fax: 304-724-3780. *Application contact:* Terry Grant, Director of Enrollment Management, 877-468-6268, Fax: 304-724-3780, E-mail: info@apus.edu.

Ashworth College, Graduate Programs, Norcross, GA 30092. Offers business administration (MBA); criminal justice (MS); health care administration (MBA, MS); human resource management (MBA, MS); international business (MBA); management (MS); marketing (MBA, MS). *Faculty:* 5 part-time/adjunct (1 woman). *Students:* 299. *Expenses:* Tuition: Full-time $9230; part-time $250 per credit hour. *Unit head:* Dr. Leslie A. Gargiulo, Vice President of Education, 770-729-8400, E-mail: lgargiulo@ashworthcollege.edu. *Application contact:* Dr. Leslie A. Gargiulo, Vice President of Education, 770-729-8400, E-mail: lgargiulo@ashworthcollege.edu.

Assumption College, Graduate School, Department of Business Studies, Worcester, MA 01609-1296. Offers accounting (MBA); business administration (CAGS); finance/economics (MBA); general business (MBA); human resources (MBA); international business (MBA); management (MBA); marketing (MBA); nonprofit leadership (MBA). Part-time and evening/weekend programs available. *Faculty:* 3 full-time (0 women), 13 part-time/adjunct (3 women). *Students:* 20 full-time (9 women), 135 part-time (70 women); includes 24 minority (19 Black or African American, non-Hispanic/Latino; 2 Asian, non-Hispanic/Latino; 3 Hispanic/Latino), 4 international. Average age 26. 85 applicants, 95% accepted. In 2010, 40 master's, 2 other advanced degrees awarded. *Entrance requirements:* For master's and CAGS, 3 letters of recommendation, resume, essay. Additional exam requirements/recommendations for international students: Required—TOEFL (minimum score 540 paper-based; 200 computer-based; 76 iBT), IELTS (minimum score 6). *Application deadline:* For fall admission, 6/1 priority date for domestic students, 5/1 priority date for international students; for spring admission, 11/1 priority date for domestic students, 9/1 priority date for international students. Applications are processed on a rolling basis. Application fee: $30. Electronic applications accepted. *Expenses:* Tuition: Part-time $503 per credit. Required fees: $20 per semester. One-time fee: $100. Part-time tuition and fees vary according to campus/location. *Financial support:* Application deadline: 6/1. *Faculty research:* Workplace diversity, dynamics of team interaction, utilization of leased employees. *Unit head:* Michael Lewis, Director, 508-767-7372, Fax: 508-767-7252, E-mail: milewis@assumption.edu. *Application contact:* Daniel Provost, Assistant Director of Graduate Student Services, 508-767-7426, Fax: 508-767-7030, E-mail: dprovost@assumption.edu.

Auburn University, Graduate School, College of Business, Department of Management, Auburn University, AL 36849. Offers human resource management (PhD); management (MS, PhD); management information systems (MS, PhD). *Accreditation:* AACSB. Part-time programs available. *Faculty:* 34

full-time (7 women), 5 part-time/adjunct (0 women). *Students:* 12 full-time (4 women), 12 part-time (2 women); includes 1 Black or African American, non-Hispanic/Latino; 2 Asian, non-Hispanic/Latino, 5 international. Average age 34. 137 applicants, 28% accepted, 20 enrolled. In 2010, 9 master's, 6 doctorates awarded. *Degree requirements:* For master's, thesis (for some programs); for doctorate, thesis/dissertation. *Entrance requirements:* For master's, GMAT, GRE General Test (MS); for doctorate, GMAT, GRE General Test. Additional exam requirements/recommendations for international students: Required—TOEFL. *Application deadline:* For fall admission, 7/7 for domestic students; for spring admission, 11/24 for domestic students. Applications are processed on a rolling basis. Application fee: $50 ($60 for international students). Electronic applications accepted. *Expenses:* Tuition, state resident: full-time $7002. Tuition, nonresident: full-time $21,898. International tuition: $22,116 full-time. Required fees: $892. Tuition and fees vary according to course load and program. *Financial support:* Teaching assistantships, Federal Work-Study available. Support available to part-time students. Financial award application deadline: 3/15; financial award applicants required to submit FAFSA. *Unit head:* Dr. Sharon Oswald, Head, 334-844-4071. *Application contact:* Dr. George Flowers, Dean of the Graduate School, 334-844-2125.

Azusa Pacific University, School of Business and Management, Azusa, CA 91702-7000. Offers business administration (MBA); diversity for strategic advantage (MA); entrepreneurship (MBA); finance (MBA); human and organizational development (MA); human resources and organizational development (MBA); human resources management (MA); international business (MBA); marketing (MBA); non-profit management (MA); organizational development and change (MA); performance improvement (MA); public administration (MA); strategic management (MBA). Part-time and evening/weekend programs available. *Faculty:* 19 full-time (5 women), 2 part-time/adjunct (1 woman). *Students:* 75 full-time (41 women), 96 part-time (46 women); includes 65 minority (15 Black or African American, non-Hispanic/Latino; 15 Asian, non-Hispanic/Latino; 34 Hispanic/Latino; 1 Native Hawaiian or other Pacific Islander, non-Hispanic/Latino), 17 international. Average age 30. In 2010, 82 master's awarded. *Degree requirements:* For master's, thesis (for some programs), final project. *Entrance requirements:* For master's, GMAT, minimum GPA of 3.0. Additional exam requirements/recommendations for international students: Required—TOEFL (minimum score 600 paper-based). *Application deadline:* For fall admission, 8/15 priority date for domestic students. Applications are processed on a rolling basis. Application fee: $45 ($65 for international students). *Expenses:* Contact institution. *Financial support:* Scholarships/grants available. *Faculty research:* Gender issues, financial risk, leadership and ethics, marketing strategy. *Unit head:* Dr. Ilene Bezjian, Dean, 626-815-3090, Fax: 626-815-3802, E-mail: ibezjian@apu.edu. *Application contact:* Dr. Ilene Bezjian, Dean, 626-815-3090, Fax: 626-815-3802, E-mail: ibezjian@apu.edu.

Baldwin-Wallace College, Graduate Programs, Division of Business, Program in Human Resources, Berea, OH 44017-2088. Offers MBA. Part-time and evening/weekend programs available. *Students:* 14 full-time (13 women), 18 part-time (15 women); includes 8 minority (4 Black or African American, non-Hispanic/Latino; 2 Hispanic/Latino; 2 Two or more races, non-Hispanic/Latino). Average age 35. 10 applicants, 70% accepted, 4 enrolled. In 2010, 13 master's awarded. *Degree requirements:* For master's, minimum overall GPA of 3.0, completion of all required courses. *Entrance requirements:* For master's, GMAT, bachelor's degree in field, work experience, minimum GPA of 3.0. Additional exam requirements/recommendations for international students: Required—TOEFL (minimum score 523 paper-based; 193 computer-based; 70 iBT). *Application deadline:* For fall admission, 7/25 priority date for domestic students, 4/30 priority date for international students; for spring admission, 12/15 priority date for domestic students, 9/30 priority date for international students. Applications are processed on a rolling basis. Application fee: $25. Electronic applications accepted. *Expenses:* Tuition: Full-time $16,750; part-time $712 per credit hour. Tuition and fees vary according to program. *Financial support:* Career-related internships or fieldwork available. Support available to part-time students. Financial award application deadline: 5/1. *Unit head:* Dr. Mary Pisnar, Director, 440-826-2392, Fax: 440-826-3868, E-mail: mpisnar@bw.edu. *Application contact:* Laura Spencer, Graduate Application Specialist, 440-826-2191, Fax: 440-826-3868, E-mail: lspencer@bw.edu.

Benedictine University, Graduate Programs, Program in Business Administration, Lisle, IL 60532-0900. Offers accounting (MBA); entrepreneurship and managing innovation (MBA); financial management (MBA); health administration (MBA); human resource management (MBA); information systems security (MBA); international business (MBA); management consulting (MBA); management information systems (MBA); marketing management (MBA); operations management and logistics (MBA); organizational leadership (MBA); MBA/MPH; MBA/MS. Part-time and evening/weekend programs available. Postbaccalaureate distance learning degree programs offered (minimal on-campus study). *Faculty:* 4 full-time (2 women), 24 part-time/adjunct (3 women). *Students:* 347 full-time (140 women), 672 part-time (360 women); includes 237 minority (155 Black or African American, non-Hispanic/Latino; 4 American Indian or Alaska Native, non-Hispanic/Latino; 43 Asian, non-Hispanic/Latino; 35 Hispanic/Latino), 21 international. Average age 34. 416 applicants, 88% accepted, 217 enrolled. In 2010, 355

master's awarded. *Entrance requirements:* For master's, GMAT. Additional exam requirements/recommendations for international students: Required—TOEFL (minimum score 550 paper-based; 213 computer-based). *Application deadline:* For fall admission, 9/1 for domestic students; for winter admission, 12/1 for domestic students; for spring admission, 2/15 for domestic students. Applications are processed on a rolling basis. Application fee: $40. Electronic applications accepted. *Financial support:* Career-related internships or fieldwork and health care benefits available. Support available to part-time students. *Faculty research:* Strategic leadership in professional organizations, sociology of professions, organizational change, social identity theory, applications to change management. *Unit head:* Dr. Sharon Borowicz, Director, 630-829-6219, E-mail: sborowicz@ben.edu. *Application contact:* Kari Gibbons, Director, Admissions, 630-829-6200, Fax: 630-829-6584, E-mail: kgibbons@ben.edu.

Briar Cliff University, Program in Human Resource Management, Sioux City, IA 51104-0100. Offers MA. Part-time and evening/weekend programs available. *Faculty:* 1 full-time (0 women), 2 part-time/adjunct (1 woman). *Students:* 1 full-time (0 women), 2 part-time (1 woman). Average age 36. 32 applicants, 66% accepted. In 2010, 9 master's awarded. *Degree requirements:* For master's, thesis optional. *Entrance requirements:* For master's, minimum undergraduate GPA of 2.77. *Application deadline:* For fall admission, 4/1 for domestic students. Application fee: $25. Electronic applications accepted. *Expenses:* Tuition: Full-time $5904; part-time $492 per credit hour. Required fees: $276; $23 per credit hour. Tuition and fees vary according to program. *Financial support:* Application deadline: 8/1. *Faculty research:* Diversity in the workplace. *Unit head:* Barb Redmond, Director, 712-279-5561, Fax: 712-279-1698, E-mail: barb.redmond@briarcliff.edu. *Application contact:* Cheryl Olson, Continuing Studies Admissions Representative, 712-279-1777, Fax: 712-279-1632, E-mail: cheryl.olson@briarcliff.edu.

Brigham Young University, Graduate Studies, Marriott School of Management, Master of Public Administration Program, Provo, UT 84602. Offers finance (MPA); human resources (MPA); local government (MPA); nonprofit management (MPA); JD/MPA. *Faculty:* 12 full-time (1 woman), 5 part-time/adjunct (0 women). *Students:* 121 full-time (58 women); includes 3 Black or African American, non-Hispanic/Latino; 1 American Indian or Alaska Native, non-Hispanic/Latino; 11 Asian, non-Hispanic/Latino; 8 Hispanic/Latino. Average age 27. 137 applicants, 64% accepted, 61 enrolled. In 2010, 47 master's awarded. *Entrance requirements:* For master's, GRE, GMAT, minimum GPA of 3.0. Additional exam requirements/recommendations for international students: Required—TOEFL (minimum score 580 paper-based; 85 iBT), IELTS (minimum score 7). *Application deadline:* For fall admission, 2/1 for domestic and international students. Application fee: $50. Electronic applications accepted. *Expenses:* Tuition: Full-time $5580; part-time $310 per credit hour. Tuition and fees vary according to program and student's religious affiliation. *Financial support:* In 2010–11, 73 students received support. Career-related internships or fieldwork and scholarships/grants available. Financial award application deadline: 4/15; financial award applicants required to submit FAFSA. *Faculty research:* Taxes, budgeting, nonprofit, ethics, decision modeling, work balance, organizational behavior. *Unit head:* Dr. David W. Hart, Director, 801-422-4221, Fax: 801-422-0311, E-mail: mpa@byu.edu. *Application contact:* Catherine Cooper, Director of Student Services, 801-422-4221, E-mail: mpa@byu.edu.

California State University, East Bay, Office of Academic Programs and Graduate Studies, College of Business and Economics, MBA Program, Hayward, CA 94542-3000. Offers entrepreneurship (MBA); finance (MBA); human resources and organizational behavior (MBA); information technology management (MBA); marketing management (MBA); operations and supply chain management (MBA); strategy and international business (MBA). Part-time and evening/weekend programs available. Postbaccalaureate distance learning degree programs offered (no on-campus study). *Faculty:* 33 full-time (9 women). *Students:* 121 full-time (58 women), 133 part-time (67 women); includes 7 Black or African American, non-Hispanic/Latino; 63 Asian, non-Hispanic/Latino; 11 Hispanic/Latino; 3 Native Hawaiian or other Pacific Islander, non-Hispanic/Latino; 5 Two or more races, non-Hispanic/Latino, 87 international. Average age 30. 284 applicants, 47% accepted, 55 enrolled. In 2010, 241 master's awarded. *Degree requirements:* For master's, comprehensive exam or thesis. *Entrance requirements:* For master's, GMAT (minimum 20th percentile verbal and quantitative section), bachelor's degree, minimum GPA of 2.75. Additional exam requirements/recommendations for international students: Required—TOEFL (minimum score 550 paper-based; 213 computer-based; 79 iBT). *Application deadline:* For fall admission, 6/30 for domestic and international students. Applications are processed on a rolling basis. Application fee: $55. Electronic applications accepted. *Financial support:* Career-related internships or fieldwork, Federal Work-Study, institutionally sponsored loans, and scholarships/grants available. Support available to part-time students. Financial award application deadline: 3/2; financial award applicants required to submit FAFSA. *Unit head:* Dr. Terri Swartz, Dean, 510-885-3291, Fax: 510-885-4884, E-mail: terri.swartz@csueastbay.edu. *Application contact:* Dr. Donna Wiley, Interim Associate Director, 510-885-2928, Fax: 510-885-4777, E-mail: donna.wiley@csueastbay.edu.

California State University, East Bay, Office of Academic Programs and Graduate Studies, College of Business and Economics, Option in Human

Resources and Organizational Behavior, Hayward, CA 94542-3000. Offers MBA. Part-time and evening/weekend programs available. *Degree requirements:* For master's, comprehensive exam or thesis. *Entrance requirements:* For master's, GMAT, minimum GPA of 2.75. Additional exam requirements/ recommendations for international students: Required—TOEFL (minimum score 550 paper-based; 213 computer-based). *Application deadline:* For fall admission, 6/30 for domestic and international students. Application fee: $55. Electronic applications accepted. *Financial support:* Fellowships, career-related internships or fieldwork, Federal Work-Study, institutionally sponsored loans, and scholarships/grants available. Support available to part-time students. Financial award application deadline: 3/2; financial award applicants required to submit FAFSA. *Unit head:* Dr. Xinjian Lu, Chair, 510-885-3307, Fax: 510-885-2660, E-mail: xinjian.lu@csueastbay.edu. *Application contact:* Dr. Donna Wiley, Interim Associate Director, 510-885-2928, Fax: 510-885-4777, E-mail: donna.wiley@csueastbay.edu.

The Catholic University of America, Metropolitan School of Professional Studies, Washington, DC 20064. Offers human resource management (MA); management (MSM). Part-time and evening/weekend programs available. *Faculty:* 44 part-time/adjunct (20 women). *Students:* 21 full-time (15 women), 153 part-time (88 women); includes 51 Black or African American, non-Hispanic/Latino; 1 American Indian or Alaska Native, non-Hispanic/Latino; 4 Asian, non-Hispanic/Latino; 16 Hispanic/Latino, 15 international. Average age 36. 176 applicants, 47% accepted, 65 enrolled. In 2010, 34 master's awarded. *Degree requirements:* For master's, minimum GPA of 3.0, capstone course. *Entrance requirements:* For master's, statement of purpose, official copies of academic transcripts, three letters of recommendation, resume. Additional exam requirements/recommendations for international students: Required— TOEFL (minimum score 237 computer-based; 93 iBT). *Application deadline:* For fall admission, 8/1 priority date for domestic students, 7/15 for international students; for spring admission, 12/1 priority date for domestic students, 10/15 for international students. Application fee: $55. *Expenses:* Tuition: Full-time $33,580; part-time $1315 per credit hour. Required fees: $80; $40 per semester hour. One-time fee: $425. *Unit head:* Dr. Sara Thompson, Dean, 202-319-5256, Fax: 202-319-6032, E-mail: thompson@cua.edu. *Application contact:* Andrew Woodall, Director of Graduate Admissions, 202-319-5057, Fax: 202-319-6533, E-mail: cua-admissions@cua.edu.

Central Michigan University, Central Michigan University Off-Campus Programs, Program in Administration, Mount Pleasant, MI 48859. Offers acquisitions administration (MSA, Certificate); general administration (MSA, Certificate); health services administration (MSA, Certificate); human resources administration (MSA, Certificate); information resource management (MSA, Certificate); international administration (MSA, Certificate); leadership (MSA, Certificate); public administration (MSA, Certificate); vehicle design and manufacturing administration (Certificate). Part-time and evening/weekend programs available. Postbaccalaureate distance learning degree programs offered (no on-campus study). *Students:* Average age 38. *Entrance requirements:* For master's, minimum GPA of 2.7 in major. *Application deadline:* Applications are processed on a rolling basis. Application fee: $50. Electronic applications accepted. *Expenses:* Tuition, state resident: full-time $8208; part-time $456 per credit hour. Tuition, non-resident: full-time $13,788; part-time $766 per credit hour. One-time fee: $25. *Financial support:* Scholarships/grants available. Support available to part-time students. Financial award applicants required to submit FAFSA. *Unit head:* Dr. Nana Korsah, Director, MSA Programs, 989-774-6525, E-mail: korsa1na@cmich.edu. *Application contact:* 877-268-4636, E-mail: cmu offcampus@cmich.edu.

Central Michigan University, College of Graduate Studies, College of Business Administration, Department of Management, Mount Pleasant, MI 48859. Offers human resource management (MBA); international business (MBA). *Faculty:* 8 full-time (2 women), 1 part-time/adjunct (0 women). *Degree requirements:* For master's, thesis or alternative. *Entrance requirements:* For master's, GMAT. *Application deadline:* Applications are processed on a rolling basis. Application fee: $35 ($45 for international students). Electronic applications accepted. *Expenses:* Tuition, state resident: full-time $8208; part-time $456 per credit hour. Tuition, nonresident: full-time $13,788; part-time $766 per credit hour. One-time fee: $25. *Financial support:* Fellowships with tuition reimbursements, research assistantships with tuition reimbursements, teaching assistantships with tuition reimbursements, unspecified assistantships and out-of-state merit awards, non-resident graduate awards available. *Faculty research:* Human resource accounting, valuation, and liability; international business and economic issues; entrepreneurial leadership; technology management and strategy; electronic commerce and neural networks. *Unit head:* Dr. Mahmood Bahaee, Chairperson, 989-774-3747, Fax: 989-774-1353, E-mail: bahae1m@cmich.edu. *Application contact:* Dr. Debasish Chakraborty, Director, MBA Program, 989-774-3337, Fax: 989-774-1320, E-mail: chakr1d@cmich.edu.

Central Michigan University, College of Graduate Studies, Interdisciplinary Administration Programs, Mount Pleasant, MI 48859. Offers acquisitions administration (MSA, Graduate Certificate); general administration (MSA, Graduate Certificate); health services administration (MSA, Graduate Certificate); human resource administration (Graduate Certificate); human resources administration (MSA); information resource management (MSA, Graduate Certificate); international administration (MSA, Graduate Certificate); leadership (MSA, Graduate Certificate); organizational communication (MSA, Graduate Certificate); public administration (MSA, Graduate Certificate); recreation and park administration (MSA); sport administration (MSA). *Accreditation:* AACSB. Part-time and evening/weekend programs available. Postbaccalaureate distance learning degree programs offered (no on-campus study). *Students:* 102 full-time (50 women), 77 part-time (51 women); includes 10 Black or African American, non-Hispanic/Latino; 3 American Indian or Alaska Native, non-Hispanic/Latino; 5 Asian, non-Hispanic/Latino, 65 international. Average age 29. *Degree requirements:* For master's, thesis or alternative. *Entrance requirements:* For master's, bachelor's degree with minimum GPA of 2.7. *Application deadline:* For fall admission, 6/1 for international students; for spring admission, 10/1 for international students. Applications are processed on a rolling basis. Application fee: $35 ($45 for international students). Electronic applications accepted. *Expenses:* Tuition, state resident: full-time $8208; part-time $456 per credit hour. Tuition, non-resident: full-time $13,788; part-time $766 per credit hour. One-time fee: $25. *Financial support:* Fellowships with tuition reimbursements, research assistantships with tuition reimbursements, career-related internships or fieldwork, Federal Work-Study, unspecified assistantships, and out-of-state merit awards, non-resident graduate awards available. *Faculty research:* Interdisciplinary studies in acquisitions administration, health services administration, sport administration, recreation and park administration, and international administration. *Unit head:* Dr. Nana Korash, Director, 989-774-6525, Fax: 989-774-2575, E-mail: msa@cmich.edu. *Application contact:* Denise Schafer, Coordinator, 989-774-4373, Fax: 989-774-2575, E-mail: schaf1dr@cmich.edu.

Claremont Graduate University, Graduate Programs, School of Behavioral and Organizational Sciences, Program in Human Resources Design, Claremont, CA 91711-6160. Offers MS. Part-time and evening/weekend programs available. *Students:* 33 full-time (20 women), 7 part-time (6 women); includes 12 minority (2 Black or African American, non-Hispanic/Latino; 3 Asian, non-Hispanic/Latino; 4 Hispanic/Latino; 1 Native Hawaiian or other Pacific Islander, non-Hispanic/Latino; 2 Two or more races, non-Hispanic/Latino), 21 international. Average age 28. In 2010, 13 master's awarded. *Entrance requirements:* For master's, GMAT or GRE General Test. Additional exam requirements/recommendations for international students: Required— TOEFL (minimum score 550 paper-based; 213 computer-based; 80 iBT). *Application deadline:* For fall admission, 1/15 priority date for domestic students. Applications are processed on a rolling basis. Application fee: $60. Electronic applications accepted. *Expenses:* Tuition: Full-time $35,748; part-time $1554 per unit. Required fees: $215 per semester. *Financial support:* Fellowships, Federal Work-Study, institutionally sponsored loans, and scholarships/grants available. Support available to part-time students. Financial award application deadline: 2/15; financial award applicants required to submit FAFSA. *Unit head:* Katie Ear, Administrative Director, 909-607-1916, Fax: 909-621-8905, E-mail: katie.ear@cgu.edu. *Application contact:* Deryn Dudley, Program Assistant, 909-607-3286, Fax: 909-621-8905, E-mail: hrd@cgu.edu.

Clemson University, Graduate School, College of Health, Education, and Human Development, Eugene T. Moore School of Education, Program in Human Resource Development, Clemson, SC 29634. Offers MHRD. Part-time and evening/weekend programs available. Postbaccalaureate distance learning degree programs offered (no on-campus study). *Students:* 2 full-time (1 woman), 70 part-time (49 women); includes 14 Black or African American, non-Hispanic/Latino; 1 American Indian or Alaska Native, non-Hispanic/Latino; 1 Hispanic/Latino. Average age 35. 51 applicants, 90% accepted, 41 enrolled. In 2010, 35 master's awarded. *Degree requirements:* For master's, comprehensive exam. *Entrance requirements:* For master's, GRE General Test, Keirsey Campbell. Additional exam requirements/recommendations for international students: Required—TOEFL; Recommended— IELTS. *Application deadline:* For fall admission, 7/1 for domestic students. Application fee: $70 ($80 for international students). Electronic applications accepted. *Expenses:* Contact institution. *Financial support:* In 2010–11, 2 students received support. Application deadline: 6/1. *Faculty research:* Organizational development, human performance improvement, attachment theory, social constructivism, technology-mediated teaching and learning, corporate universities. *Unit head:* Dr. Michael J. Padilla, Director/Associate Dean, 864-656-4444, Fax: 864-656-0311, E-mail: pmcgee@clemson.edu. *Application contact:* Dr. David Fleming, Graduate Coordinator, 864-656-1881, Fax: 864-656-0311, E-mail: dflemin@clemson.edu.

Cleveland State University, College of Graduate Studies, Nance College of Business Administration, Department of Management and Labor Relations, Cleveland, OH 44115. Offers labor relations and human resources (MLRHR). Part-time programs available. *Faculty:* 9 full-time (4 women), 10 part-time/adjunct (3 women). *Students:* 29 full-time (22 women), 40 part-time (28 women); includes 9 Black or African American, non-Hispanic/Latino; 1 Asian, non-Hispanic/Latino; 1 Hispanic/Latino; 1 Two or more races, non-Hispanic/Latino, 17 international. Average age 29. 95 applicants, 67% accepted, 24 enrolled. In 2010, 16 master's awarded. *Entrance requirements:* For master's, GMAT or GRE. Additional exam requirements/recommendations for international students: Required—TOEFL (minimum score 525 paper-based; 197

computer-based). *Application deadline:* For fall admission, 7/15 for domestic students; for spring admission, 12/15 for domestic students. Applications are processed on a rolling basis. Application fee: $30. Electronic applications accepted. *Expenses:* Tuition, state resident: full-time $8447; part-time $469 per credit hour. Tuition, nonresident: full-time $16,020; part-time $890 per credit hour. Required fees: $50. *Financial support:* In 2010–11, 3 research assistantships with full and partial tuition reimbursements (averaging $6,960 per year) were awarded; career-related internships or fieldwork, tuition waivers (full), and unspecified assistantships also available. Financial award applicants required to submit FAFSA. *Unit head:* Dr. Jeffrey C. Susbauer, Chairperson, 216-687-4747, Fax: 216-687-4708, E-mail: j.susbauer@csuohio.edu. *Application contact:* Dr. W. Benoy Joseph, Associate Dean, 216-687-2019, Fax: 216-687-9354, E-mail: w.joseph@csuohio.edu.

Concordia University, St. Paul, College of Business and Organizational Leadership, St. Paul, MN 55104-5494. Offers business and organizational leadership (MBA); criminal justice leadership (MA); health care management (MBA); human resources management (MA); leadership and management (MA). *Accreditation:* ACBSP. Evening/weekend programs available. Postbaccalaureate distance learning degree programs offered (minimal on-campus study). *Faculty:* 14 full-time (6 women), 30 part-time/adjunct (8 women). *Students:* 338 full-time (203 women), 2 part-time (1 woman); includes 24 Black or African American, non-Hispanic/Latino; 3 American Indian or Alaska Native, non-Hispanic/Latino; 11 Asian, non-Hispanic/Latino; 3 Hispanic/Latino; 3 Two or more races, non-Hispanic/Latino. Average age 34. 191 applicants, 65% accepted, 117 enrolled. In 2010, 125 master's awarded. *Application deadline:* Applications are processed on a rolling basis. Application fee: $50. Electronic applications accepted. *Expenses:* Tuition: Full-time $7500; part-time $460 per credit. Required fees: $460 per credit. Tuition and fees vary according to program. *Financial support:* Applicants required to submit FAFSA. *Unit head:* Dr. Bruce Corrie, Dean, 651-641-8226, Fax: 651-641-8807, E-mail: corrie@csp.edu. *Application contact:* Kimberly Craig, Director of Graduate and Cohort Admission, 651-603-6223, Fax: 651-603-6320, E-mail: craig@csp.edu.

Cornell University, Graduate School, Graduate Fields of Industrial and Labor Relations, Ithaca, NY 14853. Offers collective bargaining, labor law and labor history (MILR, MPS, MS, PhD); economic and social statistics (MILR); human resource studies (MILR, MPS, MS, PhD); industrial and labor relations problems (MILR, MPS, MS, PhD); international and comparative labor (MILR, MPS, MS, PhD); labor economics (MILR, MPS, MS, PhD); organizational behavior (MILR, MPS, MS, PhD). *Faculty:* 52 full-time (17 women). *Students:* 165 full-time (100 women); includes 13 Black or African American, non-Hispanic/Latino; 1 American Indian or Alaska Native, non-Hispanic/Latino; 15 Asian, non-Hispanic/Latino; 7 Hispanic/Latino; 60 international. Average age 29. 340 applicants, 29% accepted, 87 enrolled. In 2010, 68 master's, 3 doctorates awarded. *Degree requirements:* For master's, thesis (MS); for doctorate, comprehensive exam, thesis/dissertation, teaching experience. *Entrance requirements:* For master's and doctorate, GMAT or GRE General Test, 2 academic recommendations. Additional exam requirements/recommendations for international students: Required—TOEFL (minimum score 550 paper-based; 213 computer-based; 77 iBT). Application fee: $70. Electronic applications accepted. *Expenses:* Contact institution. *Financial support:* In 2010–11, 73 students received support, including 14 fellowships with full tuition reimbursements available, 26 research assistantships with full tuition reimbursements available, 30 teaching assistantships with full tuition reimbursements available; institutionally sponsored loans, scholarships/grants, health care benefits, tuition waivers (full and partial), and unspecified assistantships also available. Financial award applicants required to submit FAFSA. *Unit head:* Director of Graduate Studies, 607-255-1522. *Application contact:* Graduate Field Assistant, 607-255-1522, E-mail: ilrgradapplicant@cornell.edu.

DePaul University, Charles H. Kellstadt Graduate School of Business, Department of Management, Chicago, IL 60604-2287. Offers entrepreneurship (MBA); health sector management (MBA); human resource management (MBA, MSHR); leadership/change management (MBA); management planning and strategy (MBA); operations management (MBA). Part-time and evening/weekend programs available. *Faculty:* 36 full-time (7 women), 35 part-time/adjunct (16 women). *Students:* 267 full-time (116 women), 125 part-time (43 women); includes 76 minority (24 Black or African American, non-Hispanic/Latino; 1 American Indian or Alaska Native, non-Hispanic/Latino; 33 Asian, non-Hispanic/Latino; 13 Hispanic/Latino; 1 Native Hawaiian or other Pacific Islander, non-Hispanic/Latino; 4 Two or more races, non-Hispanic/Latino; 20 international. In 2010, 112 master's awarded. *Entrance requirements:* For master's, GMAT, GRE (MSHR), 2 letters of recommendation, resume. Additional exam requirements/recommendations for international students: Required—TOEFL (minimum score 550 paper-based; 213 computer-based). *Application deadline:* For fall admission, 7/1 for domestic students; for winter admission, 10/1 for domestic students; for spring admission, 2/1 for domestic students. Applications are processed on a rolling basis. Application fee: $60. Electronic applications accepted. *Financial support:* Research assistantships available. Financial award application deadline: 4/1. *Faculty research:* Growth management, creativity and innovation, quality management and business process design, entrepreneurship. *Application contact:*

Christopher E. Kinsella, Director of Cohort MBA Programs, 312-362-8810, Fax: 312-362-6677, E-mail: kgsb@depaul.edu.

DeSales University, Graduate Division, Program in Business Administration, Center Valley, PA 18034-9568. Offers accounting (MBA); computer information systems (MBA); finance (MBA); health care systems management (MBA); health care systems management (online) (MBA); human resource management (MBA); management (MBA); management (online) (MBA); marketing (MBA); marketing (online) (MBA); physician's track (MBA); project management (MBA); project management (online) (MBA); self-design (MBA); self-design (online) (MBA); MSN/MBA. *Accreditation:* ACBSP. Part-time programs available. Postbaccalaureate distance learning degree programs offered (no on-campus study). *Entrance requirements:* For master's, GMAT, minimum GPA of 3.0, 2 years of work experience. Additional exam requirements/recommendations for international students: Required—TOEFL. *Application deadline:* Applications are processed on a rolling basis. Application fee: $35. Electronic applications accepted. *Expenses:* Tuition: Full-time $18,200; part-time $690 per credit. Required fees: $1200. *Faculty research:* Quality improvement, executive development, productivity, cross-cultural managerial differences, leadership. *Unit head:* Dr. David Gilfoil, Director, 610-282-1100 Ext. 1828, Fax: 610-282-2869, E-mail: david.gilfoil@desales.edu. *Application contact:* Caryn Stopper, Director of Graduate Admissions, 610-282-1100 Ext. 1768, Fax: 610-282-0525, E-mail: caryn.stopper@desales.edu.

Dowling College, School of Business, Oakdale, NY 11769-1999. Offers aviation management (MBA, Certificate); banking and finance (MBA, Certificate); corporate finance (MBA); financial planning (Certificate); health care management (MBA, Certificate); human resource management (Certificate); information systems management (MBA); management and leadership (MBA); marketing (Certificate); project management (Certificate); public management (MBA, Certificate); sport, event and entertainment management (Certificate); JD/MBA. Part-time and evening/weekend programs available. *Faculty:* 10 full-time (4 women), 56 part-time/adjunct (7 women). *Students:* 295 full-time (131 women), 460 part-time (206 women); includes 219 minority (97 Black or African American, non-Hispanic/Latino; 14 Asian, non-Hispanic/Latino; 35 Hispanic/Latino; 73 Native Hawaiian or other Pacific Islander, non-Hispanic/Latino; 3 international. Average age 33. 327 applicants, 85% accepted, 160 enrolled. In 2010, 33 master's, 1 other advanced degree awarded. *Degree requirements:* For master's, comprehensive exam, thesis optional. *Entrance requirements:* For master's, minimum GPA of 2.8, 2 letters of recommendation, courses in accounting and finance or seminar in accounting/finance, resume. Additional exam requirements/recommendations for international students: Required—TOEFL (minimum score 550 paper-based). *Application deadline:* For fall admission, 9/1 priority date for domestic students; for winter admission, 1/1 priority date for domestic students; for spring admission, 2/1 priority date for domestic students. Applications are processed on a rolling basis. Application fee: $50. Electronic applications accepted. *Expenses:* Tuition: Part-time $884 per credit hour. Part-time tuition and fees vary according to degree level and campus/location. *Financial support:* Career-related internships or fieldwork and Federal Work-Study available. Support available to part-time students. Financial award application deadline: 6/30; financial award applicants required to submit FAFSA. *Faculty research:* International finance, computer applications, labor relations, executive development. *Unit head:* Antonia Loschiavo, Assistant Dean, 631-244-3266, Fax: 631-244-1018, E-mail: loschiat@dowling.edu. *Application contact:* Ronnie S. Macdonald, Assistant Vice President for Enrollment Services/Dean of Admissions, 631-244-3357, Fax: 631-244-1059, E-mail: macdonar@dowling.edu.

Eastern Michigan University, Graduate School, College of Arts and Sciences, Department of Political Science, Programs in Public Administration, Ypsilanti, MI 48197. Offers local government management (Graduate Certificate); management of public healthcare services (Graduate Certificate); public administration (MPA, Graduate Certificate); public budget management (Graduate Certificate); public land planning (Graduate Certificate); public management (Graduate Certificate); public personnel management (Graduate Certificate); public policy analysis (Graduate Certificate). *Accreditation:* NASPAA. *Students:* 28 full-time (18 women), 124 part-time (64 women); includes 50 minority (40 Black or African American, non-Hispanic/Latino; 1 American Indian or Alaska Native, non-Hispanic/Latino; 1 Asian, non-Hispanic/Latino; 6 Hispanic/Latino; 2 Two or more races, non-Hispanic/Latino, 5 international. Average age 34. In 2010, 17 master's, 17 other advanced degrees awarded. Application fee: $35. *Unit head:* Dr. Joseph Ohren, Program Director, 734-487-2522, Fax: 734-487-3340, E-mail: joseph.ohren@emich.edu. *Application contact:* Dr. Joseph Ohren, Program Director, 734-487-2522, Fax: 734-487-3340, E-mail: joseph.ohren@emich.edu.

Eastern Michigan University, Graduate School, College of Business, Department of Management, Program in Human Resources Management and Organizational Development, Ypsilanti, MI 48197. Offers MSHROD. Part-time and evening/weekend programs available. Postbaccalaureate distance learning degree programs offered (minimal on-campus study). *Students:* 24 full-time (12 women), 53 part-time (39 women); includes 18 minority (8 Black or African American, non-Hispanic/Latino; 1 American Indian or Alaska Native, non-Hispanic/Latino; 5 Asian, non-Hispanic/Latino; 4 Hispanic/

Latino), 21 international. Average age 31. In 2010, 37 master's awarded. *Degree requirements:* For master's, thesis optional. *Entrance requirements:* For master's, GMAT. Additional exam requirements/recommendations for international students: Required—TOEFL. *Application deadline:* Applications are processed on a rolling basis. Application fee: $35. *Financial support:* Fellowships, research assistantships with full tuition reimbursements, teaching assistantships with full tuition reimbursements, career-related internships or fieldwork, Federal Work-Study, institutionally sponsored loans, scholarships/grants, tuition waivers (partial), and unspecified assistantships available. Support available to part-time students. Financial award applicants required to submit FAFSA. *Unit head:* Dr. Fraya Wagner-Marsh, Advisor, 734-787-3240, Fax: 734-487-4100, E-mail: fraya.wagner@emich.edu. *Application contact:* Dr. Fraya Wagner-Marsh, Advisor, 734-787-3240, Fax: 734-487-4100, E-mail: fraya.wagner@emich.edu.

Eastern Michigan University, Graduate School, College of Business, Programs in Business Administration, Ypsilanti, MI 48197. Offers business administration (MBA, Graduate Certificate); computer information systems (Graduate Certificate); e-business (MBA, Graduate Certificate); enterprise business intelligence (MBA); entrepreneurship (MBA, Graduate Certificate); finance (MBA, Graduate Certificate); human resources (MBA); human resources management (Graduate Certificate); information systems (MBA); internal auditing (MBA); international business (MBA, Graduate Certificate); marketing management (Graduate Certificate); nonprofit management (MBA); organizational development (Graduate Certificate); supply chain management (MBA, Graduate Certificate). *Accreditation:* AACSB. Part-time programs available. Postbaccalaureate distance learning degree programs offered (no on-campus study). *Students:* 149 full-time (66 women), 456 part-time (232 women); includes 146 minority (109 Black or African American, non-Hispanic/Latino; 4 American Indian or Alaska Native, non-Hispanic/Latino; 27 Asian, non-Hispanic/Latino; 6 Hispanic/Latino), 105 international. Average age 32. 330 applicants, 64% accepted, 150 enrolled. In 2010, 128 master's, 53 other advanced degrees awarded. *Entrance requirements:* For master's, GMAT (minimum score 450), minimum cumulative undergraduate GPA of 2.75. Additional exam requirements/recommendations for international students: Required—TOEFL. *Application deadline:* For fall admission, 5/15 for domestic students, 5/1 for international students; for winter admission, 10/15 for domestic students, 10/1 for international students; for spring admission, 3/15 for domestic students, 3/1 for international students. Applications are processed on a rolling basis. Application fee: $35. *Financial support:* Fellowships, research assistantships with full tuition reimbursements, teaching assistantships with full tuition reimbursements, career-related internships or fieldwork, Federal Work-Study, institutionally sponsored loans, scholarships/grants, tuition waivers (partial), and unspecified assistantships available. Support available to part-time students. Financial award applicants required to submit FAFSA. *Unit head:* K. Michelle Henry, Interim Director, Graduate Programs, 734-487-4444, Fax: 734-483-1316, E-mail: mhenry1@emich.edu. *Application contact:* Beste Windes, Advisor, 734-487-4444, Fax: 734-483-1316, E-mail: bwindes@emich.edu.

Fairfield University, Charles F. Dolan School of Business, Fairfield, CT 06824-5195. Offers accounting (MBA, MS, CAS); accounting information systems (MBA); entrepreneurship (MBA); finance (MBA, MS, CAS); general management (MBA, CAS); human resource management (MBA, CAS); information systems and operations (MBA); information systems and operations management (CAS); international business (MBA, CAS); marketing (MBA, CAS); taxation (MBA, CAS). *Accreditation:* AACSB. Part-time and evening/weekend programs available. *Faculty:* 42 full-time (15 women), 8 part-time/adjunct (1 woman). *Students:* 89 full-time (32 women), 127 part-time (54 women); includes 4 Black or African American, non-Hispanic/Latino; 2 Asian, non-Hispanic/Latino; 4 Hispanic/Latino; 1 Two or more races, non-Hispanic/Latino, 17 international. Average age 29. 108 applicants, 62% accepted, 46 enrolled. In 2010, 79 master's awarded. *Degree requirements:* For master's, capstone course. *Entrance requirements:* For master's, GMAT (minimum score 500), 2 letters of reference, resume, minimum GPA of 3.0. Additional exam requirements/recommendations for international students: Required—TOEFL (minimum score 550 paper-based; 213 computer-based; 80 iBT). *Application deadline:* For fall admission, 5/15 for international students; for spring admission, 10/15 for international students. Applications are processed on a rolling basis. Application fee: $60. Electronic applications accepted. *Expenses:* Contact institution. *Financial support:* In 2010–11, 48 students received support. Scholarships/grants, unspecified assistantships, and merit based one-time entrance scholarship available. Financial award applicants required to submit FAFSA. *Faculty research:* Optimization strategies, international finance, consumer behavior, financial market volatility, Internet marketing, supply chain analysis, tax issues. Total annual research expenditures: $50,000. *Unit head:* Dr. Norman A. Solomon, Dean, 203-254-4000 Ext. 4070, Fax: 203-254-4105, E-mail: nsolomon@fairfield.edu. *Application contact:* Marianne Gumpper, Director of Graduate and Continuing Studies Admissions, 203-254-4184, Fax: 203-254-4073, E-mail: gradadmis@fairfield.edu.

Fairleigh Dickinson University, College at Florham, Silberman College of Business, Center for Human Resource Management Studies, Program in Human Resource Management, Madison, NJ 07940-1099. Offers MBA, MA/MBA. *Students:* 8 full-time (6 women), 8 part-time (5 women), 3 international.

Average age 30. 4 applicants, 50% accepted, 0 enrolled. In 2010, 6 master's awarded. *Application deadline:* Applications are processed on a rolling basis. Application fee: $40.

Fairleigh Dickinson University, Metropolitan Campus, Silberman College of Business, Center for Human Resources Management Studies, Program in Human Resource Management, Teaneck, NJ 07666-1914. Offers MBA, Certificate. *Students:* 5 full-time (all women), 6 part-time (5 women), 4 international. Average age 28. 5 applicants, 20% accepted, 0 enrolled. In 2010, 4 master's awarded. *Application deadline:* Applications are processed on a rolling basis. Application fee: $40. *Application contact:* Susan Brooman, University Director of Graduate Admissions, 201-692-2554, Fax: 201-692-2560, E-mail: globaleducation@fdu.edu.

Fitchburg State University, Division of Graduate and Continuing Education, Program in Business Administration, Fitchburg, MA 01420-2697. Offers accounting (MBA); human resource management (MBA); management (MBA). Part-time and evening/weekend programs available. Postbaccalaureate distance learning degree programs offered (no on-campus study). *Students:* 24 full-time (11 women), 74 part-time (46 women); includes 6 Black or African American, non-Hispanic/Latino; 1 American Indian or Alaska Native, non-Hispanic/Latino; 5 Hispanic/Latino, 13 international. Average age 33. 42 applicants, 98% accepted, 33 enrolled. In 2010, 59 master's awarded. *Entrance requirements:* For master's, GMAT, minimum GPA of 2.8, letters of recommendation, resume. Additional exam requirements/recommendations for international students: Required—TOEFL (minimum score 550 paper-based; 213 computer-based; 79 iBT). *Application deadline:* Applications are processed on a rolling basis. Application fee: $25 ($50 for international students). *Expenses:* Tuition, area resident: Part-time $150 per credit. Tuition, state resident: part-time $150 per credit. Tuition, nonresident: part-time $150 per credit. Required fees: $127 per credit. *Financial support:* In 2010–11, research assistantships with partial tuition reimbursements (averaging $5,500 per year); Federal Work-Study, scholarships/grants, and unspecified assistantships also available. Support available to part-time students. Financial award application deadline: 3/1; financial award applicants required to submit FAFSA. *Unit head:* Joseph McAloon, Chair, 978-665-3745, Fax: 978-665-3658, E-mail: gce@fitchburgstate.edu. *Application contact:* Director of Admissions, 978-665-3144, Fax: 978-665-4540, E-mail: admissions@fitchburgstate.edu.

Florida Institute of Technology, Graduate Programs, Extended Studies Division, Melbourne, FL 32901-6975. Offers acquisition and contract management (MS); aerospace engineering (MS); business administration (MBA); computer information systems (MS); computer science (MS); electrical engineering (MS); engineering management (MS); human resources management (MS); logistics management (MS), including humanitarian and disaster relief logistics; management (MS), including acquisition and contract management, e-business, human resources management, information systems, logistics management, management, transportation management; material acquisition management (MS); mechanical engineering (MS); operations research (MS); project management (MS), including information systems, operations research; public administration (MPA); quality management (MS); software engineering (MS); space systems (MS); space systems management (MS); systems management (MS), including information systems, operations research. Part-time and evening/weekend programs available. Postbaccalaureate distance learning degree programs offered (no on-campus study). *Faculty:* 11 full-time (3 women), 118 part-time/adjunct (24 women). *Students:* 69 full-time (23 women), 907 part-time (369 women); includes 385 minority (242 Black or African American, non-Hispanic/Latino; 15 American Indian or Alaska Native, non-Hispanic/Latino; 44 Asian, non-Hispanic/Latino; 52 Hispanic/Latino; 3 Native Hawaiian or other Pacific Islander, non-Hispanic/Latino; 29 Two or more races, non-Hispanic/Latino), 17 international. 517 applicants, 49% accepted, 245 enrolled. In 2010, 430 degrees awarded. *Degree requirements:* For master's, comprehensive exam (for some programs), capstone course. *Entrance requirements:* For master's, GMAT or resume showing 8 years of supervised experience, minimum GPA of 3.0, 2 letters of recommendation, resume. Additional exam requirements/recommendations for international students: Required—TOEFL (minimum score 550 paper-based; 213 computer-based; 79 iBT). *Application deadline:* For fall admission, 4/1 for international students; for spring admission, 9/30 for international students. Applications are processed on a rolling basis. Application fee: $50. Electronic applications accepted. *Expenses:* Contact institution. *Financial support:* Application deadline: 3/1. *Unit head:* Dr. Theodore Richardson, Senior Associate Dean, 321-674-8123, Fax: 321-674-7597, E-mail: trichardson@fit.edu. *Application contact:* Carolyn Farrior, Director of Graduate Admissions, Online Learning and Off-Campus Programs, 321-674-7118, Fax: 321-674-8216, E-mail: cfarrior@fit.edu.

Florida International University, Alvah H. Chapman, Jr. Graduate School of Business, Department of Management and International Business, Human Resources Management Program, Miami, FL 33199. Offers MSHRM. Part-time and evening/weekend programs available. *Students:* 35 full-time (29 women), 1 part-time (0 women); includes 7 Black or African American, non-Hispanic/Latino; 2 Asian, non-Hispanic/Latino; 20 Hispanic/Latino, 3 international. Average age 30. 112 applicants, 40% accepted. In 2010, 38 master's awarded. *Entrance requirements:* For master's, GRE (minimum score of 1000) or GMAT (minimum score of 500), minimum GPA of 3.0 (upper-level coursework); two letters of recommendation; letter of intent; minimum of five years of professional (exempt) experience, of which at least two years are in HR field. Additional exam requirements/recommendations for international students: Required—TOEFL (minimum score 550 paper-based; 213 computer-based; 80 iBT) or IELTS (minimum score 6.5). *Application deadline:* For fall admission, 6/1 for domestic students, 4/1 for international students; for spring admission, 10/1 for domestic students, 9/1 for international students. Applications are processed on a rolling basis. Application fee: $30. Electronic applications accepted. *Expenses:* Contact institution. *Financial support:* Institutionally sponsored loans and scholarships/grants available. Financial award application deadline: 3/1; financial award applicants required to submit FAFSA. *Faculty research:* Compensation, labor issues, labor law, human resource strategy. *Unit head:* Dr. Galen Kroeck, Chair, Management and International Business Department, 305-348-2791, Fax: 305-348-6146, E-mail: kroeck@fiu.edu. *Application contact:* Zuzana Hlavacova, Assistant Director, 305-348-5945, Fax: 305-348-7204, E-mail: zuzana.hlavacova@fiu.edu.

Franklin Pierce University, Graduate Studies, Rindge, NH 03461-0060. Offers curriculum and instruction (M Ed); emerging network technology (Graduate Certificate); health administration (MBA, Graduate Certificate); human resource management (MBA, Graduate Certificate); information technology management (MS); leadership (MBA, DA); nursing (MS); physical therapy (DPT); physician assistant studies (MPAS); special education (M Ed); sports management (MS). *Accreditation:* APTA. Part-time programs available. Postbaccalaureate distance learning degree programs offered (no on-campus study). *Faculty:* 28 full-time (18 women), 72 part-time/adjunct (44 women). *Students:* 100 full-time (63 women), 487 part-time (306 women); includes 42 minority (25 Black or African American, non-Hispanic/Latino; 10 Asian, non-Hispanic/Latino; 6 Hispanic/Latino; 1 Two or more races, non-Hispanic/Latino), 67 international. Average age 38. 227 applicants, 97% accepted, 185 enrolled. In 2010, 76 master's, 46 doctorates awarded. *Degree requirements:* For master's, concentrated original research projects; student teaching; fieldwork and/or internship; leadership project; PRAXIS I and II (for M Ed); for doctorate, concentrated original research projects, clinical fieldwork and/or internship, leadership project. *Entrance requirements:* For master's, minimum GPA of 2.5, 3 letters of recommendation; competencies in accounting, economics, statistics, and computer skills through life experience or undergraduate coursework (for MBA); certification/e-portfolio, minimum C grade in all education courses (for M Ed); license to practice as RN (for MS in nursing); for doctorate, GRE, BA/BS, 3 letters of recommendation, personal mission statement, interview; writing sample (for DA program)For DPT: 80 hours of observation/work in PT settings, completion of anatomy, chemistry, physics, an statistics, all > 3.0 GPAFor DA: 2.8 cum. GPA, Master's degree completion. Additional exam requirements/recommendations for international students: Required—TOEFL (minimum score 550 paper-based; 195 computer-based; 61 iBT). *Application deadline:* Applications are processed on a rolling basis. Application fee: $0. Electronic applications accepted. *Expenses:* Tuition: Part-time $573 per credit hour. Part-time tuition and fees vary according to degree level and program. *Financial support:* In 2010–11, 121 students received support, including 32 teaching assistantships with full and partial tuition reimbursements available (averaging $8,000 per year); career-related internships or fieldwork and unspecified assistantships also available. Support available to part-time students. Financial award applicants required to submit FAFSA. *Faculty research:* Evidence-based practice in sports physical therapy, human resource management in economic crisis, leadership in nursing, innovation in sports facility management, differentiated learning and understanding by design. *Unit head:* Dr. Patricia Brown, Interim Dean of Graduate and Professional Studies, 603-899-4316, Fax: 603-229-4580, E-mail: brownp@franklinpierce.edu.

Gannon University, School of Graduate Studies, College of Engineering and Business, School of Business, Program in Human Resources Management, Erie, PA 16541-0001. Offers Certificate. Part-time and evening/weekend programs available. *Students:* 3 applicants, 33% accepted, 0 enrolled. *Entrance requirements:* For degree, GMAT. Additional exam requirements/recommendations for international students: Required—TOEFL (minimum score 79 iBT). *Application deadline:* Applications are processed on a rolling basis. Application fee: $25. Electronic applications accepted. *Expenses:* Tuition: Full-time $14,670; part-time $815 per credit. Required fees: $430; $18 per credit. Tuition and fees vary according to class time, course load, degree level, campus/location and program. *Financial support:* Application deadline: 7/1. *Unit head:* Dr. Duane Prokop, Director, 814-871-7576, E-mail: prokop001@gannon.edu. *Application contact:* Kara Morgan, Assistant Director of Graduate Admissions, 814-871-5831, Fax: 814-871-5827, E-mail: graduate@gannon.edu.

George Fox University, School of Business, Newberg, OR 97132-2697. Offers finance (MBA); management (DBA); management/general (MBA); marketing (DBA); organizational strategy (MBA); strategic human resource management (MBA). MBA offered part-time and full-time, also offered in Portland, OR, and Boise, ID. Part-time and evening/weekend programs available. Postbaccalaureate distance learning degree programs offered (minimal on-campus study). *Faculty:* 9 full-time (2 women), 8 part-time/adjunct (3 women). *Students:* 21 full-time (7 women), 247 part-time (87 women); includes 4 Black or African American, non-Hispanic/Latino; 2 American Indian or Alaska Native, non-Hispanic/Latino; 13 Asian, non-Hispanic/Latino; 13 Hispanic/Latino; 2 Two or more races, non-Hispanic/Latino, 12 international. Average age 37. 101 applicants, 93% accepted, 72 enrolled. In 2010, 82 master's awarded. *Degree requirements:* For master's, capstone project; for doctorate, credit-applied research project. *Entrance requirements:* For master's, resume (5 years professional experience required); 3 professional references; interview; financial e-learning course; for doctorate, GRE or GMAT, resume; personal mission statement; academic research writing sample; official transcript from each college/university attended; three professional references. Additional exam requirements/recommendations for international students: Required—TOEFL (minimum score 577 paper-based; 233 computer-based; 90 iBT) or IELTS (minimum score 7). *Application deadline:* For fall admission, 8/1 for domestic and international students; for spring admission, 12/1 for domestic and international students. Applications are processed on a rolling basis. Application fee: $40. Electronic applications accepted. *Expenses:* Contact institution. *Financial support:* In 2010–11, 2 students received support. Applicants required to submit FAFSA. *Unit head:* Dr. Dirk Barram, Professor/Dean, 800-631-0921. *Application contact:* Robin Halverson, Admissions Counselor, 800-493-4937, Fax: 503-554-6111, E-mail: mba@georgefox.edu.

George Mason University, School of Public Policy, Program in Organization Development and Knowledge Management, Arlington, VA 22201. Offers MS. Evening/weekend programs available. *Faculty:* 66 full-time (24 women), 15 part-time/adjunct (3 women). *Students:* 64 full-time (54 women), 9 part-time (5 women); includes 7 Black or African American, non-Hispanic/Latino; 1 American Indian or Alaska Native, non-Hispanic/Latino; 2 Asian, non-Hispanic/Latino; 5 Hispanic/Latino, 3 international. Average age 34. 80 applicants, 54% accepted, 34 enrolled. In 2010, 35 master's awarded. *Degree requirements:* For master's, thesis or alternative. *Entrance requirements:* For master's, GRE (for students seeking merit-based scholarships), minimum GPA of 3.0, 2 letters of recommendation, resume. Additional exam requirements/recommendations for international students: Required—TOEFL (minimum score 570 paper-based; 230 computer-based; 88 iBT). *Application deadline:* For fall admission, 6/1 priority date for domestic students, 5/1 priority date for international students. Applications are processed on a rolling basis. Application fee: $100. Electronic applications accepted. *Expenses:* Contact institution. *Financial support:* Career-related internships or fieldwork, Federal Work-Study, scholarships/grants, unspecified assistantships, and health care benefits (full-time research or teaching assistantship recipients) available. Financial award application deadline: 3/1; financial award applicants required to submit FAFSA. *Unit head:* Dr. Ann Baker, Director, 703-993-8099, E-mail: spp@gmu.edu. *Application contact:* Tennille Haegele, Director, Graduate Admissions, 703-993-3183, Fax: 703-993-4876, E-mail: thaegele@gmu.edu.

The George Washington University, Columbian College of Arts and Sciences, Department of Organizational Sciences and Communication, Washington, DC 20052. Offers human resources management (MA); industrial/organizational psychology (PhD); organizational management (MA). Part-time and evening/weekend programs available. *Faculty:* 10 full-time (7 women), 19 part-time/adjunct (11 women). *Students:* 20 full-time (11 women), 48 part-time (42 women); includes 6 Black or African American, non-Hispanic/Latino; 2 Asian, non-Hispanic/Latino; 6 Hispanic/Latino, 6 international. Average age 29. 72 applicants, 88% accepted, 20 enrolled. In 2010, 31 master's awarded. *Degree requirements:* For master's, comprehensive exam. *Entrance requirements:* For master's, GRE General Test, minimum GPA of 3.0. Additional exam requirements/recommendations for international students: Required—TOEFL (minimum score 500 paper-based; 213 computer-based; 80 iBT). *Application deadline:* For fall admission, 1/15 priority date for domestic and international students; for spring admission, 10/1 priority date for domestic students, 9/1 priority date for international students. Applications are processed on a rolling basis. Application fee: $75. Electronic applications accepted. *Financial support:* Federal Work-Study and institutionally sponsored loans available. *Unit head:* Dr. David Costanza, Acting Director, 202-994-1875, Fax: 202-994-1881, E-mail: dconstanz@gwu.edu. *Application contact:* Information Contact, 202-994-1880, Fax: 202-994-1881.

Golden Gate University, Ageno School of Business, San Francisco, CA 94105-2968. Offers accounting (MBA); business administration (EMBA, MBA, PMBA, DBA); finance (MBA, MS, Certificate); financial planning (MS, Certificate); healthcare information systems (Certificate); human resource management (MBA, MS); human resources management (Certificate); information systems (MS); information technology (MBA); information technology management (Certificate); integrated marketing and communications (MS, Certificate); international business (MBA); management (MBA); marketing (MBA, MS, Certificate); operations supply chain management (Certificate); psychology (MA, Certificate); public administration (EMPA); public relations (MS, Certificate); technical market analysis (Certificate); JD/MBA. Part-time and evening/weekend programs available. *Faculty:* 16 full-time (4 women), 241 part-time/adjunct (72 women). *Students:* 421 full-time (235 women), 744 part-time (425 women); includes 526 minority (114 Black or African American, non-Hispanic/Latino; 2 American Indian or Alaska Native, non-Hispanic/Latino; 296 Asian, non-Hispanic/Latino; 73 Hispanic/

Latino; 29 Native Hawaiian or other Pacific Islander, non-Hispanic/Latino; 12 Two or more races, non-Hispanic/Latino), 100 international. Average age 32. 681 applicants, 78% accepted, 270 enrolled. In 2010, 550 master's, 13 doctorates awarded. *Degree requirements:* For doctorate, thesis/dissertation. *Entrance requirements:* For master's, GMAT (MBA), minimum GPA of 2.5 (MS). Additional exam requirements/recommendations for international students: Required—TOEFL. *Application deadline:* For fall admission, 5/15 for domestic and international students; for winter admission, 1/15 for domestic and international students; for spring admission, 9/15 for domestic and international students. Applications are processed on a rolling basis. Application fee: $70 ($110 for international students). Electronic applications accepted. *Expenses:* Contact institution. *Financial support:* Career-related internships or fieldwork, Federal Work-Study, institutionally sponsored loans, and scholarships/grants available. Support available to part-time students. Financial award applicants required to submit FAFSA. *Unit head:* Dr. Paul Fouts, Dean, 415-442-7026, Fax: 415-442-6579. *Application contact:* Angela Melero, Enrollment Services, 415-442-7800, Fax: 415-442-7807, E-mail: info@ggu.edu.

Goldey-Beacom College, Graduate Program, Wilmington, DE 19808-1999. Offers business administration (MBA); finance (MS); financial management (MBA); human resource management (MBA); information technology (MBA); international business management (MBA); major finance (MBA); major taxation (MBA); management (MM); marketing management (MBA); taxation (MBA, MS). *Accreditation:* ACBSP. Part-time and evening/weekend programs available. *Faculty:* 20 full-time (8 women), 28 part-time/adjunct (10 women). *Students:* 55 full-time (28 women), 393 part-time (164 women); includes 252 minority (51 Black or African American, non-Hispanic/Latino; 2 American Indian or Alaska Native, non-Hispanic/Latino; 183 Asian, non-Hispanic/Latino; 13 Hispanic/Latino; 1 Native Hawaiian or other Pacific Islander, non-Hispanic/Latino; 2 Two or more races, non-Hispanic/Latino). Average age 27. In 2010, 231 master's awarded. *Entrance requirements:* For master's, GMAT, MAT, GRE, minimum GPA of 3.0. Additional exam requirements/recommendations for international students: Required—TOEFL (minimum score 65 computer-based); Recommended—IELTS (minimum score 5). *Application deadline:* Applications are processed on a rolling basis. Electronic applications accepted. *Expenses:* Tuition: Full-time $14,796; part-time $822 per credit. Required fees: $180; $10 per credit. *Financial support:* Scholarships/grants available. Support available to part-time students. Financial award application deadline: 4/1; financial award applicants required to submit FAFSA. *Unit head:* Larry W. Eby, Director of Admissions, 302-225-6289, Fax: 302-996-5408, E-mail: ebylw@gbc.edu. *Application contact:* Ashley E. Mashington, Graduate Admissions Representative, 302-225-6259, Fax: 302-996-5408, E-mail: mashina@gbc.edu.

Grand Canyon University, College of Business, Phoenix, AZ 85017-1097. Offers accounting (MBA); corporate business administration (MBA); disaster preparedness and crisis management (MBA); executive fire service leadership (MS); finance (MBA); general management (MBA); government and policy (MPA); health care management (MPA); health systems management (MBA); human resource management (MBA); innovation (MBA); leadership (MBA, MS); management of information system (MBA); marketing (MBA); project-based (MBA); six sigma (MBA); strategic human resource management (MBA). *Accreditation:* ACBSP. Part-time and evening/weekend programs available. Postbaccalaureate distance learning degree programs offered (no on-campus study). *Faculty:* 8 full-time (3 women), 147 part-time/adjunct (49 women). *Students:* 1 full-time (0 women), 2,121 part-time (1,165 women); includes 341 minority (249 Black or African American, non-Hispanic/Latino; 17 American Indian or Alaska Native, non-Hispanic/Latino; 15 Asian, non-Hispanic/Latino; 29 Hispanic/Latino; 4 Native Hawaiian or other Pacific Islander, non-Hispanic/Latino; 27 Two or more races, non-Hispanic/Latino), 20 international. Average age 38. In 2010, 569 master's awarded. *Entrance requirements:* For master's, equivalent of two years full-time professional work experience. Additional exam requirements/recommendations for international students: Required—TOEFL (minimum score 575 paper-based; 233 computer-based; 90 iBT), IELTS (minimum score 7). *Application deadline:* For fall admission, 8/21 for domestic students, 7/2 for international students; for spring admission, 12/24 for domestic students, 11/1 for international students. Applications are processed on a rolling basis. Application fee: $0. Electronic applications accepted. *Financial support:* Federal Work-Study available. Support available to part-time students. Financial award applicants required to submit FAFSA. *Unit head:* Kim Donaldson, Dean, 602-639-6597, E-mail: kdonaldson@gcu.edu. *Application contact:* Matt Tidwell, Enrollment Manager, 602-639-6020, E-mail: mtidwell@gcu.edu.

HEC Montreal, School of Business Administration, Master of Science Programs in Administration, Program in Human Resources Management, Montréal, QC H3T 2A7, Canada. Offers M Sc. All courses are given in French. Part-time programs available. *Students:* 40 full-time (32 women), 9 part-time (8 women). 53 applicants, 43% accepted, 10 enrolled. In 2010, 24 master's awarded. *Degree requirements:* For master's, one foreign language, thesis. *Application deadline:* For fall admission, 3/15 for domestic and international students; for winter admission, 10/1 for domestic and international students. Application fee: $78 Canadian dollars. Electronic applications accepted. *Expenses:* Tuition, area resident: Part-time $68.93 per credit. Tuition, state

resident: full-time $2481.48; part-time $188.92 per credit. Tuition, nonresident: full-time $6801; part-time $482.06 per course. International tuition: $17,354.16 full-time. Required fees: $1309.50; $30.28 per credit. $93.45 per term. Tuition and fees vary according to degree level and program. *Financial support:* Fellowships, research assistantships, teaching assistantships, scholarships/grants available. Financial award application deadline: 9/2. *Unit head:* Dr. Claude Laurin, Director, 514-340-6485, Fax: 514-340-6880, E-mail: claude.laurin@hec.ca. *Application contact:* Francine Blais, Administrative Director, 514-340-6112, Fax: 514-340-6411, E-mail: francine.blais@hec.ca.

Hofstra University, Frank G. Zarb School of Business, Department of Management, Entrepreneurship and General Business, Hempstead, NY 11549. Offers business administration (MBA), including health services management, management, sports and entertainment management; general management (Advanced Certificate); human resource management (MS). Part-time and evening/weekend programs available. Postbaccalaureate distance learning degree programs offered (minimal on-campus study). *Faculty:* 7 full-time (1 woman), 6 part-time/adjunct (0 women). *Students:* 73 full-time (34 women), 169 part-time (79 women); includes 60 minority (23 Black or African American, non-Hispanic/Latino; 30 Asian, non-Hispanic/Latino; 7 Hispanic/Latino), 28 international. Average age 33. 176 applicants, 62% accepted, 62 enrolled. In 2010, 51 master's awarded. *Degree requirements:* For master's, thesis optional, capstone course (for MBA); thesis (for MS). *Entrance requirements:* For master's, GMAT/GRE, 2 letters of recommendation; resume; essay. Additional exam requirements/recommendations for international students: Required—TOEFL (minimum score 550 paper-based; 213 computer-based; 80 iBT); Recommended—IELTS (minimum score 6). *Application deadline:* Applications are processed on a rolling basis. Application fee: $70 ($75 for international students). Electronic applications accepted. *Expenses:* Contact institution. *Financial support:* In 2010–11, 12 students received support, including 11 fellowships with full and partial tuition reimbursements available (averaging $10,256 per year), 1 research assistantship with full and partial tuition reimbursement available (averaging $18,925 per year); career-related internships or fieldwork, Federal Work-Study, institutionally sponsored loans, scholarships/grants, tuition waivers (full and partial), and unspecified assistantships also available. Support available to part-time students. Financial award applicants required to submit FAFSA. *Faculty research:* Business/personal ethics, sustainability, innovation, decision-making, supply chains analysis, learning and pedagogical issues, family business, small business, entrepreneurship. *Unit head:* Dr. Mamdouh I. Farid, Chairperson, 516-463-5735, Fax: 516-463-4834, E-mail: mgbmif@hofstra.edu. *Application contact:* Carol Drummer, Dean of Graduate Admissions, 516-463-4876, Fax: 516-463-4664, E-mail: gradstudent@hofstra.edu.

Holy Family University, Graduate School, School of Business Administration, Program in Human Resources Management, Philadelphia, PA 19114. Offers MS. Part-time and evening/weekend programs available. *Faculty:* 1 full-time (0 women), 13 part-time/adjunct (7 women). *Students:* 43 part-time (28 women); includes 3 Black or African American, non-Hispanic/Latino; 1 Asian, non-Hispanic/Latino; 1 Hispanic/Latino. Average age 32. 36 applicants, 64% accepted, 13 enrolled. In 2010, 10 master's awarded. *Entrance requirements:* For master's, GMAT, BS or BA, minimum GPA of 3.0. *Application deadline:* For fall admission, 8/1 for domestic students; for winter admission, 1/1 for domestic students. Applications are processed on a rolling basis. Application fee: $25. Electronic applications accepted. *Expenses:* Tuition: Full-time $14,400; part-time $600 per credit hour. Required fees: $85 per term. *Financial support:* Application deadline: 5/1. *Unit head:* Dr. Jan Duggar, Dean of the School of Business, 267-341-3373, Fax: 215-637-5937, E-mail: jduggar@holyfamily.edu. *Application contact:* Gidget Marie Montelibano, Graduate Admissions Counselor, 267-341-3558, Fax: 215-637-1478, E-mail: gmontelibano@holyfamily.edu.

Hood College, Graduate School, Department of Economics and Management, Frederick, MD 21701-8575. Offers accounting (MBA); administration and management (MBA); finance (MBA); human resource management (MBA); information systems (MBA); marketing (MBA); public management (MBA). *Accreditation:* ACBSP. Part-time and evening/weekend programs available. *Faculty:* 4 full-time (1 woman), 9 part-time/adjunct (1 woman). *Students:* 16 full-time (9 women), 127 part-time (65 women); includes 17 Black or African American, non-Hispanic/Latino; 9 Asian, non-Hispanic/Latino; 5 Hispanic/Latino; 1 Two or more races, non-Hispanic/Latino, 10 international. Average age 32. 60 applicants, 62% accepted, 25 enrolled. In 2010, 56 master's awarded. *Degree requirements:* For master's, capstone/final research project. *Entrance requirements:* For master's, minimum GPA of 2.75, resume, letters of recommendation. Additional exam requirements/recommendations for international students: Required—TOEFL (minimum score 575 paper-based; 231 computer-based; 89 iBT). *Application deadline:* For fall admission, 7/15 for domestic and international students; for spring admission, 12/15 for domestic and international students. Applications are processed on a rolling basis. Application fee: $35. Electronic applications accepted. *Expenses:* Tuition: Full-time $6480; part-time $360 per credit. Required fees: $100; $50 per term. *Financial support:* Applicants required to submit FAFSA. *Faculty research:* Corporate strategy and sustainable competitive advantages, business ethics, entrepreneurship, investments management, economic development. *Unit head:* Dr. Anita Jose, Program Director, 301-696-3691, Fax: 301-696-3597,

E-mail: jose@hood.edu. *Application contact:* Dr. Allen P. Flora, Dean of Graduate School, 301-696-3811, Fax: 301-696-3597, E-mail: gofurther@hood.edu.

Inter American University of Puerto Rico, Bayamón Campus, Graduate School, Bayamón, PR 00957. Offers biology (MS), including environmental sciences and ecology, molecular biotechnology; electronic commerce (MBA); human resources (MBA). Part-time and evening/weekend programs available. *Faculty:* 4 full-time (1 woman), 5 part-time/adjunct (4 women). *Students:* 115 part-time (84 women); includes 49 Hispanic/Latino. Average age 31. *Degree requirements:* For master's, comprehensive exam, research project. *Entrance requirements:* For master's, EXADEP, GRE General Test, letters of recommendation. *Application deadline:* For fall admission, 7/1 for domestic students, 5/1 priority date for international students; for winter admission, 11/15 priority date for domestic and international students; for spring admission, 2/15 priority date for domestic and international students. Application fee: $31. *Expenses:* Tuition: Full-time $4424; part-time $202 per credit. Required fees: $180 per trimester. *Unit head:* Prof. Juan F. Martinez, Chancellor, 787-279-1200 Ext. 2295, Fax: 787-279-2205, E-mail: jmartinez@bc.inter.edu. *Application contact:* Carlos Alicea, Director of Admission, 787-279-1200 Ext. 2017, Fax: 787-279-2205, E-mail: calicea@bc.inter.edu.

Iona College, Hagan School of Business, Department of Management, New Rochelle, NY 10801-1890. Offers business administration (MBA); health care management (MBA); human resource management (MBA, PMC); management (MBA, PMC). Part-time and evening/weekend programs available. *Faculty:* 8 full-time (1 woman), 5 part-time/adjunct (3 women). *Students:* 33 full-time (12 women), 119 part-time (62 women); includes 20 minority (6 Black or African American, non-Hispanic/Latino; 5 Asian, non-Hispanic/Latino; 9 Hispanic/Latino), 2 international. Average age 33. 47 applicants, 83% accepted, 35 enrolled. In 2010, 74 master's, 2 other advanced degrees awarded. *Entrance requirements:* For master's, GMAT, 2 letters of recommendation; for PMC, GMAT. Additional exam requirements/recommendations for international students: Required—TOEFL (minimum score 550 paper-based; 213 computer-based). *Application deadline:* Applications are processed on a rolling basis. Application fee: $50. Electronic applications accepted. *Expenses:* Contact institution. *Financial support:* Scholarships/grants, tuition waivers (partial), and unspecified assistantships available. Support available to part-time students. Financial award application deadline: 4/15; financial award applicants required to submit FAFSA. *Faculty research:* Information systems, strategic management, corporate values and ethics. *Unit head:* Dr. Fredrica Rudell, Acting Chair, 914-637-2748, E-mail: frudell@iona.edu. *Application contact:* Ben Fan, Director of MBA Admissions, 914-633-2289, Fax: 914-637-2708, E-mail: sfan@iona.edu.

La Roche College, School of Graduate Studies and Adult Education, Program in Human Resources Management, Pittsburgh, PA 15237-5898. Offers MS, Certificate. *Accreditation:* ACBSP. Part-time and evening/weekend programs available. *Faculty:* 2 full-time (both women), 6 part-time/adjunct (2 women). *Students:* 10 full-time (6 women), 49 part-time (40 women); includes 4 Black or African American, non-Hispanic/Latino, 5 international. Average age 30. 15 applicants, 67% accepted, 8 enrolled. In 2010, 28 master's awarded. *Entrance requirements:* For master's, GMAT, GRE or MAT, minimum GPA of 3.0 during previous 2 years. Additional exam requirements/recommendations for international students: Recommended—TOEFL (minimum score 550 paper-based; 220 computer-based). *Application deadline:* For fall admission, 8/15 priority date for domestic students, 8/15 for international students; for spring admission, 12/15 priority date for domestic students, 12/15 for international students. Applications are processed on a rolling basis. Application fee: $50. Electronic applications accepted. *Expenses:* Tuition: Full-time $10,800; part-time $600 per credit. *Financial support:* Unspecified assistantships available. Financial award application deadline: 3/31; financial award applicants required to submit FAFSA. *Faculty research:* Personnel administration, human resources development. *Unit head:* Dr. Jean Forti, Coordinator, 412-536-1193, Fax: 412-536-1179, E-mail: fortij1@laroche.edu. *Application contact:* Hope Schiffgens, Director of Graduate Studies and Adult Education, 412-536-1266, Fax: 412-536-1283, E-mail: schombh1@laroche.edu.

Lasell College, Graduate and Professional Studies in Management, Newton, MA 02466-2709. Offers elder care administration (MSM, Graduate Certificate); elder care marketing (MSM, Graduate Certificate); fundraising management (MSM, Graduate Certificate); human resource management (Graduate Certificate); human resources management (MSM); management (MSM, Graduate Certificate); marketing (MSM, Graduate Certificate); non-profit management (MSM, Graduate Certificate); project management (MSM, Graduate Certificate); public relations (MSM). Part-time and evening/weekend programs available. Postbaccalaureate distance learning degree programs offered (no on-campus study). *Faculty:* 8 full-time (5 women), 7 part-time/adjunct (5 women). *Students:* 25 full-time (21 women), 97 part-time (67 women); includes 16 minority (6 Black or African American, non-Hispanic/Latino; 2 American Indian or Alaska Native, non-Hispanic/Latino; 4 Asian, non-Hispanic/Latino; 4 Hispanic/Latino), 17 international. Average age 33. 56 applicants, 52% accepted, 19 enrolled. In 2010, 65 master's, 7 other advanced degrees awarded. *Entrance requirements:* For master's and Graduate Certificate, bachelor's degree from an accredited institution. Additional exam requirements/recommendations for international students: Required—TOEFL

(minimum score 550 paper-based; 213 computer-based; 75 iBT). *Application deadline:* For fall admission, 8/31 priority date for domestic students, 6/30 priority date for international students; for spring admission, 12/31 priority date for domestic students, 10/31 priority date for international students. Applications are processed on a rolling basis. Application fee: $40. Electronic applications accepted. *Expenses:* Tuition: Part-time $550 per credit hour. Required fees: $55 per semester. *Financial support:* In 2010–11, 40 students received support. Available to part-time students. Application deadline: 8/31. *Unit head:* Dr. Joan Dolamore, Dean of Graduate and Professional Studies, 617-243-2485, Fax: 617-243-2450, E-mail: gradinfo@lasell.edu. *Application contact:* Adrienne Franciosi, Director of Graduate Admission, 617-243-2214, Fax: 617-243-2450, E-mail: gradinfo@lasell.edu.

Lewis University, College of Business, Graduate School of Management, Program in Business Administration, Romeoville, IL 60446. Offers accounting (MBA); custom elective option (MBA); e-business (MBA); finance (MBA); healthcare management (MBA); human resources management (MBA); information security (MBA); international business (MBA); management information systems (MBA); marketing (MBA); project management (MBA); technology and operations management (MBA). Part-time and evening/weekend programs available. *Students:* 119 full-time (66 women), 204 part-time (104 women); includes 55 Black or African American, non-Hispanic/Latino; 9 Asian, non-Hispanic/Latino; 30 Hispanic/Latino; 1 Native Hawaiian or other Pacific Islander, non-Hispanic/Latino, 9 international. Average age 28. In 2010, 111 master's awarded. *Entrance requirements:* For master's, interview, bachelor's degree, resume, 2 recommendations. Additional exam requirements/recommendations for international students: Required—TOEFL (minimum score 550 paper-based; 213 computer-based). *Application deadline:* For fall admission, 8/15 priority date for domestic students, 5/1 priority date for international students; for spring admission, 11/15 priority date for international students. Applications are processed on a rolling basis. Application fee: $40. Electronic applications accepted. *Expenses:* Tuition: Full-time $13,320; part-time $740 per credit hour. Tuition and fees vary according to program. *Financial support:* Career-related internships or fieldwork, Federal Work-Study, scholarships/grants, and unspecified assistantships available. Financial award application deadline: 5/1; financial award applicants required to submit FAFSA. *Unit head:* Dr. Maureen Culleeney, Academic Program Director, 815-838-0500 Ext. 5631, E-mail: culleema@lewisu.edu. *Application contact:* Michele Ryan, Director of Admission, 815-838-0500 Ext. 5384, E-mail: gsm@lewisu.edu.

Lincoln University, Graduate Studies, Oakland, CA 94612. Offers finance and investments (DBA); finance management and investment banking (MBA); general business (MBA); human resource management (MBA, DBA); international business (MBA); management information systems (MBA). Part-time and evening/weekend programs available. *Faculty:* 9 full-time (2 women), 11 part-time/adjunct (1 woman). *Students:* 297 full-time (134 women), 2 part-time (0 women). In 2010, 124 master's awarded. *Degree requirements:* For master's, research project (thesis), internship report, or comprehensive exam; for doctorate, comprehensive exam, thesis/dissertation. *Entrance requirements:* For master's, minimum GPA of 2.7; for doctorate, GMAT (minimum score: 550), GRE (minimum score: 1000), or equivalent test results (waived for master's degree with minimum cumulative GPA of 3.3). Additional exam requirements/recommendations for international students: Required—TOEFL (525 paper, 195 computer, 71 iBT) or IELTS (5.5) for MBA; TOEFL (550 paper, 213 computer, 79 iBT) or IELTS (6.0) for DBA; Recommended—IELTS. *Application deadline:* For fall admission, 7/2 priority date for domestic and international students; for spring admission, 11/25 priority date for domestic students, 11/26 priority date for international students. Applications are processed on a rolling basis. Application fee: $75. Electronic applications accepted. *Expenses:* Tuition: Full-time $6930. Required fees: $195 per semester. *Financial support:* In 2010–11, 1 teaching assistantship was awarded; career-related internships or fieldwork and scholarships/grants also available. *Unit head:* Dr. Marshall Burak, Director of Graduate Programs, 510-628-8016, Fax: 510-628-8012, E-mail: mburak@lincolnuca.edu. *Application contact:* Peggy Au, Director of Admissions and Records, 510-628-8010, Fax: 510-628-8012, E-mail: admissions@lincolnuca.edu.

Lindenwood University, Graduate Programs, College of Individualized Education, St. Charles, MO 63301-1695. Offers administration (MSA); business administration (MBA); communications (MA); criminal justice and administration (MS); gerontology (MA); health management (MS); human resource management (MS); information technology (MBA, Certificate); managing information technology (MS); writing (MFA). Part-time and evening/weekend programs available. *Faculty:* 15 full-time (8 women), 128 part-time/adjunct (53 women). *Students:* 828 full-time (527 women), 80 part-time (50 women); includes 284 minority (265 Black or African American, non-Hispanic/Latino; 3 American Indian or Alaska Native, non-Hispanic/Latino; 6 Asian, non-Hispanic/Latino; 10 Hispanic/Latino), 23 international. Average age 35. 223 applicants, 44% accepted, 87 enrolled. In 2010, 478 master's awarded. *Degree requirements:* For master's, thesis (for some programs), 1 colloquium per term. *Entrance requirements:* For master's, interview, minimum GPA of 3.0. Additional exam requirements/recommendations for international students: Required—TOEFL (minimum score 550 paper-based; 213 computer-based; 80 iBT). *Application deadline:* For fall admission, 10/2 priority date for domestic and international students; for winter admission, 1/8 priority date for domestic and international students; for spring admission, 4/8 priority date for domestic and international students. Applications are processed on a rolling basis. Application fee: $30 ($100 for international students). Electronic applications accepted. *Expenses:* Tuition: Full-time $13,260; part-time $380 per credit hour. Required fees: $340. One-time fee: $30. Tuition and fees vary according to course level and course load. *Financial support:* In 2010–11, 631 students received support. Career-related internships or fieldwork, institutionally sponsored loans, tuition waivers (partial), and unspecified assistantships available. Financial award application deadline: 6/30; financial award applicants required to submit FAFSA. *Unit head:* Dan Kemper, Dean, 636-949-4501, Fax: 636-949-4505, E-mail: dkemper@lindenwood.edu. *Application contact:* Brett Barger, Dean of Evening Admissions and Extension Campuses, 636-949-4934, Fax: 636-949-4109, E-mail: adultadmissions@lindenwood.edu.

Lindenwood University, Graduate Programs, School of Business and Entrepreneurship, St. Charles, MO 63301-1695. Offers accounting (MBA, MS); business administration (MBA); entrepreneurial studies (MBA, MS); finance (MBA, MS); human resource management (MBA); human resources (MS); international business (MBA, MS); management (MBA, MS); management information systems (MBA, MS); marketing (MBA, MS); public management (MBA, MS); sport management (MA). *Accreditation:* ACBSP. Part-time and evening/weekend programs available. *Faculty:* 20 full-time (8 women), 17 part-time/adjunct (5 women). *Students:* 179 full-time (73 women), 184 part-time (87 women); includes 27 minority (20 Black or African American, non-Hispanic/Latino; 3 Asian, non-Hispanic/Latino; 4 Hispanic/Latino), 146 international. Average age 28. 149 applicants, 73 enrolled. In 2010, 142 master's awarded. *Degree requirements:* For master's, comprehensive exam (for some programs), thesis (for some programs). *Entrance requirements:* For master's, interview, minimum GPA of 3.0, letter of recommendation. Additional exam requirements/recommendations for international students: Required—TOEFL (minimum score 550 paper-based; 213 computer-based; 80 iBT). *Application deadline:* For fall admission, 7/30 priority date for domestic students, 9/16 priority date for international students; for winter admission, 12/15 priority date for domestic and international students; for spring admission, 2/25 priority date for domestic students, 2/11 priority date for international students. Applications are processed on a rolling basis. Application fee: $30 ($100 for international students). Electronic applications accepted. *Expenses:* Tuition: Full-time $13,260; part-time $380 per credit hour. Required fees: $340. One-time fee: $30. Tuition and fees vary according to course level and course load. *Financial support:* In 2010–11, 209 students received support. Career-related internships or fieldwork, Federal Work-Study, institutionally sponsored loans, and tuition waivers (partial) available. Financial award application deadline: 6/30; financial award applicants required to submit FAFSA. *Unit head:* Roger Ellis, Dean, 636-949-4839, E-mail: rellis@lindenwood.edu. *Application contact:* Brett Barger, Dean of Evening Admissions and Extension Campuses, 636-949-4934, Fax: 636-949-4109, E-mail: adultadmissions@lindenwood.edu.

Marquette University, Graduate School of Management, Executive MBA Program, Milwaukee, WI 53201-1881. Offers economics (MBA); finance (MBA); human resources (MBA); international business (MBA); management information systems (MBA); marketing (MBA); operations and supply chain management (MBA); sports business (MBA). *Accreditation:* AACSB. *Faculty:* 3 full-time (1 woman), 2 part-time/adjunct (0 women). *Students:* 43 full-time (11 women); includes 6 minority (1 Black or African American, non-Hispanic/Latino; 4 Asian, non-Hispanic/Latino; 1 Hispanic/Latino), 3 international. Average age 37. 47 applicants, 74% accepted, 29 enrolled. In 2010, 13 master's awarded. *Degree requirements:* For master's, international trip. *Entrance requirements:* For master's, GMAT, two letters of recommendation, official transcripts from current and previous colleges/universities. Additional exam requirements/recommendations for international students: Required—TOEFL (minimum score 530 paper-based; 78 computer-based). *Application deadline:* Applications are processed on a rolling basis. Application fee: $50. Electronic applications accepted. *Expenses:* Contact institution. *Financial support:* Application deadline: 2/15. *Faculty research:* International trade and finance, customer relationship management, consumer satisfaction, customer service. *Unit head:* Dr. Jeanne Simmons, Graduate Director, 414-288-7145, Fax: 414-288-1660, E-mail: jeanne.simmons@marquette.edu. *Application contact:* Erin Fox, Assistant Director for Recruitment, 414-288-5319, Fax: 414-288-1902, E-mail: erin.fox@marquette.edu.

Marquette University, Graduate School of Management, Program in Business Administration, Milwaukee, WI 53201-1881. Offers business administration (MBA); economics (MBA); finance (MBA); human resources (MBA); international business (MBA); management information systems (MBA); marketing (MBA); operations and supply chain management (MBA); sports business (MBA); JD/MBA; MBA/MA; MBA/MSN. *Accreditation:* AACSB. Part-time and evening/weekend programs available. *Faculty:* 38 full-time (9 women), 24 part-time/adjunct (8 women). *Students:* 44 full-time (17 women), 368 part-time (105 women); includes 36 minority (4 Black or African American, non-Hispanic/Latino; 2 American Indian or Alaska Native, non-Hispanic/Latino; 20 Asian, non-Hispanic/Latino; 10 Hispanic/Latino), 30 international. Average age 31. 256 applicants, 60% accepted, 98 enrolled. In

2010, 117 master's awarded. *Entrance requirements:* For master's, GMAT, letters of recommendation. Additional exam requirements/recommendations for international students: Required—TOEFL (minimum score 530 paper-based; 78 computer-based). *Application deadline:* Applications are processed on a rolling basis. Application fee: $50. Electronic applications accepted. *Expenses:* Tuition: Full-time $16,290; part-time $905 per credit hour. Tuition and fees vary according to program. *Financial support:* In 2010–11, 4 fellowships, 11 teaching assistantships were awarded; research assistantships, Federal Work-Study, institutionally sponsored loans, scholarships/grants, and tuition waivers (full and partial) also available. Support available to part-time students. Financial award application deadline: 2/15. *Faculty research:* Ethics in the professions, services marketing, technology impact on decision-making, mentoring. *Unit head:* Dr. Jeanne Simmons, Graduate Director, 414-288-7145, Fax: 414-288-1660, E-mail: jeanne.simmons@marquette.edu. *Application contact:* Debra Leutermann, Admissions Coordinator, 414-288-8064, Fax: 414-288-1902, E-mail: debra.leutermann@marquette.edu.

Marquette University, Graduate School of Management, Program in Human Resources, Milwaukee, WI 53201-1881. Offers MSHR. Part-time and evening/weekend programs available. *Faculty:* 4 full-time (3 women), 3 part-time/adjunct (2 women). *Students:* 18 full-time (11 women), 16 part-time (12 women); includes 3 minority (2 Black or African American, non-Hispanic/Latino; 1 Asian, non-Hispanic/Latino), 16 international. Average age 26. 68 applicants, 57% accepted, 15 enrolled. In 2010, 4 master's awarded. *Entrance requirements:* For master's, GMAT or GRE General Test, letters of recommendation. Additional exam requirements/recommendations for international students: Required—TOEFL (minimum score 530 paper-based; 78 computer-based). *Application deadline:* Applications are processed on a rolling basis. Application fee: $50. Electronic applications accepted. *Expenses:* Tuition: Full-time $16,290; part-time $905 per credit hour. Tuition and fees vary according to program. *Financial support:* In 2010–11, 3 teaching assistantships were awarded; fellowships, research assistantships, Federal Work-Study, institutionally sponsored loans, and tuition waivers (full and partial) also available. Support available to part-time students. Financial award application deadline: 2/15. *Faculty research:* Diversity, mentoring. *Unit head:* Dr. Timothy Keaveny, Management Chair, 414-288-3643. *Application contact:* Dr. Timothy Keaveny, Management Chair, 414-288-3643.

Marshall University, Academic Affairs Division, Lewis College of Business, Graduate School of Management, Program in Human Resource Management, Huntington, WV 25755. Offers MS. Part-time and evening/weekend programs available. *Students:* 33 full-time (14 women), 18 part-time (12 women); includes 6 Black or African American, non-Hispanic/Latino, 18 international. Average age 27. In 2010, 49 master's awarded. *Degree requirements:* For master's, comprehensive assessment. *Entrance requirements:* For master's, GMAT or GRE General Test. *Application deadline:* Applications are processed on a rolling basis. Application fee: $40. *Financial support:* Tuition waivers (full) available. Support available to part-time students. Financial award applicants required to submit FAFSA. *Unit head:* Dr. Andrew Sikula, Associate Dean, 304-746-1956, E-mail: sikula@marshall.edu. *Application contact:* Steven Shumlas, Information Contact, 304-746-8964, Fax: 304-746-1902, E-mail: shumlas@marshall.edu.

McKendree University, Graduate Programs, Master of Business Administration Program, Lebanon, IL 62254-1299. Offers business administration (MBA); human resource management (MBA); international business (MBA). Part-time and evening/weekend programs available. Postbaccalaureate distance learning degree programs offered (no on-campus study). *Faculty:* 8 full-time (3 women), 19 part-time/adjunct (3 women). *Students:* 99 full-time (49 women), 155 part-time (63 women). Average age 36. In 2010, 37 master's awarded. *Entrance requirements:* For master's, official transcripts from all institutions attended, essay, minimum GPA of 3.0, three references, resume. Additional exam requirements/recommendations for international students: Required—TOEFL. *Application deadline:* Applications are processed on a rolling basis. Application fee: $0. Electronic applications accepted. *Expenses:* Tuition: Full-time $6750; part-time $375 per credit hour. One-time fee: $100. Tuition and fees vary according to program. *Financial support:* Application deadline: 6/30. *Unit head:* Dr. Frank Spreng, Director of MBA Program, 618-537-6902, E-mail: fspreng@mckendree.edu. *Application contact:* Patty L. Aubel, Graduate Admission Counselor, 618-537-6943, Fax: 618-537-6410, E-mail: plaubel@mckendree.edu.

Mercy College, School of Business, Program in Human Resource Management, Dobbs Ferry, NY 10522-1189. Offers MS, AC. Part-time and evening/weekend programs available. Postbaccalaureate distance learning degree programs offered (no on-campus study). *Students:* 61 full-time (53 women), 49 part-time (41 women); includes 43 Black or African American, non-Hispanic/Latino; 3 Asian, non-Hispanic/Latino; 15 Hispanic/Latino, 12 international. Average age 33. 64 applicants, 67% accepted, 27 enrolled. In 2010, 11 master's awarded. *Entrance requirements:* For master's, undergraduate transcripts, interview, two letters of reference, resume. Additional exam requirements/recommendations for international students: Required—TOEFL (minimum score 600 paper-based; 250 computer-based; 100 iBT), IELTS (minimum score 8). *Application deadline:* For fall admission, 8/1 for international students. Applications are processed on a rolling basis. Application fee: $40. Electronic applications accepted. *Expenses:* Contact institution. *Financial support:* Career-related internships or fieldwork, Federal Work-Study, scholarships/grants, and unspecified assistantships available. Support available to part-time students. Financial award applicants required to submit FAFSA. *Faculty research:* Team building, motivation, leadership, training, productivity. *Unit head:* Frederick Collette, Program Director, 914-674-7490, E-mail: hrprogram@mercy.edu. *Application contact:* Allison Gurdineer, Administrative Assistant, 914-674-7601, E-mail: agurdineer@mercy.edu.

Moravian College, Moravian College Comenius Center, Business and Management Programs, Bethlehem, PA 18018-6650. Offers accounting (MBA); general management (MBA); health care management (MBA); human resource management (MBA); leadership (MSHRM); learning and performance management (MSHRM); supply chain management (MBA). Part-time and evening/weekend programs available. *Faculty:* 6 full-time (2 women), 10 part-time/adjunct (3 women). *Students:* 67 part-time (35 women). 24 applicants, 50% accepted, 12 enrolled. In 2010, 8 master's awarded. *Entrance requirements:* For master's, GMAT. Additional exam requirements/recommendations for international students: Required—TOEFL (minimum score 550 paper-based; 260 computer-based; 90 iBT). *Application deadline:* Applications are processed on a rolling basis. Application fee: $40. *Expenses:* Contact institution. *Financial support:* In 2010–11, 1 fellowship with full tuition reimbursement was awarded. *Faculty research:* Leadership, change management, human resources. *Unit head:* Dr. William A. Kleintop, Associate Dean for Business and Management Programs, 610-507-1400, Fax: 610-861-1400, E-mail: comenius@moravian.edu. *Application contact:* Linda J. Doyle, Information Contact, 610-861-1400, Fax: 610-861-1466, E-mail: mba@moravian.edu.

National-Louis University, College of Management and Business, Chicago, IL 60603. Offers business administration (MBA); human resource management and development (MS); management (MS). Part-time and evening/weekend programs available. *Students:* 125 full-time (80 women), 8 part-time (5 women); includes 59 minority (28 Black or African American, non-Hispanic/Latino; 1 American Indian or Alaska Native, non-Hispanic/Latino; 3 Asian, non-Hispanic/Latino; 26 Hispanic/Latino; 1 Two or more races, non-Hispanic/Latino). Average age 37. In 2010, 173 master's awarded. *Entrance requirements:* For master's, college-administered critical thinking and writing skills test, minimum GPA of 3.0, resume, 3 references. Additional exam requirements/recommendations for international students: Required—TOEFL (minimum score 550 paper-based; 213 computer-based; 79 iBT). *Application deadline:* Applications are processed on a rolling basis. Application fee: $40. *Financial support:* Federal Work-Study, institutionally sponsored loans, and scholarships/grants available. Support available to part-time students. Financial award applicants required to submit FAFSA. *Unit head:* Walter Roetlger, Executive Dean, 312-261-3073, Fax: 312-261-3073, E-mail: chris.multhauf@nl.edu. *Application contact:* Dr. Larry Poselli, Vice President of Enrollment and Student Services, 800-443-5522 Ext. 5718, Fax: 312-261-3550, E-mail: larry.polselli@nl.edu.

National University, Academic Affairs, College of Letters and Sciences, Department of Professional Studies, La Jolla, CA 92037-1011. Offers forensic science (MFS), including criminalistics and investigation; public administration (MPA), including alternative dispute resolution, human resource management, organizational leadership, public finance. Part-time and evening/weekend programs available. Postbaccalaureate distance learning degree programs offered (no on-campus study). *Faculty:* 10 full-time (3 women), 110 part-time/adjunct (22 women). *Students:* 189 full-time (117 women), 284 part-time (167 women); includes 259 minority (101 Black or African American, non-Hispanic/Latino; 2 American Indian or Alaska Native, non-Hispanic/Latino; 33 Asian, non-Hispanic/Latino; 104 Hispanic/Latino; 7 Native Hawaiian or other Pacific Islander, non-Hispanic/Latino; 12 Two or more races, non-Hispanic/Latino). Average age 38. 305 applicants, 100% accepted, 192 enrolled. In 2010, 160 master's awarded. *Degree requirements:* For master's, thesis. *Entrance requirements:* For master's, interview, minimum GPA of 2.5. Additional exam requirements/recommendations for international students: Required—TOEFL (minimum score 550 paper-based; 213 computer-based; 79 iBT), IELTS (minimum score 6). *Application deadline:* Applications are processed on a rolling basis. Application fee: $60 ($65 for international students). Electronic applications accepted. *Expenses:* Tuition: Full-time $9450; part-time $350 per unit. Required fees: $350 per unit. One-time fee: $60. *Financial support:* Career-related internships or fieldwork, institutionally sponsored loans, scholarships/grants, and tuition waivers (partial) available. Support available to part-time students. Financial award application deadline: 6/30; financial award applicants required to submit FAFSA. *Unit head:* James G. Larsen, Associate Professor and Chair, 858-642-8418, Fax: 858-642-8715, E-mail: jlarson@nu.edu. *Application contact:* Dominick Giovanniello, Associate Regional Dean—San Diego, 800-NAT-UNIV, Fax: 858-541-7792, E-mail: dgiovann@nu.edu.

National University, Academic Affairs, School of Business and Management, Department of Leadership and Business Administration, La Jolla, CA 92037-1011. Offers alternative dispute resolution (MBA); e-business (MBA); financial management (MBA); human resource management (MBA); human resources management (MA); international business (MBA); knowledge management (MS); marketing (MBA); organizational leadership (MBA, MS);

technology management (MBA). Part-time and evening/weekend programs available. Postbaccalaureate distance learning degree programs offered (no on-campus study). *Faculty:* 16 full-time (4 women), 126 part-time/adjunct (39 women). *Students:* 119 full-time (81 women), 410 part-time (202 women); includes 176 minority (81 Black or African American, non-Hispanic/Latino; 1 American Indian or Alaska Native, non-Hispanic/Latino; 31 Asian, non-Hispanic/Latino; 52 Hispanic/Latino; 4 Native Hawaiian or other Pacific Islander, non-Hispanic/Latino; 7 Two or more races, non-Hispanic/Latino), 183 international. Average age 38. 219 applicants, 100% accepted, 160 enrolled. In 2010, 95 master's awarded. *Degree requirements:* For master's, thesis. *Entrance requirements:* For master's, interview, minimum GPA of 2.5. Additional exam requirements/recommendations for international students: Required—TOEFL (minimum score 550 paper-based; 213 computer-based; 79 iBT), IELTS (minimum score 6). *Application deadline:* Applications are processed on a rolling basis. Application fee: $60 ($65 for international students). Electronic applications accepted. *Expenses:* Tuition: Full-time $9450; part-time $350 per unit. Required fees: $350 per unit. One-time fee: $60. *Financial support:* Career-related internships or fieldwork, institutionally sponsored loans, scholarships/grants, and tuition waivers (partial) available. Support available to part-time students. Financial award application deadline: 6/30; financial award applicants required to submit FAFSA. *Unit head:* Dr. Bruce Buchowicz, Chair, 858-642-8439, Fax: 858-642-8406, E-mail: bbuchowicz@nu.edu. *Application contact:* Dominick Giovanniello, Associate Regional Dean—San Diego, 800-NAT-UNIV, Fax: 858-541-7792, E-mail: dgiovann@nu.edu.

New Mexico Highlands University, Graduate Studies, School of Business, Las Vegas, NM 87701. Offers business administration (MBA), including government nonprofit management, human resource management, international business, management, management information systems. *Accreditation:* ACBSP. *Faculty:* 14 full-time (3 women). *Students:* 71 full-time (44 women), 124 part-time (68 women); includes 119 minority (8 Black or African American, non-Hispanic/Latino; 18 American Indian or Alaska Native, non-Hispanic/Latino; 1 Asian, non-Hispanic/Latino; 89 Hispanic/Latino; 1 Native Hawaiian or other Pacific Islander, non-Hispanic/Latino; 2 Two or more races, non-Hispanic/Latino), 34 international. Average age 34. 128 applicants, 98% accepted, 34 enrolled. In 2010, 48 master's awarded. *Degree requirements:* For master's, comprehensive exam, thesis or alternative. *Entrance requirements:* For master's, minimum undergraduate GPA of 3.0. Additional exam requirements/recommendations for international students: Required—TOEFL (minimum score 540 paper-based; 207 computer-based). *Application deadline:* For fall admission, 8/1 priority date for domestic students. Applications are processed on a rolling basis. Application fee: $15. *Expenses:* Tuition, state resident: full-time $2544. Required fees: $624; $132 per credit hour. *Financial support:* In 2010–11, 29 students received support. Career-related internships or fieldwork, Federal Work-Study, institutionally sponsored loans, scholarships/grants, tuition waivers (full and partial), and unspecified assistantships available. Support available to part-time students. Financial award application deadline: 3/1; financial award applicants required to submit FAFSA. *Faculty research:* Real estate valuation, studying expert judgments in complex accounting, decision environments, green marketing, environmentalism, marketing research methodology. *Unit head:* Dr. Margaret Young, Dean, 505-454-3522, Fax: 505-454-3354, E-mail: young m@nmhu.edu. Application contact: Diane Trujillo, Administrative Assistant, Graduate Studies, 505-454-3266, Fax: 505-426-2117, E-mail: dtrujillo@nmhu.edu.

New York Institute of Technology, Graduate Division, School of Management, Program in Human Resources Management and Labor Relations, Old Westbury, NY 11568-8000. Offers human resources administration (Advanced Certificate); human resources management and labor relations (MS); labor relations (Advanced Certificate). Part-time and evening/weekend programs available. *Students:* 41 full-time (28 women), 62 part-time (44 women); includes 30 minority (16 Black or African American, non-Hispanic/Latino; 5 Asian, non-Hispanic/Latino; 9 Hispanic/Latino), 28 international. Average age 31. In 2010, 27 master's, 3 other advanced degrees awarded. *Degree requirements:* For master's, comprehensive exam, thesis optional. *Entrance requirements:* For master's, GRE, minimum QPA of 2.85, interview, 2 letters of recommendation. *Application deadline:* For fall admission, 7/1 priority date for domestic students; for spring admission, 12/1 priority date for domestic students. Applications are processed on a rolling basis. Application fee: $50. Electronic applications accepted. *Expenses:* Tuition: Part-time $835 per credit. *Financial support:* Fellowships, research assistantships, career-related internships or fieldwork, institutionally sponsored loans, and tuition waivers (full and partial) available. Support available to part-time students. Financial award applicants required to submit FAFSA. *Faculty research:* Ethics in industrial relations, employee relations, public sector labor relations, benefits. *Unit head:* William Ninehan, Director, 646-273-6071, Fax: 516-686-7425, E-mail: wninehan@nyit.edu. *Application contact:* Dr. Jacquelyn Nealon, Vice President for Enrollment Services, 516-686-7925, Fax: 516-686-7597, E-mail: jnealon@nyit.edu.

New York University, Robert F. Wagner Graduate School of Public Service, Program in Public Administration, New York, NY 10012-1019. Offers public administration (PhD); public and nonprofit management and policy (MPA, Advanced Certificate), including developmental administration (Advanced Certificate), financial management and public finance, human resources management (Advanced Certificate), international administration (Advanced Certificate), management (MPA), management for public and nonprofit organizations (Advanced Certificate), public policy analysis, quantitative analysis and computer applications (Advanced Certificate), urban public policy (Advanced Certificate); JD/MPA; MBA/MPA; MPA/MA. *Accreditation:* NASPAA (one or more programs are accredited). Part-time and evening/weekend programs available. *Faculty:* 32 full-time (13 women), 41 part-time/adjunct (22 women). *Students:* 400 full-time (301 women), 206 part-time (156 women); includes 43 Black or African American, non-Hispanic/Latino; 58 Asian, non-Hispanic/Latino; 36 Hispanic/Latino, 65 international. Average age 28. 1,230 applicants, 54% accepted, 219 enrolled. In 2010, 210 master's, 5 doctorates awarded. *Degree requirements:* For master's, thesis or alternative, capstone end event; for doctorate, one foreign language, thesis/dissertation. *Entrance requirements:* For master's, minimum undergraduate GPA of 3.0; for doctorate, GMAT or GRE General Test, minimum GPA of 3.5. Additional exam requirements/recommendations for international students: Required—TOEFL (minimum score 600 paper-based; 250 computer-based; 100 iBT), IELTS (minimum score 7.5), TWE (minimum score 4). *Application deadline:* For fall admission, 1/15 for domestic students, 1/4 for international students; for spring admission, 11/15 for domestic students, 10/1 for international students. Applications are processed on a rolling basis. Application fee: $80. Electronic applications accepted. *Expenses:* Contact institution. *Financial support:* In 2010–11, 176 students received support, including 171 fellowships (averaging $14,022 per year), 5 research assistantships with full tuition reimbursements available (averaging $22,440 per year); career-related internships or fieldwork, Federal Work-Study, institutionally sponsored loans, scholarships/grants, health care benefits, and unspecified assistantships also available. Support available to part-time students. Financial award application deadline: 1/5; financial award applicants required to submit FAFSA. *Unit head:* Katty Jones, Director, Program Services, 212-998-7411, Fax: 212-995-4164, E-mail: katty.jones@nyu.edu. *Application contact:* Christopher Alexander, Administrative Aide, Enrollment, 212-998-7414, Fax: 212-995-4611, E-mail: wagner.admissions@nyu.edu.

New York University, School of Continuing and Professional Studies, Division of Programs in Business, Program in Leadership and Human Capital Management, New York, NY 10012-1019. Offers benefits and compensation (Advanced Certificate); human resource development (MS); human resource management (MS, Advanced Certificate); organizational and executive coaching (Advanced Certificate); organizational effectiveness (MS). Part-time and evening/weekend programs available. Postbaccalaureate distance learning degree programs offered (no on-campus study). *Faculty:* 52 part-time/adjunct (15 women). *Students:* 21 full-time (17 women), 123 part-time (107 women); includes 19 Black or African American, non-Hispanic/Latino; 2 American Indian or Alaska Native, non-Hispanic/Latino; 6 Asian, non-Hispanic/Latino; 15 Hispanic/Latino, 18 international. Average age 31. 119 applicants, 66% accepted, 42 enrolled. In 2010, 81 master's, 28 other advanced degrees awarded. Terminal master's awarded for partial completion of doctoral program. *Degree requirements:* For master's, thesis. *Entrance requirements:* For master's, GRE General Test or GMAT (for recent graduates), 2 letters of recommendation, resume, essay, professional experience. Additional exam requirements/recommendations for international students: Required—TOEFL (minimum score 600 paper-based; 250 computer-based; 100 iBT), TWE. *Application deadline:* For fall admission, 2/1 priority date for domestic and international students; for spring admission, 10/15 priority date for domestic students, 8/15 priority date for international students. Applications are processed on a rolling basis. Application fee: $75. Electronic applications accepted. *Financial support:* In 2010–11, 106 students received support, including 106 fellowships (averaging $2,430 per year); career-related internships or fieldwork, institutionally sponsored loans, and scholarships/grants also available. Support available to part-time students. Financial award application deadline: 3/1; financial award applicants required to submit FAFSA. *Unit head:* Stephanie Bonadio, Academic Director, 212-992-3633, Fax: 212-992-3650, E-mail: sgb259@nyu.edu. *Application contact:* Assistant Director, 212-992-3600, Fax: 212-992-3650, E-mail: scps.hrmdstudent@nyu.edu.

North Central College, Graduate and Continuing Education Programs, Department of Business, Program in Business Administration, Naperville, IL 60566-7063. Offers change management (MBA); finance (MBA); human resource management (MBA); management (MBA); marketing (MBA). Part-time and evening/weekend programs available. *Faculty:* 14 full-time (4 women), 5 part-time/adjunct (1 woman). *Students:* 46 full-time (17 women), 101 part-time (46 women); includes 6 Black or African American, non-Hispanic/Latino; 1 American Indian or Alaska Native, non-Hispanic/Latino; 4 Asian, non-Hispanic/Latino; 7 Hispanic/Latino, 3 international. Average age 31. In 2010, 46 master's awarded. *Degree requirements:* For master's, project. *Entrance requirements:* For master's, interview. Additional exam requirements/recommendations for international students: Required—TOEFL (minimum score 577 paper-based; 233 computer-based; 90 iBT). *Application deadline:* For fall admission, 8/15 for domestic students; for winter admission, 12/1 for domestic students; for spring admission, 2/1 for domestic students. Application fee: $25. *Financial support:* Scholarships/grants available. Support available to part-time students. *Unit head:* Dr. Jean Clifton, MBA Program Coordinator, 630-637-5244, E-mail: jmclifton@noctrl.edu. *Application contact:* Wendy Kulpinski, Director and Graduate and Continuing Education Admission, 630-637-5808, Fax: 630-637-5844, E-mail: wekulpinski@noctrl.edu.

North Greenville University, T. Walter Brashier Graduate School, Greer, SC 29651. Offers Christian ministry (MCM); human resources (MBA). Part-time and evening/weekend programs available. Postbaccalaureate distance learning degree programs offered (no on-campus study). *Faculty:* 4 full-time (1 woman), 16 part-time/adjunct (1 woman). *Students:* 80 full-time (33 women), 148 part-time (53 women); includes 48 minority (37 Black or African American, non-Hispanic/Latino; 1 American Indian or Alaska Native, non-Hispanic/Latino; 3 Asian, non-Hispanic/Latino; 5 Hispanic/Latino; 2 Two or more races, non-Hispanic/Latino). Average age 32. 180 applicants, 98% accepted, 170 enrolled. In 2010, 29 master's awarded. *Degree requirements:* For master's, comprehensive exam (for some programs), thesis or alternative, capstone course. *Entrance requirements:* For master's, GMAT, GRE, minimum GPA of 2.25 overall, 2.5 in major. Additional exam requirements/recommendations for international students: Required—TOEFL (minimum score 550 paper-based; 213 computer-based). *Application deadline:* For fall admission, 8/1 for domestic students, 6/1 for international students; for winter admission, 1/1 for domestic students, 10/1 for international students; for spring admission, 3/1 for domestic students, 1/1 for international students. Applications are processed on a rolling basis. Application fee: $30. Electronic applications accepted. *Expenses:* Required fees: $280 per credit hour. One-time fee: $30. *Financial support:* In 2010–11, 112 students received support. Federal Work-Study, institutionally sponsored loans, scholarships/grants, and tuition waivers (partial) available. Support available to part-time students. Financial award applicants required to submit FAFSA. *Faculty research:* Organizational behavior, church growth, homiletics, human resources, business strategy. *Unit head:* Dr. Joseph Samuel Isgett, Vice President for Graduate Studies, 864-877-3052, Fax: 864-877-1653, E-mail: sisgett@ngu.edu. *Application contact:* Tawana P. Scott, Director of Graduate Enrollment, 864-877-1598, Fax: 864-877-1653, E-mail: tscott@ngu.edu.

Notre Dame de Namur University, Division of Academic Affairs, School of Business and Management, Department of Business Administration, Belmont, CA 94002-1908. Offers business administration (MBA); finance (MBA); human resource management (MBA); marketing (MBA). Part-time and evening/weekend programs available. *Faculty:* 7 full-time (1 woman), 6 part-time/adjunct (0 women). *Students:* 46 full-time (24 women), 79 part-time (54 women); includes 54 minority (3 Black or African American, non-Hispanic/Latino; 28 Asian, non-Hispanic/Latino; 20 Hispanic/Latino; 2 Native Hawaiian or other Pacific Islander, non-Hispanic/Latino; 1 Two or more races, non-Hispanic/Latino), 22 international. Average age 34. 129 applicants, 53% accepted, 37 enrolled. In 2010, 28 master's awarded. *Entrance requirements:* For master's, minimum GPA of 2.5. Additional exam requirements/recommendations for international students: Required—TOEFL (minimum score 550 paper-based; 213 computer-based; 79 iBT). *Application deadline:* For fall admission, 8/1 priority date for domestic students; for spring admission, 12/1 priority date for domestic students. Applications are processed on a rolling basis. Application fee: $60. Electronic applications accepted. *Expenses:* Tuition: Full-time $14,220; part-time $790 per credit. Required fees: $35 per semester. Tuition and fees vary according to program. *Financial support:* Available to part-time students. Applicants required to submit FAFSA. *Unit head:* Jordan Holtzman, Director, 650-508-3637, E-mail: jholtzman@ndnu.edu. *Application contact:* Candace Hallmark, Associate Director of Admissions, 650-508-3600, Fax: 650-508-3426, E-mail: grad.admit@ndnu.edu.

Notre Dame de Namur University, Division of Academic Affairs, School of Business and Management, Department of Public Administration, Belmont, CA 94002-1908. Offers human resource management (MPA); public administration (MPA); public affairs administration (MPA). Part-time and evening/weekend programs available. *Faculty:* 3 full-time (1 woman), 4 part-time/adjunct (2 women). *Students:* 13 full-time (11 women), 41 part-time (34 women); includes 4 Black or African American, non-Hispanic/Latino; 4 Asian, non-Hispanic/Latino; 12 Hispanic/Latino; 1 Native Hawaiian or other Pacific Islander, non-Hispanic/Latino, 10 international. Average age 32. 35 applicants, 49% accepted, 14 enrolled. In 2010, 13 master's awarded. *Entrance requirements:* For master's, interview, minimum GPA of 2.5. Additional exam requirements/recommendations for international students: Required—TOEFL (minimum score 550 paper-based; 213 computer-based; 79 iBT). *Application deadline:* For fall admission, 8/1 priority date for domestic students; for spring admission, 12/1 priority date for domestic students. Applications are processed on a rolling basis. Application fee: $60. Electronic applications accepted. *Expenses:* Tuition: Full-time $14,220; part-time $790 per credit. Required fees: $35 per semester. Tuition and fees vary according to program. *Financial support:* Available to part-time students. Applicants required to submit FAFSA. *Unit head:* Jordan Holtzman, Director, 650-508-3637, E-mail: jholtzman@ndnu.edu. *Application contact:* Candace Hallmark, Associate Director of Admissions, 650-508-3600, Fax: 650-508-3426, E-mail: grad.admit@ndnu.edu.

Nova Southeastern University, H. Wayne Huizenga School of Business and Entrepreneurship, Doctoral Program in Business Administration, Fort Lauderdale, FL 33314-7796. Offers accounting (DBA); decision sciences (DBA); finance (DBA); human resource management (DBA); international business (DBA); management (DBA); marketing (DBA). Part-time and evening/weekend programs available. *Faculty:* 34 full-time (11 women), 2 part-time/adjunct (1 woman). *Students:* 2 full-time (1 woman), 93 part-time (32 women); includes 9 Black or African American, non-Hispanic/Latino; 4 Asian, non-Hispanic/Latino; 11 Hispanic/Latino, 8 international. Average age 47. 66 applicants, 14% accepted, 6 enrolled. In 2010, 29 doctorates awarded. *Degree requirements:* For doctorate, comprehensive exam, thesis/dissertation. *Entrance requirements:* For doctorate, GMAT. Additional exam requirements/ recommendations for international students: Required—TOEFL (minimum score 600 paper-based; 250 computer-based; 100 iBT), IELTS (minimum score 7). *Application deadline:* Applications are processed on a rolling basis. Application fee: $50. Electronic applications accepted. *Financial support:* Available to part-time students. Applicants required to submit FAFSA. *Faculty research:* Reputation management, call centers, international social capital, corporate earnings guidance, corporate governance. *Unit head:* Kristie Tetrault, Director of Program Administration, 954-262-5120, Fax: 954-262-3849, E-mail: kristie@huizenga.nova.edu. *Application contact:* Karen Goldberg, Associate Director of Recruitment and Special Events, 954-262-5039, Fax: 954-262-3822, E-mail: karen@huizenga.nova.edu.

Nova Southeastern University, H. Wayne Huizenga School of Business and Entrepreneurship, Master's Program in Human Resources Management, Fort Lauderdale, FL 33314-7796. Offers MSHRM. Part-time and evening/ weekend programs available. Postbaccalaureate distance learning degree programs offered (minimal on-campus study). *Faculty:* 12 part-time/adjunct (3 women). *Students:* 4 full-time (all women), 355 part-time (294 women); includes 259 minority (153 Black or African American, non-Hispanic/Latino; 8 Asian, non-Hispanic/Latino; 92 Hispanic/Latino; 1 Native Hawaiian or other Pacific Islander, non-Hispanic/Latino; 5 Two or more races, non-Hispanic/ Latino), 10 international. Average age 33. 142 applicants, 63% accepted, 57 enrolled. In 2010, 95 master's awarded. *Degree requirements:* For master's, thesis or alternative. *Entrance requirements:* Additional exam requirements/ recommendations for international students: Required—TOEFL (minimum score 550 paper-based; 213 computer-based; 79 iBT), IELTS (minimum score 6). *Application deadline:* For fall admission, 8/15 for domestic and international students; for winter admission, 12/10 for domestic and international students; for spring admission, 2/10 for domestic and international students. Applications are processed on a rolling basis. Application fee: $50. Electronic applications accepted. *Financial support:* Federal Work-Study and scholarships/grants available. Support available to part-time students. Financial award applicants required to submit FAFSA. *Unit head:* Dr. Preston Jones, Executive Associate Dean, 954-262-5127, Fax: 954-262-3960, E-mail: prestonj@huizenga.nova.edu. *Application contact:* Karen Goldberg, Associate Director of Recruitment and Special Events, 954-262-5039, Fax: 954-262-3822, E-mail: karen@nova.edu.

The Ohio State University, Graduate School, Max M. Fisher College of Business, Program in Labor and Human Resources, Columbus, OH 43210. Offers MLHR, PhD. *Faculty:* 28. *Students:* 80 full-time (60 women), 40 part-time (31 women); includes 8 Black or African American, non-Hispanic/ Latino; 4 Asian, non-Hispanic/Latino; 3 Hispanic/Latino; 4 Two or more races, non-Hispanic/Latino, 23 international. Average age 28. In 2010, 34 master's, 2 doctorates awarded. *Degree requirements:* For master's, thesis optional; for doctorate, thesis/dissertation. *Entrance requirements:* For master's and doctorate, GRE General Test. Additional exam requirements/recommendations for international students: Recommended—TOEFL (minimum score 600 paper-based; 250 computer-based). *Application deadline:* For fall admission, 8/15 priority date for domestic students, 7/1 priority date for international students; for winter admission, 12/1 priority date for domestic students, 11/1 priority date for international students; for spring admission, 3/1 priority date for domestic students, 2/1 priority date for international students. Applications are processed on a rolling basis. Application fee: $40 ($50 for international students). Electronic applications accepted. *Expenses:* Tuition, state resident: full-time $10,605. Tuition, nonresident: full-time $26,535. Tuition and fees vary according to course load and program. *Financial support:* Fellowships, research assistantships, teaching assistantships, Federal Work-Study and institutionally sponsored loans available. Support available to part-time students. *Unit head:* Robert L. Heneman, Graduate Studies Committee Chair, 614-292-4587, Fax: 614-292-9006, E-mail: heneman.1@osu.edu. *Application contact:* 614-292-9444, Fax: 614-292-3895, E-mail: domestic.grad@osu.edu.

Penn State University Park, Graduate School, College of the Liberal Arts, Department of Labor Studies and Employment Relations, State College, University Park, PA 16802-1503. Offers MPS, MS. Postbaccalaureate distance learning degree programs offered.

Polytechnic Institute of NYU, Department of Technology Management, Brooklyn, NY 11201-2990. Offers construction management (Advanced Certificate); electronic business management (Advanced Certificate); entrepreneurship (Advanced Certificate); human resources management (Advanced Certificate); information management (Advanced Certificate); management (MS); management of technology (MS); organizational behavior (MS, Advanced Certificate); project management (Advanced Certificate); technology management (MBA, PhD, Advanced Certificate); telecommunications and information management (MS); telecommunications management (Advanced Certificate). Part-time and evening/weekend programs available.

Faculty: 7 full-time (2 women), 28 part-time/adjunct (4 women). *Students:* 224 full-time (93 women), 106 part-time (38 women); includes 15 Black or African American, non-Hispanic/Latino; 41 Asian, non-Hispanic/Latino; 10 Hispanic/Latino, 158 international. Average age 30. 370 applicants, 60% accepted, 120 enrolled. In 2010, 173 master's, 1 doctorate awarded. *Degree requirements:* For master's, comprehensive exam (for some programs), thesis (for some programs); for doctorate, comprehensive exam, thesis/dissertation. *Entrance requirements:* For master's, GMAT, minimum B average in undergraduate course work. Additional exam requirements/recommendations for international students: Required—TOEFL (minimum score 550 paper-based; 213 computer-based; 80 iBT); Recommended—IELTS (minimum score 6.5). *Application deadline:* For fall admission, 7/31 priority date for domestic students, 4/30 priority date for international students; for spring admission, 12/31 priority date for domestic students, 11/30 priority date for international students. Applications are processed on a rolling basis. Application fee: $75. Electronic applications accepted. *Expenses:* Tuition: Full-time $21,492; part-time $1194 per credit. Required fees: $385 per semester. Tuition and fees vary according to course load. *Financial support:* In 2010–11, 1 fellowship (averaging $26,400 per year) was awarded; research assistantships, teaching assistantships, institutionally sponsored loans, scholarships/grants, and unspecified assistantships also available. Support available to part-time students. *Unit head:* Prof. Bharadwaj Rao, Head, 718-260-3617, Fax: 718-260-3874, E-mail: brao@poly.edu. *Application contact:* JeanCarlo Bonilla, Director of Graduate Enrollment Management, 718-260-3182, Fax: 718-260-3624, E-mail: gradinfo@poly.edu.

Purdue University, Graduate School, Krannert School of Management, Doctoral Program in Organizational Behavior and Human Resource Management, West Lafayette, IN 47907-2056. Offers PhD. *Students:* 8 full-time (3 women); includes 1 Black or African American, non-Hispanic/ Latino; 1 American Indian or Alaska Native, non-Hispanic/Latino; 1 Asian, non-Hispanic/Latino, 1 international. Average age 32. 80 applicants, 3% accepted, 2 enrolled. In 2010, 3 doctorates awarded. *Degree requirements:* For doctorate, comprehensive exam, thesis/dissertation, dissertation proposal, dissertation defense. *Entrance requirements:* For doctorate, GMAT or GRE, bachelor's degree, two semesters of calculus, one semester each of linear algebra and statistics. Additional exam requirements/recommendations for international students: Required—TOEFL (minimum score 575 paper-based; 233 computer-based); Recommended—TWE. *Application deadline:* For fall admission, 1/15 priority date for domestic and international students. Application fee: $55. Electronic applications accepted. *Financial support:* In 2010–11, 1 fellowship with full tuition reimbursement (averaging $25,000 per year), research assistantships with partial tuition reimbursements (averaging $18,000 per year), teaching assistantships with partial tuition reimbursements (averaging $18,000 per year) were awarded; scholarships/grants, health care benefits, tuition waivers (full and partial), unspecified assistantships, and travel funds to present at a major conference also available. Support available to part-time students. Financial award application deadline: 1/15. *Faculty research:* Human resource management, organizational behavior. *Unit head:* Dr. Gerald J. Lynch, Dean, 765-494-4366. *Application contact:* Krannert Ph.D. Admissions, 765-494-4375, Fax: 765-494-0136, E-mail: krannertphd@purdue.edu.

Purdue University, Graduate School, Krannert School of Management, Master of Science in Human Resource Management Program, West Lafayette, IN 47907. Offers MSHRM. *Faculty:* 98 full-time (27 women), 22 part-time/ adjunct (4 women). *Students:* 43 full-time (17 women); includes 4 Black or African American, non-Hispanic/Latino; 1 Asian, non-Hispanic/Latino; 3 Hispanic/Latino, 20 international. Average age 26. 189 applicants, 36% accepted, 28 enrolled. In 2010, 25 master's awarded. *Entrance requirements:* For master's, GMAT or GRE, essays, recommendation letters, work experience/internship, minimum GPA of 3.0, four-year baccalaureate degree. Additional exam requirements/recommendations for international students: Required—TOEFL (minimum score 550 paper-based; 213 computer-based; 77 iBT), TOEFL (minimum: 550 paper, 213 computer, 77 iBT), IELTS, or Pearson PTE. *Application deadline:* For fall admission, 1/10 priority date for domestic students, 2/1 for international students. Applications are processed on a rolling basis. Application fee: $55. Electronic applications accepted. *Financial support:* In 2010–11, 8 students received support, including 6 research assistantships, 2 teaching assistantships; scholarships/grants and unspecified assistantships also available. Financial award application deadline: 2/1; financial award applicants required to submit FAFSA. *Faculty research:* Performance periods and the dynamics of the performance-risk relationship, reactions to unfair events in computer-mediated groups: a test of uncertainty management theory, influences on job search self-efficacy of spouses of military personnel, Cross-Cultural Social Intelligence: An Assessment for Employees Working in Cross-National Contexts, Will You Trust Your New Boss? The Role of Affective Reactions to Leadership Succession. *Unit head:* Dr. Gerald J. Lynch, Interim Dean, 765-494-4366. *Application contact:* Brenda Knebel, Director, Full-time Master's Admissions, 765-494-0773, Fax: 765-494-9841, E-mail: krannertmasters@purdue.edu.

Quincy University, Program in Business Administration, Quincy, IL 62301-2699. Offers business administration (MBA); human resource management (MBA). Part-time and evening/weekend programs available. *Faculty:* 5

full-time (3 women). *Students:* 8 full-time (6 women), 17 part-time (8 women); includes 1 Black or African American, non-Hispanic/Latino; 1 Hispanic/Latino. In 2010, 21 master's awarded. *Entrance requirements:* For master's, GMAT, previous course work in accounting, economics, finance, management or marketing, and statistics. Additional exam requirements/recommendations for international students: Required—TOEFL (minimum score 550 paper-based). *Application deadline:* Applications are processed on a rolling basis. Application fee: $25. Electronic applications accepted. *Expenses:* Contact institution. *Financial support:* Available to part-time students. Applicants required to submit FAFSA. *Faculty research:* Macroeconomic forecasting, business ethics/social responsibility. *Unit head:* Dr. John Palmer, Director, 217-228-5432 Ext. 3070, E-mail: palmejo@quincy.edu. *Application contact:* Jennifer Bang, Coordinator of Adult Studies, 217-228-5404, Fax: 217-228-5479, E-mail: admissions@quincy.edu.

Robert Morris University Illinois, Morris Graduate School of Management, Chicago, IL 60605. Offers accounting (MBA); accounting/finance (MBA); health care administration (MM); higher education administration (MM); human resource management (MBA); information systems (MIS); leadership (MBA); management/finance (MIS); management/human resource management (MBA). Part-time and evening/weekend programs available. *Faculty:* 9 full-time (2 women), 21 part-time/adjunct (6 women). *Students:* 275 full-time (151 women), 212 part-time (138 women); includes 170 Black or African American, non-Hispanic/Latino; 1 American Indian or Alaska Native, non-Hispanic/Latino; 21 Asian, non-Hispanic/Latino; 73 Hispanic/Latino; 2 Native Hawaiian or other Pacific Islander, non-Hispanic/Latino, 23 international. Average age 32. 172 applicants, 87% accepted, 105 enrolled. In 2010, 174 master's awarded. *Degree requirements:* For master's, 48 residency hours. *Entrance requirements:* Additional exam requirements/recommendations for international students: Required—TOEFL (minimum score 500 paper-based; 173 computer-based). *Application deadline:* Applications are processed on a rolling basis. Application fee: $50 ($100 for international students). Electronic applications accepted. *Expenses:* Tuition: Full-time $13,200; part-time $2200 per course. *Financial support:* Federal Work-Study, scholarships/grants, and tuition waivers available. Support available to part-time students. *Unit head:* Kayed Akkawi, Dean, 312-935-6025, Fax: 312-935-6020, E-mail: kakkawi@robertmorris.edu. *Application contact:* Courtney A. Kohn Sanders, Dean of Graduate Admissions, 312-935-4810, Fax: 312-935-6020, E-mail: ckohn@robertmorris.edu.

Rollins College, Hamilton Holt School, Program in Human Resources, Winter Park, FL 32789. Offers MA. Part-time and evening/weekend programs available. *Faculty:* 4 full-time (0 women), 2 part-time/adjunct (0 women). *Students:* 4 full-time (2 women), 52 part-time (46 women); includes 26 minority (13 Black or African American, non-Hispanic/Latino; 1 Asian, non-Hispanic/Latino; 12 Hispanic/Latino), 2 international. Average age 31. 42 applicants, 71% accepted, 26 enrolled. In 2010, 23 master's awarded. *Degree requirements:* For master's, thesis optional. *Entrance requirements:* For master's, GMAT or GRE, interview. Additional exam requirements/recommendations for international students: Required—TOEFL (minimum score 550 paper-based; 213 computer-based; 80 iBT). *Application deadline:* For fall admission, 4/1 for domestic students; for spring admission, 12/1 for domestic students. Application fee: $50. *Expenses:* Contact institution. *Financial support:* In 2010–11, 3 students received support. Career-related internships or fieldwork, scholarships/grants, and unspecified assistantships available. Support available to part-time students. Financial award applicants required to submit FAFSA. *Unit head:* Dr. Donald Rogers, Director, 407-646-2348, E-mail: drogers@rollins.edu. *Application contact:* Christian Ricaurte, Coordinator of Records and Registration, 407-646-2653, Fax: 407-646-1551, E-mail: cricaurte@rollins.edu.

Rutgers, The State University of New Jersey, Newark, Graduate School, Program in Public Administration, Newark, NJ 07102. Offers health care administration (MPA); human resources administration (MPA); public administration (PhD); public management (MPA); public policy analysis (MPA); urban systems and issues (MPA). *Accreditation:* NASPAA (one or more programs are accredited). Part-time and evening/weekend programs available. *Faculty:* 9 full-time (3 women). *Students:* 19 full-time (12 women), 24 part-time (11 women); includes 10 Black or African American, non-Hispanic/Latino; 14 Asian, non-Hispanic/Latino; 3 Hispanic/Latino. 46 applicants, 24% accepted, 6 enrolled. In 2010, 8 doctorates awarded. *Degree requirements:* For master's, comprehensive exam, thesis or alternative; for doctorate, thesis/dissertation. *Entrance requirements:* For master's, GRE, minimum undergraduate B average; for doctorate, GRE, MPA, minimum B average. *Application deadline:* For fall admission, 7/1 priority date for domestic students; for spring admission, 12/1 for domestic students. Applications are processed on a rolling basis. Application fee: $60. Electronic applications accepted. *Expenses:* Tuition, state resident: part-time $600 per credit. Tuition, nonresident: full-time $10,694. *Financial support:* In 2010–11, 3 fellowships (averaging $18,000 per year), 11 teaching assistantships with full and partial tuition reimbursements (averaging $23,112 per year) were awarded; career-related internships or fieldwork also available. Support available to part-time students. Financial award application deadline: 3/1. *Faculty research:* Government finance, municipal and state government, public productivity. *Unit head:* Dr. Norma Riccucci, Chairman and Director, 973-353-5093 Ext.

16, E-mail: riccucci@andromeda.rutgers.edu. *Application contact:* Gail Daniels, Assistant Dean for Student Services, 201-973-5093 Ext. 11, E-mail: gaild@andromeda.rutgers.edu.

Rutgers, The State University of New Jersey, New Brunswick, School of Management and Labor Relations, Program in Human Resource Management, Piscataway, NJ 08854-8097. Offers MHRM. Part-time and evening/weekend programs available. *Faculty:* 16 full-time (5 women), 4 part-time/adjunct (0 women). *Students:* 90 full-time (68 women), 142 part-time (104 women); includes 6 Black or African American, non-Hispanic/Latino; 41 Asian, non-Hispanic/Latino; 3 Hispanic/Latino, 62 international. Average age 33. 255 applicants, 53% accepted, 68 enrolled. In 2010, 78 master's awarded. *Entrance requirements:* For master's, GMAT or GRE General Test, 3 letters of recommendation. Additional exam requirements/recommendations for international students: Required—TOEFL (minimum score 575 paper-based; 233 computer-based). *Application deadline:* For fall admission, 3/1 priority date for domestic students, 2/1 for international students; for spring admission, 10/1 priority date for domestic students, 9/1 for international students. Applications are processed on a rolling basis. Application fee: $65. Electronic applications accepted. *Expenses:* Contact institution. *Financial support:* In 2010–11, 11 students received support, including 11 fellowships with tuition reimbursements available; research assistantships with tuition reimbursements available, teaching assistantships, career-related internships or fieldwork, Federal Work-Study, scholarships/grants, and tuition waivers (full and partial) also available. Financial award application deadline: 2/1; financial award applicants required to submit FAFSA. *Faculty research:* Human resource policy and planning, employee ownership and profit sharing, compensation and appraisal of performance, law and public policy, computers and decision making. *Unit head:* David Ferio, Director, 732-445-0862, Fax: 732-445-2830, E-mail: ferio@smlr.rutgers.edu. *Application contact:* Joanna K. Eriksen, Information Contact, 732-445-5973, Fax: 732-445-2830, E-mail: mhrm@rci.rutgers.edu.

Rutgers, The State University of New Jersey, New Brunswick, School of Management and Labor Relations, Program in Industrial Relations and Human Resources, Piscataway, NJ 08854-8097. Offers PhD. Part-time programs available. *Faculty:* 17 full-time (7 women). *Students:* 12 full-time (5 women); includes 1 Black or African American, non-Hispanic/Latino; 8 Asian, non-Hispanic/Latino. Average age 35. 31 applicants, 23% accepted, 5 enrolled. In 2010, 1 doctorate awarded. *Degree requirements:* For doctorate, comprehensive exam, thesis/dissertation. *Entrance requirements:* For doctorate, GRE or GMAT, 3 letters of recommendation. Additional exam requirements/recommendations for international students: Required—TOEFL (minimum score 575 paper-based; 233 computer-based; 91 iBT). *Application deadline:* For fall admission, 2/1 for domestic and international students. Application fee: $60. Electronic applications accepted. *Expenses:* Tuition, state resident: full-time $7200; part-time $600 per credit. Tuition, nonresident: full-time $11,124; part-time $927 per credit. *Financial support:* In 2010–11, 10 students received support, including teaching assistantships with full tuition reimbursements available (averaging $23,842 per year); health care benefits and tuition waivers (full and partial) also available. Financial award application deadline: 2/1. *Faculty research:* Strategic human resources, labor relations, organizational change, worker representation. Total annual research expenditures: $2 million. *Unit head:* Douglas Kruse, Professor/Director, 732-445-5991, Fax: 732-445-2830, E-mail: dkruse@smlr.rutgers.edu. *Application contact:* Rebecca A. Tinkhorn, Administrative Assistant, 732-445-5974, Fax: 732-445-2830, E-mail: jeriksen@rci.rutgers.edu.

Sage Graduate School, Graduate School, School of Management, Program in Business Administration, Troy, NY 12180-4115. Offers business strategy (MBA); finance (MBA); human resources (MBA); marketing (MBA); JD/MBA. Part-time and evening/weekend programs available. *Faculty:* 4 full-time (2 women), 8 part-time/adjunct (3 women). *Students:* 8 full-time (4 women), 67 part-time (45 women); includes 10 Black or African American, non-Hispanic/Latino; 2 Asian, non-Hispanic/Latino; 3 Hispanic/Latino, 1 international. Average age 31. 45 applicants, 64% accepted, 19 enrolled. In 2010, 24 master's awarded. *Entrance requirements:* For master's, minimum GPA of 2.75, resume, 2 letters of recommendation. Additional exam requirements/recommendations for international students: Required—TOEFL (minimum score 550 paper-based; 213 computer-based). *Application deadline:* Applications are processed on a rolling basis. Application fee: $40. *Expenses:* Tuition: Full-time $10,980; part-time $610 per credit hour. Tuition and fees vary according to course load, degree level and program. *Financial support:* Fellowships, research assistantships, Federal Work-Study, scholarships/grants, and unspecified assistantships available. Support available to part-time students. Financial award application deadline: 3/1; financial award applicants required to submit FAFSA. *Unit head:* Dr. Daniel Robeson, Dean, School of Management, 518-292-8637, Fax: 518-292-1964, E-mail: robesd@sage.edu. *Application contact:* Wendy D. Diefendorf, Director of Graduate and Adult Admission, 518-244-2443, Fax: 518-244-6880, E-mail: diefew@sage.edu.

St. Ambrose University, College of Business, Program in Business Administration, Davenport, IA 52803-2898. Offers business administration (DBA); health care (MBA); human resources (MBA). *Accreditation:* ACBSP. Part-time and evening/weekend programs available. *Faculty:* 17 full-time (3 women), 9 part-time/adjunct (2 women). *Students:* 52 full-time (20 women), 221 part-time (110 women); includes 16 minority (5 Black or African

American, non-Hispanic/Latino; 4 Asian, non-Hispanic/Latino; 7 Hispanic/Latino), 4 international. Average age 33. 79 applicants, 78% accepted, 51 enrolled. In 2010, 94 master's, 5 doctorates awarded. *Degree requirements:* For master's, comprehensive exam (for some programs), thesis or alternative, capstone seminar; for doctorate, comprehensive exam, thesis/dissertation, oral and written exams. *Entrance requirements:* For master's, GMAT; for doctorate, GMAT, master's degree. Additional exam requirements/recommendations for international students: Required—TOEFL. *Application deadline:* For fall admission, 8/15 priority date for domestic students; for winter admission, 12/15 for domestic students; for spring admission, 1/1 for domestic students. Applications are processed on a rolling basis. Application fee: $25. Electronic applications accepted. *Expenses:* Contact institution. *Financial support:* In 2010–11, 54 students received support, including 5 research assistantships with partial tuition reimbursements available (averaging $3,600 per year); career-related internships or fieldwork, scholarships/grants, tuition waivers (partial), and unspecified assistantships also available. Financial award application deadline: 3/15; financial award applicants required to submit FAFSA. *Unit head:* Dr. Linda K. Brown, MBA Director, 563-333-6343, Fax: 563-333-6243, E-mail: brownlindak@sau.edu. *Application contact:* Dr. Linda K. Brown, MBA Director, 563-333-6343, Fax: 563-333-6243, E-mail: brownlindak@sau.edu.

St. Edward's University, School of Management and Business, Area of Business Administration, Austin, TX 78704. Offers accounting (MBA); business management (MBA); corporate finance (MBA, Certificate); global entrepreneurship (MBA); human resource management (Certificate); management information systems (MBA, Certificate); marketing (MBA, Certificate); operations management (MBA, Certificate). Part-time and evening/weekend programs available. *Faculty:* 17 full-time (7 women), 19 part-time/adjunct (4 women). *Students:* 41 full-time (21 women), 273 part-time (135 women); includes 111 minority (19 Black or African American, non-Hispanic/Latino; 1 American Indian or Alaska Native, non-Hispanic/Latino; 8 Asian, non-Hispanic/Latino; 78 Hispanic/Latino; 1 Native Hawaiian or other Pacific Islander, non-Hispanic/Latino; 4 Two or more races, non-Hispanic/Latino), 11 international. Average age 33. 101 applicants, 77% accepted, 50 enrolled. In 2010, 115 master's awarded. *Degree requirements:* For master's, minimum of 24 resident hours. *Entrance requirements:* For master's, GMAT or GRE General Test, minimum GPA of 2.75 in last 60 hours of course work. Additional exam requirements/recommendations for international students: Required—TOEFL (minimum score 550 paper-based; 213 computer-based; 79 iBT) or IELTS (minimum score 6). *Application deadline:* For fall admission, 7/1 for domestic and international students; for spring admission, 11/1 for domestic and international students. Applications are processed on a rolling basis. Application fee: $45 ($50 for international students). Electronic applications accepted. *Expenses:* Tuition: Full-time $16,200; part-time $900 per credit hour. Required fees: $50 per trimester. Full-time tuition and fees vary according to course load and program. *Financial support:* In 2010–11, 19 students received support. Scholarships/grants available. *Faculty research:* Ethics and corporate responsibility, new hire socialization, team performance, business strategy, non-traditional marketing, social media. *Unit head:* Dr. Stan Horner, Director, 512-428-1279, Fax: 512-448-8492, E-mail: stanleyh@stedwards.edu. *Application contact:* Kelly Luna, Graduate Admissions Coordinator, 512-233-1697, Fax: 512-428-1032, E-mail: kellyl@stedwards.edu.

Saint Francis University, Graduate School of Business and Human Resource Management, Loretto, PA 15940-0600. Offers business administration (MBA); human resource management (MHRM). Part-time and evening/weekend programs available. *Faculty:* 8 full-time (2 women), 25 part-time/adjunct (12 women). *Students:* 16 full-time (8 women), 141 part-time (66 women); includes 2 Black or African American, non-Hispanic/Latino. Average age 32. 40 applicants, 88% accepted, 25 enrolled. In 2010, 67 master's awarded. *Entrance requirements:* For master's, 2 letters of recommendation, minimum GPA of 2.75. Additional exam requirements/recommendations for international students: Required—TOEFL (minimum score 550 paper-based; 213 computer-based; 57 iBT). *Application deadline:* For fall admission, 8/1 priority date for domestic and international students; for spring admission, 12/1 priority date for domestic students, 12/1 for international students. Applications are processed on a rolling basis. Application fee: $30. *Expenses:* Contact institution. *Financial support:* Fellowships with partial tuition reimbursements, career-related internships or fieldwork and unspecified assistantships available. *Unit head:* Dr. Randy Frye, Director, 814-472-3041, Fax: 814-472-3174, E-mail: rfrye@francis.edu. *Application contact:* Dr. Peter Raymond Skoner, Associate Vice President for Academic Affairs, 814-472-3085, Fax: 814-472-3365, E-mail: pskoner@francis.edu.

Saint Joseph's University, Erivan K. Haub School of Business, MS Program in Human Resources Management, Philadelphia, PA 19131-1395. Offers human resource management (MS). Part-time and evening/weekend programs available. *Students:* 1 (woman) full-time, 35 part-time (27 women); includes 12 minority (8 Black or African American, non-Hispanic/Latino; 3 Asian, non-Hispanic/Latino; 1 Two or more races, non-Hispanic/Latino). Average age 33. In 2010, 12 master's awarded. *Entrance requirements:* For master's, MAT, GRE, or GMAT, 2 letters of recommendation, resume, essay. Additional exam requirements/recommendations for international students: Required—TOEFL

(minimum score: paper 550, computer 213, iBT 79) or IELTS (6.5), Pearson Test of English (minimum 60). *Application deadline:* For fall admission, 7/15 priority date for domestic students, 5/15 priority date for international students; for spring admission, 11/15 priority date for domestic students, 10/15 priority date for international students. Applications are processed on a rolling basis. Application fee: $35. Electronic applications accepted. *Expenses:* Tuition: Part-time $729 per credit. Tuition and fees vary according to course load, degree level and program. *Financial support:* Unspecified assistantships available. Financial award application deadline: 5/1; financial award applicants required to submit FAFSA. *Unit head:* Patricia Rafferty, Director, MS in Business Intelligence and MS in Human Resource Management Programs, 610-660-1318, Fax: 610-660-1229, E-mail: patricia.rafferty@sju.edu. *Application contact:* Patricia Rafferty, Director, MS in Business Intelligence and MS in Human Resource Management Programs, 610-660-1318, Fax: 610-660-1229, E-mail: patricia.rafferty@sju.edu.

Saint Joseph's University, Erivan K. Haub School of Business, Professional MBA Program, Philadelphia, PA 19131-1395. Offers accounting (MBA); finance (MBA), including finance; general business (MBA); health and medical services administration (MBA); human resource management (MBA); international business (MBA); international marketing (MBA); management (MBA); marketing (MBA); DO/MBA. Do/MBA offered jointly with Philadelphia College of Osteopathic Medicine. Part-time and evening/weekend programs available. Postbaccalaureate distance learning degree programs offered (no on-campus study). *Students:* 47 full-time (35 women), 585 part-time (221 women); includes 92 minority (42 Black or African American, non-Hispanic/Latino; 1 American Indian or Alaska Native, non-Hispanic/Latino; 34 Asian, non-Hispanic/Latino; 12 Hispanic/Latino; 1 Native Hawaiian or other Pacific Islander, non-Hispanic/Latino; 2 Two or more races, non-Hispanic/Latino), 41 international. Average age 30. In 2010, 135 master's awarded. *Entrance requirements:* For master's, GMAT or GRE, 2 letters of recommendation, resume. Additional exam requirements/recommendations for international students: Required—TOEFL (minimum score: paper 550, computer 213, iBT 79) or IELTS (6.5), Pearson Test of English (minimum 60). *Application deadline:* For fall admission, 7/15 priority date for domestic students, 4/15 priority date for international students; for spring admission, 11/15 priority date for domestic students, 10/15 priority date for international students. Applications are processed on a rolling basis. Application fee: $35. Electronic applications accepted. *Expenses:* Tuition: Part-time $729 per credit. Tuition and fees vary according to course load, degree level and program. *Financial support:* Scholarships/grants and unspecified assistantships available. Financial award application deadline: 5/1; financial award applicants required to submit FAFSA. *Unit head:* Adele C. Foley, Associate Dean/Director, Graduate Business Programs, 610-660-1691, Fax: 610-660-1599, E-mail: afoley@sju.edu. *Application contact:* Janine N. Guerra, Assistant Director, MBA Program, 610-660-1695, Fax: 610-660-1599, E-mail: jguerra@sju.edu.

Saint Leo University, Graduate Business Studies, Saint Leo, FL 33574-6665. Offers accounting (MBA); business (MBA); health services management (MBA); human resource management (MBA); information security management (MBA); marketing (MBA); sport business (MBA). Part-time and evening/weekend programs available. Postbaccalaureate distance learning degree programs offered (no on-campus study). *Faculty:* 32 full-time (4 women), 53 part-time/adjunct (21 women). *Students:* 1,498 full-time (890 women), 10 part-time (6 women); includes 593 minority (465 Black or African American, non-Hispanic/Latino; 5 American Indian or Alaska Native, non-Hispanic/Latino; 23 Asian, non-Hispanic/Latino; 84 Hispanic/Latino; 2 Native Hawaiian or other Pacific Islander, non-Hispanic/Latino; 14 Two or more races, non-Hispanic/Latino), 14 international. Average age 38. In 2010, 557 master's awarded. *Entrance requirements:* For master's, GMAT (minimum score 500 if applicant does not have 5 years of professional work experience), bachelor's degree from regionally-accredited college or university with minimum GPA of 3.0 in the last 60 hours of coursework; 5 years of professional work experience; resume; 2 letters of recommendation. Additional exam requirements/recommendations for international students: Required—TOEFL (minimum score 550 paper-based; 213 computer-based; 80 iBT). *Application deadline:* For fall admission, 7/1 priority date for domestic and international students; for spring admission, 11/12 priority date for domestic students, 11/1 for international students. Applications are processed on a rolling basis. Application fee: $75. Electronic applications accepted. *Expenses:* Contact institution. *Financial support:* In 2010–11, 51 students received support. Career-related internships or fieldwork, Federal Work-Study, scholarships/grants, and health care benefits available. Financial award application deadline: 3/1; financial award applicants required to submit FAFSA. *Unit head:* Dr. Lorrie McGovern, Director, 352-588-7390, Fax: 352-588-8585, E-mail: mbaslu@saintleo.edu. *Application contact:* Jared Welling, Director, Graduate/Weekend and Evening Admission, 800-707-8846, Fax: 352-588-7873, E-mail: grad.admissions@saintleo.edu.

Saint Mary's University of Minnesota, Schools of Graduate and Professional Programs, Graduate School of Business and Technology, Human Resource Management Program, Winona, MN 55987-1399. Offers MA. *Unit head:* Janet Dunn, Director, 612-238-4546, E-mail: jdunn@smumn.edu. *Application contact:* Yasin Alsaidi, Director of Admissions for Graduate and Professional Programs, 612-728-5207, Fax: 612-728-5121, E-mail: yalsaidi@smumn.edu.

Saint Peter's College, Graduate Business Programs, MBA Program, Jersey City, NJ 07306-5997. Offers finance (MBA); health care administration (MBA); human resource management (MBA); international business (MBA); management (MBA); management information systems (MBA); marketing (MBA); risk management (MBA); MBA/MS. Part-time and evening/weekend programs available. *Students:* 108 applicants, 81% accepted, 62 enrolled. *Entrance requirements:* Additional exam requirements/recommendations for international students: Required—TOEFL (minimum score 79 computer-based). *Application deadline:* Applications are processed on a rolling basis. Electronic applications accepted. *Financial support:* Career-related internships or fieldwork, Federal Work-Study, and institutionally sponsored loans available. Financial award applicants required to submit FAFSA. *Faculty research:* Finance, health care management, human resource management, international business, management, management information systems, marketing, risk management. *Application contact:* Stephanie Autenrieth, Director, Graduate and Professional Studies Admission, 201-761-6474, Fax: 201-435-5270, E-mail: sautenrieth@spc.edu.

Stevens Institute of Technology, Graduate School, Wesley J. Howe School of Technology Management, Program in Management, Hoboken, NJ 07030. Offers general management (MS); global innovation management (MS); human resource management (MS); information management (MS); project management (MS); technology commercialization (MS); technology management (MS). Part-time programs available. *Students:* 15 full-time (6 women), 35 part-time (15 women); includes 1 Black or African American, non-Hispanic/Latino; 5 Asian, non-Hispanic/Latino; 6 Hispanic/Latino, 12 international. Average age 31. *Degree requirements:* For master's, thesis optional. *Entrance requirements:* For master's, GMAT, GRE General Test. Additional exam requirements/recommendations for international students: Required—TOEFL. *Application deadline:* Applications are processed on a rolling basis. Application fee: $50. Electronic applications accepted. *Financial support:* Unspecified assistantships available. *Faculty research:* Industrial economics. *Unit head:* Elizabeth Watson, Director, 201-216-5081. *Application contact:* Graduate Admissions, 800-496-4935, Fax: 201-216-8044, E-mail: gradadmissions@stevens.edu.

Stony Brook University, State University of New York, Graduate School, College of Business, Program in Business Administration, Stony Brook, NY 11794. Offers finance (MBA, Certificate); health care management (MBA, Certificate); human resource management (Certificate); human resources (MBA); information systems management (MBA, Certificate); management (MBA); marketing (MBA). *Faculty:* 14 full-time (2 women), 27 part-time/adjunct (6 women). *Students:* 182 full-time (103 women), 117 part-time (35 women); includes 11 Black or African American, non-Hispanic/Latino; 35 Asian, non-Hispanic/Latino; 10 Hispanic/Latino; 2 Two or more races, non-Hispanic/Latino, 88 international. 281 applicants, 60% accepted, 102 enrolled. In 2010, 95 master's, 1 other advanced degree awarded. Application fee: $100. *Expenses:* Tuition, state resident: full-time $8370; part-time $349 per credit. Tuition, nonresident: full-time $13,780; part-time $574 per credit. Required fees: $994. *Financial support:* In 2010–11, 2 teaching assistantships were awarded. *Unit head:* Dr. Manuel London, Interim Dean, 631-632-7180. *Application contact:* Dr. Aristotle Lekacos, Director, Graduate Program, 631-632-7171, E-mail: aristotle.lekacost@notes.cc.sunysb.edu.

Stony Brook University, State University of New York, School of Professional Development, Stony Brook, NY 11794. Offers biology-grade 7-12 (MAT); chemistry-grade 7-12 (MAT); coaching (Graduate Certificate); coaching online (Graduate Certificate); computer integrated engineering (Graduate Certificate); earth science-grade 7-12 (MAT); educational computing (Graduate Certificate); educational leadership (Advanced Certificate); English-grade 7-12 (MAT); environmental management (Graduate Certificate); environmental/occupational health and safety (Graduate Certificate); French-grade 7-12 (MAT); German-grade 7-12 (MAT); human resource management (Graduate Certificate); human resource management online (Graduate Certificate); information systems management (Graduate Certificate); Italian-grade 7-12 (MAT); liberal studies (MA); liberal studies online (MAT); mathematics-grade 7-12 (MAT); operation research (Graduate Certificate); physics-grade 7-12 (MAT); professional studies online (MPS); school administration and supervision (Graduate Certificate); school building leadership (Graduate Certificate); school district administration (Graduate Certificate); school district business leadership (Advanced Certificate); school district leadership (Graduate Certificate); social science and the professions (MPS), including environmental waste management, human resource management; social studies-grade 7-12 (MAT); Spanish-grade 7-12 (MAT); waste management (Graduate Certificate). Part-time and evening/weekend programs available. Postbaccalaureate distance learning degree programs offered. *Faculty:* 25 full-time (10 women), 105 part-time/adjunct (40 women). *Students:* 360 full-time (228 women), 1,097 part-time (729 women); includes 180 minority (65 Black or African American, non-Hispanic/Latino; 2 American Indian or Alaska Native, non-Hispanic/Latino; 30 Asian, non-Hispanic/Latino; 81 Hispanic/Latino; 1 Native Hawaiian or other Pacific Islander, non-Hispanic/Latino; 1 Two or more races, non-Hispanic/Latino), 10 international. Average age 28. In 2010, 505 master's, 187 other advanced degrees awarded. *Degree requirements:* For master's, one foreign language, thesis or alternative. *Application deadline:* Applications are processed on a

rolling basis. Application fee: $100. *Expenses:* Tuition, state resident: full-time $8370; part-time $349 per credit. Tuition, nonresident: full-time $13,780; part-time $574 per credit. Required fees: $994. *Financial support:* In 2010–11, 1 teaching assistantship was awarded; fellowships, research assistantships, career-related internships or fieldwork also available. Support available to part-time students. *Unit head:* Dr. Paul J. Edelson, Dean, 631-632-7052, Fax: 631-632-9046, E-mail: paul.edelson@stonybrook.edu. *Application contact:* Dr. Paul J. Edelson, Dean, 631-632-7052, Fax: 631-632-9046, E-mail: paul.edelson@stonybrook.edu.

Tennessee Technological University, Graduate School, College of Business, Cookeville, TN 38505. Offers accounting (MBA); finance (MBA); human resource management (MBA); international business (MBA); management information systems (MBA); risk management & insurance (MBA). *Accreditation:* AACSB. Part-time and evening/weekend programs available. *Faculty:* 28 full-time (5 women). *Students:* 58 full-time (18 women), 139 part-time (49 women); includes 10 Black or African American, non-Hispanic/Latino; 7 Asian, non-Hispanic/Latino; 7 Hispanic/Latino; 1 Native Hawaiian or other Pacific Islander, non-Hispanic/Latino. Average age 25. 211 applicants, 51% accepted, 59 enrolled. In 2010, 116 master's awarded. *Entrance requirements:* For master's, GMAT. Additional exam requirements/recommendations for international students: Required—TOEFL (minimum score 550 paper-based; 79 iBT), IELTS (minimum score 5.5). *Application deadline:* For fall admission, 8/1 for domestic and international students; for spring admission, 12/1 for domestic students, 10/1 for international students. Application fee: $25 ($30 for international students). Electronic applications accepted. *Expenses:* Tuition, state resident: full-time $7934; part-time $388 per credit hour. Tuition, nonresident: full-time $19,758; part-time $962 per credit hour. *Financial support:* In 2010–11, 5 fellowships (averaging $10,000 per year), 18 research assistantships (averaging $4,000 per year), teaching assistantships (averaging $4,000 per year) were awarded. Support available to part-time students. Financial award application deadline: 4/1. *Unit head:* Dr. Tom Timmerman, Director, 931-372-3600, Fax: 931-372-6249. *Application contact:* Shelia K. Kendrick, Coordinator of Graduate Admissions, 931-372-3808, Fax: 931-372-3497, E-mail: skendrick@tntech.edu.

Tennessee Technological University, Graduate School, Program of Professional Studies, Cookeville, TN 38505. Offers human resources leadership (MPS); strategic leadership (MPS); training and development (MPS). *Students:* 6 full-time (4 women), 25 part-time (14 women); includes 4 Black or African American, non-Hispanic/Latino; 1 American Indian or Alaska Native, non-Hispanic/Latino; 1 Hispanic/Latino. 16 applicants, 56% accepted, 6 enrolled. In 2010, 11 master's awarded. *Degree requirements:* For master's, comprehensive exam, thesis or alternative. *Entrance requirements:* For master's, GRE. Additional exam requirements/recommendations for international students: Required—TOEFL (minimum score 550 paper-based; 79 iBT), IELTS (minimum score 5.5). *Application deadline:* For fall admission, 8/1 for domestic students, 5/1 for international students; for spring admission, 12/1 for domestic students, 10/1 for international students. Application fee: $25 ($30 for international students). Electronic applications accepted. *Expenses:* Tuition, state resident: full-time $7934; part-time $388 per credit hour. Tuition, nonresident: full-time $19,758; part-time $962 per credit hour. *Financial support:* Application deadline: 4/1. *Unit head:* Dr. Susan A. Elkins, Dean, School of Interdisciplinary Studies and Extended Education, 931-372-3394, Fax: 372-372-3499, E-mail: selkins@tntech.edu. *Application contact:* Shelia K. Kendrick, Coordinator of Graduate Admissions, 931-372-3808, Fax: 931-372-3497, E-mail: skendrick@tntech.edu.

Texas A&M University, Mays Business School, Department of Management, College Station, TX 77843. Offers human resource management (MS); management (PhD). *Faculty:* 32. *Students:* 66 full-time (43 women), 2 part-time (1 woman); includes 14 minority (4 Black or African American, non-Hispanic/Latino; 1 American Indian or Alaska Native, non-Hispanic/Latino; 3 Asian, non-Hispanic/Latino; 6 Hispanic/Latino), 5 international. Average age 31. 76 applicants, 28% accepted. In 2010, 44 master's, 3 doctorates awarded. Terminal master's awarded for partial completion of doctoral program. *Degree requirements:* For master's, comprehensive exam; for doctorate, thesis/dissertation. *Entrance requirements:* For master's, GMAT or GRE; for doctorate, GMAT or GRE General Test. Additional exam requirements/recommendations for international students: Required—TOEFL. *Application deadline:* For fall admission, 3/1 priority date for domestic students; for spring admission, 8/1 for domestic students. Applications are processed on a rolling basis. Application fee: $50 ($75 for international students). *Financial support:* In 2010–11, 25 students received support; fellowships, research assistantships, teaching assistantships, career-related internships or fieldwork and institutionally sponsored loans available. Financial award application deadline: 2/1. *Faculty research:* Strategic and human resource management, business and public policy, organizational behavior, organizational theory. *Unit head:* Murray R. Barrick, Head, 979-845-0329, Fax: 979-845-9641, E-mail: mbarrick@mays.tamu.edu. *Application contact:* Kristi Mora, Senior Academic Advisor II, 979-845-6127, E-mail: kmora@mays.tamu.edu.

Texas A&M University–San Antonio, School of Business, San Antonio, TX 78224. Offers business administration (MBA); enterprise resource planning systems (MBA); finance (MBA); healthcare management (MBA); human resources management (MBA); information assurance and security (MBA);

international business (MBA); project management (MBA); supply chain management (MBA). Part-time and evening/weekend programs available. *Faculty:* 18 full-time (6 women), 1 part-time/adjunct (0 women). *Students:* 49 full-time (21 women), 195 part-time (107 women). In 2010, 20 master's awarded. *Entrance requirements:* For master's, GMAT. Additional exam requirements/recommendations for international students: Required—TOEFL (minimum score 550 paper-based; 213 computer-based; 80 iBT), IELTS (minimum score 6). *Application deadline:* For fall admission, 7/1 priority date for domestic students, 6/1 priority date for international students; for spring admission, 11/15 priority date for domestic students, 10/1 priority date for international students. Applications are processed on a rolling basis. Application fee: $35 ($50 for international students). Electronic applications accepted. *Expenses:* Tuition, state resident: full-time $2899; part-time $161 per credit hour. Tuition, nonresident: full-time $8479; part-time $471 per credit hour. Required fees: $1056; $61 per credit hour. $368 per semester. *Financial support:* Application deadline: 3/31. *Unit head:* Dr. Tracy Hurley, MBA Coordinator, 210-932-6200, E-mail: tracy.hurley@tamusa.tamus.edu. *Application contact:* Melissa A. Villanueva, Graduate Admissions Specialist, 210-932-6200, Fax: 210-932-6209, E-mail: melissa.villanueva@tamusa.tamus.edu.

Thomas Edison State College, School of Business and Management, Program in Human Resources Management, Trenton, NJ 08608-1176. Offers MSHRM, Graduate Certificate. Part-time programs available. Postbaccalaureate distance learning degree programs offered (no on-campus study). *Students:* 40 part-time (20 women); includes 21 Black or African American, non-Hispanic/Latino; 2 Asian, non-Hispanic/Latino; 10 Hispanic/Latino, 3 international. Average age 38. In 2010, 15 master's, 2 other advanced degrees awarded. *Degree requirements:* For master's, final/capstone project. *Entrance requirements:* For master's, bachelor's degree from a regionally-accredited college or university; minimum 2 letters of recommendation; 3-5 years of related working experience; current resume. Additional exam requirements/recommendations for international students: Required—TOEFL (minimum score 550 paper-based; 213 computer-based; 79 iBT). *Application deadline:* For fall admission, 8/15 priority date for domestic and international students; for winter admission, 11/15 priority date for domestic and international students; for spring admission, 2/15 priority date for domestic and international students. Applications are processed on a rolling basis. Application fee: $75. Electronic applications accepted. *Financial support:* Applicants required to submit FAFSA. *Unit head:* Dr. Susan Gilbert, Dean, School of Business and Management, 609-984-1130, Fax: 609-984-3898, E-mail: info@tesc.edu. *Application contact:* David Hoftiezer, Director of Admissions, 888-442-8372, Fax: 609-984-8447, E-mail: admissions@tesc.edu.

Tiffin University, Program in Business Administration, Tiffin, OH 44883-2161. Offers finance (MBA); general management (MBA); healthcare administration (MBA); human resources (MBA); international business (MBA); leadership (MBA); marketing (MBA); sports management (MBA). *Accreditation:* ACBSP. Part-time and evening/weekend programs available. Postbaccalaureate distance learning degree programs offered (no on-campus study). *Faculty:* 18 full-time (9 women), 22 part-time/adjunct (6 women). *Students:* 186 full-time (93 women), 250 part-time (124 women). Average age 31. 532 applicants, 86% accepted, 229 enrolled. In 2010, 340 master's awarded. *Entrance requirements:* For master's, minimum undergraduate GPA of 2.5, work experience. Additional exam requirements/recommendations for international students: Required—TOEFL (minimum score 550 paper-based; 213 computer-based). *Application deadline:* For fall admission, 8/15 for domestic students, 8/1 for international students; for spring admission, 1/9 domestic students, 12/1 for international students. Applications are processed on a rolling basis. Application fee: $0. Electronic applications accepted. *Financial support:* In 2010–11, 94 students received support. Available to part-time students. Application deadline: 7/31. *Faculty research:* Small business, executive development operations, research and statistical analysis, market research, management information systems. *Unit head:* Dr. Lillian Schumacher, Dean of the School of Business, 419-448-3053, Fax: 419-443-5002, E-mail: schumacherlb@tiffin.edu. *Application contact:* Kristi Krintzline, Director of Graduate Admissions and Student Services, 800-968-6446 Ext. 3445, Fax: 419-443-5002, E-mail: krintzlineka@tiffin.edu.

Troy University, Graduate School, College of Arts and Sciences, Program in Public Administration, Troy, AL 36082. Offers education (MPA); environmental management (MPA); government contracting (MPA); health care administration (MPA); justice administration (MPA); national security affairs (MPA); nonprofit management (MPA); public human resources management (MPA); public management (MPA). *Accreditation:* NASPAA. Part-time and evening/weekend programs available. Postbaccalaureate distance learning degree programs offered (no on-campus study). *Degree requirements:* For master's, capstone course, research methodologies course. *Entrance requirements:* For master's, GRE, MAT or GMAT, minimum undergraduate GPA of 2.5, letter of recommendation, essay. Additional exam requirements/recommendations for international students: Required—TOEFL (minimum score 523 paper-based; 193 computer-based; 70 iBT), IELTS (minimum score 6). *Application deadline:* Applications are processed on a rolling basis. Application fee: $50. Electronic applications accepted. *Expenses:* Tuition, state resident: full-time $4428; part-time $246 per credit hour. Tuition, non-resident: full-time $8856; part-time $492 per credit hour. Required fees: $432;

$24 per credit hour. $50 per term. Tuition and fees vary according to program. *Financial support:* Available to part-time students. Applicants required to submit FAFSA. *Unit head:* Dr. Ellen Rosell, Chairman, 334-670-3758, Fax: 334-670-5647, E-mail: erosell@troy.edu. *Application contact:* Brenda K. Campbell, Director of Graduate Admissions, 334-670-3178, Fax: 334-670-3733, E-mail: bcamp@troy.edu.

Troy University, Graduate School, College of Business, Program in Human Resources Management, Troy, AL 36082. Offers MS. Part-time and evening/weekend programs available. *Students:* 76 full-time (53 women), 396 part-time (326 women); includes 355 minority (338 Black or African American, non-Hispanic/Latino; 3 American Indian or Alaska Native, non-Hispanic/Latino; 3 Asian, non-Hispanic/Latino; 11 Hispanic/Latino). Average age 34. 159 applicants, 84% accepted. In 2010, 200 master's awarded. *Degree requirements:* For master's, minimum GPA of 3.0; admission to candidacy. *Entrance requirements:* For master's, GMAT (minimum score 500) or GRE General Test (minimum score 900), minimum GPA of 2.5; letter of recommendation; bachelor's degree. Additional exam requirements/recommendations for international students: Required—TOEFL (minimum score 523 paper-based; 193 computer-based; 70 iBT), IELTS (minimum score 6), or ACT compass ESL (minimum Listening, Reading, and Grammar score: 270). *Application deadline:* Applications are processed on a rolling basis. Application fee: $50. *Expenses:* Tuition, state resident: full-time $4428; part-time $246 per credit hour. Tuition, nonresident: full-time $8856; part-time $492 per credit hour. Required fees: $432; $24 per credit hour. $50 per term. Tuition and fees vary according to program. *Unit head:* Dr. Charles Durham, Associate Professor of Management, 334-241-9727, E-mail: cdurham@troy.edu. *Application contact:* Brenda K. Campbell, Director of Graduate Admissions, 334-670-3178, Fax: 334-670-3733, E-mail: bcamp@troy.edu.

Troy University, Graduate School, College of Business, Program in Management, Troy, AL 36082. Offers applied management (MSM); healthcare management (MSM); human resources management (MSM); information systems (MSM); international hospitality management (MSM); international management (MSM); leadership and organizational effectiveness (MSM); public management (MS, MSM). *Accreditation:* ACBSP. Evening/weekend programs available. *Students:* 101 full-time (62 women), 398 part-time (249 women); includes 308 minority (278 Black or African American, non-Hispanic/Latino; 8 American Indian or Alaska Native, non-Hispanic/Latino; 8 Asian, non-Hispanic/Latino; 13 Hispanic/Latino; 1 Two or more races, non-Hispanic/Latino). Average age 35. 218 applicants, 80% accepted. In 2010, 314 master's awarded. *Degree requirements:* For master's, Graduate Educational Testing Service Major Field Test, capstone exam, minimum GPA of 3.0. *Entrance requirements:* For master's, GMAT (minimum score 500) or GRE General Test (minimum score 900), minimum GPA of 2.5, bachelor's degree, letter of recommendation. Additional exam requirements/recommendations for international students: Required—TOEFL (minimum score 523 paper-based; 193 computer-based; 70 iBT), IELTS, or ACT compass ESL (minimum Listening, Reading, and Grammar score: 270). *Application deadline:* Applications are processed on a rolling basis. Application fee: $50. Electronic applications accepted. *Expenses:* Contact institution. *Unit head:* Dr. Henry M. Findley, Interim Chair/Professor, 334-670-3271, Fax: 334-670-3599, E-mail: hfindley@troy.edu. *Application contact:* Brenda K. Campbell, Director of Graduate Admissions, 334-670-3178, Fax: 334-670-3733, E-mail: bcamp@troy.edu.

TUI University, College of Business Administration, Program in Business Administration, Cypress, CA 90630. Offers business administration (PhD); conflict and negotiation management (MBA); criminal justice administration (MBA); entrepreneurship (MBA); finance (MBA); general management (MBA); government accounting (MBA); human resource management (MBA); information security and digital assurance management (MBA); information technology management (MBA); international business (MBA); logistics management (MBA); marketing (MBA); project management (MBA); public management (MBA); quality management (MBA); strategic leadership (MBA). Part-time and evening/weekend programs available. Postbaccalaureate distance learning degree programs offered (no on-campus study). *Students:* 741 full-time (200 women), 1,585 part-time (410 women). 379 applicants, 81% accepted, 300 enrolled. In 2010, 752 master's, 28 doctorates awarded. *Degree requirements:* For doctorate, comprehensive exam, thesis/dissertation, defense of dissertation. *Entrance requirements:* For master's, minimum GPA of 2.5 (students with GPA 3.0 or greater may transfer up to 30% of graduate level credits); for doctorate, minimum GPA of 3.4, curriculum vitae, course work in research methods or statistics. Additional exam requirements/recommendations for international students: Required—TOEFL. *Application deadline:* For fall admission, 10/3 for domestic and international students; for winter admission, 12/22 for domestic and international students; for spring admission, 4/3 for domestic and international students. Applications are processed on a rolling basis. Application fee: $75. Electronic applications accepted. *Expenses:* Tuition: Full-time $11,040; part-time $345 per semester hour. *Unit head:* Paul Watkins, Dean, College of Business Administration, 800-375-9878, E-mail: pwatkins@tuiu.edu. *Application contact:* Wei Ren-Finaly, Registrar, 800-375-9878, Fax: 714-827-7407, E-mail: registration@tuiu.edu.

Union Graduate College, School of Management, Schenectady, NY 12308-3107. Offers business administration (MBA); financial management (Certificate); general management (Certificate); health systems administration (MBA, Certificate); human resources (Certificate). *Accreditation:* AACSB. Part-time and evening/weekend programs available. *Faculty:* 16 full-time (3 women), 7 part-time/adjunct (2 women). *Students:* 129 full-time (61 women), 86 part-time (42 women); includes 27 minority (4 Black or African American, non-Hispanic/Latino; 16 Asian, non-Hispanic/Latino; 4 Hispanic/Latino; 3 Two or more races, non-Hispanic/Latino), 17 international. Average age 27. 115 applicants, 77% accepted, 71 enrolled. In 2010, 78 master's, 17 other advanced degrees awarded. *Degree requirements:* For master's, internship, capstone course. *Entrance requirements:* For master's, GMAT, minimum GPA of 3.0, 3 letters of recommendation. Additional exam requirements/recommendations for international students: Required—TOEFL (minimum score 550 paper-based; 213 computer-based). *Application deadline:* Applications are processed on a rolling basis. Application fee: $60. *Expenses:* Tuition: Part-time $750 per credit. One-time fee: $350 part-time. Tuition and fees vary according to course load and program. *Financial support:* Research assistantships, career-related internships or fieldwork, Federal Work-Study, scholarships/grants, health care benefits, and tuition waivers (partial) available. Support available to part-time students. Financial award applicants required to submit FAFSA. *Unit head:* Dr. Eric Lewis, Dean, 518-631-9890, Fax: 518-631-9902, E-mail: lewise@uniongraduatecollege.edu. *Application contact:* Diane Trzaskos, Admissions Coordinator, 518-631-9837, Fax: 518-631-9901, E-mail: trzaskod@uniongraduatecollege.edu.

United States International University, School of Business Administration, Nairobi, Kenya. Offers business administration (GEMBA); entrepreneurship (MBA); finance (MBA); human resource management (MBA); information technology management (MBA); integrated studies (MBA); international business administration (MBA); management and organizational development (MS); marketing (MBA); organizational development (EMS); strategic management (MBA). Part-time and evening/weekend programs available. *Faculty:* 42 full-time (8 women), 64 part-time/adjunct (14 women). *Students:* 423 full-time (227 women), 129 part-time (63 women). Average age 29. 110 applicants, 79% accepted, 78 enrolled. In 2010, 164 master's awarded. *Degree requirements:* For master's, thesis. *Entrance requirements:* For master's, GMAT, 2 letters of reference, resume. Additional exam requirements/recommendations for international students: Required—TOEFL (minimum score 550 paper-based; 213 computer-based). *Application deadline:* For fall admission, 6/30 priority date for domestic and international students; for spring admission, 9/30 for domestic and international students. Applications are processed on a rolling basis. Application fee: $50. *Financial support:* In 2010–11, 30 students received support, including 8 research assistantships (averaging $1,400 per year), 4 teaching assistantships (averaging $1,400 per year); career-related internships or fieldwork, scholarships/grants, and unspecified assistantships also available. Support available to part-time students. Financial award application deadline: 6/30; financial award applicants required to submit FAFSA. *Faculty research:* Marketing in small business enterprises, total quality management in Kenya. *Unit head:* Dr. Damary Sikalieh, Dean, 254-02-3606-415, E-mail: dsikalieh@usiu.ac.ke. *Application contact:* George Lumbasi, Director of Admissions, 254-02-3606563, Fax: 254-02-3606100, E-mail: glumbasi@usiu.ac.ke.

The University of Akron, Graduate School, College of Business Administration, Department of Management, Program in Management-Human Resources, Akron, OH 44325. Offers MSM. *Students:* 6 full-time (3 women), 5 part-time (all women); includes 2 Asian, non-Hispanic/Latino, 4 international. Average age 29. 18 applicants, 9 enrolled. *Entrance requirements:* For master's, GMAT, minimum GPA of 2.75, two letters of recommendation, statement of purpose, resume. Additional exam requirements/recommendations for international students: Required—TOEFL (minimum score 550 paper-based; 213 computer-based; 79 iBT). *Application deadline:* For fall admission, 7/15 for domestic and international students; for spring admission, 11/15 for domestic and international students. Application fee: $30 ($40 for international students). Electronic applications accepted. *Expenses:* Tuition, state resident: full-time $6800; part-time $378 per credit hour. Tuition, nonresident: full-time $11,644; part-time $647 per credit hour. Required fees: $1265. One-time fee: $30 full-time. *Application contact:* Dr. Susan Hanlon, Director of Graduate Business Programs, 330-972-7043, Fax: 330-972-6588, E-mail: shanlon@uakron.edu.

The University of Alabama in Huntsville, School of Graduate Studies, College of Business Administration, Department of Management and Marketing, Huntsville, AL 35899. Offers management (MBA), including acquisition management, finance, human resource management, logistics and supply chain management, marketing, project management. *Accreditation:* AACSB. Part-time and evening/weekend programs available. *Faculty:* 11 full-time (2 women), 4 part-time/adjunct (1 woman). *Students:* 41 full-time (17 women), 159 part-time (69 women); includes 32 minority (15 Black or African American, non-Hispanic/Latino; 6 American Indian or Alaska Native, non-Hispanic/Latino; 7 Asian, non-Hispanic/Latino; 3 Hispanic/Latino; 1 Two or more races, non-Hispanic/Latino), 14 international. Average age 31. 141 applicants, 65% accepted, 79 enrolled. In 2010, 66 master's awarded. *Degree requirements:* For master's, comprehensive exam, thesis or alternative.

Entrance requirements: For master's, GMAT (minimum score 500), minimum AACSB index of 1080. Additional exam requirements/recommendations for international students: Required—TOEFL (minimum score 550 paper-based; 213 computer-based; 62 iBT). *Application deadline:* For fall admission, 8/1 for domestic students, 4/1 for international students; for spring admission, 12/1 for domestic students, 9/1 for international students. Applications are processed on a rolling basis. Application fee: $40 ($50 for international students). Electronic applications accepted. *Expenses:* Tuition, state resident: full-time $7250; part-time $407.75 per credit hour. Tuition, nonresident: full-time $17,358; part-time $970.05 per credit hour. Required fees: $246.80 per semester. Tuition and fees vary according to course load and program. *Financial support:* In 2010–11, 3 students received support, including 1 research assistantship with full tuition reimbursement available (averaging $8,550 per year), 2 teaching assistantships with full tuition reimbursements available (averaging $8,000 per year); career-related internships or fieldwork, Federal Work-Study, institutionally sponsored loans, scholarships/grants, health care benefits, and unspecified assistantships also available. Support available to part-time students. Financial award application deadline: 4/1; financial award applicants required to submit FAFSA. *Faculty research:* Strategic human resources, corporate governance, cross-function integration and the management of research and development, determinants of team performance. Total annual research expenditures: $3 million. *Unit head:* Dr. Brent Wren, Chair, 256-824-6408, Fax: 256-824-6328, E-mail: wrenb@uah.edu. *Application contact:* Jennifer Pettitt, Director of Graduate Programs, 256-824-6681, Fax: 256-824-7571, E-mail: jennifer.pettitt@uah.edu.

University of Chicago, Booth School of Business, Full-Time MBA Program, Chicago, IL 60637. Offers accounting (MBA); analytic finance (MBA); analytic management (MBA); econometrics and statistics (MBA); economics (MBA); entrepreneurship (MBA); finance (MBA); general management (MBA); human resource management (MBA); international business (MBA); managerial and organizational behavior (MBA); marketing management (MBA); operations management (MBA); strategic management (MBA); MBA/AM; MBA/JD; MBA/MA; MBA/MD; MBA/MPP. *Accreditation:* AACSB. Part-time and evening/weekend programs available. *Faculty:* 157 full-time, 35 part-time/adjunct. *Students:* 1,177 full-time (417 women); includes 301 minority (62 Black or African American, non-Hispanic/Latino; 1 American Indian or Alaska Native, non-Hispanic/Latino; 164 Asian, non-Hispanic/Latino; 55 Hispanic/Latino; 19 Two or more races, non-Hispanic/Latino), 403 international. Average age 28. 4,299 applicants, 22% accepted, 579 enrolled. In 2010, 1,374 master's awarded. *Entrance requirements:* For master's, GMAT, 2 letters of recommendation, 3 essays, resume, interview, transcripts. Additional exam requirements/recommendations for international students: Required—TOEFL (minimum score 600 paper-based; 250 computer-based), IELTS. *Application deadline:* For fall admission, 10/10 priority date for domestic students, 10/13 priority date for international students; for winter admission, 1/5 for domestic and international students; for spring admission, 4/13 for domestic and international students. Application fee: $200. Electronic applications accepted. *Expenses:* Contact institution. *Financial support:* Fellowships available. Financial award applicants required to submit FAFSA. *Faculty research:* Finance, economics, entrepreneurship, strategy, management. *Unit head:* Stacey Kole, Deputy Dean, 773-702-7121. *Application contact:* Kurt Ahlm, Associate Dean of Admissions and Financial Aid, 773-702-7369, Fax: 773-702-9085, E-mail: admissions@chicagobooth.edu.

University of Colorado Denver, Business School, Program in Management and Organization, Denver, CO 80217. Offers communications management (MS); enterprise technology management (MS); entrepreneurship and innovation (MS); global management (MS); human resources management (MS); leadership (MS); quantitative decision methods (MS); sports and entertainment management (MS); strategic management (MS); sustainability management (MS). *Accreditation:* AACSB. Part-time and evening/weekend programs available. Postbaccalaureate distance learning degree programs offered (no on-campus study). *Students:* 34 full-time (21 women), 9 part-time (2 women); includes 3 Asian, non-Hispanic/Latino; 5 Hispanic/Latino. Average age 33. 28 applicants, 61% accepted, 10 enrolled. In 2010, 20 master's awarded. *Degree requirements:* For master's, 30 semester hours (12 of required courses, 12 of management electives, and 6 of free electives). *Entrance requirements:* For master's, GMAT. Additional exam requirements/recommendations for international students: Required—TOEFL (minimum score 525 paper-based; 197 computer-based; 71 iBT). *Application deadline:* For fall admission, 4/1 priority date for domestic students, 3/15 priority date for international students; for spring admission, 10/1 priority date for domestic and international students. Application fee: $50 ($75 for international students). Electronic applications accepted. *Expenses:* Contact institution. *Financial support:* Federal Work-Study and scholarships/grants available. Support available to part-time students. Financial award application deadline: 4/1; financial award applicants required to submit FAFSA. *Faculty research:* Human resource management, management of catastrophe, turnaround strategies. *Unit head:* Dr. Kenneth Bettenhausen, Associate Professor/Director, 303-315-8425, E-mail: kenneth.bettehausen@ucdenver.edu. *Application contact:* Shelly Townley, Admissions Director, Graduate Programs, 303-315-8202, E-mail: shelly.townley@ucdenver.edu.

University of Denver, University College, Denver, CO 80208. Offers arts and culture (MLS, Certificate), including art, literature, and culture, arts development and program management (Certificate), creative writing; environmental policy and management (MAS, Certificate), including energy and sustainability (Certificate), environmental assessment of nuclear power (Certificate), environmental health and safety (Certificate), environmental management, natural resource management (Certificate); geographic information systems (MAS, Certificate); global affairs (MLS, Certificate), including translation studies, world history and culture; healthcare leadership (MPH, Certificate), including healthcare policy, law, and ethics, medical and healthcare information technologies, strategic management of healthcare; information and communications technology (MCIS, Certificate), including database design and administration (Certificate), geographic information systems (MCIS), information security systems security (Certificate), information systems security (MCIS), project management (MCIS, MPS, Certificate), software design and administration (Certificate), software design and programming (MCIS), technology management, telecommunications technology (MCIS), Web design and development; leadership and organizations (MPS, Certificate), including human capital in organizations, philanthropic leadership, project management (MCIS, MPS, Certificate), strategic innovation and change; organizational and professional communication (MPS, Certificate), including alternative dispute resolution, organizational communication, organizational development and training, public relations and marketing; security management (MAS, Certificate), including emergency planning and response, information security (MAS), organizational security; strategic human resource management (MPS, Certificate), including global human resources (MPS), human resource management and development (MPS). Part-time and evening/weekend programs available. Postbaccalaureate distance learning degree programs offered (no on-campus study). *Faculty:* 7 full-time (2 women), 212 part-time/adjunct (83 women). *Students:* 52 full-time (19 women), 1,044 part-time (625 women); includes 196 minority (81 Black or African American, non-Hispanic/Latino; 7 American Indian or Alaska Native, non-Hispanic/Latino; 30 Asian, non-Hispanic/Latino; 66 Hispanic/Latino; 3 Native Hawaiian or other Pacific Islander, non-Hispanic/Latino; 9 Two or more races, non-Hispanic/Latino), 76 international. Average age 36. 488 applicants, 91% accepted, 339 enrolled. In 2010, 286 master's, 130 other advanced degrees awarded. *Entrance requirements:* Additional exam requirements/recommendations for international students: Required—TOEFL (minimum score 550 paper-based; 80 iBT). *Application deadline:* For fall admission, 6/22 priority date for domestic students, 6/10 priority date for international students; for winter admission, 9/15 priority date for domestic students, 9/6 priority date for international students; for spring admission, 2/3 priority date for domestic students, 12/15 priority date for international students. Applications are processed on a rolling basis. Application fee: $75. Electronic applications accepted. *Expenses:* Contact institution. *Financial support:* Applicants required to submit FAFSA. *Unit head:* Dr. James Davis, Dean, 303-871-2291, Fax: 303-871-4047, E-mail: jdavis@du.edu. *Application contact:* Information Contact, 303-871-3155, Fax: 303-871-4047, E-mail: ucolinfo@du.edu.

University of Florida, Graduate School, Warrington College of Business Administration, Hough Graduate School of Business, Programs in Business Administration, Gainesville, FL 32611. Offers accounting (MBA); arts administration (MBA); business strategy and public policy (MBA); competitive strategy (MBA); decision and information sciences (MBA); electronic commerce (MBA); finance (MBA); general business (MBA); global management (MBA); Graham-Buffett security analysis (MBA); health administration (MBA); human resources management (MBA); international studies (MBA); Latin American business (MBA); management (MBA); marketing (MBA); sports administration (MBA); JD/MBA; MBA/MS; MBA/PhD; MBA/Pharm D; MD/MBA. *Accreditation:* AACSB. Part-time and evening/weekend programs available. *Faculty:* 71 full-time (10 women). *Students:* 187 full-time (44 women), 305 part-time (83 women); includes 25 Black or African American, non-Hispanic/Latino; 2 American Indian or Alaska Native, non-Hispanic/Latino; 52 Asian, non-Hispanic/Latino; 54 Hispanic/Latino, 11 international. Average age 31. 919 applicants, 33% accepted, 225 enrolled. In 2010, 492 master's awarded. *Degree requirements:* For master's, capstone course. *Entrance requirements:* For master's, GMAT, minimum GPA of 3.0, interview. Additional exam requirements/recommendations for international students: Required—TOEFL (minimum score 550 paper-based; 213 computer-based; 80 iBT), IELTS (minimum score 6). *Application deadline:* For fall admission, 7/1 for domestic students, 1/1 for international students; for spring admission, 12/1 for domestic and international students. Applications are processed on a rolling basis. Application fee: $30. Electronic applications accepted. *Expenses:* Tuition, state resident: full-time $10,915.92. Tuition, nonresident: full-time $28,309. *Financial support:* In 2010–11, 1 student received support, including 1 teaching assistantship (averaging $20,600 per year); career-related internships or fieldwork, scholarships/grants, and unspecified assistantships also available. Support available to part-time students. Financial award applicants required to submit FAFSA. *Faculty research:* Accounting, finance, insurance, management, real estate, urban analysis marketing. *Unit head:* Prof. Alexander D. Sevilla, Assistant Dean and Director MBA Programs, 352-273-3252 Ext. 1206, E-mail: alex.sevilla@warrington.ufl.edu. *Application contact:* Prof. Kelli Gust, Associate Director of MBA Programs, 352-273-3255, Fax: 352-392-8791, E-mail: kelly.gust@warrington.ufl.edu.

University of Georgia, College of Education, Department of Lifelong Education, Administration and Policy, Athens, GA 30602. Offers adult education (M Ed, Ed D, PhD, Ed S); educational administration and policy (M Ed, PhD, Ed S); educational leadership (Ed D); human resource and organizational design (M Ed). *Accreditation:* NCATE. *Faculty:* 27 full-time (19 women). *Students:* 74 full-time (49 women), 235 part-time (163 women); includes 85 minority (70 Black or African American, non-Hispanic/Latino; 1 American Indian or Alaska Native, non-Hispanic/Latino; 6 Asian, non-Hispanic/Latino; 4 Hispanic/Latino; 1 Native Hawaiian or other Pacific Islander, non-Hispanic/Latino; 3 Two or more races, non-Hispanic/Latino), 25 international. 171 applicants, 54% accepted, 58 enrolled. In 2010, 69 master's, 27 doctorates, 12 other advanced degrees awarded. *Entrance requirements:* For master's and Ed S, GRE General Test or MAT; for doctorate, GRE General Test. *Application deadline:* For fall admission, 7/1 priority date for domestic students; for spring admission, 11/15 for domestic students. Application fee: $50. Electronic applications accepted. *Expenses:* Tuition, state resident: full-time $7200; part-time $344 per credit hour. Tuition, nonresident: full-time $21,900; part-time $944 per credit hour. Tuition and fees vary according to course load and program. *Unit head:* Dr. Janette Hill, Head, 706-542-4035, Fax: 706-542-5873, E-mail: janette@.uga.edu. *Application contact:* Dr. Kathryn Roulston, Graduate Coordinator, 706-542-2214, Fax: 706-542-5873, E-mail: roulston@uga.edu.

University of Georgia, College of Education, Department of Workforce Education, Leadership and Social Foundations, Athens, GA 30602. Offers educational leadership (Ed D); human resources and organization design (M Ed); occupational studies (MAT, Ed D, PhD, Ed S); social foundations of education (PhD). *Accreditation:* NCATE. *Faculty:* 15 full-time (7 women). *Students:* 41 full-time (26 women), 107 part-time (67 women); includes 36 minority (30 Black or African American, non-Hispanic/Latino; 1 American Indian or Alaska Native, non-Hispanic/Latino; 1 Asian, non-Hispanic/Latino; 1 Hispanic/Latino; 1 Native Hawaiian or other Pacific Islander, non-Hispanic/Latino; 2 Two or more races, non-Hispanic/Latino), 6 international. 48 applicants, 77% accepted, 25 enrolled. In 2010, 37 master's, 18 doctorates, 4 other advanced degrees awarded. *Entrance requirements:* For master's, GRE General Test, MAT; for doctorate, GRE General Test; for Ed S, GRE General Test or MAT. *Application deadline:* For fall admission, 7/1 priority date for domestic students; for spring admission, 11/15 for domestic students. Application fee: $50. Electronic applications accepted. *Expenses:* Tuition, state resident: full-time $7200; part-time $344 per credit hour. Tuition, nonresident: full-time $21,900; part-time $944 per credit hour. Tuition and fees vary according to course load and program. *Financial support:* Fellowships, research assistantships, teaching assistantships, unspecified assistantships available. *Unit head:* Dr. Roger B. Hill, Interim Head, 706-542-4100, Fax: 706-542-4054, E-mail: rbhill@uga.edu. *Application contact:* Dr. Clifton Smith, Graduate Coordinator, 706-542-4208, Fax: 706-542-4054, E-mail: csmith@uga.edu.

University of Hawaii at Manoa, Graduate Division, Shidler College of Business, Program in Business Administration, Honolulu, HI 96822. Offers Asian business studies (MBA); Chinese business studies (MBA); decision sciences (MBA); entrepreneurship (MBA); finance (MBA); finance and banking (MBA); human resources management (MBA); information management (MBA); information technology (MBA); international business (MBA); Japanese business studies (MBA); marketing (MBA); organizational behavior (MBA); organizational management (MBA); real estate (MBA); student-designed track (MBA). *Accreditation:* AACSB. Part-time and evening/weekend programs available. *Faculty:* 53 full-time (12 women). *Students:* 162 full-time (63 women), 102 part-time (43 women); includes 135 minority (1 Black or African American, non-Hispanic/Latino; 81 Asian, non-Hispanic/Latino; 5 Hispanic/Latino; 18 Native Hawaiian or other Pacific Islander, non-Hispanic/Latino; 30 Two or more races, non-Hispanic/Latino), 44 international. Average age 34. 361 applicants, 57% accepted, 172 enrolled. In 2010, 153 master's awarded. *Degree requirements:* For master's, thesis optional. *Entrance requirements:* For master's, GMAT, minimum GPA of 3.0. Additional exam requirements/recommendations for international students: Required—TOEFL (minimum score 600 paper-based; 250 computer-based; 100 iBT), IELTS (minimum score 7). *Application deadline:* For fall admission, 5/1 for domestic students, 3/1 for international students. Application fee: $60. *Expenses:* Contact institution. *Financial support:* In 2010–11, 83 fellowships (averaging $5,547 per year), 1 research assistantship (averaging $16,824 per year) were awarded. Total annual research expenditures: $427,000. *Application contact:* Daniel Port, Graduate Chair, 808-956-5565, Fax: 808-956-6889, E-mail: daniel.port@hawaii.edu.

University of Hawaii at Manoa, Graduate Division, Shidler College of Business, Program in Human Resources Management, Honolulu, HI 96822. Offers MHRM. Part-time programs available. *Students:* 10 full-time (0 women), 52 part-time (1 woman); includes 40 minority (1 Black or African American, non-Hispanic/Latino; 1 American Indian or Alaska Native, non-Hispanic/Latino; 18 Asian, non-Hispanic/Latino; 1 Hispanic/Latino; 15 Native Hawaiian or other Pacific Islander, non-Hispanic/Latino; 4 Two or more races, non-Hispanic/Latino), 4 international. Average age 35. In 2010, 44 master's awarded. *Entrance requirements:* Additional exam requirements/recommendations for international students: Required—TOEFL (minimum score 600 paper-based; 250 computer-based; 100 iBT), IELTS (minimum score 7). *Application deadline:* For fall admission, 6/1 for domestic and international students. Application fee: $60. *Expenses:* Contact institution. *Financial support:* In 2010–11, 3 students received support, including 1 fellowship (averaging $1,500 per year). *Application contact:* Richard Brislin, Director, 808-956-8135, Fax: 808-956-2774, E-mail: rbrislin@hawaii.edu.

University of Illinois at Urbana–Champaign, Graduate College, College of Education, Department of Education Policy, Organization, and Leadership, Champaign, IL 61820. Offers educational organization and leadership (Ed M, MS, Ed D, PhD, CAS); educational policy studies (Ed M, MA, PhD); human resource education (Ed M, MS, Ed D, PhD, CAS). Part-time programs available. Postbaccalaureate distance learning degree programs offered (minimal on-campus study). *Faculty:* 27 full-time (11 women), 2 part-time/adjunct (0 women). *Students:* 452 full-time (268 women), 800 part-time (516 women); includes 212 Black or African American, non-Hispanic/Latino; 4 American Indian or Alaska Native, non-Hispanic/Latino; 56 Asian, non-Hispanic/Latino; 110 Hispanic/Latino; 18 Two or more races, non-Hispanic/Latino, 128 international. 844 applicants, 58% accepted, 240 enrolled. In 2010, 402 master's, 48 doctorates, 20 other advanced degrees awarded. *Entrance requirements:* For master's, minimum GPA of 3.0; for doctorate, GRE General Test, minimum GPA of 3.0, writing samples, interview. Additional exam requirements/recommendations for international students: Required—TOEFL (minimum score 620 paper-based; 260 computer-based; 105 iBT). *Application deadline:* Applications are processed on a rolling basis. Application fee: $75 ($90 for international students). Electronic applications accepted. *Financial support:* In 2010–11, 36 fellowships, 52 research assistantships, 50 teaching assistantships were awarded; tuition waivers (full and partial) also available. *Unit head:* James Anderson, Head, 217-333-2446, Fax: 217-244-5632, E-mail: janders@illinois.edu. *Application contact:* Laura A. Ketchum, 217-333-2155, Fax: 217-244-5632, E-mail: ketchum@illinois.edu.

University of Illinois at Urbana–Champaign, Graduate College, School of Labor and Employment Relations, Champaign, IL 61820. Offers human resources and industrial relations (MHRIR, PhD); MHRIR/JD; MHRIR/MBA. Part-time programs available. *Faculty:* 15 full-time (4 women). *Students:* 169 full-time (117 women), 24 part-time (11 women); includes 40 minority (15 Black or African American, non-Hispanic/Latino; 16 Asian, non-Hispanic/Latino; 7 Hispanic/Latino; 2 Two or more races, non-Hispanic/Latino), 66 international. 262 applicants, 43% accepted, 63 enrolled. In 2010, 99 master's, 1 doctorate awarded. Terminal master's awarded for partial completion of doctoral program. *Entrance requirements:* For master's and doctorate, GRE or GMAT, minimum GPA of 3.0. Additional exam requirements/recommendations for international students: Required—TOEFL (minimum score 590 paper-based; 243 computer-based; 96 iBT) or IELTS (minimum score 6.5). Application fee: $75 ($90 for international students). Electronic applications accepted. *Financial support:* In 2010–11, 8 fellowships, 10 research assistantships, 4 teaching assistantships were awarded; tuition waivers (full and partial) also available. *Unit head:* Dr. Joel E. Cutcher-Gershenfeld, Dean, 217-333-1482, Fax: 217-244-9290, E-mail: joelcg@illinois.edu. *Application contact:* Elizabeth Barker, Director of Student Services, 217-333-2381, Fax: 217-244-9290, E-mail: ebarker@illinois.edu.

University of Louisville, Graduate School, College of Arts and Sciences, Department of Urban and Public Affairs, Louisville, KY 40208. Offers public administration (MPA), including human resources management, non-profit management, public policy and administration; urban and public affairs (PhD), including urban planning and development, urban policy and administration; urban planning (MUP), including administration of planning organizations, housing and community development, land use and environmental planning, spatial analysis. Part-time and evening/weekend programs available. *Faculty:* 22 full-time (7 women), 8 part-time/adjunct (1 woman). *Students:* 73 full-time (36 women), 31 part-time (18 women); includes 11 Black or African American, non-Hispanic/Latino; 2 Asian, non-Hispanic/Latino; 2 Hispanic/Latino; 1 Native Hawaiian or other Pacific Islander, non-Hispanic/Latino; 2 Two or more races, non-Hispanic/Latino, 11 international. Average age 31. 96 applicants, 67% accepted, 37 enrolled. In 2010, 28 master's, 5 doctorates awarded. Terminal master's awarded for partial completion of doctoral program. *Degree requirements:* For master's, internship; for doctorate, comprehensive exam, thesis/dissertation. *Entrance requirements:* For master's, GRE General Test, minimum GPA of 3.0; for doctorate, GRE General Test, master's degree in appropriate field. Additional exam requirements/recommendations for international students: Required—TOEFL (minimum score 550 paper-based; 213 computer-based; 79 iBT). *Application deadline:* For fall admission, 7/15 for domestic students; for spring admission, 11/15 for domestic students. Applications are processed on a rolling basis. Application fee: $50. Electronic applications accepted. *Expenses:* Tuition, state resident: full-time $9144; part-time $508 per credit hour. Tuition, nonresident: full-time $19,026; part-time $1057 per credit hour. Tuition and fees vary according to program and reciprocity agreements. *Financial support:* In 2010–11, 23 students received support; fellowships, research assistantships, health care benefits available. Financial award application deadline: 3/1. *Faculty research:* Housing and community development, performance-based budgeting, environmental policy and natural hazards, sustainability, real estate development, comparative urban development. *Unit head:* Dr. David Simpson, Chair, 502-852-8019, Fax: 502-852-4558, E-mail: dave.simpson@louisville.edu.

Application contact: Patty Sarley, Graduate Student Advisor, 502-852-7914, Fax: 502-852-4558, E-mail: plclea01@louisville.edu.

University of Mary, Gary Tharaldson School of Business, Bismarck, ND 58504-9652. Offers accountancy (MBA); business administration (MBA); health care (MBA); human resource management (MBA); management (MBA); project management (MPM); strategic leadership (MSSL). Part-time and evening/weekend programs available. *Faculty:* 2 full-time (0 women), 73 part-time/adjunct (27 women). *Students:* 232 full-time (123 women), 226 part-time (115 women); includes 63 minority (30 Black or African American, non-Hispanic/Latino; 23 American Indian or Alaska Native, non-Hispanic/Latino; 5 Asian, non-Hispanic/Latino; 3 Hispanic/Latino; 1 Native Hawaiian or other Pacific Islander, non-Hispanic/Latino; 1 Two or more races, non-Hispanic/Latino), 20 international. Average age 36. 209 applicants, 98% accepted, 189 enrolled. In 2010, 265 master's awarded. *Degree requirements:* For master's, strategic planning seminar. *Entrance requirements:* For master's, minimum GPA of 2.5. Additional exam requirements/recommendations for international students: Required—TOEFL (minimum score 500 paper-based; 197 computer-based; 71 iBT). *Application deadline:* Applications are processed on a rolling basis. Application fee: $40. *Expenses:* Tuition: Full-time $10,800; part-time $450 per credit. Tuition and fees vary according to course load, degree level, program and student level. *Financial support:* Application deadline: 8/1. *Unit head:* Dr. Shanda Traiser, Director of the School of Accelerated and Distance Education, 701-355-8160, Fax: 701-255-7687, E-mail: straiser@umary.edu. *Application contact:* Wayne G. Maruska, Graduate Program Advisor, 701-355-8134, Fax: 701-255-7687, E-mail: wmaruska@umary.edu.

University of Minnesota, Twin Cities Campus, Carlson School of Management, Program in Human Resources and Industrial Relations, Minneapolis, MN 55455-0213. Offers MA, PhD. *Accreditation:* AACSB. Part-time and evening/weekend programs available. *Faculty:* 11 full-time (6 women), 6 part-time/adjunct (1 woman). *Students:* 196 full-time (138 women), 92 part-time (68 women); includes 13 Black or African American, non-Hispanic/Latino; 18 Asian, non-Hispanic/Latino; 5 Hispanic/Latino, 62 international. Average age 26. 306 applicants, 44% accepted, 85 enrolled. In 2010, 96 master's, 5 doctorates awarded. Terminal master's awarded for partial completion of doctoral program. *Degree requirements:* For master's, thesis optional; for doctorate, thesis/dissertation. *Entrance requirements:* For master's, GMAT or GRE General Test; for doctorate, GRE General Test. Additional exam requirements/recommendations for international students: Required—TOEFL (minimum score 580 paper-based; 85 iBT). *Application deadline:* For fall admission, 6/15 for domestic and international students; for spring admission, 10/15 for domestic and international students. Applications are processed on a rolling basis. Application fee: $75 ($95 for international students). *Expenses:* Contact institution. *Financial support:* In 2010–11, 60 students received support, including 39 fellowships with partial tuition reimbursements available (averaging $6,500 per year), 14 research assistantships with full and partial tuition reimbursements available (averaging $12,500 per year), 7 teaching assistantships with full tuition reimbursements available (averaging $9,000 per year); career-related internships or fieldwork, Federal Work-Study, institutionally sponsored loans, and tuition waivers (full and partial) also available. Support available to part-time students. Financial award application deadline: 2/1; financial award applicants required to submit FAFSA. *Faculty research:* Staffing, training, and development; compensation and benefits; organization theory; collective bargaining. Total annual research expenditures: $200,000. *Unit head:* Theresa Glomb, Director of Graduate Studies, 612-624-4863, Fax: 612-624-8360, E-mail: tglomb@umn.edu. *Application contact:* Christina Hill, Admissions Coordinator, 612-624-5704, Fax: 612-624-8360, E-mail: hill1312@umn.edu.

University of Missouri–St. Louis, College of Business Administration, Program in Business Administration, St. Louis, MO 63121. Offers accounting (MBA); business administration (Certificate); finance (MBA); human resource management (Certificate); information systems (MBA); local government (Certificate); logistics and supply chain management (MBA, Certificate); marketing (MBA); marketing management (Certificate); operations management (MBA). *Accreditation:* AACSB. Part-time and evening/weekend programs available. *Faculty:* 30 full-time (5 women), 11 part-time/adjunct (2 women). *Students:* 132 full-time (57 women), 306 part-time (122 women); includes 55 minority (21 Black or African American, non-Hispanic/Latino; 20 Asian, non-Hispanic/Latino; 11 Hispanic/Latino; 1 Native Hawaiian or other Pacific Islander, non-Hispanic/Latino; 2 Two or more races, non-Hispanic/Latino), 6 international. Average age 30. 219 applicants, 60% accepted, 88 enrolled. In 2010, 114 master's, 9 other advanced degrees awarded. *Entrance requirements:* For master's, GMAT, 2 letters of recommendation. Additional exam requirements/recommendations for international students: Required—TOEFL (minimum score 550 paper-based; 213 computer-based). *Application deadline:* For fall admission, 7/1 for domestic students; for spring admission, 11/1 for domestic students. Applications are processed on a rolling basis. Application fee: $35 ($40 for international students). Electronic applications accepted. *Expenses:* Tuition, state resident: full-time $5522; part-time $306.80 per credit hour. Tuition, nonresident: full-time $14,253; part-time $792.10 per credit hour. Required fees: $658; $49 per credit hour. One-time fee: $12. Tuition and fees vary according to program. *Financial support:* In 2010–11, 22 research assistantships with full and partial tuition reimbursements (averaging $7,414 per year), 4 teaching assistantships with full and partial tuition reimbursements (averaging $13,950 per year) were awarded; career-related internships or fieldwork, Federal Work-Study, and institutionally sponsored loans also available. Support available to part-time students. Financial award application deadline: 4/1; financial award applicants required to submit FAFSA. *Faculty research:* Human resources, strategic management, marketing strategy, consumer behavior product development, advertising. *Unit head:* Karl Kottemann, Assistant Director, 314-516-5885, Fax: 314-516-6420, E-mail: mba@umsl.edu. *Application contact:* 314-516-5458, Fax: 314-516-6996, E-mail: gradadm@umsl.edu.

University of New Haven, Graduate School, College of Arts and Sciences, Program in Industrial and Organizational Psychology, West Haven, CT 06516-1916. Offers conflict management (MA); human resource management (MA); industrial organizational psychology (MA); organizational development (MA); psychology of conflict management (Certificate). Part-time and evening/weekend programs available. *Students:* 75 full-time (54 women), 29 part-time (19 women); includes 7 Black or African American, non-Hispanic/Latino; 1 American Indian or Alaska Native, non-Hispanic/Latino; 1 Asian, non-Hispanic/Latino; 4 Hispanic/Latino, 13 international. Average age 28. 70 applicants, 100% accepted, 33 enrolled. In 2010, 44 master's, 1 other advanced degree awarded. *Degree requirements:* For master's, thesis or alternative. *Entrance requirements:* Additional exam requirements/recommendations for international students: Required—TOEFL (minimum score 520 paper-based; 190 computer-based; 70 iBT); Recommended—IELTS (minimum score 5.5). *Application deadline:* For fall admission, 5/31 for international students; for winter admission, 10/15 for international students; for spring admission, 1/15 for international students. Applications are processed on a rolling basis. Application fee: $50. Electronic applications accepted. *Expenses:* Contact institution. *Financial support:* Research assistantships with partial tuition reimbursements, teaching assistantships with partial tuition reimbursements, career-related internships or fieldwork, Federal Work-Study, scholarships/grants, tuition waivers, and unspecified assistantships available. Support available to part-time students. Financial award applicants required to submit FAFSA. *Unit head:* Dr. Stuart D. Sidle, Coordinator, 203-932-7341. *Application contact:* Eloise Gormley, Information Contact, 203-932-7449.

University of New Haven, Graduate School, School of Business, Program in Business Administration, West Haven, CT 06516-1916. Offers accounting (MBA, Certificate), including CPA (MBA); business management (Certificate); business policy and strategy (MBA); finance (MBA), including CFA; global marketing (MBA); human resource management (Certificate); human resources management (MBA); international business (Certificate); marketing (Certificate); sports management (MBA); telecommunications management (Certificate); MBA/MPA. Part-time and evening/weekend programs available. *Students:* 158 full-time (80 women), 150 part-time (70 women); includes 36 Black or African American, non-Hispanic/Latino; 2 American Indian or Alaska Native, non-Hispanic/Latino; 19 Asian, non-Hispanic/Latino; 16 Hispanic/Latino, 82 international. Average age 32. 162 applicants, 99% accepted, 85 enrolled. In 2010, 141 master's, 16 other advanced degrees awarded. *Degree requirements:* For master's, thesis or alternative. *Entrance requirements:* For master's, GMAT. Additional exam requirements/recommendations for international students: Required—TOEFL (minimum score 520 paper-based; 190 computer-based; 70 iBT), IELTS (minimum score 5.5). *Application deadline:* For fall admission, 5/31 for international students; for winter admission, 10/15 for international students; for spring admission, 1/15 for international students. Applications are processed on a rolling basis. Application fee: $50. Electronic applications accepted. *Expenses:* Contact institution. *Financial support:* Research assistantships with partial tuition reimbursements, teaching assistantships with partial tuition reimbursements, Federal Work-Study, scholarships/grants, health care benefits, tuition waivers, and unspecified assistantships available. Support available to part-time students. Financial award applicants required to submit FAFSA. *Unit head:* Charles Coleman, Chairman, 203-932-7375. *Application contact:* Eloise Gormley, Director of Graduate Admissions, 203-932-7449, Fax: 203-932-7137, E-mail: gradinfo@newhaven.edu.

University of New Haven, Graduate School, School of Business, Program in Public Administration, West Haven, CT 06516-1916. Offers personnel and labor relations (MPA); public administration (MPA, Certificate), including city management (MPA), community-clinical services (MPA), health care management (MPA), long-term health care (MPA), personnel and labor relations (MPA), public administration (Certificate), public management (Certificate), public personnel management (Certificate); MBA/MPA. Part-time and evening/weekend programs available. *Students:* 37 full-time (19 women), 33 part-time (18 women); includes 15 Black or African American, non-Hispanic/Latino; 1 Asian, non-Hispanic/Latino; 4 Hispanic/Latino, 9 international. Average age 33. 51 applicants, 100% accepted, 35 enrolled. In 2010, 14 master's, 4 other advanced degrees awarded. *Degree requirements:* For master's, thesis or alternative. *Entrance requirements:* Additional exam requirements/recommendations for international students: Required—TOEFL (minimum score 520 paper-based; 190 computer-based; 70 iBT); Recommended—IELTS (minimum score 5.5). *Application deadline:* For fall admission, 5/31 for international students; for winter admission, 10/15 for international students; for spring admission, 1/15 for international students. Applications are processed on a rolling basis. Application fee: $50. Electronic applications accepted.

Expenses: Contact institution. *Financial support:* Research assistantships with partial tuition reimbursements, teaching assistantships with partial tuition reimbursements, career-related internships or fieldwork, Federal Work-Study, scholarships/grants, tuition waivers, and unspecified assistantships available. Support available to part-time students. Financial award application deadline: 5/1; financial award applicants required to submit FAFSA. *Unit head:* Charles Coleman, Chairman, 203-932-7375. *Application contact:* Eloise Gormley, Director of Graduate Admissions, 203-932-7449, Fax: 203-932-7137, E-mail: gradinfo@newhaven.edu.

University of New Mexico, Graduate School, College of Arts and Sciences, Department of Economics, Albuquerque, NM 87131-2039. Offers environmental/natural resources (MA, PhD); international/development (MA, PhD); labor/human resources (MA, PhD); public finance (MA, PhD). Part-time programs available. *Faculty:* 26 full-time (9 women), 7 part-time/adjunct (1 woman). *Students:* 47 full-time (14 women), 17 part-time (5 women); includes 2 American Indian or Alaska Native, non-Hispanic/Latino; 2 Asian, non-Hispanic/Latino; 8 Hispanic/Latino, 18 international. Average age 34. 75 applicants, 51% accepted, 15 enrolled. In 2010, 14 master's, 1 doctorate awarded. Terminal master's awarded for partial completion of doctoral program. *Degree requirements:* For master's, comprehensive exam, thesis (for some programs); for doctorate, comprehensive exam, thesis/dissertation. *Entrance requirements:* For master's and doctorate, GRE General Test, 3 letters of recommendation, letter of intent. Additional exam requirements/recommendations for international students: Required—TOEFL (minimum score 520 paper-based; 190 computer-based; 68 iBT). *Application deadline:* For fall admission, 3/1 priority date for domestic students, 3/1 for international students. Applications are processed on a rolling basis. Application fee: $50. Electronic applications accepted. *Expenses:* Tuition, state resident: full-time $5991; part-time $251 per credit hour. Tuition, nonresident: full-time $14,405; part-time $800.20 per credit hour. Tuition and fees vary according to course level, course load, program and reciprocity agreements. *Financial support:* In 2010–11, 47 students received support, including 3 fellowships with tuition reimbursements available (averaging $3,611 per year), 14 research assistantships with tuition reimbursements available (averaging $7,791 per year), 15 teaching assistantships (averaging $7,467 per year); career-related internships or fieldwork, Federal Work-Study, scholarships/grants, health care benefits, and unspecified assistantships also available. Support available to part-time students. Financial award application deadline: 3/1; financial award applicants required to submit FAFSA. *Faculty research:* Core theory, econometrics, public finance, international/development economics, labor/human resource economics, environmental/natural resource economics. Total annual research expenditures: $1.8 million. *Unit head:* Dr. Robert Berrens, Chair, 505-277-5304, Fax: 505-277-9445, E-mail: rberrens@unm.edu. *Application contact:* Shoshana Handel, Academic Advisor, 505-277-3056, Fax: 505-277-9445, E-mail: shandel@unm.edu.

University of North Florida, Coggin College of Business, MBA Program, Jacksonville, FL 32224. Offers accounting (MBA); construction management (MBA); e-commerce (MBA); economics (MBA); finance (MBA); human resource management (MBA); international business (MBA); logistics (MBA); management applications (MBA). *Accreditation:* AACSB. Part-time and evening/weekend programs available. *Faculty:* 17 full-time (5 women), 1 part-time/adjunct (0 women). *Students:* 137 full-time (56 women), 268 part-time (112 women); includes 17 Black or African American, non-Hispanic/Latino; 21 Asian, non-Hispanic/Latino; 12 Hispanic/Latino; 3 Two or more races, non-Hispanic/Latino, 29 international. Average age 30. 250 applicants, 57% accepted, 94 enrolled. In 2010, 173 master's awarded. *Entrance requirements:* For master's, GMAT or GRE, U.S. bachelor's degree from regionally-accredited university or equivalent foreign degree. Additional exam requirements/recommendations for international students: Required—TOEFL (minimum score 550 paper-based; 213 computer-based; 79 iBT). *Application deadline:* For fall admission, 7/1 priority date for domestic students, 5/1 for international students; for spring admission, 11/1 priority date for domestic students, 10/1 for international students. Applications are processed on a rolling basis. Application fee: $30. *Expenses:* Tuition, state resident: full-time $7646.40; part-time $318.60 per credit hour. Tuition, nonresident: full-time $23,502; part-time $979.24 per credit hour. Required fees: $1208.88; $50.37 per credit hour. Tuition and fees vary according to course load and program. *Financial support:* In 2010–11, 40 students received support; research assistantships, teaching assistantships, Federal Work-Study and tuition waivers (partial) available. Support available to part-time students. Financial award application deadline: 4/1; financial award applicants required to submit FAFSA. *Faculty research:* Performance measures, costing, and inventory issues in logistics and supply chain management; inter-organizational systems; international management and marketing practices; e-commerce; organizational learning and socialization processes. Total annual research expenditures: $9,024. *Unit head:* Dr. C. Bruce Kavan, Chair, 904-620-2780, Fax: 904-620-2832. *Application contact:* Cheryl Campbell, Graduate Advisor, 904-620-2575, Fax: 904-620-2832, E-mail: ccampbell@unf.edu.

University of Oklahoma, College of Arts and Sciences, Department of Psychology, Program in Organizational Dynamics, Tulsa, OK 74135. Offers organizational dynamics (MA), including human resource management, organizational dynamics, technical project management. Part-time and evening/

weekend programs available. *Students:* 9 full-time (4 women), 25 part-time (13 women); includes 6 minority (1 Black or African American, non-Hispanic/Latino; 1 American Indian or Alaska Native, non-Hispanic/Latino; 2 Asian, non-Hispanic/Latino; 1 Native Hawaiian or other Pacific Islander, non-Hispanic/Latino; 1 Two or more races, non-Hispanic/Latino). Average age 37. 6 applicants, 100% accepted, 6 enrolled. In 2010, 11 master's awarded. *Entrance requirements:* For master's, minimum GPA of 3.0 in last 60 hours of undergraduate course work. Additional exam requirements/recommendations for international students: Required—TOEFL (minimum score 550 paper-based; 213 computer-based; 79 iBT). *Application deadline:* For fall admission, 4/15 priority date for domestic students, 4/15 for international students; for spring admission, 11/1 for domestic students, 9/1 for international students. Applications are processed on a rolling basis. Application fee: $40 ($90 for international students). Electronic applications accepted. *Expenses:* Tuition, state resident: full-time $3893; part-time $162.20 per credit hour. Tuition, nonresident: full-time $14,167; part-time $590.30 per credit hour. Required fees: $2523; $94.60 per credit hour. Tuition and fees vary according to course load and degree level. *Financial support:* In 2010–11, 10 students received support. Scholarships/grants, health care benefits, and unspecified assistantships available. Financial award application deadline: 3/1; financial award applicants required to submit FAFSA. *Faculty research:* Academic integrity, organizational behavior, interdisciplinary teams, shared leadership. *Unit head:* Dr. Jorge Mendoza, Chair, 405-325-4511, Fax: 405-325-4737, E-mail: jmendoza@ou.edu. *Application contact:* Jennifer Kisamore, Graduate Liaison, 918-660-3603, Fax: 918-660-3383, E-mail: jkisamore@ou.edu.

University of Phoenix, School of Business, Phoenix, AZ 85034-7209. Offers accounting (MBA, MSA); business administration (MBA); energy management (MBA); global management (MBA); health care management (MBA); human resources management (MM); international management (MM); management (MM); marketing (MBA); project management (MBA); public administration (MPA); technology management (MBA). Programs are offered at the online campus. Evening/weekend programs available. Postbaccalaureate distance learning degree programs offered. *Students:* 20,237 full-time (12,641 women); includes 6,424 minority (4,376 Black or African American, non-Hispanic/Latino; 150 American Indian or Alaska Native, non-Hispanic/Latino; 546 Asian, non-Hispanic/Latino; 1,137 Hispanic/Latino; 155 Native Hawaiian or other Pacific Islander, non-Hispanic/Latino; 60 Two or more races, non-Hispanic/Latino), 1,149 international. Average age 39. *Entrance requirements:* For master's, minimum undergraduate GPA of 2.5 from accredited university, 3 years of work experience, citizen of the United States or have valid visa. Additional exam requirements/recommendations for international students: Required—TOEFL (minimum paper score 550, computer score 213, iBT 79), Test of English for International Communication, or IELTS. *Application deadline:* Applications are processed on a rolling basis. Application fee: $45. Electronic applications accepted. *Expenses:* Tuition: Full-time $16,440. One-time fee: $45 full-time. Full-time tuition and fees vary according to course load, degree level, campus/location and program. *Financial support:* Scholarships/grants available. Financial award applicants required to submit FAFSA. *Unit head:* Dr. Bill Berry, Director, 480-557-1824, E-mail: bill.berry@phoenix.edu. *Application contact:* Dr. Bill Berry, Director, 480-557-1824, E-mail: bill.berry@phoenix.edu.

University of Pittsburgh, Katz Graduate School of Business, Doctoral Program in Business Administration, Pittsburgh, PA 15260. Offers accounting (PhD); finance (PhD); information systems (PhD); marketing (PhD); operations/decision sciences/artificial intelligence (PhD); organizational behavior and human resource management (PhD); strategic planning (PhD). *Accreditation:* AACSB. *Faculty:* 50 full-time (15 women). *Students:* 51 full-time (22 women); includes 3 Black or African American, non-Hispanic/Latino; 4 Asian, non-Hispanic/Latino; 2 Hispanic/Latino, 18 international. 448 applicants, 5% accepted, 13 enrolled. In 2010, 4 doctorates awarded. *Degree requirements:* For doctorate, comprehensive exam, thesis/dissertation. *Entrance requirements:* For doctorate, GMAT or GRE, bachelor's degree, references, minimum GPA of 3.0. Additional exam requirements/recommendations for international students: Required—TOEFL, IELTS. *Application deadline:* For fall admission, 2/1 priority date for domestic and international students. Applications are processed on a rolling basis. Application fee: $50. Electronic applications accepted. *Expenses:* Tuition, state resident: full-time $17,304; part-time $701 per credit. Tuition, nonresident: full-time $29,554; part-time $1210 per credit. Required fees: $740; $214 per term. Tuition and fees vary according to program. *Financial support:* In 2010–11, 39 students received support, including 29 research assistantships with full tuition reimbursements available (averaging $1,900 per year), 10 teaching assistantships with full tuition reimbursements available (averaging $23,745 per year); fellowships, Federal Work-Study, scholarships/grants, health care benefits, and unspecified assistantships also available. Financial award application deadline: 2/1. *Faculty research:* Accounting statements and reporting, incentives and governance, corporate finance, mergers and acquisitions, information systems processes, structures and decision-making, organizational structure, knowledge management and corporate strategy, consumer behavior and marketing models. Total annual research expenditures: $362,777. *Unit head:* Dr. John E. Hulland, Director of Doctoral Program, 412-648-1534, Fax: 412-624-3633, E-mail: jhulland@katz.pitt.edu. *Application contact:* Carrie

Woods, Assistant Director, Doctoral Office, 412-648-1525, Fax: 412-624-3633, E-mail: cawoods@katz.pitt.edu.

University of Pittsburgh, Katz Graduate School of Business, Master of Business Administration Programs, Pittsburgh, PA 15260. Offers finance (MBA); information systems (MBA); marketing (MBA); operations management (MBA); organizational behavior and human resource management (MBA); organizational leadership (Certificate); six sigma (Certificate); strategy, environment and organizations (MBA); technology, innovation and entrepreneurship (Certificate); MBA/JD; MBA/MIB; MBA/MPIA; MBA/MSE; MBA/MSIS; MID/MBA. *Accreditation:* AACSB. Part-time and evening/weekend programs available. *Faculty:* 60 full-time (18 women), 22 part-time/adjunct (5 women). *Students:* 232 full-time (75 women), 458 part-time (158 women); includes 34 Black or African American, non-Hispanic/Latino; 1 American Indian or Alaska Native, non-Hispanic/Latino; 20 Asian, non-Hispanic/Latino; 9 Hispanic/Latino, 105 international. Average age 29. 697 applicants, 50% accepted, 174 enrolled. In 2010, 263 master's awarded. *Degree requirements:* For master's, minimum GPA of 3.0. *Entrance requirements:* For master's, GMAT, recommendations, undergraduate transcripts, essay responses, resume, interview, bachelor's degree. Additional exam requirements/recommendations for international students: Required—TOEFL (minimum 600 paper, 250 computer, 100 iBT) or IELTS. *Application deadline:* For fall admission, 4/1 priority date for domestic students, 2/1 priority date for international students. Application fee: $50. Electronic applications accepted. *Expenses:* Tuition, state resident: full-time $17,304; part-time $701 per credit. Tuition, nonresident: full-time $29,554; part-time $1210 per credit. Required fees: $740; $214 per term. Tuition and fees vary according to program. *Financial support:* In 2010–11, 52 students received support. Career-related internships or fieldwork and scholarships/grants available. Financial award application deadline: 3/1; financial award applicants required to submit FAFSA. *Faculty research:* Accounting statements and reporting, incentives and governance, corporate finance, mergers and acquisitions, information systems processes, structures and decision-making, organizational structure, knowledge management and corporate strategy, consumer behavior and marketing models. *Unit head:* William T. Valenta, Assistant Dean, MBA Program Director, 412-648-1610, Fax: 412-648-1659, E-mail: wtvalenta@katz.pitt.edu. *Application contact:* Cliff McCormick, Director MBA Admissions, 412-648-1700, Fax: 412-648-1659, E-mail: mba@katz.pitt.edu.

University of Puerto Rico, Mayagüez Campus, Graduate Studies, College of Business Administration, Mayagüez, PR 00681-9000. Offers business administration (MBA); finance (MBA); human resources (MBA); industrial management (MBA). Part-time and evening/weekend programs available. *Students:* 47 full-time (28 women), 36 part-time (16 women); includes 79 Hispanic/Latino, 4 international. 19 applicants, 47% accepted, 4 enrolled. In 2010, 15 master's awarded. *Degree requirements:* For master's, comprehensive exam. *Entrance requirements:* For master's, GMAT or EXADEP, bachelor's degree with courses in calculus, microeconomics, accounting and statistics. Additional exam requirements/recommendations for international students: Required—TOEFL (minimum score 500 paper-based; 173 computer-based). *Application deadline:* For fall admission, 2/15 for domestic and international students; for spring admission, 9/15 for domestic and international students. Applications are processed on a rolling basis. Application fee: $25. *Expenses:* Tuition, state resident: full-time $1188. Tuition, nonresident: full-time $1188. International tuition: $6126 full-time. Tuition and fees vary according to course level and course load. *Financial support:* In 2010–11, fellowships (averaging $12,000 per year), 2 research assistantships (averaging $15,000 per year), teaching assistantships (averaging $8,500 per year) were awarded; Federal Work-Study and institutionally sponsored loans also available. *Faculty research:* Organizational studies, management, accounting. Total annual research expenditures: $20,000. *Unit head:* Dr. Rosario Ortiz, Graduate Student Coordinator, 787-265-3800, Fax: 787-832-5320, E-mail: rosario.ortiz@upr.edu. *Application contact:* Milagros Soto, Student Administrator, 787-265-3887, Fax: 787-832-5320, E-mail: milagros.soto1@upr.edu.

University of Regina, Faculty of Graduate Studies and Research, Kenneth Levene Graduate School of Business, Program in Human Resources Management, Regina, SK S4S 0A2, Canada. Offers MHRM, Master's Certificate. Part-time programs available. *Faculty:* 51 full-time (14 women), 10 part-time/adjunct (0 women). *Students:* 17 full-time (9 women), 19 part-time (15 women). 59 applicants, 64% accepted. In 2010, 7 master's awarded. *Degree requirements:* For master's, project. *Entrance requirements:* For master's, GMAT, two years relevant work experience. Additional exam requirements/recommendations for international students: Required—TOEFL (minimum score 580 paper-based; 80 iBT). *Application deadline:* Applications are processed on a rolling basis. Application fee: $100. Electronic applications accepted. *Expenses:* Contact institution. *Financial support:* In 2010–11, 6 fellowships (averaging $18,000 per year), 2 research assistantships (averaging $16,500 per year), 5 teaching assistantships (averaging $6,759 per year) were awarded; scholarships/grants also available. Financial award application deadline: 6/15. *Faculty research:* Human behavior in organizations, labor relations and collective bargaining, organization theory, staffing organizations, human resources systems analysis. *Unit head:* Dr. Anne Lavack, 306-585-4162, Fax: 306-585-4805, E-mail: anne.lavack@uregina.ca. *Application* *contact:* Steve Wield, Manager, 306-337-8463, Fax: 306-585-5361, E-mail: steve.wield@uregina.ca.

University of Rhode Island, Graduate School, Labor Research Center, Kingston, RI 02881. Offers labor relations and human resources (MS); MS/JD. Part-time and evening/weekend programs available. *Faculty:* 1 full-time (0 women), 3 part-time/adjunct (2 women). *Students:* 24 full-time (20 women), 31 part-time (23 women); includes 14 minority (5 Black or African American, non-Hispanic/Latino; 1 Hispanic/Latino; 8 Native Hawaiian or other Pacific Islander, non-Hispanic/Latino), 3 international. In 2010, 8 master's awarded. *Entrance requirements:* For master's, GRE, MAT, GMAT, or LSAT, 2 letters of recommendation. Additional exam requirements/recommendations for international students: Required—TOEFL (minimum score 550 paper-based; 213 computer-based). *Application deadline:* For fall admission, 7/15 for domestic students, 2/1 for international students; for spring admission, 11/15 for domestic students, 7/15 for international students. Application fee: $65. Electronic applications accepted. *Expenses:* Tuition, state resident: full-time $9588; part-time $533 per credit hour. Tuition, nonresident: full-time $22,968; part-time $1276 per credit hour. Required fees: $1282; $68 per semester. Tuition and fees vary according to program. *Financial support:* In 2010–11, 2 teaching assistantships with full tuition reimbursements (averaging $13,894 per year) were awarded; institutionally sponsored loans also available. Financial award application deadline: 2/1; financial award applicants required to submit FAFSA. *Unit head:* Dr. Richard W. Scholl, Director, 401-874-4347, Fax: 401-874-2954, E-mail: rscholl@uri.edu. *Application contact:* Dr. Richard W. Scholl, Director, 401-874-4347, Fax: 401-874-2954, E-mail: rscholl@uri.edu.

University of St. Thomas, Graduate Studies, School of Education, Program in Organization Learning and Development, St. Paul, MN 55105-1096. Offers career development (Certificate); e-learning (Certificate); human resource development (Certificate); human resource management (Certificate); human resources and change leadership (MA); learning technology (Certificate); learning technology for learning development and change (MA); organization development (Ed D, Certificate). Part-time and evening/weekend programs available. Postbaccalaureate distance learning degree programs offered (minimal on-campus study). *Faculty:* 6 full-time (4 women), 15 part-time/adjunct (8 women). *Students:* 8 full-time (7 women), 156 part-time (118 women); includes 30 minority (12 Black or African American, non-Hispanic/Latino; 7 Asian, non-Hispanic/Latino; 7 Hispanic/Latino; 1 Native Hawaiian or other Pacific Islander, non-Hispanic/Latino; 3 Two or more races, non-Hispanic/Latino), 6 international. Average age 37. 165 applicants, 71% accepted, 102 enrolled. In 2010, 38 master's, 9 doctorates, 15 other advanced degrees awarded. *Degree requirements:* For doctorate, comprehensive exam, thesis/dissertation. *Entrance requirements:* For master's, minimum GPA of 3.0, 2 letters of reference, personal statement; for doctorate, minimum GPA of 3.5, interview; for Certificate, minimum graduate GPA of 3.25. Additional exam requirements/recommendations for international students: Required—TOEFL (minimum score 550 paper-based; 213 computer-based). *Application deadline:* For fall admission, 8/1 priority date for domestic and international students; for winter admission, 12/1 priority date for domestic students, 12/1 for international students; for spring admission, 12/1 priority date for domestic and international students. Applications are processed on a rolling basis. Application fee: $50. *Expenses:* Contact institution. *Financial support:* Fellowships, research assistantships, institutionally sponsored loans and scholarships/grants available. Support available to part-time students. Financial award applicants required to submit FAFSA. *Faculty research:* Workplace conflict, physician leaders, entrepreneurship education, mentoring. *Unit head:* Dr. David W. Jamieson, Department Chair, 651-962-4387, Fax: 651-962-4169, E-mail: jami9859@stthomas.edu. *Application contact:* Liz G. Knight, Department Coordinator, 651-962-4459, Fax: 651-962-4169, E-mail: egknight@stthomas.edu.

The University of Scranton, College of Graduate and Continuing Education, Department of Health Administration and Human Resources, Program in Human Resources Administration, Scranton, PA 18510. Offers human resources (MS); human resources development (MS); organizational leadership (MS). Part-time and evening/weekend programs available. *Students:* 4 full-time (3 women), 6 part-time (5 women); includes 1 Hispanic/Latino. Average age 36. In 2010, 12 master's awarded. *Degree requirements:* For master's, capstone experience. *Entrance requirements:* For master's, minimum GPA of 2.75. Additional exam requirements/recommendations for international students: Required—TOEFL (minimum score 500 paper-based; 173 computer-based), IELTS (minimum score 5.5). *Application deadline:* Applications are processed on a rolling basis. Application fee: $0. *Financial support:* Fellowships, teaching assistantships, career-related internships or fieldwork, Federal Work-Study, and unspecified assistantships available. Support available to part-time students. Financial award application deadline: 3/1. *Unit head:* Dr. Daniel West, Director, 570-941-6218, E-mail: westd1@scranton.edu. *Application contact:* Joseph M. Roback, Director of Admissions, 570-941-4385, Fax: 570-941-5928, E-mail: robackj2@scranton.edu.

University of South Carolina, The Graduate School, Darla Moore School of Business, Human Resources Program, Columbia, SC 29208. Offers MHR, JD/MHR. Part-time programs available. *Faculty:* 99 full-time (23 women), 10 part-time/adjunct (2 women). *Students:* 66 full-time (46 women); includes 8 Black or African American, non-Hispanic/Latino; 3 Hispanic/Latino, 9

international. Average age 25. 112 applicants, 59% accepted, 33 enrolled. In 2010, 48 master's awarded. *Degree requirements:* For master's, internship. *Entrance requirements:* For master's, GMAT or GRE, minimum GPA of 3.0. Additional exam requirements/recommendations for international students: Required—TOEFL (minimum score 250 computer-based; 100 iBT); Recommended—IELTS. *Application deadline:* Applications are processed on a rolling basis. Application fee: $100. Electronic applications accepted. *Expenses:* Contact institution. *Financial support:* In 2010–11, 15 students received support; fellowships, career-related internships or fieldwork, Federal Work-Study, scholarships/grants, and unspecified assistantships available. *Faculty research:* Management and compensation, performance appraisal, work values, grievance systems, union formation, group behavior. *Unit head:* Christine LaCola, Managing Director, 803-777-2730, Fax: 803-777-0414, E-mail: christine.lacola@moore.sc.edu. *Application contact:* Scott King, Director, Graduate Admissions, 803-777-6749, Fax: 803-777-0414, E-mail: scott.king@moore.sc.edu.

The University of Texas at Arlington, Graduate School, College of Business, Department of Management, Arlington, TX 76019. Offers human resources (MSHRM). Part-time and evening/weekend programs available. *Faculty:* 9 full-time (3 women). *Students:* 32 full-time (18 women), 26 part-time (19 women); includes 14 minority (9 Black or African American, non-Hispanic/Latino; 1 Asian, non-Hispanic/Latino; 3 Hispanic/Latino; 1 Two or more races, non-Hispanic/Latino), 17 international. 49 applicants, 37% accepted, 12 enrolled. In 2010, 14 master's awarded. *Degree requirements:* For master's, thesis optional. *Entrance requirements:* For master's, GMAT. Additional exam requirements/recommendations for international students: Required—TOEFL (minimum score 550 paper-based; 213 computer-based; 79 iBT). *Application deadline:* For fall admission, 6/5 priority date for domestic students, 4/1 for international students; for spring admission, 10/15 for domestic students, 9/1 for international students. Applications are processed on a rolling basis. Application fee: $35 ($50 for international students). *Expenses:* Tuition, state resident: full-time $7500. Tuition, nonresident: full-time $13,080. International tuition: $13,250 full-time. *Financial support:* In 2010–11, 4 fellowships (averaging $1,000 per year), 1 research assistantship (averaging $6,000 per year), 12 teaching assistantships (averaging $13,000 per year) were awarded; career-related internships or fieldwork, scholarships/grants, and unspecified assistantships also available. Support available to part-time students. Financial award application deadline: 6/1; financial award applicants required to submit FAFSA. *Faculty research:* Compensations, training, diversity, strategic human resources. *Unit head:* Dr. Abdul Rasheed, Chair, 817-272-3166, Fax: 817-272-3122, E-mail: abdul@uta.edu. *Application contact:* Dennis Veit, Graduate Advisor, 817-272-3865, Fax: 817-272-3122, E-mail: dveit@uta.edu.

University of Wisconsin–Madison, Graduate School, Wisconsin School of Business, Doctoral Program in Management and Human Resources, Madison, WI 53706-1380. Offers PhD. *Faculty:* 12 full-time (3 women), 3 part-time/adjunct (1 woman). *Students:* 10 full-time (4 women), 4 international. Average age 30. 58 applicants, 7% accepted, 2 enrolled. In 2010, 2 doctorates awarded. *Degree requirements:* For doctorate, comprehensive exam, thesis/dissertation. *Entrance requirements:* For doctorate, GMAT or GRE. Additional exam requirements/recommendations for international students: Required—Pearson Test of English (minimum score 73, written 80); Recommended—TOEFL (minimum score 623 paper-based; 263 computer-based; 106 iBT), IELTS (minimum score 7.5). *Application deadline:* For fall admission, 12/15 priority date for domestic and international students. Application fee: $56. Electronic applications accepted. *Expenses:* Tuition, state resident: full-time $9887; part-time $617.96 per credit. Tuition, nonresident: full-time $24,054; part-time $1503.40 per credit. Required fees: $67.63 per credit. Tuition and fees vary according to reciprocity agreements. *Financial support:* In 2010–11, 10 students received support, including 1 fellowship with tuition reimbursement available (averaging $18,756 per year), research assistantships with full tuition reimbursements available (averaging $16,506 per year), 9 teaching assistantships with full tuition reimbursements available (averaging $14,088 per year); Federal Work-Study, institutionally sponsored loans, scholarships/grants, health care benefits, and unspecified assistantships also available. Financial award application deadline: 2/1; financial award applicants required to submit FAFSA. *Faculty research:* Employee compensation, performance for work groups, small business management, venture financing, arts industry. *Unit head:* Prof. Barry Gerhart, Chair, 608-262-3895, E-mail: bgerhart@bus.wisc.edu. *Application contact:* Belle Heberling, Assistant Director for Research Programs, 608-262-3749, Fax: 608-890-0180, E-mail: phd@bus.wisc.edu.

University of Wisconsin–Madison, Graduate School, Wisconsin School of Business, Wisconsin Full-Time MBA Program, Madison, WI 53706-1380. Offers applied security analysis (MBA); arts administration (MBA); brand and product management (MBA); corporate finance and investment banking (MBA); entrepreneurial management (MBA); marketing research (MBA); operations and technology management (MBA); real estate (MBA); risk management and insurance (MBA); strategic human resource management (MBA); strategic management in the life and engineering sciences (MBA); supply chain management (MBA). *Faculty:* 32 full-time (4 women), 17 part-time/adjunct (3 women). *Students:* 242 full-time (74 women); includes 16 Black or African American, non-Hispanic/Latino; 3 American Indian or Alaska Native, non-Hispanic/Latino; 16 Asian, non-Hispanic/Latino; 12 Hispanic/Latino; 29

international. Average age 28. 526 applicants, 32% accepted, 117 enrolled. In 2010, 106 master's awarded. *Entrance requirements:* For master's, GMAT, bachelor's or equivalent degree, 2 years of work experience, letters of recommendation. Additional exam requirements/recommendations for international students: Required—TOEFL (minimum score 600 paper-based; 250 computer-based; 100 iBT), IELTS. *Application deadline:* For fall admission, 11/4 for domestic students, 11/1 for international students; for winter admission, 2/5 for domestic and international students; for spring admission, 5/15 for domestic students, 4/5 for international students. Applications are processed on a rolling basis. Application fee: $56. Electronic applications accepted. *Expenses:* Tuition, state resident: full-time $9887; part-time $617.96 per credit. Tuition, nonresident: full-time $24,054; part-time $1503.40 per credit. Required fees: $67.63 per credit. Tuition and fees vary according to reciprocity agreements. *Financial support:* In 2010–11, 103 students received support, including 13 fellowships with full and partial tuition reimbursements available (averaging $15,000 per year), 53 research assistantships with full tuition reimbursements available (averaging $8,000 per year), 35 teaching assistantships with full tuition reimbursements available (averaging $11,000 per year); scholarships/grants, health care benefits, and unspecified assistantships also available. Financial award application deadline: 4/5; financial award applicants required to submit FAFSA. *Faculty research:* Market consequences of International Financial Reporting Standards (IFRS), inter-firm relationships and strategic partnerships, application of Bayesian statistical methods and applied probability models to understanding individuals' behaviors in the context of customer relationship management (CRM) applications, liquidity provision and the structure of financial markets, strategic management of global startups. *Unit head:* Dr. Kenneth A. Kavajecz, Associate Dean of Master's Programs, 608-265-3494, Fax: 608-265-4192, E-mail: kkavajecz@bus.wisc.edu. *Application contact:* Maria Reis, Assistant Director of MBA Marketing and Recruiting, 608-262-4000, Fax: 608-265-4192, E-mail: mreis@bus.wisc.edu.

Walden University, Graduate Programs, School of Management, Minneapolis, MN 55401. Offers accounting (MS), including cpa emphasis, professional track, self-designed; accounting and management (MS), including self-designed, strategic management; applied management and decision sciences (PhD), including accounting, engineering management, finance, general applied management and decision sciences, information systems management, knowledge management, leadership and organizational change, learning management, operations research, self-designed program in applied management and design sciences; business information management (MISM); enterprise information security (MISM); entrepreneurship (MBA, DBA); finance (MBA, DBA); global management (MS); global supply chain management (DBA); health informatics (MISM); healthcare management (MBA, MS); healthcare system improvement (MBA); human resource management (MBA, MS), including functional human resource management (MS), human resource management (MS), integrating functional and strategic human resource management (MS), organizational strategy (MS); information systems (MS); information systems management (DBA); information technology (MS), including information security, software engineering; international business (MBA, DBA); IT strategy and governance (MISM); leadership (MBA, MS, DBA), including entrepreneurship (MS), general management (MS), human resources leadership (MS), innovation and technology (MS), leader development (MS), leading sustainability (MS), project management (MS), self-designed (MS); managers as leaders (MS); managing global software and service supply chains (MISM); marketing (MBA, DBA); project management (MBA, MS); research strategies (MS); risk management (MBA); self-designed (MBA, DBA); social impact management (DBA); strategy and operations (MS); sustainable futures (MBA); sustainable management (MS); technology (MBA); technology entrepreneurship (DBA); technology management (MS). Part-time and evening/weekend programs available. Postbaccalaureate distance learning degree programs offered (minimal on-campus study). *Faculty:* 22 full-time (8 women), 291 part-time/adjunct (100 women). *Students:* 3,705 full-time (1,956 women), 976 part-time (549 women); includes 2,432 minority (2,021 Black or African American, non-Hispanic/Latino; 32 American Indian or Alaska Native, non-Hispanic/Latino; 137 Asian, non-Hispanic/Latino; 193 Hispanic/Latino; 5 Native Hawaiian or other Pacific Islander, non-Hispanic/Latino; 44 Two or more races, non-Hispanic/Latino), 302 international. Average age 40. In 2010, 658 master's, 86 doctorates awarded. *Degree requirements:* For doctorate, thesis/dissertation (for some programs), residency. *Entrance requirements:* For master's, bachelor's degree or equivalent in related field; minimum GPA of 2.5; official transcripts; goal statement; access to computer and Internet; for doctorate, master's degree or equivalent in related field; minimum GPA of 3.0; 3 years of related professional/academic experience (preferred). Additional exam requirements/recommendations for international students: Required—TOEFL (minimum score 550 paper-based; 213 computer-based), IELTS (minimum score 6.5), Michigan English Language Assessment Battery (minimum score 82). *Application deadline:* Applications are processed on a rolling basis. Application fee: $50. Electronic applications accepted. *Expenses:* Tuition: Full-time $10,274; part-time $445 per credit. Tuition and fees vary according to course load, degree level and program. *Financial support:* Fellowships, Federal Work-Study, scholarships/grants, unspecified assistantships, and family tuition reduction, active duty/veteran tuition reduction, group tuition reduction, interest-free payment plans available. Support available to part-time students. Financial award applicants required to submit FAFSA.

Unit head: Dr. William Schulz, Associate Dean, 800-925-3368. *Application contact:* Jennifer Hall, Vice President of Enrollment Management, 866-4-WALDEN, E-mail: info@waldenu.edu.

West Chester University of Pennsylvania, Office of Graduate Studies, College of Business and Public Affairs, Department of Political Science, West Chester, PA 19383. Offers general public administration (MPA); human resource management (MPA, Certificate); non profit administration (Certificate); nonprofit administration (MPA); public administration (Certificate). Part-time and evening/weekend programs available. *Students:* 22 full-time (12 women), 39 part-time (31 women); includes 16 minority (12 Black or African American, non-Hispanic/Latino; 4 Hispanic/Latino), 2 international. Average age 31. 41 applicants, 88% accepted, 17 enrolled. In 2010, 22 master's awarded. *Degree requirements:* For master's, capstone project. *Entrance requirements:* For master's and Certificate, statement of professional goals, resume, two letters of reference. Additional exam requirements/recommendations for international students: Required—TOEFL (minimum score 550 paper-based; 213 computer-based; 80 iBT). *Application deadline:* For fall admission, 4/15 priority date for domestic students, 3/15 for international students; for spring admission, 10/15 for domestic students, 9/1 for international students. Applications are processed on a rolling basis. Application fee: $35. Electronic applications accepted. *Expenses:* Tuition, state resident: full-time $6966; part-time $387 per credit. Tuition, nonresident: full-time $11,146; part-time $619 per credit. Required fees: $1614.40; $133.24 per credit. Part-time tuition and fees vary according to campus/location. *Financial support:* Unspecified assistantships available. Support available to part-time students. Financial award application deadline: 2/15; financial award applicants required to submit FAFSA. *Faculty research:* Public policy, economic development, public opinion, urban politics, public administration. *Unit head:* Dr. Christopher Fiorentino, Dean, College of Business and Public Affairs, 610-436-2930, E-mail: cfiorentino@wcupa.edu. *Application contact:* Dr. Lorraine Bernotsky, Graduate Coordinator, 610-738-0576, E-mail: lbernotsky@wcupa.edu.

Widener University, School of Business Administration, Program in Human Resource Management, Chester, PA 19013-5792. Offers MHR, MS, Psy D/MHR. Part-time and evening/weekend programs available. *Faculty:* 5 full-time (1 woman), 5 part-time/adjunct (3 women). *Students:* 2 full-time (1 woman), 2 part-time (1 woman); includes 1 Black or African American, non-Hispanic/Latino; 1 American Indian or Alaska Native, non-Hispanic/Latino, 1 international. Average age 30. 38 applicants, 87% accepted. In 2010, 3 master's awarded. *Entrance requirements:* For master's, GMAT, GRE, or MAT, minimum GPA of 2.5. *Application deadline:* For fall admission, 8/1 priority date for domestic students; for spring admission, 12/1 for domestic students. Applications are processed on a rolling basis. Application fee: $25 ($300 for international students). Electronic applications accepted. *Financial support:* Research assistantships, Federal Work-Study available. Support available to part-time students. Financial award application deadline: 5/1. *Faculty research:* Training and development, collective bargaining and arbitration, business communication. *Unit head:* Dr. Caryl Carpenter, Director, 610-499-4109. *Application contact:* Ann Seltzer, Graduate Enrollment Administrator, 610-499-4305, E-mail: apseltzer@widener.edu.

Wilfrid Laurier University, Faculty of Graduate and Postdoctoral Studies, School of Business and Economics, Department of Business, Waterloo, ON N2L 3C5, Canada. Offers accounting (PhD); finance (M Fin); financial economics (PhD); marketing (PhD); operations and supply chain management (PhD); organizational behavior and human resource management (M Sc); organizational behaviour and human resource management (PhD); supply chain management (M Sc); technology management (EMTM). Part-time and evening/weekend programs available. *Faculty:* 67 full-time (20 women), 12 part-time/adjunct (4 women). *Students:* 20 full-time (11 women), 1 part-time (0 women), 5 international. 80 applicants, 28% accepted, 3 enrolled. In 2010, 6 master's, 1 doctorate awarded. *Degree requirements:* For master's, thesis optional; for doctorate, comprehensive exam, thesis/dissertation. *Entrance requirements:* For master's, GMAT, 4-year honors degree with minimum B+ average; for doctorate, GMAT, master's degree, minimum B+ average. Additional exam requirements/recommendations for international students: Required—TOEFL (minimum score 89 iBT). *Application deadline:* For fall admission, 1/15 priority date for domestic and international students. Application fee: $125. Electronic applications accepted. Tuition and fees charges are reported in Canadian dollars. *Expenses:* Tuition, area resident: Full-time $15,300 Canadian dollars; part-time $1200 Canadian dollars per credit. International tuition: $21,300 Canadian dollars full-time. Required fees: $650 Canadian dollars; $100 Canadian dollars per credit. Tuition and fees vary according to course load, degree level, campus/location and program. *Financial support:* In 2010–11, 27 fellowships, 1 research assistantship, 27 teaching assistantships were awarded; career-related internships or fieldwork, scholarships/grants, health care benefits, and unspecified assistantships also available. *Faculty research:* Financial economics, management and organizational behavior, operations and supply chain management. *Unit head:* Dr. Hamid Noori, Director, 519-884-0710 Ext. 2571, Fax: 519-884-2357, E-mail: sbephdmasters@wlu.ca. *Application contact:* Jennifer Williams, Graduate Admission and Records Officer, 519-884-0710 Ext. 3536, Fax: 519-884-1020, E-mail: gradstudies@wlu.ca.

Wilkes University, College of Graduate and Professional Studies, Jay S. Sidhu School of Business and Leadership, Wilkes-Barre, PA 18766-0002. Offers accounting (MBA); entrepreneurship (MBA); finance (MBA); health care administration (MBA); human resource management (MBA); international business (MBA); marketing (MBA); operations management (MBA); organizational leadership and development (MBA). *Accreditation:* ACBSP. Part-time and evening/weekend programs available. *Students:* 39 full-time (16 women), 146 part-time (71 women); includes 5 Black or African American, non-Hispanic/Latino; 2 Asian, non-Hispanic/Latino; 1 Hispanic/Latino; 1 Two or more races, non-Hispanic/Latino, 16 international. Average age 30. In 2010, 85 master's awarded. *Entrance requirements:* For master's, GMAT. Additional exam requirements/recommendations for international students: Required—TOEFL (minimum score 550 paper-based; 213 computer-based; 79 iBT). *Application deadline:* Applications are processed on a rolling basis. Application fee: $45 ($65 for international students). Electronic applications accepted. *Expenses:* Contact institution. *Financial support:* Federal Work-Study and unspecified assistantships available. Financial award application deadline: 3/1; financial award applicants required to submit FAFSA. *Unit head:* Dr. Paul Browne, Dean, 570-408-4701, Fax: 570-408-7846, E-mail: paul.browne@wilkes.edu. *Application contact:* Kathleen Houlihan, Director of Graduate Studies, 570-408-3235, Fax: 570-408-7846, E-mail: kathleen.houlihan@wilkes.edu.

OVERVIEW

From office supplies to clothing and household goods to car parts, consider the companies that manufacture these products. Whether that company is large or small, domestic or international, products need to be consistent in quality and an adequate supply of these goods needs to roll out of factories and assembly lines in order for any company to stay in business. And companies that manufacture goods also need to be cognizant of labor laws, safety protocols, and the relevant use of technology to keep production lines working efficiently.

Industrial managers make it possible for factory production to run smoothly. In addition to working as the upper management of personnel, they order materials and understand the logistics behind the mechanics and technologies that make production possible. Graduates of an MBA industrial management degree program have the skills to keep factories and other manufacturing companies running smoothly and efficiently and, at the same time, understand the business and legal side of the industry. The program curriculum provides students with a working knowledge of equipment maintenance, production scheduling, quality and inventory control, staffing, and production coordination. From the MBA program in industrial management, students learn how to effectively manage a manufacturing company and are prepared to successfully oversee the industrial workforce.

Required courses of study may include:

- Accounting Systems
- Business Policy
- Conflict Resolution
- Health and Safety Protocols
- Industrial Finance
- International Economics
- Labor Relations
- Product Innovation
- Quality Management
- Resource Management
- Risk Management
- Supply Chain Management

Elective courses of study may include:

- Advanced Manufacturing Technology and Management
- Business Process Management
- Change and Innovation
- Finance and Industrial Marketing
- Lean Operations
- Manufacturing Systems

Industrial managers have many responsibilities, including working with union members, overseeing a manufacturer's production, and supervising employees on a factory floor. With superior business expertise, graduates with an industrial management MBA are ready to take on responsibility for overseeing all aspects of production, ensuring production stays within budget forecasts and implementing cost-saving procedures and relevant technology.

An MBA in industrial management is a stepping stone for mid-career professionals looking to advance to senior levels within a manufacturing environment. Individuals who have earned their industrial management MBA degrees find employment as directors of organizational development, directors of organizational management, regional operations managers, organizational effectiveness managers, and directors of operations, typically in manufacturing industries such as transportation, machinery, electrical, instruments, fabricated metal, and food.

IN THIS SECTION

You'll find profiles of institutions offering graduate programs in the following fields:

HELPFUL ORGANIZATIONS/ PUBLICATIONS/BLOGS

Association for Manufacturing Excellence (AME)

http://www.ame.org/

The Association for Manufacturing Excellence (AME) is North America's premier organization for the exchange of knowledge in organizational excellence through the implementation of techniques such as lean tools, leadership, lean product development, lean supply chain, and lean accounting. Since its creation as a not-for-profit in 1985, AME has grown to have more than 5,000 members, ranging from executives to senior and middle managers.

The AME vision is to bring people together to share, learn, and grow. The AME mission is to inspire commitment to enterprise excellence through shared learning and access to best practices.

AME is a community whose members want to improve the competitiveness of their organizations and work together by sharing knowledge. AME's power is in the mentoring relationships that take place among members, providing company leaders with educational opportunities to learn leading-edge topics from leaders and fellow practitioners by attending events and through networking.

AME offers a forum whereby members can stay current with new and developing management and operational techniques. AME hosts regional best practice seminars and workshops and organizes regional and annual conferences.

Association for Manufacturing Technology (AMT)

http://www.amtonline.org/

Founded in 1902, the Association for Manufacturing Technology (AMT) represents and promotes the interests of American providers of manufacturing machinery and equipment. Its goal is to promote technological advancements and improvements in the design, manufacture, and sale of members' products in those markets and to act as an industry advocate on trade matters to governments and trade organizations throughout the world. AMT focuses its efforts on developing and implementing programs that benefit the membership as a whole and on providing support and assistance to members worldwide. AMT facilitates networking, collaboration, matchmaking, new business opportunities, and the exchange of ideas.

Since 1988, AMT has broadened its membership scope to include all of the elements of manufacturing, including design, automation, material removal, material forming, assembly, inspection and testing, and communications and control.

AMT organizes and sponsors IMTS—the International Manufacturing Technology Show—the largest industrial show in the Americas.

Manufacturing.net

http://www.manufacturing.net/

Manufacturing.net is a Web site designed for today's busy manufacturing executives, featuring daily updates covering the latest news and key topics from around the globe—regulations, industrial trends, plant openings and closings, supply chain updates, distribution and trade issues, prices, employment, finance, economic forecasts, and world events. The site is part of Advantage Business Media, an integrated business media company with a diversified portfolio of highly focused print publications, e-newsletters, specialized directories, vertical search databases, conferences, ancillary media vehicles, and associated Web-based services.

CAREER ASPIRATIONS: A PROSPECTIVE POSITION

Senior Director, Plant Operations

Job Description

This position will oversee the process of master planning and renovating the company plant, hiring/training staff, and validating and securing FDA approval of the facility. In addition, this person will develop and execute the operating plan, including the systematic transfer of volume from contract packagers to a fully integrated internal facility. He or she will also be responsible for ongoing operations of the physical plant, including manufacturing and packaging, process and facilities engineering, materials management, quality assurance/control, finance/accounting, human resources, and information systems.

Responsibilities

- Oversee all aspects of project to renovate, commission, and qualify company manufacturing/packaging facility on time and within approved capital budget.
- Oversee the execution of day-to-day manufacturing operations during start-up and on an ongoing basis.
- Develop and manage the annual facility operating budget and balance investment in working capital with impacts on service levels.
- Collaborate with human resources to develop human capital strategies; communicate and enforce corporate values, policies, and procedures.

Qualifications

- Bachelor's degree in industrial management, engineering, business administration, or other related areas
- Master's or MBA preferred
- Minimum 10 years of experience in progressive managerial assignments within a process-oriented, FDA-regulated manufacturing environment
- Prior experience as a plant/facility manager in an environment of 75+ employees
- Prior P&L responsibility required
- Prior experience working in a regulated environment with government agencies, regulations, and employment law
- Knowledge of Six Sigma and lean manufacturing tools and techniques
- Experience with federal/state prescription drug pedigree regulations—a plus

INDUSTRIAL AND MANUFACTURING MANAGEMENT

California Polytechnic State University, San Luis Obispo, Orfalea College of Business, Department of Business and Technology, San Luis Obispo, CA 93407. Offers MS. Part-time programs available. *Faculty:* 2 full-time (0 women). *Students:* 1 part-time (0 women). Average age 30. 5 applicants, 0% accepted, 0 enrolled. In 2010, 12 master's awarded. *Degree requirements:* For master's, thesis or alternative. *Entrance requirements:* For master's, GRE General Test or GMAT, minimum GPA of 2.8 in last 90 quarter units of course work, 2 letters of recommendation. Additional exam requirements/recommendations for international students: Required—TOEFL (minimum score 550 paper-based; 213 computer-based) or IELTS (minimum score 6). *Application deadline:* For fall admission, 7/1 for domestic students, 11/30 for international students. Applications are processed on a rolling basis. Application fee: $55. Electronic applications accepted. *Expenses:* Tuition, state resident: full-time $5386; part-time $3124 per year. Tuition, nonresident: full-time $11,160; part-time $248 per unit. Required fees: $2250; $614 per term. One-time fee: $2250 full-time; $1842 part-time. *Financial support:* Career-related internships or fieldwork, Federal Work-Study, institutionally sponsored loans, and scholarships/grants available. Support available to part-time students. Financial award application deadline: 3/2; financial award applicants required to submit FAFSA. *Faculty research:* Valve chain management, packing science and technology, technology entrepreneurship and innovation, industrial processes and systems. *Unit head:* Dr. Lou Tornatzky, Associate Dean/Graduate Coordinator, 805-756-2676, Fax: 805-756-6111, E-mail: ltornatzk@calpoly. edu. *Application contact:* Dr. Lou Tornatzky, Associate Dean/Graduate Coordinator, 805-756-2676, Fax: 805-756-6111, E-mail: ltornatzk@calpoly. edu.

California State University, East Bay, Office of Academic Programs and Graduate Studies, College of Business and Economics, Department of Information Technology Management, Option in Operations and Supply Chain Management, Hayward, CA 94542-3000. Offers MBA. *Degree requirements:* For master's, comprehensive exam or thesis. *Entrance requirements:* For master's, GMAT, minimum GPA of 2.75. Additional exam requirements/recommendations for international students: Required—TOEFL (minimum score 550 paper-based; 213 computer-based). *Application deadline:* For fall admission, 6/30 for domestic and international students. Application fee: $55. Electronic applications accepted. *Financial support:* Fellowships, career-related internships or fieldwork, Federal Work-Study, institutionally sponsored loans, and scholarships/grants available. Support available to part-time students. Financial award application deadline: 3/1; financial award applicants required to submit FAFSA. *Unit head:* Prof. Xinjian Lu, Chair, 510-885-3307, E-mail: xinjian.lu@csueastbay.edu. *Application contact:* Donna Wiley, Interim Associate Director, 510-885-2928, Fax: 510-885-4777, E-mail: donna. wiley@csueastbay.edu.

Central Connecticut State University, School of Graduate Studies, School of Technology, Department of Manufacturing and Construction Management, New Britain, CT 06050-4010. Offers construction management (MS, Certificate); lean manufacturing and Six Sigma (Certificate); supply chain and logistics (Certificate); technology management (MS). Part-time and evening/weekend programs available. *Faculty:* 19 full-time (4 women), 25 part-time/adjunct (1 woman). *Students:* 15 full-time (4 women), 78 part-time (16 women); includes 19 minority (10 Black or African American, non-Hispanic/Latino; 5 Asian, non-Hispanic/Latino; 3 Hispanic/Latino; 1 Two or more races, non-Hispanic/Latino), 5 international. Average age 38. 67 applicants, 76% accepted, 34 enrolled. In 2010, 24 master's awarded. *Degree requirements:* For master's, comprehensive exam, thesis or alternative; for Certificate, qualifying exam. *Entrance requirements:* For master's, minimum undergraduate GPA of 2.7. Additional exam requirements/recommendations for international students: Required—TOEFL. *Application deadline:* For fall admission, 7/1 for domestic students; for spring admission, 12/1 for domestic students. Applications are processed on a rolling basis. Application fee: $50. Electronic applications accepted. *Expenses:* Tuition, area resident: Full-time $5012; part-time $470 per credit. Tuition, state resident: full-time $7518; part-time $482 per credit. Tuition, nonresident: full-time $13,962; part-time $482 per credit. Required fees: $3772. One-time fee: $62 part-time. *Financial support:* In 2010–11, 5 students received support, including 5 research assistantships; career-related internships or fieldwork, Federal Work-Study, scholarships/grants, and unspecified assistantships also available. Support available to part-time students. Financial award application deadline: 2/15; financial award applicants required to submit FAFSA. *Faculty research:* All aspects of middle management, technical supervision in the workplace. *Unit head:* Dr. Jacob Kovel, Chair, 860-832-1830. *Application contact:* Dr. Jacob Kovel, Chair, 860-832-1830.

Central Michigan University, College of Graduate Studies, College of Science and Technology, Department of Engineering Technology, Mount Pleasant, MI 48859. Offers industrial management and technology (MA). Part-time programs available. *Faculty:* 5 full-time (0 women), 1 part-time/ adjunct (0 women). *Students:* 5 full-time (1 woman), 7 part-time (1 woman); includes 1 Asian, non-Hispanic/Latino, 5 international. Average age 29. *Degree requirements:* For master's, thesis or alternative. *Application deadline:* For fall admission, 6/1 for international students; for spring admission, 10/1 for international students. Applications are processed on a rolling basis. Application fee: $35 ($45 for international students). Electronic applications accepted. *Expenses:* Tuition, state resident: full-time $8208; part-time $456 per credit hour. Tuition, nonresident: full-time $13,788; part-time $766 per credit hour. One-time fee: $25. *Financial support:* Fellowships with tuition reimbursements, research assistantships with tuition reimbursements, teaching assistantships with tuition reimbursements, career-related internships or fieldwork, Federal Work-Study, unspecified assistantships, and out-of-state merit awards, non-resident graduate awards available. *Faculty research:* Computer applications, manufacturing process control, mechanical engineering automation, industrial technology. *Unit head:* Dr. Terence Lerch, Chairperson, 989-774-3033, Fax: 989-774-4900, E-mail: lerch1t@cmich.edu. *Application contact:* Dr. David A. Lopez, Graduate Program Coordinator, 989-774-3210, Fax: 989-774-4900, E-mail: lopez1da@cmich.edu.

Cleveland State University, College of Graduate Studies, Nance College of Business Administration, Doctor of Business Administration (DBA) Program, Cleveland, OH 44115. Offers business administration (DBA); finance (DBA); information systems (DBA); marketing (DBA); operations management (DBA). *Accreditation:* AACSB. Part-time and evening/weekend programs available. *Faculty:* 50 full-time (11 women). *Students:* 6 full-time (2 women), 31 part-time (6 women); includes 3 Black or African American, non-Hispanic/Latino; 2 Asian, non-Hispanic/Latino, 7 international. Average age 44. 7 applicants. *Degree requirements:* For doctorate, comprehensive exam, thesis/dissertation, oral dissertation defense. *Entrance requirements:* For doctorate, GMAT, MBA or equivalent. Additional exam requirements/recommendations for international students: Required—TOEFL (minimum score 550 paper-based; 213 computer-based; 79 iBT). *Application deadline:* For spring admission, 2/28 priority date for domestic and international students. Application fee: $30. Electronic applications accepted. *Expenses:* Tuition, state resident: full-time $8447; part-time $469 per credit hour. Tuition, nonresident: full-time $16,020; part-time $890 per credit hour. Required fees: $50. *Financial support:* In 2010–11, 5 research assistantships with full tuition reimbursements (averaging $11,700 per year), 1 teaching assistantship with full tuition reimbursement (averaging $11,700 per year) were awarded; tuition waivers (full) and unspecified assistantships also available. *Faculty research:* Supply chain management, international business, strategic management, risk analysis. *Unit head:* Dr. Raj Shekhar G. Javalgi, Director, 216-687-3786, Fax: 216-687-9354, E-mail: r.javalgi@csuohio.edu. *Application contact:* Brenda Wade, Administrative Secretary, 216-687-6952, Fax: 216-687-9257, E-mail: b.wade@csuohio.edu.

DePaul University, Charles H. Kellstadt Graduate School of Business, Department of Management, Chicago, IL 60604-2287. Offers entrepreneurship (MBA); health sector management (MBA); human resource management (MBA, MSHR); leadership/change management (MBA); management planning and strategy (MBA); operations management (MBA). Part-time and evening/weekend programs available. *Faculty:* 36 full-time (7 women), 35 part-time/adjunct (16 women). *Students:* 267 full-time (116 women), 125 part-time (43 women); includes 76 minority (24 Black or African American, non-Hispanic/Latino; 1 American Indian or Alaska Native, non-Hispanic/Latino; 33 Asian, non-Hispanic/Latino; 13 Hispanic/Latino; 1 Native Hawaiian or other Pacific Islander, non-Hispanic/Latino; 4 Two or more races, non-Hispanic/Latino), 20 international. In 2010, 112 master's awarded. *Entrance requirements:* For master's, GMAT, GRE (MSHR), 2 letters of recommendation, resume. Additional exam requirements/recommendations for international students: Required—TOEFL (minimum score 550 paper-based; 213 computer-based). *Application deadline:* For fall admission, 7/1 for domestic students; for winter admission, 10/1 for domestic students; for spring admission, 2/1 for domestic students. Applications are processed on a rolling basis. Application fee: $60. Electronic applications accepted. *Financial support:* Research assistantships available. Financial award application deadline: 4/1. *Faculty research:* Growth management, creativity and innovation, quality management and business process design, entrepreneurship. *Application contact:* Christopher E. Kinsella, Director of Cohort MBA Programs, 312-362-8810, Fax: 312-362-6677, E-mail: kgsb@depaul.edu.

Friends University, Graduate School, Wichita, KS 67213. Offers accounting (MBA); business administration (MBA); business law (MBL); Christian ministry (MACM); family therapy (MSFT); global leadership and management (MA); health care leadership (MHCL); management information systems (MMIS); operations management (MSOM); organization development (MSOD); teaching (MAT). Part-time and evening/weekend programs available. Postbaccalaureate distance learning degree programs offered (minimal on-campus study). *Faculty:* 14 full-time (5 women), 2 part-time/ adjunct (1 woman). *Students:* 166 full-time (122 women), 507 part-time (290 women); includes 134 minority (64 Black or African American, non-Hispanic/Latino; 6 American Indian or Alaska Native, non-Hispanic/Latino; 24 Asian, non-Hispanic/Latino; 30 Hispanic/Latino; 1 Native Hawaiian or other Pacific Islander, non-Hispanic/Latino; 9 Two or more races, non-Hispanic/Latino). Average age 38. 445 applicants, 69% accepted, 236 enrolled. In 2010, 345 master's awarded. *Degree requirements:* For master's, research project.

Entrance requirements: Additional exam requirements/recommendations for international students: Required—TOEFL (minimum score 560 paper-based; 220 computer-based). *Application deadline:* Applications are processed on a rolling basis. Application fee: $45 ($65 for international students). Electronic applications accepted. Tuition and fees vary according to course load, campus/location and program. *Financial support:* Applicants required to submit FAFSA. *Unit head:* Dr. Evelyn Hume, Dean, 800-794-6945 Ext. 5859, Fax: 316-295-5040, E-mail: evelyn_hume@friends.edu. Application contact: Jeanette Hanson, Executive Director of Adult Recruitment, 800-794-6945, Fax: 316-295-5050, E-mail: jeanette@friends.edu.

HEC Montreal, School of Business Administration, Master of Science Programs in Administration, Program in Production and Operations Management, Montréal, QC H3T 2A7, Canada. Offers M Sc. All courses are given in French. Part-time programs available. *Students:* 30 full-time (19 women), 4 part-time (0 women). 20 applicants, 80% accepted, 11 enrolled. In 2010, 10 master's awarded. *Degree requirements:* For master's, one foreign language, thesis. *Application deadline:* For fall admission, 3/15 for domestic and international students; for winter admission, 10/1 for domestic and international students. Application fee: $78 Canadian dollars. Electronic applications accepted. *Expenses:* Tuition, area resident: Part-time $68.93 per credit. Tuition, state resident: full-time $2481.48; part-time $188.92 per credit. Tuition, nonresident: full-time $6801; part-time $482.06 per course. International tuition: $17,354.16 full-time. Required fees: $1309.50; $30.28 per credit. $93.45 per term. Tuition and fees vary according to degree level and program. *Financial support:* Fellowships, research assistantships, teaching assistantships, scholarships/grants available. Financial award application deadline: 9/2. *Unit head:* Dr. Claude Laurin, Director, 514-340-6485, Fax: 514-340-6880, E-mail: claude.laurin@hec.ca. *Application contact:* Francine Blais, Administrative Director, 514-340-6112, Fax: 514-340-6411, E-mail: francine.blais@hec.ca.

Illinois Institute of Technology, Graduate College, School of Applied Technology, Program in Industrial Technology and Management, Chicago, IL 60616-3793. Offers MITO. Part-time and evening/weekend programs available. Postbaccalaureate distance learning degree programs offered (no on-campus study). *Faculty:* 2 full-time (0 women), 17 part-time/adjunct (1 woman). *Students:* 37 full-time (14 women), 19 part-time (3 women); includes 8 minority (4 Black or African American, non-Hispanic/Latino; 2 Asian, non-Hispanic/Latino; 1 Hispanic/Latino; 1 Two or more races, non-Hispanic/Latino), 34 international. Average age 28. 55 applicants, 85% accepted, 25 enrolled. In 2010, 27 master's awarded. *Entrance requirements:* For master's, GRE (minimum score 900 Quantitative and Verbal, 2.5 Analytical Writing), bachelor's degree with minimum cumulative undergraduate GPA of 3.0 (or its equivalent) from accredited institution. Additional exam requirements/recommendations for international students: Required—TOEFL (minimum score 523 paper-based; 70 iBT); Recommended—IELTS (minimum score 5.5). *Application deadline:* For fall admission, 8/1 for domestic students, 5/1 for international students; for spring admission, 12/15 for domestic students, 10/15 for international students. Applications are processed on a rolling basis. Application fee: $50. Electronic applications accepted. *Expenses:* Tuition: Full-time $18,576; part-time $1032 per credit hour. Required fees: $583 per semester. One-time fee: $150. Tuition and fees vary according to program and student level. *Financial support:* Fellowships with partial tuition reimbursements, career-related internships or fieldwork, Federal Work-Study, institutionally sponsored loans, scholarships/grants, traineeships, health care benefits, tuition waivers (partial), and unspecified assistantships available. Support available to part-time students. Financial award applicants required to submit FAFSA. *Faculty research:* Industrial logistics, industrial facilities, manufacturing technology, entrepreneurship, energy options. *Unit head:* Mazin Safit, Associate Director, 312-567-3624, Fax: 312-567-3655, E-mail: safar@iit.edu. *Application contact:* Deborah Gibson, Director, Graduate Admission, 866-472-3448, Fax: 312-567-3138, E-mail: inquiry.grad@iit.edu.

Lawrence Technological University, College of Management, Southfield, MI 48075-1058. Offers business administration (MBA, DBA); business administration international (MBA); global leadership and management (MS); global operations and project management (MS); information systems (MS); information technology (DM); operations management (MS). *Accreditation:* ACBSP. Part-time and evening/weekend programs available. *Faculty:* 14 full-time (6 women), 53 part-time/adjunct (14 women). *Students:* 7 full-time (2 women), 584 part-time (258 women); includes 137 Black or African American, non-Hispanic/Latino; 2 American Indian or Alaska Native, non-Hispanic/Latino; 51 Asian, non-Hispanic/Latino; 10 Hispanic/Latino; 8 Two or more races, non-Hispanic/Latino, 48 international. Average age 35. 431 applicants, 54% accepted, 151 enrolled. In 2010, 216 master's, 12 doctorates awarded. *Degree requirements:* For master's, thesis (for some programs). *Entrance requirements:* For master's, GMAT. Additional exam requirements/recommendations for international students: Required—TOEFL (minimum score 550 paper-based; 213 computer-based; 79 iBT). *Application deadline:* For fall admission, 6/30 priority date for domestic students, 6/30 for international students; for spring admission, 11/15 priority date for domestic students, 11/15 for international students. Applications are processed on a rolling basis. Application fee: $50. Electronic applications accepted. *Financial support:* In 2010–11, 142 students received support. Federal Work-Study and

institutionally sponsored loans available. Support available to part-time students. Financial award application deadline: 4/1; financial award applicants required to submit FAFSA. *Unit head:* Dr. Lou DeGennaro, Dean, 248-204-3050, E-mail: degennaro@ltu.edu. *Application contact:* Jane Rohrback, Director of Admissions, 248-204-3160, Fax: 248-204-2228, E-mail: admissions@ltu.edu.

Marquette University, Graduate School of Management, Executive MBA Program, Milwaukee, WI 53201-1881. Offers economics (MBA); finance (MBA); human resources (MBA); international business (MBA); management information systems (MBA); marketing (MBA); operations and supply chain management (MBA); sports business (MBA). *Accreditation:* AACSB. *Faculty:* 3 full-time (1 woman), 2 part-time/adjunct (0 women). *Students:* 43 full-time (11 women); includes 6 minority (1 Black or African American, non-Hispanic/Latino; 4 Asian, non-Hispanic/Latino; 1 Hispanic/Latino), 3 international. Average age 37. 47 applicants, 74% accepted, 29 enrolled. In 2010, 13 master's awarded. *Degree requirements:* For master's, international trip. *Entrance requirements:* For master's, GMAT, two letters of recommendation, official transcripts from current and previous colleges/universities. Additional exam requirements/recommendations for international students: Required—TOEFL (minimum score 530 paper-based; 78 computer-based). *Application deadline:* Applications are processed on a rolling basis. Application fee: $50. Electronic applications accepted. *Expenses:* Contact institution. *Financial support:* Application deadline: 2/15. *Faculty research:* International trade and finance, customer relationship management, consumer satisfaction, customer service. *Unit head:* Dr. Jeanne Simmons, Graduate Director, 414-288-7145, Fax: 414-288-1660, E-mail: jeanne.simmons@marquette.edu. *Application contact:* Erin Fox, Assistant Director for Recruitment, 414-288-5319, Fax: 414-288-1902, E-mail: erin.fox@marquette.edu.

Marquette University, Graduate School of Management, Program in Business Administration, Milwaukee, WI 53201-1881. Offers business administration (MBA); economics (MBA); finance (MBA); human resources (MBA); international business (MBA); management information systems (MBA); marketing (MBA); operations and supply chain management (MBA); sports business (MBA); JD/MBA; MBA/MA; MBA/MSN. *Accreditation:* AACSB. Part-time and evening/weekend programs available. *Faculty:* 38 full-time (9 women), 24 part-time/adjunct (8 women). *Students:* 44 full-time (17 women), 368 part-time (105 women); includes 36 minority (4 Black or African American, non-Hispanic/Latino; 2 American Indian or Alaska Native, non-Hispanic/Latino; 20 Asian, non-Hispanic/Latino; 10 Hispanic/Latino), 30 international. Average age 31. 256 applicants, 60% accepted, 98 enrolled. In 2010, 117 master's awarded. *Entrance requirements:* For master's, GMAT, letters of recommendation. Additional exam requirements/recommendations for international students: Required—TOEFL (minimum score 530 paper-based; 78 computer-based). *Application deadline:* Applications are processed on a rolling basis. Application fee: $50. Electronic applications accepted. *Expenses:* Tuition: Full-time $16,290; part-time $905 per credit hour. Tuition and fees vary according to program. *Financial support:* In 2010–11, 4 fellowships, 11 teaching assistantships were awarded; research assistantships, Federal Work-Study, institutionally sponsored loans, scholarships/grants, and tuition waivers (full and partial) also available. Support available to part-time students. Financial award application deadline: 2/15. *Faculty research:* Ethics in the professions, services marketing, technology impact on decision-making, mentoring. *Unit head:* Dr. Jeanne Simmons, Graduate Director, 414-288-7145, Fax: 414-288-1660, E-mail: jeanne.simmons@marquette.edu. *Application contact:* Debra Leutermann, Admissions Coordinator, 414-288-8064, Fax: 414-288-1902, E-mail: debra.leutermann@marquette.edu.

Milwaukee School of Engineering, Rader School of Business, Program in New Product Management, Milwaukee, WI 53202-3109. Offers MS. *Faculty:* 1 full-time (0 women), 2 part-time/adjunct (1 woman). *Students:* 1 full-time (0 women), 14 part-time (4 women); includes 2 Asian, non-Hispanic/Latino; 2 Hispanic/Latino; 1 Two or more races, non-Hispanic/Latino, 2 international. 7 applicants, 71% accepted, 4 enrolled. *Degree requirements:* For master's, thesis optional, thesis defense or capstone project. *Entrance requirements:* For master's, GRE General Test or GMAT, 2 letters of recommendation. Additional exam requirements/recommendations for international students: Recommended—TOEFL (minimum score 550 paper-based; 213 computer-based; 79 iBT), IELTS. *Application deadline:* Applications are processed on a rolling basis. Application fee: $30. Electronic applications accepted. *Expenses:* Tuition: Full-time $17,550; part-time $650 per credit. One-time fee: $75. *Financial support:* In 2010–11, 3 students received support. Applicants required to submit FAFSA. *Faculty research:* New product development, product research and design, product development. *Unit head:* Dr. Kathy Faggiani, Director, 414-277-2711, E-mail: faggiani@msoe.com. *Application contact:* Sarah K. Winchowky, Graduate Admissions Director, 800-321-6763, Fax: 414-277-7475, E-mail: wp@msoe.edu.

Northeastern State University, Graduate College, College of Business and Technology, Program in Industrial Management, Tahlequah, OK 74464-2399. Offers MS. Part-time and evening/weekend programs available. *Faculty:* 3 full-time (0 women). *Students:* 9 full-time (4 women), 11 part-time (2 women); includes 7 minority (6 American Indian or Alaska Native, non-Hispanic/Latino; 1 Asian, non-Hispanic/Latino), 2 international. In 2010, 6 master's awarded. *Degree requirements:* For master's, synergistic experience. *Entrance* *requirements:* For master's, GRE, MAT, minimum GPA of 2.5. Additional exam requirements/recommendations for international students: Required—TOEFL (minimum score 213 computer-based). *Application deadline:* For fall admission, 6/1 priority date for domestic students. Applications are processed on a rolling basis. Application fee: $0 ($25 for international students). Electronic applications accepted. *Expenses:* Tuition, state resident: part-time $144 per credit hour. Tuition, nonresident: part-time $384.05 per credit hour. Required fees: $34.90 per credit hour. Tuition and fees vary according to program. *Financial support:* Teaching assistantships, Federal Work-Study available. Financial award application deadline: 3/1. *Unit head:* Dr. Michael Turner, Chair, 918-456-5511 Ext. 2970, Fax: 918-458-2337, E-mail: turne003@nsuok.edu. *Application contact:* Dr. Michael Turner, Chair, 918-456-5511 Ext. 2970, Fax: 918-458-2337, E-mail: turne003@nsuok.edu.

Northern Illinois University, Graduate School, College of Engineering and Engineering Technology, Department of Technology, De Kalb, IL 60115-2854. Offers industrial management (MS). Part-time and evening/weekend programs available. *Faculty:* 14 full-time (1 woman), 1 part-time/adjunct (0 women). *Students:* 23 full-time (0 women), 39 part-time (6 women); includes 4 Black or African American, non-Hispanic/Latino; 2 Hispanic/Latino; 3 Two or more races, non-Hispanic/Latino, 6 international. Average age 31. 18 applicants, 72% accepted, 10 enrolled. In 2010, 15 master's awarded. *Degree requirements:* For master's, thesis optional. *Entrance requirements:* For master's, GRE General Test, minimum GPA of 2.75. Additional exam requirements/recommendations for international students: Required—TOEFL (minimum score 550 paper-based; 213 computer-based). *Application deadline:* For fall admission, 6/1 for domestic students, 5/1 for international students; for spring admission, 11/1 for domestic students, 10/1 for international students. Applications are processed on a rolling basis. Application fee: $30. Electronic applications accepted. *Expenses:* Tuition, state resident: full-time $7200; part-time $300 per credit hour. Tuition, nonresident: full-time $14,400; part-time $600 per credit hour. Required fees: $79 per credit hour. *Financial support:* In 2010–11, 1 research assistantship with full tuition reimbursement, 11 teaching assistantships with full tuition reimbursements were awarded; fellowships with full tuition reimbursements, career-related internships or fieldwork, Federal Work-Study, scholarships/grants, tuition waivers (full), and unspecified assistantships also available. Support available to part-time students. Financial award applicants required to submit FAFSA. *Faculty research:* Digital control, intelligent systems, engineering graphic design, occupational safety, ergonomics. *Unit head:* Dr. Clifford Mirman, Chair, 815-753-1349, Fax: 815-753-3702, E-mail: mirman@ceet.niu.edu. *Application contact:* Graduate School Office, 815-753-0395, E-mail: gradsch@niu.edu.

Penn State University Park, Graduate School, Intercollege Graduate Programs, Intercollege Program in Quality and Manufacturing Management, State College, University Park, PA 16802-1503. Offers MMM. *Unit head:* Dr. Jose A. Ventura, Co-Director, 814-865-5802, Fax: 814-863-4745, E-mail: jav1@psu.edu. *Application contact:* Cynthia E. Nicosia, Director, Graduate Enrollment Services, 814-865-1795, Fax: 814-865-4627, E-mail: cey1@psu.edu.

Portland State University, Graduate Studies, Maseeh College of Engineering and Computer Science, Department of Engineering and Technology Management, Portland, OR 97207-0751. Offers engineering and technology management (M Eng); engineering management (MS); manufacturing engineering (ME); manufacturing management (M Eng); systems science/engineering management (PhD); MS/MBA; MS/MS. Part-time and evening/weekend programs available. *Faculty:* 8 full-time (1 woman), 3 part-time/adjunct (2 women). *Students:* 50 full-time (13 women), 58 part-time (16 women); includes 13 Asian, non-Hispanic/Latino; 6 Hispanic/Latino, 51 international. Average age 35. 38 applicants, 76% accepted, 13 enrolled. In 2010, 42 master's awarded. *Degree requirements:* For master's, thesis optional; for doctorate, one foreign language, thesis/dissertation, oral and written exams. *Entrance requirements:* For master's, minimum GPA of 3.0 in upper-division course work, BS in civil engineering; for doctorate, GRE General Test, GRE Subject Test, minimum GPA of 3.0 in upper-division course work. Additional exam requirements/recommendations for international students: Required—TOEFL (minimum score 550 paper-based; 213 computer-based). *Application deadline:* For fall admission, 4/1 for domestic students, 3/1 for international students; for winter admission, 9/1 for domestic students, 7/1 for international students; for spring admission, 11/1 for domestic students, 9/1 for international students. Applications are processed on a rolling basis. Application fee: $50. *Expenses:* Tuition, state resident: full-time $8505; part-time $315 per credit. Tuition, nonresident: full-time $13,284; part-time $492 per credit. Required fees: $1482; $21 per credit. $99 per term. One-time fee: $120. Part-time tuition and fees vary according to course load and program. *Financial support:* In 2010–11, 3 teaching assistantships with full tuition reimbursements (averaging $8,916 per year) were awarded; research assistantships with full tuition reimbursements, career-related internships or fieldwork, Federal Work-Study, scholarships/grants, and unspecified assistantships also available. Support available to part-time students. Financial award application deadline: 3/1; financial award applicants required to submit FAFSA. *Faculty research:* Scheduling, hierarchical decision modeling, operations research, knowledge-based information systems. Total annual research expenditures: $1.1 million. *Unit head:* Dr. Dundar F. Kocaoglu, Chair, 503-725-4660, Fax: 503-725-4667, E-mail: kocaoglu@etm.pdx.edu. *Application contact:* Dr. Dundar F. Kocaoglu, Chair, 503-725-4660, Fax: 503-725-4667, E-mail: kocaoglu@etm.pdx.edu.

Purdue University, Graduate School, Krannert School of Management, Master of Science in Industrial Administration Program, West Lafayette, IN 47907. Offers MSIA. *Faculty:* 98 full-time (27 women), 22 part-time/adjunct (4 women). *Students:* 21 full-time (9 women); includes 2 Asian, non-Hispanic/Latino, 15 international. Average age 27. 77 applicants, 61% accepted, 21 enrolled. In 2010, 19 degrees awarded. *Entrance requirements:* For master's, GMAT or GRE, work experience, essays, minimum GPA of 3.0, four-year baccalaureate degree, letters of recommendation. Additional exam requirements/recommendations for international students: Required—TOEFL (minimum score 550 paper-based; 213 computer-based; 77 iBT), TOEFL (minimum: 550 paper, 213 computer, 77 iBT), IELTS, or Pearson PTE. *Application deadline:* For fall admission, 1/10 priority date for domestic students, 2/1 for international students. Applications are processed on a rolling basis. Application fee: $55. Electronic applications accepted. *Financial support:* Application deadline: 2/1. *Unit head:* Dr. Gerald J. Lynch, Interim Dean, 765-494-4366. *Application contact:* Brenda Knebel, Director, Full-time Master's Admissions, 765-494-0773, Fax: 765-494-9841, E-mail: krannertmasters@purdue.edu.

Rochester Institute of Technology, Graduate Enrollment Services, College of Applied Science and Technology, Department of Electrical, Computer and Telecommunications Engineering Technology, Program in Facility Management, Rochester, NY 14623-5603. Offers MS. Part-time programs available. Postbaccalaureate distance learning degree programs offered (no on-campus study). *Students:* 4 full-time (1 woman), 14 part-time (3 women); includes 1 Black or African American, non-Hispanic/Latino; 1 Hispanic/Latino, 1 international. Average age 39. 6 applicants, 50% accepted, 3 enrolled. In 2010, 4 master's awarded. *Degree requirements:* For master's, thesis or alternative, project. *Entrance requirements:* For master's, minimum GPA of 3.0. Additional exam requirements/recommendations for international students: Required—TOEFL (minimum score 550 paper-based; 213 computer-based; 79 iBT) or IELTS (minimum score 6.5). *Application deadline:* For fall admission, 2/15 priority date for domestic and international students; for winter admission, 11/1 priority date for domestic students, 10/1 priority date for international students; for spring admission, 2/1 priority date for domestic students, 1/1 priority date for international students. Applications are processed on a rolling basis. Electronic applications accepted. *Expenses:* Tuition: Full-time $33,234; part-time $924 per credit hour. Required fees: $219. *Financial support:* In 2010–11, 11 students received support. Career-related internships or fieldwork and scholarships/grants available. Support available to part-time students. Financial award applicants required to submit FAFSA. *Faculty research:* Sustainability. *Unit head:* Dr. Jeff Rogers, Graduate Program Director, 585-475-4185, E-mail: jwrite@rit.edu. *Application contact:* Diane Ellison, Assistant Vice President, Graduate Enrollment Services, 585-475-2229, Fax: 585-475-7164, E-mail: gradinfo@rit.edu.

Rochester Institute of Technology, Graduate Enrollment Services, Kate Gleason College of Engineering, Department of Design, Development and Manufacturing, Program in Manufacturing Leadership, Rochester, NY 14623-5603. Offers MS. Part-time and evening/weekend programs available. Postbaccalaureate distance learning degree programs offered (minimal on-campus study). *Students:* 3 full-time (all women), 18 part-time (5 women); includes 2 Black or African American, non-Hispanic/Latino; 1 Asian, non-Hispanic/Latino; 2 Hispanic/Latino, 4 international. Average age 37. 8 applicants, 88% accepted, 7 enrolled. In 2010, 13 master's awarded. *Degree requirements:* For master's, capstone. *Entrance requirements:* For master's, GMAT, minimum GPA of 2.5. Additional exam requirements/recommendations for international students: Required—TOEFL (minimum score 570 paper-based; 230 computer-based; 88 iBT) or IELTS (minimum score 6.5). *Application deadline:* For fall admission, 2/15 priority date for domestic and international students. Applications are processed on a rolling basis. Application fee: $50. *Expenses:* Tuition: Full-time $33,234; part-time $924 per credit hour. Required fees: $219. *Financial support:* In 2010–11, 7 students received support. Institutionally sponsored loans and scholarships/grants available. Support available to part-time students. Financial award applicants required to submit FAFSA. *Unit head:* Mark Smith, Graduate Program Director, 585-475-7971, Fax: 585-475-7955, E-mail: mmlmail@rit.edu. *Application contact:* Diane Ellison, Assistant Vice President, Graduate Enrollment Services, 585-475-2229, Fax: 585-475-7164, E-mail: gradinfo@rit.edu.

Southeast Missouri State University, School of Graduate Studies, Department of Industrial and Engineering Technology, Cape Girardeau, MO 63701-4799. Offers industrial management (MS); technology management (MS). Part-time programs available. Postbaccalaureate distance learning degree programs offered (no on-campus study). *Faculty:* 11 full-time (1 woman). *Students:* 42 full-time (8 women), 24 part-time (1 woman); includes 1 minority (Black or African American, non-Hispanic/Latino), 37 international. Average age 27. 60 applicants, 97% accepted, 24 enrolled. In 2010, 6 master's awarded. *Degree requirements:* For master's, comprehensive exam (for some programs), thesis (for some programs), minimum GPA of 3.0; thesis and oral exam or comprehensive exam and applied research project. *Entrance requirements:* For master's, GRE or GMAT if undergraduate GPA below 2.7, undergraduate degree in an engineering, technology, or a related field or portfolio of experience and prerequisite course work. Additional exam requirements/recommendations for international students: Required—TOEFL (minimum score 550 paper-based; 213 computer-based; 79 iBT); Recommended—IELTS (minimum score 6). *Application deadline:* For fall admission, 8/1 for domestic students, 6/1 for international students; for spring admission, 11/21 for domestic students, 10/1 for international students. Applications are processed on a rolling basis. Application fee: $25 ($35 for international students). Electronic applications accepted. *Expenses:* Tuition, state resident: full-time $4698; part-time $261 per credit hour. Tuition, nonresident: full-time $8379; part-time $465.50 per credit hour. *Financial support:* In 2010–11, 40 students received support, including 12 teaching assistantships with full tuition reimbursements available (averaging $7,600 per year); career-related internships or fieldwork, Federal Work-Study, institutionally sponsored loans, scholarships/grants, tuition waivers (full), and unspecified assistantships also available. Financial award application deadline: 6/30; financial award applicants required to submit FAFSA. *Faculty research:* Supply chain management, lean manufacturing, energy conservation, telecommunications, graphic communications, ISQ/Q5 9000, SAP (enterprise resource planning), automatic control systems. *Unit head:* Dr. Chris McGowan, Interim Chairperson, 573-651-2163, E-mail: cwmcgowan@semo.edu. *Application contact:* Gail Amick, Administrative Secretary, 573-651-2049, Fax: 573-651-2001, E-mail: gamick2@semo.edu.

Southeast Missouri State University, School of Graduate Studies, Harrison College of Business, Cape Girardeau, MO 63701-4799. Offers accounting (MBA); entrepreneurship (MBA); environmental management (MBA); financial management (MBA); general management (MBA); health administration (MBA); industrial management (MBA); international business (MBA); sport management (MBA). *Accreditation:* AACSB. Part-time and evening/weekend programs available. Postbaccalaureate distance learning degree programs offered (no on-campus study). *Faculty:* 31 full-time (10 women). *Students:* 51 full-time (24 women), 72 part-time (34 women); includes 4 minority (1 American Indian or Alaska Native, non-Hispanic/Latino; 3 Asian, non-Hispanic/Latino), 32 international. Average age 28. 71 applicants, 83% accepted, 33 enrolled. In 2010, 46 master's awarded. *Degree requirements:* For master's, variable foreign language requirement, applied research project; foreign language or 9 credit hours (for international business). *Entrance requirements:* For master's, GMAT (minimum score 400), minimum undergraduate GPA of 2.5, prerequisite courses for non-business undergraduate majors. Additional exam requirements/recommendations for international students: Required—TOEFL (minimum score 550 paper-based; 213 computer-based; 79 iBT); Recommended—IELTS (minimum score 6). *Application deadline:* For fall admission, 8/1 for domestic students, 6/1 for international students; for spring admission, 11/21 for domestic students, 10/1 for international students. Applications are processed on a rolling basis. Application fee: $25 ($35 for international students). Electronic applications accepted. *Expenses:* Tuition, state resident: full-time $4698; part-time $261 per credit hour. Tuition, nonresident: full-time $8379; part-time $465.50 per credit hour. *Financial support:* In 2010–11, 52 students received support, including 10 teaching assistantships with full tuition reimbursements available (averaging $7,600 per year); career-related internships or fieldwork, Federal Work-Study, institutionally sponsored loans, scholarships/grants, tuition waivers (full), and unspecified assistantships also available. Financial award application deadline: 6/30; financial award applicants required to submit FAFSA. *Faculty research:* Human resources, laws impacting accounting, advertising. *Unit head:* Dr. Kenneth A. Heischmidt, Director, Graduate Programs, 573-651-5116, Fax: 573-651-5032, E-mail: kheischmidt@semo.edu. *Application contact:* Gail Amick, Administrative Secretary, 573-651-2049, Fax: 573-651-2001, E-mail: gamick@semo.edu.

Stevens Institute of Technology, Graduate School, Charles V. Schaefer Jr. School of Engineering, Department of Mechanical Engineering, Program in Integrated Product Development, Hoboken, NJ 07030. Offers armament engineering (M Eng); computer and electrical engineering (M Eng); manufacturing technologies (M Eng); systems reliability and design (M Eng). *Students:* 8 part-time (1 woman). Average age 26. *Unit head:* Dr. Constantin Chassapis, Director, 201-216-5564. *Application contact:* Graduate Admissions, 800-496-4935, Fax: 201-216-8044, E-mail: gradadmissions@stevens.edu.

Texas A&M University, Mays Business School, Department of Information and Operations Management, College Station, TX 77843. Offers management information systems (MS, PhD); management science (PhD); production and operations management (PhD). *Faculty:* 14. *Students:* 148 full-time (54 women), 6 part-time (1 woman); includes 12 minority (1 Black or African American, non-Hispanic/Latino; 1 American Indian or Alaska Native, non-Hispanic/Latino; 3 Asian, non-Hispanic/Latino; 7 Hispanic/Latino), 102 international. Average age 31. In 2010, 78 master's awarded. Terminal master's awarded for partial completion of doctoral program. *Degree requirements:* For master's, comprehensive exam; for doctorate, thesis/dissertation. *Entrance requirements:* For master's, GMAT; for doctorate, GMAT or GRE General Test. Additional exam requirements/recommendations for international students: Required—TOEFL. *Application deadline:* For fall admission, 3/1 priority date for domestic students; for spring admission, 8/1 for domestic students. Applications are processed on a rolling basis. Application fee: $50 ($75 for international students). *Financial support:* In 2010–11, 51 students received support; fellowships, research assistantships, teaching assistantships, career-related internships or fieldwork, Federal Work-Study, and institutionally

sponsored loans available. Financial award application deadline: 2/1. *Unit head:* Dr. E. Powell Robinson, Head, 979-845-1616, E-mail: p-robinson@mays.tamu.edu. *Application contact:* Louise Darcey, Senior Lecturer, 979-862-1994, E-mail: ldarcey@mays.tamu.edu.

Texas Tech University, Graduate School, Jerry S. Rawls College of Business Administration, Area of Information Systems and Quantitative Sciences, Lubbock, TX 79409. Offers business statistics (MS, PhD); healthcare management (MS); management information systems (MS, PhD); production and operations management (MS, PhD); risk management (MS). Part-time programs available. *Faculty:* 15 full-time (0 women). *Students:* 73 full-time (21 women), 13 part-time (0 women); includes 5 minority (1 Black or African American, non-Hispanic/Latino; 1 Asian, non-Hispanic/Latino; 3 Hispanic/Latino), 61 international. Average age 27. 130 applicants, 75% accepted, 51 enrolled. In 2010, 31 master's, 2 doctorates awarded. Terminal master's awarded for partial completion of doctoral program. *Degree requirements:* For master's, comprehensive exam or capstone course; for doctorate, thesis/dissertation, qualifying exams. *Entrance requirements:* For master's and doctorate, GMAT, holistic profile of academic credentials. Additional exam requirements/recommendations for international students: Required—TOEFL (minimum score 550 paper-based; 213 computer-based; 79 iBT). *Application deadline:* For fall admission, 4/1 priority date for domestic students, 1/15 for international students; for spring admission, 9/1 priority date for domestic students, 6/15 priority date for international students. Applications are processed on a rolling basis. Application fee: $50 ($75 for international students). Electronic applications accepted. *Expenses:* Tuition, state resident: full-time $5495.76; part-time $228.99 per credit hour. Tuition, nonresident: full-time $12,936; part-time $538.99 per credit hour. Required fees: $2674; $36 per credit hour. $905 per semester. *Financial support:* In 2010–11, 4 research assistantships (averaging $8,800 per year), 9 teaching assistantships (averaging $18,000 per year) were awarded; Federal Work-Study, scholarships/grants, and unspecified assistantships also available. *Faculty research:* Database management systems, systems management and engineering, expert systems and adaptive knowledge-based sciences, statistical analysis and design. *Unit head:* Dr. Bradley Ewing, Area Coordinator, 806-742-3939, Fax: 806-742-3193, E-mail: bradley.ewing@ttu.edu. *Application contact:* Cynthia D. Barnes, Director, Graduate Services Center, 806-742-3184, Fax: 806-742-3958, E-mail: ba_grad@ttu.edu.

University of Arkansas, Graduate School, College of Engineering, Department of Industrial Engineering, Operations Management Program, Fayetteville, AR 72701-1201. Offers MS. Part-time and evening/weekend programs available. Postbaccalaureate distance learning degree programs offered. *Students:* 24 full-time (10 women), 434 part-time (113 women); includes 97 minority (64 Black or African American, non-Hispanic/Latino; 6 American Indian or Alaska Native, non-Hispanic/Latino; 16 Asian, non-Hispanic/Latino; 10 Hispanic/Latino; 1 Native Hawaiian or other Pacific Islander, non-Hispanic/Latino), 16 international. 137 applicants, 94% accepted. In 2010, 211 master's awarded. *Degree requirements:* For master's, thesis optional. *Application deadline:* For fall admission, 4/1 for international students; for spring admission, 10/1 for international students. Applications are processed on a rolling basis. Application fee: $0. Electronic applications accepted. *Financial support:* In 2010–11, 1 fellowship, 2 research assistantships were awarded; teaching assistantships, institutionally sponsored loans also available. *Unit head:* Dr. Kim Needy, Departmental Chair, 479-575-7426, E-mail: kneedy@uark.edu. *Application contact:* Nancy Sloan, Program Manager, 479-575-2082, E-mail: ncsloan@uark.edu.

University of California, Berkeley, Graduate Division, Haas School of Business, PhD in Business Administration Program, Berkeley, CA 94720-1500. Offers accounting (PhD); business and public policy (PhD); finance (PhD); management of organizations (PhD); marketing (PhD); operations management (PhD); real estate (PhD). *Accreditation:* AACSB. *Students:* 78 full-time (25 women); includes 12 Asian, non-Hispanic/Latino; 2 Hispanic/Latino, 32 international. Average age 30. 526 applicants, 7% accepted, 17 enrolled. In 2010, 17 doctorates awarded. *Degree requirements:* For doctorate, comprehensive exam, thesis/dissertation, written preliminary exams, oral qualifying exam. *Entrance requirements:* For doctorate, GMAT or GRE, minimum GPA of 3.0 in undergraduate and graduate coursework. Additional exam requirements/recommendations for international students: Required—TOEFL (minimum score 570 paper-based; 230 computer-based; 70 iBT), IELTS (minimum score 7). *Application deadline:* For fall admission, 12/10 for domestic and international students. Application fee: $70 ($90 for international students). Electronic applications accepted. *Financial support:* In 2010–11, 63 students received support, including 58 fellowships with full and partial tuition reimbursements available (averaging $26,000 per year); research assistantships with full and partial tuition reimbursements available, teaching assistantships with full and partial tuition reimbursements available, scholarships/grants, health care benefits, tuition waivers (full), unspecified assistantships, and transit pass, travel grants also available. Financial award application deadline: 12/10; financial award applicants required to submit FAFSA. *Faculty research:* Accounting, business and public policy, finance, management of organizations, marketing, operations and information technology management, real estate526. *Unit head:* Dr. Sunil Dutta, Director, 510-642-1229, Fax: 510-643-4255, E-mail: kimg@haas.berkeley.edu. *Application* *contact:* Kim Guilfoyle, Director, Student Affairs, 510-642-3944, Fax: 510-643-4255, E-mail: kimg@haas.berkeley.edu.

University of California, Los Angeles, Graduate Division, UCLA Anderson School of Management, Los Angeles, CA 90095-1481. Offers accounting (PhD); business administration (MBA); decisions, operations and technology management (PhD); finance (PhD); financial engineering (MFE); global economics and management (PhD); human resources and organizational behavior (PhD); marketing (PhD); strategy and policy (PhD); DDS/MBA; MBA/JD; MBA/MD; MBA/MLAS; MBA/MLIS; MBA/MPH; MBA/MPP; MBA/MSCS; MBA/MSN; MBA/MUP. *Accreditation:* AACSB. Part-time programs available. *Faculty:* 102 full-time (17 women), 43 part-time/adjunct (6 women). *Students:* 833 full-time (270 women), 1,052 part-time (271 women); includes 592 minority (25 Black or African American, non-Hispanic/Latino; 3 American Indian or Alaska Native, non-Hispanic/Latino; 482 Asian, non-Hispanic/Latino; 60 Hispanic/Latino; 6 Native Hawaiian or other Pacific Islander, non-Hispanic/Latino; 16 Two or more races, non-Hispanic/Latino), 445 international. In 2010, 735 master's, 10 doctorates awarded. *Degree requirements:* For master's, comprehensive exam, field study consulting project (for MBA); thesis/dissertation (for MFE); for doctorate, comprehensive exam, thesis/dissertation, oral and written qualifying exams. *Entrance requirements:* For master's, GMAT (MBA); GMAT or GRE General Test (MFE), minimum undergraduate GPA of 3.0; for doctorate, GMAT or GRE General Test, minimum undergraduate GPA of 3.0. Additional exam requirements/recommendations for international students: Required—TOEFL (minimum score 560 paper-based; 220 computer-based; 87 iBT), IELTS (minimum score 7). *Application deadline:* For fall admission, 10/20 for domestic and international students; for winter admission, 1/5 for domestic and international students; for spring admission, 4/13 for domestic and international students. Application fee: $200. Electronic applications accepted. *Expenses:* Contact institution. *Financial support:* Fellowships, research assistantships, teaching assistantships, career-related internships or fieldwork, institutionally sponsored loans, scholarships/grants, health care benefits, and tuition waivers (partial) available. Financial award application deadline: 3/2; financial award applicants required to submit FAFSA. *Unit head:* Judy D. Olian, Dean, UCLA Anderson School of Management, 310-825-7982, Fax: 310-206-2073. *Application contact:* Mae Jennifer Shores, Assistant Dean and Director of Full-time MBA Admissions and Financial Aid, 310-825-6944, Fax: 310-825-8582, E-mail: mba.admissions@anderson.ucla.edu.

University of Cincinnati, Graduate School, College of Business, PhD Program, Cincinnati, OH 45221. Offers accounting (PhD); finance (PhD); information systems (PhD); management (PhD); marketing (PhD); quantitative analysis and operations management (PhD). *Faculty:* 56 full-time (13 women). *Students:* 32 full-time (12 women), 9 part-time (3 women); includes 2 minority (both Hispanic/Latino), 23 international. 119 applicants, 12% accepted, 9 enrolled. In 2010, 8 doctorates awarded. *Degree requirements:* For doctorate, comprehensive exam, thesis/dissertation. *Entrance requirements:* For doctorate, GMAT, GRE, transcripts, essays, resume, letters of recommendation. Additional exam requirements/recommendations for international students: Required—TOEFL (minimum score 600 paper-based; 250 computer-based; 100 iBT). *Application deadline:* For fall admission, 2/1 for domestic and international students. Application fee: $45. Electronic applications accepted. *Expenses:* Contact institution. *Financial support:* In 2010–11, 38 students received support, including 29 research assistantships with full and partial tuition reimbursements available (averaging $14,640 per year); scholarships/grants, tuition waivers (full and partial), and unspecified assistantships also available. Financial award application deadline: 2/15; financial award applicants required to submit FAFSA. *Unit head:* Dr. Suzanne Masterson, Director, PhD Programs, 513-556-7125, Fax: 513-556-5499, E-mail: suzanne.masterson@uc.edu. *Application contact:* Deborah Schildknecht, Assistant Director, PhD Programs, 513-556-7190, Fax: 513-558-7006, E-mail: deborah.schildknecht@uc.edu.

University of Dayton, Graduate School, School of Business Administration, Dayton, OH 45469-1300. Offers accounting (MBA); business intelligence (MBA); cyber security (MBA); entrepreneurship (MBA); finance (MBA); international business (MBA); marketing (MBA); MIS (MBA); operations management (MBA); technology-enhanced business/e-commerce (MBA); JD/MBA. *Accreditation:* AACSB. Part-time and evening/weekend programs available. *Faculty:* 25 full-time (7 women), 14 part-time/adjunct (2 women). *Students:* 184 full-time (72 women), 110 part-time (34 women); includes 23 minority (7 Black or African American, non-Hispanic/Latino; 7 Asian, non-Hispanic/Latino; 8 Hispanic/Latino; 1 Two or more races, non-Hispanic/Latino), 31 international. Average age 28. 220 applicants, 85% accepted, 103 enrolled. In 2010, 113 master's awarded. *Entrance requirements:* For master's, GMAT or GRE. Additional exam requirements/recommendations for international students: Required—TOEFL (minimum score 550 paper-based; 213 computer-based; 79 iBT); Recommended—IELTS (minimum score 6.5). *Application deadline:* For fall admission, 3/1 priority date for international students; for winter admission, 7/1 priority date for international students; for spring admission, 1/1 priority date for international students. Applications are processed on a rolling basis. Application fee: $0 ($50 for international students). Electronic applications accepted. *Expenses:* Contact institution. *Financial support:* In 2010–11, 15 research assistantships with full and partial

tuition reimbursements (averaging $7,020 per year) were awarded; career-related internships or fieldwork, institutionally sponsored loans, scholarships/grants, health care benefits, and unspecified assistantships also available. Support available to part-time students. Financial award application deadline: 3/15; financial award applicants required to submit FAFSA. *Faculty research:* Management information systems, economics, finance, entrepreneurship, marketing. *Unit head:* Janice M. Glynn, Director, MBA Program, 937-229-3733, Fax: 937-229-3882, E-mail: glynn@udayton.edu. *Application contact:* Jeffrey Carter, Assistant Director, MBA Program, 937-229-3733, Fax: 937-229-3882, E-mail: jeff.carter@notes.udayton.edu.

University of Minnesota, Twin Cities Campus, Carlson School of Management, Doctoral Program in Business Administration, Minneapolis, MN 55455-0213. Offers accounting (PhD); finance (PhD); information and decision sciences (PhD); marketing and logistics management (PhD); operations and management science (PhD); strategic management and organization (PhD). *Faculty:* 100 full-time (27 women). *Students:* 73 full-time (28 women); includes 3 Asian, non-Hispanic/Latino; 3 Hispanic/Latino, 53 international. Average age 30. 319 applicants, 6% accepted, 16 enrolled. In 2010, 8 doctorates awarded. *Degree requirements:* For doctorate, comprehensive exam, thesis/dissertation, written and oral preliminary exams, proposal defense, final defense. *Entrance requirements:* For doctorate, GMAT, GRE General Test. Additional exam requirements/recommendations for international students: Required—TOEFL (minimum score 600 paper-based; 250 computer-based; 100 iBT), IELTS (minimum score 7.5). *Application deadline:* For fall admission, 12/31 for domestic students, 12/31 priority date for international students. Applications are processed on a rolling basis. Application fee: $75 ($95 for international students). Electronic applications accepted. *Financial support:* In 2010–11, 68 students received support, including 134 fellowships with full tuition reimbursements available (averaging $6,622 per year), 63 research assistantships with full tuition reimbursements available (averaging $6,750 per year), 57 teaching assistantships with full tuition reimbursements available (averaging $6,750 per year); institutionally sponsored loans, scholarships/grants, health care benefits, and unspecified assistantships also available. Financial award application deadline: 12/31. *Faculty research:* Corporate strategy, finance, entrepreneurship, marketing, information and decision science, operations, accounting, quality management. *Unit head:* Dr. Shawn P. Curley, Director of Graduate Studies and PhD Program Director, 612-624-6546, Fax: 612-624-8221, E-mail: curley@umn.edu. *Application contact:* Earlene K. Bronson, Assistant Director, PhD Program, 612-624-0875, Fax: 612-624-8221, E-mail: brons003@umn.edu.

University of Missouri–St. Louis, College of Business Administration, Program in Business Administration, St. Louis, MO 63121. Offers accounting (MBA); business administration (Certificate); finance (MBA); human resource management (Certificate); information systems (MBA); local government (Certificate); logistics and supply chain management (MBA, Certificate); marketing (MBA); marketing management (Certificate); operations management (MBA). *Accreditation:* AACSB. Part-time and evening/weekend programs available. *Faculty:* 30 full-time (5 women), 11 part-time/adjunct (2 women). *Students:* 132 full-time (57 women), 306 part-time (122 women); includes 55 minority (21 Black or African American, non-Hispanic/Latino; 20 Asian, non-Hispanic/Latino; 11 Hispanic/Latino; 1 Native Hawaiian or other Pacific Islander, non-Hispanic/Latino; 2 Two or more races, non-Hispanic/Latino), 6 international. Average age 30. 219 applicants, 60% accepted, 88 enrolled. In 2010, 114 master's, 9 other advanced degrees awarded. *Entrance requirements:* For master's, GMAT, 2 letters of recommendation. Additional exam requirements/recommendations for international students: Required—TOEFL (minimum score 550 paper-based; 213 computer-based). *Application deadline:* For fall admission, 7/1 for domestic students; for spring admission, 11/1 for domestic students. Applications are processed on a rolling basis. Application fee: $35 ($40 for international students). Electronic applications accepted. *Expenses:* Tuition, state resident: full-time $5522; part-time $306.80 per credit hour. Tuition, nonresident: full-time $14,253; part-time $792.10 per credit hour. Required fees: $658; $49 per credit hour. One-time fee: $12. Tuition and fees vary according to program. *Financial support:* In 2010–11, 22 research assistantships with full and partial tuition reimbursements (averaging $7,414 per year), 4 teaching assistantships with full and partial tuition reimbursements (averaging $13,950 per year) were awarded; career-related internships or fieldwork, Federal Work-Study, and institutionally sponsored loans also available. Support available to part-time students. Financial award application deadline: 4/1; financial award applicants required to submit FAFSA. *Faculty research:* Human resources, strategic management, marketing strategy, consumer behavior product development, advertising. *Unit head:* Karl Kottemann, Assistant Director, 314-516-5885, Fax: 314-516-6420, E-mail: mba@umsl.edu. *Application contact:* 314-516-5458, Fax: 314-516-6996, E-mail: gradadm@umsl.edu.

University of New Haven, Graduate School, Tagliatela College of Engineering, Program in Engineering and Operations Management, West Haven, CT 06516-1916. Offers MS. *Students:* 13 full-time (3 women), 24 part-time (0 women); includes 3 Black or African American, non-Hispanic/Latino; 3 Asian, non-Hispanic/Latino; 2 Hispanic/Latino, 3 international. Average age 34. 25 applicants, 92% accepted, 20 enrolled. In 2010, 8 master's awarded. *Entrance requirements:* For master's, five or more years' experience in a supervisory role in engineering, technical staff support, engineering or systems management, project management, systems engineering, manufacturing, logistics, industrial engineering, military operations, or quality assurance. Additional exam requirements/recommendations for international students: Required—TOEFL (minimum score 520 paper-based; 190 computer-based; 70 iBT); Recommended—IELTS (minimum score 5.5). *Application deadline:* For fall admission, 5/31 for international students; for winter admission, 10/15 for international students; for spring admission, 1/15 for international students. Application fee: $50. *Unit head:* Dr. Barry Farbrother, Dean, 203-932-7167. *Application contact:* Eloise Gormley, Director of Graduate Admissions, 203-932-7449, Fax: 203-932-7137, E-mail: gradinfo@newhaven.edu.

University of Pittsburgh, Katz Graduate School of Business, Master of Business Administration Programs, Pittsburgh, PA 15260. Offers finance (MBA); information systems (MBA); marketing (MBA); operations management (MBA); organizational behavior and human resource management (MBA); organizational leadership (Certificate); six sigma (Certificate); strategy, environment and organizations (MBA); technology, innovation and entrepreneurship (Certificate); MBA/JD; MBA/MIB; MBA/MPIA; MBA/MSE; MBA/MSIS; MID/MBA. *Accreditation:* AACSB. Part-time and evening/weekend programs available. *Faculty:* 60 full-time (18 women), 22 part-time/adjunct (5 women). *Students:* 232 full-time (75 women), 458 part-time (158 women); includes 34 Black or African American, non-Hispanic/Latino; 1 American Indian or Alaska Native, non-Hispanic/Latino; 20 Asian, non-Hispanic/Latino; 9 Hispanic/Latino, 105 international. Average age 29. 697 applicants, 50% accepted, 174 enrolled. In 2010, 263 master's awarded. *Degree requirements:* For master's, minimum GPA of 3.0. *Entrance requirements:* For master's, GMAT, recommendations, undergraduate transcripts, essay responses, resume, interview, bachelor's degree. Additional exam requirements/recommendations for international students: Required—TOEFL (minimum 600 paper, 250 computer, 100 iBT) or IELTS. *Application deadline:* For fall admission, 4/1 priority date for domestic students, 2/1 priority date for international students. Application fee: $50. Electronic applications accepted. *Expenses:* Tuition, state resident: full-time $17,304; part-time $701 per credit. Tuition, nonresident: full-time $29,554; part-time $1210 per credit. Required fees: $740; $214 per term. Tuition and fees vary according to program. *Financial support:* In 2010–11, 52 students received support. Career-related internships or fieldwork and scholarships/grants available. Financial award application deadline: 3/1; financial award applicants required to submit FAFSA. *Faculty research:* Accounting statements and reporting, incentives and governance, corporate finance, mergers and acquisitions, information systems processes, structures and decision-making, organizational structure, knowledge management and corporate strategy, consumer behavior and marketing models. *Unit head:* William T. Valenta, Assistant Dean, MBA Program Director, 412-648-1610, Fax: 412-648-1659, E-mail: wtvalenta@katz.pitt.edu. *Application contact:* Cliff McCormick, Director MBA Admissions, 412-648-1700, Fax: 412-648-1659, E-mail: mba@katz.pitt.edu.

University of Puerto Rico, Mayagüez Campus, Graduate Studies, College of Business Administration, Mayagüez, PR 00681-9000. Offers business administration (MBA); finance (MBA); human resources (MBA); industrial management (MBA). Part-time and evening/weekend programs available. *Students:* 47 full-time (28 women), 36 part-time (16 women); includes 79 Hispanic/Latino, 4 international. 19 applicants, 47% accepted, 4 enrolled. In 2010, 15 master's awarded. *Degree requirements:* For master's, comprehensive exam. *Entrance requirements:* For master's, GMAT or EXADEP, bachelor's degree with courses in calculus, microeconomics, accounting and statistics. Additional exam requirements/recommendations for international students: Required—TOEFL (minimum score 500 paper-based; 173 computer-based). *Application deadline:* For fall admission, 2/15 for domestic and international students; for spring admission, 9/15 for domestic and international students. Applications are processed on a rolling basis. Application fee: $25. *Expenses:* Tuition, state resident: full-time $1188. Tuition, nonresident: full-time $1188. International tuition: $6126 full-time. Tuition and fees vary according to course level and course load. *Financial support:* In 2010–11, fellowships (averaging $12,000 per year), 2 research assistantships (averaging $15,000 per year), teaching assistantships (averaging $8,500 per year) were awarded; Federal Work-Study and institutionally sponsored loans also available. *Faculty research:* Organizational studies, management, accounting. Total annual research expenditures: $20,000. *Unit head:* Dr. Rosario Ortiz, Graduate Student Coordinator, 787-265-3800, Fax: 787-832-5320, E-mail: rosario.ortiz@upr.edu. *Application contact:* Milagros Soto, Student Administrator, 787-265-3887, Fax: 787-832-5320, E-mail: milagros.soto1@upr.edu.

University of Rhode Island, Graduate School, College of Business Administration, Kingston, RI 02881. Offers accounting (MS); business administration (MBA, PhD), including finance and insurance (PhD), management (PhD), marketing (PhD), operations and supply chain management (MBA); finance (MBA); general business (MBA); management (MBA); marketing (MBA); supply chain management (MBA). *Accreditation:* AACSB. Part-time and evening/weekend programs available. *Faculty:* 54 full-time (15 women), 3 part-time/adjunct (2 women). *Students:* 82 full-time (31 women), 218 part-time (77 women); includes 31 minority (6 Black or African American, non-Hispanic/Latino; 1 American Indian or Alaska Native, non-Hispanic/Latino;

13 Asian, non-Hispanic/Latino; 11 Hispanic/Latino), 29 international. In 2010, 78 master's, 3 doctorates awarded. *Degree requirements:* For master's, comprehensive exam (for some programs), thesis optional; for doctorate, comprehensive exam, thesis/dissertation. *Entrance requirements:* For master's, GMAT or GRE, 2 letters of recommendation, resume; for doctorate, GMAT or GRE, 3 letters of recommendation, resume. Additional exam requirements/recommendations for international students: Required—TOEFL (minimum score 575 paper-based; 233 computer-based; 91 iBT). Application fee: $65. Electronic applications accepted. *Expenses:* Tuition, state resident: full-time $9588; part-time $533 per credit hour. Tuition, nonresident: full-time $22,968; part-time $1276 per credit hour. Required fees: $1282; $68 per semester. Tuition and fees vary according to program. *Financial support:* In 2010–11, 13 teaching assistantships with full and partial tuition reimbursements (averaging $12,432 per year) were awarded. Financial award applicants required to submit FAFSA. Total annual research expenditures: $9,928. *Unit head:* Dr. Mark Higgins, Dean, 401-874-4244, Fax: 401-874-4312, E-mail: markhiggins@uri.edu. *Application contact:* Lisa Lancellotta, Coordinator, MBA Programs, 401-874-4241, Fax: 401-874-4312, E-mail: mba@uri.edu.

University of Southern Indiana, Graduate Studies, College of Science and Engineering, Program in Industrial Management, Evansville, IN 47712-3590. Offers MS. Part-time and evening/weekend programs available. *Faculty:* 2 full-time (0 women). *Students:* 12 part-time (4 women). Average age 33. 2 applicants, 100% accepted, 1 enrolled. In 2010, 1 master's awarded. *Degree requirements:* For master's, project. *Entrance requirements:* For master's, minimum GPA of 2.5, BS in engineering or engineering technology. Additional exam requirements/recommendations for international students: Required—TOEFL (minimum score 550 paper-based; 213 computer-based; 79 iBT), IELTS (minimum score 6). *Application deadline:* For fall admission, 8/15 priority date for domestic students, 3/1 priority date for international students. Applications are processed on a rolling basis. Application fee: $25. Electronic applications accepted. *Expenses:* Tuition, state resident: full-time $4823; part-time $267.95 per credit hour. Tuition, nonresident: full-time $9515; part-time $528.62 per credit hour. Required fees: $220; $22.75 per term. Tuition and fees vary according to course load and reciprocity agreements. *Financial support:* Federal Work-Study, scholarships/grants, tuition waivers (full and partial), and unspecified assistantships available. Financial award application deadline: 3/1; financial award applicants required to submit FAFSA. *Unit head:* Dr. David E. Schultz, Director, 812-464-1881, E-mail: dschultz@usi.edu. *Application contact:* Dr. Peggy F. Harrel, Director, Graduate Studies, 812-465-7015, Fax: 812-464-1956, E-mail: pharrel@usi.edu.

The University of Texas at Arlington, Graduate School, College of Business, Program in Business Administration, Arlington, TX 76019. Offers accounting (PhD); business statistics (PhD); finance (MBA, PhD); information systems (MBA, PhD); management (MBA, PhD); marketing (MBA, PhD); operations management (MBA, PhD); real estate (MBA). *Accreditation:* AACSB. Part-time and evening/weekend programs available. Postbaccalaureate distance learning degree programs offered (no on-campus study). *Students:* 555 full-time (197 women), 378 part-time (144 women); includes 179 minority (55 Black or African American, non-Hispanic/Latino; 1 American Indian or Alaska Native, non-Hispanic/Latino; 58 Asian, non-Hispanic/Latino; 55 Hispanic/Latino; 10 Two or more races, non-Hispanic/Latino), 410 international. 317 applicants, 93% accepted, 196 enrolled. In 2010, 468 master's, 1 doctorate awarded. Terminal master's awarded for partial completion of doctoral program. *Degree requirements:* For master's, thesis optional; for doctorate, comprehensive exam, thesis/dissertation. *Entrance requirements:* For master's, GMAT or GRE; for doctorate, GMAT, minimum GPA of 3.0 (undergraduate), 3.4 (graduate); 30 hours of graduate course work. Additional exam requirements/recommendations for international students: Required—TOEFL (minimum score 550 paper-based; 213 computer-based; 79 iBT). *Application deadline:* For fall admission, 6/1 for domestic students, 4/1 for international students; for spring admission, 10/15 for domestic students, 9/15 for international students. Applications are processed on a rolling basis. Application fee: $35 ($50 for international students). Electronic applications accepted. *Expenses:* Tuition, state resident: full-time $7500. Tuition, nonresident: full-time $13,080. International tuition: $13,250 full-time. *Financial support:* Career-related internships or fieldwork, scholarships/grants, and unspecified assistantships available. Financial award application deadline: 6/1; financial award applicants required to submit FAFSA. *Unit head:* Dr. Edmund Prater, Director of PhD Programs, 817-272-2131, Fax: 817-272-5799. *Application contact:* Melanie McGee, Director of MBA Program, 817-272-3005, Fax: 817-272-5799, E-mail: mwmcgee@uta.edu.

The University of Toledo, College of Graduate Studies, College of Business and Innovation, Department of Information Operations and Technology Management, Toledo, OH 43606-3390. Offers information systems (MBA); manufacturing management (DME); operations management (MBA); supply chain management (Certificate). Part-time and evening/weekend programs available. *Faculty:* 12. *Students:* 36 full-time (8 women), 20 part-time (6 women); includes 4 Black or African American, non-Hispanic/Latino; 3 Asian, non-Hispanic/Latino, 23 international. Average age 32. 41 applicants, 51% accepted, 10 enrolled. In 2010, 16 master's, 4 doctorates awarded. *Degree requirements:* For doctorate, thesis/dissertation. *Entrance requirements:* For master's, doctorate, and Certificate, GMAT, 2.7 GPA on all prior academic work. Three letters of recommendation, a statement of purpose, transcripts from all prior institutions attended. Additional exam requirements/recommendations for international students: Required—TOEFL (minimum score 550 paper-based; 213 computer-based; 80 iBT), IELTS (minimum score 6.5). *Application deadline:* For fall admission, 1/15 priority date for domestic and international students. Applications are processed on a rolling basis. Application fee: $45 ($75 for international students). Electronic applications accepted. *Expenses:* Tuition, state resident: full-time $11,426; part-time $476 per credit hour. Tuition, nonresident: full-time $21,660; part-time $903 per credit hour. One-time fee: $62. *Financial support:* Research assistantships with tuition reimbursements, career-related internships or fieldwork, Federal Work-Study, institutionally sponsored loans, scholarships/grants, tuition waivers (full and partial), unspecified assistantships, and administrative assistantships available. Support available to part-time students. *Unit head:* Dr. T. S. Ragu-Nathan, Chair, 419-530-2427. *Application contact:* Graduate School Office, 419-530-4723, Fax: 419-530-4724, E-mail: grdsch@utnet.utoledo.edu.

Wake Forest University, Schools of Business, Full-time MBA Program, Winston-Salem, NC 27106. Offers consulting/general management (MBA); entrepreneurship (MBA); finance (MBA); health (MBA); marketing (MBA); operations management (MBA); JD/MBA; MD/MBA; MSA/MBA. *Accreditation:* AACSB. *Faculty:* 63 full-time (17 women), 30 part-time/adjunct (9 women). *Students:* 123 full-time (22 women); includes 9 Black or African American, non-Hispanic/Latino; 4 Asian, non-Hispanic/Latino; 2 Hispanic/Latino; 1 Two or more races, non-Hispanic/Latino, 25 international. Average age 28. In 2010, 83 master's awarded. *Degree requirements:* For master's, 65.5 total credit hours. *Entrance requirements:* For master's, GMAT or GRE, letters of recommendation, official transcripts, current resume or curriculum vitae, 2 years of work experience. Additional exam requirements/recommendations for international students: Required—TOEFL (minimum score 600 paper-based; 250 computer-based; 100 iBT), Pearson Test of English (PTE). *Application deadline:* For fall admission, 4/15 for domestic and international students. Applications are processed on a rolling basis. Application fee: $100. Electronic applications accepted. *Expenses:* Contact institution. *Financial support:* In 2010–11, 76 students received support. Career-related internships or fieldwork, scholarships/grants, and unspecified assistantships available. Financial award application deadline: 2/15; financial award applicants required to submit FAFSA. *Faculty research:* The influence of personal relationships on business decision making and management of change; drivers of perceived value and consumer behavior; impact of accounting on auditing, financial, managerial, systems and taxation stakeholders; corporate governance and executive compensation; impact of operations strategies on competitiveness. *Unit head:* Sherry Moss, Director, 336-758-5422, Fax: 336-758-5830, E-mail: admissions@mba.wfu.edu. *Application contact:* Tamara Paquee, Administrative Assistant, 336-758-5422, Fax: 336-758-5830, E-mail: admissions@mba.wfu.edu.

Washington State University, Graduate School, College of Business, Business Administration Programs, Pullman, WA 99164. Offers business administration (MBA, PhD), including accounting (PhD), finance (PhD), management and operations (PhD), management information systems (PhD), marketing (PhD). *Accreditation:* AACSB. *Faculty:* 47. *Students:* 117 full-time (42 women), 117 part-time (30 women); includes 24 minority (1 Black or African American, non-Hispanic/Latino; 17 Asian, non-Hispanic/Latino; 5 Hispanic/Latino; 1 Two or more races, non-Hispanic/Latino), 48 international. Average age 32. 347 applicants, 19% accepted, 43 enrolled. In 2010, 58 master's, 5 doctorates awarded. *Degree requirements:* For master's, comprehensive exam (for some programs), thesis (for some programs), final presentation; for doctorate, comprehensive exam, thesis/dissertation, oral and written exams. *Entrance requirements:* For master's and doctorate, GMAT, minimum GPA of 3.0, 3 letters of recommendation. Additional exam requirements/recommendations for international students: Required—TOEFL. *Application deadline:* For fall admission, 3/1 priority date for domestic students, 3/1 for international students; for spring admission, 6/1 priority date for domestic students, 6/1 for international students. Applications are processed on a rolling basis. Application fee: $50. Electronic applications accepted. *Expenses:* Tuition, state resident: full-time $8552; part-time $443 per credit. Tuition, nonresident: full-time $21,650; part-time $1083 per credit. Required fees: $846. *Financial support:* In 2010–11, 102 students received support, including 36 teaching assistantships with full and partial tuition reimbursements available (averaging $18,204 per year); career-related internships or fieldwork, Federal Work-Study, institutionally sponsored loans, health care benefits, tuition waivers (partial), unspecified assistantships, and teaching associateships also available. Financial award application deadline: 4/1. Total annual research expenditures: $344,000. *Unit head:* Dr. Eric Spangenberg, Dean, 509-335-8150, E-mail: ers@wsu.edu. *Application contact:* Graduate School Admissions, 800-GRADWSU, Fax: 509-335-1949, E-mail: gradsch@wsu.edu.

Wilkes University, College of Graduate and Professional Studies, Jay S. Sidhu School of Business and Leadership, Wilkes-Barre, PA 18766-0002. Offers accounting (MBA); entrepreneurship (MBA); finance (MBA); health care administration (MBA); human resource management (MBA); international business (MBA); marketing (MBA); operations management (MBA); organizational leadership and development (MBA). *Accreditation:* ACBSP. Part-time and evening/weekend programs available. *Students:* 39 full-time (16 women), 146 part-time (71 women); includes 5 Black or African American, non-Hispanic/Latino; 2 Asian, non-Hispanic/Latino; 1 Hispanic/Latino; 1 Two or more races, non-Hispanic/Latino, 16 international. Average age 30. In 2010, 85 master's awarded. *Entrance requirements:* For master's, GMAT. Additional exam requirements/recommendations for international students: Required—TOEFL (minimum score 550 paper-based; 213 computer-based; 79 iBT). *Application deadline:* Applications are processed on a rolling basis. Application fee: $45 ($65 for international students). Electronic applications accepted. *Expenses:* Contact institution. *Financial support:* Federal Work-Study and unspecified assistantships available. Financial award application deadline: 3/1; financial award applicants required to submit FAFSA. *Unit head:* Dr. Paul Browne, Dean, 570-408-4701, Fax: 570-408-7846, E-mail: paul.browne@wilkes.edu. *Application contact:* Kathleen Houlihan, Director of Graduate Studies, 570-408-3235, Fax: 570-408-7846, E-mail: kathleen.houlihan@wilkes.edu.

OVERVIEW

The area of risk management and insurance is a crucial part of the financing aspect of the business sector. For companies to continue to grow, they must seek out a multitude of financing options, while protecting company assets. An MBA with a concentration in insurance and risk management program is designed for students interested in addressing the needs of individuals and companies both in commercial and business liabilities. Core coursework in this program is designed to strengthen students' understanding of the principles of accounting, economics, and finance, while also gaining practical insights on strategic management. Students refine their research abilities and learn innovative techniques for analyzing and resolving complex insurance and risk management issues. Students who pursue an online MBA in insurance and risk management develop leadership, effective communication, organization, and critical-thinking skills, in addition to building expertise in understanding the legal, actuarial, financial, and economic principles that are intertwined throughout the corporate aspect of insurance and risk management.

Required courses of study may include:

- Business and Insurance Law
- Corporate Accounting
- Ethics and Leadership
- Financial Management of Property-Casualty Insurers
- Insurance and Risk Management
- Management and Organizational Behavior
- Managerial Economics
- Managing a Diverse Workforce
- Property-Casualty Insurance Contracts
- Quantitative Analysis and Decision Making for Management
- Strategic Management of Property-Casualty Insurers
- Strategic Marketing

Elective courses of study may include:

- Advanced Spreadsheets and Databases
- Employee Benefits
- Global Insurance and Risk Management
- Personal Financial Planning
- Reinsurance Principles and Practices
- Risk Assessment
- Risk Control
- Risk Financing
- Surplus Lines Insurance Operations

Graduates with an MBA in insurance and risk management are ready for professional experiences in assessing and quantifying business risks and knowing the necessary steps to reduce and control them. They have the knowledge, skills, and abilities to analyze liabilities, taxation, retirement funds, and compensation in line with an organization's policies, ethics, culture, values, and goals. Careers that develop, implement, and enforce policies and procedures within a company to mitigate risks are possibilities in positions such as consulting, risk management, employee benefit management, insurance company management, personal financial planning, and brokerage.

HELPFUL ORGANIZATIONS/ PUBLICATIONS/BLOGS

American Risk and Insurance Association (ARIA)
http://www.aria.org/

American Risk and Insurance Association (ARIA) is the premier professional association of insurance scholars and other thoughtful risk management and insurance professionals. Through ARIA, members receive valuable tools and opportunities for enlightenment, growth, and education.

Founded in 1932, the association's membership is comprised of academics, individual insurance industry representatives, students, and retirees. ARIA emphasizes research relevant to the operational concerns and functions of insurance professionals and provides resources, information, and support on important insurance issues. Those provisions come from a variety of awards, publications, and conferences, including *The Journal of Risk and Insurance, Risk Management and Insurance Review, ARIA's Annual Meeting*, and its annual *Risk Theory Seminar*.

ARIA's mission is dedicated to advancing knowledge in risk management and insurance and enhancing the career development of its members. ARIA's vision is one of an association of scholars in the field of risk management and insurance striving to be a leading advocate for risk management and insurance and education. This vision is carried out by providing recognized intellectual leadership in risk management and insurance, including premier journals in the field; supporting the intellectual growth and professional development of members and fostering relationships among members; recruiting and developing new talent in the field of risk management and insurance; nurturing relationships with industry, consumers, and policy makers; and fostering relationships with other organizations, including international organizations devoted to education and research in risk management and insurance.

ARIA's goal is to be the most widely recognized and highly respected risk management and insurance academic organization in the world by providing programs, awards, and services that expand risk management and insurance knowledge, improve academic instruction, and position its members for success.

International Association of Insurance Professionals (IAIP)
http://www.internationalinsuranceprofessionals.org/

The International Association of Insurance Professionals (IAIP) is a professional association open to individuals in the insurance and risk management industries. IAIP is best known for providing insurance education, skills enhancement, and leadership development to its members.

IAIP provides its members with the opportunity to increase business productivity and profitability by participating in educational offerings and making business connections with other industry professionals. Through the IAIP Web site, members are able to communicate with other members, access educational offerings, stay up-to-date with the latest industry and association news, find out about upcoming events, and collaborate and learn within its online community.

Society of Insurance Research (SIR)

http://www.sirnet.org/

The Society of Insurance Research (SIR) was founded in 1970 to provide a forum for the free exchange of ideas in all areas of insurance research and has expanded to marketing and planning, as well as research. The Society has since grown to include representation from many different organizations: insurance and non-insurance companies, government agencies, institutions of higher education, and trade associations. Members come from equally divergent areas: actuarial, agency, claims, consumer relations, corporate planning, education, financial planning, government relations, information services, management consulting, marketing and sales, modeling, operations, product development and analysis, reinsurance, risk management, statistical research, and underwriting.

For more than forty years, the Society of Insurance Research has served the insurance industry by providing high-caliber forums for technical education, networking, and professional growth. The activities of SIR are intended to provide opportunities to discuss current issues with fellow researchers and planners, including an annual conference and business meeting, seminars, workshops, and local networking meetings.

CAREER ASPIRATIONS: A PROSPECTIVE POSITION

Insurance Finance Transformation Senior Manager

Job Description

The Insurance Finance Transformation Senior Manager role requires the candidate to understand the business challenges of insurance clients and develop solutions to those challenges that solve the client's business and technology challenges. This is accomplished by having a deep understanding of financial management in the insurance industry and demonstrating the ability to apply financial and management reporting solutions and the ability to provide high-quality "trusted advisor" advice to customers to ensure appropriate process and technology solutions are proposed.

Requirements

- Lead project teams and ensure for successful delivery of financial reporting and performance management solutions to clients.
- Develop deep relationships within the client organization.
- Build effective cross-functional teams across diverse stakeholder groups.

Qualifications

- Bachelor's degree/MBA preferred
- Minimum 8 years of experience in financial process improvement and 5 years of experience in the insurance industry
- Minimum 4 years consulting experience at the manager or senior manager level at a consulting firm
- Experience in finance strategy consulting from a Tier 1 consulting firm
- Extensive experience reengineering financial closing, reporting, allocations, and other financial management practices for insurance organizations
- Experience defining and implementing performance metrics, management accounting methodologies, and performance management applications in financial services firms
- Exhibit working knowledge of shared services functional areas and business case
- Current management consulting experience at national or global consulting firm
- Understanding of insurance-specific management and regulatory reporting requirements and KPIs
- Ability to independently manage and grow existing client engagements
- Understanding of current events impacting the financial services industry and implications on financial management
- Ability to interact effectively with senior-level client executives
- Effective team management and leadership

ACTUARIAL SCIENCE

Ball State University, Graduate School, College of Sciences and Humanities, Department of Mathematical Sciences, Program in Actuarial Science, Muncie, IN 47306-1099. Offers MA. *Students:* 25 full-time (12 women), 8 part-time (1 woman); includes 1 Black or African American, non-Hispanic/Latino, 17 international. Average age 27. 40 applicants, 65% accepted, 8 enrolled. In 2010, 13 master's awarded. *Entrance requirements:* For master's, GMAT. Application fee: $50. *Expenses:* Tuition, state resident: full-time $6160; part-time $299 per credit hour. Tuition, nonresident: full-time $16,020; part-time $783 per credit hour. Required fees: $2278; $95 per credit hour. *Financial support:* In 2010–11, 6 teaching assistantships with full tuition reimbursements (averaging $11,450 per year) were awarded. Financial award application deadline: 3/1. *Unit head:* Dr. Sheryl Smith, Director, 765-285-8681, Fax: 765-285-1721. *Application contact:* Dr. Hanspeter Fischer, Director, 765-285-8640, Fax: 765-285-1721.

Boston University, Metropolitan College, Department of Actuarial Science, Boston, MA 02215. Offers MS. Part-time and evening/weekend programs available. *Faculty:* 1 (woman) full-time, 6 part-time/adjunct (1 woman). *Students:* 48 full-time (24 women), 40 part-time (18 women); includes 28 minority (3 Black or African American, non-Hispanic/Latino; 11 Asian, non-Hispanic/Latino; 13 Hispanic/Latino; 1 Two or more races, non-Hispanic/Latino), 50 international. Average age 25. 134 applicants, 57% accepted, 40 enrolled. In 2010, 31 master's awarded. *Entrance requirements:* For master's, prerequisite coursework in calculus. Additional exam requirements/recommendations for international students: Required—TOEFL (minimum score 550 paper-based; 213 computer-based; 84 iBT). *Application deadline:* For fall admission, 5/31 priority date for domestic students, 5/15 priority date for international students; for spring admission, 10/31 priority date for domestic students, 10/15 priority date for international students. Applications are processed on a rolling basis. Application fee: $70. Electronic applications accepted. *Expenses:* Tuition: Full-time $39,314; part-time $1228 per credit. Required fees: $40 per semester. *Financial support:* In 2010–11, 2 research assistantships with full tuition reimbursements (averaging $18,800 per year), 6 teaching assistantships with full tuition reimbursements (averaging $18,800 per year) were awarded; career-related internships or fieldwork, scholarships/grants, and unspecified assistantships also available. *Faculty research:* Survival models, life contingencies, numerical analysis, operations research, compound interest. *Unit head:* Lois K. Horwitz, Chairman, 617-353-8758, Fax: 617-353-8757, E-mail: lhorwitz@bu.edu. *Application contact:* Andrea Cozzi, Administrative Coordinator, 617-353-8758, Fax: 617-353-8757, E-mail: actuary@bu.edu.

Central Connecticut State University, School of Graduate Studies, School of Arts and Sciences, Department of Mathematical Sciences, New Britain, CT 06050-4010. Offers data mining (MS, Certificate); mathematics (MA, MS, Certificate, Sixth Year Certificate), including actuarial science (MA), computer science (MA), statistics (MA). Part-time and evening/weekend programs available. *Faculty:* 33 full-time (10 women), 65 part-time/adjunct (28 women). *Students:* 20 full-time (10 women), 131 part-time (74 women); includes 18 minority (5 Black or African American, non-Hispanic/Latino; 5 Asian, non-Hispanic/Latino; 6 Hispanic/Latino; 2 Two or more races, non-Hispanic/Latino), 8 international. Average age 37. 76 applicants, 59% accepted, 28 enrolled. In 2010, 29 master's, 4 other advanced degrees awarded. *Degree requirements:* For master's, comprehensive exam, thesis or alternative; for other advanced degree, qualifying exam. *Entrance requirements:* For master's, minimum undergraduate GPA of 2.7. Additional exam requirements/recommendations for international students: Required—TOEFL. *Application deadline:* For fall admission, 7/1 for domestic students; for spring admission, 12/1 for domestic students. Applications are processed on a rolling basis. Application fee: $50. Electronic applications accepted. *Expenses:* Tuition, area resident: Full-time $5012; part-time $470 per credit. Tuition, state resident: full-time $7518; part-time $482 per credit. Tuition, nonresident: full-time $13,962; part-time $482 per credit. Required fees: $3772. One-time fee: $62 part-time. *Financial support:* In 2010–11, 6 students received support, including 2 research assistantships; career-related internships or fieldwork, Federal Work-Study, scholarships/grants, and unspecified assistantships also available. Support available to part-time students. Financial award application deadline: 2/15; financial award applicants required to submit FAFSA. *Faculty research:* Statistics, actuarial mathematics, computer systems and engineering, computer programming techniques, operations research. *Unit head:* Dr. Jeffrey McGowan, Chair, 860-832-2835. *Application contact:* Dr. Jeffrey McGowan, Chair, 860-832-2835.

DePaul University, College of Liberal Arts and Sciences, Department of Mathematical Sciences, Chicago, IL 60614. Offers applied mathematics (MS), including actuarial science or statistics; applied statistics (MS, Certificate); mathematics education (MA). Part-time and evening/weekend programs available. *Faculty:* 23 full-time (6 women), 18 part-time/adjunct (5 women). *Students:* 111 full-time (60 women), 66 part-time (30 women); includes 16 Black or African American, non-Hispanic/Latino; 17 Asian, non-Hispanic/Latino; 16 Hispanic/Latino; 2 Two or more races, non-Hispanic/Latino, 10 international. Average age 30. 40 applicants, 100% accepted. In 2010, 30 master's awarded. *Degree requirements:* For master's, comprehensive exam.

Entrance requirements: Additional exam requirements/recommendations for international students: Required—TOEFL. *Application deadline:* For fall admission, 7/30 for domestic students, 6/30 for international students; for winter admission, 11/30 for domestic students, 10/31 for international students; for spring admission, 2/15 for domestic students. Applications are processed on a rolling basis. Application fee: $25. *Financial support:* In 2010–11, 12 students received support, including research assistantships with partial tuition reimbursements available (averaging $6,000 per year); teaching assistantships, tuition waivers (full) also available. Financial award application deadline: 4/30. *Faculty research:* Verbally prime algebras, enveloping algebras of Lie, superalgebras and related rings, harmonic analysis, estimation theory. *Unit head:* Dr. Ahmed I. Zayed, Chairperson, 773-325-7806, Fax: 773-325-7807, E-mail: azayed@depaul.edu. *Application contact:* Ann Spittle, Director of Graduate Admissions, 312-362-8300, Fax: 312-362-5749, E-mail: admitdpu@depaul.edu.

George Mason University, College of Science, Department of Mathematical Sciences, Fairfax, VA 22030. Offers actuarial sciences (Certificate); mathematics (MS, PhD). Evening/weekend programs available. *Faculty:* 30 full-time (7 women), 10 part-time/adjunct (4 women). *Students:* 10 full-time (2 women), 40 part-time (9 women); includes 8 minority (2 Black or African American, non-Hispanic/Latino; 3 Asian, non-Hispanic/Latino; 3 Hispanic/Latino), 4 international. Average age 31. 61 applicants, 48% accepted, 12 enrolled. In 2010, 1 doctorate, 6 other advanced degrees awarded. *Degree requirements:* For master's, comprehensive exam, thesis optional. *Entrance requirements:* For master's, minimum GPA of 3.0 in last 60 hours of course work. Additional exam requirements/recommendations for international students: Required—TOEFL (minimum score 570 paper-based; 230 computer-based; 88 iBT). *Application deadline:* For fall admission, 5/1 for domestic students; for spring admission, 11/1 for domestic students. Application fee: $100. Electronic applications accepted. *Expenses:* Tuition, state resident: full-time $8192; part-time $440 per credit hour. Tuition, nonresident: full-time $22,952; part-time $1055 per credit hour. Required fees: $2364; $99 per credit hour. *Financial support:* In 2010–11, 19 students received support, including 3 fellowships (averaging $18,000 per year), 4 research assistantships (averaging $16,067 per year), 12 teaching assistantships (averaging $15,748 per year); career-related internships or fieldwork, Federal Work-Study, scholarships/grants, unspecified assistantships, and health care benefits (full-time research or teaching assistantship recipients) also available. Financial award application deadline: 3/1; financial award applicants required to submit FAFSA. *Faculty research:* Nonlinear dynamics and topology, with an emphasis on global bifurcations and chaos; numerical and theoretical methods of dynamical systems. Total annual research expenditures: $522,044. *Unit head:* Klaus Fischer, Chair, 703-993-1462, Fax: 703-993-1491. *Application contact:* Dr. David Walnut, Graduate Coordinator, 703-993-1478, E-mail: dwalnut@gmu.edu.

Maryville University of Saint Louis, College of Arts and Sciences, St. Louis, MO 63141-7299. Offers actuarial science (MS); organizational leadership (MA). Part-time and evening/weekend programs available. *Faculty:* 6 full-time (all women), 1 part-time/adjunct (0 women). *Students:* 13 full-time (7 women), 13 part-time (10 women); includes 2 Black or African American, non-Hispanic/Latino; 1 Asian, non-Hispanic/Latino; 1 Two or more races, non-Hispanic/Latino, 3 international. Average age 31. In 2010, 7 master's awarded. *Entrance requirements:* For master's, GRE with minimum score of 600 (MS), strong mathematics background, 2 letters of recommendation, and personal statement (MS). Additional exam requirements/recommendations for international students: Required—TOEFL (minimum score 550 paper-based; 213 computer-based; 80 iBT). *Application deadline:* Applications are processed on a rolling basis. Application fee: $40 ($60 for international students). Electronic applications accepted. *Expenses:* Tuition: Full-time $21,100; part-time $633.50 per credit hour. Required fees: $150 per semester. *Financial support:* Application deadline: 3/1. *Unit head:* Dr. Dan Sparling, Dean, 314-529-9436, Fax: 314-529-9965, E-mail: dsparling@maryville.edu. *Application contact:* Denise Evans, Assistant Vice President, Adult and Continuing Education, 314-529-9676, Fax: 314-529-9927, E-mail: devans1@maryville.edu.

St. John's University, The Peter J. Tobin College of Business, School of Risk Management and Actuarial Science, Queens, NY 11439. Offers MBA, MS. *Students:* 67 full-time (30 women), 31 part-time (10 women); includes 23 minority (6 Black or African American, non-Hispanic/Latino; 6 Asian, non-Hispanic/Latino; 7 Hispanic/Latino; 4 Two or more races, non-Hispanic/Latino), 51 international. Average age 25. 155 applicants, 68% accepted, 54 enrolled. In 2010, 43 master's awarded. *Degree requirements:* For master's, comprehensive exam (for some programs), thesis optional. *Entrance requirements:* For master's, GMAT or GRE (MS in management of risk), 2 letters of recommendation, resume, transcripts, essay. Additional exam requirements/recommendations for international students: Required—TOEFL (minimum score 600 paper-based; 250 computer-based; 100 iBT), IELTS (minimum score 5.5). *Application deadline:* For fall admission, 5/1 priority date for domestic and international students; for spring admission, 11/1 priority date for domestic and international students. Applications are processed on a rolling basis. Application fee: $70. Electronic applications accepted. *Expenses:* Contact institution. *Financial support:* Research assistantships available. *Faculty research:* Insurance company operations and financial analysis, enterprise risk management, risk theory and modeling, credibility theory and actuarial price modeling, international insurance. Total annual research expenditures: $50,000. *Unit head:* Dr. W Jean Kwon, Chair, 212-277-5196, E-mail: kwonw@stjohns.edu. *Application contact:* Carol Swanberg, Assistant Dean, Director of Graduate Admissions, 718-990-1345, Fax: 718-990-5242, E-mail: tobingradnyc@stjohns.edu.

University of Central Florida, College of Sciences, Department of Statistics and Actuarial Science, Orlando, FL 32816. Offers SAS data mining (Certificate); statistical computing (MS). Part-time and evening/weekend programs available. *Faculty:* 10 full-time (3 women), 2 part-time/adjunct (0 women). *Students:* 29 full-time (12 women), 13 part-time (4 women); includes 3 Black or African American, non-Hispanic/Latino; 3 Asian, non-Hispanic/Latino; 1 Hispanic/Latino, 19 international. Average age 30. 59 applicants, 90% accepted, 26 enrolled. In 2010, 22 master's, 7 other advanced degrees awarded. *Degree requirements:* For master's, comprehensive exam. *Entrance requirements:* For master's, GRE General Test, minimum GPA of 3.0 in last 60 hours. Additional exam requirements/recommendations for international students: Required—TOEFL. *Application deadline:* For fall admission, 7/15 for domestic students; for spring admission, 12/1 for domestic students. Application fee: $30. Electronic applications accepted. *Expenses:* Tuition, state resident: part-time $256.56 per credit hour. Tuition, nonresident: part-time $1011.52 per credit hour. Part-time tuition and fees vary according to program. *Financial support:* In 2010–11, 13 students received support, including 1 fellowship with partial tuition reimbursement available (averaging $4,000 per year), 1 research assistantship with partial tuition reimbursement available (averaging $9,400 per year), 12 teaching assistantships with partial tuition reimbursements available (averaging $11,100 per year); career-related internships or fieldwork, Federal Work-Study, institutionally sponsored loans, tuition waivers (partial), and unspecified assistantships also available. Financial award application deadline: 3/1; financial award applicants required to submit FAFSA. *Faculty research:* Multivariate analysis, quality control, shrinkage estimation. *Unit head:* Dr. David Nickerson, Chair, 407-823-2289, Fax: 407-823-5419, E-mail: nickerson@mail.ucf.edu. *Application contact:* Dr. David Nickerson, Chair, 407-823-2289, Fax: 407-823-5419, E-mail: nickerson@mail.ucf.edu.

University of Illinois at Urbana–Champaign, Graduate College, College of Liberal Arts and Sciences, Department of Mathematics, Champaign, IL 61820. Offers applied mathematics (MS); applied mathematics: actuarial science (MS); mathematics (MA, MS, PhD); teaching of mathematics (MS). *Faculty:* 65 full-time (5 women), 4 part-time/adjunct (0 women). *Students:* 159 full-time (45 women), 35 part-time (10 women); includes 13 minority (7 Asian, non-Hispanic/Latino; 4 Hispanic/Latino; 2 Two or more races, non-Hispanic/Latino), 105 international. 454 applicants, 22% accepted, 50 enrolled. In 2010, 48 master's, 19 doctorates awarded. *Entrance requirements:* For master's and doctorate, GRE General Test, GRE Subject Test (math), minimum GPA of 3.0. Additional exam requirements/recommendations for international students: Required—TOEFL (minimum score 550 paper-based; 213 computer-based). *Application deadline:* Applications are processed on a rolling basis. Application fee: $75 ($90 for international students). Electronic applications accepted. *Financial support:* In 2010–11, 26 fellowships, 40 research assistantships, 146 teaching assistantships were awarded; tuition waivers (full and partial) also available. *Unit head:* Sheldon Katz, Chair, 217-265-6258, Fax: 217-333-9576, E-mail: katzs@illinois.edu. *Application contact:* Marci Blocher, Office Support Specialist, 217-333-3350, Fax: 217-333-9576, E-mail: mblocher@illinois.edu.

University of Northern Iowa, Graduate College, College of Natural Sciences, Department of Mathematics, Cedar Falls, IA 50614. Offers industrial mathematics (PSM), including actuarial science, continuous quality improvement, mathematical computing and modeling; mathematics (MA), including mathematics, secondary; mathematics for middle grades 4-8 (MA). Part-time programs available. *Students:* 19 full-time (13 women), 22 part-time (17 women); includes 2 minority (1 Asian, non-Hispanic/Latino; 1 Two or more races, non-Hispanic/Latino), 5 international. 20 applicants, 40% accepted, 6 enrolled. In 2010, 18 master's awarded. *Degree requirements:* For master's, comprehensive exam (for some programs), thesis or alternative. *Entrance requirements:* For master's, minimum GPA of 3.0. Additional exam requirements/recommendations for international students: Required—TOEFL (minimum score 600 paper-based; 250 computer-based; 100 iBT). *Application deadline:* For fall admission, 8/1 priority date for domestic students. Applications are processed on a rolling basis. Application fee: $50 ($70 for international students). Electronic applications accepted. *Financial support:* Career-related internships or fieldwork, Federal Work-Study, scholarships/grants, and tuition waivers (full and partial) available. Support available to part-time students. Financial award application deadline: 2/1. *Unit head:* Dr. Douglas Mupasiri, Interim Head, 319-273-2012, Fax: 319-273-2546, E-mail: douglas.mupasiri@uni.edu. *Application contact:* Laurie S. Russell, Record Analyst, 319-273-2623, Fax: 319-273-2885, E-mail: laurie.russell@uni.edu.

University of Wisconsin–Madison, Graduate School, Wisconsin School of Business, MS Program in Actuarial Science, Madison, WI 53706-1380. Offers MS. *Faculty:* 5 full-time (2 women), 1 part-time/adjunct (0 women). *Students:* 8 full-time (1 woman); includes 1 Black or African American, non-Hispanic/Latino, 2 international. Average age 24. 67 applicants, 10% accepted, 3 enrolled. In 2010, 8 master's awarded. *Entrance requirements:* For master's,

GMAT or GRE. Additional exam requirements/recommendations for international students: Required—Pearson Test of English (minimum score 73, written 80); Recommended—TOEFL (minimum score 623 paper-based; 263 computer-based; 106 iBT), IELTS (minimum score 7.5). *Application deadline:* For fall admission, 3/15 for domestic and international students. Application fee: $56. Electronic applications accepted. *Expenses:* Contact institution. *Financial support:* In 2010–11, 2 students received support, including 2 teaching assistantships with full tuition reimbursements available (averaging $9,392 per year); Federal Work-Study, institutionally sponsored loans, scholarships/grants, health care benefits, and unspecified assistantships also available. Financial award application deadline: 3/15; financial award applicants required to submit FAFSA. *Faculty research:* Fuzzy logic, business forecasting, health insurance, international insurance. *Unit head:* Prof. Marjorie Rosenberg, Chair, 608-262-1683, E-mail: mrosenberg@bus.wisc.edu. *Application contact:* Belle Heberling, Assistant Director for Research Programs, 608-262-3749, Fax: 608-890-0180, E-mail: ms@bus.wisc.edu.

INSURANCE

Florida State University, The Graduate School, College of Business, Tallahassee, FL 32306-1110. Offers accounting (M Acc), including accounting information services, assurance services, corporate accounting, taxation; business administration (MBA, PhD), including accounting (PhD), finance (PhD), management information systems (PhD), marketing (PhD), organizational behavior (PhD), risk management and insurance (PhD), strategic management (PhD); finance (MS); insurance (MSM); management information systems (MS); JD/MBA; MSW/MBA. *Accreditation:* AACSB. Part-time programs available. Postbaccalaureate distance learning degree programs offered (no on-campus study). *Faculty:* 107 full-time (31 women). *Students:* 196 full-time (76 women), 310 part-time (109 women); includes 27 Black or African American, non-Hispanic/Latino; 1 American Indian or Alaska Native, non-Hispanic/Latino; 31 Asian, non-Hispanic/Latino; 30 Hispanic/Latino. Average age 30. 702 applicants, 33% accepted, 205 enrolled. In 2010, 268 master's, 17 doctorates awarded. Terminal master's awarded for partial completion of doctoral program. *Degree requirements:* For doctorate, comprehensive exam, thesis/dissertation. *Entrance requirements:* For master's, GMAT, work experience (MBA, MS), minimum GPA of 3.0, letters of recommendation; for doctorate, GMAT, minimum graduate GPA of 3.5, letters of recommendation. Additional exam requirements/recommendations for international students: Required—TOEFL (minimum score 600 paper-based; 80 computer-based); Recommended—IELTS (minimum score 6.5). *Application deadline:* For fall admission, 6/1 for domestic students, 5/1 for international students; for spring admission, 10/1 for domestic students, 9/1 for international students. Applications are processed on a rolling basis. Application fee: $30. Electronic applications accepted. *Expenses:* Tuition, state resident: full-time $8238.24. *Financial support:* In 2010–11, 86 students received support, including 12 fellowships with full tuition reimbursements available (averaging $7,161 per year), 30 research assistantships with full tuition reimbursements available (averaging $6,000 per year), 43 teaching assistantships with full tuition reimbursements available (averaging $15,000 per year); career-related internships or fieldwork, scholarships/grants, health care benefits, tuition waivers (full and partial), and unspecified assistantships also available. Support available to part-time students. Financial award application deadline: 1/1. *Unit head:* Dr. Caryn Beck-Dudley, Dean, 850-644-3090, Fax: 850-644-0915. *Application contact:* Lisa Beverly, Director, Graduate Programs Admissions, 850-644-6458, Fax: 850-644-0588, E-mail: lbeverly@cob.fsu.edu.

St. John's University, The Peter J. Tobin College of Business, School of Risk Management and Actuarial Science, Queens, NY 11439. Offers MBA, MS. *Students:* 67 full-time (30 women), 31 part-time (10 women); includes 23 minority (6 Black or African American, non-Hispanic/Latino; 6 Asian, non-Hispanic/Latino; 7 Hispanic/Latino; 4 Two or more races, non-Hispanic/Latino), 51 international. Average age 25. 155 applicants, 68% accepted, 54 enrolled. In 2010, 43 master's awarded. *Degree requirements:* For master's, comprehensive exam (for some programs), thesis optional. *Entrance requirements:* For master's, GMAT or GRE (MS in management of risk), 2 letters of recommendation, resume, transcripts, essay. Additional exam requirements/recommendations for international students: Required—TOEFL (minimum score 600 paper-based; 250 computer-based; 100 iBT), IELTS (minimum score 5.5). *Application deadline:* For fall admission, 5/1 priority date for domestic and international students; for spring admission, 11/1 priority date for domestic and international students. Applications are processed on a rolling basis. Application fee: $70. Electronic applications accepted. *Expenses:* Contact institution. *Financial support:* Research assistantships available. *Faculty research:* Insurance company operations and financial analysis, enterprise risk management, risk theory and modeling, credibility theory and actuarial price modeling, international insurance. Total annual research expenditures: $50,000. *Unit head:* Dr. W Jean Kwon, Chair, 212-277-5196, E-mail: kwonw@stjohns.edu. *Application contact:* Carol Swanberg, Assistant Dean, Director of Graduate Admissions, 718-990-1345, Fax: 718-990-5242, E-mail: tobingradnyc@stjohns.edu.

Tennessee Technological University, Graduate School, College of Business, Cookeville, TN 38505. Offers accounting (MBA); finance (MBA); human resource management (MBA); international business (MBA); management information systems (MBA); risk management & insurance (MBA). *Accreditation:* AACSB. Part-time and evening/weekend programs available. *Faculty:* 28 full-time (5 women). *Students:* 58 full-time (18 women), 139 part-time (49 women); includes 10 Black or African American, non-Hispanic/Latino; 7 Asian, non-Hispanic/Latino; 7 Hispanic/Latino; 1 Native Hawaiian or other Pacific Islander, non-Hispanic/Latino. Average age 25. 211 applicants, 51% accepted, 59 enrolled. In 2010, 116 master's awarded. *Entrance requirements:* For master's, GMAT. Additional exam requirements/recommendations for international students: Required—TOEFL (minimum score 550 paper-based; 79 iBT), IELTS (minimum score 5.5). *Application deadline:* For fall admission, 8/1 for domestic and international students; for spring admission, 12/1 for domestic students, 10/1 for international students. Application fee: $25 ($30 for international students). Electronic applications accepted. *Expenses:* Tuition, state resident: full-time $7934; part-time $388 per credit hour. Tuition, nonresident: full-time $19,758; part-time $962 per credit hour. *Financial support:* In 2010–11, 5 fellowships (averaging $10,000 per year), 18 research assistantships (averaging $4,000 per year), teaching assistantships (averaging $4,000 per year) were awarded. Support available to part-time students. Financial award application deadline: 4/1. *Unit head:* Dr. Tom Timmerman, Director, 931-372-3600, Fax: 931-372-6249. *Application contact:* Shelia K. Kendrick, Coordinator of Graduate Admissions, 931-372-3808, Fax: 931-372-3497, E-mail: skendrick@tntech.edu.

Thomas M. Cooley Law School, Graduate Programs, Lansing, MI 48901-3038. Offers corporate law and finance (LL M); general, self-directed (LL M); insurance (LL M); intellectual property (LL M); law (JD); taxation (LL M); U. S. law for foreign attorneys (LL M). *Accreditation:* ABA. Part-time and evening/weekend programs available. Postbaccalaureate distance learning degree programs offered. *Faculty:* 127 full-time (53 women), 196 part-time/adjunct (78 women). *Students:* 718 full-time (342 women), 3,283 part-time (1,607 women); includes 1,071 minority (532 Black or African American, non-Hispanic/Latino; 19 American Indian or Alaska Native, non-Hispanic/Latino; 207 Asian, non-Hispanic/Latino; 219 Hispanic/Latino; 10 Native Hawaiian or other Pacific Islander, non-Hispanic/Latino; 84 Two or more races, non-Hispanic/Latino), 215 international. Average age 26. 4,922 applicants, 83% accepted, 1583 enrolled. In 2010, 918 first professional degrees awarded. *Degree requirements:* For master's, thesis optional; for JD, minimum of 3 credits of clinical experience. *Entrance requirements:* For JD, LSAT, CAS; for master's, JD or LL B. Additional exam requirements/recommendations for international students: Required—TOEFL. *Application deadline:* For fall admission, 9/1 for domestic and international students; for winter admission, 1/1 for domestic and international students; for spring admission, 5/1 for domestic and international students. Applications are processed on a rolling basis. Application fee: $0. Electronic applications accepted. *Expenses:* Tuition: Full-time $30,604; part-time $2186 per credit hour. Required fees: $40. *Financial support:* In 2010–11, 2,187 students received support. Federal Work-Study and scholarships/grants available. Support available to part-time students. Financial award applicants required to submit FAFSA. *Faculty research:* Wrongful convictions, civil rights, environmental law, litigation techniques, death penalty. *Unit head:* Don LeDuc, President and Dean, 517-371-5140. *Application contact:* Stephanie Gregg, Assistant Dean of Admissions, 517-371-5140, Fax: 517-334-5718, E-mail: greggs@cooley.edu.

University of Wisconsin–Madison, Graduate School, Wisconsin School of Business, Doctoral Program in Actuarial Science, Risk Management and Insurance, Madison, WI 53706-1380. Offers PhD. *Faculty:* 5 full-time (2 women), 2 part-time/adjunct (0 women). *Students:* 8 full-time (6 women); includes 1 Black or African American, non-Hispanic/Latino, 6 international. Average age 29. 27 applicants, 11% accepted, 2 enrolled. In 2010, 2 doctorates awarded. *Degree requirements:* For doctorate, comprehensive exam, thesis/dissertation. *Entrance requirements:* For doctorate, GMAT or GRE General Test. Additional exam requirements/recommendations for international students: Required—Pearson Test of English (minimum score 73, written 80); Recommended—TOEFL (minimum score 623 paper-based; 263 computer-based; 106 iBT), IELTS (minimum score 7.5). *Application deadline:* For fall admission, 12/15 priority date for domestic and international students. Application fee: $56. Electronic applications accepted. *Expenses:* Tuition, state resident: full-time $9887; part-time $617.96 per credit. Tuition, nonresident: full-time $24,054; part-time $1503.40 per credit. Required fees: $67.63 per credit. Tuition and fees vary according to reciprocity agreements. *Financial support:* In 2010–11, 6 students received support, including fellowships with full tuition reimbursements available (averaging $18,756 per year),

research assistantships with full tuition reimbursements available (averaging $16,506 per year), 7 teaching assistantships with full tuition reimbursements available (averaging $14,088 per year); Federal Work-Study, institutionally sponsored loans, scholarships/grants, health care benefits, and unspecified assistantships also available. Financial award application deadline: 2/1; financial award applicants required to submit FAFSA. *Faculty research:* Superfund, health insurance, workers compensation, employee benefits, fuzzy logic. *Unit head:* Prof. Marjorie Rosenberg, Chair, 608-262-1683, E-mail: mrosenberg@bus.wisc.edu. *Application contact:* Belle Heberling, Assistant Director for Research Programs, 608-262-3749, Fax: 608-890-0180, E-mail: phd@bus.wisc.edu.

University of Wisconsin–Madison, Graduate School, Wisconsin School of Business, Wisconsin Full-Time MBA Program, Madison, WI 53706-1380. Offers applied security analysis (MBA); arts administration (MBA); brand and product management (MBA); corporate finance and investment banking (MBA); entrepreneurial management (MBA); marketing research (MBA); operations and technology management (MBA); real estate (MBA); risk management and insurance (MBA); strategic human resource management (MBA); strategic management in the life and engineering sciences (MBA); supply chain management (MBA). *Faculty:* 32 full-time (4 women), 17 part-time/adjunct (3 women). *Students:* 242 full-time (74 women); includes 16 Black or African American, non-Hispanic/Latino; 3 American Indian or Alaska Native, non-Hispanic/Latino; 16 Asian, non-Hispanic/Latino; 12 Hispanic/Latino, 29 international. Average age 28. 526 applicants, 32% accepted, 117 enrolled. In 2010, 106 master's awarded. *Entrance requirements:* For master's, GMAT, bachelor's or equivalent degree, 2 years of work experience, letters of recommendation. Additional exam requirements/recommendations for international students: Required—TOEFL (minimum score 600 paper-based; 250 computer-based; 100 iBT), IELTS. *Application deadline:* For fall admission, 11/4 for domestic students, 11/1 for international students; for winter admission, 2/5 for domestic and international students; for spring admission, 5/15 for domestic students, 4/5 for international students. Applications are processed on a rolling basis. Application fee: $56. Electronic applications accepted. *Expenses:* Tuition, state resident: full-time $9887; part-time $617.96 per credit. Tuition, nonresident: full-time $24,054; part-time $1503.40 per credit. Tuition, nonresident: full-time $24,054; part-time $1503.40 per credit. Required fees: $67.63 per credit. Tuition and fees vary according to reciprocity agreements. *Financial support:* In 2010–11, 103 students received support, including 13 fellowships with full and partial tuition reimbursements available (averaging $15,000 per year), 53 research assistantships with full tuition reimbursements available (averaging $8,000 per year), 35 teaching assistantships with full tuition reimbursements available (averaging $11,000 per year); scholarships/grants, health care benefits, and unspecified assistantships also available. Financial award application deadline: 4/5; financial award applicants required to submit FAFSA. *Faculty research:* Market consequences of International Financial Reporting Standards (IFRS), inter-firm relationships and strategic partnerships, application of Bayesian statistical methods and applied probability models to understanding individuals' behaviors in the context of customer relationship management (CRM) applications, liquidity provision and the structure of financial markets, strategic management of global startups. *Unit head:* Dr. Kenneth A. Kavajecz, Associate Dean of Master's Programs, 608-265-3494, Fax: 608-265-4192, E-mail: kkavajecz@bus.wisc.edu. *Application contact:* Maria Reis, Assistant Director of MBA Marketing and Recruiting, 608-262-4000, Fax: 608-265-4192, E-mail: mreis@bus.wisc.edu.

Virginia Commonwealth University, Graduate School, School of Business, Program in Finance, Insurance, and Real Estate, Richmond, VA 23284-9005. Offers MS. *Faculty:* 11 full-time (0 women). *Entrance requirements:* For master's, GMAT (GRE for Finance). Additional exam requirements/recommendations for international students: Required—TOEFL (minimum score 600 paper-based; 250 computer-based; 100 iBT); Recommended—IELTS (minimum score 6.5). *Application deadline:* For fall admission, 6/1 for domestic students; for spring admission, 11/1 for domestic students. Applications are processed on a rolling basis. Application fee: $50. Electronic applications accepted. *Expenses:* Tuition, state resident: full-time $4308; part-time $479 per credit hour. Tuition, nonresident: full-time $8942; part-time $994 per credit hour. Required fees: $2000; $85 per credit hour. Tuition and fees vary according to course level, course load, degree level, campus/location and program. *Financial support:* Fellowships, research assistantships, teaching assistantships, Federal Work-Study, institutionally sponsored loans, and tuition waivers (full and partial) available. Financial award application deadline: 3/15; financial award applicants required to submit FAFSA. *Unit head:* Ed Grier, Dean, 804-828-1595, Fax: 804-828-7174, E-mail: busdean@vcu.edu. *Application contact:* Jana P. McQuaid, Assistant Dean, Masters Programs, 804-828-4622, Fax: 804-828-7174, E-mail: jpmcquaid@vcu.edu.

OVERVIEW

Today's business leaders must operate in a marketplace that is characterized by heightened competition, a scarcity of natural resources, and the increased demands of emerging economies. Moreover, business firms are seeking managerial talent with the skills to both assess global trends and mobilize global strategies. The international business MBA experience is for students looking to develop the competencies, cultural skills, and global mind set essential for success in a worldwide marketplace. These programs are designed to give graduates the ability to adapt and lead in rapidly-evolving global markets and the cross-cultural expertise that prepares them for the challenges of managing in a global economy. Students learn to examine organizations, markets, and institutions from a multinational perspective in order to better understand how culture, economics, geography, and politics impact a manager's role in industries that cross national boundaries.

In navigating both global challenges and opportunities, students in an international business MBA program not only develop a solid foundation in key business functional areas, they also delve into topics such as country and political risk analysis, social innovation investment, creativity and innovation in emerging nations, climate risks and corporate value, and localization management. Students in the international business MBA program are given the opportunity to strengthen foreign language skills, expand cultural understanding, and often gain hands-on working experience through study abroad and/or overseas internships.

Required courses of study may include:

- Economics for the Global Executive
- Global Strategic Management
- Global Strategic Marketing
- Information Systems in the Global Enterprise
- International Financial Management
- International Monetary Systems
- International Trade Basics
- Quantitative Tools for Managers
- Strategic Alliances and Joint Ventures

Elective courses of study may include:

- Competing in Global High-Technology Industries
- Environment of International Business
- Global Business and Knowledge Management
- International Accounting
- International Logistics and Transportation
- Organizational Behavior Strategies

An international business MBA is an excellent choice for students interested in a career with a large, multinational corporation or in an industry facing strong international competition. Students graduating with an MBA in international business have a wide range of career opportunities in national and international government and nongovernment agencies and organizations, the travel and leisure industry, and banking. Potential employment options include positions as international marketing managers, international trade service specialists, importers/wholesalers, freight forwarding coordinators, and directors of import/export compliance.

HELPFUL ORGANIZATIONS/ PUBLICATIONS/BLOGS

Council of the Americas (COA)

http://coa.counciloftheamericas.org/

Council of the Americas (COA) is the premier international business organization whose members share a common commitment to economic and social development, open markets, the rule of law, and democracy throughout the western hemisphere. The Council's membership consists of leading international companies representing a broad spectrum of sectors, including banking and finance, consulting services, consumer products, energy and mining, manufacturing, media, technology, and transportation. The programming and advocacy of the Council aim to inform, encourage, and promote free and integrated markets for the benefit of the companies that comprise their membership.

NASBITE International

http://nasbite.org/

NASBITE International is a professional organization for the global business community. Their members include global business educators and trainers at academic institutions; trade specialists at federal, state, and local trade assistance organizations; and practitioners who engage in or facilitate global business activity. With the mission of advancing global business practice, education, and training, NASBITE International's goals are to:

- Coordinate and administer the Certified Global Business Professional (CGBP) credential.
- Promote an exchange of information and resources among global business education and assistance professionals.
- Offer professional development for those engaged in global business education and assistance.
- Provide advocacy and leadership for global business education and assistance professionals.

Global Business Investments and Publications LLC

http://www.globip.com/

Global Business Investments and Publications LLC recognizes the fact that developments in almost every area of business are occurring fast and that there is need to keep pace with the necessary research and documentation of these developments. The Global Business Investments and Publications publishes expert, peer-reviewed journals and books related to business and investment issues that are company-, industry-, country-, and region-specific or have global implications.

CAREER ASPIRATIONS: A PROSPECTIVE POSITION

Executive Director, Global Supply Planning

Job Description

This position is responsible for defining and implementing an integrated product supply strategy for the global manufacturing network, including third-party suppliers. Specifically accountable for developing feasible master production schedules for all manufacturing sites and internal and third-party suppliers, optimizing global inventory, and meeting the company's service and cost objectives. Also responsible for managing a team of supply planning professionals located in the United States and overseas.

Requirements

- Manage API supply and inventory levels for third-party manufacturer.
- Lead the development and deployment of the global supply review process as one of the key elements of the global sales and operations planning process and manage the escalation and prioritization of the supply responses around all issues and opportunities.
- Define and implement an integrated supply strategy for the global production network, including third-party manufacturers, and develop efficient and effective inventory/supply planning processes to deploy across all global manufacturing sites.
- Actively collaborate with sales, marketing, business development, and third-party manufacturing groups in establishing supply agreements with external customers and suppliers. Ensure agreements meet the company's standards of service delivery and maintain compliance. Ensure coordination and execution of supply requirements at the respective manufacturing sites meet the contractual service and cost objectives.

Qualifications

- BS/BA in logistics, operations management, or related degree required; MBA strongly preferred
- Minimum 8 years of related work experience or an equivalent combination of education and experience
- Experience managing a globally integrated supply network, utilizing best-in-class supply planning processes and advanced planning and scheduling systems
- Experience managing joint planning and supplier relationship management methodologies in relation to a complex network of third-party manufacturers
- Strong project management skills
- Skilled in implementing challenging goals, objectives, and practices in a complex and ambiguous business environment
- Change management skills in a globally diverse, rapidly changing cross-cultural environment
- Strong strategic and analytical thinking; problem-solving and rapid decision-making capabilities
- Understanding of best practices in supply chain manufacturing management

Career Advice from a Business Professional

Mark Heiser
Financial Analyst Supervisor
Nelnet, Inc.
**MBA in International Business/
    Finance
University of Nebraska
    at Lincoln**

What drew you to this field?

I originally approached my MBA as an opportunity to further my education and acquire knowledge and skills to help me in my career. My international business emphasis was initially not part of the plan, but as opportunities to study abroad and learn business practices from companies and cultures around the world presented themselves, I became much more interested in business internationally.

What makes a day at your job interesting?

I like the variety. Working in one of our more diversified business segments means that we have many different business models to support. What drives success is really unique to each company, so every day offers the chance to be involved in a new project, venture, or analysis. With that comes the opportunity to work with a wide variety of great people who have vast amounts of experience for me to learn from.

How has your graduate education been important to your successes/accomplishments along your career path?

Besides the academics, my MBA experience instilled in me an ability to approach problems and tasks with a management mindset that reaches solutions in a more efficient fashion. In addition, the MBA program is set up to help classmates complete a variety of projects. The ability to not only work cohesively, but also challenge others to reach a common goal is crucial to our success.

In your opinion, what does the future of your field hold for someone newly entering it?

Financial Analytics on our team really deals with telling the financial story of past performance, analyzing the effects of what a current decision will be, and projecting what the future holds for our business. A person entering this field will not necessarily work on the same projects that I have, but the need for these functions will always exist and be fully integrated with Operations and top-level management.

What are the exciting developments coming in the next five years?

Like many companies, Nelnet places a high importance on innovation and diversification. Many new opportunities will present themselves to expand our service and offerings. What's exciting for me and my team is the opportunity to be involved in these opportunities at the ground floor and see them develop and succeed. In many cases, we will assist in laying out the business model, preparing pricing, and evaluating performance.

What advice would you share with new graduates entering your field?

Work hard and have a good attitude. Customers appreciate results—both accurate and timely results. Relationships with customers are always important, and a positive attitude leaves a strong impression. In addition, I would recommend that a new graduate get involved as early as possible in a wide variety of projects/tasks/activities to broaden his or her knowledge and skill set. This typically requires volunteer work for committees, projects, and so on, which I have found to be very beneficial.

INTERNATIONAL BUSINESS

American Public University System, AMU/APU Graduate Programs, Charles Town, WV 25414. Offers accounting (MBA); administration and supervision (M Ed); air warfare (MA Military Studies); asymmetrical warfare (MA Military Studies); criminal justice (MA); emergency and disaster management (MA); entrepreneurship (MBA); environmental policy and management (MS); finance (MBA); general (MBA); global business management (MBA); guidance and counseling (M Ed); history (MA); homeland security (MA); homeland security resource allocation (MBA); humanities (MA); information technology (MS); information technology management (MBA); intelligence studies (MA); international relations and conflict resolution (MA); joint warfare (MA Military Studies); land warfare (MA Military Studies); legal studies (MA); management (MA), including defense mangement, general, human resource management, organizational leadership, public administration; marketing (MBA); military history (MA); national security studies (MA); naval warfare (MA Military Studies); nonprofit management (MBA); political science (MA); psychology (MA); public administration (MA); public health (MA); security management (MA); space studies (MS); sports management (MS); strategic leadership (MA Military Studies); teaching (M Ed), including elementary, secondary social sciences; transportation and logistics management (MA). Programs offered via distance learning only. Part-time and evening/weekend programs available. Postbaccalaureate distance learning degree programs offered (no on-campus study). *Faculty:* 253 full-time (134 women), 1,208 part-time/adjunct (570 women). *Students:* 956 full-time (422 women), 8,476 part-time (2,821 women); includes 2,511 minority (1,218 Black or African American, non-Hispanic/Latino; 68 American Indian or Alaska Native, non-Hispanic/Latino; 219 Asian, non-Hispanic/Latino; 705 Hispanic/Latino; 46 Native Hawaiian or other Pacific Islander, non-Hispanic/Latino; 255 Two or more races, non-Hispanic/Latino), 107 international. Average age 35. 9,550 applicants, 100% accepted. In 2010, 1,688 master's awarded. *Degree requirements:* For master's, comprehensive exam or practicum. *Entrance requirements:* For master's, official transcript showing earned bachelor's degree from institution accredited by recognized accrediting body. Additional exam requirements/recommendations for international students: Required—TOEFL (minimum score 550 paper-based; 213 computer-based), IELTS (minimum score 6.5). *Application deadline:* Applications are processed on a rolling basis. Application fee: $0. Electronic applications accepted. *Financial support:* Applicants required to submit FAFSA. *Faculty research:* Military history, criminal justice, management performance, national security. *Unit head:* Dr. Frank McCluskey, Provost, 877-468-6268, Fax: 304-724-3780. *Application contact:* Terry Grant, Director of Enrollment Management, 877-468-6268, Fax: 304-724-3780, E-mail: info@apus.edu.

American University, Kogod School of Business, Department of International Business, Washington, DC 20016-8044. Offers international business (Certificate). Part-time and evening/weekend programs available. *Faculty:* 9 full-time (3 women). *Students:* 3 part-time (1 woman); includes 1 Hispanic/Latino. Average age 29. In 2010, 2 Certificates awarded. *Entrance requirements:* For degree, bachelor's degree. Additional exam requirements/recommendations for international students: Required—TOEFL. *Application deadline:* For fall admission, 2/1 priority date for domestic students; for spring admission, 10/1 priority date for domestic students. Applications are processed on a rolling basis. Application fee: $100. *Expenses:* Contact institution. *Financial support:* Fellowships, research assistantships with partial tuition reimbursements, career-related internships or fieldwork, Federal Work-Study, and institutionally sponsored loans available. Support available to part-time students. Financial award application deadline: 2/1; financial award applicants required to submit FAFSA. *Faculty research:* Financial risk in the multinational corporation, emerging security markets, import/export issues, joint ventures in China, Japanese management. *Unit head:* Dr. Frank DuBois, Chair, 202-885-1967, Fax: 202-885-1992, E-mail: fdubois@american.edu. *Application contact:* Shannon Demko, Associate Director of Graduate Admissions, 202-885-1994, Fax: 202-885-1108, E-mail: demko@american.edu.

American University, Kogod School of Business, Master of Business Administration Program, Washington, DC 20016-8044. Offers accounting (MBA); consulting (MBA), including information technology, international business, management; corporate finance: commercial banking (MBA); corporate finance: corporate financial management (MBA); corporate finance: investment banking (MBA), including corporate finance and private equity, trading and selling; entrepreneurship (MBA); global emerging markets (MBA), including business, finance, information technology; international trade and global supply chain management (MBA); leadership (MBA); marketing management (MBA); marketing research (MBA); real estate (MBA); MBA/JD; MBA/LL M. Part-time and evening/weekend programs available. *Faculty:* 12 full-time (5 women). *Students:* 135 full-time (62 women), 104 part-time (38 women); includes 46 minority (18 Black or African American, non-Hispanic/Latino; 1 American Indian or Alaska Native, non-Hispanic/Latino; 12 Asian, non-Hispanic/Latino; 14 Hispanic/Latino; 1 Two or more races, non-Hispanic/Latino), 34 international. Average age 27. 467 applicants, 51% accepted, 70 enrolled. In 2010, 101 master's awarded. *Entrance requirements:* For master's, GMAT. Additional exam requirements/recommendations for international students: Required—TOEFL. *Application deadline:* For fall

admission, 2/1 priority date for domestic students; for spring admission, 10/1 priority date for domestic students. Applications are processed on a rolling basis. Application fee: $100. *Expenses:* Contact institution. *Financial support:* In 2010–11, 19 students received support; fellowships, research assistantships with partial tuition reimbursements available, career-related internships or fieldwork, Federal Work-Study, and institutionally sponsored loans available. Support available to part-time students. Financial award application deadline: 2/1. *Faculty research:* Information technology, decision-aiding methodology, negotiation. *Unit head:* Dr. Stevan Holmberg, Chair, 202-885-6193, E-mail: sholmbe@american.edu. *Application contact:* Shannon Demko, Associate Director Graduate Admissions, 202-885-1994, Fax: 202-885-1108, E-mail: demko@american.edu.

The American University of Paris, Graduate Programs, Paris, France. Offers cross-cultural and sustainable business management (MA); cultural translation (MA); global communications (MA); global communications and civil society (MA); international affairs, conflict resolution and civil society development (MA); Middle East and Islamic studies (MA); Middle East and Islamic studies and international affairs (MA); public policy and international affairs (MA); public policy and international law (MA). *Faculty:* 14 full-time (3 women). *Students:* 151 full-time (110 women), 56 part-time (43 women). 271 applicants, 83% accepted, 104 enrolled. In 2010, 67 master's awarded. *Degree requirements:* For master's, thesis. *Entrance requirements:* For master's, minimum undergraduate GPA of 3.0. Additional exam requirements/recommendations for international students: Recommended—IELTS. *Application deadline:* For fall admission, 4/15 priority date for international students; for spring admission, 11/15 priority date for international students. Applications are processed on a rolling basis. Application fee: $75. Electronic applications accepted. *Financial support:* Scholarships/grants available. Financial award applicants required to submit FAFSA. *Unit head:* Dr. Celeste Schenck, President, 33-1 40 62 06 59, E-mail: president@aup.fr. *Application contact:* International Admissions Counselor, 33-1 40 62 07 20, Fax: 33-1 47 05 34 32, E-mail: admissions@aup.edu.

Ashworth College, Graduate Programs, Norcross, GA 30092. Offers business administration (MBA); criminal justice (MS); health care administration (MBA, MS); human resource management (MBA, MS); international business (MBA); management (MS); marketing (MBA, MS). *Faculty:* 5 part-time/adjunct (1 woman). *Students:* 299. *Expenses:* Tuition: Full-time $9230; part-time $250 per credit hour. *Unit head:* Dr. Leslie A. Gargiulo, Vice President of Education, 770-729-8400, E-mail: lgargiulo@ashworthcollege.edu. *Application contact:* Dr. Leslie A. Gargiulo, Vice President of Education, 770-729-8400, E-mail: lgargiulo@ashworthcollege.edu.

Assumption College, Graduate School, Department of Business Studies, Worcester, MA 01609-1296. Offers accounting (MBA); business administration (CAGS); finance/economics (MBA); general business (MBA); human resources (MBA); international business (MBA); management (MBA); marketing (MBA); nonprofit leadership (MBA). Part-time and evening/weekend programs available. *Faculty:* 3 full-time (0 women), 13 part-time/adjunct (3 women). *Students:* 20 full-time (9 women), 135 part-time (70 women); includes 24 minority (19 Black or African American, non-Hispanic/Latino; 2 Asian, non-Hispanic/Latino; 3 Hispanic/Latino), 4 international. Average age 26. 85 applicants, 95% accepted. In 2010, 40 master's, 2 other advanced degrees awarded. *Entrance requirements:* For master's and CAGS, 3 letters of recommendation, resume, essay. Additional exam requirements/recommendations for international students: Required—TOEFL (minimum score 540 paper-based; 200 computer-based; 76 iBT), IELTS (minimum score 6). *Application deadline:* For fall admission, 6/1 priority date for domestic students, 5/1 priority date for international students; for spring admission, 11/1 priority date for domestic students, 9/1 priority date for international students. Applications are processed on a rolling basis. Application fee: $30. Electronic applications accepted. *Expenses:* Tuition: Part-time $503 per credit. Required fees: $20 per semester. One-time fee: $100. Part-time tuition and fees vary according to campus/location. *Financial support:* Application deadline: 6/1. *Faculty research:* Workplace diversity, dynamics of team interaction, utilization of leased employees. *Unit head:* Michael Lewis, Director, 508-767-7372, Fax: 508-767-7252, E-mail: milewis@assumption.edu. *Application contact:* Daniel Provost, Assistant Director of Graduate Student Services, 508-767-7426, Fax: 508-767-7030, E-mail: dprovost@assumption.edu.

Avila University, School of Business, Kansas City, MO 64145-1698. Offers accounting (MBA); finance (MBA); general management (MBA); health care administration (MBA); international business (MBA); management information systems (MBA); marketing (MBA). Part-time and evening/weekend programs available. *Faculty:* 9 full-time (3 women), 24 part-time/adjunct (6 women). *Students:* 123 full-time (68 women), 87 part-time (52 women); includes 44 minority (30 Black or African American, non-Hispanic/Latino; 1 American Indian or Alaska Native, non-Hispanic/Latino; 6 Asian, non-Hispanic/Latino; 6 Hispanic/Latino; 1 Native Hawaiian or other Pacific Islander, non-Hispanic/Latino), 46 international. Average age 33. 62 applicants, 79% accepted, 49 enrolled. In 2010, 80 master's awarded. *Degree requirements:* For master's, comprehensive exam, capstone course. *Entrance requirements:* For master's, GMAT (minimum score 420), minimum GPA of 3.0, interview. Additional exam requirements/recommendations for international students: Required—TOEFL (minimum score 550 paper-based). *Application deadline:*

For fall admission, 7/30 priority date for domestic students, 7/30 for international students; for winter admission, 11/30 priority date for domestic students, 11/30 for international students; for spring admission, 2/28 priority date for domestic students, 2/28 for international students. Applications are processed on a rolling basis. Application fee: $0. Electronic applications accepted. *Expenses:* Contact institution. *Financial support:* In 2010–11, 102 students received support. Career-related internships or fieldwork and Competitive Merit Scholarship available. Support available to part-time students. Financial award applicants required to submit FAFSA. *Faculty research:* Leadership characteristics, financial hedging, group dynamics. *Unit head:* Dr. Richard Woodall, Dean, 816-501-3720, Fax: 816-501-2463, E-mail: richard.woodall@avila.edu. *Application contact:* JoAnna Giffin, MBA Admissions Director, 816-501-3601, Fax: 816-501-2463, E-mail: joanna.giffin@avila.edu.

Azusa Pacific University, School of Behavioral and Applied Sciences, Department of Higher Education and Organizational Leadership, Program in Global Leadership, Azusa, CA 91702-7000. Offers MA. *Students:* 85 part-time (46 women); includes 1 minority (Black or African American, non-Hispanic/Latino), 58 international. Average age 39. In 2010, 57 master's awarded. Application fee: $45 ($65 for international students). *Unit head:* Allyn Beekman, Administrative Director, 626-815-6000 Ext. 5530, E-mail: abeekman@apu.edu. *Application contact:* Linda Witte, Graduate Admissions Office, 626-969-3434.

Azusa Pacific University, School of Business and Management, Azusa, CA 91702-7000. Offers business administration (MBA); diversity for strategic advantage (MA); entrepreneurship (MBA); finance (MBA); human and organizational development (MA); human resources and organizational development (MBA); human resources management (MA); international business (MBA); marketing (MBA); non-profit management (MA); organizational development and change (MA); performance improvement (MA); public administration (MA); strategic management (MBA). Part-time and evening/weekend programs available. *Faculty:* 19 full-time (5 women), 2 part-time/adjunct (1 woman). *Students:* 75 full-time (41 women), 96 part-time (46 women); includes 65 minority (15 Black or African American, non-Hispanic/Latino; 15 Asian, non-Hispanic/Latino; 34 Hispanic/Latino; 1 Native Hawaiian or other Pacific Islander, non-Hispanic/Latino), 17 international. Average age 30. In 2010, 82 master's awarded. *Degree requirements:* For master's, thesis (for some programs), final project. *Entrance requirements:* For master's, GMAT, minimum GPA of 3.0. Additional exam requirements/recommendations for international students: Required—TOEFL (minimum score 600 paper-based). *Application deadline:* For fall admission, 8/15 priority date for domestic students. Applications are processed on a rolling basis. Application fee: $45 ($65 for international students). *Expenses:* Contact institution. *Financial support:* Scholarships/grants available. *Faculty research:* Gender issues, financial risk, leadership and ethics, marketing strategy. *Unit head:* Dr. Ilene Bezjian, Dean, 626-815-3090, Fax: 626-815-3802, E-mail: ibezjian@apu.edu. *Application contact:* Dr. Ilene Bezjian, Dean, 626-815-3090, Fax: 626-815-3802, E-mail: ibezjian@apu.edu.

Baldwin-Wallace College, Graduate Programs, Division of Business, Program in International Management, Berea, OH 44017-2088. Offers MBA. Part-time and evening/weekend programs available. *Students:* 25 full-time (10 women), 23 part-time (14 women); includes 16 minority (3 Black or African American, non-Hispanic/Latino; 8 Asian, non-Hispanic/Latino; 5 Hispanic/Latino), 8 international. Average age 35. 16 applicants, 69% accepted, 7 enrolled. In 2010, 20 master's awarded. *Degree requirements:* For master's, one foreign language, minimum overall GPA of 3.0, completion of all required courses. *Entrance requirements:* For master's, GMAT, interview, work experience, bachelor's degree in field. Additional exam requirements/recommendations for international students: Required—TOEFL (minimum score 523 paper-based; 193 computer-based; 70 iBT). *Application deadline:* For fall admission, 7/25 priority date for domestic students, 4/30 priority date for international students; for spring admission, 12/15 priority date for domestic students, 9/30 priority date for international students. Applications are processed on a rolling basis. Application fee: $25. Electronic applications accepted. *Expenses:* Contact institution. *Financial support:* Career-related internships or fieldwork available. Support available to part-time students. Financial award application deadline: 5/1; financial award applicants required to submit FAFSA. *Faculty research:* International finance, systems approach, international marketing. *Unit head:* Harvey Hopson, Director, 440-826-2137, Fax: 440-826-3868, E-mail: hhopson@bw.edu. *Application contact:* Laura Spencer, Graduate Application Specialist, 440-826-2191, Fax: 440-826-3868, E-mail: lspencer@bw.edu.

Benedictine University, Graduate Programs, Program in Business Administration, Lisle, IL 60532-0900. Offers accounting (MBA); entrepreneurship and managing innovation (MBA); financial management (MBA); health administration (MBA); human resource management (MBA); information systems security (MBA); international business (MBA); management consulting (MBA); management information systems (MBA); marketing management (MBA); operations management and logistics (MBA); organizational leadership (MBA); MBA/MPH; MBA/MS. Part-time and evening/weekend programs available. Postbaccalaureate distance learning degree programs offered (minimal on-campus study). *Faculty:* 4 full-time (2 women), 24 part-time/adjunct (3 women). *Students:* 347 full-time (140 women),

672 part-time (360 women); includes 237 minority (155 Black or African American, non-Hispanic/Latino; 4 American Indian or Alaska Native, non-Hispanic/Latino; 43 Asian, non-Hispanic/Latino; 35 Hispanic/Latino), 21 international. Average age 34. 416 applicants, 88% accepted, 217 enrolled. In 2010, 355 master's awarded. *Entrance requirements:* For master's, GMAT. Additional exam requirements/recommendations for international students: Required—TOEFL (minimum score 550 paper-based; 213 computer-based). *Application deadline:* For fall admission, 9/1 for domestic students; for winter admission, 12/1 for domestic students; for spring admission, 2/15 for domestic students. Applications are processed on a rolling basis. Application fee: $40. Electronic applications accepted. *Financial support:* Career-related internships or fieldwork and health care benefits available. Support available to part-time students. *Faculty research:* Strategic leadership in professional organizations, sociology of professions, organizational change, social identity theory, applications to change management. *Unit head:* Dr. Sharon Borowicz, Director, 630-829-6219, E-mail: sborowicz@ben.edu. *Application contact:* Kari Gibbons, Director, Admissions, 630-829-6200, Fax: 630-829-6584, E-mail: kgibbons@ben.edu.

Boston University, Metropolitan College, Department of Administrative Sciences, Boston, MA 02215. Offers banking and financial management (MSM); business continuity in emergency management (MSM); economics development and tourism management (MSAS); electronic commerce, systems, and technology (MSAS); financial economics (MSAS); innovation and technology (MSAS); insurance management (MSM); international market management (MSM); multinational commerce (MSAS); project management (MSM). *Accreditation:* AACSB. Part-time and evening/weekend programs available. Postbaccalaureate distance learning degree programs offered (no on-campus study). *Faculty:* 14 full-time (2 women), 22 part-time/adjunct (2 women). *Students:* 107 full-time (51 women), 786 part-time (356 women); includes 130 minority (55 Black or African American, non-Hispanic/Latino; 1 American Indian or Alaska Native, non-Hispanic/Latino; 30 Asian, non-Hispanic/Latino; 36 Hispanic/Latino; 1 Native Hawaiian or other Pacific Islander, non-Hispanic/Latino; 7 Two or more races, non-Hispanic/Latino), 175 international. Average age 33. 398 applicants, 87% accepted, 180 enrolled. In 2010, 154 master's awarded. *Degree requirements:* For master's, thesis optional. *Entrance requirements:* For master's, 1 year of work experience, minimum GPA of 3.0. Additional exam requirements/recommendations for international students: Required—TOEFL (minimum score 560 paper-based; 220 computer-based; 84 iBT). *Application deadline:* Applications are processed on a rolling basis. Application fee: $70. Electronic applications accepted. *Expenses:* Tuition: Full-time $39,314; part-time $1228 per credit. Required fees: $40 per semester. *Financial support:* In 2010–11, 15 students received support, including 7 research assistantships with partial tuition reimbursements available (averaging $10,000 per year); career-related internships or fieldwork, Federal Work-Study, and unspecified assistantships also available. *Faculty research:* International business, innovative process. *Unit head:* Dr. Kip Becker, Chairman, 617-353-3016, E-mail: adminsc@bu.edu. *Application contact:* Lucille Dicker, Administrative Sciences Department, 617-353-3016, E-mail: adminsc@bu.edu.

Brooklyn College of the City University of New York, Division of Graduate Studies, Department of Economics, Brooklyn, NY 11210-2889. Offers accounting (MS); business economics (MS), including economic analysis, global business and finance; economics (MA). Part-time and evening/weekend programs available. *Students:* 27 full-time (16 women), 163 part-time (76 women); includes 84 minority (60 Black or African American, non-Hispanic/Latino; 18 Asian, non-Hispanic/Latino; 6 Hispanic/Latino), 42 international. Average age 32. 184 applicants, 76% accepted, 68 enrolled. In 2010, 44 master's awarded. *Degree requirements:* For master's, comprehensive exam, thesis or alternative. *Entrance requirements:* For master's, GMAT (for MS), 2 letters of recommendation. Additional exam requirements/recommendations for international students: Required—TOEFL (minimum score 550 paper-based; 213 computer-based; 79 iBT). *Application deadline:* For fall admission, 3/1 priority date for domestic students, 2/1 priority date for international students; for spring admission, 11/1 priority date for domestic students, 10/1 priority date for international students. Applications are processed on a rolling basis. Application fee: $125. Electronic applications accepted. *Expenses:* Tuition, state resident: full-time $7360; part-time $310 per credit hour. Tuition, non-resident: full-time $13,800; part-time $575 per credit hour. Required fees: $190 per semester. *Financial support:* Career-related internships or fieldwork, Federal Work-Study, institutionally sponsored loans, and scholarships/grants available. Support available to part-time students. Financial award application deadline: 5/1; financial award applicants required to submit FAFSA. *Faculty research:* Econometrics, environmental economics, microeconomics, macroeconomics, taxation. *Unit head:* Dr. Emmanuel Thorne, Chairperson, 718-951-5317, E-mail: ethorne@brooklyn.cuny.edu. *Application contact:* Hernan Sierra, Graduate Admissions Coordinator, 718-951-4536, Fax: 718-951-4506, E-mail: grads@brooklyn.cuny.edu.

California Lutheran University, Graduate Studies, School of Management, Thousand Oaks, CA 91360-2787. Offers business (IMBA); computer science (MS); econometrics (MBA); economics (MS); entrepreneurship (MBA, Certificate); finance (MBA, Certificate); financial planning (MBA, Certificate); information systems and technology (MS); information technology management (MBA, Certificate); international business (MBA, Certificate); management and organization behavior (MBA); management and organizational behavior (Certificate); marketing (MBA, Certificate); microeconomics (MBA); nonprofit and social enterprise (MBA). Part-time and evening/weekend programs available. Postbaccalaureate distance learning degree programs offered (no on-campus study). *Faculty:* 12 full-time (3 women), 27 part-time/adjunct (6 women). *Students:* 350 full-time (162 women), 262 part-time (99 women); includes 21 Black or African American, non-Hispanic/Latino; 44 Asian, non-Hispanic/Latino; 56 Hispanic/Latino; 4 Native Hawaiian or other Pacific Islander, non-Hispanic/Latino; 12 Two or more races, non-Hispanic/Latino, 185 international. Average age 32. 379 applicants, 74% accepted, 138 enrolled. In 2010, 231 master's awarded. *Entrance requirements:* For master's, GMAT, interview, minimum GPA of 3.0. *Application deadline:* Applications are processed on a rolling basis. Application fee: $50. *Expenses:* Contact institution. *Unit head:* Dr. Charles Maxey, Dean, 805-493-3360. *Application contact:* 805-493-3127, Fax: 805-493-3542, E-mail: clugrad@clunet.edu.

California State University, East Bay, Office of Academic Programs and Graduate Studies, College of Business and Economics, Department of Information Technology Management, Option in Strategy and International Business, Hayward, CA 94542-3000. Offers MBA. Part-time and evening/weekend programs available. *Degree requirements:* For master's, comprehensive exam or thesis. *Entrance requirements:* For master's, GMAT, minimum GPA of 2.75. Additional exam requirements/recommendations for international students: Required—TOEFL (minimum score 550 paper-based; 213 computer-based). *Application deadline:* For fall admission, 6/30 for domestic and international students. Application fee: $55. *Financial support:* Career-related internships or fieldwork, Federal Work-Study, institutionally sponsored loans, and scholarships/grants available. Support available to part-time students. Financial award application deadline: 3/1. *Unit head:* Dr. Xinjian Lu, Chair, 510-885-3307, E-mail: xinjian.lu@csueastbay.edu. *Application contact:* Donna Wiley, Interim Associate Director, 510-885-2928, Fax: 510-885-4777, E-mail: donna.wiley@csueastbay.edu.

California State University, East Bay, Office of Academic Programs and Graduate Studies, College of Business and Economics, MBA Program, Hayward, CA 94542-3000. Offers entrepreneurship (MBA); finance (MBA); human resources and organizational behavior (MBA); information technology management (MBA); marketing management (MBA); operations and supply chain management (MBA); strategy and international business (MBA). Part-time and evening/weekend programs available. Postbaccalaureate distance learning degree programs offered (no on-campus study). *Faculty:* 33 full-time (9 women). *Students:* 121 full-time (58 women), 133 part-time (67 women); includes 7 Black or African American, non-Hispanic/Latino; 63 Asian, non-Hispanic/Latino; 11 Hispanic/Latino; 3 Native Hawaiian or other Pacific Islander, non-Hispanic/Latino; 5 Two or more races, non-Hispanic/Latino, 87 international. Average age 30. 284 applicants, 47% accepted, 55 enrolled. In 2010, 241 master's awarded. *Degree requirements:* For master's, comprehensive exam or thesis. *Entrance requirements:* For master's, GMAT (minimum 20th percentile verbal and quantitative section), bachelor's degree, minimum GPA of 2.75. Additional exam requirements/recommendations for international students: Required—TOEFL (minimum score 550 paper-based; 213 computer-based; 79 iBT). *Application deadline:* For fall admission, 6/30 for domestic and international students. Applications are processed on a rolling basis. Application fee: $55. Electronic applications accepted. *Financial support:* Career-related internships or fieldwork, Federal Work-Study, institutionally sponsored loans, and scholarships/grants available. Support available to part-time students. Financial award application deadline: 3/2; financial award applicants required to submit FAFSA. *Unit head:* Dr. Terri Swartz, Dean, 510-885-3291, Fax: 510-885-4884, E-mail: terri.swartz@csueastbay.edu. *Application contact:* Dr. Donna Wiley, Interim Associate Director, 510-885-2928, Fax: 510-885-4777, E-mail: donna.wiley@csueastbay.edu.

California State University, Fullerton, Graduate Studies, College of Business and Economics, Program in Business Administration, Fullerton, CA 92834-9480. Offers e-commerce (MBA); international business (MBA). *Accreditation:* AACSB. Part-time programs available. *Students:* 70 full-time (34 women), 88 part-time (30 women); includes 2 Black or African American, non-Hispanic/Latino; 46 Asian, non-Hispanic/Latino; 8 Hispanic/Latino; 8 Two or more races, non-Hispanic/Latino, 40 international. Average age 28. 322 applicants, 43% accepted, 50 enrolled. In 2010, 29 master's awarded. *Degree requirements:* For master's, project or thesis. *Entrance requirements:* For master's, GMAT. *Financial support:* Career-related internships or fieldwork, Federal Work-Study, institutionally sponsored loans, and scholarships/grants available. Support available to part-time students. Financial award application deadline: 3/1; financial award applicants required to submit FAFSA. *Unit head:* Dr. Anil Puri, Dean, 657-773-2592. *Application contact:* Admissions/Applications, 657-278-2371.

California State University, Los Angeles, Graduate Studies, College of Business and Economics, Department of Marketing, Los Angeles, CA 90032-8530. Offers international business (MBA, MS); marketing management (MBA, MS). Part-time and evening/weekend programs available. *Students:* 3 full-time (2 women), 9 part-time (3 women); includes 2 minority (both Asian, non-Hispanic/Latino), 7 international. Average age 27. 15 applicants, 100% accepted, 5 enrolled. In 2010, 16 master's awarded. *Degree requirements:*

For master's, comprehensive exam (MBA), thesis (MS). *Entrance requirements:* For master's, GMAT, minimum GPA of 2.5 during previous 2 years of course work. Additional exam requirements/recommendations for international students: Required—TOEFL (minimum score 550 paper-based; 213 computer-based). *Application deadline:* For fall admission, 5/1 for domestic and international students. Applications are processed on a rolling basis. Application fee: $55. Electronic applications accepted. *Financial support:* Career-related internships or fieldwork and Federal Work-Study available. Support available to part-time students. Financial award application deadline: 3/1. *Unit head:* Dr. Paul Washburn, Acting Chair, 323-343-2960, Fax: 323-343-5462, E-mail: pwashbu@calstatela.edu. *Application contact:* Dr. Alan Muchlinski, Dean of Graduate Studies, 323-343-3820, Fax: 323-343-5653, E-mail: amuchli@exchange.calstatela.edu.

California State University, Stanislaus, College of Business Administration, Department of Accounting and Finance, Turlock, CA 95382. Offers MS. Part-time and evening/weekend programs available. *Students:* 4 full-time (1 woman); includes 1 minority (Asian, non-Hispanic/Latino), 1 international. Average age 29. 8 applicants, 100% accepted, 4 enrolled. In 2010, 4 master's awarded. *Degree requirements:* For master's, comprehensive exam, thesis or alternative. *Entrance requirements:* For master's, GMAT or GRE, minimum GPA 2.50, 3 letters of reference, personal statement. Additional exam requirements/recommendations for international students: Required—TOEFL (minimum score 550 paper-based; 213 computer-based). *Application deadline:* For fall admission, 5/1 for domestic students; for spring admission, 1/7 for domestic students. Application fee: $55. Electronic applications accepted. Tuition and fees vary according to program. *Financial support:* Career-related internships or fieldwork available. Financial award application deadline: 3/1; financial award applicants required to submit FAFSA. *Unit head:* Dr. Andrew Wagner, MSBA Director, 209-667-3118, Fax: 209-667-3080, E-mail: awagner@csustan.edu. *Application contact:* Graduate School, 209-667-3129, Fax: 209-664-7025, E-mail: graduate_school@csustan.edu.

Canisius College, Graduate Division, Richard J. Wehle School of Business, Department of Management and Marketing, Buffalo, NY 14208-1098. Offers accelerated business administration (1 year) (MBA); business administration (MBA); international business (MS). *Accreditation:* AACSB. Part-time and evening/weekend programs available. *Faculty:* 35 full-time (7 women), 5 part-time/adjunct (3 women). *Students:* 95 full-time (36 women), 171 part-time (70 women); includes 26 minority (15 Black or African American, non-Hispanic/Latino; 1 American Indian or Alaska Native, non-Hispanic/Latino; 8 Asian, non-Hispanic/Latino; 2 Hispanic/Latino), 9 international. Average age 29. 149 applicants, 71% accepted, 82 enrolled. In 2010, 111 master's awarded. *Entrance requirements:* For master's, GMAT, transcripts. Additional exam requirements/recommendations for international students: Required—TOEFL. *Application deadline:* For fall admission, 7/1 priority date for domestic students; for spring admission, 11/1 priority date for domestic students. Applications are processed on a rolling basis. Application fee: $25. Electronic applications accepted. *Expenses:* Tuition: Part-time $694 per credit hour. Required fees: $11 per credit hour. $90 per semester. *Financial support:* Research assistantships, career-related internships or fieldwork, Federal Work-Study, scholarships/grants, and unspecified assistantships available. Support available to part-time students. Financial award application deadline: 7/1; financial award applicants required to submit FAFSA. *Faculty research:* Global leadership effectiveness, global supply chain management, quality management. *Unit head:* Dr. George Palumbo, Director, MBA Program, 716-888-2667, Fax: 716-888-3132, E-mail: palumbo@canisius.edu. *Application contact:* Jim Bagwell, Director, Graduate Programs, 716-888-2545, Fax: 716-888-3290, E-mail: bagwellj@canisius.edu.

Central European University, Graduate Studies, Department of Legal Studies, Budapest, Hungary. Offers comparative Constitutional law (LL M); economic and legal studies (LL M, MA); human rights (LL M, MA); international business law (LL M); legal studies (SJD). *Faculty:* 8 full-time (2 women), 1 (woman) part-time/adjunct. *Students:* 94 full-time (53 women). Average age 28. 503 applicants, 23% accepted, 88 enrolled. In 2010, 62 master's, 5 doctorates awarded. Terminal master's awarded for partial completion of doctoral program. *Degree requirements:* For master's, one foreign language, thesis; for doctorate, one foreign language, comprehensive exam, thesis/dissertation. *Entrance requirements:* For master's and doctorate, LSAT, CEU admissions exams. Additional exam requirements/recommendations for international students: Required—TOEFL (minimum score 570 paper-based; 230 computer-based). *Application deadline:* For fall admission, 1/5 for domestic and international students. Application fee: $0. Electronic applications accepted. *Expenses:* Contact institution. *Financial support:* In 2010–11, 88 students received support, including 88 fellowships with full and partial tuition reimbursements available (averaging $6,000 per year); career-related internships or fieldwork, institutionally sponsored loans, scholarships/grants, and tuition waivers (full and partial) also available. Financial award application deadline: 1/5. *Faculty research:* Institutional, constitutional and human rights in European Union law; biomedical law and reproductive rights; data protection law; Islamic banking and finance. *Unit head:* Dr. Stefan Messmann, Head, 361-327-3274, Fax: 361-327-3198, E-mail: legalst@ceu.hu. *Application contact:* Maria Balla, Coordinator, 361-327-3204, Fax: 361-327-3198, E-mail: ballam@ceu.hu.

Central Michigan University, College of Graduate Studies, College of Business Administration, Department of Management, Mount Pleasant, MI 48859. Offers human resource management (MBA); international business (MBA). *Faculty:* 8 full-time (2 women), 1 part-time/adjunct (0 women). *Degree requirements:* For master's, thesis or alternative. *Entrance requirements:* For master's, GMAT. *Application deadline:* Applications are processed on a rolling basis. Application fee: $35 ($45 for international students). Electronic applications accepted. *Expenses:* Tuition, state resident: full-time $8208; part-time $456 per credit hour. Tuition, nonresident: full-time $13,788; part-time $766 per credit hour. One-time fee: $25. *Financial support:* Fellowships with tuition reimbursements, research assistantships with tuition reimbursements, teaching assistantships with tuition reimbursements, unspecified assistantships and out-of-state merit awards, non-resident graduate awards available. *Faculty research:* Human resource accounting, valuation, and liability; international business and economic issues; entrepreneurial leadership; technology management and strategy; electronic commerce and neural networks. *Unit head:* Dr. Mahmood Bahaee, Chairperson, 989-774-3747, Fax: 989-774-1353, E-mail: bahae1m@cmich.edu. *Application contact:* Dr. Debasish Chakraborty, Director, MBA Program, 989-774-3337, Fax: 989-774-1320, E-mail: chakr1d@cmich.edu.

Central Michigan University, College of Graduate Studies, Interdisciplinary Administration Programs, Mount Pleasant, MI 48859. Offers acquisitions administration (MSA, Graduate Certificate); general administration (MSA, Graduate Certificate); health services administration (MSA, Graduate Certificate); human resource administration (Graduate Certificate); human resources administration (MSA); information resource management (MSA, Graduate Certificate); international administration (MSA, Graduate Certificate); leadership (MSA, Graduate Certificate); organizational communication (MSA, Graduate Certificate); public administration (MSA, Graduate Certificate); recreation and park administration (MSA); sport administration (MSA). *Accreditation:* AACSB. Part-time and evening/weekend programs available. Postbaccalaureate distance learning degree programs offered (no on-campus study). *Students:* 102 full-time (50 women), 77 part-time (51 women); includes 10 Black or African American, non-Hispanic/Latino; 3 American Indian or Alaska Native, non-Hispanic/Latino; 5 Asian, non-Hispanic/Latino, 65 international. Average age 29. *Degree requirements:* For master's, thesis or alternative. *Entrance requirements:* For master's, bachelor's degree with minimum GPA of 2.7. *Application deadline:* For fall admission, 6/1 for international students; for spring admission, 10/1 for international students. Applications are processed on a rolling basis. Application fee: $35 ($45 for international students). Electronic applications accepted. *Expenses:* Tuition, state resident: full-time $8208; part-time $456 per credit hour. Tuition, nonresident: full-time $13,788; part-time $766 per credit hour. One-time fee: $25. *Financial support:* Fellowships with tuition reimbursements, research assistantships with tuition reimbursements, career-related internships or fieldwork, Federal Work-Study, unspecified assistantships, and out-of-state merit awards, non-resident graduate awards available. *Faculty research:* Interdisciplinary studies in acquisitions administration, health services administration, sport administration, recreation and park administration, and international administration. *Unit head:* Dr. Nana Korash, Director, 989-774-6525, Fax: 989-774-2575, E-mail: msa@cmich.edu. *Application contact:* Denise Schafer, Coordinator, 989-774-4373, Fax: 989-774-2575, E-mail: schaf1dr@cmich.edu.

Clark University, Graduate School, Graduate School of Management, Business Administration Program, Worcester, MA 01610-1477. Offers accounting (MBA); finance (MBA); global business (MBA); health care management (MBA); management (MBA); management of information technology (MBA); marketing (MBA). *Accreditation:* AACSB. Part-time and evening/weekend programs available. *Students:* 147 full-time (75 women), 126 part-time (54 women); includes 24 minority (10 Black or African American, non-Hispanic/Latino; 1 American Indian or Alaska Native, non-Hispanic/Latino; 6 Asian, non-Hispanic/Latino; 5 Hispanic/Latino; 2 Two or more races, non-Hispanic/Latino), 99 international. Average age 30. 382 applicants, 57% accepted, 89 enrolled. In 2010, 101 master's awarded. *Degree requirements:* For master's, thesis optional. *Application deadline:* For fall admission, 6/1 priority date for domestic students; for spring admission, 12/1 priority date for domestic students. Applications are processed on a rolling basis. Application fee: $50. Electronic applications accepted. *Expenses:* Tuition: Full-time $37,000; part-time $1156 per credit hour. Required fees: $30; $1156 per credit hour. *Financial support:* In 2010–11, research assistantships with partial tuition reimbursements (averaging $4,800 per year), teaching assistantships with partial tuition reimbursements (averaging $4,800 per year) were awarded; fellowships, career-related internships or fieldwork, Federal Work-Study, institutionally sponsored loans, and tuition waivers (partial) also available. Support available to part-time students. Financial award application deadline: 5/31. *Faculty research:* Organizational development, accounting, marketing, finance, human resource management. *Unit head:* Dr. Joseph Sarkis, Dean, 508-793-7406, Fax: 508-793-8822, E-mail: clarkmba@clarku.edu. *Application contact:* Lynn Davis, Enrollment and Marketing Director, 508-793-7406, Fax: 508-793-8822, E-mail: clarkmba@clarku.edu.

Cleveland State University, College of Graduate Studies, Nance College of Business Administration, Department of Marketing, Cleveland, OH 44115. Offers global business (Graduate Certificate); marketing (MBA, DBA); marketing analytics (Graduate Certificate). *Faculty:* 12 full-time (3 women), 6 part-time/adjunct (3 women). *Students:* 4 full-time (1 woman), 11 part-time (4 women); includes 1 Black or African American, non-Hispanic/Latino, 2 international. 6 applicants, 0% accepted, 0 enrolled. *Expenses:* Tuition, state resident: full-time $8447; part-time $469 per credit hour. Tuition, nonresident: full-time $16,020; part-time $890 per credit hour. Required fees: $50. *Financial support:* In 2010–11, 4 students received support, including 4 research assistantships (averaging $9,744 per year); tuition waivers (partial) also available. Financial award application deadline: 6/30; financial award applicants required to submit FAFSA. *Unit head:* Dr. Thomas W. Whipple, Chair, 216-687-4771, Fax: 216-687-5135, E-mail: t.whipple@csuohio.edu. *Application contact:* Dr. Thomas W. Whipple, Chair, 216-687-4771, Fax: 216-687-9354, E-mail: t.whipple@csuohio.edu.

Daemen College, Department of Accounting/Information Systems, Amherst, NY 14226-3592. Offers global business (MS), including accounting, global business, management information systems, marketing. Part-time and evening/weekend programs available. *Faculty:* 1 full-time (0 women), 1 part-time/adjunct (0 women). *Students:* 19 full-time (16 women), 5 part-time (1 woman); includes 1 minority (Black or African American, non-Hispanic/Latino), 18 international. Average age 28. In 2010, 12 master's awarded. *Degree requirements:* For master's, minimum GPA of 3.0. *Entrance requirements:* For master's, GMAT if undergraduate GPA is less than 3.0, 2 letters of recommendation; goal statement; transcripts; demonstration of satisfactory oral and written English. Additional exam requirements/recommendations for international students: Required—TOEFL (minimum score 500 paper-based; 173 computer-based; 63 iBT), IELTS (minimum score 5.5). *Application deadline:* For fall admission, 3/1 priority date for domestic and international students; for spring admission, 10/1 priority date for domestic and international students. Applications are processed on a rolling basis. Application fee: $25. Electronic applications accepted. *Expenses:* Tuition: Part-time $830 per credit hour. Tuition and fees vary according to course load and reciprocity agreements. *Financial support:* Institutionally sponsored loans, scholarships/grants, and scholarships available. Financial award application deadline: 2/15; financial award applicants required to submit FAFSA. *Faculty research:* Internationalization of small business, cultural influences on business practices, international human resource practices. *Unit head:* S. Sgt. Sharlene S. Buszka, Chair, 716-839-8428, Fax: 716-839-8261, E-mail: sbuszka@daemen.edu. *Application contact:* Scott Rowe, Associate Director of Graduate Admissions, 716-839-8225, Fax: 716-839-8229, E-mail: srowe@daemen.edu.

DePaul University, Charles H. Kellstadt Graduate School of Business and College of Liberal Arts and Sciences, Department of Economics, Chicago, IL 60604-2287. Offers applied economics (MBA); business strategy (MBA); economics and policy analysis (MA); international business (MBA). Part-time and evening/weekend programs available. *Faculty:* 26 full-time (5 women), 21 part-time/adjunct (5 women). *Students:* 80 full-time (30 women), 31 part-time (12 women); includes 18 minority (8 Black or African American, non-Hispanic/Latino; 7 Asian, non-Hispanic/Latino; 3 Hispanic/Latino), 8 international. In 2010, 7 master's awarded. *Degree requirements:* For master's, thesis optional. *Entrance requirements:* For master's, GMAT (MBA), GRE (MS). Additional exam requirements/recommendations for international students: Required—TOEFL. *Application deadline:* For fall admission, 7/1 for domestic students; for winter admission, 10/1 for domestic students; for spring admission, 2/1 for domestic students. Applications are processed on a rolling basis. Application fee: $40. Electronic applications accepted. *Financial support:* In 2010–11, 3 students received support, including 2 research assistantships with partial tuition reimbursements available (averaging $9,999 per year). Support available to part-time students. *Faculty research:* Forensic economics, game theory sports, economics of education, banking in Poland and Thailand. *Unit head:* Dr. Thomas D. Donley, Chairperson, 312-362-8887, Fax: 312-362-5452, E-mail: tdonley@depaul.edu. *Application contact:* Gabriella Bucci, Director of Graduate Program in Economics, 773-362-6787, Fax: 312-362-5452, E-mail: gbucci@depaul.edu.

Dominican University of California, Graduate Programs, School of Business and Leadership, Program in Global Management, San Rafael, CA 94901-2298. Offers MBA. Part-time programs available. *Faculty:* 2 full-time (0 women), 4 part-time/adjunct (1 woman). *Students:* 21 full-time (9 women), 24 part-time (9 women); includes 14 minority (3 Black or African American, non-Hispanic/Latino; 4 Asian, non-Hispanic/Latino; 7 Hispanic/Latino), 12 international. Average age 29. 35 applicants, 63% accepted, 15 enrolled. In 2010, 11 master's awarded. *Entrance requirements:* For master's, minimum GPA of 3.0. Additional exam requirements/recommendations for international students: Required—TOEFL (minimum score 550 paper-based; 213 computer-based; 80 iBT), IELTS (minimum score 7). *Application deadline:* For fall admission, 6/15 priority date for domestic and international students; for spring admission, 11/15 priority date for domestic and international students. Applications are processed on a rolling basis. Application fee: $40. Electronic applications accepted. *Financial support:* In 2010–11, 13 students received support; fellowships, career-related internships or fieldwork, Federal Work-Study, and scholarships/grants available. Support available to part-time students. Financial award application deadline: 3/2; financial award applicants required to submit FAFSA. *Unit head:* Sue Stavn, Assistant

Dean, 415-482-2418, Fax: 415-459-3206, E-mail: sue.stavn@dominican.edu. *Application contact:* Robbie Hayes, Assistant Director, 415-458-3771, Fax: 415-485-3214, E-mail: robbie.hayes@dominican.edu.

Duquesne University, School of Leadership and Professional Advancement, Pittsburgh, PA 15282-0001. Offers leadership (MS), including business ethics, community leadership, global leadership, information technology, leadership, liberal studies, professional administration, sports leadership. Part-time and evening/weekend programs available. Postbaccalaureate distance learning degree programs offered (no on-campus study). *Faculty:* 1 full-time (0 women), 70 part-time/adjunct (35 women). *Students:* 275 full-time, 171 part-time; includes 20 Black or African American, non-Hispanic/Latino; 1 American Indian or Alaska Native, non-Hispanic/Latino; 6 Asian, non-Hispanic/Latino; 3 Hispanic/Latino. Average age 31. 161 applicants, 73% accepted, 103 enrolled. In 2010, 108 master's awarded. *Degree requirements:* For master's, capstone course. *Entrance requirements:* For master's, professional work experience, 500-word essay. Additional exam requirements/recommendations for international students: Required—TOEFL. *Application deadline:* Applications are processed on a rolling basis. Application fee: $0. Electronic applications accepted. *Expenses:* Tuition: Part-time $884 per credit. Required fees: $84 per credit. Tuition and fees vary according to course load. *Financial support:* Applicants required to submit FAFSA. *Unit head:* Dr. Dorothy Bassett, Dean, 412-396-2141, Fax: 412-396-4711, E-mail: bassettd@duq.edu. *Application contact:* Marianne Leister, Director of Student Services, 412-396-4933, Fax: 412-396-5072, E-mail: leister@duq.edu.

D'Youville College, Department of Business, Buffalo, NY 14201-1084. Offers business administration (MBA); international business (MS). Part-time and evening/weekend programs available. *Faculty:* 4 full-time (1 woman), 7 part-time/adjunct (2 women). *Students:* 63 full-time (46 women), 31 part-time (15 women); includes 24 minority (14 Black or African American, non-Hispanic/Latino; 2 American Indian or Alaska Native, non-Hispanic/Latino; 1 Asian, non-Hispanic/Latino; 6 Hispanic/Latino; 1 Two or more races, non-Hispanic/Latino), 19 international. Average age 30. 86 applicants, 62% accepted, 22 enrolled. In 2010, 19 master's awarded. *Degree requirements:* For master's, one foreign language, project or thesis. *Entrance requirements:* For master's, minimum GPA of 3.0. Additional exam requirements/recommendations for international students: Required—TOEFL (minimum score 500 paper-based; 173 computer-based). *Application deadline:* For fall admission, 5/1 priority date for international students; for spring admission, 9/1 priority date for international students. Applications are processed on a rolling basis. Application fee: $25. Electronic applications accepted. *Expenses:* Tuition: Part-time $790 per credit hour. Part-time tuition and fees vary according to degree level. *Financial support:* In 2010–11, 1 research assistantship with partial tuition reimbursement (averaging $3,000 per year) was awarded; career-related internships or fieldwork, Federal Work-Study, and scholarships/grants also available. Support available to part-time students. Financial award application deadline: 3/1; financial award applicants required to submit FAFSA. *Faculty research:* Assessment, accreditation, supply chain, online learning, adult learning. *Unit head:* Dr. Susan Kowalewski, Chair, 716-829-7839, Fax: 716-829-7760. *Application contact:* Linda Fisher, Graduate Admissions Director, 716-829-8400, Fax: 716-829-7900, E-mail: graduateadmissions@dyc.edu.

Eastern Michigan University, Graduate School, College of Arts and Sciences, Department of World Languages, Program in Language and International Trade, Ypsilanti, MI 48197. Offers MA. Evening/weekend programs available. *Students:* 3 full-time (2 women), 2 part-time (1 woman); includes 1 minority (Black or African American, non-Hispanic/Latino). Average age 27. In 2010, 1 master's awarded. *Degree requirements:* For master's, one foreign language. *Entrance requirements:* Additional exam requirements/recommendations for international students: Required—TOEFL. *Application deadline:* Applications are processed on a rolling basis. Application fee: $35. *Financial support:* Fellowships, research assistantships with full tuition reimbursements, teaching assistantships with full tuition reimbursements, career-related internships or fieldwork, Federal Work-Study, institutionally sponsored loans, scholarships/grants, tuition waivers (partial), and unspecified assistantships available. Support available to part-time students. Financial award applicants required to submit FAFSA. *Application contact:* Dr. Genevieve Peden, Program Advisor, 734-487-1498, Fax: 734-487-3411, E-mail: gpeden@emich.edu.

Eastern Michigan University, Graduate School, College of Arts and Sciences, Department of World Languages, Programs in Foreign Languages, Ypsilanti, MI 48197. Offers French (MA); German (MA); German for business (Graduate Certificate); Hispanic language and cultures (Graduate Certificate); Japanese business practices (Graduate Certificate); Spanish (MA). Part-time and evening/weekend programs available. Postbaccalaureate distance learning degree programs offered (minimal on-campus study). *Students:* 1 (woman) full-time, 12 part-time (11 women); includes 5 minority (1 Black or African American, non-Hispanic/Latino; 1 Asian, non-Hispanic/Latino; 3 Hispanic/Latino), 1 international. Average age 44. In 2010, 8 master's awarded. *Degree requirements:* For master's, one foreign language, thesis optional. *Entrance requirements:* Additional exam requirements/recommendations for international students: Required—TOEFL. *Application deadline:* Applications are processed on a rolling basis. Application fee: $35. *Financial support:* Fellowships, research assistantships with full tuition reimbursements, teaching assistantships with full tuition reimbursements, career-related internships or

fieldwork, Federal Work-Study, institutionally sponsored loans, scholarships/grants, tuition waivers (partial), and unspecified assistantships available. Support available to part-time students. Financial award applicants required to submit FAFSA. *Application contact:* Dr. Genevieve Peden, Program Advisor, 734-487-1498, Fax: 734-487-3411, E-mail: gpeden@emich.edu.

Eastern Michigan University, Graduate School, College of Business, Programs in Business Administration, Ypsilanti, MI 48197. Offers business administration (MBA, Graduate Certificate); computer information systems (Graduate Certificate); e-business (MBA, Graduate Certificate); enterprise business intelligence (MBA); entrepreneurship (MBA, Graduate Certificate); finance (MBA, Graduate Certificate); human resources (MBA); human resources management (Graduate Certificate); information systems (MBA); internal auditing (MBA); international business (MBA, Graduate Certificate); marketing management (Graduate Certificate); nonprofit management (MBA); organizational development (Graduate Certificate); supply chain management (MBA, Graduate Certificate). *Accreditation:* AACSB. Part-time programs available. Postbaccalaureate distance learning degree programs offered (no on-campus study). *Students:* 149 full-time (66 women), 456 part-time (232 women); includes 146 minority (109 Black or African American, non-Hispanic/Latino; 4 American Indian or Alaska Native, non-Hispanic/Latino; 27 Asian, non-Hispanic/Latino; 6 Hispanic/Latino), 105 international. Average age 32. 330 applicants, 64% accepted, 150 enrolled. In 2010, 128 master's, 53 other advanced degrees awarded. *Entrance requirements:* For master's, GMAT (minimum score 450), minimum cumulative undergraduate GPA of 2.75. Additional exam requirements/recommendations for international students: Required—TOEFL. *Application deadline:* For fall admission, 5/15 for domestic students, 5/1 for international students; for winter admission, 10/15 for domestic students, 10/1 for international students; for spring admission, 3/15 for domestic students, 3/1 for international students. Applications are processed on a rolling basis. Application fee: $35. *Financial support:* Fellowships, research assistantships with full tuition reimbursements, teaching assistantships with full tuition reimbursements, career-related internships or fieldwork, Federal Work-Study, institutionally sponsored loans, scholarships/grants, tuition waivers (partial), and unspecified assistantships available. Support available to part-time students. Financial award applicants required to submit FAFSA. *Unit head:* K. Michelle Henry, Interim Director, Graduate Programs, 734-487-4444, Fax: 734-483-1316, E-mail: mhenry1@emich.edu. *Application contact:* Beste Windes, Advisor, 734-487-4444, Fax: 734-483-1316, E-mail: bwindes@emich.edu.

Fairfield University, Charles F. Dolan School of Business, Fairfield, CT 06824-5195. Offers accounting (MBA, MS, CAS); accounting information systems (MBA); entrepreneurship (MBA); finance (MBA, MS, CAS); general management (MBA, CAS); human resource management (MBA, CAS); information systems and operations (MBA); information systems and operations management (CAS); international business (MBA, CAS); marketing (MBA, CAS); taxation (MBA, CAS). *Accreditation:* AACSB. Part-time and evening/weekend programs available. *Faculty:* 42 full-time (15 women), 8 part-time/adjunct (1 woman). *Students:* 89 full-time (32 women), 127 part-time (54 women); includes 4 Black or African American, non-Hispanic/Latino; 2 Asian, non-Hispanic/Latino; 4 Hispanic/Latino; 1 Two or more races, non-Hispanic/Latino, 17 international. Average age 29. 108 applicants, 62% accepted, 46 enrolled. In 2010, 79 master's awarded. *Degree requirements:* For master's, capstone course. *Entrance requirements:* For master's, GMAT (minimum score 500), 2 letters of reference, resume, minimum GPA of 3.0. Additional exam requirements/recommendations for international students: Required—TOEFL (minimum score 550 paper-based; 213 computer-based; 80 iBT). *Application deadline:* For fall admission, 5/15 for international students; for spring admission, 10/15 for international students. Applications are processed on a rolling basis. Application fee: $60. Electronic applications accepted. *Expenses:* Contact institution. *Financial support:* In 2010–11, 48 students received support. Scholarships/grants, unspecified assistantships, and merit based one-time entrance scholarship available. Financial award applicants required to submit FAFSA. *Faculty research:* Optimization strategies, international finance, consumer behavior, financial market volatility, Internet marketing, supply chain analysis, tax issues. Total annual research expenditures: $50,000. *Unit head:* Dr. Norman A. Solomon, Dean, 203-254-4000 Ext. 4070, Fax: 203-254-4105, E-mail: nsolomon@fairfield.edu. *Application contact:* Marianne Gumpper, Director of Graduate and Continuing Studies Admissions, 203-254-4184, Fax: 203-254-4073, E-mail: gradadmis@fairfield.edu.

Fairleigh Dickinson University, College at Florham, Silberman College of Business, Department of Economics, Finance, and International Business, Program in International Business, Madison, NJ 07940-1099. Offers MBA, Certificate. *Students:* 8 part-time (5 women), 1 international. Average age 33. 6 applicants, 83% accepted, 2 enrolled. In 2010, 8 master's awarded. *Application deadline:* Applications are processed on a rolling basis. Application fee: $40.

Fairleigh Dickinson University, Metropolitan Campus, Silberman College of Business, Department of Economics, Finance and International Business, Program in International Business, Teaneck, NJ 07666-1914. Offers MBA. *Students:* 6 full-time (4 women), 1 (woman) part-time, 6 international. Average age 23. 26 applicants, 42% accepted, 3 enrolled. In 2010, 2 master's awarded. *Application deadline:* Applications are processed on a rolling basis. Application fee: $40.

Florida Atlantic University, College of Business, Department of Management Programs, Boca Raton, FL 33431-0991. Offers global entrepreneurship (MBA); international business (MBA, MS); management (PhD). *Faculty:* 30 full-time (10 women), 23 part-time/adjunct (7 women). *Students:* 298 full-time (144 women), 447 part-time (192 women); includes 263 minority (81 Black or African American, non-Hispanic/Latino; 43 Asian, non-Hispanic/Latino; 124 Hispanic/Latino; 1 Native Hawaiian or other Pacific Islander, non-Hispanic/Latino; 14 Two or more races, non-Hispanic/Latino), 41 international. Average age 32. 455 applicants, 40% accepted, 138 enrolled. In 2010, 206 master's, 6 doctorates awarded. *Entrance requirements:* For master's, GMAT or GRE General Test, minimum GPA of 3.0 in last 60 hours of course work. Additional exam requirements/recommendations for international students: Required—TOEFL (minimum score 600 paper-based; 250 computer-based). *Application deadline:* For fall admission, 7/25 for domestic students, 2/15 for international students; for spring admission, 12/10 for domestic students, 7/15 for international students. Applications are processed on a rolling basis. Application fee: $30. Electronic applications accepted. *Expenses:* Tuition, area resident: Part-time $319.96 per credit. Tuition, state resident: part-time $319.96 per credit. Tuition, nonresident: part-time $926.42 per credit. *Financial support:* Research assistantships with full tuition reimbursements, career-related internships or fieldwork, tuition waivers (partial), and unspecified assistantships available. *Faculty research:* Sports administration, healthcare, policy, finance, real estate, senior living. *Unit head:* Dr. Peggy Golden, Chair, 561-297-2675, E-mail: golden@fau.edu. *Application contact:* Dr. Peggy Golden, Chair, 561-297-2675, E-mail: golden@fau.edu.

Florida International University, Alvah H. Chapman, Jr. Graduate School of Business, Department of Management and International Business, International Business Program, Miami, FL 33199. Offers MIB. Part-time and evening/weekend programs available. *Students:* 82 full-time (41 women), 33 part-time (17 women); includes 2 Black or African American, non-Hispanic/Latino; 40 Hispanic/Latino, 61 international. Average age 27. 197 applicants, 38% accepted, 74 enrolled. In 2010, 104 master's awarded. *Entrance requirements:* For master's, GRE or GMAT, minimum GPA of 3.0 (upper-level coursework), letter of intent, bachelor's degree in business administration or related area, resume, at least two years of work experience. Additional exam requirements/recommendations for international students: Required—TOEFL (minimum score 550 paper-based; 213 computer-based; 80 iBT) or IELTS (minimum score 6.5). *Application deadline:* For fall admission, 6/1 for domestic students, 4/1 for international students; for spring admission, 10/1 for domestic students, 9/1 for international students. Applications are processed on a rolling basis. Application fee: $30. Electronic applications accepted. *Expenses:* Contact institution. *Financial support:* Institutionally sponsored loans and scholarships/grants available. Financial award application deadline: 3/1; financial award applicants required to submit FAFSA. *Faculty research:* Strategy, international business, multinational corporations. *Unit head:* Dr. Galen Kroeck, Chair, Management and International Business Department, 305-348-2791, Fax: 305-348-6146, E-mail: kroeck@fiu.edu. *Application contact:* Yusimit Martinez, Coordinator, 305-348-3279, E-mail: yusimit.martinez@business.fiu.edu.

Friends University, Graduate School, Wichita, KS 67213. Offers accounting (MBA); business administration (MBA); business law (MBL); Christian ministry (MACM); family therapy (MSFT); global leadership and management (MA); health care leadership (MHCL); management information systems (MMIS); operations management (MSOM); organization development (MSOD); teaching (MAT). Part-time and evening/weekend programs available. Postbaccalaureate distance learning degree programs offered (minimal on-campus study). *Faculty:* 14 full-time (5 women), 2 part-time/adjunct (1 woman). *Students:* 166 full-time (122 women), 507 part-time (290 women); includes 134 minority (64 Black or African American, non-Hispanic/Latino; 6 American Indian or Alaska Native, non-Hispanic/Latino; 24 Asian, non-Hispanic/Latino; 30 Hispanic/Latino; 1 Native Hawaiian or other Pacific Islander, non-Hispanic/Latino; 9 Two or more races, non-Hispanic/Latino). Average age 38. 445 applicants, 69% accepted, 236 enrolled. In 2010, 345 master's awarded. *Degree requirements:* For master's, research project. *Entrance requirements:* Additional exam requirements/recommendations for international students: Required—TOEFL (minimum score 560 paper-based; 220 computer-based). *Application deadline:* Applications are processed on a rolling basis. Application fee: $45 ($65 for international students). Electronic applications accepted. Tuition and fees vary according to course load, campus/location and program. *Financial support:* Applicants required to submit FAFSA. *Unit head:* Dr. Evelyn Hume, Dean, 800-794-6945 Ext. 5859, Fax: 316-295-5040, E-mail: evelyn hume@friends.edu. Application contact: Jeanette Hanson, Executive Director of Adult Recruitment, 800-794-6945, Fax: 316-295-5050, E-mail: jeanette@friends.edu.

The George Washington University, Elliott School of International Affairs, Program in International Trade and Investment Policy, Washington, DC 20052. Offers MA, JD/MA, MBA/MA. Part-time and evening/weekend programs available. *Students:* 41 full-time (19 women), 12 part-time (9 women); includes 2 Black or African American, non-Hispanic/Latino; 5 Asian, non-Hispanic/Latino; 1 Hispanic/Latino; 2 Two or more races, non-Hispanic/Latino, 11 international. Average age 26. 93 applicants, 70% accepted, 20 enrolled. In 2010, 20 master's awarded. *Degree requirements:* For master's,

one foreign language, capstone project. *Entrance requirements:* For master's, GRE General Test, 2 years of a modern foreign language, 2 semesters of introductory economics. Additional exam requirements/recommendations for international students: Required—TOEFL. *Application deadline:* For fall admission, 2/1 for domestic students; for spring admission, 10/1 for domestic students. Application fee: $75. Electronic applications accepted. *Financial support:* In 2010–11, 11 students received support; fellowships with tuition reimbursements available, research assistantships with tuition reimbursements available, career-related internships or fieldwork, Federal Work-Study, institutionally sponsored loans, and tuition waivers available. Financial award application deadline: 1/15. *Unit head:* Steven Suranovic, Director, 202-994-7579, Fax: 202-994-5477, E-mail: smsuran@gwu.edu. *Application contact:* Jeff V. Miles, Director of Graduate Admissions, 202-994-7050, Fax: 202-994-9537, E-mail: esiagrad@gwu.edu.

The George Washington University, School of Business, Department of International Business, Washington, DC 20052. Offers MBA, PhD, MBA/MA. Part-time and evening/weekend programs available. *Degree requirements:* For doctorate, thesis/dissertation. *Entrance requirements:* For master's, GMAT; for doctorate, GMAT or GRE. Additional exam requirements/recommendations for international students: Required—TOEFL. *Application deadline:* For fall admission, 4/1 priority date for domestic students; for spring admission, 10/1 for domestic students. Applications are processed on a rolling basis. Application fee: $75. *Financial support:* Fellowships, teaching assistantships, career-related internships or fieldwork, Federal Work-Study, and institutionally sponsored loans available. Financial award application deadline: 4/1. *Faculty research:* International trade, competitiveness, business management. *Unit head:* Reid Click, Chair, 202-994-7130, E-mail: rclick@gwu.edu. *Application contact:* Kristin Williams, Assistant Vice President for Graduate and Special Enrollment Management, 202-994-0467, Fax: 202-994-0371, E-mail: ksw@gwu.edu.

Golden Gate University, Ageno School of Business, San Francisco, CA 94105-2968. Offers accounting (MBA); business administration (EMBA, MBA, PMBA, DBA); finance (MBA, MS, Certificate); financial planning (MS, Certificate); healthcare information systems (Certificate); human resource management (MBA, MS); human resources management (Certificate); information systems (MS); information technology (MBA); information technology management (Certificate); integrated marketing and communications (MS, Certificate); international business (MBA); management (MBA); marketing (MBA, MS, Certificate); operations supply chain management (Certificate); psychology (MA, Certificate); public administration (EMPA); public relations (MS, Certificate); technical market analysis (Certificate); JD/MBA. Part-time and evening/weekend programs available. *Faculty:* 16 full-time (4 women), 241 part-time/adjunct (72 women). *Students:* 421 full-time (235 women), 744 part-time (425 women); includes 526 minority (114 Black or African American, non-Hispanic/Latino; 2 American Indian or Alaska Native, non-Hispanic/Latino; 296 Asian, non-Hispanic/Latino; 73 Hispanic/Latino; 29 Native Hawaiian or other Pacific Islander, non-Hispanic/Latino; 12 Two or more races, non-Hispanic/Latino), 100 international. Average age 32. 681 applicants, 78% accepted, 270 enrolled. In 2010, 550 master's, 13 doctorates awarded. *Degree requirements:* For doctorate, thesis/dissertation. *Entrance requirements:* For master's, GMAT (MBA), minimum GPA of 2.5 (MS). Additional exam requirements/recommendations for international students: Required—TOEFL. *Application deadline:* For fall admission, 5/15 for domestic and international students; for winter admission, 1/15 for domestic and international students; for spring admission, 9/15 for domestic and international students. Applications are processed on a rolling basis. Application fee: $70 ($110 for international students). Electronic applications accepted. *Expenses:* Contact institution. *Financial support:* Career-related internships or fieldwork, Federal Work-Study, institutionally sponsored loans, and scholarships/grants available. Support available to part-time students. Financial award applicants required to submit FAFSA. *Unit head:* Dr. Paul Fouts, Dean, 415-442-7026, Fax: 415-442-6579. *Application contact:* Angela Melero, Enrollment Services, 415-442-7800, Fax: 415-442-7807, E-mail: info@ggu.edu.

Goldey-Beacom College, Graduate Program, Wilmington, DE 19808-1999. Offers business administration (MBA); finance (MS); financial management (MBA); human resource management (MBA); information technology (MBA); international business management (MBA); major finance (MBA); major taxation (MBA); management (MM); marketing management (MBA); taxation (MBA, MS). *Accreditation:* ACBSP. Part-time and evening/weekend programs available. *Faculty:* 20 full-time (8 women), 28 part-time/adjunct (10 women). *Students:* 55 full-time (28 women), 393 part-time (164 women); includes 252 minority (51 Black or African American, non-Hispanic/Latino; 2 American Indian or Alaska Native, non-Hispanic/Latino; 183 Asian, non-Hispanic/Latino; 13 Hispanic/Latino; 1 Native Hawaiian or other Pacific Islander, non-Hispanic/Latino; 2 Two or more races, non-Hispanic/Latino). Average age 27. In 2010, 231 master's awarded. *Entrance requirements:* For master's, GMAT, MAT, GRE, minimum GPA of 3.0. Additional exam requirements/recommendations for international students: Required—TOEFL (minimum score 65 computer-based); Recommended—IELTS (minimum score 5). *Application deadline:* Applications are processed on a rolling basis. Electronic applications accepted. *Expenses:* Tuition: Full-time $14,796; part-time $822 per credit.

Required fees: $180; $10 per credit. *Financial support:* Scholarships/grants available. Support available to part-time students. Financial award application deadline: 4/1; financial award applicants required to submit FAFSA. *Unit head:* Larry W. Eby, Director of Admissions, 302-225-6289, Fax: 302-996-5408, E-mail: ebylw@gbc.edu. *Application contact:* Ashley E. Mashington, Graduate Admissions Representative, 302-225-6259, Fax: 302-996-5408, E-mail: mashina@gbc.edu.

Harding University, College of Business Administration, Searcy, AR 72149-0001. Offers health care management (MBA); information technology management (MBA); international business (MBA); leadership and organizational management (MBA). *Accreditation:* ACBSP. Part-time and evening/weekend programs available. Postbaccalaureate distance learning degree programs offered (no on-campus study). *Faculty:* 30 part-time/adjunct (6 women). *Students:* 85 full-time (49 women), 133 part-time (52 women); includes 35 minority (27 Black or African American, non-Hispanic/Latino; 1 American Indian or Alaska Native, non-Hispanic/Latino; 4 Asian, non-Hispanic/Latino; 1 Hispanic/Latino; 1 Native Hawaiian or other Pacific Islander, non-Hispanic/Latino; 1 Two or more races, non-Hispanic/Latino), 29 international. Average age 30. 52 applicants, 94% accepted, 44 enrolled. In 2010, 100 master's awarded. *Degree requirements:* For master's, portfolio. *Entrance requirements:* For master's, minimum GPA of 3.0, 2 letters of recommendation, resume. Additional exam requirements/recommendations for international students: Required—TOEFL (minimum score 550 paper-based; 213 computer-based; 80 iBT). *Application deadline:* For fall admission, 8/1 priority date for domestic and international students; for spring admission, 12/1 priority date for domestic and international students. Applications are processed on a rolling basis. Application fee: $35. *Expenses:* Tuition: Full-time $10,098; part-time $561 per credit hour. Required fees: $22.50 per credit hour. *Financial support:* In 2010–11, 19 students received support. Unspecified assistantships available. Financial award application deadline: 7/30; financial award applicants required to submit FAFSA. *Unit head:* Glen Metheny, Director of Graduate Studies, 501-279-5851, Fax: 501-279-4805, E-mail: gmetheny@harding.edu. *Application contact:* Melanie Kiihnl, Recruiting Manager/Director of Marketing, 501-279-4523, Fax: 501-279-4805, E-mail: mba@harding.edu.

HEC Montreal, School of Business Administration, Master of Science Programs in Administration, Program in International Business, Montréal, QC H3T 2A7, Canada. Offers M Sc. Part-time programs available. *Students:* 65 full-time (32 women), 13 part-time (8 women). 70 applicants, 44% accepted, 18 enrolled. In 2010, 29 master's awarded. *Degree requirements:* For master's, one foreign language, thesis. *Application deadline:* For fall admission, 3/15 for domestic and international students; for winter admission, 10/1 for domestic and international students. Application fee: $78. Electronic applications accepted. *Expenses:* Tuition, area resident: Part-time $68.93 per credit. Tuition, state resident: full-time $2481.48; part-time $188.92 per credit. Tuition, nonresident: full-time $6801; part-time $482.06 per course. International tuition: $17,354.16 full-time. Required fees: $1309.50; $30.28 per credit. $93.45 per term. Tuition and fees vary according to degree level and program. *Financial support:* Research assistantships, teaching assistantships available. Financial award application deadline: 9/2. *Unit head:* Dr. Claude Laurin, Director, 514-340-6485, Fax: 514-340-6880, E-mail: claude.laurin@hec.ca. *Application contact:* Francine Blais, Administrative Director, 514-340-6112, Fax: 514-340-6411, E-mail: francine.blais@hec.ca.

Hofstra University, Frank G. Zarb School of Business, Department of Marketing and International Business, Hempstead, NY 11549. Offers business administration (MBA), including international business, marketing; marketing (MS); marketing research (MS). Part-time and evening/weekend programs available. Postbaccalaureate distance learning degree programs offered (minimal on-campus study). *Faculty:* 7 full-time (0 women), 2 part-time/adjunct (0 women). *Students:* 63 full-time (34 women), 47 part-time (24 women); includes 9 minority (1 Black or African American, non-Hispanic/Latino; 2 Asian, non-Hispanic/Latino; 6 Hispanic/Latino), 52 international. Average age 27. 150 applicants, 66% accepted, 36 enrolled. In 2010, 35 master's awarded. *Degree requirements:* For master's, capstone course (MBA), thesis (MS). *Entrance requirements:* For master's, GMAT or GRE, 2 letters of recommendation, resume, essay. Additional exam requirements/recommendations for international students: Required—TOEFL (minimum score 550 paper-based; 213 computer-based; 80 iBT); Recommended—IELTS (minimum score 6). *Application deadline:* Applications are processed on a rolling basis. Application fee: $70 ($75 for international students). Electronic applications accepted. *Expenses:* Contact institution. *Financial support:* In 2010–11, 22 students received support, including 21 fellowships with full and partial tuition reimbursements available (averaging $8,965 per year); research assistantships with full and partial tuition reimbursements available, career-related internships or fieldwork, Federal Work-Study, institutionally sponsored loans, scholarships/grants, tuition waivers (full and partial), and unspecified assistantships also available. Support available to part-time students. Financial award applicants required to submit FAFSA. *Faculty research:* Outsourcing, global alliances, retailing, Web marketing, cross-cultural age research. *Unit head:* Dr. Benny Barak, Chairperson, 516-463-5707, Fax: 516-463-4834, E-mail: mktbzb@hofstra.edu. *Application contact:* Carol Drummer,

Dean of Graduate Admissions, 516-463-4876, Fax: 516-463-4664, E-mail: gradstudent@hofstra.edu.

Iona College, Hagan School of Business, Department of Marketing and International Business, New Rochelle, NY 10801-1890. Offers international business (Certificate, PMC); marketing (MBA). Part-time and evening/weekend programs available. *Faculty:* 3 full-time (1 woman), 2 part-time/adjunct (0 women). *Students:* 14 full-time (12 women), 29 part-time (16 women); includes 9 minority (1 Black or African American, non-Hispanic/Latino; 2 Asian, non-Hispanic/Latino; 6 Hispanic/Latino). Average age 28. 18 applicants, 67% accepted, 10 enrolled. In 2010, 22 master's, 66 other advanced degrees awarded. *Entrance requirements:* For master's, GMAT, 2 letters of recommendation; for other advanced degree, GMAT. Additional exam requirements/recommendations for international students: Required—TOEFL (minimum score 550 paper-based; 213 computer-based). *Application deadline:* Applications are processed on a rolling basis. Application fee: $50. Electronic applications accepted. *Expenses:* Contact institution. *Financial support:* Scholarships/grants, tuition waivers (partial), and unspecified assistantships available. Support available to part-time students. Financial award application deadline: 4/15; financial award applicants required to submit FAFSA. *Faculty research:* Business ethics, international retailing, mega-marketing, consumer behavior and consumer confidence. *Unit head:* Dr. Frederica E. Rudell, Chair, 914-637-2748, E-mail: frudell@iona.edu. *Application contact:* Ben Fan, Director of MBA Admissions, 914-633-2289, Fax: 914-637-2708, E-mail: sfan@iona.edu.

John Marshall Law School, Graduate and Professional Programs, Chicago, IL 60604-3968. Offers comparative legal studies (LL M); employee benefits (LL M, MS); information technology (LL M, MS); intellectual property (LL M); international business and trade (LL M); law (JD); real estate (LL M, MS); taxation (LL M, MS); JD/LL M; JD/MA; JD/MBA; JD/MPA. JD/MBA offered jointly with Dominican University, JD/MA and JD/MPA with Roosevelt University. *Accreditation:* ABA. Part-time and evening/weekend programs available. *Faculty:* 65 full-time (21 women), 152 part-time/adjunct (48 women). *Students:* 1,237 full-time (567 women), 373 part-time (181 women); includes 464 minority (138 Black or African American, non-Hispanic/Latino; 12 American Indian or Alaska Native, non-Hispanic/Latino; 96 Asian, non-Hispanic/Latino; 125 Hispanic/Latino; 11 Native Hawaiian or other Pacific Islander, non-Hispanic/Latino; 82 Two or more races, non-Hispanic/Latino), 39 international. Average age 27. 3,523 applicants, 44% accepted, 351 enrolled. In 2010, 387 first professional degrees, 8 master's awarded. *Degree requirements:* For JD, 90 credits. *Entrance requirements:* For JD, LSAT; for master's, JD. Additional exam requirements/recommendations for international students: Required—TOEFL. *Application deadline:* For fall admission, 3/1 priority date for domestic and international students; for spring admission, 10/15 priority date for domestic and international students. Applications are processed on a rolling basis. Application fee: $60. Electronic applications accepted. *Expenses:* Contact institution. *Financial support:* In 2010–11, 1,350 students received support. Scholarships/grants and tuition waivers (full and partial) available. Support available to part-time students. Financial award application deadline: 6/1; financial award applicants required to submit FAFSA. *Unit head:* John Corkery, Dean, 312-427-2737. *Application contact:* William B. Powers, Associate Dean of Admission and Student Affairs, 800-537-4280, Fax: 312-427-5136, E-mail: admission@jmls.edu.

Johnson & Wales University, The Alan Shawn Feinstein Graduate School, MBA Program in Global Business Leadership, Providence, RI 02903-3703. Offers accounting (MBA); enhanced accounting (MBA); hospitality (MBA). Part-time programs available. *Faculty:* 14 full-time (3 women), 18 part-time/adjunct (4 women). *Students:* 736 full-time (433 women), 359 part-time (237 women); includes 46 minority (18 Black or African American, non-Hispanic/Latino; 5 Asian, non-Hispanic/Latino; 22 Hispanic/Latino; 1 Native Hawaiian or other Pacific Islander, non-Hispanic/Latino), 640 international. Average age 29. 397 applicants, 76% accepted, 219 enrolled. In 2010, 329 master's awarded. *Entrance requirements:* For master's, minimum GPA of 2.75. Additional exam requirements/recommendations for international students: Required—TOEFL (minimum score 550 paper-based; 210 computer-based) or IELTS (recommended); Recommended—TWE. *Application deadline:* For fall admission, 8/15 priority date for domestic students, 6/28 priority date for international students; for winter admission, 11/10 priority date for domestic students, 9/20 priority date for international students; for spring admission, 2/5 priority date for domestic students, 12/20 priority date for international students. Applications are processed on a rolling basis. *Expenses:* Tuition: Part-time $1535 per course. Part-time tuition and fees vary according to degree level and program. *Financial support:* Tuition waivers (partial) and unspecified assistantships available. Support available to part-time students. Financial award application deadline: 5/1. *Faculty research:* International banking, global economy, international trade, cultural differences. *Unit head:* Dr. Frank Sargent, Director, 401-598-1033, Fax: 401-598-1125. *Application contact:* Graduate School Admissions, 401-598-1015, Fax: 401-598-1286, E-mail: gradadm@jwu.edu.

Kean University, Nathan Weiss Graduate College, Program in Global Management, Union, NJ 07083. Offers executive management (MBA); global management (MBA). *Faculty:* 4 full-time (3 women). *Students:* 50 full-time (27 women), 46 part-time (24 women); includes 30 Black or African

American, non-Hispanic/Latino; 9 Asian, non-Hispanic/Latino; 18 Hispanic/Latino; 1 Native Hawaiian or other Pacific Islander, non-Hispanic/Latino, 17 international. Average age 32. 26 applicants, 92% accepted, 18 enrolled. In 2010, 38 master's awarded. *Degree requirements:* For master's, one foreign language, internship or study abroad. *Entrance requirements:* For master's, GMAT, minimum GPA of 3.0, 3 letters of recommendation, prerequisite business courses, transcripts, personal essay, interview; 5 years of experience, resume, and personal statement (for executive management option). Additional exam requirements/recommendations for international students: Required—TOEFL. *Application deadline:* For fall admission, 6/1 for domestic students; for spring admission, 11/1 for domestic students. Applications are processed on a rolling basis. Application fee: $75 ($150 for international students). Electronic applications accepted. *Expenses:* Tuition, state resident: full-time $10,872; part-time $500 per credit. Tuition, nonresident: full-time $14,736; part-time $614 per credit. Required fees: $2740.80; $125 per credit. Part-time tuition and fees vary according to course load and degree level. *Financial support:* In 2010–11, 17 research assistantships with full tuition reimbursements (averaging $3,263 per year) were awarded; unspecified assistantships also available. Financial award applicants required to submit FAFSA. *Unit head:* Dr. David Shani, Program Coordinator, 908-737-5980, E-mail: dshani@kean.edu. *Application contact:* Reenat Hasan, Pre-Admissions Coordinator, 908-737-5923, Fax: 908-737-5925, E-mail: rhasan@exchange.kean.edu.

Keiser University, Master of Business Administration Program, Fort Lauderdale, FL 33309. Offers accounting (MBA); health services management (MBA); international business (MBA); leadership for managers (MBA); marketing (MBA). Leadership for Managers and International Business concentrations also offered in Spanish. Part-time programs available. Postbaccalaureate distance learning degree programs offered (minimal on-campus study). *Faculty:* 8 full-time (3 women), 7 part-time/adjunct (2 women). *Students:* 18 full-time (14 women), 83 part-time (51 women); includes 30 Black or African American, non-Hispanic/Latino; 2 American Indian or Alaska Native, non-Hispanic/Latino; 2 Asian, non-Hispanic/Latino; 17 Hispanic/Latino, 1 international. Average age 42. 30 applicants, 77% accepted, 18 enrolled. In 2010, 21 degrees awarded. *Entrance requirements:* For master's, minimum GPA of 2.7 from an accredited institution. Additional exam requirements/recommendations for international students: Required—TOEFL. *Application deadline:* Applications are processed on a rolling basis. Application fee: $50. Electronic applications accepted. *Financial support:* In 2010–11, 95 students received support. Federal Work-Study available. Financial award applicants required to submit FAFSA.

Lake Forest Graduate School of Management, MBA Program, Lake Forest, IL 60045. Offers global business (MBA); healthcare management (MBA); management (MBA); marketing (MBA); organizational behavior (MBA). Part-time and evening/weekend programs available. *Faculty:* 123 part-time/adjunct (26 women). *Students:* 734 part-time (306 women); includes 156 minority (34 Black or African American, non-Hispanic/Latino; 86 Asian, non-Hispanic/Latino; 14 Hispanic/Latino; 4 Native Hawaiian or other Pacific Islander, non-Hispanic/Latino; 18 Two or more races, non-Hispanic/Latino). Average age 38. In 2010, 202 master's awarded. *Entrance requirements:* For master's, 4 years of work experience in field, interview, 2 letters of recommendation. *Application deadline:* For fall admission, 7/1 for domestic students; for winter admission, 1/5 for domestic students; for spring admission, 3/1 for domestic students. Applications are processed on a rolling basis. Application fee: $0. Electronic applications accepted. *Financial support:* In 2010–11, 290 students received support. Scholarships/grants available. Support available to part-time students. Financial award applicants required to submit FAFSA. *Unit head:* Chris Multhauf, Vice President and Degree Programs Dean, 847-574-5270, Fax: 847-295-3656, E-mail: cmulthauf@lfgsm.edu. *Application contact:* Carolyn Brune, Director of Admissions Operations, 800-737-4MBA, Fax: 847-295-3656, E-mail: admiss@lfgsm.edu.

Lawrence Technological University, College of Management, Southfield, MI 48075-1058. Offers business administration (MBA, DBA); business administration international (MBA); global leadership and management (MS); global operations and project management (MS); information systems (MS); information technology (DM); operations management (MS). *Accreditation:* ACBSP. Part-time and evening/weekend programs available. *Faculty:* 14 full-time (6 women), 53 part-time/adjunct (14 women). *Students:* 7 full-time (2 women), 584 part-time (258 women); includes 137 Black or African American, non-Hispanic/Latino; 2 American Indian or Alaska Native, non-Hispanic/Latino; 51 Asian, non-Hispanic/Latino; 10 Hispanic/Latino; 8 Two or more races, non-Hispanic/Latino, 48 international. Average age 35. 431 applicants, 54% accepted, 151 enrolled. In 2010, 216 master's, 12 doctorates awarded. *Degree requirements:* For master's, thesis (for some programs). *Entrance requirements:* For master's, GMAT. Additional exam requirements/recommendations for international students: Required—TOEFL (minimum score 550 paper-based; 213 computer-based; 79 iBT). *Application deadline:* For fall admission, 6/30 priority date for domestic students, 6/30 for international students; for spring admission, 11/15 priority date for domestic students, 11/15 for international students. Applications are processed on a rolling basis. Application fee: $50. Electronic applications accepted. *Financial support:* In 2010–11, 142 students received support. Federal Work-Study and institutionally sponsored loans available. Support available to part-time students.

Financial award application deadline: 4/1; financial award applicants required to submit FAFSA. *Unit head:* Dr. Lou DeGennaro, Dean, 248-204-3050, E-mail: degennaro@ltu.edu. *Application contact:* Jane Rohrback, Director of Admissions, 248-204-3160, Fax: 248-204-2228, E-mail: admissions@ltu.edu.

Lewis University, College of Business, Graduate School of Management, Program in Business Administration, Romeoville, IL 60446. Offers accounting (MBA); custom elective option (MBA); e-business (MBA); finance (MBA); healthcare management (MBA); human resources management (MBA); information security (MBA); international business (MBA); management information systems (MBA); marketing (MBA); project management (MBA); technology and operations management (MBA). Part-time and evening/weekend programs available. *Students:* 119 full-time (66 women), 204 part-time (104 women); includes 55 Black or African American, non-Hispanic/Latino; 9 Asian, non-Hispanic/Latino; 30 Hispanic/Latino; 1 Native Hawaiian or other Pacific Islander, non-Hispanic/Latino, 9 international. Average age 28. In 2010, 111 master's awarded. *Entrance requirements:* For master's, interview, bachelor's degree, resume, 2 recommendations. Additional exam requirements/recommendations for international students: Required—TOEFL (minimum score 550 paper-based; 213 computer-based). *Application deadline:* For fall admission, 8/15 priority date for domestic students, 5/1 priority date for international students; for spring admission, 11/15 priority date for international students. Applications are processed on a rolling basis. Application fee: $40. Electronic applications accepted. *Expenses:* Tuition: Full-time $13,320; part-time $740 per credit hour. Tuition and fees vary according to program. *Financial support:* Career-related internships or fieldwork, Federal Work-Study, scholarships/grants, and unspecified assistantships available. Financial award application deadline: 5/1; financial award applicants required to submit FAFSA. *Unit head:* Dr. Maureen Culleeney, Academic Program Director, 815-838-0500 Ext. 5631, E-mail: culleema@lewisu.edu. *Application contact:* Michele Ryan, Director of Admission, 815-838-0500 Ext. 5384, E-mail: gsm@lewisu.edu.

Lincoln University, Graduate Studies, Oakland, CA 94612. Offers finance and investments (DBA); finance management and investment banking (MBA); general business (MBA); human resource management (MBA, DBA); international business (MBA); management information systems (MBA). Part-time and evening/weekend programs available. *Faculty:* 9 full-time (2 women), 11 part-time/adjunct (1 woman). *Students:* 297 full-time (134 women), 2 part-time (0 women). In 2010, 124 master's awarded. *Degree requirements:* For master's, research project (thesis), internship report, or comprehensive exam; for doctorate, comprehensive exam, thesis/dissertation. *Entrance requirements:* For master's, minimum GPA of 2.7; for doctorate, GMAT (minimum score: 550), GRE (minimum score: 1000), or equivalent test results (waived for master's degree with minimum cumulative GPA of 3.3). Additional exam requirements/recommendations for international students: Required—TOEFL (525 paper, 195 computer, 71 iBT) or IELTS (5.5) for MBA; TOEFL (550 paper, 213 computer, 79 iBT) or IELTS (6.0) for DBA; Recommended—IELTS. *Application deadline:* For fall admission, 7/2 priority date for domestic and international students; for spring admission, 11/25 priority date for domestic students, 11/26 priority date for international students. Applications are processed on a rolling basis. Application fee: $75. Electronic applications accepted. *Expenses:* Tuition: Full-time $6930. Required fees: $195 per semester. *Financial support:* In 2010–11, 1 teaching assistantship was awarded; career-related internships or fieldwork and scholarships/grants also available. *Unit head:* Dr. Marshall Burak, Director of Graduate Programs, 510-628-8016, Fax: 510-628-8012, E-mail: mburak@lincolnuca.edu. *Application contact:* Peggy Au, Director of Admissions and Records, 510-628-8010, Fax: 510-628-8012, E-mail: admissions@lincolnuca.edu.

Lindenwood University, Graduate Programs, School of Business and Entrepreneurship, St. Charles, MO 63301-1695. Offers accounting (MBA, MS); business administration (MBA); entrepreneurial studies (MBA, MS); finance (MBA, MS); human resource management (MBA); human resources (MS); international business (MBA, MS); management (MBA, MS); management information systems (MBA, MS); marketing (MBA, MS); public management (MBA, MS); sport management (MA). *Accreditation:* ACBSP. Part-time and evening/weekend programs available. *Faculty:* 20 full-time (8 women), 17 part-time/adjunct (5 women). *Students:* 179 full-time (73 women), 184 part-time (87 women); includes 27 minority (20 Black or African American, non-Hispanic/Latino; 3 Asian, non-Hispanic/Latino; 4 Hispanic/Latino), 146 international. Average age 28. 149 applicants, 73 enrolled. In 2010, 142 master's awarded. *Degree requirements:* For master's, comprehensive exam (for some programs), thesis (for some programs). *Entrance requirements:* For master's, interview, minimum GPA of 3.0, letter of recommendation. Additional exam requirements/recommendations for international students: Required—TOEFL (minimum score 550 paper-based; 213 computer-based; 80 iBT). *Application deadline:* For fall admission, 7/30 priority date for domestic students, 9/16 priority date for international students; for winter admission, 12/15 priority date for domestic and international students; for spring admission, 2/25 priority date for domestic students, 2/11 priority date for international students. Applications are processed on a rolling basis. Application fee: $30 ($100 for international students). Electronic applications accepted. *Expenses:* Tuition: Full-time $13,260; part-time $380 per credit hour. Required fees: $340. One-time fee: $30. Tuition and fees vary according to course level and course load. *Financial support:* In 2010–11, 209 students received support. Career-related internships or fieldwork, Federal Work-Study, institutionally sponsored loans, and tuition waivers (partial) available. Financial award application deadline: 6/30; financial award applicants required to submit FAFSA. *Unit head:* Roger Ellis, Dean, 636-949-4839, E-mail: rellis@lindenwood.edu. *Application contact:* Brett Barger, Dean of Evening Admissions and Extension Campuses, 636-949-4934, Fax: 636-949-4109, E-mail: adultadmissions@lindenwood.edu.

Manhattanville College, Graduate Programs, Humanities and Social Sciences Programs, Program in International Management, Purchase, NY 10577-2132. Offers MS. Part-time and evening/weekend programs available. *Entrance requirements:* Additional exam requirements/recommendations for international students: Required—TOEFL. *Application deadline:* Applications are processed on a rolling basis. Application fee: $75. *Expenses:* Tuition: Full-time $16,110; part-time $895 per credit. Required fees: $50 per semester. *Financial support:* Career-related internships or fieldwork, Federal Work-Study, institutionally sponsored loans, and unspecified assistantships available. Financial award application deadline: 3/1; financial award applicants required to submit FAFSA. *Unit head:* Donald Richards, Dean, School of Graduate and Professional Studies, 914-323-5469, Fax: 914-694-3488, E-mail: gps@mville.edu. *Application contact:* Office of Admissions for Graduate and Professional Studies, 914-323-5418, E-mail: gps@mville.edu.

Marquette University, Graduate School of Management, Executive MBA Program, Milwaukee, WI 53201-1881. Offers economics (MBA); finance (MBA); human resources (MBA); international business (MBA); management information systems (MBA); marketing (MBA); operations and supply chain management (MBA); sports business (MBA). *Accreditation:* AACSB. *Faculty:* 3 full-time (1 woman), 2 part-time/adjunct (0 women). *Students:* 43 full-time (11 women); includes 6 minority (1 Black or African American, non-Hispanic/Latino; 4 Asian, non-Hispanic/Latino; 1 Hispanic/Latino), 3 international. Average age 37. 47 applicants, 74% accepted, 29 enrolled. In 2010, 13 master's awarded. *Degree requirements:* For master's, international trip. *Entrance requirements:* For master's, GMAT, two letters of recommendation, official transcripts from current and previous colleges/universities. Additional exam requirements/recommendations for international students: Required—TOEFL (minimum score 530 paper-based; 78 computer-based). *Application deadline:* Applications are processed on a rolling basis. Application fee: $50. Electronic applications accepted. *Expenses:* Contact institution. *Financial support:* Application deadline: 2/15. *Faculty research:* International trade and finance, customer relationship management, consumer satisfaction, customer service. *Unit head:* Dr. Jeanne Simmons, Graduate Director, 414-288-7145, Fax: 414-288-1660, E-mail: jeanne.simmons@marquette.edu. *Application contact:* Erin Fox, Assistant Director for Recruitment, 414-288-5319, Fax: 414-288-1902, E-mail: erin.fox@marquette.edu.

Marquette University, Graduate School of Management, Program in Business Administration, Milwaukee, WI 53201-1881. Offers business administration (MBA); economics (MBA); finance (MBA); human resources (MBA); international business (MBA); management information systems (MBA); marketing (MBA); operations and supply chain management (MBA); sports business (MBA); JD/MBA; MBA/MA; MBA/MSN. *Accreditation:* AACSB. Part-time and evening/weekend programs available. *Faculty:* 38 full-time (9 women), 24 part-time/adjunct (8 women). *Students:* 44 full-time (17 women), 368 part-time (105 women); includes 36 minority (4 Black or African American, non-Hispanic/Latino; 2 American Indian or Alaska Native, non-Hispanic/Latino; 20 Asian, non-Hispanic/Latino; 10 Hispanic/Latino), 30 international. Average age 31. 256 applicants, 60% accepted, 98 enrolled. In 2010, 117 master's awarded. *Entrance requirements:* For master's, GMAT, letters of recommendation. Additional exam requirements/recommendations for international students: Required—TOEFL (minimum score 530 paper-based; 78 computer-based). *Application deadline:* Applications are processed on a rolling basis. Application fee: $50. Electronic applications accepted. *Expenses:* Tuition: Full-time $16,290; part-time $905 per credit hour. Tuition and fees vary according to program. *Financial support:* In 2010–11, 4 fellowships, 11 teaching assistantships were awarded; research assistantships, Federal Work-Study, institutionally sponsored loans, scholarships/grants, and tuition waivers (full and partial) also available. Support available to part-time students. Financial award application deadline: 2/15. *Faculty research:* Ethics in the professions, services marketing, technology impact on decision-making, mentoring. *Unit head:* Dr. Jeanne Simmons, Graduate Director, 414-288-7145, Fax: 414-288-1660, E-mail: jeanne.simmons@marquette.edu. *Application contact:* Debra Leutermann, Admissions Coordinator, 414-288-8064, Fax: 414-288-1902, E-mail: debra.leutermann@marquette.edu.

McKendree University, Graduate Programs, Master of Business Administration Program, Lebanon, IL 62254-1299. Offers business administration (MBA); human resource management (MBA); international business (MBA). Part-time and evening/weekend programs available. Postbaccalaureate distance learning degree programs offered (no on-campus study). *Faculty:* 8 full-time (3 women), 19 part-time/adjunct (3 women). *Students:* 99 full-time (49 women), 155 part-time (63 women). Average age 36. In 2010, 37 master's awarded. *Entrance requirements:* For master's, official transcripts from all institutions attended, essay, minimum GPA of 3.0, three references, resume. Additional exam requirements/recommendations for international students:

Required—TOEFL. *Application deadline:* Applications are processed on a rolling basis. Application fee: $0. Electronic applications accepted. *Expenses:* Tuition: Full-time $6750; part-time $375 per credit hour. One-time fee: $100. Tuition and fees vary according to program. *Financial support:* Application deadline: 6/30. *Unit head:* Dr. Frank Spreng, Director of MBA Program, 618-537-6902, E-mail: fspreng@mckendree.edu. *Application contact:* Patty L. Aubel, Graduate Admission Counselor, 618-537-6943, Fax: 618-537-6410, E-mail: plaubel@mckendree.edu.

Milwaukee School of Engineering, Rader School of Business, Program in Marketing and Export Management, Milwaukee, WI 53202-3109. Offers MS. *Faculty:* 1 full-time (0 women), 1 part-time/adjunct (0 women). *Students:* 9 part-time (5 women); includes 1 Asian, non-Hispanic/Latino; 1 Hispanic/Latino. Average age 28. 2 applicants, 100% accepted, 2 enrolled. *Degree requirements:* For master's, thesis optional, thesis defense or capstone project. *Entrance requirements:* For master's, GRE General Test or GMAT, 2 letters of recommendation. Additional exam requirements/recommendations for international students: Recommended—TOEFL (minimum score 550 paper-based; 213 computer-based; 79 iBT), IELTS. *Application deadline:* Applications are processed on a rolling basis. Application fee: $30. Electronic applications accepted. *Expenses:* Tuition: Full-time $17,550; part-time $650 per credit. One-time fee: $75. *Financial support:* In 2010–11, 6 students received support. Applicants required to submit FAFSA. *Unit head:* Dr. Kathy Faggiani, Director, 414-277-2711, Fax: 414-277-2711, E-mail: faggiani@msoe.edu. *Application contact:* Sarah K. Winchowky, Graduate Admissions Director, 800-321-6763, Fax: 414-277-7475, E-mail: wp@msoe.edu.

Montclair State University, The Graduate School, School of Business, Department of Marketing, Montclair, NJ 07043-1624. Offers international business (MBA, Certificate); marketing (MBA). Part-time and evening/weekend programs available. *Faculty:* 10 full-time (5 women), 6 part-time/adjunct (2 women). *Students:* 6 full-time (1 woman), 40 part-time (22 women); includes 4 Black or African American, non-Hispanic/Latino; 5 Asian, non-Hispanic/Latino; 2 Hispanic/Latino. Average age 27. 50 applicants, 60% accepted, 8 enrolled. In 2010, 11 master's awarded. *Entrance requirements:* For master's, GMAT, 2 letters of recommendation, resume. Additional exam requirements/recommendations for international students: Required—TOEFL (minimum iBT score of 83) or IELTS. *Application deadline:* For fall admission, 6/1 for international students; for spring admission, 10/1 for international students. Applications are processed on a rolling basis. Application fee: $60. Electronic applications accepted. *Expenses:* Tuition, state resident: part-time $501.34 per credit. Tuition, nonresident: part-time $773.88 per credit. Required fees: $71.15 per credit. *Financial support:* In 2010–11, 5 research assistantships with tuition reimbursements (averaging $7,000 per year) were awarded; Federal Work-Study, scholarships/grants, and unspecified assistantships also available. Support available to part-time students. Financial award application deadline: 3/1; financial award applicants required to submit FAFSA. *Faculty research:* Converting service marketing to tangibility, mathematical approaches to solving marketing problems, system dynamic modeling of brand management, attitudes toward safety in leisure facilities, marketing/retailing strategy and instruction. *Unit head:* Dr. Avinandan Mukherjee, Chair, 973-655-5126. *Application contact:* Amy Aiello, Director of Graduate Admissions and Operations, 973-655-5147, Fax: 973-655-7869, E-mail: graduate.school@montclair.edu.

National University, Academic Affairs, School of Business and Management, Department of Accounting and Finance, La Jolla, CA 92037-1011. Offers accountancy (MS); corporate and international finance (MS). Part-time and evening/weekend programs available. Postbaccalaureate distance learning degree programs offered (no on-campus study). *Faculty:* 15 full-time (2 women), 149 part-time/adjunct (39 women). *Students:* 171 full-time (76 women), 410 part-time (202 women); includes 201 minority (40 Black or African American, non-Hispanic/Latino; 1 American Indian or Alaska Native, non-Hispanic/Latino; 67 Asian, non-Hispanic/Latino; 86 Hispanic/Latino; 1 Native Hawaiian or other Pacific Islander, non-Hispanic/Latino; 6 Two or more races, non-Hispanic/Latino), 147 international. Average age 33. 727 applicants, 100% accepted, 466 enrolled. In 2010, 58 master's awarded. *Degree requirements:* For master's, thesis. *Entrance requirements:* For master's, interview, minimum GPA of 2.5. Additional exam requirements/recommendations for international students: Required—TOEFL (minimum score 550 paper-based; 213 computer-based; 79 iBT), IELTS (minimum score 6). *Application deadline:* Applications are processed on a rolling basis. Application fee: $60 ($65 for international students). Electronic applications accepted. *Expenses:* Tuition: Full-time $9450; part-time $350 per unit. Required fees: $350 per unit. One-time fee: $60. *Financial support:* Career-related internships or fieldwork, institutionally sponsored loans, scholarships/grants, and tuition waivers (partial) available. Support available to part-time students. Financial award application deadline: 6/30; financial award applicants required to submit FAFSA. *Unit head:* Prof. Donald A. Schwartz, Chair and Associate Professor, 858-642-8420, Fax: 858-642-8740, E-mail: dschwartz@nu.edu. *Application contact:* Dominick Giovanniello, Associate Regional Dean—San Diego, 800-NAT-UNIV, Fax: 858-541-7792, E-mail: dgiovann@nu.edu.

National University, Academic Affairs, School of Business and Management, Department of Leadership and Business Administration, La Jolla, CA 92037-1011. Offers alternative dispute resolution (MBA); e-business (MBA);

financial management (MBA); human resource management (MBA); human resources management (MA); international business (MBA); knowledge management (MS); marketing (MBA); organizational leadership (MBA, MS); technology management (MBA). Part-time and evening/weekend programs available. Postbaccalaureate distance learning degree programs offered (no on-campus study). *Faculty:* 16 full-time (4 women), 126 part-time/adjunct (39 women). *Students:* 119 full-time (81 women), 410 part-time (202 women); includes 176 minority (81 Black or African American, non-Hispanic/Latino; 1 American Indian or Alaska Native, non-Hispanic/Latino; 31 Asian, non-Hispanic/Latino; 52 Hispanic/Latino; 4 Native Hawaiian or other Pacific Islander, non-Hispanic/Latino; 7 Two or more races, non-Hispanic/Latino), 183 international. Average age 38. 219 applicants, 100% accepted, 160 enrolled. In 2010, 95 master's awarded. *Degree requirements:* For master's, thesis. *Entrance requirements:* For master's, interview, minimum GPA of 2.5. Additional exam requirements/recommendations for international students: Required—TOEFL (minimum score 550 paper-based; 213 computer-based; 79 iBT), IELTS (minimum score 6). *Application deadline:* Applications are processed on a rolling basis. Application fee: $60 ($65 for international students). Electronic applications accepted. *Expenses:* Tuition: Full-time $9450; part-time $350 per unit. Required fees: $350 per unit. One-time fee: $60. *Financial support:* Career-related internships or fieldwork, institutionally sponsored loans, scholarships/grants, and tuition waivers (partial) available. Support available to part-time students. Financial award application deadline: 6/30; financial award applicants required to submit FAFSA. *Unit head:* Dr. Bruce Buchowicz, Chair, 858-642-8439, Fax: 858-642-8406, E-mail: bbuchowicz@nu.edu. *Application contact:* Dominick Giovanniello, Associate Regional Dean—San Diego, 800-NAT-UNIV, Fax: 858-541-7792, E-mail: dgiovann@nu.edu.

Newman University, MBA Program, Wichita, KS 67213-2097. Offers finance (MBA); international business (MBA); leadership (MBA); management (MBA); technology (MBA). Part-time programs available. *Faculty:* 4 full-time (2 women), 7 part-time/adjunct (2 women). *Students:* 33 full-time (14 women), 92 part-time (37 women); includes 28 minority (7 Black or African American, non-Hispanic/Latino; 6 Asian, non-Hispanic/Latino; 12 Hispanic/Latino; 1 Native Hawaiian or other Pacific Islander, non-Hispanic/Latino; 2 Two or more races, non-Hispanic/Latino), 24 international. Average age 32. 80 applicants, 83% accepted, 45 enrolled. In 2010, 72 master's awarded. *Degree requirements:* For master's, thesis optional. *Entrance requirements:* For master's, interview; minimum GPA of 3.0; 3 letters of recommendation; course work in algebra, statistics, macroeconomics, and financial accounting. Additional exam requirements/recommendations for international students: Required—TOEFL (minimum score 600 paper-based; 250 computer-based; 100 iBT). *Application deadline:* For fall admission, 8/1 priority date for domestic students, 7/15 priority date for international students; for winter admission, 1/1 priority date for domestic students; for spring admission, 1/1 priority date for domestic students, 11/15 priority date for international students. Applications are processed on a rolling basis. Application fee: $25 ($40 for international students). Electronic applications accepted. *Expenses:* Contact institution. *Financial support:* In 2010–11, 29 students received support. Federal Work-Study available. Financial award application deadline: 8/15; financial award applicants required to submit FAFSA. *Unit head:* Dr. George Goetz, Dean of the College of Professional Studies/Director, 316-942-4291 Ext. 2205, Fax: 316-942-4483, E-mail: smithge@newmanu.edu. *Application contact:* Linda Kay Sabala, Director of Graduate Admissions, 316-942-4291 Ext. 2230, Fax: 316-942-4483, E-mail: sabalal@newmanu.edu.

New Mexico Highlands University, Graduate Studies, School of Business, Las Vegas, NM 87701. Offers business administration (MBA), including government nonprofit management, human resource management, international business, management, management information systems. *Accreditation:* ACBSP. *Faculty:* 14 full-time (3 women). *Students:* 71 full-time (44 women), 124 part-time (68 women); includes 119 minority (8 Black or African American, non-Hispanic/Latino; 18 American Indian or Alaska Native, non-Hispanic/Latino; 1 Asian, non-Hispanic/Latino; 89 Hispanic/Latino; 1 Native Hawaiian or other Pacific Islander, non-Hispanic/Latino; 2 Two or more races, non-Hispanic/Latino), 34 international. Average age 34. 128 applicants, 98% accepted, 34 enrolled. In 2010, 48 master's awarded. *Degree requirements:* For master's, comprehensive exam, thesis or alternative. *Entrance requirements:* For master's, minimum undergraduate GPA of 3.0. Additional exam requirements/recommendations for international students: Required—TOEFL (minimum score 540 paper-based; 207 computer-based). *Application deadline:* For fall admission, 8/1 priority date for domestic students. Applications are processed on a rolling basis. Application fee: $15. *Expenses:* Tuition, state resident: full-time $2544. Required fees: $624; $132 per credit hour. *Financial support:* In 2010–11, 29 students received support. Career-related internships or fieldwork, Federal Work-Study, institutionally sponsored loans, scholarships/grants, tuition waivers (full and partial), and unspecified assistantships available. Support available to part-time students. Financial award application deadline: 3/1; financial award applicants required to submit FAFSA. *Faculty research:* Real estate valuation, studying expert judgments in complex accounting, decision environments, green marketing, environmentalism, marketing research methodology. *Unit head:* Dr. Margaret Young, Dean, 505-454-3522, Fax: 505-454-3354, E-mail: young m@nmhu.edu. Application contact: Diane Trujillo, Administrative Assistant, Graduate Studies, 505-454-3266, Fax: 505-426-2117, E-mail: dtrujillo@nmhu.edu.

New York Institute of Technology, Graduate Division, School of Management, Program in Business Administration, Old Westbury, NY 11568-8000. Offers accounting (Advanced Certificate); business administration (MBA); finance (Advanced Certificate); international business (Advanced Certificate); management of information systems (Advanced Certificate); marketing (Advanced Certificate). Part-time and evening/weekend programs available. *Students:* 454 full-time (188 women), 513 part-time (204 women); includes 49 minority (15 Black or African American, non-Hispanic/Latino; 23 Asian, non-Hispanic/Latino; 11 Hispanic/Latino), 268 international. Average age 29. In 2010, 435 master's, 1 other advanced degree awarded. *Degree requirements:* For master's, thesis (for some programs). *Entrance requirements:* For master's, minimum QPA of 2.85. Additional exam requirements/recommendations for international students: Required—TOEFL (minimum score 550 paper-based; 213 computer-based). *Application deadline:* For fall admission, 7/1 priority date for domestic students; for spring admission, 12/1 priority date for domestic students. Applications are processed on a rolling basis. Application fee: $50. Electronic applications accepted. *Expenses:* Tuition: Part-time $835 per credit. *Financial support:* Fellowships, research assistantships with partial tuition reimbursements, institutionally sponsored loans, tuition waivers (full and partial), and unspecified assistantships available. Support available to part-time students. Financial award applicants required to submit FAFSA. *Faculty research:* Instructor performance appraisal; relationship between TOEFL, GMAT, GRE, and performance in foreign students. *Unit head:* Dr. Stephen Hartman, Director, 516-686-7691, E-mail: shartman@nyit.edu. *Application contact:* Dr. Jacquelyn Nealon, Vice President for Enrollment Services, 516-686-7925, Fax: 516-686-7597, E-mail: jnealon@nyit.edu.

New York University, Graduate School of Arts and Science, Department of Politics, New York, NY 10012-1019. Offers political campaign management (MA); politics (MA, PhD); JD/MA; MBA/MA. Part-time programs available. *Faculty:* 30 full-time (4 women). *Students:* 183 full-time (92 women), 54 part-time (29 women); includes 2 Black or African American, non-Hispanic/Latino; 14 Asian, non-Hispanic/Latino; 6 Hispanic/Latino, 111 international. Average age 28. 747 applicants, 34% accepted, 78 enrolled. In 2010, 78 master's, 9 doctorates awarded. Terminal master's awarded for partial completion of doctoral program. *Degree requirements:* For master's, one foreign language, thesis or alternative; for doctorate, 2 foreign languages, comprehensive exam, thesis/dissertation. *Entrance requirements:* For master's, GRE General Test; for doctorate, GRE General Test, master's degree in political science, minimum GPA of 2.5. Additional exam requirements/recommendations for international students: Required—TOEFL. *Application deadline:* For fall admission, 12/15 priority date for domestic students. Application fee: $90. *Financial support:* Fellowships with tuition reimbursements, teaching assistantships with tuition reimbursements, career-related internships or fieldwork, Federal Work-Study, and institutionally sponsored loans available. Financial award application deadline: 12/15; financial award applicants required to submit FAFSA. *Faculty research:* Comparative politics, democratic theory and practice, rational choice, political economy, international relations. *Unit head:* Michael Gilligan, Director of PhD Program, 212-998-8500, Fax: 212-995-4184, E-mail: politics.phd@nyu.edu. *Application contact:* Shinasi Rama, Director of Master's Program, 212-998-8500, Fax: 212-995-4184, E-mail: politics.masters@nyu.edu.

New York University, School of Continuing and Professional Studies, Schack Institute of Real Estate, Program in Real Estate, New York, NY 10012-1019. Offers business of development (MS); finance and investment (MS); global real estate (MS); real estate (Advanced Certificate); strategic real estate management (MS); sustainable development (MS). Part-time and evening/weekend programs available. *Faculty:* 11 full-time (3 women), 74 part-time/adjunct (8 women). *Students:* 94 full-time (17 women), 282 part-time (63 women); includes 16 Black or African American, non-Hispanic/Latino; 2 American Indian or Alaska Native, non-Hispanic/Latino; 30 Asian, non-Hispanic/Latino; 17 Hispanic/Latino, 62 international. Average age 30. 298 applicants, 68% accepted, 111 enrolled. In 2010, 184 master's, 48 other advanced degrees awarded. *Degree requirements:* For master's, thesis, capstone. *Entrance requirements:* For master's, GRE General Test or GMAT (for recent graduates), resume, 2 letters of recommendation, essay, professional experience. Additional exam requirements/recommendations for international students: Required—TOEFL (minimum score 600 paper-based; 250 computer-based; 100 iBT), TWE. *Application deadline:* For fall admission, 2/1 priority date for domestic and international students; for spring admission, 10/15 priority date for domestic students, 8/15 priority date for international students. Applications are processed on a rolling basis. Application fee: $75. Electronic applications accepted. *Financial support:* In 2010–11, 186 students received support, including 186 fellowships (averaging $2,423 per year); scholarships/grants also available. Support available to part-time students. Financial award application deadline: 3/1; financial award applicants required to submit FAFSA. *Faculty research:* Economics and market cycles, international property rights, comparative metropolitan economies, current market trends. *Unit head:* James Stuckey, Divisional Dean, 212-992-3335, Fax: 212-992-3686, E-mail: james.stuckey@nyu.edu. *Application contact:* Jennifer Monahan, Director of Administration and Student Services, 212-992-3335, Fax: 212-992-3686, E-mail: jm189@nyu.edu.

Norwich University, School of Graduate and Continuing Studies, Program in Diplomacy, Northfield, VT 05663. Offers international commerce (MA); international conflict management (MA); international terrorism (MA). Evening/weekend programs available. *Faculty:* 44 part-time/adjunct (8 women). *Students:* 168 full-time (62 women); includes 12 Black or African American, non-Hispanic/Latino; 4 Asian, non-Hispanic/Latino; 18 Hispanic/Latino. Average age 38. 273 applicants, 74% accepted, 168 enrolled. In 2010, 168 master's awarded. *Degree requirements:* For master's, comprehensive exam, thesis optional. *Entrance requirements:* For master's, minimum undergraduate GPA of 2.75. Additional exam requirements/recommendations for international students: Required—TOEFL. *Application deadline:* For fall admission, 8/10 for domestic and international students; for winter admission, 11/7 for domestic and international students; for spring admission, 2/6 for domestic and international students. Application fee: $50. Electronic applications accepted. *Expenses:* Tuition: Full-time $17,380; part-time $645 per credit. Tuition and fees vary according to program. *Financial support:* Scholarships/grants available. Financial award applicants required to submit FAFSA. *Unit head:* Dr. Harold Kearsley, Program Director, 802-485-2730, E-mail: hkearsley@norwich.edu. *Application contact:* Sally Burkart, Application Management Team Lead, 802-485-2096, Fax: 802-485-2533, E-mail: sburkart@norwich.edu.

Nova Southeastern University, H. Wayne Huizenga School of Business and Entrepreneurship, Doctoral Program in Business Administration, Fort Lauderdale, FL 33314-7796. Offers accounting (DBA); decision sciences (DBA); finance (DBA); human resource management (DBA); international business (DBA); management (DBA); marketing (DBA). Part-time and evening/weekend programs available. *Faculty:* 34 full-time (11 women), 2 part-time/adjunct (1 woman). *Students:* 2 full-time (1 woman), 93 part-time (32 women); includes 9 Black or African American, non-Hispanic/Latino; 4 Asian, non-Hispanic/Latino, 11 Hispanic/Latino, 8 international. Average age 47. 66 applicants, 14% accepted, 6 enrolled. In 2010, 29 doctorates awarded. *Degree requirements:* For doctorate, comprehensive exam, thesis/dissertation. *Entrance requirements:* For doctorate, GMAT. Additional exam requirements/recommendations for international students: Required—TOEFL (minimum score 600 paper-based; 250 computer-based; 100 iBT), IELTS (minimum score 7). *Application deadline:* Applications are processed on a rolling basis. Application fee: $50. Electronic applications accepted. *Financial support:* Available to part-time students. Applicants required to submit FAFSA. *Faculty research:* Reputation management, call centers, international social capital, corporate earnings guidance, corporate governance. *Unit head:* Kristie Tetrault, Director of Program Administration, 954-262-5120, Fax: 954-262-3849, E-mail: kristie@huizenga.nova.edu. *Application contact:* Karen Goldberg, Associate Director of Recruitment and Special Events, 954-262-5039, Fax: 954-262-3822, E-mail: karen@huizenga.nova.edu.

Nova Southeastern University, H. Wayne Huizenga School of Business and Entrepreneurship, Program in International Business Administration, Fort Lauderdale, FL 33314-7796. Offers MIBA. Part-time and evening/weekend programs available. Postbaccalaureate distance learning degree programs offered (minimal on-campus study). *Faculty:* 4 full-time (2 women), 6 part-time/adjunct (2 women). *Students:* 30 full-time (22 women), 226 part-time (116 women); includes 37 Black or African American, non-Hispanic/Latino; 1 American Indian or Alaska Native, non-Hispanic/Latino; 11 Asian, non-Hispanic/Latino; 119 Hispanic/Latino, 41 international. Average age 31. 95 applicants, 57% accepted, 34 enrolled. In 2010, 80 master's awarded. *Degree requirements:* For master's, thesis optional. *Entrance requirements:* Additional exam requirements/recommendations for international students: Required—TOEFL (minimum score 550 paper-based; 213 computer-based; 79 iBT), IELTS (minimum score 6). *Application deadline:* For fall admission, 8/15 for domestic and international students; for winter admission, 12/10 for domestic and international students; for spring admission, 2/10 for domestic and international students. Applications are processed on a rolling basis. Application fee: $50. Electronic applications accepted. *Financial support:* Career-related internships or fieldwork, Federal Work-Study, and scholarships/grants available. Support available to part-time students. Financial award applicants required to submit FAFSA. *Unit head:* Dr. Preston Jones, Executive Associate Dean, 954-262-5127, Fax: 954-262-3960, E-mail: prestonj@huizenga.nova.edu. *Application contact:* Karen Goldberg, Associate Director of Recruitment and Special Events, 954-262-5039, Fax: 954-262-3822, E-mail: karen@nova.edu.

Old Dominion University, College of Business and Public Administration, MBA Program, Norfolk, VA 23529. Offers business and economic forecasting (MBA); financial analysis and valuation (MBA); information technology and enterprise integration (MBA); international business (MBA); maritime and port management (MBA); public administration (MBA). *Accreditation:* AACSB. Part-time and evening/weekend programs available. *Faculty:* 66 full-time (15 women), 6 part-time/adjunct (1 woman). *Students:* 74 full-time (32 women), 166 part-time (62 women); includes 45 minority (21 Black or African American, non-Hispanic/Latino; 1 American Indian or Alaska Native, non-Hispanic/Latino; 8 Asian, non-Hispanic/Latino; 10 Hispanic/Latino; 1 Native Hawaiian or other Pacific Islander, non-Hispanic/Latino; 4 Two or more races, non-Hispanic/Latino), 19 international. Average age 31. 169 applicants, 52% accepted, 61 enrolled. In 2010, 100 master's awarded. *Entrance*

requirements: For master's, GMAT, letter of reference, resume, coursework in calculus, essay. Additional exam requirements/recommendations for international students: Required—TOEFL (minimum score 550 paper-based; 213 computer-based; 80 iBT). *Application deadline:* For fall admission, 6/1 priority date for domestic students, 4/15 priority date for international students; for spring admission, 11/1 priority date for domestic students, 10/1 priority date for international students. Applications are processed on a rolling basis. Application fee: $50. Electronic applications accepted. *Expenses:* Tuition, state resident: full-time $8592; part-time $358 per credit. Tuition, nonresident: full-time $21,672; part-time $903 per credit. Required fees: $119 per semester. One-time fee: $50. *Financial support:* In 2010–11, 44 students received support, including 90 research assistantships with partial tuition reimbursements available (averaging $3,200 per year); career-related internships or fieldwork, scholarships/grants, and unspecified assistantships also available. Support available to part-time students. Financial award application deadline: 2/15; financial award applicants required to submit FAFSA. *Faculty research:* International business, buyer behavior, financial markets, strategy, operations research. *Unit head:* Dr. Larry Filer, Graduate Program Director, 757-683-3585, Fax: 757-683-5750, E-mail: mbainfo@odu.edu. *Application contact:* Shanna Wood, MBA Program Manager, 757-683-3585, Fax: 757-683-5750, E-mail: mbainfo@odu.edu.

Pacific States University, College of Business, Los Angeles, CA 90006. Offers accounting (MBA); business administration (DBA); finance (MBA); international business (MBA); management of information technology (MBA); real estate management (MBA). Part-time and evening/weekend programs available. Postbaccalaureate distance learning degree programs offered (no on-campus study). *Faculty:* 4 full-time (1 woman), 13 part-time/adjunct (0 women). *Students:* 130 full-time (55 women); includes 1 Black or African American, non-Hispanic/Latino; 7 Asian, non-Hispanic/Latino; 3 Native Hawaiian or other Pacific Islander, non-Hispanic/Latino, 115 international. Average age 31. 42 applicants, 83% accepted, 33 enrolled. In 2010, 67 master's awarded. *Degree requirements:* For doctorate, comprehensive exam, thesis/dissertation. *Entrance requirements:* For master's, minimum undergraduate GPA of 2.5 during last 90 hours of course work. Additional exam requirements/recommendations for international students: Required—TOEFL (minimum score 133 computer-based; 45 iBT), IELTS (minimum score 4.5). *Application deadline:* For fall admission, 8/15 priority date for domestic students; for winter admission, 10/15 priority date for domestic students; for spring admission, 1/15 priority date for domestic students. Applications are processed on a rolling basis. Application fee: $100. *Expenses:* Tuition: Full-time $8280; part-time $345 per credit hour. Required fees: $150 per quarter. *Financial support:* Scholarships/grants available. Financial award applicants required to submit FAFSA. *Unit head:* Dr. Chase C. Lee, Director, 888-200-0383, Fax: 323-731-2383, E-mail: admission@psuca.edu. *Application contact:* Zolzaya Enkhbayar, Assistant Director of Admissions, 323-731-2383, Fax: 323-731-7276, E-mail: admissions@psuca.edu.

Pepperdine University, Graziadio School of Business and Management, International MBA Program, Malibu, CA 90263. Offers IMBA. *Students:* 29 full-time (15 women), 1 (woman) part-time; includes 5 minority (2 Black or African American, non-Hispanic/Latino; 3 Asian, non-Hispanic/Latino), 3 international. 25 applicants, 52% accepted, 13 enrolled. In 2010, 7 master's awarded. *Entrance requirements:* For master's, GMAT or GRE, two letters of recommendation. Additional exam requirements/recommendations for international students: Required—TOEFL. *Application deadline:* For fall admission, 5/1 for domestic students, 4/1 for international students. Application fee: $75. Electronic applications accepted. *Unit head:* Dr. Linda A. Livingstone, Dean, Graziadio School of Business and Management, 310-568-5689, Fax: 310-568-5766, E-mail: linda.livingstone@pepperdine.edu. *Application contact:* Darrell Eriksen, Director of Admission and Student Accounts, Graziadio School of Business and Management, 310-568-5525, E-mail: darrell.eriksen@pepperdine.edu.

Pepperdine University, Graziadio School of Business and Management, MS in Global Business Program, Malibu, CA 90263. Offers MS. *Students:* 22 full-time (17 women); includes 2 minority (both Asian, non-Hispanic/Latino), 19 international. 70 applicants, 51% accepted, 15 enrolled. In 2010, 1 master's awarded. *Entrance requirements:* For master's, GMAT or GRE, two letters of recommendation. Additional exam requirements/recommendations for international students: Required—TOEFL. *Application deadline:* For fall admission, 5/1 for domestic students. Application fee: $75. *Unit head:* Dr. Linda A. Livingstone, Dean, Graziadio School of Business and Management, 310-568-5689, Fax: 310-568-5766, E-mail: linda.livingstone@pepperdine.edu. *Application contact:* Darrell Eriksen, Director of Admission and Student Accounts, Graziadio School of Business and Management, 310-568-5525, E-mail: darrell.eriksen@pepperdine.edu.

Portland State University, Graduate Studies, School of Business Administration, Program in International Management, Portland, OR 97207-0751. Offers MIM. Part-time and evening/weekend programs available. *Students:* 49 full-time (22 women), 75 part-time (40 women); includes 19 minority (2 Black or African American, non-Hispanic/Latino; 14 Asian, non-Hispanic/Latino; 3 Hispanic/Latino), 40 international. Average age 28. 70 applicants, 94% accepted, 48 enrolled. In 2010, 60 master's awarded. *Degree requirements:* For master's, field study trip to China and Japan. *Entrance* *requirements:* For master's, GMAT, GRE General Test, minimum GPA of 2.75, resume, 2 letters of recommendation. Additional exam requirements/recommendations for international students: Required—TOEFL (minimum score 550 paper-based; 213 computer-based). *Application deadline:* For fall admission, 4/30 priority date for domestic students, 3/1 priority date for international students. Applications are processed on a rolling basis. Application fee: $50. *Expenses:* Tuition, state resident: full-time $8505; part-time $315 per credit. Tuition, nonresident: full-time $13,284; part-time $492 per credit. Required fees: $1482; $21 per credit. $99 per term. One-time fee: $120. Part-time tuition and fees vary according to course load and program. *Financial support:* Research assistantships with tuition reimbursements, teaching assistantships, career-related internships or fieldwork, Federal Work-Study, and institutionally sponsored loans available. Support available to part-time students. Financial award application deadline: 3/1; financial award applicants required to submit FAFSA. *Unit head:* Cliff Allen, Director, 503-725-5053, Fax: 503-725-2290, E-mail: cliffa@sba.pdx.edu. *Application contact:* Cliff Allen, Director, 503-725-5053, Fax: 503-725-2290, E-mail: cliffa@sba.pdx.edu.

Providence College, Graduate Studies, School of Business, Providence, RI 02918. Offers accounting (MBA); entrepreneurship (MBA); finance (MBA); international business (MBA); management (MBA); marketing (MBA); not-for-profit organizations (MBA). Part-time and evening/weekend programs available. *Faculty:* 17 full-time (9 women), 10 part-time/adjunct (2 women). *Students:* 53 full-time (20 women), 57 part-time (22 women); includes 4 minority (1 Black or African American, non-Hispanic/Latino; 1 Asian, non-Hispanic/Latino; 2 Two or more races, non-Hispanic/Latino), 6 international. Average age 26. 72 applicants, 81% accepted. In 2010, 56 master's awarded. *Degree requirements:* For master's, thesis optional. *Entrance requirements:* For master's, GMAT. Additional exam requirements/recommendations for international students: Required—TOEFL (minimum score 550 paper-based; 213 computer-based; 80 iBT). *Application deadline:* For fall admission, 8/1 priority date for domestic and international students; for spring admission, 12/1 priority date for domestic and international students. Applications are processed on a rolling basis. Application fee: $55. *Expenses:* Contact institution. *Financial support:* In 2010–11, 34 research assistantships with full tuition reimbursements (averaging $8,400 per year) were awarded; Federal Work-Study, institutionally sponsored loans, and unspecified assistantships also available. Support available to part-time students. Financial award application deadline: 8/1; financial award applicants required to submit FAFSA. *Unit head:* Dr. MaryJane Lenon, Director, MBA Program, 401-865-2566, Fax: 401-865-2978, E-mail: mjlenon@providence.edu. *Application contact:* Katherine A. Follett, Administrative Coordinator, 401-865-2333, Fax: 401-865-2978, E-mail: kfollett@providence.edu.

Purdue University, Graduate School, Krannert School of Management, International Master's in Management Program, West Lafayette, IN 47907. Offers MBA. *Faculty:* 12 full-time (3 women), 4 part-time/adjunct (0 women). *Students:* 72 full-time (12 women); includes 2 Asian, non-Hispanic/Latino. Average age 35. 43 applicants, 88% accepted, 35 enrolled. In 2010, 42 master's awarded. *Entrance requirements:* Additional exam requirements/recommendations for international students: Required—TOEFL (minimum score 77 iBT). *Application deadline:* For fall admission, 12/1 for domestic and international students. Applications are processed on a rolling basis. Application fee: $55. Electronic applications accepted. *Financial support:* Application deadline: 3/1. *Unit head:* Charles R. Johnson, Executive Director, 877-622-5726. *Application contact:* JoAnn Whitford, Director of Admissions, 877-622-5726, E-mail: jwhitfor@purdue.edu.

Rochester Institute of Technology, Graduate Enrollment Services, E. Philip Saunders College of Business, Graduate Business Programs, Program in Management, Rochester, NY 14623-5603. Offers MS. Part-time and evening/weekend programs available. *Students:* 1 full-time (0 women), 1 part-time (0 women). Average age 25. 20 applicants, 25% accepted, 1 enrolled. In 2010, 2 master's awarded. *Degree requirements:* For master's, comprehensive exam (for some programs), thesis (for some programs). *Entrance requirements:* For master's, GMAT, minimum GPA of 2.5. Additional exam requirements/recommendations for international students: Required—TOEFL (minimum score 580 paper-based; 237 computer-based; 92 iBT) or IELTS (minimum score 7). *Application deadline:* For fall admission, 2/15 priority date for domestic and international students; for winter admission, 11/1 priority date for domestic students, 10/1 priority date for international students; for spring admission, 2/1 priority date for domestic students, 1/1 priority date for international students. Applications are processed on a rolling basis. Application fee: $50. *Expenses:* Tuition: Full-time $33,234; part-time $924 per credit hour. Required fees: $219. *Financial support:* In 2010–11, 2 students received support; research assistantships with partial tuition reimbursements available, teaching assistantships with partial tuition reimbursements available, career-related internships or fieldwork, scholarships/grants, and unspecified assistantships available. Support available to part-time students. Financial award applicants required to submit FAFSA. *Faculty research:* Strategic and managerial issues associated with manufacturing and production systems, total quality management (TQM), technology-based entrepreneurship. *Unit head:* Heather Krakehl, Graduate Program Director, 585-475-6916, Fax: 585-475-7450, E-mail: hmasch@rit.edu. *Application contact:* Diane Ellison, Assistant

Vice President, Graduate Enrollment Services, 585-475-2229, Fax: 585-475-7164, E-mail: gradinfo@rit.edu.

Rollins College, Crummer Graduate School of Business, Winter Park, FL 32789-4499. Offers entrepreneurship (MBA); finance (MBA); international business (MBA); management (MBA); marketing (MBA); operations and technology management (MBA). *Accreditation:* AACSB. Part-time and evening/weekend programs available. Postbaccalaureate distance learning degree programs offered (minimal on-campus study). *Faculty:* 22 full-time (3 women), 5 part-time/adjunct (3 women). *Students:* 303 full-time (117 women), 130 part-time (49 women); includes 111 minority (30 Black or African American, non-Hispanic/Latino; 1 American Indian or Alaska Native, non-Hispanic/Latino; 29 Asian, non-Hispanic/Latino; 50 Hispanic/Latino; 1 Two or more races, non-Hispanic/Latino), 29 international. Average age 32. 484 applicants, 42% accepted, 131 enrolled. In 2010, 223 master's awarded. *Entrance requirements:* For master's, GMAT, interview. Additional exam requirements/recommendations for international students: Required—TOEFL (minimum score 550 paper-based; 213 computer-based; 80 iBT). *Application deadline:* Applications are processed on a rolling basis. Application fee: $50. Electronic applications accepted. *Expenses:* Contact institution. *Financial support:* In 2010–11, 112 students received support, including 95 fellowships, 56 research assistantships (averaging $2,400 per year); career-related internships or fieldwork, scholarships/grants, and unspecified assistantships also available. Support available to part-time students. Financial award applicants required to submit FAFSA. *Faculty research:* Sustainability, world financial markets, international business, market research, strategic marketing. *Unit head:* Dr. Craig M. McAllaster, Dean, 407-646-2249, Fax: 407-646-1550, E-mail: cmcallaster@rollins.edu. *Application contact:* Linda Puritz, Student Admissions Office, 407-646-2405, Fax: 407-646-1550, E-mail: mba admissions@rollins.edu.

Rutgers, The State University of New Jersey, Newark, Graduate School, Program in Management, Newark, NJ 07102. Offers accounting (PhD); accounting information systems (PhD); computer information systems (PhD); finance (PhD); information technology (PhD); international business (PhD); management science (PhD); marketing (PhD); organization management (PhD). Program offered jointly with New Jersey Institute of Technology. *Accreditation:* AACSB. *Faculty:* 128 full-time (24 women), 4 part-time/adjunct (1 woman). *Students:* 95 full-time (34 women), 17 part-time (6 women); includes 9 Black or African American, non-Hispanic/Latino; 54 Asian, non-Hispanic/Latino; 3 Hispanic/Latino. 438 applicants, 14% accepted, 34 enrolled. In 2010, 10 doctorates awarded. *Degree requirements:* For doctorate, thesis/dissertation, cumulative exams. *Entrance requirements:* For doctorate, GMAT or GRE General Test, minimum undergraduate B average. Additional exam requirements/recommendations for international students: Required—TOEFL. *Application deadline:* For fall admission, 4/1 for domestic students; for spring admission, 11/1 for domestic students. Applications are processed on a rolling basis. Application fee: $60. Electronic applications accepted. *Expenses:* Tuition, state resident: part-time $600 per credit. Tuition, nonresident: full-time $10,694. *Financial support:* In 2010–11, 6 fellowships (averaging $18,000 per year), 4 research assistantships with full and partial tuition reimbursements (averaging $23,112 per year), 38 teaching assistantships with full and partial tuition reimbursements (averaging $23,112 per year) were awarded; institutionally sponsored loans and tuition waivers (full and partial) also available. Support available to part-time students. Financial award application deadline: 2/15. *Faculty research:* Technology management, leadership and teams, consumer behavior, financial and markets, logistics. *Unit head:* Dr. Glenn Shafer, Director, 973-353-1604, Fax: 973-353-5691, E-mail: gshafer@rbs.rutgers.edu. *Application contact:* Goncalo Filipe, Senior Academic Coordinator, 973-353-1002, Fax: 973-353-5691, E-mail: gfilipe@rbsmail.rutgers.edu.

Rutgers, The State University of New Jersey, Newark, Rutgers Business School–Newark and New Brunswick, Doctoral Programs in Management, Newark, NJ 07102. Offers accounting (PhD); accounting information systems (PhD); economics (PhD); finance (PhD); individualized study (PhD); information technology (PhD); international business (PhD); management science (PhD); marketing science (PhD); organizational management (PhD); science, technology and management (PhD); supply chain management (PhD). *Faculty:* 143 full-time (36 women), 2 part-time/adjunct (0 women). *Students:* 117 full-time (42 women), 1 (woman) part-time; includes 8 Black or African American, non-Hispanic/Latino; 14 Asian, non-Hispanic/Latino; 3 Hispanic/Latino, 68 international. Average age 33. 355 applicants, 14% accepted, 35 enrolled. In 2010, 8 doctorates awarded. *Degree requirements:* For doctorate, comprehensive exam, thesis/dissertation. *Entrance requirements:* For doctorate, GRE or GMAT. Additional exam requirements/recommendations for international students: Required—TOEFL (minimum score 550 paper-based; 213 computer-based; 79 iBT). *Application deadline:* For fall admission, 3/1 for domestic and international students; for spring admission, 10/15 for domestic and international students. Application fee: $65. Electronic applications accepted. *Expenses:* Tuition, state resident: part-time $600 per credit. Tuition, nonresident: full-time $10,694. *Financial support:* In 2010–11, 52 students received support, including 7 fellowships (averaging $18,000 per year), 4 research assistantships with tuition reimbursements available (averaging $23,112 per year), 41 teaching assistantships with tuition reimbursements available (averaging $23,112 per year); health care benefits also available. Financial award application deadline: 3/1. *Unit head:* Dr. Glenn Shafer, Director, 973-353-1604, Fax: 973-353-5691, E-mail: gshafer@rbs.rutgers. edu. *Application contact:* Information Contact, 973-353-5371, Fax: 973-353-5691, E-mail: phdinfo@andromeda.rutgers.edu.

St. Edward's University, School of Management and Business, Area of Business Administration, Austin, TX 78704. Offers accounting (MBA); business management (MBA); corporate finance (MBA, Certificate); global entrepreneurship (MBA); human resource management (Certificate); management information systems (MBA, Certificate); marketing (MBA, Certificate); operations management (MBA, Certificate). Part-time and evening/weekend programs available. *Faculty:* 17 full-time (7 women), 19 part-time/adjunct (4 women). *Students:* 41 full-time (21 women), 273 part-time (135 women); includes 111 minority (19 Black or African American, non-Hispanic/Latino; 1 American Indian or Alaska Native, non-Hispanic/Latino; 8 Asian, non-Hispanic/Latino; 78 Hispanic/Latino; 1 Native Hawaiian or other Pacific Islander, non-Hispanic/Latino; 4 Two or more races, non-Hispanic/Latino), 11 international. Average age 33. 101 applicants, 77% accepted, 50 enrolled. In 2010, 115 master's awarded. *Degree requirements:* For master's, minimum of 24 resident hours. *Entrance requirements:* For master's, GMAT or GRE General Test, minimum GPA of 2.75 in last 60 hours of course work. Additional exam requirements/recommendations for international students: Required—TOEFL (minimum score 550 paper-based; 213 computer-based; 79 iBT) or IELTS (minimum score 6). *Application deadline:* For fall admission, 7/1 for domestic and international students; for spring admission, 11/1 for domestic and international students. Applications are processed on a rolling basis. Application fee: $45 ($50 for international students). Electronic applications accepted. *Expenses:* Tuition: Full-time $16,200; part-time $900 per credit hour. Required fees: $50 per trimester. Full-time tuition and fees vary according to course load and program. *Financial support:* In 2010–11, 19 students received support. Scholarships/grants available. *Faculty research:* Ethics and corporate responsibility, new hire socialization, team performance, business strategy, non-traditional marketing, social media. *Unit head:* Dr. Stan Horner, Director, 512-428-1279, Fax: 512-448-8492, E-mail: stanleyh@ stedwards.edu. *Application contact:* Kelly Luna, Graduate Admissions Coordinator, 512-233-1697, Fax: 512-428-1032, E-mail: kellyl@stedwards. edu.

St. John's University, The Peter J. Tobin College of Business, Program in International Business, Queens, NY 11439. Offers MBA, Adv C. Part-time and evening/weekend programs available. *Students:* 62 full-time (40 women), 12 part-time (4 women); includes 19 minority (10 Black or African American, non-Hispanic/Latino; 3 Asian, non-Hispanic/Latino; 5 Hispanic/Latino; 1 Two or more races, non-Hispanic/Latino), 27 international. Average age 25. 84 applicants, 68% accepted, 29 enrolled. In 2010, 14 master's, 1 other advanced degree awarded. *Degree requirements:* For master's, comprehensive exam (for some programs), thesis optional. *Entrance requirements:* For master's, GMAT, 2 letters of recommendation, resume, transcripts, essay; for Adv C, GMAT, 2 letters of recommendation, resume, undergraduate transcripts, essay. Additional exam requirements/recommendations for international students: Required—TOEFL (minimum score 600 paper-based; 250 computer-based; 100 iBT), IELTS (minimum score 5.5). *Application deadline:* For fall admission, 5/1 priority date for domestic and international students; for spring admission, 11/1 priority date for domestic and international students. Applications are processed on a rolling basis. Application fee: $70. Electronic applications accepted. *Expenses:* Contact institution. *Financial support:* Research assistantships, scholarships/grants available. Support available to part-time students. Financial award application deadline: 3/1; financial award applicants required to submit FAFSA. *Unit head:* Dr. Victoria L. Shoaf, Dean, 718-990-6458, E-mail: shoafv@stjohns.edu. *Application contact:* Carol Swanberg, Assistant Dean, Director of Graduate Admissions, 718-990-1345, Fax: 718-990-5242, E-mail: tobingradnyc@stjohns.edu.

Saint Joseph's University, Erivan K. Haub School of Business, MS Program in International Marketing, Philadelphia, PA 19131. Offers MS. Part-time and evening/weekend programs available. *Students:* 24 full-time (18 women), 10 part-time (8 women); includes 4 minority (all Black or African American, non-Hispanic/Latino), 19 international. Average age 25. In 2010, 23 master's awarded. *Entrance requirements:* For master's, GMAT or GRE, 2 letters of recommendation, resume. Additional exam requirements/recommendations for international students: Required—TOEFL (minimum score: paper 550, computer 213, iBT 79) or IELTS (6.5), Pearson Test of English (minimum 60). *Application deadline:* For fall admission, 7/15 priority date for domestic students; for spring admission, 11/15 priority date for domestic students. Applications are processed on a rolling basis. Application fee: $35. Electronic applications accepted. *Expenses:* Tuition: Part-time $729 per credit. Tuition and fees vary according to course load, degree level and program. *Financial support:* In 2010–11, 2 research assistantships with partial tuition reimbursements (averaging $8,000 per year) were awarded; unspecified assistantships also available. Financial award application deadline: 5/1; financial award applicants required to submit FAFSA. *Faculty research:* Export marketing, global marketing, international marketing research, new product development, emerging markets, international consumer behavior. *Unit head:* Christine

Kaczmar-Russo, Director, 610-660-1238, Fax: 610-660-3239, E-mail: ckaczmar@sju.edu.

Saint Joseph's University, Erivan K. Haub School of Business, Professional MBA Program, Philadelphia, PA 19131-1395. Offers accounting (MBA); finance (MBA), including finance; general business (MBA); health and medical services administration (MBA); human resource management (MBA); international business (MBA); international marketing (MBA); management (MBA); marketing (MBA); DO/MBA. Do/MBA offered jointly with Philadelphia College of Osteopathic Medicine. Part-time and evening/weekend programs available. Postbaccalaureate distance learning degree programs offered (no on-campus study). *Students:* 47 full-time (35 women), 585 part-time (221 women); includes 92 minority (42 Black or African American, non-Hispanic/Latino; 1 American Indian or Alaska Native, non-Hispanic/Latino; 34 Asian, non-Hispanic/Latino; 12 Hispanic/Latino; 1 Native Hawaiian or other Pacific Islander, non-Hispanic/Latino; 2 Two or more races, non-Hispanic/Latino), 41 international. Average age 30. In 2010, 135 master's awarded. *Entrance requirements:* For master's, GMAT or GRE, 2 letters of recommendation, resume. Additional exam requirements/recommendations for international students: Required—TOEFL (minimum score: paper 550, computer 213, iBT 79) or IELTS (6.5), Pearson Test of English (minimum 60). *Application deadline:* For fall admission, 7/15 priority date for domestic students, 4/15 priority date for international students; for spring admission, 11/15 priority date for domestic students, 10/15 priority date for international students. Applications are processed on a rolling basis. Application fee: $35. Electronic applications accepted. *Expenses:* Tuition: Part-time $729 per credit. Tuition and fees vary according to course load, degree level and program. *Financial support:* Scholarships/grants and unspecified assistantships available. Financial award application deadline: 5/1; financial award applicants required to submit FAFSA. *Unit head:* Adele C. Foley, Associate Dean/Director, Graduate Business Programs, 610-660-1691, Fax: 610-660-1599, E-mail: afoley@sju. edu. *Application contact:* Janine N. Guerra, Assistant Director, MBA Program, 610-660-1695, Fax: 610-660-1599, E-mail: jguerra@sju.edu.

Saint Mary's University of Minnesota, Schools of Graduate and Professional Programs, Graduate School of Business and Technology, International Business Program, Winona, MN 55987-1399. Offers MA. *Unit head:* Dushan Knezevich, Director, 612-728-5156, E-mail: dknezevi@smumn.edu. *Application contact:* Yasin Alsaidi, Director of Admissions for Graduate and Professional Programs, 612-728-5207, E-mail: yalsaidi@smumn.edu.

Saint Peter's College, Graduate Business Programs, MBA Program, Jersey City, NJ 07306-5997. Offers finance (MBA); health care administration (MBA); human resource management (MBA); international business (MBA); management (MBA); management information systems (MBA); marketing (MBA); risk management (MBA); MBA/MS. Part-time and evening/weekend programs available. *Students:* 108 applicants, 81% accepted, 62 enrolled. *Entrance requirements:* Additional exam requirements/recommendations for international students: Required—TOEFL (minimum score 79 computer-based). *Application deadline:* Applications are processed on a rolling basis. Electronic applications accepted. *Financial support:* Career-related internships or fieldwork, Federal Work-Study, and institutionally sponsored loans available. Financial award applicants required to submit FAFSA. *Faculty research:* Finance, health care management, human resource management, international business, management, management information systems, marketing, risk management. *Application contact:* Stephanie Autenrieth, Director, Graduate and Professional Studies Admission, 201-761-6474, Fax: 201-435-5270, E-mail: sautenrieth@spc.edu.

Santa Clara University, Leavey School of Business, Program in Business Administration, Santa Clara, CA 95053. Offers accounting (MBA); entrepreneurship (MBA); executive business administration (EMBA); finance (MBA); food and agribusiness (MBA); international business (MBA); leading people and organizations (MBA); managing technology and innovation (MBA); marketing management (MBA); supply chain management (MBA). *Accreditation:* AACSB. Part-time and evening/weekend programs available. *Students:* 229 full-time (80 women), 748 part-time (244 women); includes 354 minority (14 Black or African American, non-Hispanic/Latino; 1 American Indian or Alaska Native, non-Hispanic/Latino; 287 Asian, non-Hispanic/Latino; 42 Hispanic/Latino; 5 Native Hawaiian or other Pacific Islander, non-Hispanic/Latino; 5 Two or more races, non-Hispanic/Latino), 209 international. Average age 32. 334 applicants, 76% accepted, 191 enrolled. In 2010, 307 master's awarded. *Degree requirements:* For master's, thesis or alternative. *Entrance requirements:* For master's, GMAT, GRE. Additional exam requirements/recommendations for international students: Required—TOEFL (minimum score 600 paper-based; 250 computer-based; 100 iBT). *Application deadline:* For fall admission, 6/1 for domestic and international students; for spring admission, 1/19 for domestic students, 1/17 for international students. Applications are processed on a rolling basis. Application fee: $75 ($100 for international students). Electronic applications accepted. *Expenses:* Contact institution. *Financial support:* In 2010–11, 350 students received support; fellowships with partial tuition reimbursements available, research assistantships with partial tuition reimbursements available, career-related internships or fieldwork, Federal Work-Study, institutionally sponsored loans, scholarships/grants, health care benefits, and unspecified assistantships available. Support available to part-time students. Financial award application deadline: 6/1;

financial award applicants required to submit FAFSA. *Unit head:* Elizabeth B. Ford, Senior Assistant Dean, 408-554-2752, Fax: 408-554-4571, E-mail: eford@scu.edu. *Application contact:* Molly Mulally, Assistant Director, Graduate Business Admissions, 408-554-4539, Fax: 408-554-4571, E-mail: mbaadmissions@scu.edu.

Seton Hall University, Stillman School of Business, Department of International Business, South Orange, NJ 07079-2697. Offers MBA, Certificate. Part-time and evening/weekend programs available. *Faculty:* 4 full-time (0 women), 2 part-time/adjunct (0 women). *Students:* 4 full-time (2 women), 17 part-time (10 women); includes 2 Asian, non-Hispanic/Latino; 1 Hispanic/Latino. Average age 28. 26 applicants, 85% accepted, 21 enrolled. In 2010, 10 master's awarded. *Entrance requirements:* For master's, GMAT or CPA, Advanced degree such as CPA, MS, JD, PharmD, DC, PhD., DDS, DVM, MBA from an AACSB institution, MS in a business discipline, and minimum GPA of 3.0; for Certificate, master's degree. Additional exam requirements/recommendations for international students: Required—TOEFL (minimum: 254 computer, 102 iBT), IELTS, or Pearson Test of English (PTE). *Application deadline:* For fall admission, 5/31 priority date for domestic students, 3/31 priority date for international students; for spring admission, 10/31 priority date for domestic students. Applications are processed on a rolling basis. Application fee: $75. Electronic applications accepted. *Expenses:* Contact institution. *Financial support:* In 2010–11, 16 students received support, including research assistantships with full tuition reimbursements available (averaging $35,610 per year); career-related internships or fieldwork, scholarships/grants, and unspecified assistantships also available. Support available to part-time students. Financial award application deadline: 6/30; financial award applicants required to submit FAFSA. *Faculty research:* International marketing, Asian financial markets, economics in eastern Europe and accounting in the Middle East. *Unit head:* Dr. Laurence McCarthy, 973-275-2957, Fax: 973-275-2465, E-mail: laurence.mccarthy@shu.edu. *Application contact:* Catherine Bianchi, Director of Graduate Admissions, 973-761-9262, Fax: 973-761-9208, E-mail: catherine.bianchi@shu.edu.

Seton Hall University, Stillman School of Business, Programs in Business Administration, South Orange, NJ 07079-2697. Offers accounting (MBA); finance (MBA); information technology management (MBA); international business (MBA); management (MBA); marketing (MBA); sport management (MBA); supply chain management (MBA). Part-time and evening/weekend programs available. *Faculty:* 35 full-time (8 women), 11 part-time/adjunct (1 woman). *Students:* 93 full-time (33 women), 165 part-time (76 women); includes 26 Black or African American, non-Hispanic/Latino; 39 Asian, non-Hispanic/Latino; 8 Hispanic/Latino. Average age 29. 404 applicants, 74% accepted, 258 enrolled. In 2010, 203 master's awarded. *Degree requirements:* For master's, 20 hours of community service (Social Responsibility Project). *Entrance requirements:* For master's, GMAT or CPA, Advanced degree such as PhD, MD, JD, DVM, DDS, PharmD, MBA from an AACSB institution, MS in a business discipline and a minimum GPA of 3.0. Additional exam requirements/recommendations for international students: Required—TOEFL (minimum: 254 computer, 102 iBT), IELTS or Pearson Test of English (PTE). *Application deadline:* For fall admission, 5/31 priority date for domestic students, 3/31 priority date for international students; for spring admission, 10/31 priority date for domestic students, 9/30 priority date for international students. Applications are processed on a rolling basis. Application fee: $75. Electronic applications accepted. *Financial support:* In 2010–11, research assistantships with full tuition reimbursements (averaging $35,610 per year); career-related internships or fieldwork, Federal Work-Study, scholarships/grants, and unspecified assistantships also available. Support available to part-time students. Financial award application deadline: 6/30; financial award applicants required to submit FAFSA. *Faculty research:* Financial, hedge funds, international business, legal issues, disclosure and branding. *Unit head:* Dr. Joyce A. Strawser, Associate Dean for Undergraduate and MBA Curricula, 973-761-9225, Fax: 973-761-9217, E-mail: strawsjo@shu.edu. *Application contact:* Catherine Bianchi, Director of Graduate Admissions, 973-761-9262, Fax: 973-761-9208, E-mail: catherine.bianchi@shu.edu.

Southeast Missouri State University, School of Graduate Studies, Harrison College of Business, Cape Girardeau, MO 63701-4799. Offers accounting (MBA); entrepreneurship (MBA); environmental management (MBA); financial management (MBA); general management (MBA); health administration (MBA); industrial management (MBA); international business (MBA); sport management (MBA). *Accreditation:* AACSB. Part-time and evening/weekend programs available. Postbaccalaureate distance learning degree programs offered (no on-campus study). *Faculty:* 31 full-time (10 women). *Students:* 51 full-time (24 women), 72 part-time (34 women); includes 4 minority (1 American Indian or Alaska Native, non-Hispanic/Latino; 3 Asian, non-Hispanic/Latino), 32 international. Average age 28. 71 applicants, 83% accepted, 33 enrolled. In 2010, 46 master's awarded. *Degree requirements:* For master's, variable foreign language requirement, applied research project; foreign language or 9 credit hours (for international business). *Entrance requirements:* For master's, GMAT (minimum score 400), minimum undergraduate GPA of 2.5, prerequisite courses for non-business undergraduate majors. Additional exam requirements/recommendations for international students: Required—TOEFL (minimum score 550 paper-based; 213 computer-based; 79 iBT); Recommended—IELTS (minimum score 6). *Application*

deadline: For fall admission, 8/1 for domestic students, 6/1 for international students; for spring admission, 11/21 for domestic students, 10/1 for international students. Applications are processed on a rolling basis. Application fee: $25 ($35 for international students). Electronic applications accepted. *Expenses:* Tuition, state resident: full-time $4698; part-time $261 per credit hour. Tuition, nonresident: full-time $8379; part-time $465.50 per credit hour. *Financial support:* In 2010–11, 52 students received support, including 10 teaching assistantships with full tuition reimbursements available (averaging $7,600 per year); career-related internships or fieldwork, Federal Work-Study, institutionally sponsored loans, scholarships/grants, tuition waivers (full), and unspecified assistantships also available. Financial award application deadline: 6/30; financial award applicants required to submit FAFSA. *Faculty research:* Human resources, laws impacting accounting, advertising. *Unit head:* Dr. Kenneth A. Heischmidt, Director, Graduate Programs, 573-651-5116, Fax: 573-651-5032, E-mail: kheischmidt@semo.edu. *Application contact:* Gail Amick, Administrative Secretary, 573-651-2049, Fax: 573-651-2001, E-mail: gamick@semo.edu.

Stevens Institute of Technology, Graduate School, Wesley J. Howe School of Technology Management, Program in Management, Hoboken, NJ 07030. Offers general management (MS); global innovation management (MS); human resource management (MS); information management (MS); project management (MS); technology commercialization (MS); technology management (MS). Part-time programs available. *Students:* 15 full-time (6 women), 35 part-time (15 women); includes 1 Black or African American, non-Hispanic/Latino; 5 Asian, non-Hispanic/Latino; 6 Hispanic/Latino, 12 international. Average age 31. *Degree requirements:* For master's, thesis optional. *Entrance requirements:* For master's, GMAT, GRE General Test. Additional exam requirements/recommendations for international students: Required—TOEFL. *Application deadline:* Applications are processed on a rolling basis. Application fee: $50. Electronic applications accepted. *Financial support:* Unspecified assistantships available. *Faculty research:* Industrial economics. *Unit head:* Elizabeth Watson, Director, 201-216-5081. *Application contact:* Graduate Admissions, 800-496-4935, Fax: 201-216-8044, E-mail: gradadmissions@stevens.edu.

Suffolk University, College of Arts and Sciences, Department of Economics, Boston, MA 02108-2770. Offers economic policy (MSEP); economics (MSE, PhD); international economics (MSIE); JD/MSIE. Part-time and evening/weekend programs available. *Faculty:* 13 full-time (3 women). *Students:* 25 full-time (5 women), 16 part-time (5 women); includes 3 Asian, non-Hispanic/Latino; 1 Hispanic/Latino, 16 international. Average age 27. 108 applicants, 56% accepted, 17 enrolled. In 2010, 9 master's, 3 doctorates awarded. *Degree requirements:* For doctorate, comprehensive exam, thesis/dissertation. *Entrance requirements:* For master's, GRE General Test or GMAT, 2 letters of recommendation, resume; for doctorate, GRE General Test, 3 letters of recommendation. Additional exam requirements/recommendations for international students: Required—TOEFL (minimum score 550 paper-based; 213 computer-based; 80 iBT). *Application deadline:* For fall admission, 6/15 priority date for domestic students, 6/15 for international students; for spring admission, 11/1 priority date for domestic students, 11/1 for international students. Applications are processed on a rolling basis. Application fee: $50. Electronic applications accepted. *Expenses:* Contact institution. *Financial support:* In 2010–11, 34 students received support, including 27 fellowships with full and partial tuition reimbursements available (averaging $15,298 per year); career-related internships or fieldwork, Federal Work-Study, and institutionally sponsored loans also available. Support available to part-time students. Financial award application deadline: 4/1; financial award applicants required to submit FAFSA. *Faculty research:* Trade demands, fair tax, smoking, multinational firms, charitable giving, fair tax. *Unit head:* Dr. David Tuerck, Chairperson, 617-573-8259, Fax: 617-994-4216, E-mail: dtuerck@suffolk.edu. *Application contact:* Judith Reynolds, Director of Graduate Admissions, 617-573-8302, Fax: 617-305-1733, E-mail: grad.admission@suffolk.edu.

Suffolk University, Sawyer Business School, Master of Business Administration Program, Boston, MA 02108-2770. Offers accounting (MBA); business administration (APC); corporate financial executive track (MBA); entrepreneurship (MBA); executive business administration (EMBA); finance (MBA); global business administration (GMBA); health administration (MBA); international business (MBA); marketing (MBA); organizational behavior (MBA); strategic management (MBA); taxation (MBA); JD/MBA; MBA/GDPA; MBA/MHA; MBA/MSA; MBA/MSF; MBA/MST. *Accreditation:* AACSB. Part-time and evening/weekend programs available. Postbaccalaureate distance learning degree programs offered (no on-campus study). *Faculty:* 97 full-time (30 women), 14 part-time/adjunct (3 women). *Students:* 179 full-time (65 women), 337 part-time (143 women); includes 16 Black or African American, non-Hispanic/Latino; 2 American Indian or Alaska Native, non-Hispanic/Latino; 22 Asian, non-Hispanic/Latino; 9 Hispanic/Latino; 1 Native Hawaiian or other Pacific Islander, non-Hispanic/Latino, 80 international. Average age 30. 431 applicants, 68% accepted, 128 enrolled. In 2010, 283 master's awarded. *Entrance requirements:* For master's, GMAT, minimum undergraduate GPA of 2.75 (MBA), 5 years of managerial experience (EMBA). Additional exam requirements/recommendations for international students: Required—TOEFL (minimum score 550 paper-based; 213 computer-based). *Application deadline:* For fall admission, 6/15 priority date for domestic students, 6/15 for international students; for spring admission, 11/1 priority date for domestic students, 11/1 for international students. Applications are processed on a rolling basis. Application fee: $50. Electronic applications accepted. *Financial support:* In 2010–11, 266 students received support, including 94 fellowships with full and partial tuition reimbursements available (averaging $12,635 per year); career-related internships or fieldwork, Federal Work-Study, and institutionally sponsored loans also available. Support available to part-time students. Financial award application deadline: 4/1; financial award applicants required to submit FAFSA. *Faculty research:* Foreign investments; career strategies and boundaryless careers; corporate ethics codes; interest rates, inflation, and growth options; innovation and product development performance. *Unit head:* Lillian Hallberg, Assistant Dean of Graduate Programs/Director of MBA Programs, 617-573-8306, E-mail: lhallber@suffolk.edu. *Application contact:* Judith Reynolds, Director of Graduate Admissions, 617-573-8302, Fax: 617-305-1733, E-mail: grad.admission@suffolk.edu.

Taylor University, Master of Business Administration Program, Upland, IN 46989-1001. Offers emerging business strategies (MBA); global leadership (MBA). Part-time programs available. *Faculty:* 1 full-time (0 women), 8 part-time/adjunct (0 women). *Students:* 59 full-time (15 women), 4 part-time (1 woman); includes 2 Black or African American, non-Hispanic/Latino; 2 Hispanic/Latino; 1 Two or more races, non-Hispanic/Latino, 1 international. Average age 35. 28 applicants, 79% accepted, 17 enrolled. In 2010, 37 master's awarded. *Application deadline:* Applications are processed on a rolling basis. Application fee: $100. *Expenses:* Tuition: Full-time $10,260; part-time $570 per credit hour. Required fees: $72 per semester. One-time fee: $100. *Financial support:* Applicants required to submit FAFSA. *Unit head:* Dr. Evan Wood, Interim Chair, 260-627-9663, E-mail: evwood@taylor.edu. *Application contact:* Wendy Speakman, Program Director, 866-471-6062, Fax: 260-492-0452, E-mail: wnspeakman@taylor.edu.

Tennessee Technological University, Graduate School, College of Business, Cookeville, TN 38505. Offers accounting (MBA); finance (MBA); human resource management (MBA); international business (MBA); management information systems (MBA); risk management & insurance (MBA). *Accreditation:* AACSB. Part-time and evening/weekend programs available. *Faculty:* 28 full-time (5 women). *Students:* 58 full-time (18 women), 139 part-time (49 women); includes 10 Black or African American, non-Hispanic/Latino; 7 Asian, non-Hispanic/Latino; 7 Hispanic/Latino; 1 Native Hawaiian or other Pacific Islander, non-Hispanic/Latino. Average age 25. 211 applicants, 51% accepted, 59 enrolled. In 2010, 116 master's awarded. *Entrance requirements:* For master's, GMAT. Additional exam requirements/recommendations for international students: Required—TOEFL (minimum score 550 paper-based; 79 iBT), IELTS (minimum score 5.5). *Application deadline:* For fall admission, 8/1 for domestic and international students; for spring admission, 12/1 for domestic students, 10/1 for international students. Application fee: $25 ($30 for international students). Electronic applications accepted. *Expenses:* Tuition, state resident: full-time $7934; part-time $388 per credit hour. Tuition, nonresident: full-time $19,758; part-time $962 per credit hour. *Financial support:* In 2010–11, 5 fellowships (averaging $10,000 per year), 18 research assistantships (averaging $4,000 per year), teaching assistantships (averaging $4,000 per year) were awarded. Support available to part-time students. Financial award application deadline: 4/1. *Unit head:* Dr. Tom Timmerman, Director, 931-372-3600, Fax: 931-372-6249. *Application contact:* Shelia K. Kendrick, Coordinator of Graduate Admissions, 931-372-3808, Fax: 931-372-3497, E-mail: skendrick@tntech.edu.

Texas A&M International University, Office of Graduate Studies and Research, College of Business Administration, Division of International Business and Technology Studies, Laredo, TX 78041-1900. Offers information systems (MSIS); international trade (MBA). *Faculty:* 13 full-time (1 woman), 2 part-time/adjunct (0 women). *Students:* 38 full-time (6 women), 23 part-time (6 women); includes 3 Black or African American, non-Hispanic/Latino; 1 Asian, non-Hispanic/Latino; 9 Hispanic/Latino, 46 international. Average age 26. 95 applicants, 19% accepted, 11 enrolled. In 2010, 29 master's awarded. *Degree requirements:* For master's, thesis (for some programs). *Entrance requirements:* For master's, GMAT or GRE General Test. Additional exam requirements/recommendations for international students: Required—TOEFL (minimum score 550 paper-based; 213 computer-based). *Application deadline:* For fall admission, 4/30 priority date for domestic students; for spring admission, 11/30 for domestic students, 10/1 for international students. Applications are processed on a rolling basis. Application fee: $25. *Financial support:* In 2010–11, 33 students received support. Federal Work-Study, institutionally sponsored loans, and scholarships/grants available. Support available to part-time students. *Unit head:* Dr. S. Srinivasan, Chair, 956-326-2520, Fax: 956-326-2494, E-mail: srini@tamiu.edu. *Application contact:* Imelda Lopez, Graduate Admissions Counselor, 956-326-2485, Fax: 956-326-2459, E-mail: lopez@tamiu.edu.

Texas A&M University–San Antonio, School of Business, San Antonio, TX 78224. Offers business administration (MBA); enterprise resource planning systems (MBA); finance (MBA); healthcare management (MBA); human resources management (MBA); information assurance and security (MBA); international business (MBA); project management (MBA); supply chain management (MBA). Part-time and evening/weekend programs available. *Faculty:*

18 full-time (6 women), 1 part-time/adjunct (0 women). *Students:* 49 full-time (21 women), 195 part-time (107 women). In 2010, 20 master's awarded. *Entrance requirements:* For master's, GMAT. Additional exam requirements/recommendations for international students: Required—TOEFL (minimum score 550 paper-based; 213 computer-based; 80 iBT), IELTS (minimum score 6). *Application deadline:* For fall admission, 7/1 priority date for domestic students, 6/1 priority date for international students; for spring admission, 11/15 priority date for domestic students, 10/1 priority date for international students. Applications are processed on a rolling basis. Application fee: $35 ($50 for international students). Electronic applications accepted. *Expenses:* Tuition, state resident: full-time $2899; part-time $161 per credit hour. Tuition, nonresident: full-time $8479; part-time $471 per credit hour. Required fees: $1056; $61 per credit hour. $368 per semester. *Financial support:* Application deadline: 3/31. *Unit head:* Dr. Tracy Hurley, MBA Coordinator, 210-932-6200, E-mail: tracy.hurley@tamusa.tamus.edu. *Application contact:* Melissa A. Villanueva, Graduate Admissions Specialist, 210-932-6200, Fax: 210-932-6209, E-mail: melissa.villanueva@tamusa.tamus.edu.

Texas Christian University, The Neeley School of Business at TCU, Program in International Management, Fort Worth, TX 76129-0002. Offers MBA. Evening/weekend programs available. In 2010, 21 master's awarded. *Entrance requirements:* For master's, minimum of 8 years of work experience and 5 years in management. Additional exam requirements/recommendations for international students: Required—TOEFL (minimum score 600 paper-based; 250 computer-based; 100 iBT). *Application deadline:* For spring admission, 7/15 for domestic and international students. Applications are processed on a rolling basis. Application fee: $100. Electronic applications accepted. *Expenses:* Tuition: Full-time $18,720; part-time $1040 per credit hour. Tuition and fees vary according to course load and program. *Financial support:* Institutionally sponsored loans available. Financial award application deadline: 7/15; financial award applicants required to submit FAFSA. *Faculty research:* Emerging financial markets, derivative trading activity, salesforce deployment, examining sales activity, litigation against tax practitioners. Total annual research expenditures: $2.5 million. *Unit head:* Dr. Nancy Nix, Executive Director, Executive MBA Program, 817-257-7543, Fax: 817-257-7719, E-mail: emba@tcu.edu. *Application contact:* Kevin T. Davis, Director, Executive MBA Recruiting and Corporate Relations, 817-257-4681, Fax: 817-257-7719, E-mail: kevin.davis@tcu.edu.

Texas Tech University, Graduate School, Jerry S. Rawls College of Business Administration, Programs in Business Administration, Lubbock, TX 79409. Offers agricultural business (MBA); business administration (IMBA); business statistics (MBA); entrepreneurship and innovation (MBA); general business (MBA); health organization management (MBA); international business (MBA); management and leadership skills (MBA); management information systems (MBA); marketing (MBA); real estate (MBA); JD/MBA; MBA/M Arch; MBA/MA; MBA/MD; MBA/MS; MBA/Pharm D. Part-time and evening/weekend programs available. *Faculty:* 47 full-time (8 women), 5 part-time/adjunct (0 women). *Students:* 52 full-time (13 women), 531 part-time (152 women); includes 121 minority (28 Black or African American, non-Hispanic/Latino; 3 American Indian or Alaska Native, non-Hispanic/Latino; 31 Asian, non-Hispanic/Latino; 53 Hispanic/Latino; 6 Two or more races, non-Hispanic/Latino), 49 international. Average age 30. 437 applicants, 77% accepted, 258 enrolled. In 2010, 228 master's awarded. *Degree requirements:* For master's, capstone course. *Entrance requirements:* For master's, GMAT, holistic review of academic credentials. Additional exam requirements/recommendations for international students: Required—TOEFL (minimum score 550 paper-based; 213 computer-based; 79 iBT). *Application deadline:* For fall admission, 4/1 priority date for domestic students, 1/15 for international students; for spring admission, 9/1 priority date for domestic students, 6/15 for international students. Applications are processed on a rolling basis. Application fee: $50 ($75 for international students). Electronic applications accepted. *Expenses:* Tuition, state resident: full-time $5495.76; part-time $228.99 per credit hour. Tuition, nonresident: full-time $12,936; part-time $538.99 per credit hour. Required fees: $2674; $36 per credit hour. $905 per semester. *Financial support:* In 2010–11, 25 research assistantships (averaging $8,800 per year) were awarded; teaching assistantships, career-related internships or fieldwork, Federal Work-Study, scholarships/grants, health care benefits, and unspecified assistantships also available. Support available to part-time students. Financial award applicants required to submit FAFSA. *Unit head:* Dr. W. Jay Conover, Director, 806-742-1546, Fax: 806-742-3958, E-mail: jay.conover@ttu.edu. *Application contact:* Cynthia D. Barnes, Director, Graduate Services Center, 806-742-3184, Fax: 806-742-3958, E-mail: ba_grad@ttu.edu.

Thunderbird School of Global Management, Executive MBA Program–Glendale, Glendale, AZ 85306-6000. Offers global management (MBA). Part-time and evening/weekend programs available. *Faculty:* 48 full-time (13 women). *Students:* 89 part-time (20 women); includes 3 Black or African American, non-Hispanic/Latino; 1 American Indian or Alaska Native, non-Hispanic/Latino; 10 Asian, non-Hispanic/Latino; 5 Two or more races, non-Hispanic/Latino, 17 international. Average age 37. In 2010, 48 master's awarded. *Degree requirements:* For master's, one foreign language. *Entrance requirements:* For master's, 8 years of full-time work experience, 3 years of management experience, company sponsorship, mid-management position.

Application deadline: For fall admission, 6/10 priority date for domestic students, 4/30 priority date for international students. Applications are processed on a rolling basis. Application fee: $125. Electronic applications accepted. *Expenses:* Contact institution. *Financial support:* In 2010–11, 25 students received support. Application deadline: 6/7. *Faculty research:* Management, social enterprise, cross-cultural communication, finance, marketing. *Unit head:* Barbara Carpenter, Assc VP, EMBA Programs, 602-978-7921, Fax: 602-978-7463, E-mail: barbara.carpenter@thunderbird.edu. *Application contact:* Barbara Carpenter, Assc VP, EMBA Programs, 602-978-7921, Fax: 602-978-7463, E-mail: barbara.carpenter@thunderbird.edu.

Thunderbird School of Global Management, Global MBA—Latin American Managers Program, Glendale, AZ 85306-6000. Offers GMBA. Offered jointly with Instituto Technológico y de Estudios Superiores de Monterrey. Part-time and evening/weekend programs available. Postbaccalaureate distance learning degree programs offered. *Faculty:* 48 full-time (13 women). *Students:* 286 part-time (77 women); includes 1 Asian, non-Hispanic/Latino; 3 Hispanic/Latino, 259 international. Average age 31. 217 applicants, 73% accepted, 159 enrolled. In 2010, 163 master's awarded. *Entrance requirements:* For master's, GMAT or PAEP (Pruebade Admisiona Estudios Posgrado), minimum GPA of 3.0, 2 years of work experience. Additional exam requirements/recommendations for international students: Required—TOEFL (minimum score 550 paper-based; 213 computer-based; 79 iBT). *Application deadline:* For spring admission, 4/25 priority date for domestic and international students. Application fee: $125. *Expenses:* Contact institution. *Financial support:* Scholarships/grants available. Financial award application deadline: 4/30. *Faculty research:* Globalization impact on Latin American business, doing business in Latin America, international marketing in Latin America. *Unit head:* Dr. Bert Valencia, Vice President, 602-978-7534, Fax: 602-978-7729, E-mail: globalmba@thunderbird.edu. *Application contact:* Dr. Bert Valencia, Vice President, 602-978-7534, Fax: 602-978-7729, E-mail: globalmba@thunderbird.edu.

Thunderbird School of Global Management, GMBA—On Demand Program, Glendale, AZ 85306-6000. Offers GMBA. Part-time programs available. Postbaccalaureate distance learning degree programs offered (minimal on-campus study). *Faculty:* 48 full-time (13 women). *Students:* 132 part-time (50 women); includes 3 Black or African American, non-Hispanic/Latino; 1 American Indian or Alaska Native, non-Hispanic/Latino; 6 Asian, non-Hispanic/Latino; 1 Hispanic/Latino; 5 Two or more races, non-Hispanic/Latino, 17 international. Average age 32. 81 applicants, 79% accepted, 46 enrolled. In 2010, 62 master's awarded. *Entrance requirements:* For master's, GMAT. Additional exam requirements/recommendations for international students: Required—TOEFL. *Application deadline:* For fall admission, 6/10 for domestic students, 4/30 for international students. Application fee: $125. *Expenses:* Tuition: Full-time $43,080; part-time $1436 per credit hour. Required fees: $300. Part-time tuition and fees vary according to program. *Financial support:* Scholarships/grants available. Financial award application deadline: 2/15. *Unit head:* Dr. Bert Valencia, Vice President, 602-978-7534, Fax: 602-978-7729, E-mail: globalmba@thunderbird.edu. *Application contact:* Jay Bryant, Director of Admissions, 602-978-7294, Fax: 602-439-5432, E-mail: jay.bryant@thunderbird.edu.

Thunderbird School of Global Management, Master's Programs in Global Management, Glendale, AZ 85306-6000. Offers global affairs and management (MA); global management (MS). *Accreditation:* AACSB. *Faculty:* 48 full-time (13 women). *Students:* 139 full-time (74 women); includes 2 Black or African American, non-Hispanic/Latino; 1 American Indian or Alaska Native, non-Hispanic/Latino; 5 Asian, non-Hispanic/Latino; 2 Hispanic/Latino; 5 Two or more races, non-Hispanic/Latino, 68 international. 153 applicants, 45% accepted, 69 enrolled. In 2010, 55 master's awarded. *Degree requirements:* For master's, one foreign language. *Entrance requirements:* For master's, GMAT/GRE. Additional exam requirements/recommendations for international students: Required—TOEFL. *Application deadline:* For fall admission, 6/10 for domestic students, 4/30 for international students. Application fee: $125. *Expenses:* Tuition: Full-time $43,080; part-time $1436 per credit hour. Required fees: $300. Part-time tuition and fees vary according to program. *Financial support:* Career-related internships or fieldwork, Federal Work-Study, scholarships/grants, and unspecified assistantships available. *Unit head:* Dr. Glenn Fong, Unit Head, 602-978-7156. *Application contact:* Jay Bryant, Director of Admissions, 602-978-7294, Fax: 602-439-5432, E-mail: jay.bryant@thunderbird.edu.

Tiffin University, Program in Business Administration, Tiffin, OH 44883-2161. Offers finance (MBA); general management (MBA); healthcare administration (MBA); human resources (MBA); international business (MBA); leadership (MBA); marketing (MBA); sports management (MBA). *Accreditation:* ACBSP. Part-time and evening/weekend programs available. Postbaccalaureate distance learning degree programs offered (no on-campus study). *Faculty:* 18 full-time (9 women), 22 part-time/adjunct (6 women). *Students:* 186 full-time (93 women), 250 part-time (124 women). Average age 31. 532 applicants, 86% accepted, 229 enrolled. In 2010, 340 master's awarded. *Entrance requirements:* For master's, minimum undergraduate GPA of 2.5, work experience. Additional exam requirements/recommendations for international students: Required—TOEFL (minimum score 550 paper-based; 213 computer-based). *Application deadline:* For fall admission, 8/15

for domestic students, 8/1 for international students; for spring admission, 1/9 for domestic students, 12/1 for international students. Applications are processed on a rolling basis. Application fee: $0. Electronic applications accepted. *Financial support:* In 2010–11, 94 students received support. Available to part-time students. Application deadline: 7/31. *Faculty research:* Small business, executive development operations, research and statistical analysis, market research, management information systems. *Unit head:* Dr. Lillian Schumacher, Dean of the School of Business, 419-448-3053, Fax: 419-443-5002, E-mail: schumacherlb@tiffin.edu. *Application contact:* Kristi Krintzline, Director of Graduate Admissions and Student Services, 800-968-6446 Ext. 3445, Fax: 419-443-5002, E-mail: krintzlineka@tiffin.edu.

Troy University, Graduate School, College of Business, Program in Management, Troy, AL 36082. Offers applied management (MSM); healthcare management (MSM); human resources management (MSM); information systems (MSM); international hospitality management (MSM); international management (MSM); leadership and organizational effectiveness (MSM); public management (MS, MSM). *Accreditation:* ACBSP. Evening/weekend programs available. *Students:* 101 full-time (62 women), 398 part-time (249 women); includes 308 minority (278 Black or African American, non-Hispanic/Latino; 8 American Indian or Alaska Native, non-Hispanic/Latino; 8 Asian, non-Hispanic/Latino; 13 Hispanic/Latino; 1 Two or more races, non-Hispanic/Latino). Average age 35. 218 applicants, 80% accepted. In 2010, 314 master's awarded. *Degree requirements:* For master's, Graduate Educational Testing Service Major Field Test, capstone exam, minimum GPA of 3.0. *Entrance requirements:* For master's, GMAT (minimum score 500) or GRE General Test (minimum score 900), minimum GPA of 2.5, bachelor's degree, letter of recommendation. Additional exam requirements/recommendations for international students: Required—TOEFL (minimum score 523 paper-based; 193 computer-based; 70 iBT), IELTS, or ACT compass ESL (minimum Listening, Reading, and Grammar score: 270). *Application deadline:* Applications are processed on a rolling basis. Application fee: $50. Electronic applications accepted. *Expenses:* Contact institution. *Unit head:* Dr. Henry M. Findley, Interim Chair/Professor, 334-670-3271, Fax: 334-670-3599, E-mail: hfindley@troy.edu. *Application contact:* Brenda K. Campbell, Director of Graduate Admissions, 334-670-3178, Fax: 334-670-3733, E-mail: bcamp@troy.edu.

Troy University, Graduate School, College of Education, Program in Teacher Education-Multiple Levels, Troy, AL 36082. Offers alternative 5th year art education (MS); alternative 5th year instrumental (MS); alternative 5th year physical education (MS); alternative 5th year vocal/choral (MS); traditional art education (MS); traditional gifted education (MS); traditional instrumental (MS); traditional physical education (MS); traditional reading specialist (MS); traditional vocal/choral (MS). Part-time and evening/weekend programs available. *Students:* 6 full-time (3 women), 17 part-time (9 women); includes 6 minority (all Black or African American, non-Hispanic/Latino). Average age 30. 6 applicants, 83% accepted. In 2010, 11 master's awarded. *Degree requirements:* For master's, comprehensive exam, thesis. *Entrance requirements:* For master's, minimum GPA of 2.5. Additional exam requirements/recommendations for international students: Required—TOEFL (minimum score 523 paper-based; 193 computer-based; 70 iBT), IELTS (minimum score 6). *Application deadline:* Applications are processed on a rolling basis. Application fee: $50. Electronic applications accepted. *Expenses:* Tuition, state resident: full-time $4428; part-time $246 per credit hour. Tuition, nonresident: full-time $8856; part-time $492 per credit hour. Required fees: $432; $24 per credit hour. $50 per term. Tuition and fees vary according to program. *Financial support:* Available to part-time students. Applicants required to submit FAFSA. *Unit head:* Dr. Marian Parker, Coordinator, 334-670-5661, Fax: 334-670-3548, E-mail: mjparker@troy.edu. *Application contact:* Brenda K. Campbell, Director of Graduate Admissions, 334-670-3178, Fax: 334-670-3733, E-mail: bcamp@troy.edu.

Tufts University, Fletcher School of Law and Diplomacy, Medford, MA 02155. Offers LL M, MA, MAHA, MALD, MIB, PhD, DVM/MA, JD/MALD, MALD/MA, MALD/MBA, MALD/MS, MD/MA. Postbaccalaureate distance learning degree programs offered (minimal on-campus study). *Faculty:* 37 full-time (10 women), 48 part-time/adjunct (14 women). *Students:* 541 full-time (278 women), 9 part-time (3 women); includes 73 minority (8 Black or African American, non-Hispanic/Latino; 30 Asian, non-Hispanic/Latino; 11 Hispanic/Latino; 24 Two or more races, non-Hispanic/Latino, 208 international. Average age 31. 1,875 applicants, 41% accepted, 296 enrolled. In 2010, 297 master's, 14 doctorates awarded. *Degree requirements:* For master's, one foreign language, thesis; for doctorate, one foreign language, comprehensive exam, thesis/dissertation, dissertation defense. *Entrance requirements:* For master's and doctorate, GMAT or GRE General Test. Additional exam requirements/recommendations for international students: Required—TOEFL (minimum score 600 paper-based; 250 computer-based; 100 iBT), IELTS (minimum score 7). *Application deadline:* For fall admission, 1/15 for domestic and international students; for spring admission, 10/15 for domestic and international students. Application fee: $70. Electronic applications accepted. *Expenses:* Contact institution. *Financial support:* Federal Work-Study, institutionally sponsored loans, scholarships/grants, and tuition waivers (partial) available. Financial award application deadline: 1/15; financial award applicants required to submit FAFSA. *Faculty research:* Negotiation and conflict resolution, international organizations, international business and economic law, security studies, development economics. *Unit head:* Stephen W. Bosworth, Dean, 617-627-3050, Fax: 617-627-3712. *Application contact:* Laurie A. Hurley, 617-627-3040, E-mail: fletcheradmissions@tufts.edu.

TUI University, College of Business Administration, Program in Business Administration, Cypress, CA 90630. Offers business administration (PhD); conflict and negotiation management (MBA); criminal justice administration (MBA); entrepreneurship (MBA); finance (MBA); general management (MBA); government accounting (MBA); human resource management (MBA); information security and digital assurance management (MBA); information technology management (MBA); international business (MBA); logistics management (MBA); marketing (MBA); project management (MBA); public management (MBA); quality management (MBA); strategic leadership (MBA). Part-time and evening/weekend programs available. Postbaccalaureate distance learning degree programs offered (no on-campus study). *Students:* 741 full-time (200 women), 1,585 part-time (410 women). 379 applicants, 81% accepted, 300 enrolled. In 2010, 752 master's, 28 doctorates awarded. *Degree requirements:* For doctorate, comprehensive exam, thesis/dissertation, defense of dissertation. *Entrance requirements:* For master's, minimum GPA of 2.5 (students with GPA 3.0 or greater may transfer up to 30% of graduate level credits); for doctorate, minimum GPA of 3.4, curriculum vitae, course work in research methods or statistics. Additional exam requirements/recommendations for international students: Required—TOEFL. *Application deadline:* For fall admission, 10/3 for domestic and international students; for winter admission, 12/22 for domestic and international students; for spring admission, 4/3 for domestic and international students. Applications are processed on a rolling basis. Application fee: $75. Electronic applications accepted. *Expenses:* Tuition: Full-time $11,040; part-time $345 per semester hour. *Unit head:* Paul Watkins, Dean, College of Business Administration, 800-375-9878, E-mail: pwatkins@tuiu.edu. *Application contact:* Wei Ren-Finaly, Registrar, 800-375-9878, Fax: 714-827-7407, E-mail: registration@tuiu.edu.

United States International University, School of Business Administration, Nairobi, Kenya. Offers business administration (GEMBA); entrepreneurship (MBA); finance (MBA); human resource management (MBA); information technology management (MBA); integrated studies (MBA); international business administration (MBA); management and organizational development (MS); marketing (MBA); organizational development (EMS); strategic management (MBA). Part-time and evening/weekend programs available. *Faculty:* 42 full-time (8 women), 64 part-time/adjunct (14 women). *Students:* 423 full-time (227 women), 129 part-time (63 women). Average age 29. 110 applicants, 79% accepted, 78 enrolled. In 2010, 164 master's awarded. *Degree requirements:* For master's, thesis. *Entrance requirements:* For master's, GMAT, 2 letters of reference, resume. Additional exam requirements/recommendations for international students: Required—TOEFL (minimum score 550 paper-based; 213 computer-based). *Application deadline:* For fall admission, 6/30 priority date for domestic and international students; for spring admission, 9/30 for domestic and international students. Applications are processed on a rolling basis. Application fee: $50. *Financial support:* In 2010–11, 30 students received support, including 8 research assistantships (averaging $1,400 per year), 4 teaching assistantships (averaging $1,400 per year); career-related internships or fieldwork, scholarships/grants, and unspecified assistantships also available. Support available to part-time students. Financial award application deadline: 6/30; financial award applicants required to submit FAFSA. *Faculty research:* Marketing in small business enterprises, total quality management in Kenya. *Unit head:* Dr. Damary Sikalieh, Dean, 254-02-3606-415, E-mail: dsikalieh@usiu.ac.ke. *Application contact:* George Lumbasi, Director of Admissions, 254-02-3606563, Fax: 254-02-3606100, E-mail: glumbasi@usiu.ac.ke.

Université de Sherbrooke, Faculty of Administration, Program in International Business, Sherbrooke, QC J1K 2R1, Canada. Offers M Sc. *Faculty:* 3 full-time (0 women), 3 part-time/adjunct (1 woman). *Students:* 18 full-time (8 women). Average age 23. 133 applicants, 57% accepted. In 2010, 32 master's awarded. *Degree requirements:* For master's, one foreign language, thesis. *Entrance requirements:* For master's, bachelor degree in related field Minimum GPA 3/4.3. *Application deadline:* For fall admission, 4/30 for domestic students, 1/15 for international students. Applications are processed on a rolling basis. Application fee: $70. Electronic applications accepted. *Unit head:* Prof. Julien Bilodeau, Director, Graduate programs in business, 819-821-8000 Ext. 62355. *Application contact:* Marie-Claude Drouin, Programs director's assistant, 819-821-8000 Ext. 63301.

University at Buffalo, the State University of New York, Graduate School, College of Arts and Sciences, Department of Geography, Buffalo, NY 14260. Offers earth systems science (MA); economic geography and international business and world trade (MA); environmental and earth systems science (MS); environmental modeling and analysis (MA); geographic information science (MA, Certificate); geographic information systems and science (MS); geography (MA, PhD); urban and regional geography (MA); MA/MBA. *Faculty:* 14 full-time (6 women), 1 part-time/adjunct (0 women). *Students:* 60 full-time (24 women), 49 part-time (13 women); includes 1 Black or African American, non-Hispanic/Latino; 46 Asian, non-Hispanic/Latino; 4 Hispanic/Latino, 1 international. 162 applicants, 46% accepted, 38 enrolled. In 2010, 21

master's, 5 doctorates awarded. Terminal master's awarded for partial completion of doctoral program. *Degree requirements:* For master's, thesis (for some programs), project; for doctorate, thesis/dissertation. *Entrance requirements:* For master's, GRE General Test, minimum GPA of 2.9; for doctorate, GRE General Test, minimum GPA of 3.0. Additional exam requirements/recommendations for international students: Required—TOEFL (minimum score 550 paper-based; 213 computer-based; 79 iBT). *Application deadline:* For fall admission, 7/1 priority date for domestic students, 1/10 priority date for international students; for spring admission, 12/1 priority date for domestic students, 10/1 priority date for international students. Applications are processed on a rolling basis. Application fee: $75. Electronic applications accepted. *Financial support:* In 2010–11, 19 students received support, including 7 fellowships with full tuition reimbursements available (averaging $5,714 per year), 14 teaching assistantships with full tuition reimbursements available (averaging $13,520 per year); research assistantships with full tuition reimbursements available, career-related internships or fieldwork, Federal Work-Study, institutionally sponsored loans, traineeships, health care benefits, and unspecified assistantships also available. Financial award application deadline: 1/10. *Faculty research:* International business and world trade, geographic information systems and cartography, transportation, urban and regional analysis, physical and environmental geography. Total annual research expenditures: $944,614. *Unit head:* Dr. Sharmistha Bagchi-Sen, Chairman, 716-645-0473, Fax: 716-645-2329, E-mail: geosbs@buffalo.edu. *Application contact:* Betsy Abraham, Graduate Secretary, 716-645-0471, Fax: 716-645-2329, E-mail: babraham@buffalo.edu.

The University of Akron, Graduate School, College of Business Administration, Department of Marketing, Akron, OH 44325. Offers international business (MBA); international business for international executive (MBA); strategic marketing (MBA); JD/MBA. Part-time and evening/weekend programs available. *Faculty:* 15 full-time (2 women), 6 part-time/adjunct (0 women). *Students:* 19 full-time (7 women), 24 part-time (17 women); includes 1 Asian, non-Hispanic/Latino, 14 international. Average age 29. 33 applicants, 55% accepted, 8 enrolled. In 2010, 16 master's awarded. *Entrance requirements:* For master's, GMAT, minimum GPA of 2.75, two letters of recommendation, statement of purpose, resume. Additional exam requirements/recommendations for international students: Required—TOEFL (minimum score 550 paper-based; 213 computer-based; 79 iBT). *Application deadline:* For fall admission, 7/15 for domestic and international students; for spring admission, 11/15 for domestic and international students. Application fee: $30 ($40 for international students). Electronic applications accepted. *Expenses:* Tuition, state resident: full-time $6800; part-time $378 per credit hour. Tuition, nonresident: full-time $11,644; part-time $647 per credit hour. Required fees: $1265. One-time fee: $30 full-time. *Financial support:* In 2010–11, 2 research assistantships with full tuition reimbursements, 7 teaching assistantships with full tuition reimbursements were awarded. *Faculty research:* Multi-channel marketing, direct interactive marketing, strategic retailing, marketing strategy and telemarketing. Total annual research expenditures: $38,705. *Unit head:* Dr. William Baker, Chair, 330-972-8466, E-mail: wbaker@uakron.edu. *Application contact:* Dr. Susan Hanlon, Director of Graduate Business Programs, 330-972-7043, Fax: 330-972-6588, E-mail: shanlon@uakron.edu.

The University of Akron, Graduate School, College of Business Administration, Program in International Business, Akron, OH 44325. Offers MBA, JD/MBA. Part-time and evening/weekend programs available. *Students:* 9 full-time (3 women), 10 part-time (8 women); includes 1 Asian, non-Hispanic/Latino, 8 international. Average age 28. 13 applicants, 46% accepted, 3 enrolled. In 2010, 9 master's awarded. *Entrance requirements:* For master's, GMAT, minimum GPA of 2.75, two letters of recommendation, resume, statement of purpose. Additional exam requirements/recommendations for international students: Required—TOEFL (minimum score 550 paper-based; 213 computer-based; 79 iBT). *Application deadline:* For fall admission, 7/15 for domestic and international students; for spring admission, 11/15 for domestic and international students. Application fee: $30 ($40 for international students). Electronic applications accepted. *Expenses:* Tuition, state resident: full-time $6800; part-time $378 per credit hour. Tuition, nonresident: full-time $11,644; part-time $647 per credit hour. Required fees: $1265. One-time fee: $30 full-time. *Financial support:* In 2010–11, 2 research assistantships with full tuition reimbursements, 2 teaching assistantships with full tuition reimbursements were awarded. *Application contact:* Dr. Susan Hanlon, Director of Graduate Business Programs, 330-972-7043, Fax: 330-972-6588, E-mail: shanlon@uakron.edu.

University of California, Los Angeles, Graduate Division, UCLA Anderson School of Management, Los Angeles, CA 90095-1481. Offers accounting (PhD); business administration (MBA); decisions, operations and technology management (PhD); finance (PhD); financial engineering (MFE); global economics and management (PhD); human resources and organizational behavior (PhD); marketing (PhD); strategy and policy (PhD); DDS/MBA; MBA/JD; MBA/MD; MBA/MLAS; MBA/MLIS; MBA/MPH; MBA/MPP; MBA/MSCS; MBA/MSN; MBA/MUP. *Accreditation:* AACSB. Part-time programs available. *Faculty:* 102 full-time (17 women), 43 part-time/adjunct (6 women). *Students:* 833 full-time (270 women), 1,052 part-time (271 women); includes 592 minority (25 Black or African American, non-Hispanic/Latino; 3 American Indian or Alaska Native, non-Hispanic/Latino; 482 Asian, non-Hispanic/Latino; 60 Hispanic/Latino; 6 Native Hawaiian or other Pacific Islander, non-Hispanic/Latino; 16 Two or more races, non-Hispanic/Latino), 445 international. In 2010, 735 master's, 10 doctorates awarded. *Degree requirements:* For master's, comprehensive exam, field study consulting project (for MBA); thesis/dissertation (for MFE); for doctorate, comprehensive exam, thesis/dissertation, oral and written qualifying exams. *Entrance requirements:* For master's, GMAT (MBA); GMAT or GRE General Test (MFE), minimum undergraduate GPA of 3.0; for doctorate, GMAT or GRE General Test, minimum undergraduate GPA of 3.0. Additional exam requirements/recommendations for international students: Required—TOEFL (minimum score 560 paper-based; 220 computer-based; 87 iBT), IELTS (minimum score 7). *Application deadline:* For fall admission, 10/20 for domestic and international students; for winter admission, 1/5 for domestic and international students; for spring admission, 4/13 for domestic and international students. Application fee: $200. Electronic applications accepted. *Expenses:* Contact institution. *Financial support:* Fellowships, research assistantships, teaching assistantships, career-related internships or fieldwork, institutionally sponsored loans, scholarships/grants, health care benefits, and tuition waivers (partial) available. Financial award application deadline: 3/2; financial award applicants required to submit FAFSA. *Unit head:* Judy D. Olian, Dean, UCLA Anderson School of Management, 310-825-7982, Fax: 310-206-2073. *Application contact:* Mae Jennifer Shores, Assistant Dean and Director of Full-time MBA Admissions and Financial Aid, 310-825-6944, Fax: 310-825-8582, E-mail: mba.admissions@anderson.ucla.edu.

University of Chicago, Booth School of Business, Full-Time MBA Program, Chicago, IL 60637. Offers accounting (MBA); analytic finance (MBA); analytic management (MBA); econometrics and statistics (MBA); economics (MBA); entrepreneurship (MBA); finance (MBA); general management (MBA); human resource management (MBA); international business (MBA); managerial and organizational behavior (MBA); marketing management (MBA); operations management (MBA); strategic management (MBA); MBA/AM; MBA/JD; MBA/MA; MBA/MD; MBA/MPP. *Accreditation:* AACSB. Part-time and evening/weekend programs available. *Faculty:* 157 full-time, 35 part-time/adjunct. *Students:* 1,177 full-time (417 women); includes 301 minority (62 Black or African American, non-Hispanic/Latino; 1 American Indian or Alaska Native, non-Hispanic/Latino; 164 Asian, non-Hispanic/Latino; 55 Hispanic/Latino; 19 Two or more races, non-Hispanic/Latino), 403 international. Average age 28. 4,299 applicants, 22% accepted, 579 enrolled. In 2010, 1,374 master's awarded. *Entrance requirements:* For master's, GMAT, 2 letters of recommendation, 3 essays, resume, interview, transcripts. Additional exam requirements/recommendations for international students: Required—TOEFL (minimum score 600 paper-based; 250 computer-based), IELTS. *Application deadline:* For fall admission, 10/10 priority date for domestic students, 10/13 priority date for international students; for winter admission, 1/5 for domestic and international students; for spring admission, 4/13 for domestic and international students. Application fee: $200. Electronic applications accepted. *Expenses:* Contact institution. *Financial support:* Fellowships available. Financial award applicants required to submit FAFSA. *Faculty research:* Finance, economics, entrepreneurship, strategy, management. *Unit head:* Stacey Kole, Deputy Dean, 773-702-7121. *Application contact:* Kurt Ahlm, Associate Dean of Admissions and Financial Aid, 773-702-7369, Fax: 773-702-9085, E-mail: admissions@chicagobooth.edu.

University of Colorado Denver, Business School, Program in Global Energy Management, Denver, CO 80217. Offers MS. Postbaccalaureate distance learning degree programs offered (minimal on-campus study). *Students:* 76 full-time (17 women), 2 part-time; includes 7 Black or African American, non-Hispanic/Latino; 2 American Indian or Alaska Native, non-Hispanic/Latino; 1 Asian, non-Hispanic/Latino; 4 Hispanic/Latino, 1 international. Average age 33. 41 applicants, 85% accepted, 26 enrolled. *Degree requirements:* For master's, 36 semester credit hours. *Entrance requirements:* For master's, GMAT if less than three years of experience in the energy industry and no undergraduate degree in energy sciences or engineering, minimum of 5 years' experience in energy industry. Additional exam requirements/recommendations for international students: Required—TOEFL. *Application deadline:* For fall admission, 10/1 for domestic students; for spring admission, 5/10 for domestic students. Application fee: $50. Electronic applications accepted. *Expenses:* Contact institution. *Financial support:* Application deadline: 4/1. *Unit head:* John Turner, Director, 303-605-6211, E-mail: john.turner@ucdenver.edu. *Application contact:* Shelly Townley, Admissions Coordinator, 303-556-5956, Fax: 303-556-5904, E-mail: shelly.townley@ucdenver.edu.

University of Colorado Denver, Business School, Program in International Business, Denver, CO 80217. Offers MSIB. Part-time and evening/weekend programs available. *Students:* 34 full-time (21 women), 4 part-time (2 women); includes 3 Asian, non-Hispanic/Latino; 2 Hispanic/Latino, 6 international. Average age 29. 19 applicants, 47% accepted, 7 enrolled. In 2010, 18 master's awarded. *Degree requirements:* For master's, one foreign language, 30 credit hours. *Entrance requirements:* For master's, GMAT. Additional exam requirements/recommendations for international students: Required—TOEFL (minimum score 525 paper-based; 197 computer-based; 71 iBT). *Application deadline:* For fall admission, 4/1 priority date for domestic students, 3/15 priority date for international students; for spring admission, 10/1 priority

date for domestic and international students. Application fee: $50 ($75 for international students). Electronic applications accepted. *Expenses:* Contact institution. *Financial support:* Federal Work-Study and scholarships/grants available. Support available to part-time students. Financial award application deadline: 4/1; financial award applicants required to submit FAFSA. *Faculty research:* Foreign direct investment, international business strategies, cross-cultural management, internationalization of research and development, global leadership development. *Unit head:* Dr. Manuel Serapio, Associate Professor/Director, 303-315-8436, E-mail: manuel.serapio@ucdenver.edu. *Application contact:* Shelly Townley, Admissions Director, Graduate Programs, 303-315-8202, E-mail: shelly.townley@ucdenver.edu.

University of Colorado Denver, Business School, Program in Management and Organization, Denver, CO 80217. Offers communications management (MS); enterprise technology management (MS); entrepreneurship and innovation (MS); global management (MS); human resources management (MS); leadership (MS); quantitative decision methods (MS); sports and entertainment management (MS); strategic management (MS); sustainability management (MS). *Accreditation:* AACSB. Part-time and evening/weekend programs available. Postbaccalaureate distance learning degree programs offered (no on-campus study). *Students:* 34 full-time (21 women), 9 part-time (2 women); includes 3 Asian, non-Hispanic/Latino; 5 Hispanic/Latino. Average age 33. 28 applicants, 61% accepted, 10 enrolled. In 2010, 20 master's awarded. *Degree requirements:* For master's, 30 semester hours (12 of required courses, 12 of management electives, and 6 of free electives). *Entrance requirements:* For master's, GMAT. Additional exam requirements/recommendations for international students: Required—TOEFL (minimum score 525 paper-based; 197 computer-based; 71 iBT). *Application deadline:* For fall admission, 4/1 priority date for domestic students, 3/15 priority date for international students; for spring admission, 10/1 priority date for domestic and international students. Application fee: $50 ($75 for international students). Electronic applications accepted. *Expenses:* Contact institution. *Financial support:* Federal Work-Study and scholarships/grants available. Support available to part-time students. Financial award application deadline: 4/1; financial award applicants required to submit FAFSA. *Faculty research:* Human resource management, management of catastrophe, turnaround strategies. *Unit head:* Dr. Kenneth Bettenhausen, Associate Professor/Director, 303-315-8425, E-mail: kenneth.bettehausen@ucdenver.edu. *Application contact:* Shelly Townley, Admissions Director, Graduate Programs, 303-315-8202, E-mail: shelly.townley@ucdenver.edu.

University of Colorado Denver, Business School, Program in Marketing, Denver, CO 80217. Offers brand management and marketing communication (MS); global marketing (MS); high-tech/entrepreneurial marketing (MS); Internet marketing (MS); market research (MS); marketing and business intelligence (MS); marketing for sustainability (MS); marketing in nonprofit organizations (MS); sports and entertainment marketing (MS). Part-time and evening/weekend programs available. *Students:* 31 full-time (18 women), 8 part-time (4 women); includes 3 Hispanic/Latino, 5 international. Average age 29. 46 applicants, 63% accepted, 18 enrolled. In 2010, 11 master's awarded. *Degree requirements:* For master's, 30 semester hours (18 of marketing core courses, 12 of graduate marketing electives). *Entrance requirements:* For master's, GMAT. Additional exam requirements/recommendations for international students: Required—TOEFL (minimum score 525 paper-based; 197 computer-based; 71 iBT). *Application deadline:* For fall admission, 4/1 priority date for domestic students, 3/15 priority date for international students; for spring admission, 10/1 priority date for domestic and international students. Application fee: $50 ($75 for international students). Electronic applications accepted. *Expenses:* Contact institution. *Financial support:* Federal Work-Study and scholarships/grants available. Support available to part-time students. Financial award application deadline: 4/1; financial award applicants required to submit FAFSA. *Faculty research:* Marketing issues in the Chinese environment, impact of individual difference and contextual factors on the risk-taking behaviors of managers making new-business creation decisions, Attribution Theory perspective of conflict between marketers and engineers, organizational identity and identification, international market entry strategies. *Unit head:* Dr. David Forlani, Associate Professor/Director, 303-315-8420, E-mail: david.forlani@ucdenver.edu. *Application contact:* Shelly Townley, Admissions Director, Graduate Programs, 303-315-8202, E-mail: shelly.townley@ucdenver.edu.

University of Dayton, Graduate School, School of Business Administration, Dayton, OH 45469-1300. Offers accounting (MBA); business intelligence (MBA); cyber security (MBA); entrepreneurship (MBA); finance (MBA); international business (MBA); marketing (MBA); MIS (MBA); operations management (MBA); technology-enhanced business/e-commerce (MBA); JD/MBA. *Accreditation:* AACSB. Part-time and evening/weekend programs available. *Faculty:* 25 full-time (7 women), 14 part-time/adjunct (2 women). *Students:* 184 full-time (72 women), 110 part-time (34 women); includes 23 minority (7 Black or African American, non-Hispanic/Latino; 7 Asian, non-Hispanic/Latino; 8 Hispanic/Latino; 1 Two or more races, non-Hispanic/Latino), 31 international. Average age 28. 220 applicants, 85% accepted, 103 enrolled. In 2010, 113 master's awarded. *Entrance requirements:* For master's, GMAT or GRE. Additional exam requirements/recommendations for international students: Required—TOEFL (minimum score 550 paper-based;

213 computer-based; 79 iBT); Recommended—IELTS (minimum score 6.5). *Application deadline:* For fall admission, 3/1 priority date for international students; for winter admission, 7/1 priority date for international students; for spring admission, 1/1 priority date for international students. Applications are processed on a rolling basis. Application fee: $0 ($50 for international students). Electronic applications accepted. *Expenses:* Contact institution. *Financial support:* In 2010–11, 15 research assistantships with full and partial tuition reimbursements (averaging $7,020 per year) were awarded; career-related internships or fieldwork, institutionally sponsored loans, scholarships/grants, health care benefits, and unspecified assistantships also available. Support available to part-time students. Financial award application deadline: 3/15; financial award applicants required to submit FAFSA. *Faculty research:* Management information systems, economics, finance, entrepreneurship, marketing. *Unit head:* Janice M. Glynn, Director, MBA Program, 937-229-3733, Fax: 937-229-3882, E-mail: glynn@udayton.edu. *Application contact:* Jeffrey Carter, Assistant Director, MBA Program, 937-229-3733, Fax: 937-229-3882, E-mail: jeff.carter@notes.udayton.edu.

University of Denver, Daniels College of Business, Programs in International Business/Management, Denver, CO 80208. Offers IMBA, MBA. *Accreditation:* AACSB. *Faculty:* 1 full-time (0 women), 1 part-time/adjunct (0 women). *Students:* 58 full-time (23 women), 20 part-time (9 women); includes 8 minority (1 Black or African American, non-Hispanic/Latino; 1 American Indian or Alaska Native, non-Hispanic/Latino; 1 Asian, non-Hispanic/Latino; 3 Hispanic/Latino; 2 Two or more races, non-Hispanic/Latino), 3 international. Average age 28. 98 applicants, 83% accepted, 40 enrolled. In 2010, 55 master's awarded. *Entrance requirements:* For master's, GRE General Test or GMAT. Additional exam requirements/recommendations for international students: Required—TOEFL (minimum score 570 paper-based; 88 iBT). *Application deadline:* For fall admission, 1/15 priority date for domestic students. Applications are processed on a rolling basis. Application fee: $60. Electronic applications accepted. *Expenses:* Tuition: Full-time $35,604; part-time $29,670 per year. Required fees: $687 per year. Tuition and fees vary according to program. *Financial support:* Career-related internships or fieldwork, Federal Work-Study, institutionally sponsored loans, and scholarships/grants available. Support available to part-time students. Financial award application deadline: 2/15; financial award applicants required to submit FAFSA. *Unit head:* Leslie Carter, Associate Director, 303-871-2037, E-mail: leslie.carter@du.edu. *Application contact:* Tara Stenbakken, Graduate Admissions Manager, 303-871-4211, E-mail: tara.stenbakken@du.edu.

University of Denver, Josef Korbel School of International Studies, Denver, CO 80208. Offers conflict resolution (MA); development practice (MDP); global finance, trade and economic integration (MA); global health affairs (Certificate); homeland security (Certificate); humanitarian assistance (Certificate); international development (MA); international human rights (MA); international security (MA); international studies (MA, PhD). Part-time programs available. *Faculty:* 33 full-time (13 women), 38 part-time/adjunct (11 women). *Students:* 461 full-time (279 women), 52 part-time (27 women); includes 71 minority (8 Black or African American, non-Hispanic/Latino; 3 American Indian or Alaska Native, non-Hispanic/Latino; 25 Asian, non-Hispanic/Latino; 25 Hispanic/Latino; 2 Native Hawaiian or other Pacific Islander, non-Hispanic/Latino; 8 Two or more races, non-Hispanic/Latino), 42 international. Average age 28. 1,056 applicants, 69% accepted, 259 enrolled. In 2010, 230 master's, 5 doctorates, 42 other advanced degrees awarded. *Degree requirements:* For master's, one foreign language, thesis; for doctorate, one foreign language, thesis/dissertation. *Entrance requirements:* For master's and doctorate, GRE General Test. Additional exam requirements/recommendations for international students: Required—TOEFL (minimum score 587 paper-based; 95 iBT). *Application deadline:* For fall admission, 1/15 priority date for domestic students, 12/15 priority date for international students; for winter admission, 10/15 priority date for domestic and international students. Applications are processed on a rolling basis. Application fee: $60. Electronic applications accepted. *Expenses:* Tuition: Full-time $35,604; part-time $29,670 per year. Required fees: $687 per year. Tuition and fees vary according to program. *Financial support:* In 2010–11, 1 teaching assistantship with partial tuition reimbursement (averaging $9,999 per year) was awarded; career-related internships or fieldwork, Federal Work-Study, institutionally sponsored loans, scholarships/grants, and unspecified assistantships also available. Support available to part-time students. Financial award applicants required to submit FAFSA. *Faculty research:* Human rights and international security, international politics and economics, economic-social and political development, international technology analysis and management. *Unit head:* Ambassador Christopher R. Hill, Dean, 303-871-2539, Fax: 303-871-2124, E-mail: christopher.r.hill@du.edu. *Application contact:* Brad Miller, Director of Graduate Admissions and Financial Aid, 303-871-2989, Fax: 303-871-2124, E-mail: korbeladm@du.edu.

University of Florida, Graduate School, Warrington College of Business Administration, Hough Graduate School of Business, Department of Management, Gainesville, FL 32611. Offers international business (MAIB); management (MSM, PhD). *Accreditation:* AACSB. Postbaccalaureate distance learning degree programs offered. *Faculty:* 11 full-time (2 women). *Students:* 223 full-time (103 women), 66 part-time (35 women); includes 12 Black or African American, non-Hispanic/Latino; 1 American Indian or Alaska Native,

non-Hispanic/Latino; 16 Asian, non-Hispanic/Latino; 40 Hispanic/Latino, 42 international. Average age 28. 37 applicants, 59% accepted, 15 enrolled. In 2010, 234 master's, 3 doctorates awarded. *Degree requirements:* For master's, comprehensive exam, thesis; for doctorate, comprehensive exam, thesis/dissertation. *Entrance requirements:* For master's and doctorate, GMAT or GRE General Test, minimum GPA of 3.0. Additional exam requirements/recommendations for international students: Required—TOEFL (minimum score 550 paper-based; 213 computer-based; 80 iBT), IELTS (minimum score 6). *Application deadline:* For fall admission, 1/1 for domestic and international students. Applications are processed on a rolling basis. Application fee: $30. Electronic applications accepted. *Expenses:* Tuition, state resident: full-time $10,915.92. Tuition, nonresident: full-time $28,309. *Financial support:* In 2010–11, 18 students received support, including 10 fellowships, 4 research assistantships (averaging $21,839 per year), 4 teaching assistantships (averaging $15,288 per year); unspecified assistantships also available. Financial award applicants required to submit FAFSA. *Faculty research:* Job attitudes, personality and individual differences, organizational entry and exit, knowledge management, competitive dynamics. *Unit head:* Dr. Robert E. Thomas, Chair, 352-392-0136, Fax: 352-392-6020, E-mail: rethomas@ufl.edu. *Application contact:* Dr. Jason A. Colquitt, Graduate Coordinator, 352-846-0507, Fax: 352-392-6020, E-mail: colquitt@ufl.edu.

University of Florida, Graduate School, Warrington College of Business Administration, Hough Graduate School of Business, Programs in Business Administration, Gainesville, FL 32611. Offers accounting (MBA); arts administration (MBA); business strategy and public policy (MBA); competitive strategy (MBA); decision and information sciences (MBA); electronic commerce (MBA); finance (MBA); general business (MBA); global management (MBA); Graham-Buffett security analysis (MBA); health administration (MBA); human resources management (MBA); international studies (MBA); Latin American business (MBA); management (MBA); marketing (MBA); sports administration (MBA); JD/MBA; MBA/MS; MBA/PhD; MBA/Pharm D; MD/MBA. *Accreditation:* AACSB. Part-time and evening/weekend programs available. *Faculty:* 71 full-time (10 women). *Students:* 187 full-time (44 women), 305 part-time (83 women); includes 25 Black or African American, non-Hispanic/Latino; 2 American Indian or Alaska Native, non-Hispanic/Latino; 52 Asian, non-Hispanic/Latino; 54 Hispanic/Latino, 11 international. Average age 31. 919 applicants, 33% accepted, 225 enrolled. In 2010, 492 master's awarded. *Degree requirements:* For master's, capstone course. *Entrance requirements:* For master's, GMAT, minimum GPA of 3.0, interview. Additional exam requirements/recommendations for international students: Required—TOEFL (minimum score 550 paper-based; 213 computer-based; 80 iBT), IELTS (minimum score 6). *Application deadline:* For fall admission, 7/1 for domestic students, 1/1 for international students; for spring admission, 12/1 for domestic and international students. Applications are processed on a rolling basis. Application fee: $30. Electronic applications accepted. *Expenses:* Tuition, state resident: full-time $10,915.92. Tuition, nonresident: full-time $28,309. *Financial support:* In 2010–11, 1 student received support, including 1 teaching assistantship (averaging $20,600 per year); career-related internships or fieldwork, scholarships/grants, and unspecified assistantships also available. Support available to part-time students. Financial award applicants required to submit FAFSA. *Faculty research:* Accounting, finance, insurance, management, real estate, urban analysis marketing. *Unit head:* Prof. Alexander D. Sevilla, Assistant Dean and Director MBA Programs, 352-273-3252 Ext. 1206, E-mail: alex.sevilla@warrington.ufl.edu. *Application contact:* Prof. Kelli Gust, Associate Director of MBA Programs, 352-273-3255, Fax: 352-392-8791, E-mail: kelly.gust@ warrington.ufl.edu.

University of Florida, Levin College of Law, Gainesville, FL 32611. Offers comparative law (LL M); environmental law (LL M); international taxation (LL M); law (JD); taxation (LL M, SJD). *Accreditation:* ABA. *Faculty:* 77 full-time (37 women), 36 part-time/adjunct (10 women). *Students:* 1,175 full-time (518 women), 10 part-time (1 woman); includes 74 Black or African American, non-Hispanic/Latino; 16 American Indian or Alaska Native, non-Hispanic/Latino; 73 Asian, non-Hispanic/Latino; 112 Hispanic/Latino, 33 international. Average age 24. 3,357 applicants, 24% accepted, 310 enrolled. In 2010, 382 first professional degrees awarded. *Degree requirements:* For JD, thesis/dissertation or alternative. *Entrance requirements:* LSAT. *Application deadline:* For fall admission, 1/15 for domestic and international students. Applications are processed on a rolling basis. Application fee: $30. Electronic applications accepted. *Expenses:* Tuition, state resident: full-time $10,915.92. Tuition, nonresident: full-time $28,309. *Financial support:* In 2010–11, 261 students received support, including 30 research assistantships (averaging $8,580 per year); Federal Work-Study, institutionally sponsored loans, scholarships/grants, health care benefits, and unspecified assistantships also available. Financial award application deadline: 4/7; financial award applicants required to submit FAFSA. *Faculty research:* Environmental and land use law, taxation, family law, international law, Constitutional law. *Unit head:* Robert Jerry, Dean, 352-273-0600, Fax: 352-392-8727, E-mail: jerryr@law.ufl.edu. *Application contact:* Michelle Adorno, Assistant Dean for Admissions, 352-273-0890, Fax: 352-392-4087, E-mail: madorno@law.ufl.edu.

University of Hawaii at Manoa, Graduate Division, Shidler College of Business, Program in Business Administration, Honolulu, HI 96822. Offers Asian business studies (MBA); Chinese business studies (MBA); decision sciences (MBA); entrepreneurship (MBA); finance (MBA); finance and banking (MBA); human resources management (MBA); information management (MBA); information technology (MBA); international business (MBA); Japanese business studies (MBA); marketing (MBA); organizational behavior (MBA); organizational management (MBA); real estate (MBA); student-designed track (MBA). *Accreditation:* AACSB. Part-time and evening/weekend programs available. *Faculty:* 53 full-time (12 women). *Students:* 162 full-time (63 women), 102 part-time (43 women); includes 135 minority (1 Black or African American, non-Hispanic/Latino; 81 Asian, non-Hispanic/Latino; 5 Hispanic/Latino; 18 Native Hawaiian or other Pacific Islander, non-Hispanic/Latino; 30 Two or more races, non-Hispanic/Latino), 44 international. Average age 34. 361 applicants, 57% accepted, 172 enrolled. In 2010, 153 master's awarded. *Degree requirements:* For master's, thesis optional. *Entrance requirements:* For master's, GMAT, minimum GPA of 3.0. Additional exam requirements/recommendations for international students: Required—TOEFL (minimum score 600 paper-based; 250 computer-based; 100 iBT), IELTS (minimum score 7). *Application deadline:* For fall admission, 5/1 for domestic students, 3/1 for international students. Application fee: $60. *Expenses:* Contact institution. *Financial support:* In 2010–11, 83 fellowships (averaging $5,547 per year), 1 research assistantship (averaging $16,824 per year) were awarded. Total annual research expenditures: $427,000. *Application contact:* Daniel Port, Graduate Chair, 808-956-5565, Fax: 808-956-6889, E-mail: daniel.port@hawaii.edu.

University of Hawaii at Manoa, Graduate Division, Shidler College of Business, Program in International Management, Honolulu, HI 96822. Offers Asian finance (PhD); global information technology management (PhD); international accounting (PhD); international marketing (PhD); international organization and strategy (PhD). Part-time programs available. *Students:* 30 full-time (11 women), 3 part-time (0 women); includes 7 minority (5 Asian, non-Hispanic/Latino; 2 Two or more races, non-Hispanic/Latino), 18 international. Average age 36. 65 applicants, 18% accepted, 5 enrolled. In 2010, 4 doctorates awarded. *Degree requirements:* For doctorate, comprehensive exam, thesis/dissertation. *Entrance requirements:* For doctorate, GMAT or GRE General Test, minimum GPA of 3.0. Additional exam requirements/recommendations for international students: Required—TOEFL (minimum score 600 paper-based; 250 computer-based; 100 iBT), IELTS (minimum score 7). *Application deadline:* For fall admission, 3/1 for domestic and international students. Application fee: $60. *Expenses:* Contact institution. *Financial support:* In 2010–11, 29 students received support, including 3 fellowships (averaging $5,491 per year), 25 research assistantships (averaging $17,750 per year), 1 teaching assistantship (averaging $15,558 per year). *Application contact:* Erica Okada, Graduate Chair, 808-956-6723, Fax: 808-956-6889, E-mail: imphd@hawaii.edu.

University of Houston–Victoria, School of Business Administration, Victoria, TX 77901-4450. Offers accounting (MBA); economic development and entrepreneurship (MS); finance (GMBA, MBA); general business (MBA); international business (MBA); management (GMBA, MBA); marketing (MBA). *Accreditation:* AACSB. Part-time and evening/weekend programs available. Postbaccalaureate distance learning degree programs offered (minimal on-campus study). *Faculty:* 37 full-time (11 women). *Students:* 234 full-time (108 women), 714 part-time (303 women); includes 542 minority (215 Black or African American, non-Hispanic/Latino; 1 American Indian or Alaska Native, non-Hispanic/Latino; 197 Asian, non-Hispanic/Latino; 124 Hispanic/Latino; 1 Native Hawaiian or other Pacific Islander, non-Hispanic/Latino; 4 Two or more races, non-Hispanic/Latino), 115 international. Average age 34. 362 applicants, 65% accepted, 147 enrolled. In 2010, 181 master's awarded. *Entrance requirements:* For master's, GMAT. Additional exam requirements/recommendations for international students: Required—TOEFL (minimum score 550 paper-based; 213 computer-based). *Application deadline:* For fall admission, 6/1 for international students; for spring admission, 10/1 for international students. Applications are processed on a rolling basis. Application fee: $0. Electronic applications accepted. *Expenses:* Tuition, state resident: full-time $4050; part-time $225 per credit hour. Tuition, nonresident: full-time $8730; part-time $485 per credit hour. Required fees: $810; $54 per credit hour. Tuition and fees vary according to course load. *Financial support:* In 2010–11, research assistantships with partial tuition reimbursements (averaging $2,000 per year), teaching assistantships with partial tuition reimbursements (averaging $2,000 per year) were awarded; Federal Work-Study, scholarships/grants, and unspecified assistantships also available. Support available to part-time students. Financial award application deadline: 4/15; financial award applicants required to submit FAFSA. *Faculty research:* Economic development, marketing, finance. *Unit head:* Dr. Farhang Niroomand, Dean, 361-570-4230, Fax: 361-580-5599, E-mail: niroomandf@uhv.edu. *Application contact:* Jane Mims, Assistant Dean, 361-570-4639, Fax: 361-580-5529, E-mail: mims@uhv.edu.

University of La Verne, College of Business and Public Management, Graduate Programs in Business Administration, La Verne, CA 91750-4443. Offers accounting (MBA); executive management (MBA-EP); finance (MBA, MBA-EP); health services management (MBA); information technology (MBA, MBA-EP); international business (MBA, MBA-EP); leadership (MBA-EP); managed care (MBA); management (MBA, MBA-EP); marketing (MBA, MBA-EP). Part-time and evening/weekend programs

available. *Faculty:* 34 full-time (12 women), 36 part-time/adjunct (9 women). *Students:* 412 full-time (207 women), 200 part-time (96 women); includes 423 minority (32 Black or African American, non-Hispanic/Latino; 5 American Indian or Alaska Native, non-Hispanic/Latino; 294 Asian, non-Hispanic/Latino; 92 Hispanic/Latino), 6 international. Average age 29. In 2010, 229 master's awarded. *Entrance requirements:* For master's, minimum undergraduate GPA of 3.0, 2 letters of recommendation, resume. Additional exam requirements/recommendations for international students: Required—TOEFL (minimum score 550 paper-based; 213 computer-based). *Application deadline:* Applications are processed on a rolling basis. Application fee: $50. *Expenses:* Contact institution. *Financial support:* Career-related internships or fieldwork, institutionally sponsored loans, and scholarships/grants available. Financial award application deadline: 3/2; financial award applicants required to submit FAFSA. *Unit head:* Dr. Abe Helou, Chairperson, 909-593-3511 Ext. 4211, Fax: 909-392-2704, E-mail: ihelou@laverne.edu. *Application contact:* Rina Lazarian, Program and Admission Specialist, 909-593-3511 Ext. 4819, Fax: 909-392-2704, E-mail: cbpm@ulv.edu.

University of Louisville, Graduate School, College of Business, MBA Programs, Louisville, KY 40292-0001. Offers entrepreneurship (MBA); global business (PMBA); global business (full time) (MBA). The MBA degree is offered in both a full time and part time format. The full time program is a 13 month program paired with a paid internship. The part-time program is available in an evening as well as a Saturday format. All MBA programs are cohort-based and include an international learning experience. *Accreditation:* AACSB. Part-time and evening/weekend programs available. *Faculty:* 30 full-time (7 women), 2 part-time/adjunct (0 women). *Students:* 25 full-time (9 women), 185 part-time (54 women); includes 19 minority (6 Black or African American, non-Hispanic/Latino; 1 American Indian or Alaska Native, non-Hispanic/Latino; 8 Asian, non-Hispanic/Latino; 4 Hispanic/Latino), 8 international. Average age 29. 318 applicants, 42% accepted, 111 enrolled. In 2010, 104 master's awarded. *Entrance requirements:* For master's, GMAT, 2 letters of reference, personal interview, resume, personal statement, college transcript(s). Additional exam requirements/recommendations for international students: Required—TOEFL (minimum score 557 paper-based; 213 computer-based; 83 iBT). *Application deadline:* For fall admission, 7/31 for domestic students; for spring admission, 12/1 for domestic students. Applications are processed on a rolling basis. Application fee: $50. *Expenses:* Tuition, state resident: full-time $9144; part-time $508 per credit hour. Tuition, nonresident: full-time $19,026; part-time $1057 per credit hour. Tuition and fees vary according to program and reciprocity agreements. *Financial support:* In 2010–11, 16 students received support, including 6 fellowships (averaging $3,133 per year), 10 research assistantships with full tuition reimbursements available (averaging $12,000 per year); health care benefits and unspecified assistantships also available. Financial award application deadline: 3/31; financial award applicants required to submit FAFSA. *Faculty research:* Entrepreneurship, venture capital, retailing/franchising, corporate governance and leadership, supply chain management. Total annual research expenditures: $221,322. *Unit head:* Dr. R. Charles Moyer, Dean, 502-852-6443, Fax: 502-852-7557, E-mail: charlie.moyer@louisville.edu. *Application contact:* Joshua M. Philpot, Graduate Programs Manager, 502-852-7257, Fax: 502-852-4901, E-mail: josh.philpot@louisville.edu.

University of Maryland University College, Graduate School of Management and Technology, Program in International Management, Adelphi, MD 20783. Offers MIM, Certificate. Offered evenings and weekends only. Part-time and evening/weekend programs available. Postbaccalaureate distance learning degree programs offered (no on-campus study). *Students:* 6 full-time (4 women), 223 part-time (130 women); includes 121 minority (85 Black or African American, non-Hispanic/Latino; 1 American Indian or Alaska Native, non-Hispanic/Latino; 16 Asian, non-Hispanic/Latino; 16 Hispanic/Latino; 1 Native Hawaiian or other Pacific Islander, non-Hispanic/Latino; 2 Two or more races, non-Hispanic/Latino), 6 international. Average age 35. 72 applicants, 100% accepted, 40 enrolled. In 2010, 63 master's, 11 Certificates awarded. *Degree requirements:* For master's, thesis or alternative. *Application deadline:* Applications are processed on a rolling basis. Application fee: $50. Electronic applications accepted. *Financial support:* Federal Work-Study and scholarships/grants available. Support available to part-time students. Financial award application deadline: 6/1; financial award applicants required to submit FAFSA. *Unit head:* Dr. Robert Jerome, Director, 240-684-2400, Fax: 240-684-2401, E-mail: rjerome@umuc.edu. *Application contact:* Coordinator, Graduate Admissions, 800-888-8682, Fax: 240-684-2151, E-mail: newgrad@umuc.edu.

University of Memphis, Graduate School, Fogelman College of Business and Economics, Program in Business Administration, Memphis, TN 38152. Offers accounting (MBA, PhD); economics (MBA, PhD); executive business administration (MBA); finance (PhD); finance, insurance, and real estate (MBA, MS); international business administration (IMBA); management (MBA, MS, PhD); management information systems (MBA, MS, PhD); management science (MBA); marketing (MBA, MS); marketing and supply chain management (PhD); real estate development (MS); JD/MBA. *Accreditation:* AACSB. *Faculty:* 44 full-time (9 women), 5 part-time/adjunct (0 women). *Students:* 263 full-time (106 women), 181 part-time (66 women); includes 46 Black or African American, non-Hispanic/Latino; 3 American Indian or Alaska

Native, non-Hispanic/Latino; 16 Asian, non-Hispanic/Latino; 5 Hispanic/Latino, 109 international. Average age 31. 374 applicants, 73% accepted, 119 enrolled. In 2010, 140 master's, 17 doctorates awarded. *Degree requirements:* For master's, comprehensive exam; for doctorate, comprehensive exam, thesis/dissertation. *Entrance requirements:* For master's, GMAT, resume; for doctorate, GMAT, interview, minimum GPA of 3.4, resume, letter of recommendation. Additional exam requirements/recommendations for international students: Required—TOEFL (minimum score 550 paper-based; 220 computer-based). *Application deadline:* For fall admission, 8/1 for domestic students; for spring admission, 12/1 for domestic students. Application fee: $35 ($60 for international students). *Financial support:* In 2010–11, 164 students received support; research assistantships with full tuition reimbursements available, teaching assistantships with full tuition reimbursements available, career-related internships or fieldwork, Federal Work-Study, scholarships/grants, and unspecified assistantships available. Financial award application deadline: 2/15; financial award applicants required to submit FAFSA. *Faculty research:* Competitive business strategy, finance microstructures, supply chain management innovations, health care economics, litigation risks and corporate audits. *Unit head:* Rajiv Grover, Dean, 901-678-3759, E-mail: rgrover@memphis.edu. *Application contact:* Dr. Carol V. Danehower, Associate Dean, 901-678-5402, Fax: 901-678-3579, E-mail: fcbegp@memphis.edu.

University of Michigan–Dearborn, School of Management, Dearborn, MI 48128-1491. Offers accounting (MBA, MS); finance (MBA, MS); information systems (MS); international business (MBA); management (MBA); management information systems (MBA); marketing (MBA); supply chain management (MBA); MBA/MHSA; MBA/MSE; MBA/MSF. *Accreditation:* AACSB. Part-time and evening/weekend programs available. Postbaccalaureate distance learning degree programs offered (no on-campus study). *Faculty:* 40 full-time (17 women), 2 part-time/adjunct (1 woman). *Students:* 71 full-time (26 women), 403 part-time (134 women); includes 68 minority (19 Black or African American, non-Hispanic/Latino; 1 American Indian or Alaska Native, non-Hispanic/Latino; 39 Asian, non-Hispanic/Latino; 6 Hispanic/Latino; 1 Native Hawaiian or other Pacific Islander, non-Hispanic/Latino; 2 Two or more races, non-Hispanic/Latino), 89 international. Average age 30. 185 applicants, 51% accepted, 67 enrolled. In 2010, 150 master's awarded. *Entrance requirements:* For master's, GMAT, 2 years of work experience (MBA); course work in computer applications, statistics, and pre-calculus or finite mathematics; 18 credits of accounting course work beyond introductory courses (MS in accounting). Additional exam requirements/recommendations for international students: Required—TOEFL (minimum score 560 paper-based; 220 computer-based; 84 iBT). *Application deadline:* For fall admission, 8/1 priority date for domestic students, 6/1 for international students; for winter admission, 12/1 priority date for domestic students, 10/1 for international students; for spring admission, 4/1 priority date for domestic students, 2/1 for international students. Applications are processed on a rolling basis. Application fee: $60. Electronic applications accepted. *Expenses:* Contact institution. *Financial support:* Career-related internships or fieldwork, Federal Work-Study, and scholarships/grants available. Support available to part-time students. Financial award application deadline: 9/1; financial award applicants required to submit FAFSA. *Faculty research:* Cultural diversity, buyer-supplier relations, error detection in data, economic evolution. *Unit head:* Dr. Kim Schatzel, Dean, 313-593-5248, Fax: 313-271-9835, E-mail: schatzel@umd.umich.edu. *Application contact:* Joan Doherty, Academic Advisor/Counselor, 313-593-5460, Fax: 313-271-9838, E-mail: gradbusiness@umd.umich.edu.

University of New Brunswick Saint John, Faculty of Business, Saint John, NB E2L 4L5, Canada. Offers administration (MBA); electronic commerce (MBA); international business (MBA); natural resource management (MBA). Part-time programs available. *Faculty:* 19 full-time (4 women), 14 part-time/adjunct (8 women). *Students:* 47 full-time (18 women), 55 part-time (21 women). 93 applicants, 78% accepted, 25 enrolled. In 2010, 36 master's awarded. *Entrance requirements:* For master's, GMAT, minimum GPA of 3.0. Additional exam requirements/recommendations for international students: Required—TOEFL (minimum score 580 paper-based; 237 computer-based), IELTS (minimum score 7), TWE (minimum score 4.5). *Application deadline:* For fall admission, 5/15 for domestic and international students. Applications are processed on a rolling basis. Application fee: $100. Electronic applications accepted. *Expenses:* Contact institution. *Financial support:* In 2010–11, 4 students received support. Career-related internships or fieldwork and scholarships/grants available. *Faculty research:* Business use of weblogs and podcasts to communicate, corporate governance, high-involvement work systems, international competitiveness, supply chain management and logistics. *Unit head:* Henryk Sterniczuk, Director of Graduate Studies, 506-648-5573, Fax: 506-648-5574, E-mail: sternicz@unbsj.ca. *Application contact:* Tammy Morin, Secretary, 506-648-5746, Fax: 506-648-5574, E-mail: tmorin@unbsj.ca.

University of New Haven, Graduate School, School of Business, Program in Business Administration, West Haven, CT 06516-1916. Offers accounting (MBA, Certificate), including CPA (MBA); business management (Certificate); business policy and strategy (MBA); finance (MBA), including CFA; global marketing (MBA); human resource management (Certificate); human resources management (MBA); international business (Certificate); marketing (Certificate); sports management (MBA); telecommunications management (Certificate); MBA/MPA. Part-time and evening/weekend programs available. *Students:* 158 full-time (80 women), 150 part-time (70 women); includes 36 Black or African American, non-Hispanic/Latino; 2 American Indian or Alaska Native, non-Hispanic/Latino; 19 Asian, non-Hispanic/Latino; 16 Hispanic/Latino, 82 international. Average age 32. 162 applicants, 99% accepted, 85 enrolled. In 2010, 141 master's, 16 other advanced degrees awarded. *Degree requirements:* For master's, thesis or alternative. *Entrance requirements:* For master's, GMAT. Additional exam requirements/recommendations for international students: Required—TOEFL (minimum score 520 paper-based; 190 computer-based; 70 iBT), IELTS (minimum score 5.5). *Application deadline:* For fall admission, 5/31 for international students; for winter admission, 10/15 for international students; for spring admission, 1/15 for international students. Applications are processed on a rolling basis. Application fee: $50. Electronic applications accepted. *Expenses:* Contact institution. *Financial support:* Research assistantships with partial tuition reimbursements, teaching assistantships with partial tuition reimbursements, Federal Work-Study, scholarships/grants, health care benefits, tuition waivers, and unspecified assistantships available. Support available to part-time students. Financial award applicants required to submit FAFSA. *Unit head:* Charles Coleman, Chairman, 203-932-7375. *Application contact:* Eloise Gormley, Director of Graduate Admissions, 203-932-7449, Fax: 203-932-7137, E-mail: gradinfo@newhaven.edu.

University of North Florida, Coggin College of Business, MBA Program, Jacksonville, FL 32224. Offers accounting (MBA); construction management (MBA); e-commerce (MBA); economics (MBA); finance (MBA); human resource management (MBA); international business (MBA); logistics (MBA); management applications (MBA). *Accreditation:* AACSB. Part-time and evening/weekend programs available. *Faculty:* 17 full-time (5 women), 1 part-time/adjunct (0 women). *Students:* 137 full-time (56 women), 268 part-time (112 women); includes 17 Black or African American, non-Hispanic/Latino; 21 Asian, non-Hispanic/Latino; 12 Hispanic/Latino; 3 Two or more races, non-Hispanic/Latino, 29 international. Average age 30. 250 applicants, 57% accepted, 94 enrolled. In 2010, 173 master's awarded. *Entrance requirements:* For master's, GMAT or GRE, U.S. bachelor's degree from regionally-accredited university or equivalent foreign degree. Additional exam requirements/recommendations for international students: Required—TOEFL (minimum score 550 paper-based; 213 computer-based; 79 iBT). *Application deadline:* For fall admission, 7/1 priority date for domestic students, 5/1 for international students; for spring admission, 11/1 priority date for domestic students, 10/1 for international students. Applications are processed on a rolling basis. Application fee: $30. *Expenses:* Tuition, state resident: full-time $7646.40; part-time $318.60 per credit hour. Tuition, nonresident: full-time $23,502; part-time $979.24 per credit hour. Required fees: $1208.88; $50.37 per credit hour. Tuition and fees vary according to course load and program. *Financial support:* In 2010–11, 40 students received support; research assistantships, teaching assistantships, Federal Work-Study and tuition waivers (partial) available. Support available to part-time students. Financial award application deadline: 4/1; financial award applicants required to submit FAFSA. *Faculty research:* Performance measures, costing, and inventory issues in logistics and supply chain management; inter-organizational systems; international management and marketing practices; e-commerce; organizational learning and socialization processes. Total annual research expenditures: $9,024. *Unit head:* Dr. C. Bruce Kavan, Chair, 904-620-2780, Fax: 904-620-2832. *Application contact:* Cheryl Campbell, Graduate Advisor, 904-620-2575, Fax: 904-620-2832, E-mail: ccampbell@unf.edu.

University of Pennsylvania, School of Arts and Sciences and Wharton School, Joseph H. Lauder Institute of Management and International Studies, Philadelphia, PA 19104. Offers international studies (MA); management and international studies (MBA); MBA/MA. Applications must be made concurrently and separately to the Wharton MBA program. *Students:* 125 full-time (53 women). Average age 27. In 2010, 68 master's awarded. *Degree requirements:* For master's, one foreign language, thesis. *Entrance requirements:* For master's, GMAT or GRE, advanced proficiency in a non-native language (Arabic, Chinese, French, German, Hindi, Japanese, Portuguese, Russian, or Spanish). Additional exam requirements/recommendations for international students: Required—TOEFL. *Application deadline:* For fall admission, 10/1 for domestic and international students; for winter admission, 1/3 for domestic and international students. Electronic applications accepted. *Expenses:* Contact institution. *Financial support:* Fellowships with full and partial tuition reimbursements, career-related internships or fieldwork and scholarships/grants available. *Faculty research:* Finance, marketing, strategy, operations management, multinational management. *Unit head:* Dr. Mauro Guillen, Director, 215-898-1215. *Application contact:* Marcy R. Bevan, Director of Admissions, 215-898-1215, Fax: 215-898-2067, E-mail: lauderinfo@wharton.upenn.edu.

University of Phoenix, School of Business, Phoenix, AZ 85034-7209. Offers accounting (MBA, MSA); business administration (MBA); energy management (MBA); global management (MBA); health care management (MBA); human resources management (MM); international management (MM); management (MM); marketing (MBA); project management (MBA); public administration (MPA); technology management (MBA). Programs are offered at the online campus. Evening/weekend programs available. Postbaccalaureate distance learning degree programs offered. *Students:* 20,237 full-time (12,641 women); includes 6,424 minority (4,376 Black or African American, non-Hispanic/Latino; 150 American Indian or Alaska Native, non-Hispanic/Latino; 546 Asian, non-Hispanic/Latino; 1,137 Hispanic/Latino; 155 Native Hawaiian or other Pacific Islander, non-Hispanic/Latino; 60 Two or more races, non-Hispanic/Latino), 1,149 international. Average age 39. *Entrance requirements:* For master's, minimum undergraduate GPA of 2.5 from accredited university, 3 years of work experience, citizen of the United States or have valid visa. Additional exam requirements/recommendations for international students: Required—TOEFL (minimum paper score 550, computer score 213, iBT 79), Test of English for International Communication, or IELTS. *Application deadline:* Applications are processed on a rolling basis. Application fee: $45. Electronic applications accepted. *Expenses:* Tuition: Full-time $16,440. One-time fee: $45 full-time. Full-time tuition and fees vary according to course load, degree level, campus/location and program. *Financial support:* Scholarships/grants available. Financial award applicants required to submit FAFSA. *Unit head:* Dr. Bill Berry, Director, 480-557-1824, E-mail: bill.berry@phoenix.edu. *Application contact:* Dr. Bill Berry, Director, 480-557-1824, E-mail: bill.berry@phoenix.edu.

University of Pittsburgh, Katz Graduate School of Business, Augsburg Executive Fellows Program, Pittsburgh, PA 15260. Offers MBA. *Faculty:* 60 full-time (18 women), 22 part-time/adjunct (5 women). *Students:* 27 full-time (1 woman), all international. Average age 32. *Degree requirements:* For master's, one foreign language, 7 week stay at Katz Graduate School as full-time student. *Entrance requirements:* For master's, admission to the MBA program at the University of Augsburg, Germany. Additional exam requirements/recommendations for international students: Required—TOEFL (minimum score 600 paper-based; 250 computer-based; 100 iBT) or IELTS. *Application deadline:* For spring admission, 7/1 priority date for international students. *Expenses:* Contact institution. *Faculty research:* Accounting statements and reporting, incentives and governance, corporate finance, mergers and acquisitions, information systems processes, structures and decision-making, organizational structure, knowledge management and corporate strategy, consumer behavior and marketing models. *Unit head:* William T. Valenta, Assistant Dean, MBA Programs, 412-648-1610, Fax: 412-648-1659, E-mail: wtvalenta@katz.pitt.edu. *Application contact:* Patricia Hermenault, Director, Special International and Dual Degree Programs, 412-383-8835, Fax: 412-648-1659, E-mail: hermenault@katz.pitt.edu.

University of Pittsburgh, Katz Graduate School of Business, MBA/Master of International Business Dual Degree Program, Pittsburgh, PA 15260. Offers MBA/MIB. Part-time and evening/weekend programs available. *Faculty:* 60 full-time (18 women), 22 part-time/adjunct (5 women). *Students:* 6 full-time (2 women), 2 part-time (both women); includes 2 Asian, non-Hispanic/Latino; 1 Hispanic/Latino. Average age 26. 20 applicants, 60% accepted, 4 enrolled. *Entrance requirements:* Additional exam requirements/recommendations for international students: Required—TOEFL (minimum score 600 paper-based; 250 computer-based; 100 iBT) or IELTS. *Application deadline:* For fall admission, 4/1 priority date for domestic students, 2/1 priority date for international students. Application fee: $50. Electronic applications accepted. *Expenses:* Tuition, state resident: full-time $17,304; part-time $701 per credit. Tuition, nonresident: full-time $29,554; part-time $1210 per credit. Required fees: $740; $214 per term. Tuition and fees vary according to program. *Financial support:* In 2010–11, 3 students received support. Career-related internships or fieldwork and scholarships/grants available. Financial award application deadline: 3/1; financial award applicants required to submit FAFSA. *Faculty research:* Transitional economies, incentives and governance; corporate finance, mergers and acquisitions; global information systems and structures; consumer behavior and marketing models; entrepreneurship and globalization. *Unit head:* William T. Valenta, Assistant Dean, Director of MBA Programs, 412-648-1610, Fax: 412-648-1659, E-mail: wtvalenta@katz.pitt.edu. *Application contact:* Cliff McCormick, Director MBA Admissions, 412-648-1700, Fax: 412-648-1659, E-mail: mba@katz.pitt.edu.

University of Regina, Faculty of Graduate Studies and Research, Kenneth Levene Graduate School of Business, Program in Business Administration, Regina, SK S4S 0A2, Canada. Offers business (Master's Certificate); business administration (MBA); executive business administration (MBA); international business (MBA); leadership (M Admin); organizational leadership (Master's Certificate); project management (Master's Certificate). Part-time and evening/weekend programs available. *Faculty:* 51 full-time (14 women), 10 part-time/adjunct (0 women). *Students:* 59 full-time (18 women), 19 part-time (7 women). 132 applicants, 80% accepted. In 2010, 39 master's awarded. *Degree requirements:* For master's, project. *Entrance requirements:* For master's, GMAT, two years relevant work experience. Additional exam requirements/recommendations for international students: Required—TOEFL (minimum score 580 paper-based; 80 iBT). *Application deadline:* Applications are processed on a rolling basis. Application fee: $100. Electronic applications accepted. *Financial support:* In 2010–11, 3 fellowships (averaging $18,000 per year), 3 teaching assistantships (averaging $6,759 per year) were awarded; research assistantships, scholarships/grants also available. Financial award application deadline: 6/15. *Faculty research:* Business policy and strategy, production and operations management, human behavior in organizations, financial management, social issues in business. *Unit head:* Dr. Anne Lavack, Dean, 306-585-4162, Fax: 306-585-4805,

E-mail: anne.lavack@uregina.ca. *Application contact:* Steve Wield, Manager, 306-337-8463, Fax: 306-585-5361, E-mail: steve.wield@uregina.ca.

University of San Diego, School of Business Administration, Program in Global Leadership, San Diego, CA 92110-2492. Offers MS. Postbaccalaureate distance learning degree programs offered (minimal on-campus study). *Students:* 25 full-time (10 women), 58 part-time (12 women); includes 5 Black or African American, non-Hispanic/Latino; 1 American Indian or Alaska Native, non-Hispanic/Latino; 4 Asian, non-Hispanic/Latino; 11 Hispanic/Latino; 1 Native Hawaiian or other Pacific Islander, non-Hispanic/Latino. Average age 32. In 2010, 32 master's awarded. *Entrance requirements:* For master's, minimum GPA of 3.0, minimum 2 years of work experience. Additional exam requirements/recommendations for international students: Required—TOEFL (minimum score 580 paper-based; 237 computer-based; 92 iBT), TWE. *Application deadline:* Applications are processed on a rolling basis. Application fee: $80. Electronic applications accepted. *Expenses:* Tuition: Full-time $21,744; part-time $1208 per unit. Required fees: $224. Full-time tuition and fees vary according to course load and degree level. *Financial support:* In 2010–11, 38 students received support. Scholarships/grants available. Financial award application deadline: 4/1; financial award applicants required to submit FAFSA. *Unit head:* Dr. Robert Schoultz, Director, 619-260-7459, E-mail: schoultz@sandiego.edu. *Application contact:* Stephen Pultz, Director of Admissions and Enrollment, 619-260-4506, Fax: 619-260-6836, E-mail: admissions@sandiego.edu.

University of San Francisco, School of Business and Professional Studies, Masagung Graduate School of Management, Joint Master of Global Entrepreneurship and Management Program, San Francisco, CA 94117-1080. Offers MGEM. Program offered jointly with IQS in Barcelona, Spain and Fu Jen Catholic University in Taipei, Taiwan. *Faculty:* 2 full-time (both women), 2 part-time/adjunct (0 women). *Students:* 29 full-time (17 women); includes 11 minority (1 Black or African American, non-Hispanic/Latino; 1 Asian, non-Hispanic/Latino; 6 Hispanic/Latino; 3 Two or more races, non-Hispanic/Latino), 12 international. Average age 23. 58 applicants, 71% accepted, 29 enrolled. In 2010, 29 master's awarded. *Expenses:* Tuition: Full-time $20,070; part-time $1115 per credit hour. Tuition and fees vary according to course load, degree level and program. *Financial support:* In 2010–11, 11 students received support. *Unit head:* Dr. Shenzhao Fu, 415-422-6771, Fax: 415-422-2502. *Application contact:* Kelly Brookes, Director, MBA Program, 415-422-2221, Fax: 415-422-6315, E-mail: mba@usfca.edu.

University of San Francisco, School of Business and Professional Studies, Masagung Graduate School of Management, Program in Business Administration, San Francisco, CA 94117-1080. Offers business economics (MBA); e-business (MBA); entrepreneurship (MBA); finance (MBA); international business (MBA); management (MBA); marketing (MBA); telecommunications management and policy (MBA); JD/MBA; MSN/MBA. *Accreditation:* AACSB. *Faculty:* 17 full-time (4 women), 16 part-time/adjunct (7 women). *Students:* 263 full-time (130 women), 11 part-time (6 women); includes 98 minority (3 Black or African American, non-Hispanic/Latino; 65 Asian, non-Hispanic/Latino; 18 Hispanic/Latino; 3 Native Hawaiian or other Pacific Islander, non-Hispanic/Latino; 9 Two or more races, non-Hispanic/Latino), 43 international. Average age 24. 503 applicants, 60% accepted, 80 enrolled. In 2010, 115 master's awarded. *Entrance requirements:* For master's, GMAT, minimum undergraduate GPA of 3.2. Additional exam requirements/recommendations for international students: Required—TOEFL. *Application deadline:* For fall admission, 7/1 priority date for domestic students; for spring admission, 11/30 for domestic students. Applications are processed on a rolling basis. Application fee: $55 ($65 for international students). *Expenses:* Tuition: Full-time $20,070; part-time $1115 per credit hour. Tuition and fees vary according to course load, degree level and program. *Financial support:* In 2010–11, 156 students received support; fellowships available. Financial award application deadline: 3/2; financial award applicants required to submit FAFSA. *Faculty research:* International financial markets, technology transfer licensing, international marketing, strategic planning. Total annual research expenditures: $50,000. *Unit head:* Kelly Brookes, Director, 415-422-2221, Fax: 415-422-6315. *Application contact:* Director, MBA Program, 415-422-2221, Fax: 415-422-6315, E-mail: mba@usfca.edu.

University of San Francisco, School of Law, Program in Law, San Francisco, CA 94117-1080. Offers intellectual property and technology law (LL M); international transactions and comparative law (LL M). *Faculty:* 15 full-time (7 women), 49 part-time/adjunct (18 women). *Students:* 21 full-time (13 women), 3 part-time (all women); includes 2 minority (1 Black or African American, non-Hispanic/Latino; 1 Asian, non-Hispanic/Latino), 19 international. Average age 30. 149 applicants, 71% accepted, 23 enrolled. In 2010, 14 master's awarded. *Entrance requirements:* For master's, law degree from U.S. or foreign school (intellectual property and technology law), law degree from foreign school (international transactions and comparative law). Application fee: $60. *Expenses:* Tuition: Full-time $20,070; part-time $1115 per credit hour. Tuition and fees vary according to course load, degree level and program. *Financial support:* In 2010–11, 13 students received support. *Unit head:* Eldon Reiley, Director, Fax: 415-422-5440. *Application contact:* Program Assistant, 415-422-5100, E-mail: masterlaws@usfca.edu.

The University of Scranton, College of Graduate and Continuing Education, Program in Business Administration, Scranton, PA 18510. Offers accounting (MBA); finance (MBA); general business administration (MBA); health care management (MBA); international business (MBA); management information systems (MBA); marketing (MBA); operations management (MBA). *Accreditation:* AACSB. Part-time and evening/weekend programs available. Postbaccalaureate distance learning degree programs offered (no on-campus study). *Faculty:* 34 full-time (8 women). *Students:* 251 full-time (91 women), 180 part-time (72 women); includes 41 Black or African American, non-Hispanic/Latino; 11 Asian, non-Hispanic/Latino; 7 Hispanic/Latino, 40 international. Average age 32. 386 applicants, 84% accepted. In 2010, 38 master's awarded. *Degree requirements:* For master's, capstone experience. *Entrance requirements:* For master's, GMAT, minimum GPA of 2.75. Additional exam requirements/recommendations for international students: Required—TOEFL (minimum score 500 paper-based; 173 computer-based), IELTS (minimum score 5.5). *Application deadline:* Applications are processed on a rolling basis. Application fee: $0. *Financial support:* In 2010–11, 13 students received support, including 13 teaching assistantships with full and partial tuition reimbursements available (averaging $6,430 per year); fellowships, career-related internships or fieldwork, Federal Work-Study, and unspecified assistantships also available. Support available to part-time students. Financial award application deadline: 3/1. *Faculty research:* Financial markets, strategic impact of total quality management, internal accounting controls, consumer preference, information systems and the Internet. *Unit head:* Dr. Murli Rajan, Director, 570-941-4043, Fax: 570-941-4342. *Application contact:* Joseph M. Roback, Director of Admissions, 570-941-4385, Fax: 570-941-5928, E-mail: robackj2@scranton.edu.

University of South Carolina, The Graduate School, Darla Moore School of Business, International Business Administration Program, Columbia, SC 29208. Offers IMBA. *Faculty:* 99 full-time (23 women), 10 part-time/adjunct (2 women). *Students:* 174 full-time (57 women); includes 4 Black or African American, non-Hispanic/Latino; 1 American Indian or Alaska Native, non-Hispanic/Latino; 3 Asian, non-Hispanic/Latino; 7 Hispanic/Latino, 29 international. Average age 26. 291 applicants, 69% accepted, 81 enrolled. In 2010, 86 master's awarded. *Degree requirements:* For master's, one foreign language, field consulting project/Internship. *Entrance requirements:* For master's, GMAT or GRE, Minimum two years of work experience. Additional exam requirements/recommendations for international students: Required—TOEFL (minimum score 250 computer-based; 100 iBT); Recommended—IELTS. *Application deadline:* For fall admission, 11/15 priority date for domestic and international students; for winter admission, 2/15 priority date for domestic and international students; for spring admission, 5/15 for domestic students, 5/1 priority date for international students. Applications are processed on a rolling basis. Application fee: $100. Electronic applications accepted. *Expenses:* Contact institution. *Financial support:* Fellowships, career-related internships or fieldwork, Federal Work-Study, scholarships/grants, and unspecified assistantships available. Financial award application deadline: 2/15. *Unit head:* Christine LaCola, Assistant Dean, Graduate Division, 803-777-2730, Fax: 803-777-7819, E-mail: christine.lacola@moore.sc.edu. *Application contact:* Scott King, Director, Graduate Admissions, 803-777-6749, Fax: 803-777-7819, E-mail: scott.king@moore.sc.edu.

The University of Tampa, John H. Sykes College of Business, Tampa, FL 33606-1490. Offers accounting (MS); entrepreneurship (MBA); finance (MBA, MS); information systems management (MBA); innovation management (MBA); international business (MBA); marketing (MBA, MS); non-profit management (MBA). *Accreditation:* AACSB. Part-time and evening/weekend programs available. *Faculty:* 67 full-time (24 women), 11 part-time/adjunct (4 women). *Students:* 235 full-time (89 women), 288 part-time (122 women); includes 74 minority (16 Black or African American, non-Hispanic/Latino; 2 American Indian or Alaska Native, non-Hispanic/Latino; 14 Asian, non-Hispanic/Latino; 34 Hispanic/Latino; 2 Native Hawaiian or other Pacific Islander, non-Hispanic/Latino; 6 Two or more races, non-Hispanic/Latino), 95 international. Average age 29. 457 applicants, 45% accepted, 175 enrolled. In 2010, 230 master's awarded. *Degree requirements:* For master's, capstone. *Entrance requirements:* For master's, GMAT or GRE, 4-year undergraduate degree, minimum GPA of 3.0, professional experience (for Executive MBA). Additional exam requirements/recommendations for international students: Required—TOEFL (minimum score 577 paper-based; 230 computer-based; 90 iBT); Recommended—IELTS (minimum score 7.5). *Application deadline:* Applications are processed on a rolling basis. Application fee: $40. Electronic applications accepted. *Expenses:* Tuition: Part-time $504 per credit hour. Required fees: $40 per term. *Financial support:* In 2010–11, 74 students received support. Career-related internships or fieldwork, scholarships/grants, unspecified assistantships, and grants available. Financial award applicants required to submit FAFSA. *Faculty research:* Management innovation, social marketing, value relevance of earnings and book value across industries, managerial finance, entrepreneurship. *Unit head:* Dennis Nostrand, Vice President, Enrollment/Admissions, 813-257-1808, E-mail: dnostrand@ut.edu. *Application contact:* Charlene Tobie, Associate Director of Admissions, 813-257-3566, E-mail: ctobie@ut.edu.

The University of Texas at Dallas, School of Management, Program in Accounting, Richardson, TX 75080. Offers audit and professional (MS);

financial analysis (MS); information management (MS); international audit (MS); international services (MS); managerial (MS); taxation (MS). *Accreditation:* AACSB. *Faculty:* 17 full-time (4 women), 7 part-time/adjunct (2 women). *Students:* 412 full-time (270 women), 293 part-time (149 women); includes 164 minority (22 Black or African American, non-Hispanic/Latino; 1 American Indian or Alaska Native, non-Hispanic/Latino; 102 Asian, non-Hispanic/Latino; 37 Hispanic/Latino; 2 Two or more races, non-Hispanic/Latino), 283 international. Average age 28. 570 applicants, 68% accepted, 259 enrolled. In 2010, 273 master's awarded. *Entrance requirements:* For master's, GMAT, minimum GPA of 3.0 in upper-level course work in field. Additional exam requirements/recommendations for international students: Required—TOEFL (minimum score 550 paper-based; 215 computer-based). *Application deadline:* For fall admission, 7/15 for domestic students, 5/1 priority date for international students; for spring admission, 11/15 for domestic students, 9/1 priority date for international students. Applications are processed on a rolling basis. Application fee: $50 ($100 for international students). Electronic applications accepted. *Expenses:* Tuition, state resident: full-time $10,248; part-time $569 per credit hour. Tuition, nonresident: full-time $18,544; part-time $1030 per credit hour. Tuition and fees vary according to course load. *Financial support:* In 2010–11, 260 students received support, including 1 research assistantship with partial tuition reimbursement available (averaging $10,050 per year), 10 teaching assistantships with partial tuition reimbursements available (averaging $10,050 per year); career-related internships or fieldwork, Federal Work-Study, institutionally sponsored loans, scholarships/grants, and unspecified assistantships also available. Support available to part-time students. Financial award application deadline: 4/30; financial award applicants required to submit FAFSA. *Faculty research:* Privatization and accounting/auditing, corporate performance and executive compensation, risk management, information technology in accounting. *Unit head:* Amy Troutman, Assistant Director, 972-883-6719, Fax: 972-883-6823, E-mail: amybass@utdallas.edu. *Application contact:* James Parker, Assistant Director of Graduate Recruitment, 972-883-5842, E-mail: jparker@utdallas.edu.

The University of Texas at Dallas, School of Management, Program in Business Administration, Richardson, TX 75080. Offers cohort (MBA); executive business administration (EMBA); global leadership (EMBA); global online (MBA); healthcare management (EMBA); professional business administration (MBA); project management (EMBA); MSEE/MBA. *Accreditation:* AACSB. Part-time and evening/weekend programs available. Postbaccalaureate distance learning degree programs offered (no on-campus study). *Faculty:* 78 full-time (14 women), 28 part-time/adjunct (6 women). *Students:* 426 full-time (138 women), 704 part-time (216 women); includes 333 minority (39 Black or African American, non-Hispanic/Latino; 5 American Indian or Alaska Native, non-Hispanic/Latino; 199 Asian, non-Hispanic/Latino; 84 Hispanic/Latino; 6 Two or more races, non-Hispanic/Latino), 200 international. Average age 32. 766 applicants, 51% accepted, 282 enrolled. In 2010, 503 master's awarded. *Degree requirements:* For master's, thesis optional. *Entrance requirements:* For master's, GMAT, 10 years of business experience (EMBA), minimum GPA of 3.0. Additional exam requirements/recommendations for international students: Required—TOEFL (minimum score 550 paper-based; 215 computer-based). *Application deadline:* For fall admission, 7/15 for domestic students, 5/1 priority date for international students; for spring admission, 11/15 for domestic students, 9/1 priority date for international students. Applications are processed on a rolling basis. Application fee: $50 ($100 for international students). Electronic applications accepted. *Expenses:* Contact institution. *Financial support:* In 2010–11, 265 students received support, including 2 research assistantships with partial tuition reimbursements available (averaging $11,367 per year), 39 teaching assistantships with partial tuition reimbursements available (averaging $11,528 per year); career-related internships or fieldwork, Federal Work-Study, institutionally sponsored loans, scholarships/grants, and unspecified assistantships also available. Support available to part-time students. Financial award application deadline: 4/30; financial award applicants required to submit FAFSA. *Faculty research:* Production scheduling, trade and finance, organizational decision making, life/work planning. *Unit head:* Lisa Shatz, Director, 972-883-6191, E-mail: mba@utdallas.edu. *Application contact:* James Parker, Assistant Director, 972-883-5842, E-mail: jparker@utdallas.edu.

The University of Texas at Dallas, School of Management, Program in International Management, Richardson, TX 75080. Offers MS, PhD. Part-time and evening/weekend programs available. *Faculty:* 13 full-time (3 women), 7 part-time/adjunct (2 women). *Students:* 25 full-time (11 women), 12 part-time (5 women); includes 7 minority (all Asian, non-Hispanic/Latino), 16 international. Average age 31. 95 applicants, 19% accepted, 13 enrolled. In 2010, 11 master's, 1 doctorate awarded. *Degree requirements:* For doctorate, thesis/dissertation. *Entrance requirements:* For master's and doctorate, GMAT. Additional exam requirements/recommendations for international students: Required—TOEFL (minimum score 550 paper-based; 215 computer-based). *Application deadline:* For fall admission, 7/15 for domestic students, 5/1 priority date for international students; for spring admission, 11/15 for domestic students, 9/1 priority date for international students. Applications are processed on a rolling basis. Application fee: $50 ($100 for international students). Electronic applications accepted. *Expenses:* Tuition, state resident: full-time $10,248; part-time $569 per credit hour. Tuition, nonresident: full-time $18,544; part-time $1030 per credit hour. Tuition and fees vary according to course load. *Financial support:* In 2010–11, 21 students received support, including 12 teaching assistantships with partial tuition reimbursements available (averaging $15,300 per year); research assistantships with partial tuition reimbursements available, Federal Work-Study, institutionally sponsored loans, scholarships/grants, and unspecified assistantships also available. Support available to part-time students. Financial award application deadline: 4/30; financial award applicants required to submit FAFSA. *Faculty research:* International accounting, international trade and finance, economic development, international economics. *Unit head:* Dr. Mike W. Peng, PhD Program Director, 972-883-2714, Fax: 972-883-5977, E-mail: mikepeng@utdallas.edu. *Application contact:* Dr. Habte Woldu, Master's Program Director, 972-883-6357, Fax: 972-883-5977, E-mail: wolduh@utdallas.edu.

The University of Texas at Dallas, School of Management, Program in Management and Administrative Sciences, Richardson, TX 75080. Offers electronic commerce (MS); finance (MS); healthcare administration (MS); information systems (MS); innovation and entrepreneurship (MS); international management (MS); leadership in organizations (MS); marketing (MS); operations (MS); organizations (MS); real estate (MS); strategy (MS). *Accreditation:* AACSB. Part-time and evening/weekend programs available. *Faculty:* 18 full-time (3 women), 8 part-time/adjunct (0 women). *Students:* 57 full-time (32 women), 107 part-time (49 women); includes 53 minority (14 Black or African American, non-Hispanic/Latino; 30 Asian, non-Hispanic/Latino; 8 Hispanic/Latino; 1 Two or more races, non-Hispanic/Latino), 25 international. Average age 32. 161 applicants, 67% accepted, 51 enrolled. In 2010, 27 master's awarded. *Degree requirements:* For master's, thesis optional. *Entrance requirements:* For master's, GMAT. Additional exam requirements/recommendations for international students: Required—TOEFL (minimum score 550 paper-based; 215 computer-based). *Application deadline:* For fall admission, 7/15 for domestic students, 5/1 priority date for international students; for spring admission, 11/15 for domestic students, 9/1 priority date for international students. Applications are processed on a rolling basis. Application fee: $50 ($100 for international students). Electronic applications accepted. *Expenses:* Tuition, state resident: full-time $10,248; part-time $569 per credit hour. Tuition, nonresident: full-time $18,544; part-time $1030 per credit hour. Tuition and fees vary according to course load. *Financial support:* In 2010–11, 26 students received support, including 38 teaching assistantships with partial tuition reimbursements available (averaging $11,528 per year); research assistantships with partial tuition reimbursements available, career-related internships or fieldwork, Federal Work-Study, institutionally sponsored loans, scholarships/grants, and unspecified assistantships also available. Support available to part-time students. Financial award application deadline: 4/30; financial award applicants required to submit FAFSA. *Faculty research:* Integrated and detailed knowledge of functional areas of management, analytical tools for effective appraisal and decision making. *Unit head:* Dr. Doug Eckel, Assistant Dean, 972-883-5923, E-mail: doug.eckel@utdallas.edu. *Application contact:* James Parker, Assistant Director, 972-883-5842, E-mail: jparker@utdallas.edu.

The University of Texas at El Paso, Graduate School, College of Business Administration, Programs in Business Administration, El Paso, TX 79968-0001. Offers business administration (MBA, Certificate); international business (PhD). *Accreditation:* AACSB. Part-time and evening/weekend programs available. Postbaccalaureate distance learning degree programs offered (no on-campus study). *Students:* 277 (111 women); includes 8 Black or African American, non-Hispanic/Latino; 1 American Indian or Alaska Native, non-Hispanic/Latino; 4 Asian, non-Hispanic/Latino; 177 Hispanic/Latino, 23 international. Average age 34. In 2010, 126 master's awarded. *Entrance requirements:* For master's, GMAT, minimum GPA of 2.7. Additional exam requirements/recommendations for international students: Required—TOEFL. *Application deadline:* For fall admission, 7/1 priority date for domestic students, 3/1 for international students; for spring admission, 11/1 priority date for domestic students, 9/1 for international students. Applications are processed on a rolling basis. Application fee: $15 ($65 for international students). Electronic applications accepted. *Financial support:* In 2010–11, research assistantships with partial tuition reimbursements (averaging $18,750 per year), teaching assistantships with partial tuition reimbursements (averaging $15,000 per year) were awarded; Federal Work-Study, institutionally sponsored loans, and tuition waivers (partial) also available. Financial award application deadline: 3/15; financial award applicants required to submit FAFSA. *Unit head:* Laura M. Uribarri, Director, 915-747-5379, Fax: 915-747-5147, E-mail: mba@utep.edu. *Application contact:* Dr. Charles H. Ambler, Dean of the Graduate School, 915-747-5491 Ext. 7886, Fax: 915-747-5788, E-mail: cambler@utep.edu.

See Display on this page and Close-Up on page 397.

The University of Texas at San Antonio, College of Business, General Business Program, San Antonio, TX 78249-0617. Offers accounting (PhD); business (MBA); finance (PhD); information systems (MBA); information technology (PhD); international business (MBA); management accounting (MBA); management and organization studies (PhD); management of technology (MBA); marketing (PhD); marketing management (MBA); taxation (MBA). Part-time and evening/weekend programs available. *Students:* 159 full-time (59 women), 124 part-time (43 women); includes 82 minority (9 Black or African American, non-Hispanic/Latino; 2 American Indian or

Alaska Native, non-Hispanic/Latino; 17 Asian, non-Hispanic/Latino; 50 Hispanic/Latino; 1 Native Hawaiian or other Pacific Islander, non-Hispanic/Latino; 3 Two or more races, non-Hispanic/Latino), 39 international. Average age 32. 330 applicants, 46% accepted, 105 enrolled. In 2010, 85 master's, 9 doctorates awarded. *Degree requirements:* For master's, comprehensive exam (for some programs), thesis (for some programs). *Entrance requirements:* For master's, GMAT. Additional exam requirements/recommendations for international students: Required—TOEFL (minimum score 500 paper-based; 173 computer-based; 61 iBT), IELTS (minimum score 5). *Application deadline:* For fall admission, 7/1 for domestic students, 4/1 for international students; for spring admission, 11/1 for domestic students, 9/1 for international students. Application fee: $45 ($80 for international students). *Expenses:* Tuition, state resident: full-time $4172; part-time $231.75 per credit hour. Tuition, nonresident: full-time $15,332; part-time $851.75 per credit hour. *Financial support:* In 2010–11, 282 research assistantships (averaging $13,930 per year), 74 teaching assistantships (averaging $9,284 per year) were awarded; scholarships/grants, tuition waivers, and unspecified assistantships also available. Support available to part-time students. *Unit head:* Dr. Lynda Y. de la Vinna, Dean, 210-458-4317, Fax: 210-458-4308, E-mail: lynda.delavina@utsa.edu. *Application contact:* Veronica Ramirez, Assistant Dean of the Graduate School, 210-458-4330, Fax: 210-458-4332, E-mail: graduatestudies@utsa.edu.

University of the Incarnate Word, School of Graduate Studies and Research, H-E-B School of Business and Administration, Programs in Administration, San Antonio, TX 78209-6397. Offers adult education (MAA); applied administration (MAA); communication arts (MAA); healthcare administration (MAA); instructional technology (MAA); international business (Certificate); nutrition (MAA); organizational development (MAA, Certificate); project management (Certificate); sports management (MAA). Part-time and evening/weekend programs available. Postbaccalaureate distance learning degree programs offered (no on-campus study). *Students:* 30 full-time (20 women), 64 part-time (37 women); includes 10 Black or African American, non-Hispanic/Latino; 1 Asian, non-Hispanic/Latino; 48 Hispanic/Latino, 8 international. Average age 35. In 2010, 68 master's awarded. *Degree requirements:* For master's, capstone. *Entrance requirements:* For master's, GRE, GMAT, undergraduate degree, minimum GPA of 2.5. Additional exam requirements/recommendations for international students: Required—TOEFL (minimum score 560 paper-based; 220 computer-based; 83 iBT). *Application deadline:* Applications are processed on a rolling basis. Application fee: $20. Electronic applications accepted. *Expenses:* Tuition: Part-time $725 per contact hour. Required fees: $890 per semester. *Financial support:* Federal Work-Study and scholarships/grants available. Financial award applicants required to submit FAFSA. *Unit head:* Dr. Daniel Dominguez, MAA Programs Director, 210-829-3180, Fax: 210-805-3564, E-mail: domingue@uiwtx.edu. *Application contact:* Andrea Cyterski-Acosta, Dean of Enrollment, 210-829-6005, Fax: 210-829-3921, E-mail: admis@uiwtx.edu.

University of the Incarnate Word, School of Graduate Studies and Research, H-E-B School of Business and Administration, Programs in Business Administration, San Antonio, TX 78209-6397. Offers general business (MBA); international business (MBA); international business strategy (MBA); sports management (MBA). *Accreditation:* ACBSP. Part-time and evening/weekend programs available. Postbaccalaureate distance learning degree programs offered. *Students:* 58 full-time (42 women), 32 part-time (20 women). Average age 32. In 2010, 111 master's awarded. *Degree requirements:* For master's, capstone. *Entrance requirements:* For master's, GMAT (minimum score 450), undergraduate degree with minimum overall GPA of 2.5. Additional exam requirements/recommendations for international students: Required—TOEFL (minimum score 560 paper-based; 220 computer-based; 83 iBT). *Application deadline:* Applications are processed on a rolling basis. Application fee: $20. Electronic applications accepted. *Expenses:* Tuition: Part-time $725 per contact hour. Required fees: $890 per semester. *Financial support:* Federal Work-Study and scholarships/grants available. Financial award applicants required to submit FAFSA. Total annual research expenditures: $177,763. *Unit head:* Dr. Jeannie Scott, MBA Director, 210-283-5002, Fax: 210-805-3564, E-mail: scott@uiwtx.edu. *Application contact:* Andrea Cyterski-Acosta, Dean of Enrollment, 210-829-6005, Fax: 210-829-3921, E-mail: admis@uiwtx.edu.

University of Tulsa, Graduate School, Collins College of Business, Master of Business Administration Program, Tulsa, OK 74104-3189. Offers accounting (MBA); business administration (MBA); energy management (MBA); finance (MBA); international business (MBA); management information systems (MBA); taxation (MBA); JD/MBA; MBA/MSCS; MBA/MSF. *Accreditation:* AACSB. Part-time and evening/weekend programs available. *Faculty:* 32 full-time (6 women). *Students:* 39 full-time (14 women), 40 part-time (16 women); includes 7 minority (1 Black or African American, non-Hispanic/Latino; 2 Asian, non-Hispanic/Latino; 4 Hispanic/Latino), 9 international. Average age 26. 73 applicants, 55% accepted, 18 enrolled. In 2010, 55 master's awarded. *Entrance requirements:* For master's, GMAT. Additional exam requirements/recommendations for international students: Required—TOEFL (minimum score 575 paper-based; 232 computer-based; 90 iBT), IELTS (minimum score 6.5). *Application deadline:* Applications are processed on a rolling basis. Application fee: $40. Electronic applications accepted. *Expenses:* Tuition: Full-time $16,902; part-time $939 per credit hour. Required fees: $1020; $4

per credit hour. Tuition and fees vary according to course load. *Financial support:* In 2010–11, 56 students received support, including 23 fellowships (averaging $4,872 per year), 4 research assistantships (averaging $9,323 per year), 29 teaching assistantships (averaging $10,642 per year); career-related internships or fieldwork, institutionally sponsored loans, scholarships/grants, health care benefits, tuition waivers (full and partial), and unspecified assistantships also available. Support available to part-time students. Financial award application deadline: 2/1; financial award applicants required to submit FAFSA. *Faculty research:* Accounting, energy management, finance, international business, management information systems, taxation. *Unit head:* Dr. Linda Nichols, Associate Dean of the Collins College of Business, 918-631-2242, Fax: 918-631-2142, E-mail: linda-nichols@utulsa.edu. *Application contact:* Dr. Linda Nichols, Associate Dean of the Collins College of Business, 918-631-2242, Fax: 918-631-2142, E-mail: linda-nichols@utulsa.edu.

University of Wisconsin–Milwaukee, Graduate School, College of Letters and Sciences, Interdepartmental Program in Human Resources and Labor Relations, Milwaukee, WI 53201-0413. Offers human resources and labor relations (MHRLR); international human resources and labor relations (Certificate); mediation and negotiation (Certificate). Part-time programs available. *Students:* 17 full-time (13 women), 30 part-time (23 women); includes 5 Black or African American, non-Hispanic/Latino; 1 American Indian or Alaska Native, non-Hispanic/Latino, 5 international. Average age 30. 38 applicants, 58% accepted, 8 enrolled. In 2010, 20 master's awarded. *Entrance requirements:* For master's, GMAT or GRE General Test. Additional exam requirements/recommendations for international students: Required—TOEFL (minimum score 550 paper-based; 79 iBT), IELTS (minimum score 6.5). *Application deadline:* For fall admission, 1/1 priority date for domestic students; for spring admission, 9/1 for domestic students. Applications are processed on a rolling basis. Application fee: $56 ($96 for international students). Electronic applications accepted. *Financial support:* Career-related internships or fieldwork available. Support available to part-time students. Financial award application deadline: 4/15; financial award applicants required to submit FAFSA. *Unit head:* Susan M. Donohue-Davies, Representative, 414-299-4009, Fax: 414-229-5915, E-mail: suedono@uwm.edu. *Application contact:* General Information Contact, 414-229-4982, Fax: 414-229-6967, E-mail: gradschool@uwm.edu.

Valparaiso University, Graduate School, Program in International Commerce and Policy, Valparaiso, IN 46383. Offers MS, JD/MS. Part-time and evening/weekend programs available. *Students:* 47 full-time (19 women), 9 part-time (2 women); includes 5 minority (2 Black or African American, non-Hispanic/Latino; 3 Two or more races, non-Hispanic/Latino), 43 international. Average age 24. In 2010, 49 master's awarded. *Entrance requirements:* For master's, minimum GPA of 3.0. Additional exam requirements/recommendations for international students: Required—TOEFL (minimum score 550 paper-based; 213 computer-based; 80 iBT). *Application deadline:* Applications are processed on a rolling basis. Application fee: $30 ($50 for international students). Electronic applications accepted. *Expenses:* Tuition: Full-time $9540; part-time $530 per credit hour. Required fees: $292; $95 per semester. Tuition and fees vary according to program. *Financial support:* Available to part-time students. Applicants required to submit FAFSA. *Unit head:* Dr. David L. Rowland, Dean, Graduate School and Continuing Education/Associate Provost, 219-464-5313, Fax: 219-464-5381, E-mail: david.rowland@valpo.edu. *Application contact:* Laura Groth, Coordinator of Student Services and Support, 219-464-5313, Fax: 219-464-5381, E-mail: laura.groth@valpo.edu.

Villanova University, Villanova School of Business, MBA—The Fast Track Program, Villanova, PA 19085. Offers finance (MBA); health care management (MBA); international business (MBA); management information systems (MBA); marketing (MBA); real estate (MBA); strategic management (MBA). *Accreditation:* AACSB. Part-time and evening/weekend programs available. *Faculty:* 15 full-time (2 women), 5 part-time/adjunct (0 women). *Students:* 118 part-time (34 women); includes 13 minority (2 Black or African American, non-Hispanic/Latino; 8 Asian, non-Hispanic/Latino; 3 Hispanic/Latino). Average age 30. In 2010, 35 master's awarded. *Degree requirements:* For master's, minimum GPA of 3.0. *Entrance requirements:* For master's, GMAT. Additional exam requirements/recommendations for international students: Required—TOEFL (minimum score 550 paper-based; 213 computer-based; 80 iBT). *Application deadline:* For fall admission, 6/30 for domestic and international students. Application fee: $50. Electronic applications accepted. *Expenses:* Tuition: Part-time $700 per credit. Part-time tuition and fees vary according to degree level and program. *Financial support:* Scholarships/grants available. Support available to part-time students. Financial award application deadline: 6/30; financial award applicants required to submit FAFSA. *Faculty research:* Developing and leveraging technology, ethical business practices, managing for innovation and creativity, the global political economy, strategic marketing management. *Unit head:* Meredith L. Kwiatek, Director of Graduate Recruitment & Marketing, 610-519-7016, Fax: 610-519-6273, E-mail: rachel.garonzik@villanova.edu. *Application contact:* Meredith L. Kwiatek, Assistant Director, 610-519-7016, Fax: 610-519-6273, E-mail: meredith.kwiatek@villanova.edu.

Villanova University, Villanova School of Business, MBA—The Flex Track Program, Villanova, PA 19085. Offers finance (MBA); health care management (MBA); international business (MBA); management information systems (MBA); marketing (MBA); real estate (MBA); strategic management (MBA); JD/MBA. *Accreditation:* AACSB. Part-time and evening/weekend programs available. Postbaccalaureate distance learning degree programs offered (minimal on-campus study). *Faculty:* 31 full-time (5 women), 22 part-time/adjunct (2 women). *Students:* 15 full-time (6 women), 443 part-time (150 women); includes 46 minority (5 Black or African American, non-Hispanic/Latino; 35 Asian, non-Hispanic/Latino; 6 Hispanic/Latino). Average age 30. In 2010, 133 master's awarded. *Degree requirements:* For master's, minimum GPA of 3.0. *Entrance requirements:* For master's, GMAT. Additional exam requirements/recommendations for international students: Required—TOEFL (minimum score 550 paper-based; 213 computer-based; 80 iBT). *Application deadline:* For fall admission, 6/30 for domestic and international students; for winter admission, 11/15 for domestic and international students; for spring admission, 3/30 for domestic students, 3/31 for international students. Applications are processed on a rolling basis. Application fee: $50. Electronic applications accepted. *Expenses:* Tuition: Part-time $700 per credit. Part-time tuition and fees vary according to degree level and program. *Financial support:* In 2010–11, 15 research assistantships with full tuition reimbursements (averaging $13,100 per year) were awarded; scholarships/grants and unspecified assistantships also available. Support available to part-time students. Financial award application deadline: 6/30; financial award applicants required to submit FAFSA. *Faculty research:* Developing and leveraging technology, ethical business practices, managing for innovation and creativity, the global political economy, strategic marketing management. *Unit head:* Meredith L. Kwiatek, Director of Graduate Recruitment and Marketing, 610-519-7016, Fax: 610-519-6273, E-mail: meredith.kwiatek@villanova.edu. *Application contact:* Meredith L. Kwiatek, Assistant Director, 610-519-7016, Fax: 610-519-6273, E-mail: meredith.kwiatek@villanova.edu.

Wagner College, Division of Graduate Studies, Department of Business Administration, Program in International Business, Staten Island, NY 10301-4495. Offers MBA. Part-time and evening/weekend programs available. *Faculty:* 1 full-time (0 women), 1 part-time/adjunct (0 women). *Students:* 5 full-time (3 women); includes 4 minority (1 Asian, non-Hispanic/Latino; 3 Hispanic/Latino). Average age 30. 2 applicants, 100% accepted, 1 enrolled. In 2010, 4 master's awarded. *Degree requirements:* For master's, thesis optional. *Entrance requirements:* For master's, GMAT, minimum GPA of 2.6. Additional exam requirements/recommendations for international students: Required—TOEFL (minimum score 550 paper-based; 217 computer-based; 79 iBT). *Application deadline:* For fall admission, 5/1 priority date for domestic students, 3/1 priority date for international students; for spring admission, 11/1 priority date for domestic students, 10/1 priority date for international students. Applications are processed on a rolling basis. Application fee: $50 ($80 for international students). *Expenses:* Tuition: Full-time $15,570; part-time $865 per credit. *Financial support:* Career-related internships or fieldwork, unspecified assistantships, and alumni fellowship grant available. Financial award applicants required to submit FAFSA. *Unit head:* Dr. Donald Crooks, Director, 718-390-3429, Fax: 718-420-4274, E-mail: dcrooks@wagner.edu. *Application contact:* Patricia Clancy, Assistant Coordinator of Graduate Studies, 718-420-4464, Fax: 718-390-3105, E-mail: patricia.clancy@wagner.edu.

Walden University, Graduate Programs, School of Management, Minneapolis, MN 55401. Offers accounting (MS), including cpa emphasis, professional track, self-designed; accounting and management (MS), including self-designed, strategic management; applied management and decision sciences (PhD), including accounting, engineering management, finance, general applied management and decision sciences, information systems management, knowledge management, leadership and organizational change, learning management, operations research, self-designed program in applied management and design sciences; business information management (MISM); enterprise information security (MISM); entrepreneurship (MBA, DBA); finance (MBA, DBA); global management (MS); global supply chain management (DBA); health informatics (MISM); healthcare management (MBA, MS); healthcare system improvement (MBA); human resource management (MBA, MS), including functional human resource management (MS), human resource management (MS), integrating functional and strategic human resource management (MS), organizational strategy (MS); information systems (MS); information systems management (DBA); information technology (MS), including information security, software engineering; international business (MBA, DBA); IT strategy and governance (MISM); leadership (MBA, MS, DBA), including entrepreneurship (MS), general management (MS), human resources leadership (MS), innovation and technology (MS), leader development (MS), leading sustainability (MS), project management (MS), self-designed (MS), managers as leaders (MS); managing global software and service supply chains (MISM); marketing (MBA, DBA); project management (MBA, MS); research strategies (MS); risk management (MBA); self-designed (MBA, DBA); social impact management (DBA); strategy and operations (MS); sustainable futures (MBA); sustainable management (MS); technology (MBA); technology entrepreneurship (DBA); technology management (MS). Part-time and evening/weekend programs available. Postbaccalaureate distance learning degree programs offered (minimal on-campus study). *Faculty:* 22 full-time (8 women), 291 part-time/adjunct (100 women). *Students:* 3,705 full-time (1,956 women), 976 part-time (549 women); includes 2,432 minority (2,021 Black or African American, non-Hispanic/Latino; 32 American Indian or Alaska Native, non-Hispanic/Latino; 137 Asian, non-Hispanic/Latino; 193 Hispanic/Latino; 5 Native Hawaiian or other Pacific Islander, non-Hispanic/Latino; 44 Two or more races, non-Hispanic/Latino), 302 international. Average age 40. In 2010, 658 master's, 86 doctorates awarded. *Degree requirements:* For doctorate, thesis/dissertation (for some programs), residency. *Entrance requirements:* For master's, bachelor's degree or equivalent in related field; minimum GPA of 2.5; official transcripts; goal statement; access to computer and Internet; for doctorate, master's degree or equivalent in related field; minimum GPA of 3.0; 3 years of related professional/academic experience (preferred). Additional exam requirements/recommendations for international students: Required—TOEFL (minimum score 550 paper-based; 213 computer-based), IELTS (minimum score 6.5), Michigan English Language Assessment Battery (minimum score 82). *Application deadline:* Applications are processed on a rolling basis. Application fee: $50. Electronic applications accepted. *Expenses:* Tuition: Full-time $10,274; part-time $445 per credit. Tuition and fees vary according to course load, degree level and program. *Financial support:* Fellowships, Federal Work-Study, scholarships/grants, unspecified assistantships, and family tuition reduction, active duty/veteran tuition reduction, group tuition reduction, interest-free payment plans available. Support available to part-time students. Financial award applicants required to submit FAFSA. *Unit head:* Dr. William Schulz, Associate Dean, 800-925-3368. *Application contact:* Jennifer Hall, Vice President of Enrollment Management, 866-4-WALDEN, E-mail: info@waldenu.edu.

Washington State University, Graduate School, College of Agricultural, Human, and Natural Resource Sciences, School of Economic Sciences, Department of Economics, Pullman, WA 99164. Offers applied economics (MA); economics (MA, PhD); international business economics (Certificate). *Faculty:* 26. *Students:* 48 full-time (12 women), 2 part-time (1 woman); includes 3 minority (1 American Indian or Alaska Native, non-Hispanic/Latino; 1 Asian, non-Hispanic/Latino; 1 Hispanic/Latino), 26 international. Average age 30. 97 applicants, 21% accepted, 15 enrolled. In 2010, 8 doctorates awarded. *Degree requirements:* For master's, comprehensive exam (for some programs), thesis (for some programs), oral exam; for doctorate, comprehensive exam, thesis/dissertation, oral exam, written exam, field exams. *Entrance requirements:* For master's, GRE General Test, statement of purpose, three letters of reference, copies of all transcripts; for doctorate, GRE General Test or GMAT, statement of purpose, three letters of reference, copies of all transcripts. Additional exam requirements/recommendations for international students: Required—TOEFL, IELTS. *Application deadline:* For fall admission, 1/10 priority date for domestic students, 1/10 for international students. Applications are processed on a rolling basis. Application fee: $50. *Expenses:* Tuition, state resident: full-time $8552; part-time $443 per credit. Tuition, nonresident: full-time $21,650; part-time $1083 per credit. Required fees: $846. *Financial support:* In 2010–11, 16 research assistantships (averaging $18,204 per year), 7 teaching assistantships (averaging $18,204 per year) were awarded; career-related internships or fieldwork, Federal Work-Study, institutionally sponsored loans, tuition waivers (partial), and teaching associateships also available. Financial award application deadline: 4/1; financial award applicants required to submit FAFSA. *Faculty research:* Economic theory and quantitative methods, applied microeconomics. Total annual research expenditures: $1 million. *Unit head:* Dr. Ron C. Mittelhammer, Director, 509-335-1706, Fax: 509-335-1173, E-mail: mittelha@wsu.edu. *Application contact:* Graduate School Admissions, 800-GRADWSU, Fax: 509-335-1949, E-mail: gradsch@wsu.edu.

Whitworth University, School of Global Commerce and Management, Spokane, WA 99251-0001. Offers international management (MBA, MIM). Part-time and evening/weekend programs available. *Faculty:* 5 full-time (1 woman), 11 part-time/adjunct (2 women). *Students:* 7 full-time (1 woman), 38 part-time (26 women), 6 international. Average age 31. 27 applicants, 81% accepted, 21 enrolled. In 2010, 18 master's awarded. *Degree requirements:* For master's, one foreign language, foreign language (MBA in international management, MIM). *Entrance requirements:* For master's, GMAT or GRE, minimum GPA of 3.0; two letters of recommendation; resume; completion of prerequisite courses in micro-economics, macro-economics, financial accounting, finance, and marketing. Additional exam requirements/recommendations for international students: Required—TOEFL (minimum score 213 computer-based; 88 iBT), TWE. *Application deadline:* For fall admission, 8/1 priority date for domestic and international students; for spring admission, 1/8 priority date for domestic students. Applications are processed on a rolling basis. Application fee: $35. Electronic applications accepted. Tuition and fees vary according to course load and program. *Financial support:* In 2010–11, 9 students received support; fellowships with tuition reimbursements available, career-related internships or fieldwork, Federal Work-Study, institutionally sponsored loans, and scholarships/grants available. Support available to part-time students. Financial award application deadline: 3/1; financial award applicants required to submit FAFSA. *Faculty research:* International business (European, Central America and Asian topics), entrepreneurship and business plan development. *Unit head:* John Hengesh, Director, Graduate Studies in Business, 509-777-4455, Fax: 509-777-3723, E-mail: jhengesh@whitworth.edu. *Application contact:* Bonnie Wakefield, Assistant Director, Graduate Studies in Business, 509-777-4606, Fax: 509-777-3723, E-mail: bwakefield@whitworth.edu.

Wilkes University, College of Graduate and Professional Studies, Jay S. Sidhu School of Business and Leadership, Wilkes-Barre, PA 18766-0002. Offers accounting (MBA); entrepreneurship (MBA); finance (MBA); health care administration (MBA); human resource management (MBA); international business (MBA); marketing (MBA); operations management (MBA); organizational leadership and development (MBA). *Accreditation:* ACBSP. Part-time and evening/weekend programs available. *Students:* 39 full-time (16 women), 146 part-time (71 women); includes 5 Black or African American, non-Hispanic/Latino; 2 Asian, non-Hispanic/Latino; 1 Hispanic/Latino; 1 Two or more races, non-Hispanic/Latino, 16 international. Average age 30. In 2010, 85 master's awarded. *Entrance requirements:* For master's, GMAT. Additional exam requirements/recommendations for international students: Required—TOEFL (minimum score 550 paper-based; 213 computer-based; 79 iBT). *Application deadline:* Applications are processed on a rolling basis. Application fee: $45 ($65 for international students). Electronic applications accepted. *Expenses:* Contact institution. *Financial support:* Federal Work-Study and unspecified assistantships available. Financial award application deadline: 3/1; financial award applicants required to submit FAFSA. *Unit head:* Dr. Paul Browne, Dean, 570-408-4701, Fax: 570-408-7846, E-mail: paul.browne@wilkes.edu. *Application contact:* Kathleen Houlihan, Director of Graduate Studies, 570-408-3235, Fax: 570-408-7846, E-mail: kathleen.houlihan@wilkes.edu.

Xavier University, Williams College of Business, Master of Business Administration Program, Cincinnati, OH 45207-3221. Offers business administration (Exec MBA, MBA); business intelligence (MBA); finance (MBA); international business (MBA); management information systems (MBA); marketing (MBA); MBA/MHSA; MSN/MBA. *Accreditation:* AACSB. Part-time and evening/weekend programs available. *Faculty:* 37 full-time (13 women), 9 part-time/adjunct (2 women). *Students:* 200 full-time (60 women), 735 part-time (239 women); includes 128 minority (48 Black or African American, non-Hispanic/Latino; 3 American Indian or Alaska Native, non-Hispanic/Latino; 54 Asian, non-Hispanic/Latino; 22 Hispanic/Latino; 1 Native Hawaiian or other Pacific Islander, non-Hispanic/Latino), 32 international. Average age 30. 223 applicants, 85% accepted, 139 enrolled. In 2010, 323 master's awarded. *Degree requirements:* For master's, capstone course. *Entrance requirements:* For master's, GMAT. Additional exam requirements/ recommendations for international students: Required—TOEFL (minimum score 550 paper-based; 213 computer-based; 80 iBT). *Application deadline:* For fall admission, 8/1 priority date for domestic students, 5/1 for international students; for spring admission, 12/1 priority date for domestic students, 9/1 for international students. Applications are processed on a rolling basis. Application fee: $35. Electronic applications accepted. *Expenses:* Contact institution. *Financial support:* In 2010–11, 176 students received support. Scholarships/grants, tuition waivers (partial), and unspecified assistantships available. Financial award application deadline: 3/1; financial award applicants required to submit FAFSA. *Unit head:* Dr. Hema Krishnan, Associate Dean, 513-745-3206, Fax: 513-745-3455, E-mail: krishnan@xavier.edu. *Application contact:* Anna Marie Whelan, Assistant Director, MBA Programs, 513-745-3525, Fax: 513-745-2929, E-mail: whelana@xavier.edu.

The University of Texas at El Paso

College of Business Administration
Ph.D. in International Business Program

Programs of Study

The College of Business Administration, through the departments of Economics and Finance, Information and Decision Sciences, and Marketing and Management, offers a Ph.D. degree in international business. This is one of about twenty-five such programs worldwide and is designed to prepare a new generation of faculty from diverse backgrounds to meet critical challenges projected in business education. The program is also accredited by AACSB International–The Association to Advance Collegiate Schools of Business.

The objective of the Ph.D. program is to provide opportunities to develop student competencies in research and teaching and to prepare graduates for academic careers in various business disciplines. The course work is divided between advanced research methods, a substantive international business core, and specialization courses. The areas of concentration are accounting, finance, information systems, management, and marketing.

The first two years of the program are dedicated to course work that is designed to develop the conceptual and empirical skills necessary to undertake high-quality research. Students take a minimum of four quantitative and four research methods courses, four international business substantive core courses, and four research specialization seminars. Candidacy status is achieved after successful completion of all course work and two comprehensive exams. Once admitted into candidacy, students independently conduct research by completing and defending an original dissertation. The average duration of the program is four years.

Graduates of the program are trained to plan and execute high quality research publishable in major scholarly journals. Results of their research are expected to advance both the theory and practice of international business. The Ph.D. students develop research competencies by completing course requirements and working with faculty advisors on research projects.

The College's goal is to prepare students to pursue an academic career in teaching and research. Students

selecting an academic career can choose between teaching schools (four-year colleges), research universities, or schools seeking a balance between teaching and research.

Research Facilities

Equipment and facilities are made available to graduate students from the time they start the program. Ph.D. students are provided with an office and necessary office equipment such as computers and printers. Students are provided direct access to various online academic research oriented services such as WRDS (Wharton Research Data Services), which provide instant access to financial, economic, and marketing data. The University of Texas at El Paso (UTEP) library provides Ph.D. student access to a host of online databases and journals to successfully conduct their academic research. Students are also provided with the latest statistical software tools such as SPSS, SAS, and Stata.

Financial Aid

Subject to availability of funds and academic performance, students are provided financial support in the form of teaching or research assistantships. Access to funding is very competitive and is provided to those students who demonstrate the highest probability of success in an academic setting. Accompanying the assistantship, UTEP will pay the student's health insurance after a ninety-day waiting period and provide in-state tuition rates (waiver of out-of-state tuition rates). Additional benefits are available. No specific loans are provided to Ph.D. students by the College, however, numerous financial assistance programs are available to Ph.D. students from various other sources.

Federal aid in the form of FAFSA loans are provided to eligible students. Financial aid in the form of an annual stipend of approximately $18,000 is provided to doctoral candidates as well as an office and necessary office equipment such as computers and printers. For more information about benefits, students should contact Human Resources at 915-747-5202 or visit the Web site at www.utep.edu/hresourc.

Ph.D. students attend classes in the state-of-the-art building located within the UTEP campus.

Cost of Study

The cost for a four-year Ph.D. program was approximately $15,199 for 2011–12. Stipends and merit-based benefits are available.

Living and Housing Costs

Students who wish to stay on campus can reside at the Miner Village housing complex. All rooms in Miner Village offer high-speed Internet, a basic cable package, electricity, gas, water, and refrigerated air. Room rents at Miner Village vary from $380 per person to approximately $550 per person. There are also many apartments located within walking distance of UTEP.

Student Group

Currently, there are 20 women and 26 men in the Ph.D. program. The group includes 20 U.S. nationals and 26 international students. The majority of students in the program plan to undertake a career in academics and research after graduation. All students in the program are full-time candidates.

Student Outcomes

Recent graduates have pursued academic and research careers at various universities such as Maine, John Carroll, Houston, St. John's, Southern Illinois Carbondale, American University of Sharjah, and Michigan–Flint.

Location

El Paso is located at the westernmost tip of Texas where Texas, New Mexico, and Mexico intersect. El Paso is the 5th-largest city in Texas and 23rd-largest city in the United States. It is also the second-safest city of its size (500,000+) in the nation and the largest binational community in the Western hemisphere. Bordering Ciudad Juárez, México, El Paso provides an ideal location for students of international business to study a wide range of pertinent issues and to experience a diverse social and cultural environment not available elsewhere.

The Greater El Paso region is the center for economic and cultural activity in West Texas, southern New Mexico, and northern Mexico. The region is also home to Fort Bliss (the second-largest military base in the United States), White Sands Missile Range, and Holloman Air Force Base. There is a great deal of cultural diversity within the area and ample recreational opportunities within and beyond El Paso.

The University and The College

The University of Texas at El Paso is the second-oldest academic component of the University of Texas system. It was founded by the Texas legislature in 1914 as the State School of Mines and Metallurgy, a name that reflected the scope of education offered at that time. UTEP's present 366-acre site features distinctive Bhutanese-style architecture. The campus's buildings resemble exotic oriental monasteries that are found in the small kingdom of Bhutan, which is nestled in the Himalayas. With its pivotal setting on the U.S.–Mexico border, UTEP is a nationally recognized leader in meeting the challenges of providing higher education to the country's increasing minority populations.

The University is committed to becoming the first national research university with a student demographic representative of the twenty-first century. The University strives for both excellence and affordability and Ph.D. programs play a pivotal role in the achievement of this objective. The University currently has 500 doctoral students in eighteen doctoral programs, and this number is steadily growing each year. UTEP is the only doctoral research intensive university with a predominantly Mexican-American student body.

The College of Business Administration is accredited by the Association to Advance Collegiate Schools of Business International—the only school in the El Paso metropolitan area to be awarded this distinction.

Applying

To be considered for admission to the program, applicants must have a bachelor's degree from an accredited university. A master's degree in business or a related field is preferred, but not required. A background in business, finance, accounting, economics, or statistics is helpful, but not required for admission into the program. A master's degree is not required. However, students entering the program without a master's degree and/or a business background may be required to take up to eight "leveling" graduate courses in addition to the Ph.D. course work. Students without a working knowledge of elementary calculus and statistics may also be required to take extra course work. Moreover students should demonstrate high levels of research interest in their field of specialization.

All applications must be submitted to the Graduate School. Deadline for submission of applications for a particular year generally ends by January of that year.

Correspondence and Information

Dr. Fernanda Wagstaff
Director, Ph.D. Program
The University of Texas at El Paso
Business, Room 221
500 West University Avenue
El Paso, Texas 79968-0507
United States
Phone: 915-747-5378
E-mail: fwagstaff@utep.edu
Web site: http://business.utep.edu/degrees/PHD/

Cesar Ayala
Graduate Academic Advisor
The University of Texas at El Paso
Business, Room 102
500 West University Avenue
El Paso, Texas 79968-0507
United States
Phone: 915-747-7726
E-mail: cayala3@utep.edu
Web site: http://www.utep.edu/

The Faculty

Faculty members in the UTEP Ph.D. in International Business Program hold doctoral degrees from top institutions worldwide. They bring a global perspective to the classroom and conduct research important to the global marketplace. Faculty members have recently been cited for high research productivity in the area of international business, leading their disciplines in creating relevant knowledge.

For more information about the faculty members in the UTEP Ph.D. in International Business Program, visit: http://business.utep.edu/Degrees/PHD/phd_faculty.aspx.

OVERVIEW

Information systems and technologies are fueling the transformation of corporations as they strive to meet the challenges of evolving economies and global business needs. As day-to-day business goals are increasingly affected by these systems, qualified professionals with an MBA in information systems are able to provide the high-level technical and business knowledge needed to meet these complex technology and business challenges.

The MBA information systems concentration involves the study of computer-based information systems in organizations, including information technology, knowledge management, information security, and information systems. In preparing for careers in the management, design, and implementation of information systems, students in this program learn how to understand basic concepts of IT and globalization, identify e-business strategies in a global marketplace, evaluate the value of emerging technologies and their competitive advantages, examine organizational competencies and capabilities in running high-tech firms, and identify how new ventures are exploited. The information systems MBA coursework enables students to appreciate the unique relationship between business- and corporate-level technology strategies, navigate the complexities of managing data in a global environment, and address policy and management issues surrounding information systems.

Required courses of study may include:

- Economics for Decision Making
- Financial Statement Analysis
- Marketing and Brand Management
- Problem Analysis and Research Methods
- Strategic Human Resource Management
- Strategic Management and Competitive Globalization

Elective courses may include study in:

- E-commerce: Business Models and Technology
- Data Management Systems
- Data Mining
- Information Technology and Corporate Transformation
- Modeling and Designing IT Systems
- Security and Control of Information Systems
- Telecommunications and the Internet

An MBA with an emphasis in information systems management is designed to prepare graduates for careers in the fields of configuration management, server administration, knowledge management, business systems analysis, and control systems management. With the advanced technical skills and proven business and management principles gained from this program, career opportunities include positions as IT directors, chief technology officers, management information systems directors, vice presidents of information technology, systems consultants, systems analysts, data information specialists, and information technology management consultants.

HELPFUL ORGANIZATIONS/ PUBLICATIONS/BLOGS

The Association for Information Systems (AIS)

http://aisnet.org

The Association for Information Systems (AIS) is the premier global organization for individuals and organizations who lead the research, teaching, practice, and study of information systems (IS) worldwide. Founded in 1994, AIS is an international professional society of 4,000 members from 90 countries and a key player in the advancement of the IS academic community. The AIS mission is to serve society through the advancement of knowledge and the promotion of excellence in the practice and study of information systems.

The specific purposes of AIS are to:

- Create and maintain a professional identity for IS educators, researchers, professionals, and educators.
- Promote communications and interaction among members.
- Provide a focal point for contact and relations with the bodies of government, the private sector, and the education community that influence and/or control the nature of information systems.
- Improve curricula, pedagogy, and other aspects of IS education.
- Create a vision for the future of the IS field and profession.
- Create and implement a modern, technologically sophisticated professional society.
- Establish standards of practice, ethics, and education where appropriate.
- Include professionals worldwide.

Information Resources Management Association (IRMA)

http://www.irma-international.org/

Information Resources Management Association (IRMA) is an international organization dedicated to advancing the research community by bringing together researchers, practitioners, academicians, and policy makers in information technology management. With members spanning more than 50 countries worldwide, IRMA seeks to assist organizations and professionals in enhancing the overall knowledge and understanding of effective information resources management in the early twenty-first century and beyond.

The specific aims of IRMA are to:

- Promote and encourage the association among individuals with an interest in the field of management of information resources.

- Provide resources, assistance, encouragement, and incentives to individuals either engaged in or planning to become engaged in, the field of information resources management in order to enhance professional's knowledge or information resource management issues and trends.
- Promote and publish professional and scholarly journals, periodicals, bulletins, and other forms of publications in the field of information resources management.

These objectives are accomplished through the association's diverse collection of scholarly publications, its membership, and bringing the IRM research community together.

Journal of Global Information Technology Management (JGITM)

http://www.uncg.edu/bae/jgitm/

The *Journal of Global Information Technology Management* (JGITM) is an international journal addressing international issues of IT management. The mission of JGITM is to be the premier journal on global information technology management. JGITM publishes articles and reports related to all aspects of the application of information technology for international business. The journal was founded in 1998 and publishes four issues per year to researchers, practitioners, academicians, and educators. JGTIM is a refereed international journal supported by global IT scholars worldwide.

CAREER ASPIRATIONS: A PROSPECTIVE POSITION

Vice President of Information Technology

Job Description

The Vice President of Information Technology (VP of IT) is responsible for leading a team of 3 direct reports and a span of control of at least 10 employees in managing the overall corporate technology infrastructure, including network and storage infrastructure, telecommunications infrastructure, and corporate systems. This includes managing all networks, desktop applications, and Web sites/software applications for the company. The VP of IT is responsible for creating and managing the corporate IT strategy and providing a vision and roadmap for moving forward. The position also includes management of information and physical security to protect corporate information and system integrity.

This is a key role within the company as the VP of IT will need to provide solid, scalable, and secure technical infrastructure and technology solutions that meet the capacity, security, and functional requirements for the company's current and future corporate needs. The VP of IT reports to an executive board member and will be responsible for providing strategic guidance to executive management and management of the teams providing the day-to-day IT operations.

Responsibilities

- Lead, mentor, and direct information technology department consisting of 10+ IT professionals in the operation and management of IT infrastructure, data network, business applications, Web sites, voice systems, and telecommunication services.
- Set goals and objectives for all technology aspects of the organization that align with and complement corporate objectives.
- Work with the executive team on the priority and approval in the selection, acquisition, development, and installation of major information systems.
- Provide top management in multiple states and locations with technical information and recommendations on information technology and communicate IT efforts, plans, projects, metrics, and strategy throughout the company and up and down the organizational hierarchy.
- Responsible for department budget; continually implement cost-effective strategies for company-wide savings in relation to IT and communications support.
- Negotiate and partner with vendors to minimize cost and maximize position through agreements.
- Oversee the department responsible for the requirements and planning phases of all large facility moves.
- Ensure continuous delivery of IT services through oversight of service-level agreements with end users and monitoring of IT systems' performance.
- Develop, implement, and manage business practices, procedures, policies, metrics, and personnel for all technology aspects of the company.
- Stay abreast of and advise executive staff of innovations in new business practices and technology that may impact clients and the technical operations of the company.
- Maintain security and privacy documentation.
- Lead ad hoc company IT projects as required.

(continued on next page)

CAREER ASPIRATIONS: A PROSPECTIVE POSITION (continued)

Qualifications

- A master's degree (MBA or master's in computer science or information technology) is required plus a minimum 12 years' related experience with a minimum of 5 years' supervisory experience in a multifaceted IT operation including managing corporate computing, Web site and software development, network infrastructure, and help desk services. In lieu of a master's degree, a bachelor's degree in a technical discipline with 15 years' experience managing progressively more complex systems/projects may be substituted.
- Ability to provide strategic guidance to executive management and to promote and oversee strategic IT policy and compliance relationships both internally and externally
- Excellent oral and written communication skills
- Demonstrated leadership and project management skills to drive programs and influence change
- Strong negotiating skills and record of developing partnerships with external vendors/suppliers
- Experience in general staff management skills that include mentoring, coaching, directing, delegating, evaluating, and addressing employee relations to maximize efficiency, productivity, and employee satisfaction
- Proven quality assurance and consistent measurement of IT processes and projects
- Experience in supporting the government contracting industry

Career Advice from a Business Professional

Paul Blankman, Firm Administrator
Stark & Stark Attorneys at Law
MBA in Information Science
Temple University

What drew you to this field?
I enjoyed accounting. I was around when computer courses were just being introduced at Temple. I was able to take one course before I graduated, which I enjoyed, and wanted to take more.

What makes a day at your job interesting?
Every day is different. I get involved in all aspects of running the law firm. I'm able to do this because of my education and the excellent training I received on the job with my previous employer, Price Waterhouse.

How has your graduate education been important to your successes/accomplishments along your career path?
It had virtually no significance at Price Waterhouse. Back in the day, they hired accountants with MBAs and paid about a 10% premium for them over accountants with undergraduate degrees. The salary difference disappeared over about a three-year period so that the MBAs and non-MBAs were making about the same. Public accounting firms wanted CPAs and didn't really care about MBAs. I was going at night and weekends and took some grief about being available for work. My MBA had the most impact when I decided to leave public accounting. Stark & Stark thought my CPA and MBA provided an excellent background for their needs, and I have been at Stark & Stark for the past 24 years.

What does the future of your field hold for someone newly entering it? What are the exciting developments coming in the next five years?
Computers are as important as accounting in business. If someone wants to really have the right tools, getting a higher education in both computers and accounting is a good way to go.

What advice would you share with new graduates entering your field?
The ones who were successful were the ones who worked hard (i.e., long hours) and were able to attract new clients (this is true in a law firm, too). Marketing and the ability to attract clients can be more important than being a good technician. Accountants (and lawyers) are a "dime a dozen," but the ones who bring in business are worth lots of money, partnerships, and prestige within their firms.

MANAGEMENT INFORMATION SYSTEMS

Adelphi University, School of Business, MBA Program, Garden City, NY 11530-0701. Offers finance (MBA); management information systems (MBA); management/human resource management (MBA); marketing/e-commerce (MBA). *Accreditation:* AACSB. Part-time and evening/weekend programs available. *Students:* 131 full-time (59 women), 173 part-time (73 women); includes 25 Black or African American, non-Hispanic/Latino; 20 Asian, non-Hispanic/Latino; 17 Hispanic/Latino; 3 Two or more races, non-Hispanic/Latino, 110 international. Average age 29. In 2010, 86 master's awarded. *Degree requirements:* For master's, capstone course. *Entrance requirements:* For master's, GMAT, 2 letters of recommendation. Additional exam requirements/recommendations for international students: Required—TOEFL (minimum score 550 paper-based; 213 computer-based; 80 iBT). *Application deadline:* For fall admission, 4/1 for international students; for spring admission, 11/1 for international students. Applications are processed on a rolling basis. Application fee: $50. Electronic applications accepted. *Financial support:* Research assistantships with full and partial tuition reimbursements, career-related internships or fieldwork, Federal Work-Study, institutionally sponsored loans, scholarships/grants, and unspecified assistantships available. Financial award application deadline: 3/1; financial award applicants required to submit FAFSA. *Faculty research:* Supply chain management, distribution channels, productivity benchmark analysis, data envelopment analysis, financial portfolio analysis. *Unit head:* Rakesh Gupta, 516-877-4670, Fax: 516-877-4607, E-mail: gradbusinquiries@adelphi.edu. *Application contact:* Christine Murphy, Director of Admissions, 516-877-3050, Fax: 516-877-3039, E-mail: graduateadmissions@adelphi.edu.

American Public University System, AMU/APU Graduate Programs, Charles Town, WV 25414. Offers accounting (MBA); administration and supervision (M Ed); air warfare (MA Military Studies); asymmetrical warfare (MA Military Studies); criminal justice (MA); emergency and disaster management (MA); entrepreneurship (MBA); environmental policy and management (MS); finance (MBA); general (MBA); global business management (MBA); guidance and counseling (M Ed); history (MA); homeland security (MA); homeland security resource allocation (MBA); humanities (MA); information technology (MS); information technology management (MBA); intelligence studies (MA); international relations and conflict resolution (MA); joint warfare (MA Military Studies); land warfare (MA Military Studies); legal studies (MA); management (MA), including defense mangement, general, human resource management, organizational leadership, public administration; marketing (MBA); military history (MA); national security studies (MA); naval warfare (MA Military Studies); nonprofit management (MBA); political science (MA); psychology (MA); public administration (MA); public health (MA); security management (MA); space studies (MS); sports management (MS); strategic leadership (MA Military Studies); teaching (M Ed), including elementary, secondary social sciences; transportation and logistics management (MA). Programs offered via distance learning only. Part-time and evening/weekend programs available. Postbaccalaureate distance learning degree programs offered (no on-campus study). *Faculty:* 253 full-time (134 women), 1,208 part-time/adjunct (570 women). *Students:* 956 full-time (422 women), 8,476 part-time (2,821 women); includes 2,511 minority (1,218 Black or African American, non-Hispanic/Latino; 68 American Indian or Alaska Native, non-Hispanic/Latino; 219 Asian, non-Hispanic/Latino; 705 Hispanic/Latino; 46 Native Hawaiian or other Pacific Islander, non-Hispanic/Latino; 255 Two or more races, non-Hispanic/Latino), 107 international. Average age 35. 9,550 applicants, 100% accepted. In 2010, 1,688 master's awarded. *Degree requirements:* For master's, comprehensive exam or practicum. *Entrance requirements:* For master's, official transcript showing earned bachelor's degree from institution accredited by recognized accrediting body. Additional exam requirements/recommendations for international students: Required—TOEFL (minimum score 550 paper-based; 213 computer-based), IELTS (minimum score 6.5). *Application deadline:* Applications are processed on a rolling basis. Application fee: $0. Electronic applications accepted. *Financial support:* Applicants required to submit FAFSA. *Faculty research:* Military history, criminal justice, management performance, national security. *Unit head:* Dr. Frank McCluskey, Provost, 877-468-6268, Fax: 304-724-3780. *Application contact:* Terry Grant, Director of Enrollment Management, 877-468-6268, Fax: 304-724-3780, E-mail: info@apus.edu.

American University, Kogod School of Business, Master of Business Administration Program, Washington, DC 20016-8044. Offers accounting (MBA); consulting (MBA), including information technology, international business, management; corporate finance: commercial banking (MBA); corporate finance: corporate financial management (MBA); corporate finance: investment banking (MBA), including corporate finance and private equity, trading and selling; entrepreneurship (MBA); global emerging markets (MBA), including business, finance, information technology; international trade and global supply chain management (MBA); leadership (MBA); marketing management (MBA); marketing research (MBA); real estate (MBA); MBA/JD; MBA/LL M. Part-time and evening/weekend programs available. *Faculty:* 12 full-time (5 women). *Students:* 135 full-time (62 women), 104 part-time (38 women); includes 46 minority (18 Black or African American, non-Hispanic/Latino; 1 American Indian or Alaska Native, non-Hispanic/Latino; 12 Asian, non-Hispanic/Latino; 14 Hispanic/Latino; 1 Two or more races, non-Hispanic/Latino), 34 international. Average age 27. 467 applicants, 51% accepted, 70 enrolled. In 2010, 101 master's awarded. *Entrance requirements:* For master's, GMAT. Additional exam requirements/recommendations for international students: Required—TOEFL. *Application deadline:* For fall admission, 2/1 priority date for domestic students; for spring admission, 10/1 priority date for domestic students. Applications are processed on a rolling basis. Application fee: $100. *Expenses:* Contact institution. *Financial support:* In 2010–11, 19 students received support; fellowships, research assistantships with partial tuition reimbursements available, career-related internships or fieldwork, Federal Work-Study, and institutionally sponsored loans available. Support available to part-time students. Financial award application deadline: 2/1. *Faculty research:* Information technology, decision-aiding methodology, negotiation. *Unit head:* Dr. Stevan Holmberg, Chair, 202-885-6193, E-mail: sholmbe@american.edu. *Application contact:* Shannon Demko, Associate Director Graduate Admissions, 202-885-1994, Fax: 202-885-1108, E-mail: demko@american.edu.

Arizona State University, College of Technology and Innovation, Department of Technology Management, Mesa, AZ 85212. Offers technology (aviation management and human factors) (MS); technology (environmental technology management) (MS); technology (global technology and development) (MS); technology (graphic information technology) (MS); technology (management of technology) (MS). Part-time and evening/weekend programs available. Postbaccalaureate distance learning degree programs offered (minimal on-campus study). *Faculty:* 13 full-time (3 women), 6 part-time/adjunct (2 women). *Students:* 56 full-time (16 women), 212 part-time (95 women); includes 61 minority (14 Black or African American, non-Hispanic/Latino; 8 American Indian or Alaska Native, non-Hispanic/Latino; 14 Asian, non-Hispanic/Latino; 21 Hispanic/Latino; 4 Two or more races, non-Hispanic/Latino), 27 international. Average age 36. 124 applicants, 77% accepted, 58 enrolled. In 2010, 35 master's awarded. *Degree requirements:* For master's, thesis or applied project and oral defense; interactive Program of Study (iPOS) submitted before completing 50 percent of required credit hours. *Entrance requirements:* For master's, GRE, minimum GPA of 3.0 or equivalent in last 2 years of work leading to bachelor's degree. Additional exam requirements/recommendations for international students: Required—TOEFL, IELTS, or Pearson Test of English. *Application deadline:* For fall admission, 7/1 for domestic and international students; for spring admission, 12/1 for domestic and international students. Applications are processed on a rolling basis. Application fee: $70 ($90 for international students). Electronic applications accepted. *Expenses:* Tuition, state resident: full-time $8510; part-time $608 per credit. Tuition, nonresident: full-time $16,542; part-time $919 per credit. Required fees: $339; $110 per credit. Part-time tuition and fees vary according to course load. *Financial support:* In 2010–11, 3 research assistantships with full and partial tuition reimbursements (averaging $12,729 per year), 1 teaching assistantship with full and partial tuition reimbursement (averaging $14,125 per year) were awarded; career-related internships or fieldwork, Federal Work-Study, scholarships/grants, health care benefits, tuition waivers (full and partial), and unspecified assistantships also available. Support available to part-time students. Financial award application deadline: 3/1; financial award applicants required to submit FAFSA. *Faculty research:* Digital imaging, digital publishing, Internet development/e-commerce, information aviation human factors, pilot selection, databases, multimedia, commercial digital photography, digital workflow, computer graphics modeling and animation, information design, sociotechnology, visual and technical literacy, environmental management, quality management, project management, industrial ethics, hazardous materials, environmental chemistry. Total annual research expenditures: $755,686. *Unit head:* Dr. Mitzi Montoya, Vice Provost and Dean, 480-727-1955, Fax: 480-727-1538, E-mail: mitzi.montoya@asu.edu. *Application contact:* Graduate Admissions, 480-965-6113.

Arizona State University, W. P. Carey School of Business, Department of Information Systems, Tempe, AZ 85287-4606. Offers business administration (computer information systems) (PhD); information management (MS); MBA/MS. Evening/weekend programs available. Postbaccalaureate distance learning degree programs offered (no on-campus study). *Faculty:* 23 full-time (5 women), 1 part-time/adjunct (0 women). *Students:* 71 full-time (24 women); includes 26 minority (4 Black or African American, non-Hispanic/Latino; 1 American Indian or Alaska Native, non-Hispanic/Latino; 12 Asian, non-Hispanic/Latino; 8 Hispanic/Latino; 1 Two or more races, non-Hispanic/Latino), 3 international. Average age 35. 109 applicants, 76% accepted. In 2010, 70 master's awarded. Terminal master's awarded for partial completion of doctoral program. *Degree requirements:* For master's, thesis or alternative, applied project, interactive Program of Study (iPOS) submitted before completing 50 percent of required credit hours; for doctorate, comprehensive exam, thesis/dissertation, interactive Program of Study (iPOS) submitted before completing 50 percent of required credit hours. *Entrance requirements:* For master's, 2 years of full-time related work experience, bachelor's degree in related field from accredited university, resume, essay, 2 letters of recommendation, official transcripts; for doctorate, GMAT, MBA, 2 years of full-time related work experience (recommended), bachelor's degree in related field from accredited university, 3 letters of recommendation, resume, personal statement. Additional exam requirements/recommendations for international students: Required—TOEFL (minimum score 550 paper-based; 213 computer-based; 80 iBT), IELTS (minimum score 6.5). *Application deadline:* For fall admission, 1/15 priority date for domestic and international students. Applications are processed on a rolling basis. Application fee: $70 ($90 for international students). Electronic applications accepted. *Expenses:* Contact institution. *Financial support:* Fellowships with full and partial tuition reimbursements, research assistantships with full and partial tuition reimbursements, teaching assistantships with full and partial tuition reimbursements, institutionally sponsored loans, scholarships/grants, and tuition waivers (full and partial) available. Financial award application deadline: 3/1; financial award applicants required to submit FAFSA. *Faculty research:* Strategy and technology, technology investments and firm valuation, Internet e-commerce, IT enablement for emergency preparedness and response, information supply chain, collaborative computing and security/privacy issues for e-health, enterprise information systems and their application to management control systems. Total annual research expenditures: $211,624. *Unit head:* Dr. Michael Goul, Chair, 480-965-5482, Fax: 480-727-0881, E-mail: michael.goul@asu.edu. *Application contact:* Graduate Admissions, 480-965-6113.

Arizona State University, W. P. Carey School of Business, Program in Business Administration, Tempe, AZ 85287-4906. Offers accountancy (PhD); agribusiness (PhD); business administration (MBA); finance (PhD); financial management and markets (MBA); information management (MBA); information systems (PhD); management (PhD); marketing (PhD); strategic marketing and services leadership (MBA); supply chain financial management (MBA); supply chain management (MBA, PhD); JD/MBA; MBA/M Acc; MBA/M Arch. *Accreditation:* AACSB. Part-time and evening/weekend programs available. Postbaccalaureate distance learning degree programs offered (minimal on-campus study). *Faculty:* 84 full-time (22 women), 7 part-time/adjunct (2 women). *Students:* 1,302 full-time (379 women), 86 part-time (26 women); includes 241 minority (37 Black or African American, non-Hispanic/Latino; 11 American Indian or Alaska Native, non-Hispanic/Latino; 103 Asian, non-Hispanic/Latino; 76 Hispanic/Latino; 4 Native Hawaiian or other Pacific Islander, non-Hispanic/Latino; 10 Two or more races, non-Hispanic/Latino; 171 international. Average age 31. 1,795 applicants, 44% accepted, 525 enrolled. In 2010, 734 master's, 9 doctorates awarded. Terminal master's awarded for partial completion of doctoral program. *Degree requirements:* For master's, thesis or alternative, internship, interactive Program of Study (iPOS) submitted before completing 50 percent of required credit hours; for doctorate, comprehensive exam, thesis/dissertation, interactive Program of Study (iPOS) submitted before completing 50 percent of required credit hours. *Entrance requirements:* For master's, GMAT, minimum GPA of 3.0 in last 2 years of work leading to bachelor's degree, 2 letters of recommendation, professional resume, official transcripts, 3 essays; for doctorate, GMAT or GRE, minimum GPA of 3.0 in last 2 years of work leading to bachelor's degree, 3 letters of recommendation, resume, personal statement/essay. Additional exam requirements/recommendations for international students: Required—TOEFL (minimum score 550 paper-based; 213 computer-based; 80 iBT), IELTS (minimum score 6.5). Application fee: $70 ($90 for international students). Electronic applications accepted. *Expenses:* Contact institution. *Financial support:* In 2010–11, 17 research assistantships with full and partial tuition reimbursements (averaging $18,121 per year), 153 teaching assistantships with full and partial tuition reimbursements (averaging $9,176 per year) were awarded; fellowships with full and partial tuition reimbursements, career-related internships or fieldwork, institutionally sponsored loans, scholarships/grants, and tuition waivers (full and partial) also available. Support available to part-time students. Financial award application deadline: 3/1; financial award applicants required to submit FAFSA. Total annual research expenditures: $540,779. *Unit head:* Dr. Robert E. Mittelstaedt, Dean, 480-965-2468, Fax: 480-965-5539, E-mail: mittelsr@asu.edu. *Application contact:* Graduate Admissions, 480-965-6113.

Arkansas State University, Graduate School, College of Business, Department of Computer and Information Technology, Jonesboro, State University, AR 72467. Offers business education (SCCT); business technology education (MSE); information systems and e-commerce (MS). Part-time programs available. *Faculty:* 12 full-time (1 woman). *Students:* 11 full-time (6 women), 19 part-time (16 women). Average age 35. 15 applicants, 93% accepted, 13 enrolled. In 2010, 23 master's awarded. *Degree requirements:* For master's, comprehensive exam, thesis or alternative. *Entrance requirements:* For master's, GRE General Test or MAT, appropriate bachelor's degree, official transcript, immunization records. Additional exam requirements/recommendations for international students: Required—TOEFL (minimum score 550 paper-based; 253 computer-based; 79 iBT), IELTS (minimum score 6), PTE: Pearson Test of English Academic (56). *Application deadline:* For fall admission, 7/1 for domestic and international students; for spring admission, 11/15 for domestic students, 11/14 for international students. Applications are processed on a rolling basis. Application fee: $30 ($40 for international students). Electronic applications accepted. *Expenses:* Contact institution. *Financial support:* In 2010–11, 3 students received support. Career-related internships or fieldwork, scholarships/grants, and unspecified assistantships available. Financial award application deadline: 7/1; financial award applicants required to submit FAFSA. *Unit head:* Dr. John Robertson, Chair, 870-972-3416, Fax: 870-972-3868, E-mail: jfrobert@astate.edu. *Application

contact: Dr. Andrew Sustich, Dean of the Graduate School, 870-972-3029, Fax: 870-972-3857, E-mail: sustich@astate.edu.

Auburn University, Graduate School, College of Business, Department of Management, Auburn University, AL 36849. Offers human resource management (PhD); management (MS, PhD); management information systems (MS, PhD). *Accreditation:* AACSB. Part-time programs available. *Faculty:* 34 full-time (7 women), 5 part-time/adjunct (0 women). *Students:* 12 full-time (4 women), 12 part-time (2 women); includes 1 Black or African American, non-Hispanic/Latino; 2 Asian, non-Hispanic/Latino, 5 international. Average age 34. 137 applicants, 28% accepted, 20 enrolled. In 2010, 9 master's, 6 doctorates awarded. *Degree requirements:* For master's, thesis (for some programs); for doctorate, thesis/dissertation. *Entrance requirements:* For master's, GMAT, GRE General Test (MS); for doctorate, GMAT, GRE General Test. Additional exam requirements/recommendations for international students: Required—TOEFL. *Application deadline:* For fall admission, 7/7 for domestic students; for spring admission, 11/24 for domestic students. Applications are processed on a rolling basis. Application fee: $50 ($60 for international students). Electronic applications accepted. *Expenses:* Tuition, state resident: full-time $7002. Tuition, nonresident: full-time $21,898. International tuition: $22,116 full-time. Required fees: $892. Tuition and fees vary according to course load and program. *Financial support:* Teaching assistantships, Federal Work-Study available. Support available to part-time students. Financial award application deadline: 3/15; financial award applicants required to submit FAFSA. *Unit head:* Dr. Sharon Oswald, Head, 334-844-4071. *Application contact:* Dr. George Flowers, Dean of the Graduate School, 334-844-2125.

Avila University, School of Business, Kansas City, MO 64145-1698. Offers accounting (MBA); finance (MBA); general management (MBA); health care administration (MBA); international business (MBA); management information systems (MBA); marketing (MBA). Part-time and evening/weekend programs available. *Faculty:* 9 full-time (3 women), 24 part-time/adjunct (6 women). *Students:* 123 full-time (68 women), 87 part-time (52 women); includes 44 minority (30 Black or African American, non-Hispanic/Latino; 1 American Indian or Alaska Native, non-Hispanic/Latino; 6 Asian, non-Hispanic/Latino; 6 Hispanic/Latino; 1 Native Hawaiian or other Pacific Islander, non-Hispanic/Latino); 46 international. Average age 33. 62 applicants, 79% accepted, 49 enrolled. In 2010, 80 master's awarded. *Degree requirements:* For master's, comprehensive exam, capstone course. *Entrance requirements:* For master's, GMAT (minimum score 420), minimum GPA of 3.0, interview. Additional exam requirements/recommendations for international students: Required—TOEFL (minimum score 550 paper-based). *Application deadline:* For fall admission, 7/30 priority date for domestic students, 7/30 for international students; for winter admission, 11/30 priority date for domestic students, 11/30 for international students; for spring admission, 2/28 priority date for domestic students, 2/28 for international students. Applications are processed on a rolling basis. Application fee: $0. Electronic applications accepted. *Expenses:* Contact institution. *Financial support:* In 2010–11, 102 students received support. Career-related internships or fieldwork and Competitive Merit Scholarship available. Support available to part-time students. Financial award applicants required to submit FAFSA. *Faculty research:* Leadership characteristics, financial hedging, group dynamics. *Unit head:* Dr. Richard Woodall, Dean, 816-501-3720, Fax: 816-501-2463, E-mail: richard.woodall@avila.edu. *Application contact:* JoAnna Giffin, MBA Admissions Director, 816-501-3601, Fax: 816-501-2463, E-mail: joanna.giffin@avila.edu.

Baylor University, Graduate School, Hankamer School of Business, Department of Information Systems, Waco, TX 76798. Offers information systems (MSIS); information systems management (MBA); MBA/MSIS. *Faculty:* 12 full-time (4 women). *Students:* 13 full-time (7 women), 5 part-time (2 women); includes 2 minority (1 Black or African American, non-Hispanic/Latino; 1 Hispanic/Latino), 6 international. In 2010, 8 master's awarded. *Entrance requirements:* For master's, GMAT. Additional exam requirements/recommendations for international students: Required—TOEFL. *Application deadline:* For fall admission, 8/1 for domestic students; for spring admission, 12/1 for domestic students. Applications are processed on a rolling basis. Application fee: $25. *Financial support:* Research assistantships, career-related internships or fieldwork and Federal Work-Study available. *Faculty research:* Computer personnel, group systems, information technology standards and infrastructure, international information systems, technology and the learning environment. *Unit head:* Dr. Gary Carini, Associate Dean, 254-710-4091, Fax: 254-710-1091, E-mail: gary_carini@baylor.edu. Application contact: Laurie Wilson, Director, Graduate Business Programs, 254-710-4163, Fax: 254-710-1066, E-mail: laurie_wilson@baylor.edu.

Bellarmine University, School of Continuing and Professional Studies, Louisville, KY 40205-0671. Offers MAIT. Part-time and evening/weekend programs available. *Faculty:* 1 full-time (0 women), 2 part-time/adjunct (0 women). *Students:* 13 full-time (0 women), 9 part-time (3 women); includes 2 Black or African American, non-Hispanic/Latino. Average age 30. In 2010, 6 master's awarded. *Entrance requirements:* For master's, GRE or GMAT, minimum GPA of 2.75, two letters of recommendation. Additional exam requirements/recommendations for international students: Required—TOEFL (minimum score 550 paper-based; 213 computer-based; 80 iBT). Application fee: $25. *Expenses:* Contact institution. *Unit head:* Dr. Michael D. Mattei, Dean, 502-272-8441, E-mail: mmattei@bellarmine.edu. *Application contact:*

Dr. Sara Pettingill, Dean of Graduate Admission, 502-272-8401, E-mail: spettingill@bellarmine.edu.

Benedictine University, Graduate Programs, Program in Business Administration, Lisle, IL 60532-0900. Offers accounting (MBA); entrepreneurship and managing innovation (MBA); financial management (MBA); health administration (MBA); human resource management (MBA); information systems security (MBA); international business (MBA); management consulting (MBA); management information systems (MBA); marketing management (MBA); operations management and logistics (MBA); organizational leadership (MBA); MBA/MPH; MBA/MS. Part-time and evening/weekend programs available. Postbaccalaureate distance learning degree programs offered (minimal on-campus study). *Faculty:* 4 full-time (2 women), 24 part-time/adjunct (3 women). *Students:* 347 full-time (140 women), 672 part-time (360 women); includes 237 minority (155 Black or African American, non-Hispanic/Latino; 4 American Indian or Alaska Native, non-Hispanic/Latino; 43 Asian, non-Hispanic/Latino; 35 Hispanic/Latino), 21 international. Average age 34. 416 applicants, 88% accepted, 217 enrolled. In 2010, 355 master's awarded. *Entrance requirements:* For master's, GMAT. Additional exam requirements/recommendations for international students: Required—TOEFL (minimum score 550 paper-based; 213 computer-based). *Application deadline:* For fall admission, 9/1 for domestic students; for winter admission, 12/1 for domestic students; for spring admission, 2/15 for domestic students. Applications are processed on a rolling basis. Application fee: $40. Electronic applications accepted. *Financial support:* Career-related internships or fieldwork and health care benefits available. Support available to part-time students. *Faculty research:* Strategic leadership in professional organizations, sociology of professions, organizational change, social identity theory, applications to change management. *Unit head:* Dr. Sharon Borowicz, Director, 630-829-6219, E-mail: sborowicz@ben.edu. *Application contact:* Kari Gibbons, Director, Admissions, 630-829-6200, Fax: 630-829-6584, E-mail: kgibbons@ben.edu.

Benedictine University, Graduate Programs, Program in Management Information Systems, Lisle, IL 60532-0900. Offers MS, MBA/MS, MPH/MS. Part-time programs available. *Faculty:* 2 full-time (1 woman), 6 part-time/adjunct (1 woman). *Students:* 85 full-time (24 women), 11 part-time (2 women); includes 3 minority (all Black or African American, non-Hispanic/Latino), 4 international. Average age 36. 15 applicants, 80% accepted, 5 enrolled. In 2010, 3 master's awarded. *Entrance requirements:* For master's, GMAT. Additional exam requirements/recommendations for international students: Required—TOEFL (minimum score 550 paper-based; 213 computer-based). *Application deadline:* For fall admission, 9/1 for domestic students; for winter admission, 12/1 for domestic students; for spring admission, 2/15 for domestic students. Applications are processed on a rolling basis. Application fee: $40. Electronic applications accepted. *Financial support:* Career-related internships or fieldwork and health care benefits available. Support available to part-time students. *Faculty research:* Technology management, knowledge management, electronic commerce, information security. *Unit head:* Dr. Barbara Ozog, Director, 630-829-6218, E-mail: bozog@ben.edu. *Application contact:* Kari Gibbons, Director, Admissions, 630-829-6200, Fax: 630-829-6584, E-mail: kgibbons@ben.edu.

Boston University, Metropolitan College, Department of Computer Science, Boston, MA 02215. Offers computer information systems (MS), including computer networks, database management and business intelligence, health informatics, IT project management, security; computer science (MS), including computer networks, security; telecommunications (MS), including security. Part-time and evening/weekend programs available. Postbaccalaureate distance learning degree programs offered (no on-campus study). *Faculty:* 10 full-time (0 women), 30 part-time/adjunct (3 women). *Students:* 16 full-time (2 women), 681 part-time (155 women); includes 182 minority (44 Black or African American, non-Hispanic/Latino; 1 American Indian or Alaska Native, non-Hispanic/Latino; 88 Asian, non-Hispanic/Latino; 36 Hispanic/Latino; 2 Native Hawaiian or other Pacific Islander, non-Hispanic/Latino; 11 Two or more races, non-Hispanic/Latino), 66 international. Average age 35. 273 applicants, 78% accepted, 155 enrolled. In 2010, 143 master's awarded. *Degree requirements:* For master's, thesis optional. *Entrance requirements:* For master's, 3 letters of recommendation, professional resume. Additional exam requirements/recommendations for international students: Required—TOEFL (minimum score 550 paper-based; 213 computer-based; 80 iBT). *Application deadline:* For fall admission, 6/1 priority date for international students; for spring admission, 10/1 priority date for international students. Applications are processed on a rolling basis. Application fee: $70. Electronic applications accepted. *Expenses:* Tuition: Full-time $39,314; part-time $1228 per credit. Required fees: $40 per semester. *Financial support:* In 2010–11, 9 research assistantships with partial tuition reimbursements (averaging $5,000 per year) were awarded; career-related internships or fieldwork and unspecified assistantships also available. Support available to part-time students. Financial award applicants required to submit FAFSA. *Faculty research:* Medical informatics, Web technologies, telecom and networks, security and forensics, software engineering, programming languages, multimedia and AI, information systems and IT project management. *Unit head:* Dr. Lubomir Chitkushev, Chairman, 617-353-2566, Fax: 617-353-2367, E-mail: csinfo@

bu.edu. *Application contact:* Kim Richards, Program Coordinator, 617-353-2566, Fax: 617-353-2367, E-mail: kimrich@bu.edu.

Brandeis University, Rabb School of Continuing Studies, Division of Graduate Professional Studies, Information Technology Management Program, Waltham, MA 02454-9110. Offers MS, Graduate Certificate. Part-time programs available. Postbaccalaureate distance learning degree programs offered (no on-campus study). *Faculty:* 2 full-time (both women), 33 part-time/adjunct (5 women). *Students:* 55 part-time (8 women); includes 5 Black or African American, non-Hispanic/Latino; 11 Asian, non-Hispanic/Latino. Average age 35. 10 applicants, 100% accepted, 8 enrolled. In 2010, 32 master's, 2 other advanced degrees awarded. *Entrance requirements:* For master's, resume, official transcripts, recommendations, goal statements; for Graduate Certificate, resume, official transcripts, recommendations. Additional exam requirements/recommendations for international students: Recommended—TOEFL (minimum score 600 paper-based; 250 computer-based; 100 iBT). *Application deadline:* For fall admission, 6/15 priority date for domestic students; for winter admission, 10/15 priority date for domestic students; for spring admission, 2/15 priority date for domestic students. Applications are processed on a rolling basis. Application fee: $50. Electronic applications accepted. *Unit head:* Dr. Cynthia Phillips, Program Chair, 781-736-8787, Fax: 781-736-3420, E-mail: cynthiap@brandeis.edu. *Application contact:* Frances Stearns, Associate Director of Admissions and Student Services, 781-736-8785, Fax: 781-736-3420, E-mail: fstearns@brandeis.edu.

Brigham Young University, Graduate Studies, Marriott School of Management, Information Systems Program, Provo, UT 84602. Offers MISM. *Faculty:* 13 full-time (1 woman), 4 part-time/adjunct (0 women). *Students:* 44 full-time (1 woman); includes 3 Asian, non-Hispanic/Latino; 1 Hispanic/Latino, 1 international. Average age 26. 59 applicants, 68% accepted, 40 enrolled. In 2010, 44 master's awarded. *Entrance requirements:* For master's, GMAT, minimum GPA of 3.0 in last 60 hours of course work. Additional exam requirements/recommendations for international students: Required—TOEFL (minimum score 580 paper-based; 237 computer-based). *Application deadline:* For fall admission, 3/1 for domestic and international students. Application fee: $50. Electronic applications accepted. *Expenses:* Tuition: Full-time $5580; part-time $310 per credit hour. Tuition and fees vary according to program and student's religious affiliation. *Financial support:* In 2010–11, 27 students received support; research assistantships, teaching assistantships, career-related internships or fieldwork and scholarships/grants available. Financial award application deadline: 2/15. *Faculty research:* Research standards—faculty career development in information systems, electronic commerce technology and standards, collaborative tools and methods, technology for fraud detection and prevention, ethical issues in the information systems field. *Unit head:* Dr. Marshall B. Romney, Director, 801-422-3247, Fax: 801-422-0573, E-mail: marshall romney@byu.edu. Application contact: Ann E. Sumsion, Program Assistant, 801-422-3247, Fax: 801-422-0573, E-mail: mism@byu.edu.

California Lutheran University, Graduate Studies, School of Management, Thousand Oaks, CA 91360-2787. Offers business (IMBA); computer science (MS); econometrics (MBA); economics (MS); entrepreneurship (MBA, Certificate); finance (MBA, Certificate); financial planning (MBA, Certificate); information systems and technology (MS); information technology management (MBA, Certificate); international business (MBA, Certificate); management and organization behavior (MBA); management and organizational behavior (Certificate); marketing (MBA, Certificate); microeconomics (MBA); nonprofit and social enterprise (MBA). Part-time and evening/weekend programs available. Postbaccalaureate distance learning degree programs offered (no on-campus study). *Faculty:* 12 full-time (3 women), 27 part-time/adjunct (6 women). *Students:* 350 full-time (162 women), 262 part-time (99 women); includes 21 Black or African American, non-Hispanic/Latino; 44 Asian, non-Hispanic/Latino; 56 Hispanic/Latino; 4 Native Hawaiian or other Pacific Islander, non-Hispanic/Latino; 12 Two or more races, non-Hispanic/Latino, 185 international. Average age 32. 379 applicants, 74% accepted, 138 enrolled. In 2010, 231 master's awarded. *Entrance requirements:* For master's, GMAT, interview, minimum GPA of 3.0. *Application deadline:* Applications are processed on a rolling basis. Application fee: $50. *Expenses:* Contact institution. *Unit head:* Dr. Charles Maxey, Dean, 805-493-3360. *Application contact:* 805-493-3127, Fax: 805-493-3542, E-mail: clugrad@clunet.edu.

California State Polytechnic University, Pomona, Academic Affairs, College of Business Administration, Master of Science in Business Administration Program, Pomona, CA 91768-2557. Offers information systems auditing (MS). *Students:* 2 full-time (1 woman), 12 part-time (3 women); includes 10 minority (7 Asian, non-Hispanic/Latino; 3 Hispanic/Latino), 1 international. Average age 32. 20 applicants, 35% accepted, 5 enrolled. In 2010, 5 master's awarded. *Application deadline:* Applications are processed on a rolling basis. Application fee: $55. Electronic applications accepted. *Expenses:* Tuition, state resident: full-time $5386; part-time $2850 per year. Tuition, nonresident: full-time $12,082; part-time $248 per credit. Required fees: $577; $248 per credit. $577 per year. Tuition and fees vary according to course load and program. *Unit head:* Dr. Richard S. Lapidus, Dean, 909-869-2400, E-mail: rslapidus@csupomona.edu. *Application contact:* Dr. Steven Curl, Associate Dean, 909-869-4244, E-mail: scurl@csupomona.edu.

California State University, East Bay, Office of Academic Programs and Graduate Studies, College of Business and Economics, MBA Program, Hayward, CA 94542-3000. Offers entrepreneurship (MBA); finance (MBA); human resources and organizational behavior (MBA); information technology management (MBA); marketing management (MBA); operations and supply chain management (MBA); strategy and international business (MBA). Part-time and evening/weekend programs available. Postbaccalaureate distance learning degree programs offered (no on-campus study). *Faculty:* 33 full-time (9 women). *Students:* 121 full-time (58 women), 133 part-time (67 women); includes 7 Black or African American, non-Hispanic/Latino; 63 Asian, non-Hispanic/Latino; 11 Hispanic/Latino; 3 Native Hawaiian or other Pacific Islander, non-Hispanic/Latino; 5 Two or more races, non-Hispanic/Latino, 87 international. Average age 30. 284 applicants, 47% accepted, 55 enrolled. In 2010, 241 master's awarded. *Degree requirements:* For master's, comprehensive exam or thesis. *Entrance requirements:* For master's, GMAT (minimum 20th percentile verbal and quantitative section), bachelor's degree, minimum GPA of 2.75. Additional exam requirements/recommendations for international students: Required—TOEFL (minimum score 550 paper-based; 213 computer-based; 79 iBT). *Application deadline:* For fall admission, 6/30 for domestic and international students. Applications are processed on a rolling basis. Application fee: $55. Electronic applications accepted. *Financial support:* Career-related internships or fieldwork, Federal Work-Study, institutionally sponsored loans, and scholarships/grants available. Support available to part-time students. Financial award application deadline: 3/2; financial award applicants required to submit FAFSA. *Unit head:* Dr. Terri Swartz, Dean, 510-885-3291, Fax: 510-885-4884, E-mail: terri.swartz@csueastbay.edu. *Application contact:* Dr. Donna Wiley, Interim Associate Director, 510-885-2928, Fax: 510-885-4777, E-mail: donna.wiley@csueastbay.edu.

California State University, Fullerton, Graduate Studies, College of Business and Economics, Department of Information Systems and Decision Sciences, Fullerton, CA 92834-9480. Offers information systems (MS); information systems (decision sciences) (MS); information systems (e-commerce) (MS); information technology (MS); management science (MBA). Part-time programs available. *Students:* 13 full-time (2 women), 72 part-time (16 women); includes 2 Black or African American, non-Hispanic/Latino; 24 Asian, non-Hispanic/Latino; 6 Hispanic/Latino; 3 Two or more races, non-Hispanic/Latino, 10 international. Average age 35. 120 applicants, 34% accepted, 34 enrolled. In 2010, 23 master's awarded. *Degree requirements:* For master's, project or thesis. *Entrance requirements:* For master's, GMAT, minimum AACSB index of 950. Application fee: $55. *Financial support:* Career-related internships or fieldwork, Federal Work-Study, institutionally sponsored loans, and scholarships/grants available. Support available to part-time students. Financial award application deadline: 3/1; financial award applicants required to submit FAFSA. *Unit head:* Dr. Bhushan Kapoor, Chair, 657-278-2221. *Application contact:* Admissions/Applications, 657-278-2371.

California State University, Los Angeles, Graduate Studies, College of Business and Economics, Department of Information Systems, Los Angeles, CA 90032-8530. Offers business information systems (MBA); management (MS); management information systems (MS); office management (MBA). Part-time and evening/weekend programs available. *Faculty:* 5 full-time (0 women), 1 part-time/adjunct (0 women). *Students:* 7 full-time (3 women), 14 part-time (3 women); includes 2 minority (1 Asian, non-Hispanic/Latino; 1 Hispanic/Latino), 12 international. Average age 30. 7 applicants, 100% accepted, 4 enrolled. In 2010, 10 master's awarded. *Degree requirements:* For master's, comprehensive exam (MBA), thesis (MS). *Entrance requirements:* For master's, GMAT, minimum GPA of 2.5 during previous 2 years of course work. Additional exam requirements/recommendations for international students: Required—TOEFL (minimum score 550 paper-based; 213 computer-based). *Application deadline:* For fall admission, 5/1 for domestic and international students. Applications are processed on a rolling basis. Application fee: $55. Electronic applications accepted. *Financial support:* Career-related internships or fieldwork and Federal Work-Study available. Support available to part-time students. Financial award application deadline: 3/1. *Unit head:* Dr. Adam Huarng, Chair, 323-343-2983, E-mail: ahuarng@calstatela.edu. *Application contact:* Dr. Alan Muchlinski, Dean of Graduate Studies, 323-343-3820, Fax: 323-343-5653, E-mail: amuchli@exchange.calstatela.edu.

Central European University, CEU Business School, Budapest, Hungary. Offers executive business administration (EMBA); finance (MBA); general management (MBA); information technology management (MBA); marketing (MBA); real estate management (MBA). Part-time and evening/weekend programs available. *Faculty:* 16 full-time (4 women), 2 part-time/adjunct (1 woman). *Students:* 71 full-time (30 women), 142 part-time (47 women). Average age 34. 144 applicants, 36% accepted, 32 enrolled. In 2010, 64 master's awarded. *Degree requirements:* For master's, one foreign language. *Entrance requirements:* For master's, GMAT. Additional exam requirements/recommendations for international students: Required—TOEFL (minimum score 570 paper-based; 230 computer-based); Recommended—IELTS (minimum score 6.5). *Application deadline:* For fall admission, 5/15 priority date for domestic students, 5/22 for international students; for winter admission, 11/15 priority date for domestic students, 11/10 for international students. Applications are processed on a rolling basis. Application fee: $0. Electronic applications accepted. Tuition and fees charges are reported in euros. *Expenses:* Tuition: Full-time 11,000 euros. Required fees: 250 euros. One-time fee: 200 euros full-time. Tuition and fees vary according to degree level, program, reciprocity agreements and student level. *Financial support:* In 2010–11, 4 students received support. Tuition waivers (partial) available. *Faculty research:* Social and ethical business, marketing. *Unit head:* Dr. Mel Horwitch, Dean and Managing Director, 361-887-5050, E-mail: mhorwitch@ceubusiness.com. *Application contact:* Agnes Schram, MBA Program Manager, 361-887-5511, Fax: 361-887-5133, E-mail: mba@ceubusiness.com.

Central Michigan University, Central Michigan University Off-Campus Programs, Program in Administration, Mount Pleasant, MI 48859. Offers acquisitions administration (MSA, Certificate); general administration (MSA, Certificate); health services administration (MSA, Certificate); human resources administration (MSA, Certificate); information resource management (MSA, Certificate); international administration (MSA, Certificate); leadership (MSA, Certificate); public administration (MSA, Certificate); vehicle design and manufacturing administration (Certificate). Part-time and evening/weekend programs available. Postbaccalaureate distance learning degree programs offered (no on-campus study). *Students:* Average age 38. *Entrance requirements:* For master's, minimum GPA of 2.7 in major. *Application deadline:* Applications are processed on a rolling basis. Application fee: $50. Electronic applications accepted. *Expenses:* Tuition, state resident: full-time $8208; part-time $456 per credit hour. Tuition, nonresident: full-time $13,788; part-time $766 per credit hour. One-time fee: $25. *Financial support:* Scholarships/grants available. Support available to part-time students. Financial award applicants required to submit FAFSA. *Unit head:* Dr. Nana Korsah, Director, MSA Programs, 989-774-6525, E-mail: korsa1na@cmich.edu. *Application contact:* 877-268-4636, E-mail: cmuoffcampus@cmich.edu.

Central Michigan University, College of Graduate Studies, College of Business Administration, Department of Business Information Systems, Mount Pleasant, MI 48859. Offers business computing (Graduate Certificate); information systems (MS), including enterprise software, general business, systems applications. Part-time and evening/weekend programs available. *Faculty:* 8 full-time (2 women), 3 part-time/adjunct (1 woman). *Students:* 40 full-time (13 women), 15 part-time (5 women); includes 1 Black or African American, non-Hispanic/Latino, 42 international. Average age 28. *Degree requirements:* For master's, thesis or alternative. *Application deadline:* For fall admission, 6/1 for international students; for spring admission, 10/1 for international students. Applications are processed on a rolling basis. Application fee: $35 ($45 for international students). Electronic applications accepted. *Expenses:* Tuition, state resident: full-time $8208; part-time $456 per credit hour. Tuition, nonresident: full-time $13,788; part-time $766 per credit hour. One-time fee: $25. *Financial support:* Fellowships with tuition reimbursements, research assistantships with tuition reimbursements, teaching assistantships with tuition reimbursements, career-related internships or fieldwork, Federal Work-Study, unspecified assistantships, and out-of-state merit awards, non-resident graduate awards available. *Faculty research:* Enterprise software, electronic commerce, decision support systems, ethical issues in information systems, information technology management and teaching issues. *Unit head:* Dr. Karl Smart, Chair, 989-774-6501, Fax: 989-774-3356, E-mail: smart1kl@cmich.edu. *Application contact:* Dr. Emil Boasson, Graduate Program Coordinator, 989-774-3588, Fax: 989-774-3356, E-mail: boass1e@cmich.edu.

Central Michigan University, College of Graduate Studies, Interdisciplinary Administration Programs, Mount Pleasant, MI 48859. Offers acquisitions administration (MSA, Graduate Certificate); general administration (MSA, Graduate Certificate); health services administration (MSA, Graduate Certificate); human resource administration (Graduate Certificate); human resources administration (MSA); information resource management (MSA, Graduate Certificate); international administration (MSA, Graduate Certificate); leadership (MSA, Graduate Certificate); organizational communication (MSA, Graduate Certificate); public administration (MSA, Graduate Certificate); recreation and park administration (MSA); sport administration (MSA). *Accreditation:* AACSB. Part-time and evening/weekend programs available. Postbaccalaureate distance learning degree programs offered (no on-campus study). *Students:* 102 full-time (50 women), 77 part-time (51 women); includes 10 Black or African American, non-Hispanic/Latino; 3 American Indian or Alaska Native, non-Hispanic/Latino; 5 Asian, non-Hispanic/Latino, 65 international. Average age 29. *Degree requirements:* For master's, thesis or alternative. *Entrance requirements:* For master's, bachelor's degree with minimum GPA of 2.7. *Application deadline:* For fall admission, 6/1 for international students; for spring admission, 10/1 for international students. Applications are processed on a rolling basis. Application fee: $35 ($45 for international students). Electronic applications accepted. *Expenses:* Tuition, state resident: full-time $8208; part-time $456 per credit hour. Tuition, nonresident: full-time $13,788; part-time $766 per credit hour. One-time fee: $25. *Financial support:* Fellowships with tuition reimbursements, research assistantships with tuition reimbursements, career-related internships or fieldwork, Federal Work-Study, unspecified assistantships, and out-of-state merit awards, non-resident graduate awards available. *Faculty research:* Interdisciplinary studies in acquisitions administration, health services administration, sport administration, recreation and park administration, and international administration. *Unit head:* Dr. Nana Korash, Director, 989-774-6525, Fax: 989-774-2575, E-mail: msa@cmich.edu. *Application contact:* Denise Schafer, Coordinator, 989-774-4373, Fax: 989-774-2575, E-mail: schaf1dr@cmich.edu.

Claremont Graduate University, Graduate Programs, School of Information Systems and Technology, Claremont, CA 91711-6160. Offers electronic commerce (MS, PhD); health information management (MS); information systems (Certificate); knowledge management (MS, PhD); systems development (MS, PhD); telecommunications and networking (MS, PhD); MBA/MS. Part-time programs available. *Faculty:* 6 full-time (1 woman), 1 part-time/adjunct (0 women). *Students:* 87 full-time (24 women), 22 part-time (8 women); includes 31 minority (6 Black or African American, non-Hispanic/Latino; 1 American Indian or Alaska Native, non-Hispanic/Latino; 18 Asian, non-Hispanic/Latino; 3 Hispanic/Latino; 1 Native Hawaiian or other Pacific Islander, non-Hispanic/Latino; 2 Two or more races, non-Hispanic/Latino), 37 international. Average age 37. In 2010, 30 master's, 6 doctorates awarded. *Degree requirements:* For doctorate, comprehensive exam, thesis/dissertation, portfolio. *Entrance requirements:* For master's and doctorate, GMAT, GRE General Test. Additional exam requirements/recommendations for international students: Required—TOEFL (minimum score 550 paper-based; 213 computer-based; 80 iBT). *Application deadline:* For fall admission, 2/1 priority date for domestic students. Applications are processed on a rolling basis. Application fee: $60. Electronic applications accepted. *Expenses:* Tuition: Full-time $35,748; part-time $1554 per unit. Required fees: $215 per semester. *Financial support:* Fellowships, research assistantships, teaching assistantships, Federal Work-Study, institutionally sponsored loans, and scholarships/grants available. Support available to part-time students. Financial award application deadline: 2/15; financial award applicants required to submit FAFSA. *Faculty research:* GPSS, man-machine interaction, organizational aspects of computing, implementation of information systems, information systems practice. *Unit head:* Terry Ryan, Dean, 909-607-9591, Fax: 909-621-8564, E-mail: terry.ryan@cgu.edu. *Application contact:* Matt Hutter, Director of External Affairs, 909-621-3180, Fax: 909-621-8564, E-mail: matt.hutter@cgu.edu.

Clark University, Graduate School, Graduate School of Management, Business Administration Program, Worcester, MA 01610-1477. Offers accounting (MBA); finance (MBA); global business (MBA); health care management (MBA); management (MBA); management of information technology (MBA); marketing (MBA). *Accreditation:* AACSB. Part-time and evening/weekend programs available. *Students:* 147 full-time (75 women), 126 part-time (54 women); includes 24 minority (10 Black or African American, non-Hispanic/Latino; 1 American Indian or Alaska Native, non-Hispanic/Latino; 6 Asian, non-Hispanic/Latino; 5 Hispanic/Latino; 2 Two or more races, non-Hispanic/Latino), 99 international. Average age 30. 382 applicants, 57% accepted, 89 enrolled. In 2010, 101 master's awarded. *Degree requirements:* For master's, thesis optional. *Application deadline:* For fall admission, 6/1 priority date for domestic students; for spring admission, 12/1 priority date for domestic students. Applications are processed on a rolling basis. Application fee: $50. Electronic applications accepted. *Expenses:* Tuition: Full-time $37,000; part-time $1156 per credit hour. Required fees: $30; $1156 per credit hour. *Financial support:* In 2010–11, research assistantships with partial tuition reimbursements (averaging $4,800 per year), teaching assistantships with partial tuition reimbursements (averaging $4,800 per year) were awarded; fellowships, career-related internships or fieldwork, Federal Work-Study, institutionally sponsored loans, and tuition waivers (partial) also available. Support available to part-time students. Financial award application deadline: 5/31. *Faculty research:* Organizational development, accounting, marketing, finance, human resource management. *Unit head:* Dr. Joseph Sarkis, Dean, 508-793-7406, Fax: 508-793-8822, E-mail: clarkmba@clarku.edu. *Application contact:* Lynn Davis, Enrollment and Marketing Director, 508-793-7406, Fax: 508-793-8822, E-mail: clarkmba@clarku.edu.

Cleveland State University, College of Graduate Studies, Nance College of Business Administration, Department of Computer and Information Science, Cleveland, OH 44115. Offers computer and information science (MCIS); information systems (DBA). Part-time and evening/weekend programs available. *Faculty:* 11 full-time (1 woman), 6 part-time/adjunct (2 women). *Students:* 33 full-time (13 women), 60 part-time (45 women); includes 2 Asian, non-Hispanic/Latino, 64 international. Average age 26. 283 applicants, 60% accepted, 35 enrolled. In 2010, 27 master's, 1 doctorate awarded. Terminal master's awarded for partial completion of doctoral program. *Degree requirements:* For master's, thesis optional; for doctorate, comprehensive exam, thesis/dissertation. *Entrance requirements:* For master's, GRE or GMAT, minimum GPA of 2.75; for doctorate, GRE or GMAT, MBA, MCIS or equivalent. Additional exam requirements/recommendations for international students: Required—TOEFL (minimum score 525 paper-based; 197 computer-based; 78 iBT). *Application deadline:* For fall admission, 7/15 priority date for domestic students, 5/15 priority date for international students; for spring admission, 12/15 priority date for domestic students. Applications are processed on a rolling basis. Application fee: $30. Electronic applications accepted. *Expenses:* Tuition, state resident: full-time $8447; part-time $469 per credit hour. Tuition, nonresident: full-time $16,020; part-time $890 per credit hour. Required fees: $50. *Financial support:* In 2010–11, 21 students received support, including 7

research assistantships with full and partial tuition reimbursements available (averaging $7,800 per year), 2 teaching assistantships with full and partial tuition reimbursements available (averaging $16,000 per year); career-related internships or fieldwork, tuition waivers (full), and unspecified assistantships also available. *Faculty research:* Artificial intelligence, object-oriented analysis, database design, software efficiency, distributed system, geographical information systems. Total annual research expenditures: $7,500. *Unit head:* Dr. Santosh K. Misra, Chairman, 216-687-4760, Fax: 216-687-5448, E-mail: s.misra@csuohio.edu. *Application contact:* Dr. Santosh K. Misra, Chairman, 216-687-4760, Fax: 216-687-5448, E-mail: s.misra@csuohio.edu.

Cleveland State University, College of Graduate Studies, Nance College of Business Administration, Doctor of Business Administration (DBA) Program, Cleveland, OH 44115. Offers business administration (DBA); finance (DBA); information systems (DBA); marketing (DBA); operations management (DBA). *Accreditation:* AACSB. Part-time and evening/weekend programs available. *Faculty:* 50 full-time (11 women). *Students:* 6 full-time (2 women), 31 part-time (6 women); includes 3 Black or African American, non-Hispanic/Latino; 2 Asian, non-Hispanic/Latino, 7 international. Average age 44. 7 applicants. *Degree requirements:* For doctorate, comprehensive exam, thesis/dissertation, oral dissertation defense. *Entrance requirements:* For doctorate, GMAT, MBA or equivalent. Additional exam requirements/recommendations for international students: Required—TOEFL (minimum score 550 paper-based; 213 computer-based; 79 iBT). *Application deadline:* For spring admission, 2/28 priority date for domestic and international students. Application fee: $30. Electronic applications accepted. *Expenses:* Tuition, state resident: full-time $8447; part-time $469 per credit hour. Tuition, nonresident: full-time $16,020; part-time $890 per credit hour. Required fees: $50. *Financial support:* In 2010–11, 5 research assistantships with full tuition reimbursements (averaging $11,700 per year), 1 teaching assistantship with full tuition reimbursement (averaging $11,700 per year) were awarded; tuition waivers (full) and unspecified assistantships also available. *Faculty research:* Supply chain management, international business, strategic management, risk analysis. *Unit head:* Dr. Raj Shekhar G. Javalgi, Director, 216-687-3786, Fax: 216-687-9354, E-mail: r.javalgi@csuohio.edu. *Application contact:* Brenda Wade, Administrative Secretary, 216-687-6952, Fax: 216-687-9257, E-mail: b.wade@csuohio.edu.

College of Charleston, Graduate School, School of Sciences and Mathematics, Program in Computer and Information Sciences, Charleston, SC 29424-0001. Offers MS. Program offered jointly with The Citadel, The Military College of South Carolina. Part-time and evening/weekend programs available. *Faculty:* 11 full-time (3 women), 3 part-time/adjunct (0 women). *Students:* 4 full-time (1 woman), 18 part-time (1 woman); includes 2 minority (1 Black or African American, non-Hispanic/Latino; 1 Asian, non-Hispanic/Latino), 1 international. Average age 29. 10 applicants, 60% accepted, 6 enrolled. In 2010, 9 master's awarded. *Degree requirements:* For master's, thesis optional. *Entrance requirements:* For master's, GRE. Additional exam requirements/recommendations for international students: Required—TOEFL (minimum score 81 iBT). *Application deadline:* For fall admission, 6/1 for domestic students; for spring admission, 11/1 for domestic students. Application fee: $45. Electronic applications accepted. *Financial support:* In 2010–11, research assistantships (averaging $12,400 per year); Federal Work-Study, scholarships/grants, and unspecified assistantships also available. Support available to part-time students. Financial award application deadline: 4/1; financial award applicants required to submit FAFSA. *Unit head:* Dr. Renee McCauley, Director, 843-953-3187, E-mail: mccauleyr@cofc.edu. *Application contact:* Susan Hallatt, Director of Graduate Admissions, 843-953-5614, Fax: 843-953-1434, E-mail: hallatts@cofc.edu.

The College of St. Scholastica, Graduate Studies, Department of Computer Information Systems, Duluth, MN 55811-4199. Offers MA, Certificate. Part-time programs available. Postbaccalaureate distance learning degree programs offered (minimal on-campus study). *Faculty:* 1 full-time (0 women), 4 part-time/adjunct (0 women). *Students:* 8 full-time (4 women), 15 part-time (8 women); includes 2 minority (1 American Indian or Alaska Native, non-Hispanic/Latino; 1 Two or more races, non-Hispanic/Latino). Average age 36. 21 applicants, 81% accepted, 7 enrolled. In 2010, 7 master's awarded. *Degree requirements:* For master's, thesis. *Entrance requirements:* For master's, minimum GPA of 2.8. Additional exam requirements/recommendations for international students: Required—TOEFL (minimum score 550 paper-based; 213 computer-based; 79 iBT). *Application deadline:* For fall admission, 8/1 priority date for domestic students, 8/1 for international students; for spring admission, 11/15 priority date for domestic students, 11/15 for international students. Application fee: $50. *Expenses:* Contact institution. *Financial support:* In 2010–11, 1 teaching assistantship (averaging $2,235 per year) was awarded. Support available to part-time students. Financial award applicants required to submit FAFSA. *Faculty research:* Organization acceptance of software development methodologies. *Unit head:* Brandon Olson, Program Coordinator, 218-723-6199, E-mail: bolson@css.edu. *Application contact:* Lindsay Lahti, Director of Graduate and Extended Studies Recruitment, 218-733-2240, Fax: 218-733-2275, E-mail: gradstudies@css.edu.

Colorado State University, Graduate School, College of Business, Department of Computer Information Systems, Fort Collins, CO 80523-1277. Offers MSBA. Part-time programs available. *Faculty:* 11 full-time (2 women).

Students: Average age 31. In 2010, 11 master's awarded. *Degree requirements:* For master's, thesis or alternative, project. *Entrance requirements:* For master's, GMAT, minimum GPA of 3.0. Additional exam requirements/recommendations for international students: Required—TOEFL (minimum score 565 paper-based; 227 computer-based; 86 iBT). *Application deadline:* For fall admission, 7/15 for domestic students, 4/1 for international students. Applications are processed on a rolling basis. Application fee: $50. Electronic applications accepted. *Expenses:* Tuition, state resident: full-time $7434; part-time $413 per credit. Tuition, nonresident: full-time $19,022; part-time $1057 per credit. Required fees: $1729; $88 per credit. *Financial support:* In 2010–11, 1 student received support, including 1 research assistantship (averaging $10,275 per year); fellowships, teaching assistantships with full and partial tuition reimbursements available, career-related internships or fieldwork, Federal Work-Study, scholarships/grants, traineeships, and unspecified assistantships also available. Support available to part-time students. Financial award application deadline: 3/1; financial award applicants required to submit FAFSA. *Faculty research:* Decision-making, object-oriented design, database research, electronic marketing, e-commerce. Total annual research expenditures: $75,259. *Unit head:* Dr. Jon D. Clark, Chair, 970-491-1618, Fax: 970-491-5205, E-mail: jon.clark@business.colostate.edu. *Application contact:* Dr. John Hoxmeier, Associate Dean of Graduate Programs, 970-491-2142, Fax: 970-491-5205, E-mail: john.hoxmeier@colostate.edu.

Creighton University, Graduate School, Eugene C. Eppley College of Business Administration, Omaha, NE 68178-0001. Offers business administration (MBA); information technology management (MS); securities and portfolio management (MSAPM); JD/MBA; MBA/INR; MBA/MS-ITM; MBA/MSAPM; MD/MBA; MS ITM/JD; Pharm D/MBA. *Accreditation:* AACSB. Part-time and evening/weekend programs available. Postbaccalaureate distance learning degree programs offered (minimal on-campus study). *Faculty:* 37 full-time (7 women). *Students:* 42 full-time (13 women), 268 part-time (51 women); includes 32 minority (17 Black or African American, non-Hispanic/Latino; 12 Asian, non-Hispanic/Latino; 3 Hispanic/Latino), 20 international. Average age 30. 133 applicants, 80% accepted, 100 enrolled. In 2010, 77 master's awarded. *Degree requirements:* For master's, thesis optional. *Entrance requirements:* For master's, GMAT, resume, 2 letters of recommendation. Additional exam requirements/recommendations for international students: Required—TOEFL (minimum score 550 paper-based; 213 computer-based; 80 iBT). *Application deadline:* For fall admission, 7/1 priority date for domestic students, 3/1 for international students; for winter admission, 10/1 priority date for domestic students, 7/1 for international students; for spring admission, 4/1 priority date for domestic students, 10/1 for international students. Applications are processed on a rolling basis. Application fee: $50. Electronic applications accepted. *Expenses:* Tuition: Full-time $12,168; part-time $676 per credit hour. Required fees: $131 per semester. Tuition and fees vary according to program. *Financial support:* In 2010–11, 10 fellowships with partial tuition reimbursements (averaging $8,112 per year) were awarded; career-related internships or fieldwork, tuition waivers (partial), and unspecified assistantships also available. Financial award application deadline: 3/1. *Faculty research:* Small business issues, economics. *Unit head:* Dr. Deborah Wells, Associate Dean for Graduate Programs, 402-280-2841, E-mail: deborahwells@creighton.edu. *Application contact:* Gail Hafer, Assistant Dean, 402-280-2829, Fax: 402-280-2172, E-mail: ghafer@creighton.edu.

Daemen College, Department of Accounting/Information Systems, Amherst, NY 14226-3592. Offers global business (MS), including accounting, global business, management information systems, marketing. Part-time and evening/weekend programs available. *Faculty:* 1 full-time (0 women), 1 part-time/adjunct (0 women). *Students:* 19 full-time (16 women), 5 part-time (1 woman); includes 1 minority (Black or African American, non-Hispanic/Latino), 18 international. Average age 28. In 2010, 12 master's awarded. *Degree requirements:* For master's, minimum GPA of 3.0. *Entrance requirements:* For master's, GMAT if undergraduate GPA is less than 3.0, 2 letters of recommendation; goal statement; transcripts; demonstration of satisfactory oral and written English. Additional exam requirements/recommendations for international students: Required—TOEFL (minimum score 500 paper-based; 173 computer-based; 63 iBT), IELTS (minimum score 5.5). *Application deadline:* For fall admission, 3/1 priority date for domestic and international students; for spring admission, 10/1 priority date for domestic and international students. Applications are processed on a rolling basis. Application fee: $25. Electronic applications accepted. *Expenses:* Tuition: Part-time $830 per credit hour. Tuition and fees vary according to course load and reciprocity agreements. *Financial support:* Institutionally sponsored loans, scholarships/grants, and scholarships available. Financial award application deadline: 2/15; financial award applicants required to submit FAFSA. *Faculty research:* Internationalization of small business, cultural influences on business practices, international human resource practices. *Unit head:* S. Sgt. Sharlene S. Buszka, Chair, 716-839-8428, Fax: 716-839-8261, E-mail: sbuszka@daemen.edu. *Application contact:* Scott Rowe, Associate Director of Graduate Admissions, 716-839-8225, Fax: 716-839-8229, E-mail: srowe@daemen.edu.

DePaul University, Charles H. Kellstadt Graduate School of Business, School of Accountancy and Management Information Systems, Chicago, IL 60604-2287. Offers accountancy (M Acc, MSA); business information technology (MS); e-business (MBA, MS); financial management and control (MBA);

management accounting (MBA); management information systems (MBA); taxation (MST). Part-time and evening/weekend programs available. *Faculty:* 30 full-time (9 women), 54 part-time/adjunct (7 women). *Students:* 207 full-time (112 women), 208 part-time (92 women); includes 7 Black or African American, non-Hispanic/Latino; 34 Asian, non-Hispanic/Latino; 19 Hispanic/Latino; 2 Two or more races, non-Hispanic/Latino, 76 international. In 2010, 141 master's awarded. *Entrance requirements:* For master's, GMAT, 2 letters of recommendation, resume. Additional exam requirements/recommendations for international students: Required—TOEFL (minimum score 550 paper-based; 213 computer-based). *Application deadline:* For fall admission, 7/1 for domestic students; for winter admission, 10/1 for domestic students; for spring admission, 2/1 for domestic students. Applications are processed on a rolling basis. Application fee: $60. *Financial support:* In 2010–11, 7 research assistantships with full tuition reimbursements (averaging $4,100 per year) were awarded; institutionally sponsored loans also available. Financial award application deadline: 4/2. *Faculty research:* Tax policy, property transactions, stock options as compensation, standards setting, activity-based costing in health care. *Unit head:* Kevin Stevens, Director, 312-362-6989, E-mail: kstevens@depaul.edu. *Application contact:* Christopher E. Kinsella, Director of Cohort MBA Programs, 312-362-8810, Fax: 312-362-6677, E-mail: kgsb@depaul.edu.

DePaul University, College of Computing and Digital Media, Chicago, IL 60604. Offers animation (MA, MFA); applied technology (MS); business information technology (MS); cinema (MFA); cinema production (MS); computational finance (MS); computer and information sciences (PhD); computer game development (MS); computer graphics and motion technology (MS); computer information and network security (MS); computer science (MS); e-commerce technology (MS); human-computer interaction (MS); information systems (MS); information technology (MA); information technology project management (MS); network engineering and management (MS); predictive analytics (MS); screenwriting (MFA); software engineering (MS); JD/MA; JD/MS. Part-time and evening/weekend programs available. Postbaccalaureate distance learning degree programs offered (no on-campus study). *Faculty:* 51 full-time (11 women), 50 part-time/adjunct (9 women). *Students:* 952 full-time (230 women), 927 part-time (226 women); includes 557 minority (205 Black or African American, non-Hispanic/Latino; 2 American Indian or Alaska Native, non-Hispanic/Latino; 167 Asian, non-Hispanic/Latino; 136 Hispanic/Latino; 7 Native Hawaiian or other Pacific Islander, non-Hispanic/Latino; 40 Two or more races, non-Hispanic/Latino), 292 international. Average age 31. 896 applicants, 70% accepted, 324 enrolled. In 2010, 417 master's, 6 doctorates awarded. *Degree requirements:* For master's, thesis (for some programs); for doctorate, comprehensive exam, thesis/dissertation. *Entrance requirements:* For master's, GRE or GMAT (MS in computational finance only), bachelor's degree, resume (MS in predictive analytics only), IT experience (MS in information technology project management only), portfolio review (MFA); for doctorate, GRE, master's degree in computer science. Additional exam requirements/recommendations for international students: Required—TOEFL (minimum score 550 paper-based; 213 computer-based; 80 iBT), IELTS (minimum score 6.5), Pearson Test of English (minimum score 53). *Application deadline:* For fall admission, 8/15 priority date for domestic students, 6/1 priority date for international students; for winter admission, 12/15 priority date for domestic students, 9/15 priority date for international students; for spring admission, 3/1 priority date for domestic students, 12/15 priority date for international students. Applications are processed on a rolling basis. Application fee: $25. Electronic applications accepted. *Expenses:* Contact institution. *Financial support:* In 2010–11, 102 students received support, including 4 fellowships with full tuition reimbursements available (averaging $24,435 per year), 6 research assistantships (averaging $21,100 per year), 92 teaching assistantships with full and partial tuition reimbursements available (averaging $6,904 per year); Federal Work-Study, scholarships/grants, tuition waivers (full and partial), and unspecified assistantships also available. Support available to part-time students. Financial award application deadline: 4/30; financial award applicants required to submit FAFSA. *Faculty research:* Bioinformatics, visual computing, graphics and animation, high performance and scientific computing, databases. Total annual research expenditures: $1.4 million. *Unit head:* Dr. David Miller, Dean, 312-362-8381, Fax: 312-362-5185. *Application contact:* Dr. Liz Friedman, Assistant Dean of Student Services, 312-362-8714, Fax: 312-362-5179, E-mail: efriedm2@cdm.depaul.edu.

DeSales University, Graduate Division, Program in Business Administration, Center Valley, PA 18034-9568. Offers accounting (MBA); computer information systems (MBA); finance (MBA); health care systems management (MBA); health care systems management (online) (MBA); human resource management (MBA); management (MBA); management (online) (MBA); marketing (MBA); marketing (online) (MBA); physician's track (MBA); project management (MBA); project management (online) (MBA); self-design (MBA); self-design (online) (MBA); MSN/MBA. *Accreditation:* ACBSP. Part-time programs available. Postbaccalaureate distance learning degree programs offered (no on-campus study). *Entrance requirements:* For master's, GMAT, minimum GPA of 3.0, 2 years of work experience. Additional exam requirements/recommendations for international students: Required—TOEFL. *Application deadline:* Applications are processed on a rolling basis. Application fee: $35. Electronic applications accepted.

Expenses: Tuition: Full-time $18,200; part-time $690 per credit. Required fees: $1200. *Faculty research:* Quality improvement, executive development, productivity, cross-cultural managerial differences, leadership. *Unit head:* Dr. David Gilfoil, Director, 610-282-1100 Ext. 1828, Fax: 610-282-2869, E-mail: david.gilfoil@desales.edu. *Application contact:* Caryn Stopper, Director of Graduate Admissions, 610-282-1100 Ext. 1768, Fax: 610-282-0525, E-mail: caryn.stopper@desales.edu.

Dowling College, School of Business, Oakdale, NY 11769-1999. Offers aviation management (MBA, Certificate); banking and finance (MBA, Certificate); corporate finance (MBA); financial planning (Certificate); health care management (MBA, Certificate); human resource management (Certificate); information systems management (MBA); management and leadership (MBA); marketing (Certificate); project management (Certificate); public management (MBA, Certificate); sport, event and entertainment management (Certificate); JD/MBA. Part-time and evening/weekend programs available. *Faculty:* 10 full-time (4 women), 56 part-time/adjunct (7 women). *Students:* 295 full-time (131 women), 460 part-time (206 women); includes 219 minority (97 Black or African American, non-Hispanic/Latino; 14 Asian, non-Hispanic/Latino; 35 Hispanic/Latino; 73 Native Hawaiian or other Pacific Islander, non-Hispanic/Latino), 3 international. Average age 33. 327 applicants, 85% accepted, 160 enrolled. In 2010, 33 master's, 1 other advanced degree awarded. *Degree requirements:* For master's, comprehensive exam, thesis optional. *Entrance requirements:* For master's, minimum GPA of 2.8, 2 letters of recommendation, courses in accounting and finance or seminar in accounting/finance, resume. Additional exam requirements/recommendations for international students: Required—TOEFL (minimum score 550 paper-based). *Application deadline:* For fall admission, 9/1 priority date for domestic students; for winter admission, 1/1 priority date for domestic students; for spring admission, 2/1 priority date for domestic students. Applications are processed on a rolling basis. Application fee: $50. Electronic applications accepted. *Expenses:* Tuition: Part-time $884 per credit hour. Part-time tuition and fees vary according to degree level and campus/location. *Financial support:* Career-related internships or fieldwork and Federal Work-Study available. Support available to part-time students. Financial award application deadline: 6/30; financial award applicants required to submit FAFSA. *Faculty research:* International finance, computer applications, labor relations, executive development. *Unit head:* Antonia Loschiavo, Assistant Dean, 631-244-3266, Fax: 631-244-1018, E-mail: loschiat@dowling.edu. *Application contact:* Ronnie S. Macdonald, Assistant Vice President for Enrollment Services/Dean of Admissions, 631-244-3357, Fax: 631-244-1059, E-mail: macdonar@dowling.edu.

Duquesne University, John F. Donahue Graduate School of Business, Pittsburgh, PA 15282-0001. Offers accountancy (MS); business administration (MBA); information systems management (MSISM); sustainability (MBA); JD/MBA; MBA/MA; MBA/MES; MBA/MHMS; MBA/MLLS; MBA/MS; MBA/MSN. *Accreditation:* AACSB. Part-time and evening/weekend programs available. *Faculty:* 24 full-time (5 women), 14 part-time/adjunct (0 women). *Students:* 97 full-time (45 women), 234 part-time (91 women); includes 5 Black or African American, non-Hispanic/Latino; 1 Asian, non-Hispanic/Latino; 2 Hispanic/Latino; 4 Native Hawaiian or other Pacific Islander, non-Hispanic/Latino, 29 international. Average age 31. 289 applicants, 43% accepted, 82 enrolled. In 2010, 120 master's awarded. *Entrance requirements:* For master's, GMAT, 2 letters of recommendation, current resume. Additional exam requirements/recommendations for international students: Required—TOEFL (minimum score 577 paper-based; 233 computer-based; 90 iBT); Recommended—TWE. *Application deadline:* For fall admission, 5/1 priority date for domestic students, 5/1 for international students; for spring admission, 10/1 for domestic and international students. Applications are processed on a rolling basis. Application fee: $0. Electronic applications accepted. *Expenses:* Tuition: Part-time $884 per credit. Required fees: $84 per credit. Tuition and fees vary according to course load. *Financial support:* In 2010–11, 40 students received support, including 12 fellowships with partial tuition reimbursements available, 28 research assistantships with partial tuition reimbursements available; career-related internships or fieldwork, scholarships/grants, and unspecified assistantships also available. Financial award application deadline: 7/1; financial award applicants required to submit FAFSA. *Faculty research:* International business, investment management, business ethics, technology management, supply chain management, business strategy, finance. *Unit head:* Alan R. Miciak, Dean, 412-396-5848, Fax: 412-396-5304, E-mail: miciaka@duq.edu. *Application contact:* Patricia Moore, Assistant Director, 412-396-6276, Fax: 412-396-1726, E-mail: moorep@duq.edu.

Duquesne University, School of Leadership and Professional Advancement, Pittsburgh, PA 15282-0001. Offers leadership (MS), including business ethics, community leadership, global leadership, information technology, leadership, liberal studies, professional administration, sports leadership. Part-time and evening/weekend programs available. Postbaccalaureate distance learning degree programs offered (no on-campus study). *Faculty:* 1 full-time (0 women), 70 part-time/adjunct (35 women). *Students:* 275 full-time, 171 part-time; includes 20 Black or African American, non-Hispanic/Latino; 1 American Indian or Alaska Native, non-Hispanic/Latino; 6 Asian, non-Hispanic/Latino; 3 Hispanic/Latino. Average age 31. 161 applicants, 73% accepted, 103 enrolled. In 2010, 108 master's awarded. *Degree requirements:*

For master's, capstone course. *Entrance requirements:* For master's, professional work experience, 500-word essay. Additional exam requirements/recommendations for international students: Required—TOEFL. *Application deadline:* Applications are processed on a rolling basis. Application fee: $0. Electronic applications accepted. *Expenses:* Tuition: Part-time $884 per credit. Required fees: $84 per credit. Tuition and fees vary according to course load. *Financial support:* Applicants required to submit FAFSA. *Unit head:* Dr. Dorothy Bassett, Dean, 412-396-2141, Fax: 412-396-4711, E-mail: bassettd@duq.edu. *Application contact:* Marianne Leister, Director of Student Services, 412-396-4933, Fax: 412-396-5072, E-mail: leister@duq.edu.

Eastern Michigan University, Graduate School, College of Business, Department of Computer Information Systems, Ypsilanti, MI 48197. Offers information systems (MSIS). Part-time and evening/weekend programs available. *Faculty:* 13 full-time (1 woman). *Students:* 28 full-time (9 women), 16 part-time (6 women); includes 4 minority (2 Black or African American, non-Hispanic/Latino; 2 Asian, non-Hispanic/Latino), 33 international. Average age 26. 48 applicants, 48% accepted, 6 enrolled. In 2010, 28 master's awarded. *Entrance requirements:* Additional exam requirements/recommendations for international students: Required—TOEFL. *Application deadline:* For fall admission, 5/15 priority date for domestic students, 5/1 priority date for international students; for winter admission, 10/15 priority date for domestic students, 10/1 priority date for international students; for spring admission, 3/15 priority date for domestic students, 3/1 priority date for international students. Applications are processed on a rolling basis. Application fee: $35. *Financial support:* Fellowships, research assistantships with full tuition reimbursements, teaching assistantships with full tuition reimbursements, career-related internships or fieldwork, Federal Work-Study, institutionally sponsored loans, scholarships/grants, tuition waivers (partial), and unspecified assistantships available. Support available to part-time students. Financial award applicants required to submit FAFSA. *Unit head:* Dr. S. Imtiaz Ahmad, Department Head, 734-487-2454, Fax: 734-487-1941, E-mail: imtiaz.ahmad@emich.edu. *Application contact:* Dr. S. Imtiaz Ahmad, Department Head, 734-487-2454, Fax: 734-487-1941, E-mail: imtiaz.ahmad@emich.edu.

Eastern Michigan University, Graduate School, College of Business, Programs in Business Administration, Ypsilanti, MI 48197. Offers business administration (MBA, Graduate Certificate); computer information systems (Graduate Certificate); e-business (MBA, Graduate Certificate); enterprise business intelligence (MBA); entrepreneurship (MBA, Graduate Certificate); finance (MBA, Graduate Certificate); human resources (MBA); human resources management (Graduate Certificate); information systems (MBA); internal auditing (MBA); international business (MBA, Graduate Certificate); marketing management (Graduate Certificate); nonprofit management (MBA); organizational development (Graduate Certificate); supply chain management (MBA, Graduate Certificate). *Accreditation:* AACSB. Part-time programs available. Postbaccalaureate distance learning degree programs offered (no on-campus study). *Students:* 149 full-time (66 women), 456 part-time (232 women); includes 146 minority (109 Black or African American, non-Hispanic/Latino; 4 American Indian or Alaska Native, non-Hispanic/Latino; 27 Asian, non-Hispanic/Latino; 6 Hispanic/Latino), 105 international. Average age 32. 330 applicants, 64% accepted, 150 enrolled. In 2010, 128 master's, 53 other advanced degrees awarded. *Entrance requirements:* For master's, GMAT (minimum score 450), minimum cumulative undergraduate GPA of 2.75. Additional exam requirements/recommendations for international students: Required—TOEFL. *Application deadline:* For fall admission, 5/15 for domestic students, 5/1 for international students; for winter admission, 10/15 for domestic students, 10/1 for international students; for spring admission, 3/15 for domestic students, 3/1 for international students. Applications are processed on a rolling basis. Application fee: $35. *Financial support:* Fellowships, research assistantships with full tuition reimbursements, teaching assistantships with full tuition reimbursements, career-related internships or fieldwork, Federal Work-Study, institutionally sponsored loans, scholarships/grants, tuition waivers (partial), and unspecified assistantships available. Support available to part-time students. Financial award applicants required to submit FAFSA. *Unit head:* K. Michelle Henry, Interim Director, Graduate Programs, 734-487-4444, Fax: 734-483-1316, E-mail: mhenry1@emich.edu. *Application contact:* Beste Windes, Advisor, 734-487-4444, Fax: 734-483-1316, E-mail: bwindes@emich.edu.

East Tennessee State University, School of Graduate Studies, College of Business and Technology, Department of Computer and Information Sciences, Johnson City, TN 37614. Offers applied computer science (MS); information technology (MS). Part-time and evening/weekend programs available. *Faculty:* 15 full-time (3 women). *Students:* 31 full-time (4 women), 21 part-time (4 women); includes 2 minority (1 Asian, non-Hispanic/Latino; 1 Hispanic/Latino), 9 international. Average age 30. 42 applicants, 55% accepted, 15 enrolled. In 2010, 18 master's awarded. *Degree requirements:* For master's, comprehensive exam, thesis optional, capstone. *Entrance requirements:* For master's, GRE General Test, minimum GPA of 2.5. Additional exam requirements/recommendations for international students: Required—TOEFL (minimum score 550 paper-based; 213 computer-based; 79 iBT). *Application deadline:* For fall admission, 6/1 priority date for domestic students, 4/30 for international students; for spring admission, 11/1 for domestic students, 9/30 for international students. Application fee: $25 ($35 for international students). Electronic applications accepted. *Financial support:* In 2010–11, 13 research assistantships with full tuition reimbursements (averaging $9,000 per year), 10 teaching assistantships with full tuition reimbursements (averaging $9,000 per year) were awarded; career-related internships or fieldwork, institutionally sponsored loans, scholarships/grants, and unspecified assistantships also available. Financial award application deadline: 7/1; financial award applicants required to submit FAFSA. *Faculty research:* Operating systems, database design, artificial intelligence, simulation, parallel algorithms. Total annual research expenditures: $1,270. *Unit head:* Dr. Terry Countermine, Chair, 423-439-5332, Fax: 423-439-7119, E-mail: counter@etsu.edu. *Application contact:* Dr. Terry Countermine, Chair, 423-439-5332, Fax: 423-439-7119, E-mail: counter@etsu.edu.

Emory University, Goizueta Business School, Doctoral Program in Business, Atlanta, GA 30322-1100. Offers accounting (PhD); finance (PhD); information systems (PhD); marketing (PhD); organization and management (PhD). *Faculty:* 55 full-time (11 women). *Students:* 32 full-time (17 women); includes 1 Black or African American, non-Hispanic/Latino; 17 Asian, non-Hispanic/Latino; 1 Hispanic/Latino. Average age 29. 218 applicants, 9% accepted, 9 enrolled. In 2010, 8 doctorates awarded. *Degree requirements:* For doctorate, comprehensive exam, thesis/dissertation. *Entrance requirements:* For doctorate, GMAT (strongly preferred) or GRE. Additional exam requirements/recommendations for international students: Required—TOEFL (minimum score 250 computer-based). *Application deadline:* For fall admission, 1/3 priority date for domestic students, 1/1 priority date for international students. Application fee: $50. Electronic applications accepted. *Expenses:* Tuition: Full-time $33,800. Required fees: $1300. *Financial support:* In 2010–11, 32 students received support. *Unit head:* Dr. Lawrence Benveniste, Dean, 404-727-6377, Fax: 404-727-0868, E-mail: larry_benveniste@bus.emory.edu. Application contact: Allison Gilmore, Director of Admissions & Student Services, 404-727-6353, Fax: 404-727-5337, E-mail: phd@bus.emory.edu.

Endicott College, Van Loan School of Graduate and Professional Studies, Program in Information Technology, Beverly, MA 01915-2096. Offers MSIT. *Faculty:* 4 part-time/adjunct (0 women). *Students:* 8 part-time (2 women). Average age 34. 4 applicants, 75% accepted, 3 enrolled. *Degree requirements:* For master's, thesis. *Entrance requirements:* For master's, GRE or MAT, two letters of recommendation. Additional exam requirements/recommendations for international students: Required—TOEFL. Application fee: $50. *Expenses:* Contact institution. *Financial support:* Applicants required to submit FAFSA. *Unit head:* Dr. Richard Benedetto, Associate Dean of Graduate School, 978-232-2744, Fax: 978-232-3000, E-mail: rbenedet@endicott.edu. *Application contact:* Richard Benedetto, Associate Dean of Graduate School, 978-232-2744, Fax: 978-232-3000, E-mail: rbenedet@endicott.edu.

Fairfield University, Charles F. Dolan School of Business, Fairfield, CT 06824-5195. Offers accounting (MBA, MS, CAS); accounting information systems (MBA); entrepreneurship (MBA); finance (MBA, MS, CAS); general management (MBA, CAS); human resource management (MBA, CAS); information systems and operations (MBA); information systems and operations management (CAS); international business (MBA, CAS); marketing (MBA, CAS); taxation (MBA, CAS). *Accreditation:* AACSB. Part-time and evening/weekend programs available. *Faculty:* 42 full-time (15 women), 8 part-time/adjunct (1 woman). *Students:* 89 full-time (32 women), 127 part-time (54 women); includes 4 Black or African American, non-Hispanic/Latino; 2 Asian, non-Hispanic/Latino; 4 Hispanic/Latino; 1 Two or more races, non-Hispanic/Latino, 17 international. Average age 29. 108 applicants, 62% accepted, 46 enrolled. In 2010, 79 master's awarded. *Degree requirements:* For master's, capstone course. *Entrance requirements:* For master's, GMAT (minimum score 500), 2 letters of reference, resume, minimum GPA of 3.0. Additional exam requirements/recommendations for international students: Required—TOEFL (minimum score 550 paper-based; 213 computer-based; 80 iBT). *Application deadline:* For fall admission, 5/15 for international students; for spring admission, 10/15 for international students. Applications are processed on a rolling basis. Application fee: $60. Electronic applications accepted. *Expenses:* Contact institution. *Financial support:* In 2010–11, 48 students received support. Scholarships/grants, unspecified assistantships, and merit based one-time entrance scholarship available. Financial award applicants required to submit FAFSA. *Faculty research:* Optimization strategies, international finance, consumer behavior, financial market volatility, Internet marketing, supply chain analysis, tax issues. Total annual research expenditures: $50,000. *Unit head:* Dr. Norman A. Solomon, Dean, 203-254-4000 Ext. 4070, Fax: 203-254-4105, E-mail: nsolomon@fairfield.edu. *Application contact:* Marianne Gumpper, Director of Graduate and Continuing Studies Admissions, 203-254-4184, Fax: 203-254-4073, E-mail: gradadmis@fairfield.edu.

Fairleigh Dickinson University, Metropolitan Campus, Silberman College of Business, Departments of Management, Marketing, and Entrepreneurial Studies, Program in Management, Teaneck, NJ 07666-1914. Offers management (MBA); management information systems (Certificate). *Accreditation:* AACSB. *Students:* 28 full-time (11 women), 9 part-time (3 women), 22 international. Average age 28. 100 applicants, 52% accepted, 14 enrolled. In 2010, 18 master's awarded. *Application deadline:* Applications are processed on a rolling basis. Application fee: $40. *Application contact:* Susan Brooman, University Director of Graduate Admissions, 201-692-2554, Fax: 201-692-2560, E-mail: globaleducation@fdu.edu.

Fairleigh Dickinson University, Metropolitan Campus, University College: Arts, Sciences, and Professional Studies, School of Computer Sciences and Engineering, Program in Management Information Systems, Teaneck, NJ 07666-1914. Offers MS. *Students:* 10 full-time (2 women), 13 part-time (5 women), 9 international. Average age 31. 51 applicants, 53% accepted, 7 enrolled. In 2010, 8 master's awarded. *Application deadline:* Applications are processed on a rolling basis. Application fee: $40. *Application contact:* Susan Brooman, University Director of Graduate Admissions, 201-692-2554, Fax: 201-692-2560, E-mail: globaleducation@fdu.edu.

Ferris State University, College of Business, Big Rapids, MI 49307. Offers application development (MSISM); business intelligence and informatics (MBA); database administration (MSISM); design and innovation management process (MBA); e-business (MSISM); networking (MSISM); quality management (MBA); security (MSISM). *Accreditation:* ACBSP. Part-time and evening/weekend programs available. *Faculty:* 10 full-time (3 women), 2 part-time/adjunct (both women). *Students:* 34 full-time (9 women), 112 part-time (55 women); includes 3 Black or African American, non-Hispanic/Latino; 4 American Indian or Alaska Native, non-Hispanic/Latino; 3 Asian, non-Hispanic/Latino; 3 Hispanic/Latino; 4 Two or more races, non-Hispanic/Latino, 16 international. Average age 32. 68 applicants, 35% accepted, 15 enrolled. In 2010, 62 master's awarded. *Degree requirements:* For master's, comprehensive exam, thesis (for MSISM). *Entrance requirements:* For master's, GRE or GMAT (waived if GPA is 3.5 or better), minimum GPA of 3.0 in junior/senior level classes, 2.75 overall; writing sample; 3 letters of reference; resume. Additional exam requirements/recommendations for international students: Required—TOEFL (minimum score 500 paper-based; 173 computer-based; 67 iBT). *Application deadline:* For fall admission, 7/1 priority date for domestic students, 6/15 for international students; for winter admission, 11/1 priority date for domestic students, 10/15 for international students; for spring admission, 3/1 priority date for domestic students, 2/15 for international students. Applications are processed on a rolling basis. Application fee: $30. Electronic applications accepted. *Financial support:* Career-related internships or fieldwork, Federal Work-Study, scholarships/grants, and unspecified assistantships available. Support available to part-time students. Financial award application deadline: 3/15; financial award applicants required to submit FAFSA. *Faculty research:* Quality improvement, client/server end-user computing, information management and policy, security, digital forensics. *Unit head:* Dr. David Steenstra, Department Chair, 231-591-2168, Fax: 231-591-3548, E-mail: yosts@ferris.edu. *Application contact:* Shannon Yost, Department Secretary, 231-591-2168, Fax: 231-591-3548, E-mail: yosts@ferris.edu.

Florida Atlantic University, College of Business, Department of Information Technology and Operations Management, Boca Raton, FL 33431-0991. Offers management information systems (MS). *Faculty:* 18 full-time (7 women), 5 part-time/adjunct (0 women). *Students:* 37 full-time (22 women), 38 part-time (23 women); includes 30 minority (13 Black or African American, non-Hispanic/Latino; 5 Asian, non-Hispanic/Latino; 9 Hispanic/Latino; 3 Two or more races, non-Hispanic/Latino), 5 international. Average age 30. 25 applicants, 36% accepted, 6 enrolled. In 2010, 3 master's awarded. *Degree requirements:* For master's, thesis optional. *Entrance requirements:* For master's, GMAT, minimum GPA of 3.0. Additional exam requirements/recommendations for international students: Required—TOEFL (minimum score 600 paper-based; 250 computer-based). *Application deadline:* For fall admission, 7/1 priority date for domestic students, 2/15 priority date for international students; for winter admission, 11/1 priority date for domestic students, 8/15 priority date for international students; for spring admission, 4/1 priority date for domestic students, 1/15 priority date for international students. Applications are processed on a rolling basis. Application fee: $30. Electronic applications accepted. *Expenses:* Tuition, area resident: Part-time $319.96 per credit. Tuition, state resident: part-time $319.96 per credit. Tuition, nonresident: part-time $926.42 per credit. *Financial support:* Research assistantships, teaching assistantships, career-related internships or fieldwork, Federal Work-Study, institutionally sponsored loans, tuition waivers (partial), and unspecified assistantships available. Support available to part-time students. Financial award application deadline: 3/1; financial award applicants required to submit FAFSA. *Unit head:* Dr. Paul Hart, Chair, 561-297-3675, E-mail: hart@fau.edu. *Application contact:* Dr. Paul Hart, Chair, 561-297-3675, E-mail: hart@fau.edu.

Florida Institute of Technology, Graduate Programs, Extended Studies Division, Melbourne, FL 32901-6975. Offers acquisition and contract management (MS); aerospace engineering (MS); business administration (MBA); computer information systems (MS); computer science (MS); electrical engineering (MS); engineering management (MS); human resources management (MS); logistics management (MS), including humanitarian and disaster relief logistics; management (MS), including acquisition and contract management, e-business, human resources management, information systems, logistics management, management, transportation management; material acquisition management (MS); mechanical engineering (MS); operations research (MS); project management (MS), including information systems, operations research; public administration (MPA); quality management (MS); software engineering (MS); space systems (MS); space systems management (MS); systems management (MS), including information systems, operations research. Part-time and evening/weekend programs available.

Postbaccalaureate distance learning degree programs offered (no on-campus study). *Faculty:* 11 full-time (3 women), 118 part-time/adjunct (24 women). *Students:* 69 full-time (23 women), 907 part-time (369 women); includes 385 minority (242 Black or African American, non-Hispanic/Latino; 15 American Indian or Alaska Native, non-Hispanic/Latino; 44 Asian, non-Hispanic/Latino; 52 Hispanic/Latino; 3 Native Hawaiian or other Pacific Islander, non-Hispanic/Latino; 29 Two or more races, non-Hispanic/Latino), 17 international. 517 applicants, 49% accepted, 245 enrolled. In 2010, 430 degrees awarded. *Degree requirements:* For master's, comprehensive exam (for some programs), capstone course. *Entrance requirements:* For master's, GMAT or resume showing 8 years of supervised experience, minimum GPA of 3.0, 2 letters of recommendation, resume. Additional exam requirements/recommendations for international students: Required—TOEFL (minimum score 550 paper-based; 213 computer-based; 79 iBT). *Application deadline:* For fall admission, 4/1 for international students; for spring admission, 9/30 for international students. Applications are processed on a rolling basis. Application fee: $50. Electronic applications accepted. *Expenses:* Contact institution. *Financial support:* Application deadline: 3/1. *Unit head:* Dr. Theodore Richardson, Senior Associate Dean, 321-674-8123, Fax: 321-674-7597, E-mail: trichardson@fit.edu. *Application contact:* Carolyn Farrior, Director of Graduate Admissions, Online Learning and Off-Campus Programs, 321-674-7118, Fax: 321-674-8216, E-mail: cfarrior@fit.edu.

Florida Institute of Technology, Graduate Programs, Nathan M. Bisk College of Business, Online Programs, Melbourne, FL 32901-6975. Offers accounting (MBA); accounting and finance (MBA); finance (MBA); healthcare management (MBA); information technology (MS); information technology management (MBA); Internet marketing (MBA); management (MBA); marketing (MBA); project management (MBA). Part-time and evening/weekend programs available. Postbaccalaureate distance learning degree programs offered (no on-campus study). *Faculty:* 32 part-time/adjunct (8 women). *Students:* 4 full-time (1 woman), 1,062 part-time (499 women); includes 373 minority (244 Black or African American, non-Hispanic/Latino; 8 American Indian or Alaska Native, non-Hispanic/Latino; 37 Asian, non-Hispanic/Latino; 76 Hispanic/Latino; 8 Native Hawaiian or other Pacific Islander, non-Hispanic/Latino), 39 international. Average age 37. 299 applicants, 167 enrolled. In 2010, 134 master's awarded. *Entrance requirements:* For master's, GMAT or resume showing 8 years of supervised experience, 2 letters of recommendation, resume, competency in math past college algebra. Additional exam requirements/recommendations for international students: Required—TOEFL (minimum score 550 paper-based; 213 computer-based; 79 iBT). *Application deadline:* For fall admission, 4/1 for international students; for spring admission, 9/30 for international students. Applications are processed on a rolling basis. Application fee: $50. Electronic applications accepted. *Expenses:* Contact institution. *Financial support:* Available to part-time students. Application deadline: 3/1. *Unit head:* Dr. Mary S. Bonhomme, Dean, Florida Tech Online Associate Provost for Online Learning, 321-674-8202, Fax: 321-674-8216, E-mail: bonhomme@fit.edu. *Application contact:* Carolyn Farrior, Director of Graduate Admissions Online Learning and Off Campus Programs, 321-674-7118, Fax: 321-674-8216, E-mail: cfarrior@fit.edu.

Florida International University, Alvah H. Chapman, Jr. Graduate School of Business, Department of Decision Sciences and Information Systems, Miami, FL 33199. Offers MSMIS. Part-time and evening/weekend programs available. *Faculty:* 17 full-time (7 women), 3 part-time/adjunct (1 woman). *Students:* 57 full-time (16 women), 4 part-time (0 women); includes 5 Black or African American, non-Hispanic/Latino; 39 Hispanic/Latino, 4 international. Average age 30. 159 applicants, 45% accepted. In 2010, 42 master's awarded. *Entrance requirements:* For master's, GMAT or GRE, minimum GPA of 3.0 (upper-level coursework); letter of intent; resume. Additional exam requirements/recommendations for international students: Required—TOEFL (minimum score 550 paper-based; 213 computer-based; 80 iBT) or IELTS. *Application deadline:* For fall admission, 6/1 for domestic students, 4/1 for international students; for spring admission, 10/1 for domestic students, 9/1 for international students. Applications are processed on a rolling basis. Application fee: $30. Electronic applications accepted. *Expenses:* Contact institution. *Financial support:* Institutionally sponsored loans and scholarships/grants available. Financial award application deadline: 3/1; financial award applicants required to submit FAFSA. *Faculty research:* Artificial intelligence, data warehouses, operations management. *Unit head:* Dr. Christos Koulamas, Chair, 305-348-2830, Fax: 305-348-4126, E-mail: koulamas@fiu.edu. *Application contact:* Zuzana Hlavacova, Assistant Program Director, 305-348-6852, Fax: 305-348-7204, E-mail: zuzana.hlavacova@business.fiu.edu.

Florida State University, The Graduate School, College of Business, Tallahassee, FL 32306-1110. Offers accounting (M Acc), including accounting information services, assurance services, corporate accounting, taxation; business administration (MBA, PhD), including accounting (PhD), finance (PhD), management information systems (PhD), marketing (PhD), organizational behavior (PhD), risk management and insurance (PhD), strategic management (PhD); finance (MS); insurance (MSM); management information systems (MS); JD/MBA; MSW/MBA. *Accreditation:* AACSB. Part-time programs available. Postbaccalaureate distance learning degree programs offered (no on-campus study). *Faculty:* 107 full-time (31 women). *Students:*

196 full-time (76 women), 310 part-time (109 women); includes 27 Black or African American, non-Hispanic/Latino; 1 American Indian or Alaska Native, non-Hispanic/Latino; 31 Asian, non-Hispanic/Latino; 30 Hispanic/Latino. Average age 30. 702 applicants, 33% accepted, 205 enrolled. In 2010, 268 master's, 17 doctorates awarded. Terminal master's awarded for partial completion of doctoral program. *Degree requirements:* For doctorate, comprehensive exam, thesis/dissertation. *Entrance requirements:* For master's, GMAT, work experience (MBA, MS), minimum GPA of 3.0, letters of recommendation; for doctorate, GMAT, minimum graduate GPA of 3.5, letters of recommendation. Additional exam requirements/recommendations for international students: Required—TOEFL (minimum score 600 paper-based; 80 computer-based); Recommended—IELTS (minimum score 6.5). *Application deadline:* For fall admission, 6/1 for domestic students, 5/1 for international students; for spring admission, 10/1 for domestic students, 9/1 for international students. Applications are processed on a rolling basis. Application fee: $30. Electronic applications accepted. *Expenses:* Tuition, state resident: full-time $8238.24. *Financial support:* In 2010–11, 86 students received support, including 12 fellowships with full tuition reimbursements available (averaging $7,161 per year), 30 research assistantships with full tuition reimbursements available (averaging $6,000 per year), 43 teaching assistantships with full tuition reimbursements available (averaging $15,000 per year); career-related internships or fieldwork, scholarships/grants, health care benefits, tuition waivers (full and partial), and unspecified assistantships also available. Support available to part-time students. Financial award application deadline: 1/1. *Unit head:* Dr. Caryn Beck-Dudley, Dean, 850-644-3090, Fax: 850-644-0915. *Application contact:* Lisa Beverly, Director, Graduate Programs Admissions, 850-644-6458, Fax: 850-644-0588, E-mail: lbeverly@cob.fsu.edu.

Franklin Pierce University, Graduate Studies, Rindge, NH 03461-0060. Offers curriculum and instruction (M Ed); emerging network technology (Graduate Certificate); health administration (MBA, Graduate Certificate); human resource management (MBA, Graduate Certificate); information technology management (MS); leadership (MBA, DA); nursing (MS); physical therapy (DPT); physician assistant studies (MPAS); special education (M Ed); sports management (MS). *Accreditation:* APTA. Part-time programs available. Postbaccalaureate distance learning degree programs offered (no on-campus study). *Faculty:* 28 full-time (18 women), 72 part-time/adjunct (44 women). *Students:* 100 full-time (63 women), 487 part-time (306 women); includes 42 minority (25 Black or African American, non-Hispanic/Latino; 10 Asian, non-Hispanic/Latino; 6 Hispanic/Latino; 1 Two or more races, non-Hispanic/Latino), 67 international. Average age 38. 227 applicants, 97% accepted, 185 enrolled. In 2010, 76 master's, 46 doctorates awarded. *Degree requirements:* For master's, concentrated original research projects; student teaching; fieldwork and/or internship; leadership project; PRAXIS I and II (for M Ed); for doctorate, concentrated original research projects, clinical fieldwork and/or internship, leadership project. *Entrance requirements:* For master's, minimum GPA of 2.5, 3 letters of recommendation; competencies in accounting, economics, statistics, and computer skills through life experience or undergraduate coursework (for MBA); certification/e-portfolio, minimum C grade in all education courses (for M Ed); license to practice as RN (for MS in nursing); for doctorate, GRE, BA/BS, 3 letters of recommendation, personal mission statement, interview; writing sample (for DA program)For DPT: 80 hours of observation/work in PT settings, completion of anatomy, chemistry, physics, an statistics, all > 3.0 GPAFor DA: 2.8 cum. GPA, Master's degree completion. Additional exam requirements/recommendations for international students: Required—TOEFL (minimum score 550 paper-based; 195 computer-based; 61 iBT). *Application deadline:* Applications are processed on a rolling basis. Application fee: $0. Electronic applications accepted. *Expenses:* Tuition: Part-time $573 per credit hour. Part-time tuition and fees vary according to degree level and program. *Financial support:* In 2010–11, 121 students received support, including 32 teaching assistantships with full and partial tuition reimbursements available (averaging $8,000 per year); career-related internships or fieldwork and unspecified assistantships also available. Support available to part-time students. Financial award applicants required to submit FAFSA. *Faculty research:* Evidence-based practice in sports physical therapy, human resource management in economic crisis, leadership in nursing, innovation in sports facility management, differentiated learning and understanding by design. *Unit head:* Dr. Patricia Brown, Interim Dean of Graduate and Professional Studies, 603-899-4316, Fax: 603-229-4580, E-mail: brownp@franklinpierce.edu.

Friends University, Graduate School, Wichita, KS 67213. Offers accounting (MBA); business administration (MBA); business law (MBL); Christian ministry (MACM); family therapy (MSFT); global leadership and management (MA); health care leadership (MHCL); management information systems (MMIS); operations management (MSOM); organization development (MSOD); teaching (MAT). Part-time and evening/weekend programs available. Postbaccalaureate distance learning degree programs offered (minimal on-campus study). *Faculty:* 14 full-time (5 women), 2 part-time/adjunct (1 woman). *Students:* 166 full-time (122 women), 507 part-time (290 women); includes 134 minority (64 Black or African American, non-Hispanic/Latino; 6 American Indian or Alaska Native, non-Hispanic/Latino; 24 Asian, non-Hispanic/Latino; 30 Hispanic/Latino; 1 Native Hawaiian or other Pacific Islander, non-Hispanic/Latino; 9 Two or more races, non-Hispanic/Latino). Average age 38. 445 applicants, 69% accepted, 236 enrolled. In 2010, 345 master's awarded. *Degree requirements:* For master's, research project. *Entrance requirements:* Additional exam requirements/recommendations for international students: Required—TOEFL (minimum score 560 paper-based; 220 computer-based). *Application deadline:* Applications are processed on a rolling basis. Application fee: $45 ($65 for international students). Electronic applications accepted. Tuition and fees vary according to course load, campus/location and program. *Financial support:* Applicants required to submit FAFSA. *Unit head:* Dr. Evelyn Hume, Dean, 800-794-6945 Ext. 5859, Fax: 316-295-5040, E-mail: evelyn hume@friends.edu. Application contact: Jeanette Hanson, Executive Director of Adult Recruitment, 800-794-6945, Fax: 316-295-5050, E-mail: jeanette@friends.edu.

George Mason University, Volgenau School of Engineering, Department of Computer Science, Fairfax, VA 22030. Offers biometrics (Certificate); computer games technology (Certificate); computer networking (Certificate); computer science (MS, PhD); data mining (Certificate); database management (Certificate); electronic commerce (Certificate); foundations of information systems (Certificate); information engineering (Certificate); information security and assurance (MS, Certificate); information systems (MS); intelligent agents (Certificate); software architecture (Certificate); software engineering (MS, Certificate); systems engineering (MS); Web-based software engineering (Certificate). MS program offered jointly with Old Dominion University, University of Virginia, Virginia Commonwealth University, and Virginia Polytechnic Institute and State University. Part-time and evening/weekend programs available. Postbaccalaureate distance learning degree programs offered. *Faculty:* 42 full-time (9 women), 20 part-time/adjunct (1 woman). *Students:* 124 full-time (37 women), 453 part-time (103 women); includes 14 Black or African American, non-Hispanic/Latino; 66 Asian, non-Hispanic/Latino; 13 Hispanic/Latino; 3 Two or more races, non-Hispanic/Latino, 206 international. Average age 30. 904 applicants, 53% accepted, 150 enrolled. In 2010, 203 master's, 4 doctorates, 20 other advanced degrees awarded. *Degree requirements:* For master's, thesis optional; for doctorate, comprehensive exam, thesis/dissertation. *Entrance requirements:* For master's, GRE General Test, minimum GPA of 3.0 in last 60 hours, 3 letters of recommendation; for doctorate, GRE, 4-year BA, academic work in computer science, 3 letters of recommendation, statement of career goals and aspirations. Additional exam requirements/recommendations for international students: Required—TOEFL (minimum score 570 paper-based; 230 computer-based; 88 iBT). *Application deadline:* For fall admission, 4/15 priority date for domestic students, 1/15 for international students; for spring admission, 11/15 for domestic students. Application fee: $100. Electronic applications accepted. *Expenses:* Tuition, state resident: full-time $8192; part-time $440 per credit hour. Tuition, nonresident: full-time $22,952; part-time $1055 per credit hour. Required fees: $2364; $99 per credit hour. *Financial support:* In 2010–11, 101 students received support, including 3 fellowships (averaging $18,000 per year), 52 research assistantships (averaging $15,078 per year), 47 teaching assistantships (averaging $10,983 per year); career-related internships or fieldwork, Federal Work-Study, scholarships/grants, unspecified assistantships, and health care benefits (full-time research or teaching assistantship recipients) also available. Financial award application deadline: 3/1; financial award applicants required to submit FAFSA. *Faculty research:* Artificial intelligence, image processing/graphics, parallel/distributed systems, software engineering systems. Total annual research expenditures: $1.3 million. *Unit head:* Dr. Arun Sood, Director, 703-993-1524, Fax: 703-993-1710, E-mail: asood@gmu.edu. *Application contact:* Jay Shapiro, Professor, 703-993-1485, E-mail: jshapiro@gmu.edu.

The George Washington University, School of Business, Department of Information Systems and Technology Management, Washington, DC 20052. Offers information and decision systems (PhD); information systems (MSIST); information systems development (MSIST); information systems management (MBA); information systems project management (MSIST); management information systems (MSIST); management of science, technology, and innovation (MBA, PhD). Programs also offered in Ashburn and Arlington, VA. Part-time and evening/weekend programs available. *Faculty:* 12 full-time (4 women), 5 part-time/adjunct (1 woman). *Students:* 93 full-time (33 women), 141 part-time (46 women); includes 31 Black or African American, non-Hispanic/Latino; 1 American Indian or Alaska Native, non-Hispanic/Latino; 28 Asian, non-Hispanic/Latino; 17 Hispanic/Latino; 1 Native Hawaiian or other Pacific Islander, non-Hispanic/Latino, 40 international. Average age 33. 201 applicants, 68% accepted, 67 enrolled. In 2010, 89 master's, 2 doctorates awarded. *Entrance requirements:* For master's, GMAT. Additional exam requirements/recommendations for international students: Required—TOEFL. *Application deadline:* For fall admission, 4/1 priority date for domestic students; for spring admission, 10/1 for domestic students. Applications are processed on a rolling basis. Application fee: $75. *Financial support:* In 2010–11, 35 students received support; fellowships, teaching assistantships, career-related internships or fieldwork, Federal Work-Study, institutionally sponsored loans, and tuition waivers available. Financial award application deadline: 4/1. *Faculty research:* Expert systems, decision support systems. *Unit head:* Richard G. Donnelly, Chair, 202-994-4364, E-mail: rgd@gwu.edu. *Application contact:* Kristin Williams, Assistant Vice President for Graduate and Special Enrollment Management, 202-994-0467, Fax: 202-994-0371, E-mail: ksw@gwu.edu.

Georgia College & State University, Graduate School, The J. Whitney Bunting School of Business, Milledgeville, GA 31061. Offers accountancy (MACCT); accounting (MBA); business (MBA); health services administration (MBA); information systems (MIS); management information services (MBA). *Accreditation:* AACSB. Part-time and evening/weekend programs available. Postbaccalaureate distance learning degree programs offered (no on-campus study). *Faculty:* 46 full-time (20 women). *Students:* 53 full-time (22 women), 157 part-time (53 women); includes 35 minority (18 Black or African American, non-Hispanic/Latino; 9 Asian, non-Hispanic/Latino; 5 Hispanic/Latino; 3 Two or more races, non-Hispanic/Latino), 11 international. Average age 30. 111 applicants, 83% accepted, 61 enrolled. In 2010, 121 master's awarded. *Entrance requirements:* For master's, GMAT or GRE. Additional exam requirements/recommendations for international students: Recommended—TOEFL (minimum score 550 paper-based; 213 computer-based; 79 iBT). *Application deadline:* For fall admission, 7/1 priority date for domestic students, 4/1 priority date for international students; for spring admission, 11/15 priority date for domestic students, 8/1 priority date for international students. Applications are processed on a rolling basis. Application fee: $40. Electronic applications accepted. *Expenses:* Tuition, state resident: full-time $4806; part-time $267 per hour. Tuition, nonresident: full-time $17,802; part-time $989 per hour. Tuition and fees vary according to course load. *Financial support:* In 2010–11, 33 research assistantships with full tuition reimbursements were awarded; career-related internships or fieldwork and unspecified assistantships also available. Support available to part-time students. Financial award application deadline: 3/1; financial award applicants required to submit FAFSA. *Unit head:* Dr. Matthew Liao-Troth, Dean, 478-445-5497, E-mail: matthew.liao-troth@gcsu.edu. *Application contact:* Lynn Hanson, Director of Graduate Programs, 478-445-5115, E-mail: lynn.hanson@gcsu.edu.

Golden Gate University, Ageno School of Business, San Francisco, CA 94105-2968. Offers accounting (MBA); business administration (EMBA, MBA, PMBA, DBA); finance (MBA, MS, Certificate); financial planning (MS, Certificate); healthcare information systems (Certificate); human resource management (MBA, MS); human resources management (Certificate); information systems (MS); information technology (MBA); information technology management (Certificate); integrated marketing and communications (MS, Certificate); international business (MBA); management (MBA); marketing (MBA, MS, Certificate); operations supply chain management (Certificate); psychology (MA, Certificate); public administration (EMPA); public relations (MS, Certificate); technical market analysis (Certificate); JD/MBA. Part-time and evening/weekend programs available. *Faculty:* 16 full-time (4 women), 241 part-time/adjunct (72 women). *Students:* 421 full-time (235 women), 744 part-time (425 women); includes 526 minority (114 Black or African American, non-Hispanic/Latino; 2 American Indian or Alaska Native, non-Hispanic/Latino; 296 Asian, non-Hispanic/Latino; 73 Hispanic/Latino; 29 Native Hawaiian or other Pacific Islander, non-Hispanic/Latino; 12 Two or more races, non-Hispanic/Latino), 100 international. Average age 32. 681 applicants, 78% accepted, 270 enrolled. In 2010, 550 master's, 13 doctorates awarded. *Degree requirements:* For doctorate, thesis/dissertation. *Entrance requirements:* For master's, GMAT (MBA), minimum GPA of 2.5 (MS). Additional exam requirements/recommendations for international students: Required—TOEFL. *Application deadline:* For fall admission, 5/15 for domestic and international students; for winter admission, 1/15 for domestic and international students; for spring admission, 9/15 for domestic and international students. Applications are processed on a rolling basis. Application fee: $70 ($110 for international students). Electronic applications accepted. *Expenses:* Contact institution. *Financial support:* Career-related internships or fieldwork, Federal Work-Study, institutionally sponsored loans, and scholarships/grants available. Support available to part-time students. Financial award applicants required to submit FAFSA. *Unit head:* Dr. Paul Fouts, Dean, 415-442-7026, Fax: 415-442-6579. *Application contact:* Angela Melero, Enrollment Services, 415-442-7800, Fax: 415-442-7807, E-mail: info@ggu.edu.

Goldey-Beacom College, Graduate Program, Wilmington, DE 19808-1999. Offers business administration (MBA); finance (MS); financial management (MBA); human resource management (MBA); information technology (MBA); international business management (MBA); major finance (MBA); major taxation (MBA); management (MM); marketing management (MBA); taxation (MBA, MS). *Accreditation:* ACBSP. Part-time and evening/weekend programs available. *Faculty:* 20 full-time (8 women), 28 part-time/adjunct (10 women). *Students:* 55 full-time (28 women), 393 part-time (164 women); includes 252 minority (51 Black or African American, non-Hispanic/Latino; 2 American Indian or Alaska Native, non-Hispanic/Latino; 183 Asian, non-Hispanic/Latino; 13 Hispanic/Latino; 1 Native Hawaiian or other Pacific Islander, non-Hispanic/Latino; 2 Two or more races, non-Hispanic/Latino). Average age 27. In 2010, 231 master's awarded. *Entrance requirements:* For master's, GMAT, MAT, GRE, minimum GPA of 3.0. Additional exam requirements/recommendations for international students: Required—TOEFL (minimum score 65 computer-based); Recommended—IELTS (minimum score 5). *Application deadline:* Applications are processed on a rolling basis. Electronic applications accepted. *Expenses:* Tuition: Full-time $14,796; part-time $822 per credit. Required fees: $180; $10 per credit. *Financial support:* Scholarships/grants available. Support available to part-time students. Financial award application deadline: 4/1; financial award applicants required to submit FAFSA. *Unit head:* Larry W. Eby, Director of Admissions, 302-225-6289, Fax: 302-996-5408, E-mail: ebylw@gbc.edu. *Application contact:* Ashley E. Mashington, Graduate Admissions Representative, 302-225-6259, Fax: 302-996-5408, E-mail: mashina@gbc.edu.

Grand Canyon University, College of Business, Phoenix, AZ 85017-1097. Offers accounting (MBA); corporate business administration (MBA); disaster preparedness and crisis management (MBA); executive fire service leadership (MS); finance (MBA); general management (MBA); government and policy (MPA); health care management (MPA); health systems management (MBA); human resource management (MBA); innovation (MBA); leadership (MBA, MS); management of information system (MBA); marketing (MBA); project-based (MBA); six sigma (MBA); strategic human resource management (MBA). *Accreditation:* ACBSP. Part-time and evening/weekend programs available. Postbaccalaureate distance learning degree programs offered (no on-campus study). *Faculty:* 8 full-time (3 women), 147 part-time/adjunct (49 women). *Students:* 1 full-time (0 women), 2,121 part-time (1,165 women); includes 341 minority (249 Black or African American, non-Hispanic/Latino; 17 American Indian or Alaska Native, non-Hispanic/Latino; 15 Asian, non-Hispanic/Latino; 29 Hispanic/Latino; 4 Native Hawaiian or other Pacific Islander, non-Hispanic/Latino; 27 Two or more races, non-Hispanic/Latino), 20 international. Average age 38. In 2010, 569 master's awarded. *Entrance requirements:* For master's, equivalent of two years full-time professional work experience. Additional exam requirements/recommendations for international students: Required—TOEFL (minimum score 575 paper-based; 233 computer-based; 90 iBT), IELTS (minimum score 7). *Application deadline:* For fall admission, 8/21 for domestic students, 7/2 for international students; for spring admission, 12/24 for domestic students, 11/1 for international students. Applications are processed on a rolling basis. Application fee: $0. Electronic applications accepted. *Financial support:* Federal Work-Study available. Support available to part-time students. Financial award applicants required to submit FAFSA. *Unit head:* Kim Donaldson, Dean, 602-639-6597, E-mail: kdonaldson@gcu.edu. *Application contact:* Matt Tidwell, Enrollment Manager, 602-639-6020, E-mail: mtidwell@gcu.edu.

Grantham University, Mark Skousen School of Business, Kansas City, MO 64153. Offers business administration (MBA); business intelligence (MS); information management (MBA); information management technology (MS); information technology (MS); performance improvement (MS); project management (MBA, MSIM). Part-time and evening/weekend programs available. Postbaccalaureate distance learning degree programs offered (no on-campus study). *Students:* 74 full-time (32 women), 565 part-time (177 women); includes 218 minority (142 Black or African American, non-Hispanic/Latino; 6 American Indian or Alaska Native, non-Hispanic/Latino; 31 Asian, non-Hispanic/Latino; 37 Hispanic/Latino; 1 Native Hawaiian or other Pacific Islander, non-Hispanic/Latino; 1 Two or more races, non-Hispanic/Latino). In 2010, 126 master's awarded. *Degree requirements:* For master's, capstone project. *Entrance requirements:* For master's, bachelor's degree from accredited degree-granting institution. Additional exam requirements/recommendations for international students: Required—TOEFL (minimum score 500 paper-based; 213 computer-based; 61 iBT). *Application deadline:* Applications are processed on a rolling basis. Application fee: $0. Electronic applications accepted. *Expenses:* Tuition: Full-time $7950; part-time $265 per credit hour. One-time fee: $30. *Financial support:* Institutionally sponsored loans and scholarships/grants available. *Unit head:* Niccole Buckley, Dean, 800-955-2527, Fax: 816-595-5757, E-mail: admissions@grantham.edu. *Application contact:* Dan King, Vice President of Admissions, 800-955-2527, Fax: 816-595-5757, E-mail: admissions@grantham.edu.

Harrisburg University of Science and Technology, Program in Information Systems Engineering and Management, Harrisburg, PA 17101. Offers digital government specialization (MS); digital health specialization (MS); entrepreneurship specialization (MS). Part-time programs available. *Faculty:* 1 full-time (0 women), 2 part-time/adjunct (0 women). *Students:* 4 full-time (2 women), 16 part-time (5 women); includes 5 Black or African American, non-Hispanic/Latino; 2 Hispanic/Latino. Average age 30. 18 applicants, 83% accepted, 11 enrolled. *Degree requirements:* For master's, comprehensive exam, thesis optional. *Entrance requirements:* For master's, baccalaureate degree. Additional exam requirements/recommendations for international students: Required—TOEFL (minimum score 520 paper-based; 200 computer-based; 80 iBT). *Application deadline:* For fall admission, 8/1 priority date for domestic students, 7/1 priority date for international students. Applications are processed on a rolling basis. Application fee: $0. Electronic applications accepted. *Expenses:* Tuition: Full-time $19,500; part-time $700 per credit hour. *Financial support:* In 2010–11, 2 students received support. Scholarships/grants available. Financial award applicants required to submit FAFSA. *Unit head:* Dr. Amjad Umar, Director and Professor, 717-901-5141, Fax: 717-901-3141, E-mail: aumar@harrisburgu.edu. *Application contact:* Timothy Dawson, Information Contact, 717-901-5158, Fax: 717-901-3158, E-mail: admissions@harrisburgu.edu.

HEC Montreal, School of Business Administration, Master of Science Programs in Administration, Program in Information Technologies, Montréal, QC H3T 2A7, Canada. Offers M Sc. All courses are given in French. Part-time programs available. *Students:* 26 full-time (9 women), 7 part-time (1 woman).

23 applicants, 61% accepted, 9 enrolled. In 2010, 13 master's awarded. *Degree requirements:* For master's, one foreign language, thesis. *Application deadline:* For fall admission, 3/15 for domestic and international students; for winter admission, 10/1 for domestic and international students. Application fee: $78 Canadian dollars. Electronic applications accepted. *Expenses:* Tuition, area resident: Part-time $68.93 per credit. Tuition, state resident: full-time $2481.48; part-time $188.92 per credit. Tuition, nonresident: full-time $6801; part-time $482.06 per course. International tuition: $17,354.16 full-time. Required fees: $1309.50; $30.28 per credit. $93.45 per term. Tuition and fees vary according to degree level and program. *Financial support:* Fellowships, research assistantships, teaching assistantships, scholarships/grants available. Financial award application deadline: 9/2. *Unit head:* Dr. Claude Laurin, Director, 514-340-6485, Fax: 514-340-6880, E-mail: claude.laurin@hec.ca. *Application contact:* Francine Blais, Administrative Director, 514-340-6112, Fax: 514-340-6411, E-mail: francine.blais@hec.ca.

Hodges University, Graduate Programs, Naples, FL 34119. Offers business administration (MBA); computer information technology (MS); criminal justice (MCJ); education (MPS); information systems management (MIS); interdisciplinary (MPS); legal studies (MS); management (MSM); mental health counseling (MS); psychology (MPS); public administration (MPA). Part-time and evening/weekend programs available. Postbaccalaureate distance learning degree programs offered (no on-campus study). *Faculty:* 25 full-time (9 women), 5 part-time/adjunct (4 women). *Students:* 27 full-time (15 women), 228 part-time (146 women); includes 76 minority (35 Black or African American, non-Hispanic/Latino; 5 Asian, non-Hispanic/Latino; 36 Hispanic/Latino). Average age 36. 92 applicants, 91% accepted, 81 enrolled. In 2010, 92 master's awarded. *Degree requirements:* For master's, comprehensive exam (for some programs), thesis (for some programs). *Entrance requirements:* For master's, in-house entrance exam. *Application deadline:* Applications are processed on a rolling basis. Application fee: $50. Electronic applications accepted. *Expenses:* Tuition: Full-time $16,605; part-time $615 per credit hour. Required fees: $190 per trimester. *Financial support:* In 2010–11, 200 students received support. Federal Work-Study and scholarships/grants available. Financial award application deadline: 7/9; financial award applicants required to submit FAFSA. *Unit head:* Terry McMahan, President, 239-513-1122, Fax: 239-598-6253, E-mail: tmcmahan@hodges.edu. *Application contact:* Rita Lampus, Vice President of Student Enrollment Management, 239-513-1122, Fax: 239-598-6253, E-mail: rlampus@hodges.edu.

Hofstra University, Frank G. Zarb School of Business, Department of Information Technology and Quantitative Methods, Hempstead, NY 11549. Offers business administration (MBA), including information technology, quality management; information technology (MS, Advanced Certificate). Part-time and evening/weekend programs available. Postbaccalaureate distance learning degree programs offered (minimal on-campus study). *Faculty:* 10 full-time (1 woman), 2 part-time/adjunct (0 women). *Students:* 11 full-time (1 woman), 12 part-time (4 women); includes 6 minority (1 Black or African American, non-Hispanic/Latino; 5 Asian, non-Hispanic/Latino), 4 international. Average age 29. 28 applicants, 57% accepted, 8 enrolled. In 2010, 8 master's awarded. *Degree requirements:* For master's, capstone course (for MBA); thesis (for MS). *Entrance requirements:* For master's, GMAT/GRE, 2 letters of recommendation; resume; essay; for Advanced Certificate, GMAT/GRE, 2 letters of recommendation; resume. Additional exam requirements/recommendations for international students: Required—TOEFL (minimum score 550 paper-based; 213 computer-based; 80 iBT); Recommended—IELTS (minimum score 6). *Application deadline:* Applications are processed on a rolling basis. Application fee: $70 ($75 for international students). Electronic applications accepted. *Financial support:* In 2010–11, 4 students received support, including 4 fellowships with full and partial tuition reimbursements available (averaging $11,496 per year); research assistantships with full and partial tuition reimbursements available, career-related internships or fieldwork, Federal Work-Study, institutionally sponsored loans, scholarships/grants, tuition waivers (full and partial), and unspecified assistantships also available. Support available to part-time students. Financial award applicants required to submit FAFSA. *Faculty research:* IT outsourcing, IT strategy, SAP and enterprise systems, data mining/electronic medical records, IT and crisis management, inventory theory and modeling, forecasting. *Unit head:* Dr. Mohammed H. Tafti, Chairperson, 516-463-5720, E-mail: acsmht@hofstra.edu. *Application contact:* Carol Drummer, Dean of Graduate Admissions, 516-463-4876, Fax: 516-463-4664, E-mail: gradstudent@hofstra.edu.

Holy Family University, Graduate School, School of Business Administration, Program in Information Systems Management, Philadelphia, PA 19114. Offers MS. Part-time and evening/weekend programs available. *Faculty:* 1 full-time (0 women), 4 part-time/adjunct (0 women). *Students:* 19 part-time (8 women). Average age 32. 15 applicants, 40% accepted, 4 enrolled. *Entrance requirements:* For master's, BA or BS, minimum GPA of 3.0, 2 letters of recommenation. *Application deadline:* For fall admission, 8/1 for domestic students; for winter admission, 1/1 for domestic students. Applications are processed on a rolling basis. Application fee: $25. Electronic applications accepted. *Expenses:* Tuition: Full-time $14,400; part-time $600 per credit hour. Required fees: $85 per term. *Financial support:* Application deadline: 5/1. *Unit head:*

Dr. Jan Duggar, Dean of the School of Business, 267-341-3373, Fax: 215-637-5937, E-mail: jduggar@holyfamily.edu. *Application contact:* Gidget Marie Montelibano, Graduate Admissions Counselor, 267-341-3558, Fax: 215-637-1478, E-mail: gmontelibano@holyfamily.edu.

Hood College, Graduate School, Department of Economics and Management, Frederick, MD 21701-8575. Offers accounting (MBA); administration and management (MBA); finance (MBA); human resource management (MBA); information systems (MBA); marketing (MBA); public management (MBA). *Accreditation:* ACBSP. Part-time and evening/weekend programs available. *Faculty:* 4 full-time (1 woman), 9 part-time/adjunct (1 woman). *Students:* 16 full-time (9 women), 127 part-time (65 women); includes 17 Black or African American, non-Hispanic/Latino; 9 Asian, non-Hispanic/Latino; 5 Hispanic/Latino; 1 Two or more races, non-Hispanic/Latino, 10 international. Average age 32. 60 applicants, 62% accepted, 25 enrolled. In 2010, 56 master's awarded. *Degree requirements:* For master's, capstone/final research project. *Entrance requirements:* For master's, minimum GPA of 2.75, resume, letters of recommendation. Additional exam requirements/recommendations for international students: Required—TOEFL (minimum score 575 paper-based; 231 computer-based; 89 iBT). *Application deadline:* For fall admission, 7/15 for domestic and international students; for spring admission, 12/15 for domestic and international students. Applications are processed on a rolling basis. Application fee: $35. Electronic applications accepted. *Expenses:* Tuition: Full-time $6480; part-time $360 per credit. Required fees: $100; $50 per term. *Financial support:* Applicants required to submit FAFSA. *Faculty research:* Corporate strategy and sustainable competitive advantages, business ethics, entrepreneurship, investments management, economic development. *Unit head:* Dr. Anita Jose, Program Director, 301-696-3691, Fax: 301-696-3597, E-mail: jose@hood.edu. *Application contact:* Dr. Allen P. Flora, Dean of Graduate School, 301-696-3811, Fax: 301-696-3597, E-mail: gofurther@hood.edu.

Illinois Institute of Technology, Graduate College, College of Science and Letters, Department of Computer Science, Chicago, IL 60616-3793. Offers business (MCS); computer networking and telecommunications (MCS); computer science (MCS, MS, PhD); information systems (MCS); software engineering (MCS); teaching (MST). Part-time and evening/weekend programs available. Postbaccalaureate distance learning degree programs offered (no on-campus study). *Faculty:* 29 full-time (6 women), 3 part-time/adjunct (0 women). *Students:* 262 full-time (62 women), 132 part-time (27 women); includes 13 minority (3 Black or African American, non-Hispanic/Latino; 7 Asian, non-Hispanic/Latino; 3 Hispanic/Latino), 340 international. Average age 26. 974 applicants, 71% accepted, 148 enrolled. In 2010, 138 master's, 5 doctorates awarded. Terminal master's awarded for partial completion of doctoral program. *Degree requirements:* For master's, thesis optional; for doctorate, comprehensive exam, thesis/dissertation. *Entrance requirements:* For master's, GRE General Test (minimum scores: 1000 Quantitative and Verbal, 3.0 Analytical Writing), minimum undergraduate GPA of 3.0; for doctorate, GRE General Test (minimum scores: 1100 Quantitative and Verbal, 3.5 Analytical Writing), minimum undergraduate GPA of 3.0. Additional exam requirements/recommendations for international students: Required—TOEFL (minimum score 523 paper-based; 70 iBT). *Application deadline:* For fall admission, 5/1 for domestic and international students; for spring admission, 10/15 for domestic and international students. Applications are processed on a rolling basis. Application fee: $50. Electronic applications accepted. *Expenses:* Tuition: Full-time $18,576; part-time $1032 per credit hour. Required fees: $583 per semester. One-time fee: $150. Tuition and fees vary according to program and student level. *Financial support:* In 2010–11, 15 research assistantships with full and partial tuition reimbursements (averaging $10,380 per year), 21 teaching assistantships with full and partial tuition reimbursements (averaging $12,452 per year) were awarded; fellowships with partial tuition reimbursements, career-related internships or fieldwork, Federal Work-Study, institutionally sponsored loans, scholarships/grants, traineeships, health care benefits, tuition waivers (partial), and unspecified assistantships also available. Support available to part-time students. Financial award applicants required to submit FAFSA. *Faculty research:* Algorithms, data structures, artificial intelligences, computer architecture, computer graphics, computer networking and telecommunications. Total annual research expenditures: $1.8 million. *Unit head:* Dr. Xian-He Sun, Chair/Professor, 312-567-5260, Fax: 312-567-5067, E-mail: sun@cs.iit.edu. *Application contact:* Debbie Gibson, Director, Graduate Admission, 866-472-3448, Fax: 312-567-3138, E-mail: inquiry.grad@iit.edu.

Illinois Institute of Technology, Graduate College, College of Science and Letters, Lewis Department of Humanities, Chicago, IL 60616-3793. Offers information architecture (MS); technical communication (PhD); technical communication and information design (MS). Part-time programs available. *Faculty:* 18 full-time (8 women), 16 part-time/adjunct (12 women). *Students:* 29 full-time (15 women), 16 part-time (12 women); includes 13 minority (10 Black or African American, non-Hispanic/Latino; 2 Asian, non-Hispanic/Latino; 1 Hispanic/Latino), 6 international. Average age 34. 34 applicants, 56% accepted, 11 enrolled. In 2010, 9 master's, 1 doctorate awarded. *Degree requirements:* For master's, comprehensive exam, thesis or alternative; for doctorate, comprehensive exam, thesis/dissertation. *Entrance requirements:* For master's and doctorate, GRE General Test (minimum score 500 Quantitative,

500 Verbal, and 3.0 Analytical Writing), minimum undergraduate GPA of 3.0. Additional exam requirements/recommendations for international students: Required—TOEFL (minimum score 523 paper-based; 70 iBT). *Application deadline:* For fall admission, 5/1 for domestic and international students; for spring admission, 10/15 for domestic and international students. Applications are processed on a rolling basis. Application fee: $50. Electronic applications accepted. *Expenses:* Tuition: Full-time $18,576; part-time $1032 per credit hour. Required fees: $583 per semester. One-time fee: $150. Tuition and fees vary according to program and student level. *Financial support:* In 2010–11, 4 research assistantships with partial tuition reimbursements (averaging $8,300 per year), 13 teaching assistantships with partial tuition reimbursements (averaging $7,553 per year) were awarded; fellowships with partial tuition reimbursements, career-related internships or fieldwork, Federal Work-Study, institutionally sponsored loans, scholarships/grants, health care benefits, tuition waivers (partial), and unspecified assistantships also available. Support available to part-time students. Financial award applicants required to submit FAFSA. *Faculty research:* Aesthetics, document and online design, ethics in the professions, history of art and architecture, humanizing technology. Total annual research expenditures: $180,587. *Unit head:* Dr. Maureen Flanagan, Professor and Chair, 312-567-3563, Fax: 312-567-5187, E-mail: maureen.flanagan@iit.edu. *Application contact:* Deborah Gibson, Director, Graduate Admission, 866-472-3448, Fax: 312-567-3138, E-mail: inquiry.grad@iit.edu.

Illinois Institute of Technology, Graduate College, School of Applied Technology, Program in Information Technology and Management, Chicago, IL 60616-3793. Offers MITM. Part-time and evening/weekend programs available. Postbaccalaureate distance learning degree programs offered (no on-campus study). *Faculty:* 4 full-time (2 women), 11 part-time/adjunct (2 women). *Students:* 125 full-time (33 women), 70 part-time (20 women); includes 11 minority (2 Black or African American, non-Hispanic/Latino; 8 Asian, non-Hispanic/Latino; 1 Hispanic/Latino), 143 international. Average age 27. 183 applicants, 86% accepted, 63 enrolled. In 2010, 112 master's awarded. *Entrance requirements:* For master's, GRE (minimum score 900 Quantitative and Verbal, 2.5 Analytical Writing), bachelor's degree with minimum cumulative undergraduate GPA of 3.0 (or its equivalent) from accredited institution. Additional exam requirements/recommendations for international students: Required—TOEFL (minimum score 523 paper-based; 70 iBT); Recommended—IELTS (minimum score 5.5). *Application deadline:* For fall admission, 8/1 for domestic students, 5/1 for international students; for spring admission, 12/15 for domestic students, 10/15 for international students. Applications are processed on a rolling basis. Application fee: $50. Electronic applications accepted. *Expenses:* Tuition: Full-time $18,576; part-time $1032 per credit hour. Required fees: $583 per semester. One-time fee: $150. Tuition and fees vary according to program and student level. *Financial support:* In 2010–11, 9 teaching assistantships with partial tuition reimbursements (averaging $2,658 per year) were awarded; fellowships with partial tuition reimbursements, career-related internships or fieldwork, Federal Work-Study, institutionally sponsored loans, scholarships/grants, traineeships, health care benefits, tuition waivers (partial), and unspecified assistantships also available. Support available to part-time students. Financial award applicants required to submit FAFSA. *Faculty research:* Database design, voice over IP, process engineering, object-oriented programming, computer networking, online design, system administration. *Unit head:* C. Robert Carlson, Director, 630-682-6002, Fax: 630-682-6010, E-mail: carlson@iit.edu. *Application contact:* Deborah Gibson, Director, Graduate Admission, 866-472-3448, Fax: 312-567-3138, E-mail: inquiry.grad@iit.edu.

Indiana University Bloomington, School of Public and Environmental Affairs, Public Affairs Programs, Bloomington, IN 47405-7000. Offers comparative and international affairs (MPA); economic development (MPA); energy (MPA); environmental policy (PhD); environmental policy and natural resource management (MPA); information systems (MPA); local government management (MPA); nonprofit management (MPA, Certificate); policy analysis (MPA); public finance (PhD); public financial administration (MPA); public management (MPA, PhD); public policy analysis (PhD); specialized public affairs (MPA); sustainability and sustainable development (MPA); JD/MPA; MPA/MIS; MPA/MLS; MSES/MPA. *Accreditation:* NASPAA (one or more programs are accredited). Part-time programs available. *Faculty:* 31 full-time, 15 part-time/adjunct. *Students:* 466 full-time (261 women); includes 11 Black or African American, non-Hispanic/Latino; 2 American Indian or Alaska Native, non-Hispanic/Latino; 42 Asian, non-Hispanic/Latino; 1 Hispanic/Latino, 65 international. Average age 26. 650 applicants, 218 enrolled. In 2010, 166 master's, 10 doctorates awarded. *Degree requirements:* For master's, core classes, capstone; for doctorate, comprehensive exam, thesis/dissertation. *Entrance requirements:* For master's, GRE General Test or GMAT, official transcripts, 3 letters of recommendation, resume, personal statement, departmental questions; for doctorate, GRE General Test or LSAT, official transcripts, 3 letters of recommendation, resume or curriculum vitae, statement of purpose. Additional exam requirements/recommendations for international students: Required—TOEFL (minimum score 600 paper-based; 96 iBT); Recommended—IELTS (minimum score 7). *Application deadline:* For fall admission, 5/1 priority date for domestic students, 12/1 priority date for international students. Applications are processed on a rolling basis. Application fee: $55 ($65 for international students). Electronic applications accepted. *Financial support:* Fellowships with partial tuition reimbursements, research assistantships with partial tuition reimbursements, teaching assistantships with partial tuition reimbursements, career-related internships or fieldwork, Federal Work-Study, scholarships/grants, health care benefits, unspecified assistantships, and Service Corps programs available. Financial award application deadline: 2/1; financial award applicants required to submit FAFSA. *Faculty research:* Comparative and international affairs, environmental policy and resource management, policy analysis, public finance, public management, urban management, nonprofit management, energy policy, social policy, public finance. *Unit head:* Jennifer Forney, Director of Graduate Student Services, 812-855-9485, Fax: 812-856-3665, E-mail: speampo@indiana.edu. *Application contact:* Audrey Whitaker, Admissions Assistant, 812-855-2840, E-mail: speaapps@indiana.edu.

Indiana University South Bend, School of Business and Economics, South Bend, IN 46634-7111. Offers accounting (MSA); business administration (MBA); management of information technologies (MS). Part-time and evening/weekend programs available. *Faculty:* 17 full-time (2 women), 3 part-time/adjunct (1 woman). *Students:* 61 full-time (26 women), 100 part-time (32 women); includes 16 minority (6 Black or African American, non-Hispanic/Latino; 1 American Indian or Alaska Native, non-Hispanic/Latino; 4 Asian, non-Hispanic/Latino; 4 Hispanic/Latino; 1 Two or more races, non-Hispanic/Latino), 51 international. Average age 32. 76 applicants, 58% accepted, 28 enrolled. In 2010, 67 master's awarded. *Entrance requirements:* For master's, GMAT. Additional exam requirements/recommendations for international students: Required—TOEFL (minimum score 550 paper-based; 213 computer-based). *Application deadline:* For fall admission, 7/1 priority date for domestic and international students; for spring admission, 11/1 priority date for domestic and international students. Applications are processed on a rolling basis. Application fee: $50 ($60 for international students). *Expenses:* Contact institution. *Financial support:* In 2010–11, 1 fellowship (averaging $3,846 per year) was awarded; Federal Work-Study and institutionally sponsored loans also available. Support available to part-time students. Financial award applicants required to submit FAFSA. *Faculty research:* Financial accounting, consumer research, capital budgeting research, business strategy research. *Unit head:* Robert H. Ducoffe, Dean, 574-520-4228, Fax: 574-520-4866. *Application contact:* Sharon Peterson, Secretary, 574-520-4138, Fax: 574-520-4866, E-mail: speterso@iusb.edu.

Iowa State University of Science and Technology, Graduate College, College of Business, Program in Logistics, Operations, and Management Information Systems, Ames, IA 50011. Offers information systems (MS). *Faculty:* 21 full-time (3 women). *Students:* 18 full-time (6 women), 20 part-time (7 women); includes 1 Black or African American, non-Hispanic/Latino, 25 international. 46 applicants, 33% accepted, 6 enrolled. In 2010, 8 master's awarded. *Degree requirements:* For master's, thesis or alternative. *Entrance requirements:* For master's, GMAT. Additional exam requirements/recommendations for international students: Recommended—TOEFL (minimum score 600 paper-based; 100 iBT), IELTS (minimum score 7). *Application deadline:* For fall admission, 6/1 priority date for domestic students, 3/1 priority date for international students; for spring admission, 11/1 for domestic and international students. Application fee: $40 ($90 for international students). Electronic applications accepted. *Financial support:* In 2010–11, 5 research assistantships with full and partial tuition reimbursements (averaging $2,322 per year) were awarded; teaching assistantships with full and partial tuition reimbursements, career-related internships or fieldwork, institutionally sponsored loans, scholarships/grants, health care benefits, and unspecified assistantships also available. *Unit head:* Dr. Qing Hu, Chair, 515-294-8118, E-mail: busgrad@iastate.edu. *Application contact:* Deb Johnson, Information Contact, 515-294-8118, E-mail: busgrad@iastate.edu.

John Marshall Law School, Graduate and Professional Programs, Chicago, IL 60604-3968. Offers comparative legal studies (LL M); employee benefits (LL M, MS); information technology (LL M, MS); intellectual property (LL M); international business and trade (LL M); law (JD); real estate (LL M, MS); taxation (LL M, MS); JD/LL M; JD/MA; JD/MBA; JD/MPA. JD/MBA offered jointly with Dominican University, JD/MA and JD/MPA with Roosevelt University. *Accreditation:* ABA. Part-time and evening/weekend programs available. *Faculty:* 65 full-time (21 women), 152 part-time/adjunct (48 women). *Students:* 1,237 full-time (567 women), 373 part-time (181 women); includes 464 minority (138 Black or African American, non-Hispanic/Latino; 12 American Indian or Alaska Native, non-Hispanic/Latino; 96 Asian, non-Hispanic/Latino; 125 Hispanic/Latino; 11 Native Hawaiian or other Pacific Islander, non-Hispanic/Latino; 82 Two or more races, non-Hispanic/Latino), 39 international. Average age 27. 3,523 applicants, 44% accepted, 351 enrolled. In 2010, 387 first professional degrees, 8 master's awarded. *Degree requirements:* For JD, 90 credits. *Entrance requirements:* For JD, LSAT; for master's, JD. Additional exam requirements/recommendations for international students: Required—TOEFL. *Application deadline:* For fall admission, 3/1 priority date for domestic and international students; for spring admission, 10/15 priority date for domestic and international students. Applications are processed on a rolling basis. Application fee: $60. Electronic applications accepted. *Expenses:* Contact institution. *Financial support:* In 2010–11, 1,350 students received support. Scholarships/grants and tuition waivers (full and partial) available. Support available to part-time students. Financial award application deadline: 6/1; financial award applicants required

to submit FAFSA. *Unit head:* John Corkery, Dean, 312-427-2737. *Application contact:* William B. Powers, Associate Dean of Admission and Student Affairs, 800-537-4280, Fax: 312-427-5136, E-mail: admission@jmls.edu.

The Johns Hopkins University, Carey Business School, Information Technology Programs, Baltimore, MD 21218-2699. Offers competitive intelligence (Certificate); information security management (Certificate); information systems (MS); MBA/MSIS. Part-time and evening/weekend programs available. *Faculty:* 29 full-time (6 women), 135 part-time/adjunct (29 women). *Students:* 11 full-time (3 women), 154 part-time (42 women); includes 62 minority (19 Black or African American, non-Hispanic/Latino; 1 American Indian or Alaska Native, non-Hispanic/Latino; 31 Asian, non-Hispanic/Latino; 7 Hispanic/Latino; 1 Native Hawaiian or other Pacific Islander, non-Hispanic/Latino; 3 Two or more races, non-Hispanic/Latino), 12 international. Average age 35. 53 applicants, 87% accepted, 30 enrolled. In 2010, 83 master's, 22 other advanced degrees awarded. *Degree requirements:* For master's, 36 credits including final project. *Entrance requirements:* For master's and Certificate, minimum GPA of 3.0, resume, work experience, two letters of recommendation. Additional exam requirements/recommendations for international students: Required—TOEFL (minimum score 600 paper-based; 250 computer-based; 100 iBT). *Application deadline:* For fall admission, 4/1 for international students; for spring admission, 9/15 for international students. Applications are processed on a rolling basis. Application fee: $100. Electronic applications accepted. *Financial support:* In 2010–11, 5 students received support. Scholarships/grants available. Support available to part-time students. Financial award application deadline: 4/15; financial award applicants required to submit FAFSA. *Faculty research:* Information security, healthcare information systems. Total annual research expenditures: $89,653. *Unit head:* Dr. Dipankar Chakravarti, Vice Dean of Programs, 410-234-9311, E-mail: dipankar.chakravarti@jhu.edu. *Application contact:* Robin Greenberg, Admissions Coordinator, 410-234-9227, Fax: 443-529-1554, E-mail: carey.admissions@jhu.edu.

The Johns Hopkins University, Engineering Program for Professionals, Part-time Program in Information Systems and Technology, Baltimore, MD 21218-2699. Offers MS, Post-Master's Certificate. Part-time and evening/weekend programs available. *Faculty:* 9 part-time/adjunct (1 woman). *Students:* 4 full-time (1 woman), 146 part-time (33 women); includes 64 minority (29 Black or African American, non-Hispanic/Latino; 1 American Indian or Alaska Native, non-Hispanic/Latino; 24 Asian, non-Hispanic/Latino; 8 Hispanic/Latino; 2 Two or more races, non-Hispanic/Latino), 3 international. Average age 32. 21 applicants, 90% accepted, 16 enrolled. In 2010, 42 master's awarded. *Application deadline:* Applications are processed on a rolling basis. Application fee: $75. Electronic applications accepted. *Financial support:* Institutionally sponsored loans available. *Unit head:* Dr. Thomas A. Longstaff, Program Chair, 443-778-9389, E-mail: thomas.longstaff@jhuapl.edu. *Application contact:* Priyanka Dwivedi, Admissions Manager, 410-516-2300, Fax: 410-579-8049, E-mail: pdwived1@jhu.edu.

Kent State University, Graduate School of Management, Doctoral Program in Management Systems, Kent, OH 44242. Offers PhD. *Faculty:* 20 full-time (6 women). *Students:* 16 full-time (5 women); includes 1 Black or African American, non-Hispanic/Latino, 7 international. Average age 33. 10 applicants, 40% accepted, 2 enrolled. In 2010, 3 doctorates awarded. *Degree requirements:* For doctorate, comprehensive exam, thesis/dissertation, oral defense. *Entrance requirements:* For doctorate, GMAT. Additional exam requirements/recommendations for international students: Required—TOEFL (minimum score 600 paper-based; 250 computer-based; 100 iBT). *Application deadline:* For fall admission, 2/1 for domestic students, 1/1 for international students. Application fee: $30 ($60 for international students). Electronic applications accepted. *Expenses:* Tuition, state resident: full-time $7866; part-time $437 per credit hour. Tuition, nonresident: full-time $14,022; part-time $779 per credit hour. *Financial support:* In 2010–11, 14 students received support, including 14 teaching assistantships with full tuition reimbursements available (averaging $15,000 per year); fellowships with full tuition reimbursements available, Federal Work-Study also available. Financial award application deadline: 2/1; financial award applicants required to submit FAFSA. *Unit head:* Dr. O. Felix Offodile, Chair and Professor, 330-672-2750, Fax: 330-672-2953, E-mail: foffodil@kent.edu. *Application contact:* Felecia A. Urbanek, Coordinator, Graduate Programs, 330-672-2282, Fax: 330-672-7303, E-mail: gradbus@kent.edu.

Kentucky State University, College of Professional Studies, Frankfort, KY 40601. Offers business administration (MBA), including accounting, finance, management, marketing; public administration (MPA), including human resource management, international administration and development, management information systems, nonprofit management; special education (MA). Part-time and evening/weekend programs available. Postbaccalaureate distance learning degree programs offered (minimal on-campus study). *Faculty:* 12 full-time (4 women), 2 part-time/adjunct (both women). *Students:* 88 full-time (57 women), 79 part-time (42 women); includes 104 minority (101 Black or African American, non-Hispanic/Latino; 1 Asian, non-Hispanic/Latino; 2 Hispanic/Latino), 2 international. Average age 34. 124 applicants, 62% accepted, 45 enrolled. In 2010, 38 master's awarded. *Degree requirements:* For master's, comprehensive exam, thesis optional. *Entrance requirements:* For master's, GMAT, GRE. Additional exam requirements/recommendations for international students: Required—TOEFL (minimum score 525 paper-based; 173 computer-based). *Application deadline:* Applications are processed on a rolling basis. Application fee: $30 ($100 for international students). Electronic applications accepted. *Expenses:* Tuition, state resident: full-time $5886; part-time $352 per credit hour. Tuition, nonresident: full-time $9054; part-time $528 per credit hour. Required fees: $450; $26 per credit hour. *Financial support:* In 2010–11, 46 students received support, including 4 research assistantships (averaging $10,975 per year); career-related internships or fieldwork, scholarships/grants, tuition waivers (partial), and unspecified assistantships also available. Financial award application deadline: 4/15; financial award applicants required to submit FAFSA. *Unit head:* Dr. Gashaw Lake, Dean, 502-597-6105, Fax: 502-597-6715, E-mail: gashaw.lake@kysu.edu. *Application contact:* Dr. Titilayo Ufomata, Acting Director of Graduate Studies, 502-597-6443, E-mail: titilayo.ufomata@kysu.edu.

Lawrence Technological University, College of Management, Southfield, MI 48075-1058. Offers business administration (MBA, DBA); business administration international (MBA); global leadership and management (MS); global operations and project management (MS); information systems (MS); information technology (DM); operations management (MS). *Accreditation:* ACBSP. Part-time and evening/weekend programs available. *Faculty:* 14 full-time (6 women), 53 part-time/adjunct (14 women). *Students:* 7 full-time (2 women), 584 part-time (258 women); includes 137 Black or African American, non-Hispanic/Latino; 2 American Indian or Alaska Native, non-Hispanic/Latino; 51 Asian, non-Hispanic/Latino; 10 Hispanic/Latino; 8 Two or more races, non-Hispanic/Latino; 48 international. Average age 35. 431 applicants, 54% accepted, 151 enrolled. In 2010, 216 master's, 12 doctorates awarded. *Degree requirements:* For master's, thesis (for some programs). *Entrance requirements:* For master's, GMAT. Additional exam requirements/recommendations for international students: Required—TOEFL (minimum score 550 paper-based; 213 computer-based; 79 iBT). *Application deadline:* For fall admission, 6/30 priority date for domestic students, 6/30 for international students; for spring admission, 11/15 priority date for domestic students, 11/15 for international students. Applications are processed on a rolling basis. Application fee: $50. Electronic applications accepted. *Financial support:* In 2010–11, 142 students received support. Federal Work-Study and institutionally sponsored loans available. Support available to part-time students. Financial award application deadline: 4/1; financial award applicants required to submit FAFSA. *Unit head:* Dr. Lou DeGennaro, Dean, 248-204-3050, E-mail: degennaro@ltu.edu. *Application contact:* Jane Rohrback, Director of Admissions, 248-204-3160, Fax: 248-204-2228, E-mail: admissions@ltu.edu.

Lewis University, College of Business, Graduate School of Management, Program in Business Administration, Romeoville, IL 60446. Offers accounting (MBA); custom elective option (MBA); e-business (MBA); finance (MBA); healthcare management (MBA); human resources management (MBA); information security (MBA); international business (MBA); management information systems (MBA); marketing (MBA); project management (MBA); technology and operations management (MBA). Part-time and evening/weekend programs available. *Students:* 119 full-time (66 women), 204 part-time (104 women); includes 55 Black or African American, non-Hispanic/Latino; 9 Asian, non-Hispanic/Latino; 30 Hispanic/Latino; 1 Native Hawaiian or other Pacific Islander, non-Hispanic/Latino, 9 international. Average age 28. In 2010, 111 master's awarded. *Entrance requirements:* For master's, interview, bachelor's degree, resume, 2 recommendations. Additional exam requirements/recommendations for international students: Required—TOEFL (minimum score 550 paper-based; 213 computer-based). *Application deadline:* For fall admission, 8/15 priority date for domestic students, 5/1 priority date for international students; for spring admission, 11/15 priority date for international students. Applications are processed on a rolling basis. Application fee: $40. Electronic applications accepted. *Expenses:* Tuition: Full-time $13,320; part-time $740 per credit hour. Tuition and fees vary according to program. *Financial support:* Career-related internships or fieldwork, Federal Work-Study, scholarships/grants, and unspecified assistantships available. Financial award application deadline: 5/1; financial award applicants required to submit FAFSA. *Unit head:* Dr. Maureen Culleeney, Academic Program Director, 815-838-0500 Ext. 5631, E-mail: culleema@lewisu.edu. *Application contact:* Michele Ryan, Director of Admission, 815-838-0500 Ext. 5384, E-mail: gsm@lewisu.edu.

Lincoln University, Graduate Studies, Oakland, CA 94612. Offers finance and investments (DBA); finance management and investment banking (MBA); general business (MBA); human resource management (MBA, DBA); international business (MBA); management information systems (MBA). Part-time and evening/weekend programs available. *Faculty:* 9 full-time (2 women), 11 part-time/adjunct (1 woman). *Students:* 297 full-time (134 women), 2 part-time (0 women). In 2010, 124 master's awarded. *Degree requirements:* For master's, research project (thesis), internship report, or comprehensive exam; for doctorate, comprehensive exam, thesis/dissertation. *Entrance requirements:* For master's, minimum GPA of 2.7; for doctorate, GMAT (minimum score: 550), GRE (minimum score: 1000), or equivalent test results (waived for master's degree with minimum cumulative GPA of 3.3). Additional exam requirements/recommendations for international students: Required—TOEFL (525 paper, 195 computer, 71 iBT) or IELTS (5.5) for MBA; TOEFL (550 paper, 213 computer, 79 iBT) or IELTS (6.0) for DBA;

Recommended—IELTS. *Application deadline:* For fall admission, 7/2 priority date for domestic and international students; for spring admission, 11/25 priority date for domestic students, 11/26 priority date for international students. Applications are processed on a rolling basis. Application fee: $75. Electronic applications accepted. *Expenses:* Tuition: Full-time $6930. Required fees: $195 per semester. *Financial support:* In 2010–11, 1 teaching assistantship was awarded; career-related internships or fieldwork and scholarships/grants also available. *Unit head:* Dr. Marshall Burak, Director of Graduate Programs, 510-628-8016, Fax: 510-628-8012, E-mail: mburak@lincolnuca.edu. *Application contact:* Peggy Au, Director of Admissions and Records, 510-628-8010, Fax: 510-628-8012, E-mail: admissions@lincolnuca.edu.

Lindenwood University, Graduate Programs, College of Individualized Education, St. Charles, MO 63301-1695. Offers administration (MSA); business administration (MBA); communications (MA); criminal justice and administration (MS); gerontology (MA); health management (MS); human resource management (MS); information technology (MS); managing information technology (MS); writing (MFA). Part-time and evening/weekend programs available. *Faculty:* 15 full-time (8 women), 128 part-time/adjunct (53 women). *Students:* 828 full-time (527 women), 80 part-time (50 women); includes 284 minority (265 Black or African American, non-Hispanic/Latino; 3 American Indian or Alaska Native, non-Hispanic/Latino; 6 Asian, non-Hispanic/Latino; 10 Hispanic/Latino), 23 international. Average age 35. 223 applicants, 44% accepted, 87 enrolled. In 2010, 478 master's awarded. *Degree requirements:* For master's, thesis (for some programs), 1 colloquium per term. *Entrance requirements:* For master's, interview, minimum GPA of 3.0. Additional exam requirements/recommendations for international students: Required—TOEFL (minimum score 550 paper-based; 213 computer-based; 80 iBT). *Application deadline:* For fall admission, 10/2 priority date for domestic and international students; for winter admission, 1/8 priority date for domestic and international students; for spring admission, 4/8 priority date for domestic and international students. Applications are processed on a rolling basis. Application fee: $30 ($100 for international students). Electronic applications accepted. *Expenses:* Tuition: Full-time $13,260; part-time $380 per credit hour. Required fees: $340. One-time fee: $30. Tuition and fees vary according to course level and course load. *Financial support:* In 2010–11, 631 students received support. Career-related internships or fieldwork, institutionally sponsored loans, tuition waivers (partial), and unspecified assistantships available. Financial award application deadline: 6/30; financial award applicants required to submit FAFSA. *Unit head:* Dan Kemper, Dean, 636-949-4501, Fax: 636-949-4505, E-mail: dkemper@lindenwood.edu. *Application contact:* Brett Barger, Dean of Evening Admissions and Extension Campuses, 636-949-4934, Fax: 636-949-4109, E-mail: adultadmissions@lindenwood.edu.

Lindenwood University, Graduate Programs, School of Business and Entrepreneurship, St. Charles, MO 63301-1695. Offers accounting (MBA, MS); business administration (MBA); entrepreneurial studies (MBA, MS); finance (MBA, MS); human resource management (MBA); human resources (MS); international business (MBA, MS); management (MBA, MS); management information systems (MBA, MS); marketing (MBA, MS); public management (MBA, MS); sport management (MA). *Accreditation:* ACBSP. Part-time and evening/weekend programs available. *Faculty:* 20 full-time (8 women), 17 part-time/adjunct (5 women). *Students:* 179 full-time (73 women), 184 part-time (87 women); includes 27 minority (20 Black or African American, non-Hispanic/Latino; 3 Asian, non-Hispanic/Latino; 4 Hispanic/Latino), 146 international. Average age 28. 149 applicants, 73 enrolled. In 2010, 142 master's awarded. *Degree requirements:* For master's, comprehensive exam (for some programs), thesis (for some programs). *Entrance requirements:* For master's, interview, minimum GPA of 3.0, letter of recommendation. Additional exam requirements/recommendations for international students: Required—TOEFL (minimum score 550 paper-based; 213 computer-based; 80 iBT). *Application deadline:* For fall admission, 7/30 priority date for domestic students, 9/16 priority date for international students; for winter admission, 12/15 priority date for domestic and international students; for spring admission, 2/25 priority date for domestic students, 2/11 priority date for international students. Applications are processed on a rolling basis. Application fee: $30 ($100 for international students). Electronic applications accepted. *Expenses:* Tuition: Full-time $13,260; part-time $380 per credit hour. Required fees: $340. One-time fee: $30. Tuition and fees vary according to course level and course load. *Financial support:* In 2010–11, 209 students received support. Career-related internships or fieldwork, Federal Work-Study, institutionally sponsored loans, and tuition waivers (partial) available. Financial award application deadline: 6/30; financial award applicants required to submit FAFSA. *Unit head:* Roger Ellis, Dean, 636-949-4839, E-mail: rellis@lindenwood.edu. *Application contact:* Brett Barger, Dean of Evening Admissions and Extension Campuses, 636-949-4934, Fax: 636-949-4109, E-mail: adultadmissions@lindenwood.edu.

Louisiana State University and Agricultural and Mechanical College, Graduate School, E. J. Ourso College of Business, Department of Information Systems and Decision Sciences, Baton Rouge, LA 70803. Offers MS, PhD. *Faculty:* 14 full-time (4 women). *Students:* 16 full-time (7 women), 4 part-time (1 woman); includes 2 Black or African American, non-Hispanic/Latino; 1 Asian, non-Hispanic/Latino; 1 Hispanic/Latino, 6 international.

Average age 30. 25 applicants, 32% accepted, 2 enrolled. In 2010, 1 master's, 3 doctorates awarded. Terminal master's awarded for partial completion of doctoral program. *Degree requirements:* For master's, comprehensive exam, thesis optional; for doctorate, comprehensive exam, thesis/dissertation. *Entrance requirements:* For master's, GMAT or GRE General Test; for doctorate, GMAT or GRE. Additional exam requirements/recommendations for international students: Required—TOEFL (minimum score 550 paper-based; 213 computer-based; 79 iBT). *Application deadline:* For fall admission, 1/25 priority date for domestic students, 5/15 for international students; for spring admission, 10/15 for international students. Applications are processed on a rolling basis. Application fee: $50 ($70 for international students). Electronic applications accepted. *Financial support:* In 2010–11, 19 students received support, including 1 fellowship (averaging $5,099 per year), 14 research assistantships with full and partial tuition reimbursements available (averaging $17,090 per year), 1 teaching assistantship with full and partial tuition reimbursement available (averaging $10,400 per year); Federal Work-Study, institutionally sponsored loans, scholarships/grants, health care benefits, tuition waivers (full and partial), and unspecified assistantships also available. Support available to part-time students. Financial award applicants required to submit FAFSA. *Faculty research:* Healthcare informatics, outsourcing, information systems management, operations management. Total annual research expenditures: $326,943. *Unit head:* Dr. Helmut Schneider, Department Head, 225-578-2516, Fax: 225-578-2511, E-mail: hschnei@lsu.edu. *Application contact:* Dr. Rudy Hirschheim, Graduate Adviser, 225-578-2514, Fax: 225-578-2511, E-mail: rudy@lsu.edu.

Marquette University, Graduate School of Management, Executive MBA Program, Milwaukee, WI 53201-1881. Offers economics (MBA); finance (MBA); human resources (MBA); international business (MBA); management information systems (MBA); marketing (MBA); operations and supply chain management (MBA); sports business (MBA). *Accreditation:* AACSB. *Faculty:* 3 full-time (1 woman), 2 part-time/adjunct (0 women). *Students:* 43 full-time (11 women); includes 6 minority (1 Black or African American, non-Hispanic/Latino; 4 Asian, non-Hispanic/Latino; 1 Hispanic/Latino), 3 international. Average age 37. 47 applicants, 74% accepted, 29 enrolled. In 2010, 13 master's awarded. *Degree requirements:* For master's, international trip. *Entrance requirements:* For master's, GMAT, two letters of recommendation, official transcripts from current and previous colleges/universities. Additional exam requirements/recommendations for international students: Required—TOEFL (minimum score 530 paper-based; 78 computer-based). *Application deadline:* Applications are processed on a rolling basis. Application fee: $50. Electronic applications accepted. *Expenses:* Contact institution. *Financial support:* Application deadline: 2/15. *Faculty research:* International trade and finance, customer relationship management, consumer satisfaction, customer service. *Unit head:* Dr. Jeanne Simmons, Graduate Director, 414-288-7145, Fax: 414-288-1660, E-mail: jeanne.simmons@marquette.edu. *Application contact:* Erin Fox, Assistant Director for Recruitment, 414-288-5319, Fax: 414-288-1902, E-mail: erin.fox@marquette.edu.

Marquette University, Graduate School of Management, Program in Business Administration, Milwaukee, WI 53201-1881. Offers business administration (MBA); economics (MBA); finance (MBA); human resources (MBA); international business (MBA); management information systems (MBA); marketing (MBA); operations and supply chain management (MBA); sports business (MBA); JD/MBA; MBA/MA; MBA/MSN. *Accreditation:* AACSB. Part-time and evening/weekend programs available. *Faculty:* 38 full-time (9 women), 24 part-time/adjunct (8 women). *Students:* 44 full-time (17 women), 368 part-time (105 women); includes 36 minority (4 Black or African American, non-Hispanic/Latino; 2 American Indian or Alaska Native, non-Hispanic/Latino; 20 Asian, non-Hispanic/Latino; 10 Hispanic/Latino), 30 international. Average age 31. 256 applicants, 60% accepted, 98 enrolled. In 2010, 117 master's awarded. *Entrance requirements:* For master's, GMAT, letters of recommendation. Additional exam requirements/recommendations for international students: Required—TOEFL (minimum score 530 paper-based; 78 computer-based). *Application deadline:* Applications are processed on a rolling basis. Application fee: $50. Electronic applications accepted. *Expenses:* Tuition: Full-time $16,290; part-time $905 per credit hour. Tuition and fees vary according to program. *Financial support:* In 2010–11, 4 fellowships, 11 teaching assistantships were awarded; research assistantships, Federal Work-Study, institutionally sponsored loans, scholarships/grants, and tuition waivers (full and partial) also available. Support available to part-time students. Financial award application deadline: 2/15. *Faculty research:* Ethics in the professions, services marketing, technology impact on decision-making, mentoring. *Unit head:* Dr. Jeanne Simmons, Graduate Director, 414-288-7145, Fax: 414-288-1660, E-mail: jeanne.simmons@marquette.edu. *Application contact:* Debra Leutermann, Admissions Coordinator, 414-288-8064, Fax: 414-288-1902, E-mail: debra.leutermann@marquette.edu.

Metropolitan State University, College of Management, St. Paul, MN 55106-5000. Offers business administration (MBA, DBA); information assurance security (Graduate Certificate); management information systems (MMIS); MIS generalist (Graduate Certificate); MIS systems analysis and design (Graduate Certificate); nonprofit management (MPNA); project management (Graduate Certificate); public administration (MPNA). Part-time and evening/weekend programs available. *Students:* 158 full-time (74 women), 217 part-time (114 women); includes 31 Black or African American, non-Hispanic/Latino; 26 Asian, non-Hispanic/Latino; 10 Hispanic/Latino; 6 Two or more races, non-Hispanic/Latino, 47 international. Average age 35. In 2010, 100 master's, 7 other advanced degrees awarded. *Degree requirements:* For master's, thesis optional, computer language (MMIS). *Entrance requirements:* For master's, GMAT (MBA), resume. Additional exam requirements/recommendations for international students: Required—TOEFL (minimum score 550 paper-based; 213 computer-based). *Application deadline:* For fall admission, 7/15 for international students; for winter admission, 11/15 for international students; for spring admission, 3/15 for international students. Applications are processed on a rolling basis. Application fee: $20. Electronic applications accepted. *Expenses:* Tuition, state resident: full-time $5827; part-time $291 per credit hour. Tuition, nonresident: full-time $11,654; part-time $583 per credit hour. Required fees: $10 per credit hour. Tuition and fees vary according to degree level. *Financial support:* Research assistantships with partial tuition reimbursements, career-related internships or fieldwork and Federal Work-Study available. Support available to part-time students. Financial award applicants required to submit FAFSA. *Faculty research:* Yugoslav economic system, workers' cooperatives, participative management and job enrichment, global business systems. *Unit head:* Dr. Paul Huo, Graduate Director, 612-659-7271, Fax: 612-659-7268, E-mail: carol.bormann.young@metrostate.edu. *Application contact:* Gloria B. Marcus, Recruiter/Admissions Adviser, 612-659-7258, Fax: 612-659-7268, E-mail: gloria.marcus@metrostate.edu.

Middle Tennessee State University, College of Graduate Studies, Jennings A. Jones College of Business, Department of Computer Information Systems, Murfreesboro, TN 37132. Offers MS. Part-time and evening/weekend programs available. Postbaccalaureate distance learning degree programs offered. *Faculty:* 12 full-time (3 women). *Students:* 16 full-time (5 women), 47 part-time (16 women); includes 7 Black or African American, non-Hispanic/Latino; 10 Asian, non-Hispanic/Latino; 2 Hispanic/Latino; 1 Two or more races, non-Hispanic/Latino. Average age 31. 21 applicants, 67% accepted, 14 enrolled. In 2010, 22 master's awarded. *Entrance requirements:* Additional exam requirements/recommendations for international students: Required—TOEFL (minimum score 525 paper-based; 195 computer-based; 71 iBT) or IELTS (minimum score 6). *Application deadline:* For fall admission, 6/1 for domestic and international students. Applications are processed on a rolling basis. Application fee: $25 ($30 for international students). Electronic applications accepted. *Expenses:* Tuition, state resident: full-time $4632. Tuition, nonresident: full-time $11,520. *Financial support:* In 2010–11, 8 students received support. Institutionally sponsored loans available. Support available to part-time students. Financial award application deadline: 5/1; financial award applicants required to submit FAFSA. *Faculty research:* Information technology assessment, information systems education, information technology job market, e-commerce, database technology. *Unit head:* Dr. Stanley E. Gambill, Chair, 615-898-2362, Fax: 615-898-5187, E-mail: sgambill@mtsu.edu. *Application contact:* Dr. Michael Allen, Dean and Vice Provost for Research, 615-898-2840, Fax: 615-904-8020, E-mail: mallen@mtsu.edu.

Minnesota State University Mankato, College of Graduate Studies, College of Science, Engineering and Technology, Department of Information Systems and Technology, Mankato, MN 56001. Offers database technologies (Certificate); information technology (MS). *Students:* 13 full-time (2 women), 8 part-time (3 women). *Degree requirements:* For master's, comprehensive exam, thesis or alternative. *Entrance requirements:* For master's, GRE General Test, minimum GPA of 3.0 during previous 2 years. Additional exam requirements/recommendations for international students: Required—TOEFL (minimum score 550 paper-based; 213 computer-based; 80 iBT). *Application deadline:* For fall admission, 7/1 priority date for domestic students; for spring admission, 11/1 for domestic students. Applications are processed on a rolling basis. Electronic applications accepted. *Financial support:* Research assistantships with full tuition reimbursements, teaching assistantships with full tuition reimbursements, unspecified assistantships available. Financial award application deadline: 3/15; financial award applicants required to submit FAFSA. *Unit head:* Dr. Mahbubur Syed, Graduate Coordinator, 507-389-3226. *Application contact:* 507-389-2321, E-mail: grad@mnsu.edu.

Mississippi State University, College of Business, Department of Management and Information Systems, Mississippi State, MS 39762. Offers business administration (PhD), including business information systems, management; information systems (MSIS). Part-time programs available. *Faculty:* 14 full-time (3 women). *Students:* 19 full-time (7 women), 7 part-time (2 women); includes 3 minority (1 Black or African American, non-Hispanic/Latino; 1 American Indian or Alaska Native, non-Hispanic/Latino; 1 Two or more races, non-Hispanic/Latino), 7 international. Average age 31. 55 applicants, 33% accepted, 11 enrolled. In 2010, 6 master's, 1 doctorate awarded. *Degree requirements:* For master's, comprehensive exam; for doctorate, comprehensive exam, thesis/dissertation. *Entrance requirements:* For master's, GMAT, minimum GPA of 3.0 in last 60 hours of course work; for doctorate, GMAT, minimum graduate GPA of 3.25 in last 60 hours. Additional exam requirements/recommendations for international students: Required—TOEFL (minimum score 575 paper-based; 233 computer-based; 90 iBT); Recommended—IELTS (minimum score 7). *Application deadline:* For fall admission, 7/1 for domestic students, 5/1 for international students; for spring admission, 11/1 for domestic students, 9/1 for international students.

Applications are processed on a rolling basis. Application fee: $40. Electronic applications accepted. *Expenses:* Tuition, state resident: full-time $2730.50; part-time $304 per credit hour. Tuition, nonresident: full-time $6901; part-time $767 per credit hour. *Financial support:* In 2010–11, 5 teaching assistantships (averaging $13,088 per year) were awarded; Federal Work-Study and institutionally sponsored loans also available. Financial award applicants required to submit FAFSA. *Faculty research:* Electronic commerce, management of information technology. *Unit head:* Dr. Rodney Pearson, Department Head and Professor of Information Systems, 662-325-3928, Fax: 662-325-8651, E-mail: rodney.pearson@msstate.edu. *Application contact:* Dr. Barbara Spencer, Associate Dean for Research and Outreach, 662-325-1891, Fax: 662-325-8161, E-mail: bspencer@cobian.msstate.edu.

Montclair State University, The Graduate School, School of Business, Department of Management Information Systems, Montclair, NJ 07043-1624. Offers management (MBA, Certificate); management information systems (MBA, Certificate). Part-time and evening/weekend programs available. *Faculty:* 26 full-time (8 women), 11 part-time/adjunct (2 women). *Students:* 15 full-time (8 women), 60 part-time (22 women); includes 5 Black or African American, non-Hispanic/Latino; 4 Asian, non-Hispanic/Latino; 4 Hispanic/Latino, 8 international. Average age 30. 35 applicants, 57% accepted, 12 enrolled. In 2010, 26 master's awarded. *Degree requirements:* For master's, comprehensive project. *Entrance requirements:* For master's, GMAT, 2 letters of recommendation, resume. Additional exam requirements/recommendations for international students: Required—TOEFL (minimum iBT score of 83) or IELTS. *Application deadline:* For fall admission, 6/1 for international students; for spring admission, 10/1 for international students. Applications are processed on a rolling basis. Application fee: $60. Electronic applications accepted. *Expenses:* Tuition, state resident: part-time $501.34 per credit. Tuition, nonresident: part-time $773.88 per credit. Required fees: $71.15 per credit. *Financial support:* In 2010–11, 7 research assistantships (averaging $7,000 per year) were awarded; Federal Work-Study, scholarships/grants, and unspecified assistantships also available. Support available to part-time students. Financial award application deadline: 3/1; financial award applicants required to submit FAFSA. *Faculty research:* Search engine optimization; trust and privacy online; data mining; teaching in hybrid and online environments; counterproductive work behavior and its effect on organizations, employees and customers; social identity and identification in organizations. *Unit head:* Dr. Richard Peterson, Head, 973-655-4269. *Application contact:* Amy Aiello, Director of Graduate Admissions and Operations, 973-655-5147, Fax: 973-655-7869, E-mail: graduate.school@montclair.edu.

National University, Academic Affairs, School of Engineering and Technology, Department of Applied Engineering, La Jolla, CA 92037-1011. Offers database administration (MS); engineering management (MS); environmental engineering (MS); homeland security and safety engineering (MS); system engineering (MS); wireless communications (MS). Part-time and evening/weekend programs available. Postbaccalaureate distance learning degree programs offered (no on-campus study). *Faculty:* 6 full-time (1 woman), 69 part-time/adjunct (12 women). *Students:* 82 full-time (16 women), 153 part-time (35 women); includes 87 minority (18 Black or African American, non-Hispanic/Latino; 1 American Indian or Alaska Native, non-Hispanic/Latino; 34 Asian, non-Hispanic/Latino; 28 Hispanic/Latino; 2 Native Hawaiian or other Pacific Islander, non-Hispanic/Latino; 4 Two or more races, non-Hispanic/Latino), 60 international. Average age 31. 166 applicants, 100% accepted, 106 enrolled. In 2010, 79 master's awarded. *Degree requirements:* For master's, thesis. *Entrance requirements:* For master's, interview, minimum GPA of 2.5. Additional exam requirements/recommendations for international students: Required—TOEFL (minimum score 550 paper-based; 213 computer-based; 79 iBT), IELTS (minimum score 6). *Application deadline:* Applications are processed on a rolling basis. Application fee: $60 ($65 for international students). Electronic applications accepted. *Expenses:* Tuition: Full-time $9450; part-time $350 per unit. Required fees: $350 per unit. One-time fee: $60. *Financial support:* Career-related internships or fieldwork, institutionally sponsored loans, scholarships/grants, and tuition waivers (partial) available. Support available to part-time students. Financial award application deadline: 6/30; financial award applicants required to submit FAFSA. *Unit head:* Dr. Shekar Viswanathan, Chair and Associate Professor, 858-309-8416, Fax: 858-309-3420, E-mail: sviswana@nu.edu. *Application contact:* Dominick Giovanniello, Associate Regional Dean—San Diego, 800-NAT-UNIV, Fax: 858-541-7792, E-mail: dgiovann@nu.edu.

National University, Academic Affairs, School of Engineering and Technology, Department of Computer Science and Information Systems, La Jolla, CA 92037-1011. Offers computer science (MS); information systems (MS); software engineering (MS); technology management (MS). Part-time and evening/weekend programs available. Postbaccalaureate distance learning degree programs offered (no on-campus study). *Faculty:* 8 full-time (1 woman), 90 part-time/adjunct (13 women). *Students:* 60 full-time (12 women), 146 part-time (40 women); includes 365 minority (25 Black or African American, non-Hispanic/Latino; 21 Asian, non-Hispanic/Latino; 14 Hispanic/Latino; 2 Native Hawaiian or other Pacific Islander, non-Hispanic/Latino; 303 Two or more races, non-Hispanic/Latino), 54 international. Average age 32. 138 applicants, 100% accepted, 79 enrolled. In 2010, 79 master's awarded. *Degree requirements:* For master's, thesis. *Entrance requirements:* For

master's, interview, minimum GPA of 2.5. Additional exam requirements/recommendations for international students: Required—TOEFL (minimum score 550 paper-based; 213 computer-based; 79 iBT), IELTS (minimum score 6). *Application deadline:* Applications are processed on a rolling basis. Application fee: $60 ($65 for international students). Electronic applications accepted. *Expenses:* Tuition: Full-time $9450; part-time $350 per unit. Required fees: $350 per unit. One-time fee: $60. *Financial support:* Career-related internships or fieldwork, institutionally sponsored loans, scholarships/grants, and tuition waivers (partial) available. Support available to part-time students. Financial award application deadline: 6/30; financial award applicants required to submit FAFSA. *Unit head:* Dr. Alireza M. Farahani, Chair and Instructor, 858-309-3438, Fax: 858-309-3420, E-mail: afarahan@nu.edu. *Application contact:* Dominick Giovanniello, Associate Regional Dean—San Diego, 800-NAT-UNIV, Fax: 858-541-7792, E-mail: dgiovann@nu.edu.

New Jersey Institute of Technology, Office of Graduate Studies, College of Computing Science, Department of Computer Science, Newark, NJ 07102. Offers bioinformatics (MS); computer science (MS, PhD); computing and business (MS); software engineering (MS). Part-time and evening/weekend programs available. *Faculty:* 35 full-time (2 women), 5 part-time/adjunct (1 woman). *Students:* 212 full-time (66 women), 109 part-time (14 women); includes 13 Black or African American, non-Hispanic/Latino; 3 American Indian or Alaska Native, non-Hispanic/Latino; 36 Asian, non-Hispanic/Latino; 16 Hispanic/Latino, 196 international. Average age 28. 867 applicants, 39% accepted, 116 enrolled. In 2010, 152 master's, 5 doctorates awarded. Terminal master's awarded for partial completion of doctoral program. *Degree requirements:* For master's, thesis optional; for doctorate, thesis/dissertation. *Entrance requirements:* For master's, GRE General Test; for doctorate, GRE General Test, minimum graduate GPA of 3.5. Additional exam requirements/recommendations for international students: Required—TOEFL (minimum score 550 paper-based; 213 computer-based; 79 iBT). *Application deadline:* For fall admission, 6/5 priority date for domestic students, 4/1 for international students; for spring admission, 11/15 for domestic and international students. Applications are processed on a rolling basis. Application fee: $65. Electronic applications accepted. *Expenses:* Tuition, state resident: full-time $14,724; part-time $818 per credit. Tuition, nonresident: full-time $20,304; part-time $1128 per credit. Required fees: $2272; $209 per credit. $103 per semester. One-time fee: $312 full-time; $212 part-time. *Financial support:* Fellowships with full and partial tuition reimbursements, research assistantships with full and partial tuition reimbursements, teaching assistantships with full and partial tuition reimbursements, career-related internships or fieldwork, Federal Work-Study, institutionally sponsored loans, and unspecified assistantships available. Financial award application deadline: 3/15. Total annual research expenditures: $6.4 million. *Unit head:* Dr. Michael A. Baltrush, Interim Chair, 973-596-3386, E-mail: michael.a.baltrush@njit.edu. *Application contact:* Kathryn Kelly, Director of Admissions, 973-596-3300, Fax: 973-596-3461, E-mail: admissions@njit.edu.

New Jersey Institute of Technology, Office of Graduate Studies, College of Computing Science, Program in Information Systems, Newark, NJ 07102. Offers business and information systems (MS); emergency management and business continuity (MS); information systems (MS, PhD). Part-time and evening/weekend programs available. *Students:* 86 full-time (26 women), 109 part-time (26 women); includes 23 Black or African American, non-Hispanic/Latino; 30 Asian, non-Hispanic/Latino; 14 Hispanic/Latino, 53 international. Average age 31. 275 applicants, 55% accepted, 69 enrolled. In 2010, 94 master's, 6 doctorates awarded. Terminal master's awarded for partial completion of doctoral program. *Degree requirements:* For master's, thesis optional; for doctorate, thesis/dissertation. *Entrance requirements:* For master's, GRE General Test; for doctorate, GRE General Test, minimum graduate GPA of 3.5. Additional exam requirements/recommendations for international students: Required—TOEFL (minimum score 550 paper-based; 213 computer-based; 79 iBT). *Application deadline:* For fall admission, 6/5 priority date for domestic students, 4/1 for international students; for spring admission, 11/15 for domestic and international students. Applications are processed on a rolling basis. Application fee: $65. Electronic applications accepted. *Expenses:* Tuition, state resident: full-time $14,724; part-time $818 per credit. Tuition, nonresident: full-time $20,304; part-time $1128 per credit. Required fees: $2272; $209 per credit. $103 per semester. One-time fee: $312 full-time; $212 part-time. *Financial support:* Fellowships with full and partial tuition reimbursements, research assistantships with full and partial tuition reimbursements, teaching assistantships with full and partial tuition reimbursements, career-related internships or fieldwork, Federal Work-Study, institutionally sponsored loans, and unspecified assistantships available. Financial award application deadline: 3/15. *Unit head:* Dr. Michael P. Bieber, Associate Chair, 973-596-2681, Fax: 973-596-2986, E-mail: michael.p.bieber@njit.edu. *Application contact:* Kathryn Kelly, Director of Admissions, 973-596-3300, Fax: 973-596-3461, E-mail: admissions@njit.edu.

Newman University, MBA Program, Wichita, KS 67213-2097. Offers finance (MBA); international business (MBA); leadership (MBA); management (MBA); technology (MBA). Part-time programs available. *Faculty:* 4 full-time (2 women), 7 part-time/adjunct (2 women). *Students:* 33 full-time (14 women), 92 part-time (37 women); includes 28 minority (7 Black or African American, non-Hispanic/Latino; 6 Asian, non-Hispanic/Latino; 12 Hispanic/

Latino; 1 Native Hawaiian or other Pacific Islander, non-Hispanic/Latino; 2 Two or more races, non-Hispanic/Latino), 24 international. Average age 32. 80 applicants, 83% accepted, 45 enrolled. In 2010, 72 master's awarded. *Degree requirements:* For master's, thesis optional. *Entrance requirements:* For master's, interview; minimum GPA of 3.0; 3 letters of recommendation; course work in algebra, statistics, macroeconomics, and financial accounting. Additional exam requirements/recommendations for international students: Required—TOEFL (minimum score 600 paper-based; 250 computer-based; 100 iBT). *Application deadline:* For fall admission, 8/1 priority date for domestic students, 7/15 priority date for international students; for winter admission, 1/1 priority date for domestic students; for spring admission, 1/1 priority date for domestic students, 11/15 priority date for international students. Applications are processed on a rolling basis. Application fee: $25 ($40 for international students). Electronic applications accepted. *Expenses:* Contact institution. *Financial support:* In 2010–11, 29 students received support. Federal Work-Study available. Financial award application deadline: 8/15; financial award applicants required to submit FAFSA. *Unit head:* Dr. George Goetz, Dean of the College of Professional Studies/Director, 316-942-4291 Ext. 2205, Fax: 316-942-4483, E-mail: smithge@newmanu.edu. *Application contact:* Linda Kay Sabala, Director of Graduate Admissions, 316-942-4291 Ext. 2230, Fax: 316-942-4483, E-mail: sabalal@newmanu.edu.

New Mexico Highlands University, Graduate Studies, School of Business, Las Vegas, NM 87701. Offers business administration (MBA), including government nonprofit management, human resource management, international business, management, management information systems. *Accreditation:* ACBSP. *Faculty:* 14 full-time (3 women). *Students:* 71 full-time (44 women), 124 part-time (68 women); includes 119 minority (8 Black or African American, non-Hispanic/Latino; 18 American Indian or Alaska Native, non-Hispanic/Latino; 1 Asian, non-Hispanic/Latino; 89 Hispanic/Latino; 1 Native Hawaiian or other Pacific Islander, non-Hispanic/Latino; 2 Two or more races, non-Hispanic/Latino), 34 international. Average age 34. 128 applicants, 98% accepted, 34 enrolled. In 2010, 48 master's awarded. *Degree requirements:* For master's, comprehensive exam, thesis or alternative. *Entrance requirements:* For master's, minimum undergraduate GPA of 3.0. Additional exam requirements/recommendations for international students: Required—TOEFL (minimum score 540 paper-based; 207 computer-based). *Application deadline:* For fall admission, 8/1 priority date for domestic students. Applications are processed on a rolling basis. Application fee: $15. *Expenses:* Tuition, state resident: full-time $2544. Required fees: $624; $132 per credit hour. *Financial support:* In 2010–11, 29 students received support. Career-related internships or fieldwork, Federal Work-Study, institutionally sponsored loans, scholarships/grants, tuition waivers (full and partial), and unspecified assistantships available. Support available to part-time students. Financial award application deadline: 3/1; financial award applicants required to submit FAFSA. *Faculty research:* Real estate valuation, studying expert judgments in complex accounting, decision environments, green marketing, environmentalism, marketing research methodology. *Unit head:* Dr. Margaret Young, Dean, 505-454-3522, Fax: 505-454-3354, E-mail: young m@nmhu.edu. Application contact: Diane Trujillo, Administrative Assistant, Graduate Studies, 505-454-3266, Fax: 505-426-2117, E-mail: dtrujillo@nmhu.edu.

New York Institute of Technology, Graduate Division, School of Management, Program in Business Administration, Old Westbury, NY 11568-8000. Offers accounting (Advanced Certificate); business administration (MBA); finance (Advanced Certificate); international business (Advanced Certificate); management of information systems (Advanced Certificate); marketing (Advanced Certificate). Part-time and evening/weekend programs available. *Students:* 454 full-time (188 women), 513 part-time (204 women); includes 49 minority (15 Black or African American, non-Hispanic/Latino; 23 Asian, non-Hispanic/Latino; 11 Hispanic/Latino), 268 international. Average age 29. In 2010, 435 master's, 1 other advanced degree awarded. *Degree requirements:* For master's, thesis (for some programs). *Entrance requirements:* For master's, minimum QPA of 2.85. Additional exam requirements/recommendations for international students: Required—TOEFL (minimum score 550 paper-based; 213 computer-based). *Application deadline:* For fall admission, 7/1 priority date for domestic students; for spring admission, 12/1 priority date for domestic students. Applications are processed on a rolling basis. Application fee: $50. Electronic applications accepted. *Expenses:* Tuition: Part-time $835 per credit. *Financial support:* Fellowships, research assistantships with partial tuition reimbursements, institutionally sponsored loans, tuition waivers (full and partial), and unspecified assistantships available. Support available to part-time students. Financial award applicants required to submit FAFSA. *Faculty research:* Instructor performance appraisal; relationship between TOEFL, GMAT, GRE, and performance in foreign students. *Unit head:* Dr. Stephen Hartman, Director, 516-686-7691, E-mail: shartman@nyit.edu. *Application contact:* Dr. Jacquelyn Nealon, Vice President for Enrollment Services, 516-686-7925, Fax: 516-686-7597, E-mail: jnealon@nyit.edu.

New York University, School of Continuing and Professional Studies, Division of Programs in Business, Graduate Programs in Management and Systems, New York, NY 10012-1019. Offers core business competencies (Advanced Certificate); database technologies (MS); enterprise and risk management (Advanced Certificate); enterprise risk management (MS); information technologies (Advanced Certificate); strategy and leadership (MS, Advanced Certificate); systems management (MS). Part-time and evening/weekend programs available. Postbaccalaureate distance learning degree programs offered (no on-campus study). *Faculty:* 2 full-time (0 women), 27 part-time/adjunct (6 women). *Students:* 23 full-time (11 women), 166 part-time (56 women); includes 18 Black or African American, non-Hispanic/Latino; 29 Asian, non-Hispanic/Latino; 17 Hispanic/Latino, 34 international. Average age 33. 135 applicants, 52% accepted, 39 enrolled. In 2010, 61 master's, 15 other advanced degrees awarded. *Degree requirements:* For master's, thesis, capstone project. *Entrance requirements:* For master's, GMAT or GRE General Test (for recent graduates), resume, 2 letters of recommendation, essay, professional experience. Additional exam requirements/recommendations for international students: Required—TOEFL (minimum score 600 paper-based; 250 computer-based; 100 iBT). *Application deadline:* For fall admission, 2/1 priority date for domestic and international students; for spring admission, 10/15 priority date for domestic students, 8/15 priority date for international students. Applications are processed on a rolling basis. Application fee: $75. Electronic applications accepted. *Financial support:* In 2010–11, 73 students received support, including 73 fellowships (averaging $1,803 per year); scholarships/grants also available. Support available to part-time students. Financial award application deadline: 3/1; financial award applicants required to submit FAFSA. *Unit head:* Israel Moskowitz, Academic Director, 212-992-3600, Fax: 212-992-3650, E-mail: im36@nyu.edu. *Application contact:* Helen Sapp, Assistant Director, 212-992-3640, Fax: 212-992-3650, E-mail: helen.sapp@nyu.edu.

North Central College, Graduate and Continuing Education Programs, Department of Business, Program in Management Information Systems, Naperville, IL 60566-7063. Offers MS. Part-time and evening/weekend programs available. *Faculty:* 10 full-time (2 women), 5 part-time/adjunct (0 women). *Students:* 4 full-time (1 woman), 3 part-time (1 woman); includes 1 Black or African American, non-Hispanic/Latino; 1 Asian, non-Hispanic/Latino, 2 international. Average age 34. In 2010, 2 master's awarded. *Degree requirements:* For master's, thesis optional, project. *Entrance requirements:* For master's, interview. Additional exam requirements/recommendations for international students: Required—TOEFL (minimum score 577 paper-based; 233 computer-based; 90 iBT). *Application deadline:* For fall admission, 8/15 for domestic students; for winter admission, 12/1 for domestic students; for spring admission, 2/1 for domestic students. Applications are processed on a rolling basis. Application fee: $25. *Expenses:* Contact institution. *Financial support:* Scholarships/grants available. Support available to part-time students. *Unit head:* Dr. Caroline St Clair, Program Coordinator, 630-637-5171, Fax: 630-637-5172, E-mail: cstclair@noctrl.edu. *Application contact:* Wendy Kulpinski, Director and Graduate and Continuing Education Admission, 630-637-5808, Fax: 630-637-5844, E-mail: wekulpinski@noctrl.edu.

Northeastern University, College of Computer and Information Science, Boston, MA 02115-5096. Offers computer and information science (PhD); computer science (MS); health informatics (MS); information assurance (MS). Part-time and evening/weekend programs available. *Faculty:* 28 full-time (3 women), 3 part-time/adjunct (all women). *Students:* 337 full-time (91 women), 90 part-time (52 women). 1,045 applicants, 56% accepted, 150 enrolled. In 2010, 88 master's, 7 doctorates awarded. Terminal master's awarded for partial completion of doctoral program. *Degree requirements:* For master's, thesis optional; for doctorate, comprehensive exam, thesis/dissertation. *Entrance requirements:* For master's and doctorate, GRE General Test. Additional exam requirements/recommendations for international students: Required—TOEFL or IELTS. *Application deadline:* For fall admission, 7/15 for domestic students, 5/1 for international students; for spring admission, 10/15 for domestic students, 9/1 for international students. Applications are processed on a rolling basis. Application fee: $50. Electronic applications accepted. *Expenses:* Contact institution. *Financial support:* In 2010–11, 59 students received support, including 1 fellowship, 40 research assistantships with full tuition reimbursements available (averaging $18,260 per year), 33 teaching assistantships with full tuition reimbursements available (averaging $18,260 per year); career-related internships or fieldwork, Federal Work-Study, institutionally sponsored loans, scholarships/grants, and unspecified assistantships also available. Financial award application deadline: 1/15. *Faculty research:* Programming languages, artificial intelligence, human-computer interaction, database management, network security. *Unit head:* Dr. Larry A. Finkelstein, Dean, 617-373-2462, Fax: 617-373-5121. *Application contact:* Dr. Agnes Chan, Associate Dean and Director of Graduate Program, 617-373-2462, Fax: 617-373-5121, E-mail: gradschool@ccs.neu.edu.

Northern Illinois University, Graduate School, College of Business, Department of Operations Management and Information Systems, De Kalb, IL 60115-2854. Offers management information systems (MS). Part-time programs available. *Faculty:* 11 full-time (3 women), 3 part-time/adjunct (0 women). *Students:* 27 full-time (5 women), 25 part-time (7 women); includes 1 Black or African American, non-Hispanic/Latino; 6 Asian, non-Hispanic/Latino; 1 Hispanic/Latino, 21 international. Average age 27. 33 applicants, 61% accepted, 13 enrolled. In 2010, 27 master's awarded. *Degree requirements:* For master's, computer language. *Entrance requirements:* For master's, GMAT, minimum GPA of 2.75. Additional exam requirements/recommendations for international students: Required—TOEFL (minimum score 550 paper-based; 213 computer-based). *Application deadline:* For fall admission,

6/1 for domestic students, 5/1 for international students; for spring admission, 11/1 for domestic students, 10/1 for international students. Applications are processed on a rolling basis. Application fee: $30. Electronic applications accepted. *Expenses:* Tuition, state resident: full-time $7200; part-time $300 per credit hour. Tuition, nonresident: full-time $14,400; part-time $600 per credit hour. Required fees: $79 per credit hour. *Financial support:* In 2010–11, 16 research assistantships with full tuition reimbursements were awarded; fellowships with full tuition reimbursements, teaching assistantships with full tuition reimbursements, career-related internships or fieldwork, Federal Work-Study, scholarships/grants, tuition waivers (full), and unspecified assistantships also available. Support available to part-time students. Financial award applicants required to submit FAFSA. *Faculty research:* Affordability of home ownership, Web portal competition intranet, electronic commerce, corporate-academic alliances. *Unit head:* Dr. Geoffrey Gordon, Interim chair, 815-753-1285, Fax: 815-753-7460. *Application contact:* Steve Kispert, Office of Graduate Studies in Business, 815-753-6301, E-mail: skispert@niu.edu.

Northwest Missouri State University, Graduate School, Melvin and Valorie Booth College of Business and Professional Studies, Program in Information Technology Management, Maryville, MO 64468-6001. Offers MBA. Part-time programs available. *Faculty:* 11 full-time (5 women). *Students:* 6 full-time (1 woman), 1 (woman) part-time, 4 international. 4 applicants, 0% accepted, 0 enrolled. In 2010, 1 master's awarded. *Degree requirements:* For master's, comprehensive exam. *Entrance requirements:* For master's, GMAT, minimum GPA of 2.5. Additional exam requirements/recommendations for international students: Required—TOEFL (minimum score 550 paper-based; 213 computer-based). *Application deadline:* For fall admission, 7/1 for domestic and international students; for spring admission, 12/1 for domestic students, 11/15 for international students. Application fee: $0 ($50 for international students). *Financial support:* In 2010–11, 4 research assistantships with full tuition reimbursements (averaging $6,000 per year), 1 teaching assistantship with full tuition reimbursement (averaging $6,000 per year) were awarded. Financial award application deadline: 4/1; financial award applicants required to submit FAFSA. *Unit head:* Dr. Gary Ury, Head, 660-562-1185. *Application contact:* Dr. Gregory Haddock, Dean of Graduate School, 660-562-1145, Fax: 660-562-1096, E-mail: gradsch@nwmissouri.edu.

Norwich University, School of Graduate and Continuing Studies, Program in Information Assurance, Northfield, VT 05663. Offers business continuity management (MS); managing cyber crime and digital incidents (MS). Evening/weekend programs available. *Faculty:* 18 part-time/adjunct (3 women). *Students:* 166 full-time (8 women); includes 7 Black or African American, non-Hispanic/Latino; 2 Asian, non-Hispanic/Latino; 5 Hispanic/Latino. Average age 40. In 2010, 166 master's awarded. *Entrance requirements:* For master's, minimum undergraduate GPA of 2.75. Additional exam requirements/recommendations for international students: Required—TOEFL (minimum score 550 paper-based; 212 computer-based; 83 iBT). *Application deadline:* For fall admission, 8/10 for domestic and international students; for winter admission, 11/7 for domestic and international students; for spring admission, 2/6 for domestic and international students. Application fee: $50. *Expenses:* Tuition: Full-time $17,380; part-time $645 per credit. Tuition and fees vary according to program. *Financial support:* Scholarships/grants available. Financial award applicants required to submit FAFSA. *Unit head:* Dr. Thomas Desoteaux, Program Director, 802-485-2259, E-mail: tdescote@norwich.edu. *Application contact:* Elizabeth Templeton, Administrative Director, 802-485-2757, Fax: 802-485-2533, E-mail: etemplet@norwich.edu.

Nova Southeastern University, Graduate School of Computer and Information Sciences, Program in Information Security, Fort Lauderdale, FL 33314-7796. Offers MS. *Students:* 6 full-time (1 woman), 56 part-time (9 women); includes 29 minority (8 Black or African American, non-Hispanic/Latino; 6 Asian, non-Hispanic/Latino; 15 Hispanic/Latino), 6 international. Average age 34. 55 applicants, 45% accepted. In 2010, 19 master's awarded. *Degree requirements:* For master's, thesis optional. *Entrance requirements:* Additional exam requirements/recommendations for international students: Required—TOEFL (minimum score 213 computer-based; 79 iBT), IELTS (minimum score 6). *Application deadline:* For fall admission, 8/22 for domestic students; for winter admission, 1/3 for domestic students. Applications are processed on a rolling basis. Electronic applications accepted. *Unit head:* Dr. Amon Seagull, Interim Dean, 954-262-7300. *Application contact:* 954-262-2000, Fax: 954-262-2752, E-mail: scisinfo@nova.edu.

Nova Southeastern University, Graduate School of Computer and Information Sciences, Program in Information Systems, Fort Lauderdale, FL 33314-7796. Offers MS, PhD. *Students:* 45 full-time (8 women), 235 part-time (61 women); includes 71 Black or African American, non-Hispanic/Latino; 3 American Indian or Alaska Native, non-Hispanic/Latino; 17 Asian, non-Hispanic/Latino; 28 Hispanic/Latino, 8 international. Average age 45. 60 applicants, 37% accepted. In 2010, 15 doctorates awarded. *Degree requirements:* For doctorate, thesis/dissertation. *Entrance requirements:* Additional exam requirements/recommendations for international students: Required—TOEFL (minimum score 213 computer-based; 79 iBT), IELTS (minimum score 6). *Application deadline:* For fall admission, 8/1 for domestic students. Applications are processed on a rolling basis. Electronic applications accepted. *Unit head:* Dr. Amon Seagull, Interim Dean, 954-262-7300. *Application contact:* 954-262-2000, Fax: 954-262-2752, E-mail: scisinfo@nova.edu.

Nova Southeastern University, Graduate School of Computer and Information Sciences, Program in Management Information Systems, Fort Lauderdale, FL 33314-7796. Offers information security (MS); management information systems (MS). Part-time and evening/weekend programs available. Postbaccalaureate distance learning degree programs offered (no on-campus study). *Students:* 27 full-time (6 women), 154 part-time (60 women); includes 47 Black or African American, non-Hispanic/Latino; 1 American Indian or Alaska Native, non-Hispanic/Latino; 15 Asian, non-Hispanic/Latino; 41 Hispanic/Latino; 3 Two or more races, non-Hispanic/Latino, 13 international. Average age 36. 87 applicants, 66% accepted. In 2010, 49 master's awarded. *Degree requirements:* For master's, thesis optional. *Entrance requirements:* Additional exam requirements/recommendations for international students: Required—TOEFL (minimum score 213 computer-based; 79 iBT), IELTS (minimum score 6). *Application deadline:* For fall admission, 8/22 for domestic students; for winter admission, 1/3 for domestic students. Applications are processed on a rolling basis. Application fee: $50. Electronic applications accepted. *Financial support:* Application deadline: 5/1. *Unit head:* Dr. Amon Seagull, Interim Dean. *Application contact:* 954-262-2000, Fax: 954-262-2752, E-mail: scisinfo@nova.edu.

The Ohio State University, Graduate School, Max M. Fisher College of Business, Department of Accounting and Management Information Systems, Columbus, OH 43210. Offers M Acc, MA, MS, PhD. *Accreditation:* AACSB. *Faculty:* 25. *Students:* 6 full-time (0 women), 5 part-time (2 women), 5 international. Average age 32. In 2010, 1 master's, 1 doctorate awarded. Terminal master's awarded for partial completion of doctoral program. *Degree requirements:* For doctorate, thesis/dissertation. *Entrance requirements:* For master's, GMAT (preferred) or GRE General Test; for doctorate, GMAT (preferred) or GRE. Additional exam requirements/recommendations for international students: Required—TOEFL (minimum score 600 paper-based; 250 computer-based). *Application deadline:* For fall admission, 8/15 priority date for domestic students, 7/1 priority date for international students; for winter admission, 12/1 priority date for domestic students, 11/1 priority date for international students; for spring admission, 3/1 priority date for domestic students, 2/1 priority date for international students. Applications are processed on a rolling basis. Application fee: $40 ($50 for international students). Electronic applications accepted. *Expenses:* Tuition, state resident: full-time $10,605. Tuition, nonresident: full-time $26,535. Tuition and fees vary according to course load and program. *Financial support:* Fellowships, research assistantships, teaching assistantships, career-related internships or fieldwork, Federal Work-Study, and institutionally sponsored loans available. Support available to part-time students. *Faculty research:* Artificial intelligence, protocol analysis, database design in decision-supporting systems. *Unit head:* Annette Beatty, Graduate Studies Committee Chair, 614-292-2081, Fax: 614-292-2118, E-mail: beatty.86@osu.edu. *Application contact:* 614-292-9444, Fax: 614-292-3895, E-mail: domestic.grad@osu.edu.

Oklahoma State University, Spears School of Business, Department of Management Science and Information Systems, Stillwater, OK 74078. Offers management information systems (MS); management science and information systems (PhD); telecommunications management (MS). Part-time programs available. Postbaccalaureate distance learning degree programs offered. *Faculty:* 17 full-time (3 women), 2 part-time/adjunct (0 women). *Students:* 64 full-time (12 women), 75 part-time (15 women); includes 4 Black or African American, non-Hispanic/Latino; 4 American Indian or Alaska Native, non-Hispanic/Latino; 1 Asian, non-Hispanic/Latino, 74 international. Average age 29. 252 applicants, 36% accepted, 36 enrolled. In 2010, 68 master's, 1 doctorate awarded. *Degree requirements:* For master's, thesis or alternative; for doctorate, comprehensive exam, thesis/dissertation. *Entrance requirements:* For master's and doctorate, GRE or GMAT. Additional exam requirements/recommendations for international students: Required—TOEFL (minimum score 550 paper-based; 79 iBT). *Application deadline:* For fall admission, 3/1 priority date for international students; for spring admission, 8/1 priority date for international students. Applications are processed on a rolling basis. Application fee: $40 ($75 for international students). Electronic applications accepted. *Expenses:* Tuition, state resident: full-time $3716; part-time $154.85 per credit hour. Tuition, nonresident: full-time $14,892; part-time $621 per credit hour. Required fees: $2044; $85.20 per credit hour. One-time fee: $50. Tuition and fees vary according to course load and campus/location. *Financial support:* In 2010–11, 1 research assistantship (averaging $4,200 per year), 12 teaching assistantships (averaging $12,460 per year) were awarded; career-related internships or fieldwork, Federal Work-Study, scholarships/grants, health care benefits, tuition waivers (partial), and unspecified assistantships also available. Support available to part-time students. Financial award application deadline: 3/1; financial award applicants required to submit FAFSA. *Unit head:* Dr. Rick Wilson, Head, 405-744-3551, Fax: 405-744-5180. *Application contact:* Dr. Gordon Emslie, Dean, 405-744-6368, Fax: 405-744-0355, E-mail: grad-i@okstate.edu.

Old Dominion University, College of Business and Public Administration, MBA Program, Norfolk, VA 23529. Offers business and economic forecasting (MBA); financial analysis and valuation (MBA); information technology and enterprise integration (MBA); international business (MBA); maritime and port management (MBA); public administration (MBA). *Accreditation:* AACSB. Part-time and evening/weekend programs available. *Faculty:* 66

full-time (15 women), 6 part-time/adjunct (1 woman). *Students:* 74 full-time (32 women), 166 part-time (62 women); includes 45 minority (21 Black or African American, non-Hispanic/Latino; 1 American Indian or Alaska Native, non-Hispanic/Latino; 8 Asian, non-Hispanic/Latino; 10 Hispanic/Latino; 1 Native Hawaiian or other Pacific Islander, non-Hispanic/Latino; 4 Two or more races, non-Hispanic/Latino), 19 international. Average age 31. 169 applicants, 52% accepted, 61 enrolled. In 2010, 100 master's awarded. *Entrance requirements:* For master's, GMAT, letter of reference, resume, coursework in calculus, essay. Additional exam requirements/recommendations for international students: Required—TOEFL (minimum score 550 paper-based; 213 computer-based; 80 iBT). *Application deadline:* For fall admission, 6/1 priority date for domestic students, 4/15 priority date for international students; for spring admission, 11/1 priority date for domestic students, 10/1 priority date for international students. Applications are processed on a rolling basis. Application fee: $50. Electronic applications accepted. *Expenses:* Tuition, state resident: full-time $8592; part-time $358 per credit. Tuition, nonresident: full-time $21,672; part-time $903 per credit. Required fees: $119 per semester. One-time fee: $50. *Financial support:* In 2010–11, 44 students received support, including 90 research assistantships with partial tuition reimbursements available (averaging $3,200 per year); career-related internships or fieldwork, scholarships/grants, and unspecified assistantships also available. Support available to part-time students. Financial award application deadline: 2/15; financial award applicants required to submit FAFSA. *Faculty research:* International business, buyer behavior, financial markets, strategy, operations research. *Unit head:* Dr. Larry Filer, Graduate Program Director, 757-683-3585, Fax: 757-683-5750, E-mail: mbainfo@odu.edu. *Application contact:* Shanna Wood, MBA Program Manager, 757-683-3585, Fax: 757-683-5750, E-mail: mbainfo@odu.edu.

Our Lady of the Lake University of San Antonio, School of Business and Leadership, Program in Information Systems and Security, San Antonio, TX 78207-4689. Offers MS. Postbaccalaureate distance learning degree programs offered. *Students:* 16 full-time (6 women), 28 part-time (13 women); includes 22 minority (4 Black or African American, non-Hispanic/Latino; 1 American Indian or Alaska Native, non-Hispanic/Latino; 17 Hispanic/Latino). Average age 37. In 2010, 6 master's awarded. *Expenses:* Tuition: Full-time $13,500; part-time $750 per contact hour. Required fees: $330. Tuition and fees vary according to course level, degree level and campus/location. *Unit head:* Dr. Robert Bisking, Dean, 210-434-6711, Fax: 210-434-0821. *Application contact:* Dr. Robert Bisking, Dean, 210-434-6711, Fax: 210-434-0821.

Pacific States University, College of Business, Los Angeles, CA 90006. Offers accounting (MBA); business administration (DBA); finance (MBA); international business (MBA); management of information technology (MBA); real estate management (MBA). Part-time and evening/weekend programs available. Postbaccalaureate distance learning degree programs offered (no on-campus study). *Faculty:* 4 full-time (1 woman), 13 part-time/adjunct (0 women). *Students:* 130 full-time (55 women); includes 1 Black or African American, non-Hispanic/Latino; 7 Asian, non-Hispanic/Latino; 3 Native Hawaiian or other Pacific Islander, non-Hispanic/Latino, 115 international. Average age 31. 42 applicants, 83% accepted, 33 enrolled. In 2010, 67 master's awarded. *Degree requirements:* For doctorate, comprehensive exam, thesis/dissertation. *Entrance requirements:* For master's, minimum undergraduate GPA of 2.5 during last 90 hours of course work. Additional exam requirements/recommendations for international students: Required—TOEFL (minimum score 133 computer-based; 45 iBT), IELTS (minimum score 4.5). *Application deadline:* For fall admission, 8/15 priority date for domestic students; for winter admission, 10/15 priority date for domestic students; for spring admission, 1/15 priority date for domestic students. Applications are processed on a rolling basis. Application fee: $100. *Expenses:* Tuition: Full-time $8280; part-time $345 per credit hour. Required fees: $150 per quarter. *Financial support:* Scholarships/grants available. Financial award applicants required to submit FAFSA. *Unit head:* Dr. Chase C. Lee, Director, 888-200-0383, Fax: 323-731-2383, E-mail: admission@psuca.edu. *Application contact:* Zolzaya Enkhbayar, Assistant Director of Admissions, 323-731-2383, Fax: 323-731-7276, E-mail: admissions@psuca.edu.

Pacific States University, College of Computer Science, Los Angeles, CA 90006. Offers computer science (MSCS); information systems (MSCS). Part-time and evening/weekend programs available. *Faculty:* 4 part-time/adjunct (0 women). *Students:* 16 full-time (2 women); includes 1 Asian, non-Hispanic/Latino, 14 international. Average age 27. 9 applicants, 78% accepted, 6 enrolled. In 2010, 7 master's awarded. *Entrance requirements:* For master's, bachelor's degree in physics, engineering, computer science, or applied mathematics; minimum undergraduate GPA of 2.5 during last 90 hours of course work. Additional exam requirements/recommendations for international students: Required—TOEFL (minimum score 450 paper-based; 133 computer-based; 45 iBT), IELTS (minimum score 4.5). *Application deadline:* For fall admission, 8/15 priority date for domestic students; for winter admission, 10/15 priority date for domestic students; for spring admission, 1/15 priority date for domestic students. Applications are processed on a rolling basis. Application fee: $100. *Expenses:* Tuition: Full-time $8280; part-time $345 per credit hour. Required fees: $150 per quarter. *Financial support:* Scholarships/grants available. Financial award applicants required to submit FAFSA. *Unit head:* John Ma, Director, 888-200-0383, Fax: 323-731-7276, E-mail:

admission@psuca.edu. *Application contact:* Namyoung Chah, Registrar, 323-731-2383, Fax: 323-731-7276, E-mail: registrar@psuca.edu.

Polytechnic Institute of NYU, Department of Technology Management, Brooklyn, NY 11201-2990. Offers construction management (Advanced Certificate); electronic business management (Advanced Certificate); entrepreneurship (Advanced Certificate); human resources management (Advanced Certificate); information management (Advanced Certificate); management (MS); management of technology (MS); organizational behavior (MS, Advanced Certificate); project management (Advanced Certificate); technology management (MBA, PhD, Advanced Certificate); telecommunications and information management (MS); telecommunications management (Advanced Certificate). Part-time and evening/weekend programs available. *Faculty:* 7 full-time (2 women), 28 part-time/adjunct (4 women). *Students:* 224 full-time (93 women), 106 part-time (38 women); includes 15 Black or African American, non-Hispanic/Latino; 41 Asian, non-Hispanic/Latino; 10 Hispanic/Latino, 158 international. Average age 30. 370 applicants, 60% accepted, 120 enrolled. In 2010, 173 master's, 1 doctorate awarded. *Degree requirements:* For master's, comprehensive exam (for some programs), thesis (for some programs); for doctorate, comprehensive exam, thesis/dissertation. *Entrance requirements:* For master's, GMAT, minimum B average in undergraduate course work. Additional exam requirements/recommendations for international students: Required—TOEFL (minimum score 550 paper-based; 213 computer-based; 80 iBT); Recommended—IELTS (minimum score 6.5). *Application deadline:* For fall admission, 7/31 priority date for domestic students, 4/30 priority date for international students; for spring admission, 12/31 priority date for domestic students, 11/30 priority date for international students. Applications are processed on a rolling basis. Application fee: $75. Electronic applications accepted. *Expenses:* Tuition: Full-time $21,492; part-time $1194 per credit. Required fees: $385 per semester. Tuition and fees vary according to course load. *Financial support:* In 2010–11, 1 fellowship (averaging $26,400 per year) was awarded; research assistantships, teaching assistantships, institutionally sponsored loans, scholarships/grants, and unspecified assistantships also available. Support available to part-time students. *Unit head:* Prof. Bharadwaj Rao, Head, 718-260-3617, Fax: 718-260-3874, E-mail: brao@poly.edu. *Application contact:* JeanCarlo Bonilla, Director of Graduate Enrollment Management, 718-260-3182, Fax: 718-260-3624, E-mail: gradinfo@poly.edu.

Polytechnic Institute of NYU, Westchester Graduate Center, Graduate Programs, Department of Finance and Risk Engineering, Major in Financial Engineering, Hawthorne, NY 10532-1507. Offers capital markets (MS); computational finance (MS); financial engineering (AC); financial technology (MS); financial technology management (AC); information management (AC). *Students:* 1 (woman) part-time, all international. Average age 25. In 2010, 8 master's awarded. *Degree requirements:* For master's, comprehensive exam (for some programs), thesis (for some programs). *Entrance requirements:* Additional exam requirements/recommendations for international students: Required—TOEFL (minimum score 550 paper-based; 213 computer-based; 80 iBT); Recommended—IELTS (minimum score 6.5). *Application deadline:* For fall admission, 7/31 priority date for domestic students, 4/30 priority date for international students; for spring admission, 12/31 priority date for domestic students, 11/30 priority date for international students. Applications are processed on a rolling basis. Application fee: $75. Electronic applications accepted. *Expenses:* Tuition: Full-time $21,492; part-time $1194 per credit. Required fees: $385 per semester. Tuition and fees vary according to course load. *Financial support:* Institutionally sponsored loans, scholarships/grants, and unspecified assistantships available. Support available to part-time students. *Unit head:* Dr. Charles S. Tapiero, Department Head, 718-260-3653, E-mail: ctapiero@poly.edu. *Application contact:* JeanCarlo Bonilla, Director of Graduate Enrollment Management, 718-260-3182, Fax: 718-260-3624, E-mail: gradinfo@poly.edu.

Prairie View A&M University, College of Engineering, Prairie View, TX 77446-0519. Offers computer information systems (MSCIS); computer science (MSCS); electrical engineering (MSEE, PhDEE); engineering (MS Engr). Part-time and evening/weekend programs available. *Faculty:* 19 full-time (0 women). *Students:* 89 full-time (26 women), 34 part-time (5 women); includes 45 Black or African American, non-Hispanic/Latino; 1 American Indian or Alaska Native, non-Hispanic/Latino; 13 Asian, non-Hispanic/Latino; 3 Hispanic/Latino, 53 international. Average age 32. 50 applicants, 84% accepted, 33 enrolled. In 2010, 8 master's, 2 doctorates awarded. *Degree requirements:* For master's, thesis (for some programs); for doctorate, comprehensive exam, thesis/dissertation. *Entrance requirements:* For master's, GRE General Test, bachelor's degree in engineering from an ABET accredited institution; for doctorate, GRE. Additional exam requirements/recommendations for international students: Required—TOEFL (minimum score 550 paper-based). *Application deadline:* For fall admission, 7/1 priority date for domestic and international students; for spring admission, 11/1 priority date for domestic and international students. Application fee: $50. Electronic applications accepted. *Expenses:* Tuition, state resident: full-time $3586.14; part-time $119.06 per credit hour. Tuition, nonresident: part-time $511.23 per credit hour. *Financial support:* In 2010–11, 80 students received support, including 14 fellowships (averaging $1,050 per year), 16 research assistantships (averaging $16,150 per year), 13 teaching assistantships (averaging

$14,000 per year); career-related internships or fieldwork, institutionally sponsored loans, scholarships/grants, health care benefits, tuition waivers (partial), and unspecified assistantships also available. Financial award application deadline: 3/1; financial award applicants required to submit FAFSA. *Faculty research:* Applied radiation research, thermal science, computational fluid dynamics, analog mixed signal, aerial space battlefield. Total annual research expenditures: $439,054. *Unit head:* Dr. Kendall T. Harris, Dean, 936-261-9956, Fax: 936-261-9869, E-mail: tharris@pvamu.edu. *Application contact:* Barbara A. Thompson, Administrative Assistant, 936-261-9896, Fax: 936-261-9869, E-mail: bathompson@pvamu.edu.

Quinnipiac University, School of Business, MBA Program, Hamden, CT 06518-1940. Offers chartered financial analyst (MBA); finance (MBA); healthcare management (MBA); information systems management (MBA); marketing (MBA); supply chain management (MBA); JD/MBA. *Accreditation:* AACSB. Part-time and evening/weekend programs available. *Faculty:* 25 full-time (2 women), 3 part-time/adjunct (all women). *Students:* 87 full-time (24 women), 121 part-time (46 women); includes 12 minority (1 Black or African American, non-Hispanic/Latino; 7 Asian, non-Hispanic/Latino; 4 Hispanic/Latino), 14 international. Average age 29. 119 applicants, 81% accepted, 81 enrolled. In 2010, 70 master's awarded. *Entrance requirements:* For master's, GMAT or GRE, minimum GPA of 3.0. Additional exam requirements/recommendations for international students: Required—TOEFL (minimum score 575 paper-based; 233 computer-based; 90 iBT), IELTS (minimum score 6.5). *Application deadline:* For fall admission, 7/30 priority date for domestic students, 4/30 priority date for international students; for spring admission, 12/15 priority date for domestic students, 9/15 priority date for international students. Applications are processed on a rolling basis. Application fee: $45. Electronic applications accepted. *Expenses:* Tuition: Part-time $810 per credit. Required fees: $35 per credit. *Financial support:* In 2010–11, 110 students received support. Federal Work-Study, tuition waivers (partial), and unspecified assistantships available. Support available to part-time students. Financial award application deadline: 4/15; financial award applicants required to submit FAFSA. *Faculty research:* Equity compensation, marketing relationships and public policy, corporate governance, international business, supply chain management. *Unit head:* Lisa Braiewa, MBA Program Director, 203-582-3710, Fax: 203-582-8664, E-mail: lisa.braiewa@quinnipiac.edu. *Application contact:* Jennifer Boutin, 800-462-1944, Fax: 203-582-3443, E-mail: jennifer.boutin@quinnipiac.edu.

Quinnipiac University, School of Business, Program in Information Technology, Hamden, CT 06518-1940. Offers MS. Part-time and evening/weekend programs available. *Faculty:* 3 full-time (1 woman), 1 part-time/adjunct (0 women). *Students:* 5 full-time (3 women), 21 part-time (5 women); includes 1 Black or African American, non-Hispanic/Latino; 3 Asian, non-Hispanic/Latino; 1 Hispanic/Latino, 2 international. Average age 24. 14 applicants, 93% accepted, 9 enrolled. In 2010, 15 master's awarded. *Entrance requirements:* For master's, minimum GPA of 2.75; course work in computer language programming, management, accounting foundation. Additional exam requirements/recommendations for international students: Required—TOEFL (minimum score 575 paper-based; 233 computer-based; 90 iBT), IELTS (minimum score 6.5). *Application deadline:* For fall admission, 7/30 priority date for domestic students, 4/30 priority date for international students; for spring admission, 12/15 priority date for domestic students, 9/15 priority date for international students. Applications are processed on a rolling basis. Application fee: $45. Electronic applications accepted. *Expenses:* Tuition: Part-time $810 per credit. Required fees: $35 per credit. *Financial support:* Federal Work-Study, tuition waivers (partial), and unspecified assistantships available. Support available to part-time students. Financial award application deadline: 4/15. *Faculty research:* Data management and warehousing, peer-to-peer counseling, decision support systems. *Unit head:* Lisa Braiewa, Program Director, 203-582-3710, Fax: 203-582-8664, E-mail: lisa.braiewa@quinnipiac.edu. *Application contact:* Katharina Wagner, Online Admissions Coordinator, 877-403-4277, Fax: 203-582-3352, E-mail: quonlineadmissions@quinnipiac.edu.

Rivier College, School of Graduate Studies, Department of Computer Information Systems, Nashua, NH 03060. Offers MS. Part-time programs available. *Faculty:* 3 full-time (0 women), 10 part-time/adjunct (0 women). *Students:* 3 full-time (2 women), 4 part-time (1 woman); includes 5 Asian, non-Hispanic/Latino. Average age 34. 3 applicants, 100% accepted, 2 enrolled. Application fee: $25. *Expenses:* Tuition: Part-time $456 per credit. *Financial support:* Application deadline: 2/1. *Unit head:* Dr. Paul Cunningham, Director, 603-897-8272, E-mail: pcunningham@rivier.edu. *Application contact:* Mathew Kittredge, Director of Graduate Admissions, 603-897-8229, Fax: 603-897-8810, E-mail: mkittredge@rivier.edu.

Robert Morris University Illinois, Morris Graduate School of Management, Chicago, IL 60605. Offers accounting (MBA); accounting/finance (MBA); health care administration (MM); higher education administration (MM); human resource management (MBA); information systems (MIS); leadership (MBA); management/finance (MIS); management/human resource management (MBA). Part-time and evening/weekend programs available. *Faculty:* 9 full-time (2 women), 21 part-time/adjunct (6 women). *Students:* 275 full-time (151 women), 212 part-time (138 women); includes 170 Black or African American, non-Hispanic/Latino; 1 American Indian or Alaska Native,

non-Hispanic/Latino; 21 Asian, non-Hispanic/Latino; 73 Hispanic/Latino; 2 Native Hawaiian or other Pacific Islander, non-Hispanic/Latino, 23 international. Average age 32. 172 applicants, 87% accepted, 105 enrolled. In 2010, 174 master's awarded. *Degree requirements:* For master's, 48 residency hours. *Entrance requirements:* Additional exam requirements/recommendations for international students: Required—TOEFL (minimum score 500 paper-based; 173 computer-based). *Application deadline:* Applications are processed on a rolling basis. Application fee: $50 ($100 for international students). Electronic applications accepted. *Expenses:* Tuition: Full-time $13,200; part-time $2200 per course. *Financial support:* Federal Work-Study, scholarships/grants, and tuition waivers available. Support available to part-time students. *Unit head:* Kayed Akkawi, Dean, 312-935-6025, Fax: 312-935-6020, E-mail: kakkawi@robertmorris.edu. *Application contact:* Courtney A. Kohn Sanders, Dean of Graduate Admissions, 312-935-4810, Fax: 312-935-6020, E-mail: ckohn@robertmorris.edu.

Rochester Institute of Technology, Graduate Enrollment Services, B. Thomas Golisano College of Computing and Information Sciences, Department of Networking, Security and Systems Administration, Program in Security and Information Assurance, Rochester, NY 14623-5603. Offers MS. Part-time and evening/weekend programs available. Postbaccalaureate distance learning degree programs offered (no on-campus study). *Students:* 12 full-time (1 woman), 15 part-time (3 women), 12 international. Average age 30. 29 applicants, 45% accepted, 6 enrolled. In 2010, 1 master's awarded. *Degree requirements:* For master's, thesis. *Entrance requirements:* For master's, GRE, minimum GPA of 3.0. Additional exam requirements/recommendations for international students: Required—TOEFL (minimum score 570 paper-based; 230 computer-based; 88 iBT) or IELTS (minimum score 6.5). *Application deadline:* For fall admission, 8/1 for domestic students, 7/1 for international students; for spring admission, 2/1 for domestic students. Applications are processed on a rolling basis. Electronic applications accepted. *Expenses:* Tuition: Full-time $33,234; part-time $924 per credit hour. Required fees: $219. *Financial support:* In 2010–11, 19 students received support; research assistantships with partial tuition reimbursements available, teaching assistantships with partial tuition reimbursements available, career-related internships or fieldwork, scholarships/grants, and unspecified assistantships available. Support available to part-time students. Financial award applicants required to submit FAFSA. *Unit head:* Prof. Dianne Bills, Graduate Program Director, 585-475-2700, Fax: 585-475-6584, E-mail: informaticsgrad@rit.edu. *Application contact:* Diane Ellison, Assistant Vice President, Graduate Enrollment Services, 585-475-2229, Fax: 585-475-7164, E-mail: gradinfo@rit.edu.

Rowan University, Graduate School, William G. Rohrer College of Business, Department of Marketing and Business Information Systems, Glassboro, NJ 08028-1701. Offers MBA. Part-time and evening/weekend programs available. *Faculty:* 2 full-time (1 woman), 2 part-time/adjunct (both women). *Students:* 29 full-time (26 women), 2 part-time (1 woman); includes 1 Black or African American, non-Hispanic/Latino. Average age 26. 4 applicants, 50% accepted, 1 enrolled. *Degree requirements:* For master's, comprehensive exam, thesis. *Entrance requirements:* For master's, GRE General Test. Additional exam requirements/recommendations for international students: Required—TOEFL. *Application deadline:* Applications are processed on a rolling basis. Application fee: $65 ($200 for international students). Electronic applications accepted. *Expenses:* Tuition, area resident: Part-time $602 per semester hour. Tuition, nonresident: Part-time $602 per semester hour. Required fees: $100 per semester hour. One-time fee: $10 part-time. *Unit head:* Dr. Horacio Sosa, Dean, College of Graduate and Continuing Education, 856-256-4747, Fax: 856-256-5638, E-mail: sosa@rowan.edu. *Application contact:* Karen Haynes, Graduate Coordinator, 856-256-4052, E-mail: haynes@rowan.edu.

Rutgers, The State University of New Jersey, Newark, Graduate School, Program in Management, Newark, NJ 07102. Offers accounting (PhD); accounting information systems (PhD); computer information systems (PhD); finance (PhD); information technology (PhD); international business (PhD); management science (PhD); marketing (PhD); organization management (PhD). Program offered jointly with New Jersey Institute of Technology. *Accreditation:* AACSB. *Faculty:* 128 full-time (24 women), 4 part-time/adjunct (1 woman). *Students:* 95 full-time (34 women), 17 part-time (6 women); includes 9 Black or African American, non-Hispanic/Latino; 54 Asian, non-Hispanic/Latino; 3 Hispanic/Latino. 438 applicants, 14% accepted, 34 enrolled. In 2010, 10 doctorates awarded. *Degree requirements:* For doctorate, thesis/dissertation, cumulative exams. *Entrance requirements:* For doctorate, GMAT or GRE General Test, minimum undergraduate B average. Additional exam requirements/recommendations for international students: Required—TOEFL. *Application deadline:* For fall admission, 4/1 for domestic students; for spring admission, 11/1 for domestic students. Applications are processed on a rolling basis. Application fee: $60. Electronic applications accepted. *Expenses:* Tuition, state resident: part-time $600 per credit. Tuition, nonresident: full-time $10,694. *Financial support:* In 2010–11, 6 fellowships (averaging $18,000 per year), 4 research assistantships with full and partial tuition reimbursements (averaging $23,112 per year), 38 teaching assistantships with full and partial tuition reimbursements (averaging $23,112 per year) were awarded; institutionally sponsored loans and tuition waivers (full and partial) also available. Support available to part-time students. Financial award application deadline: 2/15. *Faculty research:* Technology management, leadership and teams, consumer behavior, financial and markets, logistics. *Unit head:* Dr. Glenn Shafer, Director, 973-353-1604, Fax: 973-353-5691, E-mail: gshafer@rbs.rutgers.edu. *Application contact:* Goncalo Filipe, Senior Academic Coordinator, 973-353-1002, Fax: 973-353-5691, E-mail: gfilipe@rbsmail.rutgers.edu.

Rutgers, The State University of New Jersey, Newark, Rutgers Business School–Newark and New Brunswick, Doctoral Programs in Management, Newark, NJ 07102. Offers accounting (PhD); accounting information systems (PhD); economics (PhD); finance (PhD); individualized study (PhD); information technology (PhD); international business (PhD); management science (PhD); marketing science (PhD); organizational management (PhD); science, technology and management (PhD); supply chain management (PhD). *Faculty:* 143 full-time (36 women), 2 part-time/adjunct (0 women). *Students:* 117 full-time (42 women), 1 (woman) part-time; includes 8 Black or African American, non-Hispanic/Latino; 14 Asian, non-Hispanic/Latino; 3 Hispanic/Latino, 68 international. Average age 33. 355 applicants, 14% accepted, 35 enrolled. In 2010, 8 doctorates awarded. *Degree requirements:* For doctorate, comprehensive exam, thesis/dissertation. *Entrance requirements:* For doctorate, GRE or GMAT. Additional exam requirements/recommendations for international students: Required—TOEFL (minimum score 550 paper-based; 213 computer-based; 79 iBT). *Application deadline:* For fall admission, 3/1 for domestic and international students; for spring admission, 10/15 for domestic and international students. Application fee: $65. Electronic applications accepted. *Expenses:* Tuition, state resident: part-time $600 per credit. Tuition, nonresident: full-time $10,694. *Financial support:* In 2010–11, 52 students received support, including 7 fellowships (averaging $18,000 per year), 4 research assistantships with tuition reimbursements available (averaging $23,112 per year), 41 teaching assistantships with tuition reimbursements available (averaging $23,112 per year); health care benefits also available. Financial award application deadline: 3/1. *Unit head:* Dr. Glenn Shafer, Director, 973-353-1604, Fax: 973-353-5691, E-mail: gshafer@rbs. rutgers.edu. *Application contact:* Information Contact, 973-353-5371, Fax: 973-353-5691, E-mail: phdinfo@andromeda.rutgers.edu.

St. Edward's University, School of Management and Business, Area of Business Administration, Austin, TX 78704. Offers accounting (MBA); business management (MBA); corporate finance (MBA, Certificate); global entrepreneurship (MBA); human resource management (Certificate); management information systems (MBA, Certificate); marketing (MBA, Certificate); operations management (MBA, Certificate). Part-time and evening/weekend programs available. *Faculty:* 17 full-time (7 women), 19 part-time/adjunct (4 women). *Students:* 41 full-time (21 women), 273 part-time (135 women); includes 111 minority (19 Black or African American, non-Hispanic/Latino; 1 American Indian or Alaska Native, non-Hispanic/Latino; 8 Asian, non-Hispanic/Latino; 78 Hispanic/Latino; 1 Native Hawaiian or other Pacific Islander, non-Hispanic/Latino; 4 Two or more races, non-Hispanic/Latino), 11 international. Average age 33. 101 applicants, 77% accepted, 50 enrolled. In 2010, 115 master's awarded. *Degree requirements:* For master's, minimum of 24 resident hours. *Entrance requirements:* For master's, GMAT or GRE General Test, minimum GPA of 2.75 in last 60 hours of course work. Additional exam requirements/recommendations for international students: Required—TOEFL (minimum score 550 paper-based; 213 computer-based; 79 iBT) or IELTS (minimum score 6). *Application deadline:* For fall admission, 7/1 for domestic and international students; for spring admission, 11/1 for domestic and international students. Applications are processed on a rolling basis. Application fee: $45 ($50 for international students). Electronic applications accepted. *Expenses:* Tuition: Full-time $16,200; part-time $900 per credit hour. Required fees: $50 per trimester. Full-time tuition and fees vary according to course load and program. *Financial support:* In 2010–11, 19 students received support. Scholarships/grants available. *Faculty research:* Ethics and corporate responsibility, new hire socialization, team performance, business strategy, non-traditional marketing, social media. *Unit head:* Dr. Stan Horner, Director, 512-428-1279, Fax: 512-448-8492, E-mail: stanleyh@stedwards.edu. *Application contact:* Kelly Luna, Graduate Admissions Coordinator, 512-233-1697, Fax: 512-428-1032, E-mail: kellyl@stedwards.edu.

St. Edward's University, School of Management and Business, Program in Computer Information Systems, Austin, TX 78704. Offers MS. Part-time and evening/weekend programs available. *Students:* 8 full-time (1 woman), 20 part-time (3 women); includes 10 minority (2 Black or African American, non-Hispanic/Latino; 3 Asian, non-Hispanic/Latino; 4 Hispanic/Latino; 1 Two or more races, non-Hispanic/Latino), 2 international. Average age 39. 22 applicants, 86% accepted, 10 enrolled. In 2010, 16 master's awarded. *Degree requirements:* For master's, minimum of 24 resident hours. *Entrance requirements:* For master's, GMAT or GRE General Test, minimum GPA of 2.75 in last 60 hours of course work. Additional exam requirements/recommendations for international students: Required—TOEFL (minimum score 550 paper-based; 213 computer-based; 79 iBT) or IELTS (minimum score 6). *Application deadline:* For fall admission, 7/1 for domestic and international students; for spring admission, 11/1 for domestic and international students. Applications are processed on a rolling basis. Application fee: $45 ($50 for international students). Electronic applications accepted. *Expenses:*

Tuition: Full-time $16,200; part-time $900 per credit hour. Required fees: $50 per trimester. Full-time tuition and fees vary according to course load and program. *Financial support:* Scholarships/grants available. *Faculty research:* System design. *Unit head:* Dwight D. Daniel, Director, 512-448-8460, Fax: 512-428-8492, E-mail: dwightd@stedwards.edu. *Application contact:* Kelly Luna, Graduate Admissions Coordinator, 512-233-1697, Fax: 512-428-1032, E-mail: kellyl@stedwards.edu.

St. John's University, The Peter J. Tobin College of Business, Department of Computer Information Systems and Decision Sciences, Queens, NY 11439. Offers MBA, Adv C. Part-time and evening/weekend programs available. *Students:* 7 full-time (3 women), 6 part-time (0 women); includes 4 minority (1 Black or African American, non-Hispanic/Latino; 2 Asian, non-Hispanic/Latino; 1 Hispanic/Latino), 4 international. Average age 25. 11 applicants, 64% accepted, 4 enrolled. In 2010, 2 master's awarded. *Degree requirements:* For master's, comprehensive exam (for some programs), thesis optional. *Entrance requirements:* For master's, GMAT, 2 letters of recommendation, resume, transcripts, essay; for Adv C, GMAT, 2 letters of recommendation, resume, undergraduate transcripts, essay. Additional exam requirements/recommendations for international students: Required—TOEFL (minimum score 600 paper-based; 250 computer-based; 100 iBT), IELTS (minimum score 5.5). *Application deadline:* For fall admission, 5/1 priority date for domestic and international students; for spring admission, 11/1 priority date for domestic and international students. Applications are processed on a rolling basis. Application fee: $70. Electronic applications accepted. *Expenses:* Contact institution. *Financial support:* Research assistantships, scholarships/grants available. Support available to part-time students. Financial award application deadline: 3/1; financial award applicants required to submit FAFSA. *Unit head:* Dr. Victor Lu, Chair, 718-990-6392, Fax: 718-990-1868, E-mail: luf@stjohns.edu. *Application contact:* Carol Swanberg, Assistant Dean, Director of Graduate Admissions, 718-990-1345, Fax: 718-990-5242, E-mail: tobingradnyc@stjohns.edu.

Saint Joseph's University, Erivan K. Haub School of Business, MS Program in Business Intelligence, Philadelphia, PA 19131-1395. Offers business intelligence (MS). Part-time and evening/weekend programs available. Postbaccalaureate distance learning degree programs offered (no on-campus study). *Students:* 17 full-time (6 women), 90 part-time (21 women); includes 20 minority (8 Black or African American, non-Hispanic/Latino; 7 Asian, non-Hispanic/Latino; 4 Hispanic/Latino; 1 Two or more races, non-Hispanic/Latino), 19 international. Average age 35. In 2010, 21 master's awarded. *Entrance requirements:* For master's, GMAT or GRE, 2 letters of recommendation, resume. Additional exam requirements/recommendations for international students: Required—TOEFL (minimum score: paper 550, computer 213, iBT 79) or IELTS (6.5), Pearson Test of English (minimum 60). *Application deadline:* For fall admission, 7/15 priority date for domestic students, 4/15 priority date for international students; for spring admission, 11/15 priority date for domestic students, 10/15 priority date for international students. Applications are processed on a rolling basis. Application fee: $35. Electronic applications accepted. *Expenses:* Tuition: Part-time $729 per credit. Tuition and fees vary according to course load, degree level and program. *Financial support:* In 2010–11, teaching assistantships with partial tuition reimbursements (averaging $2,500 per year); unspecified assistantships also available. Financial award application deadline: 5/1; financial award applicants required to submit FAFSA. *Unit head:* Patricia Rafferty, Director, MS in Business Intelligence and MS in Human Resource Management Programs, 610-660-1318, Fax: 610-660-1229, E-mail: patricia.rafferty@sju.edu. *Application contact:* Patricia Rafferty, Director, MS in Business Intelligence and MS in Human Resource Management Programs, 610-660-1318, Fax: 610-660-1229, E-mail: patricia.rafferty@sju.edu.

Saint Peter's College, Graduate Business Programs, MBA Program, Jersey City, NJ 07306-5997. Offers finance (MBA); health care administration (MBA); human resource management (MBA); international business (MBA); management (MBA); management information systems (MBA); marketing (MBA); risk management (MBA); MBA/MS. Part-time and evening/weekend programs available. *Students:* 108 applicants, 81% accepted, 62 enrolled. *Entrance requirements:* Additional exam requirements/recommendations for international students: Required—TOEFL (minimum score 79 computer-based). *Application deadline:* Applications are processed on a rolling basis. Electronic applications accepted. *Financial support:* Career-related internships or fieldwork, Federal Work-Study, and institutionally sponsored loans available. Financial award applicants required to submit FAFSA. *Faculty research:* Finance, health care management, human resource management, international business, management, management information systems, marketing, risk management. *Application contact:* Stephanie Autenrieth, Director, Graduate and Professional Studies Admission, 201-761-6474, Fax: 201-435-5270, E-mail: sautenrieth@spc.edu.

Santa Clara University, Leavey School of Business, Program in Information Systems, Santa Clara, CA 95053. Offers MS. Part-time programs available. *Students:* 25 full-time (11 women), 45 part-time (11 women); includes 13 minority (11 Asian, non-Hispanic/Latino; 1 Hispanic/Latino; 1 Native Hawaiian or other Pacific Islander, non-Hispanic/Latino), 33 international. Average age 28. 38 applicants, 61% accepted, 9 enrolled. In 2010, 13 master's awarded. *Degree requirements:* For master's, capstone project. *Entrance* *requirements:* For master's, GMAT, GRE. Additional exam requirements/recommendations for international students: Required—TOEFL (minimum score 600 paper-based; 250 computer-based; 100 iBT). *Application deadline:* For fall admission, 6/1 for domestic and international students; for spring admission, 1/19 for domestic and international students. Applications are processed on a rolling basis. Application fee: $75 ($100 for international students). Electronic applications accepted. *Expenses:* Contact institution. *Financial support:* In 2010–11, 25 students received support; fellowships with partial tuition reimbursements available, research assistantships with partial tuition reimbursements available, career-related internships or fieldwork, Federal Work-Study, institutionally sponsored loans, scholarships/grants, health care benefits, and unspecified assistantships available. Support available to part-time students. Financial award application deadline: 6/1; financial award applicants required to submit FAFSA. *Unit head:* Elizabeth B. Ford, Senior Assistant Dean, 408-554-2752, Fax: 408-554-4571, E-mail: eford@scu.edu. *Application contact:* Susan Roberts, Assistant Director, MSIS Admissions, 408-551-7047, Fax: 408-554-2331, E-mail: msis-admissions@scu.edu.

Seattle Pacific University, Master's Degree in Information Systems Management (MS-ISM) Program, Seattle, WA 98119-1997. Offers MS. Part-time programs available. *Faculty:* 1 full-time (0 women). *Students:* 2 full-time (0 women), 16 part-time (5 women); includes 4 minority (3 Black or African American, non-Hispanic/Latino; 1 Asian, non-Hispanic/Latino), 4 international. Average age 30. 15 applicants, 33% accepted, 5 enrolled. In 2010, 7 master's awarded. *Entrance requirements:* For master's, GMAT, minimum GPA of 3.0. Additional exam requirements/recommendations for international students: Required—TOEFL (minimum score 225 computer-based). *Application deadline:* For fall admission, 8/1 for domestic students, 6/1 for international students; for winter admission, 11/1 for domestic and international students; for spring admission, 2/1 for domestic students, 12/1 for international students. Applications are processed on a rolling basis. Application fee: $50. Electronic applications accepted. *Financial support:* In 2010–11, 4 students received support. Applicants required to submit FAFSA. *Unit head:* Gary Karns, Associate Dean for Graduate Studies, 206-281-2948, Fax: 206-281-2733. *Application contact:* Gary Karns, Associate Dean for Graduate Studies, 206-281-2948, Fax: 206-281-2733.

Southeastern Louisiana University, College of Business, Hammond, LA 70402. Offers accounting (MBA); general (MBA); information systems for supply chain management (MBA). *Accreditation:* AACSB. Part-time and evening/weekend programs available. *Faculty:* 15 full-time (1 woman), 1 part-time/adjunct (0 women). *Students:* 52 full-time (29 women), 56 part-time (21 women); includes 12 minority (8 Black or African American, non-Hispanic/Latino; 1 Asian, non-Hispanic/Latino; 2 Hispanic/Latino; 1 Two or more races, non-Hispanic/Latino), 8 international. Average age 28. 109 applicants, 40% accepted, 25 enrolled. In 2010, 62 master's awarded. *Entrance requirements:* For master's, GMAT (minimum score 450), minimum cumulative GPA of 2.75 for all undergraduate work attempted or 3.0 on all upper-division undergraduate coursework attempted. Additional exam requirements/recommendations for international students: Required—TOEFL (minimum score 525 paper-based; 195 computer-based; 61 iBT). *Application deadline:* For fall admission, 7/15 priority date for domestic students, 6/1 priority date for international students; for spring admission, 12/1 priority date for domestic students, 10/1 priority date for international students. Applications are processed on a rolling basis. Application fee: $20 ($30 for international students). Electronic applications accepted. *Expenses:* Tuition, state resident: full-time $3533. Tuition, nonresident: full-time $12,002. Required fees: $907. Tuition and fees vary according to degree level. *Financial support:* In 2010–11, 21 students received support, including 1 research assistantship (averaging $9,000 per year); career-related internships or fieldwork, Federal Work-Study, institutionally sponsored loans, scholarships/grants, and administrative assistantships, graduate professional services assistants also available. Support available to part-time students. Financial award application deadline: 5/1; financial award applicants required to submit FAFSA. *Faculty research:* Ethical decision-making in accounting, entrepreneurship and emerging information, leadership and organizational performance. *Unit head:* Dr. Randy Settoon, Dean, 985-549-2258, Fax: 985-549-5038, E-mail: rsettoon@selu.edu. *Application contact:* Sandra Meyers, Graduate Admissions Analyst, 985-549-5620, Fax: 985-549-5882, E-mail: admissions@selu.edu.

Southeastern Louisiana University, College of Science and Technology, Program in Integrated Science and Technology, Hammond, LA 70402. Offers chemistry (MS); computer science (MS); information technology (MS); mathematics (MS); physics (MS). Part-time and evening/weekend programs available. *Faculty:* 11 full-time (3 women). *Students:* 13 full-time (5 women), 11 part-time (2 women); includes 1 minority (Asian, non-Hispanic/Latino), 8 international. Average age 32. 13 applicants, 46% accepted, 4 enrolled. In 2010, 5 degrees awarded. *Degree requirements:* For master's, thesis (for some programs), 33-36 hours. *Entrance requirements:* For master's, GRE (minimum combined score 850), 2 letters of reference; minimum GPA of 2.75; 30 hours of course work including chemistry, physics, industrial technology, or mathematics. Additional exam requirements/recommendations for international students: Required—TOEFL (minimum score 500 paper-based; 173 computer-based; 61 iBT). *Application deadline:* For fall admission, 7/15 priority date for domestic students, 6/1 priority date for international students;

for spring admission, 12/1 priority date for domestic students, 10/1 priority date for international students. Applications are processed on a rolling basis. Application fee: $20 ($30 for international students). Electronic applications accepted. *Expenses:* Tuition, state resident: full-time $3533. Tuition, nonresident: full-time $12,002. Required fees: $907. Tuition and fees vary according to degree level. *Financial support:* In 2010–11, 7 students received support, including 7 research assistantships (averaging $10,100 per year); career-related internships or fieldwork, Federal Work-Study, institutionally sponsored loans, and unspecified assistantships also available. Support available to part-time students. Financial award application deadline: 5/1; financial award applicants required to submit FAFSA. *Faculty research:* Computational statistics, medicinal chemistry, machine learning, optical interferometry, strength of materials and structure. *Unit head:* Dr. Ken Li, Coordinator, 985-549-3822, Fax: 985-549-2099, E-mail: kli@selu.edu. *Application contact:* Sandra Meyers, Graduate Admissions Analyst, 985-549-5620, Fax: 985-549-5632, E-mail: admissions@selu.edu.

Southeastern Oklahoma State University, School of Arts and Sciences, Durant, OK 74701-0609. Offers biology (MT); computer information systems (MT). Part-time and evening/weekend programs available. *Faculty:* 12 full-time (4 women), 1 part-time/adjunct (0 women). *Students:* 19 full-time (4 women), 39 part-time (6 women); includes 13 American Indian or Alaska Native, non-Hispanic/Latino; 2 Hispanic/Latino. Average age 28. 10 applicants, 100% accepted, 10 enrolled. *Degree requirements:* For master's, thesis optional. *Entrance requirements:* For master's, minimum GPA of 3.0 in last 60 hours or 2.75 overall. Additional exam requirements/recommendations for international students: Required—TOEFL (minimum score 550 paper-based; 213 computer-based). *Application deadline:* For fall admission, 8/1 for domestic students, 6/1 for international students; for spring admission, 1/5 for domestic students, 11/1 for international students. Application fee: $20 ($55 for international students). Electronic applications accepted. *Financial support:* In 2010–11, 8 students received support; fellowships, research assistantships, teaching assistantships, Federal Work-Study and institutionally sponsored loans available. Support available to part-time students. Financial award application deadline: 6/15; financial award applicants required to submit FAFSA. *Unit head:* Dr. Teresa Golden, Graduate Coordinator, 580-745-2286, E-mail: tgolden@se.edu. *Application contact:* Carrie Williamson, Graduate Secretary, 580-745-2200, Fax: 580-745-7474, E-mail: cwilliamson@se.edu.

Southern Illinois University Edwardsville, Graduate School, School of Business, Department of Computer Management and Information Systems, Edwardsville, IL 62026-0001. Offers MS. Part-time and evening/weekend programs available. *Faculty:* 9 full-time (5 women). *Students:* 7 full-time (3 women), 24 part-time (5 women); includes 3 minority (2 Black or African American, non-Hispanic/Latino; 1 Asian, non-Hispanic/Latino), 7 international. Average age 26. 29 applicants, 38% accepted. In 2010, 9 master's awarded. *Degree requirements:* For master's, thesis or alternative, final exam. *Entrance requirements:* For master's, GMAT. Additional exam requirements/recommendations for international students: Required—TOEFL (minimum score 550 paper-based; 213 computer-based; 79 iBT), IELTS (minimum score 6.5). *Application deadline:* For fall admission, 7/22 for domestic students, 6/1 for international students; for spring admission, 12/10 for domestic students, 10/1 for international students. Applications are processed on a rolling basis. Application fee: $30. Electronic applications accepted. *Expenses:* Tuition, state resident: full-time $6012; part-time $1503 per semester. Tuition, nonresident: full-time $15,030; part-time $3758 per semester. Required fees: $1711; $675 per semester. *Financial support:* In 2010–11, 5 teaching assistantships with full tuition reimbursements (averaging $8,064 per year) were awarded; fellowships, research assistantships, career-related internships or fieldwork, Federal Work-Study, institutionally sponsored loans, scholarships/grants, traineeships, and unspecified assistantships also available. Support available to part-time students. Financial award application deadline: 3/1; financial award applicants required to submit FAFSA. *Unit head:* Dr. Douglas Bock, Chair, 618-650-2504, E-mail: dbock@siue.edu. *Application contact:* Dr. Jo Ellen Moore, Director, 618-650-5816, E-mail: joemoor@siue.edu.

Southern Illinois University Edwardsville, Graduate School, School of Business, Program in Business Administration, Specialization in Management Information Systems, Edwardsville, IL 62026-0001. Offers MBA. Part-time programs available. *Students:* 13 part-time (4 women); includes 1 Black or African American, non-Hispanic/Latino. Average age 26. In 2010, 6 master's awarded. *Degree requirements:* For master's, thesis or alternative, final exam. *Entrance requirements:* For master's, GMAT. Additional exam requirements/recommendations for international students: Required—TOEFL (minimum score 550 paper-based; 213 computer-based; 79 iBT), IELTS (minimum score 6.5). *Application deadline:* For fall admission, 7/23 for domestic students, 6/1 for international students; for spring admission, 12/10 for domestic students, 10/1 for international students. Applications are processed on a rolling basis. Application fee: $30. Electronic applications accepted. *Expenses:* Tuition, state resident: full-time $6012; part-time $1503 per semester. Tuition, nonresident: full-time $15,030; part-time $3758 per semester. Required fees: $1711; $675 per semester. *Financial support:* Fellowships with full tuition reimbursements, research assistantships with full tuition reimbursements, teaching assistantships with full tuition reimbursements, career-related internships or fieldwork, Federal Work-Study, institutionally sponsored loans, scholarships/grants, traineeships, and unspecified assistantships available. Support available to part-time students. Financial award application deadline: 3/1; financial award applicants required to submit FAFSA. *Unit head:* Dr. Janice Joplin, Director, 618-650-3412, E-mail: jjoplin@siue.edu. *Application contact:* Dr. Janice Joplin, Director, 618-650-3412, E-mail: jjoplin@siue.edu.

Southern Methodist University, Cox School of Business, MBA Program, Dallas, TX 75275. Offers accounting (MBA); finance (MBA); financial consulting (MBA); general business (MBA); information technology and operations management (MBA); management (MBA); marketing (MBA); real estate (MBA); strategy and entrepreneurship (MBA). Part-time and evening/weekend programs available. *Faculty:* 59 full-time (13 women), 30 part-time/adjunct (7 women). *Students:* 359 full-time (116 women), 592 part-time (154 women); includes 215 minority (44 Black or African American, non-Hispanic/Latino; 10 American Indian or Alaska Native, non-Hispanic/Latino; 118 Asian, non-Hispanic/Latino; 39 Hispanic/Latino; 2 Native Hawaiian or other Pacific Islander, non-Hispanic/Latino; 2 Two or more races, non-Hispanic/Latino), 92 international. Average age 30. In 2010, 486 master's awarded. *Entrance requirements:* For master's, GMAT. Additional exam requirements/recommendations for international students: Required—TOEFL. *Application deadline:* Applications are processed on a rolling basis. Application fee: $0. Electronic applications accepted. *Expenses:* Contact institution. *Financial support:* Applicants required to submit FAFSA. *Faculty research:* Corporate finance, financial reporting, modeling consumer decision-making, competition between national brands and store brands, institutional determinants of firms' strategy. *Unit head:* Dr. Marci Armstrong, Associate Dean for Master's Programs, 214-768-4486, Fax: 214-768-3956, E-mail: marci@cox.smu.edu. *Application contact:* Patti Cudney, Director of MBA Admissions, 214-768-3001, Fax: 214-768-3956, E-mail: pcudney@cox.smu.edu.

Stevens Institute of Technology, Graduate School, Wesley J. Howe School of Technology Management, Doctoral Program in Technology Management, Hoboken, NJ 07030. Offers information management (PhD); technology management (PhD); telecommunications management (PhD). Part-time and evening/weekend programs available. Postbaccalaureate distance learning degree programs offered (minimal on-campus study). *Students:* 22 full-time (9 women), 66 part-time (11 women); includes 1 Black or African American, non-Hispanic/Latino; 14 Asian, non-Hispanic/Latino; 8 Hispanic/Latino, 23 international. Average age 34. 66 applicants, 70% accepted. *Entrance requirements:* Additional exam requirements/recommendations for international students: Required—TOEFL. *Application deadline:* Applications are processed on a rolling basis. Application fee: $50. Electronic applications accepted. *Financial support:* Research assistantships, teaching assistantships, institutionally sponsored loans available. *Unit head:* Richard Reilly, Director, 201-216-5383. *Application contact:* Graduate Admissions, 800-496-4935, Fax: 201-216-8044, E-mail: gradadmissions@stevens.edu.

Stevens Institute of Technology, Graduate School, Wesley J. Howe School of Technology Management, Program in Management, Hoboken, NJ 07030. Offers general management (MS); global innovation management (MS); human resource management (MS); information management (MS); project management (MS); technology commercialization (MS); technology management (MS). Part-time programs available. *Students:* 15 full-time (6 women), 35 part-time (15 women); includes 1 Black or African American, non-Hispanic/Latino; 5 Asian, non-Hispanic/Latino; 6 Hispanic/Latino, 12 international. Average age 31. *Degree requirements:* For master's, thesis optional. *Entrance requirements:* For master's, GMAT, GRE General Test. Additional exam requirements/recommendations for international students: Required—TOEFL. *Application deadline:* Applications are processed on a rolling basis. Application fee: $50. Electronic applications accepted. *Financial support:* Unspecified assistantships available. *Faculty research:* Industrial economics. *Unit head:* Elizabeth Watson, Director, 201-216-5081. *Application contact:* Graduate Admissions, 800-496-4935, Fax: 201-216-8044, E-mail: gradadmissions@stevens.edu.

Stony Brook University, State University of New York, Graduate School, College of Business, Program in Business Administration, Stony Brook, NY 11794. Offers finance (MBA, Certificate); health care management (MBA, Certificate); human resource management (Certificate); human resources (MBA); information systems management (MBA, Certificate); management (MBA); marketing (MBA). *Faculty:* 14 full-time (2 women), 27 part-time/adjunct (6 women). *Students:* 182 full-time (103 women), 117 part-time (35 women); includes 11 Black or African American, non-Hispanic/Latino; 35 Asian, non-Hispanic/Latino; 10 Hispanic/Latino; 2 Two or more races, non-Hispanic/Latino, 88 international. 281 applicants, 60% accepted, 102 enrolled. In 2010, 95 master's, 1 other advanced degree awarded. Application fee: $100. *Expenses:* Tuition, state resident: full-time $8370; part-time $349 per credit. Tuition, nonresident: full-time $13,780; part-time $574 per credit. Required fees: $994. *Financial support:* In 2010–11, 2 teaching assistantships were awarded. *Unit head:* Dr. Manuel London, Interim Dean, 631-632-7180. *Application contact:* Dr. Aristotle Lekacos, Director, Graduate Program, 631-632-7171, E-mail: aristotle.lekacost@notes.cc.sunysb.edu.

Stony Brook University, State University of New York, Graduate School, College of Engineering and Applied Sciences, Department of Computer Science, Stony Brook, NY 11794. Offers computer science (MS, PhD); information systems (Certificate); information systems engineering (MS); software engineering (Certificate). *Faculty:* 38 full-time (6 women), 3 part-time/adjunct (1 woman). *Students:* 290 full-time (54 women), 44 part-time (11 women); includes 6 Black or African American, non-Hispanic/Latino; 17 Asian, non-Hispanic/Latino; 5 Hispanic/Latino; 1 Two or more races, non-Hispanic/Latino, 279 international. Average age 25. 1,619 applicants, 23% accepted, 118 enrolled. In 2010, 96 master's, 14 doctorates awarded. *Degree requirements:* For master's, thesis or alternative; for doctorate, comprehensive exam, thesis/dissertation. *Entrance requirements:* For master's and doctorate, GRE General Test. Additional exam requirements/recommendations for international students: Required—TOEFL. *Application deadline:* For fall admission, 1/15 for domestic students. Application fee: $100. *Expenses:* Tuition, state resident: full-time $8370; part-time $349 per credit. Tuition, nonresident: full-time $13,780; part-time $574 per credit. Required fees: $994. *Financial support:* In 2010–11, 95 research assistantships, 43 teaching assistantships were awarded; fellowships also available. *Faculty research:* Artificial intelligence, computer architecture, database management systems, VLSI, operating systems. Total annual research expenditures: $6.4 million. *Unit head:* Prof. Arie Kauffman, Chairman, 631-632-8428. *Application contact:* Graduate Director, 631-632-8462, Fax: 631-632-8334.

Stony Brook University, State University of New York, School of Professional Development, Stony Brook, NY 11794. Offers biology-grade 7-12 (MAT); chemistry-grade 7-12 (MAT); coaching (Graduate Certificate); coaching online (Graduate Certificate); computer integrated engineering (Graduate Certificate); earth science-grade 7-12 (MAT); educational computing (Graduate Certificate); educational leadership (Advanced Certificate); English-grade 7-12 (MAT); environmental management (Graduate Certificate); environmental/occupational health and safety (Graduate Certificate); French-grade 7-12 (MAT); German-grade 7-12 (MAT); human resource management (Graduate Certificate); human resource management online (Graduate Certificate); information systems management (Graduate Certificate); Italian-grade 7-12 (MAT); liberal studies (MA); liberal studies online (MAT); mathematics-grade 7-12 (MAT); operation research (Graduate Certificate); physics-grade 7-12 (MAT); professional studies online (MPS); school administration and supervision (Graduate Certificate); school building leadership (Graduate Certificate); school district administration (Graduate Certificate); school district business leadership (Advanced Certificate); school district leadership (Graduate Certificate); social science and the professions (MPS), including environmental waste management, human resource management; social studies-grade 7-12 (MAT); Spanish-grade 7-12 (MAT); waste management (Graduate Certificate). Part-time and evening/weekend programs available. Postbaccalaureate distance learning degree programs offered. *Faculty:* 25 full-time (10 women), 105 part-time/adjunct (40 women). *Students:* 360 full-time (228 women), 1,097 part-time (729 women); includes 180 minority (65 Black or African American, non-Hispanic/Latino; 2 American Indian or Alaska Native, non-Hispanic/Latino; 30 Asian, non-Hispanic/Latino; 81 Hispanic/Latino; 1 Native Hawaiian or other Pacific Islander, non-Hispanic/Latino; 1 Two or more races, non-Hispanic/Latino), 10 international. Average age 28. In 2010, 505 master's, 187 other advanced degrees awarded. *Degree requirements:* For master's, one foreign language, thesis or alternative. *Application deadline:* Applications are processed on a rolling basis. Application fee: $100. *Expenses:* Tuition, state resident: full-time $8370; part-time $349 per credit. Tuition, nonresident: full-time $13,780; part-time $574 per credit. Required fees: $994. *Financial support:* In 2010–11, 1 teaching assistantship was awarded; fellowships, research assistantships, career-related internships or fieldwork also available. Support available to part-time students. *Unit head:* Dr. Paul J. Edelson, Dean, 631-632-7052, Fax: 631-632-9046, E-mail: paul.edelson@stonybrook.edu. *Application contact:* Dr. Paul J. Edelson, Dean, 631-632-7052, Fax: 631-632-9046, E-mail: paul.edelson@stonybrook.edu.

Sullivan University, School of Business, Louisville, KY 40205. Offers business administration (MBA); collaborative leadership (MSCL); conflict management (MSCM); dispute resolution (MSDR); executive business administration (EMBA); human resource leadership (MSHRL); information technology (MSMIT); management (PhD); management and information technology (MBIT); pharmacy (Pharm D). Part-time programs available. Postbaccalaureate distance learning degree programs offered (no on-campus study). *Faculty:* 13 full-time (7 women), 11 part-time/adjunct (4 women). *Students:* 429 full-time (239 women), 322 part-time (198 women); includes 244 minority (152 Black or African American, non-Hispanic/Latino; 5 American Indian or Alaska Native, non-Hispanic/Latino; 5 Hispanic/Latino; 56 Native Hawaiian or other Pacific Islander, non-Hispanic/Latino; 26 Two or more races, non-Hispanic/Latino), 15 international. In 2010, 133 master's awarded. *Entrance requirements:* Additional exam requirements/recommendations for international students: Required—TOEFL. *Application deadline:* Applications are processed on a rolling basis. Application fee: $100. *Unit head:* Dr. Eric S. Harter, Dean of Graduate School, 502-456-6504, Fax: 502-456-0040, E-mail: eharter@sullivan.edu. *Application contact:* Beverly Horsley, Admissions Officer, 502-456-6505, Fax: 502-456-0040, E-mail: bhorsley@sullivan.edu.

Syracuse University, School of Information Studies, Program in eScience, Syracuse, NY 13244. Offers CAS. Part-time and evening/weekend programs available. Postbaccalaureate distance learning degree programs offered. *Entrance requirements:* Additional exam requirements/recommendations for international students: Required—TOEFL (minimum score 100 iBT). *Application deadline:* For fall admission, 2/1 for domestic students, 2/1 priority date for international students. Applications are processed on a rolling basis. Application fee: $75. Electronic applications accepted. *Expenses:* Tuition: Part-time $1162 per credit. *Unit head:* Elizabeth Liddy, Dean, 315-443-2736. *Application contact:* Susan Corieri, Director of Enrollment Management, 315-443-2575, E-mail: ischool@syr.edu.

Syracuse University, School of Information Studies, Program in Information Management, Syracuse, NY 13244. Offers MS, DPS. Part-time and evening/weekend programs available. Postbaccalaureate distance learning degree programs offered (minimal on-campus study). *Students:* 176 full-time (62 women), 136 part-time (35 women); includes 67 minority (23 Black or African American, non-Hispanic/Latino; 4 American Indian or Alaska Native, non-Hispanic/Latino; 16 Asian, non-Hispanic/Latino; 18 Hispanic/Latino; 2 Native Hawaiian or other Pacific Islander, non-Hispanic/Latino; 4 Two or more races, non-Hispanic/Latino, 126 international. Average age 30. 467 applicants, 60% accepted, 132 enrolled. In 2010, 99 master's awarded. *Entrance requirements:* For master's, GRE General Test. Additional exam requirements/recommendations for international students: Required—TOEFL (minimum score 100 iBT). *Application deadline:* For fall admission, 2/15 priority date for domestic and international students; for spring admission, 10/15 priority date for domestic and international students. Applications are processed on a rolling basis. Application fee: $75. Electronic applications accepted. *Expenses:* Tuition: Part-time $1162 per credit. *Financial support:* Fellowships with tuition reimbursements, research assistantships with partial tuition reimbursements, teaching assistantships with partial tuition reimbursements, scholarships/grants available. Financial award application deadline: 1/1; financial award applicants required to submit FAFSA. *Unit head:* David Dischiave, Director, 315-443-4681, Fax: 315-443-6886, E-mail: ddischia@syr.edu. *Application contact:* Susan Corieri, Director of Enrollment Management, 315-443-2575, E-mail: ischool@syr.edu.

Syracuse University, School of Information Studies, Program in Information Security Management, Syracuse, NY 13244. Offers CAS. Part-time and evening/weekend programs available. Postbaccalaureate distance learning degree programs offered. *Students:* 2 full-time (0 women), 11 part-time (1 woman); includes 5 minority (2 Black or African American, non-Hispanic/Latino; 2 Asian, non-Hispanic/Latino; 1 Hispanic/Latino). Average age 37. 41 applicants, 73% accepted, 3 enrolled. In 2010, 22 CASs awarded. *Entrance requirements:* Additional exam requirements/recommendations for international students: Required—TOEFL (minimum score 100 iBT). *Application deadline:* For fall admission, 2/1 priority date for domestic and international students; for spring admission, 10/15 priority date for domestic and international students. Applications are processed on a rolling basis. Application fee: $75. Electronic applications accepted. *Expenses:* Tuition: Part-time $1162 per credit. *Financial support:* Application deadline: 1/1. *Unit head:* Joon S. Park, Head, 315-443-2911, E-mail: ischool@syr.edu. *Application contact:* Susan Corieri, Director of Enrollment Management, 315-443-2575, E-mail: ischool@syr.edu.

Syracuse University, School of Information Studies, Program in Information Systems and Telecommunications Management, Syracuse, NY 13244. Offers CAS. Part-time and evening/weekend programs available. Postbaccalaureate distance learning degree programs offered. *Students:* 2 full-time (1 woman), 7 part-time (3 women); includes 4 minority (2 Black or African American, non-Hispanic/Latino; 2 Hispanic/Latino). Average age 34. 13 applicants, 92% accepted, 3 enrolled. In 2010, 13 CASs awarded. *Entrance requirements:* Additional exam requirements/recommendations for international students: Required—TOEFL (minimum score 100 iBT). *Application deadline:* For fall admission, 2/1 priority date for domestic and international students; for spring admission, 10/15 priority date for domestic and international students. Applications are processed on a rolling basis. Application fee: $75. Electronic applications accepted. *Expenses:* Tuition: Part-time $1162 per credit. *Financial support:* Fellowships with full tuition reimbursements, research assistantships with partial tuition reimbursements, teaching assistantships with partial tuition reimbursements available. Financial award application deadline: 1/1; financial award applicants required to submit FAFSA. *Unit head:* David Dischiave, Director, 315-443-4681, Fax: 315-443-6886, E-mail: ddischia@syr.edu. *Application contact:* Susan Corieri, Director of Enrollment Management, 315-443-2575, E-mail: ischool@syr.edu.

Tennessee Technological University, Graduate School, College of Business, Cookeville, TN 38505. Offers accounting (MBA); finance (MBA); human resource management (MBA); international business (MBA); management information systems (MBA); risk management & insurance (MBA). *Accreditation:* AACSB. Part-time and evening/weekend programs available. *Faculty:* 28 full-time (5 women). *Students:* 58 full-time (18 women), 139 part-time (49 women); includes 10 Black or African American, non-Hispanic/Latino; 7 Asian, non-Hispanic/Latino; 7 Hispanic/Latino; 1 Native Hawaiian or other Pacific Islander, non-Hispanic/Latino. Average age 25. 211 applicants, 51% accepted, 59 enrolled. In 2010, 116 master's awarded. *Entrance requirements:* For master's, GMAT. Additional exam requirements/recommendations for international students: Required—TOEFL (minimum

score 550 paper-based; 79 iBT), IELTS (minimum score 5.5). *Application deadline:* For fall admission, 8/1 for domestic and international students; for spring admission, 12/1 for domestic students, 10/1 for international students. Application fee: $25 ($30 for international students). Electronic applications accepted. *Expenses:* Tuition, state resident: full-time $7934; part-time $388 per credit hour. Tuition, nonresident: full-time $19,758; part-time $962 per credit hour. *Financial support:* In 2010–11, 5 fellowships (averaging $10,000 per year), 18 research assistantships (averaging $4,000 per year), teaching assistantships (averaging $4,000 per year) were awarded. Support available to part-time students. Financial award application deadline: 4/1. *Unit head:* Dr. Tom Timmerman, Director, 931-372-3600, Fax: 931-372-6249. *Application contact:* Shelia K. Kendrick, Coordinator of Graduate Admissions, 931-372-3808, Fax: 931-372-3497, E-mail: skendrick@tntech.edu.

Texas A&M International University, Office of Graduate Studies and Research, College of Business Administration, Division of International Business and Technology Studies, Laredo, TX 78041-1900. Offers information systems (MSIS); international trade (MBA). *Faculty:* 13 full-time (1 woman), 2 part-time/adjunct (0 women). *Students:* 38 full-time (6 women), 23 part-time (6 women); includes 3 Black or African American, non-Hispanic/Latino; 1 Asian, non-Hispanic/Latino; 9 Hispanic/Latino, 46 international. Average age 26. 95 applicants, 19% accepted, 11 enrolled. In 2010, 29 master's awarded. *Degree requirements:* For master's, thesis (for some programs). *Entrance requirements:* For master's, GMAT or GRE General Test. Additional exam requirements/recommendations for international students: Required—TOEFL (minimum score 550 paper-based; 213 computer-based). *Application deadline:* For fall admission, 4/30 priority date for domestic students; for spring admission, 11/30 for domestic students, 10/1 for international students. Applications are processed on a rolling basis. Application fee: $25. *Financial support:* In 2010–11, 33 students received support. Federal Work-Study, institutionally sponsored loans, and scholarships/grants available. Support available to part-time students. *Unit head:* Dr. S. Srinivasan, Chair, 956-326-2520, Fax: 956-326-2494, E-mail: srini@tamiu.edu. *Application contact:* Imelda Lopez, Graduate Admissions Counselor, 956-326-2485, Fax: 956-326-2459, E-mail: lopez@tamiu.edu.

Texas A&M University, Mays Business School, Department of Information and Operations Management, College Station, TX 77843. Offers management information systems (MS, PhD); management science (PhD); production and operations management (PhD). *Faculty:* 14. *Students:* 148 full-time (54 women), 6 part-time (1 woman); includes 12 minority (1 Black or African American, non-Hispanic/Latino; 1 American Indian or Alaska Native, non-Hispanic/Latino; 3 Asian, non-Hispanic/Latino; 7 Hispanic/Latino), 102 international. Average age 31. In 2010, 78 master's awarded. Terminal master's awarded for partial completion of doctoral program. *Degree requirements:* For master's, comprehensive exam; for doctorate, thesis/dissertation. *Entrance requirements:* For master's, GMAT; for doctorate, GMAT or GRE General Test. Additional exam requirements/recommendations for international students: Required—TOEFL. *Application deadline:* For fall admission, 3/1 priority date for domestic students; for spring admission, 8/1 for domestic students. Applications are processed on a rolling basis. Application fee: $50 ($75 for international students). *Financial support:* In 2010–11, 51 students received support; fellowships, research assistantships, teaching assistantships, career-related internships or fieldwork, Federal Work-Study, and institutionally sponsored loans available. Financial award application deadline: 2/1. *Unit head:* Dr. E. Powell Robinson, Head, 979-845-1616, E-mail: p-robinson@mays.tamu.edu. *Application contact:* Louise Darcey, Senior Lecturer, 979-862-1994, E-mail: ldarcey@mays.tamu.edu.

Texas A&M University–San Antonio, School of Business, San Antonio, TX 78224. Offers business administration (MBA); enterprise resource planning systems (MBA); finance (MBA); healthcare management (MBA); human resources management (MBA); information assurance and security (MBA); international business (MBA); project management (MBA); supply chain management (MBA). Part-time and evening/weekend programs available. *Faculty:* 18 full-time (6 women), 1 part-time/adjunct (0 women). *Students:* 49 full-time (21 women), 195 part-time (107 women). In 2010, 20 master's awarded. *Entrance requirements:* For master's, GMAT. Additional exam requirements/recommendations for international students: Required—TOEFL (minimum score 550 paper-based; 213 computer-based; 80 iBT), IELTS (minimum score 6). *Application deadline:* For fall admission, 7/1 priority date for domestic students, 6/1 priority date for international students; for spring admission, 11/15 priority date for domestic students, 10/1 priority date for international students. Applications are processed on a rolling basis. Application fee: $35 ($50 for international students). Electronic applications accepted. *Expenses:* Tuition, state resident: full-time $2899; part-time $161 per credit hour. Tuition, nonresident: full-time $8479; part-time $471 per credit hour. Required fees: $1056; $61 per credit hour. $368 per semester. *Financial support:* Application deadline: 3/31. *Unit head:* Dr. Tracy Hurley, MBA Coordinator, 210-932-6200, E-mail: tracy.hurley@tamusa.tamus.edu. *Application contact:* Melissa A. Villanueva, Graduate Admissions Specialist, 210-932-6200, Fax: 210-932-6209, E-mail: melissa.villanueva@tamusa.tamus.edu.

Texas Southern University, Jesse H. Jones School of Business, Program in Management Information Systems, Houston, TX 77004-4584. Offers MS. *Faculty:* 12 full-time (4 women), 2 part-time/adjunct (0 women). *Students:* 23

full-time (11 women), 6 part-time (all women); includes 21 Black or African American, non-Hispanic/Latino; 5 Asian, non-Hispanic/Latino; 1 Hispanic/Latino, 1 international. Average age 32. 10 applicants, 100% accepted, 6 enrolled. In 2010, 11 master's awarded. *Application deadline:* For fall admission, 7/1 for domestic and international students; for spring admission, 11/1 for domestic and international students. Applications are processed on a rolling basis. Application fee: $50 ($75 for international students). Electronic applications accepted. *Expenses:* Tuition, state resident: full-time $1875; part-time $100 per credit hour. Tuition, nonresident: full-time $6641; part-time $343 per credit hour. Tuition and fees vary according to course level, course load and degree level. *Financial support:* In 2010–11, 2 research assistantships (averaging $3,500 per year), 2 teaching assistantships (averaging $2,050 per year) were awarded; fellowships, career-related internships or fieldwork, scholarships/grants, and unspecified assistantships also available. Financial award applicants required to submit FAFSA. *Unit head:* Jeff Brice, Chair, 713-313-7011 Ext. 1303, E-mail: bricejx@tsu.edu. *Application contact:* Bobbie J. Richardson, Executive Secretary, 713-313-7309, Fax: 713-313-7705, E-mail: richardson_bj@tsu.edu.

Texas State University–San Marcos, Graduate School, Emmett and Miriam McCoy College of Business Administration, Program in Accounting and Information Technology, San Marcos, TX 78666. Offers MS. *Faculty:* 7 full-time (2 women). *Students:* 11 full-time (3 women), 8 part-time (3 women); includes 6 minority (2 Black or African American, non-Hispanic/Latino; 2 Asian, non-Hispanic/Latino; 2 Hispanic/Latino), 3 international. Average age 32. 4 applicants, 100% accepted, 3 enrolled. In 2010, 7 master's awarded. *Degree requirements:* For master's, comprehensive exam. *Entrance requirements:* For master's, GMAT, official transcript from each college or university attended, 2 letters of recommendation, resume. Additional exam requirements/recommendations for international students: Required—TOEFL (minimum score 550 paper-based; 213 computer-based; 78 iBT). *Application deadline:* For fall admission, 6/1 for domestic and international students; for spring admission, 10/1 for domestic and international students. Application fee: $40 ($90 for international students). *Expenses:* Tuition, state resident: full-time $6024; part-time $251 per credit hour. Tuition, nonresident: full-time $13,536; part-time $564 per credit hour. Required fees: $1776; $50 per credit hour. $306 per semester. *Financial support:* In 2010–11, 5 students received support, including 6 teaching assistantships (averaging $5,098 per year); research assistantships, Federal Work-Study, institutionally sponsored loans, scholarships/grants, health care benefits, and unspecified assistantships also available. Support available to part-time students. *Unit head:* Dr. Robert Davis, Associate Dean, 512-245-3591, Fax: 512-245-7973, E-mail: rd23@txstate.edu. *Application contact:* Dr. J. Michael Willoughby, Dean of Graduate School, 512-245-2581, Fax: 512-245-8365, E-mail: gradcollege@txstate.edu.

Texas Tech University, Graduate School, Jerry S. Rawls College of Business Administration, Area of Information Systems and Quantitative Sciences, Lubbock, TX 79409. Offers business statistics (MS, PhD); healthcare management (MS); management information systems (MS, PhD); production and operations management (MS, PhD); risk management (MS). Part-time programs available. *Faculty:* 15 full-time (0 women). *Students:* 73 full-time (21 women), 13 part-time (0 women); includes 5 minority (1 Black or African American, non-Hispanic/Latino; 1 Asian, non-Hispanic/Latino; 3 Hispanic/Latino), 61 international. Average age 27. 130 applicants, 75% accepted, 51 enrolled. In 2010, 31 master's, 2 doctorates awarded. Terminal master's awarded for partial completion of doctoral program. *Degree requirements:* For master's, comprehensive exam or capstone course; for doctorate, thesis/dissertation, qualifying exams. *Entrance requirements:* For master's and doctorate, GMAT, holistic profile of academic credentials. Additional exam requirements/recommendations for international students: Required—TOEFL (minimum score 550 paper-based; 213 computer-based; 79 iBT). *Application deadline:* For fall admission, 4/1 priority date for domestic students, 1/15 for international students; for spring admission, 9/1 priority date for domestic students, 6/15 priority date for international students. Applications are processed on a rolling basis. Application fee: $50 ($75 for international students). Electronic applications accepted. *Expenses:* Tuition, state resident: full-time $5495.76; part-time $228.99 per credit hour. Tuition, nonresident: full-time $12,936; part-time $538.99 per credit hour. Required fees: $2674; $36 per credit hour. $905 per semester. *Financial support:* In 2010–11, 4 research assistantships (averaging $8,800 per year), 9 teaching assistantships (averaging $18,000 per year) were awarded; Federal Work-Study, scholarships/grants, and unspecified assistantships also available. *Faculty research:* Database management systems, systems management and engineering, expert systems and adaptive knowledge-based sciences, statistical analysis and design. *Unit head:* Dr. Bradley Ewing, Area Coordinator, 806-742-3939, Fax: 806-742-3193, E-mail: bradley.ewing@ttu.edu. *Application contact:* Cynthia D. Barnes, Director, Graduate Services Center, 806-742-3184, Fax: 806-742-3958, E-mail: ba_grad@ttu.edu.

Texas Tech University, Graduate School, Jerry S. Rawls College of Business Administration, Programs in Business Administration, Lubbock, TX 79409. Offers agricultural business (MBA); business administration (IMBA); business statistics (MBA); entrepreneurship and innovation (MBA); general business (MBA); health organization management (MBA); international business (MBA); management and leadership skills (MBA); management

information systems (MBA); marketing (MBA); real estate (MBA); JD/MBA; MBA/M Arch; MBA/MA; MBA/MD; MBA/MS; MBA/Pharm D. Part-time and evening/weekend programs available. *Faculty:* 47 full-time (8 women), 5 part-time/adjunct (0 women). *Students:* 52 full-time (13 women), 531 part-time (152 women); includes 121 minority (28 Black or African American, non-Hispanic/Latino; 3 American Indian or Alaska Native, non-Hispanic/Latino; 31 Asian, non-Hispanic/Latino; 53 Hispanic/Latino; 6 Two or more races, non-Hispanic/Latino), 49 international. Average age 30. 437 applicants, 77% accepted, 258 enrolled. In 2010, 228 master's awarded. *Degree requirements:* For master's, capstone course. *Entrance requirements:* For master's, GMAT, holistic review of academic credentials. Additional exam requirements/recommendations for international students: Required—TOEFL (minimum score 550 paper-based; 213 computer-based; 79 iBT). *Application deadline:* For fall admission, 4/1 priority date for domestic students, 1/15 for international students; for spring admission, 9/1 priority date for domestic students, 6/15 for international students. Applications are processed on a rolling basis. Application fee: $50 ($75 for international students). Electronic applications accepted. *Expenses:* Tuition, state resident: full-time $5495.76; part-time $228.99 per credit hour. Tuition, nonresident: full-time $12,936; part-time $538.99 per credit hour. Required fees: $2674; $36 per credit hour. $905 per semester. *Financial support:* In 2010–11, 25 research assistantships (averaging $8,800 per year) were awarded; teaching assistantships, career-related internships or fieldwork, Federal Work-Study, scholarships/grants, health care benefits, and unspecified assistantships also available. Support available to part-time students. Financial award applicants required to submit FAFSA. *Unit head:* Dr. W. Jay Conover, Director, 806-742-1546, Fax: 806-742-3958, E-mail: jay.conover@ttu.edu. *Application contact:* Cynthia D. Barnes, Director, Graduate Services Center, 806-742-3184, Fax: 806-742-3958, E-mail: ba_grad@ttu.edu.

Towson University, Master's Program in Applied Information Technology, Towson, MD 21252-0001. Offers applied information technology (MS, PhD); database management systems (Postbaccalaureate Certificate); information security and assurance (Postbaccalaureate Certificate); information systems management (Graduate Certificate); Internet applications development (Postbaccalaureate Certificate); networking technologies (Postbaccalaureate Certificate); software engineering (Postbaccalaureate Certificate). *Students:* 111 full-time (25 women), 232 part-time (62 women); includes 122 minority (75 Black or African American, non-Hispanic/Latino; 4 American Indian or Alaska Native, non-Hispanic/Latino; 31 Asian, non-Hispanic/Latino; 11 Hispanic/Latino; 1 Native Hawaiian or other Pacific Islander, non-Hispanic/Latino), 85 international. In 2010, 75 master's, 9 doctorates, 74 other advanced degrees awarded. *Expenses:* Tuition, state resident: part-time $324 per credit. Tuition, nonresident: part-time $681 per credit. Required fees: $95 per term. *Unit head:* Mike O'Leary, Graduate Program Director, 410-704-4757, E-mail: moleary@towson.edu. *Application contact:* Mike O'Leary, Graduate Program Director, 410-704-4757, E-mail: moleary@towson.edu.

Troy University, Graduate School, College of Business, Program in Business Administration, Troy, AL 36082. Offers accounting (EMBA, MBA); criminal justice (EMBA); finance (MBA); general management (EMBA, MBA); healthcare management (EMBA); information systems (EMBA, MBA); international economic development (MBA). *Accreditation:* ACBSP. Part-time and evening/weekend programs available. *Students:* 351 full-time (198 women), 745 part-time (452 women); includes 589 minority (425 Black or African American, non-Hispanic/Latino; 13 American Indian or Alaska Native, non-Hispanic/Latino; 129 Asian, non-Hispanic/Latino; 21 Hispanic/Latino; 1 Two or more races, non-Hispanic/Latino). Average age 29. 748 applicants, 71% accepted. In 2010, 322 master's awarded. *Degree requirements:* For master's, minimum GPA 3.0, capstone course, research course. *Entrance requirements:* For master's, GMAT (minimum score 500) or GRE General Test (minimum score 900), minimum GPA of 2.5; letter of recommendation, bachelor's degree. Additional exam requirements/recommendations for international students: Required—TOEFL (minimum score 523 paper-based; 193 computer-based; 70 iBT), IELTS (minimum score 6), or ACT compass ESL (minimum Listening, Reading, and Grammar score: 270). *Application deadline:* Applications are processed on a rolling basis. Application fee: $50. *Expenses:* Tuition, state resident: full-time $4428; part-time $246 per credit hour. Tuition, nonresident: full-time $8856; part-time $492 per credit hour. Required fees: $432; $24 per credit hour. $50 per term. Tuition and fees vary according to program. *Unit head:* Dr. Henry M. Findley, Interim Chair/Professor, 334-670-3271, Fax: 334-670-3599, E-mail: hfindley@troy.edu. *Application contact:* Brenda K. Campbell, Director of Graduate Admissions, 334-670-3178, Fax: 334-670-3733, E-mail: bcamp@troy.edu.

Troy University, Graduate School, College of Business, Program in Management, Troy, AL 36082. Offers applied management (MSM); healthcare management (MSM); human resources management (MSM); information systems (MSM); international hospitality management (MSM); international management (MSM); leadership and organizational effectiveness (MSM); public management (MS, MSM). *Accreditation:* ACBSP. Evening/weekend programs available. *Students:* 101 full-time (62 women), 398 part-time (249 women); includes 308 minority (278 Black or African American, non-Hispanic/Latino; 8 American Indian or Alaska Native, non-Hispanic/Latino; 8 Asian, non-Hispanic/Latino; 13 Hispanic/Latino; 1 Two or more races, non-Hispanic/Latino). Average age 35. 218 applicants, 80% accepted. In 2010, 314 master's awarded. *Degree requirements:* For master's, Graduate Educational Testing Service Major Field Test, capstone exam, minimum GPA of 3.0. *Entrance requirements:* For master's, GMAT (minimum score 500) or GRE General Test (minimum score 900), minimum GPA of 2.5, bachelor's degree, letter of recommendation. Additional exam requirements/recommendations for international students: Required—TOEFL (minimum score 523 paper-based; 193 computer-based; 70 iBT), IELTS, or ACT compass ESL (minimum Listening, Reading, and Grammar score: 270). *Application deadline:* Applications are processed on a rolling basis. Application fee: $50. Electronic applications accepted. *Expenses:* Contact institution. *Unit head:* Dr. Henry M. Findley, Interim Chair/Professor, 334-670-3271, Fax: 334-670-3599, E-mail: hfindley@troy.edu. *Application contact:* Brenda K. Campbell, Director of Graduate Admissions, 334-670-3178, Fax: 334-670-3733, E-mail: bcamp@troy.edu.

TUI University, College of Business Administration, Program in Business Administration, Cypress, CA 90630. Offers business administration (PhD); conflict and negotiation management (MBA); criminal justice administration (MBA); entrepreneurship (MBA); finance (MBA); general management (MBA); government accounting (MBA); human resource management (MBA); information security and digital assurance management (MBA); information technology management (MBA); international business (MBA); logistics management (MBA); marketing (MBA); project management (MBA); public management (MBA); quality management (MBA); strategic leadership (MBA). Part-time and evening/weekend programs available. Postbaccalaureate distance learning degree programs offered (no on-campus study). *Students:* 741 full-time (200 women), 1,585 part-time (410 women). 379 applicants, 81% accepted, 300 enrolled. In 2010, 752 master's, 28 doctorates awarded. *Degree requirements:* For doctorate, comprehensive exam, thesis/dissertation, defense of dissertation. *Entrance requirements:* For master's, minimum GPA of 2.5 (students with GPA 3.0 or greater may transfer up to 30% of graduate level credits); for doctorate, minimum GPA of 3.4, curriculum vitae, course work in research methods or statistics. Additional exam requirements/recommendations for international students: Required—TOEFL. *Application deadline:* For fall admission, 10/3 for domestic and international students; for winter admission, 12/22 for domestic and international students; for spring admission, 4/3 for domestic and international students. Applications are processed on a rolling basis. Application fee: $75. Electronic applications accepted. *Expenses:* Tuition: Full-time $11,040; part-time $345 per semester hour. *Unit head:* Paul Watkins, Dean, College of Business Administration, 800-375-9878, E-mail: pwatkins@tuiu.edu. *Application contact:* Wei Ren-Finaly, Registrar, 800-375-9878, Fax: 714-827-7407, E-mail: registration@tuiu.edu.

TUI University, College of Information Systems, Cypress, CA 90630. Offers business intelligence (Certificate); information technology management (MS). Part-time and evening/weekend programs available. Postbaccalaureate distance learning degree programs offered (no on-campus study). *Students:* 83 full-time (12 women), 178 part-time (30 women). 67 applicants, 84% accepted, 50 enrolled. In 2010, 116 master's awarded. *Entrance requirements:* For master's, minimum GPA of 2.5 (students with GPA 3.0 or greater may transfer up to 30% of graduate level credits); undergraduate degree completed within the past 5 years. Additional exam requirements/recommendations for international students: Required—TOEFL (minimum score 525 paper-based). *Application deadline:* For fall admission, 10/3 for domestic and international students; for winter admission, 12/22 for domestic and international students; for spring admission, 4/3 for domestic and international students. Applications are processed on a rolling basis. Application fee: $0. Electronic applications accepted. *Expenses:* Tuition: Full-time $11,040; part-time $345 per semester hour. *Unit head:* Dr. Paul Watkins, Dean, 800-509-3901, E-mail: infocis@tuiu.edu. *Application contact:* Wei Ren-Finaly, Registrar, 800-375-9878, Fax: 714-827-7407, E-mail: registration@tuiu.edu.

United States International University, School of Business Administration, Nairobi, Kenya. Offers business administration (GEMBA); entrepreneurship (MBA); finance (MBA); human resource management (MBA); information technology management (MBA); integrated studies (MBA); international business administration (MBA); management and organizational development (MS); marketing (MBA); organizational development (EMS); strategic management (MBA). Part-time and evening/weekend programs available. *Faculty:* 42 full-time (8 women), 64 part-time/adjunct (14 women). *Students:* 423 full-time (227 women), 129 part-time (63 women). Average age 29. 110 applicants, 79% accepted, 78 enrolled. In 2010, 164 master's awarded. *Degree requirements:* For master's, thesis. *Entrance requirements:* For master's, GMAT, 2 letters of reference, resume. Additional exam requirements/recommendations for international students: Required—TOEFL (minimum score 550 paper-based; 213 computer-based). *Application deadline:* For fall admission, 6/30 priority date for domestic and international students; for spring admission, 9/30 for domestic and international students. Applications are processed on a rolling basis. Application fee: $50. *Financial support:* In 2010–11, 30 students received support, including 8 research assistantships (averaging $1,400 per year), 4 teaching assistantships (averaging $1,400 per year); career-related internships or fieldwork, scholarships/grants, and unspecified assistantships also available. Support available to part-time students. Financial award

application deadline: 6/30; financial award applicants required to submit FAFSA. *Faculty research:* Marketing in small business enterprises, total quality management in Kenya. *Unit head:* Dr. Damary Sikalieh, Dean, 254-02-3606-415, E-mail: dsikalieh@usiu.ac.ke. *Application contact:* George Lumbasi, Director of Admissions, 254-02-3606563, Fax: 254-02-3606100, E-mail: glumbasi@usiu.ac.ke.

Université de Sherbrooke, Faculty of Administration, Program in Governance, Audit and Security of Information Technology, Longueuil, QC J4K0A8, Canada. Offers M Adm. Part-time and evening/weekend programs available. Postbaccalaureate distance learning degree programs offered. *Faculty:* 1 full-time (0 women), 12 part-time/adjunct (2 women). *Students:* 13 part-time (2 women). Average age 40. 47 applicants, 36% accepted, 13 enrolled. In 2010, 14 master's awarded. *Degree requirements:* For master's, thesis. *Entrance requirements:* For master's, Related work experience. *Application deadline:* For fall admission, 4/30 priority date for domestic students. Applications are processed on a rolling basis. Application fee: $70. Electronic applications accepted. *Unit head:* Prof. Julien Bilodeau, Director, Graduate programs in business, 819-821-8000 Ext. 62355, E-mail: julien.bilodeau@usherbrooke.ca. *Application contact:* Lyne Cantin, assistant to the director, 450-463-1835 Ext. 61768, Fax: 450-670-1848, E-mail: lyne.cantin@usherbrooke.ca.

Université de Sherbrooke, Faculty of Administration, Program in Management Information Systems, Sherbrooke, QC J1K 2R1, Canada. Offers M Sc. *Faculty:* 8 full-time (2 women), 1 part-time/adjunct (0 women). *Students:* 21 full-time (12 women). Average age 23. 68 applicants, 79% accepted, 21 enrolled. In 2010, 9 master's awarded. *Degree requirements:* For master's, one foreign language, thesis. *Entrance requirements:* For master's, Bachelor degree in related field Minimum 3/4.3. *Application deadline:* For fall admission, 4/30 for domestic students, 1/15 for international students. Applications are processed on a rolling basis. Application fee: $70. Electronic applications accepted. *Faculty research:* Project management in IT, IT governance, business intelligence, IT performance. *Unit head:* Prof. Julien Bilodeau, Director, Graduate programs in business, 819-821-8000 Ext. 62355. *Application contact:* Marie-Claude Drouin, Assistant to the director, 819-821-8000 Ext. 63301.

University at Buffalo, the State University of New York, Graduate School, School of Management, Buffalo, NY 14260. Offers accounting (MS); business administration (EMBA, MBA, PMBA); finance (MS), including financial engineering, financial management; information assurance (Certificate); management (PhD); management information systems (MS); supply chains and operations management (MS); Au D/MBA; JD/MBA; M Arch/MBA; MA/MBA; MD/MBA; MPH/MBA; MSW/MBA; Pharm D/MBA. *Accreditation:* AACSB. Part-time and evening/weekend programs available. *Faculty:* 65 full-time (18 women), 32 part-time/adjunct (8 women). *Students:* 626 full-time (229 women), 202 part-time (69 women); includes 43 minority (18 Black or African American, non-Hispanic/Latino; 2 American Indian or Alaska Native, non-Hispanic/Latino; 18 Asian, non-Hispanic/Latino; 5 Hispanic/Latino), 351 international. Average age 27. 1,553 applicants, 46% accepted, 400 enrolled. In 2010, 287 master's, 4 doctorates, 3 other advanced degrees awarded. *Degree requirements:* For master's, thesis (for some programs); for doctorate, comprehensive exam, thesis/dissertation. *Entrance requirements:* For master's, GMAT (MBA, MS in accounting), GRE or GMAT (for all other MS concentrations); for doctorate, GMAT or GRE. Additional exam requirements/recommendations for international students: Required—TOEFL (minimum score 230 computer-based; 95 iBT). *Application deadline:* For fall admission, 5/2 priority date for domestic students, 3/1 priority date for international students. Applications are processed on a rolling basis. Application fee: $100. Electronic applications accepted. *Expenses:* Contact institution. *Financial support:* In 2010–11, 91 students received support, including 5 fellowships with full and partial tuition reimbursements available (averaging $4,000 per year), 41 research assistantships with full and partial tuition reimbursements available (averaging $16,000 per year), 28 teaching assistantships with full and partial tuition reimbursements available (averaging $15,000 per year); career-related internships or fieldwork, Federal Work-Study, institutionally sponsored loans, scholarships/grants, health care benefits, and unspecified assistantships also available. Financial award application deadline: 2/15; financial award applicants required to submit FAFSA. *Faculty research:* Earnings management and electronic information assurance, supply chains and operations management, corporate financing and asset pricing, consumer behavior and quantitative modeling of marketing behavior, leadership and politics in organizations. Total annual research expenditures: $215,000. *Unit head:* David W. Frasier, Assistant Dean, 716-645-3204, Fax: 716-645-2341, E-mail: davidf@buffalo.edu. *Application contact:* David W. Frasier, Assistant Dean, 716-645-3204, Fax: 716-645-2341, E-mail: davidf@buffalo.edu.

The University of Akron, Graduate School, College of Business Administration, Department of Management, Program in Management-Information Systems, Akron, OH 44325. Offers MSM. *Students:* 11 full-time (4 women), 9 part-time (3 women); includes 1 Asian, non-Hispanic/Latino, 10 international. Average age 27. 19 applicants, 42% accepted, 5 enrolled. In 2010, 5 master's awarded. *Entrance requirements:* For master's, GMAT May accept GRE if applicant has two years of work experience, minimum GPA of 2.75, two letters of recommendation, statement of purpose, resume. Additional exam requirements/recommendations for international students:

Required—TOEFL (minimum score 550 paper-based; 213 computer-based; 79 iBT). *Application deadline:* For fall admission, 7/15 for domestic students, 7/1 for international students; for spring admission, 11/15 for domestic and international students. Application fee: $30 ($40 for international students). Electronic applications accepted. *Expenses:* Tuition, state resident: full-time $6800; part-time $378 per credit hour. Tuition, nonresident: full-time $11,644; part-time $647 per credit hour. Required fees: $1265. One-time fee: $30 full-time. *Unit head:* Dr. B. S. Vijayaraman, Head, 330-972-5442, E-mail: bsv@uakron.edu. *Application contact:* Dr. Susan Hanlon, Director of Graduate Business Programs, 330-972-7043, Fax: 330-972-6588, E-mail: shanlon@uakron.edu.

The University of Alabama in Huntsville, School of Graduate Studies, College of Business Administration, Department of Accounting and Finance, Huntsville, AL 35899. Offers accounting (M Acc), including CPA preparatory with an emphasis in taxation, CPA preparatory with emphasis in assurance and financial reporting, general accounting, information systems audit and control (ISAC). *Accreditation:* AACSB. Part-time and evening/weekend programs available. *Faculty:* 7 full-time (4 women), 2 part-time/adjunct (0 women). *Students:* 14 full-time (8 women), 27 part-time (14 women); includes 6 minority (all Black or African American, non-Hispanic/Latino), 3 international. Average age 33. 27 applicants, 56% accepted, 13 enrolled. In 2010, 8 master's awarded. *Degree requirements:* For master's, comprehensive exam, thesis or alternative. *Entrance requirements:* For master's, GMAT (minimum score 500), minimum AACSB index of 1080. Additional exam requirements/recommendations for international students: Required—TOEFL (minimum score 550 paper-based; 213 computer-based; 62 iBT). *Application deadline:* For fall admission, 8/1 for domestic students, 4/1 for international students; for spring admission, 12/1 for domestic students, 9/1 for international students. Applications are processed on a rolling basis. Application fee: $40 ($50 for international students). Electronic applications accepted. *Expenses:* Tuition, state resident: full-time $7250; part-time $407.75 per credit hour. Tuition, nonresident: full-time $17,358; part-time $970.05 per credit hour. Required fees: $246.80 per semester. Tuition and fees vary according to course load and program. *Financial support:* In 2010–11, 1 student received support, including 1 research assistantship with full tuition reimbursement available (averaging $14,400 per year), 1 teaching assistantship with full tuition reimbursement available (averaging $11,470 per year); career-related internships or fieldwork, Federal Work-Study, institutionally sponsored loans, scholarships/grants, health care benefits, and unspecified assistantships also available. Support available to part-time students. Financial award application deadline: 4/1; financial award applicants required to submit FAFSA. *Faculty research:* Accounting information systems, emerging technologies in accounting, behavioral accounting, state and local taxation, financial accounting. Total annual research expenditures: $17,511. *Unit head:* Dr. John Burnett, Interim Chair, 256-824-2923, Fax: 256-824-2929, E-mail: burnettj@uah.edu. *Application contact:* Jennifer Pettitt, Director of Graduate Programs, 256-824-6681, Fax: 256-824-7571, E-mail: jennifer.pettitt@uah.edu.

The University of Alabama in Huntsville, School of Graduate Studies, College of Business Administration, Department of Economics and Information Systems, Huntsville, AL 35899. Offers information systems (MSIS). Part-time and evening/weekend programs available. *Faculty:* 11 full-time (1 woman), 3 part-time/adjunct (0 women). *Students:* 3 full-time (0 women), 20 part-time (7 women); includes 4 minority (2 Black or African American, non-Hispanic/Latino; 1 American Indian or Alaska Native, non-Hispanic/Latino; 1 Asian, non-Hispanic/Latino). Average age 34. 25 applicants, 52% accepted, 8 enrolled. In 2010, 11 master's awarded. *Degree requirements:* For master's, comprehensive exam, thesis or alternative. *Entrance requirements:* For master's, GMAT (minimum score 500), minimum AACSB index of 1080. Additional exam requirements/recommendations for international students: Required—TOEFL (minimum score 550 paper-based; 213 computer-based; 62 iBT). *Application deadline:* For fall admission, 8/1 for domestic students, 4/1 for international students; for spring admission, 12/1 for domestic students, 9/1 for international students. Applications are processed on a rolling basis. Application fee: $40 ($50 for international students). Electronic applications accepted. *Expenses:* Tuition, state resident: full-time $7250; part-time $407.75 per credit hour. Tuition, nonresident: full-time $17,358; part-time $970.05 per credit hour. Required fees: $246.80 per semester. Tuition and fees vary according to course load and program. *Financial support:* Career-related internships or fieldwork, Federal Work-Study, institutionally sponsored loans, scholarships/grants, health care benefits, and unspecified assistantships available. Support available to part-time students. Financial award application deadline: 4/1; financial award applicants required to submit FAFSA. *Faculty research:* Supply chain management, incomplete contract and dynamic bargaining in technology investment, personalization at e-commerce sites, workflow management, real options modeling of technology competition. Total annual research expenditures: $513,781. *Unit head:* Dr. Allen W. Wilhite, Chair, 256-824-6591, Fax: 256-824-6328, E-mail: wilhitea@uah.edu. *Application contact:* Jennifer Pettitt, Director of Graduate Programs, 256-824-6681, Fax: 256-824-7571, E-mail: jennifer.pettitt@uah.edu.

The University of Alabama in Huntsville, School of Graduate Studies, Interdisciplinary Studies, Interdisciplinary Program in Information Assurance and Cybersecurity, Huntsville, AL 35899. Offers MS, Certificate. Part-time

and evening/weekend programs available. *Faculty:* 7 full-time (1 woman), 5 part-time/adjunct (0 women). *Students:* 1 full-time (0 women), 18 part-time (4 women); includes 4 minority (2 Black or African American, non-Hispanic/Latino; 1 American Indian or Alaska Native, non-Hispanic/Latino; 1 Asian, non-Hispanic/Latino). Average age 40. 21 applicants, 90% accepted, 16 enrolled. In 2010, 8 other advanced degrees awarded. *Degree requirements:* For master's, comprehensive exam, thesis or alternative, thesis: 24 hours course work plus 6 hour thesis. *Entrance requirements:* For master's, GRE General Test, minimum GPA of 3.0; for Certificate, GMAT, minimum GPA of 3.0. Additional exam requirements/recommendations for international students: Required—TOEFL (minimum score 550 paper-based; 213 computer-based; 62 iBT). *Application deadline:* For fall admission, 7/15 for domestic students, 4/1 for international students; for spring admission, 11/30 for domestic students, 9/1 for international students. Applications are processed on a rolling basis. Application fee: $40 ($50 for international students). Electronic applications accepted. *Expenses:* Tuition, state resident: full-time $7250; part-time $407.75 per credit hour. Tuition, nonresident: full-time $17,358; part-time $970.05 per credit hour. Required fees: $246.80 per semester. Tuition and fees vary according to course load and program. *Financial support:* Career-related internships or fieldwork, Federal Work-Study, institutionally sponsored loans, scholarships/grants, health care benefits, and unspecified assistantships available. Support available to part-time students. Financial award application deadline: 4/1; financial award applicants required to submit FAFSA. *Faculty research:* Service discovery, enterprise security, security metrics, cryptography, network security. *Unit head:* Dr. Rhonda Kay Gaede, Dean of Graduate Studies, 256-824-6002, Fax: 256-824-6405, E-mail: deangrad@uah.edu. *Application contact:* Jennifer Pettitt, College of Business Administration Director of Graduate Programs, 256-824-6681, Fax: 256-824-7572, E-mail: jennifer.pettitt@uah.edu.

The University of Arizona, Eller College of Management, Department of Management Information Systems, Tucson, AZ 85721. Offers MS. *Faculty:* 10 full-time (5 women), 2 part-time/adjunct (0 women). *Students:* 74 full-time (24 women), 4 part-time (1 woman); includes 1 Black or African American, non-Hispanic/Latino; 1 Asian, non-Hispanic/Latino; 2 Two or more races, non-Hispanic/Latino, 68 international. Average age 28. 393 applicants, 66% accepted, 58 enrolled. In 2010, 47 master's awarded. *Degree requirements:* For master's, thesis or alternative. *Entrance requirements:* For master's, GMAT or GRE General Test, 2 letters of recommendation, resume. Additional exam requirements/recommendations for international students: Required—TOEFL (minimum score 550 paper-based; 213 computer-based; 80 iBT). *Application deadline:* For fall admission, 1/15 for domestic and international students. Applications are processed on a rolling basis. Application fee: $75. Electronic applications accepted. *Expenses:* Tuition, state resident: full-time $7692. *Financial support:* In 2010–11, 15 research assistantships with full tuition reimbursements (averaging $19,504 per year), 21 teaching assistantships with full tuition reimbursements (averaging $18,570 per year) were awarded; career-related internships or fieldwork, Federal Work-Study, scholarships/grants, health care benefits, tuition waivers (partial), and unspecified assistantships also available. Financial award application deadline: 3/15. *Faculty research:* Group decision support systems, domestic and international computing issues, expert systems, data management and structures. Total annual research expenditures: $1.2 million. *Unit head:* Dr. Paul Goes, Department Head, 520-621-2429, Fax: 520-621-2775, E-mail: pgoes@eller.arizona.edu. *Application contact:* Cinda Van Winkle, 520-621-2387, E-mail: admissions_mis@eller.arizona.edu.

University of Arkansas, Graduate School, Sam M. Walton College of Business Administration, Department of Information Systems, Fayetteville, AR 72701-1201. Offers MIS. Part-time and evening/weekend programs available. *Students:* 11 full-time (3 women), 36 part-time (9 women); includes 3 minority (1 Black or African American, non-Hispanic/Latino; 2 Asian, non-Hispanic/Latino), 21 international. 47 applicants, 51% accepted. In 2010, 25 master's awarded. *Entrance requirements:* For master's, GMAT. Application fee: $40 ($50 for international students). *Financial support:* In 2010–11, 9 fellowships with tuition reimbursements, 18 research assistantships, 3 teaching assistantships were awarded. Financial award application deadline: 4/1. *Unit head:* Dr. Moez Limayem, Head, 479-575-4500, E-mail: mlimayem@uark.edu. *Application contact:* Dr. Paul Cronan, Graduate Coordinator, 479-575-6130, E-mail: cronan@uark.edu.

University of California, Los Angeles, Graduate Division, UCLA Anderson School of Management, Los Angeles, CA 90095-1481. Offers accounting (PhD); business administration (MBA); decisions, operations and technology management (PhD); finance (PhD); financial engineering (MFE); global economics and management (PhD); human resources and organizational behavior (PhD); marketing (PhD); strategy and policy (PhD); DDS/MBA; MBA/JD; MBA/MD; MBA/MLAS; MBA/MLIS; MBA/MPH; MBA/MPP; MBA/MSCS; MBA/MSN; MBA/MUP. *Accreditation:* AACSB. Part-time programs available. *Faculty:* 102 full-time (17 women), 43 part-time/adjunct (6 women). *Students:* 833 full-time (270 women), 1,052 part-time (271 women); includes 592 minority (25 Black or African American, non-Hispanic/Latino; 3 American Indian or Alaska Native, non-Hispanic/Latino; 482 Asian, non-Hispanic/Latino; 60 Hispanic/Latino; 6 Native Hawaiian or other Pacific Islander, non-Hispanic/Latino; 16 Two or more races, non-Hispanic/Latino), 445 international. In 2010, 735 master's, 10 doctorates awarded. *Degree requirements:* For master's, comprehensive exam, field study consulting project (for MBA); thesis/dissertation (for MFE); for doctorate, comprehensive exam, thesis/dissertation, oral and written qualifying exams. *Entrance requirements:* For master's, GMAT (MBA); GMAT or GRE General Test (MFE), minimum undergraduate GPA of 3.0; for doctorate, GMAT or GRE General Test, minimum undergraduate GPA of 3.0. Additional exam requirements/recommendations for international students: Required—TOEFL (minimum score 560 paper-based; 220 computer-based; 87 iBT), IELTS (minimum score 7). *Application deadline:* For fall admission, 10/20 for domestic and international students; for winter admission, 1/5 for domestic and international students; for spring admission, 4/13 for domestic and international students. Application fee: $200. Electronic applications accepted. *Expenses:* Contact institution. *Financial support:* Fellowships, research assistantships, teaching assistantships, career-related internships or fieldwork, institutionally sponsored loans, scholarships/grants, health care benefits, and tuition waivers (partial) available. Financial award application deadline: 3/2; financial award applicants required to submit FAFSA. *Unit head:* Judy D. Olian, Dean, UCLA Anderson School of Management, 310-825-7982, Fax: 310-206-2073. *Application contact:* Mae Jennifer Shores, Assistant Dean and Director of Full-time MBA Admissions and Financial Aid, 310-825-6944, Fax: 310-825-8582, E-mail: mba.admissions@anderson.ucla.edu.

University of California, Santa Cruz, Division of Graduate Studies, Jack Baskin School of Engineering, Department of Technology and Information Management, Santa Cruz, CA 95064. Offers MS, PhD. *Students:* 7 full-time (1 woman), 3 part-time (1 woman), 5 international. Average age 33. 17 applicants, 35% accepted, 3 enrolled.Terminal master's awarded for partial completion of doctoral program. *Degree requirements:* For master's, thesis, 2 seminars; for doctorate, thesis/dissertation, 2 seminars. *Entrance requirements:* For master's and doctorate, GRE General Test; GRE Subject Test preferably in computer science, engineering, physics, or mathematics (highly recommended), minimum GPA of 3.5. Additional exam requirements/recommendations for international students: Required—TOEFL (minimum score 570 paper-based; 230 computer-based; 89 iBT); Recommended—IELTS (minimum score 8). *Application deadline:* For fall admission, 1/3 for domestic and international students. Application fee: $70 ($90 for international students). Electronic applications accepted. *Financial support:* Fellowships, research assistantships, teaching assistantships, institutionally sponsored loans and tuition waivers available. Financial award applicants required to submit FAFSA. *Faculty research:* Integration of information systems, technology, and business management. *Unit head:* Carol Mullane, Graduate Program Advisor, 831-459-2576, E-mail: mullane@soe.ucsc.edu. *Application contact:* Carol Mullane, Graduate Program Advisor, 831-459-2576, E-mail: mullane@soe.ucsc.edu.

University of Cincinnati, Graduate School, College of Business, MS Program, Cincinnati, OH 45221. Offers accounting (MS); information systems (MS); marketing (MS); quantitative analysis (MS). Part-time and evening/weekend programs available. *Faculty:* 79 full-time (22 women), 71 part-time/adjunct (24 women). *Students:* 130 full-time (46 women), 87 part-time (38 women); includes 12 minority (2 Black or African American, non-Hispanic/Latino; 3 Asian, non-Hispanic/Latino; 4 Hispanic/Latino; 3 Two or more races, non-Hispanic/Latino), 89 international. 407 applicants, 53% accepted, 110 enrolled. *Degree requirements:* For master's, thesis (for some programs). *Entrance requirements:* For master's, GMAT, GRE, resume, transcripts, essays, letters of recommendation. Additional exam requirements/recommendations for international students: Required—TOEFL (minimum score 600 paper-based; 250 computer-based; 100 iBT). *Application deadline:* For fall admission, 1/15 priority date for domestic students, 4/1 for international students. Applications are processed on a rolling basis. Application fee: $45. Electronic applications accepted. *Expenses:* Contact institution. *Financial support:* In 2010–11, 10 teaching assistantships with full and partial tuition reimbursements (averaging $5,400 per year) were awarded; scholarships/grants, tuition waivers (full and partial), and unspecified assistantships also available. Financial award application deadline: 2/1; financial award applicants required to submit FAFSA. *Unit head:* Dr. David Szymanski, Dean, 513-556-7001, Fax: 513-556-4891, E-mail: will.mcintosh@uc.edu. *Application contact:* Dona Clary, Director, Graduate Programs Office, 513-556-3546, Fax: 513-558-7006, E-mail: dona.clary@uc.edu.

University of Cincinnati, Graduate School, College of Business, PhD Program, Cincinnati, OH 45221. Offers accounting (PhD); finance (PhD); information systems (PhD); management (PhD); marketing (PhD); quantitative analysis and operations management (PhD). *Faculty:* 56 full-time (13 women). *Students:* 32 full-time (12 women), 9 part-time (3 women); includes 2 minority (both Hispanic/Latino), 23 international. 119 applicants, 12% accepted, 9 enrolled. In 2010, 8 doctorates awarded. *Degree requirements:* For doctorate, comprehensive exam, thesis/dissertation. *Entrance requirements:* For doctorate, GMAT, GRE, transcripts, essays, resume, letters of recommendation. Additional exam requirements/recommendations for international students: Required—TOEFL (minimum score 600 paper-based; 250 computer-based; 100 iBT). *Application deadline:* For fall admission, 2/1 for domestic and international students. Application fee: $45. Electronic applications accepted. *Expenses:* Contact institution. *Financial support:* In 2010–11,

38 students received support, including 29 research assistantships with full and partial tuition reimbursements available (averaging $14,640 per year); scholarships/grants, tuition waivers (full and partial), and unspecified assistantships also available. Financial award application deadline: 2/15; financial award applicants required to submit FAFSA. *Unit head:* Dr. Suzanne Masterson, Director, PhD Programs, 513-556-7125, Fax: 513-556-5499, E-mail: suzanne.masterson@uc.edu. *Application contact:* Deborah Schildknecht, Assistant Director, PhD Programs, 513-556-7190, Fax: 513-558-7006, E-mail: deborah.schildknecht@uc.edu.

University of Colorado Boulder, Leeds School of Business, Division of Business Administration, Boulder, CO 80309. Offers accounting (MS, PhD); finance (PhD); information systems (PhD); marketing (PhD); operations (PhD); strategic, organizational, and entrepreneurial studies (PhD). Part-time and evening/weekend programs available. *Students:* 110 full-time (42 women), 2 part-time (1 woman); includes 6 minority (5 Asian, non-Hispanic/Latino; 1 Hispanic/Latino), 24 international. Average age 28. 342 applicants, 24 enrolled. In 2010, 48 master's, 12 doctorates awarded. *Entrance requirements:* For master's, GMAT, minimum undergraduate GPA of 3.0. *Application deadline:* For fall admission, 3/31 for domestic and international students; for spring admission, 10/31 for domestic and international students. Application fee: $50 ($60 for international students). Electronic applications accepted. *Financial support:* In 2010–11, 16 fellowships (averaging $1,038 per year), 26 research assistantships (averaging $17,558 per year), 11 teaching assistantships (averaging $12,576 per year) were awarded; career-related internships or fieldwork, Federal Work-Study, scholarships/grants, and unspecified assistantships also available. Financial award applicants required to submit FAFSA.

University of Colorado Denver, Business School, Program in Computer Science and Information Systems, Denver, CO 80217-3364. Offers PhD. *Students:* 7 full-time (0 women), 6 part-time (2 women); includes 1 Black or African American, non-Hispanic/Latino; 1 Asian, non-Hispanic/Latino, 6 international. Average age 37. 23 applicants, 13% accepted, 2 enrolled. In 2010, 4 doctorates awarded. *Degree requirements:* For doctorate, comprehensive exam, thesis/dissertation, 30 hours of CSIS courses beyond the master's level for total of 90 semester hours. *Entrance requirements:* For doctorate, GMAT or GRE General Test, letters of recommendation, portfolio essay describing applicant's motivation and initial plan for doctoral study. Additional exam requirements/recommendations for international students: Required—TOEFL (minimum score 525 paper-based; 197 computer-based; 71 iBT). *Application deadline:* For fall admission, 6/1 for domestic students, 3/15 for international students; for spring admission, 11/1 for domestic students, 10/1 for international students. Application fee: $50 ($75 for international students). Electronic applications accepted. *Expenses:* Contact institution. *Financial support:* Research assistantships, teaching assistantships, Federal Work-Study, institutionally sponsored loans, and scholarships/grants available. Support available to part-time students. Financial award application deadline: 4/1; financial award applicants required to submit FAFSA. *Faculty research:* Design science of information systems, information system economics, organizational impacts of information technology, high performance parallel and distributed systems, performance measurement and prediction. *Unit head:* Dr. Michael Mannino, Associate Professor/Co-Director, 303-315-8427, E-mail: michael.mannino@ucdenver.edu. *Application contact:* Shelly Townley, Admissions Coordinator, 303-315-8202, Fax: 303-556-5904, E-mail: shelly.townley@ucdenver.edu.

University of Colorado Denver, Business School, Program in Information Systems, Denver, CO 80217. Offers accounting and information systems audit and control (MS); business intelligence (MS); enterprise technology management (PhD); health information technology management (MS); web and mobile computing (MS). Part-time and evening/weekend programs available. Postbaccalaureate distance learning degree programs offered (no on-campus study). *Students:* 55 full-time (13 women), 30 part-time (13 women); includes 3 Black or African American, non-Hispanic/Latino; 8 Asian, non-Hispanic/Latino; 3 Hispanic/Latino, 13 international. Average age 34. 30 applicants, 80% accepted, 15 enrolled. In 2010, 13 master's awarded. *Degree requirements:* For master's, 30 credit hours. *Entrance requirements:* For master's, GMAT. Additional exam requirements/recommendations for international students: Required—TOEFL (minimum score 525 paper-based; 197 computer-based; 71 iBT). *Application deadline:* For fall admission, 4/1 priority date for domestic students, 3/15 priority date for international students; for spring admission, 10/1 priority date for domestic and international students. Application fee: $50 ($75 for international students). Electronic applications accepted. *Expenses:* Contact institution. *Financial support:* Federal Work-Study and scholarships/grants available. Support available to part-time students. Financial award application deadline: 4/1; financial award applicants required to submit FAFSA. *Faculty research:* Human-computer interaction, expert systems, database management, electronic commerce, object-oriented software development. *Unit head:* Dr. Jahangir Karimi, Director, 303-315-8430, E-mail: jahangir.karimi@ucdenver.edu. *Application contact:* Shelly Townley, Admissions Director, Graduate Programs, 303-315-8202, E-mail: shelly.townley@ucdenver.edu.

University of Dayton, Graduate School, School of Business Administration, Dayton, OH 45469-1300. Offers accounting (MBA); business intelligence (MBA); cyber security (MBA); entrepreneurship (MBA); finance (MBA);

international business (MBA); marketing (MBA); MIS (MBA); operations management (MBA); technology-enhanced business/e-commerce (MBA); JD/MBA. *Accreditation:* AACSB. Part-time and evening/weekend programs available. *Faculty:* 25 full-time (7 women), 14 part-time/adjunct (2 women). *Students:* 184 full-time (72 women), 110 part-time (34 women); includes 23 minority (7 Black or African American, non-Hispanic/Latino; 7 Asian, non-Hispanic/Latino; 8 Hispanic/Latino; 1 Two or more races, non-Hispanic/Latino), 31 international. Average age 28. 220 applicants, 85% accepted, 103 enrolled. In 2010, 113 master's awarded. *Entrance requirements:* For master's, GMAT or GRE. Additional exam requirements/recommendations for international students: Required—TOEFL (minimum score 550 paper-based; 213 computer-based; 79 iBT); Recommended—IELTS (minimum score 6.5). *Application deadline:* For fall admission, 3/1 priority date for international students; for winter admission, 7/1 priority date for international students; for spring admission, 1/1 priority date for international students. Applications are processed on a rolling basis. Application fee: $0 ($50 for international students). Electronic applications accepted. *Expenses:* Contact institution. *Financial support:* In 2010–11, 15 research assistantships with full and partial tuition reimbursements (averaging $7,020 per year) were awarded; career-related internships or fieldwork, institutionally sponsored loans, scholarships/grants, health care benefits, and unspecified assistantships also available. Support available to part-time students. Financial award application deadline: 3/15; financial award applicants required to submit FAFSA. *Faculty research:* Management information systems, economics, finance, entrepreneurship, marketing. *Unit head:* Janice M. Glynn, Director, MBA Program, 937-229-3733, Fax: 937-229-3882, E-mail: glynn@udayton.edu. *Application contact:* Jeffrey Carter, Assistant Director, MBA Program, 937-229-3733, Fax: 937-229-3882, E-mail: jeff.carter@notes.udayton.edu.

University of Denver, Daniels College of Business, Department of Information Technology and Electronic Commerce, Denver, CO 80208. Offers business intelligence (MS); information technology (IMBA, MBA). Part-time and evening/weekend programs available. *Faculty:* 6 full-time (1 woman). *Entrance requirements:* For master's, GRE General Test or GMAT. Additional exam requirements/recommendations for international students: Required—TOEFL (minimum score 570 paper-based; 88 iBT). *Application deadline:* For fall admission, 11/15 priority date for domestic students; for spring admission, 10/15 priority date for domestic students. Applications are processed on a rolling basis. Application fee: $100. Electronic applications accepted. *Expenses:* Tuition: Full-time $35,604; part-time $29,670 per year. Required fees: $687 per year. Tuition and fees vary according to program. *Financial support:* Career-related internships or fieldwork, Federal Work-Study, institutionally sponsored loans, and scholarships/grants available. Support available to part-time students. Financial award application deadline: 3/15. *Faculty research:* Cross-cultural research in information systems, electronic commerce, distributed project management, strategic information systems, management of emerging technologies. *Unit head:* Dr. Paul Bauer, Chair, 303-871-3816, E-mail: paul.bauer@du.edu. *Application contact:* Allison Sharpe, Graduate Admissions Manager, 303-871-4212, E-mail: allison.sharpe@du.edu.

University of Denver, University College, Denver, CO 80208. Offers arts and culture (MLS, Certificate), including art, literature, and culture, arts development and program management (Certificate), creative writing; environmental policy and management (MAS, Certificate), including energy and sustainability (Certificate), environmental assessment of nuclear power (Certificate), environmental health and safety (Certificate), environmental management, natural resource management (Certificate); geographic information systems (MAS, Certificate); global affairs (MLS, Certificate), including translation studies, world history and culture; healthcare leadership (MPH, Certificate), including healthcare policy, law, and ethics, medical and healthcare information technologies, strategic management of healthcare; information and communications technology (MCIS, Certificate), including database design and administration (Certificate), geographic information systems (MCIS), information security systems security (Certificate), information systems security (MCIS), project management (MCIS, MPS, Certificate), software design and administration (Certificate), software design and programming (MCIS), technology management, telecommunications technology (MCIS), Web design and development; leadership and organizations (MPS, Certificate), including human capital in organizations, philanthropic leadership, project management (MCIS, MPS, Certificate), strategic innovation and change; organizational and professional communication (MPS, Certificate), including alternative dispute resolution, organizational communication, organizational development and training, public relations and marketing; security management (MAS, Certificate), including emergency planning and response, information security (MAS), organizational security; strategic human resource management (MPS, Certificate), including global human resources (MPS), human resource management and development (MPS). Part-time and evening/weekend programs available. Postbaccalaureate distance learning degree programs offered (no on-campus study). *Faculty:* 7 full-time (2 women), 212 part-time/adjunct (83 women). *Students:* 52 full-time (19 women), 1,044 part-time (625 women); includes 196 minority (81 Black or African American, non-Hispanic/Latino; 7 American Indian or Alaska Native, non-Hispanic/Latino; 30 Asian, non-Hispanic/Latino; 66 Hispanic/Latino; 3 Native Hawaiian or other Pacific Islander, non-Hispanic/Latino; 9 Two or more races, non-Hispanic/Latino), 76

international. Average age 36. 488 applicants, 91% accepted, 339 enrolled. In 2010, 286 master's, 130 other advanced degrees awarded. *Entrance requirements:* Additional exam requirements/recommendations for international students: Required—TOEFL (minimum score 550 paper-based; 80 iBT). *Application deadline:* For fall admission, 6/22 priority date for domestic students, 6/10 priority date for international students; for winter admission, 9/15 priority date for domestic students, 9/6 priority date for international students; for spring admission, 2/3 priority date for domestic students, 12/15 priority date for international students. Applications are processed on a rolling basis. Application fee: $75. Electronic applications accepted. *Expenses:* Contact institution. *Financial support:* Applicants required to submit FAFSA. *Unit head:* Dr. James Davis, Dean, 303-871-2291, Fax: 303-871-4047, E-mail: jdavis@du.edu. *Application contact:* Information Contact, 303-871-3155, Fax: 303-871-4047, E-mail: ucolinfo@du.edu.

University of Florida, Graduate School, Warrington College of Business Administration, Hough Graduate School of Business, Department of Information Systems and Operations Management, Gainesville, FL 32611. Offers decision and information sciences (MS, PhD); supply chain management (MS). *Faculty:* 13 full-time (2 women). *Students:* 170 full-time (66 women), 20 part-time (4 women); includes 8 Black or African American, non-Hispanic/Latino; 12 Asian, non-Hispanic/Latino; 11 Hispanic/Latino, 112 international. Average age 29. 347 applicants, 78% accepted, 101 enrolled. In 2010, 42 master's, 1 doctorate awarded. Terminal master's awarded for partial completion of doctoral program. *Degree requirements:* For doctorate, thesis/dissertation. *Entrance requirements:* For master's, GMAT or GRE General Test, Minimum GPA of 3.0; for doctorate, GMAT minimum score 650 or GRE general test score 1350 (verbal and quantitative combined). Minimum GPA of 3.0. Additional exam requirements/recommendations for international students: Required—TOEFL (minimum score 550 paper-based; 213 computer-based; 80 iBT), IELTS (minimum score 6), IELTS (minimum of 6) or MELAB (minimum of 77) also required for some. *Application deadline:* For fall admission, 4/1 priority date for domestic students, 3/1 for international students; for spring admission, 10/15 for domestic students, 10/1 for international students. Applications are processed on a rolling basis. Application fee: $30. *Expenses:* Tuition: state resident: full-time $10,915.92. Tuition, nonresident: full-time $28,309. *Financial support:* In 2010–11, 14 students received support, including 1 fellowship, 6 research assistantships (averaging $16,849 per year), 7 teaching assistantships (averaging $12,325 per year); unspecified assistantships also available. Financial award application deadline: 2/1; financial award applicants required to submit FAFSA. *Faculty research:* Expert systems, nonconvex optimization, manufacturing management, production and operation management, telecommunication. *Unit head:* Dr. Gary J. Koehler, Chair, 352-846-2090, Fax: 352-392-5438, E-mail: koehler@ufl.edu. *Application contact:* Dr. Anand A. Paul, Graduate Coordinator for PhD Program, 352-392-9600, Fax: 352-392-5438, E-mail: paulaa@ufl.edu.

University of Georgia, Terry College of Business, Department of Management Information Systems, Athens, GA 30602. Offers PhD. *Faculty:* 8 full-time (2 women). *Students:* 1 (woman) full-time, 28 part-time (15 women); includes 9 Black or African American, non-Hispanic/Latino; 1 Asian, non-Hispanic/Latino. 12 applicants. *Expenses:* Tuition, state resident: full-time $7200; part-time $344 per credit hour. Tuition, nonresident: full-time $21,900; part-time $944 per credit hour. Tuition and fees vary according to course load and program. *Unit head:* Dr. Richard Watson, Head, 706-542-3706, E-mail: rwatson@terry.uga.edu. *Application contact:* Dr. Marie-Claude Bourdreau, Graduate Coordinator, 706-583-0887, E-mail: mcboudre@terry.uga.edu.

University of Hawaii at Manoa, Graduate Division, College of Social Sciences, School of Communications, Program in Telecommunication and Information Resource Management, Honolulu, HI 96822. Offers Graduate Certificate. Part-time programs available. *Students:* 1 part-time (0 women), all international. Average age 29. In 2010, 5 Graduate Certificates awarded. *Entrance requirements:* Additional exam requirements/recommendations for international students: Required—TOEFL (minimum score 500 paper-based; 173 computer-based; 61 iBT), IELTS (minimum score 5). *Application deadline:* For fall admission, 5/1 for domestic and international students; for spring admission, 10/1 for domestic and international students. Application fee: $60. *Application contact:* Norman Okamura, Director, 808-956-2895, Fax: 808-956-5591, E-mail: tirm@hawaii.edu.

University of Hawaii at Manoa, Graduate Division, Shidler College of Business, Program in Accounting, Honolulu, HI 96822. Offers accounting (M Acc); accounting law (M Acc); information systems (M Acc); taxation (M Acc). Part-time programs available. *Faculty:* 9 full-time (2 women). *Students:* 45 full-time (22 women), 33 part-time (22 women); includes 41 minority (28 Asian, non-Hispanic/Latino; 5 Native Hawaiian or other Pacific Islander, non-Hispanic/Latino; 8 Two or more races, non-Hispanic/Latino), 21 international. Average age 32. 144 applicants, 78% accepted, 72 enrolled. In 2010, 38 master's awarded. *Entrance requirements:* For master's, GMAT, bachelor's degree in accounting, minimum GPA of 3.0. Additional exam requirements/recommendations for international students: Required—TOEFL (minimum score 550 paper-based; 213 computer-based; 79 iBT), IELTS (minimum score 5). *Application deadline:* For fall admission, 5/1 for domestic students, 3/1 for international students; for spring admission, 11/1 for domestic students, 10/1 for international students. Application fee: $60.

Financial support: In 2010–11, 24 fellowships (averaging $4,662 per year), 7 research assistantships (averaging $16,478 per year) were awarded; career-related internships or fieldwork, Federal Work-Study, and tuition waivers (full) also available. *Faculty research:* International accounting, current tax topics, insurance industry financial reporting, behavioral accounting, auditing. *Application contact:* Liming Guan, Graduate Chair, 808-956-7332, Fax: 808-956-9888, E-mail: lguan@hawaii.edu.

University of Hawaii at Manoa, Graduate Division, Shidler College of Business, Program in Business Administration, Honolulu, HI 96822. Offers Asian business studies (MBA); Chinese business studies (MBA); decision sciences (MBA); entrepreneurship (MBA); finance (MBA); finance and banking (MBA); human resources management (MBA); information management (MBA); information technology (MBA); international business (MBA); Japanese business studies (MBA); marketing (MBA); organizational behavior (MBA); organizational management (MBA); real estate (MBA); student-designed track (MBA). *Accreditation:* AACSB. Part-time and evening/weekend programs available. *Faculty:* 53 full-time (12 women). *Students:* 162 full-time (63 women), 102 part-time (43 women); includes 135 minority (1 Black or African American, non-Hispanic/Latino; 81 Asian, non-Hispanic/Latino; 5 Hispanic/Latino; 18 Native Hawaiian or other Pacific Islander, non-Hispanic/Latino; 30 Two or more races, non-Hispanic/Latino), 44 international. Average age 34. 361 applicants, 57% accepted, 172 enrolled. In 2010, 153 master's awarded. *Degree requirements:* For master's, thesis optional. *Entrance requirements:* For master's, GMAT, minimum GPA of 3.0. Additional exam requirements/recommendations for international students: Required—TOEFL (minimum score 600 paper-based; 250 computer-based; 100 iBT), IELTS (minimum score 7). *Application deadline:* For fall admission, 5/1 for domestic students, 3/1 for international students. Application fee: $60. *Expenses:* Contact institution. *Financial support:* In 2010–11, 83 fellowships (averaging $5,547 per year), 1 research assistantship (averaging $16,824 per year) were awarded. Total annual research expenditures: $427,000. *Application contact:* Daniel Port, Graduate Chair, 808-956-5565, Fax: 808-956-6889, E-mail: daniel.port@hawaii.edu.

University of Hawaii at Manoa, Graduate Division, Shidler College of Business, Program in International Management, Honolulu, HI 96822. Offers Asian finance (PhD); global information technology management (PhD); international accounting (PhD); international marketing (PhD); international organization and strategy (PhD). Part-time programs available. *Students:* 30 full-time (11 women), 3 part-time (0 women); includes 7 minority (5 Asian, non-Hispanic/Latino; 2 Two or more races, non-Hispanic/Latino), 18 international. Average age 36. 65 applicants, 18% accepted, 5 enrolled. In 2010, 4 doctorates awarded. *Degree requirements:* For doctorate, comprehensive exam, thesis/dissertation. *Entrance requirements:* For doctorate, GMAT or GRE General Test, minimum GPA of 3.0. Additional exam requirements/recommendations for international students: Required—TOEFL (minimum score 600 paper-based; 250 computer-based; 100 iBT), IELTS (minimum score 7). *Application deadline:* For fall admission, 3/1 for domestic and international students. Application fee: $60. *Expenses:* Contact institution. *Financial support:* In 2010–11, 29 students received support, including 3 fellowships (averaging $5,491 per year), 25 research assistantships (averaging $17,750 per year), 1 teaching assistantship (averaging $15,558 per year). *Application contact:* Erica Okada, Graduate Chair, 808-956-6723, Fax: 808-956-6889, E-mail: imphd@hawaii.edu.

The University of Kansas, Graduate Studies, School of Engineering, Department of Electrical Engineering and Computer Science, Program in Information Technology, Lawrence, KS 66045. Offers MS. Part-time and evening/weekend programs available. *Faculty:* 35. *Students:* 2 full-time (1 woman), 20 part-time (4 women); includes 1 minority (Asian, non-Hispanic/Latino), 3 international. Average age 34. 25 applicants, 24% accepted, 3 enrolled. In 2010, 8 master's awarded. *Degree requirements:* For master's, thesis optional, exam. *Entrance requirements:* For master's, GRE. Additional exam requirements/recommendations for international students: Required—TOEFL (minimum score 600 paper-based; 250 computer-based; 100 iBT). *Application deadline:* For fall admission, 3/1 priority date for domestic students, 3/1 for international students; for spring admission, 10/1 priority date for domestic students, 10/1 for international students. Applications are processed on a rolling basis. Application fee: $55 ($65 for international students). Electronic applications accepted. *Expenses:* Tuition, state resident: full-time $7092; part-time $295.50 per credit hour. Tuition, nonresident: full-time $16,590; part-time $691.25 per credit hour. Required fees: $858; $71.49 per credit hour. Tuition and fees vary according to course load, campus/location and program. *Faculty research:* Information security and privacy, game theory, graph theory, software process improvement, resilient and survivable networks, object orientation technology. *Unit head:* Dr. Glenn Prescott, Chairperson, 785-864-4620, Fax: 785-864-3226. *Application contact:* Pam Shadoin, Assistant to Graduate Director, 785-864-4487, Fax: 785-864-3226, E-mail: graduate@eecs.ku.edu.

University of La Verne, College of Business and Public Management, Graduate Programs in Business Administration, La Verne, CA 91750-4443. Offers accounting (MBA); executive management (MBA-EP); finance (MBA, MBA-EP); health services management (MBA); information technology (MBA, MBA-EP); international business (MBA, MBA-EP);

leadership (MBA-EP); managed care (MBA); management (MBA, MBA-EP); marketing (MBA, MBA-EP). Part-time and evening/weekend programs available. *Faculty:* 34 full-time (12 women), 36 part-time/adjunct (9 women). *Students:* 412 full-time (207 women), 200 part-time (96 women); includes 423 minority (32 Black or African American, non-Hispanic/Latino; 5 American Indian or Alaska Native, non-Hispanic/Latino; 294 Asian, non-Hispanic/Latino; 92 Hispanic/Latino), 6 international. Average age 29. In 2010, 229 master's awarded. *Entrance requirements:* For master's, minimum undergraduate GPA of 3.0, 2 letters of recommendation, resume. Additional exam requirements/recommendations for international students: Required—TOEFL (minimum score 550 paper-based; 213 computer-based). *Application deadline:* Applications are processed on a rolling basis. Application fee: $50. *Expenses:* Contact institution. *Financial support:* Career-related internships or fieldwork, institutionally sponsored loans, and scholarships/grants available. Financial award application deadline: 3/2; financial award applicants required to submit FAFSA. *Unit head:* Dr. Abe Helou, Chairperson, 909-593-3511 Ext. 4211, Fax: 909-392-2704, E-mail: ihelou@laverne.edu. *Application contact:* Rina Lazarian, Program and Admission Specialist, 909-593-3511 Ext. 4819, Fax: 909-392-2704, E-mail: cbpm@ulv.edu.

University of La Verne, Regional Campus Administration, Graduate Programs, Central Coast/Vandenberg Air Force Base Campuses, La Verne, CA 91750-4443. Offers business (MBA-EP), including health services management, information technology; health administration (MHA); leadership and management (MS). *Faculty:* 12 part-time/adjunct (7 women). *Students:* 26 full-time (13 women), 33 part-time (16 women); includes 18 minority (6 Black or African American, non-Hispanic/Latino; 2 American Indian or Alaska Native, non-Hispanic/Latino; 2 Asian, non-Hispanic/Latino; 8 Hispanic/Latino). Average age 36. In 2010, 4 master's awarded. *Entrance requirements:* For master's, 2 letters of recommendation, resume. *Application deadline:* Applications are processed on a rolling basis. Application fee: $50. *Expenses:* Contact institution. *Financial support:* Institutionally sponsored loans available. Financial award application deadline: 3/2; financial award applicants required to submit FAFSA. *Unit head:* Kitt Vincent, Director, Central Coast Campus, 805-542-9690 Ext. 6043, Fax: 805-542-9735, E-mail: kvincent@laverne.edu. *Application contact:* Kitt Vincent, Director, Central Coast Campus, 805-542-9690 Ext. 6043, Fax: 805-542-9735, E-mail: kvincent@laverne.edu.

University of La Verne, Regional Campus Administration, Graduate Programs, Inland Empire Campus, Rancho Cucamonga, CA 91730. Offers business (MBA-EP), including health services management, information technology, management, marketing; leadership and management (MS). *Faculty:* 3 full-time (2 women), 22 part-time/adjunct (9 women). *Students:* 27 full-time (17 women), 100 part-time (68 women); includes 14 Black or African American, non-Hispanic/Latino; 1 American Indian or Alaska Native, non-Hispanic/Latino; 22 Asian, non-Hispanic/Latino; 36 Hispanic/Latino. Average age 39. In 2010, 20 master's awarded. *Entrance requirements:* For master's, 2 letters of recommendation, resume. *Application deadline:* Applications are processed on a rolling basis. Application fee: $50. *Expenses:* Contact institution. *Financial support:* Institutionally sponsored loans available. Financial award application deadline: 3/2; financial award applicants required to submit FAFSA. *Unit head:* Allan Stout, Director, 909-484-3858 Ext. 6002, Fax: 909-484-9469, E-mail: astout@laverne.edu. *Application contact:* Allan Stout, Director, 909-484-3858 Ext. 6002, Fax: 909-484-9469, E-mail: astout@laverne.edu.

University of Maine, Graduate School, Interdisciplinary Program in Information Systems, Orono, ME 04469. Offers MS. Part-time programs available. *Faculty:* 4 full-time (1 woman), 3 part-time/adjunct (1 woman). *Students:* 2 full-time (0 women), 1 part-time (0 women); includes 1 minority (Hispanic/Latino). Average age 30. 8 applicants, 50% accepted, 3 enrolled. In 2010, 1 master's awarded. *Entrance requirements:* For master's, GRE General Test or GMAT. Additional exam requirements/recommendations for international students: Required—TOEFL. *Application deadline:* For fall admission, 2/1 priority date for domestic students. Applications are processed on a rolling basis. Application fee: $65. Electronic applications accepted. *Expenses:* Tuition, state resident: full-time $400. Tuition, nonresident: full-time $1050. *Financial support:* In 2010–11, 4 teaching assistantships with tuition reimbursements (averaging $12,790 per year) were awarded; Federal Work-Study also available. *Unit head:* Dr. Owen Smith, Associate Dean of the Graduate School, 207-581-4358, Fax: 207-581-4357, E-mail: graduate@maine.edu. *Application contact:* Dr. Owen Smith, Associate Dean of the Graduate School, 207-581-4358, Fax: 207-581-4357, E-mail: graduate@maine.edu.

University of Mary Hardin-Baylor, Graduate Studies in Business Administration, Belton, TX 76513. Offers accounting (MBA); information systems management (MBA); management (MBA). Part-time and evening/weekend programs available. *Faculty:* 6 full-time (3 women), 2 part-time/adjunct (0 women). *Students:* 29 full-time (10 women), 26 part-time (13 women); includes 12 minority (3 Black or African American, non-Hispanic/Latino; 9 Hispanic/Latino), 23 international. Average age 29. 71 applicants, 72% accepted, 27 enrolled. In 2010, 7 master's awarded. *Degree requirements:* For master's, comprehensive exam. *Entrance requirements:* For master's, GMAT, minimum GPA of 3.0, work experience, interview. *Application deadline:* For fall admission, 6/1 priority date for domestic students; for spring admission, 11/1 for domestic students. Applications are processed on a rolling basis. Application fee: $35 ($135 for international students). Electronic applications accepted. *Financial support:* Federal Work-Study and scholarships (for some active duty military personnel only) available. Financial award applicants required to submit FAFSA. *Unit head:* Dr. Terry Fox, Program Director, 254-295-5406, E-mail: terry.fox@umhb.edu. *Application contact:* Dr. Terry Fox, Program Director, 254-295-5406, E-mail: terry.fox@umhb.edu.

University of Mary Hardin-Baylor, Graduate Studies in Information Systems, Belton, TX 76513. Offers MS. Part-time and evening/weekend programs available. *Faculty:* 3 full-time (1 woman). *Students:* 47 full-time (16 women), 8 part-time (3 women); includes 1 minority (Black or African American, non-Hispanic/Latino), 52 international. Average age 23. 148 applicants, 100% accepted, 32 enrolled. In 2010, 2 master's awarded. *Degree requirements:* For master's, comprehensive exam. *Entrance requirements:* For master's, GMAT, minimum GPA of 3.0, work experience, interview. *Application deadline:* For fall admission, 6/1 priority date for domestic students; for spring admission, 11/1 for domestic students. Applications are processed on a rolling basis. Application fee: $35 ($135 for international students). Electronic applications accepted. *Financial support:* Federal Work-Study and scholarships (for some active duty military personnel only) available. Support available to part-time students. Financial award applicants required to submit FAFSA. *Unit head:* Dr. Nancy Bonner, Graduate Program Director, 254-295-5405, E-mail: nbonner@umhb.edu. *Application contact:* Dr. Nancy Bonner, Graduate Program Director, 254-295-5405, E-mail: nbonner@umhb.edu.

University of Maryland University College, Graduate School of Management and Technology, Program in Financial Management and Information Systems, Adelphi, MD 20783. Offers MS, Certificate. Part-time and evening/weekend programs available. Postbaccalaureate distance learning degree programs offered (no on-campus study). *Students:* 7 full-time (2 women), 168 part-time (84 women); includes 112 minority (89 Black or African American, non-Hispanic/Latino; 17 Asian, non-Hispanic/Latino; 5 Hispanic/Latino; 1 Two or more races, non-Hispanic/Latino), 4 international. Average age 33. 39 applicants, 100% accepted, 28 enrolled. In 2010, 30 master's awarded. *Degree requirements:* For master's, thesis or alternative. *Application deadline:* Applications are processed on a rolling basis. Application fee: $50. Electronic applications accepted. *Financial support:* Federal Work-Study and scholarships/grants available. Support available to part-time students. Financial award application deadline: 6/1; financial award applicants required to submit FAFSA. *Unit head:* Dr. Jayanta Sen, Director, 240-684-2400, Fax: 240-684-2401, E-mail: jsen@umuc.edu. *Application contact:* Coordinator, Graduate Admissions, 800-888-8682, Fax: 240-684-2151, E-mail: newgrad@umuc.edu.

University of Mary Washington, College of Business, Fredericksburg, VA 22401-5300. Offers business administration (MBA); management information systems (MSMIS). Part-time and evening/weekend programs available. *Faculty:* 11 full-time (4 women), 9 part-time/adjunct (1 woman). *Students:* 107 full-time (57 women), 253 part-time (123 women); includes 78 Black or African American, non-Hispanic/Latino; 1 American Indian or Alaska Native, non-Hispanic/Latino; 8 Asian, non-Hispanic/Latino; 13 Hispanic/Latino, 5 international. Average age 36. 131 applicants, 56% accepted, 53 enrolled. In 2010, 85 master's awarded. *Entrance requirements:* For master's, GMAT or GRE, minimum GPA of 3.0. Additional exam requirements/recommendations for international students: Required—TOEFL (minimum score 570 paper-based; 230 computer-based; 88 iBT), IELTS (minimum score 6.5). *Application deadline:* For fall admission, 6/1 priority date for domestic students, 6/1 for international students; for spring admission, 10/1 for domestic and international students. Application fee: $50. Electronic applications accepted. *Financial support:* Available to part-time students. Application deadline: 3/15. *Faculty research:* Management of IT offshoring, boundary theory and co-creation matrix: hermeneutics perspectives, text and image mining, queuing theory and supply chain, organizational learning. *Unit head:* Dr. Larry W. Penwell, Acting Dean, 540-654-1561, E-mail: lpenwell@umw.edu. *Application contact:* Matthew E. Mejia, Associate Dean of Admissions, 540-286-8088, Fax: 540-286-8085, E-mail: mmejia@umw.edu.

University of Memphis, Graduate School, Fogelman College of Business and Economics, Program in Business Administration, Memphis, TN 38152. Offers accounting (MBA, PhD); economics (MBA, PhD); executive business administration (MBA); finance (PhD); finance, insurance, and real estate (MBA, MS); international business administration (IMBA); management (MBA, MS, PhD); management information systems (MBA, MS, PhD); management science (MBA); marketing (MBA, MS); marketing and supply chain management (PhD); real estate development (MS); JD/MBA. *Accreditation:* AACSB. *Faculty:* 44 full-time (9 women), 5 part-time/adjunct (0 women). *Students:* 263 full-time (106 women), 181 part-time (66 women); includes 46 Black or African American, non-Hispanic/Latino; 3 American Indian or Alaska Native, non-Hispanic/Latino; 16 Asian, non-Hispanic/Latino; 5 Hispanic/Latino, 109 international. Average age 31. 374 applicants, 73% accepted, 119 enrolled. In 2010, 140 master's, 17 doctorates awarded. *Degree requirements:* For master's, comprehensive exam; for doctorate, comprehensive exam, thesis/dissertation. *Entrance requirements:* For master's, GMAT, resume; for doctorate, GMAT, interview, minimum GPA of 3.4, resume, letter of recommendation. Additional exam requirements/recommendations for international students: Required—TOEFL (minimum score 550 paper-based; 220

computer-based). *Application deadline:* For fall admission, 8/1 for domestic students; for spring admission, 12/1 for domestic students. Application fee: $35 ($60 for international students). *Financial support:* In 2010–11, 164 students received support; research assistantships with full tuition reimbursements available, teaching assistantships with full tuition reimbursements available, career-related internships or fieldwork, Federal Work-Study, scholarships/grants, and unspecified assistantships available. Financial award application deadline: 2/15; financial award applicants required to submit FAFSA. *Faculty research:* Competitive business strategy, finance microstructures, supply chain management innovations, health care economics, litigation risks and corporate audits. *Unit head:* Rajiv Grover, Dean, 901-678-3759, E-mail: rgrover@memphis.edu. *Application contact:* Dr. Carol V. Danehower, Associate Dean, 901-678-5402, Fax: 901-678-3579, E-mail: fcbegp@memphis.edu.

University of Michigan–Dearborn, School of Management, Dearborn, MI 48128-1491. Offers accounting (MBA, MS); finance (MBA, MS); information systems (MS); international business (MBA); management (MBA); management information systems (MBA); marketing (MBA); supply chain management (MBA); MBA/MHSA; MBA/MSE; MBA/MSF. *Accreditation:* AACSB. Part-time and evening/weekend programs available. Postbaccalaureate distance learning degree programs offered (no on-campus study). *Faculty:* 40 full-time (17 women), 2 part-time/adjunct (1 woman). *Students:* 71 full-time (26 women), 403 part-time (134 women); includes 68 minority (19 Black or African American, non-Hispanic/Latino; 1 American Indian or Alaska Native, non-Hispanic/Latino; 39 Asian, non-Hispanic/Latino; 6 Hispanic/Latino; 1 Native Hawaiian or other Pacific Islander, non-Hispanic/Latino; 2 Two or more races, non-Hispanic/Latino), 89 international. Average age 30. 185 applicants, 51% accepted, 67 enrolled. In 2010, 150 master's awarded. *Entrance requirements:* For master's, GMAT, 2 years of work experience (MBA); course work in computer applications, statistics, and pre-calculus or finite mathematics; 18 credits of accounting course work beyond introductory courses (MS in accounting). Additional exam requirements/recommendations for international students: Required—TOEFL (minimum score 560 paper-based; 220 computer-based; 84 iBT). *Application deadline:* For fall admission, 8/1 priority date for domestic students, 6/1 for international students; for winter admission, 12/1 priority date for domestic students, 10/1 for international students; for spring admission, 4/1 priority date for domestic students, 2/1 for international students. Applications are processed on a rolling basis. Application fee: $60. Electronic applications accepted. *Expenses:* Contact institution. *Financial support:* Career-related internships or fieldwork, Federal Work-Study, and scholarships/grants available. Support available to part-time students. Financial award application deadline: 9/1; financial award applicants required to submit FAFSA. *Faculty research:* Cultural diversity, buyer-supplier relations, error detection in data, economic evolution. *Unit head:* Dr. Kim Schatzel, Dean, 313-593-5248, Fax: 313-271-9835, E-mail: schatzel@umd.umich.edu. *Application contact:* Joan Doherty, Academic Advisor/Counselor, 313-593-5460, Fax: 313-271-9838, E-mail: gradbusiness@umd.umich.edu.

University of Minnesota, Twin Cities Campus, Carlson School of Management, Carlson Full-Time MBA Program, Minneapolis, MN 55455. Offers finance (MBA); information technology (MBA); management (MBA); marketing (MBA); medical industry orientation (MBA); supply chain and operations (MBA); JD/MBA; MBA/MPP; MD/MBA; MHA/MBA; Pharm D/MBA. *Accreditation:* AACSB. *Faculty:* 52 full-time (14 women), 20 part-time/adjunct (3 women). *Students:* 170 full-time (62 women); includes 1 Black or African American, non-Hispanic/Latino; 1 American Indian or Alaska Native, non-Hispanic/Latino; 9 Asian, non-Hispanic/Latino; 8 Hispanic/Latino, 36 international. Average age 28. 452 applicants, 30% accepted, 71 enrolled. In 2010, 105 master's awarded. *Entrance requirements:* For master's, GMAT. Additional exam requirements/recommendations for international students: Required—TOEFL (minimum score 580 paper-based; 240 computer-based; 84 iBT), IELTS (minimum score 7), or Pearson Test of English (PTE). *Application deadline:* For fall admission, 4/1 for domestic students, 2/1 for international students. Application fee: $60 ($90 for international students). Electronic applications accepted. *Expenses:* Contact institution. *Financial support:* In 2010–11, 95 students received support, including 95 fellowships with full and partial tuition reimbursements available (averaging $21,235 per year); research assistantships with partial tuition reimbursements available, teaching assistantships with partial tuition reimbursements available, career-related internships or fieldwork, Federal Work-Study, institutionally sponsored loans, scholarships/grants, health care benefits, and unspecified assistantships also available. Financial award application deadline: 4/1; financial award applicants required to submit FAFSA. *Faculty research:* Finance and accounting: financial reporting, asset pricing models and corporate finance; information and decision sciences: on-line auctions, information transparency and recommender systems; marketing: psychological influences on consumer behavior, brand equity, pricing and marketing channels; operations: lean manufacturing, quality management and global supply chains; strategic management and organization: global strategy, networks, entrepreneurship and innovation, sustainability. *Unit head:* Kathryn J. Carlson, Assistant Dean, MBA Programs and Graduate Business Career Center, 612-625-5555, Fax: 612-625-1012, E-mail: mba@umn.edu. *Application contact:* Daniel Bursch, Director of Admissions & Recruiting, 612-625-5555, Fax: 612-625-1012, E-mail: mba@umn.edu.

University of Minnesota, Twin Cities Campus, Carlson School of Management, Carlson Part-Time MBA Program, Minneapolis, MN 55455. Offers finance (MBA); information technology (MBA); management (MBA); marketing (MBA); supply chain and operations (MBA). Part-time and evening/weekend programs available. *Faculty:* 67 full-time (18 women), 23 part-time/adjunct (2 women). *Students:* 1,520 part-time (490 women); includes 16 Black or African American, non-Hispanic/Latino; 3 American Indian or Alaska Native, non-Hispanic/Latino; 87 Asian, non-Hispanic/Latino; 14 Hispanic/Latino, 94 international. Average age 29. 306 applicants, 70% accepted, 186 enrolled. In 2010, 401 master's awarded. *Entrance requirements:* For master's, GMAT. Additional exam requirements/recommendations for international students: Required—TOEFL (minimum score 580 paper-based; 240 computer-based; 84 iBT), IELTS (minimum score 7), or Pearson Test of English (PTE). *Application deadline:* For fall admission, 5/1 priority date for domestic and international students; for spring admission, 11/1 priority date for domestic and international students. Application fee: $60 ($90 for international students). Electronic applications accepted. *Expenses:* Contact institution. *Financial support:* Applicants required to submit FAFSA. *Faculty research:* Finance and accounting: financial reporting, asset pricing models and corporate finance; information and decision sciences: on-line auctions, information transparency and recommender systems; marketing: psychological influences on consumer behavior, brand equity, pricing and marketing channels; operations: lean manufacturing, quality management and global supply chains; strategic management and organization: global Strategy, networks, entrepreneurship and innovation, sustainability. *Unit head:* Kathryn J. Carlson, Assistant Dean, MBA Programs and Graduate Business Career Center, 612-624-2039, Fax: 612-625-1012, E-mail: mba@umn.edu. *Application contact:* Daniel Bursch, Director of Admissions & Recruiting, 612-625-5555, Fax: 612-625-1012, E-mail: mba@umn.edu.

University of Minnesota, Twin Cities Campus, Carlson School of Management, Doctoral Program in Business Administration, Minneapolis, MN 55455-0213. Offers accounting (PhD); finance (PhD); information and decision sciences (PhD); marketing and logistics management (PhD); operations and management science (PhD); strategic management and organization (PhD). *Faculty:* 100 full-time (27 women). *Students:* 73 full-time (28 women); includes 3 Asian, non-Hispanic/Latino; 3 Hispanic/Latino, 53 international. Average age 30. 319 applicants, 6% accepted, 16 enrolled. In 2010, 8 doctorates awarded. *Degree requirements:* For doctorate, comprehensive exam, thesis/dissertation, written and oral preliminary exams, proposal defense, final defense. *Entrance requirements:* For doctorate, GMAT, GRE General Test. Additional exam requirements/recommendations for international students: Required—TOEFL (minimum score 600 paper-based; 250 computer-based; 100 iBT), IELTS (minimum score 7.5). *Application deadline:* For fall admission, 12/31 for domestic students, 12/31 priority date for international students. Applications are processed on a rolling basis. Application fee: $75 ($95 for international students). Electronic applications accepted. *Financial support:* In 2010–11, 68 students received support, including 134 fellowships with full tuition reimbursements available (averaging $6,622 per year), 63 research assistantships with full tuition reimbursements available (averaging $6,750 per year), 57 teaching assistantships with full tuition reimbursements available (averaging $6,750 per year); institutionally sponsored loans, scholarships/grants, health care benefits, and unspecified assistantships also available. Financial award application deadline: 12/31. *Faculty research:* Corporate strategy, finance, entrepreneurship, marketing, information and decision science, operations, accounting, quality management. *Unit head:* Dr. Shawn P. Curley, Director of Graduate Studies and PhD Program Director, 612-624-6546, Fax: 612-624-8221, E-mail: curley@umn.edu. *Application contact:* Earlene K. Bronson, Assistant Director, PhD Program, 612-624-0875, Fax: 612-624-8221, E-mail: brons003@umn.edu.

University of Mississippi, Graduate School, School of Business Administration, Oxford, University, MS 38677. Offers business administration (MBA, PhD); systems management (MS); JD/MBA. *Accreditation:* AACSB. *Students:* 96 full-time (30 women), 49 part-time (8 women); includes 17 minority (8 Black or African American, non-Hispanic/Latino; 2 Asian, non-Hispanic/Latino; 2 Hispanic/Latino; 5 Two or more races, non-Hispanic/Latino), 16 international. In 2010, 46 master's, 9 doctorates awarded. *Degree requirements:* For doctorate, thesis/dissertation. *Entrance requirements:* For master's, GMAT, minimum GPA of 3.0; for doctorate, GMAT. Additional exam requirements/recommendations for international students: Required—TOEFL. *Application deadline:* For fall admission, 2/1 for domestic students; for spring admission, 10/1 for domestic students. Applications are processed on a rolling basis. Application fee: $25. Electronic applications accepted. *Financial support:* Fellowships, career-related internships or fieldwork, scholarships/grants, tuition waivers (full), and unspecified assistantships available. Financial award application deadline: 3/1; financial award applicants required to submit FAFSA. *Unit head:* Dr. Ken Cyree, Dean, 662-915-5820, Fax: 662-915-5821, E-mail: info@bus.olemiss.edu. *Application contact:* Dr. Christy M. Wyandt, Associate Dean, 662-915-7474, Fax: 662-915-7577, E-mail: cwyandt@olemiss.edu.

University of Missouri–St. Louis, College of Business Administration, Program in Business Administration, St. Louis, MO 63121. Offers accounting (MBA); business administration (Certificate); finance (MBA); human resource

management (Certificate); information systems (MBA); local government (Certificate); logistics and supply chain management (MBA, Certificate); marketing (MBA); marketing management (Certificate); operations management (MBA). *Accreditation:* AACSB. Part-time and evening/weekend programs available. *Faculty:* 30 full-time (5 women), 11 part-time/adjunct (2 women). *Students:* 132 full-time (57 women), 306 part-time (122 women); includes 55 minority (21 Black or African American, non-Hispanic/Latino; 20 Asian, non-Hispanic/Latino; 11 Hispanic/Latino; 1 Native Hawaiian or other Pacific Islander, non-Hispanic/Latino; 2 Two or more races, non-Hispanic/Latino), 6 international. Average age 30. 219 applicants, 60% accepted, 88 enrolled. In 2010, 114 master's, 9 other advanced degrees awarded. *Entrance requirements:* For master's, GMAT, 2 letters of recommendation. Additional exam requirements/recommendations for international students: Required—TOEFL (minimum score 550 paper-based; 213 computer-based). *Application deadline:* For fall admission, 7/1 for domestic students; for spring admission, 11/1 for domestic students. Applications are processed on a rolling basis. Application fee: $35 ($40 for international students). Electronic applications accepted. *Expenses:* Tuition, state resident: full-time $5522; part-time $306.80 per credit hour. Tuition, nonresident: full-time $14,253; part-time $792.10 per credit hour. Required fees: $658; $49 per credit hour. One-time fee: $12. Tuition and fees vary according to program. *Financial support:* In 2010–11, 22 research assistantships with full and partial tuition reimbursements (averaging $7,414 per year), 4 teaching assistantships with full and partial tuition reimbursements (averaging $13,950 per year) were awarded; career-related internships or fieldwork, Federal Work-Study, and institutionally sponsored loans also available. Support available to part-time students. Financial award application deadline: 4/1; financial award applicants required to submit FAFSA. *Faculty research:* Human resources, strategic management, marketing strategy, consumer behavior product development, advertising. *Unit head:* Karl Kottemann, Assistant Director, 314-516-5885, Fax: 314-516-6420, E-mail: mba@umsl.edu. *Application contact:* 314-516-5458, Fax: 314-516-6996, E-mail: gradadm@umsl.edu.

University of Missouri–St. Louis, College of Business Administration, Program in Information Systems, St. Louis, MO 63121. Offers information systems (MSIS, PhD); logistics and supply chain management (PhD). Part-time and evening/weekend programs available. *Faculty:* 8 full-time (0 women). *Students:* 10 full-time (3 women), 13 part-time (1 woman); includes 5 minority (4 Black or African American, non-Hispanic/Latino; 1 Hispanic/Latino), 4 international. Average age 31. 16 applicants, 25% accepted, 1 enrolled. In 2010, 6 master's, 2 doctorates awarded. *Entrance requirements:* For master's, GMAT, 2 letters of recommendation; for doctorate, GMAT or GRE, 3 letters of recommendation. Additional exam requirements/recommendations for international students: Required—TOEFL (minimum score 550 paper-based; 213 computer-based). *Application deadline:* For fall admission, 7/1 priority date for domestic and international students; for spring admission, 12/1 priority date for domestic and international students. Applications are processed on a rolling basis. Application fee: $35 ($40 for international students). Electronic applications accepted. *Expenses:* Tuition, state resident: full-time $5522; part-time $306.80 per credit hour. Tuition, nonresident: full-time $14,253; part-time $792.10 per credit hour. Required fees: $658; $49 per credit hour. One-time fee: $12. Tuition and fees vary according to program. *Financial support:* Career-related internships or fieldwork, Federal Work-Study, and institutionally sponsored loans available. Support available to part-time students. Financial award application deadline: 4/1; financial award applicants required to submit FAFSA. *Faculty research:* International information systems, telecommunications, systems development, information systems sourcing. *Unit head:* Karl Kottemann, Assistant Director, 314-516-5885, Fax: 314-516-6420, E-mail: mba@umsl.edu. *Application contact:* 314-516-5458, Fax: 314-516-6996, E-mail: gradadm@umsl.edu.

University of Nebraska at Omaha, Graduate Studies, College of Information Science and Technology, Department of Information Systems and Quantitative Analysis, Omaha, NE 68182. Offers information systems and quantitative analysis (Certificate); information technology (PhD); management information systems (MS). Part-time and evening/weekend programs available. *Faculty:* 13 full-time (6 women). *Students:* 61 full-time (20 women), 87 part-time (32 women); includes 15 minority (6 Black or African American, non-Hispanic/Latino; 5 Asian, non-Hispanic/Latino; 3 Hispanic/Latino; 1 Two or more races, non-Hispanic/Latino), 75 international. Average age 37. 164 applicants, 35% accepted, 41 enrolled. In 2010, 36 master's, 5 doctorates, 21 other advanced degrees awarded. *Degree requirements:* For master's, comprehensive exam, thesis (for some programs); for doctorate, comprehensive exam, thesis/dissertation. *Entrance requirements:* For master's, GMAT or GRE General Test; for doctorate, GMAT or GRE General Test, letters of recommendation. Additional exam requirements/recommendations for international students: Required—TOEFL (minimum score 575 paper-based; 230 computer-based; 89 iBT). *Application deadline:* For fall admission, 3/15 for domestic students; for spring admission, 10/1 for domestic students. Applications are processed on a rolling basis. Application fee: $45. Electronic applications accepted. *Financial support:* In 2010–11, 80 students received support; fellowships, research assistantships with tuition reimbursements available, teaching assistantships with tuition reimbursements available, career-related internships or fieldwork, Federal Work-Study, scholarships/grants, tuition waivers (partial), and unspecified assistantships available. Financial award application deadline:

3/1; financial award applicants required to submit FAFSA. *Unit head:* Dr. Ilze Zigurs, Chairperson, 402-554-3770. *Application contact:* Carla Frakes, Information Contact, 402-554-2423.

University of Nevada, Las Vegas, Graduate College, College of Business, Department of Management Information Systems, Las Vegas, NV 89154-6034. Offers MS, Certificate. *Faculty:* 7 full-time (1 woman). *Students:* 26 full-time (12 women), 21 part-time (6 women); includes 20 minority (3 Black or African American, non-Hispanic/Latino; 7 Asian, non-Hispanic/Latino; 4 Hispanic/Latino; 6 Two or more races, non-Hispanic/Latino), 13 international. Average age 33. 55 applicants, 75% accepted, 21 enrolled. In 2010, 9 master's, 1 other advanced degree awarded. *Entrance requirements:* For master's and Certificate, GMAT or GRE. Additional exam requirements/recommendations for international students: Required—TOEFL (minimum score 550 paper-based; 213 computer-based; 80 iBT), IELTS (minimum score 7). *Application deadline:* For fall admission, 6/15 priority date for domestic students, 6/15 for international students; for spring admission, 11/15 priority date for domestic students, 11/15 for international students. Applications are processed on a rolling basis. Application fee: $60 ($95 for international students). Electronic applications accepted. *Expenses:* Tuition, area resident: Part-time $239.50 per credit. Tuition, state resident: part-time $239.50 per credit. Tuition, nonresident: part-time $503 per credit. Required fees: $108 per semester. Tuition and fees vary according to course load, program and reciprocity agreements. *Financial support:* In 2010–11, 5 students received support, including 4 research assistantships with partial tuition reimbursements available (averaging $10,000 per year), 1 teaching assistantship with partial tuition reimbursement available (averaging $10,000 per year); institutionally sponsored loans, scholarships/grants, health care benefits, and unspecified assistantships also available. Financial award application deadline: 3/1. *Faculty research:* Software engineering, human computer interaction, virtual team and virtual worlds, computer self-efficacy, IT outsourcing. *Unit head:* Dr. Marcus Rothenberger, Chair/ Assistant Professor, 702-895-3676, Fax: 702-895-0802, E-mail: marcus.rothenberger@unlv.edu. *Application contact:* Graduate College Admissions Evaluator, 702-895-3320, Fax: 702-895-4180, E-mail: gradcollege@unlv.edu.

University of North Florida, College of Computing, Engineering, and Construction, School of Computing, Jacksonville, FL 32224. Offers computer science (MS); information systems (MS); software engineering (MS). Part-time programs available. *Faculty:* 15 full-time (4 women). *Students:* 12 full-time (4 women), 35 part-time (14 women); includes 5 Black or African American, non-Hispanic/Latino; 2 Asian, non-Hispanic/Latino; 2 Hispanic/Latino; 2 Two or more races, non-Hispanic/Latino, 14 international. Average age 32. 45 applicants, 58% accepted, 11 enrolled. In 2010, 5 master's awarded. *Degree requirements:* For master's, thesis. *Entrance requirements:* For master's, GRE General Test, minimum GPA of 3.0 in last 60 hours of course work. Additional exam requirements/recommendations for international students: Required—TOEFL (minimum score 500 paper-based; 173 computer-based; 61 iBT). *Application deadline:* For fall admission, 7/1 for domestic students, 5/1 for international students; for spring admission, 11/1 for domestic students, 10/1 for international students. Applications are processed on a rolling basis. Application fee: $30. Electronic applications accepted. *Expenses:* Tuition, state resident: full-time $7646.40; part-time $318.60 per credit hour. Tuition, nonresident: full-time $23,502; part-time $979.24 per credit hour. Required fees: $1208.88; $50.37 per credit hour. Tuition and fees vary according to course load and program. *Financial support:* In 2010–11, 9 students received support, including 1 teaching assistantship (averaging $2,000 per year); Federal Work-Study, scholarships/grants, and unspecified assistantships also available. Financial award application deadline: 4/1; financial award applicants required to submit FAFSA. Total annual research expenditures: $62,830. *Unit head:* Dr. Neal Coulter, Dean, 904-620-1350, E-mail: ncoulter@unf.edu. *Application contact:* Lillith Richardson, Assistant Director, The Graduate School, 904-620-1360, Fax: 904-620-1362, E-mail: graduateschool@unf.edu.

University of North Texas, Toulouse Graduate School, College of Business Administration, Department of Information Technology and Decision Sciences, Denton, TX 76203. Offers business computer information systems (PhD); decision technologies (MS); information technology (MS); management science (PhD). Part-time and evening/weekend programs available. *Degree requirements:* For doctorate, comprehensive exam, thesis/dissertation. *Entrance requirements:* For master's, GMAT; for doctorate, GMAT or GRE General Test. Additional exam requirements/recommendations for international students: Recommended—TOEFL (minimum score 550 paper-based; 213 computer-based; 79 iBT). *Application deadline:* Applications are processed on a rolling basis. Electronic applications accepted. *Expenses:* Tuition, state resident: full-time $4298; part-time $239 per credit hour. Tuition, nonresident: full-time $10,782; part-time $549 per credit hour. Required fees: $1292; $270 per credit hour. *Financial support:* Fellowships, research assistantships, teaching assistantships, career-related internships or fieldwork and Federal Work-Study available. Financial award application deadline: 4/1; financial award applicants required to submit FAFSA. *Faculty research:* Large scale IS, business intelligence, security, applied statistics, quality and reliability management. *Unit head:* Chair. *Application contact:* Graduate Advisor, 940-565-4149, Fax: 940-565-4935, E-mail: itdsrecp@unt.edu.

University of Oklahoma, Gaylord College of Journalism and Mass Communication, Program in Journalism and Mass Communication, Norman, OK 73019-0390. Offers advertising and public relations (MA); information gathering and distribution (MA); mass communication management and policy (MA); professional writing (MA); telecommunications and new technologies (MA). Part-time programs available. *Students:* 21 full-time (16 women), 26 part-time (13 women); includes 7 minority (4 Black or African American, non-Hispanic/Latino; 2 American Indian or Alaska Native, non-Hispanic/Latino; 1 Hispanic/Latino), 6 international. Average age 27. 29 applicants, 76% accepted, 10 enrolled. In 2010, 20 master's awarded. *Degree requirements:* For master's, thesis optional. *Entrance requirements:* For master's, GRE General Test, minimum GPA of 3.2, 9 hours of course work in journalism, course work in statistics. Additional exam requirements/recommendations for international students: Required—TOEFL (minimum score 600 paper-based; 250 computer-based; 100 iBT), TWE (minimum score 5). *Application deadline:* For fall admission, 2/1 for domestic students, 4/1 for international students; for spring admission, 11/1 for domestic students, 9/1 for international students. Application fee: $40 ($90 for international students). Electronic applications accepted. *Expenses:* Tuition, state resident: full-time $3893; part-time $162.20 per credit hour. Tuition, nonresident: full-time $14,167; part-time $590.30 per credit hour. Required fees: $2523; $94.60 per credit hour. Tuition and fees vary according to course load and degree level. *Financial support:* In 2010–11, 30 students received support. Career-related internships or fieldwork, scholarships/grants, health care benefits, and unspecified assistantships available. *Faculty research:* Organizational management, strategic communications, rhetorical theories and mass communication, interactive messaging and audience response; mass media history and law. *Unit head:* Dr. Joe Foote, Dean, 405-325-2721, Fax: 405-325-7565, E-mail: jfoote@ou.edu. *Application contact:* Kelly Storm, Graduate Advisor, 405-325-2722, Fax: 405-325-7565, E-mail: kstorm@ou.edu.

University of Oklahoma, Michael F. Price College of Business, Division of Management Information Systems, Norman, OK 73019. Offers MS, PhD, Graduate Certificate. Part-time and evening/weekend programs available. *Faculty:* 9 full-time (3 women). *Students:* 17 full-time (3 women), 18 part-time (3 women); includes 4 minority (1 Black or African American, non-Hispanic/Latino; 3 Asian, non-Hispanic/Latino), 6 international. Average age 28. 14 applicants, 79% accepted, 10 enrolled. In 2010, 6 master's awarded. *Entrance requirements:* Additional exam requirements/recommendations for international students: Required—TOEFL (minimum score 550 paper-based; 213 computer-based; 79 iBT). *Application deadline:* For fall admission, 3/15 for domestic students, 3/1 for international students; for spring admission, 11/1 for domestic students, 9/1 for international students. Applications are processed on a rolling basis. Application fee: $40 ($90 for international students). Electronic applications accepted. *Expenses:* Tuition, state resident: full-time $3893; part-time $162.20 per credit hour. Tuition, nonresident: full-time $14,167; part-time $590.30 per credit hour. Required fees: $2523; $94.60 per credit hour. Tuition and fees vary according to course load and degree level. *Financial support:* In 2010–11, 24 students received support, including 11 research assistantships with full tuition reimbursements available (averaging $11,603 per year), 4 teaching assistantships with full tuition reimbursements available (averaging $11,021 per year); scholarships/grants and unspecified assistantships also available. Financial award applicants required to submit FAFSA. *Faculty research:* IT enabled teams, business value of IT, knowledge management, technology adoption. Total annual research expenditures: $97,911. *Unit head:* Laku Chidambaram, Director, 405-325-5721, Fax: 405-325-2096, E-mail: laku@ou.edu. *Application contact:* Amber Hasbrook, Academic Counselor, 405-325-4107, Fax: 405-325-7753, E-mail: amber.hasbrook@ou.edu.

University of Phoenix, College of Information Systems and Technology, Phoenix, AZ 85034-7209. Offers information systems (MIS). Programs are offered at the online campus. Evening/weekend programs available. Postbaccalaureate distance learning degree programs offered. *Students:* 1,816 full-time (630 women); includes 580 minority (364 Black or African American, non-Hispanic/Latino; 15 American Indian or Alaska Native, non-Hispanic/Latino; 60 Asian, non-Hispanic/Latino; 112 Hispanic/Latino; 20 Native Hawaiian or other Pacific Islander, non-Hispanic/Latino; 9 Two or more races, non-Hispanic/Latino), 124 international. Average age 40. *Entrance requirements:* For master's, minimum undergraduate GPA of 2.5 from accredited university, 3 years of work experience, citizen of the United States or have valid visa. Additional exam requirements/recommendations for international students: Required—TOEFL (minimum paper score 550, computer score 213, iBT 79), Test of English for International Communication, or IELTS. *Application deadline:* Applications are processed on a rolling basis. Application fee: $45. Electronic applications accepted. *Expenses:* Tuition: Full-time $16,440. One-time fee: $45 full-time. Full-time tuition and fees vary according to course load, degree level, campus/location and program. *Financial support:* Scholarships/grants available. Financial award applicants required to submit FAFSA. *Unit head:* Dr. Blair Sith, Dean/Executive Director, 480-557-1241, E-mail: blair.smitha@phoenix.edu. *Application contact:* Dr. Blair Sith, Dean/Executive Director, 480-557-1241, E-mail: blair.smitha@phoenix.edu.

University of Phoenix–Northern Virginia Campus, College of Information Systems and Technology, Reston, VA 20190. Offers MIS. Evening/weekend programs available. Postbaccalaureate distance learning degree programs offered. *Students:* 8 full-time (0 women); includes 3 Black or African American, non-Hispanic/Latino. Average age 38. *Entrance requirements:* For master's, 3 years working experience, a minimum GPA of 2.5 from an accredited university, must be a citizen of the United States or have a valid visa. Specific requirements may vary by program. Additional exam requirements/ recommendations for international students: Required—TOEFL (minimum score 213 paper, 79 iBT), TOEIC, IELTS or Berlitz. *Application deadline:* Applications are processed on a rolling basis. Application fee: $45. Electronic applications accepted. *Expenses:* Tuition: Full-time $16,440. One-time fee: $45 full-time. Full-time tuition and fees vary according to course load, degree level, campus/location and program. *Financial support:* Scholarships/ grants available. Financial award applicants required to submit FAFSA. *Unit head:* Dr. Blair Smith, Dean/Executive Director, 480-557-1241, E-mail: blair. smith@phoenix.edu. *Application contact:* Dr. Blair Smith, Dean/Executive Director, 480-557-1241, E-mail: blair.smith@phoenix.edu.

University of Pittsburgh, Katz Graduate School of Business, Doctoral Program in Business Administration, Pittsburgh, PA 15260. Offers accounting (PhD); finance (PhD); information systems (PhD); marketing (PhD); operations/decision sciences/artificial intelligence (PhD); organizational behavior and human resource management (PhD); strategic planning (PhD). *Accreditation:* AACSB. *Faculty:* 50 full-time (15 women). *Students:* 51 full-time (22 women); includes 3 Black or African American, non-Hispanic/ Latino; 4 Asian, non-Hispanic/Latino; 2 Hispanic/Latino, 18 international. 448 applicants, 5% accepted, 13 enrolled. In 2010, 4 doctorates awarded. *Degree requirements:* For doctorate, comprehensive exam, thesis/dissertation. *Entrance requirements:* For doctorate, GMAT or GRE, bachelor's degree, references, minimum GPA of 3.0. Additional exam requirements/recommendations for international students: Required—TOEFL, IELTS. *Application deadline:* For fall admission, 2/1 priority date for domestic and international students. Applications are processed on a rolling basis. Application fee: $50. Electronic applications accepted. *Expenses:* Tuition, state resident: full-time $17,304; part-time $701 per credit. Tuition, nonresident: full-time $29,554; part-time $1210 per credit. Required fees: $740; $214 per term. Tuition and fees vary according to program. *Financial support:* In 2010–11, 39 students received support, including 29 research assistantships with full tuition reimbursements available (averaging $1,900 per year), 10 teaching assistantships with full tuition reimbursements available (averaging $23,745 per year); fellowships, Federal Work-Study, scholarships/grants, health care benefits, and unspecified assistantships also available. Financial award application deadline: 2/1. *Faculty research:* Accounting statements and reporting, incentives and governance, corporate finance, mergers and acquisitions, information systems processes, structures and decision-making, organizational structure, knowledge management and corporate strategy, consumer behavior and marketing models. Total annual research expenditures: $362,777. *Unit head:* Dr. John E. Hulland, Director of Doctoral Program, 412-648-1534, Fax: 412-624-3633, E-mail: jhulland@katz.pitt.edu. *Application contact:* Carrie Woods, Assistant Director, Doctoral Office, 412-648-1525, Fax: 412-624-3633, E-mail: cawoods@katz.pitt.edu.

University of Pittsburgh, Katz Graduate School of Business, Master of Business Administration Programs, Pittsburgh, PA 15260. Offers finance (MBA); information systems (MBA); marketing (MBA); operations management (MBA); organizational behavior and human resource management (MBA); organizational leadership (Certificate); six sigma (Certificate); strategy, environment and organizations (MBA); technology, innovation and entrepreneurship (Certificate); MBA/JD; MBA/MIB; MBA/MPIA; MBA/ MSE; MBA/MSIS; MID/MBA. *Accreditation:* AACSB. Part-time and evening/weekend programs available. *Faculty:* 60 full-time (18 women), 22 part-time/adjunct (5 women). *Students:* 232 full-time (75 women), 458 part-time (158 women); includes 34 Black or African American, non-Hispanic/Latino; 1 American Indian or Alaska Native, non-Hispanic/Latino; 20 Asian, non-Hispanic/Latino; 9 Hispanic/Latino, 105 international. Average age 29. 697 applicants, 50% accepted, 174 enrolled. In 2010, 263 master's awarded. *Degree requirements:* For master's, minimum GPA of 3.0. *Entrance requirements:* For master's, GMAT, recommendations, undergraduate transcripts, essay responses, resume, interview, bachelor's degree. Additional exam requirements/recommendations for international students: Required— TOEFL (minimum 600 paper, 250 computer, 100 iBT) or IELTS. *Application deadline:* For fall admission, 4/1 priority date for domestic students, 2/1 priority date for international students. Application fee: $50. Electronic applications accepted. *Expenses:* Tuition, state resident: full-time $17,304; part-time $701 per credit. Tuition, nonresident: full-time $29,554; part-time $1210 per credit. Required fees: $740; $214 per term. Tuition and fees vary according to program. *Financial support:* In 2010–11, 52 students received support. Career-related internships or fieldwork and scholarships/grants available. Financial award application deadline: 3/1; financial award applicants required to submit FAFSA. *Faculty research:* Accounting statements and reporting, incentives and governance, corporate finance, mergers and acquisitions, information systems processes, structures and decision-making, organizational structure, knowledge management and corporate strategy, consumer behavior and marketing models. *Unit head:* William T. Valenta, Assistant Dean, MBA Program

Director, 412-648-1610, Fax: 412-648-1659, E-mail: wtvalenta@katz.pitt. edu. *Application contact:* Cliff McCormick, Director MBA Admissions, 412-648-1700, Fax: 412-648-1659, E-mail: mba@katz.pitt.edu.

University of Pittsburgh, Katz Graduate School of Business, MBA/MS in Management of Information Systems Program, Pittsburgh, PA 15206. Offers MBA/MS. Part-time and evening/weekend programs available. *Faculty:* 60 full-time (18 women), 22 part-time/adjunct (5 women). *Students:* 10 full-time (1 woman), 20 part-time (7 women); includes 4 Black or African American, non-Hispanic/Latino; 2 Asian, non-Hispanic/Latino; 1 Hispanic/Latino. Average age 29. 24 applicants, 63% accepted, 6 enrolled. *Entrance requirements:* Additional exam requirements/recommendations for international students: Required—TOEFL (minimum score 600 paper-based; 250 computer-based; 100 iBT) or IELTS. *Application deadline:* For fall admission, 4/1 priority date for domestic students, 2/1 priority date for international students. Application fee: $50. Electronic applications accepted. *Expenses:* Tuition, state resident: full-time $17,304; part-time $701 per credit. Tuition, nonresident: full-time $29,554; part-time $1210 per credit. Required fees: $740; $214 per term. Tuition and fees vary according to program. *Financial support:* In 2010–11, 2 students received support. Career-related internships or fieldwork and scholarships/grants available. Financial award application deadline: 3/1; financial award applicants required to submit FAFSA. *Faculty research:* Social media and their impacts on organizations, information technology adoption and diffusion, economics of information systems, software acquisition and implementation, human-computer interaction. *Unit head:* William T. Valenta, Assistant Dean/Director of MBA Programs, 412-648-1610, Fax: 412-648-1659, E-mail: wtvalenta@katz.pitt.edu. *Application contact:* Cliff McCormick, Director, MBA Admissions, 412-648-1700, Fax: 412-648-1659, E-mail: mba@katz.pitt.edu.

University of St. Thomas, Graduate Studies, Graduate Programs in Software, Saint Paul, MN 55105. Offers advanced studies in software engineering (Certificate); business analysis (Certificate); computer security (Certificate); information systems (Certificate); software design and development (Certificate); software engineering (MS); software management (MS); software systems (MSS); MS/MBA. Part-time and evening/weekend programs available. *Faculty:* 5 full-time (0 women), 16 part-time/adjunct (1 woman). *Students:* 26 full-time (9 women), 297 part-time (75 women); includes 31 Black or African American, non-Hispanic/Latino; 52 Asian, non-Hispanic/Latino; 6 Hispanic/Latino; 2 Two or more races, non-Hispanic/ Latino, 69 international. Average age 34. 106 applicants, 96% accepted, 67 enrolled. In 2010, 40 master's, 4 other advanced degrees awarded. *Degree requirements:* For master's, thesis optional. *Entrance requirements:* For master's, bachelor's degree earned in U.S. or equivalent international degree. Additional exam requirements/recommendations for international students: Required—TOEFL (minimum score 80 iBT). *Application deadline:* For fall admission, 8/1 priority date for domestic students, 5/1 priority date for international students; for spring admission, 1/1 priority date for domestic students, 10/1 priority date for international students. Applications are processed on a rolling basis. Application fee: $30. *Expenses:* Contact institution. *Financial support:* Federal Work-Study, institutionally sponsored loans, and scholarships/grants available. Financial award application deadline: 4/1. *Faculty research:* Data mining, distributed databases, computer security. *Unit head:* Dr. Bhabani Misra, Director, 651-962-5508, Fax: 651-962-5543, E-mail: bsmisra@stthomas.edu. *Application contact:* Douglas J. Stubeda, Assistant Director, 651-962-5503, Fax: 651-962-5543, E-mail: djstubeda@stthomas. edu.

University of San Francisco, School of Business and Professional Studies, Program in Information Systems, San Francisco, CA 94117-1080. Offers MS. Part-time and evening/weekend programs available. *Faculty:* 1 full-time (0 women), 12 part-time/adjunct (3 women). *Students:* 56 full-time (15 women), 4 part-time (3 women); includes 28 minority (2 Black or African American, non-Hispanic/Latino; 18 Asian, non-Hispanic/Latino; 6 Hispanic/Latino; 2 Two or more races, non-Hispanic/Latino), 9 international. Average age 39. 43 applicants, 65% accepted, 18 enrolled. In 2010, 27 master's awarded. *Degree requirements:* For master's, thesis. *Entrance requirements:* For master's, minimum GPA of 3.0. Application fee: $55 ($65 for international students). *Expenses:* Tuition: Full-time $20,070; part-time $1115 per credit hour. Tuition and fees vary according to course load, degree level and program. *Financial support:* In 2010–11, 25 students received support. Application deadline: 3/2. *Unit head:* Dr. Moira Gunn, Director, 415-422-2592. *Application contact:* Advising Office, 415-422-6000, E-mail: graduate@usfca.edu.

The University of Scranton, College of Graduate and Continuing Education, Program in Business Administration, Scranton, PA 18510. Offers accounting (MBA); finance (MBA); general business administration (MBA); health care management (MBA); international business (MBA); management information systems (MBA); marketing (MBA); operations management (MBA). *Accreditation:* AACSB. Part-time and evening/weekend programs available. Postbaccalaureate distance learning degree programs offered (no on-campus study). *Faculty:* 34 full-time (8 women). *Students:* 251 full-time (91 women), 180 part-time (72 women); includes 41 Black or African American, non-Hispanic/Latino; 11 Asian, non-Hispanic/Latino; 7 Hispanic/Latino, 40 international. Average age 32. 386 applicants, 84% accepted. In 2010, 38 master's awarded. *Degree requirements:* For master's, capstone experience. *Entrance* *requirements:* For master's, GMAT, minimum GPA of 2.75. Additional exam requirements/recommendations for international students: Required—TOEFL (minimum score 500 paper-based; 173 computer-based), IELTS (minimum score 5.5). *Application deadline:* Applications are processed on a rolling basis. Application fee: $0. *Financial support:* In 2010–11, 13 students received support, including 13 teaching assistantships with full and partial tuition reimbursements available (averaging $6,430 per year); fellowships, career-related internships or fieldwork, Federal Work-Study, and unspecified assistantships also available. Support available to part-time students. Financial award application deadline: 3/1. *Faculty research:* Financial markets, strategic impact of total quality management, internal accounting controls, consumer preference, information systems and the Internet. *Unit head:* Dr. Murli Rajan, Director, 570-941-4043, Fax: 570-941-4342. *Application contact:* Joseph M. Roback, Director of Admissions, 570-941-4385, Fax: 570-941-5928, E-mail: robackj2@scranton.edu.

University of South Alabama, Graduate School, School of Computer and Information Sciences, Mobile, AL 36688-0002. Offers computer science (MS); information systems (MS). Part-time and evening/weekend programs available. *Faculty:* 9 full-time (0 women). *Students:* 81 full-time (23 women), 20 part-time (4 women); includes 7 minority (4 Black or African American, non-Hispanic/Latino; 2 Asian, non-Hispanic/Latino; 1 Hispanic/Latino), 68 international. 164 applicants, 71% accepted, 31 enrolled. In 2010, 20 master's awarded. *Degree requirements:* For master's, thesis optional, project. *Entrance requirements:* For master's, GRE General Test. *Application deadline:* For fall admission, 7/15 priority date for domestic students, 6/15 priority date for international students; for spring admission, 12/1 for domestic students, 11/1 priority date for international students. Applications are processed on a rolling basis. Application fee: $35. *Expenses:* Tuition, state resident: part-time $300 per credit hour. Tuition, nonresident: part-time $600 per credit hour. Required fees: $150 per semester. *Financial support:* Research assistantships, career-related internships or fieldwork and institutionally sponsored loans available. Support available to part-time students. Financial award application deadline: 4/1. *Faculty research:* Numerical analysis, artificial intelligence, simulation, medical applications, software engineering. *Unit head:* Dr. Roy Daigle, Director of Graduate Studies, 251-460-6390. *Application contact:* Dr. B. Keith Harrison, Dean of the Graduate School, 251-460-6310, Fax: 251-461-1513, E-mail: kharriso@usouthal.edu.

University of Southern Mississippi, Graduate School, College of Business, School of Accountancy and Information Systems, Hattiesburg, MS 39406-0001. Offers accountancy (MPA). *Accreditation:* AACSB. Part-time and evening/weekend programs available. *Faculty:* 7 full-time (4 women), 2 part-time/adjunct (both women). *Students:* 21 full-time (13 women), 2 part-time (1 woman); includes 1 Black or African American, non-Hispanic/Latino, 1 international. Average age 26. 29 applicants, 79% accepted, 19 enrolled. In 2010, 14 master's awarded. *Degree requirements:* For master's, comprehensive exam. *Entrance requirements:* For master's, GMAT, minimum GPA of 2.75 on last 60 hours. Additional exam requirements/recommendations for international students: Required—TOEFL, IELTS. *Application deadline:* For fall admission, 7/15 priority date for domestic students, 7/15 for international students; for spring admission, 11/15 priority date for domestic students, 11/15 for international students. Applications are processed on a rolling basis. Application fee: $50. Electronic applications accepted. *Financial support:* In 2010–11, 7 research assistantships with full tuition reimbursements (averaging $7,200 per year) were awarded; Federal Work-Study, institutionally sponsored loans, scholarships/grants, health care benefits, and unspecified assistantships also available. Support available to part-time students. Financial award application deadline: 3/15; financial award applicants required to submit FAFSA. *Faculty research:* Bank liquidity, subchapter S corporations, internal auditing, governmental accounting, inflation accounting. *Unit head:* Dr. Skip Hughes, Director, 601-266-4322, Fax: 601-266-4639. *Application contact:* Dr. Michael Dugan, Director of Graduate Studies, 601-266-4641, Fax: 601-266-5814.

University of South Florida, Graduate School, College of Business, Department of Business Administration, Tampa, FL 33620-9951. Offers accounting (PhD); entrepreneurship (MBA); finance (PhD); information systems (PhD); leadership and organizational effectiveness (MSM); management and organization (MBA); marketing (PhD). *Accreditation:* AACSB. Part-time and evening/weekend programs available. *Faculty:* 1 (woman) full-time. *Students:* 148 full-time (48 women), 190 part-time (61 women); includes 70 minority (7 Black or African American, non-Hispanic/Latino; 1 American Indian or Alaska Native, non-Hispanic/Latino; 26 Asian, non-Hispanic/Latino; 36 Hispanic/Latino), 62 international. Average age 30. 452 applicants, 29% accepted, 80 enrolled. In 2010, 146 master's, 5 doctorates awarded. *Degree requirements:* For master's, comprehensive exam, thesis (for some programs); for doctorate, comprehensive exam, thesis/dissertation, 90 credit hours, minimum GPA of 3.0. *Entrance requirements:* For master's, GMAT, minimum GPA of 3.0 in last 60 hours of course work, 2 years of work experience, resume; for doctorate, GMAT, letters of recommendation, personal statement. Additional exam requirements/recommendations for international students: Required—TOEFL (minimum score 550 paper-based; 213 computer-based; 79 iBT). *Application deadline:* For fall admission, 6/1 for domestic students, 1/2 for international students; for spring admission, 10/15 for domestic students, 6/1 for international students. Application fee: $30. *Financial support:*

Scholarships/grants, health care benefits, and unspecified assistantships available. Financial award applicants required to submit FAFSA. *Unit head:* Irene Hurst, Program Director, 813-974-3335, Fax: 813-974-4518, E-mail: hurst@coba.usf.edu. *Application contact:* Wendy Baker, Assistant Director, Graduate Studies, 813-974-3335, Fax: 813-974-4518, E-mail: wbaker@usf.edu.

University of South Florida, Graduate School, College of Business, Information Systems and Decision Sciences Department, Tampa, FL 33620-9951. Offers business administration (PhD), including management information systems; management information systems (MS). Part-time programs available. *Faculty:* 1 full-time (0 women). *Students:* 45 full-time (19 women), 43 part-time (11 women); includes 5 Black or African American, non-Hispanic/Latino; 5 Asian, non-Hispanic/Latino; 8 Hispanic/Latino, 30 international. Average age 28. 112 applicants, 59% accepted, 32 enrolled. In 2010, 32 master's awarded. Terminal master's awarded for partial completion of doctoral program. *Degree requirements:* For master's, thesis or alternative, 33 credit hours, minimum GPA of 3.0; for doctorate, comprehensive exam, thesis/dissertation. *Entrance requirements:* For master's, GMAT or GRE, minimum GPA of 3.0, industry experience (preferred); for doctorate, GMAT, letters of recommendation, personal statement. Additional exam requirements/recommendations for international students: Required—TOEFL (minimum score 550 paper-based; 213 computer-based; 79 iBT). *Application deadline:* For fall admission, 6/1 for domestic students, 1/2 for international students; for spring admission, 10/30 for domestic students, 6/1 for international students. Applications are processed on a rolling basis. Application fee: $30. Electronic applications accepted. *Financial support:* In 2010–11, 4 research assistantships with tuition reimbursements (averaging $15,002 per year), 23 teaching assistantships with tuition reimbursements (averaging $14,943 per year) were awarded; scholarships/grants, health care benefits, and unspecified assistantships also available. Financial award applicants required to submit FAFSA. *Faculty research:* Business intelligence, software engineering, health informatics, information technology adoption, organizational impacts of IT. Total annual research expenditures: $178,922. *Unit head:* Dr. Kaushal Chari, Chairperson /Program Director, 813-974-5524, Fax: 813-974-6749, E-mail: kchari@usf.edu. *Application contact:* Mike Walters, Program Coordinator, 813-974-5524, Fax: 813-974-6749, E-mail: msmis@coba.usf.edu.

The University of Tampa, John H. Sykes College of Business, Tampa, FL 33606-1490. Offers accounting (MS); entrepreneurship (MBA); finance (MBA, MS); information systems management (MBA); innovation management (MBA); international business (MBA); marketing (MBA, MS); nonprofit management (MBA). *Accreditation:* AACSB. Part-time and evening/weekend programs available. *Faculty:* 67 full-time (24 women), 11 part-time/adjunct (4 women). *Students:* 235 full-time (89 women), 288 part-time (122 women); includes 74 minority (16 Black or African American, non-Hispanic/Latino; 2 American Indian or Alaska Native, non-Hispanic/Latino; 14 Asian, non-Hispanic/Latino; 34 Hispanic/Latino; 2 Native Hawaiian or other Pacific Islander, non-Hispanic/Latino; 6 Two or more races, non-Hispanic/Latino), 95 international. Average age 29. 457 applicants, 45% accepted, 175 enrolled. In 2010, 230 master's awarded. *Degree requirements:* For master's, capstone. *Entrance requirements:* For master's, GMAT or GRE, 4-year undergraduate degree, minimum GPA of 3.0, professional experience (for Executive MBA). Additional exam requirements/recommendations for international students: Required—TOEFL (minimum score 577 paper-based; 230 computer-based; 90 iBT); Recommended—IELTS (minimum score 7.5). *Application deadline:* Applications are processed on a rolling basis. Application fee: $40. Electronic applications accepted. *Expenses:* Tuition: Part-time $504 per credit hour. Required fees: $40 per term. *Financial support:* In 2010–11, 74 students received support. Career-related internships or fieldwork, scholarships/grants, unspecified assistantships, and grants available. Financial award applicants required to submit FAFSA. *Faculty research:* Management innovation, social marketing, value relevance of earnings and book value across industries, managerial finance, entrepreneurship. *Unit head:* Dennis Nostrand, Vice President, Enrollment/Admissions, 813-257-1808, E-mail: dnostrand@ut.edu. *Application contact:* Charlene Tobie, Associate Director of Admissions, 813-257-3566, E-mail: ctobie@ut.edu.

The University of Texas at Arlington, Graduate School, College of Business, Department of Information Systems and Operations Management, Arlington, TX 76019. Offers information systems (MS, PhD). Part-time and evening/weekend programs available. *Faculty:* 5 full-time (1 woman). *Students:* 43 full-time (17 women), 23 part-time (4 women); includes 21 minority (4 Black or African American, non-Hispanic/Latino; 1 American Indian or Alaska Native, non-Hispanic/Latino; 8 Asian, non-Hispanic/Latino; 6 Hispanic/Latino; 2 Two or more races, non-Hispanic/Latino), 17 international. 78 applicants, 58% accepted, 24 enrolled. In 2010, 36 master's, 2 doctorates awarded. *Degree requirements:* For master's, thesis optional; for doctorate, comprehensive exam, thesis/dissertation. *Entrance requirements:* For master's, GMAT, minimum GPA of 3.0. Additional exam requirements/recommendations for international students: Required—TOEFL (minimum score 550 paper-based; 213 computer-based; 79 iBT). *Application deadline:* For fall admission, 6/1 for domestic students, 4/1 for international students; for spring admission, 10/15 for domestic students, 9/15 for international students. Applications are processed on a rolling basis. Application fee: $35 ($50 for international students). *Expenses:* Tuition, state resident: full-time $7500. Tuition, nonresident: full-time $13,080. International tuition: $13,250 full-time. *Financial support:* In 2010–11, 7 students received support, including 15 teaching assistantships (averaging $14,000 per year); research assistantships, career-related internships or fieldwork, scholarships/grants, and unspecified assistantships also available. Support available to part-time students. Financial award application deadline: 6/1; financial award applicants required to submit FAFSA. *Faculty research:* Database modeling, strategic issues in information systems, simulations, production operations management. *Unit head:* Dr. R. C. Baker, Chair, 817-272-3502, Fax: 817-272-5801, E-mail: rcbaker@uta.edu. *Application contact:* Dr. Carolyn Davis, Graduate Advisor, 817-272-7399, Fax: 817-272-5801, E-mail: carolynd@exchange.uta.edu.

The University of Texas at Arlington, Graduate School, College of Business, Program in Business Administration, Arlington, TX 76019. Offers accounting (PhD); business statistics (PhD); finance (MBA, PhD); information systems (MBA, PhD); management (MBA, PhD); marketing (MBA, PhD); operations management (MBA, PhD); real estate (MBA). *Accreditation:* AACSB. Part-time and evening/weekend programs available. Postbaccalaureate distance learning degree programs offered (no on-campus study). *Students:* 555 full-time (197 women), 378 part-time (144 women); includes 179 minority (55 Black or African American, non-Hispanic/Latino; 1 American Indian or Alaska Native, non-Hispanic/Latino; 58 Asian, non-Hispanic/Latino; 55 Hispanic/Latino; 10 Two or more races, non-Hispanic/Latino), 410 international. 317 applicants, 93% accepted, 196 enrolled. In 2010, 468 master's, 1 doctorate awarded. Terminal master's awarded for partial completion of doctoral program. *Degree requirements:* For master's, thesis optional; for doctorate, comprehensive exam, thesis/dissertation. *Entrance requirements:* For master's, GMAT or GRE; for doctorate, GMAT, minimum GPA of 3.0 (undergraduate), 3.4 (graduate); 30 hours of graduate course work. Additional exam requirements/recommendations for international students: Required—TOEFL (minimum score 550 paper-based; 213 computer-based; 79 iBT). *Application deadline:* For fall admission, 6/1 for domestic students, 4/1 for international students; for spring admission, 10/15 for domestic students, 9/15 for international students. Applications are processed on a rolling basis. Application fee: $35 ($50 for international students). Electronic applications accepted. *Expenses:* Tuition, state resident: full-time $7500. Tuition, nonresident: full-time $13,080. International tuition: $13,250 full-time. *Financial support:* Career-related internships or fieldwork, scholarships/grants, and unspecified assistantships available. Financial award application deadline: 6/1; financial award applicants required to submit FAFSA. *Unit head:* Dr. Edmund Prater, Director of PhD Programs, 817-272-2131, Fax: 817-272-5799. *Application contact:* Melanie McGee, Director of MBA Program, 817-272-3005, Fax: 817-272-5799, E-mail: mwmcgee@uta.edu.

The University of Texas at Dallas, School of Management, Program in Accounting, Richardson, TX 75080. Offers audit and professional (MS); financial analysis (MS); information management (MS); international audit (MS); international services (MS); managerial (MS); taxation (MS). *Accreditation:* AACSB. *Faculty:* 17 full-time (4 women), 7 part-time/adjunct (2 women). *Students:* 412 full-time (270 women), 293 part-time (149 women); includes 164 minority (22 Black or African American, non-Hispanic/Latino; 1 American Indian or Alaska Native, non-Hispanic/Latino; 102 Asian, non-Hispanic/Latino; 37 Hispanic/Latino; 2 Two or more races, non-Hispanic/Latino), 283 international. Average age 28. 570 applicants, 68% accepted, 259 enrolled. In 2010, 273 master's awarded. *Entrance requirements:* For master's, GMAT, minimum GPA of 3.0 in upper-level course work in field. Additional exam requirements/recommendations for international students: Required—TOEFL (minimum score 550 paper-based; 215 computer-based). *Application deadline:* For fall admission, 7/15 for domestic students, 5/1 priority date for international students; for spring admission, 11/15 for domestic students, 9/1 priority date for international students. Applications are processed on a rolling basis. Application fee: $50 ($100 for international students). Electronic applications accepted. *Expenses:* Tuition, state resident: full-time $10,248; part-time $569 per credit hour. Tuition, nonresident: full-time $18,544; part-time $1030 per credit hour. Tuition and fees vary according to course load. *Financial support:* In 2010–11, 260 students received support, including 1 research assistantship with partial tuition reimbursement available (averaging $10,050 per year), 10 teaching assistantships with partial tuition reimbursements available (averaging $10,050 per year); career-related internships or fieldwork, Federal Work-Study, institutionally sponsored loans, scholarships/grants, and unspecified assistantships also available. Support available to part-time students. Financial award application deadline: 4/30; financial award applicants required to submit FAFSA. *Faculty research:* Privatization and accounting/auditing, corporate performance and executive compensation, risk management, information technology in accounting. *Unit head:* Amy Troutman, Assistant Director, 972-883-6719, Fax: 972-883-6823, E-mail: amybass@utdallas.edu. *Application contact:* James Parker, Assistant Director of Graduate Recruitment, 972-883-5842, E-mail: jparker@utdallas.edu.

The University of Texas at Dallas, School of Management, Program in Information Systems and Operations Management, Richardson, TX 75080. Offers information technology management (MS), including enterprise systems, health care systems, information security. Part-time and evening/weekend programs available. *Faculty:* 20 full-time (1 woman), 4 part-time/adjunct (1 woman). *Students:* 171 full-time (59 women), 109 part-time (37 women); includes 28 minority (2 Black or African American, non-Hispanic/Latino; 20 Asian, non-Hispanic/Latino; 6 Hispanic/Latino), 214 international. Average age 27. 404 applicants, 68% accepted, 103 enrolled. In 2010, 92 master's awarded. *Degree requirements:* For master's, thesis optional. *Entrance requirements:* For master's, GMAT. Additional exam requirements/recommendations for international students: Required—TOEFL (minimum score 550 paper-based; 215 computer-based). *Application deadline:* For fall admission, 7/15 for domestic students, 5/1 priority date for international students; for spring admission, 11/15 for domestic students, 9/1 priority date for international students. Applications are processed on a rolling basis. Application fee: $50 ($100 for international students). Electronic applications accepted. *Expenses:* Tuition, state resident: full-time $10,248; part-time $569 per credit hour. Tuition, nonresident: full-time $18,544; part-time $1030 per credit hour. Tuition and fees vary according to course load. *Financial support:* In 2010–11, 71 students received support, including 2 research assistantships with partial tuition reimbursements available (averaging $10,800 per year), 10 teaching assistantships with partial tuition reimbursements available (averaging $10,125 per year); career-related internships or fieldwork, Federal Work-Study, institutionally sponsored loans, scholarships/grants, and unspecified assistantships also available. Support available to part-time students. Financial award application deadline: 4/30; financial award applicants required to submit FAFSA. *Faculty research:* Technology marketing, measuring information work productivity, electronic commerce, decision support systems, data quality. *Unit head:* Dr. Mark Thouin, Director, 972-883-4011, E-mail: mark.thouin@utdallas.edu. *Application contact:* James Parker, Assistant Director, 972-883-5842, E-mail: jparker@utdallas.edu.

The University of Texas at Dallas, School of Management, Program in Management and Administrative Sciences, Richardson, TX 75080. Offers electronic commerce (MS); finance (MS); healthcare administration (MS); information systems (MS); innovation and entrepreneurship (MS); international management (MS); leadership in organizations (MS); marketing (MS); operations (MS); organizations (MS); real estate (MS); strategy (MS). *Accreditation:* AACSB. Part-time and evening/weekend programs available. *Faculty:* 18 full-time (3 women), 8 part-time/adjunct (0 women). *Students:* 57 full-time (32 women), 107 part-time (49 women); includes 53 minority (14 Black or African American, non-Hispanic/Latino; 30 Asian, non-Hispanic/Latino; 8 Hispanic/Latino; 1 Two or more races, non-Hispanic/Latino), 25 international. Average age 32. 161 applicants, 67% accepted, 51 enrolled. In 2010, 27 master's awarded. *Degree requirements:* For master's, thesis optional. *Entrance requirements:* For master's, GMAT. Additional exam requirements/recommendations for international students: Required—TOEFL (minimum score 550 paper-based; 215 computer-based). *Application deadline:* For fall admission, 7/15 for domestic students, 5/1 priority date for international students; for spring admission, 11/15 for domestic students, 9/1 priority date for international students. Applications are processed on a rolling basis. Application fee: $50 ($100 for international students). Electronic applications accepted. *Expenses:* Tuition, state resident: full-time $10,248; part-time $569 per credit hour. Tuition, nonresident: full-time $18,544; part-time $1030 per credit hour. Tuition and fees vary according to course load. *Financial support:* In 2010–11, 26 students received support, including 38 teaching assistantships with partial tuition reimbursements available (averaging $11,528 per year); research assistantships with partial tuition reimbursements available, career-related internships or fieldwork, Federal Work-Study, institutionally sponsored loans, scholarships/grants, and unspecified assistantships also available. Support available to part-time students. Financial award application deadline: 4/30; financial award applicants required to submit FAFSA. *Faculty research:* Integrated and detailed knowledge of functional areas of management, analytical tools for effective appraisal and decision making. *Unit head:* Dr. Doug Eckel, Assistant Dean, 972-883-5923, E-mail: doug.eckel@utdallas.edu. *Application contact:* James Parker, Assistant Director, 972-883-5842, E-mail: jparker@utdallas.edu.

The University of Texas at Dallas, School of Management, Programs in Management Science, Richardson, TX 75080. Offers accounting (PhD); finance (PhD); information systems (PhD); marketing (PhD); operations management (PhD). *Accreditation:* AACSB. Part-time and evening/weekend programs available. *Faculty:* 12 full-time (3 women), 3 part-time/adjunct (0 women). *Students:* 77 full-time (27 women), 11 part-time (4 women); includes 5 minority (all Asian, non-Hispanic/Latino), 72 international. Average age 32. 223 applicants, 9% accepted. In 2010, 16 doctorates awarded. *Degree requirements:* For doctorate, thesis/dissertation. *Entrance requirements:* For doctorate, GMAT, minimum GPA of 3.0. Additional exam requirements/recommendations for international students: Required—TOEFL (minimum score 550 paper-based; 215 computer-based). *Application deadline:* For fall admission, 7/15 for domestic students, 5/1 priority date for international students; for spring admission, 11/15 for domestic students, 9/1 priority date for international students. Applications are processed on a rolling basis. Application fee: $50 ($100 for international students). Electronic applications accepted. *Expenses:* Tuition, state resident: full-time $10,248; part-time $569 per credit hour. Tuition, nonresident: full-time $18,544; part-time $1030 per credit hour. Tuition and fees vary according to course load. *Financial support:* In 2010–11, 56 students received support, including 1 research assistantship with partial tuition reimbursement available (averaging $13,050 per year), 58 teaching assistantships with partial tuition reimbursements available (averaging $14,772 per year); career-related internships or fieldwork, Federal Work-Study, institutionally sponsored loans, scholarships/grants, and unspecified assistantships also available. Support available to part-time students. Financial award application deadline: 4/30; financial award applicants required to submit FAFSA. *Faculty research:* Empirical generalizations in marketing, diffusion of generations of technology, stochastic brand-choice theory, acceptance of trade deals by supermarkets, nonparametric estimations of market share response. *Unit head:* Dr. Sumit Sarkar, Program Director, 972-883-2745, Fax: 972-883-5977, E-mail: som phd.@utdallas.edu. Application contact: Dr. LeeAnne Sloane, Program Coordinator, 972-883-2745, Fax: 972-883-5977, E-mail: som_phd@utdallas.edu.

The University of Texas at San Antonio, College of Business, Department of Information Systems and Technology Management, San Antonio, TX 78249-0617. Offers information technology (MSIT); management technology (MSMOT), including information assurance. *Faculty:* 10 full-time (3 women), 1 part-time/adjunct (0 women). *Students:* 23 full-time (1 woman), 71 part-time (20 women); includes 33 minority (3 Black or African American, non-Hispanic/Latino; 3 Asian, non-Hispanic/Latino; 23 Hispanic/Latino; 1 Native Hawaiian or other Pacific Islander, non-Hispanic/Latino; 3 Two or more races, non-Hispanic/Latino), 7 international. Average age 32. 51 applicants, 61% accepted, 22 enrolled. In 2010, 48 master's awarded. *Degree requirements:* For master's, comprehensive exam (for some programs), thesis (for some programs). *Entrance requirements:* For master's, GMAT, minimum GPA of 3.0. Additional exam requirements/recommendations for international students: Required—TOEFL (minimum score 500 paper-based; 173 computer-based; 61 iBT), IELTS (minimum score 5). *Application deadline:* For fall admission, 7/1 for domestic students, 4/1 for international students; for spring admission, 11/1 for domestic students, 9/1 for international students. Applications are processed on a rolling basis. Application fee: $45 ($80 for international students). Electronic applications accepted. *Expenses:* Tuition, state resident: full-time $4172; part-time $231.75 per credit hour. Tuition, nonresident: full-time $15,332; part-time $851.75 per credit hour. *Financial support:* In 2010–11, 7 students received support, including 7 research assistantships (averaging $10,400 per year), 8 teaching assistantships (averaging $7,800 per year); scholarships/grants, tuition waivers (partial), and unspecified assistantships also available. Support available to part-time students. *Faculty research:* Infrastructure assurance, digital forensics, management of technology, e-commerce, technology transfer. Total annual research expenditures: $162,886. *Unit head:* Dr. Glenn Dietrich, Chair, 210-458-5354, Fax: 210-458-6305, E-mail: gdietrich@utsa.edu. *Application contact:* Veronica Ramirez, Assistant Dean of the Graduate School, 210-458-4330, Fax: 210-458-4332, E-mail: graduatestudies@utsa.edu.

The University of Texas at San Antonio, College of Business, General Business Program, San Antonio, TX 78249-0617. Offers accounting (PhD); business (MBA); finance (PhD); information systems (MBA); information technology (PhD); international business (MBA); management accounting (MBA); management and organization studies (PhD); management of technology (MBA); marketing (PhD); marketing management (MBA); taxation (MBA). Part-time and evening/weekend programs available. *Students:* 159 full-time (59 women), 124 part-time (43 women); includes 82 minority (9 Black or African American, non-Hispanic/Latino; 2 American Indian or Alaska Native, non-Hispanic/Latino; 17 Asian, non-Hispanic/Latino; 50 Hispanic/Latino; 1 Native Hawaiian or other Pacific Islander, non-Hispanic/Latino; 3 Two or more races, non-Hispanic/Latino), 39 international. Average age 32. 330 applicants, 46% accepted, 105 enrolled. In 2010, 85 master's, 9 doctorates awarded. *Degree requirements:* For master's, comprehensive exam (for some programs), thesis (for some programs). *Entrance requirements:* For master's, GMAT. Additional exam requirements/recommendations for international students: Required—TOEFL (minimum score 500 paper-based; 173 computer-based; 61 iBT), IELTS (minimum score 5). *Application deadline:* For fall admission, 7/1 for domestic students, 4/1 for international students; for spring admission, 11/1 for domestic students, 9/1 for international students. Application fee: $45 ($80 for international students). *Expenses:* Tuition, state resident: full-time $4172; part-time $231.75 per credit hour. Tuition, nonresident: full-time $15,332; part-time $851.75 per credit hour. *Financial support:* In 2010–11, 282 research assistantships (averaging $13,930 per year), 74 teaching assistantships (averaging $9,284 per year) were awarded; scholarships/grants, tuition waivers, and unspecified assistantships also available. Support available to part-time students. *Unit head:* Dr. Lynda Y. de la Vinna, Dean, 210-458-4317, Fax: 210-458-4308, E-mail: lynda.delavina@utsa.edu. *Application contact:* Veronica Ramirez, Assistant Dean of the Graduate School, 210-458-4330, Fax: 210-458-4332, E-mail: graduatestudies@utsa.edu.

The University of Toledo, College of Graduate Studies, College of Business and Innovation, Department of Information Operations and Technology Management, Toledo, OH 43606-3390. Offers information systems (MBA); manufacturing management (DME); operations management (MBA); supply chain management (Certificate). Part-time and evening/weekend programs available. *Faculty:* 12. *Students:* 36 full-time (8 women), 20 part-time (6 women); includes 4 Black or African American, non-Hispanic/Latino; 3 Asian, non-Hispanic/Latino, 23 international. Average age 32. 41 applicants, 51%

accepted, 10 enrolled. In 2010, 16 master's, 4 doctorates awarded. *Degree requirements:* For doctorate, thesis/dissertation. *Entrance requirements:* For master's, doctorate, and Certificate, GMAT, 2.7 GPA on all prior academic work. Three letters of recommendation, a statement of purpose, transcripts from all prior institutions attended. Additional exam requirements/recommendations for international students: Required—TOEFL (minimum score 550 paper-based; 213 computer-based; 80 iBT), IELTS (minimum score 6.5). *Application deadline:* For fall admission, 1/15 priority date for domestic and international students. Applications are processed on a rolling basis. Application fee: $45 ($75 for international students). Electronic applications accepted. *Expenses:* Tuition, state resident: full-time $11,426; part-time $476 per credit hour. Tuition, nonresident: full-time $21,660; part-time $903 per credit hour. One-time fee: $62. *Financial support:* Research assistantships with tuition reimbursements, career-related internships or fieldwork, Federal Work-Study, institutionally sponsored loans, scholarships/grants, tuition waivers (full and partial), unspecified assistantships, and administrative assistantships available. Support available to part-time students. *Unit head:* Dr. T. S. Ragu-Nathan, Chair, 419-530-2427. *Application contact:* Graduate School Office, 419-530-4723, Fax: 419-530-4724, E-mail: grdsch@utnet.utoledo.edu.

University of Tulsa, Graduate School, Collins College of Business, Master of Business Administration Program, Tulsa, OK 74104-3189. Offers accounting (MBA); business administration (MBA); energy management (MBA); finance (MBA); international business (MBA); management information systems (MBA); taxation (MBA); JD/MBA; MBA/MSCS; MBA/MSF. *Accreditation:* AACSB. Part-time and evening/weekend programs available. *Faculty:* 32 full-time (6 women). *Students:* 39 full-time (14 women), 40 part-time (16 women); includes 7 minority (1 Black or African American, non-Hispanic/Latino; 2 Asian, non-Hispanic/Latino; 4 Hispanic/Latino), 9 international. Average age 26. 73 applicants, 55% accepted, 18 enrolled. In 2010, 55 master's awarded. *Entrance requirements:* For master's, GMAT. Additional exam requirements/recommendations for international students: Required—TOEFL (minimum score 575 paper-based; 232 computer-based; 90 iBT), IELTS (minimum score 6.5). *Application deadline:* Applications are processed on a rolling basis. Application fee: $40. Electronic applications accepted. *Expenses:* Tuition: Full-time $16,902; part-time $939 per credit hour. Required fees: $1020; $4 per credit hour. Tuition and fees vary according to course load. *Financial support:* In 2010–11, 56 students received support, including 23 fellowships (averaging $4,872 per year), 4 research assistantships (averaging $9,323 per year), 29 teaching assistantships (averaging $10,642 per year); career-related internships or fieldwork, institutionally sponsored loans, scholarships/grants, health care benefits, tuition waivers (full and partial), and unspecified assistantships also available. Support available to part-time students. Financial award application deadline: 2/1; financial award applicants required to submit FAFSA. *Faculty research:* Accounting, energy management, finance, international business, management information systems, taxation. *Unit head:* Dr. Linda Nichols, Associate Dean of the Collins College of Business, 918-631-2242, Fax: 918-631-2142, E-mail: linda-nichols@utulsa.edu. *Application contact:* Dr. Linda Nichols, Associate Dean of the Collins College of Business, 918-631-2242, Fax: 918-631-2142, E-mail: linda-nichols@utulsa.edu.

University of Utah, Graduate School, David Eccles School of Business, Department of Operations and Information Systems, Salt Lake City, UT 84112-1107. Offers information systems (MS). *Faculty:* 14 full-time (2 women). *Students:* 39 full-time (5 women), 15 part-time (0 women); includes 4 Asian, non-Hispanic/Latino; 3 Hispanic/Latino, 9 international. Average age 29. 68 applicants, 68% accepted, 33 enrolled. In 2010, 2 master's awarded. *Entrance requirements:* For master's, GMAT/GRE, minimum undergraduate GPA of 3.0. Additional exam requirements/recommendations for international students: Required—TOEFL (minimum score 600 paper-based; 250 computer-based; 100 iBT), IELTS (minimum score 7). *Application deadline:* For fall admission, 3/1 priority date for domestic and international students. Applications are processed on a rolling basis. Application fee: $55 ($65 for international students). Electronic applications accepted. *Expenses:* Tuition, area resident: Part-time $179.19 per credit hour. Tuition, state resident: full-time $4384. Tuition, nonresident: full-time $16,684; part-time $630.67 per credit hour. Required fees: $350 per semester. Tuition and fees vary according to course load, degree level and program. *Financial support:* In 2010–11, 4 students received support. Unspecified assistantships and graduate assistantships available. Financial award application deadline: 3/1; financial award applicants required to submit FAFSA. *Faculty research:* Data management, IT security, economics of information systems, Web and data mining, applications and management of IT in healthcare. *Unit head:* Dr. Olivia Sheng, Head, 801-585-9071, E-mail: actos@business.utah.edu. *Application contact:* Andrea Chmelik, Academic Coordinator, 801-585-1719, Fax: 801-581-3666, E-mail: andrea.chmelik@business.utah.edu.

University of Virginia, McIntire School of Commerce, Program in Management of Information Technology, Charlottesville, VA 22903. Offers MS. *Students:* 32 full-time (5 women), 35 part-time (9 women); includes 4 Black or African American, non-Hispanic/Latino; 11 Asian, non-Hispanic/Latino; 3 Hispanic/Latino; 1 Two or more races, non-Hispanic/Latino, 5 international. Average age 36. In 2010, 79 master's awarded. *Entrance requirements:* For master's, GMAT, 2 recommendations. Additional exam requirements/recommendations for international students: Required—TOEFL (minimum score 620 paper-based; 270 computer-based). *Application deadline:* For fall admission, 9/15 priority date for domestic students, 1/15 for international students. Applications are processed on a rolling basis. Application fee: $75. Electronic applications accepted. *Expenses:* Contact institution. *Financial support:* Fellowships, Federal Work-Study available. Financial award application deadline: 2/15; financial award applicants required to submit FAFSA. *Unit head:* Stefano Grazioli, Director, 434-982-2973, E-mail: grazioli@virginia.edu. *Application contact:* Matthew Miller, Assistant Director of Graduate Marketing and Admissions, 434-982-2245, Fax: 434-924-4511, E-mail: msmit@virginia.edu.

University of Wisconsin–Madison, Graduate School, Wisconsin School of Business, Doctoral Program in Accounting and Information Systems, Madison, WI 53706-1380. Offers PhD. *Accreditation:* AACSB. *Faculty:* 12 full-time (4 women), 5 part-time/adjunct (2 women). *Students:* 11 full-time (6 women), 1 international. Average age 30. 82 applicants, 11% accepted, 5 enrolled. In 2010, 4 doctorates awarded. *Degree requirements:* For doctorate, comprehensive exam, thesis/dissertation. *Entrance requirements:* For doctorate, GMAT or GRE. Additional exam requirements/recommendations for international students: Required—Pearson Test of English (minimum score 73, written 80); Recommended—TOEFL (minimum score 623 paper-based; 263 computer-based; 106 iBT), IELTS (minimum score 7.5). *Application deadline:* For fall admission, 12/15 priority date for domestic and international students. Application fee: $56. Electronic applications accepted. *Expenses:* Tuition, state resident: full-time $9887; part-time $617.96 per credit. Tuition, nonresident: full-time $24,054; part-time $1503.40 per credit. Required fees: $67.63 per credit. Tuition and fees vary according to reciprocity agreements. *Financial support:* In 2010–11, 11 students received support, including 1 fellowship with full tuition reimbursement available (averaging $18,756 per year), research assistantships with full tuition reimbursements available (averaging $16,506 per year), 9 teaching assistantships with full tuition reimbursements available (averaging $14,088 per year); Federal Work-Study, institutionally sponsored loans, scholarships/grants, health care benefits, and unspecified assistantships also available. Financial award application deadline: 2/1. *Faculty research:* Auditing, financial reporting, economic theory, strategy, computer models. *Unit head:* Prof. Jon Davis, Chair, 608-263-4264. *Application contact:* Belle Heberling, Assistant Director for Research Programs, 608-262-3749, Fax: 608-890-0180, E-mail: phd@bus.wisc.edu.

University of Wisconsin–Madison, Graduate School, Wisconsin School of Business, Doctoral Program in Operations and Information Management, Madison, WI 53706-1380. Offers information systems (PhD); operations management (PhD). *Faculty:* 8 full-time (0 women), 1 part-time/adjunct (0 women). *Students:* 2 full-time (0 women), 1 international. Average age 32. 23 applicants, 0% accepted, 0 enrolled. In 2010, 3 doctorates awarded. *Degree requirements:* For doctorate, comprehensive exam, thesis/dissertation. *Entrance requirements:* For doctorate, GMAT or GRE General Test. Additional exam requirements/recommendations for international students: Required—Pearson Test of English (minimum score 73, written 80); Recommended—TOEFL (minimum score 623 paper-based; 263 computer-based; 106 iBT), IELTS (minimum score 7.5). *Application deadline:* For fall admission, 12/15 priority date for domestic and international students. Application fee: $56. Electronic applications accepted. *Expenses:* Tuition, state resident: full-time $9887; part-time $617.96 per credit. Tuition, nonresident: full-time $24,054; part-time $1503.40 per credit. Required fees: $67.63 per credit. Tuition and fees vary according to reciprocity agreements. *Financial support:* In 2010–11, 4 students received support, including fellowships with full tuition reimbursements available (averaging $18,756 per year), research assistantships with full tuition reimbursements available (averaging $16,506 per year), 2 teaching assistantships with full tuition reimbursements available (averaging $14,088 per year); Federal Work-Study, institutionally sponsored loans, scholarships/grants, health care benefits, and unspecified assistantships also available. Financial award application deadline: 2/1; financial award applicants required to submit FAFSA. *Faculty research:* Supply-chain management, reorganization of the factory, creating continuous innovation, transportation economics, organizational economics. *Unit head:* Prof. James G. Morris, Chair, 608-262-1284, E-mail: jmorris@bus.wisc.edu. *Application contact:* Belle Heberling, Assistant Director for Research Programs, 608-262-3749, Fax: 608-890-0180, E-mail: phd@bus.wisc.edu.

Valparaiso University, Graduate School, Program in Information Technology, Valparaiso, IN 46383. Offers MS. Part-time and evening/weekend programs available. *Students:* 28 full-time (5 women), 13 part-time (4 women); includes 1 minority (Asian, non-Hispanic/Latino), 33 international. Average age 27. In 2010, 7 master's awarded. *Entrance requirements:* For master's, minimum GPA of 3.0; minor or equivalent in computer science, information technology, or a related field. Additional exam requirements/recommendations for international students: Required—TOEFL (minimum score 550 paper-based; 213 computer-based; 80 iBT). *Application deadline:* For fall admission, 4/15 priority date for domestic students. Applications are processed on a rolling basis. Application fee: $30 ($50 for international students). Electronic applications accepted. *Expenses:* Tuition: Full-time $9540; part-time $530 per credit hour. Required fees: $292; $95 per semester. Tuition and fees vary according to program. *Financial support:* Available to part-time students. Applicants required to submit FAFSA. *Unit head:* Dr. David L. Rowland, Dean, Graduate

School and Continuing Education/Associate Provost, 219-464-5313, Fax: 219-464-5381, E-mail: david.rowland@valpo.edu. *Application contact:* Laura Groth, Coordinator of Student Services and Support, 219-464-5313, Fax: 219-464-5381, E-mail: laura.groth@valpo.edu.

Villanova University, Villanova School of Business, MBA—The Fast Track Program, Villanova, PA 19085. Offers finance (MBA); health care management (MBA); international business (MBA); management information systems (MBA); marketing (MBA); real estate (MBA); strategic management (MBA). *Accreditation:* AACSB. Part-time and evening/weekend programs available. *Faculty:* 15 full-time (2 women), 5 part-time/adjunct (0 women). *Students:* 118 part-time (34 women); includes 13 minority (2 Black or African American, non-Hispanic/Latino; 8 Asian, non-Hispanic/Latino; 3 Hispanic/Latino). Average age 30. In 2010, 35 master's awarded. *Degree requirements:* For master's, minimum GPA of 3.0. *Entrance requirements:* For master's, GMAT. Additional exam requirements/recommendations for international students: Required—TOEFL (minimum score 550 paper-based; 213 computer-based; 80 iBT). *Application deadline:* For fall admission, 6/30 for domestic and international students. Application fee: $50. Electronic applications accepted. *Expenses:* Tuition: Part-time $700 per credit. Part-time tuition and fees vary according to degree level and program. *Financial support:* Scholarships/grants available. Support available to part-time students. Financial award application deadline: 6/30; financial award applicants required to submit FAFSA. *Faculty research:* Developing and leveraging technology, ethical business practices, managing for innovation and creativity, the global political economy, strategic marketing management. *Unit head:* Meredith L. Kwiatek, Director of Graduate Recruitment & Marketing, 610-519-7016, Fax: 610-519-6273, E-mail: rachel.garonzik@villanova.edu. *Application contact:* Meredith L. Kwiatek, Assistant Director, 610-519-7016, Fax: 610-519-6273, E-mail: meredith.kwiatek@villanova.edu.

Villanova University, Villanova School of Business, MBA—The Flex Track Program, Villanova, PA 19085. Offers finance (MBA); health care management (MBA); international business (MBA); management information systems (MBA); marketing (MBA); real estate (MBA); strategic management (MBA); JD/MBA. *Accreditation:* AACSB. Part-time and evening/weekend programs available. Postbaccalaureate distance learning degree programs offered (minimal on-campus study). *Faculty:* 31 full-time (5 women), 22 part-time/adjunct (2 women). *Students:* 15 full-time (6 women), 443 part-time (150 women); includes 46 minority (5 Black or African American, non-Hispanic/Latino; 35 Asian, non-Hispanic/Latino; 6 Hispanic/Latino). Average age 30. In 2010, 133 master's awarded. *Degree requirements:* For master's, minimum GPA of 3.0. *Entrance requirements:* For master's, GMAT. Additional exam requirements/recommendations for international students: Required—TOEFL (minimum score 550 paper-based; 213 computer-based; 80 iBT). *Application deadline:* For fall admission, 6/30 for domestic and international students; for winter admission, 11/15 for domestic and international students; for spring admission, 3/30 for domestic students, 3/31 for international students. Applications are processed on a rolling basis. Application fee: $50. Electronic applications accepted. *Expenses:* Tuition: Part-time $700 per credit. Part-time tuition and fees vary according to degree level and program. *Financial support:* In 2010–11, 15 research assistantships with full tuition reimbursements (averaging $13,100 per year) were awarded; scholarships/grants and unspecified assistantships also available. Support available to part-time students. Financial award application deadline: 6/30; financial award applicants required to submit FAFSA. *Faculty research:* Developing and leveraging technology, ethical business practices, managing for innovation and creativity, the global political economy, strategic marketing management. *Unit head:* Meredith L. Kwiatek, Director of Graduate Recruitment and Marketing, 610-519-7016, Fax: 610-519-6273, E-mail: meredith.kwiatek@villanova.edu. *Application contact:* Meredith L. Kwiatek, Assistant Director, 610-519-7016, Fax: 610-519-6273, E-mail: meredith.kwiatek@villanova.edu.

Virginia Commonwealth University, Graduate School, School of Business, Program in Information Systems, Richmond, VA 23284-9005. Offers MS, PhD. *Faculty:* 13 full-time (3 women). *Students:* 27 full-time (8 women), 22 part-time (4 women); includes 19 minority (13 Black or African American, non-Hispanic/Latino; 2 Asian, non-Hispanic/Latino; 2 Hispanic/Latino; 2 Two or more races, non-Hispanic/Latino), 5 international. 20 applicants, 40% accepted, 6 enrolled. In 2010, 32 master's awarded. *Degree requirements:* For doctorate, thesis/dissertation. *Entrance requirements:* For master's, GMAT. Additional exam requirements/recommendations for international students: Required—TOEFL (minimum score 600 paper-based; 250 computer-based; 100 iBT); Recommended—IELTS (minimum score 6.5). *Application deadline:* For fall admission, 7/15 for domestic students; for spring admission, 11/1 for domestic students. Applications are processed on a rolling basis. Application fee: $50. Electronic applications accepted. *Expenses:* Tuition, state resident: full-time $4308; part-time $479 per credit hour. Tuition, nonresident: full-time $8942; part-time $994 per credit hour. Required fees: $2000; $85 per credit hour. Tuition and fees vary according to course level, course load, degree level, campus/location and program. *Financial support:* Fellowships, research assistantships, teaching assistantships, Federal Work-Study, institutionally sponsored loans, and tuition waivers (full and partial) available. Financial award application deadline: 3/15; financial award applicants required to submit FAFSA. *Unit head:* Dr. Richard Redmond, Chair,

804-828-1737, Fax: 804-828-3199, E-mail: rtredmon@vcu.edu. *Application contact:* Jana P. McQuaid, Assistant Dean, Masters Programs, 804-828-4622, Fax: 804-828-7174, E-mail: jpmcquaid@vcu.edu.

Virginia Polytechnic Institute and State University, Graduate School, Intercollege, Program in Information Technology, Blacksburg, VA 24061. Offers MIT. *Students:* 11 full-time (3 women), 274 part-time (58 women); includes 32 Black or African American, non-Hispanic/Latino; 1 American Indian or Alaska Native, non-Hispanic/Latino; 35 Asian, non-Hispanic/Latino; 9 Hispanic/Latino, 24 international. Average age 34. 99 applicants, 77% accepted, 56 enrolled. In 2010, 78 master's awarded. *Degree requirements:* For master's, comprehensive exam (for some programs), thesis (for some programs). *Entrance requirements:* For master's, GRE. Additional exam requirements/recommendations for international students: Required—TOEFL (minimum score 550 paper-based; 213 computer-based). *Application deadline:* For fall admission, 7/1 for domestic and international students; for spring admission, 12/1 for domestic and international students. Applications are processed on a rolling basis. Application fee: $65. Electronic applications accepted. *Expenses:* Tuition, state resident: full-time $9399; part-time $488 per credit hour. Tuition, nonresident: full-time $17,854; part-time $957.75 per credit hour. Required fees: $1534. Full-time tuition and fees vary according to program. *Financial support:* Career-related internships or fieldwork, Federal Work-Study, scholarships/grants, health care benefits, and unspecified assistantships available. Financial award application deadline: 1/15. Total annual research expenditures: $125,985. *Unit head:* Dr. Thomas T. Sheehan, UNIT HEAD, 703-538-8361, Fax: 703-538-8415, E-mail: thsheeha@vt.edu. *Application contact:* Cindy Rubens, Contact, 703-818-8464, Fax: 703-538-8415, E-mail: crubens@vt.edu.

Virginia Polytechnic Institute and State University, Graduate School, Pamplin College of Business, Department of Business Information Technology, Blacksburg, VA 24061. Offers PhD. *Faculty:* 22 full-time (6 women). *Students:* 8 full-time (1 woman), 2 part-time (0 women); includes 1 Black or African American, non-Hispanic/Latino, 4 international. Average age 34. 11 applicants, 27% accepted, 2 enrolled. In 2010, 3 doctorates awarded. *Degree requirements:* For doctorate, comprehensive exam (for some programs), thesis/dissertation (for some programs). *Entrance requirements:* For doctorate, GRE. Additional exam requirements/recommendations for international students: Required—TOEFL (minimum score 550 paper-based; 213 computer-based). *Application deadline:* For fall admission, 7/1 for domestic and international students; for spring admission, 12/1 for domestic students, 11/1 for international students. Applications are processed on a rolling basis. Application fee: $65. Electronic applications accepted. *Expenses:* Tuition, state resident: full-time $9399; part-time $488 per credit hour. Tuition, nonresident: full-time $17,854; part-time $957.75 per credit hour. Required fees: $1534. Full-time tuition and fees vary according to program. *Financial support:* In 2010–11, 1 research assistantship with full tuition reimbursement (averaging $15,674 per year), 5 teaching assistantships with full tuition reimbursements (averaging $17,873 per year) were awarded; career-related internships or fieldwork, Federal Work-Study, scholarships/grants, health care benefits, and unspecified assistantships also available. Financial award application deadline: 1/15. *Faculty research:* Mathematical programming, computer simulation, decision support systems, production/operations research, information technology. *Unit head:* Dr. Bernard W. Taylor, UNIT HEAD, 540-231-6596, Fax: 540-231-7916, E-mail: betaylo3@vt.edu. *Application contact:* Cliff Ragsdale, Contact, 540-231-4697, Fax: 540-231-7916, E-mail: cragsdal@vt.edu.

Walden University, Graduate Programs, School of Management, Minneapolis, MN 55401. Offers accounting (MS), including cpa emphasis, professional track, self-designed; accounting and management (MS), including self-designed, strategic management; applied management and decision sciences (PhD), including accounting, engineering management, finance, general applied management and decision sciences, information systems management, knowledge management, leadership and organizational change, learning management, operations research, self-designed program in applied management and design sciences; business information management (MISM); enterprise information security (MISM); entrepreneurship (MBA, DBA); finance (MBA, DBA); global management (MS); global supply chain management (DBA); health informatics (MISM); healthcare management (MBA, MS); healthcare system improvement (MBA); human resource management (MBA, MS), including functional human resource management (MS), human resource management (MS), integrating functional and strategic human resource management (MS), organizational strategy (MS); information systems (MS); information systems management (DBA); information technology (MS), including information security, software engineering; international business (MBA, DBA); IT strategy and governance (MISM); leadership (MBA, MS, DBA), including entrepreneurship (MS), general management (MS), human resources leadership (MS), innovation and technology (MS), leader development (MS), leading sustainability (MS), project management (MS), self-designed (MS); managers as leaders (MS); managing global software and service supply chains (MISM); marketing (MBA, DBA); project management (MBA, MS); research strategies (MS); risk management (MBA); self-designed (MBA, DBA); social impact management (DBA); strategy and operations (MS); sustainable futures (MBA); sustainable management (MS); technology (MBA); technology entrepreneurship (DBA); technology management (MS).

Part-time and evening/weekend programs available. Postbaccalaureate distance learning degree programs offered (minimal on-campus study). *Faculty:* 22 full-time (8 women), 291 part-time/adjunct (100 women). *Students:* 3,705 full-time (1,956 women), 976 part-time (549 women); includes 2,432 minority (2,021 Black or African American, non-Hispanic/Latino; 32 American Indian or Alaska Native, non-Hispanic/Latino; 137 Asian, non-Hispanic/Latino; 193 Hispanic/Latino; 5 Native Hawaiian or other Pacific Islander, non-Hispanic/Latino; 44 Two or more races, non-Hispanic/Latino), 302 international. Average age 40. In 2010, 658 master's, 86 doctorates awarded. *Degree requirements:* For doctorate, thesis/dissertation (for some programs), residency. *Entrance requirements:* For master's, bachelor's degree or equivalent in related field; minimum GPA of 2.5; official transcripts; goal statement; access to computer and Internet; for doctorate, master's degree or equivalent in related field; minimum GPA of 3.0; 3 years of related professional/academic experience (preferred). Additional exam requirements/recommendations for international students: Required—TOEFL (minimum score 550 paper-based; 213 computer-based), IELTS (minimum score 6.5), Michigan English Language Assessment Battery (minimum score 82). *Application deadline:* Applications are processed on a rolling basis. Application fee: $50. Electronic applications accepted. *Expenses:* Tuition: Full-time $10,274; part-time $445 per credit. Tuition and fees vary according to course load, degree level and program. *Financial support:* Fellowships, Federal Work-Study, scholarships/grants, unspecified assistantships, and family tuition reduction, active duty/veteran tuition reduction, group tuition reduction, interest-free payment plans available. Support available to part-time students. Financial award applicants required to submit FAFSA. *Unit head:* Dr. William Schulz, Associate Dean, 800-925-3368. *Application contact:* Jennifer Hall, Vice President of Enrollment Management, 866-4-WALDEN, E-mail: info@waldenu.edu.

Washington State University, Graduate School, College of Business, Business Administration Programs, Pullman, WA 99164. Offers business administration (MBA, PhD), including accounting (PhD), finance (PhD), management and operations (PhD), management information systems (PhD), marketing (PhD). *Accreditation:* AACSB. *Faculty:* 47. *Students:* 117 full-time (42 women), 117 part-time (30 women); includes 24 minority (1 Black or African American, non-Hispanic/Latino; 17 Asian, non-Hispanic/Latino; 5 Hispanic/Latino; 1 Two or more races, non-Hispanic/Latino), 48 international. Average age 32. 347 applicants, 19% accepted, 43 enrolled. In 2010, 58 master's, 5 doctorates awarded. *Degree requirements:* For master's, comprehensive exam (for some programs), thesis (for some programs), final presentation; for doctorate, comprehensive exam, thesis/dissertation, oral and written exams. *Entrance requirements:* For master's and doctorate, GMAT, minimum GPA of 3.0, 3 letters of recommendation. Additional exam requirements/recommendations for international students: Required—TOEFL. *Application deadline:* For fall admission, 3/1 priority date for domestic students, 3/1 for international students; for spring admission, 6/1 priority date for domestic students, 6/1 for international students. Applications are processed on a rolling basis. Application fee: $50. Electronic applications accepted. *Expenses:* Tuition, state resident: full-time $8552; part-time $443 per credit. Tuition, nonresident: full-time $21,650; part-time $1083 per credit. Required fees: $846. *Financial support:* In 2010–11, 102 students received support, including 36 teaching assistantships with full and partial tuition reimbursements available (averaging $18,204 per year); career-related internships or fieldwork, Federal Work-Study, institutionally sponsored loans, health care benefits, tuition waivers (partial), unspecified assistantships, and teaching associateships also available. Financial award application deadline: 4/1. Total annual research expenditures: $344,000. *Unit head:* Dr. Eric Spangenberg, Dean, 509-335-8150, E-mail: ers@wsu.edu. *Application contact:* Graduate School Admissions, 800-GRADWSU, Fax: 509-335-1949, E-mail: gradsch@wsu.edu.

Washington State University, Graduate School, College of Business, Department of Accounting, Pullman, WA 99164. Offers accounting and information systems (M Acc); accounting and taxation (M Acc). *Accreditation:* AACSB. *Faculty:* 9. *Students:* 47 full-time (25 women), 13 part-time (5 women); includes 7 minority (2 American Indian or Alaska Native, non-Hispanic/Latino; 4 Asian, non-Hispanic/Latino; 1 Hispanic/Latino), 19 international. Average age 27. 123 applicants, 37% accepted, 45 enrolled. In 2010, 28 master's awarded. *Degree requirements:* For master's, comprehensive exam (for some programs), thesis (for some programs), oral exam, research paper. *Entrance requirements:* For master's, GMAT (minimum score of 600), resume; statement of purpose identifying area of interest, experiences, and intended research focus; minimum GPA of 3.25. Additional exam requirements/recommendations for international students: Required—TOEFL (minimum score 580 paper-based; 237 computer-based), IELTS. *Application deadline:* For fall admission, 1/10 priority date for domestic students, 1/10 for international students. Applications are processed on a rolling basis. Application fee: $50. Electronic applications accepted. *Expenses:* Tuition, state resident: full-time $8552; part-time $443 per credit. Tuition, nonresident: full-time $21,650; part-time $1083 per credit. Required fees: $846. *Financial support:* In 2010–11, research assistantships (averaging $13,917 per year), 7 teaching assistantships with tuition reimbursements (averaging $18,204 per year) were awarded; Federal Work-Study, institutionally sponsored loans, tuition waivers (partial), and teaching associateships also available. Financial award application deadline: 3/1. *Faculty research:* Ethics, taxation, auditing. *Unit head:* Dr. John

Sweeney, Chair, 509-335-8541, Fax: 509-335-4275, E-mail: jtsweeney@wsu.edu. *Application contact:* Graduate School Admissions, 800-GRADWSU, Fax: 509-335-1949, E-mail: gradsch@wsu.edu.

West Chester University of Pennsylvania, Office of Graduate Studies, College of Arts and Sciences, Department of Computer Science, West Chester, PA 19383. Offers computer science (MS); computer security (Certificate); information systems (Certificate); Web technology (Certificate). Part-time and evening/weekend programs available. *Students:* 10 full-time (1 woman), 9 part-time (1 woman); includes 2 minority (1 Black or African American, non-Hispanic/Latino; 1 Hispanic/Latino), 6 international. Average age 29. 23 applicants, 57% accepted, 5 enrolled. In 2010, 11 master's, 1 other advanced degree awarded. *Degree requirements:* For master's, thesis optional. *Entrance requirements:* For master's, GRE, two letters of recommendation; for Certificate, BS. Additional exam requirements/recommendations for international students: Required—TOEFL (minimum score 550 paper-based; 213 computer-based; 80 iBT). *Application deadline:* For fall admission, 4/15 priority date for domestic students, 3/15 for international students; for spring admission, 10/15 for domestic students, 9/1 for international students. Applications are processed on a rolling basis. Application fee: $35. Electronic applications accepted. *Expenses:* Tuition, state resident: full-time $6966; part-time $387 per credit. Tuition, nonresident: full-time $11,146; part-time $619 per credit. Required fees: $1614.40; $133.24 per credit. Part-time tuition and fees vary according to campus/location. *Financial support:* Unspecified assistantships available. Support available to part-time students. Financial award application deadline: 2/15; financial award applicants required to submit FAFSA. *Faculty research:* Automata theory, compilers, non well-founded sets, security in sensor and mobile ad-hoc networks, intrusion detection, security and trust in pervasive computing, economic modeling of security protocols. *Unit head:* Dr. James Fabrey, Chair, 610-436-2204, E-mail: jfabrey@wcupa.edu. *Application contact:* Dr. Afrand Agah, Graduate Coordinator, 610-436-4419, E-mail: aagah@wcupa.edu.

Worcester Polytechnic Institute, Graduate Studies, School of Business, Worcester, MA 01609-2280. Offers information technology (MS), including information security management; management (Graduate Certificate); marketing and technological innovation (MS); operations design and leadership (MS); technology (MBA). *Accreditation:* AACSB. Part-time and evening/weekend programs available. Postbaccalaureate distance learning degree programs offered (minimal on-campus study). *Faculty:* 13 full-time (7 women), 9 part-time/adjunct (2 women). *Students:* 112 full-time (53 women), 135 part-time (33 women); includes 5 Black or African American, non-Hispanic/Latino; 1 Hispanic/Latino; 15 Native Hawaiian or other Pacific Islander, non-Hispanic/Latino, 105 international. 396 applicants, 67% accepted, 79 enrolled. In 2010, 69 degrees awarded. *Degree requirements:* For master's, thesis optional. *Entrance requirements:* For master's, GMAT (MBA), GMAT or GRE General Test (MS), resume; for Graduate Certificate, GMAT or GRE General Test, statement of purpose, 3 letters of recommendation. Additional exam requirements/recommendations for international students:

Required—TOEFL (minimum score 550 paper-based; 213 computer-based; 79 iBT), IELTS (minimum score 6.5). *Application deadline:* For fall admission, 6/1 priority date for domestic and international students; for spring admission, 11/1 priority date for domestic students, 10/1 priority date for international students. Applications are processed on a rolling basis. Application fee: $70. Electronic applications accepted. *Expenses:* Tuition: Full-time $20,862; part-time $1159 per term. One-time fee: $15. *Financial support:* Career-related internships or fieldwork, institutionally sponsored loans, scholarships/grants, and unspecified assistantships available. Financial award application deadline: 6/1; financial award applicants required to submit FAFSA. *Faculty research:* Organizational aesthetics, resistance in organizations, dynamics of product innovation, economic approaches to productivity, corporate earnings forecasts and value relevance, ERP implementation, improving Web accessibility, information quality assessment, measuring strategic and transactional IT, website quality, service operations modeling, healthcare operations and performance analysis, loan process design. *Unit head:* Dr. Mark Rice, Dean, 508-831-4665, Fax: 508-831-5218, E-mail: rice@wpi.edu. *Application contact:* Alyssa Bates, Director, Graduate Management Programs, 508-831-4665, Fax: 508-831-5720, E-mail: ajbates@wpi.edu.

Xavier University, Williams College of Business, Master of Business Administration Program, Cincinnati, OH 45207-3221. Offers business administration (Exec MBA, MBA); business intelligence (MBA); finance (MBA); international business (MBA); management information systems (MBA); marketing (MBA); MBA/MHSA; MSN/MBA. *Accreditation:* AACSB. Part-time and evening/weekend programs available. *Faculty:* 37 full-time (13 women), 9 part-time/adjunct (2 women). *Students:* 200 full-time (60 women), 735 part-time (239 women); includes 128 minority (48 Black or African American, non-Hispanic/Latino; 3 American Indian or Alaska Native, non-Hispanic/Latino; 54 Asian, non-Hispanic/Latino; 22 Hispanic/Latino; 1 Native Hawaiian or other Pacific Islander, non-Hispanic/Latino), 32 international. Average age 30. 223 applicants, 85% accepted, 139 enrolled. In 2010, 323 master's awarded. *Degree requirements:* For master's, capstone course. *Entrance requirements:* For master's, GMAT. Additional exam requirements/recommendations for international students: Required—TOEFL (minimum score 550 paper-based; 213 computer-based; 80 iBT). *Application deadline:* For fall admission, 8/1 priority date for domestic students, 5/1 for international students; for spring admission, 12/1 priority date for domestic students, 9/1 for international students. Applications are processed on a rolling basis. Application fee: $35. Electronic applications accepted. *Expenses:* Contact institution. *Financial support:* In 2010–11, 176 students received support. Scholarships/grants, tuition waivers (partial), and unspecified assistantships available. Financial award application deadline: 3/1; financial award applicants required to submit FAFSA. *Unit head:* Dr. Hema Krishnan, Associate Dean, 513-745-3206, Fax: 513-745-3455, E-mail: krishnan@xavier.edu. *Application contact:* Anna Marie Whelan, Assistant Director, MBA Programs, 513-745-3525, Fax: 513-745-2929, E-mail: whelana@xavier.edu.

OVERVIEW

Businesses today operate in a highly competitive global marketplace, and business leaders must always be cognizant of and proactive with the business' vision, objectives, and policies. The MBA with a strategic management specialization focuses on the process of strategically positioning an organization for success. This degree program prepares graduates to effectively analyze operations, address competition, survive volatile markets, and evolve operations in a fast-paced business environment by understanding the importance of defining a corporate strategy and implementing technology methodologies.

Within the strategic management MBA curriculum, students learn how to recognize, analyze, respond to, and strategically plan for changing laws and regulations; financial and economic challenges; technological changes; organizational, as well as socio-cultural issues; and domestic and international trends. The formal and systematic management methods of directing and motivating group efforts toward achieving the organization's primary objective are covered, as are the changes that occur in the industry along with the developmentation of an analytical framework for evaluating organizational and competitive strategy responses. A strategic management MBA prepares graduates for multifunctional line responsibilities and planning assignments, including preparing environmental and industry analysis studies, investigating business opportunities, and making strategic assessments.

Required courses may include study in:

- Accounting and Finance Concepts for Managers
- The Economics of Management
- Enterprise Management in a Global Environment
- Ethical and Legal Environment of Business
- Decision Points in Marketing and Operations
- Developing Effective Organizations
- Managing Change
- Strategy Formulation

Elective courses may include study in:

- Achieving Social Impact
- Building and Managing Professional Sales Organizations
- Controllership
- Global Management
- Global Value Chain Strategies
- Information Systems Management
- Leadership: Explored and Applied
- Professional Communications
- Social Entrepreneurship
- Strategy Implementation and Management

The strategic management MBA is key for success in the management and leadership of businesses, both domestically and globally. Strategic management MBA graduates will have developed the critical thinking necessary to plan and manage international resource strategies or to undertake international management consultancy. With strategy needed in every department of any organization, graduates can look to fill roles in HR strategy, financial strategy, and management strategy, oftentimes at a consultant level.

IN THIS SECTION

You'll find profiles of institutions offering graduate programs in the following fields:

You'll also find a Close-Up—in-depth information—from the following institution:

HELPFUL ORGANIZATIONS/ PUBLICATIONS/BLOGS

The International Society of Sustainability Professionals (ISSP)

http://www.sustainabilityprofessionals.org/

The International Society of Sustainability Professionals (ISSP) is a nonprofit, member-driven association for professionals who are committed to making sustainability standard practice. Members share resources and best practices and develop themselves professionally. Special reports, salary surveys, and the knowledge competency study are just a sampling of the content offered to members.

ISSP is the premier global professional association supporting sustainability practitioners through the following:

- Research—investigating cutting-edge concepts and practices in the field of sustainability
- Resources—sharing best practices from around the world
- Professional Development—enhancing careers through career coaching, job postings, and learning events

The Association for Public Policy Analysis & Management (APPAM)

http://www.appam.org/

The Association for Public Policy Analysis & Management (APPAM) is a nonprofit organization dedicated to improving public policy and management by fostering excellence in research, analysis, and education. With more than 1,500 academic, practitioner, organizational, and institutional members, APPAM promotes its mission through its annual Fall Research Conference, its journal—*Journal of Policy Analysis and Management (JPAM),* its award programs, and various activities including international and national conferences and workshops.

Strategic Management Society (SMS)

http://strategicmanagement.net/

Founded in London in 1981, the Strategic Management Society (SMS) brings together the worlds of reflective practice and thoughtful scholarship. The Society consists of 2,600 members from more than 60 different countries. Membership, composed of academics, business practitioners, and consultants, focuses on the development and dissemination of insights on the strategic management process, as well as on fostering contacts and interchange around the world.

The SMS holds its annual meeting at various sites worldwide, typically alternating between North America and Europe. Each conference addresses a current theme, with specific tracks addressing sub-themes, and presents multiple sessions by leading experts in the field from around the world. The SMS has responded to membership interest in special topics through its introduction of a series of smaller, regionally based Special Conferences, addressing more specific industry or subject themes.

CAREER ASPIRATIONS: A PROSPECTIVE POSITION

Director of Commercial Sustainability, ABC Mineral Company

Job Description

The Director of Commercial Sustainability's chief function is to increase the long-term sustainability of our company's largest market—filtration—by developing a suite of useful and economical outlets for spent filter cake worldwide.

Responsibilities

- Develop/implement sustainable solutions for spent cake reuse and recycle with company customers, using both internal and external resources.
- Become a subject matter expert on diatomaceous earth and its use in various filtration processes.
- Develop and implement sustainable and economic outlets for spent filter cake.
- Understand regulatory disposal and reuse restrictions/barriers for spent cake globally.
- Develop key partnerships with existing companies worldwide that currently process spent filter cake.
- Develop a strong understanding of the current state of knowledge and what uses already exist for spent cake.
- Identify potential partners/universities/customers to assist efforts in determining uses for spent cake.
- Identify and recommend focused regions and markets for research.
- Work with filtration customers to build consensus on best uses for spent cake and potential end-users.

Qualifications

- Technically adept with raw materials and capable of developing sustainable strategies across industries
- Strong project engineering/project management background
- A technical degree (preferably in chemical or mechanical engineering); an advanced degree or an MBA preferred
- Proven track record of delivering results and developing creative solutions to problems using both internal and external resources
- History of working with groups of customers to find common solutions to problems
- Excellent economic modeling and analytical skills
- Excellent strategic thinking capabilities and ability to see and take advantage of new and emerging market trends
- Ability to work with a high degree of autonomy
- Ability to work and influence across industries
- Experience working internationally and domestically
- Experience working in an industrial environment heavily influenced by government regulations
- Excellent communication (written and verbal) and presentation skills

MANAGEMENT STRATEGY AND POLICY

American Public University System, AMU/APU Graduate Programs, Charles Town, WV 25414. Offers accounting (MBA); administration and supervision (M Ed); air warfare (MA Military Studies); asymmetrical warfare (MA Military Studies); criminal justice (MA); emergency and disaster management (MA); entrepreneurship (MBA); environmental policy and management (MS); finance (MBA); general (MBA); global business management (MBA); guidance and counseling (M Ed); history (MA); homeland security (MA); homeland security resource allocation (MBA); humanities (MA); information technology (MS); information technology management (MBA); intelligence studies (MA); international relations and conflict resolution (MA); joint warfare (MA Military Studies); land warfare (MA Military Studies); legal studies (MA); management (MA), including defense mangement, general, human resource management, organizational leadership, public administration; marketing (MBA); military history (MA); national security studies (MA); naval warfare (MA Military Studies); nonprofit management (MBA); political science (MA); psychology (MA); public administration (MA); public health (MA); security management (MA); space studies (MS); sports management (MS); strategic leadership (MA Military Studies); teaching (M Ed), including elementary, secondary social sciences; transportation and logistics management (MA). Programs offered via distance learning only. Part-time and evening/weekend programs available. Postbaccalaureate distance learning degree programs offered (no on-campus study). *Faculty:* 253 full-time (134 women), 1,208 part-time/adjunct (570 women). *Students:* 956 full-time (422 women), 8,476 part-time (2,821 women); includes 2,511 minority (1,218 Black or African American, non-Hispanic/Latino; 68 American Indian or Alaska Native, non-Hispanic/Latino; 219 Asian, non-Hispanic/Latino; 705 Hispanic/Latino; 46 Native Hawaiian or other Pacific Islander, non-Hispanic/Latino; 255 Two or more races, non-Hispanic/Latino), 107 international. Average age 35. 9,550 applicants, 100% accepted. In 2010, 1,688 master's awarded. *Degree requirements:* For master's, comprehensive exam or practicum. *Entrance requirements:* For master's, official transcript showing earned bachelor's degree from institution accredited by recognized accrediting body. Additional exam requirements/recommendations for international students: Required—TOEFL (minimum score 550 paper-based; 213 computer-based), IELTS (minimum score 6.5). *Application deadline:* Applications are processed on a rolling basis. Application fee: $0. Electronic applications accepted. *Financial support:* Applicants required to submit FAFSA. *Faculty research:* Military history, criminal justice, management performance, national security. *Unit head:* Dr. Frank McCluskey, Provost, 877-468-6268, Fax: 304-724-3780. *Application contact:* Terry Grant, Director of Enrollment Management, 877-468-6268, Fax: 304-724-3780, E-mail: info@apus.edu.

Azusa Pacific University, School of Business and Management, Azusa, CA 91702-7000. Offers business administration (MBA); diversity for strategic advantage (MA); entrepreneurship (MBA); finance (MBA); human and organizational development (MA); human resources and organizational development (MBA); human resources management (MA); international business (MBA); marketing (MBA); non-profit management (MA); organizational development and change (MA); performance improvement (MA); public administration (MA); strategic management (MBA). Part-time and evening/weekend programs available. *Faculty:* 19 full-time (5 women), 2 part-time/adjunct (1 woman). *Students:* 75 full-time (41 women), 96 part-time (46 women); includes 65 minority (15 Black or African American, non-Hispanic/Latino; 15 Asian, non-Hispanic/Latino; 34 Hispanic/Latino; 1 Native Hawaiian or other Pacific Islander, non-Hispanic/Latino), 17 international. Average age 30. In 2010, 82 master's awarded. *Degree requirements:* For master's, thesis (for some programs), final project. *Entrance requirements:* For master's, GMAT, minimum GPA of 3.0. Additional exam requirements/recommendations for international students: Required—TOEFL (minimum score 600 paper-based). *Application deadline:* For fall admission, 8/15 priority date for domestic students. Applications are processed on a rolling basis. Application fee: $45 ($65 for international students). *Expenses:* Contact institution. *Financial support:* Scholarships/grants available. *Faculty research:* Gender issues, financial risk, leadership and ethics, marketing strategy. *Unit head:* Dr. Ilene Bezjian, Dean, 626-815-3090, Fax: 626-815-3802, E-mail: ibezjian@apu.edu. *Application contact:* Dr. Ilene Bezjian, Dean, 626-815-3090, Fax: 626-815-3802, E-mail: ibezjian@apu.edu.

Boston University, Metropolitan College, Department of Computer Science, Boston, MA 02215. Offers computer information systems (MS), including computer networks, database management and business intelligence, health informatics, IT project management, security; computer science (MS), including computer networks, security; telecommunications (MS), including security. Part-time and evening/weekend programs available. Postbaccalaureate distance learning degree programs offered (no on-campus study). *Faculty:* 10 full-time (0 women), 30 part-time/adjunct (3 women). *Students:* 16 full-time (2 women), 681 part-time (155 women); includes 182 minority (44 Black or African American, non-Hispanic/Latino; 1 American Indian or Alaska Native, non-Hispanic/Latino; 88 Asian, non-Hispanic/Latino; 36 Hispanic/Latino; 2 Native Hawaiian or other Pacific Islander, non-Hispanic/Latino; 11

Two or more races, non-Hispanic/Latino), 66 international. Average age 35. 273 applicants, 78% accepted, 155 enrolled. In 2010, 143 master's awarded. *Degree requirements:* For master's, thesis optional. *Entrance requirements:* For master's, 3 letters of recommendation, professional resume. Additional exam requirements/recommendations for international students: Required—TOEFL (minimum score 550 paper-based; 213 computer-based; 80 iBT). *Application deadline:* For fall admission, 6/1 priority date for international students; for spring admission, 10/1 priority date for international students. Applications are processed on a rolling basis. Application fee: $70. Electronic applications accepted. *Expenses:* Tuition: Full-time $39,314; part-time $1228 per credit. Required fees: $40 per semester. *Financial support:* In 2010–11, 9 research assistantships with partial tuition reimbursements (averaging $5,000 per year) were awarded; career-related internships or fieldwork and unspecified assistantships also available. Support available to part-time students. Financial award applicants required to submit FAFSA. *Faculty research:* Medical informatics, Web technologies, telecom and networks, security and forensics, software engineering, programming languages, multimedia and AI, information systems and IT project management. *Unit head:* Dr. Lubomir Chitkushev, Chairman, 617-353-2566, Fax: 617-353-2367, E-mail: csinfo@bu.edu. *Application contact:* Kim Richards, Program Coordinator, 617-353-2566, Fax: 617-353-2367, E-mail: kimrich@bu.edu.

California State University, East Bay, Office of Academic Programs and Graduate Studies, College of Business and Economics, Department of Information Technology Management, Option in Strategy and International Business, Hayward, CA 94542-3000. Offers MBA. Part-time and evening/weekend programs available. *Degree requirements:* For master's, comprehensive exam or thesis. *Entrance requirements:* For master's, GMAT, minimum GPA of 2.75. Additional exam requirements/recommendations for international students: Required—TOEFL (minimum score 550 paper-based; 213 computer-based). *Application deadline:* For fall admission, 6/30 for domestic and international students. Application fee: $55. *Financial support:* Career-related internships or fieldwork, Federal Work-Study, institutionally sponsored loans, and scholarships/grants available. Support available to part-time students. Financial award application deadline: 3/1. *Unit head:* Dr. Xinjian Lu, Chair, 510-885-3307, E-mail: xinjian.lu@csueastbay.edu. *Application contact:* Donna Wiley, Interim Associate Director, 510-885-2928, Fax: 510-885-4777, E-mail: donna.wiley@csueastbay.edu.

California State University, East Bay, Office of Academic Programs and Graduate Studies, College of Business and Economics, MBA Program, Hayward, CA 94542-3000. Offers entrepreneurship (MBA); finance (MBA); human resources and organizational behavior (MBA); information technology management (MBA); marketing management (MBA); operations and supply chain management (MBA); strategy and international business (MBA). Part-time and evening/weekend programs available. Postbaccalaureate distance learning degree programs offered (no on-campus study). *Faculty:* 33 full-time (9 women). *Students:* 121 full-time (58 women), 133 part-time (67 women); includes 7 Black or African American, non-Hispanic/Latino; 63 Asian, non-Hispanic/Latino; 11 Hispanic/Latino; 3 Native Hawaiian or other Pacific Islander, non-Hispanic/Latino; 5 Two or more races, non-Hispanic/Latino, 87 international. Average age 30. 284 applicants, 47% accepted, 55 enrolled. In 2010, 241 master's awarded. *Degree requirements:* For master's, comprehensive exam or thesis. *Entrance requirements:* For master's, GMAT (minimum 20th percentile verbal and quantitative section), bachelor's degree, minimum GPA of 2.75. Additional exam requirements/recommendations for international students: Required—TOEFL (minimum score 550 paper-based; 213 computer-based; 79 iBT). *Application deadline:* For fall admission, 6/30 for domestic and international students. Applications are processed on a rolling basis. Application fee: $55. Electronic applications accepted. *Financial support:* Career-related internships or fieldwork, Federal Work-Study, institutionally sponsored loans, and scholarships/grants available. Support available to part-time students. Financial award application deadline: 3/2; financial award applicants required to submit FAFSA. *Unit head:* Dr. Terri Swartz, Dean, 510-885-3291, Fax: 510-885-4884, E-mail: terri.swartz@csueastbay.edu. *Application contact:* Dr. Donna Wiley, Interim Associate Director, 510-885-2928, Fax: 510-885-4777, E-mail: donna.wiley@csueastbay.edu.

Claremont Graduate University, Graduate Programs, Peter F. Drucker and Masatoshi Ito Graduate School of Management, Program in Executive Management, Claremont, CA 91711-6160. Offers advanced management (MS); executive management (EMBA); leadership (Certificate); management (MA, PhD, Certificate); strategy (Certificate). *Accreditation:* AACSB. Part-time programs available. *Students:* 35 full-time (18 women), 76 part-time (29 women); includes 7 Black or African American, non-Hispanic/Latino; 1 American Indian or Alaska Native, non-Hispanic/Latino; 26 Asian, non-Hispanic/Latino; 21 Hispanic/Latino; 2 Two or more races, non-Hispanic/Latino. Average age 44. In 2010, 31 master's, 1 doctorate, 71 other advanced degrees awarded. *Entrance requirements:* Additional exam requirements/recommendations for international students: Required—TOEFL (minimum score 550 paper-based; 213 computer-based; 80 iBT). *Application deadline:* For fall admission, 2/15 priority date for domestic students. Applications are processed on a rolling basis. Application fee: $60. Electronic applications accepted. *Expenses:* Contact institution. *Financial support:* Federal Work-Study, institutionally sponsored loans, and scholarships/grants available. Support available to part-time students. Financial award application deadline: 2/15; financial award applicants required to submit FAFSA. *Faculty research:* Strategy and leadership, brand management, cost management and control, organizational transformation, general management. *Unit head:* Christina Wassenaar, Director, 909-607-7812, Fax: 909-607-9104, E-mail: christina.wassenaar@cgu.edu. *Application contact:* Albert Ramos, Admissions Coordinator, 909-621-8067, Fax: 909-621-8551, E-mail: albert.ramos@cgu.edu.

DePaul University, Charles H. Kellstadt Graduate School of Business and College of Liberal Arts and Sciences, Department of Economics, Chicago, IL 60604-2287. Offers applied economics (MBA); business strategy (MBA); economics and policy analysis (MA); international business (MBA). Part-time and evening/weekend programs available. *Faculty:* 26 full-time (5 women), 21 part-time/adjunct (5 women). *Students:* 80 full-time (30 women), 31 part-time (12 women); includes 18 minority (8 Black or African American, non-Hispanic/Latino; 7 Asian, non-Hispanic/Latino; 3 Hispanic/Latino), 8 international. In 2010, 7 master's awarded. *Degree requirements:* For master's, thesis optional. *Entrance requirements:* For master's, GMAT (MBA), GRE (MS). Additional exam requirements/recommendations for international students: Required—TOEFL. *Application deadline:* For fall admission, 7/1 for domestic students; for winter admission, 10/1 for domestic students; for spring admission, 2/1 for domestic students. Applications are processed on a rolling basis. Application fee: $40. Electronic applications accepted. *Financial support:* In 2010–11, 3 students received support, including 2 research assistantships with partial tuition reimbursements available (averaging $9,999 per year). Support available to part-time students. *Faculty research:* Forensic economics, game theory sports, economics of education, banking in Poland and Thailand. *Unit head:* Dr. Thomas D. Donley, Chairperson, 312-362-8887, Fax: 312-362-5452, E-mail: tdonley@depaul.edu. *Application contact:* Gabriella Bucci, Director of Graduate Program in Economics, 773-362-6787, Fax: 312-362-5452, E-mail: gbucci@depaul.edu.

DePaul University, Charles H. Kellstadt Graduate School of Business, Department of Management, Chicago, IL 60604-2287. Offers entrepreneurship (MBA); health sector management (MBA); human resource management (MBA, MSHR); leadership/change management (MBA); management planning and strategy (MBA); operations management (MBA). Part-time and evening/weekend programs available. *Faculty:* 36 full-time (7 women), 35 part-time/adjunct (16 women). *Students:* 267 full-time (116 women), 125 part-time (43 women); includes 76 minority (24 Black or African American, non-Hispanic/Latino; 1 American Indian or Alaska Native, non-Hispanic/Latino; 33 Asian, non-Hispanic/Latino; 13 Hispanic/Latino; 1 Native Hawaiian or other Pacific Islander, non-Hispanic/Latino; 4 Two or more races, non-Hispanic/Latino), 20 international. In 2010, 112 master's awarded. *Entrance requirements:* For master's, GMAT, GRE (MSHR), 2 letters of recommendation, resume. Additional exam requirements/recommendations for international students: Required—TOEFL (minimum score 550 paper-based; 213 computer-based). *Application deadline:* For fall admission, 7/1 for domestic students; for winter admission, 10/1 for domestic students; for spring admission, 2/1 for domestic students. Applications are processed on a rolling basis. Application fee: $60. Electronic applications accepted. *Financial support:* Research assistantships available. Financial award application deadline: 4/1. *Faculty research:* Growth management, creativity and innovation, quality management and business process design, entrepreneurship. *Application contact:* Christopher E. Kinsella, Director of Cohort MBA Programs, 312-362-8810, Fax: 312-362-6677, E-mail: kgsb@depaul.edu.

DePaul University, Charles H. Kellstadt Graduate School of Business, Department of Marketing, Chicago, IL 60604-2287. Offers brand management (MBA); customer relationship management (MBA); integrated marketing communication (MBA); marketing analysis (MSMA); marketing and management (MBA); marketing strategy and analysis (MBA); marketing strategy and planning (MBA); new product management (MBA); sales leadership (MBA). Part-time and evening/weekend programs available. *Faculty:* 23 full-time (4 women), 15 part-time/adjunct (6 women). *Students:* 173 full-time (86 women), 73 part-time (36 women); includes 26 minority (5 Black or African American, non-Hispanic/Latino; 16 Asian, non-Hispanic/Latino; 4 Hispanic/Latino; 1 Native Hawaiian or other Pacific Islander, non-Hispanic/Latino), 26 international. In 2010, 88 master's awarded. *Entrance requirements:* For master's, GMAT, 2 letters of recommendation, resume. Additional exam requirements/recommendations for international students: Required—TOEFL (minimum score 550 paper-based; 213 computer-based). *Application deadline:* For fall admission, 7/1 for domestic students; for winter admission, 10/1 for domestic students; for spring admission, 2/1 for domestic students. Applications are processed on a rolling basis. Application fee: $60. Electronic applications accepted. *Financial support:* In 2010–11, 6 research assistantships with partial tuition reimbursements (averaging $2,500 per year) were awarded. Financial award application deadline: 4/30. *Faculty research:* International and marketing role in developing economics, Internet marketing, direct marketing, consumer behavior, new product development processes. Total annual research expenditures: $100,000. *Unit head:* Dr. Suzanne Louise Fogel, Chairperson and Associate Professor of Marketing, 312-362-5150, Fax: 312-362-5647, E-mail: sfogel@depaul.edu. *Application contact:* Director of MBA Programs, 312-362-8810, Fax: 312-362-6677, E-mail: kgsb@depaul.edu.

Dominican University of California, Graduate Programs, School of Business and Leadership, Program in Strategic Leadership, San Rafael, CA 94901-2298. Offers MBA. Part-time and evening/weekend programs available. *Faculty:* 1 full-time (0 women), 1 part-time/adjunct (0 women). *Students:* 1 full-time (0 women), 12 part-time (5 women); includes 3 minority (all Hispanic/Latino). Average age 32. 8 applicants, 13% accepted, 0 enrolled. In 2010, 8 master's awarded. *Degree requirements:* For master's, thesis or alternative, practicum. *Entrance requirements:* For master's, minimum GPA of 3.0. Additional exam requirements/recommendations for international students: Required—TOEFL (minimum score 550 paper-based; 213 computer-based; 80 iBT), IELTS (minimum score 7). *Application deadline:* For fall admission, 6/15 priority date for domestic and international students. Applications are processed on a rolling basis. Application fee: $40. Electronic applications accepted. *Expenses:* Contact institution. *Financial support:* Fellowships, scholarships/grants available. Support available to part-time students. Financial award application deadline: 3/2; financial award applicants required to submit FAFSA. *Unit head:* Sue Stavn, Assistant Dean, 415-482-2418, Fax: 415-459-3206, E-mail: sue.stavn@dominican.edu. *Application contact:* Robbie Hayes, Director, 415-458-3771, Fax: 415-485-3214, E-mail: robbie.hayes@dominican.edu.

Duquesne University, School of Leadership and Professional Advancement, Pittsburgh, PA 15282-0001. Offers leadership (MS), including business ethics, community leadership, global leadership, information technology, leadership, liberal studies, professional administration, sports leadership. Part-time and evening/weekend programs available. Postbaccalaureate distance learning degree programs offered (no on-campus study). *Faculty:* 1 full-time (0 women), 70 part-time/adjunct (35 women). *Students:* 275 full-time, 171 part-time; includes 20 Black or African American, non-Hispanic/Latino; 1 American Indian or Alaska Native, non-Hispanic/Latino; 6 Asian, non-Hispanic/Latino; 3 Hispanic/Latino. Average age 31. 161 applicants, 73% accepted, 103 enrolled. In 2010, 108 master's awarded. *Degree requirements:* For master's, capstone course. *Entrance requirements:* For master's, professional work experience, 500-word essay. Additional exam requirements/recommendations for international students: Required—TOEFL. *Application deadline:* Applications are processed on a rolling basis. Application fee: $0. Electronic applications accepted. *Expenses:* Tuition: Part-time $884 per credit. Required fees: $84 per credit. Tuition and fees vary according to course load. *Financial support:* Applicants required to submit FAFSA. *Unit head:* Dr. Dorothy Bassett, Dean, 412-396-2141, Fax: 412-396-4711, E-mail: bassettd@duq.edu. *Application contact:* Marianne Leister, Director of Student Services, 412-396-4933, Fax: 412-396-5072, E-mail: leister@duq.edu.

East Tennessee State University, School of Graduate Studies, Division of Cross-Disciplinary Studies, Johnson City, TN 37614. Offers archival studies (MALS); strategic leadership (MPS); training and development (MPS). Part-time programs available. Postbaccalaureate distance learning degree programs offered (no on-campus study). *Faculty:* 2 full-time (1 woman). *Students:* 14 full-time (9 women), 61 part-time (51 women); includes 11 minority (5 Black or African American, non-Hispanic/Latino; 1 American Indian or Alaska Native, non-Hispanic/Latino; 3 Hispanic/Latino; 2 Two or more races, non-Hispanic/Latino). Average age 42. 47 applicants, 66% accepted, 25 enrolled. In 2010, 14 master's, 2 other advanced degrees awarded. *Degree requirements:* For master's, comprehensive exam, professional project. *Entrance requirements:* For master's, GRE General Test, minimum GPA of 2.75, professional portfolio. Additional exam requirements/recommendations for international students: Required—TOEFL (minimum score 550 paper-based; 213 computer-based; 79 iBT). *Application deadline:* For fall admission, 6/1 for domestic students, 4/30 for international students; for spring admission, 11/1 for domestic students, 9/30 for international students. Application fee: $25 ($35 for international students). Electronic applications accepted. *Financial support:* In 2010–11, 2 research assistantships with full tuition reimbursements (averaging $5,500 per year) were awarded; teaching assistantships with full tuition reimbursements, institutionally sponsored loans, scholarships/grants, and unspecified assistantships also available. Financial award application deadline: 7/1; financial award applicants required to submit FAFSA. *Unit head:* Dr. Rick E. Osborn, Associate Dean, 423-439-4223, Fax: 423-439-7091, E-mail: osbornr@etsu.edu. *Application contact:* Admissions and Records Clerk, 423-439-4221, Fax: 423-439-5624, E-mail: gradsch@etsu.edu.

Florida State University, The Graduate School, College of Business, Tallahassee, FL 32306-1110. Offers accounting (M Acc), including accounting information services, assurance services, corporate accounting, taxation; business administration (MBA, PhD), including accounting (PhD), finance (PhD), management information systems (PhD), marketing (PhD), organizational behavior (PhD), risk management and insurance (PhD), strategic management (PhD); finance (MS); insurance (MSM); management information systems (MS); JD/MBA; MSW/MBA. *Accreditation:* AACSB. Part-time programs available. Postbaccalaureate distance learning degree programs offered (no on-campus study). *Faculty:* 107 full-time (31 women). *Students:* 196 full-time (76 women), 310 part-time (109 women); includes 27 Black or African American, non-Hispanic/Latino; 1 American Indian or Alaska Native, non-Hispanic/Latino; 31 Asian, non-Hispanic/Latino; 30 Hispanic/Latino. Average age 30. 702 applicants, 33% accepted, 205 enrolled. In 2010, 268 master's, 17 doctorates awarded. Terminal master's awarded for partial completion of doctoral program. *Degree requirements:* For doctorate, comprehensive exam, thesis/dissertation. *Entrance requirements:* For master's, GMAT, work experience (MBA, MS), minimum GPA of 3.0, letters of recommendation; for doctorate, GMAT, minimum graduate GPA of 3.5, letters of recommendation. Additional exam requirements/recommendations for international students: Required—TOEFL (minimum score 600 paper-based; 80 computer-based); Recommended—IELTS (minimum score 6.5). *Application deadline:* For fall admission, 6/1 for domestic students, 5/1 for international students; for spring admission, 10/1 for domestic students, 9/1 for international students. Applications are processed on a rolling basis. Application fee: $30. Electronic applications accepted. *Expenses:* Tuition, state resident: full-time $8238.24. *Financial support:* In 2010–11, 86 students received support, including 12 fellowships with full tuition reimbursements available (averaging $7,161 per year), 30 research assistantships with full tuition reimbursements available (averaging $6,000 per year), 43 teaching assistantships with full tuition reimbursements available (averaging $15,000 per year); career-related internships or fieldwork, scholarships/grants, health care benefits, tuition waivers (full and partial), and unspecified assistantships also available. Support available to part-time students. Financial award application deadline: 1/1. *Unit head:* Dr. Caryn Beck-Dudley, Dean, 850-644-3090, Fax: 850-644-0915. *Application contact:* Lisa Beverly, Director, Graduate Programs Admissions, 850-644-6458, Fax: 850-644-0588, E-mail: lbeverly@cob.fsu.edu.

Franklin Pierce University, Graduate Studies, Rindge, NH 03461-0060. Offers curriculum and instruction (M Ed); emerging network technology (Graduate Certificate); health administration (MBA, Graduate Certificate); human resource management (MBA, Graduate Certificate); information technology management (MS); leadership (MBA, DA); nursing (MS); physical therapy (DPT); physician assistant studies (MPAS); special education (M Ed); sports management (MS). *Accreditation:* APTA. Part-time programs available. Postbaccalaureate distance learning degree programs offered (no on-campus study). *Faculty:* 28 full-time (18 women), 72 part-time/adjunct (44 women). *Students:* 100 full-time (63 women), 487 part-time (306 women); includes 42 minority (25 Black or African American, non-Hispanic/Latino; 10 Asian, non-Hispanic/Latino; 6 Hispanic/Latino; 1 Two or more races, non-Hispanic/Latino), 67 international. Average age 38. 227 applicants, 97% accepted, 185 enrolled. In 2010, 76 master's, 46 doctorates awarded. *Degree requirements:* For master's, concentrated original research projects; student teaching; fieldwork and/or internship; leadership project; PRAXIS I and II (for M Ed); for doctorate, concentrated original research projects, clinical fieldwork and/or internship, leadership project. *Entrance requirements:* For master's, minimum GPA of 2.5, 3 letters of recommendation; competencies in accounting, economics, statistics, and computer skills through life experience or undergraduate coursework (for MBA); certification/e-portfolio, minimum C grade in all education courses (for M Ed); license to practice as RN (for MS in nursing); for doctorate, GRE, BA/BS, 3 letters of recommendation, personal mission statement, interview; writing sample (for DA program)For DPT: 80 hours of observation/work in PT settings, completion of anatomy, chemistry, physics, an statistics, all > 3.0 GPAFor DA: 2.8 cum. GPA, Master's degree completion. Additional exam requirements/recommendations for international students: Required—TOEFL (minimum score 550 paper-based; 195 computer-based; 61 iBT). *Application deadline:* Applications are processed on a rolling basis. Application fee: $0. Electronic applications accepted. *Expenses:* Tuition: Part-time $573 per credit hour. Part-time tuition and fees vary according to degree level and program. *Financial support:* In 2010–11, 121 students received support, including 32 teaching assistantships with full and partial tuition reimbursements available (averaging $8,000 per year); career-related internships or fieldwork and unspecified assistantships also available. Support available to part-time students. Financial award applicants required to submit FAFSA. *Faculty research:* Evidence-based practice in sports physical therapy, human resource management in economic crisis, leadership in nursing, innovation in sports facility management, differentiated learning and understanding by design. *Unit head:* Dr. Patricia Brown, Interim Dean of Graduate and Professional Studies, 603-899-4316, Fax: 603-229-4580, E-mail: brownp@franklinpierce.edu.

The George Washington University, School of Business, Department of Strategic Management and Public Policy, Washington, DC 20052. Offers MBA, PhD. Part-time and evening/weekend programs available. *Faculty:* 15 full-time (4 women), 6 part-time/adjunct (1 woman). *Students:* 231 full-time (101 women), 4 part-time (1 woman); includes 9 Black or African American, non-Hispanic/Latino; 1 American Indian or Alaska Native, non-Hispanic/Latino; 23 Asian, non-Hispanic/Latino; 6 Hispanic/Latino; 1 Two or more races, non-Hispanic/Latino, 71 international. Average age 28. 574 applicants, 54% accepted. In 2010, 92 master's awarded. *Degree requirements:* For doctorate, thesis/dissertation. *Entrance requirements:* For master's, GMAT; for doctorate, GMAT or GRE. Additional exam requirements/recommendations for international students: Required—TOEFL. *Application deadline:* For fall admission, 4/1 priority date for domestic students; for spring admission, 10/1 for domestic students. Applications are processed on a rolling basis. Application fee: $75. *Financial support:* In 2010–11, 1 student received support; fellowships, teaching assistantships, career-related internships or fieldwork, Federal Work-Study, and institutionally sponsored loans available. Financial award application deadline: 4/1. *Unit head:* Dr. Mark Starik, Chair, 202-994-6677, E-mail: starik@gwu.edu. *Application contact:* Kristin Williams, Asst VP Gradpec Enrlmnt Mgmt, 202-994-0467, Fax: 202-994-0371, E-mail: ksw@gwu.edu.

Grantham University, Mark Skousen School of Business, Kansas City, MO 64153. Offers business administration (MBA); business intelligence (MS); information management (MBA); information management technology (MS); information technology (MS); performance improvement (MS); project management (MBA, MSIM). Part-time and evening/weekend programs available. Postbaccalaureate distance learning degree programs offered (no on-campus study). *Students:* 74 full-time (32 women), 565 part-time (177 women); includes 218 minority (142 Black or African American, non-Hispanic/Latino; 6 American Indian or Alaska Native, non-Hispanic/Latino; 31 Asian, non-Hispanic/Latino; 37 Hispanic/Latino; 1 Native Hawaiian or other Pacific Islander, non-Hispanic/Latino; 1 Two or more races, non-Hispanic/Latino). In 2010, 126 master's awarded. *Degree requirements:* For master's, capstone project. *Entrance requirements:* For master's, bachelor's degree from accredited degree-granting institution. Additional exam requirements/recommendations for international students: Required—TOEFL (minimum score 500 paper-based; 213 computer-based; 61 iBT). *Application deadline:* Applications are processed on a rolling basis. Application fee: $0. Electronic applications accepted. *Expenses:* Tuition: Full-time $7950; part-time $265 per credit hour. One-time fee: $30. *Financial support:* Institutionally sponsored loans and scholarships/grants available. *Unit head:* Niccole Buckley, Dean, 800-955-2527, Fax: 816-595-5757, E-mail: admissions@grantham.edu. *Application contact:* Dan King, Vice President of Admissions, 800-955-2527, Fax: 816-595-5757, E-mail: admissions@grantham.edu.

HEC Montreal, School of Business Administration, Master of Science Programs in Administration, Program in Business Intelligence, Montréal, QC H3T 2A7, Canada. Offers M Sc. All courses are given in French. Part-time programs available. *Students:* 18 full-time (8 women), 10 part-time (3 women). 22 applicants, 59% accepted, 8 enrolled. In 2010, 5 master's awarded. *Degree requirements:* For master's, one foreign language, thesis. *Application deadline:* For fall admission, 3/15 for domestic and international students; for winter admission, 9/15 for domestic and international students. Application fee: $78 Canadian dollars. Electronic applications accepted. *Expenses:* Tuition, area resident: Part-time $68.93 per credit. Tuition, state resident: full-time $2481.48; part-time $188.92 per credit. Tuition, nonresident: full-time $6801; part-time $482.06 per course. International tuition: $17,354.16 full-time. Required fees: $1309.50; $30.28 per credit. $93.45 per term. Tuition and fees vary according to degree level and program. *Financial support:* Fellowships, research assistantships, teaching assistantships, scholarships/grants available. Financial award application deadline: 9/2. *Unit head:* Dr. Claude Laurin, Director, 514-340-6485, Fax: 514-340-6880, E-mail: claude.laurin@hec.ca. *Application contact:* Francine Blais, Administrative Director, 514-340-6112, Fax: 514-340-6411, E-mail: francine.blais@hec.ca.

HEC Montreal, School of Business Administration, Master of Science Programs in Administration, Program in Strategy, Montréal, QC H3T 2A7, Canada. Offers M Sc. Part-time programs available. *Students:* 17 full-time (9 women), 5 part-time (3 women). 29 applicants, 69% accepted, 14 enrolled. *Degree requirements:* For master's, one foreign language, thesis. *Application deadline:* For fall admission, 3/15 for domestic and international students; for winter admission, 9/15 for domestic and international students. Application fee: $78. Electronic applications accepted. *Expenses:* Tuition, area resident: Part-time $68.93 per credit. Tuition, state resident: full-time $2481.48; part-time $188.92 per credit. Tuition, nonresident: full-time $6801; part-time $482.06 per course. International tuition: $17,354.16 full-time. Required fees: $1309.50; $30.28 per credit. $93.45 per term. Tuition and fees vary according to degree level and program. *Financial support:* Scholarships/grants available. Financial award application deadline: 9/2. *Unit head:* Claude Laurin, Director, 514-340-6485, Fax: 514-340-6880, E-mail: claude.laurin@hec.ca. *Application contact:* Francine Blais, Administrative Director, 514-340-6112, Fax: 514-340-6411, E-mail: francine.blais@hec.ca.

Lamar University, College of Graduate Studies, College of Business, Beaumont, TX 77710. Offers accounting (MBA); experiential business and entrepreneurship (MBA); financial management (MBA); healthcare administration (MBA); information systems (MBA); management (MBA). *Accreditation:* AACSB. Part-time and evening/weekend programs available. *Faculty:* 17 full-time (4 women), 4 part-time/adjunct (0 women). *Students:* 79 full-time (37 women), 56 part-time (22 women); includes 14 Black or African American, non-Hispanic/Latino; 8 Asian, non-Hispanic/Latino; 12 Hispanic/Latino, 18 international. Average age 28. 103 applicants, 70% accepted, 40 enrolled. In 2010, 49 master's awarded. *Degree requirements:* For master's, comprehensive exam (for some programs), thesis optional. *Entrance requirements:* For master's, GMAT. Additional exam requirements/recommendations for international students: Required—TOEFL (minimum score 525 paper-based; 197 computer-based). *Application deadline:* For fall admission, 3/15 priority date for domestic students; for spring admission, 10/1 priority date for domestic students. Applications are processed on a rolling basis. Application fee: $25 ($50 for international students). *Expenses:* Tuition, state resident: full-time $4160; part-time $208 per credit hour. Tuition, nonresident: full-time $10,360; part-time $518 per credit hour. *Financial support:* In 2010–11, 12 students received support, including 4 research assistantships with partial tuition reimbursements available; fellowships with tuition reimbursements available, career-related internships or fieldwork, Federal Work-Study, institutionally sponsored loans, scholarships/grants, and tuition waivers (partial) also available. Support available to part-time students. Financial award application deadline: 4/1; financial award applicants required to submit FAFSA. *Faculty research:* Marketing, finance, quantitative methods, management information systems, legal, environmental. *Unit head:* Dr. Enrique R. Venta, Dean, 409-880-8604, Fax: 409-880-8088, E-mail: henry.venta@lamar.edu. *Application contact:* Dr. Brad Mayer, Professor and Associate Dean, 409-880-2383, Fax: 409-880-8605, E-mail: bradley.mayer@lamar.edu.

LeTourneau University, School of Graduate and Professional Studies, Longview, TX 75607-7001. Offers business administration (MBA); counseling (MA); curriculum and instruction (M Ed); educational administration (M Ed); engineering (M Sc); psychology (MA); strategic leadership (MSL); teaching and learning (M Ed). Part-time and evening/weekend programs available. Postbaccalaureate distance learning degree programs offered (no on-campus study). *Faculty:* 9 full-time (1 woman), 62 part-time/adjunct (26 women). *Students:* 329 full-time (233 women); includes 152 Black or African American, non-Hispanic/Latino; 1 American Indian or Alaska Native, non-Hispanic/Latino; 5 Asian, non-Hispanic/Latino; 23 Hispanic/Latino. Average age 36. 138 applicants, 90% accepted, 120 enrolled. In 2010, 129 master's awarded. *Entrance requirements:* For master's, GRE (for MA in counseling and M Sc in engineering), minimum GPA of 2.8. Additional exam requirements/recommendations for international students: Required—TOEFL. *Application deadline:* Applications are processed on a rolling basis. Application fee: $0. Electronic applications accepted. *Expenses:* Tuition: Full-time $13,020; part-time $620 per credit hour. *Financial support:* Applicants required to submit FAFSA. *Unit head:* Dr. Carol Green, Vice President, 903-233-4010, Fax: 903-233-3227, E-mail: carolgreen@letu.edu. *Application contact:* Chris Fontaine, Assistant Vice President for Enrollment Management and Marketing, 903-233-4071, Fax: 903-233-3227, E-mail: chrisfontaine@letu.edu.

Manhattanville College, Graduate Programs, Humanities and Social Sciences Programs, Program in Leadership and Strategic Management, Purchase, NY 10577-2132. Offers MS. Part-time and evening/weekend programs available. In 2010, 14 master's awarded. *Degree requirements:* For master's, thesis. *Entrance requirements:* For master's, 2 letters of recommendation, interview. Additional exam requirements/recommendations for international students: Required—TOEFL. *Application deadline:* Applications are processed on a rolling basis. Application fee: $75. *Expenses:* Tuition: Full-time $16,110; part-time $895 per credit. Required fees: $50 per semester. *Financial support:* Career-related internships or fieldwork, Federal Work-Study, institutionally sponsored loans, and unspecified assistantships available. Financial award applicants required to submit FAFSA. *Unit head:* Donald Richards, Interim Dean, School of Graduate and Professional Studies, 914-323-5469, Fax: 914-694-3488, E-mail: gps@mville.edu. *Application contact:* Office of Admissions for Graduate and Professional Studies, 914-323-5418, E-mail: gps@mville.edu.

Middle Tennessee State University, College of Graduate Studies, University College, Murfreesboro, TN 37132. Offers M Ed, MPS, MSN, Graduate Certificate. Part-time and evening/weekend programs available. Postbaccalaureate distance learning degree programs offered. *Students:* 1 (woman) full-time, 184 part-time (144 women); includes 28 Black or African American, non-Hispanic/Latino; 1 American Indian or Alaska Native, non-Hispanic/Latino; 3 Hispanic/Latino; 5 Two or more races, non-Hispanic/Latino. Average age 38. 41 applicants, 78% accepted, 32 enrolled. In 2010, 38 master's, 1 other advanced degree awarded. *Entrance requirements:* Additional exam requirements/recommendations for international students: Required—TOEFL (minimum score 525 paper-based; 195 computer-based; 71 iBT) or IELTS (minimum score 6). *Application deadline:* For fall admission, 6/1 for domestic and international students. Applications are processed on a rolling basis. Application fee: $25 ($30 for international students). *Expenses:* Tuition, state resident: full-time $4632. Tuition, nonresident: full-time $11,520. *Financial support:* In 2010–11, 4 students received support. Application deadline: 5/1. *Unit head:* Dr. Mike Boyle, Dean, 615-898-2177, Fax: 615-896-7925, E-mail: mboyle@mtsu.edu. *Application contact:* Dr. Michael Allen, Dean and Vice Provost for Research, 615-898-2840, Fax: 615-904-8020, E-mail: mallen@mtsu.edu.

Mountain State University, School of Graduate Studies, Program in Strategic Leadership, Beckley, WV 25802-9003. Offers MSSL. Part-time and evening/weekend programs available. Postbaccalaureate distance learning degree programs offered (no on-campus study). *Faculty:* 8 full-time (3 women), 14 part-time/adjunct (4 women). *Students:* 282 full-time (154 women), 6 part-time (5 women); includes 60 minority (42 Black or African American, non-Hispanic/Latino; 3 Asian, non-Hispanic/Latino; 15 Hispanic/Latino), 5 international. Average age 38. 303 applicants, 42% accepted, 108 enrolled. In 2010, 291 master's awarded. *Degree requirements:* For master's, thesis or alternative. *Entrance requirements:* Additional exam requirements/recommendations for international students: Required—TOEFL (minimum score 550 paper-based; 213 computer-based); Recommended—IELTS (minimum score 6.5). *Application deadline:* For fall admission, 5/31 priority date for domestic and international students. Applications are processed on a rolling basis. Application fee: $25 ($50 for international students). Electronic applications accepted. *Expenses:* Tuition: Full-time $4800; part-time $400 per credit hour.

Required fees: $2250; $2250 per credit hour. Tuition and fees vary according to degree level and program. *Financial support:* Federal Work-Study, scholarships/grants, and unspecified assistantships available. Support available to part-time students. Financial award applicants required to submit FAFSA. *Unit head:* Dr. William White, Dean, School of Leadership and Professional Development/Interim Dean, School of Graduate Studies, 304-929-1658, Fax: 304-929-1637, E-mail: wwhite@mountainstate.edu. *Application contact:* Anita Diaz, Enrollment Coordinator for Graduate Studies, 304-929-1731, Fax: 304-929-1710, E-mail: adiaz@mountainstate.edu.

New York University, School of Continuing and Professional Studies, Division of Programs in Business, Graduate Programs in Management and Systems, New York, NY 10012-1019. Offers core business competencies (Advanced Certificate); database technologies (MS); enterprise and risk management (Advanced Certificate); enterprise risk management (MS); information technologies (Advanced Certificate); strategy and leadership (MS, Advanced Certificate); systems management (MS). Part-time and evening/weekend programs available. Postbaccalaureate distance learning degree programs offered (no on-campus study). *Faculty:* 2 full-time (0 women), 27 part-time/adjunct (6 women). *Students:* 23 full-time (11 women), 166 part-time (56 women); includes 18 Black or African American, non-Hispanic/Latino; 29 Asian, non-Hispanic/Latino; 17 Hispanic/Latino, 34 international. Average age 33. 135 applicants, 52% accepted, 39 enrolled. In 2010, 61 master's, 15 other advanced degrees awarded. *Degree requirements:* For master's, thesis, capstone project. *Entrance requirements:* For master's, GMAT or GRE General Test (for recent graduates), resume, 2 letters of recommendation, essay, professional experience. Additional exam requirements/recommendations for international students: Required—TOEFL (minimum score 600 paper-based; 250 computer-based; 100 iBT). *Application deadline:* For fall admission, 2/1 priority date for domestic and international students; for spring admission, 10/15 priority date for domestic students, 8/15 priority date for international students. Applications are processed on a rolling basis. Application fee: $75. Electronic applications accepted. *Financial support:* In 2010–11, 73 students received support, including 73 fellowships (averaging $1,803 per year); scholarships/grants also available. Support available to part-time students. Financial award application deadline: 3/1; financial award applicants required to submit FAFSA. *Unit head:* Israel Moskowitz, Academic Director, 212-992-3600, Fax: 212-992-3650, E-mail: im36@nyu.edu. *Application contact:* Helen Sapp, Assistant Director, 212-992-3640, Fax: 212-992-3650, E-mail: helen.sapp@nyu.edu.

New York University, School of Continuing and Professional Studies, Schack Institute of Real Estate, Program in Real Estate, New York, NY 10012-1019. Offers business of development (MS); finance and investment (MS); global real estate (MS); real estate (Advanced Certificate); strategic real estate management (MS); sustainable development (MS). Part-time and evening/weekend programs available. *Faculty:* 11 full-time (3 women), 74 part-time/adjunct (8 women). *Students:* 94 full-time (17 women), 282 part-time (63 women); includes 16 Black or African American, non-Hispanic/Latino; 2 American Indian or Alaska Native, non-Hispanic/Latino; 30 Asian, non-Hispanic/Latino; 17 Hispanic/Latino, 62 international. Average age 30. 298 applicants, 68% accepted, 111 enrolled. In 2010, 184 master's, 48 other advanced degrees awarded. *Degree requirements:* For master's, thesis, capstone. *Entrance requirements:* For master's, GRE General Test or GMAT (for recent graduates), resume, 2 letters of recommendation, essay, professional experience. Additional exam requirements/recommendations for international students: Required—TOEFL (minimum score 600 paper-based; 250 computer-based; 100 iBT), TWE. *Application deadline:* For fall admission, 2/1 priority date for domestic and international students; for spring admission, 10/15 priority date for domestic students, 8/15 priority date for international students. Applications are processed on a rolling basis. Application fee: $75. Electronic applications accepted. *Financial support:* In 2010–11, 186 students received support, including 186 fellowships (averaging $2,423 per year); scholarships/grants also available. Support available to part-time students. Financial award application deadline: 3/1; financial award applicants required to submit FAFSA. *Faculty research:* Economics and market cycles, international property rights, comparative metropolitan economies, current market trends. *Unit head:* James Stuckey, Divisional Dean, 212-992-3335, Fax: 212-992-3686, E-mail: james.stuckey@nyu.edu. *Application contact:* Jennifer Monahan, Director of Administration and Student Services, 212-992-3335, Fax: 212-992-3686, E-mail: jm189@nyu.edu.

North Central College, Graduate and Continuing Education Programs, Department of Business, Program in Business Administration, Naperville, IL 60566-7063. Offers change management (MBA); finance (MBA); human resource management (MBA); management (MBA); marketing (MBA). Part-time and evening/weekend programs available. *Faculty:* 14 full-time (4 women), 5 part-time/adjunct (1 woman). *Students:* 46 full-time (17 women), 101 part-time (46 women); includes 6 Black or African American, non-Hispanic/Latino; 1 American Indian or Alaska Native, non-Hispanic/Latino; 4 Asian, non-Hispanic/Latino; 7 Hispanic/Latino, 3 international. Average age 31. In 2010, 46 master's awarded. *Degree requirements:* For master's, project. *Entrance requirements:* For master's, interview. Additional exam requirements/recommendations for international students: Required—TOEFL (minimum score 577 paper-based; 233 computer-based; 90 iBT). *Application deadline:*

For fall admission, 8/15 for domestic students; for winter admission, 12/1 for domestic students; for spring admission, 2/1 for domestic students. Application fee: $25. *Financial support:* Scholarships/grants available. Support available to part-time students. *Unit head:* Dr. Jean Clifton, MBA Program Coordinator, 630-637-5244, E-mail: jmclifton@noctrl.edu. *Application contact:* Wendy Kulpinski, Director and Graduate and Continuing Education Admission, 630-637-5808, Fax: 630-637-5844, E-mail: wekulpinski@noctrl.edu.

Regent University, Graduate School, School of Global Leadership and Entrepreneurship, Virginia Beach, VA 23464-9800. Offers business administration (MBA); management (MA); organizational leadership (MA, PhD, Certificate); strategic foresight (MA); strategic leadership (DSL). Part-time and evening/weekend programs available. Postbaccalaureate distance learning degree programs offered (minimal on-campus study). *Faculty:* 13 full-time (3 women), 9 part-time/adjunct (3 women). *Students:* 30 full-time (11 women), 499 part-time (184 women); includes 125 Black or African American, non-Hispanic/Latino; 4 American Indian or Alaska Native, non-Hispanic/Latino; 10 Asian, non-Hispanic/Latino; 15 Hispanic/Latino, 93 international. Average age 41. 157 applicants, 66% accepted, 64 enrolled. In 2010, 86 master's, 30 doctorates awarded. *Degree requirements:* For master's, thesis or alternative, 3 credit hour culminating experience; for doctorate, thesis/dissertation. *Entrance requirements:* For master's, GRE, GMAT, minimum undergraduate GPA of 2.75, computer literacy survey, 2 recommendations, resume, transcripts, essay; for doctorate, GRE, GMAT, sample of writing, minimum 3 years of relevant experience, computer literacy survey, 2 recommendations, resume, essay, transcripts; for Certificate, writing sample, resume, transcripts. Additional exam requirements/recommendations for international students: Required—TOEFL (minimum score 577 paper-based; 233 computer-based). *Application deadline:* For fall admission, 5/1 priority date for domestic students; for spring admission, 10/1 priority date for domestic students. Applications are processed on a rolling basis. Application fee: $50. Electronic applications accepted. *Expenses:* Contact institution. *Financial support:* Career-related internships or fieldwork, scholarships/grants, and tuition waivers (full and partial) available. Support available to part-time students. Financial award application deadline: 9/1. *Faculty research:* Servant leadership, ethics and values, telecommuting and family values, organizational communications, distance education. *Unit head:* Dr. Bruce Winston, Dean, 757-352-4306, Fax: 757-352-4634, E-mail: brucwin@regent.edu. *Application contact:* Matthew Chadwick, Director of Enrollment Support Services, 800-373-5504, Fax: 757-352-4381, E-mail: admissions@regent.edu.

Sage Graduate School, Graduate School, School of Management, Program in Business Administration, Troy, NY 12180-4115. Offers business strategy (MBA); finance (MBA); human resources (MBA); marketing (MBA); JD/MBA. Part-time and evening/weekend programs available. *Faculty:* 4 full-time (2 women), 8 part-time/adjunct (3 women). *Students:* 8 full-time (4 women), 67 part-time (45 women); includes 10 Black or African American, non-Hispanic/Latino; 2 Asian, non-Hispanic/Latino; 3 Hispanic/Latino, 1 international. Average age 31. 45 applicants, 64% accepted, 19 enrolled. In 2010, 24 master's awarded. *Entrance requirements:* For master's, minimum GPA of 2.75, resume, 2 letters of recommendation. Additional exam requirements/recommendations for international students: Required—TOEFL (minimum score 550 paper-based; 213 computer-based). *Application deadline:* Applications are processed on a rolling basis. Application fee: $40. *Expenses:* Tuition: Full-time $10,980; part-time $610 per credit hour. Tuition and fees vary according to course load, degree level and program. *Financial support:* Fellowships, research assistantships, Federal Work-Study, scholarships/grants, and unspecified assistantships available. Support available to part-time students. Financial award application deadline: 3/1; financial award applicants required to submit FAFSA. *Unit head:* Dr. Daniel Robeson, Dean, School of Management, 518-292-8637, Fax: 518-292-1964, E-mail: robesd@sage.edu. *Application contact:* Wendy D. Diefendorf, Director of Graduate and Adult Admission, 518-244-2443, Fax: 518-244-6880, E-mail: diefew@sage.edu.

Saint Joseph's University, Erivan K. Haub School of Business, MS Program in Business Intelligence, Philadelphia, PA 19131-1395. Offers business intelligence (MS). Part-time and evening/weekend programs available. Postbaccalaureate distance learning degree programs offered (no on-campus study). *Students:* 17 full-time (6 women), 90 part-time (21 women); includes 20 minority (8 Black or African American, non-Hispanic/Latino; 7 Asian, non-Hispanic/Latino; 4 Hispanic/Latino; 1 Two or more races, non-Hispanic/Latino), 19 international. Average age 35. In 2010, 21 master's awarded. *Entrance requirements:* For master's, GMAT or GRE, 2 letters of recommendation, resume. Additional exam requirements/recommendations for international students: Required—TOEFL (minimum score: paper 550, computer 213, iBT 79) or IELTS (6.5), Pearson Test of English (minimum 60). *Application deadline:* For fall admission, 7/15 priority date for domestic students, 4/15 priority date for international students; for spring admission, 11/15 priority date for domestic students, 10/15 priority date for international students. Applications are processed on a rolling basis. Application fee: $35. Electronic applications accepted. *Expenses:* Tuition: Part-time $729 per credit. Tuition and fees vary according to course load, degree level and program. *Financial support:* In 2010–11, teaching assistantships with partial tuition reimbursements (averaging $2,500 per year); unspecified assistantships also available. Financial award application deadline: 5/1; financial award applicants required

to submit FAFSA. *Unit head:* Patricia Rafferty, Director, MS in Business Intelligence and MS in Human Resource Management Programs, 610-660-1318, Fax: 610-660-1229, E-mail: patricia.rafferty@sju.edu. *Application contact:* Patricia Rafferty, Director, MS in Business Intelligence and MS in Human Resource Management Programs, 610-660-1318, Fax: 610-660-1229, E-mail: patricia.rafferty@sju.edu.

Southern Methodist University, Cox School of Business, MBA Program, Dallas, TX 75275. Offers accounting (MBA); finance (MBA); financial consulting (MBA); general business (MBA); information technology and operations management (MBA); management (MBA); marketing (MBA); real estate (MBA); strategy and entrepreneurship (MBA). Part-time and evening/weekend programs available. *Faculty:* 59 full-time (13 women), 30 part-time/adjunct (7 women). *Students:* 359 full-time (116 women), 592 part-time (154 women); includes 215 minority (44 Black or African American, non-Hispanic/Latino; 10 American Indian or Alaska Native, non-Hispanic/Latino; 118 Asian, non-Hispanic/Latino; 39 Hispanic/Latino; 2 Native Hawaiian or other Pacific Islander, non-Hispanic/Latino; 2 Two or more races, non-Hispanic/Latino), 92 international. Average age 30. In 2010, 486 master's awarded. *Entrance requirements:* For master's, GMAT. Additional exam requirements/recommendations for international students: Required—TOEFL. *Application deadline:* Applications are processed on a rolling basis. Application fee: $0. Electronic applications accepted. *Expenses:* Contact institution. *Financial support:* Applicants required to submit FAFSA. *Faculty research:* Corporate finance, financial reporting, modeling consumer decision-making, competition between national brands and store brands, institutional determinants of firms' strategy. *Unit head:* Dr. Marci Armstrong, Associate Dean for Master's Programs, 214-768-4486, Fax: 214-768-3956, E-mail: marci@cox.smu.edu. *Application contact:* Patti Cudney, Director of MBA Admissions, 214-768-3001, Fax: 214-768-3956, E-mail: pcudney@cox.smu.edu.

Stevens Institute of Technology, Graduate School, Wesley J. Howe School of Technology Management, Program in Management, Hoboken, NJ 07030. Offers general management (MS); global innovation management (MS); human resource management (MS); information management (MS); project management (MS); technology commercialization (MS); technology management (MS). Part-time programs available. *Students:* 15 full-time (6 women), 35 part-time (15 women); includes 1 Black or African American, non-Hispanic/Latino; 5 Asian, non-Hispanic/Latino; 6 Hispanic/Latino, 12 international. Average age 31. *Degree requirements:* For master's, thesis optional. *Entrance requirements:* For master's, GMAT, GRE General Test. Additional exam requirements/recommendations for international students: Required—TOEFL. *Application deadline:* Applications are processed on a rolling basis. Application fee: $50. Electronic applications accepted. *Financial support:* Unspecified assistantships available. *Faculty research:* Industrial economics. *Unit head:* Elizabeth Watson, Director, 201-216-5081. *Application contact:* Graduate Admissions, 800-496-4935, Fax: 201-216-8044, E-mail: gradadmissions@stevens.edu.

Suffolk University, Sawyer Business School, Master of Business Administration Program, Boston, MA 02108-2770. Offers accounting (MBA); business administration (APC); corporate financial executive track (MBA); entrepreneurship (MBA); executive business administration (EMBA); finance (MBA); global business administration (GMBA); health administration (MBA); international business (MBA); marketing (MBA); organizational behavior (MBA); strategic management (MBA); taxation (MBA); JD/MBA; MBA/GDPA; MBA/MHA; MBA/MSA; MBA/MSF; MBA/MST. *Accreditation:* AACSB. Part-time and evening/weekend programs available. Postbaccalaureate distance learning degree programs offered (no on-campus study). *Faculty:* 97 full-time (30 women), 14 part-time/adjunct (3 women). *Students:* 179 full-time (65 women), 337 part-time (143 women); includes 16 Black or African American, non-Hispanic/Latino; 2 American Indian or Alaska Native, non-Hispanic/Latino; 22 Asian, non-Hispanic/Latino; 9 Hispanic/Latino; 1 Native Hawaiian or other Pacific Islander, non-Hispanic/Latino, 80 international. Average age 30. 431 applicants, 68% accepted, 128 enrolled. In 2010, 283 master's awarded. *Entrance requirements:* For master's, GMAT, minimum undergraduate GPA of 2.75 (MBA), 5 years of managerial experience (EMBA). Additional exam requirements/recommendations for international students: Required—TOEFL (minimum score 550 paper-based; 213 computer-based). *Application deadline:* For fall admission, 6/15 priority date for domestic students, 6/15 for international students; for spring admission, 11/1 priority date for domestic students, 11/1 for international students. Applications are processed on a rolling basis. Application fee: $50. Electronic applications accepted. *Financial support:* In 2010–11, 266 students received support, including 94 fellowships with full and partial tuition reimbursements available (averaging $12,635 per year); career-related internships or fieldwork, Federal Work-Study, and institutionally sponsored loans also available. Support available to part-time students. Financial award application deadline: 4/1; financial award applicants required to submit FAFSA. *Faculty research:* Foreign investments; career strategies and boundaryless careers; corporate ethics codes; interest rates, inflation, and growth options; innovation and product development performance. *Unit head:* Lillian Hallberg, Assistant Dean of Graduate Programs/Director of MBA Programs, 617-573-8306, E-mail: lhallber@suffolk.edu. *Application contact:* Judith Reynolds, Director of Graduate Admissions, 617-573-8302, Fax: 617-305-1733, E-mail: grad. admission@suffolk.edu.

Taylor University, Master of Business Administration Program, Upland, IN 46989-1001. Offers emerging business strategies (MBA); global leadership (MBA). Part-time programs available. *Faculty:* 1 full-time (0 women), 8 part-time/adjunct (0 women). *Students:* 59 full-time (15 women), 4 part-time (1 woman); includes 2 Black or African American, non-Hispanic/Latino; 2 Hispanic/Latino; 1 Two or more races, non-Hispanic/Latino, 1 international. Average age 35. 28 applicants, 79% accepted, 17 enrolled. In 2010, 37 master's awarded. *Application deadline:* Applications are processed on a rolling basis. Application fee: $100. *Expenses:* Tuition: Full-time $10,260; part-time $570 per credit hour. Required fees: $72 per semester. One-time fee: $100. *Financial support:* Applicants required to submit FAFSA. *Unit head:* Dr. Evan Wood, Interim Chair, 260-627-9663, E-mail: evwood@taylor.edu. *Application contact:* Wendy Speakman, Program Director, 866-471-6062, Fax: 260-492-0452, E-mail: wnspeakman@taylor.edu.

Tennessee Technological University, Graduate School, Program of Professional Studies, Cookeville, TN 38505. Offers human resources leadership (MPS); strategic leadership (MPS); training and development (MPS). *Students:* 6 full-time (4 women), 25 part-time (14 women); includes 4 Black or African American, non-Hispanic/Latino; 1 American Indian or Alaska Native, non-Hispanic/Latino; 1 Hispanic/Latino. 16 applicants, 56% accepted, 6 enrolled. In 2010, 11 master's awarded. *Degree requirements:* For master's, comprehensive exam, thesis or alternative. *Entrance requirements:* For master's, GRE. Additional exam requirements/recommendations for international students: Required—TOEFL (minimum score 550 paper-based; 79 iBT), IELTS (minimum score 5.5). *Application deadline:* For fall admission, 8/1 for domestic students, 5/1 for international students; for spring admission, 12/1 for domestic students, 10/1 for international students. Application fee: $25 ($30 for international students). Electronic applications accepted. *Expenses:* Tuition, state resident: full-time $7934; part-time $388 per credit hour. Tuition, nonresident: full-time $19,758; part-time $962 per credit hour. *Financial support:* Application deadline: 4/1. *Unit head:* Dr. Susan A. Elkins, Dean, School of Interdisciplinary Studies and Extended Education, 931-372-3394, Fax: 372-372-3499, E-mail: selkins@tntech.edu. *Application contact:* Shelia K. Kendrick, Coordinator of Graduate Admissions, 931-372-3808, Fax: 931-372-3497, E-mail: skendrick@tntech.edu.

Towson University, Program in Management and Leadership Development, Towson, MD 21252-0001. Offers Certificate. Part-time and evening/weekend programs available. *Students:* 8 full-time (6 women), 22 part-time (18 women); includes 13 minority (10 Black or African American, non-Hispanic/Latino; 1 American Indian or Alaska Native, non-Hispanic/Latino; 2 Asian, non-Hispanic/Latino). Average age 34. In 2010, 4 Certificates awarded. *Entrance requirements:* For degree, minimum GPA of 3.0, letter of intent. Application fee: $50. *Expenses:* Tuition, state resident: part-time $324 per credit. Tuition, nonresident: part-time $681 per credit. Required fees: $95 per term. *Unit head:* Alan Clardy, Graduate Program Director, 410-704-3069, E-mail: aclardy@towson.edu. *Application contact:* The Graduate School, 410-704-2501, Fax: 410-704-2501, E-mail: grads@towson.edu.

United States International University, School of Business Administration, Nairobi, Kenya. Offers business administration (GEMBA); entrepreneurship (MBA); finance (MBA); human resource management (MBA); information technology management (MBA); integrated studies (MBA); international business administration (MBA); management and organizational development (MS); marketing (MBA); organizational development (EMS); strategic management (MBA). Part-time and evening/weekend programs available. *Faculty:* 42 full-time (8 women), 64 part-time/adjunct (14 women). *Students:* 423 full-time (227 women), 129 part-time (63 women). Average age 29. 110 applicants, 79% accepted, 78 enrolled. In 2010, 164 master's awarded. *Degree requirements:* For master's, thesis. *Entrance requirements:* For master's, GMAT, 2 letters of reference, resume. Additional exam requirements/recommendations for international students: Required—TOEFL (minimum score 550 paper-based; 213 computer-based). *Application deadline:* For fall admission, 6/30 priority date for domestic and international students; for spring admission, 9/30 for domestic and international students. Applications are processed on a rolling basis. Application fee: $50. *Financial support:* In 2010–11, 30 students received support, including 6 research assistantships (averaging $1,400 per year), 4 teaching assistantships (averaging $1,400 per year); career-related internships or fieldwork, scholarships/grants, and unspecified assistantships also available. Support available to part-time students. Financial award application deadline: 6/30; financial award applicants required to submit FAFSA. *Faculty research:* Marketing in small business enterprises, total quality management in Kenya. *Unit head:* Dr. Damary Sikalieh, Dean, 254-02-3606-415, E-mail: dsikalieh@usiu.ac.ke. *Application contact:* George Lumbasi, Director of Admissions, 254-02-3606563, Fax: 254-02-3606100, E-mail: glumbasi@usiu.ac.ke.

The University of Arizona, Eller College of Management, Department of Management, Tucson, AZ 85721. Offers PhD. Evening/weekend programs available. *Faculty:* 14 full-time (3 women). *Students:* 98 full-time (29 women), 18 part-time (6 women); includes 2 Asian, non-Hispanic/Latino; 4 Hispanic/Latino; 7 Two or more races, non-Hispanic/Latino, 54 international.

Average age 31. 373 applicants, 29% accepted, 47 enrolled. In 2010, 10 doctorates awarded. *Entrance requirements:* Additional exam requirements/recommendations for international students: Required—TOEFL (minimum score 550 paper-based; 213 computer-based; 79 iBT). *Application deadline:* For fall admission, 1/15 for domestic and international students. Applications are processed on a rolling basis. Application fee: $75. Electronic applications accepted. *Expenses:* Tuition, state resident: full-time $7692. *Financial support:* In 2010–11, 8 research assistantships with full tuition reimbursements (averaging $25,023 per year) were awarded; teaching assistantships with full tuition reimbursements, career-related internships or fieldwork, Federal Work-Study, institutionally sponsored loans, scholarships/grants, health care benefits, tuition waivers (partial), and unspecified assistantships also available. Financial award application deadline: 3/15. *Faculty research:* Organizational behavior, human resources, decision-making, health economics and finance, immigration. Total annual research expenditures: $147,455. *Unit head:* Dr. Stephen Gilliland, Department Head, 520-621-9324, Fax: 520-621-4171, E-mail: sgill@eller.arizona.edu. *Application contact:* Information Contact, 520-621-1053, Fax: 520-621-4171.

University of California, Los Angeles, Graduate Division, UCLA Anderson School of Management, Los Angeles, CA 90095-1481. Offers accounting (PhD); business administration (MBA); decisions, operations and technology management (PhD); finance (PhD); financial engineering (MFE); global economics and management (PhD); human resources and organizational behavior (PhD); marketing (PhD); strategy and policy (PhD); DDS/MBA; MBA/JD; MBA/MD; MBA/MLAS; MBA/MLIS; MBA/MPH; MBA/MPP; MBA/MSCS; MBA/MSN; MBA/MUP. *Accreditation:* AACSB. Part-time programs available. *Faculty:* 102 full-time (17 women), 43 part-time/adjunct (6 women). *Students:* 833 full-time (270 women), 1,052 part-time (271 women); includes 592 minority (25 Black or African American, non-Hispanic/Latino; 3 American Indian or Alaska Native, non-Hispanic/Latino; 482 Asian, non-Hispanic/Latino; 60 Hispanic/Latino; 6 Native Hawaiian or other Pacific Islander, non-Hispanic/Latino; 16 Two or more races, non-Hispanic/Latino), 445 international. In 2010, 735 master's, 10 doctorates awarded. *Degree requirements:* For master's, comprehensive exam, field study consulting project (for MBA); thesis/dissertation (for MFE); for doctorate, comprehensive exam, thesis/dissertation, oral and written qualifying exams. *Entrance requirements:* For master's, GMAT (MBA); GMAT or GRE General Test (MFE), minimum undergraduate GPA of 3.0; for doctorate, GMAT or GRE General Test, minimum undergraduate GPA of 3.0. Additional exam requirements/recommendations for international students: Required—TOEFL (minimum score 560 paper-based; 220 computer-based; 87 iBT), IELTS (minimum score 7). *Application deadline:* For fall admission, 10/20 for domestic and international students; for winter admission, 1/5 for domestic and international students; for spring admission, 4/13 for domestic and international students. Application fee: $200. Electronic applications accepted. *Expenses:* Contact institution. *Financial support:* Fellowships, research assistantships, teaching assistantships, career-related internships or fieldwork, institutionally sponsored loans, scholarships/grants, health care benefits, and tuition waivers (partial) available. Financial award application deadline: 3/2; financial award applicants required to submit FAFSA. *Unit head:* Judy D. Olian, Dean, UCLA Anderson School of Management, 310-825-7982, Fax: 310-206-2073. *Application contact:* Mae Jennifer Shores, Assistant Dean and Director of Full-time MBA Admissions and Financial Aid, 310-825-6944, Fax: 310-825-8582, E-mail: mba.admissions@anderson.ucla.edu.

University of Chicago, Booth School of Business, Full-Time MBA Program, Chicago, IL 60637. Offers accounting (MBA); analytic finance (MBA); analytic management (MBA); econometrics and statistics (MBA); economics (MBA); entrepreneurship (MBA); finance (MBA); general management (MBA); human resource management (MBA); international business (MBA); managerial and organizational behavior (MBA); marketing management (MBA); operations management (MBA); strategic management (MBA); MBA/AM; MBA/JD; MBA/MA; MBA/MD; MBA/MPP. *Accreditation:* AACSB. Part-time and evening/weekend programs available. *Faculty:* 157 full-time, 35 part-time/adjunct. *Students:* 1,177 full-time (417 women); includes 301 minority (62 Black or African American, non-Hispanic/Latino; 1 American Indian or Alaska Native, non-Hispanic/Latino; 164 Asian, non-Hispanic/Latino; 55 Hispanic/Latino; 19 Two or more races, non-Hispanic/Latino), 403 international. Average age 28. 4,299 applicants, 22% accepted, 579 enrolled. In 2010, 1,374 master's awarded. *Entrance requirements:* For master's, GMAT, 2 letters of recommendation, 3 essays, resume, interview, transcripts. Additional exam requirements/recommendations for international students: Required—TOEFL (minimum score 600 paper-based; 250 computer-based), IELTS. *Application deadline:* For fall admission, 10/10 priority date for domestic students, 10/13 priority date for international students; for winter admission, 1/5 for domestic and international students; for spring admission, 4/13 for domestic and international students. Application fee: $200. Electronic applications accepted. *Expenses:* Contact institution. *Financial support:* Fellowships available. Financial award applicants required to submit FAFSA. *Faculty research:* Finance, economics, entrepreneurship, strategy, management. *Unit head:* Stacey Kole, Deputy Dean, 773-702-7121. *Application contact:* Kurt Ahlm, Associate Dean of Admissions and Financial Aid, 773-702-7369, Fax: 773-702-9085, E-mail: admissions@chicagobooth. edu.

University of Colorado Denver, Business School, Program in Management and Organization, Denver, CO 80217. Offers communications management (MS); enterprise technology management (MS); entrepreneurship and innovation (MS); global management (MS); human resources management (MS); leadership (MS); quantitative decision methods (MS); sports and entertainment management (MS); strategic management (MS); sustainability management (MS). *Accreditation:* AACSB. Part-time and evening/weekend programs available. Postbaccalaureate distance learning degree programs offered (no on-campus study). *Students:* 34 full-time (21 women), 9 part-time (2 women); includes 3 Asian, non-Hispanic/Latino; 5 Hispanic/Latino. Average age 33. 28 applicants, 61% accepted, 10 enrolled. In 2010, 20 master's awarded. *Degree requirements:* For master's, 30 semester hours (12 of required courses, 12 of management electives, and 6 of free electives). *Entrance requirements:* For master's, GMAT. Additional exam requirements/recommendations for international students: Required—TOEFL (minimum score 525 paper-based; 197 computer-based; 71 iBT). *Application deadline:* For fall admission, 4/1 priority date for domestic students, 3/15 priority date for international students; for spring admission, 10/1 priority date for domestic and international students. Application fee: $50 ($75 for international students). Electronic applications accepted. *Expenses:* Contact institution. *Financial support:* Federal Work-Study and scholarships/grants available. Support available to part-time students. Financial award application deadline: 4/1; financial award applicants required to submit FAFSA. *Faculty research:* Human resource management, management of catastrophe, turnaround strategies. *Unit head:* Dr. Kenneth Bettenhausen, Associate Professor/Director, 303-315-8425, E-mail: kenneth.bettehausen@ucdenver.edu. *Application contact:* Shelly Townley, Admissions Director, Graduate Programs, 303-315-8202, E-mail: shelly.townley@ucdenver.edu.

University of Dayton, Graduate School, School of Business Administration, Dayton, OH 45469-1300. Offers accounting (MBA); business intelligence (MBA); cyber security (MBA); entrepreneurship (MBA); finance (MBA); international business (MBA); marketing (MBA); MIS (MBA); operations management (MBA); technology-enhanced business/e-commerce (MBA); JD/MBA. *Accreditation:* AACSB. Part-time and evening/weekend programs available. *Faculty:* 25 full-time (7 women), 14 part-time/adjunct (2 women). *Students:* 184 full-time (72 women), 110 part-time (34 women); includes 23 minority (7 Black or African American, non-Hispanic/Latino; 7 Asian, non-Hispanic/Latino; 8 Hispanic/Latino; 1 Two or more races, non-Hispanic/Latino), 31 international. Average age 28. 220 applicants, 85% accepted, 103 enrolled. In 2010, 113 master's awarded. *Entrance requirements:* For master's, GMAT or GRE. Additional exam requirements/recommendations for international students: Required—TOEFL (minimum score 550 paper-based; 213 computer-based; 79 iBT); Recommended—IELTS (minimum score 6.5). *Application deadline:* For fall admission, 3/1 priority date for international students; for winter admission, 7/1 priority date for international students; for spring admission, 1/1 priority date for international students. Applications are processed on a rolling basis. Application fee: $0 ($50 for international students). Electronic applications accepted. *Expenses:* Contact institution. *Financial support:* In 2010–11, 15 research assistantships with full and partial tuition reimbursements (averaging $7,020 per year) were awarded; career-related internships or fieldwork, institutionally sponsored loans, scholarships/grants, health care benefits, and unspecified assistantships also available. Support available to part-time students. Financial award application deadline: 3/15; financial award applicants required to submit FAFSA. *Faculty research:* Management information systems, economics, finance, entrepreneurship, marketing. *Unit head:* Janice M. Glynn, Director, MBA Program, 937-229-3733, Fax: 937-229-3882, E-mail: glynn@udayton.edu. *Application contact:* Jeffrey Carter, Assistant Director, MBA Program, 937-229-3733, Fax: 937-229-3882, E-mail: jeff.carter@notes.udayton.edu.

University of Denver, Daniels College of Business, Department of Information Technology and Electronic Commerce, Denver, CO 80208. Offers business intelligence (MS); information technology (IMBA, MBA). Part-time and evening/weekend programs available. *Faculty:* 6 full-time (1 woman). *Entrance requirements:* For master's, GRE General Test or GMAT. Additional exam requirements/recommendations for international students: Required—TOEFL (minimum score 570 paper-based; 88 iBT). *Application deadline:* For fall admission, 11/15 priority date for domestic students; for spring admission, 10/15 priority date for domestic students. Applications are processed on a rolling basis. Application fee: $100. Electronic applications accepted. *Expenses:* Tuition: Full-time $35,604; part-time $29,670 per year. Required fees: $687 per year. Tuition and fees vary according to program. *Financial support:* Career-related internships or fieldwork, Federal Work-Study, institutionally sponsored loans, and scholarships/grants available. Support available to part-time students. Financial award application deadline: 3/15. *Faculty research:* Cross-cultural research in information systems, electronic commerce, distributed project management, strategic information systems, management of emerging technologies. *Unit head:* Dr. Paul Bauer, Chair, 303-871-3816, E-mail: paul.bauer@du.edu. *Application contact:* Allison Sharpe, Graduate Admissions Manager, 303-871-4212, E-mail: allison.sharpe@du.edu.

University of Denver, Daniels College of Business, Department of Statistics and Operations Technology, Denver, CO 80208. Offers business intelligence (MS); data mining (MS). *Faculty:* 7 full-time (2 women). *Entrance requirements:* Additional exam requirements/recommendations for international students: Required—TOEFL (minimum score 570 paper-based; 88 iBT). *Application deadline:* For fall admission, 1/15 priority date for domestic students. Applications are processed on a rolling basis. Application fee: $60. Electronic applications accepted. *Expenses:* Tuition: Full-time $35,604; part-time $29,670 per year. Required fees: $687 per year. Tuition and fees vary according to program. *Financial support:* Career-related internships or fieldwork, Federal Work-Study, institutionally sponsored loans, and scholarships/grants available. Support available to part-time students. Financial award application deadline: 2/15; financial award applicants required to submit FAFSA. *Unit head:* Dr. Anthony Hayter, Professor, 303-871-4341, E-mail: anthony.hayter@du.edu. *Application contact:* Information Contact, 303-871-3416.

University of Florida, Graduate School, Warrington College of Business Administration, Hough Graduate School of Business, Programs in Business Administration, Gainesville, FL 32611. Offers accounting (MBA); arts administration (MBA); business strategy and public policy (MBA); competitive strategy (MBA); decision and information sciences (MBA); electronic commerce (MBA); finance (MBA); general business (MBA); global management (MBA); Graham-Buffett security analysis (MBA); health administration (MBA); human resources management (MBA); international studies (MBA); Latin American business (MBA); management (MBA); marketing (MBA); sports administration (MBA); JD/MBA; MBA/MS; MBA/PhD; MBA/Pharm D; MD/MBA. *Accreditation:* AACSB. Part-time and evening/weekend programs available. *Faculty:* 71 full-time (10 women). *Students:* 187 full-time (44 women), 305 part-time (83 women); includes 25 Black or African American, non-Hispanic/Latino; 2 American Indian or Alaska Native, non-Hispanic/Latino; 52 Asian, non-Hispanic/Latino; 54 Hispanic/Latino, 11 international. Average age 31. 919 applicants, 33% accepted, 225 enrolled. In 2010, 492 master's awarded. *Degree requirements:* For master's, capstone course. *Entrance requirements:* For master's, GMAT, minimum GPA of 3.0, interview. Additional exam requirements/recommendations for international students: Required—TOEFL (minimum score 550 paper-based; 213 computer-based; 80 iBT), IELTS (minimum score 6). *Application deadline:* For fall admission, 7/1 for domestic students, 1/1 for international students; for spring admission, 12/1 for domestic and international students. Applications are processed on a rolling basis. Application fee: $30. Electronic applications accepted. *Expenses:* Tuition, state resident: full-time $10,915.92. Tuition, non-resident: full-time $28,309. *Financial support:* In 2010–11, 1 student received support, including 1 teaching assistantship (averaging $20,600 per year); career-related internships or fieldwork, scholarships/grants, and unspecified assistantships also available. Support available to part-time students. Financial award applicants required to submit FAFSA. *Faculty research:* Accounting, finance, insurance, management, real estate, urban analysis marketing. *Unit head:* Prof. Alexander D. Sevilla, Assistant Dean and Director MBA Programs, 352-273-3252 Ext. 1206, E-mail: alex.sevilla@warrington.ufl.edu. *Application contact:* Prof. Kelli Gust, Associate Director of MBA Programs, 352-273-3255, Fax: 352-392-8791, E-mail: kelly.gust@warrington.ufl.edu.

University of Illinois at Urbana–Champaign, Graduate College, College of Education, Department of Education Policy, Organization, and Leadership, Champaign, IL 61820. Offers educational organization and leadership (Ed M, MS, Ed D, PhD, CAS); educational policy studies (Ed M, MA, PhD); human resource education (Ed M, MS, Ed D, PhD, CAS). Part-time programs available. Postbaccalaureate distance learning degree programs offered (minimal on-campus study). *Faculty:* 27 full-time (11 women), 2 part-time/adjunct (0 women). *Students:* 452 full-time (268 women), 800 part-time (516 women); includes 212 Black or African American, non-Hispanic/Latino; 4 American Indian or Alaska Native, non-Hispanic/Latino; 56 Asian, non-Hispanic/Latino; 110 Hispanic/Latino; 18 Two or more races, non-Hispanic/Latino, 128 international. 844 applicants, 58% accepted, 240 enrolled. In 2010, 402 master's, 48 doctorates, 20 other advanced degrees awarded. *Entrance requirements:* For master's, minimum GPA of 3.0; for doctorate, GRE General Test, minimum GPA of 3.0, writing samples, interview. Additional exam requirements/recommendations for international students: Required—TOEFL (minimum score 620 paper-based; 260 computer-based; 105 iBT). *Application deadline:* Applications are processed on a rolling basis. Application fee: $75 ($90 for international students). Electronic applications accepted. *Financial support:* In 2010–11, 36 fellowships, 52 research assistantships, 50 teaching assistantships were awarded; tuition waivers (full and partial) also available. *Unit head:* James Anderson, Head, 217-333-2446, Fax: 217-244-5632, E-mail: janders@illinois.edu. *Application contact:* Laura A. Ketchum, 217-333-2155, Fax: 217-244-5632, E-mail: ketchum@illinois.edu.

The University of Iowa, Henry B. Tippie College of Business, Henry B. Tippie School of Management, Iowa City, IA 52242-1316. Offers corporate finance (MBA); investment management (MBA); marketing (MBA); process and operations excellence (MBA); strategic management and innovation (MBA); JD/MBA; MBA/MA; MBA/MD; MBA/MHA; MBA/MSN. *Accreditation:* AACSB. Part-time and evening/weekend programs available. *Faculty:* 110 full-time (25 women), 19 part-time/adjunct (1 woman). *Students:* 242 full-time (46 women), 809 part-time (277 women); includes 95 minority (15 Black or African American, non-Hispanic/Latino; 3 American Indian or

Alaska Native, non-Hispanic/Latino; 56 Asian, non-Hispanic/Latino; 21 Hispanic/Latino), 132 international. Average age 31. 652 applicants, 66% accepted, 380 enrolled. In 2010, 333 master's awarded. *Degree requirements:* For master's, minimum GPA of 2.75. *Entrance requirements:* For master's, GMAT, quality work experience and leadership as shown through resume, references, and essays. Additional exam requirements/recommendations for international students: Required—TOEFL (minimum score 600 paper-based; 250 computer-based; 100 iBT), IELTS (minimum score 7). *Application deadline:* For fall admission, 7/30 for domestic students, 4/15 for international students; for spring admission, 12/15 for domestic and international students. Applications are processed on a rolling basis. Application fee: $60 ($100 for international students). Electronic applications accepted. *Expenses:* Contact institution. *Financial support:* In 2010–11, 111 students received support, including 121 fellowships (averaging $8,285 per year), 87 research assistantships with partial tuition reimbursements available (averaging $8,288 per year), 25 teaching assistantships with partial tuition reimbursements available (averaging $11,326 per year); career-related internships or fieldwork, scholarships/grants, health care benefits, and unspecified assistantships also available. Financial award application deadline: 4/15; financial award applicants required to submit FAFSA. *Faculty research:* Capital markets, econometrics, optimization, investments and empirical corporate finance, Iowa electronic markets. *Unit head:* Prof. Jarjisu Sa-Aadu, Associate Dean, MBA Programs, 800-622-4692, Fax: 319-335-3604, E-mail: jsa-aadu@uiowa.edu. *Application contact:* Jodi Schafer, Director of Admissions and Financial Aid, 319-335-0864, Fax: 319-335-3604, E-mail: jodi-schafer@uiowa.edu.

University of Mary, Gary Tharaldson School of Business, Bismarck, ND 58504-9652. Offers accountancy (MBA); business administration (MBA); health care (MBA); human resource management (MBA); management (MBA); project management (MPM); strategic leadership (MSSL). Part-time and evening/weekend programs available. *Faculty:* 2 full-time (0 women), 73 part-time/adjunct (27 women). *Students:* 232 full-time (123 women), 226 part-time (115 women); includes 63 minority (30 Black or African American, non-Hispanic/Latino; 23 American Indian or Alaska Native, non-Hispanic/Latino; 5 Asian, non-Hispanic/Latino; 3 Hispanic/Latino; 1 Native Hawaiian or other Pacific Islander, non-Hispanic/Latino; 1 Two or more races, non-Hispanic/Latino), 20 international. Average age 36. 209 applicants, 98% accepted, 189 enrolled. In 2010, 265 master's awarded. *Degree requirements:* For master's, strategic planning seminar. *Entrance requirements:* For master's, minimum GPA of 2.5. Additional exam requirements/recommendations for international students: Required—TOEFL (minimum score 500 paper-based; 197 computer-based; 71 iBT). *Application deadline:* Applications are processed on a rolling basis. Application fee: $40. *Expenses:* Tuition: Full-time $10,800; part-time $450 per credit. Tuition and fees vary according to course load, degree level, program and student level. *Financial support:* Application deadline: 8/1. *Unit head:* Dr. Shanda Traiser, Director of the School of Accelerated and Distance Education, 701-355-8160, Fax: 701-255-7687, E-mail: straiser@umary.edu. *Application contact:* Wayne G. Maruska, Graduate Program Advisor, 701-355-8134, Fax: 701-255-7687, E-mail: wmaruska@umary.edu.

University of Minnesota, Twin Cities Campus, Carlson School of Management, Doctoral Program in Business Administration, Minneapolis, MN 55455-0213. Offers accounting (PhD); finance (PhD); information and decision sciences (PhD); marketing and logistics management (PhD); operations and management science (PhD); strategic management and organization (PhD). *Faculty:* 100 full-time (27 women). *Students:* 73 full-time (28 women); includes 3 Asian, non-Hispanic/Latino; 3 Hispanic/Latino, 53 international. Average age 30. 319 applicants, 6% accepted, 16 enrolled. In 2010, 8 doctorates awarded. *Degree requirements:* For doctorate, comprehensive exam, thesis/dissertation, written and oral preliminary exams, proposal defense, final defense. *Entrance requirements:* For doctorate, GMAT, GRE General Test. Additional exam requirements/recommendations for international students: Required—TOEFL (minimum score 600 paper-based; 250 computer-based; 100 iBT), IELTS (minimum score 7.5). *Application deadline:* For fall admission, 12/31 for domestic students, 12/31 priority date for international students. Applications are processed on a rolling basis. Application fee: $75 ($95 for international students). Electronic applications accepted. *Financial support:* In 2010–11, 68 students received support, including 134 fellowships with full tuition reimbursements available (averaging $6,622 per year), 63 research assistantships with full tuition reimbursements available (averaging $6,750 per year), 57 teaching assistantships with full tuition reimbursements available (averaging $6,750 per year); institutionally sponsored loans, scholarships/grants, health care benefits, and unspecified assistantships also available. Financial award application deadline: 12/31. *Faculty research:* Corporate strategy, finance, entrepreneurship, marketing, information and decision science, operations, accounting, quality management. *Unit head:* Dr. Shawn P. Curley, Director of Graduate Studies and PhD Program Director, 612-624-6546, Fax: 612-624-8221, E-mail: curley@umn.edu. *Application contact:* Earlene K. Bronson, Assistant Director, PhD Program, 612-624-0875, Fax: 612-624-8221, E-mail: brons003@umn.edu.

University of New Haven, Graduate School, School of Business, Program in Business Administration, West Haven, CT 06516-1916. Offers accounting (MBA, Certificate), including CPA (MBA); business management (Certificate); business policy and strategy (MBA); finance (MBA), including CFA; global marketing (MBA); human resource management (Certificate); human resources management (MBA); international business (Certificate); marketing (Certificate); sports management (MBA); telecommunications management (Certificate); MBA/MPA. Part-time and evening/weekend programs available. *Students:* 158 full-time (80 women), 150 part-time (70 women); includes 36 Black or African American, non-Hispanic/Latino; 2 American Indian or Alaska Native, non-Hispanic/Latino; 19 Asian, non-Hispanic/Latino; 16 Hispanic/Latino, 82 international. Average age 32. 162 applicants, 99% accepted, 85 enrolled. In 2010, 141 master's, 16 other advanced degrees awarded. *Degree requirements:* For master's, thesis or alternative. *Entrance requirements:* For master's, GMAT. Additional exam requirements/recommendations for international students: Required—TOEFL (minimum score 520 paper-based; 190 computer-based; 70 iBT), IELTS (minimum score 5.5). *Application deadline:* For fall admission, 5/31 for international students; for winter admission, 10/15 for international students; for spring admission, 1/15 for international students. Applications are processed on a rolling basis. Application fee: $50. Electronic applications accepted. *Expenses:* Contact institution. *Financial support:* Research assistantships with partial tuition reimbursements, teaching assistantships with partial tuition reimbursements, Federal Work-Study, scholarships/grants, health care benefits, tuition waivers, and unspecified assistantships available. Support available to part-time students. Financial award applicants required to submit FAFSA. *Unit head:* Charles Coleman, Chairman, 203-932-7375. *Application contact:* Eloise Gormley, Director of Graduate Admissions, 203-932-7449, Fax: 203-932-7137, E-mail: gradinfo@newhaven.edu.

University of Pittsburgh, Katz Graduate School of Business, Master of Business Administration Programs, Pittsburgh, PA 15260. Offers finance (MBA); information systems (MBA); marketing (MBA); operations management (MBA); organizational behavior and human resource management (MBA); organizational leadership (Certificate); six sigma (Certificate); strategy, environment and organizations (MBA); technology, innovation and entrepreneurship (Certificate); MBA/JD; MBA/MIB; MBA/MPIA; MBA/MSE; MBA/MSIS; MID/MBA. *Accreditation:* AACSB. Part-time and evening/weekend programs available. *Faculty:* 60 full-time (18 women), 22 part-time/adjunct (5 women). *Students:* 232 full-time (75 women), 458 part-time (158 women); includes 34 Black or African American, non-Hispanic/Latino; 1 American Indian or Alaska Native, non-Hispanic/Latino; 20 Asian, non-Hispanic/Latino; 9 Hispanic/Latino, 105 international. Average age 29. 697 applicants, 50% accepted, 174 enrolled. In 2010, 263 master's awarded. *Degree requirements:* For master's, minimum GPA of 3.0. *Entrance requirements:* For master's, GMAT, recommendations, undergraduate transcripts, essay responses, resume, interview, bachelor's degree. Additional exam requirements/recommendations for international students: Required—TOEFL (minimum 600 paper, 250 computer, 100 iBT) or IELTS. *Application deadline:* For fall admission, 4/1 priority date for domestic students, 2/1 priority date for international students. Application fee: $50. Electronic applications accepted. *Expenses:* Tuition, state resident: full-time $17,304; part-time $701 per credit. Tuition, nonresident: full-time $29,554; part-time $1210 per credit. Required fees: $740; $214 per term. Tuition and fees vary according to program. *Financial support:* In 2010–11, 52 students received support. Career-related internships or fieldwork and scholarships/grants available. Financial award application deadline: 3/1; financial award applicants required to submit FAFSA. *Faculty research:* Accounting statements and reporting, incentives and governance, corporate finance, mergers and acquisitions, information systems processes, structures and decision-making, organizational structure, knowledge management and corporate strategy, consumer behavior and marketing models. *Unit head:* William T. Valenta, Assistant Dean, MBA Program Director, 412-648-1610, Fax: 412-648-1659, E-mail: wtvalenta@katz.pitt.edu. *Application contact:* Cliff McCormick, Director MBA Admissions, 412-648-1700, Fax: 412-648-1659, E-mail: mba@katz.pitt.edu.

The University of Texas at Dallas, School of Management, Program in Management and Administrative Sciences, Richardson, TX 75080. Offers electronic commerce (MS); finance (MS); healthcare administration (MS); information systems (MS); innovation and entrepreneurship (MS); international management (MS); leadership in organizations (MS); marketing (MS); operations (MS); organizations (MS); real estate (MS); strategy (MS). *Accreditation:* AACSB. Part-time and evening/weekend programs available. *Faculty:* 18 full-time (3 women), 8 part-time/adjunct (0 women). *Students:* 57 full-time (32 women), 107 part-time (49 women); includes 53 minority (14 Black or African American, non-Hispanic/Latino; 30 Asian, non-Hispanic/Latino; 8 Hispanic/Latino; 1 Two or more races, non-Hispanic/Latino), 25 international. Average age 32. 161 applicants, 67% accepted, 51 enrolled. In 2010, 27 master's awarded. *Degree requirements:* For master's, thesis optional. *Entrance requirements:* For master's, GMAT. Additional exam requirements/recommendations for international students: Required—TOEFL (minimum score 550 paper-based; 215 computer-based). *Application deadline:* For fall admission, 7/15 for domestic students, 5/1 priority date for international students; for spring admission, 11/15 for domestic students, 9/1 priority date for international students. Applications are processed on a rolling basis. Application fee: $50 ($100 for international students). Electronic applications accepted. *Expenses:* Tuition, state resident: full-time $10,248; part-time $569 per credit hour. Tuition, nonresident: full-time $18,544; part-time $1030 per credit hour. Tuition and fees vary according to course load. *Financial support:* In 2010–11, 26 students received support, including 38 teaching assistantships with partial tuition reimbursements available (averaging $11,528 per year); research assistantships with partial tuition reimbursements available, career-related internships or fieldwork, Federal Work-Study, institutionally sponsored loans, scholarships/grants, and unspecified assistantships also available. Support available to part-time students. Financial award application deadline: 4/30; financial award applicants required to submit FAFSA. *Faculty research:* Integrated and detailed knowledge of functional areas of management, analytical tools for effective appraisal and decision making. *Unit head:* Dr. Doug Eckel, Assistant Dean, 972-883-5923, E-mail: doug.eckel@utdallas.edu. *Application contact:* James Parker, Assistant Director, 972-883-5842, E-mail: jparker@utdallas.edu.

The University of Texas at Dallas, School of Management, Programs in Management Science, Richardson, TX 75080. Offers accounting (PhD); finance (PhD); information systems (PhD); marketing (PhD); operations management (PhD). *Accreditation:* AACSB. Part-time and evening/weekend programs available. *Faculty:* 12 full-time (3 women), 3 part-time/adjunct (0 women). *Students:* 77 full-time (27 women), 11 part-time (4 women); includes 5 minority (all Asian, non-Hispanic/Latino), 72 international. Average age 32. 223 applicants, 9% accepted. In 2010, 16 doctorates awarded. *Degree requirements:* For doctorate, thesis/dissertation. *Entrance requirements:* For doctorate, GMAT, minimum GPA of 3.0. Additional exam requirements/recommendations for international students: Required—TOEFL (minimum score 550 paper-based; 215 computer-based). *Application deadline:* For fall admission, 7/15 for domestic students, 5/1 priority date for international students; for spring admission, 11/15 for domestic students, 9/1 priority date for international students. Applications are processed on a rolling basis. Application fee: $50 ($100 for international students). Electronic applications accepted. *Expenses:* Tuition, state resident: full-time $10,248; part-time $569 per credit hour. Tuition, nonresident: full-time $18,544; part-time $1030 per credit hour. Tuition and fees vary according to course load. *Financial support:* In 2010–11, 56 students received support, including 1 research assistantship with partial tuition reimbursement available (averaging $13,050 per year), 58 teaching assistantships with partial tuition reimbursements available (averaging $14,772 per year); career-related internships or fieldwork, Federal Work-Study, institutionally sponsored loans, scholarships/grants, and unspecified assistantships also available. Support available to part-time students. Financial award application deadline: 4/30; financial award applicants required to submit FAFSA. *Faculty research:* Empirical generalizations in marketing, diffusion of generations of technology, stochastic brand-choice theory, acceptance of trade deals by supermarkets, nonparametric estimations of market share response. *Unit head:* Dr. Sumit Sarkar, Program Director, 972-883-2745, Fax: 972-883-5977, E-mail: som_phd.@utdallas.edu. Application contact: Dr. LeeAnne Sloane, Program Coordinator, 972-883-2745, Fax: 972-883-5977, E-mail: som_phd@utdallas.edu.

University of West Florida, College of Professional Studies, Department of Professional and Community Leadership, Program in Administration, Pensacola, FL 32514-5750. Offers acquisition and contract administration (MSA); biomedical/pharmaceutical (MSA); criminal justice administration (MSA); database administration (MSA); education leadership (MSA); healthcare administration (MSA); human performance technology (MSA); leadership (MSA); nursing administration (MSA); public administration (MSA); software engineering administration (MSA). Part-time and evening/weekend programs available. Postbaccalaureate distance learning degree programs offered (no on-campus study). *Students:* 26 full-time (24 women), 185 part-time (115 women); includes 30 Black or African American, non-Hispanic/Latino; 1 American Indian or Alaska Native, non-Hispanic/Latino; 5 Asian, non-Hispanic/Latino; 13 Hispanic/Latino; 1 Native Hawaiian or other Pacific Islander, non-Hispanic/Latino, 2 international. Average age 34. 139 applicants, 70% accepted, 80 enrolled. In 2010, 60 master's awarded. *Entrance requirements:* For master's, GRE General Test, letter of intent, names of references. Additional exam requirements/recommendations for international students: Required—TOEFL (minimum score 550 paper-based; 213 computer-based). *Application deadline:* For fall admission, 6/1 for domestic students, 5/15 for international students; for spring admission, 10/1 for domestic and international students. Applications are processed on a rolling basis. Application fee: $30. *Expenses:* Tuition, state resident: full-time $4982; part-time $208 per credit hour. Tuition, nonresident: full-time $20,059; part-time $836 per credit hour. Required fees: $1365; $57 per credit hour. *Financial support:* Unspecified assistantships available. Financial award application deadline: 4/15; financial award applicants required to submit FAFSA. *Unit head:* Dr. Karen Rasmussen, Chairperson, 850-474-2301, Fax: 850-474-2804, E-mail: krasmuss@uwf.edu. *Application contact:* Terry McCray, Assistant Director of Graduate Admissions, 850-473-7718, Fax: 850-473-7714, E-mail: gradadmissions@uwf.edu.

University of Wisconsin–Madison, Graduate School, Wisconsin School of Business, Wisconsin Full-Time MBA Program, Madison, WI 53706-1380. Offers applied security analysis (MBA); arts administration (MBA); brand and product management (MBA); corporate finance and investment banking (MBA); entrepreneurial management (MBA); marketing research (MBA); operations and technology management (MBA); real estate (MBA); risk management and insurance (MBA); strategic human resource management (MBA); strategic management in the life and engineering sciences (MBA); supply

chain management (MBA). *Faculty:* 32 full-time (4 women), 17 part-time/adjunct (3 women). *Students:* 242 full-time (74 women); includes 16 Black or African American, non-Hispanic/Latino; 3 American Indian or Alaska Native, non-Hispanic/Latino; 16 Asian, non-Hispanic/Latino; 12 Hispanic/Latino, 29 international. Average age 28. 526 applicants, 32% accepted, 117 enrolled. In 2010, 106 master's awarded. *Entrance requirements:* For master's, GMAT, bachelor's or equivalent degree, 2 years of work experience, letters of recommendation. Additional exam requirements/recommendations for international students: Required—TOEFL (minimum score 600 paper-based; 250 computer-based; 100 iBT), IELTS. *Application deadline:* For fall admission, 11/4 for domestic students, 11/1 for international students; for winter admission, 2/5 for domestic and international students; for spring admission, 5/15 for domestic students, 4/5 for international students. Applications are processed on a rolling basis. Application fee: $56. Electronic applications accepted. *Expenses:* Tuition, state resident: full-time $9887; part-time $617.96 per credit. Tuition, nonresident: full-time $24,054; part-time $1503.40 per credit. Required fees: $67.63 per credit. Tuition and fees vary according to reciprocity agreements. *Financial support:* In 2010–11, 103 students received support, including 13 fellowships with full and partial tuition reimbursements available (averaging $15,000 per year), 53 research assistantships with full tuition reimbursements available (averaging $8,000 per year), 35 teaching assistantships with full tuition reimbursements available (averaging $11,000 per year); scholarships/grants, health care benefits, and unspecified assistantships also available. Financial award application deadline: 4/5; financial award applicants required to submit FAFSA. *Faculty research:* Market consequences of International Financial Reporting Standards (IFRS), inter-firm relationships and strategic partnerships, application of Bayesian statistical methods and applied probability models to understanding individuals' behaviors in the context of customer relationship management (CRM) applications, liquidity provision and the structure of financial markets, strategic management of global startups. *Unit head:* Dr. Kenneth A. Kavajecz, Associate Dean of Master's Programs, 608-265-3494, Fax: 608-265-4192, E-mail: kkavajecz@bus.wisc.edu. *Application contact:* Maria Reis, Assistant Director of MBA Marketing and Recruiting, 608-262-4000, Fax: 608-265-4192, E-mail: mreis@bus.wisc.edu.

Villanova University, Villanova School of Business, MBA—The Fast Track Program, Villanova, PA 19085. Offers finance (MBA); health care management (MBA); international business (MBA); management information systems (MBA); marketing (MBA); real estate (MBA); strategic management (MBA). *Accreditation:* AACSB. Part-time and evening/weekend programs available. *Faculty:* 15 full-time (2 women), 5 part-time/adjunct (0 women). *Students:* 118 part-time (34 women); includes 13 minority (2 Black or African American, non-Hispanic/Latino; 8 Asian, non-Hispanic/Latino; 3 Hispanic/Latino). Average age 30. In 2010, 35 master's awarded. *Degree requirements:* For master's, minimum GPA of 3.0. *Entrance requirements:* For master's, GMAT. Additional exam requirements/recommendations for international students: Required—TOEFL (minimum score 550 paper-based; 213 computer-based; 80 iBT). *Application deadline:* For fall admission, 6/30 for domestic and international students. Application fee: $50. Electronic applications accepted. *Expenses:* Tuition: Part-time $700 per credit. Part-time tuition and fees vary according to degree level and program. *Financial support:* Scholarships/grants available. Support available to part-time students. Financial award application deadline: 6/30; financial award applicants required to submit FAFSA. *Faculty research:* Developing and leveraging technology, ethical business practices, managing for innovation and creativity, the global political economy, strategic marketing management. *Unit head:* Meredith L. Kwiatek, Director of Graduate Recruitment & Marketing, 610-519-7016, Fax: 610-519-6273, E-mail: rachel. garonzik@villanova.edu. *Application contact:* Meredith L. Kwiatek, Assistant Director, 610-519-7016, Fax: 610-519-6273, E-mail: meredith.kwiatek@villanova.edu.

Villanova University, Villanova School of Business, MBA—The Flex Track Program, Villanova, PA 19085. Offers finance (MBA); health care management (MBA); international business (MBA); management information systems (MBA); marketing (MBA); real estate (MBA); strategic management (MBA); JD/MBA. *Accreditation:* AACSB. Part-time and evening/weekend programs available. Postbaccalaureate distance learning degree programs offered (minimal on-campus study). *Faculty:* 31 full-time (5 women), 22 part-time/adjunct (2 women). *Students:* 15 full-time (6 women), 443 part-time (150 women); includes 46 minority (5 Black or African American, non-Hispanic/Latino; 35 Asian, non-Hispanic/Latino; 6 Hispanic/Latino). Average age 30. In 2010, 133 master's awarded. *Degree requirements:* For master's, minimum GPA of 3.0. *Entrance requirements:* For master's, GMAT. Additional exam requirements/recommendations for international students: Required—TOEFL (minimum score 550 paper-based; 213 computer-based; 80 iBT). *Application deadline:* For fall admission, 6/30 for domestic and international students; for winter admission, 11/15 for domestic and international students; for spring admission, 3/30 for domestic students, 3/31 for international students. Applications are processed on a rolling basis. Application fee: $50. Electronic applications accepted. *Expenses:* Tuition: Part-time $700 per credit. Part-time tuition and fees vary according to degree level and program. *Financial support:* In 2010–11, 15 research assistantships with full tuition reimbursements (averaging $13,100 per year) were awarded; scholarships/grants and unspecified assistantships also available. Support available to part-time students. Financial award application deadline: 6/30; financial award applicants required to submit FAFSA. *Faculty research:* Developing and leveraging technology, ethical business practices, managing for innovation and creativity, the global political economy, strategic marketing management. *Unit head:* Meredith L. Kwiatek, Director of Graduate Recruitment and Marketing, 610-519-7016, Fax: 610-519-6273, E-mail: meredith.kwiatek@villanova.edu. *Application contact:* Meredith L. Kwiatek, Assistant Director, 610-519-7016, Fax: 610-519-6273, E-mail: meredith.kwiatek@villanova.edu.

Walden University, Graduate Programs, School of Management, Minneapolis, MN 55401. Offers accounting (MS), including cpa emphasis, professional track, self-designed; accounting and management (MS), including self-designed, strategic management; applied management and decision sciences (PhD), including accounting, engineering management, finance, general applied management and decision sciences, information systems management, knowledge management, leadership and organizational change, learning management, operations research, self-designed program in applied management and design sciences; business information management (MISM); enterprise information security (MISM); entrepreneurship (MBA, DBA); finance (MBA, DBA); global management (MS); global supply chain management (DBA); health informatics (MISM); healthcare management (MBA, MS); healthcare system improvement (MBA); human resource management (MBA, MS), including functional human resource management (MS), human resource management (MS), integrating functional and strategic human resource management (MS), organizational strategy (MS); information systems (MS); information systems management (DBA); information technology (MS), including information security, software engineering; international business (MBA, DBA); IT strategy and governance (MISM); leadership (MBA, MS, DBA), including entrepreneurship (MS), general management (MS), human resources leadership (MS), innovation and technology (MS), leader development (MS), leading sustainability (MS), project management (MS), self-designed (MS); managers as leaders (MS); managing global software and service supply chains (MISM); marketing (MBA, DBA); project management (MBA, MS); research strategies (MS); risk management (MBA); self-designed (MBA, DBA); social impact management (DBA); strategy and operations (MS); sustainable futures (MBA); sustainable management (MS); technology (MBA); technology entrepreneurship (DBA); technology management (MS). Part-time and evening/weekend programs available. Postbaccalaureate distance learning degree programs offered (minimal on-campus study). *Faculty:* 22 full-time (8 women), 291 part-time/adjunct (100 women). *Students:* 3,705 full-time (1,956 women), 976 part-time (549 women); includes 2,432 minority (2,021 Black or African American, non-Hispanic/Latino; 32 American Indian or Alaska Native, non-Hispanic/Latino; 137 Asian, non-Hispanic/Latino; 193 Hispanic/Latino; 5 Native Hawaiian or other Pacific Islander, non-Hispanic/Latino; 44 Two or more races, non-Hispanic/Latino; 302 international. Average age 40. In 2010, 658 master's, 86 doctorates awarded. *Degree requirements:* For doctorate, thesis/dissertation (for some programs), residency. *Entrance requirements:* For master's, bachelor's degree or equivalent in related field; minimum GPA of 2.5; official transcripts; goal statement; access to computer and Internet; for doctorate, master's degree or equivalent in related field; minimum GPA of 3.0; 3 years of related professional/academic experience (preferred). Additional exam requirements/recommendations for international students: Required—TOEFL (minimum score 550 paper-based; 213 computer-based), IELTS (minimum score 6.5), Michigan English Language Assessment Battery (minimum score 82). *Application deadline:* Applications are processed on a rolling basis. Application fee: $50. Electronic applications accepted. *Expenses:* Tuition: Full-time $10,274; part-time $445 per credit. Tuition and fees vary according to course load, degree level and program. *Financial support:* Fellowships, Federal Work-Study, scholarships/grants, unspecified assistantships, and family tuition reduction, active duty/veteran tuition reduction, group tuition reduction, interest-free payment plans available. Support available to part-time students. Financial award applicants required to submit FAFSA. *Unit head:* Dr. William Schulz, Associate Dean, 800-925-3368. *Application contact:* Jennifer Hall, Vice President of Enrollment Management, 866-4-WALDEN, E-mail: info@waldenu.edu.

Xavier University, Williams College of Business, Master of Business Administration Program, Cincinnati, OH 45207-3221. Offers business administration (Exec MBA, MBA); business intelligence (MBA); finance (MBA); international business (MBA); management information systems (MBA); marketing (MBA); MBA/MHSA; MSN/MBA. *Accreditation:* AACSB. Part-time and evening/weekend programs available. *Faculty:* 37 full-time (13 women), 9 part-time/adjunct (2 women). *Students:* 200 full-time (60 women), 735 part-time (239 women); includes 128 minority (48 Black or African American, non-Hispanic/Latino; 3 American Indian or Alaska Native, non-Hispanic/Latino; 54 Asian, non-Hispanic/Latino; 22 Hispanic/Latino; 1 Native Hawaiian or other Pacific Islander, non-Hispanic/Latino), 32 international. Average age 30. 223 applicants, 85% accepted, 139 enrolled. In 2010, 323 master's awarded. *Degree requirements:* For master's, capstone course. *Entrance requirements:* For master's, GMAT. Additional exam requirements/recommendations for international students: Required—TOEFL (minimum score 550 paper-based; 213 computer-based; 80 iBT). *Application deadline:* For fall admission, 8/1 priority date for domestic students, 5/1 for international students; for spring admission, 12/1 priority date for domestic students, 9/1 for international students. Applications are processed on a rolling basis. Application fee: $35. Electronic applications accepted. *Expenses:* Contact

institution. *Financial support:* In 2010–11, 176 students received support. Scholarships/grants, tuition waivers (partial), and unspecified assistantships available. Financial award application deadline: 3/1; financial award applicants required to submit FAFSA. *Unit head:* Dr. Hema Krishnan, Associate Dean, 513-745-3206, Fax: 513-745-3455, E-mail: krishnan@xavier.edu. *Application contact:* Anna Marie Whelan, Assistant Director, MBA Programs, 513-745-3525, Fax: 513-745-2929, E-mail: whelana@xavier.edu.

SUSTAINABILITY MANAGEMENT

Baldwin-Wallace College, Graduate Programs, Division of Business, Program in Sustainability, Berea, OH 44017-2088. Offers MBA. Part-time and evening/weekend programs available. *Students:* 1 (woman) part-time. Average age 30. 1 applicant, 100% accepted, 1 enrolled. *Degree requirements:* For master's, minimum overall GPA of 3.0, completion of all required courses. *Entrance requirements:* For master's, GMAT, bachelor's degree, minimum GPA of 3.0. Additional exam requirements/recommendations for international students: Required—TOEFL (minimum score 523 paper-based; 193 computer-based; 70 iBT). *Application deadline:* For fall admission, 7/25 for domestic students, 4/30 for international students; for spring admission, 12/15 for domestic students, 9/30 for international students. Application fee: $25. *Expenses:* Tuition: Full-time $16,750; part-time $712 per credit hour. Tuition and fees vary according to program. *Financial support:* Application deadline: 5/1. *Unit head:* Ven Ochaya, Director, 440-826-2391, Fax: 440-826-3868, E-mail: vochaya@bw.edu. *Application contact:* Laura Spencer, Graduate Application Specialist, 440-826-2191, Fax: 440-826-3868, E-mail: lspencer@bw.edu.

Bard College, Bard Center for Environmental Policy, Annandale-on-Hudson, NY 12504. Offers climate science and policy (MS, Professional Certificate), including agriculture (MS), ecosystems (MS); environmental policy (MS, Professional Certificate); sustainability (MBA); MS/JD; MS/MAT. Part-time programs available. *Faculty:* 10 full-time (5 women), 6 part-time/adjunct (3 women). *Students:* 58 full-time (41 women). Average age 26. 75 applicants, 77% accepted, 28 enrolled. In 2010, 13 master's awarded. *Degree requirements:* For master's, thesis, 4-month, full-time internship. *Entrance requirements:* For master's, GRE, coursework in statistics, chemistry and one other semester of college science; personal statement; curriculum vitae; 3 letters of recommendation; sample of written work. Additional exam requirements/recommendations for international students: Required—TOEFL (minimum score 600 paper-based; 250 computer-based; 100 iBT). *Application deadline:* For winter admission, 1/15 priority date for domestic and international students; for spring admission, 5/15 for domestic and international students. Applications are processed on a rolling basis. Application fee: $65. Electronic applications accepted. *Expenses:* Contact institution. *Financial support:* In 2010–11, 58 students received support, including 58 fellowships (averaging $7,000 per year), 6 research assistantships (averaging $6,000 per year), 1 teaching assistantship (averaging $6,000 per year); career-related internships or fieldwork, scholarships/grants, tuition waivers (full), and unspecified assistantships also available. Support available to part-time students. Financial award application deadline: 2/15; financial award applicants required to submit FAFSA. *Faculty research:* Climate and agriculture, alternative energy, environmental economics, environmental toxicology, EPA law, sustainable development, international relations, literature and composition, human rights, agronomy, advocacy, leadership. *Unit head:* Dr. Eban Goodstein, Director, 845-758-7067, Fax: 845-758-7636, E-mail: ebangood@bard.edu. *Application contact:* Molly Williams, Admissions Coordinator, 845-758-7071, Fax: 845-758-7636, E-mail: mwilliam@bard.edu.

Cleary University, Online Program in Business Administration, Ann Arbor, MI 48105-2659. Offers financial planning (MBA); financial planning (Graduate Certificate); green business strategy (MBA, Graduate Certificate); management (MBA); nonprofit management (MBA, Graduate Certificate); organizational leadership (MBA); public accounting (MBA). Part-time and evening/weekend programs available. Postbaccalaureate distance learning degree programs offered (no on-campus study). *Faculty:* 1 (woman) full-time, 20 part-time/adjunct (8 women). *Students:* 1 (woman) full-time, 115 part-time (67 women); includes 30 minority (21 Black or African American, non-Hispanic/Latino; 1 American Indian or Alaska Native, non-Hispanic/Latino; 6 Asian, non-Hispanic/Latino; 2 Hispanic/Latino), 7 international. Average age 34. 62 applicants, 77% accepted, 36 enrolled. In 2010, 22 master's awarded. *Degree requirements:* For master's, thesis. *Entrance requirements:* For master's, bachelor's degree; minimum GPA of 2.5; professional resume indicating minimum 2 years management or related experience; undergraduate degree from an accredited college or university with at least 18 quarter hours (or 12 semester hours) of accounting study (for MBA in accounting). Additional exam requirements/recommendations for international students: Required—TOEFL (minimum score 550 paper-based; 213 computer-based; 79 iBT), Michigan English Language Assessment Battery (minimum score: 75). *Application deadline:* For fall admission, 8/15 for domestic students, 7/15 for international students; for spring admission, 4/2 for domestic students, 1/2 for international students. Applications are processed on a rolling basis. Application fee: $50. Electronic applications accepted. *Financial support:* In 2010–11, 80 students received support, including 80 fellowships (averaging

$12,501 per year); Federal Work-Study and scholarships/grants also available. Support available to part-time students. Financial award application deadline: 8/15; financial award applicants required to submit FAFSA. *Unit head:* Dr. Vincent Linder, Provost and Vice President for Academic Affairs, 800-686-1883, Fax: 734-332-4646, E-mail: vlinder@cleary.edu. *Application contact:* Carrie Bonofiglio, Director of Student Recruiting, 800-686-1883, Fax: 517-552-7805, E-mail: cbono@cleary.edu.

Colorado State University, Graduate School, College of Business, Program in Global Social and Sustainable Enterprise, Fort Collins, CO 80523-1201. Offers MSBA. *Students:* 41 full-time (25 women), 2 part-time (1 woman); includes 1 Black or African American, non-Hispanic/Latino; 1 American Indian or Alaska Native, non-Hispanic/Latino; 3 Asian, non-Hispanic/Latino; 2 Hispanic/Latino, 16 international. Average age 32. *Degree requirements:* For master's, variable foreign language requirement, comprehensive exam (for some programs), thesis, practicum. *Entrance requirements:* For master's, GMAT or GRE, 3 recommendations, current resume, minimum cumulative GPA of 3.0. Additional exam requirements/recommendations for international students: Required—TOEFL (minimum score 567 paper-based; 227 computer-based; 80 iBT); Recommended—IELTS (minimum score 6). *Application deadline:* For fall admission, 3/31 priority date for domestic students, 3/30 priority date for international students. Application fee: $50. *Expenses:* Tuition, state resident: full-time $7434; part-time $413 per credit. Tuition, nonresident: full-time $19,022; part-time $1057 per credit. Required fees: $1729; $88 per credit. *Financial support:* Fellowships with tuition reimbursements, research assistantships with tuition reimbursements, teaching assistantships, scholarships/grants and unspecified assistantships available. Financial award application deadline: 3/31; financial award applicants required to submit FAFSA. *Faculty research:* Entrepreneurial and collective decision making, entrepreneurship and sustainability, cooperative business analysis, organizational behavior, risk management. *Unit head:* Carl Hammerdorfer, Director, 970-491-8734, E-mail: carl.hammerdorfer@business.colostate.edu. *Application contact:* Sandy Dahlberg, Program Advisor, 970-491-6937, E-mail: sandy.dahlberg@colostate.edu.

Columbia University, School of Continuing Education, Program in Sustainability Management, New York, NY 10027. Offers MS. Program offered in collaboration with Columbia University's Earth Institute. Part-time programs available. Electronic applications accepted.

See Display on this page and Close-Up on page 459.

Dominican University of California, Graduate Programs, School of Business and Leadership, Green Business Administration Program, San Rafael, CA 94901-2298. Offers sustainable enterprise (MBA). Part-time and evening/weekend programs available. *Faculty:* 4 full-time (3 women), 12 part-time/adjunct (7 women). *Students:* 56 full-time (30 women), 58 part-time (34 women); includes 28 minority (3 Black or African American, non-Hispanic/Latino; 7 Asian, non-Hispanic/Latino; 11 Hispanic/Latino; 7 Two or more races, non-Hispanic/Latino). Average age 35. 46 applicants, 70% accepted, 21 enrolled. In 2010, 36 master's awarded. *Entrance requirements:* Additional exam requirements/recommendations for international students: Required—TOEFL (minimum score 550 paper-based; 213 computer-based; 80 iBT), IELTS (minimum score 7). *Application deadline:* For fall admission, 6/15 priority date for domestic and international students; for spring admission, 11/15 priority date for domestic and international students. Applications are processed on a rolling basis. Application fee: $40. Electronic applications accepted. *Financial support:* In 2010–11, 43 students received support; fellowships, scholarships/grants available. Financial award application deadline: 3/2; financial award applicants required to submit FAFSA. *Unit head:* Joey Shepp, Director, 415-482-1822, Fax: 415-459-3206, E-mail: joey.shepp@dominican.edu. *Application contact:* Robbie Hayes, Assistant Director, 415-458-3771, Fax: 415-485-3214, E-mail: robbie.hayes@dominican.edu.

Duquesne University, John F. Donahue Graduate School of Business, Pittsburgh, PA 15282-0001. Offers accountancy (MS); business administration (MBA); information systems management (MSISM); sustainability (MBA); JD/MBA; MBA/MA; MBA/MES; MBA/MHMS; MBA/MLLS; MBA/MS; MBA/MSN. *Accreditation:* AACSB. Part-time and evening/weekend programs available. *Faculty:* 24 full-time (5 women), 14 part-time/adjunct (0 women). *Students:* 97 full-time (45 women), 234 part-time (91 women); includes 5 Black or African American, non-Hispanic/Latino; 1 Asian, non-Hispanic/Latino; 2 Hispanic/Latino; 4 Native Hawaiian or other Pacific Islander, non-Hispanic/Latino, 29 international. Average age 31. 289 applicants, 43% accepted, 82 enrolled. In 2010, 120 master's awarded. *Entrance requirements:* For master's, GMAT, 2 letters of recommendation, current resume. Additional exam requirements/recommendations for international students: Required—TOEFL (minimum score 577 paper-based; 233 computer-based; 90 iBT); Recommended—TWE. *Application deadline:* For fall admission, 5/1 priority date for domestic students, 5/1 for international students; for spring admission, 10/1 for domestic and international students. Applications are processed on a rolling basis. Application fee: $0. Electronic applications accepted. *Expenses:* Tuition: Part-time $884 per credit. Required fees: $84 per credit. Tuition and fees vary according to course load. *Financial support:* In 2010–11, 40 students received support, including 12 fellowships with partial tuition reimbursements available, 28 research assistantships with partial tuition reimbursements available; career-related internships or fieldwork, scholarships/

grants, and unspecified assistantships also available. Financial award application deadline: 7/1; financial award applicants required to submit FAFSA. *Faculty research:* International business, investment management, business ethics, technology management, supply chain management, business strategy, finance. *Unit head:* Alan R. Miciak, Dean, 412-396-5848, Fax: 412-396-5304, E-mail: miciaka@duq.edu. *Application contact:* Patricia Moore, Assistant Director, 412-396-6276, Fax: 412-396-1726, E-mail: moorep@duq.edu.

Fairleigh Dickinson University, College at Florham, Silberman College of Business, Certificate Program in Managing Sustainability, Madison, NJ 07940-1099. Offers Certificate. *Unit head:* Director, 973-443-8802, E-mail: daniel twomey@fdu.edu. Application contact: Susan Brooman, University Director of Graduate Admissions.

Illinois Institute of Technology, Stuart School of Business, Program in Business Administration, Chicago, IL 60616-3793. Offers financial management (MBA); innovation and emerging enterprises (MBA); management science (MBA); marketing (MBA); sustainability (MBA); JD/MBA; M Des/MBA; MBA/MS. *Accreditation:* AACSB. Part-time and evening/weekend programs available. *Faculty:* 37 full-time (4 women), 21 part-time/adjunct (5 women). *Students:* 153 full-time (66 women), 30 part-time (12 women); includes 17 minority (3 Black or African American, non-Hispanic/Latino; 9 Asian, non-Hispanic/Latino; 3 Hispanic/Latino; 2 Two or more races, non-Hispanic/Latino), 119 international. Average age 27. 334 applicants, 77% accepted, 63 enrolled. In 2010, 40 master's awarded. *Entrance requirements:* For master's, GRE (minimum score 1000) or GMAT (500). Additional exam requirements/recommendations for international students: Required—TOEFL (minimum score 600 paper-based; 85 iBT); Recommended—IELTS (minimum score 7). *Application deadline:* For fall admission, 8/1 for domestic students, 5/1 for international students; for spring admission, 12/15 for domestic students, 10/15 for international students. Applications are processed on a rolling basis. Application fee: $75. Electronic applications accepted. *Expenses:* Contact institution. *Financial support:* Career-related internships or fieldwork, Federal Work-Study, institutionally sponsored loans, scholarships/grants, traineeships, health care benefits, and tuition waivers (partial) available. Support available to part-time students. Financial award applicants required to submit FAFSA. *Faculty research:* Global management and marketing strategy, technological innovation, management science, financial management, knowledge management. *Unit head:* M. Krishna Erramilli, Interim Director, 312-906-6573, Fax: 312-906-6549. *Application contact:* Deborah Gibson, Director, Graduate Admission, 866-472-3448, Fax: 312-472-3448, E-mail: inquiry.grad@iit.edu.

Indiana University Bloomington, School of Public and Environmental Affairs, Public Affairs Programs, Bloomington, IN 47405-7000. Offers comparative and international affairs (MPA); economic development (MPA); energy (MPA); environmental policy (PhD); environmental policy and natural resource management (MPA); information systems (MPA); local government management (MPA); nonprofit management (MPA, Certificate); policy analysis (MPA); public finance (PhD); public financial administration (MPA); public management (MPA, PhD); public policy analysis (PhD); specialized public affairs (MPA); sustainability and sustainable development (MPA); JD/MPA; MPA/MIS; MPA/MLS; MSES/MPA. *Accreditation:* NASPAA (one or more programs are accredited). Part-time programs available. *Faculty:* 31 full-time, 15 part-time/adjunct. *Students:* 466 full-time (261 women); includes 11 Black or African American, non-Hispanic/Latino; 2 American Indian or Alaska Native, non-Hispanic/Latino; 42 Asian, non-Hispanic/Latino; 1 Hispanic/Latino, 65 international. Average age 26. 650 applicants, 218 enrolled. In 2010, 166 master's, 10 doctorates awarded. *Degree requirements:* For master's, core classes, capstone; for doctorate, comprehensive exam, thesis/dissertation. *Entrance requirements:* For master's, GRE General Test or GMAT, official transcripts, 3 letters of recommendation, resume, personal statement, departmental questions; for doctorate, GRE General Test or LSAT, official transcripts, 3 letters of recommendation, resume or curriculum vitae, statement of purpose. Additional exam requirements/recommendations for international students: Required—TOEFL (minimum score 600 paper-based; 96 iBT); Recommended—IELTS (minimum score 7). *Application deadline:* For fall admission, 5/1 priority date for domestic students, 12/1 priority date for international students. Applications are processed on a rolling basis. Application fee: $55 ($65 for international students). Electronic applications accepted. *Financial support:* Fellowships with partial tuition reimbursements, research assistantships with partial tuition reimbursements, teaching assistantships with partial tuition reimbursements, career-related internships or fieldwork, Federal Work-Study, scholarships/grants, health care benefits, unspecified assistantships, and Service Corps programs available. Financial award application deadline: 2/1; financial award applicants required to submit FAFSA. *Faculty research:* Comparative and international affairs, environmental policy and resource management, policy analysis, public finance, public management, urban management, nonprofit management, energy policy, social policy, public finance. *Unit head:* Jennifer Forney, Director of Graduate Student Services, 812-855-9485, Fax: 812-856-3665, E-mail: speampo@indiana.edu. *Application contact:* Audrey Whitaker, Admissions Assistant, 812-855-2840, E-mail: speaapps@indiana.edu.

Lipscomb University, MBA Program, Nashville, TN 37204-3951. Offers accounting (MBA); business administration (general) (MBA); conflict management (MBA); financial services (MBA); healthcare management (MBA); leadership (MBA); nonprofit management (MBA); sports administration (MBA); sustainable practice (MBA). *Accreditation:* ACBSP. Part-time and evening/weekend programs available. *Faculty:* 17 full-time (5 women), 3 part-time/adjunct (0 women). *Students:* 52 full-time (30 women), 79 part-time (36 women); includes 20 Black or African American, non-Hispanic/Latino; 1 American Indian or Alaska Native, non-Hispanic/Latino; 1 Asian, non-Hispanic/Latino; 7 Hispanic/Latino. Average age 32. 151 applicants, 47% accepted, 45 enrolled. In 2010, 70 master's awarded. *Entrance requirements:* For master's, GMAT, interview, 2 references, resume. Additional exam requirements/recommendations for international students: Required—TOEFL (minimum score 570 paper-based; 230 computer-based). *Application deadline:* For fall admission, 2/1 for international students; for winter admission, 6/1 for international students. Applications are processed on a rolling basis. Application fee: $50 ($75 for international students). Electronic applications accepted. *Expenses:* Contact institution. *Financial support:* Career-related internships or fieldwork, Federal Work-Study, scholarships/grants, tuition waivers (partial), and unspecified assistantships available. Support available to part-time students. Financial award application deadline: 7/1; financial award applicants required to submit FAFSA. *Faculty research:* Impact of spirituality on organization commitment, leadership, psychological empowerment, training. *Unit head:* Dr. Mike Kendrick, Interim Chair of Graduate Business Studies, 615-966-1833, Fax: 615-966-1818, E-mail: mikekendrick@lipscomb.edu. *Application contact:* Emily Landsdell, 615-966-5284, E-mail: emily.lansdell@lipscomb.edu.

Marlboro College, Graduate School, Program in Business Administration, Marlboro, VT 05344. Offers managing for sustainability (MBA). Part-time and evening/weekend programs available. Postbaccalaureate distance learning degree programs offered (minimal on-campus study). *Faculty:* 1 full-time (0 women), 9 part-time/adjunct (5 women). *Students:* 30 full-time (20 women), 7 part-time (2 women); includes 1 Black or African American, non-Hispanic/Latino. Average age 37. In 2010, 3 master's awarded. *Degree requirements:* For master's, 60 credits including capstone project. *Entrance requirements:* For master's, letter of intent, essay, transcripts, 2 letters of recommendation. *Application deadline:* For winter admission, 10/30 priority date for domestic students. Applications are processed on a rolling basis. Application fee: $0. Electronic applications accepted. *Expenses:* Tuition: Full-time $14,280; part-time $680 per credit. Tuition and fees vary according to course load and program. *Financial support:* In 2010–11, 1 student received support. Applicants required to submit FAFSA. *Unit head:* Ralph Meima, Program Director, 802-251-7690, Fax: 802-258-9201, E-mail: rmeima@gradschool.marlboro.edu. *Application contact:* Joe Heslin, Associate Director of Admissions, 802-258-9209, Fax: 802-258-9201, E-mail: jheslin@gradcenter.marlboro.edu.

Rochester Institute of Technology, Graduate Enrollment Services, Golisano Institute for Sustainability, Rochester, NY 14623-5603. Offers M Arch, PhD. *Students:* 11 full-time (7 women), 1 part-time (0 women); includes 1 Black or African American, non-Hispanic/Latino; 1 Hispanic/Latino, 5 international. Average age 31. 45 applicants, 24% accepted, 6 enrolled. *Degree requirements:* For master's, comprehensive exam, thesis. *Entrance requirements:* For master's, GRE. Additional exam requirements/recommendations for international students: Required—TOEFL (minimum score 600 paper-based; 250 computer-based; 100 iBT) or IELTS (minimum score 6.5). *Application deadline:* For fall admission, 1/15 priority date for domestic and international students. Application fee: $50. *Expenses:* Tuition: Full-time $33,234; part-time $924 per credit hour. Required fees: $219. *Financial support:* In 2010–11, 12 students received support. *Faculty research:* Remanufacturing and resource recovery, sustainable production, sustainable mobility, systems modernization and sustainment, pollution prevention. *Unit head:* Dr. Nabil Nasr, Assistant Provost and Director, 585-475-2602, E-mail: info@sustainability.rit.edu. *Application contact:* Diane Ellison, Assistant Vice President, Graduate Enrollment Services, 585-475-2229, Fax: 585-475-7164, E-mail: gradinfo@rit.edu.

University of Colorado Denver, Business School, Program in Management and Organization, Denver, CO 80217. Offers communications management (MS); enterprise technology management (MS); entrepreneurship and innovation (MS); global management (MS); human resources management (MS); leadership (MS); quantitative decision methods (MS); sports and entertainment management (MS); strategic management (MS); sustainability management (MS). *Accreditation:* AACSB. Part-time and evening/weekend programs available. Postbaccalaureate distance learning degree programs offered (no on-campus study). *Students:* 34 full-time (21 women), 9 part-time (2 women); includes 3 Asian, non-Hispanic/Latino; 5 Hispanic/Latino. Average age 33. 28 applicants, 61% accepted, 10 enrolled. In 2010, 20 master's awarded. *Degree requirements:* For master's, 30 semester hours (12 of required courses, 12 of management electives, and 6 of free electives). *Entrance requirements:* For master's, GMAT. Additional exam requirements/recommendations for international students: Required—TOEFL (minimum score 525 paper-based; 197 computer-based; 71 iBT). *Application deadline:* For fall admission, 4/1 priority date for domestic students, 3/15 priority date for international students; for spring admission, 10/1 priority date for domestic and international students. Application fee: $50 ($75 for international students). Electronic applications accepted. *Expenses:* Contact institution. *Financial support:* Federal

Work-Study and scholarships/grants available. Support available to part-time students. Financial award application deadline: 4/1; financial award applicants required to submit FAFSA. *Faculty research:* Human resource management, management of catastrophe, turnaround strategies. *Unit head:* Dr. Kenneth Bettenhausen, Associate Professor/Director, 303-315-8425, E-mail: kenneth. bettehausen@ucdenver.edu. *Application contact:* Shelly Townley, Admissions Director, Graduate Programs, 303-315-8202, E-mail: shelly.townley@ ucdenver.edu.

University of Maine, Graduate School, College of Business, Public Policy and Health, The Maine Business School, Orono, ME 04469. Offers accounting (MBA); business and sustainability (MBA); finance (MBA); management (MBA). *Accreditation:* AACSB. Part-time and evening/weekend programs available. *Faculty:* 23 full-time (8 women), 2 part-time/adjunct (both women). *Students:* 53 full-time (24 women), 15 part-time (5 women); includes 4 minority (1 American Indian or Alaska Native, non-Hispanic/Latino; 2 Asian, non-Hispanic/Latino; 1 Hispanic/Latino), 3 international. Average age 29. 42 applicants, 69% accepted, 25 enrolled. In 2010, 25 degrees awarded. *Entrance requirements:* For master's, GMAT. Additional exam requirements/recommendations for international students: Required—TOEFL (minimum score 550 paper-based; 213 computer-based). *Application deadline:* For fall admission, 6/1 priority date for domestic and international students; for spring admission, 11/1 priority date for domestic and international students. Applications are processed on a rolling basis. Application fee: $65. Electronic applications accepted. *Expenses:* Contact institution. *Financial support:* In 2010–11, 16 students received support, including 4 teaching assistantships with tuition reimbursements available (averaging $12,790 per year); career-related internships or fieldwork, Federal Work-Study, institutionally sponsored loans, scholarships/grants, tuition waivers (full and partial), and unspecified assistantships also available. Financial award application deadline: 3/1. *Faculty research:* Entrepreneurship, investment management, international markets, decision support systems, strategic planning. *Unit head:* Dr. Nory Jones, Director of Graduate Programs, 207-581-1971, Fax: 207-581-1930, E-mail: mba@maine. edu. *Application contact:* Scott G. Delcourt, Associate Dean of the Graduate School, 207-581-3291, Fax: 207-581-3232, E-mail: graduate@maine.edu.

University of Portland, Dr. Robert B. Pamplin, Jr. School of Business, Portland, OR 97203-5798. Offers business administration (MBA); entrepreneurship (MBA); finance (MBA, MS); health care management (MBA); marketing (MBA); nonprofit management (EMBA); operations and technology management (MBA); sustainability (MBA). *Accreditation:* AACSB. Part-time and evening/weekend programs available. *Faculty:* 12 full-time (2 women), 7 part-time/adjunct (2 women). *Students:* 55 full-time (24 women), 81 part-time (29 women); includes 18 minority (2 Black or African American, non-Hispanic/Latino; 8 Asian, non-Hispanic/Latino; 5 Hispanic/Latino; 3 Two or more races, non-Hispanic/Latino), 23 international. Average age 30. In 2010, 55 master's awarded. *Entrance requirements:* For master's, GMAT, minimum GPA of 3.0, resume, 2 letters of recommendation. Additional exam requirements/ recommendations for international students: Required—TOEFL (minimum score 570 paper-based; 89 iBT), IELTS (minimum score 7). *Application deadline:* For fall admission, 7/15 priority date for domestic and international students; for spring admission, 12/15 priority date for domestic and international students. Applications are processed on a rolling basis. Application fee: $50. *Expenses:* Contact institution. *Financial support:* Federal Work-Study, scholarships/grants, and tuition waivers (partial) available. Support available to part-time students. Financial award application deadline: 3/1; financial award applicants required to submit FAFSA. *Unit head:* Dr. Howard Feldman, Associate Dean, 503-943-7224, E-mail: feldman@up.edu. *Application contact:* Melissa McCarthy, Academic Specialist, 503-943-7225, E-mail: mccarthy@up.edu.

Walden University, Graduate Programs, School of Management, Minneapolis, MN 55401. Offers accounting (MS), including cpa emphasis, professional track, self-designed; accounting and management (MS), including self-designed, strategic management; applied management and decision sciences (PhD), including accounting, engineering management, finance, general applied management and decision sciences, information systems management, knowledge management, leadership and organizational change, learning management, operations research, self-designed program in applied management and design sciences; business information management (MISM); enterprise information security (MISM); entrepreneurship (MBA, DBA); finance (MBA, DBA); global management (MS); global supply chain management (DBA); health informatics (MISM); healthcare management (MBA, MS); healthcare system improvement (MBA); human resource management (MBA, MS), including functional human resource management (MS), human resource management (MS), integrating functional and strategic human resource management (MS), organizational strategy (MS); information systems (MS); information systems management (DBA); information technology (MS), including information security, software engineering; international business (MBA, DBA); IT strategy and governance (MISM); leadership (MBA, MS, DBA), including entrepreneurship (MS), general management (MS), human resources leadership (MS), innovation and technology (MS), leader development (MS), leading sustainability (MS), project management (MS), self-designed (MS); managers as leaders (MS); managing global software and service supply chains (MISM); marketing (MBA, DBA); project management (MBA, MS); research strategies (MS); risk management (MBA); self-designed (MBA, DBA); social impact management (DBA); strategy and operations (MS); sustainable futures (MBA); sustainable management (MS); technology (MBA); technology entrepreneurship (DBA); technology management (MS). Part-time and evening/weekend programs available. Postbaccalaureate distance learning degree programs offered (minimal on-campus study). *Faculty:* 22 full-time (8 women), 291 part-time/adjunct (100 women). *Students:* 3,705 full-time (1,956 women), 976 part-time (549 women); includes 2,432 minority (2,021 Black or African American, non-Hispanic/Latino; 32 American Indian or Alaska Native, non-Hispanic/Latino; 137 Asian, non-Hispanic/Latino; 193 Hispanic/Latino; 5 Native Hawaiian or other Pacific Islander, non-Hispanic/Latino; 44 Two or more races, non-Hispanic/Latino), 302 international. Average age 40. In 2010, 658 master's, 86 doctorates awarded. *Degree requirements:* For doctorate, thesis/dissertation (for some programs), residency. *Entrance requirements:* For master's, bachelor's degree or equivalent in related field; minimum GPA of 2.5; official transcripts; goal statement; access to computer and Internet; for doctorate, master's degree or equivalent in related field; minimum GPA of 3.0; 3 years of related professional/academic experience (preferred). Additional exam requirements/recommendations for international students: Required—TOEFL (minimum score 550 paper-based; 213 computer-based), IELTS (minimum score 6.5), Michigan English Language Assessment Battery (minimum score 82). *Application deadline:* Applications are processed on a rolling basis. Application fee: $50. Electronic applications accepted. *Expenses:* Tuition: Full-time $10,274; part-time $445 per credit. Tuition and fees vary according to course load, degree level and program. *Financial support:* Fellowships, Federal Work-Study, scholarships/ grants, unspecified assistantships, and family tuition reduction, active duty/ veteran tuition reduction, group tuition reduction, interest-free payment plans available. Support available to part-time students. Financial award applicants required to submit FAFSA. *Unit head:* Dr. William Schulz, Associate Dean, 800-925-3368. *Application contact:* Jennifer Hall, Vice President of Enrollment Management, 866-4-WALDEN, E-mail: info@waldenu.edu.

Columbia University

MASTER OF SCIENCE IN
Sustainability Management

THE EARTH INSTITUTE | ⚜ COLUMBIA UNIVERSITY
COLUMBIA UNIVERSITY | School of Continuing Education

Programs of Study

The Master of Science (M.S.) in sustainability management program is cosponsored by Columbia University's Earth Institute and School of Continuing Education. The program's curriculum includes specially developed courses coordinated with some new and existing courses at the University, taught by faculty and researchers who are leaders in the fields of earth science, engineering, architecture, and environmental policy and management. The program utilizes environmental and sustainable development research to provide practical training to a new generation of professionals who will address critical interdisciplinary issues.

The program draws upon the Earth Institute's years of experience in bridging research and practice in the field of sustainability. In response to the increasing global challenges all organizations face, from limiting carbon emissions to managing water resources, the program melds academic leadership, scientific rigor, and professional practice to form a unique interdisciplinary community dedicated to making lasting advances in global sustainability practice. The program draws upon the most sophisticated environmental measurement tools, cutting-edge environmental science, and world-class management and policy studies to help students fully understand the systematic role of sustainability in any organization. Taking a bold and innovative approach to sustainability that prioritizes the protection of the Earth's systems and resources, as well as the spread of social and economic opportunities for all people, the sustainability management program seeks to train a new generation of problem solvers. Graduates of this program should be able to appreciate environmental services, climate, water, and energy to maximize efficient usage and minimize negative impacts.

The M.S. in sustainability management is a 36-point professional degree program that includes five required areas of study: integrative courses in sustainability management, economics and quantitative analysis, the physical dimensions of sustainability management, the public policy environment of sustainability management, and general and financial management.

The degree may be completed on a full- or part-time basis. Full-time students will complete the degree in three intensive semesters (fall, spring, and summer). Part-time students, taking two to three courses per semester, can complete the program over two academic years. Students must complete all requirements within three years with an overall grade point average of 3.0 (B) or better. Graduates receive a unique Master of Science degree and an essential set of skills and knowledge, as well as access to the placement services and networking opportunities presented by Columbia University, the School of Continuing Education, and the Earth Institute.

Research Facilities

The Earth Institute is a $135-million-a-year operation with over 700 environmental scientists, managers, policy analysts, lawyers, engineers, and other experts working all over the world on issues of sustainable development and environmental management.

Financial Aid

All School of Continuing Education students may arrange a private loan to help cover their educational expenses. Students enrolled in this program may be eligible for the Federal Stafford Loan. Students are strongly encouraged to research and apply for scholarship funds from outside sources to help supplement the cost of their education, such as those that may be available from philanthropic, fraternal or nonprofit organizations as well as corporations.

Cost of Study

The tuition for fall 2011–spring 2012 was $1502 per point. A student enrolled in the program on a full-time basis will enroll in 12 points per semester. The degree requires the completion of 36 points. There is a student activities fee of $30 per semester and a University facilities fee of $393 per term for full-time students and $211 per semester for part-time students. A one-time transcript fee of $95 is required of all new students. The health services fee is $450 per semester.

Living and Housing Costs

Graduate students have three main housing opportunities: University Apartment Housing (UAH), International House, and off-campus listings. UAH operates Columbia-owned apartments and dormitory-style suites within walking distance of the campus. Students must be enrolled on a full-time basis to be eligible for UAH. International House, a privately owned student residence near the campus, has accommodations for about 500 graduate students, both international and American, who attend various area colleges and universities. There are also a number of off-campus housing opportunities. The University operates the Off-Campus Housing Assistance (OCHA) program, which lists rooms and apartments in rental properties not owned or operated by the University. More information about this service can be found at http://www.columbia.edu/cu/ire/ocha.

Student Outcomes

Sustainability management students will gain the skills necessary to analyze an organization's work processes and operations in order to understand how it can reduce resource utilization and environmental impact; demonstrate a working knowledge of the processes through which sustainability rules and regulations are created by governments and implemented by organizations; clearly show an ability to apply their understanding of the basic principles and theories of sustainability management as a frame for strategic planning, and the management of people, finances and operations toward sustainability goals; and display an ability to work collaboratively to develop strategies promoting wide-ranging sustainable solutions and to effectively communicate these plans in a professional environment.

Location

Columbia University is located on the Upper West Side of Manhattan. The main entrance to the Morningside Heights campus is on 116th Street and Broadway.

The University

By royal charter of King George II of England, Columbia University was founded in 1754 as King's College. It is the oldest institution of higher learning in New York State and the fifth oldest in the nation. A private, nonsectarian institution, Columbia University is organized into fifteen schools and is associated with more than seventy research and public service institutions and twenty-two scholarly journals.

Applying

Admission to the program is highly selective. The early admissions application deadline for spring admission is October 1. The regular application deadline for spring admission is November 1. The early admissions application deadline for the fall admission is January 15. The regular application deadline for fall admission is May 1. For more specific details regarding applying to the program, and a link to the online application form, potential applicants may visit Columbia's School of Continuing Education Web site at http://ce.columbia.edu/Sustainability-Management/Apply-Program.

Correspondence and Information

Office of Admissions
Columbia University School of Continuing Education
203 Lewisohn Hall
2970 Broadway, Mail Code 4119
New York, New York 10027-6902
United States
Phone: 212-854-9666
E-mail: ce-info@columbia.edu
Web site: http://ce.columbia.edu/Sustainability-Management/
About-the-Program

The Faculty

Courses are taught by an expert faculty, including renowned practitioners in fields ranging from environmental law to alternative energy financing and researchers who are leaders in the fields of earth science, engineering, and environmental management. The program utilizes environmental and sustainable development research and practitioner experience to provide practical training in sustainability management to a new generation of professionals who will address critical interdisciplinary issues.

Additional information about the faculty members can be found at:
http://ce.columbia.edu/Sustainability-Management/Faculty

Web Sites for Additional Information

Video: http://ce.columbia.edu/files/ce/multimedia/SUMA_InfoSession/SUMA_promo_video.html

About the Applying to the Program: http://ce.columbia.edu/Sustainability-Management/Apply-Program

About the Sustainability Management Program: http://ce.columbia.edu/Sustainability-Management/About-the-Program

About the Sustainability Management Program Video: http://www.earth.columbia.edu/videos/watch/302

About the Program Director: http://earth.columbia.edu/articles/view/2252

About the Program Courses: http://ce.columbia.edu/Sustainability-Management/Course-Descriptions

About the Program's Students: http://earth.columbia.edu/articles/view/2805

Program Events: http://earth.columbia.edu/articles/view/1774

Faculty Profiles: http://earth.columbia.edu/articles/view/2248

Student Profiles: http://earth.columbia.edu/articles/view/2331

Marketing

OVERVIEW

Within both the public and private sectors, strategic decision makers describe marketing as a fundamental approach to general management decision making and a necessary set of business functions. Marketing professionals provide critical input in such areas as markets, competitors, and portfolios of operating technologies. Both businesses and noncommercial institutions attempt to anticipate, manage, and satisfy demands for goods and services. As such, the field of marketing is a valuable preparation for many types of management careers, including consulting, entrepreneurial management, and line management. It also benefits entrepreneurs who have goals of starting their own businesses.

An MBA with a concentration in marketing exposes students to a variety of subjects, including consumer behavior and product management, multinational business policy, and legal responsibility. In building a strong portfolio of marketing skills, the MBA in marketing encourages students to delve into the basic disciplines essential to understanding consumer and organizational buying patterns and develop successful marketing strategies. Within MBA marketing programs, students learn ways to successfully conceive, promote, price, and distribute products and services.

Required courses may include study in:

- Business-to-Business Marketing
- Consumer and Buyer Behavior
- Customer Data Analysis and Relationship Marketing
- International Marketing
- Marketing Channels and Logistics
- Marketing Promotion and Communication
- Market Research and Analysis
- New Products: Planning, Developing, and Marketing
- Strategic Marketing

Elective courses may include study in:

- Brand Management
- Consulting
- Consumer Behavior
- Customer Equity Management
- International Marketing
- Marketing High Technology Products
- Marketing Research Methods
- Models for Marketing Decisions
- Product Management
- Service Marketing

Students with a marketing MBA prepare themselves for employment in corporate or not-for-profit management or in marketing fields that range from product management, advertising, and sales and account management to retailing, e-business, distribution management, finance, and strategic marketing planning. Qualified marketing MBA graduates can look forward to careers as brand managers, chief marketing officers, directors of channel marketing, directors of product marketing, international marketing managers, marketing analysts,

marketing communications managers, MBA program directors, segment marketing managers, senior analysts for new product marketing research, senior marketing managers, or vice presidents of marketing and sales. They will find opportunities in large and small organizations representing a spectrum of industrial, consumer goods, service, electronic commerce, and consulting firms in public- and private-sector institutions.

HELPFUL ORGANIZATIONS/ PUBLICATIONS/BLOGS

American Marketing Association (AMA)

http://www.marketingpower.com/Pages/default.aspx

The American Marketing Association (AMA) is the professional association for organizations and individuals who are leading the practice, teaching, and development of marketing worldwide. The organization's principal roles are to:

- Serve as a conduit to foster knowledge sharing.
- Promote/support marketing practice and thought leadership.
- Assist marketers in deepening their marketing expertise, elevating their careers, and achieving better results through relevant information, comprehensive education, and targeted networking.

Marketing Research Association (MRA)

http://www.mra-net.org/

The Marketing Research Association (MRA), based in Glastonbury, CT, was formed in 1954. MRA has a fully operational headquarters with a full-time staff. MRA's activities are governed by a volunteer Board of Directors. MRA is a self-managed, not-for-profit organization providing programs and services for members to:

- Enhance their professional development.
- Stay connected with the marketing research community.
- Gain insight into information about trends occurring in the industry.
- Network with fellow researchers.

MRA currently has approximately 3,000 members internationally, representing all segments of the research profession.

European Society for Opinion and Market Research (ESOMAR)

http://www.esomar.org/

Founded in 1948, European Society for Opinion and Market Research (ESOMAR) is the essential organization for encouraging, advancing, and elevating market research worldwide. With more than 4,800 members from over 120 countries, ESOMAR's aim is to promote the value of market and opinion research in illuminating real issues and bringing about effective decision-making. ESOMAR creates and manages a comprehensive program of industry-specific and thematic conferences, publications, and communications. The Society also actively advocates self-regulation and the worldwide code of practice.

The objects of the ESOMAR are:

- Internationally, to promote the development and use of marketing, social, and opinion research, as being recognized forms of scientific endeavor, as an important basis for effective management decision in both public and private sectors alike.
- To further the professional interest of members wherever they may reside and work.

- To encourage the highest technical standards and levels of professional conduct among its members.
- To establish a code or codes of ethical practice and professional standards.
- To study and advise on national and/or international legislation and judicial decisions which may appear to affect members in their professional capacity.
- To provide the means, through meetings, congresses, seminars, publications, and other activities by which all members may extend their knowledge, widen their experience, and advance their professional status.
- To engage in any other activity or activities as may be considered with the interest of members.

The Forrester Blog

http://blogs.forrester.com/market_insights

This blog is a roll-up of all the posts from analysts who serve Market Insights professionals.

CAREER ASPIRATIONS: A PROSPECTIVE POSITION

Director, Product Marketing-Recovery Services

Job Description

The Director of Product Marketing will be part of the product marketing team, which reports into the marketing strategy group. The marketing strategy group thinks strategically about the industry and business to complement and inform product development, product management, and marketing operations.

The Director of Product Marketing-Recovery Services is responsible for developing strategies to increase market share of the company's offerings in the areas of managed recovery and cloud storage.

Responsibilities

- Serve as the marketing functional team lead/single-point-of-contact in support of the line of business product management on new product development efforts.
- Develop marketing plans highlighting service positioning, target market, recommended go-to-market strategy, and tactics (including recommended channels, analyst relations communications strategy, lead generation tactics, and market segments to address for in-year revenue generation and multiyear pipeline development).
- Develop sales enablement tools related to new services introductions, including customer-facing presentations, case studies, and industry-specific value propositions (where applicable).
- Lead integrated marketing campaign efforts jointly with the marketing operations team to support new business demand generation and customer cross-selling efforts. Campaign responsibilities include: identification of service(s) to be promoted, target market, special promotional offers, messaging for differentiation, etc.
- Collaborate with Market Insights team in the design and testing of market research to support value proposition development for existing and new service offerings.
- Track substitute offerings and competitors, competitive offerings, and competitive pricing at the individual service level. Understand competitive dynamics, market segmentation criteria, and main market value drivers.
- Directly contribute to thought leadership development through blogs, speaking engagements at industry and customer events, white-paper-type content development, etc.
- Interact with industry analysts to understand emerging market trends and influences. Incorporate findings to inform value proposition and go-to-market initiatives.

Qualifications

- At least 7 years of experience in product marketing or product management in a storage or virtualization technology-related field
- Deep technology and market knowledge (vendors, technologies, market drivers) in area of storage, virtualization, and cloud. Understanding of client-server, web-enabled application, and multi-tenant architectures. Understanding of IT recovery components and processes.
- MBA preferred; strong understanding of market and customer segmentation frameworks and hands-on experience with segmentation projects required. Ability to switch between technical and business benefit-level discussion.
- Strong written and verbal communication skills, including strong PowerPoint and Microsoft Excel skills. Strong project management skills. Microsoft Project experience.
- Demonstrated strong performance in prior roles

Career Advice from Business Professionals

Susan J. Brelus
Chief Marketing Officer
Thompson Hine LLP
MBA in Marketing
Case Western Reserve University
Weatherhead School of Management

What drew you to this field?

I love the analytical aspects of marketing coupled with the creativity. Understanding customer/client needs is at the heart of every business. Marketing is centered on this fundamental core and challenges business leaders to develop the right product/service to fulfill those needs and create a compelling vehicle to reach the target audience through promotion and distribution.

What makes a day at your job interesting?

It is dynamic! Every day poses new challenges. My job encompasses strategic thinking as well as tactical execution. I love that combination of developing a plan and thinking through all of the supporting pillars to see it through to fruition.

How has your graduate education been important to your successes and accomplishments along your career path?

The credential opened doors that would otherwise not have been available. When I entered graduate school, I wanted to position myself to go into product management. At the time, it was near impossible to pursue that career path in a major corporation without an MBA degree. The program was personally fulfilling, because it gave me an opportunity to interact with peers from other business disciplines, including those who had a bit of work and life experience under their belts, and learn from those interactions. It was a very stimulating and interactive learning environment.

In your opinion, what does the future of your field hold for someone newly entering it?

Marketing will always be core to business, so the opportunities are limitless.

What are the exciting developments coming in the next five years?

Technology continues to be an incredible enabler, and smart marketers will find more ways to harness it to their advantage. Global business also continues to offer new markets, opportunities, and challenges.

What advice would you share with new graduates entering your field?

When I started out in the products world, I had no idea other industries, such as professional services, had sophisticated marketing organizations. My eyes were opened when a friend asked me if I would interview for a CMO position at a global law firm. I thought, "A law firm??? What kind of marketing would a law firm need and why would I want to do that?" Twelve years later, I'm still doing that, and I love it. It is a fascinating position where I work with incredibly smart lawyers who are schooled in a completely different manner than a business professional. It is a great collaboration that is intellectually stimulating and more creative than I would have ever anticipated. The legal industry is big business, and law firms require talented business professionals to manage the business side of law. My other piece of advice is to take risks. I have taken a number of risks over the course of my career, moving from a Fortune 10 company to a Silicon Valley start-up and moving between different industries. The marketing principles remain the same across all of these settings, but the path you take to the market and to your customers can vary significantly. Taking risks moving to new opportunities can provide great perspective and be very intellectually invigorating. Learning a new market and unlocking its potential is a thrill!

Gail C. Cohen
VP Business Development
Matrix, a Division of L'Oréal USA
M.M. in Marketing and Management
Northwestern University
Kellogg Graduate School of
    Management

What drew you to this field?
Marketing/business development provides you with the incredible opportunity to touch your end user and see the fruits of your labor on products on shelves or in program offerings. It's a dynamic, fast-paced field that is constantly challenging but almost always rewarding.

What makes a day at your job interesting?
Each day is a new challenge and a new opportunity to connect with our users (stylists and clients) in a way that breaks through the clutter and truly resonates with all constituents. Our industry is driven by products, education, and passion. It's always a challenge to see that the combination of those three items becomes a part of every program we develop.

How has your graduate education been important to your successes/accomplishments along your career path?
My undergraduate degree was in accounting, yet I always enjoyed the marketing and business development aspects of the companies I audited. My graduate degree provided the credentials to make the move from accounting to marketing/business development and truly opened that first door. I've been able to leverage the core learning from graduate school and use that as a base to build upon with continued real-world experience.

In your opinion, what does the future of your field hold for someone newly entering it?
I think there is tremendous opportunity for someone entering this field, as new and creative ideas are critical for growth. It's a challenging, demanding, yet rewarding path.

What are the exciting developments coming in the next five years?
I believe that social networking will continue to evolve and heavily influence/challenge traditional marketing/business development models.

What advice would you share with new graduates entering your field?
Keep an open mind and maintain your 'can do' attitude.

MARKETING

Adelphi University, School of Business, MBA Program, Garden City, NY 11530-0701. Offers finance (MBA); management information systems (MBA); management/human resource management (MBA); marketing/e-commerce (MBA). *Accreditation:* AACSB. Part-time and evening/weekend programs available. *Students:* 131 full-time (59 women), 173 part-time (73 women); includes 25 Black or African American, non-Hispanic/Latino; 20 Asian, non-Hispanic/Latino; 17 Hispanic/Latino; 3 Two or more races, non-Hispanic/Latino, 110 international. Average age 29. In 2010, 86 master's awarded. *Degree requirements:* For master's, capstone course. *Entrance requirements:* For master's, GMAT, 2 letters of recommendation. Additional exam requirements/recommendations for international students: Required—TOEFL (minimum score 550 paper-based; 213 computer-based; 80 iBT). *Application deadline:* For fall admission, 4/1 for international students; for spring admission, 11/1 for international students. Applications are processed on a rolling basis. Application fee: $50. Electronic applications accepted. *Financial support:* Research assistantships with full and partial tuition reimbursements, career-related internships or fieldwork, Federal Work-Study, institutionally sponsored loans, scholarships/grants, and unspecified assistantships available. Financial award application deadline: 3/1; financial award applicants required to submit FAFSA. *Faculty research:* Supply chain management, distribution channels, productivity benchmark analysis, data envelopment analysis, financial portfolio analysis. *Unit head:* Rakesh Gupta, 516-877-4670, Fax: 516-877-4607, E-mail: gradbusinquiries@adelphi.edu. *Application contact:* Christine Murphy, Director of Admissions, 516-877-3050, Fax: 516-877-3039, E-mail: graduateadmissions@adelphi.edu.

American Public University System, AMU/APU Graduate Programs, Charles Town, WV 25414. Offers accounting (MBA); administration and supervision (M Ed); air warfare (MA Military Studies); asymmetrical warfare (MA Military Studies); criminal justice (MA); emergency and disaster management (MA); entrepreneurship (MBA); environmental policy and management (MS); finance (MBA); general (MBA); global business management (MBA); guidance and counseling (M Ed); history (MA); homeland security (MA); homeland security resource allocation (MBA); humanities (MA); information technology (MS); information technology management (MBA); intelligence studies (MA); international relations and conflict resolution (MA); joint warfare (MA Military Studies); land warfare (MA Military Studies); legal studies (MA); management (MA), including defense mangement, general, human resource management, organizational leadership, public administration; marketing (MBA); military history (MA); national security studies (MA); naval warfare (MA Military Studies); nonprofit management (MBA); political science (MA); psychology (MA); public administration (MA); public health (MA); security management (MA); space studies (MS); sports management (MS); strategic leadership (MA Military Studies); teaching (M Ed), including elementary, secondary social sciences; transportation and logistics management (MA). Programs offered via distance learning only. Part-time and evening/weekend programs available. Postbaccalaureate distance learning degree programs offered (no on-campus study). *Faculty:* 253 full-time (134 women), 1,208 part-time/adjunct (570 women). *Students:* 956 full-time (422 women), 8,476 part-time (2,821 women); includes 2,511 minority (1,218 Black or African American, non-Hispanic/Latino; 68 American Indian or Alaska Native, non-Hispanic/Latino; 219 Asian, non-Hispanic/Latino; 705 Hispanic/Latino; 46 Native Hawaiian or other Pacific Islander, non-Hispanic/Latino; 255 Two or more races, non-Hispanic/Latino), 107 international. Average age 35. 9,550 applicants, 100% accepted. In 2010, 1,688 master's awarded. *Degree requirements:* For master's, comprehensive exam or practicum. *Entrance requirements:* For master's, official transcript showing earned bachelor's degree from institution accredited by recognized accrediting body. Additional exam requirements/recommendations for international students: Required—TOEFL (minimum score 550 paper-based; 213 computer-based), IELTS (minimum score 6.5). *Application deadline:* Applications are processed on a rolling basis. Application fee: $0. Electronic applications accepted. *Financial support:* Applicants required to submit FAFSA. *Faculty research:* Military history, criminal justice, management performance, national security. *Unit head:* Dr. Frank McCluskey, Provost, 877-468-6268, Fax: 304-724-3780. *Application contact:* Terry Grant, Director of Enrollment Management, 877-468-6268, Fax: 304-724-3780, E-mail: info@apus.edu.

American University, Kogod School of Business, Master of Business Administration Program, Washington, DC 20016-8044. Offers accounting (MBA); consulting (MBA), including information technology, international business, management; corporate finance: commercial banking (MBA); corporate finance: corporate financial management (MBA); corporate finance: investment banking (MBA), including corporate finance and private equity, trading and selling; entrepreneurship (MBA); global emerging markets (MBA), including business, finance, information technology; international trade and global supply chain management (MBA); leadership (MBA); marketing management (MBA); marketing research (MBA); real estate (MBA); MBA/JD; MBA/LL M. Part-time and evening/weekend programs available. *Faculty:* 12 full-time (5 women). *Students:* 135 full-time (62 women), 104 part-time (38 women); includes 46 minority (18 Black or African American, non-Hispanic/Latino; 1 American Indian or Alaska Native, non-Hispanic/

Latino; 12 Asian, non-Hispanic/Latino; 14 Hispanic/Latino; 1 Two or more races, non-Hispanic/Latino), 34 international. Average age 27. 467 applicants, 51% accepted, 70 enrolled. In 2010, 101 master's awarded. *Entrance requirements:* For master's, GMAT. Additional exam requirements/recommendations for international students: Required—TOEFL. *Application deadline:* For fall admission, 2/1 priority date for domestic students; for spring admission, 10/1 priority date for domestic students. Applications are processed on a rolling basis. Application fee: $100. *Expenses:* Contact institution. *Financial support:* In 2010–11, 19 students received support; fellowships, research assistantships with partial tuition reimbursements available, career-related internships or fieldwork, Federal Work-Study, and institutionally sponsored loans available. Support available to part-time students. Financial award application deadline: 2/1. *Faculty research:* Information technology, decision-aiding methodology, negotiation. *Unit head:* Dr. Stevan Holmberg, Chair, 202-885-6193, E-mail: sholmbe@american.edu. *Application contact:* Shannon Demko, Associate Director Graduate Admissions, 202-885-1994, Fax: 202-885-1108, E-mail: demko@american.edu.

Arizona State University, W. P. Carey School of Business, Department of Marketing, Tempe, AZ 85287-4106. Offers business administration (marketing) (PhD); real estate development (MRED). Part-time and evening/weekend programs available. Postbaccalaureate distance learning degree programs offered. *Faculty:* 23 full-time (6 women), 3 part-time/adjunct (0 women). *Students:* 42 full-time (6 women); includes 13 minority (2 Black or African American, non-Hispanic/Latino; 3 Asian, non-Hispanic/Latino; 7 Hispanic/Latino; 1 Two or more races, non-Hispanic/Latino), 6 international. Average age 33. 73 applicants, 85% accepted, 41 enrolled. In 2010, 38 master's awarded. *Degree requirements:* For master's, thesis or alternative, capstone project, interactive Program of Study (iPOS) submitted before completing 50 percent of required credit hours; for doctorate, comprehensive exam, thesis/dissertation, interactive Program of Study (iPOS) submitted before completing 50 percent of required credit hours. *Entrance requirements:* For master's, GMAT, GRE, or LSAT, minimum GPA of 3.0 in last 2 years of work leading to bachelor's degree, 3 personal references, resume, official transcripts, personal statement; for doctorate, GMAT, minimum GPA of 3.0 in last 2 years of work leading to bachelor's degree, 3 letters of recommendation, personal statement/essay. Additional exam requirements/recommendations for international students: Required—TOEFL (minimum score 550 paper-based; 213 computer-based; 80 iBT), IELTS (minimum score 6.5). *Application deadline:* For fall admission, 1/15 for domestic and international students. Application fee: $70 ($90 for international students). Electronic applications accepted. *Expenses:* Contact institution. *Financial support:* Fellowships with full and partial tuition reimbursements, research assistantships with full and partial tuition reimbursements, teaching assistantships with full and partial tuition reimbursements, career-related internships or fieldwork, institutionally sponsored loans, scholarships/grants, and tuition waivers (full and partial) available. Financial award application deadline: 3/1; financial award applicants required to submit FAFSA. *Faculty research:* Service marketing and management, strategic marketing, customer portfolio management, characteristics and skills of high-performing managers, market orientation, market segmentation, consumer behavior, marketing strategy, new product development, management of innovation, social influences on consumption, e-commerce, market research methodology. Total annual research expenditures: $213,495. *Unit head:* Mark Stapp, Executive Director, 480-727-9287, Fax: 480-727-9288, E-mail: mark.stapp@asu.edu. *Application contact:* Graduate Admissions, 480-965-6113.

Arizona State University, W. P. Carey School of Business, Program in Business Administration, Tempe, AZ 85287-4906. Offers accountancy (PhD); agribusiness (PhD); business administration (MBA); finance (PhD); financial management and markets (MBA); information management (MBA); information systems (PhD); management (PhD); marketing (PhD); strategic marketing and services leadership (MBA); supply chain financial management (MBA); supply chain management (MBA, PhD); JD/MBA; MBA/M Acc; MBA/M Arch. *Accreditation:* AACSB. Part-time and evening/weekend programs available. Postbaccalaureate distance learning degree programs offered (minimal on-campus study). *Faculty:* 84 full-time (22 women), 7 part-time/adjunct (2 women). *Students:* 1,302 full-time (379 women), 86 part-time (26 women); includes 241 minority (37 Black or African American, non-Hispanic/Latino; 11 American Indian or Alaska Native, non-Hispanic/Latino; 103 Asian, non-Hispanic/Latino; 76 Hispanic/Latino; 4 Native Hawaiian or other Pacific Islander, non-Hispanic/Latino; 10 Two or more races, non-Hispanic/Latino), 171 international. Average age 31. 1,795 applicants, 44% accepted, 525 enrolled. In 2010, 734 master's, 9 doctorates awarded. Terminal master's awarded for partial completion of doctoral program. *Degree requirements:* For master's, thesis or alternative, internship, interactive Program of Study (iPOS) submitted before completing 50 percent of required credit hours; for doctorate, comprehensive exam, thesis/dissertation, interactive Program of Study (iPOS) submitted before completing 50 percent of required credit hours. *Entrance requirements:* For master's, GMAT, minimum GPA of 3.0 in last 2 years of work leading to bachelor's degree, 2 letters of recommendation, professional resume, official transcripts, 3 essays; for doctorate, GMAT or GRE, minimum GPA of 3.0 in last 2 years of work leading to bachelor's degree, 3 letters of recommendation, resume, personal statement/essay. Additional exam requirements/recommendations for international students: Required—TOEFL (minimum score 550 paper-based; 213 computer-based; 80 iBT), IELTS (minimum score 6.5). Application fee: $70 ($90 for international students). Electronic applications accepted. *Expenses:* Contact institution. *Financial support:* In 2010–11, 17 research assistantships with full and partial tuition reimbursements (averaging $18,121 per year), 153 teaching assistantships with full and partial tuition reimbursements (averaging $9,176 per year) were awarded; fellowships with full and partial tuition reimbursements, career-related internships or fieldwork, institutionally sponsored loans, scholarships/grants, and tuition waivers (full and partial) also available. Support available to part-time students. Financial award application deadline: 3/1; financial award applicants required to submit FAFSA. Total annual research expenditures: $540,779. *Unit head:* Dr. Robert E. Mittelstaedt, Dean, 480-965-2468, Fax: 480-965-5539, E-mail: mittelsr@asu.edu. *Application contact:* Graduate Admissions, 480-965-6113.

Ashworth College, Graduate Programs, Norcross, GA 30092. Offers business administration (MBA); criminal justice (MS); health care administration (MBA, MS); human resource management (MBA, MS); international business (MBA); management (MS); marketing (MBA, MS). *Faculty:* 5 part-time/adjunct (1 woman). *Students:* 299. *Expenses:* Tuition: Full-time $9230; part-time $250 per credit hour. *Unit head:* Dr. Leslie A. Gargiulo, Vice President of Education, 770-729-8400, E-mail: lgargiulo@ashworthcollege.edu. *Application contact:* Dr. Leslie A. Gargiulo, Vice President of Education, 770-729-8400, E-mail: lgargiulo@ashworthcollege.edu.

Assumption College, Graduate School, Department of Business Studies, Worcester, MA 01609-1296. Offers accounting (MBA); business administration (CAGS); finance/economics (MBA); general business (MBA); human resources (MBA); international business (MBA); management (MBA); marketing (MBA); nonprofit leadership (MBA). Part-time and evening/weekend programs available. *Faculty:* 3 full-time (0 women), 13 part-time/adjunct (3 women). *Students:* 20 full-time (9 women), 135 part-time (70 women); includes 24 minority (19 Black or African American, non-Hispanic/Latino; 2 Asian, non-Hispanic/Latino; 3 Hispanic/Latino), 4 international. Average age 26. 85 applicants, 95% accepted. In 2010, 40 master's, 2 other advanced degrees awarded. *Entrance requirements:* For master's and CAGS, 3 letters of recommendation, resume, essay. Additional exam requirements/recommendations for international students: Required—TOEFL (minimum score 540 paper-based; 200 computer-based; 76 iBT), IELTS (minimum score 6). *Application deadline:* For fall admission, 6/1 priority date for domestic students, 5/1 priority date for international students; for spring admission, 11/1 priority date for domestic students, 9/1 priority date for international students. Applications are processed on a rolling basis. Application fee: $30. Electronic applications accepted. *Expenses:* Tuition: Part-time $503 per credit. Required fees: $20 per semester. One-time fee: $100. Part-time tuition and fees vary according to campus/location. *Financial support:* Application deadline: 6/1. *Faculty research:* Workplace diversity, dynamics of team interaction, utilization of leased employees. *Unit head:* Michael Lewis, Director, 508-767-7372, Fax: 508-767-7252, E-mail: milewis@assumption.edu. *Application contact:* Daniel Provost, Assistant Director of Graduate Student Services, 508-767-7426, Fax: 508-767-7030, E-mail: dprovost@assumption.edu.

Avila University, School of Business, Kansas City, MO 64145-1698. Offers accounting (MBA); finance (MBA); general management (MBA); health care administration (MBA); international business (MBA); management information systems (MBA); marketing (MBA). Part-time and evening/weekend programs available. *Faculty:* 9 full-time (3 women), 24 part-time/adjunct (6 women). *Students:* 123 full-time (68 women), 87 part-time (52 women); includes 44 minority (30 Black or African American, non-Hispanic/Latino; 1 American Indian or Alaska Native, non-Hispanic/Latino; 6 Asian, non-Hispanic/Latino; 6 Hispanic/Latino; 1 Native Hawaiian or other Pacific Islander, non-Hispanic/Latino), 46 international. Average age 33. 62 applicants, 79% accepted, 49 enrolled. In 2010, 80 master's awarded. *Degree requirements:* For master's, comprehensive exam, capstone course. *Entrance requirements:* For master's, GMAT (minimum score 420), minimum GPA of 3.0, interview. Additional exam requirements/recommendations for international students: Required—TOEFL (minimum score 550 paper-based). *Application deadline:* For fall admission, 7/30 priority date for domestic students, 7/30 for international students; for winter admission, 11/30 priority date for domestic students, 11/30 for international students; for spring admission, 2/28 priority date for domestic students, 2/28 for international students. Applications are processed on a rolling basis. Application fee: $0. Electronic applications accepted. *Expenses:* Contact institution. *Financial support:* In 2010–11, 102 students received support. Career-related internships or fieldwork and Competitive Merit Scholarship available. Support available to part-time students. Financial award applicants required to submit FAFSA. *Faculty research:* Leadership characteristics, financial hedging, group dynamics. *Unit head:* Dr. Richard Woodall, Dean, 816-501-3720, Fax: 816-501-2463, E-mail: richard.woodall@avila.edu. *Application contact:* JoAnna Giffin, MBA Admissions Director, 816-501-3601, Fax: 816-501-2463, E-mail: joanna.giffin@avila.edu.

Azusa Pacific University, School of Business and Management, Azusa, CA 91702-7000. Offers business administration (MBA); diversity for strategic advantage (MA); entrepreneurship (MBA); finance (MBA); human and organizational development (MA); human resources and organizational development (MBA); human resources management (MA); international business (MBA); marketing (MBA); non-profit management (MA); organizational development

and change (MA); performance improvement (MA); public administration (MA); strategic management (MBA). Part-time and evening/weekend programs available. *Faculty:* 19 full-time (5 women), 2 part-time/adjunct (1 woman). *Students:* 75 full-time (41 women), 96 part-time (46 women); includes 65 minority (15 Black or African American, non-Hispanic/Latino; 15 Asian, non-Hispanic/Latino; 34 Hispanic/Latino; 1 Native Hawaiian or other Pacific Islander, non-Hispanic/Latino), 17 international. Average age 30. In 2010, 82 master's awarded. *Degree requirements:* For master's, thesis (for some programs), final project. *Entrance requirements:* For master's, GMAT, minimum GPA of 3.0. Additional exam requirements/recommendations for international students: Required—TOEFL (minimum score 600 paper-based). *Application deadline:* For fall admission, 8/15 priority date for domestic students. Applications are processed on a rolling basis. Application fee: $45 ($65 for international students). *Expenses:* Contact institution. *Financial support:* Scholarships/grants available. *Faculty research:* Gender issues, financial risk, leadership and ethics, marketing strategy. *Unit head:* Dr. Ilene Bezjian, Dean, 626-815-3090, Fax: 626-815-3802, E-mail: ibezjian@apu.edu. *Application contact:* Dr. Ilene Bezjian, Dean, 626-815-3090, Fax: 626-815-3802, E-mail: ibezjian@apu.edu.

Benedictine University, Graduate Programs, Program in Business Administration, Lisle, IL 60532-0900. Offers accounting (MBA); entrepreneurship and managing innovation (MBA); financial management (MBA); health administration (MBA); human resource management (MBA); information systems security (MBA); international business (MBA); management consulting (MBA); management information systems (MBA); marketing management (MBA); operations management and logistics (MBA); organizational leadership (MBA); MBA/MPH; MBA/MS. Part-time and evening/weekend programs available. Postbaccalaureate distance learning degree programs offered (minimal on-campus study). *Faculty:* 4 full-time (2 women), 24 part-time/adjunct (3 women). *Students:* 347 full-time (140 women), 672 part-time (360 women); includes 237 minority (155 Black or African American, non-Hispanic/Latino; 4 American Indian or Alaska Native, non-Hispanic/Latino; 43 Asian, non-Hispanic/Latino; 35 Hispanic/Latino), 21 international. Average age 34. 416 applicants, 88% accepted, 217 enrolled. In 2010, 355 master's awarded. *Entrance requirements:* For master's, GMAT. Additional exam requirements/recommendations for international students: Required—TOEFL (minimum score 550 paper-based; 213 computer-based). *Application deadline:* For fall admission, 9/1 for domestic students; for winter admission, 12/1 for domestic students; for spring admission, 2/15 for domestic students. Applications are processed on a rolling basis. Application fee: $40. Electronic applications accepted. *Financial support:* Career-related internships or fieldwork and health care benefits available. Support available to part-time students. *Faculty research:* Strategic leadership in professional organizations, sociology of professions, organizational change, social identity theory, applications to change management. *Unit head:* Dr. Sharon Borowicz, Director, 630-829-6219, E-mail: sborowicz@ben.edu. *Application contact:* Kari Gibbons, Director, Admissions, 630-829-6200, Fax: 630-829-6584, E-mail: kgibbons@ben.edu.

Bentley University, McCallum Graduate School of Business, Program in Marketing Analytics, Waltham, MA 02452-4705. Offers MSMA. Part-time and evening/weekend programs available. *Faculty:* 74 full-time (22 women), 21 part-time/adjunct (5 women). *Students:* 37 full-time (26 women), 21 part-time (16 women); includes 5 minority (4 Asian, non-Hispanic/Latino; 1 Hispanic/Latino), 38 international. Average age 26. 107 applicants, 62% accepted, 29 enrolled. *Entrance requirements:* For master's, GMAT or GRE General Test. Additional exam requirements/recommendations for international students: Required—TOEFL, TOEFL (minimum score 600 paper-based; 250 computer-based; 100 iBT) or IELTS (minimum score 7). *Application deadline:* For fall admission, 12/1 priority date for domestic and international students; for spring admission, 10/1 priority date for domestic and international students. Application fee: $50. Electronic applications accepted. *Expenses:* Tuition: Full-time $28,224; part-time $1176 per credit. Required fees: $404. Part-time tuition and fees vary according to course load. *Financial support:* In 2010–11, 11 students received support. Scholarships/grants and unspecified assistantships available. Financial award application deadline: 6/1; financial award applicants required to submit CSS PROFILE or FAFSA. *Faculty research:* Marketing information processing, blogging and social media, customer lifetime value and customer relationship management, measuring and improving productivity, online consumer behavior. *Unit head:* Dr. Paul Berger, Director, 781-891-2746, E-mail: pberger@bentley.edu. *Application contact:* Sharon Hill, Director of Graduate Admissions, 781-891-2108, Fax: 781-891-2464, E-mail: bentleygraduateadmissions@bentley.edu.

California Lutheran University, Graduate Studies, School of Management, Thousand Oaks, CA 91360-2787. Offers business (IMBA); computer science (MS); econometrics (MBA); economics (MS); entrepreneurship (MBA, Certificate); finance (MBA, Certificate); financial planning (MBA, Certificate); information systems and technology (MS); information technology management (MBA, Certificate); international business (MBA, Certificate); management and organization behavior (MBA); management and organizational behavior (Certificate); marketing (MBA, Certificate); microeconomics (MBA); nonprofit and social enterprise (MBA). Part-time and evening/weekend programs available. Postbaccalaureate distance learning degree programs offered (no on-campus study). *Faculty:* 12 full-time (3 women), 27 part-time/adjunct (6 women). *Students:* 350 full-time (162 women), 262 part-time (99 women); includes 21 Black or African American, non-Hispanic/Latino; 44 Asian, non-Hispanic/Latino; 56 Hispanic/Latino; 4 Native Hawaiian or other Pacific Islander, non-Hispanic/Latino; 12 Two or more races, non-Hispanic/Latino, 185 international. Average age 32. 379 applicants, 74% accepted, 138 enrolled. In 2010, 231 master's awarded. *Entrance requirements:* For master's, GMAT, interview, minimum GPA of 3.0. *Application deadline:* Applications are processed on a rolling basis. Application fee: $50. *Expenses:* Contact institution. *Unit head:* Dr. Charles Maxey, Dean, 805-493-3360. *Application contact:* 805-493-3127, Fax: 805-493-3542, E-mail: clugrad@clunet.edu.

California State University, East Bay, Office of Academic Programs and Graduate Studies, College of Business and Economics, Department of Marketing, Option in Marketing Management, Hayward, CA 94542-3000. Offers MBA. Part-time and evening/weekend programs available. *Degree requirements:* For master's, comprehensive exam or thesis. *Entrance requirements:* For master's, GMAT, minimum GPA of 2.75. Additional exam requirements/recommendations for international students: Required—TOEFL (minimum score 550 paper-based; 213 computer-based). *Application deadline:* For fall admission, 6/30 for domestic and international students. Application fee: $55. Electronic applications accepted. *Financial support:* Fellowships, teaching assistantships, career-related internships or fieldwork, Federal Work-Study, institutionally sponsored loans, and scholarships/grants available. Support available to part-time students. Financial award application deadline: 3/1; financial award applicants required to submit FAFSA. *Unit head:* Dr. Nan Maxwell, Chair, 510-885-4336, E-mail: nan.maxwell.@csueastbay.edu. *Application contact:* Donna Wiley, Interim Associate Director, 510-885-2928, Fax: 510-885-4777, E-mail: donna.wiley@csueastbay.edu.

California State University, East Bay, Office of Academic Programs and Graduate Studies, College of Business and Economics, MBA Program, Hayward, CA 94542-3000. Offers entrepreneurship (MBA); finance (MBA); human resources and organizational behavior (MBA); information technology management (MBA); marketing management (MBA); operations and supply chain management (MBA); strategy and international business (MBA). Part-time and evening/weekend programs available. Postbaccalaureate distance learning degree programs offered (no on-campus study). *Faculty:* 33 full-time (9 women). *Students:* 121 full-time (58 women), 133 part-time (67 women); includes 7 Black or African American, non-Hispanic/Latino; 63 Asian, non-Hispanic/Latino; 11 Hispanic/Latino; 3 Native Hawaiian or other Pacific Islander, non-Hispanic/Latino; 5 Two or more races, non-Hispanic/Latino, 87 international. Average age 30. 284 applicants, 47% accepted, 55 enrolled. In 2010, 241 master's awarded. *Degree requirements:* For master's, comprehensive exam or thesis. *Entrance requirements:* For master's, GMAT (minimum 20th percentile verbal and quantitative section), bachelor's degree, minimum GPA of 2.75. Additional exam requirements/recommendations for international students: Required—TOEFL (minimum score 550 paper-based; 213 computer-based; 79 iBT). *Application deadline:* For fall admission, 6/30 for domestic and international students. Applications are processed on a rolling basis. Application fee: $55. Electronic applications accepted. *Financial support:* Career-related internships or fieldwork, Federal Work-Study, institutionally sponsored loans, and scholarships/grants available. Support available to part-time students. Financial award application deadline: 3/2; financial award applicants required to submit FAFSA. *Unit head:* Dr. Terri Swartz, Dean, 510-885-3291, Fax: 510-885-4884, E-mail: terri.swartz@csueastbay.edu. *Application contact:* Dr. Donna Wiley, Interim Associate Director, 510-885-2928, Fax: 510-885-4777, E-mail: donna.wiley@csueastbay.edu.

California State University, Fullerton, Graduate Studies, College of Business and Economics, Department of Marketing, Fullerton, CA 92834-9480. Offers marketing (MBA). Part-time programs available. *Students:* 21 full-time (12 women), 19 part-time (9 women); includes 1 Black or African American, non-Hispanic/Latino; 6 Asian, non-Hispanic/Latino; 1 Hispanic/Latino, 15 international. Average age 27. 65 applicants, 26% accepted, 5 enrolled. In 2010, 9 master's awarded. *Degree requirements:* For master's, project or thesis. *Entrance requirements:* For master's, GMAT, minimum AACSB index of 950. Application fee: $55. *Financial support:* Career-related internships or fieldwork, Federal Work-Study, institutionally sponsored loans, and scholarships/grants available. Support available to part-time students. Financial award application deadline: 3/1; financial award applicants required to submit FAFSA. *Unit head:* Dr. Irene Lange, Chair, 657-278-2223. *Application contact:* Admissions/Applications, 657-278-2371.

California State University, Los Angeles, Graduate Studies, College of Business and Economics, Department of Marketing, Los Angeles, CA 90032-8530. Offers international business (MBA, MS); marketing management (MBA, MS). Part-time and evening/weekend programs available. *Students:* 3 full-time (2 women), 9 part-time (3 women); includes 2 minority (both Asian, non-Hispanic/Latino), 7 international. Average age 27. 15 applicants, 100% accepted, 5 enrolled. In 2010, 16 master's awarded. *Degree requirements:* For master's, comprehensive exam (MBA), thesis (MS). *Entrance requirements:* For master's, GMAT, minimum GPA of 2.5 during previous 2 years of course work. Additional exam requirements/recommendations for international students: Required—TOEFL (minimum score 550 paper-based; 213

computer-based). *Application deadline:* For fall admission, 5/1 for domestic and international students. Applications are processed on a rolling basis. Application fee: $55. Electronic applications accepted. *Financial support:* Career-related internships or fieldwork and Federal Work-Study available. Support available to part-time students. Financial award application deadline: 3/1. *Unit head:* Dr. Paul Washburn, Acting Chair, 323-343-2960, Fax: 323-343-5462, E-mail: pwashbu@calstatela.edu. *Application contact:* Dr. Alan Muchlinski, Dean of Graduate Studies, 323-343-3820, Fax: 323-343-5653, E-mail: amuchli@exchange.calstatela.edu.

Canisius College, Graduate Division, Richard J. Wehle School of Business, Department of Management and Marketing, Buffalo, NY 14208-1098. Offers accelerated business administration (1 year) (MBA); business administration (MBA); international business (MS). *Accreditation:* AACSB. Part-time and evening/weekend programs available. *Faculty:* 35 full-time (7 women), 5 part-time/adjunct (3 women). *Students:* 95 full-time (36 women), 171 part-time (70 women); includes 26 minority (15 Black or African American, non-Hispanic/Latino; 1 American Indian or Alaska Native, non-Hispanic/Latino; 8 Asian, non-Hispanic/Latino; 2 Hispanic/Latino), 9 international. Average age 29. 149 applicants, 71% accepted, 82 enrolled. In 2010, 111 master's awarded. *Entrance requirements:* For master's, GMAT, transcripts. Additional exam requirements/recommendations for international students: Required—TOEFL. *Application deadline:* For fall admission, 7/1 priority date for domestic students; for spring admission, 11/1 priority date for domestic students. Applications are processed on a rolling basis. Application fee: $25. Electronic applications accepted. *Expenses:* Tuition: Part-time $694 per credit hour. Required fees: $11 per credit hour. $90 per semester. *Financial support:* Research assistantships, career-related internships or fieldwork, Federal Work-Study, scholarships/grants, and unspecified assistantships available. Support available to part-time students. Financial award application deadline: 7/1; financial award applicants required to submit FAFSA. *Faculty research:* Global leadership effectiveness, global supply chain management, quality management. *Unit head:* Dr. George Palumbo, Director, MBA Program, 716-888-2667, Fax: 716-888-3132, E-mail: palumbo@canisius.edu. *Application contact:* Jim Bagwell, Director, Graduate Programs, 716-888-2545, Fax: 716-888-3290, E-mail: bagwellj@canisius.edu.

Central European University, CEU Business School, Budapest, Hungary. Offers executive business administration (EMBA); finance (MBA); general management (MBA); information technology management (MBA); marketing (MBA); real estate management (MBA). Part-time and evening/weekend programs available. *Faculty:* 16 full-time (4 women), 2 part-time/adjunct (1 woman). *Students:* 71 full-time (30 women), 142 part-time (47 women). Average age 34. 144 applicants, 36% accepted, 32 enrolled. In 2010, 64 master's awarded. *Degree requirements:* For master's, one foreign language. *Entrance requirements:* For master's, GMAT. Additional exam requirements/recommendations for international students: Required—TOEFL (minimum score 570 paper-based; 230 computer-based); Recommended—IELTS (minimum score 6.5). *Application deadline:* For fall admission, 5/15 priority date for domestic students, 5/22 for international students; for winter admission, 11/15 priority date for domestic students, 11/10 for international students. Applications are processed on a rolling basis. Application fee: $0. Electronic applications accepted. Tuition and fees charges are reported in euros. *Expenses:* Tuition: Full-time 11,000 euros. Required fees: 250 euros. One-time fee: 200 euros full-time. Tuition and fees vary according to degree level, program, reciprocity agreements and student level. *Financial support:* In 2010–11, 4 students received support. Tuition waivers (partial) available. *Faculty research:* Social and ethical business, marketing. *Unit head:* Dr. Mel Horwitch, Dean and Managing Director, 361-887-5050, E-mail: mhorwitch@ceubusiness.com. *Application contact:* Agnes Schram, MBA Program Manager, 361-887-5511, Fax: 361-887-5133, E-mail: mba@ceubusiness.com.

Central Michigan University, College of Graduate Studies, College of Business Administration, Department of Marketing and Hospitality Services Administration, Mount Pleasant, MI 48859. Offers marketing (MBA). Part-time and evening/weekend programs available. *Faculty:* 8 full-time (2 women), 1 part-time/adjunct (0 women). *Degree requirements:* For master's, thesis or alternative. *Entrance requirements:* For master's, GMAT. *Application deadline:* For fall admission, 6/1 for international students; for spring admission, 10/1 for international students. Applications are processed on a rolling basis. Application fee: $35 ($45 for international students). Electronic applications accepted. *Expenses:* Tuition, state resident: full-time $8208; part-time $456 per credit hour. Tuition, nonresident: full-time $13,788; part-time $766 per credit hour. One-time fee: $25. *Financial support:* Fellowships with tuition reimbursements, research assistantships with tuition reimbursements, teaching assistantships with tuition reimbursements, unspecified assistantships and out-of-state merit awards, non-resident graduate awards available. *Faculty research:* Consumer preferences and market assessment, marketing research and new product development, business economics and forecasting, SAP/marketing and logistics, services marketing and hospitality organizations. *Unit head:* Dr. Richard Divine, Chairperson, 989-774-3701, Fax: 989-774-7406, E-mail: divin1rl@cmich.edu. *Application contact:* Dr. Debasish Chakraborty, Director, MBA Program, 989-774-3337, Fax: 989-774-1320, E-mail: chakr1d@cmich.edu.

Clark University, Graduate School, Graduate School of Management, Business Administration Program, Worcester, MA 01610-1477. Offers accounting (MBA); finance (MBA); global business (MBA); health care management (MBA); management (MBA); management of information technology (MBA); marketing (MBA). *Accreditation:* AACSB. Part-time and evening/weekend programs available. *Students:* 147 full-time (75 women), 126 part-time (54 women); includes 24 minority (10 Black or African American, non-Hispanic/Latino; 1 American Indian or Alaska Native, non-Hispanic/Latino; 6 Asian, non-Hispanic/Latino; 5 Hispanic/Latino; 2 Two or more races, non-Hispanic/Latino), 99 international. Average age 30. 382 applicants, 57% accepted, 89 enrolled. In 2010, 101 master's awarded. *Degree requirements:* For master's, thesis optional. *Application deadline:* For fall admission, 6/1 priority date for domestic students; for spring admission, 12/1 priority date for domestic students. Applications are processed on a rolling basis. Application fee: $50. Electronic applications accepted. *Expenses:* Tuition: Full-time $37,000; part-time $1156 per credit hour. Required fees: $30; $1156 per credit hour. *Financial support:* In 2010–11, research assistantships with partial tuition reimbursements (averaging $4,800 per year), teaching assistantships with partial tuition reimbursements (averaging $4,800 per year) were awarded; fellowships, career-related internships or fieldwork, Federal Work-Study, institutionally sponsored loans, and tuition waivers (partial) also available. Support available to part-time students. Financial award application deadline: 5/31. *Faculty research:* Organizational development, accounting, marketing, finance, human resource management. *Unit head:* Dr. Joseph Sarkis, Dean, 508-793-7406, Fax: 508-793-8822, E-mail: clarkmba@clarku.edu. *Application contact:* Lynn Davis, Enrollment and Marketing Director, 508-793-7406, Fax: 508-793-8822, E-mail: clarkmba@clarku.edu.

Clemson University, Graduate School, College of Business and Behavioral Science, Department of Marketing, Clemson, SC 29634. Offers marketing (MS). *Faculty:* 15 full-time (3 women). *Students:* 10 full-time (6 women); includes 1 Two or more races, non-Hispanic/Latino, 3 international. Average age 25. 114 applicants, 17% accepted, 10 enrolled. In 2010, 13 master's awarded. *Entrance requirements:* For master's, GMAT, minimum GPA of 3.0, letters of recommendation. Additional exam requirements/recommendations for international students: Required—TOEFL. *Application deadline:* Applications are processed on a rolling basis. Application fee: $70 ($80 for international students). Electronic applications accepted. *Expenses:* Tuition, state resident: full-time $6492; part-time $400 per credit hour. Tuition, nonresident: full-time $13,634; part-time $800 per credit hour. Required fees: $262 per semester. Part-time tuition and fees vary according to course load and program. *Financial support:* In 2010–11, 6 students received support, including 6 teaching assistantships with partial tuition reimbursements available (averaging $6,797 per year); career-related internships or fieldwork, institutionally sponsored loans, scholarships/grants, health care benefits, and unspecified assistantships also available. Support available to part-time students. Financial award applicants required to submit FAFSA. *Unit head:* Dr. Greg Pickett, Head, 864-656-5294, E-mail: pgregor@clemson.edu. *Application contact:* Dr. Thomas Baker, Program Contact, 864-656-2397, Fax: 864-656-0138, E-mail: tbaker2@clemson.edu.

Cleveland State University, College of Graduate Studies, Nance College of Business Administration, Department of Marketing, Cleveland, OH 44115. Offers global business (Graduate Certificate); marketing (MBA, DBA); marketing analytics (Graduate Certificate). *Faculty:* 12 full-time (3 women), 6 part-time/adjunct (3 women). *Students:* 4 full-time (1 woman), 11 part-time (4 women); includes 1 Black or African American, non-Hispanic/Latino, 2 international. 6 applicants, 0% accepted, 0 enrolled. *Expenses:* Tuition, state resident: full-time $8447; part-time $469 per credit hour. Tuition, non-resident: full-time $16,020; part-time $890 per credit hour. Required fees: $50. *Financial support:* In 2010–11, 4 students received support, including 4 research assistantships (averaging $9,744 per year); tuition waivers (partial) also available. Financial award application deadline: 6/30; financial award applicants required to submit FAFSA. *Unit head:* Dr. Thomas W. Whipple, Chair, 216-687-4771, Fax: 216-687-5135, E-mail: t.whipple@csuohio.edu. *Application contact:* Dr. Thomas W. Whipple, Chair, 216-687-4771, Fax: 216-687-9354, E-mail: t.whipple@csuohio.edu.

Cleveland State University, College of Graduate Studies, Nance College of Business Administration, Doctor of Business Administration (DBA) Program, Cleveland, OH 44115. Offers business administration (DBA); finance (DBA); information systems (DBA); marketing (DBA); operations management (DBA). *Accreditation:* AACSB. Part-time and evening/weekend programs available. *Faculty:* 50 full-time (11 women). *Students:* 6 full-time (2 women), 31 part-time (6 women); includes 3 Black or African American, non-Hispanic/Latino; 2 Asian, non-Hispanic/Latino, 7 international. Average age 44. 7 applicants. *Degree requirements:* For doctorate, comprehensive exam, thesis/dissertation, oral dissertation defense. *Entrance requirements:* For doctorate, GMAT, MBA or equivalent. Additional exam requirements/recommendations for international students: Required—TOEFL (minimum score 550 paper-based; 213 computer-based; 79 iBT). *Application deadline:* For spring admission, 2/28 priority date for domestic and international students. Application fee: $30. Electronic applications accepted. *Expenses:* Tuition, state resident: full-time $8447; part-time $469 per credit hour. Tuition, non-resident: full-time $16,020; part-time $890 per credit hour. Required fees:

$50. *Financial support:* In 2010–11, 5 research assistantships with full tuition reimbursements (averaging $11,700 per year), 1 teaching assistantship with full tuition reimbursement (averaging $11,700 per year) were awarded; tuition waivers (full) and unspecified assistantships also available. *Faculty research:* Supply chain management, international business, strategic management, risk analysis. *Unit head:* Dr. Raj Shekhar G. Javalgi, Director, 216-687-3786, Fax: 216-687-9354, E-mail: r.javalgi@csuohio.edu. *Application contact:* Brenda Wade, Administrative Secretary, 216-687-6952, Fax: 216-687-9257, E-mail: b.wade@csuohio.edu.

Cornell University, Graduate School, Graduate Field of Management, Ithaca, NY 14853. Offers accounting (PhD); behavioral decision theory (PhD); finance (PhD); marketing (PhD); organizational behavior (PhD); production and operations management (PhD). *Accreditation:* AACSB. *Faculty:* 55 full-time (9 women). *Students:* 41 full-time (12 women); includes 5 Asian, non-Hispanic/Latino, 23 international. Average age 29. 436 applicants, 4% accepted, 12 enrolled. In 2010, 5 doctorates awarded. *Degree requirements:* For doctorate, comprehensive exam, thesis/dissertation. *Entrance requirements:* For doctorate, GMAT or GRE General Test. Additional exam requirements/recommendations for international students: Required—TOEFL (minimum score 600 paper-based; 250 computer-based; 77 iBT). *Application deadline:* For fall admission, 1/3 for domestic students. Application fee: $70. Electronic applications accepted. *Expenses:* Contact institution. *Financial support:* In 2010–11, 38 students received support, including 4 fellowships with full tuition reimbursements available, 34 research assistantships with full tuition reimbursements available, 1 teaching assistantship with full tuition reimbursement available; institutionally sponsored loans, scholarships/grants, health care benefits, tuition waivers (full and partial), and unspecified assistantships also available. Financial award applicants required to submit FAFSA. *Faculty research:* Operations and manufacturing. *Unit head:* Director of Graduate Studies, 607-255-3669. *Application contact:* Graduate Field Assistant, 607-255-9431, E-mail: js_phd@cornell.edu.

Daemen College, Department of Accounting/Information Systems, Amherst, NY 14226-3592. Offers global business (MS), including accounting, global business, management information systems, marketing. Part-time and evening/weekend programs available. *Faculty:* 1 full-time (0 women), 1 part-time/adjunct (0 women). *Students:* 19 full-time (16 women), 5 part-time (1 woman); includes 1 minority (Black or African American, non-Hispanic/Latino), 18 international. Average age 28. In 2010, 12 master's awarded. *Degree requirements:* For master's, minimum GPA of 3.0. *Entrance requirements:* For master's, GMAT if undergraduate GPA is less than 3.0, 2 letters of recommendation; goal statement; transcripts; demonstration of satisfactory oral and written English. Additional exam requirements/recommendations for international students: Required—TOEFL (minimum score 500 paper-based; 173 computer-based; 63 iBT), IELTS (minimum score 5.5). *Application deadline:* For fall admission, 3/1 priority date for domestic and international students; for spring admission, 10/1 priority date for domestic and international students. Applications are processed on a rolling basis. Application fee: $25. Electronic applications accepted. *Expenses:* Tuition: Part-time $830 per credit hour. Tuition and fees vary according to course load and reciprocity agreements. *Financial support:* Institutionally sponsored loans, scholarships/grants, and scholarships available. Financial award application deadline: 2/15; financial award applicants required to submit FAFSA. *Faculty research:* Internationalization of small business, cultural influences on business practices, international human resource practices. *Unit head:* S. Sgt. Sharlene S. Buszka, Chair, 716-839-8428, Fax: 716-839-8261, E-mail: sbuszka@daemen.edu. *Application contact:* Scott Rowe, Associate Director of Graduate Admissions, 716-839-8225, Fax: 716-839-8229, E-mail: srowe@daemen.edu.

DePaul University, Charles H. Kellstadt Graduate School of Business, Department of Marketing, Chicago, IL 60604-2287. Offers brand management (MBA); customer relationship management (MBA); integrated marketing communication (MBA); marketing analysis (MSMA); marketing and management (MBA); marketing strategy and analysis (MBA); marketing strategy and planning (MBA); new product management (MBA); sales leadership (MBA). Part-time and evening/weekend programs available. *Faculty:* 23 full-time (4 women), 15 part-time/adjunct (6 women). *Students:* 173 full-time (86 women), 73 part-time (36 women); includes 26 minority (5 Black or African American, non-Hispanic/Latino; 16 Asian, non-Hispanic/Latino; 4 Hispanic/Latino; 1 Native Hawaiian or other Pacific Islander, non-Hispanic/Latino), 26 international. In 2010, 88 master's awarded. *Entrance requirements:* For master's, GMAT, 2 letters of recommendation, resume. Additional exam requirements/recommendations for international students: Required—TOEFL (minimum score 550 paper-based; 213 computer-based). *Application deadline:* For fall admission, 7/1 for domestic students; for winter admission, 10/1 for domestic students; for spring admission, 2/1 for domestic students. Applications are processed on a rolling basis. Application fee: $60. Electronic applications accepted. *Financial support:* In 2010–11, 6 research assistantships with partial tuition reimbursements (averaging $2,500 per year) were awarded. Financial award application deadline: 4/30. *Faculty research:* International and marketing role in developing economics, Internet marketing, direct marketing, consumer behavior, new product development processes. Total annual research expenditures: $100,000. *Unit head:* Dr. Suzanne Louise Fogel, Chairperson and Associate Professor of Marketing, 312-362-5150, Fax:

312-362-5647, E-mail: sfogel@depaul.edu. *Application contact:* Director of MBA Programs, 312-362-8810, Fax: 312-362-6677, E-mail: kgsb@depaul.edu.

DeSales University, Graduate Division, Program in Business Administration, Center Valley, PA 18034-9568. Offers accounting (MBA); computer information systems (MBA); finance (MBA); health care systems management (MBA); health care systems management (online) (MBA); human resource management (MBA); management (MBA); management (online) (MBA); marketing (MBA); marketing (online) (MBA); physician's track (MBA); project management (MBA); project management (online) (MBA); self-design (MBA); self-design (online) (MBA); MSN/MBA. *Accreditation:* ACBSP. Part-time programs available. Postbaccalaureate distance learning degree programs offered (no on-campus study). *Entrance requirements:* For master's, GMAT, minimum GPA of 3.0, 2 years of work experience. Additional exam requirements/recommendations for international students: Required—TOEFL. *Application deadline:* Applications are processed on a rolling basis. Application fee: $35. Electronic applications accepted. *Expenses:* Tuition: Full-time $18,200; part-time $690 per credit. Required fees: $1200. *Faculty research:* Quality improvement, executive development, productivity, cross-cultural managerial differences, leadership. *Unit head:* Dr. David Gilfoil, Director, 610-282-1100 Ext. 1828, Fax: 610-282-2869, E-mail: david.gilfoil@desales.edu. *Application contact:* Caryn Stopper, Director of Graduate Admissions, 610-282-1100 Ext. 1768, Fax: 610-282-0525, E-mail: caryn.stopper@desales.edu.

Dowling College, School of Business, Oakdale, NY 11769-1999. Offers aviation management (MBA, Certificate); banking and finance (MBA, Certificate); corporate finance (MBA); financial planning (Certificate); health care management (MBA, Certificate); human resource management (Certificate); information systems management (MBA); management and leadership (MBA); marketing (Certificate); project management (Certificate); public management (MBA, Certificate); sport, event and entertainment management (Certificate); JD/MBA. Part-time and evening/weekend programs available. *Faculty:* 10 full-time (4 women), 56 part-time/adjunct (7 women). *Students:* 295 full-time (131 women), 460 part-time (206 women); includes 219 minority (97 Black or African American, non-Hispanic/Latino; 14 Asian, non-Hispanic/Latino; 35 Hispanic/Latino; 73 Native Hawaiian or other Pacific Islander, non-Hispanic/Latino), 3 international. Average age 33. 327 applicants, 85% accepted, 160 enrolled. In 2010, 33 master's, 1 other advanced degree awarded. *Degree requirements:* For master's, comprehensive exam, thesis optional. *Entrance requirements:* For master's, minimum GPA of 2.8, 2 letters of recommendation, courses in accounting and finance or seminar in accounting/finance, resume. Additional exam requirements/recommendations for international students: Required—TOEFL (minimum score 550 paper-based). *Application deadline:* For fall admission, 9/1 priority date for domestic students; for winter admission, 1/1 priority date for domestic students; for spring admission, 2/1 priority date for domestic students. Applications are processed on a rolling basis. Application fee: $50. Electronic applications accepted. *Expenses:* Tuition: Part-time $884 per credit hour. Part-time tuition and fees vary according to degree level and campus/location. *Financial support:* Career-related internships or fieldwork and Federal Work-Study available. Support available to part-time students. Financial award application deadline: 6/30; financial award applicants required to submit FAFSA. *Faculty research:* International finance, computer applications, labor relations, executive development. *Unit head:* Antonia Loschiavo, Assistant Dean, 631-244-3266, Fax: 631-244-1018, E-mail: loschiat@dowling.edu. *Application contact:* Ronnie S. Macdonald, Assistant Vice President for Enrollment Services/Dean of Admissions, 631-244-3357, Fax: 631-244-1059, E-mail: macdonar@dowling.edu.

Eastern Michigan University, Graduate School, Academic Affairs Division, Program in Integrated Marketing Communications, Ypsilanti, MI 48197. Offers MS. *Students:* 36 full-time (28 women), 47 part-time (33 women); includes 23 minority (19 Black or African American, non-Hispanic/Latino; 2 American Indian or Alaska Native, non-Hispanic/Latino; 1 Asian, non-Hispanic/Latino; 1 Hispanic/Latino), 1 international. Average age 32. 58 applicants, 41% accepted, 18 enrolled. In 2010, 30 master's awarded. *Unit head:* K. Michelle Henry, Interim Director, Graduate Programs, 734-487-4444, Fax: 734-487-1316, E-mail: mhenry1@emich.edu. *Application contact:* Graduate Advisor.

Eastern Michigan University, Graduate School, College of Business, Programs in Business Administration, Ypsilanti, MI 48197. Offers business administration (MBA, Graduate Certificate); computer information systems (Graduate Certificate); e-business (MBA, Graduate Certificate); enterprise business intelligence (MBA); entrepreneurship (MBA, Graduate Certificate); finance (MBA, Graduate Certificate); human resources (MBA); human resources management (Graduate Certificate); information systems (MBA); internal auditing (MBA); international business (MBA, Graduate Certificate); marketing management (Graduate Certificate); nonprofit management (MBA); organizational development (Graduate Certificate); supply chain management (MBA, Graduate Certificate). *Accreditation:* AACSB. Part-time programs available. Postbaccalaureate distance learning degree programs offered (no on-campus study). *Students:* 149 full-time (66 women), 456 part-time (232 women); includes 146 minority (109 Black or African

American, non-Hispanic/Latino; 4 American Indian or Alaska Native, non-Hispanic/Latino; 27 Asian, non-Hispanic/Latino; 6 Hispanic/Latino), 105 international. Average age 32. 330 applicants, 64% accepted, 150 enrolled. In 2010, 128 master's, 53 other advanced degrees awarded. *Entrance requirements:* For master's, GMAT (minimum score 450), minimum cumulative undergraduate GPA of 2.75. Additional exam requirements/recommendations for international students: Required—TOEFL. *Application deadline:* For fall admission, 5/15 for domestic students, 5/1 for international students; for winter admission, 10/15 for domestic students, 10/1 for international students; for spring admission, 3/15 for domestic students, 3/1 for international students. Applications are processed on a rolling basis. Application fee: $35. *Financial support:* Fellowships, research assistantships with full tuition reimbursements, teaching assistantships with full tuition reimbursements, career-related internships or fieldwork, Federal Work-Study, institutionally sponsored loans, scholarships/grants, tuition waivers (partial), and unspecified assistantships available. Support available to part-time students. Financial award applicants required to submit FAFSA. *Unit head:* K. Michelle Henry, Interim Director, Graduate Programs, 734-487-4444, Fax: 734-483-1316, E-mail: mhenry1@emich.edu. *Application contact:* Beste Windes, Advisor, 734-487-4444, Fax: 734-483-1316, E-mail: bwindes@emich.edu.

Emory University, Goizueta Business School, Doctoral Program in Business, Atlanta, GA 30322-1100. Offers accounting (PhD); finance (PhD); information systems (PhD); marketing (PhD); organization and management (PhD). *Faculty:* 55 full-time (11 women). *Students:* 32 full-time (17 women); includes 1 Black or African American, non-Hispanic/Latino; 17 Asian, non-Hispanic/Latino; 1 Hispanic/Latino. Average age 29. 218 applicants, 9% accepted, 9 enrolled. In 2010, 8 doctorates awarded. *Degree requirements:* For doctorate, comprehensive exam, thesis/dissertation. *Entrance requirements:* For doctorate, GMAT (strongly preferred) or GRE. Additional exam requirements/recommendations for international students: Required—TOEFL (minimum score 250 computer-based). *Application deadline:* For fall admission, 1/3 priority date for domestic students, 1/1 priority date for international students. Application fee: $50. Electronic applications accepted. *Expenses:* Tuition: Full-time $33,800. Required fees: $1300. *Financial support:* In 2010–11, 32 students received support. *Unit head:* Dr. Lawrence Benveniste, Dean, 404-727-6377, Fax: 404-727-0868, E-mail: larry_benveniste@bus.emory.edu. Application contact: Allison Gilmore, Director of Admissions & Student Services, 404-727-6353, Fax: 404-727-5337, E-mail: phd@bus.emory.edu.

Fairfield University, Charles F. Dolan School of Business, Fairfield, CT 06824-5195. Offers accounting (MBA, MS, CAS); accounting information systems (MBA); entrepreneurship (MBA); finance (MBA, MS, CAS); general management (MBA, CAS); human resource management (MBA, CAS); information systems and operations (MBA); information systems and operations management (CAS); international business (MBA, CAS); marketing (MBA, CAS); taxation (MBA, CAS). *Accreditation:* AACSB. Part-time and evening/weekend programs available. *Faculty:* 42 full-time (15 women), 8 part-time/adjunct (1 woman). *Students:* 89 full-time (32 women), 127 part-time (54 women); includes 4 Black or African American, non-Hispanic/Latino; 2 Asian, non-Hispanic/Latino; 4 Hispanic/Latino; 1 Two or more races, non-Hispanic/Latino, 17 international. Average age 29. 108 applicants, 62% accepted, 46 enrolled. In 2010, 79 master's awarded. *Degree requirements:* For master's, capstone course. *Entrance requirements:* For master's, GMAT (minimum score 500), 2 letters of reference, resume, minimum GPA of 3.0. Additional exam requirements/recommendations for international students: Required—TOEFL (minimum score 550 paper-based; 213 computer-based; 80 iBT). *Application deadline:* For fall admission, 5/15 for international students; for spring admission, 10/15 for international students. Applications are processed on a rolling basis. Application fee: $60. Electronic applications accepted. *Expenses:* Contact institution. *Financial support:* In 2010–11, 48 students received support. Scholarships/grants, unspecified assistantships, and merit based one-time entrance scholarship available. Financial award applicants required to submit FAFSA. *Faculty research:* Optimization strategies, international finance, consumer behavior, financial market volatility, Internet marketing, supply chain analysis, tax issues. Total annual research expenditures: $50,000. *Unit head:* Dr. Norman A. Solomon, Dean, 203-254-4000 Ext. 4070, Fax: 203-254-4105, E-mail: nsolomon@fairfield.edu. *Application contact:* Marianne Gumpper, Director of Graduate and Continuing Studies Admissions, 203-254-4184, Fax: 203-254-4073, E-mail: gradadmis@fairfield.edu.

Fairleigh Dickinson University, College at Florham, Silberman College of Business, Departments of Management, Marketing, and Entrepreneurial Studies, Program in Marketing, Madison, NJ 07940-1099. Offers MBA, Certificate. *Students:* 7 full-time (4 women), 26 part-time (11 women), 2 international. Average age 29. 9 applicants, 56% accepted, 5 enrolled. In 2010, 16 master's awarded. *Entrance requirements:* For master's, GMAT. *Application deadline:* Applications are processed on a rolling basis. Application fee: $40.

Fairleigh Dickinson University, Metropolitan Campus, Silberman College of Business, Departments of Management, Marketing, and Entrepreneurial Studies, Program in Marketing, Teaneck, NJ 07666-1914. Offers MBA, Certificate. *Students:* 24 full-time (16 women), 8 part-time (3 women), 25 international. Average age 24. 42 applicants, 50% accepted, 7 enrolled. In 2010, 14 master's awarded. *Application deadline:* Applications are processed on a rolling basis. Application fee: $40. *Application contact:* Susan Brooman,

University Director of Graduate Admissions, 201-692-2554, Fax: 201-692-2560, E-mail: globaleducation@fdu.edu.

Florida Institute of Technology, Graduate Programs, Nathan M. Bisk College of Business, Online Programs, Melbourne, FL 32901-6975. Offers accounting (MBA); accounting and finance (MBA); finance (MBA); healthcare management (MBA); information technology (MS); information technology management (MBA); Internet marketing (MBA); management (MBA); marketing (MBA); project management (MBA). Part-time and evening/weekend programs available. Postbaccalaureate distance learning degree programs offered (no on-campus study). *Faculty:* 32 part-time/adjunct (8 women). *Students:* 4 full-time (1 woman), 1,062 part-time (499 women); includes 373 minority (244 Black or African American, non-Hispanic/Latino; 8 American Indian or Alaska Native, non-Hispanic/Latino; 37 Asian, non-Hispanic/Latino; 76 Hispanic/Latino; 8 Native Hawaiian or other Pacific Islander, non-Hispanic/Latino), 39 international. Average age 37. 299 applicants, 167 enrolled. In 2010, 134 master's awarded. *Entrance requirements:* For master's, GMAT or resume showing 8 years of supervised experience, 2 letters of recommendation, resume, competency in math past college algebra. Additional exam requirements/recommendations for international students: Required—TOEFL (minimum score 550 paper-based; 213 computer-based; 79 iBT). *Application deadline:* For fall admission, 4/1 for international students; for spring admission, 9/30 for international students. Applications are processed on a rolling basis. Application fee: $50. Electronic applications accepted. *Expenses:* Contact institution. *Financial support:* Available to part-time students. Application deadline: 3/1. *Unit head:* Dr. Mary S. Bonhomme, Dean, Florida Tech Online Associate Provost for Online Learning, 321-674-8202, Fax: 321-674-8216, E-mail: bonhomme@fit.edu. *Application contact:* Carolyn Farrior, Director of Graduate Admissions Online Learning and Off Campus Programs, 321-674-7118, Fax: 321-674-8216, E-mail: cfarrior@fit.edu.

Florida State University, The Graduate School, College of Business, Tallahassee, FL 32306-1110. Offers accounting (M Acc), including accounting information services, assurance services, corporate accounting, taxation; business administration (MBA, PhD), including accounting (PhD), finance (PhD), management information systems (PhD), marketing (PhD), organizational behavior (PhD), risk management and insurance (PhD), strategic management (PhD); finance (MS); insurance (MSM); management information systems (MS); JD/MBA; MSW/MBA. *Accreditation:* AACSB. Part-time programs available. Postbaccalaureate distance learning degree programs offered (no on-campus study). *Faculty:* 107 full-time (31 women). *Students:* 196 full-time (76 women), 310 part-time (109 women); includes 27 Black or African American, non-Hispanic/Latino; 1 American Indian or Alaska Native, non-Hispanic/Latino; 31 Asian, non-Hispanic/Latino; 30 Hispanic/Latino. Average age 30. 702 applicants, 33% accepted, 205 enrolled. In 2010, 268 master's, 17 doctorates awarded. Terminal master's awarded for partial completion of doctoral program. *Degree requirements:* For doctorate, comprehensive exam, thesis/dissertation. *Entrance requirements:* For master's, GMAT, work experience (MBA, MS), minimum GPA of 3.0, letters of recommendation; for doctorate, GMAT, minimum graduate GPA of 3.5, letters of recommendation. Additional exam requirements/recommendations for international students: Required—TOEFL (minimum score 600 paper-based; 80 computer-based); Recommended—IELTS (minimum score 6.5). *Application deadline:* For fall admission, 6/1 for domestic students, 5/1 for international students; for spring admission, 10/1 for domestic students, 9/1 for international students. Applications are processed on a rolling basis. Application fee: $30. Electronic applications accepted. *Expenses:* Tuition, state resident: full-time $8238.24. *Financial support:* In 2010–11, 86 students received support, including 12 fellowships with full tuition reimbursements available (averaging $7,161 per year), 30 research assistantships with full tuition reimbursements available (averaging $6,000 per year), 43 teaching assistantships with full tuition reimbursements available (averaging $15,000 per year); career-related internships or fieldwork, scholarships/grants, health care benefits, tuition waivers (full and partial), and unspecified assistantships also available. Support available to part-time students. Financial award application deadline: 1/1. *Unit head:* Dr. Caryn Beck-Dudley, Dean, 850-644-3090, Fax: 850-644-0915. *Application contact:* Lisa Beverly, Director, Graduate Programs Admissions, 850-644-6458, Fax: 850-644-0588, E-mail: lbeverly@cob.fsu.edu.

Florida State University, The Graduate School, College of Communication and Information, School of Communication, Tallahassee, FL 32306. Offers corporate and public communication (MS); integrated marketing communication (MA, MS); mass communication (PhD); media and communication studies (MA, MS); speech communication (PhD). Part-time programs available. *Faculty:* 24 full-time (9 women), 6 part-time/adjunct (1 woman). *Students:* 147 full-time (94 women), 63 part-time (38 women); includes 92 minority (26 Black or African American, non-Hispanic/Latino; 2 American Indian or Alaska Native, non-Hispanic/Latino; 45 Asian, non-Hispanic/Latino; 16 Hispanic/Latino; 1 Native Hawaiian or other Pacific Islander, non-Hispanic/Latino; 2 Two or more races, non-Hispanic/Latino). Average age 24. 268 applicants, 57% accepted, 79 enrolled. In 2010, 103 master's, 4 doctorates awarded. *Degree requirements:* For master's, thesis (for some programs); for doctorate, comprehensive exam, thesis/dissertation. *Entrance requirements:* For master's, GRE General Test, minimum GPA of 3.0; for doctorate, GRE General Test, minimum GPA of 3.3 in graduate course work. Additional exam requirements/recommendations for international students: Required—TOEFL (minimum score 600 paper-based; 250 computer-based; 100 iBT). *Application deadline:* For fall admission, 7/1 priority date for domestic students, 5/1 priority date for international students; for spring admission, 11/1 priority date for domestic and international students. Applications are processed on a rolling basis. Application fee: $30. Electronic applications accepted. *Expenses:* Tuition, state resident: full-time $8238.24. *Financial support:* In 2010–11, 52 students received support, including 1 fellowship with full tuition reimbursement available, 8 research assistantships with full tuition reimbursements available (averaging $14,000 per year), 40 teaching assistantships with full tuition reimbursements available (averaging $5,000 per year); career-related internships or fieldwork, Federal Work-Study, institutionally sponsored loans, scholarships/grants, tuition waivers (partial), and unspecified assistantships also available. Support available to part-time students. Financial award application deadline: 2/1; financial award applicants required to submit FAFSA. *Faculty research:* Communication technology and policy, marketing communication, communication content and effect, new communication/information technologies. Total annual research expenditures: $400,000. *Unit head:* Dr. Stephen D. McDowell, Director, 850-644-2276, Fax: 850-644-8642, E-mail: steve.mcdowell@cci.fsu.edu. *Application contact:* Natashia Hinson-Turner, Graduate Coordinator, 850-644-8746, Fax: 850-644-8642, E-mail: natashia.turner@cci.fsu.edu.

Franklin University, Marketing and Communications Program, Columbus, OH 43215-5399. Offers MS. Part-time and evening/weekend programs available. *Students:* 109 full-time (77 women), 37 part-time (28 women); includes 21 minority (17 Black or African American, non-Hispanic/Latino; 3 Asian, non-Hispanic/Latino; 1 Hispanic/Latino), 2 international. Average age 34. In 2010, 33 master's awarded. *Entrance requirements:* For master's, minimum undergraduate GPA of 2.75. Additional exam requirements/recommendations for international students: Required—TOEFL (minimum score 550 paper-based; 213 computer-based). *Application deadline:* For fall admission, 8/1 priority date for domestic students, 6/1 for international students; for winter admission, 12/1 priority date for domestic students, 10/1 for international students; for spring admission, 4/15 priority date for domestic students, 2/1 for international students. Applications are processed on a rolling basis. Application fee: $30. Electronic applications accepted. *Expenses:* Tuition: Full-time $9720; part-time $540 per credit hour. One-time fee: $30. Tuition and fees vary according to program. *Financial support:* Application deadline: 6/30. *Unit head:* Dr. Doug Ross, Program Chair, 614-947-6149. *Application contact:* Graduate Services Office, 614-797-4700, Fax: 614-224-7723, E-mail: gradschl@franklin.edu.

Gannon University, School of Graduate Studies, College of Engineering and Business, School of Business, Program in Marketing, Erie, PA 16541-0001. Offers Certificate. Part-time and evening/weekend programs available. *Students:* 2 part-time (both women). Average age 44. 3 applicants, 100% accepted, 2 enrolled. In 2010, 1 Certificate awarded. *Entrance requirements:* For degree, GMAT. Additional exam requirements/recommendations for international students: Required—TOEFL (minimum score 79 iBT). *Application deadline:* Applications are processed on a rolling basis. Application fee: $25. Electronic applications accepted. *Expenses:* Tuition: Full-time $14,670; part-time $815 per credit. Required fees: $430; $18 per credit. Tuition and fees vary according to class time, course load, degree level, campus/location and program. *Financial support:* Application deadline: 7/1. *Unit head:* Dr. Duane Prokop, Director, 814-871-7576, E-mail: prokop001@gannon.edu. *Application contact:* Kara Morgan, Assistant Director of Graduate Admissions, 814-871-5831, Fax: 814-871-5827, E-mail: graduate@gannon.edu.

George Fox University, School of Business, Newberg, OR 97132-2697. Offers finance (MBA); management (DBA); management/general (MBA); marketing (DBA); organizational strategy (MBA); strategic human resource management (MBA). MBA offered part-time and full-time, also offered in Portland, OR, and Boise, ID. Part-time and evening/weekend programs available. Postbaccalaureate distance learning degree programs offered (minimal on-campus study). *Faculty:* 9 full-time (2 women), 8 part-time/adjunct (3 women). *Students:* 21 full-time (7 women), 247 part-time (87 women); includes 4 Black or African American, non-Hispanic/Latino; 2 American Indian or Alaska Native, non-Hispanic/Latino; 13 Asian, non-Hispanic/Latino; 13 Hispanic/Latino; 2 Two or more races, non-Hispanic/Latino, 12 international. Average age 37. 101 applicants, 93% accepted, 72 enrolled. In 2010, 82 master's awarded. *Degree requirements:* For master's, capstone project; for doctorate, credit-applied research project. *Entrance requirements:* For master's, resume (5 years professional experience required); 3 professional references; interview; financial e-learning course; for doctorate, GRE or GMAT, resume; personal mission statement; academic research writing sample; official transcript from each college/university attended; three professional references. Additional exam requirements/recommendations for international students: Required—TOEFL (minimum score 577 paper-based; 233 computer-based; 90 iBT) or IELTS (minimum score 7). *Application deadline:* For fall admission, 8/1 for domestic and international students; for spring admission, 12/1 for domestic and international students. Applications are processed on a rolling basis. Application fee: $40. Electronic applications accepted. *Expenses:* Contact institution. *Financial support:* In 2010–11, 2 students received support. Applicants required to submit FAFSA. *Unit head:* Dr. Dirk Barram, Professor/Dean, 800-631-0921. *Application contact:* Robin Halverson, Admissions Counselor, 800-493-4937, Fax: 503-554-6111, E-mail: mba@georgefox.edu.

Golden Gate University, Ageno School of Business, San Francisco, CA 94105-2968. Offers accounting (MBA); business administration (EMBA, MBA, PMBA, DBA); finance (MBA, MS, Certificate); financial planning (MS, Certificate); healthcare information systems (Certificate); human resource management (MBA, MS); human resources management (Certificate); information systems (MS); information technology (MBA); information technology management (Certificate); integrated marketing and communications (MS, Certificate); international business (MBA); management (MBA); marketing (MBA, MS, Certificate); operations supply chain management (Certificate); psychology (MA, Certificate); public administration (EMPA); public relations (MS, Certificate); technical market analysis (Certificate); JD/MBA. Part-time and evening/weekend programs available. *Faculty:* 16 full-time (4 women), 241 part-time/adjunct (72 women). *Students:* 421 full-time (235 women), 744 part-time (425 women); includes 526 minority (114 Black or African American, non-Hispanic/Latino; 2 American Indian or Alaska Native, non-Hispanic/Latino; 296 Asian, non-Hispanic/Latino; 73 Hispanic/Latino; 29 Native Hawaiian or other Pacific Islander, non-Hispanic/Latino; 12 Two or more races, non-Hispanic/Latino), 100 international. Average age 32. 681 applicants, 78% accepted, 270 enrolled. In 2010, 550 master's, 13 doctorates awarded. *Degree requirements:* For doctorate, thesis/dissertation. *Entrance requirements:* For master's, GMAT (MBA), minimum GPA of 2.5 (MS). Additional exam requirements/recommendations for international students: Required—TOEFL. *Application deadline:* For fall admission, 5/15 for domestic and international students; for winter admission, 1/15 for domestic and international students; for spring admission, 9/15 for domestic and international students. Applications are processed on a rolling basis. Application fee: $70 ($110 for international students). Electronic applications accepted. *Expenses:* Contact institution. *Financial support:* Career-related internships or fieldwork, Federal Work-Study, institutionally sponsored loans, and scholarships/grants available. Support available to part-time students. Financial award applicants required to submit FAFSA. *Unit head:* Dr. Paul Fouts, Dean, 415-442-7026, Fax: 415-442-6579. *Application contact:* Angela Melero, Enrollment Services, 415-442-7800, Fax: 415-442-7807, E-mail: info@ggu.edu.

Goldey-Beacom College, Graduate Program, Wilmington, DE 19808-1999. Offers business administration (MBA); finance (MS); financial management (MBA); human resource management (MBA); information technology (MBA); international business management (MBA); major finance (MBA); major taxation (MBA); management (MM); marketing management (MBA); taxation (MBA, MS). *Accreditation:* ACBSP. Part-time and evening/weekend programs available. *Faculty:* 20 full-time (8 women), 28 part-time/adjunct (10 women). *Students:* 55 full-time (28 women), 393 part-time (164 women); includes 252 minority (51 Black or African American, non-Hispanic/Latino; 2 American Indian or Alaska Native, non-Hispanic/Latino; 183 Asian, non-Hispanic/Latino; 13 Hispanic/Latino; 1 Native Hawaiian or other Pacific Islander, non-Hispanic/Latino; 2 Two or more races, non-Hispanic/Latino). Average age 27. In 2010, 231 master's awarded. *Entrance requirements:* For master's, GMAT, MAT, GRE, minimum GPA of 3.0. Additional exam requirements/recommendations for international students: Required—TOEFL (minimum score 65 computer-based); Recommended—IELTS (minimum score 5). *Application deadline:* Applications are processed on a rolling basis. Electronic applications accepted. *Expenses:* Tuition: Full-time $14,796; part-time $822 per credit. Required fees: $180; $10 per credit. *Financial support:* Scholarships/grants available. Support available to part-time students. Financial award application deadline: 4/1; financial award applicants required to submit FAFSA. *Unit head:* Larry W. Eby, Director of Admissions, 302-225-6289, Fax: 302-996-5408, E-mail: ebylw@gbc.edu. *Application contact:* Ashley E. Mashington, Graduate Admissions Representative, 302-225-6259, Fax: 302-996-5408, E-mail: mashina@gbc.edu.

Grand Canyon University, College of Business, Phoenix, AZ 85017-1097. Offers accounting (MBA); corporate business administration (MBA); disaster preparedness and crisis management (MBA); executive fire service leadership (MS); finance (MBA); general management (MBA); government and policy (MPA); health care management (MPA); health systems management (MBA); human resource management (MBA); innovation (MBA); leadership (MBA, MS); management of information system (MBA); marketing (MBA); project-based (MBA); six sigma (MBA); strategic human resource management (MBA). *Accreditation:* ACBSP. Part-time and evening/weekend programs available. Postbaccalaureate distance learning degree programs offered (no on-campus study). *Faculty:* 8 full-time (3 women), 147 part-time/adjunct (49 women). *Students:* 1 full-time (0 women), 2,121 part-time (1,165 women); includes 341 minority (249 Black or African American, non-Hispanic/Latino; 17 American Indian or Alaska Native, non-Hispanic/Latino; 15 Asian, non-Hispanic/Latino; 29 Hispanic/Latino; 4 Native Hawaiian or other Pacific Islander, non-Hispanic/Latino; 27 Two or more races, non-Hispanic/Latino), 20 international. Average age 38. In 2010, 569 master's awarded. *Entrance requirements:* For master's, equivalent of two years full-time professional work experience. Additional exam requirements/recommendations

for international students: Required—TOEFL (minimum score 575 paper-based; 233 computer-based; 90 iBT), IELTS (minimum score 7). *Application deadline:* For fall admission, 8/21 for domestic students, 7/2 for international students; for spring admission, 12/24 for domestic students, 11/1 for international students. Applications are processed on a rolling basis. Application fee: $0. Electronic applications accepted. *Financial support:* Federal Work-Study available. Support available to part-time students. Financial award applicants required to submit FAFSA. *Unit head:* Kim Donaldson, Dean, 602-639-6597, E-mail: kdonaldson@gcu.edu. *Application contact:* Matt Tidwell, Enrollment Manager, 602-639-6020, E-mail: mtidwell@gcu.edu.

HEC Montreal, School of Business Administration, Master of Science Programs in Administration, Program in Marketing, Montréal, QC H3T 2A7, Canada. Offers M Sc. All courses are given in French. Part-time programs available. *Students:* 97 full-time (57 women), 22 part-time (15 women). 115 applicants, 65% accepted, 38 enrolled. In 2010, 25 master's awarded. *Degree requirements:* For master's, one foreign language, thesis. *Application deadline:* For fall admission, 3/15 for domestic and international students; for winter admission, 10/1 for domestic and international students. Application fee: $78 Canadian dollars. Electronic applications accepted. *Expenses:* Tuition, area resident: Part-time $68.93 per credit. Tuition, state resident: full-time $2481.48; part-time $188.92 per credit. Tuition, nonresident: full-time $6801; part-time $482.06 per course. International tuition: $17,354.16 full-time. Required fees: $1309.50; $30.28 per credit. $93.45 per term. Tuition and fees vary according to degree level and program. *Financial support:* Fellowships, research assistantships, teaching assistantships, scholarships/grants available. Financial award application deadline: 9/2. *Unit head:* Dr. Claude Laurin, Director, 514-340-6485, Fax: 514-340-6880, E-mail: claude.laurin@hec.ca. *Application contact:* Francine Blais, Administrative Director, 514-340-6112, Fax: 514-340-6411, E-mail: francine.blais@hec.ca.

Hofstra University, Frank G. Zarb School of Business, Department of Marketing and International Business, Hempstead, NY 11549. Offers business administration (MBA), including international business, marketing; marketing (MS); marketing research (MS). Part-time and evening/weekend programs available. Postbaccalaureate distance learning degree programs offered (minimal on-campus study). *Faculty:* 7 full-time (0 women), 2 part-time/adjunct (0 women). *Students:* 63 full-time (34 women), 47 part-time (24 women); includes 9 minority (1 Black or African American, non-Hispanic/Latino; 2 Asian, non-Hispanic/Latino; 6 Hispanic/Latino), 52 international. Average age 27. 150 applicants, 66% accepted, 36 enrolled. In 2010, 35 master's awarded. *Degree requirements:* For master's, capstone course (MBA), thesis (MS). *Entrance requirements:* For master's, GMAT or GRE, 2 letters of recommendation, resume, essay. Additional exam requirements/recommendations for international students: Required—TOEFL (minimum score 550 paper-based; 213 computer-based; 80 iBT); Recommended—IELTS (minimum score 6). *Application deadline:* Applications are processed on a rolling basis. Application fee: $70 ($75 for international students). Electronic applications accepted. *Expenses:* Contact institution. *Financial support:* In 2010–11, 22 students received support, including 21 fellowships with full and partial tuition reimbursements (averaging $8,965 per year); research assistantships with full and partial tuition reimbursements available, career-related internships or fieldwork, Federal Work-Study, institutionally sponsored loans, scholarships/grants, tuition waivers (full and partial), and unspecified assistantships also available. Support available to part-time students. Financial award applicants required to submit FAFSA. *Faculty research:* Outsourcing, global alliances, retailing, Web marketing, cross-cultural age research. *Unit head:* Dr. Benny Barak, Chairperson, 516-463-5707, Fax: 516-463-4834, E-mail: mktbzb@hofstra.edu. *Application contact:* Carol Drummer, Dean of Graduate Admissions, 516-463-4876, Fax: 516-463-4664, E-mail: gradstudent@hofstra.edu.

Holy Names University, Graduate Division, Department of Business, Oakland, CA 94619-1699. Offers energy and environment management (MBA); finance (MBA); management and leadership (MBA); marketing (MBA); sports management (MBA). Part-time and evening/weekend programs available. *Faculty:* 3 full-time (2 women), 4 part-time/adjunct (1 woman). *Students:* 67 full-time (40 women); includes 28 Black or African American, non-Hispanic/Latino; 7 Asian, non-Hispanic/Latino; 5 Hispanic/Latino, 2 international. Average age 33. 24 applicants, 75% accepted, 7 enrolled. In 2010, 29 master's awarded. *Entrance requirements:* For master's, minimum undergraduate GPA of 2.6 overall, 3.0 in major. Additional exam requirements/recommendations for international students: Required—TOEFL (minimum score 550 paper-based; 213 computer-based; 80 iBT). *Application deadline:* For fall admission, 8/1 priority date for domestic students, 8/1 for international students; for spring admission, 12/1 priority date for domestic students, 12/1 for international students. Applications are processed on a rolling basis. Application fee: $0. *Expenses:* Tuition: Full-time $13,788; part-time $766 per credit. Required fees: $340; $170 per semester. *Financial support:* In 2010–11, 19 students received support. Available to part-time students. Application deadline: 3/2. *Faculty research:* Business ethics, sustainable economics, accounting models, cross-cultural management, diversity in organizations. *Unit head:* Dr. Marcia Frideger, Program Director, 510-436-1205, E-mail: frideger@hnu.edu. *Application contact:* 800-430-1351, Fax: 510-436-1325, E-mail: admissions@hnu.edu.

Hood College, Graduate School, Department of Economics and Management, Frederick, MD 21701-8575. Offers accounting (MBA); administration and management (MBA); finance (MBA); human resource management (MBA); information systems (MBA); marketing (MBA); public management (MBA). *Accreditation:* ACBSP. Part-time and evening/weekend programs available. *Faculty:* 4 full-time (1 woman), 9 part-time/adjunct (1 woman). *Students:* 16 full-time (9 women), 127 part-time (65 women); includes 17 Black or African American, non-Hispanic/Latino; 9 Asian, non-Hispanic/Latino; 5 Hispanic/Latino; 1 Two or more races, non-Hispanic/Latino, 10 international. Average age 32. 60 applicants, 62% accepted, 25 enrolled. In 2010, 56 master's awarded. *Degree requirements:* For master's, capstone/final research project. *Entrance requirements:* For master's, minimum GPA of 2.75, resume, letters of recommendation. Additional exam requirements/recommendations for international students: Required—TOEFL (minimum score 575 paper-based; 231 computer-based; 89 iBT). *Application deadline:* For fall admission, 7/15 for domestic and international students; for spring admission, 12/15 for domestic and international students. Applications are processed on a rolling basis. Application fee: $35. Electronic applications accepted. *Expenses:* Tuition: Full-time $6480; part-time $360 per credit. Required fees: $100; $50 per term. *Financial support:* Applicants required to submit FAFSA. *Faculty research:* Corporate strategy and sustainable competitive advantages, business ethics, entrepreneurship, investments management, economic development. *Unit head:* Dr. Anita Jose, Program Director, 301-696-3691, Fax: 301-696-3597, E-mail: jose@hood.edu. *Application contact:* Dr. Allen P. Flora, Dean of Graduate School, 301-696-3811, Fax: 301-696-3597, E-mail: gofurther@hood.edu.

Illinois Institute of Technology, Stuart School of Business, Program in Business Administration, Chicago, IL 60616-3793. Offers financial management (MBA); innovation and emerging enterprises (MBA); management science (MBA); marketing (MBA); sustainability (MBA); JD/MBA; M Des/MBA; MBA/MS. *Accreditation:* AACSB. Part-time and evening/weekend programs available. *Faculty:* 37 full-time (4 women), 21 part-time/adjunct (5 women). *Students:* 153 full-time (66 women), 30 part-time (12 women); includes 17 minority (3 Black or African American, non-Hispanic/Latino; 9 Asian, non-Hispanic/Latino; 3 Hispanic/Latino; 2 Two or more races, non-Hispanic/Latino), 119 international. Average age 27. 334 applicants, 77% accepted, 63 enrolled. In 2010, 40 master's awarded. *Entrance requirements:* For master's, GRE (minimum score 1000) or GMAT (500). Additional exam requirements/recommendations for international students: Required—TOEFL (minimum score 600 paper-based; 85 iBT); Recommended—IELTS (minimum score 7). *Application deadline:* For fall admission, 8/1 for domestic students, 5/1 for international students; for spring admission, 12/15 for domestic students, 10/15 for international students. Applications are processed on a rolling basis. Application fee: $75. Electronic applications accepted. *Expenses:* Contact institution. *Financial support:* Career-related internships or fieldwork, Federal Work-Study, institutionally sponsored loans, scholarships/grants, traineeships, health care benefits, and tuition waivers (partial) available. Support available to part-time students. Financial award applicants required to submit FAFSA. *Faculty research:* Global management and marketing strategy, technological innovation, management science, financial management, knowledge management. *Unit head:* M. Krishna Erramilli, Interim Director, 312-906-6573, Fax: 312-906-6549. *Application contact:* Deborah Gibson, Director, Graduate Admission, 866-472-3448, Fax: 312-472-3448, E-mail: inquiry.grad@iit.edu.

Illinois Institute of Technology, Stuart School of Business, Program in Marketing Communication, Chicago, IL 60661. Offers MS, MBA/MS. Part-time and evening/weekend programs available. *Faculty:* 37 full-time (4 women), 21 part-time/adjunct (5 women). *Students:* 62 full-time (44 women), 3 part-time (2 women); includes 1 minority (Hispanic/Latino), 63 international. Average age 24. 198 applicants, 75% accepted, 32 enrolled. In 2010, 13 master's awarded. *Entrance requirements:* For master's, GRE (minimum score 1000) or GMAT (500). Additional exam requirements/recommendations for international students: Required—TOEFL (minimum score 600 paper-based; 85 iBT); Recommended—IELTS (minimum score 7). *Application deadline:* For fall admission, 8/1 for domestic students, 5/1 for international students; for spring admission, 12/15 for domestic students, 10/15 for international students. Applications are processed on a rolling basis. Application fee: $75. Electronic applications accepted. *Expenses:* Contact institution. *Financial support:* Career-related internships or fieldwork, Federal Work-Study, institutionally sponsored loans, scholarships/grants, traineeships, health care benefits, and tuition waivers (partial) available. Support available to part-time students. Financial award applicants required to submit FAFSA. *Unit head:* Dr. Krishna Erramilli, Professor, 312-906-6573, Fax: 312-906-6549, E-mail: krish@stuart.iit.edu. *Application contact:* Deborah Gibson, Director, Graduate Admission, 866-472-3448, Fax: 312-567-3138, E-mail: inquiry.grad@iit.edu.

Iona College, Hagan School of Business, Department of Marketing and International Business, New Rochelle, NY 10801-1890. Offers international business (Certificate, PMC); marketing (MBA). Part-time and evening/weekend programs available. *Faculty:* 3 full-time (1 woman), 2 part-time/adjunct (0 women). *Students:* 14 full-time (12 women), 29 part-time (16 women); includes 9 minority (1 Black or African American, non-Hispanic/Latino; 2 Asian, non-Hispanic/Latino; 6 Hispanic/Latino). Average age 28.

18 applicants, 67% accepted, 10 enrolled. In 2010, 22 master's, 66 other advanced degrees awarded. *Entrance requirements:* For master's, GMAT, 2 letters of recommendation; for other advanced degree, GMAT. Additional exam requirements/recommendations for international students: Required—TOEFL (minimum score 550 paper-based; 213 computer-based). *Application deadline:* Applications are processed on a rolling basis. Application fee: $50. Electronic applications accepted. *Expenses:* Contact institution. *Financial support:* Scholarships/grants, tuition waivers (partial), and unspecified assistantships available. Support available to part-time students. Financial award application deadline: 4/15; financial award applicants required to submit FAFSA. *Faculty research:* Business ethics, international retailing, mega-marketing, consumer behavior and consumer confidence. *Unit head:* Dr. Frederica E. Rudell, Chair, 914-637-2748, E-mail: frudell@iona.edu. *Application contact:* Ben Fan, Director of MBA Admissions, 914-633-2289, Fax: 914-637-2708, E-mail: sfan@iona.edu.

The Johns Hopkins University, Carey Business School, Marketing Programs, Baltimore, MD 21218-2699. Offers MS. Part-time and evening/weekend programs available. *Faculty:* 29 full-time (6 women), 135 part-time/adjunct (29 women). *Students:* 46 full-time (34 women), 72 part-time (53 women); includes 24 minority (13 Black or African American, non-Hispanic/Latino; 6 Asian, non-Hispanic/Latino; 2 Hispanic/Latino; 3 Two or more races, non-Hispanic/Latino), 40 international. Average age 29. 56 applicants, 75% accepted, 28 enrolled. In 2010, 70 master's awarded. *Degree requirements:* For master's, research project (MS). *Entrance requirements:* For master's, minimum GPA of 3.0, resume, work experience, two letters of recommendation. Additional exam requirements/recommendations for international students: Required—TOEFL (minimum score 600 paper-based; 250 computer-based; 100 iBT). *Application deadline:* For fall admission, 4/1 for international students; for spring admission, 9/15 for international students. Applications are processed on a rolling basis. Application fee: $100. Electronic applications accepted. *Financial support:* In 2010–11, 6 students received support. Scholarships/grants available. Support available to part-time students. Financial award application deadline: 4/15; financial award applicants required to submit FAFSA. *Faculty research:* Consumer behavior and advertising. *Unit head:* Dr. Dipankar Chakravarti, Vice Dean of Programs, 410-234-9311, E-mail: dipankar.chakravarti@jhu.edu. *Application contact:* Robin Greenberg, Admissions Coordinator, 410-234-9227, Fax: 443-529-1554, E-mail: carey.admissions@jhu.edu.

Keiser University, Master of Business Administration Program, Fort Lauderdale, FL 33309. Offers accounting (MBA); health services management (MBA); international business (MBA); leadership for managers (MBA); marketing (MBA). Leadership for Managers and International Business concentrations also offered in Spanish. Part-time programs available. Postbaccalaureate distance learning degree programs offered (minimal on-campus study). *Faculty:* 8 full-time (3 women), 7 part-time/adjunct (2 women). *Students:* 18 full-time (14 women), 83 part-time (51 women); includes 30 Black or African American, non-Hispanic/Latino; 2 American Indian or Alaska Native, non-Hispanic/Latino; 2 Asian, non-Hispanic/Latino; 17 Hispanic/Latino, 1 international. Average age 42. 30 applicants, 77% accepted, 18 enrolled. In 2010, 21 degrees awarded. *Entrance requirements:* For master's, minimum GPA of 2.7 from an accredited institution. Additional exam requirements/recommendations for international students: Required—TOEFL. *Application deadline:* Applications are processed on a rolling basis. Application fee: $50. Electronic applications accepted. *Financial support:* In 2010–11, 95 students received support. Federal Work-Study available. Financial award applicants required to submit FAFSA.

Kent State University, Graduate School of Management, Doctoral Program in Marketing, Kent, OH 44242. Offers PhD. *Faculty:* 13 full-time (3 women). *Students:* 11 full-time (9 women); includes 1 Asian, non-Hispanic/Latino, 4 international. Average age 32. 17 applicants, 24% accepted, 3 enrolled. *Degree requirements:* For doctorate, comprehensive exam, thesis/dissertation, oral defense. *Entrance requirements:* For doctorate, GMAT. Additional exam requirements/recommendations for international students: Required—TOEFL (minimum score 600 paper-based; 250 computer-based; 100 iBT). *Application deadline:* For fall admission, 2/1 for domestic students, 1/1 for international students. Application fee: $30 ($60 for international students). Electronic applications accepted. *Expenses:* Tuition, state resident: full-time $7866; part-time $437 per credit hour. Tuition, nonresident: full-time $14,022; part-time $779 per credit hour. *Financial support:* In 2010–11, 11 students received support, including 11 teaching assistantships with full tuition reimbursements available (averaging $15,000 per year); fellowships with full tuition reimbursements available, Federal Work-Study also available. Financial award application deadline: 2/1; financial award applicants required to submit FAFSA. *Faculty research:* Advertising effects, satisfaction, international marketing, high-tech marketing, personality and consumer behavior. *Unit head:* Dr. Pamela Grimm, Chair and Associate Professor, 330-672-2170, Fax: 330-672-5006, E-mail: pgrimm@kent.edu. *Application contact:* Felecia A. Urbanek, Coordinator, Graduate Programs, 330-672-2282, Fax: 330-672-7303, E-mail: gradbus@kent.edu.

Kentucky State University, College of Professional Studies, Frankfort, KY 40601. Offers business administration (MBA), including accounting, finance, management, marketing; public administration (MPA), including human resource management, international administration and development, management information systems, nonprofit management; special education (MA). Part-time and evening/weekend programs available. Postbaccalaureate distance learning degree programs offered (minimal on-campus study). *Faculty:* 12 full-time (4 women), 2 part-time/adjunct (both women). *Students:* 88 full-time (57 women), 79 part-time (42 women); includes 104 minority (101 Black or African American, non-Hispanic/Latino; 1 Asian, non-Hispanic/Latino; 2 Hispanic/Latino), 2 international. Average age 34. 124 applicants, 62% accepted, 45 enrolled. In 2010, 38 master's awarded. *Degree requirements:* For master's, comprehensive exam, thesis optional. *Entrance requirements:* For master's, GMAT, GRE. Additional exam requirements/recommendations for international students: Required—TOEFL (minimum score 525 paper-based; 173 computer-based). *Application deadline:* Applications are processed on a rolling basis. Application fee: $30 ($100 for international students). Electronic applications accepted. *Expenses:* Tuition, state resident: full-time $5886; part-time $352 per credit hour. Tuition, nonresident: full-time $9054; part-time $528 per credit hour. Required fees: $450; $26 per credit hour. *Financial support:* In 2010–11, 46 students received support, including 4 research assistantships (averaging $10,975 per year); career-related internships or fieldwork, scholarships/grants, tuition waivers (partial), and unspecified assistantships also available. Financial award application deadline: 4/15; financial award applicants required to submit FAFSA. *Unit head:* Dr. Gashaw Lake, Dean, 502-597-6105, Fax: 502-597-6715, E-mail: gashaw.lake@kysu.edu. *Application contact:* Dr. Titilayo Ufomata, Acting Director of Graduate Studies, 502-597-6443, E-mail: titilayo.ufomata@kysu.edu.

Lake Forest Graduate School of Management, MBA Program, Lake Forest, IL 60045. Offers global business (MBA); healthcare management (MBA); management (MBA); marketing (MBA); organizational behavior (MBA). Part-time and evening/weekend programs available. *Faculty:* 123 part-time/adjunct (26 women). *Students:* 734 part-time (306 women); includes 156 minority (34 Black or African American, non-Hispanic/Latino; 86 Asian, non-Hispanic/Latino; 14 Hispanic/Latino; 4 Native Hawaiian or other Pacific Islander, non-Hispanic/Latino; 18 Two or more races, non-Hispanic/Latino). Average age 38. In 2010, 202 master's awarded. *Entrance requirements:* For master's, 4 years of work experience in field, interview, 2 letters of recommendation. *Application deadline:* For fall admission, 7/1 for domestic students; for winter admission, 1/5 for domestic students; for spring admission, 3/1 for domestic students. Applications are processed on a rolling basis. Application fee: $0. Electronic applications accepted. *Financial support:* In 2010–11, 290 students received support. Scholarships/grants available. Support available to part-time students. Financial award applicants required to submit FAFSA. *Unit head:* Chris Multhauf, Vice President and Degree Programs Dean, 847-574-5270, Fax: 847-295-3656, E-mail: cmulthauf@lfgsm.edu. *Application contact:* Carolyn Brune, Director of Admissions Operations, 800-737-4MBA, Fax: 847-295-3656, E-mail: admiss@lfgsm.edu.

Lasell College, Graduate and Professional Studies in Communication, Newton, MA 02466-2709. Offers integrated marketing communication (MSC, Graduate Certificate); public relations (MSC, Graduate Certificate). Part-time and evening/weekend programs available. Postbaccalaureate distance learning degree programs offered (minimal on-campus study). *Faculty:* 2 full-time (both women), 2 part-time/adjunct (both women). *Students:* 8 full-time (all women), 25 part-time (22 women); includes 3 minority (all Black or African American, non-Hispanic/Latino), 2 international. Average age 28. 24 applicants, 83% accepted, 13 enrolled. In 2010, 10 master's awarded. *Entrance requirements:* For master's and Graduate Certificate, bachelor's degree from an accredited institution. Additional exam requirements/recommendations for international students: Required—TOEFL (minimum score 550 paper-based; 213 computer-based; 75 iBT), IELTS. *Application deadline:* For fall admission, 8/31 priority date for domestic students, 6/30 priority date for international students; for spring admission, 12/31 priority date for domestic students, 10/31 priority date for international students. Applications are processed on a rolling basis. Application fee: $40. Electronic applications accepted. *Expenses:* Tuition: Part-time $550 per credit hour. Required fees: $55 per semester. *Financial support:* In 2010–11, 2 students received support. Available to part-time students. Application deadline: 8/31. *Unit head:* Dr. Joan Dolamore, Dean of Graduate and Professional Studies, 617-243-2485, Fax: 617-243-2450, E-mail: gradinfo@lasell.edu. *Application contact:* Adrienne Franciosi, Director of Graduate Admission, 617-243-2214, Fax: 617-243-2450, E-mail: gradinfo@lasell.edu.

Lasell College, Graduate and Professional Studies in Management, Newton, MA 02466-2709. Offers elder care administration (MSM, Graduate Certificate); elder care marketing (MSM, Graduate Certificate); fundraising management (MSM, Graduate Certificate); human resource management (Graduate Certificate); human resources management (MSM); management (MSM, Graduate Certificate); marketing (MSM, Graduate Certificate); non-profit management (MSM, Graduate Certificate); project management (MSM, Graduate Certificate); public relations (MSM). Part-time and evening/weekend programs available. Postbaccalaureate distance learning degree programs offered (no on-campus study). *Faculty:* 8 full-time (5 women), 7 part-time/adjunct (5 women). *Students:* 25 full-time (21 women), 97 part-time (67 women); includes 16 minority (6 Black or African American, non-Hispanic/Latino; 2 American Indian or Alaska Native, non-Hispanic/Latino; 4 Asian,

non-Hispanic/Latino; 4 Hispanic/Latino), 17 international. Average age 33. 56 applicants, 52% accepted, 19 enrolled. In 2010, 65 master's, 7 other advanced degrees awarded. *Entrance requirements:* For master's and Graduate Certificate, bachelor's degree from an accredited institution. Additional exam requirements/recommendations for international students: Required—TOEFL (minimum score 550 paper-based; 213 computer-based; 75 iBT). *Application deadline:* For fall admission, 8/31 priority date for domestic students, 6/30 priority date for international students; for spring admission, 12/31 priority date for domestic students, 10/31 priority date for international students. Applications are processed on a rolling basis. Application fee: $40. Electronic applications accepted. *Expenses:* Tuition: Part-time $550 per credit hour. Required fees: $55 per semester. *Financial support:* In 2010–11, 40 students received support. Available to part-time students. Application deadline: 8/31. *Unit head:* Dr. Joan Dolamore, Dean of Graduate and Professional Studies, 617-243-2485, Fax: 617-243-2450, E-mail: gradinfo@lasell.edu. *Application contact:* Adrienne Franciosi, Director of Graduate Admission, 617-243-2214, Fax: 617-243-2450, E-mail: gradinfo@lasell.edu.

Lewis University, College of Business, Graduate School of Management, Program in Business Administration, Romeoville, IL 60446. Offers accounting (MBA); custom elective option (MBA); e-business (MBA); finance (MBA); healthcare management (MBA); human resources management (MBA); information security (MBA); international business (MBA); management information systems (MBA); marketing (MBA); project management (MBA); technology and operations management (MBA). Part-time and evening/weekend programs available. *Students:* 119 full-time (66 women), 204 part-time (104 women); includes 55 Black or African American, non-Hispanic/Latino; 9 Asian, non-Hispanic/Latino; 30 Hispanic/Latino; 1 Native Hawaiian or other Pacific Islander, non-Hispanic/Latino, 9 international. Average age 28. In 2010, 111 master's awarded. *Entrance requirements:* For master's, interview, bachelor's degree, resume, 2 recommendations. Additional exam requirements/recommendations for international students: Required—TOEFL (minimum score 550 paper-based; 213 computer-based). *Application deadline:* For fall admission, 8/15 priority date for domestic students, 5/1 priority date for international students; for spring admission, 11/15 priority date for international students. Applications are processed on a rolling basis. Application fee: $40. Electronic applications accepted. *Expenses:* Tuition: Full-time $13,320; part-time $740 per credit hour. Tuition and fees vary according to program. *Financial support:* Career-related internships or fieldwork, Federal Work-Study, scholarships/grants, and unspecified assistantships available. Financial award application deadline: 5/1; financial award applicants required to submit FAFSA. *Unit head:* Dr. Maureen Culleeney, Academic Program Director, 815-838-0500 Ext. 5631, E-mail: culleema@lewisu.edu. *Application contact:* Michele Ryan, Director of Admission, 815-838-0500 Ext. 5384, E-mail: gsm@lewisu.edu.

Lindenwood University, Graduate Programs, School of Business and Entrepreneurship, St. Charles, MO 63301-1695. Offers accounting (MBA, MS); business administration (MBA); entrepreneurial studies (MBA, MS); finance (MBA, MS); human resource management (MBA); human resources (MS); international business (MBA, MS); management (MBA, MS); management information systems (MBA, MS); marketing (MBA, MS); public management (MBA, MS); sport management (MA). *Accreditation:* ACBSP. Part-time and evening/weekend programs available. *Faculty:* 20 full-time (8 women), 17 part-time/adjunct (5 women). *Students:* 179 full-time (73 women), 184 part-time (87 women); includes 27 minority (20 Black or African American, non-Hispanic/Latino; 3 Asian, non-Hispanic/Latino; 4 Hispanic/Latino), 146 international. Average age 28. 149 applicants, 73 enrolled. In 2010, 142 master's awarded. *Degree requirements:* For master's, comprehensive exam (for some programs), thesis (for some programs). *Entrance requirements:* For master's, interview, minimum GPA of 3.0, letter of recommendation. Additional exam requirements/recommendations for international students: Required—TOEFL (minimum score 550 paper-based; 213 computer-based; 80 iBT). *Application deadline:* For fall admission, 7/30 priority date for domestic students, 9/16 priority date for international students; for winter admission, 12/15 priority date for domestic and international students; for spring admission, 2/25 priority date for domestic students, 2/11 priority date for international students. Applications are processed on a rolling basis. Application fee: $30 ($100 for international students). Electronic applications accepted. *Expenses:* Tuition: Full-time $13,260; part-time $380 per credit hour. Required fees: $340. One-time fee: $30. Tuition and fees vary according to course level and course load. *Financial support:* In 2010–11, 209 students received support. Career-related internships or fieldwork, Federal Work-Study, institutionally sponsored loans, and tuition waivers (partial) available. Financial award application deadline: 6/30; financial award applicants required to submit FAFSA. *Unit head:* Roger Ellis, Dean, 636-949-4839, E-mail: rellis@lindenwood.edu. *Application contact:* Brett Barger, Dean of Evening Admissions and Extension Campuses, 636-949-4934, Fax: 636-949-4109, E-mail: adultadmissions@lindenwood.edu.

Louisiana State University and Agricultural and Mechanical College, Graduate School, E. J. Ourso College of Business, Department of Marketing, Baton Rouge, LA 70803. Offers business administration (PhD), including marketing. Part-time programs available. *Faculty:* 10 full-time (2 women). *Students:* 6 full-time (5 women), 3 part-time (1 woman), 4 international.

Average age 31. 1 applicant, 100% accepted, 1 enrolled. In 2010, 4 doctorates awarded. *Degree requirements:* For doctorate, thesis/dissertation. *Entrance requirements:* Additional exam requirements/recommendations for international students: Required—TOEFL (minimum score 550 paper-based; 213 computer-based; 79 iBT) or IELTS (minimum score 6.5). *Application deadline:* For fall admission, 1/25 priority date for domestic students, 5/15 for international students; for spring admission, 10/15 for international students. Applications are processed on a rolling basis. Application fee: $50 ($70 for international students). Electronic applications accepted. *Financial support:* In 2010–11, 8 students received support, including 6 teaching assistantships with full and partial tuition reimbursements available (averaging $16,800 per year); fellowships, research assistantships with partial tuition reimbursements available, career-related internships or fieldwork, Federal Work-Study, institutionally sponsored loans, scholarships/grants, health care benefits, and unspecified assistantships also available. Support available to part-time students. Financial award applicants required to submit FAFSA. *Faculty research:* Consumer behavior, marketing strategy, global marketing, e-commerce, branding/brand equity. Total annual research expenditures: $5,050. *Unit head:* Dr. Alvin C. Burns, Chair, 225-578-8786, Fax: 225-578-8616, E-mail: alburns@lsu.edu. *Application contact:* Dr. Ron Niedrich, Graduate Adviser, 225-578-9068, Fax: 225-578-8616, E-mail: niedrich@lsu.edu.

Manhattanville College, Graduate Programs, Humanities and Social Sciences Programs, Program in Integrated Marketing Communications, Purchase, NY 10577-2132. Offers MS. Part-time and evening/weekend programs available. *Entrance requirements:* Additional exam requirements/recommendations for international students: Required—TOEFL. *Application deadline:* Applications are processed on a rolling basis. Application fee: $75. *Expenses:* Tuition: Full-time $16,110; part-time $895 per credit. Required fees: $50 per semester. *Financial support:* Career-related internships or fieldwork, Federal Work-Study, institutionally sponsored loans, and unspecified assistantships available. Financial award applicants required to submit FAFSA. *Unit head:* Donald Richards, Dean, School of Graduate and Professional Studies, 914-323-5469, Fax: 914-694-3488, E-mail: gps@mville.edu. *Application contact:* Office of Admissions, Graduate and Professional Studies, 914-323-5418, E-mail: gps@mville.edu.

Marquette University, Graduate School of Management, Executive MBA Program, Milwaukee, WI 53201-1881. Offers economics (MBA); finance (MBA); human resources (MBA); international business (MBA); management information systems (MBA); marketing (MBA); operations and supply chain management (MBA); sports business (MBA). *Accreditation:* AACSB. *Faculty:* 3 full-time (1 woman), 2 part-time/adjunct (0 women). *Students:* 43 full-time (11 women); includes 6 minority (1 Black or African American, non-Hispanic/Latino; 4 Asian, non-Hispanic/Latino; 1 Hispanic/Latino), 3 international. Average age 37. 47 applicants, 74% accepted, 29 enrolled. In 2010, 13 master's awarded. *Degree requirements:* For master's, international trip. *Entrance requirements:* For master's, GMAT, two letters of recommendation, official transcripts from current and previous colleges/universities. Additional exam requirements/recommendations for international students: Required—TOEFL (minimum score 530 paper-based; 78 computer-based). *Application deadline:* Applications are processed on a rolling basis. Application fee: $50. Electronic applications accepted. *Expenses:* Contact institution. *Financial support:* Application deadline: 2/15. *Faculty research:* International trade and finance, customer relationship management, consumer satisfaction, customer service. *Unit head:* Dr. Jeanne Simmons, Graduate Director, 414-288-7145, Fax: 414-288-1660, E-mail: jeanne.simmons@marquette.edu. *Application contact:* Erin Fox, Assistant Director for Recruitment, 414-288-5319, Fax: 414-288-1902, E-mail: erin.fox@marquette.edu.

Marquette University, Graduate School of Management, Program in Business Administration, Milwaukee, WI 53201-1881. Offers business administration (MBA); economics (MBA); finance (MBA); human resources (MBA); international business (MBA); management information systems (MBA); marketing (MBA); operations and supply chain management (MBA); sports business (MBA); JD/MBA; MBA/MA; MBA/MSN. *Accreditation:* AACSB. Part-time and evening/weekend programs available. *Faculty:* 38 full-time (9 women), 24 part-time/adjunct (8 women). *Students:* 44 full-time (17 women), 368 part-time (105 women); includes 36 minority (4 Black or African American, non-Hispanic/Latino; 2 American Indian or Alaska Native, non-Hispanic/Latino; 20 Asian, non-Hispanic/Latino; 10 Hispanic/Latino), 30 international. Average age 31. 256 applicants, 60% accepted, 98 enrolled. In 2010, 117 master's awarded. *Entrance requirements:* For master's, GMAT, letters of recommendation. Additional exam requirements/recommendations for international students: Required—TOEFL (minimum score 530 paper-based; 78 computer-based). *Application deadline:* Applications are processed on a rolling basis. Application fee: $50. Electronic applications accepted. *Expenses:* Tuition: Full-time $16,290; part-time $905 per credit hour. Tuition and fees vary according to program. *Financial support:* In 2010–11, 4 fellowships, 11 teaching assistantships were awarded; research assistantships, Federal Work-Study, institutionally sponsored loans, scholarships/grants, and tuition waivers (full and partial) also available. Support available to part-time students. Financial award application deadline: 2/15. *Faculty research:* Ethics in the professions, services marketing, technology impact on decision-making, mentoring. *Unit head:* Dr. Jeanne Simmons, Graduate Director, 414-288-7145,

Fax: 414-288-1660, E-mail: jeanne.simmons@marquette.edu. *Application contact:* Debra Leutermann, Admissions Coordinator, 414-288-8064, Fax: 414-288-1902, E-mail: debra.leutermann@marquette.edu.

Marylhurst University, Department of Business Administration, Marylhurst, OR 97036-0261. Offers finance (MBA); general management (MBA); government policy and administration (MBA); green development (MBA); health care management (MBA); marketing (MBA); natural and organic resources (MBA); nonprofit management (MBA); organizational behavior (MBA); real estate (MBA); renewable energy (MBA); sustainable business (MBA). Part-time and evening/weekend programs available. Postbaccalaureate distance learning degree programs offered (no on-campus study). *Faculty:* 3 full-time (0 women), 36 part-time/adjunct (6 women). *Students:* 27 full-time (13 women), 727 part-time (373 women); includes 167 minority (47 Black or African American, non-Hispanic/Latino; 6 American Indian or Alaska Native, non-Hispanic/Latino; 36 Asian, non-Hispanic/Latino; 51 Hispanic/Latino; 6 Native Hawaiian or other Pacific Islander, non-Hispanic/Latino; 21 Two or more races, non-Hispanic/Latino), 7 international. Average age 38. 262 applicants, 91% accepted, 194 enrolled. In 2010, 289 master's awarded. *Degree requirements:* For master's, comprehensive exam, capstone course. *Entrance requirements:* For master's, GMAT (if GPA less than 3.0 and fewer than 5 years of work experience), interview, resume, 2 letters of recommendation. Additional exam requirements/recommendations for international students: Recommended—TOEFL (minimum score 550 paper-based; 213 computer-based; 80 iBT). *Application deadline:* For fall admission, 9/11 priority date for domestic and international students; for winter admission, 12/15 priority date for domestic and international students; for spring admission, 3/15 priority date for domestic students, 3/17 priority date for international students. Applications are processed on a rolling basis. Application fee: $50. Electronic applications accepted. *Expenses:* Tuition: Full-time $13,932; part-time $516 per credit. Tuition and fees vary according to course load and program. *Financial support:* Scholarships/grants available. Support available to part-time students. Financial award applicants required to submit FAFSA. *Unit head:* Bob Hanks, Director of Business and Real Estate Programs, 503-636-8141, Fax: 503-697-5597, E-mail: mba@marylhurst.edu. *Application contact:* Maruska Lynch, Graduate Admissions Specialist, 800-634-9982 Ext. 6322, Fax: 503-699-6320, E-mail: admissions@marylhurst.edu.

Maryville University of Saint Louis, The John E. Simon School of Business, St. Louis, MO 63141-7299. Offers accounting (MBA, PGC); business studies (PGC); management (MBA, PGC); marketing (MBA, PGC); process and project management (MBA, PGC); sport and entertainment management (MBA, PGC). *Accreditation:* ACBSP. Part-time and evening/weekend programs available. *Faculty:* 7 full-time (4 women), 13 part-time/adjunct (5 women). *Students:* 16 full-time (8 women), 119 part-time (57 women); includes 15 minority (9 Black or African American, non-Hispanic/Latino; 3 Asian, non-Hispanic/Latino; 3 Hispanic/Latino), 5 international. Average age 31. In 2010, 60 master's awarded. *Entrance requirements:* For master's, GMAT (unless applicant possesses undergraduate business degree with minimum cumulative GPA of 3.0, or has completed master's degree from accredited university or one early access course prior to undergraduate degree). Additional exam requirements/recommendations for international students: Required—TOEFL (minimum score 563 paper-based; 85 iBT), If you took the revised TOEFL (after Sept. 24, 2005), you will be admitted into our MBA program with a speaking sub-score of 23, a writing sub-score of 20, reading and listening scores of 21 or higher and a combined score of 79 or higher. *Application deadline:* Applications are processed on a rolling basis. Application fee: $40 ($60 for international students). Electronic applications accepted. *Expenses:* Tuition: Full-time $21,100; part-time $633.50 per credit hour. Required fees: $150 per semester. *Financial support:* Career-related internships or fieldwork, Federal Work-Study, tuition waivers (partial), and campus employment available. Financial award application deadline: 3/1; financial award applicants required to submit FAFSA. *Faculty research:* International business, e-marketing, strategic planning, interpersonal management skills, financial analysis. *Unit head:* Dr. Pamela Horwitz, Dean, 314-529-9418, Fax: 314-529-9975, E-mail: horwitz@maryville.edu. *Application contact:* Kathy Dougherty, Director of MBA Programs, 314-529-9382, Fax: 314-529-9975, E-mail: business@maryville.edu.

Middle Tennessee State University, College of Graduate Studies, Jennings A. Jones College of Business, Department of Management and Marketing, Murfreesboro, TN 37132. Offers MBA. *Accreditation:* AACSB. Part-time and evening/weekend programs available. Postbaccalaureate distance learning degree programs offered. *Faculty:* 18 full-time (4 women). *Students:* 33 full-time (6 women), 343 part-time (136 women); includes 53 Black or African American, non-Hispanic/Latino; 1 American Indian or Alaska Native, non-Hispanic/Latino; 38 Asian, non-Hispanic/Latino; 10 Hispanic/Latino; 3 Two or more races, non-Hispanic/Latino. Average age 29. 213 applicants, 66% accepted, 140 enrolled. In 2010, 109 master's awarded. *Degree requirements:* For master's, comprehensive exam. *Entrance requirements:* Additional exam requirements/recommendations for international students: Required—TOEFL (minimum score 525 paper-based; 195 computer-based; 71 iBT) or IELTS (minimum score 6). *Application deadline:* For fall admission, 6/1 for domestic and international students. Applications are processed on a rolling basis. Application fee: $25 ($30 for international students). Electronic applications accepted. *Expenses:* Tuition, state resident: full-time $4632. Tuition, nonresident: full-time $11,520. *Financial support:* In 2010–11, 8 students received support. Institutionally sponsored loans available. Support available to part-time students. Financial award application deadline: 5/1; financial award applicants required to submit FAFSA. *Faculty research:* International business, business strategy, organizational culture/leadership, consumer behavior, services marketing. *Unit head:* Dr. Jill M. Austin, Chair, 615-898-2736, Fax: 615-898-5308, E-mail: jaustin@mtsu.edu. *Application contact:* Dr. Michael Allen, Dean and Vice Provost for Research, 615-898-2840, Fax: 615-904-8020, E-mail: mallen@mtsu.edu.

Milwaukee School of Engineering, Rader School of Business, Program in Marketing and Export Management, Milwaukee, WI 53202-3109. Offers MS. *Faculty:* 1 full-time (0 women), 1 part-time/adjunct (0 women). *Students:* 9 part-time (5 women); includes 1 Asian, non-Hispanic/Latino; 1 Hispanic/Latino. Average age 28. 2 applicants, 100% accepted, 2 enrolled. *Degree requirements:* For master's, thesis optional, thesis defense or capstone project. *Entrance requirements:* For master's, GRE General Test or GMAT, 2 letters of recommendation. Additional exam requirements/recommendations for international students: Recommended—TOEFL (minimum score 550 paper-based; 213 computer-based; 79 iBT), IELTS. *Application deadline:* Applications are processed on a rolling basis. Application fee: $30. Electronic applications accepted. *Expenses:* Tuition: Full-time $17,550; part-time $650 per credit. One-time fee: $75. *Financial support:* In 2010–11, 6 students received support. Applicants required to submit FAFSA. *Unit head:* Dr. Kathy Faggiani, Director, 414-277-2711, Fax: 414-277-2711, E-mail: faggiani@msoe.edu. *Application contact:* Sarah K. Winchowky, Graduate Admissions Director, 800-321-6763, Fax: 414-277-7475, E-mail: wp@msoe.edu.

Mississippi State University, College of Business, Department of Marketing, Quantitative Analysis and Business Law, Mississippi State, MS 39762. Offers business administration (MBA, PhD), including marketing. Part-time and evening/weekend programs available. *Faculty:* 10 full-time (3 women). *Students:* 5 full-time (4 women); includes 1 minority (Black or African American, non-Hispanic/Latino), 1 international. Average age 28. 16 applicants, 6% accepted, 1 enrolled. *Degree requirements:* For doctorate, comprehensive exam, thesis/dissertation. *Entrance requirements:* For doctorate, GMAT, minimum GPA of 2.75 in last 60 undergraduate hours. Additional exam requirements/recommendations for international students: Required—TOEFL (minimum score 575 paper-based; 233 computer-based; 90 iBT); Recommended—IELTS (minimum score 6.5). *Application deadline:* For fall admission, 7/1 for domestic students, 5/1 for international students; for spring admission, 11/1 for domestic students, 9/1 for international students. Applications are processed on a rolling basis. Application fee: $40. Electronic applications accepted. *Expenses:* Tuition, state resident: full-time $2730.50; part-time $304 per credit hour. Tuition, nonresident: full-time $6901; part-time $767 per credit hour. *Financial support:* In 2010–11, 2 teaching assistantships (averaging $12,270 per year) were awarded; Federal Work-Study, institutionally sponsored loans, and scholarships/grants also available. Financial award application deadline: 4/1; financial award applicants required to submit FAFSA. *Unit head:* Dr. Jason Lueg, Associate Professor and Department Head, 662-325-3163, Fax: 662-325-7012, E-mail: jlueg@cobilan.msstate.edu. *Application contact:* Dr. Barbara Spencer, Associate Dean for Research and Outreach, 662-325-1891, Fax: 662-325-8161, E-mail: gsbi@cobilan.msstate.edu.

Montclair State University, The Graduate School, School of Business, Department of Marketing, Montclair, NJ 07043-1624. Offers international business (MBA, Certificate); marketing (MBA). Part-time and evening/weekend programs available. *Faculty:* 10 full-time (5 women), 6 part-time/adjunct (2 women). *Students:* 6 full-time (1 woman), 40 part-time (22 women); includes 4 Black or African American, non-Hispanic/Latino; 5 Asian, non-Hispanic/Latino; 2 Hispanic/Latino. Average age 27. 50 applicants, 60% accepted, 8 enrolled. In 2010, 11 master's awarded. *Entrance requirements:* For master's, GMAT, 2 letters of recommendation, resume. Additional exam requirements/recommendations for international students: Required—TOEFL (minimum iBT score of 83) or IELTS. *Application deadline:* For fall admission, 6/1 for international students; for spring admission, 10/1 for international students. Applications are processed on a rolling basis. Application fee: $60. Electronic applications accepted. *Expenses:* Tuition, state resident: part-time $501.34 per credit. Tuition, nonresident: part-time $773.88 per credit. Required fees: $71.15 per credit. *Financial support:* In 2010–11, 5 research assistantships with tuition reimbursements (averaging $7,000 per year) were awarded; Federal Work-Study, scholarships/grants, and unspecified assistantships also available. Support available to part-time students. Financial award application deadline: 3/1; financial award applicants required to submit FAFSA. *Faculty research:* Converting service marketing to tangibility, mathematical approaches to solving marketing problems, system dynamic modeling of brand management, attitudes toward safety in leisure facilities, marketing/retailing strategy and instruction. *Unit head:* Dr. Avinandan Mukherjee, Chair, 973-655-5126. *Application contact:* Amy Aiello, Director of Graduate Admissions and Operations, 973-655-5147, Fax: 973-655-7869, E-mail: graduate.school@montclair.edu.

National University, Academic Affairs, School of Business and Management, Department of Leadership and Business Administration, La Jolla, CA 92037-1011. Offers alternative dispute resolution (MBA); e-business (MBA); financial management (MBA); human resource management (MBA); human resources management (MA); international business (MBA); knowledge management (MS); marketing (MBA); organizational leadership (MBA, MS); technology management (MBA). Part-time and evening/weekend programs available. Postbaccalaureate distance learning degree programs offered (no on-campus study). *Faculty:* 16 full-time (4 women), 126 part-time/adjunct (39 women). *Students:* 119 full-time (81 women), 410 part-time (202 women); includes 176 minority (81 Black or African American, non-Hispanic/Latino; 1 American Indian or Alaska Native, non-Hispanic/Latino; 31 Asian, non-Hispanic/Latino; 52 Hispanic/Latino; 4 Native Hawaiian or other Pacific Islander, non-Hispanic/Latino; 7 Two or more races, non-Hispanic/Latino), 183 international. Average age 38. 219 applicants, 100% accepted, 160 enrolled. In 2010, 95 master's awarded. *Degree requirements:* For master's, thesis. *Entrance requirements:* For master's, interview, minimum GPA of 2.5. Additional exam requirements/recommendations for international students: Required—TOEFL (minimum score 550 paper-based; 213 computer-based; 79 iBT), IELTS (minimum score 6). *Application deadline:* Applications are processed on a rolling basis. Application fee: $60 ($65 for international students). Electronic applications accepted. *Expenses:* Tuition: Full-time $9450; part-time $350 per unit. Required fees: $350 per unit. One-time fee: $60. *Financial support:* Career-related internships or fieldwork, institutionally sponsored loans, scholarships/grants, and tuition waivers (partial) available. Support available to part-time students. Financial award application deadline: 6/30; financial award applicants required to submit FAFSA. *Unit head:* Dr. Bruce Buchowicz, Chair, 858-642-8439, Fax: 858-642-8406, E-mail: bbuchowicz@nu.edu. *Application contact:* Dominick Giovanniello, Associate Regional Dean—San Diego, 800-NAT-UNIV, Fax: 858-541-7792, E-mail: dgiovann@nu.edu.

New Mexico State University, Graduate School, College of Business, Department of Marketing, Las Cruces, NM 88003-8001. Offers business administration (PhD), including marketing. *Faculty:* 8 full-time (1 woman). *Students:* 7 full-time (3 women), 1 part-time (0 women); includes 3 minority (all Hispanic/Latino), 2 international. Average age 34. 1 applicant, 100% accepted, 1 enrolled. In 2010, 1 doctorate awarded. *Degree requirements:* For doctorate, comprehensive exam, thesis/dissertation, 15 credits in marketing, 21 in methods, 12 in support area. *Entrance requirements:* For doctorate, GMAT, MBA or equivalent. Additional exam requirements/recommendations for international students: Required—TOEFL. *Application deadline:* For fall admission, 3/1 priority date for domestic and international students. *Expenses:* Tuition, state resident: full-time $4536; part-time $242 per credit. Tuition, nonresident: full-time $15,816; part-time $712 per credit. Required fees: $636 per term. *Financial support:* In 2010–11, 4 students received support, including 7 teaching assistantships (averaging $21,268 per year); research assistantships, scholarships/grants and health care benefits also available. Financial award application deadline: 3/1. *Unit head:* Dr. Elise Pookie Sautter, Head, 575-646-3341, Fax: 575-646-1498, E-mail: esautter@nmsu.edu. *Application contact:* Dr. Kelly Tian, Director, 575-646-3341, Fax: 575-646-1498, E-mail: ktian@nmsu.edu.

New York Institute of Technology, Graduate Division, School of Management, Program in Business Administration, Old Westbury, NY 11568-8000. Offers accounting (Advanced Certificate); business administration (MBA); finance (Advanced Certificate); international business (Advanced Certificate); management of information systems (Advanced Certificate); marketing (Advanced Certificate). Part-time and evening/weekend programs available. *Students:* 454 full-time (188 women), 513 part-time (204 women); includes 49 minority (15 Black or African American, non-Hispanic/Latino; 23 Asian, non-Hispanic/Latino; 11 Hispanic/Latino), 268 international. Average age 29. In 2010, 435 master's, 1 other advanced degree awarded. *Degree requirements:* For master's, thesis (for some programs). *Entrance requirements:* For master's, minimum QPA of 2.85. Additional exam requirements/recommendations for international students: Required—TOEFL (minimum score 550 paper-based; 213 computer-based). *Application deadline:* For fall admission, 7/1 priority date for domestic students; for spring admission, 12/1 priority date for domestic students. Applications are processed on a rolling basis. Application fee: $50. Electronic applications accepted. *Expenses:* Tuition: Part-time $835 per credit. *Financial support:* Fellowships, research assistantships with partial tuition reimbursements, institutionally sponsored loans, tuition waivers (full and partial), and unspecified assistantships available. Support available to part-time students. Financial award applicants required to submit FAFSA. *Faculty research:* Instructor performance appraisal; relationship between TOEFL, GMAT, GRE, and performance in foreign students. *Unit head:* Dr. Stephen Hartman, Director, 516-686-7691, E-mail: shartman@nyit.edu. *Application contact:* Dr. Jacquelyn Nealon, Vice President for Enrollment Services, 516-686-7925, Fax: 516-686-7597, E-mail: jnealon@nyit.edu.

New York University, School of Continuing and Professional Studies, Division of Programs in Business, Program in Integrated Marketing, New York, NY 10012-1019. Offers brand management (MS); digital marketing (MS); marketing analytics (MS). Part-time and evening/weekend programs available. *Faculty:* 2 full-time (1 woman), 22 part-time/adjunct (7 women). *Students:* 36 full-time (29 women), 51 part-time (40 women); includes 6 Black or African American, non-Hispanic/Latino; 4 Asian, non-Hispanic/Latino; 11 Hispanic/Latino, 38 international. Average age 29. 225 applicants, 32%

accepted, 25 enrolled. In 2010, 36 master's awarded. *Degree requirements:* For master's, comprehensive exam, thesis, capstone; writing of complete business plan. *Entrance requirements:* For master's, GRE General Test or GMAT required for all applicants, resume, 2 letters of recommendation, essay, professional experience. Additional exam requirements/recommendations for international students: Required—TOEFL (minimum score 600 paper-based; 250 computer-based; 100 iBT). *Application deadline:* For fall admission, 2/1 priority date for domestic and international students; for spring admission, 10/15 priority date for domestic students, 8/15 priority date for international students. Applications are processed on a rolling basis. Application fee: $75. Electronic applications accepted. *Financial support:* In 2010–11, 44 students received support, including 44 fellowships (averaging $2,547 per year); career-related internships or fieldwork, institutionally sponsored loans, and scholarships/grants also available. Support available to part-time students. Financial award application deadline: 3/1; financial award applicants required to submit FAFSA. *Faculty research:* Branding, digital marketing, Web analytics, consumer behavior, customer loyalty, campaign planning and management. *Unit head:* Dr. Marjorie Kalter, Academic Director, 212-992-3221, Fax: 212-992-3676, E-mail: mk99@nyu.edu. *Application contact:* Fadia Angrand, Assistant Director, 212-992-3221, Fax: 212-992-3676, E-mail: fs20@nyu.edu.

New York University, School of Continuing and Professional Studies, The Preston Robert Tisch Center for Hospitality, Tourism, and Sports Management, Program in Sports Business, New York, NY 10012-1019. Offers collegiate and professional sports operations (MS); marketing and media (MS); sports business (Advanced Certificate). Part-time and evening/weekend programs available. *Faculty:* 12 full-time (5 women), 13 part-time/adjunct (2 women). *Students:* 19 full-time (10 women), 37 part-time (9 women); includes 4 Black or African American, non-Hispanic/Latino; 1 Asian, non-Hispanic/Latino; 3 Hispanic/Latino, 14 international. Average age 28. 143 applicants, 27% accepted, 21 enrolled. In 2010, 35 master's, 13 other advanced degrees awarded. *Degree requirements:* For master's, thesis. *Entrance requirements:* For master's, GMAT or GRE General Test (for recent graduates), resume, 2 letters of recommendation, essay, professional experience. Additional exam requirements/recommendations for international students: Required—TOEFL (minimum score 600 paper-based; 250 computer-based; 100 iBT), TWE. *Application deadline:* For fall admission, 2/1 priority date for domestic and international students; for spring admission, 10/15 priority date for domestic students, 8/15 priority date for international students. Applications are processed on a rolling basis. Application fee: $75. Electronic applications accepted. *Financial support:* In 2010–11, 35 students received support, including 35 fellowships (averaging $3,256 per year); career-related internships or fieldwork, Federal Work-Study, institutionally sponsored loans, and scholarships/grants also available. Support available to part-time students. Financial award application deadline: 3/1; financial award applicants required to submit FAFSA. *Faculty research:* Implications of college football's bowl coalition series from a legal, economic, and academic perspective; social history of sports. *Unit head:* Bjorn Hanson, Divisional Dean, Clinical Professor, HVS Chair, 212-998-9101, Fax: 212-995-4677. *Application contact:* Sandra Dove-Lowther, Academic Services Director, 212-998-9087, Fax: 212-995-4676, E-mail: sd2@nyu.edu.

North Central College, Graduate and Continuing Education Programs, Department of Business, Program in Business Administration, Naperville, IL 60566-7063. Offers change management (MBA); finance (MBA); human resource management (MBA); management (MBA); marketing (MBA). Part-time and evening/weekend programs available. *Faculty:* 14 full-time (4 women), 5 part-time/adjunct (1 woman). *Students:* 46 full-time (17 women), 101 part-time (46 women); includes 6 Black or African American, non-Hispanic/Latino; 1 American Indian or Alaska Native, non-Hispanic/Latino; 4 Asian, non-Hispanic/Latino; 7 Hispanic/Latino, 3 international. Average age 31. In 2010, 46 master's awarded. *Degree requirements:* For master's, project. *Entrance requirements:* For master's, interview. Additional exam requirements/recommendations for international students: Required—TOEFL (minimum score 577 paper-based; 233 computer-based; 90 iBT). *Application deadline:* For fall admission, 8/15 for domestic students; for winter admission, 12/1 for domestic students; for spring admission, 2/1 for domestic students. Application fee: $25. *Financial support:* Scholarships/grants available. Support available to part-time students. *Unit head:* Dr. Jean Clifton, MBA Program Coordinator, 630-637-5244, E-mail: jmclifton@noctrl.edu. *Application contact:* Wendy Kulpinski, Director and Graduate and Continuing Education Admission, 630-637-5808, Fax: 630-637-5844, E-mail: wekulpinski@noctrl.edu.

Northeastern Illinois University, Graduate College, College of Business and Management, Chicago, IL 60625-4699. Offers accounting (MSA); finance (MBA); management (MBA); marketing (MBA). Part-time and evening/weekend programs available. *Faculty:* 24 full-time (3 women), 13 part-time/adjunct (4 women). *Students:* 41 full-time (19 women), 69 part-time (32 women); includes 23 minority (4 Black or African American, non-Hispanic/Latino; 1 American Indian or Alaska Native, non-Hispanic/Latino; 11 Asian, non-Hispanic/Latino; 6 Hispanic/Latino; 1 Two or more races, non-Hispanic/Latino), 21 international. Average age 31. 112 applicants, 75% accepted, 80 enrolled. In 2010, 34 master's awarded. *Degree requirements:* For master's, thesis optional. *Entrance requirements:* For master's, GMAT, minimum GPA of 2.75. Additional exam requirements/recommendations for international students: Required—TOEFL (minimum score 550 paper-based;

213 computer-based; 79 iBT). *Application deadline:* For fall admission, 4/1 priority date for domestic students; for spring admission, 8/15 for domestic students. Applications are processed on a rolling basis. Application fee: $30. Electronic applications accepted. *Financial support:* In 2010–11, 20 students received support, including 6 research assistantships with full and partial tuition reimbursements available (averaging $6,600 per year); career-related internships or fieldwork, Federal Work-Study, institutionally sponsored loans, scholarships/grants, tuition waivers (full and partial), and unspecified assistantships also available. Support available to part-time students. *Faculty research:* Perception of accountants and non-accountants toward future of the accounting industry, asynchronous learning outcomes, cost and efficiency of financial markets, impact of deregulation on airline industry, analysis of derivational instruments. *Unit head:* Dr. Amy B. Hietapelto, Dean, 773-442-6105. *Application contact:* Dr. Amy B. Hietapelto, Dean, 773-442-6105.

Notre Dame de Namur University, Division of Academic Affairs, School of Business and Management, Department of Business Administration, Belmont, CA 94002-1908. Offers business administration (MBA); finance (MBA); human resource management (MBA); marketing (MBA). Part-time and evening/weekend programs available. *Faculty:* 7 full-time (1 woman), 6 part-time/adjunct (0 women). *Students:* 46 full-time (24 women), 79 part-time (54 women); includes 54 minority (3 Black or African American, non-Hispanic/Latino; 28 Asian, non-Hispanic/Latino; 20 Hispanic/Latino; 2 Native Hawaiian or other Pacific Islander, non-Hispanic/Latino; 1 Two or more races, non-Hispanic/Latino), 22 international. Average age 34. 129 applicants, 53% accepted, 37 enrolled. In 2010, 28 master's awarded. *Entrance requirements:* For master's, minimum GPA of 2.5. Additional exam requirements/recommendations for international students: Required—TOEFL (minimum score 550 paper-based; 213 computer-based; 79 iBT). *Application deadline:* For fall admission, 8/1 priority date for domestic students; for spring admission, 12/1 priority date for domestic students. Applications are processed on a rolling basis. Application fee: $60. Electronic applications accepted. *Expenses:* Tuition: Full-time $14,220; part-time $790 per credit. Required fees: $35 per semester. Tuition and fees vary according to program. *Financial support:* Available to part-time students. Applicants required to submit FAFSA. *Unit head:* Jordan Holtzman, Director, 650-508-3637, E-mail: jholtzman@ndnu.edu. *Application contact:* Candace Hallmark, Associate Director of Admissions, 650-508-3600, Fax: 650-508-3426, E-mail: grad.admit@ndnu.edu.

Nova Southeastern University, H. Wayne Huizenga School of Business and Entrepreneurship, Doctoral Program in Business Administration, Fort Lauderdale, FL 33314-7796. Offers accounting (DBA); decision sciences (DBA); finance (DBA); human resource management (DBA); international business (DBA); management (DBA); marketing (DBA). Part-time and evening/weekend programs available. *Faculty:* 34 full-time (11 women), 2 part-time/adjunct (1 woman). *Students:* 2 full-time (1 woman), 93 part-time (32 women); includes 9 Black or African American, non-Hispanic/Latino; 4 Asian, non-Hispanic/Latino; 11 Hispanic/Latino, 8 international. Average age 47. 66 applicants, 14% accepted, 6 enrolled. In 2010, 29 doctorates awarded. *Degree requirements:* For doctorate, comprehensive exam, thesis/dissertation. *Entrance requirements:* For doctorate, GMAT. Additional exam requirements/recommendations for international students: Required—TOEFL (minimum score 600 paper-based; 250 computer-based; 100 iBT), IELTS (minimum score 7). *Application deadline:* Applications are processed on a rolling basis. Application fee: $50. Electronic applications accepted. *Financial support:* Available to part-time students. Applicants required to submit FAFSA. *Faculty research:* Reputation management, call centers, international social capital, corporate earnings guidance, corporate governance. *Unit head:* Kristie Tetrault, Director of Program Administration, 954-262-5120, Fax: 954-262-3849, E-mail: kristie@huizenga.nova.edu. *Application contact:* Karen Goldberg, Associate Director of Recruitment and Special Events, 954-262-5039, Fax: 954-262-3822, E-mail: karen@huizenga.nova.edu.

The Ohio State University, Graduate School, Max M. Fisher College of Business, Program in Marketing, Columbus, OH 43210. Offers MBA, MS, PhD. *Students:* 1 full-time (0 women), 16 part-time (10 women); includes 1 Asian, non-Hispanic/Latino, 2 international. Average age 35. *Entrance requirements:* Additional exam requirements/recommendations for international students: Required—TOEFL. *Expenses:* Tuition, state resident: full-time $10,605. Tuition, nonresident: full-time $26,535. Tuition and fees vary according to course load and program. *Application contact:* Graduate Admissions, 614-292-9444, Fax: 614-292-3895, E-mail: domestic.grad@osu.edu.

Oklahoma State University, Spears School of Business, Department of Marketing, Stillwater, OK 74078. Offers business administration (PhD), including marketing; marketing (MBA). Part-time programs available. *Faculty:* 17 full-time (4 women), 13 part-time/adjunct (3 women). *Students:* 7 full-time (0 women), 5 part-time (1 woman); includes 1 Asian, non-Hispanic/Latino, 5 international. Average age 34. *Degree requirements:* For master's, thesis or alternative; for doctorate, comprehensive exam, thesis/dissertation. *Entrance requirements:* For master's and doctorate, GRE or GMAT. Additional exam requirements/recommendations for international students: Required—TOEFL (minimum score 550 paper-based; 79 iBT). *Application deadline:* For fall admission, 3/1 priority date for international students; for spring admission, 8/1 priority date for international students. Applications are processed on a rolling basis. Application fee: $40 ($75 for international students). Electronic applications accepted. *Expenses:* Tuition, state resident: full-time $3716; part-time $154.85 per credit hour. Tuition, nonresident: full-time $14,892; part-time $621 per credit hour. Required fees: $2044; $85.20 per credit hour. One-time fee: $50. Tuition and fees vary according to course load and campus/location. *Financial support:* In 2010–11, 4 research assistantships (averaging $15,288 per year), 6 teaching assistantships (averaging $22,735 per year) were awarded; career-related internships or fieldwork, Federal Work-Study, scholarships/grants, health care benefits, tuition waivers (partial), and unspecified assistantships also available. Support available to part-time students. Financial award application deadline: 3/1; financial award applicants required to submit FAFSA. *Faculty research:* Decision-making (consumer, managerial, cross-functional), communication effects, services marketing, public policy and marketing, corporate image. *Unit head:* Dr. Joshua L. Wiener, Head, 405-744-5192, Fax: 405-744-5180. *Application contact:* Dr. Gordon Emslie, Dean, 405-744-6368, Fax: 405-744-0355, E-mail: grad-i@okstate.edu.

Old Dominion University, College of Business and Public Administration, Doctoral Program in Business Administration, Norfolk, VA 23529. Offers finance (PhD); information technology (PhD); marketing (PhD); strategic management (PhD). *Accreditation:* AACSB. *Faculty:* 21 full-time (2 women). *Students:* 36 full-time (13 women), 1 part-time (0 women); includes 5 minority (2 Black or African American, non-Hispanic/Latino; 2 Asian, non-Hispanic/Latino; 1 Native Hawaiian or other Pacific Islander, non-Hispanic/Latino), 28 international. Average age 35. 42 applicants, 69% accepted, 10 enrolled. In 2010, 5 doctorates awarded. *Degree requirements:* For doctorate, comprehensive exam, thesis/dissertation. *Entrance requirements:* For doctorate, GMAT. Additional exam requirements/recommendations for international students: Required—TOEFL (minimum score 550 paper-based; 213 computer-based; 79 iBT). *Application deadline:* For fall admission, 4/1 priority date for domestic and international students. Application fee: $50. Electronic applications accepted. *Expenses:* Tuition, state resident: full-time $8592; part-time $358 per credit. Tuition, nonresident: full-time $21,672; part-time $903 per credit. Required fees: $119 per semester. One-time fee: $50. *Financial support:* In 2010–11, 27 students received support, including 2 fellowships with full tuition reimbursements available (averaging $7,500 per year), 32 research assistantships with full tuition reimbursements available (averaging $7,500 per year), 12 teaching assistantships with full tuition reimbursements available (averaging $7,500 per year); scholarships/grants and unspecified assistantships also available. Financial award application deadline: 4/1; financial award applicants required to submit FAFSA. *Faculty research:* International business, buyer behavior, financial markets, strategy, operations research. *Unit head:* Dr. John B. Ford, Graduate Program Director, 757-683-3587, Fax: 757-683-4076, E-mail: jford@odu.edu. *Application contact:* Katrina Davenport, Program Coordinator, 757-683-5138, Fax: 757-683-4076, E-mail: kdavenpo@odu.edu.

Providence College, Graduate Studies, School of Business, Providence, RI 02918. Offers accounting (MBA); entrepreneurship (MBA); finance (MBA); international business (MBA); management (MBA); marketing (MBA); not-for-profit organizations (MBA). Part-time and evening/weekend programs available. *Faculty:* 17 full-time (9 women), 10 part-time/adjunct (2 women). *Students:* 53 full-time (20 women), 57 part-time (22 women); includes 4 minority (1 Black or African American, non-Hispanic/Latino; 1 Asian, non-Hispanic/Latino; 2 Two or more races, non-Hispanic/Latino), 6 international. Average age 26. 72 applicants, 81% accepted. In 2010, 56 master's awarded. *Degree requirements:* For master's, thesis optional. *Entrance requirements:* For master's, GMAT. Additional exam requirements/recommendations for international students: Required—TOEFL (minimum score 550 paper-based; 213 computer-based; 80 iBT). *Application deadline:* For fall admission, 8/1 priority date for domestic and international students; for spring admission, 12/1 priority date for domestic and international students. Applications are processed on a rolling basis. Application fee: $55. *Expenses:* Contact institution. *Financial support:* In 2010–11, 34 research assistantships with full tuition reimbursements (averaging $8,400 per year) were awarded; Federal Work-Study, institutionally sponsored loans, and unspecified assistantships also available. Support available to part-time students. Financial award application deadline: 8/1; financial award applicants required to submit FAFSA. *Unit head:* Dr. MaryJane Lenon, Director, MBA Program, 401-865-2566, Fax: 401-865-2978, E-mail: mjlenon@providence.edu. *Application contact:* Katherine A. Follett, Administrative Coordinator, 401-865-2333, Fax: 401-865-2978, E-mail: kfollett@providence.edu.

Quinnipiac University, School of Business, MBA Program, Hamden, CT 06518-1940. Offers chartered financial analyst (MBA); finance (MBA); healthcare management (MBA); information systems management (MBA); marketing (MBA); supply chain management (MBA); JD/MBA. *Accreditation:* AACSB. Part-time and evening/weekend programs available. *Faculty:* 25 full-time (2 women), 3 part-time/adjunct (all women). *Students:* 87 full-time (24 women), 121 part-time (46 women); includes 12 minority (1 Black or African American, non-Hispanic/Latino; 7 Asian, non-Hispanic/Latino; 4 Hispanic/Latino), 14 international. Average age 29. 119 applicants, 81% accepted, 81 enrolled. In 2010, 70 master's awarded. *Entrance requirements:* For master's,

GMAT or GRE, minimum GPA of 3.0. Additional exam requirements/recommendations for international students: Required—TOEFL (minimum score 575 paper-based; 233 computer-based; 90 iBT), IELTS (minimum score 6.5). *Application deadline:* For fall admission, 7/30 priority date for domestic students, 4/30 priority date for international students; for spring admission, 12/15 priority date for domestic students, 9/15 priority date for international students. Applications are processed on a rolling basis. Application fee: $45. Electronic applications accepted. *Expenses:* Tuition: Part-time $810 per credit. Required fees: $35 per credit. *Financial support:* In 2010–11, 110 students received support. Federal Work-Study, tuition waivers (partial), and unspecified assistantships available. Support available to part-time students. Financial award application deadline: 4/15; financial award applicants required to submit FAFSA. *Faculty research:* Equity compensation, marketing relationships and public policy, corporate governance, international business, supply chain management. *Unit head:* Lisa Braiewa, MBA Program Director, 203-582-3710, Fax: 203-582-8664, E-mail: lisa.braiewa@quinnipiac.edu. *Application contact:* Jennifer Boutin, 800-462-1944, Fax: 203-582-3443, E-mail: jennifer.boutin@quinnipiac.edu.

Rollins College, Crummer Graduate School of Business, Winter Park, FL 32789-4499. Offers entrepreneurship (MBA); finance (MBA); international business (MBA); management (MBA); marketing (MBA); operations and technology management (MBA). *Accreditation:* AACSB. Part-time and evening/weekend programs available. Postbaccalaureate distance learning degree programs offered (minimal on-campus study). *Faculty:* 22 full-time (3 women), 5 part-time/adjunct (3 women). *Students:* 303 full-time (117 women), 130 part-time (49 women); includes 111 minority (30 Black or African American, non-Hispanic/Latino; 1 American Indian or Alaska Native, non-Hispanic/Latino; 29 Asian, non-Hispanic/Latino; 50 Hispanic/Latino; 1 Two or more races, non-Hispanic/Latino), 29 international. Average age 32. 484 applicants, 42% accepted, 131 enrolled. In 2010, 223 master's awarded. *Entrance requirements:* For master's, GMAT, interview. Additional exam requirements/recommendations for international students: Required—TOEFL (minimum score 550 paper-based; 213 computer-based; 80 iBT). *Application deadline:* Applications are processed on a rolling basis. Application fee: $50. Electronic applications accepted. *Expenses:* Contact institution. *Financial support:* In 2010–11, 112 students received support, including 95 fellowships, 56 research assistantships (averaging $2,400 per year); career-related internships or fieldwork, scholarships/grants, and unspecified assistantships also available. Support available to part-time students. Financial award applicants required to submit FAFSA. *Faculty research:* Sustainability, world financial markets, international business, market research, strategic marketing. *Unit head:* Dr. Craig M. McAllaster, Dean, 407-646-2249, Fax: 407-646-1550, E-mail: cmcallaster@rollins.edu. *Application contact:* Linda Puritz, Student Admissions Office, 407-646-2405, Fax: 407-646-1550, E-mail: mbaadmissions@rollins.edu.

Rowan University, Graduate School, William G. Rohrer College of Business, Department of Marketing and Business Information Systems, Glassboro, NJ 08028-1701. Offers MBA. Part-time and evening/weekend programs available. *Faculty:* 2 full-time (1 woman), 2 part-time/adjunct (both women). *Students:* 29 full-time (26 women), 2 part-time (1 woman); includes 1 Black or African American, non-Hispanic/Latino. Average age 26. 4 applicants, 50% accepted, 1 enrolled. *Degree requirements:* For master's, comprehensive exam, thesis. *Entrance requirements:* For master's, GRE General Test. Additional exam requirements/recommendations for international students: Required—TOEFL. *Application deadline:* Applications are processed on a rolling basis. Application fee: $65 ($200 for international students). Electronic applications accepted. *Expenses:* Tuition, area resident: Part-time $602 per semester hour. Tuition, nonresident: part-time $602 per semester hour. Required fees: $100 per semester hour. One-time fee: $10 part-time. *Unit head:* Dr. Horacio Sosa, Dean, College of Graduate and Continuing Education, 856-256-4747, Fax: 856-256-5638, E-mail: sosa@rowan.edu. *Application contact:* Karen Haynes, Graduate Coordinator, 856-256-4052, E-mail: haynes@rowan.edu.

Rutgers, The State University of New Jersey, Newark, Graduate School, Program in Management, Newark, NJ 07102. Offers accounting (PhD); accounting information systems (PhD); computer information systems (PhD); finance (PhD); information technology (PhD); international business (PhD); management science (PhD); marketing (PhD); organization management (PhD). Program offered jointly with New Jersey Institute of Technology. *Accreditation:* AACSB. *Faculty:* 128 full-time (24 women), 4 part-time/adjunct (1 woman). *Students:* 95 full-time (34 women), 17 part-time (6 women); includes 9 Black or African American, non-Hispanic/Latino; 54 Asian, non-Hispanic/Latino; 3 Hispanic/Latino. 438 applicants, 14% accepted, 34 enrolled. In 2010, 10 doctorates awarded. *Degree requirements:* For doctorate, thesis/dissertation, cumulative exams. *Entrance requirements:* For doctorate, GMAT or GRE General Test, minimum undergraduate B average. Additional exam requirements/recommendations for international students: Required—TOEFL. *Application deadline:* For fall admission, 4/1 for domestic students; for spring admission, 11/1 for domestic students. Applications are processed on a rolling basis. Application fee: $60. Electronic applications accepted. *Expenses:* Tuition, state resident: part-time $600 per credit. Tuition, nonresident: full-time $10,694. *Financial support:* In 2010–11, 6 fellowships (averaging $18,000 per year), 4 research assistantships with full and partial tuition reimbursements (averaging $23,112 per year), 38 teaching assistantships with full and partial tuition reimbursements (averaging $23,112 per year) were awarded; institutionally sponsored loans and tuition waivers (full and partial) also available. Support available to part-time students. Financial award application deadline: 2/15. *Faculty research:* Technology management, leadership and teams, consumer behavior, financial and markets, logistics. *Unit head:* Dr. Glenn Shafer, Director, 973-353-1604, Fax: 973-353-5691, E-mail: gshafer@rbs.rutgers.edu. *Application contact:* Goncalo Filipe, Senior Academic Coordinator, 973-353-1002, Fax: 973-353-5691, E-mail: gfilipe@rbsmail.rutgers.edu.

Rutgers, The State University of New Jersey, Newark, Rutgers Business School–Newark and New Brunswick, Doctoral Programs in Management, Newark, NJ 07102. Offers accounting (PhD); accounting information systems (PhD); economics (PhD); finance (PhD); individualized study (PhD); information technology (PhD); international business (PhD); management science (PhD); marketing science (PhD); organizational management (PhD); science, technology and management (PhD); supply chain management (PhD). *Faculty:* 143 full-time (36 women), 2 part-time/adjunct (0 women). *Students:* 117 full-time (42 women), 1 (woman) part-time; includes 8 Black or African American, non-Hispanic/Latino; 14 Asian, non-Hispanic/Latino; 3 Hispanic/Latino, 68 international. Average age 33. 355 applicants, 14% accepted, 35 enrolled. In 2010, 8 doctorates awarded. *Degree requirements:* For doctorate, comprehensive exam, thesis/dissertation. *Entrance requirements:* For doctorate, GRE or GMAT. Additional exam requirements/recommendations for international students: Required—TOEFL (minimum score 550 paper-based; 213 computer-based; 79 iBT). *Application deadline:* For fall admission, 3/1 for domestic and international students; for spring admission, 10/15 for domestic and international students. Application fee: $65. Electronic applications accepted. *Expenses:* Tuition, state resident: part-time $600 per credit. Tuition, nonresident: full-time $10,694. *Financial support:* In 2010–11, 52 students received support, including 7 fellowships (averaging $18,000 per year), 4 research assistantships with tuition reimbursements available (averaging $23,112 per year), 41 teaching assistantships with tuition reimbursements available (averaging $23,112 per year); health care benefits also available. Financial award application deadline: 3/1. *Unit head:* Dr. Glenn Shafer, Director, 973-353-1604, Fax: 973-353-5691, E-mail: gshafer@rbs.rutgers.edu. *Application contact:* Information Contact, 973-353-5371, Fax: 973-353-5691, E-mail: phdinfo@andromeda.rutgers.edu.

Sage Graduate School, Graduate School, School of Management, Program in Business Administration, Troy, NY 12180-4115. Offers business strategy (MBA); finance (MBA); human resources (MBA); marketing (MBA); JD/MBA. Part-time and evening/weekend programs available. *Faculty:* 4 full-time (2 women), 8 part-time/adjunct (3 women). *Students:* 8 full-time (4 women), 67 part-time (45 women); includes 10 Black or African American, non-Hispanic/Latino; 2 Asian, non-Hispanic/Latino; 3 Hispanic/Latino, 1 international. Average age 31. 45 applicants, 64% accepted, 19 enrolled. In 2010, 24 master's awarded. *Entrance requirements:* For master's, minimum GPA of 2.75, resume, 2 letters of recommendation. Additional exam requirements/recommendations for international students: Required—TOEFL (minimum score 550 paper-based; 213 computer-based). *Application deadline:* Applications are processed on a rolling basis. Application fee: $40. *Expenses:* Tuition: Full-time $10,980; part-time $610 per credit hour. Tuition and fees vary according to course load, degree level and program. *Financial support:* Fellowships, research assistantships, Federal Work-Study, scholarships/grants, and unspecified assistantships available. Support available to part-time students. Financial award application deadline: 3/1; financial award applicants required to submit FAFSA. *Unit head:* Dr. Daniel Robeson, Dean, School of Management, 518-292-8637, Fax: 518-292-1964, E-mail: robesd@sage.edu. *Application contact:* Wendy D. Diefendorf, Director of Graduate and Adult Admission, 518-244-2443, Fax: 518-244-6880, E-mail: diefew@sage.edu.

St. Edward's University, School of Management and Business, Area of Business Administration, Austin, TX 78704. Offers accounting (MBA); business management (MBA); corporate finance (MBA, Certificate); global entrepreneurship (MBA); human resource management (Certificate); management information systems (MBA, Certificate); marketing (MBA, Certificate); operations management (MBA, Certificate). Part-time and evening/weekend programs available. *Faculty:* 17 full-time (7 women), 19 part-time/adjunct (4 women). *Students:* 41 full-time (21 women), 273 part-time (135 women); includes 111 minority (19 Black or African American, non-Hispanic/Latino; 1 American Indian or Alaska Native, non-Hispanic/Latino; 8 Asian, non-Hispanic/Latino; 78 Hispanic/Latino; 1 Native Hawaiian or other Pacific Islander, non-Hispanic/Latino; 4 Two or more races, non-Hispanic/Latino), 11 international. Average age 33. 101 applicants, 77% accepted, 50 enrolled. In 2010, 115 master's awarded. *Degree requirements:* For master's, minimum of 24 resident hours. *Entrance requirements:* For master's, GMAT or GRE General Test, minimum GPA of 2.75 in last 60 hours of course work. Additional exam requirements/recommendations for international students: Required—TOEFL (minimum score 550 paper-based; 213 computer-based; 79 iBT) or IELTS (minimum score 6). *Application deadline:* For fall admission, 7/1 for domestic and international students; for spring admission, 11/1 for domestic and international students. Applications are processed on a rolling basis. Application fee: $45 ($50 for international students). Electronic

applications accepted. *Expenses:* Tuition: Full-time $16,200; part-time $900 per credit hour. Required fees: $50 per trimester. Full-time tuition and fees vary according to course load and program. *Financial support:* In 2010–11, 19 students received support. Scholarships/grants available. *Faculty research:* Ethics and corporate responsibility, new hire socialization, team performance, business strategy, non-traditional marketing, social media. *Unit head:* Dr. Stan Horner, Director, 512-428-1279, Fax: 512-448-8492, E-mail: stanleyh@stedwards.edu. *Application contact:* Kelly Luna, Graduate Admissions Coordinator, 512-233-1697, Fax: 512-428-1032, E-mail: kellyl@stedwards.edu.

St. John's University, The Peter J. Tobin College of Business, Department of Marketing, Queens, NY 11439. Offers MBA, Adv C. Part-time and evening/weekend programs available. *Students:* 58 full-time (31 women), 28 part-time (14 women); includes 16 minority (4 Black or African American, non-Hispanic/Latino; 1 American Indian or Alaska Native, non-Hispanic/Latino; 7 Asian, non-Hispanic/Latino; 4 Hispanic/Latino), 37 international. Average age 26. 81 applicants, 68% accepted, 28 enrolled. In 2010, 25 master's awarded. *Degree requirements:* For master's, comprehensive exam (for some programs), thesis optional. *Entrance requirements:* For master's, GMAT, 2 letters of recommendation, resume, transcripts, essay; for Adv C, GMAT, 2 letters of recommendation, resume, undergraduate transcripts, essay. Additional exam requirements/recommendations for international students: Required—TOEFL (minimum score 600 paper-based; 250 computer-based; 100 iBT), IELTS (minimum score 5.5). *Application deadline:* For fall admission, 5/1 priority date for domestic and international students; for spring admission, 11/1 priority date for domestic and international students. Applications are processed on a rolling basis. Application fee: $70. Electronic applications accepted. *Expenses:* Contact institution. *Financial support:* Research assistantships, scholarships/grants available. Support available to part-time students. Financial award application deadline: 3/1; financial award applicants required to submit FAFSA. *Faculty research:* Global brand management, China's stimulus plan, measuring attitude, marketing in India, consumer decision making. *Unit head:* Dr. A. Noel Doherty, Acting Chair, 718-990-7370, Fax: 718-990-1868, E-mail: dohertya@stjohns.edu. *Application contact:* Carol Swanberg, Assistant Dean, Director of Graduate Admissions, 718-990-1345, Fax: 718-990-5242, E-mail: tobingradnyc@stjohns.edu.

Saint Joseph's University, Erivan K. Haub School of Business, Executive Master's in Food Marketing Program, Philadelphia, PA 19131-1395. Offers MBA, MS. Part-time programs available. *Students:* 1 (woman) full-time, 62 part-time (27 women); includes 5 minority (2 Black or African American, non-Hispanic/Latino; 1 Asian, non-Hispanic/Latino; 2 Hispanic/Latino). Average age 37. In 2010, 13 master's awarded. *Entrance requirements:* For master's, 4 years of industry experience, interview or GMAT/GRE, 2 letters of recommendation, resume. Additional exam requirements/recommendations for international students: Required—TOEFL (minimum score: paper 550, computer 213, iBT 79) or IELTS (6.5), Pearson Test of English (minimum 60). *Application deadline:* For fall admission, 7/15 priority date for domestic students, 4/15 priority date for international students; for spring admission, 11/15 priority date for domestic students, 10/15 priority date for international students. Applications are processed on a rolling basis. Application fee: $0. Electronic applications accepted. *Expenses:* Contact institution. *Financial support:* In 2010–11, research assistantships with partial tuition reimbursements (averaging $4,000 per year), teaching assistantships (averaging $4,000 per year) were awarded; fellowships, institutionally sponsored loans, tuition waivers (partial), and unspecified assistantships also available. Financial award application deadline: 5/1; financial award applicants required to submit FAFSA. *Faculty research:* Marketing strategy, obesity, business ethics, bio-defense, international food marketing. *Unit head:* Christine Hartmann, Director, 610-660-1659, Fax: 610-660-3153, E-mail: chartman@sju.edu. *Application contact:* Amanda Basile, Program Administrator, 610-660-3151, Fax: 610-660-3153, E-mail: abasile@sju.edu.

Saint Joseph's University, Erivan K. Haub School of Business, MS Program in International Marketing, Philadelphia, PA 19131. Offers MS. Part-time and evening/weekend programs available. *Students:* 24 full-time (18 women), 10 part-time (8 women); includes 4 minority (all Black or African American, non-Hispanic/Latino), 19 international. Average age 25. In 2010, 23 master's awarded. *Entrance requirements:* For master's, GMAT or GRE, 2 letters of recommendation, resume. Additional exam requirements/recommendations for international students: Required—TOEFL (minimum score: paper 550, computer 213, iBT 79) or IELTS (6.5), Pearson Test of English (minimum 60). *Application deadline:* For fall admission, 7/15 priority date for domestic students; for spring admission, 11/15 priority date for domestic students. Applications are processed on a rolling basis. Application fee: $35. Electronic applications accepted. *Expenses:* Tuition: Part-time $729 per credit. Tuition and fees vary according to course load, degree level and program. *Financial support:* In 2010–11, 2 research assistantships with partial tuition reimbursements (averaging $8,000 per year) were awarded; unspecified assistantships also available. Financial award application deadline: 5/1; financial award applicants required to submit FAFSA. *Faculty research:* Export marketing, global marketing, international marketing research, new product development, emerging markets, international consumer behavior. *Unit head:* Christine

Kaczmar-Russo, Director, 610-660-1238, Fax: 610-660-3239, E-mail: ckaczmar@sju.edu.

Saint Joseph's University, Erivan K. Haub School of Business, Pharmaceutical and Healthcare Marketing MBA for Executives Program, Philadelphia, PA 19131-1395. Offers executive pharmaceutical marketing (Post Master's Certificate); pharmaceutical marketing (MBA). Part-time and evening/weekend programs available. Postbaccalaureate distance learning degree programs offered (minimal on-campus study). *Students:* 7 full-time (2 women), 101 part-time (57 women); includes 23 minority (8 Black or African American, non-Hispanic/Latino; 9 Asian, non-Hispanic/Latino; 5 Hispanic/Latino; 1 Two or more races, non-Hispanic/Latino), 1 international. Average age 38. In 2010, 34 master's awarded. *Entrance requirements:* For master's, 4 years of industry experience, letter of recommendation, resume, interview; for Post Master's Certificate, MBA, 4 years of industry experience, resume. Additional exam requirements/recommendations for international students: Required—TOEFL (minimum score: paper 550, computer 213, iBT 79) or IELTS (6.5), Pearson Test of English (minimum 60). *Application deadline:* For fall admission, 7/15 priority date for domestic students, 4/15 priority date for international students; for spring admission, 11/15 priority date for domestic students, 10/15 priority date for international students. Applications are processed on a rolling basis. Electronic applications accepted. *Expenses:* Tuition: Part-time $729 per credit. Tuition and fees vary according to course load, degree level and program. *Financial support:* Scholarships/grants available. Financial award applicants required to submit FAFSA. *Faculty research:* Pharmaceutical strategy, Internet and pharmaceuticals, pharmaceutical promotion. *Unit head:* Terese W. Waldron, Director, 610-660-3150, Fax: 610-660-5160, E-mail: twaldron@sju.edu. *Application contact:* Christine Anderson, Senior Manager, Executive Relations and Industry Outreach, 610-660-3157, Fax: 610-660-3160, E-mail: christine.anderson@sju.edu.

Saint Joseph's University, Erivan K. Haub School of Business, Professional MBA Program, Philadelphia, PA 19131-1395. Offers accounting (MBA); finance (MBA), including finance (MBA); general business (MBA); health and medical services administration (MBA); human resource management (MBA); international business (MBA); international marketing (MBA); management (MBA); marketing (MBA); DO/MBA. Do/MBA offered jointly with Philadelphia College of Osteopathic Medicine. Part-time and evening/weekend programs available. Postbaccalaureate distance learning degree programs offered (no on-campus study). *Students:* 47 full-time (35 women), 585 part-time (221 women); includes 92 minority (42 Black or African American, non-Hispanic/Latino; 1 American Indian or Alaska Native, non-Hispanic/Latino; 34 Asian, non-Hispanic/Latino; 12 Hispanic/Latino; 1 Native Hawaiian or other Pacific Islander, non-Hispanic/Latino; 2 Two or more races, non-Hispanic/Latino), 41 international. Average age 30. In 2010, 135 master's awarded. *Entrance requirements:* For master's, GMAT or GRE, 2 letters of recommendation, resume. Additional exam requirements/recommendations for international students: Required—TOEFL (minimum score: paper 550, computer 213, iBT 79) or IELTS (6.5), Pearson Test of English (minimum 60). *Application deadline:* For fall admission, 7/15 priority date for domestic students, 4/15 priority date for international students; for spring admission, 11/15 priority date for domestic students, 10/15 priority date for international students. Applications are processed on a rolling basis. Application fee: $35. Electronic applications accepted. *Expenses:* Tuition: Part-time $729 per credit. Tuition and fees vary according to course load, degree level and program. *Financial support:* Scholarships/grants and unspecified assistantships available. Financial award application deadline: 5/1; financial award applicants required to submit FAFSA. *Unit head:* Adele C. Foley, Associate Dean/Director, Graduate Business Programs, 610-660-1691, Fax: 610-660-1599, E-mail: afoley@sju.edu. *Application contact:* Janine N. Guerra, Assistant Director, MBA Program, 610-660-1695, Fax: 610-660-1599, E-mail: jguerra@sju.edu.

Saint Leo University, Graduate Business Studies, Saint Leo, FL 33574-6665. Offers accounting (MBA); business (MBA); health services management (MBA); human resource management (MBA); information security management (MBA); marketing (MBA); sport business (MBA). Part-time and evening/weekend programs available. Postbaccalaureate distance learning degree programs offered (no on-campus study). *Faculty:* 32 full-time (4 women), 53 part-time/adjunct (21 women). *Students:* 1,498 full-time (890 women), 10 part-time (6 women); includes 593 minority (465 Black or African American, non-Hispanic/Latino; 5 American Indian or Alaska Native, non-Hispanic/Latino; 23 Asian, non-Hispanic/Latino; 84 Hispanic/Latino; 2 Native Hawaiian or other Pacific Islander, non-Hispanic/Latino; 14 Two or more races, non-Hispanic/Latino), 14 international. Average age 38. In 2010, 557 master's awarded. *Entrance requirements:* For master's, GMAT (minimum score 500 if applicant does not have 5 years of professional work experience), bachelor's degree from regionally-accredited college or university with minimum GPA of 3.0 in the last 60 hours of coursework; 5 years of professional work experience; resume; 2 letters of recommendation. Additional exam requirements/recommendations for international students: Required—TOEFL (minimum score 550 paper-based; 213 computer-based; 80 iBT). *Application deadline:* For fall admission, 7/1 priority date for domestic and international students; for spring admission, 11/12 priority date for domestic students, 11/1 for international students. Applications are processed on a rolling basis. Application fee: $75. Electronic applications accepted. *Expenses:* Contact institution.

Financial support: In 2010–11, 51 students received support. Career-related internships or fieldwork, Federal Work-Study, scholarships/grants, and health care benefits available. Financial award application deadline: 3/1; financial award applicants required to submit FAFSA. *Unit head:* Dr. Lorrie McGovern, Director, 352-588-7390, Fax: 352-588-8585, E-mail: mbaslu@saintleo.edu. *Application contact:* Jared Welling, Director, Graduate/Weekend and Evening Admission, 800-707-8846, Fax: 352-588-7873, E-mail: grad.admissions@saintleo.edu.

Saint Peter's College, Graduate Business Programs, MBA Program, Jersey City, NJ 07306-5997. Offers finance (MBA); health care administration (MBA); human resource management (MBA); international business (MBA); management (MBA); management information systems (MBA); marketing (MBA); risk management (MBA); MBA/MS. Part-time and evening/weekend programs available. *Students:* 108 applicants, 81% accepted, 62 enrolled. *Entrance requirements:* Additional exam requirements/recommendations for international students: Required—TOEFL (minimum score 79 computer-based). *Application deadline:* Applications are processed on a rolling basis. Electronic applications accepted. *Financial support:* Career-related internships or fieldwork, Federal Work-Study, and institutionally sponsored loans available. Financial award applicants required to submit FAFSA. *Faculty research:* Finance, health care management, human resource management, international business, management, management information systems, marketing, risk management. *Application contact:* Stephanie Autenrieth, Director, Graduate and Professional Studies Admission, 201-761-6474, Fax: 201-435-5270, E-mail: sautenrieth@spc.edu.

Santa Clara University, Leavey School of Business, Program in Business Administration, Santa Clara, CA 95053. Offers accounting (MBA); entrepreneurship (MBA); executive business administration (EMBA); finance (MBA); food and agribusiness (MBA); international business (MBA); leading people and organizations (MBA); managing technology and innovation (MBA); marketing management (MBA); supply chain management (MBA). *Accreditation:* AACSB. Part-time and evening/weekend programs available. *Students:* 229 full-time (80 women), 748 part-time (244 women); includes 354 minority (14 Black or African American, non-Hispanic/Latino; 1 American Indian or Alaska Native, non-Hispanic/Latino; 287 Asian, non-Hispanic/Latino; 42 Hispanic/Latino; 5 Native Hawaiian or other Pacific Islander, non-Hispanic/Latino; 5 Two or more races, non-Hispanic/Latino), 209 international. Average age 32. 334 applicants, 76% accepted, 191 enrolled. In 2010, 307 master's awarded. *Degree requirements:* For master's, thesis or alternative. *Entrance requirements:* For master's, GMAT, GRE. Additional exam requirements/recommendations for international students: Required—TOEFL (minimum score 600 paper-based; 250 computer-based; 100 iBT). *Application deadline:* For fall admission, 6/1 for domestic and international students; for spring admission, 1/19 for domestic students, 1/17 for international students. Applications are processed on a rolling basis. Application fee: $75 ($100 for international students). Electronic applications accepted. *Expenses:* Contact institution. *Financial support:* In 2010–11, 350 students received support; fellowships with partial tuition reimbursements available, research assistantships with partial tuition reimbursements available, career-related internships or fieldwork, Federal Work-Study, institutionally sponsored loans, scholarships/grants, health care benefits, and unspecified assistantships available. Support available to part-time students. Financial award application deadline: 6/1; financial award applicants required to submit FAFSA. *Unit head:* Elizabeth B. Ford, Senior Assistant Dean, 408-554-2752, Fax: 408-554-4571, E-mail: eford@scu.edu. *Application contact:* Molly Mulally, Assistant Director, Graduate Business Admissions, 408-554-4539, Fax: 408-554-4571, E-mail: mbaadmissions@scu.edu.

Seton Hall University, Stillman School of Business, Programs in Business Administration, South Orange, NJ 07079-2697. Offers accounting (MBA); finance (MBA); information technology management (MBA); international business (MBA); management (MBA); marketing (MBA); sport management (MBA); supply chain management (MBA). Part-time and evening/weekend programs available. *Faculty:* 35 full-time (8 women), 11 part-time/adjunct (1 woman). *Students:* 93 full-time (33 women), 165 part-time (76 women); includes 26 Black or African American, non-Hispanic/Latino; 39 Asian, non-Hispanic/Latino; 8 Hispanic/Latino. Average age 29. 404 applicants, 74% accepted, 258 enrolled. In 2010, 203 master's awarded. *Degree requirements:* For master's, 20 hours of community service (Social Responsibility Project). *Entrance requirements:* For master's, GMAT or CPA, Advanced degree such as PhD, MD, JD, DVM, DDS, PharmD, MBA from an AACSB institution, MS in a business discipline and a minimum GPA of 3.0. Additional exam requirements/recommendations for international students: Required—TOEFL (minimum: 254 computer, 102 iBT), IELTS or Pearson Test of English (PTE). *Application deadline:* For fall admission, 5/31 priority date for domestic students, 3/31 priority date for international students; for spring admission, 10/31 priority date for domestic students, 9/30 priority date for international students. Applications are processed on a rolling basis. Application fee: $75. Electronic applications accepted. *Financial support:* In 2010–11, research assistantships with full tuition reimbursements (averaging $35,610 per year); career-related internships or fieldwork, Federal Work-Study, scholarships/grants, and unspecified assistantships also available. Support available to part-time students. Financial award application deadline: 6/30; financial award applicants required to submit FAFSA. *Faculty research:* Financial, hedge funds, international business, legal issues, disclosure and branding. *Unit head:* Dr. Joyce A. Strawser, Associate Dean for Undergraduate and MBA Curricula, 973-761-9225, Fax: 973-761-9217, E-mail: strawsjo@shu.edu. *Application contact:* Catherine Bianchi, Director of Graduate Admissions, 973-761-9262, Fax: 973-761-9208, E-mail: catherine.bianchi@shu.edu.

Southern Methodist University, Cox School of Business, MBA Program, Dallas, TX 75275. Offers accounting (MBA); finance (MBA); financial consulting (MBA); general business (MBA); information technology and operations management (MBA); management (MBA); marketing (MBA); real estate (MBA); strategy and entrepreneurship (MBA). Part-time and evening/weekend programs available. *Faculty:* 59 full-time (13 women), 30 part-time/adjunct (7 women). *Students:* 359 full-time (116 women), 592 part-time (154 women); includes 215 minority (44 Black or African American, non-Hispanic/Latino; 10 American Indian or Alaska Native, non-Hispanic/Latino; 118 Asian, non-Hispanic/Latino; 39 Hispanic/Latino; 2 Native Hawaiian or other Pacific Islander, non-Hispanic/Latino; 2 Two or more races, non-Hispanic/Latino), 92 international. Average age 30. In 2010, 486 master's awarded. *Entrance requirements:* For master's, GMAT. Additional exam requirements/recommendations for international students: Required—TOEFL. *Application deadline:* Applications are processed on a rolling basis. Application fee: $0. Electronic applications accepted. *Expenses:* Contact institution. *Financial support:* Applicants required to submit FAFSA. *Faculty research:* Corporate finance, financial reporting, modeling consumer decision-making, competition between national brands and store brands, institutional determinants of firms' strategy. *Unit head:* Dr. Marci Armstrong, Associate Dean for Master's Programs, 214-768-4486, Fax: 214-768-3956, E-mail: marci@cox.smu.edu. *Application contact:* Patti Cudney, Director of MBA Admissions, 214-768-3001, Fax: 214-768-3956, E-mail: pcudney@cox.smu.edu.

Southwest Minnesota State University, Department of Business and Public Affairs, Marshall, MN 56258. Offers leadership (MBA); management (MBA); marketing (MBA). Part-time and evening/weekend programs available. Postbaccalaureate distance learning degree programs offered (no on-campus study). *Faculty:* 11 full-time (3 women), 1 (woman) part-time/adjunct. *Students:* 27 full-time (15 women), 82 part-time (38 women); includes 7 minority (3 Black or African American, non-Hispanic/Latino; 1 Asian, non-Hispanic/Latino; 2 Hispanic/Latino; 1 Two or more races, non-Hispanic/Latino), 21 international. Average age 30. 49 applicants, 55% accepted, 18 enrolled. In 2010, 20 master's awarded. *Degree requirements:* For master's, thesis. *Entrance requirements:* For master's, GMAT (minimum score: 450). Additional exam requirements/recommendations for international students: Recommended—TOEFL (minimum score 550 paper-based; 213 computer-based; 79 iBT), IELTS. *Application deadline:* For fall admission, 8/28 for domestic students, 6/15 for international students; for spring admission, 1/15 for domestic students, 12/15 for international students. Applications are processed on a rolling basis. Application fee: $30. Electronic applications accepted. *Financial support:* Institutionally sponsored loans and unspecified assistantships available. Support available to part-time students. Financial award application deadline: 3/1; financial award applicants required to submit FAFSA. *Unit head:* Dr. Daniel Campagna, Dean of Professional Studies, 507-537-6251, E-mail: daniel.campagna@smsu.edu. *Application contact:* Cori Ann Dahlager, Graduate Office Coordinator, 507-537-6819, Fax: 507-537-6227, E-mail: coriann.dahlager@smsu.edu.

Stony Brook University, State University of New York, Graduate School, College of Business, Program in Business Administration, Stony Brook, NY 11794. Offers finance (MBA, Certificate); health care management (MBA, Certificate); human resource management (Certificate); human resources (MBA); information systems management (MBA, Certificate); management (MBA); marketing (MBA). *Faculty:* 14 full-time (2 women), 27 part-time/adjunct (6 women). *Students:* 182 full-time (103 women), 117 part-time (35 women); includes 11 Black or African American, non-Hispanic/Latino; 35 Asian, non-Hispanic/Latino; 10 Hispanic/Latino; 2 Two or more races, non-Hispanic/Latino, 88 international. 281 applicants, 60% accepted, 102 enrolled. In 2010, 95 master's, 1 other advanced degree awarded. Application fee: $100. *Expenses:* Tuition, state resident: full-time $8370; part-time $349 per credit. Tuition, nonresident: full-time $13,780; part-time $574 per credit. Required fees: $994. *Financial support:* In 2010–11, 2 teaching assistantships were awarded. *Unit head:* Dr. Manuel London, Interim Dean, 631-632-7180. *Application contact:* Dr. Aristotle Lekacos, Director, Graduate Program, 631-632-7171, E-mail: aristotle.lekacost@notes.cc.sunysb.edu.

Suffolk University, Sawyer Business School, Master of Business Administration Program, Boston, MA 02108-2770. Offers accounting (MBA); business administration (APC); corporate financial executive track (MBA); entrepreneurship (MBA); executive business administration (EMBA); finance (MBA); global business administration (GMBA); health administration (MBA); international business (MBA); marketing (MBA); organizational behavior (MBA); strategic management (MBA); taxation (MBA); JD/MBA; MBA/GDPA; MBA/MHA; MBA/MSA; MBA/MSF; MBA/MST. *Accreditation:* AACSB. Part-time and evening/weekend programs available. Postbaccalaureate distance learning degree programs offered (no on-campus study). *Faculty:* 97 full-time (30 women), 14 part-time/adjunct (3 women). *Students:* 179 full-time (65 women), 337 part-time (143 women); includes

16 Black or African American, non-Hispanic/Latino; 2 American Indian or Alaska Native, non-Hispanic/Latino; 22 Asian, non-Hispanic/Latino; 9 Hispanic/Latino; 1 Native Hawaiian or other Pacific Islander, non-Hispanic/Latino, 80 international. Average age 30. 431 applicants, 68% accepted, 128 enrolled. In 2010, 283 master's awarded. *Entrance requirements:* For master's, GMAT, minimum undergraduate GPA of 2.75 (MBA), 5 years of managerial experience (EMBA). Additional exam requirements/recommendations for international students: Required—TOEFL (minimum score 550 paper-based; 213 computer-based). *Application deadline:* For fall admission, 6/15 priority date for domestic students, 6/15 for international students; for spring admission, 11/1 priority date for domestic students, 11/1 for international students. Applications are processed on a rolling basis. Application fee: $50. Electronic applications accepted. *Financial support:* In 2010–11, 266 students received support, including 94 fellowships with full and partial tuition reimbursements available (averaging $12,635 per year); career-related internships or fieldwork, Federal Work-Study, and institutionally sponsored loans also available. Support available to part-time students. Financial award application deadline: 4/1; financial award applicants required to submit FAFSA. *Faculty research:* Foreign investments; career strategies and boundaryless careers; corporate ethics codes; interest rates, inflation, and growth options; innovation and product development performance. *Unit head:* Lillian Hallberg, Assistant Dean of Graduate Programs/Director of MBA Programs, 617-573-8306, E-mail: lhallber@suffolk.edu. *Application contact:* Judith Reynolds, Director of Graduate Admissions, 617-573-8302, Fax: 617-305-1733, E-mail: grad.admission@suffolk.edu.

Texas A&M University, Mays Business School, Department of Marketing, College Station, TX 77843. Offers MS, PhD. *Faculty:* 10. *Students:* 63 full-time (45 women), 3 part-time (all women); includes 8 minority (2 Black or African American, non-Hispanic/Latino; 3 Asian, non-Hispanic/Latino; 3 Hispanic/Latino), 12 international. Average age 30. 53 applicants, 25% accepted. In 2010, 29 master's, 3 doctorates awarded. Terminal master's awarded for partial completion of doctoral program. *Degree requirements:* For master's, comprehensive exam; for doctorate, thesis/dissertation. *Entrance requirements:* For master's, GMAT; for doctorate, GMAT or GRE General Test. Additional exam requirements/recommendations for international students: Required—TOEFL. *Application deadline:* For fall admission, 3/1 priority date for domestic students. Applications are processed on a rolling basis. Application fee: $50 ($75 for international students). *Financial support:* In 2010–11, 16 students received support; fellowships, research assistantships, teaching assistantships, career-related internships or fieldwork and institutionally sponsored loans available. Financial award application deadline: 2/1. *Faculty research:* Consumer behavior, innovation and product management, international marketing, marketing management and strategy, services marketing. *Unit head:* Rajan Varadarajan, Head, 979-845-5809, E-mail: rvaradarajan@mays.tamu.edu. *Application contact:* Stephen W. McDaniel, Advisor, 979-845-5801, E-mail: smcdaniel@mays.tamu.edu.

Texas Tech University, Graduate School, Jerry S. Rawls College of Business Administration, Area of Marketing, Lubbock, TX 79409. Offers PhD. Part-time programs available. *Faculty:* 11 full-time (3 women). *Students:* 7 full-time (3 women), 5 international. Average age 34. 14 applicants, 36% accepted, 2 enrolled. *Degree requirements:* For doctorate, thesis/dissertation, qualifying exams. *Entrance requirements:* For doctorate, GMAT, holistic profile of academic credentials. Additional exam requirements/recommendations for international students: Required—TOEFL (minimum score 550 paper-based; 213 computer-based; 79 iBT). *Application deadline:* For fall admission, 2/1 priority date for domestic students, 1/15 for international students. Applications are processed on a rolling basis. Application fee: $50 ($75 for international students). Electronic applications accepted. *Expenses:* Tuition, state resident: full-time $5495.76; part-time $228.99 per credit hour. Tuition, nonresident: full-time $12,936; part-time $538.99 per credit hour. Required fees: $2674; $36 per credit hour. $905 per semester. *Financial support:* In 2010–11, 12 research assistantships (averaging $8,800 per year), 4 teaching assistantships (averaging $18,000 per year) were awarded; Federal Work-Study and scholarships/grants also available. *Faculty research:* Consumer behavior, macro-marketing, marketing strategy and strategic planning. *Unit head:* Dr. Robert McDonald, Area Coordinator, 806-742-1175, Fax: 806-742-2199, E-mail: bob.mcdonald@ttu.edu. *Application contact:* Cynthia D. Barnes, Director, Graduate Services Center, 806-742-3184, Fax: 806-742-3958, E-mail: ba_grad@ttu.edu.

Texas Tech University, Graduate School, Jerry S. Rawls College of Business Administration, Programs in Business Administration, Lubbock, TX 79409. Offers agricultural business (MBA); business administration (IMBA); business statistics (MBA); entrepreneurship and innovation (MBA); general business (MBA); health organization management (MBA); international business (MBA); management and leadership skills (MBA); management information systems (MBA); marketing (MBA); real estate (MBA); JD/MBA; MBA/M Arch; MBA/MA; MBA/MD; MBA/MS; MBA/Pharm D. Part-time and evening/weekend programs available. *Faculty:* 47 full-time (8 women), 5 part-time/adjunct (0 women). *Students:* 52 full-time (13 women), 531 part-time (152 women); includes 121 minority (28 Black or African American, non-Hispanic/Latino; 3 American Indian or Alaska Native, non-Hispanic/Latino; 31 Asian, non-Hispanic/Latino; 53 Hispanic/Latino; 6 Two or more races, non-Hispanic/Latino), 49 international. Average age 30. 437 applicants, 77% accepted, 258 enrolled. In 2010, 228 master's awarded. *Degree requirements:* For master's, capstone course. *Entrance requirements:* For master's, GMAT, holistic review of academic credentials. Additional exam requirements/recommendations for international students: Required—TOEFL (minimum score 550 paper-based; 213 computer-based; 79 iBT). *Application deadline:* For fall admission, 4/1 priority date for domestic students, 1/15 for international students; for spring admission, 9/1 priority date for domestic students, 6/15 for international students. Applications are processed on a rolling basis. Application fee: $50 ($75 for international students). Electronic applications accepted. *Expenses:* Tuition, state resident: full-time $5495.76; part-time $228.99 per credit hour. Tuition, nonresident: full-time $12,936; part-time $538.99 per credit hour. Required fees: $2674; $36 per credit hour. $905 per semester. *Financial support:* In 2010–11, 25 research assistantships (averaging $8,800 per year) were awarded; teaching assistantships, career-related internships or fieldwork, Federal Work-Study, scholarships/grants, health care benefits, and unspecified assistantships also available. Support available to part-time students. Financial award applicants required to submit FAFSA. *Unit head:* Dr. W. Jay Conover, Director, 806-742-1546, Fax: 806-742-3958, E-mail: jay.conover@ttu.edu. *Application contact:* Cynthia D. Barnes, Director, Graduate Services Center, 806-742-3184, Fax: 806-742-3958, E-mail: ba_grad@ttu.edu.

Tiffin University, Program in Business Administration, Tiffin, OH 44883-2161. Offers finance (MBA); general management (MBA); healthcare administration (MBA); human resources (MBA); international business (MBA); leadership (MBA); marketing (MBA); sports management (MBA). *Accreditation:* ACBSP. Part-time and evening/weekend programs available. Postbaccalaureate distance learning degree programs offered (no on-campus study). *Faculty:* 18 full-time (9 women), 22 part-time/adjunct (6 women). *Students:* 186 full-time (93 women), 250 part-time (124 women). Average age 31. 532 applicants, 86% accepted, 229 enrolled. In 2010, 340 master's awarded. *Entrance requirements:* For master's, minimum undergraduate GPA of 2.5, work experience. Additional exam requirements/recommendations for international students: Required—TOEFL (minimum score 550 paper-based; 213 computer-based). *Application deadline:* For fall admission, 8/15 for domestic students, 8/1 for international students; for spring admission, 1/9 for domestic students, 12/1 for international students. Applications are processed on a rolling basis. Application fee: $0. Electronic applications accepted. *Financial support:* In 2010–11, 94 students received support. Available to part-time students. Application deadline: 7/31. *Faculty research:* Small business, executive development operations, research and statistical analysis, market research, management information systems. *Unit head:* Dr. Lillian Schumacher, Dean of the School of Business, 419-448-3053, Fax: 419-443-5002, E-mail: schumacherlb@tiffin.edu. *Application contact:* Kristi Krintzline, Director of Graduate Admissions and Student Services, 800-968-6446 Ext. 3445, Fax: 419-443-5002, E-mail: krintzlineka@tiffin.edu.

TUI University, College of Business Administration, Program in Business Administration, Cypress, CA 90630. Offers business administration (PhD); conflict and negotiation management (MBA); criminal justice administration (MBA); entrepreneurship (MBA); finance (MBA); general management (MBA); government accounting (MBA); human resource management (MBA); information security and digital assurance management (MBA); information technology management (MBA); international business (MBA); logistics management (MBA); marketing (MBA); project management (MBA); public management (MBA); quality management (MBA); strategic leadership (MBA). Part-time and evening/weekend programs available. Postbaccalaureate distance learning degree programs offered (no on-campus study). *Students:* 741 full-time (200 women), 1,585 part-time (410 women). 379 applicants, 81% accepted, 300 enrolled. In 2010, 752 master's, 28 doctorates awarded. *Degree requirements:* For doctorate, comprehensive exam, thesis/dissertation, defense of dissertation. *Entrance requirements:* For master's, minimum GPA of 2.5 (students with GPA 3.0 or greater may transfer up to 30% of graduate level credits); for doctorate, minimum GPA of 3.4, curriculum vitae, course work in research methods or statistics. Additional exam requirements/recommendations for international students: Required—TOEFL. *Application deadline:* For fall admission, 10/3 for domestic and international students; for winter admission, 12/22 for domestic and international students; for spring admission, 4/3 for domestic and international students. Applications are processed on a rolling basis. Application fee: $75. Electronic applications accepted. *Expenses:* Tuition: Full-time $11,040; part-time $345 per semester hour. *Unit head:* Paul Watkins, Dean, College of Business Administration, 800-375-9878, E-mail: pwatkins@tuiu.edu. *Application contact:* Wei Ren-Finaly, Registrar, 800-375-9878, Fax: 714-827-7407, E-mail: registration@tuiu.edu.

United States International University, School of Business Administration, Nairobi, Kenya. Offers business administration (GEMBA); entrepreneurship (MBA); finance (MBA); human resource management (MBA); information technology management (MBA); integrated studies (MBA); international business administration (MBA); management and organizational development (MS); marketing (MBA); organizational development (EMS); strategic management (MBA). Part-time and evening/weekend programs available. *Faculty:* 42 full-time (8 women), 64 part-time/adjunct (14 women). *Students:* 423 full-time (227 women), 129 part-time (63 women). Average age 29. 110 applicants, 79% accepted, 78 enrolled. In 2010, 164 master's awarded. *Degree requirements:* For master's, thesis. *Entrance requirements:* For master's, GMAT, 2 letters of reference, resume. Additional exam requirements/recommendations for international students: Required—TOEFL (minimum score 550 paper-based; 213 computer-based). *Application deadline:* For fall admission, 6/30 priority date for domestic and international students; for spring admission, 9/30 for domestic and international students. Applications are processed on a rolling basis. Application fee: $50. *Financial support:* In 2010–11, 30 students received support, including 8 research assistantships (averaging $1,400 per year), 4 teaching assistantships (averaging $1,400 per year); career-related internships or fieldwork, scholarships/grants, and unspecified assistantships also available. Support available to part-time students. Financial award application deadline: 6/30; financial award applicants required to submit FAFSA. *Faculty research:* Marketing in small business enterprises, total quality management in Kenya. *Unit head:* Dr. Damary Sikalieh, Dean, 254-02-3606-415, E-mail: dsikalieh@usiu.ac.ke. *Application contact:* George Lumbasi, Director of Admissions, 254-02-3606563, Fax: 254-02-3606100, E-mail: glumbasi@usiu.ac.ke.

Université de Sherbrooke, Faculty of Administration, Program in Marketing, Sherbrooke, QC J1K 2R1, Canada. Offers M Sc. *Faculty:* 8 full-time (5 women), 1 part-time/adjunct (0 women). *Students:* 19 full-time (16 women). Average age 23. 91 applicants, 38% accepted, 19 enrolled. In 2010, 18 master's awarded. *Degree requirements:* For master's, one foreign language, thesis. *Entrance requirements:* For master's, bachelor degree in related field Minimum GPA 3/4.3. *Application deadline:* For fall admission, 4/30 for domestic students, 1/15 for international students. Applications are processed on a rolling basis. Application fee: $70. Electronic applications accepted. *Faculty research:* Consumer behavior, sales force, branding, prices management. *Unit head:* Prof. Julien Bilodeau, Director, Graduate programs in business, 819-821-8000 Ext. 62355. *Application contact:* Marie-Claude Drouin, Programs Assistant Director, 819-821-8000 Ext. 63301.

The University of Akron, Graduate School, College of Business Administration, Department of Marketing, Akron, OH 44325. Offers international business (MBA); international business for international executive (MBA); strategic marketing (MBA); JD/MBA. Part-time and evening/weekend programs available. *Faculty:* 15 full-time (2 women), 6 part-time/adjunct (0 women). *Students:* 19 full-time (7 women), 24 part-time (17 women); includes 1 Asian, non-Hispanic/Latino, 14 international. Average age 29. 33 applicants, 55% accepted, 8 enrolled. In 2010, 16 master's awarded. *Entrance requirements:* For master's, GMAT, minimum GPA of 2.75, two letters of recommendation, statement of purpose, resume. Additional exam requirements/recommendations for international students: Required—TOEFL (minimum score 550 paper-based; 213 computer-based; 79 iBT). *Application deadline:* For fall admission, 7/15 for domestic and international students; for spring admission, 11/15 for domestic and international students. Application fee: $30 ($40 for international students). Electronic applications accepted. *Expenses:* Tuition, state resident: full-time $6800; part-time $378 per credit hour. Tuition, nonresident: full-time $11,644; part-time $647 per credit hour. Required fees: $1265. One-time fee: $30 full-time. *Financial support:* In 2010–11, 2 research assistantships with full tuition reimbursements, 7 teaching assistantships with full tuition reimbursements were awarded. *Faculty research:* Multi-channel marketing, direct interactive marketing, strategic retailing, marketing strategy and telemarketing. Total annual research expenditures: $38,705. *Unit head:* Dr. William Baker, Chair, 330-972-8466, E-mail: wbaker@uakron.edu. *Application contact:* Dr. Susan Hanlon, Director of Graduate Business Programs, 330-972-7043, Fax: 330-972-6588, E-mail: shanlon@uakron.edu.

The University of Alabama, Graduate School, Manderson Graduate School of Business, Department of Management and Marketing, Program in Marketing, Tuscaloosa, AL 35487. Offers MS, PhD. *Accreditation:* AACSB. *Faculty:* 25 full-time (7 women), 1 part-time/adjunct (0 women). *Students:* 63 full-time (33 women), 6 part-time (3 women); includes 8 minority (3 Black or African American, non-Hispanic/Latino; 3 Hispanic/Latino; 2 Two or more races, non-Hispanic/Latino), 16 international. Average age 26. 110 applicants, 55% accepted, 38 enrolled. In 2010, 47 master's awarded. Terminal master's awarded for partial completion of doctoral program. *Degree requirements:* For master's, internship; for doctorate, comprehensive exam, thesis/dissertation. *Entrance requirements:* For master's, GRE or GMAT; for doctorate, GRE or GMAT, minimum GPA of 3.0. Additional exam requirements/recommendations for international students: Required—TOEFL (minimum score 600 paper-based) or IELTS (minimum score 6.5). *Application deadline:* For fall admission, 4/1 priority date for domestic and international students; for spring admission, 2/1 priority date for domestic and international students. Applications are processed on a rolling basis. Application fee: $50 ($60 for international students). Electronic applications accepted. *Expenses:* Tuition, state resident: full-time $7900. Tuition, nonresident: full-time $20,500. *Financial support:* In 2010–11, 1 fellowship with full tuition reimbursement (averaging $15,000 per year), 5 research assistantships with full tuition reimbursements (averaging $25,000 per year), 5 teaching assistantships with full tuition reimbursements (averaging $25,000 per year) were awarded; scholarships/grants, health care benefits, and unspecified assistantships also available. *Faculty research:* Relationship marketing, consumer behavior, services marketing, professional selling, supply chain management. *Unit head:* Dr. Robert M. Morgan, Department Head, 205-348-6183, Fax: 205-348-6695, E-mail: rmorgan@cba.ua.edu. *Application contact:* Courtney Cox, Office Associate II, 205-348-6183, Fax: 205-348-6695, E-mail: crhodes@cba.ua.edu.

The University of Alabama in Huntsville, School of Graduate Studies, College of Business Administration, Department of Management and Marketing, Huntsville, AL 35899. Offers management (MBA), including acquisition management, finance, human resource management, logistics and supply chain management, marketing, project management. *Accreditation:* AACSB. Part-time and evening/weekend programs available. *Faculty:* 11 full-time (2 women), 4 part-time/adjunct (1 woman). *Students:* 41 full-time (17 women), 159 part-time (69 women); includes 32 minority (15 Black or African American, non-Hispanic/Latino; 6 American Indian or Alaska Native, non-Hispanic/Latino; 7 Asian, non-Hispanic/Latino; 3 Hispanic/Latino; 1 Two or more races, non-Hispanic/Latino), 14 international. Average age 31. 141 applicants, 65% accepted, 79 enrolled. In 2010, 66 master's awarded. *Degree requirements:* For master's, comprehensive exam, thesis or alternative. *Entrance requirements:* For master's, GMAT (minimum score 500), minimum AACSB index of 1080. Additional exam requirements/recommendations for international students: Required—TOEFL (minimum score 550 paper-based; 213 computer-based; 62 iBT). *Application deadline:* For fall admission, 8/1 for domestic students, 4/1 for international students; for spring admission, 12/1 for domestic students, 9/1 for international students. Applications are processed on a rolling basis. Application fee: $40 ($50 for international students). Electronic applications accepted. *Expenses:* Tuition, state resident: full-time $7250; part-time $407.75 per credit hour. Tuition, nonresident: full-time $17,358; part-time $970.05 per credit hour. Required fees: $246.80 per semester. Tuition and fees vary according to course load and program. *Financial support:* In 2010–11, 3 students received support, including 1 research assistantship with full tuition reimbursement available (averaging $8,550 per year), 2 teaching assistantships with full tuition reimbursements available (averaging $8,000 per year); career-related internships or fieldwork, Federal Work-Study, institutionally sponsored loans, scholarships/grants, health care benefits, and unspecified assistantships also available. Support available to part-time students. Financial award application deadline: 4/1; financial award applicants required to submit FAFSA. *Faculty research:* Strategic human resources, corporate governance, cross-function integration and the management of research and development, determinants of team performance. Total annual research expenditures: $3 million. *Unit head:* Dr. Brent Wren, Chair, 256-824-6408, Fax: 256-824-6328, E-mail: wrenb@uah.edu. *Application contact:* Jennifer Pettitt, Director of Graduate Programs, 256-824-6681, Fax: 256-824-7571, E-mail: jennifer.pettitt@uah.edu.

The University of Arizona, Eller College of Management, Department of Marketing, Tucson, AZ 85721. Offers MS, PhD. *Faculty:* 10 full-time (3 women), 1 part-time/adjunct (0 women). *Degree requirements:* For doctorate, comprehensive exam, thesis/dissertation. *Entrance requirements:* For doctorate, GMAT (minimum score 600). Additional exam requirements/recommendations for international students: Required—TOEFL (minimum score 600 paper-based). *Application deadline:* For fall admission, 3/1 for domestic students, 12/1 for international students. Applications are processed on a rolling basis. Application fee: $75. Electronic applications accepted. *Expenses:* Tuition, state resident: full-time $7692. *Financial support:* In 2010–11, 11 teaching assistantships with full tuition reimbursements (averaging $24,306 per year) were awarded; research assistantships with full tuition reimbursements, career-related internships or fieldwork, Federal Work-Study, scholarships/grants, health care benefits, tuition waivers (partial), and unspecified assistantships also available. Financial award application deadline: 2/1. *Faculty research:* Consumer behavior, customer relationship management, research methods, brand strategy, public policy. *Unit head:* Dr. Robert F. Lusch, Head, 520-621-7480, Fax: 520-621-7483, E-mail: rlusch@eller.arizona.edu. *Application contact:* Audrey L. Hambleton, Graduate Secretary, 520-621-1321, Fax: 520-621-7483, E-mail: audrey@eller.arizona.edu.

University of California, Berkeley, Graduate Division, Haas School of Business, PhD in Business Administration Program, Berkeley, CA 94720-1500. Offers accounting (PhD); business and public policy (PhD); finance (PhD); management of organizations (PhD); marketing (PhD); operations management (PhD); real estate (PhD). *Accreditation:* AACSB. *Students:* 78 full-time (25 women); includes 12 Asian, non-Hispanic/Latino; 2 Hispanic/Latino, 32 international. Average age 30. 526 applicants, 7% accepted, 17 enrolled. In 2010, 17 doctorates awarded. *Degree requirements:* For doctorate, comprehensive exam, thesis/dissertation, written preliminary exams, oral qualifying exam. *Entrance requirements:* For doctorate, GMAT or GRE, minimum GPA of 3.0 in undergraduate and graduate coursework. Additional exam requirements/recommendations for international students: Required—TOEFL (minimum score 570 paper-based; 230 computer-based; 70 iBT), IELTS (minimum score 7). *Application deadline:* For fall admission, 12/10 for domestic and international students. Application fee: $70 ($90 for international students). Electronic applications accepted. *Financial support:* In 2010–11, 63 students received support, including 58 fellowships with full and partial tuition reimbursements available (averaging $26,000 per year); research assistantships with full and partial tuition reimbursements available, teaching assistantships with full and partial tuition reimbursements available,

scholarships/grants, health care benefits, tuition waivers (full), unspecified assistantships, and transit pass, travel grants also available. Financial award application deadline: 12/10; financial award applicants required to submit FAFSA. *Faculty research:* Accounting, business and public policy, finance, management of organizations, marketing, operations and information technology management, real estate526. *Unit head:* Dr. Sunil Dutta, Director, 510-642-1229, Fax: 510-643-4255, E-mail: kimg@haas.berkeley.edu. *Application contact:* Kim Guilfoyle, Director, Student Affairs, 510-642-3944, Fax: 510-643-4255, E-mail: kimg@haas.berkeley.edu.

University of California, Los Angeles, Graduate Division, UCLA Anderson School of Management, Los Angeles, CA 90095-1481. Offers accounting (PhD); business administration (MBA); decisions, operations and technology management (PhD); finance (PhD); financial engineering (MFE); global economics and management (PhD); human resources and organizational behavior (PhD); marketing (PhD); strategy and policy (PhD); DDS/MBA; MBA/JD; MBA/MD; MBA/MLAS; MBA/MLIS; MBA/MPH; MBA/MPP; MBA/MSCS; MBA/MSN; MBA/MUP. *Accreditation:* AACSB. Part-time programs available. *Faculty:* 102 full-time (17 women), 43 part-time/adjunct (6 women). *Students:* 833 full-time (270 women), 1,052 part-time (271 women); includes 592 minority (25 Black or African American, non-Hispanic/Latino; 3 American Indian or Alaska Native, non-Hispanic/Latino; 482 Asian, non-Hispanic/Latino; 60 Hispanic/Latino; 6 Native Hawaiian or other Pacific Islander, non-Hispanic/Latino; 16 Two or more races, non-Hispanic/Latino), 445 international. In 2010, 735 master's, 10 doctorates awarded. *Degree requirements:* For master's, comprehensive exam, field study consulting project (for MBA); thesis/dissertation (for MFE); for doctorate, comprehensive exam, thesis/dissertation, oral and written qualifying exams. *Entrance requirements:* For master's, GMAT (MBA); GMAT or GRE General Test (MFE), minimum undergraduate GPA of 3.0; for doctorate, GMAT or GRE General Test, minimum undergraduate GPA of 3.0. Additional exam requirements/recommendations for international students: Required—TOEFL (minimum score 560 paper-based; 220 computer-based; 87 iBT), IELTS (minimum score 7). *Application deadline:* For fall admission, 10/20 for domestic and international students; for winter admission, 1/5 for domestic and international students; for spring admission, 4/13 for domestic and international students. Application fee: $200. Electronic applications accepted. *Expenses:* Contact institution. *Financial support:* Fellowships, research assistantships, teaching assistantships, career-related internships or fieldwork, institutionally sponsored loans, scholarships/grants, health care benefits, and tuition waivers (partial) available. Financial award application deadline: 3/2; financial award applicants required to submit FAFSA. *Unit head:* Judy D. Olian, Dean, UCLA Anderson School of Management, 310-825-7982, Fax: 310-206-2073. *Application contact:* Mae Jennifer Shores, Assistant Dean and Director of Full-time MBA Admissions and Financial Aid, 310-825-6944, Fax: 310-825-8582, E-mail: mba.admissions@anderson.ucla.edu.

University of Chicago, Booth School of Business, Full-Time MBA Program, Chicago, IL 60637. Offers accounting (MBA); analytic finance (MBA); analytic management (MBA); econometrics and statistics (MBA); economics (MBA); entrepreneurship (MBA); finance (MBA); general management (MBA); human resource management (MBA); international business (MBA); managerial and organizational behavior (MBA); marketing management (MBA); operations management (MBA); strategic management (MBA); MBA/AM; MBA/JD; MBA/MA; MBA/MD; MBA/MPP. *Accreditation:* AACSB. Part-time and evening/weekend programs available. *Faculty:* 157 full-time, 35 part-time/adjunct. *Students:* 1,177 full-time (417 women); includes 301 minority (62 Black or African American, non-Hispanic/Latino; 1 American Indian or Alaska Native, non-Hispanic/Latino; 164 Asian, non-Hispanic/Latino; 55 Hispanic/Latino; 19 Two or more races, non-Hispanic/Latino), 403 international. Average age 28. 4,299 applicants, 22% accepted, 579 enrolled. In 2010, 1,374 master's awarded. *Entrance requirements:* For master's, GMAT, 2 letters of recommendation, 3 essays, resume, interview, transcripts. Additional exam requirements/recommendations for international students: Required—TOEFL (minimum score 600 paper-based; 250 computer-based), IELTS. *Application deadline:* For fall admission, 10/10 priority date for domestic students, 10/13 priority date for international students; for winter admission, 1/5 for domestic and international students; for spring admission, 4/13 for domestic and international students. Application fee: $200. Electronic applications accepted. *Expenses:* Contact institution. *Financial support:* Fellowships available. Financial award applicants required to submit FAFSA. *Faculty research:* Finance, economics, entrepreneurship, strategy, management. *Unit head:* Stacey Kole, Deputy Dean, 773-702-7121. *Application contact:* Kurt Ahlm, Associate Dean of Admissions and Financial Aid, 773-702-7369, Fax: 773-702-9085, E-mail: admissions@chicagobooth.edu.

University of Cincinnati, Graduate School, College of Business, MS Program, Cincinnati, OH 45221. Offers accounting (MS); information systems (MS); marketing (MS); quantitative analysis (MS). Part-time and evening/weekend programs available. *Faculty:* 79 full-time (22 women), 71 part-time/adjunct (24 women). *Students:* 130 full-time (46 women), 87 part-time (38 women); includes 12 minority (2 Black or African American, non-Hispanic/Latino; 3 Asian, non-Hispanic/Latino; 4 Hispanic/Latino; 3 Two or more races, non-Hispanic/Latino), 89 international. 407 applicants, 53% accepted, 110 enrolled.

Degree requirements: For master's, thesis (for some programs). *Entrance requirements:* For master's, GMAT, GRE, resume, transcripts, essays, letters of recommendation. Additional exam requirements/recommendations for international students: Required—TOEFL (minimum score 600 paper-based; 250 computer-based; 100 iBT). *Application deadline:* For fall admission, 1/15 priority date for domestic students, 4/1 for international students. Applications are processed on a rolling basis. Application fee: $45. Electronic applications accepted. *Expenses:* Contact institution. *Financial support:* In 2010–11, 10 teaching assistantships with full and partial tuition reimbursements (averaging $5,400 per year) were awarded; scholarships/grants, tuition waivers (full and partial), and unspecified assistantships also available. Financial award application deadline: 2/1; financial award applicants required to submit FAFSA. *Unit head:* Dr. David Szymanski, Dean, 513-556-7001, Fax: 513-556-4891, E-mail: will.mcintosh@uc.edu. *Application contact:* Dona Clary, Director, Graduate Programs Office, 513-556-3546, Fax: 513-558-7006, E-mail: dona.clary@uc.edu.

University of Cincinnati, Graduate School, College of Business, PhD Program, Cincinnati, OH 45221. Offers accounting (PhD); finance (PhD); information systems (PhD); management (PhD); marketing (PhD); quantitative analysis and operations management (PhD). *Faculty:* 56 full-time (13 women). *Students:* 32 full-time (12 women), 9 part-time (3 women); includes 2 minority (both Hispanic/Latino), 23 international. 119 applicants, 12% accepted, 9 enrolled. In 2010, 8 doctorates awarded. *Degree requirements:* For doctorate, comprehensive exam, thesis/dissertation. *Entrance requirements:* For doctorate, GMAT, GRE, transcripts, essays, resume, letters of recommendation. Additional exam requirements/recommendations for international students: Required—TOEFL (minimum score 600 paper-based; 250 computer-based; 100 iBT). *Application deadline:* For fall admission, 2/1 for domestic and international students. Application fee: $45. Electronic applications accepted. *Expenses:* Contact institution. *Financial support:* In 2010–11, 38 students received support, including 29 research assistantships with full and partial tuition reimbursements available (averaging $14,640 per year); scholarships/grants, tuition waivers (full and partial), and unspecified assistantships also available. Financial award application deadline: 2/15; financial award applicants required to submit FAFSA. *Unit head:* Dr. Suzanne Masterson, Director, PhD Programs, 513-556-7125, Fax: 513-556-5499, E-mail: suzanne.masterson@uc.edu. *Application contact:* Deborah Schildknecht, Assistant Director, PhD Programs, 513-556-7190, Fax: 513-558-7006, E-mail: deborah.schildknecht@uc.edu.

University of Colorado Boulder, Leeds School of Business, Division of Business Administration, Boulder, CO 80309. Offers accounting (MS, PhD); finance (PhD); information systems (PhD); marketing (PhD); operations (PhD); strategic, organizational, and entrepreneurial studies (PhD). Part-time and evening/weekend programs available. *Students:* 110 full-time (42 women), 2 part-time (1 woman); includes 6 minority (5 Asian, non-Hispanic/Latino; 1 Hispanic/Latino), 24 international. Average age 28. 342 applicants, 24 enrolled. In 2010, 48 master's, 12 doctorates awarded. *Entrance requirements:* For master's, GMAT, minimum undergraduate GPA of 3.0. *Application deadline:* For fall admission, 3/31 for domestic and international students; for spring admission, 10/31 for domestic and international students. Application fee: $50 ($60 for international students). Electronic applications accepted. *Financial support:* In 2010–11, 16 fellowships (averaging $1,038 per year), 26 research assistantships (averaging $17,558 per year), 11 teaching assistantships (averaging $12,576 per year) were awarded; career-related internships or fieldwork, Federal Work-Study, scholarships/grants, and unspecified assistantships also available. Financial award applicants required to submit FAFSA.

University of Colorado Denver, Business School, Program in Marketing, Denver, CO 80217. Offers brand management and marketing communication (MS); global marketing (MS); high-tech/entrepreneurial marketing (MS); Internet marketing (MS); market research (MS); marketing and business intelligence (MS); marketing for sustainability (MS); marketing in nonprofit organizations (MS); sports and entertainment marketing (MS). Part-time and evening/weekend programs available. *Students:* 31 full-time (18 women), 8 part-time (4 women); includes 3 Hispanic/Latino, 5 international. Average age 29. 46 applicants, 63% accepted, 18 enrolled. In 2010, 11 master's awarded. *Degree requirements:* For master's, 30 semester hours (18 of marketing core courses, 12 of graduate marketing electives). *Entrance requirements:* For master's, GMAT. Additional exam requirements/recommendations for international students: Required—TOEFL (minimum score 525 paper-based; 197 computer-based; 71 iBT). *Application deadline:* For fall admission, 4/1 priority date for domestic students, 3/15 priority date for international students; for spring admission, 10/1 priority date for domestic and international students. Application fee: $50 ($75 for international students). Electronic applications accepted. *Expenses:* Contact institution. *Financial support:* Federal Work-Study and scholarships/grants available. Support available to part-time students. Financial award application deadline: 4/1; financial award applicants required to submit FAFSA. *Faculty research:* Marketing issues in the Chinese environment, impact of individual difference and contextual factors on the risk-taking behaviors of managers making new-business creation decisions, Attribution Theory perspective of conflict between marketers and engineers, organizational identity and identification , international market entry strategies. *Unit head:* Dr. David Forlani, Associate Professor/Director,

303-315-8420, E-mail: david.forlani@ucdenver.edu. *Application contact:* Shelly Townley, Admissions Director, Graduate Programs, 303-315-8202, E-mail: shelly.townley@ucdenver.edu.

University of Dayton, Graduate School, School of Business Administration, Dayton, OH 45469-1300. Offers accounting (MBA); business intelligence (MBA); cyber security (MBA); entrepreneurship (MBA); finance (MBA); international business (MBA); marketing (MBA); MIS (MBA); operations management (MBA); technology-enhanced business/e-commerce (MBA); JD/MBA. *Accreditation:* AACSB. Part-time and evening/weekend programs available. *Faculty:* 25 full-time (7 women), 14 part-time/adjunct (2 women). *Students:* 184 full-time (72 women), 110 part-time (34 women); includes 23 minority (7 Black or African American, non-Hispanic/Latino; 7 Asian, non-Hispanic/Latino; 8 Hispanic/Latino; 1 Two or more races, non-Hispanic/Latino), 31 international. Average age 28. 220 applicants, 85% accepted, 103 enrolled. In 2010, 113 master's awarded. *Entrance requirements:* For master's, GMAT or GRE. Additional exam requirements/recommendations for international students: Required—TOEFL (minimum score 550 paper-based; 213 computer-based; 79 iBT); Recommended—IELTS (minimum score 6.5). *Application deadline:* For fall admission, 3/1 priority date for international students; for winter admission, 7/1 priority date for international students; for spring admission, 1/1 priority date for international students. Applications are processed on a rolling basis. Application fee: $0 ($50 for international students). Electronic applications accepted. *Expenses:* Contact institution. *Financial support:* In 2010–11, 15 research assistantships with full and partial tuition reimbursements (averaging $7,020 per year) were awarded; career-related internships or fieldwork, institutionally sponsored loans, scholarships/grants, health care benefits, and unspecified assistantships also available. Support available to part-time students. Financial award application deadline: 3/15; financial award applicants required to submit FAFSA. *Faculty research:* Management information systems, economics, finance, entrepreneurship, marketing. *Unit head:* Janice M. Glynn, Director, MBA Program, 937-229-3733, Fax: 937-229-3882, E-mail: glynn@udayton.edu. *Application contact:* Jeffrey Carter, Assistant Director, MBA Program, 937-229-3733, Fax: 937-229-3882, E-mail: jeff.carter@notes.udayton.edu.

University of Denver, Daniels College of Business, Department of Marketing, Denver, CO 80208. Offers IMBA, MBA, MS. Part-time and evening/weekend programs available. *Faculty:* 10 full-time (4 women), 6 part-time/adjunct (3 women). *Students:* 23 full-time (15 women), 23 part-time (15 women); includes 2 minority (1 Black or African American, non-Hispanic/Latino; 1 Hispanic/Latino), 30 international. Average age 25. 190 applicants, 63% accepted, 28 enrolled. In 2010, 27 master's awarded. *Entrance requirements:* For master's, GRE General Test or GMAT. Additional exam requirements/recommendations for international students: Required—TOEFL (minimum score 570 paper-based; 88 iBT). *Application deadline:* For fall admission, 11/15 priority date for domestic students; for spring admission, 10/1 priority date for domestic students. Applications are processed on a rolling basis. Application fee: $100. Electronic applications accepted. *Expenses:* Tuition: Full-time $35,604; part-time $29,670 per year. Required fees: $687 per year. Tuition and fees vary according to program. *Financial support:* In 2010–11, 5 teaching assistantships with full and partial tuition reimbursements (averaging $1,572 per year) were awarded; career-related internships or fieldwork, Federal Work-Study, institutionally sponsored loans, scholarships/grants, and unspecified assistantships also available. Support available to part-time students. Financial award application deadline: 3/15; financial award applicants required to submit FAFSA. *Faculty research:* Social policy issues in marketing, price bundling, marketing to the disabled, marketing to the elderly, international marketing and logistics. *Unit head:* Dr. Carol Johnson, Chair, 303-871-2276, Fax: 303-871-2323, E-mail: carol.johnson@du.edu. *Application contact:* Soumontha A. Colwell-Chanthaphonh, Assistant Director of Graduate Student Recruitment and Admissions, 303-871-2338, Fax: 303-871-2323, E-mail: soumontha.chanthaphonh@du.edu.

University of Florida, Graduate School, Warrington College of Business Administration, Hough Graduate School of Business, Department of Marketing, Gainesville, FL 32611. Offers MS, PhD. *Faculty:* 10 full-time (2 women). *Students:* 6 full-time (3 women), 2 part-time (1 woman); includes 1 Asian, non-Hispanic/Latino, 4 international. Average age 29. 38 applicants, 3% accepted, 1 enrolled. In 2010, 3 doctorates awarded. Terminal master's awarded for partial completion of doctoral program. *Degree requirements:* For master's, comprehensive exam, thesis optional; for doctorate, comprehensive exam, thesis/dissertation. *Entrance requirements:* For master's, GMAT or GRE General Test, minimum GPA of 3.0; for doctorate, GMAT (or GRE General Test, minimum GPA of 3.0. Additional exam requirements/recommendations for international students: Required—TOEFL (minimum score 550 paper-based; 213 computer-based; 80 iBT), IELTS (minimum score 6). *Application deadline:* For fall admission, 2/1 for domestic and international students. Applications are processed on a rolling basis. Application fee: $30. Electronic applications accepted. *Expenses:* Tuition, state resident: full-time $10,915.92. Tuition, nonresident: full-time $28,309. *Financial support:* In 2010–11, 5 students received support, including 5 research assistantships (averaging $26,368 per year); career-related internships or fieldwork, institutionally sponsored loans, and unspecified assistantships also available. Financial award application deadline: 2/1; financial award applicants required to submit FAFSA. *Faculty research:* Consumer behavior, decision-making, behavioral decision theory, marketing models, marketing strategy. *Unit head:* Dr. Joseph W. Alba, Chair, 352-273-3280, Fax: 352-846-0457, E-mail: joe.alba@warrington.ufl.edu. *Application contact:* Dr. Lyle A. Brenner, Graduate Coordinator, 352-273-3272, Fax: 352-846-0457, E-mail: lbrenner@ufl.edu.

University of Florida, Graduate School, Warrington College of Business Administration, Hough Graduate School of Business, Programs in Business Administration, Gainesville, FL 32611. Offers accounting (MBA); arts administration (MBA); business strategy and public policy (MBA); competitive strategy (MBA); decision and information sciences (MBA); electronic commerce (MBA); finance (MBA); general business (MBA); global management (MBA); Graham-Buffett security analysis (MBA); health administration (MBA); human resources management (MBA); international studies (MBA); Latin American business (MBA); management (MBA); marketing (MBA); sports administration (MBA); JD/MBA; MBA/MS; MBA/PhD; MBA/Pharm D; MD/MBA. *Accreditation:* AACSB. Part-time and evening/weekend programs available. *Faculty:* 71 full-time (10 women). *Students:* 187 full-time (44 women), 305 part-time (83 women); includes 25 Black or African American, non-Hispanic/Latino; 2 American Indian or Alaska Native, non-Hispanic/Latino; 52 Asian, non-Hispanic/Latino; 54 Hispanic/Latino, 11 international. Average age 31. 919 applicants, 33% accepted, 225 enrolled. In 2010, 492 master's awarded. *Degree requirements:* For master's, capstone course. *Entrance requirements:* For master's, GMAT, minimum GPA of 3.0, interview. Additional exam requirements/recommendations for international students: Required—TOEFL (minimum score 550 paper-based; 213 computer-based; 80 iBT), IELTS (minimum score 6). *Application deadline:* For fall admission, 7/1 for domestic students, 1/1 for international students; for spring admission, 12/1 for domestic and international students. Applications are processed on a rolling basis. Application fee: $30. Electronic applications accepted. *Expenses:* Tuition, state resident: full-time $10,915.92. Tuition, nonresident: full-time $28,309. *Financial support:* In 2010–11, 1 student received support, including 1 teaching assistantship (averaging $20,600 per year); career-related internships or fieldwork, scholarships/grants, and unspecified assistantships also available. Support available to part-time students. Financial award applicants required to submit FAFSA. *Faculty research:* Accounting, finance, insurance, management, real estate, urban analysis marketing. *Unit head:* Prof. Alexander D. Sevilla, Assistant Dean and Director MBA Programs, 352-273-3252 Ext. 1206, E-mail: alex.sevilla@warrington.ufl.edu. *Application contact:* Prof. Kelli Gust, Associate Director of MBA Programs, 352-273-3255, Fax: 352-392-8791, E-mail: kelly.gust@ warrington.ufl.edu.

University of Hawaii at Manoa, Graduate Division, Shidler College of Business, Program in Business Administration, Honolulu, HI 96822. Offers Asian business studies (MBA); Chinese business studies (MBA); decision sciences (MBA); entrepreneurship (MBA); finance (MBA); finance and banking (MBA); human resources management (MBA); information management (MBA); information technology (MBA); international business (MBA); Japanese business studies (MBA); marketing (MBA); organizational behavior (MBA); organizational management (MBA); real estate (MBA); student-designed track (MBA). *Accreditation:* AACSB. Part-time and evening/weekend programs available. *Faculty:* 53 full-time (12 women). *Students:* 162 full-time (63 women), 102 part-time (43 women); includes 135 minority (1 Black or African American, non-Hispanic/Latino; 81 Asian, non-Hispanic/Latino; 5 Hispanic/Latino; 18 Native Hawaiian or other Pacific Islander, non-Hispanic/Latino; 30 Two or more races, non-Hispanic/Latino), 44 international. Average age 34. 361 applicants, 57% accepted, 172 enrolled. In 2010, 153 master's awarded. *Degree requirements:* For master's, thesis optional. *Entrance requirements:* For master's, GMAT, minimum GPA of 3.0. Additional exam requirements/recommendations for international students: Required—TOEFL (minimum score 600 paper-based; 250 computer-based; 100 iBT), IELTS (minimum score 7). *Application deadline:* For fall admission, 5/1 for domestic students, 3/1 for international students. Application fee: $60. *Expenses:* Contact institution. *Financial support:* In 2010–11, 83 fellowships (averaging $5,547 per year), 1 research assistantship (averaging $16,824 per year) were awarded. Total annual research expenditures: $427,000. *Application contact:* Daniel Port, Graduate Chair, 808-956-5565, Fax: 808-956-6889, E-mail: daniel.port@hawaii.edu.

University of Hawaii at Manoa, Graduate Division, Shidler College of Business, Program in International Management, Honolulu, HI 96822. Offers Asian finance (PhD); global information technology management (PhD); international accounting (PhD); international marketing (PhD); international organization and strategy (PhD). Part-time programs available. *Students:* 30 full-time (11 women), 3 part-time (0 women); includes 7 minority (5 Asian, non-Hispanic/Latino; 2 Two or more races, non-Hispanic/Latino), 18 international. Average age 36. 65 applicants, 18% accepted, 5 enrolled. In 2010, 4 doctorates awarded. *Degree requirements:* For doctorate, comprehensive exam, thesis/dissertation. *Entrance requirements:* For doctorate, GMAT or GRE General Test, minimum GPA of 3.0. Additional exam requirements/recommendations for international students: Required—TOEFL (minimum score 600 paper-based; 250 computer-based; 100 iBT), IELTS (minimum score 7). *Application deadline:* For fall admission, 3/1 for domestic and international students. Application fee: $60. *Expenses:* Contact institution. *Financial support:* In 2010–11, 29 students received support, including 3 fellowships

(averaging $5,491 per year), 25 research assistantships (averaging $17,750 per year), 1 teaching assistantship (averaging $15,558 per year). *Application contact:* Erica Okada, Graduate Chair, 808-956-6723, Fax: 808-956-6889, E-mail: imphd@hawaii.edu.

University of Houston, Bauer College of Business, Marketing Program, Houston, TX 77204. Offers PhD. Part-time and evening/weekend programs available. *Faculty:* 8 full-time (1 woman), 4 part-time/adjunct (0 women). *Degree requirements:* For doctorate, comprehensive exam, thesis/dissertation. *Entrance requirements:* For doctorate, GMAT or GRE. *Expenses:* Tuition, state resident: full-time $8592; part-time $358 per credit hour. Tuition, nonresident: full-time $16,032; part-time $668 per credit hour. Required fees: $2889. Tuition and fees vary according to course load and program. *Financial support:* In 2010–11, 17 fellowships with partial tuition reimbursements (averaging $2,400 per year), 15 teaching assistantships with partial tuition reimbursements (averaging $17,824 per year) were awarded; career-related internships or fieldwork, Federal Work-Study, institutionally sponsored loans, scholarships/grants, health care benefits, and unspecified assistantships also available. Support available to part-time students. Financial award application deadline: 2/1; financial award applicants required to submit FAFSA. *Faculty research:* Accountancy and taxation, finance, international business, management. *Unit head:* Dr. Edward Blair, Chairperson, 713-743-4555, Fax: 713-743-4572, E-mail: blair@uh.edu.

University of Houston–Victoria, School of Business Administration, Victoria, TX 77901-4450. Offers accounting (MBA); economic development and entrepreneurship (MS); finance (GMBA, MBA); general business (MBA); international business (MBA); management (GMBA, MBA); marketing (MBA). *Accreditation:* AACSB. Part-time and evening/weekend programs available. Postbaccalaureate distance learning degree programs offered (minimal on-campus study). *Faculty:* 37 full-time (11 women). *Students:* 234 full-time (108 women), 714 part-time (303 women); includes 542 minority (215 Black or African American, non-Hispanic/Latino; 1 American Indian or Alaska Native, non-Hispanic/Latino; 197 Asian, non-Hispanic/Latino; 124 Hispanic/Latino; 1 Native Hawaiian or other Pacific Islander, non-Hispanic/Latino; 4 Two or more races, non-Hispanic/Latino), 115 international. Average age 34. 362 applicants, 65% accepted, 147 enrolled. In 2010, 181 master's awarded. *Entrance requirements:* For master's, GMAT. Additional exam requirements/recommendations for international students: Required—TOEFL (minimum score 550 paper-based; 213 computer-based). *Application deadline:* For fall admission, 6/1 for international students; for spring admission, 10/1 for international students. Applications are processed on a rolling basis. Application fee: $0. Electronic applications accepted. *Expenses:* Tuition, state resident: full-time $4050; part-time $225 per credit hour. Tuition, nonresident: full-time $8730; part-time $485 per credit hour. Required fees: $810; $54 per credit hour. Tuition and fees vary according to course load. *Financial support:* In 2010–11, research assistantships with partial tuition reimbursements (averaging $2,000 per year), teaching assistantships with partial tuition reimbursements (averaging $2,000 per year) were awarded; Federal Work-Study, scholarships/grants, and unspecified assistantships also available. Support available to part-time students. Financial award application deadline: 4/15; financial award applicants required to submit FAFSA. *Faculty research:* Economic development, marketing, finance. *Unit head:* Dr. Farhang Niroomand, Dean, 361-570-4230, Fax: 361-580-5599, E-mail: niroomandf@ uhv.edu. *Application contact:* Jane Mims, Assistant Dean, 361-570-4639, Fax: 361-580-5529, E-mail: mims@uhv.edu.

The University of Iowa, Henry B. Tippie College of Business, Department of Marketing, Iowa City, IA 52242-1316. Offers PhD. *Faculty:* 15 full-time (4 women), 6 part-time/adjunct (0 women). *Students:* 12 full-time (5 women); includes 1 American Indian or Alaska Native, non-Hispanic/Latino; 1 Asian, non-Hispanic/Latino, 10 international. Average age 35. 27 applicants, 11% accepted, 2 enrolled. *Degree requirements:* For doctorate, comprehensive exam, thesis/dissertation, thesis defense. *Entrance requirements:* For doctorate, GMAT or GRE, minimum undergraduate GPA of 2.7. Additional exam requirements/recommendations for international students: Required—TOEFL (minimum score 600 paper-based; 250 computer-based; 100 iBT). *Application deadline:* For fall admission, 1/15 for domestic and international students. Applications are processed on a rolling basis. Application fee: $60 ($100 for international students). Electronic applications accepted. *Financial support:* In 2010–11, 12 students received support, including 1 fellowship with full tuition reimbursement available (averaging $20,000 per year), 11 teaching assistantships with full tuition reimbursements available (averaging $16,575 per year); institutionally sponsored loans, scholarships/grants, health care benefits, unspecified assistantships, and 10 partial fellowships (averaging $1800 per year) also available. Financial award application deadline: 1/15. *Faculty research:* Judgments and decision making under certainty; consumer behavior: cognitive neuroscience, attitudes and evaluation; hierarchical Bayesian estimation; marketing-finance interface; advertising effects. *Unit head:* Prof. Gary J. Russell, Department Executive Officer, 319-335-1013, Fax: 319-335-1956, E-mail: gary-j-russell@uiowa.edu. *Application contact:* Renea L. Jay, PhD Program Coordinator, 319-335-0830, Fax: 319-335-1956, E-mail: renea-jay@uiowa.edu.

The University of Iowa, Henry B. Tippie College of Business, Henry B. Tippie School of Management, Iowa City, IA 52242-1316. Offers corporate finance

(MBA); investment management (MBA); marketing (MBA); process and operations excellence (MBA); strategic management and innovation (MBA); JD/MBA; MBA/MA; MBA/MD; MBA/MHA; MBA/MSN. *Accreditation:* AACSB. Part-time and evening/weekend programs available. *Faculty:* 110 full-time (25 women), 19 part-time/adjunct (1 woman). *Students:* 242 full-time (46 women), 809 part-time (277 women); includes 95 minority (15 Black or African American, non-Hispanic/Latino; 3 American Indian or Alaska Native, non-Hispanic/Latino; 56 Asian, non-Hispanic/Latino; 21 Hispanic/Latino), 132 international. Average age 31. 652 applicants, 66% accepted, 380 enrolled. In 2010, 333 master's awarded. *Degree requirements:* For master's, minimum GPA of 2.75. *Entrance requirements:* For master's, GMAT, quality work experience and leadership as shown through resume, references, and essays. Additional exam requirements/recommendations for international students: Required—TOEFL (minimum score 600 paper-based; 250 computer-based; 100 iBT), IELTS (minimum score 7). *Application deadline:* For fall admission, 7/30 for domestic students, 4/15 for international students; for spring admission, 12/15 for domestic and international students. Applications are processed on a rolling basis. Application fee: $60 ($100 for international students). Electronic applications accepted. *Expenses:* Contact institution. *Financial support:* In 2010–11, 111 students received support, including 121 fellowships (averaging $8,285 per year), 87 research assistantships with partial tuition reimbursements available (averaging $8,288 per year), 25 teaching assistantships with partial tuition reimbursements available (averaging $11,326 per year); career-related internships or fieldwork, scholarships/grants, health care benefits, and unspecified assistantships also available. Financial award application deadline: 4/15; financial award applicants required to submit FAFSA. *Faculty research:* Capital markets, econometrics, optimization, investments and empirical corporate finance, Iowa electronic markets. *Unit head:* Prof. Jarjisu Sa-Aadu, Associate Dean, MBA Programs, 800-622-4692, Fax: 319-335-3604, E-mail: jsa-aadu@uiowa.edu. *Application contact:* Jodi Schafer, Director of Admissions and Financial Aid, 319-335-0864, Fax: 319-335-3604, E-mail: jodi-schafer@uiowa.edu.

University of La Verne, College of Business and Public Management, Graduate Programs in Business Administration, La Verne, CA 91750-4443. Offers accounting (MBA); executive management (MBA-EP); finance (MBA, MBA-EP); health services management (MBA); information technology (MBA, MBA-EP); international business (MBA, MBA-EP); leadership (MBA-EP); managed care (MBA); management (MBA, MBA-EP); marketing (MBA, MBA-EP). Part-time and evening/weekend programs available. *Faculty:* 34 full-time (12 women), 36 part-time/adjunct (9 women). *Students:* 412 full-time (207 women), 200 part-time (96 women); includes 423 minority (32 Black or African American, non-Hispanic/Latino; 5 American Indian or Alaska Native, non-Hispanic/Latino; 294 Asian, non-Hispanic/Latino; 92 Hispanic/Latino), 6 international. Average age 29. In 2010, 229 master's awarded. *Entrance requirements:* For master's, minimum undergraduate GPA of 3.0, 2 letters of recommendation, resume. Additional exam requirements/recommendations for international students: Required—TOEFL (minimum score 550 paper-based; 213 computer-based). *Application deadline:* Applications are processed on a rolling basis. Application fee: $50. *Expenses:* Contact institution. *Financial support:* Career-related internships or fieldwork, institutionally sponsored loans, and scholarships/grants available. Financial award application deadline: 3/2; financial award applicants required to submit FAFSA. *Unit head:* Dr. Abe Helou, Chairperson, 909-593-3511 Ext. 4211, Fax: 909-392-2704, E-mail: ihelou@laverne.edu. *Application contact:* Rina Lazarian, Program and Admission Specialist, 909-593-3511 Ext. 4819, Fax: 909-392-2704, E-mail: cbpm@ulv.edu.

University of La Verne, Regional Campus Administration, Graduate Programs, Inland Empire Campus, Rancho Cucamonga, CA 91730. Offers business (MBA-EP), including health services management, information technology, management, marketing; leadership and management (MS). *Faculty:* 3 full-time (2 women), 22 part-time/adjunct (9 women). *Students:* 27 full-time (17 women), 100 part-time (68 women); includes 14 Black or African American, non-Hispanic/Latino; 1 American Indian or Alaska Native, non-Hispanic/Latino; 22 Asian, non-Hispanic/Latino; 36 Hispanic/Latino. Average age 39. In 2010, 20 master's awarded. *Entrance requirements:* For master's, 2 letters of recommendation, resume. *Application deadline:* Applications are processed on a rolling basis. Application fee: $50. *Expenses:* Contact institution. *Financial support:* Institutionally sponsored loans available. Financial award application deadline: 3/2; financial award applicants required to submit FAFSA. *Unit head:* Allan Stout, Director, 909-484-3858 Ext. 6002, Fax: 909-484-9469, E-mail: astout@laverne.edu. *Application contact:* Allan Stout, Director, 909-484-3858 Ext. 6002, Fax: 909-484-9469, E-mail: astout@laverne.edu.

University of Massachusetts Dartmouth, Graduate School, Charlton College of Business, Program in Business Administration, North Dartmouth, MA 02747-2300. Offers accounting (Postbaccalaureate Certificate); business administration (MBA); e-commerce (PMC); finance (PMC); general management (PMC); leadership (PMC); management (Postbaccalaureate Certificate); marketing (PMC); supply chain management (PMC). *Accreditation:* AACSB. Part-time programs available. *Faculty:* 40 full-time (13 women), 28 part-time/adjunct (8 women). *Students:* 99 full-time (38 women), 123 part-time (62 women); includes 4 Black or African American, non-Hispanic/Latino; 2 American Indian or Alaska Native, non-Hispanic/Latino; 3 Asian, non-Hispanic/Latino; 8 Hispanic/Latino; 1 Two or more races, non-Hispanic/Latino, 45 international. Average age 30. 185 applicants, 76% accepted, 79 enrolled. In 2010, 79 master's, 12 other advanced degrees awarded. *Entrance requirements:* For master's, GMAT, resume, letters of recommendation. Additional exam requirements/recommendations for international students: Required—TOEFL (minimum score 500 paper-based; 200 computer-based; 72 iBT). *Application deadline:* For fall admission, 6/1 for domestic students, 5/1 for international students; for spring admission, 10/1 for domestic students, 8/1 for international students. Application fee: $40 ($60 for international students). Electronic applications accepted. *Expenses:* Tuition, state resident: full-time $2071; part-time $86 per credit. Tuition, nonresident: full-time $8099; part-time $337 per credit. Required fees: $9446; $394 per credit. One-time fee: $75. Part-time tuition and fees vary according to class time, course load, degree level and reciprocity agreements. *Financial support:* In 2010–11, 1 research assistantship with full tuition reimbursement (averaging $6,000 per year) was awarded; teaching assistantships, Federal Work-Study and unspecified assistantships also available. Support available to part-time students. Financial award application deadline: 3/1; financial award applicants required to submit FAFSA. *Faculty research:* Global business environment, e-commerce, managing diversity, agile manufacturing, green business. Total annual research expenditures: $29,538. *Unit head:* Dr. Norm Barber, Assistant Dean, 508-999-8543, E-mail: nbarber@umassd.edu. *Application contact:* Elan Turcotte-Shamski, Graduate Admissions Officer, 508-999-8604, Fax: 508-999-8183, E-mail: graduate@umassd.edu.

University of Memphis, Graduate School, Fogelman College of Business and Economics, Program in Business Administration, Memphis, TN 38152. Offers accounting (MBA, PhD); economics (MBA, PhD); executive business administration (MBA); finance (PhD); finance, insurance, and real estate (MBA, MS); international business administration (IMBA); management (MBA, MS, PhD); management information systems (MBA, MS, PhD); management science (MBA); marketing (MBA, MS); marketing and supply chain management (PhD); real estate development (MS); JD/MBA. *Accreditation:* AACSB. *Faculty:* 44 full-time (9 women), 5 part-time/adjunct (0 women). *Students:* 263 full-time (106 women), 181 part-time (66 women); includes 46 Black or African American, non-Hispanic/Latino; 3 American Indian or Alaska Native, non-Hispanic/Latino; 16 Asian, non-Hispanic/Latino; 5 Hispanic/Latino, 109 international. Average age 31. 374 applicants, 73% accepted, 119 enrolled. In 2010, 140 master's, 17 doctorates awarded. *Degree requirements:* For master's, comprehensive exam; for doctorate, comprehensive exam, thesis/dissertation. *Entrance requirements:* For master's, GMAT, resume; for doctorate, GMAT, interview, minimum GPA of 3.4, resume, letter of recommendation. Additional exam requirements/recommendations for international students: Required—TOEFL (minimum score 550 paper-based; 220 computer-based). *Application deadline:* For fall admission, 8/1 for domestic students; for spring admission, 12/1 for domestic students. Application fee: $35 ($60 for international students). *Financial support:* In 2010–11, 164 students received support; research assistantships with full tuition reimbursements available, teaching assistantships with full tuition reimbursements available, career-related internships or fieldwork, Federal Work-Study, scholarships/grants, and unspecified assistantships available. Financial award application deadline: 2/15; financial award applicants required to submit FAFSA. *Faculty research:* Competitive business strategy, finance microstructures, supply chain management innovations, health care economics, litigation risks and corporate audits. *Unit head:* Rajiv Grover, Dean, 901-678-3759, E-mail: rgrover@memphis.edu. *Application contact:* Dr. Carol V. Danehower, Associate Dean, 901-678-5402, Fax: 901-678-3579, E-mail: fcbegp@memphis.edu.

University of Michigan–Dearborn, School of Management, Dearborn, MI 48128-1491. Offers accounting (MBA, MS); finance (MBA, MS); information systems (MS); international business (MBA); management (MBA); management information systems (MBA); marketing (MBA); supply chain management (MBA); MBA/MHSA; MBA/MSE; MBA/MSF. *Accreditation:* AACSB. Part-time and evening/weekend programs available. Postbaccalaureate distance learning degree programs offered (no on-campus study). *Faculty:* 40 full-time (17 women), 2 part-time/adjunct (1 woman). *Students:* 71 full-time (26 women), 403 part-time (134 women); includes 68 minority (19 Black or African American, non-Hispanic/Latino; 1 American Indian or Alaska Native, non-Hispanic/Latino; 39 Asian, non-Hispanic/Latino; 6 Hispanic/Latino; 1 Native Hawaiian or other Pacific Islander, non-Hispanic/Latino; 2 Two or more races, non-Hispanic/Latino), 89 international. Average age 30. 185 applicants, 51% accepted, 67 enrolled. In 2010, 150 master's awarded. *Entrance requirements:* For master's, GMAT, 2 years of work experience (MBA); course work in computer applications, statistics, and pre-calculus or finite mathematics; 18 credits of accounting course work beyond introductory courses (MS in accounting). Additional exam requirements/recommendations for international students: Required—TOEFL (minimum score 560 paper-based; 220 computer-based; 84 iBT). *Application deadline:* For fall admission, 8/1 priority date for domestic students, 6/1 for international students; for winter admission, 12/1 priority date for domestic students, 10/1 for international students; for spring admission, 4/1 priority date for domestic students, 2/1 for international students. Applications are processed on a rolling basis. Application fee: $60. Electronic applications accepted. *Expenses:* Contact institution. *Financial support:* Career-related internships or fieldwork, Federal Work-Study, and scholarships/grants available. Support available to part-time students. Financial award application deadline: 9/1; financial award applicants required to submit FAFSA. *Faculty research:* Cultural diversity, buyer-supplier relations, error detection in data, economic evolution. *Unit head:* Dr. Kim Schatzel, Dean, 313-593-5248, Fax: 313-271-9835, E-mail: schatzel@umd.umich.edu. *Application contact:* Joan Doherty, Academic Advisor/Counselor, 313-593-5460, Fax: 313-271-9838, E-mail: gradbusiness@umd.umich.edu.

University of Minnesota, Twin Cities Campus, Carlson School of Management, Carlson Full-Time MBA Program, Minneapolis, MN 55455. Offers finance (MBA); information technology (MBA); management (MBA); marketing (MBA); medical industry orientation (MBA); supply chain and operations (MBA); JD/MBA; MBA/MPP; MD/MBA; MHA/MBA; Pharm D/MBA. *Accreditation:* AACSB. *Faculty:* 52 full-time (14 women), 20 part-time/adjunct (3 women). *Students:* 170 full-time (62 women); includes 1 Black or African American, non-Hispanic/Latino; 1 American Indian or Alaska Native, non-Hispanic/Latino; 9 Asian, non-Hispanic/Latino; 8 Hispanic/Latino, 36 international. Average age 28. 452 applicants, 30% accepted, 71 enrolled. In 2010, 105 master's awarded. *Entrance requirements:* For master's, GMAT. Additional exam requirements/recommendations for international students: Required—TOEFL (minimum score 580 paper-based; 240 computer-based; 84 iBT), IELTS (minimum score 7), or Pearson Test of English (PTE). *Application deadline:* For fall admission, 4/1 for domestic students, 2/1 for international students. Application fee: $60 ($90 for international students). Electronic applications accepted. *Expenses:* Contact institution. *Financial support:* In 2010–11, 95 students received support, including 95 fellowships with full and partial tuition reimbursements available (averaging $21,235 per year); research assistantships with partial tuition reimbursements available, teaching assistantships with partial tuition reimbursements available, career-related internships or fieldwork, Federal Work-Study, institutionally sponsored loans, scholarships/grants, health care benefits, and unspecified assistantships also available. Financial award application deadline: 4/1; financial award applicants required to submit FAFSA. *Faculty research:* Finance and accounting: financial reporting, asset pricing models and corporate finance; information and decision sciences: on-line auctions, information transparency and recommender systems; marketing: psychological influences on consumer behavior, brand equity, pricing and marketing channels; operations: lean manufacturing, quality management and global supply chains; strategic management and organization: global strategy, networks, entrepreneurship and innovation, sustainability. *Unit head:* Kathryn J. Carlson, Assistant Dean, MBA Programs and Graduate Business Career Center, 612-625-5555, Fax: 612-625-1012, E-mail: mba@umn.edu. *Application contact:* Daniel Bursch, Director of Admissions & Recruiting, 612-625-5555, Fax: 612-625-1012, E-mail: mba@umn.edu.

University of Minnesota, Twin Cities Campus, Carlson School of Management, Carlson Part-Time MBA Program, Minneapolis, MN 55455. Offers finance (MBA); information technology (MBA); management (MBA); marketing (MBA); supply chain and operations (MBA). Part-time and evening/weekend programs available. *Faculty:* 67 full-time (18 women), 23 part-time/adjunct (2 women). *Students:* 1,520 part-time (490 women); includes 16 Black or African American, non-Hispanic/Latino; 3 American Indian or Alaska Native, non-Hispanic/Latino; 87 Asian, non-Hispanic/Latino; 14 Hispanic/Latino, 94 international. Average age 29. 306 applicants, 70% accepted, 186 enrolled. In 2010, 401 master's awarded. *Entrance requirements:* For master's, GMAT. Additional exam requirements/recommendations for international students: Required—TOEFL (minimum score 580 paper-based; 240 computer-based; 84 iBT), IELTS (minimum score 7), or Pearson Test of English (PTE). *Application deadline:* For fall admission, 5/1 priority date for domestic and international students; for spring admission, 11/1 priority date for domestic and international students. Application fee: $60 ($90 for international students). Electronic applications accepted. *Expenses:* Contact institution. *Financial support:* Applicants required to submit FAFSA. *Faculty research:* Finance and accounting: financial reporting, asset pricing models and corporate finance; information and decision sciences: on-line auctions, information transparency and recommender systems; marketing: psychological influences on consumer behavior, brand equity, pricing and marketing channels; operations: lean manufacturing, quality management and global supply chains; strategic management and organization: global Strategy, networks, entrepreneurship and innovation, sustainability. *Unit head:* Kathryn J. Carlson, Assistant Dean, MBA Programs and Graduate Business Career Center, 612-624-2039, Fax: 612-625-1012, E-mail: mba@umn.edu. *Application contact:* Daniel Bursch, Director of Admissions & Recruiting, 612-625-5555, Fax: 612-625-1012, E-mail: mba@umn.edu.

University of Minnesota, Twin Cities Campus, Carlson School of Management, Doctoral Program in Business Administration, Minneapolis, MN 55455-0213. Offers accounting (PhD); finance (PhD); information and decision sciences (PhD); marketing and logistics management (PhD); operations and management science (PhD); strategic management and organization (PhD). *Faculty:* 100 full-time (27 women). *Students:* 73 full-time (28 women); includes 3 Asian, non-Hispanic/Latino; 3 Hispanic/Latino, 53 international. Average age 30. 319 applicants, 6% accepted, 16 enrolled. In 2010, 8 doctorates awarded. *Degree requirements:* For doctorate, comprehensive exam, thesis/dissertation, written and oral preliminary exams, proposal defense,

final defense. *Entrance requirements:* For doctorate, GMAT, GRE General Test. Additional exam requirements/recommendations for international students: Required—TOEFL (minimum score 600 paper-based; 250 computer-based; 100 iBT), IELTS (minimum score 7.5). *Application deadline:* For fall admission, 12/31 for domestic students, 12/31 priority date for international students. Applications are processed on a rolling basis. Application fee: $75 ($95 for international students). Electronic applications accepted. *Financial support:* In 2010–11, 68 students received support, including 134 fellowships with full tuition reimbursements available (averaging $6,622 per year), 63 research assistantships with full tuition reimbursements available (averaging $6,750 per year), 57 teaching assistantships with full tuition reimbursements available (averaging $6,750 per year); institutionally sponsored loans, scholarships/grants, health care benefits, and unspecified assistantships also available. Financial award application deadline: 12/31. *Faculty research:* Corporate strategy, finance, entrepreneurship, marketing, information and decision science, operations, accounting, quality management. *Unit head:* Dr. Shawn P. Curley, Director of Graduate Studies and PhD Program Director, 612-624-6546, Fax: 612-624-8221, E-mail: curley@umn.edu. *Application contact:* Earlene K. Bronson, Assistant Director, PhD Program, 612-624-0875, Fax: 612-624-8221, E-mail: brons003@umn.edu.

University of Missouri–St. Louis, College of Business Administration, Program in Business Administration, St. Louis, MO 63121. Offers accounting (MBA); business administration (Certificate); finance (MBA); human resource management (Certificate); information systems (MBA); local government (Certificate); logistics and supply chain management (MBA, Certificate); marketing (MBA); marketing management (Certificate); operations management (MBA). *Accreditation:* AACSB. Part-time and evening/weekend programs available. *Faculty:* 30 full-time (5 women), 11 part-time/adjunct (2 women). *Students:* 132 full-time (57 women), 306 part-time (122 women); includes 55 minority (21 Black or African American, non-Hispanic/Latino; 20 Asian, non-Hispanic/Latino; 11 Hispanic/Latino; 1 Native Hawaiian or other Pacific Islander, non-Hispanic/Latino; 2 Two or more races, non-Hispanic/Latino), 6 international. Average age 30. 219 applicants, 60% accepted, 88 enrolled. In 2010, 114 master's, 9 other advanced degrees awarded. *Entrance requirements:* For master's, GMAT, 2 letters of recommendation. Additional exam requirements/recommendations for international students: Required—TOEFL (minimum score 550 paper-based; 213 computer-based). *Application deadline:* For fall admission, 7/1 for domestic students; for spring admission, 11/1 for domestic students. Applications are processed on a rolling basis. Application fee: $35 ($40 for international students). Electronic applications accepted. *Expenses:* Tuition, state resident: full-time $5522; part-time $306.80 per credit hour. Tuition, nonresident: full-time $14,253; part-time $792.10 per credit hour. Required fees: $658; $49 per credit hour. One-time fee: $12. Tuition and fees vary according to program. *Financial support:* In 2010–11, 22 research assistantships with full and partial tuition reimbursements (averaging $7,414 per year), 4 teaching assistantships with full and partial tuition reimbursements (averaging $13,950 per year) were awarded; career-related internships or fieldwork, Federal Work-Study, and institutionally sponsored loans also available. Support available to part-time students. Financial award application deadline: 4/1; financial award applicants required to submit FAFSA. *Faculty research:* Human resources, strategic management, marketing strategy, consumer behavior product development, advertising. *Unit head:* Karl Kottemann, Assistant Director, 314-516-5885, Fax: 314-516-6420, E-mail: mba@umsl.edu. *Application contact:* 314-516-5458, Fax: 314-516-6996, E-mail: gradadm@umsl.edu.

University of New Brunswick Fredericton, School of Graduate Studies, Faculty of Forestry and Environmental Management, Fredericton, NB E3B 5A3, Canada. Offers ecological foundations of forest management (PhD); environmental management (MEM); forest engineering (M Sc FE, MFE); forest products marketing (MBA); forest resources (M Sc F, MF, PhD). Part-time programs available. *Faculty:* 22 full-time (3 women), 1 part-time/adjunct (0 women). *Students:* 68 full-time (29 women), 7 part-time (2 women). In 2010, 20 master's, 4 doctorates awarded. *Degree requirements:* For master's, thesis; for doctorate, thesis/dissertation. *Entrance requirements:* For master's and doctorate, minimum GPA of 3.0. Additional exam requirements/recommendations for international students: Required—TWE (minimum score 4), TOEFL (minimum score 580 paper-based) or IELTS. *Application deadline:* For fall admission, 3/1 priority date for domestic students. Application fee: $50 Canadian dollars. Electronic applications accepted. *Expenses:* Tuition, area resident: Full-time $3708; part-time $927 per term. International tuition: $6300 full-time. Required fees: $50 per term. *Financial support:* In 2010–11, 54 research assistantships, 46 teaching assistantships were awarded. *Faculty research:* Forest machines, soils, and ecosystems; integrated forest management; forest meteorology; wood engineering; stream ecosystems dynamics; forest and natural resources policy; forest operations planning; wood technology and mechanics; forest road construction and engineering; forest, wildlife, insect, bird, and fire ecology; remote sensing; insect impacts; Silviculture; LiDAR analytics; integrated pest management; forest tree genetics; genetic resource conservation and sustainable management. *Unit head:* Dr. John Kershaw, Director of Graduate Studies, 506-453-4933, Fax: 506-453-3538, E-mail: kershaw@unb.ca. *Application contact:* Faith Sharpe, Graduate Secretary, 506-458-7520, Fax: 506-453-3538, E-mail: fsharpe@unb.ca.

University of New Haven, Graduate School, School of Business, Program in Business Administration, West Haven, CT 06516-1916. Offers accounting (MBA, Certificate), including CPA (MBA); business management (Certificate); business policy and strategy (MBA); finance (MBA), including CFA; global marketing (MBA); human resource management (Certificate); human resources management (MBA); international business (Certificate); marketing (Certificate); sports management (MBA); telecommunications management (Certificate); MBA/MPA. Part-time and evening/weekend programs available. *Students:* 158 full-time (80 women), 150 part-time (70 women); includes 36 Black or African American, non-Hispanic/Latino; 2 American Indian or Alaska Native, non-Hispanic/Latino; 19 Asian, non-Hispanic/Latino; 16 Hispanic/Latino, 82 international. Average age 32. 162 applicants, 99% accepted, 85 enrolled. In 2010, 141 master's, 16 other advanced degrees awarded. *Degree requirements:* For master's, thesis or alternative. *Entrance requirements:* For master's, GMAT. Additional exam requirements/recommendations for international students: Required—TOEFL (minimum score 520 paper-based; 190 computer-based; 70 iBT), IELTS (minimum score 5.5). *Application deadline:* For fall admission, 5/31 for international students; for winter admission, 10/15 for international students; for spring admission, 1/15 for international students. Applications are processed on a rolling basis. Application fee: $50. Electronic applications accepted. *Expenses:* Contact institution. *Financial support:* Research assistantships with partial tuition reimbursements, teaching assistantships with partial tuition reimbursements, Federal Work-Study, scholarships/grants, health care benefits, tuition waivers, and unspecified assistantships available. Support available to part-time students. Financial award applicants required to submit FAFSA. *Unit head:* Charles Coleman, Chairman, 203-932-7375. *Application contact:* Eloise Gormley, Director of Graduate Admissions, 203-932-7449, Fax: 203-932-7137, E-mail: gradinfo@newhaven.edu.

The University of North Carolina at Charlotte, Graduate School, Belk College of Business, Program in Business Administration, Charlotte, NC 28223-0001. Offers business administration (PhD); Hong Kong (MBA); MBA-plus (Post-Master's Certificate); Mexico (MBA); real estate finance and development (Certificate); sports marketing and management (MBA); Taiwan (MBA); U. S. (MBA). *Accreditation:* AACSB. Part-time and evening/weekend programs available. *Faculty:* 34 full-time (10 women). *Students:* 142 full-time (55 women), 307 part-time (96 women); includes 69 minority (33 Black or African American, non-Hispanic/Latino; 22 Asian, non-Hispanic/Latino; 12 Hispanic/Latino; 2 Two or more races, non-Hispanic/Latino), 145 international. Average age 30. 265 applicants, 82% accepted, 126 enrolled. In 2010, 227 master's, 1 doctorate awarded. *Degree requirements:* For master's, thesis or alternative; for doctorate, thesis/dissertation. *Entrance requirements:* For master's, GMAT, minimum GPA of 3.0 in undergraduate major, 2.8 overall. Additional exam requirements/recommendations for international students: Required—TOEFL (minimum score 557 paper-based; 220 computer-based; 83 iBT). *Application deadline:* For fall admission, 7/15 for domestic students, 5/1 for international students; for spring admission, 11/15 for domestic students, 10/1 for international students. Applications are processed on a rolling basis. Application fee: $55. Electronic applications accepted. *Expenses:* Tuition, state resident: full-time $3464. Tuition, nonresident: full-time $14,297. Required fees: $2094. Tuition and fees vary according to course load. *Financial support:* In 2010–11, 68 students received support, including 2 research assistantships (averaging $18,000 per year), 65 teaching assistantships (averaging $12,142 per year); career-related internships or fieldwork, Federal Work-Study, institutionally sponsored loans, scholarships/grants, and administrative assistantship also available. Support available to part-time students. Financial award application deadline: 4/1; financial award applicants required to submit FAFSA. Total annual research expenditures: $86,745. *Unit head:* Jeremiah Nelson, Interim Director, MBA Program, 704-687-6058, Fax: 704-687-4014, E-mail: jeremiah.nelson@uncc.edu. *Application contact:* Kathy B. Giddings, Director of Graduate Admissions, 704-687-5503, Fax: 704-687-3279, E-mail: gradadm@uncc.edu.

University of North Texas, Toulouse Graduate School, College of Business Administration, Department of Marketing and Logistics, Denton, TX 76203-5017. Offers PhD. Part-time programs available. *Degree requirements:* For doctorate, comprehensive exam, thesis/dissertation, referred publication. *Entrance requirements:* For doctorate, GMAT (minimum score: 550). Additional exam requirements/recommendations for international students: Recommended—TOEFL (minimum score 550 paper-based; 213 computer-based; 79 iBT). *Application deadline:* Applications are processed on a rolling basis. *Expenses:* Tuition, state resident: full-time $4298; part-time $239 per credit hour. Tuition, nonresident: full-time $10,782; part-time $549 per credit hour. Required fees: $1292; $270 per credit hour. *Financial support:* Fellowships, teaching assistantships, career-related internships or fieldwork, Federal Work-Study, and institutionally sponsored loans available. Financial award applicants required to submit FAFSA. *Faculty research:* Promotion, distribution channels, international distribution, sales management, consumer behavior, services marketing, NPD. *Application contact:* Graduate Advisor, 940-565-4419, Fax: 940-565-3837, E-mail: jeff.lewin@unt.edu.

University of Phoenix, School of Business, Phoenix, AZ 85034-7209. Offers accounting (MBA, MSA); business administration (MBA); energy management (MBA); global management (MBA); health care management (MBA); human resources management (MM); international management

(MM); management (MM); marketing (MBA); project management (MBA); public administration (MPA); technology management (MBA). Programs are offered at the online campus. Evening/weekend programs available. Postbaccalaureate distance learning degree programs offered. *Students:* 20,237 full-time (12,641 women); includes 6,424 minority (4,376 Black or African American, non-Hispanic/Latino; 150 American Indian or Alaska Native, non-Hispanic/Latino; 546 Asian, non-Hispanic/Latino; 1,137 Hispanic/Latino; 155 Native Hawaiian or other Pacific Islander, non-Hispanic/Latino; 60 Two or more races, non-Hispanic/Latino), 1,149 international. Average age 39. *Entrance requirements:* For master's, minimum undergraduate GPA of 2.5 from accredited university, 3 years of work experience, citizen of the United States or have valid visa. Additional exam requirements/recommendations for international students: Required—TOEFL (minimum paper score 550, computer score 213, iBT 79), Test of English for International Communication, or IELTS. *Application deadline:* Applications are processed on a rolling basis. Application fee: $45. Electronic applications accepted. *Expenses:* Tuition: Full-time $16,440. One-time fee: $45 full-time. Full-time tuition and fees vary according to course load, degree level, campus/location and program. *Financial support:* Scholarships/grants available. Financial award applicants required to submit FAFSA. *Unit head:* Dr. Bill Berry, Director, 480-557-1824, E-mail: bill.berry@phoenix.edu. *Application contact:* Dr. Bill Berry, Director, 480-557-1824, E-mail: bill.berry@phoenix.edu.

University of Pittsburgh, Katz Graduate School of Business, Doctoral Program in Business Administration, Pittsburgh, PA 15260. Offers accounting (PhD); finance (PhD); information systems (PhD); marketing (PhD); operations/decision sciences/artificial intelligence (PhD); organizational behavior and human resource management (PhD); strategic planning (PhD). *Accreditation:* AACSB. *Faculty:* 50 full-time (15 women). *Students:* 51 full-time (22 women); includes 3 Black or African American, non-Hispanic/Latino; 4 Asian, non-Hispanic/Latino; 2 Hispanic/Latino, 18 international. 448 applicants, 5% accepted, 13 enrolled. In 2010, 4 doctorates awarded. *Degree requirements:* For doctorate, comprehensive exam, thesis/dissertation. *Entrance requirements:* For doctorate, GMAT or GRE, bachelor's degree, references, minimum GPA of 3.0. Additional exam requirements/recommendations for international students: Required—TOEFL, IELTS. *Application deadline:* For fall admission, 2/1 priority date for domestic and international students. Applications are processed on a rolling basis. Application fee: $50. Electronic applications accepted. *Expenses:* Tuition, state resident: full-time $17,304; part-time $701 per credit. Tuition, nonresident: full-time $29,554; part-time $1210 per credit. Required fees: $740; $214 per term. Tuition and fees vary according to program. *Financial support:* In 2010–11, 39 students received support, including 29 research assistantships with full tuition reimbursements available (averaging $1,900 per year), 10 teaching assistantships with full tuition reimbursements available (averaging $23,745 per year); fellowships, Federal Work-Study, scholarships/grants, health care benefits, and unspecified assistantships also available. Financial award application deadline: 2/1. *Faculty research:* Accounting statements and reporting, incentives and governance, corporate finance, mergers and acquisitions, information systems processes, structures and decision-making, organizational structure, knowledge management and corporate strategy, consumer behavior and marketing models. Total annual research expenditures: $362,777. *Unit head:* Dr. John E. Hulland, Director of Doctoral Program, 412-648-1534, Fax: 412-624-3633, E-mail: jhulland@katz.pitt.edu. *Application contact:* Carrie Woods, Assistant Director, Doctoral Office, 412-648-1525, Fax: 412-624-3633, E-mail: cawoods@katz.pitt.edu.

University of Pittsburgh, Katz Graduate School of Business, Master of Business Administration Programs, Pittsburgh, PA 15260. Offers finance (MBA); information systems (MBA); marketing (MBA); operations management (MBA); organizational behavior and human resource management (MBA); organizational leadership (Certificate); six sigma (Certificate); strategy, environment and organizations (MBA); technology, innovation and entrepreneurship (Certificate); MBA/JD; MBA/MIB; MBA/MPIA; MBA/MSE; MBA/MSIS; MID/MBA. *Accreditation:* AACSB. Part-time and evening/weekend programs available. *Faculty:* 60 full-time (18 women), 22 part-time/adjunct (5 women). *Students:* 232 full-time (75 women), 458 part-time (158 women); includes 34 Black or African American, non-Hispanic/Latino; 1 American Indian or Alaska Native, non-Hispanic/Latino; 20 Asian, non-Hispanic/Latino; 9 Hispanic/Latino, 105 international. Average age 29. 697 applicants, 50% accepted, 174 enrolled. In 2010, 263 master's awarded. *Degree requirements:* For master's, minimum GPA of 3.0. *Entrance requirements:* For master's, GMAT, recommendations, undergraduate transcripts, essay responses, resume, interview, bachelor's degree. Additional exam requirements/recommendations for international students: Required—TOEFL (minimum 600 paper, 250 computer, 100 iBT) or IELTS. *Application deadline:* For fall admission, 4/1 priority date for domestic students, 2/1 priority date for international students. Application fee: $50. Electronic applications accepted. *Expenses:* Tuition, state resident: full-time $17,304; part-time $701 per credit. Tuition, nonresident: full-time $29,554; part-time $1210 per credit. Required fees: $740; $214 per term. Tuition and fees vary according to program. *Financial support:* In 2010–11, 52 students received support. Career-related internships or fieldwork and scholarships/grants available. Financial award application deadline: 3/1; financial award applicants required to submit FAFSA. *Faculty research:* Accounting statements and reporting, incentives and governance, corporate finance, mergers and acquisitions, information systems processes, structures and decision-making, organizational structure, knowledge management and corporate strategy, consumer behavior and marketing models. *Unit head:* William T. Valenta, Assistant Dean, MBA Program Director, 412-648-1610, Fax: 412-648-1659, E-mail: wtvalenta@katz.pitt.edu. *Application contact:* Cliff McCormick, Director MBA Admissions, 412-648-1700, Fax: 412-648-1659, E-mail: mba@katz.pitt.edu.

University of Portland, Dr. Robert B. Pamplin, Jr. School of Business, Portland, OR 97203-5798. Offers business administration (MBA); entrepreneurship (MBA); finance (MBA, MS); health care management (MBA); marketing (MBA); nonprofit management (EMBA); operations and technology management (MBA); sustainability (MBA). *Accreditation:* AACSB. Part-time and evening/weekend programs available. *Faculty:* 12 full-time (2 women), 7 part-time/adjunct (2 women). *Students:* 55 full-time (24 women), 81 part-time (29 women); includes 18 minority (2 Black or African American, non-Hispanic/Latino; 8 Asian, non-Hispanic/Latino; 5 Hispanic/Latino; 3 Two or more races, non-Hispanic/Latino), 23 international. Average age 30. In 2010, 55 master's awarded. *Entrance requirements:* For master's, GMAT, minimum GPA of 3.0, resume, 2 letters of recommendation. Additional exam requirements/recommendations for international students: Required—TOEFL (minimum score 570 paper-based; 89 iBT), IELTS (minimum score 7). *Application deadline:* For fall admission, 7/15 priority date for domestic and international students; for spring admission, 12/15 priority date for domestic and international students. Applications are processed on a rolling basis. Application fee: $50. *Expenses:* Contact institution. *Financial support:* Federal Work-Study, scholarships/grants, and tuition waivers (partial) available. Support available to part-time students. Financial award application deadline: 3/1; financial award applicants required to submit FAFSA. *Unit head:* Dr. Howard Feldman, Associate Dean, 503-943-7224, E-mail: feldman@up.edu. *Application contact:* Melissa McCarthy, Academic Specialist, 503-943-7225, E-mail: mccarthy@up.edu.

University of Rhode Island, Graduate School, College of Business Administration, Kingston, RI 02881. Offers accounting (MS); business administration (MBA, PhD), including finance and insurance (PhD), management (PhD), marketing (PhD), operations and supply chain management (MBA); finance (MBA); general business (MBA); management (MBA); marketing (MBA); supply chain management (MBA). *Accreditation:* AACSB. Part-time and evening/weekend programs available. *Faculty:* 54 full-time (15 women), 3 part-time/adjunct (2 women). *Students:* 82 full-time (31 women), 218 part-time (77 women); includes 31 minority (6 Black or African American, non-Hispanic/Latino; 1 American Indian or Alaska Native, non-Hispanic/Latino; 13 Asian, non-Hispanic/Latino; 11 Hispanic/Latino), 29 international. In 2010, 78 master's, 3 doctorates awarded. *Degree requirements:* For master's, comprehensive exam (for some programs), thesis optional; for doctorate, comprehensive exam, thesis/dissertation. *Entrance requirements:* For master's, GMAT or GRE, 2 letters of recommendation, resume; for doctorate, GMAT or GRE, 3 letters of recommendation, resume. Additional exam requirements/recommendations for international students: Required—TOEFL (minimum score 575 paper-based; 233 computer-based; 91 iBT). Application fee: $65. Electronic applications accepted. *Expenses:* Tuition, state resident: full-time $9588; part-time $533 per credit hour. Tuition, nonresident: full-time $22,968; part-time $1276 per credit hour. Required fees: $1282; $68 per semester. Tuition and fees vary according to program. *Financial support:* In 2010–11, 13 teaching assistantships with full and partial tuition reimbursements (averaging $12,432 per year) were awarded. Financial award applicants required to submit FAFSA. Total annual research expenditures: $9,928. *Unit head:* Dr. Mark Higgins, Dean, 401-874-4244, Fax: 401-874-4312, E-mail: markhiggins@uri.edu. *Application contact:* Lisa Lancellotta, Coordinator, MBA Programs, 401-874-4241, Fax: 401-874-4312, E-mail: mba@uri.edu.

University of San Francisco, School of Business and Professional Studies, Masagung Graduate School of Management, Program in Business Administration, San Francisco, CA 94117-1080. Offers business economics (MBA); e-business (MBA); entrepreneurship (MBA); finance (MBA); international business (MBA); management (MBA); marketing (MBA); telecommunications management and policy (MBA); JD/MBA; MSN/MBA. *Accreditation:* AACSB. *Faculty:* 17 full-time (4 women), 16 part-time/adjunct (7 women). *Students:* 263 full-time (130 women), 11 part-time (6 women); includes 98 minority (3 Black or African American, non-Hispanic/Latino; 65 Asian, non-Hispanic/Latino; 18 Hispanic/Latino; 3 Native Hawaiian or other Pacific Islander, non-Hispanic/Latino; 9 Two or more races, non-Hispanic/Latino), 43 international. Average age 29. 503 applicants, 60% accepted, 80 enrolled. In 2010, 115 master's awarded. *Entrance requirements:* For master's, GMAT, minimum undergraduate GPA of 3.2. Additional exam requirements/recommendations for international students: Required—TOEFL. *Application deadline:* For fall admission, 7/1 priority date for domestic students; for spring admission, 11/30 for domestic students. Applications are processed on a rolling basis. Application fee: $55 ($65 for international students). *Expenses:* Tuition: Full-time $20,070; part-time $1115 per credit hour. Tuition and fees vary according to course load, degree level and program. *Financial support:* In 2010–11, 156 students received support; fellowships available. Financial award application deadline: 3/2; financial award applicants required to submit FAFSA. *Faculty research:* International financial markets, technology transfer

licensing, international marketing, strategic planning. Total annual research expenditures: $50,000. *Unit head:* Kelly Brookes, Director, 415-422-2221, Fax: 415-422-6315. *Application contact:* Director, MBA Program, 415-422-2221, Fax: 415-422-6315, E-mail: mba@usfca.edu.

The University of Scranton, College of Graduate and Continuing Education, Program in Business Administration, Scranton, PA 18510. Offers accounting (MBA); finance (MBA); general business administration (MBA); health care management (MBA); international business (MBA); management information systems (MBA); marketing (MBA); operations management (MBA). *Accreditation:* AACSB. Part-time and evening/weekend programs available. Postbaccalaureate distance learning degree programs offered (no on-campus study). *Faculty:* 34 full-time (8 women). *Students:* 251 full-time (91 women), 180 part-time (72 women); includes 41 Black or African American, non-Hispanic/Latino; 11 Asian, non-Hispanic/Latino; 7 Hispanic/Latino, 40 international. Average age 32. 386 applicants, 84% accepted. In 2010, 38 master's awarded. *Degree requirements:* For master's, capstone experience. *Entrance requirements:* For master's, GMAT, minimum GPA of 2.75. Additional exam requirements/recommendations for international students: Required—TOEFL (minimum score 500 paper-based; 173 computer-based), IELTS (minimum score 5.5). *Application deadline:* Applications are processed on a rolling basis. Application fee: $0. *Financial support:* In 2010–11, 13 students received support, including 13 teaching assistantships with full and partial tuition reimbursements available (averaging $6,430 per year); fellowships, career-related internships or fieldwork, Federal Work-Study, and unspecified assistantships also available. Support available to part-time students. Financial award application deadline: 3/1. *Faculty research:* Financial markets, strategic impact of total quality management, internal accounting controls, consumer preference, information systems and the Internet. *Unit head:* Dr. Murli Rajan, Director, 570-941-4043, Fax: 570-941-4342. *Application contact:* Joseph M. Roback, Director of Admissions, 570-941-4385, Fax: 570-941-5928, E-mail: robackj2@scranton.edu.

University of South Florida, Graduate School, College of Business, Department of Business Administration, Tampa, FL 33620-9951. Offers accounting (PhD); entrepreneurship (MBA); finance (PhD); information systems (PhD); leadership and organizational effectiveness (MSM); management and organization (MSM); marketing (PhD). *Accreditation:* AACSB. Part-time and evening/weekend programs available. *Faculty:* 1 (woman) full-time. *Students:* 148 full-time (48 women), 190 part-time (61 women); includes 70 minority (7 Black or African American, non-Hispanic/Latino; 1 American Indian or Alaska Native, non-Hispanic/Latino; 26 Asian, non-Hispanic/Latino; 36 Hispanic/Latino), 62 international. Average age 30. 452 applicants, 29% accepted, 80 enrolled. In 2010, 146 master's, 5 doctorates awarded. *Degree requirements:* For master's, comprehensive exam, thesis (for some programs); for doctorate, comprehensive exam, thesis/dissertation, 90 credit hours, minimum GPA of 3.0. *Entrance requirements:* For master's, GMAT, minimum GPA of 3.0 in last 60 hours of course work, 2 years of work experience, resume; for doctorate, GMAT, letters of recommendation, personal statement. Additional exam requirements/recommendations for international students: Required—TOEFL (minimum score 550 paper-based; 213 computer-based; 79 iBT). *Application deadline:* For fall admission, 6/1 for domestic students, 1/2 for international students; for spring admission, 10/15 for domestic students, 6/1 for international students. Application fee: $30. *Financial support:* Scholarships/grants, health care benefits, and unspecified assistantships available. Financial award applicants required to submit FAFSA. *Unit head:* Irene Hurst, Program Director, 813-974-3335, Fax: 813-974-4518, E-mail: hurst@coba.usf.edu. *Application contact:* Wendy Baker, Assistant Director, Graduate Studies, 813-974-3335, Fax: 813-974-4518, E-mail: wbaker@usf.edu.

University of South Florida, Graduate School, College of Business, Department of Marketing, Tampa, FL 33620-9951. Offers business administration (PhD), including marketing; marketing (MSM). Part-time and evening/weekend programs available. *Faculty:* 1 (woman) full-time. *Students:* 22 full-time (15 women), 12 part-time (10 women); includes 2 Black or African American, non-Hispanic/Latino; 1 American Indian or Alaska Native, non-Hispanic/Latino; 2 Asian, non-Hispanic/Latino; 4 Hispanic/Latino; 1 Two or more races, non-Hispanic/Latino, 5 international. Average age 29. 54 applicants, 43% accepted, 12 enrolled. In 2010, 4 master's, 1 doctorate awarded. Terminal master's awarded for partial completion of doctoral program. *Degree requirements:* For master's, thesis (for some programs); for doctorate, comprehensive exam, thesis/dissertation, 90 credit hours, minimum GPA of 3.0. *Entrance requirements:* For master's, GMAT, letter of recommendation, work experience (desirable); for doctorate, GMAT, letter of recommendation. Additional exam requirements/recommendations for international students: Required—TOEFL (minimum score 550 paper-based; 213 computer-based; 79 iBT). *Application deadline:* For fall admission, 6/1 for domestic students, 1/2 for international students; for spring admission, 10/15 for domestic students, 6/1 for international students. Applications are processed on a rolling basis. Application fee: $30. Electronic applications accepted. *Financial support:* In 2010–11, 5 research assistantships (averaging $14,943 per year), 5 teaching assistantships (averaging $14,942 per year) were awarded; health care benefits and unspecified assistantships also available. *Faculty research:* Consumer behavior, supply chain management, reverse logistics (product returns), pricing, branding. Total annual research expenditures: $56,918. *Unit head:* Dr. Miriam Stamps, Chairperson, 813-974-6205, Fax: 813-974-6175, E-mail: mstamps@usf.edu. *Application contact:* Dr. Paul Solomon, Professor, 813-974-5995, Fax: 813-974-6175, E-mail: psolomon@usf.edu.

The University of Tampa, John H. Sykes College of Business, Tampa, FL 33606-1490. Offers accounting (MS); entrepreneurship (MBA); finance (MBA, MS); information systems management (MBA); innovation management (MBA); international business (MBA); marketing (MBA, MS); nonprofit management (MBA). *Accreditation:* AACSB. Part-time and evening/weekend programs available. *Faculty:* 67 full-time (24 women), 11 part-time/adjunct (4 women). *Students:* 235 full-time (89 women), 288 part-time (122 women); includes 74 minority (16 Black or African American, non-Hispanic/Latino; 2 American Indian or Alaska Native, non-Hispanic/Latino; 14 Asian, non-Hispanic/Latino; 34 Hispanic/Latino; 2 Native Hawaiian or other Pacific Islander, non-Hispanic/Latino; 6 Two or more races, non-Hispanic/Latino), 95 international. Average age 29. 457 applicants, 45% accepted, 175 enrolled. In 2010, 230 master's awarded. *Degree requirements:* For master's, capstone. *Entrance requirements:* For master's, GMAT or GRE, 4-year undergraduate degree, minimum GPA of 3.0, professional experience (for Executive MBA). Additional exam requirements/recommendations for international students: Required—TOEFL (minimum score 577 paper-based; 230 computer-based; 90 iBT); Recommended—IELTS (minimum score 7.5). *Application deadline:* Applications are processed on a rolling basis. Application fee: $40. Electronic applications accepted. *Expenses:* Tuition: Part-time $504 per credit hour. Required fees: $40 per term. *Financial support:* In 2010–11, 74 students received support. Career-related internships or fieldwork, scholarships/grants, unspecified assistantships, and grants available. Financial award applicants required to submit FAFSA. *Faculty research:* Management innovation, social marketing, value relevance of earnings and book value across industries, managerial finance, entrepreneurship. *Unit head:* Dennis Nostrand, Vice President, Enrollment/Admissions, 813-257-1808, E-mail: dnostrand@ut.edu. *Application contact:* Charlene Tobie, Associate Director of Admissions, 813-257-3566, E-mail: ctobie@ut.edu.

The University of Texas at Arlington, Graduate School, College of Business, Department of Marketing, Arlington, TX 76019. Offers marketing (PhD); marketing research (MS). Part-time programs available. *Faculty:* 7 full-time (1 woman). *Students:* 27 full-time (16 women), 12 part-time (5 women); includes 3 minority (1 Black or African American, non-Hispanic/Latino; 1 Asian, non-Hispanic/Latino; 1 Hispanic/Latino), 20 international. 41 applicants, 44% accepted, 11 enrolled. In 2010, 11 master's, 1 doctorate awarded. *Degree requirements:* For master's, thesis optional; for doctorate, comprehensive exam, thesis/dissertation. *Entrance requirements:* For master's, GMAT, GRE. Additional exam requirements/recommendations for international students: Required—TOEFL (minimum score 550 paper-based; 213 computer-based; 79 iBT). *Application deadline:* For fall admission, 6/1 for domestic students, 4/1 for international students; for spring admission, 10/15 for domestic students, 9/15 for international students. Applications are processed on a rolling basis. Application fee: $35 ($50 for international students). Electronic applications accepted. *Expenses:* Tuition, state resident: full-time $7500. Tuition, nonresident: full-time $13,080. International tuition: $13,250 full-time. *Financial support:* In 2010–11, 8 teaching assistantships (averaging $14,000 per year) were awarded; career-related internships or fieldwork, scholarships/grants, and unspecified assistantships also available. Support available to part-time students. Financial award application deadline: 6/1; financial award applicants required to submit FAFSA. *Faculty research:* Marketing strategy, marketing research, international marketing. Total annual research expenditures: $30,000. *Unit head:* Dr. Greg Frazier, Interim Chair, 817-272-0264, Fax: 817-272-2854, E-mail: frazier@uta.edu. *Application contact:* Dr. Robert Rogers, MS Program Director, 817-272-2340, Fax: 817-272-2854, E-mail: msmr@uta.edu.

The University of Texas at Arlington, Graduate School, College of Business, Program in Business Administration, Arlington, TX 76019. Offers accounting (PhD); business statistics (PhD); finance (MBA, PhD); information systems (MBA, PhD); management (MBA, PhD); marketing (MBA, PhD); operations management (MBA, PhD); real estate (MBA). *Accreditation:* AACSB. Part-time and evening/weekend programs available. Postbaccalaureate distance learning degree programs offered (no on-campus study). *Students:* 555 full-time (197 women), 378 part-time (144 women); includes 179 minority (55 Black or African American, non-Hispanic/Latino; 1 American Indian or Alaska Native, non-Hispanic/Latino; 58 Asian, non-Hispanic/Latino; 55 Hispanic/Latino; 10 Two or more races, non-Hispanic/Latino), 410 international. 317 applicants, 93% accepted, 196 enrolled. In 2010, 468 master's, 1 doctorate awarded. Terminal master's awarded for partial completion of doctoral program. *Degree requirements:* For master's, thesis optional; for doctorate, comprehensive exam, thesis/dissertation. *Entrance requirements:* For master's, GMAT or GRE; for doctorate, GMAT, minimum GPA of 3.0 (undergraduate), 3.4 (graduate); 30 hours of graduate course work. Additional exam requirements/recommendations for international students: Required—TOEFL (minimum score 550 paper-based; 213 computer-based; 79 iBT). *Application deadline:* For fall admission, 6/1 for domestic students, 4/1 for international students; for spring admission, 10/15 for domestic students, 9/15 for international students. Applications are processed on a rolling basis. Application

fee: $35 ($50 for international students). Electronic applications accepted. *Expenses:* Tuition, state resident: full-time $7500. Tuition, nonresident: full-time $13,080. International tuition: $13,250 full-time. *Financial support:* Career-related internships or fieldwork, scholarships/grants, and unspecified assistantships available. Financial award application deadline: 6/1; financial award applicants required to submit FAFSA. *Unit head:* Dr. Edmund Prater, Director of PhD Programs, 817-272-2131, Fax: 817-272-5799. *Application contact:* Melanie McGee, Director of MBA Program, 817-272-3005, Fax: 817-272-5799, E-mail: mwmcgee@uta.edu.

The University of Texas at Dallas, School of Management, Program in Management and Administrative Sciences, Richardson, TX 75080. Offers electronic commerce (MS); finance (MS); healthcare administration (MS); information systems (MS); innovation and entrepreneurship (MS); international management (MS); leadership in organizations (MS); marketing (MS); operations (MS); organizations (MS); real estate (MS); strategy (MS). *Accreditation:* AACSB. Part-time and evening/weekend programs available. *Faculty:* 18 full-time (3 women), 8 part-time/adjunct (0 women). *Students:* 57 full-time (32 women), 107 part-time (49 women); includes 53 minority (14 Black or African American, non-Hispanic/Latino; 30 Asian, non-Hispanic/Latino; 8 Hispanic/Latino; 1 Two or more races, non-Hispanic/Latino), 25 international. Average age 32. 161 applicants, 67% accepted, 51 enrolled. In 2010, 27 master's awarded. *Degree requirements:* For master's, thesis optional. *Entrance requirements:* For master's, GMAT. Additional exam requirements/recommendations for international students: Required—TOEFL (minimum score 550 paper-based; 215 computer-based). *Application deadline:* For fall admission, 7/15 for domestic students, 5/1 priority date for international students; for spring admission, 11/15 for domestic students, 9/1 priority date for international students. Applications are processed on a rolling basis. Application fee: $50 ($100 for international students). Electronic applications accepted. *Expenses:* Tuition, state resident: full-time $10,248; part-time $569 per credit hour. Tuition, nonresident: full-time $18,544; part-time $1030 per credit hour. Tuition and fees vary according to course load. *Financial support:* In 2010–11, 26 students received support, including 38 teaching assistantships with partial tuition reimbursements available (averaging $11,528 per year); research assistantships with partial tuition reimbursements available, career-related internships or fieldwork, Federal Work-Study, institutionally sponsored loans, scholarships/grants, and unspecified assistantships also available. Support available to part-time students. Financial award application deadline: 4/30; financial award applicants required to submit FAFSA. *Faculty research:* Integrated and detailed knowledge of functional areas of management, analytical tools for effective appraisal and decision making. *Unit head:* Dr. Doug Eckel, Assistant Dean, 972-883-5923, E-mail: doug.eckel@utdallas.edu. *Application contact:* James Parker, Assistant Director, 972-883-5842, E-mail: jparker@utdallas.edu.

The University of Texas at Dallas, School of Management, Programs in Management Science, Richardson, TX 75080. Offers accounting (PhD); finance (PhD); information systems (PhD); marketing (PhD); operations management (PhD). *Accreditation:* AACSB. Part-time and evening/weekend programs available. *Faculty:* 12 full-time (3 women), 3 part-time/adjunct (0 women). *Students:* 77 full-time (27 women), 11 part-time (4 women); includes 5 minority (all Asian, non-Hispanic/Latino), 72 international. Average age 32. 223 applicants, 9% accepted. In 2010, 16 doctorates awarded. *Degree requirements:* For doctorate, thesis/dissertation. *Entrance requirements:* For doctorate, GMAT, minimum GPA of 3.0. Additional exam requirements/recommendations for international students: Required—TOEFL (minimum score 550 paper-based; 215 computer-based). *Application deadline:* For fall admission, 7/15 for domestic students, 5/1 priority date for international students; for spring admission, 11/15 for domestic students, 9/1 priority date for international students. Applications are processed on a rolling basis. Application fee: $50 ($100 for international students). Electronic applications accepted. *Expenses:* Tuition, state resident: full-time $10,248; part-time $569 per credit hour. Tuition, nonresident: full-time $18,544; part-time $1030 per credit hour. Tuition and fees vary according to course load. *Financial support:* In 2010–11, 56 students received support, including 1 research assistantship with partial tuition reimbursement available (averaging $13,050 per year), 58 teaching assistantships with partial tuition reimbursements available (averaging $14,772 per year); career-related internships or fieldwork, Federal Work-Study, institutionally sponsored loans, scholarships/grants, and unspecified assistantships also available. Support available to part-time students. Financial award application deadline: 4/30; financial award applicants required to submit FAFSA. *Faculty research:* Empirical generalizations in marketing, diffusion of generations of technology, stochastic brand-choice theory, acceptance of trade deals by supermarkets, nonparametric estimations of market share response. *Unit head:* Dr. Sumit Sarkar, Program Director, 972-883-2745, Fax: 972-883-5977, E-mail: som phd.@utdallas.edu. Application contact: Dr. LeeAnne Sloane, Program Coordinator, 972-883-2745, Fax: 972-883-5977, E-mail: som_phd@utdallas.edu.

The University of Texas at San Antonio, College of Business, General Business Program, San Antonio, TX 78249-0617. Offers accounting (PhD); business (MBA); finance (PhD); information systems (MBA); information technology (PhD); international business (MBA); management accounting (MBA); management and organization studies (PhD); management of technology (MBA); marketing (PhD); marketing management (MBA); taxation (MBA). Part-time and evening/weekend programs available. *Students:* 159 full-time (59 women), 124 part-time (43 women); includes 82 minority (9 Black or African American, non-Hispanic/Latino; 2 American Indian or Alaska Native, non-Hispanic/Latino; 17 Asian, non-Hispanic/Latino; 50 Hispanic/Latino; 1 Native Hawaiian or other Pacific Islander, non-Hispanic/Latino; 3 Two or more races, non-Hispanic/Latino), 39 international. Average age 32. 330 applicants, 46% accepted, 105 enrolled. In 2010, 85 master's, 9 doctorates awarded. *Degree requirements:* For master's, comprehensive exam (for some programs), thesis (for some programs). *Entrance requirements:* For master's, GMAT. Additional exam requirements/recommendations for international students: Required—TOEFL (minimum score 500 paper-based; 173 computer-based; 61 iBT), IELTS (minimum score 5). *Application deadline:* For fall admission, 7/1 for domestic students, 4/1 for international students; for spring admission, 11/1 for domestic students, 9/1 for international students. Application fee: $45 ($80 for international students). *Expenses:* Tuition, state resident: full-time $4172; part-time $231.75 per credit hour. Tuition, nonresident: full-time $15,332; part-time $851.75 per credit hour. *Financial support:* In 2010–11, 282 research assistantships (averaging $13,930 per year), 74 teaching assistantships (averaging $9,284 per year) were awarded; scholarships/grants, tuition waivers, and unspecified assistantships also available. Support available to part-time students. *Unit head:* Dr. Lynda Y. de la Vinna, Dean, 210-458-4317, Fax: 210-458-4308, E-mail: lynda.delavina@utsa.edu. *Application contact:* Veronica Ramirez, Assistant Dean of the Graduate School, 210-458-4330, Fax: 210-458-4332, E-mail: graduatestudies@utsa.edu.

University of the Cumberlands, Graduate Programs in Education, Williamsburg, KY 40769-1372. Offers all grades (P-12) (M Ed); business and marketing (MA Ed, MAT); director of pupil personnel (Certificate); director of special education (Certificate); educational administration and supervision (Ed S); educational leadership (Ed D); elementary education (MA Ed, MAT); instructional leadership—principalship (MA Ed); instructional leadership—school principal (Certificate); middle school education (MA Ed, MAT); reading and writing (MA Ed); school counseling (MA Ed); school superintendent (Certificate); secondary education (MA Ed, MAT); special education (MAT); supervisor of instruction (Certificate); teacher leader (MA Ed). Part-time and evening/weekend programs available. Postbaccalaureate distance learning degree programs offered. *Faculty:* 33 full-time (15 women), 26 part-time/adjunct (12 women). *Students:* 1,198 full-time (818 women), 260 part-time (168 women); includes 44 Black or African American, non-Hispanic/Latino; 4 American Indian or Alaska Native, non-Hispanic/Latino; 7 Asian, non-Hispanic/Latino; 10 Hispanic/Latino, 2 international. Average age 33. In 2010, 291 master's, 97 other advanced degrees awarded. *Degree requirements:* For master's, comprehensive exam. *Application deadline:* Applications are processed on a rolling basis. Application fee: $30. Electronic applications accepted. *Expenses:* Tuition: Full-time $6984; part-time $291 per credit hour. Required fees: $50 per term. Tuition and fees vary according to course level, course load and program. *Financial support:* Unspecified assistantships available. *Unit head:* Dr. Robert Heffern, Department Chair, 800-549-2200 Ext. 4588, Fax: 606-539-4588, E-mail: robert.heffern@ucumberlands.edu. *Application contact:* Donna Stanfill, Director of Graduate Admissions, 606-539-4390.

University of Virginia, McIntire School of Commerce, Program in Commerce, Charlottesville, VA 22903. Offers financial services (MSC); marketing and management (MSC). *Students:* 85 full-time (36 women); includes 4 Asian, non-Hispanic/Latino; 3 Hispanic/Latino; 4 Two or more races, non-Hispanic/Latino, 11 international. Average age 22. 193 applicants, 68% accepted. In 2010, 42 master's awarded. *Entrance requirements:* For master's, GMAT, 2 letters of recommendation; prerequisite course work in financial accounting, microeconomics, and introduction to business. Additional exam requirements/recommendations for international students: Required—TOEFL (minimum score 600 paper-based; 250 computer-based; 100 iBT), IELTS (minimum score 7). *Application deadline:* For fall admission, 9/15 priority date for domestic students, 1/15 priority date for international students. Applications are processed on a rolling basis. Application fee: $75. Electronic applications accepted. *Expenses:* Contact institution. *Financial support:* Scholarships/grants available. Financial award application deadline: 3/1; financial award applicants required to submit CSS PROFILE or FAFSA. *Unit head:* Ira C. Harris, Head, 434-924-8816, Fax: 434-924-7074, E-mail: ich3x@comm.virginia.edu. *Application contact:* Emma Jean Candelier, Assistant Director, Commerce Graduate Marketing and Admissions, 434-243-4992, Fax: 434-924-7074, E-mail: mscommerce@virginia.edu.

University of Wisconsin–Madison, Graduate School, Wisconsin School of Business, Doctoral Program in Marketing, Madison, WI 53706-1380. Offers PhD. *Faculty:* 13 full-time (3 women), 2 part-time/adjunct (0 women). *Students:* 9 full-time (7 women); includes 1 Asian, non-Hispanic/Latino, 4 international. Average age 31. 59 applicants, 3% accepted, 2 enrolled. In 2010, 1 doctorate awarded. *Degree requirements:* For doctorate, comprehensive exam, thesis/dissertation. *Entrance requirements:* For doctorate, GMAT or GRE. Additional exam requirements/recommendations for international students: Required—Pearson Test of English (minimum score 73, written 80); Recommended—TOEFL (minimum score 623 paper-based; 263

computer-based; 106 iBT), IELTS (minimum score 7.5). *Application deadline:* For fall admission, 12/15 priority date for domestic and international students. Application fee: $56. Electronic applications accepted. *Expenses:* Tuition, state resident: full-time $9887; part-time $617.96 per credit. Tuition, nonresident: full-time $24,054; part-time $1503.40 per credit. Required fees: $67.63 per credit. Tuition and fees vary according to reciprocity agreements. *Financial support:* In 2010–11, 9 students received support, including fellowships with full tuition reimbursements available (averaging $18,756 per year), research assistantships with full tuition reimbursements available (averaging $16,506 per year), 8 teaching assistantships with full tuition reimbursements available (averaging $14,088 per year); Federal Work-Study, institutionally sponsored loans, scholarships/grants, health care benefits, and unspecified assistantships also available. Financial award application deadline: 2/1; financial award applicants required to submit FAFSA. *Faculty research:* Marketing strategy, consumer behavior, channels of distribution, advertising, price promotions. *Unit head:* Prof. Jack Nevin, Chair, 608-262-8912, Fax: 608-262-0394, E-mail: jnevin@bus.wisc.edu. *Application contact:* Belle Heberling, Assistant Director for Research Programs, 608-262-3749, Fax: 608-890-0180, E-mail: phd@bus.wisc.edu.

Villanova University, Villanova School of Business, MBA—The Fast Track Program, Villanova, PA 19085. Offers finance (MBA); health care management (MBA); international business (MBA); management information systems (MBA); marketing (MBA); real estate (MBA); strategic management (MBA). *Accreditation:* AACSB. Part-time and evening/weekend programs available. *Faculty:* 15 full-time (2 women), 5 part-time/adjunct (0 women). *Students:* 118 part-time (34 women); includes 13 minority (2 Black or African American, non-Hispanic/Latino; 8 Asian, non-Hispanic/Latino; 3 Hispanic/Latino). Average age 30. In 2010, 35 master's awarded. *Degree requirements:* For master's, minimum GPA of 3.0. *Entrance requirements:* For master's, GMAT. Additional exam requirements/recommendations for international students: Required—TOEFL (minimum score 550 paper-based; 213 computer-based; 80 iBT). *Application deadline:* For fall admission, 6/30 for domestic and international students. Application fee: $50. Electronic applications accepted. *Expenses:* Tuition: Part-time $700 per credit. Part-time tuition and fees vary according to degree level and program. *Financial support:* Scholarships/grants available. Support available to part-time students. Financial award application deadline: 6/30; financial award applicants required to submit FAFSA. *Faculty research:* Developing and leveraging technology, ethical business practices, managing for innovation and creativity, the global political economy, strategic marketing management. *Unit head:* Meredith L. Kwiatek, Director of Graduate Recruitment & Marketing, 610-519-7016, Fax: 610-519-6273, E-mail: rachel.garonzik@villanova.edu. *Application contact:* Meredith L. Kwiatek, Assistant Director, 610-519-7016, Fax: 610-519-6273, E-mail: meredith.kwiatek@villanova.edu.

Villanova University, Villanova School of Business, MBA—The Flex Track Program, Villanova, PA 19085. Offers finance (MBA); health care management (MBA); international business (MBA); management information systems (MBA); marketing (MBA); real estate (MBA); strategic management (MBA); JD/MBA. *Accreditation:* AACSB. Part-time and evening/weekend programs available. Postbaccalaureate distance learning degree programs offered (minimal on-campus study). *Faculty:* 31 full-time (5 women), 22 part-time/adjunct (2 women). *Students:* 15 full-time (6 women), 443 part-time (150 women); includes 46 minority (5 Black or African American, non-Hispanic/Latino; 35 Asian, non-Hispanic/Latino; 6 Hispanic/Latino). Average age 30. In 2010, 133 master's awarded. *Degree requirements:* For master's, minimum GPA of 3.0. *Entrance requirements:* For master's, GMAT. Additional exam requirements/recommendations for international students: Required—TOEFL (minimum score 550 paper-based; 213 computer-based; 80 iBT). *Application deadline:* For fall admission, 6/30 for domestic and international students; for winter admission, 11/15 for domestic and international students; for spring admission, 3/30 for domestic students, 3/31 for international students. Applications are processed on a rolling basis. Application fee: $50. Electronic applications accepted. *Expenses:* Tuition: Part-time $700 per credit. Part-time tuition and fees vary according to degree level and program. *Financial support:* In 2010–11, 15 research assistantships with full tuition reimbursements (averaging $13,100 per year) were awarded; scholarships/grants and unspecified assistantships also available. Support available to part-time students. Financial award application deadline: 6/30; financial award applicants required to submit FAFSA. *Faculty research:* Developing and leveraging technology, ethical business practices, managing for innovation and creativity, the global political economy, strategic marketing management. *Unit head:* Meredith L. Kwiatek, Director of Graduate Recruitment and Marketing, 610-519-7016, Fax: 610-519-6273, E-mail: meredith.kwiatek@villanova.edu. *Application contact:* Meredith L. Kwiatek, Assistant Director, 610-519-7016, Fax: 610-519-6273, E-mail: meredith.kwiatek@villanova.edu.

Virginia Commonwealth University, Graduate School, School of Business, Program in Marketing and Business Law, Richmond, VA 23284-9005. Offers MS. *Faculty:* 9 full-time (3 women). *Entrance requirements:* For master's, GMAT. Additional exam requirements/recommendations for international students: Required—TOEFL (minimum score 600 paper-based; 250 computer-based; 100 iBT); Recommended—IELTS (minimum score 6.5). *Application deadline:* For fall admission, 6/1 for domestic students; for spring admission,

11/1 for domestic students. Applications are processed on a rolling basis. Application fee: $50. Electronic applications accepted. *Expenses:* Tuition, state resident: full-time $4308; part-time $479 per credit hour. Tuition, nonresident: full-time $8942; part-time $994 per credit hour. Required fees: $2000; $85 per credit hour. Tuition and fees vary according to course level, course load, degree level, campus/location and program. *Financial support:* Fellowships, research assistantships, teaching assistantships, Federal Work-Study, institutionally sponsored loans, and tuition waivers (full and partial) available. Financial award application deadline: 3/15; financial award applicants required to submit FAFSA. *Unit head:* Dr. Michael W. Little, Chair, 804-828-3190, E-mail: mwlittle@vcu.edu. *Application contact:* Jana P. McQuaid, Assistant Dean, Masters Programs, 804-828-4622, Fax: 804-828-7174, E-mail: jpmcquaid@vcu.edu.

Virginia Polytechnic Institute and State University, Graduate School, Pamplin College of Business, Department of Marketing, Blacksburg, VA 24061. Offers MS, PhD. *Faculty:* 15 full-time (7 women). *Students:* 7 full-time (4 women), 3 international. Average age 31. 17 applicants, 12% accepted, 2 enrolled. In 2010, 1 doctorate awarded. *Degree requirements:* For master's, comprehensive exam (for some programs), thesis (for some programs); for doctorate, comprehensive exam (for some programs), thesis/dissertation (for some programs). *Entrance requirements:* For master's and doctorate, GRE. Additional exam requirements/recommendations for international students: Required—TOEFL (minimum score 550 paper-based; 213 computer-based). *Application deadline:* For fall admission, 7/1 for domestic and international students; for spring admission, 12/1 for domestic and international students. Applications are processed on a rolling basis. Application fee: $65. Electronic applications accepted. *Expenses:* Tuition, state resident: full-time $9399; part-time $488 per credit hour. Tuition, nonresident: full-time $17,854; part-time $957.75 per credit hour. Required fees: $1534. Full-time tuition and fees vary according to program. *Financial support:* In 2010–11, 6 teaching assistantships with full tuition reimbursements (averaging $13,692 per year) were awarded; career-related internships or fieldwork, Federal Work-Study, scholarships/grants, health care benefits, and unspecified assistantships also available. Financial award application deadline: 1/15; financial award applicants required to submit CSS PROFILE. *Faculty research:* Consumer behavior, marketing research, channels of distribution, advertising, marketing strategy. Total annual research expenditures: $117,647. *Unit head:* Dr. Kent Nakamoto, UNIT HEAD, 540-231-6949, Fax: 540-231-4487, E-mail: nakamoto@vt.edu. *Application contact:* David Brinberg, Contact, 540-231-7639, Fax: 540-231-4487, E-mail: dbrinber@vt.edu.

Wagner College, Division of Graduate Studies, Department of Business Administration, Program in Marketing, Staten Island, NY 10301-4495. Offers MBA. Part-time and evening/weekend programs available. *Faculty:* 1 (woman) part-time/adjunct. *Students:* 8 full-time (5 women), 6 part-time (2 women); includes 2 minority (both Hispanic/Latino), 1 international. Average age 30. 9 applicants, 100% accepted, 5 enrolled. In 2010, 7 master's awarded. *Degree requirements:* For master's, thesis optional. *Entrance requirements:* For master's, GMAT, minimum GPA of 2.6. Additional exam requirements/recommendations for international students: Required—TOEFL (minimum score 550 paper-based; 217 computer-based; 79 iBT). *Application deadline:* For fall admission, 4/1 priority date for domestic students, 3/1 priority date for international students; for spring admission, 11/1 priority date for domestic students, 10/1 priority date for international students. Applications are processed on a rolling basis. Application fee: $50 ($80 for international students). *Expenses:* Tuition: Full-time $15,570; part-time $865 per credit. *Financial support:* Career-related internships or fieldwork, unspecified assistantships, and alumni fellowship grant available. Financial award applicants required to submit FAFSA. *Unit head:* Prof. Donald Crooks, Director, 718-390-3429, Fax: 718-420-4274, E-mail: dcrooks@wagner.edu. *Application contact:* Patricia Clancy, Assistant Coordinator of Graduate Studies, 718-420-4464, Fax: 718-390-3105, E-mail: patricia.clancy@wagner.edu.

Wake Forest University, Schools of Business, Full-time MBA Program, Winston-Salem, NC 27106. Offers consulting/general management (MBA); entrepreneurship (MBA); finance (MBA); health (MBA); marketing (MBA); operations management (MBA); JD/MBA; MD/MBA; MSA/MBA. *Accreditation:* AACSB. *Faculty:* 63 full-time (17 women), 30 part-time/adjunct (9 women). *Students:* 123 full-time (22 women); includes 9 Black or African American, non-Hispanic/Latino; 4 Asian, non-Hispanic/Latino; 2 Hispanic/Latino; 1 Two or more races, non-Hispanic/Latino, 25 international. Average age 28. In 2010, 83 master's awarded. *Degree requirements:* For master's, 65.5 total credit hours. *Entrance requirements:* For master's, GMAT or GRE, letters of recommendation, official transcripts, current resume or curriculum vitae, 2 years of work experience. Additional exam requirements/recommendations for international students: Required—TOEFL (minimum score 600 paper-based; 250 computer-based; 100 iBT), Pearson Test of English (PTE). *Application deadline:* For fall admission, 4/15 for domestic and international students. Applications are processed on a rolling basis. Application fee: $100. Electronic applications accepted. *Expenses:* Contact institution. *Financial support:* In 2010–11, 76 students received support. Career-related internships or fieldwork, scholarships/grants, and unspecified assistantships available. Financial award application deadline: 2/15; financial award applicants required to submit FAFSA. *Faculty research:* The influence of personal

relationships on business decision making and management of change; drivers of perceived value and consumer behavior; impact of accounting on auditing, financial, managerial, systems and taxation stakeholders; corporate governance and executive compensation; impact of operations strategies on competitiveness. *Unit head:* Sherry Moss, Director, 336-758-5422, Fax: 336-758-5830, E-mail: admissions@mba.wfu.edu. *Application contact:* Tamara Paquee, Administrative Assistant, 336-758-5422, Fax: 336-758-5830, E-mail: admissions@mba.wfu.edu.

Walden University, Graduate Programs, School of Management, Minneapolis, MN 55401. Offers accounting (MS), including cpa emphasis, professional track, self-designed; accounting and management (MS), including self-designed, strategic management; applied management and decision sciences (PhD), including accounting, engineering management, finance, general applied management and decision sciences, information systems management, knowledge management, leadership and organizational change, learning management, operations research, self-designed program in applied management and design sciences; business information management (MISM); enterprise information security (MISM); entrepreneurship (MBA, DBA); finance (MBA, DBA); global management (MS); global supply chain management (DBA); health informatics (MISM); healthcare management (MBA, MS); healthcare system improvement (MBA); human resource management (MBA, MS), including functional human resource management (MS), human resource management (MS), integrating functional and strategic human resource management (MS), organizational strategy (MS); information systems (MS); information systems management (DBA); information technology (MS), including information security, software engineering; international business (MBA, DBA); IT strategy and governance (MISM); leadership (MBA, MS, DBA), including entrepreneurship (MS), general management (MS), human resources leadership (MS), innovation and technology (MS), leader development (MS), leading sustainability (MS), project management (MS), self-designed (MS); managers as leaders (MS); managing global software and service supply chains (MISM); marketing (MBA, DBA); project management (MBA, MS); research strategies (MS); risk management (MBA); self-designed (MBA, DBA); social impact management (DBA); strategy and operations (MS); sustainable futures (MBA); sustainable management (MS); technology (MBA); technology entrepreneurship (DBA); technology management (MS). Part-time and evening/weekend programs available. Postbaccalaureate distance learning degree programs offered (minimal on-campus study). *Faculty:* 22 full-time (8 women), 291 part-time/adjunct (100 women). *Students:* 3,705 full-time (1,956 women), 976 part-time (549 women); includes 2,432 minority (2,021 Black or African American, non-Hispanic/Latino; 32 American Indian or Alaska Native, non-Hispanic/Latino; 137 Asian, non-Hispanic/Latino; 193 Hispanic/Latino; 5 Native Hawaiian or other Pacific Islander, non-Hispanic/Latino; 44 Two or more races, non-Hispanic/Latino), 302 international. Average age 40. In 2010, 658 master's, 86 doctorates awarded. *Degree requirements:* For doctorate, thesis/dissertation (for some programs), residency. *Entrance requirements:* For master's, bachelor's degree or equivalent in related field; minimum GPA of 2.5; official transcripts; goal statement; access to computer and Internet; for doctorate, master's degree or equivalent in related field; minimum GPA of 3.0; 3 years of related professional/academic experience (preferred). Additional exam requirements/recommendations for international students: Required—TOEFL (minimum score 550 paper-based; 213 computer-based), IELTS (minimum score 6.5), Michigan English Language Assessment Battery (minimum score 82). *Application deadline:* Applications are processed on a rolling basis. Application fee: $50. Electronic applications accepted. *Expenses:* Tuition: Full-time $10,274; part-time $445 per credit. Tuition and fees vary according to course load, degree level and program. *Financial support:* Fellowships, Federal Work-Study, scholarships/grants, unspecified assistantships, and family tuition reduction, active duty/veteran tuition reduction, group tuition reduction, interest-free payment plans available. Support available to part-time students. Financial award applicants required to submit FAFSA. *Unit head:* Dr. William Schulz, Associate Dean, 800-925-3368. *Application contact:* Jennifer Hall, Vice President of Enrollment Management, 866-4-WALDEN, E-mail: info@waldenu.edu.

Walsh University, Graduate Studies, MBA Program, North Canton, OH 44720-3396. Offers health care management (MBA); integrated marketing communications (MBA); management (MBA). Part-time and evening/weekend programs available. *Faculty:* 8 full-time (3 women), 21 part-time/adjunct (4 women). *Students:* 22 full-time (8 women), 132 part-time (68 women); includes 13 minority (10 Black or African American, non-Hispanic/Latino; 3 Hispanic/Latino). Average age 34. 60 applicants, 98% accepted, 49 enrolled. In 2010, 57 master's awarded. *Entrance requirements:* For master's, GMAT, minimum GPA of 3.0. Additional exam requirements/recommendations for international students: Required—TOEFL (minimum score 500 paper-based; 173 computer-based; 61 iBT). *Application deadline:* For fall admission, 7/15 priority date for domestic students. Applications are processed on a rolling basis. Application fee: $25. Electronic applications accepted. *Expenses:* Tuition: Full-time $13,080; part-time $545 per credit hour. *Financial support:* In 2010–11, 98 students received support, including 9 research assistantships with partial tuition reimbursements available (averaging $5,518 per year); tuition waivers (partial), unspecified assistantships, and tuition discounts also available. Financial award application deadline: 12/31. *Faculty research:* Patient and physician satisfaction, advancing and improving learning with information technology, consumer-driven healthcare, branding and the service industry, service provider training and customer satisfaction. *Unit head:* Dr. Michael A. Petrochuk, Director of the MBA Program and Assistant Professor, 330-244-4764, Fax: 330-490-7359, E-mail: mpetrochuk@walsh.edu. *Application contact:* Christine Haver, Assistant Director for Graduate and Transfer Admissions, 330-490-7177, Fax: 330-244-4925, E-mail: chaver@walsh.edu.

Washington State University, Graduate School, College of Business, Business Administration Programs, Pullman, WA 99164. Offers business administration (MBA, PhD), including accounting (PhD), finance (PhD), management and operations (PhD), management information systems (PhD), marketing (PhD). *Accreditation:* AACSB. *Faculty:* 47. *Students:* 117 full-time (42 women), 117 part-time (30 women); includes 24 minority (1 Black or African American, non-Hispanic/Latino; 17 Asian, non-Hispanic/Latino; 5 Hispanic/Latino; 1 Two or more races, non-Hispanic/Latino), 48 international. Average age 32. 347 applicants, 19% accepted, 43 enrolled. In 2010, 58 master's, 5 doctorates awarded. *Degree requirements:* For master's, comprehensive exam (for some programs), thesis (for some programs), final presentation; for doctorate, comprehensive exam, thesis/dissertation, oral and written exams. *Entrance requirements:* For master's and doctorate, GMAT, minimum GPA of 3.0, 3 letters of recommendation. Additional exam requirements/recommendations for international students: Required—TOEFL. *Application deadline:* For fall admission, 3/1 priority date for domestic students, 3/1 for international students; for spring admission, 6/1 priority date for domestic students, 6/1 for international students. Applications are processed on a rolling basis. Application fee: $50. Electronic applications accepted. *Expenses:* Tuition, state resident: full-time $8552; part-time $443 per credit. Tuition, nonresident: full-time $21,650; part-time $1083 per credit. Required fees: $846. *Financial support:* In 2010–11, 102 students received support, including 36 teaching assistantships with full and partial tuition reimbursements available (averaging $18,204 per year); career-related internships or fieldwork, Federal Work-Study, institutionally sponsored loans, health care benefits, tuition waivers (partial), unspecified assistantships, and teaching associateships also available. Financial award application deadline: 4/1. Total annual research expenditures: $344,000. *Unit head:* Dr. Eric Spangenberg, Dean, 509-335-8150, E-mail: ers@wsu.edu. *Application contact:* Graduate School Admissions, 800-GRADWSU, Fax: 509-335-1949, E-mail: gradsch@wsu.edu.

West Chester University of Pennsylvania, Office of Graduate Studies, College of Business and Public Affairs, Department of Marketing, West Chester, PA 19383. Offers MBA. Part-time and evening/weekend programs available. *Students:* 1 (woman) part-time. Average age 46. In 2010, 1 master's awarded. *Entrance requirements:* Additional exam requirements/recommendations for international students: Required—TOEFL (minimum score 550 paper-based; 213 computer-based; 80 iBT). *Application deadline:* For fall admission, 4/15 for domestic students, 3/15 for international students; for spring admission, 10/15 for domestic students, 9/1 for international students. Applications are processed on a rolling basis. Application fee: $35. Electronic applications accepted. *Expenses:* Tuition, state resident: full-time $6966; part-time $387 per credit. Tuition, nonresident: full-time $11,146; part-time $619 per credit. Required fees: $1614.40; $133.24 per credit. Part-time tuition and fees vary according to campus/location. *Financial support:* Unspecified assistantships available. Support available to part-time students. Financial award application deadline: 2/15; financial award applicants required to submit FAFSA. *Unit head:* Dr. Paul Christ, MBA Director and Graduate Coordinator, 610-425-5000 Ext. 3232, E-mail: mba@wcupa.edu. *Application contact:* Office of Graduate Studies, 610-436-2943, Fax: 610-436-2763, E-mail: gradstudy@wcupa.edu.

Wilfrid Laurier University, Faculty of Graduate and Postdoctoral Studies, School of Business and Economics, Department of Business, Waterloo, ON N2L 3C5, Canada. Offers accounting (PhD); finance (M Fin); financial economics (PhD); marketing (PhD); operations and supply chain management (PhD); organizational behavior and human resource management (M Sc); organizational behaviour and human resource management (PhD); supply chain management (M Sc); technology management (EMTM). Part-time and evening/weekend programs available. *Faculty:* 67 full-time (20 women), 12 part-time/adjunct (4 women). *Students:* 20 full-time (11 women), 1 part-time (0 women), 5 international. 80 applicants, 28% accepted, 3 enrolled. In 2010, 6 master's, 1 doctorate awarded. *Degree requirements:* For master's, thesis optional; for doctorate, comprehensive exam, thesis/dissertation. *Entrance requirements:* For master's, GMAT, 4-year honors degree with minimum B+ average; for doctorate, GMAT, master's degree, minimum B+ average. Additional exam requirements/recommendations for international students: Required—TOEFL (minimum score 89 iBT). *Application deadline:* For fall admission, 1/15 priority date for domestic and international students. Application fee: $125. Electronic applications accepted. Tuition and fees charges are reported in Canadian dollars. *Expenses:* Tuition, area resident: Full-time $15,300 Canadian dollars; part-time $1200 Canadian dollars per credit. International tuition: $21,300 Canadian dollars full-time. Required fees: $650 Canadian dollars; $100 Canadian dollars per credit. Tuition and fees vary according to course load, degree level, campus/location and program. *Financial support:* In 2010–11, 27 fellowships, 1 research assistantship, 27

teaching assistantships were awarded; career-related internships or fieldwork, scholarships/grants, health care benefits, and unspecified assistantships also available. *Faculty research:* Financial economics, management and organizational behavior, operations and supply chain management. *Unit head:* Dr. Hamid Noori, Director, 519-884-0710 Ext. 2571, Fax: 519-884-2357, E-mail: sbephdmasters@wlu.ca. *Application contact:* Jennifer Williams, Graduate Admission and Records Officer, 519-884-0710 Ext. 3536, Fax: 519-884-1020, E-mail: gradstudies@wlu.ca.

Wilkes University, College of Graduate and Professional Studies, Jay S. Sidhu School of Business and Leadership, Wilkes-Barre, PA 18766-0002. Offers accounting (MBA); entrepreneurship (MBA); finance (MBA); health care administration (MBA); human resource management (MBA); international business (MBA); marketing (MBA); operations management (MBA); organizational leadership and development (MBA). *Accreditation:* ACBSP. Part-time and evening/weekend programs available. *Students:* 39 full-time (16 women), 146 part-time (71 women); includes 5 Black or African American, non-Hispanic/Latino; 2 Asian, non-Hispanic/Latino; 1 Hispanic/Latino; 1 Two or more races, non-Hispanic/Latino, 16 international. Average age 30. In 2010, 85 master's awarded. *Entrance requirements:* For master's, GMAT. Additional exam requirements/recommendations for international students: Required—TOEFL (minimum score 550 paper-based; 213 computer-based; 79 iBT). *Application deadline:* Applications are processed on a rolling basis. Application fee: $45 ($65 for international students). Electronic applications accepted. *Expenses:* Contact institution. *Financial support:* Federal Work-Study and unspecified assistantships available. Financial award application deadline: 3/1; financial award applicants required to submit FAFSA. *Unit head:* Dr. Paul Browne, Dean, 570-408-4701, Fax: 570-408-7846, E-mail: paul.browne@wilkes.edu. *Application contact:* Kathleen Houlihan, Director of Graduate Studies, 570-408-3235, Fax: 570-408-7846, E-mail: kathleen.houlihan@wilkes.edu.

Worcester Polytechnic Institute, Graduate Studies, School of Business, Worcester, MA 01609-2280. Offers information technology (MS), including information security management; management (Graduate Certificate); marketing and technological innovation (MS); operations design and leadership (MS); technology (MBA). *Accreditation:* AACSB. Part-time and evening/weekend programs available. Postbaccalaureate distance learning degree programs offered (minimal on-campus study). *Faculty:* 13 full-time (7 women), 9 part-time/adjunct (2 women). *Students:* 112 full-time (53 women), 135 part-time (33 women); includes 5 Black or African American, non-Hispanic/Latino; 1 Hispanic/Latino; 15 Native Hawaiian or other Pacific Islander, non-Hispanic/Latino, 105 international. 396 applicants, 67% accepted, 79 enrolled. In 2010, 69 degrees awarded. *Degree requirements:* For master's, thesis optional. *Entrance requirements:* For master's, GMAT (MBA), GMAT or GRE General Test (MS), resume; for Graduate Certificate, GMAT or GRE General Test, statement of purpose, 3 letters of recommendation. Additional exam requirements/recommendations for international students: Required—TOEFL (minimum score 550 paper-based; 213 computer-based; 79 iBT), IELTS (minimum score 6.5). *Application deadline:* For fall admission, 6/1 priority date for domestic and international students; for spring admission, 11/1 priority date for domestic students, 10/1 priority date for international students. Applications are processed on a rolling basis. Application fee: $70. Electronic applications accepted. *Expenses:* Tuition: Full-time $20,862; part-time $1159 per term. One-time fee: $15. *Financial support:* Career-related internships or fieldwork, institutionally sponsored loans, scholarships/grants, and unspecified assistantships available. Financial award application deadline: 6/1; financial award applicants required to submit FAFSA. *Faculty research:* Organizational aesthetics, resistance in organizations, dynamics of product innovation, economic approaches to productivity, corporate earnings forecasts and value relevance, ERP implementation, improving Web accessibility, information quality assessment, measuring strategic and transactional IT, website quality, service operations modeling, healthcare operations and performance analysis, loan process design. *Unit head:* Dr. Mark Rice, Dean, 508-831-4665, Fax: 508-831-5218, E-mail: rice@wpi.edu. *Application contact:* Alyssa Bates, Director, Graduate Management Programs, 508-831-4665, Fax: 508-831-5720, E-mail: ajbates@wpi.edu.

Xavier University, Williams College of Business, Master of Business Administration Program, Cincinnati, OH 45207-3221. Offers business administration (Exec MBA, MBA); business intelligence (MBA); finance (MBA); international business (MBA); management information systems (MBA); marketing (MBA); MBA/MHSA; MSN/MBA. *Accreditation:* AACSB. Part-time and evening/weekend programs available. *Faculty:* 37 full-time (13 women), 9 part-time/adjunct (2 women). *Students:* 200 full-time (60 women), 735 part-time (239 women); includes 128 minority (48 Black or African American, non-Hispanic/Latino; 3 American Indian or Alaska Native, non-Hispanic/Latino; 54 Asian, non-Hispanic/Latino; 22 Hispanic/Latino; 1 Native Hawaiian or other Pacific Islander, non-Hispanic/Latino), 32 international. Average age 30. 223 applicants, 85% accepted, 139 enrolled. In 2010, 323 master's awarded. *Degree requirements:* For master's, capstone course. *Entrance requirements:* For master's, GMAT. Additional exam requirements/recommendations for international students: Required—TOEFL (minimum score 550 paper-based; 213 computer-based; 80 iBT). *Application deadline:* For fall admission, 8/1 priority date for domestic students, 5/1 for international students; for spring admission, 12/1 priority date for domestic students, 9/1 for international students. Applications are processed on a rolling basis. Application fee: $35. Electronic applications accepted. *Expenses:* Contact institution. *Financial support:* In 2010–11, 176 students received support. Scholarships/grants, tuition waivers (partial), and unspecified assistantships available. Financial award application deadline: 3/1; financial award applicants required to submit FAFSA. *Unit head:* Dr. Hema Krishnan, Associate Dean, 513-745-3206, Fax: 513-745-3455, E-mail: krishnan@xavier.edu. *Application contact:* Anna Marie Whelan, Assistant Director, MBA Programs, 513-745-3525, Fax: 513-745-2929, E-mail: whelana@xavier.edu.

Yale University, Yale School of Management and Graduate School of Arts and Sciences, Doctoral Program in Management, New Haven, CT 06520. Offers accounting (PhD); financial economics (PhD); marketing (PhD); organizations and management (PhD). *Accreditation:* AACSB. *Faculty:* 68 full-time (12 women), 1 (woman) part-time/adjunct. *Students:* 32 full-time (9 women); includes 3 Asian, non-Hispanic/Latino, 16 international. Average age 28. 441 applicants, 4% accepted, 6 enrolled. In 2010, 9 doctorates awarded. *Degree requirements:* For doctorate, comprehensive exam, thesis/dissertation. *Entrance requirements:* For doctorate, GMAT or GRE General Test. Additional exam requirements/recommendations for international students: Required—TOEFL, IELTS. *Application deadline:* For fall admission, 1/2 for domestic and international students. Application fee: $100. Electronic applications accepted. *Expenses:* Contact institution. *Financial support:* In 2010–11, 30 students received support, including 30 fellowships with full tuition reimbursements available, 30 research assistantships with full tuition reimbursements available, 30 teaching assistantships with full tuition reimbursements available; institutionally sponsored loans, scholarships/grants, and health care benefits also available. Financial award application deadline: 1/2. *Faculty research:* Pricing of options and futures, term structure of interest rates, use of accounting numbers in debt contracts, product differentiation, e-commerce and marketing, behavioral finance. *Unit head:* Carla Mills, Registrar, 203-432-3955, Fax: 203-432-0342, E-mail: carla.mills@yale.edu. *Application contact:* Carla Mills, Registrar, 203-432-3955, Fax: 203-432-0342, E-mail: carla.mills@yale.edu.

York College of Pennsylvania, Department of Business Administration, York, PA 17405-7199. Offers accounting (MBA); continuous improvement (MBA); finance (MBA); management (MBA); marketing (MBA). *Accreditation:* ACBSP. Part-time and evening/weekend programs available. *Faculty:* 11 full-time (2 women), 5 part-time/adjunct (1 woman). *Students:* 20 full-time (6 women), 111 part-time (44 women); includes 4 Black or African American, non-Hispanic/Latino; 1 Asian, non-Hispanic/Latino; 4 Hispanic/Latino, 2 international. Average age 30. 53 applicants, 91% accepted, 40 enrolled. In 2010, 45 master's awarded. *Entrance requirements:* For master's, GMAT. Additional exam requirements/recommendations for international students: Required—TOEFL (minimum score 530 paper-based; 200 computer-based; 72 iBT). *Application deadline:* For fall admission, 7/15 priority date for domestic students; for spring admission, 12/15 priority date for domestic students. Applications are processed on a rolling basis. Application fee: $60. Electronic applications accepted. *Expenses:* Tuition: Full-time $11,520; part-time $640 per credit hour. Required fees: $1500; $660 per year. *Financial support:* Scholarships/grants available. Financial award application deadline: 4/15; financial award applicants required to submit FAFSA. *Unit head:* Dr. David Greisler, MBA Director, 717-815-6410, Fax: 717-600-3999, E-mail: dgreisle@ycp.edu. *Application contact:* Brenda Adams, Assistant Director, MBA Program, 717-815-1749, Fax: 717-600-3999, E-mail: badams@ycp.edu.

MARKETING RESEARCH

American University, Kogod School of Business, Master of Business Administration Program, Washington, DC 20016-8044. Offers accounting (MBA); consulting (MBA), including information technology, international business, management; corporate finance: commercial banking (MBA); corporate finance: corporate financial management (MBA); corporate finance: investment banking (MBA), including corporate finance and private equity, trading and selling; entrepreneurship (MBA); global emerging markets (MBA), including business, finance, information technology; international trade and global supply chain management (MBA); leadership (MBA); marketing management (MBA); marketing research (MBA); real estate (MBA); MBA/JD; MBA/LL M. Part-time and evening/weekend programs available. *Faculty:* 12 full-time (5 women). *Students:* 135 full-time (62 women), 104 part-time (38 women); includes 46 minority (18 Black or African American, non-Hispanic/Latino; 1 American Indian or Alaska Native, non-Hispanic/Latino; 12 Asian, non-Hispanic/Latino; 14 Hispanic/Latino; 1 Two or more races, non-Hispanic/Latino), 34 international. Average age 27. 467 applicants, 51% accepted, 70 enrolled. In 2010, 101 master's awarded. *Entrance requirements:* For master's, GMAT. Additional exam requirements/recommendations for international students: Required—TOEFL. *Application deadline:* For fall admission, 2/1 priority date for domestic students; for spring admission, 10/1 priority date for domestic students. Applications are processed on a rolling basis. Application fee: $100. *Expenses:* Contact institution. *Financial support:* In 2010–11, 19 students received support; fellowships, research assistantships

with partial tuition reimbursements available, career-related internships or fieldwork, Federal Work-Study, and institutionally sponsored loans available. Support available to part-time students. Financial award application deadline: 2/1. *Faculty research:* Information technology, decision-aiding methodology, negotiation. *Unit head:* Dr. Stevan Holmberg, Chair, 202-885-6193, E-mail: sholmbe@american.edu. *Application contact:* Shannon Demko, Associate Director Graduate Admissions, 202-885-1994, Fax: 202-885-1108, E-mail: demko@american.edu.

Hofstra University, Frank G. Zarb School of Business, Department of Marketing and International Business, Hempstead, NY 11549. Offers business administration (MBA), including international business, marketing; marketing (MS); marketing research (MS). Part-time and evening/weekend programs available. Postbaccalaureate distance learning degree programs offered (minimal on-campus study). *Faculty:* 7 full-time (0 women), 2 part-time/adjunct (0 women). *Students:* 63 full-time (34 women), 47 part-time (24 women); includes 9 minority (1 Black or African American, non-Hispanic/Latino; 2 Asian, non-Hispanic/Latino; 6 Hispanic/Latino), 52 international. Average age 27. 150 applicants, 66% accepted, 36 enrolled. In 2010, 35 master's awarded. *Degree requirements:* For master's, capstone course (MBA), thesis (MS). *Entrance requirements:* For master's, GMAT or GRE, 2 letters of recommendation, resume, essay. Additional exam requirements/recommendations for international students: Required—TOEFL (minimum score 550 paper-based; 213 computer-based; 80 iBT); Recommended—IELTS (minimum score 6). *Application deadline:* Applications are processed on a rolling basis. Application fee: $70 ($75 for international students). Electronic applications accepted. *Expenses:* Contact institution. *Financial support:* In 2010–11, 22 students received support, including 21 fellowships with full and partial tuition reimbursements available (averaging $8,965 per year); research assistantships with full and partial tuition reimbursements available, career-related internships or fieldwork, Federal Work-Study, institutionally sponsored loans, scholarships/grants, tuition waivers (full and partial), and unspecified assistantships also available. Support available to part-time students. Financial award applicants required to submit FAFSA. *Faculty research:* Outsourcing, global alliances, retailing, Web marketing, cross-cultural age research. *Unit head:* Dr. Benny Barak, Chairperson, 516-463-5707, Fax: 516-463-4834, E-mail: mktbzb@hofstra.edu. *Application contact:* Carol Drummer, Dean of Graduate Admissions, 516-463-4876, Fax: 516-463-4664, E-mail: gradstudent@hofstra.edu.

Marquette University, Graduate School of Management, Department of Economics, Milwaukee, WI 53201-1881. Offers business economics (MSAE); financial economics (MSAE); international economics (MSAE); marketing research (MSAE); real estate economics (MSAE). Part-time and evening/weekend programs available. *Faculty:* 13 full-time (4 women), 3 part-time/adjunct (0 women). *Students:* 29 full-time (11 women), 33 part-time (8 women); includes 5 minority (2 Black or African American, non-Hispanic/Latino; 1 Asian, non-Hispanic/Latino; 1 Hispanic/Latino; 1 Two or more races, non-Hispanic/Latino), 17 international. Average age 25. 96 applicants, 73% accepted, 27 enrolled. In 2010, 15 master's awarded. *Degree requirements:* For master's, comprehensive exam, professional project. *Entrance requirements:* For master's, GMAT or GRE General Test. Additional exam requirements/recommendations for international students: Required—TOEFL (minimum score 530 paper-based; 78 computer-based). *Application deadline:* Applications are processed on a rolling basis. Application fee: $50. Electronic applications accepted. *Expenses:* Tuition: Full-time $16,290; part-time $905 per credit hour. Tuition and fees vary according to program. *Financial support:* In 2010–11, 2 fellowships, 7 teaching assistantships were awarded; research assistantships, Federal Work-Study, institutionally sponsored loans, scholarships/grants, and tuition waivers (full and partial) also available. Support available to part-time students. Financial award application deadline: 2/15. *Faculty research:* Monetary and fiscal policy in open economy, housing and regional migration, political economy of taxation and state/local government. Total annual research expenditures: $15,656. *Unit head:* Dr. Abdur Chowdhury, Chair, 414-288-6915, Fax: 414-288-5757. *Application contact:* Farrokh Nourzad, Information Contact, 414-288-3570.

Southern Illinois University Edwardsville, Graduate School, School of Business, Department of Management and Marketing, Edwardsville, IL 62026. Offers marketing research (MMR). Part-time and evening/weekend programs available. *Faculty:* 17 full-time (6 women). *Students:* 18 full-time (6 women), 8 part-time (2 women); includes 4 minority (2 Black or African American, non-Hispanic/Latino; 1 Asian, non-Hispanic/Latino; 1 Hispanic/Latino), 14 international. Average age 26. 19 applicants, 74% accepted. In 2010, 19 master's awarded. *Degree requirements:* For master's, comprehensive exam, final exam. *Entrance requirements:* For master's, GMAT. Additional exam requirements/recommendations for international students: Required—TOEFL (minimum score 550 paper-based; 213 computer-based; 79 iBT), IELTS (minimum score 6.5). *Application deadline:* For fall admission, 7/22 for domestic students, 6/1 for international students; for spring admission, 12/10 for domestic students, 10/1 for international students. Applications are processed on a rolling basis. Application fee: $30. Electronic applications accepted. *Expenses:* Tuition, state resident: full-time $6012; part-time $1503 per semester. Tuition, non-resident: full-time $15,030; part-time $3758 per semester. Required fees: $1711; $675 per semester. *Financial support:* In 2010–11, fellowships with full tuition reimbursements (averaging $8,364 per year), 5 research assistantships with full tuition reimbursements (averaging $8,064 per year), 18 teaching assistantships with full tuition reimbursements (averaging $8,064 per year) were awarded; career-related internships or fieldwork, Federal Work-Study, institutionally sponsored loans, scholarships/grants, traineeships, and unspecified assistantships also available. Support available to part-time students. Financial award application deadline: 3/1; financial award applicants required to submit FAFSA. *Unit head:* Dr. Ralph Giacobbe, Chair, 618-650-2750, E-mail: rgiacob@siue.edu. *Application contact:* Dr. Madhav Segal, Program Director, 618-650-2601, E-mail: msegal@siue.edu.

University of Colorado Denver, Business School, Program in Marketing, Denver, CO 80217. Offers brand management and marketing communication (MS); global marketing (MS); high-tech/entrepreneurial marketing (MS); Internet marketing (MS); market research (MS); marketing and business intelligence (MS); marketing for sustainability (MS); marketing in nonprofit organizations (MS); sports and entertainment marketing (MS). Part-time and evening/weekend programs available. *Students:* 31 full-time (18 women), 8 part-time (4 women); includes 3 Hispanic/Latino, 5 international. Average age 29. 46 applicants, 63% accepted, 18 enrolled. In 2010, 11 master's awarded. *Degree requirements:* For master's, 30 semester hours (18 of marketing core courses, 12 of graduate marketing electives). *Entrance requirements:* For master's, GMAT. Additional exam requirements/recommendations for international students: Required—TOEFL (minimum score 525 paper-based; 197 computer-based; 71 iBT). *Application deadline:* For fall admission, 4/1 priority date for domestic students, 3/15 priority date for international students; for spring admission, 10/1 priority date for domestic and international students. Application fee: $50 ($75 for international students). Electronic applications accepted. *Expenses:* Contact institution. *Financial support:* Federal Work-Study and scholarships/grants available. Support available to part-time students. Financial award application deadline: 4/1; financial award applicants required to submit FAFSA. *Faculty research:* Marketing issues in the Chinese environment, impact of individual difference and contextual factors on the risk-taking behaviors of managers making new-business creation decisions, Attribution Theory perspective of conflict between marketers and engineers, organizational identity and identification , international market entry strategies. *Unit head:* Dr. David Forlani, Associate Professor/Director, 303-315-8420, E-mail: david.forlani@ucdenver.edu. *Application contact:* Shelly Townley, Admissions Director, Graduate Programs, 303-315-8202, E-mail: shelly.townley@ucdenver.edu.

University of Georgia, Terry College of Business, Program in Marketing Research, Athens, GA 30602. Offers MMR. *Students:* 21 full-time (13 women); includes 1 Asian, non-Hispanic/Latino; 1 Hispanic/Latino, 2 international. In 2010, 27 master's awarded. *Entrance requirements:* For master's, GMAT or GRE General Test. *Application deadline:* For fall admission, 7/1 priority date for domestic students; for spring admission, 11/15 for domestic students. Application fee: $50. Electronic applications accepted. *Expenses:* Tuition, state resident: full-time $7200; part-time $344 per credit hour. Tuition, nonresident: full-time $21,900; part-time $944 per credit hour. Tuition and fees vary according to course load and program. *Financial support:* Research assistantships available. *Unit head:* Dr. Charlotte Mason, Head, 706-542-3776, E-mail: cmason@terry.uga.edu. *Application contact:* Dr. Thomas Leigh, Graduate Coordinator, 706-542-3763, Fax: 706-542-3738, E-mail: tleight@terry.uga.edu.

The University of Texas at Arlington, Graduate School, College of Business, Department of Marketing, Arlington, TX 76019. Offers marketing (PhD); marketing research (MS). Part-time programs available. *Faculty:* 7 full-time (1 woman). *Students:* 27 full-time (16 women), 12 part-time (5 women); includes 3 minority (1 Black or African American, non-Hispanic/Latino; 1 Asian, non-Hispanic/Latino; 1 Hispanic/Latino), 20 international. 41 applicants, 44% accepted, 11 enrolled. In 2010, 11 master's, 1 doctorate awarded. *Degree requirements:* For master's, thesis optional; for doctorate, comprehensive exam, thesis/dissertation. *Entrance requirements:* For master's, GMAT, GRE. Additional exam requirements/recommendations for international students: Required—TOEFL (minimum score 550 paper-based; 213 computer-based; 79 iBT). *Application deadline:* For fall admission, 6/1 for domestic students, 4/1 for international students; for spring admission, 10/15 for domestic students, 9/15 for international students. Applications are processed on a rolling basis. Application fee: $35 ($50 for international students). Electronic applications accepted. *Expenses:* Tuition, state resident: full-time $7500. Tuition, nonresident: full-time $13,080. International tuition: $13,250 full-time. *Financial support:* In 2010–11, 8 teaching assistantships (averaging $14,000 per year) were awarded; career-related internships or fieldwork, scholarships/grants, and unspecified assistantships also available. Support available to part-time students. Financial award application deadline: 6/1; financial award applicants required to submit FAFSA. *Faculty research:* Marketing strategy, marketing research, international marketing. Total annual research expenditures: $30,000. *Unit head:* Dr. Greg Frazier, Interim Chair, 817-272-0264, Fax: 817-272-2854, E-mail: frazier@uta.edu. *Application contact:* Dr. Robert Rogers, MS Program Director, 817-272-2340, Fax: 817-272-2854, E-mail: msmr@uta.edu.

University of Wisconsin–Madison, Graduate School, Wisconsin School of Business, Wisconsin Full-Time MBA Program, Madison, WI 53706-1380. Offers applied security analysis (MBA); arts administration (MBA); brand and product management (MBA); corporate finance and investment banking (MBA); entrepreneurial management (MBA); marketing research (MBA); operations and technology management (MBA); real estate (MBA); risk management and insurance (MBA); strategic human resource management (MBA); strategic management in the life and engineering sciences (MBA); supply chain management (MBA). *Faculty:* 32 full-time (4 women), 17 part-time/adjunct (3 women). *Students:* 242 full-time (74 women); includes 16 Black or African American, non-Hispanic/Latino; 3 American Indian or Alaska Native, non-Hispanic/Latino; 16 Asian, non-Hispanic/Latino; 12 Hispanic/Latino, 29 international. Average age 28. 526 applicants, 32% accepted, 117 enrolled. In 2010, 106 master's awarded. *Entrance requirements:* For master's, GMAT, bachelor's or equivalent degree, 2 years of work experience, letters of recommendation. Additional exam requirements/recommendations for international students: Required—TOEFL (minimum score 600 paper-based; 250 computer-based; 100 iBT), IELTS. *Application deadline:* For fall admission, 11/4 for domestic students, 11/1 for international students; for winter admission, 2/5 for domestic and international students; for spring admission, 5/15 for domestic students, 4/5 for international students. Applications are processed on a rolling basis. Application fee: $56. Electronic applications accepted. *Expenses:* Tuition, state resident: full-time $9887; part-time $617.96 per credit. Tuition, nonresident: full-time $24,054; part-time $1503.40 per credit. Required fees: $67.63 per credit. Tuition and fees vary according to reciprocity agreements. *Financial support:* In 2010–11, 103 students received support, including 13 fellowships with full and partial tuition reimbursements available (averaging $15,000 per year), 53 research assistantships with full tuition reimbursements available (averaging $8,000 per year), 35 teaching assistantships with full tuition reimbursements available (averaging $11,000 per year); scholarships/grants, health care benefits, and unspecified assistantships also available. Financial award application deadline: 4/5; financial award applicants required to submit FAFSA. *Faculty research:* Market consequences of International Financial Reporting Standards (IFRS), inter-firm relationships and strategic partnerships, application of Bayesian statistical methods and applied probability models to understanding individuals' behaviors in the context of customer relationship management (CRM) applications, liquidity provision and the structure of financial markets, strategic management of global startups. *Unit head:* Dr. Kenneth A. Kavajecz, Associate Dean of Master's Programs, 608-265-3494, Fax: 608-265-4192, E-mail: kkavajecz@bus.wisc.edu. *Application contact:* Maria Reis, Assistant Director of MBA Marketing and Recruiting, 608-262-4000, Fax: 608-265-4192, E-mail: mreis@bus.wisc.edu.

OVERVIEW

In nonprofit organizations, employers need professionals with strong communication and fundraising skills who can mobilize public support for their causes. An MBA in nonprofit management is designed for students who seek to use core business management skills to address society's most challenging humanitarian and social problems in the global economy. It is a benchmark for individuals who seek employment in the world of civic or charitable causes. This course of study prepares students with the financial, operational, leadership, and entrepreneurial skills to lead and manage in today's changing, and challenging, nonprofit environment.

An MBA program in nonprofit management provides students with the principals of accounting, business law, business management, human resources management, public administration, and taxation and their application to nonprofit organizations—all designed to develop the skills specific to management work in charitable and civic organizations. These programs also guide students through the unique challenges of nonprofits, such as generating operating finance, attracting high-caliber professionals, maintaining goodwill services, and finding meaningful success-measuring tools.

Required courses may include study in:

- Executive Leadership
- Global Sustainability
- Government, Society, and the New Entrepreneur
- Human Resource Management
- Law and Public Affairs
- Leading the Mission-Driven Organization
- Management in the Nonprofit Sector
- Marketing Social Change
- Negotiations
- Public Management Economics
- Public Policy Analysis
- Public Program Evaluation
- Social Entrepreneurship
- Statistical Analysis
- Strategic Fundraising and Corporate Philanthropy
- Urban Management

Elective courses may include study in:

- Business
- Entrepreneurship
- Leadership
- Negotiations
- Real Estate Development
- Starting New Ventures

An MBA in nonprofit management prepares graduates to head nonprofit corporations, foundations, educational institutions, and associations. Graduates are prepared to be strategic and effective leaders in the government, nonprofit, or private sector, understanding the interchange across the sectors and how they all work together to improve social and economic conditions worldwide.

Jobs are increasingly plentiful in the nonprofit sector, and the field is growing fast—Americans are giving more than ever to charitable causes: nearly $300 billion in 2010, according to the Giving USA Foundation (www.aafrc.org). Career options for qualified nonprofit management MBA graduates include associate director, controller, corporate tax manager, director of administration, director of market risk, director of development, and executive director.

IN THIS SECTION

You'll find profiles of institutions offering graduate programs in the following field:

HELPFUL ORGANIZATIONS/ PUBLICATIONS/BLOGS

Independent Sector (IS)

http://www.independentsector.org/

Independent Sector (IS) is the leadership forum for charities, foundations, and corporate giving programs committed to advancing the common good in America and around the world. This nonpartisan coalition of approximately 600 organizations leads, strengthens, and mobilizes the charitable community in order to fulfill its vision of a just and inclusive society and a healthy democracy of active citizens, effective institutions, and vibrant communities.

Independent Sector serves as the premier meeting ground for the leaders of America's charitable and philanthropic sector. Since 1980, Independent Sector has sponsored ground-breaking research; fought for public policies that support a dynamic, independent sector; and created unparalleled resources so staff, boards, and volunteers can improve their organizations and better serve their communities.

Independent Sector fulfills its mission by:

- Convening opportunities for sector leaders to work together on key issues.
- Promoting policies that enable the nonprofit and philanthropic community to engage with public officials on a nonpartisan basis. IS is currently focusing on issues such as protecting advocacy rights of nonprofits, promoting tax incentives for charitable giving, and addressing federal and state budget concerns.
- Supporting the development and dissemination of strategies to strengthen volunteering, voting, giving, and other forms of citizen engagement.
- Encouraging the sector to meet the highest standards of ethical practice and effectiveness. To that end, IS has convened the Panel on the Nonprofit Sector, which is making recommendations in the areas of governance, fiduciary responsibility, government oversight, self-regulation, and financial accountability.
- Serving as the voice of the independent sector to the media, government, business, and international voluntary communities.

Nonprofit Quarterly

http://www.nonprofitquarterly.org/

The *Nonprofit Quarterly*'s overarching editorial goal is to strengthen the role of nonprofit organizations to activate democracy. *Nonprofit Quarterly* believes that open societies require venues for individuals to undertake public projects together that are larger than friends and family but smaller than the state and that range from community arts and group homes to environmental advocacy. Nonprofits naturally fill this role, particularly when their efforts engage the ideas, energy, and speech of members of their community. *Nonprofit Quarterly* is committed to provide a forum for the critical thinking and exploration needed to help nonprofits stay true to this democratic calling—and to achieve their potential as effective, powerful, and influential organizations in concert with their constituencies.

The American Society of Association Executives (ASAE)

http://www.asaecenter.org/

The American Society of Association Executives (ASAE) is a membership organization of more than 22,000 association executives and industry partners representing more than 11,000 organizations. ASAE members manage leading trade associations, individual membership societies, and voluntary organizations across the United States and in nearly 50 countries around the world. ASAE believes associations have the power to transform society for the better and is passionate about helping association professionals achieve previously unimaginable levels of performance. With support of the ASAE Foundation, a separate nonprofit entity, ASAE is the premier source of learning, knowledge, and future-oriented research for the association and the nonprofit community. It provides resources, education, ideas, and advocacy to enhance the power and performance of the association and nonprofit community.

CAREER ASPIRATIONS: A PROSPECTIVE POSITION

Director of Advice: Nonprofit Market

Job Description

A leading provider of multi-manager investment strategies with more than $161 billion in assets under management worldwide is creating a new role: Director of Advice: Nonprofit Market. There is an immediate need for a qualified individual to focus upon the success in the foundation and nonprofit market and to help maximize the company's competitive advantage. This individual will act as an expert in the nonprofit market, contributing internally to ensure effective delivery and positioning of competitive solutions and externally as a market-recognized professional and advocate for the company with integral participation in sales agendas and existing client relationships.

Responsibilities

- Research needs and develop thought leadership for a variety of nonprofits with key sub-markets, including education endowments, community foundations, and private foundations.
- Help establish a point of view on best practices, including investment policy statement, spending policies, portfolio construction, and reporting requirements.
- Act as liaison among fulfillment groups (sales, service, solutions, and investment management units) with the objective of ensuring awareness of the needs of the nonprofit market and of how to best serve it.
- Monitor the efficacy of investment solutions in meeting client goals, and develop recommendations for improvement.
- Maintain an understanding of current and emerging competitive offerings and help create solutions and positioning that best contribute to the company's success.
- Develop key nonprofit and investment industry contacts and act as expert for media contact, conferences, and thought leadership content.
- Play an active role in key strategic sales and client service/retention agendas.

Qualifications

- Minimum of 7 years of financial services experience and preferably 3 years of institutional asset management or related experience
- Experience in working with nonprofits, with emphasis in education endowments, public charities, and/or private foundations mandatory
- CFA or MBA
- Strong project management skills
- Strong oral and written communication skills
- Proven ability to prioritize and manage multiple agendas

NONPROFIT MANAGEMENT

American Public University System, AMU/APU Graduate Programs, Charles Town, WV 25414. Offers accounting (MBA); administration and supervision (M Ed); air warfare (MA Military Studies); asymmetrical warfare (MA Military Studies); criminal justice (MA); emergency and disaster management (MA); entrepreneurship (MBA); environmental policy and management (MS); finance (MBA); general (MBA); global business management (MBA); guidance and counseling (M Ed); history (MA); homeland security (MA); homeland security resource allocation (MBA); humanities (MA); information technology (MS); information technology management (MBA); intelligence studies (MA); international relations and conflict resolution (MA); joint warfare (MA Military Studies); land warfare (MA Military Studies); legal studies (MA); management (MA), including defense mangement, general, human resource management, organizational leadership, public administration; marketing (MBA); military history (MA); national security studies (MA); naval warfare (MA Military Studies); nonprofit management (MBA); political science (MA); psychology (MA); public administration (MA); public health (MA); security management (MA); space studies (MS); sports management (MS); strategic leadership (MA Military Studies); teaching (M Ed), including elementary, secondary social sciences; transportation and logistics management (MA). Programs offered via distance learning only. Part-time and evening/weekend programs available. Postbaccalaureate distance learning degree programs offered (no on-campus study). *Faculty:* 253 full-time (134 women), 1,208 part-time/adjunct (570 women). *Students:* 956 full-time (422 women), 8,476 part-time (2,821 women); includes 2,511 minority (1,218 Black or African American, non-Hispanic/Latino; 68 American Indian or Alaska Native, non-Hispanic/Latino; 219 Asian, non-Hispanic/Latino; 705 Hispanic/Latino; 46 Native Hawaiian or other Pacific Islander, non-Hispanic/Latino; 255 Two or more races, non-Hispanic/Latino), 107 international. Average age 35. 9,550 applicants, 100% accepted. In 2010, 1,688 master's awarded. *Degree requirements:* For master's, comprehensive exam or practicum. *Entrance requirements:* For master's, official transcript showing earned bachelor's degree from institution accredited by recognized accrediting body. Additional exam requirements/recommendations for international students: Required—TOEFL (minimum score 550 paper-based; 213 computer-based), IELTS (minimum score 6.5). *Application deadline:* Applications are processed on a rolling basis. Application fee: $0. Electronic applications accepted. *Financial support:* Applicants required to submit FAFSA. *Faculty research:* Military history, criminal justice, management performance, national security. *Unit head:* Dr. Frank McCluskey, Provost, 877-468-6268, Fax: 304-724-3780. *Application contact:* Terry Grant, Director of Enrollment Management, 877-468-6268, Fax: 304-724-3780, E-mail: info@apus.edu.

American University, School of Public Affairs, Department of Public Administration, Washington, DC 20016-8070. Offers advanced organization development (Certificate); fundamentals of organization development (Certificate); key executive leadership (MPA); leadership for organizational change (Certificate); non-profit management (Certificate); organization development (MSOD); organizational change (Certificate); public administration (MPA, PhD); public financial management (Certificate); public management (Certificate); public policy (MPP); public policy analysis (Certificate); LL M/MPA; MPA/JD; MPP/JD; MPP/LL M. Part-time and evening/weekend programs available. *Faculty:* 22 full-time (12 women), 12 part-time/adjunct (5 women). *Students:* 220 full-time (135 women), 248 part-time (159 women); includes 107 minority (71 Black or African American, non-Hispanic/Latino; 4 American Indian or Alaska Native, non-Hispanic/Latino; 18 Asian, non-Hispanic/Latino; 14 Hispanic/Latino), 19 international. Average age 30. 858 applicants, 73% accepted, 175 enrolled. In 2010, 205 master's, 8 doctorates awarded. *Degree requirements:* For master's, comprehensive exam; for doctorate, comprehensive exam, thesis/dissertation. *Entrance requirements:* For master's, GRE, statement of purpose; 2 recommendations; for doctorate, GRE, 3 recommendations; for Certificate, bachelor's degree. Additional exam requirements/recommendations for international students: Required—TOEFL. *Application deadline:* For fall admission, 2/1 for domestic students; for spring admission, 11/1 for domestic students. Application fee: $55. *Financial support:* Fellowships, research assistantships, teaching assistantships, career-related internships or fieldwork, Federal Work-Study, and institutionally sponsored loans available. Financial award application deadline: 2/1. *Faculty research:* Urban management, conservation politics, state and local budgeting, tax policy. *Unit head:* Dr. Robert Durant, Chair, 202-885-2509, E-mail: durant@american.edu. *Application contact:* Dr. Robert Durant, Chair, 202-885-2509, E-mail: durant@american.edu.

Arizona State University, College of Public Programs, School of Community Resources and Development, Phoenix, AZ 85004-0685. Offers community resources and development (PhD); nonprofit leadership and management (Graduate Certificate); nonprofit studies (MNpS); recreation and tourism studies (MS). Part-time and evening/weekend programs available. *Faculty:* 19 full-time (8 women), 2 part-time/adjunct (both women). *Students:* 53 full-time (35 women), 72 part-time (55 women); includes 28 minority (6 Black or African American, non-Hispanic/Latino; 5 American Indian or Alaska Native, non-Hispanic/Latino; 1 Asian, non-Hispanic/Latino; 16 Hispanic/Latino), 12 international. Average age 33. 90 applicants, 73% accepted, 45 enrolled.

In 2010, 37 master's, 3 other advanced degrees awarded. Terminal master's awarded for partial completion of doctoral program. *Degree requirements:* For master's, thesis or alternative, interactive Program of Study (iPOS) submitted before completing 50 percent of required credit hours; for doctorate, comprehensive exam, thesis/dissertation, interactive Program of Study (iPOS) submitted before completing 50 percent of required credit hours. *Entrance requirements:* For master's and doctorate, GRE, minimum GPA of 3.0 or equivalent in last 2 years of work leading to bachelor's degree. Additional exam requirements/recommendations for international students: Required—TOEFL, IELTS, or Pearson Test of English. *Application deadline:* For fall admission, 3/1 for domestic and international students; for spring admission, 10/1 for domestic and international students. Application fee: $70 ($90 for international students). Electronic applications accepted. *Expenses:* Contact institution. *Financial support:* In 2010–11, 6 research assistantships with full and partial tuition reimbursements (averaging $8,949 per year), 5 teaching assistantships with full and partial tuition reimbursements (averaging $9,774 per year) were awarded; fellowships with full tuition reimbursements, career-related internships or fieldwork, Federal Work-Study, institutionally sponsored loans, scholarships/grants, and tuition waivers (full and partial) also available. Financial award application deadline: 3/1; financial award applicants required to submit FAFSA. Total annual research expenditures: $2.5 million. *Unit head:* Dr. Kathleen Andereck, Director, 602-496-1056, E-mail: kandereck@asu.edu. *Application contact:* Graduate Admissions, 480-965-6113.

Arizona State University, College of Public Programs, School of Public Affairs, Phoenix, AZ 85004-0687. Offers public administration (nonprofit administration) (MPA); public administration (urban management) (MPA); public affairs (PhD); public policy (MPP); MPA/MSW. *Accreditation:* NASPAA (one or more programs are accredited). Part-time and evening/weekend programs available. *Faculty:* 19 full-time (7 women), 1 part-time/adjunct (0 women). *Students:* 149 full-time (96 women), 106 part-time (62 women); includes 62 minority (14 Black or African American, non-Hispanic/Latino; 5 American Indian or Alaska Native, non-Hispanic/Latino; 9 Asian, non-Hispanic/Latino; 32 Hispanic/Latino; 2 Two or more races, non-Hispanic/Latino), 34 international. Average age 32. 227 applicants, 71% accepted, 87 enrolled. In 2010, 68 master's, 4 doctorates awarded. Terminal master's awarded for partial completion of doctoral program. *Degree requirements:* For master's, thesis or alternative, policy analysis or capstone project; interactive Program of Study (iPOS) submitted before completing 50 percent of required credit hours; for doctorate, comprehensive exam, thesis/dissertation, interactive Program of Study (iPOS) submitted before completing 50 percent of required credit hours. *Entrance requirements:* For master's, GRE, minimum GPA of 3.0 or equivalent in last 2 years of work leading to bachelor's degree; for doctorate, GRE, minimum GPA of 3.0 or equivalent in last 2 years of work leading to bachelor's degree, 3 letters of recommendation, resume, statement of goals, samples of research reports. Additional exam requirements/recommendations for international students: Required—TOEFL (minimum score 600 paper-based; 213 computer-based; 100 iBT), IELTS (minimum score 6.5). *Application deadline:* For fall admission, 1/15 for domestic and international students. Application fee: $70 ($90 for international students). Electronic applications accepted. *Expenses:* Contact institution. *Financial support:* In 2010–11, 16 research assistantships with full and partial tuition reimbursements (averaging $14,106 per year), 2 teaching assistantships with full and partial tuition reimbursements (averaging $9,913 per year) were awarded; fellowships with full tuition reimbursements, career-related internships or fieldwork, Federal Work-Study, institutionally sponsored loans, scholarships/grants, and tuition waivers (full and partial) also available. Financial award application deadline: 3/1; financial award applicants required to submit FAFSA. Total annual research expenditures: $621,146. *Unit head:* Dr. Jonathan Koppell, Director, 602-496-1101, E-mail: koppell@asu.edu. *Application contact:* Graduate Admissions, 480-965-6113.

Assumption College, Graduate School, Department of Business Studies, Worcester, MA 01609-1296. Offers accounting (MBA); business administration (CAGS); finance/economics (MBA); general business (MBA); human resources (MBA); international business (MBA); management (MBA); marketing (MBA); nonprofit leadership (MBA). Part-time and evening/weekend programs available. *Faculty:* 3 full-time (0 women), 13 part-time/adjunct (3 women). *Students:* 20 full-time (9 women), 135 part-time (70 women); includes 24 minority (19 Black or African American, non-Hispanic/Latino; 2 Asian, non-Hispanic/Latino; 3 Hispanic/Latino), 4 international. Average age 26. 85 applicants, 95% accepted. In 2010, 40 master's, 2 other advanced degrees awarded. *Entrance requirements:* For master's and CAGS, 3 letters of recommendation, resume, essay. Additional exam requirements/recommendations for international students: Required—TOEFL (minimum score 540 paper-based; 200 computer-based; 76 iBT), IELTS (minimum score 6). *Application deadline:* For fall admission, 6/1 priority date for domestic students, 5/1 priority date for international students; for spring admission, 11/1 priority date for domestic students, 9/1 priority date for international students. Applications are processed on a rolling basis. Application fee: $30. Electronic applications accepted. *Expenses:* Tuition: Part-time $503 per credit. Required fees: $20 per semester. One-time fee: $100. Part-time tuition and fees vary according to campus/location. *Financial support:* Application deadline: 6/1. *Faculty research:* Workplace diversity, dynamics of team interaction, utilization of leased employees. *Unit head:* Michael Lewis, Director, 508-767-7372, Fax:

508-767-7252, E-mail: milewis@assumption.edu. *Application contact:* Daniel Provost, Assistant Director of Graduate Student Services, 508-767-7426, Fax: 508-767-7030, E-mail: dprovost@assumption.edu.

Avila University, Program in Organizational Development, Kansas City, MO 64145-1698. Offers fundraising (Graduate Certificate); management (MA), including fundraising, project management; organizational development (MS); project management (Graduate Certificate). Part-time and evening/weekend programs available. Postbaccalaureate distance learning degree programs offered (no on-campus study). *Faculty:* 2 full-time (1 woman), 10 part-time/adjunct (7 women). *Students:* 72 full-time (61 women), 36 part-time (24 women); includes 35 minority (28 Black or African American, non-Hispanic/Latino; 2 American Indian or Alaska Native, non-Hispanic/Latino; 2 Asian, non-Hispanic/Latino; 2 Hispanic/Latino; 1 Native Hawaiian or other Pacific Islander, non-Hispanic/Latino), 4 international. Average age 36. 47 applicants, 64% accepted, 27 enrolled. In 2010, 18 master's awarded. *Degree requirements:* For master's, thesis optional. *Entrance requirements:* For master's, 2 letters of recommendation, minimum GPA of 3.25 during last 60 hours, resume. Additional exam requirements/recommendations for international students: Required—TOEFL. *Application deadline:* Applications are processed on a rolling basis. Application fee: $0. Electronic applications accepted. *Expenses:* Tuition: Full-time $5580; part-time $465 per credit hour. Required fees: $348; $29 per credit hour. *Financial support:* In 2010–11, 69 students received support. Unspecified assistantships available. Support available to part-time students. Financial award applicants required to submit FAFSA. *Unit head:* Dr. Steve Iliff, Dean, 816-501-3737, Fax: 816-941-4650, E-mail: advantage@avila.edu. *Application contact:* Linda Dubar, School of Professional Studies, 816-501-3737, Fax: 816-941-4650, E-mail: advantage@avila.edu.

Azusa Pacific University, School of Business and Management, Azusa, CA 91702-7000. Offers business administration (MBA); diversity for strategic advantage (MA); entrepreneurship (MBA); finance (MBA); human and organizational development (MA); human resources and organizational development (MBA); human resources management (MA); international business (MBA); marketing (MBA); non-profit management (MA); organizational development and change (MA); performance improvement (MA); public administration (MA); strategic management (MBA). Part-time and evening/weekend programs available. *Faculty:* 19 full-time (5 women), 2 part-time/adjunct (1 woman). *Students:* 75 full-time (41 women), 96 part-time (46 women); includes 65 minority (15 Black or African American, non-Hispanic/Latino; 15 Asian, non-Hispanic/Latino; 34 Hispanic/Latino; 1 Native Hawaiian or other Pacific Islander, non-Hispanic/Latino), 17 international. Average age 30. In 2010, 82 master's awarded. *Degree requirements:* For master's, thesis (for some programs), final project. *Entrance requirements:* For master's, GMAT, minimum GPA of 3.0. Additional exam requirements/recommendations for international students: Required—TOEFL (minimum score 600 paper-based). *Application deadline:* For fall admission, 8/15 priority date for domestic students. Applications are processed on a rolling basis. Application fee: $45 ($65 for international students). *Expenses:* Contact institution. *Financial support:* Scholarships/grants available. *Faculty research:* Gender issues, financial risk, leadership and ethics, marketing strategy. *Unit head:* Dr. Ilene Bezjian, Dean, 626-815-3090, Fax: 626-815-3802, E-mail: ibezjian@apu.edu. *Application contact:* Dr. Ilene Bezjian, Dean, 626-815-3090, Fax: 626-815-3802, E-mail: ibezjian@apu.edu.

Bernard M. Baruch College of the City University of New York, School of Public Affairs, Program in Public Administration, New York, NY 10010-5585. Offers health care policy (MPA); nonprofit administration (MPA); policy analysis and evaluation (MPA); public management (MPA); MS/MPA. *Accreditation:* NASPAA. Part-time and evening/weekend programs available. *Faculty:* 71 full-time (27 women), 51 part-time/adjunct (23 women). *Students:* 180 full-time (125 women), 491 part-time (327 women); includes 152 Black or African American, non-Hispanic/Latino; 2 American Indian or Alaska Native, non-Hispanic/Latino; 68 Asian, non-Hispanic/Latino; 107 Hispanic/Latino; 18 Two or more races, non-Hispanic/Latino. Average age 33. 482 applicants, 68% accepted, 233 enrolled. In 2010, 203 master's awarded. *Degree requirements:* For master's, thesis, capstone. *Entrance requirements:* For master's, GRE General Test. Additional exam requirements/recommendations for international students: Required—TOEFL. *Application deadline:* For fall admission, 4/1 priority date for domestic and international students; for spring admission, 11/15 priority date for domestic and international students. Applications are processed on a rolling basis. Application fee: $125. Electronic applications accepted. *Expenses:* Contact institution. *Financial support:* In 2010–11, 31 students received support, including 8 fellowships (averaging $1,500 per year), 23 research assistantships (averaging $12,000 per year); career-related internships or fieldwork, Federal Work-Study, scholarships/grants, tuition waivers (partial), and unspecified assistantships also available. Support available to part-time students. Financial award application deadline: 5/15; financial award applicants required to submit FAFSA. *Faculty research:* Urbanization, population and poverty in the developing world, housing and community development, labor unions and housing, government-nongovernment relations, immigration policy, social network analysis, cross-sectoral governance, comparative healthcare systems, program evaluation, social welfare policy, health outcomes, educational policy and leadership, transnationalism, infant health, welfare reform, racial/ethnic disparities in health, urban politics,

homelessness, race and ethnic relations. Total annual research expenditures: $2.6 million. *Unit head:* David Birdsell, Dean, 646-660-6700, Fax: 646-660-6721, E-mail: david.birdsell@baruch.cuny.edu. *Application contact:* Michael J. Lovaglio, Director of Student Affairs and Graduate Admissions, 646-660-6750, Fax: 646-660-6751, E-mail: michael.lovaglio@baruch.cuny.edu.

Brandeis University, The Heller School for Social Policy and Management, Program in Nonprofit Management, Waltham, MA 02454-9110. Offers child, youth, and family management (MBA); health care management (MBA); social impact management (MBA); social policy and management (MBA); sustainable development (MBA); MBA/MA; MBA/MD. MBA/MD program offered in conjunction with Tufts University School of Medicine. *Accreditation:* AACSB. Part-time programs available. *Faculty:* 36 full-time, 107 part-time/adjunct. *Students:* 58 full-time (39 women), 5 part-time (3 women); includes 2 Black or African American, non-Hispanic/Latino; 11 Asian, non-Hispanic/Latino; 2 Hispanic/Latino, 4 international. Average age 27. 116 applicants, 57% accepted, 34 enrolled. In 2010, 21 master's awarded. *Degree requirements:* For master's, team consulting project. *Entrance requirements:* For master's, GMAT (preferred) or GRE, 2 letters of recommendation, problem statement analysis, 3-5 years of professional experience. Additional exam requirements/recommendations for international students: Required—TOEFL (minimum score 600 paper-based; 250 computer-based; 100 iBT). *Application deadline:* For fall admission, 3/15 for domestic and international students. Applications are processed on a rolling basis. Application fee: $55. Electronic applications accepted. *Expenses:* Contact institution. *Financial support:* Scholarships/grants and tuition waivers (partial) available. Financial award application deadline: 3/15; financial award applicants required to submit FAFSA. *Faculty research:* Health care; children and families; elder and disabled services; social impact management; organizations in the non-profit, for-profit, or public sector. *Unit head:* Dr. Brenda Anderson, Program Director, 781-736-8423, E-mail: banderson@brandeis.edu. *Application contact:* Shana Mongan, Assistant Director for Admissions and Financial Aid, 781-736-4229, E-mail: mongan@brandeis.edu.

Brigham Young University, Graduate Studies, Marriott School of Management, Master of Public Administration Program, Provo, UT 84602. Offers finance (MPA); human resources (MPA); local government (MPA); nonprofit management (MPA); JD/MPA. *Faculty:* 12 full-time (1 woman), 5 part-time/adjunct (0 women). *Students:* 121 full-time (58 women); includes 3 Black or African American, non-Hispanic/Latino; 1 American Indian or Alaska Native, non-Hispanic/Latino; 11 Asian, non-Hispanic/Latino; 8 Hispanic/Latino. Average age 27. 137 applicants, 64% accepted, 61 enrolled. In 2010, 47 master's awarded. *Entrance requirements:* For master's, GRE, GMAT, minimum GPA of 3.0. Additional exam requirements/recommendations for international students: Required—TOEFL (minimum score 580 paper-based; 85 iBT), IELTS (minimum score 7). *Application deadline:* For fall admission, 2/1 for domestic and international students. Application fee: $50. Electronic applications accepted. *Expenses:* Tuition: Full-time $5580; part-time $310 per credit hour. Tuition and fees vary according to program and student's religious affiliation. *Financial support:* In 2010–11, 73 students received support. Career-related internships or fieldwork and scholarships/grants available. Financial award application deadline: 4/15; financial award applicants required to submit FAFSA. *Faculty research:* Taxes, budgeting, nonprofit, ethics, decision modeling, work balance, organizational behavior. *Unit head:* Dr. David W. Hart, Director, 801-422-4221, Fax: 801-422-0311, E-mail: mpa@byu.edu. *Application contact:* Catherine Cooper, Director of Student Services, 801-422-4221, E-mail: mpa@byu.edu.

California Lutheran University, Graduate Studies, School of Management, Thousand Oaks, CA 91360-2787. Offers business (IMBA); computer science (MS); econometrics (MBA); economics (MS); entrepreneurship (MBA, Certificate); finance (MBA, Certificate); financial planning (MBA, Certificate); information systems and technology (MS); information technology management (MBA, Certificate); international business (MBA, Certificate); management and organization behavior (MBA); management and organizational behavior (Certificate); marketing (MBA, Certificate); microeconomics (MBA); nonprofit and social enterprise (MBA). Part-time and evening/weekend programs available. Postbaccalaureate distance learning degree programs offered (no on-campus study). *Faculty:* 12 full-time (3 women), 27 part-time/adjunct (6 women). *Students:* 350 full-time (162 women), 262 part-time (99 women); includes 21 Black or African American, non-Hispanic/Latino; 44 Asian, non-Hispanic/Latino; 56 Hispanic/Latino; 4 Native Hawaiian or other Pacific Islander, non-Hispanic/Latino; 12 Two or more races, non-Hispanic/Latino, 185 international. Average age 32. 379 applicants, 74% accepted, 138 enrolled. In 2010, 231 master's awarded. *Entrance requirements:* For master's, GMAT, interview, minimum GPA of 3.0. *Application deadline:* Applications are processed on a rolling basis. Application fee: $50. *Expenses:* Contact institution. *Unit head:* Dr. Charles Maxey, Dean, 805-493-3360. *Application contact:* 805-493-3127, Fax: 805-493-3542, E-mail: clugrad@clunet.edu.

Cambridge College, School of Management, Cambridge, MA 02138-5304. Offers business negotiation and conflict resolution (M Mgt); general business (M Mgt); health care informatics (M Mgt); health care management (M Mgt); leadership in human and organizational dynamics (M Mgt); non-profit and public organization management (M Mgt); small business development (M Mgt); technology management (M Mgt). Part-time and evening/weekend programs available. *Faculty:* 6 full-time (3 women), 54 part-time/adjunct (26 women). *Students:* 222 full-time (121 women), 175 part-time (110 women); includes 127 minority (89 Black or African American, non-Hispanic/Latino; 2 American Indian or Alaska Native, non-Hispanic/Latino; 9 Asian, non-Hispanic/Latino; 25 Hispanic/Latino; 2 Two or more races, non-Hispanic/Latino), 125 international. Average age 37. In 2010, 221 master's awarded. *Degree requirements:* For master's, thesis, seminars. *Entrance requirements:* For master's, resume, 2 professional references. Additional exam requirements/recommendations for international students: Required—TOEFL (minimum score 550 paper-based; 213 computer-based; 79 iBT); Recommended—IELTS (minimum score 6). *Application deadline:* Applications are processed on a rolling basis. Application fee: $30. Electronic applications accepted. *Expenses:* Contact institution. *Financial support:* Career-related internships or fieldwork, Federal Work-Study, and scholarships/grants available. Financial award applicants required to submit FAFSA. *Faculty research:* Negotiation, mediation and conflict resolution; leadership; management of diverse organizations; case studies and simulation methodologies for management education, digital as a second language: social networking for digital immigrants, non-profit and public management. *Unit head:* Dr. Mary Ann Joseph, Acting Dean, 617-873-0227, E-mail: maryann.joseph@cambridgecollege.edu. *Application contact:* Elaine M. Lapomardo, Dean of Enrollment Management, 617-873-0274, Fax: 617-349-3561, E-mail: elaine.lapomardo@cambridgecollege.edu.

Carlos Albizu University, Miami Campus, Graduate Programs, Miami, FL 33172-2209. Offers clinical psychology (Psy D); entrepreneurship (MBA); exceptional student education (MS); industrial/organizational psychology (MS); marriage and family therapy (MS); mental health counseling (MS); nonprofit management (MBA); organizational management (MBA); psychology (MS); school counseling (MS); teaching English as a second language (MS). *Accreditation:* APA. Part-time and evening/weekend programs available. *Faculty:* 21 full-time (12 women), 37 part-time/adjunct (18 women). *Students:* 496 full-time (400 women), 242 part-time (192 women); includes 590 minority (58 Black or African American, non-Hispanic/Latino; 2 American Indian or Alaska Native, non-Hispanic/Latino; 5 Asian, non-Hispanic/Latino; 523 Hispanic/Latino; 2 Two or more races, non-Hispanic/Latino), 15 international. Average age 36. 141 applicants, 84% accepted, 118 enrolled. In 2010, 159 master's, 20 doctorates awarded. Terminal master's awarded for partial completion of doctoral program. *Degree requirements:* For master's, one foreign language, comprehensive exam, integrative project (MBA), research project (exceptional student education, teaching English as a second language); for doctorate, one foreign language, comprehensive exam, internship, project. *Entrance requirements:* For master's, 3 letters of recommendation, interview, minimum GPA of 3.0, resume, statement of purpose, official transcripts; for doctorate, 3 letters of recommendation, minimum GPA of 3.0, resume, interview. *Application deadline:* For fall admission, 8/1 priority date for domestic students; for spring admission, 11/30 priority date for domestic students. Applications are processed on a rolling basis. Application fee: $50. Electronic applications accepted. *Expenses:* Tuition: Full-time $9360; part-time $520 per credit. Required fees: $298 per term. Tuition and fees vary according to course load, degree level and program. *Financial support:* In 2010–11, 106 students received support. Federal Work-Study, scholarships/grants, and tuition discounts available. Financial award application deadline: 6/1; financial award applicants required to submit FAFSA. *Faculty research:* Psychotherapy, forensic psychology, neuropsychology, marketing strategy, entrepreneurship, special education. *Unit head:* Dr. Carmen S. Roca, Chancellor, 305-593-1223 Ext. 120, Fax: 305-629-8052, E-mail: croca@albizu.edu. *Application contact:* Vanessa Almendarez, Secretary, 305-593-1223 Ext. 137, Fax: 305-593-1854, E-mail: valmendarez@albizu.edu.

Cleary University, Online Program in Business Administration, Ann Arbor, MI 48105-2659. Offers financial planning (MBA); financial planning (Graduate Certificate); green business strategy (MBA, Graduate Certificate); management (MBA); nonprofit management (MBA, Graduate Certificate); organizational leadership (MBA); public accounting (MBA). Part-time and evening/weekend programs available. Postbaccalaureate distance learning degree programs offered (no on-campus study). *Faculty:* 1 (woman) full-time, 20 part-time/adjunct (8 women). *Students:* 1 (woman) full-time, 115 part-time (67 women); includes 30 minority (21 Black or African American, non-Hispanic/Latino; 1 American Indian or Alaska Native, non-Hispanic/Latino; 6 Asian, non-Hispanic/Latino; 2 Hispanic/Latino), 7 international. Average age 34. 62 applicants, 77% accepted, 36 enrolled. In 2010, 22 master's awarded. *Degree requirements:* For master's, thesis. *Entrance requirements:* For master's, bachelor's degree; minimum GPA of 2.5; professional resume indicating minimum 2 years management or related experience; undergraduate degree from an accredited college or university with at least 18 quarter hours (or 12 semester hours) of accounting study (for MBA in accounting). Additional exam requirements/recommendations for international students: Required—TOEFL (minimum score 550 paper-based; 213 computer-based; 79 iBT), Michigan English Language Assessment Battery (minimum score: 75). *Application deadline:* For fall admission, 8/15 for domestic students, 7/15 for international students; for spring admission, 4/2 for domestic students, 1/2 for international students. Applications are processed on a rolling basis. Application fee: $50. Electronic applications accepted. *Financial support:* In 2010–11, 80 students received support, including 80 fellowships (averaging $12,501 per year); Federal Work-Study and scholarships/grants also available.

Support available to part-time students. Financial award application deadline: 8/15; financial award applicants required to submit FAFSA. *Unit head:* Dr. Vincent Linder, Provost and Vice President for Academic Affairs, 800-686-1883, Fax: 734-332-4646, E-mail: vlinder@cleary.edu. *Application contact:* Carrie Bonofiglio, Director of Student Recruiting, 800-686-1883, Fax: 517-552-7805, E-mail: cbono@cleary.edu.

Cleveland State University, College of Graduate Studies, Maxine Goodman Levin College of Urban Affairs, Program in Nonprofit Administration and Leadership, Cleveland, OH 44115. Offers geographic information systems (Certificate); local and urban management (Certificate); nonprofit administration and leadership (MNAL); nonprofit management (Certificate); urban economic development (Certificate). Part-time and evening/weekend programs available. *Faculty:* 10 full-time (9 women), 8 part-time/adjunct (4 women). *Students:* 11 full-time (10 women), 20 part-time (17 women); includes 7 Black or African American, non-Hispanic/Latino; 2 Asian, non-Hispanic/Latino. Average age 35. 35 applicants, 57% accepted, 14 enrolled. *Degree requirements:* For master's, thesis or alternative, capstone course. *Entrance requirements:* For master's, GRE (minimum 40th percentile verbal and quantitative, 4.0 analytical writing), minimum GPA of 3.0. Additional exam requirements/recommendations for international students: Required—TOEFL (minimum score 525 paper-based; 197 computer-based; 65 iBT). *Application deadline:* For fall admission, 7/15 priority date for domestic students, 5/15 for international students; for spring admission, 11/1 for international students. Applications are processed on a rolling basis. Application fee: $30. Electronic applications accepted. *Expenses:* Tuition, state resident: full-time $8447; part-time $469 per credit hour. Tuition, nonresident: full-time $16,020; part-time $890 per credit hour. Required fees: $50. *Financial support:* In 2010–11, 5 students received support, including research assistantships with full and partial tuition reimbursements available (averaging $6,960 per year); career-related internships or fieldwork, Federal Work-Study, scholarships/grants, tuition waivers (full and partial), and unspecified assistantships also available. Support available to part-time students. Financial award application deadline: 3/1; financial award applicants required to submit FAFSA. *Faculty research:* Human resource management, volunteerism, performance measurement in nonprofits, government-nonprofit partnerships. *Unit head:* Dr. Jennifer Alexander, Director, 216-687-5011, Fax: 216-687-2013, E-mail: j.k.alexander@csuohio.edu. *Application contact:* Joan Demko, Graduate Academic Support Specialist, 216-523-7522, Fax: 216-687-5398, E-mail: urbanprograms@csuohio.edu.

Cleveland State University, College of Graduate Studies, Maxine Goodman Levin College of Urban Affairs, Program in Public Administration, Cleveland, OH 44115. Offers geographic information systems (Certificate); local and urban management (Certificate); non-profit management (Certificate); public administration (MPA); urban real estate development (Certificate); JD/MPA. *Accreditation:* NASPAA. Part-time and evening/weekend programs available. *Faculty:* 26 full-time (10 women), 14 part-time/adjunct (8 women). *Students:* 36 full-time (22 women), 70 part-time (41 women); includes 26 Black or African American, non-Hispanic/Latino; 1 American Indian or Alaska Native, non-Hispanic/Latino; 1 Asian, non-Hispanic/Latino; 2 Hispanic/Latino; 1 Two or more races, non-Hispanic/Latino, 4 international. Average age 36. 82 applicants, 41% accepted, 15 enrolled. In 2010, 37 master's, 8 other advanced degrees awarded. *Degree requirements:* For master's, thesis or alternative, capstone course. *Entrance requirements:* For master's, GRE General Test (minimum 40th percentile verbal and quantitative, 4.0 writing), minimum GPA of 3.0. Additional exam requirements/recommendations for international students: Required—TOEFL (minimum score 525 paper-based; 197 computer-based; 65 iBT). *Application deadline:* For fall admission, 7/15 priority date for domestic students, 5/15 for international students; for spring admission, 11/1 for international students. Applications are processed on a rolling basis. Application fee: $30. Electronic applications accepted. *Expenses:* Tuition, state resident: full-time $8447; part-time $469 per credit hour. Tuition, nonresident: full-time $16,020; part-time $890 per credit hour. Required fees: $50. *Financial support:* In 2010–11, 10 students received support, including 7 research assistantships with full and partial tuition reimbursements available (averaging $6,960 per year), 3 teaching assistantships with full and partial tuition reimbursements available (averaging $6,960 per year); career-related internships or fieldwork, institutionally sponsored loans, tuition waivers (full and partial), and unspecified assistantships also available. Financial award application deadline: 3/1; financial award applicants required to submit FAFSA. *Faculty research:* Health care administration, public management, economic development, city management, nonprofit management. *Unit head:* Dr. Jennifer Alexander, Director, 216-687-5011, Fax: 216-687-2013, E-mail: j.k.alexander@csuohio.edu. *Application contact:* Joan Demko, Graduate Academic Support Specialist, 216-523-7522, Fax: 216-687-5398, E-mail: urbanprograms@csuohio.edu.

Cleveland State University, College of Graduate Studies, Maxine Goodman Levin College of Urban Affairs, Program in Urban Studies, Cleveland, OH 44115. Offers geographic information systems (Certificate); local and urban management (Certificate); nonprofit management (Certificate); urban economic development (Certificate); urban real estate development and finance (Certificate); urban studies (MS); urban studies and public affairs (PhD). PhD program offered jointly with The University of Akron. Part-time and evening/

weekend programs available. *Faculty:* 26 full-time (10 women), 20 part-time/adjunct (11 women). *Students:* 16 full-time (10 women), 35 part-time (18 women); includes 7 Black or African American, non-Hispanic/Latino, 17 international. Average age 37. 90 applicants, 38% accepted, 18 enrolled. In 2010, 6 master's, 7 doctorates, 6 other advanced degrees awarded. *Degree requirements:* For master's, thesis or alternative, exit project, capstone course; for doctorate, comprehensive exam, thesis/dissertation. *Entrance requirements:* For master's, GRE General Test, minimum GPA of 3.0; for doctorate, GRE General Test, minimum GPA of 3.5. Additional exam requirements/recommendations for international students: Required—TOEFL (minimum score 525 paper-based; 197 computer-based; 65 iBT). *Application deadline:* For fall admission, 7/15 priority date for domestic students, 5/15 for international students; for spring admission, 11/1 for international students. Applications are processed on a rolling basis. Application fee: $30. Electronic applications accepted. *Expenses:* Tuition, state resident: full-time $8447; part-time $469 per credit hour. Tuition, nonresident: full-time $16,020; part-time $890 per credit hour. Required fees: $50. *Financial support:* In 2010–11, 15 students received support, including 11 research assistantships with full tuition reimbursements available (averaging $7,000 per year), 4 teaching assistantships with full and partial tuition reimbursements available (averaging $7,000 per year); career-related internships or fieldwork, Federal Work-Study, institutionally sponsored loans, scholarships/grants, tuition waivers (full and partial), and unspecified assistantships also available. Support available to part-time students. Financial award application deadline: 3/1; financial award applicants required to submit FAFSA. *Faculty research:* Environmental issues, economic development, urban and public policy, public management. *Unit head:* Dr. Sugie Lee, Director, 216-687-2381, Fax: 216-687-9342, E-mail: s.lee56@csuohio.edu. *Application contact:* Joan Demko, Graduate Academic Support Specialist, 216-523-7522, Fax: 216-687-5398, E-mail: urbanprograms@csuohio.edu.

The College at Brockport, State University of New York, School of Education and Human Services, Department of Public Administration, Brockport, NY 14420-2997. Offers arts administration (AGC); nonprofit management (AGC); public administration (MPA), including general public administration, health care management, nonprofit management, public safety. *Accreditation:* NASPAA. Part-time and evening/weekend programs available. *Students:* 26 full-time (17 women), 80 part-time (64 women); includes 12 Black or African American, non-Hispanic/Latino; 2 Asian, non-Hispanic/Latino; 5 Hispanic/Latino. 48 applicants, 79% accepted, 27 enrolled. In 2010, 49 master's, 2 other advanced degrees awarded. *Degree requirements:* For master's, thesis or alternative. *Entrance requirements:* For master's, GRE or minimum GPA of 3.0, letters of recommendation, statement of objectives; current resume. Additional exam requirements/recommendations for international students: Required—TOEFL (minimum score 550 paper-based; 213 computer-based; 79 iBT). *Application deadline:* For fall admission, 3/1 priority date for domestic and international students; for spring admission, 10/1 priority date for domestic and international students. Application fee: $50. Electronic applications accepted. *Financial support:* In 2010–11, teaching assistantships with full tuition reimbursements (averaging $6,000 per year); Federal Work-Study, scholarships/grants, and unspecified assistantships also available. Support available to part-time students. Financial award application deadline: 3/15; financial award applicants required to submit FAFSA. *Faculty research:* E-government, performance management, nonprofits and policy implementation, Medicaid and disabilities. *Unit head:* Dr. Ed Downey, Chairperson, 585-395-2375, Fax: 585-395-2172, E-mail: edowney@brockport.edu. *Application contact:* Dr. Ed Downey, Chairperson, 585-395-2375, Fax: 585-395-2172, E-mail: edowney@brockport.edu.

Daemen College, Program in Executive Leadership and Change, Amherst, NY 14226-3592. Offers business (MS); health professions (MS); not-for-profit organizations (MS). Part-time and evening/weekend programs available. *Faculty:* 1 full-time (0 women), 4 part-time/adjunct (1 woman). *Students:* 8 full-time (5 women), 12 part-time (9 women); includes 3 minority (all Black or African American, non-Hispanic/Latino). Average age 38. In 2010, 5 master's awarded. *Degree requirements:* For master's, thesis, cohort learning sequence (2 years for weekend cohort; 3 years for weeknight cohort). *Entrance requirements:* For master's, 2 letters of recommendation, interview, goal statement, official transcripts, resume. Additional exam requirements/recommendations for international students: Required—TOEFL (minimum score 500 paper-based; 173 computer-based; 63 iBT), IELTS (minimum score 5.5). *Application deadline:* For fall admission, 3/1 priority date for domestic and international students; for spring admission, 10/1 priority date for domestic and international students. Applications are processed on a rolling basis. Application fee: $25. Electronic applications accepted. *Expenses:* Tuition: Part-time $830 per credit hour. Tuition and fees vary according to course load and reciprocity agreements. *Financial support:* In 2010–11, 1 student received support. Institutionally sponsored loans available. Financial award application deadline: 2/15; financial award applicants required to submit FAFSA. *Unit head:* Dr. John S. Frederick, Executive Director, 716-839-8342, Fax: 716-839-8261, E-mail: jfrederi@daemen.edu. *Application contact:* Scott Rowe, Associate Director of Graduate Admissions, 716-839-8225, Fax: 716-839-8229, E-mail: srowe@daemen.edu.

DePaul University, School of Public Service, Chicago, IL 60604. Offers financial administration management (Certificate); health administration (Certificate); health law and policy (MS); international public services (MS); leadership and policy studies (MS); metropolitan planning (Certificate); public administration (MPA); public service management (MS), including association management, fundraising and philanthropy, healthcare administration, higher education administration, metropolitan planning; public services (Certificate); JD/MS. Part-time and evening/weekend programs available. Postbaccalaureate distance learning degree programs offered (minimal on-campus study). *Faculty:* 14 full-time (3 women), 43 part-time/adjunct (24 women). *Students:* 372 full-time (256 women), 324 part-time (237 women); includes 156 Black or African American, non-Hispanic/Latino; 33 Asian, non-Hispanic/Latino; 65 Hispanic/Latino; 18 Two or more races, non-Hispanic/Latino, 18 international. Average age 26. 162 applicants, 100% accepted, 94 enrolled. In 2010, 108 master's awarded. *Degree requirements:* For master's, thesis or integrative seminar. *Entrance requirements:* For master's, minimum GPA of 2.7. Additional exam requirements/recommendations for international students: Required—TOEFL (minimum score 550 paper-based; 213 computer-based; 80 iBT), IELTS (minimum score 6.5). *Application deadline:* Applications are processed on a rolling basis. Application fee: $40. Electronic applications accepted. *Financial support:* In 2010–11, 60 students received support, including 3 research assistantships with full tuition reimbursements available (averaging $7,000 per year); career-related internships or fieldwork, Federal Work-Study, institutionally sponsored loans, scholarships/grants, tuition waivers (partial), and unspecified assistantships also available. Support available to part-time students. Financial award application deadline: 7/1; financial award applicants required to submit FAFSA. *Faculty research:* Government financing, transportation, leadership, health care, volunteerism and organizational behavior, non-profit organizations. Total annual research expenditures: $20,000. *Unit head:* Dr. J. Patrick Murphy, Director, 312-362-5608, Fax: 312-362-5506, E-mail: jpmurphy@depaul.edu. *Application contact:* Megan B. Balderston, Director of Admissions and Marketing, 312-362-5565, Fax: 312-362-5506, E-mail: pubserv@depaul.edu.

Eastern Michigan University, Graduate School, College of Business, Programs in Business Administration, Ypsilanti, MI 48197. Offers business administration (MBA, Graduate Certificate); computer information systems (Graduate Certificate); e-business (MBA, Graduate Certificate); enterprise business intelligence (MBA); entrepreneurship (MBA, Graduate Certificate); finance (MBA, Graduate Certificate); human resources (MBA); human resources management (Graduate Certificate); information systems (MBA); internal auditing (MBA); international business (MBA, Graduate Certificate); marketing management (Graduate Certificate); nonprofit management (MBA); organizational development (Graduate Certificate); supply chain management (MBA, Graduate Certificate). *Accreditation:* AACSB. Part-time programs available. Postbaccalaureate distance learning degree programs offered (no on-campus study). *Students:* 149 full-time (66 women), 456 part-time (232 women); includes 146 minority (109 Black or African American, non-Hispanic/Latino; 4 American Indian or Alaska Native, non-Hispanic/Latino; 27 Asian, non-Hispanic/Latino; 6 Hispanic/Latino), 105 international. Average age 32. 330 applicants, 64% accepted, 150 enrolled. In 2010, 128 master's, 53 other advanced degrees awarded. *Entrance requirements:* For master's, GMAT (minimum score 450), minimum cumulative undergraduate GPA of 2.75. Additional exam requirements/recommendations for international students: Required—TOEFL. *Application deadline:* For fall admission, 5/15 for domestic students, 5/1 for international students; for winter admission, 10/15 for domestic students, 10/1 for international students; for spring admission, 3/15 for domestic students, 3/1 for international students. Applications are processed on a rolling basis. Application fee: $35. *Financial support:* Fellowships, research assistantships with full tuition reimbursements, teaching assistantships with full tuition reimbursements, career-related internships or fieldwork, Federal Work-Study, institutionally sponsored loans, scholarships/grants, tuition waivers (partial), and unspecified assistantships available. Support available to part-time students. Financial award applicants required to submit FAFSA. *Unit head:* K. Michelle Henry, Interim Director, Graduate Programs, 734-487-4444, Fax: 734-483-1316, E-mail: mhenry1@emich.edu. *Application contact:* Beste Windes, Advisor, 734-487-4444, Fax: 734-483-1316, E-mail: bwindes@emich.edu.

Eastern Michigan University, Graduate School, College of Health and Human Services, Interdisciplinary Program in Non-Profit Management, Ypsilanti, MI 48197. Offers Graduate Certificate. *Students:* 7 part-time (all women); includes 4 minority (all Black or African American, non-Hispanic/Latino). Average age 35. 5 applicants, 60% accepted, 2 enrolled. In 2010, 9 Graduate Certificates awarded. *Unit head:* Dr. Marcia Bombyk, Program Coordinator, 734-487-4173, Fax: 734-487-8536, E-mail: marcia.bombyk@emich.edu. *Application contact:* Dr. Marcia Bombyk, Program Coordinator, 734-487-4173, Fax: 734-487-8536, E-mail: marcia.bombyk@emich.edu.

East Tennessee State University, School of Graduate Studies, College of Arts and Sciences, Department of Economics, Finance, and Urban Studies, Johnson City, TN 37614. Offers city management (MCM); not-for-profit (MPA); planning and development (MPA); public financial management (MPA). Part-time programs available. *Faculty:* 1 full-time (0 women). *Students:* 15 full-time (5 women), 8 part-time (4 women); includes 1 Black or African

American, non-Hispanic/Latino, 2 international. Average age 30. 19 applicants, 42% accepted, 7 enrolled. In 2010, 14 master's awarded. *Degree requirements:* For master's, comprehensive exam, internship, capstone, research report. *Entrance requirements:* For master's, GRE General Test, minimum GPA of 2.5. Additional exam requirements/recommendations for international students: Required—TOEFL (minimum score 550 paper-based; 213 computer-based; 79 iBT). *Application deadline:* For fall admission, 6/1 priority date for domestic students, 4/30 for international students; for spring admission, 11/1 for domestic students, 9/30 for international students. Application fee: $25 ($35 for international students). Electronic applications accepted. *Financial support:* In 2010–11, 9 research assistantships with full tuition reimbursements (averaging $5,500 per year) were awarded; career-related internships or fieldwork, institutionally sponsored loans, scholarships/grants, and unspecified assistantships also available. Financial award application deadline: 7/1; financial award applicants required to submit FAFSA. Total annual research expenditures: $6,519. *Unit head:* Dr. Weixing Chen, Chair, 423-439-6632, Fax: 423-439-4348, E-mail: chen@etsu.edu. *Application contact:* Dr. Weixing Chen, Chair, 423-439-6632, Fax: 423-439-4348, E-mail: chen@etsu.edu.

Fairleigh Dickinson University, Metropolitan Campus, Anthony J. Petrocelli College of Continuing Studies, Public Administration Institute, Teaneck, NJ 07666-1914. Offers public administration (MPA, Certificate); public nonprofit management (Certificate). *Students:* 116 full-time (49 women), 123 part-time (64 women), 97 international. Average age 32. 165 applicants, 76% accepted, 56 enrolled. In 2010, 104 master's awarded. *Application deadline:* Applications are processed on a rolling basis. Application fee: $40. *Unit head:* Dr. William Roberts, Director, 201-692-2000. *Application contact:* Susan Brooman, University Director of Graduate Admissions, 201-692-2554, Fax: 201-692-2560, E-mail: globaleducation@fdu.edu.

Florida Atlantic University, College of Design and Social Inquiry, School of Public Administration, Program in Nonprofit Management, Boca Raton, FL 33431-0991. Offers MNM. *Students:* 10 full-time (all women), 17 part-time (14 women); includes 8 minority (5 Black or African American, non-Hispanic/Latino; 2 Hispanic/Latino; 1 Two or more races, non-Hispanic/Latino). Average age 32. 34 applicants, 65% accepted, 8 enrolled. In 2010, 8 master's awarded. *Degree requirements:* For master's, thesis optional. *Entrance requirements:* For master's, GRE, minimum GPA of 3.0. Additional exam requirements/recommendations for international students: Required—TOEFL. *Application deadline:* For fall admission, 7/1 priority date for domestic students, 2/15 for international students; for spring admission, 11/1 priority date for domestic students, 7/15 for international students. Application fee: $30. *Expenses:* Tuition, area resident: Part-time $319.96 per credit. Tuition, state resident: part-time $319.96 per credit. Tuition, nonresident: part-time $926.42 per credit. *Financial support:* Career-related internships or fieldwork and institutionally sponsored loans available. *Faculty research:* Governance, nonprofit management, resource development, public and private nonprofit enterprise, accounting for government. *Unit head:* Dr. Ron Nyhan, Coordinator, 954-762-5664, E-mail: rcnyhan@fau.edu. *Application contact:* Dr. Ron Nyhan, Coordinator, 954-762-5664, E-mail: rcnyhan@fau.edu.

George Mason University, College of Humanities and Social Sciences, Department of Public and International Affairs, Fairfax, VA 22030. Offers association management (Certificate); biodefense (MS, PhD); emergency management and homeland security (Certificate); nonprofit management (Certificate); political science (MA, PhD); public administration (MPA); public management (Certificate). *Accreditation:* NASPAA (one or more programs are accredited). *Faculty:* 38 full-time (14 women), 31 part-time/adjunct (8 women). *Students:* 134 full-time (76 women), 319 part-time (176 women); includes 63 minority (29 Black or African American, non-Hispanic/Latino; 9 Asian, non-Hispanic/Latino; 21 Hispanic/Latino; 1 Native Hawaiian or other Pacific Islander, non-Hispanic/Latino; 3 Two or more races, non-Hispanic/Latino), 16 international. Average age 31. 574 applicants, 58% accepted, 144 enrolled. In 2010, 140 master's, 3 doctorates, 11 other advanced degrees awarded. *Entrance requirements:* For master's, GRE General Test, minimum GPA of 3.0 in last 60 hours of course work. Additional exam requirements/recommendations for international students: Required—TOEFL (minimum score 570 paper-based; 230 computer-based; 88 iBT). *Application deadline:* For fall admission, 3/1 priority date for domestic students; for spring admission, 10/15 for domestic students. Application fee: $100. Electronic applications accepted. *Expenses:* Tuition, state resident: full-time $8192; part-time $440 per credit hour. Tuition, nonresident: full-time $22,952; part-time $1055 per credit hour. Required fees: $2364; $99 per credit hour. *Financial support:* In 2010–11, 30 students received support, including 3 fellowships with full tuition reimbursements available (averaging $18,000 per year), 10 research assistantships with full and partial tuition reimbursements available (averaging $12,271 per year), 18 teaching assistantships with full and partial tuition reimbursements available (averaging $10,428 per year); career-related internships or fieldwork, Federal Work-Study, scholarships/grants, unspecified assistantships, and health care benefits (full-time research or teaching assistantship recipients) also available. Financial award application deadline: 3/1; financial award applicants required to submit FAFSA. *Faculty research:* The Rehnquist Court and economic liberties; intersection of economic development with high-tech industry, telecommunications, and entrepreneurism; political economy of development; violence, terrorism and U. S. foreign policy; international

security issues. Total annual research expenditures: $696,997. *Unit head:* Dr. Priscilla Regan, Chair, 703-993-1419, Fax: 703-993-1399, E-mail: pregan@gmu.edu. *Application contact:* Peg Koback, Information Contact, 703-993-9466, E-mail: mkoback@gmu.edu.

Hamline University, School of Business, St. Paul, MN 55104-1284. Offers business (MBA); nonprofit management (MA); public administration (MA, DPA); JD/MA; JD/MBA; LL M/MA; LL M/MBA; MA/MA; MBA/MA. Part-time and evening/weekend programs available. *Faculty:* 20 full-time (8 women), 42 part-time/adjunct (12 women). *Students:* 509 full-time (234 women), 130 part-time (74 women); includes 102 minority (55 Black or African American, non-Hispanic/Latino; 6 American Indian or Alaska Native, non-Hispanic/Latino; 29 Asian, non-Hispanic/Latino; 10 Hispanic/Latino; 2 Two or more races, non-Hispanic/Latino), 66 international. Average age 32. 244 applicants, 73% accepted, 139 enrolled. In 2010, 293 master's, 3 doctorates awarded. *Degree requirements:* For master's, thesis (for some programs); for doctorate, comprehensive exam, thesis/dissertation. *Entrance requirements:* For master's, personal statement, official transcripts, curriculum vitae, letters of recommendation, writing sample; for doctorate, personal statement, curriculum vitae, official transcripts, letters of recommendation, writing sample. Additional exam requirements/recommendations for international students: Required—TOEFL (minimum score 80 iBT). *Application deadline:* For fall admission, 6/1 for international students; for spring admission, 10/1 for international students. Applications are processed on a rolling basis. Application fee: $0. Electronic applications accepted. *Expenses:* Tuition: Full-time $7248; part-time $453 per credit hour. Required fees: $7 per credit hour. One-time fee: $210. Tuition and fees vary according to degree level, campus/location and program. *Financial support:* Federal Work-Study and scholarships/grants available. Support available to part-time students. Financial award applicants required to submit FAFSA. *Faculty research:* Liberal arts-based business programs, experiential learning, organizational process/politics, gender differences, social equity. *Unit head:* Nancy Hellerud, Interim Dean, 651-523-2284, Fax: 651-523-3098, E-mail: nhellerud@gw.hamline.edu. *Application contact:* Rae A. Lenway, Director, Graduate Recruitment and Admission, 651-523-2900, Fax: 651-523-3058, E-mail: rlenway@gw.hamline.edu.

High Point University, Norcross Graduate School, High Point, NC 27262-3598. Offers business administration (MBA); educational leadership (M Ed); elementary education (M Ed); history (MA); nonprofit management (MA); secondary math (M Ed); special education (M Ed); strategic communication (MA); teaching elementary education k-6 (MAT); teaching secondary mathematics 9-12 (MAT). *Accreditation:* ACBSP; NCATE. Part-time and evening/weekend programs available. *Faculty:* 30 full-time (11 women), 5 part-time/adjunct (1 woman). *Students:* 17 full-time (10 women), 292 part-time (198 women); includes 107 minority (100 Black or African American, non-Hispanic/Latino; 1 Asian, non-Hispanic/Latino; 6 Hispanic/Latino), 19 international. 249 applicants, 69% accepted, 141 enrolled. *Degree requirements:* For master's, comprehensive exam (for some programs), thesis (for some programs). *Entrance requirements:* For master's, GMAT (MBA), GRE, MAT, minimum GPA of 3.0. Additional exam requirements/recommendations for international students: Required—TOEFL (minimum score 550 paper-based). *Application deadline:* For fall admission, 4/15 priority date for domestic and international students; for spring admission, 10/15 priority date for domestic and international students. Applications are processed on a rolling basis. Application fee: $50. Electronic applications accepted. *Expenses:* Tuition: Full-time $11,520; part-time $640 per hour. Required fees: $90; $150 per semester. Part-time tuition and fees vary according to program. *Financial support:* Federal Work-Study available. Support available to part-time students. Financial award application deadline: 3/1; financial award applicants required to submit FAFSA. *Unit head:* Tracy Collum, Associate Dean, 336-767-4840, Fax: 336-841-9024, E-mail: tcollum@highpoint.edu. *Application contact:* Tracy Collum, Associate Dean, 336-767-4840, Fax: 336-841-9024, E-mail: tcollum@highpoint.edu.

Indiana University Bloomington, School of Public and Environmental Affairs, Public Affairs Programs, Bloomington, IN 47405-7000. Offers comparative and international affairs (MPA); economic development (MPA); energy (MPA); environmental policy (PhD); environmental policy and natural resource management (MPA); information systems (MPA); local government management (MPA); nonprofit management (MPA, Certificate); policy analysis (MPA); public finance (PhD); public financial administration (MPA); public management (MPA, PhD); public policy analysis (PhD); specialized public affairs (MPA); sustainability and sustainable development (MPA); JD/MPA; MPA/MIS; MPA/MLS; MSES/MPA. *Accreditation:* NASPAA (one or more programs are accredited). Part-time programs available. *Faculty:* 31 full-time, 15 part-time/adjunct. *Students:* 466 full-time (261 women); includes 11 Black or African American, non-Hispanic/Latino; 2 American Indian or Alaska Native, non-Hispanic/Latino; 42 Asian, non-Hispanic/Latino; 1 Hispanic/Latino, 65 international. Average age 26. 650 applicants, 218 enrolled. In 2010, 166 master's, 10 doctorates awarded. *Degree requirements:* For master's, core classes, capstone; for doctorate, comprehensive exam, thesis/dissertation. *Entrance requirements:* For master's, GRE General Test or GMAT, official transcripts, 3 letters of recommendation, resume, personal statement, departmental questions; for doctorate, GRE General Test or LSAT, official transcripts, 3 letters of recommendation, resume or curriculum vitae, statement of purpose. Additional exam requirements/recommendations for international students: Required—TOEFL (minimum score 600 paper-based; 96 iBT); Recommended—IELTS (minimum score 7). *Application deadline:* For fall admission, 5/1 priority date for domestic students, 12/1 priority date for international students. Applications are processed on a rolling basis. Application fee: $55 ($65 for international students). Electronic applications accepted. *Financial support:* Fellowships with partial tuition reimbursements, research assistantships with partial tuition reimbursements, teaching assistantships with partial tuition reimbursements, career-related internships or fieldwork, Federal Work-Study, scholarships/grants, health care benefits, unspecified assistantships, and Service Corps programs available. Financial award application deadline: 2/1; financial award applicants required to submit FAFSA. *Faculty research:* Comparative and international affairs, environmental policy and resource management, policy analysis, public finance, public management, urban management, nonprofit management, energy policy, social policy, public finance. *Unit head:* Jennifer Forney, Director of Graduate Student Services, 812-855-9485, Fax: 812-856-3665, E-mail: speampo@indiana.edu. *Application contact:* Audrey Whitaker, Admissions Assistant, 812-855-2840, E-mail: speaapps@indiana.edu.

Indiana University Northwest, School of Public and Environmental Affairs, Gary, IN 46408-1197. Offers criminal justice (MPA); environmental affairs (Graduate Certificate); health services administration (MPA); human services administration (MPA); nonprofit management (Graduate Certificate); public management (MPA, Graduate Certificate). *Accreditation:* NASPAA (one or more programs are accredited). Part-time programs available. *Faculty:* 5 full-time (3 women). *Students:* 9 full-time (6 women), 127 part-time (96 women); includes 96 minority (81 Black or African American, non-Hispanic/Latino; 1 American Indian or Alaska Native, non-Hispanic/Latino; 2 Asian, non-Hispanic/Latino; 10 Hispanic/Latino; 2 Two or more races, non-Hispanic/Latino). Average age 38. 43 applicants, 95% accepted, 40 enrolled. In 2010, 37 master's, 24 other advanced degrees awarded. *Entrance requirements:* For master's, GRE General Test or GMAT, letters of recommendation. *Application deadline:* For fall admission, 8/15 priority date for domestic students. Applications are processed on a rolling basis. Application fee: $25. *Financial support:* Career-related internships or fieldwork, Federal Work-Study, and tuition waivers (partial) available. Support available to part-time students. Financial award application deadline: 3/1. *Faculty research:* Employment in income security policies, evidence in criminal justice, equal employment law, social welfare policy and welfare reform, public finance in developing countries. *Unit head:* George Assibey-Mensah, Interim Dean/Division Director, 219-980-6695, Fax: 219-980-6737. *Application contact:* Sandra Hall Smith, Secretary, 219-980-6695, Fax: 219-980-6737, E-mail: shsmith@iun.edu.

Indiana University–Purdue University Indianapolis, School of Public and Environmental Affairs, Indianapolis, IN 46202. Offers criminal justice and public safety (MSCJPS); public affairs (MPA), including criminal justice, nonprofit management, policy analysis, public management; public management (Graduate Certificate); JD/MPA; MATS/MM; MLS/NMC; MLS/PMC. *Accreditation:* CAHME (one or more programs are accredited); NASPAA. Part-time and evening/weekend programs available. Postbaccalaureate distance learning degree programs offered (no on-campus study). *Faculty:* 23 full-time (7 women). *Students:* 81 full-time (47 women), 205 part-time (142 women); includes 30 Black or African American, non-Hispanic/Latino; 6 Asian, non-Hispanic/Latino; 8 Hispanic/Latino, 9 international. Average age 31. 217 applicants, 73% accepted, 136 enrolled. In 2010, 77 degrees awarded. *Entrance requirements:* For master's, GRE General Test, GMAT or LSAT, minimum GPA of 3.0 (preferred). Additional exam requirements/recommendations for international students: Required—All international applicants to IUPUI whose native language is not English must demonstrate proficiency in English as a second language through an accepted examination and an accepted score. *Application deadline:* For fall admission, 5/15 priority date for domestic students; for spring admission, 2/15 priority date for domestic students. Applications are processed on a rolling basis. Application fee: $50 ($65 for international students). Electronic applications accepted. *Financial support:* In 2010–11, 1 fellowship with full tuition reimbursement (averaging $14,000 per year), 4 research assistantships with full tuition reimbursements (averaging $12,000 per year) were awarded; teaching assistantships, career-related internships or fieldwork, Federal Work-Study, institutionally sponsored loans, and scholarships/grants also available. Support available to part-time students. Financial award application deadline: 3/1; financial award applicants required to submit FAFSA. *Faculty research:* Nonprofit and public management, public policy, urban and environmental policy, disaster preparedness and recovery, vehicular safety, homicide, and offender rehabilitation and re-entry. Total annual research expenditures: $1.6 million. *Unit head:* Dr. Terry L. Baumer, Executive Associate Dean, 317-274-2016, Fax: 317-274-5153.

Indiana University South Bend, School of Public and Environmental Affairs, South Bend, IN 46634-7111. Offers health systems administration and policy (MPA); health systems management (Certificate); nonprofit management (Certificate); public and community services administration and policy (MPA); public management (Certificate); urban affairs (Certificate). *Accreditation:* NASPAA. Part-time and evening/weekend programs available. *Faculty:* 4 full-time (1 woman). *Students:* 1 full-time (0 women), 9 part-time (7 women); includes 1 minority (Black or African American, non-Hispanic/

Latino). Average age 43. 2 applicants, 0% accepted, 0 enrolled. In 2010, 11 master's awarded. *Entrance requirements:* For master's, GRE General Test, minimum undergraduate GPA of 2.5. *Application deadline:* For fall admission, 7/1 priority date for domestic students; for spring admission, 11/1 for domestic students. Applications are processed on a rolling basis. Application fee: $50 ($60 for international students). *Financial support:* Fellowships, research assistantships, career-related internships or fieldwork, Federal Work-Study, and institutionally sponsored loans available. Support available to part-time students. Financial award application deadline: 3/1; financial award applicants required to submit FAFSA. *Unit head:* Leda M. Hall, Dean, 574-520-4803. *Application contact:* Leda M. Hall, Dean, 574-520-4803.

Kean University, College of Business and Public Management, Program in Public Administration, Union, NJ 07083. Offers environmental management (MPA); health services administration (MPA); non-profit management (MPA); public administration (MPA). *Accreditation:* NASPAA. Part-time and evening/weekend programs available. *Faculty:* 7 full-time (4 women). *Students:* 61 full-time (41 women), 82 part-time (48 women); includes 61 Black or African American, non-Hispanic/Latino; 7 Asian, non-Hispanic/Latino; 19 Hispanic/Latino, 5 international. Average age 31. 70 applicants, 76% accepted, 36 enrolled. In 2010, 44 master's awarded. *Degree requirements:* For master's, thesis, internship, research seminar. *Entrance requirements:* For master's, minimum GPA of 3.0, 2 letters of recommendation, interview, writing sample, transcripts. *Application deadline:* For fall admission, 6/1 for domestic students; for spring admission, 11/1 for domestic students. Application fee: $75 ($150 for international students). Electronic applications accepted. *Expenses:* Tuition, state resident: full-time $10,872; part-time $500 per credit. Tuition, nonresident: full-time $14,736; part-time $614 per credit. Required fees: $2740.80; $125 per credit. Part-time tuition and fees vary according to course load and degree level. *Financial support:* In 2010–11, 11 research assistantships with full tuition reimbursements (averaging $3,263 per year) were awarded; unspecified assistantships also available. Financial award applicants required to submit FAFSA. *Unit head:* Dr. Patricia Moore, Program Coordinator, 908-737-4314, E-mail: pmoore@kean.edu. *Application contact:* Reenat Hasan, Pre-Admissions Coordinator, 908-737-5923, Fax: 908-737-5925, E-mail: hasanr@kean.edu.

Kentucky State University, College of Professional Studies, Frankfort, KY 40601. Offers business administration (MBA), including accounting, finance, management, marketing; public administration (MPA), including human resource management, international administration and development, management information systems, nonprofit management; special education (MA). Part-time and evening/weekend programs available. Postbaccalaureate distance learning degree programs offered (minimal on-campus study). *Faculty:* 12 full-time (4 women), 2 part-time/adjunct (both women). *Students:* 88 full-time (57 women), 79 part-time (42 women); includes 104 minority (101 Black or African American, non-Hispanic/Latino; 1 Asian, non-Hispanic/Latino; 2 Hispanic/Latino), 2 international. Average age 34. 124 applicants, 62% accepted, 45 enrolled. In 2010, 38 master's awarded. *Degree requirements:* For master's, comprehensive exam, thesis optional. *Entrance requirements:* For master's, GMAT, GRE. Additional exam requirements/recommendations for international students: Required—TOEFL (minimum score 525 paper-based; 173 computer-based). *Application deadline:* Applications are processed on a rolling basis. Application fee: $30 ($100 for international students). Electronic applications accepted. *Expenses:* Tuition, state resident: full-time $5886; part-time $352 per credit hour. Tuition, nonresident: full-time $9054; part-time $528 per credit hour. Required fees: $450; $26 per credit hour. *Financial support:* In 2010–11, 46 students received support, including 4 research assistantships (averaging $10,975 per year); career-related internships or fieldwork, scholarships/grants, tuition waivers (partial), and unspecified assistantships also available. Financial award application deadline: 4/15; financial award applicants required to submit FAFSA. *Unit head:* Dr. Gashaw Lake, Dean, 502-597-6105, Fax: 502-597-6715, E-mail: gashaw.lake@kysu.edu. *Application contact:* Dr. Titilayo Ufomata, Acting Director of Graduate Studies, 502-597-6443, E-mail: titilayo.ufomata@kysu.edu.

Lasell College, Graduate and Professional Studies in Management, Newton, MA 02466-2709. Offers elder care administration (MSM, Graduate Certificate); elder care marketing (MSM, Graduate Certificate); fundraising management (MSM, Graduate Certificate); human resource management (Graduate Certificate); human resources management (MSM); management (MSM, Graduate Certificate); marketing (MSM, Graduate Certificate); non-profit management (MSM, Graduate Certificate); project management (MSM, Graduate Certificate); public relations (MSM). Part-time and evening/weekend programs available. Postbaccalaureate distance learning degree programs offered (no on-campus study). *Faculty:* 8 full-time (5 women), 7 part-time/adjunct (5 women). *Students:* 25 full-time (21 women), 97 part-time (67 women); includes 16 minority (6 Black or African American, non-Hispanic/Latino; 2 American Indian or Alaska Native, non-Hispanic/Latino; 4 Asian, non-Hispanic/Latino; 4 Hispanic/Latino), 17 international. Average age 33. 56 applicants, 52% accepted, 19 enrolled. In 2010, 65 master's, 7 other advanced degrees awarded. *Entrance requirements:* For master's and Graduate Certificate, bachelor's degree from an accredited institution. Additional exam requirements/recommendations for international students: Required—TOEFL (minimum score 550 paper-based; 213 computer-based; 75 iBT). *Application* *deadline:* For fall admission, 8/31 priority date for domestic students, 6/30 priority date for international students; for spring admission, 12/31 priority date for domestic students, 10/31 priority date for international students. Applications are processed on a rolling basis. Application fee: $40. Electronic applications accepted. *Expenses:* Tuition: Part-time $550 per credit hour. Required fees: $55 per semester. *Financial support:* In 2010–11, 40 students received support. Available to part-time students. Application deadline: 8/31. *Unit head:* Dr. Joan Dolamore, Dean of Graduate and Professional Studies, 617-243-2485, Fax: 617-243-2450, E-mail: gradinfo@lasell.edu. *Application contact:* Adrienne Franciosi, Director of Graduate Admission, 617-243-2214, Fax: 617-243-2450, E-mail: gradinfo@lasell.edu.

Lasell College, Graduate and Professional Studies in Sport Management, Newton, MA 02466-2709. Offers sport hospitality management (MS, Graduate Certificate); sport leadership (MS, Graduate Certificate); sport non-profit management (MS, Graduate Certificate). Part-time programs available. Postbaccalaureate distance learning degree programs offered (no on-campus study). *Faculty:* 1 full-time (0 women), 4 part-time/adjunct (3 women). *Students:* 3 full-time (2 women), 10 part-time (0 women); includes 1 minority (Black or African American, non-Hispanic/Latino). Average age 28. 12 applicants, 58% accepted, 4 enrolled. *Entrance requirements:* For master's and Graduate Certificate, bachelor's degree from an accredited institution. Additional exam requirements/recommendations for international students: Required—TOEFL (minimum score 550 paper-based; 213 computer-based; 75 iBT), IELTS. *Application deadline:* For fall admission, 8/31 priority date for domestic students, 6/30 priority date for international students; for spring admission, 12/31 priority date for domestic students, 10/31 priority date for international students. Applications are processed on a rolling basis. Application fee: $40. Electronic applications accepted. *Expenses:* Tuition: Part-time $550 per credit hour. Required fees: $55 per semester. *Financial support:* In 2010–11, 2 students received support. Available to part-time students. Application deadline: 8/31. *Unit head:* Dr. Joan Dolamore, Dean of Graduate and Professional Studies, 617-243-2485, Fax: 617-243-2450, E-mail: gradinfo@lasell.edu. *Application contact:* Adrienne Franciosi, Director of Graduate Admission, 617-243-2214, Fax: 617-243-2450, E-mail: gradinfo@lasell.edu.

Lindenwood University, Graduate Programs, School of Human Services, St. Charles, MO 63301-1695. Offers nonprofit administration (MA); public administration (MPA). Part-time programs available. *Faculty:* 2 full-time (1 woman), 9 part-time/adjunct (4 women). *Students:* 7 full-time (3 women), 22 part-time (19 women); includes 7 Black or African American, non-Hispanic/Latino. Average age 33. *Degree requirements:* For master's, minimum cumulative GPA of 3.0, directed internship, capstone project. *Entrance requirements:* Additional exam requirements/recommendations for international students: Required—TOEFL (minimum score 550 paper-based; 213 computer-based; 80 iBT). *Application deadline:* For fall admission, 8/27 priority date for domestic and international students; for spring admission, 1/28 priority date for domestic and international students. Applications are processed on a rolling basis. Application fee: $30 ($100 for international students). Electronic applications accepted. *Expenses:* Tuition: Full-time $13,260; part-time $380 per credit hour. Required fees: $340. One-time fee: $30. Tuition and fees vary according to course level and course load. *Financial support:* Career-related internships or fieldwork, institutionally sponsored loans, tuition waivers, and unspecified assistantships available. Financial award application deadline: 6/30; financial award applicants required to submit FAFSA. *Unit head:* Carla Mueller, Dean, 636-949-4731, E-mail: cmueller@lindenwood.edu. *Application contact:* Brett Barger, Dean of Evening Admissions and Extension Campuses, 636-949-4934, Fax: 636-949-4109, E-mail: adultadmissions@lindenwood.edu.

Lipscomb University, MBA Program, Nashville, TN 37204-3951. Offers accounting (MBA); business administration (general) (MBA); conflict management (MBA); financial services (MBA); healthcare management (MBA); leadership (MBA); nonprofit management (MBA); sports administration (MBA). *Accreditation:* ACBSP. Part-time and evening/weekend programs available. *Faculty:* 17 full-time (5 women), 3 part-time/adjunct (0 women). *Students:* 52 full-time (30 women), 79 part-time (36 women); includes 20 Black or African American, non-Hispanic/Latino; 1 American Indian or Alaska Native, non-Hispanic/Latino; 1 Asian, non-Hispanic/Latino; 7 Hispanic/Latino. Average age 32. 151 applicants, 47% accepted, 45 enrolled. In 2010, 70 master's awarded. *Entrance requirements:* For master's, GMAT, interview, 2 references, resume. Additional exam requirements/recommendations for international students: Required—TOEFL (minimum score 570 paper-based; 230 computer-based). *Application deadline:* For fall admission, 2/1 for international students; for winter admission, 6/1 for international students. Applications are processed on a rolling basis. Application fee: $50 ($75 for international students). Electronic applications accepted. *Expenses:* Contact institution. *Financial support:* Career-related internships or fieldwork, Federal Work-Study, scholarships/grants, tuition waivers (partial), and unspecified assistantships available. Support available to part-time students. Financial award application deadline: 7/1; financial award applicants required to submit FAFSA. *Faculty research:* Impact of spirituality on organization commitment, leadership, psychological empowerment, training. *Unit head:* Dr. Mike Kendrick, Interim Chair of Graduate Business Studies, 615-966-1833, Fax: 615-966-1818, E-mail: mikekendrick@lipscomb.edu. *Application contact:* Emily Landsdell, 615-966-5284, E-mail: emily.lansdell@lipscomb.edu.

Marquette University, Graduate School, Program in Public Service, Milwaukee, WI 53201-1881. Offers criminal justice administration (MLS); dispute resolution (MDR, MLS); engineering (MLS); health care administration (MLS); law enforcement leadership and management (Certificate); leadership studies (Certificate); non-profit sector (MLS); public service (MAPS, MLS); sports leadership (MLS). Part-time and evening/weekend programs available. Postbaccalaureate distance learning degree programs offered (no on-campus study). *Faculty:* 3 full-time (2 women), 29 part-time/adjunct (11 women). *Students:* 27 full-time (13 women), 134 part-time (84 women); includes 29 minority (21 Black or African American, non-Hispanic/Latino; 1 American Indian or Alaska Native, non-Hispanic/Latino; 1 Asian, non-Hispanic/Latino; 6 Hispanic/Latino), 1 international. Average age 38. 108 applicants, 78% accepted, 36 enrolled. In 2010, 11 master's, 12 Certificates awarded. *Degree requirements:* For master's, comprehensive exam (for some programs). *Entrance requirements:* For master's, GRE General Test (preferred), GMAT, or LSAT, official transcripts from all current and previous colleges/universities except Marquette, three letters of recommendation, statement of purpose. Additional exam requirements/recommendations for international students: Required—TOEFL. *Application deadline:* Applications are processed on a rolling basis. Application fee: $50. Electronic applications accepted. *Expenses:* Tuition: Full-time $16,290; part-time $905 per credit hour. Tuition and fees vary according to program. *Financial support:* In 2010–11, 1 fellowship, 1 research assistantship were awarded; teaching assistantships. Financial award application deadline: 2/15. *Unit head:* Dr. Johnette Caulfield, Adjunct Assistant Professor and Director of Graduate Programs, 414-288-5556, E-mail: jay.caulfield@marquette.edu. *Application contact:* Erin Fox, Assistant Director for Recruitment, 414-288-5319, Fax: 414-288-1902, E-mail: erin.fox@marquette.edu.

Marylhurst University, Department of Business Administration, Marylhurst, OR 97036-0261. Offers finance (MBA); general management (MBA); government policy and administration (MBA); green development (MBA); health care management (MBA); marketing (MBA); natural and organic resources (MBA); nonprofit management (MBA); organizational behavior (MBA); real estate (MBA); renewable energy (MBA); sustainable business (MBA). Part-time and evening/weekend programs available. Postbaccalaureate distance learning degree programs offered (no on-campus study). *Faculty:* 3 full-time (0 women), 36 part-time/adjunct (6 women). *Students:* 27 full-time (13 women), 727 part-time (373 women); includes 167 minority (47 Black or African American, non-Hispanic/Latino; 6 American Indian or Alaska Native, non-Hispanic/Latino; 36 Asian, non-Hispanic/Latino; 51 Hispanic/Latino; 6 Native Hawaiian or other Pacific Islander, non-Hispanic/Latino; 21 Two or more races, non-Hispanic/Latino), 7 international. Average age 38. 262 applicants, 91% accepted, 194 enrolled. In 2010, 289 master's awarded. *Degree requirements:* For master's, comprehensive exam, capstone course. *Entrance requirements:* For master's, GMAT (if GPA less than 3.0 and fewer than 5 years of work experience), interview, resume, 2 letters of recommendation. Additional exam requirements/recommendations for international students: Recommended—TOEFL (minimum score 550 paper-based; 213 computer-based; 80 iBT). *Application deadline:* For fall admission, 9/11 priority date for domestic and international students; for winter admission, 12/15 priority date for domestic and international students; for spring admission, 3/15 priority date for domestic students, 3/17 priority date for international students. Applications are processed on a rolling basis. Application fee: $50. Electronic applications accepted. *Expenses:* Tuition: Full-time $13,932; part-time $516 per credit. Tuition and fees vary according to course load and program. *Financial support:* Scholarships/grants available. Support available to part-time students. Financial award applicants required to submit FAFSA. *Unit head:* Bob Hanks, Director of Business and Real Estate Programs, 503-636-8141, Fax: 503-697-5597, E-mail: mba@marylhurst.edu. *Application contact:* Maruska Lynch, Graduate Admissions Specialist, 800-634-9982 Ext. 6322, Fax: 503-699-6320, E-mail: admissions@marylhurst.edu.

Metropolitan State University, College of Management, St. Paul, MN 55106-5000. Offers business administration (MBA, DBA); information assurance security (Graduate Certificate); management information systems (MMIS); MIS generalist (Graduate Certificate); MIS systems analysis and design (Graduate Certificate); nonprofit management (MPNA); project management (Graduate Certificate); public administration (MPNA). Part-time and evening/weekend programs available. *Students:* 158 full-time (74 women), 217 part-time (114 women); includes 31 Black or African American, non-Hispanic/Latino; 26 Asian, non-Hispanic/Latino; 10 Hispanic/Latino; 6 Two or more races, non-Hispanic/Latino, 47 international. Average age 35. In 2010, 100 master's, 7 other advanced degrees awarded. *Degree requirements:* For master's, thesis optional, computer language (MMIS). *Entrance requirements:* For master's, GMAT (MBA), resume. Additional exam requirements/recommendations for international students: Required—TOEFL (minimum score 550 paper-based; 213 computer-based). *Application deadline:* For fall admission, 7/15 for international students; for winter admission, 11/15 for international students; for spring admission, 3/15 for international students. Applications are processed on a rolling basis. Application fee: $20. Electronic applications accepted. *Expenses:* Tuition, state resident: full-time $5827; part-time $291 per credit hour. Tuition, nonresident: full-time $11,654; part-time $583 per credit hour. Required fees: $10 per credit hour. Tuition and fees vary according to degree level. *Financial support:* Research assistantships with partial tuition reimbursements, career-related internships or fieldwork and Federal Work-Study available. Support available to part-time students. Financial award applicants required to submit FAFSA. *Faculty research:* Yugoslav economic system, workers' cooperatives, participative management and job enrichment, global business systems. *Unit head:* Dr. Paul Huo, Graduate Director, 612-659-7271, Fax: 612-659-7268, E-mail: carol.bormann.young@metrostate.edu. *Application contact:* Gloria B. Marcus, Recruiter/Admissions Adviser, 612-659-7258, Fax: 612-659-7268, E-mail: gloria.marcus@metrostate.edu.

New Mexico Highlands University, Graduate Studies, School of Business, Las Vegas, NM 87701. Offers business administration (MBA), including government nonprofit management, human resource management, international business, management, management information systems. *Accreditation:* ACBSP. *Faculty:* 14 full-time (3 women). *Students:* 71 full-time (44 women), 124 part-time (68 women); includes 119 minority (8 Black or African American, non-Hispanic/Latino; 18 American Indian or Alaska Native, non-Hispanic/Latino; 1 Asian, non-Hispanic/Latino; 89 Hispanic/Latino; 1 Native Hawaiian or other Pacific Islander, non-Hispanic/Latino; 2 Two or more races, non-Hispanic/Latino), 34 international. Average age 34. 128 applicants, 98% accepted, 34 enrolled. In 2010, 48 master's awarded. *Degree requirements:* For master's, comprehensive exam, thesis or alternative. *Entrance requirements:* For master's, minimum undergraduate GPA of 3.0. Additional exam requirements/recommendations for international students: Required—TOEFL (minimum score 540 paper-based; 207 computer-based). *Application deadline:* For fall admission, 8/1 priority date for domestic students. Applications are processed on a rolling basis. Application fee: $15. *Expenses:* Tuition, state resident: full-time $2544. Required fees: $624; $132 per credit hour. *Financial support:* In 2010–11, 29 students received support. Career-related internships or fieldwork, Federal Work-Study, institutionally sponsored loans, scholarships/grants, tuition waivers (full and partial), and unspecified assistantships available. Support available to part-time students. Financial award application deadline: 3/1; financial award applicants required to submit FAFSA. *Faculty research:* Real estate valuation, studying expert judgments in complex accounting, decision environments, green marketing, environmentalism, marketing research methodology. *Unit head:* Dr. Margaret Young, Dean, 505-454-3522, Fax: 505-454-3354, E-mail: young_m@nmhu.edu. Application contact: Diane Trujillo, Administrative Assistant, Graduate Studies, 505-454-3266, Fax: 505-426-2117, E-mail: dtrujillo@nmhu.edu.

New Mexico Highlands University, Graduate Studies, School of Social Work, Las Vegas, NM 87701. Offers bilingual/bicultural social work practice (MSW); clinical practice (MSW); government non-profit management (MSW). *Accreditation:* CSWE. Part-time programs available. *Faculty:* 11 full-time (3 women). *Students:* 260 full-time (216 women), 102 part-time (88 women); includes 13 Black or African American, non-Hispanic/Latino; 22 American Indian or Alaska Native, non-Hispanic/Latino; 3 Asian, non-Hispanic/Latino; 142 Hispanic/Latino; 4 Two or more races, non-Hispanic/Latino, 8 international. Average age 36. 222 applicants, 99% accepted, 164 enrolled. In 2010, 133 master's awarded. *Degree requirements:* For master's, comprehensive exam, thesis or alternative. *Entrance requirements:* For master's, minimum undergraduate GPA of 3.0. Additional exam requirements/recommendations for international students: Required—TOEFL (minimum score 540 paper-based; 207 computer-based). *Application deadline:* For fall admission, 8/1 priority date for domestic students. Applications are processed on a rolling basis. Application fee: $15. *Expenses:* Tuition, state resident: full-time $2544. Required fees: $624; $132 per credit hour. *Financial support:* In 2010–11, 17 students received support. Career-related internships or fieldwork, Federal Work-Study, institutionally sponsored loans, scholarships/grants, tuition waivers (partial), and unspecified assistantships available. Support available to part-time students. Financial award application deadline: 3/1; financial award applicants required to submit FAFSA. *Faculty research:* Treatment attrition among domestic violence batterers, children's health and mental health, Dejando Huellas: meeting the bilingual/bicultural needs of the Latino mental health patient, impact of culture on the therapeutic process, effects of generational gang involvement on adolescents' future. *Unit head:* Dr. Alfredo Garcia, Dean, 505-891-9053, Fax: 505-454-3290, E-mail: a_garcia@nmhu.edu. Application contact: LouAnn Romero, Administrative Assistant, Graduate Studies, 505-454-3087, E-mail: laromero@nmhu.edu.

New York University, Robert F. Wagner Graduate School of Public Service, Program in Public Administration, New York, NY 10012-1019. Offers public administration (PhD); public and nonprofit management and policy (MPA, Advanced Certificate), including developmental administration (Advanced Certificate), financial management and public finance, human resources management (Advanced Certificate), international administration (Advanced Certificate), management (MPA), management for public and nonprofit organizations (Advanced Certificate), public policy analysis, quantitative analysis and computer applications (Advanced Certificate), urban public policy (Advanced Certificate); JD/MPA; MBA/MPA; MPA/MA. *Accreditation:* NASPAA (one or more programs are accredited). Part-time and evening/weekend programs available. *Faculty:* 32 full-time (13 women), 41 part-time/

adjunct (22 women). *Students:* 400 full-time (301 women), 206 part-time (156 women); includes 43 Black or African American, non-Hispanic/Latino; 58 Asian, non-Hispanic/Latino; 36 Hispanic/Latino, 65 international. Average age 28. 1,230 applicants, 54% accepted, 219 enrolled. In 2010, 210 master's, 5 doctorates awarded. *Degree requirements:* For master's, thesis or alternative, capstone end event; for doctorate, one foreign language, thesis/dissertation. *Entrance requirements:* For master's, minimum undergraduate GPA of 3.0; for doctorate, GMAT or GRE General Test, minimum GPA of 3.5. Additional exam requirements/recommendations for international students: Required—TOEFL (minimum score 600 paper-based; 250 computer-based; 100 iBT), IELTS (minimum score 7.5), TWE (minimum score 4). *Application deadline:* For fall admission, 1/15 for domestic students, 1/4 for international students; for spring admission, 11/15 for domestic students, 10/1 for international students. Applications are processed on a rolling basis. Application fee: $80. Electronic applications accepted. *Expenses:* Contact institution. *Financial support:* In 2010–11, 176 students received support, including 171 fellowships (averaging $14,022 per year), 5 research assistantships with full tuition reimbursements available (averaging $22,440 per year); career-related internships or fieldwork, Federal Work-Study, institutionally sponsored loans, scholarships/grants, health care benefits, and unspecified assistantships also available. Support available to part-time students. Financial award application deadline: 1/5; financial award applicants required to submit FAFSA. *Unit head:* Katty Jones, Director, Program Services, 212-998-7411, Fax: 212-995-4164, E-mail: katty.jones@nyu.edu. *Application contact:* Christopher Alexander, Administrative Aide, Enrollment, 212-998-7414, Fax: 212-995-4611, E-mail: wagner.admissions@nyu.edu.

New York University, School of Continuing and Professional Studies, The George Heyman Jr. Center for Philanthropy and Fundraising, New York, NY 10012-1019. Offers fundraising (MS), including fundraising, grantmaking. Part-time and evening/weekend programs available. *Faculty:* 1 full-time (0 women), 17 part-time/adjunct (9 women). *Students:* 8 full-time (all women), 20 part-time (13 women); includes 4 Black or African American, non-Hispanic/Latino; 2 Asian, non-Hispanic/Latino, 4 international. Average age 33. 24 applicants, 63% accepted, 12 enrolled. In 2010, 12 master's awarded. *Degree requirements:* For master's, thesis, capstone project. *Entrance requirements:* For master's, GRE General Test or GMAT (for recent graduates), 2 letters of recommendation, resume, essay, professional experience. Additional exam requirements/recommendations for international students: Required—TOEFL (minimum score 600 paper-based; 250 computer-based; 100 iBT), TWE. *Application deadline:* For fall admission, 2/1 priority date for domestic and international students; for spring admission, 10/15 priority date for domestic students, 8/15 priority date for international students. Applications are processed on a rolling basis. Application fee: $75. Electronic applications accepted. *Financial support:* In 2010–11, 23 students received support, including 23 fellowships (averaging $2,443 per year); scholarships/grants also available. Financial award application deadline: 3/1; financial award applicants required to submit FAFSA. *Unit head:* Levine Naomi, Chair and Executive Director, 212-998-6770, Fax: 212-995-4784. *Application contact:* Mayelly Moreno, 212-998-6777, Fax: 212-995-4784, E-mail: mm172@nyu.edu.

North Central College, Graduate and Continuing Education Programs, Department of Leadership Studies, Naperville, IL 60566-7063. Offers higher education leadership (MLS); professional leadership (MLS); social entrepreneurship (MLS); sports leadership (MLS). Part-time and evening/weekend programs available. *Faculty:* 7 full-time (1 woman), 7 part-time/adjunct (1 woman). *Students:* 28 full-time (15 women), 32 part-time (21 women); includes 5 Black or African American, non-Hispanic/Latino; 3 Hispanic/Latino; 1 Two or more races, non-Hispanic/Latino. Average age 28. In 2010, 2 master's awarded. *Degree requirements:* For master's, project. *Entrance requirements:* For master's, interview. Additional exam requirements/recommendations for international students: Required—TOEFL (minimum score 570 paper-based; 233 computer-based; 90 iBT). *Application deadline:* For fall admission, 8/15 for domestic students; for winter admission, 12/1 for domestic students; for spring admission, 2/1 for domestic students. Applications are processed on a rolling basis. Application fee: $25. *Expenses:* Contact institution. *Financial support:* Scholarships/grants available. Support available to part-time students. *Unit head:* Dr. Thomas Cavanagh, Head, 630-637-5285. *Application contact:* Wendy Kulpinski, Director and Graduate and Continuing Education Admissions, 630-637-5808, Fax: 630-637-5844, E-mail: wekulpinski@noctrl.edu.

Northern Kentucky University, Office of Graduate Programs, College of Arts and Sciences, Program in Public Administration, Highland Heights, KY 41099. Offers non-profit management (Certificate); public administration (MPA). *Accreditation:* NASPAA. Part-time and evening/weekend programs available. *Faculty:* 5 full-time (2 women), 1 (woman) part-time/adjunct. *Students:* 12 full-time (5 women), 89 part-time (50 women); includes 19 minority (17 Black or African American, non-Hispanic/Latino; 1 Asian, non-Hispanic/Latino; 1 Hispanic/Latino), 1 international. Average age 34. 45 applicants, 62% accepted, 24 enrolled. In 2010, 20 master's, 7 other advanced degrees awarded. *Degree requirements:* For master's, capstone. *Entrance requirements:* For master's, GRE, GMAT or MAT, 2 letters of recommendation, writing sample, minimum GPA of 2.75, essay, resume (for those in-career).

Additional exam requirements/recommendations for international students: Required—TOEFL (minimum score 550 paper-based; 213 computer-based; 79 iBT); Recommended—IELTS (minimum score 6.5). *Application deadline:* For fall admission, 7/1 for domestic students, 6/1 for international students; for spring admission, 12/1 for domestic students, 10/1 for international students. Applications are processed on a rolling basis. Application fee: $40. Electronic applications accepted. *Expenses:* Tuition, state resident: full-time $7254; part-time $403 per credit hour. Tuition, nonresident: full-time $12,492; part-time $694 per credit hour. Tuition and fees vary according to degree level and program. *Financial support:* Unspecified assistantships available. Financial award applicants required to submit FAFSA. *Faculty research:* Non-profit management, human resource management, local government, budgeting and finance, urban planning. *Unit head:* Dr. Shamima Ahmed, Director, 859-572-6402, Fax: 859-572-6184, E-mail: ahmed@nku.edu. *Application contact:* Beth Devantier, MPA Coordinator, 859-572-5326, Fax: 859-572-6184, E-mail: devantier@nku.edu.

North Park University, School of Business and Nonprofit Management, Chicago, IL 60625-4895. Offers MBA, MHEA, MHRM, MM, MNA. Part-time and evening/weekend programs available. Postbaccalaureate distance learning degree programs offered (no on-campus study). *Faculty:* 12 full-time (5 women), 40 part-time/adjunct (22 women). *Students:* 12 full-time (5 women), 338 part-time (185 women). Average age 34. 130 applicants, 77% accepted, 87 enrolled. In 2010, 85 master's awarded. *Entrance requirements:* For master's, GMAT, GRE. Additional exam requirements/recommendations for international students: Required—TOEFL. *Application deadline:* For fall admission, 8/1 priority date for domestic students, 7/1 for international students; for spring admission, 12/15 for domestic students, 12/1 for international students. Applications are processed on a rolling basis. Application fee: $30. *Expenses:* Contact institution. *Financial support:* In 2010–11, 98 students received support. Scholarships/grants available. Support available to part-time students. Financial award application deadline: 8/15; financial award applicants required to submit FAFSA. *Unit head:* Dr. Wesley E. Lindahl, Dean, 773-784-3000. *Application contact:* Dr. Christopher Nicholson, Director of Admissions for Graduate and Continuing Education, 773-244-5518, Fax: 773-255-4953, E-mail: cnicholson@northpark.edu.

Our Lady of the Lake University of San Antonio, School of Business and Leadership, Program in Nonprofit Management, San Antonio, TX 78207-4689. Offers MS. Part-time and evening/weekend programs available. Postbaccalaureate distance learning degree programs offered. *Students:* 36 part-time (27 women); includes 14 minority (3 Black or African American, non-Hispanic/Latino; 11 Hispanic/Latino). Average age 39. In 2010, 10 master's awarded. *Expenses:* Tuition: Full-time $13,500; part-time $750 per contact hour. Required fees: $330. Tuition and fees vary according to course level, degree level and campus/location. *Unit head:* Dr. Robert Bisking, Dean, 210-434-6711, Fax: 210-434-0821. *Application contact:* Dr. Robert Bisking, Dean, 210-434-6711, Fax: 210-434-0821.

Providence College, Graduate Studies, School of Business, Providence, RI 02918. Offers accounting (MBA); entrepreneurship (MBA); finance (MBA); international business (MBA); management (MBA); marketing (MBA); not-for-profit organizations (MBA). Part-time and evening/weekend programs available. *Faculty:* 17 full-time (9 women), 10 part-time/adjunct (2 women). *Students:* 53 full-time (20 women), 57 part-time (22 women); includes 4 minority (1 Black or African American, non-Hispanic/Latino; 1 Asian, non-Hispanic/Latino; 2 Two or more races, non-Hispanic/Latino), 6 international. Average age 26. 72 applicants, 81% accepted. In 2010, 56 master's awarded. *Degree requirements:* For master's, thesis optional. *Entrance requirements:* For master's, GMAT. Additional exam requirements/recommendations for international students: Required—TOEFL (minimum score 550 paper-based; 213 computer-based; 80 iBT). *Application deadline:* For fall admission, 8/1 priority date for domestic and international students; for spring admission, 12/1 priority date for domestic and international students. Applications are processed on a rolling basis. Application fee: $55. *Expenses:* Contact institution. *Financial support:* In 2010–11, 34 research assistantships with full tuition reimbursements (averaging $8,400 per year) were awarded; Federal Work-Study, institutionally sponsored loans, and unspecified assistantships also available. Support available to part-time students. Financial award application deadline: 8/1; financial award applicants required to submit FAFSA. *Unit head:* Dr. MaryJane Lenon, Director, MBA Program, 401-865-2566, Fax: 401-865-2978, E-mail: mjlenon@providence.edu. *Application contact:* Katherine A. Follett, Administrative Coordinator, 401-865-2333, Fax: 401-865-2978, E-mail: kfollett@providence.edu.

San Francisco State University, Division of Graduate Studies, College of Behavioral and Social Sciences, Public Administration Program, San Francisco, CA 94132-1722. Offers nonprofit administration (MPA); policy making and analysis (MPA); public management (MPA); urban administration (MPA). *Accreditation:* NASPAA. *Unit head:* Dr. Genie Stowers, Chair, 415-817-4457, Fax: 415-338-1980, E-mail: gstowers@sfsu.edu. *Application contact:* Bridget McCracken, Director of Academic Services, 415-817-4455, E-mail: mpa@sfsu.edu.

Suffolk University, Sawyer Business School, Department of Public Administration, Boston, MA 02108-2770. Offers nonprofit management

(MPA); public administration (CASPA); state and local government (MPA); JD/MPA; MPA/MS. *Accreditation:* NASPAA (one or more programs are accredited). Part-time and evening/weekend programs available. *Faculty:* 9 full-time (4 women), 5 part-time/adjunct (2 women). *Students:* 30 full-time (17 women), 102 part-time (65 women); includes 12 Black or African American, non-Hispanic/Latino; 1 American Indian or Alaska Native, non-Hispanic/Latino; 3 Asian, non-Hispanic/Latino; 8 Hispanic/Latino; 2 Two or more races, non-Hispanic/Latino, 5 international. Average age 31. 76 applicants, 87% accepted, 28 enrolled. In 2010, 62 master's awarded. *Entrance requirements:* Additional exam requirements/recommendations for international students: Required—TOEFL (minimum score 550 paper-based; 213 computer-based; 80 iBT). *Application deadline:* For fall admission, 6/15 priority date for domestic students, 6/15 for international students; for spring admission, 11/1 priority date for domestic students, 11/1 for international students. Applications are processed on a rolling basis. Application fee: $50. Electronic applications accepted. *Expenses:* Contact institution. *Financial support:* In 2010–11, 93 students received support, including 52 fellowships with full and partial tuition reimbursements available (averaging $9,356 per year); career-related internships or fieldwork and Federal Work-Study also available. Support available to part-time students. Financial award application deadline: 4/1; financial award applicants required to submit FAFSA. *Faculty research:* Local government, health care, federal policy, mental health, HIV/AIDS. *Unit head:* Dr. Richard Beinecke, Chair, 617-573-8062, Fax: 617-227-4618, E-mail: rbeineck@suffolk.edu. *Application contact:* Judith Reynolds, Director of Graduate Admissions, 617-573-8302, Fax: 617-305-1733, E-mail: grad.admission@suffolk.edu.

Texas A&M University, Bush School of Government and Public Service, College Station, TX 77843. Offers advanced international affairs (Certificate); China studies (Certificate); homeland security (Certificate); international affairs (MPIA); national security affairs (Certificate); nonprofit management (Certificate); public service and administration (MPSA). *Accreditation:* NASPAA. *Faculty:* 45. *Students:* 215 full-time (98 women), 93 part-time (32 women); includes 20 Black or African American, non-Hispanic/Latino; 2 American Indian or Alaska Native, non-Hispanic/Latino; 14 Asian, non-Hispanic/Latino; 30 Hispanic/Latino, 15 international. Average age 24. In 2010, 93 master's awarded. *Degree requirements:* For master's, summer internship. *Entrance requirements:* For master's, GRE (preferred) or GMAT. *Application deadline:* For fall admission, 1/24 for domestic and international students. Application fee: $50 ($75 for international students). Electronic applications accepted. *Financial support:* In 2010–11, fellowships (averaging $11,000 per year), research assistantships (averaging $11,250 per year) were awarded; career-related internships or fieldwork, Federal Work-Study, and institutionally sponsored loans also available. Financial award application deadline: 2/1; financial award applicants required to submit FAFSA. *Faculty research:* Public policy, presidential studies, public leadership, economic policy, social policy. *Unit head:* Ryan C. Crocker, Dean, 979-862-8007, E-mail: rcrocker@bushschool.tamu.edu. *Application contact:* Kathryn Meyer, Director of Recruiting, 979-458-4767, Fax: 979-845-4155, E-mail: kmeyer@bushschool.tamu.edu.

Troy University, Graduate School, College of Arts and Sciences, Program in Public Administration, Troy, AL 36082. Offers education (MPA); environmental management (MPA); government contracting (MPA); health care administration (MPA); justice administration (MPA); national security affairs (MPA); nonprofit management (MPA); public human resources management (MPA); public management (MPA). *Accreditation:* NASPAA. Part-time and evening/weekend programs available. Postbaccalaureate distance learning degree programs offered (no on-campus study). *Degree requirements:* For master's, capstone course, research methodologies course. *Entrance requirements:* For master's, GRE, MAT or GMAT, minimum undergraduate GPA of 2.5, letter of recommendation, essay. Additional exam requirements/recommendations for international students: Required—TOEFL (minimum score 523 paper-based; 193 computer-based; 70 iBT), IELTS (minimum score 6). *Application deadline:* Applications are processed on a rolling basis. Application fee: $50. Electronic applications accepted. *Expenses:* Tuition, state resident: full-time $4428; part-time $246 per credit hour. Tuition, nonresident: full-time $8856; part-time $492 per credit hour. Required fees: $432; $24 per credit hour. $50 per term. Tuition and fees vary according to program. *Financial support:* Available to part-time students. Applicants required to submit FAFSA. *Unit head:* Dr. Ellen Rosell, Chairman, 334-670-3758, Fax: 334-670-5647, E-mail: erosell@troy.edu. *Application contact:* Brenda K. Campbell, Director of Graduate Admissions, 334-670-3178, Fax: 334-670-3733, E-mail: bcamp@troy.edu.

University of Central Florida, College of Health and Public Affairs, Department of Public Administration, Orlando, FL 32816. Offers emergency management and homeland security (Certificate); non-profit management (MNM, Certificate); public administration (MPA, Certificate); research administration (MS); urban and regional planning (Certificate). *Accreditation:* NASPAA. Part-time and evening/weekend programs available. *Faculty:* 14 full-time (5 women), 9 part-time/adjunct (3 women). *Students:* 103 full-time (70 women), 271 part-time (208 women); includes 125 minority (85 Black or African American, non-Hispanic/Latino; 1 American Indian or Alaska Native, non-Hispanic/Latino; 13 Asian, non-Hispanic/Latino; 22 Hispanic/Latino;

2 Native Hawaiian or other Pacific Islander, non-Hispanic/Latino; 2 Two or more races, non-Hispanic/Latino), 8 international. Average age 31. 258 applicants, 69% accepted, 138 enrolled. In 2010, 101 master's, 25 other advanced degrees awarded. *Degree requirements:* For master's, comprehensive exam, thesis or alternative, research report. *Entrance requirements:* For master's, GRE General Test. *Application deadline:* For fall admission, 7/1 for domestic students; for spring admission, 12/1 for domestic students. Application fee: $30. Electronic applications accepted. *Expenses:* Tuition, state resident: part-time $256.56 per credit hour. Tuition, nonresident: part-time $1011.52 per credit hour. Part-time tuition and fees vary according to program. *Financial support:* In 2010–11, 13 students received support, including 1 fellowship with partial tuition reimbursement available (averaging $10,000 per year), 11 research assistantships with partial tuition reimbursements available (averaging $5,900 per year), 2 teaching assistantships with partial tuition reimbursements available (averaging $7,100 per year); career-related internships or fieldwork, Federal Work-Study, institutionally sponsored loans, tuition waivers (partial), and unspecified assistantships also available. Financial award application deadline: 3/1; financial award applicants required to submit FAFSA. *Unit head:* Dr. Mary Ann Feldheim, Chair, 407-823-3693, Fax: 407-823-5651, E-mail: mfeldhei@mail.ucf.edu. *Application contact:* Dr. Mary Ann Feldheim, Chair, 407-823-3693, Fax: 407-823-5651, E-mail: mfeldhei@mail.ucf.edu.

University of Colorado Denver, Business School, Program in Marketing, Denver, CO 80217. Offers brand management and marketing communication (MS); global marketing (MS); high-tech/entrepreneurial marketing (MS); Internet marketing (MS); market research (MS); marketing and business intelligence (MS); marketing for sustainability (MS); marketing in nonprofit organizations (MS); sports and entertainment marketing (MS). Part-time and evening/weekend programs available. *Students:* 31 full-time (18 women), 8 part-time (4 women); includes 3 Hispanic/Latino, 5 international. Average age 29. 46 applicants, 63% accepted, 18 enrolled. In 2010, 11 master's awarded. *Degree requirements:* For master's, 30 semester hours (18 of marketing core courses, 12 of graduate marketing electives). *Entrance requirements:* For master's, GMAT. Additional exam requirements/recommendations for international students: Required—TOEFL (minimum score 525 paper-based; 197 computer-based; 71 iBT). *Application deadline:* For fall admission, 4/1 priority date for domestic students, 3/15 priority date for international students; for spring admission, 10/1 priority date for domestic and international students. Application fee: $50 ($75 for international students). Electronic applications accepted. *Expenses:* Contact institution. *Financial support:* Federal Work-Study and scholarships/grants available. Support available to part-time students. Financial award application deadline: 4/1; financial award applicants required to submit FAFSA. *Faculty research:* Marketing issues in the Chinese environment, impact of individual difference and contextual factors on the risk-taking behaviors of managers making new-business creation decisions, Attribution Theory perspective of conflict between marketers and engineers, organizational identity and identification, international market entry strategies. *Unit head:* Dr. David Forlani, Associate Professor/Director, 303-315-8420, E-mail: david.forlani@ucdenver.edu. *Application contact:* Shelly Townley, Admissions Director, Graduate Programs, 303-315-8202, E-mail: shelly.townley@ucdenver.edu.

University of Colorado Denver, School of Public Affairs, Program in Public Affairs and Administration, Denver, CO 80127. Offers public administration (MPA), including domestic violence, emergency management and homeland security, environmental policy, management and law, homeland security and defense, local government, nonprofit management, public administration; public affairs (PhD). *Accreditation:* NASPAA. Part-time and evening/weekend programs available. Postbaccalaureate distance learning degree programs offered (no on-campus study). *Faculty:* 19 full-time (9 women), 14 part-time/adjunct (5 women). *Students:* 317 full-time (181 women), 167 part-time (100 women); includes 15 Black or African American, non-Hispanic/Latino; 2 American Indian or Alaska Native, non-Hispanic/Latino; 18 Asian, non-Hispanic/Latino; 29 Hispanic/Latino; 1 Two or more races, non-Hispanic/Latino, 36 international. Average age 30. 270 applicants, 66% accepted, 118 enrolled. In 2010, 119 master's, 4 doctorates awarded. *Degree requirements:* For master's, thesis or alternative, 36-39 credit hours; for doctorate, comprehensive exam, thesis/dissertation, minimum of 66 semester hours, including at least 30 hours of doctoral dissertation credits. *Entrance requirements:* For master's and doctorate, GRE, resume, essay, transcripts, recommendations. Additional exam requirements/recommendations for international students: Required—TOEFL (minimum score 550 paper-based; 223 computer-based). *Application deadline:* For fall admission, 2/1 for domestic students; for spring admission, 10/15 priority date for domestic students. Application fee: $50 ($75 for international students). Electronic applications accepted. *Expenses:* Contact institution. *Financial support:* Fellowships with partial tuition reimbursements, research assistantships with partial tuition reimbursements, teaching assistantships with partial tuition reimbursements, Federal Work-Study and scholarships/grants available. Support available to part-time students. Financial award application deadline: 4/1; financial award applicants required to submit FAFSA. *Faculty research:* Housing, education and the social and economic issues of vulnerable populations; nonprofit governance and management; education finance, effectiveness and reform; P-20 (preschool through graduate school) education initiatives; municipal government accountability. *Unit head:*

Dr. Mary Guy, Program Director, 303-315-2007, Fax: 303-315-2229, E-mail: mary.guy@ucdenver.edu. *Application contact:* Annie Davies, Director of Marketing, Community Outreach and Alumni Affairs, 303-315-2896, Fax: 303-315-2229, E-mail: annie.davies@ucdenver.edu.

University of Georgia, School of Social Work, Institute for Non-Profit Organizations, Athens, GA 30602. Offers MA, Certificate. *Students:* 28 full-time (19 women), 4 part-time (2 women); includes 2 Black or African American, non-Hispanic/Latino, 1 international. 25 applicants, 80% accepted, 17 enrolled. In 2010, 18 master's awarded. *Application deadline:* For fall admission, 7/1 priority date for domestic students; for spring admission, 11/15 for domestic students. Application fee: $50. *Expenses:* Tuition, state resident: full-time $7200; part-time $344 per credit hour. Tuition, nonresident: full-time $21,900; part-time $944 per credit hour. Tuition and fees vary according to course load and program. *Unit head:* Dr. Michelle Mohr Carney, Director, 706-542-5429, Fax: 706-542-3282, E-mail: mmcarney@uga.edu. *Application contact:* Dr. Michelle Mohr Carney, Director, 706-542-5429, Fax: 706-542-3282, E-mail: mmcarney@uga.edu.

University of La Verne, College of Business and Public Management, Program in Organizational Management and Leadership, La Verne, CA 91750-4443. Offers nonprofit management (Certificate); organizational leadership (Certificate); organizational management and leadership (MS). Part-time programs available. *Faculty:* 34 full-time (12 women), 36 part-time/adjunct (9 women). *Students:* 92 full-time (44 women), 70 part-time (46 women); includes 9 Black or African American, non-Hispanic/Latino; 31 Asian, non-Hispanic/Latino; 35 Hispanic/Latino. Average age 32. In 2010, 58 master's awarded. *Degree requirements:* For master's, thesis or research project. *Entrance requirements:* For master's, minimum undergraduate GPA of 2.75, 2 letters of recommendation, interview, resume. Additional exam requirements/recommendations for international students: Required—TOEFL (minimum score 550 paper-based; 213 computer-based). *Application deadline:* Applications are processed on a rolling basis. Application fee: $50. *Expenses:* Contact institution. *Financial support:* Institutionally sponsored loans available. Financial award application deadline: 3/2; financial award applicants required to submit FAFSA. *Unit head:* Dr. Kathy Duncan, Chairperson, 909-593-3511 Ext. 4415, E-mail: kduncan2@laverne.edu. *Application contact:* Program and Admissions Specialist, 909-593-3511 Ext. 4819, Fax: 909-392-2761, E-mail: cbpm@laverne.edu.

University of Louisville, Graduate School, College of Arts and Sciences, Department of Urban and Public Affairs, Louisville, KY 40208. Offers public administration (MPA), including human resources management, non-profit management, public policy and administration; urban and public affairs (PhD), including urban planning and development, urban policy and administration; urban planning (MUP), including administration of planning organizations, housing and community development, land use and environmental planning, spatial analysis. Part-time and evening/weekend programs available. *Faculty:* 22 full-time (7 women), 8 part-time/adjunct (1 woman). *Students:* 73 full-time (36 women), 31 part-time (18 women); includes 11 Black or African American, non-Hispanic/Latino; 2 Asian, non-Hispanic/Latino; 2 Hispanic/Latino; 1 Native Hawaiian or other Pacific Islander, non-Hispanic/Latino; 2 Two or more races, non-Hispanic/Latino, 11 international. Average age 31. 96 applicants, 67% accepted, 37 enrolled. In 2010, 28 master's, 5 doctorates awarded. Terminal master's awarded for partial completion of doctoral program. *Degree requirements:* For master's, internship; for doctorate, comprehensive exam, thesis/dissertation. *Entrance requirements:* For master's, GRE General Test, minimum GPA of 3.0; for doctorate, GRE General Test, master's degree in appropriate field. Additional exam requirements/recommendations for international students: Required—TOEFL (minimum score 550 paper-based; 213 computer-based; 79 iBT). *Application deadline:* For fall admission, 7/15 for domestic students; for spring admission, 11/15 for domestic students. Applications are processed on a rolling basis. Application fee: $50. Electronic applications accepted. *Expenses:* Tuition, state resident: full-time $9144; part-time $508 per credit hour. Tuition, nonresident: full-time $19,026; part-time $1057 per credit hour. Tuition and fees vary according to program and reciprocity agreements. *Financial support:* In 2010–11, 23 students received support; fellowships, research assistantships, health care benefits available. Financial award application deadline: 3/1. *Faculty research:* Housing and community development, performance-based budgeting, environmental policy and natural hazards, sustainability, real estate development, comparative urban development. *Unit head:* Dr. David Simpson, Chair, 502-852-8019, Fax: 502-852-4558, E-mail: dave.simpson@louisville.edu. *Application contact:* Patty Sarley, Graduate Student Advisor, 502-852-7914, Fax: 502-852-4558, E-mail: plclea01@louisville.edu.

University of Maryland, Baltimore County, Graduate School, College of Arts, Humanities and Social Sciences, Department of Sociology and Anthropology, Baltimore, MD 21250. Offers applied sociology (MA, Postbaccalaureate Certificate), including applied sociology (MA), nonprofit sector (Postbaccalaureate Certificate). Part-time and evening/weekend programs available. *Faculty:* 16 full-time (10 women), 2 part-time/adjunct (both women). *Students:* 33 full-time (25 women), 23 part-time (19 women); includes 8 Black or African American, non-Hispanic/Latino; 5 Asian, non-Hispanic/Latino; 4 Hispanic/Latino, 1 international. Average age 26. 40 applicants, 93% accepted, 23 enrolled. In 2010, 27 master's awarded. *Degree* *requirements:* For master's, thesis or alternative. *Entrance requirements:* For master's, minimum GPA of 3.0, undergraduate statistics course. Additional exam requirements/recommendations for international students: Required—TOEFL. *Application deadline:* For fall admission, 7/15 for domestic students; for spring admission, 12/15 for domestic students. Applications are processed on a rolling basis. Application fee: $70. Electronic applications accepted. *Financial support:* In 2010–11, 11 students received support, including 7 research assistantships with full and partial tuition reimbursements available (averaging $12,500 per year), 4 teaching assistantships with full and partial tuition reimbursements available (averaging $12,500 per year); scholarships/grants, health care benefits, unspecified assistantships, and tuition remission also available. Financial award application deadline: 2/14; financial award applicants required to submit FAFSA. *Faculty research:* Sociology of aging, medical sociology, migration. *Unit head:* Dr. J. Kevin Eckert, Chairperson, 410-455-2076, Fax: 410-455-1154, E-mail: eckert@umbc.edu. *Application contact:* Dr. William G. Rothstein, Director, 410-455-2078, Fax: 410-455-1154, E-mail: rothstei@umbc.edu.

University of Memphis, Graduate School, College of Arts and Sciences, Division of Public and Nonprofit Administration, Memphis, TN 38152. Offers nonprofit administration (MPA); public management and policy (MPA); urban management and planning (MPA). *Accreditation:* NASPAA. Part-time and evening/weekend programs available. Postbaccalaureate distance learning degree programs offered (minimal on-campus study). *Faculty:* 5 full-time (2 women), 1 (woman) part-time/adjunct. *Students:* 18 full-time (15 women), 43 part-time (33 women); includes 35 Black or African American, non-Hispanic/Latino; 1 Hispanic/Latino; 1 Two or more races, non-Hispanic/Latino. Average age 34. 32 applicants, 88% accepted, 9 enrolled. In 2010, 17 master's awarded. *Degree requirements:* For master's, comprehensive exam, thesis or alternative, internship. *Entrance requirements:* For master's, GRE General Test, GMAT, or MAT, minimum GPA of 3.0. Additional exam requirements/recommendations for international students: Required—TOEFL. *Application deadline:* For fall admission, 7/1 for domestic students, 5/15 for international students; for spring admission, 12/1 for domestic students, 9/15 for international students. Applications are processed on a rolling basis. Application fee: $35 ($60 for international students). *Financial support:* In 2010–11, 37 students received support; fellowships, research assistantships with full tuition reimbursements available, career-related internships or fieldwork, Federal Work-Study, scholarships/grants, and unspecified assistantships available. Support available to part-time students. Financial award application deadline: 2/15; financial award applicants required to submit FAFSA. *Faculty research:* Nonprofit organization governance, local government management, community collaboration, urban problems, accountability. *Unit head:* Dr. Charles Menifield, Director, 901-678-5527, Fax: 901-678-2981, E-mail: cmenifld@memphis.edu. *Application contact:* Dr. Charles Menifield, Graduate Admissions Coordinator, 901-678-3360, Fax: 901-678-2981, E-mail: cmenifld@memphis.edu.

University of Michigan–Dearborn, College of Arts, Sciences, and Letters, Master of Public Administration Program, Dearborn, MI 48128. Offers assessment and evaluation (Certificate); nonprofit leadership (Certificate); public administration (MPA). Part-time and evening/weekend programs available. *Faculty:* 3 full-time (1 woman), 9 part-time/adjunct (2 women). *Students:* 21 full-time (13 women), 59 part-time (44 women); includes 26 minority (20 Black or African American, non-Hispanic/Latino; 1 American Indian or Alaska Native, non-Hispanic/Latino; 2 Asian, non-Hispanic/Latino; 1 Hispanic/Latino; 1 Native Hawaiian or other Pacific Islander, non-Hispanic/Latino; 1 Two or more races, non-Hispanic/Latino). Average age 35. 36 applicants, 86% accepted, 31 enrolled. In 2010, 22 master's awarded. *Degree requirements:* For master's, assessment seminar. *Entrance requirements:* For master's, GRE or minimum undergraduate GPA of 3.0, 3 letters of recommendation. Additional exam requirements/recommendations for international students: Required—TOEFL, TWE. *Application deadline:* For fall admission, 8/1 for domestic students, 4/1 for international students; for winter admission, 12/1 for domestic students, 11/1 for international students; for spring admission, 4/1 for domestic students, 3/1 for international students. Applications are processed on a rolling basis. Application fee: $60. *Financial support:* Career-related internships or fieldwork and Federal Work-Study available. Support available to part-time students. Financial award applicants required to submit FAFSA. *Faculty research:* Federal, state, and local agency management; independent sector management; educational administration. *Unit head:* Dr. Paul Draus, Director, 313-583-6539, Fax: 313-583-6700, E-mail: draus@umich.edu. *Application contact:* Carol Ligienza, Graduate Programs Coordinator, 313-593-1183, Fax: 313-583-6700, E-mail: caslgrad@umd.umich.edu.

University of Missouri–St. Louis, College of Arts and Sciences, School of Social Work, St. Louis, MO 63121. Offers gerontology (MS, Certificate), including gerontology, long term care administration (Certificate); nonprofit organization management and leadership (Certificate); social work (MSW). *Accreditation:* CSWE. *Faculty:* 10 full-time (8 women), 5 part-time/adjunct (3 women). *Students:* 66 full-time (60 women), 69 part-time (62 women); includes 18 minority (16 Black or African American, non-Hispanic/Latino; 1 Asian, non-Hispanic/Latino; 1 Hispanic/Latino), 2 international. Average age 31. In 2010, 50 master's, 3 other advanced degrees awarded. *Entrance requirements:* For master's, 3 letters of recommendation. Additional exam requirements/recommendations for international students: Required—TOEFL (minimum score 550 paper-based; 213 computer-based). *Application deadline:* For fall admission, 2/15 for domestic and international students. Application fee: $35 ($40 for international students). Electronic applications accepted. *Expenses:* Tuition, state resident: full-time $5522; part-time $306.80 per credit hour. Tuition, nonresident: full-time $14,253; part-time $792.10 per credit hour. Required fees: $658; $49 per credit hour. One-time fee: $12. Tuition and fees vary according to program. *Financial support:* In 2010–11, 1 research assistantship with full and partial tuition reimbursement (averaging $9,900 per year), 7 teaching assistantships with full and partial tuition reimbursements (averaging $8,360 per year) were awarded. Financial award applicants required to submit FAFSA. *Faculty research:* Family violence, child abuse/neglect, immigration, community economic development. *Unit head:* Dr. Lois Pierce, Graduate Program Director, 314-516-6364, Fax: 314-516-5816, E-mail: socialwork@umsl.edu. *Application contact:* 314-516-5458, Fax: 314-516-6996, E-mail: gradadm@umsl.edu.

University of Missouri–St. Louis, Graduate School, Program in Public Policy Administration, St. Louis, MO 63121. Offers health policy (MPPA); local government management (MPPA); managing human resources and organization (MPPA); nonprofit organization management (MPPA); nonprofit organization management and leadership (Certificate); policy research and analysis (MPPA). *Accreditation:* NASPAA. Part-time and evening/weekend programs available. *Faculty:* 9 full-time (4 women), 8 part-time/adjunct (6 women). *Students:* 36 full-time (21 women), 59 part-time (33 women); includes 17 minority (13 Black or African American, non-Hispanic/Latino; 2 American Indian or Alaska Native, non-Hispanic/Latino; 1 Asian, non-Hispanic/Latino; 1 Hispanic/Latino), 11 international. Average age 31. 60 applicants, 68% accepted, 24 enrolled. In 2010, 23 master's, 17 Certificates awarded. *Entrance requirements:* For master's, 3 letters of recommendation. Additional exam requirements/recommendations for international students: Required—TOEFL (minimum score 550 paper-based; 213 computer-based). *Application deadline:* For fall admission, 7/1 priority date for domestic and international students; for spring admission, 12/1 priority date for domestic and international students. Applications are processed on a rolling basis. Application fee: $35 ($40 for international students). Electronic applications accepted. *Expenses:* Tuition, state resident: full-time $5522; part-time $306.80 per credit hour. Tuition, nonresident: full-time $14,253; part-time $792.10 per credit hour. Required fees: $658; $49 per credit hour. One-time fee: $12. Tuition and fees vary according to program. *Financial support:* In 2010–11, 3 research assistantships with full and partial tuition reimbursements (averaging $12,000 per year) were awarded; career-related internships or fieldwork also available. Financial award application deadline: 4/1; financial award applicants required to submit FAFSA. *Faculty research:* Urban policy, public finance, evaluation. *Unit head:* Dr. Brady Baybeck, Director, 314-516-5145, Fax: 314-516-5210, E-mail: baybeck@umsl.edu. *Application contact:* 314-516-5458, Fax: 314-516-6996, E-mail: gradadm@umsl.edu.

University of Nevada, Las Vegas, Graduate College, Greenspun College of Urban Affairs, School of Environmental and Public Affairs, Las Vegas, NV 89154-4030. Offers crisis and emergency management (MS); environmental science (MS, PhD); non-profit management (Certificate); public administration (MPA); public affairs (PhD); public management (Certificate). Part-time programs available. *Faculty:* 6 full-time (2 women). *Students:* 55 full-time (27 women), 95 part-time (55 women); includes 63 minority (17 Black or African American, non-Hispanic/Latino; 2 American Indian or Alaska Native, non-Hispanic/Latino; 5 Asian, non-Hispanic/Latino; 20 Hispanic/Latino; 19 Two or more races, non-Hispanic/Latino), 8 international. Average age 35. 67 applicants, 72% accepted, 35 enrolled. In 2010, 61 master's, 2 doctorates, 24 other advanced degrees awarded. *Degree requirements:* For master's, comprehensive exam (for some programs), thesis; for doctorate, comprehensive exam (for some programs), thesis/dissertation. *Entrance requirements:* Additional exam requirements/recommendations for international students: Required—TOEFL (minimum score 550 paper-based; 213 computer-based; 80 iBT), IELTS (minimum score 7). *Application deadline:* For fall admission, 2/15 priority date for domestic and international students; for spring admission, 11/15 priority date for domestic and international students. Applications are processed on a rolling basis. Application fee: $60 ($95 for international students). Electronic applications accepted. *Expenses:* Tuition, area resident: Part-time $239.50 per credit. Tuition, state resident: part-time $239.50 per credit. Tuition, nonresident: part-time $503 per credit. Required fees: $108 per semester. Tuition and fees vary according to course load, program and reciprocity agreements. *Financial support:* In 2010–11, 9 students received support, including 6 research assistantships with partial tuition reimbursements available (averaging $13,850 per year), 3 teaching assistantships with partial tuition reimbursements available (averaging $10,666 per year); institutionally sponsored loans, scholarships/grants, health care benefits, and unspecified assistantships also available. Financial award application deadline: 3/1. *Faculty research:* Environmental decision-making and management; budgeting and human resource/workforce management; urban design, sustainability and governance; participatory simulation modeling of environmental issues; public and non-profit management. Total annual research expenditures: $1.1 million. *Unit head:* Dr. Ed Weber, Chair/Associate Professor, 702-895-4440, Fax: 702-895-4436, E-mail: edward.weber@unlv.edu. *Application contact:* Graduate College Admissions Evaluator, 702-895-3320, Fax: 702-895-4180, E-mail: gradcollege@unlv.edu.

The University of North Carolina at Charlotte, Graduate School, College of Arts and Sciences, Department of Political Science, Charlotte, NC 28223-0001. Offers emergency management (Certificate); non-profit management (Certificate); public administration (MPA, PhD), including arts administration (MPA), emergency management (MPA), non-profit management (MPA), public finance (MPA), urban management and policy (PhD); public finance (Certificate); public policy (PhD); urban management and policy (Certificate). *Accreditation:* NASPAA. Part-time and evening/weekend programs available. *Faculty:* 19 full-time (8 women), 3 part-time/adjunct (2 women). *Students:* 51 full-time (37 women), 75 part-time (49 women); includes 32 minority (26 Black or African American, non-Hispanic/Latino; 1 Asian, non-Hispanic/Latino; 2 Hispanic/Latino; 3 Two or more races, non-Hispanic/Latino), 11 international. Average age 29. 99 applicants, 72% accepted, 42 enrolled. In 2010, 15 master's, 5 doctorates awarded. *Degree requirements:* For master's, thesis or alternative; for doctorate, thesis/dissertation. *Entrance requirements:* For master's, GRE General Test or MAT, minimum GPA of 3.0 in undergraduate major, 2.75 overall. Additional exam requirements/recommendations for international students: Required—TOEFL (minimum score 557 paper-based; 220 computer-based; 83 iBT). *Application deadline:* For fall admission, 7/1 for domestic students, 5/1 for international students; for spring admission, 11/1 for domestic students, 10/1 for international students. Applications are processed on a rolling basis. Application fee: $55. Electronic applications accepted. *Expenses:* Tuition, state resident: full-time $3464. Tuition, non-resident: full-time $14,297. Required fees: $2094. Tuition and fees vary according to course load. *Financial support:* In 2010–11, 22 students received support, including 16 research assistantships (averaging $6,943 per year), 6 teaching assistantships (averaging $9,380 per year); career-related internships or fieldwork, Federal Work-Study, institutionally sponsored loans, scholarships/grants, unspecified assistantships, and administrative assistantship also available. Support available to part-time students. Financial award application deadline: 4/1; financial award applicants required to submit FAFSA. *Faculty research:* Terrorism, public administration, nonprofit and arts administration, educational policy, social policy. Total annual research expenditures: $242,404. *Unit head:* Dr. Theodore S. Arrington, Chair, 704-687-2571, Fax: 704-687-3497, E-mail: tarrngtn@uncc.edu. *Application contact:* Kathy B. Giddings, Director of Graduate Admissions, 704-687-5503, Fax: 704-687-3279, E-mail: gradadm@uncc.edu.

University of Northern Iowa, Graduate College, Program in Philanthropy and Nonprofit Development, Cedar Falls, IA 50614. Offers MA. *Students:* 10 part-time (all women); includes 1 minority (Black or African American, non-Hispanic/Latino). 2 applicants, 50% accepted, 0 enrolled. In 2010, 5 master's awarded. *Entrance requirements:* For master's, minimum GPA of 3.0; 3 letters of recommendation; experience in the philanthropy and/or nonprofit areas. Additional exam requirements/recommendations for international students: Required—TOEFL (minimum score 500 paper-based; 180 computer-based; 61 iBT). *Application deadline:* Applications are processed on a rolling basis. Application fee: $50 ($70 for international students). Electronic applications accepted. *Financial support:* Application deadline: 2/1. *Unit head:* Dr. Rodney Dieser, Coordinator, 319-273-7775, Fax: 319-273-5958, E-mail: rodney.dieser@uni.edu. *Application contact:* Laurie S. Russell, Record Analyst, 319-273-2623, Fax: 319-273-2885, E-mail: laurie.russell@uni.edu.

University of North Florida, College of Arts and Sciences, Department of Political Science and Public Administration, Jacksonville, FL 32224. Offers nonprofit management (Graduate Certificate); public administration (MPA). *Accreditation:* NASPAA. Part-time programs available. *Faculty:* 11 full-time (3 women), 1 part-time/adjunct (0 women). *Students:* 27 full-time (15 women), 48 part-time (27 women); includes 11 Black or African American, non-Hispanic/Latino; 3 Asian, non-Hispanic/Latino; 7 Hispanic/Latino; 1 Native Hawaiian or other Pacific Islander, non-Hispanic/Latino; 2 Two or more races, non-Hispanic/Latino, 1 international. Average age 30. 38 applicants, 55% accepted, 13 enrolled. In 2010, 27 master's awarded. *Degree requirements:* For master's, thesis or alternative, internship. *Entrance requirements:* For master's, GRE General Test, minimum GPA of 3.0 in last 60 hours, 2 letters of recommendation, interview. Additional exam requirements/recommendations for international students: Required—TOEFL (minimum score 500 paper-based; 173 computer-based; 61 iBT). *Application deadline:* For fall admission, 7/1 priority date for domestic students, 5/1 for international students; for spring admission, 11/1 priority date for domestic students, 10/1 for international students. Applications are processed on a rolling basis. Application fee: $30. Electronic applications accepted. *Expenses:* Tuition, state resident: full-time $7646.40; part-time $318.60 per credit hour. Tuition, nonresident: full-time $23,502; part-time $979.24 per credit hour. Required fees: $1208.88; $50.37 per credit hour. Tuition and fees vary according to course load and program. *Financial support:* In 2010–11, 20 students received support, including 1 research assistantship (averaging $2,354 per year), 2 teaching assistantships (averaging $3,667 per year); career-related internships or fieldwork, Federal Work-Study, scholarships/grants, tuition waivers (partial), and unspecified assistantships also available. Financial award application deadline: 4/1; financial award applicants required to submit FAFSA. *Faculty research:* America's usage of the Internet, use of information communication technologies by educators and children. Total annual research expenditures: $23,372. *Unit head:* Dr. Matthew T. Corrigan, Chair, 904-620-2977, Fax: 904-620-2979, E-mail: mcorriga@unf.edu. *Application contact:* Lillith

Richardson, Assistant Director, The Graduate School, 904-620-1360, Fax: 907-620-1362, E-mail: graduateschool@unf.edu.

University of Notre Dame, Mendoza College of Business, Program in Nonprofit Administration, Notre Dame, IN 46556. Offers MNA. *Accreditation:* AACSB. Part-time programs available. Postbaccalaureate distance learning degree programs offered (minimal on-campus study). *Faculty:* 8 full-time (0 women), 9 part-time/adjunct (5 women). *Students:* 10 full-time (5 women), 55 part-time (34 women); includes 1 Asian, non-Hispanic/Latino; 1 Hispanic/Latino, 4 international. Average age 30. 40 applicants, 93% accepted, 29 enrolled. In 2010, 20 master's awarded. *Degree requirements:* For master's, thesis. *Entrance requirements:* For master's, GRE General Test, work experience. Additional exam requirements/recommendations for international students: Required—TOEFL (minimum score 600 paper-based; 250 computer-based). *Application deadline:* For winter admission, 1/15 for domestic students; for spring admission, 3/31 for domestic students. Application fee: $60. Electronic applications accepted. *Expenses:* Contact institution. *Financial support:* In 2010–11, 13 students received support, including 32 fellowships (averaging $2,500 per year); institutionally sponsored loans and scholarships/grants also available. Support available to part-time students. *Unit head:* Thomas J. Harvey, Director, 574-631-7593, Fax: 574-631-6532, E-mail: harvey.18@nd.edu. *Application contact:* Kimberly M. Brennan, Program Manager, 574-631-3639, Fax: 574-631-6532, E-mail: brennan.53@nd.edu.

University of Pittsburgh, Graduate School of Public and International Affairs, Public Policy and Management Program for Mid-Career Professionals, Pittsburgh, PA 15260. Offers development planning (MPPM); international development (MPPM); international political economy (MPPM); international security studies (MPPM); management of non profit organizations (MPPM); metropolitan management and regional development (MPPM); policy analysis and evaluation (MPPM). Part-time programs available. *Faculty:* 30 full-time (12 women), 67 part-time/adjunct (25 women). *Students:* 14 full-time (1 woman), 34 part-time (17 women), 8 international. Average age 38. 31 applicants, 74% accepted, 15 enrolled. In 2010, 14 master's awarded. *Degree requirements:* For master's, thesis optional, capstone seminar. *Entrance requirements:* For master's, 2 letters of recommendation, resume, 5 years of supervisory or budgetary experience. Additional exam requirements/recommendations for international students: Required—TOEFL (minimum score 600 paper-based; 250 computer-based; 100 iBT), TWE (minimum score 4); Recommended—IELTS (minimum score 7). *Application deadline:* For fall admission, 6/1 priority date for domestic students, 2/15 for international students; for spring admission, 1/1 priority date for domestic students, 8/1 for international students. Applications are processed on a rolling basis. Application fee: $50. Electronic applications accepted. *Expenses:* Tuition, state resident: full-time $17,304; part-time $701 per credit. Tuition, nonresident: full-time $29,554; part-time $1210 per credit. Required fees: $740; $214 per term. Tuition and fees vary according to program. *Financial support:* In 2010–11, 14 students received support. Scholarships/grants and tuition waivers (partial) available. Support available to part-time students. Financial award application deadline: 2/1. *Faculty research:* Nonprofit management, urban and regional affairs, policy analysis and evaluation, security and intelligence studies, global political economy, nongovernmental organizations, civil society, development planning and environmental sustainability, human security. Total annual research expenditures: $892,349. *Unit head:* Dr. George Dougherty, Director, Executive Education, 412-648-7603, Fax: 412-648-2605, E-mail: gwdjr@pitt.edu. *Application contact:* Michael T. Rizzi, Associate Director of Student Services, 412-648-7640, Fax: 412-648-7641, E-mail: rizzim@pitt.edu.

University of Portland, Dr. Robert B. Pamplin, Jr. School of Business, Portland, OR 97203-5798. Offers business administration (MBA); entrepreneurship (MBA); finance (MBA, MS); health care management (MBA); marketing (MBA); nonprofit management (EMBA); operations and technology management (MBA); sustainability (MBA). *Accreditation:* AACSB. Part-time and evening/weekend programs available. *Faculty:* 12 full-time (2 women), 7 part-time/adjunct (2 women). *Students:* 55 full-time (24 women), 81 part-time (29 women); includes 18 minority (2 Black or African American, non-Hispanic/Latino; 8 Asian, non-Hispanic/Latino; 5 Hispanic/Latino; 3 Two or more races, non-Hispanic/Latino), 23 international. Average age 30. In 2010, 55 master's awarded. *Entrance requirements:* For master's, GMAT, minimum GPA of 3.0, resume, 2 letters of recommendation. Additional exam requirements/recommendations for international students: Required—TOEFL (minimum score 570 paper-based; 89 iBT), IELTS (minimum score 7). *Application deadline:* For fall admission, 7/15 priority date for domestic and international students; for spring admission, 12/15 priority date for domestic and international students. Applications are processed on a rolling basis. Application fee: $50. *Expenses:* Contact institution. *Financial support:* Federal Work-Study, scholarships/grants, and tuition waivers (partial) available. Support available to part-time students. Financial award application deadline: 3/1; financial award applicants required to submit FAFSA. *Unit head:* Dr. Howard Feldman, Associate Dean, 503-943-7224, E-mail: feldman@up.edu. *Application contact:* Melissa McCarthy, Academic Specialist, 503-943-7225, E-mail: mccarthy@up.edu.

University of San Diego, School of Leadership and Education Sciences, Department of Leadership Studies, San Diego, CA 92110-2492. Offers higher education leadership (MA); leadership studies (MA, PhD); nonprofit leadership and management (MA, Certificate). Part-time and evening/weekend programs available. *Faculty:* 9 full-time (5 women), 23 part-time/adjunct (14 women). *Students:* 23 full-time (12 women), 189 part-time (137 women); includes 73 minority (9 Black or African American, non-Hispanic/Latino; 1 American Indian or Alaska Native, non-Hispanic/Latino; 13 Asian, non-Hispanic/Latino; 45 Hispanic/Latino; 2 Native Hawaiian or other Pacific Islander, non-Hispanic/Latino; 3 Two or more races, non-Hispanic/Latino), 3 international. Average age 35. 186 applicants, 53% accepted, 72 enrolled. In 2010, 69 master's, 9 doctorates awarded. *Degree requirements:* For master's, thesis (for some programs), portfolio; for doctorate, comprehensive exam, thesis/dissertation. *Entrance requirements:* For master's, minimum GPA of 3.0, interview; for doctorate, GRE, master's degree, minimum GPA of 3.5 (recommended), interview, writing sample, resume. Additional exam requirements/recommendations for international students: Required—TOEFL (minimum score 580 paper-based; 237 computer-based; 83 iBT), TWE. *Application deadline:* For fall admission, 3/1 for domestic and international students. Application fee: $45. Electronic applications accepted. *Expenses:* Tuition: Full-time $21,744; part-time $1208 per unit. Required fees: $224. Full-time tuition and fees vary according to course load and degree level. *Financial support:* In 2010–11, 182 students received support. Career-related internships or fieldwork, Federal Work-Study, institutionally sponsored loans, unspecified assistantships, and stipends available. Support available to part-time students. Financial award application deadline: 4/1; financial award applicants required to submit FAFSA. *Faculty research:* Educational leadership, higher education policy and relations, organizational leadership, nonprofits and philanthropy, peace studies. *Unit head:* Dr. Cheryl Getz, Graduate Program Director, 619-260-4289, Fax: 619-260-6835, E-mail: cgetz@sandiego.edu. *Application contact:* Stephen Pultz, Director of Admissions and Enrollment, 619-260-4506, Fax: 619-260-6836, E-mail: admissions@sandiego.edu.

University of San Francisco, School of Business and Professional Studies, Program in Nonprofit Administration, San Francisco, CA 94117-1080. Offers MNA. *Faculty:* 6 part-time/adjunct (5 women). *Students:* 63 full-time (47 women), 11 part-time (9 women); includes 22 minority (7 Black or African American, non-Hispanic/Latino; 5 Asian, non-Hispanic/Latino; 6 Hispanic/Latino; 4 Two or more races, non-Hispanic/Latino), 4 international. Average age 37. 44 applicants, 80% accepted, 22 enrolled. In 2010, 35 master's awarded. *Degree requirements:* For master's, thesis optional. *Entrance requirements:* For master's, minimum GPA of 3.0. Application fee: $55 ($65 for international students). *Expenses:* Tuition: Full-time $20,070; part-time $1115 per credit hour. Tuition and fees vary according to course load, degree level and program. *Financial support:* In 2010–11, 37 students received support. Application deadline: 3/2. *Faculty research:* Philanthropy in ethnic communities. *Unit head:* Dr. Kathleen Fletcher, Director, 415-422-5121. *Application contact:* 415-422-6000, E-mail: graduate@usfca.edu.

University of Southern California, Graduate School, School of Policy, Planning, and Development, Master of Public Administration Program, Los Angeles, CA 90089. Offers nonprofit management and policy (Graduate Certificate); political management (Graduate Certificate); public administration (MPA); public management (Graduate Certificate); MPA/JD; MPA/M Pl; MPA/MA; MPA/MAJCS; MPA/MS; MPA/MSW. *Accreditation:* NASPAA (one or more programs are accredited). Part-time and evening/weekend programs available. Postbaccalaureate distance learning degree programs offered (minimal on-campus study). *Faculty:* 51 full-time (12 women), 100 part-time/adjunct (30 women). *Students:* 171 full-time (117 women), 37 part-time (16 women); includes 79 minority (14 Black or African American, non-Hispanic/Latino; 29 Asian, non-Hispanic/Latino; 31 Hispanic/Latino; 5 Two or more races, non-Hispanic/Latino), 37 international. 297 applicants, 64% accepted, 90 enrolled. In 2010, 71 master's awarded. Terminal master's awarded for partial completion of doctoral program. *Degree requirements:* For master's, capstone, internship. *Entrance requirements:* For master's, GRE, GMAT. Additional exam requirements/recommendations for international students: Required—TOEFL (minimum score 600 paper-based; 250 computer-based; 100 iBT). *Application deadline:* For fall admission, 12/15 priority date for domestic and international students; for spring admission, 11/1 for domestic and international students. Applications are processed on a rolling basis. Application fee: $85. Electronic applications accepted. *Expenses:* Tuition: Full-time $31,240; part-time $1420 per unit. Required fees: $600. One-time fee: $35 full-time. Full-time tuition and fees vary according to degree level and program. *Financial support:* In 2010–11, 99 students received support, including 2 research assistantships with full tuition reimbursements available (averaging $19,612 per year); scholarships/grants and tuition waivers (full and partial) also available. Financial award application deadline: 12/15. *Faculty research:* Collaborative governance and decision-making, nonprofit management, environmental management, institutional analysis, local government, civic engagement. Total annual research expenditures: $6.2 million. *Unit head:* Dr. Shui Yan Tang, Director, 213-740-0379, Fax: 213-740-0001, E-mail: stang@usc.edu. *Application contact:* Marisol R. Gonzalez, Director of Recruitment and Admission, 213-740-0550, Fax: 213-740-7573, E-mail: marisolr@usc.edu.

The University of Tampa, John H. Sykes College of Business, Tampa, FL 33606-1490. Offers accounting (MS); entrepreneurship (MBA); finance (MBA, MS); information systems management (MBA); innovation management (MBA); international business (MBA); marketing (MBA, MS); nonprofit management (MBA). *Accreditation:* AACSB. Part-time and evening/weekend programs available. *Faculty:* 67 full-time (24 women), 11 part-time/adjunct (4 women). *Students:* 235 full-time (89 women), 288 part-time (122 women); includes 74 minority (16 Black or African American, non-Hispanic/Latino; 2 American Indian or Alaska Native, non-Hispanic/Latino; 14 Asian, non-Hispanic/Latino; 34 Hispanic/Latino; 2 Native Hawaiian or other Pacific Islander, non-Hispanic/Latino; 6 Two or more races, non-Hispanic/Latino), 95 international. Average age 29. 457 applicants, 45% accepted, 175 enrolled. In 2010, 230 master's awarded. *Degree requirements:* For master's, capstone. *Entrance requirements:* For master's, GMAT or GRE, 4-year undergraduate degree, minimum GPA of 3.0, professional experience (for Executive MBA). Additional exam requirements/recommendations for international students: Required—TOEFL (minimum score 577 paper-based; 230 computer-based; 90 iBT); Recommended—IELTS (minimum score 7.5). *Application deadline:* Applications are processed on a rolling basis. Application fee: $40. Electronic applications accepted. *Expenses:* Tuition: Part-time $504 per credit hour. Required fees: $40 per term. *Financial support:* In 2010–11, 74 students received support. Career-related internships or fieldwork, scholarships/grants, unspecified assistantships, and grants available. Financial award applicants required to submit FAFSA. *Faculty research:* Management innovation, social marketing, value relevance of earnings and book value across industries, managerial finance, entrepreneurship. *Unit head:* Dennis Nostrand, Vice President, Enrollment/Admissions, 813-257-1808, E-mail: dnostrand@ut.edu. *Application contact:* Charlene Tobie, Associate Director of Admissions, 813-257-3566, E-mail: ctobie@ut.edu.

The University of Tennessee at Chattanooga, Graduate School, College of Arts and Sciences, Department of Political Science, Chattanooga, TN 37403. Offers local government management (MPA); non profit management (MPA); public administration (MPA); public administration and non-profit management (Postbaccalaureate Certificate). Part-time and evening/weekend programs available. *Faculty:* 4 full-time (0 women). *Students:* 11 full-time (8 women), 18 part-time (10 women); includes 2 minority (both Black or African American, non-Hispanic/Latino). Average age 28. 32 applicants, 66% accepted, 17 enrolled. In 2010, 21 master's, 1 other advanced degree awarded. *Degree requirements:* For master's, comprehensive exam, thesis or alternative, internship. *Entrance requirements:* For master's, GRE General Test. Additional exam requirements/recommendations for international students: Required—TOEFL (minimum score 550 paper-based; 213 computer-based; 79 iBT), IELTS (minimum score 6). *Application deadline:* For fall admission, 8/1 priority date for domestic students, 6/1 for international students; for spring admission, 12/1 priority date for domestic students, 10/1 for international students. Applications are processed on a rolling basis. Application fee: $35. Electronic applications accepted. *Financial support:* In 2010–11, 6 research assistantships with full and partial tuition reimbursements (averaging $5,500 per year) were awarded; career-related internships or fieldwork, scholarships/grants, and unspecified assistantships also available. Support available to part-time students. *Faculty research:* Organizational cultures and renewal, management theory, public policy, policy analysis, nonprofit organization. Total annual research expenditures: $35,240. *Unit head:* Dr. Fouad M. Moughrabi, Head, 423-425-4281, Fax: 423-425-2373, E-mail: fouad-moughrabi@utc.edu. *Application contact:* Dr. Jerald Ainsworth, Dean of Graduate Studies, 423-425-4478, Fax: 423-425-5223, E-mail: jerald-ainsworth@utc.edu.

The University of Toledo, College of Graduate Studies, College of Language, Literature and Social Sciences, Department of Political Science and Public Administration, Toledo, OH 43606-3390. Offers health care administration (Certificate); management of non-profit organizations (Certificate); political science (MA); public administration (MPA), including health care policy, municipal administration, public administration. Part-time programs available. *Faculty:* 9. *Students:* 21 full-time (11 women), 13 part-time (8 women); includes 7 minority (5 Black or African American, non-Hispanic/Latino; 2 Hispanic/Latino), 2 international. Average age 30. 34 applicants, 59% accepted, 16 enrolled. In 2010, 14 master's, 7 other advanced degrees awarded. *Degree requirements:* For master's, thesis. *Entrance requirements:* For master's, GRE General Test, A minimum 2.7 cumulative point-hour ratio (on a 4.0 scale) for all previous academic work, a statement of purpose, 3 letters of recommendation and transcripts from all prior institutions attended; for Certificate, A minimum 2.7 cumulative point-hour ratio (on a 4.0 scale) for all previous academic work, a statement of purpose, 3 letters of recommendation and transcripts from all prior institutions attended. Additional exam requirements/recommendations for international students: Required—TOEFL (minimum score 550 paper-based; 213 computer-based; 80 iBT), IELTS (minimum score 6.5). *Application deadline:* For fall admission, 1/15 priority date for domestic and international students. Applications are processed on a rolling basis. Application fee: $45 ($75 for international students). Electronic applications accepted. *Expenses:* Tuition, state resident: full-time $11,426; part-time $476 per credit hour. Tuition, nonresident: full-time $21,660; part-time $903 per credit hour. One-time fee: $62. *Financial support:* Research assistantships with tuition reimbursements, teaching assistantships with tuition reimbursements, career-related internships or fieldwork, Federal Work-Study, institutionally sponsored loans, scholarships/grants, tuition waivers (full), and unspecified assistantships available. Support available to part-time students. *Faculty research:* Economic development, health care, Third World, criminal justice, Eastern Europe. *Unit head:* Dr. Mark E. Denham, Chair, 419-530-4151, E-mail: mark.denham@utoledo.edu. *Application contact:* Graduate School Office, 419-530-4723, Fax: 419-530-4724, E-mail: grdsch@utnet.utoledo.edu.

University of Wisconsin–Milwaukee, Graduate School, School of Social Welfare, Department of Social Work, Milwaukee, WI 53201-0413. Offers applied gerontology (Certificate); marriage and family therapy (Certificate); non-profit management (Certificate); social work (MSW, PhD). *Accreditation:* CSWE. Part-time programs available. *Faculty:* 19 full-time (10 women). *Students:* 214 full-time (196 women), 109 part-time (97 women); includes 35 Black or African American, non-Hispanic/Latino; 1 American Indian or Alaska Native, non-Hispanic/Latino; 6 Asian, non-Hispanic/Latino; 5 Hispanic/Latino. Average age 30. 351 applicants, 55% accepted, 95 enrolled. In 2010, 105 master's awarded. *Degree requirements:* For master's, thesis or alternative. *Entrance requirements:* For doctorate, GRE, bachelor's degree. Additional exam requirements/recommendations for international students: Required—TOEFL (minimum score 550 paper-based; 79 iBT), IELTS (minimum score 6.5). *Application deadline:* For fall admission, 1/1 priority date for domestic students; for spring admission, 9/1 for domestic students. Applications are processed on a rolling basis. Application fee: $56 ($96 for international students). Electronic applications accepted. *Financial support:* In 2010–11, 5 fellowships, 4 research assistantships, 3 teaching assistantships were awarded; career-related internships or fieldwork, health care benefits, unspecified assistantships, and project assistantships also available. Support available to part-time students. Financial award application deadline: 4/15; financial award applicants required to submit FAFSA. *Unit head:* Deborah Padgett, Representative—MSW, 414-229-4851, Fax: 414-229-5311, E-mail: dpadgett@uwm.edu. *Application contact:* Steve McMurtry, Representative—PhD, 414-229-2249, Fax: 414-229-6967, E-mail: mcmurtry@uwm.edu.

University of Wisconsin–Milwaukee, Graduate School, Sheldon B. Lubar School of Business, Program in Nonprofit Management and Leadership, Milwaukee, WI 53201-0413. Offers MS, Certificate. *Faculty:* 11 full-time (6 women). *Students:* 16 full-time (11 women), 38 part-time (29 women); includes 6 Black or African American, non-Hispanic/Latino; 2 American Indian or Alaska Native, non-Hispanic/Latino; 1 Asian, non-Hispanic/Latino. Average age 34. 23 applicants, 70% accepted, 12 enrolled. In 2010, 9 master's awarded. *Entrance requirements:* For master's, GRE/GMAT. Additional exam requirements/recommendations for international students: Required—TOEFL (minimum score 550 paper-based; 213 computer-based; 79 iBT), IELTS (minimum score 6.5). *Application deadline:* Applications are processed on a rolling basis. Application fee: $56 ($96 for international students). Electronic applications accepted. *Financial support:* Fellowships, research assistantships, teaching assistantships, health care benefits and unspecified assistantships available. Financial award applicants required to submit FAFSA. *Unit head:* Douglas Ihrke, Representative, 414-229-3176, E-mail: dihrke@uwm.edu. *Application contact:* Douglas Ihrke, Representative, 414-229-3176, E-mail: dihrke@uwm.edu.

Virginia Commonwealth University, Graduate School, College of Humanities and Sciences, Program in Nonprofit Management, Richmond, VA 23284-9005. Offers Graduate Certificate. Part-time programs available. *Students:* 1 full-time (0 women), 5 part-time (all women); includes 2 minority (1 Black or African American, non-Hispanic/Latino; 1 Two or more races, non-Hispanic/Latino). 12 applicants, 42% accepted, 5 enrolled. In 2010, 7 Graduate Certificates awarded. *Entrance requirements:* For degree, None. Additional exam requirements/recommendations for international students: Required—TOEFL (minimum score 600 paper-based; 250 computer-based; 100 iBT); Recommended—IELTS (minimum score 6.5). Application fee: $50. Electronic applications accepted. *Expenses:* Tuition, state resident: full-time $4308; part-time $479 per credit hour. Tuition, nonresident: full-time $8942; part-time $994 per credit hour. Required fees: $2000; $85 per credit hour. Tuition and fees vary according to course level, course load, degree level, campus/location and program. *Unit head:* Dr. Niraj Verma, Director of the L. Douglas Wilder School of Government and Public Affairs, 804-828-2292. *Application contact:* Lisbeth D. Dannenbrink, 804-828-6837, E-mail: lddannenbrin@vcu.edu.

Virginia Polytechnic Institute and State University, Graduate School, College of Architecture and Urban Studies, School of Public and International Affairs, Blacksburg, VA 24061. Offers economic development (Certificate); government and international affairs (MPIA, PhD); homeland security policy (Certificate); local government management (Certificate); nonprofit and non-governmental organization management (Certificate); planning, governance and globalization (PhD); public administration and public affairs (MPA, PhD); urban and regional planning (MURPL). *Accreditation:* ACSP. *Faculty:* 31 full-time (9 women). *Students:* 114 full-time (66 women), 105 part-time (54 women); includes 11 Black or African American, non-Hispanic/Latino; 1 American Indian or Alaska Native, non-Hispanic/Latino; 7 Asian, non-Hispanic/Latino; 8 Hispanic/Latino, 19 international. Average age 31. 166 applicants, 67% accepted, 53 enrolled. In 2010, 41 master's, 3 doctorates awarded. *Degree requirements:* For master's, comprehensive exam (for some programs), thesis (for some programs); for doctorate, comprehensive exam (for some programs), thesis/dissertation (for some programs). *Entrance requirements:* For master's and doctorate, GRE. Additional exam requirements/

recommendations for international students: Required—TOEFL (minimum score 550 paper-based; 213 computer-based). *Application deadline:* For fall admission, 7/1 for domestic and international students; for spring admission, 12/1 for domestic and international students. Applications are processed on a rolling basis. Application fee: $65. Electronic applications accepted. *Expenses:* Tuition, state resident: full-time $9399; part-time $488 per credit hour. Tuition, nonresident: full-time $17,854; part-time $957.75 per credit hour. Required fees: $1534. Full-time tuition and fees vary according to program. *Financial support:* In 2010–11, 1 teaching assistantship with full tuition reimbursement (averaging $21,395 per year) was awarded; career-related internships or fieldwork, Federal Work-Study, scholarships/grants, health care benefits, and unspecified assistantships also available. Financial award application deadline: 1/15. *Faculty research:* Design theory, environmental planning, town planning, transportation planning. Total annual research expenditures: $610,749. *Unit head:* Dr. Karen M. Hult, UNIT HEAD, 540-231-5351, Fax: 540-231-9938, E-mail: khult@vt.edu. *Application contact:* Krystal D. Wright, Contact, 540-231-2291, Fax: 540-231-9938, E-mail: garch@vt.edu.

Walden University, Graduate Programs, School of Counseling and Social Service, Minneapolis, MN 55401. Offers career counseling (MS); counselor education and supervision (PhD), including consultation, counseling and social change, forensic mental health counseling, general program, nonprofit management and leadership, trauma and crisis; human services (PhD), including clinical social work, counseling, criminal justice, disaster, crisis and intervention, family studies and intervention strategies, general program, human services administration, public health, self-designed, social policy analysis and planning; marriage, couple, and family counseling (MS), including forensic counseling, trauma and crisis counseling; mental health counseling (MS), including forensic counseling. Part-time and evening/weekend programs available. Postbaccalaureate distance learning degree programs offered (minimal on-campus study). *Faculty:* 25 full-time (17 women), 241 part-time/adjunct (162 women). *Students:* 2,687 full-time (2,269 women), 536 part-time (473 women); includes 1,582 minority (1,319 Black or African American, non-Hispanic/Latino; 34 American Indian or Alaska Native, non-Hispanic/Latino; 29 Asian, non-Hispanic/Latino; 142 Hispanic/Latino; 58 Two or more races, non-Hispanic/Latino), 47 international. Average age 38. In 2010, 182 master's, 8 doctorates awarded. *Degree requirements:* For master's, residency (for some programs); for doctorate, thesis/dissertation, residency. *Entrance requirements:* For master's, bachelor's degree or equivalent in related field, minimum GPA of 2.5; for doctorate, master's degree or equivalent in related field; minimum GPA of 3.0; official transcripts; three years' related professional/academic experience (preferred); access to computer and Internet. Additional exam requirements/recommendations for international students: Required—TOEFL (minimum score 550 paper-based; 213 computer-based), IELTS (minimum score 6.5), TOEFL (minimum score 550 paper-based; 213 computer-based), IELTS (minimum score 6.5), or Michigan English Language Assessment Battery (minimum score 82). *Application deadline:* Applications are processed on a rolling basis. Application fee: $50. Electronic applications accepted. *Expenses:* Tuition: Full-time $10,274; part-time $445 per credit. Tuition and fees vary according to course load, degree level and program. *Financial support:* Fellowships, Federal Work-Study, scholarships/grants, unspecified assistantships, and family tuition reduction, active duty/veteran tuition reduction, group tuition reduction, interest-free payment plans available. Support available to part-time students. Financial award applicants required to submit FAFSA. *Unit head:* Dr. Savitri Dixon-Saxon, Associate Dean, 800-925-3368. *Application contact:* Jennifer Hall, Vice President of Enrollment Management, 866-4-WALDEN, E-mail: info@waldenu.edu.

Walden University, Graduate Programs, School of Psychology, Minneapolis, MN 55401. Offers clinical child psychology (Post-Doctoral Certificate); clinical psychology (MS, Post-Doctoral Certificate), including counseling (MS); counseling psychology (Post-Doctoral Certificate); forensic psychology (MS), including forensic psychology in the community, general program, mental health applications, program planning and evaluation in forensic settings, psychology and legal systems; general psychology (Post-Doctoral Certificate); health psychology (Post-Doctoral Certificate); organizational psychology (Post-Doctoral Certificate); organizational psychology and development (Postbaccalaureate Certificate); psychology (MS, PhD), including clinical psychology (PhD), counseling psychology (PhD), crisis management and response (MS), general program (MS), general psychology (PhD), health psychology, leadership development and coaching (MS), media psychology (MS), organizational psychology (PhD), organizational psychology and development (MS), organizational psychology and nonprofit management (MS), program evaluation and research (MS), psychology of culture (MS), psychology, public administration, and social change (MS), social psychology (MS), terrorism and security (MS); teaching online (Post-Master's Certificate). Part-time and evening/weekend programs available. Postbaccalaureate distance learning degree programs offered (minimal on-campus study). *Faculty:* 41 full-time (25 women), 254 part-time/adjunct (131 women). *Students:* 3,463 full-time (2,737 women), 1,400 part-time (1,130 women); includes 1,491 Black or African American, non-Hispanic/Latino; 59 American Indian or Alaska Native, non-Hispanic/Latino; 89 Asian, non-Hispanic/Latino; 283 Hispanic/Latino; 76 Two or more races, non-Hispanic/Latino, 126 international. Average age 40. In 2010, 559 master's, 100 doctorates awarded. Terminal master's awarded for partial completion of doctoral program. *Degree requirements:* For master's, thesis optional; for doctorate, thesis/dissertation, residency. *Entrance requirements:* For master's, bachelor's degree or equivalent in related field; minimum GPA of 2.5; official transcripts; goal statement; access to computer and Internet; for doctorate, master's degree or equivalent in related field; minimum GPA of 3.0; 3 years of related professional/academic experience (preferred). Additional exam requirements/recommendations for international students: Required—TOEFL (minimum score 550 paper-based; 213 computer-based), IELTS (minimum score 6.5), TOEFL (minimum score 550 paper-based; 213 computer-based), IELTS (minimum score 6.5), or Michigan English Language Assessment Battery (minimum score 82). *Application deadline:* Applications are processed on a rolling basis. Application fee: $50. Electronic applications accepted. *Expenses:* Tuition: Full-time $10,274; part-time $445 per credit. Tuition and fees vary according to course load, degree level and program. *Financial support:* In 2010–11, 1 fellowship was awarded; Federal Work-Study, scholarships/grants, unspecified assistantships, and family tuition reduction, active duty/veteran tuition reduction, group tuition reduction, interest-free payment plans also available. Support available to part-time students. Financial award applicants required to submit FAFSA. *Unit head:* Dr. Melanie Storms, Associate Dean, 800-925-3368. *Application contact:* Jennifer Hall, Vice President of Enrollment Management, 866-4-WALDEN, E-mail: info@waldenu.edu.

Walden University, Graduate Programs, School of Public Policy and Administration, Minneapolis, MN 55401. Offers criminal justice (MPA); emergency management (MPA); government management (Postbaccalaureate Certificate); health policy (MPA); homeland security policy (MPA); homeland security policy and coordination (MPA); interdisciplinary policy studies (MPA); international nongovernmental organizations (ngos) (MPA); law and public policy (MPA); local government management for sustainable communities (MPA); nonprofit management (Postbaccalaureate Certificate); nonprofit management and leadership (MPA, MS); policy analysis (MPA); public management and leadership (MPA); public policy and administration (MPA, PhD), including criminal justice (PhD), emergency management (PhD), health policy (PhD), health services (PhD), homeland security policy (PhD), homeland security policy and coordination (PhD), interdisciplinary policy studies (PhD), international nongovernmental organizations (PhD), law and public policy (PhD), local government management for sustainable communities (PhD), nonprofit management and leadership (PhD), policy analysis (PhD), public management and leadership (PhD), terrorism, mediation, and peace (PhD); terrorism, mediation, and peace (MPA). Part-time and evening/weekend programs available. Postbaccalaureate distance learning degree programs offered (minimal on-campus study). *Faculty:* 10 full-time (5 women), 117 part-time/adjunct (49 women). *Students:* 1,408 full-time (901 women), 599 part-time (392 women); includes 1,022 Black or African American, non-Hispanic/Latino; 11 American Indian or Alaska Native, non-Hispanic/Latino; 37 Asian, non-Hispanic/Latino; 64 Hispanic/Latino; 26 Two or more races, non-Hispanic/Latino, 47 international. Average age 40. In 2010, 311 master's, 23 doctorates awarded. *Degree requirements:* For doctorate, thesis/dissertation, residency. *Entrance requirements:* For master's, bachelor's degree or equivalent in related field, minimum GPA of 2.5; for doctorate, master's degree or equivalent in related field; minimum GPA of 3.0; official transcripts; three years of related professional/academic experience (preferred); access to computer and Internet. Additional exam requirements/recommendations for international students: Required—TOEFL (minimum score 550 paper-based; 213 computer-based), IELTS (minimum score 6.5), TOEFL (minimum score 550 paper-based; 213 computer-based), IELTS (minimum score 6.5), or Michigan English Language Assessment Battery (minimum score 82). *Application deadline:* Applications are processed on a rolling basis. Application fee: $50. Electronic applications accepted. *Expenses:* Tuition: Full-time $10,274; part-time $445 per credit. Tuition and fees vary according to course load, degree level and program. *Financial support:* Fellowships with tuition reimbursements, Federal Work-Study, scholarships/grants, unspecified assistantships,

and family tuition reduction, active duty/veteran tuition reduction, group tuition reduction, interest-free payment plans available. Support available to part-time students. Financial award applicants required to submit FAFSA. *Unit head:* Dr. Mark Gordon, Associate Dean, 800-925-3368. *Application contact:* Jennifer Hall, Vice President of Enrollment Management, 866-4-WALDEN, E-mail: info@waldenu.edu.

West Chester University of Pennsylvania, Office of Graduate Studies, College of Business and Public Affairs, Department of Political Science, West Chester, PA 19383. Offers general public administration (MPA); human resource management (MPA, Certificate); non profit administration (Certificate); nonprofit administration (MPA); public administration (Certificate). Part-time and evening/weekend programs available. *Students:* 22 full-time (12 women), 39 part-time (31 women); includes 16 minority (12 Black or African American, non-Hispanic/Latino; 4 Hispanic/Latino), 2 international. Average age 31. 41 applicants, 88% accepted, 17 enrolled. In 2010, 22 master's awarded. *Degree requirements:* For master's, capstone project. *Entrance requirements:* For master's and Certificate, statement of professional goals, resume, two letters of reference. Additional exam requirements/recommendations for international students: Required—TOEFL (minimum score 550 paper-based; 213 computer-based; 80 iBT). *Application deadline:* For fall admission, 4/15 priority date for domestic students, 3/15 for international students; for spring admission, 10/15 for domestic students, 9/1 for international students. Applications are processed on a rolling basis. Application fee: $35. Electronic applications accepted. *Expenses:* Tuition, state resident: full-time $6966; part-time $387 per credit. Tuition, nonresident: full-time $11,146; part-time $619 per credit. Required fees: $1614.40; $133.24 per credit. Part-time tuition and fees vary according to campus/location. *Financial support:* Unspecified assistantships available. Support available to part-time students. Financial award application deadline: 2/15; financial award applicants required to submit FAFSA. *Faculty research:* Public policy, economic development, public opinion, urban politics, public administration. *Unit head:* Dr. Christopher Fiorentino, Dean, College of Business and Public Affairs, 610-436-2930, E-mail: cfiorentino@wcupa.edu. *Application contact:* Dr. Lorraine Bernotsky, Graduate Coordinator, 610-738-0576, E-mail: lbernotsky@wcupa.edu.

Worcester State University, Graduate Studies, Program in Non-Profit Management, Worcester, MA 01602-2597. Offers MS. Part-time and evening/weekend programs available. *Faculty:* 1 (woman) full-time, 2 part-time/adjunct (1 woman). *Students:* 7 full-time (3 women), 23 part-time (12 women); includes 1 Black or African American, non-Hispanic/Latino; 1 Asian, non-Hispanic/Latino; 2 Hispanic/Latino; 1 Two or more races, non-Hispanic/Latino, 3 international. Average age 34. 20 applicants, 65% accepted, 8 enrolled. In 2010, 6 master's awarded. *Degree requirements:* For master's, comprehensive exam (for some programs), thesis optional. *Entrance requirements:* For master's, GRE General Test or MAT. Additional exam requirements/recommendations for international students: Required—TOEFL (minimum score 500 paper-based; 61 iBT). *Application deadline:* Applications are processed on a rolling basis. Application fee: $40. Electronic applications accepted. *Expenses:* Tuition, state resident: full-time $2700; part-time $150 per credit. Tuition, nonresident: full-time $2700; part-time $150 per credit. Required fees: $2016; $112 per credit. *Financial support:* In 2010–11, 1 student received support, including 1 research assistantship with full tuition reimbursement available (averaging $4,800 per year); career-related internships or fieldwork, scholarships/grants, and unspecified assistantships also available. Financial award application deadline: 3/1; financial award applicants required to submit FAFSA. *Faculty research:* Politics of human services, models of supervision. *Unit head:* Dr. Shiko Gathuo, Coordinator, 508-929-8892, Fax: 508-929-8144, E-mail: agathuo@worcester.edu. *Application contact:* Sara Grady, Assistant Dean of Continuing Education, 508-929-8787, Fax: 508-929-8100, E-mail: sara.grady@worcester.edu.

OVERVIEW

The study of organizational behavior examines the behavioral aspects of management and leadership—how power and influence, norms and values, and incentives and rewards shape individual and group behavior in organizations. Most large businesses and corporations understand that much of their success depends on their employees' motivation. Professionals with an MBA in organizational studies are trained to focus on the human aspects of a company's productivity by providing in-depth knowledge behind the dynamics of how people best work together and on how individuals and groups make decisions. They have a talent for motivating employees and are well versed in team dynamics and employee compensation issues and possess the traits that encompass an effective leader.

Course work towards this degree is designed to provide professionals with an enhanced ability to interpret the work experiences they have accrued and sharpen their ability to make effective decisions, motivate and lead subordinates, and understand the processes underlying human interaction in organizations. This often includes instruction in the management of cross-functional teams and a diverse workforce, project management, technology application, organization theory, industrial and organizational psychology, social psychology, sociology of organizations, reinforcement and incentive theory, employee relations strategies, organizational power and influence, organization stratification and hierarchy, and leadership styles.

Required courses may include study in:
- Behavioral Issues and Ethics in Management
- Contemporary Marketing Perspectives
- Corporate Financial Management
- Decision Analysis
- Global Strategic Management
- Managerial Economics
- Strategic Profitability Analysis: Accounting for Managers

Elective courses may include study in:
- Managing for Internal Innovation
- Managing the Service Organization
- Situational and Transformational Leadership
- Strategic Human Resources Management

MBA courses in organizational studies help students to understand behavior at both the individual and organization levels. Topics at the individual level cover individual motivation and behavior; decision-making; interpersonal communication and influence; small group behavior; and individual, dyadic, and inter-group conflict and cooperation. At the organization level, topics include organizational growth, organizational change, organizational learning, organizations and leadership, power, social networks, and social responsibility.

An MBA in organizational studies prepares individuals for management and leadership responsibilities in business, government, and nonprofit entities and provides the framework for diagnosing and dealing with the problems and opportunities that typically arise in organizational settings. Career paths include positions such as compensation and benefits analyst, job analysis specialist, director of human resources, EEO/diversity manager, industrial relations director, job evaluation specialist, labor relations director, management analyst, organizational development director, and recruiter.

HELPFUL ORGANIZATIONS/ PUBLICATIONS/BLOGS

Journal of Organizational Behavior Management (JOBM)

http://www.obmnetwork.com/publications/jobm

The *Journal of Organizational Behavior Management (JOBM)* is the only professional journal devoted to behavior management in organizations. This innovative journal serves as a tool for improving productivity and the quality of working life. Top researchers provide proven methods—backed by facts, not opinions—to show the best practical ways to apply behavior management in the workplace.

The *Journal of Organizational Behavior Management*—the official journal of the OBM Network—publishes research and review articles, case studies, discussions, and book reviews on the topics that are critical to today's organization development practitioners and human resource managers. Beyond the general principles of organizational systems and structure, the *Journal of Organizational Behavior Management* focuses on specific concerns, such as:

- Employee safety and training.
- Stress, health, and employee productivity.
- Evaluation of employee satisfaction and feedback systems.
- Use of monetary and nonmonetary incentives.
- Self-management procedures.
- Programmed instruction, behavioral modeling, and computer-aided instruction.
- Positive and negative side effects of OBM interventions.

The *Journal of Organizational Behavior Management* occasionally produces thematic issues that concentrate on a single, highly relevant topic. Past thematic issues have focused on organizational culture and rule-governed behavior; pay for performance; OBM and statistical process control; computers, people, and productivity; behavioral systems analysis; and improving staff effectiveness.

European Group for Organizational Studies (EGOS)

http://www.egosnet.org/

The European Group for Organizational Studies (EGOS), with more than 1,800 members representing 44 countries from all over the world, is a scholarly association that aims to further the theoretical and/

or empirical advancement of knowledge about organizations, organizing, and the contexts in which organizations operate. EGOS has its identity and intellectual roots in the social sciences. It encourages an analytical and theoretical approach towards organizations. EGOS embraces diversity of all kinds, including a pluralistic approach to understanding organizations from the perspective of the social sciences as well as the humanities.

EGOS emphasizes broad themes and issue-based research. The association provides a forum for identifying and discussing key issues in organizational theory and practice. Critical reflection on the most recent ideas and theoretical approaches is at the core of the association's activities. EGOS, moreover, offers a stimulating intellectual environment for younger scholars, running well-attended PhD and post-doctoral workshops at the beginning of the annual EGOS Colloquium.

Group & Organization Management (GOM)

http://gom.sagepub.com/

Group & Organization Management (*GOM*) is a peer-reviewed bimonthly publication, which publishes the work of scholars and professionals who extend management and organization theory and address the implications for practitioners. Innovation, conceptual sophistication, methodological rigor, and cutting-edge scholarship are the driving principles. From individual behavior to organizational strategy and functioning, GOM features both empirical and theoretical articles spanning various levels of analysis in organizations.

CAREER ASPIRATIONS: A PROSPECTIVE POSITION

Chief Operating Officer

Job Description

Reporting directly to the CEO, the Chief Operating Officer will ensure that the organization continues to deliver exceptional performance while meeting its ambitious growth goals. This is an ideal opportunity for an innovative, entrepreneurial, and driven leader with experience leading a business unit or innovative mission-driven organization, to play a role in growing a premier education reform organization that transforms the lives of children across the state.

Responsibilities

- Drive operational excellence across all departments including operations (human resources, technology, data/compliance), fundraising, marketing, recruitment, and finance.
- Hire, manage, and develop best-in-class leaders throughout the organization, providing ongoing mentorship and opportunities for professional development.
- Identify gaps and implement process improvements to support efficient and effective departments in both school and central office operations.
- Develop robust systems that will enable excellence across the organization as it grows in both scale and complexity.
- Conduct and/or oversee analysis to drive organizational decision making.
- Serve as organizational leader, partnering with CEO, department heads, and staff to deliver best-in-class results.

Qualifications

The ideal candidate will have a track record of success in leading cross-functional teams to achieve ambitious goals in a high-growth, entrepreneurial setting. The COO must be exceptionally polished, professional, and articulate with a high level of comfort building and refining operational process and supporting and developing senior leaders. Finally, he or she must be a genuinely kind individual who thrives leading a highly motivated, committed team.

- 10+ years of progressively increasing operational management experience in the context of a growing organization or business
- Demonstrated ability to develop, implement, and manage business systems and processes to support a growing multi-million dollar organization
- Proactive, entrepreneurial style with the ability to take initiative, recognize opportunities, and develop and implement focused plans for executing on those opportunities
- Excellent organizational, project management, and time management skills; able to oversee multiple, high-priority work streams
- Strong critical thinking and problem-solving skills, able to use quantitative and qualitative information to drive decision making
- Exceptional verbal and written communication skills, with an ability to communicate clearly and work effectively with a variety of staff at all levels across the organization
- Commitment to teamwork with a willingness to be hands-on and do whatever it takes to support the success of the organization
- Bachelor's degree required; MBA or master's degree in related field preferred

ORGANIZATIONAL BEHAVIOR

Amridge University, Graduate and Professional Programs, Montgomery, AL 36117. Offers behavioral leadership and management (MA); Biblical exposition (MA); biblical studies (MA, PhD); family therapy (D Min); historical and theological studies (MA); leadership and management (MS); marriage and family therapy (M Div, MA, PhD); ministerial leadership (M Div, MS); pastoral counseling (M Div, MS); practical ministry (MA); professional counseling (M Div, MA, PhD); theology (D Min). Part-time and evening/weekend programs available. Postbaccalaureate distance learning degree programs offered (no on-campus study). *Faculty:* 39 full-time (6 women), 39 part-time/adjunct (5 women). *Students:* 119 full-time (54 women), 260 part-time (149 women); includes 160 minority (153 Black or African American, non-Hispanic/Latino; 1 Asian, non-Hispanic/Latino; 6 Hispanic/Latino). Average age 35. *Degree requirements:* For master's, one foreign language, comprehensive exam (for some programs), thesis (for some programs); for doctorate, comprehensive exam (for some programs), thesis/dissertation; for M Div, comprehensive exam (for some programs). *Entrance requirements:* For M Div, master's, and doctorate, GRE General Test or MAT. Additional exam requirements/recommendations for international students: Required—TOEFL. *Application deadline:* For fall admission, 9/1 priority date for domestic students; for spring admission, 1/1 priority date for domestic students. Applications are processed on a rolling basis. Application fee: $75. Electronic applications accepted. *Financial support:* Federal Work-Study and scholarships/grants available. Support available to part-time students. Financial award applicants required to submit FAFSA. *Faculty research:* Homiletics, hermeneutics, ancient Near Eastern history. *Unit head:* Director of Enrollment Management, 800-351-4040 Ext. 7513, Fax: 334-387-3878. *Application contact:* Ora Davis, Admissions Officer, 334-387-3877 Ext. 7524, Fax: 334-387-3878, E-mail: admissions@amridgeuniversity.edu.

Benedictine University, Graduate Programs, Program in Management and Organizational Behavior, Lisle, IL 60532-0900. Offers MS, MBA/MS, MPH/MS. Part-time and evening/weekend programs available. *Faculty:* 1 full-time (0 women), 15 part-time/adjunct (7 women). *Students:* 42 full-time (27 women), 122 part-time (90 women); includes 40 minority (29 Black or African American, non-Hispanic/Latino; 1 American Indian or Alaska Native, non-Hispanic/Latino; 5 Asian, non-Hispanic/Latino; 5 Hispanic/Latino), 4 international. Average age 40. 75 applicants, 85% accepted, 31 enrolled. In 2010, 33 master's awarded. *Entrance requirements:* For master's, GMAT. Additional exam requirements/recommendations for international students: Required—TOEFL (minimum score 550 paper-based; 213 computer-based). *Application deadline:* For fall admission, 9/1 for domestic students; for winter admission, 12/1 for domestic students; for spring admission, 2/15 for domestic students. Applications are processed on a rolling basis. Application fee: $40. Electronic applications accepted. *Financial support:* Career-related internships or fieldwork and health care benefits available. Support available to part-time students. *Faculty research:* Organizational change, transformation, development, learning organizations, career transitions for academics. *Unit head:* Dr. Peter F. Sorensen, Director, 630-829-6220, Fax: 630-960-1126, E-mail: psorensen@ben.edu. *Application contact:* Kari Gibbons, Director, Admissions, 630-829-6200, Fax: 630-829-6584, E-mail: kgibbons@ben.edu.

Boston College, Carroll School of Management, Department of Organization Studies, Chestnut Hill, MA 02467-3800. Offers PhD. *Faculty:* 12 full-time (6 women). *Students:* 20 full-time (14 women); includes 1 Black or African American, non-Hispanic/Latino; 1 Hispanic/Latino, 7 international. Average age 32. 73 applicants, 4% accepted, 3 enrolled. In 2010, 2 doctorates awarded. *Degree requirements:* For doctorate, comprehensive exam, thesis/dissertation, teaching experience. *Entrance requirements:* For doctorate, GMAT or GRE, letters of recommendation, resume, transcripts. Additional exam requirements/recommendations for international students: Required—TOEFL. *Application deadline:* For spring admission, 2/1 for domestic and international students. Application fee: $50. *Financial support:* In 2010–11, 20 fellowships, 20 research assistantships with full tuition reimbursements were awarded. Financial award application deadline: 3/1; financial award applicants required to submit FAFSA. *Faculty research:* Organizational transformation, mergers and acquisitions, managerial effectiveness, organizational change, organizational structure. *Unit head:* Dr. Jeffrey L. Ringuest, Associate Dean, Graduate Programs, 617-552-9100, Fax: 617-552-0514, E-mail: gsomdean@bc.edu. *Application contact:* Shelley A. Burt, Director of Graduate Enrollment, 617-552-3920, Fax: 617-552-8078, E-mail: bcmba@bc.edu.

Brooklyn College of the City University of New York, Division of Graduate Studies, Department of Psychology, Program in Industrial and Organizational Psychology, Brooklyn, NY 11210-2889. Offers human relations (MA); organizational behavior (MA). *Students:* 6 full-time (5 women), 100 part-time (78 women); includes 63 minority (42 Black or African American, non-Hispanic/Latino; 8 Asian, non-Hispanic/Latino; 13 Hispanic/Latino), 10 international. Average age 30. 93 applicants, 69% accepted, 41 enrolled. In 2010, 39 master's awarded. *Degree requirements:* For master's, comprehensive exam, thesis. *Entrance requirements:* For master's, 2 letters of recommendation. Additional exam requirements/recommendations for international students: Required—TOEFL (minimum score 520 paper-based; 190 computer-based; 69 iBT). *Application deadline:* For fall admission, 3/1 priority date for domestic students, 2/1 for international students. Applications are processed on a rolling basis. Electronic applications accepted. *Expenses:* Tuition, state resident: full-time $7360; part-time $310 per credit hour. Tuition, nonresident: full-time $13,800; part-time $575 per credit hour. Required fees: $190 per semester. *Unit head:* Benzion Chanowitz, Graduate Advisor, 718-951-5601, E-mail: bchanowitz@brooklyn.cuny.edu. *Application contact:* Hernan Sierra, Graduate Admissions Coordinator, 718-951-4536, Fax: 718-951-4506, E-mail: grads@brooklyn.cuny.edu.

California Lutheran University, Graduate Studies, School of Management, Thousand Oaks, CA 91360-2787. Offers business (IMBA); computer science (MS); econometrics (MBA); economics (MS); entrepreneurship (MBA, Certificate); finance (MBA, Certificate); financial planning (MBA, Certificate); information systems and technology (MS); information technology management (MBA, Certificate); international business (MBA, Certificate); management and organization behavior (MBA); management and organizational behavior (Certificate); marketing (MBA, Certificate); microeconomics (MBA); nonprofit and social enterprise (MBA). Part-time and evening/weekend programs available. Postbaccalaureate distance learning degree programs offered (no on-campus study). *Faculty:* 12 full-time (3 women), 27 part-time/adjunct (6 women). *Students:* 350 full-time (162 women), 262 part-time (99 women); includes 21 Black or African American, non-Hispanic/Latino; 44 Asian, non-Hispanic/Latino; 56 Hispanic/Latino; 4 Native Hawaiian or other Pacific Islander, non-Hispanic/Latino; 12 Two or more races, non-Hispanic/Latino, 185 international. Average age 32. 379 applicants, 74% accepted, 138 enrolled. In 2010, 231 master's awarded. *Entrance requirements:* For master's, GMAT, interview, minimum GPA of 3.0. *Application deadline:* Applications are processed on a rolling basis. Application fee: $50. *Expenses:* Contact institution. *Unit head:* Dr. Charles Maxey, Dean, 805-493-3360. *Application contact:* 805-493-3127, Fax: 805-493-3542, E-mail: clugrad@clunet.edu.

Cornell University, Graduate School, Graduate Field of Management, Ithaca, NY 14853. Offers accounting (PhD); behavioral decision theory (PhD); finance (PhD); marketing (PhD); organizational behavior (PhD); production and operations management (PhD). *Accreditation:* AACSB. *Faculty:* 55 full-time (9 women). *Students:* 41 full-time (12 women); includes 5 Asian, non-Hispanic/Latino, 23 international. Average age 29. 436 applicants, 4% accepted, 12 enrolled. In 2010, 5 doctorates awarded. *Degree requirements:* For doctorate, comprehensive exam, thesis/dissertation. *Entrance requirements:* For doctorate, GMAT or GRE General Test. Additional exam requirements/recommendations for international students: Required—TOEFL (minimum score 600 paper-based; 250 computer-based; 77 iBT). *Application deadline:* For fall admission, 1/3 for domestic students. Application fee: $70. Electronic applications accepted. *Expenses:* Contact institution. *Financial support:* In 2010–11, 38 students received support, including 4 fellowships with full tuition reimbursements available, 34 research assistantships with full tuition reimbursements available, 1 teaching assistantship with full tuition reimbursement available; institutionally sponsored loans, scholarships/grants, health care benefits, tuition waivers (full and partial), and unspecified assistantships also available. Financial award applicants required to submit FAFSA. *Faculty research:* Operations and manufacturing. *Unit head:* Director of Graduate Studies, 607-255-3669. *Application contact:* Graduate Field Assistant, 607-255-9431, E-mail: js_phd@cornell.edu.

Cornell University, Graduate School, Graduate Fields of Industrial and Labor Relations, Ithaca, NY 14853. Offers collective bargaining, labor law and labor history (MILR, MPS, MS, PhD); economic and social statistics (MILR); human resource studies (MILR, MPS, MS, PhD); industrial and labor relations problems (MILR, MPS, MS, PhD); international and comparative labor (MILR, MPS, MS, PhD); labor economics (MILR, MPS, MS, PhD); organizational behavior (MILR, MPS, MS, PhD). *Faculty:* 52 full-time (17 women). *Students:* 165 full-time (100 women); includes 13 Black or African American, non-Hispanic/Latino; 1 American Indian or Alaska Native, non-Hispanic/Latino; 15 Asian, non-Hispanic/Latino; 7 Hispanic/Latino, 60 international. Average age 29. 340 applicants, 29% accepted, 87 enrolled. In 2010, 68 master's, 3 doctorates awarded. *Degree requirements:* For master's, thesis (MS); for doctorate, comprehensive exam, thesis/dissertation, teaching experience. *Entrance requirements:* For master's and doctorate, GMAT or GRE General Test, 2 academic recommendations. Additional exam requirements/recommendations for international students: Required—TOEFL (minimum score 550 paper-based; 213 computer-based; 77 iBT). Application fee: $70. Electronic applications accepted. *Expenses:* Contact institution. *Financial support:* In 2010–11, 73 students received support, including 14 fellowships with full tuition reimbursements available, 26 research assistantships with full tuition reimbursements available, 30 teaching assistantships with full tuition reimbursements available; institutionally sponsored loans, scholarships/grants, health care benefits, tuition waivers (full and partial), and unspecified assistantships also available. Financial award applicants required to submit FAFSA. *Unit head:* Director of Graduate Studies, 607-255-1522. *Application contact:* Graduate Field Assistant, 607-255-1522, E-mail: ilrgradapplicant@cornell.edu.

Fairleigh Dickinson University, College at Florham, Maxwell Becton College of Arts and Sciences, Department of Psychology, Program in Organizational Behavior, Madison, NJ 07940-1099. Offers organizational behavior (MA); organizational leadership (Certificate). *Students:* 2 full-time (both women), 18 part-time (8 women). Average age 38. 7 applicants, 100% accepted, 7 enrolled. In 2010, 6 master's awarded. Application fee: $40. *Application contact:* Susan

Brooman, University Director, Graduate Admissions, 973-443-8905, Fax: 973-443-8088, E-mail: grad@fdu.edu.

Florida Institute of Technology, Graduate Programs, College of Psychology and Liberal Arts, School of Psychology, Melbourne, FL 32901-6975. Offers applied behavior analysis (MS); applied behavior analysis and organizational behavior management (MS); behavior analysis (PhD); clinical psychology (Psy D); industrial/organizational psychology (MS, PhD); organizational behavior management (MS). *Accreditation:* APA (one or more programs are accredited). Part-time programs available. *Faculty:* 21 full-time (10 women), 6 part-time/adjunct (2 women). *Students:* 220 full-time (167 women), 11 part-time (10 women); includes 25 minority (5 Black or African American, non-Hispanic/Latino; 4 Asian, non-Hispanic/Latino; 16 Hispanic/Latino), 22 international. Average age 27. 378 applicants, 42% accepted, 77 enrolled. In 2010, 57 master's, 13 doctorates awarded. Terminal master's awarded for partial completion of doctoral program. *Degree requirements:* For master's, comprehensive exam (for some programs), thesis (for some programs), BCBA certification, final exam; for doctorate, comprehensive exam, thesis/dissertation, internship, full time resident of school for 4 years (8 semesters, 3 summers). *Entrance requirements:* For master's, GRE General Test, 3 letters of recommendation, minimum GPA of 3.0, resume, statement of objectives; for doctorate, GRE General Test, GRE Subject Test (psychology), 3 letters of recommendation, minimum GPA of 3.2, resume, statement of objectives. Additional exam requirements/recommendations for international students: Required—TOEFL (minimum score 550 paper-based; 213 computer-based; 79 iBT). *Application deadline:* For fall admission, 4/1 for international students; for spring admission, 9/30 for international students. Applications are processed on a rolling basis. Application fee: $50. Electronic applications accepted. *Expenses:* Tuition: Part-time $1040 per credit hour. Tuition and fees vary according to campus/location. *Financial support:* In 2010–11, 4 fellowships with full and partial tuition reimbursements (averaging $3,775 per year), 32 research assistantships with full and partial tuition reimbursements (averaging $5,602 per year), 8 teaching assistantships with full and partial tuition reimbursements (averaging $4,570 per year) were awarded; career-related internships or fieldwork, institutionally sponsored loans, tuition waivers (partial), unspecified assistantships, and tuition remissions also available. Support available to part-time students. Financial award application deadline: 3/1; financial award applicants required to submit FAFSA. *Faculty research:* Addictions, neuropsychology, child abuse, assessment, psychological trauma. Total annual research expenditures: $1.8 million. *Unit head:* Dr. Mary Beth Kenkel, Dean, 321-674-8142, Fax: 321-674-7105, E-mail: mkenkel@fit.edu. *Application contact:* Cheryl A. Brown, Associate Director of Graduate Admissions, 321-674-7581, Fax: 321-723-9468, E-mail: cbrown@fit.edu.

Florida State University, The Graduate School, College of Business, Tallahassee, FL 32306-1110. Offers accounting (M Acc), including accounting information services, assurance services, corporate accounting, taxation; business administration (MBA, PhD), including accounting (PhD), finance (PhD), management information systems (PhD), marketing (PhD), organizational behavior (PhD), risk management and insurance (PhD), strategic management (PhD); finance (MS); insurance (MSM); management information systems (MS); JD/MBA; MSW/MBA. *Accreditation:* AACSB. Part-time programs available. Postbaccalaureate distance learning degree programs offered (no on-campus study). *Faculty:* 107 full-time (31 women). *Students:* 196 full-time (76 women), 310 part-time (109 women); includes 27 Black or African American, non-Hispanic/Latino; 1 American Indian or Alaska Native, non-Hispanic/Latino; 31 Asian, non-Hispanic/Latino; 30 Hispanic/Latino. Average age 30. 702 applicants, 33% accepted, 205 enrolled. In 2010, 268 master's, 17 doctorates awarded. Terminal master's awarded for partial completion of doctoral program. *Degree requirements:* For doctorate, comprehensive exam, thesis/dissertation. *Entrance requirements:* For master's, GMAT, work experience (MBA, MS), minimum GPA of 3.0, letters of recommendation; for doctorate, GMAT, minimum graduate GPA of 3.5, letters of recommendation. Additional exam requirements/recommendations for international students: Required—TOEFL (minimum score 600 paper-based; 80 computer-based); Recommended—IELTS (minimum score 6.5). *Application deadline:* For fall admission, 6/1 for domestic students, 5/1 for international students; for spring admission, 10/1 for domestic students, 9/1 for international students. Applications are processed on a rolling basis. Application fee: $30. Electronic applications accepted. *Expenses:* Tuition, state resident: full-time $8238.24. *Financial support:* In 2010–11, 86 students received support, including 12 fellowships with full tuition reimbursements available (averaging $7,161 per year), 30 research assistantships with full tuition reimbursements available (averaging $6,000 per year), 43 teaching assistantships with full tuition reimbursements available (averaging $15,000 per year); career-related internships or fieldwork, scholarships/grants, health care benefits, tuition waivers (full and partial), and unspecified assistantships also available. Support available to part-time students. Financial award application deadline: 1/1. *Unit head:* Dr. Caryn Beck-Dudley, Dean, 850-644-3090, Fax: 850-644-0915. *Application contact:* Lisa Beverly, Director, Graduate Programs Admissions, 850-644-6458, Fax: 850-644-0588, E-mail: lbeverly@cob.fsu.edu.

Lake Forest Graduate School of Management, MBA Program, Lake Forest, IL 60045. Offers global business (MBA); healthcare management (MBA); management (MBA); marketing (MBA); organizational behavior (MBA).

Part-time and evening/weekend programs available. *Faculty:* 123 part-time/adjunct (26 women). *Students:* 734 part-time (306 women); includes 156 minority (34 Black or African American, non-Hispanic/Latino; 86 Asian, non-Hispanic/Latino; 14 Hispanic/Latino; 4 Native Hawaiian or other Pacific Islander, non-Hispanic/Latino; 18 Two or more races, non-Hispanic/Latino). Average age 38. In 2010, 202 master's awarded. *Entrance requirements:* For master's, 4 years of work experience in field, interview, 2 letters of recommendation. *Application deadline:* For fall admission, 7/1 for domestic students; for winter admission, 1/5 for domestic students; for spring admission, 3/1 for domestic students. Applications are processed on a rolling basis. Application fee: $0. Electronic applications accepted. *Financial support:* In 2010–11, 290 students received support. Scholarships/grants available. Support available to part-time students. Financial award applicants required to submit FAFSA. *Unit head:* Chris Multhauf, Vice President and Degree Programs Dean, 847-574-5270, Fax: 847-295-3656, E-mail: cmulthauf@lfgsm.edu. *Application contact:* Carolyn Brune, Director of Admissions Operations, 800-737-4MBA, Fax: 847-295-3656, E-mail: admiss@lfgsm.edu.

Marylhurst University, Department of Business Administration, Marylhurst, OR 97036-0261. Offers finance (MBA); general management (MBA); government policy and administration (MBA); green development (MBA); health care management (MBA); marketing (MBA); natural and organic resources (MBA); nonprofit management (MBA); organizational behavior (MBA); real estate (MBA); renewable energy (MBA); sustainable business (MBA). Part-time and evening/weekend programs available. Postbaccalaureate distance learning degree programs offered (no on-campus study). *Faculty:* 3 full-time (0 women), 36 part-time/adjunct (6 women). *Students:* 27 full-time (13 women), 727 part-time (373 women); includes 167 minority (47 Black or African American, non-Hispanic/Latino; 6 American Indian or Alaska Native, non-Hispanic/Latino; 36 Asian, non-Hispanic/Latino; 51 Hispanic/Latino; 6 Native Hawaiian or other Pacific Islander, non-Hispanic/Latino; 21 Two or more races, non-Hispanic/Latino), 7 international. Average age 38. 262 applicants, 91% accepted, 194 enrolled. In 2010, 289 master's awarded. *Degree requirements:* For master's, comprehensive exam, capstone course. *Entrance requirements:* For master's, GMAT (if GPA less than 3.0 and fewer than 5 years of work experience), interview, resume, 2 letters of recommendation. Additional exam requirements/recommendations for international students: Recommended—TOEFL (minimum score 550 paper-based; 213 computer-based; 80 iBT). *Application deadline:* For fall admission, 9/11 priority date for domestic and international students; for winter admission, 12/15 priority date for domestic and international students; for spring admission, 3/15 priority date for domestic students, 3/17 priority date for international students. Applications are processed on a rolling basis. Application fee: $50. Electronic applications accepted. *Expenses:* Tuition: Full-time $13,932; part-time $516 per credit. Tuition and fees vary according to course load and program. *Financial support:* Scholarships/grants available. Support available to part-time students. Financial award applicants required to submit FAFSA. *Unit head:* Bob Hanks, Director of Business and Real Estate Programs, 503-636-8141, Fax: 503-697-5597, E-mail: mba@marylhurst.edu. *Application contact:* Maruska Lynch, Graduate Admissions Specialist, 800-634-9982 Ext. 6322, Fax: 503-699-6320, E-mail: admissions@marylhurst.edu.

Polytechnic Institute of NYU, Department of Finance and Risk Engineering, Brooklyn, NY 11201-2990. Offers financial engineering (MS, Advanced Certificate), including capital markets (MS), computational finance (MS), financial technology (MS); financial technology management (Advanced Certificate); organizational behavior (Advanced Certificate); risk management (Advanced Certificate); technology management (Advanced Certificate). Part-time and evening/weekend programs available. *Faculty:* 6 full-time (1 woman), 24 part-time/adjunct (5 women). *Students:* 126 full-time (45 women), 61 part-time (15 women); includes 4 Black or African American, non-Hispanic/Latino; 17 Asian, non-Hispanic/Latino; 1 Hispanic/Latino, 130 international. Average age 27. 528 applicants, 44% accepted, 67 enrolled. In 2010, 154 master's awarded. *Degree requirements:* For master's, comprehensive exam (for some programs), thesis (for some programs). *Entrance requirements:* For master's, GMAT, minimum B average in undergraduate course work. Additional exam requirements/recommendations for international students: Required—TOEFL (minimum score 550 paper-based; 213 computer-based; 80 iBT); Recommended—IELTS (minimum score 6.5). *Application deadline:* For fall admission, 7/31 priority date for domestic students, 4/30 priority date for international students; for spring admission, 12/31 priority date for domestic students, 11/30 priority date for international students. Applications are processed on a rolling basis. Application fee: $75. Electronic applications accepted. *Expenses:* Tuition: Full-time $21,492; part-time $1194 per credit. Required fees: $385 per semester. Tuition and fees vary according to course load. *Financial support:* Institutionally sponsored loans, scholarships/grants, and unspecified assistantships available. Support available to part-time students. Financial award applicants required to submit FAFSA. *Unit head:* Prof. Charles S. Tapiero, Academic Director, 718-260-3653, Fax: 718-260-3874, E-mail: ctapiero@poly.edu. *Application contact:* JeanCarlo Bonilla, Director, Graduate Enrollment Management, 718-260-3182, Fax: 718-260-3624.

Polytechnic Institute of NYU, Department of Technology Management, Major in Organizational Behavior, Brooklyn, NY 11201-2990. Offers MS. Part-time and evening/weekend programs available. *Students:* 34 full-time (26 women), 12 part-time (8 women); includes 9 Black or African American, non-Hispanic/Latino; 6 Asian, non-Hispanic/Latino; 4 Hispanic/Latino, 14 international. Average age 29. 54 applicants, 70% accepted, 24 enrolled. In 2010, 25 master's awarded. *Degree requirements:* For master's, comprehensive exam (for some programs), thesis (for some programs). *Entrance requirements:* For master's, GMAT, minimum B average in undergraduate course work. Additional exam requirements/recommendations for international students: Required—TOEFL (minimum score 550 paper-based; 213 computer-based; 80 iBT); Recommended—IELTS (minimum score 6.5). *Application deadline:* For fall admission, 7/31 priority date for domestic students, 4/30 priority date for international students; for spring admission, 12/31 priority date for domestic students, 11/30 priority date for international students. Applications are processed on a rolling basis. Application fee: $75. Electronic applications accepted. *Expenses:* Tuition: Full-time $21,492; part-time $1194 per credit. Required fees: $385 per semester. Tuition and fees vary according to course load. *Financial support:* Applicants required to submit FAFSA. *Unit head:* Prof. Bharadwaj Rao, Head, 718-260-3617, Fax: 718-260-3874, E-mail: brao@poly.edu. *Application contact:* JeanCarlo Bonilla, Director of Graduate Enrollment Management, 718-260-3182, Fax: 718-260-3624.

Purdue University, Graduate School, Krannert School of Management, Doctoral Program in Organizational Behavior and Human Resource Management, West Lafayette, IN 47907-2056. Offers PhD. *Students:* 8 full-time (3 women); includes 1 Black or African American, non-Hispanic/Latino; 1 American Indian or Alaska Native, non-Hispanic/Latino; 1 Asian, non-Hispanic/Latino, 1 international. Average age 32. 80 applicants, 3% accepted, 2 enrolled. In 2010, 3 doctorates awarded. *Degree requirements:* For doctorate, comprehensive exam, thesis/dissertation, dissertation proposal, dissertation defense. *Entrance requirements:* For doctorate, GMAT or GRE, bachelor's degree, two semesters of calculus, one semester each of linear algebra and statistics. Additional exam requirements/recommendations for international students: Required—TOEFL (minimum score 575 paper-based; 233 computer-based); Recommended—TWE. *Application deadline:* For fall admission, 1/15 priority date for domestic and international students. Application fee: $55. Electronic applications accepted. *Financial support:* In 2010–11, 1 fellowship with full tuition reimbursement (averaging $25,000 per year), research assistantships with partial tuition reimbursements (averaging $18,000 per year), teaching assistantships with partial tuition reimbursements (averaging $18,000 per year) were awarded; scholarships/grants, health care benefits, tuition waivers (full and partial), unspecified assistantships, and travel funds to present at a major conference also available. Support available to part-time students. Financial award application deadline: 1/15. *Faculty research:* Human resource management, organizational behavior. *Unit head:* Dr. Gerald J. Lynch, Dean, 765-494-4366. *Application contact:* Krannert Ph.D. Admissions, 765-494-4375, Fax: 765-494-0136, E-mail: krannertphd@purdue.edu.

Saybrook University, Graduate College of Psychology and Humanistic Studies, San Francisco, CA 94111-1920. Offers clinical psychology (Psy D); human science (MA, PhD), including consciousness and spirituality, humanistic and transpersonal psychology, integrative health studies, organizational systems, social transformation, transformative social change (MA); organizational systems (MA, PhD), including consciousness and spirituality, humanistic and transpersonal psychology, integrative health studies, leadership of sustainable systems (MA), organizational systems, social transformation; psychology (MA, PhD), including clinical psychology (PhD), consciousness and spirituality, creativity studies (MA), humanistic and transpersonal psychology, integrative health studies, Jungian studies, marriage and family therapy (MA), organizational systems, social transformation. Postbaccalaureate distance learning degree programs offered (minimal on-campus study). *Faculty:* 15 full-time (5 women), 83 part-time/adjunct (34 women). *Students:* 479 full-time (333 women); includes 30 Black or African American, non-Hispanic/Latino; 1 American Indian or Alaska Native, non-Hispanic/Latino; 13 Asian, non-Hispanic/Latino; 18 Hispanic/Latino, 18 international. Average age 43. 280 applicants, 52% accepted, 105 enrolled. In 2010, 28 master's, 43 doctorates awarded. Terminal master's awarded for partial completion of doctoral program. *Degree requirements:* For master's, thesis or alternative; for doctorate, thesis/dissertation. *Entrance requirements:* Additional exam requirements/recommendations for international students: Required—TOEFL (minimum score 580 paper-based; 237 computer-based; 93 iBT). *Application deadline:* For fall admission, 6/1 priority date for domestic students; for spring admission, 12/16 priority date for domestic students. Application fee: $50. Electronic applications accepted. *Financial support:* In 2010–11, 335 students received support. Scholarships/grants available. Financial award applicants required to submit FAFSA. *Faculty research:* Humanistic theory, health studies, organizational systems, consciousness and spirituality, social transformation. Total annual research expenditures: $90,000. *Unit head:* Mark Schulman, President, 800-825-4480, Fax: 415-433-9271. *Application contact:* Director of Admissions, 800-825-4480, Fax: 415-433-9271, E-mail: admissions@saybrook.edu.

Saybrook University, LIOS Graduate College, Leadership and Organization Development Track, San Francisco, CA 94111-1920. Offers MA. Program offered jointly with Bastyr University. *Faculty:* 10 full-time (6 women), 5 part-time/adjunct (2 women). *Students:* 48 full-time. Average age 40. 50 applicants, 98% accepted, 40 enrolled. In 2010, 19 master's awarded. *Degree requirements:* For master's, thesis (for some programs), oral exams. *Entrance*

requirements: For master's, bachelor's degree from an accredited college or university. *Application deadline:* Applications are processed on a rolling basis. Application fee: $65. *Financial support:* In 2010–11, 32 students received support. Career-related internships or fieldwork, Federal Work-Study, and scholarships/grants available. Financial award applicants required to submit FAFSA. *Faculty research:* Cross-functional work teams, communication, management authority, employee influence, systems theory. *Unit head:* Dr. Shelley Drogin, Head, 425-939-8181, Fax: 425-939-8110, E-mail: sdrogin@lios.org. *Application contact:* Jennifer Herron, Director, Academic Admissions, 425-939-8124, Fax: 425-939-8110.

Silver Lake College, Division of Graduate Studies, Program in Management and Organizational Behavior, Manitowoc, WI 54220-9319. Offers MS. Part-time and evening/weekend programs available. Postbaccalaureate distance learning degree programs offered (minimal on-campus study). *Faculty:* 27 part-time/adjunct (14 women). *Students:* 15 full-time (13 women), 52 part-time (31 women); includes 7 minority (6 American Indian or Alaska Native, non-Hispanic/Latino; 1 Asian, non-Hispanic/Latino). Average age 38. 33 applicants, 94% accepted, 18 enrolled. In 2010, 39 master's awarded. *Degree requirements:* For master's, thesis optional. *Entrance requirements:* For master's, minimum undergraduate GPA of 3.0, statement of purpose, three letters of recommendation, professional resume. Additional exam requirements/recommendations for international students: Required—TOEFL. *Application deadline:* For fall admission, 8/1 priority date for domestic students; for spring admission, 12/1 priority date for domestic students. Applications are processed on a rolling basis. Application fee: $0. Electronic applications accepted. *Expenses:* Tuition: Part-time $425 per credit. Required fees: $10 per semester. *Financial support:* Career-related internships or fieldwork, Federal Work-Study, and scholarships/grants available. Support available to part-time students. Financial award application deadline: 6/30; financial award applicants required to submit FAFSA. *Unit head:* Suzanne M. Lawrence, Director, 920-686-6198, Fax: 920-684-7082, E-mail: law@silver.sl.edu. *Application contact:* Cindy St. John, Interim Director of Admissions, 800-236-4752 Ext. 350, Fax: 920-686-6350, E-mail: cynthia.st.john@sl.edu.

Suffolk University, Sawyer Business School, Master of Business Administration Program, Boston, MA 02108-2770. Offers accounting (MBA); business administration (APC); corporate financial executive track (MBA); entrepreneurship (MBA); executive business administration (EMBA); finance (MBA); global business administration (GMBA); health administration (MBA); international business (MBA); marketing (MBA); organizational behavior (MBA); strategic management (MBA); taxation (MBA); JD/MBA; MBA/GDPA; MBA/MHA; MBA/MSA; MBA/MSF; MBA/MST. *Accreditation:* AACSB. Part-time and evening/weekend programs available. Postbaccalaureate distance learning degree programs offered (no on-campus study). *Faculty:* 97 full-time (30 women), 14 part-time/adjunct (3 women). *Students:* 179 full-time (65 women), 337 part-time (143 women); includes 16 Black or African American, non-Hispanic/Latino; 2 American Indian or Alaska Native, non-Hispanic/Latino; 22 Asian, non-Hispanic/Latino; 9 Hispanic/Latino; 1 Native Hawaiian or other Pacific Islander, non-Hispanic/Latino, 80 international. Average age 30. 431 applicants, 68% accepted, 128 enrolled. In 2010, 283 master's awarded. *Entrance requirements:* For master's, GMAT, minimum undergraduate GPA of 2.75 (MBA), 5 years of managerial experience (EMBA). Additional exam requirements/recommendations for international students: Required—TOEFL (minimum score 550 paper-based; 213 computer-based). *Application deadline:* For fall admission, 6/15 priority date for domestic students, 6/15 for international students; for spring admission, 11/1 priority date for domestic students, 11/1 for international students. Applications are processed on a rolling basis. Application fee: $50. Electronic applications accepted. *Financial support:* In 2010–11, 266 students received support, including 94 fellowships with full and partial tuition reimbursements available (averaging $12,635 per year); career-related internships or fieldwork, Federal Work-Study, and institutionally sponsored loans also available. Support available to part-time students. Financial award application deadline: 4/1; financial award applicants required to submit FAFSA. *Faculty research:* Foreign investments; career strategies and boundaryless careers; corporate ethics codes; interest rates, inflation, and growth options; innovation and product development performance. *Unit head:* Lillian Hallberg, Assistant Dean of Graduate Programs/Director of MBA Programs, 617-573-8306, E-mail: lhallber@suffolk.edu. *Application contact:* Judith Reynolds, Director of Graduate Admissions, 617-573-8302, Fax: 617-305-1733, E-mail: grad.admission@suffolk.edu.

Towson University, Program in Organizational Change, Towson, MD 21252-0001. Offers CAS. *Students:* 17 full-time (12 women), 62 part-time (50 women); includes 20 minority (19 Black or African American, non-Hispanic/Latino; 1 American Indian or Alaska Native, non-Hispanic/Latino), 2 international. Average age 35. In 2010, 1 CAS awarded. *Entrance requirements:* For degree, GRE or MAT, 2 letters of recommendation, minimum GPA of 3.5. Additional exam requirements/recommendations for international students: Required—TOEFL (minimum score 550 paper-based; 213 computer-based). *Application deadline:* Applications are processed on a rolling basis. Application fee: $50. Electronic applications accepted. *Expenses:* Tuition, state resident: part-time $324 per credit. Tuition, nonresident: part-time $681 per credit. Required fees: $95 per term. *Faculty research:* Leadership, school administration, change, social responsibility. *Unit head:* Jane Neapolitan,

Assistant Dean, 410-704-4954, Fax: 410-704-2733, E-mail: jneapolitan@towson.edu. *Application contact:* 410-704-2501, Fax: 410-704-4675, E-mail: grads@towson.edu.

Université de Sherbrooke, Faculty of Administration, Program in Organizational Change and Intervention, Sherbrooke, QC J1K 2R1, Canada. Offers M Sc. *Faculty:* 8 full-time (2 women), 5 part-time/adjunct (2 women). *Students:* 19 full-time (16 women). Average age 24. 74 applicants, 74% accepted, 19 enrolled. In 2010, 23 master's awarded. *Degree requirements:* For master's, one foreign language, thesis. *Entrance requirements:* For master's, bachelor degree in related field Minimum GPA 3/4.3. *Application deadline:* For fall admission, 4/30 for domestic students, 1/15 for international students. Applications are processed on a rolling basis. Application fee: $70. Electronic applications accepted. *Faculty research:* Organizational change, organizational communication, process approaches and qualitative research, organizational behavior. *Unit head:* Prof. Julien Bilodeau, Director, Graduate programs in business, 819-821-8000 Ext. 62355. *Application contact:* Marie-Claude Drouin, Programs Assistant Director, 819-821-8000 Ext. 63301.

University of California, Berkeley, Graduate Division, Haas School of Business, PhD in Business Administration Program, Berkeley, CA 94720-1500. Offers accounting (PhD); business and public policy (PhD); finance (PhD); management of organizations (PhD); marketing (PhD); operations management (PhD); real estate (PhD). *Accreditation:* AACSB. *Students:* 78 full-time (25 women); includes 12 Asian, non-Hispanic/Latino; 2 Hispanic/Latino, 32 international. Average age 30. 526 applicants, 7% accepted, 17 enrolled. In 2010, 17 doctorates awarded. *Degree requirements:* For doctorate, comprehensive exam, thesis/dissertation, written preliminary exams, oral qualifying exam. *Entrance requirements:* For doctorate, GMAT or GRE, minimum GPA of 3.0 in undergraduate and graduate coursework. Additional exam requirements/recommendations for international students: Required—TOEFL (minimum score 570 paper-based; 230 computer-based; 70 iBT), IELTS (minimum score 7). *Application deadline:* For fall admission, 12/10 for domestic and international students. Application fee: $70 ($90 for international students). Electronic applications accepted. *Financial support:* In 2010–11, 63 students received support, including 58 fellowships with full and partial tuition reimbursements available (averaging $26,000 per year); research assistantships with full and partial tuition reimbursements available, teaching assistantships with full and partial tuition reimbursements available, scholarships/grants, health care benefits, tuition waivers (full), unspecified assistantships, and transit pass, travel grants also available. Financial award application deadline: 12/10; financial award applicants required to submit FAFSA. *Faculty research:* Accounting, business and public policy, finance, management of organizations, marketing, operations and information technology management, real estate526. *Unit head:* Dr. Sunil Dutta, Director, 510-642-1229, Fax: 510-643-4255, E-mail: kimg@haas.berkeley.edu. *Application contact:* Kim Guilfoyle, Director, Student Affairs, 510-642-3944, Fax: 510-643-4255, E-mail: kimg@haas.berkeley.edu.

University of California, Los Angeles, Graduate Division, UCLA Anderson School of Management, Los Angeles, CA 90095-1481. Offers accounting (PhD); business administration (MBA); decisions, operations and technology management (PhD); finance (PhD); financial engineering (MFE); global economics and management (PhD); human resources and organizational behavior (PhD); marketing (PhD); strategy and policy (PhD); DDS/MBA; MBA/JD; MBA/MD; MBA/MLAS; MBA/MLIS; MBA/MPH; MBA/MPP; MBA/MSCS; MBA/MSN; MBA/MUP. *Accreditation:* AACSB. Part-time programs available. *Faculty:* 102 full-time (17 women), 43 part-time/adjunct (6 women). *Students:* 833 full-time (270 women), 1,052 part-time (271 women); includes 592 minority (25 Black or African American, non-Hispanic/Latino; 3 American Indian or Alaska Native, non-Hispanic/Latino; 482 Asian, non-Hispanic/Latino; 60 Hispanic/Latino; 6 Native Hawaiian or other Pacific Islander, non-Hispanic/Latino; 16 Two or more races, non-Hispanic/Latino, 445 international. In 2010, 735 master's, 10 doctorates awarded. *Degree requirements:* For master's, comprehensive exam, field study consulting project (for MBA); thesis/dissertation (for MFE); for doctorate, comprehensive exam, thesis/dissertation, oral and written qualifying exams. *Entrance requirements:* For master's, GMAT (MBA); GMAT or GRE General Test (MFE), minimum undergraduate GPA of 3.0; for doctorate, GMAT or GRE General Test, minimum undergraduate GPA of 3.0. Additional exam requirements/recommendations for international students: Required—TOEFL (minimum score 560 paper-based; 220 computer-based; 87 iBT), IELTS (minimum score 7). *Application deadline:* For fall admission, 10/20 for domestic and international students; for winter admission, 1/5 for domestic and international students; for spring admission, 4/13 for domestic and international students. Application fee: $200. Electronic applications accepted. *Expenses:* Contact institution. *Financial support:* Fellowships, research assistantships, teaching assistantships, career-related internships or fieldwork, institutionally sponsored loans, scholarships/grants, health care benefits, and tuition waivers (partial) available. Financial award application deadline: 3/2; financial award applicants required to submit FAFSA. *Unit head:* Judy D. Olian, Dean, UCLA Anderson School of Management, 310-825-7982, Fax: 310-206-2073. *Application contact:* Mae Jennifer Shores, Assistant Dean and Director of Full-time MBA Admissions and Financial Aid, 310-825-6944, Fax: 310-825-8582, E-mail: mba.admissions@anderson.ucla.edu.

University of Chicago, Booth School of Business, Full-Time MBA Program, Chicago, IL 60637. Offers accounting (MBA); analytic finance (MBA); analytic

management (MBA); econometrics and statistics (MBA); economics (MBA); entrepreneurship (MBA); finance (MBA); general management (MBA); human resource management (MBA); international business (MBA); managerial and organizational behavior (MBA); marketing management (MBA); operations management (MBA); strategic management (MBA); MBA/AM; MBA/JD; MBA/MA; MBA/MD; MBA/MPP. *Accreditation:* AACSB. Part-time and evening/weekend programs available. *Faculty:* 157 full-time, 35 part-time/adjunct. *Students:* 1,177 full-time (417 women); includes 301 minority (62 Black or African American, non-Hispanic/Latino; 1 American Indian or Alaska Native, non-Hispanic/Latino; 164 Asian, non-Hispanic/Latino; 55 Hispanic/Latino; 19 Two or more races, non-Hispanic/Latino), 403 international. Average age 28. 4,299 applicants, 22% accepted, 579 enrolled. In 2010, 1,374 master's awarded. *Entrance requirements:* For master's, GMAT, 2 letters of recommendation, 3 essays, resume, interview, transcripts. Additional exam requirements/recommendations for international students: Required—TOEFL (minimum score 600 paper-based; 250 computer-based), IELTS. *Application deadline:* For fall admission, 10/10 priority date for domestic students, 10/13 priority date for international students; for winter admission, 1/5 for domestic and international students; for spring admission, 4/13 for domestic and international students. Application fee: $200. Electronic applications accepted. *Expenses:* Contact institution. *Financial support:* Fellowships available. Financial award applicants required to submit FAFSA. *Faculty research:* Finance, economics, entrepreneurship, strategy, management. *Unit head:* Stacey Kole, Deputy Dean, 773-702-7121. *Application contact:* Kurt Ahlm, Associate Dean of Admissions and Financial Aid, 773-702-7369, Fax: 773-702-9085, E-mail: admissions@chicagobooth.edu.

University of Hawaii at Manoa, Graduate Division, Shidler College of Business, Program in Business Administration, Honolulu, HI 96822. Offers Asian business studies (MBA); Chinese business studies (MBA); decision sciences (MBA); entrepreneurship (MBA); finance (MBA); finance and banking (MBA); human resources management (MBA); information management (MBA); information technology (MBA); international business (MBA); Japanese business studies (MBA); marketing (MBA); organizational behavior (MBA); organizational management (MBA); real estate (MBA); student-designed track (MBA). *Accreditation:* AACSB. Part-time and evening/weekend programs available. *Faculty:* 53 full-time (12 women). *Students:* 162 full-time (63 women), 102 part-time (43 women); includes 135 minority (1 Black or African American, non-Hispanic/Latino; 81 Asian, non-Hispanic/Latino; 5 Hispanic/Latino; 18 Native Hawaiian or other Pacific Islander, non-Hispanic/Latino; 30 Two or more races, non-Hispanic/Latino), 44 international. Average age 34. 361 applicants, 57% accepted, 172 enrolled. In 2010, 153 master's awarded. *Degree requirements:* For master's, thesis optional. *Entrance requirements:* For master's, GMAT, minimum GPA of 3.0. Additional exam requirements/recommendations for international students: Required—TOEFL (minimum score 600 paper-based; 250 computer-based; 100 iBT), IELTS (minimum score 7). *Application deadline:* For fall admission, 5/1 for domestic students, 3/1 for international students. Application fee: $60. *Expenses:* Contact institution. *Financial support:* In 2010–11, 83 fellowships (averaging $5,547 per year), 1 research assistantship (averaging $16,824 per year) were awarded. Total annual research expenditures: $427,000. *Application contact:* Daniel Port, Graduate Chair, 808-956-5565, Fax: 808-956-6889, E-mail: daniel.port@hawaii.edu.

University of Oklahoma, College of Arts and Sciences, Department of Psychology, Program in Organizational Dynamics, Tulsa, OK 74135. Offers organizational dynamics (MA), including human resource management, organizational dynamics, technical project management. Part-time and evening/weekend programs available. *Students:* 9 full-time (4 women), 25 part-time (13 women); includes 6 minority (1 Black or African American, non-Hispanic/Latino; 1 American Indian or Alaska Native, non-Hispanic/Latino; 2 Asian, non-Hispanic/Latino; 1 Native Hawaiian or other Pacific Islander, non-Hispanic/Latino; 1 Two or more races, non-Hispanic/Latino). Average age 37. 6 applicants, 100% accepted, 6 enrolled. In 2010, 11 master's awarded. *Entrance requirements:* For master's, minimum GPA of 3.0 in last 60 hours of undergraduate course work. Additional exam requirements/recommendations for international students: Required—TOEFL (minimum score 550 paper-based; 213 computer-based; 79 iBT). *Application deadline:* For fall admission, 4/15 priority date for domestic students, 4/15 for international students; for spring admission, 11/1 for domestic students, 9/1 for international students. Applications are processed on a rolling basis. Application fee: $40 ($90 for international students). Electronic applications accepted. *Expenses:* Tuition, state resident: full-time $3893; part-time $162.20 per credit hour. Tuition, nonresident: full-time $14,167; part-time $590.30 per credit hour. Required fees: $2523; $94.60 per credit hour. Tuition and fees vary according to course load and degree level. *Financial support:* In 2010–11, 10 students received support. Scholarships/grants, health care benefits, and unspecified assistantships available. Financial award application deadline: 3/1; financial award applicants required to submit FAFSA. *Faculty research:* Academic integrity, organizational behavior, interdisciplinary teams, shared leadership. *Unit head:* Dr. Jorge Mendoza, Chair, 405-325-4511, Fax: 405-325-4737, E-mail: jmendoza@ou.edu. *Application contact:* Jennifer Kisamore, Graduate Liaison, 918-660-3603, Fax: 918-660-3383, E-mail: jkisamore@ou.edu.

University of Pennsylvania, School of Arts and Sciences, Graduate Group in Organizational Dynamics, Philadelphia, PA 19104. Offers MS. Part-time and evening/weekend programs available. *Students:* 46 full-time (24 women), 155 part-time (86 women); includes 17 Black or African American, non-Hispanic/Latino; 8 Asian, non-Hispanic/Latino, 10 international. 71 applicants, 83% accepted, 48 enrolled. In 2010, 34 master's awarded. *Degree requirements:* For master's, thesis. *Application deadline:* For fall admission, 12/1 priority date for domestic students. Application fee: $70. Electronic applications accepted. *Expenses:* Tuition: Full-time $25,660; part-time $4758 per course. Required fees: $2152; $270 per course. Tuition and fees vary according to course load, degree level and program. *Financial support:* Scholarships/grants available. Support available to part-time students. Financial award application deadline: 12/15. *Unit head:* Director. *Application contact:* Director.

University of Pittsburgh, Katz Graduate School of Business, Doctoral Program in Business Administration, Pittsburgh, PA 15260. Offers accounting (PhD); finance (PhD); information systems (PhD); marketing (PhD); operations/decision sciences/artificial intelligence (PhD); organizational behavior and human resource management (PhD); strategic planning (PhD). *Accreditation:* AACSB. *Faculty:* 50 full-time (15 women). *Students:* 51 full-time (22 women); includes 3 Black or African American, non-Hispanic/Latino; 4 Asian, non-Hispanic/Latino; 2 Hispanic/Latino, 18 international. 448 applicants, 5% accepted, 13 enrolled. In 2010, 4 doctorates awarded. *Degree requirements:* For doctorate, comprehensive exam, thesis/dissertation. *Entrance requirements:* For doctorate, GMAT or GRE, bachelor's degree, references, minimum GPA of 3.0. Additional exam requirements/recommendations for international students: Required—TOEFL, IELTS. *Application deadline:* For fall admission, 2/1 priority date for domestic and international students. Applications are processed on a rolling basis. Application fee: $50. Electronic applications accepted. *Expenses:* Tuition, state resident: full-time $17,304; part-time $701 per credit. Tuition, nonresident: full-time $29,554; part-time $1210 per credit. Required fees: $740; $214 per term. Tuition and fees vary according to program. *Financial support:* In 2010–11, 39 students received support, including 29 research assistantships with full tuition reimbursements available (averaging $1,900 per year), 10 teaching assistantships with full tuition reimbursements available (averaging $23,745 per year); fellowships, Federal Work-Study, scholarships/grants, health care benefits, and unspecified assistantships also available. Financial award application deadline: 2/1. *Faculty research:* Accounting statements and reporting, incentives and governance, corporate finance, mergers and acquisitions, information systems processes, structures and decision-making, organizational structure, knowledge management and corporate strategy, consumer behavior and marketing models. Total annual research expenditures: $362,777. *Unit head:* Dr. John E. Hulland, Director of Doctoral Program, 412-648-1534, Fax: 412-624-3633, E-mail: jhulland@katz.pitt.edu. *Application contact:* Carrie Woods, Assistant Director, Doctoral Office, 412-648-1525, Fax: 412-624-3633, E-mail: cawoods@katz.pitt.edu.

University of Pittsburgh, Katz Graduate School of Business, Master of Business Administration Programs, Pittsburgh, PA 15260. Offers finance (MBA); information systems (MBA); marketing (MBA); operations management (MBA); organizational behavior and human resource management (MBA); organizational leadership (Certificate); six sigma (Certificate); strategy, environment and organizations (MBA); technology, innovation and entrepreneurship (Certificate); MBA/JD; MBA/MIB; MBA/MPIA; MBA/MSE; MBA/MSIS; MID/MBA. *Accreditation:* AACSB. Part-time and evening/weekend programs available. *Faculty:* 60 full-time (18 women), 22 part-time/adjunct (5 women). *Students:* 232 full-time (75 women), 458 part-time (158 women); includes 34 Black or African American, non-Hispanic/Latino; 1 American Indian or Alaska Native, non-Hispanic/Latino; 20 Asian, non-Hispanic/Latino; 9 Hispanic/Latino, 105 international. Average age 29. 697 applicants, 50% accepted, 174 enrolled. In 2010, 263 master's awarded. *Degree requirements:* For master's, minimum GPA of 3.0. *Entrance requirements:* For master's, GMAT, recommendations, undergraduate transcripts, essay responses, resume, interview, bachelor's degree. Additional exam requirements/recommendations for international students: Required—TOEFL (minimum 600 paper, 250 computer, 100 iBT) or IELTS. *Application deadline:* For fall admission, 4/1 priority date for domestic students, 2/1 priority date for international students. Application fee: $50. Electronic applications accepted. *Expenses:* Tuition, state resident: full-time $17,304; part-time $701 per credit. Tuition, nonresident: full-time $29,554; part-time $1210 per credit. Required fees: $740; $214 per term. Tuition and fees vary according to program. *Financial support:* In 2010–11, 52 students received support. Career-related internships or fieldwork and scholarships/grants available. Financial award application deadline: 3/1; financial award applicants required to submit FAFSA. *Faculty research:* Accounting statements and reporting, incentives and governance, corporate finance, mergers and acquisitions, information systems processes, structures and decision-making, organizational structure, knowledge management and corporate strategy, consumer behavior and marketing models. *Unit head:* William T. Valenta, Assistant Dean, MBA Program Director, 412-648-1610, Fax: 412-648-1659, E-mail: wtvalenta@katz.pitt.edu. *Application contact:* Cliff McCormick, Director MBA Admissions, 412-648-1700, Fax: 412-648-1659, E-mail: mba@katz.pitt.edu.

Wilfrid Laurier University, Faculty of Graduate and Postdoctoral Studies, School of Business and Economics, Department of Business, Waterloo, ON N2L 3C5, Canada. Offers accounting (PhD); finance (M Fin); financial economics (PhD); marketing (PhD); operations and supply chain management (PhD); organizational behavior and human resource management (M Sc); organizational behaviour and human resource management (PhD); supply chain management (M Sc); technology management (EMTM). Part-time and evening/weekend programs available. *Faculty:* 67 full-time (20 women), 12 part-time/adjunct (4 women). *Students:* 20 full-time (11 women), 1 part-time (0 women), 5 international. 80 applicants, 28% accepted, 3 enrolled. In 2010, 6 master's, 1 doctorate awarded. *Degree requirements:* For master's, thesis optional; for doctorate, comprehensive exam, thesis/dissertation. *Entrance requirements:* For master's, GMAT, 4-year honors degree with minimum B+ average; for doctorate, GMAT, master's degree, minimum B+ average. Additional exam requirements/recommendations for international students: Required—TOEFL (minimum score 89 iBT). *Application deadline:* For fall admission, 1/15 priority date for domestic and international students. Application fee: $125. Electronic applications accepted. Tuition and fees charges are reported in Canadian dollars. *Expenses:* Tuition, area resident: Full-time $15,300 Canadian dollars; part-time $1200 Canadian dollars per credit. International tuition: $21,300 Canadian dollars full-time. Required fees: $650 Canadian dollars; $100 Canadian dollars per credit. Tuition and fees vary according to course load, degree level, campus/location and program. *Financial support:* In 2010–11, 27 fellowships, 1 research assistantship, 27 teaching assistantships were awarded; career-related internships or fieldwork, scholarships/grants, health care benefits, and unspecified assistantships also available. *Faculty research:* Financial economics, management and organizational behavior, operations and supply chain management. *Unit head:* Dr. Hamid Noori, Director, 519-884-0710 Ext. 2571, Fax: 519-884-2357, E-mail: sbephdmasters@wlu.ca. *Application contact:* Jennifer Williams, Graduate Admission and Records Officer, 519-884-0710 Ext. 3536, Fax: 519-884-1020, E-mail: gradstudies@wlu.ca.

ORGANIZATIONAL MANAGEMENT

Adler Graduate School, Program in Adlerian Counseling and Psychotherapy, Richfield, MN 55423. Offers art therapy (MA); clinical mental health counseling (MA); marriage and family therapy (MA); non-clinical Adlerian studies (MA); online Adlerian studies (MA); organizational wellness and transformation (MA); parent coaching (Certificate); personal and professional life coaching (Certificate); school counseling (MA). Part-time and evening/weekend programs available. *Faculty:* 11 full-time (4 women), 48 part-time/adjunct (28 women). *Students:* 442 part-time (361 women). Average age 37. *Degree requirements:* For master's, thesis or alternative, 500-700 hour internship (depending on license choice). *Entrance requirements:* For master's, minimum undergraduate GPA of 3.0, 12 credits of course work in psychology or related field. *Application deadline:* Applications are processed on a rolling basis. Application fee: $50. *Expenses:* Tuition: Part-time $455 per credit. *Financial support:* Career-related internships or fieldwork and tuition waivers available. Support available to part-time students. Financial award applicants required to submit FAFSA. *Unit head:* Dr. Dan Haugen, President, 612-861-7554 Ext. 107, Fax: 612-861-7559, E-mail: haugen@alfredadler.edu. *Application contact:* Evelyn B. Haas, Director of Student Services and Admissions, 612-861-7554 Ext. 103, Fax: 612-861-7559, E-mail: ev@alfredadler.edu.

The American College, Graduate Programs, Bryn Mawr, PA 19010-2105. Offers financial services (MSFS); leadership (MSM). Part-time and evening/weekend programs available. Postbaccalaureate distance learning degree programs offered (minimal on-campus study). *Faculty:* 20 full-time, 7 part-time/adjunct. *Students:* 629 part-time (141 women). *Application deadline:* Applications are processed on a rolling basis. Application fee: $335. Electronic applications accepted. *Financial support:* Scholarships/grants available. Support available to part-time students. *Faculty research:* Retirement counseling, social security, aging, family composition, inflation. *Unit head:* Dr. Walter J. Woerheide, Vice President for Academics and Dean, 610-526-1398, Fax: 610-526-1359, E-mail: walt.woerheide@theamericancollege.edu. *Application contact:* Joanne F. Patterson, Associate Director of Graduate School Administration, 610-526-1366, Fax: 610-526-1359, E-mail: joanne.patterson@theamericancollege.edu.

American Public University System, AMU/APU Graduate Programs, Charles Town, WV 25414. Offers accounting (MBA); administration and supervision (M Ed); air warfare (MA Military Studies); asymmetrical warfare (MA Military Studies); criminal justice (MA); emergency and disaster management (MA); entrepreneurship (MBA); environmental policy and management (MS); finance (MBA); general (MBA); global business management (MBA); guidance and counseling (M Ed); history (MA); homeland security (MA); homeland security resource allocation (MBA); humanities (MA); information technology (MS); information technology management (MBA); intelligence studies (MA); international relations and conflict resolution (MA); joint warfare (MA Military Studies); land warfare (MA Military Studies); legal studies (MA); management (MA), including defense mangement, general, human resource management, organizational leadership, public administration; marketing (MBA); military history (MA); national security studies (MA);

naval warfare (MA Military Studies); nonprofit management (MBA); political science (MA); psychology (MA); public administration (MA); public health (MA); security management (MA); space studies (MS); sports management (MS); strategic leadership (MA Military Studies); teaching (M Ed), including elementary, secondary social sciences; transportation and logistics management (MA). Programs offered via distance learning only. Part-time and evening/weekend programs available. Postbaccalaureate distance learning degree programs offered (no on-campus study). *Faculty:* 253 full-time (134 women), 1,208 part-time/adjunct (570 women). *Students:* 956 full-time (422 women), 8,476 part-time (2,821 women); includes 2,511 minority (1,218 Black or African American, non-Hispanic/Latino; 68 American Indian or Alaska Native, non-Hispanic/Latino; 219 Asian, non-Hispanic/Latino; 705 Hispanic/Latino; 46 Native Hawaiian or other Pacific Islander, non-Hispanic/Latino; 255 Two or more races, non-Hispanic/Latino), 107 international. Average age 35. 9,550 applicants, 100% accepted. In 2010, 1,688 master's awarded. *Degree requirements:* For master's, comprehensive exam or practicum. *Entrance requirements:* For master's, official transcript showing earned bachelor's degree from institution accredited by recognized accrediting body. Additional exam requirements/recommendations for international students: Required—TOEFL (minimum score 550 paper-based; 213 computer-based), IELTS (minimum score 6.5). *Application deadline:* Applications are processed on a rolling basis. Application fee: $0. Electronic applications accepted. *Financial support:* Applicants required to submit FAFSA. *Faculty research:* Military history, criminal justice, management performance, national security. *Unit head:* Dr. Frank McCluskey, Provost, 877-468-6268, Fax: 304-724-3780. *Application contact:* Terry Grant, Director of Enrollment Management, 877-468-6268, Fax: 304-724-3780, E-mail: info@apus.edu.

Amridge University, Graduate and Professional Programs, Montgomery, AL 36117. Offers behavioral leadership and management (MA); Biblical exposition (MA); biblical studies (MA, PhD); family therapy (D Min); historical and theological studies (MA); leadership and management (MS); marriage and family therapy (M Div, MA, PhD); ministerial leadership (M Div, MS); pastoral counseling (M Div, MS); practical ministry (MA); professional counseling (M Div, MA, PhD); theology (D Min). Part-time and evening/weekend programs available. Postbaccalaureate distance learning degree programs offered (no on-campus study). *Faculty:* 39 full-time (6 women), 39 part-time/adjunct (5 women). *Students:* 119 full-time (54 women), 260 part-time (149 women); includes 160 minority (153 Black or African American, non-Hispanic/Latino; 1 Asian, non-Hispanic/Latino; 6 Hispanic/Latino). Average age 35. *Degree requirements:* For master's, one foreign language, comprehensive exam (for some programs), thesis (for some programs); for doctorate, comprehensive exam (for some programs), thesis/dissertation; for M Div, comprehensive exam (for some programs). *Entrance requirements:* For M Div, master's, and doctorate, GRE General Test or MAT. Additional exam requirements/recommendations for international students: Required—TOEFL. *Application deadline:* For fall admission, 9/1 priority date for domestic students; for spring admission, 1/1 priority date for domestic students. Applications are processed on a rolling basis. Application fee: $75. Electronic applications accepted. *Financial support:* Federal Work-Study and scholarships/grants available. Support available to part-time students. Financial award applicants required to submit FAFSA. *Faculty research:* Homiletics, hermeneutics, ancient Near Eastern history. *Unit head:* Director of Enrollment Management, 800-351-4040 Ext. 7513, Fax: 334-387-3878. *Application contact:* Ora Davis, Admissions Officer, 334-387-3877 Ext. 7524, Fax: 334-387-3878, E-mail: admissions@amridgeuniversity.edu.

Avila University, Program in Organizational Development, Kansas City, MO 64145-1698. Offers fundraising (Graduate Certificate); management (MA), including fundraising, project management; organizational development (MS); project management (Graduate Certificate). Part-time and evening/weekend programs available. Postbaccalaureate distance learning degree programs offered (no on-campus study). *Faculty:* 2 full-time (1 woman), 10 part-time/adjunct (7 women). *Students:* 72 full-time (61 women), 36 part-time (24 women); includes 35 minority (28 Black or African American, non-Hispanic/Latino; 2 American Indian or Alaska Native, non-Hispanic/Latino; 2 Asian, non-Hispanic/Latino; 2 Hispanic/Latino; 1 Native Hawaiian or other Pacific Islander, non-Hispanic/Latino), 4 international. Average age 36. 47 applicants, 64% accepted, 27 enrolled. In 2010, 18 master's awarded. *Degree requirements:* For master's, thesis optional. *Entrance requirements:* For master's, 2 letters of recommendation, minimum GPA of 3.25 during last 60 hours, resume. Additional exam requirements/recommendations for international students: Required—TOEFL. *Application deadline:* Applications are processed on a rolling basis. Application fee: $0. Electronic applications accepted. *Expenses:* Tuition: Full-time $5580; part-time $465 per credit hour. Required fees: $348; $29 per credit hour. *Financial support:* In 2010–11, 69 students received support. Unspecified assistantships available. Support available to part-time students. Financial award applicants required to submit FAFSA. *Unit head:* Dr. Steve Iliff, Dean, 816-501-3737, Fax: 816-941-4650, E-mail: advantage@avila.edu. *Application contact:* Linda Dubar, School of Professional Studies, 816-501-3737, Fax: 816-941-4650, E-mail: advantage@avila.edu.

Azusa Pacific University, Center for Adult and Professional Studies, Azusa, CA 91702-7000. Offers leadership and organizational studies (MA). Postbaccalaureate distance learning degree programs offered. *Students:* 1 full-time (0 women), 89 part-time (50 women); includes 29 minority (10 Black

or African American, non-Hispanic/Latino; 4 Asian, non-Hispanic/Latino; 15 Hispanic/Latino), 1 international. Average age 38. In 2010, 42 master's awarded. Application fee: $45 ($65 for international students). *Unit head:* Dr. Fred G. Garlett, Dean, 626-815-5301, E-mail: fgarlett@apu.edu. *Application contact:* Linda Witte, Graduate Admissions Office, 626-969-3434.

Azusa Pacific University, School of Behavioral and Applied Sciences, Department of Higher Education and Organizational Leadership, Program in Organizational Leadership, Azusa, CA 91702-7000. Offers MA. *Students:* 1 (woman) full-time, 120 part-time (58 women); includes 3 Black or African American, non-Hispanic/Latino; 6 Asian, non-Hispanic/Latino; 6 Hispanic/Latino, 30 international. In 2010, 53 master's awarded. *Unit head:* Dr. Dennis A. Sheridan, Director, 626-815-5485, Fax: 626-815-3868. *Application contact:* Linda Witte, Graduate Admissions Office, 626-969-3434.

Azusa Pacific University, School of Business and Management, Azusa, CA 91702-7000. Offers business administration (MBA); diversity for strategic advantage (MA); entrepreneurship (MBA); finance (MBA); human and organizational development (MA); human resources and organizational development (MBA); human resources management (MA); international business (MBA); marketing (MBA); non-profit management (MA); organizational development and change (MA); performance improvement (MA); public administration (MA); strategic management (MBA). Part-time and evening/weekend programs available. *Faculty:* 19 full-time (5 women), 2 part-time/adjunct (1 woman). *Students:* 75 full-time (41 women), 96 part-time (46 women); includes 65 minority (15 Black or African American, non-Hispanic/Latino; 15 Asian, non-Hispanic/Latino; 34 Hispanic/Latino; 1 Native Hawaiian or other Pacific Islander, non-Hispanic/Latino), 17 international. Average age 30. In 2010, 82 master's awarded. *Degree requirements:* For master's, thesis (for some programs), final project. *Entrance requirements:* For master's, GMAT, minimum GPA of 3.0. Additional exam requirements/recommendations for international students: Required—TOEFL (minimum score 600 paper-based). *Application deadline:* For fall admission, 8/15 priority date for domestic students. Applications are processed on a rolling basis. Application fee: $45 ($65 for international students). *Expenses:* Contact institution. *Financial support:* Scholarships/grants available. *Faculty research:* Gender issues, financial risk, leadership and ethics, marketing strategy. *Unit head:* Dr. Ilene Bezjian, Dean, 626-815-3090, Fax: 626-815-3802, E-mail: ibezjian@apu.edu. *Application contact:* Dr. Ilene Bezjian, Dean, 626-815-3090, Fax: 626-815-3802, E-mail: ibezjian@apu.edu.

Benedictine University, Graduate Programs, Program in Business Administration, Lisle, IL 60532-0900. Offers accounting (MBA); entrepreneurship and managing innovation (MBA); financial management (MBA); health administration (MBA); human resource management (MBA); information systems security (MBA); international business (MBA); management consulting (MBA); management information systems (MBA); marketing management (MBA); operations management and logistics (MBA); organizational leadership (MBA); MBA/MPH; MBA/MS. Part-time and evening/weekend programs available. Postbaccalaureate distance learning degree programs offered (minimal on-campus study). *Faculty:* 4 full-time (2 women), 24 part-time/adjunct (3 women). *Students:* 347 full-time (140 women), 672 part-time (360 women); includes 237 minority (155 Black or African American, non-Hispanic/Latino; 4 American Indian or Alaska Native, non-Hispanic/Latino; 43 Asian, non-Hispanic/Latino; 35 Hispanic/Latino), 21 international. Average age 34. 416 applicants, 88% accepted, 217 enrolled. In 2010, 355 master's awarded. *Entrance requirements:* For master's, GMAT. Additional exam requirements/recommendations for international students: Required—TOEFL (minimum score 550 paper-based; 213 computer-based). *Application deadline:* For fall admission, 9/1 for domestic students; for winter admission, 12/1 for domestic students; for spring admission, 2/15 for domestic students. Applications are processed on a rolling basis. Application fee: $40. Electronic applications accepted. *Financial support:* Career-related internships or fieldwork and health care benefits available. Support available to part-time students. *Faculty research:* Strategic leadership in professional organizations, sociology of professions, organizational change, social identity theory, applications to change management. *Unit head:* Dr. Sharon Borowicz, Director, 630-829-6219, E-mail: sborowicz@ben.edu. *Application contact:* Kari Gibbons, Director, Admissions, 630-829-6200, Fax: 630-829-6584, E-mail: kgibbons@ben.edu.

Benedictine University, Graduate Programs, Program in Organizational Development, Lisle, IL 60532-0900. Offers PhD. Evening/weekend programs available. *Faculty:* 2 full-time (0 women), 2 part-time/adjunct (1 woman). *Students:* 50 full-time (34 women), 29 part-time (17 women); includes 19 minority (13 Black or African American, non-Hispanic/Latino; 5 Asian, non-Hispanic/Latino; 1 Hispanic/Latino), 8 international. Average age 44. 23 applicants, 52% accepted, 11 enrolled. *Degree requirements:* For doctorate, thesis/dissertation. *Entrance requirements:* Additional exam requirements/recommendations for international students: Required—TOEFL (minimum score 550 paper-based). *Application deadline:* For fall admission, 9/1 for domestic students; for winter admission, 12/1 for domestic students; for spring admission, 2/15 for domestic students. Application fee: $40. Electronic applications accepted. *Financial support:* Career-related internships or fieldwork and health care benefits available. *Faculty research:* Change management, appreciative inquiry, innovation and organization design, global and international organization development, organization renewal. *Unit head:* Dr. Peter F. Sorensen,

Director, 630-829-6220, Fax: 630-960-1126, E-mail: psorensen@ben.edu. *Application contact:* Kari Gibbons, Director, Admissions, 630-829-6200, Fax: 630-829-6584, E-mail: kgibbons@ben.edu.

Bethel University, Graduate School, Program in Organizational Leadership, St. Paul, MN 55112-6999. Offers MA. Evening/weekend programs available. *Faculty:* 5 full-time (1 woman), 12 part-time/adjunct (5 women). *Students:* 71 full-time (44 women), 31 part-time (19 women); includes 3 Black or African American, non-Hispanic/Latino; 2 Two or more races, non-Hispanic/Latino, 4 international. Average age 36. 22 applicants, 100% accepted, 17 enrolled. In 2010, 34 master's awarded. *Degree requirements:* For master's, thesis. *Entrance requirements:* For master's, baccalaureate degree, interview, minimum GPA of 3.0, letters of reference, statement of purpose essay. Additional exam requirements/recommendations for international students: Required—TOEFL (minimum score 550 paper-based; 213 computer-based; 80 iBT). *Application deadline:* For fall admission, 6/15 priority date for domestic students; for winter admission, 12/1 priority date for domestic students. Applications are processed on a rolling basis. Electronic applications accepted. *Expenses:* Tuition: Full-time $5400; part-time $450 per credit. Tuition and fees vary according to course level, course load, degree level and program. *Financial support:* Applicants required to submit FAFSA. *Unit head:* Nikki Daniels, Assistant Dean, 651-635-8000, Fax: 651-635-8039, E-mail: n-daniels@bethel.edu. *Application contact:* Paul Ives, Director of Admissions, 651-635-8000, Fax: 651-635-8004, E-mail: gs@bethel.edu.

Biola University, School of Professional Studies, La Mirada, CA 90639-0001. Offers Christian apologetics (MA); organizational leadership (MA). Part-time and evening/weekend programs available. *Faculty:* 4 full-time (0 women), 40 part-time/adjunct (12 women). *Students:* 5 full-time (2 women), 44 part-time (22 women); includes 6 Black or African American, non-Hispanic/Latino; 6 Asian, non-Hispanic/Latino; 6 Hispanic/Latino. 184 applicants, 65% accepted. In 2010, 72 master's awarded. *Entrance requirements:* For master's, minimum undergraduate GPA of 3.0. Additional exam requirements/recommendations for international students: Required—TOEFL (minimum score 550 paper-based; 213 computer-based). *Application deadline:* For fall admission, 7/1 for domestic students; for spring admission, 12/1 for domestic students. Applications are processed on a rolling basis. Application fee: $45. Electronic applications accepted. *Financial support:* Institutionally sponsored loans and scholarships/grants available. Support available to part-time students. Financial award application deadline: 3/2; financial award applicants required to submit FAFSA. *Unit head:* Dr. Ed Norman, Dean, 562-903-4715, E-mail: ed.norman@biola.edu. *Application contact:* Roy M. Allinson, Director of Graduate Admissions, 562-903-4752, Fax: 562-903-4709, E-mail: admissions@biola.edu.

Boston College, Carroll School of Management, Department of Organization Studies, Chestnut Hill, MA 02467-3800. Offers PhD. *Faculty:* 12 full-time (6 women). *Students:* 20 full-time (14 women); includes 1 Black or African American, non-Hispanic/Latino; 1 Hispanic/Latino, 7 international. Average age 32. 73 applicants, 4% accepted, 3 enrolled. In 2010, 2 doctorates awarded. *Degree requirements:* For doctorate, comprehensive exam, thesis/dissertation, teaching experience. *Entrance requirements:* For doctorate, GMAT or GRE, letters of recommendation, resume, transcripts. Additional exam requirements/recommendations for international students: Required—TOEFL. *Application deadline:* For spring admission, 2/1 for domestic and international students. Application fee: $50. *Financial support:* In 2010-11, 20 fellowships, 20 research assistantships with full tuition reimbursements were awarded. Financial award application deadline: 3/1; financial award applicants required to submit FAFSA. *Faculty research:* Organizational transformation, mergers and acquisitions, managerial effectiveness, organizational change, organizational structure. *Unit head:* Dr. Jeffrey L. Ringuest, Associate Dean, Graduate Programs, 617-552-9100, Fax: 617-552-0514, E-mail: gsomdean@bc.edu. *Application contact:* Shelley A. Burt, Director of Graduate Enrollment, 617-552-3920, Fax: 617-552-8078, E-mail: bcmba@bc.edu.

Brenau University, Sydney O. Smith Graduate School, School of Business and Mass Communication, Gainesville, GA 30501. Offers accounting (MBA); business administration (MBA); healthcare management (MBA); organizational leadership (MS); project management (MBA). Part-time and evening/weekend programs available. Postbaccalaureate distance learning degree programs offered (no on-campus study). *Faculty:* 12 full-time (7 women), 24 part-time/adjunct (10 women). *Students:* 124 full-time (89 women), 348 part-time (250 women); includes 130 Black or African American, non-Hispanic/Latino; 2 American Indian or Alaska Native, non-Hispanic/Latino; 7 Asian, non-Hispanic/Latino; 13 Hispanic/Latino; 9 Two or more races, non-Hispanic/Latino, 42 international. Average age 35. In 2010, 125 master's awarded. *Degree requirements:* For master's, comprehensive exam (for some programs). *Entrance requirements:* For master's, resume, minimum undergraduate GPA of 2.5. Additional exam requirements/recommendations for international students: Required—TOEFL (minimum score 500 paper-based; 173 computer-based; 61 iBT); Recommended—IELTS (minimum score 5). *Application deadline:* Applications are processed on a rolling basis. Electronic applications accepted. *Expenses:* Contact institution. *Financial support:* In 2010-11, 1 student received support. Application deadline: 7/15. *Unit head:* Dr. William S. Lightfoot, Dean, 770-538-5330, Fax: 770-537-4701, E-mail: wlightfoot@brenau.edu. *Application contact:* Christina White, Graduate Admissions Specialist, 770-718-5320, Fax: 770-718-5338, E-mail: cwhite@brenau.edu.

Cabrini College, Graduate and Professional Studies, Radnor, PA 19087-3698. Offers education (M Ed); organization leadership (MS). Part-time and evening/weekend programs available. *Faculty:* 4 full-time (3 women), 141 part-time/adjunct (87 women). *Students:* 175 full-time (119 women), 1,850 part-time (1,423 women); includes 273 minority (186 Black or African American, non-Hispanic/Latino; 3 American Indian or Alaska Native, non-Hispanic/Latino; 24 Asian, non-Hispanic/Latino; 48 Hispanic/Latino; 5 Native Hawaiian or other Pacific Islander, non-Hispanic/Latino; 7 Two or more races, non-Hispanic/Latino), 3 international. Average age 34. 724 applicants, 74% accepted, 496 enrolled. In 2010, 728 master's awarded. *Degree requirements:* For master's, thesis optional. *Entrance requirements:* For master's, GRE and/or MAT (in some cases), letter of recommendation, minimum GPA of 2.5. *Application deadline:* For fall admission, 7/29 priority date for domestic students, 7/29 for international students; for spring admission, 12/9 for domestic and international students. Applications are processed on a rolling basis. Application fee: $50. Electronic applications accepted. *Expenses:* Tuition: Part-time $575 per credit. *Financial support:* Career-related internships or fieldwork and unspecified assistantships available. Support available to part-time students. Financial award applicants required to submit FAFSA. *Unit head:* Dr. Dennis R. Dougherty, Interim Dean, 610-902-8501, Fax: 610-902-8522, E-mail: dennis.dougherty@cabrini.edu. *Application contact:* Bruce D. Bryde, Director of Enrollment and Recruiting, 610-902-8291, Fax: 610-902-8522, E-mail: bruce.d.bryde@cabrini.edu.

California College of the Arts, Graduate Programs, Program in Design Strategy, San Francisco, CA 94107. Offers MBA. *Accreditation:* NASAD. *Faculty:* 4 full-time (1 woman), 17 part-time/adjunct (6 women). *Students:* 72 full-time (39 women), 2 part-time (both women); includes 26 minority (5 Black or African American, non-Hispanic/Latino; 15 Asian, non-Hispanic/Latino; 6 Hispanic/Latino), 8 international. Average age 32. 151 applicants, 58% accepted, 51 enrolled. In 2010, 23 master's awarded. *Degree requirements:* For master's, thesis. *Entrance requirements:* Additional exam requirements/recommendations for international students: Required—TOEFL (minimum score 600 paper-based; 250 computer-based; 100 iBT). *Application deadline:* For fall admission, 1/5 for domestic and international students. Application fee: $70. *Expenses:* Tuition: Full-time $38,550; part-time $1285 per unit. One-time fee: $185 full-time. *Financial support:* In 2010-11, 3 fellowships (averaging $18,000 per year) were awarded. *Unit head:* Nathan Shedroff, Program Chair, 800-447-1ART, E-mail: nshedroff@cca.edu. *Application contact:* Heidi Geis, Assistant Director of Graduate Admissions, 415-703-9523 Ext. 9533, Fax: 415-703-9539, E-mail: hgeis@cca.edu.

California State University, East Bay, Office of Academic Programs and Graduate Studies, College of Business and Economics, MBA Program, Hayward, CA 94542-3000. Offers entrepreneurship (MBA); finance (MBA); human resources and organizational behavior (MBA); information technology management (MBA); marketing management (MBA); operations and supply chain management (MBA); strategy and international business (MBA). Part-time and evening/weekend programs available. Postbaccalaureate distance learning degree programs offered (no on-campus study). *Faculty:* 33 full-time (9 women). *Students:* 121 full-time (58 women), 133 part-time (67 women); includes 7 Black or African American, non-Hispanic/Latino; 63 Asian, non-Hispanic/Latino; 11 Hispanic/Latino; 3 Native Hawaiian or other Pacific Islander, non-Hispanic/Latino; 5 Two or more races, non-Hispanic/Latino, 87 international. Average age 30. 284 applicants, 47% accepted, 55 enrolled. In 2010, 241 master's awarded. *Degree requirements:* For master's, comprehensive exam or thesis. *Entrance requirements:* For master's, GMAT (minimum 20th percentile verbal and quantitative section), bachelor's degree, minimum GPA of 2.75. Additional exam requirements/recommendations for international students: Required—TOEFL (minimum score 550 paper-based; 213 computer-based; 79 iBT). *Application deadline:* For fall admission, 6/30 for domestic and international students. Applications are processed on a rolling basis. Application fee: $55. Electronic applications accepted. *Financial support:* Career-related internships or fieldwork, Federal Work-Study, institutionally sponsored loans, and scholarships/grants available. Support available to part-time students. Financial award application deadline: 3/2; financial award applicants required to submit FAFSA. *Unit head:* Dr. Terri Swartz, Dean, 510-885-3291, Fax: 510-885-4884, E-mail: terri.swartz@csueastbay.edu. *Application contact:* Dr. Donna Wiley, Interim Associate Director, 510-885-2928, Fax: 510-885-4777, E-mail: donna.wiley@csueastbay.edu.

Cambridge College, School of Management, Cambridge, MA 02138-5304. Offers business negotiation and conflict resolution (M Mgt); general business (M Mgt); health care informatics (M Mgt); health care management (M Mgt); leadership in human and organizational dynamics (M Mgt); non-profit and public organization management (M Mgt); small business development (M Mgt); technology management (M Mgt). Part-time and evening/weekend programs available. *Faculty:* 6 full-time (3 women), 54 part-time/adjunct (26 women). *Students:* 222 full-time (121 women), 175 part-time (110 women); includes 127 minority (89 Black or African American, non-Hispanic/Latino; 2 American Indian or Alaska Native, non-Hispanic/Latino; 9 Asian, non-Hispanic/Latino; 25 Hispanic/Latino; 2 Two or more races, non-Hispanic/Latino), 125 international. Average age 37. In 2010, 221 master's awarded. *Degree requirements:* For master's, thesis, seminars. *Entrance requirements:* For master's, resume, 2 professional references. Additional exam requirements/

recommendations for international students: Required—TOEFL (minimum score 550 paper-based; 213 computer-based; 79 iBT); Recommended—IELTS (minimum score 6). *Application deadline:* Applications are processed on a rolling basis. Application fee: $30. Electronic applications accepted. *Expenses:* Contact institution. *Financial support:* Career-related internships or fieldwork, Federal Work-Study, and scholarships/grants available. Financial award applicants required to submit FAFSA. *Faculty research:* Negotiation, mediation and conflict resolution; leadership; management of diverse organizations; case studies and simulation methodologies for management education, digital as a second language: social networking for digital immigrants, non-profit and public management. *Unit head:* Dr. Mary Ann Joseph, Acting Dean, 617-873-0227, E-mail: maryann.joseph@cambridgecollege.edu. *Application contact:* Elaine M. Lapomardo, Dean of Enrollment Management, 617-873-0274, Fax: 617-349-3561, E-mail: elaine.lapomardo@cambridgecollege.edu.

Carlos Albizu University, Miami Campus, Graduate Programs, Miami, FL 33172-2209. Offers clinical psychology (Psy D); entrepreneurship (MBA); exceptional student education (MS); industrial/organizational psychology (MS); marriage and family therapy (MS); mental health counseling (MS); non-profit management (MBA); organizational management (MBA); psychology (MS); school counseling (MS); teaching English as a second language (MS). *Accreditation:* APA. Part-time and evening/weekend programs available. *Faculty:* 21 full-time (12 women), 37 part-time/adjunct (18 women). *Students:* 496 full-time (400 women), 242 part-time (192 women); includes 590 minority (58 Black or African American, non-Hispanic/Latino; 2 American Indian or Alaska Native, non-Hispanic/Latino; 5 Asian, non-Hispanic/Latino; 523 Hispanic/Latino; 2 Two or more races, non-Hispanic/Latino), 15 international. Average age 36. 141 applicants, 84% accepted, 118 enrolled. In 2010, 159 master's, 20 doctorates awarded. Terminal master's awarded for partial completion of doctoral program. *Degree requirements:* For master's, one foreign language, comprehensive exam, integrative project (MBA), research project (exceptional student education, teaching English as a second language); for doctorate, one foreign language, comprehensive exam, internship, project. *Entrance requirements:* For master's, 3 letters of recommendation, interview, minimum GPA of 3.0, resume, statement of purpose, official transcripts; for doctorate, 3 letters of recommendation, minimum GPA of 3.0, resume, interview. *Application deadline:* For fall admission, 8/1 priority date for domestic students; for spring admission, 11/30 priority date for domestic students. Applications are processed on a rolling basis. Application fee: $50. Electronic applications accepted. *Expenses:* Tuition: Full-time $9360; part-time $520 per credit. Required fees: $298 per term. Tuition and fees vary according to course load, degree level and program. *Financial support:* In 2010–11, 106 students received support. Federal Work-Study, scholarships/grants, and tuition discounts available. Financial award application deadline: 6/1; financial award applicants required to submit FAFSA. *Faculty research:* Psychotherapy, forensic psychology, neuropsychology, marketing strategy, entrepreneurship, special education. *Unit head:* Dr. Carmen S. Roca, Chancellor, 305-593-1223 Ext. 120, Fax: 305-629-8052, E-mail: croca@albizu.edu. *Application contact:* Vanessa Almendarez, Secretary, 305-593-1223 Ext. 137, Fax: 305-593-1854, E-mail: valmendarez@albizu.edu.

Carlow University, School for Social Change, Pittsburgh, PA 15213-3165. Offers counseling psychology (Psy D); professional counseling (MS); professional counseling: school counseling (MS). *Accreditation:* APA. Part-time and evening/weekend programs available. *Students:* 206 full-time (184 women), 21 part-time (18 women); includes 41 Black or African American, non-Hispanic/Latino; 1 American Indian or Alaska Native, non-Hispanic/Latino; 2 Asian, non-Hispanic/Latino; 3 Hispanic/Latino. Average age 31. 298 applicants, 36% accepted, 71 enrolled. In 2010, 50 master's awarded. *Entrance requirements:* Additional exam requirements/recommendations for international students: Required—TOEFL (minimum score 550 paper-based; 213 computer-based). *Application deadline:* For fall admission, 6/15 priority date for domestic and international students; for spring admission, 11/15 priority date for domestic and international students. Applications are processed on a rolling basis. Application fee: $20. Electronic applications accepted. *Expenses:* Tuition: Full-time $9900; part-time $660 per credit. Tuition and fees vary according to course load, degree level and program. *Financial support:* Federal Work-Study available. Financial award application deadline: 4/1; financial award applicants required to submit FAFSA. *Unit head:* Dr. Robert A. Reed, Chair, Department of Psychology and Counseling, 412-575-6349, E-mail: reedra@carlow.edu. *Application contact:* Jo Danhires, Administrative Assistant of Admissions, 412-578-6059, Fax: 412-578-6321, E-mail: gradstudies@carlow.edu.

Cleary University, Online Program in Business Administration, Ann Arbor, MI 48105-2659. Offers financial planning (MBA); financial planning (Graduate Certificate); green business strategy (MBA, Graduate Certificate); management (MBA); nonprofit management (MBA, Graduate Certificate); organizational leadership (MBA); public accounting (MBA). Part-time and evening/weekend programs available. Postbaccalaureate distance learning degree programs offered (no on-campus study). *Faculty:* 1 (woman) full-time, 20 part-time/adjunct (8 women). *Students:* 1 (woman) full-time, 115 part-time (67 women); includes 30 minority (21 Black or African American, non-Hispanic/Latino; 1 American Indian or Alaska Native, non-Hispanic/Latino; 6 Asian, non-Hispanic/Latino; 2 Hispanic/Latino), 7 international. Average age 34. 62 applicants, 77% accepted, 36 enrolled. In 2010, 22 master's awarded. *Degree requirements:* For master's, thesis. *Entrance requirements:* For master's, bachelor's degree; minimum GPA of 2.5; professional resume indicating minimum 2 years management or related experience; undergraduate degree from an accredited college or university with at least 18 quarter hours (or 12 semester hours) of accounting study (for MBA in accounting). Additional exam requirements/recommendations for international students: Required—TOEFL (minimum score 550 paper-based; 213 computer-based; 79 iBT), Michigan English Language Assessment Battery (minimum score: 75). *Application deadline:* For fall admission, 8/15 for domestic students, 7/15 for international students; for spring admission, 4/2 for domestic students, 1/2 for international students. Applications are processed on a rolling basis. Application fee: $50. Electronic applications accepted. *Financial support:* In 2010–11, 80 students received support, including 80 fellowships (averaging $12,501 per year); Federal Work-Study and scholarships/grants also available. Support available to part-time students. Financial award application deadline: 8/15; financial award applicants required to submit FAFSA. *Unit head:* Dr. Vincent Linder, Provost and Vice President for Academic Affairs, 800-686-1883, Fax: 734-332-4646, E-mail: vlinder@cleary.edu. *Application contact:* Carrie Bonofiglio, Director of Student Recruiting, 800-686-1883, Fax: 517-552-7805, E-mail: cbono@cleary.edu.

College of Mount St. Joseph, Master of Science in Organizational Leadership Program, Cincinnati, OH 45233-1670. Offers MS. Part-time and evening/weekend programs available. *Faculty:* 6 full-time (3 women), 1 part-time/adjunct (0 women). *Students:* 66 part-time (48 women); includes 10 minority (8 Black or African American, non-Hispanic/Latino; 1 American Indian or Alaska Native, non-Hispanic/Latino; 1 Asian, non-Hispanic/Latino). Average age 41. 7 applicants, 57% accepted, 2 enrolled. In 2010, 7 master's awarded. *Degree requirements:* For master's, integrative project. *Entrance requirements:* For master's, minimum GPA of 3.0, interview, 3 years of work experience, 3 letters of reference, resume. Additional exam requirements/recommendations for international students: Required—TOEFL (minimum score 560 paper-based; 220 computer-based; 83 iBT). *Application deadline:* Applications are processed on a rolling basis. Application fee: $50. Electronic applications accepted. *Expenses:* Contact institution. *Financial support:* In 2010–11, 2 students received support. Application deadline: 6/1. *Faculty research:* Gender and cultural effects on management education, group identity formation, leadership skill development, methods for improving instructional effectiveness, technology-based productivity improvement. *Unit head:* Daryl Smith, Chair, 513-244-4920, Fax: 513-244-4270, E-mail: daryl smith@mail.msj.edu. Application contact: Marilyn Hoskins, Assistant Director of Graduate Recruitment, 513-244-4723, Fax: 513-244-4629, E-mail: marilyn_hoskins@mail.msj.edu.

Colorado State University, Graduate School, College of Business, Program in Management Practice, Fort Collins, CO 80523-1201. Offers MMP. *Students:* 41 full-time (25 women), 7 part-time (4 women); includes 5 minority (1 Black or African American, non-Hispanic/Latino; 2 Asian, non-Hispanic/Latino; 2 Hispanic/Latino), 8 international. Average age 27. 31 applicants, 97% accepted, 25 enrolled. In 2010, 25 master's awarded. *Entrance requirements:* For master's, GMAT or GRE, minimum cumulative GPA of 3.0, current resume, 3 recommendations. Additional exam requirements/recommendations for international students: Required—TOEFL (minimum score 565 paper-based; 227 computer-based; 86 iBT) or IELTS (minimum score 6.5). *Application deadline:* For fall admission, 7/15 for domestic students, 6/1 for international students; for spring admission, 12/5 for domestic students, 11/1 for international students. Applications are processed on a rolling basis. Application fee: $50. Electronic applications accepted. *Expenses:* Tuition, state resident: full-time $7434; part-time $413 per credit. Tuition, nonresident: full-time $19,022; part-time $1057 per credit. Required fees: $1729; $88 per credit. *Financial support:* Fellowships with partial tuition reimbursements, research assistantships with partial tuition reimbursements, teaching assistantships, unspecified assistantships available. Financial award application deadline: 4/1; financial award applicants required to submit FAFSA. *Faculty research:* Ethical behavior in the marketplace, sustainable entrepreneurship, corporate entrepreneurship, logistics in market orientation, organizational communication. *Unit head:* Dr. John Hoxmeier, Associate Dean, 970-491-2142, Fax: 970-491-0269, E-mail: john.hoxmeier@colostate.edu. *Application contact:* Tonja Rosales, Admissions Coordinator, 970-491-4661, Fax: 970-491-3481, E-mail: tonja.rosales@colostate.edu.

Columbus State University, Graduate Studies, D. Abbott Turner College of Business and Computer Science, Columbus, GA 31907-5645. Offers applied computer science (MS); business administration (MBA); modeling and simulation (Certificate); organizational leadership (MS). *Accreditation:* AACSB. *Faculty:* 15 full-time (2 women). *Students:* 36 full-time (9 women), 145 part-time (54 women); includes 43 minority (19 Black or African American, non-Hispanic/Latino; 3 American Indian or Alaska Native, non-Hispanic/Latino; 12 Asian, non-Hispanic/Latino; 3 Hispanic/Latino; 6 Two or more races, non-Hispanic/Latino), 11 international. Average age 33. 133 applicants, 61% accepted, 58 enrolled. In 2010, 59 master's awarded. *Entrance requirements:* For master's, GMAT, GRE. Additional exam requirements/recommendations for international students: Required—TOEFL (minimum score 550 paper-based; 213 computer-based; 79 iBT). *Application deadline:* For fall admission, 6/30 for domestic students, 5/1 for international students; for spring admission, 11/1 for domestic and international students. Applications are processed on a rolling basis. Application fee: $30. Electronic applications accepted. *Expenses:* Tuition, state resident: full-time $5573; part-time $232 per semester hour. Tuition, nonresident: full-time $13,968; part-time $582 per semester hour. Required fees: $1300; $650 per semester. Tuition and fees vary according to degree level and program. *Financial support:* In 2010–11, 62 students received support, including 11 research assistantships (averaging $3,000 per year). Financial award application deadline: 5/1. *Unit head:* Dr. Linda U. Hadley, Dean, 706-568-2044, Fax: 706-568-2184, E-mail: hadley_linda@colstate.edu. Application contact: Katie Thornton, Graduate Admissions Specialist, 706-568-2035, Fax: 706-568-2462, E-mail: thornton_katie@colstate.edu.

Concordia University, St. Paul, College of Business and Organizational Leadership, St. Paul, MN 55104-5494. Offers business and organizational leadership (MBA); criminal justice leadership (MA); health care management (MBA); human resources management (MA); leadership and management (MA). *Accreditation:* ACBSP. Evening/weekend programs available. Postbaccalaureate distance learning degree programs offered (minimal on-campus study). *Faculty:* 14 full-time (6 women), 30 part-time/adjunct (8 women). *Students:* 338 full-time (203 women), 2 part-time (1 woman); includes 24 Black or African American, non-Hispanic/Latino; 3 American Indian or Alaska Native, non-Hispanic/Latino; 11 Asian, non-Hispanic/Latino; 3 Hispanic/Latino; 3 Two or more races, non-Hispanic/Latino. Average age 34. 191 applicants, 65% accepted, 117 enrolled. In 2010, 125 master's awarded. *Application deadline:* Applications are processed on a rolling basis. Application fee: $50. Electronic applications accepted. *Expenses:* Tuition: Full-time $7500; part-time $460 per credit. Required fees: $460 per credit. Tuition and fees vary according to program. *Financial support:* Applicants required to submit FAFSA. *Unit head:* Dr. Bruce Corrie, Dean, 651-641-8226, Fax: 651-641-8807, E-mail: corrie@csp.edu. *Application contact:* Kimberly Craig, Director of Graduate and Cohort Admission, 651-603-6223, Fax: 651-603-6320, E-mail: craig@csp.edu.

Duquesne University, School of Leadership and Professional Advancement, Pittsburgh, PA 15282-0001. Offers leadership (MS), including business ethics, community leadership, global leadership, information technology, leadership, liberal studies, professional administration, sports leadership. Part-time and evening/weekend programs available. Postbaccalaureate distance learning degree programs offered (no on-campus study). *Faculty:* 1 full-time (0 women), 70 part-time/adjunct (35 women). *Students:* 275 full-time, 171 part-time; includes 20 Black or African American, non-Hispanic/Latino; 1 American Indian or Alaska Native, non-Hispanic/Latino; 6 Asian, non-Hispanic/Latino; 3 Hispanic/Latino. Average age 31. 161 applicants, 73% accepted, 103 enrolled. In 2010, 108 master's awarded. *Degree requirements:* For master's, capstone course. *Entrance requirements:* For master's, professional work experience, 500-word essay. Additional exam requirements/recommendations for international students: Required—TOEFL. *Application deadline:* Applications are processed on a rolling basis. Application fee: $0. Electronic applications accepted. *Expenses:* Tuition: Part-time $884 per credit. Required fees: $84 per credit. Tuition and fees vary according to course load. *Financial support:* Applicants required to submit FAFSA. *Unit head:* Dr. Dorothy Bassett, Dean, 412-396-2141, Fax: 412-396-4711, E-mail: bassettd@duq.edu. *Application contact:* Marianne Leister, Director of Student Services, 412-396-4933, Fax: 412-396-5072, E-mail: leister@duq.edu.

Eastern Connecticut State University, School of Education and Professional Studies/Graduate Division, Program in Organizational Management, Willimantic, CT 06226-2295. Offers MS. Part-time and evening/weekend programs available. *Faculty:* 3 full-time (1 woman), 1 part-time/adjunct (0 women). *Students:* 2 full-time (both women), 31 part-time (15 women); includes 5 minority (3 Black or African American, non-Hispanic/Latino; 2 Hispanic/Latino). Average age 40. 9 applicants, 44% accepted, 3 enrolled. In 2010, 9 master's awarded. *Degree requirements:* For master's, comprehensive exam or thesis. *Entrance requirements:* For master's, minimum GPA of 2.7. Additional exam requirements/recommendations for international students: Required—TOEFL (minimum score 550 paper-based; 213 computer-based). *Application deadline:* For fall admission, 7/6 priority date for domestic and international students; for spring admission, 11/3 priority date for domestic and international students. Applications are processed on a rolling basis. Application fee: $50. *Expenses:* Tuition, state resident: full-time $5012; part-time $3440 per year. Tuition, nonresident: full-time $13,962; part-time $3488 per year. Required fees: $4147; $80 per semester. *Financial support:* Teaching assistantships, career-related internships or fieldwork, scholarships/grants, and unspecified assistantships available. Support available to part-time students. Financial award application deadline: 3/15; financial award applicants required to submit FAFSA. *Unit head:* Dr. Elizabeth Scott, Advisor, 860-465-5366, Fax: 860-465-4459, E-mail: scotte@easternct.edu. *Application contact:* Graduate Division, School of Education and Professional Studies, 860-465-5292, E-mail: graduateadmissions@easternct.edu.

Eastern Michigan University, Graduate School, College of Business, Department of Management, Program in Human Resources Management and Organizational Development, Ypsilanti, MI 48197. Offers MSHROD. Part-time and evening/weekend programs available. Postbaccalaureate distance learning degree programs offered (minimal on-campus study). *Students:* 24 full-time (12 women), 53 part-time (39 women); includes 18 minority (8 Black or African American, non-Hispanic/Latino; 1 American Indian or Alaska Native,

non-Hispanic/Latino; 5 Asian, non-Hispanic/Latino; 4 Hispanic/Latino), 21 international. Average age 31. In 2010, 37 master's awarded. *Degree requirements:* For master's, thesis optional. *Entrance requirements:* For master's, GMAT. Additional exam requirements/recommendations for international students: Required—TOEFL. *Application deadline:* Applications are processed on a rolling basis. Application fee: $35. *Financial support:* Fellowships, research assistantships with full tuition reimbursements, teaching assistantships with full tuition reimbursements, career-related internships or fieldwork, Federal Work-Study, institutionally sponsored loans, scholarships/grants, tuition waivers (partial), and unspecified assistantships available. Support available to part-time students. Financial award applicants required to submit FAFSA. *Unit head:* Dr. Fraya Wagner-Marsh, Advisor, 734-787-3240, Fax: 734-487-4100, E-mail: fraya.wagner@emich.edu. *Application contact:* Dr. Fraya Wagner-Marsh, Advisor, 734-787-3240, Fax: 734-487-4100, E-mail: fraya.wagner@emich.edu.

Eastern Michigan University, Graduate School, College of Business, Programs in Business Administration, Ypsilanti, MI 48197. Offers business administration (MBA, Graduate Certificate); computer information systems (Graduate Certificate); e-business (MBA, Graduate Certificate); enterprise business intelligence (MBA); entrepreneurship (MBA, Graduate Certificate); finance (MBA, Graduate Certificate); human resources (MBA); human resources management (Graduate Certificate); information systems (MBA); internal auditing (MBA); international business (MBA, Graduate Certificate); marketing management (Graduate Certificate); nonprofit management (MBA); organizational development (Graduate Certificate); supply chain management (MBA, Graduate Certificate). *Accreditation:* AACSB. Part-time programs available. Postbaccalaureate distance learning degree programs offered (no on-campus study). *Students:* 149 full-time (66 women), 456 part-time (232 women); includes 146 minority (109 Black or African American, non-Hispanic/Latino; 4 American Indian or Alaska Native, non-Hispanic/Latino; 27 Asian, non-Hispanic/Latino; 6 Hispanic/Latino), 105 international. Average age 32. 330 applicants, 64% accepted, 150 enrolled. In 2010, 128 master's, 53 other advanced degrees awarded. *Entrance requirements:* For master's, GMAT (minimum score 450), minimum cumulative undergraduate GPA of 2.75. Additional exam requirements/recommendations for international students: Required—TOEFL. *Application deadline:* For fall admission, 5/15 for domestic students, 5/1 for international students; for winter admission, 10/15 for domestic students, 10/1 for international students; for spring admission, 3/15 for domestic students, 3/1 for international students. Applications are processed on a rolling basis. Application fee: $35. *Financial support:* Fellowships, research assistantships with full tuition reimbursements, teaching assistantships with full tuition reimbursements, career-related internships or fieldwork, Federal Work-Study, institutionally sponsored loans, scholarships/grants, tuition waivers (partial), and unspecified assistantships available. Support available to part-time students. Financial award applicants required to submit FAFSA. *Unit head:* K. Michelle Henry, Interim Director, Graduate Programs, 734-487-4444, Fax: 734-483-1316, E-mail: mhenry1@emich.edu. *Application contact:* Beste Windes, Advisor, 734-487-4444, Fax: 734-483-1316, E-mail: bwindes@emich.edu.

Emory University, Goizueta Business School, Doctoral Program in Business, Atlanta, GA 30322-1100. Offers accounting (PhD); finance (PhD); information systems (PhD); marketing (PhD); organization and management (PhD). *Faculty:* 55 full-time (11 women). *Students:* 32 full-time (17 women); includes 1 Black or African American, non-Hispanic/Latino; 17 Asian, non-Hispanic/Latino; 1 Hispanic/Latino. Average age 29. 218 applicants, 9% accepted, 9 enrolled. In 2010, 8 doctorates awarded. *Degree requirements:* For doctorate, comprehensive exam, thesis/dissertation. *Entrance requirements:* For doctorate, GMAT (strongly preferred) or GRE. Additional exam requirements/recommendations for international students: Required—TOEFL (minimum score 250 computer-based). *Application deadline:* For fall admission, 1/3 priority date for domestic students, 1/1 priority date for international students. Application fee: $50. Electronic applications accepted. *Expenses:* Tuition: Full-time $33,800. Required fees: $1300. *Financial support:* In 2010–11, 32 students received support. *Unit head:* Dr. Lawrence Benveniste, Dean, 404-727-6377, Fax: 404-727-0868, E-mail: larry_benveniste@bus.emory.edu. Application contact: Allison Gilmore, Director of Admissions & Student Services, 404-727-6353, Fax: 404-727-5337, E-mail: phd@bus.emory.edu.

Endicott College, Apicius International School of Hospitality, Florence, MA 50122, Italy. Offers organizational management (M Ed). Program held entirely in Florence, Italy. *Degree requirements:* For master's, thesis. *Entrance requirements:* For master's, MAT or GRE, 250-500 word essay explaining professional goals, official transcripts of all academic work, bachelor's degree, two letters of recommendation, personal interview. *Application deadline:* For fall admission, 6/30 for domestic and international students. Application fee: $50. *Financial support:* Applicants required to submit FAFSA. *Application contact:* Dr. Mary Huegel, Dean of Graduate and Professional Studies, 978-232-2084, Fax: 978-232-3000, E-mail: mhuegel@endicott.edu.

Endicott College, Van Loan School of Graduate and Professional Studies, Program in Organizational Management, Beverly, MA 01915-2096. Offers M Ed. Part-time and evening/weekend programs available. *Faculty:* 3 full-time (1 woman), 5 part-time/adjunct (1 woman). *Students:* 65 full-time (40 women), 9 part-time (7 women); includes 2 Black or African American, non-Hispanic/

Latino; 1 Asian, non-Hispanic/Latino; 2 Hispanic/Latino; 1 Native Hawaiian or other Pacific Islander, non-Hispanic/Latino, 1 international. Average age 37. 7 applicants, 71% accepted, 5 enrolled. In 2010, 47 master's awarded. *Degree requirements:* For master's, thesis. *Entrance requirements:* For master's, GRE or MAT, letters of recommendation. Additional exam requirements/recommendations for international students: Required—TOEFL. *Application deadline:* Applications are processed on a rolling basis. Application fee: $50. *Expenses:* Contact institution. *Financial support:* Career-related internships or fieldwork, Federal Work-Study, institutionally sponsored loans, and tuition waivers (partial) available. Financial award applicants required to submit FAFSA. *Unit head:* Richard Benedetto, Associate Dean of Graduate School, 978-232-2744, Fax: 978-232-3000, E-mail: rbenedet@endicott.edu. *Application contact:* Richard Benedetto, Associate Dean of Graduate School, 978-232-2744, Fax: 978-232-3000, E-mail: rbenedet@endicott.edu.

Evangel University, Organizational Leadership Program, Springfield, MO 65802. Offers MOL. Part-time and evening/weekend programs available. Postbaccalaureate distance learning degree programs offered (minimal on-campus study). *Faculty:* 5 full-time (1 woman), 7 part-time/adjunct (0 women). *Students:* 61 full-time (37 women), 8 part-time (3 women); includes 1 Black or African American, non-Hispanic/Latino; 1 Asian, non-Hispanic/Latino. Average age 37. 20 applicants, 60% accepted, 8 enrolled. In 2010, 8 master's awarded. *Degree requirements:* For master's, comprehensive exam, thesis, capstone project. *Entrance requirements:* For master's, GMAT or GRE. Additional exam requirements/recommendations for international students: Required—TOEFL (minimum score 550 paper-based; 213 computer-based). *Application deadline:* For fall admission, 7/15 priority date for domestic and international students; for spring admission, 11/15 priority date for domestic and international students. Applications are processed on a rolling basis. Application fee: $25. Electronic applications accepted. *Financial support:* In 2010–11, 9 students received support. Career-related internships or fieldwork and scholarships/grants available. Support available to part-time students. Financial award application deadline: 3/1; financial award applicants required to submit FAFSA. *Unit head:* Dr. Jeff Fulks, Director of Graduate Studies, 417-865-2815 Ext. 8260, Fax: 417-575-5484, E-mail: fulksj@evangel.edu. *Application contact:* Charity H. Fahlstrom, Admissions Representative, Graduate and Professional Studies Admissions, 417-865-2815 Ext. 7227, Fax: 417-575-5484, E-mail: fahlstromc@evangel.edu.

Fairleigh Dickinson University, College at Florham, Maxwell Becton College of Arts and Sciences, Department of Psychology, Program in Organizational Behavior, Madison, NJ 07940-1099. Offers organizational behavior (MA); organizational leadership (Certificate). *Students:* 2 full-time (both women), 18 part-time (8 women). Average age 38. 7 applicants, 100% accepted, 7 enrolled. In 2010, 6 master's awarded. Application fee: $40. *Application contact:* Susan Brooman, University Director, Graduate Admissions, 973-443-8905, Fax: 973-443-8088, E-mail: grad@fdu.edu.

Fielding Graduate University, Graduate Programs, School of Human and Organization Development, Santa Barbara, CA 93105-3538. Offers evidence-based coaching (Certificate); human and organizational systems (PhD); human development (PhD); integral studies (Certificate); organization management and development (MA, Certificate). Postbaccalaureate distance learning degree programs offered (minimal on-campus study). *Faculty:* 25 full-time (11 women), 11 part-time/adjunct (3 women). *Students:* 455 full-time (325 women), 148 part-time (112 women); includes 124 minority (69 Black or African American, non-Hispanic/Latino; 6 American Indian or Alaska Native, non-Hispanic/Latino; 19 Asian, non-Hispanic/Latino; 20 Hispanic/Latino; 10 Two or more races, non-Hispanic/Latino), 65 international. Average age 48. 179 applicants, 94% accepted, 109 enrolled. In 2010, 49 master's, 32 doctorates, 55 other advanced degrees awarded. Terminal master's awarded for partial completion of doctoral program. *Degree requirements:* For master's, thesis or alternative; for doctorate, comprehensive exam, thesis/dissertation. *Entrance requirements:* For master's, minimum GPA of 2.5, letter of recommendation; for doctorate, 2 letters of recommendation, writing sample, resume, self-assessment statement. *Application deadline:* For fall admission, 3/1 for domestic and international students; for spring admission, 9/1 for domestic and international students. Application fee: $75. Electronic applications accepted. *Expenses:* Contact institution. *Financial support:* In 2010–11, 27 students received support. Scholarships/grants and health care benefits available. Support available to part-time students. *Unit head:* Dr. Charles McClintock, Dean, 805-898-2930, Fax: 805-687-4590, E-mail: cmcclintock@fielding.edu. *Application contact:* Carmen Kuchera, Admission Counselor, 800-340-1099, Fax: 805-687-9793, E-mail: hodadmissions@fielding.edu.

Gannon University, School of Graduate Studies, College of Humanities, Education, and Social Sciences, School of Humanities, Program in Organizational Learning and Leadership, Erie, PA 16541-0001. Offers PhD. Part-time and evening/weekend programs available. *Students:* 2 full-time (1 woman), 43 part-time (22 women); includes 1 Black or African American, non-Hispanic/Latino. Average age 42. 18 applicants, 67% accepted, 11 enrolled. *Degree requirements:* For doctorate, thesis/dissertation. *Entrance requirements:* For doctorate, GRE (verbal, quantitative and written sections taken within the last 3 years), minimum graduate GPA of 3.5, 2 years post-baccalaureate work experience. Additional exam requirements/recommendations for international students: Required—TOEFL (minimum score 79 iBT). *Application deadline:* For spring admission, 2/1 for domestic students. Application fee: $50. Electronic applications accepted. *Expenses:* Tuition: Full-time $14,670; part-time $815 per credit. Required fees: $430; $18 per credit. Tuition and fees vary according to class time, course load, degree level, campus/location and program. *Financial support:* Scholarships/grants and unspecified assistantships available. Financial award applicants required to submit FAFSA. *Unit head:* Dr. David B. Barker, Director, 814-871-7700, E-mail: barker002@gannon.edu. *Application contact:* Kara Morgan, Director of Graduate Recruitment, 814-871-5831, Fax: 814-871-5827, E-mail: graduate@gannon.edu.

George Fox University, School of Business, Newberg, OR 97132-2697. Offers finance (MBA); management (DBA); management/general (MBA); marketing (DBA); organizational strategy (MBA); strategic human resource management (MBA). MBA offered part-time and full-time, also offered in Portland, OR, and Boise, ID. Part-time and evening/weekend programs available. Postbaccalaureate distance learning degree programs offered (minimal on-campus study). *Faculty:* 9 full-time (2 women), 8 part-time/adjunct (3 women). *Students:* 21 full-time (7 women), 247 part-time (87 women); includes 4 Black or African American, non-Hispanic/Latino; 2 American Indian or Alaska Native, non-Hispanic/Latino; 13 Asian, non-Hispanic/Latino; 13 Hispanic/Latino; 2 Two or more races, non-Hispanic/Latino, 12 international. Average age 37. 101 applicants, 93% accepted, 72 enrolled. In 2010, 82 master's awarded. *Degree requirements:* For master's, capstone project; for doctorate, credit-applied research project. *Entrance requirements:* For master's, resume (5 years professional experience required); 3 professional references; interview; financial e-learning course; for doctorate, GRE or GMAT, resume; personal mission statement; academic research writing sample; official transcript from each college/university attended; three professional references. Additional exam requirements/recommendations for international students: Required—TOEFL (minimum score 577 paper-based; 233 computer-based; 90 iBT) or IELTS (minimum score 7). *Application deadline:* For fall admission, 8/1 for domestic and international students; for spring admission, 12/1 for domestic and international students. Applications are processed on a rolling basis. Application fee: $40. Electronic applications accepted. *Expenses:* Contact institution. *Financial support:* In 2010–11, 2 students received support. Applicants required to submit FAFSA. *Unit head:* Dr. Dirk Barram, Professor/Dean, 800-631-0921. *Application contact:* Robin Halverson, Admissions Counselor, 800-493-4937, Fax: 503-554-6111, E-mail: mba@georgefox.edu.

George Mason University, School of Public Policy, Program in Organization Development and Knowledge Management, Arlington, VA 22201. Offers MS. Evening/weekend programs available. *Faculty:* 66 full-time (24 women), 15 part-time/adjunct (3 women). *Students:* 64 full-time (54 women), 9 part-time (5 women); includes 7 Black or African American, non-Hispanic/Latino; 1 American Indian or Alaska Native, non-Hispanic/Latino; 2 Asian, non-Hispanic/Latino; 5 Hispanic/Latino, 3 international. Average age 34. 80 applicants, 54% accepted, 34 enrolled. In 2010, 35 master's awarded. *Degree requirements:* For master's, thesis or alternative. *Entrance requirements:* For master's, GRE (for students seeking merit-based scholarships), minimum GPA of 3.0, 2 letters of recommendation, resume. Additional exam requirements/recommendations for international students: Required—TOEFL (minimum score 570 paper-based; 230 computer-based; 88 iBT). *Application deadline:* For fall admission, 6/1 priority date for domestic students, 5/1 priority date for international students. Applications are processed on a rolling basis. Application fee: $100. Electronic applications accepted. *Expenses:* Contact institution. *Financial support:* Career-related internships or fieldwork, Federal Work-Study, scholarships/grants, unspecified assistantships, and health care benefits (full-time research or teaching assistantship recipients) available. Financial award application deadline: 3/1; financial award applicants required to submit FAFSA. *Unit head:* Dr. Ann Baker, Director, 703-993-8099, E-mail: spp@gmu.edu. *Application contact:* Tennille Haegele, Director, Graduate Admissions, 703-993-3183, Fax: 703-993-4876, E-mail: thaegele@gmu.edu.

The George Washington University, Columbian College of Arts and Sciences, Department of Organizational Sciences and Communication, Washington, DC 20052. Offers human resources management (MA); industrial/organizational psychology (PhD); organizational management (MA). Part-time and evening/weekend programs available. *Faculty:* 10 full-time (7 women), 19 part-time/adjunct (11 women). *Students:* 20 full-time (11 women), 48 part-time (42 women); includes 6 Black or African American, non-Hispanic/Latino; 2 Asian, non-Hispanic/Latino; 6 Hispanic/Latino, 6 international. Average age 29. 72 applicants, 88% accepted, 20 enrolled. In 2010, 31 master's awarded. *Degree requirements:* For master's, comprehensive exam. *Entrance requirements:* For master's, GRE General Test, minimum GPA of 3.0. Additional exam requirements/recommendations for international students: Required—TOEFL (minimum score 500 paper-based; 213 computer-based; 80 iBT). *Application deadline:* For fall admission, 1/15 priority date for domestic and international students; for spring admission, 10/1 priority date for domestic students, 9/1 priority date for international students. Applications are processed on a rolling basis. Application fee: $75. Electronic applications accepted. *Financial support:* Federal Work-Study and institutionally sponsored loans available. *Unit head:* Dr. David Costanza, Acting Director, 202-994-1875, Fax: 202-994-1881, E-mail: dconstanz@gwu.edu. *Application contact:* Information Contact, 202-994-1880, Fax: 202-994-1881.

Grand Canyon University, College of Doctoral Studies, Phoenix, AZ 85017-1097. Offers business administration (DBA); general psychology (PhD), including cognition and instruction, industrial and organizational psychology; organizational leadership (Ed D, PhD), including behavioral health (PhD), education and effective schools (PhD), higher education (PhD), instructional leadership (PhD), organizational development (Ed D). *Faculty:* 2 full-time (1 woman), 12 part-time/adjunct (5 women). *Students:* 968 part-time (711 women); includes 316 minority (283 Black or African American, non-Hispanic/Latino; 12 American Indian or Alaska Native, non-Hispanic/Latino; 3 Asian, non-Hispanic/Latino; 11 Hispanic/Latino; 1 Native Hawaiian or other Pacific Islander, non-Hispanic/Latino; 6 Two or more races, non-Hispanic/Latino). *Degree requirements:* For doctorate, comprehensive exam, thesis/dissertation. *Entrance requirements:* For doctorate, minimum GPA of 3.4 on earned advanced degree from regionally-accredited institution; transcripts; goals statement. Application fee: $0. *Unit head:* Dr. Hank Radda, Dean, 602-639-7255, E-mail: hank.radda@gcu.edu. *Application contact:* Hector Leal, Associate Vice President of Internet Enrollment, 800-639-7144, E-mail: hector.leal@.gcu.edu.

Grantham University, College of Arts and Sciences, Kansas City, MO 64153. Offers case management (MSN); health systems management (MS); healthcare administration (MHA); nursing (MSN); nursing education (MSN); nursing informatics (MSN); nursing management and organizational leadership (MSN). Part-time and evening/weekend programs available. Postbaccalaureate distance learning degree programs offered (no on-campus study). *Students:* 40 full-time (20 women), 389 part-time (152 women); includes 181 minority (139 Black or African American, non-Hispanic/Latino; 4 American Indian or Alaska Native, non-Hispanic/Latino; 13 Asian, non-Hispanic/Latino; 24 Hispanic/Latino; 1 Two or more races, non-Hispanic/Latino). *Degree requirements:* For master's, thesis (for some programs), capstone project. *Entrance requirements:* For master's, bachelor's degree from accredited degree-granting institution. Additional exam requirements/recommendations for international students: Required—TOEFL (minimum score 500 paper-based; 213 computer-based; 61 iBT). *Application deadline:* Applications are processed on a rolling basis. Electronic applications accepted. *Expenses:* Tuition: Full-time $7950; part-time $265 per credit hour. One-time fee: $30. *Financial support:* Institutionally sponsored loans and scholarships/grants available. *Unit head:* Dr. Paul Illian, Dean, 800-955-2527, Fax: 816-595-5757, E-mail: admissions@grantham.edu. *Application contact:* Dan King, Vice President of Enrollment Management, 800-955-2527, Fax: 816-595-5757, E-mail: admissions@grantham.edu.

Harding University, College of Business Administration, Searcy, AR 72149-0001. Offers health care management (MBA); information technology management (MBA); international business (MBA); leadership and organizational management (MBA). *Accreditation:* ACBSP. Part-time and evening/weekend programs available. Postbaccalaureate distance learning degree programs offered (no on-campus study). *Faculty:* 30 part-time/adjunct (6 women). *Students:* 85 full-time (49 women), 133 part-time (52 women); includes 35 minority (27 Black or African American, non-Hispanic/Latino; 1 American Indian or Alaska Native, non-Hispanic/Latino; 4 Asian, non-Hispanic/Latino; 1 Hispanic/Latino; 1 Native Hawaiian or other Pacific Islander, non-Hispanic/Latino; 1 Two or more races, non-Hispanic/Latino), 29 international. Average age 30. 52 applicants, 94% accepted, 44 enrolled. In 2010, 100 master's awarded. *Degree requirements:* For master's, portfolio. *Entrance requirements:* For master's, minimum GPA of 3.0, 2 letters of recommendation, resume. Additional exam requirements/recommendations for international students: Required—TOEFL (minimum score 550 paper-based; 213 computer-based; 80 iBT). *Application deadline:* For fall admission, 8/1 priority date for domestic and international students; for spring admission, 12/1 priority date for domestic and international students. Applications are processed on a rolling basis. Application fee: $35. *Expenses:* Tuition: Full-time $10,098; part-time $561 per credit hour. Required fees: $22.50 per credit hour. *Financial support:* In 2010–11, 19 students received support. Unspecified assistantships available. Financial award application deadline: 7/30; financial award applicants required to submit FAFSA. *Unit head:* Glen Metheny, Director of Graduate Studies, 501-279-5851, Fax: 501-279-4805, E-mail: gmetheny@harding.edu. *Application contact:* Melanie Kiihnl, Recruiting Manager/Director of Marketing, 501-279-4523, Fax: 501-279-4805, E-mail: mba@harding.edu.

HEC Montreal, School of Business Administration, Master of Science Programs in Administration, Program in Organizational Development, Montréal, QC H3T 2A7, Canada. Offers M Sc. Part-time programs available. *Students:* 33 full-time (22 women), 13 part-time (12 women). 58 applicants, 50% accepted, 20 enrolled. *Degree requirements:* For master's, one foreign language, thesis. *Application deadline:* For fall admission, 3/15 for domestic and international students; for winter admission, 10/1 for domestic and international students. Application fee: $78. Electronic applications accepted. *Expenses:* Tuition, area resident: Part-time $68.93 per credit. Tuition, state resident: full-time $2481.48; part-time $188.92 per credit. Tuition, nonresident: full-time $6801; part-time $482.06 per course. International tuition: $17,354.16 full-time. Required fees: $1309.50; $30.28 per credit. $93.45 per term. Tuition and fees vary according to degree level and program. *Financial support:* Research assistantships, teaching assistantships, scholarships/grants available. Financial award application deadline: 9/2. *Unit head:* Claude Laurin, Director, 514-340-6485, Fax: 514-340-6880, E-mail: claude.laurin@hec.ca. *Application contact:* Francine Blais, Administrative Director, 514-340-6112, Fax: 514-340-6411, E-mail: francine.blais@hec.ca.

HEC Montreal, School of Business Administration, Master of Science Programs in Administration, Program in Organizational Studies, Montréal, QC H3T 2A7, Canada. Offers M Sc. Part-time programs available. *Students:* 1 full-time (0 women), 1 (woman) part-time. 6 applicants, 100% accepted. *Degree requirements:* For master's, one foreign language, thesis. *Application deadline:* For fall admission, 3/15 for domestic and international students; for winter admission, 10/1 for domestic and international students. Application fee: $78. Electronic applications accepted. *Expenses:* Tuition, area resident: Part-time $68.93 per credit. Tuition, state resident: full-time $2481.48; part-time $188.92 per credit. Tuition, nonresident: full-time $6801; part-time $482.06 per course. International tuition: $17,354.16 full-time. Required fees: $1309.50; $30.28 per credit. $93.45 per term. Tuition and fees vary according to degree level and program. *Financial support:* Research assistantships, teaching assistantships, scholarships/grants available. Financial award application deadline: 9/2. *Unit head:* Claude Laurin, Director, 514-340-6485, Fax: 514-340-6880, E-mail: claude.laurin@hec.ca. *Application contact:* Francine Blais, Administrative Director, 514-340-6112, Fax: 514-340-6411, E-mail: francine.blais@hec.ca.

Immaculata University, College of Graduate Studies, Program in Organization Studies, Immaculata, PA 19345. Offers MA. Part-time and evening/weekend programs available. *Students:* 2 full-time (0 women), 21 part-time (18 women). Average age 35. 8 applicants, 50% accepted, 4 enrolled. In 2010, 8 master's awarded. *Degree requirements:* For master's, comprehensive exam, thesis optional. *Entrance requirements:* For master's, GMAT, GRE General Test, MAT, minimum GPA of 3.0. Additional exam requirements/recommendations for international students: Required—TOEFL, IELTS. *Application deadline:* Applications are processed on a rolling basis. Application fee: $50. Electronic applications accepted. *Financial support:* Application deadline: 5/1. *Unit head:* Dr. Janice Jacobs, Chair, 610-647-4400 Ext. 3452, Fax: 610-993-8550, E-mail: jjacobs@immaculata.edu. *Application contact:* 610-647-4400 Ext. 3211, Fax: 610-993-8550, E-mail: graduate@immaculata.edu.

Indiana University–Purdue University Fort Wayne, College of Engineering, Technology, and Computer Science, Department of Organizational Leadership and Supervision, Fort Wayne, IN 46805-1499. Offers human resources (MS); leadership (MS); organizational leadership and supervision (Certificate). Part-time programs available. *Faculty:* 5 full-time (2 women). *Students:* 3 full-time (all women), 34 part-time (22 women); includes 5 minority (all Black or African American, non-Hispanic/Latino), 2 international. Average age 35. 10 applicants, 90% accepted, 8 enrolled. In 2010, 1 master's awarded. *Entrance requirements:* For master's, GRE or GMAT (if undergraduate GPA is below 3.0), current resume, 2 recent letters of recommendation, essay. Additional exam requirements/recommendations for international students: Required—TOEFL (minimum score 550 paper-based; 213 computer-based; 77 iBT); Recommended—TWE. *Application deadline:* For fall admission, 5/15 for domestic students, 4/1 for international students; for spring admission, 11/15 for domestic students, 10/1 for international students. Applications are processed on a rolling basis. Application fee: $55 ($60 for international students). Electronic applications accepted. *Expenses:* Tuition, state resident: full-time $4824; part-time $268 per credit. Tuition, nonresident: full-time $11,625; part-time $646 per credit. Required fees: $555; $30.85 per credit. Tuition and fees vary according to course load. *Financial support:* In 2010–11, 1 teaching assistantship with partial tuition reimbursement (averaging $12,740 per year) was awarded; scholarships/grants also available. Support available to part-time students. Financial award application deadline: 3/1; financial award applicants required to submit FAFSA. *Faculty research:* Hate crimes compared with ethnicity and religion. *Unit head:* Dr. Kimberly McDonald, Chair, 260-481-6418, Fax: 260-481-6417, E-mail: mcdonalk@ipfw.edu. *Application contact:* Dr. Linda Hite, Director of Graduate Studies, 260-481-6416, Fax: 260-481-6417, E-mail: hitel@ipfw.edu.

Judson University, Graduate Programs, Elgin, IL 60123-1498. Offers architecture (M Arch); literacy (M Ed); organizational leadership (MA); teaching (M Ed). Part-time and evening/weekend programs available. Postbaccalaureate distance learning degree programs offered (no on-campus study). *Faculty:* 18 full-time (7 women), 27 part-time/adjunct (9 women). *Students:* 59 full-time (38 women), 46 part-time (23 women); includes 16 minority (8 Black or African American, non-Hispanic/Latino; 1 Asian, non-Hispanic/Latino; 7 Hispanic/Latino), 2 international. Average age 32. In 2010, 76 master's awarded. *Degree requirements:* For master's, comprehensive exam (for some programs), thesis. *Entrance requirements:* For master's, interviews, written essays, portfolios (depending on program of study). Additional exam requirements/recommendations for international students: Required—TOEFL (minimum score 550 paper-based; 213 computer-based). *Application deadline:* Applications are processed on a rolling basis. Application fee: $40. Electronic applications accepted. *Expenses:* Tuition: Full-time $18,000; part-time $1000 per credit hour. Required fees: $200 per term. Tuition and fees vary according to course load, program and student level. *Financial support:* Applicants required to submit FAFSA. *Faculty research:* Leadership, sustainable design, sustainability management, bilingual education, literacy. *Unit head:* Dr. Dale H. Simmons, Provost and Vice-President for Academic Affairs, 847-628-1000, E-mail: dsimmons@judsonu.edu. *Application contact:* Maria Aguirre, Assistant to the Registrar for Graduate Programs, 847-628-1160, E-mail: maguirre@judsonu.edu.

Lewis University, College of Arts and Sciences, Program in Organizational Leadership, Romeoville, IL 60446. Offers higher education/student services (MA); organizational management (MA); public administration (MA); training and development (MA). Part-time and evening/weekend programs available. Postbaccalaureate distance learning degree programs offered (no on-campus study). *Faculty:* 2 full-time (0 women), 9 part-time/adjunct (2 women). *Students:* 18 full-time (8 women), 151 part-time (111 women); includes 44 Black or African American, non-Hispanic/Latino; 1 Asian, non-Hispanic/Latino; 11 Hispanic/Latino. Average age 36. In 2010, 51 master's awarded. *Entrance requirements:* For master's, bachelor's degree, at least 25 years of age, minimum of 3 years of work experience, minimum GPA of 3.0, letter of recommendation, interview. Additional exam requirements/recommendations for international students: Required—TOEFL (minimum score 550 paper-based; 213 computer-based). *Application deadline:* For fall admission, 5/1 priority date for international students; for spring admission, 11/15 priority date for international students. Applications are processed on a rolling basis. Application fee: $40. Electronic applications accepted. *Expenses:* Tuition: Full-time $13,320; part-time $740 per credit hour. Tuition and fees vary according to program. *Financial support:* Federal Work-Study, scholarships/grants, tuition waivers, and unspecified assistantships available. Financial award application deadline: 5/1; financial award applicants required to submit FAFSA. *Unit head:* Dr. Rich Walsh, Director, 815-838-0500, E-mail: walshri@lewisu.edu. *Application contact:* Julie Nickel, Assistant Director, Graduate and Adult Admission, 815-836-5574, Fax: 815-836-5578, E-mail: nickelju@lewisu.edu.

Malone University, Graduate Program in Organizational Leadership, Canton, OH 44709. Offers MAOL. Part-time and evening/weekend programs available. *Faculty:* 6 full-time (4 women), 3 part-time/adjunct (0 women). *Students:* 22 full-time (14 women), 14 part-time (9 women); includes 5 Black or African American, non-Hispanic/Latino. Average age 39. 61 applicants, 77% accepted, 36 enrolled. *Entrance requirements:* For master's, minimum GPA of 3.0. Additional exam requirements/recommendations for international students: Required—TOEFL (minimum score 550 paper-based; 213 computer-based; 79 iBT). *Expenses:* Contact institution. *Financial support:* Tuition waivers (partial) available. Support available to part-time students. Financial award application deadline: 6/30. *Unit head:* Dr. Mary E. Quinn, Director, 330-471-8556, Fax: 330-471-8343, E-mail: mquinn@malone.edu. *Application contact:* Mona J. McAuliffe, Corporate Recruiter for Graduate and Professional Studies, 330-471-8623, Fax: 330-471-8343, E-mail: mmcauliffe@malone.edu.

Manhattanville College, Graduate Programs, Humanities and Social Sciences Programs, Program in Organizational Management and Human Resource Development, Purchase, NY 10577-2132. Offers MS. Part-time and evening/weekend programs available. In 2010, 25 master's awarded. *Degree requirements:* For master's, thesis. *Entrance requirements:* For master's, interview, 2 letters of recommendation. Additional exam requirements/recommendations for international students: Required—TOEFL. *Application deadline:* Applications are processed on a rolling basis. Application fee: $75. *Expenses:* Tuition: Full-time $16,110; part-time $895 per credit. Required fees: $50 per semester. *Financial support:* Career-related internships or fieldwork, Federal Work-Study, institutionally sponsored loans, and unspecified assistantships available. Financial award application deadline: 3/1; financial award applicants required to submit FAFSA. *Unit head:* Dr. Don Richards, Interim Dean, School of Graduate and Professional Studies, 914-323-5469, Fax: 914-694-3488, E-mail: gps@mivlle.edu. *Application contact:* Office of Admissions for Graduate and Professional Studies, 914-323-5418, E-mail: gps@mville.edu.

Marian University, Business Division, Fond du Lac, WI 54935-4699. Offers organizational leadership and quality (MS). Part-time and evening/weekend programs available. *Faculty:* 17 part-time/adjunct (1 woman). *Students:* 11 full-time (6 women), 111 part-time (79 women); includes 7 Black or African American, non-Hispanic/Latino; 3 Asian, non-Hispanic/Latino; 4 Hispanic/Latino. Average age 38. 36 applicants, 92% accepted, 33 enrolled. In 2010, 52 master's awarded. *Degree requirements:* For master's, comprehensive group project. *Entrance requirements:* For master's, 3 years of managerial experience, minimum GPA of 2.75, letters of professional reference. *Application deadline:* Applications are processed on a rolling basis. Application fee: $25. Electronic applications accepted. *Expenses:* Contact institution. *Financial support:* In 2010–11, 8 students received support. Institutionally sponsored loans available. Support available to part-time students. Financial award application deadline: 3/1; financial award applicants required to submit FAFSA. *Faculty research:* Organizational values, statistical decision making, learning organization, quality planning, customer research. *Unit head:* Donna Innes, Dean of PACE, 920-923-8760, Fax: 920-923-7167, E-mail: dinnes@marianuniversity.edu. *Application contact:* Tracy Qualman, Director of Marketing and Admission, 920-923-7159, Fax: 920-923-7167, E-mail: tqualmann@marianuniversity.edu.

Maryville University of Saint Louis, College of Arts and Sciences, St. Louis, MO 63141-7299. Offers actuarial science (MS); organizational leadership (MA). Part-time and evening/weekend programs available. *Faculty:* 6 full-time (all women), 1 part-time/adjunct (0 women). *Students:* 13 full-time (7 women), 13 part-time (10 women); includes 2 Black or African American, non-Hispanic/Latino; 1 Asian, non-Hispanic/Latino; 1 Two or more races, non-Hispanic/Latino, 3 international. Average age 31. In 2010, 7 master's awarded. *Entrance requirements:* For master's, GRE with minimum score of 600 (MS), strong mathematics background, 2 letters of recommendation, and personal statement (MS). Additional exam requirements/recommendations for international students: Required—TOEFL (minimum score 550 paper-based; 213 computer-based; 80 iBT). *Application deadline:* Applications are processed on a rolling basis. Application fee: $40 ($60 for international students). Electronic applications accepted. *Expenses:* Tuition: Full-time $21,100; part-time $633.50 per credit hour. Required fees: $150 per semester. *Financial support:* Application deadline: 3/1. *Unit head:* Dr. Dan Sparling, Dean, 314-529-9436, Fax: 314-529-9965, E-mail: dsparling@maryville.edu. *Application contact:* Denise Evans, Assistant Vice President, Adult and Continuing Education, 314-529-9676, Fax: 314-529-9927, E-mail: devans1@maryville.edu.

Medaille College, Program in Business Administration—Amherst, Amherst, NY 14221. Offers business administration (MBA); organizational leadership (MA). Evening/weekend programs available. *Faculty:* 8 full-time (3 women), 14 part-time/adjunct (4 women). *Students:* 222 full-time (126 women), 1 (woman) part-time; includes 24 Black or African American, non-Hispanic/Latino; 3 Asian, non-Hispanic/Latino; 6 Hispanic/Latino; 1 Two or more races, non-Hispanic/Latino. Average age 31. In 2010, 143 master's awarded. *Degree requirements:* For master's, thesis or alternative. *Entrance requirements:* For master's, GMAT, minimum undergraduate GPA of 2.7, 3 years of work experience. Additional exam requirements/recommendations for international students: Required—TOEFL (minimum score 550 paper-based; 213 computer-based). *Application deadline:* Applications are processed on a rolling basis. Application fee: $100. *Expenses:* Contact institution. *Financial support:* In 2010–11, 180 students received support. Federal Work-Study available. Financial award applicants required to submit FAFSA. *Unit head:* Jennifer Bavifard, Associate Dean for Special Programs, 716-631-1061 Ext. 150, Fax: 716-631-1380, E-mail: jbavifar@medaille.edu. *Application contact:* Jacqueline Matheny, Executive Director of Marketing and Enrollment, 716-932-2541, Fax: 716-632-1811, E-mail: jmatheny@medaille.edu.

Medaille College, Program in Business Administration—Rochester, Rochester, NY 14623. Offers business administration (MBA); organizational leadership (MA). Evening/weekend programs available. *Faculty:* 3 full-time (2 women), 40 part-time/adjunct (20 women). *Students:* 37 full-time (26 women); includes 9 Black or African American, non-Hispanic/Latino; 5 Hispanic/Latino. Average age 36. 31 applicants, 90% accepted, 25 enrolled. In 2010, 27 master's awarded. *Degree requirements:* For master's, thesis or alternative. *Entrance requirements:* For master's, GMAT, 3 years of work experience, minimum undergraduate GPA of 2.7. Additional exam requirements/recommendations for international students: Required—TOEFL (minimum score 550 paper-based; 213 computer-based). *Application deadline:* Applications are processed on a rolling basis. Application fee: $100. *Expenses:* Contact institution. *Financial support:* In 2010–11, 37 students received support. Federal Work-Study available. Financial award applicants required to submit FAFSA. *Unit head:* Jennifer Bavifard, Branch Campus Director, 716-932-2591, Fax: 716-631-1380, E-mail: jbavifard@medaille.edu. *Application contact:* Jane Rowlands, Marketing Support, 585-272-0030, Fax: 585-272-0057, E-mail: jrowlands@medaille.edu.

Mercy College, School of Business, Program in Organizational Leadership, Dobbs Ferry, NY 10522-1189. Offers MS. Part-time and evening/weekend programs available. Postbaccalaureate distance learning degree programs offered (no on-campus study). *Students:* 112 full-time (82 women), 2 part-time (1 woman); includes 57 Black or African American, non-Hispanic/Latino; 3 Asian, non-Hispanic/Latino; 30 Hispanic/Latino; 2 Two or more races, non-Hispanic/Latino. Average age 36. 139 applicants, 77% accepted, 69 enrolled. In 2010, 62 master's awarded. *Entrance requirements:* For master's, assessment by program director, resume, 2 letters of reference, interview. Additional exam requirements/recommendations for international students: Required—TOEFL (minimum score 600 paper-based; 250 computer-based; 100 iBT), IELTS (minimum score 8). *Application deadline:* For fall admission, 8/1 for international students. Applications are processed on a rolling basis. Application fee: $40. Electronic applications accepted. *Expenses:* Contact institution. *Financial support:* Career-related internships or fieldwork, Federal Work-Study, scholarships/grants, and unspecified assistantships available. Support available to part-time students. Financial award applicants required to submit FAFSA. *Faculty research:* Organizational behavior, strategic management, collaborative relationship. *Unit head:* Benjamin Manyindo, Program Director, 212-615-3330, E-mail: bmanyindo@mercy.edu. *Application contact:* Carolyn Bow, Assistant Director, 914-674-7285, E-mail: cbow@mercy.edu.

Misericordia University, College of Professional Studies and Social Sciences, Program in Organizational Management, Dallas, PA 18612-1098. Offers MS. Part-time and evening/weekend programs available. Postbaccalaureate distance learning degree programs offered. *Faculty:* 3 full-time (1 woman), 9 part-time/adjunct (1 woman). *Students:* 71 part-time (45 women); includes 2 minority (1 Black or African American, non-Hispanic/Latino; 1 Two or more races, non-Hispanic/Latino). Average age 34. 23 applicants, 87% accepted, 18 enrolled. In 2010, 23 master's awarded. *Entrance requirements:* For master's, GRE General Test, MAT (35th percentile or higher), or minimum undergraduate GPA of 2.79. *Application deadline:* Applications are processed on a rolling basis. Application fee: $25. Electronic applications accepted. *Expenses:* Contact institution. *Financial support:* In 2010–11, 40 students received support. Career-related internships or fieldwork and scholarships/grants available. Support available to part-time students. Financial award application deadline: 6/30; financial award applicants required to submit FAFSA. *Unit head:* Dr. John Sumansky, Director of Graduate Business Programs, 570-674-6158, E-mail: jsumansk@ misericordia.edu. *Application contact:* Larree Brown, Assistant Director of Admissions, Part-Time Undergraduate and Graduate Programs, 570-674-6451, Fax: 570-674-6232, E-mail: lbrown@misericordia.edu.

Mountain State University, School of Graduate Studies, Program in Executive Leadership, Beckley, WV 25802-9003. Offers DEL. *Faculty:* 2 full-time (1 woman), 5 part-time/adjunct (2 women). *Students:* 35 full-time (20 women); includes 10 minority (8 Black or African American, non-Hispanic/Latino; 2 Hispanic/Latino). Average age 35. 21 applicants, 67% accepted, 12 enrolled. *Entrance requirements:* For doctorate, discussion paper, resume, official transcripts from all colleges/universities attended, master's degree, 2 professional references. Application fee: $75. *Expenses:* Tuition: Full-time $4800; part-time $400 per credit hour. Required fees: $2250; $2250 per credit hour. Tuition and fees vary according to degree level and program. *Unit head:* Dr. William White, Dean, School of Leadership and Professional Development/Interim Dean, School of Graduate Studies, 304-929-1658, E-mail: wwhite@mountainstate. edu. *Application contact:* Anita Diaz, Enrollment Coordinator of Graduate Studies, 304-929-1731, Fax: 304-929-1710, E-mail: adiaz@mountainstate.edu.

National University, Academic Affairs, College of Letters and Sciences, Department of Professional Studies, La Jolla, CA 92037-1011. Offers forensic science (MFS), including criminalistics and investigation; public administration (MPA), including alternative dispute resolution, human resource management, organizational leadership, public finance. Part-time and evening/weekend programs available. Postbaccalaureate distance learning degree programs offered (no on-campus study). *Faculty:* 10 full-time (3 women), 110 part-time/adjunct (22 women). *Students:* 189 full-time (117 women), 284 part-time (167 women); includes 259 minority (101 Black or African American, non-Hispanic/Latino; 2 American Indian or Alaska Native, non-Hispanic/Latino; 33 Asian, non-Hispanic/Latino; 104 Hispanic/Latino; 7 Native Hawaiian or other Pacific Islander, non-Hispanic/Latino; 12 Two or more races, non-Hispanic/Latino). Average age 38. 305 applicants, 100% accepted, 192 enrolled. In 2010, 160 master's awarded. *Degree requirements:* For master's, thesis. *Entrance requirements:* For master's, interview, minimum GPA of 2.5. Additional exam requirements/ recommendations for international students: Required—TOEFL (minimum score 550 paper-based; 213 computer-based; 79 iBT), IELTS (minimum score 6). *Application deadline:* Applications are processed on a rolling basis. Application fee: $60 ($65 for international students). Electronic applications accepted. *Expenses:* Tuition: Full-time $9450; part-time $350 per unit. Required fees: $350 per unit. One-time fee: $60. *Financial support:* Career-related internships or fieldwork, institutionally sponsored loans, scholarships/ grants, and tuition waivers (partial) available. Support available to part-time students. Financial award application deadline: 6/30; financial award applicants required to submit FAFSA. *Unit head:* James G. Larsen, Associate Professor and Chair, 858-642-8418, Fax: 858-642-8715, E-mail: jlarson@nu.edu. *Application contact:* Dominick Giovanniello, Associate Regional Dean—San Diego, 800-NAT-UNIV, Fax: 858-541-7792, E-mail: dgiovann@nu.edu.

National University, Academic Affairs, School of Business and Management, Department of Leadership and Business Administration, La Jolla, CA 92037-1011. Offers alternative dispute resolution (MBA); e-business (MBA); financial management (MBA); human resource management (MBA); human resources management (MA); international business (MBA); knowledge management (MS); marketing (MBA); organizational leadership (MBA, MS); technology management (MBA). Part-time and evening/weekend programs available. Postbaccalaureate distance learning degree programs offered (no on-campus study). *Faculty:* 16 full-time (4 women), 126 part-time/adjunct (39 women). *Students:* 119 full-time (81 women), 410 part-time (202 women); includes 176 minority (81 Black or African American, non-Hispanic/Latino; 1 American Indian or Alaska Native, non-Hispanic/Latino; 31 Asian, non-Hispanic/Latino; 52 Hispanic/Latino; 4 Native Hawaiian or other Pacific Islander, non-Hispanic/ Latino; 7 Two or more races, non-Hispanic/Latino), 183 international. Average age 38. 219 applicants, 100% accepted, 160 enrolled. In 2010, 95 master's awarded. *Degree requirements:* For master's, thesis. *Entrance requirements:* For master's, interview, minimum GPA of 2.5. Additional exam requirements/ recommendations for international students: Required—TOEFL (minimum score 550 paper-based; 213 computer-based; 79 iBT), IELTS (minimum score 6). *Application deadline:* Applications are processed on a rolling basis. Application fee: $60 ($65 for international students). Electronic applications accepted. *Expenses:* Tuition: Full-time $9450; part-time $350 per unit. Required fees: $350 per unit. One-time fee: $60. *Financial support:* Career-related internships or fieldwork, institutionally sponsored loans, scholarships/grants, and tuition waivers (partial) available. Support available to part-time students. Financial award application deadline: 6/30; financial award applicants required to submit FAFSA. *Unit head:* Dr. Bruce Buchowicz, Chair, 858-642-8439, Fax: 858-642-8406, E-mail: bbuchowicz@nu.edu. *Application contact:* Dominick Giovanniello, Associate Regional Dean—San Diego, 800-NAT-UNIV, Fax: 858-541-7792, E-mail: dgiovann@nu.edu.

National University, Academic Affairs, School of Business and Management, Department of Management and Marketing, La Jolla, CA 92037-1011. Offers e-business (MS); knowledge management (MS); management (MA); organizational leadership (MS). Part-time and evening/weekend programs available. Postbaccalaureate distance learning degree programs offered (no on-campus

study). *Faculty:* 16 full-time (4 women), 110 part-time/adjunct (34 women). *Students:* 364 full-time (165 women), 458 part-time (212 women); includes 278 minority (71 Black or African American, non-Hispanic/Latino; 4 American Indian or Alaska Native, non-Hispanic/Latino; 99 Asian, non-Hispanic/Latino; 91 Hispanic/Latino; 4 Native Hawaiian or other Pacific Islander, non-Hispanic/ Latino; 9 Two or more races, non-Hispanic/Latino), 195 international. Average age 34. 157 applicants, 100% accepted, 134 enrolled. In 2010, 321 master's awarded. *Degree requirements:* For master's, thesis. *Entrance requirements:* For master's, interview, minimum GPA of 2.5. Additional exam requirements/ recommendations for international students: Required—TOEFL (minimum score 550 paper-based; 213 computer-based; 79 iBT), IELTS (minimum score 6). *Application deadline:* Applications are processed on a rolling basis. Application fee: $60 ($65 for international students). Electronic applications accepted. *Expenses:* Tuition: Full-time $9450; part-time $350 per unit. Required fees: $350 per unit. One-time fee: $60. *Financial support:* Career-related internships or fieldwork, institutionally sponsored loans, scholarships/ grants, and tuition waivers (partial) available. Support available to part-time students. Financial award application deadline: 6/30; financial award applicants required to submit FAFSA. *Unit head:* Dr. Ramon Corona, Chair and Professor, 858-642-8427, Fax: 858-642-8406, E-mail: rcorona@nu.edu. *Application contact:* Dominick Giovanniello, Associate Regional Dean—San Diego, 800-NAT-UNIV, Fax: 858-541-7792, E-mail: dgiovann@nu.edu.

Newman University, MBA Program, Wichita, KS 67213-2097. Offers finance (MBA); international business (MBA); leadership (MBA); management (MBA); technology (MBA). Part-time programs available. *Faculty:* 4 full-time (2 women), 7 part-time/adjunct (2 women). *Students:* 33 full-time (14 women), 92 part-time (37 women); includes 28 minority (7 Black or African American, non-Hispanic/Latino; 6 Asian, non-Hispanic/Latino; 12 Hispanic/Latino; 1 Native Hawaiian or other Pacific Islander, non-Hispanic/Latino; 2 Two or more races, non-Hispanic/Latino), 24 international. Average age 32. 80 applicants, 83% accepted, 45 enrolled. In 2010, 72 master's awarded. *Degree requirements:* For master's, thesis optional. *Entrance requirements:* For master's, interview; minimum GPA of 3.0; 3 letters of recommendation; course work in algebra, statistics, macroeconomics, and financial accounting. Additional exam requirements/recommendations for international students: Required— TOEFL (minimum score 600 paper-based; 250 computer-based; 100 iBT). *Application deadline:* For fall admission, 8/1 priority date for domestic students, 7/15 priority date for international students; for winter admission, 1/1 priority date for domestic students; for spring admission, 1/1 priority date for domestic students, 11/15 priority date for international students. Applications are processed on a rolling basis. Application fee: $25 ($40 for international students). Electronic applications accepted. *Expenses:* Contact institution. *Financial support:* In 2010–11, 29 students received support. Federal Work-Study available. Financial award application deadline: 8/15; financial award applicants required to submit FAFSA. *Unit head:* Dr. George Goetz, Dean of the College of Professional Studies/Director, 316-942-4291 Ext. 2205, Fax: 316-942-4483, E-mail: smithge@newmanu.edu. *Application contact:* Linda Kay Sabala, Director of Graduate Admissions, 316-942-4291 Ext. 2230, Fax: 316-942-4483, E-mail: sabalal@newmanu.edu.

North Central College, Graduate and Continuing Education Programs, Department of Leadership Studies, Naperville, IL 60566-7063. Offers higher education leadership (MLS); professional leadership (MLS); social entrepreneurship (MLS); sports leadership (MLS). Part-time and evening/weekend programs available. *Faculty:* 7 full-time (1 woman), 7 part-time/adjunct (1 woman). *Students:* 28 full-time (15 women), 32 part-time (21 women); includes 5 Black or African American, non-Hispanic/Latino; 3 Hispanic/Latino; 1 Two or more races, non-Hispanic/Latino. Average age 28. In 2010, 2 master's awarded. *Degree requirements:* For master's, project. *Entrance requirements:* For master's, interview. Additional exam requirements/recommendations for international students: Required—TOEFL (minimum score 570 paper-based; 233 computer-based; 90 iBT). *Application deadline:* For fall admission, 8/15 for domestic students; for winter admission, 12/1 for domestic students; for spring admission, 2/1 for domestic students. Applications are processed on a rolling basis. Application fee: $25. *Expenses:* Contact institution. *Financial support:* Scholarships/grants available. Support available to part-time students. *Unit head:* Dr. Thomas Cavanagh, Head, 630-637-5285. *Application contact:* Wendy Kulpinski, Director and Graduate and Continuing Education Admissions, 630-637-5808, Fax: 630-637-5844, E-mail: wekulpinski@noctrl. edu.

Northern Kentucky University, Office of Graduate Programs, College of Business, Program in Executive Leadership and Organizational Change, Highland Heights, KY 41099. Offers MS. Part-time and evening/weekend programs available. *Students:* 47 part-time (26 women); includes 7 minority (5 Black or African American, non-Hispanic/Latino; 1 Asian, non-Hispanic/ Latino; 1 Hispanic/Latino). Average age 40. 38 applicants, 66% accepted, 24 enrolled. In 2010, 20 master's awarded. *Degree requirements:* For master's, field research project. *Entrance requirements:* For master's, minimum GPA of 2.5; essay on professional career objective; 3 letters of recommendation, 1 from a current organization; 3 years of professional or managerial work experience. Additional exam requirements/recommendations for international students: Required—TOEFL (minimum score 600 paper-based; 213 computer-based; 79 iBT); Recommended—IELTS (minimum score 6.5). *Application deadline:* For fall admission, 6/15 for domestic students, 6/1 priority date for international students. Application fee: $40. Electronic applications accepted. *Expenses:* Tuition, state resident: full-time $7254; part-time $403 per credit hour. Tuition, nonresident: full-time $12,492; part-time $694 per credit hour. Tuition and fees vary according to degree level and program. *Financial support:* Unspecified assistantships available. Financial award applicants required to submit FAFSA. *Faculty research:* Leadership and development, organizational change, field research, team and conflict management, strategy development and systems thinking. *Unit head:* Dr. Kenneth Rhee, Program Director, 859-572-6310, Fax: 859-572-7694, E-mail: rhee@nku.edu. *Application contact:* Amberly Hurst-Nutini, Coordinator, 859-572-5947, Fax: 859-572-7694, E-mail: hurstam@nku.edu.

Northwest University, School of Business and Management, Kirkland, WA 98033. Offers business administration (MBA); social entrepreneurship (MA). Evening/weekend programs available. *Faculty:* 6 full-time (1 woman), 7 part-time/adjunct (3 women). *Students:* 41 full-time (20 women), 3 part-time (1 woman); includes 10 minority (5 Black or African American, non-Hispanic/Latino; 3 Asian, non-Hispanic/Latino; 2 Hispanic/Latino), 9 international. Average age 34. 21 applicants, 86% accepted, 18 enrolled. In 2010, 11 master's awarded. *Degree requirements:* For master's, formalized research. *Entrance requirements:* For master's, GMAT, 4 foundation courses. Additional exam requirements/recommendations for international students: Required—TOEFL (minimum score 550 paper-based). *Application deadline:* For fall admission, 8/1 for domestic and international students; for spring admission, 12/1 for domestic and international students. Applications are processed on a rolling basis. Application fee: $75. Electronic applications accepted. Tuition and fees vary according to program. *Financial support:* Federal Work-Study, scholarships/grants, health care benefits, and tuition waivers (full) available. Financial award applicants required to submit FAFSA. *Unit head:* Dr. Teresa Gillespie, Dean, 425-889-5290, E-mail: teresa.gillespie@northwestu.edu. *Application contact:* Aaron Oosterwyk, Director of Graduate and Professional Studies Enrollment, 425-889-7799, Fax: 425-803-3059, E-mail: aaron.oosterwyk@northwestu.edu.

Norwich University, School of Graduate and Continuing Studies, Program in Business Administration, Northfield, VT 05663. Offers finance (MBA); organizational leadership (MBA); project management (MBA). *Accreditation:* ACBSP. Evening/weekend programs available. *Faculty:* 26 part-time/adjunct (0 women). *Students:* 108 full-time (45 women); includes 17 minority (5 Black or African American, non-Hispanic/Latino; 3 American Indian or Alaska Native, non-Hispanic/Latino; 4 Asian, non-Hispanic/Latino; 5 Hispanic/Latino), 4 international. Average age 36. 187 applicants, 84% accepted, 95 enrolled. In 2010, 389 master's awarded. *Degree requirements:* For master's, comprehensive exam (for some programs), thesis optional. *Entrance requirements:* For master's, minimum undergraduate GPA of 2.75. Additional exam requirements/recommendations for international students: Required—TOEFL (minimum score 550 paper-based; 213 computer-based; 83 iBT). *Application deadline:* For fall admission, 8/10 for domestic and international students; for winter admission, 11/7 for domestic and international students; for spring admission, 2/6 for domestic and international students. Application fee: $50. *Expenses:* Tuition: Full-time $17,380; part-time $645 per credit. Tuition and fees vary according to program. *Financial support:* Scholarships/grants available. Financial award applicants required to submit FAFSA. *Unit head:* Dr. Jose Cordova, Faculty Director, 802-485-2567, Fax: 802-485-2533, E-mail: jcordova@norwich.edu. *Application contact:* Bernice Fousek, Student Services Coordinator, 802-485-2748, Fax: 802-485-2533, E-mail: bfousek@norwich.edu.

Norwich University, School of Graduate and Continuing Studies, Program in Organizational Leadership, Northfield, VT 05663. Offers MSOL. Evening/weekend programs available. *Faculty:* 9 part-time/adjunct (4 women). *Students:* 29 full-time (12 women); includes 3 Black or African American, non-Hispanic/Latino; 1 Hispanic/Latino. Average age 43. 60 applicants, 80% accepted, 29 enrolled. In 2010, 29 master's awarded. *Entrance requirements:* Additional exam requirements/recommendations for international students: Required—TOEFL (minimum score 550 paper-based; 212 computer-based; 83 iBT). *Application deadline:* For fall admission, 8/10 for domestic and international students; for winter admission, 11/7 for domestic and international students; for spring admission, 2/6 for domestic and international students. Application fee: $50. *Expenses:* Tuition: Full-time $17,380; part-time $645 per credit. Tuition and fees vary according to program. *Financial support:* Applicants required to submit FAFSA. *Unit head:* Donal Hartman, Program Director, 802-485-2767, Fax: 802-485-2533, E-mail: hartmand@norwich.edu. *Application contact:* Alec Adams, Associate Program Director, 802-485-2567, Fax: 802-485-2533, E-mail: aadams@norwich.edu.

Norwich University, School of Graduate and Continuing Studies, Program in Public Administration, Northfield, VT 05663. Offers continuity of government operations (MPA); criminal justice (MPA); fiscal management (MPA); leadership (MPA); organizational leadership (MPA); public works administration (MPA). Evening/weekend programs available. *Faculty:* 12 part-time/adjunct (5 women). *Students:* 64 full-time (21 women); includes 4 Black or African American, non-Hispanic/Latino; 2 Two or more races, non-Hispanic/Latino. Average age 37. 189 applicants, 81% accepted. In 2010, 64 master's awarded. *Entrance requirements:* Additional exam requirements/recommendations for

international students: Required—TOEFL (minimum score 550 paper-based; 212 computer-based; 83 iBT). *Application deadline:* For fall admission, 8/10 for domestic and international students; for winter admission, 11/7 for domestic and international students; for spring admission, 2/6 for domestic and international students. Application fee: $50. *Expenses:* Tuition: Full-time $17,380; part-time $645 per credit. Tuition and fees vary according to program. *Financial support:* Scholarships/grants available. Financial award applicants required to submit FAFSA. *Unit head:* Donal Hartman, Program Director, 802-485-2567, Fax: 802-485-2533, E-mail: dhartman@norwich.edu. *Application contact:* Chris Ormsby, Associate Program Director, 802-249-7809, Fax: 802-485-2533, E-mail: cormsby@norwich.edu.

Nova Southeastern University, Fischler School of Education and Human Services, Program in Education, Fort Lauderdale, FL 33314-7796. Offers educational leadership (Ed D); health care education (Ed D); higher education leadership (Ed D); human services administration (Ed D); instructional leadership (Ed D); instructional technology and distance education (Ed D); organizational leadership (Ed D); special education (Ed D); speech language pathology (Ed D). Part-time and evening/weekend programs available. Postbaccalaureate distance learning degree programs offered (minimal on-campus study). *Faculty:* 114 full-time (68 women), 170 part-time/adjunct (83 women). *Students:* 2,632 full-time (2,011 women), 1,384 part-time (1,012 women); includes 2,578 minority (1,881 Black or African American, non-Hispanic/Latino; 14 American Indian or Alaska Native, non-Hispanic/Latino; 57 Asian, non-Hispanic/Latino; 608 Hispanic/Latino; 2 Native Hawaiian or other Pacific Islander, non-Hispanic/Latino; 16 Two or more races, non-Hispanic/Latino), 27 international. Average age 44. 585 applicants, 67% accepted, 318 enrolled. In 2010, 457 doctorates awarded. *Degree requirements:* For doctorate, thesis/dissertation. *Entrance requirements:* For doctorate, MAT or GRE, master's degree, 2 letters of recommendation, work experience. Additional exam requirements/recommendations for international students: Recommended—TOEFL (minimum score 79 iBT), IELTS (minimum score 6). *Application deadline:* Applications are processed on a rolling basis. Application fee: $50. Electronic applications accepted. *Financial support:* Scholarships/grants and tuition waivers (full) available. Financial award application deadline: 4/15; financial award applicants required to submit FAFSA. *Unit head:* Dr. H. Wells Singleton, Dean, 800-986-3223 Ext. 28730, Fax: 954-262-3894, E-mail: singlew@nova.edu. *Application contact:* Lenny Jacobskind, Director of School-Wide Recruiting, 800-986-3223 Ext. 28538, Fax: 954-262-2914, E-mail: lenny@nova.edu.

Nova Southeastern University, Fischler School of Education and Human Services, Program in Organizational Leadership, Fort Lauderdale, FL 33314-7796. Offers Ed D. Part-time and evening/weekend programs available. Postbaccalaureate distance learning degree programs offered (minimal on-campus study). *Faculty:* 39 full-time (17 women), 29 part-time/adjunct (12 women). *Students:* 152 full-time (114 women), 4 part-time (3 women); includes 91 Black or African American, non-Hispanic/Latino; 1 American Indian or Alaska Native, non-Hispanic/Latino; 2 Asian, non-Hispanic/Latino; 11 Hispanic/Latino, 1 international. 10 applicants, 90% accepted, 7 enrolled. In 2010, 79 doctorates awarded. *Degree requirements:* For doctorate, thesis/dissertation. *Entrance requirements:* For doctorate, MAT or GRE, master's degree, minimum GPA of 3.0, letter of recommendation. Additional exam requirements/recommendations for international students: Recommended—TOEFL (minimum score 79 iBT), IELTS (minimum score 6). *Application deadline:* Applications are processed on a rolling basis. Application fee: $50. Electronic applications accepted. *Financial support:* Tuition waivers (full) available. Financial award application deadline: 1/7; financial award applicants required to submit FAFSA. *Unit head:* Dr. H. Wells Singleton, Dean, 800-986-3223 Ext. 28730, Fax: 954-262-3894, E-mail: singlew@nova.edu. *Application contact:* Lenny Jacobskind, Director of School-Wide Recruiting, 800-986-3223 Ext. 28538, Fax: 954-262-2914, E-mail: lenny@nova.edu.

Nyack College, School of Business and Leadership, Nyack, NY 10960-3698. Offers business administration (MBA); organizational leadership (MS). Evening/weekend programs available. *Students:* 112 full-time (72 women), 7 part-time (5 women); includes 96 minority (83 Black or African American, non-Hispanic/Latino; 3 Asian, non-Hispanic/Latino; 7 Hispanic/Latino; 3 Two or more races, non-Hispanic/Latino), 6 international. Average age 40. In 2010, 53 master's awarded. *Degree requirements:* For master's, thesis (for some programs). *Entrance requirements:* For master's, GMAT (MBA only), resume. *Application deadline:* Applications are processed on a rolling basis. Application fee: $50. Electronic applications accepted. *Expenses:* Contact institution. *Unit head:* Dr. Anita Underwood, Dean, 845-675-4511, Fax: 845-353-5812. *Application contact:* Traci Piescki, Director of Admissions, 800-541-6891, Fax: 845-348-3912, E-mail: admissions.grad@nyack.edu.

Our Lady of the Lake University of San Antonio, School of Business and Leadership, Program in Leadership Studies, San Antonio, TX 78207-4689. Offers PhD. *Faculty:* 5 full-time (1 woman), 5 part-time/adjunct (1 woman). *Students:* 26 full-time (17 women), 182 part-time (107 women); includes 124 minority (24 Black or African American, non-Hispanic/Latino; 1 Asian, non-Hispanic/Latino; 95 Hispanic/Latino; 2 Native Hawaiian or other Pacific Islander, non-Hispanic/Latino; 2 Two or more races, non-Hispanic/Latino). Average age 41. In 2010, 12 doctorates awarded. *Degree requirements:* For doctorate, thesis/dissertation, internship, qualifying exam. *Entrance requirements:* For doctorate, GRE General Test or MAT, interview. *Application deadline:* For fall admission, 3/1 for domestic students. Application fee: $25 ($50 for international students). *Expenses:* Tuition: Full-time $13,500; part-time $750 per contact hour. Required fees: $330. Tuition and fees vary according to course level, degree level and campus/location. *Unit head:* Dr. Robert Bisking, Chair, 210-434-6711, E-mail: biskr@lake.ollusa.edu. *Application contact:* Dr. Robert Bisking, Chair, 210-434-6711, E-mail: biskr@lake.ollusa.edu.

Our Lady of the Lake University of San Antonio, School of Business and Leadership, Program in Organizational Leadership, San Antonio, TX 78207-4689. Offers MS. *Students:* 2 full-time (both women), 55 part-time (39 women); includes 31 minority (7 Black or African American, non-Hispanic/Latino; 22 Hispanic/Latino; 1 Native Hawaiian or other Pacific Islander, non-Hispanic/Latino; 1 Two or more races, non-Hispanic/Latino). Average age 36. In 2010, 16 master's awarded. *Expenses:* Tuition: Full-time $13,500; part-time $750 per contact hour. Required fees: $330. Tuition and fees vary according to course level, degree level and campus/location. *Unit head:* Dr. Robert Bisking, Dean, 210-434-6711 Ext. 2281, Fax: 210-434-0821, E-mail: rbisking@ollusa.edu. *Application contact:* Dr. Robert Bisking, Dean, 210-434-6711 Ext. 2281, Fax: 210-434-0821, E-mail: rbisking@ollusa.edu.

Oxford Graduate School, Graduate Programs, Dayton, TN 37321-6736. Offers family life education (M Litt); organizational leadership (M Litt); sociological integration of religion and society (D Phil). *Faculty:* 10 full-time (2 women), 22 part-time/adjunct (7 women). *Students:* 105 full-time (40 women). *Application contact:* Joanne Phillips, Information Contact, 423-775-6596, Fax: 423-775-6599, E-mail: oxfordgraduateschool@ogs.edu.

Palm Beach Atlantic University, MacArthur School of Leadership, West Palm Beach, FL 33416-4708. Offers organizational leadership (MS). Part-time and evening/weekend programs available. *Faculty:* 5 full-time (2 women), 3 part-time/adjunct (0 women). *Students:* 5 full-time (all women), 83 part-time (56 women); includes 34 minority (20 Black or African American, non-Hispanic/Latino; 1 American Indian or Alaska Native, non-Hispanic/Latino; 1 Asian, non-Hispanic/Latino; 12 Hispanic/Latino), 1 international. Average age 37. 46 applicants, 91% accepted, 35 enrolled. In 2010, 32 master's awarded. *Entrance requirements:* For master's, GRE, minimum GPA of 3.0. Additional exam requirements/recommendations for international students: Required—TOEFL (minimum score 550 paper-based; 213 computer-based). *Application deadline:* For fall admission, 7/15 priority date for domestic students; for spring admission, 11/15 priority date for domestic students. Applications are processed on a rolling basis. Application fee: $45. Electronic applications accepted. *Expenses:* Tuition: Full-time $8280; part-time $460 per credit hour. Required fees: $99 per semester. Tuition and fees vary according to course load, degree level and campus/location. *Financial support:* Tuition waivers (partial) available. Financial award applicants required to submit FAFSA. *Unit head:* Dr. Jim Laub, Dean, 561-803-2302, E-mail: jim laub@pba.edu. Application contact: Graduate Admissions, 888-468-6722, E-mail: grad@pba.edu.

Pepperdine University, Graduate School of Education and Psychology, Division of Education, MA Program in Social Entrepreneurship and Change, Malibu, CA 90263. Offers MA. *Faculty:* 50 full-time (29 women), 114 part-time/adjunct (68 women). *Students:* 24 part-time (20 women); includes 13 minority (5 Black or African American, non-Hispanic/Latino; 4 Asian, non-Hispanic/Latino; 3 Hispanic/Latino; 1 Native Hawaiian or other Pacific Islander, non-Hispanic/Latino). 31 applicants, 81% accepted, 24 enrolled. *Entrance requirements:* For master's, two letters of recommendation, one- to two-page statement of educational purpose. Additional exam requirements/recommendations for international students: Required—TOEFL. *Application deadline:* For fall admission, 6/1 priority date for domestic students. Application fee: $55. *Unit head:* Dr. Margaret J. Weber, Dean, 310-568-5600, E-mail: margaret.weber@pepperdine.edu. *Application contact:* Jennifer Agatep, Admissions Manager, Education, 310-258-2849, E-mail: jennifer.agatep@pepperdine.edu.

Pepperdine University, Graziadio School of Business and Management, MS in Organization Development Program, Malibu, CA 90263. Offers MSOD. Program consists of four week-long sessions per year at different locations in Northern California, Southern California and abroad. Part-time programs available. *Students:* 65 part-time (47 women); includes 17 minority (6 Black or African American, non-Hispanic/Latino; 2 American Indian or Alaska Native, non-Hispanic/Latino; 6 Asian, non-Hispanic/Latino; 3 Hispanic/Latino), 8 international. 42 applicants, 81% accepted, 30 enrolled. In 2010, 27 master's awarded. *Entrance requirements:* For master's, GMAT or GRE, two letters of recommendation. Additional exam requirements/recommendations for international students: Required—TOEFL. Application fee: $75. *Unit head:* Dr. Linda A. Livingstone, Dean, 310-568-5689, Fax: 310-568-5766, E-mail: linda.livingstone@pepperdine.edu. *Application contact:* Darrell Eriksen, Director of Admission and Student Accounts, 310-568-5525, E-mail: darrell.eriksen@pepperdine.edu.

Philadelphia Biblical University, School of Business and Leadership, Langhorne, PA 19047-2990. Offers organizational leadership (MSOL). Part-time and evening/weekend programs available. *Faculty:* 2 full-time (0 women). *Students:* 3 full-time (1 woman), 26 part-time (10 women); includes 11 Black or African American, non-Hispanic/Latino; 1 Asian, non-Hispanic/Latino; 1 Hispanic/Latino, 2 international. Average age 42. 18 applicants, 78% accepted, 12 enrolled. In 2010, 14 master's awarded. *Entrance requirements:* Additional exam requirements/recommendations for international students:

Required—TOEFL (minimum score 550 paper-based; 213 computer-based). *Application deadline:* Applications are processed on a rolling basis. Application fee: $25. Electronic applications accepted. *Expenses:* Tuition: Full-time $10,710; part-time $595 per credit. Tuition and fees vary according to program. *Financial support:* In 2010–11, 2 students received support. Scholarships/grants available. Support available to part-time students. Financial award applicants required to submit FAFSA. *Unit head:* Dr. William Bowles, Chair, Graduate Programs, 215-702-4871, Fax: 215-702-4248, E-mail: wbowles@pbu.edu. *Application contact:* Timothy Nessler, Assistant Director, Graduate Admissions, 800-572-2472, Fax: 215-702-4248, E-mail: tnessler@pbu.edu.

Point Park University, School of Business, Pittsburgh, PA 15222-1984. Offers business (MBA); organizational leadership (MA). Part-time and evening/weekend programs available. *Faculty:* 11 full-time, 14 part-time/adjunct. *Students:* 121 full-time (69 women), 272 part-time (137 women); includes 107 minority (86 Black or African American, non-Hispanic/Latino; 1 American Indian or Alaska Native, non-Hispanic/Latino; 9 Asian, non-Hispanic/Latino; 5 Hispanic/Latino; 6 Two or more races, non-Hispanic/Latino), 23 international. Average age 32. 356 applicants, 73% accepted, 166 enrolled. In 2010, 168 master's awarded. *Degree requirements:* For master's, comprehensive exam (for some programs), thesis or alternative. *Entrance requirements:* For master's, minimum QPA of 2.75; 2 letters of recommendation; resume (MA). Additional exam requirements/recommendations for international students: Required—TOEFL (minimum score 550 paper-based; 79 iBT). *Application deadline:* Applications are processed on a rolling basis. Application fee: $30. Electronic applications accepted. *Expenses:* Tuition: Full-time $12,456; part-time $692 per credit. Required fees: $630; $35 per credit. *Financial support:* In 2010–11, 48 students received support, including 5 teaching assistantships with full tuition reimbursements available (averaging $6,400 per year); scholarships/grants also available. Financial award application deadline: 4/15; financial award applicants required to submit FAFSA. *Faculty research:* Technology issues, foreign direct investment, multinational corporate issues, cross-cultural international organizations/administrations, regional integration issues. *Unit head:* Dr. Angela Isaac, Dean, 412-392-8011, Fax: 412-392-8048, E-mail: aisaac@pointpark.edu. *Application contact:* Marty M. Paonessa, Associate Director, Graduate and Adult Enrollment, 412-392-3915, Fax: 412-392-6164, E-mail: mpaonessa@pointpark.edu.

Quinnipiac University, School of Business, Program in Organizational Leadership, Hamden, CT 06518-1940. Offers MS. Part-time and evening/weekend programs available. *Faculty:* 4 full-time (1 woman), 1 part-time/adjunct (0 women). *Students:* 7 full-time (5 women), 160 part-time (103 women); includes 16 minority (8 Black or African American, non-Hispanic/Latino; 1 Asian, non-Hispanic/Latino; 6 Hispanic/Latino; 1 Two or more races, non-Hispanic/Latino). 73 applicants, 93% accepted, 58 enrolled. In 2010, 22 master's awarded. *Entrance requirements:* Additional exam requirements/recommendations for international students: Required—TOEFL (minimum score 575 paper-based; 233 computer-based; 90 iBT), IELTS (minimum score 6.5). *Application deadline:* Applications are processed on a rolling basis. Application fee: $45. Electronic applications accepted. *Expenses:* Tuition: Part-time $810 per credit. Required fees: $35 per credit. *Unit head:* Lisa Braiewa, Director of Online Master's Programs, School of Business, 203-582-3710, Fax: 203-582-8664, E-mail: lisa.braiewa@quinnipiac.edu. *Application contact:* Valerie Schlesinger, Director of Admissions for QU Online, 203-582-8949, Fax: 203-582-3443, E-mail: valerie.schlesinger@quinnipiac.edu.

Regent University, Graduate School, School of Global Leadership and Entrepreneurship, Virginia Beach, VA 23464-9800. Offers business administration (MBA); management (MA); organizational leadership (MA, PhD, Certificate); strategic foresight (MA); strategic leadership (DSL). Part-time and evening/weekend programs available. Postbaccalaureate distance learning degree programs offered (minimal on-campus study). *Faculty:* 13 full-time (3 women), 9 part-time/adjunct (3 women). *Students:* 30 full-time (11 women), 499 part-time (184 women); includes 125 Black or African American, non-Hispanic/Latino; 4 American Indian or Alaska Native, non-Hispanic/Latino; 10 Asian, non-Hispanic/Latino; 15 Hispanic/Latino, 93 international. Average age 41. 157 applicants, 66% accepted, 64 enrolled. In 2010, 86 master's, 30 doctorates awarded. *Degree requirements:* For master's, thesis or alternative, 3 credit hour culminating experience; for doctorate, thesis/dissertation. *Entrance requirements:* For master's, GRE, GMAT, minimum undergraduate GPA of 2.75, computer literacy survey, 2 recommendations, resume, transcripts, essay; for doctorate, GRE, GMAT, sample of writing, minimum 3 years of relevant experience, computer literacy survey, 2 recommendations, resume, essay, transcripts; for Certificate, writing sample, resume, transcripts. Additional exam requirements/recommendations for international students: Required—TOEFL (minimum score 577 paper-based; 233 computer-based). *Application deadline:* For fall admission, 5/1 priority date for domestic students; for spring admission, 10/1 priority date for domestic students. Applications are processed on a rolling basis. Application fee: $50. Electronic applications accepted. *Expenses:* Contact institution. *Financial support:* Career-related internships or fieldwork, scholarships/grants, and tuition waivers (full and partial) available. Support available to part-time students. Financial award application deadline: 9/1. *Faculty research:* Servant leadership, ethics and values, telecommuting and family values, organizational communications, distance education. *Unit head:* Dr. Bruce Winston, Dean, 757-352-4306, Fax: 757-352-4634, E-mail:

brucwin@regent.edu. *Application contact:* Matthew Chadwick, Director of Enrollment Support Services, 800-373-5504, Fax: 757-352-4381, E-mail: admissions@regent.edu.

Rutgers, The State University of New Jersey, Newark, Rutgers Business School–Newark and New Brunswick, Doctoral Programs in Management, Newark, NJ 07102. Offers accounting (PhD); accounting information systems (PhD); economics (PhD); finance (PhD); individualized study (PhD); information technology (PhD); international business (PhD); management science (PhD); marketing science (PhD); organizational management (PhD); science, technology and management (PhD); supply chain management (PhD). *Faculty:* 143 full-time (36 women), 2 part-time/adjunct (0 women). *Students:* 117 full-time (42 women), 1 (woman) part-time; includes 8 Black or African American, non-Hispanic/Latino; 14 Asian, non-Hispanic/Latino; 3 Hispanic/Latino, 68 international. Average age 33. 355 applicants, 14% accepted, 35 enrolled. In 2010, 8 doctorates awarded. *Degree requirements:* For doctorate, comprehensive exam, thesis/dissertation. *Entrance requirements:* For doctorate, GRE or GMAT. Additional exam requirements/recommendations for international students: Required—TOEFL (minimum score 550 paper-based; 213 computer-based; 79 iBT). *Application deadline:* For fall admission, 3/1 for domestic and international students; for spring admission, 10/15 for domestic and international students. Application fee: $65. Electronic applications accepted. *Expenses:* Tuition, state resident: part-time $600 per credit. Tuition, nonresident: full-time $10,694. *Financial support:* In 2010–11, 52 students received support, including 7 fellowships (averaging $18,000 per year), 4 research assistantships with tuition reimbursements available (averaging $23,112 per year), 41 teaching assistantships with tuition reimbursements available (averaging $23,112 per year); health care benefits also available. Financial award application deadline: 3/1. *Unit head:* Dr. Glenn Shafer, Director, 973-353-1604, Fax: 973-353-5691, E-mail: gshafer@rbs.rutgers.edu. *Application contact:* Information Contact, 973-353-5371, Fax: 973-353-5691, E-mail: phdinfo@andromeda.rutgers.edu.

Sage Graduate School, Graduate School, School of Management, Program in Organization Management, Troy, NY 12180-4115. Offers organization management (MS); public administration (MS). Part-time and evening/weekend programs available. *Faculty:* 4 full-time (2 women), 8 part-time/adjunct (3 women). *Students:* 9 full-time (5 women), 43 part-time (29 women); includes 12 minority (10 Black or African American, non-Hispanic/Latino; 1 Asian, non-Hispanic/Latino; 1 Hispanic/Latino). Average age 32. 26 applicants, 69% accepted, 15 enrolled. In 2010, 19 master's awarded. *Degree requirements:* For master's, capstone seminar. *Entrance requirements:* For master's, minimum GPA of 2.75. Additional exam requirements/recommendations for international students: Required—TOEFL (minimum score 550 paper-based; 213 computer-based). *Application deadline:* Applications are processed on a rolling basis. Application fee: $40. *Expenses:* Tuition: Full-time $10,980; part-time $610 per credit hour. Tuition and fees vary according to course load, degree level and program. *Financial support:* Fellowships, research assistantships, Federal Work-Study, scholarships/grants, tuition waivers (partial), and unspecified assistantships available. Support available to part-time students. Financial award application deadline: 3/1; financial award applicants required to submit FAFSA. *Unit head:* Dr. Daniel Robeson, Dean, School of Management, 518-292-8637, Fax: 518-292-1964, E-mail: robesd@sage.edu. *Application contact:* Wendy D. Diefendorf, Director of Graduate and Adult Admission, 518-244-2443, Fax: 518-244-6880, E-mail: diefew@sage.edu.

St. Ambrose University, College of Business, Program in Organizational Leadership, Davenport, IA 52801. Offers MOL. Part-time and evening/weekend programs available. *Faculty:* 5 full-time (0 women), 4 part-time/adjunct (1 woman). *Students:* 22 full-time (14 women), 95 part-time (67 women); includes 15 minority (10 Black or African American, non-Hispanic/Latino; 2 American Indian or Alaska Native, non-Hispanic/Latino; 3 Hispanic/Latino). Average age 37. 38 applicants, 74% accepted, 27 enrolled. In 2010, 44 master's awarded. *Degree requirements:* For master's, comprehensive exam (for some programs), thesis or alternative, integration projects. *Entrance requirements:* Additional exam requirements/recommendations for international students: Required—TOEFL. *Application deadline:* For fall admission, 8/15 priority date for domestic students; for winter admission, 12/15 priority date for domestic students; for spring admission, 1/1 priority date for domestic students. Applications are processed on a rolling basis. Application fee: $25. Electronic applications accepted. *Expenses:* Contact institution. *Financial support:* In 2010–11, 50 students received support, including 10 research assistantships (averaging $3,343 per year); scholarships/grants, tuition waivers (partial), and unspecified assistantships also available. Financial award application deadline: 3/15; financial award applicants required to submit FAFSA. *Unit head:* Dr. Ron O. Wastyn, Director, 563-322-1014, Fax: 563-324-0842, E-mail: wastynronaldo@sau.edu. *Application contact:* Megan M. Gisi, Program Coordinator, 563-322-1051, Fax: 563-324-0842, E-mail: gisimeganm@sau.edu.

St. Catherine University, Graduate Programs, Program in Organizational Leadership, St. Paul, MN 55105. Offers MA. Part-time and evening/weekend programs available. *Faculty:* 8 full-time (7 women), 20 part-time/adjunct (14 women). *Students:* 17 full-time (all women), 176 part-time (167 women); includes 30 minority (11 Black or African American, non-Hispanic/Latino; 9 Asian, non-Hispanic/Latino; 4 Hispanic/Latino; 6 Two or more races,

non-Hispanic/Latino), 1 international. Average age 40. 45 applicants, 78% accepted, 29 enrolled. In 2010, 38 master's awarded. *Degree requirements:* For master's, thesis. *Entrance requirements:* For master's, GMAT, GRE General Test or MAT, 2 years of work experience, minimum GPA of 3.0. Additional exam requirements/recommendations for international students: Required—TOEFL (minimum score 600 paper-based; 250 computer-based; 100 iBT). *Application deadline:* For fall admission, 8/1 priority date for domestic students; for winter admission, 12/1 priority date for domestic students; for spring admission, 3/1 priority date for domestic students. Applications are processed on a rolling basis. Application fee: $35. *Expenses:* Tuition: Part-time $763 per credit. Part-time tuition and fees vary according to degree level and program. *Financial support:* In 2010–11, 66 students received support; research assistantships, career-related internships or fieldwork and institutionally sponsored loans available. Support available to part-time students. Financial award application deadline: 4/1; financial award applicants required to submit FAFSA. *Faculty research:* Ethics. *Unit head:* Rebecca Hawthorne, Director, 651-690-6420, Fax: 651-690-6024. *Application contact:* 651-690-6933, Fax: 651-690-6064.

St. Edward's University, School of Management and Business, Program in Organizational Leadership and Ethics, Austin, TX 78704. Offers MS. Part-time and evening/weekend programs available. *Students:* 42 part-time (29 women); includes 21 minority (6 Black or African American, non-Hispanic/Latino; 1 American Indian or Alaska Native, non-Hispanic/Latino; 14 Hispanic/Latino). Average age 37. 11 applicants, 100% accepted, 10 enrolled. In 2010, 20 master's awarded. *Degree requirements:* For master's, minimum of 24 hours in residence. *Entrance requirements:* For master's, GMAT or GRE General Test, minimum GPA of 2.75 in last 60 hours of course work. Additional exam requirements/recommendations for international students: Required—TOEFL (minimum score 550 paper-based; 213 computer-based; 79 iBT) or IELTS (minimum score 6). *Application deadline:* For fall admission, 7/1 for domestic and international students; for spring admission, 11/1 for domestic and international students. Applications are processed on a rolling basis. Application fee: $45 ($50 for international students). Electronic applications accepted. *Expenses:* Tuition: Full-time $16,200; part-time $900 per credit hour. Required fees: $50 per trimester. Full-time tuition and fees vary according to course load and program. *Financial support:* Scholarships/grants available. *Faculty research:* Spirituality and work, Asian (Eastern) ethics, Birkman Method impact on college retention. *Unit head:* Dr. Tom Sechrest, Director, 512-637-1954, Fax: 512-448-8492, E-mail: thomasl@stedwards.edu. *Application contact:* Kay Lynn Arnold, Assistant Director of Admission, 512-233-1636, Fax: 512-428-1032, E-mail: kayla@stedwards.edu.

St. Edward's University, School of Management and Business, Program in Organization Development, Austin, TX 78704. Offers MA. *Expenses:* Tuition: Full-time $16,200; part-time $900 per credit hour. Required fees: $50 per trimester. Full-time tuition and fees vary according to course load and program. *Unit head:* Marsha Kelliher, Dean, 512-448-8588, Fax: 512-448-8492, E-mail: marshak@stedwards.edu. *Application contact:* Kelly Luna, Graduate Admissions Coordinator, 512-233-1697, Fax: 512-428-1032, E-mail: kellyl@stedwards.edu.

Saint Joseph's University, College of Arts and Sciences, Department of Education, Philadelphia, PA 19131-1395. Offers educational leadership (Ed D); elementary education (MS); instructional technology (MS); organizational development and leadership (MS); professional education (MS); reading specialist (MS); secondary education (MS); special education (MS). Part-time and evening/weekend programs available. *Faculty:* 25 full-time (18 women), 69 part-time/adjunct (43 women). *Students:* 126 full-time (98 women), 963 part-time (729 women); includes 168 minority (116 Black or African American, non-Hispanic/Latino; 3 American Indian or Alaska Native, non-Hispanic/Latino; 18 Asian, non-Hispanic/Latino; 24 Hispanic/Latino; 1 Native Hawaiian or other Pacific Islander, non-Hispanic/Latino; 6 Two or more races, non-Hispanic/Latino), 6 international. Average age 33. 304 applicants, 92% accepted, 230 enrolled. In 2010, 217 master's, 14 doctorates awarded. *Entrance requirements:* For master's, 2 letters of recommendation, minimum GPA of 3.0, official transcripts, personal statement; for doctorate, GRE, master's degree from accredited institution, minimum graduate GPA of 3.5, computer competence, commitment to participate in cohort, interview with program director. Additional exam requirements/recommendations for international students: Required—TOEFL (minimum score 550 paper-based; 213 computer-based; 79 iBT). *Application deadline:* For fall admission, 7/15 priority date for domestic students, 4/15 for international students; for winter admission, 11/15 for domestic students, 1/15 for international students; for spring admission, 11/15 priority date for domestic students, 10/15 for international students. Applications are processed on a rolling basis. Application fee: $35. Electronic applications accepted. *Expenses:* Contact institution. *Financial support:* Unspecified assistantships available. Financial award applicants required to submit FAFSA. *Faculty research:* Early childhood course design, public education professional development. Total annual research expenditures: $91,900. *Unit head:* Dr. Teri Sosa, Director of Graduate Education, 610-660-3162, E-mail: tsosa@sju.edu. *Application contact:* Kate McConnell, Director, Graduate College of Arts and Sciences Admissions and Retention, 610-660-3184, Fax: 610-660-3230, E-mail: kate.mcconnell@sju.edu.

Saint Joseph's University, College of Arts and Sciences, Organization Development and Leadership Programs, Philadelphia, PA 19131-1395. Offers adult learning and training (MS, Certificate); organization dynamics and leadership (MS, Certificate); organizational psychology and development (MS, Certificate). Part-time and evening/weekend programs available. Postbaccalaureate distance learning degree programs offered (no on-campus study). *Faculty:* 1 (woman) full-time, 6 part-time/adjunct (3 women). *Students:* 20 full-time (10 women), 112 part-time (81 women); includes 32 Black or African American, non-Hispanic/Latino; 1 American Indian or Alaska Native, non-Hispanic/Latino; 2 Asian, non-Hispanic/Latino; 6 Hispanic/Latino; 3 Two or more races, non-Hispanic/Latino, 11 international. Average age 36. 57 applicants, 84% accepted, 42 enrolled. In 2010, 23 master's awarded. *Entrance requirements:* For master's, GRE (if GPA less than 2.7), minimum GPA of 2.7, 2 letters of recommendation, resume. Additional exam requirements/recommendations for international students: Required—TOEFL (minimum score 550 paper-based; 213 computer-based; 79 iBT). *Application deadline:* For fall admission, 7/15 priority date for domestic students, 4/15 for international students; for winter admission, 1/15 for international students; for spring admission, 11/15 priority date for domestic students, 10/15 for international students. Applications are processed on a rolling basis. Application fee: $35. Electronic applications accepted. *Expenses:* Tuition: Part-time $729 per credit. Tuition and fees vary according to course load, degree level and program. *Financial support:* Applicants required to submit FAFSA. *Unit head:* Dr. Felice Tilin, Director, 610-660-1575, E-mail: ftilin@sju.edu. *Application contact:* Kate McConnell, Director, Graduate College of Arts and Sciences Admissions and Retention, 610-660-3184, Fax: 610-660-3230, E-mail: kate.mcconnell@sju.edu.

Saint Mary's University of Minnesota, Schools of Graduate and Professional Programs, Graduate School of Business and Technology, Organizational Leadership Program, Winona, MN 55987-1399. Offers MA. *Unit head:* Viki Kimsal, Director, 507-238-4510, E-mail: vkimsal@smumn.edu. *Application contact:* Yasin Alsaidi, Director of Admissions for Graduate and Professional Programs, 612-728-5207, Fax: 612-728-5121, E-mail: yalsaidi@smumn.edu.

Santa Clara University, Leavey School of Business, Program in Business Administration, Santa Clara, CA 95053. Offers accounting (MBA); entrepreneurship (MBA); executive business administration (EMBA); finance (MBA); food and agribusiness (MBA); international business (MBA); leading people and organizations (MBA); managing technology and innovation (MBA); marketing management (MBA); supply chain management (MBA). *Accreditation:* AACSB. Part-time and evening/weekend programs available. *Students:* 229 full-time (80 women), 748 part-time (244 women); includes 354 minority (14 Black or African American, non-Hispanic/Latino; 1 American Indian or Alaska Native, non-Hispanic/Latino; 287 Asian, non-Hispanic/Latino; 42 Hispanic/Latino; 5 Native Hawaiian or other Pacific Islander, non-Hispanic/Latino; 5 Two or more races, non-Hispanic/Latino), 209 international. Average age 32. 334 applicants, 76% accepted, 191 enrolled. In 2010, 307 master's awarded. *Degree requirements:* For master's, thesis or alternative. *Entrance requirements:* For master's, GMAT, GRE. Additional exam requirements/recommendations for international students: Required—TOEFL (minimum score 600 paper-based; 250 computer-based; 100 iBT). *Application deadline:* For fall admission, 6/1 for domestic and international students; for spring admission, 1/19 for domestic students, 1/17 for international students. Applications are processed on a rolling basis. Application fee: $75 ($100 for international students). Electronic applications accepted. *Expenses:* Contact institution. *Financial support:* In 2010–11, 350 students received support; fellowships with partial tuition reimbursements available, research assistantships with partial tuition reimbursements available, career-related internships or fieldwork, Federal Work-Study, institutionally sponsored loans, scholarships/grants, health care benefits, and unspecified assistantships available. Support available to part-time students. Financial award application deadline: 6/1; financial award applicants required to submit FAFSA. *Unit head:* Elizabeth B. Ford, Senior Assistant Dean, 408-554-2752, Fax: 408-554-4571, E-mail: eford@scu.edu. *Application contact:* Molly Mulally, Assistant Director, Graduate Business Admissions, 408-554-4539, Fax: 408-554-4571, E-mail: mbaadmissions@scu.edu.

Saybrook University, Graduate College of Psychology and Humanistic Studies, San Francisco, CA 94111-1920. Offers clinical psychology (Psy D); human science (MA, PhD), including consciousness and spirituality, humanistic and transpersonal psychology, integrative health studies, organizational systems, social transformation, transformative social change (MA); organizational systems (MA, PhD), including consciousness and spirituality, humanistic and transpersonal psychology, integrative health studies, leadership of sustainable systems (MA), organizational systems, social transformation; psychology (MA, PhD), including clinical psychology (PhD), consciousness and spirituality, creativity studies (MA), humanistic and transpersonal psychology, integrative health studies, Jungian studies, marriage and family therapy (MA), organizational systems, social transformation. Postbaccalaureate distance learning degree programs offered (minimal on-campus study). *Faculty:* 15 full-time (5 women), 83 part-time/adjunct (34 women). *Students:* 479 full-time (333 women); includes 30 Black or African American, non-Hispanic/Latino; 1 American Indian or Alaska Native, non-Hispanic/Latino; 13 Asian, non-Hispanic/Latino; 18 Hispanic/Latino, 18 international. Average age 43. 280 applicants, 52% accepted, 105 enrolled. In 2010, 28 master's, 43 doctorates awarded. Terminal master's awarded for partial completion of doctoral program. *Degree requirements:* For master's, thesis or alternative; for doctorate,

thesis/dissertation. *Entrance requirements:* Additional exam requirements/recommendations for international students: Required—TOEFL (minimum score 580 paper-based; 237 computer-based; 93 iBT). *Application deadline:* For fall admission, 6/1 priority date for domestic students; for spring admission, 12/16 priority date for domestic students. Application fee: $50. Electronic applications accepted. *Financial support:* In 2010–11, 335 students received support. Scholarships/grants available. Financial award applicants required to submit FAFSA. *Faculty research:* Humanistic theory, health studies, organizational systems, consciousness and spirituality, social transformation. Total annual research expenditures: $90,000. *Unit head:* Mark Schulman, President, 800-825-4480, Fax: 415-433-9271. *Application contact:* Director of Admissions, 800-825-4480, Fax: 415-433-9271, E-mail: admissions@saybrook.edu.

Saybrook University, LIOS Graduate College, Leadership and Organization Development Track, San Francisco, CA 94111-1920. Offers MA. Program offered jointly with Bastyr University. *Faculty:* 10 full-time (6 women), 5 part-time/adjunct (2 women). *Students:* 48 full-time. Average age 40. 50 applicants, 98% accepted, 40 enrolled. In 2010, 19 master's awarded. *Degree requirements:* For master's, thesis (for some programs), oral exams. *Entrance requirements:* For master's, bachelor's degree from an accredited college or university. *Application deadline:* Applications are processed on a rolling basis. Application fee: $65. *Financial support:* In 2010–11, 32 students received support. Career-related internships or fieldwork, Federal Work-Study, and scholarships/grants available. Financial award applicants required to submit FAFSA. *Faculty research:* Cross-functional work teams, communication, management authority, employee influence, systems theory. *Unit head:* Dr. Shelley Drogin, Head, 425-939-8181, Fax: 425-939-8110, E-mail: sdrogin@lios.org. *Application contact:* Jennifer Herron, Director, Academic Admissions, 425-939-8124, Fax: 425-939-8110.

Shenandoah University, School of Education and Human Development, Winchester, VA 22601-5195. Offers administrative leadership (D Ed); advanced professional teaching English to speakers of other languages (Certificate); education (MSE); elementary education (Certificate); middle school education (Certificate); organizational leadership (MS, D Prof); professional studies (Certificate), including administration and supervision, ESL teacher education, reading specialist, special education; professional teaching English to speakers of other languages (Certificate); public management (Certificate); school reform (Certificate); secondary education (Certificate). *Accreditation:* Teacher Education Accreditation Council. Part-time and evening/weekend programs available. Postbaccalaureate distance learning degree programs offered (minimal on-campus study). *Faculty:* 14 full-time (8 women), 25 part-time/adjunct (20 women). *Students:* 22 full-time (14 women), 369 part-time (267 women); includes 27 minority (12 Black or African American, non-Hispanic/Latino; 4 Asian, non-Hispanic/Latino; 10 Hispanic/Latino; 1 Two or more races, non-Hispanic/Latino), 13 international. Average age 38. 270 applicants, 91% accepted, 187 enrolled. In 2010, 111 master's, 7 doctorates, 45 other advanced degrees awarded. *Degree requirements:* For master's, comprehensive exam (for some programs), thesis (for some programs), internship; for doctorate, comprehensive exam, thesis/dissertation; for Certificate, full time teaching in area for 1 year. *Entrance requirements:* For master's, minimum GPA of 3.0 or satisfactory GRE, 3 letters of recommendation, valid teaching license, writing sample; for doctorate, minimum graduate GPA of 3.5, 3 years of teaching experience, 3 letters of recommendation, writing samples, interview, resume; for Certificate, minimum undergraduate GPA of 3.0, essay, 3 letters of recommendation. Additional exam requirements/recommendations for international students: Required—TOEFL (minimum score 550 paper-based; 213 computer-based; 79 iBT), IELTS (minimum score 6.5), Sakae Institute of Study Abroad (550). *Application deadline:* For fall admission, 7/1 for domestic and international students; for spring admission, 10/15 for domestic and international students. Application fee: $30. Electronic applications accepted. *Expenses:* Tuition: Full-time $17,352; part-time $723 per credit. Tuition and fees vary according to course load and program. *Financial support:* Application deadline: 3/15. *Unit head:* Dr. Steven E. Humphries, Director, 540-535-3574, E-mail: shumphri@su.edu. *Application contact:* David Anthony, Dean of Admissions, 540-665-4581, Fax: 540-665-4627, E-mail: admit@su.edu.

Shippensburg University of Pennsylvania, School of Graduate Studies, College of Arts and Sciences, Department of Sociology and Anthropology, Shippensburg, PA 17257-2299. Offers organizational development and leadership (MS), including business, communications, education, environmental management, higher education, historical administration, individual and organizational development, public organizations, social structures and organizations. Part-time and evening/weekend programs available. *Faculty:* 3 full-time (all women). *Students:* 18 full-time (13 women), 46 part-time (33 women); includes 11 minority (6 Black or African American, non-Hispanic/Latino; 3 Asian, non-Hispanic/Latino; 2 Two or more races, non-Hispanic/Latino), 2 international. Average age 32. 56 applicants, 55% accepted, 20 enrolled. In 2010, 28 master's awarded. *Degree requirements:* For master's, capstone experience including internship. *Entrance requirements:* For master's, interview (if GPA less than 2.75), resume, personal goals statement. Additional exam requirements/recommendations for international students: Required—TOEFL (minimum score 580 paper-based; 237 computer-based); Recommended—IELTS (minimum score 6). *Application deadline:* For fall admission, 3/1 for international students; for spring admission, 7/1 for international students. Applications are processed on a rolling basis. Application fee: $30. Electronic applications accepted. *Expenses:* Tuition, state resident: full-time $6966. Tuition, nonresident: full-time $11,146. Required fees: $1802. *Financial support:* In 2010–11, 8 research assistantships with full tuition reimbursements (averaging $5,000 per year) were awarded; career-related internships or fieldwork, scholarships/grants, unspecified assistantships, and resident hall director and student payroll positions also available. Support available to part-time students. Financial award applicants required to submit FAFSA. *Unit head:* Dr. Barbara Denison, Chairperson, 717-477-1735, Fax: 717-477-4011, E-mail: bjdeni@ship.edu. *Application contact:* Jeremy R. Goshorn, Associate Dean of Graduate Admissions, 717-477-1231, Fax: 717-477-4016, E-mail: jrgoshorn@ship.edu.

Southwestern College, Fifth-Year Graduate Programs, Winfield, KS 67156-2499. Offers leadership (MS); management (MBA); music (MA), including education, performance. Part-time programs available. *Faculty:* 9 full-time (1 woman), 8 part-time/adjunct (2 women). *Students:* 9 full-time (3 women), 8 part-time (3 women), 6 international. Average age 25. 10 applicants, 90% accepted, 9 enrolled. In 2010, 26 master's awarded. *Entrance requirements:* For master's, baccalaureate degree, minimum GPA of 3.0. Additional exam requirements/recommendations for international students: Required—TOEFL (minimum score 550 paper-based; 213 computer-based). *Application deadline:* For fall admission, 4/1 priority date for domestic students; for spring admission, 12/1 priority date for domestic students. Applications are processed on a rolling basis. Electronic applications accepted. *Expenses:* Tuition: Full-time $7470; part-time $415 per credit hour. Tuition and fees vary according to program. *Financial support:* In 2010–11, 6 students received support. Federal Work-Study, tuition waivers (partial), and unspecified assistantships available. Financial award application deadline: 4/1; financial award applicants required to submit FAFSA. *Unit head:* Dr. James Sheppard, Vice President for Academic Affairs, 620-229-6227, Fax: 620-229-6224, E-mail: james.sheppard@sckans. edu. *Application contact:* Marla Sexson, Director of Admissions, 800-846-1543 Ext. 6364, Fax: 620-229-6344, E-mail: marla.sexson@sckans.edu.

Spring Arbor University, School of Graduate and Professional Studies, Spring Arbor, MI 49283-9799. Offers counseling (MAC); family studies (MAFS); nursing (MSN); organizational management (MAOM). Part-time and evening/weekend programs available. Postbaccalaureate distance learning degree programs offered (no on-campus study). *Faculty:* 16 full-time (7 women), 100 part-time/adjunct (56 women). *Students:* 407 full-time (324 women), 357 part-time (293 women); includes 171 Black or African American, non-Hispanic/Latino; 3 American Indian or Alaska Native, non-Hispanic/Latino; 9 Asian, non-Hispanic/Latino; 19 Hispanic/Latino, 2 international. Average age 39. In 2010, 279 master's awarded. *Entrance requirements:* For master's, bachelor's degree from regionally-accredited college or university, minimum GPA of 3.0 for at least the last two years of the bachelor's degree, at least two recommendations from professional/academic individuals. Additional exam requirements/recommendations for international students: Required—TOEFL (minimum score 600 paper-based; 220 computer-based). *Application deadline:* Applications are processed on a rolling basis. Application fee: $40. Electronic applications accepted. *Expenses:* Tuition: Full-time $6300; part-time $525 per credit hour. Required fees: $240; $120 per semester. Tuition and fees vary according to course load and program. *Financial support:* Scholarships/grants available. Support available to part-time students. Financial award applicants required to submit FAFSA. *Unit head:* Natalie Gianetti, Dean, 517-750-1200 Ext. 1343, Fax: 517-750-6602, E-mail: gianetti@arbor.edu. *Application contact:* Greg Bentle, Coordinator of Graduate Recruitment, 517-750-6763, Fax: 517-750-6624, E-mail: gbentle@arbor.edu.

State University of New York College at Potsdam, School of Education and Professional Studies, Program in Information and Communication Technology, Potsdam, NY 13676. Offers educational technology specialist (MS Ed); organizational performance, leadership and technology (MS Ed). Part-time and evening/weekend programs available. Postbaccalaureate distance learning degree programs offered. *Faculty:* 4 full-time (1 woman), 2 part-time/adjunct (1 woman). *Students:* 27 full-time (12 women), 49 part-time (35 women); includes 5 minority (4 Black or African American, non-Hispanic/Latino; 1 American Indian or Alaska Native, non-Hispanic/Latino), 9 international. 34 applicants, 97% accepted, 31 enrolled. In 2010, 23 master's awarded. *Degree requirements:* For master's, thesis optional, culminating experience. *Entrance requirements:* For master's, minimum GPA of 3.0 in last 60 hours of course work. Additional exam requirements/recommendations for international students: Required—TOEFL (minimum score 550 paper-based; 213 computer-based; 80 iBT), IELTS (minimum score 6). *Application deadline:* For fall admission, 4/1 for domestic and international students; for winter admission, 10/15 for domestic and international students; for spring admission, 3/1 for domestic and international students. Applications are processed on a rolling basis. Application fee: $50. *Financial support:* Fellowships, teaching assistantships, career-related internships or fieldwork, Federal Work-Study, scholarships/grants, and unspecified assistantships available. Support available to part-time students. Financial award application deadline: 3/1; financial award applicants required to submit FAFSA. *Unit head:* Dr. Timothy V. Fossum, Chairperson, 315-267-2056, Fax: 315-267-3207, E-mail: fossumtv@potsdam. edu. *Application contact:* Peter Cutler, Graduate Admissions Counselor, 315-267-3154, Fax: 315-267-4802, E-mail: cutlerpj@potsdam.edu.

Suffolk University, College of Arts and Sciences, Department of Education and Human Services, Boston, MA 02108-2770. Offers administration of higher education (M Ed, CAGS), including administration of higher education (M Ed), leadership (CAGS); human resource, learning and performance (MS, CAGS, Graduate Certificate), including global human resources (Graduate Certificate), human resources (MS, Graduate Certificate), organizational development (CAGS, Graduate Certificate), organizational learning and development (MS, Graduate Certificate); mental health counseling (MS, CAGS); school counseling (M Ed, CAGS); school teaching (M Ed, CAGS), including foundations of education (M Ed), middle school teaching (M Ed), secondary school teaching (M Ed); MPA/MSMHC; MS/Certificate. Part-time and evening/weekend programs available. *Faculty:* 8 full-time (4 women), 9 part-time/adjunct (3 women). *Students:* 62 full-time (49 women), 126 part-time (94 women); includes 6 Black or African American, non-Hispanic/Latino; 1 American Indian or Alaska Native, non-Hispanic/Latino; 3 Asian, non-Hispanic/Latino; 5 Hispanic/Latino, 7 international. Average age 28. 170 applicants, 78% accepted, 61 enrolled. In 2010, 80 master's, 2 other advanced degrees awarded. *Entrance requirements:* For master's, GRE General Test or MAT, 2 letters of recommendation, resume. Additional exam requirements/recommendations for international students: Required—TOEFL (minimum score 550 paper-based; 213 computer-based; 80 iBT). *Application deadline:* For fall admission, 6/15 priority date for domestic students, 6/15 for international students; for spring admission, 11/1 priority date for domestic students, 11/1 for international students. Applications are processed on a rolling basis. Application fee: $50. Electronic applications accepted. *Expenses:* Contact institution. *Financial support:* In 2010–11, 110 students received support, including 34 fellowships with full and partial tuition reimbursements available (averaging $10,596 per year); career-related internships or fieldwork, Federal Work-Study, and institutionally sponsored loans also available. Support available to part-time students. Financial award application deadline: 4/1; financial award applicants required to submit FAFSA. *Faculty research:* Predicting competent Head Start preschools, cultural differences. *Unit head:* Dr. Donna Qualters, Interim Chair & Director, 617-573-8264 Ext. 8261, Fax: 617-305-1743, E-mail: dqualters@suffolk.edu. *Application contact:* Judith Reynolds, Director of Graduate Admissions, 617-573-8302, Fax: 617-305-1733, E-mail: grad.admission@suffolk.edu.

Syracuse University, Maxwell School of Citizenship and Public Affairs, Program in Leadership of International and Non-governmental Organizations, Syracuse, NY 13244. Offers CAS. Part-time programs available. *Students:* 1 (woman) part-time, all international. Average age 29. 6 applicants, 100% accepted, 1 enrolled. In 2010, 6 CASs awarded. *Degree requirements:* For CAS, seminar. *Entrance requirements:* Additional exam requirements/recommendations for international students: Required—TOEFL (minimum score 100 iBT). *Application deadline:* For fall admission, 2/1 for domestic and international students. Application fee: $75. Electronic applications accepted. *Expenses:* Tuition: Part-time $1162 per credit. *Unit head:* Michael Wasylenko, Interim Dean, 315-443-2253, Fax: 315-443-3385. *Application contact:* Michael Wasylenko, Interim Dean, 315-443-2253, Fax: 315-443-3385.

Teachers College, Columbia University, Graduate Faculty of Education, Department of Organization and Leadership, Program in Social and Organizational Psychology, New York, NY 10027-6696. Offers change leadership (MA); social-organizational psychology (MA). *Faculty:* 8 full-time (5 women), 22 part-time/adjunct (10 women). *Students:* 122 full-time (71 women), 113 part-time (85 women); includes 59 minority (11 Black or African American, non-Hispanic/Latino; 20 Asian, non-Hispanic/Latino; 23 Hispanic/Latino; 1 Native Hawaiian or other Pacific Islander, non-Hispanic/Latino; 4 Two or more races, non-Hispanic/Latino), 40 international. Average age 28. 202 applicants, 62% accepted, 69 enrolled. In 2010, 111 master's awarded. Terminal master's awarded for partial completion of doctoral program. *Degree requirements:* For master's, comprehensive exam. *Entrance requirements:* For master's, GRE, MAT, or GMAT, minimum GPA of 3.0. *Application deadline:* For fall admission, 1/15 priority date for domestic students. Application fee: $65. Electronic applications accepted. *Expenses:* Tuition: Full-time $28,272; part-time $1178 per credit. Required fees: $756; $378 per semester. *Financial support:* Fellowships, research assistantships, career-related internships or fieldwork, Federal Work-Study, institutionally sponsored loans, and tuition waivers (full and partial) available. Support available to part-time students. Financial award application deadline: 2/1. *Faculty research:* Conflict resolution, human resource and organization development, management competence, organizational culture, leadership. *Unit head:* Dr. W. Warner Burke, Director of the Graduate Programs in Social-Organizational Psychology, 212-678-3831, E-mail: wwb3@columbia.edu. *Application contact:* Lynda Hallmark, Program Manager of the Social-Organizational Psychology Program, 212-678-3273, Fax: 212-678-3273, E-mail: hallmark@tc.edu.

Thomas Edison State College, School of Business and Management, Program in Organizational Leadership, Trenton, NJ 08608-1176. Offers Graduate Certificate. Part-time programs available. Postbaccalaureate distance learning degree programs offered (no on-campus study). *Students:* 41 part-time (20 women); includes 8 Black or African American, non-Hispanic/Latino; 1 Asian, non-Hispanic/Latino, 2 international. Average age 42. In 2010, 6 Graduate Certificates awarded. *Entrance requirements:* Additional exam requirements/recommendations for international students: Required—TOEFL (minimum score 550 paper-based; 213 computer-based; 79 iBT). *Application deadline:*

For fall admission, 8/15 priority date for domestic and international students; for winter admission, 11/15 priority date for domestic and international students; for spring admission, 2/15 priority date for domestic and international students. Applications are processed on a rolling basis. Application fee: $75. Electronic applications accepted. *Financial support:* Applicants required to submit FAFSA. *Unit head:* Dr. Susan Gilbert, Dean, School of Business and Management, 609-984-1130, Fax: 609-984-3898, E-mail: info@tesc.edu. *Application contact:* David Hoftiezer, Director of Admissions, 888-442-8372, Fax: 609-984-8447, E-mail: admissions@tesc.edu.

Trevecca Nazarene University, Graduate Division, Graduate Business Programs, Major in Management, Nashville, TN 37210-2877. Offers MSM. Evening/weekend programs available. *Students:* 69 full-time (31 women), 2 part-time (both women); includes 22 minority (19 Black or African American, non-Hispanic/Latino; 1 American Indian or Alaska Native, non-Hispanic/Latino; 1 Native Hawaiian or other Pacific Islander, non-Hispanic/Latino; 1 Two or more races, non-Hispanic/Latino). In 2010, 16 master's awarded. *Entrance requirements:* For master's, GMAT, proficiency exam (quantitative skills), minimum GPA of 2.5, resume, 2 letters of recommendation, employer letter of recommendation, written business analysis. Additional exam requirements/recommendations for international students: Required—TOEFL (minimum score 550 paper-based; 213 computer-based). *Application deadline:* Applications are processed on a rolling basis. Application fee: $25. *Expenses:* Contact institution. *Financial support:* Applicants required to submit FAFSA. *Unit head:* Dr. Jon Burch, Director of Graduate Management Program, 615-248-1529, E-mail: management@trevecca.edu. *Application contact:* College of Lifelong Learning, 615-248-1200, E-mail: cll@trevecca.edu.

Trevecca Nazarene University, Graduate Division, Graduate Organizational Leadership Program, Nashville, TN 37210-2877. Offers MOL. Postbaccalaureate distance learning degree programs offered (no on-campus study). *Faculty:* 1 (woman) full-time. *Students:* 17 full-time (7 women); includes 3 Black or African American, non-Hispanic/Latino. *Degree requirements:* For master's, capstone course. *Entrance requirements:* For master's, resume, writing sample (selected topics), minimum undergraduate GPA of 2.5. Additional exam requirements/recommendations for international students: Required—TOEFL (minimum score 550 paper-based; 213 computer-based). *Financial support:* Applicants required to submit FAFSA. *Unit head:* Dr. David Phillips, Dean, College of Lifelong Learning, 615-248-1200, E-mail: cll@trevecca.edu. *Application contact:* Glenda Bolling, College of Lifelong Learning, 615-248-1200, E-mail: cll@trevecca.edu.

Troy University, Graduate School, College of Business, Program in Management, Troy, AL 36082. Offers applied management (MSM); healthcare management (MSM); human resources management (MSM); information systems (MSM); international hospitality management (MSM); international management (MSM); leadership and organizational effectiveness (MSM); public management (MS, MSM). *Accreditation:* ACBSP. Evening/weekend programs available. *Students:* 101 full-time (62 women), 398 part-time (249 women); includes 308 minority (278 Black or African American, non-Hispanic/Latino; 8 American Indian or Alaska Native, non-Hispanic/Latino; 8 Asian, non-Hispanic/Latino; 13 Hispanic/Latino; 1 Two or more races, non-Hispanic/Latino). Average age 35. 218 applicants, 80% accepted. In 2010, 314 master's awarded. *Degree requirements:* For master's, Graduate Educational Testing Service Major Field Test, capstone exam, minimum GPA of 3.0. *Entrance requirements:* For master's, GMAT (minimum score 500) or GRE General Test (minimum score 900), minimum GPA of 2.5, bachelor's degree, letter of recommendation. Additional exam requirements/recommendations for international students: Required—TOEFL (minimum score 523 paper-based; 193 computer-based; 70 iBT), IELTS, or ACT compass ESL (minimum Listening, Reading, and Grammar score: 270). *Application deadline:* Applications are processed on a rolling basis. Application fee: $50. Electronic applications accepted. *Expenses:* Contact institution. *Unit head:* Dr. Henry M. Findley, Interim Chair/Professor, 334-670-3271, Fax: 334-670-3599, E-mail: hfindley@troy.edu. *Application contact:* Brenda K. Campbell, Director of Graduate Admissions, 334-670-3178, Fax: 334-670-3733, E-mail: bcamp@troy.edu.

United States International University, School of Business Administration, Nairobi, Kenya. Offers business administration (GEMBA); entrepreneurship (MBA); finance (MBA); human resource management (MBA); information technology management (MBA); integrated studies (MBA); international business administration (MBA); management and organizational development (MS); marketing (MBA); organizational development (EMS); strategic management (MBA). Part-time and evening/weekend programs available. *Faculty:* 42 full-time (8 women), 64 part-time/adjunct (14 women). *Students:* 423 full-time (227 women), 129 part-time (63 women). Average age 29. 110 applicants, 79% accepted, 78 enrolled. In 2010, 164 master's awarded. *Degree requirements:* For master's, thesis. *Entrance requirements:* For master's, GMAT, 2 letters of reference, resume. Additional exam requirements/recommendations for international students: Required—TOEFL (minimum score 550 paper-based; 213 computer-based). *Application deadline:* For fall admission, 6/30 priority date for domestic and international students; for spring admission, 9/30 for domestic and international students. Applications are processed on a rolling basis. Application fee: $50. *Financial support:* In 2010–11, 30 students received support, including 8 research assistantships (averaging $1,400 per year), 4 teaching assistantships (averaging $1,400 per year); career-related internships

or fieldwork, scholarships/grants, and unspecified assistantships also available. Support available to part-time students. Financial award application deadline: 6/30; financial award applicants required to submit FAFSA. *Faculty research:* Marketing in small business enterprises, total quality management in Kenya. *Unit head:* Dr. Damary Sikalieh, Dean, 254-02-3606-415, E-mail: dsikalieh@usiu.ac.ke. *Application contact:* George Lumbasi, Director of Admissions, 254-02-3606563, Fax: 254-02-3606100, E-mail: glumbasi@usiu.ac.ke.

University of Colorado Boulder, Leeds School of Business, Division of Business Administration, Boulder, CO 80309. Offers accounting (MS, PhD); finance (PhD); information systems (PhD); marketing (PhD); operations (PhD); strategic, organizational, and entrepreneurial studies (PhD). Part-time and evening/weekend programs available. *Students:* 110 full-time (42 women), 2 part-time (1 woman); includes 6 minority (5 Asian, non-Hispanic/Latino; 1 Hispanic/Latino), 24 international. Average age 28. 342 applicants, 24 enrolled. In 2010, 48 master's, 12 doctorates awarded. *Entrance requirements:* For master's, GMAT, minimum undergraduate GPA of 3.0. *Application deadline:* For fall admission, 3/31 for domestic and international students; for spring admission, 10/31 for domestic and international students. Application fee: $50 ($60 for international students). Electronic applications accepted. *Financial support:* In 2010–11, 16 fellowships (averaging $1,038 per year), 26 research assistantships (averaging $17,558 per year), 11 teaching assistantships (averaging $12,576 per year) were awarded; career-related internships or fieldwork, Federal Work-Study, scholarships/grants, and unspecified assistantships also available. Financial award applicants required to submit FAFSA.

University of Denver, University College, Denver, CO 80208. Offers arts and culture (MLS, Certificate), including art, literature, and culture, arts development and program management (Certificate), creative writing; environmental policy and management (MAS, Certificate), including energy and sustainability (Certificate), environmental assessment of nuclear power (Certificate), environmental health and safety (Certificate), environmental management, natural resource management (Certificate); geographic information systems (MAS, Certificate); global affairs (MLS, Certificate), including translation studies, world history and culture; healthcare leadership (MPH, Certificate), including healthcare policy, law, and ethics, medical and healthcare information technologies, strategic management of healthcare; information and communications technology (MCIS, Certificate), including database design and administration (Certificate), geographic information systems (MCIS), information security systems security (Certificate), information systems security (MCIS), project management (MCIS, MPS, Certificate), software design and administration (Certificate), software design and programming (MCIS), technology management, telecommunications technology (MCIS), Web design and development; leadership and organizations (MPS, Certificate), including human capital in organizations, philanthropic leadership, project management (MCIS, MPS, Certificate), strategic innovation and change; organizational and professional communication (MPS, Certificate), including alternative dispute resolution, organizational communication, organizational development and training, public relations and marketing; security management (MAS, Certificate), including emergency planning and response, information security (MAS), organizational security; strategic human resource management (MPS, Certificate), including global human resources (MPS), human resource management and development (MPS). Part-time and evening/weekend programs available. Postbaccalaureate distance learning degree programs offered (no on-campus study). *Faculty:* 7 full-time (2 women), 212 part-time/adjunct (83 women). *Students:* 52 full-time (19 women), 1,044 part-time (625 women); includes 196 minority (81 Black or African American, non-Hispanic/Latino; 7 American Indian or Alaska Native, non-Hispanic/Latino; 30 Asian, non-Hispanic/Latino; 66 Hispanic/Latino; 3 Native Hawaiian or other Pacific Islander, non-Hispanic/Latino; 9 Two or more races, non-Hispanic/Latino), 76 international. Average age 36. 488 applicants, 91% accepted, 339 enrolled. In 2010, 286 master's, 130 other advanced degrees awarded. *Entrance requirements:* Additional exam requirements/recommendations for international students: Required—TOEFL (minimum score 550 paper-based; 80 iBT). *Application deadline:* For fall admission, 6/22 priority date for domestic students, 6/10 priority date for international students; for winter admission, 9/15 priority date for domestic students, 9/6 priority date for international students; for spring admission, 2/3 priority date for domestic students, 12/15 priority date for international students. Applications are processed on a rolling basis. Application fee: $75. Electronic applications accepted. *Expenses:* Contact institution. *Financial support:* Applicants required to submit FAFSA. *Unit head:* Dr. James Davis, Dean, 303-871-2291, Fax: 303-871-4047, E-mail: jdavis@du.edu. *Application contact:* Information Contact, 303-871-3155, Fax: 303-871-4047, E-mail: ucolinfo@du.edu.

The University of Findlay, Graduate and Professional Studies, College of Business, Findlay, OH 45840-3653. Offers health care management (MBA); hospitality management (MBA); organizational leadership (MBA); public management (MBA). Part-time and evening/weekend programs available. Postbaccalaureate distance learning degree programs offered (no on-campus study). *Faculty:* 20 full-time (5 women), 6 part-time/adjunct (0 women). *Students:* 25 full-time (11 women), 239 part-time (112 women); includes 15 minority (5 Black or African American, non-Hispanic/Latino; 9 Asian, non-Hispanic/Latino; 1 Hispanic/Latino), 98 international. Average age 25. 93 applicants, 86% accepted, 70 enrolled. In 2010, 283 master's awarded. *Degree* *requirements:* For master's, thesis, cumulative project. *Entrance requirements:* For master's, GMAT or GRE, minimum undergraduate GPA of 3.0. Additional exam requirements/recommendations for international students: Required—TOEFL (minimum score 550 paper-based; 213 computer-based; 80 iBT). *Application deadline:* Applications are processed on a rolling basis. Application fee: $25. Electronic applications accepted. *Expenses:* Contact institution. *Financial support:* In 2010–11, 8 research assistantships with full and partial tuition reimbursements (averaging $4,200 per year) were awarded; career-related internships or fieldwork, Federal Work-Study, health care benefits, and unspecified assistantships also available. Financial award application deadline: 4/1; financial award applicants required to submit FAFSA. *Faculty research:* Health care management, operations and logistics management. *Unit head:* Dr. Paul Sears, Dean, College of Business, 419-434-4704, Fax: 419-434-4822. *Application contact:* Heather Riffle, Assistant Director, Graduate and Professional Studies, 419-434-4640, Fax: 419-434-5517, E-mail: riffle@findlay.edu.

University of Hawaii at Manoa, Graduate Division, Shidler College of Business, Program in Business Administration, Honolulu, HI 96822. Offers Asian business studies (MBA); Chinese business studies (MBA); decision sciences (MBA); entrepreneurship (MBA); finance (MBA); finance and banking (MBA); human resources management (MBA); information management (MBA); information technology (MBA); international business (MBA); Japanese business studies (MBA); marketing (MBA); organizational behavior (MBA); organizational management (MBA); real estate (MBA); student-designed track (MBA). *Accreditation:* AACSB. Part-time and evening/weekend programs available. *Faculty:* 53 full-time (12 women). *Students:* 162 full-time (63 women), 102 part-time (43 women); includes 135 minority (1 Black or African American, non-Hispanic/Latino; 81 Asian, non-Hispanic/Latino; 5 Hispanic/Latino; 18 Native Hawaiian or other Pacific Islander, non-Hispanic/Latino; 30 Two or more races, non-Hispanic/Latino), 44 international. Average age 34. 361 applicants, 57% accepted, 172 enrolled. In 2010, 153 master's awarded. *Degree requirements:* For master's, thesis optional. *Entrance requirements:* For master's, GMAT, minimum GPA of 3.0. Additional exam requirements/recommendations for international students: Required—TOEFL (minimum score 600 paper-based; 250 computer-based; 100 iBT), IELTS (minimum score 7). *Application deadline:* For fall admission, 5/1 for domestic students, 3/1 for international students. Application fee: $60. *Expenses:* Contact institution. *Financial support:* In 2010–11, 83 fellowships (averaging $5,547 per year), 1 research assistantship (averaging $16,824 per year) were awarded. Total annual research expenditures: $427,000. *Application contact:* Daniel Port, Graduate Chair, 808-956-5565, Fax: 808-956-6889, E-mail: daniel.port@hawaii.edu.

University of Hawaii at Manoa, Graduate Division, Shidler College of Business, Program in International Management, Honolulu, HI 96822. Offers Asian finance (PhD); global information technology management (PhD); international accounting (PhD); international marketing (PhD); international organization and strategy (PhD). Part-time programs available. *Students:* 30 full-time (11 women), 3 part-time (0 women); includes 7 minority (5 Asian, non-Hispanic/Latino; 2 Two or more races, non-Hispanic/Latino), 18 international. Average age 36. 65 applicants, 18% accepted, 5 enrolled. In 2010, 4 doctorates awarded. *Degree requirements:* For doctorate, comprehensive exam, thesis/dissertation. *Entrance requirements:* For doctorate, GMAT or GRE General Test, minimum GPA of 3.0. Additional exam requirements/recommendations for international students: Required—TOEFL (minimum score 600 paper-based; 250 computer-based; 100 iBT), IELTS (minimum score 7). *Application deadline:* For fall admission, 3/1 for domestic and international students. Application fee: $60. *Expenses:* Contact institution. *Financial support:* In 2010–11, 29 students received support, including 3 fellowships (averaging $5,491 per year), 25 research assistantships (averaging $17,750 per year), 1 teaching assistantship (averaging $15,558 per year). *Application contact:* Erica Okada, Graduate Chair, 808-956-6723, Fax: 808-956-6889, E-mail: imphd@hawaii.edu.

The University of Kansas, University of Kansas Medical Center, School of Nursing, Kansas City, KS 66160. Offers clinical research management (PMC); family nurse practitioner (PMC); health care informatics (PMC); health professions educator (PMC); nurse midwife (PMC); nursing (MS, DNP, PhD); organizational leadership (PMC); psychiatric/mental health nurse practitioner (PMC); public health nursing (PMC). *Accreditation:* AACN; ACNM/DOA. Part-time programs available. Postbaccalaureate distance learning degree programs offered (minimal on-campus study). *Faculty:* 77. *Students:* 54 full-time (51 women), 307 part-time (283 women); includes 49 minority (22 Black or African American, non-Hispanic/Latino; 3 American Indian or Alaska Native, non-Hispanic/Latino; 9 Asian, non-Hispanic/Latino; 11 Hispanic/Latino; 4 Two or more races, non-Hispanic/Latino), 6 international. Average age 38. 142 applicants, 45% accepted, 62 enrolled. In 2010, 78 master's, 7 doctorates, 17 other advanced degrees awarded. Terminal master's awarded for partial completion of doctoral program. *Degree requirements:* For master's, thesis optional, general oral exam; for doctorate, one foreign language, thesis/dissertation, comprehensive oral and written exam. *Entrance requirements:* For master's, bachelor's degree in nursing, minimum GPA of 3.0, RN license, 1 year of clinical experience; for doctorate, GRE General Test, master's degree in nursing, minimum GPA of 3.5. Additional exam requirements/recommendations for international

students: Required—TOEFL. *Application deadline:* For fall admission, 4/1 for domestic and international students; for spring admission, 9/1 for domestic and international students. Application fee: $60. Electronic applications accepted. *Expenses:* Tuition, state resident: full-time $7092; part-time $295.50 per credit hour. Tuition, nonresident: full-time $16,590; part-time $691.25 per credit hour. Required fees: $858; $71.49 per credit hour. Tuition and fees vary according to course load, campus/location and program. *Financial support:* Research assistantships with full and partial tuition reimbursements, teaching assistantships with full and partial tuition reimbursements, traineeships available. Financial award application deadline: 2/14; financial award applicants required to submit FAFSA. *Faculty research:* Breastfeeding practices of teen mothers, national database of nursing quality indicators, caregiving of families of patients using technology in the home, self care talk intervention partnership between caregivers of stroke survivors and nurses, smoking cessation. Total annual research expenditures: $5.4 million. *Unit head:* Dr. Karen L. Miller, Dean, 913-588-1601, Fax: 913-588-1660, E-mail: kmiller@kumc.edu. *Application contact:* Dr. Rita K. Clifford, Associate Dean, Student Affairs, 913-588-1619, Fax: 913-588-1615, E-mail: rcliffor@kumc.edu.

University of La Verne, College of Business and Public Management, Program in Organizational Management and Leadership, La Verne, CA 91750-4443. Offers nonprofit management (Certificate); organizational leadership (Certificate); organizational management and leadership (MS). Part-time programs available. *Faculty:* 34 full-time (12 women), 36 part-time/adjunct (9 women). *Students:* 92 full-time (44 women), 70 part-time (46 women); includes 9 Black or African American, non-Hispanic/Latino; 31 Asian, non-Hispanic/Latino; 35 Hispanic/Latino. Average age 32. In 2010, 58 master's awarded. *Degree requirements:* For master's, thesis or research project. *Entrance requirements:* For master's, minimum undergraduate GPA of 2.75, 2 letters of recommendation, interview, resume. Additional exam requirements/recommendations for international students: Required—TOEFL (minimum score 550 paper-based; 213 computer-based). *Application deadline:* Applications are processed on a rolling basis. Application fee: $50. *Expenses:* Contact institution. *Financial support:* Institutionally sponsored loans available. Financial award application deadline: 3/2; financial award applicants required to submit FAFSA. *Unit head:* Dr. Kathy Duncan, Chairperson, 909-593-3511 Ext. 4415, E-mail: kduncan2@laverne.edu. *Application contact:* Program and Admissions Specialist, 909-593-3511 Ext. 4819, Fax: 909-392-2761, E-mail: cbpm@laverne.edu.

University of La Verne, Regional Campus Administration, Graduate Programs, Central Coast/Vandenberg Air Force Base Campuses, La Verne, CA 91750-4443. Offers business (MBA-EP), including health services management, information technology; health administration (MHA); leadership and management (MS). *Faculty:* 12 part-time/adjunct (7 women). *Students:* 26 full-time (13 women), 33 part-time (16 women); includes 18 minority (6 Black or African American, non-Hispanic/Latino; 2 American Indian or Alaska Native, non-Hispanic/Latino; 2 Asian, non-Hispanic/Latino; 8 Hispanic/Latino). Average age 36. In 2010, 4 master's awarded. *Entrance requirements:* For master's, 2 letters of recommendation, resume. *Application deadline:* Applications are processed on a rolling basis. Application fee: $50. *Expenses:* Contact institution. *Financial support:* Institutionally sponsored loans available. Financial award application deadline: 3/2; financial award applicants required to submit FAFSA. *Unit head:* Kitt Vincent, Director, Central Coast Campus, 805-542-9690 Ext. 6043, Fax: 805-542-9735, E-mail: kvincent@laverne.edu. *Application contact:* Kitt Vincent, Director, Central Coast Campus, 805-542-9690 Ext. 6043, Fax: 805-542-9735, E-mail: kvincent@laverne.edu.

University of La Verne, Regional Campus Administration, Graduate Programs, Inland Empire Campus, Rancho Cucamonga, CA 91730. Offers business (MBA-EP), including health services management, information technology, management, marketing; leadership and management (MS). *Faculty:* 3 full-time (2 women), 22 part-time/adjunct (9 women). *Students:* 27 full-time (17 women), 100 part-time (68 women); includes 14 Black or African American, non-Hispanic/Latino; 1 American Indian or Alaska Native, non-Hispanic/Latino; 22 Asian, non-Hispanic/Latino; 36 Hispanic/Latino. Average age 39. In 2010, 20 master's awarded. *Entrance requirements:* For master's, 2 letters of recommendation, resume. *Application deadline:* Applications are processed on a rolling basis. Application fee: $50. *Expenses:* Contact institution. *Financial support:* Institutionally sponsored loans available. Financial award application deadline: 3/2; financial award applicants required to submit FAFSA. *Unit head:* Allan Stout, Director, 909-484-3858 Ext. 6002, Fax: 909-484-9469, E-mail: astout@laverne.edu. *Application contact:* Allan Stout, Director, 909-484-3858 Ext. 6002, Fax: 909-484-9469, E-mail: astout@laverne.edu.

University of La Verne, Regional Campus Administration, Graduate Programs, Kern County Campus, Bakersfield, CA 93301. Offers business (MBA-EP); health administration (MHA); leadership and management (MS). *Faculty:* 16 part-time/adjunct (7 women). *Students:* 8 full-time (5 women), 7 part-time (2 women); includes 8 minority (1 Black or African American, non-Hispanic/Latino; 3 Asian, non-Hispanic/Latino; 4 Hispanic/Latino). Average age 35. In 2010, 2 master's awarded. *Entrance requirements:* For master's, 2 letters of recommendation, resume. *Application deadline:* Applications are processed on a rolling basis. Application fee: $50. *Expenses:* Contact institution. *Financial support:* Institutionally sponsored loans available. Financial award application deadline: 3/2; financial award applicants required to submit FAFSA. *Unit* *head:* Nora Dominguez, Interim Director, 661-328-1430 Ext. 6024, E-mail: ndominguez@laverne.edu. *Application contact:* Nora Dominguez, Interim Director, 661-328-1430 Ext. 6024, E-mail: ndominguez@laverne.edu.

University of Massachusetts Dartmouth, Graduate School, Charlton College of Business, Program in Business Administration, North Dartmouth, MA 02747-2300. Offers accounting (Postbaccalaureate Certificate); business administration (MBA); e-commerce (PMC); finance (PMC); general management (PMC); leadership (PMC); management (Postbaccalaureate Certificate); marketing (PMC); supply chain management (PMC). *Accreditation:* AACSB. Part-time programs available. *Faculty:* 40 full-time (13 women), 28 part-time/adjunct (8 women). *Students:* 99 full-time (38 women), 123 part-time (62 women); includes 4 Black or African American, non-Hispanic/Latino; 2 American Indian or Alaska Native, non-Hispanic/Latino; 3 Asian, non-Hispanic/Latino; 8 Hispanic/Latino; 1 Two or more races, non-Hispanic/Latino, 45 international. Average age 30. 185 applicants, 76% accepted, 79 enrolled. In 2010, 79 master's, 12 other advanced degrees awarded. *Entrance requirements:* For master's, GMAT, resume, letters of recommendation. Additional exam requirements/recommendations for international students: Required—TOEFL (minimum score 500 paper-based; 200 computer-based; 72 iBT). *Application deadline:* For fall admission, 6/1 for domestic students, 5/1 for international students; for spring admission, 10/1 for domestic students, 8/1 for international students. Application fee: $40 ($60 for international students). Electronic applications accepted. *Expenses:* Tuition, state resident: full-time $2071; part-time $86 per credit. Tuition, nonresident: full-time $8099; part-time $337 per credit. Required fees: $9446; $394 per credit. One-time fee: $75. Part-time tuition and fees vary according to class time, course load, degree level and reciprocity agreements. *Financial support:* In 2010–11, 1 research assistantship with full tuition reimbursement (averaging $6,000 per year) was awarded; teaching assistantships, Federal Work-Study and unspecified assistantships also available. Support available to part-time students. Financial award application deadline: 3/1; financial award applicants required to submit FAFSA. *Faculty research:* Global business environment, e-commerce, managing diversity, agile manufacturing, green business. Total annual research expenditures: $29,538. *Unit head:* Dr. Norm Barber, Assistant Dean, 508-999-8543, E-mail: nbarber@umassd. edu. *Application contact:* Elan Turcotte-Shamski, Graduate Admissions Officer, 508-999-8604, Fax: 508-999-8183, E-mail: graduate@umassd.edu.

University of New Haven, Graduate School, College of Arts and Sciences, Program in Industrial and Organizational Psychology, West Haven, CT 06516-1916. Offers conflict management (MA); human resource management (MA); industrial organizational psychology (MA); organizational development (MA); psychology of conflict management (Certificate). Part-time and evening/weekend programs available. *Students:* 75 full-time (54 women), 29 part-time (19 women); includes 7 Black or African American, non-Hispanic/Latino; 1 American Indian or Alaska Native, non-Hispanic/Latino; 1 Asian, non-Hispanic/Latino; 4 Hispanic/Latino, 13 international. Average age 28. 70 applicants, 100% accepted, 33 enrolled. In 2010, 44 master's, 1 other advanced degree awarded. *Degree requirements:* For master's, thesis or alternative. *Entrance requirements:* Additional exam requirements/recommendations for international students: Required—TOEFL (minimum score 520 paper-based; 190 computer-based; 70 iBT); Recommended—IELTS (minimum score 5.5). *Application deadline:* For fall admission, 5/31 for international students; for winter admission, 10/15 for international students; for spring admission, 1/15 for international students. Applications are processed on a rolling basis. Application fee: $50. Electronic applications accepted. *Expenses:* Contact institution. *Financial support:* Research assistantships with partial tuition reimbursements, teaching assistantships with partial tuition reimbursements, career-related internships or fieldwork, Federal Work-Study, scholarships/grants, tuition waivers, and unspecified assistantships available. Support available to part-time students. Financial award applicants required to submit FAFSA. *Unit head:* Dr. Stuart D. Sidle, Coordinator, 203-932-7341. *Application contact:* Eloise Gormley, Information Contact, 203-932-7449.

University of Pennsylvania, School of Arts and Sciences, Graduate Group in Organizational Dynamics, Philadelphia, PA 19104. Offers MS. Part-time and evening/weekend programs available. *Students:* 46 full-time (24 women), 155 part-time (86 women); includes 17 Black or African American, non-Hispanic/Latino; 8 Asian, non-Hispanic/Latino, 10 international. 71 applicants, 83% accepted, 48 enrolled. In 2010, 34 master's awarded. *Degree requirements:* For master's, thesis. *Application deadline:* For fall admission, 12/1 priority date for domestic students. Application fee: $70. Electronic applications accepted. *Expenses:* Tuition: Full-time $25,660; part-time $4758 per course. Required fees: $2152; $270 per course. Tuition and fees vary according to course load, degree level and program. *Financial support:* Scholarships/grants available. Support available to part-time students. Financial award application deadline: 12/15. *Unit head:* Director. *Application contact:* Director.

University of Phoenix, School of Advanced Studies, Phoenix, AZ 85034-7209. Offers business administration (DBA); education (Ed D); educational leadership (Ed D), including curriculum and instruction, educational technology; health administration (DHA); higher education administration (PhD); industrial organizational psychology (PhD); nursing (PhD); organizational leadership and technology (DM), including information systems and technology, organizational leadership. Evening/weekend programs available. Postbaccalaureate distance learning degree programs offered. *Students:* 6,882 full-time (4,598

women); includes 2,871 minority (2,251 Black or African American, non-Hispanic/Latino; 50 American Indian or Alaska Native, non-Hispanic/Latino; 133 Asian, non-Hispanic/Latino; 378 Hispanic/Latino; 46 Native Hawaiian or other Pacific Islander, non-Hispanic/Latino; 13 Two or more races, non-Hispanic/Latino), 375 international. Average age 46. *Degree requirements:* For doctorate, thesis/dissertation. *Entrance requirements:* For doctorate, master's degree from accredited university, minimum master's GPA of 3.0, 3 years' professional work experience, laptop computer, membership in research library. Additional exam requirements/recommendations for international students: Required—TOEFL (minimum paper score 550, computer score 213, iBT 79), Test of English for International Communication, or IELTS. *Application deadline:* Applications are processed on a rolling basis. Application fee: $45. Electronic applications accepted. *Expenses:* Contact institution. *Financial support:* Scholarships/grants available. Financial award applicants required to submit FAFSA. *Unit head:* Dr. Jeremy Moreland, Dean/Executive Director, 480-557-3231, E-mail: jeremy.moreland@phoenix.edu. *Application contact:* Dr. Jeremy Moreland, Dean/Executive Director, 480-557-3231, E-mail: jeremy.moreland@phoenix. edu.

University of Regina, Faculty of Graduate Studies and Research, Kenneth Levene Graduate School of Business, Program in Business Administration, Regina, SK S4S 0A2, Canada. Offers business (Master's Certificate); business administration (MBA); executive business administration (MBA); international business (MBA); leadership (M Admin); organizational leadership (Master's Certificate); project management (Master's Certificate). Part-time and evening/weekend programs available. *Faculty:* 51 full-time (14 women), 10 part-time/adjunct (0 women). *Students:* 59 full-time (18 women), 19 part-time (7 women). 132 applicants, 80% accepted. In 2010, 39 master's awarded. *Degree requirements:* For master's, project. *Entrance requirements:* For master's, GMAT, two years relevant work experience. Additional exam requirements/recommendations for international students: Required—TOEFL (minimum score 580 paper-based; 80 iBT). *Application deadline:* Applications are processed on a rolling basis. Application fee: $100. Electronic applications accepted. *Expenses:* Contact institution. *Financial support:* In 2010–11, 3 fellowships (averaging $18,000 per year), 3 teaching assistantships (averaging $6,759 per year) were awarded; research assistantships, scholarships/grants also available. Financial award application deadline: 6/15. *Faculty research:* Business policy and strategy, production and operations management, human behavior in organizations, financial management, social issues in business. *Unit head:* Dr. Anne Lavack, Dean, 306-585-4162, Fax: 306-585-4805, E-mail: anne.lavack@uregina.ca. *Application contact:* Steve Wield, Manager, 306-337-8463, Fax: 306-585-5361, E-mail: steve.wield@uregina.ca.

University of St. Thomas, Graduate Studies, School of Education, Program in Organization Learning and Development, St. Paul, MN 55105-1096. Offers career development (Certificate); e-learning (Certificate); human resource development (Certificate); human resource management (Certificate); human resources and change leadership (MA); learning technology (Certificate); learning technology for learning development and change (MA); organization development (Ed D, Certificate). Part-time and evening/weekend programs available. Postbaccalaureate distance learning degree programs offered (minimal on-campus study). *Faculty:* 6 full-time (4 women), 15 part-time/adjunct (8 women). *Students:* 8 full-time (7 women), 156 part-time (118 women); includes 30 minority (12 Black or African American, non-Hispanic/Latino; 7 Asian, non-Hispanic/Latino; 7 Hispanic/Latino; 1 Native Hawaiian or other Pacific Islander, non-Hispanic/Latino; 3 Two or more races, non-Hispanic/Latino), 6 international. Average age 37. 165 applicants, 71% accepted, 102 enrolled. In 2010, 38 master's, 9 doctorates, 15 other advanced degrees awarded. *Degree requirements:* For doctorate, comprehensive exam, thesis/dissertation. *Entrance requirements:* For master's, minimum GPA of 3.0, 2 letters of reference, personal statement; for doctorate, minimum GPA of 3.5, interview; for Certificate, minimum graduate GPA of 3.25. Additional exam requirements/recommendations for international students: Required—TOEFL (minimum score 550 paper-based; 213 computer-based). *Application deadline:* For fall admission, 8/1 priority date for domestic and international students; for winter admission, 12/1 priority date for domestic students, 12/1 for international students; for spring admission, 12/1 priority date for domestic and international students. Applications are processed on a rolling basis. Application fee: $50. *Expenses:* Contact institution. *Financial support:* Fellowships, research assistantships, institutionally sponsored loans and scholarships/grants available. Support available to part-time students. Financial award applicants required to submit FAFSA. *Faculty research:* Workplace conflict, physician leaders, entrepreneurship education, mentoring. *Unit head:* Dr. David W. Jamieson, Department Chair, 651-962-4387, Fax: 651-962-4169, E-mail: jami9859@stthomas.edu. *Application contact:* Liz G. Knight, Department Coordinator, 651-962-4459, Fax: 651-962-4169, E-mail: egknight@stthomas.edu.

University of San Francisco, School of Business and Professional Studies, Program in Organization Development, San Francisco, CA 94117-1080. Offers MS. Part-time and evening/weekend programs available. *Faculty:* 4 full-time (1 woman), 10 part-time/adjunct (3 women). *Students:* 150 full-time (114 women), 1 (woman) part-time; includes 76 minority (16 Black or African American, non-Hispanic/Latino; 2 American Indian or Alaska Native, non-Hispanic/Latino; 25 Asian, non-Hispanic/Latino; 22 Hispanic/Latino; 2 Native Hawaiian or other Pacific Islander, non-Hispanic/Latino; 9 Two or more races, non-Hispanic/Latino), 4 international. Average age 38. 84 applicants, 80% accepted, 51 enrolled. In 2010, 62 master's awarded. *Degree requirements:* For master's, thesis. *Entrance requirements:* For master's, minimum GPA of 3.0. Application fee: $55 ($65 for international students). *Expenses:* Tuition: Full-time $20,070; part-time $1115 per credit hour. Tuition and fees vary according to course load, degree level and program. *Financial support:* In 2010–11, 107 students received support. Application deadline: 3/2. *Unit head:* Dr. Sharon Wagner, Head, 415-422-6886. *Application contact:* 415-422-6000, E-mail: graduate@usfca.edu.

The University of Scranton, College of Graduate and Continuing Education, Department of Health Administration and Human Resources, Program in Human Resources Administration, Scranton, PA 18510. Offers human resources (MS); human resources development (MS); organizational leadership (MS). Part-time and evening/weekend programs available. *Students:* 4 full-time (3 women), 6 part-time (5 women); includes 1 Hispanic/Latino. Average age 36. In 2010, 12 master's awarded. *Degree requirements:* For master's, capstone experience. *Entrance requirements:* For master's, minimum GPA of 2.75. Additional exam requirements/recommendations for international students: Required—TOEFL (minimum score 500 paper-based; 173 computer-based), IELTS (minimum score 5.5). *Application deadline:* Applications are processed on a rolling basis. Application fee: $0. *Financial support:* Fellowships, teaching assistantships, career-related internships or fieldwork, Federal Work-Study, and unspecified assistantships available. Support available to part-time students. Financial award application deadline: 3/1. *Unit head:* Dr. Daniel West, Director, 570-941-6218, E-mail: westd1@scranton.edu. *Application contact:* Joseph M. Roback, Director of Admissions, 570-941-4385, Fax: 570-941-5928, E-mail: robackj2@scranton.edu.

University of Southern California, Graduate School, School of Policy, Planning, and Development, Executive Master of Leadership Program, Los Angeles, CA 90089. Offers EML. Part-time and evening/weekend programs available. *Faculty:* 51 full-time (12 women), 100 part-time/adjunct (30 women). *Students:* 13 full-time (4 women), 38 part-time (11 women); includes 28 minority (7 Black or African American, non-Hispanic/Latino; 4 Asian, non-Hispanic/Latino; 15 Hispanic/Latino; 2 Native Hawaiian or other Pacific Islander, non-Hispanic/Latino). 43 applicants, 79% accepted, 29 enrolled. In 2010, 23 master's awarded. *Entrance requirements:* Additional exam requirements/recommendations for international students: Required—TOEFL (minimum score 600 paper-based; 250 computer-based; 100 iBT). *Application deadline:* For fall admission, 2/1 for domestic and international students. Applications are processed on a rolling basis. Application fee: $85. Electronic applications accepted. *Expenses:* Contact institution. *Financial support:* In 2010–11, 2 students received support. Scholarships/grants and tuition waivers (partial) available. Financial award application deadline: 2/1. *Faculty research:* Strategic planning, organizational transformation, strategic management, leadership. Total annual research expenditures: $6.2 million. *Unit head:* Dr. Robert Myrtle, Director, 213-740-0378, Fax: 213-740-1801, E-mail: myrtle@usc.edu. *Application contact:* Marisol Rios Gonzalez, Director of Recruitment and Admission, 213-740-0550, Fax: 213-740-7573, E-mail: sppd@usc.edu.

The University of Texas at Dallas, School of Management, Program in Management and Administrative Sciences, Richardson, TX 75080. Offers electronic commerce (MS); finance (MS); healthcare administration (MS); information systems (MS); innovation and entrepreneurship (MS); international management (MS); leadership in organizations (MS); marketing (MS); operations (MS); organizations (MS); real estate (MS); strategy (MS). *Accreditation:* AACSB. Part-time and evening/weekend programs available. *Faculty:* 18 full-time (3 women), 8 part-time/adjunct (0 women). *Students:* 57 full-time (32 women), 107 part-time (49 women); includes 53 minority (14 Black or African American, non-Hispanic/Latino; 30 Asian, non-Hispanic/Latino; 8 Hispanic/Latino; 1 Two or more races, non-Hispanic/Latino), 25 international. Average age 32. 161 applicants, 67% accepted, 51 enrolled. In 2010, 27 master's awarded. *Degree requirements:* For master's, thesis optional. *Entrance requirements:* For master's, GMAT. Additional exam requirements/recommendations for international students: Required—TOEFL (minimum score 550 paper-based; 215 computer-based). *Application deadline:* For fall admission, 7/15 for domestic students, 5/1 priority date for international students; for spring admission, 11/15 for domestic students, 9/1 priority date for international students. Applications are processed on a rolling basis. Application fee: $50 ($100 for international students). Electronic applications accepted. *Expenses:* Tuition, state resident: full-time $10,248; part-time $569 per credit hour. Tuition, nonresident: full-time $18,544; part-time $1030 per credit hour. Tuition and fees vary according to course load. *Financial support:* In 2010–11, 26 students received support, including 38 teaching assistantships with partial tuition reimbursements available (averaging $11,528 per year); research assistantships with partial tuition reimbursements available, career-related internships or fieldwork, Federal Work-Study, institutionally sponsored loans, scholarships/grants, and unspecified assistantships also available. Support available to part-time students. Financial award application deadline: 4/30; financial award applicants required to submit FAFSA. *Faculty research:* Integrated and detailed knowledge of functional areas of management, analytical tools for effective appraisal and decision making. *Unit head:* Dr. Doug Eckel, Assistant Dean, 972-883-5923, E-mail: doug.eckel@utdallas.edu. *Application contact:* James Parker, Assistant Director, 972-883-5842, E-mail: jparker@utdallas.edu.

The University of Texas at San Antonio, College of Business, General Business Program, San Antonio, TX 78249-0617. Offers accounting (PhD); business (MBA); finance (PhD); information systems (MBA); information technology (PhD); international business (MBA); management accounting (MBA); management and organization studies (PhD); management of technology (MBA); marketing (PhD); marketing management (MBA); taxation (MBA). Part-time and evening/weekend programs available. *Students:* 159 full-time (59 women), 124 part-time (43 women); includes 82 minority (9 Black or African American, non-Hispanic/Latino; 2 American Indian or Alaska Native, non-Hispanic/Latino; 17 Asian, non-Hispanic/Latino; 50 Hispanic/Latino; 1 Native Hawaiian or other Pacific Islander, non-Hispanic/Latino; 3 Two or more races, non-Hispanic/Latino), 39 international. Average age 32. 330 applicants, 46% accepted, 105 enrolled. In 2010, 85 master's, 9 doctorates awarded. *Degree requirements:* For master's, comprehensive exam (for some programs), thesis (for some programs). *Entrance requirements:* For master's, GMAT. Additional exam requirements/recommendations for international students: Required—TOEFL (minimum score 500 paper-based; 173 computer-based; 61 iBT), IELTS (minimum score 5). *Application deadline:* For fall admission, 7/1 for domestic students, 4/1 for international students; for spring admission, 11/1 for domestic students, 9/1 for international students. Application fee: $45 ($80 for international students). *Expenses:* Tuition, state resident: full-time $4172; part-time $231.75 per credit hour. Tuition, nonresident: full-time $15,332; part-time $851.75 per credit hour. *Financial support:* In 2010–11, 282 research assistantships (averaging $13,930 per year), 74 teaching assistantships (averaging $9,284 per year) were awarded; scholarships/grants, tuition waivers, and unspecified assistantships also available. Support available to part-time students. *Unit head:* Dr. Lynda Y. de la Vinna, Dean, 210-458-4317, Fax: 210-458-4308, E-mail: lynda.delavina@utsa.edu. *Application contact:* Veronica Ramirez, Assistant Dean of the Graduate School, 210-458-4330, Fax: 210-458-4332, E-mail: graduatestudies@utsa.edu.

University of the Incarnate Word, School of Graduate Studies and Research, Dreeben School of Education, Programs in Education, San Antonio, TX 78209-6397. Offers adult education (M Ed, MA); cross-cultural education (M Ed, MA); early childhood literacy (M Ed, MA); general education (M Ed, MA); higher education (PhD); instructional technology (M Ed, MA); international education and entrepreneurship (PhD); kinesiology (M Ed, MA); literacy (M Ed, MA); organizational leadership (PhD); organizational learning and learning (M Ed, MA); reading (M Ed, MA); special education (M Ed, MA); teacher leadership (M Ed, MA). Part-time and evening/weekend programs available. *Students:* 14 full-time (5 women), 230 part-time (151 women); includes 25 Black or African American, non-Hispanic/Latino; 2 American Indian or Alaska Native, non-Hispanic/Latino; 2 Asian, non-Hispanic/Latino; 98 Hispanic/Latino, 31 international. Average age 41. In 2010, 20 master's, 13 doctorates awarded. *Degree requirements:* For master's, capstone; for doctorate, thesis/dissertation, qualifying exam. *Entrance requirements:* For master's, baccalaureate degree; minimum foundation GPA of 2.5; interview; for doctorate, master's degree; interview; supervised writing sample. Additional exam requirements/recommendations for international students: Required—TOEFL (minimum score 560 paper-based; 220 computer-based; 83 iBT). *Application deadline:* Applications are processed on a rolling basis. Application fee: $20. Electronic applications accepted. *Expenses:* Tuition: Part-time $725 per contact hour. Required fees: $890 per semester. *Financial support:* Federal Work-Study and scholarships/grants available. Financial award applicants required to submit FAFSA. *Unit head:* Dr. Denise Staudt, Dean, Dreeben School of Education, 210-829-2762, E-mail: staudt@uiwtx.edu. *Application contact:* Andrea Cyterski-Acosta, Dean of Enrollment, 210-829-6005, Fax: 210-829-3921, E-mail: admis@uiwtx.edu.

University of the Incarnate Word, School of Graduate Studies and Research, H-E-B School of Business and Administration, Programs in Administration, San Antonio, TX 78209-6397. Offers adult education (MAA); applied administration (MAA); communication arts (MAA); healthcare administration (MAA); instructional technology (MAA); international business (Certificate); nutrition (MAA); organizational development (MAA, Certificate); project management (Certificate); sports management (MAA). Part-time and evening/weekend programs available. Postbaccalaureate distance learning degree programs offered (no on-campus study). *Students:* 30 full-time (20 women), 64 part-time (37 women); includes 10 Black or African American, non-Hispanic/Latino; 1 Asian, non-Hispanic/Latino; 48 Hispanic/Latino, 8 international. Average age 35. In 2010, 68 master's awarded. *Degree requirements:* For master's, capstone. *Entrance requirements:* For master's, GRE, GMAT, undergraduate degree, minimum GPA of 2.5. Additional exam requirements/recommendations for international students: Required—TOEFL (minimum score 560 paper-based; 220 computer-based; 83 iBT). *Application deadline:* Applications are processed on a rolling basis. Application fee: $20. Electronic applications accepted. *Expenses:* Tuition: Part-time $725 per contact hour. Required fees: $890 per semester. *Financial support:* Federal Work-Study and scholarships/grants available. Financial award applicants required to submit FAFSA. *Unit head:* Dr. Daniel Dominguez, MAA Programs Director, 210-829-3180, Fax: 210-805-3564, E-mail: domingue@uiwtx.edu. *Application contact:* Andrea Cyterski-Acosta, Dean of Enrollment, 210-829-6005, Fax: 210-829-3921, E-mail: admis@uiwtx.edu.

Vanderbilt University, Peabody College, Department of Leadership, Policy, and Organizations, Nashville, TN 37240-1001. Offers education policy (MPP);

educational leadership and policy (Ed D); higher education (M Ed); higher education, leadership and policy (Ed D); international education policy and management (M Ed); leadership and organizational performance (M Ed). Part-time and evening/weekend programs available. *Faculty:* 38 full-time (16 women), 11 part-time/adjunct (3 women). *Students:* 163 full-time (114 women), 103 part-time (55 women); includes 34 minority (17 Black or African American, non-Hispanic/Latino; 3 Asian, non-Hispanic/Latino; 8 Hispanic/Latino; 6 Two or more races, non-Hispanic/Latino, 23 international. Average age 30. 439 applicants, 56% accepted, 124 enrolled. In 2010, 73 master's, 21 doctorates awarded. *Degree requirements:* For master's, comprehensive exam, thesis optional; for doctorate, thesis/dissertation, qualifying exams, residency. *Entrance requirements:* For master's and doctorate, GRE General Test. Additional exam requirements/recommendations for international students: Required—TOEFL (minimum score 550 paper-based; 213 computer-based). *Application deadline:* For fall admission, 12/31 priority date for domestic and international students; for spring admission, 11/1 priority date for domestic and international students. Applications are processed on a rolling basis. Application fee: $0. Electronic applications accepted. *Financial support:* In 2010–11, 179 students received support, including 5 fellowships with full and partial tuition reimbursements available, 52 research assistantships with full and partial tuition reimbursements available, 2 teaching assistantships with full and partial tuition reimbursements available; Federal Work-Study, institutionally sponsored loans, scholarships/grants, tuition waivers (partial), and unspecified assistantships also available. Support available to part-time students. Financial award application deadline: 2/1; financial award applicants required to submit FAFSA. *Faculty research:* Education policy and leadership, international and comparative education management and policy, higher education policy, accountability, teacher and leader effectiveness. *Unit head:* Dr. Ellen B. Goldring, Chair, 615-322-8000, Fax: 615-343-7094, E-mail: ellen.b.goldring@vanderbilt.edu. *Application contact:* Rosie Moody, Educational Coordinator, 615-322-8019, Fax: 615-343-7094, E-mail: rosie.moody@vanderbilt.edu.

Walden University, Graduate Programs, School of Management, Minneapolis, MN 55401. Offers accounting (MS), including cpa emphasis, professional track, self-designed; accounting and management (MS), including self-designed, strategic management; applied management and decision sciences (PhD), including accounting, engineering management, finance, general applied management and decision sciences, information systems management, knowledge management, leadership and organizational change, learning management, operations research, self-designed program in applied management and design sciences; business information management (MISM); enterprise information security (MISM); entrepreneurship (MBA, DBA); finance (MBA, DBA); global management (MS); global supply chain management (DBA); health informatics (MISM); healthcare management (MBA, MS); healthcare system improvement (MBA); human resource management (MBA, MS), including functional human resource management (MS), human resource management (MS), integrating functional and strategic human resource management (MS), organizational strategy (MS); information systems (MS); information systems management (DBA); information technology (MS), including information security, software engineering; international business (MBA, DBA); IT strategy and governance (MISM); leadership (MBA, MS, DBA), including entrepreneurship (MS), general management (MS), human resources leadership (MS), innovation and technology (MS), leader development (MS), leading sustainability (MS), project management (MS), self-designed (MS), managers as leaders (MS); managing global software and service supply chains (MISM); marketing (MBA, DBA); project management (MBA, MS); research strategies (MS); risk management (MBA); self-designed (MBA, DBA); social impact management (DBA); strategy and operations (MS); sustainable futures (MBA); sustainable management (MS); technology (MBA); technology entrepreneurship (DBA); technology management (MS). Part-time and evening/weekend programs available. Postbaccalaureate distance learning degree programs offered (minimal on-campus study). *Faculty:* 22 full-time (8 women), 291 part-time/adjunct (100 women). *Students:* 3,705 full-time (1,956 women), 976 part-time (549 women); includes 2,432 minority (2,021 Black or African American, non-Hispanic/Latino; 32 American Indian or Alaska Native, non-Hispanic/Latino; 137 Asian, non-Hispanic/Latino; 193 Hispanic/Latino; 5 Native Hawaiian or other Pacific Islander, non-Hispanic/Latino; 44 Two or more races, non-Hispanic/Latino), 302 international. Average age 40. In 2010, 658 master's, 86 doctorates awarded. *Degree requirements:* For doctorate, thesis/dissertation (for some programs), residency. *Entrance requirements:* For master's, bachelor's degree or equivalent in related field; minimum GPA of 2.5; official transcripts; goal statement; access to computer and Internet; for doctorate, master's degree or equivalent in related field; minimum GPA of 3.0; 3 years of related professional/academic experience (preferred). Additional exam requirements/recommendations for international students: Required—TOEFL (minimum score 550 paper-based; 213 computer-based), IELTS (minimum score 6.5), Michigan English Language Assessment Battery (minimum score 82). *Application deadline:* Applications are processed on a rolling basis. Application fee: $50. Electronic applications accepted. *Expenses:* Tuition: Full-time $10,274; part-time $445 per credit. Tuition and fees vary according to course load, degree level and program. *Financial support:* Fellowships, Federal Work-Study, scholarships/grants, unspecified assistantships, and family tuition reduction, active duty/veteran tuition reduction, group tuition reduction, interest-free payment plans available. Support available to part-time students.

Financial award applicants required to submit FAFSA. *Unit head:* Dr. William Schulz, Associate Dean, 800-925-3368. *Application contact:* Jennifer Hall, Vice President of Enrollment Management, 866-4-WALDEN, E-mail: info@waldenu.edu.

Walden University, Graduate Programs, School of Public Policy and Administration, Minneapolis, MN 55401. Offers criminal justice (MPA); emergency management (MPA); government management (Postbaccalaureate Certificate); health policy (MPA); homeland security policy (MPA); homeland security policy and coordination (MPA); interdisciplinary policy studies (MPA); international nongovernmental organizations (ngos) (MPA); law and public policy (MPA); local government management for sustainable communities (MPA); nonprofit management (Postbaccalaureate Certificate); nonprofit management and leadership (MPA, MS); policy analysis (MPA); public management and leadership (MPA); public policy and administration (MPA, PhD), including criminal justice (PhD), emergency management (PhD), health policy (PhD), health services (PhD), homeland security policy (PhD), homeland security policy and coordination (PhD), interdisciplinary policy studies (PhD), international nongovernmental organizations (PhD), law and public policy (PhD), local government management for sustainable communities (PhD), nonprofit management and leadership (PhD), policy analysis (PhD), public management and leadership (PhD), terrorism, mediation, and peace (PhD); terrorism, mediation, and peace (MPA). Part-time and evening/weekend programs available. Postbaccalaureate distance learning degree programs offered (minimal on-campus study). *Faculty:* 10 full-time (5 women), 117 part-time/adjunct (49 women). *Students:* 1,408 full-time (901 women), 599 part-time (392 women); includes 1,022 Black or African American, non-Hispanic/Latino; 11 American Indian or Alaska Native, non-Hispanic/Latino; 37 Asian, non-Hispanic/Latino; 64 Hispanic/Latino; 26 Two or more races, non-Hispanic/Latino, 47 international. Average age 40. In 2010, 311 master's, 23 doctorates awarded. *Degree requirements:* For doctorate, thesis/dissertation, residency. *Entrance requirements:* For master's, bachelor's degree or equivalent in related field, minimum GPA of 2.5; for doctorate, master's degree or equivalent in related field; minimum GPA of 3.0; official transcripts; three years of related professional/academic experience (preferred); access to computer and Internet. Additional exam requirements/recommendations for international students: Required—TOEFL (minimum score 550 paper-based; 213 computer-based), IELTS (minimum score 6.5), TOEFL (minimum score 550 paper-based; 213 computer-based), IELTS (minimum score 6.5), or Michigan English Language Assessment Battery (minimum score 82). *Application deadline:* Applications are processed on a rolling basis. Application fee: $50. Electronic applications accepted. *Expenses:* Tuition: Full-time $10,274; part-time $445 per credit. Tuition and fees vary according to course load, degree level and program. *Financial support:* Fellowships with tuition reimbursements, Federal Work-Study, scholarships/grants, unspecified assistantships, and family tuition reduction, active duty/veteran tuition reduction, group tuition reduction, interest-free payment plans available. Support available to part-time students. Financial award applicants required to submit FAFSA. *Unit head:* Dr. Mark Gordon, Associate Dean, 800-925-3368. *Application contact:* Jennifer Hall, Vice President of Enrollment Management, 866-4-WALDEN, E-mail: info@waldenu.edu.

Wilfrid Laurier University, Faculty of Graduate and Postdoctoral Studies, Faculty of Social Work, Waterloo, ON N2L 3C5, Canada. Offers Aboriginal studies (MSW); community, policy, planning and organizations (MSW); critical social policy and organizational studies (PhD); individuals, families and groups (MSW); social work practice (individuals, families, groups and communities) (PhD); social work practice: individuals, families, groups and communities (PhD). Part-time programs available. *Faculty:* 20 full-time (13 women), 50 part-time/adjunct (36 women). *Students:* 271 full-time (227 women), 111 part-time (100 women), 1 international. 621 applicants, 40% accepted, 132 enrolled. In 2010, 164 master's, 5 doctorates awarded. *Degree requirements:* For master's, thesis optional; for doctorate, thesis/dissertation. *Entrance requirements:* For master's, course work in social science, research methodology, and statistics; honors BA with a minimum B average; for doctorate, master's degree in social work, minimum A- average. Additional exam requirements/recommendations for international students: Required—TOEFL (minimum score 89 iBT). *Application deadline:* For fall admission, 1/15 priority date for domestic and international students. Application fee: $125. Electronic applications accepted. *Expenses:* Contact institution. *Financial support:* Career-related internships or fieldwork, scholarships/grants, health care benefits, and unspecified assistantships available. *Unit head:* Dr. Cheryl-Anne Cait, Associate Dean, 519-884-1970 Ext. 5224, E-mail: ccait@wlu.ca. *Application contact:* Rosemary Springett, Graduate Admission and Records Officer, 519-884-0710 Ext. 3078, E-mail: gradstudies@wlu.ca.

Wilkes University, College of Graduate and Professional Studies, Jay S. Sidhu School of Business and Leadership, Wilkes-Barre, PA 18766-0002. Offers accounting (MBA); entrepreneurship (MBA); finance (MBA); health care administration (MBA); human resource management (MBA); international business (MBA); marketing (MBA); operations management (MBA); organizational leadership and development (MBA). *Accreditation:* ACBSP. Part-time and evening/weekend programs available. *Students:* 39 full-time (16 women), 146 part-time (71 women); includes 5 Black or African American, non-Hispanic/Latino; 2 Asian, non-Hispanic/Latino; 1 Hispanic/Latino; 1 Two or more races, non-Hispanic/Latino, 16 international. Average age 30. In 2010, 85 master's awarded. *Entrance requirements:* For master's, GMAT. Additional exam requirements/recommendations for international students: Required—TOEFL (minimum score 550 paper-based; 213 computer-based; 79 iBT). *Application deadline:* Applications are processed on a rolling basis. Application fee: $45 ($65 for international students). Electronic applications accepted. *Expenses:* Contact institution. *Financial support:* Federal Work-Study and unspecified assistantships available. Financial award application deadline: 3/1; financial award applicants required to submit FAFSA. *Unit head:* Dr. Paul Browne, Dean, 570-408-4701, Fax: 570-408-7846, E-mail: paul.browne@wilkes.edu. *Application contact:* Kathleen Houlihan, Director of Graduate Studies, 570-408-3235, Fax: 570-408-7846, E-mail: kathleen.houlihan@wilkes.edu.

Woodbury University, School of Business and Management, Program in Organizational Leadership, Burbank, CA 91504-1099. Offers MA. Evening/weekend programs available. *Faculty:* 1 (woman) full-time, 10 part-time/adjunct (6 women). *Students:* 51 full-time (28 women), 19 part-time (13 women); includes 23 minority (7 Black or African American, non-Hispanic/Latino; 3 Asian, non-Hispanic/Latino; 13 Hispanic/Latino), 8 international. Average age 39. 74 applicants, 46% accepted, 26 enrolled. In 2010, 74 master's awarded. *Entrance requirements:* For master's, GRE General Test (if GPA less than 2.5), 3 recommendations, essay, resume, academic transcripts. Additional exam requirements/recommendations for international students: Required—TOEFL (minimum score 550 paper-based; 220 computer-based; 83 iBT), IELTS (minimum score 6.5). *Application deadline:* For fall admission, 8/1 priority date for domestic students; for spring admission, 12/1 priority date for domestic students. Applications are processed on a rolling basis. Application fee: $35. *Expenses:* Tuition: Full-time $10,548; part-time $879 per credit. Required fees: $8 per credit. $50 per semester. One-time fee: $110. *Financial support:* In 2010–11, 1 student received support. Scholarships/grants available. *Unit head:* Paul Decker, Director of the Institute for Excellence in Teaching and Learning, 818-252-5267, E-mail: paul.decker@woodbury.edu. *Application contact:* Ruth Lorenzana, Director of Admissions, 800-784-9663, Fax: 818-767-7520, E-mail: admissions@woodbury.edu.

Worcester Polytechnic Institute, Graduate Studies, School of Business, Worcester, MA 01609-2280. Offers information technology (MS), including information security management; management (Graduate Certificate); marketing and technological innovation (MS); operations design and leadership (MS); technology (MBA). *Accreditation:* AACSB. Part-time and evening/weekend programs available. Postbaccalaureate distance learning degree programs offered (minimal on-campus study). *Faculty:* 13 full-time (7 women), 9 part-time/adjunct (2 women). *Students:* 112 full-time (53 women), 135 part-time (33 women); includes 5 Black or African American, non-Hispanic/Latino; 1 Hispanic/Latino; 15 Native Hawaiian or other Pacific Islander, non-Hispanic/Latino, 105 international. 396 applicants, 67% accepted, 79 enrolled. In 2010, 69 degrees awarded. *Degree requirements:* For master's, thesis optional. *Entrance requirements:* For master's, GMAT (MBA), GMAT or GRE General Test (MS), resume; for Graduate Certificate, GMAT or GRE General Test, statement of purpose, 3 letters of recommendation. Additional exam requirements/recommendations for international students: Required—TOEFL (minimum score 550 paper-based; 213 computer-based; 79 iBT), IELTS (minimum score 6.5). *Application deadline:* For fall admission, 6/1 priority date for domestic and international students; for spring admission, 11/1 priority date for domestic students, 10/1 priority date for international students. Applications are processed on a rolling basis. Application fee: $70. Electronic applications accepted. *Expenses:* Tuition: Full-time $20,862; part-time $1159 per term. One-time fee: $15. *Financial support:* Career-related internships or fieldwork, institutionally sponsored loans, scholarships/grants, and unspecified assistantships available.

Financial award application deadline: 6/1; financial award applicants required to submit FAFSA. *Faculty research:* Organizational aesthetics, resistance in organizations, dynamics of product innovation, economic approaches to productivity, corporate earnings forecasts and value relevance, ERP implementation, improving Web accessibility, information quality assessment, measuring strategic and transactional IT, website quality, service operations modeling, healthcare operations and performance analysis, loan process design. *Unit head:* Dr. Mark Rice, Dean, 508-831-4665, Fax: 508-831-5218, E-mail: rice@wpi.edu. *Application contact:* Alyssa Bates, Director, Graduate Management Programs, 508-831-4665, Fax: 508-831-5720, E-mail: ajbates@wpi.edu.

Worcester State University, Graduate Studies, Program in Management, Worcester, MA 01602-2597. Offers accounting (MS); managerial leadership (MS). Part-time and evening/weekend programs available. *Faculty:* 1 (woman) full-time, 1 part-time/adjunct (0 women). *Students:* 7 full-time (2 women), 12 part-time (5 women); includes 1 Black or African American, non-Hispanic/Latino; 1 Two or more races, non-Hispanic/Latino, 4 international. Average age 28. 21 applicants, 76% accepted, 11 enrolled. In 2010, 4 master's awarded. *Degree requirements:* For master's, comprehensive exam (for some programs), thesis optional. *Entrance requirements:* Additional exam requirements/recommendations for international students: Required—TOEFL (minimum score 500 paper-based; 61 iBT). *Application deadline:* Applications are processed on a rolling basis. Application fee: $40. Electronic applications accepted. *Expenses:* Tuition, state resident: full-time $2700; part-time $150 per credit. Tuition, nonresident: full-time $2700; part-time $150 per credit. Required fees: $2016; $112 per credit. *Financial support:* In 2010–11, 2 students received support, including 2 research assistantships with full tuition reimbursements available (averaging $4,800 per year); career-related internships or fieldwork, scholarships/grants, and unspecified assistantships also available. Financial award application deadline: 3/1; financial award applicants required to submit FAFSA. *Unit head:* Dr. Laurie Dahlin, Coordinator, 508-929-9084, Fax: 508-929-8048, E-mail: ldahlin@worcester.edu. *Application contact:* Sara Grady, Assistant Dean of Continuing Education, 508-929-8787, Fax: 508-929-8100, E-mail: sara.grady@worcester.edu.

Yale University, Yale School of Management and Graduate School of Arts and Sciences, Doctoral Program in Management, New Haven, CT 06520. Offers accounting (PhD); financial economics (PhD); marketing (PhD); organizations and management (PhD). *Accreditation:* AACSB. *Faculty:* 68 full-time (12 women), 1 (woman) part-time/adjunct. *Students:* 32 full-time (9 women); includes 3 Asian, non-Hispanic/Latino, 16 international. Average age 28. 441 applicants, 4% accepted, 6 enrolled. In 2010, 9 doctorates awarded. *Degree requirements:* For doctorate, comprehensive exam, thesis/dissertation. *Entrance requirements:* For doctorate, GMAT or GRE General Test. Additional exam requirements/recommendations for international students: Required—TOEFL, IELTS. *Application deadline:* For fall admission, 1/2 for domestic and international students. Application fee: $100. Electronic applications accepted. *Expenses:* Contact institution. *Financial support:* In 2010–11, 30 students received support, including 30 fellowships with full tuition reimbursements available, 30 research assistantships with full tuition reimbursements available, 30 teaching assistantships with full tuition reimbursements available; institutionally sponsored loans, scholarships/grants, and health care benefits also available. Financial award application deadline: 1/2. *Faculty research:* Pricing of options and futures, term structure of interest rates, use of accounting numbers in debt contracts, product differentiation, e-commerce and marketing, behavioral finance. *Unit head:* Carla Mills, Registrar, 203-432-3955, Fax: 203-432-0342, E-mail: carla.mills@yale.edu. *Application contact:* Carla Mills, Registrar, 203-432-3955, Fax: 203-432-0342, E-mail: carla.mills@yale.edu.

Project Management

OVERVIEW

Project management involves the application of knowledge, skills, tools, and techniques shaped by the specifications and requirements of particular projects. While these skills have long been recognized as important in engineering and development, new industries now realize careful project management is vital. Project management professionals need to be organized, have an eye for detail, and possess the confidence and skill to manage a project from start to finish in an efficient manner. A Project Management MBA enables students to acquire the skills, knowledge, and confidence required to successfully manage projects of all sizes in a business environment.

A Project Management MBA covers a wide range of specialist areas, ranging from organizational skills and communications to strategy, techniques, and leadership skills. Those professionals with significant project, program, or general management responsibilities should look at these programs as an excellent way to move their careers forward as rigorous project management training and education further help develop professional competence. The knowledge gained from a Project Management MBA program enhances skills applicable to projects regardless of size, scope, or industry and prepares general managers to use project principles in all business operations.

Required courses may include study in:

- Bridging Strategy and Tactics in Project Management
- Managerial Economics
- Managing Projects for Competitive Advantage
- Marketing Management
- Organizational Skills for Project Management
- Project Estimation and Risk Management
- Project Planning and Control
- Project Teams
- Strategic Issues

Elective courses may include study in:

- Advanced Project Management Practices and Professional Exam Preparation
- Contract and Procurement Management
- Managing Quality
- Managing Software Development Projects
- Project Management Systems
- Project Risk Management

Project management is an increasingly crucial responsibility in today's business environment. Key positions are plentiful but often require the skill and training of a graduate degree. In addition to achieving general MBA learning outcomes, an MBA Project Management graduate will be able to evaluate project costs; analyze issues related to procurement and risk management; engage in practical exercises that increase organizational skills within the project management arena; and develop the necessary tools to effectively plan, measure, and control projects. With an MBA in Project Management, professionals can look forward to careers in environmental project management, senior program management, quality assurance management, and project management consulting.

HELPFUL ORGANIZATIONS/ PUBLICATIONS/BLOGS

Project Management Institute (PMI)

http://www.pmi.org/

Project Management Institute (PMI) is one of the world's largest professional membership associations, with half a million members and credential holders in more than 185 countries. It is a not-for-profit organization that advances the project management profession through globally recognized standards and certifications, collaborative communities, an extensive research program, and professional development opportunities.

PMI offers five certifications that recognize knowledge and competency, including the Project Management Professional (PMP)® credential held by more than 370,000 practitioners worldwide.

PMI's 12 standards for project, program, and portfolio management are the most widely recognized standards in the profession and increasingly the model for project management in business and government. They are developed and updated by thousands of PMI volunteers with experience in every type of project and provide a common language for project management around the world.

Most of PMI's activity takes place in more than 250 geographic chapters and 30 industry- or interest-based communities of practice. These communities, open to PMI members and led by volunteers, support the knowledge sharing and professional networking that are central to PMI's mission.

PMI offers a wide range of professional development opportunities, from SeminarsWorld® and e-learning courses to PMI global congresses and other events.

The PMI Research Program advances the science, practice, and profession of project management. It expands project management's body of knowledge through research projects, symposiums, and surveys and shares it through publications, research conferences, and working sessions.

PMI is governed by a 15-member volunteer Board of Directors. Each year, PMI members elect five directors to three-year terms. Three directors elected by others on the board serve one-year terms as officers. Day-to-day PMI operations are guided by the Executive Management Group and professional staff at the Global Operations Center in Newtown Square, PA, USA.

International Project Management Association (IPMA)®

http://www.ipma.ch/

The International Project Management Association (IPMA)® is a world leading nonprofit making project management organization. IPMA represents more than 50 project management associations from all continents of the world. IPMA actively promotes project management to businesses and organizations around the world. In order to increase the recognition of the profession, IPMA certifies project managers, awards successful project teams and research projects, and provides a number of project management publications. Through IPMA, project managers from all cultures and all parts of the world can network, share ideas, and bring project management forward in cooperation.

In order to increase the status of project management and make more organizations discover its benefits and profitability, IPMA is strongly engaged in setting professional standards and improving the methods of certification. Through IPMA Web sites and international events, the Association enables project managers from around the world to share ideas and take active part in the progression of project management.

Project Management Magazine

http://www.projectmanagementmagazine.com/

Project Management Magazine is a monthly digital magazine focused on research case studies and best practices in project management.

CAREER ASPIRATIONS: A PROSPECTIVE POSITION

Product Director

Job Description

The Product Director will be responsible for working with the marketing and tech teams to obtain product vision and develop requirements, track progress, and keep the process moving along effectively and efficiently.

With direction from senior and executive management, this position directs and coordinates the identification and prioritization, development, and implementation of all technical, database, and marketing projects throughout the company.

Responsibilities

- Evaluate product development scope and understand user needs and completive set.
- Provide clear and best-in-class requirements and work collaboratively with engineering to develop multiple key platforms, including the learning system, acquisitions, reporting, and customer care.
- Effectively integrate the product with third-party social applications.
- Integrate usability studies, user research, and market analysis into product requirements in order to ensure that products satisfy customer needs.
- Provide strategic direction for organization-wide program and project development and implementation activities to ensure that the business objectives are met in a timely and appropriate manner.
- In conjunction with key organizational leadership, define high-level project scope and objectives from which to make decisions concerning project prioritization, development, and implementation.
- Define and track key deliverables as projects and releases move through the pipeline.
- Define and scope social/sharing strategy.
- Work with instructors, students, and other stakeholders to ensure their needs are being met.
- Determine metrics of success for each product and follow-up with post-mortem analysis of product misses and successes.
- Direct and maintain accountability for all department projects from original concept through final implementation.
- Lead and direct the interface with all areas affected by the project(s), including end users, marketing, and technology.
- Conduct project meetings and maintain responsibility for project tracking and analysis. Provide project status reports to senior and executive management as requested.
- Provide direction and guidance to project managers in team and business analysis staff to assist them in their role and understanding of more complex project management.
- Provide technical and analytical guidance to project team.
- Recommend and take action to direct the analysis and solutions of problems. Clear pathway for project team to ensure they have the appropriate resources to function in their assigned role.

Qualifications

- A knack for turning requirements into written product and feature recommendations and functional specs
- Demonstrable ability to work in an agile, collaborative development environment
- Strong familiarity with social platforms
- A keen eye for great design
- BA in business, marketing, database management, or social sciences required. MBA preferred.
- 4–7 years experience in online product management and/or project management experience on progressively responsible and complex projects required. Experience with responsibility for comprehensive and complex projects required.
- Thorough knowledge and understanding of commonly used concepts, practices, and procedures within a particular field respective to the information systems to enable incumbent to direct and manage highly complex and comprehensive projects
- Ability to team with individuals across the organization
- Strong interpersonal, written, and verbal communication skills with demonstrated ability to work in a team environment
- Great attention to detail, while not losing view on the bigger vision and mission
- Experience defining system scope and multiple project objectives, as well as prioritizing, directing, and assigning the activities of team members on highly complex and comprehensive projects required
- Must have a relatively high level of analytical ability to strategize and prioritize organizational projects

PROJECT MANAGEMENT

American Graduate University, Program in Project Management, Covina, CA 91724. Offers MPM, Certificate. Part-time programs available. Postbaccalaureate distance learning degree programs offered (no on-campus study). *Faculty:* 2 full-time (1 woman), 15 part-time/adjunct (2 women). *Students:* 250 part-time. In 2010, 14 master's awarded. *Entrance requirements:* For master's, 2 letters of recommendation, proctor designation. Additional exam requirements/recommendations for international students: Required— TOEFL. *Application deadline:* Applications are processed on a rolling basis. Application fee: $50. Electronic applications accepted. *Expenses:* Tuition: Part-time $275 per credit. *Unit head:* Paul McDonald, President, 626-966-4576 Ext. 1006, E-mail: paulmcdonald@agu.edu. *Application contact:* Marie Sirney, Director of Admissions, 626-966-4576 Ext. 1003, Fax: 626-915-1709, E-mail: mariesirney@agu.edu.

Avila University, Program in Organizational Development, Kansas City, MO 64145-1698. Offers fundraising (Graduate Certificate); management (MA), including fundraising, project management; organizational development (MS); project management (Graduate Certificate). Part-time and evening/ weekend programs available. Postbaccalaureate distance learning degree programs offered (no on-campus study). *Faculty:* 2 full-time (1 woman), 10 part-time/adjunct (7 women). *Students:* 72 full-time (61 women), 36 part-time (24 women); includes 35 minority (28 Black or African American, non-Hispanic/ Latino; 2 American Indian or Alaska Native, non-Hispanic/Latino; 2 Asian, non-Hispanic/Latino; 2 Hispanic/Latino; 1 Native Hawaiian or other Pacific Islander, non-Hispanic/Latino), 4 international. Average age 36. 47 applicants, 64% accepted, 27 enrolled. In 2010, 18 master's awarded. *Degree requirements:* For master's, thesis optional. *Entrance requirements:* For master's, 2 letters of recommendation, minimum GPA of 3.25 during last 60 hours, resume. Additional exam requirements/recommendations for international students: Required—TOEFL. *Application deadline:* Applications are processed on a rolling basis. Application fee: $0. Electronic applications accepted. *Expenses:* Tuition: Full-time $5580; part-time $465 per credit hour. Required fees: $348; $29 per credit hour. *Financial support:* In 2010–11, 69 students received support. Unspecified assistantships available. Support available to part-time students. Financial award applicants required to submit FAFSA. *Unit head:* Dr. Steve Iliff, Dean, 816-501-3737, Fax: 816-941-4650, E-mail: advantage@ avila.edu. *Application contact:* Linda Dubar, School of Professional Studies, 816-501-3737, Fax: 816-941-4650, E-mail: advantage@avila.edu.

Boston University, Metropolitan College, Department of Administrative Sciences, Boston, MA 02215. Offers banking and financial management (MSM); business continuity in emergency management (MSM); economics development and tourism management (MSAS); electronic commerce, systems, and technology (MSAS); financial economics (MSAS); innovation and technology (MSAS); insurance management (MSM); international market management (MSM); multinational commerce (MSAS); project management (MSM). *Accreditation:* AACSB. Part-time and evening/weekend programs available. Postbaccalaureate distance learning degree programs offered (no on-campus study). *Faculty:* 14 full-time (2 women), 22 part-time/adjunct (2 women). *Students:* 107 full-time (51 women), 786 part-time (356 women); includes 130 minority (55 Black or African American, non-Hispanic/Latino; 1 American Indian or Alaska Native, non-Hispanic/Latino; 30 Asian, non-His-panic/Latino; 36 Hispanic/Latino; 1 Native Hawaiian or other Pacific Islander, non-Hispanic/Latino; 7 Two or more races, non-Hispanic/Latino), 175 international. Average age 33. 398 applicants, 87% accepted, 180 enrolled. In 2010, 154 master's awarded. *Degree requirements:* For master's, thesis optional. *Entrance requirements:* For master's, 1 year of work experience, minimum GPA of 3.0. Additional exam requirements/recommendations for international students: Required—TOEFL (minimum score 560 paper-based; 220 computer-based; 84 iBT). *Application deadline:* Applications are processed on a rolling basis. Application fee: $70. Electronic applications accepted. *Expenses:* Tuition: Full-time $39,314; part-time $1228 per credit. Required fees: $40 per semester. *Financial support:* In 2010–11, 15 students received support, including 7 research assistantships with partial tuition reimbursements available (averaging $10,000 per year); career-related internships or fieldwork, Federal Work-Study, and unspecified assistantships also available. *Faculty research:* International business, innovative process. *Unit head:* Dr. Kip Becker, Chairman, 617-353-3016, E-mail: adminsc@bu.edu. *Application contact:* Lucille Dicker, Administrative Sciences Department, 617-353-3016, E-mail: adminsc@bu.edu.

Boston University, Metropolitan College, Department of Computer Science, Boston, MA 02215. Offers computer information systems (MS), including computer networks, database management and business intelligence, health informatics, IT project management, security; computer science (MS), including computer networks, security; telecommunications (MS), including security. Part-time and evening/weekend programs available. Postbaccalaureate distance learning degree programs offered (no on-campus study). *Faculty:* 10 full-time (0 women), 30 part-time/adjunct (3 women). *Students:* 16 full-time (2 women), 681 part-time (155 women); includes 182 minority (44 Black or African American, non-Hispanic/Latino; 1 American Indian or Alaska Native, non-Hispanic/Latino; 88 Asian, non-Hispanic/Latino; 36 Hispanic/ Latino; 2 Native Hawaiian or other Pacific Islander, non-Hispanic/Latino; 11

Two or more races, non-Hispanic/Latino), 66 international. Average age 35. 273 applicants, 78% accepted, 155 enrolled. In 2010, 143 master's awarded. *Degree requirements:* For master's, thesis optional. *Entrance requirements:* For master's, 3 letters of recommendation, professional resume. Additional exam requirements/recommendations for international students: Required— TOEFL (minimum score 550 paper-based; 213 computer-based; 80 iBT). *Application deadline:* For fall admission, 6/1 priority date for international students; for spring admission, 10/1 priority date for international students. Applications are processed on a rolling basis. Application fee: $70. Electronic applications accepted. *Expenses:* Tuition: Full-time $39,314; part-time $1228 per credit. Required fees: $40 per semester. *Financial support:* In 2010–11, 9 research assistantships with partial tuition reimbursements (averaging $5,000 per year) were awarded; career-related internships or fieldwork and unspecified assistantships also available. Support available to part-time students. Financial award applicants required to submit FAFSA. *Faculty research:* Medical informatics, Web technologies, telecom and networks, security and forensics, software engineering, programming languages, multimedia and AI, information systems and IT project management. *Unit head:* Dr. Lubomir Chitkushev, Chairman, 617-353-2566, Fax: 617-353-2367, E-mail: csinfo@ bu.edu. *Application contact:* Kim Richards, Program Coordinator, 617-353-2566, Fax: 617-353-2367, E-mail: kimrich@bu.edu.

Brandeis University, Rabb School of Continuing Studies, Division of Graduate Professional Studies, Program in Management of Projects and Programs, Waltham, MA 02454-9110. Offers MS, Graduate Certificate. Part-time programs available. Postbaccalaureate distance learning degree programs offered (no on-campus study). *Faculty:* 2 full-time (both women), 33 part-time/adjunct (5 women). *Students:* 35 part-time (14 women); includes 1 Black or African American, non-Hispanic/Latino; 6 Asian, non-Hispanic/ Latino; 1 Hispanic/Latino. Average age 35. 6 applicants, 100% accepted, 5 enrolled. In 2010, 27 master's, 4 other advanced degrees awarded. *Degree requirements:* For master's, thesis. *Entrance requirements:* For master's, resume, official transcripts, recommendations, goal statements; for Graduate Certificate, resume, official transcripts, recommendations. Additional exam requirements/recommendations for international students: Recommended— TOEFL (minimum score 600 paper-based; 250 computer-based; 100 iBT). *Application deadline:* For fall admission, 6/15 priority date for domestic students; for winter admission, 10/15 priority date for domestic students; for spring admission, 2/15 priority date for domestic students. Applications are processed on a rolling basis. Application fee: $50. Electronic applications accepted. *Unit head:* Anne Marando, Program Chair, 781-736-8787, Fax: 781-736-3420, E-mail: marando@brandeis.edu. *Application contact:* Frances Stearns, Associate Director of Admissions and Student Services, 781-736-8785, Fax: 781-736-3420, E-mail: fstearns@brandeis.edu.

Brandeis University, Rabb School of Continuing Studies, Division of Graduate Professional Studies, Virtual Team Management and Communication Program, Waltham, MA 02454-9110. Offers MS, Graduate Certificate. Part-time programs available. Postbaccalaureate distance learning degree programs offered (no on-campus study). *Faculty:* 2 full-time (both women), 33 part-time/adjunct (5 women). *Students:* 6 part-time (2 women); includes 1 Black or African American, non-Hispanic/Latino. Average age 35. 3 applicants, 100% accepted, 3 enrolled. *Entrance requirements:* For master's, resume, official transcripts, recommendations, goal statements; for Graduate Certificate, resume, recommendations. Additional exam requirements/recommendations for international students: Recommended—TOEFL (minimum score 600 paper-based; 250 computer-based; 100 iBT). *Application deadline:* For fall admission, 6/15 priority date for domestic students; for winter admission, 10/15 priority date for domestic students; for spring admission, 2/15 priority date for domestic students. Applications are processed on a rolling basis. Application fee: $50. Electronic applications accepted. *Unit head:* Dr. Aline Yurik, Program Chair, 781-736-8787, Fax: 781-736-3420, E-mail: ayurik@brandeis.edu. *Application contact:* Frances Stearns, Associate Director of Admissions and Student Services, 781-736-8785, Fax: 781-736-3420, E-mail: fstearns@brandeis.edu.

Brenau University, Sydney O. Smith Graduate School, School of Business and Mass Communication, Gainesville, GA 30501. Offers accounting (MBA); business administration (MBA); healthcare management (MBA); organizational leadership (MS); project management (MBA). Part-time and evening/ weekend programs available. Postbaccalaureate distance learning degree programs offered (no on-campus study). *Faculty:* 12 full-time (7 women), 24 part-time/adjunct (10 women). *Students:* 124 full-time (89 women), 348 part-time (250 women); includes 130 Black or African American, non-Hispanic/Latino; 2 American Indian or Alaska Native, non-Hispanic/Latino; 7 Asian, non-His-panic/Latino; 13 Hispanic/Latino; 9 Two or more races, non-Hispanic/Latino, 42 international. Average age 35. In 2010, 125 master's awarded. *Degree requirements:* For master's, comprehensive exam (for some programs). *Entrance requirements:* For master's, resume, minimum undergraduate GPA of 2.5. Additional exam requirements/recommendations for international students: Required—TOEFL (minimum score 500 paper-based; 173 computer-based; 61 iBT); Recommended—IELTS (minimum score 5). *Application deadline:* Applications are processed on a rolling basis. Electronic applications accepted. *Expenses:* Contact institution. *Financial support:* In 2010–11, 1 student received support. Application deadline: 7/15. *Unit head:* Dr. William S. Lightfoot, Dean, 770-538-5330, Fax: 770-537-4701, E-mail: wlightfoot@

brenau.edu. *Application contact:* Christina White, Graduate Admissions Specialist, 770-718-5320, Fax: 770-718-5338, E-mail: cwhite@brenau.edu.

Christian Brothers University, School of Business, Memphis, TN 38104-5581. Offers business (MBA); financial planning (Certificate); project management (Certificate). Part-time and evening/weekend programs available. *Faculty:* 1 full-time (0 women), 5 part-time/adjunct (1 woman). *Students:* 11 full-time (4 women), 180 part-time (67 women); includes 57 minority (40 Black or African American, non-Hispanic/Latino; 8 Asian, non-Hispanic/Latino; 7 Hispanic/Latino; 2 Two or more races, non-Hispanic/Latino), 9 international. Average age 35. In 2010, 46 master's awarded. *Entrance requirements:* For master's, GMAT, GRE. Additional exam requirements/recommendations for international students: Required—TOEFL. *Application deadline:* Applications are processed on a rolling basis. Application fee: $50. *Expenses:* Tuition: Full-time $11,520; part-time $640 per credit hour. Required fees: $140; $140 per course. $70 per semester. Tuition and fees vary according to program. *Financial support:* Institutionally sponsored loans available. Support available to part-time students. *Unit head:* Dr. Scott Lawyer, Director, 901-321-3104, Fax: 901-321-3566, E-mail: mlawyer@cbu.edu. *Application contact:* Dr. Scott Lawyer, Director, Graduate Business Programs, 901-321-3104, Fax: 901-321-3566, E-mail: mlawyer@cbu.edu.

Colorado Christian University, Program in Business Administration, Lakewood, CO 80226. Offers corporate training (MBA); information security (MA); leadership (MBA); project management (MBA). Part-time and evening/weekend programs available. Postbaccalaureate distance learning degree programs offered (minimal on-campus study). *Faculty:* 10 full-time (7 women), 35 part-time/adjunct (17 women). *Students:* 65 full-time (33 women), 35 part-time (19 women); includes 6 Black or African American, non-Hispanic/Latino; 2 Asian, non-Hispanic/Latino; 9 Hispanic/Latino. Average age 37. 25 applicants, 20% accepted. *Degree requirements:* For master's, thesis optional. *Entrance requirements:* For master's, GMAT, 2 letters of recommendation, resume. Additional exam requirements/recommendations for international students: Required—TOEFL. *Application deadline:* For fall admission, 8/25 priority date for domestic and international students; for spring admission, 1/12 priority date for domestic and international students. Applications are processed on a rolling basis. Application fee: $40. Electronic applications accepted. *Expenses:* Contact institution. *Financial support:* In 2010–11, 27 students received support. Scholarships/grants and tuition waivers (full and partial) available. Support available to part-time students. Financial award application deadline: 3/1; financial award applicants required to submit FAFSA. *Unit head:* Dr. Mellani Day, Dean of Business and Technology, 303-963-3300, Fax: 303-963-3301, E-mail: agsadmission@ccu.edu. *Application contact:* Dr. Mellani Day, Dean of Business and Technology, 303-963-3300, Fax: 303-963-3301, E-mail: agsadmission@ccu.edu.

DeSales University, Graduate Division, Program in Business Administration, Center Valley, PA 18034-9568. Offers accounting (MBA); computer information systems (MBA); finance (MBA); health care systems management (MBA); health care systems management (online) (MBA); human resource management (MBA); management (MBA); management (online) (MBA); marketing (MBA); marketing (online) (MBA); physician's track (MBA); project management (MBA); project management (online) (MBA); self-design (MBA); self-design (online) (MBA); MSN/MBA. *Accreditation:* ACBSP. Part-time programs available. Postbaccalaureate distance learning degree programs offered (no on-campus study). *Entrance requirements:* For master's, GMAT, minimum GPA of 3.0, 2 years of work experience. Additional exam requirements/recommendations for international students: Required—TOEFL. *Application deadline:* Applications are processed on a rolling basis. Application fee: $35. Electronic applications accepted. *Expenses:* Tuition: Full-time $18,200; part-time $690 per credit. Required fees: $1200. *Faculty research:* Quality improvement, executive development, productivity, cross-cultural managerial differences, leadership. *Unit head:* Dr. David Gilfoil, Director, 610-282-1100 Ext. 1828, Fax: 610-282-2869, E-mail: david.gilfoil@desales.edu. *Application contact:* Caryn Stopper, Director of Graduate Admissions, 610-282-1100 Ext. 1768, Fax: 610-282-0525, E-mail: caryn.stopper@desales.edu.

Dowling College, School of Business, Oakdale, NY 11769-1999. Offers aviation management (MBA, Certificate); banking and finance (MBA, Certificate); corporate finance (MBA); financial planning (Certificate); health care management (MBA, Certificate); human resource management (Certificate); information systems management (MBA); management and leadership (MBA); marketing (Certificate); project management (Certificate); public management (MBA, Certificate); sport, event and entertainment management (Certificate); JD/MBA. Part-time and evening/weekend programs available. *Faculty:* 10 full-time (4 women), 56 part-time/adjunct (7 women). *Students:* 295 full-time (131 women), 460 part-time (206 women); includes 219 minority (97 Black or African American, non-Hispanic/Latino; 14 Asian, non-Hispanic/Latino; 35 Hispanic/Latino; 73 Native Hawaiian or other Pacific Islander, non-Hispanic/Latino), 3 international. Average age 33. 327 applicants, 85% accepted, 160 enrolled. In 2010, 33 master's, 1 other advanced degree awarded. *Degree requirements:* For master's, comprehensive exam, thesis optional. *Entrance requirements:* For master's, minimum GPA of 2.8, 2 letters of recommendation, courses in accounting and finance or seminar in accounting/finance, resume. Additional exam requirements/recommendations

for international students: Required—TOEFL (minimum score 550 paper-based). *Application deadline:* For fall admission, 9/1 priority date for domestic students; for winter admission, 1/1 priority date for domestic students; for spring admission, 2/1 priority date for domestic students. Applications are processed on a rolling basis. Application fee: $50. Electronic applications accepted. *Expenses:* Tuition: Part-time $884 per credit hour. Part-time tuition and fees vary according to degree level and campus/location. *Financial support:* Career-related internships or fieldwork and Federal Work-Study available. Support available to part-time students. Financial award application deadline: 6/30; financial award applicants required to submit FAFSA. *Faculty research:* International finance, computer applications, labor relations, executive development. *Unit head:* Dr. Antonia Loschiavo, Assistant Dean, 631-244-3266, Fax: 631-244-1018, E-mail: loschiat@dowling.edu. *Application contact:* Ronnie S. Macdonald, Assistant Vice President for Enrollment Services/Dean of Admissions, 631-244-3357, Fax: 631-244-1059, E-mail: macdonar@dowling.edu.

Embry-Riddle Aeronautical University–Worldwide, Worldwide Headquarters, Program in Project Management, Daytona Beach, FL 32114-3900. Offers MSPM. Part-time and evening/weekend programs available. Postbaccalaureate distance learning degree programs offered. *Faculty:* 4 full-time (1 woman), 50 part-time/adjunct (15 women). *Students:* 192 full-time (43 women), 110 part-time (27 women); includes 63 minority (30 Black or African American, non-Hispanic/Latino; 1 American Indian or Alaska Native, non-Hispanic/Latino; 8 Asian, non-Hispanic/Latino; 21 Hispanic/Latino; 3 Two or more races, non-Hispanic/Latino). Average age 35. 118 applicants, 77% accepted, 69 enrolled. In 2010, 51 master's awarded. *Degree requirements:* For master's, thesis (for some programs). *Application deadline:* Applications are processed on a rolling basis. Application fee: $50. Electronic applications accepted. *Financial support:* In 2010–11, 74 students received support. *Unit head:* Dr. Kees Rietsema, Chair, 602-904-1285, E-mail: rietsd37@erau.edu. *Application contact:* Linda Dammer, Director of Admissions, 386-226-6396 Ext. 1, Fax: 386-226-6984, E-mail: worldwide@erau.edu.

Florida Institute of Technology, Graduate Programs, Extended Studies Division, Melbourne, FL 32901-6975. Offers acquisition and contract management (MS); aerospace engineering (MS); business administration (MBA); computer information systems (MS); computer science (MS); electrical engineering (MS); engineering management (MS); human resources management (MS); logistics management (MS), including humanitarian and disaster relief logistics; management (MS), including acquisition and contract management, e-business, human resources management, information systems, logistics management, management, transportation management; material acquisition management (MS); mechanical engineering (MS); operations research (MS); project management (MS), including information systems, operations research; public administration (MPA); quality management (MS); software engineering (MS); space systems (MS); space systems management (MS); systems management (MS), including information systems, operations research. Part-time and evening/weekend programs available. Postbaccalaureate distance learning degree programs offered (no on-campus study). *Faculty:* 11 full-time (3 women), 118 part-time/adjunct (24 women). *Students:* 69 full-time (23 women), 907 part-time (369 women); includes 385 minority (242 Black or African American, non-Hispanic/Latino; 15 American Indian or Alaska Native, non-Hispanic/Latino; 44 Asian, non-Hispanic/Latino; 52 Hispanic/Latino; 3 Native Hawaiian or other Pacific Islander, non-Hispanic/Latino; 29 Two or more races, non-Hispanic/Latino), 17 international. 517 applicants, 49% accepted, 245 enrolled. In 2010, 430 degrees awarded. *Degree requirements:* For master's, comprehensive exam (for some programs), capstone course. *Entrance requirements:* For master's, GMAT or resume showing 8 years of supervised experience, minimum GPA of 3.0, 2 letters of recommendation, resume. Additional exam requirements/recommendations for international students: Required—TOEFL (minimum score 550 paper-based; 213 computer-based; 79 iBT). *Application deadline:* For fall admission, 4/1 for international students; for spring admission, 9/30 for international students. Applications are processed on a rolling basis. Application fee: $50. Electronic applications accepted. *Expenses:* Contact institution. *Financial support:* Application deadline: 3/1. *Unit head:* Dr. Theodore Richardson, Senior Associate Dean, 321-674-8123, Fax: 321-674-7597, E-mail: trichardson@fit.edu. *Application contact:* Carolyn Farrior, Director of Graduate Admissions, Online Learning and Off-Campus Programs, 321-674-7118, Fax: 321-674-8216, E-mail: cfarrior@fit.edu.

Florida Institute of Technology, Graduate Programs, Nathan M. Bisk College of Business, Online Programs, Melbourne, FL 32901-6975. Offers accounting (MBA); accounting and finance (MBA); finance (MBA); healthcare management (MBA); information technology (MS); information technology management (MBA); Internet marketing (MBA); management (MBA); marketing (MBA); project management (MBA). Part-time and evening/weekend programs available. Postbaccalaureate distance learning degree programs offered (no on-campus study). *Faculty:* 32 part-time/adjunct (8 women). *Students:* 4 full-time (1 woman), 1,062 part-time (499 women); includes 373 minority (244 Black or African American, non-Hispanic/Latino; 8 American Indian or Alaska Native, non-Hispanic/Latino; 37 Asian, non-Hispanic/Latino; 76 Hispanic/Latino; 8 Native Hawaiian or other Pacific Islander, non-Hispanic/Latino), 39 international. Average age 37. 299 applicants, 167 enrolled. In 2010, 134 master's awarded. *Entrance requirements:* For master's, GMAT or resume showing 8 years of supervised experience, 2 letters of recommendation, resume, competency in math past college algebra. Additional exam requirements/recommendations for international students: Required—TOEFL (minimum score 550 paper-based; 213 computer-based; 79 iBT). *Application deadline:* For fall admission, 4/1 for international students; for spring admission, 9/30 for international students. Applications are processed on a rolling basis. Application fee: $50. Electronic applications accepted. *Expenses:* Contact institution. *Financial support:* Available to part-time students. Application deadline: 3/1. *Unit head:* Dr. Mary S. Bonhomme, Dean, Florida Tech Online Associate Provost for Online Learning, 321-674-8202, Fax: 321-674-8216, E-mail: bonhomme@fit.edu. *Application contact:* Carolyn Farrior, Director of Graduate Admissions Online Learning and Off Campus Programs, 321-674-7118, Fax: 321-674-8216, E-mail: cfarrior@fit.edu.

The George Washington University, School of Business, Department of Decision Sciences, Washington, DC 20052. Offers project management (MS). *Faculty:* 16 full-time (1 woman), 2 part-time/adjunct (0 women). *Students:* 18 full-time (6 women), 207 part-time (82 women); includes 25 Black or African American, non-Hispanic/Latino; 1 American Indian or Alaska Native, non-Hispanic/Latino; 16 Asian, non-Hispanic/Latino; 13 Hispanic/Latino, 28 international. Average age 39. 89 applicants, 91% accepted, 49 enrolled. In 2010, 77 master's awarded. Application fee: $75. *Financial support:* Tuition waivers available. *Unit head:* Srinivas Prasad, Chair, 202-994-2078, Fax: 202-994-6382, E-mail: prasad@gwu.edu. *Application contact:* Kristin Williams, Asst VP Gradpec Enrlmnt Mgmt, 202-994-0467, Fax: 202-994-0371, E-mail: ksw@gwu.edu.

The George Washington University, School of Business, Department of Information Systems and Technology Management, Washington, DC 20052. Offers information and decision systems (PhD); information systems (MSIST); information systems development (MSIST); information systems management (MBA); information systems project management (MSIST); management information systems (MSIST); management of science, technology, and innovation (MBA, PhD). Programs also offered in Ashburn and Arlington, VA. Part-time and evening/weekend programs available. *Faculty:* 12 full-time (4 women), 5 part-time/adjunct (1 woman). *Students:* 93 full-time (33 women), 141 part-time (46 women); includes 31 Black or African American, non-Hispanic/Latino; 1 American Indian or Alaska Native, non-Hispanic/Latino; 28 Asian, non-Hispanic/Latino; 17 Hispanic/Latino; 1 Native Hawaiian or other Pacific Islander, non-Hispanic/Latino, 40 international. Average age 33. 201 applicants, 68% accepted, 67 enrolled. In 2010, 89 master's, 2 doctorates awarded. *Entrance requirements:* For master's, GMAT. Additional exam requirements/recommendations for international students: Required—TOEFL. *Application deadline:* For fall admission, 4/1 priority date for domestic students; for spring admission, 10/1 for international students. Applications are processed on a rolling basis. Application fee: $75. *Financial support:* In 2010–11, 35 students received support; fellowships, teaching assistantships, career-related internships or fieldwork, Federal Work-Study, institutionally sponsored loans, and tuition waivers available. Financial award application deadline: 4/1. *Faculty research:* Expert systems, decision support systems. *Unit head:* Richard G. Donnelly, Chair, 202-994-4364, E-mail: rgd@gwu.edu. *Application contact:* Kristin Williams, Assistant Vice President for Graduate and Special Enrollment Management, 202-994-0467, Fax: 202-994-0371, E-mail: ksw@gwu.edu.

Grantham University, Mark Skousen School of Business, Kansas City, MO 64153. Offers business administration (MBA); business intelligence (MS); information management (MBA); information management technology (MS); information technology (MS); performance improvement (MS); project management (MBA, MSIM). Part-time and evening/weekend programs available. Postbaccalaureate distance learning degree programs offered (no on-campus study). *Students:* 74 full-time (32 women), 565 part-time (177 women); includes 218 minority (142 Black or African American, non-Hispanic/Latino; 6 American Indian or Alaska Native, non-Hispanic/Latino; 31 Asian, non-Hispanic/Latino; 37 Hispanic/Latino; 1 Native Hawaiian or other Pacific Islander, non-Hispanic/Latino; 1 Two or more races, non-Hispanic/Latino). In 2010, 126 master's awarded. *Degree requirements:* For master's, capstone project. *Entrance requirements:* For master's, bachelor's degree from accredited degree-granting institution. Additional exam requirements/recommendations for international students: Required—TOEFL (minimum score 500 paper-based; 213 computer-based; 61 iBT). *Application deadline:* Applications are processed on a rolling basis. Application fee: $0. Electronic applications accepted. *Expenses:* Tuition: Full-time $7950; part-time $265 per credit hour. One-time fee: $30. *Financial support:* Institutionally sponsored loans and scholarships/grants available. *Unit head:* Niccole Buckley, Dean, 800-955-2527, Fax: 816-595-5757, E-mail: admissions@grantham.edu. *Application contact:* Dan King, Vice President of Admissions, 800-955-2527, Fax: 816-595-5757, E-mail: admissions@grantham.edu.

Harrisburg University of Science and Technology, Program in Project Management, Harrisburg, PA 17101. Offers construction services (MS); governmental services (MS); information technology (MS). Part-time and evening/weekend programs available. *Faculty:* 1 full-time (0 women), 3 part-time/adjunct (0 women). *Students:* 11 part-time (2 women); includes 1 Black or African American, non-Hispanic/Latino; 1 Asian, non-Hispanic/Latino; 1

Hispanic/Latino, 1 international. Average age 30. 24 applicants, 75% accepted. In 2010, 7 master's awarded. *Entrance requirements:* For master's, BS, BBA. Additional exam requirements/recommendations for international students: Required—TOEFL (minimum score 520 paper-based; 200 computer-based; 80 iBT). *Application deadline:* For fall admission, 8/1 priority date for domestic students, 7/1 priority date for international students. Applications are processed on a rolling basis. Application fee: $0. Electronic applications accepted. *Expenses:* Tuition: Full-time $19,500; part-time $700 per credit hour. *Financial support:* Scholarships/grants available. Financial award applicants required to submit FAFSA. *Unit head:* Dr. Amjad Umar, Director and Professor, 717-901-5141, Fax: 717-901-3141, E-mail: aumar@harrisburgu.edu. *Application contact:* Timothy Dawson, Information Contact, 717-901-5158, Fax: 717-901-3158, E-mail: admissions@harrisburgu.edu.

Lasell College, Graduate and Professional Studies in Management, Newton, MA 02466-2709. Offers elder care administration (MSM, Graduate Certificate); elder care marketing (MSM, Graduate Certificate); fundraising management (MSM, Graduate Certificate); human resource management (Graduate Certificate); human resources management (MSM); management (MSM, Graduate Certificate); marketing (MSM, Graduate Certificate); non-profit management (MSM, Graduate Certificate); project management (MSM, Graduate Certificate); public relations (MSM). Part-time and evening/weekend programs available. Postbaccalaureate distance learning degree programs offered (no on-campus study). *Faculty:* 8 full-time (5 women), 7 part-time/adjunct (5 women). *Students:* 25 full-time (21 women), 97 part-time (67 women); includes 16 minority (6 Black or African American, non-Hispanic/Latino; 2 American Indian or Alaska Native, non-Hispanic/Latino; 4 Asian, non-Hispanic/Latino; 4 Hispanic/Latino), 17 international. Average age 33. 56 applicants, 52% accepted, 19 enrolled. In 2010, 65 master's, 7 other advanced degrees awarded. *Entrance requirements:* For master's and Graduate Certificate, bachelor's degree from an accredited institution. Additional exam requirements/recommendations for international students: Required—TOEFL (minimum score 550 paper-based; 213 computer-based; 75 iBT). *Application deadline:* For fall admission, 8/31 priority date for domestic students, 6/30 priority date for international students; for spring admission, 12/31 priority date for domestic students, 10/31 priority date for international students. Applications are processed on a rolling basis. Application fee: $40. Electronic applications accepted. *Expenses:* Tuition: Part-time $550 per credit hour. Required fees: $55 per semester. *Financial support:* In 2010–11, 40 students received support. Available to part-time students. Application deadline: 8/31. *Unit head:* Dr. Joan Dolamore, Dean of Graduate and Professional Studies, 617-243-2485, Fax: 617-243-2450, E-mail: gradinfo@lasell.edu. *Application contact:* Adrienne Franciosi, Director of Graduate Admission, 617-243-2214, Fax: 617-243-2450, E-mail: gradinfo@lasell.edu.

Lawrence Technological University, College of Management, Southfield, MI 48075-1058. Offers business administration (MBA, DBA); business administration international (MBA); global leadership and management (MS); global operations and project management (MS); information systems (MS); information technology (DM); operations management (MS). *Accreditation:* ACBSP. Part-time and evening/weekend programs available. *Faculty:* 14 full-time (6 women), 53 part-time/adjunct (14 women). *Students:* 7 full-time (2 women), 584 part-time (258 women); includes 137 Black or African American, non-Hispanic/Latino; 2 American Indian or Alaska Native, non-Hispanic/Latino; 51 Asian, non-Hispanic/Latino; 10 Hispanic/Latino; 8 Two or more races, non-Hispanic/Latino, 48 international. Average age 35. 431 applicants, 54% accepted, 151 enrolled. In 2010, 216 master's, 12 doctorates awarded. *Degree requirements:* For master's, thesis (for some programs). *Entrance requirements:* For master's, GMAT. Additional exam requirements/recommendations for international students: Required—TOEFL (minimum score 550 paper-based; 213 computer-based; 79 iBT). *Application deadline:* For fall admission, 6/30 priority date for domestic students, 6/30 for international students; for spring admission, 11/15 priority date for domestic students, 11/15 for international students. Applications are processed on a rolling basis. Application fee: $50. Electronic applications accepted. *Financial support:* In 2010–11, 142 students received support. Federal Work-Study and institutionally sponsored loans available. Support available to part-time students. Financial award application deadline: 4/1; financial award applicants required to submit FAFSA. *Unit head:* Dr. Lou DeGennaro, Dean, 248-204-3050, E-mail: degennaro@ltu.edu. *Application contact:* Jane Rohrback, Director of Admissions, 248-204-3160, Fax: 248-204-2228, E-mail: admissions@ltu.edu.

Lehigh University, College of Business and Economics, Bethlehem, PA 18015. Offers accounting (MS), including accounting and information analysis; business administration (MBA); economics (MS, PhD), including economics, health and bio-pharmaceutical economics (MS); entrepreneurship (Certificate); finance (MS), including analytical finance; project management (Certificate); supply chain management (Certificate); MBA/E; MBA/M Ed. *Accreditation:* AACSB. Part-time and evening/weekend programs available. Postbaccalaureate distance learning degree programs offered (minimal on-campus study). *Faculty:* 43 full-time (10 women), 19 part-time/adjunct (4 women). *Students:* 164 full-time (82 women), 242 part-time (72 women); includes 37 minority (6 Black or African American, non-Hispanic/Latino; 25 Asian, non-Hispanic/Latino; 5 Hispanic/Latino; 1 Native Hawaiian or other Pacific Islander, non-Hispanic/Latino), 110 international. Average age 29.

790 applicants, 35% accepted, 158 enrolled. In 2010, 159 master's, 3 doctorates awarded. Terminal master's awarded for partial completion of doctoral program. *Degree requirements:* For master's, thesis optional; for doctorate, comprehensive exam, thesis/dissertation, proposal defense. *Entrance requirements:* For master's, GMAT, GRE General Test; MCAT, DAT (health and biopharmaceutical economics); for doctorate, GMAT or GRE General Test. Additional exam requirements/recommendations for international students: Required—TOEFL (minimum score 600 paper-based; 250 computer-based; 94 iBT). *Application deadline:* For fall admission, 7/15 for domestic students, 5/1 for international students; for spring admission, 12/1 for domestic and international students. Applications are processed on a rolling basis. Application fee: $100. Electronic applications accepted. *Expenses:* Contact institution. *Financial support:* In 2010–11, 93 students received support, including 2 fellowships with full tuition reimbursements available (averaging $16,000 per year), 39 research assistantships with full and partial tuition reimbursements available (averaging $2,269 per year), 17 teaching assistantships with full tuition reimbursements available (averaging $13,840 per year); career-related internships or fieldwork, scholarships/grants, health care benefits, tuition waivers (full and partial), and unspecified assistantships also available. Support available to part-time students. Financial award application deadline: 1/15. *Faculty research:* Public finance, energy, investments, activity-based costing, management information systems. *Unit head:* Paul R. Brown, Dean, 610-758-6725, Fax: 610-758-4499, E-mail: prb207@lehigh.edu. *Application contact:* Corinn McBride, Director of Recruitment and Admissions, 610-758-3418, Fax: 610-758-5283, E-mail: com207@lehigh.edu.

Lewis University, College of Business, Graduate School of Management, Program in Business Administration, Romeoville, IL 60446. Offers accounting (MBA); custom elective option (MBA); e-business (MBA); finance (MBA); healthcare management (MBA); human resources management (MBA); information security (MBA); international business (MBA); management information systems (MBA); marketing (MBA); project management (MBA); technology and operations management (MBA). Part-time and evening/weekend programs available. *Students:* 119 full-time (66 women), 204 part-time (104 women); includes 55 Black or African American, non-Hispanic/Latino; 9 Asian, non-Hispanic/Latino; 30 Hispanic/Latino; 1 Native Hawaiian or other Pacific Islander, non-Hispanic/Latino, 9 international. Average age 28. In 2010, 111 master's awarded. *Entrance requirements:* For master's, interview, bachelor's degree, resume, 2 recommendations. Additional exam requirements/recommendations for international students: Required—TOEFL (minimum score 550 paper-based; 213 computer-based). *Application deadline:* For fall admission, 8/15 priority date for domestic students, 5/1 priority date for international students; for spring admission, 11/15 priority date for international students. Applications are processed on a rolling basis. Application fee: $40. Electronic applications accepted. *Expenses:* Tuition: Full-time $13,320; part-time $740 per credit hour. Tuition and fees vary according to program. *Financial support:* Career-related internships or fieldwork, Federal Work-Study, scholarships/grants, and unspecified assistantships available. Financial award application deadline: 5/1; financial award applicants required to submit FAFSA. *Unit head:* Dr. Maureen Culleeney, Academic Program Director, 815-838-0500 Ext. 5631, E-mail: culleema@lewisu.edu. *Application contact:* Michele Ryan, Director of Admission, 815-838-0500 Ext. 5384, E-mail: gsm@lewisu.edu.

Marlboro College, Graduate School, Program in Information Technologies, Marlboro, VT 05344. Offers information technologies (MS); open source Web development (Certificate); project management (Certificate). Part-time and evening/weekend programs available. Postbaccalaureate distance learning degree programs offered (minimal on-campus study). *Faculty:* 5 part-time/adjunct (4 women). *Students:* 4 full-time (2 women), 11 part-time (6 women); includes 1 Black or African American, non-Hispanic/Latino. Average age 40. 9 applicants, 100% accepted, 8 enrolled. In 2010, 12 master's awarded. *Degree requirements:* For master's, 30 credits including capstone project. *Entrance requirements:* For master's, letter of intent, 2 letters of recommendation, transcripts. *Application deadline:* For fall admission, 7/1 priority date for domestic students; for winter admission, 11/1 priority date for domestic students; for spring admission, 3/1 priority date for domestic students. Applications are processed on a rolling basis. Application fee: $0. Electronic applications accepted. *Expenses:* Tuition: Full-time $14,280; part-time $680 per credit. Tuition and fees vary according to course load and program. *Financial support:* Applicants required to submit FAFSA. *Unit head:* Sean Conley, Associate Dean of the Graduate School. *Application contact:* Joe Heslin, Associate Director of Admissions, 802-258-9209, Fax: 802-258-9201, E-mail: jheslin@gradschool.marlboro.edu.

Maryville University of Saint Louis, The John E. Simon School of Business, St. Louis, MO 63141-7299. Offers accounting (MBA, PGC); business studies (PGC); management (MBA, PGC); marketing (MBA, PGC); process and project management (MBA, PGC); sport and entertainment management (MBA, PGC). *Accreditation:* ACBSP. Part-time and evening/weekend programs available. *Faculty:* 7 full-time (4 women), 13 part-time/adjunct (5 women). *Students:* 16 full-time (8 women), 119 part-time (57 women); includes 15 minority (9 Black or African American, non-Hispanic/Latino; 3 Asian, non-Hispanic/Latino; 3 Hispanic/Latino), 5 international. Average age 31. In 2010, 60 master's awarded. *Entrance requirements:* For

master's, GMAT (unless applicant possesses undergraduate business degree with minimum cumulative GPA of 3.0, or has completed master's degree from accredited university or one early access course prior to undergraduate degree). Additional exam requirements/recommendations for international students: Required—TOEFL (minimum score 563 paper-based; 85 iBT), If you took the revised TOEFL (after Sept. 24, 2005), you will be admitted into our MBA program with a speaking sub-score of 23, a writing sub-score of 20, reading and listening scores of 21 or higher and a combined score of 79 or higher. *Application deadline:* Applications are processed on a rolling basis. Application fee: $40 ($60 for international students). Electronic applications accepted. *Expenses:* Tuition: Full-time $21,100; part-time $633.50 per credit hour. Required fees: $150 per semester. *Financial support:* Career-related internships or fieldwork, Federal Work-Study, tuition waivers (partial), and campus employment available. Financial award application deadline: 3/1; financial award applicants required to submit FAFSA. *Faculty research:* International business, e-marketing, strategic planning, interpersonal management skills, financial analysis. *Unit head:* Dr. Pamela Horwitz, Dean, 314-529-9418, Fax: 314-529-9975, E-mail: horwitz@maryville.edu. *Application contact:* Kathy Dougherty, Director of MBA Programs, 314-529-9382, Fax: 314-529-9975, E-mail: business@maryville.edu.

Metropolitan State University, College of Management, St. Paul, MN 55106-5000. Offers business administration (MBA, DBA); information assurance security (Graduate Certificate); management information systems (MMIS); MIS generalist (Graduate Certificate); MIS systems analysis and design (Graduate Certificate); nonprofit management (MPNA); project management (Graduate Certificate); public administration (MPNA). Part-time and evening/weekend programs available. *Students:* 158 full-time (74 women), 217 part-time (114 women); includes 31 Black or African American, non-Hispanic/Latino; 26 Asian, non-Hispanic/Latino; 10 Hispanic/Latino; 6 Two or more races, non-Hispanic/Latino, 47 international. Average age 35. In 2010, 100 master's, 7 other advanced degrees awarded. *Degree requirements:* For master's, thesis optional, computer language (MMIS). *Entrance requirements:* For master's, GMAT (MBA), resume. Additional exam requirements/recommendations for international students: Required—TOEFL (minimum score 550 paper-based; 213 computer-based). *Application deadline:* For fall admission, 7/15 for international students; for winter admission, 11/15 for international students; for spring admission, 3/15 for international students. Applications are processed on a rolling basis. Application fee: $20. Electronic applications accepted. *Expenses:* Tuition, state resident: full-time $5827; part-time $291 per credit hour. Tuition, nonresident: full-time $11,654; part-time $583 per credit hour. Required fees: $10 per credit hour. Tuition and fees vary according to degree level. *Financial support:* Research assistantships with partial tuition reimbursements, career-related internships or fieldwork and Federal Work-Study available. Support available to part-time students. Financial award applicants required to submit FAFSA. *Faculty research:* Yugoslav economic system, workers' cooperatives, participative management and job enrichment, global business systems. *Unit head:* Dr. Paul Huo, Graduate Director, 612-659-7271, Fax: 612-659-7268, E-mail: carol.bormann.young@metrostate.edu. *Application contact:* Gloria B. Marcus, Recruiter/Admissions Adviser, 612-659-7258, Fax: 612-659-7268, E-mail: gloria.marcus@metrostate.edu.

Mississippi State University, College of Business, Graduate Studies in Business, Mississippi State, MS 39762. Offers business administration (MBA); project management (MBA). MBA (accounting) is only available at the Meridian branch campus. *Accreditation:* AACSB. Part-time and evening/weekend programs available. Postbaccalaureate distance learning degree programs offered (no on-campus study). *Students:* 99 full-time (37 women), 245 part-time (79 women); includes 34 minority (17 Black or African American, non-Hispanic/Latino; 3 American Indian or Alaska Native, non-Hispanic/Latino; 1 Asian, non-Hispanic/Latino; 10 Hispanic/Latino; 1 Native Hawaiian or other Pacific Islander, non-Hispanic/Latino; 2 Two or more races, non-Hispanic/Latino), 20 international. Average age 29. 218 applicants, 64% accepted, 105 enrolled. In 2010, 154 master's awarded. Terminal master's awarded for partial completion of doctoral program. *Degree requirements:* For master's, comprehensive exam (for some programs), thesis optional. *Entrance requirements:* For master's, GMAT, minimum GPA of 3.0 in last 60 hours of course work. Additional exam requirements/recommendations for international students: Required—TOEFL (minimum score 575 paper-based; 233 computer-based; 90 iBT); Recommended—IELTS (minimum score 6.5). *Application deadline:* For fall admission, 7/1 for domestic students, 5/1 for international students; for spring admission, 11/1 for domestic students, 9/1 for international students. Applications are processed on a rolling basis. Application fee: $40. Electronic applications accepted. *Expenses:* Tuition, state resident: full-time $2730.50; part-time $304 per credit hour. Tuition, nonresident: full-time $6901; part-time $767 per credit hour. *Financial support:* In 2010–11, 1 research assistantship with full tuition reimbursement (averaging $11,779 per year), 34 teaching assistantships with full tuition reimbursements (averaging $10,024 per year) were awarded; Federal Work-Study, institutionally sponsored loans, scholarships/grants, and unspecified assistantships also available. Financial award application deadline: 4/1; financial award applicants required to submit FAFSA. *Unit head:* Dr. Barbara Spencer, Director, 662-325-1891, Fax: 662-325-8161, E-mail: gsbi@cobilan.msstate.edu. *Application contact:* Dr. Barbara Spencer, Director, 662-325-1891, Fax: 662-325-8161, E-mail: gsbi@cobilan.msstate.edu.

Montana Tech of The University of Montana, Graduate School, Project Engineering and Management Program, Butte, MT 59701-8997. Offers MPEM. Part-time and evening/weekend programs available. Postbaccalaureate distance learning degree programs offered (no on-campus study). *Faculty:* 1 full-time (0 women), 7 part-time/adjunct (1 woman). *Students:* 16 part-time (4 women); includes 1 American Indian or Alaska Native, non-Hispanic/Latino, 1 international. 5 applicants, 40% accepted, 0 enrolled. *Degree requirements:* For master's, comprehensive exam, final project presentation. *Entrance requirements:* For master's, minimum GPA of 3.0. Additional exam requirements/recommendations for international students: Required—TOEFL (minimum score 550 paper-based; 213 computer-based; 71 iBT). *Application deadline:* For fall admission, 4/1 priority date for domestic students, 3/1 priority date for international students; for spring admission, 10/1 priority date for domestic students, 7/1 priority date for international students. Applications are processed on a rolling basis. Application fee: $30. Electronic applications accepted. *Expenses:* Tuition, state resident: full-time $5084. Tuition, nonresident: full-time $15,104. *Financial support:* Application deadline: 4/1. *Unit head:* Dr. Kumar Ganesan, Director, 406-496-4239, Fax: 406-496-4650, E-mail: kganesan@mtech.edu. *Application contact:* Fred Sullivan, Administrator, Graduate School, 406-496-4304, Fax: 406-496-4710, E-mail: fsullivan@mtech.edu.

Norwich University, School of Graduate and Continuing Studies, Program in Business Administration, Northfield, VT 05663. Offers finance (MBA); organizational leadership (MBA); project management (MBA). *Accreditation:* ACBSP. Evening/weekend programs available. *Faculty:* 26 part-time/adjunct (0 women). *Students:* 108 full-time (45 women); includes 17 minority (5 Black or African American, non-Hispanic/Latino; 3 American Indian or Alaska Native, non-Hispanic/Latino; 4 Asian, non-Hispanic/Latino; 5 Hispanic/Latino), 4 international. Average age 36. 187 applicants, 84% accepted, 95 enrolled. In 2010, 389 master's awarded. *Degree requirements:* For master's, comprehensive exam (for some programs), thesis optional. *Entrance requirements:* For master's, minimum undergraduate GPA of 2.75. Additional exam requirements/recommendations for international students: Required—TOEFL (minimum score 550 paper-based; 213 computer-based; 83 iBT). *Application deadline:* For fall admission, 8/10 for domestic and international students; for winter admission, 11/7 for domestic and international students; for spring admission, 2/6 for domestic and international students. Application fee: $50. *Expenses:* Tuition: Full-time $17,380; part-time $645 per credit. Tuition and fees vary according to program. *Financial support:* Scholarships/grants available. Financial award applicants required to submit FAFSA. *Unit head:* Dr. Jose Cordova, Faculty Director, 802-485-2567, Fax: 802-485-2533, E-mail: jcordova@norwich.edu. *Application contact:* Bernice Fousek, Student Services Coordinator, 802-485-2748, Fax: 802-485-2533, E-mail: bfousek@norwich.edu.

Polytechnic Institute of NYU, Department of Technology Management, Brooklyn, NY 11201-2990. Offers construction management (Advanced Certificate); electronic business management (Advanced Certificate); entrepreneurship (Advanced Certificate); human resources management (Advanced Certificate); information management (Advanced Certificate); management (MS); management of technology (MS); organizational behavior (MS, Advanced Certificate); project management (Advanced Certificate); technology management (MBA, PhD, Advanced Certificate); telecommunications and information management (MS); telecommunications management (Advanced Certificate). Part-time and evening/weekend programs available. *Faculty:* 7 full-time (2 women), 28 part-time/adjunct (4 women). *Students:* 224 full-time (93 women), 106 part-time (38 women); includes 15 Black or African American, non-Hispanic/Latino; 41 Asian, non-Hispanic/Latino; 10 Hispanic/Latino, 158 international. Average age 30. 370 applicants, 60% accepted, 120 enrolled. In 2010, 173 master's, 1 doctorate awarded. *Degree requirements:* For master's, comprehensive exam (for some programs), thesis (for some programs); for doctorate, comprehensive exam, thesis/dissertation. *Entrance requirements:* For master's, GMAT, minimum B average in undergraduate course work. Additional exam requirements/recommendations for international students: Required—TOEFL (minimum score 550 paper-based; 213 computer-based; 80 iBT); Recommended—IELTS (minimum score 6.5). *Application deadline:* For fall admission, 7/31 priority date for domestic students, 4/30 priority date for international students; for spring admission, 12/31 priority date for domestic students, 11/30 priority date for international students. Applications are processed on a rolling basis. Application fee: $75. Electronic applications accepted. *Expenses:* Tuition: Full-time $21,492; part-time $1194 per credit. Required fees: $385 per semester. Tuition and fees vary according to course load. *Financial support:* In 2010–11, 1 fellowship (averaging $26,400 per year) was awarded; research assistantships, teaching assistantships, institutionally sponsored loans, scholarships/grants, and unspecified assistantships also available. Support available to part-time students. *Unit head:* Prof. Bharadwaj Rao, Head, 718-260-3617, Fax: 718-260-3874, E-mail: brao@poly.edu. *Application contact:* JeanCarlo Bonilla, Director of Graduate Enrollment Management, 718-260-3182, Fax: 718-260-3624, E-mail: gradinfo@poly.edu.

Rowan University, Graduate School, College of Engineering, Department of Civil and Environmental Engineering, Program in Project Management, Glassboro, NJ 08028-1701. Offers MS. *Students:* 40 part-time (12 women); includes 1 Black or African American, non-Hispanic/Latino; 2 Asian, non-Hispanic/Latino; 1 Hispanic/Latino. Average age 28. 15 applicants, 100% accepted, 12 enrolled. *Entrance requirements:* For master's, GRE General Test. Additional exam requirements/recommendations for international students: Required—TOEFL. *Application deadline:* Applications are processed on a rolling basis. Application fee: $65 ($200 for international students). Electronic applications accepted. *Expenses:* Tuition, area resident: Part-time $602 per semester hour. Tuition, nonresident: part-time $602 per semester hour. Required fees: $100 per semester hour. One-time fee: $10 part-time. *Unit head:* Kauser Jahan, Chair, 856-256-5323, E-mail: jahan@rowan.edu. *Application contact:* Dr. Ralph Dusseau, Program Adviser, 856-256-5332.

St. Edward's University, School of Management and Business, Program in Project Management, Austin, TX 78704. Offers MS. Part-time and evening/weekend programs available. *Students:* 2 full-time (both women), 33 part-time (15 women); includes 18 minority (3 Black or African American, non-Hispanic/Latino; 1 American Indian or Alaska Native, non-Hispanic/Latino; 1 Asian, non-Hispanic/Latino; 13 Hispanic/Latino), 1 international. Average age 36. 17 applicants, 76% accepted, 11 enrolled. In 2010, 14 master's awarded. *Degree requirements:* For master's, minimum of 24 resident hours. *Entrance requirements:* For master's, GMAT or GRE General Test, minimum GPA of 2.75 in last 60 hours of course work. Additional exam requirements/recommendations for international students: Required—TOEFL (minimum score 550 paper-based; 213 computer-based; 79 iBT) or IELTS (minimum score 6). *Application deadline:* For fall admission, 7/1 for domestic and international students; for spring admission, 11/1 for domestic and international students. Applications are processed on a rolling basis. Application fee: $45 ($50 for international students). Electronic applications accepted. *Expenses:* Tuition: Full-time $16,200; part-time $900 per credit hour. Required fees: $50 per trimester. Full-time tuition and fees vary according to course load and program. *Financial support:* Scholarships/grants available. *Unit head:* Dr. John S. Loucks, Director, 512-448-8630, Fax: 512-448-8492, E-mail: johnsl@stedwards.edu. *Application contact:* Kay L. Arnold, Assistant Director of Admissions, 512-233-1636, Fax: 512-428-1032, E-mail: kayla@stedwards.edu.

Saint Mary's University of Minnesota, Schools of Graduate and Professional Programs, Graduate School of Business and Technology, Project Management Program, Winona, MN 55987-1399. Offers MS, Certificate. *Unit head:* Dr. Gerald Ellis, Director, 612-728-5178, E-mail: gellis@smumn.edu. *Application contact:* Yasin Alsaidi, Director of Admissions for Graduate and Professional Programs, 612-728-5207, Fax: 612-728-5121, E-mail: yalsaidi@smumn.edu.

Southern Illinois University Edwardsville, Graduate School, School of Business, Program in Business Administration, Edwardsville, IL 62026. Offers management information systems (MBA); project management (MBA). *Accreditation:* AACSB. Part-time and evening/weekend programs available. *Students:* 25 full-time (12 women), 130 part-time (46 women); includes 14 minority (6 Black or African American, non-Hispanic/Latino; 1 Asian, non-Hispanic/Latino; 3 Hispanic/Latino; 1 Native Hawaiian or other Pacific Islander, non-Hispanic/Latino; 3 Two or more races, non-Hispanic/Latino), 9 international. Average age 26. 83 applicants, 63% accepted. In 2010, 59 master's awarded. *Degree requirements:* For master's, comprehensive exam. *Entrance requirements:* For master's, GMAT. Additional exam requirements/recommendations for international students: Required—TOEFL (minimum score 550 paper-based; 213 computer-based; 79 iBT), IELTS (minimum score 6.5). *Application deadline:* For fall admission, 7/22 for domestic students, 6/1 for international students; for spring admission, 12/10 for domestic students, 10/1 for international students. Applications are processed on a rolling basis. Application fee: $30. Electronic applications accepted. *Expenses:* Tuition, state resident: full-time $6012; part-time $1503 per semester. Tuition, nonresident: full-time $15,030; part-time $3758 per semester. Required fees: $1711; $675 per semester. *Financial support:* In 2010–11, 1 research assistantship with full tuition reimbursement (averaging $8,064 per year), 31 teaching assistantships with full tuition reimbursements (averaging $8,064 per year) were awarded; fellowships with full tuition reimbursements, career-related internships or fieldwork, Federal Work-Study, institutionally sponsored loans, scholarships/grants, traineeships, and unspecified assistantships also available. Support available to part-time students. Financial award application deadline: 3/1; financial award applicants required to submit FAFSA. *Unit head:* Dr. Janice Joplin, Director, 618-650-2485, E-mail: jjoplin@siue.edu. *Application contact:* Dr. Janice Joplin, Director, 618-650-2485, E-mail: jjoplin@siue.edu.

Stevens Institute of Technology, Graduate School, Wesley J. Howe School of Technology Management, Program in Management, Hoboken, NJ 07030. Offers general management (MS); global innovation management (MS); human resource management (MS); information management (MS); project management (MS); technology commercialization (MS); technology management (MS). Part-time programs available. *Students:* 15 full-time (6 women), 35 part-time (15 women); includes 1 Black or African American, non-Hispanic/Latino; 5 Asian, non-Hispanic/Latino; 6 Hispanic/Latino, 12 international. Average age 31. *Degree requirements:* For master's, thesis optional. *Entrance requirements:* For master's, GMAT, GRE General Test. Additional exam requirements/recommendations for international students: Required—TOEFL. *Application deadline:* Applications are processed on a rolling basis. Application fee: $50. Electronic applications accepted. *Financial support:* Unspecified assistantships available. *Faculty research:* Industrial economics. *Unit head:* Elizabeth Watson, Director, 201-216-5081. *Application contact:* Graduate Admissions, 800-496-4935, Fax: 201-216-8044, E-mail: gradadmissions@stevens.edu.

Texas A&M University–San Antonio, School of Business, San Antonio, TX 78224. Offers business administration (MBA); enterprise resource planning systems (MBA); finance (MBA); healthcare management (MBA); human resources management (MBA); information assurance and security (MBA); international business (MBA); project management (MBA); supply chain management (MBA). Part-time and evening/weekend programs available. *Faculty:* 18 full-time (6 women), 1 part-time/adjunct (0 women). *Students:* 49 full-time (21 women), 195 part-time (107 women). In 2010, 20 master's awarded. *Entrance requirements:* For master's, GMAT. Additional exam requirements/recommendations for international students: Required—TOEFL (minimum score 550 paper-based; 213 computer-based; 80 iBT), IELTS (minimum score 6). *Application deadline:* For fall admission, 7/1 priority date for domestic students, 6/1 priority date for international students; for spring admission, 11/15 priority date for domestic students, 10/1 priority date for international students. Applications are processed on a rolling basis. Application fee: $35 ($50 for international students). Electronic applications accepted. *Expenses:* Tuition, state resident: full-time $2899; part-time $161 per credit hour. Tuition, nonresident: full-time $8479; part-time $471 per credit hour. Required fees: $1056; $61 per credit hour. $368 per semester. *Financial support:* Application deadline: 3/31. *Unit head:* Dr. Tracy Hurley, MBA Coordinator, 210-932-6200, E-mail: tracy.hurley@tamusa.tamus.edu. *Application contact:* Melissa A. Villanueva, Graduate Admissions Specialist, 210-932-6200, Fax: 210-932-6209, E-mail: melissa.villanueva@tamusa.tamus.edu.

TUI University, College of Business Administration, Program in Business Administration, Cypress, CA 90630. Offers business administration (PhD); conflict and negotiation management (MBA); criminal justice administration (MBA); entrepreneurship (MBA); finance (MBA); general management (MBA); government accounting (MBA); human resource management (MBA); information security and digital assurance management (MBA); information technology management (MBA); international business (MBA); logistics management (MBA); marketing (MBA); project management (MBA); public management (MBA); quality management (MBA); strategic leadership (MBA). Part-time and evening/weekend programs available. Postbaccalaureate distance learning degree programs offered (no on-campus study). *Students:* 741 full-time (200 women), 1,585 part-time (410 women). 379 applicants, 81% accepted, 300 enrolled. In 2010, 752 master's, 28 doctorates awarded. *Degree requirements:* For doctorate, comprehensive exam, thesis/dissertation, defense of dissertation. *Entrance requirements:* For master's, minimum GPA of 2.5 (students with GPA 3.0 or greater may transfer up to 30% of graduate level credits); for doctorate, minimum GPA of 3.4, curriculum vitae, course work in research methods or statistics. Additional exam requirements/recommendations for international students: Required—TOEFL. *Application deadline:* For fall admission, 10/3 for domestic and international students; for winter admission, 12/22 for domestic and international students; for spring admission, 4/3 for domestic and international students. Applications are processed on a rolling basis. Application fee: $75. Electronic applications accepted. *Expenses:* Tuition: Full-time $11,040; part-time $345 per semester hour. *Unit head:* Paul Watkins, Dean, College of Business Administration, 800-375-9878, E-mail: pwatkins@tuiu.edu. *Application contact:* Wei Ren-Finaly, Registrar, 800-375-9878, Fax: 714-827-7407, E-mail: registration@tuiu.edu.

Université du Québec en Outaouais, Graduate Programs, Program in Project Management, Gatineau, QC J8X 3X7, Canada. Offers M Sc, MA, DESS, Diploma. Programs offered jointly with Université du Québec à Chicoutimi, Université du Québec à Rimouski, Université du Québec à Trois-Rivières, Université du Québec en Abitibi-Témiscamingue, and Université du Québec à Montréal. Part-time and evening/weekend programs available. *Students:* 169 full-time, 193 part-time, 45 international. *Degree requirements:* For master's, thesis (for some programs). *Entrance requirements:* For master's, appropriate bachelor's degree, proficiency in French. *Application deadline:* For fall admission, 6/1 priority date for domestic students, 3/1 for international students; for winter admission, 11/1 priority date for domestic students, 10/1 for international students. Application fee: $30 Canadian dollars. *Financial support:* Fellowships, research assistantships, teaching assistantships available. *Unit head:* Sebastien Azondekon, Director, 819-595-3900 Ext. 1936, Fax: 819-773-1747, E-mail: sebastien.azondekon@uqo.ca. *Application contact:* Registrar Office, 819-773-1850, Fax: 819-773-1835, E-mail: registraire@ugo.ca.

The University of Alabama in Huntsville, School of Graduate Studies, College of Business Administration, Department of Management and Marketing, Huntsville, AL 35899. Offers management (MBA), including acquisition management, finance, human resource management, logistics and supply chain management, marketing, project management. *Accreditation:* AACSB. Part-time and evening/weekend programs available. *Faculty:* 11 full-time (2 women), 4 part-time/adjunct (1 woman). *Students:* 41 full-time (17 women), 159 part-time (69 women); includes 32 minority (15 Black or African American, non-Hispanic/Latino; 6 American Indian or Alaska Native, non-Hispanic/Latino; 7 Asian, non-Hispanic/Latino; 3 Hispanic/Latino; 1 Two or more races, non-Hispanic/Latino), 14 international. Average age 31. 141 applicants, 65% accepted, 79 enrolled. In 2010, 66 master's awarded. *Degree requirements:* For master's, comprehensive exam, thesis or alternative. *Entrance requirements:* For master's, GMAT (minimum score 500), minimum AACSB index of 1080. Additional exam requirements/recommendations for international students: Required—TOEFL (minimum score 550 paper-based; 213 computer-based; 62 iBT). *Application deadline:* For fall admission, 8/1 for domestic students, 4/1 for international students; for spring admission, 12/1 for domestic students, 9/1 for international students. Applications are processed on a rolling basis. Application fee: $40 ($50 for international students). Electronic applications accepted. *Expenses:* Tuition, state resident: full-time $7250; part-time $407.75 per credit hour. Tuition, nonresident: full-time $17,358; part-time $970.05 per credit hour. Required fees: $246.80 per semester. Tuition and fees vary according to course load and program. *Financial support:* In 2010–11, 3 students received support, including 1 research assistantship with full tuition reimbursement available (averaging $8,550 per year), 2 teaching assistantships with full tuition reimbursements available (averaging $8,000 per year); career-related internships or fieldwork, Federal Work-Study, institutionally sponsored loans, scholarships/grants, health care benefits, and unspecified assistantships also available. Support available to part-time students. Financial award application deadline: 4/1; financial award applicants required to submit FAFSA. *Faculty research:* Strategic human resources, corporate governance, cross-function integration and the management of research and development, determinants of team performance. Total annual research expenditures: $3 million. *Unit head:* Dr. Brent Wren, Chair, 256-824-6408, Fax: 256-824-6328, E-mail: wrenb@uah.edu. *Application contact:* Jennifer Pettitt, Director of Graduate Programs, 256-824-6681, Fax: 256-824-7571, E-mail: jennifer.pettitt@uah.edu.

University of Denver, University College, Denver, CO 80208. Offers arts and culture (MLS, Certificate), including art, literature, and culture, arts development and program management (Certificate), creative writing; environmental policy and management (MAS, Certificate), including energy and sustainability (Certificate), environmental assessment of nuclear power (Certificate), environmental health and safety (Certificate), environmental management, natural resource management (Certificate); geographic information systems (MAS, Certificate); global affairs (MLS, Certificate), including translation studies, world history and culture; healthcare leadership (MPH, Certificate), including healthcare policy, law, and ethics, medical and healthcare information technologies, strategic management of healthcare; information and communications technology (MCIS, Certificate), including database design and administration (Certificate), geographic information systems (MCIS), information security systems security (Certificate), information systems security (MCIS), project management (MCIS, MPS, Certificate), software design and administration (Certificate), software design and programming (MCIS), technology management, telecommunications technology (MCIS), Web design and development; leadership and organizations (MPS, Certificate), including human capital in organizations, philanthropic leadership, project management (MCIS, MPS, Certificate), strategic innovation and change; organizational and professional communication (MPS, Certificate), including alternative dispute resolution, organizational communication, organizational development and training, public relations and marketing; security management (MAS, Certificate), including emergency planning and response, information security (MAS), organizational security; strategic human resource management (MPS, Certificate), including global human resources (MPS), human resource management and development (MPS). Part-time and evening/weekend programs available. Postbaccalaureate distance learning degree programs offered (no on-campus study). *Faculty:* 7 full-time (2 women), 212 part-time/adjunct (83 women). *Students:* 52 full-time (19 women), 1,044 part-time (625 women); includes 196 minority (81 Black or African American, non-Hispanic/Latino; 7 American Indian or Alaska Native, non-Hispanic/Latino; 30 Asian, non-Hispanic/Latino; 66 Hispanic/Latino; 3 Native Hawaiian or other Pacific Islander, non-Hispanic/Latino; 9 Two or more races, non-Hispanic/Latino), 76 international. Average age 36. 488 applicants, 91% accepted, 339 enrolled. In 2010, 286 master's, 130 other advanced degrees awarded. *Entrance requirements:* Additional exam requirements/recommendations for international students: Required—TOEFL (minimum score 550 paper-based; 80 iBT). *Application deadline:* For fall admission, 6/22 priority date for domestic students, 6/10 priority date for international students; for winter admission, 9/15 priority date for domestic students, 9/6 priority date for international students; for spring admission, 2/3 priority date for domestic students, 12/15 priority date for international students. Applications are processed on a rolling basis. Application fee: $75. Electronic applications accepted. *Expenses:* Contact institution. *Financial support:* Applicants required to submit FAFSA. *Unit head:* Dr. James Davis, Dean, 303-871-2291, Fax: 303-871-4047, E-mail: jdavis@du.edu. *Application contact:* Information Contact, 303-871-3155, Fax: 303-871-4047, E-mail: ucolinfo@du.edu.

University of Houston, College of Technology, Department of Information and Logistics Technology, Houston, TX 77204. Offers information security (MS); supply chain and logistics technology (MS); technology project management (MS). Part-time programs available. *Faculty:* 6 full-time (3 women), 6 part-time/adjunct (2 women). *Students:* 80 full-time (30 women), 75 part-time (29 women); includes 35 minority (12 Black or African American, non-Hispanic/Latino; 9 Asian, non-Hispanic/Latino; 11 Hispanic/Latino; 1 Native Hawaiian or other Pacific Islander, non-Hispanic/Latino; 2 Two or more races, non-Hispanic/Latino), 73 international. Average age 31. 60 applicants, 92%

accepted, 35 enrolled. In 2010, 22 master's awarded. *Degree requirements:* For master's, project or thesis (most programs). *Entrance requirements:* For master's, GMAT. Additional exam requirements/recommendations for international students: Required—TOEFL (minimum score 550 paper-based; 79 iBT). *Application deadline:* For fall admission, 7/1 for domestic students, 4/1 for international students; for spring admission, 12/1 for domestic students, 10/1 for international students. Applications are processed on a rolling basis. Application fee: $75 ($150 for international students). Electronic applications accepted. *Expenses:* Tuition, state resident: full-time $8592; part-time $358 per credit hour. Tuition, nonresident: full-time $16,032; part-time $668 per credit hour. Required fees: $2889. Tuition and fees vary according to course load and program. *Financial support:* In 2010–11, 10 research assistantships with partial tuition reimbursements (averaging $8,380 per year), 15 teaching assistantships with partial tuition reimbursements (averaging $8,078 per year) were awarded. *Unit head:* Michael Gibson, Chairperson, 713-743-5116, E-mail: mlgibson@uh.edu. *Application contact:* Tiffany Roosa, Graduate Advisor, 713-743-4100, Fax: 713-743-4151, E-mail: troosa@uh.edu.

University of Mary, Gary Tharaldson School of Business, Bismarck, ND 58504-9652. Offers accountancy (MBA); business administration (MBA); health care (MBA); human resource management (MBA); management (MBA); project management (MPM); strategic leadership (MSSL). Part-time and evening/weekend programs available. *Faculty:* 2 full-time (0 women), 73 part-time/adjunct (27 women). *Students:* 232 full-time (123 women), 226 part-time (115 women); includes 63 minority (30 Black or African American, non-Hispanic/Latino; 23 American Indian or Alaska Native, non-Hispanic/Latino; 5 Asian, non-Hispanic/Latino; 3 Hispanic/Latino; 1 Native Hawaiian or other Pacific Islander, non-Hispanic/Latino; 1 Two or more races, non-Hispanic/Latino), 20 international. Average age 36. 209 applicants, 98% accepted, 189 enrolled. In 2010, 265 master's awarded. *Degree requirements:* For master's, strategic planning seminar. *Entrance requirements:* For master's, minimum GPA of 2.5. Additional exam requirements/recommendations for international students: Required—TOEFL (minimum score 500 paper-based; 197 computer-based; 71 iBT). *Application deadline:* Applications are processed on a rolling basis. Application fee: $40. *Expenses:* Tuition: Full-time $10,800; part-time $450 per credit. Tuition and fees vary according to course load, degree level, program and student level. *Financial support:* Application deadline: 8/1. *Unit head:* Dr. Shanda Traiser, Director of the School of Accelerated and Distance Education, 701-355-8160, Fax: 701-255-7687, E-mail: straiser@umary.edu. *Application contact:* Wayne G. Maruska, Graduate Program Advisor, 701-355-8134, Fax: 701-255-7687, E-mail: wmaruska@umary.edu.

University of Michigan–Dearborn, College of Engineering and Computer Science, Department of Industrial and Manufacturing Systems Engineering, Dearborn, MI 48128-1491. Offers engineering management (MS); industrial and systems engineering (MSE); information systems and technology (MS); information systems engineering (PhD); program and project management (MS); MBA/MSE. Part-time and evening/weekend programs available. *Faculty:* 13 full-time (0 women), 3 part-time/adjunct (0 women). *Students:* 23 full-time (8 women), 142 part-time (40 women); includes 14 Black or African American, non-Hispanic/Latino; 27 Asian, non-Hispanic/Latino; 8 Hispanic/Latino, 23 international. Average age 35. 81 applicants, 58% accepted, 47 enrolled. In 2010, 57 master's awarded. *Degree requirements:* For master's, thesis optional. *Entrance requirements:* For master's, bachelor's degree in applied mathematics, computer science, engineering, or physical science; minimum GPA of 3.0. Additional exam requirements/recommendations for international students: Required—TOEFL (minimum score 560 paper-based; 220 computer-based; 84 iBT). *Application deadline:* For fall admission, 8/1 priority date for domestic students, 4/1 for international students; for winter admission, 12/1 priority date for domestic students, 8/1 for international students; for spring admission, 4/1 for domestic students, 12/1 for international students. Applications are processed on a rolling basis. Application fee: $60. Electronic applications accepted. *Financial support:* Fellowships, research assistantships, teaching assistantships, Federal Work-Study available. Financial award application deadline: 4/1; financial award applicants required to submit FAFSA. *Faculty research:* Health care systems, data and knowledge management, human factors engineering, machine diagnostics, precision machining. *Unit head:* Dr. Armen Zakarian, Chair, 313-593-5361, Fax: 313-593-3692, E-mail: zakarian@umd.umich.edu. *Application contact:* Joey W. Woods, Graduate Program Assistant, 313-593-5361, Fax: 313-593-3692, E-mail: jwwoods@umd.umich.edu.

University of Oklahoma, College of Arts and Sciences, Department of Psychology, Program in Organizational Dynamics, Tulsa, OK 74135. Offers organizational dynamics (MA), including human resource management, organizational dynamics, technical project management. Part-time and evening/weekend programs available. *Students:* 9 full-time (4 women), 25 part-time (13 women); includes 6 minority (1 Black or African American, non-Hispanic/Latino; 1 American Indian or Alaska Native, non-Hispanic/Latino; 2 Asian, non-Hispanic/Latino; 1 Native Hawaiian or other Pacific Islander, non-Hispanic/Latino; 1 Two or more races, non-Hispanic/Latino). Average age 37. 6 applicants, 100% accepted, 6 enrolled. In 2010, 11 master's awarded. *Entrance requirements:* For master's, minimum GPA of 3.0 in last 60 hours of undergraduate course work. Additional exam requirements/recommendations for international students: Required—TOEFL (minimum score 550

paper-based; 213 computer-based; 79 iBT). *Application deadline:* For fall admission, 4/15 priority date for domestic students, 4/15 for international students; for spring admission, 11/1 for domestic students, 9/1 for international students. Applications are processed on a rolling basis. Application fee: $40 ($90 for international students). Electronic applications accepted. *Expenses:* Tuition, state resident: full-time $3893; part-time $162.20 per credit hour. Tuition, nonresident: full-time $14,167; part-time $590.30 per credit hour. Required fees: $2523; $94.60 per credit hour. Tuition and fees vary according to course load and degree level. *Financial support:* In 2010–11, 10 students received support. Scholarships/grants, health care benefits, and unspecified assistantships available. Financial award application deadline: 3/1; financial award applicants required to submit FAFSA. *Faculty research:* Academic integrity, organizational behavior, interdisciplinary teams, shared leadership. *Unit head:* Dr. Jorge Mendoza, Chair, 405-325-4511, Fax: 405-325-4737, E-mail: jmendoza@ou.edu. *Application contact:* Jennifer Kisamore, Graduate Liaison, 918-660-3603, Fax: 918-660-3383, E-mail: jkisamore@ou.edu.

University of Phoenix, School of Business, Phoenix, AZ 85034-7209. Offers accounting (MBA, MSA); business administration (MBA); energy management (MBA); global management (MBA); health care management (MBA); human resources management (MM); international management (MM); management (MM); marketing (MBA); project management (MBA); public administration (MPA); technology management (MBA). Programs are offered at the online campus. Evening/weekend programs available. Postbaccalaureate distance learning degree programs offered. *Students:* 20,237 full-time (12,641 women); includes 6,424 minority (4,376 Black or African American, non-Hispanic/Latino; 150 American Indian or Alaska Native, non-Hispanic/Latino; 546 Asian, non-Hispanic/Latino; 1,137 Hispanic/Latino; 155 Native Hawaiian or other Pacific Islander, non-Hispanic/Latino; 60 Two or more races, non-Hispanic/Latino), 1,149 international. Average age 39. *Entrance requirements:* For master's, minimum undergraduate GPA of 2.5 from accredited university, 3 years of work experience, citizen of the United States or have valid visa. Additional exam requirements/recommendations for international students: Required—TOEFL (minimum paper score 550, computer score 213, iBT 79), Test of English for International Communication, or IELTS. *Application deadline:* Applications are processed on a rolling basis. Application fee: $45. Electronic applications accepted. *Expenses:* Tuition: Full-time $16,440. One-time fee: $45 full-time. Full-time tuition and fees vary according to course load, degree level, campus/location and program. *Financial support:* Scholarships/grants available. Financial award applicants required to submit FAFSA. *Unit head:* Dr. Bill Berry, Director, 480-557-1824, E-mail: bill.berry@phoenix.edu. *Application contact:* Dr. Bill Berry, Director, 480-557-1824, E-mail: bill.berry@phoenix.edu.

University of Regina, Faculty of Graduate Studies and Research, Kenneth Levene Graduate School of Business, Program in Business Administration, Regina, SK S4S 0A2, Canada. Offers business (Master's Certificate); business administration (MBA); executive business administration (MBA); international business (MBA); leadership (M Admin); organizational leadership (Master's Certificate); project management (Master's Certificate). Part-time and evening/weekend programs available. *Faculty:* 51 full-time (14 women), 10 part-time/adjunct (0 women). *Students:* 59 full-time (18 women), 19 part-time (7 women). 132 applicants, 80% accepted. In 2010, 39 master's awarded. *Degree requirements:* For master's, project. *Entrance requirements:* For master's, GMAT, two years relevant work experience. Additional exam requirements/recommendations for international students: Required—TOEFL (minimum score 580 paper-based; 80 iBT). *Application deadline:* Applications are processed on a rolling basis. Application fee: $100. Electronic applications accepted. *Expenses:* Contact institution. *Financial support:* In 2010–11, 3 fellowships (averaging $18,000 per year), 3 teaching assistantships (averaging $6,759 per year) were awarded; research assistantships, scholarships/grants also available. Financial award application deadline: 6/15. *Faculty research:* Business policy and strategy, production and operations management, human behavior in organizations, financial management, social issues in business. *Unit head:* Dr. Anne Lavack, Dean, 306-585-4162, Fax: 306-585-4805, E-mail: anne.lavack@uregina.ca. *Application contact:* Steve Wield, Manager, 306-337-8463, Fax: 306-585-5361, E-mail: steve.wield@uregina.ca.

University of San Francisco, School of Business and Professional Studies, Program in Project Management, San Francisco, CA 94117-1080. Offers MS. *Faculty:* 1 (woman) full-time, 5 part-time/adjunct (3 women). *Students:* 36 full-time (22 women), 1 part-time (0 women); includes 19 minority (1 Black or African American, non-Hispanic/Latino; 9 Asian, non-Hispanic/Latino; 3 Hispanic/Latino; 2 Native Hawaiian or other Pacific Islander, non-Hispanic/Latino; 4 Two or more races, non-Hispanic/Latino), 2 international. Average age 34. 37 applicants, 57% accepted, 13 enrolled. In 2010, 11 master's awarded. *Expenses:* Tuition: Full-time $20,070; part-time $1115 per credit hour. Tuition and fees vary according to course load, degree level and program. *Financial support:* In 2010–11, 25 students received support. *Unit head:* Dr. Linda Henderson, Director, 415-422-2592. *Application contact:* Dr. Linda Henderson, Director, 415-422-2592.

The University of Tennessee at Chattanooga, Graduate School, College of Engineering and Computer Science, Program in Engineering Management, Chattanooga, TN 37403. Offers engineering management (MS); fundamentals of engineering management (Graduate Certificate); power systems management (Graduate Certificate); project and value management (Graduate Certificate); quality management (Graduate Certificate). Postbaccalaureate distance learning degree programs offered (no on-campus study). *Faculty:* 4 full-time (1 woman). *Students:* 15 full-time (4 women), 77 part-time (13 women); includes 8 Black or African American, non-Hispanic/Latino; 1 Asian, non-Hispanic/Latino; 1 Hispanic/Latino, 11 international. Average age 32. 29 applicants, 100% accepted. In 2010, 23 master's, 20 other advanced degrees awarded. *Degree requirements:* For master's, thesis. *Entrance requirements:* For master's, GRE General Test, letters of recommendation; minimum undergraduate GPA of 2.5 overall or 3.0 in senior year. Additional exam requirements/recommendations for international students: Required—TOEFL (minimum score 550 paper-based; 213 computer-based; 79 iBT), IELTS (minimum score 6). *Application deadline:* For fall admission, 8/1 priority date for domestic students, 6/1 for international students; for spring admission, 12/1 priority date for domestic students, 10/1 for international students. Applications are processed on a rolling basis. Application fee: $35. Electronic applications accepted. *Financial support:* In 2010–11, 5 research assistantships with full and partial tuition reimbursements (averaging $5,500 per year) were awarded; career-related internships or fieldwork, scholarships/grants, and unspecified assistantships also available. Support available to part-time students. *Faculty research:* Plant layout design, lean manufacturing, six sigma, value management, product development. *Unit head:* Dr. Neslihan Alp, Director, 423-425-4032, Fax: 423-425-5229, E-mail: neslihan-alp@utc.edu. *Application contact:* Dr. Jerald Ainsworth, Dean of Graduate Studies, 423-425-4478, Fax: 423-425-5223, E-mail: jerald-ainsworth@utc.edu.

The University of Texas at Dallas, School of Management, Program in Business Administration, Richardson, TX 75080. Offers cohort (MBA); executive business administration (EMBA); global leadership (EMBA); global online (MBA); healthcare management (EMBA); professional business administration (MBA); project management (EMBA); MSEE/MBA. *Accreditation:* AACSB. Part-time and evening/weekend programs available. Postbaccalaureate distance learning degree programs offered (no on-campus study). *Faculty:* 78 full-time (14 women), 28 part-time/adjunct (6 women). *Students:* 426 full-time (138 women), 704 part-time (216 women); includes 333 minority (39 Black or African American, non-Hispanic/Latino; 5 American Indian or Alaska Native, non-Hispanic/Latino; 199 Asian, non-Hispanic/Latino; 84 Hispanic/Latino; 6 Two or more races, non-Hispanic/Latino), 200 international. Average age 32. 766 applicants, 51% accepted, 282 enrolled. In 2010, 503 master's awarded. *Degree requirements:* For master's, thesis optional. *Entrance requirements:* For master's, GMAT, 10 years of business experience (EMBA), minimum GPA of 3.0. Additional exam requirements/recommendations for international students: Required—TOEFL (minimum score 550 paper-based; 215 computer-based). *Application deadline:* For fall admission, 7/15 for domestic students, 5/1 priority date for international students; for spring admission, 11/15 for domestic students, 9/1 priority date for international students. Applications are processed on a rolling basis. Application fee: $50 ($100 for international students). Electronic applications accepted. *Expenses:* Contact institution. *Financial support:* In 2010–11, 265 students received support, including 2 research assistantships with partial tuition reimbursements available (averaging $11,367 per year), 39 teaching assistantships with partial tuition reimbursements available (averaging $11,528 per year); career-related internships or fieldwork, Federal Work-Study, institutionally sponsored loans, scholarships/grants, and unspecified assistantships also available. Support available to part-time students. Financial award application deadline: 4/30; financial award applicants required to submit FAFSA. *Faculty research:* Production scheduling, trade and finance, organizational decision making, life/work planning. *Unit head:* Lisa Shatz, Director, 972-883-6191, E-mail: mba@utdallas.edu. *Application contact:* James Parker, Assistant Director, 972-883-5842, E-mail: jparker@utdallas.edu.

University of the Incarnate Word, School of Graduate Studies and Research, H-E-B School of Business and Administration, Programs in Administration, San Antonio, TX 78209-6397. Offers adult education (MAA); applied administration (MAA); communication arts (MAA); healthcare administration (MAA); instructional technology (MAA); international business (Certificate); nutrition (MAA); organizational development (MAA, Certificate); project management (Certificate); sports management (MAA). Part-time and evening/weekend programs available. Postbaccalaureate distance learning degree programs offered (no on-campus study). *Students:* 30 full-time (20 women), 64 part-time (37 women); includes 10 Black or African American, non-Hispanic/Latino; 1 Asian, non-Hispanic/Latino; 48 Hispanic/Latino, 8 international. Average age 35. In 2010, 68 master's awarded. *Degree requirements:* For master's, capstone. *Entrance requirements:* For master's, GRE, GMAT, undergraduate degree, minimum GPA of 2.5. Additional exam requirements/recommendations for international students: Required—TOEFL (minimum score 560 paper-based; 220 computer-based; 83 iBT). *Application deadline:* Applications are processed on a rolling basis. Application fee: $20. Electronic applications accepted. *Expenses:* Tuition: Part-time $725 per contact hour. Required fees: $890 per semester. *Financial support:* Federal Work-Study and scholarships/grants available. Financial award applicants required to submit FAFSA. *Unit head:* Dr. Daniel Dominguez, MAA Programs Director, 210-829-3180, Fax: 210-805-3564, E-mail: domingue@uiwtx.edu. *Application contact:* Andrea Cyterski-Acosta, Dean of Enrollment, 210-829-6005, Fax: 210-829-3921, E-mail: admis@uiwtx.edu.

University of Wisconsin–Platteville, School of Graduate Studies, Distance Learning Center, Online Master of Science in Project Management Program, Platteville, WI 53818-3099. Offers MS. Part-time and evening/weekend programs available. Postbaccalaureate distance learning degree programs offered (no on-campus study). *Students:* 3 full-time (0 women), 199 part-time (68 women); includes 30 minority (15 Black or African American, non-Hispanic/Latino; 2 American Indian or Alaska Native, non-Hispanic/Latino; 7 Asian, non-Hispanic/Latino; 4 Hispanic/Latino; 2 Native Hawaiian or other Pacific Islander, non-Hispanic/Latino), 21 international. 100 applicants, 62% accepted, 38 enrolled. In 2010, 50 master's awarded. *Degree requirements:* For master's, thesis or alternative. *Entrance requirements:* Additional exam requirements/recommendations for international students: Required—TOEFL (minimum score 500 paper-based; 173 computer-based; 61 iBT). *Application deadline:* For fall admission, 7/1 priority date for domestic students; for spring admission, 11/1 priority date for domestic students. Applications are processed on a rolling basis. Application fee: $56. Electronic applications accepted. *Expenses:* Tuition, state resident: full-time $7000. Tuition, nonresident: full-time $16,800. Required fees: $756. *Unit head:* William Haskins, Coordinator, 608-342-1961, Fax: 608-342-1466, E-mail: haskinsd@uwplatt.edu. *Application contact:* William Haskins, Coordinator, 608-342-1961, Fax: 608-342-1466, E-mail: haskinsd@uwplatt.edu.

Walden University, Graduate Programs, School of Management, Minneapolis, MN 55401. Offers accounting (MS), including cpa emphasis, professional track, self-designed; accounting and management (MS), including self-designed, strategic management; applied management and decision sciences (PhD), including accounting, engineering management, finance, general applied management and decision sciences, information systems management, knowledge management, leadership and organizational change, learning management, operations research, self-designed program in applied management and design sciences; business information management (MISM); enterprise information security (MISM); entrepreneurship (MBA, DBA); finance (MBA, DBA); global management (MS); global supply chain management (DBA); health informatics (MISM); healthcare management (MBA, MS); healthcare system improvement (MBA); human resource management (MBA, MS), including functional human resource management (MS), human resource management (MS), integrating functional and strategic human resource management (MS), organizational strategy (MS); information systems (MS); information systems management (DBA); information technology (MS), including information security, software engineering; international business (MBA, DBA); IT strategy and governance (MISM); leadership (MBA, MS, DBA), including entrepreneurship (MS), general management (MS), human resources leadership (MS), innovation and technology (MS), leader development (MS), leading sustainability (MS), project management (MS), self-designed (MS); managers as leaders (MS); managing global software and service supply chains (MISM); marketing (MBA, DBA); project management (MBA, MS); research strategies (MS); risk management (MBA); self-designed (MBA, DBA); social impact management (DBA); strategy and operations (MS); sustainable futures (MBA); sustainable management (MS); technology (MBA); technology entrepreneurship (DBA); technology management (MS). Part-time and evening/weekend programs available. Postbaccalaureate distance learning degree programs offered (minimal on-campus study). *Faculty:* 22 full-time (8 women), 291 part-time/adjunct (100 women). *Students:* 3,705 full-time (1,956 women), 976 part-time (549 women); includes 2,432 minority (2,021 Black or African American, non-Hispanic/Latino; 32 American Indian or Alaska Native, non-Hispanic/Latino; 137 Asian, non-Hispanic/Latino; 193 Hispanic/Latino; 5 Native Hawaiian or other Pacific Islander, non-Hispanic/Latino; 44 Two or more races, non-Hispanic/Latino), 302 international. Average age 40. In 2010, 658 master's, 86 doctorates awarded. *Degree requirements:* For doctorate, thesis/dissertation (for some programs), residency. *Entrance requirements:* For master's, bachelor's degree or equivalent in related field; minimum GPA of 2.5; official transcripts; goal statement; access to computer and Internet; for doctorate, master's degree or equivalent in related field; minimum GPA of 3.0; 3 years of related professional/academic experience (preferred). Additional exam requirements/recommendations for international students: Required—TOEFL (minimum score 550 paper-based; 213 computer-based), IELTS (minimum score 6.5), Michigan English Language Assessment Battery (minimum score 82). *Application deadline:* Applications are processed on a rolling basis. Application fee: $50. Electronic applications accepted. *Expenses:* Tuition: Full-time $10,274; part-time $445 per credit. Tuition and fees vary according to course load, degree level and program. *Financial support:* Fellowships, Federal Work-Study, scholarships/grants, unspecified assistantships, and family tuition reduction, active duty/veteran tuition reduction, group tuition reduction, interest-free payment plans available. Support available to part-time students. Financial award applicants required to submit FAFSA. *Unit head:* Dr. William Schulz, Associate Dean, 800-925-3368. *Application contact:* Jennifer Hall, Vice President of Enrollment Management, 866-4-WALDEN, E-mail: info@waldenu.edu.

Quality Management

OVERVIEW

The quality management emphasis within an MBA program is designed to provide learners with the skills and knowledge needed to advance quality within both service and manufacturing organizations and prepare them for careers in the fields of total quality management, quality control management, business analysis, project management, project controlling, and project implementation management.

At the overview level, an MBA in quality management covers the foundations of the quality movement, the critical concepts of quality, and a thorough understanding of continuous improvement practices by using the definition and measurement of outcomes and techniques to achieve increased quality of organizational activities. Students pursuing this track can expect to cover topics such as information technology project management, human factors and team management dynamics, quality design for Six Sigma, and total quality management. Relevant theories and quality improvement processes are often explored in conjunction with application to real-world environments and problems. Learners may be expected to develop a comprehension of and demonstrate the ability to use major audit procedures, as well as mastering the historical view of quality management and how it has shaped organizational competitiveness.

Required courses may include study in:

- Business Process Management
- Contemporary Issues in Quality Management
- Economics for Decision-Making
- Financial Statement Analysis
- Marketing and Brand Management
- Problem Analysis and Research Methods
- Six Sigma Quality Management
- Strategic Human Resource Management
- Strategic Management and Competitive Globalization
- Statistical Quality Control

Elective courses may include study in:

- Human Factors and Team Dynamics
- Information Systems in Project Management
- Project Management for Professionals
- Quality Design for Six Sigma
- Total Quality Management

Some program course work may lead to professional quality and project management industry certifications. Students completing this program can expect to be able to assume a leadership role advancing quality in organizations. Therefore, individuals with leadership aspirations and oriented task management who are looking for a career in business management are likely to be successful program candidates and graduates.

IN THIS SECTION

You'll find profiles of institutions offering graduate programs in the following field:

HELPFUL ORGANIZATIONS/ PUBLICATIONS/BLOGS

American Society for Quality (ASQ)

http://asq.org/index.aspx

Established in 1946, the American Society for Quality (ASQ) marked the 25th anniversary of its International Team Excellence Award at the World Conference on Quality and Improvement in 2010. ASQ's participation and influence in international standards includes its role as the administrator of the U.S. Technical Advisory Group of the ISO 26000 standard on social responsibility.

Headquartered in Milwaukee, WI, ASQ supports membership services and business operations through ASQ Global, ASQ China, ASQ Mexico, and ASQ India; with ASQ WorldPartners® around the globe; and through its work with ANAB and RABQSA.

ASQ is a global community of experts and the leading authority on quality in all fields, organizations, and industries. As a professional association, ASQ advances the professional development, credentials, knowledge, and information services, membership community, and advocacy on behalf of its more than 85,000 members worldwide. As champion of the quality movement, ASQ members are driven by a sense of responsibility to enrich their lives, improve their workplaces and communities, and make the world a better place by applying quality tools, techniques, and systems.

International Organization for Standardization (ISO)

http://www.iso.org/iso/home.html

The International Organization for Standardization (ISO) is the world's largest developer and publisher of International Standards. ISO is a network of the national standards institutes of 162 countries, one member per country, with a Central Secretariat in Geneva, Switzerland, that coordinates the system. ISO is a nongovernmental organization that forms a bridge between the public and private sectors. On the one hand, many of its member institutes are part of the governmental structure of their countries or are mandated by their government. On the other hand, other members have their roots uniquely in the private sector, having been set up by national partnerships of industry associations. Therefore, ISO enables a consensus to be reached on solutions that meet both the requirements of business and the broader needs of society.

Society of Quality Assurance (SQA)

http://www.sqa.org/

The Society of Quality Assurance (SQA) is a professional membership organization dedicated to promoting and advancing the principles and knowledge of quality assurance essential to human, animal, and environmental health. Current membership of the Society is nearly 2,500 active and affiliate members in more than 30 countries working in industry, government, academia, and consulting. The Society includes general membership, special interest and administrative committees, regional chapters, and specialty sections.

According to its vision statement, SQA will be the premier quality assurance professional organization, known as the innovative leader in:

- Providing professional development, education, and training.
- Creating collaborative relationships with governmental authorities, professional organizations, academia, and industry.
- Participating in the regulatory processes related to human, animal, and environmental health.

The professionals in the Society are challenged to perform duties relating to quality assurance of:

- Nonclinical laboratory studies subject to the Good Laboratory Practice (GLP) regulations of the U.S. Environmental Protection Agency (EPA) and the U.S. Food and Drug Administration (FDA).
- Clinical studies subject to Good Clinical Practice (GCP) regulations of the FDA and International Conference on Harmonization (ICH).
- Current Good Manufacturing Practices (cGMP) worldwide.

CAREER ASPIRATIONS: A PROSPECTIVE POSITION

Assistant Vice President, Medical Management

Job Description

As a member of the Managed Care Management Team, you will manage the Medical Management Department, which includes Product Management and the Nurse Case Managers. You will also provide guidance and be responsible for all aspects of the program and provide leadership and direction to ensure that the company is recognized as best in class and maintain a competitive advantage in the property and casualty insurance and self-insured markets.

Responsibilities

- Develop the strategic vision for the medical management programs and services; design and implement medical management services that align with and complement the organization's service strategy, model, and reputation.
- Responsible for medical management services profit/loss for the organization; use cost/benefit analysis and program evaluation to develop the operational model, staffing levels, and information technology investments.
- Identify, negotiate with, and evaluate strategic business partners for services to supplement and complement the organization's medical management services.
- Oversee the development of the outcome data and management information needed to validate the impact of the organization's medical management services for internal and external customers.
- Oversee the development and implementation of the medical management quality assurance (QA) program and report out on QA trends.
- Submit recommendations regarding medical management services billing strategy.
- Monitor medical management services industry to ensure the organization's services remain competitive.
- Represent the Managed Care Services Department at customer meetings, on interdepartmental committees, and through professional organizations, including periodic consultations with practitioners in the field.
- Supervise case management managers, case management nurses, and medical corporate specialists.

Qualifications

- Bachelor's degree required; MBA or equivalent master's degree is preferred
- Postgraduate experience in direct patient care is preferred
- Current, unrestricted registered nursing or physical or occupational therapy license is preferred
- Strong national worker's compensation experience is required
- CCM, CMAC, CDMS designations are preferred
- Minimum 3–5 years of senior management responsibilities
- Minimum of 10 years of managed care experience
- Prior experience working collaboratively with cross-function business units to launch, implement, and evaluate projects
- Proven project management experience with the ability to work on multiple projects simultaneously and to effectively prioritize
- Demonstrated management and leadership skills with a proven track record of successful group dynamics and interpersonal relationships
- Strong analytical skills are required with the ability to solve complex problems
- Prior experience establishing and maintaining quality management processes
- Effective communication skills with demonstrated interpersonal skills and the ability to influence; direct both verbally and in written communications with internal and external parties on a wide variety of issues

QUALITY MANAGEMENT

California State University, Dominguez Hills, College of Extended and International Education, Program in Quality Assurance, Carson, CA 90747-0001. Offers MS. Part-time and evening/weekend programs available. Postbaccalaureate distance learning degree programs offered (no on-campus study). *Faculty:* 18 part-time/adjunct (4 women). *Students:* 5 full-time (4 women), 248 part-time (132 women); includes 25 Black or African American, non-Hispanic/Latino; 1 American Indian or Alaska Native, non-Hispanic/Latino; 41 Asian, non-Hispanic/Latino; 23 Hispanic/Latino; 2 Native Hawaiian or other Pacific Islander, non-Hispanic/Latino, 19 international. Average age 41. 117 applicants, 73% accepted, 66 enrolled. In 2010, 57 master's awarded. *Degree requirements:* For master's, thesis. *Entrance requirements:* For master's, minimum GPA of 2.75. Additional exam requirements/recommendations for international students: Required—TOEFL. *Application deadline:* For fall admission, 6/1 priority date for domestic and international students; for spring admission, 10/1 priority date for domestic and international students. Application fee: $55. Electronic applications accepted. *Expenses:* Contact institution. *Faculty research:* Six Sigma, lean thinking, risk management, quality management. *Unit head:* Dr. Milton Krivokuca, Coordinator, 310-243-3880, Fax: 310-516-4423, E-mail: mkrivokuca@csudh.edu. *Application contact:* Rodger Hamrick, Program Assistant, 310-243-3880, E-mail: rhamrick@csudh.edu.

Eastern Michigan University, Graduate School, College of Technology, School of Engineering Technology, Program in Quality Management, Ypsilanti, MI 48197. Offers quality (MS, Graduate Certificate); quality management (MS). Part-time and evening/weekend programs available. Postbaccalaureate distance learning degree programs offered (minimal on-campus study). *Students:* 7 full-time (2 women), 108 part-time (40 women); includes 20 minority (12 Black or African American, non-Hispanic/Latino; 4 Asian, non-Hispanic/Latino; 4 Hispanic/Latino), 5 international. Average age 42. In 2010, 24 master's, 7 other advanced degrees awarded. *Entrance requirements:* Additional exam requirements/recommendations for international students: Required—TOEFL. *Application deadline:* Applications are processed on a rolling basis. Application fee: $35. *Financial support:* Fellowships, research assistantships with full tuition reimbursements, teaching assistantships with full tuition reimbursements, career-related internships or fieldwork, Federal Work-Study, institutionally sponsored loans, scholarships/grants, tuition waivers (partial), and unspecified assistantships available. Support available to part-time students. Financial award applicants required to submit FAFSA. *Unit head:* Dr. Walter Tucker, Program Coordinator, 734-487-2040, Fax: 734-487-8755, E-mail: walter.tucker@emich.edu. *Application contact:* Dr. Walter Tucker, Program Coordinator, 734-487-2040, Fax: 734-487-8755, E-mail: walter.tucker@emich.edu.

Ferris State University, College of Business, Big Rapids, MI 49307. Offers application development (MSISM); business intelligence and informatics (MBA); database administration (MSISM); design and innovation management process (MBA); e-business (MSISM); networking (MSISM); quality management (MBA); security (MSISM). *Accreditation:* ACBSP. Part-time and evening/weekend programs available. *Faculty:* 10 full-time (3 women), 2 part-time/adjunct (both women). *Students:* 34 full-time (9 women), 112 part-time (55 women); includes 3 Black or African American, non-Hispanic/Latino; 4 American Indian or Alaska Native, non-Hispanic/Latino; 3 Asian, non-Hispanic/Latino; 3 Hispanic/Latino; 4 Two or more races, non-Hispanic/Latino, 16 international. Average age 32. 68 applicants, 35% accepted, 15 enrolled. In 2010, 62 master's awarded. *Degree requirements:* For master's, comprehensive exam, thesis (for MSISM). *Entrance requirements:* For master's, GRE or GMAT (waived if GPA is 3.5 or better), minimum GPA of 3.0 in junior/senior level classes, 2.75 overall; writing sample; 3 letters of reference; resume. Additional exam requirements/recommendations for international students: Required—TOEFL (minimum score 500 paper-based; 173 computer-based; 67 iBT). *Application deadline:* For fall admission, 7/1 priority date for domestic students, 6/15 for international students; for winter admission, 11/1 priority date for domestic students, 10/15 for international students; for spring admission, 3/1 priority date for domestic students, 2/15 for international students. Applications are processed on a rolling basis. Application fee: $30. Electronic applications accepted. *Financial support:* Career-related internships or fieldwork, Federal Work-Study, scholarships/grants, and unspecified assistantships available. Support available to part-time students. Financial award application deadline: 3/15; financial award applicants required to submit FAFSA. *Faculty research:* Quality improvement, client/server end-user computing, information management and policy, security, digital forensics. *Unit head:* Dr. David Steenstra, Department Chair, 231-591-2168, Fax: 231-591-3548, E-mail: yosts@ferris.edu. *Application contact:* Shannon Yost, Department Secretary, 231-591-2168, Fax: 231-591-3548, E-mail: yosts@ferris.edu.

Florida Institute of Technology, Graduate Programs, Extended Studies Division, Melbourne, FL 32901-6975. Offers acquisition and contract management (MS); aerospace engineering (MS); business administration (MBA); computer information systems (MS); computer science (MS); electrical engineering (MS); engineering management (MS); human resources management (MS); logistics management (MS), including humanitarian and disaster relief logistics; management (MS), including acquisition and contract management, e-business, human resources management, information systems, logistics management, management, transportation management; material acquisition management (MS); mechanical engineering (MS); operations research (MS); project management (MS), including information systems, operations research; public administration (MPA); quality management (MS); software engineering (MS); space systems (MS); space systems management (MS); systems management (MS), including information systems, operations research. Part-time and evening/weekend programs available. Postbaccalaureate distance learning degree programs offered (no on-campus study). *Faculty:* 11 full-time (3 women), 118 part-time/adjunct (24 women). *Students:* 69 full-time (23 women), 907 part-time (369 women); includes 385 minority (242 Black or African American, non-Hispanic/Latino; 15 American Indian or Alaska Native, non-Hispanic/Latino; 44 Asian, non-Hispanic/Latino; 52 Hispanic/Latino; 3 Native Hawaiian or other Pacific Islander, non-Hispanic/Latino; 29 Two or more races, non-Hispanic/Latino), 17 international. 517 applicants, 49% accepted, 245 enrolled. In 2010, 430 degrees awarded. *Degree requirements:* For master's, comprehensive exam (for some programs), capstone course. *Entrance requirements:* For master's, GMAT or resume showing 8 years of supervised experience, minimum GPA of 3.0, 2 letters of recommendation, resume. Additional exam requirements/recommendations for international students: Required—TOEFL (minimum score 550 paper-based; 213 computer-based; 79 iBT). *Application deadline:* For fall admission, 4/1 for international students; for spring admission, 9/30 for international students. Applications are processed on a rolling basis. Application fee: $50. Electronic applications accepted. *Expenses:* Contact institution. *Financial support:* Application deadline: 3/1. *Unit head:* Dr. Theodore Richardson, Senior Associate Dean, 321-674-8123, Fax: 321-674-7597, E-mail: trichardson@fit.edu. *Application contact:* Carolyn Farrior, Director of Graduate Admissions, Online Learning and Off-Campus Programs, 321-674-7118, Fax: 321-674-8216, E-mail: cfarrior@fit.edu.

Hofstra University, Frank G. Zarb School of Business, Department of Information Technology and Quantitative Methods, Hempstead, NY 11549. Offers business administration (MBA), including information technology, quality management; information technology (MS, Advanced Certificate). Part-time and evening/weekend programs available. Postbaccalaureate distance learning degree programs offered (minimal on-campus study). *Faculty:* 10 full-time (1 woman), 2 part-time/adjunct (0 women). *Students:* 11 full-time (1 woman), 12 part-time (4 women); includes 6 minority (1 Black or African American, non-Hispanic/Latino; 5 Asian, non-Hispanic/Latino), 4 international. Average age 29. 28 applicants, 57% accepted, 8 enrolled. In 2010, 8 master's awarded. *Degree requirements:* For master's, capstone course (for MBA); thesis (for MS). *Entrance requirements:* For master's, GMAT/GRE, 2 letters of recommendation; resume; essay; for Advanced Certificate, GMAT/GRE, 2 letters of recommendation; resume. Additional exam requirements/recommendations for international students: Required—TOEFL (minimum score 550 paper-based; 213 computer-based; 80 iBT); Recommended—IELTS (minimum score 6). *Application deadline:* Applications are processed on a rolling basis. Application fee: $70 ($75 for international students). Electronic applications accepted. *Expenses:* Contact institution. *Financial support:* In 2010–11, 4 students received support, including 4 fellowships with full and partial tuition reimbursements available (averaging $11,496 per year); research assistantships with full and partial tuition reimbursements available, career-related internships or fieldwork, Federal Work-Study, institutionally sponsored loans, scholarships/grants, tuition waivers (full and partial), and unspecified assistantships also available. Support available to part-time students. Financial award applicants required to submit FAFSA. *Faculty research:* IT outsourcing, IT strategy, SAP and enterprise systems, data mining/electronic medical records, IT and crisis management, inventory theory and modeling, forecasting. *Unit head:* Dr. Mohammed H. Tafti, Chairperson, 516-463-5720, E-mail: acsmht@hofstra.edu. *Application contact:* Carol Drummer, Dean of Graduate Admissions, 516-463-4876, Fax: 516-463-4664, E-mail: gradstudent@hofstra.edu.

Marian University, Business Division, Fond du Lac, WI 54935-4699. Offers organizational leadership and quality (MS). Part-time and evening/weekend programs available. *Faculty:* 17 part-time/adjunct (1 woman). *Students:* 11 full-time (6 women), 111 part-time (79 women); includes 7 Black or African American, non-Hispanic/Latino; 3 Asian, non-Hispanic/Latino; 4 Hispanic/Latino. Average age 38. 36 applicants, 92% accepted, 33 enrolled. In 2010, 52 master's awarded. *Degree requirements:* For master's, comprehensive group project. *Entrance requirements:* For master's, 3 years of managerial experience, minimum GPA of 2.75, letters of professional reference. *Application deadline:* Applications are processed on a rolling basis. Application fee: $25. Electronic applications accepted. *Expenses:* Contact institution. *Financial support:* In 2010–11, 8 students received support. Institutionally sponsored loans available. Support available to part-time students. Financial award application deadline: 3/1; financial award applicants required to submit FAFSA. *Faculty research:* Organizational values, statistical decision making, learning organization, quality planning, customer research. *Unit head:* Donna Innes, Dean of PACE, 920-923-8760, Fax: 920-923-7167, E-mail: dinnes@marianuniversity.edu. *Application contact:* Tracy Qualman, Director of Marketing and Admission, 920-923-7159, Fax: 920-923-7167, E-mail: tqualmann@marianuniversity.edu.

Penn State University Park, Graduate School, Intercollege Graduate Programs, Intercollege Program in Quality and Manufacturing Management, State College, University Park, PA 16802-1503. Offers MMM. *Unit head:* Dr. Jose A. Ventura, Co-Director, 814-865-5802, Fax: 814-863-4745, E-mail: jav1@psu.edu. *Application contact:* Cynthia E. Nicosia, Director, Graduate Enrollment Services, 814-865-1795, Fax: 814-865-4627, E-mail: cey1@psu.edu.

Southern Polytechnic State University, School of Engineering Technology and Management, Department of Industrial Engineering Technology, Marietta, GA 30060-2896. Offers quality assurance (MS, Graduate Certificate). Part-time and evening/weekend programs available. Postbaccalaureate distance learning degree programs offered (minimal on-campus study). *Faculty:* 2 full-time (1 woman), 5 part-time/adjunct (4 women). *Students:* 12 full-time (5 women), 63 part-time (23 women); includes 19 Black or African American, non-Hispanic/Latino; 4 Asian, non-Hispanic/Latino; 4 Hispanic/Latino; 1 Two or more races, non-Hispanic/Latino, 5 international. Average age 40. 31 applicants, 97% accepted, 24 enrolled. In 2010, 19 master's, 1 other advanced degree awarded. *Degree requirements:* For master's and Graduate Certificate, comprehensive exam (for some programs). *Entrance requirements:* For master's, 3 reference forms, minimum GPA of 2.7, statement of purpose; for Graduate Certificate, minimum GPA of 2.7, statement of purpose. Additional exam requirements/recommendations for international students: Required—TOEFL (minimum score 550 paper-based; 213 computer-based; 79 iBT), IELTS (minimum score 6.5). *Application deadline:* For fall admission, 7/1 priority date for domestic students, 5/1 priority date for international students; for spring admission, 11/1 priority date for domestic students, 9/1 priority date for international students. Applications are processed on a rolling basis. Application fee: $20. Electronic applications accepted. *Expenses:* Tuition, state resident: full-time $3690; part-time $205 per semester hour. Tuition, nonresident: full-time $13,428; part-time $746 per semester hour. Required fees: $598 per semester. *Financial support:* In 2010–11, 1 research assistantship with partial tuition reimbursement (averaging $1,500 per year) was awarded; career-related internships or fieldwork, scholarships/grants, and unspecified assistantships also available. Support available to part-time students. Financial award application deadline: 5/1; financial award applicants required to submit FAFSA. *Faculty research:* Application on industrial engineering to public sector, investigation of the response model method in robust design, effectiveness of online education, learning community, physical and mechanical properties of shape-wear garments to their functional performance, the advantage of tablet computer technology in a distance learning format, health care, BRIGE: Optimization Models for Public Health Policy. *Unit head:* Tom Ball, Chair, 678-915-7162, Fax: 678-915-4991, E-mail: tball@spsu.edu. *Application contact:* Nikki Palamiotis, Director of Graduate Studies, 678-915-4276, Fax: 678-915-7292, E-mail: npalamio@spsu.edu.

Stevens Institute of Technology, Graduate School, Charles V. Schaefer Jr. School of Engineering, Department of Civil, Environmental, and Ocean Engineering, Program in Construction Management, Hoboken, NJ 07030. Offers construction accounting/estimating (Certificate); construction engineering (Certificate); construction law/disputes (Certificate); construction management (MS); construction/quality management (Certificate). *Students:* 23 full-time (4 women), 29 part-time (3 women); includes 2 Black or African American, non-Hispanic/Latino; 6 Asian, non-Hispanic/Latino, 18 international. Average age 28. 21 applicants, 100% accepted. *Degree requirements:* For master's, thesis optional. *Entrance requirements:* For master's, GMAT, GRE General Test. Additional exam requirements/recommendations for international students: Required—TOEFL. *Application deadline:* Applications are processed on a rolling basis. Application fee: $50. Electronic applications accepted. *Unit head:* Henry Dobbelaar, Head, 201-216-5340. *Application contact:* Dr. David A. Vaccari, Director, 201-216-5570, Fax: 201-216-5352, E-mail: dvaccari@stevens.edu.

TUI University, College of Business Administration, Program in Business Administration, Cypress, CA 90630. Offers business administration (PhD); conflict and negotiation management (MBA); criminal justice administration (MBA); entrepreneurship (MBA); finance (MBA); general management (MBA); government accounting (MBA); human resource management (MBA); information security and digital assurance management (MBA); information technology management (MBA); international business (MBA); logistics management (MBA); marketing (MBA); project management (MBA); public management (MBA); quality management (MBA); strategic leadership (MBA). Part-time and evening/weekend programs available. Postbaccalaureate distance learning degree programs offered (no on-campus study). *Students:* 741 full-time (200 women), 1,585 part-time (410 women). 379 applicants, 81% accepted, 300 enrolled. In 2010, 752 master's, 28 doctorates awarded. *Degree requirements:* For doctorate, comprehensive exam, thesis/dissertation, defense of dissertation. *Entrance requirements:* For master's, minimum GPA of 2.5 (students with GPA 3.0 or greater may transfer up to 30% of graduate level credits); for doctorate, minimum GPA of 3.4, curriculum vitae, course work in research methods or statistics. Additional exam requirements/recommendations for international students: Required—TOEFL. *Application deadline:* For fall admission, 10/3 for domestic and international students; for winter admission, 12/22 for domestic and international students; for spring admission, 4/3 for domestic and international students. Applications are processed on a rolling basis. Application fee: $75. Electronic applications accepted. *Expenses:*

Tuition: Full-time $11,040; part-time $345 per semester hour. *Unit head:* Paul Watkins, Dean, College of Business Administration, 800-375-9878, E-mail: pwatkins@tuiu.edu. *Application contact:* Wei Ren-Finaly, Registrar, 800-375-9878, Fax: 714-827-7407, E-mail: registration@tuiu.edu.

TUI University, College of Health Sciences, Program in Health Sciences, Cypress, CA 90630. Offers clinical research administration (MS, Certificate); emergency and disaster management (MS, Certificate); environmental health science (Certificate); health care administration (PhD); health care management (MS), including health informatics; health education (MS, Certificate); health informatics (Certificate); health sciences (PhD); international health (MS); international health: educator or researcher option (PhD); international health: practitioner option (PhD); law and expert witness studies (MS, Certificate); public health (MS); quality assurance (Certificate). Part-time and evening/weekend programs available. Postbaccalaureate distance learning degree programs offered (no on-campus study). *Students:* 322 full-time (170 women), 709 part-time (357 women). 227 applicants, 80% accepted, 164 enrolled. In 2010, 366 master's, 29 doctorates awarded. *Degree requirements:* For doctorate, comprehensive exam, thesis/dissertation, defense of dissertation. *Entrance requirements:* For master's, minimum GPA of 2.5 (students with GPA 3.0 or greater may transfer up to 30% of graduate level credits); for doctorate, minimum GPA of 3.4, curriculum vitae, course work in research methods or statistics. Additional exam requirements/recommendations for international students: Required—TOEFL. *Application deadline:* For fall admission, 10/3 for domestic and international students; for winter admission, 12/22 for domestic and international students; for spring admission, 4/3 for domestic and international students. Applications are processed on a rolling basis. Application fee: $75. Electronic applications accepted. *Expenses:* Tuition: Full-time $11,040; part-time $345 per semester hour. *Unit head:* Dr. Michaela Tanasescu, Dean, 714-816-0366, Fax: 714-226-9844, E-mail: infocoe@tuiu.edu. *Application contact:* Wei Ren-Finaly, Registrar, 800-375-9878, Fax: 714-827-7407, E-mail: registration@tuiu.edu.

The University of Alabama, Graduate School, College of Human Environmental Sciences, Program in Human Environmental Science, Tuscaloosa, AL 35487. Offers family financial planning and counseling (MS); interactive technology (MS); quality management (MS); restaurant and meeting management (MS); rural community health (MS); sport management (MS). *Faculty:* 1 full-time (0 women). *Students:* 67 full-time (39 women), 86 part-time (52 women); includes 47 minority (40 Black or African American, non-Hispanic/Latino; 3 Hispanic/Latino; 4 Two or more races, non-Hispanic/Latino), 1 international. Average age 34. 112 applicants, 78% accepted, 64 enrolled. In 2010, 64 master's awarded. *Degree requirements:* For master's, comprehensive exam. *Entrance requirements:* For master's, GRE (for some specializations), minimum GPA of 3.0. Additional exam requirements/recommendations for international students: Required—TOEFL. *Application deadline:* Applications are processed on a rolling basis. Application fee: $50 ($60 for international students). Electronic applications accepted. *Expenses:* Tuition, state resident: full-time $7900. Tuition, nonresident: full-time $20,500. *Faculty research:* Hospitality management, sports medicine education, technology and education. *Unit head:* Dr. Milla D. Boschung, Dean, 205-348-6250, Fax: 205-348-1786, E-mail: mboschun@ches.ua.edu. *Application contact:* Dr. Stuart Usdan, Associate Dean, 205-348-6150, Fax: 205-348-3789, E-mail: susdan@ches.ua.edu.

The University of Tennessee at Chattanooga, Graduate School, College of Engineering and Computer Science, Program in Engineering Management, Chattanooga, TN 37403. Offers engineering management (MS); fundamentals of engineering management (Graduate Certificate); power systems management (Graduate Certificate); project and value management (Graduate Certificate); quality management (Graduate Certificate). Postbaccalaureate distance learning degree programs offered (no on-campus study). *Faculty:* 4 full-time (1 woman). *Students:* 15 full-time (4 women), 77 part-time (13 women); includes 8 Black or African American, non-Hispanic/Latino; 1 Asian, non-Hispanic/Latino; 1 Hispanic/Latino, 11 international. Average age 32. 29 applicants, 100% accepted, 20 enrolled. In 2010, 23 master's, 20 other advanced degrees awarded. *Degree requirements:* For master's, thesis. *Entrance requirements:* For master's, GRE General Test, letters of recommendation; minimum undergraduate GPA of 2.5 overall or 3.0 in senior year. Additional exam requirements/recommendations for international students: Required—TOEFL (minimum score 550 paper-based; 213 computer-based; 79 iBT), IELTS (minimum score 6). *Application deadline:* For fall admission, 8/1 priority date for domestic students, 6/1 for international students; for spring admission, 12/1 priority date for domestic students, 10/1 for international students. Applications are processed on a rolling basis. Application fee: $35. Electronic applications accepted. *Financial support:* In 2010–11, 5 research assistantships with full and partial tuition reimbursements (averaging $5,500 per year) were awarded; career-related internships or fieldwork, scholarships/grants, and unspecified assistantships also available. Support available to part-time students. *Faculty research:* Plant layout design, lean manufacturing, six sigma, value management, product development. *Unit head:* Dr. Neslihan Alp, Director, 423-425-4032, Fax: 423-425-5229, E-mail: neslihan-alp@utc.edu. *Application contact:* Dr. Jerald Ainsworth, Dean of Graduate Studies, 423-425-4478, Fax: 423-425-5223, E-mail: jerald-ainsworth@utc.edu.

Quantitative Analysis

OVERVIEW

An MBA in quantitative analysis trains potential candidates in various aspects of finance, with the main emphasis of the degree on equipping candidates in mathematics, reinsurance, and financial analysis and the use of quantitative skills such as mathematics, probability, statistics, and computer science to solve business problems. To help facilitate this, students also develop a thorough understanding of the problems faced by, and the terminology used in, the various areas of modern business.

Required courses may include study in:

- Decision-making and Decision Analysis
- Distribution and Network Models
- Integer Models
- Linear Programming and Applications
- Project Scheduling
- Risk Analysis
- Sensitivity Analysis

Elective courses may include study in:

- Data Analysis and Optimization
- Games and Auctions
- Management Decision Models
- Managerial Quantitative Analysis

With recent advances in technology, it's no surprise to learn of a 48-percent increase in interest in this degree. Usually positioned as a mathematical and analytical degree, the pursuit of an MBA in quantitative analysis is an ideal choice for candidates who are adept in numerical or quantitative techniques and possess exceptional skills in mathematics and finance. However, candidates should note that the work of quantitative analysis is not restricted to management in that it also includes divergent fields such as risk management and derivatives pricing. With an MBA in quantitative analysis, graduates can look towards careers as management scientists, operations research analysts, and systems analysts.

IN THIS SECTION

You'll find profiles of institutions offering graduate programs in the following field:

HELPFUL ORGANIZATIONS/ PUBLICATIONS/BLOGS

Society of Quantitative Analysts (SQA)

http://www.sqa-us.org/

The Society of Quantitative Analysts (SQA), founded in 1972, is a not-for-profit organization focused on education and communication to support members of the quantitative investment practitioner community. The SQA seeks to encourage the dissemination of leading-edge ideas and innovations relevant to the work of the quantitative investment practitioner. The knowledge of such ideas and innovations can assist portfolio and risk managers, strategists, analysts, traders, regulators, and asset owners in performing their functions and responding to the ever-quickening pace of change. The Society welcomes the participation of academics and students and provides forums for the presentation of theory and practice by practitioners, academics, and regulators with an emphasis on the new and controversial.

The principal mission of the SQA is to encourage the dissemination and discussion of leading-edge ideas and innovations related to the work of the quantitatively oriented investment professional, including analytical techniques and technologies for investment research and management such as:

- Practical applications by investment practitioners.
- Academic presentations of theories in finance and economics.
- Concepts from other disciplines that might provide inspiration to the investment practitioner.
- Regulatory issues that can impact investment practice.

The Society holds monthly meetings in New York City from September through June. Monthly meetings consist of one-hour talks on a specific topic. The Society also organizes a half-day seminar in the fall on a topic of current interest and a full-day "Fuzzy Day" seminar in the spring on an exploratory topic. The Society also provides opportunities for communication and interaction among its members and with members of similar societies. All SQA events provide time for members to meet and share ideas, opinions, and experiences.

The SQA continues to be a pioneer in the use of quantitative investment techniques. Membership in the SQA brings a number of benefits, including access to the members-only section of the SQA Web site, reduced fees for all SQA events, reduced fees for other events of interest to quantitative practitioners, discounts on a wide range of investment journals, access to presentation materials from past SQA programs, and continuing education credits from the CFA Institute.

American Society for Quantitative Analysis (ASQA)

http://www.asqa.org/

The mission of the American Society for Quantitative Analysis (ASQA) Web site is to provide support, resources, and information for quantitative analysts in a variety of fields. The ASQA provides the latest news and topical updates of interest to its members, as well as acting to facilitate information exchange between ASQA members through the development of the QuantBase information-sharing retrieval/exchange system.

Journal of Financial and Quantitative Analysis (JFQA)

http://journals.cambridge.org/action/displayJournal?jid=JFQ

The *Journal of Financial and Quantitative Analysis* (*JFQA*) publishes theoretical and empirical research in financial economics. Topics include corporate finance, investments, capital and security markets, and quantitative methods of particular relevance to financial researchers. The *JFQA* serves an international community of sophisticated finance scholars—academics and practitioners—and has an impressive circulation to 3,000 libraries, firms, and individuals in 70 nations. The *JFQA* prints less than 10 percent of the more than 600 unsolicited manuscripts submitted annually. An intensive blind review process and exacting editorial standards contribute to the *JFQA*'s reputation as a top finance journal.

CAREER ASPIRATIONS: A PROSPECTIVE POSITION

Quantitative ETF Analyst

Job Description

This position will offer the individual the chance to be part of a cutting-edge asset management team focused on product development from idea generation to investable product.

Responsibilities

- Factor model creation, attribution analysis, optimization, and backtesting of new strategies.
- Conduct academic research to generate proposed new factors.
- Write white papers on the subject of asset allocation and indices within product line.
- Interact with product development and distribution teams at major financial institutions.
- Monitor the performance of new and existing strategies.
- Manage/maintain proprietary databases and integrating additional data sources.

Qualifications

- BS in economics, finance, accounting, or related field; MS, MBA, or CFA preferred
- 1 to 3 years of experience in equity markets
- Strong understanding of quantitative modeling and domestic/international markets
- Financial modeling and/or security analysis experience

QUANTITATIVE ANALYSIS

Lehigh University, College of Business and Economics, Department of Finance, Bethlehem, PA 18015. Offers analytical finance (MS). *Faculty:* 8 full-time (2 women). *Students:* 55 full-time (31 women), 26 part-time (8 women); includes 7 minority (6 Asian, non-Hispanic/Latino; 1 Native Hawaiian or other Pacific Islander, non-Hispanic/Latino), 46 international. Average age 26. 367 applicants, 18% accepted, 40 enrolled. In 2010, 36 master's awarded. *Degree requirements:* For master's, capstone project. *Entrance requirements:* For master's, GMAT or GRE, bachelor's degree from a mathematically rigorous program, minimum GPA of 3.0. Additional exam requirements/recommendations for international students: Required—TOEFL (minimum score 600 paper-based; 250 computer-based; 94 iBT). *Application deadline:* For fall admission, 7/15 for domestic students, 2/15 for international students. Applications are processed on a rolling basis. Application fee: $100. Electronic applications accepted. *Expenses:* Contact institution. Total annual research expenditures: $67,063. *Unit head:* Richard Kish, Department Chair, 610-758-4205, E-mail: rjk7@lehigh.edu. *Application contact:* Corinn McBride, Director of Recruitment and Admissions, 610-758-3418, Fax: 610-758-5283, E-mail: com207@lehigh.edu.

New York University, Robert F. Wagner Graduate School of Public Service, Program in Public Administration, New York, NY 10012-1019. Offers public administration (PhD); public and nonprofit management and policy (MPA, Advanced Certificate), including developmental administration (Advanced Certificate), financial management and public finance, human resources management (Advanced Certificate), international administration (Advanced Certificate), management (MPA), management for public and nonprofit organizations (Advanced Certificate), public policy analysis, quantitative analysis and computer applications (Advanced Certificate), urban public policy (Advanced Certificate); JD/MPA; MBA/MPA; MPA/MA. *Accreditation:* NASPAA (one or more programs are accredited). Part-time and evening/weekend programs available. *Faculty:* 32 full-time (13 women), 41 part-time/adjunct (22 women). *Students:* 400 full-time (301 women), 206 part-time (156 women); includes 43 Black or African American, non-Hispanic/Latino; 58 Asian, non-Hispanic/Latino; 36 Hispanic/Latino, 65 international. Average age 28. 1,230 applicants, 54% accepted, 219 enrolled. In 2010, 210 master's, 5 doctorates awarded. *Degree requirements:* For master's, thesis or alternative, capstone end event; for doctorate, one foreign language, thesis/dissertation. *Entrance requirements:* For master's, minimum undergraduate GPA of 3.0; for doctorate, GMAT or GRE General Test, minimum GPA of 3.5. Additional exam requirements/recommendations for international students: Required—TOEFL (minimum score 600 paper-based; 250 computer-based; 100 iBT), IELTS (minimum score 7.5), TWE (minimum score 4). *Application deadline:* For fall admission, 1/15 for domestic students, 1/4 for international students; for spring admission, 11/15 for domestic students, 10/1 for international students. Applications are processed on a rolling basis. Application fee: $80. Electronic applications accepted. *Expenses:* Contact institution. *Financial support:* In 2010–11, 176 students received support, including 171 fellowships (averaging $14,022 per year), 5 research assistantships with full tuition reimbursements available (averaging $22,440 per year); career-related internships or fieldwork, Federal Work-Study, institutionally sponsored loans, scholarships/grants, health care benefits, and unspecified assistantships also available. Support available to part-time students. Financial award application deadline: 1/5; financial award applicants required to submit FAFSA. *Unit head:* Katty Jones, Director, Program Services, 212-998-7411, Fax: 212-995-4164, E-mail: katty.jones@nyu.edu. *Application contact:* Christopher Alexander, Administrative Aide, Enrollment, 212-998-7414, Fax: 212-995-4611, E-mail: wagner.admissions@nyu.edu.

Oklahoma State University, Spears School of Business, Department of Finance, Stillwater, OK 74078. Offers finance (PhD); quantitative financial economics (MS). Part-time programs available. *Faculty:* 13 full-time (1 woman), 5 part-time/adjunct (0 women). *Students:* 20 full-time (8 women), 9 part-time (2 women); includes 1 Black or African American, non-Hispanic/Latino; 1 Asian, non-Hispanic/Latino, 14 international. Average age 29. 59 applicants, 32% accepted, 8 enrolled. In 2010, 9 master's, 1 doctorate awarded. *Degree requirements:* For master's, thesis or alternative; for doctorate, comprehensive exam, thesis/dissertation. *Entrance requirements:* For master's and doctorate, GRE or GMAT. Additional exam requirements/recommendations for international students: Required—TOEFL (minimum score 550 paper-based; 79 iBT). *Application deadline:* For fall admission, 3/1 priority date for international students; for spring admission, 8/1 priority date for international students. Applications are processed on a rolling basis. Application fee: $40 ($75 for international students). Electronic applications accepted. *Expenses:* Tuition, state resident: full-time $3716; part-time $154.85 per credit hour. Tuition, nonresident: full-time $14,892; part-time $621 per credit hour. Required fees: $2044; $85.20 per credit hour. One-time fee: $50. Tuition and fees vary according to course load and campus/location. *Financial support:* In 2010–11, 13 research assistantships (averaging $8,749 per year), 5 teaching assistantships (averaging $21,587 per year) were awarded; career-related internships or fieldwork, Federal Work-Study, scholarships/grants, health care benefits, tuition waivers (partial), and unspecified assistantships also available. Support available to part-time students. Financial award application

deadline: 3/1; financial award applicants required to submit FAFSA. *Faculty research:* Corporate risk management, derivatives banking, investments and securities issuance, corporate governance, banking. *Unit head:* Dr. John Polonchek, Head, 405-744-5199, Fax: 405-744-5180. *Application contact:* Dr. Gordon Emslie, Dean, 405-744-6368, Fax: 405-744-0355, E-mail: grad-i@okstate.edu.

St. John's University, The Peter J. Tobin College of Business, Department of Computer Information Systems and Decision Sciences, Queens, NY 11439. Offers MBA, Adv C. Part-time and evening/weekend programs available. *Students:* 7 full-time (3 women), 6 part-time (0 women); includes 4 minority (1 Black or African American, non-Hispanic/Latino; 2 Asian, non-Hispanic/Latino; 1 Hispanic/Latino), 4 international. Average age 25. 11 applicants, 64% accepted, 4 enrolled. In 2010, 2 master's awarded. *Degree requirements:* For master's, comprehensive exam (for some programs), thesis optional. *Entrance requirements:* For master's, GMAT, 2 letters of recommendation, resume, transcripts, essay; for Adv C, GMAT, 2 letters of recommendation, resume, undergraduate transcripts, essay. Additional exam requirements/recommendations for international students: Required—TOEFL (minimum score 600 paper-based; 250 computer-based; 100 iBT), IELTS (minimum score 5.5). *Application deadline:* For fall admission, 5/1 priority date for domestic and international students; for spring admission, 11/1 priority date for domestic and international students. Applications are processed on a rolling basis. Application fee: $70. Electronic applications accepted. *Expenses:* Contact institution. *Financial support:* Research assistantships, scholarships/grants available. Support available to part-time students. Financial award application deadline: 3/1; financial award applicants required to submit FAFSA. *Unit head:* Dr. Victor Lu, Chair, 718-990-6392, Fax: 718-990-1868, E-mail: luf@stjohns.edu. *Application contact:* Carol Swanberg, Assistant Dean, Director of Graduate Admissions, 718-990-1345, Fax: 718-990-5242, E-mail: tobingradnyc@stjohns.edu.

Texas Tech University, Graduate School, Jerry S. Rawls College of Business Administration, Area of Information Systems and Quantitative Sciences, Lubbock, TX 79409. Offers business statistics (MS, PhD); healthcare management (MS); management information systems (MS, PhD); production and operations management (MS, PhD); risk management (MS). Part-time programs available. *Faculty:* 15 full-time (0 women). *Students:* 73 full-time (21 women), 13 part-time (0 women); includes 5 minority (1 Black or African American, non-Hispanic/Latino; 1 Asian, non-Hispanic/Latino; 3 Hispanic/Latino), 61 international. Average age 27. 130 applicants, 75% accepted, 51 enrolled. In 2010, 31 master's, 2 doctorates awarded. Terminal master's awarded for partial completion of doctoral program. *Degree requirements:* For master's, comprehensive exam or capstone course; for doctorate, thesis/dissertation, qualifying exams. *Entrance requirements:* For master's and doctorate, GMAT, holistic profile of academic credentials. Additional exam requirements/recommendations for international students: Required—TOEFL (minimum score 550 paper-based; 213 computer-based; 79 iBT). *Application deadline:* For fall admission, 4/1 priority date for domestic students, 1/15 for international students; for spring admission, 9/1 priority date for domestic students, 6/15 priority date for international students. Applications are processed on a rolling basis. Application fee: $50 ($75 for international students). Electronic applications accepted. *Expenses:* Tuition, state resident: full-time $5495.76; part-time $228.99 per credit hour. Tuition, nonresident: full-time $12,936; part-time $538.99 per credit hour. Required fees: $2674; $36 per credit hour. $905 per semester. *Financial support:* In 2010–11, 4 research assistantships (averaging $8,800 per year), 9 teaching assistantships (averaging $18,000 per year) were awarded; Federal Work-Study, scholarships/grants, and unspecified assistantships also available. *Faculty research:* Database management systems, systems management and engineering, expert systems and adaptive knowledge-based sciences, statistical analysis and design. *Unit head:* Dr. Bradley Ewing, Area Coordinator, 806-742-3939, Fax: 806-742-3193, E-mail: bradley.ewing@ttu.edu. *Application contact:* Cynthia D. Barnes, Director, Graduate Services Center, 806-742-3184, Fax: 806-742-3958, E-mail: ba_grad@ttu.edu.

University of California, Santa Barbara, Graduate Division, College of Letters and Sciences, Division of Mathematics, Life, and Physical Sciences, Department of Geography, Santa Barbara, CA 93106-4060. Offers cognitive science (PhD); geography (MA, PhD); quantitative methods in the social sciences (PhD); transportation (PhD); MA/PhD. *Faculty:* 23 full-time (4 women), 11 part-time/adjunct (4 women). *Students:* 71 full-time (32 women); includes 2 Black or African American, non-Hispanic/Latino; 14 Asian, non-Hispanic/Latino; 6 Hispanic/Latino. Average age 31. 82 applicants, 33% accepted, 18 enrolled. In 2010, 3 master's, 13 doctorates awarded. Terminal master's awarded for partial completion of doctoral program. *Degree requirements:* For master's, comprehensive exam (for some programs), thesis or alternative; for doctorate, comprehensive exam, thesis/dissertation. *Entrance requirements:* For master's and doctorate, GRE (minimum verbal/quantitative score 1100). Additional exam requirements/recommendations for international students: Required—TOEFL (minimum score 550 paper-based; 80 iBT), IELTS (minimum score 7). *Application deadline:* For fall admission, 2/1 for domestic and international students. Application fee: $70 ($90 for international students). Electronic applications accepted. *Financial support:* In 2010–11, 61 students received support, including 49 fellowships with full and partial tuition reimbursements available (averaging $8,958 per year), 32 research assistantships with full and partial tuition reimbursements available (averaging $10,335 per year), 29 teaching assistantships with partial tuition reimbursements available (averaging $9,384 per year). Financial award applicants required to submit FAFSA. *Faculty research:* Earth system science, human environment relations, modeling, measurement and computation. *Unit head:* Dr. Dar Alexander Roberts, Professor/Chair, 805-880-2531, Fax: 805-893-2578, E-mail: dar@geog.ucsb.edu. *Application contact:* Jose Luis Saleta, Student Programs Manager, 805-456-2829, Fax: 805-893-2578, E-mail: saleta@geog.ucsb.edu.

University of California, Santa Barbara, Graduate Division, College of Letters and Sciences, Division of Mathematics, Life, and Physical Sciences, Department of Statistics and Applied Probability, Santa Barbara, CA 93106-3110. Offers financial mathematics and statistics (PhD); quantitative methods in the social sciences (PhD); statistics (MA), including applied statistics, mathematical statistics; statistics and applied probability (PhD); MA/PhD. *Faculty:* 11 full-time (3 women). *Students:* 49 full-time (17 women); includes 30 Asian, non-Hispanic/Latino; 2 Hispanic/Latino. Average age 29. 195 applicants, 20% accepted, 14 enrolled. In 2010, 16 master's, 2 doctorates awarded. Terminal master's awarded for partial completion of doctoral program. *Degree requirements:* For master's, comprehensive exam, thesis (for some programs); for doctorate, comprehensive exam, thesis/dissertation. *Entrance requirements:* For master's and doctorate, GRE General Test. Additional exam requirements/recommendations for international students: Required—TOEFL (minimum score 550 paper-based; 80 iBT), IELTS (minimum score 7). *Application deadline:* For fall admission, 1/1 priority date for domestic and international students; for winter admission, 11/1 priority date for domestic and international students; for spring admission, 2/1 priority date for domestic and international students. Application fee: $70 ($90 for international students). Electronic applications accepted. *Financial support:* In 2010–11, 23 students received support, including 6 fellowships with full tuition reimbursements available (averaging $11,285 per year), 1 research assistantship with full and partial tuition reimbursement available (averaging $2,790 per year), 28 teaching assistantships with partial tuition reimbursements available (averaging $14,557 per year). Financial award application deadline: 1/1; financial award applicants required to submit FAFSA. *Faculty research:* Bayesian inference, financial mathematics, stochastic processes, environmental statistics, biostatistical modeling. Total annual research expenditures: $139,480. *Unit head:* Dr. Yuedong Wang, Chair, 805-893-4870, E-mail: yeudong@pstat.ucsb.edu. *Application contact:* Rickie R. Smith, Graduate Program Assistant, 805-893-2129, Fax: 805-893-2334, E-mail: smith@pstat.ucsb.edu.

University of California, Santa Barbara, Graduate Division, College of Letters and Sciences, Division of Social Sciences, Department of Communication, Santa Barbara, CA 93106-4020. Offers cognitive science (PhD); feminist studies (PhD); quantitative methods in the social science (PhD); society and technology (PhD); MA/PhD. *Faculty:* 20 full-time (9 women). *Students:* 39 full-time (26 women); includes 3 Black or African American, non-Hispanic/Latino; 5 Asian, non-Hispanic/Latino; 6 Hispanic/Latino. Average age 30. 169 applicants, 6% accepted, 5 enrolled. In 2010, 3 doctorates awarded. Terminal master's awarded for partial completion of doctoral program. *Degree requirements:* For doctorate, comprehensive exam, thesis/dissertation. *Entrance requirements:* For doctorate, GRE. Additional exam requirements/recommendations for international students: Required—TOEFL (minimum score 550 paper-based; 80 iBT), IELTS (minimum score 7). *Application deadline:* For fall admission, 12/1 for domestic and international students. Application fee: $70 ($90 for international students). Electronic applications accepted. *Financial support:* In 2010–11, 39 students received support, including 39 fellowships with full and partial tuition reimbursements available (averaging $6,045 per year), 5 research assistantships with full and partial tuition reimbursements available (averaging $9,646 per year), 29 teaching assistantships with partial tuition reimbursements available (averaging $14,294 per year); career-related internships or fieldwork, health care benefits, and tuition waivers (full and partial) also available. Support available to part-time students. Financial award application deadline: 12/1. *Faculty research:* Interpersonal, intercultural, organizational, health, media. *Unit head:* Prof. Linda L. Putnam, Professor, 805-893-7935, Fax: 805-893-7102, E-mail: lputnam@comm.ucsb.edu. *Application contact:* Nancy Siris-Rawls, Graduate Program Assistant, 805-893-3046, Fax: 805-893-7102, E-mail: nsiris@comm.ucsb.edu.

University of California, Santa Barbara, Graduate Division, College of Letters and Sciences, Division of Social Sciences, Department of Sociology, Santa Barbara, CA 93106-9430. Offers feminist studies (PhD); global studies (PhD); language, interaction and social organization (PhD); quantitative methods in the social sciences (PhD); technology and society (PhD); MA/PhD. *Faculty:* 35 full-time (14 women). *Students:* 71 full-time (44 women); includes 5 Black or African American, non-Hispanic/Latino; 4 Asian, non-Hispanic/Latino; 21 Hispanic/Latino. Average age 30. 162 applicants, 8% accepted, 6 enrolled. In 2010, 13 doctorates awarded. Terminal master's awarded for partial completion of doctoral program. *Degree requirements:* For doctorate, comprehensive exam, thesis/dissertation. *Entrance requirements:* For doctorate, GRE General Test. Additional exam requirements/recommendations for international students: Required—TOEFL (minimum score 550 paper-based;

80 iBT), IELTS (minimum score 7). *Application deadline:* For fall admission, 12/1 for domestic and international students. Application fee: $70 ($90 for international students). Electronic applications accepted. *Financial support:* In 2010–11, 60 students received support, including 40 fellowships with full and partial tuition reimbursements available (averaging $10,059 per year), 4 research assistantships with full and partial tuition reimbursements available (averaging $10,166 per year), 43 teaching assistantships with full and partial tuition reimbursements available (averaging $11,913 per year); career-related internships or fieldwork, Federal Work-Study, institutionally sponsored loans, scholarships/grants, health care benefits, tuition waivers (full and partial), and unspecified assistantships also available. Financial award application deadline: 12/1. *Faculty research:* Feminist studies/sexualities, race ethnicity, global, culture, conversation analysis. *Unit head:* Prof. Verta Taylor, Chair, 805-893-3118, Fax: 805-893-3324. *Application contact:* Sharon Applegate, Graduate Program Assistant, 805-893-3328, Fax: 805-893-3324, E-mail: grad-soc@soc.ucsb.edu.

University of Cincinnati, Graduate School, College of Business, MS Program, Cincinnati, OH 45221. Offers accounting (MS); information systems (MS); marketing (MS); quantitative analysis (MS). Part-time and evening/weekend programs available. *Faculty:* 79 full-time (22 women), 71 part-time/adjunct (24 women). *Students:* 130 full-time (46 women), 87 part-time (38 women); includes 12 minority (2 Black or African American, non-Hispanic/Latino; 3 Asian, non-Hispanic/Latino; 4 Hispanic/Latino; 3 Two or more races, non-Hispanic/Latino), 89 international. 407 applicants, 53% accepted, 110 enrolled. *Degree requirements:* For master's, thesis (for some programs). *Entrance requirements:* For master's, GMAT, GRE, resume, transcripts, essays, letters of recommendation. Additional exam requirements/recommendations for international students: Required—TOEFL (minimum score 600 paper-based; 250 computer-based; 100 iBT). *Application deadline:* For fall admission, 1/15 priority date for domestic students, 4/1 for international students. Applications are processed on a rolling basis. Application fee: $45. Electronic applications accepted. *Expenses:* Contact institution. *Financial support:* In 2010–11, 10 teaching assistantships with full and partial tuition reimbursements (averaging $5,400 per year) were awarded; scholarships/grants, tuition waivers (full and partial), and unspecified assistantships also available. Financial award application deadline: 2/1; financial award applicants required to submit FAFSA. *Unit head:* Dr. David Szymanski, Dean, 513-556-7001, Fax: 513-556-4891, E-mail: will.mcintosh@uc.edu. *Application contact:* Dona Clary, Director, Graduate Programs Office, 513-556-3546, Fax: 513-558-7006, E-mail: dona.clary@uc.edu.

University of Cincinnati, Graduate School, College of Business, PhD Program, Cincinnati, OH 45221. Offers accounting (PhD); finance (PhD); information systems (PhD); management (PhD); marketing (PhD); quantitative analysis and operations management (PhD). *Faculty:* 56 full-time (13 women). *Students:* 32 full-time (12 women), 9 part-time (3 women); includes 2 minority (both Hispanic/Latino), 23 international. 119 applicants, 12% accepted, 9 enrolled. In 2010, 8 doctorates awarded. *Degree requirements:* For doctorate, comprehensive exam, thesis/dissertation. *Entrance requirements:* For doctorate, GMAT, GRE, transcripts, essays, resume, letters of recommendation. Additional exam requirements/recommendations for international students: Required—TOEFL (minimum score 600 paper-based; 250 computer-based; 100 iBT). *Application deadline:* For fall admission, 2/1 for domestic and international students. Application fee: $45. Electronic applications accepted. *Expenses:* Contact institution. *Financial support:* In 2010–11, 38 students received support, including 29 research assistantships with full and partial tuition reimbursements available (averaging $14,640 per year); scholarships/grants, tuition waivers (full and partial), and unspecified assistantships also available. Financial award application deadline: 2/15; financial award applicants required to submit FAFSA. *Unit head:* Dr. Suzanne Masterson, Director, PhD Programs, 513-556-7125, Fax: 513-556-5499, E-mail: suzanne.masterson@uc.edu. *Application contact:* Deborah Schildknecht, Assistant Director, PhD Programs, 513-556-7190, Fax: 513-558-7006, E-mail: deborah.schildknecht@uc.edu.

University of Colorado Denver, Business School, Program in Decision Sciences, Denver, CO 80217. Offers MS. Part-time and evening/weekend programs available. *Students:* 7 full-time (5 women); includes 1 minority (Hispanic/Latino), 1 international. Average age 31. 6 applicants, 83% accepted, 3 enrolled. *Degree requirements:* For master's, 30 semester hours (18 of required courses and 12 of electives). *Entrance requirements:* For master's, GMAT. Additional exam requirements/recommendations for international students: Required—TOEFL (minimum score 525 paper-based; 197 computer-based; 71 iBT). *Application deadline:* For fall admission, 4/1 priority date for domestic students, 3/15 priority date for international students; for spring admission, 10/1 priority date for domestic and international students. Application fee: $50 ($75 for international students). Electronic applications accepted. *Expenses:* Contact institution. *Financial support:* Federal Work-Study and scholarships/grants available. Support available to part-time students. Financial award application deadline: 4/1; financial award applicants required to submit FAFSA. *Faculty research:* Quantitative business analysis, quantitative methods and modeling, business intelligence, forecasting, quality and Six Sigma, optimization, project management, data mining, supply chain management. *Unit head:* Marlene Smith, Associate Professor/Director,

303-315-8421, E-mail: ma.smith@ucdenver.edu. *Application contact:* Shelly Townley, Admissions Coordinator, 303-556-5956, Fax: 303-556-5904, E-mail: shelly.townley@ucdenver.edu.

University of Colorado Denver, Business School, Program in Management and Organization, Denver, CO 80217. Offers communications management (MS); enterprise technology management (MS); entrepreneurship and innovation (MS); global management (MS); human resources management (MS); leadership (MS); quantitative decision methods (MS); sports and entertainment management (MS); strategic management (MS); sustainability management (MS). *Accreditation:* AACSB. Part-time and evening/weekend programs available. Postbaccalaureate distance learning degree programs offered (no on-campus study). *Students:* 34 full-time (21 women), 9 part-time (2 women); includes 3 Asian, non-Hispanic/Latino; 5 Hispanic/Latino. Average age 33. 28 applicants, 61% accepted, 10 enrolled. In 2010, 20 master's awarded. *Degree requirements:* For master's, 30 semester hours (12 of required courses, 12 of management electives, and 6 of free electives). *Entrance requirements:* For master's, GMAT. Additional exam requirements/recommendations for international students: Required—TOEFL (minimum score 525 paper-based; 197 computer-based; 71 iBT). *Application deadline:* For fall admission, 4/1 priority date for domestic students, 3/15 priority date for international students; for spring admission, 10/1 priority date for domestic and international students. Application fee: $50 ($75 for international students). Electronic applications accepted. *Expenses:* Contact institution. *Financial support:* Federal Work-Study and scholarships/grants available. Support available to part-time students. Financial award application deadline: 4/1; financial award applicants required to submit FAFSA. *Faculty research:* Human resource management, management of catastrophe, turnaround strategies. *Unit head:* Dr. Kenneth Bettenhausen, Associate Professor/Director, 303-315-8425, E-mail: kenneth.bettehausen@ucdenver.edu. *Application contact:* Shelly Townley, Admissions Director, Graduate Programs, 303-315-8202, E-mail: shelly.townley@ucdenver.edu.

University of Florida, Graduate School, Warrington College of Business Administration, Hough Graduate School of Business, Programs in Business Administration, Gainesville, FL 32611. Offers accounting (MBA); arts administration (MBA); business strategy and public policy (MBA); competitive strategy (MBA); decision and information sciences (MBA); electronic commerce (MBA); finance (MBA); general business (MBA); global management (MBA); Graham-Buffett security analysis (MBA); health administration (MBA); human resources management (MBA); international studies (MBA); Latin American business (MBA); management (MBA); marketing (MBA); sports administration (MBA); JD/MBA; MBA/MS; MBA/PhD; MBA/Pharm D; MD/MBA. *Accreditation:* AACSB. Part-time and evening/weekend programs available. *Faculty:* 71 full-time (10 women). *Students:* 187 full-time (44 women), 305 part-time (83 women); includes 25 Black or African American, non-Hispanic/Latino; 2 American Indian or Alaska Native, non-Hispanic/Latino; 52 Asian, non-Hispanic/Latino; 54 Hispanic/Latino, 11 international. Average age 31. 919 applicants, 33% accepted, 225 enrolled. In 2010, 492 master's awarded. *Degree requirements:* For master's, capstone course. *Entrance requirements:* For master's, GMAT, minimum GPA of 3.0, interview. Additional exam requirements/recommendations for international students: Required—TOEFL (minimum score 550 paper-based; 213 computer-based; 80 iBT), IELTS (minimum score 6). *Application deadline:* For fall admission, 7/1 for domestic students, 1/1 for international students; for spring admission, 12/1 for domestic and international students. Applications are processed on a rolling basis. Application fee: $30. Electronic applications accepted. *Expenses:* Tuition, state resident: full-time $10,915.92. Tuition, nonresident: full-time $28,309. *Financial support:* In 2010–11, 1 student received support, including 1 teaching assistantship (averaging $20,600 per year); career-related internships or fieldwork, scholarships/grants, and unspecified assistantships also available. Support available to part-time students. Financial award applicants required to submit FAFSA. *Faculty research:* Accounting, finance, insurance, management, real estate, urban analysis marketing. *Unit head:* Prof. Alexander D. Sevilla, Assistant Dean and Director MBA Programs, 352-273-3252 Ext. 1206, E-mail: alex.sevilla@warrington.ufl.edu. *Application contact:* Prof. Kelli Gust, Associate Director of MBA Programs, 352-273-3255, Fax: 352-392-8791, E-mail: kelly.gust@warrington.ufl.edu.

University of Medicine and Dentistry of New Jersey, UMDNJ–School of Public Health (UMDNJ, Rutgers, NJIT) Newark Campus, Newark, NJ 07107-1709. Offers clinical epidemiology (Certificate); dental public health (MPH); general public health (Certificate); public policy and oral health services administration (Certificate); quantitative methods (MPH); urban health (MPH); DMD/MPH; MD/MPH; MS/MPH. *Accreditation:* CEPH. Part-time and evening/weekend programs available. *Degree requirements:* For master's, thesis, internship. *Entrance requirements:* For master's, GRE General Test. Additional exam requirements/recommendations for international students: Required—TOEFL. *Application deadline:* For fall admission, 5/1 for domestic students; for spring admission, 10/1 for domestic students. Application fee: $115. Electronic applications accepted. *Application contact:* Yvette J. Holding-Ford, Information Contact, 973-972-7212, Fax: 973-972-8032, E-mail: holdinys@umdnj.edu.

University of North Texas, Toulouse Graduate School, College of Business Administration, Department of Information Technology and Decision Sciences, Denton, TX 76203. Offers business computer information systems (PhD); decision technologies (MS); information technology (MS); management science (PhD). Part-time and evening/weekend programs available. *Degree requirements:* For doctorate, comprehensive exam, thesis/dissertation. *Entrance requirements:* For master's, GMAT; for doctorate, GMAT or GRE General Test. Additional exam requirements/recommendations for international students: Recommended—TOEFL (minimum score 550 paper-based; 213 computer-based; 79 iBT). *Application deadline:* Applications are processed on a rolling basis. Electronic applications accepted. *Expenses:* Tuition, state resident: full-time $4298; part-time $239 per credit hour. Tuition, nonresident: full-time $10,782; part-time $549 per credit hour. Required fees: $1292; $270 per credit hour. *Financial support:* Fellowships, research assistantships, teaching assistantships, career-related internships or fieldwork and Federal Work-Study available. Financial award application deadline: 4/1; financial award applicants required to submit FAFSA. *Faculty research:* Large scale IS, business intelligence, security, applied statistics, quality and reliability management. *Unit head:* Chair. *Application contact:* Graduate Advisor, 940-565-4149, Fax: 940-565-4935, E-mail: itdsrecp@unt.edu.

University of Pittsburgh, Katz Graduate School of Business, Doctoral Program in Business Administration, Pittsburgh, PA 15260. Offers accounting (PhD); finance (PhD); information systems (PhD); marketing (PhD); operations/decision sciences/artificial intelligence (PhD); organizational behavior and human resource management (PhD); strategic planning (PhD). *Accreditation:* AACSB. *Faculty:* 50 full-time (15 women). *Students:* 51 full-time (22 women); includes 3 Black or African American, non-Hispanic/Latino; 4 Asian, non-Hispanic/Latino; 2 Hispanic/Latino, 18 international. 448 applicants, 5% accepted, 13 enrolled. In 2010, 4 doctorates awarded. *Degree requirements:* For doctorate, comprehensive exam, thesis/dissertation. *Entrance requirements:* For doctorate, GMAT or GRE, bachelor's degree, references, minimum GPA of 3.0. Additional exam requirements/recommendations for international students: Required—TOEFL, IELTS. *Application deadline:* For fall admission, 2/1 priority date for domestic and international students. Applications are processed on a rolling basis. Application fee: $50. Electronic applications accepted. *Expenses:* Tuition, state resident: full-time $17,304; part-time $701 per credit. Tuition, nonresident: full-time $29,554; part-time $1210 per credit. Required fees: $740; $214 per term. Tuition and fees vary according to program. *Financial support:* In 2010–11, 39 students received support, including 29 research assistantships with full tuition reimbursements available (averaging $1,900 per year), 10 teaching assistantships with full tuition reimbursements available (averaging $23,745 per year); fellowships, Federal Work-Study, scholarships/grants, health care benefits, and unspecified assistantships also available. Financial award application deadline: 2/1. *Faculty research:* Accounting statements and reporting, incentives and governance, corporate finance, mergers and acquisitions, information systems processes, structures and decision-making, organizational structure, knowledge management and corporate strategy, consumer behavior and marketing models. Total annual research expenditures: $362,777. *Unit head:* Dr. John E. Hulland, Director of Doctoral Program, 412-648-1534, Fax: 412-624-3633, E-mail: jhulland@katz.pitt.edu. *Application contact:* Carrie Woods, Assistant Director, Doctoral Office, 412-648-1525, Fax: 412-624-3633, E-mail: cawoods@katz.pitt.edu.

University of Southern California, Graduate School, Dana and David Dornsife College of Letters, Arts and Sciences, Department of Psychology, Los Angeles, CA 90089. Offers brain and cognitive science (PhD); clinical science (PhD); developmental psychology (PhD); human behavior (MHB); quantitative methods (PhD); social psychology (PhD). *Accreditation:* APA. *Faculty:* 34 full-time (10 women), 15 part-time/adjunct (9 women). *Students:* 105 full-time (65 women), 3 part-time (all women); includes 32 minority (4 Black or African American, non-Hispanic/Latino; 17 Asian, non-Hispanic/Latino; 9 Hispanic/Latino; 2 Two or more races, non-Hispanic/Latino), 22 international. 543 applicants, 5% accepted, 14 enrolled. In 2010, 17 master's, 12 doctorates awarded. *Degree requirements:* For doctorate, comprehensive exam, thesis/dissertation, one-year internship (for clinical science students). *Entrance requirements:* For doctorate, GRE. Additional exam requirements/recommendations for international students: Recommended—TOEFL (minimum score 600 paper-based; 250 computer-based; 100 iBT). *Application deadline:* For fall admission, 12/1 for domestic and international students. Application fee: $85. Electronic applications accepted. *Expenses:* Tuition: Full-time $31,240; part-time $1420 per unit. Required fees: $600. One-time fee: $35 full-time. Full-time tuition and fees vary according to degree level and program. *Financial support:* In 2010–11, 85 students received support, including 30 fellowships with full tuition reimbursements available (averaging $24,000 per year), 12 research assistantships with full tuition reimbursements available (averaging $19,250 per year), 40 teaching assistantships with full tuition reimbursements available (averaging $19,250 per year); scholarships/grants, traineeships, health care benefits, and unspecified assistantships also available. Financial award application deadline: 12/1. *Faculty research:* Affective neuroscience; children and families; vision, culture and ethnicity; intergroup relations; aggression and violence; language and reading development; substance abuse. *Unit head:* Dr. Margaret Gatz, Chair and Professor, 213-740-2212, Fax: 213-746-9028, E-mail: gatz@usc.edu. *Application contact:* Irene Takaragawa, Graduate Advisor, 213-740-2205, Fax: 213-746-9082, E-mail: itakarag@usc.edu.

The University of Texas at Arlington, Graduate School, College of Business, Department of Finance and Real Estate, Arlington, TX 76019. Offers finance (PhD); quantitative finance (MS); real estate (MS). Part-time and evening/weekend programs available. *Faculty:* 3 full-time (1 woman). *Students:* 48 full-time (10 women), 31 part-time (9 women); includes 18 minority (1 Black or African American, non-Hispanic/Latino; 1 American Indian or Alaska Native, non-Hispanic/Latino; 11 Asian, non-Hispanic/Latino; 4 Hispanic/Latino; 1 Two or more races, non-Hispanic/Latino), 28 international. 37 applicants, 70% accepted, 18 enrolled. In 2010, 24 master's, 1 doctorate awarded. *Degree requirements:* For master's, thesis optional; for doctorate, comprehensive exam, thesis/dissertation. *Entrance requirements:* For master's, GMAT, minimum GPA of 3.0. Additional exam requirements/recommendations for international students: Required—TOEFL (minimum score 550 paper-based; 213 computer-based; 79 iBT). *Application deadline:* For fall admission, 6/1 priority date for domestic students, 4/1 for international students; for spring admission, 10/15 for domestic students, 9/15 for international students. Applications are processed on a rolling basis. Application fee: $35 ($50 for international students). *Expenses:* Tuition, state resident: full-time $7500. Tuition, nonresident: full-time $13,080. International tuition: $13,250 full-time. *Financial support:* In 2010–11, 10 teaching assistantships (averaging $14,000 per year) were awarded; career-related internships or fieldwork, Federal Work-Study, institutionally sponsored loans, and unspecified assistantships also available. Financial award application deadline: 6/1; financial award applicants required to submit FAFSA. *Unit head:* Dr. David Diltz, Chair, 817-272-3705, Fax: 817-272-2252, E-mail: diltz@uta.edu. *Application contact:* Dr. Fred Forgey, Graduate Advisor, 817-272-0359, Fax: 817-272-2252, E-mail: realestate@uta.edu.

The University of Texas at Arlington, Graduate School, College of Business, Program in Business Administration, Arlington, TX 76019. Offers accounting (PhD); business statistics (PhD); finance (MBA, PhD); information systems (MBA, PhD); management (MBA, PhD); marketing (MBA, PhD); operations management (MBA, PhD); real estate (MBA). *Accreditation:* AACSB. Part-time and evening/weekend programs available. Postbaccalaureate distance learning degree programs offered (no on-campus study). *Students:* 555 full-time (197 women), 378 part-time (144 women); includes 179 minority (55 Black or African American, non-Hispanic/Latino; 1 American Indian or Alaska Native, non-Hispanic/Latino; 58 Asian, non-Hispanic/Latino; 55 Hispanic/Latino; 10 Two or more races, non-Hispanic/Latino), 410 international. 317 applicants, 93% accepted, 196 enrolled. In 2010, 468 master's, 1 doctorate awarded. Terminal master's awarded for partial completion of doctoral program. *Degree requirements:* For master's, thesis optional; for doctorate, comprehensive exam, thesis/dissertation. *Entrance requirements:* For master's, GMAT or GRE; for doctorate, GMAT, minimum GPA of 3.0 (undergraduate), 3.4 (graduate); 30 hours of graduate course work. Additional exam requirements/recommendations for international students: Required—TOEFL (minimum score 550 paper-based; 213 computer-based; 79 iBT). *Application deadline:* For fall admission, 6/1 for domestic students, 4/1 for international students; for spring admission, 10/15 for domestic students, 9/15 for international students. Applications are processed on a rolling basis. Application fee: $35 ($50 for international students). Electronic applications accepted. *Expenses:* Tuition, state resident: full-time $7500. Tuition, nonresident: full-time $13,080. International tuition: $13,250 full-time. *Financial support:* Career-related internships or fieldwork, scholarships/grants, and unspecified assistantships available. Financial award application deadline: 6/1; financial award applicants required to submit FAFSA. *Unit head:* Dr. Edmund Prater, Director of PhD Programs, 817-272-2131, Fax: 817-272-5799. *Application contact:* Melanie McGee, Director of MBA Program, 817-272-3005, Fax: 817-272-5799, E-mail: mwmcgee@uta.edu.

Virginia Commonwealth University, Graduate School, School of Business, Program in Decision Sciences, Richmond, VA 23284-9005. Offers MBA, MS. *Entrance requirements:* For master's, GMAT. Additional exam requirements/recommendations for international students: Required—TOEFL (minimum score 600 paper-based; 250 computer-based; 100 iBT). *Application deadline:* For fall admission, 6/1 for domestic students; for spring admission, 11/1 for domestic students. Applications are processed on a rolling basis. Application fee: $50. Electronic applications accepted. *Expenses:* Tuition, state resident: full-time $4308; part-time $479 per credit hour. Tuition, nonresident: full-time $8942; part-time $994 per credit hour. Required fees: $2000; $85 per credit hour. Tuition and fees vary according to course level, course load, degree level, campus/location and program. *Financial support:* Fellowships, research assistantships, teaching assistantships, Federal Work-Study, institutionally sponsored loans, and tuition waivers (full and partial) available. Financial award application deadline: 3/15; financial award applicants required to submit FAFSA. *Unit head:* Dr. Jose Dula, Interim Chair, Department of Management, 804-828-6002, Fax: 804-828-8884, E-mail: jdula@vcu.edu. *Application contact:* Jana P. McQuaid, Assistant Dean, Masters Programs, 804-828-4622, Fax: 804-828-7174, E-mail: jpmcquaid@vcu.edu.

Walden University, Graduate Programs, School of Management, Minneapolis, MN 55401. Offers accounting (MS), including cpa emphasis, professional track, self-designed; accounting and management (MS), including self-designed, strategic management; applied management and decision sciences (PhD), including accounting, engineering management, finance, general applied management and decision sciences, information systems management, knowledge management, leadership and organizational change, learning management, operations research, self-designed program in applied management and design sciences; business information management (MISM); enterprise information security (MISM); entrepreneurship (MBA, DBA); finance (MBA, DBA); global management (MS); global supply chain management (DBA); health informatics (MISM); healthcare management (MBA, MS); healthcare system improvement (MBA); human resource management (MBA, MS), including functional human resource management (MS), human resource management (MS), integrating functional and strategic human resource management (MS), organizational strategy (MS); information systems (MS); information systems management (DBA); information technology (MS), including information security, software engineering; international business (MBA, DBA); IT strategy and governance (MISM); leadership (MBA, MS, DBA), including entrepreneurship (MS), general management (MS), human resources leadership (MS), innovation and technology (MS), leader development (MS), leading sustainability (MS), project management (MS), self-designed (MS); managers as leaders (MS); managing global software and service supply chains (MISM); marketing (MBA, DBA); project management (MBA, MS); research strategies (MS); risk management (MBA); self-designed (MBA, DBA); social impact management (DBA); strategy and operations (MS); sustainable futures (MBA); sustainable management (MS); technology (MBA); technology entrepreneurship (DBA); technology management (MS). Part-time and evening/weekend programs available. Postbaccalaureate distance learning degree programs offered (minimal on-campus study). *Faculty:* 22 full-time (8 women), 291 part-time/adjunct (100 women). *Students:* 3,705 full-time (1,956 women), 976 part-time (549 women); includes 2,432 minority (2,021 Black or African American, non-Hispanic/Latino; 32 American Indian or Alaska Native, non-Hispanic/Latino; 137 Asian, non-Hispanic/Latino; 193 Hispanic/Latino; 5 Native Hawaiian or other Pacific Islander, non-Hispanic/Latino; 44 Two or more races, non-Hispanic/Latino), 302 international. Average age 40. In 2010, 658 master's, 86 doctorates awarded. *Degree requirements:* For doctorate, thesis/dissertation (for some programs), residency. *Entrance requirements:* For master's, bachelor's degree or equivalent in related field; minimum GPA of 2.5; official transcripts; goal statement; access to computer and Internet; for doctorate, master's degree or equivalent in related field; minimum GPA of 3.0; 3 years of related professional/academic experience (preferred). Additional exam requirements/recommendations for international students: Required—TOEFL (minimum score 550 paper-based; 213 computer-based), IELTS (minimum score 6.5), Michigan English Language Assessment Battery (minimum score 82). *Application deadline:* Applications are processed on a rolling basis. Application fee: $50. Electronic applications accepted. *Expenses:* Tuition: Full-time $10,274; part-time $445 per credit. Tuition and fees vary according to course load, degree level and program. *Financial support:* Fellowships, Federal Work-Study, scholarships/grants, unspecified assistantships, and family tuition reduction, active duty/veteran tuition reduction, group tuition reduction, interest-free payment plans available. Support available to part-time students. Financial award applicants required to submit FAFSA. *Unit head:* Dr. William Schulz, Associate Dean, 800-925-3368. *Application contact:* Jennifer Hall, Vice President of Enrollment Management, 866-4-WALDEN, E-mail: info@waldenu.edu.

Real Estate

OVERVIEW

An MBA real estate program is often broadly defined to include appraisal, development, corporate real estate, leasing, brokerage, property management, and institutional investment. The focus of a program tends to be primarily commercial (office or retail) and industrial, with some exposure to housing policy issues. Through a strong analytical focus combined with hands-on field experience, students can expect their MBA real estate coursework to cover a significant amount of theory, methodology, and application case material, as well as subject matter from related fields, such as architecture, law, public policy, and city planning.

Required courses may include study in:

- Business and Legal Issues in Real Estate Development
- Housing and the Urban Economy
- Real Estate Finance and Securitization
- Real Estate Investment Analysis

Elective courses may include study in:

- Bargaining, Negotiation, and Dispute Settlement for Managers
- Contemporary Topics, Venture Creation
- Corporate Finance Theory and Practice
- Entrepreneurial Management
- Fixed Income and Derivative Securities
- Investment Analysis and Strategies
- Money and Capital Markets
- Multinational Business Finance
- Real Estate Law and Transactions
- Security Analysis
- Urban Economics
- Valuation and Market Analysis

Careers choices for graduates with a real estate MBA include opportunities in development, private equity, leasing, mortgage lending, investment banking, property management, government housing agencies, construction finance, corporate real estate, lending and portfolio or asset management, and institutional investment. A real estate MBA opens doors across various spaces, including residential, office, industrial, hospitality, and retail and various firms, including real estate investment trusts, real estate operating companies, developers, financial institutions, investment banks, and consulting companies.

IN THIS SECTION

You'll find profiles of institutions offering graduate programs in the following field:

HELPFUL ORGANIZATIONS/ PUBLICATIONS/BLOGS

National Real Estate Investors Association (REIA)

http://www.nationalreia.com/

The National Real Estate Investors Association (REIA) is a 501(c)(6) trade association made up of local associations or investment clubs throughout the United States. Members represent national local investor associations, property owner associations, apartment associations, and landlord associations.

The stated mission of the organization is to develop, support, and promote local real estate investor organizations while serving the interests of the real estate investment industry through networking, education, leadership on legislative issues, and promoting professionalism and standards of excellence in the industry. The stated vision of the organization is to be the source for the independent real estate investment industry where the key focus areas will be legislation, funding, membership, education, administration/governance, and information/communication.

National Association of Real Estate Investment Managers (NAREIM)

http://www.nareim.org/

The National Association of Real Estate Investment Managers (NAREIM) is the leading association for companies engaged in the real estate investment management business. NAREIM members manage investment capital on behalf of third-party investors in commercial real estate assets. Investment sectors include office, retail, multi-family, industrial properties and hotels. NAREIM members serve the investment goals of public and corporate pension funds, foundations, endowments, insurance companies, and individuals, both domestic and foreign. Collectively, they manage over $1 trillion of real estate investment assets around the world. NAREIM members range from the largest institutional firms in the world with fully integrated service platforms to specialized entrepreneurial firms. NAREIM members invest in all four quadrants of real estate: public equity, private equity, public debt, and private debt.

NAREIM provides the organizational platform, programs, information, and tools to help real estate investment managers:

- Establish important relationships with fellow industry leaders.
- Benchmark their companies relative to their peers.
- Maximize their understanding of what is happening in their industry.
- Enhance the skills and knowledge base of their operations teams.

NAREIM members create and add value by providing:

- Timely and skilled acquisition/disposition services.
- Expert asset and portfolio management.
- Experienced development services.
- Risk aligned structured debt investment.
- Loan origination.

NAREIM is also the established voice of real estate investment managers with federal lawmakers on policies and regulations affecting the industry.

Journal of Real Estate Portfolio Management (JREPM)

http://business.fullerton.edu/finance/jrepm/

The *Journal of Real Estate Portfolio Management (JREPM)* is a publication of the American Real Estate Society (ARES). The focus of the journal is to investigate and expand the frontiers of knowledge that cover business decision-making applications or scholarly real estate research. ARES has a special interest in research that can be useful to the business decision-maker in areas such as development, finance, management, market analysis, marketing, and valuation.

CAREER ASPIRATIONS: A PROSPECTIVE POSITION

Vice President Finance/Chief Financial Officer

Job Description

Real estate development and investment company is seeking an experienced senior financial professional who is a creative, strategic thinker and a very hands-on, energetic team player. The candidate will report directly to the CEO/COO and will operate as an integral part of a small senior management team running a successful real estate business with a very stable portfolio. Only candidates with extensive real estate backgrounds (at least 7 years) will be considered.

Responsibilities

- Financial Reporting and Oversight: Oversight of the preparation of financial reports/budgets and general ledger. Implement and strengthen internal controls and accounting infrastructure to keep pace with growth strategy.
- Management: Oversee, motivate, and develop accounting department of 5 people in two offices. Knowledge and experience with financial software packages, ADP Payroll, MS Excel, and other financial-related software.
- Financing: Lead real estate financings for both development projects and existing property portfolio, including managing legal documentation, negotiations with lenders, and deal structuring. Important that candidates have the initiative and gravitas to maintain and grow relationships with lenders and equity investment partners.
- Tax: Oversee preparation of property tax returns in conjunction with outside accountants. Perform tax planning and analysis for acquisitions and portfolio properties, including experience with 1031 and other tax-efficient transaction structures.
- Insurance: Procure and manage insurance coverage for property portfolio working with third-party consultants.
- Acquisitions/Divestitures: Participate in identifying deals and acquisition due diligence of new investment opportunities, including financial modeling and analysis and overall property analysis.
- Strategic Planning: Provide strategic, operational, and financial analysis and advice for all areas of company operations. Oversee annual property reporting, including debt schedules, tenant/leasing summaries, capital improvement forecasts, and other summary schedules.
- General: Direct experience with leasing, property management, and development preferred. CFO/VP will be involved in these functional areas based on background.

Qualifications

- Entrepreneurial: A candidate who is comfortable rolling up his/her sleeves and being resourceful in solving problems, as well as proposing new ways of thinking about existing portfolio assets and new acquisitions. Candidates who are used to having 30 direct reports will not thrive in this job, although position requires both management skills as well as ability to fit in culturally with existing senior management team.
- Clever Idea Generator: A problem-solver and creative thinker who can apply previous experience to come up with solutions to financial issues affecting company and its real estate. This is not a job for a straight-and-narrow financial type who can't think outside the box and generate new ideas to help the company.
- Shrewd Negotiator: Candidate will play a front line role representing the company with banks, investors, tenants, vendors, and others and will have to be an experienced negotiator who can effectively advocate the company's interests.
- Integrity: Candidate must have unblemished history of high integrity in previous professional positions.
- Interpersonal Fit: Candidate will be able to fit in culturally with fellow employees who have long-term relationships. Collegial, team-oriented environment. Hard work expected.
- Experience/Qualifications: 7+ years real estate experience, CPA, MBA, or other relevant graduate degree preferred.

REAL ESTATE

American University, Kogod School of Business, Master of Business Administration Program, Washington, DC 20016-8044. Offers accounting (MBA); consulting (MBA), including information technology, international business, management; corporate finance: commercial banking (MBA); corporate finance: corporate financial management (MBA); corporate finance: investment banking (MBA), including corporate finance and private equity, trading and selling; entrepreneurship (MBA); global emerging markets (MBA), including business, finance, information technology; international trade and global supply chain management (MBA); leadership (MBA); marketing management (MBA); marketing research (MBA); real estate (MBA); MBA/JD; MBA/LL M. Part-time and evening/weekend programs available. *Faculty:* 12 full-time (5 women). *Students:* 135 full-time (62 women), 104 part-time (38 women); includes 46 minority (18 Black or African American, non-Hispanic/Latino; 1 American Indian or Alaska Native, non-Hispanic/Latino; 12 Asian, non-Hispanic/Latino; 14 Hispanic/Latino; 1 Two or more races, non-Hispanic/Latino), 34 international. Average age 27. 467 applicants, 51% accepted, 70 enrolled. In 2010, 101 master's awarded. *Entrance requirements:* For master's, GMAT. Additional exam requirements/recommendations for international students: Required—TOEFL. *Application deadline:* For fall admission, 2/1 priority date for domestic students; for spring admission, 10/1 priority date for domestic students. Applications are processed on a rolling basis. Application fee: $100. *Expenses:* Contact institution. *Financial support:* In 2010–11, 19 students received support; fellowships, research assistantships with partial tuition reimbursements available, career-related internships or fieldwork, Federal Work-Study, and institutionally sponsored loans available. Support available to part-time students. Financial award application deadline: 2/1. *Faculty research:* Information technology, decision-aiding methodology, negotiation. *Unit head:* Dr. Stevan Holmberg, Chair, 202-885-6193, E-mail: sholmbe@american.edu. *Application contact:* Shannon Demko, Associate Director Graduate Admissions, 202-885-1994, Fax: 202-885-1108, E-mail: demko@american.edu.

Arizona State University, W. P. Carey School of Business, Department of Marketing, Tempe, AZ 85287-4106. Offers business administration (marketing) (PhD); real estate development (MRED). Part-time and evening/weekend programs available. Postbaccalaureate distance learning degree programs offered. *Faculty:* 23 full-time (6 women), 3 part-time/adjunct (0 women). *Students:* 42 full-time (6 women); includes 13 minority (2 Black or African American, non-Hispanic/Latino; 3 Asian, non-Hispanic/Latino; 7 Hispanic/Latino; 1 Two or more races, non-Hispanic/Latino), 6 international. Average age 33. 73 applicants, 85% accepted, 41 enrolled. In 2010, 38 master's awarded. *Degree requirements:* For master's, thesis or alternative, capstone project, interactive Program of Study (iPOS) submitted before completing 50 percent of required credit hours; for doctorate, comprehensive exam, thesis/dissertation, interactive Program of Study (iPOS) submitted before completing 50 percent of required credit hours. *Entrance requirements:* For master's, GMAT, GRE, or LSAT, minimum GPA of 3.0 in last 2 years of work leading to bachelor's degree, 3 personal references, resume, official transcripts, personal statement; for doctorate, GMAT, minimum GPA of 3.0 in last 2 years of work leading to bachelor's degree, 3 letters of recommendation, personal statement/essay. Additional exam requirements/recommendations for international students: Required—TOEFL (minimum score 550 paper-based; 213 computer-based; 80 iBT), IELTS (minimum score 6.5). *Application deadline:* For fall admission, 1/15 for domestic and international students. Application fee: $70 ($90 for international students). Electronic applications accepted. *Expenses:* Contact institution. *Financial support:* Fellowships with full and partial tuition reimbursements, research assistantships with full and partial tuition reimbursements, teaching assistantships with full and partial tuition reimbursements, career-related internships or fieldwork, institutionally sponsored loans, scholarships/grants, and tuition waivers (full and partial) available. Financial award application deadline: 3/1; financial award applicants required to submit FAFSA. *Faculty research:* Service marketing and management, strategic marketing, customer portfolio management, characteristics and skills of high-performing managers, market orientation, market segmentation, consumer behavior, marketing strategy, new product development, management of innovation, social influences on consumption, e-commerce, market research methodology. Total annual research expenditures: $213,495. *Unit head:* Mark Stapp, Executive Director, 480-727-9287, Fax: 480-727-9288, E-mail: mark.stapp@asu.edu. *Application contact:* Graduate Admissions, 480-965-6113.

Central European University, CEU Business School, Budapest, Hungary. Offers executive business administration (EMBA); finance (MBA); general management (MBA); information technology management (MBA); marketing (MBA); real estate management (MBA). Part-time and evening/weekend programs available. *Faculty:* 16 full-time (4 women), 2 part-time/adjunct (1 woman). *Students:* 71 full-time (30 women), 142 part-time (47 women). Average age 34. 144 applicants, 36% accepted, 32 enrolled. In 2010, 64 master's awarded. *Degree requirements:* For master's, one foreign language. *Entrance requirements:* For master's, GMAT. Additional exam requirements/recommendations for international students: Required—TOEFL (minimum score 570 paper-based; 230 computer-based); Recommended—IELTS (minimum score 6.5). *Application deadline:* For fall admission, 5/15

priority date for domestic students, 5/22 for international students; for winter admission, 11/15 priority date for domestic students, 11/10 for international students. Applications are processed on a rolling basis. Application fee: $0. Electronic applications accepted. Tuition and fees charges are reported in euros. *Expenses:* Tuition: Full-time 11,000 euros. Required fees: 250 euros. One-time fee: 200 euros full-time. Tuition and fees vary according to degree level, program, reciprocity agreements and student level. *Financial support:* In 2010–11, 4 students received support. Tuition waivers (partial) available. *Faculty research:* Social and ethical business, marketing. *Unit head:* Dr. Mel Horwitch, Dean and Managing Director, 361-887-5050, E-mail: mhorwitch@ceubusiness.com. *Application contact:* Agnes Schram, MBA Program Manager, 361-887-5511, Fax: 361-887-5133, E-mail: mba@ceubusiness.com.

Clemson University, Graduate School, College of Architecture, Arts, and Humanities, Department of Planning and Landscape Architecture and College of Business and Behavioral Science, Program in Real Estate Development, Clemson, SC 29634. Offers MRED. *Students:* 39 full-time (6 women), 1 part-time (0 women); includes 1 Hispanic/Latino. Average age 27. 54 applicants, 54% accepted, 20 enrolled. In 2010, 20 master's awarded. *Entrance requirements:* For master's, GRE or GMAT, 3 letters of recommendation, resume, personal statement. Additional exam requirements/recommendations for international students: Required—TOEFL (minimum score 600 paper-based). *Application deadline:* For fall admission, 2/15 priority date for domestic and international students. Applications are processed on a rolling basis. Application fee: $70 ($80 for international students). Electronic applications accepted. *Expenses:* Tuition, state resident: full-time $6492; part-time $400 per credit hour. Tuition, nonresident: full-time $13,634; part-time $800 per credit hour. Required fees: $262 per semester. Part-time tuition and fees vary according to course load and program. *Financial support:* In 2010–11, 1 student received support, including 1 fellowship with partial tuition reimbursement available (averaging $200 per year); research assistantships with partial tuition reimbursements available, teaching assistantships with partial tuition reimbursements available, career-related internships or fieldwork, scholarships/grants, health care benefits, and unspecified assistantships also available. *Faculty research:* Real estate education, real estate investment/finance, sustainability, public private partnership, historic preservation. *Unit head:* Dr. Elaine M. Worzala, Interim Director, 864-656-4258, Fax: 864-656-7519, E-mail: eworzal@clemson.edu. *Application contact:* Amy Matthews, Program Coordinator, 864-656-4257, Fax: 864-656-7519, E-mail: matthe3@clemson.edu.

Cleveland State University, College of Graduate Studies, Maxine Goodman Levin College of Urban Affairs, Program in Environmental Studies, Cleveland, OH 44115. Offers environmental studies (MAES); geographic information systems (Certificate); urban real estate development and finance (Certificate); JD/MAES. Part-time and evening/weekend programs available. *Faculty:* 26 full-time (10 women), 3 part-time/adjunct (0 women). *Students:* 12 full-time (5 women), 23 part-time (12 women); includes 1 Asian, non-Hispanic/Latino, 4 international. 16 applicants, 50% accepted, 6 enrolled. In 2010, 7 master's awarded. *Degree requirements:* For master's, thesis or alternative, exit project. *Entrance requirements:* For master's, GRE General Test (minimum score: verbal and quantitative 40th percentile, analytical writing 4.0), minimum GPA of 3.0. Additional exam requirements/recommendations for international students: Required—TOEFL (minimum score 525 paper-based; 197 computer-based; 65 iBT). *Application deadline:* For fall admission, 7/15 priority date for domestic students, 5/15 for international students; for spring admission, 11/1 for international students. Applications are processed on a rolling basis. Application fee: $30. Electronic applications accepted. *Expenses:* Tuition, state resident: full-time $8447; part-time $469 per credit hour. Tuition, nonresident: full-time $16,020; part-time $890 per credit hour. Required fees: $50. *Financial support:* In 2010–11, 1 student received support, including 1 research assistantship with full and partial tuition reimbursement available (averaging $6,960 per year); career-related internships or fieldwork, Federal Work-Study, scholarships/grants, tuition waivers (full and partial), and unspecified assistantships also available. Support available to part-time students. Financial award application deadline: 3/1; financial award applicants required to submit FAFSA. *Faculty research:* Environmental policy and administration, environmental planning, geographic information systems (GIS), urban sustainability planning and management, energy policy, land re-use. *Unit head:* Dr. Sanda Kaufman, Director, 216-687-2367, Fax: 216-687-9342, E-mail: s.kaufman@csuohio.edu. *Application contact:* Joan Demko, Graduate Academic Support Specialist, 216-523-7522, Fax: 216-687-5398, E-mail: urbanprograms@csuohio.edu.

Cleveland State University, College of Graduate Studies, Maxine Goodman Levin College of Urban Affairs, Program in Public Administration, Cleveland, OH 44115. Offers geographic information systems (Certificate); local and urban management (Certificate); non-profit management (Certificate); public administration (MPA); urban real estate development (Certificate); JD/MPA. *Accreditation:* NASPAA. Part-time and evening/weekend programs available. *Faculty:* 26 full-time (10 women), 14 part-time/adjunct (8 women). *Students:* 36 full-time (22 women), 70 part-time (41 women); includes 26 Black or African American, non-Hispanic/Latino; 1 American Indian or Alaska Native, non-Hispanic/Latino; 1 Asian, non-Hispanic/Latino; 2 Hispanic/Latino; 1

Two or more races, non-Hispanic/Latino, 4 international. Average age 36. 82 applicants, 41% accepted, 15 enrolled. In 2010, 37 master's, 8 other advanced degrees awarded. *Degree requirements:* For master's, thesis or alternative, capstone course. *Entrance requirements:* For master's, GRE General Test (minimum 40th percentile verbal and quantitative, 4.0 writing), minimum GPA of 3.0. Additional exam requirements/recommendations for international students: Required—TOEFL (minimum score 525 paper-based; 197 computer-based; 65 iBT). *Application deadline:* For fall admission, 7/15 priority date for domestic students, 5/15 for international students; for spring admission, 11/1 for international students. Applications are processed on a rolling basis. Application fee: $30. Electronic applications accepted. *Expenses:* Tuition, state resident: full-time $8447; part-time $469 per credit hour. Tuition, nonresident: full-time $16,020; part-time $890 per credit hour. Required fees: $50. *Financial support:* In 2010–11, 10 students received support, including 7 research assistantships with full and partial tuition reimbursements available (averaging $6,960 per year), 3 teaching assistantships with full and partial tuition reimbursements available (averaging $6,960 per year); career-related internships or fieldwork, institutionally sponsored loans, tuition waivers (full and partial), and unspecified assistantships also available. Financial award application deadline: 3/1; financial award applicants required to submit FAFSA. *Faculty research:* Health care administration, public management, economic development, city management, nonprofit management. *Unit head:* Dr. Jennifer Alexander, Director, 216-687-5011, Fax: 216-687-2013, E-mail: j.k.alexander@csuohio.edu. *Application contact:* Joan Demko, Graduate Academic Support Specialist, 216-523-7522, Fax: 216-687-5398, E-mail: urbanprograms@csuohio.edu.

Cleveland State University, College of Graduate Studies, Maxine Goodman Levin College of Urban Affairs, Program in Urban Planning, Design, and Development, Cleveland, OH 44115. Offers geographic information systems (Certificate); local and urban management (Certificate); urban economic development (Certificate); urban planning, design, and development (MUPDD); urban real estate development and finance (Certificate); JD/MUPDD. *Accreditation:* ACSP. Part-time and evening/weekend programs available. *Faculty:* 32 full-time (19 women), 8 part-time/adjunct (4 women). *Students:* 30 full-time (10 women), 28 part-time (17 women); includes 6 Black or African American, non-Hispanic/Latino; 3 Hispanic/Latino, 5 international. Average age 38. 72 applicants, 56% accepted, 21 enrolled. In 2010, 24 master's, 9 Certificates awarded. *Degree requirements:* For master's, thesis or alternative, project or thesis. *Entrance requirements:* For master's, GRE General Test (minimum 50th percentile verbal and quantitative, 4.0 analytical writing), minimum GPA of 3.0. Additional exam requirements/recommendations for international students: Required—TOEFL (minimum score 525 paper-based; 197 computer-based; 65 iBT). *Application deadline:* For fall admission, 7/15 priority date for domestic students, 5/15 for international students; for spring admission, 11/1 for international students. Applications are processed on a rolling basis. Application fee: $30. Electronic applications accepted. *Expenses:* Tuition, state resident: full-time $8447; part-time $469 per credit hour. Tuition, nonresident: full-time $16,020; part-time $890 per credit hour. Required fees: $50. *Financial support:* In 2010–11, 15 students received support, including 10 research assistantships with full and partial tuition reimbursements available (averaging $6,960 per year), 5 teaching assistantships with full and partial tuition reimbursements available (averaging $6,960 per year); career-related internships or fieldwork, Federal Work-Study, tuition waivers (full and partial), and unspecified assistantships also available. Support available to part-time students. Financial award application deadline: 3/1. *Faculty research:* Housing and neighborhood development, urban housing policy, environmental sustainability, economic development, metropolitan change, GIS and planning decision support, PPGIS. *Unit head:* Dr. Dennis Keating, Director, 216-687-2298, Fax: 216-687-2013, E-mail: w.keating@csuohio.edu. *Application contact:* Joan Demkow, Graduate Program Coordinator, 216-523-7522, Fax: 216-687-5398, E-mail: urbanprograms@csuohio.edu.

Cleveland State University, College of Graduate Studies, Maxine Goodman Levin College of Urban Affairs, Program in Urban Studies, Cleveland, OH 44115. Offers geographic information systems (Certificate); local and urban management (Certificate); nonprofit management (Certificate); urban economic development (Certificate); urban real estate development and finance (Certificate); urban studies (MS); urban studies and public affairs (PhD). PhD program offered jointly with The University of Akron. Part-time and evening/weekend programs available. *Faculty:* 26 full-time (10 women), 20 part-time/adjunct (11 women). *Students:* 16 full-time (10 women), 35 part-time (18 women); includes 7 Black or African American, non-Hispanic/Latino, 17 international. Average age 37. 90 applicants, 38% accepted, 18 enrolled. In 2010, 6 master's, 7 doctorates, 6 other advanced degrees awarded. *Degree requirements:* For master's, thesis or alternative, exit project, capstone course; for doctorate, comprehensive exam, thesis/dissertation. *Entrance requirements:* For master's, GRE General Test, minimum GPA of 3.0; for doctorate, GRE General Test, minimum GPA of 3.5. Additional exam requirements/recommendations for international students: Required—TOEFL (minimum score 525 paper-based; 197 computer-based; 65 iBT). *Application deadline:* For fall admission, 7/15 priority date for domestic students, 5/15 for international students; for spring admission, 11/1 for international students. Applications are processed on a rolling basis. Application fee: $30. Electronic applications

accepted. *Expenses:* Tuition, state resident: full-time $8447; part-time $469 per credit hour. Tuition, nonresident: full-time $16,020; part-time $890 per credit hour. Required fees: $50. *Financial support:* In 2010–11, 15 students received support, including 11 research assistantships with full tuition reimbursements available (averaging $7,000 per year), 4 teaching assistantships with full and partial tuition reimbursements available (averaging $7,000 per year); career-related internships or fieldwork, Federal Work-Study, institutionally sponsored loans, scholarships/grants, tuition waivers (full and partial), and unspecified assistantships also available. Support available to part-time students. Financial award application deadline: 3/1; financial award applicants required to submit FAFSA. *Faculty research:* Environmental issues, economic development, urban and public policy, public management. *Unit head:* Dr. Sugie Lee, Director, 216-687-2381, Fax: 216-687-9342, E-mail: s.lee56@csuohio.edu. *Application contact:* Joan Demko, Graduate Academic Support Specialist, 216-523-7522, Fax: 216-687-5398, E-mail: urbanprograms@csuohio.edu.

Cornell University, Graduate School, Graduate Fields of Architecture, Art and Planning, Field of Real Estate, Ithaca, NY 14853-0001. Offers MPSRE. *Faculty:* 17 full-time (0 women). *Students:* 48 full-time (7 women); includes 3 Black or African American, non-Hispanic/Latino; 4 Asian, non-Hispanic/Latino; 3 Hispanic/Latino, 11 international. Average age 27. 137 applicants, 32% accepted, 32 enrolled. In 2010, 23 master's awarded. *Degree requirements:* For master's, project paper. *Entrance requirements:* For master's, GMAT, 2 letters of recommendation, resume. Additional exam requirements/recommendations for international students: Required—TOEFL (minimum score 600 paper-based; 250 computer-based; 77 iBT). *Application deadline:* For fall admission, 1/15 for domestic students. Application fee: $70. Electronic applications accepted. *Expenses:* Tuition: Full-time $29,500. Required fees: $76. Tuition and fees vary according to degree level and program. *Financial support:* In 2010–11, 1 fellowship with full tuition reimbursement, 1 research assistantship with full tuition reimbursement were awarded; teaching assistantships with full tuition reimbursements, institutionally sponsored loans, scholarships/grants, health care benefits, and unspecified assistantships also available. Financial award applicants required to submit FAFSA. *Faculty research:* Smart growth, economic development, urban redevelopment, development financing, securitization of real estate. *Unit head:* Director of Graduate Studies, 607-255-7110, Fax: 607-255-0242. *Application contact:* Graduate Field Assistant, 607-255-7110, Fax: 607-255-0242, E-mail: real_estate@cornell.edu.

DePaul University, Charles H. Kellstadt Graduate School of Business, Department of Finance, Chicago, IL 60604-2287. Offers behavioral finance (MBA); computational finance (MS); finance (MBA, MSF); financial analysis (MBA); financial management and control (MBA); international marketing and finance (MBA); managerial finance (MBA); real estate (MS); real estate finance and investment (MBA); strategy, execution and valuation (MBA). Part-time and evening/weekend programs available. *Faculty:* 26 full-time (5 women), 23 part-time/adjunct (2 women). *Students:* 454 full-time (138 women), 190 part-time (41 women); includes 85 minority (13 Black or African American, non-Hispanic/Latino; 53 Asian, non-Hispanic/Latino; 17 Hispanic/Latino; 2 Two or more races, non-Hispanic/Latino), 129 international. In 2010, 239 master's awarded. *Entrance requirements:* For master's, GMAT, 2 letters of recommendation, resume. Additional exam requirements/recommendations for international students: Required—TOEFL (minimum score 550 paper-based; 213 computer-based; 80 iBT). *Application deadline:* For fall admission, 7/1 for domestic students, 6/1 for international students; for winter admission, 10/1 for domestic students, 9/1 for international students; for spring admission, 2/1 for domestic students, 1/1 for international students. Applications are processed on a rolling basis. Application fee: $60. Electronic applications accepted. *Financial support:* In 2010–11, 8 students received support, including 6 research assistantships with partial tuition reimbursements available (averaging $4,340 per year); scholarships/grants and unspecified assistantships also available. Financial award application deadline: 4/1; financial award applicants required to submit FAFSA. *Faculty research:* Derivatives, valuation, international finance, real estate, corporate finance. *Unit head:* Ali M. Fatemi, Professor and Chair, 312-362-8826, Fax: 312-362-6566, E-mail: afatemi@depaul.edu. *Application contact:* Christopher E. Kinsella, Director of Cohort MBA Programs, 312-362-8810, Fax: 312-362-6677, E-mail: kgsb@depaul.edu.

DePaul University, Charles H. Kellstadt Graduate School of Business, Department of Real Estate, Chicago, IL 60604-2287. Offers real estate (MS); real estate finance and investment (MBA). Part-time and evening/weekend programs available. *Faculty:* 6 full-time (1 woman), 10 part-time/adjunct (1 woman). *Students:* 59 full-time (16 women), 29 part-time (7 women); includes 11 minority (3 Black or African American, non-Hispanic/Latino; 5 Asian, non-Hispanic/Latino; 2 Hispanic/Latino; 1 Native Hawaiian or other Pacific Islander, non-Hispanic/Latino), 3 international. *Entrance requirements:* For master's, essay, 3 letters of recommendation. Additional exam requirements/recommendations for international students: Required—TOEFL, GMAT; Recommended—IELTS. *Financial support:* In 2010–11, 2 teaching assistantships with full and partial tuition reimbursements (averaging $1 per year) were awarded; career-related internships or fieldwork and scholarships/grants also available. Financial award applicants required to submit FAFSA. *Unit* *head:* Susanne Cannon, Chairman/Director, 312-362-5905, Fax: 312-362-5907, E-mail: scannon@depaul.edu. *Application contact:* Melissa Carnwell, Director of Recruiting and Admission, 312-362-8810, Fax: 312-362-6677, E-mail: kgsb@depaul.edu.

Florida International University, Alvah H. Chapman, Jr. Graduate School of Business, Department of Finance and Real Estate, Miami, FL 33199. Offers finance (MSF); international real estate (MS); real estate (MS). Part-time and evening/weekend programs available. *Faculty:* 19 full-time (3 women), 10 part-time/adjunct (2 women). *Students:* 74 full-time (22 women), 3 part-time (2 women); includes 6 Black or African American, non-Hispanic/Latino; 1 Asian, non-Hispanic/Latino; 31 Hispanic/Latino, 18 international. Average age 29. 317 applicants, 30% accepted. In 2010, 121 master's awarded. *Entrance requirements:* For master's, GMAT or GRE, minimum GPA of 3.0 (upper-level coursework); letter of intent; resume. Additional exam requirements/recommendations for international students: Required—TOEFL (minimum score 550 paper-based; 213 computer-based; 80 iBT) or IELTS (minimum score 6.5). *Application deadline:* For fall admission, 6/1 for domestic students, 4/1 for international students; for spring admission, 10/1 for domestic students, 9/1 for international students. Applications are processed on a rolling basis. Application fee: $30. Electronic applications accepted. *Expenses:* Contact institution. *Financial support:* Institutionally sponsored loans and scholarships/grants available. Financial award application deadline: 3/1; financial award applicants required to submit FAFSA. *Faculty research:* Investment, corporate and international finance, commercial real estate. *Unit head:* Dr. Chun-Hao Chang, Chair, Finance and Real Estate Department, 305-348-2680, Fax: 305-348-4245, E-mail: chun-hao.chang@fiu.edu. *Application contact:* Isabel Lopez, Assistant Director, Finance and Real Estate Graduate Programs, 305-348-4198, E-mail: lopezi@fiu.edu.

Florida International University, Alvah H. Chapman, Jr. Graduate School of Business, Program in Real Estate, Miami, FL 33199. Offers international real estate (MS); real estate (MS). Part-time and evening/weekend programs available. *Students:* 15 full-time (1 woman); includes 1 Black or African American, non-Hispanic/Latino; 5 Hispanic/Latino, 3 international. Average age 27. 35 applicants, 60% accepted. In 2010, 16 master's awarded. *Entrance requirements:* For master's, GMAT or GRE, letter of intent; resume. Additional exam requirements/recommendations for international students: Required—TOEFL (minimum score 550 paper-based; 213 computer-based; 80 iBT) or IELTS (minimum score 6.5). *Application deadline:* For fall admission, 4/1 for domestic and international students. Application fee: $30. Electronic applications accepted. *Expenses:* Contact institution. *Financial support:* Institutionally sponsored loans and scholarships/grants available. Financial award application deadline: 3/1; financial award applicants required to submit FAFSA. *Faculty research:* International real estate, real estate investments, commercial real estate. *Unit head:* Dr. Chun-Hao Chang, Chair, Finance and Real Estate Department, 305-348-2680, Fax: 305-348-4245, E-mail: chun-hao.chang@fiu.edu. *Application contact:* Isabel Lopez, Assistant Director, Finance and Real Estate Graduate Programs, 305-348-4198, E-mail: lopezi@fiu.edu.

George Mason University, School of Management, Fairfax, VA 22030. Offers accounting (MS); business administration (EMBA, MBA); real estate development (MS); taxation (MS); technology management (MS). Part-time and evening/weekend programs available. *Faculty:* 80 full-time (26 women), 51 part-time/adjunct (15 women). *Students:* 188 full-time (70 women), 353 part-time (111 women); includes 18 Black or African American, non-Hispanic/Latino; 1 American Indian or Alaska Native, non-Hispanic/Latino; 52 Asian, non-Hispanic/Latino; 17 Hispanic/Latino; 2 Two or more races, non-Hispanic/Latino, 40 international. Average age 31. 467 applicants, 58% accepted, 164 enrolled. In 2010, 203 master's awarded. *Entrance requirements:* For master's, GMAT. Additional exam requirements/recommendations for international students: Required—TOEFL (minimum score 570 paper-based; 230 computer-based; 88 iBT). *Application deadline:* Applications are processed on a rolling basis. Application fee: $100. Electronic applications accepted. *Expenses:* Tuition, state resident: full-time $8192; part-time $440 per credit hour. Tuition, nonresident: full-time $22,952; part-time $1055 per credit hour. Required fees: $2364; $99 per credit hour. *Financial support:* In 2010–11, 38 students received support, including 21 research assistantships with full and partial tuition reimbursements available (averaging $7,176 per year), 20 teaching assistantships with full and partial tuition reimbursements available (averaging $7,255 per year); career-related internships or fieldwork, Federal Work-Study, scholarships/grants, unspecified assistantships, and health care benefits (full-time research or teaching assistantship recipients) also available. Support available to part-time students. Financial award application deadline: 3/1; financial award applicants required to submit FAFSA. *Faculty research:* Current leading global issues: offshore outsourcing, international financial risk, comparative systems of innovation. Total annual research expenditures: $482,158. *Unit head:* Jorge Haddock, Dean, 703-993-1875, E-mail: jhaddock@gmu.edu. *Application contact:* Melanie Pflugshaupt, Administrative Coordinator to Dean's Office, 703-993-3638, E-mail: mpflugsh@gmu.edu.

The George Washington University, School of Business, Department of Finance, Washington, DC 20052. Offers finance (MSF, PhD); finance and investments (MBA); real estate and urban development (MBA). Part-time and evening/weekend programs available. *Faculty:* 17 full-time (4 women),

9 part-time/adjunct (2 women). *Students:* 71 full-time (27 women), 42 part-time (15 women); includes 7 Black or African American, non-Hispanic/Latino; 8 Asian, non-Hispanic/Latino; 5 Hispanic/Latino; 1 Two or more races, non-Hispanic/Latino, 64 international. Average age 30. 602 applicants, 23% accepted, 65 enrolled. In 2010, 52 master's awarded. *Degree requirements:* For doctorate, thesis/dissertation. *Entrance requirements:* For master's, GMAT; for doctorate, GMAT or GRE. Additional exam requirements/recommendations for international students: Required—TOEFL. *Application deadline:* For fall admission, 4/1 priority date for domestic students; for spring admission, 10/1 for domestic students. Applications are processed on a rolling basis. Application fee: $75. *Financial support:* In 2010–11, 38 students received support; fellowships, teaching assistantships, career-related internships or fieldwork, Federal Work-Study, and institutionally sponsored loans available. Financial award application deadline: 4/1. *Unit head:* Mark S. Klock, Chair, 202-994-5996, E-mail: klock@gwu.edu. *Application contact:* Kristin Williams, Asst VP Gradpec Enrlmnt Mgmt, 202-994-0467, Fax: 202-994-0371, E-mail: ksw@gwu.edu.

Hofstra University, Frank G. Zarb School of Business, Department of Finance, Hempstead, NY 11549. Offers banking (Advanced Certificate); business administration (MBA), including finance, real estate management; corporate finance (Advanced Certificate); finance (MS); investment management (Advanced Certificate); quantitative finance (MS). Part-time and evening/weekend programs available. Postbaccalaureate distance learning degree programs offered (minimal on-campus study). *Faculty:* 12 full-time (2 women), 2 part-time/adjunct (1 woman). *Students:* 180 full-time (68 women), 99 part-time (26 women); includes 24 minority (6 Black or African American, non-Hispanic/Latino; 10 Asian, non-Hispanic/Latino; 8 Hispanic/Latino), 13 international. Average age 27. 329 applicants, 73% accepted, 102 enrolled. In 2010, 76 master's awarded. *Degree requirements:* For master's, capstone course (for MBA); thesis (for MS). *Entrance requirements:* For master's, GMAT/GRE, 2 letters of recommendation; resume; essay. Additional exam requirements/recommendations for international students: Required—TOEFL (minimum score 550 paper-based; 213 computer-based; 80 iBT); Recommended—IELTS (minimum score 6). *Application deadline:* Applications are processed on a rolling basis. Application fee: $70 ($75 for international students). Electronic applications accepted. *Expenses:* Contact institution. *Financial support:* In 2010–11, 41 students received support, including 38 fellowships with full and partial tuition reimbursements available (averaging $10,353 per year), 1 research assistantship with full and partial tuition reimbursement available (averaging $9,375 per year); Federal Work-Study, institutionally sponsored loans, scholarships/grants, and tuition waivers (full and partial) also available. Support available to part-time students. Financial award applicants required to submit FAFSA. *Faculty research:* International finance, investments, banking, real estate, derivatives. *Unit head:* Dr. Nancy W. White, Chairperson, 516-463-5699, Fax: 516-463-4834, E-mail: finnwh@hofstra.edu. *Application contact:* Carol Drummer, Dean of Graduate Admissions, 516-463-4876, Fax: 516-463-4664, E-mail: gradstudent@hofstra.edu.

John Marshall Law School, Graduate and Professional Programs, Chicago, IL 60604-3968. Offers comparative legal studies (LL M); employee benefits (LL M, MS); information technology (LL M, MS); intellectual property (LL M); international business and trade (LL M); law (JD); real estate (LL M, MS); taxation (LL M, MS); JD/LL M; JD/MA; JD/MBA; JD/MPA. JD/MBA offered jointly with Dominican University, JD/MA and JD/MPA with Roosevelt University. *Accreditation:* ABA. Part-time and evening/weekend programs available. *Faculty:* 65 full-time (21 women), 152 part-time/adjunct (48 women). *Students:* 1,237 full-time (567 women), 373 part-time (181 women); includes 464 minority (138 Black or African American, non-Hispanic/Latino; 12 American Indian or Alaska Native, non-Hispanic/Latino; 96 Asian, non-Hispanic/Latino; 125 Hispanic/Latino; 11 Native Hawaiian or other Pacific Islander, non-Hispanic/Latino; 82 Two or more races, non-Hispanic/Latino), 39 international. Average age 27. 3,523 applicants, 44% accepted, 351 enrolled. In 2010, 387 first professional degrees, 8 master's awarded. *Degree requirements:* For JD, 90 credits. *Entrance requirements:* For JD, LSAT; for master's, JD. Additional exam requirements/recommendations for international students: Required—TOEFL. *Application deadline:* For fall admission, 3/1 priority date for domestic and international students; for spring admission, 10/15 priority date for domestic and international students. Applications are processed on a rolling basis. Application fee: $60. Electronic applications accepted. *Expenses:* Contact institution. *Financial support:* In 2010–11, 1,350 students received support. Scholarships/grants and tuition waivers (full and partial) available. Support available to part-time students. Financial award application deadline: 6/1; financial award applicants required to submit FAFSA. *Unit head:* John Corkery, Dean, 312-427-2737. *Application contact:* William B. Powers, Associate Dean of Admission and Student Affairs, 800-537-4280, Fax: 312-427-5136, E-mail: admission@jmls.edu.

The Johns Hopkins University, Carey Business School, The Edward St. John Department of Real Estate, Baltimore, MD 21218-2699. Offers MS. Part-time and evening/weekend programs available. *Faculty:* 29 full-time (6 women), 135 part-time/adjunct (29 women). *Students:* 15 full-time (3 women), 106 part-time (24 women); includes 27 minority (17 Black or African American, non-Hispanic/Latino; 7 Asian, non-Hispanic/Latino; 3 Hispanic/Latino), 2 international. Average age 32. 76 applicants, 66% accepted, 33 enrolled. In

2010, 78 master's awarded. *Degree requirements:* For master's, 36 credits including final project. *Entrance requirements:* For master's, GMAT, GRE, or LSAT (full-time only), minimum GPA of 3.0, resume, work experience, two letters of recommendation. Additional exam requirements/recommendations for international students: Required—TOEFL (minimum score 600 paper-based; 250 computer-based; 100 iBT). *Application deadline:* For fall admission, 4/1 for international students; for spring admission, 9/15 for international students. Applications are processed on a rolling basis. Application fee: $100. Electronic applications accepted. *Financial support:* In 2010–11, 14 students received support. Scholarships/grants available. Support available to part-time students. Financial award application deadline: 4/15; financial award applicants required to submit FAFSA. *Unit head:* Dr. Michael Anikeeff, Director, Edward St. John Real Estate Program, 410-234-9404, E-mail: mikea@jhu.edu. *Application contact:* Robin Greenberg, Admissions Coordinator, 410-234-9227, Fax: 443-529-1554, E-mail: carey.admissions@jhu.edu.

Marquette University, Graduate School of Management, Department of Economics, Milwaukee, WI 53201-1881. Offers business economics (MSAE); financial economics (MSAE); international economics (MSAE); marketing research (MSAE); real estate economics (MSAE). Part-time and evening/weekend programs available. *Faculty:* 13 full-time (4 women), 3 part-time/adjunct (0 women). *Students:* 29 full-time (11 women), 33 part-time (8 women); includes 5 minority (2 Black or African American, non-Hispanic/Latino; 1 Asian, non-Hispanic/Latino; 1 Hispanic/Latino; 1 Two or more races, non-Hispanic/Latino), 17 international. Average age 25. 96 applicants, 73% accepted, 27 enrolled. In 2010, 15 master's awarded. *Degree requirements:* For master's, comprehensive exam, professional project. *Entrance requirements:* For master's, GMAT or GRE General Test. Additional exam requirements/recommendations for international students: Required—TOEFL (minimum score 530 paper-based; 78 computer-based). *Application deadline:* Applications are processed on a rolling basis. Application fee: $50. Electronic applications accepted. *Expenses:* Tuition: Full-time $16,290; part-time $905 per credit hour. Tuition and fees vary according to program. *Financial support:* In 2010–11, 2 fellowships, 7 teaching assistantships were awarded; research assistantships, Federal Work-Study, institutionally sponsored loans, scholarships/grants, and tuition waivers (full and partial) also available. Support available to part-time students. Financial award application deadline: 2/15. *Faculty research:* Monetary and fiscal policy in open economy, housing and regional migration, political economy of taxation and state/local government. Total annual research expenditures: $15,656. *Unit head:* Dr. Abdur Chowdhury, Chair, 414-288-6915, Fax: 414-288-5757. *Application contact:* Farrokh Nourzad, Information Contact, 414-288-3570.

Marylhurst University, Department of Business Administration, Marylhurst, OR 97036-0261. Offers finance (MBA); general management (MBA); government policy and administration (MBA); green development (MBA); health care management (MBA); marketing (MBA); natural and organic resources (MBA); nonprofit management (MBA); organizational behavior (MBA); real estate (MBA); renewable energy (MBA); sustainable business (MBA). Part-time and evening/weekend programs available. Postbaccalaureate distance learning degree programs offered (no on-campus study). *Faculty:* 3 full-time (0 women), 36 part-time/adjunct (6 women). *Students:* 27 full-time (13 women), 727 part-time (373 women); includes 167 minority (47 Black or African American, non-Hispanic/Latino; 6 American Indian or Alaska Native, non-Hispanic/Latino; 36 Asian, non-Hispanic/Latino; 51 Hispanic/Latino; 6 Native Hawaiian or other Pacific Islander, non-Hispanic/Latino; 21 Two or more races, non-Hispanic/Latino), 7 international. Average age 38. 262 applicants, 91% accepted, 194 enrolled. In 2010, 289 master's awarded. *Degree requirements:* For master's, comprehensive exam, capstone course. *Entrance requirements:* For master's, GMAT (if GPA less than 3.0 and fewer than 5 years of work experience), interview, resume, 2 letters of recommendation. Additional exam requirements/recommendations for international students: Recommended—TOEFL (minimum score 550 paper-based; 213 computer-based; 80 iBT). *Application deadline:* For fall admission, 9/11 priority date for domestic and international students; for winter admission, 12/15 priority date for domestic and international students; for spring admission, 3/15 priority date for domestic students, 3/17 priority date for international students. Applications are processed on a rolling basis. Application fee: $50. Electronic applications accepted. *Expenses:* Tuition: Full-time $13,932; part-time $516 per credit. Tuition and fees vary according to course load and program. *Financial support:* Scholarships/grants available. Support available to part-time students. Financial award applicants required to submit FAFSA. *Unit head:* Bob Hanks, Director of Business and Real Estate Programs, 503-636-8141, Fax: 503-697-5597, E-mail: mba@marylhurst.edu. *Application contact:* Maruska Lynch, Graduate Admissions Specialist, 800-634-9982 Ext. 6322, Fax: 503-699-6320, E-mail: admissions@marylhurst.edu.

Massachusetts Institute of Technology, School of Architecture and Planning, Center for Real Estate, Cambridge, MA 02139-4307. Offers real estate development (MSRED). *Faculty:* 4 full-time (0 women), 4 part-time/adjunct (1 woman). *Students:* 25 full-time (6 women); includes 1 minority (Hispanic/Latino), 10 international. Average age 31. 103 applicants, 35% accepted, 23 enrolled. In 2010, 30 master's awarded. *Degree requirements:* For master's, thesis. *Entrance requirements:* For master's, GMAT. Additional exam requirements/recommendations for international students: Required—TOEFL (minimum score 600 paper-based; 250 computer-based; IELTS (minimum score 7.5). *Application deadline:* For fall admission, 1/2 for domestic students, 1/5 for international students. Application fee: $75. Electronic applications accepted. *Expenses:* Tuition: Full-time $38,940; part-time $605 per unit. Required fees: $272. *Financial support:* In 2010–11, 12 students received support, including 3 fellowships; institutionally sponsored loans, scholarships/grants, and health care benefits also available. *Faculty research:* Real estate finance and investment, real estate development, urban design, planning, project management, infrastructure delivery methods, urban economics, entrepreneurship, strategic planning, housing, leadership development. *Unit head:* Prof. Brian A. Ciochetti, Director, 617-253-4373, Fax: 617-258-6991. *Application contact:* Maria Vieira, Associate Director of Education, 617-253-4373, Fax: 617-258-6991, E-mail: mit-cre@mit.edu.

Monmouth University, The Graduate School, Leon Hess Business School, West Long Branch, NJ 07764-1898. Offers accounting (MBA, Post-Master's Certificate); business (MBA); finance (MBA); healthcare management (MBA, Post-Master's Certificate); real estate (MBA). *Accreditation:* AACSB. Part-time and evening/weekend programs available. *Faculty:* 27 full-time (9 women), 7 part-time/adjunct (1 woman). *Students:* 87 full-time (31 women), 144 part-time (69 women); includes 6 Black or African American, non-Hispanic/Latino; 14 Asian, non-Hispanic/Latino; 8 Hispanic/Latino; 2 Two or more races, non-Hispanic/Latino, 17 international. Average age 29. 181 applicants, 78% accepted, 81 enrolled. In 2010, 88 master's awarded. *Degree requirements:* For master's, capstone course. *Entrance requirements:* For master's, GMAT, minimum GPA of 3.0 in major, 2.75 overall. Additional exam requirements/recommendations for international students: Required—TOEFL (minimum score 550 paper-based; 213 computer-based; 79 iBT), IELTS (minimum score 5), Michigan English Language Assessment Battery (minimum score 77), Cambridge A, B, C. *Application deadline:* For fall admission, 7/15 priority date for domestic students, 6/1 for international students; for spring admission, 11/15 priority date for domestic students, 11/1 for international students. Applications are processed on a rolling basis. Application fee: $50. Electronic applications accepted. *Expenses:* Tuition: Full-time $19,572; part-time $816 per credit. Required fees: $628; $157 per semester. *Financial support:* In 2010–11, 166 students received support, including 161 fellowships (averaging $1,741 per year), 17 research assistantships (averaging $10,505 per year); career-related internships or fieldwork, scholarships/grants, and unspecified assistantships also available. Support available to part-time students. Financial award applicants required to submit FAFSA. *Faculty research:* Information technology and marketing, behavioral research in accounting, human resources, management of technology. *Unit head:* Douglas Stives, MBA Program Director, 732-263-5894, Fax: 732-263-5517, E-mail: dstives@monmouth.edu. *Application contact:* Kevin Roane, Director, Office of Graduate Admission, 732-571-3452, Fax: 732-263-5123, E-mail: gradadm@monmouth.edu.

New York University, School of Continuing and Professional Studies, Schack Institute of Real Estate, New York, NY 10012-1019. Offers construction management (MS, Advanced Certificate), including construction management (Advanced Certificate), construction management for the development process (MS), project management (MS); real estate (MS, Advanced Certificate), including business of development (MS), finance and investment (MS), real estate (Advanced Certificate), strategic real estate management (MS), sustainable development (MS). Part-time and evening/weekend programs available. *Faculty:* 16 full-time (4 women), 93 part-time/adjunct (10 women). *Students:* 109 full-time (21 women), 327 part-time (71 women); includes 18 Black or African American, non-Hispanic/Latino; 3 American Indian or Alaska Native, non-Hispanic/Latino; 33 Asian, non-Hispanic/Latino; 20 Hispanic/Latino, 74 international. Average age 31. 351 applicants, 67% accepted, 126 enrolled. In 2010, 216 master's, 64 other advanced degrees awarded. *Degree requirements:* For master's, thesis. *Entrance requirements:* For master's, GRE General Test or GMAT (for recent graduates), resume, 2 letters of recommendation, essay, professional experience. Additional exam requirements/recommendations for international students: Required—TOEFL (minimum score 600 paper-based; 250 computer-based; 100 iBT), TWE. *Application deadline:* For fall admission, 2/1 priority date for domestic and international students; for spring admission, 10/15 priority date for domestic students, 8/15 priority date for international students. Applications are processed on a rolling basis. Application fee: $75. Electronic applications accepted. *Financial support:* In 2010–11, 222 students received support, including 222 fellowships (averaging $2,202 per year); scholarships/grants also available. Support available to part-time students. Financial award application deadline: 3/1; financial award applicants required to submit FAFSA. *Faculty research:* Project financial management, sustainable design, impact of large-scale development projects, economics and market cycles, international property rights, comparative metropolitan economies, current market trends. *Unit head:* James Stuckey, Divisional Dean, 212-992-3335, Fax: 212-992-3686, E-mail: james.stuckey@nyu.edu. *Application contact:* Jennifer Monahan, Director of Administration and Student Services, 212-992-3335, Fax: 212-992-3686, E-mail: jm189@nyu.edu.

Nova Southeastern University, H. Wayne Huizenga School of Business and Entrepreneurship, Program in Real Estate Development, Fort Lauderdale,

FL 33314-7796. Offers MS. Evening/weekend programs available. *Faculty:* 1 full-time (0 women), 4 part-time/adjunct (0 women). *Students:* 5 full-time (2 women), 27 part-time (5 women); includes 2 Black or African American, non-Hispanic/Latino; 9 Hispanic/Latino, 2 international. Average age 32. 39 applicants, 54% accepted, 14 enrolled. *Entrance requirements:* Additional exam requirements/recommendations for international students: Required— TOEFL (minimum score 550 paper-based; 213 computer-based; 79 iBT), IELTS (minimum score 6). *Application deadline:* For fall admission, 7/1 for domestic and international students; for winter admission, 10/1 for domestic and international students; for spring admission, 1/1 for domestic and international students. Applications are processed on a rolling basis. Application fee: $50. Electronic applications accepted. *Financial support:* Federal Work-Study and scholarships/grants available. Support available to part-time students. Financial award applicants required to submit FAFSA. *Unit head:* Dr. Preston Jones, Executive Associate Dean, 954-262-5127, Fax: 954-262-3960, E-mail: prestonj@huizenga.nova.edu. *Application contact:* Karen Goldberg, Associate Director of Recruitment and Special Events, 954-262-5039, Fax: 954-262-3822, E-mail: karen@nova.edu.

Pacific States University, College of Business, Los Angeles, CA 90006. Offers accounting (MBA); business administration (DBA); finance (MBA); international business (MBA); management of information technology (MBA); real estate management (MBA). Part-time and evening/weekend programs available. Postbaccalaureate distance learning degree programs offered (no on-campus study). *Faculty:* 4 full-time (1 woman), 13 part-time/adjunct (0 women). *Students:* 130 full-time (55 women); includes 1 Black or African American, non-Hispanic/Latino; 7 Asian, non-Hispanic/Latino; 3 Native Hawaiian or other Pacific Islander, non-Hispanic/Latino, 115 international. Average age 31. 42 applicants, 83% accepted, 33 enrolled. In 2010, 67 master's awarded. *Degree requirements:* For doctorate, comprehensive exam, thesis/dissertation. *Entrance requirements:* For master's, minimum undergraduate GPA of 2.5 during last 90 hours of course work. Additional exam requirements/recommendations for international students: Required—TOEFL (minimum score 133 computer-based; 45 iBT), IELTS (minimum score 4.5). *Application deadline:* For fall admission, 8/15 priority date for domestic students; for winter admission, 10/15 priority date for domestic students; for spring admission, 1/15 priority date for domestic students. Applications are processed on a rolling basis. Application fee: $100. *Expenses:* Tuition: Full-time $8280; part-time $345 per credit hour. Required fees: $150 per quarter. *Financial support:* Scholarships/grants available. Financial award applicants required to submit FAFSA. *Unit head:* Dr. Chase C. Lee, Director, 888-200-0383, Fax: 323-731-2383, E-mail: admission@psuca.edu. *Application contact:* Zolzaya Enkhbayar, Assistant Director of Admissions, 323-731-2383, Fax: 323-731-7276, E-mail: admissions@psuca.edu.

Southern Methodist University, Cox School of Business, MBA Program, Dallas, TX 75275. Offers accounting (MBA); finance (MBA); financial consulting (MBA); general business (MBA); information technology and operations management (MBA); management (MBA); marketing (MBA); real estate (MBA); strategy and entrepreneurship (MBA). Part-time and evening/weekend programs available. *Faculty:* 59 full-time (13 women), 30 part-time/adjunct (7 women). *Students:* 359 full-time (116 women), 592 part-time (154 women); includes 215 minority (44 Black or African American, non-Hispanic/Latino; 10 American Indian or Alaska Native, non-Hispanic/Latino; 118 Asian, non-Hispanic/Latino; 39 Hispanic/Latino; 2 Native Hawaiian or other Pacific Islander, non-Hispanic/Latino; 2 Two or more races, non-Hispanic/Latino), 92 international. Average age 30. In 2010, 486 master's awarded. *Entrance requirements:* For master's, GMAT. Additional exam requirements/recommendations for international students: Required—TOEFL. *Application deadline:* Applications are processed on a rolling basis. Application fee: $0. Electronic applications accepted. *Expenses:* Contact institution. *Financial support:* Applicants required to submit FAFSA. *Faculty research:* Corporate finance, financial reporting, modeling consumer decision-making, competition between national brands and store brands, institutional determinants of firms' strategy. *Unit head:* Dr. Marci Armstrong, Associate Dean for Master's Programs, 214-768-4486, Fax: 214-768-3956, E-mail: marci@cox.smu.edu. *Application contact:* Patti Cudney, Director of MBA Admissions, 214-768-3001, Fax: 214-768-3956, E-mail: pcudney@cox.smu.edu.

Texas A&M University, Mays Business School, Real Estate Program, College Station, TX 77843. Offers MRE. *Entrance requirements:* For master's, GMAT or GRE, letters of reference, interview. Additional exam requirements/recommendations for international students: Required—TOEFL. *Application deadline:* For fall admission, 3/15 priority date for domestic students, 2/15 for international students; for spring admission, 10/15 priority date for domestic students, 9/15 for international students. Application fee: $50 ($75 for international students). Electronic applications accepted. *Financial support:* Fellowships, scholarships/grants available. Financial award application deadline: 2/1. *Unit head:* Angela Degelman, Program Coordinator, 979-845-4858, Fax: 979-845-3884, E-mail: adegelman@mays.tamu.edu. *Application contact:* Angela Degelman, Program Coordinator, 979-845-4858, Fax: 979-845-3884, E-mail: adegelman@mays.tamu.edu.

Texas Tech University, Graduate School, Jerry S. Rawls College of Business Administration, Programs in Business Administration, Lubbock, TX 79409. Offers agricultural business (MBA); business administration (IMBA); business statistics (MBA); entrepreneurship and innovation (MBA); general business (MBA); health organization management (MBA); international business (MBA); management and leadership skills (MBA); management information systems (MBA); marketing (MBA); real estate (MBA); JD/MBA; MBA/M Arch; MBA/MA; MBA/MD; MBA/MS; MBA/Pharm D. Part-time and evening/weekend programs available. *Faculty:* 47 full-time (8 women), 5 part-time/adjunct (0 women). *Students:* 52 full-time (13 women), 531 part-time (152 women); includes 121 minority (28 Black or African American, non-Hispanic/Latino; 3 American Indian or Alaska Native, non-Hispanic/Latino; 31 Asian, non-Hispanic/Latino; 53 Hispanic/Latino; 6 Two or more races, non-Hispanic/Latino), 49 international. Average age 30. 437 applicants, 77% accepted, 258 enrolled. In 2010, 228 master's awarded. *Degree requirements:* For master's, capstone course. *Entrance requirements:* For master's, GMAT, holistic review of academic credentials. Additional exam requirements/recommendations for international students: Required—TOEFL (minimum score 550 paper-based; 213 computer-based; 79 iBT). *Application deadline:* For fall admission, 4/1 priority date for domestic students, 1/15 for international students; for spring admission, 9/1 priority date for domestic students, 6/15 for international students. Applications are processed on a rolling basis. Application fee: $50 ($75 for international students). Electronic applications accepted. *Expenses:* Tuition, state resident: full-time $5495.76; part-time $228.99 per credit hour. Tuition, nonresident: full-time $12,936; part-time $538.99 per credit hour. Required fees: $2674; $36 per credit hour. $905 per semester. *Financial support:* In 2010–11, 25 research assistantships (averaging $8,800 per year) were awarded; teaching assistantships, career-related internships or fieldwork, Federal Work-Study, scholarships/grants, health care benefits, and unspecified assistantships also available. Support available to part-time students. Financial award applicants required to submit FAFSA. *Unit head:* Dr. W. Jay Conover, Director, 806-742-1546, Fax: 806-742-3958, E-mail: jay.conover@ttu.edu. *Application contact:* Cynthia D. Barnes, Director, Graduate Services Center, 806-742-3184, Fax: 806-742-3958, E-mail: ba_grad@ttu.edu.

University of California, Berkeley, Graduate Division, Haas School of Business, PhD in Business Administration Program, Berkeley, CA 94720-1500. Offers accounting (PhD); business and public policy (PhD); finance (PhD); management of organizations (PhD); marketing (PhD); operations management (PhD); real estate (PhD). *Accreditation:* AACSB. *Students:* 78 full-time (25 women); includes 12 Asian, non-Hispanic/Latino; 2 Hispanic/Latino, 32 international. Average age 30. 526 applicants, 7% accepted, 17 enrolled. In 2010, 17 doctorates awarded. *Degree requirements:* For doctorate, comprehensive exam, thesis/dissertation, written preliminary exams, oral qualifying exam. *Entrance requirements:* For doctorate, GMAT or GRE, minimum GPA of 3.0 in undergraduate and graduate coursework. Additional exam requirements/recommendations for international students: Required— TOEFL (minimum score 570 paper-based; 230 computer-based; 70 iBT), IELTS (minimum score 7). *Application deadline:* For fall admission, 12/10 for domestic and international students. Application fee: $70 ($90 for international students). Electronic applications accepted. *Financial support:* In 2010–11, 63 students received support, including 58 fellowships with full and partial tuition reimbursements available (averaging $26,000 per year); research assistantships with full and partial tuition reimbursements available, teaching assistantships with full and partial tuition reimbursements available, scholarships/grants, health care benefits, tuition waivers (full), unspecified assistantships, and transit pass, travel grants also available. Financial award application deadline: 12/10; financial award applicants required to submit FAFSA. *Faculty research:* Accounting, business and public policy, finance, management of organizations, marketing, operations and information technology management, real estate526. *Unit head:* Dr. Sunil Dutta, Director, 510-642-1229, Fax: 510-643-4255, E-mail: kimg@haas.berkeley.edu. *Application contact:* Kim Guilfoyle, Director, Student Affairs, 510-642-3944, Fax: 510-643-4255, E-mail: kimg@haas.berkeley.edu.

University of Central Florida, College of Business Administration, Dr. P. Phillips School of Real Estate, Program in Real Estate, Orlando, FL 32816. Offers MSRE. *Students:* 22 full-time (6 women), 2 part-time (1 woman); includes 4 minority (2 Black or African American, non-Hispanic/Latino; 1 American Indian or Alaska Native, non-Hispanic/Latino; 1 Asian, non-Hispanic/Latino), 2 international. Average age 36. 35 applicants, 77% accepted, 24 enrolled. *Expenses:* Tuition, state resident: part-time $256.56 per credit hour. Tuition, nonresident: part-time $1011.52 per credit hour. Part-time tuition and fees vary according to program. *Financial support:* In 2010–11, 2 students received support, including 2 teaching assistantships (averaging $3,900 per year). *Application contact:* Judy Ryder, Director, Graduate Admissions, 407-823-2364, Fax: 407-823-0219, E-mail: jryder@bus.ucf.edu.

University of Denver, Daniels College of Business, Franklin L. Burns School of Real Estate and Construction Management, Denver, CO 80208. Offers construction management (IMBA, MS); real estate (IMBA, MBA, MS); real estate and construction management (EMS). Part-time and evening/weekend programs available. *Faculty:* 8 full-time (1 woman), 8 part-time/adjunct (2 women). *Students:* 40 full-time (8 women), 65 part-time (11 women); includes 11 minority (4 Black or African American, non-Hispanic/Latino; 3 Asian, non-Hispanic/Latino; 4 Hispanic/Latino), 14 international. Average age 32. 91 applicants, 77% accepted, 41 enrolled. In 2010, 62 master's awarded.

Entrance requirements: For master's, GRE General Test or GMAT. Additional exam requirements/recommendations for international students: Required—TOEFL (minimum score 570 paper-based; 88 iBT). *Application deadline:* For fall admission, 11/15 priority date for domestic students; for spring admission, 10/15 priority date for domestic students. Applications are processed on a rolling basis. Application fee: $100. Electronic applications accepted. *Expenses:* Tuition: Full-time $35,604; part-time $29,670 per year. Required fees: $687 per year. Tuition and fees vary according to program. *Financial support:* In 2010–11, 3 teaching assistantships with full and partial tuition reimbursements (averaging $1,966 per year) were awarded; career-related internships or fieldwork, Federal Work-Study, institutionally sponsored loans, scholarships/grants, and unspecified assistantships also available. Support available to part-time students. Financial award application deadline: 3/15; financial award applicants required to submit FAFSA. *Unit head:* Dr. Mark Levine, Director, 303-871-2142, E-mail: mark.levine@du.edu. *Application contact:* Victoria Chen, Graduate Admissions Manager, 303-871-3826, E-mail: victoria.chen@du.edu.

University of Florida, Graduate School, Warrington College of Business Administration, Hough Graduate School of Business, Department of Finance, Insurance and Real Estate, Gainesville, FL 32611. Offers business administration (MS), including entrepreneurship, real estate and urban analysis; finance (PhD); financial services (Certificate); real estate and urban analysis (PhD); JD/MBA. *Faculty:* 13 full-time (0 women). *Students:* 56 full-time (13 women), 2 part-time (0 women); includes 2 Black or African American, non-Hispanic/Latino; 2 Asian, non-Hispanic/Latino; 1 Hispanic/Latino, 16 international. Average age 27. 245 applicants, 34% accepted, 58 enrolled. In 2010, 105 master's awarded. Terminal master's awarded for partial completion of doctoral program. *Degree requirements:* For master's, comprehensive exam, thesis; for doctorate, comprehensive exam, thesis/dissertation. *Entrance requirements:* For master's, GMAT or GRE General Test, minimum GPA of 3.0 for last 60 hours of undergraduate degree, work experience (preferred); for doctorate, GMAT or GRE General Test, minimum GPA of 3.0. Additional exam requirements/recommendations for international students: Required—TOEFL (minimum score 550 paper-based; 213 computer-based; 80 iBT), IELTS (minimum score 6). *Application deadline:* For fall admission, 1/15 priority date for domestic students, 1/15 for international students. Applications are processed on a rolling basis. Application fee: $30. Electronic applications accepted. *Expenses:* Tuition, state resident: full-time $10,915.92. Tuition, nonresident: full-time $28,309. *Financial support:* In 2010–11, 18 students received support, including 6 fellowships, 12 research assistantships (averaging $20,699 per year), 2 teaching assistantships; career-related internships or fieldwork, scholarships/grants, and unspecified assistantships also available. Financial award application deadline: 1/15; financial award applicants required to submit FAFSA. *Faculty research:* Banking, empirical corporate finance, hedge funds. *Unit head:* Dr. Mahendrarajah Nimalendran, Chair, 352-392-9526, Fax: 352-392-0301, E-mail: nimal@ufl.edu. *Application contact:* Mark J. Flannery, Graduate Coordinator, 352-392-3184, Fax: 352-392-0301, E-mail: flannery@ufl.edu.

University of Hawaii at Manoa, Graduate Division, Shidler College of Business, Program in Business Administration, Honolulu, HI 96822. Offers Asian business studies (MBA); Chinese business studies (MBA); decision sciences (MBA); entrepreneurship (MBA); finance (MBA); finance and banking (MBA); human resources management (MBA); information management (MBA); information technology (MBA); international business (MBA); Japanese business studies (MBA); marketing (MBA); organizational behavior (MBA); organizational management (MBA); real estate (MBA); student-designed track (MBA). *Accreditation:* AACSB. Part-time and evening/weekend programs available. *Faculty:* 53 full-time (12 women). *Students:* 162 full-time (63 women), 102 part-time (43 women); includes 135 minority (1 Black or African American, non-Hispanic/Latino; 81 Asian, non-Hispanic/Latino; 5 Hispanic/Latino; 18 Native Hawaiian or other Pacific Islander, non-Hispanic/Latino; 30 Two or more races, non-Hispanic/Latino), 44 international. Average age 34. 361 applicants, 57% accepted, 172 enrolled. In 2010, 153 master's awarded. *Degree requirements:* For master's, thesis optional. *Entrance requirements:* For master's, GMAT, minimum GPA of 3.0. Additional exam requirements/recommendations for international students: Required—TOEFL (minimum score 600 paper-based; 250 computer-based; 100 iBT), IELTS (minimum score 7). *Application deadline:* For fall admission, 5/1 for domestic students, 3/1 for international students. Application fee: $60. *Expenses:* Contact institution. *Financial support:* In 2010–11, 83 fellowships (averaging $5,547 per year), 1 research assistantship (averaging $16,824 per year) were awarded. Total annual research expenditures: $427,000. *Application contact:* Daniel Port, Graduate Chair, 808-956-5565, Fax: 808-956-6889, E-mail: daniel.port@hawaii.edu.

University of Maryland, College Park, Academic Affairs, School of Architecture, Planning and Preservation, Program in Real Estate Development, College Park, MD 20742. Offers MRED. *Students:* 36 full-time (12 women), 49 part-time (14 women); includes 24 minority (17 Black or African American, non-Hispanic/Latino; 2 Asian, non-Hispanic/Latino; 2 Hispanic/Latino; 3 Two or more races, non-Hispanic/Latino), 6 international. 98 applicants, 50% accepted, 30 enrolled. In 2010, 33 master's awarded. *Application deadline:* For fall admission, 3/15 for domestic students, 2/1 for international students; for spring admission, 10/1 for domestic students, 6/1 for international students. Application fee: $75. *Expenses:* Tuition, state resident: part-time $471 per credit hour. Tuition, nonresident: part-time $1016 per credit hour. Required fees: $337 per term. *Financial support:* In 2010–11, 2 fellowships (averaging $10,831 per year), 9 teaching assistantships (averaging $14,968 per year) were awarded. *Unit head:* Dr. Margaret McFarland, Director, 301-405-6709, E-mail: mmcf@umd.edu. *Application contact:* Dr. Charles A. Caramello, Dean of Graduate School, 301-405-0358, Fax: 301-314-9305.

University of Memphis, Graduate School, Fogelman College of Business and Economics, Program in Business Administration, Memphis, TN 38152. Offers accounting (MBA, PhD); economics (MBA, PhD); executive business administration (MBA); finance (PhD); finance, insurance, and real estate (MBA, MS); international business administration (IMBA); management (MBA, MS, PhD); management information systems (MBA, MS, PhD); management science (MBA); marketing (MBA, MS); marketing and supply chain management (PhD); real estate development (MS); JD/MBA. *Accreditation:* AACSB. *Faculty:* 44 full-time (9 women), 5 part-time/adjunct (0 women). *Students:* 263 full-time (106 women), 181 part-time (66 women); includes 46 Black or African American, non-Hispanic/Latino; 3 American Indian or Alaska Native, non-Hispanic/Latino; 16 Asian, non-Hispanic/Latino; 5 Hispanic/Latino, 109 international. Average age 31. 374 applicants, 73% accepted, 119 enrolled. In 2010, 140 master's, 17 doctorates awarded. *Degree requirements:* For master's, comprehensive exam; for doctorate, comprehensive exam, thesis/dissertation. *Entrance requirements:* For master's, GMAT, resume; for doctorate, GMAT, interview, minimum GPA of 3.4, resume, letter of recommendation. Additional exam requirements/recommendations for international students: Required—TOEFL (minimum score 550 paper-based; 220 computer-based). *Application deadline:* For fall admission, 8/1 for domestic students; for spring admission, 12/1 for domestic students. Application fee: $35 ($60 for international students). *Financial support:* In 2010–11, 164 students received support; research assistantships with full tuition reimbursements available, teaching assistantships with full tuition reimbursements available, career-related internships or fieldwork, Federal Work-Study, scholarships/grants, and unspecified assistantships available. Financial award application deadline: 2/15; financial award applicants required to submit FAFSA. *Faculty research:* Competitive business strategy, finance microstructures, supply chain management innovations, health care economics, litigation risks and corporate audits. *Unit head:* Rajiv Grover, Dean, 901-678-3759, E-mail: rgrover@memphis.edu. *Application contact:* Dr. Carol V. Danehower, Associate Dean, 901-678-5402, Fax: 901-678-3579, E-mail: fcbegp@memphis.edu.

The University of North Carolina at Charlotte, Graduate School, Belk College of Business, Program in Business Administration, Charlotte, NC 28223-0001. Offers business administration (PhD); Hong Kong (MBA); MBA-plus (Post-Master's Certificate); Mexico (MBA); real estate finance and development (Certificate); sports marketing and management (MBA); Taiwan (MBA); U. S. (MBA). *Accreditation:* AACSB. Part-time and evening/weekend programs available. *Faculty:* 34 full-time (10 women). *Students:* 142 full-time (55 women), 307 part-time (96 women); includes 69 minority (33 Black or African American, non-Hispanic/Latino; 22 Asian, non-Hispanic/Latino; 12 Hispanic/Latino; 2 Two or more races, non-Hispanic/Latino), 145 international. Average age 30. 265 applicants, 82% accepted, 126 enrolled. In 2010, 227 master's, 1 doctorate awarded. *Degree requirements:* For master's, thesis or alternative; for doctorate, thesis/dissertation. *Entrance requirements:* For master's, GMAT, minimum GPA of 3.0 in undergraduate major, 2.8 overall. Additional exam requirements/recommendations for international students: Required—TOEFL (minimum score 557 paper-based; 220 computer-based; 83 iBT). *Application deadline:* For fall admission, 7/15 for domestic students, 5/1 for international students; for spring admission, 11/15 for domestic students, 10/1 for international students. Applications are processed on a rolling basis. Application fee: $55. Electronic applications accepted. *Expenses:* Tuition, state resident: full-time $3464. Tuition, nonresident: full-time $14,297. Required fees: $2094. Tuition and fees vary according to course load. *Financial support:* In 2010–11, 68 students received support, including 2 research assistantships (averaging $18,000 per year), 65 teaching assistantships (averaging $12,142 per year); career-related internships or fieldwork, Federal Work-Study, institutionally sponsored loans, scholarships/grants, and administrative assistantship also available. Support available to part-time students. Financial award application deadline: 4/1; financial award applicants required to submit FAFSA. Total annual research expenditures: $86,745. *Unit head:* Jeremiah Nelson, Interim Director, MBA Program, 704-687-6058, Fax: 704-687-4014, E-mail: jeremiah.nelson@uncc.edu. *Application contact:* Kathy B. Giddings, Director of Graduate Admissions, 704-687-5503, Fax: 704-687-3279, E-mail: gradadm@uncc.edu.

University of North Texas, Toulouse Graduate School, College of Business Administration, Department of Finance, Insurance, Real Estate, and Law, Denton, TX 76203. Offers finance (PhD); finance, insurance, real estate, and law (MS); real estate (MS). Part-time programs available. *Degree requirements:* For master's, thesis optional; for doctorate, comprehensive exam, thesis/dissertation. *Entrance requirements:* For master's, GMAT; for doctorate, GMAT or GRE General Test. Additional exam requirements/recommendations for international students: Recommended—TOEFL (minimum score 550 paper-based; 213 computer-based; 79 iBT). *Expenses:* Tuition, state resident:

full-time $4298; part-time $239 per credit hour. Tuition, nonresident: full-time $10,782; part-time $549 per credit hour. Required fees: $1292; $270 per credit hour. *Financial support:* Fellowships, research assistantships, teaching assistantships, career-related internships or fieldwork and tuition waivers (partial) available. Financial award application deadline: 4/1; financial award applicants required to submit FAFSA. *Faculty research:* Financial impact of regulation, risk management, taxes and valuation, bankruptcy, real financial options. *Application contact:* PhD Advisor, 940-565-2511, Fax: 940-565-4234, E-mail: john.kensinger@unt.edu.

University of St. Thomas, Graduate Studies, Opus College of Business, Master of Science in Real Estate Program, Minneapolis, MN 55403. Offers MS. Part-time and evening/weekend programs available. *Students:* 22 part-time (9 women); includes 1 minority (Asian, non-Hispanic/Latino), 1 international. Average age 32. In 2010, 6 master's awarded. *Entrance requirements:* For master's, GMAT. Additional exam requirements/recommendations for international students: Required—TOEFL (minimum 80 iBT), IELTS (minimum 6.5), or Michigan English Language Assessment Battery. *Application deadline:* For fall admission, 6/1 for domestic students, 4/15 for international students; for spring admission, 11/1 for domestic students, 10/1 for international students. Applications are processed on a rolling basis. Application fee: $40. Electronic applications accepted. *Unit head:* Herb Tousley, Director, 651-962-4289, E-mail: msrealestate@stthomas.edu. *Application contact:* Susan Eckstein, Program Manager, 651-962-4289, Fax: 651-962-4410, E-mail: msrealestate@stthomas.edu.

University of San Diego, School of Business Administration, San Diego, CA 92110-2492. Offers accountancy and taxation (MS), including accountancy, taxation; business administration (MBA); executive leadership (MS); global leadership (MS); international business administration (IMBA); real estate (MS); supply chain management (MS, Certificate); taxation (MS); JD/IMBA; JD/MBA; MBA/MSRE. *Accreditation:* AACSB. Part-time and evening/weekend programs available. *Faculty:* 53 full-time (7 women), 14 part-time/adjunct (6 women). *Students:* 207 full-time (85 women), 269 part-time (93 women); includes 98 minority (10 Black or African American, non-Hispanic/Latino; 2 American Indian or Alaska Native, non-Hispanic/Latino; 30 Asian, non-Hispanic/Latino; 46 Hispanic/Latino; 2 Native Hawaiian or other Pacific Islander, non-Hispanic/Latino; 8 Two or more races, non-Hispanic/Latino), 41 international. Average age 31. 591 applicants, 54% accepted, 216 enrolled. In 2010, 239 master's awarded. *Degree requirements:* For master's, variable foreign language requirement. *Entrance requirements:* For master's, GMAT, minimum GPA of 3.0. Additional exam requirements/recommendations for international students: Required—TOEFL (minimum score 580 paper-based; 237 computer-based; 92 iBT), TWE. Application fee: $80. Electronic applications accepted. *Expenses:* Tuition: Full-time $21,744; part-time $1208 per unit. Required fees: $224. Full-time tuition and fees vary according to course load and degree level. *Financial support:* In 2010-11, 247 students received support. Career-related internships or fieldwork, Federal Work-Study, institutionally sponsored loans, scholarships/grants, and unspecified assistantships available. Support available to part-time students. Financial award application deadline: 4/1; financial award applicants required to submit FAFSA. *Unit head:* Dr. David Pyke, Dean, 619-260-4886, E-mail: sbadean@sandiego.edu. *Application contact:* Stephen Pultz, Director of Admissions and Enrollment, 619-260-4506, Fax: 619-260-6836, E-mail: admissions@sandiego.edu.

University of Southern California, Graduate School, School of Policy, Planning, and Development, Master of Real Estate Development Program, Los Angeles, CA 90089. Offers MRED, M Pl/MRED, JD/MRED, MBA/MRED. Part-time programs available. *Faculty:* 51 full-time (12 women), 100 part-time/adjunct (30 women). *Students:* 38 full-time (3 women), 11 part-time (1 woman); includes 12 minority (1 Black or African American, non-Hispanic/Latino; 6 Asian, non-Hispanic/Latino; 3 Hispanic/Latino; 2 Two or more races, non-Hispanic/Latino), 3 international. 156 applicants, 50% accepted, 49 enrolled. In 2010, 53 master's awarded. *Degree requirements:* For master's, comprehensive exam. *Entrance requirements:* For master's, GRE, GMAT. Additional exam requirements/recommendations for international students: Required—TOEFL (minimum score 600 paper-based; 250 computer-based; 100 iBT). *Application deadline:* For fall admission, 2/1 for domestic and international students. Application fee: $85. Electronic applications accepted. *Expenses:* Contact institution. *Financial support:* In 2010-11, 11 students received support. Scholarships/grants and tuition waivers (partial) available. Financial award application deadline: 2/1; financial award applicants required to submit CSS PROFILE or FAFSA. *Faculty research:* Urban development, urban economics, real estate finance, housing markets. Total annual research expenditures: $6.2 million. *Unit head:* Dr. Christian Redfearn, Director, Graduate Programs in Real Estate Development, 213-821-1364, Fax: 213-740-0001, E-mail: redfearn@usc.edu. *Application contact:* Marisol R. Gonzalez, Director of Recruitment and Admission, 213-740-0550, Fax: 213-740-7573, E-mail: marisolr@usc.edu.

University of South Florida, Graduate School, College of Business, Department of Finance, Tampa, FL 33620-9951. Offers business (PhD), including finance; finance (MS); real estate (MS). Part-time and evening/weekend programs available. *Faculty:* 2 full-time (0 women). *Students:* 30 full-time (11 women), 10 part-time (4 women); includes 2 Black or African American, non-Hispanic/Latino; 5 Asian, non-Hispanic/Latino; 1 Hispanic/

Latino, 9 international. Average age 27. 119 applicants, 40% accepted, 20 enrolled. In 2010, 4 master's, 1 doctorate awarded. Terminal master's awarded for partial completion of doctoral program. *Degree requirements:* For master's, thesis or alternative, 30 credits, minimum GPA of 3.0; for doctorate, comprehensive exam, thesis/dissertation. *Entrance requirements:* For master's, GMAT, minimum GPA of 3.0; for doctorate, GMAT, letters of recommendation, personal statement. Additional exam requirements/recommendations for international students: Required—TOEFL (minimum score 550 paper-based; 213 computer-based; 79 iBT). *Application deadline:* For fall admission, 6/1 for domestic students, 1/2 for international students; for spring admission, 10/15 for domestic students, 6/1 for international students. Application fee: $30. Electronic applications accepted. *Financial support:* In 2010-11, 10 research assistantships (averaging $14,943 per year), 6 teaching assistantships with tuition reimbursements (averaging $14,943 per year) were awarded; scholarships/grants, health care benefits, and unspecified assistantships also available. Financial award application deadline: 6/30. *Faculty research:* Corporate governance, international finance, asset pricing models, risk management, market efficiency. Total annual research expenditures: $110,581. *Unit head:* Dr. Scott Besley, Chairperson, 813-974-2081, Fax: 813-974-3084, E-mail: sbesley@coba.usf.edu. *Application contact:* Dr. Scott Besley, Chairperson, 813-974-2081, Fax: 813-974-3084, E-mail: sbesley@coba.usf.edu.

The University of Texas at Arlington, Graduate School, College of Business, Department of Finance and Real Estate, Arlington, TX 76019. Offers finance (PhD); quantitative finance (MS); real estate (MS). Part-time and evening/weekend programs available. *Faculty:* 3 full-time (1 woman). *Students:* 48 full-time (10 women), 31 part-time (9 women); includes 18 minority (1 Black or African American, non-Hispanic/Latino; 1 American Indian or Alaska Native, non-Hispanic/Latino; 11 Asian, non-Hispanic/Latino; 4 Hispanic/Latino; 1 Two or more races, non-Hispanic/Latino), 28 international. 37 applicants, 70% accepted, 18 enrolled. In 2010, 24 master's, 1 doctorate awarded. *Degree requirements:* For master's, thesis optional; for doctorate, comprehensive exam, thesis/dissertation. *Entrance requirements:* For master's, GMAT, minimum GPA of 3.0. Additional exam requirements/recommendations for international students: Required—TOEFL (minimum score 550 paper-based; 213 computer-based; 79 iBT). *Application deadline:* For fall admission, 6/1 priority date for domestic students, 4/1 for international students; for spring admission, 10/15 for domestic students, 9/15 for international students. Applications are processed on a rolling basis. Application fee: $35 ($50 for international students). *Expenses:* Tuition, state resident: full-time $7500. Tuition, nonresident: full-time $13,080. International tuition: $13,250 full-time. *Financial support:* In 2010-11, 10 teaching assistantships (averaging $14,000 per year) were awarded; career-related internships or fieldwork, Federal Work-Study, institutionally sponsored loans, and unspecified assistantships also available. Financial award application deadline: 6/1; financial award applicants required to submit FAFSA. *Unit head:* Dr. David Diltz, Chair, 817-272-3705, Fax: 817-272-2252, E-mail: diltz@uta.edu. *Application contact:* Dr. Fred Forgey, Graduate Advisor, 817-272-0359, Fax: 817-272-2252, E-mail: realestate@uta.edu.

The University of Texas at Arlington, Graduate School, College of Business, Program in Business Administration, Arlington, TX 76019. Offers accounting (PhD); business statistics (PhD); finance (MBA, PhD); information systems (MBA, PhD); management (MBA, PhD); marketing (MBA, PhD); operations management (MBA, PhD); real estate (MBA). *Accreditation:* AACSB. Part-time and evening/weekend programs available. Postbaccalaureate distance learning degree programs offered (no on-campus study). *Students:* 555 full-time (197 women), 378 part-time (144 women); includes 179 minority (55 Black or African American, non-Hispanic/Latino; 1 American Indian or Alaska Native, non-Hispanic/Latino; 58 Asian, non-Hispanic/Latino; 55 Hispanic/Latino; 10 Two or more races, non-Hispanic/Latino), 410 international. 317 applicants, 93% accepted, 196 enrolled. In 2010, 468 master's, 1 doctorate awarded. Terminal master's awarded for partial completion of doctoral program. *Degree requirements:* For master's, thesis optional; for doctorate, comprehensive exam, thesis/dissertation. *Entrance requirements:* For master's, GMAT or GRE; for doctorate, GMAT, minimum GPA of 3.0 (undergraduate), 3.4 (graduate); 30 hours of graduate course work. Additional exam requirements/recommendations for international students: Required—TOEFL (minimum score 550 paper-based; 213 computer-based; 79 iBT). *Application deadline:* For fall admission, 6/1 for domestic students, 4/1 for international students; for spring admission, 10/15 for domestic students, 9/15 for international students. Applications are processed on a rolling basis. Application fee: $35 ($50 for international students). Electronic applications accepted. *Expenses:* Tuition, state resident: full-time $7500. Tuition, nonresident: full-time $13,080. International tuition: $13,250 full-time. *Financial support:* Career-related internships or fieldwork, scholarships/grants, and unspecified assistantships available. Financial award application deadline: 6/1; financial award applicants required to submit FAFSA. *Unit head:* Dr. Edmund Prater, Director of PhD Programs, 817-272-2131, Fax: 817-272-5799. *Application contact:* Melanie McGee, Director of MBA Program, 817-272-3005, Fax: 817-272-5799, E-mail: mwmcgee@uta.edu.

The University of Texas at Dallas, School of Management, Program in Management and Administrative Sciences, Richardson, TX 75080. Offers electronic commerce (MS); finance (MS); healthcare administration (MS); information systems (MS); innovation and entrepreneurship (MS); international management (MS); leadership in organizations (MS); marketing (MS); operations (MS); organizations (MS); real estate (MS); strategy (MS). *Accreditation:* AACSB. Part-time and evening/weekend programs available. *Faculty:* 18 full-time (3 women), 8 part-time/adjunct (0 women). *Students:* 57 full-time (32 women), 107 part-time (49 women); includes 53 minority (14 Black or African American, non-Hispanic/Latino; 30 Asian, non-Hispanic/Latino; 8 Hispanic/Latino; 1 Two or more races, non-Hispanic/Latino), 25 international. Average age 32. 161 applicants, 67% accepted, 51 enrolled. In 2010, 27 master's awarded. *Degree requirements:* For master's, thesis optional. *Entrance requirements:* For master's, GMAT. Additional exam requirements/recommendations for international students: Required—TOEFL (minimum score 550 paper-based; 215 computer-based). *Application deadline:* For fall admission, 7/15 for domestic students, 5/1 priority date for international students; for spring admission, 11/15 for domestic students, 9/1 priority date for international students. Applications are processed on a rolling basis. Application fee: $50 ($100 for international students). Electronic applications accepted. *Expenses:* Tuition, state resident: full-time $10,248; part-time $569 per credit hour. Tuition, nonresident: full-time $18,544; part-time $1030 per credit hour. Tuition and fees vary according to course load. *Financial support:* In 2010–11, 26 students received support, including 38 teaching assistantships with partial tuition reimbursements available (averaging $11,528 per year); research assistantships with partial tuition reimbursements available, career-related internships or fieldwork, Federal Work-Study, institutionally sponsored loans, scholarships/grants, and unspecified assistantships also available. Support available to part-time students. Financial award application deadline: 4/30; financial award applicants required to submit FAFSA. *Faculty research:* Integrated and detailed knowledge of functional areas of management, analytical tools for effective appraisal and decision making. *Unit head:* Dr. Doug Eckel, Assistant Dean, 972-883-5923, E-mail: doug.eckel@utdallas.edu. *Application contact:* James Parker, Assistant Director, 972-883-5842, E-mail: jparker@utdallas.edu.

The University of Texas at San Antonio, College of Business, Department of Finance, San Antonio, TX 78249-0617. Offers business finance (MBA); construction science and management (MS); finance (MS); real estate finance (MBA). Part-time and evening/weekend programs available. *Faculty:* 10 full-time (1 woman). *Students:* 24 full-time (6 women), 58 part-time (11 women); includes 21 minority (1 Black or African American, non-Hispanic/Latino; 4 Asian, non-Hispanic/Latino; 15 Hispanic/Latino; 1 Two or more races, non-Hispanic/Latino), 8 international. Average age 29. 56 applicants, 52% accepted, 17 enrolled. In 2010, 38 master's awarded. *Degree requirements:* For master's, comprehensive exam (for some programs), thesis (for some programs). *Entrance requirements:* For master's, GMAT, minimum GPA of 3.0. Additional exam requirements/recommendations for international students: Required—TOEFL (minimum score 500 paper-based; 173 computer-based; 61 iBT), IELTS (minimum score 5). *Application deadline:* For fall admission, 7/1 for domestic students, 4/1 for international students; for spring admission, 11/1 for domestic students, 9/1 for international students. Applications are processed on a rolling basis. Application fee: $45 ($85 for international students). Electronic applications accepted. *Expenses:* Tuition, state resident: full-time $4172; part-time $231.75 per credit hour. Tuition, nonresident: full-time $15,332; part-time $851.75 per credit hour. *Financial support:* In 2010–11, 6 students received support, including 7 research assistantships (averaging $16,052 per year), 38 teaching assistantships (averaging $9,767 per year); career-related internships or fieldwork, scholarships/grants, tuition waivers, and unspecified assistantships also available. Support available to part-time students. *Faculty research:* Capital markets, corporate finance, asset pricing and investments, international finance, real estate, finance. *Unit head:* Dr. Lalatendu Misra, Chair, 210-458-6315, Fax: 210-458-6320, E-mail: kfairchild@utsa.edu. *Application contact:* Veronica Ramirez, Assistant Dean of the Graduate School, 210-458-4330, Fax: 210-458-4332, E-mail: graduatestudies@utsa.edu.

University of Utah, Graduate School, David Eccles School of Business, Program in Real Estate Development, Salt Lake City, UT 84112-1107. Offers MRED. *Students:* 19 full-time (2 women), 9 part-time (0 women), 1 international. Average age 34. 26 applicants, 23% accepted, 3 enrolled. *Entrance requirements:* For master's, GMAT or GRE, minimum undergraduate GPA of 3.0. Additional exam requirements/recommendations for international students: Required—TOEFL (minimum score 600 paper-based; 250 computer-based; 100 iBT), IELTS (minimum score 7). *Application deadline:* For fall admission, 4/1 priority date for domestic and international students. Applications are processed on a rolling basis. Application fee: $55 ($65 for international students). Electronic applications accepted. *Expenses:* Contact institution. *Financial support:* Scholarships/grants and unspecified assistantships available. *Unit head:* Buzz Welch, Program Director, 801-581-7463, E-mail: buzz.welch@utah.edu. *Application contact:* Carly Brisbay, MRED Senior Admissions Coordinator, 801-581-7785, Fax: 801-581-3666, E-mail: mredsadmissions@business.utah.edu.

University of Wisconsin–Madison, Graduate School, Wisconsin School of Business, Doctoral Program in Real Estate and Urban Land Economics, Madison, WI 53706-1380. Offers PhD. *Faculty:* 6 full-time (0 women), 5

part-time/adjunct (0 women). *Students:* 5 full-time (all women), all international. Average age 27. 13 applicants, 8% accepted, 1 enrolled. *Degree requirements:* For doctorate, comprehensive exam, thesis/dissertation. *Entrance requirements:* For doctorate, GMAT or GRE. Additional exam requirements/recommendations for international students: Recommended—TOEFL (minimum score 623 paper-based; 263 computer-based; 106 iBT), IELTS (minimum score 7.5). *Application deadline:* For fall admission, 12/15 priority date for domestic and international students. Application fee: $56. Electronic applications accepted. *Expenses:* Tuition, state resident: full-time $9887; part-time $617.96 per credit. Tuition, nonresident: full-time $24,054; part-time $1503.40 per credit. Required fees: $67.63 per credit. Tuition and fees vary according to reciprocity agreements. *Financial support:* In 2010–11, 5 students received support, including fellowships with full tuition reimbursements available (averaging $18,756 per year), research assistantships with full tuition reimbursements available (averaging $16,506 per year), 5 teaching assistantships with full tuition reimbursements available (averaging $14,088 per year); career-related internships or fieldwork, Federal Work-Study, institutionally sponsored loans, scholarships/grants, health care benefits, and unspecified assistantships also available. Financial award application deadline: 2/1; financial award applicants required to submit FAFSA. *Faculty research:* Real estate finance, real estate equity investments, zoning restructurings, home ownership, international real estate and public policy. *Unit head:* Prof. Francois Ortalo-Magne, Chair, 608-262-7867, Fax: 608-265-2738, E-mail: fom@bus.wisc.edu. *Application contact:* Belle Heberling, Assistant Director for Research Programs, 608-262-3749, Fax: 608-890-0180, E-mail: phd@bus.wisc.edu.

University of Wisconsin–Madison, Graduate School, Wisconsin School of Business, Wisconsin Full-Time MBA Program, Madison, WI 53706-1380. Offers applied security analysis (MBA); arts administration (MBA); brand and product management (MBA); corporate finance and investment banking (MBA); entrepreneurial management (MBA); marketing research (MBA); operations and technology management (MBA); real estate (MBA); risk management and insurance (MBA); strategic human resource management (MBA); strategic management in the life and engineering sciences (MBA); supply chain management (MBA). *Faculty:* 32 full-time (4 women), 17 part-time/adjunct (3 women). *Students:* 242 full-time (74 women); includes 16 Black or African American, non-Hispanic/Latino; 3 American Indian or Alaska Native, non-Hispanic/Latino; 16 Asian, non-Hispanic/Latino; 12 Hispanic/Latino, 29 international. Average age 28. 526 applicants, 32% accepted, 117 enrolled. In 2010, 106 master's awarded. *Entrance requirements:* For master's, GMAT, bachelor's or equivalent degree, 2 years of work experience, letters of recommendation. Additional exam requirements/recommendations for international students: Required—TOEFL (minimum score 600 paper-based; 250 computer-based; 100 iBT), IELTS. *Application deadline:* For fall admission, 11/4 for domestic students, 11/1 for international students; for winter admission, 2/5 for domestic and international students; for spring admission, 5/15 for domestic students, 4/5 for international students. Applications are processed on a rolling basis. Application fee: $56. Electronic applications accepted. *Expenses:* Tuition, state resident: full-time $9887; part-time $617.96 per credit. Tuition, nonresident: full-time $24,054; part-time $1503.40 per credit. Required fees: $67.63 per credit. Tuition and fees vary according to reciprocity agreements. *Financial support:* In 2010–11, 103 students received support, including 13 fellowships with full and partial tuition reimbursements available (averaging $15,000 per year), 53 research assistantships with full tuition reimbursements available (averaging $8,000 per year), 35 teaching assistantships with full tuition reimbursements available (averaging $11,000 per year); scholarships/grants, health care benefits, and unspecified assistantships also available. Financial award application deadline: 4/5; financial award applicants required to submit FAFSA. *Faculty research:* Market consequences of International Financial Reporting Standards (IFRS), inter-firm relationships and strategic partnerships, application of Bayesian statistical methods and applied probability models to understanding individuals' behaviors in the context of customer relationship management (CRM) applications, liquidity provision and the structure of financial markets, strategic management of global startups. *Unit head:* Dr. Kenneth A. Kavajecz, Associate Dean of Master's Programs, 608-265-3494, Fax: 608-265-4192, E-mail: kkavajecz@bus.wisc.edu. *Application contact:* Maria Reis, Assistant Director of MBA Marketing and Recruiting, 608-262-4000, Fax: 608-265-4192, E-mail: mreis@bus.wisc.edu.

University of Wisconsin–Milwaukee, Graduate School, School of Architecture and Urban Planning, Department of Urban Planning, Milwaukee, WI 53201-0413. Offers geographic information systems (Certificate); real estate development (Certificate); urban planning (MUP); M Arch/MUP; MPA/MUP; MUP/MS. *Accreditation:* ACSP. Part-time programs available. *Faculty:* 5 full-time (2 women). *Students:* 40 full-time (14 women), 28 part-time (11 women); includes 3 Black or African American, non-Hispanic/Latino; 1 American Indian or Alaska Native, non-Hispanic/Latino; 3 Asian, non-Hispanic/Latino; 1 Hispanic/Latino, 3 international. Average age 29. 75 applicants, 72% accepted, 28 enrolled. In 2010, 21 master's awarded. *Degree requirements:* For master's, comprehensive exam, thesis or alternative. *Entrance requirements:* For master's, GRE General Test. Additional exam requirements/recommendations for international students: Required—TOEFL (minimum score 550 paper-based; 213 computer-based; 79 iBT), IELTS (minimum score 6.5). *Application deadline:* For fall admission, 1/1 priority date for domestic students; for spring admission, 9/1 for domestic students. Applications are processed on a rolling basis. Application fee: $56 ($96 for international students). Electronic applications accepted. *Financial support:* Fellowships, research assistantships, teaching assistantships, career-related internships or fieldwork, health care benefits, and unspecified assistantships available. Support available to part-time students. Financial award application deadline: 4/15; financial award applicants required to submit FAFSA. *Unit head:* Joan Simuncak, Representative, 414-229-4015, Fax: 414-229-6976, E-mail: joanarch@uwm.edu. *Application contact:* General Information Contact, 414-229-4982, Fax: 414-229-6967, E-mail: gradschool@uwm.edu.

Villanova University, Villanova School of Business, MBA—The Fast Track Program, Villanova, PA 19085. Offers finance (MBA); health care management (MBA); international business (MBA); management information systems (MBA); marketing (MBA); real estate (MBA); strategic management (MBA). *Accreditation:* AACSB. Part-time and evening/weekend programs available. *Faculty:* 15 full-time (2 women), 5 part-time/adjunct (0 women). *Students:* 118 part-time (34 women); includes 13 minority (2 Black or African American, non-Hispanic/Latino; 8 Asian, non-Hispanic/Latino; 3 Hispanic/Latino). Average age 30. In 2010, 35 master's awarded. *Degree requirements:* For master's, minimum GPA of 3.0. *Entrance requirements:* For master's, GMAT. Additional exam requirements/recommendations for international students: Required—TOEFL (minimum score 550 paper-based; 213 computer-based; 80 iBT). *Application deadline:* For fall admission, 6/30 for domestic and international students. Application fee: $50. Electronic applications accepted. *Expenses:* Tuition: Part-time $700 per credit. Part-time tuition and fees vary according to degree level and program. *Financial support:* Scholarships/grants available. Support available to part-time students. Financial award application deadline: 6/30; financial award applicants required to submit FAFSA. *Faculty research:* Developing and leveraging technology, ethical business practices, managing for innovation and creativity, the global political economy, strategic marketing management. *Unit head:* Meredith L. Kwiatek, Director of Graduate Recruitment & Marketing, 610-519-7016, Fax: 610-519-6273, E-mail: rachel.garonzik@villanova.edu. *Application contact:* Meredith L. Kwiatek, Assistant Director, 610-519-7016, Fax: 610-519-6273, E-mail: meredith.kwiatek@villanova.edu.

Villanova University, Villanova School of Business, MBA—The Flex Track Program, Villanova, PA 19085. Offers finance (MBA); health care management (MBA); international business (MBA); management information systems (MBA); marketing (MBA); real estate (MBA); strategic management (MBA); JD/MBA. *Accreditation:* AACSB. Part-time and evening/weekend programs available. Postbaccalaureate distance learning degree programs offered (minimal on-campus study). *Faculty:* 31 full-time (5 women), 22 part-time/adjunct (2 women). *Students:* 15 full-time (6 women), 443 part-time (150 women); includes 46 minority (5 Black or African American, non-Hispanic/Latino; 35 Asian, non-Hispanic/Latino; 6 Hispanic/Latino). Average age 30. In 2010, 133 master's awarded. *Degree requirements:* For master's, minimum GPA of 3.0. *Entrance requirements:* For master's, GMAT. Additional exam requirements/recommendations for international students: Required—TOEFL (minimum score 550 paper-based; 213 computer-based; 80 iBT). *Application deadline:* For fall admission, 6/30 for domestic and international students; for winter admission, 11/15 for domestic and international students; for spring admission, 3/30 for domestic students, 3/31 for international students. Applications are processed on a rolling basis. Application fee: $50. Electronic

applications accepted. *Expenses:* Tuition: Part-time $700 per credit. Part-time tuition and fees vary according to degree level and program. *Financial support:* In 2010–11, 15 research assistantships with full tuition reimbursements (averaging $13,100 per year) were awarded; scholarships/grants and unspecified assistantships also available. Support available to part-time students. Financial award application deadline: 6/30; financial award applicants required to submit FAFSA. *Faculty research:* Developing and leveraging technology, ethical business practices, managing for innovation and creativity, the global political economy, strategic marketing management. *Unit head:* Meredith L. Kwiatek, Director of Graduate Recruitment and Marketing, 610-519-7016, Fax: 610-519-6273, E-mail: meredith.kwiatek@villanova.edu. *Application contact:* Meredith L. Kwiatek, Assistant Director, 610-519-7016, Fax: 610-519-6273, E-mail: meredith.kwiatek@villanova.edu.

Virginia Commonwealth University, Graduate School, School of Business, Program in Finance, Insurance, and Real Estate, Richmond, VA 23284-9005. Offers MS. *Faculty:* 11 full-time (0 women). *Entrance requirements:* For master's, GMAT (GRE for Finance). Additional exam requirements/recommendations for international students: Required—TOEFL (minimum score 600 paper-based; 250 computer-based; 100 iBT); Recommended—IELTS (minimum score 6.5). *Application deadline:* For fall admission, 6/1 for domestic students; for spring admission, 11/1 for domestic students. Applications are processed on a rolling basis. Application fee: $50. Electronic applications accepted. *Expenses:* Tuition, state resident: full-time $4308; part-time $479 per credit hour. Tuition, nonresident: full-time $8942; part-time $994 per credit hour. Required fees: $2000; $85 per credit hour. Tuition and fees vary according to course level, course load, degree level, campus/location and program. *Financial support:* Fellowships, research assistantships, teaching assistantships, Federal Work-Study, institutionally sponsored loans, and tuition waivers (full and partial) available. Financial award application deadline: 3/15; financial award applicants required to submit FAFSA. *Unit head:* Ed Grier, Dean, 804-828-1595, Fax: 804-828-7174, E-mail: busdean@vcu.edu. *Application contact:* Jana P. McQuaid, Assistant Dean, Masters Programs, 804-828-4622, Fax: 804-828-7174, E-mail: jpmcquaid@vcu.edu.

Virginia Commonwealth University, Graduate School, School of Business, Program in Real Estate and Urban Land Development, Richmond, VA 23284-9005. Offers Certificate. In 2010, 5 Certificates awarded. *Entrance requirements:* Additional exam requirements/recommendations for international students: Required—TOEFL (minimum score 600 paper-based; 250 computer-based; 100 iBT); Recommended—IELTS (minimum score 6.5). *Application deadline:* For fall admission, 6/1 for domestic students; for winter admission, 11/1 for domestic students. Applications are processed on a rolling basis. Application fee: $50. Electronic applications accepted. *Expenses:* Tuition, state resident: full-time $4308; part-time $479 per credit hour. Tuition, nonresident: full-time $8942; part-time $994 per credit hour. Required fees: $2000; $85 per credit hour. Tuition and fees vary according to course level, course load, degree level, campus/location and program. *Financial support:* Fellowships, research assistantships, teaching assistantships, Federal Work-Study, institutionally sponsored loans, and tuition waivers (full and partial) available. Financial award application deadline: 3/15; financial award applicants required to submit FAFSA. *Unit head:* Dr. Nanda Rangan, Chair, 804-827-7410, E-mail: nkrangan@vcu.edu. *Application contact:* Jana P. McQuaid, Assistant Dean, Masters Programs, 804-828-4622, Fax: 804-828-7174, E-mail: jpmcquaid@vcu.edu.

OVERVIEW

The demand for managers who can create competitive advantages for their organizations by delivering customer value through effective supply chain management has never been greater. An MBA in this field is for students interested in learning how to apply the detailed functional aspects of logistics and supply chain management from a global and domestic perspective. Teachings in this area emphasize an understanding of the latest tools and systems, including real-time, e-supply chain technologies; product design; warehousing; distribution, procurements, and contracting decisions; optimization planning software; and modeling and analysis applications.

The MBA with an emphasis in transportation management program is well suited for individuals who possess the aptitude for leadership, analytical thinking, and personal relationships. These programs are characterized by the study of theoretical and conceptual aspects of transportation management, as well as practical applications.

Required courses may include study in:

- Applied Managerial Accounting
- Applied Managerial Decision-Making
- Applied Managerial Economics
- Applied Managerial Finance
- Applied Managerial Marketing
- Graduate Research Methods
- Leadership and Ethical Decision-Making
- Strategic Management in Dynamic Environments

Elective courses may include study in:

- International Logistics and Transportation Management
- Logistics Management
- Managing Technology in the Supply Chain
- Managing the Real-time Supply Chain
- Models of Operations Management
- Transportation Management

Economists and employers single out supply chain management for its strong growth potential. In fact, *U.S. News & World Report* describes it as one of the 20 hottest job tracks of this century. According to the U.S. Department of Commerce and Bureau of Labor Statistics, material handling and logistics is also one of America's largest and fastest growing industries. The consumption of material handling and logistics equipment and systems in America exceeds $156 billion per year with more than 700,000 workers employed in the field. Careers in material handling and logistics involve a broad array of equipment and systems that aid in forecasting, resource allocation, production planning, flow and process management, inventory management, customer delivery, after-sales support and service, and a host of other activities and processes basic to business. Solutions include sophisticated techniques that expedite information flow such as satellite tracking systems and the electronic transmission of order and shipping information.

HELPFUL ORGANIZATIONS/ PUBLICATIONS/BLOGS

Supply Chain Council (SCC)

http://supply-chain.org/

Supply Chain Council (SCC) is a global nonprofit organization whose framework, improvement methodology, training, certification, and benchmarking tools help member organizations make dramatic, rapid, and sustainable improvements in supply chain performance.

The Supply Chain Operations Reference (SCOR®) is the world standard for supply chain management, a model that provides a unique framework for defining and linking performance metrics, processes, best practices, and people into a unified structure.

Material Handling Industry of America (MHIA)

http://www.mhia.org/

Material Handling Industry of America (MHIA) is the largest U.S. material handling and logistics association representing the leading providers of material handling and logistics solutions.

MHIA members are material handling and logistics equipment, systems, and software manufacturers; consultants; systems integrators and simulators; third-party logistics providers; and publishers. MHIA provides educational, business development, networking, and solution sourcing opportunities for its 800 member companies and for the larger community of manufacturing, distribution, logistics, and supply chain professionals.

Logistics Business Magazine

http://www.logisticsbusiness.com/Magazine/Default.aspx

Logistics Business Magazine is the only pan-European journal dedicated to the best-in-class application of all aspects of technology and services spanning the entire supply chain—from materials handling and warehousing equipment to transport and distribution technology, services, and packaging.

Published quarterly, in February, May, September, and November, *Logistics Business Magazine* is read by high-level logistics decision-makers in end-user blue-chip organizations, operational management in third-party logistics and warehousing companies, purchasers and specifiers in systems integrators, and dealers and technical management in major materials handling original equipment manufacturers (OEM).

CAREER ASPIRATIONS: A PROSPECTIVE POSITION

Commodity Manager, Systems Components

Job Description

This high-growth and leadership position in the renewable energy business offers outstanding opportunities to individuals seeking an exciting work environment in one of the most important industries for the twenty-first century. This company is a leader in the development and manufacturing of thin film solar modules used in grid-connected solar power plants, as well as a provider of complete solar generation solutions for U.S. utilities. The company culture is one where teamwork, continuous improvement, achievement of results, and environmental responsibility are core values.

Responsibilities

- Perform role of global commodity team leader for assigned categories.
- Develop, advocate, and implement a global sourcing strategy with specific negotiation strategies to achieve cost, quality, lead time, delivery performance, flexibility, supply assurance, and risk mitigation objectives.
- Develop and foster relationships with key suppliers and negotiate and administer contracts within key areas of spending.
- Coordinate aggregation of all sites' demands and develop forward-looking forecasts for supplier planning and cost reduction.
- Proactively and relentlessly manage global supplier base, ensuring supply with no adverse impact on EPC business results.
- Drive continuous improvement in supplier base along identified vectors and in line with commodity strategy.
- Develop and implement cost-reduction programs through the use of Cost-of-Ownership analysis, cost build-up analysis, value stream integration, and supplier competition.
- Measure and report supply performance (TQRDC) within defined spend category.
- Generate monthly supplier scorecard and track and report on spend category industry trends.
- Effectively communicate with senior executives both internally and externally.
- Demonstrate expert project management skills in leading cross-functional teams.
- Conduct business dealings with the highest level of integrity and regard for legal and environmental issues.
- Work on issues of diverse scope and increased complexity where analysis of situation or data requires evaluation of a variety of factors, including an understanding of current business trends.
- Follow processes and operational policies in selecting methods and techniques for obtaining solutions.
- Develop and administer project plan schedules and performance requirements.
- Exercise judgment within defined procedures and policies to determine appropriate action.
- Work on issues where analysis of situations or data requires an in-depth knowledge of organizational objectives.
- Conduct presentations concerning specific projects, objectives, and schedules.

Job Qualifications

- Experience with aluminum, steel, electrical components, wiring and wire harness, electronic assemblies, and fasteners/fastening systems
- Low-cost country/region strategy sourcing track record. Asia sourcing experience preferred
- Exposure working in an engineered systems/project-based business model
- Experience partnering with contract manufacturers
- BS/BA degree plus 8 years of experience in a related technical or business field or MBA plus 3 years of experience in a related technical or business field. Specific education in supply chain management (SCM) preferred
- ISM and APICS certification preferred
- Decision-making skills, including selecting, evaluating, and developing category plan objectives in areas of technology, quality, cost, flexibility, delivery, and service
- Ability to prioritize tasks consistent with achieving overall supply management organizational goals
- Ability to drive sourcing decisions based on team consensus to weighted scorecard
- Ability to independently assess, define, and solve complex supply chain and procurement issues
- Ability to apply appropriate competitive cost benchmarks, financial analysis, and risk management techniques to solve complex issues
- Ability to influence diverse group of people to achieve mutually beneficial solutions
- Understands and demonstrates advanced project management skills
- Demonstrated ability to handle multiple projects at the same time
- Ability to close advanced projects on time with minimal supervision
- Able to effectively lead team of peers and subordinates
- Ability to interact with functional peers and functional peer group managers, requiring the ability to gain cooperation of others
- Ability to interact (including negotiations) with senior-level leaders regarding matters of significance to the organization
- Able to build strong relationships and drive commodity strategy with suppliers in North America, Asia, and Europe

Career Advice from a Business Professional

Brian Korenstein
Associate Manager
Bristol-Myers Squibb
MBA in Supply Chain
Rutgers Business School

What drew you to this field?

Working in pharma since my undergrad graduation from Rutgers University, I never really considered working in supply chain until I started taking my first couple of supply chain classes in the Rutgers MBA program. Learning about supply chains, value chains, and logistics got me wondering about how BMS was able to supply so many products to different customers (wholesalers, distributors, hospitals, pharmacies, government agencies, etc.) and to so many markets around the world. Where and how are these products produced? What does BMS's distribution and transportation networks look like? These are the types of questions that really got me interested in moving into a supply chain role.

What makes a day at your job interesting?

Currently, I'm handling some of the supply chain operations in a group known as External Manufacturing. This group manages third-party manufacturers that produce BMS products. What makes the job interesting is that it is fast-paced, ever-changing, and I'm constantly learning new things about how our products are manufactured, packaged, and transported. It seems that the trend in pharma has been that companies are doing less of their own manufacturing, and more outsourcing to contract manufacturers. With that said, I have been fortunate enough to work on several manufacturing transfers to third-parties in which I've been involved with setting up new supply chain networks to ensure a seamless supply of products to our customers.

How has your graduate education been important to your successes/accomplishments along your career path?

The Rutgers MBA program has a comprehensive set of core classes that has given me a solid foundation of basic business knowledge ranging from finance and marketing to information management. This knowledge has helped me to become a well-rounded employee at BMS. Along my career path, I have worked on several cross-functional teams and the Rutgers MBA program has helped me to build knowledge in many of these areas, which in turn has helped me to become a more effective member of these teams. Working with people from finance, marketing, and IT, I can not only understand their requests better as a result of my education, but I can perhaps help them understand their requests better as well.

In your opinion, what does the future of your field hold for someone newly entering it?

I believe that now is a great time to be entering the supply chain field. Companies have been stressing the importance of building an effective and efficient supply chain more than ever before. We're in a time where suppliers and customers are tightly integrated into every company's operations, and supply chain is at the heart of these relationships. In addition, there is increasing pressure to achieve high customer service levels (in terms of product delivery) while maintaining inventory levels as low as possible, and this places a great amount of reliance on the supply chain function of an organization. In the future, I see supply chain as having an even more critical role as technological developments will allow companies to seamlessly share more information with each other.

What are the exciting developments coming in the next five years?

Over the next few years, technological developments in supply chain are expected to premiere, which will make company's manufacturing, logistics, and distribution networks even more robust. MRP systems, such as SAP (used by BMS) will allow companies to share critical information with suppliers and customers through data interfaces. BMS will be implementing some of these enhancements which will allow us to do things like "what-if" analyses to analyze various potential supply-related issues and scenarios. This type of technology will enable us to make good decisions when we come across typical supply chain–related issues, such as problems with securing raw materials, manufacturing issues, quality issues, etc.

What advice would you share with new graduates entering your field?

Supply Chain is a dynamic and robust field that crosses multiple industries in virtually every manufacturing and service organization. My advice to someone entering this field would be to ask lots of questions and strive to achieve a solid understanding of your company's manufacturing, logistics, and distribution networks. In addition, never assume that the current process is the best way to do things—always be looking for improvements!

AVIATION MANAGEMENT

Arizona State University, College of Technology and Innovation, Department of Technology Management, Mesa, AZ 85212. Offers technology (aviation management and human factors) (MS); technology (environmental technology management) (MS); technology (global technology and development) (MS); technology (graphic information technology) (MS); technology (management of technology) (MS). Part-time and evening/weekend programs available. Postbaccalaureate distance learning degree programs offered (minimal on-campus study). *Faculty:* 13 full-time (3 women), 6 part-time/adjunct (2 women). *Students:* 56 full-time (16 women), 212 part-time (95 women); includes 61 minority (14 Black or African American, non-Hispanic/Latino; 8 American Indian or Alaska Native, non-Hispanic/Latino; 14 Asian, non-Hispanic/Latino; 21 Hispanic/Latino; 4 Two or more races, non-Hispanic/Latino), 27 international. Average age 36. 124 applicants, 77% accepted, 58 enrolled. In 2010, 35 master's awarded. *Degree requirements:* For master's, thesis or applied project and oral defense; interactive Program of Study (iPOS) submitted before completing 50 percent of required credit hours. *Entrance requirements:* For master's, GRE, minimum GPA of 3.0 or equivalent in last 2 years of work leading to bachelor's degree. Additional exam requirements/recommendations for international students: Required—TOEFL, IELTS, or Pearson Test of English. *Application deadline:* For fall admission, 7/1 for domestic and international students; for spring admission, 12/1 for domestic and international students. Applications are processed on a rolling basis. Application fee: $70 ($90 for international students). Electronic applications accepted. *Expenses:* Tuition: state resident: full-time $8510; part-time $608 per credit. Tuition, nonresident: full-time $16,542; part-time $919 per credit. Required fees: $339; $110 per credit. Part-time tuition and fees vary according to course load. *Financial support:* In 2010–11, 3 research assistantships with full and partial tuition reimbursements (averaging $12,729 per year), 1 teaching assistantship with full and partial tuition reimbursement (averaging $14,125 per year) were awarded; career-related internships or fieldwork, Federal Work-Study, scholarships/grants, health care benefits, tuition waivers (full and partial), and unspecified assistantships also available. Support available to part-time students. Financial award application deadline: 3/1; financial award applicants required to submit FAFSA. *Faculty research:* Digital imaging, digital publishing, Internet development/e-commerce, information aviation human factors, pilot selection, databases, multimedia, commercial digital photography, digital workflow, computer graphics modeling and animation, information design, sociotechnology, visual and technical literacy, environmental management, quality management, project management, industrial ethics, hazardous materials, environmental chemistry. Total annual research expenditures: $755,686. *Unit head:* Dr. Mitzi Montoya, Vice Provost and Dean, 480-727-1955, Fax: 480-727-1538, E-mail: mitzi.montoya@asu.edu. *Application contact:* Graduate Admissions, 480-965-6113.

Dowling College, School of Business, Oakdale, NY 11769-1999. Offers aviation management (MBA, Certificate); banking and finance (MBA, Certificate); corporate finance (MBA); financial planning (Certificate); health care management (MBA, Certificate); human resource management (Certificate); information systems management (MBA); management and leadership (MBA); marketing (Certificate); project management (Certificate); public management (MBA, Certificate); sport, event and entertainment management (Certificate); JD/MBA. Part-time and evening/weekend programs available. *Faculty:* 10 full-time (4 women), 56 part-time/adjunct (7 women). *Students:* 295 full-time (131 women), 460 part-time (206 women); includes 219 minority (97 Black or African American, non-Hispanic/Latino; 14 Asian, non-Hispanic/Latino; 35 Hispanic/Latino; 73 Native Hawaiian or other Pacific Islander, non-Hispanic/Latino), 3 international. Average age 33. 327 applicants, 85% accepted, 160 enrolled. In 2010, 33 master's, 1 other advanced degree awarded. *Degree requirements:* For master's, comprehensive exam, thesis optional. *Entrance requirements:* For master's, minimum GPA of 2.8, 2 letters of recommendation, courses in accounting and finance or seminar in accounting/finance, resume. Additional exam requirements/recommendations for international students: Required—TOEFL (minimum score 550 paper-based). *Application deadline:* For fall admission, 9/1 priority date for domestic students; for winter admission, 1/1 priority date for domestic students; for spring admission, 2/1 priority date for domestic students. Applications are processed on a rolling basis. Application fee: $50. Electronic applications accepted. *Expenses:* Tuition: Part-time $884 per credit hour. Part-time tuition and fees vary according to degree level and campus/location. *Financial support:* Career-related internships or fieldwork and Federal Work-Study available. Support available to part-time students. Financial award application deadline: 6/30; financial award applicants required to submit FAFSA. *Faculty research:* International finance, computer applications, labor relations, executive development. *Unit head:* Antonia Loschiavo, Assistant Dean, 631-244-3266, Fax: 631-244-1018, E-mail: loschiat@dowling.edu. *Application contact:* Ronnie S. Macdonald, Assistant Vice President for Enrollment Services/Dean of Admissions, 631-244-3357, Fax: 631-244-1059, E-mail: macdonar@dowling.edu.

Embry-Riddle Aeronautical University–Daytona, Daytona Beach Campus Graduate Program, Department of Business Administration, Daytona Beach, FL 32114-3900. Offers business administration (MBA); business

administration aviation management (MBA-AM). *Accreditation:* ACBSP. Part-time programs available. Postbaccalaureate distance learning degree programs offered (minimal on-campus study). *Faculty:* 12 full-time (3 women), 3 part-time/adjunct (1 woman). *Students:* 102 full-time (29 women), 59 part-time (16 women); includes 19 minority (9 Black or African American, non-Hispanic/Latino; 4 Asian, non-Hispanic/Latino; 6 Hispanic/Latino), 56 international. Average age 29. 96 applicants, 50% accepted, 32 enrolled. In 2010, 39 master's awarded. *Degree requirements:* For master's, thesis or alternative. *Entrance requirements:* For master's, minimum GPA of 2.5. Additional exam requirements/recommendations for international students: Required—TOEFL (minimum score 550 paper-based; 213 computer-based; 79 iBT). *Application deadline:* For fall admission, 8/1 priority date for domestic students; for spring admission, 12/1 priority date for domestic students. Applications are processed on a rolling basis. Application fee: $50. *Expenses:* Tuition: Full-time $14,040; part-time $1170 per credit hour. *Financial support:* In 2010–11, 35 students received support, including 20 research assistantships with partial tuition reimbursements available (averaging $2,882 per year), 3 teaching assistantships (averaging $2,452 per year); career-related internships or fieldwork, Federal Work-Study, and unspecified assistantships also available. Support available to part-time students. Financial award application deadline: 4/15; financial award applicants required to submit FAFSA. *Faculty research:* Aircraft safety operations analysis, energy consumption analysis, statistical analysis of general aviation accidents, airport funding strategies, industry assessment and marketing analysis for ENAER aerospace. *Unit head:* Dr. Dawna Rhoades, MBA Program Coordinator, 386-226-7756, E-mail: dawna.rhoades@erau.edu. *Application contact:* Keith Deaton, Director, International and Graduate Admissions, 800-388-3728, Fax: 386-226-7070, E-mail: graduate.admissions@erau.edu.

See Display on the next page and Close-Up on page 590.

Embry-Riddle Aeronautical University–Worldwide, Worldwide Headquarters, Program in Management, Daytona Beach, FL 32114-3900. Offers MSM, MSM/MBAA. Part-time and evening/weekend programs available. Postbaccalaureate distance learning degree programs offered. *Faculty:* 4 full-time (1 woman), 50 part-time/adjunct (15 women). *Students:* 409 full-time (103 women), 328 part-time (89 women); includes 196 minority (91 Black or African American, non-Hispanic/Latino; 5 American Indian or Alaska Native, non-Hispanic/Latino; 34 Asian, non-Hispanic/Latino; 52 Hispanic/Latino; 3 Native Hawaiian or other Pacific Islander, non-Hispanic/Latino; 11 Two or more races, non-Hispanic/Latino), 2 international. Average age 34. 173 applicants, 77% accepted, 100 enrolled. In 2010, 104 master's awarded. *Degree requirements:* For master's, thesis optional. *Entrance requirements:* For master's, GMAT. *Application deadline:* Applications are processed on a rolling basis. Application fee: $50. Electronic applications accepted. *Financial support:* In 2010–11, 188 students received support. Applicants required to submit FAFSA. *Unit head:* Dr. Kees Rietsema, Chair, 602-904-1285, E-mail: rietsd37@erau.edu. *Application contact:* Linda Dammer, Director of Admissions, 386-226-6396 Ext. 1, Fax: 386-226-6984, E-mail: worldwide@erau.edu.

Lewis University, College of Arts and Sciences, Program in Aviation and Transportation, Romeoville, IL 60446. Offers administration (MS); safety and security (MS). Part-time and evening/weekend programs available. Postbaccalaureate distance learning degree programs offered (minimal on-campus study). *Faculty:* 2 full-time (0 women), 1 part-time/adjunct (0 women). *Students:* 7 full-time (2 women), 13 part-time (1 woman); includes 3 Black or African American, non-Hispanic/Latino; 1 Hispanic/Latino, 1 international. Average age 37. In 2010, 4 master's awarded. *Entrance requirements:* For master's, bachelor's degree, minimum GPA of 3.0, personal statement, 3 letters of recommendation. Additional exam requirements/recommendations for international students: Required—TOEFL (minimum score 550 paper-based; 213 computer-based). *Application deadline:* For fall admission, 5/1 priority date for international students; for spring admission, 11/15 priority date for international students. Applications are processed on a rolling basis. Application fee: $40. Electronic applications accepted. *Expenses:* Tuition: Full-time $13,320; part-time $740 per credit hour. Tuition and fees vary according to program. *Financial support:* Application deadline: 5/1. *Unit head:* Dr. Randal DeMik, Head, 815-838-0500 Ext. 5559, E-mail: demikra@lewisu.edu. *Application contact:* Julie Nickel, Assistant Director, Graduate and Adult Admission, 815-836-5574, E-mail: nickelju@lewisu.edu.

Middle Tennessee State University, College of Graduate Studies, College of Basic and Applied Sciences, Department of Aerospace, Program in Aviation Administration, Murfreesboro, TN 37132. Offers MS. Part-time and evening/weekend programs available. Postbaccalaureate distance learning degree programs offered. *Students:* 6 full-time (0 women), 18 part-time (4 women); includes 5 Black or African American, non-Hispanic/Latino; 1 Asian, non-Hispanic/Latino. Average age 29. 8 applicants, 75% accepted, 6 enrolled. In 2010, 4 master's awarded. *Degree requirements:* For master's, one foreign language, comprehensive exam. *Entrance requirements:* For master's, GRE or MAT. Additional exam requirements/recommendations for international students: Required—TOEFL (minimum score 525 paper-based; 195 computer-based; 71 iBT) or IELTS (minimum score 6). *Application deadline:* For fall admission, 6/1 for domestic and international students. Applications are processed on a rolling basis. Application fee: $25 ($30 for international students).

Expenses: Tuition, state resident: full-time $4632. Tuition, nonresident: full-time $11,520. *Financial support:* Institutionally sponsored loans available. Support available to part-time students. Financial award application deadline: 5/1. *Unit head:* Dr. Wayne Dornan, Chair, 615-898-2788, E-mail: wdornan@mtsu.edu. *Application contact:* Dr. Wayne Dornan, Chair, 615-898-2788, E-mail: wdornan@mtsu.edu.

Southeastern Oklahoma State University, Department of Aviation Science, Durant, OK 74701-0609. Offers aerospace administration and logistics (MS). Part-time and evening/weekend programs available. *Students:* 51 full-time (8 women), 65 part-time (12 women); includes 9 Black or African American, non-Hispanic/Latino; 6 American Indian or Alaska Native, non-Hispanic/Latino; 7 Asian, non-Hispanic/Latino; 12 Hispanic/Latino, 2 international. Average age 30. 117 applicants, 99% accepted, 116 enrolled. *Entrance requirements:* For master's, minimum GPA of 3.0 in last 60 hours or 2.75 overall. Additional exam requirements/recommendations for international students: Required—TOEFL (minimum score 550 paper-based; 213 computer-based). *Application deadline:* For fall admission, 8/1 for domestic students, 6/1 for international students; for spring admission, 1/5 for domestic students, 11/1 for international students. Application fee: $20 ($55 for international students). Electronic applications accepted. *Financial support:* Federal Work-Study and institutionally sponsored loans available. Support available to part-time students. Financial award application deadline: 6/15. *Unit head:* Dr. David Conway, Director, 580-745-3240, Fax: 580-924-0741, E-mail: dconway@se.edu. *Application contact:* Carrie Williamson, Administrative Assistant, Graduate Office, 580-745-2200, Fax: 580-745-7474, E-mail: cwilliamson@se.edu.

LOGISTICS

American Public University System, AMU/APU Graduate Programs, Charles Town, WV 25414. Offers accounting (MBA); administration and supervision (M Ed); air warfare (MA Military Studies); asymmetrical warfare (MA Military Studies); criminal justice (MA); emergency and disaster management (MA); entrepreneurship (MBA); environmental policy and management (MS); finance (MBA); general (MBA); global business management (MBA); guidance and counseling (M Ed); history (MA); homeland security (MA); homeland security resource allocation (MBA); humanities (MA); information technology (MS); information technology management (MBA); intelligence studies (MA); international relations and conflict resolution (MA); joint warfare (MA Military Studies); land warfare (MA Military Studies); legal studies (MA); management (MA), including defense mangement, general, human resource management, organizational leadership, public administration; marketing (MBA); military history (MA); national security studies (MA); naval warfare (MA Military Studies); nonprofit management (MBA); political science (MA); psychology (MA); public administration (MA); public health (MA); security management (MA); space studies (MS); sports management (MS); strategic leadership (MA Military Studies); teaching (M Ed), including elementary, secondary social sciences; transportation and logistics management (MA). Programs offered via distance learning only. Part-time and evening/weekend programs available. Postbaccalaureate distance learning degree programs offered (no on-campus study). *Faculty:* 253 full-time (134 women), 1,208 part-time/adjunct (570 women). *Students:* 956 full-time (422 women), 8,476 part-time (2,821 women); includes 2,511 minority (1,218 Black or African American, non-Hispanic/Latino; 68 American Indian or Alaska Native, non-Hispanic/Latino; 219 Asian, non-Hispanic/Latino; 705 Hispanic/Latino; 46 Native Hawaiian or other Pacific Islander, non-Hispanic/Latino; 255 Two or more races, non-Hispanic/Latino), 107 international. Average age 35. 9,550 applicants, 100% accepted. In 2010, 1,688 master's awarded. *Degree requirements:* For master's, comprehensive exam or practicum. *Entrance requirements:* For master's, official transcript showing earned bachelor's degree from institution accredited by recognized accrediting body. Additional exam requirements/recommendations for international students: Required—TOEFL (minimum score 550 paper-based; 213 computer-based), IELTS (minimum score 6.5). *Application deadline:* Applications are processed on a rolling basis. Application fee: $0. Electronic applications accepted. *Financial support:* Applicants required to submit FAFSA. *Faculty research:* Military history, criminal justice, management performance, national security. *Unit head:* Dr. Frank McCluskey, Provost, 877-468-6268, Fax: 304-724-3780. *Application contact:* Terry Grant, Director of Enrollment Management, 877-468-6268, Fax: 304-724-3780, E-mail: info@apus.edu.

Benedictine University, Graduate Programs, Program in Business Administration, Lisle, IL 60532-0900. Offers accounting (MBA); entrepreneurship and managing innovation (MBA); financial management (MBA); health administration (MBA); human resource management (MBA); information systems security (MBA); international business (MBA); management consulting (MBA); management information systems (MBA); marketing management (MBA); operations management and logistics (MBA); organizational leadership (MBA); MBA/MPH; MBA/MS. Part-time and evening/weekend programs available. Postbaccalaureate distance learning degree programs offered (minimal on-campus study). *Faculty:* 4 full-time (2 women), 24 part-time/adjunct (3 women). *Students:* 347 full-time (140 women), 672 part-time (360 women); includes 237 minority (155 Black or African American, non-Hispanic/Latino; 4 American Indian or Alaska Native, non-Hispanic/Latino; 43 Asian, non-Hispanic/Latino; 35 Hispanic/Latino), 21 international. Average age 34. 416 applicants, 88% accepted, 217 enrolled. In 2010, 355 master's awarded. *Entrance requirements:* For master's, GMAT. Additional exam requirements/recommendations for international students: Required—TOEFL (minimum score 550 paper-based; 213 computer-based). *Application deadline:* For fall admission, 9/1 for domestic students; for winter admission, 12/1 for domestic students; for spring admission, 2/15 for domestic students. Applications are processed on a rolling basis. Application fee: $40. Electronic applications accepted. *Financial support:* Career-related internships or fieldwork and health care benefits available. Support available to part-time students. *Faculty research:* Strategic leadership in professional organizations, sociology of professions, organizational change, social identity theory, applications to change management. *Unit head:* Dr. Sharon Borowicz, Director, 630-829-6219, E-mail: sborowicz@ben.edu. *Application contact:* Kari Gibbons, Director, Admissions, 630-829-6200, Fax: 630-829-6584, E-mail: kgibbons@ben.edu.

California State University, Long Beach, Graduate Studies, College of Liberal Arts, Department of Economics, Long Beach, CA 90840. Offers economics (MA); global logistics (MA). Part-time programs available. *Faculty:* 5 full-time (2 women), 1 part-time/adjunct (0 women). *Students:* 13 full-time (5 women), 17 part-time (11 women); includes 1 Black or African American, non-Hispanic/Latino; 5 Asian, non-Hispanic/Latino; 2 Hispanic/Latino, 8 international. Average age 29. 101 applicants, 57% accepted, 17 enrolled. In 2010, 22 master's awarded. *Degree requirements:* For master's, comprehensive exam or thesis. *Entrance requirements:* For master's, GRE General Test, GRE Subject Test, minimum GPA of 3.0. *Application deadline:* For fall admission, 4/1 for domestic students. Applications are processed on a rolling basis. Application fee: $55. Electronic applications accepted. *Financial support:* Federal Work-Study, institutionally sponsored loans, and scholarships/grants available. Financial award application deadline: 3/2. *Faculty research:* Trade and development, economic forecasting, resource economics. *Unit head:* Dr. Joseph P. Magaddino, Chair, 562-985-5061, Fax: 562-985-5804, E-mail: magaddin@csulb.edu. *Application contact:* Dr. Alejandra C. Edwards, Graduate Advisor, 562-985-5969, Fax: 562-985-5804, E-mail: acoxedwa@csulb.edu.

Case Western Reserve University, School of Graduate Studies, Case School of Engineering, Department of Electrical Engineering and Computer Science, Cleveland, OH 44106. Offers computer engineering (MS, PhD); computing and information sciences (MS, PhD); electrical engineering (MS, PhD); systems and control engineering (MS, PhD). Part-time and evening/weekend programs available. Postbaccalaureate distance learning degree programs offered (minimal on-campus study). *Faculty:* 33 full-time (2 women). *Students:* 190 full-time (31 women), 26 part-time (4 women); includes 3 Black or African American, non-Hispanic/Latino; 6 Asian, non-Hispanic/Latino, 128 international. In 2010, 32 master's, 13 doctorates awarded. Terminal master's awarded for partial completion of doctoral program. *Degree requirements:* For master's, thesis; for doctorate, thesis/dissertation, qualifying exam, teaching experience. *Entrance requirements:* For master's and doctorate, GRE General Test. Additional exam requirements/recommendations for international students: Required—TOEFL. *Application deadline:* For fall admission, 2/1 for domestic students; for spring admission, 11/1 for domestic students. Applications are processed on a rolling basis. Application fee: $50. *Financial support:* Fellowships with full and partial tuition reimbursements, research assistantships with full and partial tuition reimbursements, teaching assistantships, career-related internships or fieldwork, Federal Work-Study, and institutionally sponsored loans available. Support available to part-time students. Financial award application deadline: 3/1; financial award applicants required to submit FAFSA. *Faculty research:* Applied artificial intelligence, automation, computer-aided design and testing of digital systems. Total annual research expenditures: $6.8 million. *Unit head:* Michael Branicky, Department Chair, 216-368-6888, E-mail: branicky@case.edu. *Application contact:* David Easler, Student Affairs Coordinator, 216-368-4080, Fax: 216-368-2801, E-mail: david.easler@case.edu.

Central Connecticut State University, School of Graduate Studies, School of Technology, Department of Manufacturing and Construction Management, New Britain, CT 06050-4010. Offers construction management (MS, Certificate); lean manufacturing and Six Sigma (Certificate); supply chain and logistics (Certificate); technology management (MS). Part-time and evening/weekend programs available. *Faculty:* 19 full-time (4 women), 25 part-time/adjunct (1 woman). *Students:* 15 full-time (4 women), 78 part-time (16 women); includes 19 minority (10 Black or African American, non-Hispanic/Latino; 5 Asian, non-Hispanic/Latino; 3 Hispanic/Latino; 1 Two or more races, non-Hispanic/Latino), 5 international. Average age 38. 67 applicants, 76% accepted, 34 enrolled. In 2010, 24 master's awarded. *Degree requirements:* For master's, comprehensive exam, thesis or alternative; for Certificate, qualifying exam. *Entrance requirements:* For master's, minimum undergraduate GPA of 2.7. Additional exam requirements/recommendations for international students: Required—TOEFL. *Application deadline:* For fall admission, 7/1 for domestic students; for spring admission, 12/1 for domestic students. Applications are processed on a rolling basis. Application fee: $50. Electronic applications accepted. *Expenses:* Tuition, area resident: Full-time $5012; part-time $470 per credit. Tuition, state resident: full-time $7518;

part-time $482 per credit. Tuition, nonresident: full-time $13,962; part-time $482 per credit. Required fees: $3772. One-time fee: $62 per part-time. *Financial support:* In 2010–11, 5 students received support, including 5 research assistantships; career-related internships or fieldwork, Federal Work-Study, scholarships/grants, and unspecified assistantships also available. Support available to part-time students. Financial award application deadline: 2/15; financial award applicants required to submit FAFSA. *Faculty research:* All aspects of middle management, technical supervision in the workplace. *Unit head:* Dr. Jacob Kovel, Chair, 860-832-1830. *Application contact:* Dr. Jacob Kovel, Chair, 860-832-1830.

Central Michigan University, Central Michigan University Off-Campus Programs, Program in Business Administration, Mount Pleasant, MI 48859. Offers logistics management (MBA, Certificate); SAP (MBA, Certificate); value-driven organization (MBA). Part-time and evening/weekend programs available. *Entrance requirements:* For master's, GMAT. *Expenses:* Tuition, state resident: full-time $8208; part-time $456 per credit hour. Tuition, nonresident: full-time $13,788; part-time $766 per credit hour. One-time fee: $25. *Financial support:* Scholarships/grants available. Support available to part-time students. *Unit head:* Dr. Debabish Chakraborty, 989-774-3678, E-mail: chakt1d@cmich.edu. *Application contact:* Off-Campus Programs Call Center, 877-268-4636.

Embry-Riddle Aeronautical University–Worldwide, Worldwide Headquarters, Program in Logistics and Supply Chain Management, Daytona Beach, FL 32114-3900. Offers MSLSCM. *Faculty:* 4 full-time (1 woman), 50 part-time/adjunct (15 women). *Students:* 44 full-time (14 women), 57 part-time (21 women); includes 42 minority (21 Black or African American, non-Hispanic/Latino; 2 American Indian or Alaska Native, non-Hispanic/Latino; 5 Asian, non-Hispanic/Latino; 11 Hispanic/Latino; 3 Two or more races, non-Hispanic/Latino). Average age 35. 86 applicants, 66% accepted, 28 enrolled. In 2010, 1 master's awarded. *Degree requirements:* For master's, thesis (for some programs). Application fee: $50. *Financial support:* In 2010–11, 23 students received support. *Unit head:* Dr. Kees Rietsema, Chair, 602-904-1285, E-mail: rietsd37@erau.edu. *Application contact:* Linda Dammer, Director of Admissions, 386-226-6396 Ext. 1, Fax: 386-226-6984, E-mail: worldwide@erau.edu.

Florida Institute of Technology, Graduate Programs, Extended Studies Division, Melbourne, FL 32901-6975. Offers acquisition and contract management (MS); aerospace engineering (MS); business administration (MBA); computer information systems (MS); computer science (MS); electrical engineering (MS); engineering management (MS); human resources management (MS); logistics management (MS), including humanitarian and disaster relief logistics; management (MS), including acquisition and contract management, e-business, human resources management, information systems, logistics management, management, transportation management; material acquisition management (MS); mechanical engineering (MS); operations research (MS); project management (MS), including information systems, operations research; public administration (MPA); quality management (MS); software engineering (MS); space systems (MS); space systems management (MS); systems management (MS), including information systems, operations research. Part-time and evening/weekend programs available. Postbaccalaureate distance learning degree programs offered (no on-campus study). *Faculty:* 11 full-time (3 women), 118 part-time/adjunct (24 women). *Students:* 69 full-time (23 women), 907 part-time (369 women); includes 385 minority (242 Black or African American, non-Hispanic/Latino; 15 American Indian or Alaska Native, non-Hispanic/Latino; 44 Asian, non-Hispanic/Latino; 52 Hispanic/Latino; 3 Native Hawaiian or other Pacific Islander, non-Hispanic/Latino; 29 Two or more races, non-Hispanic/Latino), 17 international. 517 applicants, 49% accepted, 245 enrolled. In 2010, 430 degrees awarded. *Degree requirements:* For master's, comprehensive exam (for some programs), capstone course. *Entrance requirements:* For master's, GMAT or resume showing 8 years of supervised experience, minimum GPA of 3.0, 2 letters of recommendation, resume. Additional exam requirements/recommendations for international students: Required—TOEFL (minimum score 550 paper-based; 213 computer-based; 79 iBT). *Application deadline:* For fall admission, 4/1 for international students; for spring admission, 9/30 for international students. Applications are processed on a rolling basis. Application fee: $50. Electronic applications accepted. *Expenses:* Contact institution. *Financial support:* Application deadline: 3/1. *Unit head:* Dr. Theodore Richardson, Senior Associate Dean, 321-674-8123, Fax: 321-674-7597, E-mail: trichardson@fit.edu. *Application contact:* Carolyn Farrior, Director of Graduate Admissions, Online Learning and Off-Campus Programs, 321-674-7118, Fax: 321-674-8216, E-mail: cfarrior@fit.edu.

George Mason University, School of Public Policy, Program in Transportation Policy, Operations and Logistics, Arlington, VA 22201. Offers MA. Part-time programs available. Postbaccalaureate distance learning degree programs offered (no on-campus study). *Faculty:* 66 full-time (24 women), 15 part-time/adjunct (3 women). *Students:* 10 full-time (1 woman), 32 part-time (7 women); includes 2 Black or African American, non-Hispanic/Latino; 1 Two or more races, non-Hispanic/Latino, 3 international. Average age 33. 29 applicants, 45% accepted, 6 enrolled. In 2010, 19 master's awarded. *Degree requirements:* For master's, thesis or alternative. *Entrance requirements:* For master's, GRE (for students seeking merit-based scholarships), minimum undergraduate GPA of 3.0, resume, 2 letters of recommendation. Additional exam requirements/recommendations for international students: Required—TOEFL (minimum score 570 paper-based; 230 computer-based; 88 iBT). *Application deadline:* For fall admission, 6/1 priority date for domestic students, 5/1 priority date for international students; for spring admission, 12/1 priority date for domestic students, 11/1 priority date for international students. Applications are processed on a rolling basis. Application fee: $100. Electronic applications accepted. *Expenses:* Contact institution. *Financial support:* In 2010–11, 1 research assistantship (averaging $16,150 per year) was awarded; career-related internships or fieldwork, Federal Work-Study, scholarships/grants, unspecified assistantships, and health care benefits (full-time research or teaching assistantship recipients) also available. Financial award application deadline: 3/1; financial award applicants required to submit FAFSA. *Unit head:* Dr. Jonathan Gifford, Director, 703-993-8099, E-mail: spp@gmu.edu. *Application contact:* Tennille Haegele, Director, Graduate Admissions, 703-993-3183, Fax: 703-993-4876, E-mail: thaegele@gmu.edu.

Georgia College & State University, Graduate School, College of Arts and Sciences, Department of Government and Sociology, Logistics Education Center, Milledgeville, GA 31061. Offers logistics management (MSA). Part-time and evening/weekend programs available. *Students:* 7 full-time (5 women), 79 part-time (35 women); includes 24 minority (19 Black or African American, non-Hispanic/Latino; 3 Hispanic/Latino; 2 Two or more races, non-Hispanic/Latino). Average age 34. 26 applicants, 96% accepted, 20 enrolled. In 2010, 32 master's awarded. *Entrance requirements:* For master's, MAT, GRE, GMAT, immunization record, transcripts. Additional exam requirements/recommendations for international students: Recommended—TOEFL (minimum score 550 paper-based; 213 computer-based; 79 iBT). *Application deadline:* For fall admission, 7/1 priority date for domestic students, 4/1 priority date for international students; for spring admission, 11/15 priority date for domestic students, 9/1 priority date for international students. Applications are processed on a rolling basis. Application fee: $40. Electronic applications accepted. *Expenses:* Tuition, state resident: full-time $4806; part-time $267 per hour. Tuition, nonresident: full-time $17,802; part-time $989 per hour. Tuition and fees vary according to course load. *Financial support:* Application deadline: 3/1. *Unit head:* Glen Easterly, Director of Robins Center/Coordinator of Logistics Program, 478-327-7376, Fax: 478-926-2468, E-mail: glenn.easterly@gcsu.edu. *Application contact:* Glen Easterly, Director of Robins Center/Coordinator of Logistics Program, 478-327-7376, Fax: 478-926-2468, E-mail: glenn.easterly@gcsu.edu.

Georgia Southern University, Jack N. Averitt College of Graduate Studies, College of Business Administration, Program in Logistics/Supply Chain Management, Statesboro, GA 30460. Offers PhD. *Students:* 9 full-time (4 women); includes 1 Asian, non-Hispanic/Latino; 1 Hispanic/Latino; 1 Two or more races, non-Hispanic/Latino, 2 international. Average age 34. 27 applicants, 44% accepted, 5 enrolled. *Degree requirements:* For doctorate, comprehensive exam, thesis/dissertation. *Entrance requirements:* For doctorate, GMAT or GRE, letters of reference. Additional exam requirements/recommendations for international students: Required—TOEFL (minimum score 550 paper-based; 213 computer-based; 80 iBT). *Application deadline:* For fall admission, 3/15 priority date for domestic and international students. Application fee: $50. Electronic applications accepted. *Expenses:* Tuition, state resident: full-time $6000; part-time $250 per semester hour. Tuition, nonresident: full-time $23,976; part-time $999 per semester hour. Required fees: $1644. *Financial support:* In 2010–11, 9 students received support. Career-related internships or fieldwork, Federal Work-Study, scholarships/grants, traineeships, and unspecified assistantships available. Support available to part-time students. Financial award application deadline: 4/15; financial award applicants required to submit FAFSA. *Unit head:* Dr. Ron Shiffler, Dean, 912-478-5106, Fax: 912-478-0292, E-mail: shiffler@georgiasouthern.edu. *Application contact:* Dr. Stephen Rutner, Graduate Program Director, 912-478-0511, Fax: 912-478-1523, E-mail: srutner@georgiasouthern.edu.

HEC Montreal, School of Business Administration, Master of Science Programs in Administration, Program in Logistics, Montréal, QC H3T 2A7, Canada. Offers M Sc. All courses are given in French. Part-time programs available. *Students:* 16 full-time (9 women), 3 part-time (1 woman). 22 applicants, 55% accepted, 6 enrolled. In 2010, 7 master's awarded. *Degree requirements:* For master's, one foreign language, thesis. *Application deadline:* For fall admission, 3/15 for domestic and international students; for winter admission, 10/1 for domestic and international students. Application fee: $78 Canadian dollars. Electronic applications accepted. *Expenses:* Tuition, area resident: Part-time $68.93 per credit. Tuition, state resident: full-time $2481.48; part-time $188.92 per credit. Tuition, nonresident: full-time $6801; part-time $482.06 per course. International tuition: $17,354.16 full-time. Required fees: $1309.50; $30.28 per credit. $93.45 per term. Tuition and fees vary according to degree level and program. *Financial support:* Fellowships, research assistantships, teaching assistantships, scholarships/grants available. Financial award application deadline: 9/2. *Unit head:* Dr. Claude Laurin, Director, 514-340-6485, Fax: 514-340-6880, E-mail: claude.laurin@hec.ca. *Application contact:* Francine Blais, Administrative Director, 514-340-6112, Fax: 514-340-6411, E-mail: francine.blais@hec.ca.

Massachusetts Institute of Technology, School of Engineering, Engineering Systems Division, Cambridge, MA 02139-4307. Offers engineering and management (SM); engineering systems (SM, PhD); logistics (M Eng); technology and policy (SM); technology, management and policy (PhD); SM/MBA. *Faculty:* 22 full-time (7 women). *Students:* 271 full-time (78 women); includes 39 minority (5 Black or African American, non-Hispanic/Latino; 27 Asian, non-Hispanic/Latino; 6 Hispanic/Latino; 1 Two or more races, non-Hispanic/Latino), 105 international. Average age 31. 927 applicants, 28% accepted, 185 enrolled. In 2010, 169 master's, 10 doctorates awarded. *Degree requirements:* For master's, thesis; for doctorate, comprehensive exam, thesis/dissertation. *Entrance requirements:* For master's, GRE General Test (or GMAT for some programs); for doctorate, GRE General Test. Additional exam requirements/recommendations for international students: Required—IELTS (minimum score 7.5). Application fee: $75. *Expenses:* Contact institution. *Financial support:* In 2010–11, 217 students received support, including 36 fellowships with tuition reimbursements available (averaging $25,594 per year), 95 research assistantships with tuition reimbursements available (averaging $27,695 per year), 15 teaching assistantships with tuition reimbursements available (averaging $25,802 per year); career-related internships or fieldwork, Federal Work-Study, institutionally sponsored loans, scholarships/grants, health care benefits, and unspecified assistantships also available. *Faculty research:* Critical infrastructures, extended enterprises, energy and sustainability, health care delivery, humans and technology, uncertainty and dynamics, design and implementation, networks and flows, policy and standards. Total annual research expenditures: $13.2 million. *Unit head:* Prof. Yossi Sheffi, Director, 617-253-1764, E-mail: esdinquiries@mit.edu. *Application contact:* Graduate Admissions, 617-253-1182, E-mail: esdgrad@mit.edu.

North Dakota State University, College of Graduate and Interdisciplinary Studies, College of Engineering and Architecture, Department of Civil Engineering, Fargo, ND 58108. Offers civil engineering (MS, PhD); environmental engineering (MS, PhD); transportation and logistics (PhD). PhD in transportation and logistics offered jointly with Upper Great Plains Transportation Institute. Part-time programs available. Postbaccalaureate distance learning degree programs offered (minimal on-campus study). *Students:* 28 full-time (2 women), 19 part-time (3 women); includes 1 American Indian or Alaska Native, non-Hispanic/Latino, 24 international. 37 applicants, 57% accepted, 12 enrolled. In 2010, 1 master's, 3 doctorates awarded. *Degree requirements:* For master's, thesis; for doctorate, comprehensive exam, thesis/dissertation. *Entrance requirements:* Additional exam requirements/recommendations for international students: Required—TOEFL (minimum score 525 paper-based; 197 computer-based; 71 iBT). *Application deadline:* For fall admission, 7/1 priority date for domestic students, 1/15 priority date for international students; for spring admission, 5/1 priority date for international students. Applications are processed on a rolling basis. Application fee: $45 ($60 for international students). *Financial support:* Fellowships with full tuition reimbursements, research assistantships with full tuition reimbursements, teaching assistantships with full tuition reimbursements, career-related internships or fieldwork, Federal Work-Study, and institutionally sponsored loans available. Support available to part-time students. Financial award application deadline: 1/15. *Faculty research:* Wastewater, solid waste, composites, nanotechnology. Total annual research expenditures: $800,000. *Unit head:* Dr. Eakalak Khan, Chair, 701-231-7244, Fax: 701-231-6185, E-mail: eakalak.khan@ndsu.edu. *Application contact:* Dr. Kalpana Katti, Professor and Graduate Program Coordinator, 701-231-9504, Fax: 701-231-6185, E-mail: kalpana.katti@ndsu.edu.

North Dakota State University, College of Graduate and Interdisciplinary Studies, Interdisciplinary Program in Transportation and Logistics, Fargo, ND 58108. Offers PhD. *Students:* 15 full-time (4 women), 7 part-time (0 women); includes 1 Black or African American, non-Hispanic/Latino, 9 international. 6 applicants, 67% accepted, 4 enrolled. In 2010, 2 doctorates awarded. *Entrance requirements:* For doctorate, 1 year of calculus, statistics and probability, minimum GPA of 3.0. Additional exam requirements/recommendations for international students: Required—TOEFL (minimum score 550 paper-based; 213 computer-based; 79 iBT). *Application deadline:* For fall admission, 5/1 priority date for domestic students. Applications are processed on a rolling basis. Application fee: $45 ($60 for international students). *Financial support:* Research assistantships with full tuition reimbursements available. *Faculty research:* Supply chain optimization, spatial analysis of transportation networks, advanced traffic analysis, transportation demand, railroad/intermodal freight. *Unit head:* Dr. Denver Tolliver, Director, 701-231-7190, Fax: 701-231-1945, E-mail: denver.tolliver@ndsu.nodak.edu. *Application contact:* Dr. Denver Tolliver, Director, 701-231-7190, Fax: 701-231-1945, E-mail: denver.tolliver@ndsu.nodak.edu.

The Ohio State University, Graduate School, Max M. Fisher College of Business, Program in Business Logistics Engineering, Columbus, OH 43210. Offers MBLE. *Students:* 32 full-time (19 women), 16 part-time (8 women), 46 international. Average age 24. In 2010, 26 master's awarded. *Entrance requirements:* For master's, GRE or GMAT. Additional exam requirements/recommendations for international students: Required—TOEFL. *Application deadline:* Applications are processed on a rolling basis. Application fee: $40 ($50 for international students). Electronic applications accepted. *Expenses:* Tuition, state resident: full-time $10,605. Tuition, nonresident: full-time $26,535. Tuition and fees vary according to course load and program. *Unit* *head:* Walter Zinn, Graduate Studies Committee Chair, 416-292-0797, Fax: 416-292-9006, E-mail: zinn.13@osu.edu. *Application contact:* Graduate Admissions, 614-292-9444, Fax: 614-292-3895, E-mail: domestic.grad@osu.edu.

Stevens Institute of Technology, Graduate School, School of Systems and Enterprises, Program in Systems Design and Operational Effectiveness, Hoboken, NJ 07030. Offers M Eng. *Students:* 42 part-time (11 women); includes 1 Black or African American, non-Hispanic/Latino; 3 Asian, non-Hispanic/Latino. Average age 37.*Unit head:* Dr. Charles L. Suffel, Dean of the Graduate School, 201-216-5234, Fax: 201-216-8044, E-mail: csuffel@stevens-tech.edu. *Application contact:* Graduate Admissions, 800-496-4935, Fax: 201-216-8044, E-mail: gradadmissions@stevens.edu.

Stevens Institute of Technology, Graduate School, School of Systems and Enterprises, Program in Systems Engineering, Hoboken, NJ 07030. Offers agile systems and enterprises (Certificate); systems and supportability engineering (Certificate); systems engineering (M Eng, PhD); systems engineering management (Certificate). *Students:* 34 full-time (11 women), 156 part-time (29 women); includes 5 Black or African American, non-Hispanic/Latino; 19 Asian, non-Hispanic/Latino; 10 Hispanic/Latino, 20 international. Average age 34.*Unit head:* Dr. Charles L. Suffel, Dean of the Graduate School, 201-216-5234, Fax: 201-216-8044, E-mail: csuffel@stevens-tech.edu. *Application contact:* Graduate Admissions, 800-496-4935, Fax: 201-216-8044, E-mail: gradadmissions@stevens.edu.

TUI University, College of Business Administration, Program in Business Administration, Cypress, CA 90630. Offers business administration (PhD); conflict and negotiation management (MBA); criminal justice administration (MBA); entrepreneurship (MBA); finance (MBA); general management (MBA); government accounting (MBA); human resource management (MBA); information security and digital assurance management (MBA); information technology management (MBA); international business (MBA); logistics management (MBA); marketing (MBA); project management (MBA); public management (MBA); quality management (MBA); strategic leadership (MBA). Part-time and evening/weekend programs available. Postbaccalaureate distance learning degree programs offered (no on-campus study). *Students:* 741 full-time (200 women), 1,585 part-time (410 women). 379 applicants, 81% accepted, 300 enrolled. In 2010, 752 master's, 28 doctorates awarded. *Degree requirements:* For doctorate, comprehensive exam, thesis/dissertation, defense of dissertation. *Entrance requirements:* For master's, minimum GPA of 2.5 (students with GPA 3.0 or greater may transfer up to 30% of graduate level credits); for doctorate, minimum GPA of 3.4, curriculum vitae, course work in research methods or statistics. Additional exam requirements/recommendations for international students: Required—TOEFL. *Application deadline:* For fall admission, 10/3 for domestic and international students; for winter admission, 12/22 for domestic and international students; for spring admission, 4/3 for domestic and international students. Applications are processed on a rolling basis. Application fee: $75. Electronic applications accepted. *Expenses:* Tuition: Full-time $11,040; part-time $345 per semester hour. *Unit head:* Paul Watkins, Dean, College of Business Administration, 800-375-9878, E-mail: pwatkins@tuiu.edu. *Application contact:* Wei Ren-Finaly, Registrar, 800-375-9878, Fax: 714-827-7407, E-mail: registration@tuiu.edu.

University at Buffalo, the State University of New York, Graduate School, School of Management, Buffalo, NY 14260. Offers accounting (MS); business administration (EMBA, MBA, PMBA); finance (MS), including financial engineering, financial management; information assurance (Certificate); management (PhD); management information systems (MS); supply chains and operations management (MS); Au D/MBA; JD/MBA; M Arch/MBA; MA/MBA; MD/MBA; MPH/MBA; MSW/MBA; Pharm D/MBA. *Accreditation:* AACSB. Part-time and evening/weekend programs available. *Faculty:* 65 full-time (18 women), 32 part-time/adjunct (8 women). *Students:* 626 full-time (229 women), 202 part-time (69 women); includes 43 minority (18 Black or African American, non-Hispanic/Latino; 2 American Indian or Alaska Native, non-Hispanic/Latino; 18 Asian, non-Hispanic/Latino; 5 Hispanic/Latino), 351 international. Average age 27. 1,553 applicants, 46% accepted, 400 enrolled. In 2010, 287 master's, 4 doctorates, 3 other advanced degrees awarded. *Degree requirements:* For master's, thesis (for some programs); for doctorate, comprehensive exam, thesis/dissertation. *Entrance requirements:* For master's, GMAT (MBA, MS in accounting), GRE or GMAT (for all other MS concentrations); for doctorate, GMAT or GRE. Additional exam requirements/recommendations for international students: Required—TOEFL (minimum score 230 computer-based; 95 iBT). *Application deadline:* For fall admission, 5/2 priority date for domestic students, 3/1 priority date for international students. Applications are processed on a rolling basis. Application fee: $100. Electronic applications accepted. *Expenses:* Contact institution. *Financial support:* In 2010–11, 91 students received support, including 5 fellowships with full and partial tuition reimbursements available (averaging $4,000 per year), 41 research assistantships with full and partial tuition reimbursements available (averaging $16,000 per year), 28 teaching assistantships with full and partial tuition reimbursements available (averaging $15,000 per year); career-related internships or fieldwork, Federal Work-Study, institutionally sponsored loans, scholarships/grants, health care benefits, and unspecified assistantships also available. Financial award application deadline: 2/15; financial award

applicants required to submit FAFSA. *Faculty research:* Earnings management and electronic information assurance, supply chains and operations management, corporate financing and asset pricing, consumer behavior and quantitative modeling of marketing behavior, leadership and politics in organizations. Total annual research expenditures: $215,000. *Unit head:* David W. Frasier, Assistant Dean, 716-645-3204, Fax: 716-645-2341, E-mail: davidf@buffalo.edu. *Application contact:* David W. Frasier, Assistant Dean, 716-645-3204, Fax: 716-645-2341, E-mail: davidf@buffalo.edu.

The University of Alabama in Huntsville, School of Graduate Studies, College of Business Administration, Department of Management and Marketing, Huntsville, AL 35899. Offers management (MBA), including acquisition management, finance, human resource management, logistics and supply chain management, marketing, project management. *Accreditation:* AACSB. Part-time and evening/weekend programs available. *Faculty:* 11 full-time (2 women), 4 part-time/adjunct (1 woman). *Students:* 41 full-time (17 women), 159 part-time (69 women); includes 32 minority (15 Black or African American, non-Hispanic/Latino; 6 American Indian or Alaska Native, non-Hispanic/Latino; 7 Asian, non-Hispanic/Latino; 3 Hispanic/Latino; 1 Two or more races, non-Hispanic/Latino), 14 international. Average age 31. 141 applicants, 65% accepted, 79 enrolled. In 2010, 66 master's awarded. *Degree requirements:* For master's, comprehensive exam, thesis or alternative. *Entrance requirements:* For master's, GMAT (minimum score 500), minimum AACSB index of 1080. Additional exam requirements/recommendations for international students: Required—TOEFL (minimum score 550 paper-based; 213 computer-based; 62 iBT). *Application deadline:* For fall admission, 8/1 for domestic students, 4/1 for international students; for spring admission, 12/1 for domestic students, 9/1 for international students. Applications are processed on a rolling basis. Application fee: $40 ($50 for international students). Electronic applications accepted. *Expenses:* Tuition, state resident: full-time $7250; part-time $407.75 per credit hour. Tuition, nonresident: full-time $17,358; part-time $970.05 per credit hour. Required fees: $246.80 per semester. Tuition and fees vary according to course load and program. *Financial support:* In 2010–11, 3 students received support, including 1 research assistantship with full tuition reimbursement available (averaging $8,550 per year), 2 teaching assistantships with full tuition reimbursements available (averaging $8,000 per year); career-related internships or fieldwork, Federal Work-Study, institutionally sponsored loans, scholarships/grants, health care benefits, and unspecified assistantships also available. Support available to part-time students. Financial award application deadline: 4/1; financial award applicants required to submit FAFSA. *Faculty research:* Strategic human resources, corporate governance, cross-function integration and the management of research and development, determinants of team performance. Total annual research expenditures: $3 million. *Unit head:* Dr. Brent Wren, Chair, 256-824-6408, Fax: 256-824-6328, E-mail: wrenb@uah.edu. *Application contact:* Jennifer Pettitt, Director of Graduate Programs, 256-824-6681, Fax: 256-824-7571, E-mail: jennifer.pettitt@uah.edu.

University of Houston, College of Technology, Department of Information and Logistics Technology, Houston, TX 77204. Offers information security (MS); supply chain and logistics technology (MS); technology project management (MS). Part-time programs available. *Faculty:* 6 full-time (3 women), 6 part-time/adjunct (2 women). *Students:* 80 full-time (30 women), 75 part-time (29 women); includes 35 minority (12 Black or African American, non-Hispanic/Latino; 9 Asian, non-Hispanic/Latino; 11 Hispanic/Latino; 1 Native Hawaiian or other Pacific Islander, non-Hispanic/Latino; 2 Two or more races, non-Hispanic/Latino), 73 international. Average age 31. 60 applicants, 92% accepted, 35 enrolled. In 2010, 22 master's awarded. *Degree requirements:* For master's, project or thesis (most programs). *Entrance requirements:* For master's, GMAT. Additional exam requirements/recommendations for international students: Required—TOEFL (minimum score 550 paper-based; 79 iBT). *Application deadline:* For fall admission, 7/1 for domestic students, 4/1 for international students; for spring admission, 12/1 for domestic students, 10/1 for international students. Applications are processed on a rolling basis. Application fee: $75 ($150 for international students). Electronic applications accepted. *Expenses:* Tuition, state resident: full-time $8592; part-time $358 per credit hour. Tuition, nonresident: full-time $16,032; part-time $668 per credit hour. Required fees: $2889. Tuition and fees vary according to course load and program. *Financial support:* In 2010–11, 10 research assistantships with partial tuition reimbursements (averaging $8,380 per year), 15 teaching assistantships with partial tuition reimbursements (averaging $8,078 per year) were awarded. *Unit head:* Michael Gibson, Chairperson, 713-743-5116, E-mail: mlgibson@uh.edu. *Application contact:* Tiffany Roosa, Graduate Advisor, 713-743-4100, Fax: 713-743-4151, E-mail: troosa@uh.edu.

University of Louisville, J. B. Speed School of Engineering, Department of Industrial Engineering, Louisville, KY 40292-0001. Offers engineering management (M Eng); industrial engineering (M Eng, MS, PhD); logistics and distribution (Certificate). *Accreditation:* ABET (one or more programs are accredited). Part-time programs available. *Faculty:* 10 full-time (1 woman). *Students:* 45 full-time (11 women), 26 part-time (7 women); includes 5 Black or African American, non-Hispanic/Latino; 1 Asian, non-Hispanic/Latino; 1 Hispanic/Latino; 1 Two or more races, non-Hispanic/Latino, 18 international. Average age 28. 56 applicants, 32% accepted, 7 enrolled. In 2010, 25 master's, 4 doctorates awarded. Terminal master's awarded for partial completion of doctoral program. *Degree requirements:* For master's, comprehensive exam (for some programs), thesis or alternative; for doctorate, comprehensive exam, thesis/dissertation, minimum GPA of 3.0. *Entrance requirements:* For master's and doctorate, GRE General Test. Additional exam requirements/recommendations for international students: Required—TOEFL (minimum score 550 paper-based; 213 computer-based; 80 iBT), IELTS (minimum score 6.5). *Application deadline:* For fall admission, 5/1 priority date for domestic and international students; for spring admission, 11/1 priority date for domestic and international students. Applications are processed on a rolling basis. Application fee: $50. Electronic applications accepted. *Expenses:* Tuition, state resident: full-time $9144; part-time $508 per credit hour. Tuition, non-resident: full-time $19,026; part-time $1057 per credit hour. Tuition and fees vary according to program and reciprocity agreements. *Financial support:* In 2010–11, 15 students received support, including 7 fellowships with full tuition reimbursements available (averaging $20,000 per year), 2 research assistantships with full tuition reimbursements available (averaging $20,000 per year), 6 teaching assistantships with full tuition reimbursements available (averaging $20,000 per year). Financial award application deadline: 1/25; financial award applicants required to submit FAFSA. *Faculty research:* Optimization, computer simulation, logistics and distribution, ergonomics and human factors, advanced manufacturing process. Total annual research expenditures: $748,000. *Unit head:* Dr. John S. Usher, Chair, 502-852-6342, Fax: 502-852-5633, E-mail: usher@louisville.edu. *Application contact:* Dr. Michael Day, Associate Dean, 502-852-6195, Fax: 502-852-7294, E-mail: day@louisville.edu.

University of Minnesota, Twin Cities Campus, Carlson School of Management, Doctoral Program in Business Administration, Minneapolis, MN 55455-0213. Offers accounting (PhD); finance (PhD); information and decision sciences (PhD); marketing and logistics management (PhD); operations and management science (PhD); strategic management and organization (PhD). *Faculty:* 100 full-time (27 women). *Students:* 73 full-time (28 women); includes 3 Asian, non-Hispanic/Latino; 3 Hispanic/Latino, 53 international. Average age 30. 319 applicants, 6% accepted, 16 enrolled. In 2010, 8 doctorates awarded. *Degree requirements:* For doctorate, comprehensive exam, thesis/dissertation, written and oral preliminary exams, proposal defense, final defense. *Entrance requirements:* For doctorate, GMAT, GRE General Test. Additional exam requirements/recommendations for international students: Required—TOEFL (minimum score 600 paper-based; 250 computer-based; 100 iBT), IELTS (minimum score 7.5). *Application deadline:* For fall admission, 12/31 for domestic students, 12/31 priority date for international students. Applications are processed on a rolling basis. Application fee: $75 ($95 for international students). Electronic applications accepted. *Financial support:* In 2010–11, 68 students received support, including 134 fellowships with full tuition reimbursements available (averaging $6,622 per year), 63 research assistantships with full tuition reimbursements available (averaging $6,750 per year), 57 teaching assistantships with full tuition reimbursements available (averaging $6,750 per year); institutionally sponsored loans, scholarships/grants, health care benefits, and unspecified assistantships also available. Financial award application deadline: 12/31. *Faculty research:* Corporate strategy, finance, entrepreneurship, marketing, information and decision science, operations, accounting, quality management. *Unit head:* Dr. Shawn P. Curley, Director of Graduate Studies and PhD Program Director, 612-624-6546, Fax: 612-624-8221, E-mail: curley@umn.edu. *Application contact:* Earlene K. Bronson, Assistant Director, PhD Program, 612-624-0875, Fax: 612-624-8221, E-mail: brons003@umn.edu.

University of Missouri–St. Louis, College of Business Administration, Program in Business Administration, St. Louis, MO 63121. Offers accounting (MBA); business administration (Certificate); finance (MBA); human resource management (Certificate); information systems (MBA); local government (Certificate); logistics and supply chain management (MBA, Certificate); marketing (MBA); marketing management (Certificate); operations management (MBA). *Accreditation:* AACSB. Part-time and evening/weekend programs available. *Faculty:* 30 full-time (5 women), 11 part-time/adjunct (2 women). *Students:* 132 full-time (57 women), 306 part-time (122 women); includes 55 minority (21 Black or African American, non-Hispanic/Latino; 20 Asian, non-Hispanic/Latino; 11 Hispanic/Latino; 1 Native Hawaiian or other Pacific Islander, non-Hispanic/Latino; 2 Two or more races, non-Hispanic/Latino), 6 international. Average age 30. 219 applicants, 60% accepted, 88 enrolled. In 2010, 114 master's, 9 other advanced degrees awarded. *Entrance requirements:* For master's, GMAT, 2 letters of recommendation. Additional exam requirements/recommendations for international students: Required—TOEFL (minimum score 550 paper-based; 213 computer-based). *Application deadline:* For fall admission, 7/1 for domestic students; for spring admission, 11/1 for domestic students. Applications are processed on a rolling basis. Application fee: $35 ($40 for international students). Electronic applications accepted. *Expenses:* Tuition, state resident: full-time $5522; part-time $306.80 per credit hour. Tuition, nonresident: full-time $14,253; part-time $792.10 per credit hour. Required fees: $658; $49 per credit hour. One-time fee: $12. Tuition and fees vary according to program. *Financial support:* In 2010–11, 22 research assistantships with full and partial tuition reimbursements (averaging $7,414 per year), 4 teaching assistantships with full and partial tuition reimbursements (averaging $13,950 per year) were awarded; career-related internships or fieldwork, Federal Work-Study, and institutionally sponsored

loans also available. Support available to part-time students. Financial award application deadline: 4/1; financial award applicants required to submit FAFSA. *Faculty research:* Human resources, strategic management, marketing strategy, consumer behavior product development, advertising. *Unit head:* Karl Kottemann, Assistant Director, 314-516-5885, Fax: 314-516-6420, E-mail: mba@umsl.edu. *Application contact:* 314-516-5458, Fax: 314-516-6996, E-mail: gradadm@umsl.edu.

University of Missouri–St. Louis, College of Business Administration, Program in Information Systems, St. Louis, MO 63121. Offers information systems (MSIS, PhD); logistics and supply chain management (PhD). Part-time and evening/weekend programs available. *Faculty:* 8 full-time (0 women). *Students:* 10 full-time (3 women), 13 part-time (1 woman); includes 5 minority (4 Black or African American, non-Hispanic/Latino; 1 Hispanic/Latino), 4 international. Average age 31. 16 applicants, 25% accepted, 1 enrolled. In 2010, 6 master's, 2 doctorates awarded. *Entrance requirements:* For master's, GMAT, 2 letters of recommendation; for doctorate, GMAT or GRE, 3 letters of recommendation. Additional exam requirements/recommendations for international students: Required—TOEFL (minimum score 550 paper-based; 213 computer-based). *Application deadline:* For fall admission, 7/1 priority date for domestic and international students; for spring admission, 12/1 priority date for domestic and international students. Applications are processed on a rolling basis. Application fee: $35 ($40 for international students). Electronic applications accepted. *Expenses:* Tuition, state resident: full-time $5522; part-time $306.80 per credit hour. Tuition, nonresident: full-time $14,253; part-time $792.10 per credit hour. Required fees: $658; $49 per credit hour. One-time fee: $12. Tuition and fees vary according to program. *Financial support:* Career-related internships or fieldwork, Federal Work-Study, and institutionally sponsored loans available. Support available to part-time students. Financial award application deadline: 4/1; financial award applicants required to submit FAFSA. *Faculty research:* International information systems, telecommunications, systems development, information systems sourcing. *Unit head:* Karl Kottemann, Assistant Director, 314-516-5885, Fax: 314-516-6420, E-mail: mba@umsl.edu. *Application contact:* 314-516-5458, Fax: 314-516-6996, E-mail: gradadm@umsl.edu.

University of New Hampshire, Graduate School, College of Engineering and Physical Sciences, Department of Mechanical Engineering, Durham, NH 03824. Offers mechanical engineering (MS, PhD); systems design (PhD). Part-time programs available. *Faculty:* 14 full-time (1 woman). *Students:* 18 full-time (2 women), 34 part-time (4 women); includes 1 minority (Two or more races, non-Hispanic/Latino), 12 international. Average age 29. 45 applicants, 69% accepted, 13 enrolled. In 2010, 11 master's, 1 doctorate awarded. *Degree requirements:* For master's, thesis or alternative; for doctorate, thesis/dissertation. *Entrance requirements:* For master's and doctorate, GRE. Additional exam requirements/recommendations for international students: Required—TOEFL (minimum score 550 paper-based; 213 computer-based; 80 iBT). *Application deadline:* For fall admission, 4/1 priority date for domestic students, 4/1 for international students; for spring admission, 12/1 for domestic students. Applications are processed on a rolling basis. Application fee: $65. Electronic applications accepted. *Financial support:* In 2010–11, 32 students received support, including 1 fellowship, 14 research assistantships, 15 teaching assistantships; Federal Work-Study, scholarships/grants, and tuition waivers (full and partial) also available. Support available to part-time students. Financial award application deadline: 2/15. *Faculty research:* Solid mechanics, dynamics, materials science, dynamic systems, automatic control. *Unit head:* Dr. Todd Gross, Chairperson, 603-862-2445. *Application contact:* Tracey Harvey, Administrative Assistant, 603-862-1353, E-mail: mechanical.engineering@unh.edu.

University of North Florida, Coggin College of Business, MBA Program, Jacksonville, FL 32224. Offers accounting (MBA); construction management (MBA); e-commerce (MBA); economics (MBA); finance (MBA); human resource management (MBA); international business (MBA); logistics (MBA); management applications (MBA). *Accreditation:* AACSB. Part-time and evening/weekend programs available. *Faculty:* 17 full-time (5 women), 1 part-time/adjunct (0 women). *Students:* 137 full-time (56 women), 268 part-time (112 women); includes 17 Black or African American, non-Hispanic/Latino; 21 Asian, non-Hispanic/Latino; 12 Hispanic/Latino; 3 Two or more races, non-Hispanic/Latino, 29 international. Average age 30. 250 applicants, 57% accepted, 94 enrolled. In 2010, 173 master's awarded. *Entrance requirements:* For master's, GMAT or GRE, U.S. bachelor's degree from regionally-accredited university or equivalent foreign degree. Additional exam requirements/recommendations for international students: Required—TOEFL (minimum score 550 paper-based; 213 computer-based; 79 iBT). *Application deadline:* For fall admission, 7/1 priority date for domestic students, 5/1 for international students; for spring admission, 11/1 priority date for domestic students, 10/1 for international students. Applications are processed on a rolling basis. Application fee: $30. *Expenses:* Tuition, state resident: full-time $7646.40; part-time $318.60 per credit hour. Tuition, nonresident: full-time $23,502; part-time $979.24 per credit hour. Required fees: $1208.88; $50.37 per credit hour. Tuition and fees vary according to course load and program. *Financial support:* In 2010–11, 40 students received support; research assistantships, teaching assistantships, Federal Work-Study and tuition waivers (partial) available. Support available to part-time students. Financial award application deadline: 4/1; financial award applicants required to submit FAFSA. *Faculty research:* Performance measures, costing, and inventory issues in logistics and supply chain management; inter-organizational systems; international management and marketing practices; e-commerce; organizational learning and socialization processes. Total annual research expenditures: $9,024. *Unit head:* Dr. C. Bruce Kavan, Chair, 904-620-2780, Fax: 904-620-2832. *Application contact:* Cheryl Campbell, Graduate Advisor, 904-620-2575, Fax: 904-620-2832, E-mail: ccampbell@unf.edu.

The University of Texas at Arlington, Graduate School, College of Engineering, Department of Industrial and Manufacturing Systems Engineering, Program in Logistics, Arlington, TX 76019. Offers MS. *Students:* 5 full-time (2 women), 5 part-time (1 woman); includes 1 minority (Black or African American, non-Hispanic/Latino), 8 international. 7 applicants, 100% accepted, 5 enrolled. In 2010, 7 master's awarded. *Degree requirements:* For master's, comprehensive exam, thesis optional. *Entrance requirements:* For master's, GRE, GMAT, minimum GPA of 3.0. Additional exam requirements/recommendations for international students: Required—TOEFL (minimum score 550 paper-based; 213 computer-based). *Application deadline:* For fall admission, 6/6 for domestic students, 4/4 for international students; for spring admission, 10/15 for domestic students, 9/5 for international students. Application fee: $35 ($50 for international students). *Expenses:* Tuition, state resident: full-time $7500. Tuition, nonresident: full-time $13,080. International tuition: $13,250 full-time. *Financial support:* Fellowships, research assistantships, teaching assistantships, career-related internships or fieldwork, Federal Work-Study, institutionally sponsored loans, scholarships/grants, and unspecified assistantships available. Financial award application deadline: 6/1; financial award applicants required to submit FAFSA. *Unit head:* Dr. Donald H. Liles, Chair, 817-272-3092, Fax: 817-272-3406, E-mail: dliles@uta.edu. *Application contact:* Dr. Jamie Rogers, Graduate Advisor, 817-272-2495, Fax: 817-272-3406, E-mail: jrogers@uta.edu.

SUPPLY CHAIN MANAGEMENT

American University, Kogod School of Business, Master of Business Administration Program, Washington, DC 20016-8044. Offers accounting (MBA); consulting (MBA), including information technology, international business, management; corporate finance: commercial banking (MBA); corporate finance: corporate financial management (MBA); corporate finance: investment banking (MBA), including corporate finance and private equity, trading and selling; entrepreneurship (MBA); global emerging markets (MBA), including business, finance, information technology; international trade and global supply chain management (MBA); leadership (MBA); marketing management (MBA); marketing research (MBA); real estate (MBA); MBA/JD; MBA/LL M. Part-time and evening/weekend programs available. *Faculty:* 12 full-time (5 women). *Students:* 135 full-time (62 women), 104 part-time (38 women); includes 46 minority (18 Black or African American, non-Hispanic/Latino; 1 American Indian or Alaska Native, non-Hispanic/Latino; 12 Asian, non-Hispanic/Latino; 14 Hispanic/Latino; 1 Two or more races, non-Hispanic/Latino), 34 international. Average age 27. 467 applicants, 51% accepted, 70 enrolled. In 2010, 101 master's awarded. *Entrance requirements:* For master's, GMAT. Additional exam requirements/recommendations for international students: Required—TOEFL. *Application deadline:* For fall admission, 2/1 priority date for domestic students; for spring admission, 10/1 priority date for domestic students. Applications are processed on a rolling basis. Application fee: $100. *Expenses:* Contact institution. *Financial support:* In 2010–11, 19 students received support; fellowships, research assistantships with partial tuition reimbursements available, career-related internships or fieldwork, Federal Work-Study, and institutionally sponsored loans available. Support available to part-time students. Financial award application deadline: 2/1. *Faculty research:* Information technology, decision-aiding methodology, negotiation. *Unit head:* Dr. Stevan Holmberg, Chair, 202-885-6193, E-mail: sholmbe@american.edu. *Application contact:* Shannon Demko, Associate Director Graduate Admissions, 202-885-1994, Fax: 202-885-1108, E-mail: demko@american.edu.

Arizona State University, W. P. Carey School of Business, Program in Business Administration, Tempe, AZ 85287-4906. Offers accountancy (PhD); agribusiness (PhD); business administration (MBA); finance (PhD); financial management and markets (MBA); information management (MBA); information systems (PhD); management (PhD); marketing (PhD); strategic marketing and services leadership (MBA); supply chain financial management (MBA); supply chain management (MBA, PhD); JD/MBA; MBA/M Acc; MBA/M Arch. *Accreditation:* AACSB. Part-time and evening/weekend programs available. Postbaccalaureate distance learning degree programs offered (minimal on-campus study). *Faculty:* 84 full-time (22 women), 7 part-time/adjunct (2 women). *Students:* 1,302 full-time (379 women), 86 part-time (26 women); includes 241 minority (37 Black or African American, non-Hispanic/Latino; 11 American Indian or Alaska Native, non-Hispanic/Latino; 103 Asian, non-Hispanic/Latino; 76 Hispanic/Latino; 4 Native Hawaiian or other Pacific Islander, non-Hispanic/Latino; 10 Two or more races, non-Hispanic/Latino), 171 international. Average age 31. 1,795 applicants, 44% accepted, 525 enrolled. In 2010, 734 master's, 9 doctorates awarded. Terminal master's

awarded for partial completion of doctoral program. *Degree requirements:* For master's, thesis or alternative, internship, interactive Program of Study (iPOS) submitted before completing 50 percent of required credit hours; for doctorate, comprehensive exam, thesis/dissertation, interactive Program of Study (iPOS) submitted before completing 50 percent of required credit hours. *Entrance requirements:* For master's, GMAT, minimum GPA of 3.0 in last 2 years of work leading to bachelor's degree, 2 letters of recommendation, professional resume, official transcripts, 3 essays; for doctorate, GMAT or GRE, minimum GPA of 3.0 in last 2 years of work leading to bachelor's degree, 3 letters of recommendation, resume, personal statement/essay. Additional exam requirements/recommendations for international students: Required—TOEFL (minimum score 550 paper-based; 213 computer-based; 80 iBT), IELTS (minimum score 6.5). Application fee: $70 ($90 for international students). Electronic applications accepted. *Expenses:* Contact institution. *Financial support:* In 2010–11, 17 research assistantships with full and partial tuition reimbursements (averaging $18,121 per year), 153 teaching assistantships with full and partial tuition reimbursements (averaging $9,176 per year) were awarded; fellowships with full and partial tuition reimbursements, career-related internships or fieldwork, institutionally sponsored loans, scholarships/grants, and tuition waivers (full and partial) also available. Support available to part-time students. Financial award application deadline: 3/1; financial award applicants required to submit FAFSA. Total annual research expenditures: $540,779. *Unit head:* Dr. Robert E. Mittelstaedt, Dean, 480-965-2468, Fax: 480-965-5539, E-mail: mittelsr@asu.edu. *Application contact:* Graduate Admissions, 480-965-6113.

California State University, East Bay, Office of Academic Programs and Graduate Studies, College of Business and Economics, Department of Information Technology Management, Option in Operations and Supply Chain Management, Hayward, CA 94542-3000. Offers MBA. *Degree requirements:* For master's, comprehensive exam or thesis. *Entrance requirements:* For master's, GMAT, minimum GPA of 2.75. Additional exam requirements/recommendations for international students: Required—TOEFL (minimum score 550 paper-based; 213 computer-based). *Application deadline:* For fall admission, 6/30 for domestic and international students. Application fee: $55. Electronic applications accepted. *Financial support:* Fellowships, career-related internships or fieldwork, Federal Work-Study, institutionally sponsored loans, and scholarships/grants available. Support available to part-time students. Financial award application deadline: 3/1; financial award applicants required to submit FAFSA. *Unit head:* Prof. Xinjian Lu, Chair, 510-885-3307, E-mail: xinjian.lu@csueastbay.edu. *Application contact:* Donna Wiley, Interim Associate Director, 510-885-2928, Fax: 510-885-4777, E-mail: donna.wiley@csueastbay.edu.

California State University, East Bay, Office of Academic Programs and Graduate Studies, College of Business and Economics, MBA Program, Hayward, CA 94542-3000. Offers entrepreneurship (MBA); finance (MBA); human resources and organizational behavior (MBA); information technology management (MBA); marketing management (MBA); operations and supply chain management (MBA); strategy and international business (MBA). Part-time and evening/weekend programs available. Postbaccalaureate distance learning degree programs offered (no on-campus study). *Faculty:* 33 full-time (9 women). *Students:* 121 full-time (58 women), 133 part-time (67 women); includes 7 Black or African American, non-Hispanic/Latino; 63 Asian, non-Hispanic/Latino; 11 Hispanic/Latino; 3 Native Hawaiian or other Pacific Islander, non-Hispanic/Latino; 5 Two or more races, non-Hispanic/Latino, 87 international. Average age 30. 284 applicants, 47% accepted, 55 enrolled. In 2010, 241 master's awarded. *Degree requirements:* For master's, comprehensive exam or thesis. *Entrance requirements:* For master's, GMAT (minimum 20th percentile verbal and quantitative section), bachelor's degree, minimum GPA of 2.75. Additional exam requirements/recommendations for international students: Required—TOEFL (minimum score 550 paper-based; 213 computer-based; 79 iBT). *Application deadline:* For fall admission, 6/30 for domestic and international students. Applications are processed on a rolling basis. Application fee: $55. Electronic applications accepted. *Financial support:* Career-related internships or fieldwork, Federal Work-Study, institutionally sponsored loans, and scholarships/grants available. Support available to part-time students. Financial award application deadline: 3/2; financial award applicants required to submit FAFSA. *Unit head:* Dr. Terri Swartz, Dean, 510-885-3291, Fax: 510-885-4884, E-mail: terri.swartz@csueastbay.edu. *Application contact:* Dr. Donna Wiley, Interim Associate Director, 510-885-2928, Fax: 510-885-4777, E-mail: donna.wiley@csueastbay.edu.

Central Connecticut State University, School of Graduate Studies, School of Technology, Department of Manufacturing and Construction Management, New Britain, CT 06050-4010. Offers construction management (MS, Certificate); lean manufacturing and Six Sigma (Certificate); supply chain and logistics (Certificate); technology management (MS). Part-time and evening/weekend programs available. *Faculty:* 19 full-time (4 women), 25 part-time/adjunct (1 woman). *Students:* 15 full-time (4 women), 78 part-time (16 women); includes 19 minority (10 Black or African American, non-Hispanic/Latino; 5 Asian, non-Hispanic/Latino; 3 Hispanic/Latino; 1 Two or more races, non-Hispanic/Latino), 5 international. Average age 38. 67 applicants, 76% accepted, 34 enrolled. In 2010, 24 master's awarded. *Degree requirements:* For master's, comprehensive exam, thesis or alternative; for

Certificate, qualifying exam. *Entrance requirements:* For master's, minimum undergraduate GPA of 2.7. Additional exam requirements/recommendations for international students: Required—TOEFL. *Application deadline:* For fall admission, 7/1 for domestic students; for spring admission, 12/1 for domestic students. Applications are processed on a rolling basis. Application fee: $50. Electronic applications accepted. *Expenses:* Tuition, area resident: Full-time $5012; part-time $470 per credit. Tuition, state resident: full-time $7518; part-time $482 per credit. Tuition, nonresident: full-time $13,962; part-time $482 per credit. Required fees: $3772. One-time fee: $62 part-time. *Financial support:* In 2010–11, 5 students received support, including 5 research assistantships; career-related internships or fieldwork, Federal Work-Study, scholarships/grants, and unspecified assistantships also available. Support available to part-time students. Financial award application deadline: 2/15; financial award applicants required to submit FAFSA. *Faculty research:* All aspects of middle management, technical supervision in the workplace. *Unit head:* Dr. Jacob Kovel, Chair, 860-832-1830. *Application contact:* Dr. Jacob Kovel, Chair, 860-832-1830.

Eastern Michigan University, Graduate School, College of Business, Programs in Business Administration, Ypsilanti, MI 48197. Offers business administration (MBA, Graduate Certificate); computer information systems (Graduate Certificate); e-business (MBA, Graduate Certificate); enterprise business intelligence (MBA); entrepreneurship (MBA, Graduate Certificate); finance (MBA, Graduate Certificate); human resources (MBA); human resources management (Graduate Certificate); information systems (MBA); internal auditing (MBA); international business (MBA, Graduate Certificate); marketing management (Graduate Certificate); nonprofit management (MBA); organizational development (Graduate Certificate); supply chain management (MBA, Graduate Certificate). *Accreditation:* AACSB. Part-time programs available. Postbaccalaureate distance learning degree programs offered (no on-campus study). *Students:* 149 full-time (66 women), 456 part-time (232 women); includes 146 minority (109 Black or African American, non-Hispanic/Latino; 4 American Indian or Alaska Native, non-Hispanic/Latino; 27 Asian, non-Hispanic/Latino; 6 Hispanic/Latino), 105 international. Average age 32. 330 applicants, 64% accepted, 150 enrolled. In 2010, 128 master's, 53 other advanced degrees awarded. *Entrance requirements:* For master's, GMAT (minimum score 450), minimum cumulative undergraduate GPA of 2.75. Additional exam requirements/recommendations for international students: Required—TOEFL. *Application deadline:* For fall admission, 5/15 for domestic students, 5/1 for international students; for winter admission, 10/15 for domestic students, 10/1 for international students; for spring admission, 3/15 for domestic students, 3/1 for international students. Applications are processed on a rolling basis. Application fee: $35. *Financial support:* Fellowships, research assistantships with full tuition reimbursements, teaching assistantships with full tuition reimbursements, career-related internships or fieldwork, Federal Work-Study, institutionally sponsored loans, scholarships/grants, tuition waivers (partial), and unspecified assistantships available. Support available to part-time students. Financial award applicants required to submit FAFSA. *Unit head:* K. Michelle Henry, Interim Director, Graduate Programs, 734-487-4444, Fax: 734-483-1316, E-mail: mhenry1@emich.edu. *Application contact:* Beste Windes, Advisor, 734-487-4444, Fax: 734-483-1316, E-mail: bwindes@emich.edu.

Elmhurst College, Graduate Programs, Program in Supply Chain Management, Elmhurst, IL 60126-3296. Offers MS. Part-time and evening/weekend programs available. *Faculty:* 2 full-time (0 women), 3 part-time/adjunct (0 women). *Students:* 40 part-time (13 women); includes 13 minority (7 Black or African American, non-Hispanic/Latino; 2 Asian, non-Hispanic/Latino; 4 Hispanic/Latino), 1 international. Average age 38. 41 applicants, 63% accepted, 21 enrolled. In 2010, 21 master's awarded. *Entrance requirements:* For master's, 3 recommendations, resume, statement of purpose. Additional exam requirements/recommendations for international students: Required—TOEFL (minimum score 550 paper-based; 213 computer-based). *Application deadline:* Applications are processed on a rolling basis. Application fee: $0. Electronic applications accepted. *Expenses:* Tuition: Part-time $785 per credit hour. Required fees: $60 per year. Tuition and fees vary according to program. *Financial support:* In 2010–11, 5 students received support. Federal Work-Study and scholarships/grants available. Support available to part-time students. Financial award application deadline: 6/1; financial award applicants required to submit FAFSA. *Unit head:* Elizabeth D. Kuebler, Director of Adult and Graduate Admission, 630-617-3300, Fax: 630-617-5501, E-mail: sal@elmhurst.edu. *Application contact:* Elizabeth D. Kuebler, Director of Adult and Graduate Admission, 630-617-3300, Fax: 630-617-5501, E-mail: sal@elmhurst.edu.

Embry-Riddle Aeronautical University–Worldwide, Worldwide Headquarters, Program in Logistics and Supply Chain Management, Daytona Beach, FL 32114-3900. Offers MSLSCM. *Faculty:* 4 full-time (1 woman), 50 part-time/adjunct (15 women). *Students:* 44 full-time (14 women), 57 part-time (21 women); includes 42 minority (21 Black or African American, non-Hispanic/Latino; 2 American Indian or Alaska Native, non-Hispanic/Latino; 5 Asian, non-Hispanic/Latino; 11 Hispanic/Latino; 3 Two or more races, non-Hispanic/Latino). Average age 35. 86 applicants, 66% accepted, 28 enrolled. In 2010, 1 master's awarded. *Degree requirements:* For master's, thesis (for some programs). Application fee: $50. *Financial support:* In 2010–11, 27 students received support. *Unit head:* Dr. Kees Rietsema, Chair, 602-904-1285, E-mail: rietsd37@erau.edu. *Application contact:* Linda Dammer, Director of Admissions, 386-226-6396 Ext. 1, Fax: 386-226-6984, E-mail: worldwide@erau.edu.

Florida Institute of Technology, Graduate Programs, Extended Studies Division, Melbourne, FL 32901-6975. Offers acquisition and contract management (MS); aerospace engineering (MS); business administration (MBA); computer information systems (MS); computer science (MS); electrical engineering (MS); engineering management (MS); human resources management (MS); logistics management (MS), including humanitarian and disaster relief logistics; management (MS), including acquisition and contract management, e-business, human resources management, information systems, logistics management, management, transportation management; material acquisition management (MS); mechanical engineering (MS); operations research (MS); project management (MS), including information systems, operations research; public administration (MPA); quality management (MS); software engineering (MS); space systems (MS); space systems management (MS); systems management (MS), including information systems, operations research. Part-time and evening/weekend programs available. Postbaccalaureate distance learning degree programs offered (no on-campus study). *Faculty:* 11 full-time (3 women), 118 part-time/adjunct (24 women). *Students:* 69 full-time (23 women), 907 part-time (369 women); includes 385 minority (242 Black or African American, non-Hispanic/Latino; 15 American Indian or Alaska Native, non-Hispanic/Latino; 44 Asian, non-Hispanic/Latino; 52 Hispanic/Latino; 3 Native Hawaiian or other Pacific Islander, non-Hispanic/Latino; 29 Two or more races, non-Hispanic/Latino), 17 international. 517 applicants, 49% accepted, 245 enrolled. In 2010, 430 degrees awarded. *Degree requirements:* For master's, comprehensive exam (for some programs), capstone course. *Entrance requirements:* For master's, GMAT or resume showing 8 years of supervised experience, minimum GPA of 3.0, 2 letters of recommendation, resume. Additional exam requirements/recommendations for international students: Required—TOEFL (minimum score 550 paper-based; 213 computer-based; 79 iBT). *Application deadline:* For fall admission, 4/1 for international students; for spring admission, 9/30 for international students. Applications are processed on a rolling basis. Application fee: $50. Electronic applications accepted. *Expenses:* Contact institution. *Financial support:* Application deadline: 3/1. *Unit head:* Dr. Theodore Richardson, Senior Associate Dean, 321-674-8123, Fax: 321-674-7597, E-mail: trichardson@fit.edu. *Application contact:* Carolyn Farrior, Director of Graduate Admissions, Online Learning and Off-Campus Programs, 321-674-7118, Fax: 321-674-8216, E-mail: cfarrior@fit.edu.

Georgia Southern University, Jack N. Averitt College of Graduate Studies, College of Business Administration, Program in Logistics/Supply Chain Management, Statesboro, GA 30460. Offers PhD. *Students:* 9 full-time (4 women); includes 1 Asian, non-Hispanic/Latino; 1 Hispanic/Latino; 1 Two or more races, non-Hispanic/Latino, 2 international. Average age 34. 27 applicants, 44% accepted, 5 enrolled. *Degree requirements:* For doctorate, comprehensive exam, thesis/dissertation. *Entrance requirements:* For doctorate, GMAT or GRE, letters of reference. Additional exam requirements/recommendations for international students: Required—TOEFL (minimum score 550 paper-based; 213 computer-based; 80 iBT). *Application deadline:* For fall admission, 3/15 priority date for domestic and international students. Application fee: $50. Electronic applications accepted. *Expenses:* Tuition, state resident: full-time $6000; part-time $250 per semester hour. Tuition, nonresident: full-time $23,976; part-time $999 per semester hour. Required fees: $1644. *Financial support:* In 2010–11, 9 students received support. Career-related internships or fieldwork, Federal Work-Study, scholarships/grants, traineeships, and unspecified assistantships available. Support available to part-time students. Financial award application deadline: 4/15; financial award applicants required to submit FAFSA. *Unit head:* Dr. Ron Shiffler, Dean, 912-478-5106, Fax: 912-478-0292, E-mail: shiffler@georgiasouthern.edu. *Application contact:* Dr. Stephen Rutner, Graduate Program Director, 912-478-0511, Fax: 912-478-1523, E-mail: srutner@georgiasouthern.edu.

Golden Gate University, Ageno School of Business, San Francisco, CA 94105-2968. Offers accounting (MBA); business administration (EMBA, MBA, PMBA, DBA); finance (MBA, MS, Certificate); financial planning (MS, Certificate); healthcare information systems (Certificate); human resource management (MBA, MS); human resources management (Certificate); information systems (MS); information technology (MBA); information technology management (Certificate); integrated marketing and communications (MS, Certificate); international business (MBA); management (MBA); marketing (MBA, MS, Certificate); operations supply chain management (Certificate); psychology (MA, Certificate); public administration (EMPA); public relations (MS, Certificate); technical market analysis (Certificate); JD/MBA. Part-time and evening/weekend programs available. *Faculty:* 16 full-time (4 women), 241 part-time/adjunct (72 women). *Students:* 421 full-time (235 women), 744 part-time (425 women); includes 526 minority (114 Black or African American, non-Hispanic/Latino; 2 American Indian or Alaska Native, non-Hispanic/Latino; 296 Asian, non-Hispanic/Latino; 73 Hispanic/Latino; 29 Native Hawaiian or other Pacific Islander, non-Hispanic/Latino; 12 Two or more races, non-Hispanic/Latino), 100 international. Average age 32. 681 applicants, 78% accepted, 270 enrolled. In 2010, 550 master's, 13 doctorates awarded. *Degree requirements:* For doctorate, thesis/dissertation. *Entrance requirements:* For master's, GMAT (MBA), minimum GPA of 2.5 (MS). Additional exam requirements/recommendations for international students: Required—TOEFL. *Application deadline:* For fall admission, 5/15 for domestic and international students; for winter admission, 1/15 for domestic and international students; for spring admission, 9/15 for domestic and international students. Applications are processed on a rolling basis. Application fee: $70 ($110 for international students). Electronic applications accepted. *Expenses:* Contact institution. *Financial support:* Career-related internships or fieldwork, Federal Work-Study, institutionally sponsored loans, and scholarships/grants available. Support available to part-time students. Financial award applicants required to submit FAFSA. *Unit head:* Dr. Paul Fouts, Dean, 415-442-7026, Fax: 415-442-6579. *Application contact:* Angela Melero, Enrollment Services, 415-442-7800, Fax: 415-442-7807, E-mail: info@ggu.edu.

HEC Montreal, School of Business Administration, Diploma Programs in Administration, Program in Supply Chain Management, Montréal, QC H3T 2A7, Canada. Offers Diploma. Part-time programs available. *Students:* 27 full-time (14 women), 96 part-time (25 women). 67 applicants, 75% accepted, 35 enrolled. In 2010, 30 Diplomas awarded. *Degree requirements:* For Diploma, one foreign language. *Entrance requirements:* For degree, 2 years of working experience, letters of recommendation. *Application deadline:* For fall admission, 4/15 for domestic and international students; for winter admission, 9/15 for domestic and international students. Application fee: $78 Canadian dollars. Electronic applications accepted. *Expenses:* Tuition, area resident: Part-time $68.93 per credit. Tuition, state resident: full-time $2481.48; part-time $188.92 per credit. Tuition, nonresident: full-time $6801; part-time $482.06 per course. International tuition: $17,354.16 full-time. Required fees: $1309.50; $30.28 per credit. $93.45 per term. Tuition and fees vary according to degree level and program. *Financial support:* Research assistantships, teaching assistantships available. Financial award application deadline: 9/2. *Unit head:* Silvia Ponce, Director, 514-340-6393, Fax: 514-340-6915, E-mail: silvia.ponce@hec.ca. *Application contact:* Marie Deshaies, Senior Student Advisor, 514-340-6135, Fax: 514-340-6411, E-mail: marie.deshaies@hec.ca.

Lehigh University, College of Business and Economics, Bethlehem, PA 18015. Offers accounting (MS), including accounting and information analysis; business administration (MBA); economics (MS, PhD), including economics, health and bio-pharmaceutical economics (MS); entrepreneurship (Certificate); finance (MS), including analytical finance; project management (Certificate); supply chain management (Certificate); MBA/E; MBA/M Ed. *Accreditation:* AACSB. Part-time and evening/weekend programs available. Postbaccalaureate distance learning degree programs offered (minimal on-campus study). *Faculty:* 43 full-time (10 women), 19 part-time/adjunct (4 women). *Students:* 164 full-time (82 women), 242 part-time (72 women); includes 37 minority (6 Black or African American, non-Hispanic/Latino; 25 Asian, non-Hispanic/Latino; 5 Hispanic/Latino; 1 Native Hawaiian or other Pacific Islander, non-Hispanic/Latino), 110 international. Average age 29. 790 applicants, 35% accepted, 158 enrolled. In 2010, 159 master's, 3 doctorates awarded. Terminal master's awarded for partial completion of doctoral program. *Degree requirements:* For master's, thesis optional; for doctorate, comprehensive exam, thesis/dissertation, proposal defense. *Entrance requirements:* For master's, GMAT, GRE General Test; MCAT, DAT (health and biopharmaceutical economics); for doctorate, GMAT or GRE General Test. Additional exam requirements/recommendations for international students: Required—TOEFL (minimum score 600 paper-based; 250 computer-based; 94 iBT). *Application deadline:* For fall admission, 7/15 for domestic students, 5/1 for international students; for spring admission, 12/1 for domestic and international students. Applications are processed on a rolling basis. Application fee: $100. Electronic applications accepted. *Expenses:* Contact institution. *Financial support:* In 2010–11, 93 students received support, including 2 fellowships with full tuition reimbursements available (averaging $16,000 per year), 39 research assistantships with full and partial tuition reimbursements available (averaging $2,269 per year), 17 teaching assistantships with full tuition reimbursements available (averaging $13,840 per year); career-related internships or fieldwork, scholarships/grants, health care benefits, tuition waivers (full and partial), and unspecified assistantships also available. Support available to part-time students. Financial award application deadline: 1/15. *Faculty research:* Public finance, energy, investments, activity-based costing, management information systems. *Unit head:* Paul R. Brown, Dean, 610-758-6725, Fax: 610-758-4499, E-mail: prb207@lehigh.edu. *Application contact:* Corinn McBride, Director of Recruitment and Admissions, 610-758-3418, Fax: 610-758-5283, E-mail: com207@lehigh.edu.

Marquette University, Graduate School of Management, Executive MBA Program, Milwaukee, WI 53201-1881. Offers economics (MBA); finance (MBA); human resources (MBA); international business (MBA); management information systems (MBA); marketing (MBA); operations and supply chain management (MBA); sports business (MBA). *Accreditation:* AACSB. *Faculty:* 3 full-time (1 woman), 2 part-time/adjunct (0 women). *Students:* 43 full-time (11 women); includes 6 minority (1 Black or African American, non-Hispanic/Latino; 4 Asian, non-Hispanic/Latino; 1 Hispanic/Latino), 3 international. Average age 37. 47 applicants, 74% accepted, 29 enrolled. In 2010, 13 master's awarded. *Degree requirements:* For master's, international trip. *Entrance requirements:* For master's, GMAT, two letters of recommendation, official transcripts from current and previous colleges/universities. Additional exam requirements/recommendations for international students: Required—TOEFL (minimum score 530 paper-based; 78 computer-based). *Application deadline:* Applications are processed on a rolling basis. Application fee: $50. Electronic applications accepted. *Expenses:* Contact institution. *Financial support:* Application deadline: 2/15. *Faculty research:* International trade and finance, customer relationship management, consumer satisfaction, customer service. *Unit head:* Dr. Jeanne Simmons, Graduate Director, 414-288-7145, Fax: 414-288-1660, E-mail: jeanne.simmons@marquette.edu. *Application contact:* Erin Fox, Assistant Director for Recruitment, 414-288-5319, Fax: 414-288-1902, E-mail: erin.fox@marquette.edu.

Marquette University, Graduate School of Management, Program in Business Administration, Milwaukee, WI 53201-1881. Offers business administration (MBA); economics (MBA); finance (MBA); human resources (MBA); international business (MBA); management information systems (MBA); marketing (MBA); operations and supply chain management (MBA); sports business (MBA); JD/MBA; MBA/MA; MBA/MSN. *Accreditation:* AACSB. Part-time and evening/weekend programs available. *Faculty:* 38 full-time (9 women), 24 part-time/adjunct (8 women). *Students:* 44 full-time (17 women), 368 part-time (105 women); includes 36 minority (4 Black or African American, non-Hispanic/Latino; 2 American Indian or Alaska Native, non-Hispanic/Latino; 20 Asian, non-Hispanic/Latino; 10 Hispanic/Latino), 30 international. Average age 31. 256 applicants, 60% accepted, 98 enrolled. In 2010, 117 master's awarded. *Entrance requirements:* For master's, GMAT, letters of recommendation. Additional exam requirements/recommendations for international students: Required—TOEFL (minimum score 530 paper-based; 78 computer-based). *Application deadline:* Applications are processed on a rolling basis. Application fee: $50. Electronic applications accepted. *Expenses:* Tuition: Full-time $16,290; part-time $905 per credit hour. Tuition and fees vary according to program. *Financial support:* In 2010–11, 4 fellowships, 11 teaching assistantships were awarded; research assistantships, Federal Work-Study, institutionally sponsored loans, scholarships/grants, and tuition waivers (full and partial) also available. Support available to part-time students. Financial award application deadline: 2/15. *Faculty research:* Ethics in the professions, services marketing, technology impact on decision-making, mentoring. *Unit head:* Dr. Jeanne Simmons, Graduate Director, 414-288-7145, Fax: 414-288-1660, E-mail: jeanne.simmons@marquette.edu. *Application contact:* Debra Leutermann, Admissions Coordinator, 414-288-8064, Fax: 414-288-1902, E-mail: debra.leutermann@marquette.edu.

Moravian College, Moravian College Comenius Center, Business and Management Programs, Bethlehem, PA 18018-6650. Offers accounting (MBA); general management (MBA); health care management (MBA); human resource management (MBA); leadership (MSHRM); learning and performance management (MSHRM); supply chain management (MBA). Part-time and evening/weekend programs available. *Faculty:* 6 full-time (2 women), 10 part-time/adjunct (3 women). *Students:* 67 part-time (35 women). 24 applicants, 50% accepted, 12 enrolled. In 2010, 8 master's awarded. *Entrance requirements:* For master's, GMAT. Additional exam requirements/recommendations for international students: Required—TOEFL (minimum score 550 paper-based; 260 computer-based; 90 iBT). *Application deadline:* Applications are processed on a rolling basis. Application fee: $40. *Expenses:* Contact institution. *Financial support:* In 2010–11, 1 fellowship with full tuition reimbursement was awarded. *Faculty research:* Leadership, change management, human resources. *Unit head:* Dr. William A. Kleintop, Associate Dean for Business and Management Programs, 610-507-1400, Fax: 610-861-1400, E-mail: comenius@moravian.edu. *Application contact:* Linda J. Doyle, Information Contact, 610-861-1400, Fax: 610-861-1466, E-mail: mba@moravian.edu.

Quinnipiac University, School of Business, MBA Program, Hamden, CT 06518-1940. Offers chartered financial analyst (MBA); finance (MBA); healthcare management (MBA); information systems management (MBA); marketing (MBA); supply chain management (MBA); JD/MBA. *Accreditation:* AACSB. Part-time and evening/weekend programs available. *Faculty:* 25 full-time (2 women), 3 part-time/adjunct (all women). *Students:* 87 full-time (24 women), 121 part-time (46 women); includes 12 minority (1 Black or African American, non-Hispanic/Latino; 7 Asian, non-Hispanic/Latino; 4 Hispanic/Latino), 14 international. Average age 29. 119 applicants, 81% accepted, 81 enrolled. In 2010, 70 master's awarded. *Entrance requirements:* For master's, GMAT or GRE, minimum GPA of 3.0. Additional exam requirements/recommendations for international students: Required—TOEFL (minimum score 575 paper-based; 233 computer-based; 90 iBT), IELTS (minimum score 6.5). *Application deadline:* For fall admission, 7/30 priority date for domestic students, 4/30 priority date for international students; for spring admission, 12/15 priority date for domestic students, 9/15 priority date for international students. Applications are processed on a rolling basis. Application fee: $45. Electronic applications accepted. *Expenses:* Tuition: Part-time $810 per credit. Required fees: $35 per credit. *Financial support:* In 2010–11, 110 students received support. Federal Work-Study, tuition waivers (partial), and unspecified assistantships available. Support available to part-time students. Financial award application deadline: 4/15; financial award applicants required to submit FAFSA. *Faculty research:* Equity compensation, marketing relationships and public policy, corporate governance, international business, supply chain management. *Unit head:* Lisa Braiewa, MBA Program Director, 203-582-3710, Fax: 203-582-8664, E-mail: lisa.braiewa@quinnipiac.edu. *Application contact:* Jennifer Boutin, 800-462-1944, Fax: 203-582-3443, E-mail: jennifer.boutin@quinnipiac.edu.

Quinnipiac University, School of Business, MBA—Supply Chain Management Track, Hamden, CT 06518-1940. Offers MBA. Part-time and evening/weekend programs available. *Faculty:* 25 full-time (2 women), 3 part-time/adjunct (all women). *Entrance requirements:* For master's, GMAT or GRE. Additional exam requirements/recommendations for international students: Required—TOEFL (minimum score 575 paper-based; 233 computer-based; 90 iBT), IELTS (minimum score 6.5). *Application deadline:* For fall admission, 7/31 priority date for domestic students, 4/30 priority date for international students; for spring admission, 12/15 priority date for domestic students, 9/15 priority date for international students. Applications are processed on a rolling basis. Electronic applications accepted. *Expenses:* Tuition: Part-time $810 per credit. Required fees: $35 per credit. *Financial support:* Federal Work-Study available. Support available to part-time students. *Unit head:* Lisa Braiewa, MBA Program Director, 203-582-3710, Fax: 203-582-8664. *Application contact:* Jennifer Boutin, 800-462-1944, Fax: 203-582-3443, E-mail: jennifer.boutin@quinnipiac.edu.

Rutgers, The State University of New Jersey, Newark, Rutgers Business School–Newark and New Brunswick, Doctoral Programs in Management, Newark, NJ 07102. Offers accounting (PhD); accounting information systems (PhD); economics (PhD); finance (PhD); individualized study (PhD); information technology (PhD); international business (PhD); management science (PhD); marketing science (PhD); organizational management (PhD); science, technology and management (PhD); supply chain management (PhD). *Faculty:* 143 full-time (36 women), 2 part-time/adjunct (0 women). *Students:* 117 full-time (42 women), 1 (woman) part-time; includes 8 Black or African American, non-Hispanic/Latino; 14 Asian, non-Hispanic/Latino; 3 Hispanic/Latino, 68 international. Average age 33. 355 applicants, 14% accepted, 35 enrolled. In 2010, 8 doctorates awarded. *Degree requirements:* For doctorate, comprehensive exam, thesis/dissertation. *Entrance requirements:* For doctorate, GRE or GMAT. Additional exam requirements/recommendations for international students: Required—TOEFL (minimum score 550 paper-based; 213 computer-based; 79 iBT). *Application deadline:* For fall admission, 3/1 for domestic and international students; for spring admission, 10/15 for domestic and international students. Application fee: $65. Electronic applications accepted. *Expenses:* Tuition, state resident: part-time $600 per credit. Tuition, nonresident: full-time $10,694. *Financial support:* In 2010–11, 52 students received support, including 7 fellowships (averaging $18,000 per year), 4 research assistantships with tuition reimbursements available (averaging $23,112 per year), 41 teaching assistantships with tuition reimbursements available (averaging $23,112 per year); health care benefits also available. Financial award application deadline: 3/1. *Unit head:* Dr. Glenn Shafer, Director, 973-353-1604, Fax: 973-353-5691, E-mail: gshafer@rbs.rutgers.edu. *Application contact:* Information Contact, 973-353-5371, Fax: 973-353-5691, E-mail: phdinfo@andromeda.rutgers.edu.

Santa Clara University, Leavey School of Business, Program in Business Administration, Santa Clara, CA 95053. Offers accounting (MBA); entrepreneurship (MBA); executive business administration (EMBA); finance (MBA); food and agribusiness (MBA); international business (MBA); leading people and organizations (MBA); managing technology and innovation (MBA); marketing management (MBA); supply chain management (MBA). *Accreditation:* AACSB. Part-time and evening/weekend programs available. *Students:* 229 full-time (80 women), 748 part-time (244 women); includes 354 minority (14 Black or African American, non-Hispanic/Latino; 1 American Indian or Alaska Native, non-Hispanic/Latino; 287 Asian, non-Hispanic/Latino; 42 Hispanic/Latino; 5 Native Hawaiian or other Pacific Islander, non-Hispanic/Latino; 5 Two or more races, non-Hispanic/Latino), 209 international. Average age 32. 334 applicants, 76% accepted, 191 enrolled. In 2010, 307 master's awarded. *Degree requirements:* For master's, thesis or alternative. *Entrance requirements:* For master's, GMAT, GRE. Additional exam requirements/recommendations for international students: Required—TOEFL (minimum score 600 paper-based; 250 computer-based; 100 iBT). *Application deadline:* For fall admission, 6/1 for domestic and international students; for spring admission, 1/19 for domestic students, 1/17 for international students. Applications are processed on a rolling basis. Application fee: $75 ($100 for international students). Electronic applications accepted. *Expenses:* Contact institution. *Financial support:* In 2010–11, 350 students received support; fellowships with partial tuition reimbursements available, research assistantships with partial tuition reimbursements available, career-related internships or fieldwork, Federal Work-Study, institutionally sponsored loans, scholarships/grants, health care benefits, and unspecified assistantships available. Support available to part-time students. Financial award application deadline: 6/1; financial award applicants required to submit FAFSA. *Unit head:* Elizabeth B. Ford, Senior Assistant Dean, 408-554-2752, Fax: 408-554-4571, E-mail: eford@scu.edu. *Application contact:* Molly Mulally, Assistant Director, Graduate Business Admissions, 408-554-4539, Fax: 408-554-4571, E-mail: mbaadmissions@scu.edu.

Seton Hall University, Stillman School of Business, Programs in Business Administration, South Orange, NJ 07079-2697. Offers accounting (MBA); finance (MBA); information technology management (MBA); international business (MBA); management (MBA); marketing (MBA); sport management (MBA); supply chain management (MBA). Part-time and evening/weekend programs available. *Faculty:* 35 full-time (8 women), 11 part-time/adjunct (1 woman). *Students:* 93 full-time (33 women), 165 part-time (76 women); includes 26 Black or African American, non-Hispanic/Latino; 39 Asian, non-Hispanic/Latino; 8 Hispanic/Latino. Average age 29. 404 applicants, 74% accepted, 258 enrolled. In 2010, 203 master's awarded. *Degree requirements:* For master's, 20 hours of community service (Social Responsibility Project). *Entrance requirements:* For master's, GMAT or CPA, Advanced degree such as PhD, MD, JD, DVM, DDS, PharmD, MBA from an AACSB institution, MS in a business discipline and a minimum GPA of 3.0. Additional exam requirements/recommendations for international students: Required—TOEFL (minimum: 254 computer, 102 iBT), IELTS or Pearson Test of English (PTE). *Application deadline:* For fall admission, 5/31 priority date for domestic students, 3/31 priority date for international students; for spring admission, 10/31 priority date for domestic students, 9/30 priority date for international students. Applications are processed on a rolling basis. Application fee: $75. Electronic applications accepted. *Financial support:* In 2010–11, research assistantships with full tuition reimbursements (averaging $35,610 per year); career-related internships or fieldwork, Federal Work-Study, scholarships/grants, and unspecified assistantships also available. Support available to part-time students. Financial award application deadline: 6/30; financial award applicants required to submit FAFSA. *Faculty research:* Financial, hedge funds, international business, legal issues, disclosure and branding. *Unit head:* Dr. Joyce A. Strawser, Associate Dean for Undergraduate and MBA Curricula, 973-761-9225, Fax: 973-761-9217, E-mail: strawsjo@shu.edu. *Application contact:* Catherine Bianchi, Director of Graduate Admissions, 973-761-9262, Fax: 973-761-9208, E-mail: catherine.bianchi@shu.edu.

Southeastern Louisiana University, College of Business, Hammond, LA 70402. Offers accounting (MBA); general (MBA); information systems for supply chain management (MBA). *Accreditation:* AACSB. Part-time and evening/weekend programs available. *Faculty:* 15 full-time (1 woman), 1 part-time/adjunct (0 women). *Students:* 52 full-time (29 women), 56 part-time (21 women); includes 12 minority (8 Black or African American, non-Hispanic/Latino; 1 Asian, non-Hispanic/Latino; 2 Hispanic/Latino; 1 Two or more races, non-Hispanic/Latino), 8 international. Average age 28. 109 applicants, 40% accepted, 25 enrolled. In 2010, 62 master's awarded. *Entrance requirements:* For master's, GMAT (minimum score 450), minimum cumulative GPA of 2.75 for all undergraduate work attempted or 3.0 on all upper-division undergraduate coursework attempted. Additional exam requirements/recommendations for international students: Required—TOEFL (minimum score 525 paper-based; 195 computer-based; 61 iBT). *Application deadline:* For fall admission, 7/15 priority date for domestic students, 6/1 priority date for international students; for spring admission, 12/1 priority date for domestic students, 10/1 priority date for international students. Applications are processed on a rolling basis. Application fee: $20 ($30 for international students). Electronic applications accepted. *Expenses:* Tuition, state resident: full-time $3533. Tuition, nonresident: full-time $12,002. Required fees: $907. Tuition and fees vary according to degree level. *Financial support:* In 2010–11, 21 students received support, including 1 research assistantship (averaging $9,000 per year); career-related internships or fieldwork, Federal Work-Study, institutionally sponsored loans, scholarships/grants, and administrative assistantships, graduate professional services assistants also available. Support available to part-time students. Financial award application deadline: 5/1; financial award applicants required to submit FAFSA. *Faculty research:* Ethical decision-making in accounting, entrepreneurship and emerging information, leadership and organizational performance. *Unit head:* Dr. Randy Settoon, Dean, 985-549-2258, Fax: 985-549-5038, E-mail: rsettoon@selu.edu. *Application contact:* Sandra Meyers, Graduate Admissions Analyst, 985-549-5620, Fax: 985-549-5882, E-mail: admissions@selu.edu.

Texas A&M University–San Antonio, School of Business, San Antonio, TX 78224. Offers business administration (MBA); enterprise resource planning systems (MBA); finance (MBA); healthcare management (MBA); human resources management (MBA); information assurance and security (MBA); international business (MBA); project management (MBA); supply chain management (MBA). Part-time and evening/weekend programs available. *Faculty:* 18 full-time (6 women), 1 part-time/adjunct (0 women). *Students:* 49 full-time (21 women), 195 part-time (107 women). In 2010, 20 master's awarded. *Entrance requirements:* For master's, GMAT. Additional exam requirements/recommendations for international students: Required—TOEFL (minimum score 550 paper-based; 213 computer-based; 80 iBT), IELTS (minimum score 6). *Application deadline:* For fall admission, 7/1 priority date for domestic students, 6/1 priority date for international students; for spring admission, 11/15 priority date for domestic students, 10/1 priority date for international students. Applications are processed on a rolling basis. Application fee: $35 ($50 for international students). Electronic applications accepted. *Expenses:* Tuition, state resident: full-time $2899; part-time $161 per credit hour. Tuition, nonresident: full-time $8479; part-time $471 per credit hour. Required fees: $1056; $61 per credit hour. $368 per semester. *Financial support:* Application deadline: 3/31. *Unit head:* Dr. Tracy Hurley,

MBA Coordinator, 210-932-6200, E-mail: tracy.hurley@tamusa.tamus.edu. *Application contact:* Melissa A. Villanueva, Graduate Admissions Specialist, 210-932-6200, Fax: 210-932-6209, E-mail: melissa.villanueva@tamusa.tamus.edu.

The University of Akron, Graduate School, College of Business Administration, Department of Management, Program in Management-Supply Chain Management, Akron, OH 44325. Offers MSM. *Students:* 1 (woman) full-time. Average age 28. 13 applicants, 69% accepted. In 2010, 6 master's awarded. *Entrance requirements:* For master's, GMAT, minimum GPA of 2.75, two letters of recommendation, statement of purpose, resume. Additional exam requirements/recommendations for international students: Required—TOEFL (minimum score 550 paper-based; 213 computer-based; 79 iBT). *Application deadline:* For fall admission, 7/15 for domestic and international students; for spring admission, 11/15 for domestic and international students. Application fee: $30 ($40 for international students). Electronic applications accepted. *Expenses:* Tuition, state resident: full-time $6800; part-time $378 per credit hour. Tuition, nonresident: full-time $11,644; part-time $647 per credit hour. Required fees: $1265. One-time fee: $30 full-time. *Unit head:* Chair. *Application contact:* Dr. Susan Hanlon, Director of Graduate Business Programs, 330-972-7043, Fax: 330-972-6588, E-mail: shanlon@uakron.edu.

The University of Alabama in Huntsville, School of Graduate Studies, College of Business Administration, Department of Management and Marketing, Huntsville, AL 35899. Offers management (MBA), including acquisition management, finance, human resource management, logistics and supply chain management, marketing, project management. *Accreditation:* AACSB. Part-time and evening/weekend programs available. *Faculty:* 11 full-time (2 women), 4 part-time/adjunct (1 woman). *Students:* 41 full-time (17 women), 159 part-time (69 women); includes 32 minority (15 Black or African American, non-Hispanic/Latino; 6 American Indian or Alaska Native, non-Hispanic/Latino; 7 Asian, non-Hispanic/Latino; 3 Hispanic/Latino; 1 Two or more races, non-Hispanic/Latino), 14 international. Average age 31. 141 applicants, 65% accepted, 79 enrolled. In 2010, 66 master's awarded. *Degree requirements:* For master's, comprehensive exam, thesis or alternative. *Entrance requirements:* For master's, GMAT (minimum score 500), minimum AACSB index of 1080. Additional exam requirements/recommendations for international students: Required—TOEFL (minimum score 550 paper-based; 213 computer-based; 62 iBT). *Application deadline:* For fall admission, 8/1 for domestic students, 4/1 for international students; for spring admission, 12/1 for domestic students, 9/1 for international students. Applications are processed on a rolling basis. Application fee: $40 ($50 for international students). Electronic applications accepted. *Expenses:* Tuition, state resident: full-time $7250; part-time $407.75 per credit hour. Tuition, nonresident: full-time $17,358; part-time $970.05 per credit hour. Required fees: $246.80 per semester. Tuition and fees vary according to course load and program. *Financial support:* In 2010–11, 3 students received support, including 1 research assistantship with full tuition reimbursement available (averaging $8,550 per year), 2 teaching assistantships with full tuition reimbursements available (averaging $8,000 per year); career-related internships or fieldwork, Federal Work-Study, institutionally sponsored loans, scholarships/grants, health care benefits, and unspecified assistantships also available. Support available to part-time students. Financial award application deadline: 4/1; financial award applicants required to submit FAFSA. *Faculty research:* Strategic human resources, corporate governance, cross-function integration and the management of research and development, determinants of team performance. Total annual research expenditures: $3 million. *Unit head:* Dr. Brent Wren, Chair, 256-824-6408, Fax: 256-824-6328, E-mail: wrenb@uah.edu. *Application contact:* Jennifer Pettitt, Director of Graduate Programs, 256-824-6681, Fax: 256-824-7571, E-mail: jennifer.pettitt@uah.edu.

University of Florida, Graduate School, Warrington College of Business Administration, Hough Graduate School of Business, Department of Information Systems and Operations Management, Gainesville, FL 32611. Offers decision and information sciences (MS, PhD); supply chain management (MS). *Faculty:* 13 full-time (2 women). *Students:* 170 full-time (66 women), 20 part-time (4 women); includes 8 Black or African American, non-Hispanic/Latino; 12 Asian, non-Hispanic/Latino; 11 Hispanic/Latino, 112 international. Average age 29. 347 applicants, 78% accepted, 101 enrolled. In 2010, 42 master's, 1 doctorate awarded. Terminal master's awarded for partial completion of doctoral program. *Degree requirements:* For doctorate, thesis/dissertation. *Entrance requirements:* For master's, GMAT or GRE General Test, Minimum GPA of 3.0; for doctorate, GMAT minimum score 650 or GRE general test score 1350 (verbal and quantitative combined). Minimum GPA of 3.0. Additional exam requirements/recommendations for international students: Required—TOEFL (minimum score 550 paper-based; 213 computer-based; 80 iBT), IELTS (minimum score 6), IELTS (minimum of 6) or MELAB (minimum of 77) also required for some. *Application deadline:* For fall admission, 4/1 priority date for domestic students, 3/1 for international students; for spring admission, 10/15 for domestic students, 10/1 for international students. Applications are processed on a rolling basis. Application fee: $30. *Expenses:* Tuition, state resident: full-time $10,915.92. Tuition, nonresident: full-time $28,309. *Financial support:* In 2010–11, 14 students received support, including 1 fellowship, 6 research assistantships (averaging $16,849 per year), 7 teaching assistantships (averaging $12,325 per year); unspecified

assistantships also available. Financial award application deadline: 2/1; financial award applicants required to submit FAFSA. *Faculty research:* Expert systems, nonconvex optimization, manufacturing management, production and operation management, telecommunication. *Unit head:* Dr. Gary J. Koehler, Chair, 352-846-2090, Fax: 352-392-5438, E-mail: koehler@ufl.edu. *Application contact:* Dr. Anand A. Paul, Graduate Coordinator for PhD Program, 352-392-9600, Fax: 352-392-5438, E-mail: paulaa@ufl.edu.

University of Houston, College of Technology, Department of Information and Logistics Technology, Houston, TX 77204. Offers information security (MS); supply chain and logistics technology (MS); technology project management (MS). Part-time programs available. *Faculty:* 6 full-time (3 women), 6 part-time/adjunct (2 women). *Students:* 80 full-time (30 women), 75 part-time (29 women); includes 35 minority (12 Black or African American, non-Hispanic/Latino; 9 Asian, non-Hispanic/Latino; 11 Hispanic/Latino; 1 Native Hawaiian or other Pacific Islander, non-Hispanic/Latino; 2 Two or more races, non-Hispanic/Latino), 73 international. Average age 31. 60 applicants, 92% accepted, 35 enrolled. In 2010, 22 master's awarded. *Degree requirements:* For master's, project or thesis (most programs). *Entrance requirements:* For master's, GMAT. Additional exam requirements/recommendations for international students: Required—TOEFL (minimum score 550 paper-based; 79 iBT). *Application deadline:* For fall admission, 7/1 for domestic students, 4/1 for international students; for spring admission, 12/1 for domestic students, 10/1 for international students. Applications are processed on a rolling basis. Application fee: $75 ($150 for international students). Electronic applications accepted. *Expenses:* Tuition, state resident: full-time $8592; part-time $358 per credit hour. Tuition, nonresident: full-time $16,032; part-time $668 per credit hour. Required fees: $2889. Tuition and fees vary according to course load and program. *Financial support:* In 2010–11, 10 research assistantships with partial tuition reimbursements (averaging $8,380 per year), 15 teaching assistantships with partial tuition reimbursements (averaging $8,078 per year) were awarded. *Unit head:* Michael Gibson, Chairperson, 713-743-5116, E-mail: mlgibson@uh.edu. *Application contact:* Tiffany Roosa, Graduate Advisor, 713-743-4100, Fax: 713-743-4151, E-mail: troosa@uh.edu.

University of Louisville, J. B. Speed School of Engineering, Department of Industrial Engineering, Louisville, KY 40292-0001. Offers engineering management (M Eng); industrial engineering (M Eng, MS, PhD); logistics and distribution (Certificate). *Accreditation:* ABET (one or more programs are accredited). Part-time programs available. *Faculty:* 10 full-time (1 woman). *Students:* 45 full-time (11 women), 26 part-time (7 women); includes 5 Black or African American, non-Hispanic/Latino; 1 Asian, non-Hispanic/Latino; 1 Hispanic/Latino; 1 Two or more races, non-Hispanic/Latino, 18 international. Average age 28. 56 applicants, 32% accepted, 7 enrolled. In 2010, 25 master's, 4 doctorates awarded. Terminal master's awarded for partial completion of doctoral program. *Degree requirements:* For master's, comprehensive exam (for some programs), thesis or alternative; for doctorate, comprehensive exam, thesis/dissertation, minimum GPA of 3.0. *Entrance requirements:* For master's and doctorate, GRE General Test. Additional exam requirements/recommendations for international students: Required—TOEFL (minimum score 550 paper-based; 213 computer-based; 80 iBT), IELTS (minimum score 6.5). *Application deadline:* For fall admission, 5/1 priority date for domestic and international students; for spring admission, 11/1 priority date for domestic and international students. Applications are processed on a rolling basis. Application fee: $50. Electronic applications accepted. *Expenses:* Tuition, state resident: full-time $9144; part-time $508 per credit hour. Tuition, nonresident: full-time $19,026; part-time $1057 per credit hour. Tuition and fees vary according to program and reciprocity agreements. *Financial support:* In 2010–11, 15 students received support, including 7 fellowships with full tuition reimbursements available (averaging $20,000 per year), 2 research assistantships with full tuition reimbursements available (averaging $20,000 per year), 6 teaching assistantships with full tuition reimbursements available (averaging $20,000 per year). Financial award application deadline: 1/25; financial award applicants required to submit FAFSA. *Faculty research:* Optimization, computer simulation, logistics and distribution, ergonomics and human factors, advanced manufacturing process. Total annual research expenditures: $748,000. *Unit head:* Dr. John S. Usher, Chair, 502-852-6342, Fax: 502-852-5633, E-mail: usher@louisville.edu. *Application contact:* Dr. Michael Day, Associate Dean, 502-852-6195, Fax: 502-852-7294, E-mail: day@louisville.edu.

University of Massachusetts Dartmouth, Graduate School, Charlton College of Business, Program in Business Administration, North Dartmouth, MA 02747-2300. Offers accounting (Postbaccalaureate Certificate); business administration (MBA); e-commerce (PMC); finance (PMC); general management (PMC); leadership (PMC); management (Postbaccalaureate Certificate); marketing (PMC); supply chain management (PMC). *Accreditation:* AACSB. Part-time programs available. *Faculty:* 40 full-time (13 women), 28 part-time/adjunct (8 women). *Students:* 99 full-time (38 women), 123 part-time (62 women); includes 4 Black or African American, non-Hispanic/Latino; 2 American Indian or Alaska Native, non-Hispanic/Latino; 3 Asian, non-Hispanic/Latino; 8 Hispanic/Latino; 1 Two or more races, non-Hispanic/Latino, 45 international. Average age 30. 185 applicants, 76% accepted, 79 enrolled. In 2010, 79 master's, 12 other advanced degrees awarded. *Entrance requirements:* For master's, GMAT, resume, letters of recommendation. Additional exam requirements/recommendations for international students: Required—TOEFL (minimum score 500 paper-based; 200 computer-based; 72 iBT). *Application deadline:* For fall admission, 6/1 for domestic students, 5/1 for international students; for spring admission, 10/1 for domestic students, 8/1 for international students. Application fee: $40 ($60 for international students). Electronic applications accepted. *Expenses:* Tuition, state resident: full-time $2071; part-time $86 per credit. Tuition, nonresident: full-time $8099; part-time $337 per credit. Required fees: $9446; $394 per credit. One-time fee: $75. Part-time tuition and fees vary according to class time, course load, degree level and reciprocity agreements. *Financial support:* In 2010–11, 1 research assistantship with full tuition reimbursement (averaging $6,000 per year) was awarded; teaching assistantships, Federal Work-Study and unspecified assistantships also available. Support available to part-time students. Financial award application deadline: 3/1; financial award applicants required to submit FAFSA. *Faculty research:* Global business environment, e-commerce, managing diversity, agile manufacturing, green business. Total annual research expenditures: $29,538. *Unit head:* Dr. Norm Barber, Assistant Dean, 508-999-8543, E-mail: nbarber@umassd.edu. *Application contact:* Elan Turcotte-Shamski, Graduate Admissions Officer, 508-999-8604, Fax: 508-999-8183, E-mail: graduate@umassd.edu.

University of Memphis, Graduate School, Fogelman College of Business and Economics, Program in Business Administration, Memphis, TN 38152. Offers accounting (MBA, PhD); economics (MBA, PhD); executive business administration (MBA); finance (PhD); finance, insurance, and real estate (MBA, MS); international business administration (IMBA); management (MBA, MS, PhD); management information systems (MBA, MS, PhD); management science (MBA); marketing (MBA, MS); marketing and supply chain management (PhD); real estate development (MS); JD/MBA. *Accreditation:* AACSB. *Faculty:* 44 full-time (9 women), 5 part-time/adjunct (0 women). *Students:* 263 full-time (106 women), 181 part-time (66 women); includes 46 Black or African American, non-Hispanic/Latino; 3 American Indian or Alaska Native, non-Hispanic/Latino; 16 Asian, non-Hispanic/Latino; 5 Hispanic/Latino, 109 international. Average age 31. 374 applicants, 73% accepted, 119 enrolled. In 2010, 140 master's, 17 doctorates awarded. *Degree requirements:* For master's, comprehensive exam; for doctorate, comprehensive exam, thesis/dissertation. *Entrance requirements:* For master's, GMAT, resume; for doctorate, GMAT, interview, minimum GPA of 3.4, resume, letter of recommendation. Additional exam requirements/recommendations for international students: Required—TOEFL (minimum score 550 paper-based; 220 computer-based). *Application deadline:* For fall admission, 8/1 for domestic students; for spring admission, 12/1 for domestic students. Application fee: $35 ($60 for international students). *Financial support:* In 2010–11, 164 students received support; research assistantships with full tuition reimbursements available, teaching assistantships with full tuition reimbursements available, career-related internships or fieldwork, Federal Work-Study, scholarships/grants, and unspecified assistantships available. Financial award application deadline: 2/15; financial award applicants required to submit FAFSA. *Faculty research:* Competitive business strategy, finance microstructures, supply chain management innovations, health care economics, litigation risks and corporate audits. *Unit head:* Rajiv Grover, Dean, 901-678-3759, E-mail: rgrover@memphis.edu. *Application contact:* Dr. Carol V. Danehower, Associate Dean, 901-678-5402, Fax: 901-678-3579, E-mail: fcbegp@memphis.edu.

University of Michigan–Dearborn, School of Management, Dearborn, MI 48128-1491. Offers accounting (MBA, MS); finance (MBA, MS); information systems (MS); international business (MBA); management (MBA); management information systems (MBA); marketing (MBA); supply chain management (MBA); MBA/MHSA; MBA/MSE; MBA/MSF. *Accreditation:* AACSB. Part-time and evening/weekend programs available. Postbaccalaureate distance learning degree programs offered (no on-campus study). *Faculty:* 40 full-time (17 women), 2 part-time/adjunct (1 woman). *Students:* 71 full-time (26 women), 403 part-time (134 women); includes 68 minority (19 Black or African American, non-Hispanic/Latino; 1 American Indian or Alaska Native, non-Hispanic/Latino; 39 Asian, non-Hispanic/Latino; 6 Hispanic/Latino; 1 Native Hawaiian or other Pacific Islander, non-Hispanic/Latino; 2 Two or more races, non-Hispanic/Latino), 89 international. Average age 30. 185 applicants, 51% accepted, 67 enrolled. In 2010, 150 master's awarded. *Entrance requirements:* For master's, GMAT, 2 years of work experience (MBA); course work in computer applications, statistics, and pre-calculus or finite mathematics; 18 credits of accounting course work beyond introductory courses (MS in accounting). Additional exam requirements/recommendations for international students: Required—TOEFL (minimum score 560 paper-based; 220 computer-based; 84 iBT). *Application deadline:* For fall admission, 8/1 priority date for domestic students, 6/1 for international students; for winter admission, 12/1 priority date for domestic students, 10/1 for international students; for spring admission, 4/1 priority date for domestic students, 2/1 for international students. Applications are processed on a rolling basis. Application fee: $60. Electronic applications accepted. *Expenses:* Contact institution. *Financial support:* Career-related internships or fieldwork, Federal Work-Study, and scholarships/grants available. Support available to part-time students. Financial award application deadline: 9/1; financial award applicants required to submit FAFSA. *Faculty research:* Cultural diversity, buyer-supplier relations, error detection in data, economic evolution. *Unit head:* Dr. Kim Schatzel, Dean, 313-593-5248, Fax: 313-271-9835, E-mail: schatzel@umd.

umich.edu. *Application contact:* Joan Doherty, Academic Advisor/Counselor, 313-593-5460, Fax: 313-271-9838, E-mail: gradbusiness@umd.umich.edu.

University of Minnesota, Twin Cities Campus, Carlson School of Management, Carlson Full-Time MBA Program, Minneapolis, MN 55455. Offers finance (MBA); information technology (MBA); management (MBA); marketing (MBA); medical industry orientation (MBA); supply chain and operations (MBA); JD/MBA; MBA/MPP; MD/MBA; MHA/MBA; Pharm D/MBA. *Accreditation:* AACSB. *Faculty:* 52 full-time (14 women), 20 part-time/adjunct (3 women). *Students:* 170 full-time (62 women); includes 1 Black or African American, non-Hispanic/Latino; 1 American Indian or Alaska Native, non-Hispanic/Latino; 9 Asian, non-Hispanic/Latino; 8 Hispanic/Latino, 36 international. Average age 28. 452 applicants, 30% accepted, 71 enrolled. In 2010, 105 master's awarded. *Entrance requirements:* For master's, GMAT. Additional exam requirements/recommendations for international students: Required—TOEFL (minimum score 580 paper-based; 240 computer-based; 84 iBT), IELTS (minimum score 7), or Pearson Test of English (PTE). *Application deadline:* For fall admission, 4/1 for domestic students, 2/1 for international students. Application fee: $60 ($90 for international students). Electronic applications accepted. *Expenses:* Contact institution. *Financial support:* In 2010–11, 95 students received support, including 95 fellowships with full and partial tuition reimbursements available (averaging $21,235 per year); research assistantships with partial tuition reimbursements available, teaching assistantships with partial tuition reimbursements available, career-related internships or fieldwork, Federal Work-Study, institutionally sponsored loans, scholarships/grants, health care benefits, and unspecified assistantships also available. Financial award application deadline: 4/1; financial award applicants required to submit FAFSA. *Faculty research:* Finance and accounting: financial reporting, asset pricing models and corporate finance; information and decision sciences: on-line auctions, information transparency and recommender systems; marketing: psychological influences on consumer behavior, brand equity, pricing and marketing channels; operations: lean manufacturing, quality management and global supply chains; strategic management and organization: global strategy, networks, entrepreneurship and innovation, sustainability. *Unit head:* Kathryn J. Carlson, Assistant Dean, MBA Programs and Graduate Business Career Center, 612-625-5555, Fax: 612-625-1012, E-mail: mba@umn.edu. *Application contact:* Daniel Bursch, Director of Admissions & Recruiting, 612-625-5555, Fax: 612-625-1012, E-mail: mba@umn.edu.

University of Minnesota, Twin Cities Campus, Carlson School of Management, Carlson Part-Time MBA Program, Minneapolis, MN 55455. Offers finance (MBA); information technology (MBA); management (MBA); marketing (MBA); supply chain and operations (MBA). Part-time and evening/weekend programs available. *Faculty:* 67 full-time (18 women), 23 part-time/adjunct (2 women). *Students:* 1,520 part-time (490 women); includes 16 Black or African American, non-Hispanic/Latino; 3 American Indian or Alaska Native, non-Hispanic/Latino; 87 Asian, non-Hispanic/Latino; 14 Hispanic/Latino, 94 international. Average age 29. 306 applicants, 70% accepted, 186 enrolled. In 2010, 401 master's awarded. *Entrance requirements:* For master's, GMAT. Additional exam requirements/recommendations for international students: Required—TOEFL (minimum score 580 paper-based; 240 computer-based; 84 iBT), IELTS (minimum score 7), or Pearson Test of English (PTE). *Application deadline:* For fall admission, 5/1 priority date for domestic and international students; for spring admission, 11/1 priority date for domestic and international students. Application fee: $60 ($90 for international students). Electronic applications accepted. *Expenses:* Contact institution. *Financial support:* Applicants required to submit FAFSA. *Faculty research:* Finance and accounting: financial reporting, asset pricing models and corporate finance; information and decision sciences: on-line auctions, information transparency and recommender systems; marketing: psychological influences on consumer behavior, brand equity, pricing and marketing channels; operations: lean manufacturing, quality management and global supply chains; strategic management and organization: global Strategy, networks, entrepreneurship and innovation, sustainability. *Unit head:* Kathryn J. Carlson, Assistant Dean, MBA Programs and Graduate Business Career Center, 612-624-2039, Fax: 612-625-1012, E-mail: mba@umn.edu. *Application contact:* Daniel Bursch, Director of Admissions & Recruiting, 612-625-5555, Fax: 612-625-1012, E-mail: mba@umn.edu.

University of Missouri–St. Louis, College of Business Administration, Program in Business Administration, St. Louis, MO 63121. Offers accounting (MBA); business administration (Certificate); finance (MBA); human resource management (Certificate); information systems (MBA); local government (Certificate); logistics and supply chain management (MBA, Certificate); marketing (MBA); marketing management (Certificate); operations management (MBA). *Accreditation:* AACSB. Part-time and evening/weekend programs available. *Faculty:* 30 full-time (5 women), 11 part-time/adjunct (2 women). *Students:* 132 full-time (57 women), 306 part-time (122 women); includes 55 minority (21 Black or African American, non-Hispanic/Latino; 20 Asian, non-Hispanic/Latino; 11 Hispanic/Latino; 1 Native Hawaiian or other Pacific Islander, non-Hispanic/Latino; 2 Two or more races, non-Hispanic/Latino), 6 international. Average age 30. 219 applicants, 60% accepted, 88 enrolled. In 2010, 114 master's, 9 other advanced degrees awarded. *Entrance requirements:* For master's, GMAT, 2 letters of recommendation. Additional exam requirements/recommendations for international students: Required—TOEFL (minimum score 550 paper-based; 213 computer-based). *Application deadline:* For fall admission, 7/1 for domestic students; for spring admission, 11/1 for domestic students. Applications are processed on a rolling basis. Application fee: $35 ($40 for international students). Electronic applications accepted. *Expenses:* Tuition, state resident: full-time $5522; part-time $306.80 per credit hour. Tuition, nonresident: full-time $14,253; part-time $792.10 per credit hour. Required fees: $658; $49 per credit hour. One-time fee: $12. Tuition and fees vary according to program. *Financial support:* In 2010–11, 22 research assistantships with full and partial tuition reimbursements (averaging $7,414 per year), 4 teaching assistantships with full and partial tuition reimbursements (averaging $13,950 per year) were awarded; career-related internships or fieldwork, Federal Work-Study, and institutionally sponsored loans also available. Support available to part-time students. Financial award application deadline: 4/1; financial award applicants required to submit FAFSA. *Faculty research:* Human resources, strategic management, marketing strategy, consumer behavior product development, advertising. *Unit head:* Karl Kottemann, Assistant Director, 314-516-5885, Fax: 314-516-6420, E-mail: mba@umsl.edu. *Application contact:* 314-516-5458, Fax: 314-516-6996, E-mail: gradadm@umsl.edu.

University of Missouri–St. Louis, College of Business Administration, Program in Information Systems, St. Louis, MO 63121. Offers information systems (MSIS, PhD); logistics and supply chain management (PhD). Part-time and evening/weekend programs available. *Faculty:* 8 full-time (0 women). *Students:* 10 full-time (3 women), 13 part-time (1 woman); includes 5 minority (4 Black or African American, non-Hispanic/Latino; 1 Hispanic/Latino), 4 international. Average age 31. 16 applicants, 25% accepted, 1 enrolled. In 2010, 6 master's, 2 doctorates awarded. *Entrance requirements:* For master's, GMAT, 2 letters of recommendation; for doctorate, GMAT or GRE, 3 letters of recommendation. Additional exam requirements/recommendations for international students: Required—TOEFL (minimum score 550 paper-based; 213 computer-based). *Application deadline:* For fall admission, 7/1 priority date for domestic and international students; for spring admission, 12/1 priority date for domestic and international students. Applications are processed on a rolling basis. Application fee: $35 ($40 for international students). Electronic applications accepted. *Expenses:* Tuition, state resident: full-time $5522; part-time $306.80 per credit hour. Tuition, nonresident: full-time $14,253; part-time $792.10 per credit hour. Required fees: $658; $49 per credit hour. One-time fee: $12. Tuition and fees vary according to program. *Financial support:* Career-related internships or fieldwork, Federal Work-Study, and institutionally sponsored loans available. Support available to part-time students. Financial award application deadline: 4/1; financial award applicants required to submit FAFSA. *Faculty research:* International information systems, telecommunications, systems development, information systems sourcing. *Unit head:* Karl Kottemann, Assistant Director, 314-516-5885, Fax: 314-516-6420, E-mail: mba@umsl.edu. *Application contact:* 314-516-5458, Fax: 314-516-6996, E-mail: gradadm@umsl.edu.

University of Rhode Island, Graduate School, College of Business Administration, Kingston, RI 02881. Offers accounting (MS); business administration (MBA, PhD), including finance and insurance (PhD), management (PhD), marketing (PhD), operations and supply chain management (MBA); finance (MBA); general business (MBA); management (MBA); marketing (MBA); supply chain management (MBA). *Accreditation:* AACSB. Part-time and evening/weekend programs available. *Faculty:* 54 full-time (15 women), 3 part-time/adjunct (2 women). *Students:* 82 full-time (31 women), 218 part-time (77 women); includes 31 minority (6 Black or African American, non-Hispanic/Latino; 1 American Indian or Alaska Native, non-Hispanic/Latino; 13 Asian, non-Hispanic/Latino; 11 Hispanic/Latino), 29 international. In 2010, 78 master's, 3 doctorates awarded. *Degree requirements:* For master's, comprehensive exam (for some programs), thesis optional; for doctorate, comprehensive exam, thesis/dissertation. *Entrance requirements:* For master's, GMAT or GRE, 2 letters of recommendation, resume; for doctorate, GMAT or GRE, 3 letters of recommendation, resume. Additional exam requirements/recommendations for international students: Required—TOEFL (minimum score 575 paper-based; 233 computer-based; 91 iBT). Application fee: $65. Electronic applications accepted. *Expenses:* Tuition, state resident: full-time $9588; part-time $533 per credit hour. Tuition, nonresident: full-time $22,968; part-time $1276 per credit hour. Required fees: $1282; $68 per semester. Tuition and fees vary according to program. *Financial support:* In 2010–11, 13 teaching assistantships with full and partial tuition reimbursements (averaging $12,432 per year) were awarded. Financial award applicants required to submit FAFSA. Total annual research expenditures: $9,928. *Unit head:* Dr. Mark Higgins, Dean, 401-874-4244, Fax: 401-874-4312, E-mail: mark higgins@uri.edu. *Application contact:* Lisa Lancellotta, Coordinator, MBA Programs, 401-874-4241, Fax: 401-874-4312, E-mail: mba@uri.edu.

University of San Diego, School of Business Administration, Program in Supply Chain Management, San Diego, CA 92110-2492. Offers MS, Certificate. Postbaccalaureate distance learning degree programs offered (minimal on-campus study). *Students:* 16 full-time (6 women), 57 part-time (19 women); includes 3 Black or African American, non-Hispanic/Latino; 2 Asian, non-Hispanic/Latino; 3 Hispanic/Latino; 1 Two or more races, non-Hispanic/Latino, 3 international. Average age 36. In 2010, 19 master's, 28 other advanced degrees awarded. *Degree requirements:* For master's,

capstone course. *Entrance requirements:* Additional exam requirements/recommendations for international students: Required—TOEFL (minimum score 580 paper-based; 237 computer-based; 92 iBT), TWE. Application fee: $80. *Expenses:* Tuition: Full-time $21,744; part-time $1208 per unit. Required fees: $224. Full-time tuition and fees vary according to course load and degree level. *Financial support:* In 2010–11, 11 students received support. Scholarships/grants available. Financial award application deadline: 4/1; financial award applicants required to submit FAFSA. *Unit head:* Lauren Lukens, Director, MS Program, 619-260-7901, E-mail: msscm@sandiego.edu. *Application contact:* Stephen Pultz, Director of Admissions and Enrollment, 619-260-4506, Fax: 619-260-6836, E-mail: admissions@sandiego.edu.

University of Southern California, Graduate School, Viterbi School of Engineering, Daniel J. Epstein Department of Industrial and Systems Engineering, Los Angeles, CA 90089. Offers digital supply chain management (MS); engineering management (MS); engineering technology communication (Graduate Certificate); health systems operations (Graduate Certificate); industrial and systems engineering (MS, PhD, Engr); manufacturing engineering (MS); operations research engineering (MS); optimization and supply chain management (Graduate Certificate); product development engineering (MS); safety systems and security (MS); systems architecting and engineering (MS, Graduate Certificate); systems safety and security (Graduate Certificate); transportation systems (Graduate Certificate); MS/MBA. Part-time and evening/weekend programs available. Postbaccalaureate distance learning degree programs offered (no on-campus study). *Faculty:* 12 full-time (2 women), 21 part-time/adjunct (2 women). *Students:* 224 full-time (69 women), 143 part-time (32 women); includes 63 minority (6 Black or African American, non-Hispanic/Latino; 35 Asian, non-Hispanic/Latino; 17 Hispanic/Latino; 5 Two or more races, non-Hispanic/Latino), 253 international. 669 applicants, 45% accepted, 155 enrolled. In 2010, 98 master's, 7 doctorates awarded. Terminal master's awarded for partial completion of doctoral program. *Degree requirements:* For master's, thesis optional; for doctorate, thesis/dissertation. *Entrance requirements:* For master's and doctorate, GRE General Test. *Application deadline:* For fall admission, 12/1 priority date for domestic students, 11/1 priority date for international students; for spring admission, 9/15 priority date for domestic and international students. Applications are processed on a rolling basis. Application fee: $85. Electronic applications accepted. *Expenses:* Tuition: Full-time $31,240; part-time $1420 per unit. Required fees: $600. One-time fee: $35 full-time. Full-time tuition and fees vary according to degree level and program. *Financial support:* In 2010–11, fellowships with full tuition reimbursements (averaging $30,000 per year), research assistantships with full tuition reimbursements (averaging $20,000 per year), teaching assistantships with full tuition reimbursements (averaging $20,000 per year) were awarded; career-related internships or fieldwork, scholarships/grants, health care benefits, and unspecified assistantships also available. Financial award application deadline: 12/1; financial award applicants required to submit CSS PROFILE or FAFSA. *Faculty research:* Health systems, music cognition and retrieval, transportation and logistics, manufacturing and automation, engineering systems design, risk and economic analysis. Total annual research expenditures: $1 million. *Unit head:* Dr. F. Stan Settles, Chair, 213-740-4893, E-mail: isedept@usc.edu. *Application contact:* Evelyn Felina, Director of Student Affairs, 213-740-7549, E-mail: efelina@usc.edu.

The University of Texas at Dallas, School of Management, Program in Supply Chain Management, Richardson, TX 75080. Offers MS. Part-time and evening/weekend programs available. *Faculty:* 11 full-time (1 woman), 2 part-time/adjunct (1 woman). *Students:* 72 full-time (34 women), 21 part-time (10 women); includes 16 minority (1 Black or African American, non-Hispanic/Latino; 11 Asian, non-Hispanic/Latino; 4 Hispanic/Latino), 64 international. Average age 27. 142 applicants, 70% accepted, 49 enrolled. In 2010, 19 master's awarded. *Degree requirements:* For master's, thesis optional. *Entrance requirements:* For master's, GMAT, minimum GPA of 3.0 in upper-level coursework in field. Additional exam requirements/recommendations for international students: Required—TOEFL (minimum score 550 paper-based; 215 computer-based). *Application deadline:* For fall admission, 7/15 for domestic students, 5/1 priority date for international students; for spring admission, 11/15 for domestic students, 9/1 priority date for international students. Applications are processed on a rolling basis. Application fee: $50 ($100 for international students). Electronic applications accepted. *Expenses:* Tuition, state resident: full-time $10,248; part-time $569 per credit hour. Tuition, nonresident: full-time $18,544; part-time $1030 per credit hour. Tuition and fees vary according to course load. *Financial support:* In 2010–11, 37 students received support; research assistantships with partial tuition reimbursements available, teaching assistantships with partial tuition reimbursements available, career-related internships or fieldwork, Federal Work-Study, institutionally sponsored loans, scholarships/grants, and unspecified assistantships available. Support available to part-time students. Financial award application deadline: 4/30; financial award applicants required to submit FAFSA. *Faculty research:* Inventory control and risk management. *Unit head:* Shawn Alborz, Director, 972-883-6455, E-mail: salborz@utdallas.edu. *Application contact:* David B. Ritchey, Director of Advising, 972-883-2750, Fax: 972-883-6425, E-mail: davidr@utdallas.edu.

The University of Toledo, College of Graduate Studies, College of Business and Innovation, Department of Information Operations and Technology Management, Toledo, OH 43606-3390. Offers information systems (MBA); manufacturing management (DME); operations management (MBA); supply chain management (Certificate). Part-time and evening/weekend programs available. *Faculty:* 12. *Students:* 36 full-time (8 women), 20 part-time (6 women); includes 4 Black or African American, non-Hispanic/Latino; 3 Asian, non-Hispanic/Latino, 23 international. Average age 32. 41 applicants, 51% accepted, 10 enrolled. In 2010, 16 master's, 4 doctorates awarded. *Degree requirements:* For doctorate, thesis/dissertation. *Entrance requirements:* For master's, doctorate, and Certificate, GMAT, 2.7 GPA on all prior academic work. Three letters of recommendation, a statement of purpose, transcripts from all prior institutions attended. Additional exam requirements/recommendations for international students: Required—TOEFL (minimum score 550 paper-based; 213 computer-based; 80 iBT), IELTS (minimum score 6.5). *Application deadline:* For fall admission, 1/15 priority date for domestic and international students. Applications are processed on a rolling basis. Application fee: $45 ($75 for international students). Electronic applications accepted. *Expenses:* Tuition, state resident: full-time $11,426; part-time $476 per credit hour. Tuition, nonresident: full-time $21,660; part-time $903 per credit hour. One-time fee: $62. *Financial support:* Research assistantships with tuition reimbursements, career-related internships or fieldwork, Federal Work-Study, institutionally sponsored loans, scholarships/grants, tuition waivers (full and partial), unspecified assistantships, and administrative assistantships available. Support available to part-time students. *Unit head:* Dr. T. S. Ragu-Nathan, Chair, 419-530-2427. *Application contact:* Graduate School Office, 419-530-4723, Fax: 419-530-4724, E-mail: grdsch@utnet.utoledo.edu.

University of Wisconsin–Madison, Graduate School, Wisconsin School of Business, Wisconsin Full-Time MBA Program, Madison, WI 53706-1380. Offers applied security analysis (MBA); arts administration (MBA); brand and product management (MBA); corporate finance and investment banking (MBA); entrepreneurial management (MBA); marketing research (MBA); operations and technology management (MBA); real estate (MBA); risk management and insurance (MBA); strategic human resource management (MBA); strategic management in the life and engineering sciences (MBA); supply chain management (MBA). *Faculty:* 32 full-time (4 women), 17 part-time/adjunct (3 women). *Students:* 242 full-time (74 women); includes 16 Black or African American, non-Hispanic/Latino; 3 American Indian or Alaska Native, non-Hispanic/Latino; 16 Asian, non-Hispanic/Latino; 12 Hispanic/Latino, 29 international. Average age 28. 526 applicants, 32% accepted, 117 enrolled. In 2010, 106 master's awarded. *Entrance requirements:* For master's, GMAT, bachelor's or equivalent degree, 2 years of work experience, letters of recommendation. Additional exam requirements/recommendations for international students: Required—TOEFL (minimum score 600 paper-based; 250 computer-based; 100 iBT), IELTS. *Application deadline:* For fall admission, 11/4 for domestic students, 11/1 for international students; for winter admission, 2/5 for domestic and international students; for spring admission, 5/15 for domestic students, 4/5 for international students. Applications are processed on a rolling basis. Application fee: $56. Electronic applications accepted. *Expenses:* Tuition, state resident: full-time $9887; part-time $617.96 per credit. Tuition, nonresident: full-time $24,054; part-time $1503.40 per credit. Required fees: $67.63 per credit. Tuition and fees vary according to reciprocity agreements. *Financial support:* In 2010–11, 103 students received support, including 13 fellowships with full and partial tuition reimbursements available (averaging $15,000 per year), 53 research assistantships with full tuition reimbursements available (averaging $8,000 per year), 35 teaching assistantships with full tuition reimbursements available (averaging $11,000 per year); scholarships/grants, health care benefits, and unspecified assistantships also available. Financial award application deadline: 4/5; financial award applicants required to submit FAFSA. *Faculty research:* Market consequences of International Financial Reporting Standards (IFRS), inter-firm relationships and strategic partnerships, application of Bayesian statistical methods and applied probability models to understanding individuals' behaviors in the context of customer relationship management (CRM) applications, liquidity provision and the structure of financial markets, strategic management of global startups. *Unit head:* Dr. Kenneth A. Kavajecz, Associate Dean of Master's Programs, 608-265-3494, Fax: 608-265-4192, E-mail: kkavajecz@bus.wisc.edu. *Application contact:* Maria Reis, Assistant Director of MBA Marketing and Recruiting, 608-262-4000, Fax: 608-265-4192, E-mail: mreis@bus.wisc.edu.

Walden University, Graduate Programs, School of Management, Minneapolis, MN 55401. Offers accounting (MS), including cpa emphasis, professional track, self-designed; accounting and management (MS), including self-designed, strategic management; applied management and decision sciences (PhD), including accounting, engineering management, finance, general applied management and decision sciences, information systems management, knowledge management, leadership and organizational change, learning management, operations research, self-designed program in applied management and design sciences; business information management (MISM); enterprise information security (MISM); entrepreneurship (MBA, DBA); finance (MBA, DBA); global management (MS); global supply chain management (DBA); health informatics (MISM); healthcare management (MBA, MS); healthcare system improvement (MBA); human resource management (MBA, MS), including functional human resource management (MS), human resource management (MS), integrating functional and strategic human resource management (MS), organizational strategy (MS); information systems (MS); information systems management (DBA); information technology (MS), including information security, software engineering; international business (MBA, DBA); IT strategy and governance (MISM); leadership (MBA, MS, DBA), including entrepreneurship (MS), general management (MS), human resources leadership (MS), innovation and technology (MS), leader development (MS), leading sustainability (MS), project management (MS), self-designed (MS); managers as leaders (MS); managing global software and service supply chains (MISM); marketing (MBA, DBA); project management (MBA, MS); research strategies (MS); risk management (MBA); self-designed (MBA, DBA); social impact management (DBA); strategy and operations (MS); sustainable futures (MBA); sustainable management (MS); technology (MBA); technology entrepreneurship (DBA); technology management (MS). Part-time and evening/weekend programs available. Postbaccalaureate distance learning degree programs offered (minimal on-campus study). *Faculty:* 22 full-time (8 women), 291 part-time/adjunct (100 women). *Students:* 3,705 full-time (1,956 women), 976 part-time (549 women); includes 2,432 minority (2,021 Black or African American, non-Hispanic/Latino; 32 American Indian or Alaska Native, non-Hispanic/Latino; 137 Asian, non-Hispanic/Latino; 193 Hispanic/Latino; 5 Native Hawaiian or other Pacific Islander, non-Hispanic/Latino; 44 Two or more races, non-Hispanic/Latino), 302 international. Average age 40. In 2010, 658 master's, 86 doctorates awarded. *Degree requirements:* For doctorate, thesis/dissertation (for some programs), residency. *Entrance requirements:* For master's, bachelor's degree or equivalent in related field; minimum GPA of 2.5; official transcripts; goal statement; access to computer and Internet; for doctorate, master's degree or equivalent in related field; minimum GPA of 3.0; 3 years of related professional/academic experience (preferred). Additional exam requirements/recommendations for international students: Required—TOEFL (minimum score 550 paper-based; 213 computer-based), IELTS (minimum score 6.5), Michigan English Language Assessment Battery (minimum score 82). *Application deadline:* Applications are processed on a rolling basis. Application fee: $50. Electronic applications accepted. *Expenses:* Tuition: Full-time $10,274; part-time $445 per credit. Tuition and fees vary according to course load, degree level and program. *Financial support:* Fellowships, Federal Work-Study, scholarships/grants, unspecified assistantships, and family tuition reduction, active duty/veteran tuition reduction, group tuition reduction, interest-free payment plans available. Support available to part-time students. Financial award applicants required to submit FAFSA. *Unit head:* Dr. William Schulz, Associate Dean, 800-925-3368. *Application contact:* Jennifer Hall, Vice President of Enrollment Management, 866-4-WALDEN, E-mail: info@waldenu.edu.

Washington University in St. Louis, Olin Business School, Program in Supply Chain Management, St. Louis, MO 63130-4899. Offers MS. Part-time programs available. *Faculty:* 79 full-time (17 women), 42 part-time/adjunct (7 women). *Students:* 15 full-time (7 women), 3 part-time (2 women); includes 1 minority (Black or African American, non-Hispanic/Latino), 14 international. Average age 26. 72 applicants, 51% accepted, 15 enrolled. In 2010, 5 master's awarded. *Entrance requirements:* For master's, GMAT or GRE. Additional exam requirements/recommendations for international students: Required—TOEFL. *Application deadline:* For fall admission, 11/1 for domestic and international students; for winter admission, 1/31 for domestic and international students; for spring admission, 2/28 for domestic students. Application fee: $100. Electronic applications accepted. *Financial support:* Applicants required to submit FAFSA. *Unit head:* Joseph Peter Fox, Associate Dean and Director of MBA Programs, 314-935-6322, Fax: 314-935-4464, E-mail: fox@wustl.edu. *Application contact:* Dr. Gary Hochberg, Director, Specialized Master's Programs, 314-935-6380, Fax: 314-935-4464, E-mail: hochberg@wustl.edu.

Wilfrid Laurier University, Faculty of Graduate and Postdoctoral Studies, School of Business and Economics, Department of Business, Waterloo, ON N2L 3C5, Canada. Offers accounting (PhD); finance (M Fin); financial economics (PhD); marketing (PhD); operations and supply chain management (PhD); organizational behavior and human resource management (M Sc); organizational behaviour and human resource management (PhD); supply chain management (M Sc); technology management (EMTM). Part-time and evening/weekend programs available. *Faculty:* 67 full-time (20 women), 12 part-time/adjunct (4 women). *Students:* 20 full-time (11 women), 1 part-time (0 women), 5 international. 80 applicants, 28% accepted, 3 enrolled. In 2010, 6 master's, 1 doctorate awarded. *Degree requirements:* For master's, thesis optional; for doctorate, comprehensive exam, thesis/dissertation. *Entrance requirements:* For master's, GMAT, 4-year honors degree with minimum B+ average; for doctorate, GMAT, master's degree, minimum B+ average. Additional exam requirements/recommendations for international students: Required—TOEFL (minimum score 89 iBT). *Application deadline:* For fall admission, 1/15 priority date for domestic and international students. Application fee: $125. Electronic applications accepted. Tuition and fees charges are reported in Canadian dollars. *Expenses:* Tuition, area resident: Full-time $15,300 Canadian dollars; part-time $1200 Canadian dollars per credit. International tuition: $21,300 Canadian dollars full-time. Required fees: $650 Canadian dollars; $100 Canadian dollars per credit. Tuition and fees vary according to course load, degree level, campus/location and program. *Financial support:* In 2010–11, 27 fellowships, 1 research assistantship, 27 teaching assistantships were awarded; career-related internships or fieldwork, scholarships/grants, health care benefits, and unspecified assistantships also available. *Faculty research:* Financial economics, management and organizational behavior, operations and supply chain management. *Unit head:* Dr. Hamid Noori, Director, 519-884-0710 Ext. 2571, Fax: 519-884-2357, E-mail: sbephdmasters@wlu.ca. *Application contact:* Jennifer Williams, Graduate Admission and Records Officer, 519-884-0710 Ext. 3536, Fax: 519-884-1020, E-mail: gradstudies@wlu.ca.

TRANSPORTATION MANAGEMENT

American Public University System, AMU/APU Graduate Programs, Charles Town, WV 25414. Offers accounting (MBA); administration and supervision (M Ed); air warfare (MA Military Studies); asymmetrical warfare (MA Military Studies); criminal justice (MA); emergency and disaster management (MA); entrepreneurship (MBA); environmental policy and management (MS); finance (MBA); general (MBA); global business management (MBA); guidance and counseling (M Ed); history (MA); homeland security (MA); homeland security resource allocation (MBA); humanities (MA); information technology (MS); information technology management (MBA); intelligence studies (MA); international relations and conflict resolution (MA); joint warfare (MA Military Studies); land warfare (MA Military Studies); legal studies (MA); management (MA), including defense mangement, general, human resource management, organizational leadership, public administration; marketing (MBA); military history (MA); national security studies (MA); naval warfare (MA Military Studies); nonprofit management (MBA); political science (MA); psychology (MA); public administration (MA); public health (MA); security management (MA); space studies (MS); sports management (MS); strategic leadership (MA Military Studies); teaching (M Ed), including elementary, secondary social sciences; transportation and logistics management (MA). Programs offered via distance learning only. Part-time and evening/weekend programs available. Postbaccalaureate distance learning degree programs offered (no on-campus study). *Faculty:* 253 full-time (134 women), 1,208 part-time/adjunct (570 women). *Students:* 956 full-time (422 women), 8,476 part-time (2,821 women); includes 2,511 minority (1,218 Black or African American, non-Hispanic/Latino; 68 American Indian or Alaska Native, non-Hispanic/Latino; 219 Asian, non-Hispanic/Latino; 705 Hispanic/Latino; 46 Native Hawaiian or other Pacific Islander, non-Hispanic/Latino; 255 Two or more races, non-Hispanic/Latino), 107 international. Average age 35. 9,550 applicants, 100% accepted. In 2010, 1,688 master's awarded. *Degree requirements:* For master's, comprehensive exam or practicum. *Entrance requirements:* For master's, official transcript showing earned bachelor's degree from institution accredited by recognized accrediting body. Additional exam requirements/recommendations for international students: Required—TOEFL (minimum score 550 paper-based; 213 computer-based), IELTS (minimum score 6.5). *Application deadline:* Applications are processed on a rolling basis. Application fee: $0. Electronic applications accepted. *Financial support:* Applicants required to submit FAFSA. *Faculty research:* Military history, criminal justice, management performance, national security. *Unit head:* Dr. Frank McCluskey, Provost, 877-468-6268, Fax: 304-724-3780. *Application contact:* Terry Grant, Director of Enrollment Management, 877-468-6268, Fax: 304-724-3780, E-mail: info@apus.edu.

Florida Institute of Technology, Graduate Programs, Extended Studies Division, Melbourne, FL 32901-6975. Offers acquisition and contract management (MS); aerospace engineering (MS); business administration (MBA); computer information systems (MS); computer science (MS); electrical engineering (MS); engineering management (MS); human resources management (MS); logistics management (MS), including humanitarian and disaster relief logistics; management (MS), including acquisition and contract management, e-business, human resources management, information systems, logistics management, management, transportation management; material acquisition management (MS); mechanical engineering (MS); operations research (MS); project management (MS), including information systems, operations research; public administration (MPA); quality management (MS); software engineering (MS); space systems (MS); space systems management (MS); systems management (MS), including information systems, operations research. Part-time and evening/weekend programs available. Postbaccalaureate distance learning degree programs offered (no on-campus study). *Faculty:* 11 full-time (3 women), 118 part-time/adjunct (24 women). *Students:* 69 full-time (23 women), 907 part-time (369 women); includes 385 minority (242 Black or African American, non-Hispanic/Latino; 15 American Indian or Alaska Native, non-Hispanic/Latino; 44 Asian, non-Hispanic/Latino; 52 Hispanic/Latino; 3 Native Hawaiian or other Pacific Islander, non-Hispanic/Latino; 29 Two or more races, non-Hispanic/Latino), 17 international. 517 applicants, 49% accepted, 245 enrolled. In 2010, 430 degrees awarded. *Degree requirements:* For master's, comprehensive exam (for some programs), capstone course. *Entrance requirements:* For master's, GMAT or resume showing 8 years of supervised experience, minimum GPA of 3.0, 2 letters of recommendation, resume. Additional exam requirements/recommendations for international students: Required—TOEFL (minimum score 550 paper-based; 213 computer-based; 79 iBT). *Application deadline:* For fall admission, 4/1

for international students; for spring admission, 9/30 for international students. Applications are processed on a rolling basis. Application fee: $50. Electronic applications accepted. *Expenses:* Contact institution. *Financial support:* Application deadline: 3/1. *Unit head:* Dr. Theodore Richardson, Senior Associate Dean, 321-674-8123, Fax: 321-674-7597, E-mail: trichardson@fit.edu. *Application contact:* Carolyn Farrior, Director of Graduate Admissions, Online Learning and Off-Campus Programs, 321-674-7118, Fax: 321-674-8216, E-mail: cfarrior@fit.edu.

George Mason University, School of Public Policy, Program in Transportation Policy, Operations and Logistics, Arlington, VA 22201. Offers MA. Part-time programs available. Postbaccalaureate distance learning degree programs offered (no on-campus study). *Faculty:* 66 full-time (24 women), 15 part-time/adjunct (3 women). *Students:* 10 full-time (1 woman), 32 part-time (7 women); includes 2 Black or African American, non-Hispanic/Latino; 1 Two or more races, non-Hispanic/Latino, 3 international. Average age 33. 29 applicants, 45% accepted, 6 enrolled. In 2010, 19 master's awarded. *Degree requirements:* For master's, thesis or alternative. *Entrance requirements:* For master's, GRE (for students seeking merit-based scholarships), minimum undergraduate GPA of 3.0, resume, 2 letters of recommendation. Additional exam requirements/recommendations for international students: Required—TOEFL (minimum score 570 paper-based; 230 computer-based; 88 iBT). *Application deadline:* For fall admission, 6/1 priority date for domestic students, 5/1 priority date for international students; for spring admission, 12/1 priority date for domestic students, 11/1 priority date for international students. Applications are processed on a rolling basis. Application fee: $100. Electronic applications accepted. *Expenses:* Contact institution. *Financial support:* In 2010–11, 1 research assistantship (averaging $16,150 per year) was awarded; career-related internships or fieldwork, Federal Work-Study, scholarships/grants, unspecified assistantships, and health care benefits (full-time research or teaching assistantship recipients) also available. Financial award application deadline: 3/1; financial award applicants required to submit FAFSA. *Unit head:* Dr. Jonathan Gifford, Director, 703-993-8099, E-mail: spp@gmu.edu. *Application contact:* Tennille Haegele, Director, Graduate Admissions, 703-993-3183, Fax: 703-993-4876, E-mail: thaegele@gmu.edu.

Iowa State University of Science and Technology, Graduate College, College of Design, Department of Community and Regional Planning, Ames, IA 50011. Offers community and regional planning (MCRP); transportation (MS); M Arch/MCRP; MBA/MCRP; MCRP/MLA; MCRP/MPA. *Accreditation:* ACSP (one or more programs are accredited). Part-time programs available. *Faculty:* 11 full-time (4 women), 1 part-time/adjunct (0 women). *Students:* 26 full-time (14 women), 26 part-time (9 women); includes 3 Black or African American, non-Hispanic/Latino; 1 Hispanic/Latino, 6 international. Average age 31. 44 applicants, 55% accepted, 16 enrolled. In 2010, 10 master's awarded. *Degree requirements:* For master's, thesis or alternative. *Entrance requirements:* For master's, GRE General Test. Additional exam requirements/recommendations for international students: Required—TOEFL (minimum score 550 paper-based; 79 iBT), IELTS (minimum score 6.5). *Application deadline:* For fall admission, 1/1 priority date for domestic and international students. Applications are processed on a rolling basis. Application fee: $40 ($90 for international students). Electronic applications accepted. *Financial support:* In 2010–11, 3 research assistantships with full and partial tuition reimbursements (averaging $13,788 per year), 13 teaching assistantships with full and partial tuition reimbursements (averaging $3,886 per year) were awarded; career-related internships or fieldwork, institutionally sponsored loans, tuition waivers (partial), and unspecified assistantships also available. Support available to part-time students. Financial award application deadline: 2/1; financial award applicants required to submit FAFSA. *Faculty research:* Economic development, housing, land use, geographic information systems planning in developing nations, regional and community revitalization, transportation planning in developing countries. *Unit head:* Dr. Douglas Johnston, Chair, 515-294-8958, Fax: 515-294-2348, E-mail: landarch@iastate.edu. *Application contact:* Dr. Francis Owusu, Director of Graduate Education, 515-294-7769, E-mail: crp@iastate.edu.

Iowa State University of Science and Technology, Graduate College, Interdisciplinary Programs, Program in Transportation, Ames, IA 50011. Offers MS. *Students:* 2 full-time (1 woman), 5 part-time (1 woman); includes 1 Black or African American, non-Hispanic/Latino, 1 international. In 2010, 2 master's awarded. *Degree requirements:* For master's, thesis. *Entrance requirements:* For master's, GMAT or GRE General Test. Additional exam requirements/recommendations for international students: Required—TOEFL (minimum score 550 paper-based; 82 iBT), IELTS (minimum score 6.5). *Application deadline:* For fall admission, 7/15 priority date for domestic students, 2/15 priority date for international students. Application fee: $40 ($90 for international students). Electronic applications accepted. *Financial support:* Research assistantships with full and partial tuition reimbursements, teaching assistantships, scholarships/grants, health care benefits, and unspecified assistantships available. *Unit head:* Dr. Nadia Gkritza, Supervisory Committee Chair, 515-294-2343, Fax: 515-294-0467. *Application contact:* Information Contact, 515-294-5836, Fax: 515-294-2592, E-mail: grad_admissions@iastate.edu.

New Jersey Institute of Technology, Office of Graduate Studies, Newark College of Engineering, Interdisciplinary Program in Transportation, Newark, NJ 07102. Offers MS, PhD. Part-time and evening/weekend programs available. *Students:* 24 full-time (4 women), 14 part-time (4 women); includes 4 Black or African American, non-Hispanic/Latino; 8 Asian, non-Hispanic/Latino; 4 Hispanic/Latino, 11 international. Average age 32. 63 applicants, 40% accepted, 13 enrolled. In 2010, 6 master's, 2 doctorates awarded. Terminal master's awarded for partial completion of doctoral program. *Degree requirements:* For master's, thesis or alternative; for doctorate, thesis/dissertation, residency. *Entrance requirements:* For master's, GRE General Test; for doctorate, GRE General Test, minimum graduate GPA of 3.5. Additional exam requirements/recommendations for international students: Required—TOEFL (minimum score 550 paper-based; 213 computer-based; 79 iBT). *Application deadline:* For fall admission, 6/5 priority date for domestic students, 4/1 for international students; for spring admission, 11/15 for domestic and international students. Applications are processed on a rolling basis. Application fee: $65. Electronic applications accepted. *Expenses:* Tuition, state resident: full-time $14,724; part-time $818 per credit. Tuition, nonresident: full-time $20,304; part-time $1128 per credit. Required fees: $2272; $209 per credit. $103 per semester. One-time fee: $312 full-time; $212 part-time. *Financial support:* Fellowships with full and partial tuition reimbursements, research assistantships with full and partial tuition reimbursements, teaching assistantships with full and partial tuition reimbursements, career-related internships or fieldwork, Federal Work-Study, institutionally sponsored loans, and unspecified assistantships available. Financial award application deadline: 3/15. *Faculty research:* Transportation planning, administration, and policy; intelligent vehicle highway systems; bridge maintenance. *Unit head:* Dr. Athanassios Bladikas, Director, 973-596-3653, E-mail: athanassios.bladikas@njit.edu. *Application contact:* Kathryn Kelly, Director of Admissions, 973-596-3300, Fax: 973-596-3461, E-mail: admissions@njit.edu.

North Dakota State University, College of Graduate and Interdisciplinary Studies, College of Engineering and Architecture, Department of Civil Engineering, Fargo, ND 58108. Offers civil engineering (MS, PhD); environmental engineering (MS, PhD); transportation and logistics (PhD). PhD in transportation and logistics offered jointly with Upper Great Plains Transportation Institute. Part-time programs available. Postbaccalaureate distance learning degree programs offered (minimal on-campus study). *Students:* 28 full-time (2 women), 19 part-time (3 women); includes 1 American Indian or Alaska Native, non-Hispanic/Latino, 24 international. 37 applicants, 57% accepted, 12 enrolled. In 2010, 1 master's, 3 doctorates awarded. *Degree requirements:* For master's, thesis; for doctorate, comprehensive exam, thesis/dissertation. *Entrance requirements:* Additional exam requirements/recommendations for international students: Required—TOEFL (minimum score 525 paper-based; 197 computer-based; 71 iBT). *Application deadline:* For fall admission, 7/1 priority date for domestic students, 1/15 priority date for international students; for spring admission, 5/1 priority date for international students. Applications are processed on a rolling basis. Application fee: $45 ($60 for international students). *Financial support:* Fellowships with full tuition reimbursements, research assistantships with full tuition reimbursements, teaching assistantships with full tuition reimbursements, career-related internships or fieldwork, Federal Work-Study, and institutionally sponsored loans available. Support available to part-time students. Financial award application deadline: 1/15. *Faculty research:* Wastewater, solid waste, composites, nanotechnology. Total annual research expenditures: $800,000. *Unit head:* Dr. Eakalak Khan, Chair, 701-231-7244, Fax: 701-231-6185, E-mail: eakalak.khan@ndsu.edu. *Application contact:* Dr. Kalpana Katti, Professor and Graduate Program Coordinator, 701-231-9504, Fax: 701-231-6185, E-mail: kalpana.katti@ndsu.edu.

North Dakota State University, College of Graduate and Interdisciplinary Studies, Interdisciplinary Program in Transportation and Logistics, Fargo, ND 58108. Offers PhD. *Students:* 15 full-time (4 women), 7 part-time (0 women); includes 1 Black or African American, non-Hispanic/Latino, 9 international. 6 applicants, 67% accepted, 4 enrolled. In 2010, 2 doctorates awarded. *Entrance requirements:* For doctorate, 1 year of calculus, statistics and probability, minimum GPA of 3.0. Additional exam requirements/recommendations for international students: Required—TOEFL (minimum score 550 paper-based; 213 computer-based; 79 iBT). *Application deadline:* For fall admission, 5/1 priority date for domestic students. Applications are processed on a rolling basis. Application fee: $45 ($60 for international students). *Financial support:* Research assistantships with full tuition reimbursements available. *Faculty research:* Supply chain optimization, spatial analysis of transportation networks, advanced traffic analysis, transportation demand, railroad/intermodal freight. *Unit head:* Dr. Denver Tolliver, Director, 701-231-7190, Fax: 701-231-1945, E-mail: denver.tolliver@ndsu.nodak.edu. *Application contact:* Dr. Denver Tolliver, Director, 701-231-7190, Fax: 701-231-1945, E-mail: denver.tolliver@ndsu.nodak.edu.

Polytechnic Institute of NYU, Department of Civil Engineering, Major in Transportation Management, Brooklyn, NY 11201-2990. Offers MS. Part-time and evening/weekend programs available. *Students:* 3 full-time (2 women), 26 part-time (8 women); includes 9 Black or African American,

non-Hispanic/Latino; 1 American Indian or Alaska Native, non-Hispanic/Latino; 2 Asian, non-Hispanic/Latino, 2 international. Average age 39. 10 applicants, 90% accepted, 6 enrolled. In 2010, 4 master's awarded. *Degree requirements:* For master's, comprehensive exam (for some programs), thesis (for some programs). *Entrance requirements:* Additional exam requirements/recommendations for international students: Required—TOEFL (minimum score 550 paper-based; 213 computer-based; 80 iBT); Recommended—IELTS (minimum score 6.5). *Application deadline:* For fall admission, 7/31 priority date for domestic students, 4/30 priority date for international students; for spring admission, 12/31 priority date for domestic students, 10/30 priority date for international students. Applications are processed on a rolling basis. Application fee: $75. Electronic applications accepted. *Expenses:* Tuition: Full-time $21,492; part-time $1194 per credit. Required fees: $385 per semester. Tuition and fees vary according to course load. *Financial support:* Fellowships, research assistantships, teaching assistantships, institutionally sponsored loans, scholarships/grants, and unspecified assistantships available. Support available to part-time students. Financial award applicants required to submit FAFSA. *Unit head:* Dr. Lawrence Chiarelli, Head, 718-260-4040, Fax: 718-260-3433, E-mail: lchiarel@poly.edu. *Application contact:* JeanCarlo Bonilla, Director, Graduate Enrollment Management, 718-260-3182, Fax: 718-260-3624, E-mail: gradinfo@poly.edu.

Texas Southern University, School of Science and Technology, Program in Transportation, Planning and Management, Houston, TX 77004-4584. Offers MS. Part-time and evening/weekend programs available. *Faculty:* 4 full-time (2 women). *Students:* 36 full-time (15 women), 17 part-time (9 women); includes 24 Black or African American, non-Hispanic/Latino; 24 Asian, non-Hispanic/Latino; 2 Hispanic/Latino. Average age 31. 17 applicants, 88% accepted, 11 enrolled. In 2010, 9 master's awarded. *Degree requirements:* For master's, comprehensive exam, thesis optional. *Entrance requirements:* For master's, GRE General Test, minimum GPA of 2.5. Additional exam requirements/recommendations for international students: Required—TOEFL. *Application deadline:* For fall admission, 7/1 for domestic and international students; for spring admission, 11/1 for domestic and international students. Applications are processed on a rolling basis. Application fee: $50 ($75 for international students). Electronic applications accepted. *Expenses:* Tuition, state resident: full-time $1875; part-time $100 per credit hour. Tuition, nonresident: full-time $6641; part-time $343 per credit hour. Tuition and fees vary according to course level, course load and degree level. *Financial support:* In 2010–11, 21 research assistantships (averaging $5,677 per year), 6 teaching assistantships (averaging $4,449 per year) were awarded; fellowships with partial tuition reimbursements, career-related internships or fieldwork, scholarships/grants, and unspecified assistantships also available. Financial award application deadline: 5/1. *Faculty research:* Highway traffic operations, transportation and policy planning, air quality in transportation, transportation modeling. Total annual research expenditures: $500,000. *Unit head:* Dr. Yi Qi, Interim Chair, 713-313-6809, E-mail: qiy@tsu.edu. *Application contact:* Paula Eakins, Administrative Assistant, 713-313-1841, E-mail: eakins_pl@tsu.edu.

University of California, Santa Barbara, Graduate Division, College of Letters and Sciences, Division of Mathematics, Life, and Physical Sciences, Department of Geography, Santa Barbara, CA 93106-4060. Offers cognitive science (PhD); geography (MA, PhD); quantitative methods in the social sciences (PhD); transportation (PhD); MA/PhD. *Faculty:* 23 full-time (4 women), 11 part-time/adjunct (4 women). *Students:* 71 full-time (32 women); includes 2 Black or African American, non-Hispanic/Latino; 14 Asian, non-Hispanic/Latino; 6 Hispanic/Latino. Average age 31. 82 applicants, 33% accepted, 18 enrolled. In 2010, 3 master's, 13 doctorates awarded. Terminal master's awarded for partial completion of doctoral program. *Degree requirements:* For master's, comprehensive exam (for some programs), thesis or alternative; for doctorate, comprehensive exam, thesis/dissertation. *Entrance requirements:* For master's and doctorate, GRE (minimum verbal/quantitative score 1100). Additional exam requirements/recommendations for international students: Required—TOEFL (minimum score 550 paper-based; 80 iBT), IELTS (minimum score 7). *Application deadline:* For fall admission, 2/1 for domestic and international students. Application fee: $70 ($90 for international students). Electronic applications accepted. *Financial support:* In 2010–11, 61 students received support, including 49 fellowships with full and partial tuition reimbursements available (averaging $8,958 per year), 32 research assistantships with full and partial tuition reimbursements available (averaging $10,335 per year), 29 teaching assistantships with partial tuition reimbursements available (averaging $9,384 per year). Financial award applicants required to submit FAFSA. *Faculty research:* Earth system science, human environment relations, modeling, measurement and computation. *Unit head:* Dr. Dar Alexander Roberts, Professor/Chair, 805-880-2531, Fax: 805-893-2578, E-mail: dar@geog.ucsb.edu. *Application contact:* Jose Luis Saleta, Student Programs Manager, 805-456-2829, Fax: 805-893-2578, E-mail: saleta@geog.ucsb.edu.

Aeronautical University

DAYTONA BEACH, FLORIDA

COLLEGE OF BUSINESS

Master of Business Administration

Program of Study

The Embry-Riddle M.B.A. provides graduates with a world-class management education in an aviation/aerospace context. Professional managers who have earned their M.B.A. at Embry-Riddle Aeronautical University (ERAU) understand the imperatives of change, globalization, technological innovation, and increasingly sophisticated and demanding customers that mark the strategic and operational environments of today's airlines, airports, and aerospace firms.

The Master of Business Administration (M.B.A.) degree program is designed to develop managers who can apply the concepts of modern management techniques to the challenges of the aviation/aerospace industry. The M.B.A. is offered as a full-time residential program on the Daytona Beach campus.

The M.B.A. curriculum combines a strong traditional business core with specializations in airport management, airline management, finance, aviation human resources, and aviation system management. The development of versatility and analytical resourcefulness are two of the key aims of the M.B.A. program. The program is fashioned to stress pragmatic solutions to the managerial, technical, and operational problems likely to arise in the aviation/aerospace industry as a result of the frequent and sweeping changes that occur in technology as well as in the domestic and international regulations with which the industry must abide. For those seeking a broader view of the global challenges airlines and airports face, the M.B.A. in Aviation Management is also offered on the Daytona Beach campus.

M.B.A. degree candidates must complete a minimum of 33 credit hours of course work consisting of 21 hours of core curriculum and 12 hours of specified electives. The M.B.A. program can usually be completed in sixteen to twenty-four months based on how the student progresses through the curriculum.

Research Facilities

A cluster of servers (UNIX and IBM) and PCs supported by a telecommunications network provide the faculty and students with the latest advances in information management and computing facilities. These are augmented by academic student labs, the Applied Aviation Simulation Lab, and the Total Airspace and Airport Modeler (TAMM) Research Lab. Extensive modern computer facilities and Internet access are available to all students.

Financial Aid

Scholarships are awarded to outstanding graduate students during the admissions process. Assistantships are also available on a limited basis. Students may apply for financial aid by calling 800-943-6279 (toll-free). All graduate programs are approved for U.S. Veterans Administration education benefits.

Cost of Study

In 2011–12, tuition costs for the residential M.B.A. program were $1190 per credit hour. The estimated cost of books and supplies was $1200 per semester.

Living and Housing Costs

On-campus housing is available on a limited basis to graduate students on the Daytona Beach campus. Single students who share rent and utility expenses can expect off-campus room and board expenses of $4000 per semester.

Student Group

ERAU's graduate programs on the Daytona Beach campus currently enroll approximately 600 students. The students in the programs on the Daytona Beach campus possess various cultural origins—many are from other countries, 25 percent are women, and 23 percent are members of U.S. minority groups. The M.B.A. program attracts students with diverse academic backgrounds and common scholastic abilities that enrich the program. The majority of incoming students have business degrees, although all degrees are welcomed with many engineers and air science students currently enrolled. The average age of incoming students is 28.

The recently opened College of Business building on the Daytona Beach campus, part of a major infrastructure program bringing new academic and student facilities across the campus.

Student Outcomes

In addition to contacts gained from internships with leading airlines, airports, and aerospace firms, the M.B.A. degree program conducts placement activities for its graduates. Years of research and consulting have allowed the faculty to cultivate contacts within the aviation industry, and its network provides job opportunities for graduates. The Career Services Office sponsors an annual industry Career Expo, which attracts more than 100 major companies such as Boeing, Federal Express, Delta, and United Airlines. In addition, the Career Resource Center offers corporate profiles, job postings, and development information. The office also assists with resume development and interview preparation.

Location

The Daytona Beach, Florida, campus is located next to the Daytona Beach International Airport and 10 minutes from the Daytona beaches. Within an hour's drive of Orlando and destinations such as Disney World, EPCOT, Universal Studios, SeaWorld, Kennedy Space Center, and St. Augustine.

The University

Since its founding in 1926, Embry-Riddle Aeronautical University has built a reputation for high-quality education within the field of aviation and has become a world leader in aerospace higher education. The University is comprised of the eastern campus in Daytona Beach, Florida; the western campus in Prescott, Arizona; and the WorldWide Campus, with off-campus programs.

Applying

A desired minimum bachelor degree cumulative GPA of 3.0 (4.0 scale) and a minimum score of 500 on the GMAT are the requirements for full admission consideration for the M.B.A. program. GRE scores may be submitted in lieu of the GMAT. Applications not meeting these qualifications may be considered for conditional admission with enhanced student oversight as an applicant matriculates into the program. Applications are accepted on a rolling basis and should be completed sixty days prior to the start of a semester for U.S. citizens, resident aliens, and international students. For international applicants the required minimum IELTS score is 6.0, or a TOEFL score of 550 or 79 on the TOFEL-IBT.

Correspondence and Information

Office of International and Graduate Admissions
Embry-Riddle Aeronautical University
600 South Clyde Morris Boulevard
Daytona Beach, Florida 32114-3900
United States
Phone: 386-226-6176 (outside the United States)
**   800-388-3728 (toll-free within the United States)**
Fax: 386-226-7070
E-mail: graduate.admissions@erau.edu
Web site: http://www.embryriddle.edu/graduate

The Faculty

The College of Business faculty takes pride in bringing relevant, real-world problems, issues, and experiences into the classrooms. Faculty members give a high priority to preparing students for the leadership roles they will eventually assume. The faculty members accomplish this not only by excellence in teaching but also by advising students on their business research and consulting projects. Many members of the faculty serve as consultants to a variety of industries, and their diverse backgrounds provide a rich, multicultural teaching field, with an emphasis on global standards and practices.

In addition, the Embry-Riddle faculty members are the go-to references for print and broadcast journalists on questions of aviation. When the question concerns aviation business, the savvy journalist calls the experts at the Embry-Riddle College of Business. For issues such as airline mergers, acquisitions, bankruptcies, or the general state of the aviation business, members of the COB faculty have provided information to scores of journalists for countless articles and broadcasts. Such is the reputation of the faculty of the College of Business.

For detailed information about the College of Business faculty members, visit http://daytonabeach.erau.edu/cob/departments/faculty/index.html

Students at work in the Applied Aviation Simulation Lab, which contains multiple servers to aid students in completing research projects for airlines and airports across the globe.

Appendixes

GMAT Practice Test

Index of Close-Ups and Displays

ANALYTICAL WRITING ASSESSMENT

Analysis of an Issue

1 QUESTION • 30 MINUTES

Directions: Using a word processor, compose a response to the following statement and directive. Do not use any spell-checking or grammar-checking functions.

"No business should sacrifice the quality of its products or services for the sake of maximizing profits."

Discuss the extent to which you agree or disagree with the foregoing statement. Support your perspective using reasons and/or examples from your experience, observation, reading, or academic studies.

Analysis of an Argument

1 QUESTION • 30 MINUTES

Directions: Using a word processor, compose an essay for the following argument and directive. Do not use any spell-checking or grammar-checking functions.

The following is excerpted from an editorial appearing in a local newspaper:

"In order to prevent a decline of Oak City's property values and in rents that Oak City property owners can command, the residents of Oak City must speak out against the approval of a new four-year private college in their town. After all, in the nearby town of Mapleton the average rent for apartments has decreased by ten percent since its new community college opened last year, while the average value of Mapleton's single-family homes has declined by an even greater percentage over the same time period."

Discuss how well reasoned you find this argument. In your discussion be sure to analyze the line of reasoning and the use of evidence in the argument. For example, you may need to consider what questionable assumptions underlie the thinking and what alternative explanations or counterexamples might weaken the conclusion. You can also discuss what sort of evidence would strengthen or refute the argument, what changes in the argument would make it more logically sound, and what, if anything, would help you better evaluate its conclusion.

QUANTITATIVE SECTION

37 QUESTIONS • 75 MINUTES

Directions for Problem Solving Questions: *(These directions will appear on your screen before your first Problem Solving question.)*

Solve this problem and indicate the best of the answer choices given.

Numbers: All numbers used are real numbers.

Figures: A figure accompanying a Problem Solving question is intended to provide information useful in solving the problem. Figures are drawn as accurately as possible EXCEPT when it is stated in a specific problem that its figure is not drawn to scale. Straight lines may sometimes appear jagged. All figures lie on a plane unless otherwise indicated.

To review these directions for subsequent questions of this type, click on HELP.

Directions for Data Sufficiency Questions: * *(These directions will appear on your screen before your first Data Sufficiency question.)*

This Data Sufficiency problem consists of a question and two statements, labeled (1) and (2), in which certain data are given. You have to decide whether the data given in the statements are *sufficient* for answering the question. Using the data given in the statements *plus* your knowledge of mathematics and everyday facts (such as the number of days in July or the meaning of *counterclockwise*), you must indicate whether:

- **(A)** Statement (1) ALONE is sufficient, but statement (2) alone is not sufficient to answer the question asked;

- **(B)** Statement (2) ALONE is sufficient, but statement (1) alone is not sufficient to answer the question asked;

- **(C)** BOTH statements (1) and (2) TOGETHER are sufficient to answer the question asked, but NEITHER statement ALONE is sufficient;

- **(D)** EACH statement ALONE is sufficient to answer the question asked;

- **(E)** Statements (1) and (2) TOGETHER are NOT sufficient to answer the question asked, and additional data specific to the problem are needed.

Numbers: All numbers used are real numbers.

Figures: A figure accompanying a Data Sufficiency problem will conform to the information given in the question, but will not necessarily conform to the additional information in statements (1) and (2).

Lines shown as straight can be assumed to be straight and lines that appear jagged can also be assumed to be straight.

You may assume that positions of points, angles, regions, etc., exist in the order shown and that angle measures are greater than zero.

All figures lie in a plane unless otherwise indicated.

Note: In Data Sufficiency problems that ask you for the value of a quantity, the data given in the statements are sufficient only when it is possible to determine exactly one numerical value for the quantity.

To review these directions for subsequent questions of this type, click on HELP.

---

*Editors' Note: In this Practice Test, the following are Data Sufficiency Questions: 3, 4, 5, 15, 17, 18, 20, 21, 24, 26, 27, 33, 34, and 35.

1. What is the sum of $\sqrt{0.49}$, $\frac{3}{4}$, and 80%?

   (A) 0.425
   (B) 1.59
   (C) 1.62
   (D) 2.04
   (E) 2.25

2. If the value of *XYZ* Company stock drops from $25 per share to $21 per share, what is the percent of decrease?

   (A) 4
   (B) 8
   (C) 12
   (D) 16
   (E) 20

3. How many buses are required to transport 175 students to the museum?

   (1) No two buses have the same carrying capacity.

   (2) The average capacity of a bus is 55 students.

4. The storage capacity of disk drive A is 85% that of disk drive B. What percentage of drive B's storage capacity is currently used?

   (1) Disk drive B holds 3 more gigabytes than disk drive A.

   (2) 8.5 gigabytes of disk drive B's storage capacity is currently used.

5. Eight square window panes of equal size are to be pieced together to form a rectangular French door. What is the perimeter of the door, excluding framing between and around the panes?

   (1) The area of each pane is 1 square foot.

   (2) The area of the door, excluding framing between and around the panes, is 8 square feet.

6. The denominator of a certain fraction is twice as great as the numerator. If 4 were added to both the numerator and denominator, the new fraction would be $\frac{5}{8}$. What is the denominator of the fraction?

   (A) 3
   (B) 6
   (C) 9
   (D) 12
   (E) 13

7. If $0.2t = 2.2 - 0.6s$ and $0.5s = 0.2t + 1.1$, then $s =$

   (A) 1
   (B) 3
   (C) 10
   (D) 11
   (E) 30

QUESTIONS 8-9 REFER TO THE FOLLOWING GRAPH:

AREA OF WAREHOUSE UNITS A, B, C, AND D (AS PORTIONS OF TOTAL WAREHOUSE AREA)

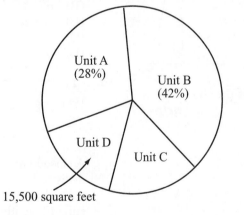

15,500 square feet

Total: 140,000 square feet

8. By approximately how many square feet does the size of Unit A exceed that of Unit C?

   (A) 9000
   (B) 11,000
   (C) 12,600
   (D) 15,500
   (E) 19,000

9. The combined area of Unit B and Unit D is approximately

   (A) 51,000 square feet.
   (B) 57,500 square feet.
   (C) 70,000 square feet.
   (D) 74,500 square feet.
   (E) 108,000 square feet.

10. Carrie's current age is 24 years greater than her son Benjamin's age. In 8 years, Carrie's age will be twice Benjamin's age at that time. What is Carrie's current age?

   (A) 32
   (B) 40
   (C) 48
   (D) 52
   (E) 66

11.

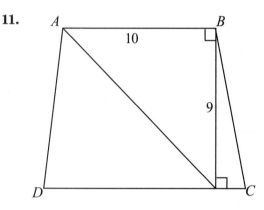

In the figure above, if the length of $\overline{DC}$ is 12, what is the area of $ABCD$?

   (A) 99
   (B) 108
   (C) 112
   (D) 120
   (E) $50\sqrt{3}$

12. $\dfrac{\sqrt[3]{81x^7}}{\sqrt{9x^4}} - \dfrac{\sqrt{162x^5}}{\sqrt[3]{27x^6}} =$

   (A) $3x^3 - \dfrac{1}{3}$

   (B) $\sqrt[3]{2x} - 3$

   (C) $\sqrt[3]{3x} - 3\sqrt{2x}$

   (D) $3x^2 - \sqrt{2}$

   (E) $9x - \sqrt{3}$

13. If the average (arithmetic mean) of the first sixteen positive integers is subtracted from the average (arithmetic mean) of the next sixteen positive integers, what is the result?

   (A) 0
   (B) 16
   (C) 32
   (D) 64
   (E) 128

14. If $a > b$, and if $c > d$, then

   (A) $a - b > c - d$
   (B) $a - c > b - d$
   (C) $c + d < a - b$
   (D) $a - c < b + d$
   (E) $b + d < a + c$

15.

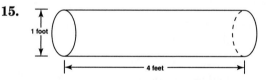

A closed cardboard box is to be designed for packing the cylindrical tube shown above. Will the entire tube fit inside the box?

   (1) The empty box contains 3 cubic feet.

   (2) The total surface area of the box is 14 square feet.

16. If x and y are negative integers, and if $x - y = 1$, what is the least possible value of xy?

(A) 0
(B) 1
(C) 2
(D) 3
(E) 4

17. A certain jar contains 20 jellybeans; each jellybean is either black, pink, or yellow. Does the jar contain more pink jellybeans than yellow jellybeans?

(1) The jar contains more black jellybeans than pink jellybeans.

(2) The jar contains 6 pink jellybeans.

18. Is the value of $a^2 - b^2$ greater than the value of $(3a + 3b)(2a - 2b)$?

(1) $b < a$

(2) $a < -1$

19. If $\blacktriangleleft x \blacktriangleright = (x + 2) - (x + 1) - (x - 1) - (x - 2)$, what is the value of $\blacktriangleleft -100 \blacktriangleright - \blacktriangleleft 100 \blacktriangleright$?

(A) -196
(B) -1
(C) 0
(D) 6
(E) 400

20.

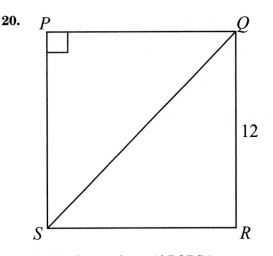

In the figure above, if $PQRS$ is a rectangle, and if the length of $\overline{QR}$ is 12, is $PQRS$ a square?

(1) The length of $\overline{SQ}$ is $12\sqrt{2}$.

(2) The length of $\overline{PS}$ is 12.

21. If a computer dealer bought a particular computer system for $10,000 and sold the computer system to a customer, how much did the customer pay for the computer system?

(1) The dealer's profit from the sale was 50%.

(2) The amount that the dealer paid for the computer system was two thirds the amount that the customer paid for the computer system.

22. Which of the following distribution of numbers has the greatest standard deviation?

(A) $\{-3, 1, 2\}$
(B) $\{-2, -1, 1, 2\}$
(C) $\{3, 5, 7\}$
(D) $\{-1, 2, 3, 4\}$
(E) $\{0, 2, 4\}$

23. Patrons at a certain restaurant can select two of three appetizers—fruit, soup, and salad—along with two of three vegetables—carrots, squash, and peas. What is the statistical probability that any patron will select fruit, salad, squash, and peas?

(A) $\dfrac{1}{12}$

(B) $\dfrac{1}{9}$

(C) $\dfrac{1}{6}$

(D) $\dfrac{1}{3}$

(E) $\dfrac{1}{2}$

24. If bin A contains exactly twice as many potatoes as bin B, and if bin A contains exactly 11 more potatoes than bin C, does bin B contain more potatoes than bin C?

(1) The difference between the number of potatoes in bin A and the number in bin C is greater than the number of potatoes in bin B.

(2) If one potato were added to bin A and to bin C, bin A would contain exactly twice as many potatoes as bin C.

25. One of two ropes equal in length is cut into three segments to form the largest possible triangular area. The other rope is cut into four segments to form the largest possible rectangular area. Which of the following most closely approximates the ratio of the triangle's area to the rectangle's area?

(A) 1:2
(B) 2:3
(C) 3:4
(D) 1:1
(E) 4:3

26. Code letters X, Y, and Z each represent one digit in the three-digit prime number XYZ. If neither X nor Y is an odd integer, what is the number represented by XYZ ?

(1) The sum of the three digits is 7.

(2) $X - Y > 2$

27. If $abcd \neq 0$, and if $0 < c < b < a < 1$, is it true that $\dfrac{a^4 bc}{d^2} < 1$?

(1) $a = \sqrt{d}$

(2) $d > 0$

28. If $x > 0$, and if $x + 3$ is a multiple of 3, which of the following is not a multiple of 3?

(A) x
(B) $x + 6$
(C) $3x + 5$
(D) $2x + 6$
(E) $6x + 18$

29. If one dollar can buy m pieces of paper, how many dollars are needed to buy p reams of paper? (*Note:* 1 ream = 500 pieces of paper.)

(A) $\dfrac{p}{500m}$

(B) $\dfrac{m}{500p}$

(C) $\dfrac{500}{p + m}$

(D) $\dfrac{500p}{m}$

(E) $500m(p - m)$

QUESTIONS 30–31 REFER TO THE FOLLOWING CHART:

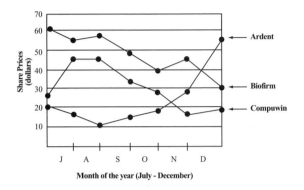

**SHARE PRICES OF COMMON STOCK
(ARDENT, BIOFIRM AND COMPUWIN CORPORATIONS)**

Month of the year (July - December)

30. At the end of September, the combined share price of Ardent stock and Biofirm stock exceeded the share price of Compuwin stock by approximately

(A) 20%
(B) 35%
(C) 50%
(D) 100%
(E) 150%

31. During which of the following months did the aggregate share price of stock in all three companies change the LEAST?

(A) July
(B) August
(C) October
(D) November
(E) December

32.

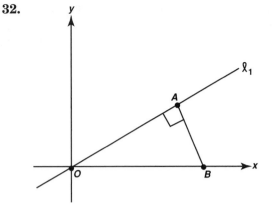

On the xy-plane above, if the equation of l_1 is $y=\dfrac{1}{2}x$ and if point B is defined by the xy-coordinate pair (5,0), what is the area of $\triangle OAB$?

(A) 4
(B) $3\sqrt{2}$
(C) $2\sqrt{5}$
(D) 5
(E) 7

33. In a group of 30 students, 18 are enrolled in an English class and 16 are enrolled in an Algebra class. How many students are enrolled in both an English and Algebra class?

(1) 20 are enrolled in exactly one of these two classes.

(2) 3 are not enrolled in either of these classes.

34. Total revenue from the sale of adult and student tickets was $180. If twice as many student tickets as adult tickets were sold, and if 27 tickets were sold altogether, what was the total revenue from the sale of student tickets?

(1) The price of each adult ticket was $10.

(2) The price of each student ticket was 50% of the price of each adult ticket.

35. If a, b, c, and d are integers, is the sum of ab and cd an odd integer?

(1) a and c are both even integers.

(2) b is an even integer and d is an odd integer.

36.

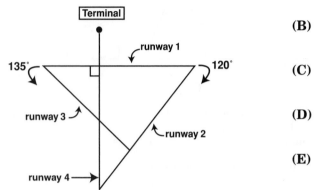

As shown in the figure above, from runway 1, airplanes must turn either 120° to the right onto runway 2 or 135° to the left onto runway 3. Which of the following does NOT indicate a complete turn from one runway to another?

(A) 30°
(B) 55°
(C) 60°
(D) 75°
(E) 105°

37. A legislature passed a bill into law by a 5:3 margin. No legislator abstained. What part of the votes cast were cast in favor of the motion?

(A) $\dfrac{3}{8}$

(B) $\dfrac{2}{5}$

(C) $\dfrac{8}{15}$

(D) $\dfrac{3}{5}$

(E) $\dfrac{5}{8}$

VERBAL SECTION

41 QUESTIONS • 75 MINUTES

Directions for Sentence Correction Questions: *(These directions will appear on your screen before your first Sentence Correction question.)*

This question presents a sentence, all or part of which is underlined. Beneath the sentence you will find five ways of phrasing the underlined part. The first of these repeats the original; the other four are different. If you think the original is best, choose the first answer; otherwise choose one of the others.

This question tests correctness and effectiveness of expression. In choosing your answer, follow the requirements of Standard Written English; that is, pay attention to grammar, choice of words, and sentence construction. Choose the answer that produces the most effective sentence; this answer should be clear and exact, without awkwardness, ambiguity, redundancy, or grammatical error.

Directions for Critical Reasoning Questions: *(These directions will appear on your screen before your first Critical Reasoning question.)*

For this question, select the best of the answer choices given.

Directions for Reading Comprehension Questions: *(These directions will appear on your screen before your first group of Reading Comprehension questions.)*

The questions in this group are based on the content of a passage. After reading the passage, choose the best answer to each question. Answer all the questions following the passage on the basis of what is *stated* or *implied* in the passage.

1. Either interest rates or the supply of money <u>can, along with the level of government spending, be factors contributing to</u> the amount of monetary inflation.

   (A) can, along with the level of government spending, be factors contributing to

   (B) along with the level of government spending, can one or the other be contributing factors in

   (C) can, along with the level of government spending, contribute as factors to

   (D) can be a contributing factor to, along with the level of government spending

   (E) can contribute, along with the level of government spending, to

2. During his prolific career, Beethoven composed dozens of symphonies, <u>out of which he never completed some of them.</u>

   (A) out of which he never completed some of them.

   (B) of which some of them were never completed by him.

   (C) which some he never completed.

   (D) some of which he never completed.

   (E) but some were not completed by him.

3. The space program's missions to Mars have confirmed that the soil composition on that planet is similar <u>to that on our planet.</u>

   (A) to that on our planet.
   (B) to our planet.
   (C) with the soil on our planet.
   (D) to this composition on our planet.
   (E) to our planet's soil's composition.

4. According to life-insurance company statistics, nine out of ten alcoholics die before the age of seventy-five, as opposed to seven out of ten non-alcoholics. A recent report issued by the State Medical Board recounts these statistics and concludes that alcohol addiction increases a person's susceptibility to life-threatening diseases, thereby reducing life expectancy.

The conclusion drawn by the State Medical Board depends on which of the following assumptions?

   (A) People who are predisposed to life-threatening diseases are more likely than other people to become alcoholic.
   (B) The statistics cited exclude deaths due to other alcohol-related events such as automobile accidents.
   (C) Alcoholism does not also increase a person's susceptibility to diseases that are not life-threatening.
   (D) The life expectancy of that portion of the general population not characterized by alcoholism increases over time.
   (E) The author of the report is not biased in his or her personal opinion about the morality of alcohol consumption.

5. For the purpose of stimulating innovation at TechCorp, one of the company's long-standing goals has been to obtain at least 50 percent of its annual revenues from sales of products that are no more than three years old. Last year, TechCorp achieved this goal, despite the fact that the company introduced no new products during the year.

Which of the following, if true, best explains the results described above?

   (A) None of the company's competitors introduced any new products during the last year.
   (B) Scientists at the company report that they are close to breakthroughs that should result in several new products during the coming year.
   (C) Sales of some of the company's older products were discontinued during that last year.
   (D) The company has introduced very few new products during the last three years.
   (E) Company spending on research and development has increased sharply over the past five years.

QUESTIONS 6–8 ARE BASED ON THE FOLLOWING PASSAGE:

Line   The Pan-American land bridge, or isthmus, connecting North and South America was formed volcanically long after dinosaurs became extinct. The

5   isthmus cleaved populations of marine organisms, creating sister species. These twin species, called "geminates," then evolved independently. Scientists observe, for example, that Pacific pistol

10   shrimp no longer mate with those from the Atlantic Ocean. Yet the two oceans had already begun to form their distinctive personalities long before the isthmus was fully formed. As the

15   seabed rose, Pacific waters grew cooler, their upswelling currents carrying rich nutrients, while the Atlantic side grew shallower, warmer, and nutrient poor. In fact, it was these new conditions,

20 and not so much the fully formed isthmus, that spawned changes in the shrimp population.

For terrestrial life, the impact of the isthmus was more immediate. Animals
25 traversed the newly formed bridge in both directions, although North American creatures proved better colonizers—more than half of South America's mammals trace direct
30 lineage to this so-called Great American Biotic Exchange. Only three animals—the armadillo, opossum, and hedgehog—survive as transplants in the north today.

6. Which of the following statements finds the LEAST support in the passage?

(A) Population divergences resulting from the formation of the Pan-American isthmus were more a process than an event.

(B) The divergence in ocean temperature during the formation of the Pan-American isthmus resulted in a divergence in the ocean's nutrient value.

(C) Genetic differences among pistol shrimp have grown to the point that there are now at least two distinct species of these shrimp.

(D) The part of ocean that is now the Pacific grew deeper due to the geologic forces that created the Pan-American isthmus.

(E) Not until the Pan-American isthmus was fully formed did geminate marine organisms begin to develop in that area of the ocean.

7. The author mentions the mating habits of pistol shrimp in order to show that

(A) some species of marine organisms inhabiting the Pacific Ocean are now entirely distinct from those in the Atlantic Ocean.

(B) twin species of marine organisms can each survive even though one species can no longer mate with the other.

(C) since the formation of the Pan-American isthmus, some marine geminates no longer mate with their sister species.

(D) geminate species that do not mate with one another are considered separate species.

(E) the evolutionary impact of the Pan-American isthmus was greater for marine organisms than for land animals.

8. Which of the following statements is most readily inferable from the information in the passage?

(A) Species of marine organisms in the Atlantic Ocean number fewer today than before the formation of the Pan-American isthmus.

(B) The number of terrestrial animal species in South America today exceeds the number prior to the formation of the Pan-American isthmus.

(C) Of the indigenous North American species that migrated south across the Pan-American isthmus, more than three survive to this day.

(D) Since the formation of the Pan-American isthmus, fewer terrestrial animals have traveled north across the isthmus than south.

(E) As the Pan-American isthmus began to form, most pistol shrimp migrated west to what is now the Pacific Ocean.

9. That which is self-evident cannot be disputed, and that in itself is self-evident.

- **(A)** That which is self-evident cannot be disputed, and that in
- **(B)** That that is self-evident cannot be disputed, of which
- **(C)** It is self-evident that which cannot be disputed, and this fact
- **(D)** The self-evident cannot be disputed, and this fact
- **(E)** That which is self-evident cannot be disputed, a fact which

10. People who discontinue regular exercise typically claim that exercising amounted to wasted time for them. But this claim is born of laziness, in light of the overwhelming evidence that regular exercise improves one's health.

Which of the following statements, if true, would most seriously weaken the argument above?

- **(A)** Exercise has been shown to not only improve one's health, but also to increase longevity, or life span.
- **(B)** People who have discontinued regular exercise now make productive use of the time they formerly devoted to exercise.
- **(C)** People who are in good health are more likely to exercise regularly than people who are in poor health.
- **(D)** A person need not exercise every day to experience improved health from the exercise.
- **(E)** People who are in poor health are less likely to exercise than other people.

11. Very few software engineers have left MicroFirm Corporation to seek employment elsewhere. Thus, unless CompTech Corporation increases the salaries of its software engineers to the same level as those of Micro-Firm's, these CompTech employees are likely to leave CompTech for another employer.

The flawed reasoning in the argument above is most similar to the reasoning in which of the following arguments?

- **(A)** Robert does not gamble, and he has never been penniless. Therefore, if Gina refrains from gambling she will also avoid being penniless.
- **(B)** If Dan throws a baseball directly at the window, the window pane will surely break. The window pane is not broken, so Dan has not thrown a baseball directly at it.
- **(C)** If a piano sits in a humid room the piano will need tuning within a week. This piano needs tuning; therefore, it must have sat in a humid room for at least a week.
- **(D)** Diligent practice results in perfection. Thus, one must practice diligently in order to achieve perfection.
- **(E)** More expensive cars are stolen than inexpensive cars. Accordingly, owners of expensive cars should carry auto theft insurance, whereas owners of inexpensive cars should not.

12. The technique of "ping-ponging," which permits overdubbing of audio sound tracks, has not been used as much from the time of the advent of computer-based recording.

- **(A)** as much from the time of
- **(B)** as much since
- **(C)** as much as
- **(D)** much as after
- **(E)** much because of

13. The volatility of a balanced portfolio of stocks and bonds, less than eighty percent of the overall stock market.

- **(A)** The volatility of a balanced portfolio of stocks and bonds, less than eighty percent of the overall stock market.
- **(B)** A balanced portfolio of stocks and bonds is less than eighty percent as volatile as the overall stock market.
- **(C)** A balanced portfolio of stocks and bonds is less than eighty percent as volatile as that of the overall stock market.
- **(D)** Volatility is less than eighty percent for a balanced portfolio of stocks and bonds compared to the overall stock market.
- **(E)** The volatility of a balanced portfolio of stocks and bonds is less than eighty percent of the overall stock market.

14. In 19th-century Europe, a renewed interest in Middle Eastern architecture was kindled not only by increased trade but also by increased tourism and improved diplomatic relations.

- **(A)** not only by increased trade but also by
- **(B)** by not only increased trade but also by
- **(C)** not only by increased trade but also
- **(D)** not only by increased trade but
- **(E)** by increased trade and also by

QUESTIONS 15–17 ARE BASED ON THE FOLLOWING PASSAGE:

Line Historians sometimes forget that no matter how well they might come to know a particular historical figure, they are not free to claim a godlike
5 knowledge of the figure or of the events surrounding the figure's life. Richard III, one of England's monarchs, is an apt case because we all think we "know" what he was like. In his play
10 *Richard III*, Shakespeare provided a portrait of a monster of a man, twisted in both body and soul. Shakespeare's great artistry and vivid depiction of Richard has made us accept this
15 creature for the man. We are prepared, therefore, to interpret all the events around him in such a way as to justify our opinion of him.

We accept that Richard executed his
20 brother Clarence, even though the records of the time show that Richard pleaded for his brother's life. We assume that Richard supervised the death of King Henry VI, overlooking
25 that there is no proof that Henry was actually murdered. And we recoil at Richard's murdering his two nephews, children of his brother's wife Elizabeth; yet we forget that Elizabeth had spent
30 her time on the throne plotting to replace her husband's family in power with her own family. Once we appreciate the historical context, especially the actions of Richard's opponents, we
35 no longer see his actions as monstrous. Richard becomes, if not lovable, at least understandable. What's more, when we account for the tone of the times during which Richard lived, as
40 illuminated in literary works of that era such as Machiavelli's *The Prince*, Richard's actions seem to us all the more reasonable.

15. With which of the following statements would the author of the passage most likely agree?

- **(A)** In *Richard III*, Shakespeare portrays the king as more noble than he actually was.
- **(B)** The deeds of Elizabeth were even more evil than those of Richard III.
- **(C)** Richard III may have been innocent of some of the crimes that Shakespeare leads us to believe he committed.
- **(D)** Richard III may have had a justifiable reason for killing Henry VI.
- **(E)** Shakespeare was unaware of many of the historical facts about the life of Richard III.

16. The author of the passage refers to Shakespeare's "great artistry and vivid depiction of Richard" (lines 12–14) most probably in order to

   (A) make the point that studying *Richard III* is the best way to understand Richard as a historical figure.
   (B) explain why *Richard III* is widely acclaimed as one of Shakespeare's greatest works.
   (C) contrast Shakespeare's depiction of Richard with how Richard might have described himself.
   (D) illustrate how historians might become prejudiced in their view of historical figures.
   (E) point out that historians should never rely on fictional works to understand and interpret historical events.

17. It can be inferred from the passage information that Machiavelli's *The Prince* helps show

   (A) that, in his play *Richard III*, Shakespeare's depiction of the king was historically accurate.
   (B) that Richard's actions were an accurate reflection of the times in which he lived.
   (C) that different authors often depict the same historical figures in very different ways.
   (D) that Machiavelli was more astute than Shakespeare as an observer of human nature.
   (E) that Richard's actions as a king are not surprising in light of his earlier actions as a prince.

18. PharmaCorp, which manufactures the drug Aidistan, claims that Aidistan is more effective than the drug Betatol in treating Puma Syndrome. To support its claim, PharmaCorp cites the fact that one of every two victims of Puma Syndrome is treated successfully with Aidistan alone, as opposed to one out of every three treated with Betatol alone. However, PharmaCorp's claim cannot be taken seriously in light of the fact that the presence of Gregg's Syndrome has been known to render Puma Syndrome more resistant to any treatment.

Which of the following, if true, would most support the allegation that PharmaCorp's claim cannot be taken seriously?

   (A) Among people who suffer from both Puma Syndrome and Gregg's Syndrome, fewer are treated with Aidistan than with Betatol.
   (B) Among people who suffer from both Puma Syndrome and Gregg's Syndrome, fewer are treated with Betatol than with Aidistan.
   (C) Gregg's Syndrome reduces Aidistan's effectiveness in treating Puma Syndrome more than Betatol's effectiveness in treating the same syndrome.
   (D) Betatol is less effective than Aidistan in treating Gregg's Syndrome.
   (E) Neither Aidistan nor Betatol is effective in treating Gregg's Syndrome.

19. *City official:* In order to revitalize our city's downtown business district, we should increase the number of police officers that patrol the district during business hours. Three years ago, the city reduced the total size of its police force by nearly 20 percent. Since then, retail businesses in the district have experienced a steady decline in revenue.

Any of the following, if true, would be an effective criticism of the city official's recommendation EXCEPT:

(A) Two years ago, the city established more rigorous standards for the retention and hiring of its police officers.

(B) New businesses offering products or services similar to those in the district have emerged outside the district recently.

(C) The number of people who reside in the district has not changed significantly over the last three years.

(D) Businesses operating in the city but outside the district have experienced declining revenues during the last three years.

(E) Some of the city's police officers patrol areas outside as well as inside the district.

20. Which of the following provides the most logical completion of the passage below?

More and more consumers are being attracted to sport utility vehicles because they are safer to drive than regular cars and because of the feeling of power a person experiences when driving a sport utility vehicle. In its current advertising campaign, Jupiter Auto Company emphasizes the low price of its new sport utility vehicle compared to the price of other such vehicles. However, this marketing strategy is unwise because _____.

(A) Jupiter's sport utility vehicle is not as safe as those produced by competing automobile manufacturers.

(B) if Jupiter reduces the price of its sport utility vehicle even further, Jupiter would sell even more of these vehicles.

(C) the retail price of Jupiter's most expensive luxury car is less than that of its new sport utility vehicle.

(D) most consumers who purchase sport utility vehicles are also concerned about the reliability of their vehicle.

(E) consumers who purchase sport utility vehicles associate affordability with lack of safety.

21. Since City X reduced the frequency with which its service vehicles pick up recyclable materials from residences for transport to its recycling center, the volume of material that its service vehicles transport to landfills for permanent disposal has increased to unmanageable levels. However, the city cannot increase the frequency of either its trash pickup or its recycling pickup at city residences.

Based only the information above, which of the following strategies seems most appropriate for City X in the interest of reducing the volume of material that the city's service vehicles transport to landfills?

(A) Provide larger recycling containers to the residents of the city.

(B) Establish a community program to increase awareness of the benefits of recycling.

(C) Establish additional recycling centers as near as possible to the city's residential areas.

(D) Provide incentives to the city's residents to reuse, rather than discard for pickup by the city's service vehicles, whatever they can.

(E) Ease restrictions on the types of materials the city's service vehicles will pick up for transport to its recycling center.

22. The pesticide Azocide, introduced to central valley farms three summers ago, has proven ineffective <u>because other pesticides' chemical compositions already in wide use</u> neutralizing its desired effect.

(A) because other pesticides' chemical compositions already in wide use

(B) because of the chemical compositions of the pesticides already in wide use

(C) due to other pesticides already in wide use, whose chemical compositions have been

(D) since, due to the chemical compositions of other pesticides already in use, those pesticides have been

(E) because of other pesticides and their chemical compositions already in use, which have been

23. To relieve anxiety, moderate exercise can be equally <u>effective as, and</u> less addictive than, most sedatives.

(A) effective as, and

(B) as effective as, while being

(C) effectively equal to, but

(D) as effective as, and

(E) effective, and

24. The government's means <u>of disposal of</u> war surplus following <u>World War II</u> met with vociferous objections by industrialists, prominent advisors, and many others.

(A) of disposal of

(B) in disposing

(C) for the disposition of

(D) used in disposing

(E) of disposing

25. No nation in the world has experienced as significant a decline in its Yucaipa tree population as our nation. Yet only our nation imposes a law prohibiting the use of Yucaipa tree-bark oil in cosmetics. The purpose of this law in the first place was to help maintain the Yucaipa tree population, at least in this nation. But the law is clearly unnecessary and therefore should be repealed.

Which of the following, if true, would most seriously weaken the conclusion drawn in the passage?

(A) This nation contains more Yucaipa trees than any other nation.

(B) Yucaipa tree-bark oil is not used for any consumer goods other than cosmetics.

(C) The demand for cosmetics containing Yucaipa tree-bark oil is expected to decline in the future in other nations while continuing unabated in this nation.

(D) In other countries, labor used to harvest Yucaipa trees for cosmetics is less expensive than comparable labor in this nation.

(E) In this nation, some wild animals eat Yucaipa tree bark, thereby contributing to their destruction.

26. Some official Web sites of regionally accredited colleges have received the highest possible rating from the Federal Department of Education. However, all official Web sites of nationally accredited colleges have received the highest possible rating from the same department.

Which of the following, if added to the statements above, would provide most support for the conclusion that all Web sites administered by individuals holding advanced degrees in educational technology have received the highest possible rating from the Federal Department of Education?

(A) Only official Web sites of nationally accredited colleges are administered by individuals holding advanced degrees in educational technology.

(B) All Web sites of nationally accredited colleges are administered by individuals holding advanced degrees in educational technology.

(C) Only Web sites that have not received the highest possible rating from the Federal Department of Education are administered by individuals not holding advanced degrees in educational technology.

(D) All official Web sites of nationally accredited colleges are administered by individuals holding advanced degrees in educational technology.

(E) No Web site administered by individuals holding advanced degrees in educational technology is an official Web site of a regionally accredited college.

27. The time it takes for a star to change its brightness is directly related to <u>the luminosity of it.</u>

(A) the luminosity of it.
(B) the luminosity of its brightness.
(C) the luminosity of a star.
(D) luminosity of it.
(E) its luminosity.

QUESTIONS 28–30 ARE BASED ON THE FOLLOWING PASSAGE:

Line   Diseases associated with aging in
women are difficult to correlate
explicitly with estrogen deficiency
because aging and genetics are impor-
5   tant influences in the development of
such diseases. A number of studies,
however, indicate a profound effect of
estrogen deficiency in syndromes such
as cardiovascular disease (including
10   atherosclerosis and stroke) and os-
teoporosis—the loss and increasing
fragility of bone in aging individuals.

The amount of bone in the elderly
skeleton—a key determinant in its
15   susceptibility to fractures—is believed
to be a function of two major factors.
The first is the peak amount of bone
mass attained, determined to a large
extent by genetic inheritance. The
20   marked effect of gender is obvious—
elderly men experience only one-half as
many hip fractures per capita as
elderly women. However, African
American women have a lower inci-
25   dence of osteoporotic fractures than
Caucasian women. Other important
variables include diet, exposure to
sunlight, and physical activity. The
second major factor is the rate of bone
30   loss after peak bone mass has been
attained. While many of the variables
that affect peak bone mass also affect
rates of bone loss, additional factors
influencing bone loss include physi-
35   ological stresses such as pregnancy and
lactation. It is hormonal status,
however, reflected primarily by estrogen and progesterone levels, that may
exert the greatest effect on rates of
40   decline in skeletal mass.

28. Based upon the passage, which of the following is LEAST clearly a factor affecting the rate of decline in bone mass?

   (A) Gender
   (B) Exposure to sunlight
   (C) Progesterone levels
   (D) Age
   (E) Estrogen levels

29. In discussing the "marked effect of gender" (line 20), the author assumes all of the following EXCEPT:

   (A) the difference in incidence of hip fractures is not due instead to different rates of bone loss.
   (B) the incidence of hip fractures among elderly men as compared to elderly women is representa- tive of the total number of bone fractures among elderly men as compared to elderly women.
   (C) elderly women are not more accident-prone than elderly men.
   (D) the population upon which the cited statistic is based includes both African Americans and Caucasians.
   (E) men achieve peak bone mass at the same age as women.

30. It can be inferred from the passage that the peak amount of bone mass in women

   (A) is not affected by either preg- nancy or lactation.
   (B) is determined primarily by diet.
   (C) depends partly upon hormonal status.
   (D) may play a role in determining the rate of decrease in estrogen and progesterone levels.
   (E) is not dependent upon genetic makeup.

31. Vining University's teacher credential program should be credited for the high grade-point averages of high school students who enroll in classes taught by Vining graduates. More new graduates of Vining's credential program accept entry-level positions at Franklin High School than at any other high school. And during the most recent academic year, just prior to which many of Franklin's teachers transferred to Valley View High School, the median grade point average of the students at Franklin has declined while at Valley View it has increased.

The argument above depends on which of the following assumptions?

(A) The two high schools employ different methods of computing student grade point averages.

(B) Neither high school has a peer tutoring program that would afford the school an advantage over the other in terms of student academic performance.

(C) Just prior to last year, more teachers transferred from Franklin to Valley View than from Valley View to Franklin.

(D) The teachers who transferred from Franklin to Valley View were replaced with teachers who are also graduates of Vining University's teacher credential program.

(E) The teachers who transferred from Franklin to Valley View last year were graduates of Vining's teacher credential program.

32. More airplane accidents are caused by pilot error than any other single factor. The military recently stopped requiring its pilots to obtain immunization shots against chemical warfare agents. These shots are known to cause unpredictable dizzy spells, which can result in pilot error. Since many military pilots also pilot commercial passenger airliners, the reason for the military's decision must have been to reduce the number of commercial airline accidents.

Which of the following, if true, provides most support for the conclusion drawn above?

(A) Recently, more pilots have been volunteering for the immunization shots.

(B) All commercial airline flights are piloted by two co-pilots, whereas military flights are usually piloted by only one.

(C) Chemical warfare is likely to escalate in the future.

(D) Military pilots are choosing to resign rather than obtain the immunization shots.

(E) Recently, the number of military pilots also piloting commercial airliners has declined.

33. <u>While few truly great artists consider themselves visionary, many lesser talents boast about their own destiny to lead the way to higher artistic ground.</u>

(A) While few truly great artists consider themselves visionary, many lesser talents boast about their own destiny to lead the way to higher artistic ground.

(B) While many lesser talents boast about their own destinies to lead the way to higher ground, few truly great artists consider themselves as visionary.

(C) Many lesser talents boast about their own destiny to lead the way to higher artistic ground while few truly great artists consider themselves as being visionary.

(D) Few truly great artists consider himself or herself a visionary while many lesser talents boast about their own destinies to lead the way to higher artistic ground.

(E) While many lesser talents boast about their own destiny, few truly great artists consider themselves visionary, to lead the way to higher artistic ground.

34. <u>History shows that while simultaneously attaining</u> global or even regional dominance, a country generally succumbs to erosion of its social infrastructure.

(A) History shows that while simultaneously attaining

(B) History would show that, while attaining

(C) History bears out that, in the course of attaining

(D) During the course of history, the attainment of

(E) Throughout history, during any country's attaining

35. *Connie:* This season, new episodes of my favorite television program are even more entertaining than previous episodes; so the program should be even more popular this season than last season.

Karl: I disagree. After all, we both know that the chief aim of television networks is to maximize advertising revenue by increasing the popularity of their programs. But this season the television networks that compete with the one that shows your favorite program are showing reruns of old programs during the same time slot as your favorite program.

Which of the following, if true, would provide the most support for Karl's response to Connie's argument?

(A) What Connie considers entertaining does not necessarily coincide with what most television viewers consider entertaining.

(B) Entertaining television shows are not necessarily popular as well.

(C) Television networks generally schedule their most popular shows during the same time slots as their competitors' most popular shows.

(D) Certain educational programs that are not generally considered entertaining are nevertheless among the most popular programs.

(E) The most common reason for a network to rerun a television program is that a great number of television viewers request the rerun.

QUESTIONS 36–39 ARE BASED ON THE FOLLOWING PASSAGE:

(The following passage was written in 1991.)

Line One of the cornerstones of economic reform in the formerly Communist states is privatization, which can be approached either gradually or rapidly.

5 Under the gradual approach, a state bureau would decide if and when an enterprise is prepared for privatization and which form is most suitable for it. However, gradual privatization would

10 only prolong the core problems of inefficiency and misallocation of both labor and capital. Under one of two approaches to rapid privatization, shares of an enterprise would be

15 distributed among the enterprise's employees so that the employees would become the owners of the enterprise. This socialist-reform approach discriminates in favor of workers who

20 happen to be employed by a modern and efficient enterprise as well as by placing workers' property at great risk by requiring them to invest their property in the same enterprise in

25 which they are employed rather than permitting them to diversify their investments.

A better approach involves distribution of shares in enterprises, free of

30 charge, among all the people by means of vouchers—a kind of investment money. Some critics charge that voucher holders would not be interested in how their enterprises are

35 managed, as may be true of small corporate shareholders in capitalist countries who pay little attention to their investments until the corporation's profits fail to meet expectations,

40 at which time these shareholders rush to sell their securities. While the resulting fall in stock prices can cause serious problems for a corporation, it is this very pressure that drives private

45 firms toward efficiency and profitability. Other detractors predict that most people will sell their vouchers to foreign capitalists. These skeptics ignore the capacity of individuals to

50 consider their own future—that is, to compare the future flow of income secured by a voucher to the benefits of immediate consumption. Even if an individual should decide to sell, the

55 aim of voucher privatization is not to secure equality of property but rather equality of opportunity.

36. Which of the following is NOT mentioned in the passage as a possible adverse consequence of rapid privatization?

(A) Undue prolongation of inefficiency and misallocation

(B) Loss of ownership in domestic private enterprises to foreign concerns

(C) Financial devastation for employees of private enterprises

(D) Inequitable distribution of wealth among employees of various enterprises

(E) Instability in stock prices

37. Which of the following would the author probably agree is the LEAST desirable outcome of economic reform in formerly Communist countries?

(A) Effective allocation of labor

(B) Equitable distribution of property among citizens

(C) Financial security of citizens

(D) Equal opportunity for financial success among citizens

(E) Financial security of private enterprises

38. In responding to those "skeptics" who claim that people will sell their vouchers to foreign capitalists (lines 47–50), the author implies that

(A) foreign capitalists will not be willing to pay a fair price for the vouchers.

(B) the future flow of income is likely in many cases to exceed the present exchange value of a voucher.

(C) foreign investment in a nation's enterprises may adversely affect currency exchange rates.

(D) although the skeptics are correct, their point is irrelevant in evaluating the merits of voucher privatization.

(E) foreign capitalists are less interested in the success of voucher privatization than in making a profit.

39. Which of the following is LEAST accurate in characterizing the author's method of argumentation in discussing the significance of falling stock prices (lines 42–46)?

(A) Describing a paradox that supports the author's position

(B) Asserting that one drawback of an approach is outweighed by countervailing considerations

(C) Rebutting an opposing position by suggesting an alternative explanation

(D) Discrediting an opposing argument by questioning its relevance

(E) Characterizing an argument against a course of action instead as an argument in its favor

40. Currently, the supply of office buildings in this state far exceeds demand, while demand for single-family housing far exceeds supply. As a result, real estate developers have curtailed office building construction until demand meets supply and have Stepped up construction of single-family housing. The state legislature recently enacted a law eliminating a state income tax on corporations whose primary place of business is this state. In response, many large private employers from other states have already begun to relocate to this state and, according to a reliable study, this trend will continue during the next five years.

Which of the following predictions is best supported by the information above?

(A) During the next five years, fewer new office buildings than single-family houses will be constructed in the state.

(B) Five years from now, the available supply of single-family housing in the state will exceed demand.

(C) Five years from now, the per capita income of the state's residents will exceed current levels.

(D) During the next five years, the cost of purchasing new single-family residential housing will decrease.

(E) During the next five years, the number of state residents working at home as opposed to working in office buildings will decrease.

41. Humans naturally crave to do good, act reasonably, and <u>to think decently, these</u> urges must have a global purpose in order to have meaning.

(A) to think decently, these

(B) think decently, yet these

(C) to decently think, and these

(D) thinking decently, but these

(E) think decent, these

ANSWER KEYS AND EXPLANATIONS

See Appendix B for score conversion tables to determine your score. Be sure to keep a tally of correct and incorrect answers for each test section.

Analysis of an Issue—Evaluation and Scoring

Evaluate your Issue-Analysis essay on a scale of 1 to 6 (6 being the highest score) according to the following five criteria:

1. Does your essay develop a position on the issue through the use of incisive reasons and persuasive examples?

2. Are your essay's ideas conveyed clearly and articulately?

3. Does your essay maintain proper focus on the issue, and is it well organized?

4. Does your essay demonstrate proficiency, fluency, and maturity in its use of sentence structure, vocabulary, and idiom?

5. Does your essay demonstrate command of the elements of Standard Written English, including grammar, word usage, spelling, and punctuation?

Analysis of an Argument—Evaluation and Scoring

Evaluate your Argument-Analysis essay on a scale of 1 to 6 (6 being the highest score) according to the following five criteria:

1 Does your essay identify the key features of the argument and analyze each one in a thoughtful manner?

2 Does your essay support each point of its critique with insightful reasons and examples?

3 Does your essay develop its ideas in a clear, organized manner, with appropriate transitions to help connect ideas?

4 Does your essay demonstrate proficiency, fluency, and maturity in its use of sentence structure, vocabulary, and idiom?

5 Does your essay demonstrate command of the elements of Standard Written English, including grammar, word usage, spelling, and punctuation?

The following series of questions, which serve to identify the Argument's five distinct problems, will help you evaluate your essay in terms of criteria 1 and 2. To earn a score of 4 or higher, your essay should identify at least three of these problems and, for each one, provide at least one example or counterexample that supports your critique. (Your examples need not be the same as the ones below.) Identifying and discussing at least four of the problems would help earn you an even higher score.

- Does the Argument draw a *questionable analogy* between Oak City's circumstances and Mapleton's? (Perhaps the percentage of students needing off-campus housing, which might affect property values, is significantly greater in one town than the other.)

- Does the Argument draw a *questionable analogy* between four-year colleges and community colleges? (Perhaps a four-year college would bring greater prestige or higher culture to the town.)

- Is the presence of Mapleton's new community college necessarily the *actual cause* of the decline in Mapleton's property values and rents? (Perhaps some other recent development is responsible instead.)

- Is it *necessary* to refuse the new college in order to prevent a decline in property values and rents? (Perhaps Oak City can counteract downward pressure on property values and rents through some other means.)

Quantitative Section

1.	E	9.	D	17.	E	24.	D	31.	B
2.	D	10.	B	18.	C	25.	C	32.	D
3.	B	11.	A	19.	E	26.	E	33.	D
4.	C	12.	C	20.	A	27.	A	34.	D
5.	E	13.	B	21.	D	28.	C	35.	A
6.	D	14.	E	22.	A	29.	D	36.	B
7.	B	15.	D	23.	B	30.	D	37.	E
8.	C	16.	C						

1. **The correct answer is (E).** Since the answer choices are expressed in decimal terms, convert all three terms in the question to decimals, then add:

$$\sqrt{0.49} = 0.7$$

$$\frac{3}{4} = 0.75$$

$$80\% = 0.8$$

$$0.7 + 0.75 + 0.8 = 2.25$$

2. **The correct answer is (D).** The amount of the decrease is $4. The percent of the decrease is $\frac{4}{25}$, or $\frac{16}{100}$, or 16%.

3. **The correct answer is (B).** Statement (2) provides an average of 55 students per bus. Thus, since $(55)(4) = 220 > 175$, this means that 4 buses would be required.

4. **The correct answer is (C).** To answer the question, you need to know drive B's total capacity as well as the amount (number of gigabytes) of drive B's capacity currently used. Statement (1), together with the information given in the question stem, provides the former, while Statement (2) provides the latter. [The storage capacities of drives A and B are 17 and 20, respectively. Of drive B's 20 gigabyte capacity, 42.5% (8.5 gigabytes) is currently used.]

5. **The correct answer is (E).** You could piece together the panes into either a single column (or row) of 8 panes or into 2 adjacent columns (or rows) of 4 panes each. In the first case, the door's perimeter would be 18. In the second case, the door's perimeter would be 12. Thus, statement (1) alone is insufficient to answer the question. Statement (2) alone is insufficient for the same reason. Both statements together still fail to provide sufficient information to determine the shape (or perimeter) of the door.

6. **The correct answer is (D).** One way to solve this problem is to substitute each answer choice in turn into the given fraction. You can also solve the problem algebraically. Let $\frac{x}{2x}$ represent the original fraction. Add 4 to both the numerator and denominator, then cross-multiply to solve for x:

$$\frac{x + 4}{2x + 4} = \frac{5}{8}$$
$$8x + 32 = 10x + 20$$
$$12 = 2x$$
$$6 = x$$

The original denominator is $2x$, or 12.

7. **The correct answer is (B).** Because the t-terms are the same ($0.2t$), the quickest way to solve for s is with the addition-subtraction method. Manipulate both equations so that corresponding terms "line up," then add the two equations:

$$0.2t + 0.6s = 2.2$$
$$\underline{-\ 0.2t + 0.5s = 1.1}$$
$$1.1s = 3.3$$
$$s = 3$$

8. **The correct answer is (C).** To determine the size of Unit C, first determine the size of Unit D as a percentage of the total warehouse size. Unit D occupies 15,500 square feet, or approximately 11%, of the total 140,000 square feet in the warehouse. Thus, Unit C occupies 19% of that total ($100\% - 28\% - 42\% - 11\% = 19\%$). The question asks for the difference in size between Unit A (28%) and Unit D (19%). That difference is 9% of the 140,000 total square feet, or 12,600 square feet.

9. **The correct answer is (D).** The size of Unit B is 42% of 140,000 square feet, or about 59,000 square feet. Thus, the combined size of Unit B and Unit D is approximately 74,500 square feet.

10. **The correct answer is (B).** One way to solve this problem is to substitute each answer choice, in turn, for Carrie's current age. You can also solve the problem by setting up an algebraic equation. Letting x equal Benjamin's present age, you can express Benjamin's age eight years from now as $x + 8$. Similarly, you can express Carrie's present age as ($x + 24$), and her age eight years from now as ($x + 32$). Set up the following equation relating Carrie's age and Benjamin's age eight years from now:

$$x + 32 = 2(x + 8)$$
$$x + 32 = 2x + 16$$
$$16 = x$$

Benjamin's current age is 16 and Carrie's current age is 40.

11. **The correct answer is (A).** Because of the two right angles indicated in the figure, $AB \parallel DC$, $ABCD$ is a trapezoid. The area of a trapezoid $= \frac{1}{2}h(b_1 + b_2)$, where h is the height and each b is a parallel base (side):

$$A = \frac{1}{2}(9)(10 + 12) = 99$$

12. **The correct answer is (C).** Simplify all four terms by removing perfect squares or cubes. Then, for each fraction, divide common factors:

$$\frac{\sqrt[3]{81x^7}}{\sqrt{9x^4}} - \frac{\sqrt{162x^5}}{\sqrt[3]{27x^6}} = \frac{(3x^2)\sqrt[3]{3x}}{3x^2} - \frac{(9x^2)\sqrt{2x}}{3x^2} = \sqrt[3]{3x} - 3\sqrt{2x}$$

13. **The correct answer is (B).** Since each of the two series is strictly arithmetic (all terms are evenly spaced), for each series the mean is the same as the median: exactly midway between the least and greatest numbers.

Mean of first series: $\dfrac{1 + 16}{2} = \dfrac{17}{2}$

Mean of second series: $\dfrac{17 + 32}{2} = \dfrac{49}{2}$

Now, do the subtraction: $\dfrac{49}{2} - \dfrac{17}{2} = \dfrac{32}{2}$, or 16.

14. **The correct answer is (E).** If unequal quantities (c and d) are added to unequal quantities of the same order (a and b), the result is an inequality of the same order. Choice (E) essentially states this rule.

15. **The correct answer is (D).** First, you need to determine the volume of the cylindrical tube. The tube's radius (r) is $\frac{1}{2}$ and its length is 4. Apply the formula for the volume of a right cylinder ($V = \pi r^2 h$):

$$V = \pi\left(\frac{1}{2}\right)^2 (4) = \pi\left(\frac{1}{4}\right)(4) = \pi$$

The tube's volume is π (approximately 3.1) cubic feet. Regardless of its shape, the tube will not fit into a box containing only 3 cubic feet. Thus, given statement (1) alone, you can answer the question. (The answer is *no*.) Statement (2) alone allows for an infinite variety of box shapes. However, no shape with a surface area of 14 will accommodate the tube. How do you know this? Assume that the box's dimensions are $3 \times 1 \times 1$. It's total surface area is exactly 14, yet it's too short (only 3 feet long) to accommodate the tube, which is 4 feet long. Visualize altering the box's shape (making it either "fatter" or "skinnier") while maintaining a surface area of 14. To increase its length, you must sacrifice surface area of the base (and vice versa). In any case, a box with surface area of 14 cannot accommodate the tube. Thus, statement (2) alone suffices to answer the question. (Again, the answer is *no*.)

16. **The correct answer is (C).** Using negative integers with the least absolute value yields the least product. Start with -1, then decrease the values of x and y if necessary. The first two values that satisfy the equation are: $y = -2$, $x = -1$ $[-1 - (-2) = 1]$. Accordingly, $xy = 2$.

17. **The correct answer is (E).** Neither statement (1) nor (2) alone provides any information about the number of yellow jellybeans. Considering both statements together, however, we know that the jar must contain 7 or more black jellybeans (along with exactly 6 pink jellybeans). Accordingly, the jar can contain a maximum of 7 yellow jellybeans. If the jar contains either 6 or 7 yellow jellybeans, the answer to the question is *no*. However, if the jar contains 5 or fewer yellow jellybeans, the answer to the question is *yes*.

18. **The correct answer is (C).** The expression $a^2 - b^2$ can also be expressed in its factored form: $(a + b)(a - b)$. Notice the similarity between this form and the binomial expression given in the question. Factor out the constants (numbers) in the binomial so that it more closely resembles the factored form of $a^2 - b^2$:

$$(3a + 3b)(2a - 2b) = 6(a + b)(a - b) = 6(a^2 - b^2)$$

So the question is asking: Is $a^2 - b^2$ greater than $6(a^2 - b^2)$? Considering statement (1) alone, $(a^2 - b^2)$ might be either positive or negative, depending on whether the absolute value of b is less than a or greater than a. Accordingly, $(6)(a^2 - b^2)$ might be either greater or less than $(a^2 - b^2)$, and statement (1) alone does not suffice to answer the question. Considering statement (2) alone, whether $(a^2 - b^2)$ is positive or negative depends on the value of b, and therefore $(6)(a^2 - b^2)$ might be either greater or less than $(a^2 - b^2)$. Thus, statement (2) alone does not suffice to answer the question. However, both statements together do suffice to answer the question. Given that $b < a < -1$, $(a^2 - b^2)$ must be a negative number. Multiplying this negative number by 6 yields an even lesser number (to the left on the real number line). Therefore, $6(a^2 - b^2) < a^2 - b^2$. (The answer to the question is *yes*.)

19. **The correct answer is (E).** Apply the defined operation to -100 and to 100 in turn, by substituting each value for x in the operation:

$$\blacktriangleleft -100 \blacktriangleright = -98 - (-99) - (-101) - (-102) = -98 + 99 + 101 + 102 = 204$$

$$\blacktriangleleft 100 \blacktriangleright = 102 - 101 - 99 - 98 = -196$$

Then combine the two results:

$$\blacktriangleleft -100 \blacktriangleright - \blacktriangleleft 100 \blacktriangleright = 204 - (-196) = 204 + 196 = 400$$

20. **The correct answer is (A).** Given statement (1) alone, ΔQRS must be a $1{:}1{:}\sqrt{2}$ triangle. Accordingly, $\overline{QR} \cong \overline{SR}$. Since $PQRS$ is a rectangle, $\overline{QR}$ and $\overline{SR}$ are congruent to their respective opposite sides. Thus, all four sides are congruent, and $PQRS$ must be a square. Statement (2) alone provides no new information. We already know that $PQRS$ is a rectangle and, accordingly, that the length of $\overline{PS}$ is 12. $\overline{PQ}$ and $\overline{SR}$ could be any length, so the rectangle might, but need not, be a square.

21. **The correct answer is (D).** Consider statement (1) alone. If the dealer earned a 50% profit from the sale to the customer, determining the amount the customer paid is a simple matter of adding 50% of $10,000 to $10,000. Thus, statement (1) alone suffices to answer the question. Consider statement (2) alone. If the dealer's cost was two thirds the amount the customer paid, then the customer paid $\frac{3}{2}$ of dealer's cost. Determining how much the customer paid is a simple matter of multiplying $10,000 by $\frac{3}{2}$. Thus, statement (2) alone suffices to answer the question.

22. **The correct answer is (A).** Computing standard deviation involves these steps:

    Step 1: Compute the arithmetic mean (simple average) of all terms in the set

    Step 2: Compute the difference between the mean and each term

    Step 3: Square each difference you computed in Step (2)

    Step 4: Compute the mean of the squares you computed in Step (3)

    Step 5: Compute the non-negative square root of the mean you computed in Step (4)

    Applying Steps 1−4 to each of the five answer choices yields the following results:

    (A) $\frac{14}{3}$ **(B)** $\frac{5}{2}$ **(C)** $\frac{8}{3}$ **(D)** $\frac{7}{2}$ **(E)** $\frac{8}{3}$

    Choice (A) is the only fraction that exceeds 4. [There's no need to compute the square roots of any of these fractions (Step 5), since their relative values would remain the same.]

23. **The correct answer is (B).** In each set are three distinct member pairs. Thus the probability of selecting any pair is one in three, or $\frac{1}{3}$. Accordingly, the probability of selecting fruit and salad from the appetizer menu along with squash and peas from the vegetable menu is $\frac{1}{3} \times \frac{1}{3} = \frac{1}{9}$.

24. **The correct answer is (D).** Statement (1) says essentially: $A - C > B$. Given that bin A contains exactly twice as many potatoes as bin B, you can substitute $2B$ for A in the inequality, then determine the relationship between the number of potatoes in bins B and C:

$$A - C > B$$
$$2B - C > B$$
$$B - C > 0$$
$$B > C$$

Thus, statement (1) alone suffices to answer the question. (The answer is *yes*.) Given statement (2) alone, C must be less than $\frac{1}{2}A$. (If you're not certain of this, use a few simple numbers to confirm it.) Given that $B = \frac{1}{2}A$, you can conclude from statement (2) alone that $B > C$. Statement (2) alone also suffices to answer the question. (Notice that you can answer the question with either statement alone without the additional fact that bin A contains *exactly* 11 more potatoes than bin C. This additional information appears to make the problem more complicated than it really is.)

25. **The correct answer is (C).** The largest possible rectangular area is formed by a square, the area of which is the square of any side. (The length of each side is one-fourth the rope's length.) The largest possible triangular area is formed by an equilateral triangle, the area of which is defined as follows (s = the length of any side):

$$Area = \frac{s^2\sqrt{3}}{4}$$

One way to compare the two areas is to substitute a hypothetical value for the length of the ropes. Assume the length of each rope before it was cut was 12. The length of each of the triangle's sides is 4, while the length of the square's sides is 3:

The triangle's area $= \dfrac{4^2\sqrt{3}}{4} = 4\sqrt{3} \approx 4(1.7) \approx 6.8$

The square's area $= 3^2 = 9$

The ratio of 6.8 to 9 is approximately 3 to 4.

26. **The correct answer is (E).** Any multiple-digit prime number must end in an odd digit other than 5 (1, 3, 7, or 9). Considering statement (1) alone, Z must be either 1 or 3, and five possibilities emerge:

601
421
241
403
223

Statement (2) alone allows for many possibilities, since Z can be either 1, 3, 7 or 9. Statements (1) and (2) together eliminate only three of the possibilities, leaving more than one answer.

27. **The correct answer is (A).** Given statement (1), $a^2 = d$. Substituting a^2 for d in the fraction: $\dfrac{a^4bc}{a^4}$, or simply bc. Given that b and c are both positive but less than 1, $bc < 1$, and statement (1) alone suffices to answer the question. (The answer to the question is *yes*.) However, statement (2) alone is insufficient to answer the question. Even if d is greater than zero, statement (2) fails to provide sufficient information to determine the relative values of the numerator and denominator. A sufficiently small d-value relative to the values of a, b, and c results in a quotient greater than 1, whereas a sufficiently greater relative d-value results in a quotient less than 1.

28. **The correct answer is (C).** $3x$ is a multiple of 3; thus, adding 5 to that number yields a number that is not a multiple of 3. None of the other choices fits the bill. Choice (A) is incorrect because $x > 0$ and therefore must equal 3 or some multiple of 3. Choices (B), (D), and (E) are incorrect because any integer multiplied by 3 is a multiple of 3, and any multiple of 3 (such as 6 or 18) added to a multiple of 3 is also a multiple of 3.

29. **The correct answer is (D).** The number of dollars increases proportionately with the number of pieces of paper. The question is essentially asking: "1 is to m as what is to p?" First, set up a proportion (equate two ratios, or fractions). Then convert pieces of paper to reams (divide m by 500) or reams to pieces (multiply p by 500). (The second conversion method is used below.) Cross-multiply to solve for x:

$$\frac{1}{m} = \frac{x}{500p}$$

$$mx = 500p$$

$$x = \frac{500p}{m}$$

30. **The correct answer is (D).** At the end of September the approximate share prices of the three companies' stocks were as follows:

  Ardent stock: $15
  Biofirm stock: $49
  Compuwin stock: $34

The aggregate price of Ardent stock and Biofirm stock was $64, which exceeds the price of Compuwin stock ($34) by approximately 100%.

31. **The correct answer is (B).** During August, the price of Biofirm stock and Compuwin stock increased by a combined amount of about $5. During the same month the price of Ardent stock decreased by about $6. The net aggregate change is nearly zero.

32. **The correct answer is (D).** The key to this problem involves perpendicular lines and the concept of slope. The slope of l_1 is $\frac{1}{2}$, which means that every 2 units from left to right (the line's "run") corresponds to 1 unit upward (vertically) on the plane (the line's "rise"). Since the angle at point A is a right angle, the slope of $\overline{AB}$ must be -2 (a "drop" or "negative rise" of 2 units for every 1 unit from left to right). Drawing a plumb line down from point A reveals that, in order to attain these slopes, the height (altitude) of ΔOAB must be 2:

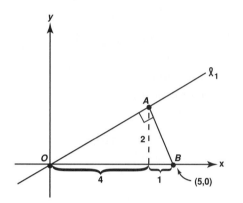

The area of any triangle is defined as one-half the product of its base and height (altitude). Given a base ($\overline{OB}$) of 5 and an altitude of 2, the area of ΔOAB must equal 5.

33. **The correct answer is (D).** Using the variables to represent portions of these intersecting circles, we know that $x + y = 18$ and $y + z = 16$. Through subtraction, we get $x - z = 2$. Using statement (1) only, $x + z = 20$, and combined with $x - z = 2$, we find that $x = 11$ and $z = 9$. We know that $y = 7$ by substituting into $x + y = 18$ or $y + z = 16$. Using statement (2) only, $w = 3$, so $x + y + z = 27$. Combine this equation with $x + y = 18$, and $y + z = 16$. If $x + y = 18$, then $x = 18 - y$. If $y + z = 16$, then $z = 16 - y$. Substitute into $x + y + z = 27$ to get $18 - y + y + 16 - y = 27$, so $y = 7$. Thus, statements (1) and (2) are each sufficient to establish that 7 students are enrolled in both English and Algebra classes.

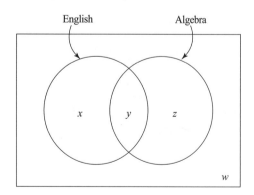

34. The correct answer is (D). Given that twice as many student tickets as adult tickets were sold, two thirds (18) of the 27 tickets sold were student tickets, while one third (9) were adult tickets. You can express the ticket sales revenue by way of the following equation (A = adult ticket price, S = student ticket price):

$$9A + 18S = \$180$$

Statement (1) provides the value of A, which allows you to determine the value of S (the answer to the question):

$$9(10) + 18S = 180$$
$$18S = 90$$
$$S = 5$$

Statement (2) allows you to substitute $2S$ for A in the equation above, thereby allowing you to determine the value of S (the answer to the question):

$$9(2S) + 18S = \$180$$
$$36S = \$180$$
$$S = \$5$$

35. The correct answer is (A). The product of an even integer and any other integer is always even. Therefore, statement (1) alone establishes that ab and cd are both even and, accordingly, that $ab + cd$ is even (the sum of two even integers is always even). Given statement (2) alone, however, although ab must be even, cd might be either odd or even, depending on the value of c. Accordingly, $ab + cd$ might be either odd or even, and statement (2) alone does not suffice to answer the question.

36. The correct answer is (B). The key to this problem is in determining the interior angles of the various triangles formed by the runways. The interior angle formed by the 120° turn from runway 1 to 2 is 60° (a 180° turn would reverse the airplane's direction). Similarly, the interior angle formed by the 135° turn from runway 1 to 3 is 45° (180° − 135°). Two triangle "angle triplets" emerge: a 45°-45°-90° triplet and a 30°-60°-90° triplet, as shown in the next figure. Since the sum of the measures of any triangle's interior angles is 180°, the remaining angles can also be determined:

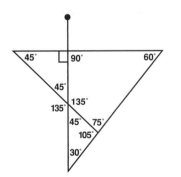

The only angle measure listed among the answer choices that does not appear in the figure above is 55°.

37. **The correct answer is (E).** You can answer this question without knowing the total number of legislators who voted, because the question involves ratios only. Think of the legislature as containing 8 voters divided into two parts: $\frac{5}{8} + \frac{3}{8} = \frac{8}{8}$. For every 5 votes in favor, 3 were cast against the motion. Thus, 5 out of every 8 votes, or $\frac{5}{8}$, were cast in favor of the motion.

Verbal Section

1. E	10. B	18. A	26. A	34. C
2. D	11. D	19. C	27. E	35. E
3. A	12. B	20. E	28. B	36. A
4. B	13. B	21. D	29. E	37. E
5. C	14. A	22. C	30. A	38. B
6. E	15. C	23. D	31. E	39. C
7. A	16. D	24. E	32. C	40. A
8. C	17. B	25. D	33. A	41. B
9. D				

1. **The correct answer is (E).** The original sentence is faulty in two respects. First, the sentence treats the compound subject (*interest rates* and *the supply of money*) as singular by using *either . . . or*; the predicate should agree by also referring to the subject in the singular form, using *a factor* rather than *factors*. Second, the verb phrase *can . . . be* is improperly split. Third, the phrase *can . . . be factors contributing to* is redundant and wordy. Choice (E) remedies all the original sentence problems by uniting the verb parts, rewording the predicate to agree in form with the subject, and removing the redundant language.

2. **The correct answer is (D).** The original version is wordy and very awkward. Choice (D) is clear and concise.

3. **The correct answer is (A).** The original version is perfectly fine. The phrase *similar to* sets up a comparison between soil composition on Mars and soil composition on Earth. The relative pronoun *that* is proper here to refer to the latter.

4. **The correct answer is (B).** The argument relies on the assumption that alcoholics die relatively young only because alcoholism increases a person's susceptibility to life-threatening diseases and not for other reasons as well. Choice (B) provides explicitly that those other possible reasons were ruled out in compiling the insurance statistics cited in the report.

5. **The correct answer is (C).** Choice (C) helps explain last year's sales results by suggesting that sales of products three years old and older could have fallen sharply during the year. Thus, the proportion of sales produced by newer products could have grown, even without popular new products.

6. **The correct answer is (E).** It can reasonably be inferred that the "new conditions" that sparked the divergence in pistol shrimp are an aspect of the two oceans' "distinctive personalities," which the author states began to emerge "long before the isthmus was fully formed." Choice (E) contradicts the inference.

7. **The correct answer is (A).** The author discusses pistol shrimp as an example of twin species or geminates. Thus, choice (A) expresses the author's immediate purpose in mentioning the mating habits of pistol shrimp.

8. **The correct answer is (C).** The second paragraph provides ample support for this inference. The author states that the terrestrial species migrating south were "better colonizers" than the ones migrating north, that *more than half* of those in the south today came from the north, and that *only three* animal species migrating north across the isthmus survive today. It is readily inferable, then, that more than three species that migrated south across the isthmus survive today.

9. **The correct answer is (D).** The original sentence contains a vague pronoun reference. It is unclear as to what the second *that* refers. Choice (D) restates the idea of the first clause of the original sentence more succinctly and clearly, as well as making it clear by the use of the phrase, *and this fact*, that the latter part of the sentence refers to the earlier part.

10. **The correct answer is (B).** The conclusion of the argument is that the claim made by those who have discontinued regular exercise is born of laziness; in other words, these people are making this claim because they are lazy. One effective way to refute the argument is to provide convincing evidence that directly contradicts the conclusion. Choice (B) provides just such evidence, by showing that these people are not in fact lazy.

11. **The correct answer is (D).** The original argument's line of reasoning is essentially as follows:

    Premise: The well-paid engineers at CompTech do not quit their jobs.

    Conclusion: If MicroFirm engineers are not well-paid, they will quit their jobs.

    You can express this argument symbolically as follows:

    Premise: All As are Bs.

    Conclusion: If not A, then not B.

    The reasoning is fallacious (flawed), because it fails to account for other possible reasons why MicroFirm engineers have not left their jobs. (Some Bs might not be As.) Choice (D) is the only answer choice that demonstrates the same essential pattern of flawed reasoning. To recognize the similarity, rephrase the argument's sentence structure to match the essence of the original argument:

    Premise: All people who practice diligently (A) achieve perfection (B).

    Conclusion: If one does not practice diligently (not A) one cannot achieve perfection (not B).

12. **The correct answer is (B).** In the original version, *the advent* and *from the time of* are redundant. Also, *since* is more appropriate than *from* to express the sentence's intended meaning. Choice (B) corrects both problems.

13. **The correct answer is (B).** The original sentence is not a complete sentence. Choice (B) completes the sentence without committing any errors in grammar or diction.

14. **The correct answer is (A).** The original sentence properly uses the correlative *not only . . . but also*. The two modifying phrases (*not only by increased* and *but also by increased*) are grammatically parallel.

15. **The correct answer is (C).** Shakespeare depicts Richard III as a monster with a twisted soul—a depiction that leads us to believe that Richard could well have been responsible for the deaths of both his brother Clarence and Henry VI. However, the author of the passage tells us that there is historical evidence that Richard did not kill his brother and that there is no proof that Henry VI was actually murdered.

16. **The correct answer is (D).** In the passage, the author first tells us that historians sometimes think they know a historical figure better than they really do. Then the passage's author explains how this can happen by providing an illustrative example—a biographical work (*Richard III*) that is so compelling in its development of the main character that even a historian can be unduly influenced by it.

17. **The correct answer is (B).** According to the passage, Machiavelli's *The Prince* provides information about the tone of the times in which Richard lived. The passage's final sentence tells us that Richard's actions seem "reasonable" in light of the tone of the times—in other words, that his actions reflected the times.

18. **The correct answer is (A).** This argument relies on the assumption that Gregg's Syndrome is more prevalent among Puma Syndrome victims who take Betatol than among those who take Aidistan. Choice (A) essentially affirms this assumption, although it expresses it in a somewhat different way. Given that Gregg's Syndrome renders any Puma Syndrome treatment less effective, if victims who have both syndromes are treated with Betatol while victims who have only Puma Syndrome are treated with Aidistan, then Aidistan will appear to be more effective, although the absence of Gregg's Syndrome might in fact be the key factor that explains the differing results.

19. **The correct answer is (C).** In all likelihood, the district's residents contribute to the revenues of businesses there by purchasing goods and services from them. A net loss in the number of district residents would provide an alternative explanation for the loss of revenue. Choice (C) rules out this possibility, thereby *strengthening* the claim that the loss in revenue was due to the city's reduction in its police force and, accordingly, that increasing the size of the force will reverse the decline in revenues.

20. **The correct answer is (E).** The passage boils down to the following:

> *Premise:* People buy sport utility vehicles because they believe these vehicles are safe.

> *Conclusion:* To sell a vehicle, a manufacturer should not emphasize affordability.

Choice (E) provides the assumption needed to render the argument logically convincing:

> *Premise:* People buy sport utility vehicles because they believe these vehicles are safe.

> *Premise (E):* People do not believe that affordable vehicles are safe.

> *Conclusion:* To sell a sport utility vehicle, a manufacturer should not emphasize its affordability.

21. **The correct answer is (D).** Regardless of the reason for the increase in the volume of material transported to landfills, reducing the volume of material available for transport to landfills would serve the stated objective. Choice (D) suggests a plan of action that, if successful, would help.

22. **The correct answer is (C).** The original sentence is faulty in two respects. First, it improperly uses *because* instead of *because of*. Second, the construction leaves it unclear as to whether the modifying phrase *already in wide use* refers to *other pesticides* or to *chemical compositions*. Choice (C) corrects the misuse of *because* by replacing it with *due to* (an alternative to *because of*).

23. **The correct answer is (D).** Instead of using the proper idiom *equal . . . to* or the proper correlative pair *as . . . as*, the original version attempts to make a comparison by using the improper *equal . . . as*. Choice (D) corrects this error with the correlative pair *as . . . as*.

24. **The correct answer is (E).** The original sentence uses *of* twice; the result is wordy and awkward. Choice (E) is idiomatically proper and more concise than the original version.

25. **The correct answer is (D).** Choice (D) weakens the argument by providing some evidence that in this nation it would be comparatively expensive to produce cosmetics with Yucaipa tree-bark oil and, accordingly, that the tree population in this nation might not be significantly depleted even if the law were repealed.

26. The correct answer is (A). You can rephrase choice (A) as follows: *All* Web sites administered by individuals holding advanced degrees in educational technology are official Web sites of nationally accredited colleges. In other words, the following two symbolic statements are logically equivalent:

Only A are B.

All B are A.

Given that all Web sites of nationally accredited colleges have received the highest possible rating from the Department, and given that all Web sites administered by individuals holding advanced degrees in educational technology are official Web sites of nationally accredited colleges, it follows logically that all Web sites administered by individuals holding advanced degrees in educational technology have received the highest possible rating from the Department. To follow the logical steps, it helps to express the premises and conclusion symbolically:

Premise: All A are C.

Premise: All B are A.

Conclusion: All B are C.

27. The correct answer is (E). The original version is grammatically correct, but the pronoun reference is vague. (To what does it refer?) Choice (E) clarifies the pronoun reference by using the possessive *its luminosity*.

28. The correct answer is (B). Exposure to sunlight was mentioned as one factor determining peak bone mass. Although the passage states that "many of the factors that affect the attainment of peak bone mass also affect rates of bone loss," it is unwarranted to infer that exposure to sunlight is one such factor.

29. The correct answer is (E). As long as the population upon which the cited statistic was based excluded those who had not yet achieved peak bone mass, it does not make a difference whether the men in the group achieved their peak bone mass at a different age than the women.

30. The correct answer is (A). In lines 17–28, the author lists various factors affecting peak bone mass, then asserts that many of these factors also affect the rate of bone loss. In mentioning pregnancy and lactation as "additional factors" (line 33) affecting bone loss, the author implies that these two factors do not also affect peak bone mass.

31. The correct answer is (E). The argument relies on two important assumptions. One is that the teachers who transferred from Franklin to Valley View were Vining graduates; the other is that teachers who transferred from Valley View to Franklin were not Vining graduates. If neither or only one were the case, then it would be unreasonable to conclude that Vining graduates are responsible for high academic performance. Admittedly, these assumptions involve a matter of degree; for example, the greater the percentage of Vining alumni among the teachers transferring from Franklin to Valley View, the stronger the argument's conclusion. And admittedly, choice (E) does not acknowledge this fact. Nevertheless, choice (E) provides the essence of one of these two crucial assumptions.

32. **The correct answer is (C).** The argument concludes that the reason for the military's decision was to reduce pilot error during commercial flights. Choice (C) is the only answer choice that supports this conclusion. Given that chemical warfare is likely to escalate in the future, it would seem that the military would *continue* to require immunization shots. But the military stopped requiring the shots. So the military's decision must have been based on some factor outweighing the potential danger of chemical warfare to pilots. One such possible factor is the increased danger of commercial airline accidents resulting from the immunization shots.

33. **The correct answer is (A).** The original sentence contains no grammatical errors, ambiguous references, or idiomatically improper words or phrases. The word *visionary*, used as an adjective here, is proper, although you could use the word *visionaries* (a noun) instead.

34. **The correct answer is (C).** The original sentence is unclear in meaning; the use of the word *simultaneously* suggests that two or more items are attained. If the sentence had continued with the phrase *global and regional dominance*, the use of the word *simultaneously* would have made more sense. Choice (C) excludes the confusing word *simultaneously* and properly sets off the prepositional phrase beginning with *in the course* with commas to clarify the sentence's meaning.

35. **The correct answer is (E).** Karl's response relies on two alternative but interrelated assumptions: (1) the reruns are likely to be popular enough to compete with Connie's favorite program, and (2) Connie's favorite program will not in fact be popular. Choice (E) provides evidence that helps affirm both of these assumptions by suggesting that the reruns might very well be popular enough to draw the viewing audience away from Connie's favorite program, thus rendering it less popular. Admittedly, choice (E) would provide even greater support if it explicitly indicated that one popular program can draw viewers away from another. Nevertheless, choice (E) is the best among the five answer choices.

36. **The correct answer is (A).** The author foresees prolonged inefficiency and misallocation as a consequence of gradual, not rapid, privatization (lines 9–12).

37. **The correct answer is (E).** In the third paragraph the author suggests a willingness to place a private enterprise at risk for the broader purpose of achieving a free-market system. While advocating voucher privatization, the author admits that this approach may very well result in the instability of stock prices; yet, the author seems to view the insecurity caused by market pressures as "good" for private enterprises in that it will drive them to efficiency—a sort of sink-or-swim approach.

38. **The correct answer is (B).** The author responds to the skeptics' claim by pointing out that people are likely to weigh the future flow of income from a voucher against the benefits of selling their vouchers now and using the proceeds for consumption. If people were not likely, at least in many cases, to hold their vouchers after weighing these two alternatives, the author would not have made this argument. Thus, the author is implying that, in many cases, the future flow of income from a voucher will exceed the present value of the voucher.

39. **The correct answer is (C).** Although the author does respond to what might be one undesired result of voucher privatization—falling stock prices, as well as explain the cause of falling stock prices—the author does not offer an "alternative" explanation for this phenomenon, as suggested by choice (C). Moreover, the author's purpose in discussing falling stock prices is not to explain their cause, but rather to acknowledge that what appears to be an undesirable consequence of voucher privatization may actually help bring about a desirable result.

40. **The correct answer is (A).** The passage indicates that developers have curtailed construction of new office buildings until demand grows to meet supply, while Stepping up construction of single-family houses. This evidence in itself strongly supports choice (A). Admittedly, it is possible that an influx of businesses from other states will deplete the current oversupply of office buildings and create sufficient demand for new ones. Nevertheless, choice (A) is the best of the five choices.

41. **The correct answer is (B).** The original sentence lacks proper parallelism; *to* should be omitted. Also, the original sentence is composed of two main clauses (each of which could stand on its own as a complete sentence) separated only by a comma. This comma splice should be corrected by inserting an appropriate connecting word, such as *but*, *yet*, or *although*. Choice (B) corrects both problems.

Index of Close-Ups and Displays

Special Advertising Section

Saint Louis University, John Cook School of Business

St. Mary's University, Bill Greehey School of Business

Thomas Jefferson University School of Population Health

University of Medicine & Dentistry of New Jersey

The Winston Preparatory Schools

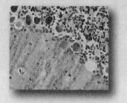
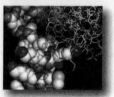

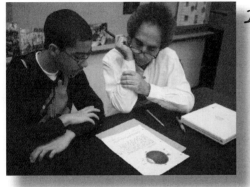

NOTES

NOTES

NOTES